A

THE
COLLINS
SCHOOL
DICTIONARY

HarperCollins*Publishers*

First Published 1989
© HarperCollins Publishers 1989
Latest Reprint 1991

ISBN 0 00433127-3 Hardback (School Edition)
ISBN 0 00433229-6 Vinyl Cover (Net Edition)

British Library Cataloguing in Publication Data
Collins school dictionary.
1. English language. Dictionaries
423

NOTE

Computer typeset by Barbers Ltd.
Wrotham, England

Printed and bound in Great Britain
by HarperCollins Manufacturing
P.O. Box, Glasgow G4 0NB

CONTENTS

EDITORIAL TEAM

CHIEF EDITOR
Patrick Hanks

MANAGING EDITORS
Marian Makins, Gwyneth Fox

TEXT EDITORS
Diana Adams, Alice Grandison

CHIEF COMPILER
Deborah Kirby

COMPILERS
**Stephen Bullon, Sheila Dignen, Ann Hewings, Janet Hilsdon,
Helen Liebeck, Elaine Pollard, Christina Rammell,
Sue Sutton, John Todd**

ETYMOLOGIES
**Ela Bullon, Malcolm Coulthard, Sheila Dignen, Margaret Ellis,
Ann Hewings, Janet Hilsdon, Flavia Hodges, Rosamund Moon,
Hannah Stone, Janet Whitcut**

SIMILAR WORDS
Lorna Knight, Catherine Forde

Acknowledgments

The editors and compilers wish to thank all the teachers and English advisers who helped in the planning of this book, in particular, Kate Barnett, King Edward VI Grammar School, Camp Hill, Birmingham, who also helped greatly by piloting sections of the text in class; Alan Jones, Hampton School, Middlesex; J. Stewart, Paisley Grammar School; and Don Summers, Smithycroft Secondary School, Glasgow.

We are also indebted to Professor Brian Cox for his advice on the role of a dictionary in the National Curriculum for England and Wales, and to the pioneering work of the Cobuild project in the University of Birmingham, directed by John Sinclair, Professor of Modern English Language. We were fortunate in being able to use the 20-million word collection of current English texts held on computer in the University of Birmingham, as well as a computerized corpus of school textbooks.

FOREWORD

THE COLLINS SCHOOL DICTIONARY reflects a new consensus about the best ways of helping young people to understand and to use the English language. Its approach to the explanation of words and to grammar is that favoured by the Kingman Report of 1988 and by the 1989 Report of the National Curriculum English Working Group, which I had the privilege to chair. Under the provisions of the Education Reform Act of 1988, the National Curriculum sets out programmes of study for English in all State schools in England and Wales. Using this dictionary will help pupils acquire a better understanding of how their language works, in line with the recommendations of our report.

Sometimes, in the past, pupils were expected to learn dictionary definitions off by heart, without understanding how words are used in practice. This is why, in this dictionary, words are generally explained in a way that shows typical *use* as well as meaning. Consider, for example, the words **legislate** and **legalize.** The explanations for these two words begin as follows:

> When a government legislates, it ...
> To legalize something that is illegal means to ...

The explanations are worded in this way to show verb use, and to show such matters as transitivity and intransitivity, rather than discussing them in the abstract. They go further, for they show typical context ("a government") and presupposition (to be legalized, a thing must be illegal to start with). In this way, the dictionary holds up models of standard usage for the user. The definitions of words are also often followed by examples of their current use. Children need to understand how words are used in actual conversation and writing; this emphasis on language in use is of central importance in the programmes of study in the National Curriculum. When I was teaching in Brazil I found these words printed on an advertisement for a hotel restaurant: "Music to rear or to dance". After a moment when I imagined the dancers rearing up like performing bears, I realized the words referred to background music. The explanation and examples in this dictionary will help its readers to use words more appropriately than the Brazilian hotelier.

The National Curriculum also requires pupils to acquire an understanding of the variety of origins of English words, and for this reason clear, simple etymologies are given for many entries. The lists of similar words given after some entries can be used to help pupils extend their vocabulary, and to appreciate fine distinctions in meaning and usage.

The Introduction to the dictionary provides a simple, invaluable guide to the basic terminology that all secondary pupils need in order to discuss language. During the last forty years or so teachers have changed their minds twice about the teaching of linguistic terms. When I was at school in the 1930s and 1940s we were taught grammar by learning rules off by heart, and by spending tedious hours on parsing and clause analysis. Teachers began to realize that such exercises had little influence on the way children used language in their speech and writing, and so in the 1950s and 1960s there was a reaction against these methods. Many teachers of English felt then that the learning by rote of the rules of grammar repressed children's abilities to write expressively and imaginatively. In many classrooms children were positively discouraged from using terms such as 'noun', 'verb', or 'preposition' when they were discussing their writings.

By 1980 it had become clear that this reaction to the old-fashioned teaching of grammar had gone much too far, and that it was absurd for children not to use any linguistic terms. In the National Curriculum Report we say that teachers must explain grammatical terms in language which children can understand, just as they must explain any other unfamiliar words in books children read. In the process of editing and redrafting written work, teachers and pupils will be helped by descriptive technical language. Teaching of language must involve talking about language, since learning without that activity is slow and inefficient.

It would be a wonderful improvement if all school-leavers could understand and use the grammatical terms explained in the Introduction to this dictionary. This must not mean a return to learning definitions by rote, for pupils should use words such as 'noun' or 'verb' in discussions of their own writing, not in exercises out of context.

In our National Curriculum Report we defined two related strands in the development of reading skills. Young people need to read as widely as possible, particularly great literature, for this is how they develop a feeling for language. At the same time they must learn what are called information-retrieval skills, must know how to use an index or a thesaurus or a dictionary. I am always amazed when I receive important letters, for example from students applying for university admission, which include spelling errors. Why have they not learnt to check difficult words in a dictionary? This new Collins dictionary will help young people to gain confidence in their use of vocabulary, to extend their reading and writing skills. I believe the new consensus in the teaching of English, reflected in this dictionary as well as in the National Curriculum, will have great success in raising standards of literacy and in helping all of us to know more about the English language.

Brian Cox

INTRODUCTION: LANGUAGE AND THE DICTIONARY

What is a dictionary for? Dictionaries give information about words: about their spelling and meaning, for example, and where they came from—but also about how they are used. In order to understand how words are used, we need to know both something about the words and something about the patterns of language that they fit into. This introduction summarizes some of the main points about the structure and use of English.

I: GRAMMAR: THE STRUCTURE OF LANGUAGE

When we set out to communicate an idea or ask a question, we put words together into a structure. We don't just shout the words out at random. Suppose somebody said to you: 'Book your home at Peter left!' You might just be able to understand what they intended to say. But you would also know that there was something funny about what they had said: perhaps this person is a foreigner, or an invader from outer space. The words themselves are all right, but the structure is all wrong.

Of course, we don't need to study the *structure* of English in order to understand a familiar English sentence such as 'Peter left your book at home!' Every English speaker has been instinctively practising the structures of English all his or her life. Like so many things, it seems obvious if you know it already!

However, there are several good reasons for studying the structures and the names of the parts of English, as well as being able to use them instinctively. For example, when we come to study a foreign language, we want to know how the foreign language differs from English. In order to describe the differences, we need to be able to say something about the structures of English in the first place. Also, studying grammar—the structure of languages—can help you to think logically and work out the details of complicated ideas. And if we are trying to learn to use an unfamiliar word, we need to know whether the word is a noun, adjective, or verb, as well as what it means.

For all of these reasons, this dictionary gives information about the grammar of words. For example, it tells you what **part of speech** each word belongs to. The main parts of speech are: verb, noun, pronoun, adjective, adverb, preposition, conjunction, determiner, and interjection. In this section of the introduction, we give a brief summary of how each of these parts of speech is used, introducing some of the technical terms of grammar.

sentences and clauses

English speech and writing is made up of **sentences,** and each sentence is made up of one or more **clauses.**

The sentence

> Peter left your book at home

consists of one clause. The sentence

> Peter left your book at home | because he forgot |
> that you wanted it

consists of three clauses. 'Peter left your book at home' is a **main clause.** 'Because he forgot' and 'that you wanted it' are **subordinate clauses.**

subject, verb, object

The typical structure of an English clause is: **subject, verb, object.** Each clause is built around a verb. (The verbs in the three-clause sentence just quoted are 'left', 'forgot', and 'wanted'.) Typically, the verb tells you what was done, and the subject tells you who or what did it.

INTRODUCTION

The subject of a clause or sentence is a noun or pronoun, and normally it comes in front of the verb. (The subjects of the three clauses just quoted are 'Peter', 'he', and 'you'.)

A clause can also have an object. This too is a noun or pronoun. For example, the clause

> Chris patted her dog

has an object ('dog').

Some clauses do not have an object at all. For example, the clauses

> Peter departed

and

> Peter left

have a subject ('Peter') and a verb ('departed', 'left'), but no object.

phrases
To be more precise, we can say that the subject or object of a clause is not just a noun, but a **noun phrase,** and the clause is built not just around a verb, but around a **verb phrase.**
So, in the clause

> The proud owner was patting her prize-winning pet,

the verb phrase is 'was patting', the subject is 'The proud owner', and the object is 'her prize-winning pet'.

adjuncts
Finally, there are some parts of a clause that are neither subject, verb, nor object. We call these **adjuncts** or **adverbial phrases.** These typically give information about time, place, and manner. For example, the sentence

> Maria left school in a hurry yesterday

contains two adjuncts: 'in a hurry' and 'yesterday'.

the basic structure of English
English sentences can be very complicated, but the vast majority are variations on this basic theme of subject, verb, object, and adjunct.

We can now go on to describe in a little more detail the role of each of the parts of speech, in relation to the basic structure just outlined.

adjectives
An adjective is a word that modifies the meaning of a noun. Some examples of adjectives are 'strong', 'red', and 'medical', as in *a strong woman;   that red book; medical treatment.*

Comparative and superlative. Adjectives can be used in three different forms: the basic word (e.g. *strong*), the comparative (e.g. *stronger*), and the superlative (e.g. *strongest*).

A different way of forming the comparative and superlative of an adjective is to use *more* for the comparative and *most* for the superlative. This is done with some adjectives that have two syllables and all that have three or more syllables (e.g. *faithful, more faithful, most faithful* and *beautiful, more beautiful, most beautiful*).

adverbs

There are several different kinds of adverb, and several different ways in which adverbs can be used. The main types are as follows:

1. Most adverbs can modify the meaning of a verb, e.g. 'quickly' in *She walked quickly past,* or 'cheerfully' in *Tom greeted her cheerfully.*

2. Many adverbs can also be used to modify the meaning of an adjective, e.g. 'dangerously' in *dangerously ill patients.* There is a small group of adverbs that can be used only to modify the meaning of an adjective (or occasionally another adverb). Examples are 'very', 'rather', and 'totally'. Adverbs used in this way are sometimes called **adverbs of degree.**

3. Some adverbs are used to comment on the meaning of a whole statement, introducing the opinion of the writer or speaker. These are sometimes called **sentence adverbs.** For example, 'unfortunately' is a sentence adverb in *Unfortunately, he did not recognize her.*

4. Some adverbs are used to give structure to the argument in an essay or speech, and to organize the way the sentences are put together. These are words such as 'therefore', 'however', 'furthermore', and 'anyway'.

5. The words 'when', 'where', 'why', and 'how' are sometimes referred to as **interrogative adverbs** when they are used at the beginning of a main clause, to ask a question.

conjunctions

Conjunctions are words such as 'and', 'or', and 'but', which are used to join together two sentences, phrases, or words. These are sometimes called **coordinating conjunctions.**

Some other words, such as 'if', 'when', 'because', and 'how', are used to join a subordinate clause to a main clause, as in *If it happens, I shall be very pleased.* They are therefore called **subordinating conjunctions.**

determiners

A determiner is a word that introduces a noun phrase, saying more about what the noun phrase as a whole refers to. The main types of determiner are as follows:

1. The most common determiners are 'the', called the **definite article,** and 'a' (or 'an'), called the **indefinite article.** The definite article tells you that you should already know what the noun refers to. For example, the statement *Amy had the idea* would only be used if we had already been told what the idea was—or if we are going to be told there and then what the idea was: *Amy had the idea of going to the match.*

The indefinite article, 'a' or 'an', is used to mention one particular thing when it is being first introduced into the conversation or text, for example, *Suddenly, Amy had an idea....*

2. Another group of determiners consists of the words 'this' and 'that', 'these' and 'those', sometimes called **demonstratives.**

3. A third group consists of the words 'his', 'her', 'its', 'my', 'your', 'our', and 'their', sometimes called **possessives.**

interjections

Interjections, also called exclamations, are utterances expressing reactions such as alarm, surprise, anger, pleasure, etc., for example 'Oh', 'bother', and 'hurrah'. Unlike other words, they often stand alone, instead of being fitted into clauses and sentences.

nouns

Nouns are words that refer to people, things, and abstract ideas. 'Student', 'dog', 'desk', 'money', 'health', and 'information' are all nouns. There are three main types of noun:

1. Countable nouns in the singular are always used with a determiner. Countable nouns have a plural form, usually ending in '-s', which can be used with or without a determiner. So, for example, 'student' is a countable noun: you can talk about 'a student' or 'the student'. You can talk about 'four students', and you can also talk about 'students' in general. You cannot talk about 'student' in the singular without a determiner.

Some nouns, for example 'scissors' and 'police', are normally used only in the plural. In this dictionary, these are described as **plural nouns,** and given a plural definition. In other cases, such as 'tadpole', the definition is in the plural, but the description simply says 'noun'. This means that the noun can be used in either the singular or the plural, although the plural is rather more common.

2. Uncountable nouns (sometimes called **mass nouns**) are used to talk about general concepts: you can talk about 'health', 'money', or 'information' in general. These nouns do not have a plural form, and cannot be counted: you cannot talk about 'eight moneys' or 'three informations'. Uncountable nouns cannot be used with the indefinite article, either: you cannot talk about 'a health' or 'an information'.

In this dictionary, the distinction between countable nouns and uncountable nouns is made in the way in which they are explained, rather than in the grammatical labels used. Thus, the explanation of 'student' begins "A student is...", showing that it is a countable noun. The explanation of 'money' begins "Money is...", showing that the noun is uncountable.

3. Another main class of nouns is **proper nouns:** names such as 'John', 'London', and 'Baxter'. Although proper nouns are very common in the language as a whole, they are not common in dictionaries, since proper nouns refer to individuals, not to general classes of items that can be explained in a dictionary.

prepositions

A preposition is a word such as 'by', 'on', 'with', or 'from', used in front of a noun phrase or a pronoun to form a prepositional phrase. A prepositional phrase expresses the relation of a noun to the rest of the sentence. Examples are 'by' in *The book is by a well-known writer* and 'on' in *She put the flowers on the table.*

pronouns

Pronouns are single words used to refer to people or things without naming or describing them. There are five main classes of pronouns:

1. Personal pronouns refer to people or things. When the pronoun is the subject of a sentence, the forms 'I', 'you', 'he', 'she', 'it', 'we', and 'they' are used. When the pronoun is the object of a verb or of a preposition, the forms 'me', 'you', 'him', 'her', 'it', 'us', and 'them' are used.

2. Possessive pronouns are the words 'mine', 'yours', 'his', 'hers', 'ours', and 'theirs', used to identify ownership, as in *This towel is mine, that's yours.* Possessive pronouns should be carefully distinguished from possessive determiners (see **determiners,** paragraph 3).

3. Relative pronouns, such as 'who' and 'which', introduce **relative clauses.** Relative clauses modify nouns, for example in *people who make me laugh* or *the dodo, which is now extinct.*

(The words 'who' and 'which' can also be used to ask questions, in which case they are referred to as **interrogative pronouns.**)

4. Reflexive pronouns refer back to a noun or personal pronoun earlier in the same clause. They are formed with '-self' or '-selves'. Examples are *She hurt herself; they did it for themselves.* Reflexive pronouns can also be used for emphasis, as in *The Head Teacher himself did not know the answer.*

5. Indefinite pronouns are used to refer to a possible person or thing, without being specific about who or what they are. Examples are 'anyone', 'anything', 'somebody', 'nobody', and 'everything'.

verbs
Verbs are words that describe actions and states.

1. Types of verb: there are three different types of English verb: **main verbs, auxiliary verbs,** and **modal verbs.**

Main verbs, such as 'walk', 'talk', 'expect', 'grow', and 'think', carry the main meaning of the action. All well-formed English sentences have a main verb.

The auxiliary verbs 'be', 'have', and 'do', and the auxiliary modals 'shall' and 'will' are used in forming **tenses.** The verb 'be' is also used in forming **passives.**

The modal verbs are 'can', 'could', 'may', 'might', 'must', 'ought to', 'should', and 'would'. They refer to such matters as the possibility or necessity of an action, for example *He can do it; she might do it; you must do it.*

2. Tense. The form of a verb or verb phrase that refers to the time of the action is called its tense. Tenses are formed either by choosing a particular form of the main verb, for example one ending in *-ed,* or by using an auxiliary verb with a form of the main verb. English has two kinds of tenses: **simple tenses** and **continuous tenses.** Examples of simple tenses are 'catches' in *Rashid catches the bus to school most days* and 'caught' in *Rashid caught the bus to school yesterday.* Examples of continuous tenses are 'is catching' and 'was catching' in *Rashid is catching the bus this morning* and *Rashid was catching the bus when Shona drove by.*

English also has two ways of looking at the past: a simple past tense is used to recount a past event. An example of the simple past is 'ran' in *Sarah ran a marathon last year.* Another way of talking about the same event would be to use a **perfect tense,** formed with the auxiliary verb 'have', e.g. *Sarah has run a marathon.* The perfect tense is often said to look at past events from the point of view of present relevance.

3. Verb forms: most verbs in English have four different forms. Some have five. The forms are:

The base form, e.g. 'talk', 'expect', 'grow', 'think', 'swim'.

The third person present singular, e.g. 'talks', 'expects', 'grows', 'thinks', 'swims'.

The present participle, e.g. 'talking', 'expecting', 'growing', 'thinking', 'swimming'.

The past tense, e.g. 'talked', 'expected', 'grew', 'thought', 'swam'.

The past participle, e.g. 'talked', 'expected', 'grown', 'thought', 'swum'.

The past tense and the past participle are identical for most verbs, but for a few, e.g. *grew/grown* and *swam/swum,* they are different. The past tense is used as in *He grew some prize vegetables.* The past participle is used for perfect tenses, as in *He has grown some prize vegetables,* and for the passive, as in *Some prize vegetables were grown.*

4. Transitive and intransitive. A noun phrase or pronoun coming after a verb is called its **direct object.** When a verb has a direct object, it is called a transitive verb. 'Helped' in *The teacher helped Rebecca* is a transitive verb, because there is a direct object, 'Rebecca'.

A verb that does not have a direct object is called **intransitive.** 'Laugh' is an intransitive verb, as in *She laughed* or *She was laughing at him.*

Some verbs require more than one object. In the sentence *John gave Peter a book,* 'a book' is the direct object, and 'Peter' is the indirect object. It is called an indirect object because you can use a prepositional phrase to express the same meaning: *John gave a book to Peter.*

5. Active and passive. Notice the relationship between the following two sentences:

> The teacher helped Rebecca.
> Rebecca was helped by the teacher.

They have the same meaning, but in the first one, 'The teacher' is the subject, while in the second, 'Rebecca' is the subject, so the focus is different. The verb in the first sentence is in the **active voice.** In the second sentence, the verb, formed with 'was', is in the **passive voice.** The direct object of an active verb can always be made the subject of a passive verb.

The passive voice can be very useful when you want to talk about an action or event, but do not know (or do not want to say) who did it. Compare *Darren stole my pen* (active voice) with *My pen has been stolen* (passive voice).

6. Phrasal verbs. Some verbs are used with an adverb or preposition to form a special kind of verb, called a **phrasal verb.** Phrasal verbs are expressions like 'take in', 'take off', 'take over'; 'run down'; 'break in', and so on. The meaning of a phrasal verb is often very different from the meaning of the verb and the adverb used on their own. Phrasal verbs are explained as separate entries in this dictionary, immediately after the entry for the verb from which they are formed.

words belonging to more than one part-of-speech class
Many words can belong to more than one part-of-speech class. For instance, 'fall' can be a verb, as in *She saw a tree fall across the road,* or a noun, as in *a fall of snow.* In this dictionary the part-of-speech class is stated after the first relevant definition number.

idiomatic phrases
Sometimes a word is so often used in a particular phrase that it has a separate meaning from the ordinary sense of the word. In such cases, the phrase is printed in bold type in the explanation. Thus, at the entry for 'feather' the dictionary explains what is meant if someone **feathers their nest.**

II: EXPLANATIONS: THE WORDING OF DEFINITIONS AND EXAMPLES
The explanations in this dictionary have two purposes: one is to tell you what each word means, supposing that you have read it in a book or newspaper or heard it used and do not recognize it. The other is to help you to use unfamiliar words correctly and naturally, by showing the word in use in its normal context. The explanations are worded to show the word in use. So, for example, a typical verb definition begins 'If you earn money, you...' A typical noun definition begins 'A vehicle is....'

In some cases, it was felt that an example of the word used in a wider context would help the dictionary users. These examples are based on a detailed study at the University of Birmingham of how words are actually used.

INTRODUCTION

Of course, there are many more words in the language than are recorded in this dictionary. There are many technical terms or rare or literary words. To understand them you need to go to a much bigger dictionary, or perhaps to a special-subject dictionary. This dictionary records all the words that a pupil needs for everyday use.

III: SIMILAR WORDS

Many words in English have meanings that are very similar. This dictionary will help you to distinguish between them, and to choose the one that is most suitable. Similar words are listed in groups at the end of some entries, so that you can look them all up and compare the explanations.

IV: CONTEXT OF USE

Not all words are equally appropriate in all contexts of use. A boy who told his friends that he had "sustained an injury" while playing football would probably be laughed at: the form of words is much too formal and literary for the context. We might read in a newspaper that the Archbishop of Canterbury had sustained an injury after slipping on a wet pavement, but that would not make the form of words appropriate for everyday use among friends.

This dictionary gives guidance on the appropriate level of use for particular words and meanings, if they are not generally appropriate for all contexts. The main guidelines given are as follows:

Informal — Although the word or meaning may be widely used, especially in conversation, it is not suitable in formal contexts such as a written examination paper or a formal academic lecture.

Examples: *bash, uptight, advert, scary, showbiz, suck up to, a sucker* (=a person who is easily fooled)

Formal — The word or meaning is characteristically used in written English rather than in ordinary conversation, and typically occurs in an official context. Formal words and expressions often have a less formal counterpart.

Examples: *efficacious, succour, sustain an injury, valedictory, veracity, vitiate, volition*

Literary — The word or meaning is not used in everyday modern English, but is found in the literature of the past, and may sometimes still be in modern literature. Literary words are always rather formal and, like formal words, they usually have a nonliterary equivalent.

Examples: *sylvan, vanquish, vengeful, behold, brigand, serpent, sepulchral*

Old-fashioned — The word was in use in the fairly recent past, but is now no longer common in everyday English. Such words have in many cases been replaced by a more modern everyday equivalent.

Examples: *suitor, vouchsafe, scoundrel, stripling*

Technical The word or meaning is used in a specialist field, for example biology, computing, or science. Wherever possible, the dictionary tells you which subject field or technical area the word is used in. Thus, *suture* is described as 'a medical word', and *vacuole* as used 'in biology'.

Offensive The word or sense may be regarded as hurtful or derogatory by the person described or referred to, even if the speaker uses the word without any unkind intention.

Examples: *swine, slut*

In addition to the above, the dictionary mentions the main points where American English differs from British English. For example, it records that 'vacation' is the American word for a holiday, and that in American English the path for pedestrians beside a street is called the 'sidewalk'.

V: THE PRONUNCIATION OF ENGLISH
There are many different accents to be heard throughout the English-speaking world. In the USA, Scotland, Ireland, Devonshire, and elsewhere, for example, the letter 'r' is sounded distinctly in words such as 'fern' and 'arm', while in the speech of Southeast England it is not. In many places, words like 'castle' and 'fast' are pronounced with a short 'a' sound, not the long 'a' of Southeast England. For speakers with these accents, 'aunt' may sound exactly like 'ant'.

It used to be claimed in the past that the accent of Southeast England was the so-called correct one, and that other regional accents were somehow wrong. Now, however, many people think that to say that someone's accent is wrong is like saying that someone's facial appearance or choice of dress is wrong. What really matters is the ability to communicate clearly, lucidly, and coherently with other English speakers. Details of accent are secondary to this, and only become important when the accent makes it difficult for other people to understand what is being said.

In this book, occasional guidance is given on the pronunciation of difficult words, especially where the spelling might be misleading. The transcriptions are designed to be as neutral as possible, so that they can give help to speakers of many accents, not just Southeastern British English.

VI: ETYMOLOGY: WHERE DID OUR WORDS COME FROM?
English words are derived from a large number of different languages, and in many cases their development is a complex series of stages reflecting our linguistic and cultural heritage. In this dictionary, etymologies are given in square brackets at the end of many entries. These tell you a little about where English words came from, and they also record some of the changes in meaning that have taken place. It is important to remember, when reading the literature of the past, that words do change their meanings. The next few paragraphs describe the main sources from which English words are derived.

Old English
English is basically a Germanic language, like German, Dutch, Swedish, and Danish. It was brought to England by invaders from the continent of Europe in the 5th and 6th centuries AD. These invaders were called Angles and Saxons, and so Old English is sometimes called Anglo-Saxon. Their language was very different from modern

English, and only about 8 per cent of the words still in everyday use are descended directly from Old English words. They tend to be very basic words. Examples are 'become' (Old English *becuman*), 'behind' (Old English *behindan*), 'man' (Old English *mann*), 'woman' (Old English *wifmann*), 'neck' (Old English *hnecca*), 'broad' (Old English *brād*), 'holiday' (Old English *hāligdæg*), and 'make' (Old English *macian*).

Scandinavian influences
In the 9th and 10th centuries, Scandinavian settlers from Denmark and Norway established settlements in northern and central England. They too contributed words to English: words such as 'bubble', 'scare', and 'rap'.

French
The Norman invasion of 1066 completely changed the character of English. The Normans spoke French, and for three hundred years the language of the court and the administration in England was Norman French. To them we owe about 20 per cent of our modern vocabulary: words such as 'noble', 'common', 'caution', 'beef', 'bacon', and 'pork', as well as legal terms such as 'malice', 'mortgage', and 'forfeit'.

In the Norman period, Old English had become the language of the peasantry, a conquered people. It is sometimes said that English owed its survival to the upbringing of Norman lords by English-speaking servant women. No doubt it owed something as well to the poet Geoffrey Chaucer, who established English as a literary language in the European tradition, alongside Italian and French. He used Italian and French writers as his models, rather than Old English writers.

Latin
Throughout the Middle Ages, there was another language spoken in England, namely Latin, the language of monks, priests, and scholars. From the earliest times, Latin words had been gradually taken into English. In the 16th century, shortly before it finally went out of use as a spoken language among scholars, Latin poured thousands of new words into English. Words of Latin origin make up the language of traditional learning: words such as 'consider', 'explain', 'ignore', 'interest', 'propel', and 'temperature'.

Of course, French is itself largely derived from Latin, so that in some cases, a word could come into English from French, and then, a century or two later, a Latin form of the same word could be borrowed, giving rise to two different English words. Thus, the word 'sample' came into English in the 13th century via French from Latin *exemplum*, to be followed a century later by 'example', taken directly from Latin.

No less than 30 per cent of present-day English words are derived directly from Latin, while a further 9 per cent came in via French.

By Shakespeare's day, some 70 per cent of our present-day English vocabulary was already in use. Shakespeare also used a few words which have gone out of use since. His influence on the language has been enormous. Generations of writers have read his plays and absorbed his language. In some cases, when we use an expression such as "a foregone conclusion" or "to be sick of something" we are unconsciously quoting a phrase that was coined by Shakespeare.

Greek
A more recent source of English words is ancient Greek, the language of the earliest and most influential European philosophy, but also the language of the early Christian Church and the New Testament. A few Greek words crept into English during the first thousand years of its existence, via Latin. These were mostly Church terms such as 'bishop' (ultimately from Greek *episkopos* meaning 'overseer') and 'ecclesiastic' (from Greek *ecclesia* meaning 'assembly'). From the 17th century onwards, ancient Greek came to be widely used for words to denote new scientific and technical concepts:

words such as 'psychology', 'phonetic', 'symbol', 'haemoglobin', 'phase', and 'telegraph'. Some 13 per cent of English words are derived from Greek.

Other sources
Old English, French, Latin, and Greek are the main sources of our modern English words. Over the centuries, however, English has come into contact with other languages from all over the world, and has borrowed words from many of them. Thus, sailors in medieval times borrowed words such as 'skipper' and 'hoist' from Dutch. The early settlers in North America took words such as 'caucus', 'squaw', 'raccoon', and 'skunk' from the American Indians. From the Australian Aborigines we get terms such as 'boomerang' and 'kangaroo'; 'bungalow' comes from Hindi, the most common language of India; 'average' from Arabic. Closer to home, terms such as 'whisky' and 'slogan' are taken from Gaelic, the ancient Celtic language of Scotland and Ireland.

VII: PUNCTUATION
When we speak, we convey part of our meaning by the tone of voice we use and the 'tune' or **intonation** of what we say. In writing, we can get something of the same effect by using punctuation marks. Correct use of punctuation is important, because it can greatly help the reader to understand the writer's intention. The punctuation marks are as follows:

apostrophe
An apostrophe (') is usually used to indicate possession. In the singular -'s is used (e.g. *Peter's dog*). In the plural the apostrophe is added to the end of the word (e.g. *the neighbours' dog*). Plurals that do not end in -s take -'s to show possession (e.g. *children's toys*). Proper names ending in -s either add an apostrophe alone (e.g. *Jesus' life, Keats' poetry*) or add -'s (e.g. *Thomas's house, Mrs Jones's garden*).

brackets
Brackets are put round a part of a sentence that could be omitted while still leaving an intelligible statement, e.g. *That house over there (with the blue door) is ours.*

capital letters
Capital letters are used at the beginning of a sentence, and for proper names and titles of people and organizations, e.g. *Ms Robertson, Dr Smith, South America, British Rail.*

colon
A colon is used to introduce a following statement, e.g. *Take it or leave it: the choice is yours.* It is also used to introduce a list, quotation, or summary.
(Compare **semicolon.**)

comma
1. A comma is used to make a division between two groups of words in a sentence, e.g. *She ran off, her tennis racket swinging loosely at her side.*

2. Commas are also used to divide units in a series of nouns, adjectives, or phrases, e.g. *The cupboard was full of records, cassettes, and compact discs.* A comma is not normally placed between an adjective and a noun, e.g. *It was a long, hot, humid day* (not *...hot, humid, day*).

3. Commas are also used to mark off a word or phrase in a sentence which adds a comment but is not an essential part of the sentence. Dashes and brackets can be used for the same purpose. Commas give the lightest degree of separation, dashes produce a jerky effect, and brackets cut off part of a sentence most firmly, e.g.

He hurried home, taking a short cut, but still arrived too late.

It's a long time — over two years — since we last met.

They both went to the Youth Club (unaware of each other's plans) and met there.

4. Commas are also used to separate a relative clause that adds some information about a noun, but is not an essential part of the meaning, e.g. *The dodo, which is now extinct, inhabited Mauritius.* Here the clause 'which is now extinct' adds a comment on 'dodo'. It is an addition, not an essential part, so it is separated off by commas. Compare this with *I like people who make me laugh.* Here the words 'people who make me laugh' are to be interpreted as a whole. The clause is therefore not separated off by commas.

5. When addressing a person, commas are used before and after the person's name or title, e.g. *I think, Lee, you should try for the prize.*

exclamation mark
An exclamation mark is used after an interjection (or exclamation) such as *Oh! Bother!* or *Hurrah!* It is not normally used after an ordinary statement.

full stop
A full stop marks the end of a sentence.

Full stops are also often used after abbreviations and initial letters standing for a whole word (e.g. *Dec.* for 'December', *fig.* for 'figure', *a.m.* for 'ante meridiem'). Abbreviations that include the first and last letters of a word are equally acceptable with or without the full stop (e.g. *Dr, Mr, ft* or *Dr., Mr., ft.*). It is usual to write certain names or titles, such as BBC, USA, TUC, without full stops.

hyphen
Compound words, like 'layby' and 'fire engine', may often be spelled with a hyphen in them. Words with a prefix such as 'non-' or 'anti-' are sometimes spelled with a hyphen. When a compound adjective comes before a noun it is often hyphenated to stress that the constituent parts are not being used independently, e.g. *She has a red-striped jumper; this is a user-friendly dictionary.*

inverted commas (quotation marks, quotes, speech marks)
1. Inverted commas are used for direct quotation, not for indirect speech.
It is usual to have a comma before and after a quotation if the sentence continues after the quotation, e.g. *She said, "Let's go," and set off down the street.*

2. Single quotation marks can be used to indicate a title or quotation within a speech, e.g. *"I really enjoyed reading 'Romeo and Juliet' last term," she said, "and now I want to see a live performance."* Where such a distinction is not required, either single or double quotation marks may be used. Nowadays the single style is more often used.

question mark
A question mark is used at the end of direct questions, but not after reported ones. Thus, you use a question mark at the end of 'Where are you going?', but not after 'He asked where I was going'.

semicolon
A semicolon can be used instead of a full stop or instead of a conjunction between two sentences that are closely related, e.g. *I arrived home late; the house was in darkness.*

PWH

A

a, an
(determiner) The indefinite articles 'a' and 'an' are used when you are talking about one of something, especially something that you have not mentioned before, e.g. *a book... an orange... There was a book on the table.* Compare **the**.

aback
(adverb) If you are taken aback, you are very surprised and slightly shocked.

abacus, abacuses
(noun) An abacus is a frame with beads that slide along rods, used for calculating.
[from Greek *abax* meaning 'board covered with sand for doing sums on']

abandon, abandons, abandoning, abandoned
1 (verb) If you abandon someone or something, you leave them or give them up permanently.
2 If you abandon yourself to an emotion, you do not try to control it, e.g. *She abandoned herself to her grief.*
3 (noun) If you do something with abandon, you do it in a rather wild uncontrolled way.
abandoned (adjective), **abandonment** (noun).
[from Old French *a bandon* meaning 'under the control of something outside oneself']

Similar words: (sense 1) desert, forsake, quit

abase, abases, abasing, abased
(verb; a formal word) If you abase yourself, you act in a humble way towards someone.

abashed
(adjective) ashamed and embarrassed.

abate, abates, abating, abated
(verb) If something abates, it becomes less, e.g. *The storm had largely abated.*
abatement (noun).
[from French *abattre* meaning 'to beat down']

abattoir, abattoirs (pronounced ab-a-twah)
(noun) An abattoir is a place where animals are killed for meat.
[a French word]

abbess, abbesses
(noun) An abbess is a nun in charge of all the nuns in a convent.

abbey, abbeys
(noun) An abbey is a large church with a community of monks or nuns attached to it.

abbot, abbots
(noun) An abbot is the monk or priest in charge of all the monks in a monastery.
[from Latin *abbat*, originally from Aramaic *abba* meaning 'father']

abbreviate, abbreviates, abbreviating, abbreviated
(verb) To abbreviate something means to make it shorter.
[from Latin *brevis* meaning 'brief']

abbreviation, abbreviations
(noun) An abbreviation is a short form of a word or phrase.

abdicate, abdicates, abdicating, abdicated
1 (verb) If a king or queen abdicates, he or she resigns.
2 (a formal use) If you abdicate your responsibilities or your rights, you give them up.
abdication (noun).
[from Latin *abdicare*, meaning 'to renounce']

abdomen, abdomens
(noun) Your abdomen is the front part of your body below your chest, containing your stomach and intestines.
abdominal (adjective).

abduct, abducts, abducting, abducted
(verb) To abduct someone means to take them away by force.
abduction (noun).
[from Latin *abducere* meaning 'to lead away']

aberration, aberrations
(noun) An aberration is anything that is not normal or usual, e.g. *His political victory was not just an aberration.*
[from Latin *aberrare* meaning 'to wander away']

abet, abets, abetting, abetted
(verb) If you abet someone, you help them to commit a crime or to do something wrong.
[from Old French *abeter* meaning 'to entice']

abeyance
(noun; a formal word) If something is in abeyance, it is temporarily not happening.
[originally a legal term meaning 'ownership not decided']

abhor, abhors, abhorring, abhorred
(verb; a formal word) If you abhor something, you hate it.
abhorrence (noun), **abhorrent** (adjective).
[from Latin *abhorrere* meaning 'to shudder at']

abide, abides, abiding, abided
1 (verb) If you can't abide something, you dislike it very much.
2 If you abide by a decision, agreement, or law, you accept it and act in accordance with it.
3 If something abides, it remains or continues to happen for a long time.
[from Old English *bidan* meaning 'to wait']

ability, abilities
(noun) Your ability to do something is the quality of intelligence or skill that you have that enables you to do it, e.g. *the ability to read.*

Similar words: capacity, facility, faculty, competence

abject
1 (adjective) very bad, e.g. *abject poverty.*
2 Someone who is abject has no self-respect.
abjectly (adverb).
[from Latin *abjectus* meaning 'thrown away']

ablaze
(adjective) on fire or in flames.

able, abler, ablest
1 (adjective) If you are able to do something, you can do it.
2 Someone who is able is very clever or talented.

Similar words: (sense 1) capable, fit
(sense 2) capable, competent

able-bodied
(adjective) physically fit and with no injuries or disabilities.

ablution, ablutions
(noun; a formal or humorous word) Your ablutions are the act of washing yourself.
[from Latin *abluere* meaning 'to wash away']

ably (pronounced **ay**-blee)
(adverb) skilfully and successfully, e.g. *She was ably assisted by her husband.*

abnormal
(adjective) not normal or usual, e.g. *Not all abnormal skin growths are signs of cancer.*
abnormally (adverb).

abnormality, abnormalities
(noun) An abnormality is something that is not normal or usual.

Similar words: aberration, irregularity, deviation

aboard
(preposition and adverb) on a ship or plane.

abode, abodes
(noun; an old-fashioned word) Your abode is your home.
[originally meaning 'the place where someone abides']

abolish, abolishes, abolishing, abolished
(verb) To abolish something means to put an end to it officially.
abolition (noun).
[from Latin *abolere* meaning 'to destroy']

Similar words: do away with, repeal, revoke

abominable
(adjective) very unpleasant or shocking.
abominably (adverb).

abominate, abominates, abominating, abominated
(verb; a formal word) If you abominate something, you hate it very much.
[from Latin *abominare* meaning 'to regard as a bad omen']

abomination, abominations
(noun) An abomination is a thing, person, or action that is shockingly unpleasant.

Aborigine, Aborigines (pronounced ab-or-**rij**-in-ee)
(noun) An Aborigine is someone descended from the people who lived in Australia before Europeans arrived.
Aboriginal (adjective).
[borrowed from *aborigines*, the Latin word for the pre-Roman inhabitants of Italy]

abort, aborts, aborting, aborted
1 (verb) If a pregnant woman aborts, the pregnancy ends too soon and the baby dies.
2 If a plan or activity is aborted, it is stopped before it is finished.
abortion (noun).
[from Latin *aboriri* meaning 'to miscarry']

abortive
(adjective) unsuccessful, e.g. *an abortive attempt.*

abound, abounds, abounding, abounded
(verb) If things abound, there are very large numbers of them.
[from Latin *abundare* meaning 'to overflow']

about
1 (preposition and adverb) of or concerning.
2 present or in a place, e.g. *Is John about?*
3 approximately and not exactly.
4 (adverb) in different directions, e.g. *He was waving his arms about.*
5 (phrase) If you are **about to** do something, you are just going to do it.

about-turn, about-turns
(noun) If you do an about-turn, you completely change your attitude or opinion.

above
1 (preposition and adverb) directly over or higher than something, e.g. *above the trees.*
2 greater than a level or amount, e.g. *The temperature never rises above 10°C.*

above board
(adjective) completely open, honest, and legal, e.g. *Was the deal above board?*
[an allusion to the difficulty of cheating at cards with your hands above the table]

abrasion, abrasions
(noun) An abrasion is an area where your skin has been broken or scraped.

abrasive
1 (adjective) An abrasive substance is rough and can be used to clean hard surfaces.
2 Someone who is abrasive is unpleasant and rude, e.g. *an abrasive manner.*
[from Latin *abradare* meaning 'to scrape away']

abreast
(adjective after noun) If people or things are abreast, they are side by side, e.g. *We marched four abreast.*

abridge, abridges, abridging, abridged
(verb) To abridge something such as a piece of writing means to make it shorter.
abridgement (noun).

abroad
(adverb) in a foreign country.

abrupt
1 (adjective) sudden, quick, and unexpected, e.g. *The interview came to an abrupt end.*
2 rude, unfriendly, and impolite.
abruptly (adverb), **abruptness** (noun).
[from Latin *abruptus* meaning 'broken off']

abscess, abscesses (pronounced **ab**-sess)
(noun) An abscess is a painful swelling that contains pus.

abscond, absconds, absconding, absconded
(verb; a formal word) If you abscond, you leave suddenly and secretly after doing something wrong.
[from Latin *abscondere* meaning 'to hide away']

abseil, abseils, abseiling, abseiled
(verb) If you abseil down a cliff or mountain, you go down it by sliding down a rope.
[from German *ab* meaning 'down' and *Seil* meaning 'rope']

absent, absents, absenting, absented
1 (adjective) Something that is absent is not present in a place or situation.
2 (verb; a formal use) If you absent yourself, you keep away from a place.
absence (noun).

Similar words: (sense 1) away, elsewhere

absentee, absentees
(noun) An absentee is someone who is not present in a place when they should be present.

absently
(adverb) If you do something absently, you are not paying attention and are thinking about something else.

absent-minded
(adjective) rather vague and forgetful.
absent-mindedly (adverb), **absent-mindedness** (noun).

absolute
1 (adjective) total and complete, e.g. *absolute secrecy.*
2 having complete and unlimited power and authority, e.g. *an absolute ruler.*
3 Absolute rules and principles are believed to be true and valid in all situations.
absolutely (adverb).
[from Latin *absolutus* meaning 'freed']

absolute zero
(noun) Absolute zero is the lowest temperature possible, and is equal to 0 kelvins, or -273.15° centigrade.

absolution
(noun; a formal word) In Christianity, absolution is formal forgiveness for sins.

absolve, absolves, absolving, absolved
(verb) To absolve someone of something means to state officially that they are not guilty of it or not to blame for it.
[from Latin *absolvere* meaning 'to free']

absorb, absorbs, absorbing, absorbed
1 (verb) If something absorbs liquid or gas, it soaks it up.
2 To absorb a shock, change, or effect means to deal with it or cope with it.
[from Latin *absorbere* meaning 'to suck']

Similar words: (sense 1) digest, assimilate, take in

absorbed
(adjective) If you are absorbed in something, it gets all your attention.

absorbent
(adjective) Absorbent materials soak up liquid easily.

absorption
1 (noun) An absorption is a great interest in something, e.g. *an absorption with politics.*
2 Absorption is the soaking up of a liquid.

abstain, abstains, abstaining, abstained
1 (verb) If you abstain from something, you do not do it or have it, e.g. *to abstain from alcohol.*
2 If you abstain in a vote, you do not vote.
abstainer (noun), **abstention** (noun).

abstemious
(adjective) Someone who is abstemious does not eat or drink too much.

abstinence
(noun) Abstinence is deliberately not doing something that you enjoy.

abstract, abstracts, abstracting, abstracted
1 (adjective) based on thoughts and ideas rather than physical objects or events.
2 Abstract art is a style of art which uses shapes rather than representing people or objects.
3 Abstract nouns refer to qualities or ideas rather than to physical objects.
4 (verb) If you abstract information from a piece of writing, you summarize the main points.
abstraction (noun).
[from Latin *abstractus* meaning 'removed']

abstracted
(adjective) rather vague and not paying attention, usually because you are thinking.

abstruse
(adjective; a formal word) difficult to understand, e.g. *an abstruse legal argument.*
[from Latin *abstrusus* meaning 'concealed']

absurd
(adjective) ridiculous and stupid.
absurdly (adverb), **absurdity** (noun).

Similar words: ludicrous, preposterous, ridiculous

abundance
(noun) Something that exists in abundance exists in large numbers, e.g. *an abundance of fish.*
abundant (adjective), **abundantly** (adverb).

Similar words: profusion, proliferation, plenty, wealth

abuse, abuses, abusing, abused
1 (noun) Abuse is insults and rude words directed towards someone.
2 The abuse of something is the wrong use of it, e.g. *the abuse of power... drug abuse.*
3 (verb) If you abuse someone, you speak insultingly to them.
4 To abuse someone also means to treat them cruelly and violently.
5 If you abuse something, you use it wrongly or for a bad purpose, e.g. *People in power should not abuse their privileges.*

Similar words: (sense 2) misuse, ill-treatment, maltreatment, harm
(sense 4) ill-treat, maltreat, misuse

abusive
(adjective) rude, offensive, and unkind.
abusively (adverb), **abusiveness** (noun).

abut, abuts, abutting, abutted
(verb) If land or a building abuts on something, it is next to it, e.g. *an enormous garden which abuts onto the graveyard.*
[from Old French *abouter* meaning 'to join at the ends']

abysmal (pronounced ab-**biz**-ml)
(adjective) very bad indeed, e.g. *abysmal wages.*
abysmally (adverb).

abyss, abysses
(noun) An abyss is a very deep hole.
[from Greek *abussos* meaning 'bottomless']

Similar words: gulf, void, chasm, pit

acacia, acacias (pronounced a-**kay**-sha)
(noun) An acacia is a type of thorny shrub.

academic, academics
1 (adjective) Academic work is work done in a school, college, or university.
2 (noun) An academic is someone who teaches or does research in a college or university.
academically (adverb).

academy, academies
1 (noun) An academy is a school or college, usually one that specializes in one particular subject, e.g. *the Royal Academy of Music.*
2 An academy is also a society of scientists, artists, writers, or musicians. e.g. *the Royal Academy.*
[from Greek *akadēmeia*, the name of the grove where Plato taught]

accede, accedes, acceding, acceded (pronounced ak-**seed**)
(verb; a formal word) If you accede to something, you agree to it, e.g. *She was prepared to accede to his wishes.*

accelerate, accelerates, accelerating, accelerated
(verb) To accelerate means to go faster.

acceleration, accelerations
(noun) Acceleration is the rate at which the speed of something is increasing.

accelerator, accelerators
(noun) The accelerator in a vehicle is the pedal which you press to make it go faster.

accent, accents
1 (noun) An accent is a way of pronouncing a language, e.g. *She has a Scottish accent.*
2 An accent is also a mark placed above or below a letter in some languages, which affects the way the letter is pronounced.
3 An accent on something is an emphasis on it, e.g. *This season's accent is on glamour.*

accentuate, accentuates, accentuating, accentuated
(verb) To accentuate a feature of something means to make it more noticeable.
accentuation (noun).

accept, accepts, accepting, accepted
1 (verb) If you accept something, you say yes to it or take it from someone.

2 If you accept a situation, you realize that it cannot be changed, e.g. *The astronaut accepts danger as part of his job.*
3 If you accept a statement or story, you believe that it is true, e.g. *I do not accept that there has been any racial discrimination in this school.*
4 If a group accepts you, they treat you as one of the group.
acceptance (noun), **acceptable** (adjective), **acceptably** (adverb), **acceptability** (noun).
[from Latin *ad* meaning 'to' and *capere* meaning 'to take']

access
(noun) Access is the right or opportunity to use something or to enter a place.
[from Latin *accessus* meaning 'an approach']

accessible
1 (adjective) easily reached or seen, e.g. *The cave was accessible only at low tide.*
2 easily understood and used, e.g. *to make computers more accessible to ordinary people.*
accessibility (noun).

accession
(noun) A ruler's accession is the time when he or she becomes the ruler of a country.

accessory, accessories
1 (noun) An accessory is an extra part.
2 An accessory to a crime is someone who helps another person commit the crime.

accident, accidents
1 (noun) An accident is an event in which people are injured or killed.
2 Something that happens by accident happens by chance.
[from Latin *accidere* meaning 'to happen']

accidental
(adjective) happening by chance.
accidentally (adverb).

Similar words: inadvertent, unplanned, unintentional

acclaim, acclaims, acclaiming, acclaimed (a formal word)
1 (verb) To acclaim someone or something means to praise them a lot, e.g. *The speech was acclaimed by everyone present.*
2 (noun) Acclaim is great praise.
[from Latin *acclamare* meaning 'to shout applause']

acclamation
(noun) Acclamation is noisy and enthusiastic approval, for example clapping and cheering.

acclimatize, acclimatizes, acclimatizing, acclimatized; also spelled acclimatise
(verb) To acclimatize to something such as a foreign climate means to become used to it.
acclimatization (noun).

accolade, accolades
(noun; a formal word) An accolade is great praise or an award that is given to someone.

accommodate, accommodates, accommodating, accommodated
1 (verb) If you accommodate someone, you provide them with a place to sleep, live, or work.

2 If a place can accommodate a number of things or people, it has enough room for them.
[from Latin *accomodare* meaning 'to make something fit in']

accommodating
(adjective) willing to help and to adjust to new situations.

accommodation
(noun) Accommodation is a place provided for someone to sleep, work, or live in.

Similar words: board, lodging, lodgings, housing

accompaniment, accompaniments
1 (noun) The accompaniment to a song or tune is the music that is played to go with it.
2 An accompaniment to something is another thing that comes with it, e.g. *This sauce can be served as an accompaniment to fish.*

accompanist, accompanists
(noun) An accompanist is a pianist who accompanies a singer or musician.

accompany, accompanies, accompanying, accompanied
1 (verb) If you accompany someone, you go with them.
2 If one thing accompanies another, the two things exist at the same time, e.g. *High inflation was accompanied by economic decline.*
3 If you accompany a singer or musician, you play the piano or another instrument while they sing or play the main tune.
[from Old French *compaing* meaning 'companion']

accomplice, accomplices
(noun) An accomplice is a person who helps someone else to commit a crime.
[from *complice*, an old word meaning 'associate']

Similar words: partner, henchman, accessory

accomplish, accomplishes, accomplishing, accomplished
(verb) If you accomplish something, you succeed in doing it.
[from Latin *complere* meaning 'to fill up']

accomplished
(adjective) very talented at something, e.g. *She is an accomplished musician.*

accomplishment, accomplishments
1 (noun) Someone's accomplishments are the skills that they have acquired.
2 The accomplishment of something is the finishing of it.

accord, accords, according, accorded
1 (verb) If you accord someone or something a particular treatment, you treat them in that way, e.g. *The speech was accorded a standing ovation.*
2 (a formal use) If one thing accords with another, the two things are consistent with each other, e.g. *a description of Steve that didn't accord with my own view of him.*
3 (noun) Accord is agreement.
4 (phrase) If you do something **of your own**

accord, you do it willingly and not because you have been forced to do it.

accordance
(phrase) If you act **in accordance with** a rule or belief, you act in the way that the rule or belief says you should.

accordingly
(adverb) in a way that is appropriate for the circumstances, e.g. *The street had changed its character, and the shops had changed accordingly.*

according to
1 (preposition) If something is true according to a particular person, that person says that it is true.
2 If something is done according to a principle or plan, that principle or plan is used as the basis for it.

accordion, accordions
(noun) An accordion is a musical instrument shaped like an expanding box. It is played by squeezing the two sides together while pressing the keys on it.

accost, accosts, accosting, accosted
(verb) If someone accosts you, especially someone you do not know, they come up and speak to you.
[from Latin *costa* meaning 'side']

account, accounts, accounting, accounted
1 (noun) An account is a written or spoken report of something.
2 (plural noun) Accounts are records of money spent and received by a person or business.
3 (noun) If you have a bank account, you can leave money in the bank and take it out when you need it.
4 (phrase) If you **take something into account**, you include it in your planning.
5 **On account of** means because of.
6 If something must **on no account** be done, it must not be done under any circumstances.
7 If something is **of no account**, it does not matter.
8 (verb) To account for something means to explain it, e.g. *If she wasn't feeling well, that might account for her strange mood.*
9 If something accounts for a particular amount of something, it is that amount, e.g. *Tea accounted for three fifths of Sri Lanka's exports.*
[from Old French *conter* meaning 'to count']

accountable
(adjective) If you are accountable for something, you are responsible for it and have to explain your actions, e.g. *a public corporation that is fully accountable to Parliament.*
accountability (noun).

accountancy
(noun) Accountancy is the job of keeping or inspecting financial accounts.

accountant, accountants
(noun) An accountant is a person whose job is to keep or inspect financial accounts.

accounting
(noun) Accounting is the process of keeping and checking financial accounts.

accoutrements (pronounced a-**koo**-tre-ments)
(plural noun; a formal word) Accoutrements are the things that someone has with them when they travel or take part in an activity.
[from Old French *accoustrer* meaning 'to clothe']

accredited
(adjective) officially appointed or recognized, e.g. *an accredited representative.*

accretion, accretions
(noun; a formal word) An accretion of something is a gradual increase in the amount of it.

accrue, accrues, accruing, accrued
(verb) If money or interest accrues, it increases or accumulates gradually.

accumulate, accumulates, accumulating, accumulated
(verb) If you accumulate things, you gather or collect them over a period of time. When things accumulate, they come together in one place. **accumulation** (noun), **accumulative** (adjective).
[from Latin *cumulus* meaning 'heap']

accurate
(adjective) completely true, correct, or precise. **accurately** (adverb), **accuracy** (noun).
[from Latin *accurare* meaning 'to perform carefully']

Similar words: exact, precise, correct, true

accursed
(adjective; a formal word) under a curse.

accusative
(noun and adjective) In the grammar of some languages, the accusative is the form of a noun when it is the direct object of a verb.

accuse, accuses, accusing, accused
(verb) If you accuse someone of doing something wrong, you say that they have done it. **accusation** (noun), **accuser** (noun).
[from Latin *causa* meaning 'lawsuit']

accustom, accustoms, accustoming, accustomed
(verb) If you accustom yourself to something new or different, you get used to it.

Similar words: acclimatize, condition, familiarize

ace, aces
1 (noun) In a pack of cards, an ace is a card with a single symbol on it.
2 (adjective; an informal use) good or skilful, e.g. *an ace marksman.*
3 (noun) In tennis, an ace is a serve that is so good that the other player cannot return the ball.
[from Latin *as* meaning 'a unit']

acerbic (pronounced as-**ser**-bik)
(adjective; a formal word) Acerbic remarks are harsh, bitter, and unpleasant.
[from Latin *acerbus* meaning 'sour' or 'bitter']

acetic acid (pronounced as-**seet**-ik **ass**-id)
(noun) Acetic acid is a clear colourless acid. It is the main ingredient in vinegar.
[from Latin *acetum* meaning 'vinegar']

acetylene (pronounced as-**set**-til-een)
(noun) Acetylene is a colourless gas that burns with a very hot flame. Acetylene is often used for cutting and welding metals.

ache, aches, aching, ached
1 (verb) If you ache, you feel a continuous dull pain in a part of your body.
2 If you are aching for something or aching to do something, you want it very much.
3 (noun) An ache is a continuous dull pain.

achieve, achieves, achieving, achieved
(verb) If you achieve something, you successfully do it or cause it to happen.
[from Old French *achever* meaning 'to bring to a conclusion']

Similar words: accomplish, attain, realize, fulfil

achievement, achievements
(noun) An achievement is something which you succeed in doing, especially after a lot of effort.

Achilles heel (pronounced ak-**kil**-eez heel)
(noun) Someone's Achilles heel is the weakest point in their character. In Greek mythology, the hero Achilles was dipped by his mother in the river Styx as a baby in order to make him invulnerable. His only weak point was the heel that she held him by.

Achilles tendon, Achilles tendons
(noun) The Achilles tendon is the tendon that connects the heel to the calf muscles in your leg.

acid, acids
1 (noun) An acid is a substance with a pH value of less than 7. There are many different acids; some are used in chemical processes and others in household substances.
2 (adjective) Acid tastes are sharp or sour.
3 Acid comments are unkind and critical.
4 (phrase) Something that is an **acid test** is used as a way of testing whether something is true or not, or whether it is of good quality or not.
5 (noun; an informal use) Acid also means the drug LSD.
acidly (adverb), **acidic** (adjective), **acidity** (noun).
[from Latin *acidus* meaning 'sour']

acid rain
(noun) Acid rain is rain polluted by acid in the atmosphere which has come from factories.

acknowledge, acknowledges, acknowledging, acknowledged
1 (verb) If you acknowledge a fact or situation, you agree or admit that it is true.
2 If you acknowledge someone, you show that you have seen and recognized them.
3 If you acknowledge a message or letter, you tell the person who sent it that you have received it.
acknowledgment or **acknowledgement** (noun).

Similar words: (sense 1) accept, admit, grant

acme (pronounced **ak**-mee)
(noun; a formal word) The acme of something is the highest point of its achievement.
[from Greek *akme* meaning 'point']

acne (pronounced **ak**-nee)
(noun) Acne consists of painful, lumpy spots that cover someone's face.
[from Greek *akme* meaning 'point' or 'spot']

acolyte, acolytes (pronounced **ak**-o-lite)
(a formal word)
1 (noun) An acolyte is someone who assists a priest in a religious ceremony.
2 An acolyte is also a follower of an important person.
[from Greek *acolouthos* meaning 'follower']

acorn, acorns
(noun) An acorn is the fruit of the oak tree, consisting of a pale oval nut in a cup-shaped base.

acoustic (pronounced a-**koo**-stik)
1 (adjective) relating to sound or hearing.
2 An acoustic guitar does not have its sound amplified electronically.

acoustics
(noun) The acoustics of a room are its structural features which determine how clearly you can hear sounds made in it.
[from Greek *akouein* meaning 'to hear']

acquaint, acquaints, acquainting, acquainted
1 (verb) If you acquaint someone with something, you tell them about it.
2 If you are acquainted with someone, you know them slightly but not well.
[from Latin *accognoscere* meaning 'to know perfectly']

acquaintance, acquaintances
(noun) An acquaintance is someone you know slightly but not well.

acquiesce, acquiesces, acquiescing, acquiesced
(pronounced ak-**wee**-ess)
(verb; a formal word) If you acquiesce in someone's plan or suggestion, you agree to it.
acquiescent (adjective), **acquiescence** (noun).
[from Latin *quiescere* meaning 'to be quiet']

acquire, acquires, acquiring, acquired
1 (verb) If you acquire something, you obtain it.
2 (phrase) If something is an **acquired taste** for you, you learn to like it after some time.
[from Latin *quaerere* meaning 'to seek' or 'to get']

acquisition, acquisitions
(noun) An acquisition is something that you have obtained.

acquisitive
(adjective) keen on acquiring new possessions.

acquit, acquits, acquitting, acquitted
1 (verb) If someone is acquitted of a crime, they have been tried in a court and found not guilty.
2 If you acquit yourself well on a particular occasion, you behave or perform well.
acquittal (noun).

Similar words: (sense 1) clear, exonerate, absolve

acre, acres
(noun) An acre is a unit for measuring areas of land. One acre is equal to 4840 square yards or about 4047 square metres.
[from Old English *æcer* meaning 'field']

acreage (pronounced **ay**-ker-rij)
(noun) The acreage of a piece of land is the area of it measured in acres.

acrid
(adjective) sharp and bitter, e.g. *the acrid smell of burnt wood.*

acrimony (pronounced **ak**-rim-on-ee)
(noun; a formal word) Acrimony is bitterness and anger.
acrimonious (adjective).

acrobat, acrobats
(noun) An acrobat is an entertainer who performs gymnastic tricks.
acrobatic (adjective), **acrobatics** (plural noun).
[from Greek *akrobates* meaning 'someone who walks on tiptoe']

acronym, acronyms
(noun) An acronym is a word made up of the initial letters of a phrase. An example of an acronym is OPEC, which stands for 'Organization of Petroleum Exporting Countries'.

across
1 (preposition and adverb) going from one side of something to the other.
2 on the other side of a road or river.

acrylic (pronounced a-**kril**-lik)
(noun) Acrylic is a type of man-made cloth.

act, acts, acting, acted
1 (verb) If you act, you do something, e.g. *We have to act quickly.*
2 If you act in a particular way, you behave in that way.
3 If one thing acts on another, it has an effect on the second thing.
4 If one thing acts as something else, it has the function or does the job of the second thing, e.g. *We hired a student to act as our interpreter.*
5 If you act in a play or film, you play a part.
6 (noun) An act is a single thing that someone does, e.g. *an act of violence.*
7 An Act of Parliament is a law passed by the government.
8 In a play, ballet, or opera, an act is one of the main parts that it is divided into.
9 In a television or stage show, an act is one of the separate short performances in it by different performers.
[from Latin *actum* meaning 'something done']

Similar words: (sense 5) perform, enact, play
(sense 6) action, deed
(sense 7) bill, law, statute, decree, legislation

acting
1 (noun) Acting is the profession of performing in plays or films.
2 (adjective) Acting is used before the title of a job to show that someone is doing that job temporarily, e.g. *the acting head of Department.*

Similar words: (sense 2) temporary, provisional

actinide, actinides
(noun) An actinide is any element in the actinide series.

actinide series
(noun) The actinide series is a class of 15 radioactive elements whose atomic numbers range from 89 to 103.

action, actions
1 (noun) An action is something you do for a particular purpose, e.g. *The government took action to stop the strike.*
2 An action is also a physical movement.
3 In law, an action is a legal proceeding, e.g. *a libel action.*
4 Action is fighting in a war or battle, e.g. *He was killed in action.*

activate, activates, activating, activated
(verb) To activate something means to cause it to start working.

Similar words: actuate, set in motion, trigger

active
1 (adjective) Active people are full of energy and are always busy doing things.
2 happening now and energetically, e.g. *The project is under active discussion.*
3 In grammar, a verb in the active voice is one where the subject does the action, rather than having it done to them. Compare **passive**.
actively (adverb).

activist, activists
(noun) A political activist is a person who tries to bring about political and social change.

activity, activities
1 (noun) Activity is a situation in which a lot of things are happening at the same time.
2 An activity is something that you do for pleasure, e.g. *outdoor activities and hobbies.*
3 The activities of a group or organization are the things that they do to achieve their aims.

Act of God, Acts of God
(noun) In insurance law, an Act of God is a natural event that causes damage, such as an earthquake, for which nobody can be held responsible.

actor, actors
(noun) An actor is a man or woman whose profession is acting in plays, television, or films.

Similar words: actress, player

actress, actresses
(noun) An actress is a woman whose profession is acting.

actual
(adjective) real or genuine, and not imaginary.
actually (adverb).

actuary, actuaries
(noun) An actuary is a person whose job is to calculate insurance risks.
[from Latin *actuarius* meaning 'shorthand writer']

actuate, actuates, actuating, actuated
(verb) To actuate something means to cause it to start.

acumen
(noun) Acumen is the ability to make good decisions quickly, e.g. *good business acumen.*
[from Latin *acuere* meaning 'to sharpen']

acupuncture
(noun) Acupuncture is the treatment of illness or pain by sticking small needles into specific places in a person's body. It originates from China.
[from Latin *acus* meaning 'needle' added to 'puncture']

acute
1 (adjective) severe or intense, e.g. *acute pain.*
2 very bright and intelligent, e.g. *an acute mind.*
3 An acute angle is less than 90°.
4 In French and some other languages, an acute accent is an upward-sloping line placed over a vowel to indicate a change in pronunciation, as in the word *blasé.*

ad, ads
(noun; an informal word) An ad is an advertisement.

AD
You use AD in dates to indicate the number of years after the birth of Jesus Christ.
[from Latin *anno Domini* meaning 'in the year of our Lord']

adage, adages (pronounced ad-dij)
(noun) An adage is a saying or proverb that expresses some general truth about life.

adagio (pronounced ad-ah-jee-oh)
In music, adagio is an instruction to play or sing something slowly.
[an Italian word]

adamant
(adjective) If you are adamant, you are determined not to change your mind.
adamantly (adverb).
[from Latin *adamas* meaning 'diamond']

Adam's apple, Adam's apples
(noun) The Adam's apple is the larynx, a lump that sticks out at the front of the neck.
[from the story that a piece of the forbidden apple got stuck in Adam's throat]

adapt, adapts, adapting, adapted
1 (verb) If you adapt to a new situation, you change so that you can deal with it successfully.
2 If you adapt something, you change it so that it is suitable for a new purpose or situation.
adaptable (adjective), **adaptation** (noun).

adaptor, adaptors; also spelled adapter
(noun) An adaptor is a type of electric plug which can be used to connect two or more plugs to one socket.

add, adds, adding, added
1 (verb) If you add something to a number of things, you put it with the things.
2 If you add numbers together or add them up, you calculate the total.

adder, adders
(noun) An adder is a small poisonous snake with

a black zigzag pattern on its back. Adders are the only poisonous snakes in Britain.
[from Middle English *a naddre*]

addict, addicts
(noun) An addict is someone who cannot stop taking harmful drugs.
addicted (adjective), **addiction** (noun).
[from Latin *addicere* meaning 'to agree to']

addictive
(adjective) If a drug is addictive, the people who take it find that they cannot stop taking it.

addition, additions
1 (noun) An addition is something that has been added to something else, e.g. *The last addition to the house was in the early 18th century.*
2 Addition is the process of adding numbers together.

Similar words: (sense 1) adjunct, postscript

additional
(adjective) extra or more, e.g. *An additional problem is that he is blind.*
additionally (adverb).

additive, additives
(noun) Additives are things that are added to something, usually in order to improve it.

address, addresses, addressing, addressed
1 (noun) Your address is the number of the house where you live, together with the name of the street and the town or village.
2 (verb) If a letter is addressed to you, it has your name and address written on it.
3 (noun) An address is also a speech given to a group of people.
4 (verb) If you address a problem or task, you start to deal with it.

adenoids
(plural noun) Your adenoids are the soft lumpy tissue at the back of your throat.

adept
(adjective) very skilful or clever at doing something, e.g. *Chimpanzees are adept climbers.*

adequate
(adjective) enough in amount or good enough for a purpose, e.g. *an adequate answer.*
adequately (adverb), **adequacy** (noun).
[from Latin *adaequare* meaning 'to make equal']

Similar words: sufficient, satisfactory, enough

adhere, adheres, adhering, adhered
1 (verb) If one thing adheres to another, it sticks firmly to it.
2 If you adhere to a rule or agreement, you do exactly what it says.
3 If you adhere to an opinion or belief, you firmly hold that opinion or belief.
adherence (noun).

adherent, adherents
(noun) An adherent of a particular belief is someone who holds that belief.

adhesion
(noun) The adhesion of one thing to another is the fact that it is sticking to it.

adhesive, adhesives
1 (noun) Adhesive is any substance that is used to stick two things together, for example glue.
2 (adjective) Adhesive substances are sticky and able to stick to things.

ad hoc
(adjective and adverb) An ad hoc arrangement is made only when it becomes necessary, rather than in advance, e.g. *Emergency teams were reinforced by ad hoc groups of local citizens.*
[a Latin expression meaning 'to this']

adieu, adieux or adieus (pronounced ad-yoo)
(noun and exclamation; an old-fashioned word) Adieu means goodbye.
[from Old French *à Dieu* meaning 'to God']

ad infinitum (pronounced add in-fin-nite-um)
(adverb) If something is done ad infinitum, it is done again and again, e.g. *Your father heard it from his father, and so on ad infinitum.*
[two Latin words meaning 'to infinity']

adjacent (pronounced ad-jay-sent)
(adjective; a formal word) If two things are adjacent, they are next to each other, e.g. *She sat on a chair adjacent to mine.*

adjective, adjectives
(noun) An adjective is a word that adds to the description given by a noun. For example, in 'They live in a large white Georgian house', 'large', 'white', and 'Georgian' are all adjectives.
adjectival (adjective).
[from Latin *adjicere* meaning 'to throw to']

adjoin, adjoins, adjoining, adjoined
(verb) If one room adjoins another, they are next to each other and are connected.

adjourn, adjourns, adjourning, adjourned
1 (verb) If a meeting or trial is adjourned, it stops for a time, e.g. *The trial was adjourned until the next morning.*
2 If people adjourn to another place, they go there together after a meeting, e.g. *We adjourned to the pub.*
adjournment (noun).
[from Old French *à* meaning 'to' and *jour* meaning 'day']

adjudge, adjudges, adjudging, adjudged
(verb; a formal word) To adjudge someone means to make a particular judgment about them, e.g. *He was adjudged guilty.*

adjudicate, adjudicates, adjudicating, adjudicated
(verb; a formal word) To adjudicate on a question or dispute means to make an official decision about it.
adjudication (noun), **adjudicator** (noun).
[from Latin *judicare* meaning 'to act as judge']

adjunct, adjuncts
1 (noun) An adjunct is something that is added or attached to something else.
2 In grammar, an adjunct is one of the main elements of a clause, expressing ideas of time, place, manner, or possibility. In the clause 'The children sang beautifully this morning', 'beautifully' and 'this morning' are both adjuncts.

adjust, adjusts, adjusting, adjusted
1 (verb) If you adjust something, you slightly change its position or alter it in some other way.
2 If you adjust to a new situation, you get used to it, often by slightly changing your attitude.
adjustable (adjective), **adjustment** (noun).

adjutant, adjutants (pronounced add-jew-tnt)
(noun) An adjutant is an army officer who deals with administrative work.
[from Latin *adjutare* meaning 'to help']

ad-lib, ad-libs, ad-libbing, ad-libbed
1 (verb) If you ad-lib, you say something that has not been prepared beforehand, e.g. *He had lost his script, so he had to ad-lib.*
2 (noun) An ad-lib is a comment that has not been prepared beforehand.
[short for Latin *ad libitum* meaning 'according to desire']

administer, administers, administering, administered
1 (verb) To administer an organization means to be responsible for managing it.
2 To administer the law or administer justice means to put it into practice and apply it.
3 If medicine or a punishment is administered to someone, it is given to them.

administration, administrations
1 (noun) Administration is the work of organizing and supervising an organization.
2 Administration is also the process of administering something, e.g. *the administration of justice.*
3 The administration is the group of people that manages an organization or a country.
administrative (adjective), **administrator** (noun).

admirable
(adjective) very good and deserving to be admired.
admirably (adverb).

admiral, admirals
1 (noun) An admiral is the commander of a navy.
2 Admiral is also the highest naval rank.
[from Arabic *amir* meaning 'commander']

Admiralty
(noun) The Admiralty is the government department in charge of the Navy.

admire, admires, admiring, admired
(verb) If you admire someone or something, you like, respect, and approve of them.
admiration (noun), **admirer** (noun), **admiring** (adjective), **admiringly** (adverb).
[from Latin *admirari* meaning 'to wonder at']

admissible
(adjective; a formal word) allowed to be used, e.g. *This evidence was not admissible.*

admission, admissions
1 (noun) If you are allowed admission to a place, you are allowed to go in.
2 If you make an admission of something bad such as guilt or laziness, you agree, often reluctantly, that it is true.

admit, admits, admitting, admitted
1 (verb) If you admit something, you agree, often reluctantly, that it is true.
2 To admit someone or something to a place means to allow them to enter it.
3 If you are admitted to hospital, you are taken there to stay there until you are better.
4 If you admit someone to an organization, you allow them to join it.
[from Latin *ad* meaning 'to' and *mittere* meaning 'to send']

admittance
(noun) Admittance is the right to enter a place.

admittedly
(adverb) People use 'admittedly' to show that what they are saying contrasts with something they have already said, and weakens their argument, e.g. *He chose to marry a poor, though admittedly pretty, girl.*

admonish, admonishes, admonishing, admonished
(verb; a formal word) If you admonish someone, you tell them off very sternly.
[from Latin *monere* meaning 'to advise']

ad nauseam (pronounced ad naw-zee-am)
(adverb) If something happens ad nauseam, it happens again and again so that it becomes very boring or very annoying.
[two Latin words meaning 'to sickness']

ado
(phrase) If you do something **without further ado**, you do it at once without delaying any longer.

adolescent, adolescents
(noun) An adolescent is a young person who is no longer a child but who is not yet an adult.
adolescence (noun).
[from Latin *adolescere* meaning 'to grow up']

adopt, adopts, adopting, adopted
1 (verb) If you adopt a child that is not your own, you take him or her into your family as your son or daughter.
2 (a formal use) If you adopt a particular attitude, you start to have it, e.g. *I adopted a dignified attitude to show my displeasure.*
adoption (noun).
[from Latin *adoptare* meaning 'to choose for oneself']

adorable
(adjective) sweet, pretty, and attractive.

adore, adores, adoring, adored
(verb) If you adore someone, you feel deep love and admiration for them.
adoration (noun).
[from Latin *adorare* meaning 'to pray to']

adorn, adorns, adorning, adorned
(verb) To adorn someone or something means to decorate them or make them beautiful, e.g. *The desk was adorned with a vase of fresh flowers.*
adornment (noun).

adrenal gland, adrenal glands (pronounced a-dree-nal gland)
(noun) Your adrenal glands are the two glands situated at the top of your kidneys, which secrete various hormones, including adrenalin.

adrenalin or **adrenaline** (pronounced
a-**dren**-al-in)
(noun) Adrenalin is a hormone which is
produced by your body when you are angry,
nervous, or excited. Adrenalin makes your heart
beat faster, and gives you more energy.

adrift
1 (adjective and adverb) If a boat is adrift, it is
floating on the water without being controlled.
2 If a plan goes adrift, it goes wrong.

adroit (pronounced a-**droyt**)
(adjective) quick and skilful in actions and
behaviour, e.g. *She is an adroit negotiator.*
adroitly (adverb), **adroitness** (noun).
[from French *à droit* meaning 'rightly']

adulation (pronounced ad-yoo-**lay**-shn)
(noun) Adulation is excessive admiration and
praise for someone.
adulatory (adjective).
[from Latin *adulari* meaning 'to flatter']

adult, adults
(noun) An adult is a mature and fully developed
person or animal.
[from Latin *adolescere* meaning 'to grow up']

adulterate, adulterates, adulterating, adulterated
(verb) To adulterate something means to spoil it
by adding something inferior, e.g. *The wine was
adulterated with grape juice.*
adulteration (noun).
[from Latin *adulterare* meaning 'to corrupt']

adultery
(noun) Adultery is sexual intercourse between a
married person and someone who he or she is not
married to.
adulterer (noun), **adulterous** (adjective).

adulthood
(noun) Someone's adulthood is the time during
their life when they are an adult.

advance, advances, advancing, advanced
1 (verb) To advance means to move forward.
2 (noun) An advance is a forward movement,
especially by an army.
3 Advance in something is progress in it, e.g.
technological advance.
4 (verb) To advance a cause or interest means to
help it to be successful.
5 If you advance someone a sum of money, you
lend it to them.
6 (noun) An advance is also a sum of money that
is lent to someone.
7 To make advances to someone means to try to
start a sexual relationship with them.
8 (adjective) done or happening before an event,
e.g. *We had no advance warning.*
9 (phrase) If you do something **in advance**, you
do it before something else happens, e.g. *We
booked well in advance to get a good seat.*
advancement (noun).

Similar words: (sense 3) progress, development

advantage, advantages
1 (noun) An advantage is a benefit or something
that puts you in a better position.

2 In tennis, the umpire says 'Advantage' to
indicate the first point won after deuce.
3 (phrase) If you **take advantage of** someone, you
treat them unfairly for your own benefit.
4 If you **take advantage of** something, you make
use of it.

advantageous
(adjective) likely to be useful or to benefit you in
some way, e.g. *an advantageous marriage.*

advent
1 (noun) The advent of something is its start or
its coming into existence, e.g. *This process was
inconceivable before the advent of computers.*
2 Advent is the season just before Christmas in
the Christian calendar.
[from Latin *advenire* meaning 'to come']

adventure, adventures
(noun) An adventure is a series of events that
are unusual, exciting, and often dangerous.

adventurer, adventurers
(noun) An adventurer is someone who enjoys
doing dangerous and exciting things.

adventurous
(adjective) willing to take risks and do new and
exciting things.

adverb, adverbs
(noun) An adverb is a word that adds
information about a verb or a following adjective
or other adverb, for example saying how, when,
or where something is done. 'Slowly', 'now', and
'here' are all adverbs.
adverbial (adjective).
[from Latin *adverbium* meaning 'added word']

adversary, adversaries (ad-ver-sar-ee)
(noun) Your adversary is someone who is your
enemy or who opposes what you are doing.

adverse
(adjective) unfavourable to you or opposite to
what you want or need, e.g. *adverse weather.*
adversely (adverb).

adversity, adversities
(noun) Adversity is a time of danger or difficulty.

advert, adverts
(noun; an informal word) An advert is an
advertisement.

advertise, advertises, advertising, advertised
1 (verb) If you advertise something, you tell
people about it in a newspaper or poster, or on
TV.
2 To advertise means to make an announcement
in a newspaper or poster, or on TV.
advertiser (noun), **advertising** (noun).
[from Latin *advertere* meaning 'to turn one's
attention to']

Similar words: publicize, promote, push, plug

advertisement, advertisements (pronounced
ad-**ver**-tiz-ment)
(noun) An advertisement is an announcement
about something in a newspaper or poster, or on
TV, e.g. *an advertisement for a trainee chef.*

Similar words: advert, commercial, promotion, plug

advice

(noun) Advice is an opinion or suggestion from someone about what you should do.
[from Latin *ad visum* meaning 'according to one's view']

Similar words: guidance, counsel, instruction

advisable

(adjective) sensible and likely to achieve the result you want, e.g. *It is advisable to take out medical insurance.*
advisably (adverb), **advisability** (noun).

advise, advises, advising, advised

1 (verb) If you advise someone to do something, you tell them that you think they should do it.
2 (a formal use) If you advise someone of something, you inform them of it.
adviser (noun), **advisory** (adjective).

Similar words: (sense 1) recommend, counsel, guide

advocate, advocates, advocating, advocated

1 (verb) If you advocate a course of action or plan, you support it publicly.
2 (noun) An advocate of something is someone who supports it publicly.
3 (a formal use) An advocate is a lawyer who represents clients in court.
advocacy (noun).
[from Latin *advocatus* meaning 'legal witness']

aegis (pronounced **ee**-jiss)

(noun) If something is done under the aegis of a person or organization, it is done with their official support and backing, e.g. *The concert was held under the aegis of the school governors.*
[from Greek *aigis*, the protective shield of Zeus]

aerate, aerates, aerating, aerated (pronounced air-rate)

(verb) To aerate a liquid means to add air to it.
aeration (noun).

aerial, aerials (pronounced air-ee-al)

1 (adjective) Aerial means happening in the air or above the ground, e.g. *aerial photography.*
2 (noun) An aerial is a piece of wire for receiving television or radio signals.

aerobatics

(noun) Aerobatics are skilful movements by a small aeroplane, for example diving and making loops.
aerobatic (noun).

aerobics

(noun) Aerobics is a type of fast physical exercise, which increases the oxygen in your blood and strengthens your heart and lungs.
aerobic (adjective).

aerodrome, aerodromes

(noun) An aerodrome is a place where small aeroplanes can land and take off.

aerodynamic

(adjective) having a streamlined shape that moves easily through the air.

aerodynamics

(noun) Aerodynamics is the scientific study of the way air flows around moving objects.

aerofoil, aerofoils

(noun) An aerofoil is a flap on the wing or tail of an aeroplane, which is lifted or dropped to control the aeroplane when it is flying.

aerogram, aerograms; also spelled aerogramme

(noun) An aerogram is an air-mail letter that consists of a single sheet of very light paper.

aeronautics

(noun) Aeronautics is the science of designing and building aircraft.
aeronautical (adjective).

aeroplane, aeroplanes

(noun) An aeroplane is a vehicle with wings and engines that enable it to fly.

aerosol, aerosols

(noun) An aerosol is a small metal container in which liquid is kept under pressure so that it can be forced out as a spray.

aerospace

(adjective) involved in making and designing aeroplanes, rockets, and spacecraft.

aesthete or esthete (pronounced **eess**-theet)

(noun; a formal word) An aesthete is someone who appreciates beautiful things.

aesthetic or esthetic (pronounced eess-**thet**-ik)

(adjective; a formal word) relating to the appreciation of beauty or art.
aesthetically (adverb), **aesthetics** (noun).
[from Greek *aisthesthai* meaning 'to perceive']

afar

(adjective; a literary word) From afar means from a long way away.

affable

(adjective) pleasant and easy to talk to.
affably (adverb), **affability** (noun).
[from Latin *affabilis* meaning 'easy to talk to']

affair, affairs

1 (noun) An affair is an event or series of events, e.g. *The wedding was a quiet affair.*
2 (plural noun) Your affairs are your private and personal life, e.g. *Why had she meddled in his affairs?*
3 (noun) To have an affair means to have a secret sexual or romantic relationship, especially when one of the people is married.
[from Old French *à faire* meaning 'to do']

affect, affects, affecting, affected

1 (verb) If something affects you, it influences you or changes you in some way.
2 (a formal use) If you affect a particular way of behaving, you behave in that way, e.g. *She affected a lisp.*
[from Latin *afficere* meaning 'to act upon']

Similar words: (sense 1) influence, change

affectation, affectations

(noun) An affectation is behaviour that is not genuine but is put on to impress people.

affected

(adjective) rather artificial and not genuine, e.g. *a very affected and mannered actress.*

affecting
(adjective) very moving and making you feel sad, e.g. *a most affecting farewell scene.*

affection, affections
1 (noun) Affection is a feeling of love and fondness for someone.
2 (plural noun) Your affections are feelings of love that you have for someone.

affectionate
(adjective) full of love, care, and fondness for someone, e.g. *an affectionate parent.*
affectionately (adverb).

affidavit, affidavits (rhymes with gave it)
(noun) An affidavit is a formal written statement, made under oath, which may be used as evidence in a court of law.
[a Latin word meaning 'he has sworn']

affiliate, affiliates, affiliating, affiliated
1 (verb) If a group affiliates itself to another, larger group, it forms a close association with it, e.g. *Our union is affiliated to the Labour Party.*
2 (noun) An affiliate is an organization which has a close link with another, larger group.
affiliation (noun).
[from Latin *affiliare* meaning 'to adopt as a son']

affinity, affinities
(noun) An affinity is a close similarity or understanding between two things, groups, or people, e.g. *There are no political affinities between us.*
[from Latin *affinis* meaning 'related']

affirm, affirms, affirming, affirmed
(verb) If you affirm an idea or belief, you clearly indicate your support for it, e.g. *They affirm a policy of religious toleration.*
affirmation (noun).

affirmative
(adjective) An affirmative word or gesture is one that means yes.

affix, affixes, affixing, affixed
1 (verb; a formal use) To affix something somewhere means to stick or attach it there.
2 (noun) In grammar, an affix is a prefix or suffix added to a word.

afflict, afflicts, afflicting, afflicted
(verb) If pain, illness, or sorrow afflicts someone, it causes them to suffer, e.g. *He had been afflicted with blindness.*
affliction (noun).
[from Latin *affligere* meaning 'to knock against']

affluent
(adjective) having a lot of money and possessions.
affluence (noun).
[from Latin *affluere* meaning 'to flow towards']

afford, affords, affording, afforded
1 (verb) If you can afford to do something, you have enough money to do it.
2 If you afford the time or energy to do something, you find the time or energy to do it.
3 If you cannot afford something to happen, it would be harmful or embarrassing for you if it happened, e.g. *We can't afford another scandal.*

[from Old English *geforthian* meaning 'to further' or 'to promote']

afforestation
(noun) Afforestation is the planting of large numbers of trees to form forests.

affray
(noun; a formal word) An affray is a noisy and violent fight.

affront, affronts, affronting, affronted
1 (verb) If you are affronted by something, you are insulted and angered by it.
2 (noun) An affront is something that you feel is an insult, e.g. *Apartheid is an affront to humanity.*
[from Old French *afronter* meaning 'to strike in the face']

Afghan, Afghans (pronounced af-gan)
1 (adjective) belonging or relating to Afghanistan.
2 (noun) An Afghan is someone who comes from Afghanistan.

afield
(adverb) Far afield means a long way away, e.g. *tennis tournaments as far afield as Brazil.*

afloat
1 (adverb and adjective) floating on water.
2 successful and not likely to fail, e.g. *They kept the company afloat during the recession.*

afoot
(adjective and adverb) happening or being planned, especially secretly, e.g. *There are plans afoot to publish the diaries.*

afraid
1 (adjective) If you are afraid, you are very frightened.
2 If you are afraid that something might happen, you are worried that it might happen.
[from *affraied*, the past participle of *affray* meaning 'to frighten']

Similar words: (sense 1) fearful, frightened, scared

afresh
(adverb) again and in a new way, e.g. *to start afresh.*

Africa
(noun) Africa is the second largest continent. It is almost surrounded by sea, with the Atlantic on its west side, the Mediterranean to the north and the Indian Ocean and the Red Sea to the east.

African, Africans
1 (adjective) belonging or relating to Africa.
2 (noun) An African is someone, especially a black person, who comes from Africa.

Afrikaans (pronounced af-rik-ahns)
(noun) Afrikaans is a language spoken in South Africa. It is based on 17th-century Dutch.
[a Dutch word meaning 'African']

Afrikaner, Afrikaners
(noun) An Afrikaner is a white South African of Dutch descent.

afro, afros
(noun) An afro is a hairstyle in which hair is a great mass of very small curls.

aft
(adverb and adjective) towards the back of a ship or boat.

after
1 (preposition and adverb) later than a particular time, date, or event.
2 behind and following someone or something, e.g. *She ran after him.*
3 (preposition) searching for someone, e.g. *The police are after them.*
4 trying to get something for yourself, e.g. *He's after a promotion.*
5 If you are named after someone, you have been given the same name as them.
6 If you ask after someone, you ask how they are.

Similar words: (sense 1) afterwards, thereafter

afterbirth
(noun) The afterbirth is the placenta and other membranes that come out of a female's womb soon after she has given birth.

aftereffect, aftereffects
(noun) The aftereffects of a situation or event are the conditions that result from it, e.g. *They died from the aftereffects of radiation.*

afterlife
(noun) The afterlife is a life that some people believe begins when you die.

aftermath
(noun) The aftermath of a disaster is the situation that comes after it.
[from *after* + *math* meaning 'a second mowing'; originally referring to a second crop from the same field]

afternoon, afternoons
(noun) The afternoon is the part of the day between noon and about tea-time.

aftershave
(noun) Aftershave is a pleasant-smelling liquid that men put on their faces after shaving.

afterthought, afterthoughts
(noun) An afterthought is something that you do or say as an addition to something else that you have already done or said.

afterwards
(adverb) after an event, date, or time.

again
1 (adverb) happening one more time, e.g. *Try again in half an hour.*
2 returning to the same state or place as before, e.g. *His blister began to hurt him again.*
3 in addition to an amount that has already been mentioned, e.g. *I could eat twice as much again.*

Similar words: (sense 2) once more, afresh, anew

against
1 (preposition) touching and leaning on, e.g. *He leaned against a tree.*
2 in opposition to, e.g. *the Test match against Australia.*

3 in comparison with, e.g. *The pound is now at its lowest rate against the dollar.*
4 in order to prevent, e.g. *precautions against burglary.*

agar (pronounced **ay**-gahr)
(noun) Agar is a jelly-like substance made from seaweed. It is used for growing cultures in biological experiments.
[a Malay word]

agate
(noun) Agate is a semiprecious type of quartz.

age, ages, ageing, aged
1 (noun) The age of something or someone is the number of years that they have lived or existed.
2 (phrase) When you **come of age**, you become legally an adult.
3 (noun) Age is the quality of being old, e.g. *Age has great status in some cultures.*
4 (verb) To age means to grow old or to appear older.
5 (noun) An age is a particular period in history, e.g. *the Bronze Age.*
6 (plural noun; an informal use) Ages means a very long time, e.g. *I haven't seen you for ages.*

aged
1 (rhymes with **raged**) having a particular age, e.g. *women aged 60 and over.*
2 (pronounced **ay**-dgid) very old, e.g. *his aged aunt.*

agency, agencies
(noun) An agency is an organization or business which provides certain services on behalf of other businesses, e.g. *an advertising agency.*
[from Latin *agere* meaning 'to do']

agenda, agendas
(noun) An agenda is a list of items to be discussed at a meeting.
[a Latin word meaning 'things to be done']

agent, agents
1 (noun) An agent is someone who arranges work or business for other people, especially actors or singers.
2 An agent is also someone who works for their country's secret service.
3 Something that is an agent has an effect on a situation or thing, e.g. *chemical drying agents.*

agent provocateur, agents provocateurs
(pronounced **ah**-zhon pro-vok-a-**ter**)
(noun) An agent provocateur is someone employed by the government or the police to encourage trouble-makers to break the law, so that they can be arrested.
[a French expression]

age of consent
(noun) The age of consent is the age at which a person can legally marry or have sex.

age-old
(adjective) having existed for a very long time, e.g. *the age-old exploitation of servants.*

agglomeration, agglomerations
(noun) An agglomeration is a large group of things that have been gathered together.

[from Latin *glomerare* meaning 'to wind into a ball']

aggrandizement (pronounced ag-**grand**-iz-ment); also spelled **aggrandisement** (noun; a formal word) If you do something for your own aggrandizement, you do it to increase your own importance or power.

aggravate, aggravates, aggravating, aggravated
1 (verb) To aggravate a bad situation means to make it worse.
2 (an informal use) If someone or something aggravates you, they make you annoyed.
aggravating (adjective), **aggravation** (noun).
[from Latin *aggravare* meaning 'to make heavier']

aggregate, aggregates
1 (noun) An aggregate is a total that is made up of several smaller amounts.
2 Aggregate is the sand and grit that is mixed with cement to make concrete.
aggregation (noun).
[from Latin *aggregare* meaning 'to add to a flock']

aggression
(noun) Aggression is violent and hostile behaviour.
[from Latin *aggressare* meaning 'to attack']

aggressive
1 (adjective) full of anger, hostility, and violence.
2 determined and eager to succeed, e.g. *aggressive salesmen*.
aggressively (adverb), **aggressiveness** (noun).

Similar words: (sense 1) hostile, antagonistic, pugnacious, belligerent, truculent

aggressor, aggressors
(noun) An aggressor is a person or country that starts a fight or a war.

aggrieved
(adjective) upset and angry about the way you have been treated.

aghast (pronounced a-**gast**)
(adjective) shocked and horrified.
[from Middle English *agast*]

agile
1 (adjective) able to move quickly and easily, e.g. *He was as agile as a monkey*.
2 quick and intelligent, e.g. *an agile mind*.
agilely (adverb), **agility** (noun).

agitate, agitates, agitating, agitated
1 (verb) If you agitate for something, you campaign energetically to get it.
2 If something agitates you, it worries you.
3 If you agitate something, you stir or shake it vigorously.
agitation (noun), **agitator** (noun).

aglow
(adjective) glowing with light or warmth.

AGM, AGMs
(noun) An AGM is a meeting held once a year by an organization for all its members. AGM is an abbreviation for 'annual general meeting'.

agnostic, agnostics
(noun and adjective) Someone who is an agnostic believes that it is impossible to know definitely whether God exists or not.
agnosticism (noun).
[from Greek *agnōstos* meaning 'unknown']

ago
(adverb) in the past, e.g. *We met two years ago*.

agog
(adjective) excited and eager to know more, e.g. *The village is agog: a body has been found*.

agonize, agonizes, agonizing, agonized; also spelled **agonise**
(verb) If you agonize about something, you worry and think anxiously about it.

agonizing or **agonising**
(adjective) extremely painful, either physically or mentally, e.g. *an agonizing dilemma*.

Similar words: excruciating, painful

agony
(noun) very great physical or mental pain.
[from Greek *agōnia* meaning 'struggle']

Similar words: anguish, torment, suffering, hell

agoraphobia (pronounced a-gor-a-**foe**-bee-a)
(noun) Agoraphobia is the fear of open spaces.
agoraphobic (adjective).
[from Greek *agora* meaning 'market place' + *phobia*]

agrarian (pronounced ag-**rare**-ee-an)
(adjective; a formal word) relating to farming and agriculture, e.g. *agrarian societies*.
[from Latin *ager* meaning 'field']

agree, agrees, agreeing, agreed
1 (verb) If you agree with someone, you have the same opinion as them.
2 If you agree to do something, you say that you will do it.
3 If two stories or totals agree, they are the same.
4 Food that doesn't agree with you makes you ill.

Similar words: (sense 1) concur, accord
(sense 2) assent, acquiesce

agreeable
1 (adjective) pleasant or enjoyable, e.g. *The fungus has an agreeable flavour*.
2 If you are agreeable to something, you are willing to allow it or to do it, e.g. *He was perfectly agreeable to the revised plan*.
agreeably (adverb).

agreement, agreements
1 (noun) An agreement is a joint decision that has been reached by two or more people.
2 Two people who are in agreement have the same opinion about something.

Similar words: (sense 1) arrangement, contract, deal, covenant, bargain, compact, pact, treaty
(sense 2) concord, accordance, accord, harmony

agriculture
(noun) Agriculture means the same as farming.
agricultural (adjective).
[from Latin *ager* meaning 'field' and *cultura* meaning 'culture']

aground

(adverb) If a boat runs aground, it becomes stuck in a shallow part of the sea, a lake, or a river.

ahead

1 (adverb) in front, e.g. *She looked ahead.*
2 more advanced than someone or something else, e.g. *His research is ahead of the rest.*
3 in the future, e.g. *We need to plan ahead.*

ahoy

(interjection) 'Ahoy!' is a shout used by sailors to attract attention.

aid, aids, aiding, aided

1 (noun) Aid is money or equipment that is provided for people in need.
2 Aid is also help or support, e.g. *a report compiled with the aid of experts.*
3 An aid is something that makes a task easier, e.g. *teaching aids.*
4 (verb; a formal use) If you aid someone, you help or support them.
5 If something aids a process, it makes it easier.
[from Latin *adjutare* meaning 'to help']

aide, aides

(noun) An aide is an assistant to an important person, especially in the government or the army, e.g. *the president and his aides.*

aide-de-camp, aides-de-camp (pronounced aid-de-**kom**)

(noun) An aide-de-camp is an army officer who acts as an assistant to an officer of higher rank.
[a French expression meaning 'camp assistant']

AIDS

(noun) AIDS is a disease which destroys the body's natural system of immunity to diseases. AIDS is an abbreviation for 'acquired immune deficiency syndrome'.

aileron, ailerons (pronounced ale-er-on)

(noun) An aileron is a flap on the back edge of an aeroplane's wing, which can be raised or lowered to control the plane's movement.
[from French *aile* meaning 'wing']

ailing

1 (adjective) sick or ill, and not getting better.
2 getting into difficulties, especially financially.
[from Old English *egle* meaning 'troublesome' or 'painful']

ailment, ailments

(noun) An ailment is a minor illness.

aim, aims, aiming, aimed

1 (verb) If you aim an object or weapon at someone or something, you point it at them.
2 If you aim to do something, you are planning or hoping to do it.
3 If you aim an action at a particular group, you intend them to be influenced by it, e.g. *an anti-smoking campaign aimed at teenagers.*
4 (noun) Your aim is what you intend to achieve.
5 If you take aim, you point an object or weapon at someone or something.

Similar words: (sense 1) point, direct, level
(sense 2) aspire, intend
(sense 3) direct, level
(sense 4) goal, intention, purpose, ambition, intent, objective, aspiration, object, end, target

aimless

(adjective) having no clear purpose or plan.
aimlessly (adverb), **aimlessness** (noun).

air, airs, airing, aired

1 (noun) Air is the mixture of oxygen and other gases which we breathe and which forms the earth's atmosphere.
2 An air that someone or something has is the impression that they give, e.g. *an air of defiance.*
3 (plural noun) If you give yourself airs, you behave as if you were more important than you really are.
4 (noun) An air is a simple tune.
5 (verb) If you air your opinions, you talk about them to other people.
6 If you air clothing, you put it somewhere warm to make sure that it is completely dry.
7 (phrase) If a radio or television programme is **on the air**, it is being broadcast. If it is **off the air**, it is no longer being broadcast.
[from Greek *aēr* meaning 'the lower atmosphere']

airbed, airbeds

(noun) An airbed is a plastic or rubber mattress which is filled with air before being used.

airborne

(adjective) in the air and flying.

air brake, air brakes

(noun) An air brake is a type of brake on large vehicles, operated by means of compressed air.

air commodore, air commodores

(noun) An air commodore is an RAF officer of the rank immediately above group captain.

air-conditioning

(noun) Air-conditioning is a system of providing cool, dry, clean air in buildings.
air-conditioned (adjective).

aircraft

(noun) An aircraft is any vehicle which can fly.

aircraft carrier, aircraft carriers

(noun) An aircraft carrier is a warship with a deck on which aircraft take off and land.

aircraftsman, aircraftsmen

(noun) An aircraftsman is an airman of the lowest rank in the RAF.

aircrew

(noun) The aircrew on a plane are the pilot and the rest of the crew.

airfield, airfields

(noun) An airfield is an open area of ground with runways where small aircraft take off and land.

air force, air forces

(noun) An air force is the part of a country's armed services that fights using aircraft.

air gun, air guns

(noun) An air gun is a gun which fires pellets by means of air pressure.

air hostess, air hostesses
(noun) An air hostess is a woman whose job is to look after passengers on an aircraft.

airing cupboard, airing cupboards
(noun) An airing cupboard is a warm, dry cupboard, usually containing a hot-water tank, in which you can air washed clothes.

airless
(adjective) having no wind, breeze, or fresh air.

air letter, air letters
(noun) An air letter is a letter sent by air mail.

airlift, airlifts
(noun) An airlift is an operation to move people or goods by air, especially in an emergency.

airline, airlines
(noun) An airline is a company which provides air travel.

airlock, airlocks
1 (noun) An airlock is a compartment between places that do not have the same pressure, for example in a spacecraft or a submarine.
2 An airlock is also a bubble of air in a pipe which prevents water from flowing through it.

air mail
(noun) Air mail is the system of sending letters and parcels by air.

airman, airmen
(noun) An airman is a man who serves in his country's air force.

air marshal, air marshals
(noun) The four most senior ranks in the RAF are Marshal of the Royal Air Force, Air Chief Marshal, Air Marshal, and Air Vice Marshal.

air pocket, air pockets
(noun) An air pocket is a downward current of air in which an aircraft loses height suddenly.

airport, airports
(noun) An airport is a place where people go to catch planes.

air raid, air raids
(noun) An air raid is an attack by enemy aircraft, in which bombs are dropped.

airship, airships
(noun) An airship was a large, light aircraft, consisting of a rigid balloon filled with gas and powered by an engine, with a passenger compartment underneath.

airspace
(noun) A country's airspace is the air above it considered to belong to that country.

airstrip, airstrips
(noun) An airstrip is a stretch of land that has been cleared for aircraft to take off and land.

airtight
(adjective) not letting air in or out.

air-traffic control
(noun) Air-traffic control is an organization that gives instructions to pilots by radio about their course and height.

airy
1 (adjective) full of fresh air and light.
2 light-hearted and casual, e.g. *an airy gesture*.
airily (adverb).

aisle, aisles (rhymes with **mile**)
(noun) An aisle is a long narrow gap that people can walk along between rows of seats or shelves.
[from Latin *ala* meaning 'wing']

ajar
(adjective) A door or window that is ajar is slightly open.
[from Old English *on char* meaning 'on the turn']

akimbo
(adverb; an old-fashioned word) If you stand with arms akimbo, you stand with your hands on your hips and your elbows pointing outwards.
[from Middle English *in kenebowe* meaning 'in a sharp curve']

akin
(adjective; a formal word) similar to, e.g. *She answered with something akin to anger.*

alabaster
(noun) Alabaster is a type of smooth stone used for making ornaments.
[from Latin *alabaster* meaning 'vase for perfume']

à la carte (rhymes with **tart**)
(adjective and adverb) An à la carte menu gives a choice of dishes for each course of a meal.
[a French expression meaning 'according to the card']

alacrity
(noun; a formal word) Alacrity is eager willingness, e.g. *He accepted with alacrity.*
[from Latin *alacer* meaning 'lively']

à la mode (rhymes with **road**)
(adjective and adverb; a formal expression) very fashionable, e.g. *She always dresses à la mode.*
[a French expression meaning 'according to the fashion']

alarm, alarms, alarming, alarmed
1 (noun) Alarm is a feeling of fear, anxiety, and worry, e.g. *She looked round in alarm.*
2 An alarm is an automatic device used to warn people of something, e.g. *fire alarms.*
3 (verb) If something alarms you, it makes you worried and anxious.
alarming (adjective).
[from Italian *all'arme* meaning 'to arms']

alarm clock, alarm clocks
(noun) An alarm clock is a clock that can be set to make a noise at a certain time to wake you up.

alas
(adverb) unfortunately or regrettably, e.g. *I am, alas, unable to publish your story.*

Albanian, Albanians
1 (adjective) belonging or relating to Albania.
2 (noun) An Albanian is someone who comes from Albania.
3 Albanian is the main language spoken in Albania.

albatross, albatrosses
1 (noun) An albatross is a large white seabird. It has the largest wingspan of any bird in the world.
2 If you describe something as an albatross, you mean that it is a commitment that causes a great deal of difficulty, e.g. *Nationalization was an electoral albatross.*
[sense 1 is from Portuguese *alcatraz* meaning 'pelican'; sense 2 is from the dead albatross hung around the sailor's neck in Coleridge's poem 'The Ancient Mariner']

albeit (pronounced awl-**bee**-it)
(conjunction; a formal word) although, e.g. *They published two journals, albeit irregularly.*

albino, albinos
(noun) An albino is a person or animal without any of the pigment melanin in their body, so that they have pale skin, white hair, and pink eyes.
albinism (noun).
[from Latin *albus* meaning 'white']

album, albums
1 (noun) An album is a record with about 25 minutes of music or speech on each side.
2 An album is also a book in which you keep a collection of things such as photographs or stamps.

albumen (pronounced **al**-byoo-men)
(noun) Albumen is the white of an egg.

albumin (pronounced **al**-byoo-min)
(noun) Albumin is a water-soluble protein found in egg white and blood plasma.

alchemy (pronounced **al**-kem-ee)
(noun) Alchemy was a medieval science that attempted to change ordinary metals into gold.
alchemist (noun).
[an Arabic word]

alcohol
(noun) Alcohol is any drink that can make people drunk; also the colourless flammable liquid found in these drinks, produced by fermenting sugar. Alcohol is sometimes used as a solvent.

alcoholic, alcoholics
1 (adjective) An alcoholic drink contains alcohol.
2 (noun) An alcoholic is someone who is addicted to alcohol.
alcoholism (noun).

alcove, alcoves
(noun) An alcove is an area of a room which is set back slightly from the main part.
[from Arabic *al-qubbah* meaning 'arch']

alder, alders
(noun) An alder is a type of small tree that grows near rivers. It is related to the birch.

ale
(noun) Ale is a type of beer.

alert, alerts, alerting, alerted
1 (adjective) paying full attention to what is happening, e.g. *an alert guard dog.*
2 (noun) An alert is a situation in which people prepare themselves for danger, e.g. *a nuclear alert.*

3 (verb) If you alert someone to a problem or danger, you warn them of it.
alertness (noun).

Similar words: (sense 1) watchful, vigilant, attentive

alfalfa
(noun) Alfalfa is a plant grown to feed cattle. It has clusters of small purple flowers.
[from Arabic *al-fasfasah* meaning 'the best fodder']

algae (pronounced **al**-jee)
(plural noun) Algae are plants that grow in water or on damp surfaces. They have chlorophyll but not roots, stems, or leaves.
[from Latin *alga* meaning 'seaweed']

algebra
(noun) Algebra is a branch of mathematics in which symbols and letters are used instead of numbers, in order to express general relationships between quantities.
algebraic (adjective).
[from Arabic *al-jabr* meaning 'reunion']

Algerian, Algerians
1 (adjective) belonging or relating to Algeria.
2 (noun) An Algerian is someone who comes from Algeria.

algorithm, algorithms
(noun) An algorithm is a mathematical procedure for solving a particular problem.
[from *al-Khuwarizmi*, the name of a 9th century Arab mathematician]

alias, aliases (pronounced **ay**-lee-ass)
(noun) An alias is a false name used by a criminal, e.g. *Bryan Procter, alias Barry Cornwall.*
[from Latin *alias* meaning 'otherwise']

Similar words: assumed name, pseudonym

alibi, alibis (pronounced **al**-li-bye)
(noun) An alibi is evidence proving that you were somewhere else when a crime was committed.
[from Latin *alibi* meaning 'elsewhere']

alien, aliens (pronounced **ay**-lee-an)
1 (adjective) not normal, and therefore strange and slightly frightening, e.g. *a totally alien environment and culture.*
2 If something is alien to your beliefs or behaviour, it is not the way you normally think or behave.
3 (noun) An alien is someone who is not a citizen of the country in which he or she lives.
4 In science fiction, an alien is a creature from outer space.
[from Latin *alienus* meaning 'foreign']

alienate, alienates, alienating, alienated
(verb) If you alienate someone, you do something that makes them become unsympathetic to you, e.g. *The Government alienated the unions.*
alienation (noun).

alight, alights, alighting, alighted
1 (adjective) Something that is alight is burning.

2 (verb) If a bird or insect alights somewhere, it lands there.
3 (a formal use) When passengers alight from a vehicle, they get out of it at the end of a journey.

align, aligns, aligning, aligned (pronounced a-**line**)
1 (verb) If you align yourself with a particular group, you support them politically.
2 If you align things, you place them in a straight line, e.g. *The building blocks were neatly aligned.*
alignment (noun).

alike
1 (adjective) Things that are alike are similar in some way.
2 (adverb) If people or things are treated alike, they are treated in a similar way.

alimentary canal, alimentary canals
(noun) Your alimentary canal is the passage in your body through which food passes from your mouth to your anus.
[from Latin *alimentum* meaning 'food']

alimony (pronounced **al**-li-mon-ee)
(noun) Alimony is money that someone has to pay regularly to their wife or husband after they are divorced.
[from Latin *alimonia* meaning 'sustenance']

alive
1 (adjective) living.
2 lively and active, and full of interest.

Similar words: (sense 1) living, live, animate
---

alkali, alkalis (pronounced al-kal-**eye**)
(noun) In chemistry, an alkali is a substance with a pH value of more than 7.
alkaline (adjective), **alkalinity** (noun).
[from Arabic *al-qili* meaning 'ashes']

alkaloid, alkaloids
(noun) An alkaloid is a substance containing nitrogen, which is obtained from plants. Many alkaloids are used in medicines, for example codeine, morphine, and quinine.

all
1 (adjective, pronoun, and adverb) used when referring to the whole of something, e.g. *Can you eat all that?... She ate it all... It is all quiet.*
2 (adverb) All is also used when saying that the two sides in a game or contest have the same score, e.g. *The score is six all.*

Allah
(proper noun) Allah is the Muslim name for God.

allay, allays, allaying, allayed
(verb) To allay someone's fears or suspicions means to cause them to be felt less strongly.

allege, alleges, alleging, alleged (pronounced a-**lej**)
(verb) If you allege that something is true, you say it is true but do not provide any proof, e.g. *They alleged that the figures were invented.*
allegation (noun), **alleged** (adjective).

allegiance, allegiances (pronounced al-**lee**-jenss)
(noun) Allegiance is loyal support for a person or organization.

allegory, allegories (pronounced al-li-**gor**-ee)
(noun) An allegory is a piece of writing or art in which the characters and events are symbols for something else. Allegories usually make some moral, religious, or political point.
allegorical (adjective).
[from Greek *allegoria* meaning 'speaking otherwise']

allegro
In music, allegro is an instruction to play or sing something quickly.
[an Italian word]

alleluia, alleluias (pronounced al-li-**loo**-yah)
(noun) Alleluia is an exclamation of praise and thanks to God.
[a Hebrew word]

allergy, allergies (pronounced **al**-er-jee)
(noun) An allergy is an abnormal physical sensitivity that someone has to something, so that they become ill when they eat it or are exposed to it, e.g. *She has an allergy to milk.*
allergic (adjective).

alleviate, alleviates, alleviating, alleviated
(verb) To alleviate pain or a problem means to make it less severe, e.g. *measures to help alleviate high unemployment.*
alleviation (noun).

alley, alleys
(noun) An alley is a narrow passage between buildings.
[from Old French *aler* meaning 'to go']

alliance, alliances
(noun) An alliance is a group of people, organizations, or countries working together for similar aims.

Similar words: association, league, affiliation, confederation, union, coalition
---

allied
1 (adjective) united by political or military agreements, e.g. *the Allied forces.*
2 similar or related to something else, e.g. *the coal and allied industries.*

alligator, alligators
(noun) An alligator is a large reptile with powerful jaws, sharp teeth, and a strong tail. Alligators live in lakes and rivers in the Southern United States and China. They are similar to crocodiles, except that they have shorter snouts.
[from Spanish *el lagarto* meaning 'lizard']

alliteration
(noun; a literary word) Alliteration is the use of several words together which all begin with the same sound, for example 'the forest's ferny floor'.
alliterative (adjective).

allocate, allocates, allocating, allocated
(verb) If you allocate something, you decide that it should be given to a person or place, or used for a particular purpose, e.g. *Modern houses had been allocated to people with young children.*
allocation (noun).

allot, allots, allotting, allotted
(verb) If something is allotted to you, it is given to you as your share, e.g. *They were allotted humble living quarters.*

allotment, allotments
1 (noun) An allotment is a piece of land which people can rent to grow vegetables on.
2 An allotment of something is a share of it.

allow, allows, allowing, allowed
1 (verb) If you allow something to happen, you let it happen.
2 If you allow a period of time or an amount of something, you set it aside for a particular purpose, e.g. *Allow 4 metres for the skirt... She allowed two hours for the journey.*
3 (a formal use) If you allow that something is true, you admit that it is true, e.g. *He allowed that even world leaders could make mistakes.*
allowable (adjective).

allowance, allowances
1 (noun) An allowance is money that is given regularly to someone for a particular purpose, e.g. *a maternity allowance.*
2 (phrase) If you **make allowances** for something, you take it into account in your plans or actions, e.g. *They made no allowances for ill health.*

alloy, alloys
(noun) An alloy is a mixture of two or more metals, e.g. *aluminium alloys.*
[from Old French *aloier* meaning 'to combine']

all right or **alright**
Some people say that **all right** is the only correct spelling.
1 (adjective) If something is all right, it is satisfactory or acceptable.
2 If someone is all right, they are safe and not harmed.
3 You say 'all right' to agree to something.

all-rounder, all-rounders
(noun) An all-rounder is someone who is good at lots of different things, especially in sport.

allude, alludes, alluding, alluded
(verb) If you allude to something, you refer to it in an indirect way.
[from Latin *alludere* meaning 'to play with']

allure
(noun) The allure of something is a pleasing or exciting quality that makes it attractive, e.g. *the allure of money.*
alluring (adjective).
[from Old French *lure* meaning 'bait']

allusion, allusion
(noun) An allusion to something is an indirect reference to it or comment about it, e.g. *English literature is full of classical allusions.*
allusive (adjective).

alluvium
(noun) Alluvium is a fine, fertile soil consisting of mud and silt that has been deposited by flowing water on a plain or at the mouth of a river.
alluvial (adjective).
[from Latin *alluvio* meaning 'overflowing']

ally, allies, allying, allied
1 (noun) An ally is a person, organization, or country that helps and supports another.
2 (verb) If you ally yourself with someone, you agree to help and support each other.

Similar words: (sense 1) confederate, associate (sense 2) associate, affiliate

alma mater
(noun) A person's alma mater is their old school, college, or university.
[a Latin expression meaning 'generous mother']

almanac, almanacs
(noun) An almanac is a book published every year giving information about the movements of the planets, times of sunrise and sunset, tides, and important anniversaries.

almighty
1 (adjective) very great or serious, e.g. *She made the most almighty fuss.*
2 (proper noun) The Almighty is another name for God.

almond, almonds
(noun) An almond is a pale brown oval nut.

almost
(adverb) very nearly, but not completely or exactly, e.g. *I almost forgot... He's almost blind.*

Similar words: nearly, all but, practically, virtually

alms
(plural noun; an old-fashioned word) Alms are gifts of money, food, or clothing to poor people.
[from Greek *eleēmosunē* meaning 'pity']

almshouse, almshouses
(noun) An almshouse was a house built by a church or charity, where very old and poor people used to live for free.

aloe, aloes
1 (noun) Aloe is an African plant with long thorny leaves and bright red flowers. It is used in medicines and cosmetics.
2 **Bitter aloes** is a drug made from the leaves of this plant, used as a laxative.

aloft
(adverb) up in the air or in a high position, e.g. *a poster carried aloft in a demonstration.*

alone
(adjective and adverb) not with other people or things, e.g. *I wanted to be alone... She was left to bring up her children alone.*

Similar words: solitary, lonely, unaccompanied

along
1 (preposition) moving, happening, or existing continuously from one end to the other of something, or at various points beside it, e.g. *The current passes along this wire... the houses along the Lanark Road.*
2 (adverb) moving forward or making progress, e.g. *The soldiers trudged along.*
3 with someone, e.g. *She always took her children along.*
4 (phrase) **All along** means from the beginning of

a period of time right up to now, e.g. *Perhaps they had been mistaken all along.*

alongside
(preposition and adverb) next to something, e.g. *A car drew up alongside mine.*

aloof
(adjective) separate from someone or something, distant, and not involved with them.

aloud
(adverb) When you read or speak aloud, you speak loudly enough for other people to hear you.

Similar words: out loud, audibly

alpaca, alpacas (pronounced al-**pak**-a)
(noun) An alpaca is a South American animal that is related to the llama; also used of the wool obtained from this animal.
[from a South American Indian language]

alphabet, alphabets
(noun) An alphabet is a set of letters in a fixed order that is used in writing a language.
alphabetical (adjective), **alphabetically** (adverb).
[from *alpha + beta*, the first two letters of the Greek alphabet]

alpine
(adjective) existing in or relating to high mountains, e.g. *alpine meadows... alpine plants.*
[from *the Alps*, a mountain range in central Europe]

already
(adverb) having happened before the present time or earlier than expected, e.g. *I've already read that book... She was already in bed.*

alright another spelling of **all right**.

Alsatian, Alsatians (pronounced al-**say**-shn)
(noun) An Alsatian is a type of large, fierce dog. Alsatians are used as guard dogs and police dogs.

also
(adverb) in addition to an action, situation, person, or thing that has just been mentioned.

altar, altars
(noun) An altar is a table in a church or temple, on which religious rites are performed.

alter, alters, altering, altered
(verb) If something alters or if you alter it, it changes.
alteration (noun).

altercation, altercations
(noun; a formal word) An altercation is a noisy argument or disagreement.

alter ego, alter egos
1 (noun) Your alter ego is another side to your personality, which people do not normally see.
2 An alter ego is also a close and intimate friend.
[a Latin expression meaning 'other self']

alternate, alternates, alternating, alternated
1 (verb) If one thing alternates with another, the two things regularly occur one after the other.
2 (adjective) If something happens on alternate days, it happens on the first day but not the second, and happens again on the third day but

not the fourth, and so on, e.g. *We meet on alternate Mondays.*
alternately (adverb), **alternation** (noun).

alternating current, alternating currents
(noun) An alternating current is a current that regularly changes its direction, so that the electrons flow first one way and then the other.

alternative, alternatives
1 (noun) An alternative is something that you can do or have instead of something else, e.g. *We must develop alternatives to oil fuels.*
2 (adjective) Alternative plans, arrangements, or processes can happen or be done instead of what is already happening or being done.
alternatively (adverb).

alternator, alternators
(noun) An alternator is an electrical device that generates an alternating current.

although
(conjunction) in spite of the fact that, e.g. *I skipped lunch although I was hungry.*

altimeter, altimeters
(noun) An altimeter is a device used for measuring altitude. It works rather like a barometer, by measuring air pressure.

altitude, altitudes
(noun) The altitude of something is its height above sea level, e.g. *The plane climbed to an altitude of 31,000 feet.*
[from Latin *altus* meaning 'high']

alto, altos
1 (noun) An alto is a person who sings the second highest part in four-part harmony.
2 (adjective) An alto musical instrument has a range of notes that are of medium pitch.
[an Italian word meaning 'high'; altos were originally men with high singing voices]

altogether
1 (adverb) completely or entirely, e.g. *For years we did without a bathroom altogether.*
2 in total; used of amounts, e.g. *I get £120 a week altogether.*

altruism
(noun; a formal word) Altruism is unselfish concern for other people.
altruist (noun), **altruistic** (adjective).
[from Italian *altrui* meaning 'others']

aluminium
(noun) Aluminium is a light silvery-white metallic element. It is used to make aircraft and other equipment, usually in the form of aluminium alloys. The atomic number of aluminium is 13 and its symbol is Al.

always
(adverb) all the time or for ever, e.g. *I shall always love you... He's always complaining.*

alyssum (pronounced al-**liss**-um)
(noun) Alyssum is a small garden plant with very small white flowers.

am the first person singular, present tense of **be**.

a.m.
used to specify times between 12 midnight and

12 noon, e.g. *We get up at 6 a.m.* It is an abbreviation for the Latin phrase 'ante meridiem', which means 'before noon'.

amalgam, amalgams
1 (noun) An amalgam is a combination or mixture of two or more things.
2 Amalgam is an alloy of mercury and another metal, usually silver, used in dental fillings.
[from Greek *malagma* meaning 'softening']

amalgamate, amalgamates, amalgamating, amalgamated
(verb) If two organizations amalgamate, they join together to form one new organization.
amalgamation (noun).

amass, amasses, amassing, amassed
(verb) If you amass something such as money, information, or goods, you collect large quantities of it, e.g. *He amassed a huge collection of Indian art.*

amateur, amateurs
(noun) An amateur is someone who does something as a hobby rather than as a job.
[from Latin *amator* meaning 'lover']

amateurish
(adjective) not skilfully made or done.
amateurishly (adverb).

amaze, amazes, amazing, amazed
(verb) If something amazes you, it surprises you very much.
amazement (noun).

Similar words: surprise, astonish, astound, stagger, flabbergast, dumbfound

amazing
(adjective) very surprising, remarkable, or difficult to believe.
amazingly (adverb).

Similar words: incredible, fabulous, wonderful

ambassador, ambassadors
(noun) An ambassador is a person sent to a foreign country as the representative of his or her own government.

amber
1 (noun) Amber is a hard, yellowish-brown fossilized resin. It is used for making jewellery and ornaments.
2 (noun and adjective) orange-brown.
[from Arabic *anbar*]

ambidextrous
(adjective) Someone who is ambidextrous is able to use both hands equally skilfully.

ambience
(noun; a formal word) The ambience of a place is its atmosphere.
[from French *ambiant* meaning 'surrounding']

ambiguous
(adjective) A word or phrase that is ambiguous has more than one meaning.
ambiguously (adjective), **ambiguity** (noun).

ambition, ambitions
1 (noun) If you have an ambition to achieve something, you want very much to achieve it.
2 Ambition is a great desire for success, power, and wealth, e.g. *a man of ambition.*

ambitious
1 (adjective) Someone who is ambitious has a strong desire for success, power, and wealth.
2 An ambitious plan or project is on a large scale and requires a lot of effort and work, e.g. *an ambitious development programme.*

ambivalent
(adjective) having or showing two conflicting attitudes or emotions.
ambivalence (noun).

amble, ambles, ambling, ambled
(verb) If you amble, you walk slowly and in a relaxed and leisurely manner.
[from Latin *ambulare* meaning 'to walk']

ambulance, ambulances
(noun) An ambulance is a vehicle for taking sick and injured people to hospital.

ambush, ambushes, ambushing, ambushed
1 (verb) To ambush someone means to attack them after hiding and lying in wait for them.
2 (noun) An ambush is an attack on someone after hiding and lying in wait for them.
[from Old French *embuschier* meaning 'to hide in a wood']

ameba another spelling of **amoeba.**

ameliorate, ameliorates, ameliorating, ameliorated
(verb; a formal word) To ameliorate something means to make it become better.
amelioration (noun).
[from Latin *melior* meaning 'better']

amen
(interjection) Amen is said by Christians at the end of a prayer. It means 'so be it'.
[a Hebrew word]

amenable (pronounced am-**mee**-na-bl)
(adjective) willing to listen to comments and suggestions, or to cooperate with someone, e.g. *She was amenable to whatever I suggested.*
amenably (adverb), **amenability** (noun).

amend, amends, amending, amended
1 (verb) To amend something that has been written or said means to alter it slightly, e.g. *Last year the regulations were amended.*
2 (plural noun) If you make amends for something bad that you have done, you say you are sorry and try to make up for it in some way.
amendment (noun).

amenity, amenities (pronounced am-**mee**-nit-ee)
(noun) Amenities are things that are available for the public to use, such as sports facilities, cinemas, or shopping centres.

America
(noun) America refers to the United States, or to the whole of North, South, and Central America.

American, Americans
1 (adjective) belonging or relating to the United

States, or to the whole of North, South, and Central America.
2 (noun) An American is someone who comes from the United States.

amethyst, amethysts
(noun) An amethyst is a type of purple semiprecious stone, used in making jewellery.
[from Greek *amethustos* meaning 'not drunk'. It was thought to prevent intoxication]

amiable
(adjective) pleasant, friendly, and kind, e.g. *He was in an amiable mood.*
amiably (adverb), **amiability** (noun).

amicable
(adjective) fairly friendly.
amicably (adverb).
[from Latin *amicus* meaning 'friend']

amid or **amidst**
(preposition; a formal word) surrounded by, e.g. *Tombstones stood amid the grass.*

amidships
(adverb) at or near the middle of a ship or boat.

amino acid, amino acids
(noun) An amino acid is a compound containing an amino group, which forms a part of protein molecules.

amiss
1 (adjective) If something is amiss, there is something wrong.
2 (phrase) If you **take something amiss**, you are upset or hurt by it, e.g. *You mustn't take anything I say amiss.*

amity
(noun; a formal word) Amity is a state of peace and friendship.
[from Latin *amicus* meaning 'friend']

ammeter, ammeters
(noun) An ammeter is an instrument for measuring the strength of an electric current.

ammonia
(noun) Ammonia is a colourless, strong-smelling gas or alkaline liquid. It is used in household cleaning materials, explosives, and fertilizers. It has the chemical formula NH_3.

ammunition
1 (noun) Ammunition is anything that can be fired from a gun or other weapon, for example bullets, rockets, and shells.
2 Ammunition is also information that you can use against somebody, e.g. *The letters might be used as ammunition against him.*

amnesia
(noun) Amnesia is loss of memory.
amnesiac (adjective).

amnesty
(noun) An amnesty is an official pardon for political or other prisoners.
[from Greek *amnestos* meaning 'forgetting']

amniotic
(adjective) The amniotic sac is the protective membrane surrounding a baby in its mother's womb. It is filled with amniotic fluid, which protects the baby.
[from Greek *amnos* meaning 'lamb']

amoeba, amoebas or amoebae (pronounced am-**mee**-ba); also spelled **ameba**
(noun) Amoebas are the smallest kind of living creature. They consist of one cell, which reproduces by dividing into two.
[from Greek *amoibē* meaning 'change']

amok (pronounced am-**muk**)
(phrase) If a person or animal **runs amok**, they behave in a violent and uncontrolled way.
[a Malay word]

among or **amongst**
1 (preposition) surrounded by, e.g. *We stood among piles of wooden boxes.*
2 in the company of, e.g. *I was among friends.*
3 between more than two, e.g. *The estate was divided among the brothers.*

Similar words: (sense 1) amid, amidst

amoral
(adjective) Someone who is amoral has no moral standards by which to live or on which to base their behaviour.

amorous
(adjective) passionately affectionate, e.g. *He was always sweet, welcoming, and amorous.*
amorously (adverb), **amorousness** (noun).
[from Latin *amor* meaning 'love']

amorphous
(adjective; a formal word) having no definite shape or structure.
amorphously (adverb), **amorphousness** (noun).

amount, amounts, amounting, amounted
1 (noun) An amount of something is how much there is of it.
2 (verb) If something amounts to a particular total, all the parts of it add up to that total, e.g. *fees which amounted to £2,000... His attitude towards her amounted to loathing.*

Similar words: (sense 1) quantity, measure, degree

amp, amps
(noun) An amp is the same as an ampere.

ampere, amperes (pronounced **am**-pair)
(noun) The ampere is the SI unit of electrical current. One ampere of current is produced by one volt of electrical force when the resistance is one ohm. The ampere is named after the French physicist A.M. Ampère (1775-1836).

amphetamine, amphetamines
(noun) Amphetamine is a drug that increases people's energy and makes them excited. It can have dangerous and unpleasant side-effects.

amphibian, amphibians
(noun) An amphibian is a creature that lives partly on land and partly in water. Amphibians lay their eggs in water, which develop into larvae (called tadpoles). The fully adult form usually lives on land. Frogs, toads, and newts are amphibians.

amphibious
1 (adjective) An amphibious animal, such as a frog, lives partly on land and partly in the water.
2 An amphibious military operation uses boats to land soldiers on an enemy shore.
3 An amphibious vehicle is able to move on both land and water.
[from Greek *amphibios* meaning 'having a double life']

amphitheatre, amphitheatres
(noun) An amphitheatre is a large, semicircular open area with sloping sides covered with rows of seats. Amphitheatres were built originally by the Greeks and Romans for theatrical performances.

ample
(adjective) If there is an ample amount of something, there is more than enough of it.
amply (adverb).

amplifier, amplifiers
(noun) An amplifier is a piece of equipment in a radio or stereo system which causes sounds or signals to become louder.

amplify, amplifies, amplifying, amplified
1 (verb) If you amplify a sound, you make it louder.
2 If you amplify something such as an idea or opinion, you explain it more fully.
amplification (noun).

amplitude
(noun) In physics, the amplitude of a wave is the extent to which its curve moves away from a mid-point.

amputate, amputates, amputating, amputated
(verb) To amputate an arm or a leg means to cut it off as a surgical operation.
amputation (noun).
[from Latin *putare* meaning 'to trim']

amulet, amulets (pronounced **am**-yoo-let)
(noun) An amulet is a small charm or other object worn for good luck or to ward off bad luck.

amuse, amuses, amusing, amused
1 (verb) If something amuses you, you think it is funny.
2 If you amuse yourself, you find things to do which stop you from being bored.
amused (adjective), **amusing** (adjective).

amusement, amusements
1 (noun) Amusement is the state of thinking that something is funny.
2 Amusement is also the pleasure you get from being entertained or from doing something interesting.
3 Amusements are ways of passing the time pleasantly.

an
(determiner) 'An' is used instead of 'a' in front of words that begin with a vowel sound.

anabolic steroid, anabolic steroids
(noun) Anabolic steroids are drugs which cause muscles and bones to grow. They can be used for medical purposes, but they are sometimes taken illegally by athletes to improve their performance.

anachronism, anachronisms (pronounced an-**ak**-kron-ism)
(noun) An anachronism is something that belongs or seems to belong to another time.
anachronistic (adjective).
[from Greek *anakhronismos* meaning 'mistake in time']

anaemia or **anemia** (pronounced a-**nee**-mee-a)
(noun) Anaemia is a medical condition resulting from too few red cells in a person's blood. People with anaemia look pale and feel very tired.
anaemic or **anemic** (adjective).
[from Greek *anaimia* meaning 'lack of blood']

anaesthetic, anaesthetics (pronounced an-niss-**thet**-ik); also spelled **anesthetic**
(noun) An anaesthetic is a substance that stops you feeling pain. A general anaesthetic stops you from feeling pain in the whole of your body by putting you to sleep, and a local anaesthetic makes just one part of your body go numb.
[from Greek *anaisthēsia* meaning 'lack of feeling']

anaesthetist, anaesthetists
(noun) An anaesthetist is a doctor who is specially trained to give anaesthetics.

anaesthetize, anaesthetizes, anaesthetizing, anaesthetized; also spelled **anesthetize** or **anaesthetise**
(verb) To anaesthetize someone means to give them an anaesthetic to make them unconscious.

anagram, anagrams
(noun) An anagram is a word or phrase formed by reordering the letters of another word or phrase. For example, 'triangle' is an anagram of 'integral'.

anal (pronounced **ay**-nl)
(adjective) relating to the anus.

analgesic, analgesics (pronounced an-al-**jee**-sik)
(noun) An analgesic is a substance that relieves pain.

analogy, analogies (pronounced an-**al**-o-jee)
(noun) An analogy is a comparison showing that two things are similar in some ways.
analogous (adjective).

analyse, analyses, analysing, analysed
(verb) To analyse something means to investigate it carefully in order to understand it or find out what it consists of.

analysis, analyses
(noun) Analysis is the process of investigating something in order to understand it or find out what it consists of, e.g. *chemical analysis... a calm analysis of the situation.*
[from Greek *analusis* meaning 'dissolving']

analyst, analysts
(noun) An analyst is a person whose job is to analyse things to find out about them.

analytic or **analytical**
(adjective) using logical reasoning, e.g. *her acute analytical powers.*
analytically (adverb).

anarchism (pronounced **an**-nar-kizm)
(noun) Anarchism is the political belief that all governments should be abolished.
anarchist (noun), **anarchistic** (adjective).

anarchy (pronounced **an**-nar-kee)
(noun) Anarchy is a situation where nobody obeys laws or rules.
[from Greek *anarkhos* meaning 'without a ruler']

anathema (pronounced an-**ath**-im-ma)
(noun; a formal word) If something is anathema to you, you hate it or dislike it intensely.

anatomy
1 (noun) Anatomy is the study of the structure of the human body or of the bodies of animals.
2 An animal's anatomy is the structure of its body.
anatomical (adjective), **anatomically** (adverb).
[from Greek *anatemnein* meaning 'to dissect']

ancestor, ancestors
(noun) Your ancestors are the members of your family who lived many years ago and from whom you are descended.
ancestral (adjective).
[from Latin *antecessor* meaning 'one who goes before']

Similar words: forefather, predecessor, progenitor

ancestry, ancestries
(noun) Your ancestry consists of the people from whom you are descended, e.g. *American citizens of Irish ancestry.*

Similar words: lineage, stock, pedigree

anchor, anchors, anchoring, anchored
1 (noun) An anchor is a heavy, hooked object that is dropped from a boat into the water at the end of a chain, to keep the boat in one place.
2 (verb) To anchor a boat or another object means to stop it from moving by dropping an anchor or attaching it to something solid.

anchorage, anchorages
(noun) An anchorage is a place where a boat or ship can safely anchor.

anchovy, anchovies
(noun) An anchovy is a type of small edible fish with a very strong salty taste.

ancient (pronounced **ayn**-shent)
1 (adjective) existing or happening in the distant past, e.g. *ancient Greece and Rome.*
2 very old or having a very long history, e.g. *an ancient Catholic family.*

ancillary (pronounced an-**sil**-lar-ee)
1 (adjective) The ancillary workers in an institution are the people such as cooks and cleaners, whose work supports the main work of the institution.
2 Something that is ancillary is an extra part of something else, e.g. *I had a smaller ancillary sleeping tent.*
[from Latin *ancilla* meaning 'maidservant']

and
(conjunction) You use 'and' to link two or more words or phrases together.

andante (pronounced an-**dan**-tee)
In music, andante is an instruction to play or sing something moderately slowly.
[an Italian word]

androgynous (pronounced an-**droj**-in-uss)
(adjective; a formal word) having both male and female characteristics.
[from Greek *anēr* meaning 'man' and *gunē* meaning 'woman']

anecdote, anecdotes
(noun) An anecdote is a short, entertaining story about a person or event.
anecdotal (adjective).
[from Greek *anekdotos* meaning 'unpublished']

anemia another spelling of **anaemia.**

anemic another spelling of **anaemic.**

anemometer, anemometers
(noun) An anemometer is an instrument used for recording the speed and direction of winds.

anemone, anemones (pronounced an-**em**-on-ee)
(noun) An anemone is a plant with large red, purple, or white flowers and feathery leaves.
[from Greek *amenos* meaning 'wind'; its other name is 'windflower']

aneroid barometer, aneroid barometers
(noun) An aneroid barometer measures air pressure by means of a surface fitted over a vacuum chamber. The surface moves in response to external air pressure.

anesthetic another spelling of **anaesthetic.**

anesthetize another spelling of **anaesthetize.**

anew
(adverb) If you do something anew, you do it again, e.g. *starting life anew in a fresh place.*

angel, angels
(noun) Angels are spiritual beings that some people believe live in heaven and act as messengers for God.
angelic (adjective).
[from Greek *angelos* meaning 'messenger']

angelica
(noun) Angelica is a type of sweet-scented plant that is crystallized and used for decorating cakes and puddings.

anger, angers, angering, angered
1 (noun) Anger is the strong feeling that you get when you feel that someone has behaved in an unfair, cruel, or insulting way.
2 (verb) If something angers you, it makes you feel angry.

Similar words: (sense 1) fury, rage, wrath, ire (sense 2) enrage, infuriate, incense, madden

angina (pronounced an-**jy**-na)
(noun) Angina is a brief but very severe heart

pain, caused by lack of blood supply to the heart.
It is also known as 'angina pectoris'.

angle, angles, angling, angled
1 (noun) An angle is the distance between two
lines at the point where they join together.
Angles are measured in degrees.
2 An angle is also the direction from which you
look at something, e.g. *The house was
photographed from all angles.*
3 (phrase) If something is **at an angle**, it is not in
a vertical or horizontal position, e.g. *an old table
leaning at an angle.*
4 (noun) An angle on something is a particular
way of considering it, e.g. *the play's socialist
angle.*
5 (verb) If you angle for something, you try to
make someone offer it to you without asking for
it directly.

Anglican, Anglicans
(noun and adjective) An Anglican is a member of
one of the churches belonging to the Anglican
Communion, a group of Protestant churches
which includes the Church of England.
[from Latin *Anglicus* meaning 'English']

angling
(noun) Angling is the sport of fishing using a rod.
angler (noun).
[from Old English *angul* meaning 'fish-hook']

Anglo-
(prefix) Anglo- means involving England or
Britain, e.g. *the Anglo-Irish treaty.*

Anglo-Saxon, Anglo-Saxons
1 (noun) The Anglo-Saxons were a race of people
who settled in England from the fifth century
AD and were the dominant people until the
Norman invasion in 1066. They were composed
of three West Germanic tribes, the Angles,
Saxons, and Jutes.
2 Anglo-Saxon is another name for **Old English.**

Angolan, Angolans (pronounced ang-**goh**-ln)
1 (adjective) belonging or relating to Angola.
2 (noun) An Angolan is someone who comes from
Angola.

angora
(adjective and noun) An angora goat or rabbit is
a breed with long silky hair.
[from *Angora*, the former name of Ankara in
Turkey]

angry, angrier, angriest
(adjective) very cross or annoyed.

Similar words: furious, enraged, incensed, infuriated,
irate, livid, wrathful

anguish
(noun) Anguish is extreme mental or physical
suffering.
anguished (adjective).
[from Old French *angoisse* meaning 'strangling']

angular
(adjective) Angular things have straight lines
and sharp points, e.g. *his angular face.*

animal, animals
(noun) An animal is any living being except a
plant, or any mammal except a human being.
[from Latin *anima* meaning 'life' or 'soul']

Similar words: brute, beast, creature

animate, animates, animating, animated
1 (verb) To animate something means to make it
lively and interesting.
2 (adjective) Something which is animate has
life, in contrast to things like stones or machines
that do not have life.

animated
1 (adjective) lively and interesting, e.g. *an
animated discussion.*
2 An animated film has been made using
animation, e.g. *an animated cartoon.*
animatedly (adverb).

animation
1 (noun) Animation is a method of film-making
in which a series of drawings are photographed.
When the film is projected, the characters in the
drawings appear to move.
2 Someone who has animation shows liveliness
in the way they speak and act, e.g. *She talked
with animation about her art.*
animator (noun).

animosity, animosities
(noun) Animosity is a feeling of strong dislike
and anger towards someone.

ankle, ankles
(noun) Your ankle is the joint, made up of seven
bones, which connects your foot to your leg.

annals
(noun) The annals of a nation or society are its
recorded history, e.g. *the annals of military
history.*
[from Latin *(libri) annales* meaning 'yearly
(books)']

annex, annexes, annexing, annexed; also spelled
annexe
1 (noun) An annex is an extra building which is
joined to a larger main building.
2 (verb) If one country annexes another, it seizes
the other country and takes control of it.
annexation (noun).

annihilate, annihilates, annihilating, annihilated
(pronounced an-**nye**-ill-ate)
(verb) If something is annihilated, it is
completely destroyed.
annihilation (noun).
[from Latin *annihilare* meaning 'to bring to
nothing']

anniversary, anniversaries
(noun) An anniversary is a date which is
remembered or celebrated because something
special happened on that date in a previous year.
[from Latin *anniversarius* meaning 'returning
annually']

annotate, annotates, annotating, annotated
(verb) If you annotate a book or a diagram, you
write notes and comments on it.
annotation (noun).

announce, announces, announcing, announced
(verb) If you announce something, you tell people about it publicly or officially, e.g. *The Prime Minister announced her resignation.*
announcement (noun).
[from Latin *nuntius* meaning 'messenger']

Similar words: broadcast, proclaim

announcer, announcers
(noun) An announcer is someone who introduces programmes on radio and television.

annoy, annoys, annoying, annoyed
(verb) If someone or something annoys you, they irritate you and make you fairly angry.
annoyance (noun), **annoyed** (adjective).

Similar words: vex, gall, irk, bait, aggravate

annual, annuals
1 (adjective) happening or done every year or once a year, e.g. *her annual holiday.*
2 happening or calculated over a period of one year, e.g. *an annual income of £12,000.*
3 (noun) An annual is a book or magazine published regularly once a year.
4 An annual is also a plant that grows, flowers, and dies within one year.
annually (adverb).
[from Latin *annus* meaning 'year']

annuity, annuities
(noun) An annuity is a fixed sum of money paid to someone every year from an investment or insurance policy.

annul, annuls, annulling, annulled
(verb) If a marriage or contract is annulled, it is declared invalid, so that legally it is considered never to have existed.
annulment (noun).
[from Latin *annullare* meaning 'to bring to nothing']

Similar words: dissolve, nullify, invalidate, rescind

anode, anodes
(noun) An anode is the positive electrode in a cell or battery. Negatively charged ions move towards the anode and positively charged ions move away from it towards the cathode.

anodyne, anodynes
1 (noun; a technical use) An anodyne is a drug that relieves pain.
2 (adjective) Something that is anodyne seems neutral and not dangerous or distressing, e.g. *They kept the conversation on a safely anodyne level.*

anoint, anoints, anointing, anointed
(verb) To anoint someone means to put oil on them as part of a ceremony.
anointment (noun).

anomaly, anomalies (pronounced an-**nom**-al-ee)
(noun) Something is an anomaly if it is unusual or different from what is considered normal.
anomalous (adjective).
[from Greek *anōmalos* meaning 'uneven']

anon
(adverb) Anon is an old-fashioned word meaning quite soon, e.g. *Well, see you anon.*
anon. an abbreviation for **anonymous**.

anonymous
(adjective) If something is anonymous, nobody knows who did it or who is responsible for it, e.g. *The donor preferred to remain anonymous.*
anonymously (adverb), **anonymity** (noun).

anorak, anoraks
(noun) An anorak is a warm waterproof jacket, usually with a hood.
[an Eskimo word]

anorexia
(noun) Anorexia is a psychological illness in which the person refuses to eat because they are frightened of becoming fat. It often leads to great weakness and sometimes death.
[from Greek *an-* + *orexis* meaning 'no appetite']

another
(determiner and pronoun) Another thing or person means an additional thing or person.

answer, answers, answering, answered
1 (verb) If you answer someone, you reply to them using words or actions or in writing.
2 If you answer for something, you are responsible for it, e.g. *You'll have to answer to the authorities for this blunder.*
3 Someone or something that answers to a description has the characteristics described.
4 (noun) An answer is the reply you give when you answer someone.
5 An answer is also a solution to a problem.
6 (phrase) If you say that someone has **a lot to answer for**, you mean that they are responsible for a lot of trouble.

Similar words: (sense 1) respond, rejoin, riposte (sense 4) response, retort, rejoinder

answerable
(adjective) If you are answerable to someone for something, you are responsible for it, e.g. *We are answerable for the actions of our children.*

answering machine, answering machines
(noun) An answering machine is a machine which records telephone calls while you are out.

ant, ants
(noun) Ants are small insects that live in large groups.

antagonism
(noun) Antagonism is hatred or hostility.

antagonist, antagonists
(noun) An antagonist is an enemy or opponent.

antagonistic
(adjective) Someone who is antagonistic towards you shows hate or hostility.
antagonistically (adverb).

antagonize, antagonizes, antagonizing, antagonized; also spelled **antagonise**
(verb) If someone is antagonized, they are made to feel anger and hostility.
[from Greek *antagōnizesthai* meaning 'to struggle against']

Antarctic
(noun) The Antarctic is the region south of the Antarctic Circle.

Antarctic Circle
(noun) The Antarctic Circle is an imaginary circle around the southern part of the world at latitude 66° 32′ S.

ante-
(prefix) Ante- means before, e.g. *antenatal care.*

anteater, anteaters
(noun) An anteater is a South American animal with a long snout that eats termites and ants.

antecedent, antecedents (pronounced an-tis-**see**-dent)
1 (noun) An antecedent of a thing or event is something which happened or existed before it and is related or similar to it in some way, e.g. *the prehistoric antecedents of the horse.*
2 Your antecedents are your ancestors, the relatives from whom you are descended.
[from Latin *antecedere* meaning 'to go before']

antechamber, antechambers
(noun) An antechamber is a small room leading to a bigger room.

antediluvian (pronounced an-tid-dill-**oo**-vee-an)
(adjective) extremely old-fashioned, e.g. *antediluvian ideas.*
[from Latin *ante-* + *diluvium* meaning 'before the flood']

antelope, antelopes
(noun) An antelope is an animal which looks like a deer. Antelope live in Africa and Asia.

antenatal
(adjective) concerned with the care of pregnant women and their unborn children, e.g. *the antenatal clinic.*

antenna, antennae or antennas
1 (noun) The antennae of insects and certain other animals are the two long, thin parts attached to their heads which they use to feel with. The plural is 'antennae'.
2 In American English, an antenna is a radio or television aerial. The plural is 'antennas'.

anthem, anthems
(noun) An anthem is a hymn written for a special occasion such as a coronation.

anther, anthers
(noun) In a flower, an anther is the part of the stamen that makes pollen grains.
[from Greek *anthos* meaning 'flower']

anthology, anthologies
(noun) An anthology is a collection of poems, songs, or extracts from literature written by various authors and published in one book.
[from Greek *anthologia* meaning 'flower gathering']

anthracite
(noun) Anthracite is a type of very hard, slow-burning coal which gives off little smoke but a lot of heat.

anthrax
(noun) Anthrax is a highly infectious disease of cattle, causing fever, a swollen throat, and painful boils. It can be caught by humans.
[from Greek *anthrax* meaning 'carbuncle']

anthropoid
(adjective) An anthropoid creature is very like a human being, e.g. *an anthropoid ape.*

anthropology
(noun) Anthropology is the study of human beings and their society and culture.
anthropological (adjective), **anthropologist** (noun).
[from Greek *anthrōpos* meaning 'human being']

anthropomorphic
(adjective; a formal word) If you are being anthropomorphic about an animal or object, you think of it as having human qualities and feelings.
anthropomorphism (noun).

anti-
(prefix) opposed to, against, or opposite to something, e.g. *an anti-apartheid demonstration.*

anti-aircraft
(adjective) Anti-aircraft weapons or systems are designed to destroy enemy aircraft.

antibiotic, antibiotics
(noun) Antibiotics are drugs or chemicals that are used in medicines to kill bacteria and cure infections. An example is penicillin.

antibody, antibodies
(noun) Antibodies are proteins produced in the blood which neutralize antigens and so protect against disease.

anticipate, anticipates, anticipating, anticipated
(verb) If you anticipate an event, you are expecting it and are prepared for it, e.g. *The secretary had anticipated the question.*
anticipation (noun).
[from Latin *anticipare* meaning 'to take before']

anticlimax, anticlimaxes
(noun) If something is an anticlimax, it disappoints you because it is not as exciting as expected, or because it occurs after something that was very exciting.

anticlockwise
(adjective and adverb) moving in the opposite direction to the hands of a clock.

antics
(plural noun) Antics are funny or silly ways of behaving.

anticyclone, anticyclones
(noun) An anticyclone is an area of high air pressure which causes settled weather.

antidote, antidotes
(noun) An antidote is a chemical substance that counteracts the effect of a poison.

antifreeze
(noun) Antifreeze is a substance which is added to the water in a car radiator to stop it freezing.

antigen, antigens
(noun) An antigen is a foreign substance, such as a virus, that has entered the body.

antihistamine, antihistamines
(noun) An antihistamine is a drug used to treat an allergy.

antimacassar, antimacassars
(noun) An antimacassar is a cloth which covers the back or arms of a chair to protect it.
[from *anti-* + *macassar*, a type of hair oil]

antioxidant, antioxidants
(noun) An antioxidant is a chemical added to substances, especially foods, in order to prevent them deteriorating because of oxidation.

antipathy
(noun) Antipathy is a strong feeling of dislike or hostility towards something or someone.
antipathetic (adjective).

antiperspirant, antiperspirants
(noun) An antiperspirant is a substance which stops you sweating when you put it on your skin.

antipodes (pronounced an-**tip**-pod-eez)
(plural noun) The antipodes are any two points on the earth's surface that are situated directly opposite each other. Australia and New Zealand are sometimes called the Antipodes.
antipodean (adjective).
[from Greek *antipous* meaning 'with the feet opposite']

antiquarian
(adjective) relating to or involving old and rare objects, e.g. *antiquarian bookshops*.

antiquated
(adjective) very old-fashioned and out of date.

antique, antiques (pronounced an-**teek**)
1 (noun) An antique is an object from the past that is collected because of its value or beauty.
2 (adjective) from or concerning the past, e.g. *antique furniture*.

antiquity, antiquities
1 (noun) Antiquity is the distant past, especially the time of the ancient Egyptians, Greeks, and Romans.
2 Antiquities are interesting works of art and buildings from the distant past.
3 The antiquity of something is its great age.

anti-Semitism
(noun) Anti-Semitism is hatred of Jewish people.
anti-Semitic (adjective), **anti-Semite** (noun).

antiseptic
(adjective) Something that is antiseptic kills germs.

antisocial
1 (adjective) An antisocial person is unwilling to meet and be friendly with other people.
2 Antisocial behaviour is annoying or upsetting to other people, e.g. *Smoking is antisocial*.

antithesis, antitheses (pronounced an-**tith**-iss-iss)
(noun; a formal word) The antithesis of something is its exact opposite, e.g. *He is the antithesis of a contented man*.
[from a Greek word meaning 'opposition']

antitoxin, antitoxins
(noun) An antitoxin is a substance produced by the body to reduce the effect of a poison.

antler, antlers
(noun) A male deer's antlers are the branched horns on its head.

antonym, antonyms
(noun) An antonym is a word which means the opposite of another word. For example, 'hot' is the antonym of 'cold'.
[from *anti-* meaning 'opposite' and Greek *onoma* meaning 'name']

anus, anuses
(noun) The anus is the opening at the end of the alimentary canal through which faeces leave the body.

anvil, anvils
(noun) An anvil is a heavy iron block on which hot metal is beaten into shape.

anxiety, anxieties
(noun) Anxiety is nervousness or worry.

anxious
1 (adjective) If you are anxious, you are nervous or worried.
2 If you are anxious to do something or anxious that something should happen, you very much want to do it or want it to happen.
anxiously (adverb).

any
1 (determiner and pronoun) one, some or several, e.g. *Do you have any books I could read?*
2 even the smallest amount or even one, e.g. *I don't want any breakfast... Don't sell him any.*
3 whatever or whichever, no matter what or which, e.g. *Any of them will do.*

anybody
(pronoun) any person.

anyhow
1 (adverb) in any case.
2 in a careless or untidy way, e.g. *They were packed together anyhow*.

anyone
(pronoun) any person.

anything
(pronoun) any object, event, situation, or action.

anyway
(adverb) in any case.

anywhere
(adverb) in, at, or to any place.

aorta (pronounced ay-**or**-ta)
(noun) The aorta is the main artery in the body, which carries blood away from the heart.
[from Greek *aortē* meaning 'something lifted']

apart
1 (adverb and adjective) When something is apart from something else, there is a space or a distance between them, e.g. *They lived apart from each other... The cars were two feet apart*.
2 (adverb) If you take something apart, you separate it into pieces.

Similar words: (sense 1) separate, asunder

apartheid (pronounced ap-**par**-tide)
(noun) In South Africa, apartheid is the
government policy and laws which keep people
of different races apart.
[an Afrikaans word]

apartment, apartments
(noun) An apartment is a set of rooms for living
in, usually on one floor of a building.

apathetic
(adjective) not interested in anything.
apathetically (adverb).

Similar words: indifferent, languid, uninterested,
half-hearted

apathy (pronounced **ap**-path-ee)
(noun) Apathy is a state of mind in which you do
not care about anything.
[from Greek *apathēs* meaning 'without feeling']

Similar words: indifference, torpor, langour

ape, apes, aping, aped
1 (noun) Apes are primates with a very short tail
or no tail. They are closely related to man. Apes
include chimpanzees, gorillas, and gibbons.
2 (verb) If you ape someone's speech or
behaviour, you imitate it.

apéritif, apéritifs (pronounced ap-per-it-**teef**)
(noun) An apéritif is an alcoholic drink drunk
before a meal.
[a French word]

aperture, apertures (pronounced **app**-er-chure)
(noun) An aperture is a narrow hole or opening.

apex, apexes or apices
(noun) The apex of something is its pointed top.

aphid, aphids
(noun) An aphid is a small insect that feeds by
sucking the juices from plants.

aphorism, aphorisms
(noun) An aphorism is a short, clever sentence
that expresses a general truth.

aphrodisiac, aphrodisiacs
(noun) An aphrodisiac is a food, drink, or drug
which makes people want to have sex.
[from Greek *aphrodisios* meaning 'belonging to
Aphrodite, the goddess of love']

apiary, apiaries (pronounced **ape**-yer-ee)
(noun) An apiary is a place where bees are kept,
usually in beehives.
[from Latin *apis* meaning 'bee']

apiculture (pronounced **ape**-ik-kul-cher)
(noun) Apiculture is beekeeping.

apiece
(adverb) If people have a particular number of
things apiece, they have that number each.

aplomb (pronounced uh-**plom**)
(noun) If you do something with aplomb, you do
it with great confidence.

apocalypse (pronounced uh-**pok**-ka-lips)
1 (noun) The Apocalypse is the total destruction
and end of the world.

2 The apocalypse of something such as a
civilization is its total destruction.
apocalyptic (adjective).
[from Greek *apokaluptein* meaning 'to reveal';
the way the world will end is considered to be
revealed in the last book of the Bible, called
'Apocalypse' or 'Revelation']

Apocrypha
(noun) The Apocrypha is a collection of fourteen
books included in some versions of the Bible as
an appendix to the Old Testament. They are not
found in Hebrew scripture, but in Greek sources.
[from Latin *apocryphus* meaning 'hidden']

apocryphal
(adjective) A story that is apocryphal is
generally believed not to have really happened.

apolitical (pronounced ay-poll-**it**-i-kl)
(adjective) not interested in politics.

apologetic
(adjective) showing or saying that you are sorry
for what you have said or done.
apologetically (adverb).

apologize, apologizes, apologizing, apologized;
also spelled **apologise**
(verb) When you apologize to someone, you say
that you are sorry for something that you have
said or done.

apology, apologies
(noun) An apology is something you say or write
to tell someone that you are sorry for something
you have said or done.

apoplexy (pronounced **ap**-pop-plex-ee)
(noun; an old-fashioned word) Apoplexy is the
same as a stroke, a bursting of a blood vessel in
the brain, which, it was once thought, could be
caused by excessive rage or frustration.
apoplectic (adjective).

apostate, apostates (pronounced a-**poss**-tate)
(noun) An apostate is a person who has
abandoned his or her religious faith or political
beliefs.
apostasy (noun).
[from Greek *apostasis* meaning 'desertion']

apostle, apostles
(noun) The Apostles are the twelve disciples who
were chosen by Christ.
apostolic (adjective).
[from Greek *apostolos* meaning 'messenger']

apostrophe, apostrophes (pronounced
ap-**poss**-troff-ee)
(noun) An apostrophe is a punctuation mark that
is used to show that one or more letters have
been missed out of a word. An example is 'he's'
for 'he is'. Apostrophes are also used with -s at
the end of a noun to show that what follows
belongs to or relates to the noun, e.g. *my
brother's books*. If the noun already has an -s at
the end, for example because it is plural, you just
add the apostrophe, e.g. *my brothers' books*,
referring to more than one brother.

apothecary, apothecaries (pronounced
ap-**poth**-ik-ar-ee)

(noun; an old-fashioned word) An apothecary is the same as a chemist.
[from Greek *apothēkē* meaning 'storehouse']

appal, appals, appalling, appalled
(verb) If something appals you, it shocks you because it is very bad.
[from Old French *apalir* meaning 'to turn pale']

appalling
(adjective) so bad as to be shocking, e.g. *They lived in appalling conditions.*

apparatus
(noun) The apparatus for a particular task is the equipment used for it.
[from Latin *apparare* meaning 'to make ready']

apparel (rhymes with **barrel**)
(noun; an old-fashioned word) A person's apparel is the clothing that he or she is wearing.

apparent
1 (adjective) seeming real rather than actually being real, e.g. *his apparent success.*
2 clear and obvious, e.g. *It became apparent that she wasn't going to turn up.*
apparently (adverb).
[from Latin *apparere* meaning 'to appear']

Similar words: (sense 1) ostensible, seeming

apparition, apparitions
(noun) An apparition is something that you think you see but that is not really there.

appeal, appeals, appealing, appealed
1 (verb) If you appeal for something, you make a serious and urgent request for it, e.g. *The police appealed for calm.*
2 If you appeal to someone in authority against a decision, you formally ask them to change it.
3 If something appeals to you, you find it attractive or interesting.
4 (noun) The appeal of something is the quality it has which people find attractive or interesting, e.g. *What is the appeal of water polo?*
appealing (adjective).

appear, appears, appearing, appeared
1 (verb) When something which you could not see appears, it moves (or you move) so that you can see it.
2 When something new appears, it begins to exist.
3 When an actor or actress appears in a film, play, or show, they take part in it.
4 If something appears to be a certain way, it seems or looks that way, e.g. *He appeared to be having a good time.*

Similar words: (sense 1) materialize, show, emerge (sense 2) emerge, turn up

appearance, appearances
1 (noun) The appearance of someone in a place is their arrival there, especially when it is unexpected.
2 The appearance of something new is the time when it begins to exist, e.g. *the appearance of computer technology.*
3 Someone's or something's appearance is the

way they look to other people, e.g. *Girls seem to take more care of their appearance than boys.*

appease, appeases, appeasing, appeased
(verb) If you try to appease someone, you try to calm them down when they are angry, for example by giving them what they want.
appeasement (noun).

appellation, appellations
(noun; a formal word) An appellation is a name or title.

append, appends, appending, appended
(verb) If you append something, you add it on to something else, e.g. *He appended his signature at the bottom of the page.*
[from Latin *pendere* meaning 'to hang']

appendage, appendages
(noun) An appendage is a less important part attached to a main part.

appendectomy, appendectomies; also spelled **appendicectomy**
(noun) An appendectomy is an operation to take out a person's appendix.

appendicitis (pronounced app-end-i-**site**-uss)
(noun) Appendicitis is a painful illness in which a person's appendix becomes infected.

appendix, appendices
1 (noun) Your appendix is a small closed tube forming part of your digestive system. It has no particular purpose.
2 An appendix to a book is extra information that is placed after the end of the main text.
[a Latin word meaning 'appendage']

appertain, appertains, appertaining, appertained
(verb; a formal word) If something appertains to something else, it belongs to it or is relevant to it, e.g. *facts appertaining to this case.*

appetite, appetites
1 (noun) Your appetite is your desire to eat.
2 If you have an appetite for something, you have a strong desire for it and enjoyment of it, e.g. *He has an amazing appetite for hard work.*
[from Latin *appetere* meaning 'to desire']

appetizer, appetizers; also spelled **appetiser**
(noun) An appetizer is a small amount of food served just before a meal in order to give people an appetite.

appetizing or **appetising**
(adjective) Food that is appetizing looks and smells good, and makes you want to eat it.

applaud, applauds, applauding, applauded
1 (verb) When a group of people applaud, they clap their hands in approval or praise.
2 When an action or attitude is applauded, people praise it.
[from Latin *applaudere* meaning 'to clap']

applause
(noun) Applause is clapping by a group of people.

apple, apples
(noun) An apple is a round fruit with smooth skin and firm white flesh.

appliance, appliances
(noun) An appliance is any device or machine

that is designed to do a particular job, especially in the home, e.g. *electrical appliances.*

applicable
(adjective) Something that is applicable to a situation is relevant to it, e.g. *This rule is applicable only to sixth-formers.*

applicant, applicants
(noun) An applicant is someone who is applying for something, e.g. *There were more than twenty applicants for the job.*

application, applications
1 (noun) An application for something is a formal request for it, usually in writing.
2 The application of a rule, system, or skill is the use of it in a particular situation.
3 To do something with application means to do it with a lot of hard work and concentration.

applied
(adjective) to do with or designed for practical use, e.g. *applied mathematics.*

appliqué (pronounced ap-**plee**-kay)
(noun) Appliqué is the art of decorating material by sewing other pieces of material on top of it.
[a French word meaning 'applied']

apply, applies, applying, applied
1 (verb) If you apply for something, you formally ask for it, usually by writing a letter.
2 If you apply a rule, system, or skill, you use it in a situation or an activity, e.g. *She applied her common sense to the problem.*
3 If something applies to a person or a situation, it is relevant to that person or situation, e.g. *The rule applies only to motorcyclists.*
4 If you apply something to a surface, you put it on, e.g. *Apply the glue to the corners.*

appoint, appoints, appointing, appointed
1 (verb) If you appoint someone to a job or position, you formally choose them for it.
2 If you appoint a time or place for something to happen, you decide when or where it will happen.
appointed (adjective).
[from Old French *apointier* meaning 'to arrange']

appointment, appointments
1 (noun) An appointment is an arrangement you have with someone to meet or visit them.
2 The appointment of a person to do a particular job is the choosing of that person to do it.
3 An appointment is also a job or a position of responsibility, e.g. *She has applied for an appointment in London.*

Similar words: (sense 1) engagement, date, booking

apportion, apportions, apportioning, apportioned
(verb) If you apportion something, you divide it, e.g. *The head apportioned the blame fairly.*

apposite (pronounced **app**-o-zit)
(adjective) well suited for a particular purpose, e.g. *an apposite reply.*
[from Latin *appositus* meaning 'place near']

apposition
(noun) When one word or phrase is in apposition to another, it comes next to it and tells you more about it.

appraise, appraises, appraising, appraised
(verb) If you appraise something, you think about it carefully and form an opinion about it.
appraisal (noun).

appreciable (pronounced a-**pree**-shuh-bl)
(adjective) large enough or important enough to be noticed, e.g. *an appreciable increase.*
appreciably (adverb).

appreciate, appreciates, appreciating, appreciated
1 (verb) If you appreciate something, you like it because you recognize its good qualities, e.g. *She appreciates good food.*
2 If you appreciate a situation or problem, you understand it and know what it involves.
3 If you appreciate something that someone has done for you, you are grateful to them for it, e.g. *I really appreciate you coming to visit me.*
4 If something appreciates over a period of time, its value increases, e.g. *Our house appreciated by 50% in six months.*
appreciation (noun).
[from Latin *pretium* meaning 'price']

Similar words: (sense 1) esteem, value, prize

appreciative
(adjective) thankful and grateful, e.g. *She was very appreciative of the gifts we sent.*
appreciatively (adverb).

apprehend, apprehends, apprehending, apprehended
1 (verb) When the police apprehend someone, they arrest them and take them into custody.
2 (a formal use) If you apprehend something, you understand it fully, e.g. *We often fail to apprehend the real nature of change.*
[from Latin *apprehendere* meaning 'to seize']

apprehensive
(adjective) afraid that something bad may happen, e.g. *I'm very apprehensive about my driving test.*
apprehensively (adverb), apprehension (noun).

apprentice, apprentices
(noun) An apprentice is a person who works for a period of time with a skilled craftsman in order to learn a skill or trade.
apprenticeship (noun).
[from Old French *aprendre* meaning 'to learn']

approach, approaches, approaching, approached
1 (verb) To approach something means to come nearer to it.
2 When a future event approaches, it gradually gets nearer, e.g. *As nightfall approached we arrived at the next village.*
3 (noun) The approach of something is the process of it coming closer, e.g. *the approach of winter.*
4 (verb) If you approach someone about something, you ask them about it.
5 If you approach a situation or problem in a particular way, you think about it or deal with it in that way.
6 (noun) An approach to a situation or problem is a way of thinking about it or dealing with it.

7 (verb) If something approaches a particular level or state, it almost reaches that level or state, e.g. *The temperature was approaching 95°.*
8 (noun) An approach to a place is a road or path that leads to it.
approaching (adjective).

approbation
(noun; a formal word) Approbation is approval of something.

appropriate, appropriates, appropriating, appropriated
1 (adjective) suitable or acceptable for a particular situation, e.g. *Jeans are not appropriate for a formal dinner party.*
2 (verb) If you appropriate something which does not belong to you, you take it without permission.
3 (a formal use) If goods or funds are appropriated for a particular purpose, they are put aside for that purpose, e.g. *The cash has already been appropriated for the youth club.*
appropriately (adverb), **appropriation** (noun).
[from Latin *appropriare* meaning 'to make one's own']

approval
1 (noun) Approval is agreement given to a plan or request, e.g. *The development scheme doesn't have government approval yet.*
2 Approval is also admiration for someone, e.g. *Janet looked at her young son with approval.*

Similar words: (sense 1) authorization, sanction, approbation, blessing, okay

approve, approves, approving, approved
1 (verb) If you approve of something, you think that it is right or good.
2 If you approve of someone, you like them and think they are all right, e.g. *My parents don't approve of my new girlfriend.*
3 If someone in a position of authority approves a plan or idea, they formally agree to it.
approved (adjective), **approving** (adjective).
[from Latin *probare* meaning 'to test']

Similar words: (sense 1) applaud, commend (sense 3) authorize, sanction

approximate, approximates, approximating, approximated
1 (adjective) almost accurate or exact, e.g. *The approximate value of the house is £90,000.*
2 (verb) If something approximates to a particular number or size, it is close to it.
3 If something approximates to something else, it is similar to it, but not exactly the same, e.g. *The fashions of the eighties approximate to those of twenty years ago.*
approximately (adverb).
[from Latin *proximus* meaning 'nearest']

Similar words: (sense 1) close, near, rough

approximation, approximations
(noun) An approximation is a vague or unreliable version or description, e.g. *His story was an approximation of what really happened.*

appurtenances
(plural noun; a formal word) Appurtenances are extra features or additions to something.
[from Old French *apartenir* meaning 'to belong to']

après-ski
(noun) Après-ski is social activities and entertainment after a day's skiing.
[a French expression meaning 'after skiing']

apricot, apricots
(noun) An apricot is a small, soft, yellowish-orange fruit.
[from Latin *praecox* meaning 'early ripening']

April
(noun) April is the fourth month of the year. It has 30 days.

apron, aprons
1 (noun) An apron is a piece of clothing worn over the front of normal clothing to protect it.
2 An apron is also a hard-surfaced area in front of an aircraft hangar or terminal building.
[from Middle English *a napron*]

apropos
(phrase) Something that is **apropos of** a subject is relevant to it.
[from French *à propos* meaning 'to the purpose']

apse, apses
(noun) An apse in a church is a domed recess in the east wall.

apt
1 (adjective) suitable or relevant, e.g. *a very apt remark.*
2 having a particular tendency, e.g. *He's apt to make silly remarks in public.*
3 You can describe a person as apt when they have an ability to learn quickly, e.g. *an apt pupil.*

aptitude
(noun) Someone's aptitude for something is their ability to learn it quickly and to do it well, e.g. *She has an aptitude for figures.*

aqualung, aqualungs
(noun) An aqualung is a piece of equipment used by divers to enable them to breathe under water. It consists of a bottle of air connected by tubes to a face mask.

aquamarine, aquamarines
1 (noun and adjective) greenish-blue.
2 (noun) An aquamarine is a clear greenish-blue stone used in making jewellery.
[from Latin *aqua marina* meaning 'sea water']

aquarium, aquaria or aquariums
(noun) An aquarium is a glass tank filled with water in which fish are kept.

Aquarius
(noun) Aquarius is the eleventh sign of the zodiac, represented by a person carrying water. People born between January 20th and February 18th are born under this sign.

aquatic
1 (adjective) An aquatic animal or plant lives or grows in water.
2 involving water, e.g. *aquatic sports.*

aqueduct, aqueducts
(noun) An aqueduct is a long bridge with many arches carrying a water supply over a valley.

aquiline
(adjective) An aquiline nose is curved or hooked like an eagle's beak.
[from Latin *aquila* meaning 'eagle']

Arab, Arabs
(noun) An Arab is a member of a group of people who used to live in Arabia but who now live throughout the Middle East and North Africa.

Arabic
(noun) Arabic is a language spoken by many people in the Middle East and North Africa. It is the official language of several countries including Egypt, Libya, and Iraq. There are many dialects of Arabic.

arable
(adjective) Arable land is suitable for growing crops.

arachnid, arachnids (pronounced ar-**rak**-nid)
(noun) An arachnid is an animal such as a spider, with simple eyes and four pairs of legs.

arbiter, arbiters
(noun) The arbiter of something is the person who decides about it.

arbitrary
(adjective) An arbitrary decision or action is one that is not based on a plan or system.
arbitrarily (adverb).

arbitrate, arbitrates, arbitrating, arbitrated
(verb) When someone arbitrates between two people or groups who are in disagreement, they consider the facts and decide who is right.
arbitration (noun), **arbitrator** (noun).

arboreal (pronounced ahr-**bore**-ee-al)
(adjective) An animal that is arboreal lives mainly in the tops of trees.
[from Latin *arbor* meaning 'tree']

arbour, arbours
(noun; a literary word) An arbour is a shelter in a garden made of leaves and stems growing close together over a light framework.

arc, arcs, arcing, arced
1 (noun) An arc is a smoothly curving line.
2 In geometry, an arc is a section of the circumference of a circle.
3 (verb) When an electric current arcs, it jumps across a gap between two contact points and produces a line of sparks.
4 (noun) An arc is a line of sparks that occurs when an electric current flows between two contact points separated by a gap.
[from Latin *arcus* meaning 'bow']

arcade, arcades
(noun) An arcade is a covered passageway where there are shops or market stalls.

arcane
(adjective) mysterious and difficult to understand.

arch, arches, arching, arched
1 (noun) An arch is a structure that has a curved top supported on either side by a pillar or wall.
2 An arch is also anything that is curved like an arch, e.g. *the arch of your foot.*
3 (verb) When something arches, it forms a curved line or shape.
4 (adjective) most important, e.g. *our arch enemy.*
5 An arch look is mysterious and mischievous.

archaeology or **archeology** (pronounced ar-kee-**ol**-loj-ee)
(noun) Archaeology is the study of the past by digging up and examining the remains of buildings, tools, and other things.
archaeological (adjective), **archaeologist** (noun).
[from Greek *arkhaios* meaning 'ancient']

archaic (pronounced ar-**kay**-ik)
(adjective) very old or old-fashioned.

archangel, archangels (pronounced ark-**ain**-jel)
(noun) An archangel is an angel of the highest rank.

archbishop, archbishops
(noun) An archbishop is a bishop of the highest rank in a Christian Church.

archdeacon, archdeacons
(noun) An archdeacon is an Anglican clergyman ranking just below a bishop.

archeology another spelling of **archaeology.**

archer, archers
(noun) An archer is someone who shoots with a bow and arrow, especially for sport.

archery
(noun) Archery is a sport in which people shoot at a target with a bow and arrow.

archetype, archetypes (pronounced **ark**-i-type)
(noun) An archetype is anything that is a perfect example of its kind, e.g. *He is the archetype of a first class athlete.*
archetypal (adjective).

archipelago, archipelagos (pronounced ar-kip-**pel**-lag-oh)
(noun) An archipelago is a group of small islands.
[from Italian *arcipelago* meaning 'chief sea'; originally referring to the Aegean Sea]

architect, architects (pronounced **ar**-kit-tekt)
(noun) An architect is a person who designs buildings.
[from Greek *arkhitektōn* meaning 'chief builder']

architecture
(noun) Architecture is the art or practice of designing buildings.
architectural (adjective).

archive, archives (pronounced **ar**-kive)
(noun) Archives are collections of documents and records about the history of a family, organization, or some other group of people.

archway, archways
(noun) An archway is a passage or entrance under an arch.

arctic
1 (noun) The Arctic is the region north of the Arctic Circle.
2 (adjective) Arctic means very cold indeed, e.g. *arctic temperatures.*
[from Greek *arktos* meaning 'bear'; originally it referred to the northern constellation of the Great Bear]

Arctic Circle
(noun) The Arctic Circle is an imaginary circle around the northern part of the world at latitude 66° 32′ N.

ardent
(adjective) full of enthusiasm and passion.
ardently (adverb).
[from Latin *ardere* meaning 'to burn']

ardour
(noun) Ardour is a strong and passionate feeling of love or enthusiasm.

arduous (pronounced ard-yoo-uss)
(adjective) tiring and needing a lot of effort, e.g. *Writing an essay can be an arduous exercise.*

area, areas
1 (noun) An area is a particular part of a place, country, or the world, e.g. *a run-down area of Birmingham.*
2 The area of a piece of ground or a surface is the amount of space that it covers, measured in square feet or square metres.
3 An area of knowledge, interest, or activity is a particular kind of subject or activity.
[from Latin *area* meaning 'piece of flat ground']

Similar words: (sense 1) district, locality, neighbourhood, vicinity, zone

arena, arenas
1 (noun) An arena is a place where sports and other public events take place.
2 A particular arena is the centre of attention or activity in a particular situation, e.g. *He entered the arena of politics at an early age.*
[from Latin *harena* meaning 'sand', hence the sandy centre of an amphitheatre where gladiators fought]

areola, areolas or areolae (pronounced ar-ee-o-la)
(noun; a technical word) An areola is a dark area of skin around a nipple.

Argentinian, Argentinians (pronounced ar-jen-tin-ee-an)
1 (adjective) belonging or relating to Argentina.
2 (noun) An Argentinian is someone who comes from Argentina.

argon
(noun) Argon is a chemical element found as a colourless, odourless gas in the earth's atmosphere. It is used in electric lights. Argon's atomic number is 18 and its symbol is Ar.

argot, argots (pronounced ar-goh)
(noun) An argot is a special vocabulary used by a particular group of people, which other people find difficult to understand.
[a French word]

arguable
1 (adjective) An arguable idea, point, or comment is not necessarily true or correct and should be questioned.
2 If you say that something is arguable, you mean that it is possible to argue that it is true.
arguably (adverb).

argue, argues, arguing, argued
1 (verb) If you argue with someone about something, you disagree with them about it, sometimes in an angry way.
2 If you argue that something is the case, you give reasons why you think it is so, e.g. *Some people argue that the NHS should be abolished.*
[from Latin *arguere* meaning 'to make clear' or 'to accuse']

argument, arguments
1 (noun) An argument is a disagreement between two people which causes a quarrel.
2 An argument is also a point or a set of reasons that you use to try to convince people about something.

argumentative
(adjective) An argumentative person is always arguing or disagreeing with other people.

aria, arias (pronounced ah-ree-a)
(noun) An aria is a song sung by one of the leading singers in an opera or choral work.
[an Italian word meaning 'tune']

arid
1 (adjective) Arid land is very dry because it has very little rain.
2 An arid topic or piece of writing is dull and uninteresting, e.g. *What an arid book!*
aridity (noun).

Aries (pronounced air-reez)
(noun) Aries is the first sign of the zodiac, represented by a ram. People born between March 21st and April 19th are born under this sign.

arise, arises, arising, arose, arisen
1 (verb) When something such as an opportunity, problem, or new state of affairs arises, it begins to exist.
2 (a formal use) To arise also means to stand up from a sitting, kneeling, or lying position.

aristocracy, aristocracies
(noun) The aristocracy is a class of people who have a high social rank and special titles.
[from Greek *aristos* meaning 'best']

aristocrat, aristocrats
(noun) An aristocrat is someone whose family has a high social rank, and who has a title.
aristocratic (adjective).

arithmetic
(noun) Arithmetic is the part of mathematics which is to do with the addition, subtraction, multiplication, and division of numbers.
arithmetic (adjective), **arithmetically** (adverb).
[from Greek *arithmos* meaning 'number']

ark
1 (noun) In the Bible, the ark was the boat built

by Noah for his family and the animals during the Flood.

2 The Ark of the Covenant was the symbol of the presence of God to the Hebrew people. It took the form of a box covered with gold.

3 In Judaism, the ark is the cupboard at the front of a synagogue in which the Torah scrolls are kept.

[senses 2 and 3 are from Latin *arca* meaning 'box']

arm, arms, arming, armed
1 (noun) Your arms are the part of your body between your shoulder and your wrist.
2 The arm of an object is any part which looks like or works like an arm.
3 An arm of an organization is a section of it, e.g. *the political arm of the Students' Union.*
4 (plural noun) Arms are weapons used in a war.
5 (verb) To arm someone means to provide them with weapons as a preparation for war.

armada, armadas (pronounced ar-**mah**-da)
(noun) An armada is a large fleet of warships. In 1588, the Spanish Armada was sent against England by Philip II of Spain, but was defeated in the Channel by the English and destroyed.
[a Spanish word]

armadillo, armadillos
(noun) An armadillo is a mammal from South America which is covered with strong bony plates like armour.
[a Spanish word meaning 'little armed man']

Armageddon
(noun) In Christianity, Armageddon is the final battle between good and evil at the end of the world.
[from Hebrew *har megiddon*, the mountain district of Megiddo, the site of many battles]

armament, armaments
(noun) Armaments are the weapons and military equipment that belong to a country.

armature
(noun) The armature in an electric motor is a coiled wire surrounding an iron core, which vibrates or revolves to create electric current.

armchair, armchairs
(noun) An armchair is a comfortable chair with a support on each side for your arms.

armed
1 (adjective) A person who is armed is carrying a weapon or weapons.
2 If you are armed with something such as information, skill, or a tool, you have it ready to be used, e.g. *Armed with a set of spanners he went out to mend his bike.*

armistice, armistices (pronounced **ar**-miss-tiss)
(noun) An armistice is an agreement in a war to stop fighting in order to discuss peace.
[from Latin *arma* meaning 'weapons' and *sistere* meaning 'to stop']

armorial
(adjective; a formal word) concerned with heraldry and coats of arms.

armour
1 (noun) In the past, armour was metal clothing worn for protection in battle.
2 In modern warfare, tanks are often referred to as armour.

armoured
(adjective) covered with thick steel for protection from gunfire and other missiles, e.g. *an armoured car.*

armour-plate
(noun) Armour-plate is a heavy, tough steel used for protecting warships and tanks.

armoury, armouries
(noun) An armoury is a place where weapons are stored.

armpit, armpits
(noun) Your armpit is the area under your arm where your arm joins your shoulder.

army, armies
(noun) An army is a large group of soldiers organized into divisions for fighting on land.
[from Latin *armata* meaning 'armed forces']

aroma, aromas
(noun) An aroma is a strong, pleasant smell.
aromatic (adjective).
[a Greek word meaning 'spice']

around
1 (preposition) placed at various points in a place or area, e.g. *There are many fire extinguishers around the building.*
2 from place to place inside an area, e.g. *We walked around the shopping centre.*
3 at approximately the time or place mentioned, e.g. *It happened around March sometime.*
4 (adverb) here and there, e.g. *There were cushions scattered around.*

arouse, arouse, arousing, aroused
1 (verb) If something arouses a feeling in you, it causes you to begin to have this feeling, e.g. *The letter aroused in me a strong feeling of jealousy.*
2 When something or someone arouses you from sleep, they wake you up.
arousal (noun).

arpeggio, arpeggios (pronounced ar-**pej**-ee-oh)
(noun) In music, an arpeggio is a chord in which the notes are played one after the other.
[from Italian *arpeggiare* meaning 'to play the harp']

arraign, arraigns, arraigning, arraigned
(verb; a formal word) To arraign someone means to bring them before a court of law to answer a charge made against them.
arraignment (noun).

arrange, arranges, arranging, arranged
1 (verb) If you arrange to do something, you make plans for it.
2 If you arrange something for someone, you make it possible for them to have it or do it, e.g. *The bank manager has arranged a loan for me.*
3 If you arrange objects, you set them out in a particular position, e.g. *The chairs were arranged in a circle.*
arrangement (noun).

[from Old French *arangier* meaning 'to put in a row']

arrant
(adjective; an old-fashioned word) complete and absolute, e.g. *an arrant thief*.
[from *errant* meaning 'wandering', used originally to describe thieves and rogues]

array, arrays, arraying, arrayed
1 (noun) An array of different things is a large number of them displayed together.
2 (verb) If things are arrayed somewhere, they are displayed there in an attractive way.
[from Old French *arayer* meaning 'to arrange']

arrears
1 (plural noun) Arrears are amounts of money that you owe, e.g. *rent arrears*.
2 (phrase) If you are paid **in arrears**, you are paid at the end of the period for which the payment is due.
[from Old French *arere* meaning 'backwards']

arrest, arrests, arresting, arrested
1 (verb) If the police arrest someone, they take them into custody to decide whether to charge them with an offence.
2 (noun) An arrest is the act of taking a person into custody.
3 (verb) If you arrest something, you stop it happening, e.g. *Doctors tried to arrest the disease with drugs*.
4 If something arrests your attention, it interests or surprises you so that you stop and look at it.
arresting (adjective).
[from Latin *restare* meaning 'to remain']

Similar words: (sense 1) apprehend, detain, stop

arrival, arrivals
1 (noun) An arrival is the act or time of arriving, e.g. *The arrival of the plane was delayed*.
2 An arrival is something or someone that has arrived, e.g. *We welcomed all the new arrivals*.

arrive, arrives, arriving, arrived
1 (verb) When you arrive at a place, you reach it at the end of your journey.
2 When something such as a piece of news arrives, it is brought to you, e.g. *News of the disaster arrived this morning*.
3 When you arrive at an idea, decision, or conclusion, you reach it or decide on it, e.g. *The committee arrived at their decision last night*.
4 When a moment, event, or new thing arrives, it begins to happen, e.g. *The holidays arrived*.

arrogant
(adjective) Someone who is arrogant behaves as if they are better than other people.
arrogantly (adverb), **arrogance** (noun).
[from Latin *arrogare* meaning 'to lay claim to']

arrow, arrows
1 (noun) An arrow is a long, thin weapon with a sharp point at one end, shot from a bow.
2 An arrow is a sign showing a direction.

arrowroot
(noun) Arrowroot is a type of starch used in cooking; also the plant from which it is obtained.

arsenal, arsenals
(noun) An arsenal is a place where weapons and ammunition are stored or produced.
[from Italian *arsenale* meaning 'dockyard', originally in Venice]

arsenic
(noun) Arsenic is a strongly poisonous element used in insecticides and weedkillers. Arsenic's atomic number is 33 and its symbol is As.

arson
(noun) Arson is the crime of deliberately setting fire to something, especially a building.

art, arts
1 (noun) Art is the creation of objects such as paintings and sculptures, which are thought to be beautiful or which express a particular idea; also used to refer to the objects themselves.
2 (plural noun) The arts are literature, music, painting, and sculpture, considered together.
3 (noun) An activity is an art when it requires a lot of skill or ability, e.g. *the art of conversation*.

artefact, artefacts (pronounced ar-tif-fact)
(noun) An artefact is any ornament, tool, or other object that is made by people.

artery, arteries
1 (noun) Your arteries are the tubes that carry oxygenated blood from your heart to the rest of your body.
2 An artery is also a main road or major section of any system of communication or transport.
arterial (adjective).

artesian well, artesian wells
(noun) An artesian well is a well in which water is continually forced upwards under pressure.
[from *Artois*, a French province where these wells were common]

artful
(adjective) clever and skilful, often in a cunning way.
artfully (adverb).

arthritis
(noun) Arthritis is a condition in which the joints in someone's body become swollen and painful.
arthritic (adjective).

artichoke, artichokes
1 (noun) A globe artichoke is a round green vegetable that has a cluster of fleshy leaves, the bottom part of which you can eat.
2 A Jerusalem artichoke is a small yellowish-white vegetable that grows underground and looks like a potato.
[from Arabic *al-kharshuf*]

article, articles
1 (noun) An article is a particular object or item, e.g. *She bought three articles of clothing*.
2 An article is also a piece of writing in a newspaper or magazine.
3 In English grammar, 'a' and 'the' are sometimes called articles: 'a' (or 'an') is the indefinite article; 'the' is the definite article.

articulate, articulates, articulating, articulated
1 (verb) When you articulate your ideas or

feelings, you express in words what you think or feel, e.g. *He could not articulate his grief.*
2 When you articulate a sound or word, you speak it clearly and distinctly.
3 (adjective) If you are articulate, you are able to express yourself well in words.
articulation (noun).

articulated
(adjective) An articulated lorry has two sections, a tractor and a trailer, joined together.
[from Latin *articulatus* meaning 'jointed']

artifact another spelling of **artefact**.

artificial
1 (adjective) created by people rather than occurring naturally, e.g. *artificial flowers.*
2 pretending to have attitudes and feelings which other people realize are not real, e.g. *an artificial smile.*
artificially (adverb), **artificiality** (noun).

artificial insemination
(noun) Artificial insemination is the placing of sperm into a female in order to make her pregnant without direct contact with the male.

artificial intelligence
(noun) Artificial intelligence is the study of how to make computers do things that are considered to be specifically human activities, especially in the areas of thought, language, and vision.

artillery
1 (noun) Artillery consists of large, powerful guns such as cannons.
2 The artillery is the branch of an army which uses large, powerful guns.

artisan, artisans
(noun) An artisan is a skilled workman.

artist, artists
1 (noun) An artist is a person who draws or paints or produces other works of art.
2 An artist is also a person who is very skilled at a particular activity.

artiste, artistes (pronounced ar-**teest**)
(noun) An artiste is a professional entertainer, for example a singer or a dancer.
[a French word meaning 'artist']

artistic
1 (adjective) able to create good paintings, sculpture, or other works of art.
2 concerning or involving art or artists.
artistically (adverb).

artistry
(noun) Artistry is the degree of creative skill of an artist, writer, actor, or musician, e.g. *He played the piece with great artistry.*

artless
(adjective) without deceit or cunning
artlessly (adverb), **artlessness** (noun).

arty
(adjective; an informal word) interested in painting, sculpture, and other works of art.

as
1 (conjunction) at the same time that, e.g. *She laughed as she left the room.*

2 in the way that, e.g. *laughing and joking, as children do.*
3 because, e.g. *As I won't be here tomorrow, don't bother to cook a meal.*
4 You use the structure **as ... as** when you are comparing things that are similar, e.g. *He was out of the door as quick as a flash.*
5 (preposition) You use 'as' when you are saying what role someone or something has, e.g. *He worked as a clerk for most of his life.*
6 You use **as if** or **as though** when you are giving a possible explanation for something, e.g. *She looked at me as if I were stupid.*

asbestos
(noun) Asbestos is a grey heat-resistant material used in the past to make fireproof articles. It is now known to cause lung disease.
[from Greek *asbestos* meaning 'inextinguishable']

ascend, ascends, ascending, ascended
(pronounced ass-**end**)
(verb; a formal word) To ascend means to move or lead upwards, e.g. *stairs ascending to the attic.*

ascendancy
(noun) If one group has ascendancy over another, it has more power or influence than the other.

ascendant
1 (adjective) rising or moving upwards.
2 (phrase) Someone or something that is **in the ascendant** is increasing in power or popularity.

ascent, ascents
(noun) An ascent is an upward journey, for example up a mountain.

ascertain, ascertains, ascertaining, ascertained
(pronounced **ass**-er-tain)
(verb; a formal word) If you ascertain that something is the case, you find out that it is the case, e.g. *I ascertained that John had left.*
[from Old French *acertener* meaning 'to make certain']

ascetic, ascetics (pronounced ass-**set**-ik)
1 (adjective) People who are ascetic have a way of life that is simple and strict, usually because of their religious beliefs.
2 (noun) An ascetic is a person who has a strict and simple way of life.
ascetically (adverb), **asceticism** (noun).
[from Greek *askētēs* meaning 'monk' or 'hermit']

ASCI
(noun) ASCI is a set of 128 letters, numbers, and symbols which make up the computer alphabet. ASCI stands for 'American Standard Code for Information Exchange'.

ascribe, ascribes, ascribing, ascribed
1 (verb) If you ascribe an event or state of affairs to a particular factor, you consider that it is caused by that factor, e.g. *Stomach pains can often be ascribed to worry.*
2 If you ascribe a quality to someone, you consider that they possess it.
3 If a work of art is ascribed to a particular

artist, it is considered to have been created by that artist.
[from Latin *ascribere* meaning 'to enrol']

aseptic
(adjective) clean and free from germs.

asexual
1 (adjective) having no sex or sexual organs.
2 involving no sexual activity or processes.

ash, ashes
1 (noun) An ash is a tree with grey bark and hard tough wood used for timber.
2 Ash is the grey or black powdery remains of anything that has been burnt.

ashamed
1 (adjective) feeling embarrassed or guilty.
2 If you are ashamed of someone, you feel embarrassed to be connected with them.

ashen
(adjective) grey or pale, e.g. *His face was ashen.*

ashore
(adverb) on land or onto the land.

ashtray, ashtrays
(noun) An ashtray is a small dish for ash from cigarettes, pipes, and cigars.

Asia
(noun) Asia is the largest continent. It has Europe on its western side, with the Arctic to the north, the Pacific to the east, and the Indian Ocean to the south. Asia includes several island groups, including Japan, Indonesia, and the Philippines.

Asian, Asians
1 (adjective) belonging or relating to Asia.
2 (noun) An Asian is someone who comes from India, Pakistan, Bangladesh, Sri Lanka, or from some other part of Asia.

aside, asides
1 (adverb) If you move something aside, you move it to one side.
2 (noun) An aside is a comment that does not form part of the conversation or dialogue.

asinine
(adjective) stupid.
[from Latin *asinus* meaning 'ass']

ask, asks, asking, asked
1 (verb) If you ask someone a question, you put a question to them.
2 If you ask someone to do something, you tell them that you want them to do it.
3 If you ask for something, you say that you would like to have it.
4 If you ask someone's permission or forgiveness, you try to obtain it.
5 If you ask someone somewhere, you invite them there, e.g. *They were asked to the party.*
6 If someone asks something of you, they expect it of you, e.g. *You're asking too much of me.*
7 (phrase) If you say that someone is **asking for trouble**, you mean that they are doing something that will get them into trouble.

askance
1 (adverb) If you look askance at someone or something, you glance at them sideways.
2 If you look askance at a situation, you regard it with doubt or mistrust.

askew
(adjective) not straight or level.

asleep
(adjective) sleeping.

asp, asps
(noun) An asp is a type of small poisonous snake.

asparagus
(noun) Asparagus is a vegetable that has long soft-tipped shoots which are cooked and eaten.

aspect, aspects
1 (noun) An aspect of something is one of its distinctive features, e.g. *The most interesting aspect of photography is developing your prints.*
2 The aspect of a building is the direction it faces, e.g. *a house with a southern aspect.*
3 If something acquires a new aspect, it acquires a new appearance or quality.
[from Latin *aspicere* meaning 'to look at']

aspen, aspens
(noun) An aspen is a kind of poplar tree whose leaves are attached to the stem by long, flat stalks so that they quiver in the breeze.

asperity
(noun; a formal word) If you speak to someone with asperity, you speak to them in a harsh or severe way.
[from Latin *asper* meaning 'rough']

aspersion, aspersions
(noun) If you cast aspersions on someone or something, you make critical or damaging remarks about them.

asphalt
(noun) Asphalt is a mixture of bitumen, oil, and small stones used to make road surfaces and playgrounds.

asphyxia (pronounced ass-**fiks**-ee-a)
(noun) Asphyxia is not being able to get enough oxygen or not being able to breathe at all.
[from Greek *asphuxia* meaning 'stopping of the pulse']

asphyxiate, asphyxiates, asphyxiating, asphyxiated
(verb) If a person asphyxiates, they cannot breathe or cannot get enough oxygen.
asphyxiation (noun).

aspic
(noun) Aspic is a clear jelly made from meat or fish juices.

aspirant, aspirants (pronounced ass-pir-nt)
(noun; a formal word) An aspirant is a person with a desire to achieve a particular ambition.

aspirate, aspirates, aspirating, aspirated
(verb) To aspirate a word means to pronounce it with an 'h' sound at the beginning.

aspiration, aspirations
(noun) Someone's aspirations are their desires and ambitions.

aspire, aspires, aspiring, aspired
(verb) If you aspire to something, you have an ambition to achieve it, e.g. *She had always aspired to becoming a first-class gymnast.*
aspiring (adjective).

aspirin, aspirins
1 (noun) Aspirin is a white crystalline drug used to relieve pain, fever, and colds.
2 An aspirin is a tablet of this drug.

ass, asses
1 (noun) An ass is a donkey.
2 You can call someone an ass if you think they are stupid.

assail, assails, assailing, assailed
(verb; a formal word) To assail someone means to attack them physically, mentally, or with words, e.g. *He was assailed by doubts.*
[from Latin *assalire* meaning 'to leap upon']

assailant, assailants
(noun) An assailant is someone who attacks another person.

assassin, assassins
(noun) An assassin is someone who has murdered a political or religious leader.
[from Arabic *hashshashin* meaning 'people who eat hashish'; the name comes from a medieval Muslim sect who ate hashish and went about murdering Crusaders]

assassinate, assassinates, assassinating, assassinated
(verb) To assassinate a political or religious leader means to murder him or her.
assassination (noun).

assault, assaults, assaulting, assaulted
1 (noun) An assault is a violent physical attack on someone.
2 (verb) To assault someone means to attack them violently.
[from Latin *assalire* meaning 'to leap upon']

assemble, assembles, assembling, assembled
1 (verb) To assemble means to gather together.
2 If you assemble something, you fit the parts of it together.
[from Latin *simul* meaning 'together']

assembly, assemblies
1 (noun) An assembly is a group of people who have gathered together for a meeting.
2 The assembly of an object is the fitting together of its parts, e.g. *instructions for the assembly of a barbecue.*

assembly line, assembly lines
(noun) An assembly line is an arrangement of machines in a factory, in which each machine makes one part of a product. The product is passed along from machine to machine.

assent, assents, assenting, assented (pronounced as-**sent**)
1 (noun) If you give your assent to something, you agree to it or say yes to it.
2 (verb) If you assent to something, you agree to it or say yes to it.
[from Latin *sentire* meaning 'to feel' or 'to think']

assert, asserts, asserting, asserted
1 (verb) If you assert a fact, belief, or opinion, you state it firmly and forcefully.
2 If you assert yourself, you speak and behave in a forceful way, so that people pay attention to you and your opinions.
[from Latin *asserere* meaning 'to join to oneself']

assertive
(adjective) If you are assertive, you speak and behave in a forceful way, so that people pay attention to you and your opinions.
assertively (adverb), **assertiveness** (noun).

assess, assesses, assessing, assessed
(verb) If you assess something, you consider it carefully and make a judgment about it.
assessment (noun).
[from Latin *assidere* meaning 'to sit beside']

Similar words: appraise, evaluate, size up

assessor, assessors
(noun) An assessor is someone whose job is to assess the value of something.

asset, assets
1 (noun) An asset is a person or thing that is considered useful, e.g. *As editor he was a major asset to the paper.*
2 (plural noun) The assets of a person or company are all the things they own that could be sold to raise money.
[from Old French *asez* meaning 'enough']

assiduous
(adjective) working very hard and paying great attention to detail.
assiduously (adverb), **assiduity** (noun).
[from Latin *assidere* meaning 'to sit beside']

assign, assigns, assigning, assigned
1 (verb) To assign something to someone means to give it to them officially or to make them responsible for it.
2 If someone is assigned to do something, they are officially told to do it.
[from Latin *signare* meaning 'to mark out']

Similar words: (sense 1) allocate, allot
(sense 2) appoint

assignation, assignations
(pronounced ass-ig-**nay**-shn)
(noun) If you have an assignation with someone, especially a lover, you meet him or her secretly.

assignment, assignments
(noun) An assignment is a job or task that someone is given to do.

assimilate, assimilates, assimilating, assimilated
1 (verb) If you assimilate ideas or experiences, you learn and understand them.
2 When people are assimilated into a group or community, they become part of it.
assimilation (noun).
[from Latin *assimilare* meaning 'to make alike']

assist, assists, assisting, assisted
(verb) To assist someone means to help them do something.
assistance (noun).
[from French *assister* meaning 'to be present']

assistant, assistants
(noun) An assistant is someone whose job is to help another person in their work.

assizes
(noun) Up to 1971, the assizes were the principal sessions of a county court, held four times a year to hear civil and criminal cases. They were attended by special travelling judges.
[from Old French *asseoir* meaning 'to sit']

associate, associates, associating, associated
1 (verb) If you associate one thing with another, you connect the two things in your mind.
2 If you associate with a group of people, you spend a lot of time with them, e.g. *He spent his adolescence associating with criminals.*
3 (noun) Your associates are the people you work with or spend a lot of time with.
[from Latin *associare* meaning 'to join with']

Similar words: (sense 2) fraternize, hobnob, consort

association, associations
1 (noun) An association is an organization for people who have similar interests, jobs, or aims.
2 Your association with a person, group, or organization is the connection or involvement that you have with them.
3 An association between two things is a link that you make in your mind between them, e.g. *The name has many strange associations.*

assonance
(noun) Assonance is similarity of sounds, for example in poetry.

assorted
(adjective) Assorted things vary in size, shape, and colour, e.g. *assorted sweets.*

assortment, assortments
(noun) An assortment is a group of similar things that vary in size, shape, and colour, e.g. *a splendid assortment of travelling rugs.*

assuage, assuages, assuaging, assuaged
(pronounced ass-**wage**)
(verb; a formal word) To assuage a need, desire, or feeling means to make it less intense or to satisfy it, e.g. *I tried to calm the woman but could not assuage her terror.*
[from Old French *assouagier* meaning 'to sweeten']

assume, assumes, assuming, assumed
1 (verb) If you assume that something is true, you accept that it is true even though you have not thought about it, e.g. *They assumed that he had married for money.*
2 To assume responsibility for something means to put yourself in charge of it.
3 If you assume a particular appearance, you start to have it, e.g. *Her eyes assumed a weary, indifferent look.*
[from Latin *assumere* meaning 'to take up']

Similar words: (sense 2) adopt, take up, undertake (sense 3) adopt, affect

assumption, assumptions
1 (noun) An assumption is a belief that something is true, without thinking about it.
2 Assumption of power or responsibility is the taking of it.

assurance, assurances
1 (noun) An assurance is something said about a situation which is intended to make people less worried, e.g. *the Government's assurances about the safety of nuclear power.*
2 Assurance is a feeling of confidence, e.g. *He was speaking now with more assurance.*
3 Life assurance is a type of insurance that pays money to your dependants when you die.

assure, assures, assuring, assured
1 (verb) If you assure someone that something is true, you tell them that it is true.
2 If you assure yourself of something by what you do, you are certain to get it as a result, e.g. *This film assured him a place in movie history.*
[from Latin *assecurare* meaning 'to secure' or 'to make sure']

assured
(adjective) very confident, e.g. *the assured voice of a man who inspires confidence in others.*

assuredly
(adverb) certainly or definitely.

asterisk, asterisks
(noun) An asterisk is the symbol '∗' used in printing and writing.
[from Greek *asterikos* meaning 'small star']

astern
(adverb and adjective; a nautical word) backwards or at the back.

asteroid, asteroids
(noun) An asteroid is one of the large number of very small planets that move around the sun between the orbits of Jupiter and Mars.
[from Greek *asteroeidēs* meaning 'starlike']

asthma (pronounced **ass**-ma)
(noun) Asthma is a disease of the chest which causes wheezing and difficulty in breathing.
asthmatic (adjective).
[from Greek *azein* meaning 'to breathe hard']

astigmatism
(noun) Astigmatism is a defect in the lens of an eye, which results in distorted vision.
astigmatic (adjective).
[from Greek *a* meaning 'not' and *stigma* meaning 'focus']

astir
(adverb and adjective; a literary word) moving or happening, e.g. *revolution astir in Peru.*

astonish, astonishes, astonishing, astonished
(verb) If something astonishes you, it surprises you very much.
astonished (adjective), **astonishing** (adjective), **astonishingly** (adverb), **astonishment** (noun).

astound, astounds, astounding, astounded
(verb) If something astounds you, it shocks and amazes you.
astounded (adjective), **astounding** (adjective).

astrakhan (pronounced ass-trak-**kan**)
(noun) Astrakhan is black or grey curly fur from the skins of young lambs from Astrakhan in the Soviet Union. It is used for making coats.

astray
1 (phrase) To **lead someone astray** means to influence them to do something wrong.
2 If something **goes astray**, it gets lost, e.g. *The letter had gone astray.*

astride
(preposition) with one leg on either side of something, e.g. *He was sitting astride a chair.*

astringent, astringents (pronounced ass-**trin**-jent)
1 (noun) An astringent is a substance that causes body tissues to contract. It stops bleeding.
2 (adjective) Astringent comments are harsh and severe, e.g. *an astringent attack on the President.*
astringency (noun).
[from Latin *astringens* meaning 'drawing tight']

astrology
(noun) Astrology is the study of the sun, moon, and stars in order to predict the future.
astrological (adjective), **astrologer** (noun).

astronaut, astronauts
(noun) An astronaut is a person who operates a spacecraft.
[from Greek *astron* meaning 'star' and *nautēs* meaning 'sailor']

astronomical
1 (adjective) involved with or relating to astronomy.
2 extremely large in amount or value, e.g. *The house was sold at an astronomical price.*
astronomically (adverb).

astronomy
(noun) Astronomy is the scientific study of stars and planets.
astronomer (noun).

astrophysics
(noun) Astrophysics is the scientific study of the physics and chemistry of stars and planets.

astute
(adjective) clever and quick at understanding situations and behaviour, e.g. *an astute businesswoman.*
[from Latin *astutus* meaning 'cunning']

asunder
(adverb; a literary word) If something is torn asunder, it is violently torn apart.

asylum, asylums (pronounced ass-**eye**-lum)
1 (noun; an old-fashioned use) An asylum was a hospital for mental patients.
2 Political asylum is protection given by a government to someone who has fled from their own country for political reasons.
[from Greek *asulon* meaning 'refuge']

asymmetrical or **asymmetric**
(pronounced ay-sim-**met**-ri-kl)
(adjective) not symmetrical or unbalanced.
asymmetry (noun).

at
1 (preposition) used to say where someone or something is, e.g. *I met him at the airport.*
2 used to mention the direction something is going in, e.g. *They threw stones at the wall.*
3 used to say when something happens, e.g. *The party starts at 9 o'clock.*
4 used to mention the rate, price, or value of something, e.g. *The book is published at £7.95.*
5 used to describe the state or activity of someone or something, e.g. *He looked at ease.*

atavism
(noun) Atavism is the recurrence in an individual plant or animal of primitive characteristics that were present in an ancestor but have not occurred in intermediate generations.
atavistic (adjective).

atheist, atheists (pronounced **ayth**-ee-ist)
(noun) An atheist is someone who believes that there is no God.
atheistic (adjective), **atheism** (noun).
[from Greek *atheos* meaning 'godless']

athlete, athletes
(noun) An athlete is someone who is good at sport and takes part in sporting events.
[from Greek *athlos* meaning 'contest']

athlete's foot
(noun) Athlete's foot is a fungal infection of the skin of the feet, especially between the toes.

athletic
1 (adjective) strong, healthy, and good at sports.
2 involving athletes or athletics, e.g. *the athletic traditions of this school.*

athletics
(noun) Sporting events such as running, jumping, and throwing are called athletics.

Atlantic
(noun) The Atlantic is the ocean separating North and South America from Europe and Africa.
[from the *Atlas* mountains in Libya; the Atlantic lies to the west of these mountains]

atlas, atlases
(noun) An atlas is a book of maps.
[from the giant *Atlas* in Greek mythology, who supported the sky on his shoulders]

atmosphere, atmospheres
1 (noun) The atmosphere is the air and other gases that surround a planet; also the air in a particular place, e.g. *pollution of the atmosphere... a smoky atmosphere.*
2 The atmosphere of a place is its general mood, e.g. *a slightly spooky atmosphere.*
atmospheric (adjective).

atoll, atolls
(noun) An atoll is a circular coral reef that surrounds a lagoon.
[from *atolu*, a word from the Maldive Islands]

atom, atoms
(noun) An atom is the smallest part of an element that can take part in a chemical reaction. [from Greek *atomos* meaning 'indivisible'; it was thought at one time that the atom could not be split]

atom bomb, atom bombs
(noun) An atom bomb is an extremely powerful bomb which explodes because of nuclear energy that comes from splitting atoms.

atomic
(adjective) relating to atoms or to the power released by splitting atoms, e.g. *atomic energy.*

atomic number, atomic numbers
(noun) The atomic number of a chemical element is a number used to classify it, which is equal to the number of protons in the nucleus of the atom of the element.

atomic weight, atomic weights
(noun) The atomic weight of a chemical element is the weight of an atom of the element relative to the weight of carbon 12.

atomize, atomizes, atomizing, atomized; also spelled **atomise**
(verb) To atomize something means to reduce it to atoms or very small particles.

atomizer, atomizers; also spelled **atomiser**
(noun) An atomizer is a device for turning a liquid such as perfume into a fine spray.

atone, atones, atoning, atoned
(verb; a formal word) If you atone for something wrong that you have done, you say you are sorry and try to make everything better again.
atonement (noun).
[from *at one* meaning 'in harmony']

atrocious
(adjective) extremely bad, e.g. *He spoke French with an atrocious accent.*
atrociously (adverb).

atrocity, atrocities
(noun) An atrocity is an extremely cruel and shocking act.

atrophy, atrophies, atrophying, atrophied
(pronounced **at**-troff-ee)
(verb; a formal word) To atrophy means to waste away, e.g. *Muscles atrophy when they are not used.*
[from Greek *atrophos* meaning 'ill-fed']

attach, attaches, attaching, attached
(verb) If you attach something to something else, you join or fasten the two things together.

attaché, attachés (pronounced at-**tash**-ay)
(noun) An attaché is a member of staff in an embassy, e.g. *the French Cultural Attaché.*
[a French word]

attaché case, attaché cases
(noun) An attaché case is a small flat briefcase.

attached
(adjective) If you are attached to someone, you are very fond of them.

attachment, attachments
1 (noun) Attachment to someone is a feeling of love and affection for them.
2 Attachment to a cause or ideal is a strong belief in it and support for it.
3 An attachment for a tool or machine is a piece of equipment that can be attached to it to do a particular job.

attack, attacks, attacking, attacked
1 (verb) To attack someone means to use violence against them so as to hurt or kill them.
2 (noun) An attack is violent physical action against someone.
3 (verb) If you attack someone or their ideas, you criticize them strongly, e.g. *He attacked the press for misleading the public.*
4 (noun) An attack on someone or on their ideas is strong criticism of them.
5 (verb) If a disease or chemical attacks something, it damages or destroys it, e.g. *Radiation can attack the cells in living tissue.*
6 (noun) An attack of an illness is a short time in which you suffer badly with it.
7 (verb) In a game such as football or hockey, to attack means to get the ball into a position from which a goal can be scored.
attacker (noun).

Similar words: (sense 1) assault, assail, set about (sense 2) assault, offensive, onslaught (sense 3) assail, set about

attain, attains, attaining, attained
(verb; a formal word) If you attain something, you manage to achieve it, e.g. *He eventually attained high office.*
attainable (adjective), **attainment** (noun).

attempt, attempts, attempting, attempted
1 (verb) If you attempt to do something, you try to do it or achieve it, but may not succeed, e.g. *He attempted to blackmail me.*
2 (noun) An attempt is an act of trying to do something, e.g. *She made no attempt to talk.*

attend, attends, attending, attended
1 (verb) If you attend an event, you are present at it.
2 To attend school, church, or hospital means to go there regularly.
3 If you attend to something, you deal with it, e.g. *I had some business to attend to.*
4 (a formal use) If something attends an event or situation, it happens at the same time as it, e.g. *the publicity which attended her activities.*
attendance (noun).
[from Latin *attendere* meaning 'to stretch towards']

attendant, attendants
1 (noun) An attendant is someone whose job is to serve people in a shop, museum, or garage.
2 (adjective) happening at the same time, e.g. *nuclear energy and its attendant dangers.*

attention, attentions
1 (noun) Attention is the thought, care, or interest that you give to something, e.g. *She was the centre of attention... The roof needs attention.*

2 (phrase) When soldiers or the police **stand to attention**, they stand straight up with their feet together and arms at their sides.

attentive
(adjective) paying close attention to something, e.g. *an attentive audience.*
attentively (adverb), **attentiveness** (noun).

attenuate, attenuates, attenuating, attenuated
(verb; a formal word) To attenuate something means to weaken it or make it less.
attenuation (noun).
[from Latin *tenuis* meaning 'thin']

attest, attests, attesting, attested
(verb; a formal word) To attest something means to show or declare that it is true.
attestation (noun).
[from Latin *testare* meaning 'to bear witness']

attic, attics
(noun) An attic is a room at the top of a house immediately below the roof.

attire
(noun; a formal word) Attire is clothing, e.g. *It was not really suitable attire for a wedding.*

attitude, attitudes
1 (noun) Your attitude to someone or something is the way you think and feel about them and behave towards them.
2 Your attitude is also the way that you are sitting, standing, or lying.

attorney, attorneys (pronounced at-**turn**-ee)
(noun; an American word) An attorney is the same as a lawyer.
[from Old French *atorné* meaning 'appointed']

attract, attracts, attracting, attracted
1 (verb) If something attracts people, it interests them and makes them want to go to it, e.g. *The show attracted large crowds this year.*
2 If someone attracts you, you like and admire them, e.g. *What really attracted me to her was her sense of humour.*
3 If something attracts something else, it pulls it towards it, like a magnet.
[from Latin *trahere* meaning 'to pull']

attraction, attractions
1 (noun) Attraction is a feeling of liking someone very much and wanting to be with them, e.g. *physical attraction.*
2 An attraction is something that people visit for interest or pleasure, e.g. *Buckingham Palace is one of London's major tourist attractions.*

attractive
1 (adjective) interesting and possibly advantageous, e.g. *an attractive idea.*
2 pleasant to look at or be with, e.g. *an attractive girl... an attractive personality.*
attractively (adverb), **attractiveness** (noun).

Similar words: (sense 1) appealing
(sense 2) appealing, engaging, winsome

attribute, attributes, attributing, attributed
1 (verb) If you attribute something to a circumstance, person, or thing, you believe that it was caused or created by that circumstance,

person, or thing, e.g. *He attributed these attacks to 'bad luck'... The painting is attributed to Rembrandt.*
2 (noun) An attribute is a quality or feature that someone or something has.
attribution (noun), **attributable** (adjective).
[from Latin *attribuere* meaning 'to associate with']

Similar words: (sense 1) ascribe, charge, impute

attrition
(noun) Attrition is the constant wearing down of an enemy, e.g. *a war of attrition.*
[from Latin *attritio* meaning 'rubbing away']

attuned
(adjective) accustomed or well adjusted to something, e.g. *His eyes became attuned to the darkness.*

atypical (pronounced ay-**tip**-i-kl)
(adjective) not like other similar things, e.g. *My weeks are atypical: I work when others rest.*
atypically (adverb).

aubergine, aubergines (pronounced oh-ber-jeen)
(noun) An aubergine is a dark purple, pear-shaped vegetable with shiny skin and pale flesh. It is also called an **egg plant.**
[from Arabic *al-badindjan* meaning 'aubergine']

auburn
(adjective) Auburn hair is reddish brown.
[from Old French *alborne* meaning 'blond']

auction, auctions, auctioning, auctioned
1 (noun) An auction is a public sale in which goods are sold to the person who offers the highest price.
2 (verb) To auction something means to sell it in an auction.
[from Latin *auctio* meaning 'increasing']

auctioneer, auctioneers
(noun) An auctioneer is the person in charge of an auction.

audacious
(adjective) very daring, e.g. *audacious decisions.*
audaciously (adverb), **audacity** (noun).

audible
(adjective) loud enough to be heard, e.g. *Her reply was barely audible.*
audibly (adverb), **audibility** (noun).
[from Latin *audire* meaning 'to hear']

audience, audiences
1 (noun) An audience is the group of people who are watching or listening to a performance.
2 An audience is also a private or formal meeting with an important person, e.g. *an audience with the Pope.*
[from Latin *audientia* meaning 'hearing']

audio
(adjective) used in recording and reproducing sound, e.g. *audio equipment.*

audiovisual
(adjective) involving both recorded sound and pictures, e.g. *audiovisual aids for teaching.*

audit, audits, auditing, audited
1 (verb) To audit a set of financial accounts means to examine them officially to check that they are correct.
2 (noun) An audit is an official examination of an organization's accounts.
auditor (noun).

audition, auditions
(noun) An audition is a short performance given by an actor or musician, so that a director can decide whether they are suitable for a part in a play or film or for a place in an orchestra.
[from Latin *auditus* meaning 'act of hearing']

auditorium, auditoriums or **auditoria**
(noun) In a theatre or concert hall, the auditorium is the part where the audience sits.

auditory
(adjective; a technical word) relating to hearing, e.g. *the auditory nerve*.

au fait (pronounced oh **fay**)
(adjective; a formal word) well informed or knowing all about something, e.g. *Is he au fait with the company's financial position?*
[a French expression meaning 'to the point']

augment, augments, augmenting, augmented
(verb; a formal word) To augment something means to add something to it.

augur, augurs, auguring, augured
(verb; a formal word) If something augurs well, it is a sign that good things are going to happen.
[The *augurs* were Roman priests who foretold the future]

august (pronounced aw-**gust**)
(adjective; a formal word) dignified, magnificent, and impressive, e.g. *the august buildings of Westminster*.

August (pronounced **aw**-gust)
(noun) August is the eighth month of the year. It has 31 days.
[from the name of the Roman emperor *Augustus*]

aunt, aunts
(noun) Your aunt is the sister of your mother or father, or the wife of your uncle.

au pair, au pairs (pronounced oh **pair**)
(noun) An au pair is a young foreign girl who lives with a family to help with the children and housework and to learn the language.
[a French expression meaning 'on equal terms']

aura, auras
(noun) An aura is an atmosphere that surrounds a person or thing, e.g. *There was an aura of glamour and prestige about her*.
[from Greek *aura* meaning 'breeze']

aural (rhymes with **floral**)
(adjective) relating to or done through the sense of hearing, e.g. *an aural comprehension test*.

aurora borealis (pronounced aw-**roh**-ra bor-ee-**ay**-liss)
(noun) The aurora borealis consists of bands of glowing coloured light sometimes seen in the sky in the Arctic. It is caused by charged particles discharged from the sun hitting the earth's atmosphere at an acute angle. A similar phenomenon in the Antarctic is called the **aurora australis**.
[from Latin meaning 'northern dawn']

auspices (pronounced **aw**-spiss-eez)
(noun; a formal word) If you do something under the auspices of a person or organization, you do it with their support, e.g. *a conference held under the auspices of the United Nations*.

auspicious
(adjective; a formal word) favourable and seeming to promise success, e.g. *It was an auspicious start to the year*.
[from Latin *auspicium* meaning 'prophecy by watching birds']

austere
(adjective) plain and simple, and without luxury, e.g. *an austere monastic life*.
austerity (noun).
[from Latin *austerus* meaning 'sour']

Australasia (pronounced ost-ral-**lay**-sha)
(noun) Australasia consists of Australia, New Zealand, and neighbouring islands in the Pacific.
Australasian (adjective).

Australia
(noun) Australia is the smallest continent and the largest island in the world, situated between the Indian Ocean and the Pacific.

Australian, Australians
1 (adjective) belonging or relating to Australia.
2 (noun) An Australian is someone who comes from Australia.

Austrian, Austrians
1 (adjective) belonging or relating to Austria.
2 (noun) An Austrian is someone who comes from Austria.

authentic
(adjective) real and genuine.
authentically (adverb), **authenticity** (noun).
[from Latin *authenticus* meaning 'coming from the author']

authenticate, authenticates, authenticating, authenticated
(verb) To authenticate something means to establish that it is genuine.
authentication (noun).

author, authors
(noun) The author of a book is the person who wrote it.
authorship (noun).

authoritarian
(adjective) believing in strict obedience, e.g. *She has very authoritarian parents*.
authoritarianism (noun).

authoritative
1 (adjective) having authority, e.g. *an authoritative voice*.
2 generally accepted as being reliable and accurate, e.g. *an authoritative report*.
authoritatively (adverb).

authority, authorities
1 (noun) Authority is the power to control

people, e.g. *the authority of the State... He spoke with authority.*
2 (plural noun) The authorities are the people who have the power to make decisions.
3 (noun) An authority is a local government department, e.g. *the Local Education Authority.*
4 Someone who is an authority on something knows a lot about it, e.g. *She is the world's greatest authority on African fish.*

authorize, authorizes, authorizing, authorized; also spelled **authorise**
(verb) To authorize something means to give official permission for it to happen.
authorization (noun).

autism
(noun) Autism is a mental condition which some children are born with, in which they do not respond normally to other people.
autistic (adjective).

auto-
(prefix) Auto- means 'self' or 'same'.

autobiography, autobiographies
(noun) Someone's autobiography is an account of their life which they have written themselves.
autobiographical (adjective).

autocrat, autocrats
(noun) An autocrat is a ruler who has absolute power.
autocratic (adjective), **autocracy** (noun).
[from Greek *auto* meaning 'self' and *kratos* meaning 'power']

autocue, autocues
(noun) An autocue is a piece of equipment that displays words for a newsreader or television presenter to read while looking at the camera.

autograph, autographs
(noun) An autograph is the signature of a famous person.
[from Greek *auto* meaning 'self' and *graphos* meaning 'written']

automate, automates, automating, automated
(verb) To automate a factory or industrial process means to install machines to do the work instead of people.
automation (noun).

automatic, automatics
1 (adjective) An automatic machine is programmed to perform tasks without needing a person to operate it, e.g. *The airliner was flying on automatic pilot.*
2 Automatic actions or reactions take place without involving conscious thought.
3 A process or punishment that is automatic always happens as a direct result of something, e.g. *This offence carries an automatic fine.*
4 (noun) An automatic is a gun that has a mechanism for continuous reloading and firing.
5 An automatic is also a car in which the gears change automatically as the car's speed changes.
automatically (adverb).

Similar words: (sense 1) mechanical, mechanized

automaton, automatons or automata
(pronounced aw-**tom**-mat-on)
1 (noun) An automaton is a robot.
2 If you describe someone as an automaton, you mean that they act mechanically without thinking about what they are doing.

automobile, automobiles
(noun; an American or formal word) An automobile is a car.
[from *auto-* + *mobile* meaning 'self-moving']

autonomous (pronounced aw-**ton**-nom-uss)
(adjective) self-controlling or self-governing, e.g. *The Republic has nine autonomous regions.*
autonomy (noun).

autopsy, autopsies
(noun) An autopsy is a medical examination of a dead body to discover the cause of death.
[from Greek *autopsia* meaning 'seeing with one's own eyes']

autumn, autumns
(noun) Autumn is the season between summer and winter, when the weather becomes cooler.
autumnal (adjective).

auxiliary, auxiliaries
1 (noun) An auxiliary is a person employed to help other members of staff, e.g. *nursing auxiliaries.*
2 (adjective) Auxiliary equipment is used when necessary in addition to the main equipment, e.g. *Auxiliary scaffolding had been erected.*
[from Latin *auxilium* meaning 'help']

avail, avails, availing, availed
1 (phrase) If something that you do is **of no avail** or **to no avail,** it is not successful or helpful.
2 (verb; a formal use) If you avail yourself of something, you make use of it.

available
1 (adjective) Something that is available can to obtained, e.g. *now available in paperback.*
2 Someone who is available is ready for work or free for people to talk to, e.g. *The Minister was not available for comment.*
availability (noun).

Similar words: (sense 1) obtainable, accessible, attainable

avalanche, avalanches (pronounced av-a-lahnsh)
(noun) An avalanche is a huge mass of snow and ice that falls down a mountainside.

avant-garde (pronounced av-vong-**gard**)
(adjective) extremely modern or experimental, especially in art, literature, or music.
[from French *avant-garde* meaning 'vanguard']

Similar words: progressive, experimental, innovative

avarice
(noun; a formal word) Avarice is greed for money and possessions.
avaricious (adjective).

avenge, avenges, avenging, avenged
(verb) If you avenge something harmful that someone has done to you or your family, you

punish or harm the other person in return, e.g.
He was determined to avenge his father's death.
avenger (noun).

avenue, avenues
1 (noun) An avenue is a street, especially one
with trees along it.
2 You can say that a way of getting something
done is an avenue, e.g. *explore every avenue.*
[from French *avenir* meaning 'to approach']

average, averages, averaging, averaged
1 (noun) An average is a result obtained by
adding several amounts together and then
dividing the total by the number of different
amounts, e.g. *Six pupils were examined in a
total of 39 subjects, an average of 6.5 subjects
per pupil.*
2 (adjective) Average means standard, normal,
or usual, e.g. *the average day's work.*
3 (verb) To average a number means to produce
that number over a period of time, e.g. *House
price increases averaged around 20%.*
4 (phrase) You say **on average** when mentioning
what usually happens in a situation, e.g. *On
average women's pay is lower than men's.*
[sense 1 is from Italian *avaria* meaning 'damage
to ships or cargo'; the loss was shared equally
among all concerned]

Similar words: (sense 2) ordinary, middling

averse
(adjective) unwilling to do something, e.g. *He
was averse to giving advice to his superiors.*

aversion, aversions
(noun) If you have an aversion to someone or
something, you dislike them very much.

avert, averts, averting, averted
1 (verb) If you avert an unpleasant event, you
prevent it from happening.
2 If you avert your eyes from something, you
turn your eyes away from it.
[from Latin *avertere* meaning 'to turn from']

aviary, aviaries
(noun) An aviary is a large cage or group of
cages in which birds are kept.
[from Latin *avis* meaning 'bird']

aviation
(noun) Aviation is the science of flying aircraft.

aviator, aviators
(noun; an old-fashioned word) An aviator is a
pilot of an aircraft.

avid
(adjective) eager and enthusiastic for something.
avidly (adverb).

avocado, avocados
(noun) An avocado is a pear-shaped fruit, with
dark green skin, soft greenish yellow flesh, and a
large stone.
[from a South American Indian word *ahuacatl*
meaning 'testicle', from its shape]

avoid, avoids, avoiding, avoided
1 (verb) If you avoid doing something, you make
a deliberate effort not to do it.

2 If you avoid someone, you keep away from
them.
avoidable (adjective), **avoidance** (noun).

Similar words: (sense 1) evade, shirk, side-step,
dodge
(sense 2) elude, dodge

avow, avows, avowing, avowed
(verb; a formal word) If you avow something,
you admit it or declare it.
avowal (noun), **avowed** (adjective).

avuncular
(adjective) friendly and helpful in manner
towards younger people, rather like an uncle.
[from Latin *avunculus* meaning 'uncle']

await, awaits, awaiting, awaited
1 (verb) If you await something, you expect it.
2 If something awaits you, it will happen to you
in the future.

awake, awakes, awaking, awoke, awoken
1 (adjective) Someone who is awake is not
sleeping.
2 (verb) When you awake, you wake up.
3 If you are awoken by something, it wakes you
up.

awaken, awakens, awakening, awakened
(verb) If something awakens an emotion or
interest in you, you start to feel this emotion or
interest.

award, awards, awarding, awarded
1 (noun) An award is a prize or certificate for
doing something well.
2 An award is also a sum of money that an
organization gives to students for training or
study.
3 (verb) If you award someone something, you
give it to them formally or officially.
[from Old French *eswarder* meaning 'to decide']

aware
(adjective) If you are aware of something, you
know about it or realize that it is there.
awareness (noun).

Similar words: conscious, mindful, knowing

awash
(adjective and adverb) covered with water, e.g.
In the monsoon the whole place is awash.

away
1 (adverb) moving from a place, e.g. *I drove
away.*
2 at a distance from a place, e.g. *London is sixty
miles away.*
3 in its proper place, e.g. *Tom put the book away.*
4 not at home, school, or work, e.g. *She was away
at the time.*
5 continuously or repeatedly, e.g. *He was
working away in the library.*

awe
(noun; a formal word) Awe is a feeling of great
respect mixed with amazement and sometimes
slight fear.
awesome (adjective).
[an Old Germanic word meaning 'fear']

awful
1 (adjective) very unpleasant or very bad.
2 (an informal use) very great, e.g. *It took an awful lot of courage.*
awfully (adverb).

Similar words: (sense 1) ghastly, nasty, lousy

awhile
(adverb) for a short time, e.g. *Wait awhile.*

awkward
1 (adjective) clumsy and uncomfortable, e.g. *an awkward gesture.*
2 embarrassed, shy, or nervous, e.g. *Meeting strangers made him diffident and awkward.*
[from Old Norse *ofugr* meaning 'turned the wrong way']

awning, awnings
(noun) An awning is a large roof of canvas or plastic attached to a building or vehicle, to shelter people from the sun and rain.

awoke the past tense of **awake.**

awry (pronounced a-rye)
1 (adjective) crooked, e.g. *His tie was awry.*
2 wrong or not as planned, e.g. *A strike threw all the schedules awry.*

axe, axes, axing, axed
1 (noun) An axe is a tool with a handle and a sharp blade, used for chopping wood.
2 (verb) To axe something means to end it.

axiom, axioms
(noun) An axiom is a statement or saying that is generally accepted to be true.
axiomatic (adjective).
[from Greek *axios* meaning 'worthwhile']

axis, axes (pronounced **ak**-siss)
1 (noun) An axis is an imaginary line through the centre of something, around which it moves.
2 An axis is also one of the two sides of a graph.

axle, axles
(noun) An axle is the long bar that connects a pair of wheels on a vehicle.

ayatollah, ayatollahs
(noun) An ayatollah is an Islamic religious leader in Iran.
[from Arabic *ayatullah* meaning 'manifestation of God']

aye or **ay** (rhymes with **lie**)
In some dialects of English, especially in Northern England and Scotland, aye means yes.

azalea, azaleas (pronounced a-**zayl**-ya)
(noun) An azalea is a type of garden shrub, related to the rhododendron, with brightly coloured sweet-smelling flowers.
[from Greek *azaleos* meaning 'dry'; it was thought to grow best in dry places]

azure (pronounced **az**-yoor)
(adjective; a literary word) bright blue, e.g. *the azure sky.*

B

BA, BAs
(noun) A BA is a university degree in a subject such as languages, literature, history, or a social science; also used to refer to someone who has such a degree. BA is an abbreviation for 'Bachelor of Arts'.

babble, babbles, babbling, babbled
1 (verb) When someone babbles, they talk in a confused or excited way.
2 When a baby babbles, it makes meaningless sounds.
3 When a stream babbles, it makes a continuous bubbling sound.

babe, babes
(noun; an old-fashioned word) A babe is a baby.

babel (pronounced bay-bl)
(noun) A babel of voices or other sounds is a confused mixture of them.
[from the Tower of Babel in the Bible; see Genesis, chapter 11]

baboon, baboons
(noun) A baboon is an African monkey with a pointed face, large teeth, and a long tail.
[from Old French *baboue* meaning 'grimace']

baby, babies
(noun) A baby is a child in the first year or two of its life.
babyhood (noun), **babyish** (adjective).

Similar words: babe, infant

baby-sit, baby-sits, baby-sitting, baby-sat
(verb) To baby-sit for someone means to look after their children while that person is out.
baby-sitter (noun), **baby-sitting** (noun).

bachelor, bachelors
(noun) A bachelor is a man who has never been married.
bachelorhood (noun).
[from Old French *bacheler* meaning 'young man']

Bachelor of Arts, Bachelors of Arts
(noun) A Bachelor of Arts is a university degree in a subject such as languages, literature, history, or a social science; also used to refer to someone who has such a degree.

Bachelor of Science, Bachelors of Science
(noun) A Bachelor of Science is a university degree in a science subject; also used to refer to someone who has such a degree.

bacillus (pronounced bas-sil-uss), bacilli
(pronounced bas-sil-eye)
(noun; a technical word) Bacilli are rod-shaped bacteria.
[from Latin *baculus* meaning 'rod' or 'stick']

back, backs, backing, backed
1 (adverb) When people or things move back, they move in the opposite direction from the one in which they are facing, e.g. *He stepped back.*
2 When people or things go back to a place or state, they return to it, e.g. *I went back to sleep.*
3 If you get something back, you get it into your possession again.
4 If you do something back to someone, you do to them what they have done to you, e.g. *I stared back at her.*
5 Something that is kept back or set back is kept or set at a distance from something else, e.g. *The house is set back from the road... The police kept the crowd back.*
6 Back also means in the past, e.g. *It happened back in 1968.*
7 (noun) Your back is the rear part of your body.
8 The back of something is the part that is at the rear, e.g. *the back of the house.*
9 (adjective) The back parts of something are the ones near the rear, e.g. *the back wheels of the car.*
10 (verb) If a building backs onto something, its back faces in that direction.
11 When a car backs, it moves backwards.
12 To back a person or organization means to support, encourage, or finance that person or organization.
13 If you back a horse in a race, you bet money on it.
14 (noun) In a game such as football or hockey, a back is a player in a defending position.
15 (phrase) If something is **back to front**, the back part is where the front should be.
16 If you do or say something nasty **behind someone's back**, you do it without letting them know about it.
17 If you **put someone's back up**, you do or say something that annoys them.

back down
(phrasal verb) If you back down on a demand or claim, you withdraw and give up.

back out
(phrasal verb) If you back out of a promise or commitment, you decide not to do what you had promised or agreed to do.

back up
1 (phrasal verb) If you back up a claim or story, you produce evidence to show that it is true.
2 If you back someone up, you support them against their critics or enemies.

backbencher, backbenchers
(noun) A backbencher is a Member of Parliament who is not a government minister and who does not have an official position as a spokesperson for an opposition party.

backbone, backbones
(noun) A backbone is the column of linked bones along the middle of a person's or animal's back.

Similar words: spine, vertebrae

backcloth, backcloths
(noun) In a theatre, a backcloth is a cloth with scenery painted on it, hung at the back of the stage.

backdate, backdates, backdating, backdated
(verb) If an arrangement is backdated, it is made effective from a date earlier than the one on which it is completed or signed, e.g. *Their pay rise has been backdated to last April.*

backdrop, backdrops
(noun) A backdrop is a backcloth.

backer, backers
(noun) The backers of a project are the people who give it financial help.

backfire, backfires, backfiring, backfired
1 (verb) If a plan backfires, it produces an opposite result to the one intended.
2 When a car backfires, there is a small but noisy explosion in its exhaust pipe.

background, backgrounds
1 (noun) Your background is the kind of home you come from and the education you have had, e.g. *She comes from a working-class background.*
2 The background to an event consists of the circumstances which surround it and caused it to happen.
3 The background in a picture consists of the less noticeable things in it which are behind the main things.
4 Sounds in the background are sounds which you can hear but do not pay attention to, e.g. *The TV was blaring in the background... background music.*

backhand, backhands
(noun and adjective) Backhand is a stroke in tennis, squash, or badminton made in front of your body with the back of your hand facing in the direction that you hit the ball.

backhanded
(adjective) A backhanded compliment is one which contains indirect or implied criticism.

backing, backings
1 (noun) Backing is support or help, e.g. *This move has the backing of the government.*
2 The backing to a pop song is the music that accompanies it.

backlash
(noun) A backlash is a hostile reaction to a new development or a new policy.

backlog, backlogs
(noun) A backlog is a number of things that have accumulated and that must be dealt with.

backpack, backpacks
(noun) A backpack is a large bag that hikers or campers carry on their backs.

backside, backsides
(noun; an informal word) Your backside is the part of your body that you sit on.

Similar words: bottom, rear, rump, posterior

backsliding
(noun) Backsliding is a return to bad habits or bad behaviour after a period of being good.

backstroke
(noun) Backstroke is a swimming stroke in which you lie on your back, kick your legs, and move your arms back over your head.

backward
1 (adjective) Backward means behind you, e.g. *Without a backward glance, he walked away.*
2 A backward country or society is one that does not have modern industries or technology.
3 A backward child is one who has not progressed as far in learning as other children of the same age.
backwardness (noun).

Similar words: (sense 3) slow, retarded

backwards
1 (adverb) Backwards means behind you, e.g. *She glanced backwards.*
2 If you do something backwards, you do it the opposite of the usual way, e.g. *I can recite the alphabet backwards.*
3 (an informal use) If you know something backwards, you know it very well.

backwater, backwaters
(noun) A place that is a backwater is isolated and has not been affected by the important events and changes that have happened in other places.

bacon
(noun) Bacon is meat from the back or sides of a pig, which has been salted and sometimes smoked.

bacteria
(plural noun) Bacteria are very tiny organisms which live in air, water, soil, plants, and the bodies of animals. Some bacteria provide food for plants, others cause diseases such as typhoid.
bacterial (adjective).
[from Greek *baktērion* meaning 'little rod'; some bacteria are rod-shaped]

bacteriology
(noun) Bacteriology is the study of bacteria.
bacteriologist (noun).

bad, worse, worst
1 (adjective) Anything that you disapprove of or that harms or upsets you can be described as bad, e.g. *I have some bad news...Is the pain bad?*
2 insufficient or of poor quality, e.g. *bad light... The pay was bad... bad roads.*
3 evil or immoral in character or behaviour, e.g. *a bad person.*
4 not skilful at something, e.g. *I was bad at sports.*
5 Bad food is not suitable for eating, because it has started to decay.
6 Bad language consists of swear words.
7 If you have a bad temper, you become angry easily.
8 People who have bad manners behave in a rude and unacceptable way.
badly (adverb), **badness** (noun).

Similar words: (sense 3) evil, wicked, wrong, sinful (sense 5) rotten, decayed, off, putrid

bade a form of the past tense of **bid.**

badge, badges
(noun) A badge is a piece of plastic, metal, or

other material with a design or message on it that you can pin to your clothes.

badger, badgers, badgering, badgered
1 (noun) A badger is a wild animal that has a white head with two black stripes on it. Badgers live underground and come out to feed at night.
2 (verb) If you badger someone, you keep asking them questions or pestering them to do something.

badminton
(noun) Badminton is a game in which two or four players use rackets to hit a shuttlecock over a high net. It was first played at Badminton House in Gloucestershire.

baffle, baffles, baffling, baffled
(verb) If something baffles you, you cannot understand it or cannot think of an answer to it, e.g. *The second question baffled her completely.*
baffled (adjective), **baffling** (adjective), **bafflingly** (adverb), **bafflement** (noun).

bag, bags, bagging, bagged
1 (noun) A bag is a container, usually made of plastic, cloth, or paper, which is used for carrying things in.
2 (an informal use) Bags of something is a lot of it, e.g. *There's bags of room.*
3 (verb; an informal use) If you bag something, you get it before anyone else can get it.
[from Old Norse *baggi* meaning 'bundle']

baggage
(noun) Your baggage is all the suitcases and bags that you have when you are travelling.

baggy, baggier, baggiest
(adjective) Baggy clothing hangs loosely because it is too big.

bagpipes
(plural noun) Bagpipes are a musical instrument played by squeezing air out of a leather bag through pipes, on which a tune is played.

bail, bails, bailing, bailed
1 (noun) Bail is a sum of money paid to a court to allow an accused person to go free until the time of his or her trial, e.g. *He was released on bail.*
2 In cricket, the bails are the two small pieces of wood placed on top of the stumps to form the wicket.
3 (verb) If you bail water from a boat, you remove it using a container.
[Sense 1 is from Old French *bail* meaning 'custody'; sense 2 is from Old French *baile* meaning 'cross-beam'; sense 3 is from Old French *baille* meaning 'bucket']

bail out or **bale out**
(phrasal verb) To bail out of an aircraft means to jump out of it with a parachute.

bailiff, bailiffs
1 (noun) A bailiff is a law officer who makes sure that the decisions of a court are obeyed, especially by removing someone's property if they fail to pay a fine or money that they owe.
2 A bailiff is also a person employed to look after land or property for the owner.
[from Old French *baillif* meaning 'custodian']

bairn, bairns
(noun) In Scotland and Northern England a child is often called a bairn.
[from Old Norse *barn* meaning 'child']

bait, baits, baiting, baited
1 (noun) Bait is a small amount of food placed on a hook or in a trap, to tempt a fish or wild animal to eat it so that it gets caught.
2 (verb) If you bait a hook or trap, you put bait on it to catch a fish or wild animal.
3 (noun) Bait is also something intended to tempt a person to do something, e.g. *The possibility of promotion was the bait.*
[from the Old Norse verb *beita* meaning 'to hunt']

baize
(noun) Baize is a thick woollen material, usually green, used for covering snooker tables.
[from Old French *bai*, meaning 'reddish brown'; this was probably the original colour of the material]

bake, bakes, baking, baked
1 (verb) To bake food means to cook it in an oven without using liquid or fat.
2 To bake earth or clay means to heat it until it becomes hard.

baker, bakers
(noun) A baker is a person who bakes and sells bread and cakes.

bakery, bakeries
(noun) A bakery is a building where bread and cakes are baked and sold.

balaclava, balaclavas
(noun) A balaclava is a close-fitting woollen hood that covers every part of your head except your face. Balaclava is the name of a place in Russia; at a battle there in the Crimean War in 1854, British soldiers wore these hoods to protect themselves from the cold.

balalaika, balalaikas (pronounced bal-lal-**eye**-ka)
(noun) A balalaika is a musical instrument used in Russian folk music. It has a triangular body and three strings, which are plucked or strummed.

balance, balances, balancing, balanced
1 (verb) When something balances, it remains steady and does not fall over.
2 (noun) Balance is the state that a person or thing is in when upright and steady, e.g. *She nearly lost her balance.*
3 (phrase) If something is **off balance**, it is in an unsteady position and likely to fall.
4 (noun) Balance is also a situation in which all the things involved have a stable relationship with each other, e.g. *the ecological balance of the lake.*
5 (verb) If you balance a budget or balance the books, you make sure that no more money is spent than is earned.
6 (noun) The balance in someone's bank account is the amount of money that they have in it.
7 When you have paid part of the cost of something, the balance is the amount still remaining to be paid.
8 A country's balance of payments is the

difference between the amount it spends on imports and the amount it receives from exports.
9 (phrase) When something is **in the balance**, it is uncertain whether it will happen or continue.
[from Latin *bilanx* meaning 'having two scales']

balanced
(adjective) A balanced account or report presents information in a fair and objective way.

balcony, balconies
1 (noun) A balcony is a platform on the outside of a building with a wall or railing round it.
2 In a theatre or cinema, the balcony is an area of upstairs seats.
[from Italian *balcone*]

bald, balder, baldest
1 (adjective) A bald person has little or no hair on the top of their head.
2 A bald statement or question is made in the simplest way without any attempt to be polite.
baldly (adverb), **baldness** (noun).
[from Middle English *ballede* meaning 'having a white patch']

bale, bales, baling, baled
1 (noun) A bale is a large quantity of something such as cloth, paper, or hay tied in a tight bundle.
2 (verb) If you bale water from a boat, you remove it using a container; also spelled **bail**
[sense 1 has the same origin as **ball** 1]

bale out or **bail out**
(phrasal verb) To bale out of an aircraft means to jump out of it with a parachute.

baleful
(adjective) having harmful effects or showing harmful intentions, e.g. *a baleful influence... his baleful gaze.*
balefully (adverb).
[from Old English *balu* meaning 'evil']

balk, balks, balking, balked; also spelled **baulk**
1 (verb) If you balk at something, you object to it and may refuse to do it or refuse to let it happen, e.g. *He balked at shooting down innocent civilians.*
2 If you are balked, you are prevented from doing or getting what you want, e.g. *She was balked of the chance to see Gordon.*
[from Old English *balca* meaning 'ridge']

Balkans
(noun) The Balkans or Balkan States are a group of countries in south-east Europe, including Yugoslavia, Romania, Bulgaria, Albania, and Greece.
Balkan (adjective).

ball, balls
1 (noun) A ball is any object shaped like a sphere, especially one of those used in games such as tennis, cricket, and football.
2 The ball of your foot or thumb is the rounded part where your toes join your foot or your thumb joins your hand.
3 A ball is also a large formal social event at which people dance.
4 (informal phrase) Someone who is **on the ball** is alert and quick to understand what is going on.

5 If you are **having a ball**, you are enjoying yourself very much.
[sense 1 is from Old Norse *bollr* meaning 'round object'; sense 2 is from French *baler* meaning 'to dance']

Similar words: (sense 1) globe, orb, sphere

ballad, ballads
1 (noun) A ballad is a long song or poem which tells a story.
2 A ballad is also a slow, romantic pop song.
[from Old French *ballade* meaning 'song for dancing to']

ballast
1 (noun) Ballast is any heavy material placed in a ship to make it more stable.
2 Ballast is also small pieces of rock spread on the ground as a foundation for a railway line or a road.

ball bearings
(plural noun) Ball bearings are small metal balls placed between the parts of a wheel or a machine in order to allow them to move smoothly against each other.

ballcock, ballcocks
(noun) A ballcock is a piece of equipment in a water tank, consisting of a floating ball attached to a hinged rod. When you use water from the tank, the ball sinks and the rod opens a hole through which water enters to fill the tank again.

ballerina, ballerinas
(noun) A ballerina is a woman ballet dancer.

ballet, ballets (pronounced **bal**-lay)
1 (noun) Ballet is a type of very skilled artistic dancing with carefully planned movements.
2 A ballet is an artistic work performed by ballet dancers.
[from Italian *balletto* meaning 'little dance']

ballistics
(noun) Ballistics is the study of the motion of missiles after they have been fired.
ballistic (adjective).
[from Latin *ballista*, a kind of giant catapult for hurling rocks at city walls, from Greek *ballein* meaning 'to throw']

balloon, balloons
1 (noun) A balloon is a small bag made of thin rubber that you blow into until it becomes larger and rounder. Balloons are used as toys or decorations.
2 A balloon is also a large, strong bag filled with gas or hot air, which travels through the air carrying passengers in a basket or compartment underneath.
[from Italian *ballone* meaning 'large round object']

ballot, ballots, balloting, balloted
1 (noun) A ballot is a secret vote in which people choose a candidate in an election or express their opinion about something.
2 (verb) When a group of people are balloted, they are asked questions to find out what they think about a particular problem or question.

[from Italian *ballotta* meaning 'little round object'; in medieval Venice votes were cast by dropping black or white pebbles or balls into a box]

ballpoint, ballpoints
(noun) A ballpoint is a pen with a small metal ball at the end which transfers the ink onto the paper.

ballroom, ballrooms
(noun) A ballroom is a very large room used for dancing or formal balls.

ballroom dancing
(noun) Ballroom dancing is a type of dancing in which a man and a woman dance together using fixed sequences of steps and movements.

balm (pronounced **bahm**)
(noun; an old-fashioned word) Balm is a soothing ointment made from a fragrant oily resin produced by certain kinds of tropical trees. Another word for balm is **balsam.**

balmy, balmier, balmiest
(adjective) mild and pleasant, e.g. *The air was warm and balmy... a balmy day.*

balsa
(noun) Balsa is very lightweight wood from a South American tree, used to make such things as model aeroplanes.
[from Spanish *balsa* meaning 'raft']

balsam (pronounced **bol**-sam)
(noun) Balsam is the same as balm.

balustrade, balustrades
(noun) A balustrade is a railing or wall on a balcony or staircase.

bamboo
(noun) Bamboo is a tall tropical plant with hard, hollow stems used for making furniture. It is a species of giant grass. The young shoots can be eaten.
[from South Indian *bambus*]

ban, bans, banning, banned
1 (verb) If something is banned, or if you are banned from doing it or using it, you are not allowed to do it or use it.
2 (noun) If there is a ban on something, it is not allowed.
[from Old English *bannan* meaning 'to proclaim aloud']

Similar words: (sense 1) forbid, bar, prohibit, proscribe, outlaw
(sense 2) embargo, prohibition, proscription

banal (pronounced ba-**nahl**)
(adjective) very ordinary or obvious, and therefore not effective or interesting, e.g. *His remarks are totally banal... a banal little song.*
banality (noun).
[Old French *banal* referred to military service which all tenants had to do; hence the word came to mean 'common to everyone' or 'ordinary']

banana, bananas
(noun) A banana is a long curved fruit with a yellow skin and cream-coloured flesh.
[from a West African language, via Portuguese]

band, bands, banding, banded
1 (noun) A band is a group of musicians who play jazz or pop music together, or a group who play brass instruments together; also used to refer to any group of people who have joined together for a particular purpose, e.g. *a band of revolutionaries.*
2 A band is a narrow strip of something used to hold things together or worn as a decoration round someone's head or wrist, e.g. *a rubber band... a head band.*
3 A band of numbers or values is a particular range of them, e.g. *All the applicants were in the 25 to 35 age band.*
bandsman (noun).

band together
(phrasal verb) When people band together, they join together for a particular purpose.

bandage, bandages, bandaging, bandaged
1 (noun) A bandage is a strip of cloth wrapped round a wound to protect it.
2 (verb) If you bandage a wound, you tie a bandage round it.

bandit, bandits
(noun; an old-fashioned word) A bandit was a member of an armed gang who lived by robbing travellers, especially in southern Europe and in Spanish-speaking countries.
[from Italian *bandito* meaning 'man who has been banished or outlawed']

bandstand, bandstands
(noun) A bandstand is a platform, usually with a roof, where a military band or brass band can play in the open air.

bandwagon
(phrase) To **jump on the bandwagon** means to become involved in something because it is fashionable or likely to be successful.

bandy, bandies, bandying, bandied
1 (verb) If a word, name, or idea is bandied about, many people use it or mention it.
2 If you **bandy words** with someone, you argue with them.
[from Old French *bander* meaning 'to hit a tennis ball back and forth']

bandy-legged
(adjective) Someone who is bandy-legged has legs that curve outwards at the knees.

bane
(noun; a literary word) Someone or something that is the bane of a person or organization causes a lot of trouble for them, e.g. *He is regarded as the bane of Whitehall... the bane of my life.*
[from Old English *bana* meaning 'murderer']

bang, bangs, banging, banged
1 (verb) If you bang something, you hit it or put it somewhere violently, so that it makes a loud noise, e.g. *Don't bang the door.*
2 If you bang a part of your body against something, you accidentally bump it, e.g. *I banged my head on a shelf.*
3 (noun) A bang is a sudden, short, loud noise.
4 A bang is also a hard or painful bump.

5 (phrase) If something **goes with a bang**, it is very successful and impressive.
6 (adverb; an informal use) If something is bang in a particular position, that is exactly where it is, e.g. *The university is bang in the middle of the old town.*

banger, bangers
1 (noun; an informal use) A banger is a sausage.
2 (an informal use) A banger is also an old car in poor condition.
3 A banger is also a small firework that makes a loud noise.

Bangladeshi, Bangladeshis (pronounced bang-glad-**desh**-ee)
1 (adjective) belonging or relating to Bangladesh.
2 (noun) A Bangladeshi is someone who comes from Bangladesh.

bangle, bangles
(noun) A bangle is an ornamental band or chain worn round someone's wrist or ankle.
[from Hindi *bangri* meaning 'bracelet']

banish, banishes, banishing, banished
1 (verb) To banish someone means to send them into exile.
2 To banish something means to get rid of it, e.g. *She tried to banish the thought.*
banishment (noun).
[from Old French *banir* meaning 'to send away' or 'ban']

Similar words: (sense 1) exile, deport, transport

banister, banisters; also spelled **bannister**
(noun) A banister is a rail supported by posts along the side of a staircase.

banjo, banjos or **banjoes**
(noun) A banjo is a musical instrument with a long neck, a hollow circular body, and four or more strings which you pluck or strum.

bank, banks, banking, banked
1 (noun) A bank is an institution where you can keep your money, and which lends money and offers other financial services.
2 (verb) If you bank with a particular bank, you have an account with it.
3 When you bank money, you pay it into a bank.
4 (noun) A bank of something is a store of it kept ready for use, e.g. *a blood bank... a bank of data.*
5 The bank of a river or lake is the raised ground along its edge.
6 A bank is also the sloping side of an area of raised ground.
7 A bank of something is also a long row or mass of it, e.g. *We made our way between banks of snow.*
8 (verb) If you bank on something happening, you expect it and rely on it.
9 When a plane banks, it tilts so that one of its wings is higher than the other, in order to turn.
banker (noun), **banking** (noun).
[senses 1-4 are from Italian *banca* meaning 'bench', applied to a money-changer's table; senses 5-9 are from Old Norse *banki* meaning 'ridge' or 'bank']

bank holiday, bank holidays
(noun) A bank holiday is a public holiday, when banks are closed by law.

banknote, banknotes
(noun) A banknote is a piece of paper money.

bankrupt, bankrupts, bankrupting, bankrupted
1 (adjective) When someone is declared bankrupt, they are legally recognized as not having enough money to pay their debts. Their property can then be sold, and the money used to repay some of what they owe.
2 (verb) To bankrupt someone means to make them bankrupt, e.g. *Another failure like this will bankrupt us.*
3 (noun) A bankrupt is someone who has been declared bankrupt.
bankruptcy (noun).
[from Italian *banca* meaning 'bank' + *rotta* meaning 'broken']

banner, banners
1 (noun) A banner is a piece of cloth with writing or a design on it, stretched high above the ground or carried in a procession.
2 (adjective) A banner headline is a headline printed right across the front page of a newspaper.
[from Old French *baniere* meaning 'flag']

bannister another spelling of **banister**.

banns
(plural noun) When the banns are read in a Christian church, the clergyman announces that two people intend to get married.
[from the Old English verb *bannan* meaning 'to proclaim']

banquet, banquets
(noun) A banquet is a grand formal dinner, often followed by speeches.
[from Old French *banquet*, originally meaning 'little bench']

banshee, banshees
(noun) In Irish folklore, a banshee was a female spirit who wailed outside a house when someone was going to die.

bantam, bantams
(noun) A bantam is a small breed of chicken. They were originally bred in a village in Java called Bantam.

banter
(noun) Banter is friendly joking and teasing.

Bantu (pronounced **ban**-too)
1 (noun) Bantu is the name of a large group of languages, including Swahili, Xhosa, and Zulu, spoken in eastern and southern Africa.
2 The Bantu are the people who speak these languages.

banyan, banyans
(noun) A banyan is an Indian fruit tree whose branches go down into the ground to form additional trunks.
[from an Indian word meaning 'merchant'; so called because merchants used to gather under these trees]

bap, baps
(noun) A bap is a kind of soft bread roll.

baptism
(noun) Baptism is the ceremony in which someone is baptized.

Baptist, Baptists
(noun and adjective) Baptists are members of a Protestant church who believe that people should be baptized when they are adults rather than when they are babies.

baptize, baptizes, baptizing, baptized; also spelled baptise
(verb) In the Christian religion, when someone is baptized, water is sprinkled on them, or they are immersed in water, as a sign that they have become a Christian.
[from Greek *baptein* meaning 'to dip in water']

bar, bars, barring, barred
1 (noun) A bar is a room in a pub or hotel where drinks are served; also used of the counter on which drinks are served.
2 A bar is also a small shop or stall where you can buy food and drink, e.g. *a sandwich bar*.
3 A bar is a long, straight piece of metal.
4 Bars are strong, thin, vertical pieces of metal fixed over a window to prevent people getting in or out, or made into a door or cage.
5 A bar is also a piece of something made in a rectangular shape, e.g. *a bar of soap*.
6 (verb) If you bar a door, you place something across it to prevent it being opened.
7 If you bar someone's way, you stop them going somewhere by standing in front of them.
8 If someone is barred from a place, they are not allowed to go there.
9 If something is barred, it is forbidden by a rule or law, e.g. *The use of these additives is now barred*.
10 (phrase) If there are **no holds barred** when people are competing for something, they do not observe any rules in their attempts to get it.
11 (noun) The Bar is the profession of a barrister, e.g. *That year I was called to the Bar.*
12 (preposition; a formal use) except, e.g. *We go there every day bar Tuesdays... He is the best sprinter in Europe, bar none.*
13 (noun) The bars in a piece of music are the many short parts of equal length that the piece is divided into.
14 In meteorology, a bar is a unit of pressure, equivalent to 100,000 newtons per square metre.

barb, barbs
(noun) A barb is a sharp backward curving point on the end of an arrow or fish-hook.
[from Latin *barba* meaning 'beard']

barbarian, barbarians
(noun) A barbarian was a member of a wild and uncivilized tribe in former times.
[from Greek *barbaros* meaning 'foreigner', originally 'person saying *bar-bar*']

barbaric
(adjective) cruel or brutal, e.g. *the barbaric sport of hunting*.
barbarity (noun).

barbarous
1 (adjective) cruel or brutal.
2 wild and uncivilized, e.g. *barbarous tribes*.
barbarism (noun).

barbecue, barbecues, barbecuing, barbecued
1 (noun) A barbecue is a grill with a charcoal fire on which you cook food, usually outdoors; also an outdoor party where you eat food cooked on a barbecue.
2 (verb) When food is barbecued, it is cooked over a charcoal grill, usually outdoors.
[from a Caribbean word meaning 'framework']

barbed
(adjective) A barbed remark is one that seems straightforward but is really malicious or spiteful.

barbed wire
(noun) Barbed wire is strong wire with sharp points sticking out of it, used to make fences.

barbell, barbells
(noun) A barbell is a metal rod to which heavy discs are attached at each end, used for weightlifting.

barber, barbers
(noun) A barber is a man who cuts men's hair.
[from Old French *barbe* meaning 'beard']

barbershop
(noun) Barbershop is a type of singing in close harmony, usually performed by four men.

barbiturate, barbiturates
(noun) A barbiturate is a drug that people take to make them calm or to put them to sleep.

bard, bards
(noun) A bard is a Celtic poet; also used as a literary word for any poet, especially Shakespeare.

bare, bares, baring, bared
1 (adjective) If a part of your body is bare, it is not covered by any clothing.
2 If something is bare, it has nothing on top of it or inside it, e.g. *bare floorboards... The room was bare.*
3 When trees are bare, they have no leaves on them.
4 (verb) If you bare something, you uncover it, e.g. *She bared her teeth... He bared his arm.*
5 (phrase) If you do something **with your bare hands**, you do it without using any tools or weapons.
6 (adjective) The bare minimum or bare essentials means the very least that is needed, e.g. *She packed the bare minimum of clothes.*
[from Old English *bær* meaning 'naked']

Similar words: (sense 1) naked, nude
(sense 2) stark

bareback
(adverb and adjective) Riding a horse without using a saddle.

barefoot
(adjective and adverb) not wearing anything on your feet.

barely
(adverb) only just, e.g. *He was so drunk he could barely stand.*

bargain, bargains, bargaining, bargained
1 (noun) A bargain is an agreement in which two people or groups discuss and agree what each will do, pay, or receive in a matter which affects them both.
2 (verb) When people bargain with each other, they discuss and agree terms about what each will do, pay, or receive in a matter which involves both.
3 (noun) A bargain is also something which is sold at a low price and which is good value.
4 (phrase) **Into the bargain** means as well or in addition, e.g. *He was a good man, and a clever one into the bargain.*
[from Old French *bargaigner* meaning 'to trade']

bargain for
(phrasal verb) If you had not bargained for or on something, you were not prepared for it.

barge, barges, barging, barged
1 (noun) A barge is a boat with a flat bottom. Barges are used for carrying heavy loads, especially on canals.
2 (verb; an informal use) If you barge into a place, you push into it in a rough or rude away.

baritone, baritones
(noun) A baritone is a man with a fairly deep singing voice, between that of a tenor and a bass.
[from Greek *barus* meaning 'heavy' + *tonos* meaning 'tone']

barium (pronounced **bare-ree-um**)
(noun) Barium is a soft, silvery-white chemical element. Its compounds are used in making glass. Its atomic number is 56 and its symbol is Ba.
[from Greek *barus* meaning 'heavy']

barium meal, barium meals
(noun) A barium meal is a preparation of barium sulphate fed to a patient before an X-ray of the stomach and intestines. Barium is opaque to X-rays, so any object in the patient's intestines will show up in the X-ray.

bark, barks, barking, barked
1 (verb) When a dog barks, it makes a short, loud noise, once or several times.
2 (noun) A bark is the short, loud noise that a dog makes.
3 (informal phrase) If you say that **someone's bark is worse than their bite**, you mean they are not so unpleasant or hostile as they seem.
4 If someone is **barking up the wrong tree**, they are using the wrong methods to try and solve a problem.
5 (noun) The bark of a tree is the tough material on the outside of its trunk and branches.

barley
(noun) Barley is a cereal that is grown for food. It is also used for making beer and whisky.

barmaid, barmaids
(noun) A barmaid is a woman who serves drinks in a pub or bar.

barman, barmen
(noun) A barman is a man who serves drinks in a pub or bar.

bar mitzvah
(noun) A Jewish boy's bar mitzvah is a ceremony that takes place on his 13th birthday, after which he is regarded as an adult.
[a Hebrew phrase meaning 'son of the law']

barmy, barmier, barmiest
(adjective; an informal word) mad or very foolish.

barn, barns
(noun) A barn is a large farm building used for storing crops or animal food.
[from Old English *bere ærn* meaning 'barley room']

barnacle, barnacles
(noun) A barnacle is a small shellfish that fixes itself to rocks and to the bottom of boats.

barometer, barometers
(noun) A barometer is an instrument that measures atmospheric pressure and shows when the weather is changing.
[from Greek *baros* + *metron*, meaning 'weight measurer']

baron, barons
1 (noun) A baron is a member of the lowest rank of the nobility.
2 A baron is also someone who is very powerful, e.g. *a press baron.*
baronial (adjective).

baroness, baronesses
(noun) A baroness is a woman who has the rank of baron, or who is the wife of a baron.

baronet, baronets
(noun) A baronet is a man who is given the title 'baronet' by the King or Queen, and who can pass this title on to his son. Baronets are addressed as 'Sir'.
baronetcy (noun).

baroque (pronounced ba-**rok**)
(adjective) Baroque describes an elaborate, highly ornamental style of architecture and art which flourished in Europe in the 17th and 18th centuries.

barrack, barracks, barracking, barracked
(verb) If you barrack someone who is making a speech, you interrupt them by shouting at them.

barracks
(noun) A barracks is a building where soldiers live.
[from Spanish *barraca* meaning 'hut']

barracuda, barracudas
(noun) A barracuda is a large, fierce, fast-swimming tropical fish with sharp teeth, which attacks man.
[from Spanish, from a South American Indian language]

barrage, barrages
1 (noun) A barrage of questions or complaints is a lot of them all coming at the same time.
2 A barrage is continuous artillery fire over a

wide area, intended to keep the enemy from
moving.
3 A barrage across a river is an artificial barrier
to control the flow of water.
[from French *barrer* meaning 'to obstruct']

Similar words: (sense 1) bombardment, volley
(sense 2) bombardment, fusillade, salvo, volley

barrel, barrels
1 (noun) A barrel is a wooden container for
liquids, with rounded sides and flat ends.
2 The barrel of a gun is the long cylindrical part
through which the bullet or shell is fired.
3 (phrase) If you are **scraping the bottom of the
barrel**, you are using the last remaining and least
satisfactory resources.
[from Old French *baril* meaning 'barrel']

barrel organ, barrel organs
(noun) A barrel organ was a musical instrument
which used to be played in the street by a person
called an organ grinder. It was played by turning
a handle, so that pins projecting from a cylinder
could operate a row of small organ pipes in order
to play tunes.

barren
1 (adjective) Barren land has soil of such poor
quality that plants cannot grow on it.
2 A barren female is physically incapable of
having offspring.
barrenness (noun).

Similar words: (sense 1) infertile, desert
(sense 2) sterile, infertile, childless

barricade, barricades, barricading, barricaded
1 (noun) A barricade is a temporary barrier
placed across a road to stop people getting past.
2 (verb) If you barricade yourself inside a room
or building, you put something heavy against the
door to stop people getting in.
[from Old French *barriquer* meaning 'to block
with barrels']

barrier, barriers
1 (noun) A barrier is a fence or wall that
prevents people or animals getting from one area
to another.
2 Something that is a barrier prevents two
people or groups from agreeing or
communicating, or prevents something from
being achieved, e.g. *These attitudes have always
been a barrier to progress.*
[from French *barrière* meaning 'bar']

Similar words: (sense 1) barricade, bar, railing

barring
(preposition) provided that something is not the
case or does not happen, e.g. *We should finish the
job tomorrow, barring accidents.*

barrister, barristers
(noun) A barrister is a lawyer who can speak in a
higher court on behalf of the defence or the
prosecution.

barrow, barrows
1 (noun) A barrow is a cart, in particular a large

covered cart from which fruit or other goods are
sold in the street.
2 A barrow is also a mound of earth or stones
built over a grave in prehistoric times.
[sense 1 is from Old English *bearwe* meaning
'carrier'; sense 2 is from Germanic *berg* meaning
'hill' or 'mountain']

barter, barters, bartering, bartered
1 (verb) If you barter goods, you exchange them
for other goods, rather than selling them for
money.
2 (noun) Barter is the activity of bartering goods.

basalt (pronounced **bas**-solt)
(noun) Basalt is a dark-coloured volcanic rock.

base, bases, basing, based
1 (noun) The base of something is its lowest part,
often the part which supports the rest.
2 A base is a place from which operations or
activities are organized, directed, and supplied.
3 (verb) To base something on something else
means to use the second thing as a foundation or
starting point of the first, e.g. *The film is based
on a story by Pushkin.*
4 If you are based somewhere, it is the main
place from which your work is organized.
5 (noun) In chemistry, a base is any compound
that reacts with an acid to form a salt.
6 In mathematics, a base is a system of counting
and expressing numbers. The decimal system
uses base 10, and the binary system uses base 2.
7 (adjective; a literary use) A base act is one
which is shocking and contemptible.
[senses 1-6 are from Greek *basis;* sense 7 is from
Latin *bassus* meaning 'low']

Similar words: (sense 1) bottom, foot, foundation
(sense 7) low, mean, ignoble, dishonourable

baseball
(noun) Baseball is a game played by two teams of
nine players. Each player hits a ball with a bat
and tries to run round four points, called bases,
before the other team can get the ball back.

baseless
(adjective) A story or belief that is baseless is
not based on facts and is therefore untrue.

basement, basements
(noun) The basement of a building is a floor built
wholly or partly below the ground.

base metal, base metals
(noun) A base metal is a metal, such as iron or
copper, that is not a precious metal.

bases
1 (pronounced **bay**-seez) the plural of **basis**.
2 (pronounced **bay**-siz) the plural of **base**.

bash, bashes, bashing, bashed
1 (verb; an informal word) If you bash someone
or bash into them, you hit them hard.
2 (noun) A bash is a hard blow.
3 (phrase) If you **have a bash** at something, you
try to do it.

bashful
(adjective) shy and easily embarrassed.
bashfully (adverb), **bashfulness** (noun).

basic, basics
1 (adjective) The basic aspects of something are the most important ones, e.g. *They never solved the basic economic problems.*
2 (plural noun) The basics of something are the most important aspects of it, e.g. *For a year I learned the basics of journalism.*
3 (adjective) Something that is basic has only the necessary features and no extras or luxuries, e.g. *The facilities are very basic.*
basically (adverb).

Similar words: (sense 1) elementary, fundamental, key, primary, rudimentary

basil
(noun) Basil is a herb used for flavouring in cooking.
[from Greek *basilikon* 'the royal herb'; from *basileus* meaning 'king']

basilica, basilicas
(noun) A basilica is an oblong church with a semicircular end called an apse.
[from Greek *basilikē* meaning 'royal hall']

basin, basins
1 (noun) A basin is a deep bowl used for mixing or storing food.
2 The basin of a river is all the area round it from which water runs into it.

basis, bases
1 (noun) The basis of something is the foundation or main principle from which it can be further developed, e.g. *This was the basis of the final design.*
2 The basis for a belief is the facts that provide a reason for it, e.g. *There is no basis for this assumption.*
[from Greek *basis* meaning 'foundation' or 'pedestal']

Similar words: (sense 1) groundwork, foundation (sense 2) foundation

bask, basks, basking, basked
1 (verb) If you bask in the sun, you sit or lie in it, enjoying its warmth.
2 (a literary use) If you bask in someone's approval or favour, you have it and enjoy it.
[from Old Norse *bathask* meaning 'to bathe oneself']

basket, baskets
(noun) A basket is a container made of thin strips of cane woven together.

basketball
(noun) Basketball is a game in which two teams, usually of five players each, try to score goals by throwing a large ball through one of two circular nets suspended high up at each end of the court.

Basque, Basques (pronounced **bask**)
1 (noun) Basque is a language spoken in northern Spain. It is not related to any other language.
2 A Basque is a person who comes from the part of northern Spain where Basque is spoken.

bas-relief (**bas** rhyming with **gas** or **ha**)
(noun) Bas-relief is a type of sculpture on a flat surface, in which the figures project slightly from the background.
[a French term, from Italian *basso rilievo* meaning 'low projection']

bass, basses (rhymes with **lace**)
1 (noun) A bass is a man who sings the lowest part in four-part harmony.
2 A bass is also a musical instrument that provides the rhythm and lowest part in the harmonies for a rock group or jazz band. A bass may be either a large guitar or a very large member of the violin family: see **double bass**.
[from Italian *basso* meaning 'low']

bass, basses (rhymes with **gas**)
(noun) A bass is a type of edible sea fish.

basset hound, basset hounds
(noun) A basset hound is a smooth-haired dog with a large body, long ears, and short legs.

bassoon, bassoons
(noun) A bassoon is a large woodwind instrument that can produce a wide range of notes, including very low ones.

bastard, bastards
1 (noun; an old-fashioned use) A bastard is someone whose parents were not married at the time he or she was born.
2 (an offensive use) People sometimes call someone a bastard when they dislike them or are very angry with them.

baste, bastes, basting, basted
(verb) When you baste meat that is roasting, you pour hot fat over it so that it does not become dry while cooking.

bastion, bastions
1 (noun; a literary word) A bastion is a projecting part of the walls of a fortification, which enables defenders to fire along the lines of the outside walls.
2 A bastion is also something that protects a system or way of life, e.g. *one of the last bastions of privilege.*

bat, bats, batting, batted
1 (noun) A bat is a specially shaped piece of wood with a handle, used for hitting the ball in a game such as cricket, baseball, or table tennis.
2 (verb) In cricket, when someone is batting, it is their turn to try to hit the ball and score runs.
3 (phrase) If you do something **off your own bat**, you do it without anyone else suggesting it.
4 If someone **did not bat an eyelid**, they showed no surprise.
5 (noun) A bat is also a small, flying nocturnal animal that looks like a mouse with wings.
[senses 1-4 are from Old English *batt* meaning 'club' or 'stick'; sense 5 is from Middle English *bakke*]

batch, batches
(noun) A batch is a group of things of the same kind produced or dealt with together.
[originally referring to a batch of loaves baked together, from Old English *bacan* meaning 'to bake']

bated
(phrase) **With bated breath** means very anxiously.

bath, baths, bathing, bathed
1 (noun) A bath is a long container which you fill with water and sit in to wash yourself.
2 (verb) To bath means to wash in a bath.

bathe, bathes, bathing, bathed
1 (verb) When you bathe, you swim or play in the sea or in a river or lake.
2 When you bathe a wound, you wash it gently.
3 (a literary use) If a place is bathed in light, a lot of light reaches it, e.g. *The garden was bathed in sunshine.*
bather (noun), **bathing** (noun).

bathos (pronounced **bay**-thoss)
(noun; a literary word) Bathos is a sudden change in speech or writing from a serious or important tone or subject to a silly or trivial one.
[from Greek *bathos* meaning 'depth', with reference to the sudden plunge from seriousness to silliness]

bathroom, bathrooms
(noun) A bathroom is a room with a bath, a washbasin, and often a toilet in it. In American English, 'the bathroom' is a euphemism for the toilet.

baths
(noun) The baths is a public swimming pool.

batik
(noun) Batik is a process in which designs are printed on cloth by putting wax on parts of it, so that these parts are not coloured when the rest is dyed.
[from Javanese *mbatik* meaning 'painting']

batman, batmen
(noun) A batman is an army officer's personal servant.
[from *bât*, a French word meaning 'pack-saddle']

baton, batons
1 (noun) A baton is a light, thin stick that a conductor uses to direct an orchestra or choir.
2 In athletics, the baton is a short stick passed from one runner to another in a relay race.
3 A baton is also a short stick used by policemen in some countries as a weapon, lighter than a truncheon.
[a French word]

batsman, batsmen
(noun) In cricket, the batsman is the person who is batting.

battalion, battalions
(noun) A battalion is an army unit consisting of three or more companies.
[from Italian *battaglione* meaning 'large company of soldiers', from *battaglia* meaning 'battle']

batten, battens, battening, battened
(noun) A batten is a strip of wood that is fixed to something to strengthen it or hold it firm.
[from French *bâton* meaning 'stick']

batten down
(phrasal verb) If you batten something down, you make it secure by fixing battens across it.

batter, batters, battering, battered
1 (verb) To batter someone or something means to hit them many times, e.g. *The ship was being battered by the waves.*
2 (noun) Batter is a mixture of flour, eggs, and milk, used to make food such as pancakes, or to coat food such as fish before frying it.

battery, batteries
1 (noun) A battery is an apparatus for storing and producing electricity in a piece of equipment such as a torch, a radio, or a car.
2 A battery is also a group of heavy guns operating as a single unit.
3 A battery of things or people is a large group of them.
4 (adjective) A battery hen is one of a large number of hens kept in small cages for the mass production of eggs.
[from Old French *batterie* meaning 'a beating', hence 'bombardment by a group of heavy guns', hence 'group of guns or other apparatus operating as a single unit']

battle, battles, battling, battled
1 (noun) A battle is a fight between armies, ships, or planes; also used of a struggle between two people or groups with conflicting aims.
2 A battle for something difficult is a determined attempt to obtain or achieve it, e.g. *the battle for women's rights.*
3 (verb) If you battle for something, you fight against difficulties to achieve it.
[from Latin *battalia* meaning 'military exercises']

battlefield, battlefields
(noun) A battlefield is a place where a battle is or has been fought.

battlements
(plural noun) The battlements of a castle or fortress consist of a wall built round the top, with gaps through which guns or arrows could be fired.

battleship, battleships
(noun) A battleship is a large, heavily armoured warship.

batty, battier, battiest
(adjective; an informal word) crazy or eccentric.

bauble, baubles
(noun) A bauble is a pretty but cheap ornament or piece of jewellery.
[from Old French *baubel* meaning 'toy']

baulk another spelling of balk.

bauxite (pronounced **bawk**-site)
(noun) Bauxite is a type of clay containing aluminium oxide, from which aluminium is made.
[named after *Les Baux*, the place in France where it was discovered]

bawdy, bawdier, bawdiest
(adjective) A bawdy joke, story, or song contains humorous references to sex.
[from Middle English *baude* meaning 'brothel keeper']

bawl, bawls, bawling, bawled
1 (verb; an informal word) To bawl at someone means to shout at them loudly and harshly.
2 When a child is bawling, it is crying very loudly and angrily.

bay, bays, baying, bayed
1 (noun) A bay is a part of a coastline where the land curves inwards.
2 A bay is also a space or area used for a particular purpose, e.g. *a loading bay.*
3 Bay is a kind of tree similar to the laurel. Bay leaves are used for flavouring in cooking.
4 A horse that is a bay is a reddish brown colour.
5 (phrase) If you **keep something at bay**, you prevent it from reaching you, e.g. *The invaders were kept at bay.*
6 (verb) When a hound or wolf bays, it makes a deep howling noise as, for instance, when it is hunting for something.
[senses 1 and 2 from Old French *baie;* sense 3 from Latin *baca* meaning 'berry'; sense 4 from Old French *bai* meaning 'reddish brown'; sense 5 from Old French *abaiier* meaning 'to bark or howl']

Similar words: (sense 1) cove, gulf, inlet

bayonet, bayonets
(noun) A bayonet is a sharp blade that can be fixed to the end of a rifle and used for stabbing.
[named after *Bayonne* in France, where it originated]

bay window, bay windows
(noun) A bay window is a window that sticks out from the outside wall of a house.

bazaar, bazaars
1 (noun) A bazaar is an area with many small shops and stalls, especially in Eastern countries.
2 A bazaar is also a sale of various goods to raise money for charity, e.g. *a Christmas bazaar.*
[from Persian *bazar* meaning 'market']

B.B.C. an abbreviation for **British Broadcasting Corporation.**

B.C.
B.C. means 'before Christ', e.g. *in the year 55 B.C.*

be, am, is, are; was, were; been, being
1 (auxiliary verb) Be is used with a present participle to form the continuous tense, e.g. *We are living just outside Glasgow... I am doing my best.*
2 Be is also used to say that something will happen, e.g. *We're going to St Andrews for our holidays.*
3 Be is used to form the passive voice, e.g. *He was arrested the following day... New plans are being made.*
4 (verb) Be is used to express the relationship between the subject of a sentence and its complement or adjunct, e.g. *Her name is Melanie... I am fourteen years old... She was not at home.*
5 To be yourself means to behave in a way that is natural to you.
6 (phrase; a rather formal use) You say **be that**

as it may when you want to change the subject without giving an opinion about what has just been said, e.g. *Be that as it may, we still have to find £53,000 from somewhere.*

beach, beaches
(noun) A beach is an area of sand or pebbles next to the sea.

Similar words: seaside, shore, seashore, strand, coast

beachcomber, beachcombers
(noun) A beachcomber is a person who wanders along beaches looking for useful or valuable things washed up by the sea.

beacon, beacons
(noun) In the past a beacon was a light or fire on a hill, which acted as a signal or warning.
[from Old English *beacen* meaning 'sign']

bead, beads
1 (noun) Beads are small pieces of coloured glass, wood, or plastic with a hole through the middle, strung together to make necklaces and bracelets.
2 Beads of sweat or other liquid are drops of it.
[from Old English *bed* meaning 'prayer'; beads on a string were used for counting prayers]

beady
(adjective) Beady eyes are small and bright like beads.

beagle, beagles
(noun) A beagle is a short-haired dog with long ears and short legs. Beagles are kept as pets or used for hunting hares.

beak, beaks
(noun) A bird's beak is the hard part of its mouth that sticks out.
[from Old French *bec* meaning 'beak']

beaker, beakers
(noun) A beaker is a cup for drinking out of, usually made of plastic and without a handle.
[from Old Norse *bikarr* meaning 'cup']

beam, beams, beaming, beamed
1 (verb) If you beam, you smile broadly because you are happy.
2 (noun) A beam is a happy smile.
3 A beam of light is a band of light from something such as a torch.
4 A beam is also a long, thick bar of wood, concrete, or metal, especially one that supports a roof.

bean, beans
1 (noun) Beans are the pods of a climbing plant, or the seeds inside these pods, which are eaten as a vegetable; also used of some other seeds, for example the seeds from which coffee is made.
2 (informal phrase) If someone is **full of beans**, they are very lively and energetic.
3 If you **spill the beans**, you reveal something that people have been trying to keep secret.

beansprouts
(plural noun) Beansprouts are small shoots grown from certain kinds of beans. You can eat them cooked or raw.

bear, bears, bearing, bore, borne
1 (noun) A bear is a large, strong wild animal with thick fur and sharp claws.
2 (verb; a formal use) To bear something means to carry it or support its weight, e.g. *His ankle was now strong enough to bear his weight.*
3 If something bears a mark or typical feature, it has it, e.g. *The scene bore all the marks of a country wedding.*
4 If you can bear something difficult, you accept it and are able to deal with it, e.g *It was painful, but he bore it in silence.*
5 If you can't bear someone or something, you dislike them very much.
6 (a formal use) When a plant or tree bears flowers, fruit, or leaves, it produces them.
7 To bear left or bear right means to turn left or right.
8 (phrase) If you **bring pressure to bear** on someone, you try to persuade them to do something.
9 If someone **bears a grudge** or **bears malice** towards someone else, they continue to have hostile feelings towards that person.
bearable (adjective), **bearably** (adverb).

bear down
(phrasal verb) If something large bears down on you, it moves quickly towards you.

bear out
(phrasal verb) To bear someone out or to bear out their story or report means to support what they are saying, e.g. *These claims are not borne out by the evidence.*

bear up
(phrasal verb) If you bear up when you are having problems, you remain brave and cheerful.

bear with
(phrasal verb) If you ask someone to bear with you, you are asking them to be patient.

beard, beards
(noun) A man's beard is the hair that grows on his chin and cheeks.
bearded (adjective).

bearer, bearers
1 (noun) The bearer of something such as a document is the person who is taking it somewhere, or who has it in his or her possession.
2 At a funeral, the bearers are the people who carry the coffin.

bearing, bearings
1 (noun) Someone's bearing is the way in which they move or stand.
2 If something has a bearing on a situation, it is relevant to it.
3 (phrases) To **get your bearings** means to find out where you are or what is happening. To **lose your bearings** means not to know where you are or what is happening.

beast, beasts
1 (noun; an old-fashioned use) A beast is an animal, especially a large one.
2 (an informal use) If you call someone a beast, you mean that they are unkind, cruel, or spiteful.

beastly, beastlier, beastliest
(adjective; an old-fashioned informal word) unkind, cruel, or spiteful.
beastliness (noun).
[from Latin *bestia* meaning 'animal']

beat, beats, beating, beaten
1 (verb) To beat someone or something means to hit them hard and repeatedly, e.g. *His father used to beat him... The rain was beating against the window.*
2 If you beat eggs, cream, or butter, you mix them vigorously using a fork or a whisk.
3 When a bird or insect beats its wings, it moves them up and down.
4 When your heart is beating, it is pumping blood with a regular rhythm.
5 (noun) The beat of your heart is its regular pumping action.
6 The beat of a piece of music is its main rhythm.
7 (phrase) If you **beat time** to a piece of music, you move your hand or foot up and down in time with the music.
8 (verb) If you beat someone in a race, game, or competition, you defeat them or do better than them.
9 (an informal use) If something beats you, you cannot understand it, e.g. *It beats me where they get the money from.*
10 (noun) A police officer's beat is the area which he or she walks around when on duty.
beater (noun), **beating** (noun).

Similar words: (sense 1) thrash, batter, pound, buffet (sense 8) conquer, overcome, vanquish, defeat, lick, trounce

beat down
(phrasal verb) When the sun beats down, it is very hot and bright.

beat up
(phrasal verb) To beat someone up means to hit or kick them violently until they are severely hurt.

Beaufort scale (pronounced **boh-fort**)
(noun) The Beaufort scale is a scale for measuring the speed of wind, ranging from 0 (calm) to 12 (hurricane force). It was devised by Sir Francis Beaufort (1774-1857), an English admiral.

beautician, beauticians
(noun) A beautician is a person whose job is giving people beauty treatments.

beautiful
(adjective) very attractive or pleasing, e.g. *a beautiful girl... beautiful gardens... beautiful cooking... a beautiful shot.*
beautifully (adverb).

Similar words: glamorous, gorgeous, lovely, exquisite, ravishing

beautify, beautifies, beautifying, beautified
(verb; a formal word) To beautify something means to make it look beautiful.
beautification (noun).

beauty, beauties
1 (noun) Beauty is the quality of being beautiful.
2 (a rather old-fashioned use) A beauty is a beautiful woman.
3 The beauty of an idea or plan is what makes it attractive or worthwhile, e.g. *That's the beauty of the plan—it's so simple.*
[from Old French *biau* meaning 'beautiful']

beaver, beavers
(noun) A beaver is an amphibious rodent with a big, flat tail. Beavers build dams in streams.

becalm
(verb) When a sailing ship is becalmed, it is unable to sail on, because there is no wind.

because
1 (conjunction) Because is used with a clause that gives the reason for something, e.g. *I went home because I was tired.*
2 (preposition) **Because of** is used with a noun that gives the reason for something, e.g. *He retired last month because of ill health.*
[from Middle English *bi + cause* meaning 'by cause of']

beck, becks
(noun) If you are at someone's beck and call, you are always available to do what they ask.
[from Middle English *beknen* meaning 'to beckon']

beckon, beckons, beckoning, beckoned
1 (verb) If you beckon to someone, you signal with your hand that you want them to come to you.
2 If you say that something beckons, you mean that you find it very attractive, e.g. *The night life of the city beckoned.*

become, becomes, becoming, became
1 (verb) To become something means to start feeling or being that thing, e.g. *She became very angry... We became good friends.*
2 (phrase) If you ask **what has become of** someone or something, you are asking where they are and what has happened to them.
3 (verb; an old-fashioned use) If something becomes you, it suits you and seems right for you, e.g. *Sarcasm doesn't become you.*
becoming (adjective).
[from Old English *becuman* meaning 'to happen']

becquerel, becquerels (pronounced bek-er-**rel**)
(noun) A becquerel is a unit of radioactive activity. It is named after the French physicist A.H. Becquerel (1852-1908).

bed, beds, bedding, bedded
1 (noun) A bed is a piece of furniture that you lie on when you sleep.
2 A bed in a garden is an area of ground in which plants are grown.
3 The sea bed or a river bed is the ground at the bottom of the sea or a river.
4 A bed is also a layer of rock, e.g. *horizontal beds of sandstone.*
5 (verb) If you bed down somewhere, you sleep there for the night.

bedclothes
(plural noun) Bedclothes are the sheets and covers that you put over you when you get into bed.

bedding
(noun) Bedding is sheets, blankets, and other covers that are used on beds.

bedevil, bedevils, bedevilling, bedevilled
(pronounced bid-**dev**-il)
(verb) If you are bedevilled by something, you are constantly troubled or tormented by it, e.g. *He has been bedevilled by injuries.*

bedfellow, bedfellows
(noun) Bedfellows are two things or people that are associated in some way, e.g. *Heavy drinking and puritanical moral attitudes make strange bedfellows.*

bedlam
(noun) You can refer to a noisy and disorderly place or situation as bedlam, e.g. *Inside the house it was bedlam.*
[from *Bedlam*, a shortened form of the Hospital of St. Mary of Bethlehem in London, which was an institution for the insane or mentally ill]

Bedouin, Bedouins (pronounced **bed**-oo-in)
(noun) A Bedouin is a member of any of the nomadic tribes of Arabs who live in the deserts of north Africa and the Middle East.

bedpan, bedpans
(noun) A bedpan is a shallow bowl shaped like a toilet seat, which is used instead of a toilet by people who are too ill to get out of bed.

bedraggled
(adjective) A bedraggled person or animal is in a messy state, as a result of being soaked or handled roughly.

bedridden
(adjective) Someone who is bedridden is so ill or disabled that they cannot get out of bed.

bedrock
1 (noun) Bedrock is the solid rock under the soil.
2 The bedrock of something is the foundation and principles on which it is based, e.g. *Family values are the bedrock of the nation.*

bedroom, bedrooms
(noun) A bedroom is a room used for sleeping in.

bedsitter, bedsitters
(noun) A bedsitter is a rented furnished room in a house, where you can live and sleep.

bedsore, bedsores
(noun) A bedsore is a sore caused by staying too long in one position in bed.

bedspread, bedspreads
(noun) A bedspread is a cover put over a bed, on top of the sheets and blankets.

bedstead, bedsteads
(noun) A bedstead is the metal or wooden frame of an old-fashioned bed.

bee, bees
1 (noun) A bee is an insect that buzzes as it flies. Bees make honey and live in large groups.
2 (phrase) If you have **a bee in your bonnet** about something, you are obsessed with it and keep mentioning it.

beech, beeches
(noun) A beech is a deciduous tree with a smooth grey trunk and shiny leaves. Its wood is often used for furniture.

beef, beefs, beefing, beefed
1 (noun) Beef is the meat of a cow, bull, or ox.
2 (verb; an informal use) If you beef about something, you complain.
[from Old French *boef* meaning 'ox' or 'bull']

Beefeater, Beefeaters
(noun) Beefeaters are the guards at the Tower of London. They wear 16th-century costume.

beefy, beefier, beefiest
(adjective; an informal word) A beefy man is strong and muscular.

beehive, beehives
(noun) A beehive is a natural or artificial structure in which bees live and make their honey.

beeline
(phrase; an informal use) If you **make a beeline** for a place, you go there as quickly and directly as possible.

been the past participle of **be**.

beer
(noun) Beer is an alcoholic drink made from malted barley and flavoured with hops.

beet
(noun) Beet is a plant with an edible root and leaves. Sugar is made from the root of one type of beet, and another type is used as food for farm animals.

beetle, beetles
(noun) A beetle is a flying insect with hard forewings which cover its body when it is not flying.
[from Old English *bitan* meaning 'to bite']

beetroot, beetroots
(noun) A beetroot is the round, dark red root of a type of beet. It is cooked and eaten, especially cold as a salad vegetable or preserved in vinegar.

befall, befalls, befalling, befell
(verb; an old-fashioned word) If something befalls you, it happens to you, e.g. *A similar fate befell my cousin.*
[from Old English *befeallan* meaning 'to happen']

befit, befits, befitting, befitted
(verb; a literary word) If something befits you, it is suitable or appropriate for you, e.g. *He was courteous, as befitted a young man in his position.*
befitting (adjective), **befittingly** (adverb).

before
1 (adverb, preposition, and conjunction) Before is used to refer to a previous time, e.g. *It had rained the night before... the day before yesterday... Before I sign this document, I want to know what it means.*
2 (adverb) If you have done something before, you have done it on a previous occasion, e.g. *Have you been to Greece before?*
3 (preposition; a formal use) Before also means

in front of, e.g. *You will appear before the magistrate.*

Similar words: (sense 2) earlier, formerly, previously, sooner, beforehand

beforehand
(adverb) before, e.g. *They got married without telling anyone beforehand.*

befriend, befriends, befriending, befriended
(verb) If you befriend someone, you act in a kind and helpful way and so become friends with them.

beg, begs, begging, begged
1 (verb) If you beg someone to do something, you ask them very earnestly to do it.
2 When people beg, they ask for food or money, because they are very poor.

Similar words: (sense 1) beseech, entreat, implore, plead

beget, begets, begetting, begot, begotten
(verb; an old-fashioned word) To beget something means to cause it to happen or be created, e.g. *Poverty begets crime.*

beggar, beggars
(noun) A beggar is someone who lives by asking people for money or food.

beggarly
(adjective) A beggarly sum of money is very small and inadequate.

begin, begins, beginning, began, begun
(verb) If you begin to do something, you start doing it. When something begins, it starts.

Similar words: initiate, launch, start, commence

beginner, beginners
(noun) A beginner is someone who has just started learning to do something and cannot do it very well yet.

Similar words: learner, novice, recruit, fledgling, tyro

beginning, beginnings
(noun) The beginning of something is the first part of it or the time when it starts, e.g. *I say this at the beginning of my book... There have been four accidents since the beginning of the year.*

begonia, begonias (pronounced be-**go**-nya)
(noun) A begonia is a garden plant or house plant with brightly coloured flowers. Begonia is named after Michel Bégon (1638-1710), a French patron of botany.

begot the past tense of **beget**.

begotten the past participle of **beget**.

begrudge, begrudges, begrudging, begrudged
(verb) If you begrudge someone something, you are angry or envious because they have it, e.g. *I do not begrudge them their success.*

beguile, beguiles, beguiling, beguiled (rhymes with **mile**)
1 (verb) If someone beguiles you into doing something, they trick you into doing it.
2 To beguile someone also means to charm or

amuse them, e.g. *He beguiled us with stories of his travels.*
beguiling (adjective), **beguilingly** (adverb).

behalf
(phrase) To do something **on someone else's behalf** means to do it for their benefit or as their representative.
[from Old English *be* meaning 'by' and *halfe* meaning 'side']

behave, behaves, behaving, behaved
1 (verb) If you behave in a particular way, you act in that way, e.g. *He has been behaving very strangely lately.*
2 To behave yourself means to act correctly or properly.

behaviour
(noun) Your behaviour is the way in which you behave.

behead, beheads, beheading, beheaded
(verb) To behead someone means to cut their head off.
beheading (noun).

beheld the past tense of **behold.**

behest
(phrase; an old-fashioned expression) If you do something **at someone's behest**, you do it because they have asked or ordered you to.
[from Old English *behæs* meaning 'command' or 'vow']

behind, behinds
1 (preposition) at the back of, e.g. *hiding behind the screen.*
2 responsible for or causing, e.g. *These were the reasons behind his statement... the man behind the new scheme.*
3 supporting someone, e.g. *We are all behind you.*
4 (adverb) If you stay behind, you remain somewhere after other people have gone.
5 If you leave something behind, you do not take it with you.
6 If you are behind with your work, you have not done as much of it as you ought to have done.
7 (noun; an informal use) Your behind is your bottom.
[from Old English *behindan* meaning 'at a place in the rear']

behold, beholds, beholding, beheld
(verb; a literary word) To behold something means to notice it or look at it.
beholder (noun).

beige (pronounced **bayj**)
(noun and adjective) pale brown.
[a French word, referring to undyed wool]

being, beings
1 Being is the present participle of **be.**
2 (phrase) If something is **in being**, it exists, e.g. *laws already in being... The Polytechnic came into being in 1971.*
3 (noun) A being is a living creature, e.g. *Beings from outer space.*

belated
(adjective; a formal word) A belated action

happens later than it should have done, e.g. *Please accept my belated thanks for your gift.*
belatedly (adverb).

belch, belches, belching, belched
1 (verb) If you belch, you make a sudden noise in your throat because air has risen up from your stomach.
2 (noun) A belch is the noise you make when you belch.
3 (verb) If something belches smoke or fire, it sends it out in large amounts, e.g. *The engine belched flames.*

beleaguered
1 (adjective) besieged, e.g. *the beleaguered garrison.*
2 surrounded or beset, e.g. *listening to a beleaguered government minister making lame excuses.*
[from Dutch *be* meaning 'completely' and *leger* meaning 'siege']

belfry, belfries
(noun) The belfry is the part of a church tower where the bells are.
[from Old French *berfrei* meaning 'tower'; because towers often contained bells this word was later changed to *belfrey*]

Belgian, Belgians
1 (adjective) belonging or relating to Belgium.
2 (noun) A Belgian is someone who comes from Belgium.

belie, belies, belying, belied (pronounced bil-**lie**)
(verb) To belie something means to show that it is untrue, or to make it difficult to believe, e.g. *Their attitudes belie their words... Her appearance belied her seventy years.*

belief, beliefs
1 (noun) A belief is a feeling of certainty that something exists or is true.
2 A belief is also one of the principles of a religion or moral system.

Similar words: (sense 2) creed, doctrine, ideology, philosophy

believe, believes, believing, believed
1 (verb) If you believe that something is true, you accept that it is true.
2 If you believe someone, you accept that they are telling the truth.
3 If you believe in things such as God and miracles, you accept that they exist or happen.
4 If you believe in something such as a plan or system, you are in favour of it, e.g. *He continued to believe in democracy.*
believable (adjective), **believer** (noun).

belittle, belittles, belittling, belittled
(verb) If you belittle someone or something, you make them seem unimportant, e.g. *I'm not trying to belittle his efforts.*
belittlement (noun).

Similar words: disparage, decry, denigrate

bell, bells
1 (noun) A bell is a hollow metal object shaped

like an inverted cup. It has a piece inside called a clapper that hits the sides, producing a loud ringing sound.
2 A bell is also any piece of equipment that makes a sound when required, in order to attract attention.
3 (phrase; an informal use) If something **rings a bell**, it reminds you of something, though you cannot remember exactly what.

bellicose
(adjective; a literary word) eager to start a fight or an argument.
bellicosity (noun).
[from Latin *bellicosus* meaning 'warlike']

belligerent, belligerents
1 (adjective) hostile and aggressive.
2 (noun) A belligerent is one of the nations or other groups that are involved in a war.
belligerently (adverb), **belligerence** (noun).
[from Latin *bellum gerere* meaning 'to wage war']

bellow, bellows, bellowing, bellowed
1 (verb) When an animal such as a bull bellows, it makes a loud, deep roaring noise.
2 If someone bellows, they shout in a loud, deep voice.
3 (noun) A bellow is a loud, deep roar.
4 (plural noun) Bellows are a piece of equipment used for blowing air into a fire to make it burn more fiercely.

belly, bellies
1 (noun) Your belly is your stomach or the front of your body below your chest.
2 An animal's belly is the underneath part of its body.
[from Old English *belig* meaning 'bulge' or 'bag']

belly dance, belly dances
(noun) A belly dance is a Middle Eastern dance performed by a woman, in which the dancer moves her hips and abdomen vigorously.
belly dancer (noun).

belong, belongs, belonging, belonged
1 (verb) If something belongs to you, it is yours and you own it.
2 To belong to a group means to be a member of it.
3 If something belongs in a particular place, that is where it should be, e.g. *The plates belong over there.*

belongings
(noun) Your belongings are the things that you own.

beloved (pronounced bil-**luv**-id)
1 (adjective) A beloved person or thing is one that you feel a great affection for.
2 (noun; an old-fashioned use) Someone's beloved is the person they love.

Similar words: (sense 1) adored, cherished, dear

below
1 (preposition and adverb) If something is below a line or the surface of something else, it is lower down, e.g. *Fifteen fathoms below the surface of the ocean... His office was on the floor below.*

2 In a piece of writing, below refers to something mentioned further on, e.g. *See below.*
3 Below also means at or to a lower point, level, or rate, e.g. *The temperature fell below freezing.*
4 If someone is below you in an organization, they have a lower rank than you and you have authority over them.

belt, belts, belting, belted
1 (noun) A belt is a strip of leather or cloth that you fasten round your waist to hold your trousers or skirt up.
2 In a machine, a belt is a circular strip of rubber that drives moving parts or carries objects along.
3 A belt of land or sea is a long, narrow area of it.
4 (verb; informal uses) To belt someone means to hit them very hard.
5 If someone is belting along, they are moving very fast.

bemoan, bemoans, bemoaning, bemoaned
(verb; a literary word) If you bemoan something, you express sorrow or dissatisfaction about it, e.g. *They were bemoaning their fate.*

bemused
(adjective) If you are bemused, you are puzzled or confused.

bench, benches
1 (noun) A bench is a long seat that two or more people can sit on.
2 In Parliament, the benches are the seats occupied by particular groups of MPs, e.g. *There was laughter on the Opposition benches.*
3 In a court, the bench is the place where the judges or magistrates sit.
4 A bench is also a long, narrow table in a factory, workshop, or laboratory.

Similar words: (sense 1) form, pew

bend, bends, bending, bent
1 (verb) When you bend, you move your head and shoulders forwards and downwards.
2 When you bend something, you use force to make it curved or angular.
3 (noun) A bend in a road, river, or pipe is a curved part of it.
4 (phrase) If someone is **bending over backwards** to help you, they are trying very hard to help you.
5 If you **bend the rules**, you interpret them in a way that allows you to do what you want.
bent (adjective).

Similar words: (senses 1 and 2) bow, curve, flex, buckle, crook
(sense 3): curve, bow, crook

beneath
1 an old-fashioned word for **underneath**.
2 (phrase) If someone thinks that something is beneath them, they think that it is too trivial or unimportant for them to bother with it.

benediction
(noun) A benediction is a blessing, especially one pronounced formally by a Christian clergyman at the end of a service.
[from Latin *benedicere* meaning 'to bless']

benefactor, benefactors
(noun) A benefactor is a person who helps someone by giving them money.
[from Latin *bene facere* meaning 'to do well']

Similar words: patron, sponsor

beneficial
(adjective) Something that is beneficial is good for people, e.g. *the beneficial effects of exercise.*
beneficially (adverb).
[from Latin *beneficium* meaning 'kindness']

Similar words: advantageous, profitable, favourable

beneficiary, beneficiaries
(noun) A beneficiary of something is someone who receives money or other benefits from it, e.g. *the beneficiaries of the will.*

benefit, benefits, benefiting, benefited
1 (noun) The benefits of something are the advantages that it brings to people, e.g. *the benefits of modern technology.*
2 (verb) If you benefit from something, it helps you.
3 (phrase) If you do something **for someone's benefit**, you do it specially for them or so that they will notice.
4 If you **have had the benefit** of something, it has been valuable or useful to you, e.g. *She had the benefit of a good education.*
5 If you **give someone the benefit of the doubt**, you accept that they are innocent because you cannot be sure that they are guilty.
6 (noun) Benefit is money given by the government to people who are poor, ill, or unemployed.
[from Latin *benefactum* meaning 'good deed']

Similar words: (sense 1) asset, good, profit, gain (sense 2) profit, gain

benevolent
(adjective) kind and helpful.
benevolence (noun), **benevolently** (adverb).
[from Latin *bene volere* meaning 'to wish well']

Bengali, Bengalis (pronounced ben-**gaw**-lee)
1 (adjective) belonging or relating to Bengal, a former province of India, now divided into Bangladesh and the Indian state of West Bengal.
2 (noun) A Bengali is someone who comes from Bengal.
3 Bengali is the official language of Bangladesh. It is also spoken in West Bengal.

benign (pronounced be-**nine**)
1 (adjective) Someone who is benign is kind, gentle, and harmless.
2 A benign tumour is one that will not cause death or serious illness.
benignly (adverb).
[from Latin *bene gignere* meaning 'to produce good']

bent
1 Bent is the past participle and past tense of **bend.**
2 (phrase) If you are **bent on** doing something, you are determined to do it.

3 (noun) If you have a bent for something, you are naturally good at it.
4 (adjective; an informal use) If someone is bent, they are dishonest.

bequeath, bequeaths, bequeathed, bequeathing
(verb; a formal word) If someone bequeaths money or property to you, they give it to you in their will, so that it is yours after they have died.
[from Old English *becwethan* meaning 'to say about']

bequest, bequests
(noun; a formal word) A bequest is a legal gift of money or property by someone who has died.

berate, berates, berating, berated
(verb; a formal word) If you berate someone, you scold them angrily, e.g. *He berated me for my lack of care.*

bereaved
(adjective; a formal word) You say that someone is bereaved when a close relative of theirs has recently died.
bereavement (noun).
[from Old English *bereafian* meaning 'to take forcible possession of something']

bereft
(adjective; a literary word) If you are bereft of something, you no longer have it, e.g. *The survivors were bereft of hope.*

beret, berets (pronounced **ber**-ray)
(noun) A beret is a circular flat hat with no brim.
[a French word, from Latin *birettum* meaning 'cap']

berry, berries
(noun) Berries are small, round fruit that grow on bushes or trees.

berserk
(phrase) If someone **goes berserk**, they lose control of themselves and become very violent.
[from Icelandic *berserkr*, a kind of Viking who wore a shirt (*serkr*) made from the skin of a bear (*björn*). They worked themselves into a frenzy before battle]

berth, berths
1 (noun) A berth is a space in a harbour where a ship stays when it is being loaded or unloaded.
2 In a boat, train, or caravan, a berth is a bed.
3 (phrase) If you **give something a wide berth**, you avoid it because it is unpleasant or dangerous,

beryl
(noun) Beryl is a hard, transparent, crystalline mineral found in many different varieties; emerald is one of them.

beryllium (pronounced be-**ril**-lee-um)
(noun) Beryllium is a lightweight grey metallic element used in the manufacture of nuclear reactors and space vehicles. Its atomic number is 4 and its symbol is Be.

beseech, beseeches, beseeching, beseeched or besought
(verb; a literary word) If you beseech someone to

do something, you ask them very earnestly to do it, e.g. *I beseech you to go with her.*
beseeching (adjective), **beseechingly** (adverb).

beset
(adjective; a formal word) If you are beset by difficulties, problems, or doubts, you have a lot of them.

beside
1 (preposition) If one thing is beside something else, they are next to each other.
2 (phrase) If you are **beside yourself** with anger or excitement, you are very angry or excited.

Similar words: (sense 1) adjacent to, alongside, next to

besides
(preposition and adverb) in addition, e.g. *What languages do you know besides English?*

besiege, besieges, besieging, besieged
1 (verb) When soldiers besiege a place, they surround it and wait for the people inside to surrender.
2 If you are besieged by people, problems, or questions, there are a lot of them around you and they keep troubling you.

besought a past tense and past participle of **beseech.**

best
1 the superlative of **good** and **well.**
2 (adverb) The thing that you like best is the thing that you prefer to everything else.

Similar words: (sense 1) finest, top, first-rate

bestial
(adjective; a literary word) Bestial behaviour is unpleasant and disgusting, e.g. *his bestial habits.*
bestially (adverb), **bestiality** (noun).
[from Latin *bestia* meaning 'animal']

best man
(noun) The best man at a wedding is the man who acts as the bridegroom's attendant and supporter.

bestow, bestows, bestowing, bestowed
(verb; a formal word) If you bestow something on someone, you give it to them.

best seller, best sellers
(noun) A best seller is a book of which very many copies have been sold.

bet, bets, betting
1 (verb) If you bet on a future event, you make an agreement which means you receive money if something happens and lose money if it does not.
2 (noun) A bet is the act of betting on something, or the amount of money that you agree to risk.
3 (informal phrase) If you tell someone that something is **a good bet** or is **their best bet**, you mean that it is a good thing or the best thing for them to do.
4 You say **I bet** to indicate that you are sure that something is or will be so, e.g. *I bet she won't turn up.*
5 You bet is an emphatic way of saying yes.
betting (noun).

betel (pronounced **beetle**)
(noun) Betel refers to the leaves and nuts of the betel tree. They are chewed by Asians as an aid to digestion or as a narcotic.

bête noire (pronounced bet **nwar**)
(noun) If you say that someone or something is your bête noire, you mean that you dislike them more than anyone or anything else.
[a French phrase meaning literally 'black beast']

betray, betrays, betraying, betrayed
1 (verb) If you betray someone who trusts you, you do something which harms them, such as helping their enemies.
2 If you betray a secret, you tell it to someone you should not tell it to.
3 If you betray your feelings or thoughts, you show them without intending to.
betrayal (noun), **betrayer** (noun).
[from Old English *be* meaning 'completely' and Old French *trair* meaning 'to deliver up']

Similar words: (sense 1) double-cross, give away (senses 2 and 3) give away

betrothal, betrothals
(noun; an old-fashioned word) A betrothal is an engagement to be married.
betrothed (adjective).
[from Old English *treuthe* meaning 'loyalty' or 'truth']

better
1 the comparative of **good** and **well.**
2 (adverb) If you like one thing better than another, you like it more than the other thing.
3 (adjective) If you are better after an illness, you are no longer ill.

Similar words: (sense 1) finer, greater, superior

between
1 (preposition and adverb) If something is between two other things, it is situated or happens in the space or time that separates them, e.g. *Reading is between London and Bristol... We are open between ten and twelve.*
2 A relationship, discussion, or difference between two people or things involves only those two.
3 If something is between two other things in size or quality, it is more than one and less than the other.
4 If you must choose between two things, you must choose one or the other.
5 If something stands between you and what you want, it prevents you from getting it, e.g. *Only two people stood between her and the power she craved.*

beverage, beverages
(noun; a formal word) A beverage is a drink.
[from Old French *beivre* meaning 'to drink']

bevy, bevies
(noun) A bevy of things or people is a group of them, e.g. *a bevy of reporters.*

bewail, bewails, bewailing, bewailed
(verb; a literary word) If you bewail something,

you express great sorrow about it, e.g. *They bewail the ingratitude of their children.*

beware
(verb) If you tell someone to beware of something, you are warning them that it might be dangerous or harmful.

Similar words: be careful, look out, watch out

bewilder, bewilders, bewildering, bewildered
(verb) If something bewilders you, it is so confusing or difficult that you cannot understand it.
bewildered (adjective), **bewildering** (adjective), **bewilderment** (noun).

bewitch, bewitches, bewitching, bewitched
1 (verb) To bewitch someone means to cast a spell on them.
2 If something bewitches you, you are so excited or attracted by it that you cannot pay attention to anything else.
bewitched (adjective), **bewitching** (adjective).

beyond
1 (preposition) If something is beyond a certain place, it is on the other side of it, e.g. *She lived somewhere beyond Exeter.*
2 If something extends or continues beyond a particular point, it extends or continues further than that point, e.g. *Many children remain at school beyond the age of 16.*
3 If someone or something is beyond understanding, control, or help, they cannot be understood, controlled, or helped.
[from Old English *begeondan* meaning 'beyond']

bi-
(prefix) Bi- means twice or two.

biannual
(adjective) occurring twice a year.
biannually (adverb).
[from Latin *bis* meaning 'twice' and *annus* meaning 'year']

bias
1 (noun) Someone who shows bias favours one person or thing unfairly in preference to others.
2 In the game of bowls, bias is the weight on one side of a bowl which makes it run in a curve rather than in a straight line.

Similar words: (sense 1) bigotry, discrimination, slant, prejudice, predisposition

biased or biassed
(adjective) favouring one person or thing unfairly in preference to others, e.g. *a biased judgement.*

Similar words: prejudiced, predisposed, weighted, one-sided, bigoted, partisan

bib, bibs
(noun) A bib is a piece of cloth or plastic which is tied under the chin of very young children when they are eating, to keep their clothes clean.
[from Middle English *bibben* meaning 'to drink']

Bible, Bibles
(noun) The Bible is the sacred book of the Jewish and Christian religions.
biblical (adjective).
[from Greek *biblia* meaning 'the books']

bibliography, bibliographies
(noun) A bibliography is a list of books on a particular subject, or a list of the other books and articles referred to in a book or article.
bibliographical (adjective).
[from Greek *biblos* meaning 'book' and *graphein* meaning 'to write']

bicarbonate of soda
(noun) Bicarbonate of soda is a white powder used in baking to make cakes rise.

bicentenary, bicentenaries
(noun) The bicentenary of an event is its two-hundredth anniversary.
bicentennial (adjective).
[from Latin *bis* meaning 'two' and *centum* meaning 'hundred']

biceps
(noun) Your biceps are the large muscles on your upper arms.

bicker, bickers, bickering, bickered
(verb) When people bicker, they argue or quarrel about unimportant things.

bicycle, bicycles
(noun) A bicycle is a two-wheeled vehicle which you ride by sitting on it and pushing two pedals with your feet.
[from Latin *bis* meaning 'two' and Greek *kuklos* meaning 'wheel']

bid, bids, bidding, bade, bidden, bid
In paragraph 3, the past tense and past participle is 'bid'; in paragraph 4, the past tense is 'bade' and the past participle is 'bidden'.
1 (noun) A bid is an attempt to obtain or do something, e.g. *He made a bid for power.*
2 A bid is also an offer to buy something for a certain sum of money.
3 (verb) If you bid for something, you offer to pay a certain sum of money for it.
4 (an old-fashioned use) If you bid someone good morning, you say good morning to them. If you bid them farewell, you say goodbye to them.

bidder
(phrase) If you sell something to **the highest bidder**, you sell it to the person who offers most money for it.

bide, bides, biding, bided
(phrase) If you **bide your time**, you wait for a good opportunity before doing something.

bidet, bidets (pronounced **bee**-day)
(noun) A bidet is a low basin in a bathroom which is used for washing your bottom in.
[a French word meaning 'small horse']

biennial
1 (adjective) happening or done once every two years.
2 (noun) A biennial is a plant that lives for two

years, producing flowers and dying in the second year.
biennially (adverb).
[from Latin *bis* meaning 'two' and *annus* meaning 'year']

bier, biers (pronounced **beer**)
(noun) A bier is a stand or frame on which a corpse or coffin is placed at a funeral.
[from Old English *beran* meaning 'to carry']

bifocals
(plural noun) Bifocals are glasses with lenses made in two halves, the upper halves for looking at distant objects and the lower ones for reading.

big, bigger, biggest
(adjective) large in size, extent, or importance.
biggish (adjective), **bigness** (noun).

Similar words: large, considerable, sizeable, substantial

bigamy
(noun) Bigamy is the crime of marrying someone when you are already married to someone else.
bigamist (noun), **bigamous** (adjective),
[from Latin *bis* meaning 'twice' and Greek *gamos* meaning 'married']

bigot, bigots
(noun) A bigot is someone who has strong and unreasonable opinions which they refuse to change.
bigoted (adjective), **bigotry** (noun).

big top, big tops
(noun) A big top is a large round tent that a circus uses for its performances.

bike, bikes
(noun; an informal word) A bike is a bicycle or motorcycle.

bikini, bikinis
(noun) A bikini is a small two-piece swimming costume worn by women.

bilateral
(adjective) A bilateral agreement is one made between two groups or countries.
bilaterally (adverb).

bilberry, bilberries
(noun) Bilberries are edible bluish-black berries that grow on small bushes.

bile
(noun) Bile is a bitter yellow liquid produced by the liver which helps the digestion of fat. In the Middle Ages, it was believed to cause anger.

bilge
1 (noun) The bilge of a ship is its lowest part, where dirty water collects.
2 (an informal use) If you refer to something as bilge, you mean that it is silly rubbish.
[a 16th century word, probably a variant of *bulge*]

bilingual
(adjective) involving or using two languages, e.g. *bilingual street signs... The children were brought up to be bilingual.*
bilingually (adverb), **bilingualism** (noun).

[from Latin *bis* meaning 'two' and *lingua* meaning 'tongue']

bilious
(adjective) If you feel bilious, you feel sick and have a headache.
biliousness (noun).

bill, bills
1 (noun) A bill is a written statement of how much is owed for goods or services.
2 In America, a bill is a piece of paper money, e.g. *a dollar bill.*
3 In Parliament, a bill is a formal statement of a proposed new law that is discussed and then voted on.
4 A bill is also a notice or a poster.
5 A bird's bill is its beak.
[senses 1 to 4 from Latin *bulla* meaning 'document']

Similar words: (sense 1) invoice, reckoning

billboard, billboards
(noun) A billboard is a large board on which advertisements are displayed.

billet, billets, billeting, billeted
1 (verb) When soldiers are billeted in a building, arrangements are made for them to stay there.
2 (noun) A billet is a building where soldiers are billeted.
[from Latin *bulla* meaning 'document', because documents were needed for people to provide board and lodging for soldiers]

billiards
(noun) Billiards is a game played on a large table, in which a long, leather-tipped stick called a cue is used to strike one of three balls. The aim is to hit a second ball with the first so that either the third ball is also hit or one of the balls goes into one of the six pockets at the edges of the table.

billion, billions
(noun) A billion is a thousand million. Formerly, a billion was a million million.
billionth (adjective).

billow, billows, billowing, billowed
1 (verb) When things made of cloth billow, they swell out and flap slowly in the wind.
2 When smoke or cloud billows, it spreads upwards and outwards.
3 (noun) A billow is a large wave.

bin, bins
(noun) A bin is a container, especially one that you put rubbish in.
[from Old English *binne* meaning 'basket']

binary (pronounced **by**-nar-ee)
(adjective) The binary system expresses numbers using only two digits, 0 and 1.
[from Latin *binarius* meaning 'two together']

bind, binds, binding, bound
1 (verb) If you bind something, you tie rope or string round it so that it is held firmly.
2 If something binds you to a course of action, it compels you to act in that way, e.g. *This oath binds you to secrecy.*

3 When a book is bound, the pages are joined together and the cover is put on.

binder, binders
(noun) A binder is a hard cover with metal rings inside, which is used to hold loose pieces of paper.

binding, bindings
1 (adjective) If a promise or agreement is binding, it must be obeyed or carried out.
2 (noun) The binding of a book is its cover.
3 Binding is a strip of material that you put round the edge of something to strengthen or decorate it.

bindweed
(noun) Bindweed is a plant with white flowers, which climbs and twists around other plants as it grows.

binge, binges
(noun; an informal word) A binge is a wild bout of excessive drinking or eating.
[from a dialect word *binge* meaning 'to soak']

bingo
(noun) Bingo is a game in which each player has a card with numbers on. Someone calls out numbers and, if you are the first person to have all your numbers called, you win a prize.

binoculars
(plural noun) Binoculars are an instrument with lenses for both eyes, which you look through in order to see distant objects.
[from Latin *bis* meaning 'two' and *ocularis* meaning 'of the eye']

binomial
(adjective; a term in algebra) containing two terms, e.g. $x + y$ *is a binomial expression.*
[from Latin *bis* meaning 'two' and *nomen* meaning 'name']

biochemistry
(noun) Biochemistry is the study of the chemistry of living things.
biochemical (adjective), **biochemically** (adverb), **biochemist** (noun).
[from Greek *bios* meaning 'life' and Arabic *kimiya* meaning 'transmutation']

biodegradable
(adjective) capable of being decomposed naturally by the action of bacteria, e.g. *Most plastics are not biodegradable.*
[from Greek *bios* meaning 'life' and Latin *degradare* meaning 'to reduce to a lower status']

biography, biographies
(noun) A biography is an account of someone's life, written by someone else. Compare **autobiography.**
biographer (noun), **biographical** (adjective).
[from Greek *bios* meaning 'life' and *graphein* meaning 'to write']

biology
(noun) Biology is the study of living things.
biological (adjective), **biologically** (adverb), **biologist** (noun).
[from Greek *bios* + *logos* meaning 'life study']

bionic
(adjective) having a part of the body that is operated electronically.

biopsy, biopsies
(noun) A biopsy is an examination under a microscope of tissue from a living body, usually in order to help diagnose a disease.
[from Greek *bios* meaning 'life' and *opsis* meaning 'viewing']

biped, bipeds (pronounced **by**-ped)
(noun; a formal word) Any creature with two feet can be referred to as a biped.
[from Latin *bis* + *pedes* meaning 'two feet']

biplane, biplanes
(noun) A biplane is an early type of plane with two pairs of wings, one above the other.

birch, birches
(noun) A birch is a tall deciduous tree with thin branches and thin, peeling, often silvery bark.

bird, birds
(noun) A bird is a creature with feathers and wings. Most birds can fly; female birds lay eggs.

bird of prey, birds of prey
(noun) A bird of prey is a bird that kills other birds and small animals for food. Eagles, hawks, and owls are birds of prey.

birth, births
1 (noun) The birth of a baby is its emergence from its mother's womb at the beginning of its life.
2 The birth of something is its beginning, e.g. *the birth of television.*

birth control is the same as contraception.

birthday, birthdays
(noun) Your birthday is the anniversary of the date on which you were born.

birthmark, birthmarks
(noun) A birthmark is a mark on someone's skin that has been there since they were born.

biscuit, biscuits
(noun) A biscuit is a small flat cake made of baked dough.
[from Old French *bes* + *cuit* meaning 'twice-cooked']

bisect, bisects, bisecting, bisected
(verb) To bisect a line, angle, or area means to divide it in half.
[from Latin *bis* meaning 'two' and *secare* meaning 'to cut']

bisexual
(adjective) sexually attracted by members of both sexes.

bishop, bishops
1 (noun) A bishop is a high-ranking clergyman in some Christian Churches.
2 In chess, a bishop is a piece that is moved diagonally across the board.
[from Greek *episkopos* meaning 'overseer']

bison
(noun) A bison is a large hairy animal, related to cattle, with a large head and shoulders. Bison

used to be very common on the prairies in North America, but they are now almost extinct.

bistro, bistros (pronounced **bee**-stroh)
(noun) A bistro is a small informal restaurant.
[a French word]

bit, bits
1 (noun) A bit of something is a small amount of it, e.g. *a bit of cheese.*
2 In computing, a bit is the smallest unit of information held in a computer's memory. It is either 1 or 0. Several bits form a byte.
3 A horse's bit is a metal bar that fits in its mouth and is attached to the reins to help a rider to control the horse.
4 (informal phrase) If you do something **bit by bit**, you do it in many short stages.
5 A bit means slightly or to a small extent, e.g. *He's a bit deaf.*
6 If you do something **for a bit**, you do it for a short time, e.g. *Can't we stay here for a bit?*
7 Bit is also the past tense of **bite**.
[from Old English *bita* meaning 'piece bitten off']

Similar words: (sense 1) fragment, piece, part, scrap

bitch, bitches
1 (noun) A bitch is a female dog.
2 (an offensive use) People sometimes refer to a woman as a bitch, meaning that they think she behaves in an unpleasant way.
bitchy (adjective).

bite, bites, biting, bit, bitten
1 (verb) If you bite something, you use your teeth to cut into it or through it.
2 (noun) A bite is a small amount that you bite off something with your teeth.
3 (verb) When an insect or a snake bites you, it pierces your skin with its mouth, causing pain and often swelling or itching.
4 (noun) A bite is also the injury you get when an insect or snake bites you.
[from Old English *bitan* meaning 'to bite']

biting
1 (adjective) A biting wind is an extremely cold wind.
2 Biting sarcasm is sharp and clever in a way that makes people feel uncomfortable.

bitter, bitterest
1 (adjective) If someone is bitter, they feel angry and resentful.
2 A bitter disappointment or experience makes people feel angry or unhappy for a long time afterwards.
3 In a bitter argument or war, people argue or fight fiercely and angrily, e.g. *a bitter struggle for supremacy.*
4 A bitter wind is an extremely cold wind.
5 Something that tastes bitter has a sharp, unpleasant taste.
6 (noun) Bitter is a kind of beer with a slightly bitter taste.
bitterly (adverb), **bitterness** (noun).
[from Old English *bitan* meaning 'to bite']

Similar words: (sense 1) embittered, sour, acrimonious, resentful
(sense 3) acrimonious
(sense 5) sour, astringent, acid, acrid, sharp

bittern, bitterns
(noun) A bittern is a long-legged wading bird like a heron, with an unusual booming cry.

bitumen (pronounced **bit**-you-men)
(noun) Bitumen is a black sticky substance obtained from tar or petrol and used in making roads.

bivouac, bivouacs (pronounced **biv**-oo-ak)
(noun) A bivouac is a temporary camp in the open air, without tents.
[an 18th century word, from French *bivouac*]

bizarre (pronounced biz-**zahr**)
(adjective) very strange or eccentric, sometimes in an interesting or amusing way.
[a French word]

blab, blabs, blabbing, blabbed
(verb; an informal word) When someone blabs, they give away secrets by talking carelessly.

black, blacker, blackest; blacks, blacking, blacked
1 (noun and adjective) Black is the darkest possible colour. A surface that is completely black reflects no light at all.
2 Someone who is black is a Negro or a member of some other race of people with dark skins.
3 (adjective) Black coffee or tea has no milk or cream added to it.
4 If you describe a situation as black, you mean that it is bad and not likely to improve, e.g. *Things are not so black as he suggested.*
5 Black humour involves jokes about death or suffering.
6 (verb) When a group such as a trade union blacks goods or people, it refuses to handle the goods or deal with the people.
blackness (noun).

Similar words: (sense 1) pitch-black, ebony, sable

black out
(phrasal verb) If you black out, you lose consciousness.

black belt, black belts
(noun) A black belt is a high level of skill in judo or karate; also a person who has achieved this level.

blackberry, blackberries
(noun) Blackberries are small black fruits that grow on prickly bushes called brambles.

blackbird, blackbirds
(noun) A blackbird is a common European bird. The male has black feathers and a bright yellow beak; the female has browr feathers.

blackboard, blackboards
(noun) A blackboard is a dark-coloured board in a classroom, which teachers write on using chalk.

black box
(noun) A black box is an electronic device in an aircraft which collects and stores information

during flights. This information can be used to
provide evidence if an accident occurs.

blackcurrant, blackcurrants
(noun) Blackcurrants are very small dark purple
fruit that grow in bunches on bushes.

blacken, blackens, blackening, blackened
1 (verb) To blacken something means to make it
black, e.g. *His face was blackened with charcoal.*
2 (phrase) If someone **blackens your name**, they
harm it by saying bad things about you.

blackguard, blackguards (say **blag**-gard)
(noun; an old-fashioned word) A blackguard is a
wicked person, usually a man, who is immoral
and has no principles.

blackhead, blackheads
(noun) A blackhead is a very small black spot on
the skin caused by a pore being blocked with dirt.

blackleg, blacklegs
(noun; a term of abuse) A blackleg is someone
who goes on working when their workmates are
on strike.

blacklist, blacklists, blacklisting, blacklisted
1 (noun) A blacklist is a list of people or
organizations who are thought to be
untrustworthy or to have done something wrong,
and who are therefore discriminated against.
2 (verb) When someone is blacklisted, they are
put on a blacklist.

blackmail, blackmails, blackmailing, blackmailed
1 (verb) If someone blackmails another person,
they threaten to reveal something unpleasant
about that person unless they are given money or
something is done that they want doing.
2 (noun) Blackmail is the practice of
blackmailing people.
blackmailer (noun).

black market
(noun) If something is bought or sold on the
black market, it is bought or sold illegally, often
at an excessively high price.
black marketeer (noun).

blackout, blackouts
(noun) If you have a blackout, you temporarily
lose consciousness.

black sheep
(noun) The black sheep of a family is a member
of it who is no good.

blacksmith, blacksmiths
(noun) A blacksmith is a person whose job is
making things out of metal, especially
horseshoes.

bladder, bladders
(noun) Your bladder is the part of your body
where urine is held until it leaves your body.

blade, blades
1 (noun) The blade of a knife, axe, or saw is the
sharp part that is used for cutting.
2 The blades of a propeller are the thin, flat
parts that turn round.

3 The blade of an oar is the thin, flat part that
you dip into and out of the water when rowing.
4 A blade of grass is a single piece of it.
[from Old Norse *blath* meaning 'leaf']

blame, blames, blaming, blamed
1 (verb) If someone blames you for something
bad that has happened, they say that you caused
it or are responsible for it.
2 (noun) The blame for something bad that
happens is the responsibility for causing it or
letting it happen.
[from medieval Latin *blasphemare* meaning 'to
reproach', from Greek *blasphēmein;* see
blaspheme]

Similar words: (sense 1) accuse, charge, hold
responsible

blameless
(adjective) Someone who is blameless has not
done anything wrong.

blanch, blanches, blanching, blanched
1 (verb) If you blanch, you suddenly become
very pale.
2 When you blanch vegetables, you cook them
for a minute or two in boiling water before you
freeze them.
[from Old French *blanchir* meaning 'to make
white']

blancmange (pronounced blam-**monj**)
(noun) Blancmange is a cold, jelly-like pudding
made from milk, sugar, cornflour, and flavouring.
[from Old French *blanc manger* meaning 'white
food']

bland, blander, blandest
(adjective) mild, tasteless, and dull, e.g.*bland
food... a bland reply.*
blandly (adverb).
[from Latin *blandus* meaning 'flattering']

blandishment, blandishments
(noun) Blandishments are pleasant things that
someone might say to you in order to persuade
you to do something.
[from the Latin verb *blandiri* meaning 'to flatter']

blank, blanker, blankest
1 (adjective) Something that is blank has nothing
on it, e.g. *a blank sheet of paper.*
2 If you look blank, your face shows no feeling,
understanding, or interest.
3 (noun) If your mind or memory is a blank, you
cannot think of anything or remember anything.
4 (phrase) If you **draw a blank** when you are
looking for someone or something, you fail to
find them.
[from Old French *blanc* meaning 'white']

Similar words: (sense 2) expressionless, vacant,
impassive, vacuous

blanket, blankets
1 (noun) A blanket is a large rectangle of thick
cloth that is put on a bed to keep people warm.
2 A blanket of something such as snow is a thick
covering of it.
3 (adjective) Blanket coverage or blanket

acceptance of something involves all parts of it, without any exceptions.
[from Old French *blancquete* meaning 'little white thing']

blank verse
(noun) Poetry in which the lines do not rhyme is called blank verse.

blare, blares, blaring, blared
(verb) To blare means to make a loud, unpleasant noise, e.g. *The radio was blaring in the background.*

blasé (pronounced blah-zay)
(adjective) bored or unimpressed by things that other people find exciting, e.g. *He watched the proceedings with a blasé air of complete detachment.*
[a French word]

blaspheme, blasphemes, blaspheming, blasphemed
(verb) When people blaspheme, they say rude or disrespectful things about God, or they use God's name as a swear word.
[from Greek *blapsis* meaning 'evil' and *phēmein* meaning 'to speak']

blasphemy, blasphemies
(noun) Blasphemy is speech or behaviour that shows disrespect for God or for things people regard as holy.
blasphemous (adjective).

Similar words: impiety, sacrilege, profanity

blast, blasts, blasting, blasted
1 (verb) When people blast a hole in something, they make the hole with an explosion.
2 (noun) A blast is a big explosion, especially one caused by a bomb.
3 A blast of air or wind is a sudden strong rush of it.
4 A blast is also a short, sharp sound made by a whistle or wind instrument.
5 (phrase) If a machine is working **at full blast**, it is working at its greatest speed or to its full capacity.

blastoff
(noun) Blastoff is the moment when a rocket or space shuttle leaves the ground and rises into the air.

blatant
(adjective) done in an obvious way, without any attempt at concealment, e.g. *blatant discrimination.*
[from *blattant* meaning 'extremely noisy'; coined by Edmund Spenser in 1596 to describe a monster in 'The Faerie Queen']

blaze, blazes, blazing, blazed
1 (noun) A blaze is a large, hot fire.
2 A blaze of light is a very bright light, e.g. *a blaze of sunlight.*
3 A blaze of publicity or attention is a lot of it.
4 (verb) When a fire blazes, it burns strongly and brightly.
5 If something blazes with light or colour, it is extremely bright.

6 If your eyes are blazing, they look very bright because you are excited or angry.
[from Old English *blæse* meaning 'bright flame']

blazer, blazers
(noun) A blazer is a jacket, especially one worn as part of a uniform by schoolchildren or members of a sports team.

bleach, bleaches, bleaching, bleached
1 (verb) To bleach material or hair means to make it white or pale, usually by using a chemical.
2 (noun) Bleach is a chemical that is used to make material white or to kill germs.
[from Old English *blæcan* meaning 'to make pale']

bleak, bleaker, bleakest
1 (adjective) If a situation is bleak, it is bad and depressing and seems unlikely to improve.
2 If a place is bleak, it is cold, bare, and exposed to the wind.
[from Old English *blac* meaning 'pale']

bleary
(adjective) If your eyes look bleary, they are red and watery, usually because you are tired.
blearily (adverb).

bleat, bleats, bleating, bleated
1 (verb) When sheep or goats bleat, they make a high-pitched sound.
2 (noun) A bleat is the high-pitched sound that a sheep or goat makes.

bleed, bleeds, bleeding, bled
(verb) When you bleed, you lose blood as a result of an injury or illness.

bleep, bleeps
(noun) A bleep is a short high-pitched sound made by an electrical device such as an alarm.

blemish, blemishes, blemishing, blemished
1 (noun) A blemish is a mark that spoils the appearance of something.
2 (verb) If something blemishes your reputation, it spoils it.
[from Old French *blemir* meaning 'to make pale']

blench, blenches, blenching, blenched
(verb) If you blench at something, you recoil from it because you are afraid.

blend, blends, blending, blended
1 (verb) When you blend two or more substances, you mix them together to form a single substance.
2 When colours or sounds blend, they combine in a pleasing way.
3 (noun) A blend of things is a mixture of them, especially one that is pleasing.

blender, blenders
(noun) A blender is a machine used for mixing liquids and foods at high speed.

bless, blesses, blessing, blessed or blest
(verb) When a priest blesses people or things, he asks for God's favour and protection for them.
[from Old English *blædsian* meaning 'to sprinkle with sacrificial blood']

Similar words: consecrate, sanctify

blessed

1 (adjective; pronounced **bless**-id) People use blessed to describe something that they are glad about, e.g. *a blessed sense of relief as the hurricane retreated.*
2 (pronounced **blest**) If someone is blessed with a particular quality or skill, they have it, e.g. *I am blessed with a good memory.*
blessedly (adverb).

blessing, blessings

1 (noun) A blessing is something good that you are thankful for, e.g. *Good health is the greatest blessing.*
2 (phrase) If something is done **with someone's blessing**, they approve of it and support it.
3 If something is **a blessing in disguise**, it seems at first as if it will cause problems, but turns out in fact to be a good thing.

Similar words: (sense 1) boon, bounty, godsend

blew the past tense of **blow**.

blight, blights, blighting, blighted

1 (noun) Blight is any disease that makes plants wither, usually caused by bacteria or by fungi.
2 A blight is something that damages or spoils other things, e.g. *the blight of pollution.*
3 (verb) When something is blighted, it is spoiled or seriously harmed, e.g. *His career had been blighted.*

blind, blinds, blinding, blinded

1 (adjective) Someone who is blind cannot see.
2 If someone is blind to a particular fact, they fail to recognize it or understand it.
3 You say that someone's actions or beliefs are blind when they ignore the facts or behave in an unreasonable way, e.g. *their blind pursuit of their plans... He was in a blind rage.*
4 A blind corner is one where drivers and cyclists cannot see what is coming.
5 (verb) If something blinds you, you become unable to see, either for a short time or permanently.
6 If something blinds you to a fact or situation, it prevents you from realizing that it exists.
7 (noun) A blind is a roll of cloth or paper that you pull down over a window to keep out the light.
blindly (adverb), **blindness** (noun).

blindfold, blindfolds, blindfolding, blindfolded

1 (noun) A blindfold is a strip of cloth tied over someone's eyes so that they cannot see.
2 (verb) To blindfold someone means to tie a blindfold over their eyes.

blinding

(adjective) A blinding light is so bright that it hurts your eyes, e.g. *There came a blinding flash.*

blindingly

(adverb; an informal use) If something is blindingly obvious, it is very obvious indeed.

blind man's buff

(noun) Blind man's buff is a game in which a child with a piece of cloth tied over his or her eyes tries to catch other children.

blind spot

(noun) If you have a blind spot about something, you cannot understand it, e.g. *I'm afraid I have a blind spot about economics.*

blink, blinks, blinking, blinked

(verb) When you blink, you close your eyes rapidly for a moment. Blinking is an involuntary action that keeps the eyes moist.

blinkers

1 (noun) Blinkers are two pieces of leather placed at the side of a horse's eyes so that it can only see straight ahead.
2 (phrase) If you say that someone is **wearing blinkers**, you mean that they are considering only a narrow point of view and ignoring other factors.
blinkered (adjective).

bliss

(noun) Bliss is a state of complete happiness.
blissful (adjective), **blissfully** (adverb).

blister, blisters, blistering, blistered

1 (noun) A blister is a swelling on your skin containing watery liquid, caused by a burn or rubbing.
2 (verb) If someone's skin blisters, blisters appear on it as result of burning or rubbing.
[from Old French *blestre*]

blistering

1 (adjective) Blistering heat is very hot.
2 A blistering remark expresses great anger or criticism.

blithe

1 (adjective) casual and done without serious thought, e.g. *her blithe disregard of all our warnings.*
2 (an old-fashioned use) carefree and cheerful.
blithely (adverb).

blitz, blitzes, blitzing, blitzed

1 (noun) A blitz is a sudden intensive bombing attack by aircraft on a city or town.
2 (verb) When a city, town, or building is blitzed, it is bombed by aircraft and is damaged or destroyed.
[from German *Blitzkrieg* meaning 'lightning war']

blizzard, blizzards

(noun) A blizzard is a heavy snowstorm with strong winds.

bloated

(adjective) Something that is bloated is much larger than normal, often because there is a lot of liquid or gas inside it.

bloater, bloaters

(noun) A bloater is a herring that has been salted in brine and then smoked.

blob, blobs

(noun) A blob of a thick or sticky liquid is a small amount of it.

bloc, blocs

(noun) A group of countries with similar aims and interests acting together is often called a bloc, e.g. *the Soviet bloc.*
[a French word]

block, blocks, blocking, blocked
1 (noun) A block of flats or offices is a large building containing flats or offices.
2 In a town, a block is an area of land or buildings with streets on all its sides, e.g. *I'm going for a walk round the block.*
3 A block of a substance is a large rectangular piece of it, e.g. *a block of ice cream.*
4 If you have a mental block about something, you are briefly unable to remember it.
5 (verb) To block a road, channel, or pipe means to put something across it so that nothing can get through.
6 If something blocks your view, it is in the way and prevents you from seeing what you want to see.
7 If someone blocks something, they prevent it from happening, e.g. *The council blocked his plans.*
[from French *bloc* meaning 'block']

Similar words: (sense 3) bar, brick, chunk, square (sense 5) obstruct, clog, bung, choke (senses 6 and 7) obstruct

blockade, blockades, blockading, blockaded
1 (noun) A blockade is an action that prevents goods from reaching a place.
2 (verb) When a place is blockaded, goods are prevented from reaching it.

blockage, blockages
(noun) When there is a blockage in a pipe, tube, or tunnel, something is blocking it.

Similar words: obstruction, impediment, stoppage

block capitals or **block letters**
(noun) Block capitals are simple clear capital letters.

bloke, blokes
(noun; an informal word) A bloke is a man.

blonde, blondes
1 (adjective) Blonde hair is pale yellow in colour. The spelling 'blond' is used when referring to men.
2 (noun) A blonde is a woman with blonde hair.
[from Latin *blondus* meaning 'yellow']

blood
1 (noun) Blood is the red liquid that is pumped by the heart round the bodies of human beings and other mammals.
2 Blood is sometimes used to refer to someone's race or ancestors, e.g. *There was Irish blood on his mother's side.*
3 (phrase) If there is **bad blood** between people, they feel hatred and enmity towards each other.
4 If something cruel is done in **cold blood**, it is done deliberately and without emotion.
5 New people introduced into an organization can be referred to as **new blood**.

blood bank, blood banks
(noun) A blood bank is a store of blood kept until it is needed for blood transfusions.

blood bath
(noun) A blood bath is a massacre, in which a lot of people are violently killed.

bloodcurdling
(adjective) very frightening and horrible, e.g. *a bloodcurdling shriek.*

blood donor, blood donors
(noun) A blood donor is someone who gives blood from his or her body to be used for blood transfusions.

bloodhound, bloodhounds
(noun) A bloodhound is a large dog with an excellent sense of smell. Bloodhounds were used to follow fugitives or to find people when they were lost.

bloodless
1 (adjective) If someone's face or skin is bloodless, it is very pale.
2 In a bloodless coup or revolution, nobody is killed.

blood pressure
(noun) Your blood pressure is a measure of the force with which your blood is being pumped round your body.

bloodshed
(noun) When there is bloodshed, people are killed or wounded.

bloodshot
(adjective) If a person's eyes are bloodshot, the white parts have become red because tiny blood vessels have burst in their eyes.

blood sport, blood sports
(noun) Blood sports are sports such as hunting, shooting, and fishing, in which animals are killed.

bloodstained
(adjective) covered with blood.

bloodstream
(noun) Your bloodstream is your blood as it flows round your body.

bloodthirsty
(adjective) Someone who is bloodthirsty is eager to use violence or to see other people use violence.

blood transfusion, blood transfusions
(noun) A blood transfusion is a process in which blood is injected into the body of someone who has lost a lot of blood, for example through injury.

blood vessel, blood vessels
(noun) Your blood vessels are the narrow tubes in your body through which your blood flows.

bloody, bloodier, bloodiest
1 (adjective and adverb) Bloody is a common swear word, used to express anger or annoyance.
2 (adjective) A bloody event is one in which a lot of people are killed, e.g. *a bloody massacre.*
3 Bloody also means covered with blood, e.g. *He returned with bloody hands.*
bloodily (adverb).

bloody-minded
(adjective) Someone who is being bloody-minded is deliberately being difficult instead of helpful.
bloody-mindedness (noun).

bloom, blooms, blooming, bloomed
1 (noun) A bloom is a flower on a plant.

2 (verb) When a plant blooms, it produces flowers.
[from Old Norse *blom* meaning 'flower']

blossom, blossoms, blossoming, blossomed
1 (noun) Blossom is the growth of flowers that appears on a tree before the fruit.
2 (verb) When a tree blossoms, it produces blossom.
3 When a person blossoms, they develop attractive qualities and become happy and successful.

blot, blots, blotting, blotted
1 (noun) A blot is a drop of ink that has been spilled on a surface.
2 A blot on someone's reputation is a mistake or piece of bad behaviour that spoils their good name.

blot out
(phrasal verb) To blot something out means to be in front of it and prevent it from being seen, e.g. *A huge dust cloud blotted out the sun.*

blotch, blotches
(noun) A blotch is a discoloured area or stain.
blotchy (adjective).

blotting paper
(noun) Blotting paper is thick, soft paper used for drying ink on a freshly written page.

blouse, blouses
(noun) A blouse is a light garment, similar to a shirt, worn by a girl or a woman on the upper part of their body.
[a French word]

blow, blows, blowing, blew, blown
1 (verb) When the wind blows, the air moves.
2 If something blows or is blown somewhere, the wind moves it there.
3 If you blow a whistle or horn, you make a sound by blowing into it.
4 (noun) If you give someone a blow, you hit them.
5 A blow is also something that makes you very disappointed or unhappy, e.g. *Losing his job was a terrible blow to him.*
6 (phrase) If you **strike a blow** for a cause or principle, you do something which makes it more likely to succeed, e.g. *He felt that he had struck a blow for liberty.*
7 (phrase) If people **come to blows**, they start fighting.

blow out
(phrasal verb) If you blow out a flame or candle, you blow at it so that it stops burning.

blow over
(phrasal verb) If trouble or an argument blows over, it comes to an end.

blow up
1 (phrasal verb) To blow something up means to destroy it with an explosion.
2 To blow up a balloon or a tyre means to fill it with air.
3 To blow up a photograph means to enlarge it.

blow-by-blow
(adjective) A blow-by-blow account of an event describes every stage of it in detail.

blowlamp, blowlamps
(noun) A blowlamp is a hand-held device that produces a hot flame, used for example to heat metal or to burn off old paint.

blowout, blowouts
1 (noun) A blowout is a sudden uncontrolled escape of gas or oil from a well.
2 A blowout is also a sudden loss of air from a tyre because of a puncture.

blowzy, blowzier, blowziest
(adjective) A blowzy woman is rather fat, untidy, and red-faced.

blubber
(noun) Blubber is the thick insulating layer of fat beneath the skin of animals such as whales and seals.

bludgeon, bludgeons, bludgeoning, bludgeoned
(verb) To bludgeon someone means to hit them several times with a heavy object.

blue, bluer, bluest
1 (adjective and noun) Blue is the colour of the sky on a clear, sunny day.
2 (phrase) If something happens **out of the blue**, it happens suddenly and unexpectedly.
3 (adjective) Blue films, stories, and jokes are about sex.
bluish or **blueish** (adjective).

bluebell, bluebells
(noun) A bluebell is a woodland plant with blue, bell-shaped flowers on an upright stem.

blueberry, blueberries
(noun) Blueberries are the same as bilberries.

blue blood
(noun) Someone who has blue blood belongs to a royal or noble family.
blue-blooded (adjective).

bluebottle, bluebottles
(noun) A bluebottle is a large fly with a shiny dark-blue body, which buzzes as it flies.

blue-collar
(adjective) Blue-collar workers do manual work as opposed to office work.

blueprint, blueprints
1 (noun) A blueprint is a photographic print of an architect's or engineer's plan. It consists of white lines on a blue background.
2 A blueprint for something is a plan of how it is expected to work, e.g. *a blueprint for a better society.*

blues
(noun) The blues is a type of music which is similar to jazz, but is always slow and sad.

bluetit, bluetits
(noun) A bluetit is a common small bird with bluish wings and head, a yellow breast, and a white face.

bluff, bluffs, bluffing, bluffed
1 (noun) A bluff is an attempt to make someone

believe that you will do something when you do not really intend to do it.

2 (phrase) If you **call someone's bluff**, you tell them to do what they are threatening to do, because you are sure that they will not really do it.

3 (verb) If you are bluffing, you are trying to make someone believe that you will do something, although you do not really intend to do it.

4 (adjective) If someone has a bluff manner, they are rather rough and outspoken but they mean to be kind and friendly.

[from Dutch *bluffen* meaning to boast]

blunder, blunders, blundering, blundered
1 (verb) If you blunder, you make a silly mistake.
2 (noun) A blunder is a silly mistake.
[related to Old Norse *blunda* meaning 'to close one's eyes']

blunderbuss, blunderbusses
(noun) In the past, a blunderbuss was a type of gun with a short wide barrel and a wide opening, used to scatter shot at close range.

blunt, blunter, bluntest
1 (adjective) A blunt object has a rounded point or edge, rather than a sharp one.
2 If you are blunt, you say exactly what you think, without trying to be polite.

Similar words: (sense 2) brusque, outspoken, abrupt, tactless

blur, blurs, blurring, blurred
1 (noun) A blur is a shape or area which you cannot see clearly because it has no distinct outline or because it is moving very fast.
2 (verb) To blur the differences between things means to make them no longer clear, e.g. *They tried to blur the distinction between art and reality.*
blurred (adjective).

blurb
(noun) The blurb about a product is information about it written to make people interested in it.
[coined in the 20th century by Gelett Burgess, an American humorist]

blurt out, blurts out, blurting out, blurted out
(verb) If you blurt something out, you say it suddenly, after trying to keep quiet or keep it a secret, e.g. *She suddenly blurted out, 'I'm not going.'*

blush, blushes, blushing, blushed
1 (verb) If you blush, your face becomes redder than usual, because you are ashamed or embarrassed.
2 (noun) A blush is the red colour on someone's face when they blush.
[from Old English *blyscan* meaning 'to glow']

Similar words: (sense 1) colour, flush, redden

bluster, blusters, blustering, blustered
1 (verb) When someone blusters, they behave aggressively because they are angry or offended.
2 (noun) Bluster is aggressive behaviour by someone who is angry or offended.

[from Low German *blüsteren* meaning 'to blow violently']

blustery
(adjective) Blustery weather is rough and windy.

B.O. an abbreviation for **body odour.**

boa, boas
(noun) A boa, or a boa constrictor, is a large snake that kills its prey by coiling round it and crushing it.

boar, boars
(noun) A boar is a male wild pig, or a male domestic pig used for breeding.

board, boards, boarding, boarded
1 (noun) A board is a long flat piece of wood.
2 In chess and similar games, the board is the piece of wood or stiff cardboard marked with squares on which you play.
3 The board of a company or organization is the group of people who control it.
4 Board is the food provided when you stay somewhere, e.g. *board and lodging.*
5 (verb) If you board a train, ship, or aircraft, you get on it.
6 (phrase) If you are **on board** a train, ship, or aircraft, you are on it or in it.
7 Something that is **above board** is open, fair, and honest.

Similar words: (sense 3) committee, council, panel

board up
(phrasal verb) If you board up a door or window, you cover it by fixing pieces of wood across it.

boarder, boarders
1 (noun) A boarder is a pupil who lives at school during term time.
2 A boarder is also a lodger.

boarding house, boarding houses
(noun) A boarding house is a house in which people pay to stay for a short time.

boarding school, boarding schools
(noun) A boarding school is a school where the pupils live during the term.

boardroom, boardrooms
(noun) A boardroom is a room where the board of a company meets.

boast, boasts, boasting, boasted
1 (verb) If you boast about your possessions or achievements, you talk about them proudly, especially to impress other people.
2 (noun) A boast is something that you say which shows that you are proud of what you own or have done.
boastful (adjective), **boastfully** (adverb).

Similar words: (sense 1) brag, crow, blow your own trumpet

boat, boats
1 (noun) A boat is a small vehicle for travelling across water.
2 (phrase) If someone is **rocking the boat**, they are upsetting a calm situation and causing trouble.

3 When people are **in the same boat**, they are all in the same unpleasant situation.

boater, boaters
(noun) A boater is an old-fashioned kind of hard straw hat with a flat top and a flat brim.

boatswain, boatswains (pronounced **boh**-sn)
(noun) A boatswain on a ship is the officer who looks after the ship's maintenance and equipment.
[from Old English *bat swan* meaning 'boat servant']

bob, bobs, bobbing, bobbed
1 (verb) When something bobs, it moves up and down, e.g. *The boat bobbed gently on the lake.*
2 (noun) A bob is a woman's hair style in which her hair is cut level with her chin.
[sense 2 from Middle English *bobbe* meaning 'bunch of flowers']

bobbin, bobbins
(noun) A bobbin is a small round object on which thread or wool is wound.
[from Old French *bobine*]

bobble, bobbles
(noun) A bobble is a small ball of material used for decorating clothes or furniture.

bobby, bobbies
(noun; an old-fashioned informal word) A bobby is a policeman. Bobbies were named after Robert Peel, who founded the Metropolitan Police Force in 1828.

bode, bodes, boding, boded
(phrase; a literary use) If something **bodes ill** or **bodes no good**, it makes you think that something bad will happen.
[from Old English *bodian* meaning 'to announce']

bodice, bodices
(noun) A bodice is the upper part of a dress.

bodily
1 (adjective) relating to the body, e.g. *the bodily functions.*
2 (adverb) involving the whole of someone's body, e.g. *He picked her up bodily.*

body, bodies
1 (noun) Your body is either all your physical parts or just your trunk, excluding your head and limbs.
2 A body is a person's dead body.
3 The body of a car or aircraft is the main part of it, excluding the engine.
4 A body of people is also an organized group.

Similar words: (sense 1) figure, form, frame, build, physique

bodyguard, bodyguards
(noun) A bodyguard is a person or group of people employed to protect someone.

bodywork
(noun) The bodywork of a motor vehicle is the outer part of it.

Boer, Boers (pronounced **boh**-er)
(noun) A Boer is a descendant of the Dutch people who went to live in South Africa.

bog, bogs
(noun) A bog is an area of land which is wet and permanently spongy.
[from Gaelic *bogach* meaning 'swamp']

Similar words: fen, marsh, mire, morass, quagmire, swamp

bogged down
(adjective) If you are bogged down in something, you are unable to make progress.

boggle, boggles, boggling, boggled
(verb) If your mind boggles at something, you find it difficult to imagine or understand.

bogus
(adjective) not genuine, e.g. *a bogus Scottish accent.*
[from the name of a machine that made counterfeit money]

bohemian (pronounced boh-**hee**-mee-an)
(adjective) Someone who is bohemian lives in an exotic and unconventional way, and is usually involved with music, art, and literature.

boil, boils, boiling, boiled
1 (verb) When a hot liquid boils, bubbles appear in it and it starts to change into vapour.
2 When you boil a kettle, you heat it until the water in it boils.
3 When you boil food, you cook it in boiling water.
4 (phrase) If something **boils down to** a particular point, that point is the most important aspect of it.
5 When a liquid **comes to the boil**, it starts to boil.
6 (noun) A boil is a red swelling on your skin.
[from Latin *bullire* meaning 'to bubble']

Similar words: (sense 6) pustule, carbuncle

boiler, boilers
(noun) A boiler is a piece of equipment which burns fuel to provide hot water.

boiling
1 (adjective; an informal word) very hot.
2 very angry.

boisterous
(adjective) Someone who is boisterous is noisy, lively, and rather rough.
boisterously (adverb), **boisterousness** (noun).

Similar words: riotous, uproarious, rowdy, rollicking

bold, bolder, boldest
1 (adjective) confident and not shy or embarrassed, e.g. *Mary was surprisingly bold for a girl of her age.*
2 not afraid of risk or danger.
3 clear and noticeable, e.g. *bold handwriting... bold colours.*
boldly (adverb), **boldness** (noun).
[from Old Norse *ballr* meaning 'dangerous' or 'terrible']

Similar words: (sense 1) brash, brazen, forward, pert (sense 3) conspicuous, eye-catching, striking

bolero, boleros (pronounced **boll**-er-roh)
(noun) A bolero is a short jacket that does not
reach the waist, usually part of a woman's outfit.

bollard, bollards
(noun) A bollard is a short, thick post used to
keep vehicles out of a road or traffic lane.

bolster, bolsters, bolstering, bolstered
(verb) To bolster something means to support it
or make it stronger, e.g. *I needed something to
bolster up my courage.*

bolt, bolts, bolting, bolted
1 (noun) A bolt is a metal object which screws
into a nut and is used to fasten things together.
2 A bolt is also a metal bar that you slide across
a door or window in order to fasten it.
3 (verb) If you bolt things together, you fasten
them together using a bolt. If you bolt a door or
window, you fasten it using a bolt.
4 To bolt means to escape or run away.
5 To bolt food means to eat it very quickly.
6 (phrase) If you are sitting or standing **bolt
upright**, you are sitting or standing very straight.
[from Old English *bolt* meaning 'arrow']

bomb, bombs, bombing, bombed
1 (noun) A bomb is a container fitted with
incendiary material that explodes when it hits
something or is activated by a timing mechanism.
2 Nuclear weapons are sometimes referred to as
the bomb, e.g. *Ban the bomb!*
3 (verb) When a place is bombed, it is attacked
with bombs.
[from Greek *bombos* meaning 'a booming sound']

Similar words: (sense 3) bombard, blitz, shell, blast

bombard, bombards, bombarding, bombarded
(verb) To bombard a place means to attack it
with heavy gunfire or bombs.
bombardment (noun).

bombastic
(adjective) Bombastic statements or threats are
intended to impress people rather than to
express meaning clearly.
bombastically (adverb), **bombast** (noun).
[from Old French *bombace* meaning 'cotton wool']

bomber, bombers
(noun) A bomber is an aircraft that drops bombs.

bombshell, bombshells
(noun) A bombshell is a sudden piece of shocking
or upsetting news.

bona fide (pronounced boh-na **fie**-dee)
(adjective) genuine, e.g. *a bona fide excuse.*
[a Latin expression meaning 'in good faith']

bonanza, bonanzas
(noun) An event or thing from which people
suddenly become rich is called a bonanza.
[a Spanish word literally meaning 'calm sea' and
therefore 'good luck']

bond, bonds, bonding, bonded
1 (noun) A bond is a close relationship between
people, e.g. *the bond between mother and child.*
2 A bond is also a certificate which records that
you have lent money to a business and that it
will repay you the loan with interest.

3 (a literary use) Bonds are chains or ropes used
to tie a prisoner up.
4 In chemistry, a bond is the means by which
atoms or groups of atoms are combined in
molecules.
5 Bonds are also feelings or obligations that
force you to behave in a particular way, e.g. *the
bonds of party discipline.*
6 (verb) When two things bond or are bonded,
they become closely linked or attached.
[from Old Norse *band* meaning 'something that
binds']

Similar words: (sense 1) link, connection, tie
(sense 5) tie

bondage
(noun) Bondage is the condition of being
someone's slave.

bone, bones
1 (noun) Bones are the hard parts that form the
framework of a person's or animal's body.
2 (phrase) If you **make no bones** about doing
something, especially something unpleasant or
difficult, you do not hesitate or have any doubts
about doing it.
boneless (adjective).

bone china
(noun) Bone china is very fine porcelain
containing powdered bone.

bonfire, bonfires
(noun) A bonfire is a fire made out of doors,
usually to burn rubbish.
[from 'bone' + 'fire'; bones were used as fuel in
the Middle Ages]

bongos
(plural noun) Bongos are small drums, usually in
pairs, played by tapping with the fingers.

bonhomie (pronounced **bon**-nom-ee)
(noun) Bonhomie is warm, happy friendliness.
[from French *bonhomme* meaning 'good-natured
fellow']

bonnet, bonnets
1 (noun) The bonnet of a car is the metal cover
over the engine.
2 A bonnet is also a baby's or woman's hat tied
under the chin.
[from Old French *bonet* meaning 'hat']

bonny, bonnier, bonniest
(adjective; a Scottish and Northern English
word) nice to look at.
[from Old French *bon* meaning 'good']

bonsai, bonsais (pronounced **bon**-sigh)
1 (noun) A bonsai is a dwarf tree, which is kept
small by artificial methods of cultivation.
2 Bonsai is the art of growing such trees,
originating in Japan.
[from Japanese *bon* meaning 'bowl' and *sai*
meaning 'to plant']

bonus, bonuses
1 (noun) A bonus is an amount of money added
to your usual pay.
2 Something that is a bonus is a good thing that

you get in addition to something else, e.g. *Having John in the team was an unexpected bonus.*
[from Latin *bonus* meaning 'good']

bony, bonier, boniest
(adjective) Bony people or animals are thin, with very little flesh covering their bones.

boo, boos, booing, booed
1 (noun) A boo is a shout of disapproval.
2 (verb) When people boo, they shout 'boo' to show their disapproval.

booby prize, booby prizes
(noun) A booby prize is a prize given to the person who comes last in a competition.

booby trap, booby traps
(noun) A booby trap is a bomb which is hidden or disguised and which is set off by being touched.

book, books, booking, booked
1 (noun) A book is a number of pages held together inside a cover.
2 An organization's books are records of money that it has earned and spent.
3 (verb) When you book something such as a room, you arrange to have it or use it at a particular time.
4 (phrase) If you are **in someone's bad books**, they are displeased with you. If you are **in their good books**, they are pleased with you.
[from Old English *boc*; this word was derived from an Old Germanic word meaning 'beech', because books used to be written on beech bark]

bookcase, bookcases
(noun) A bookcase is a piece of furniture with shelves for books.

bookie, bookies
(noun; an informal word) A bookie is a bookmaker.

booking, bookings
(noun) A booking is an arrangement to book something such as a hotel room.

book-keeping
(noun) Book-keeping is the keeping of a record of the money spent and received by a business or other organization.

booklet, booklets
(noun) A booklet is a small book with a paper cover.

bookmaker, bookmakers
(noun) A bookmaker is a person who makes a living by taking people's bets and paying them when they win.

bookmark, bookmarks
(noun) A bookmark is a piece of card or other material which you put between the pages of a book to mark your place.

bookworm, bookworms
1 (noun) A bookworm is a person who is very fond of reading.
2 A bookworm is also a type of insect that feeds on the binding paste of books.

boom, booms, booming, boomed
1 (noun) A boom is a rapid increase in something, e.g. *the population boom.*

2 (verb) When something booms, it increases rapidly, e.g. *Profits are booming.*
3 (noun) A boom is also a loud deep echoing sound, e.g. *the boom of the drum.*
4 (verb) To boom means to make a loud deep echoing sound, e.g. *'Nonsense!' he boomed.*
5 (noun) The boom of a boat is a pole that sticks out from the mast to hold the bottom of the sail outstretched.
[sense 5 is from Dutch *boom* meaning 'tree']

boomerang, boomerangs
(noun) A boomerang is a curved piece of wood thrown as a weapon by Australian aborigines. It is supposed to come back to you if you throw it correctly.
[an Australian Aboriginal word]

boon, boons
(noun) Something that is a boon makes life better or easier, e.g. *Having her mother to help was a boon.*
[from Old Norse *bon* meaning 'request']

boor, boors
(noun) Someone who is a boor behaves in a rough, impolite way.
boorish (adjective), **boorishly** (adverb).
[from Old English *gebur* meaning 'peasant']

boost, boosts, boosting, boosted
1 (verb) To boost something means to cause it to improve or increase, e.g. *Winning will boost their morale... The new technology should boost food production.*
2 (noun) A boost is an improvement or increase, e.g. *a boost to the economy.*
booster (noun).

boot, boots, booting, booted
1 (noun) Boots are strong shoes that cover your ankle and sometimes your calf.
2 (verb) If you boot something somewhere, you kick it there.
3 (noun) The boot of a car is a covered space, usually at the back, for carrying things in.
4 (phrase; an old-fashioned literary use) **To boot** means also or in addition, e.g. *She was an unaccompanied female, and a foreigner to boot.*
[sense 1 is from Old French *bote*; sense 4 is from Old English *bot* meaning 'compensation']

booth, booths
1 (noun) A booth is a small area separated by a screen from a public area where, for example, you can make a phone call.
2 A booth is also a tent or stall where you can buy goods or watch some kind of entertainment.

booty
(noun) Booty is valuable things taken from a place, especially by soldiers after a battle.
[from Old German *buite* meaning 'exchange']

booze, boozes, boozing, boozed (an informal word)
1 (noun) Booze is alcoholic drink.
2 (verb) When people booze, they drink alcohol.
boozer (noun), **boozy** (adjective).
[from Old Dutch *busen* meaning 'to drink to excess']

borax
(noun) Borax is a white powdery mineral, used in making glass and as a cleaning chemical.
[from Arabic *buraq*]

border, borders, bordering, bordered
1 (noun) The border between two countries is the dividing line between them.
2 A border is also a strip or band round the edge of something, e.g. *It's painted white with a gold border.*
3 In a garden, a border is a long flower bed.
4 (verb) To border something means to form a border or boundary along the side of it, e.g. *Huge elm trees bordered the road.*
[from Old French *bordure*, originally from Germanic *bort* meaning 'the side of a ship']

border on
(phrasal verb) If something borders on a particular state or condition, it is almost in that state or condition.

borderline
(adjective) only just acceptable as a member of a class or group, e.g. *a borderline case.*

bore, bores, boring, bored
1 (verb) If something bores you, you find it dull and uninteresting.
2 (noun) A bore is someone or something that bores you.
3 (verb) If you bore a hole in something, you make it using a tool such as a drill.
4 Bore is also the past tense of **bear**.
[sense 3 from Old English *borian* meaning 'to pierce']

bored
(adjective) If you are bored, you are impatient because you find something uninteresting or because you have nothing to do.
boredom (noun).

boring
(adjective) dull and uninteresting.

Similar words: monotonous, humdrum, tedious

born
1 (verb) When a baby is born, it comes out of its mother's womb at the beginning of its life.
2 To be born also means to come into existence, e.g. *It was here that the cotton industry was born.*
3 (adjective) You use born to mean that someone has a natural ability to do something well, e.g. *He is a born writer.*
[from Old English *boren*, past participle of *beran* meaning 'to bear']

borne the past participle of **bear**.

boron
(noun) Boron is a hard, crystalline chemical element, used in hardening steel. Its atomic number is 5 and its symbol is B.
[from *borax* + *carbon*]

borough, boroughs (pronounced **bur-uh**)
(noun) A borough is a town, or a district within a large town, that has its own council.
[from Old English *burg* meaning 'fortified place']

borrow, borrows, borrowing, borrowed
(verb) If you borrow something that belongs to someone else, or borrow something from someone, you use it for a period of time with their permission.
borrower (noun).

borstal, borstals
(noun; an old-fashioned word) Borstals are prisons for young criminals. They are now officially known as 'youth custody centres'.
[from *Borstal*, the village in Kent where the first borstal was set up]

borzoi, borzois
(noun) A borzoi is a tall, fast-moving dog with a silky coat, originally used in Russia for hunting wolves.
[a Russian word]

bosom, bosoms
1 (noun) A woman's bosom is her breasts.
2 (a literary use) Strong feelings are sometimes described as being in your bosom, e.g. *She continued to nurse a deep hatred in her bosom.*
3 (adjective) A bosom friend is a very close friend.
bosomy (adjective).

boss, bosses, bossing, bossed
1 (noun) Someone's boss is the person in charge of the organization where they work.
2 (verb) If someone bosses you around, they keep telling you what to do.
[from Dutch *baas* meaning 'master']

boss-eyed
(adjective) Someone who is boss-eyed has a squint, so that their eyes seems to be looking different ways.

bossy, bossier, bossiest
(adjective) A bossy person enjoys telling other people what to do.
bossily (adverb), **bossiness** (noun).

Similar words: overbearing, domineering, dictatorial

bosun another spelling of **boatswain**.

botany
(noun) Botany is the scientific study of plants.
botanic (adjective), **botanical** (adjective), **botanist** (noun).
[from Greek *botane* meaning 'plant']

botch, botches, botching, botched
(verb; an informal word) If you botch something, you do it badly or clumsily.

Similar words: bungle, mismanage, mess up, muff

both
(determiner and pronoun) Both is used when saying something about two things or people.

bother, bothers, bothering, bothered
1 (verb) If you do not bother to do something, you do not do it because it involves too much effort or it seems unnecessary.
2 If something bothers you, you are worried or concerned about it. If you do not bother about it, you are not concerned about it, e.g. *I did not bother what I looked like.*

3 If you bother someone, you interrupt them when they are busy.
4 (noun) Bother is trouble, fuss, or difficulty.
bothersome (adjective).
[from Old Irish *bodhraim* meaning 'to deafen', hence to bewilder or confuse with noise]

bottle, bottles, bottling, bottled
1 (noun) A bottle is a glass or plastic container for keeping liquids in.
2 (verb) To bottle something means to store it in bottles.
[from Medieval Latin *butticula* meaning 'a little cask']

bottle up
(phrasal verb) If you bottle up strong feelings, you do not express or show them.

bottleneck, bottlenecks
(noun) A bottleneck is a narrow section of road or an awkward junction where traffic has to slow down or stop, often causing a traffic jam.

bottom, bottoms
1 (noun) The bottom of something is its lowest part.
2 Your bottom is your buttocks.
3 (adjective) The bottom thing in a series of things is the lowest one.
4 (phrase) If you **get to the bottom of** something, you find out the real truth about it.
bottomless (adjective).

botulism (pronounced **bot**-yoo-lizm)
(noun) Botulism is a serious disease caused by eating contaminated food.
[from Latin *botulus* meaning 'sausage'; used originally to describe poisoning from eating contaminated sausage]

bougainvillea, bougainvilleas (pronounced boo-gan-**vill**-ee-a)
(noun) A bougainvillea is a tropical climbing plant with small red or purple flowers.

bough, boughs (rhymes with **now**)
(noun) A bough is a large branch of a tree.
[from Old English *bog* meaning 'arm' or 'twig']

bought the past tense and past participle of **buy**.

boulder, boulders
(noun) A boulder is a large rounded rock.

boulevard, boulevards (pronounced **boo**-le-vard)
(noun) A boulevard is a wide street in a city, usually with trees along each side.
[a French word]

bounce, bounces, bouncing, bounced
1 (verb) When an object bounces, it springs back from something after hitting it. If you bounce an object, such as a ball, you throw it against a surface to make it do this.
2 To bounce also means to move up and down, e.g. *the rucksack bounced on my shoulders.*
3 If a cheque bounces, the bank refuses to accept it because there is not enough money in the account.

Similar words: (sense 1) rebound, recoil, ricochet

bouncy
(adjective) Someone who is bouncy is lively and enthusiastic.

bound, bounds, bounding, bounded
1 (adjective) If you say that something is bound to happen, you mean that it is certain to happen.
2 If a plane, ship, or bus is bound for a place, it is going there.
3 If someone is bound by an agreement or regulation, they must obey it.
4 (plural noun) Bounds are limits which restrict what can be done, e.g. *the bounds of possibility.*
5 (noun) A bound is a large leap.
6 (phrase) If a place is **out of bounds**, you are forbidden to go there.
7 If one thing is **bound up with** another, it is closely connected with it.
8 (verb) When animals or people bound, they move quickly with large leaps, e.g. *The goats bounded off.*
9 Bound is also the past tense and past participle of **bind**.
[sense 2 is from Old Norse *buinn* meaning 'prepared'; sense 3 is the past participle of 'bind'; sense 4 is from Old French *bunde* meaning boundary; sense 8 is from Old French *bondir* meaning 'to jump']

boundary, boundaries
1 (noun) A boundary is a line that separates an area from other areas.
2 In cricket, the boundary is the line indicating the edge of the pitch. If a batsman hits the ball beyond this line, he scores a boundary.

boundless
(adjective) without end or limit, e.g. *her boundless energy.*

bountiful
(adjective; a literary word) freely available in large amounts, e.g. *a bountiful supply.*
bountifully (adverb), **bountifulness** (noun).

bounty
1 (noun; a literary word) Bounty is a generous supply, e.g. *the bounty of nature.*
2 Someone's bounty is their generosity in giving a lot of something.
[from Latin *bonitas* meaning 'goodness']

bouquet, bouquets (pronounced boo-**kay**)
1 (noun) A bouquet is an attractively arranged bunch of flowers.
2 The bouquet of a wine is its smell.
[a French word; originally from Old French *bosc* meaning 'forest']

bourgeois (pronounced **boor**-jhwah)
(adjective) belonging to or typical of the urban middle class in a society.
[a French word; originally from Old French *borjois* meaning 'citizen']

bourgeoisie (pronounced boor-jhwah-**zee**)
(noun) The bourgeoisie is the urban middle class in a society.

bout, bouts
1 (noun) If you have a bout of something such as an illness, you have it for a short time, e.g. *recovering from a bout of malaria.*

2 If you have a bout of doing something, you do it enthusiastically for a short time, e.g. *a bout of writing.*
3 A bout is also a boxing or wrestling match.

boutique, boutiques (pronounced boo-**teek**)
(noun) A boutique is a small shop that sells fashionable clothes, shoes, or jewellery.
[a French word]

bovine
1 (adjective; a technical use) relating to cattle.
2 (an informal use) Someone who is bovine is slow and rather stupid.
[from Latin *bovinus* meaning 'to do with cows']

bow, bows, bowing, bowed (rhymes with **now**)
1 (verb) When you bow, you bend your body downwards briefly to show respect.
2 (noun) A bow is the movement you make when you bow.
3 (verb) If you bow to something, you give in to it, e.g. *He bowed to public opinion.*
4 (noun) The bow of a ship is its front part.
[sense 1 is from Old English *bugan* meaning 'to bend'; sense 4 is from Dutch *boeg* meaning 'shoulder', hence the front of a ship]

bow, bows (rhymes with **low**)
1 (noun) A bow is a knot with two loops and two loose ends.
2 A bow is also a long flexible piece of wood used for shooting arrows.
3 The bow of a violin or other stringed instrument is a long piece of wood with horsehair stretched along it, which you move over the strings to play the instrument.
[from Old English *boga* meaning 'arch' or 'bow']

bowdlerize, bowdlerizes, bowdlerizing, bowdlerized; also spelled **bowdlerise**
(verb) To bowdlerize a text means to remove words or passages from it that are regarded as indecent.
bowdlerization (noun).
[from the name of Thomas Bowdler, who in 1818 published an expurgated edition of Shakespeare]

bowel, bowels
(noun) Your bowels are the tubes in the lower part of your body, through which waste matter from digested food goes on its way to being excreted through the anus.
[from Latin *botellus* meaning 'little sausage']

bower, bowers (rhymes with **flower**)
(noun; a literary word) A bower is a shady, leafy shelter.
[from Old English *bur* meaning 'dwelling' or 'lady's apartment']

bowl, bowls, bowling, bowled
1 (noun) A bowl is a circular container with a wide uncovered top, used especially in cooking or for serving food.
2 A bowl is also the hollow, rounded part of various things, e.g. *a lavatory bowl... the bowl of his pipe.*
3 A bowl is a large heavy ball used in the game of bowls or tenpin bowling.
4 (verb) In cricket, to bowl means to throw the ball towards the batsman; if a batsman is

bowled, or bowled out, his wicket is knocked over by the ball and he is out.
bowler (noun).
[sense 1 from Old English *bolla* meaning 'cup'; sense 3 from French *boule* meaning 'ball']

bowl over
(phrasal verb) If you are bowled over by something, you are very surprised and impressed by it, e.g. *I was bowled over by the beauty of Malawi.*

bow-legged
(adjective) Someone who is bow-legged has legs that curve outwards at the knees.

bowling
(noun) Bowling is a game in which you roll a heavy ball down an alley towards a group of wooden objects called pins and try to knock them down.

bowling alley, bowling alleys
(noun) A bowling alley is a track down which you roll a ball in bowling; also a building containing these tracks.

bowling green, bowling greens
(noun) A bowling green is an area of smooth short grass on which bowls is played.

bowls
(noun) Bowls is a game in which heavy balls, which are biased so that they do not run straight, are rolled over a green so as to end up as near as possible to a small ball called the jack.
[from French *boule* meaning 'ball']

bow tie, bow ties (rhymes with **low**)
(noun) A bow tie is a man's tie in the form of a bow, worn especially on formal occasions as part of evening dress.

bow window, bow windows (rhymes with **low**)
(noun) A bow window is a curving window that projects slightly from the wall.

box, boxes, boxing, boxed
1 (noun) A box is a container with a firm base and sides and usually a lid.
2 On a form, a box is a rectangular space which you have to fill in.
3 In a theatre, a box is a small separate area where a few people can watch the performance together.
4 Box is a dense slow-growing evergreen tree often used for hedges.
5 (verb) To box means to fight someone according to the rules of boxing.
[sense 1 from Latin *buxus*, the Latin name of the box tree; hence a wooden container]

box in
(phrasal verb) If you are boxed in, you cannot move away, because you are surrounded by other people or other cars.

boxer, boxers
1 (noun) A boxer is a man who boxes.
2 A boxer is also a breed of medium-sized, smooth-haired dog with a flat face.

boxing
(noun) Boxing is a sport in which two men fight using their fists, wearing padded gloves.

box office, box offices
(noun) In a theatre or cinema, the box office is the place where tickets are sold.

boy, boys
(noun) A boy is a male child.
boyhood (noun), **boyish** (adjective), **boyishly** (adverb).

Similar words: stripling, lad, youngster, youth

boycott, boycotts, boycotting, boycotted
1 (verb) If you boycott a person, organization, product, or event, you refuse to have anything to do with it, e.g. *He urged them to boycott the election.*
2 (noun) A boycott is the boycotting of a person, organization, product, or event, e.g. *an Olympic boycott.*
[from the name of Captain C.C. Boycott (1832-97), an Irish land agent, who offended the tenants, so that they refused to pay their rents]

Similar words: (sense 1) black, blacklist, ostracize

boyfriend, boyfriends
(noun) Someone's boyfriend is the man or boy with whom they are having a romantic or sexual relationship.

bra, bras
(noun; an informal word) A bra is a piece of underwear worn by a woman to support her breasts. The formal word is **brassière.**

brace, braces, bracing, braced
1 (verb) When you brace yourself, you stiffen your body in order to steady yourself or avoid falling over, e.g. *The taxi swung round a bend and he braced himself with his foot.*
2 If you brace yourself for something unpleasant or difficult, you prepare yourself to face it and deal with it, e.g. *She braced herself to read the letter.*
3 (plural noun) Braces are a pair of straps fastened to someone's trousers and passing over their shoulders.
4 (noun) A brace is an object fastened to something to straighten or support it.
5 A brace is also two things of the same kind, e.g. *a brace of geese.*
[from Old French *brace* meaning 'two arms']

bracelet, bracelets
(noun) A bracelet is a chain or band worn around someone's wrist as an ornament.
[from Old French *bracel* meaning 'little arm']

bracing
(adjective) Something that is bracing makes you feel fit and full of energy, e.g. *the bracing mountain air.*

bracken
(noun) Bracken is a plant like a large fern that grows on hills and in woods.

bracket, brackets, bracketing, bracketed
1 (noun) Brackets are a pair of written marks, ( ), or [ ], placed round a word, expression, or sentence that is not part of the main text, or to show that the items inside the brackets belong together.

2 A bracket is a range, for example of ages or prices, e.g. *the 14-16 age bracket.*
3 A bracket is also a piece of metal or wood fastened to a wall to support something such as a shelf.
4 (verb) When you bracket two things together, you consider them to be similar or related, e.g. *Current affairs, should that be bracketed with documentary?*

brackish
(adjective) Brackish water is slightly salty.
[from Dutch *brac* meaning 'salty']

bract, bracts
(noun) A bract is a leaf-like part at the base of a flower.
[from Latin *bractea* meaning 'thin metal plate' or 'goldleaf']

brag, brags, bragging, bragged
(verb) When someone brags, they talk in a boastful way about something that they own or something that they have done, e.g. *He bragged that he had just stolen a watch.*

braggart, braggarts
(noun) A braggart is someone who brags.

brahmin, brahmins (pronounced **brah**-min)
(noun) A brahmin is a member of the highest or priestly caste in Hindu society.

braid, braids, braiding, braided
1 (noun) Braid is a strip of contrasting cloth or twisted threads used to decorate clothes or curtains.
2 A braid is a length of hair which has been plaited and tied.
3 (verb) To braid hair or thread means to plait it.
[from Old English *bredgan* meaning 'to weave together']

Braille
(noun) Braille is a system of printing for blind people in which letters are represented by raised dots that can be felt with the fingers. It was invented by the French inventor Louis Braille in the 19th century.

brain, brains
1 (noun) Your brain is the mass of nerve tissue inside your head that controls your body and enables you to think and feel; also used to refer to your mind and the way that you think, e.g. *He has a clever brain.*
2 If you say that someone has brains, you mean that they are very intelligent, e.g. *He'd got brains but wouldn't use them.*
3 (phrase) If you **pick someone's brains**, you get ideas or information from them.
4 The brains behind something is the person organizing it.
5 (verb; an informal use) To brain someone means to hit them hard on the head.
[from Old English *brægen* meaning 'brain']

brainchild
(noun; an informal word) Someone's brainchild is something that they have invented or created.

brainwash, brainwashes, brainwashing, brainwashed

(verb) If people are brainwashed into believing something, they accept it unthinkingly because it is repeatedly or systematically presented to them.
brainwashing (noun).

brainwave, brainwaves
(noun; an informal expression) If you have a brainwave, you suddenly think of a clever idea.

brainy, brainier, brainiest
(adjective; an informal word) clever.

braise, braises, braising, braised
(verb) To braise food means to fry it for a short time, then cook it slowly in a little liquid.
[from French *braiser*, originally from *braise* meaning 'hot coals']

brake, brakes, braking, braked
1 (noun) A brake is a device for making a vehicle stop or slow down.
2 (verb) When a driver brakes, he or she makes a vehicle stop or slow down by using its brakes.

brake horsepower
(noun) The brake horsepower of an engine is the power that it produces, measured by the force needed to stop it with brakes.

bramble, brambles
(noun) A bramble is a wild, thorny bush that produces blackberries.

bran
(noun) Bran is the ground husks that are left over after flour has been made from wheat grains.

branch, branches, branching, branched
1 (noun) The branches of a tree are the parts that grow out from its trunk.
2 A branch of a business or other organization is one of its offices, shops, or local groups.
3 A branch of a subject is one of its areas of study or activity, e.g. *specialists in certain branches of medicine*.
4 (verb) A road that branches off from another road starts from it at a fork and goes off in a different direction.
[from Old French *branche*, originally from Latin *branca* meaning 'paw' or 'foot']

branch out
(phrasal verb) To branch out means to develop a new field of activity.

brand, brands, branding, branded
1 (noun) A brand of something is a particular kind of it, e.g. *his favourite brand of whisky*.
2 (verb) When an animal is branded, a permanent mark is burned on its skin to show who owns it.
3 If you are branded as something bad, you have a reputation for it, e.g. *He had been branded a traitor*.
[from Old English *brand* meaning 'piece of burning wood']

brandish, brandishes, brandishing, brandished
(verb; a literary word) If you brandish something, you wave it vigorously, e.g. *They brandished their spears*.

[from Old French *brandir* meaning 'to hold or use a sword']

brand-new
(adjective) completely new.

brandy
(noun) Brandy is a strong alcoholic drink, consisting of spirits distilled from wine.
[from Dutch *brandewijn* meaning 'burnt wine']

brash, brasher, brashest
(adjective) self-confident and aggressive, e.g. *a brash young man*.

brass
1 (noun and adjective) Brass is a yellow-coloured metal made from copper and zinc.
2 In an orchestra, the brass section consists of wind instruments such as trumpets, trombones, and French horns.

brassière, brassières
(noun; a formal word) A brassière is a bra.

brat, brats
(noun; an informal word) An irritating child may be referred to as a brat.

bravado (pronounced bra-**vah**-doh)
(noun) Bravado is a display of courage intended to impress other people.
[from Old Italian *bravare* meaning 'to challenge']

brave, braver, bravest; braves, braving, braved
1 (adjective) A brave person is willing to do dangerous things and does not show any fear.
2 (verb) If you brave a difficult or dangerous situation, you put up with it in order to achieve something, e.g. *Farmers braved wintry conditions to rescue the sheep*.
bravely (adverb), **bravery** (noun).
[from Italian *bravo* meaning 'courageous' or 'wild']

Similar words: (sense 1) courageous, fearless, plucky, heroic, valiant, intrepid, valorous

---

bravo
People shout 'Bravo!' to express appreciation when something has been done well.
[an Italian word meaning 'splendid']

brawl, brawls, brawling, brawled
1 (noun) A brawl is a rough fight.
2 (verb) When people brawl, they take part in a rough fight.

brawn
1 (noun) Brawn is physical strength, e.g. *He is all brawn and no brain*.
2 Brawn is also food made from pieces of pork in the jelly of the meat pressed together.
brawny (adjective).
[from Old French *braon* meaning 'slice of meat']

bray, brays, braying, brayed
1 (verb) When a donkey brays, it makes a loud, harsh sound.
2 (noun) A bray is the sound a donkey makes.

brazen
(adjective) When someone's behaviour is brazen,

they do not care if other people think they are behaving wrongly.

brazenly (adverb), **brazenness** (noun).
[from Old English *bræsen* meaning 'made of brass']

brazier, braziers
(noun) A brazier is a metal container in which coal or charcoal is burned to keep people warm out of doors.
[from Old French *braise* meaning 'hot coals']

Brazilian, Brazilians
1 (adjective) belonging or relating to Brazil.
2 (noun) A Brazilian is someone who comes from Brazil.

breach, breaches, breaching, breached
1 (verb; a formal word) If you breach an agreement or law, you break it.
2 (noun) A breach of an agreement or law is an action that breaks it, e.g. *a breach of contract.*
3 A breach is a gap or break.
4 (verb) To breach a barrier means to make a gap in it, e.g. *They succeeded in breaching the city wall.*
[from Old English *bræc* meaning 'to breach']

Similar words: (sense 2) contravention, infringement, transgression, violation

bread
(noun) Bread is a common food made from flour and water, usually leavened with yeast, and baked.

breadth
(noun) The breadth of something is the distance between its two sides.
[from Old English *brad* meaning 'broad']

breadwinner, breadwinners
(noun) The breadwinner in a family is the person who earns the money.

break, breaks, breaking, broke, broken
1 (verb) When an object breaks, it is damaged and separates into pieces.
2 If you break a rule, promise, or agreement, you fail to keep it.
3 To break something means to end or interrupt it, e.g. *Radio contact was broken.*
4 When a boy's voice breaks, it becomes permanently deeper.
5 (noun) A break is a short period during which you rest or do something different.
6 When there is a break between people or groups, they stop being involved with each other, e.g. *his break with the Labour Party.*
7 (phrase) To **break a fall** means to weaken its effect.
8 When you **break the news**, you give a piece of bad news to someone.
9 To **break a record** means to do better than the previous recorded best.
10 When a company or project **breaks even**, it makes just enough money to cover its costs, but not enough to make a profit.

breakable (adjective).
[from Old English *brecan* meaning 'to break']

Similar words: (sense 1) smash, shatter, snap, fracture, crack
(sense 2) transgress, violate, contravene, infringe

break down
1 (phrasal verb) When a machine or a vehicle breaks down, it stops working.
2 When a system, plan, or negotiation breaks down, it ends because of problems or disagreements.
3 If someone breaks down, they start crying.

break in
1 (phrasal verb) If someone breaks in, they get into a building by force.
2 To break in a young horse means to train it.

break off
1 (phrasal verb) If you break off, you suddenly stop what you are saying or doing.
2 When someone breaks off a relationship, they end it.

break out
(phrasal verb) If something such as a fight or disease breaks out, it begins suddenly.

break up
1 (phrasal verb) If something breaks up, it ends, e.g. *The party had broken up.*
2 When schools or the pupils in them break up, the school term ends and the pupils start their holidays.

breakage, breakages
(noun) A breakage is the act of breaking something; also a thing that has been broken.

breakaway
(adjective) A breakaway group is one that has separated from a larger group.

breakdown, breakdowns
1 (noun) The breakdown of something such as a system is its failure, e.g. *a breakdown in communications.*
2 If someone has a breakdown, they become so depressed that they cannot cope with life.
3 If a driver has a breakdown, his or her car stops working.
4 A breakdown of something complex is a summary of its important points, e.g. *Give me a breakdown of what happened.*

breaker, breakers
(noun) Breakers are big sea waves.

breakfast, breakfasts, breakfasting, breakfasted
1 (noun) Breakfast is the first meal of the day.
2 (verb; a formal use) When you breakfast, you eat the first meal of the day.
[from *break one's fast*]

break-in, break-ins
(noun) A break-in is the illegal entering of a building, especially by a burglar.

breakneck
(adjective; an informal word) Someone or something that is travelling at breakneck speed is travelling dangerously fast.

breakthrough, breakthroughs
(noun) A breakthrough is a sudden important

development, e.g. *a breakthrough in the peace negotiations.*

breakwater, breakwaters
(noun) A breakwater is a wall extending into the sea which protects a harbour or beach from the force of the waves.

breast, breasts
1 (noun) A woman's breasts are the two soft, round fleshy parts on her chest, which secrete milk after she has had a baby.
2 (a literary or old-fashioned use) The human breast is the upper front part of the body, sometimes regarded as the place where emotions are felt, e.g. *What a panic was in his breast!*

breast-feed, breast-feeds, breast-feeding, breast-fed
(verb) If a woman is breast-feeding her baby, she is feeding it with milk from her breasts.

breaststroke
(noun) Breaststroke is a swimming stroke in which you lie on your front, moving your arms horizontally through the water and kicking both legs at the same time.

breath, breaths
1 (noun) Your breath is the air you take into your lungs and let out again when you breathe.
2 (phrase) If you are **out of breath**, you are breathing with difficulty after doing something energetic.
3 If you **hold your breath**, you stop breathing for a short time.
4 If you say that something **takes your breath away**, you mean that it is very surprising or beautiful.
5 If you say something **under your breath**, you say it in a very quiet voice.
[from Old English *bræth* meaning 'odour' or 'vapour']

breathalyse, breathalyses, breathalysing, breathalysed
(verb) When the police breathalyse a driver, they ask the driver to breathe into a device that shows if he or she has drunk too much alcohol.

breathe, breathes, breathing, breathed
(verb) When you breathe, you take air into your lungs and let it out again.

breathless
(adjective) If you are breathless, you are out of breath.
breathlessly (adverb), **breathlessness** (noun).

breathtaking
(adjective) If you say that something is breathtaking, you mean that it is very beautiful or exciting.

bred the past tense and past participle of **breed**.

breeches (pronounced **brit**-chiz)
(noun) Breeches are trousers reaching to just below the knee, nowadays worn especially for riding.
[from Old English *brec* meaning 'leg coverings']

breed, breeds, breeding, bred
1 (noun) A breed of a species of pet animal or farm animal is a particular type of it.

2 (verb) Someone who breeds animals or plants keeps them in order to produce more animals or plants with particular qualities.
3 When animals breed, they mate and produce offspring.
4 When one thing breeds another, it causes it, e.g. *These rumours bred fear in the townships.*
5 (phrase) Someone who was **born and bred** in a place was born there and spent their childhood there.

Similar words: (sense 3) procreate, multiply, reproduce

breeze, breezes
(noun) A breeze is a gentle wind.
[probably from Old Spanish *briza* meaning 'north-east wind']

breeze block, breeze blocks
(noun) Breeze blocks are large, light bricks for building, made from the cinders of coke or coal.

brethren
(plural noun; an old-fashioned word) Brethren is the plural form of brothers, now used mainly in religious contexts.

Breton
(noun) Breton is a language spoken in Brittany in north-west France.

brevity
(noun; a formal word) Brevity means shortness, e.g. *the brevity of his account...the brevity of human life.*
[from Latin *brevitas* meaning 'shortness']

brew, brews, brewing, brewed
1 (verb) If you brew a pot of tea or coffee, you make it by pouring hot water over it.
2 To brew beer means to make it, by boiling and fermenting malt.
3 If an unpleasant situation is brewing, it is about to happen, e.g. *There's trouble brewing in the factory.*
brewer (noun).

brewery, breweries
(noun) A brewery is a place where beer is made, or a company that makes it.

briar, briars
(noun) A briar is a wild rose that grows on a dense prickly bush.
[from French *bruyère* meaning 'heath']

bribe, bribes, bribing, bribed
1 (noun) A bribe is money or something valuable given to an official to persuade him or her to make a favourable decision.
2 (verb) To bribe someone means to give them a bribe.
bribery (noun).
[from Old French *briber* meaning 'to beg']

bric-a-brac
(noun) Bric-a-brac consists of small ornaments or pieces of furniture of no great value.
[from a French phrase *à bric et à brac* meaning 'at random']

brick, bricks
(noun) Bricks are rectangular blocks of baked clay used for building walls.

bricklayer, bricklayers
(noun) A bricklayer is someone whose job is to build brick walls.

bride, brides
(noun) A bride is a woman who is getting married or who has just got married.
bridal (adjective).

bridegroom, bridegrooms
(noun) A bridegroom is a man who is getting married or who has just got married.

bridesmaid, bridesmaids
(noun) A bridesmaid is a girl or woman who helps and accompanies a bride on her wedding day.

bridge, bridges
1 (noun) A bridge is a structure built over a river, road, or railway so that vehicles and people can cross.
2 A ship's bridge is the high part from which it is steered and controlled.
3 Bridge is a card game for four players based on whist.
[from Old Norse *bryggja* meaning 'gangway']

bridle, bridles
1 (noun) A bridle is a set of straps round a horse's head and mouth, which the rider uses to control the horse.
2 (verb) If a person bridles, they show that they are offended by drawing back their head stiffly.

bridle path, bridle paths
(noun) A bridle path is a path for use by people riding horses.

bridleway, bridleways
(noun) A bridleway is the same as a bridle path.

brief, briefer, briefest; briefs, briefing, briefed
1 (adjective) Something that is brief lasts only a short time.
2 (verb) When you brief someone who is about to undertake a task, you give them all the necessary instructions and information about it.
3 (noun) A brief is a set of instructions about a task.
briefly (adverb).
[sense 1 from Old French *bref* meaning 'short'; sense 3 from Latin *breve* meaning 'summary']

Similar words: (sense 1) short, momentary, quick, fleeting, cursory

briefcase, briefcases
(noun) A briefcase is a small flat case for carrying papers.

briefing, briefings
(noun) A briefing is a meeting at which information and instructions are given.

brier another spelling of **briar**.

brigade, brigades
(noun) A brigade is an army unit consisting of three battalions.
[from Italian *brigare* meaning 'to fight']

brigadier, brigadiers (pronounced brig-ad-**ear**)
(noun) A brigadier is an army officer of the rank immediately above colonel.

brigand, brigands
(noun; a literary word) A brigand is an armed thief, especially one who robs travellers.
[from Old Italian *brigante* meaning 'fighter']

bright, brighter, brightest
1 (adjective) strong and noticeable, e.g. *a bright light... a bright colour.*
2 clever, e.g. *my brightest pupil... a bright idea.*
3 cheerful, e.g. *a bright smile.*
brightly (adverb), **brightness** (noun).

Similar words: (sense 1) bold, vivid, brilliant, dazzling

brighten, brightens, brightening, brightened
1 (verb) If something brightens, it becomes brighter, e.g. *The sky brightened.*
2 If someone brightens, they suddenly look happier.

brighten up
(phrasal verb) To brighten something up means to make it more attractive and cheerful, e.g. *These flowers will brighten up the garden.*

brilliant
1 (adjective) A brilliant light or colour is extremely bright.
2 A brilliant person is extremely clever.
3 A brilliant career is extremely successful.
brilliantly (adverb), **brilliance** (noun).
[from French *brillant* meaning 'shining']

brim, brims, brimming, brimmed
1 (noun) The brim of a hat is the wide part that sticks outwards at the bottom.
2 (phrase) If a container is filled **to the brim**, it is filled right to the top.
3 (verb) To brim with a liquid means to be full of it, e.g. *Her eyes brimmed with tears.*
[from Old Norse *barmr* meaning 'edge']

brine
(noun) Brine is salt water.
briny (adjective).

bring, brings, bringing, brought
1 (verb) If you bring something or someone with you when you go to a place, you take them with you, e.g. *Please bring your calculator to every lesson.*
2 To bring something to a particular state or condition means to cause it to be like that, e.g. *Printing brought the cost of books down.*
3 (phrase) If you **cannot bring yourself** to do something, you refuse to do it because you think it is wrong.

bring about
(phrasal verb) To bring something about means to cause it to happen, e.g. *Better working conditions might bring about a change in attitudes.*

bring off
(phrasal verb) If you bring off something difficult, you succeed in doing it.

bring out
1 (phrasal verb) To bring out a new product means to produce it and offer it for sale.
2 If something brings out a particular kind of behaviour, it causes it to occur, e.g. *These situations bring out the worst in everybody.*

bring up
1 (phrasal verb) To bring up children means to look after them while they grow up.
2 If you bring up a subject, you introduce it into the conversation, e.g. *Julia brought up the question of a replacement for Mrs Higgs.*

brink
(noun) If you are on the brink of something, you are just about to do it or to experience it.

brisk, brisker, briskest
1 (adjective) If someone's manner is brisk, it shows that they want to get things done quickly and efficiently.
2 A brisk action is done quickly and energetically, e.g. *I went for a brisk walk.*
briskly (adverb), **briskness** (noun).

bristle, bristles, bristling, bristled
1 (noun) Bristles are strong animal hairs used to make brushes.
2 (verb) If the hairs on an animal's body bristle, they rise up, because it is frightened.
bristly (adjective).

British
(adjective) belonging or relating to the United Kingdom of Great Britain and Northern Ireland.

British Isles
(noun) The British Isles are a group of islands in western Europe consisting of Great Britain, Ireland, the Isle of Man, Orkney, the Shetland Islands, the Channel Islands, and the other islands close to these.

Briton, Britons
(noun) A Briton is someone who comes from the United Kingdom of Great Britain and Northern Ireland.

brittle
(adjective) An object that is brittle is hard but breaks easily.
brittleness (noun).

broach, broaches, broaching, broached
(verb) When you broach a subject, you introduce it into a discussion.

broad, broader, broadest
1 (adjective) wide, e.g. *a broad avenue.*
2 having many different aspects or concerning many different people, e.g. *The syllabus is a broad one... The organization has a broad appeal.*
3 general rather than detailed, e.g. *He gave a broad outline of the project.*
4 If someone has a broad accent, the way that they speak makes it very clear where they come from, e.g. *She had a broad Yorkshire accent.*

broad bean, broad beans
(noun) Broad beans are light-green beans with thick flat edible seeds.

broadcast, broadcasts, broadcasting, broadcast or broadcasted
1 (verb) To broadcast something means to send it out by radio waves, so that it can be seen on television or heard on radio.
2 (noun) A broadcast is a programme or announcement on radio or television.
broadcaster (noun), **broadcasting** (noun).

broaden, broadens, broadening, broadened
1 (verb) When something broadens, it becomes wider, e.g. *Further on, the stream broadened.*
2 To broaden something means to cause it to involve more things or concern more people, e.g. *We must broaden the scope of the campaign.*
3 If an experience broadens your mind, it gives you a better understanding of other people, e.g. *Travel broadens the mind.*

broadly
1 (adverb) true to a large extent or in most cases, e.g. *I was broadly in favour of the suggestion... This is, broadly speaking, the best way of pruning roses.*
2 If you smile broadly, you smile with your mouth stretched wide.

broad-minded
(adjective) Someone who is broad-minded is tolerant of behaviour that other people may find upsetting or immoral.

Similar words: liberal, open-minded, tolerant, permissive

brocade
(noun) Brocade is a thick, expensive material, often made of silk, with a raised pattern.
[from Spanish *brocado* meaning 'embossed fabric']

broccoli
(noun) Broccoli is a vegetable with green stalks and green or purple flower buds.
[an Italian word meaning 'little sprouts']

brochure, brochures (pronounced broh-sher)
(noun) A brochure is a booklet with pictures in it which gives information about a product or service.
[from French *brocher* meaning 'to bind books']

brogue, brogues (pronounced broag)
1 (noun) A brogue is a strong accent, especially an Irish one.
2 Brogues are thick leather shoes.
[from Irish Gaelic *brog* meaning 'boot' or 'shoe']

broke
1 the past tense of **break**.
2 (adjective; an informal use) If you are broke, you have no money.

Similar words: (sense 2) bankrupt, insolvent, penniless

broken the past participle of **break**.

broker, brokers
(noun) A broker is a person whose job is to buy and sell shares for other people.
[from Anglo-French *brocour* meaning 'wine-seller']

brolly, brollies
(noun; an informal word) A brolly is an umbrella.

bromine
(noun) Bromine is a heavy, corrosive liquid element used in fumigants and dyes. Its atomic number is 35 and its symbol is Br.

bronchial tube, bronchial tubes
(noun) Your bronchial tubes are the two tubes which connect your windpipe to your lungs. [from Greek *bronkhus* meaning 'windpipe']

bronchitis
(noun) Bronchitis is an illness in which your bronchial tubes become infected, making you cough.

brontosaurus, brontosauruses
(noun) A brontosaurus was a type of very large, four-footed, herbivorous dinosaur, with a long neck and a long tail.

bronze
(noun) Bronze is a yellowish-brown metal which is a mixture of copper and tin; also the yellowish-brown colour of this metal.

bronzed
(adjective) attractively sun tanned.

brooch, brooches (rhymes with **coach**)
(noun) A brooch is a piece of jewellery with a pin at the back for attaching to a dress or blouse. [from Old French *broche* meaning 'long needle']

brood, broods, brooding, brooded
1 (noun) A brood is a family of baby birds.
2 (verb) If you brood about something, you keep thinking about it in a serious or unhappy way.

brook, brooks
(noun) A brook is a stream.

broom, brooms
1 (noun) A broom is a long-handled brush.
2 Broom is a shrub with yellow flowers.

broomstick, broomsticks
(noun) A broomstick is the handle of a broom.

broth
(noun) Broth is soup, usually with vegetables in it.

brothel, brothels
(noun) A brothel is a house where men pay to have sex with prostitutes.

brother, brothers
(noun) Your brother is a boy or man who has the same parents as you.
brotherly (adjective).

brotherhood, brotherhoods
1 (noun) Brotherhood is the affection and loyalty that brothers or close male friends feel for each other.
2 A brotherhood is an organization or group of men with common interests, jobs, or beliefs.

brother-in-law, brothers-in-law
(noun) Someone's brother-in-law is the brother of their husband or wife, or their sister's husband.

brought the past tense and past participle of **bring**.

brow, brows
1 (noun) Your brow is your forehead.
2 Your brows are your eyebrows.
3 The brow of a hill is the top of it.

browbeat, browbeats, browbeating, browbeaten
(verb) If someone is browbeating you, they are trying in a persistent or unpleasant way to persuade you to do something.

brown, browner, brownest
(adjective and noun) Brown is the colour of earth or wood.

browned off
(adjective; an informal use) Someone who is browned off is feeling fed up.

brownie, brownies
(noun) A brownie is a junior member of the Girl Guides.

browse, browses, browsing, browsed
1 (verb) If you browse through a book, you look through it in a casual way.
2 If you browse in a shop, you look at the things in it for interest rather than because you want to buy something.
3 When animals such as deer are browsing, they are nibbling at the young shoots and leaves of trees.
[sense 3 from French *broust* meaning 'bud' or 'young shoot']

bruise, bruises, bruising, bruised
1 (noun) A bruise is a purple mark that appears on your skin after something has hit it.
2 (verb) If something bruises you, it hits you so that a bruise appears on your skin.
[from Old English *brysan* meaning 'to crush']

brunette, brunettes
(noun) A brunette is a girl or woman with dark brown hair.
[from French *brunet* meaning 'dark' or 'brownish']

brunt
(phrase) If you **bear the brunt** of something unpleasant, you are the person who suffers most, e.g. *The infantry bore the brunt of the attack.*

brush, brushes, brushing, brushed
1 (noun) A brush is an object with bristles which you use for cleaning things, painting, or tidying your hair.
2 (verb) If you brush something, you clean it or tidy it with a brush.
3 To brush against something means to touch it while passing it, e.g. *Her hair brushed his cheek.*

brush up
(phrasal verb) If you brush up on a subject, you improve your knowledge of it, e.g. *They need to brush up their French.*

brusque (pronounced **broosk**)
(adjective) Someone who is brusque deals with people quickly and without considering their feelings.
brusquely (adverb), **brusqueness** (noun).
[a French word, originally from Italian *brusco* meaning 'rough']

brussels sprout, brussels sprouts
(noun) Brussels sprouts are vegetables that look like tiny cabbages.

brutal
(adjective) Brutal behaviour is cruel and violent, e.g. *their brutal treatment of prisoners.*
brutally (adverb), **brutality** (noun).

brute, brutes
1 (noun) A man who is a brute is rough and insensitive.
2 A brute is also a large animal.
3 (adjective) Brute force is strength alone, without any skill, e.g. *He had to use brute force to break the door open.*
brutish (adjective).
[from Latin *brutus* meaning 'heavy' or 'stupid']

BSc, BScs
(noun) A BSc is a university degree in a science subject; also used to refer to someone who has such a degree. BSc is an abbreviation for 'Bachelor of Science'.

BST an abbreviation for **British Summer Time.**

bubble, bubbles, bubbling, bubbled
1 (noun) A bubble is a ball of air in a liquid.
2 A bubble is also a hollow, delicate ball of soapy liquid floating on the surface of a liquid or in the air.
3 (verb) When a liquid bubbles, bubbles form in it.
4 If you are bubbling with something like excitement, you are full of it.
bubbly (adjective).

bubonic plague (pronounced byoo-**bon**-ik)
(noun) Bubonic plague is a disease transmitted by fleas on rats. Until a cure was discovered in the 19th century, it was a widespread cause of epidemics and death. Swellings, called buboes, appeared in the armpits and groin of people who caught it.
[from Greek *boubon* meaning 'groin']

buccaneer, buccaneers
(noun; a literary word) Buccaneers were French or English pirates who attacked Spanish shipping in the West Indies in the 17th and 18th centuries.
[from French *boucan* meaning 'framework on which meat is smoked'; hunters who lived on smoked meat later became pirates]

buck, bucks, bucking, bucked
1 (noun) A buck is the male of various animals, including the deer and the rabbit.
2 (verb) If a horse bucks, it jumps straight up in the air with all four feet off the ground.
3 (informal phrase) If you **pass the buck**, you pass the responsibility for something to someone else.
[from Old English *bucca* meaning 'male goat']

bucket, buckets
(noun) A bucket is a cylindrical metal or plastic container with a handle.

buckle, buckles, buckling, buckled
1 (noun) A buckle is a fastening on the end of a belt or strap.

2 (verb) If you buckle a belt or strap, you fasten it.
3 If something buckles, it becomes bent because of severe heat or pressure.
[from Latin *buccula* meaning 'helmet strap']

bucolic
(adjective; a literary word) relating to the countryside or country life.
[from Greek *boukolos* meaning 'cowherd']

bud, buds, budding, budded
1 (noun) A bud is a small, tight swelling on a tree or plant, consisting of overlapping undeveloped petals or leaves which develop into a flower or a cluster of leaves.
2 (verb) When a tree or plant buds, new buds appear on it.
3 (phrase) To **nip something in the bud** means to put an end to it at an early stage.

Buddhism
(noun) Buddhism is an Eastern religion which teaches that the way to end suffering is by overcoming your desires. It was founded in the 6th century BC by the Buddha (a title meaning 'the enlightened one'), Gautama Siddhartha, a nobleman and religious teacher of northern India.
Buddhist (noun and adjective).

budding
(adjective) just beginning to develop, e.g. *a budding poet.*

buddleia, buddleias (pronounced **bud**-lee-a)
(noun) A buddleia is a bush with scented mauve or yellow flowers, which attract butterflies. Buddleia is named after A. Buddle, an 18th century botanist.

budge, budges, budging, budged
(verb) If something will not budge, you cannot move it.

budgerigar, budgerigars
(noun) A budgerigar is a small brightly coloured pet bird. Budgerigars originated in Australia.
[an Australian Aboriginal name, from *budgeri* + *gar* meaning 'good cockatoo']

budget, budgets, budgeting, budgeted
1 (noun) A budget is a plan showing how much money will be available in a given period, usually a year, and how it will be spent.
2 (verb) If you budget for something, you plan your money carefully, so as to be able to afford it.
3 (adjective) cheap, e.g. *budget prices... budget travel.*
budgetary (adjective).
[from Old French *bougette* meaning 'small leather bag']

budgie, budgies
(noun; an informal word) A budgie is a budgerigar.

buff, buffs
1 (adjective) a pale brown colour.
2 (noun; an informal use) A buff is someone who knows a lot about a subject, e.g. *a film buff.*

buffalo, buffaloes
1 (noun) A buffalo is a wild animal of Africa, like a large cow with long curved horns.
2 Buffalo is also another name for the American bison.
[from Greek *boubalos* meaning 'wild ox']

buffer, buffers
(noun) Buffers on a train or at the end of a railway line are metal discs on springs that reduce shock when they are hit.

buffet, buffets (pronounced **boof**-ay)
1 (noun) A buffet is a cafe at a station.
2 A buffet is also a cold meal at a party or public occasion.
[a French word meaning 'sideboard']

buffet, buffets, buffeting, buffeted (pronounced **buff**-it)
(verb) If the wind or sea buffets a place or person, it strikes them violently and repeatedly.
[from Old French *buffet* meaning 'light blow']

buffoon, buffoons
(noun) A buffoon is someone who says or does silly things.
[from Italian *buffare* meaning 'to puff out the cheeks']

bug, bugs, bugging, bugged
1 (noun) A bug is an insect, especially one that infests dirty houses.
2 A bug in a computer program is a small error which means that the program will not work properly.
3 (an informal use) A bug is also a virus or minor infection, e.g. *I've got a stomach bug.*
4 (verb) If a place is bugged, tiny microphones are hidden there to pick up what people are saying.

Similar words: (sense 3) germ, virus, infection

bugle, bugles
(noun) A bugle is a simple brass instrument that looks like a small trumpet.
bugler (noun).

build, builds, building, built
1 (verb) To build something such as a house or a bridge means to make it from its parts.
2 To build something such as an organization means to form it gradually.
3 To build on something means to base new developments on it, e.g. *an economy built on tourism.*
4 (noun) Your build is the shape of your body.
builder (noun).

Similar words: (sense 1) construct, erect, assemble

build up
(phrasal verb) If something builds up, more and more gradually accumulates, e.g. *Mud had built up in the lake.*

building, buildings
(noun) A building is a structure with walls and a roof.

building society, building societies
(noun) A building society is an organization in which some people invest their money, while others borrow from it to buy a house.

build-up, build-ups
(noun) A build-up is a gradual increase in something, e.g. *a build-up of nuclear weapons.*

built-up
(adjective) A built-up area is one where there are many buildings.

bulb, bulbs
1 (noun) A bulb is the glass part of an electric lamp.
2 A bulb is also an onion-shaped root that grows into a flower or plant.
[from Greek *bolbos* meaning 'onion']

bulbous
(adjective) round and fat in an ugly way, e.g. *his bulbous nose.*

Bulgarian, Bulgarians
1 (adjective) belonging or relating to Bulgaria.
2 (noun) A Bulgarian is someone who comes from Bulgaria.
3 Bulgarian is the main language spoken in Bulgaria.

bulge, bulges, bulging, bulged
1 (verb) If something bulges, it sticks out from a surface.
2 (noun) A bulge is a lump on a normally flat surface.

bulk, bulks
1 (noun) A bulk is a large mass of something, e.g. *the dark bulk of the building.*
2 The bulk of something is most of it, e.g. *The bulk of the population are poor and illiterate.*
3 (phrase) To buy something in bulk means to buy it in large quantities.
[from Old Norse *bulki* meaning 'cargo']

bulky, bulkier, bulkiest
(adjective) large and heavy, e.g. *a bulky load.*

Similar words: cumbersome, unwieldy

bull, bulls
(noun) A bull is the male of some species of animals, including domestic cattle, elephants, seals, and whales.

bulldog, bulldogs
(noun) A bulldog is a dog with a large square head and short hair.

bulldozer, bulldozers
(noun) A bulldozer is a large, powerful tractor with a broad blade in front, which is used for moving earth or knocking things down.

bullet, bullets
(noun) A bullet is a small piece of metal fired from a gun.
[from French *boulette* meaning 'small ball']

bulletin, bulletins
1 (noun) A bulletin is a short news report on radio or television.
2 A bulletin is also a leaflet or small newspaper regularly produced by a group or organization.
[from Italian *bulletino* meaning 'small Papal edict']

bullfight, bullfights
(noun) A bullfight is a public entertainment, popular in Spain, in which a man makes a bull angry so that it rushes at him until it is exhausted, and then he kills it with a sword.
bullfighter (noun), **bullfighting** (noun).

bullfinch, bullfinches
(noun) A bullfinch is a small bird with a short bill and a black head. The male has a red breast. Bullfinches often damage fruit trees by eating the buds.

bullion
(noun) Bullion is gold or silver in the form of lumps or bars.
[from Old French *bouillir* meaning 'to boil'; metals are refined by being heated]

bullock, bullocks
(noun) A bullock is a young castrated bull.

bull's-eye, bull's-eyes
(noun) A bull's-eye is the small circular area at the centre of a target, which people aim at when shooting.

bully, bullies, bullying, bullied
1 (noun) A bully is someone who uses their strength or power to hurt or frighten other people.
2 (verb) If someone bullies you into doing something, they make you do it by using force or threats.
[a 16th century word meaning 'fine fellow' or 'hired ruffian']

bulrush, bulrushes
(noun) Bulrushes are tall, stiff reeds that grow on the edges of rivers.

bulwark, bulwarks
1 (noun) A bulwark is a large mound or barricade built in order to protect people.
2 A bulwark is also anything that protects you from something unpleasant, e.g. *I saw my savings as a bulwark against unemployment.*

bumblebee, bumblebees
(noun) A bumblebee is a large hairy bee.

bump, bumps, bumping, bumped
1 (verb) If you bump into something, you knock into it with a jolt.
2 (noun) A bump is a soft or dull noise made by something knocking into something else.
3 A bump on a surface is a raised, uneven part.
bumpy (adjective).

Similar words: (sense 3) lump, hump, bulge, protuberance

---

bump off
(phrasal verb; an informal use) To bump someone off means to kill them.

bumper, bumpers
1 (noun) Bumpers are bars on the front and back of a vehicle which protect it if there is a collision.
2 (adjective) A bumper crop or harvest is larger than usual.

bumpkin, bumpkins
(noun) A bumpkin is a country person who is considered to be stupid or ignorant.

bumptious
(adjective) Bumptious people are always expressing their own opinions and ideas in a self-important way.
bumptiousness (noun).

bun, buns
(noun) A bun is a small, round cake.

bunch, bunches, bunching, bunched
1 (noun) A bunch of people or things is a group of them.
2 A bunch of flowers is a number of them held or tied together.
3 A bunch of bananas or grapes is a group of them growing on the same stem.
4 (verb) When people bunch together or bunch up, they stay very close to each other.

bundle, bundles, bundling, bundled
1 (noun) A bundle is a number of things tied together or wrapped up in a cloth.
2 (verb) If you bundle someone or something somewhere, you push them there quickly and roughly, e.g. *They bundled him into an ambulance.*

bung, bungs, bunging, bunged
1 (noun) A bung is a piece of wood, cork, or rubber used to close a hole in something such as a barrel.
2 (verb; an informal use) If you bung something somewhere, you put it there quickly and carelessly.

bungalow, bungalows
(noun) A bungalow is a one-storeyed house.
[from Hindi *bangla* meaning 'house']

bunged up
(adjective; an informal use) If a hole is bunged up, it is blocked.

bungle, bungles, bungling, bungled
(verb) To bungle something means to make mistakes and fail to do it properly.
bungler (noun).

bunion, bunions
(noun) A bunion is a painful lump on the first joint of a person's big toe.

bunk, bunks
1 (noun) A bunk is a bed fixed to a wall in a ship or caravan.
2 (an informal use) If you describe something written or spoken as bunk, you mean it is silly or untrue.
3 (phrase; an informal use) If someone **does a bunk**, they leave a place without telling anyone.

bunker, bunkers
1 (noun) On a golf course, a bunker is a large hole filled with sand.
2 A coal bunker is a storage place for coal.
3 A bunker is also an underground shelter with strong walls to protect it from bombing and gunfire.

Bunsen burner, Bunsen burners
(noun) A Bunsen burner is a kind of gas burner used in scientific laboratories. It was invented by R.W. von Bunsen (1811-99), a German scientist.

bunting
(noun) Bunting is a series of rows of small coloured flags displayed on streets and buildings on special occasions.

buoy, buoys, buoying, buoyed (pronounced boy)
(noun) A buoy is a floating object anchored to the bottom of the sea, marking a channel or warning of an obstruction.

buoy up
(phrasal verb) To buoy someone up means to keep them cheerful in a difficult situation.

buoyant
1 (adjective) able to float.
2 lively and cheerful, e.g. *She's in a buoyant mood.*
buoyancy (noun).
[from Spanish *boyar* meaning 'to float']

burble, burbles, burbling, burbled
(verb) To burble means to makes an indistinct, continuous bubbling sound.

burden, burdens
1 (noun) A burden is a heavy load.
2 If something is a burden to you, it causes you a lot of worry or hard work.
burdensome (adjective).
[from Old English *byrthen* meaning 'load' or 'weight']

Similar words: (sense 1) encumbrance, weight (sense 2) load, encumbrance, onus, weight, millstone

bureau, bureaux (pronounced byoo-roh)
1 (noun) A bureau is a writing desk with shelves and drawers.
2 A bureau is also an office that provides a service, e.g. *a travel bureau.*
[a French word meaning 'desk' or 'office']

bureaucracy
(noun) Bureaucracy is the complex system of rules and routine procedures which operate in government departments.
bureaucratic (adjective).
[from French *bureau* meaning 'office' and Greek *kratos* meaning 'power']

Similar words: red tape, officialdom

bureaucrat, bureaucrats
(noun) A bureaucrat is a person who works in a government department, especially one who is excessively concerned with rules and procedures.

burgeon, burgeons, burgeoning, burgeoned
(verb; a literary word) To burgeon means to grow or develop rapidly, e.g. *a burgeoning manufacturing industry.*

burglar, burglars
(noun) A burglar is a thief who breaks into a building.
burglary (noun).

burgle, burgles, burgling, burgled
(verb) If your house is burgled, someone breaks into it and steals things.

burial, burials
(noun) A burial is a ceremony held when a dead person is buried.
[from Old English *byrgels* meaning 'tomb']

burlesque, burlesques (pronounced burl-esk)
(noun) A burlesque is a piece of writing or acting that caricatures or satirizes something serious.
[from Italian *burla* meaning 'jest' or 'nonsense']

burly, burlier, burliest
(adjective) A burly man has a broad body and strong muscles.
[from Middle English *borli* meaning 'stately' or 'imposing']

Similar words: beefy, brawny

Burmese (pronounced bur-meez)
1 (adjective) belonging or relating to Burma.
2 (noun) A Burmese is someone who comes from Burma.
3 Burmese is the main language spoken in Burma.

burn, burns, burning, burned or burnt
1 (verb) If something is burning, it is on fire.
2 To burn something means to destroy it with fire.
3 If you burn yourself or are burned, you are injured by fire or by something hot.
4 If you are burning with emotion, you feel it very strongly, e.g. *She was burning with indignation.*
5 (noun) A burn is an injury caused by fire or by something hot.

Similar words: (sense 1) blaze, flame (sense 2) incinerate

burnish, burnishes, burnishing, burnished
(verb) To burnish metal means to polish it until it shines.
[from Old french *brunir* meaning 'to make brown']

burp, burps, burping, burped
1 (verb) If you burp, you make a noise because air from your stomach has been forced up through your throat.
2 (noun) A burp is the noise that you make when you burp.

burrow, burrows, burrowing, burrowed
1 (noun) A burrow is a tunnel or hole in the ground dug by a rabbit or other small animal.
2 (verb) When an animal burrows, it digs a burrow.

bursar, bursars
(noun) A bursar is a person who manages the finances of a school or college.
[from Latin *bursa* meaning 'purse']

bursary, bursaries
(noun) A bursary is a sum of money given to someone to enable them to study in a college or university.

burst, bursts, bursting, burst
1 (verb) When something bursts, it splits open because of pressure from inside it.
2 If you burst into a room, you enter it suddenly.
3 To burst means to happen or come suddenly

and with force, e.g. *Mrs Campbell burst into tears... a blinding flash burst down out of the sky.*
4 (an informal use) If you are bursting with something, you find it difficult to keep it to yourself, e.g. *She was bursting with the news.*
5 (noun) A burst of something is a short period of it, e.g. *a burst of speed... a burst of rifle fire.*

Similar words: (sense 5) outbreak, spurt, spate

bury, buries, burying, buried
1 (verb) When a dead person is buried, their body is put into a grave and covered with earth.
2 To bury something means to put it in a hole in the ground and cover it up.
3 If you are buried under something, you are covered by it, e.g. *People were buried under the rubble.*
4 If you bury yourself in something, you concentrate hard on it, e.g. *He buried himself in his work.*

bus, buses
(noun) A bus is a large motor vehicle that carries passengers.
[from Latin *omnibus* meaning 'for all'; buses were originally called omnibuses]

bush, bushes
1 (noun) A bush is a large plant with many stems branching out from ground level.
2 The wild, uncultivated parts of some hot countries are referred to as the bush.

Bushman, Bushmen
1 (noun) A Bushman is a member of a group of people in southern Africa who live by hunting and gathering food.
2 Bushman is the language spoken by Bushmen.

bushy, bushier, bushiest
(adjective) Bushy hair or fur grows very thickly, e.g. *bushy eyebrows... a bushy tail.*

business, businesses
1 (noun) A business is an organization which produces or sells goods or provides a service.
2 Business is work relating to the buying and selling of goods and services.
3 You can refer to any event, situation, or activity as a business, e.g. *This whole business has upset me... She got down to the business of clearing up.*
4 (phrase) If a company goes **out of business**, it stops trading because it is not making any money.
5 If you say that someone **has no business** to do something, you mean that they have no right to do it.
businessman (noun), **businesswoman** (noun).
[from Old English *bisignis* meaning 'attentiveness' or 'diligence']

Similar words: (sense 1) company, enterprise, concern, firm

businesslike
(adjective) dealing wih things in an efficient way.

busker, buskers
(noun) A busker is someone who plays music or

sings for money in the street or in some other public place.

bust, busts, busting, bust or busted
1 (noun) A bust is a statue of someone's head and shoulders, e.g. *a bust of Shakespeare.*
2 A woman's bust is her chest and her breasts.
3 (verb; an informal use) If you bust something, you break it.
4 (adjective; an informal use) broken, e.g. *The TV's bust.*
5 (an informal use) If a business goes bust, it becomes bankrupt and closes down.
[sense 1 from Italian *busto* meaning 'sculpture']

bustle, bustles, bustling, bustled
1 (verb) When people bustle, they move in a busy, hurried way.
2 (noun) Bustle is busy, noisy activity, e.g. *the bustle of the airport.*
[from *buskle* meaning 'to prepare energetically']

Similar words: (sense 2) hurly-burly, activity, flurry

busy, busier, busiest; busies, busying, busied
1 (adjective) If you are busy, you are in the middle of doing something and are not free to do something else.
2 A busy place is full of people doing things or moving about, e.g. *a busy office.*
3 (verb) If you busy yourself with something, you occupy yourself by doing it.
busily (adverb).
[from Old English *bisig* meaning 'busy']

Similar words: (sense 1) employed, engaged, occupied

busybody, busybodies
(noun) A busybody is someone who interferes in other people's affairs.

but
1 (conjunction) used to contrast what you say next with what you have just said, e.g. *We were poor, but we were happy.*
2 used when apologizing, e.g. *I'm sorry, but I can't come tonight.*
3 except, e.g. *You do nothing but complain.*
4 (phrase) **But for** means 'If it had not been for', e.g. *But for your help, we would not be here.*
5 (adverb; an old-fashioned use) only, nothing better than, e.g. *We are but poor pilgrims.*
[from Old English *butan* meaning 'without' or 'except']

butcher, butchers
(noun) A butcher is a shopkeeper who sells meat.
[from Old French *bouchier* meaning 'butcher']

butler, butlers
(noun) A butler is the chief male servant in a rich household.
[from Old French *bouteillier* meaning 'person who deals with bottles']

butt, butts, butting, butted
1 (noun) The butt of a weapon is the thick end of its handle.
2 A butt is also a large barrel.
3 If you are the butt of teasing or criticism, people keep teasing or criticizing you.

4 (verb) If you butt something, you ram it with
your head.
[sense 1 from *butt* meaning 'buttock'; sense 2
from Old French *botte* meaning 'cask'; sense 3
from Old French *ut* meaning 'target'; sense 4
from Old French *boter* meaning 'to strike']

butt in
(phrasal verb) If you butt in, you join in a
private conversation or activity without being
asked to.

butter, butters, buttering, buttered
1 (noun) Butter is a yellowish substance made
from cream, which is spread on bread and used
in cooking.
2 (verb) To butter bread means to spread butter
on it.

buttercup, buttercups
(noun) A buttercup is a wild plant with bright
yellow flowers.

butterfly, butterflies
1 (noun) A butterfly is a type of insect with large
colourful wings and a thin body.
2 Butterfly is a swimming stroke in which you lie
on your front and bring both arms together over
your head.

buttocks
(plural noun) Your buttocks are the part of your
body that you sit on.
[from Old English *buttuc* meaning 'rounded
slope']

button, buttons, buttoning, buttoned
1 (noun) Buttons are small, hard objects sewn on
to a piece of clothing, used to fasten it.
2 (verb) If you button a piece of clothing, you
fasten it using its buttons.
3 (noun) A button is also a small object on a piece
of equipment that you press to operate the
equipment.

**buttonhole, buttonholes, buttonholing,
buttonholed**
1 (noun) A buttonhole is a hole that you push a
button through to fasten a piece of clothing.
2 A buttonhole is also a flower worn in your
lapel.
3 (verb) If you buttonhole someone, you stop
them and make them listen to you.

buttress, buttresses, buttressing, buttressed
1 (noun) A buttress is one of a set of stone or
brick supports for a wall.
2 (verb) To buttress a wall means to support it
with a buttress.

buxom
(adjective) A buxom woman is large, healthy,
and attractive.

buy, buys, buying, bought
(verb) If you buy something, you obtain it by
paying for it.
buyer (noun).

buzz, buzzes, buzzing, buzzed
1 (verb) If something buzzes, it makes a
continuous humming sound, like a bumblebee.

2 (noun) A buzz is the sound something makes
when it buzzes.

Similar words: drone, hum

buzzard, buzzards
(noun) A buzzard is a large brown and white bird
of prey with broad rounded wings.

buzzer, buzzers
(noun) A buzzer is a device that makes a buzzing
sound, to attract attention.

by
1 (preposition and adverb) going past, e.g. *We
drove by his house... She laughed as we ran by.*
2 (preposition) located next to, e.g. *I sat by her
bed.*
3 before a particular time, e.g. *I want these
finished by Monday.*
4 used to indicate who or what has done
something, e.g. *a new novel by Kingsley Amis...
written by a computer.*
5 used to indicate how something is done, e.g. *He
earned some money by selling souvenirs... I
always go home by bus.*
6 also used to give the measurements of a
rectangular area, e.g. *The room is sixteen feet by
twelve.*
7 used when talking about amounts or
quantities, e.g. *Our grant was cut by 20 per cent.*
8 (phrase) If you are **by yourself**, you are alone.
If you do something **by yourself**, you do it
without help from anyone else.

by-election, by-elections
(noun) A by-election is an election held to choose
a new member of parliament after the previous
member has resigned or died.

bygone
(adjective; a literary word) happening or
existing a long time ago, e.g. *empires established
in bygone centuries.*

by-law, by-laws
(noun) A by-law is a law passed by a local
authority, which applies only in its area.

bypass, bypasses
(noun) A bypass is a main road which takes
traffic round a town rather than through it.

by-product, by-products
(noun) A by-product is something which is
created during the manufacture of something
else.

bystander, bystanders
(noun) A bystander is someone who sees
something happen but does not take part in it.

byte, bytes
(noun) A byte is a unit of storage in a computer,
often representing a single letter or figure.

byword, bywords
(noun) Someone or something that is a byword
for a quality is well known as having that
quality, e.g. *The regime had become a byword
for repression and cruelty.*

C

cab, cabs
1 (noun) A cab is a taxi.
2 In a lorry, bus, or train, the cab is where the driver sits.
[from French *cabriolet* meaning 'light two-wheeled carriage'. Cabs were originally horse-drawn]

cabal, cabals
(noun) A cabal is a small group of people who meet secretly for political reasons.

cabaret, cabarets (pronounced **kab**-bar-ray)
(noun) A cabaret is an entertainment performed in restaurants or nightclubs, consisting of dancing, singing, or comedy acts.
[from French *cabaret* meaning 'tavern']

cabbage, cabbages
(noun) A cabbage is a large green leafy vegetable.
[from Norman French *cabache* meaning 'head']

cabin, cabins
1 (noun) A cabin is a room in a ship where a passenger sleeps.
2 In a plane, the cabin is the area where the passengers or the crew sit.
3 A cabin is also a small house, usually in the country and often made of wood.
[from Latin *capanna* meaning 'hut']

cabinet, cabinets
1 (noun) A cabinet is a small cupboard.
2 The cabinet in a government is a group of ministers who advise the leader and decide policies.

cable, cables, cabling, cabled
1 (noun) A cable is a strong, thick rope or chain.
2 An electric cable is a bundle of wires with a rubber covering, which carries electricity.
3 A cable is also a message sent abroad by means of electricity.
4 (verb) If you cable someone, you send them a message or money by cable.
[from Latin *capulum* meaning 'horse's halter']

cable car, cable cars
(noun) A cable car is a vehicle pulled by a moving cable, for taking people up mountains.

cable television
(noun) Cable television is a special television service which people receive by cable from a central receiver.

cacao (pronounced ka-**kah**-oh)
(noun) A cacao is a type of small tropical evergreen tree, whose berries are used to produce chocolate and cocoa.

cache, caches (pronounced **kash**)
(noun) A cache is a store of things hidden away, e.g. *a cache of weapons*.
[from French *cacher* meaning 'to hide']

cachet (pronounced **kash**-shay)
(noun; a formal word) Cachet is a quality of distinction and prestige, e.g. *My visit to*

Hollywood had given me a certain cachet in her eyes.

cackle, cackles, cackling, cackled
1 (verb) If you cackle, you laugh harshly.
2 (noun) A cackle is a harsh triumphant laugh.
3 (verb) When hens cackle, they make a shrill broken squawking noise after laying an egg.

cacophony (pronounced kak-**koff**-fon-nee)
(noun; a formal word) A cacophony is a loud, unpleasant noise, e.g. *a cacophony of laughter*.
cacophonous (adjective).
[from Greek *kakos* + *phōnē* meaning 'bad sound']

cactus, cacti or cactuses
(noun) A cactus is a thick, fleshy plant that grows in deserts and is usually covered in spikes.

cad, cads
(noun; an old-fashioned word) If you describe a man as a cad, you mean that he treats people badly and unfairly.

cadaverous (pronounced kad-**dav**-russ)
(adjective; a formal word) pale, thin, and unhealthy, e.g. *a cadaverous young man*.
[from *cadaver*, an old word meaning 'corpse']

caddie, caddies; also spelled **caddy**
1 (noun) A caddie is a person who carries golf clubs for a golf player.
2 A tea caddy is a box or tin for keeping tea in.
[sense 1 is from French *cadet* meaning 'junior officer']

cadence, cadences
1 (noun) The cadence of someone's voice is the way it goes up and down as they speak.
2 In music, a cadence is a group of chords at the end of a phrase.

cadenza, cadenzas (pronounced kad-**den**-za)
(noun) In a piece of orchestral music, a cadenza is an elaborate solo passage for a solo instrument.

cadet, cadets
(noun) A cadet is a young person being trained in the army, navy, air force, or police.

cadge, cadges, cadging, cadged
(verb) If you cadge something off someone, you get it from them and don't give them anything in return, e.g. *He lived by cadging money off relatives*.
cadger (noun).

cadmium
(noun) Cadmium is a soft, bluish-white metallic element. It is used in electroplating, alloys, and as a neutron absorber in the control of nuclear fission. Its atomic number is 48 and its symbol is Cd.

caesarean, caesareans (pronounced siz-**air**-ee-an); also spelled **caesarian** and **cesarean** or **cesarian**
(noun) A caesarean or caesarean section is an operation in which a baby is lifted out of a

woman's womb through an opening cut in her abdomen.

caesium or **cesium**
(noun) Caesium is a silvery-white metallic element, used in photocells and in radiotherapy. Its atomic number is 55 and its symbol is Cs.

caesura, caesuras or **caesurae** (pronounced siz-**yoor**-ra)
(noun) A caesura is a pause in a line of poetry.
[from Latin *caesus* meaning 'cut']

cafe, cafes (pronounced **kaf**-fay)
(noun) A cafe is a place where you can buy light meals, snacks, and drinks.

cafeteria, cafeterias (pronounced kaf-fit-**ee**-ree-ya)
(noun) A cafeteria is a restaurant where you serve yourself.

caffeine or **caffein** (pronounced **kaf**-feen)
(noun) Caffeine is a chemical stimulant found in coffee, tea, and cocoa, which makes you more active and keeps you awake.

caftan another spelling of **kaftan**.

cage, cages
(noun) A cage is a boxlike structure made of wire or bars in which birds or animals are kept.
caged (adjective).
[from Latin *cavea* meaning 'enclosure']

cagey, cagier, cagiest (pronounced **kay**-jee)
(adjective; an informal word) cautious and not direct or open, e.g. *He's being very cagey about the whole affair.*
cagily (adverb), **caginess** (noun).

cagoule, cagoules (pronounced ka-**gool**)
(noun) A cagoule is a lightweight waterproof jacket with a hood.

cahoots
(phrase; an informal use) If you are **in cahoots** with someone, you are working closely with them on a secret plan.

cairn, cairns
(noun) A cairn is a pile of stones built as a memorial or a landmark.
[from Gaelic *carn* meaning 'heap of stones' or 'hill']

cajole, cajoles, cajoling, cajoled
(verb) If you cajole someone into doing something, you persuade them to do it by saying nice things to them.
[from French *cajoler* meaning 'to coax']

cake, cakes, caking, caked
1 (noun) A cake is a sweet food made by baking flour, eggs, fat, and sugar.
2 A cake of a hard substance such as soap is a block of it.
3 (verb) If something cakes or is caked, it forms or becomes covered with a solid layer, e.g. *His shoes were caked with mud.*
[from Old Norse *kaka* meaning 'oatcake']

calamity, calamities
(noun) A calamity is an event that causes disaster or distress.
calamitous (adjective).
[from Latin *calamitas* meaning 'injury']

calcium (pronounced **kal**-see-um)
(noun) Calcium is a soft white element found in bones and teeth. Its atomic number is 20 and its symbol is Ca.
[from Latin *calx* meaning 'lime']

calculate, calculates, calculating, calculated
1 (verb) If you calculate something, you work it out, usually by doing some arithmetic, e.g. *Calculate the total number of votes.*
2 If something is calculated, it is deliberately planned to have a particular effect, e.g. *His attitude was calculated to discourage familiarity.*
calculation (noun).
[from Latin *calculus* meaning 'stone' or 'pebble'. The Romans used pebbles to count with]

calculating
(adjective) carefully planning situations to get what you want, e.g. *a cold, calculating criminal.*

calculator, calculators
(noun) A calculator is a small electronic machine used for doing mathematical calculations.

calculus
(noun) Calculus is a branch of mathematics concerned with variable quantities.

calendar, calendars
1 (noun) A calendar is a chart showing the date of each day in a particular year.
2 A particular calendar is a system of dividing time into fixed periods of days, months, and years, e.g. *the Muslim calendar.*
[from Latin *kalendae*, the day of the month on which interest on debts was due]

calf, calves
1 (noun) A calf is a young cow, elephant, giraffe, buffalo, whale, or seal.
2 Your calf is the thick part at the back of your leg below your knee.
[sense 1 from Old English *cælf*; sense 2 from Old Norse *kalfi*]

calibrate, calibrates, calibrating, calibrated
(verb) To calibrate an instrument means to mark it or adjust it so that it measures something accurately.
calibrated (adjective), **calibration** (noun).

calibre, calibres (pronounced **kal**-lib-ber)
1 (noun) A person's calibre is their ability or intelligence, e.g. *a director of high calibre.*
2 The calibre of a gun is the width of the inside of the barrel of the gun.
[from Arabic *qalib* meaning 'cobbler's last']

calico
(noun) Calico is a plain white cotton fabric.
[from *Calicut*, the town in India where it was first sold]

call, calls, calling, called
1 (verb) If someone or something is called by a

particular name, that is their name, e.g. *They called the baby Anthony.*
2 If you call people or situations something, you use words to describe your opinion of them, e.g. *He called me a liar.*
3 If you call something, you say it loudly.
4 If you call someone, you telephone them.
5 If you call on someone, you pay them a short visit, e.g. *I called round but you were out.*
6 If you call a meeting, you arrange for it to take place.
7 If someone is called before a court of law, they are ordered to appear there, e.g. *She was called as a witness in the case.*
8 (noun) If you get a call from someone, they telephone you or pay you a visit.
9 A call is a cry or shout, e.g. *a call for help.*
10 A call for something is a demand or desire for it, e.g. *There is little call for that type of book.*
11 (phrase) If someone such as a doctor is on **call**, they are ready to go to work if they are needed.

Similar words: (sense 1) name, label, christen, dub, term
(sense 7) summon

call off
(phrasal verb) If you call something off, you cancel it.

call up
(phrasal verb) If someone is called up, they are ordered to join the army, navy, or air force.

call box, call boxes
(noun) A call box is a telephone kiosk.

calligraphy
(noun) Calligraphy is the art of beautiful handwriting.
[from Greek *kalos* + *graphein* meaning 'beautiful writing']

calling
1 (noun) A calling is a profession or career.
2 If you have a calling to a particular job, you have a strong feeling that you should do it, e.g. *his calling to become a priest.*

Similar words: (sense 2) vocation, mission

calliper, callipers; also spelled caliper
1 (noun) Callipers are instruments consisting of two long pieces of metal hinged at one end. They are used to measure the size of things.
2 Callipers are also supports worn round someone's leg when they cannot walk properly.

callous
(adjective) cruel and showing no concern for other people's feelings.
callously (adverb), **callousness** (noun).

Similar words: heartless, unfeeling, hardened

callow
(adjective) immature or lacking experience, e.g. *a callow youth.*
[from Old English *calu* meaning 'unfledged']

callus, calluses
(noun) A callus is an area of hard, thick skin caused by rubbing, usually on the feet or hands.

calm, calmer, calmest; calms, calming, calmed
1 (adjective) Someone who is calm is quiet and does not show any worry or excitement, e.g. *Her voice was calm.*
2 If the weather or the sea is calm, it is still because there is no strong wind.
3 (noun) Calm is a state of quietness and peacefulness, e.g. *the calm of the countryside.*
4 (verb) To calm someone means to make them less upset or excited.
calmly (adverb), **calmness** (noun).
[from Latin *cauma* meaning 'heat of the day']

Similar words: (sense 1) cool, unflappable, composed
(sense 3) calmness, stillness, tranquillity, composure
(sense 4) allay, placate, quieten, lull, soothe

Calor gas
(noun; a trademark) Calor gas is butane gas liquefied in portable metal containers, used for cooking and heating.

calorie, calories
1 (noun) A calorie is a unit of measurement for the energy value of food, e.g. *a diet of 1,500 calories a day.*
2 A calorie is also a unit of heat equal to about 4.187 joules. This sense of calorie is now rarely used.
calorific (adjective).
[from Latin *calor* meaning 'heat']

calumny, calumnies
(noun; a formal word) A calumny is a false statement intended to damage someone's reputation.
[from Latin *calumnia* meaning 'deception' or 'slander']

calve, calves, calving, calved
(verb) When cows or some other animals calve, they give birth to a calf.

calves the plural of calf.

calypso, calypsos (pronounced kal-**lip**-soh)
(noun) A calypso is a type of song from the West Indies, with a topical subject and a lively rhythm.

calyx, calyxes or calyces (pronounced **kay**-lix)
(noun; a technical word) In a flower, a calyx is the ring of petal-like sepals that protects the developing bud.

cam, cams
(noun) A cam is the part of an engine which changes circular motion into motion up and down or from side to side.

camaraderie (pronounced kam-mer-**rah**-der-ree)
(noun) Camaraderie is a feeling of trust and friendship.

camber, cambers
(noun) A camber is a gradual downwards slope from the centre of a road to each side of it.
[from Old French *cambre* meaning 'curved']

camel, camels
(noun) A camel is a large mammal with either

one or two humps on its back. Camels live in hot desert areas and are used for carrying things. [from Hebrew *gamal*]

camellia, camellias (pronounced kam-**meel**-ya) (noun) A camellia is a shrub with shiny leaves and large rose-like flowers.

cameo, cameos
1 (noun) A cameo is a short descriptive piece of writing or acting.
2 A cameo is also a brooch with a raised stone design on a flat stone of another colour.

camera, cameras
1 (noun) A camera is a piece of equipment used for taking photographs or for filming.
2 (phrase; a legal expression) If a trial is held **in camera**, the public are not allowed to attend. [from Latin *camera* meaning 'vault']

camomile or **chamomile**
(noun) Camomile is a plant with a strong smell and daisy-like flowers which are used in medicine and to make herbal tea. [from Greek *khamaimēlon* meaning 'apple on the ground']

camouflage, camouflages, camouflaging, camouflaged (pronounced **kam**-mof-flahj)
1 (noun) Camouflage is a way of avoiding being seen by having the same colour or appearance as the surroundings.
2 (verb) To camouflage something means to hide it or disguise it using camouflage. [from Italian *camuffare* meaning 'to disguise' or 'to deceive']

camp, camps, camping, camped
1 (noun) A camp is a place where people live in tents or stay in tents on holiday.
2 A camp is also a collection of buildings used for a particular group of people such as soldiers or prisoners.
3 A particular camp is a group of people who support a particular idea or belief.
4 (verb) If you camp, you stay in a tent.
5 (adjective; informal uses) exaggerated or vulgar in style, e.g. *camp theatre*.
6 If a man is described as camp, he behaves or dresses in an affected way which makes people think he is homosexual.
camper (noun), **camping** (noun). [from Latin *campus* meaning 'field']

campaign, campaigns, campaigning, campaigned (pronounced kam-**pane**)
1 (noun) A campaign is a planned set of actions aimed at achieving a particular result, e.g. *the campaign against world hunger*.
2 (verb) To campaign means to carry out a campaign, e.g. *He campaigned for reform*.
campaigner (noun).

Similar words: (sense 1) movement, crusade

camphor (pronounced **kam**-for)
(noun) Camphor is a white solid with a strong smell, used in medicines and for making celluloid. [from Arabic *kafur* meaning 'chalk']

campus, campuses
(noun) A campus is the area of land and the buildings that make up a university or college.

can, could
1 (verb) If you can do something, it is possible for you to do it or you are allowed to do it, e.g. *Can I go please?... I can't stay long*.
2 If you can do something, you have the skill or ability to do it, e.g. *She can play the piano well*.

can, cans, canning, canned
1 (noun) A can is a metal container, often a sealed one with food or drink inside.
2 (verb) To can food or drink means to seal it in cans. [from Old English *canne* meaning 'vessel for liquid']

Canadian, Canadians
1 (adjective) belonging or relating to Canada.
2 (noun) A Canadian is someone who comes from Canada.

canal, canals
(noun) A canal is a long, narrow man-made channel of water. [from Latin *canalis* meaning 'channel' or 'water-pipe']

canapé, canapés (pronounced **kan**-nap-pay)
(noun) Canapés are savoury snacks handed round at parties, consisting of thin bread or toast with cheese, fish, or meat on top.

canary, canaries
(noun) A canary is a small yellow bird, often kept in a cage as a pet.

can-can, can-cans
(noun) The can-can is a lively dance which originated in Paris, in which women kick their legs high in the air to fast music.

cancel, cancels, cancelling, cancelled
1 (verb) If you cancel something that has been arranged, you stop it from happening.
2 If you cancel a cheque or an agreement, you make sure that it is no longer valid.
3 If you cancel something written, you cross it out.
cancellation (noun). [from Latin *cancellare* meaning 'to cross out']

cancer, cancers
1 (noun) Cancer is a serious disease in which abnormal cells in a part of the body increase rapidly, producing growths.
2 Cancer is also the fourth sign of the zodiac, represented by a crab. People born between June 21st and July 22nd are born under this sign.
cancerous (adjective). [from Latin *cancer* meaning 'crab']

Similar words: (sense 1) tumour, carcinoma

candela, candelas
(noun) The candela is the SI unit of luminous intensity. [from Latin *candela* meaning 'candle']

candelabra or **candelabrum, candelabras**
(noun) A candelabra is an ornamental holder for a number of candles.

candid
(adjective) honest and frank, e.g. *I'll be candid with you.*
candidly (adverb), **candour** (noun).
[from Latin *candidus* meaning 'white']

candidate, candidates
1 (noun) A candidate for a job is a person who is being considered for that job.
2 A candidate is also a person taking an examination.
candidacy (noun).
[from Latin *candidatus* meaning 'white-robed'. In Rome, a candidate wore a white toga]

candied
(adjective) covered or cooked in sugar, e.g. *candied peel.*

candle, candles
(noun) A candle is a stick of hard wax with a wick through the middle. The lighted wick gives a flame that provides light.
[from Latin *candere* meaning 'to shine with a white light']

candlestick, candlesticks
(noun) A candlestick is a holder for a candle.

candy, candies
(noun; used especially in American English) Candies are sweets.
[from Arabic *qand* meaning 'cane sugar']

cane, canes, caning, caned
1 (noun) Cane is the long, hollow stems of a plant such as bamboo.
2 Cane is also strips of cane used for weaving things such as baskets and chairs.
3 A cane is a long narrow stick, often one used to beat people as a punishment.
4 (verb) To cane someone means to beat them with a cane as a punishment.
[from Greek *kanna* meaning 'reed']

canine, canines (pronounced **kay**-nine)
1 (adjective) relating to dogs.
2 (noun) A canine, or a canine tooth, is one of the pointed teeth near the front of the mouth in humans and some animals.
[from Latin *canis* meaning 'dog']

canister, canisters
(noun) A canister is a container with a lid, used for storing foods such as sugar or tea.
[from Greek *kanastron* meaning 'wicker basket']

canker, cankers
(noun) Canker is a disease which causes sores around the mouth or ears of animals or people.

cannabis
(noun) Cannabis is a drug made from the hemp plant, which some people smoke. It is illegal in many countries.
[from Latin *cannabis* meaning 'hemp']

canned
1 (adjective) Canned food is preserved in cans.
2 Canned music or laughter on a television or radio show is recorded beforehand.

cannibal, cannibals
(noun) A cannibal is a person who eats the flesh of other human beings; also used of animals that eat animals of their own type.
cannibalism (noun).

cannibalize, cannibalizes, cannibalizing, cannibalized; also spelled cannibalise
(verb) To cannibalize a machine means to take parts from it to repair another machine.

cannon, cannons, cannoning, cannoned
1 (noun) A cannon is a large gun, usually on wheels, used in battles to fire heavy metal balls.
2 (verb) To cannon into people or things means to collide into them with force.
[from Italian *canna* meaning 'tube']

canny
(adjective) clever and cautious, e.g. *a canny businessman.*
cannily (adverb).

canoe, canoes (pronounced ka-**noo**)
(noun) A canoe is a small, narrow boat that you row using a paddle.
canoeing (noun), **canoeist** (noun).
[from Spanish *canoa* meaning 'boat']

canon, canons
1 (noun) A canon is a member of the clergy who is attached to a cathedral.
2 A canon is also a basic rule or principle, e.g. *the traditional canons of artistic judgment.*
3 In literature, a canon is all the writings by a particular author which are known to be genuine.
[from Greek *kanōn* meaning 'measuring rod' or 'rule']

canonize, canonizes, canonizing, canonized; also spelled canonise
(verb) If a dead person is canonized, he or she is declared a saint.

canopy, canopies
(noun) A canopy is a cover for something, used for shelter or decoration, e.g. *a throne with a silk canopy.*
[from Greek *kōnōpeion* meaning 'bed with a mosquito net']

cant
(noun) Cant consists of moral or religious statements made by someone who does not believe what they are saying.
[from Latin *cantare* meaning 'to sing']

cantankerous
(adjective) Cantankerous people are quarrelsome and bad-tempered.

canteen, canteens
1 (noun) A canteen is the part of a factory or other workplace where the workers can go to eat.
2 A canteen of cutlery is a set of cutlery in a box.
[from Italian *cantina* meaning 'cellar']

canter, canters, cantering, cantered
(verb) When a horse canters, it moves at a speed between a gallop and a trot.

cantilever, cantilevers
(noun) A cantilever is a long beam or bar fixed at only one end and supporting a bridge or other structure at the other end.

canton, cantons
(noun) A canton is a political and administrative region of a country, especially in Switzerland.

canvas, canvases
1 (noun) Canvas is strong, heavy cotton or linen cloth used for making things such as sails, tents, and bags.
2 A canvas is a piece of canvas on which an artist does a painting.
[from Latin *cannabis* meaning 'hemp']

canvass, canvasses, canvassing, canvassed
1 (verb) If you canvass people or a place, you go round trying to persuade people to vote for a particular candidate or party in an election, e.g. *He had canvassed for Mr Foot in the election.*
2 If you canvass opinion, you find out what people think about a particular subject by asking them.
3 (noun) A canvass is the activity of canvassing.

canyon, canyons
(noun) A canyon is a narrow river valley with steep sides.

cap, caps, capping, capped
1 (noun) A cap is a soft, flat hat usually worn by men or boys, often with a peak at the front.
2 A cap is also the lid or top of a bottle.
3 Caps are small explosives used in toy guns.
4 (verb) To cap something means to cover it with something, e.g. *chocolates capped with a cherry.*
5 If you cap a story or a joke that someone has just told, you tell a better one.
[from Latin *cappa* meaning 'hood']

capable
1 (adjective) able to do something, e.g. *a poison capable of causing death.*
2 skilful or talented, e.g. *a capable cricketer.*
capably (adverb), **capability** (noun).
[from Latin *capabilis* meaning 'able to take in']

capacious (pronounced kap-**pay**-shus)
(adjective; a formal word) having a lot of space or room.

capacity, capacities (pronounced kap-**pas**-sit-tee)
1 (noun) The capacity of something is the maximum amount that it can hold or produce, e.g. *a tank with a capacity of 10 gallons.*
2 A person's capacity is their power or ability to do something, e.g. *her vast capacity for learning.*
3 You can also refer to someone's position or role as their capacity, e.g. *He is here in his capacity as adviser.*

cape, capes
1 (noun) A cape is a short cloak with no sleeves.
2 A cape is also a large piece of land sticking out into the sea, e.g. *the southern cape of India.*

caper, capers, capering, capered
1 (noun) Capers are the flower buds of a spiky Mediterranean shrub, which are pickled and used to flavour food.
2 A caper is also a light-hearted practical joke, e.g. *more capers from the Carry-On team.*
3 (verb) If you caper, you dance or leap about playfully.

capillary, capillaries (pronounced kap-**pill**-lar-ree)
1 (noun) Capillaries are very thin blood vessels.
2 (adjective) Capillary tubes are very thin tubes used in scientific equipment.
[from Latin *capillus* meaning 'hair']

capital, capitals
1 (noun) The capital of a country is its main city or town where the government meets.
2 A capital or capital letter is a larger letter used at the beginning of a sentence or a name.
3 Capital is the amount of money or property owned or used by a business.
4 Capital is also a sum of money that you save or invest in order to gain interest.
5 (adjective) involving or requiring the punishment of death, e.g. *capital punishment.*
6 (noun) In architecture, a capital is the top part of a stone column, often decorated.
[from Latin *caput* meaning 'head']

capitalism
(noun) Capitalism is an economic and political system where business and industry are owned by private individuals and not by the state.
capitalist (adjective and noun).

Similar words: free enterprise, private enterprise

capitalize, capitalizes, capitalizing, capitalized; also spelled **capitalise**
(verb) If you capitalize on a situation, you use it to get an advantage.

capitulate, capitulates, capitulating, capitulated
(verb) To capitulate means to give in and stop fighting or resisting, e.g. *The government was forced to capitulate to their demands.*
capitulation (noun).

cappuccino, cappuccinos (pronounced kap-poot-**sheen**-oh)
(noun) Cappuccino is coffee made with frothy milk.

caprice, caprices (pronounced kap-**prees**)
1 (noun) A caprice is an unexpected change of mind or action.
2 Caprice is also a tendency in a person to change unexpectedly, e.g. *He altered unpredictably according to caprice.*

capricious (pronounced kap-**prish**-uss)
(adjective) often changing unexpectedly, e.g. *capricious behaviour.*
capriciously (adverb), **capriciousness** (noun).

Capricorn
(noun) Capricorn is the tenth sign of the zodiac, represented by a goat. People born between December 22nd and January 19th are born under this sign.
[from Latin *caper* meaning 'goat' and *cornu* meaning 'horn']

capsicum, capsicums
(noun) A capsicum is a type of hollow green, red, or yellow vegetable, with small white seeds.

capsize, capsizes, capsizing, capsized
(verb) If a boat capsizes, it turns upside down.

capsule, capsules
1 (noun) A capsule is a small container with powdered medicine inside which you swallow.
2 A capsule is also the part of a spacecraft in which astronauts travel.
[from Latin *capsula* meaning 'little box']

captain, captains, captaining, captained
1 (noun) The captain of a ship is the officer in charge of it, especially a naval officer.
2 The captain of an aeroplane is the pilot.
3 In the army, a captain is an officer of the rank immediately above lieutenant.
4 In the navy, a captain is an officer of the rank immediately above commander.
5 The captain of a sports team is its leader, e.g. *captain of the hockey team.*
6 (verb) If you captain a group of people, you are their leader.
[from Latin *caput* meaning 'head']

Similar words: (sense 1) skipper, commander, master

caption, captions
(noun) A caption is a title or description printed underneath a picture or photograph.
[from Latin *captio* meaning 'seizure'; a caption seizes your attention]

captivate, captivates, captivating, captivated
(verb) To captivate someone means to fascinate them or attract them so that they cannot take their attention away, e.g. *He was captivated by a beautiful blonde.*
captivating (adjective).

captive, captives
1 (noun) A captive is a person who has been captured and kept prisoner.
2 (adjective) imprisoned or enclosed, e.g. *captive animals.*
captivity (noun).

captor, captors
(noun) The captor of a person or animal is someone who has captured them.

capture, captures, capturing, captured
1 (verb) To capture someone means to take them prisoner.
2 To capture something means to take control of it, e.g. *stories that capture the imagination.*
3 To capture a quality or mood means to succeed in representing or describing it, e.g. *His pictures capture beautifully the atmosphere of the town.*
4 (noun) The capture of someone or something is the capturing of them.
[from Latin *capere* meaning 'to take']

car, cars
1 (noun) A car is a four-wheeled road vehicle with room for a small number of people.
2 A car is also a railway carriage used for a particular purpose, e.g. *the dining car.*
[from Latin *carra* meaning 'wagon']

carafe, carafes (pronounced kar-**raf**)
(noun) A carafe is a glass bottle for serving water or wine.
[from Arabic *gharrafah* meaning 'vessel for liquid']

caramel, caramels
1 (noun) A caramel is a chewy sweet made from sugar, butter, and milk.
2 Caramel is burnt sugar used for colouring or flavouring food.

carat, carats
1 (noun) A carat is a unit for measuring the weight of diamonds and other precious stones, equal to 0.2 grams.
2 A carat is also a unit for measuring the purity of gold. The purest gold is 24 carats.

caravan, caravans
1 (noun) A caravan is a vehicle pulled by a car in which people live or spend their holidays.
2 A caravan is also a group of people and animals travelling together, usually across a desert.
[from Persian *karwan*]

caraway
(noun) Caraway is a plant with strong-smelling seeds that are used for cooking.

carbide
(noun) In chemistry, carbide is a compound of carbon and one other element, especially a metal.

carbine, carbines
(noun) A carbine is a light automatic rifle.
[from French *carabine* meaning 'rifle']

carbohydrate, carbohydrates
(noun) Carbohydrate is an organic compound containing carbon, hydrogen, and oxygen, found in food such as sugar and bread. Carbohydrate gives you energy.

carbon
(noun) Carbon is a chemical element that is pure in diamonds and also found in coal. All living things contain carbon. Its atomic number is 6 and its symbol is C.
[from Latin *carbo* meaning 'charcoal']

carbon copy, carbon copies
(noun) A carbon copy is a copy of a piece of writing made using carbon paper.

carbon dioxide
(noun) Carbon dioxide is a colourless, odourless gas that humans and animals breathe out. It is used in industry, for example in making fizzy drinks and in fire extinguishers.

carbon monoxide
(noun) Carbon monoxide is a colourless, poisonous gas formed when carbon burns in a very small amount of air.

carbon paper
(noun) Carbon paper is a type of thin paper with a dark chemical coating on one side. You put it between two sheets of paper so that writing on the top sheet also appears on the bottom sheet.

carbuncle, carbuncles
(noun) A carbuncle is a large swelling like a boil under the skin.
[from Latin *carbunculus* meaning 'little coal']

carburettor, carburettors (pronounced **kahr**-bur-ret-ter)
(noun) The carburettor in a vehicle is the part of

the engine in which air and petrol are mixed together.

carcass, carcasses; also spelled **carcase**
(noun) A carcass is the body of a dead animal.

carcinogen, carcinogens (pronounced kahr-**sin**-ne-jen)
(noun; a technical word) A carcinogen is a substance that produces cancer.
carcinogenic (adjective).

carcinoma, carcinomas (pronounced kahr-sin-**noh**-ma)
(noun; a medical word) A carcinoma is a cancerous tumour or growth.

card, cards
1 (noun) A card is a piece of stiff paper, plastic, or thin cardboard with information or a message on it, e.g. *my membership card.*
2 A card is also a playing card, e.g. *a pack of cards.*
3 When you play cards, you play any game using playing cards.
4 Card is strong, stiff paper or thin cardboard.
5 (phrase) If something is **on the cards**, it is very likely to happen.
[from Greek *khartēs* meaning 'papyrus leaf']

cardamon
(noun) Cardamon is a spice from the seeds of an Asian plant, used in cooking.

cardboard
(noun) Cardboard is thick, stiff paper.

cardiac
(adjective; a medical word) relating to the heart, e.g. *cardiac failure.*
[from Greek *kardia* meaning 'heart']

cardigan, cardigans
(noun) A cardigan is a knitted jacket that fastens up the front. It is named after the 7th Earl of Cardigan (1797-1868).

cardinal, cardinals
1 (noun) In the Roman Catholic church, a cardinal is one of the high-ranking members of the clergy who elect and advise the Pope.
2 (adjective) extremely important, e.g. *The family is a cardinal feature of our society.*
[from Latin *cardo* meaning 'hinge'. When something is important, other things hinge on it]

cardinal number, cardinal numbers
(noun) A cardinal number is a whole number signifying quantity as opposed to a number signifying the order of things.

cardinal point, cardinal points
(noun) The cardinal points are the main points of the compass, north, south, east, and west.

care, cares, caring, cared
1 (verb) If you care about something, you are concerned about it and interested in it.
2 If you care about someone, you feel affection towards them.
3 If you care for someone, you look after them.
4 If you don't care for something, you don't like it.
5 (noun) Care is a feeling of concern or worry.
6 Care of someone or something is treatment for

them or looking after them, e.g. *the care of mental patients.*
7 If you do something with care, you do it with close attention.
8 (phrase) Children who are **in care** are living in a home owned by the state, often because their parents are dead or are unable to look after them properly.
9 If someone sends something to you **care of** another person, they send it to the other person to be passed on to you.
[from Germanic *kara* meaning 'grief']

Similar words: (sense 3) attend, nurse, tend

career, careers, careering, careered
1 (noun) Someone's career is the series of jobs that they have in life, usually in the same occupation, e.g. *his career as a journalist.*
2 (verb) To career somewhere means to move very quickly, often out of control, e.g. *A car came careering round the corner.*
[from Latin *carraria* meaning 'paved road']

careerist, careerists
(noun) A careerist is someone who considers success in their career to be more important than anything else.

carefree
(adjective) having no worries or responsibilities.

careful
1 (adjective) acting sensibly and with care, e.g. *a careful driver.*
2 complete and well done, e.g. *a careful copy.*
carefully (adverb), **carefulness** (noun).

Similar words: (sense 1) cautious, chary, circumspect, watchful, wary

careless
1 (adjective) doing something badly without enough attention, e.g. *Her work is careless.*
2 relaxed and unconcerned, e.g. *She put a careless hand to her hair.*
carelessly (adverb), **carelessness** (noun).

Similar words: (sense 1) thoughtless, haphazard, negligent, lax, slipshod, cavalier, slapdash, sloppy, neglectful

caress, caresses, caressing, caressed
1 (verb) If you caress someone, you stroke them gently and affectionately.
2 (noun) A caress is a gentle, affectionate stroke.
[from Latin *carus* meaning 'dear']

Similar words: (sense 1) fondle, stroke

caretaker, caretakers
1 (noun) A caretaker is a person whose job is to look after a large building such as a school.
2 (adjective) having an important position for a short time until a new person is appointed, e.g. *a caretaker manager.*

careworn
(adjective) tired and troubled.

cargo, cargoes
(noun) Cargo is the goods carried on a ship or plane.
[from Spanish *cargar* meaning 'to load up']

Similar words: freight, shipment, consignment, load

Caribbean
1 (noun) The Caribbean consists of the Caribbean Sea east of Central America and the islands adjoining it.
2 (adjective) relating to or typical of the Caribbean, e.g. *a Caribbean atmosphere.*

caribou, caribou or caribous (pronounced kar-rib-boo)
(noun) A caribou is a large North American deer.

caricature, caricatures, caricaturing, caricatured
1 (noun) A caricature is a drawing or description of someone that exaggerates striking parts of their appearance or personality.
2 (verb) To caricature someone means to give a caricature of them.
[from Latin *caricare* meaning 'to exaggerate']

caries (pronounced care-reez)
(noun; a formal word) Dental caries is decay in teeth.

carmine
(adjective) deep bright red.

carnage (pronounced kahr-nij)
(noun) Carnage is the violent killing of large numbers of people.

carnal
(adjective; a formal word) sexual and sensual rather than spiritual, e.g. *his carnal desires.*
[from Latin *caro* meaning 'flesh']

carnation, carnations
(noun) A carnation is a plant with long stems and white, pink, or red flowers.
[from Latin *carnatio* meaning 'fleshiness'. Carnations were originally flesh-coloured]

carnival, carnivals
(noun) A carnival is a special occasion when there are celebrations and entertainments such as processions and dancing.

carnivore, carnivores
(noun) A carnivore is an animal that eats meat.
carnivorous (adjective).

carol, carols
(noun) A carol is a religious song sung at Christmas time.

carouse, carouses, carousing, caroused
(verb) When people carouse, they enjoy themselves drinking together.
carousal (noun).
[from German *gar aus trinken* meaning 'to drink completely']

carousel, carousels (pronounced kar-ros-sel)
(noun) A carousel is a merry-go-round.

carp, carps, carping, carped
1 (noun) A carp is a large edible freshwater fish.
2 (verb) To carp means to complain about unimportant things.

[sense 1 from Latin *carpa* meaning 'carp'; sense 2 from Old Norse *karpa* meaning 'to boast']

carpel, carpels
(noun) In a flower, the carpel is the seed-bearing part.
[from Greek *karpos* meaning 'fruit']

carpenter, carpenters
(noun)A carpenter is a person whose job is making and repairing wooden structures.
carpentry (noun).
[from Latin *carpentarius* meaning 'wagon-maker']

carpet, carpets, carpeting, carpeted
1 (noun) A carpet is a thick covering for a floor, usually made of a material like wool.
2 (verb) To carpet a floor means to cover it with a carpet.
[from Latin *carpeta* meaning 'carded wool']

carriage, carriages
1 (noun) A carriage is one of the separate sections of a passenger train.
2 A carriage is also an old-fashioned vehicle for carrying passengers, usually pulled by horses.
3 On a machine, a carriage is a movable supporting part, e.g. *a typewriter carriage.*
4 Someone's carriage is the way they hold their head and body.
5 Carriage is the cost of transporting something, e.g. *It costs £9.90 including carriage.*
[from Old French *carier* meaning 'to convey']

carriageway, carriageways
(noun) A carriageway is one of the sides of a road which traffic travels along in one direction only.

carrier, carriers
1 (noun) A carrier is a vehicle or other structure that is used for carrying things, e.g. *a weapons carrier.*
2 A carrier of a germ or disease is a person or animal that can pass it on to others.

carrier bag, carrier bags
(noun) A carrier bag is a bag made of plastic or paper, which is used for carrying shopping in.

carrion
(noun) Carrion is the decaying flesh of dead animals.
[from Latin *caro* meaning 'flesh']

carrot, carrots
(noun) A carrot is a long, thin orange root vegetable.

carry, carries, carrying, carried
1 (verb) To carry something means to hold it and take it somewhere.
2 When a vehicle carries people, they travel in it.
3 A person or animal that carries a germ is capable of passing it on to other people or animals, e.g. *Rats carry nasty diseases.*
4 To carry a quality means to involve it, e.g. *This job carries a lot of risk.*
5 In a meeting, if a proposal is carried, it is accepted by a majority of the people there.
6 If a sound carries, it can be heard far away, e.g. *His voice carried right to the back row.*

7 If someone carries people with them, they make the people support them or believe in them, e.g. *He carries his audience with him.*
8 The way that you carry yourself is the way you move and hold your body.
[from Old French *carier* meaning 'to take by vehicle']

Similar words: (sense 2) bear, convey, relay, take

carry away
(phrasal verb) If you are carried away, you are so excited by something that you do not behave sensibly.

carry on
1 (phrasal verb) To carry on doing something means to continue doing it.
2 If you carry on an activity, you take part in it, e.g. *How can we carry on a conversation here?*

carry out
(phrasal verb) To carry something out means to do it and complete it, e.g. *They carried out a survey.*

cart, carts
1 (noun) A cart is a vehicle with wheels, used to carry goods and often pulled by horses or cattle.
2 (phrase) If you **put the cart before the horse**, you do things in the wrong order.
[from Old Norse *kartr* meaning 'carriage']

carte blanche (pronounced kart **blahnsh**)
(noun) If you have carte blanche, you have been given full power to do as you wish, e.g. *They gave him carte blanche to publish his proposals.*

cartilage
(noun) Cartilage is strong, flexible body tissue found around the joints and in the nose and ears.
[from Latin *cartilago* meaning 'gristle']

cartography (pronounced kahr-**tog**-raf-fee)
(noun) Cartography is the art of drawing maps.
cartographer (noun).
[from Greek *khartēs* meaning 'papyrus leaf' and *graphein* meaning 'to write' or 'to draw']

carton, cartons
(noun) A carton is a cardboard or plastic container.

cartoon, cartoons
1 (noun) A cartoon is a drawing or a series of drawings which are funny or make a political point.
2 A cartoon is also a film in which the characters and scenes are drawn rather than being real people and objects.
cartoonist (noun).
[from Italian *cartone* meaning 'sketch on stiff paper']

cartridge, cartridges
1 (noun) A cartridge is a tube containing a bullet and an explosive substance, used in guns.
2 A cartridge is also a thin plastic tube containing ink that you put inside a pen.
3 On a record player, a cartridge is the part of the arm that holds the needle.
[from French *cartouche*]

cartridge paper
(noun) Cartridge paper is thick, strong paper used for drawing on.

cartwheel, cartwheels
1 (noun) A cartwheel is an acrobatic movement in which you throw yourself sideways onto one hand and move round in a circle with arms and legs stretched until you land on your feet again.
2 A cartwheel is also the wheel of a cart.

carve, carves, carving, carved
1 (verb) To carve an object means to cut it out of a substance such as stone or wood.
2 To carve meat means to cut slices from it.
[from Old English *ceorfan* meaning 'to cut into']

Similar words: (sense 1) sculpt, engrave, whittle

carving, carvings
(noun) A carving is a carved object.

cascade, cascades, cascading, cascaded
1 (noun) A cascade is a waterfall or group of waterfalls.
2 (verb) To cascade means to flow downwards quickly, e.g. *The water cascaded over the rocks.*
[from Italian *cascare* meaning 'to fall']

case, cases
1 (noun) A case is a particular situation, event, or example, e.g. *a case of mistaken identity.*
2 A case is also a container for something, or a suitcase, e.g. *a glasses case.*
3 Doctors sometimes refer to a patient as a case.
4 Police detectives refer to a crime they are investigating as a case.
5 In an argument, the case for an idea is the facts and reasons used to support it.
6 In law, a case is a trial or other legal inquiry.
7 In grammar, the case of a noun or pronoun is the form of it which shows its relationship with other words in a sentence, e.g. *the accusative case.*
8 (phrase) You say **in that case** to indicate that you are assuming something to be true, e.g. *'I don't want to go.'* — *'In that case neither do I.'*
9 You say **in case** to explain something that you do because a particular thing might happen, e.g. *I've got some money in case you run out.*
[from Latin *casus* meaning 'event']

Similar words: (sense 1) instance, circumstance

cased
(adjective) An object that is cased in something is covered by it, e.g. *a ball cased in mud.*

case history
(noun) A person's case history is information about their history, background and problems which is used by a doctor or social worker.

casement, casements
(noun) A casement is a window that opens on hinges at one side.

cash, cashes, cashing, cashed
1 (noun) Cash is money in the form of notes and coins rather than cheques.
2 (verb) If you cash a cheque, you take it to a bank and exchange it for money.
[from Italian *cassa* meaning 'money-box']

cash dispenser, cash dispensers
(noun) A cash dispenser is a machine in the wall of some banks where you can take out money at any time using a special card.

cashew, cashews (pronounced **kash**-oo)
(noun) Cashews are curved, edible nuts.

cashier, cashiers
(noun) A cashier is the person that customers pay in a shop or get money from in a bank.

cashmere
(noun) Cashmere is very soft, fine wool from goats in the Kashmir area.

cash register, cash registers
(noun) A cash register is a machine in a shop which records sales, and where the money is kept.

casing, casings
(noun) A casing is a protective covering for something.

casino, casinos (pronounced kass-**ee**-noh)
(noun) A casino is a place where people go to play gambling games.

cask, casks
(noun) A cask is a wooden barrel.
[from Spanish *casco* meaning 'helmet']

casket, caskets
(noun) A casket is a small decorative box for jewellery or other valuables.
[from Old French *cassette* meaning 'little box']

cassava
(noun) Cassava is a South American plant with thick roots from which flour is obtained.

casserole, casseroles
(noun) A casserole is a dish made by cooking a mixture of meat and vegetables slowly in an oven; also used of the pot a casserole is cooked in.
[from Old French *casse* meaning 'ladle' or 'dripping pan']

cassette, cassettes
(noun) A cassette is a small flat container with magnetic tape inside, which is used for recording and playing back sounds.
[from Old French *cassette* meaning 'little box']

cassette recorder, cassette recorders
(noun) A cassette recorder or cassette player is a machine used for recording and playing cassettes.

cassock, cassocks
(noun) A cassock is a long robe, usually black, that is worn by some members of the clergy.
[from Italian *casacca* meaning 'long coat']

cast, casts, casting, cast
1 (noun) The cast of a play or film is all the people who act in it.
2 (verb) To cast actors means to choose them for roles in a play or film.
3 To cast something means to throw it.
4 If you cast your eyes somewhere, you look there, e.g. *He cast a nervous glance over his shoulder.*
5 If you cast doubt or suspicion on something, you make people unsure about it.

6 When people cast their votes in an election, they vote.
7 To cast an object means to make it by pouring liquid into a mould and leaving it to harden, e.g. *a statue cast in bronze.*
8 (noun) A cast is an object made in this way, e.g. *casts taken from the inside of the skull.*
[from Old Norse *kasta* meaning 'to throw']

Similar words: (sense 1) actors, company, dramatis personae

cast about
(phrasal verb; a literary use) To cast about for something means to look for it.

cast off
1 (phrasal verb) If you cast off, you untie the rope fastening a boat to a harbour wall, shore, or quay.
2 In knitting, to cast off stitches means to take them off the needle and finish the edge of the knitting.

cast on
(phrasal verb) In knitting, to cast on stitches means to make them on a needle.

castanets
(plural noun) Castanets are a Spanish musical instrument consisting of two small round pieces of wood that are clicked together with the fingers.
[from Spanish *castañetas* meaning 'little chestnuts']

castaway, castaways
(noun) A castaway is a person who has been shipwrecked.

caste, castes
1 (noun) A caste is one of the four hereditary classes into which Hindu society is divided.
2 Caste is a system of social classes decided according to family, wealth, and position.
[from Portuguese *casto* meaning 'pure']

caster sugar or **castor sugar**
(noun) Caster sugar is very fine white sugar used in cooking.

castigate, castigates, castigating, castigated
(verb; a formal word) To castigate someone means to criticize them severely.
[from Latin *castum* + *agere* meaning 'to compel to be pure']

cast iron
1 (noun) Cast iron is iron which is made into objects by casting. It contains carbon.
2 (adjective) A cast-iron excuse or guarantee is absolutely certain and firm.

castle, castles
1 (noun) A castle is a large building with walls or ditches round it to protect it from attack.
2 In chess, a castle is the same as a rook.
[from Latin *castellum* meaning 'little fort']

cast-off, cast-offs
(noun) A cast-off is a piece of outgrown or discarded clothing that has been passed on to someone else.

castor, castors; also spelled **caster**
(noun) A castor is a small wheel fitted to
furniture so that it can be moved easily.

castor oil
(noun) Castor oil is a thick oil that comes from
the seeds of the castor oil plant. It is used as a
laxative.

castrate, castrates, castrating, castrated
(verb) To castrate a male animal means to
remove its testicles so that it can no longer
produce sperm.
castration (noun).

casual
1 (adjective) happening by chance without
planning, e.g. *a casual meeting.*
2 careless or without interest, e.g. *a casual
glance... He had a casual attitude.*
3 Casual clothes are suitable for informal
occasions.
4 Casual work is not regular or permanent, e.g.
They employ casual labourers at peak season.
casually (adverb), **casualness** (noun).
[from Latin *casualis* meaning 'happening by
chance']

Similar words: (sense 2) nonchalant, blasé,
unconcerned

casualty, casualties
(noun) A casualty is a person killed or injured in
an accident or war, e.g. *The casualties were
taken to hospital.*

cat, cats
1 (noun) A cat is a small furry mammal kept as a
pet.
2 A cat is also any of the family of mammals that
includes lions and tigers, e.g. *the big cats.*
3 (phrase) If you **let the cat out of the bag,** you
reveal a secret, often by mistake.
[from Latin *cattus*]

cataclysm, cataclysms (pronounced **kat**-a-klism)
(noun; a formal word) A cataclysm is a disaster
or violent upheaval in society.
cataclysmic (adjective).
[from Greek *kataklusmos* meaning 'deluge']

catacomb, catacombs (pronounced **kat**-a-koom)
(noun) Catacombs are underground passages
with places where dead bodies are buried.
[from Latin *catacumbas*, an underground
cemetery near Rome]

Catalan, Catalans
1 (noun) Catalan is a language spoken by many
people in Catalonia in north-eastern Spain.
2 A Catalan is someone who comes from
Catalonia.

catalogue, catalogues, cataloguing, catalogued
1 (noun) A catalogue is a book containing a list
of goods that you can buy in a shop or through
the post, together with prices and illustrations.
2 A catalogue is also a list of things such as the
objects in a museum or the books in a library.
3 (verb) To catalogue a collection of things
means to list them in a catalogue.
[from Greek *katalegein* meaning 'to list']

catalyst, catalysts (pronounced **kat**-a-list)
1 (noun) In chemistry, a catalyst is a substance
that speeds up a chemical reaction without
changing itself.
2 A catalyst is also something that causes a
change to happen, e.g. *Their demonstration
acted as a catalyst in setting off the revolution.*
[from Greek *kataluein* meaning 'to dissolve']

catamaran, catamarans
(noun) A catamaran is a sailing boat with two
parallel hulls connected to each other.
[from Tamil *kattumaram* meaning 'tied logs']

catapult, catapults, catapulting, catapulted
1 (noun) A catapult is a Y-shaped object with a
piece of elastic tied between the two top ends
used for shooting small stones.
2 (verb) To catapult something means to shoot it
or throw it violently through the air.
3 If someone is catapulted into a situation, they
suddenly find themselves unexpectedly in that
situation, e.g. *She was catapulted to fame.*
[from Greek *kata-* + *pallein* meaning 'to hurl
down']

cataract, cataracts
1 (noun) A cataract is an area of the lens of
someone's eye that has become white instead of
clear, so that they cannot see properly.
2 A cataract is also a large waterfall.
[from Greek *katarassein* meaning 'to dash down']

catarrh (pronounced kat-**tahr**)
(noun) Catarrh is a condition in which you get a
lot of mucus in your nose and throat, for
example when you have a cold.
[from Greek *katarrhein* meaning 'to flow down']

catastrophe, catastrophes (pronounced
kat-**tass**-trif-fee)
(noun) A catastrophe is a terrible disaster.
catastrophic (adjective).
[from Greek *katastrephein* meaning 'to overturn']

catcall, catcalls
(noun) A catcall is a loud high-pitched cry made
to express disapproval.

catch, catches, catching, caught
1 (verb) To catch an animal means to stop it
from moving freely after chasing or trapping it,
e.g. *He caught three fish in his net.*
2 If you catch a ball moving in the air, you grasp
hold of it when it comes near you.
3 When the police catch criminals, they find
them and arrest them.
4 If you catch someone doing something they
should not be doing, you discover them doing it,
e.g. *They were caught smoking behind the sheds.*
5 If something catches you, it hits you, e.g. *His
shoe caught me in the belly.*
6 If something catches on an object, it sticks to it
or gets trapped, e.g. *My skirt caught on a
bramble.*
7 If you catch a bus or train, you get on it and
travel somewhere.
8 If you catch a sound, look, or quality, you hear
it, notice it, or understand it, e.g. *I caught a brief
smile from Jane... I couldn't catch his meaning.*

9 If something catches your attention or interest, you notice it or become interested in it.
10 If a fire catches, it starts burning.
11 If you catch a cold or a disease, you become infected with it.
12 (noun) A catch is an act of catching or something that is caught, e.g. *a catch of fish.*
13 A catch is also a hook that fastens or locks a door or window.
14 If there is a catch in something, there is a problem or hidden complication.
[from Latin *captiare* meaning 'to take captive']

Similar words: (sense 1) bag, entrap, ensnare, snare (sense 3) capture, seize, apprehend, take prisoner (sense 11) contract, go down with, develop

catch on
1 (phrasal verb) If you catch on to something, you understand it.
2 If something catches on, it becomes popular, e.g. *Short skirts have caught on.*

catch out
(phrasal verb) To catch someone out means to trick them or trap them.

catch up
1 (phrasal verb) To catch up with someone in front of you means to reach the place where they are by moving slightly faster than them.
2 To catch up with someone also means to reach the same level or standard as them.

catching
(adjective) tending to spread very quickly, e.g. *Is measles catching?*

catchment area, catchment areas
(noun) A catchment area is the area that a school, hospital, or other institution serves.

catch phrase, catch phrases
(noun) A catch phrase is a phrase that is often used by a famous person, and is therefore popular and well-known.

catch 22
(noun and adjective) A catch 22 situation is one in which it is impossible for you to do anything because there are things which prevent any attempt from succeeding.

catchword, catchwords
(noun) A catchword is the same as a catch phrase.

catchy, catchier, catchiest
(adjective) attractive and easily remembered, e.g. *a catchy tune.*

catechism, catechisms (pronounced kat-ik-kizm)
(noun) A catechism is a set of questions and answers which summarizes the main beliefs of a religion.
[from Greek *katekhein* meaning 'to instruct orally']

categorical
(adjective) absolutely certain and direct, e.g. *a categorical denial.*
categorically (adverb).

categorize, categorizes, categorizing, categorized; also spelled categorise
(verb) To categorize things means to arrange them in different categories.
categorization (noun).

category, categories
(noun) A category of things is a set of them with a particular characteristic in common, e.g. *jobs in two categories, office and manual.*

cater, caters, catering, catered
(verb) To cater for people means to provide them with what they need, especially food.
[from Medieval English *catour* meaning 'buyer']

caterer, caterers
(noun) A caterer is a person or business that provides food for parties and groups.

caterpillar, caterpillars
(noun) A caterpillar is the larva of a butterfly or moth. It looks like a type of small coloured worm and feeds on plants.
[from Old French *catepelose* meaning 'hairy cat']

caterwaul, caterwauls, caterwauling, caterwauled
(verb) To caterwaul means to wail or howl loudly.

catharsis, catharses (pronounced kath-ar-siss)
(noun; a formal word) Catharsis is the release of strong emotions and feelings by expressing them through drama, art, or literature.
[from Greek *kathairein* meaning 'to purge' or 'to purify']

cathedral, cathedrals
(noun) A cathedral is the main church in an area that has a bishop in charge of it.
[from Greek *kathedra* meaning 'seat']

catheter, catheters (pronounced kath-thit-ter)
(noun) A catheter is a thin hollow tube used to drain fluids from a patient's body, especially urine.
[from Greek *kathienai* meaning 'to send down']

cathode, cathodes
(noun; a technical word) A cathode is a negative electrode.
[from Greek *kathodos* meaning 'way down']

cathode-ray tube, cathode-ray tubes
(noun) A cathode-ray tube is a tube used in televisions and computers, in which an image is produced by sending a beam of electrons onto a fluorescent screen.

Catholic, Catholics
1 (noun and adjective) A Catholic is a Roman Catholic.
2 (adjective) Catholic also means having a wide range of interests or tastes, e.g. *a catholic taste in music.*
Catholicism (noun).
[from Greek *katholikos* meaning 'universal']

catkin, catkins
(noun) A catkin is a long, thin, soft flower on trees such as birch and willow.
[from Old Dutch *katteken* meaning 'kitten']

cat's-eye, cat's-eyes
(noun; a trademark) Cat's-eyes are small pieces

of glass or plastic set into a road to reflect light so that drivers can see the road at night.

cattle
(plural noun) Cattle are cows and bulls kept by farmers.

cattle grid, cattle grids
(noun) A cattle grid is a grid of metal bars set into the surface of a road so that cattle and sheep cannot get across.

catty, cattier, cattiest
(adjective) unpleasant and spiteful.
cattiness (noun).

catwalk, catwalks
(noun) A catwalk is a narrow pathway that people walk along, for example along a bridge or over a stage.

Caucasian, Caucasians (pronounced kaw-**kayz**-yn)
(noun) A Caucasian is a person belonging to the race of people with fair or light-brown skin, who originally come from Europe, north Africa, south-west Asia, and India.
[from *Caucasia*, a region in the USSR]

caucus, caucuses (pronounced **kaw**-kuss)
(noun) A caucus is a small group within a political party which discusses policy.
[from Algonquian Indian *caucauasu* meaning 'adviser']

caught the past tense and past participle of catch.

cauldron, cauldrons
(noun) A cauldron is a large, round metal cooking pot, especially one that sits over a fire.
[from Latin *caldarium* meaning 'hot bath']

cauliflower, cauliflowers
(noun) A cauliflower is a large, round, white vegetable surrounded by green leaves.
[from Italian *caoli* + *fiore* meaning 'cabbage flowers']

cause, causes, causing, caused
1 (noun) The cause of something is the thing that makes it happen, e.g. *What was the cause of death?*
2 A cause is an aim or principle which a group of people are working for, e.g. *The money went towards a good cause.*
3 If you have cause for something, you have a reason for it, e.g. *I have no cause to go back.*
4 (verb) To cause something means to make it happen, e.g. *They were causing a disturbance.*
causal (adjective).
[from Latin *causa* meaning 'cause' or 'reason']

Similar words: (sense 4) bring about, give rise to, lead to, effect, induce

causeway, causeways
(noun) A causeway is a raised path or road across water or marshland.
[from Latin *calciatus* meaning 'paved with limestone']

caustic
1 (adjective) capable of destroying substances by chemical action, e.g. *caustic cleaning fluid.*
2 bitter or sarcastic, e.g. *caustic remarks.*
[from Greek *kaiein* meaning 'to burn']

cauterize, cauterizes, cauterizing, cauterized; also spelled cauterise
(verb) To cauterize a wound means to burn it in order to help it heal.
[from Latin *cauterium* meaning 'branding-iron']

caution, cautions, cautioning, cautioned
1 (noun) Caution is great care which you take to avoid danger, e.g. *They proceeded with caution.*
2 A caution is a warning, e.g. *They were let off with a caution.*
3 (verb) If someone cautions you, they warn you, usually not to do something again, e.g. *He was caught asleep on duty and cautioned.*
cautionary (adjective).
[from Latin *cavere* meaning 'to beware']

cautious
(adjective) acting very carefully to avoid danger, e.g. *a cautious driver.*
cautiously (adverb), cautiousness (noun).

cavalcade, cavalcades
(noun) A cavalcade is a procession of people on horses or in cars or carriages.

cavalier (pronounced kav-val-**eer**)
(adjective) arrogant and behaving without sensitivity, e.g. *a cavalier attitude.*

cavalry
(noun) The cavalry is the part of an army that uses armoured vehicles or horses.

cave, caves, caving, caved
1 (noun) A cave is a large hole in rock, that is underground or in the side of a cliff.
2 (verb) If a roof caves in, it collapses inwards.
[from Latin *cava* meaning 'hollows']

caveman, cavemen
(noun) Cavemen were people who lived in caves in prehistoric times.

cavern, caverns
(noun) A cavern is a large cave.

cavernous
(adjective) large, deep, and hollow, e.g. *a cavernous building... cavernous eyes.*

caviar or caviare (pronounced **kav**-vee-ar)
(noun) Caviar is the tiny salted eggs of a fish called the sturgeon, eaten as a delicacy.

cavil, cavils, cavilling, cavilled
(verb) To cavil means to complain about unimportant things.
[from Latin *cavillari* meaning 'to jeer']

cavity, cavities
(noun) A cavity is a small hole in something solid, e.g. *a tooth cavity.*

cavort, cavorts, cavorting, cavorted
(verb) When people cavort, they jump around excitedly.

caw, caws, cawing, cawed
1 (verb) When a crow or rook caws, it makes a harsh sound.

2 (noun) A caw is the harsh sound that a crow or rook makes.

cayenne pepper
(noun) Cayenne pepper is a very hot red spice made from ground dried peppers.

CB, CBs
(noun) A CB is a range of radio waves which the general public can use to send messages to one another. CB is an abbreviation for 'Citizens' Band'.

CBE, CBEs
(noun) A CBE is an honour granted by the King or Queen. CBE is an abbreviation for 'Commander of the Order of the British Empire', e.g. *Graham Jones, CBE.*

cc an abbreviation for 'cubic centimetres'.

cease, ceases, ceasing, ceased
1 (verb) If something ceases, it stops happening. **2** If you cease to do something, or cease doing it, you stop doing it.
[from Latin *cedere* meaning 'to yield']

cease-fire, cease-fires
(noun) A cease-fire is an agreement between groups that are fighting each other to stop for a period and discuss peace.

ceaseless
(adjective) going on without stopping, e.g. *the ceaseless drone of traffic.*
ceaselessly (adverb).

cedar, cedars
(noun) A cedar is a large evergreen tree with wide branches and needle-shaped leaves.
[from Greek *kedros* meaning 'cedar' or 'juniper']

cede, cedes, ceding, ceded (pronounced **seed**)
(verb) To cede something means to give it up to someone else, e.g. *The colony was ceded to Spain.*
[from Latin *cedere* meaning 'to yield']

cedilla, cedillas (pronounced sid-**dil**-la)
(noun) In French and Portuguese, a cedilla is a symbol written under the letter 'c' to indicate that it is pronounced like an 's' rather than a 'k', as in the word *garçon.*
[an Old Spanish word meaning 'little z']

ceilidh, ceilidhs (pronounced **kay**-lee)
(noun) A ceilidh is an informal evening of folk music, singing, and dancing, originating from Scotland and Ireland.

ceiling, ceilings
1 (noun) A ceiling is the top inside surface of a room.
2 A ceiling is also a top limit for things such as prices, e.g. *a ceiling on wage increases.*

celebrate, celebrates, celebrating, celebrated
1 (verb) If you celebrate or celebrate something, you do something special and enjoyable in honour of it, e.g. *We had champagne to celebrate my promotion.*
2 When a priest celebrates Mass, he performs the actions and ceremonies of the Mass.
celebration (noun), **celebratory** (adjective).
[from Latin *celeber* meaning 'renowned']

Similar words: (sense 1) rejoice, exult

celebrated
(adjective) famous, e.g. *a celebrated actress.*

celebrity, celebrities
(noun) A celebrity is a famous person.

celery
(noun) Celery is a vegetable with long pale green stalks.
[from Greek *selinon* meaning 'parsley']

celestial (pronounced sil-**lest**-yal)
(adjective; a formal word) concerning the sky or heaven, e.g. *celestial bodies.*
[from Latin *caelum* meaning 'the heavens']

celibate, celibates (pronounced **sel**-lib-bit)
1 (adjective) Someone who is celibate does not marry or have sex, often because of their religious beliefs.
2 (noun) A celibate is a person who is celibate.
celibacy (noun).
[from Latin *caelebs* meaning 'unmarried']

cell, cells
1 (noun) In biology, a cell is the smallest part of an animal or plant that can exist by itself. Each cell contains a nucleus.
2 In a prison or police station, a cell is a small room which a prisoner is locked in.
3 A cell is also a device that produces electricity using energy from chemicals, heat, or light.
4 A cell is also a small group of people set up to work together as part of a larger organization.
cellular (adjective).
[from Latin *cella* meaning 'monk's cell']

cellar, cellars
(noun) A cellar is an underground room below a building, often used to store wine.
[from Latin *cellarium* meaning 'foodstore']

cello, cellos (pronounced **chel**-loh)
(noun) A cello is a large musical stringed instrument which you play sitting down, holding the instrument upright with your knees.
cellist (noun).

cellophane
(noun) Cellophane is thin, transparent plastic material used to wrap food or other things to protect them.

celluloid (pronounced **sel**-yul-loyd)
(noun) Celluloid is a type of plastic.

cellulose
(noun) Cellulose is a substance found in the cell walls of plants and used to make paper, plastic, and other materials.

Celsius (pronounced **sel**-see-yuss)
Celsius is a scale for measuring temperature in which water freezes at 0 degrees (0°C) and boils at 100 degrees (100°C). It is named after Anders Celsius (1701-1744), who invented it. Celsius is the same as 'Centigrade'.

Celtic (pronounced **kel**-tik)
(adjective) A Celtic language is a member of a group of languages that includes Gaelic, Welsh, and Breton.

cement, cements, cementing, cemented
1 (noun) Cement is a fine powder made from limestone and clay, which is mixed with sand and water to make mortar or concrete.
2 (verb) To cement things means to stick them together with cement or cover them with cement.
3 Something that cements a relationship makes it stronger, e.g. *contracts to cement the companies' alliance.*
[from Latin *caementum* meaning 'quarried stone']

cemetery, cemeteries
(noun) A cemetery is an area of land where dead people are buried.
[from Greek *koimētērion* meaning 'dormitory']

cenotaph, cenotaphs (pronounced **sen**-not-ahf)
(noun) A cenotaph is a monument built in memory of dead people, especially soldiers buried elsewhere.
[from Greek *kenos + taphos* meaning 'empty tomb']

censor, censors, censoring, censored
1 (noun) A censor is a person officially appointed to examine books or films and to cut or ban parts that are considered obscene, too violent, or politically unacceptable.
2 (verb) If someone censors a book or film, they cut or ban parts of it that are considered unsuitable for the public.
censorship (noun).

Similar words: (sense 2) cut, expurgate

censorious (pronounced sen-**saw**-ree-uss)
(adjective) very critical of other people.

censure, censures, censuring, censured
(pronounced **sen**-sher)
1 (noun) Censure is strong disapproval of something.
2 (verb) To censure someone means to criticize them severely.

census, censuses
(noun) A census is an official survey of the population of a country.

cent, cents
(noun) The cent is a unit of currency in the USA and in some other countries. In the USA, a cent is worth one hundredth of a dollar.
[from Latin *centum* meaning 'hundred']

centaur, centaurs (pronounced **sen**-tawr)
(noun) In Greek mythology, a centaur is a creature with the top half of a man and the lower body and legs of a horse.

centenarian, centenarians (pronounced sen-ten-**nair**-ee-en)
(noun) A centenarian is a person who is a hundred years old or more.

centenary, centenaries (pronounced sen-**teen**-er-ee)
(noun) A centenary is the 100th anniversary of something.

centi-
(prefix) Centi- is used to form words that have 'hundred' as part of their meaning, e.g. *centimetre.*
[from Latin *centum* meaning 'hundred']

Centigrade
Centigrade is another name for 'Celsius'.

centilitre, centilitres
(noun) A centilitre is a unit of liquid volume equal to one hundredth of a litre.

centime, centimes (pronounced **sonn**-team)
(noun) The centime is a unit of currency in France, Belgium, Switzerland, and some other countries. A centime is worth one hundredth of the country's main currency.

centimetre, centimetres
(noun) A centimetre is a unit of length equal to ten millimetres or one hundredth of a metre.

centipede, centipedes
(noun) A centipede is a small, wormlike creature with a body in segments and many pairs of legs.
[from Latin *centum + pedes* meaning 'a hundred feet']

central
1 (adjective) in or near the centre of an object or area, e.g. *houses around a central courtyard.*
2 main or most important, e.g. *the central character in the book.*
centrally (adverb), **centrality** (noun).

Central America
(noun) Central America is another name for the Isthmus of Panama, the area of land joining North America to South America.
Central American (adjective).

central heating
(noun) Central heating is a system of heating a building in which water or air is heated in a tank and travels through pipes and radiators round the building.

centralize, centralizes, centralizing, centralized; also spelled **centralise**
(verb) To centralize a system means to bring the organization of it under the control of one central group.
centralization (noun).

Similar words: concentrate, rationalize

centre, centres, centring, centred
1 (noun) The centre of an object or area is the middle of it.
2 A centre is a building where people go for activities, meetings, or help, e.g. *an arts centre.*
3 Someone or something that is the centre of attention attracts a lot of attention.
4 In politics, the centre is the group with political beliefs considered to be between the two extremes of left and right wing.
5 A centre in a sports team is a player whose position is in the central area of the playing field.
6 (verb) To centre something means to move it so that it is balanced or at the centre of something else, e.g. *He centred himself on the raft.*
7 If something centres on or around a particular thing, that thing is the main subject of attention, e.g. *The workers' demands centred around pay.*

[from Latin *centrum* meaning 'stationary point of pair of compasses']

Similar words: (sense 1) heart, hub, middle

centre of gravity, centres of gravity
(noun) The centre of gravity in an object is the point at which it balances perfectly.

centrifugal (pronounced sen-trif-**yoo**-gl)
(adjective) In physics, centrifugal force is the force that makes rotating objects move outwards.
[from Latin *centrum* + *fugere* meaning 'to flee from the centre']

centripetal (pronounced sen-**trip**-pee-tl)
(adjective) In physics, centripetal force is the force that makes rotating objects move inwards.
[from Latin *centrum* + *petere* meaning 'to seek the centre']

centurion, centurions
(noun) A centurion was a Roman officer in charge of a hundred soldiers.

century, centuries
1 (noun) A century is a period of one hundred years.
2 In cricket, a century is one hundred runs scored by a batsman.
[from Latin *centum* meaning 'hundred']

ceramic, ceramics (pronounced sir-**ram**-mik)
1 (noun) Ceramic is a hard material made by baking clay to a very high temperature.
2 A ceramic is an object made from ceramic.
3 Ceramics is the art of making objects out of clay.
[from Greek *keramos* meaning 'potter's clay']

cereal, cereals
1 (noun) A cereal is a plant that produces edible grain, such as wheat, maize, oats, or rice.
2 A cereal is also a food made from grain, often eaten with milk for breakfast.
[from Latin *cerealis* meaning 'concerning the growing of grain']

cerebral (pronounced **ser**-reb-ral)
(adjective; a formal word) relating to the brain, e.g. *a cerebral haemorrhage*.
[from Latin *cerebrum* meaning 'brain']

cerebral palsy
(noun) Cerebral palsy is an illness caused by damage to a baby's brain before it is born, which makes its muscles and limbs very weak.

ceremonial, ceremonials
1 (adjective) relating to a ceremony, e.g. *ceremonial dances*.
2 (noun) The ceremonial of a formal occasion is the traditional clothing and customs of the occasion, e.g. *the ceremonial of the wedding*.
ceremonially (adverb).

ceremonious
(adjective) extremely formal or polite, e.g. *He bid a ceremonious farewell*.
ceremoniously (adverb).

ceremony, ceremonies
1 (noun) A ceremony is a set of formal actions performed at a special occasion or important public event, e.g. *a wedding ceremony*.

2 Ceremony is very formal and polite behaviour, e.g. *She was received with respectful ceremony*.
3 (phrase) If someone tells you **not to stand on ceremony**, they mean you should not behave formally, e.g. *Help yourself to food; we never stand on ceremony here*.
[from Latin *caerimonia* meaning 'holy ritual']

Similar words: (sense 1) rite, ritual, ceremonial

certain
1 (adjective) definite and with no doubt at all.
2 You use certain to refer to a specific person or thing, e.g. *We met on a certain day*.
3 You use certain to suggest that a quality is noticeable but not clearly definable, e.g. *His suit gave him a certain distinction*.
[from Latin *certus* meaning 'sure' or 'decided']

certainly
1 (adverb) without doubt, e.g. *There will certainly be an economic crisis*.
2 of course, e.g. *'May I borrow your pen?'*—*'Certainly.'*

certainty, certainties
1 (noun) Certainty is the state of being certain.
2 A certainty is something that is known without doubt, e.g. *The result was a certainty*.

certifiable
(adjective) A person who is certifiable is considered mad and can be declared insane.

certificate, certificates
(noun) A certificate is a document stating particular facts, e.g. *a marriage certificate*.

certify, certifies, certifying, certified
1 (verb) To certify something means to declare formally that it is true, e.g. *a letter certifying payment*.
2 To certify someone means to declare officially that they are insane.
[from Latin *certus* + *facere* meaning 'to make sure']

certitude
(noun; a formal word) Certitude is a feeling of certainty.

cervical (pronounced **ser**-vik-kl)
1 (adjective; a technical word) relating to the cervix.
2 relating to the neck.

cervix, cervixes or **cervices**
(noun; a technical word) The cervix is the entrance to the womb at the top of the vagina.
[from Latin *cervix* meaning 'neck']

cessation
(noun; a formal word) The cessation of something is the stopping of it, e.g. *Both sides wanted a cessation of hostilities*.
[from Latin *cessare* meaning 'to desist']

cesspit, cesspits
(noun) A cesspit is the same as a cesspool.

cesspool, cesspools
(noun) A cesspool is a tank in the ground into which waste water and sewage flow.
[from Old French *souspirail* meaning 'air-hole']

cf. means 'compare'. It is written to mention something that should be considered in connection with the subject being discussed.

chafe, chafes, chafing, chafed
1 (verb) If your skin chafes, it becomes sore by something rubbing against it.
2 If you chafe at something, you feel irritated or impatient with it, e.g. *They chafed at the restrictions imposed on them.*
[from Old French *chaufer* meaning 'to warm']

chaff
(noun) Chaff is the outer parts of grain separated from the seeds by beating.

chaffinch, chaffinches
(noun) A chaffinch is a small European bird with black and white wings. The male has a reddish body.

chagrin (pronounced **shag**-rin)
(noun; a formal word) Chagrin is a feeling of annoyance or disappointment.
chagrined (adjective).

chain, chains, chaining, chained
1 (noun) A chain is a number of metal rings connected together in a line, e.g. *a bicycle chain.*
2 A chain of things is a number of them in a series or connected to each other, e.g. *a chain of islands... Were you involved in this chain of events?... a chain of hotels.*
3 (verb) If you chain one thing to another, you fasten them together with a chain, e.g. *Demonstrators chained themselves to a fence.*
[from Latin *catena* meaning 'chain']

chain reaction, chain reactions
(noun) A chain reaction is a rapid series of events in which each event causes the next one.

chain saw, chain saws
(noun) A chain saw is a large saw with teeth fixed in a chain that is driven round by a motor.

chain-smoke, chain-smokes, chain-smoking, chain-smoked
(verb) To chain-smoke means to smoke cigarettes continually.
chain-smoker (noun).

chain store, chain stores
(noun) A chain store is a large shop that is part of a chain of shops owned by one company.

chair, chairs, chairing, chaired
1 (noun) A chair is a seat with a back and four legs for one person.
2 A chair at university is a professor's post.
3 The chair of a meeting is the person in charge who decides when each person may speak.
4 (verb) The person who chairs a meeting is in charge of it.
[from Greek *kathedra* meaning 'seat']

chair lift, chair lifts
(noun) A chair lift is a line of chairs that hang from a moving cable and carry people up and down a mountain.

chairman, chairmen
1 (noun) The chairman of a meeting is the person in charge who decides when each person may speak.

2 The chairman of a company or committee is the head of it.
chairperson (noun), **chairwoman** (noun), **chairmanship** (noun).

chaise longue, chaises longues (pronounced shayz **long**)
(noun) A chaise longue is a type of couch with a single armrest. 'Chaise longue' is French for 'long chair'.

chalet, chalets (pronounced **shall**-lay)
(noun) A chalet is a wooden house with a sloping roof, especially in a mountain area or a holiday camp.

chalice, chalices (pronounced **chal**-liss)
(noun) A chalice is a gold or silver cup used in Christian churches to hold the Communion wine.

chalk, chalks, chalking, chalked
1 (noun) Chalk is a soft white rock consisting of calcium carbonate and containing minute fossils. Small sticks of chalk are used for writing or drawing on a blackboard.
2 (verb) To chalk something means to mark it with chalk.
3 To chalk up a result means to achieve it, e.g. *They have already chalked up four wins.*
chalky (adjective).
[from Greek *khalix* meaning 'pebble']

challenge, challenges, challenging, challenged
1 (noun) A challenge is something that is new and exciting but requires a lot of effort, e.g. *Mount Everest presented a challenge to Hillary.*
2 A challenge is also a suggestion from someone to compete with them.
3 A challenge to something is a questioning of whether it is correct or true, e.g. *the challenge to authority.*
4 (verb) If someone challenges you, they suggest that you compete with them in some way, e.g. *He challenged me to a race.*
5 If you challenge something, you question whether it is correct or true, e.g. *challenging the government's authority.*
6 If someone such as a soldier challenges you, they order you to stop and say who you are or why you are there.
challenger (noun), **challenging** (adjective).

Similar words: (sense 5) defy, contradict, dispute

chamber, chambers
1 (noun) A chamber is a large room, especially one used for formal meetings, e.g. *the Council Chamber.*
2 A Chamber is also a group of people appointed to decide laws or administrative matters.
3 (plural noun) Chambers are a room where judges hear cases that are not being heard in an open court.
4 (noun) A chamber is also a hollow place or compartment inside something, especially inside an animal's body or inside a gun, e.g. *the chambers of the heart.*
[from Greek *kamara* meaning 'vault']

chamberlain, chamberlains (pronounced **chaim**-ber-lin) (noun) A chamberlain is the person in charge of the household affairs of a king or queen.

chambermaid, chambermaids
(noun) A chambermaid is a woman who works in a hotel cleaning and tidying the bedrooms.

chamber music
(noun) Chamber music is classical music written for a small group of instruments.

chamber of commerce, chambers of commerce
(noun) A chamber of commerce is an organization of businessmen who work together to improve business in their region.

chamber pot, chamber pots
(noun) A chamber pot is a bowl that people used to keep in their bedrooms to urinate into during the night.

chameleon, chameleons (pronounced kam-**mee**-lee-on)
(noun) A chameleon is a lizard which is able to change the colour of its skin to match the colour of its surroundings.
[from Greek *khamai* + *leōn* meaning 'ground lion']

chamois leather, chamois leathers (pronounced **sham**-mee)
(noun) A chamois leather is a soft leather cloth used for polishing. It used to be made from the skin of a kind of goat called a chamois.

chamomile another spelling of **camomile.**

champ, champs, champing, champed
1 (verb) To champ means to eat noisily.
2 (phrase) If you are **champing at the bit,** you are very impatient to start something.

champagne, champagnes (pronounced sham-**pain**)
(noun) Champagne is a sparkling white wine, called after the region of France where it is made.

champion, champions, championing, championed
1 (noun) A champion is a person who wins a competition.
2 A champion of a cause or principle is someone who supports or defends it, e.g. *a champion of human rights.*
3 (verb) Someone who champions a cause or principle supports or defends it.
[from Latin *campus* meaning 'battlefield']

championship, championships
(noun) A championship is a competition to find the champion of a sport; also the title or status of a champion.

chance, chances, chancing, chanced
1 (noun) The chance of something happening is how possible or likely it is, e.g. *Has he got a chance of winning?*
2 A chance to do something is an opportunity to do it, e.g. *She left before I had a chance to explain.*
3 A chance is also a possibility that something dangerous or unpleasant may happen, e.g. *If you want to make money you've got to take chances.*
4 (verb) If you chance something, you try it although you are taking a risk.

5 (noun) Chance is also the way things happen unexpectedly without being planned, e.g. *We met purely by chance.*
6 (verb) If you chance to do something or chance on something, you do it or find it by chance, e.g. *I chanced on an old school-friend in the street.*
[from Old French *cheoir* meaning 'to occur']

Similar words: (sense 5) accident, coincidence, fluke

chancel, chancels
(noun) In a church, the chancel is the part containing the altar, where the clergy and choir sit.
[from Latin *cancelli* meaning 'lattice']

chancellor, chancellors
1 (noun) In some European countries, the Chancellor is the head of government.
2 In Britain, the Chancellor is the Chancellor of the Exchequer.
3 A chancellor is also the honorary head of a British university.
[from Latin *cancellarius* meaning 'porter' or 'secretary']

Chancellor of the Exchequer
(noun) The Chancellor of the Exchequer is the minister responsible for finance and taxes.

chancy, chancier, chanciest
(adjective; an informal word) risky or uncertain.

chandelier, chandeliers (pronounced shan-del-**leer**)
(noun) A chandelier is an ornamental frame hanging from a ceiling with branches that hold several light bulbs or candles.

chandler, chandlers
(noun) A chandler is a person who sells equipment for ships and sailing.

change, changes, changing, changed
1 (noun) A change in something is a difference or alteration, e.g. *He doesn't like changes in his life... It made a change walking to work.*
2 A change of something is a replacement by something else, e.g. *The car needs an oil change.*
3 (verb) When something changes or when you change it, it becomes different, e.g. *My ideas have changed since then.*
4 If you change something, you exchange it for something else, e.g. *Can I change this for a larger size?*
5 When you change, you put on different clothes.
6 To change money means to exchange it for smaller coins of the same total value, or to exchange it for foreign currency.
7 (noun) Change is money you get back when you have paid more than the actual price of something.
8 Change is also small coins rather than notes, e.g. *Have you got change for a fiver?*
changeless (adjective).
[from Latin *cambire* meaning 'to swap' or 'to barter']

Similar words: (sense 1) adjustment, modification, alteration
(sense 3) adapt, alter, modify, transform, convert

changeable
(adjective) likely to change all the time.

Similar words: inconsistent, volatile, unpredictable, erratic, unreliable, fickle, mercurial, variable, capricious

changeling, changelings
(noun) In fairy stories, a changeling is a fairy child exchanged by the fairies for a real child.

change of life
(noun) The change of life is the menopause.

changeover, changeovers
(noun) A changeover is a change from one system or activity to another, e.g. *the changeover from manual to computer operation.*

channel, channels, channelling, channelled
1 (noun) A channel is a wavelength used to receive programmes broadcast by a television or radio station; also the station itself, e.g. *He switched to the other channel.*
2 A channel is also a passage along which water flows or along which something is carried.
3 The Channel or the English Channel is the stretch of sea between England and France.
4 A channel is also a method of achieving something, e.g. *I applied through all the correct channels.*
5 (verb) To channel something such as money or energy means to control and direct it in a particular way, e.g. *Funds must be channelled through the project.*
[from Latin *canalis* meaning 'pipe']

chant, chants, chanting, chanted
1 (noun) A chant is a group of words repeated over and over again, e.g. *a football chant.*
2 A chant is also a religious song sung on only a few notes with very little melody.
3 (verb) If people chant a group of words, they repeat them over and over again, e.g. *thousands of demonstrators chanting outside.*
4 To chant also means to sing a religious song.
[from Latin *cantare* meaning 'to sing']

chaos (pronounced kay-oss)
(noun) Chaos is a state of complete disorder and confusion.
chaotic (adjective).
[from Greek *khaos* meaning 'formlessness']

chap, chaps, chapping, chapped
1 (noun; an informal use) A chap is a man.
2 (verb) If your skin chaps, it becomes dry and cracked, usually as a result of cold or wind.
[sense 1 from *chapman* an old word meaning 'customer' or 'buyer']
chapped (adjective).

chapel, chapels
1 (noun) A chapel is a section of a church or cathedral with its own altar, used for private prayer or special services.
2 A chapel is also a type of small church.
[from Latin *capella* meaning 'small cloak'; originally used of the place where St Martin's cloak was kept as a relic]

chaperone, chaperones, chaperoning, chaperoned (pronounced shap-per-rone); also spelled chaperon
1 (noun) A chaperone is an older woman who accompanies a young unmarried woman on social occasions, or any person who accompanies a group of younger people.
2 (verb) To chaperone a person or group means to accompany them somewhere and be responsible for them.
[from Old French *chape* meaning 'hood', i.e. a protective cover]

chaplain, chaplains
(noun) A chaplain is a member of the Christian clergy attached to an institution such as a hospital, school, or prison.
chaplaincy (noun).

chapter, chapters
1 (noun) A chapter is one of the parts into which a book is divided.
2 A chapter in someone's life or in history is a particular period in it, e.g. *A new chapter of my career was about to begin.*
3 In a cathedral, the chapter is the group of Christian clergy who work there.
[from Latin *capitulum* meaning 'little head']

char, chars, charring, charred
(verb) If something chars, it gets partly burned and goes black.
charred (adjective).

character, characters
1 (noun) The character of a person or place is all the qualities which combine to form their personality or atmosphere.
2 A person or place that has character has an interesting, attractive, or admirable quality, e.g. *an old house of great character.*
3 The characters in a film, play, or book are the people in it.
4 You can refer to a person as a character, especially when you are describing a particular quality they have, e.g. *an unpleasant character.*
5 A character is also a letter, number, or other written symbol.
[from Greek *kharaktēr* meaning 'engraver's tool']

Similar words: (sense 1) identity, nature, personality

characteristic, characteristics
1 (noun) A characteristic is a quality that is typical of a particular person or thing, e.g. *Impatience is one of his characteristics.*
2 (adjective) Characteristic means typical of a particular person or thing, e.g. *stone walls characteristic of this area.*
characteristically (adverb).

Similar words: (sense 1) attribute, property, feature, quality, trait
(sense 2) distinctive, distinguishing, idiosyncratic

characterization
(noun) Characterization is the way people are portrayed in books, plays, or films.

characterize, characterizes, characterizing, characterized; also spelled characterise
1 (verb) A quality that characterizes something is typical of it, e.g. *the bright reds and yellows that characterize her designs.*

2 To characterize someone or something means to describe their characteristics.

characterless
(adjective) dull and uninteresting, e.g. *a characterless new town.*

charade, charades (pronounced shar-**rahd**)
1 (noun) A charade is a ridiculous and unnecessary activity or pretence.
2 Charades is a game in which players act a word or phrase for other players to guess.
[from Provençal *charrado* meaning 'chat']

charcoal
(noun) Charcoal is a black form of carbon made by burning wood without air, used as a fuel and also for drawing.

charge, charges, charging, charged
1 (verb) If someone charges you money, they ask you to pay it for something that you have bought or received, e.g. *They charged £2 admission.*
2 (noun) A charge is the price that you have to pay for something.
3 A charge is a formal accusation that a person is guilty of a crime and has to go to court.
4 (verb) To charge someone means to accuse them formally of having committed a crime.
5 (a formal use) To charge someone to do something means to order them to do it.
6 (noun) To have charge or be in charge of someone or something means to be responsible for them and be in control of them.
7 A charge is also an explosive put in a gun or other weapon.
8 An electrical charge is the amount of electricity that something carries.
9 (verb) To charge a battery means to pass an electrical current through it to make it store electricity.
10 To charge somewhere means to rush forward, often in order to attack someone, e.g. *The bull charged at him.*
[from Old French *chargier* meaning 'to load']

charger, chargers
1 (noun) A charger is a device for charging or recharging batteries.
2 In the past, a charger was a horse ridden into battle by a knight.

chariot, chariots
(noun) A chariot is a two-wheeled open vehicle pulled by horses, which was used in ancient times for racing and fighting.
[from Old French *char* meaning 'light vehicle']

charisma (pronounced kar-**riz**-ma)
(noun) Charisma is a special ability to attract or influence people by your personality.
charismatic (adjective).
[from Greek *kharis* meaning 'grace' or 'charm']

charity, charities
1 (noun) Charity is money or other help given to poor, disabled, or ill people, e.g. *Even when homeless he was too proud to accept charity.*
2 A charity is an organization that raises money to help people who are ill, poor, or disabled.

3 Charity is also a kind, sympathetic attitude towards people.
charitable (adjective).
[from Latin *caritas* meaning 'love' or 'affection']

charlady, charladies
(noun; an old-fashioned word) A charlady or charwoman is a woman who works as a cleaner.

charlatan, charlatans (pronounced **shar**-lat-tn)
(noun) A charlatan is someone who pretends to have skill or knowledge that they do not really have.
[from Italian *ciarlare* meaning 'to chatter']

charm, charms, charming, charmed
1 (noun) Charm is an attractive and pleasing quality that some people and things have, e.g. *narrow cobbled streets full of charm.*
2 (verb) If you charm someone, you use your charm to please them.
3 (noun) A charm is a small ornament worn on a bracelet.
4 A charm is also a magical spell or an object that is supposed to bring good luck.
[from Latin *carmen* meaning 'song' or 'incantation']

Similar words: (sense 2) bewitch, delight, enchant

charmer, charmers
(noun) A charmer is someone who uses their personal charm to influence people.

charming
(adjective) very pleasant and attractive, e.g. *a charming girl... a charming house.*
charmingly (adverb).

chart, charts, charting, charted
1 (noun) A chart is a diagram or table showing information, e.g. *a chart showing the fall in birth rate over 10 years.*
2 A chart is also a map of the sea or stars.
3 (verb) To chart an area means to make a map of it.
4 If you chart a course of action, you plan it.
[from Greek *khartēs* meaning 'papyrus']

charter, charters, chartering, chartered
1 (noun) A charter is a document stating the rights or aims of a group or organization as laid down by the government, e.g. *the charter of the University.*
2 (verb) To charter transport such as a plane or boat means to hire it for private use.
chartered (adjective).

chary (pronounced **chair**-ee)
(adjective) very cautious and wary.
charily (adverb), **chariness** (noun).

chase, chases, chasing, chased
1 (verb) If you chase someone or something, you run or go after them in order to catch them or drive them away.
2 (noun) A chase is the activity of chasing or hunting someone or something, e.g. *a car chase.*
[from Old French *chacier* meaning 'to hunt']

Similar words: (sense 1) hound, pursue, run after

chasm, chasms (pronounced **kazm**)
1 (noun) A chasm is a deep crack in the earth's surface.
2 A chasm is also a very large difference between two ideas or groups of people, e.g. *a society with a chasm between rich and poor.*
[from Greek *khasma* meaning 'yawn' or 'gulf']

chassis (pronounced **shas**-ee)
The plural is also **chassis**.
(noun) The chassis of a vehicle is the frame on which it is built.
[from French *chassis* meaning 'window-frame']

chaste (pronounced **chayst**)
1 (adjective; an old-fashioned use) not having sex with anyone outside marriage.
2 very simple in style, e.g. *chaste houses.*
chastely (adverb), **chastity** (noun).
[from Latin *castus* meaning 'pure']

chasten, chastens, chastening, chastened
(pronounced **chay**-sn)
(verb; a literary word) If you are chastened by an experience, it makes you regret that you have behaved badly or foolishly.

chastise, chastises, chastising, chastised
(verb; a formal word) If someone chastises you, they scold you or punish you for something that you have done.
chastisement (noun).

chat, chats, chatting, chatted
1 (noun) A chat is a friendly talk with someone, usually about things that are not very important.
2 (verb) When people chat, they talk to each other in a friendly way.

Similar words: gossip, natter, chatter

chat up
(phrasal verb; an informal use) If you chat up a member of the opposite sex, you talk to them in a friendly way, because you are attracted to them.

chateau, chateaux (pronounced **shat**-toe)
(noun) A chateau is a large country house or castle in France.

chattel, chattels
(noun; an old-fashioned word) Your chattels are the things you own.
[from Latin *capitale* meaning 'wealth']

chatter, chatters, chattering, chattered
1 (verb) When people chatter, they talk very fast.
2 (noun) Chatter is a lot of fast unimportant talk.
3 (verb) If your teeth are chattering, they are knocking together and making a clicking noise because you are cold.

chatterbox, chatterboxes
(noun; an informal word) A chatterbox is a person who talks too much.

chatty, chattier, chattiest
(adjective) talkative and friendly.

chauffeur, chauffeurs (pronounced **show**-fur)
(noun) A chauffeur is a person whose job is to drive another person's car.
[from French *chauffeur* meaning 'stoker' or 'fireman']

chauvinist, chauvinists (pronounced **show**-vin-ist)
1 (noun) A chauvinist is a person who thinks their country is always right. Nicolas Chauvin was an extreme French patriot.
2 A male chauvinist is a man who believes that men are superior to women.
chauvinistic (adjective), **chauvinism** (noun).

cheap, cheaper, cheapest
1 (adjective) Something that is cheap costs very little money, and is usually of poor quality.
2 A cheap joke or cheap remark is unfair and unkind.
cheaply (adverb).
[from Old English *ceap* meaning 'price' or 'bargain']

Similar words: (sense 1) inexpensive, reasonable, cut-price

cheat, cheats, cheating, cheated
1 (verb) If someone cheats, they do wrong or unfair things in order to win or get something that they want.
2 If you are cheated of or out of something, you do not get what you are entitled to, e.g. *They felt cheated of victory.*
3 (noun) A cheat is a person who cheats.

Similar words: (sense 1) swindle, deceive, double-cross, hoodwink, con, defraud

check, checks, checking, checked
1 (noun) A check is an inspection to make sure that everything is all right.
2 Checks are different coloured squares which form a pattern.
3 In chess, check is a position in which a player's king is threatened with capture.
4 (verb) To check something means to examine it in order to make sure that everything is all right.
5 To check the growth, movement, or spread of something means to make it stop, e.g. *The government's first aim was to check rising prices.*
6 If you check yourself, you suddenly stop yourself from doing what you were going to do.
7 (phrase) If you keep something such as an emotion **in check**, you keep it under control.
8 (adjective) Check or checked means marked with a pattern of squares, e.g. *check trousers.*

check in
(phrasal verb) When you check in at a hotel or airport, you arrive and sign your name or show your ticket.

check out
1 (phrasal verb) When you check out of a hotel, you pay the bill and leave.
2 If you check something out, you inspect it and find out whether everything about it is right.

check up on
(phrasal verb) To check up on someone means to find out whether they are doing what they should be doing, or whether what they have said is true.

checkmate
(noun) In chess, checkmate is a situation where one player cannot stop their king being captured in the next move and so loses the game.
[from Arabic *shah mat* meaning 'the King is dead']

checkout, checkouts
(noun) A checkout is a counter in a supermarket where the customers pay for their goods.

checkpoint, checkpoints
(noun) A checkpoint is a place where traffic has to stop in order to be checked.

checkup, checkups
(noun) A checkup is an examination by a doctor to see if your health is all right.

cheek, cheeks
1 (noun) Your cheeks are the sides of your face below your eyes.
2 Cheek is speech or behaviour that is rude or disrespectful, e.g. *I've had enough of your cheek.*

Similar words: (sense 2) gall, impertinence, insolence, nerve, effrontery, impudence

cheeky, cheekier, cheekiest
(adjective) rather rude and disrespectful, often in an amusing way.

cheer, cheers, cheering, cheered
1 (verb) When people cheer, they shout with approval or in order to show support for a person or team.
2 (noun) A cheer is a shout of approval or support.
3 (verb) If something cheers you, it makes you feel happier.

Similar words: (sense 3) hearten, gladden, uplift

cheer up
(phrasal verb) When you cheer up, you feel more cheerful.

cheerful
1 (adjective) happy and in good spirits, e.g. *She's in a cheerful mood.*
2 bright and pleasant-looking, e.g. *cheerful colours... a cheerful fire.*
cheerfully (adverb), **cheerfulness** (noun).

Similar words: (sense 1) bright, breezy, jolly, jovial, hearty, cheery, jocular, merry

cheerio
Cheerio is a friendly way of saying goodbye.

cheery, cheerier, cheeriest
(adjective) happy and cheerful, e.g. *a cheery smile.*

cheese, cheeses
(noun) Cheese is a hard or creamy food made from the thick soft part of milk (curds) that separates from the watery part (whey) when milk turns sour.
[from Latin *caseus*]

cheesecake, cheesecakes
(noun) Cheesecake is a dessert consisting of a layer of biscuit covered with a mixture of cream cheese.

cheeseparing
(adjective) excessively mean with money, e.g. *the cheeseparing attitude of some employers.*

cheetah, cheetahs
(noun) A cheetah is one of the largest members of the cat family. It has a black-spotted light brown coat. Cheetahs are found in Africa and are the fastest land animals.
[from Sanskrit *citra + kaya* meaning 'speckled body']

chef, chefs
(noun) A chef is a head cook in a restaurant or hotel.

chemical, chemicals
1 (adjective) involved in chemistry or using chemicals, e.g. *the chemical composition of water... a ban on chemical weapons.*
2 (noun) Chemicals are substances manufactured by chemistry. Some are used as fertilizers or to kill weeds, and others are used in industry.
chemically (adverb).
[from Greek *khēmeia* meaning 'alchemy']

chemist, chemists
1 (noun) A chemist is a person who is qualified to make up drugs and medicines prescribed by a doctor.
2 A chemist or a chemist's is a shop where medicines and cosmetics are sold.
3 A chemist is also a person qualified in chemistry who works in industry or in a university, e.g. *a research chemist at ICI.*

chemistry
(noun) Chemistry is the scientific study of substances and the ways in which they change when they are combined with other substances.

chemotherapy (pronounced keem-oh-**ther**-a-pee)
(noun) Chemotherapy is a way of treating diseases such as cancer by using chemicals.

cheque, cheques
(noun) A cheque is a printed form on which you write an amount of money that you have to pay. You sign the cheque and your bank pays the money from your account.

chequebook, chequebooks
(noun) A chequebook is a book of printed cheques.

chequered (pronounced **chek**-kerd)
1 (adjective) covered with a pattern of squares.
2 A chequered career is a varied career that has both good and bad parts.

cherish, cherishes, cherishing, cherished
1 (verb) If you cherish something, you care deeply about it and want to keep it or look after it lovingly, e.g. *It was one of his most cherished possessions.*
2 If you cherish a memory or hope, you have it in your mind and care deeply about it, e.g. *He secretly cherishes the hope that she will return.*

Similar words: (sense 1) treasure
(sense 2) foster, treasure, nurture, cultivate

cherry, cherries
1 (noun) A cherry is a small, juicy fruit with a red or black skin and a hard stone in the centre.
2 A cherry is also a tree that produces cherries. Its wood is used for furniture.

cherub, cherubs or **cherubim**
(noun) A cherub is an angel, shown in pictures as a plump, naked child with wings.
cherubic (adjective).

chess
(noun) Chess is a board game for two people in which each player has 16 pieces and tries to move his or her pieces so that the other player's king cannot escape.

chessboard, chessboards
(noun) A chessboard is a board divided into 64 squares of two alternating colours on which chess is played.

chest, chests
1 (noun) A chest is a large wooden box with a hinged lid.
2 Your chest is the front part of your body between your shoulders and your waist.
3 (an informal phrase) If you **get something off your chest**, you tell someone about it because it has been worrying you.
[from Latin *cista* meaning 'box' or 'basket']

chestnut, chestnuts
1 (noun) Chestnuts are reddish-brown nuts that grow inside a prickly green outer covering. Some chestnuts can be eaten.
2 A chestnut is a tree that produces these nuts.
3 (adjective) A chestnut horse or chestnut hair is reddish-brown in colour.

chest of drawers, chests of drawers
(noun) A chest of drawers is a piece of furniture with drawers in it, used for storing clothes.

chevron, chevrons (pronounced **shev**-ron)
(noun) A chevron is a V-shape which is worn on the sleeve by sergeants, corporals, and other noncommissioned officers to show their rank.
[from Latin *capreoli* meaning 'two pieces of wood forming a rafter']

chew, chews, chewing, chewed
(verb) When you chew something, you use your teeth to break it up in your mouth before swallowing it.

chewing gum
(noun) Chewing gum is a kind of sweet that you chew and keep in your mouth for a long time, but which you do not swallow.

chic (pronounced **sheek**)
(adjective) elegant and fashionable, e.g. *a chic black coat... a chic dinner party.*

chick, chicks
(noun) A chick is a young bird, especially a young chicken.

chicken, chickens, chickening, chickened
1 (noun) A chicken is a bird kept on a farm for its eggs and meat; also the meat of this bird, e.g. *We're having chicken for dinner.*
2 (adjective; an informal use) Someone who is chicken is cowardly or easily scared.

3 (verb; an informal use) If you chicken out of something, you do not do it because you are afraid.

chickenpox
(noun) Chickenpox is an illness which produces a fever and blister-like spots on the skin.

chickpea, chickpeas
(noun) Chickpeas are yellow pealike seeds used in cooking. They come from a bushy plant that grows in the Mediterranean region, Asia, and Africa.

chicory
(noun) Chicory is a plant with bitter leaves that are used in salads, and roots that are roasted and used in some types of coffee.

chide, chides, chiding, chided
(verb; an old-fashioned word) To chide someone means to tell them off.
[from Old English *cidan* meaning 'to scold']

chief, chiefs
1 (noun) The leader of a group or organization is its chief.
2 (adjective) most important, e.g. *the chief reason for resigning... the chief steward.*
chiefly (adverb).

chieftain, chieftains
(noun) A chieftain is the leader of a tribe or clan.

chiffon (pronounced **shif**-fon)
(noun) Chiffon is a very thin lightweight cloth made of silk or nylon, e.g. *a chiffon scarf.*
[from French *chiffe* meaning 'rag']

chihuahua, chihuahuas (pronounced chi-**wah**-wah)
(noun) A chihuahua is a breed of very small dog with short hair and pointed ears.

chilblain, chilblains
(noun) A chilblain is a sore, itchy swelling, usually on the foot or hand, caused by poor circulation of the blood.

child, children
1 (noun) A child is a young person who is not yet an adult.
2 Someone's child is their son or daughter, e.g. *He is married with two children.*
3 (an informal phrase) If you say that something is **child's play**, you mean it is very easy.

Similar words: (sense 1) kid, juvenile, youngster, minor, nipper, toddler, tot
(sense 2) offspring, issue, progeny, descendant

childhood, childhoods
(noun) Someone's childhood is the time of their life during which they are a child.

childish
(adjective) immature and foolish, e.g. *He was annoyed by her childish behaviour.*
childishly (adverb), **childishness** (noun).

Similar words: babyish, infantile, juvenile, puerile

childless
(adjective) having no children, e.g. *a childless couple.*

childlike
(adjective) like a child in appearance or behaviour, e.g. *her childlike innocence.*

childminder, childminders
(noun) A childminder is a person who is qualified and paid to look after other people's children while they are at work.

childproof
(adjective) Something that is childproof is designed to stop children from hurting themselves on it or damaging it.

Chilean, Chileans
1 (adjective) belonging or relating to Chile.
2 (noun) A Chilean is someone who comes from Chile.

chill, chills, chilling, chilled
1 (verb) To chill something means to make it cold, e.g. *The wine should be chilled.*
2 If something chills you, it makes you feel worried or frightened, e.g. *chilling reports about the war.*
3 (noun) A chill is a feverish cold.
4 A chill is also a feeling of cold, e.g. *the chill of the night.*

chilli, chillies
(noun) A chilli is the red or green seed pod of a type of pepper which has a very hot, spicy taste and is used for flavouring in cooking.

chilly, chillier, chilliest
1 (adjective) rather cold, e.g. *a chilly afternoon.*
2 unfriendly and without enthusiasm, e.g. *He got a very chilly reception.*

chime, chimes, chiming, chimed
1 (verb) When a bell chimes, it makes a clear ringing sound.
2 (noun) Chimes are a set of bells or other objects which make ringing sounds.
[from Old English *chymbe* meaning 'bell']

chimney, chimneys
(noun) A chimney is a vertical pipe or other hollow structure above a fireplace or furnace through which smoke from a fire escapes.
[from Greek *kaminos* meaning 'fireplace' or 'oven']

chimney stack, chimney stacks
(noun) A chimney stack is the part of a chimney that is above the roof of a building.

chimney sweep, chimney sweeps
(noun) A chimney sweep is a person whose job is cleaning the soot out of chimneys.

chimpanzee, chimpanzees
(noun) A chimpanzee is a small ape with dark fur that lives in forests in central Africa.

chin, chins
(noun) Your chin is the part of your face below your mouth.

china
(noun) China is items like cups, saucers, and plates made from very fine clay.

Chinese
1 (adjective) belonging or relating to China.
2 (noun) A Chinese is someone who comes from China.
3 Chinese refers to any of a group of related languages and dialects spoken by Chinese people.

chink, chinks
1 (noun) A chink is a small, narrow opening, e.g. *a chink in the curtains... a chink of light.*
2 A chink is also a short, light, ringing sound, like one made by glasses touching each other.

chintz
(noun) Chintz is a type of brightly patterned cotton fabric, used for making curtains and covering furniture.
[from Hindi *chint* meaning 'brightly coloured']

chip, chips, chipping, chipped
1 (noun) Chips are thin strips of fried potato.
2 In electronics, a chip is a tiny piece of silicon inside a computer which is used to form electronic circuits.
3 A chip is also a small piece broken off an object, or the mark made when a piece breaks off, e.g. *a mug with a chip in it.*
4 (verb) If you chip an object, you break a small piece off it.
5 In some gambling games, chips are counters used to represent money.
6 (phrase) If you say that someone is **a chip off the old block**, you mean they are very like one of their parents in behaviour.
7 Someone who has **a chip on their shoulder** behaves aggressively because they have a grudge or feel sensitive about something.

chipboard
(noun) Chipboard is a material made from wood scraps pressed together into hard sheets.

chipmunk, chipmunks
(noun) A chipmunk is a small rodent with a striped back, found in North America.

chipolata, chipolatas
(noun) A chipolata is a type of small, spicy sausage.

chiropodist, chiropodists (pronounced kir-**rop**-pod-dist)
(noun) A chiropodist is a person whose job is treating people's feet.
chiropody (noun).
[from Greek *kheir* meaning 'hand' and *podes* meaning 'feet']

chirp, chirps, chirping, chirped
1 (verb) To chirp means to make a short, high-pitched sound, e.g. *birds chirping in the trees.*
2 (noun) A chirp is a short, high-pitched sound.

chirpy, chirpier, chirpiest
(adjective; an informal word) lively and cheerful, e.g. *She seems much chirpier now.*

chirrup, chirrups, chirruping, chirruped
(verb) Chirrup means the same as chirp.

chisel, chisels, chiselling, chiselled
1 (noun) A chisel is a tool with a long metal blade and a sharp edge at the end which is used for cutting and shaping wood, stone, or metal.

2 (verb) To chisel wood, stone, or metal means to cut or shape it using a chisel.
[from Latin *caesus* meaning 'a cut']

chit, chits
(noun) A chit is a small note such as a receipt or a voucher.
[from Hindi *cittha* meaning 'note']

chivalry (pronounced **shiv**-val-ree)
1 (noun) Chivalry is polite, kind, helpful behaviour, especially by men towards women.
2 In medieval times, chivalry was a system with strict ideals about courage, honour, and loyalty which was followed by knights.
chivalrous (adjective).
[from Latin *caballarius* meaning 'horseman']

chive, chives
(noun) Chives are grasslike hollow leaves that have a mild onion flavour. Chives are used for flavouring in cooking.

chivvy, chivvies, chivvying, chivvied
(verb) If you chivvy someone, you keep urging them to do something.

chlorinate, chlorinates, chlorinating, chlorinated
(verb) To chlorinate something, especially water, means to treat it with chlorine.

chlorine (pronounced **klaw**-reen)
(noun) Chlorine is a chemical element which is a poisonous greenish-yellow gas with a strong, unpleasant smell. It is used to disinfect water and to make bleach. Its atomic number is 17 and its symbol is Cl.

chloroform (pronounced **klor**-rof-form)
(noun) Chloroform is a colourless liquid with a strong, sweet smell used in cleaning products. In the past it was used as an anaesthetic.

chlorophyll (pronounced **klor**-rof-fil)
(noun) Chlorophyll is a green pigment in plants which traps the energy from sunlight and makes photosynthesis possible.
[from Greek *khlōros* meaning 'green']

chloroplast
(noun) Chloroplast is a substance containing chlorophyll and other pigments, which occurs in plants that carry out photosynthesis.

chock, chocks
(noun) A chock is a block or wedge for placing behind wheels or heavy objects, in order to stop them moving.

chock-a-block or **chock-full**
(adjective) completely full.

chocolate, chocolates
1 (noun) Chocolate is a sweet food made from cacao seeds. A chocolate is a sweet made of chocolate.
2 (adjective) dark brown.
[from Aztec *xococ + atl* meaning 'bitter water']

choice, choices; choicer, choicest
1 (noun) A choice is a range of different things that are available to choose from, e.g. *We had a choice of five types of vegetable.*
2 A choice is also something that you choose, e.g. *Who is your choice for leader of the party?*

3 Choice is the power or right to choose, e.g. *I don't want to go but I have no choice.*
4 (adjective) Choice means of very high quality, e.g. *choice food and drink.*

Similar words: (sense 1) selection, variety, alternative, option
(sense 4) select, prize, hand-picked

choir, choirs (pronounced **kwire**)
(noun) A choir is a group of singers, for example in a church.

choke, chokes, choking, choked
1 (verb) If you choke, you stop being able to breathe properly, usually because something is blocking your windpipe, e.g. *He choked on his drink.*
2 If things choke a place, they fill it so much that it is blocked or clogged up, e.g. *The stream was choked with leaves.*
3 (noun) The choke in a car engine is the control that reduces the amount of air going into the engine, and so makes the car easier to start.

choke back
(phrasal verb) If you choke back a strong emotion, you force yourself not to show it, e.g. *She choked back her tears.*

cholera (pronounced **kol**-ler-ra)
(noun) Cholera is a serious disease causing severe diarrhoea and vomiting. It is caused by infected food or water.
[from Greek *kholera* meaning 'jaundice']

cholesterol (pronounced kol-**less**-ter-rol)
(noun) Cholesterol is a substance found in all animal fats, tissues, and blood.
[from Greek *kholē* meaning 'bile' and *stereos* meaning 'hard']

choose, chooses, choosing, chose, chosen
(verb) To choose something means to decide to have it or do it, e.g. *He can afford to go anywhere he chooses.*

Similar words: pick, select, opt for, take

choosy, choosier, choosiest
(adjective) fussy and difficult to satisfy, e.g. *She's very choosy about what music she listens to.*

chop, chops, chopping, chopped
1 (verb) To chop something means to cut it with quick, heavy strokes using an axe or a knife.
2 (noun) A chop is a small piece of lamb or pork containing a bone, usually cut from the ribs.
3 (phrase) If you **chop and change**, you keep changing your mind or what you do.

Similar words: (sense 1) hack, hew, lop

chopper, choppers
(noun; an informal word) A chopper is a helicopter.

choppy, choppier, choppiest
(adjective) Choppy water has a lot of waves because it is windy.

chopstick, chopsticks
(noun) Chopsticks are a pair of thin sticks used by people in the Far East for eating food.

choral
(adjective) relating to singing by a choir, e.g. *a concert of choral music.*

chord, chords
1 (noun) A chord is a group of three or more musical notes played together.
2 In geometry, a chord is a straight line connecting two points on a curve.
[from Greek *khordē* meaning 'gut' or 'string']

chore, chores
(noun) A chore is an unpleasant job that has to be done, e.g. *household chores.*
[from Old English *cierr* meaning 'job']

choreography (pronounced kor-ree-**og**-raf-fee)
(noun) Choreography is the art of composing dance steps and movements.
choreographer (noun).
[from Greek *khoreia* meaning 'dance' and *graphein* meaning 'to write']

chorister, choristers (pronounced **kor**-riss-ter)
(noun) A chorister is a singer in a church choir, especially a male singer.

chortle, chortles, chortling, chortled
(verb) To chortle means to laugh with amusement.

chorus, choruses, chorusing, chorused
1 (noun) A chorus is a large group of singers; also a piece of music for a large group of singers.
2 The chorus of a song is a part which is repeated after each verse.
3 (verb) If people chorus something, they all speak or sing it at the same time.
[from Greek *khoros*, the group of actors who gave the commentary in Classical plays]

chow, chows
(noun) A chow is a breed of dog with a thick coat and curly tail, originally from China.

Christ
(noun) Christ is the name for Jesus. Christians believe that Jesus is the son of God.

christen, christens, christening, christened
(verb) When a baby is christened, it is named by a clergyman in a religious ceremony as a sign that it is a member of the Christian church.

Christian, Christians
1 (noun) A Christian is a person who believes in Jesus Christ and his teachings.
2 (adjective) relating to Christ and his teachings, e.g. *the Christian faith.*
3 good, kind, and considerate, e.g. *She was a very Christian woman.*
Christianity (noun).

Christian name, Christian names
(noun) Someone's Christian name is the name given to them when they were born or christened.

Christmas, Christmases
(noun) Christmas is the Christian festival celebrating the birth of Christ, falling on December 25th.

chrome (pronounced **krome**)
(noun) Chrome is metal plated with chromium.

chromium (pronounced **krome**-me-um)
(noun) Chromium is a hard shiny metallic element, used to make steel alloys and to cover other metals to increase hardness and prevent rusting. Its atomic number is 24 and its symbol is Cr.

chromosome, chromosomes
(noun) In biology, a chromosome is one of a number of rod-shaped parts in the nucleus of a cell which contains genes that determine the characteristics of an animal or plant.
[from Greek *khrōma* meaning 'colour' and *sōma* meaning 'body']

chronic (pronounced **kron**-nik)
1 (adjective) never stopping or lasting a very long time, e.g. *He has chronic asthma.*
2 (an informal use) very bad, severe, or unpleasant, e.g. *It was a really chronic film.*
chronically (adverb).

chronicle, chronicles, chronicling, chronicled
1 (noun) A chronicle is a record of a series of events described in the order in which they happened.
2 (verb) To chronicle a series of events means to record or describe them in the order in which they happened, e.g. *His book chronicles the war years of 1914-18.*

chronological (pronounced kron-nol-**loj**-i-kl)
(adjective) arranged in the order in which things happened, e.g. *His paintings are displayed in chronological order.*
chronologically (adverb).

Similar words: consecutive, historical

chronology (pronounced kron-**nol**-loj-jee)
(noun) The chronology of events is the order in which they happened.
[from Greek *khronos* meaning 'time' and *legein* meaning 'to say']

chronometer, chronometers (pronounced kron-**nom**-mit-ter)
(noun) A chronometer is an extremely accurate type of clock, used especially in navigation, diving, and mountaineering.
[from Greek *khronos* meaning 'time' and *metron* meaning 'a measure']

chrysalis, chrysalises (pronounced **kriss**-sal-liss)
(noun) A chrysalis is a butterfly or moth when it is developing from being a caterpillar to being a fully grown adult. It has a hard protective covering.

chrysanthemum, chrysanthemums (pronounced kriss-**an**-thim-mum)
(noun) A chrysanthemum is a plant with large, brightly coloured flowers.
[from Greek *khrusos* + *anthemon* meaning 'gold flower']

chubby, chubbier, chubbiest
(adjective) plump and round, e.g. *a chubby baby.*

chuck, chucks, chucking, chucked
(verb; an informal word) To chuck something means to throw it casually.

chuckle, chuckles, chuckling, chuckled
(verb) When you chuckle, you laugh quietly.

chug, chugs, chugging, chugged
(verb) When a machine or engine chugs, it makes a continuous dull thudding sound.

chum, chums
(noun; an informal word) A chum is a friend.

chump, chumps
(noun) If you call someone a chump, you mean that they have been rather silly or foolish.

chunk, chunks
(noun) A chunk of something solid is a thick piece of it.

Similar words: block, hunk, lump, knob

chunky, chunkier, chunkiest
1 (adjective) Someone who is chunky is broad and heavy but usually short.
2 in a chunk or in chunks, e.g. *chunky dogfood.*

church, churches
1 (noun) A church is a building where Christians go for religious sevices and worship.
2 In the Christian religion, a church is one of the groups with their own particular beliefs, customs, and clergy, e.g. *the Episcopal Church.*
[from Greek *kuriakon* meaning 'master's house']

Church of England
(noun) The Church of England is the Anglican church in England, where it is the state church, with the King or Queen as its head.

churchyard, churchyards
(noun) A churchyard is an area of land around a church, often used as a graveyard.

churlish
(adjective) bad-tempered and unfriendly.
[from Old English *ceorl* meaning 'commoner']

churn, churns, churning, churned
1 (noun) A churn is a container used for making milk or cream into butter.
2 (verb) To churn something means to stir it vigorously, for example when making milk into butter.

churn out
(phrasal verb) If you churn things out, you produce them quickly in large numbers, e.g. *We are all churning out ideas for the next show.*

chute, chutes (pronounced **shoot**)
(noun) A chute is a steep slope or channel used to slide things down, e.g. *a laundry chute.*
[from Old French *cheoite* meaning 'fallen']

chutney
(noun) Chutney is a strong-tasting thick sauce made from fruit, vinegar, and spices.

cicada, cicadas (pronounced sik-**kah**-da)
(noun) A cicada is a large insect that lives in hot countries. The male cicada makes a loud high-pitched vibrating noise.

CID
(noun) The CID is the detective branch of the British police force. CID is an abbreviation for 'Criminal Investigation Department'.

cider
(noun) Cider is an alcoholic drink made from apples.
[from Hebrew *shekhar* meaning 'strong drink']

cigar, cigars
(noun) A cigar is a roll of dried tobacco leaves which people smoke.
[from Mayan *sicar* meaning 'to smoke']

cigarette, cigarettes
(noun) A cigarette is a thin roll of tobacco covered in thin paper which people smoke.

cilia
(plural noun; a technical word) Cilia are small hairlike projections on the surface of a cell or micro-organism, which beat regularly in order to move either the organism or the surrounding fluid.

cinder, cinders
(noun) Cinders are small pieces of burnt material left after something such as wood or coal has burned.

cine camera, cine cameras (pronounced **sin**-nee)
(noun) A cine camera is a camera that takes moving film rather than still photographs.

cinema, cinemas
1 (noun) A cinema is a place where people go to watch films.
2 Cinema is the business of making films.
[from Greek *kinema* meaning 'motion']

cinematography
(noun) Cinematography is the technique of making films.

cinnamon
(noun) Cinnamon is a sweet spice which comes from the bark of an Asian tree. It is used for flavouring in cooking.

cipher, ciphers (pronounced **sy**-fer); also spelled **cypher**
1 (noun) A cipher is a secret code or system of writing used to send secret messages.
2 A cipher is also a person with no power or importance.
[from Arabic *sifr* meaning 'zero' or 'empty']

circa (pronounced **sir**-ka)
(preposition; a formal word) about or approximately; used especially before dates, e.g. *a Victorian cabinet, circa 1880.*

circle, circles, circling, circled
1 (noun) A circle is a completely regular round shape. Every point on its edge is the same distance from the centre.
2 (verb) To circle means to move round and round as though going round the edge of a circle, e.g. *A plane was circling overhead.*
3 (noun) A circle of people is a group of them with the same interest or profession, e.g. *a new work being widely discussed in music circles.*
4 In a theatre, the circle is an area of seats on an upper floor.
5 (phrase) To **come full circle** means to end up in the same situation you were in to start with.

circuit, circuits (pronounced sir-kit)
1 (noun) A circuit is any closed line or path, often circular, for example a racing track; also the distance round this path, e.g. *The race is ten circuits of the track.*
2 An electrical circuit is a complete route around which an electric current can flow.

circuitous (pronounced sir-**kyoo**-it-tuss) (adjective; a formal word) A circuitous route is long, complicated, and indirect.

circular, circulars
1 (adjective) in the shape of a circle.
2 A circular argument or theory is not valid because it uses a statement to prove a conclusion and the conclusion to prove the statement.
3 (noun) A circular is a letter or advertisement sent to a lot of people at the same time.
circularity (noun).

circulate, circulates, circulating, circulated
1 (verb) When something circulates or when you circulate it, it moves easily around an area, e.g. *Open a window and let the air circulate.*
2 When you circulate something among people, you pass it round or tell it to all the people, e.g. *A letter was circulated to all the club members.*

Similar words: (sense 2) spread, disseminate

circulation, circulations
1 (noun) The circulation of something is the act of circulating it or the action of it circulating, e.g. *the circulation of books... traffic circulation.*
2 The circulation of a newspaper or magazine is the number of copies that are sold of each issue.
3 Your circulation is the movement of blood through your body.

circumcise, circumcises, circumcising, circumcised
(verb) If a boy or man is circumcised, the foreskin at the end of his penis is removed. This is carried out mainly as part of a Muslim or Jewish religious ceremony.
circumcision (noun).
[from Latin *circum* meaning 'circle' and *caesum* meaning 'cut']

circumference, circumferences
(noun) The circumference of a circle is its outer line or edge; also the length of this line.

circumflex, circumflexes
(noun) In French and some other languages, a circumflex is a mark like an inverted 'v' placed over some vowels to indicate a change in pronunciation, for example in the word *rôle.*

circumspect
(adjective; a formal word) cautious and careful not to take risks.
circumspectly (adverb), **circumspection** (noun).
[from Latin *circumspicere* meaning 'to look round']

circumstance, circumstances
1 (noun) The circumstances of a situation or event are the conditions that affect what happens, e.g. *the country's political circumstances.*
2 Someone's circumstances are their position and conditions in life, e.g. *His change in circumstances brought him confidence.*
[from Latin *circumstare* meaning 'to surround']

circumstantial
(adjective; a formal word) Circumstantial evidence makes it seem likely that something happened, but does not prove it.

circumvent, circumvents, circumventing, circumvented
(verb; a formal word) To circumvent a rule means to avoid having to obey it, often in a dishonest way.
[from Latin *circumvenire* meaning 'to deceive']

circus, circuses
(noun) A circus is a show given by a travelling group of entertainers such as clowns, acrobats, and specially trained animals.
[from Latin *circus* meaning 'circle']

cirrhosis (pronounced si-**roh**-siss)
(noun) Cirrhosis is a disease of the liver, often caused by drinking too much alcohol.
[from Greek *kirrhos* meaning 'orange-coloured']

cirrus
(noun; a meteorological word) Cirrus is a type of thin cloud high up in the sky.
[from Latin *cirrus* meaning 'curly' or 'fringed']

cistern, cisterns
(noun) A cistern is a tank in which water is stored, for example one in the roof of a house.
[from Latin *cista* meaning 'box']

citadel, citadels
(noun) A citadel is a fortress in or near a city.

cite, cites, citing, cited
1 (verb; a formal word) If you cite something, you quote it or refer to it, e.g. *He cited several examples to prove his point.*
2 If someone is cited in a legal action, they are officially summoned to appear in court.
3 If someone is cited for something good that they have done, they are given official written praise for it, e.g. *soldiers cited for bravery.*
citation (noun).

citizen, citizens
(noun) The citizens of a country or city are the people who live in it or belong to it.
citizenship (noun).

citric acid
(noun) Citric acid is a type of weak water-soluble acid, found especially in citrus fruits.

citrus fruit, citrus fruits
(noun) Citrus fruits are juicy, sharp-tasting fruits such as oranges, lemons, and grapefruit.

city, cities
1 (noun) A city is a large town where many people live and work.
2 The City is the part of London which contains the main British financial institutions such as the Stock Exchange.
[from Latin *civitas* meaning 'citizenship']

Similar words: (sense 1) town, conurbation, metropolis

civic
(adjective) relating to a city or citizens, e.g.
Birmingham civic offices... civic responsibilities.

civil
1 (adjective) relating to the citizens of a country,
e.g. *civil rights... civil disturbances.*
2 relating to people or things that are not
connected with the armed forces, e.g. *a civil
airliner.*
3 polite, e.g. *She gave a civil answer.*
civilly (adverb), **civility** (noun).

civil engineering
(noun) Civil engineering is the design and
construction of roads, bridges, and public
buildings.

civilian, civilians
(noun) A civilian is a person who is not in the
armed forces.

civilization, civilizations; also spelled civilisation
1 (noun) A civilization is a society which has a
highly developed organization, culture, and way
of life, e.g. *ancient Greek civilization.*
2 Civilization is an advanced state of social
organization, culture, and way of life.

civilize, civilizes, civilizing, civilized; also spelled civilise
(verb) To civilize a society or group of people
means to educate them and develop their social
organization, culture, and way of life.
civilized (adjective).

civil servant, civil servants
(noun) A civil servant is a person who works in
the civil service.

civil service
(noun) The civil service is the staff who work in
government departments responsible for the
administration of a country.

civil war, civil wars
(noun) A civil war is a war between groups of
people who live in the same country.

cl an abbreviation for 'centilitres'.

clad
(adjective; a literary word) Someone who is clad
in particular clothes is wearing them.

cladding
(noun) Cladding is a covering of tiles, boards, or
concrete fixed to the outside of a building, often
to protect it from the weather.

claim, claims, claiming, claimed
1 (verb) If you claim that something is true or is
the case, you say that it is, although some people
may not believe you, e.g. *He claimed to be a
British citizen.*
2 If you claim something, you ask for it because
it belongs to you or you have a right to it, e.g.
You may claim expenses for the journey.
3 (noun) A claim is a statement that something is
the case, or that you have a right to something,
e.g. *He put in a claim for £10.*
[from Latin *clamare* meaning 'to cry out']

Similar words: (sense 1) allege, assert, profess

claimant, claimants
(noun) A claimant is someone who is making a
claim, especially for money.

clairvoyant, clairvoyants
1 (adjective) able to know about things that will
happen in the future.
2 (noun) A clairvoyant is a person who is, or
claims to be, clairvoyant.
clairvoyance (noun).
[from French *clair* + *voyant* meaning
'clear-seeing']

clam, clams
(noun) A clam is a type of mollusc, which lives in
sand under the sea and has two shells that shut
together tightly. Many types of clam are edible.

clamber, clambers, clambering, clambered
(verb) If you clamber somewhere, you climb
there with difficulty.

clammy, clammier, clammiest
(adjective) unpleasantly damp and sticky, e.g.
cold, clammy hands.
[from Old English *clæman* meaning 'to smear']

clamour, clamours, clamouring, clamoured
1 (verb) If people clamour for something, they
demand it noisily or angrily, e.g. *hundreds of
children clamouring for attention.*
2 (noun) Clamour is noisy or angry shouts or
demands by a lot of people.
clamorous (adjective).

clamp, clamps, clamping, clamped
1 (noun) A clamp is an object with movable parts
that are used to hold two things firmly together.
2 (verb) To clamp things together means to
fasten them or hold them firmly with a clamp.
3 To clamp down on something means to become
stricter in controlling it, e.g. *The authorities are
clamping down on crime.*
[from Old English *clamm* meaning 'fetter']

clan, clans
(noun) A clan is a group of families related to
each other by being descended from the same
ancestor, especially in Scotland.

clandestine
(adjective) secret and hidden, e.g. *clandestine
meetings at night.*
[from Latin *clam* meaning 'secretly']

clang, clangs, clanging, clanged
(verb) When something metal clangs or when
you clang it, it makes a loud, deep sound.

clanger, clangers
(noun; an informal word) If you drop a clanger,
you make an embarrassing mistake.

clank, clanks, clanking, clanked
(verb) If something metal clanks, it makes a loud
noise.

clap, claps, clapping, clapped
1 (verb) When you clap, you hit your hands
together loudly, for example at the end of a
concert or play to show your appreciation.
2 If you clap someone on the back or shoulder,
you hit them in a friendly way.
3 If you clap something somewhere, you put it

there quickly and firmly, e.g. *He clapped his cap on his head.*
4 (noun) A clap is a sound made by clapping your hands.
5 A clap of thunder is a sudden loud noise of thunder.

clapper, clappers
(noun) A clapper is a small piece of metal that hangs inside a bell and strikes the side to make the bell sound.

claptrap
(noun; an informal word) Claptrap is foolish or insincere talk.

claret, clarets
(noun) Claret is a type of red wine, especially one from the Bordeaux region of France.

clarify, clarifies, clarifying, clarified
1 (verb) To clarify something means to make it clear and easier to understand, e.g. *Would you clarify that last point you made?*
2 To clarify a substance such as butter means to remove the impurities from it by heating. **clarification** (noun).
[from Latin *clarus* + *facere* meaning 'to make clear']

clarinet, clarinets
(noun) A clarinet is a woodwind instrument with a straight tube and a single reed in its mouthpiece.

clarinettist, clarinettists
(noun) A clarinettist is a person who plays the clarinet.

clarion call, clarion calls
(noun) A clarion call is a strong encouragement to people to do something.

clarity
(noun) The clarity of something is its clearness.
[from Latin *clarus* meaning 'clear']

clash, clashes, clashing, clashed
1 (verb) If people clash with each other, they fight or argue.
2 Ideas or styles that clash are so different that they do not go together.
3 If two events clash, they happen at the same time so you cannot go to both.
4 When metal objects clash, they hit each other with a loud noise.
5 (noun) A clash is a fight or argument.
6 A clash of ideas, styles, or events is a situation in which they do not go together.
7 A clash of metal objects is a loud noise made when they hit each other.

clasp, clasps, clasping, clasped
1 (verb) To clasp something means to hold it tightly or fasten it, e.g. *He sat clasping his knees.*
2 (noun) A clasp is a fastening such as a hook or catch.

class, classes, classing, classed
1 (noun) A class of people or things is a group of them of a particular type or quality, e.g. *the middle class.*
2 A class is a group of pupils or students taught together, or a lesson that they have together.

3 Someone who has class is elegant in appearance or behaviour.
4 (verb) To class something means to arrange it in a particular group or to consider it as belonging to a particular group, e.g. *Her job is classed as part-time despite the long hours.*

Similar words: (sense 1) group, category, order, set

classic, classics
1 (adjective) typical and therefore a good model or example of something, e.g. *The place has a classic country village atmosphere.*
2 of very high quality, e.g. *a classic film.*
3 simple in style and form, e.g. *a classic tailored suit.*
4 (noun) Something that is considered a classic is of the highest quality, e.g. *the classics of English literature.*
5 Classics is the study of the literature of ancient Greece and Rome.
[from Latin *classicus* meaning 'of the first rank']

classical
1 (adjective) traditional in style, form, and content, e.g. *classical ballet.*
2 characteristic of the style of ancient Greece and Rome, e.g. *classical architecture.*
3 Classical music is serious music considered to be of lasting value.
classically (adverb).

classicist, classicists
(noun) A classicist is a person who studies classics.

classified
(adjective) officially declared secret by the government, e.g. *classified information.*

classify, classifies, classifying, classified
(verb) To classify things means to arrange them into groups with similar characteristics, e.g. *Books are classified according to subject area.*
classification (noun).

classy, classier, classiest
(adjective; an informal word) stylish and elegant.

clatter, clatters, clattering, clattered
1 (noun) A clatter is a loud rattling noise made by hard things hitting each other.
2 (verb) When things clatter, they hit each other with a loud rattling noise.

clause, clauses
1 (noun) A clause is a section of a legal document.
2 In grammar, a clause is a group of words with a subject and a verb, which may be a complete sentence or one of the parts of a sentence.
[from Latin *clausa* meaning 'end of sentence']

claustrophobia (pronounced klos-trof-**foe**-bee-ya)
(noun) Claustrophobia is a fear of being in enclosed spaces.
claustrophobic (adjective).
[from Latin *claustrum* meaning 'cloister' and Greek *phobos* meaning 'fear']

claw, claws, clawing, clawed
1 (noun) An animal's claws are hard, curved nails at the end of its feet.
2 The claws of a crab or lobster are the two jointed parts, used for grasping things.
3 (verb) If an animal claws something, it digs its claws into it.

clay
(noun) Clay is a type of earth that is soft and sticky when wet and hard when baked dry. It is used to make pottery and bricks.
[from Old English *clæg* meaning 'mud']

clean, cleaner, cleanest; cleans, cleaning, cleaned
1 (adjective) free from dirt or other unwanted substances or marks.
2 (verb) To clean something means to make it clean.
3 (adjective) Clean humour is decent and not offensive.
4 Clean also means free from fault or error, e.g. *a clean driving licence... a clean bill of health.*
5 A clean movement is skilful and accurate.
6 (an informal phrase) If you **come clean**, you tell people about something that you have been keeping secret.
cleanly (adverb), **cleaner** (noun).

cleanliness (pronounced klen-lin-ness)
(noun) Cleanliness is the practice or habit of keeping yourself and your surroundings clean.

cleanse, cleanses, cleansing, cleansed
(pronounced **klenz**)
(verb) To cleanse something means to make it completely clean and free from impurities.

clear, clearer, clearest; clears, clearing, cleared
1 (adjective) easy to understand, see, or hear, e.g. *a clear explanation.*
2 easy to see through, e.g. *clear water.*
3 free from obstructions or unwanted things, e.g. *Move out when the road is clear.*
4 (verb) To clear an area means to remove unwanted things from it.
5 When fog or mist clears, it disappears.
6 If you clear a fence or other obstacle, you jump over it without touching it.
7 If someone is cleared of a crime, they are proved to be not guilty.
8 (phrase) If someone is **in the clear**, they are free from blame, suspicion, or danger.
clearly (adverb).
[from Latin *clarus* meaning 'clear' or 'bright']

Similar words: (sense 1) distinct, lucid, coherent

clear out
1 (phrasal verb; an informal use) To clear out means to leave, e.g. *Clear out of here and leave me alone!*
2 If you clear out a room or cupboard, you tidy it and throw away unwanted things.

clear up
1 (phrasal verb) If you clear up, you tidy a place and put things away.
2 When a problem or misunderstanding is cleared up, it is solved or settled.

3 When the weather clears up, it becomes brighter.

clearance
1 (noun) Clearance is the removal of old buildings in an area.
2 If someone is given clearance to do something, they get official permission to do it.

clear-cut
(adjective) definite and distinct, e.g. *clear-cut differences between the parties.*

clearing, clearings
(noun) A clearing is an area of bare ground in a forest.

clearway, clearways
(noun) A clearway is a road on which cars are not allowed to park.

cleavage, cleavages
(noun) A woman's cleavage is the space between her breasts.

cleaver, cleavers
(noun) A cleaver is a knife with a large square blade, used especially by butchers.

clef, clefs
(noun) In written music, a clef is a symbol at the beginning of each line which indicates the pitch of the notes.
[from Latin *clavis* meaning 'key']

cleft, clefts
(noun) A cleft in a rock is a narrow opening.

cleft palate, cleft palates
(noun) Someone with a cleft palate was born with a narrow opening along the roof of their mouth which makes it difficult for them to speak.

clematis
(noun) Clematis is a climbing plant with large purple or white flowers.

clemency
(noun; a formal word) Clemency is kind treatment, especially from a person in authority.
[from Latin *clementia* meaning 'mildness']

clementine, clementines
(noun) A clementine is a type of small citrus fruit bred from the orange and the tangerine.

clench, clenches, clenching, clenched
1 (verb) When you clench your fist, you curl your fingers up tightly.
2 If you clench something in your hand, you hold it very tightly.
3 When you clench your teeth, you squeeze them together tightly.

clergy
(plural noun) The clergy are the ministers of the Christian Church.
[from Old French *clergie* meaning 'priesthood']

clergyman, clergymen
(noun) A clergyman is a male member of the clergy.

cleric, clerics
(noun; a formal word) A cleric is a member of the clergy.

clerical
1 (adjective) relating to work done in an office, e.g. *a job requiring clerical skills.*
2 relating to the clergy.

clerk, clerks (pronounced **klahrk**)
(noun) A clerk is a person whose job is keeping records or accounts in an office, bank, or law court.
[from Latin *clericus* meaning 'priest']

clever, cleverer, cleverest
1 (adjective) intelligent and quick to understand things.
2 very effective or skilful, e.g. *a book with a clever plot... a clever device.*
cleverly (adverb), **cleverness** (noun).

Similar words: (sense 1) brainy, smart, bright, brilliant, intelligent

cliché, clichés (pronounced **klee-shay**)
(noun) A cliché is an idea or phrase which is no longer effective because it has been used so much.

click, clicks, clicking, clicked
1 (verb) When something clicks or when you click it, it makes a short snapping sound.
2 (noun) A click is a sound of something clicking, e.g. *The door shut with a click.*
3 (verb; an informal use) When something clicks, you suddenly understand it.

client, clients
(noun) A client is someone who pays a professional person or company to receive a service, e.g. *a solicitor's clients.*
[from Latin *cliens* meaning 'a dependant']

clientele (pronounced klee-on-**tell**)
(plural noun) The clientele of a place are its customers.

cliff, cliffs
(noun) A cliff is a steep high rock face by the sea.

cliffhanger, cliffhangers
(noun) A cliffhanger is a situation that is tense and exciting because you do not know what is going to happen, for example in a book or film.

climactic
(adjective; a formal word) bringing a climax, e.g. *Her death is the climactic point of the film.*

climate, climates
1 (noun) The climate of a place is the typical weather conditions there, e.g. *hot climates.*
2 The climate of opinion is the general attitude and opinion of people at a particular time, e.g. *The climate of opinion is against privatization.*
climatic (adjective).

climax, climaxes
(noun) The climax of a process, story, or piece of music is the most exciting moment in it, usually near the end.
[from Greek *klimax* meaning 'ladder']

climb, climbs, climbing, climbed
1 (verb) To climb means to move upwards.
2 (noun) A climb is a movement upwards, e.g. *a long climb up the hill... a climb in house prices.*
3 (verb) If you climb somewhere, you move there with difficulty, e.g. *She climbed out of the truck.*
climber (noun).

Similar words: (sense 1) ascend, scale, mount

climb down
(phrasal verb) If you climb down in an argument, you give in slightly, e.g. *They refused to climb down over the issue of overtime.*

clinch, clinches, clinching, clinched
(verb) If you clinch an agreement or an argument, you settle it in a definite way, e.g. *He clinched a deal with a record company.*

cling, clings, clinging, clung
(verb) To cling to something means to hold onto it or stay closely attached to it, e.g. *She clung to the rope for dear life... old men clinging to traditional methods.*

clingfilm
(noun; a trademark) Clingfilm is a clear thin plastic used for wrapping food. Clingfilm sticks to itself.

clinic, clinics
(noun) A clinic is a building, often part of a hospital, where people go for medical treatment.
[from Latin *clinicus* meaning 'person on sickbed']

clinical
1 (adjective) relating to the medical treatment of patients, e.g. *clinical tests.*
2 Clinical behaviour or thought is logical and unemotional, e.g. *Her attitude was impersonal and clinical.*
clinically (adverb).

clink, clinks, clinking, clinked
(verb) When glass or metal objects clink, they make a gentle sound by touching each other.

clip, clips, clipping, clipped
1 (noun) A clip is a small metal or plastic object used for holding things together.
2 (verb) If you clip things together, you fasten them with clips.
3 If you clip something, you cut bits from it to shape it, e.g. *a neatly clipped hedge.*
4 (noun) A clip of a film is a short piece of it shown by itself.
[from Old Norse *klippa* meaning 'to cut']

clipboard, clipboards
(noun) A clipboard is a board with a clip at the top to keep papers in place.

clipper, clippers
1 (noun) Clippers are a tool used for cutting.
2 In the past, a clipper was a fast sailing ship.

clipping, clippings
(noun) A clipping is an article cut from a newspaper or magazine.

clique, cliques (rhymes with **seek**)
(noun) A clique is a small group of people who stick together and do not mix with other people.
cliquey (adjective).

Similar words: faction, sect, coterie, circle

clitoris, clitorises (pronounced **klit**-tor-riss)
(noun) A woman's clitoris is a small highly sensitive piece of flesh near the opening of her vagina.
[from Greek *kleiein* meaning 'to close']

cloak, cloaks, cloaking, cloaked
1 (noun) A cloak is a wide, loose coat without sleeves.
2 (verb) To cloak something means to cover or hide it, e.g. *hills cloaked in mist.*
[from Latin *clocca* meaning 'bell']

cloak-and-dagger
(adjective) involving mystery and secrecy.

cloakroom, cloakrooms
(noun) In a public building, a cloakroom is a room for coats, or a room with toilets and washbasins.

clobber, clobbers, clobbering, clobbered (an informal word)
1 (noun) You can call someone's belongings their clobber.
2 (verb) If you clobber someone, you hit them.

cloche, cloches (pronounced **klosh**)
(noun) A cloche is a glass or plastic covering put over garden plants for protection.
[from Latin *clocca* meaning 'bell']

clock, clocks, clocking, clocked
1 (noun) A clock is an instrument that measures and shows the time.
2 (phrase) If you work **round the clock**, you work all day and night.
[from Latin *clocca* meaning 'bell']

clock in
(phrasal verb) When workers clock in, they record their time of arrival at work.

clock up
(phrasal verb) To clock up an amount means to reach it, e.g. *He has clocked up 1000 miles of cycling.*

clockwise
(adjective and adverb) in the same direction as the hands on a clock.

clockwork
1 (noun) Toys that work by clockwork move when they are wound up with a key.
2 (phrase) If something happens **like clockwork**, it happens with no problems or delays.

clod, clods
(noun) A clod of earth is a lump of it.

clog, clogs, clogging, clogged
1 (verb) When something clogs a hole, it blocks it, e.g. *The drain was clogged with mud.*
2 (noun) Clogs are heavy wooden shoes.

cloister, cloisters
(noun) A cloister is a covered area for walking around a square in a monastery or a cathedral.

cloistered
(adjective) Someone who has a cloistered life lives quietly away from other people.

clone, clones, cloning, cloned
1 (noun) In biology, a clone is an animal or plant that has been produced artificially from the cells of another animal or plant and is therefore identical to it.
2 (verb) To clone an animal or plant means to produce it as a clone.
[from Greek *klōn* meaning 'twig' or 'shoot']

clop, clops, clopping, clopped
(verb) When a horse clops, its hoofs make a noise on the ground.

close, closes, closing, closed; closer, closest
1 (verb) To close something means to shut it.
2 If you close a meeting, conversation, or event, you bring it to an end.
3 (noun) The close of a period of time is the end of it, e.g. *The evening drew to a close.*
4 (adjective and adverb) near to something, e.g. *Move closer.*
5 (adjective) People who are close to each other are very friendly and know each other well.
6 Close inspection or attention is very careful and thorough.
7 If a competition is close, the competitors are nearly equal and the winner wins by only a small amount.
8 If the atmosphere is close, it is uncomfortably warm with not enough air.
9 (an informal phrase) If something is a **close shave** or a **close call**, there is very nearly an accident or disaster.
closely (adverb), **closeness** (noun), **closed** (adjective).
[from Latin *clausus* meaning 'shut up']

Similar words: (sense 4) near, at hand, nearby

close down
(phrasal verb) If a business closes down, all work stops there permanently.

close in
(phrasal verb) If people close in on you, they come nearer and nearer and surround you.

closed shop, closed shops
(noun) A closed shop is a factory or other business whose employees have to be members of a trade union.

closet, closets, closeting, closeted
1 (noun) A closet is a cupboard.
2 (verb) If you closet yourself or are closeted somewhere, you hide yourself away alone or in private with another person.
3 (adjective) Closet beliefs or habits are kept private and secret, e.g. *closet alcoholics.*

close-up, close-ups
(noun) A close-up is a detailed close view of something, especially a photograph taken close to the subject.

closure, closures (pronounced **klohz**-yur)
1 (noun) The closure of a business is the permanent shutting of it.
2 The closure of a road is the blocking of it.

clot, clots, clotting, clotted
1 (noun) A clot is a lump, especially one that forms when blood thickens.
2 (verb) When a substance such as blood clots, it thickens and forms a lump.

3 (noun; an informal use) If you call someone a clot, you mean that they have done something stupid.

cloth, cloths
1 (noun) Cloth is fabric made by a process such as weaving.
2 A cloth is a piece of cloth used for wiping or protecting things.

Similar words: (sense 1) material, textiles, fabric

clothe, clothes, clothing, clothed
1 (plural noun) Clothes are the things people wear on their bodies.
2 (verb) To clothe someone means to give them clothes to wear.

Similar words: (sense 1) clothing, garb, garments, gear, apparel, attire, array, dress
(sense 2) dress, attire, array, garb

clothing
(noun) Clothing is the clothes people wear.

cloud, clouds, clouding, clouded
1 (noun) A cloud is a mass of water vapour that forms in the air and is seen as a white or grey patch in the sky.
2 A cloud of smoke or dust is a mass of it floating in the air.
3 (verb) If something clouds or is clouded, it becomes cloudy or difficult to see through, e.g. *The sky clouded over.*
4 Something that clouds an issue makes it more confusing.
5 (phrase) If someone is **under a cloud**, they are in disgrace.
[from Old English *clud* meaning 'hill']

cloudburst, cloudbursts
(noun) A cloudburst is a sudden very heavy fall of rain.

cloudy, cloudier, cloudiest
1 (adjective) full of clouds, e.g. *a cloudy sky.*
2 difficult to see through, e.g. *cloudy water.*

Similar words: (sense 1) dull, overcast

clout, clouts, clouting, clouted (an informal word)
1 (verb) If you clout someone, you hit them.
2 (noun) A clout is a hit, e.g. *a clout on the head.*
3 Someone who has clout has influence.

clove, cloves
1 (noun) Cloves are small, strong-smelling dried flower buds from a tropical tree, used as a spice in cooking.
2 A clove of garlic is one of the separate sections of the bulb, used in cooking.
[from Old English *clufu* meaning 'bulb']

cloven hoof, cloven hooves
(noun) An animal with cloven hooves has hooves divided into two parts.

clover
1 (noun) Clover is a small plant with leaves made up of three lobes, and clustered pink or white flowers in a ball shape.
2 (phrase) Someone who is **in clover** is living in luxury and comfort.

clown, clowns, clowning, clowned
1 (noun) A clown is a circus performer who wears funny clothes and make-up and does silly things to make people laugh.
2 You can refer to any funny or silly person as a clown.
3 (verb) If you clown, you do silly things to make people laugh.
clownish (adjective).

Similar words: (sense 2) buffoon, jester, joker, fool

cloying
(adjective) unpleasantly sickly, sweet, or sentimental, e.g. *cloying perfume.*

club, clubs, clubbing, clubbed
1 (noun) A club is an organization of people with a particular interest, who meet regularly; also the place where they meet.
2 A club is also a thick, heavy stick used as a weapon.
3 In golf, a club is a stick with a shaped head that a player uses to hit the ball.
4 (verb) To club someone means to hit them hard with a heavy object.
5 (noun) Clubs is one of the four suits in a pack of playing cards. It is marked by a black symbol in the shape of a clover leaf.
6 (verb) If people club together, they all join together to give money to buy something.
[senses 2-5 from Old Norse *klubba* meaning 'wooden bludgeon']

Similar words: (sense 1) guild, association, society
(sense 2) bludgeon, cudgel, cosh, truncheon

cluck, clucks, clucking, clucked
(verb) When a hen clucks, it makes a short repeated high-pitched sound.

clue, clues
(noun) A clue to a problem, mystery, or puzzle is something that provides help in solving it.

clueless
(adjective; an informal word) stupid.

clump, clumps, clumping, clumped
1 (noun) A clump of plants, people, or buildings is a small group of them close together.
2 (verb) If you clump about, you walk with heavy footsteps.
[from Old English *clympe* meaning 'bunch']

clumsy, clumsier, clumsiest
1 (adjective) moving awkwardly and carelessly.
2 said or done without thought or tact, e.g. *His clumsy remark upset her.*
clumsily (adverb), **clumsiness** (noun).

Similar words: (sense 1) awkward, gauche, ungainly
(sense 2) awkward, gauche, maladroit, inept

cluster, clusters, clustering, clustered
1 (noun) A cluster of things is a group of them together, e.g. *clusters of flowers on the tree.*
2 (verb) If people cluster together, they stay together in a close group.
[from Old English *clyster* meaning 'bunch of grapes']

clutch, clutches, clutching, clutched
1 (verb) If you clutch something, you hold it tightly or seize it.
2 (plural noun) If you are in someone's clutches, they have power or control over you.
3 (noun) In a car, the clutch is the foot pedal that you press when changing gear.
4 A clutch of things, especially hens' eggs, is a group of them produced at one time.
[senses 1-3 are from Germanic *klukjan* meaning 'to grasp'; sense 4 is from Old Norse *klekja* meaning 'to hatch']

clutter, clutters, cluttering, cluttered
1 (noun) Clutter is an untidy mess.
2 (verb) Things that clutter a place fill it and make it untidy.

cm an abbreviation for 'centimetres'.

CND
(noun) CND is an organization which opposes the development and use of nuclear weapons. CND is an abbreviation for 'Campaign for Nuclear Disarmament'.

co-
(prefix) Co- means together, e.g. *We co-wrote the song.*
[from Latin *con* meaning 'together']

c/o
You write c/o before an address when writing to someone who is staying at the address for a short time. It is an abbreviation for 'care of'.

coach, coaches, coaching, coached
1 (noun) A coach is a long motor vehicle used for taking passengers on long journeys.
2 The coaches of a train are the separate sections that carry passengers.
3 A coach is also a four-wheeled enclosed vehicle pulled by horses, which people used to travel in.
4 (verb) If someone coaches you, they teach you and help you to get better at a sport or a subject.
5 (noun) Someone's coach is a person who coaches them in a sport or a subject.
[from Hungarian *kocsi szekér* meaning 'wagon of Kocs' (the village where coaches were first made)]

Similar words: (sense 4) train, instruct
(sense 5) trainer, instructor, tutor

coagulate, coagulates, coagulating, coagulated
(pronounced koh-**ag**-yool-late)
(verb) When a liquid coagulates, it gets thicker.
coagulation (noun).
[from Latin *coagulum* meaning 'rennet']

coal, coals
1 (noun) Coal is a hard black rock obtained from under the earth and burned as a fuel. It consists of layers of decomposed vegetation deposits containing carbon.
2 Coals are burning pieces of coal.
3 (phrase) If you say someone is **carrying coals to Newcastle**, you mean they are supplying something unnecessarily because it is already there.

coalesce, coalesces, coalescing, coalesced
(pronounced koh-al-**less**)

(verb) If things coalesce, they join together, e.g. *The two groups coalesced to form one unit.*

coalfield, coalfields
(noun) A coalfield is a region where there is coal underground.

coalition, coalitions
(noun) A coalition is a temporary alliance, especially between different political parties in order to form a government.

coarse, coarser, coarsest
1 (adjective) Something that is coarse is rough in texture, often consisting of large particles, e.g. *coarse cloth... coarse sand.*
2 Someone who is coarse talks or behaves in a rude or rather offensive way.
coarsely (adverb), **coarseness** (noun).

coarsen, coarsens, coarsening, coarsened
(verb) If someone or something coarsens, they become coarse.

coast, coasts, coasting, coasted
1 (noun) A coast is the edge of the land where it meets the sea.
2 (phrase) If you say that **the coast is clear**, you mean there is no longer any danger.
3 (verb) A vehicle that is coasting is moving without engine power.
coastal (adjective).
[from Latin *costa* meaning 'side' or 'rib']

coastguard, coastguards
(noun) A coastguard is an official who watches the sea near a coast to get help for sailors when they need it, and to prevent smuggling.

coastline, coastlines
(noun) A coastline is the outline of a coast, especially its appearance as seen from the sea or air, e.g. *a rocky coastline.*

coat, coats, coating, coated
1 (noun) A coat is a piece of clothing with sleeves which you wear outside over your other clothes.
2 An animal's coat is the fur or hair on its body.
3 A coat of paint or varnish is a layer of it.
4 (verb) To coat something means to cover it with a thin layer of a substance, e.g. *The nuts are then coated in chocolate.*
coating (noun).
[from Germanic *kotta* meaning 'garment']

coat hanger, coat hangers
(noun) A coat hanger is a curved piece of wood, metal, or plastic that you hang clothes on.

coat of arms, coats of arms
(noun) A coat of arms is a shield with a design on it, used as an emblem of a noble family, a town, or an organization.

coax, coaxes, coaxing, coaxed
(verb) If you coax someone to do something, you gently persuade them to do it.

Similar words: persuade, wheedle, cajole, talk into

cobalt
(noun) Cobalt is a hard silvery-white metallic element which is used in alloys and for

producing a blue dye. Its atomic number is 27 and its symbol is Co.

cobble, cobbles, cobbling, cobbled
1 (noun) Cobbles or cobblestones are stones with a rounded surface that were used in the past for making roads.
2 (verb) If you cobble something together, you make it roughly, e.g. *We managed to cobble together a letter of reply.*

cobbler, cobblers
(noun; an old-fashioned word) A cobbler is a person whose job is making or mending shoes.

cobra, cobras (pronounced **koh**-bra)
(noun) A cobra is a type of large poisonous snake from Africa and Asia. It spreads the skin at the back of its head into a hood when it is alarmed.

cobweb, cobwebs
(noun) A cobweb is the very thin net that a spider spins for catching insects.
[from Old English *coppe* + *webb* meaning 'spider-web']

cocaine
(noun) Cocaine is an addictive drug. It is sometimes used as an anaesthetic.
[from Spanish *coca* meaning 'preparation of coca leaves']

coccyx, coccyxes (pronounced **kok**-siks)
(noun) In anatomy, the coccyx is the small triangular bone at the bottom of the spine in humans and some apes.
[from Greek *kokkux* meaning 'cuckoo'; the bone looks like a cuckoo's beak]

cochineal (pronounced koch-chin-**neel**)
(noun) Cochineal is a red substance obtained from an insect and used for colouring food.
[from Greek *kokkos* meaning 'berry']

cock, cocks
(noun) A cock is an adult male chicken; also used of any male bird.

cockatoo, cockatoos
(noun) A cockatoo is a type of parrot with a crest, found in Australia and New Guinea.

cockerel, cockerels
(noun) A cockerel is a young cock.

cockeyed
(adjective; an informal word) A cockeyed idea or scheme is silly and unlikely to succeed.

cockle, cockles
(noun) Cockles are a kind of small shellfish.
[from Old French *coquille* meaning 'shell']

Cockney, Cockneys
(noun) A Cockney is a person born in the East End of London.
[from Middle English *cokeney* meaning 'cock's egg']

cockpit, cockpits
(noun) The cockpit of a small plane is the place where the pilot sits.

cockroach, cockroaches
(noun) A cockroach is a large dark-coloured insect often found in dirty rooms.
[from Spanish *cucaracha*]

cocktail, cocktails
(noun) A cocktail is an alcoholic drink made from several ingredients.

cocky, cockier, cockiest
(adjective; an informal word) cheeky or too self-confident.
cockily (adverb), **cockiness** (noun).

cocoa
(noun) Cocoa is a brown powder made from the seeds of a tropical tree and used for making chocolate; also a hot drink made from this powder.

coconut, coconuts
(noun) A coconut is a very large nut with white flesh, milky juice, and a hard hairy shell.

cocoon, cocoons
(noun) A cocoon is a silky covering over the silkworm or the larvae of certain other insects.
[from Provençal *coucoun* meaning 'eggshell']

cod
(noun) A cod is a large edible fish.

coddle, coddles, coddling, coddled
(verb) If you coddle someone, you treat them too kindly, or protect them too much.

code, codes
1 (noun) A code is a system of replacing the letters or words in a message with other letters or words, so that nobody can understand the message unless they know the system.
2 A code is also a group of numbers and letters which is used to identify something, e.g. *Your course code is E5L21.*
3 A code of behaviour is a set of rules about how people should behave.
coded (adjective).
[from Latin *codex* meaning 'book']

codify, codifies, codifying, codified
(verb) To codify a system of rules means to define and present them in a clear, ordered way.
codification (noun).

coeducation
(noun) Coeducation is the system of educating boys and girls together at the same school.
coeducational (adjective).

coerce, coerces, coercing, coerced (pronounced koh-**erss**)
(verb; a formal word) If you coerce someone into doing something, you make them do it against their will.
coercion (noun).
[from Latin *coercere* meaning 'to restrain']

coexist, coexists, coexisting, coexisted
(verb) When two or more things coexist, they exist together in the same place or at the same time.
coexistence (noun), **coexistent** (adjective).

coffee
(noun) Coffee is a substance made by roasting and grinding the beans of a tropical shrub; also a hot drink made from this substance.
[from Arabic *qahwah* meaning 'wine' or 'coffee']

coffin, coffins
(noun) A coffin is a box in which a dead body is buried or cremated.
[from Greek *kophinos* meaning 'basket']

cog, cogs
(noun) A cog is a wheel with teeth which turns another wheel or part of a machine.

cogent (pronounced **koh**-jent)
(adjective; a formal word) A cogent reason or argument is a convincing one.
cogently (adverb), **cogency** (noun).
[from Latin *cogere* meaning 'to draw together']

cogitate, cogitates, cogitating, cogitated
(verb; a formal word) To cogitate means to think deeply.
cogitation (noun).
[from Latin *cogitare* meaning 'to think']

cognac (pronounced **kon**-yak)
(noun) Cognac is a kind of brandy, named after the district in France where it is produced.

cognition
(noun; a formal word) Cognition is the process of knowing, learning, or understanding things.
cognitive (adjective).
[from Latin *cognoscere* meaning 'to get to know']

cohabit, cohabits, cohabiting, cohabited
(verb; a formal word) Two people who cohabit live together and have a sexual relationship but are not married.
cohabitation (noun).
[from Latin *co-* + *habitare* meaning 'to live with']

coherent
1 (adjective) If something such as a theory is coherent, its parts fit together well and do not contradict each other.
2 If someone is coherent, what they are saying makes sense and is not jumbled or confused.
coherently (adverb), **coherence** (noun).
[from Latin *co-* + *haerere* meaning 'to adhere together']

cohesive
(adjective) If something is cohesive, its parts fit together well and form a united whole, e.g. *The poor do not see themselves as a cohesive group.*
cohesively (adverb), **cohesion** (noun).

coiffure (pronounced kwah-**fyoor**)
(noun; a formal word) A woman's coiffure is her hairstyle.
[from Old French *coiffe* meaning 'cap' or 'helmet']

coil, coils, coiling, coiled
1 (noun) A coil of rope or wire is a length of it wound into a series of loops; also one of the loops.
2 The coil is a contraceptive device placed inside a woman's womb.
3 (verb) If something coils, it turns into a series of loops.
[from Old French *coillir* meaning 'to collect up']

coin, coins, coining, coined
1 (noun) A coin is a small metal disc which is used as money.

2 (verb) If you coin a word or a phrase, you invent it.
[from Old French *coignier* meaning 'to mint']

coinage
(noun) The coinage of a country is the coins that are used there.

coincide, coincides, coinciding, coincided
1 (verb) If two events coincide, they happen at about the same time.
2 When two people's ideas or opinions coincide, they agree, e.g. *His ideas coincided with mine.*
[from Latin *co-* meaning 'with' and *incidere* meaning 'to occur']

coincidence, coincidences
1 (noun) A coincidence is the fact that two things are surprisingly the same, e.g. *My name's George Taylor too. What a coincidence!*
2 A coincidence is also what happens when two similar things occur at the same time by chance, e.g. *By coincidence she was on the same train.*
coincidental (adjective), **coincidentally** (adverb).

coitus (pronounced **koh**-ee-tuss)
(noun) Coitus is sexual intercourse.

coke
(noun) Coke is a grey fuel produced from coal.

colander, colanders (pronounced **kol**-an-der)
(noun) A colander is a bowl-shaped container with holes in it, used for washing or draining food.
[from Provençal *colador* meaning 'sieve']

cold, colder, coldest; colds
1 (adjective) Something that is cold has a very low temperature.
2 If it is cold, the air temperature is very low.
3 (noun) You can refer to cold weather as the cold, e.g. *Her fingers were stiff from the cold.*
4 (adjective) Someone who is cold does not show much affection.
5 (noun) A cold is a minor illness which makes you sneeze and often gives you a sore throat.
coldly (adverb), **coldness** (noun).

cold-blooded
1 (adjective) Someone who is cold-blooded does not show any pity, e.g. *a cold-blooded murderer.*
2 A cold-blooded animal has a body temperature that changes according to the surrounding temperature.
cold-bloodedly (adverb), **cold-bloodedness** (noun).

cold war
(noun) Cold war is a state of extreme unfriendliness between countries not actually at war.

coleslaw
(noun) Coleslaw is a salad of chopped cabbage and other vegetables in mayonnaise.
[from Dutch *koolsla* meaning 'cabbage salad']

colic
(noun) Colic is pain in a baby's stomach and bowels.

collaborate, collaborates, collaborating, collaborated
(verb) When people collaborate, they work

together to produce something, e.g. *George and I are collaborating on a new book.*
collaboration (noun), **collaborator** (noun).
[from Latin *co-* + *laborare* meaning 'to work together']

collage, collages (pronounced kol-lahj)
(noun) A collage is a picture made by sticking pieces of paper or cloth onto a surface.
[from French *colle* meaning 'glue']

collapse, collapses, collapsing, collapsed
1 (verb) If something such as a building collapses, it falls down suddenly. If a person collapses, they fall down suddenly because they are ill.
2 If something such as a system collapses, it suddenly fails completely, e.g. *Their marriage had collapsed.*
3 (noun) The collapse of something is what happens when it collapses, e.g. *a company on the verge of collapse.*
[from Latin *collapsus* meaning 'fallen in ruins']

Similar words: (sense 1) fall down, give way

collapsible
(adjective) A collapsible object can be folded flat when it is not in use, e.g. *a collapsible bed.*

collar, collars, collaring, collared
1 (noun) The collar of a shirt or coat is the part round the neck which is usually folded over.
2 A collar is also a leather band round the neck of a dog or cat.
3 (verb; an informal use) If someone collars you, they catch you, e.g. *I was collared by the police.*
[from Latin *collum* meaning 'neck']

collarbone, collarbones
(noun) Your collarbones are the two long bones which run from the base of your neck to your shoulders.

collate, collates, collating, collated
(verb) When you collate pieces of information, you gather them together and examine them.
[from Latin *collatus* meaning 'brought together']

collateral
(noun) Collateral is money or property which is used as a guarantee that someone will repay a loan.

colleague, colleagues
(noun) A person's colleagues are the people he or she works with.
[from Latin *com-* meaning 'with' and *legare* meaning 'to choose']

Similar words: associate, work-mate

collect, collects, collecting, collected
1 (verb) To collect things means to gather them together for a special purpose or as a hobby, e.g. *collecting firewood... Do you collect antiques?*
2 If you collect someone or something from a place, you call there and take them away, e.g. *I have to collect the children from school.*
3 When things collect in a place, they gather

there over a period of time, e.g. *Damp leaves collected in the gutters.*
collector (noun).
[from Latin *colligere* meaning 'to gather together']

collected
(adjective) calm and self-controlled.

collection, collections
1 (noun) A collection of things is a group of them acquired over a period of time, e.g. *my stamp collection.*
2 Collection is the collecting of something, e.g. *tax collection.*
3 A collection is also the organized collecting of money, for example for charity, or the sum of money collected.

Similar words: (sense 1) anthology, compilation, set

collective, collectives
1 (adjective) involving every member of a group of people, e.g. *a collective decision.*
2 (noun) A collective is a group of people who share the responsibility both for running something and for doing the work.
collectively (adverb).

college, colleges
1 (noun) A college is a place where students study after they have left school.
2 A college is also one of the institutions into which some universities are divided, e.g. *Jesus College, Cambridge.*
collegiate (adjective).
[from Latin *collegium* meaning 'band' or 'company']

collide, collides, colliding, collided
(verb) If a moving object collides with something, it hits it.
[from Latin *collidere* meaning 'to clash together']

collie, collies
(noun) A collie is a kind of large wavy-haired sheepdog.

colliery, collieries
(noun) A colliery is a coal mine.

collision, collisions
(noun) A collision occurs when a moving object hits something.

Similar words: accident, smash, crash, impact

colloquial (pronounced kol-loh-kwee-al)
(adjective) Colloquial words and phrases are informal and used especially in conversation.
colloquially (adverb), **colloquialism** (noun).
[from Latin *colloqui* meaning 'to talk with']

Similar words: informal, vernacular

collude, colludes, colluding, colluded
(verb; a formal word) To collude with someone means to cooperate with them secretly and dishonestly.
collusion (noun).
[from Latin *colludere* meaning 'to play together']

cologne (pronounced kol-lone)
(noun) Cologne is a kind of weak perfume,

named after the German city where it was first made.

colon, colons
1 (noun) A colon is the punctuation mark (:).
2 Your colon is the part of your intestine above your rectum.
[from Greek *kōlon* meaning 'limb']

colonel, colonels (pronounced **kur-nl**)
(noun) A colonel is an army officer of the rank immediately above lieutenant-colonel.
[from Italian *colonnello* meaning 'column of soldiers']

colonize, colonizes, colonizing, colonized; also spelled **colonise**
(verb) When people colonize a place, they go to live there and take control of it, e.g. *the Europeans who colonized North America*.
colonization (noun), **colonist** (noun).

colonnade, colonnades
(noun) A colonnade is a row of evenly spaced columns.

colony, colonies
(noun) A colony is a country controlled by a more powerful country.
colonial (adjective).
[from Latin *colere* meaning 'to settle']

Similar words: settlement, outpost, province

colossal
(adjective) very large indeed.
colossally (adverb).
[from Greek *kolossos* meaning 'huge statue']

colour, colours, colouring, coloured
1 (noun) The colour of something is the appearance that it has as a result of reflecting light.
2 Someone's colour is the normal colour of their skin.
3 Colour is also a quality that makes something interesting or exciting, e.g. *The visitors brought some colour to our dull lives*.
4 (verb) If something colours your opinion, it affects the way you think about something.
coloured (adjective), **colourful** (adjective), **colourfully** (adverb), **colourless** (adjective), **colouring** (noun), **coloration** (noun).
[from Latin *color* meaning 'colour']

Similar words: (sense 1) shade, tint, hue

colour blind
(adjective) Someone who is colour blind cannot distinguish between colours.

colt, colts
(noun) A colt is a young male horse.

column, columns
1 (noun) A column is a tall solid upright cylinder, especially one supporting a part of a building.
2 A column is also a group of people moving in a long line, two or more abreast.
3 In a newspaper or magazine, a column is a vertical section of writing.
[from Latin *columen* meaning 'peak']

columnist, columnists
(noun) A columnist is a journalist who writes a regular article in a newspaper or magazine.

coma, comas
(noun) Someone who is in a coma is in a state of deep unconsciousness.
[from Greek *kōma* meaning 'heavy sleep']

comb, combs, combing, combed
1 (noun) A comb is a flat object with pointed teeth used for tidying your hair.
2 (verb) When you comb your hair, you tidy it with a comb.
3 If you comb a place, you search it thoroughly to try to find someone or something.

combat, combats, combating, combated
1 (noun) Combat is fighting, e.g. *unarmed combat*.
2 (verb) To combat something means to try to stop it happening or developing, e.g. *the problem of combating disease*.
[from Latin *com-* meaning 'together' and *battuere* meaning 'to hit']

combatant, combatants
(noun) The combatants in a fight or battle are the people fighting it.

combination, combinations
1 (noun) A combination of things is a mixture of them, e.g. *a combination of these techniques*.
2 A combination is a series of letters or numbers used to open a combination lock.

combination lock, combination locks
(noun) A combination lock is a lock which can only be opened by turning dials to a particular series of letters or numbers.

combine, combines, combining, combined
1 (verb) To combine things means to cause them to exist together, e.g. *We intend to combine liberty with order*.
2 To combine things also means to join them together to make a single thing, e.g. *The two teams were combined*.
3 If something combines two qualities or features, it has them both, e.g. *Carbon fibre combines flexibility with strength*.
4 (noun) A combine is a group of people or organizations working or acting together.
[from Latin *com-* meaning 'together' and *bini* meaning 'two by two']

combustible
(adjective) Something that is combustible catches fire easily.

combustion
(noun) Combustion is the act of burning something or the process of burning.
[from Latin *comburere* meaning 'to burn up']

come, comes, coming, came, come
1 (verb) To come to a place means to move there or arrive there.
2 To come to a place also means to extend as far as that place, e.g. *Her hair came down to her waist*.
3 Come is used to say that someone or something enters or reaches a particular state, e.g. *They*

came to power the next year... The jug came apart in my hands.

4 When a particular time or event comes, it happens, e.g. *Spring came late last year.*

5 If you come from a place, you were born there or it is your home.

6 Something that comes from something else is derived from it or was a part of it, e.g. *The word 'idea' comes from Greek.*

7 If a feeling or situation comes from doing something, it is the result of it, e.g. *the warm glow that comes from working cooperatively.*

8 (phrase) A time or event **to come** is a future time or event, e.g. *We will see many changes in the years to come.*

Similar words: (sense 7) issue, emanate, originate

come about
(phrasal verb) The way something comes about is the way it happens, e.g. *This discovery came about through a mistake.*

come across
(phrasal verb) If you come across something, you find it by chance.

come by
(phrasal verb) To come by something means to find it or obtain it, e.g. *Jobs were hard to come by.*

come into
(phrasal verb) If someone comes into property or money, they inherit it.

come off
(phrasal verb) If something comes off, it succeeds, e.g. *I hadn't expected his plan to come off.*

come on
(phrasal verb) If something is coming on, it is making progress, e.g. *My new book is coming on well.*

come round
1 (phrasal verb) To come round means to recover consciousness.

2 To come round to an idea or situation means to eventually accept it.

3 When a regular event comes round, it happens, e.g. *Beginning of term came round too quickly.*

come to
(phrasal verb) To come to means to recover consciousness.

come up
(phrasal verb) If something comes up in a conversation or meeting, it is mentioned or discussed.

come up against
(phrasal verb) If you come up against a problem, you are faced with it and have to deal with it.

come up with
(phrasal verb) If you come up with a plan or idea, you suggest it.

comeback, comebacks
(noun) To make a comeback means to be popular or successful again.

comedian, comedians
(noun) A comedian is an entertainer whose job is to make people laugh, especially by telling jokes or funny stories.

Similar words: humorist, comic, wit, entertainer

comedienne, comediennes (pronounced kom-mee-dee-**en**)
(noun) A comedienne is a female comedian.

comedy, comedies
1 (noun) A comedy is a light-hearted play or film with a happy ending.

2 Comedy is something that amuses people in books, plays, films, or real life.
[from Greek *kōmos* meaning 'village festival' and *aeidein* meaning 'to sing']

comely (pronounced **kum**-lee)
(adjective; an old-fashioned word) A comely woman is attractive.
[from Old English *cymlic* meaning 'beautiful']

comet, comets
(noun) A comet is an object that travels around the sun leaving a bright trail behind it.
[from Greek *komētēs* meaning 'long-haired']

comfort, comforts, comforting, comforted
1 (noun) Comfort is the state of being physically relaxed, e.g. *She longed to stretch out in comfort.*

2 Comfort is also a feeling of relief from worries or unhappiness, e.g. *I found comfort in his words.*

3 (plural noun) Comforts are things which make your life easier and more pleasant, e.g. *I longed for the comforts of home.*

4 (verb) To comfort someone means to make them less worried or unhappy.
[from Latin *confortare* meaning 'to strengthen']

comfortable
1 (adjective) If you are comfortable, you are physically relaxed.

2 Something that is comfortable makes you feel relaxed, e.g. *a comfortable chair.*

3 If you feel comfortable in a particular situation, you are not afraid or embarrassed.

4 You can say that someone is comfortable when they have enough money to live without financial problems.
comfortably (adverb).

comic, comics
1 (adjective) funny, e.g. *a comic sight.*

2 (noun) A comic is someone who tells jokes.

3 A comic is also a magazine that contains stories told in pictures.

comical
(adjective) funny, e.g. *a comical expression.*
comically (adverb).

comma, commas
(noun) A comma is the punctuation mark (,).
[from Greek *koptein* meaning 'to cut']

command, commands, commanding, commanded
1 (verb) To command someone to do something means to order them to do it.

2 (noun) A command is an order to do something.

3 (verb) If you command something such as respect, you receive it because of your personal

qualities, e.g. *He could no longer command obedience.*
4 An officer who commands part of an army or navy is in charge of it.
5 (phrase) Someone who is **in command** of a ship or part of an army is in charge of it.
6 (noun) Your command of something is your knowledge of it and your ability to use this knowledge, e.g. *a good command of French.*
[from Latin *com-* + *mandare* meaning 'to entrust with']

Similar words: (sense 1) bid, charge, direct, order

commandant, commandants (pronounced **kom**-man-dant)
(noun) A commandant is an army officer in charge of a place or group of people.

commandeer, commandeers, commandeering, commandeered (pronounced kom-man-**deer**)
(verb) If soldiers commandeer something, they officially take it so that they can use it.

Similar words: appropriate, requisition, annexe

commander, commanders
1 (noun) A commander is an officer in charge of a military operation or organization.
2 In the navy, a commander is an officer of the rank immediately above lieutenant-commander.

commandment, commandments
(noun) The commandments are ten rules of behaviour that, according to the Old Testament, we should obey. They were given to Moses by God.

commando, commandos
(noun) A commando is a small group of specially trained soldiers; also a member of this group.

commemorate, commemorates, commemorating, commemorated
1 (verb) An object that commemorates a person or an event has been placed somewhere to remind people about the person or event.
2 If you commemorate an event, you do something special to show that you remember it.
commemorative (adjective), **commemoration** (noun).
[from Latin *com-* meaning 'with' and *memorare* meaning 'to remind']

Similar words: (sense 2) celebrate, observe, keep

commence, commences, commencing, commenced
(verb; a formal word) To commence means to begin.
commencement (noun).

commend, commends, commending, commended
(verb) To commend someone or something means to praise them, e.g. *I was commended for my report.*
commendation (noun), **commendable** (adjective).
[from Latin *com-* + *mandare* meaning 'to entrust with']

commensurate (pronounced kom-**men**-sur-ret)
(adjective; a formal word) suitable or in

proportion to something, e.g. *a job commensurate with her experience.*
[from Latin *com-* meaning 'with' and *mensurare* meaning 'to measure']

comment, comments, commenting, commented
1 (verb) If you comment on something, you make a remark about it.
2 (noun) A comment is a remark about something, e.g. *They made rude comments about my hair.*
[from Latin *commentum* meaning 'invention']

Similar words: (sense 1) remark, mention, note

commentary, commentaries
(noun) A commentary is a description of an event which is broadcast on radio or television while the event is taking place.

commentator, commentators
(noun) A commentator is someone who gives a radio or television commentary.

commerce
(noun) Commerce is the buying and selling of goods.
[from Latin *commercium* meaning 'trade']

commercial, commercials
1 (adjective) relating to commerce.
2 Commercial activities involve producing goods on a large scale in order to make money, e.g. *the commercial breeding of goats.*
3 Commercial television and radio are paid for by advertisements between the programmes.
4 (noun) A commercial is an advertisement on television or radio.
commercially (adverb).

commercialized or **commercialised**
(adjective) You say that something is commercialized when it is used for making a lot of money.
commercialization (noun).

commercial traveller, commercial travellers
(noun) A commercial traveller is someone who travels around and meets people in order to sell goods or take orders.

commiserate, commiserates, commiserating, commiserated
(verb) If you commiserate with someone, you show them sympathy when something unpleasant has happened to them.
commiseration (noun).
[from Latin *com-* meaning 'together' and *miserari* meaning 'to bewail' or 'to pity']

commission, commissions, commissioning, commissioned
1 (verb) If someone commissions a piece of work, they formally ask someone to do it, e.g. *I was commissioned to write another book.*
2 (noun) A commission is a piece of work that has been commissioned.
3 Commission is money paid to a salesman each time a sale is made.
4 A commission is also an official body appointed to investigate or control something.

[from Latin *commissio* meaning 'a bringing together']

commissionaire, commissionaires
(noun) A commissionaire is a man employed by a hotel or theatre to open doors and help customers.

commit, commits, committing, committed
1 (verb) To commit a crime or sin means to do it.
2 If you commit yourself, you state an opinion or state that you will do something.
3 If someone is committed to hospital or prison, they are officially sent there.
committal (noun).
[from Latin *committere* meaning 'to put together']

Similar words: (sense 1) perpetrate, carry out

commitment, commitments
1 (noun) Commitment is a strong belief in an idea or system.
2 A commitment is something that regularly takes up some of your time, e.g. *She has family commitments.*

committed
(adjective) A committed person has strong beliefs, e.g. *a committed Christian.*

committee, committees
(noun) A committee is a group of people who make decisions on behalf of a larger group.

commodious
(adjective; a formal word) A commodious house or room is large and spacious.
[from Latin *commodus* meaning 'convenient']

commodity, commodities
(noun; a formal word) Commodities are things that are sold.

commodore, commodores
(noun) A commodore is a navy officer of the rank immediately above captain.
[from Old French *commander* meaning 'to command']

common, commoner, commonest; commons
1 (adjective) Something that is common exists in large numbers or happens often, e.g. *Durand is a common name there.*
2 If something is common to two or more people, they all have it or use it, e.g. *We share a common language.*
3 Common is used to indicate that something is of the ordinary kind and not special.
4 If something is common knowledge or a common belief, it is widely known or believed.
5 If you describe someone as common, you mean they do not have good taste or good manners.
6 (noun) A common is an area of grassy land where everyone can go.
7 (phrase) If two things or people have something **in common**, they both have it.
commonly (adverb).
[from Latin *communis* meaning 'general' or 'universal']

Similar words: (sense 4) popular, prevalent
(sense 5) vulgar, coarse, plebeian

commoner, commoners
(noun) A commoner is someone who is not a member of the nobility.

Common Market
(noun) The Common Market is the EEC.

commonplace
(adjective) Something that is commonplace is not surprising because it happens often or can be seen in many places, e.g. *Air travel had become commonplace.*

common sense
(noun) Your common sense is your natural ability to behave sensibly and make sound judgments.

Similar words: practicality, good sense

Commonwealth
(noun) The Commonwealth consists of an association of countries around the world that are or used to be ruled by Britain.

commotion
(noun) A commotion is a lot of noise and excitement.
[from Latin *commovere* meaning 'to throw into disorder']

communal
(adjective) shared by a group of people, e.g. *a communal dining-room.*
communally (adverb).

commune, communes (pronounced **kom**-yoon)
(noun) A commune is a group of people who live together and share everything.
[from Old French *comuner* meaning 'to hold in common']

communicate, communicates, communicating, communicated
1 (verb) When people communicate with each other, they exchange information, usually by talking or writing to each other.
2 If you communicate an idea or a feeling to someone, you make them aware of it.
[from Latin *communicare* meaning 'to share']

Similar words: (sense 2) convey, transmit, impart

communication, communications
1 (noun) Communication is the process by which people or animals exchange information.
2 (plural noun) Communications are the systems by which people communicate or broadcast information, especially using electricity or radio waves, e.g. *a communications satellite.*
3 (noun; a formal use) A communication is a letter or other message, e.g. *I refer to your communication of 28th July.*

communicative
(adjective) Someone who is communicative is willing to talk to people.

communion
1 (noun) Communion is the sharing of thoughts and feelings.
2 In Christianity, Communion is a religious service in which people share bread and wine in

remembrance of the death and resurrection of Jesus Christ.
[from Latin *communio* meaning 'general participation']

communiqué, communiqués (pronounced kom-**yoo**-nik-kay)
(noun) A communiqué is an official statement or announcement.

communism
(noun) Communism is the doctrine that the state should control the means of production and that there should be no private property.
communist (adjective and noun).
[from Old French *commun* meaning 'common']

community, communities
(noun) A community is all the people living in a particular area; also used to refer to particular groups within a society, e.g. *support from the local community... the black community.*

commute, commutes, commuting, commuted
(verb) People who commute travel a long distance to work every day.
commuter (noun).

compact, compacts
1 (adjective) taking up very litle space, e.g. *a compact kitchen.*
2 (noun) A compact is a small flat round case containing face-powder and a mirror.
3 (verb) To compact something means to press it down so that it becomes more dense.
4 (noun) A compact between people is an agreement.
compactly (adverb), **compactness** (noun).
[senses 1-3 are from Latin *com-* + *pangere* meaning 'to fasten together'; sense 4 is from Latin *compacisci* meaning 'to agree']

Similar words: (sense 1) dense, solid, compressed

compact disc, compact discs
(noun) A compact disc is a type of record with superior sound reproduction, played using a laser on a special machine.

companion, companions
(noun) A companion is someone you travel or spend time with.
companionship (noun).
[from Latin *com-* meaning 'together' and *panis* meaning 'bread'. A companion was originally someone you shared a meal with]

companionable
(adjective) Someone who is companionable is friendly and pleasant to be with.

company, companies
1 (noun) A company is a business that sells goods or provides a service, e.g. *an oil company.*
2 A company is also a group of actors, opera singers, or dancers, e.g. *the Royal Shakespeare Company.*
3 If you have company, you have a friend or visitor with you, e.g. *She enjoyed his company.*
4 (phrase) If you **keep someone company**, you spend time with them.

5 If you **part company** with someone, you stop associating with them.

Similar words: (sense 3) companionship, fellowship, society

comparable (pronounced **kom**-pra-bl)
(adjective) If two things are comparable, they are similar in size or quality, e.g. *Their achievements are not comparable.*
comparably (adverb), **comparability** (noun).

Similar words: commensurate, on a par

comparative
1 (adjective) You add comparative to indicate that something is true only when compared with what is normal, e.g. *We spent the night in comparative safety.*
2 In a comparative study, two or more things are compared.
3 (noun) In grammar, the comparative is the form of an adjective which indicates that the person or thing described has more of a particular quality than someone or something else. For example, **quicker, better,** and **easier** are all comparatives.
comparatively (adverb).

compare, compares, comparing, compared
1 (verb) When you compare things, you consider them together and see in what ways they are different or similar.
2 If you compare one thing to another, you say it is like the other thing, e.g. *As an essayist he is often compared to Hazlitt.*
[from Latin *compar* meaning 'similar']

comparison, comparisons
(noun) When you make a comparison, you consider two things together and see in what ways they are different or similar.

compartment, compartments
1 (noun) A compartment is a section of a railway carriage.
2 A compartment is also one of the separate parts of an object, e.g. *the inner compartment of his wallet.*
[from Latin *compartiri* meaning 'to share']

compass, compasses
1 (noun) A compass is an instrument with a magnetic needle for finding directions.
2 (plural noun) Compasses are a hinged instrument for drawing circles.
3 (noun) The compass of something is its range, e.g. *Her voice has a compass of three octaves.*

compassion
(noun) Compassion is pity and sympathy for someone who is suffering.
compassionate (adjective), **compassionately** (adverb).
[from Latin *compati* meaning 'to suffer with']

compatible
(adjective) If people or things are compatible, they can live or exist together successfully.
compatibility (noun).
[from Latin *compati* meaning 'to be in sympathy with']

Similar words: suited, well-matched

compatriot, compatriots
(noun) Your compatriots are people from your own country.
[from Latin *com-* meaning 'with' and *patria* meaning 'fatherland']

compel, compels, compelling, compelled
(verb) To compel someone to do something means to force them to do it.
[from Latin *compellere* meaning 'to drive together']

compelling
(adjective) A compelling argument or reason makes you believe that something is true or should be done, e.g. *I had no compelling reason to stay.*

compensate, compensates, compensating, compensated
1 (verb) To compensate someone means to give them money to replace something lost, damaged, or destroyed.
2 If one thing compensates for another, it cancels out its bad effects, e.g. *The view compensated for the hard climb.*
compensatory (adjective), **compensation** (noun).
[from Latin *com-* meaning 'with' and *pendere* meaning 'to weigh']

Similar words: recompense, make up for

compere, comperes, compering, compered
(pronounced **kom**-pare)
1 (noun) The compere of a show is the person who introduces the guests or performers.
2 (verb) To compere a show means to act as its compere.
[from French *compère* meaning 'godfather']

compete, competes, competing, competed
1 (verb) When people or firms compete, each tries to prove that they or their products are the best.
2 If you compete in a contest or game, you take part in it.
[from Latin *competere* meaning 'to strive together']

competent
(adjective) Someone who is competent at something can do it satisfactorily, e.g. *a competent swimmer.*
competently (adverb), **competence** (noun).

competition, competitions
1 (noun) When there is competition between people or groups, they are all trying to get something that not everyone can have, e.g. *Competition for places was keen.*
2 When there is competition between firms, each firm is trying to get people to buy its own goods rather than the others'.
3 A competition is an event in which people take part to find who is best at something.

competitive
1 (adjective) A competitive situation is one in which people or firms are competing with each other, e.g. *a highly competitive society.*
2 A competitive person is eager to be more successful than others.
3 Goods sold at competitive prices are cheaper than other goods of the same kind.
competitively (adverb).

competitor, competitors
(noun) A competitor is a person or firm that is competing to become the most successful.

compilation, compilations
1 (noun) A compilation is a book, record, or programme consisting of several items that were originally produced separately, e.g. *a compilation of Victorian poetry.*
2 The compilation of something such as a report is the compiling of it.

compile, compiles, compiling, compiled
(verb) When someone compiles a book or report, they make it by putting together several items.
[from Latin *compilare* meaning 'to pile together']

complacent
(adjective) If someone is complacent, they are self-satisfied and unconcerned about a serious situation.
complacently (adverb), **complacency** (noun).
[from Latin *complacens* meaning 'very pleasing']

Similar words: self-satisfied, smug

complain, complains, complaining, complained
1 (verb) If you complain, you say that you are not satisfied with something.
2 If you complain of pain or illness, you say that you have it.
[from Latin *com-* + *plangere* meaning 'to bewail greatly']

Similar words: (sense 1) grizzle, groan, grouse, grumble, carp, moan, whine

complaint, complaints
1 (noun) If you make a complaint, you complain about something, e.g. *There were the usual complaints of violence.*
2 A complaint is also an illness, e.g. *She has a minor urinary complaint.*

complement, complements, complementing, complemented
1 (verb) If one thing complements another, the two things go well together, e.g. *Chinese medicine and Western medicine can sometimes complement each other.*
2 (noun) If one thing is a complement to another, it complements it.
complementary (adjective).
[from Latin *complere* meaning 'to fill up']

complete, completes, completing, completed
1 (adjective) to the greatest degree possible, e.g. *They were in complete agreement.*
2 If something is complete, none of it is missing, e.g. *a complete skeleton.*
3 When a task is complete, it is finished, e.g. *The harvesting was complete.*
4 (verb) If you complete something, you finish it.

5 If something completes a set, it is the last item needed to make it a full set.
6 If you complete a form, you fill it in.
completely (adverb), **completion** (noun).
[from Latin *completus* meaning 'filled up']

Similar words: (sense 1) absolute, thorough, utter, outright, total
(sense 2) entire, whole, full

complex, complexes
1 (adjective) Something that is complex has many different parts, e.g. *complex patterns*.
2 (noun) A complex is a group of buildings, roads, or other things connected with each other in some way, e.g. *a leisure complex*.
3 If someone has a complex, they have a continuing emotional problem because of a past experience, e.g. *a guilt complex*.
complexity (noun).
[from Latin *complecti* meaning 'to entwine']

Similar words: (sense 1) complicated, intricate, involved

complexion, complexions
(noun) Your complexion is the quality of the skin on your face, e.g. *a beautiful complexion*.
[from Latin *complexio* meaning 'bodily characteristics']

compliant
(adjective) Someone who is compliant willingly does what they are asked to do.

complicate, complicates, complicating, complicated
(verb) To complicate something means to make it more difficult to understand or deal with.
[from Latin *complicare* meaning 'to fold together']

complicated
(adjective) Something that is complicated has so many parts or aspects that it is difficult to understand or deal with.

complication, complications
(noun) A complication is a circumstance that makes a situation more difficult to deal with, e.g. *An added complication is that we are running out of money*.

complicity (pronounced kom-**pliss**-sit-tee)
(noun; a formal word) Complicity is involvement in an illegal activity or plan, e.g. *I suspected him of complicity in the robbery*.

compliment, compliments, complimenting, complimented
1 (noun) If you pay someone a compliment, you tell them you admire something about them.
2 (verb) If you compliment someone, you pay them a compliment.
3 (plural noun; a formal use) When someone sends their compliments, they formally express their good wishes, e.g. *His Excellency sends his compliments and regrets he is unable to attend*.
[from Spanish *cumplir* meaning 'to do what is fitting']

complimentary
1 (adjective) If you are complimentary about something, you express admiration for it.
2 A complimentary seat, ticket, or publication is given to you free.

comply, complies, complying, complied
(verb) If you comply with an order or rule, you obey it.
compliance (noun).
[from Spanish *cumplir* meaning 'to do what is fitting']

component, components
(noun) The components of something are the parts it is made of.
[from Latin *componere* meaning 'to put together']

compose, composes, composing, composed
1 (verb) If something is composed of particular things or people, it is made up of them.
2 To compose a piece of music, letter, or speech means to write it.
3 If you compose yourself, you become calm after being angry, excited, or upset.
[from Latin *componere* meaning 'to put together']

composed
(adjective) calm and in control of your feelings.

composer, composers
(noun) A composer is someone who writes music.

composite, composites
1 (adjective; a formal word) made up of different parts or things, e.g. *a composite fee*.
2 (noun) A composite is something made up of different parts or things, e.g. *His work is a composite of styles*.

composition, compositions
1 (noun) The composition of something is the things it consists of, e.g. *the composition of the atmosphere*.
2 The composition of a poem or piece of music is the writing of it.
3 A composition is a piece of music or writing.

compositor, compositors
(noun) A compositor is someone who sets up the text and illustrations of a book or newspaper before printing.

compost
(noun) Compost is a mixture of decaying plants and manure added to soil to help plants grow.
[from Latin *compositus* meaning 'put together']

composure
(noun) Someone's composure is their ability to stay calm, e.g. *He had recovered his composure*.

compound, compounds, compounding, compounded
1 (noun) A compound is an enclosed area of land with buildings used for a particular purpose, e.g. *a prison compound*.
2 In chemistry, a compound is a substance consisting of two or more different substances or chemical elements.
3 (adjective) consisting of two or more parts, e.g. *Butterflies have compound eyes*.
4 (verb) To compound something means to put together different parts to make a whole.

5 To compound a problem means to make it worse by adding to it, e.g. *Her uncertainty was now compounded by fear.*
[from Latin *componere* meaning 'to put together']

comprehend, comprehends, comprehending, comprehended
(verb; a formal word) To comprehend something means to understand or appreciate it, e.g. *a failure to comprehend what was happening.*
comprehension (noun).
[from Latin *comprehendere* meaning 'to seize']

comprehensible
(adjective) able to be understood.
comprehensibly (adverb).

comprehensive, comprehensives
1 (adjective) Something that is comprehensive includes everything necessary or relevant, e.g. *a comprehensive list.*
2 (noun) A comprehensive is a school where children of all abilities are taught together.
comprehensively (adverb).

compress, compresses, compressing, compressed
(verb) To compress something means to squeeze it or shorten it so that it takes up less space, e.g. *compressed air.*
compression (noun).
[from Latin *comprimere* meaning 'to squeeze together']

comprise, comprises, comprising, comprised
(verb; a formal word) What something comprises is what it consists of, e.g. *The Privy Council comprised 283 members.*
[from French *compris* meaning 'included']

compromise, compromises, compromising, compromised
1 (noun) A compromise is an agreement in which people accept less than they originally wanted, e.g. *At last a compromise was reached.*
2 (verb) When people compromise, they agree to accept less than they originally wanted.
3 If you compromise yourself or your beliefs, you behave in a way that makes people doubt your honesty or sincerity.
compromising (adjective).
[from Latin *compromissum* meaning 'mutual decision to accept arbiter's judgment']

compulsion, compulsions
1 (noun) A compulsion is a very strong desire to do something.
2 If someone uses compulsion to get you to do something, they force you to do it, for example by threatening you.

compulsive
1 (adjective) You use compulsive to describe someone who cannot stop doing something, e.g. *a compulsive gambler.*
2 If you find something such as a book or television programme compulsive, you cannot stop reading it or watching it.
compulsively (adverb).

compulsory
(adjective) If something is compulsory, you have to do it, e.g. *compulsory games.*

Similar words: mandatory, obligatory

compunction
(noun; a formal word) If you do something without compunction, you do it without feeling ashamed or guilty, e.g. *I could have shot him without compunction.*
[from Latin *compungere* meaning 'to sting']

compute, computes, computing, computed
(verb) To compute a figure or amount means to calculate it.
computation (noun).
[from Latin *computare* meaning 'to calculate']

computer, computers
(noun) A computer is an electronic machine that can quickly make calculations or store and retrieve information.

computerize, computerizes, computerizing, computerized; also spelled computerise
(verb) When a system or process is computerized, the work starts being done by computers.
computerization (noun).

computing
(noun) Computing is the use of computers and the writing of programs for them.

comrade, comrades
1 (noun) A soldier's comrades are his fellow soldiers, especially in battle.
2 Socialists and communists often address each other as 'comrade'.
comradeship (noun).
[from Spanish *camarada* meaning 'sharer of a billet']

con, cons, conning, conned (an informal word)
1 (verb) If someone cons you, they trick you into doing or believing something.
2 (noun) A con is a trick in which someone deceives you into doing or believing something. Con is short for 'confidence trick'.

concave
(adjective) A concave surface curves inwards, rather than being level or bulging outwards.
[from Latin *concavus* meaning 'arched']

conceal, conceals, concealing, concealed
(verb) To conceal something means to hide it, e.g. *He might be concealing his feelings.*
concealed (adjective), **concealment** (noun).
[from Latin *con- + celare* meaning 'to hide thoroughly']

concede, concedes, conceding, conceded
(pronounced kon-**seed**)
1 (verb) If you concede something, you admit that it is true, e.g. *The company conceded that an error had been made.*
2 When someone concedes defeat, they accept that they have lost something such as a contest or an election.
[from Latin *concedere* meaning 'to yield']

conceit

(noun) Conceit is someone's excessive pride in their appearance, abilities, or achievements.

Similar words: arrogance, vanity, pride

conceited

(adjective) Someone who is conceited is too proud of their appearance, abilities, or achievements.
conceitedly (adverb).

Similar words: bumptious, cocky, arrogant, big-headed, vain

conceivable

(adjective) If something is conceivable, you can believe that it could exist or be true, e.g. *It is conceivable that he drowned.*
conceivably (adverb).

conceive, conceives, conceiving, conceived

1 (verb) If you can conceive of something, you can imagine it or believe it, e.g. *We could not conceive of such a thing happening.*
2 If you conceive something such as a plan, you think of it and work out how it could be done.
3 When a woman conceives, she becomes pregnant.
[from Latin *concipere* meaning 'to take in']

concentrate, concentrates, concentrating, concentrated

1 (verb) If you concentrate on something, you give it all your attention.
2 When something is concentrated in one place, it is all there rather than being distributed among several places, e.g. *Modern industry has been concentrated in a few large urban centres.*
3 (noun) A concentrate is a liquid or substance from which unnecessary substances have been removed to make it stronger or purer.
concentration (noun).

concentrated

(adjective) A concentrated liquid has been made stronger by having water removed from it, e.g. *concentrated orange juice.*

concentration camp, concentration camps

(noun) A concentration camp is a prison camp, especially one in Nazi Germany during World War Two.

concentric

(adjective) Concentric circles have the same centre.

concept, concepts

(noun) A concept is an idea or abstract principle, e.g. *the concept of justice.*
conceptual (adjective), conceptually (adverb).

conception, conceptions

1 (noun) Your conception of something is the idea you have of it.
2 Conception is the process by which a woman becomes pregnant.

concern, concerns, concerning, concerned

1 (noun) Concern is a feeling of worry about something or someone, e.g. *public concern over Britain's poor economic performance.*
2 (verb) If something concerns you or if you are concerned about it, it worries you, e.g. *Her disappearance concerned him deeply.*
3 You also say that something concerns you if it affects or involves you, e.g. *What I have to say concerns all of you.*
4 (phrase) If something is of concern to you, it is important to you.
5 (noun) If something is your concern, it is your responsibility.
6 (verb) If a book or talk concerns or is concerned with a subject, it is about that subject.
7 (noun) A concern is also a business, e.g. *a West German chemical concern.*
concerned (adjective).
[from Latin *concernere* meaning 'to mingle together']

Similar words: (sense 3) pertain to, regard, relate to, involve

concerning

(preposition) You use concerning to indicate what something is about, e.g. *questions concerning his private life.*

concert, concerts

(noun) A concert is a public performance by musicians.
[from French *concerter* meaning 'to bring into agreement']

concerted

(adjective) A concerted action is done by several people together, e.g. *We made a concerted effort.*

concertina, concertinas, concertinaing, concertinaed

1 (noun) A concertina is a musical instrument like an accordion, played by pressing buttons at each end.
2 (verb) To concertina means to fold up like a concertina, e.g. *The front of the car concertinaed.*

concerto, concertos or concerti (pronounced kon-cher-toe)

(noun) A concerto is a piece of music for a solo instrument and an orchestra.

concession, concessions

(noun) If you make a concession, you agree to let someone have or do something, e.g. *As a special concession, we were allowed to go home early.*

conciliate, conciliates, conciliating, conciliated

(verb; a formal word) To conciliate means to try to end a quarrel or disagreement.
conciliation (noun), conciliator (noun), conciliatory (adjective).
[from Latin *concilium* meaning 'council']

concise

(adjective) giving all the necessary information using the minimum number of words, e.g. *a concise summary.*
concisely (adverb), conciseness (noun).
[from Latin *concisus* meaning 'cut up' or 'cut short']

Similar words: short, pithy, terse, compact, succinct

conclude, concludes, concluding, concluded
1 (verb) If you conclude that something is true, you decide that it is true because of other things that you know are true.
2 When you conclude something, you finish it, e.g. *I will conclude this chapter with a quotation from Orwell.*
3 When a treaty or business deal is concluded, it is finally arranged or settled.
concluding (adjective), **conclusion** (noun).
[from Latin *concludere* meaning 'to enclose']

conclusive
(adjective) Facts that are conclusive show that something is certainly true.
conclusively (adverb).

concoct, concocts, concocting, concocted
1 (verb) If you concoct an excuse or explanation, you invent one.
2 If you concoct something, you make it by mixing several things together, e.g. *Nancy had concocted a red wine sauce.*
concoction (noun).
[from Latin *con-* + *coquere* meaning 'to cook together']

concourse, concourses
(noun) A concourse is a wide hall in a building where people walk about or gather together.
[from Latin *concurrere* meaning 'to run together']

concrete
1 (noun) Concrete is a solid building material made by mixing cement, sand, and water.
2 (adjective) definite, rather than general or vague, e.g. *concrete proposals.*
3 real and physical, rather than abstract, e.g. *concrete reminders of his existence.*
[from Latin *concretus* meaning 'grown together']

concubine, concubines (pronounced **kong**-kyoo-bine)
(noun; an old-fashioned word) A man's concubine is his mistress.
[from Latin *concumbere* meaning 'to lie together']

concur, concurs, concurring, concurred
(verb; a formal word) To concur means to agree, e.g. *The judge concurred with earlier findings.*
concurrence (noun).
[from Latin *concurrere* meaning 'to run together']

concurrent
(adjective) If things are concurrent, they happen at the same time.
concurrently (adverb).

concussed
(adjective) confused or unconscious because of a blow to the head.
concussion (noun).
[from Latin *concussus* meaning 'violently shaken']

condemn, condemns, condemning, condemned
1 (verb) If you condemn something, you say it is bad and unacceptable, e.g. *The archbishop condemned all acts of terrorism.*
2 If someone is condemned to a punishment, they are given it, e.g. *He was condemned to death.*
3 If you are condemned to something unpleasant,

you must suffer it, e.g. *She was condemned to a life of drudgery.*
4 When a building is condemned, it is going to be pulled down because it is unsafe.
condemned (adjective), **condemnation** (noun).
[from Latin *condemnare*]

Similar words: (sense 1) censure, damn, criticize
(sense 2) sentence
(sense 3) doom

condensation
(noun) Condensation is a coating of tiny drops formed on a surface by steam or vapour.

condense, condenses, condensing, condensed
1 (verb) If you condense a piece of writing or a speech, you shorten it by removing the less important parts.
2 When a gas or vapour condenses, it changes into a liquid.
[from Latin *condensare* meaning 'to make thick']

condescend, condescends, condescending, condescended
(verb) If you condescend to do something, you do it showing that you think you are superior to the other people involved, e.g. *She condescended to have dinner with us.*
condescension (noun).
[from Latin *condescendere* meaning 'to show humility']

condescending
(adjective) If you are condescending, you show by your behaviour that you think you are superior to other people.
condescendingly (adverb).

Similar words: patronizing, superior

condiment, condiments
(noun) Condiments are substances like salt, pepper, and mustard that you add to food that you are eating to give it more flavour.
[from Latin *condire* meaning 'to pickle']

condition, conditions, conditioning, conditioned
1 (noun) The condition of someone or something is the state they are in.
2 (plural noun) The conditions in which something is done are the location and other factors likely to affect it, e.g. *The experiment was carried out in the most difficult conditions.*
3 A condition is a requirement that must be fulfilled for something else to be possible, e.g. *Living here is a condition of your job.*
4 You can refer to an illness or other medical problem as a condition, e.g. *a heart condition.*
5 (phrase) If you are **out of condition**, you are unfit.
6 (verb) If someone is conditioned to behave or think in a certain way, they do it as a result of their upbringing or training.
conditioning (noun).
[from Latin *condicere* meaning 'to discuss' or 'to agree']

Similar words: (sense 3) precondition, prerequisite, provision, proviso, requirement, stipulation

conditional

(adjective) If one thing is conditional on another, it can only happen if the other thing happens, e.g. *Their support is conditional on further cuts in public expenditure.*
conditionally (adverb).

conditioner, conditioners

(noun) A conditioner is a thick liquid that you can put on your hair after washing it to make it soft and shiny.

condolence, condolences

(noun) Condolence is sympathy expressed for a bereaved person, e.g. *letters of condolence.*

condom, condoms

(noun) A condom is a rubber sheath worn by a man on his penis as a contraceptive.

condone, condones, condoning, condoned

(verb) If you condone someone's bad behaviour, you accept it and do not try to stop it, e.g. *We cannot condone the massacre of innocent people.*
[from Latin *condonare* meaning 'to forgive a fault' or 'to overlook']

conducive (pronounced kon-joo-siv)

(adjective) If something is conducive to something else, it makes it likely to happen, e.g. *Competition is not conducive to happiness.*

conduct, conducts, conducting, conducted

1 (verb) To conduct an activity or task means to carry it out, e.g. *We are conducting a survey of the region.*
2 (noun) If you take part in the conduct of an activity or task, you help to carry it out, e.g. *the conduct of the war.*
3 (verb; a formal use) The way you conduct yourself is the way you behave.
4 (noun) Your conduct is your behaviour.
5 (verb) When someone conducts an orchestra or choir, they stand in front of it and direct it.
6 If something conducts heat or electricity, heat or electricity can pass through it.
conduction (noun), **conductance** (noun).
[from Latin *conducere* meaning 'to draw together']

conductor, conductors

1 (noun) A conductor is someone who conducts an orchestra or choir.
2 A bus conductor is someone who moves round a bus selling tickets.
3 A conductor of heat or electricity is a substance that conducts it.

conductress, conductresses

(noun) A conductress is a female bus conductor.

conduit, conduits (pronounced kon-dit)

(noun) A conduit is a small tunnel, pipe, or channel for water or electrical wires.
[from Latin *conductus* meaning 'channel']

cone, cones

1 (noun) A cone is a regular three-dimensional shape with a circular base and a point at the top.
2 A fir cone or pine cone is the fruit of a fir or pine tree, consisting of a cluster of woody scales containing seeds.
conical (adjective).
[from Greek *kōnus* meaning 'pine cone']

confectioner, confectioners

(noun) A confectioner is someone who makes or sells sweets.

confectionery

(noun) Confectionery is sweets.
[from Latin *confectus* meaning 'done' or 'made']

confederate, confederates

(noun) Someone's confederates are the people they are working with in a secret activity.
[from Latin *con-* meaning 'together' and *foedus* meaning 'treaty']

confederation, confederations

(noun) A confederation is an organization or alliance formed for business or political purposes.

confer, confers, conferring, conferred

(verb) When people confer, they discuss something in order to make a decision.
[from Latin *conferre* meaning 'to gather together']

conference, conferences

(noun) A conference is a meeting at which formal discussions take place.

Similar words: convention, symposium, congress

confess, confesses, confessing, confessed

(verb) If you confess to something, you admit it, e.g. *Bianchi had confessed to the murder.*
[from Latin *confiteri* meaning 'to admit']

Similar words: admit, come clean, own up

confession, confessions

1 (noun) If you make a confession, you admit you have done something wrong.
2 Confession is the act of confessing something, especially a religious act in which people confess their sins to a priest.

Similar words: (sense 1) admission, revelation

confessional, confessionals

(noun) A confessional is a small room in some churches where people confess their sins to a priest.

confetti

(noun) Confetti is small pieces of coloured paper thrown over the bride and groom at a wedding.
[from Italian *confetto* meaning 'a sweet']

confidant, confidants (pronounced kon-fid-dant); spelled confidante for a female.

(noun; a formal word) Your confidant is a person you discuss your private problems with.

confide, confides, confiding, confided

(verb) If you confide a secret to someone, you tell it to them, e.g. *He confided to me that he didn't really want the job.*
confiding (adjective), **confidingly** (adverb).
[from Latin *confidere* meaning 'to trust']

confidence, confidences
1 (noun) If you have confidence in someone, you feel you can trust them.
2 Someone who has confidence is sure of their own abilities, qualities, or ideas.
3 A confidence is a secret you tell someone.
4 (phrase) If you **take someone into your confidence**, you tell them a secret.

Similar words: (sense 2) aplomb, assurance, certainty, self-assurance, self-possession, conviction

confidence trick, confidence tricks
(noun) A confidence trick is the same as a con.
confidence trickster (noun).

confident
1 (adjective) If you are confident about something, you are sure it will happen the way you want it to, e.g. *He was confident that the scheme would succeed.*
2 People who are confident are sure of their own abilities, qualities, or ideas.
confidently (adverb).

Similar words: (sense 1) certain, sure, positive
(sense 2) self-assured, assured

confidential
1 (adjective) Confidential information is meant to be kept secret.
2 If you talk in a confidential way, you lower your voice because you are telling someone a secret.
confidentially (adverb), **confidentiality** (noun).

configuration, configurations
(noun; a formal word) A configuration is an arrangement of a group of things.
[from Latin *configuratio* meaning 'model']

confine, confines, confining, confined
1 (verb) If something is confined to one place, person, or thing, it exists only in that place or affects only that person or thing.
2 If you confine yourself to doing or saying something, it is the only thing you do or say, e.g. *They confined themselves to discussing the weather.*
3 If you are confined to a place, you cannot leave it, e.g. *The troops were confined to barracks.*
4 (plural noun) The confines of a place are its boundaries, e.g. *within the confines of the Palace.*
confinement (noun).
[from Latin *con-* meaning 'with' and *finis* meaning 'boundary']

confined
(adjective) A confined space is small and enclosed by walls.

confirm, confirms, confirming, confirmed
1 (verb) To confirm something means to say or show that it is true, e.g. *She asked if it was my car and I confirmed that it was.*
2 If you confirm an arrangement or appointment, you say it is definite.
3 When someone is confirmed, they are formally accepted as a member of a Christian church.
confirmation (noun), **confirmatory** (adjective).
[from Latin *confirmare* meaning 'to establish']

Similar words: (sense 1) authenticate, validate, ratify, substantiate

confirmed
(adjective) You use confirmed to describe someone who has a habit, belief, or way of life that is unlikely to change, e.g. *a confirmed bachelor.*

Similar words: inveterate, hardened

confiscate, confiscates, confiscating, confiscated
(verb) To confiscate something means to take it away from someone as a punishment.
confiscation (noun).
[from Latin *confiscare* meaning 'to seize for the public treasury']

conflagration, conflagrations
(noun; a formal word) A conflagration is a large fire.
[from Latin *conflagrare* meaning 'to be burnt up']

conflict, conflicts, conflicting, conflicted
1 (noun) Conflict is disagreement and argument, e.g. *They came into conflict with the islanders.*
2 A conflict is a war or battle.
3 When there is a conflict of ideas or interests, people have different ideas or interests which cannot all be satisfied.
4 (verb) When ideas or interests conflict, they are different and cannot all be satisfied.
[from Latin *confligere* meaning 'to fight' or 'to contend']

Similar words: (sense 1) dissension, disagreement
(sense 3) clash, variance
(sense 4) disagree, clash, be at variance

conform, conforms, conforming, conformed
1 (verb) If you conform, you behave the way people expect you to.
2 If something conforms to a law or to someone's wishes, it is what is required or wanted.
conformist (noun and adjective).

Similar words: (sense 2) comply, correspond

confront, confronts, confronting, confronted
1 (verb) If you are confronted with a problem or task, you have to deal with it.
2 If you confront someone, you meet them face to face like an enemy.
3 If you confront someone with evidence or a fact, you present it to them in order to accuse them of something.
[from Latin *confrontari* meaning 'to stand face to face with']

confrontation, confrontations
(noun) A confrontation is a serious dispute or fight, e.g. *a confrontation with the unions.*

confuse, confuses, confusing, confused
1 (verb) If you confuse two things, you mix them up and think one of them is the other, e.g. *You must be confusing me with my sister.*
2 To confuse someone means to make them uncertain about what is happening or what to do.

3 To confuse a situation means to make it more complicated.
confused (adjective), **confusing** (adjective), **confusion** (noun).
[from Latin *confundere* meaning 'to pour together']

Similar words: (sense 2) bewilder, fuddle

congeal, congeals, congealing, congealed
(pronounced kon-**jeel**)
(verb) When a liquid congeals, it becomes very thick and sticky.
[from Latin *con-* + *gelare* meaning 'to freeze thoroughly']

Similar words: jell, clot, coagulate, curdle

congenial (kon-**jeen**-yal)
(adjective) If something is congenial, it is pleasant and suits you, e.g. *congenial company.*

congenital
(adjective; a medical word) If someone has a congenital disease or handicap, they have had it from birth but did not inherit it.
congenitally (adverb).
[from Latin *congenitus* meaning 'born together with']

conger, congers
(noun) A conger is a type of large seawater eel.

congested
(adjective) When a road is congested, it is so full of traffic that normal movement is impossible.
congestion (noun).
[from Latin *congestus* meaning 'pressed together']

conglomerate, conglomerates
(noun) A conglomerate is a large business organization consisting of several companies.

conglomeration, conglomerations
(noun) A conglomeration is a group of many different things, e.g. *a conglomeration of buildings.*
[from Latin *con-* + *glomerare* meaning 'to wind into a ball']

Congolese
(adjective) belonging or relating to the Republic of the Congo.

congratulate, congratulates, congratulating, congratulated
(verb) If you congratulate someone, you express pleasure at something good that has happened to them, or praise them for something they have achieved.
congratulation (noun), **congratulatory** (adjective).
[from Latin *con-* + *gratulari* meaning 'to rejoice with']

congregate, congregates, congregating, congregated
(verb) When people congregate, they gather together somewhere.
[from Latin *congregare* meaning 'to collect into a flock']

congregation, congregations
(noun) In a church, the congregation are the people attending a service.

congress, congresses
1 (noun) A congress is a large meeting held to discuss ideas or policies, e.g. *a writers' congress.*
2 In the United States, Congress is the elected group of politicians responsible for law making.
[from Latin *congredi* meaning 'to meet with']

congruent
(adjective) Two triangles are congruent if they are exactly the same shape and size.

conical
(adjective) shaped like a cone.

conifer, conifers
(noun) A conifer is a tree that has needle-like leaves and produces brown cones.
coniferous (adjective).
[from Latin *conus* meaning 'cone' and *ferre* meaning 'to bear']

conjecture, conjectures
1 (noun) Conjecture is guesswork about the nature of something, e.g. *The exact figure is a matter for conjecture.*
2 A conjecture is a guess.
conjectural (adjective).
[from Latin *conjicere* meaning 'to throw together']

conjugal (pronounced **kon**-joo-gl)
(adjective; a formal word) relating to marriage, e.g. *conjugal happiness.*
[from Latin *conjunx* meaning 'married person']

conjunction, conjunctions
1 (noun; a formal use) A conjunction of things is a combination of them, e.g. *a conjunction of personal and social factors.*
2 (phrase) If two or more things are done in conjunction, they are done together.
3 (noun) In grammar, a conjunction is a word that links two other words or two clauses, for example 'and', 'but', 'while', and 'that'.
conjunctive (adjective).
[from Latin *conjunctus* meaning 'united']

conjurer, conjurers
(noun) A conjurer is someone who entertains people by doing magic tricks.
conjuring (noun).
[from Latin *conjurare* meaning 'to conspire']

conjure up, conjures up, conjuring up, conjured up
(phrasal verb) If something conjures up a memory or idea, it creates it in your mind, e.g. *The name conjured up a picture of snow-capped peaks.*

conker, conkers
(noun) Conkers are hard brown nuts from a horse chestnut tree.

connect, connects, connecting, connected
1 (verb) To connect two things means to join them together.
2 If your train connects with another one, it gets somewhere in time for you to transfer to the other train.
3 If you connect something with something else, you think of them as being linked, e.g. *There is no evidence to connect Griffiths with the murder.*

[from Latin *connectere* meaning 'to bind together']

connection, connections; also spelled **connexion**
1 (noun) A connection is a link or relationship that exists between things.
2 A connection is also the point where two wires or pipes are joined together, e.g. *a loose connection.*
3 If you get a connection on a rail journey, you get off one train and catch another one.
4 (plural noun) Someone's connections are the people they know, e.g. *He has valuable business connections.*

connive, connives, conniving, connived
(verb) If you connive at something, you let it happen although you know it is wrong.
connivance (noun).
[from Latin *connivere* meaning 'to blink']

connoisseur, connoisseurs (pronounced kon-nis-**sir**)
(noun) A connoisseur is someone who knows a lot about the arts, or about food or drink, e.g. *a connoisseur of Italian opera.*
[from Old French *connoistre* meaning 'to know']

connotation, connotations
(noun) The connotations of a word or name are what it makes you think of, e.g. *Nowadays Dallas has connotations of wealth and glamour.*

connubial (pronounced kon-**yoo**-bee-al)
(adjective; a formal word) relating to marriage.
[from Latin *conubium* meaning 'marriage']

conquer, conquers, conquering, conquered
1 (verb) To conquer people means to take control of their country by force.
2 If you conquer something difficult or dangerous, you succeed in getting control of it, e.g. *the effort to conquer cancer.*
conqueror (noun).
[from Latin *conquirere* meaning 'to search for']

conquest, conquests
1 (noun) Conquest is the conquering of a country or group of people.
2 Conquests are lands captured by conquest.

conscience, consciences
1 (noun) Your conscience is the part of your mind that tells you what is right and wrong.
2 If you have a guilty conscience, you feel guilty because you have done something wrong.
[from Latin *conscire* meaning 'to know']

Similar words: (sense 1) scruples, principles

conscientious (pronounced kon-shee-**en**-shus)
(adjective) Someone who is conscientious is very careful to do their work properly.
conscientiously (adverb), **conscientiousness** (noun).

Similar words: thorough, painstaking, dedicated, scrupulous, meticulous

conscientious objector, conscientious objectors
(noun) A conscientious objector is someone who refuses to join the armed forces for moral or religious reasons.

conscious
1 (adjective) If you are conscious of something, you are aware of it, e.g. *She became conscious of Rudolph looking at her.*
2 A conscious action or effort is done deliberately, e.g. *He made a conscious effort to look happy.*
3 Someone who is conscious is awake, rather than asleep or unconscious, e.g. *He was now fully conscious.*
consciously (adverb), **consciousness** (noun).
[from Latin *conscius* meaning 'sharing knowledge']

conscript, conscripts, conscripting, conscripted
1 (verb) When someone is conscripted, they are officially made to join a country's armed forces.
2 (noun) A conscript is someone who has been conscripted.
conscription (noun).
[from Latin *conscribere* meaning 'to enrol']

consecrate, consecrates, consecrating, consecrated
(verb) When a place or object is consecrated, it is officially declared to be holy, e.g. *The church was consecrated in 1065.*
consecrated (adjective), **consecration** (noun).
[from Latin *consecrare* meaning 'to make holy']

consecutive
(adjective) Consecutive events or periods of time happen one after the other, e.g. *three consecutive victories... four consecutive days.*
consecutively (adverb).
[from Latin *consecutus* meaning 'having followed']

consensus
(noun) Consensus is general agreement among a group of people, e.g. *The consensus was that we should move on.*

consent, consents, consenting, consented
1 (noun) Consent is permission to do something, e.g. *She married without her parents' consent.*
2 Consent is also agreement between two or more people, e.g. *By common consent they stopped.*
3 (verb) If you consent to something, you agree to it or allow it.
[from Latin *consentire* meaning 'to agree']

consequence, consequences
1 (noun) The consequences of something are its results or effects.
2 (phrase) If one thing happens **in consequence** of another, it happens as a result of it, e.g. *He fell out with his boss and lost his job in consequence.*
3 (noun; a formal use) If something is of consequence, it is important.

consequent
(adjective) Consequent describes something as being the result of something else, e.g. *the shortage of land and the consequent rise in house prices.*
consequently (adverb).
[from Latin *consequi* meaning 'to pursue']

consequential
1 (adjective; a formal word) Consequential means the same as consequent, e.g. *overcrowding and the consequential lack of privacy.*
2 Consequential also means important, e.g. *a highly consequential event.*

conservation
(noun) Conservation is the preservation of the environment.
conservationist (noun and adjective).

conservative, conservatives
1 (noun) A Conservative is someone with right-wing views.
2 (adjective) Conservative views and policies are right-wing ones.
3 Someone who is conservative is not willing to accept changes or new ideas.
4 A conservative estimate or guess is a cautious or moderate one.
conservatively (adverb), **conservatism** (noun).

conservatory, conservatories
(noun) A conservatory is a room with glass walls and a glass roof in which plants are kept.

conserve, conserves, conserving, conserved
(verb) If you conserve a supply of something, you make it last, e.g. *We must conserve our strength.*
[from Latin *conservare* meaning 'to preserve']

consider, considers, considering, considered
1 (verb) If you consider something to be the case, you think or judge it to be so, e.g. *They consider themselves to be lucky.*
2 To consider something means to think about it carefully, e.g. *I stopped to consider what to do.*
3 If you consider someone's needs, wishes, or feelings, you take account of them.
[from Latin *considerare* meaning 'to inspect']

Similar words: (sense 2) contemplate, deliberate, mull over, ponder, reflect, weigh

considerable
(adjective) A considerable amount of something is a lot of it, e.g. *The building suffered considerable damage.*
considerably (adverb).

considerate
(adjective) Someone who is considerate pays attention to other people's needs, wishes, and feelings.
considerately (adverb).

consideration, considerations
1 (noun) Consideration is careful thought about something, e.g. *After much consideration, they agreed to go.*
2 If you show consideration for someone, you take account of their needs, wishes, and feelings.
3 A consideration is something that has to be taken into account, e.g. *An important consideration is the amount of time it will take.*

Similar words: (sense 1) contemplation, deliberation, reflection

considered
(adjective) A considered opinion or judgment is arrived at by careful thought.

considering
(conjunction and preposition) You say considering to indicate that you are taking something into account, e.g. *Considering that he received no help, his results are very good.*

consign, consigns, consigning, consigned
(verb; a formal word) To consign something to a particular place means to send or put it there.
[from Latin *consignare* meaning 'to put one's seal to']

consignment, consignments
(noun) A consignment of goods is a load of them being delivered somewhere.

consist, consists, consisting, consisted
(verb) What something consists of is its different parts or members, e.g. *The committee consists of scientists and engineers.*

Similar words: comprise, constitute, be composed of

consistency, consistencies
1 (noun) Consistency is the quality of being consistent.
2 The consistency of a substance is its degree of thickness or smoothness.

consistent
1 (adjective) If you are consistent, you keep doing something the same way, e.g. *the consistent support of my colleagues.*
2 If something such as a statement or argument is consistent, there are no contradictions in it.
consistently (adverb).

console, consoles, consoling, consoled
1 (verb) To console someone who is unhappy means to make them more cheerful, e.g. *I was consoled by the thought of the money.*
2 (noun) A console is a panel with switches or knobs for operating a machine.
consolation (noun), **consolatory** (adjective).
[sense 1 from Latin *consolari* meaning 'to comfort']

consolidate, consolidates, consolidating, consolidated
(verb) To consolidate something you have gained or achieved means to make it more secure.
consolidation (noun).
[from Latin *consolidare* meaning 'to make firm']

consommé (pronounced kon-**som**-may)
(noun) Consommé is a thin, clear soup.
[from French *consommer* meaning 'to use up']

consonant, consonants
(noun) A consonant is a sound such as 'p' or 'm' which you make by stopping the air flowing freely through your mouth.
[from Latin *consonare* meaning 'to sound at the same time']

consort, consorts, consorting, consorted
1 (verb; a formal word) If you consort with someone, you spend a lot of time with them.

2 (noun) The wife or husband of the ruling monarch is his or her consort.
[from Latin *consors* meaning 'sharer' or 'partner']

consortium, consortiums
(noun) A consortium is a group of businesses working together.

conspicuous
(adjective) If something is conspicuous, people can see or notice it very easily.
conspicuously (adverb).
[from Latin *conspicere* meaning 'to perceive']

conspiracy, conspiracies
(noun) When there is a conspiracy, a group of people plan something illegal, often for a political purpose.

conspirator, conspirators
(noun) A conspirator is someone involved in a conspiracy.

conspiratorial
(adjective) If someone's behaviour is conspiratorial, they behave as if they are sharing a secret with you, e.g. *a conspiratorial smile*.
conspiratorially (adverb).

conspire, conspires, conspiring, conspired
1 (verb) When people conspire, they plan together to do something illegal, often for a political purpose.
2 (a literary use) When events conspire towards a particular result, they seem to work together to cause it, e.g. *Everything had conspired to make him happy*.
[from Latin *conspirare* meaning 'to plot']

constable, constables
(noun) A constable is a police officer of the lowest rank.
[from Latin *comes stabuli* meaning 'officer of the stable']

constabulary, constabularies
(noun) The constabulary of an area is its police force.

constant, constants
1 (adjective) Something that is constant happens all the time or is always there, e.g. *He was in constant pain*.
2 If an amount or level is constant, it stays the same, e.g. *a constant temperature*.
3 People who are constant remain loyal to a person or idea.
4 (noun) A constant is a number or quantity that does not change.
constantly (adverb), **constancy** (noun).
[from Latin *constare* meaning 'to stand firm']

Similar words: (sense 2) unchanging, consistent, immutable

constellation, constellations
(noun) A constellation is a group of stars.
[from Latin *con-* meaning 'together' and *stellae* meaning 'stars']

consternation
(noun) Consternation is great anxiety or fear, e.g. *We looked at each other in consternation*.

[from Latin *consternere* meaning 'to scatter' or 'to throw down']

constipated
(adjective) Someone who is constipated is unable to defecate.
constipation (noun).
[from Latin *constipare* meaning 'to press together']

constituency, constituencies
(noun) A constituency is a town or area represented by an MP.

constituent, constituents
1 (noun) An MP's constituents are the voters who live in his or her constituency.
2 The constituents of something are its parts, e.g. *the constituents of living matter*.

constitute, constitutes, constituting, constituted
(verb) If a group of things constitute something, they are what it consists of, e.g. *Conifers constitute about a third of the world's forests*.
[from Latin *constituere* meaning 'to cause to stand']

constitution, constitutions
1 (noun) The constitution of a country is the system of laws which formally states people's rights and duties.
2 Your constitution is your health, e.g. *He has a strong constitution*.
3 (a formal use) The constitution of something is what it consists of.
constitutional (adjective), **constitutionally** (adverb).

constrain, constrains, constraining, constrained
(verb; a formal word) To constrain someone means to limit their freedom of action.
[from Latin *constringere* meaning 'to bind together' or 'to restrain']

constraint, constraints
(noun) A constraint is something that limits someone's freedom of action, e.g. *The constraint on most doctors is lack of time*.

constrict, constricts, constricting, constricted
(verb) To constrict something means to squeeze it tightly.
constriction (noun), **constricting** (adjective).

construct, constructs, constructing, constructed
1 (verb) To construct something means to build or make it.
2 (noun; a formal use) A construct is something built or made, e.g. *vast constructs of cogs, screws, and wheels*.
3 (verb) In geometry, to construct something such as a line or an angle means to draw it according to particular requirements.
[from Latin *construere* meaning 'to heap together' or 'to build']

construction, constructions
1 (noun) The construction of something is the building or making of it, e.g. *the construction of the Panama Canal*.
2 A construction is something built or made, e.g. *a complicated construction of wood and glass*.

constructive

(adjective) Constructive criticisms and comments are helpful.
constructively (adverb).

construe, construes, construing, construed

(pronounced kon-**stroo**)
(verb; a formal word) If you construe something in a particular way, you interpret it that way, e.g. *A show of emotion is construed as weakness.*

consul, consuls

1 (noun) A consul is an official who lives in a foreign city and who looks after people there who are citizens of his or her own country.
2 In ancient Rome, a consul was one of two annually elected chief magistrates.
consular (adjective).
[from Latin *consulere* meaning 'to consult']

consulate, consulates

(noun) A consulate is the place where a consul works.

consult, consults, consulting, consulted

1 (verb) If you consult someone, you ask for their opinion or advice.
2 When people consult each other, they exchange ideas and opinions.
3 If you consult a book or map, you refer to it for information.
[from Latin *consultare* meaning 'to consider' or 'to reflect']

Similar words: (senses 1 and 2) confer, converse, take counsel

consultancy, consultancies

(noun) A consultancy is an organization whose members give expert advice on a subject.

consultant, consultants

1 (noun) A consultant is an experienced doctor who specializes in one type of medicine.
2 A consultant is also someone who gives expert advice, e.g. *a firm of public relations consultants.*

consultation, consultations

1 (noun) A consultation is a meeting held to discuss something.
2 Consultation is discussion or the seeking of advice, e.g. *decisions taken after consultation with the unions.*
3 Consultation is also reference to a book or something similar for information, e.g. *Keep the handbook near for frequent consultation.*
consultative (adjective).

consume, consumes, consuming, consumed

1 (verb; a formal word) If you consume something, you eat or drink it.
2 To consume fuel or energy means to use it up.
[from Latin *consumere* meaning 'to take altogether']

Similar words: (sense 2) utilize, eat up, use

consumer, consumers

(noun) A consumer is someone who buys things or uses services, e.g. *The consumer is entitled to value for money.*

consuming

(adjective) A consuming passion or interest is more important to you than anything else.

consummate, consummates, consummating, consummated (pronounced **kons**-yum-mate)

1 (verb; a formal word) If two people consummate a marriage or relationship, they make it complete by having sex.
2 To consummate something means to make it complete.
3 (adjective) You use consummate to describe someone who is very good at something, e.g. *a consummate liar... a fighter of consummate skill.*
consummation (noun), **consummately** (adverb).
[from Latin *consummare* meaning 'to add together' or 'to complete']

consumption

1 (noun) The consumption of fuel or food is the using of it, or the amount used, e.g. *the high fuel consumption of the aircraft.*
2 (an old-fashioned use) Consumption is tuberculosis.

contact, contacts, contacting, contacted

1 (noun) If you are in contact with someone, you regularly meet them, talk to them, or write to them.
2 When things are in contact, they are touching each other.
3 (verb) If you contact someone, you telephone them or write to them.
4 (noun) A contact is someone you know in a place or organization from whom you can get help or information.
[from Latin *contactus* meaning 'a touch']

Similar words: (sense 3) get in touch with, get hold of, reach

contact lens, contact lenses

(noun) Contact lenses are small plastic lenses that you put in your eyes instead of wearing glasses, to help you see better.

contagion (pronounced kon-**tay**-jn)

(noun; a formal word) Contagion is the spreading of infectious disease by physical contact.

contagious

(adjective) A contagious disease can be caught by touching people or things infected with it.

contain, contains, containing, contained

1 (verb) If a substance contains something, that thing is a part of it, e.g. *chemical compounds containing mercury.*
2 The things a box or room contains are the things inside it.
3 (a formal use) To contain something also means to stop it increasing or spreading, e.g. *measures to contain population growth.*
containment (noun).
[from Latin *con-* + *tenere* meaning 'to hold together']

container, containers

1 (noun) A container is something such as a box or a bottle that you keep things in.
2 Containers are also large sealed metal boxes for transporting things by road, rail, or ship.

Similar words: (sense 1) holder, receptacle, canister, carton, repository, vessel

contaminate, contaminates, contaminating, contaminated
(verb) If something is contaminated by dirt, chemicals, or radiation, it is made impure and harmful, e.g. *contaminated drinking water.*
contamination (noun), **contaminant** (noun).
[from Latin *contaminare* meaning 'to defile']

contemplate, contemplates, contemplating, contemplated
1 (verb) To contemplate means to think carefully about something for a long time.
2 If you contemplate doing something, you consider doing it, e.g. *Lawrence contemplated publishing the book.*
3 If you contemplate something, you look at it for a long time, e.g. *They contemplated each other in silence.*
contemplation (noun), **contemplative** (adjective).
[from Latin *contemplari* meaning 'to regard']

contemporary, contemporaries
1 (adjective) functioning, produced, or happening now, e.g. *contemporary writers.*
2 functioning, produced, or happening at the time you are talking about, e.g. *a contemporary account of the trial.*
3 (noun) Someone's contemporaries are other people living or active at the same time as them, e.g. *Darwin's contemporary, Sir James Simpson.*
[from Latin *con-* meaning 'together' and *tempus* meaning 'time']

contempt
(noun) If you treat someone or something with contempt, you show no respect for them at all, e.g. *She looked at him with contempt.*
[from Latin *contemnere* meaning 'to condemn']

contemptible
(adjective) not worthy of any respect, e.g. *his contemptible lack of courage.*

contemptuous
(adjective) showing contempt.
contemptuously (adverb).

contend, contends, contending, contended
1 (verb) To contend with a difficulty means to deal with it, e.g. *I have enough to contend with already.*
2 (a formal use) If you contend that something is true, you say firmly that it is true.
3 When people contend for something, they compete for it, e.g. *Three parties are contending for power.*
contender (noun).
[from Latin *contendere* meaning 'to stretch' or 'to strive']

content, contents, contenting, contented
1 (plural noun) The contents of something are the things inside it.
2 (noun) The content of an article or speech is what is expressed in it.
3 Content is used to refer to the proportion of something that a substance contains, e.g. *Spinach has a very high iron content.*
4 (adjective) happy and satisfied with your life.
5 willing to do or have something, e.g. *She was content to pay the fine.*
6 (verb) If you content yourself with doing something, you do it and do not try to do anything else, e.g. *He contented himself with staring out of the window.*
[from Latin *continere* meaning 'to contain' or 'to hold back']

contented
(adjective) happy and satisfied with your life.
contentedly (adverb), **contentment** (noun).

contention, contentions (a formal word)
1 (noun) Someone's contention is the idea or opinion they are expressing, e.g. *My contention is that all people are equal.*
2 Contention is disagreement and argument about something, e.g. *What had brought about all this contention?*

contentious
(adjective) causing disagreement and argument, e.g. *His contentious view is that mental illness is a myth.*

contest, contests, contesting, contested
1 (noun) A contest is a competition or game, e.g. *a fishing contest.*
2 A contest is also a struggle for power, e.g. *the contest for the deputy leadership.*
3 (verb) If you contest a statement or decision, you object to it formally.
[from Latin *contestari* meaning 'to call to witness']

Similar words: (sense 1) match, championship, tournament, game, competition

contestant, contestants
(noun) The contestants in a competition are the people taking part in it.

Similar words: competitor, participant, player

context, contexts
1 (noun) The context of something consists of matters related to it which help to explain it, e.g. *We must examine these ideas in the context of recent events.*
2 The context of a word or sentence consists of the words or sentences before and after it.
contextual (adjective).
[from Latin *contextus* meaning 'connected']

continent, continents
1 (noun) A continent is a very large area of land, such as Africa or Asia.
2 The Continent is the mainland of Europe.
continental (adjective).
[from Latin *terra continens* meaning 'continuous land']

contingency, contingencies (pronounced kon-**tin**-jen-see)
(noun) A contingency is something that might happen in the future, e.g. *He was ready for all contingencies.*
[from Latin *contingere* meaning 'to happen']

contingent, contingents

1 (noun) A contingent is a group of people representing a country or organization, e.g. *the Dutch contingent*.
2 A contingent is also a group of police or soldiers.
3 (adjective; a formal use) If something is contingent on something else, it depends on it in order to happen or exist, e.g. *The raid was contingent on the weather*.

Similar words: (sense 1) deputation, detachment, lobby, delegation

continual

1 (adjective) happening all the time without stopping, e.g. *a continual increase in cost*.
2 happening again and again, e.g. *her continual warnings*.
continually (adverb).

Similar words: incessant, continuous, persistent, constant, nonstop, unremitting

continuation, continuations

1 (noun) The continuation of something is the continuing of it.
2 Something that is a continuation of an event follows it and seems like a part of it.

Similar words: extension, prolongation, perpetuation

continue, continues, continuing, continued

1 (verb) If you continue to do something, you keep doing it.
2 If something continues, it does not stop.
3 You also say something continues when it starts again after stopping, e.g. *The performance continued*.
4 If a road or path continues, it goes on beyond a particular place.
continuance (noun).
[from Latin *continuare* meaning 'to join together']

Similar words: (senses 2-4) carry on, go on, proceed

continuous

1 (adjective) Continuous means happening or existing without stopping.
2 A continuous line or surface has no gaps or holes in it.
continuously (adverb), **continuity** (noun).

contorted

(adjective) twisted into an unnatural, unattractive shape, e.g. *His face was contorted with pain*.
[from Latin *contortus* meaning 'twisted']

contortion, contortions

(noun) Contortions are movements in which you twist your body into unusual positions.

contour, contours

1 (noun) The contours of something are its general shape.
2 On a map, a contour is a line joining points of equal height.
[from Italian *contornare* meaning 'to draw in outline']

contra-

(prefix) Contra- means against or opposite to, e.g. *a contra-indication*.
[from Latin *contra* meaning 'against']

contraband

(noun) Contraband consists of goods smuggled into a country.

contraception

(noun) Contraception refers to methods of preventing pregnancy.
[from Latin *contra-* meaning 'against' and *concipere* meaning 'to conceive']

contraceptive, contraceptives

(noun) A contraceptive is a device or pill for preventing pregnancy.

contract, contracts, contracting, contracted

1 (noun) A contract is a written legal agreement concerning the sale of something or work done for money.
2 (verb) When something contracts, it gets smaller or shorter.
3 (a formal use) If you contract an illness, you get it, e.g. *She contracted breast cancer*.
contractual (adjective), **contraction** (noun).
[from Latin *contrahere* meaning 'to draw together']

contractor, contractors

(noun) A contractor is a person or company who does work for other people or companies, e.g. *a haulage contractor*.

contradict, contradicts, contradicting, contradicted

(verb) If you contradict someone, you say that what they have just said is not true, and that something else is.
contradiction (noun), **contradictory** (adjective).
[from Latin *contra-* + *dicere* meaning 'to speak against']

contralto, contraltos

(noun) A contralto is a woman with a low singing voice. Contraltos usually sing the second highest part in four-part harmony.

contraption, contraptions

(noun) A contraption is a strange-looking device or machine.

contrary

1 (adjective) Contrary ideas or opinions are opposed to each other and cannot be held by the same person, e.g. *opinions contrary to their own*.
2 (phrase) You say **on the contrary** when you are contradicting what someone has just said, e.g. *'You'll get tired of it.' — 'On the contrary, I shall enjoy it.'*
3 Evidence or statements **to the contrary** contradict what you are saying or what someone else has said, e.g. *This method, despite statements to the contrary, is perfectly safe.*

contrast, contrasts, contrasting, contrasted

1 (noun) A contrast is a great difference between things, e.g. *the contrast between his public image and his private life*.
2 If one thing is a contrast to another, it is very

different from it, e.g. *Our new home was a complete contrast to the old one.*
3 (verb) If you contrast things, you describe or emphasize the differences between them, e.g. *The book contrasts methods used in different countries.*
4 If one thing contrasts with another, it is very different from it, e.g. *contrasting attitudes.*
[from Latin *contra-* + *stare* meaning 'to stand against']

contravene, contravenes, contravening, contravened
(verb; a formal word) If you contravene a law or rule, you do something that it forbids.
contravention (noun).
[from Latin *contra-* + *venire* meaning 'to come against']

contribute, contributes, contributing, contributed
1 (verb) If you contribute to something, you do things to help it succeed, e.g. *The elderly have much to contribute to the community.*
2 If you contribute money, you give it to help to pay for something.
3 If something contributes to an event or situation, it is one of its causes, e.g. *Soaring land prices contribute to the high cost of housing.*
4 People who contribute to a book or magazine write things that are published in it.
contribution (noun), **contributor** (noun), **contributory** (adjective).
[from Latin *contribuere*]

Similar words: (sense 2) donate, give

contrite
(adjective; a literary word) If you are contrite, you are ashamed of something you have done.
contritely (adverb), **contrition** (noun).
[from Latin *contritus* meaning 'worn out' or 'well used']

contrivance, contrivances
1 (noun) A contrivance is a strange-looking device or machine.
2 A contrivance is also a dishonest scheme, e.g. *a contrivance to raise prices.*

contrive, contrives, contriving, contrived
(verb; a formal word) If you contrive to do something difficult, you succeed in doing it, e.g. *I contrived to squeeze past him.*

contrived
(adjective) Something that is contrived is unnatural, e.g. *a contrived ending to the play.*

control, controls, controlling, controlled
1 (noun) Control of a country or organization is the power to make the important decisions about how it is run.
2 Your control over something is your ability to make it work the way you want it to.
3 (verb) To control a country or organization means to have the power to make decisions about how it is run.
4 To control something such as a machine or system means to make it work the way you want it to.

5 If you control yourself, you make yourself behave calmly when you are angry or upset.
6 (noun) The controls on a machine are knobs or other devices used to operate it.
7 (phrase) If something is **out of control**, nobody has any power over it.
controller (noun).

Similar words: (sense 5) curb, restrain, check, hold back

controversial
(adjective) Something that is controversial causes a lot of discussion and argument, because many people disapprove of it.

Similar words: contentious, provocative, outrageous

controversy, controversies (pronounced **kon**-triv-ver-see)
(noun) Controversy is discussion and argument because many people disapprove of something.
[from Latin *controversus* meaning 'turned in an opposite direction']

conundrum, conundrums
(noun; a formal word) A conundrum is a puzzling problem.

conurbation, conurbations
(noun; a formal word) A conurbation is a very large urban area formed by towns spreading towards each other.
[from Latin *con-* meaning 'together' and *urbs* meaning 'city']

convalesce, convalesces, convalescing, convalesced
(verb) When people convalesce, they rest and regain their health after an illness or operation.
convalescent (adjective), **convalescence** (noun).
[from Latin *convalescere* meaning 'to become strong']

convection
(noun) Convection is the process by which heat travels through gases and liquids.
[from Latin *con-* meaning 'with' and *vectus* meaning 'carried']

convector, convectors
(noun) A convector or convector heater is a heater that heats a room using hot air.

convene, convenes, convening, convened
1 (verb; a formal word) To convene a meeting means to arrange for it to take place.
2 When people convene, they come together for a meeting.
[from Latin *convenire* meaning 'to come together']

convenience, conveniences
1 (noun) The convenience of something is the fact that it is easy to use or that it makes something easy to do, e.g. *the convenience of living in town.*
2 A convenience is something useful, e.g. *a house with every modern convenience.*

convenient
(adjective) If something is convenient, it is easy to use or it makes something easy to do.
conveniently (adverb).
[from Latin *conveniens* meaning 'appropriate']

Similar words: handy, serviceable, useful

convent, convents
(noun) A convent is a building where nuns live, or a school run by nuns.
[from Latin *conventus* meaning 'meeting']

convention, conventions
1 (noun) A convention is an accepted way of behaving or doing something.
2 A convention is also a large meeting of an organization or political group, especially one to form an agreement, e.g. *the Geneva Convention*.
[from Latin *conventio* meaning 'agreement' or 'assembly']

conventional
1 (adjective) You say that people are conventional when there is nothing unusual about their way of life.
2 Conventional methods and products are the ones that are usually used.
3 Conventional wars and weapons are non-nuclear.
conventionally (adverb).

converge, converges, converging, converged
(verb) To converge means to meet or join at a particular place.
convergence (noun), **convergent** (adjective).
[from Latin *con-* + *vergere* meaning 'to bend together']

conversant
(adjective; a formal word) If you are conversant with something, you are familiar with it.

conversation, conversations
(noun) If you have a conversation with someone, you spend time talking to them.
conversational (adjective), **conversationally** (adverb), **conversationalist** (noun).

converse, converses, conversing, conversed
1 (verb; a formal use) When people converse, they talk to each other.
2 (noun) The converse of something is its opposite, e.g. *What you can do, a machine can do. The converse, however, is not true.*
3 (adjective) Converse is used to describe things which are the opposite of other things, e.g. *the converse process.*
conversely (adverb).
[from Latin *conversare* meaning 'to turn constantly']

convert, converts, converting, converted
1 (verb) To convert one thing into another means to change it so that it becomes the other thing.
2 If someone converts you, they persuade you to change your religious or political beliefs.
3 (noun) A convert is someone who has changed their religious or political beliefs.
conversion (noun), **convertible** (adjective).
[from Latin *convertere* meaning 'to turn round']

convex
(adjective) A convex surface bulges outwards, rather than being level or curving inwards.
[from Latin *convexus* meaning 'vaulted' or 'rounded']

convey, conveys, conveying, conveyed
1 (verb) To convey information or ideas means to cause them to be known or understood.
2 (a formal use) To convey someone or something to a place means to transport them there, e.g. *the truck conveying the work crew.*

conveyance, conveyances
(noun; an old-fashioned word) A conveyance is a vehicle.

conveyor belt, conveyor belts
(noun) A conveyor belt is a moving strip used in factories for moving objects along.

convict, convicts, convicting, convicted
1 (verb) To convict someone of a crime means to find them guilty, e.g. *He was convicted of spying.*
2 (noun) A convict is someone serving a prison sentence.
[from Latin *convictus* meaning 'convicted of crime']

conviction, convictions
1 (noun) A conviction is a strong belief or opinion.
2 The conviction of someone is what happens when they are found guilty in a court of law.

convince, convinces, convincing, convinced
(verb) To convince someone of something means to persuade them that it is true.
[from Latin *convincere* meaning 'to demonstrate conclusively']

Similar words: sway, persuade

convincing
(adjective) Convincing is used to describe things or people that can make you believe something is true, e.g. *a convincing explanation.*
convincingly (adverb).

Similar words: persuasive, cogent, plausible, credible, believable

convivial
(adjective; a formal word) enjoyable and friendly, e.g. *a convivial evening.*
convivially (adverb), **conviviality** (noun).
[from Latin *convivialis* meaning 'relating to a feast']

convoluted (pronounced kon-vol-**yoo**-tid)
(adjective) Something that is convoluted has many twists and bends, e.g. *a long and convoluted road... convoluted sentences.*
convolution (noun).
[from Latin *convolutus* meaning 'rolled together']

convoy, convoys
(noun) A convoy is a group of vehicles or ships travelling together.
[from Old French *convoier* meaning 'to convey']

convulse, convulses, convulsing, convulsed
(verb) If you convulse, your body shakes
violently, e.g. *He convulsed in pain.*
[from Latin *convellere* meaning 'to tear up']

convulsion, convulsions
(noun) If someone has convulsions, their muscles
move violently and uncontrollably.
convulsive (adjective).

coo, coos, cooing, cooed
(verb) When pigeons and doves coo, they make a
soft flutelike sound.

cook, cooks, cooking, cooked
1 (verb) To cook food means to prepare it for
eating by heating it.
2 (noun) A cook is someone who prepares and
cooks food, often as their job.
[from Latin *coquere*]

cook up
(phrasal verb) To cook up a dishonest plan or
scheme means to invent it.

cooker, cookers
(noun) A cooker is a device for cooking food.

cookery
(noun) Cookery is the activity of preparing and
cooking food.

cool, cooler, coolest; cools, cooling, cooled
1 (adjective) Something cool has a low
temperature but is not cold.
2 (verb) When something cools or when you cool
it, it becomes less warm.
3 (adjective) If you are cool in a difficult
situation, you stay calm and unemotional.
4 If your behaviour towards someone is cool, you
are not friendly to them.
coolly (adverb), **coolness** (noun).

coolant, coolants
(noun) A coolant is a liquid used to keep a
machine cool while it is operating.

coop, coops
(noun) A coop is a cage for chickens or rabbits.

cooped up
(adjective) kept in a place which is too small or
which does not allow enough freedom, e.g. *I
hated being cooped up in the flat all day.*

cooperate, cooperates, cooperating, cooperated
(pronounced koh-**op**-er-ate)
1 (verb) When people cooperate, they work or
act together.
2 To cooperate also means to do what someone
asks.
cooperation (noun).
[from Latin *co-* + *operari* meaning 'to work
with']

cooperative, cooperatives (pronounced
koh-**op**-er-ut-tiv)
1 (noun) A cooperative is a business or
organization run by the people who work for it,
and who share its benefits or profits.
2 (adjective) A cooperative activity is done by
people working together.
3 Someone who is cooperative does what you ask
them to.
cooperatively (adverb).

coopt, coopts, coopting, coopted
(pronounced koh-**opt**)
(verb) If the people in a group coopt you, they
make you a member.
[from Latin *cooptare* meaning 'to elect']

coordinate, coordinates, coordinating,
coordinated (pronounced koh-**or**-din-ate)
(verb) To coordinate an activity means to
organize the people or things involved in it, e.g.
Emergency services were coordinated centrally.
coordination (noun), **coordinator** (noun).

coot, coots
(noun) A coot is a black water bird with a white
patch on its forehead.

cop, cops
(noun; an informal word) A cop is a policeman.

cope, copes, coping, coped
(verb) If you cope with a problem or task, you
deal with it successfully.

copious
(adjective; a formal word) existing or produced
in large quantities, e.g. *She made copious notes.*
copiously (adverb).
[from Latin *copia* meaning 'abundance']

copper, coppers
1 (noun) Copper is a reddish-brown metallic
element. Its atomic number is 29 and its symbol
is Cu.
2 Coppers are brown metal coins of low value.
[from Greek *Kupris* meaning Cyprus, where
copper originally came from]

coppice, coppices (pronounced **kop**-piss)
(noun) A coppice is a small group of trees
growing close together.

copse, copses
(noun) A copse is a coppice.

copulate, copulates, copulating, copulated
(verb; a formal word) To copulate means to have
sex.
copulation (noun).
[from Latin *co-* + *apere* meaning 'to fasten
together']

copy, copies, copying, copied
1 (noun) A copy is something made to look like
something else.
2 A copy of a book, newspaper, or record is one
of many identical ones produced at the same
time.
3 (verb) If you copy what someone does, you do
the same thing.
4 If you copy something, you make a copy of it.
copier (noun).

Similar words: (sense 1) facsimile, reproduction,
replica
(sense 4) duplicate, replicate

---

copyright, copyrights
(noun) If someone has the copyright on a piece of
writing or music, it cannot be copied or
performed without their permission.

copywriter, copywriters
(noun) A copywriter is someone who writes the words for advertisements.
copywriting (noun).

coracle, coracles
(noun) A coracle is a simple round rowing boat made of woven sticks covered with skins.
[from Welsh *corwgl* meaning 'boat' or 'carcass']

coral, corals
(noun) Coral is a hard substance that forms in the sea from the skeletons of tiny animals called corals. Coral is used to make jewellery.
[from Greek *korallion*]

cor anglais, cors anglais (pronounced kohr ong-**glay**)
(noun) A cor anglais is a woodwind instrument with a double reed. It has a slightly lower pitch than an oboe.

cord, cords
1 (noun) Cord is strong, thick string.
2 Electrical wire covered in rubber or plastic is also called cord.
[from Greek *khordē* meaning 'gut' or 'string']

cordial
1 (adjective) warm and friendly, e.g. *He gave a cordial response.*
2 (noun) Cordial is a sweet drink made from fruit juice.
cordially (adverb), **cordiality** (noun).

cordite
(noun) Cordite is an explosive substance used in guns and bombs.

cordon, cordons, cordoning, cordoned
1 (noun) A cordon is a line or ring of police or soldiers preventing people entering or leaving a place.
2 (verb) If police or soldiers cordon off an area, they stop people entering or leaving by forming themselves into a line or ring.
[from Old French *cordon* meaning 'little cord']

corduroy
(noun) Corduroy is a thick cloth with parallel raised lines on the outside.

core, cores
1 (noun) The core of a fruit such as an apple is its hard central part.
2 The core of an object or a place is its most central part, e.g. *the earth's core.*
3 The core of something is its most important part, e.g. *the core of the problem.*

coriander (pronounced kor-ree-**an**-der)
(noun) Coriander is a plant with seeds that are used as a spice and leaves that are used as a herb for flavouring in cooking.

cork, corks
1 (noun) Cork is the very light, spongelike bark of a Mediterranean tree.
2 A cork is a piece of cork pushed into the end of a bottle to close it.
[from Latin *cortex* meaning 'bark']

corkscrew, corkscrews
(noun) A corkscrew is a device for pulling corks out of bottles.

corm, corms
(noun) A corm is a fleshy part of the stem of some types of plant which grows beneath the soil and is used for reproduction.
[from Greek *kormos* meaning 'tree trunk with branches lopped off']

cormorant, cormorants
(noun) A cormorant is a dark-coloured bird with a long neck, which dives into the sea to catch fish.

corn, corns
1 (noun) Corn refers to crops such as wheat and barley and to their seeds.
2 A corn is a small painful area of hard skin on your foot.

cornea, corneas (pronounced **kor**-nee-a)
(noun) The cornea is the transparent skin that covers the outside of your eyeball.
[from Latin *cornea tela* meaning 'horny web']

corner, corners, cornering, cornered
1 (noun) A corner is a place where two sides or edges of something meet, e.g. *the corner of the page... a street corner.*
2 (verb) To corner a person or animal means to get them into a place they cannot escape from.

cornet, cornets
(noun) A cornet is a small brass instrument used in brass and military bands.
[from Latin *cornu* meaning 'horn']

cornflour
(noun) Cornflour is a fine white flour made from maize and used in cooking to thicken soups, gravy, and sauces.

cornflower, cornflowers
(noun) A cornflower is a small plant with bright flowers, usually blue.

cornice, cornices
(noun) A cornice is a decorative strip of plaster, wood, or stone along the top edge of a wall.

cornucopia (pronounced kor-nyoo-**koe**-pee-ya)
(noun; a formal word) A cornucopia of good things is a large number of them.
[from Latin *cornu copiae* meaning 'horn of plenty']

corny, cornier, corniest
(adjective) very obvious or sentimental and not at all original, e.g. *a corny joke.*

Similar words: banal, trite, hackneyed

corollary, corollaries
(noun; a formal word) A corollary of something is an idea, argument, or fact that necessarily results from it, e.g. *This change is the inevitable corollary of social revolution.*

coronary, coronaries
(noun) If someone has a coronary, blood cannot reach their heart because of a blood clot.

coronation, coronations
(noun) A coronation is the ceremony at which a king or queen is crowned.
[from Latin *corona* meaning 'crown']

coroner, coroners
(noun) A coroner is an official who investigates the deaths of people who have died in a violent or unusual way.

coronet, coronets
(noun) A coronet is a small crown.

corporal, corporals
(noun) A corporal is a non-commissioned officer in the army or air force, immediately below sergeant in rank.

corporal punishment
(noun) Corporal punishment is the punishing of people by beating them.
[from Latin *corpus* meaning 'body']

corporate
(adjective; a formal word) belonging to or done by all members of a group together, e.g. *a corporate achievement*.
[from Latin *corpus* meaning 'body']

corporation, corporations
1 (noun) A corporation is a group of people responsible for running a city.
2 A corporation is also a large business.

corps (rhymes with **more**)
1 (noun) A corps is a part of an army with special duties, e.g. *the Royal Army Ordnance Corps*.
2 A corps is also a small group of people who do a special job, e.g. *the diplomatic corps*.

corpse, corpses
(noun) A corpse is a dead body.
[from Latin *corpus* meaning 'body']

corpulent (pronounced **kor**-pyul-lent)
(adjective; a formal word) Someone who is corpulent is fat.
[from Latin *corpulentus* meaning 'fleshy']

corpuscle, corpuscles (pronounced **kor**-pus-sl)
(noun) A corpuscle is a red or white blood cell.
[from Latin *corpusculum* meaning 'little body']

correct, corrects, correcting, corrected
1 (adjective) If something is correct, there are no mistakes in it.
2 The correct thing in a particular situation is the right one, e.g. *I hope you've brought the correct fuse*.
3 Correct behaviour is considered to be socially acceptable.
4 (verb) If you correct something which is wrong, you make it right.
correctly (adverb), **correction** (noun), **corrective** (adjective and noun), **correctness** (noun).
[from Latin *corrigere* meaning 'to put right']

Similar words: (sense 4) rectify, redress, remedy, emend

correlate, correlates, correlating, correlated
(verb) If two things correlate or are correlated, they are closely connected or strongly influence each other, e.g. *Power is not always correlated with income*.
correlation (noun), **correlative** (adjective).

correspond, corresponds, corresponding, corresponded
1 (verb) If one thing corresponds to another, it has a similar purpose, function, or status.
2 If numbers or amounts correspond, they are the same.
3 When people correspond, they write to each other.

correspondence
1 (noun) Correspondence is the writing of letters; also the letters written.
2 If there is a correspondence between two things, they are closely related or very similar.

correspondence course, correspondence courses
(noun) If you take a correspondence course, you study at home, receiving your work by post.

correspondent, correspondents
(noun) A correspondent is a newspaper, television, or radio reporter.

corresponding
1 (adjective) You use corresponding to describe a change that results from a change in something else, e.g. *a rise in inflation with corresponding wage increases*.
2 You also use corresponding to describe something which has a similar purpose, function, or status to something else, e.g. *a degree or corresponding professional qualification*.

corridor, corridors
(noun) A corridor is a passage in a building or train.
[from Old Italian *corridore* meaning 'place for running']

corrie, corries
(noun; a technical word) A corrie is a circular hollow on a hillside.

corroborate, corroborates, corroborating, corroborated
(verb; a formal word) To corroborate an idea, account, or argument means to provide evidence to support it.
corroboration (noun), **corroborative** (adjective).
[from Latin *corroborare* meaning 'to strengthen']

corrode, corrodes, corroding, corroded
(verb) When metal corrodes, it is gradually destroyed by a chemical or rust.
corrosion (noun), **corrosive** (adjective).
[from Latin *corrodere* meaning 'to gnaw away']

corrugated
(adjective) Corrugated metal or cardboard is produced in parallel folds to make it stronger.
[from Latin *corrugare* meaning 'to wrinkle up']

corrupt, corrupts, corrupting, corrupted
1 (adjective) Corrupt people act dishonestly or illegally in return for money or power.
2 (verb) To corrupt someone means to make them dishonest or immoral, e.g. *Young prisoners are corrupted by hardened criminals*.
[from Latin *corruptus* meaning 'weakened']

Similar words: (sense 1) depraved, immoral (sense 2) debauch, deprave, pervert

corruption

1 (noun) Corruption is dishonesty and illegal behaviour by people in positions of power.
2 The corruption of someone is the process of making them behave in a way that is morally or sexually wrong.
3 (a formal use) Corruption is also immoral sexual behaviour.

Similar words: (sense 3) debauchery, immorality, vice, depravity

corset, corsets
(noun) Corsets are stiff underwear worn by some women round their hips and waist to make them look slimmer.
[from Old French *corset* meaning 'little bodice']

cortege, corteges (pronounced kor-**tayj**)
(noun) A cortege is a procession of people or vehicles going to a funeral.
[from Italian *corteggiare* meaning 'to attend']

cortex, cortices
(noun) The cortex of the brain or other organ is its outer layer.
[from Latin *cortex* meaning 'bark']

cortisone (pronounced **kor**-tis-sone)
(noun) Cortisone is a hormone used in treating arthritis, allergies, and some skin diseases.

cosine, cosines
(noun) In mathematics a cosine is a function of an angle. If B is the right angle in a right-angled triangle ABC, the cosine of the angle at A is AB divided by AC.

cosmetic, cosmetics
1 (noun) Cosmetics are substances such as lipstick and face powder.
2 (adjective) Cosmetic measures or changes improve the appearance of something without changing its basic character.
[from Greek *kosmein* meaning 'to arrange']

cosmetic surgery
(noun) Cosmetic surgery is surgery carried out to make people look more attractive.

cosmic
(adjective) belonging or relating to the universe.
[from Greek *kosmos* meaning 'order' or 'universe']

cosmology
(noun) Cosmology is the study of the origin and nature of the universe.

cosmonaut, cosmonauts
(noun) A cosmonaut is a Soviet astronaut.
[from Greek *kosmos* meaning 'universe' and *nautes* meaning 'sailor']

cosmopolitan, cosmopolitans
1 (adjective) A cosmopolitan place is full of people from many countries.
2 (noun) A cosmopolitan is someone who has travelled or lived in many countries.
[from Greek *kosmos* meaning 'universe' and *politēs* meaning 'citizen']

cosmos
(noun) The cosmos is the universe.

cosset, cossets, cosseting, cosseted
(verb) If you cosset someone, you spoil them and protect them too much.

cost, costs, costing, cost
1 (noun) The cost of something is the amount of money needed to buy it, do it, or make it.
2 The cost of achieving something is what is lost in achieving it, e.g. *The cost in human life had been enormous.*
3 (verb) What something costs is the amount you must pay for it.
4 If a mistake costs you something, you lose that thing because of the mistake, e.g. *One slip could have cost him his life.*
5 (phrase) You say something must be done **at all costs** to emphasize the importance of doing it.
[from Latin *constare* meaning 'to cost']

cost-effective
(adjective) If something is cost-effective, it saves or makes a lot of money compared to the costs involved.

costly, costlier, costliest
(adjective) expensive, e.g. *costly jewels.*

cost of living
(noun) The cost of living in a country is the average amount each person needs to spend on food, housing, and clothing.

cost price
(noun) When something is sold at cost price, someone sells it for what he or she paid for it, without making a profit.

costume, costumes
1 (noun) A costume is a set of clothes worn by an actor.
2 Costume is the clothing worn in a particular place or during a particular period, e.g. *17th-century costume.*

costume jewellery
(noun) Costume jewellery is decorative jewellery made from cheap materials.

cosy, cosier, cosiest; cosies
1 (adjective) warm and comfortable, e.g. *their cosy flat.*
2 Cosy activities are pleasant and friendly, e.g. *a cosy chat.*
3 (noun) A cosy is a soft cover put over a teapot to keep the tea warm.
cosily (adverb), **cosiness** (noun).

cot, cots
(noun) A cot is a small bed for a baby, with bars or panels round it to stop the baby falling out.
[from Hindi *khat* meaning 'bedstead']

cottage, cottages
(noun) A cottage is a small house in the country.

cottage cheese
(noun) Cottage cheese is a type of soft white lumpy cheese made from skimmed milk.

cottage industry, cottage industries
(noun) A cottage industry is a small business run from someone's home, such as the making of clothes or pottery.

cotton, cottons, cottoning, cottoned
1 (noun) Cotton is cloth made from the soft fibres of the cotton plant.
2 Cotton is also thread used for sewing.
3 (verb) If you cotton on to something, you understand it or realize it.
[from Arabic *qutn*]

cotton wool
(noun) Cotton wool is soft fluffy cotton, often used for dressing wounds.

cotyledon, cotyledons (pronounced kot-til-**lee**-dn)
(noun) A cotyledon is the first leaf of a new plant.
[from Greek *kotulē* meaning 'cup' or 'hollow']

couch, couches, couching, couched
1 (noun) A couch is a long, soft piece of furniture which more than one person can sit on.
2 A doctor's couch is a flat bed in his or her consulting room.
3 (verb) If a statement is couched in a particular type of language, it is expressed in that language, e.g. *a resolution couched in forthright terms.*
[from French *coucher* meaning 'to lie down']

cougar, cougars (pronounced **koo**-gar)
(noun) A cougar is the same as a puma.

cough, coughs, coughing, coughed
1 (verb) When you cough, you force air out of your throat with a sudden harsh noise.
2 (noun) A cough is an illness that makes you cough a lot; also the noise you make when you cough.

cough up
(phrasal verb) If you get someone to cough up money, you get them to give it to you.

could
1 You use could to say that you were able or allowed to do something, e.g. *I could just hear.*
2 You also use could to say that something might happen or might be the case, e.g. *The river could overflow.*
3 You use could when you are asking for something politely, e.g. *Could you pass the salt, please?*

council, councils
1 (noun) A council is a group of people elected to look after the affairs of a town, district, or county, e.g. *Wiltshire County Council.*
2 Some other groups have Council as part of their name, e.g. *the Arts Council.*
[from Latin *concilium* meaning 'assembly']

councillor, councillors
(noun) A councillor is an elected member of a local council.

counsel, counsels, counselling, counselled
1 (noun; a formal use) To give someone counsel means to give them advice.
2 (verb) To counsel people means to give them advice about their problems.
3 (noun) A counsel is a lawyer who gives advice on a legal case and fights the case in court.
counselling (noun), **counsellor** (noun).

count, counts, counting, counted
1 (verb) To count means to say all the numbers in order up to a particular number.
2 If you count all the things in a group, you add them up to see how many there are.
3 (noun) A count is a number reached by counting.
4 (phrases) If you **keep count**, you keep a record of how often something happens. If you **lose count** of something, you cannot remember how often it has happened.
5 (verb) What counts in a situation is whatever is most important.
6 If something counts against you, it is a factor which could cause you to be punished or rejected.
7 To count as something means to be regarded as that thing, e.g. *These benefits count as income.*
8 What something counts for is whatever importance is given to it, e.g. *Honesty counts for very little here.*
9 (noun; a formal use) If something is wrong on a particular count, it is wrong in that respect.
10 (verb) If you can count on someone or something, you can rely on them.
11 (noun) A count is a European nobleman.
[senses 1-10 from Latin *computare* meaning 'to calculate'; sense 11 from Latin *comes* meaning 'companion' or 'associate']

Similar words: (sense 2) calculate, reckon, compute, enumerate, number, tally, tot up
(sense 3) calculation, computation, enumeration, reckoning, tally

---

countdown, countdowns
(noun) Countdown is the counting aloud of numbers in reverse order before something happens, especially before a spacecraft is launched.

countenance, countenances, countenancing, countenanced (a formal word)
1 (noun) Someone's countenance is their face.
2 (verb) To countenance something means to allow or accept it, e.g. *I will not countenance behaviour of this sort.*

counter, counters, countering, countered
1 (noun) A counter is a small, flat, round object used in board games.
2 A counter in a shop is a long, flat surface over which goods are sold.
3 (verb) If you counter something that is being done, you take action to make it less effective, e.g. *We could counter this with a denial.*
[senses 1-2 from Latin *computare* meaning 'to calculate'; sense 3 from Latin *contra* meaning 'against']

counteract, counteracts, counteracting, counteracted
(verb) To counteract something means to reduce its effect by producing an opposite effect.

counterattack, counterattacks, counterattacking, counterattacked
1 (verb) To counterattack means to attack someone who has attacked you.
2 (noun) A counterattack is an attack on someone who has attacked you.

counterbalance, counterbalances, counterbalancing, counterbalanced
(verb) To counterbalance something means to balance or correct it by producing an equal but opposite effect, e.g. *Losses in the cities were counterbalanced by gains in the country.*

counterfeit, counterfeits, counterfeiting, counterfeited (pronounced **kown**-ter-fit)
1 (adjective) Something counterfeit is not genuine but has been made to look genuine to deceive people, e.g. *a counterfeit coin.*
2 (verb) To counterfeit something means to make a counterfeit version of it.
counterfeiter (noun).
[from Old French *contrefaire* meaning 'to copy']

counterfoil, counterfoils
(noun) The counterfoil of a cheque or receipt is the part that you keep.

countermand, countermands, countermanding, countermanded
(verb; a formal word) To countermand an order means to cancel it, usually by giving a new order.

counterpane, counterpanes
(noun; an old-fashioned word) A counterpane is a bedspread.
[from Latin *culcita puncta* meaning 'quilted mattress']

counterpart, counterparts
(noun) The counterpart of a person or thing is another person or thing with a similar function in a different place, e.g. *The Foreign Secretary met his Angolan counterpart last week.*

counterpoint
(noun) In music, counterpoint is a technique in which two or more themes are written to be played or sung together.

counterproductive
(adjective) If something is counterproductive, it has the opposite effect from what you intend.

countersign, countersigns, countersigning, countersigned
(verb) To countersign a document means to sign it after someone else has, to confirm that their signature is genuine.

countertenor, countertenors
(noun) A countertenor is a man who sings with a high voice similar to a low female singing voice.

countess, countesses
(noun) A countess is the wife of a count or earl, or a woman with the same rank as a count or earl.

counting
(preposition) You say 'counting' when including something in a calculation, e.g. *36,600,000 Americans, not counting children.*

countless
(adjective) too many to count, e.g. *He sent countless letters to the newspapers.*

Similar words: innumerable, incalculable, untold

country, countries
1 (noun) A country is one of the political areas the world is divided into.

2 The country is land away from towns and cities.
3 Country is used to refer to an area with particular features or associations, e.g. *hilly country... Now we're in James Herriot country.*

Similar words: (sense 1) nation, state, land

countryman, countrymen
(noun) Your countrymen are people from your own country.

countryside
(noun) The countryside is land away from towns and cities.

county, counties
(noun) A county is a region with its own local government.
[from Old French *conté* meaning 'land belonging to a count']

Similar words: province, shire

coup, coups (rhymes with **you**)
(noun) When there is a coup, a group of people seize power in a country.
[from French *coup* meaning 'a blow']

Similar words: coup d'état, overthrow, takeover

coup d'état, coups d'état (pronounced koo day-**tah**)
(noun) A coup d'état is a coup.

couple, couples, coupling, coupled
1 (noun) You refer to two people as a couple when they are married or are having a sexual or romantic relationship.
2 A couple of things or people means two of them, e.g. *a couple of years ago.*
3 (verb) If one thing is coupled with another, the two things are done or dealt with together, e.g. *Strong protests were made, coupled with demands for an official inquiry.*
[from Latin *copula* meaning 'bond']

couplet, couplets
(noun) A couplet is two lines of poetry together, especially two that rhyme.

coupon, coupons
1 (noun) A coupon is a piece of printed paper which, when you hand it in, entitles you to pay less than usual for something.
2 A coupon is also a form you fill in to ask for information or to enter a competition.
[from Old French *colpon* meaning 'piece cut off']

courage
(noun) Courage is the quality shown by people who do things knowing they are dangerous or likely to make them unpopular.
courageous (adjective), **courageously** (adverb).

courgette, courgettes (pronounced koor-**jet**)
(noun) A courgette is a type of small vegetable marrow with dark green skin and pale flesh.
[from French *courgette* meaning 'little marrow']

courier, couriers (pronounced **koo**-ree-er)
1 (noun) A courier is someone employed by a travel company to look after people on holiday.

2 A courier is also someone employed to deliver special letters quickly.
[from Old Italian *correre* meaning 'to run']

course, courses
1 (noun) A course is a series of lessons or lectures.
2 A series of medical treatments is also called a course, e.g. *a course of injections.*
3 A course is one of the parts of a meal.
4 A course or a course of action is one of the things you can do in a situation.
5 A course is also a piece of land where a sport such as golf is played.
6 The course of a ship or aircraft is the route it takes.
7 You can refer to the way events develop as the course of history or the course of events, e.g. *ideas that change the course of history.*
8 If something happens in the course of a period of time, it happens during that period, e.g. *in the course of the next few weeks.*
9 (phrase) If you do something as **a matter of course**, you do it as part of your normal work or way of life, e.g. *He flies overseas as a matter of course.*

Similar words: (sense 5) circuit, track

court, courts, courting, courted
1 (noun) A court is a place where legal matters are decided by a judge and jury or a magistrate. The judge and jury or magistrate can also be referred to as the court.
2 A court is a place where a game such as tennis or badminton is played.
3 A king or queen's court is the place where they live and carry out ceremonial duties.
4 (verb; an old-fashioned use) If a man and woman are courting, they are spending a lot of time together because they intend to get married.

court card, court cards
(noun) In a pack of cards, the court cards are the kings, queens, and jacks.

courteous (pronounced **kur**-tee-yuss)
(adjective) Courteous behaviour is polite, respectful, and considerate.
courteously (adverb).
[from Old French *corteis* meaning 'courtly-mannered']

courtesy
1 (noun) Courtesy is polite, respectful, considerate behaviour.
2 (phrase) If something is done **by courtesy of** someone, it is done with their permission.

courtier, courtiers
(noun) Courtiers were noblemen and noblewomen at the court of a king or queen.

court-martial, court-martials, court-martialling, court-martialled
1 (noun) A court martial is a military trial.
2 (verb) If a member of the armed forces is court-martialled, he or she is tried by a court martial.

court of appeal, courts of appeal
(noun) A court of appeal is a court of law that deals with appeals against legal judgments.

courtship
(noun; a formal word) Courtship is the activity of courting or the period of time during which a man and a woman are courting.

courtyard, courtyards
(noun) A courtyard is a flat area of ground surrounded by buildings or walls.

cousin, cousins
(noun) Your cousin is the child of your uncle or aunt.

couture (pronounced koo-**toor**)
(noun) Couture is high fashion design and dressmaking.
[from Latin *consuere* meaning 'to stitch together']

couturier, couturiers (pronounced koo-**toor**-ree-ay)
(noun) A couturier is a person who designs, makes, and sells fashion clothes.

cove, coves
(noun) A cove is a small bay.

covenant, covenants (pronounced **kuv**-vi-nant)
(noun) A covenant is a formal written agreement or promise.
[from Latin *convenire* meaning 'to come together']

cover, covers, covering, covered
1 (verb) If you cover something, you put something else over it to protect it or hide it.
2 If something covers something else, it forms a layer over it, e.g. *Snow covered the ground.*
3 (noun) A cover is something put over an object to protect it or keep it warm.
4 The cover of a book or magazine is its outside.
5 (verb) If you cover a particular distance, you travel that distance, e.g. *I covered about twenty miles a day.*
6 An insurance policy that covers something guarantees that money will be paid if that thing is lost or harmed.
7 (noun) Insurance cover is a guarantee that money will be paid if something is lost or harmed.
8 (verb) To cover a topic means to discuss it in a lecture, course, or book.
9 If the media cover an event, they report on it.
10 (noun) In the open, cover consists of trees, rocks, or other places where you can shelter or hide.
11 If respectable or normal behaviour is a cover for secret or illegal activities, it is intended to hide these activities.
[from Latin *cooperire* meaning 'to cover completely']

cover up
(phrasal verb) If you cover up something you do not want people to know about, you hide it from them, e.g. *She tried to cover up for her boss.*
cover-up (noun).

coverage
(noun) The coverage of something in the news is the reporting of it.

cover charge, cover charges
(noun) A cover charge is a fixed charge added to the bill in some restaurants.

covert (pronounced **kuv**-vert)
(adjective; a formal word) Covert activities are secret, rather than open.
covertly (adverb).

covet, covets, coveting, coveted (pronounced **kuv**-vit)
(verb; a formal word) If you covet something, you want it very much.

covetous
(adjective; a formal word) Covetous feelings and behaviour involve a strong desire to have something.
covetously (adverb), **covetousness** (noun).

cow, cows
(noun) A cow is a large animal kept on farms for its milk.

coward, cowards
(noun) A coward is someone who is easily frightened and who avoids dangerous or difficult situations.
cowardly (adjective), **cowardice** (noun).

cowboy, cowboys
(noun) A cowboy is a man employed to look after cattle in America.

cowed
(adjective) Someone who is cowed is afraid to do something because they have been threatened or bullied.

cower, cowers, cowering, cowered
(verb) When someone cowers, they crouch or move backwards because they are afraid.

Similar words: shrink, cringe, quail

cowl, cowls
(noun) A monk's cowl is a large, loose hood.
[from Latin *cucullus* meaning 'hood']

cowslip, cowslips
(noun) A cowslip is a small wild plant with yellow flowers.
[from Old English *cu* + *slyppe* meaning 'cow dung']

cox, coxes
(noun) A cox is a coxswain.

coxswain, coxswains (pronounced **kok**-sn)
(noun) The coxswain of a boat is the person who steers it.

coy, coyer, coyest
(adjective) If someone is coy, they pretend to be shy and modest.
coyly (adverb), **coyness** (noun).

coyote, coyotes (pronounced **koy**-yote)
(noun) A coyote is a North American animal like a small wolf.

coypu, coypus
(noun) A coypu is an animal like a small beaver with a rat-like tail. Coypus originally came from South America, and are now bred in captivity for their soft fur.

crab, crabs
(noun) A crab is a sea creature with four pairs of legs, two pincers, and a flat, round body covered by a shell.

crack, cracks, cracking, cracked
1 (verb) If something cracks, it becomes damaged, with lines appearing on its surface.
2 (noun) A crack is one of the lines appearing on something when it cracks.
3 A crack is also a narrow gap.
4 (verb) If you crack a joke, you tell it.
5 If you crack a problem or code, you solve it.
6 (adjective) A crack soldier or sportsman is highly trained and skilful.
7 (phrase; an informal use) If you **have a crack** at something, you try to do it.
8 If you do something **at the crack of dawn**, you do it very early in the morning.

Similar words: (sense 3) chink, cleft, crevice, cranny, fissure

crack down
(phrasal verb) If the authorities crack down on a group of people, they become stricter in making them obey the law.
crackdown (noun).

crack up
(phrasal verb) If someone cracks up, they become mentally ill as a result of emotional strain.

cracker, crackers
1 (noun) A cracker is a thin, crisp biscuit that is often eaten with cheese.
2 A cracker is also a paper-covered tube that pulls apart with a bang and usually has a toy and paper hat inside.

crackle, crackles, crackling, crackled
1 (verb) If something crackles, it makes a rapid series of short, harsh noises.
2 (noun) A crackle is a short, harsh noise.

crackling
(noun) Crackling is the crisp brown skin of roast pork.

cradle, cradles, cradling, cradled
1 (noun) A cradle is a box-shaped bed for a baby.
2 (a literary use) The cradle of something is the place where it began, e.g. *Ironbridge — the cradle of the Industrial Revolution.*
3 (verb) If you cradle something in your arms or hands, you hold it there carefully.
[from Old English *cradol* meaning 'little basket']

craft, crafts
1 (noun) A craft is an activity such as weaving, carving, or pottery.
2 Any skilful occupation can be referred to as a craft, e.g. *the writer's craft.*
3 Craft is cunning or crafty behaviour.
4 You can also refer to a boat, plane, or spacecraft as a craft.

craftsman, craftsmen
(noun) A craftsman is a man whose job is to make things skilfully with his hands.
craftsmanship (noun).

crafty, craftier, craftiest
(adjective) Someone who is crafty gets what they want by tricking people in a clever way.
craftily (adverb), **craftiness** (noun).
[from Old English *cræftig* meaning 'skilful']

crag, crags
(noun) A crag is a steep rugged rock or peak.

craggy, craggier, craggiest
(adjective) A craggy mountain or cliff is steep and rocky.

cram, crams, cramming, crammed
1 (verb) If you cram people or things into a place, you put more in than there is room for.
2 When students cram for an examination, they learn as much as possible just before it.

Similar words: (sense 1) jam, crowd, overcrowd, stuff, pack

cramp, cramps
(noun) Cramp or cramps is a pain caused by a muscle contracting.

cramped
(adjective) If a room or building is cramped, it is not big enough for the people or things in it.

cranberry, cranberries
(noun) Cranberries are sour-tasting red berries, often made into a sauce or jelly for eating with poultry.

crane, cranes, craning, craned
1 (noun) A crane is a machine that moves heavy things by lifting them in the air.
2 A crane is also a large bird with a long neck and long legs.
3 (verb) If you crane your neck, you extend your head in a particular direction to see or hear something better.

cranefly, craneflies
(noun) A cranefly is a flying insect with long legs. It is also called a daddy-long-legs.

cranium, craniums (pronounced **kray**-nee-um)
(noun) Your cranium is the round part of your skull that contains your brain.
cranial (adjective).
[from Greek *kranion* meaning 'skull']

crank, cranks, cranking, cranked
1 (noun) A crank is someone with strange ideas who behaves in an odd way.
2 A crank is a device you turn to make something move, e.g. *He turned the crank to reel in the fish.*
3 (verb) If you crank something, you make it move by turning a handle.
cranky (adjective).

cranny, crannies
(noun) A cranny is a very narrow opening in a wall or rock, e.g. *nooks and crannies.*

crash, crashes, crashing, crashed
1 (noun) A crash is an accident in which a moving vehicle hits something violently.
2 (verb) When a vehicle crashes, it hits something and is badly damaged.
3 (noun) A crash is a sudden loud noise, e.g. *a crash of thunder.*

4 The sudden failure of a business or financial institution is also called a crash.

crash helmet, crash helmets
(noun) A crash helmet is a helmet worn by motor cyclists for protection when they are riding.

crass, crasser, crassest
(adjective) Crass behaviour is stupid and insensitive.
[from Latin *crassus* meaning 'thick' or 'stupid']

crate, crates
(noun) A crate is a large box used for transporting or storing things.
[from Latin *cratis* meaning 'wickerwork']

crater, craters
(noun) A crater is a wide hole in the ground caused by something hitting it or by an explosion, e.g. *the craters of the moon.*
[from Greek *kratēr* meaning 'mixing-bowl']

cravat, cravats
(noun) A cravat is a piece of cloth a man wears round his neck tucked into his shirt collar.
[from Serbo-Croat *Hrvat* meaning 'Croat'. Croat soldiers wore cravats during the Thirty Years' War]

crave, craves, craving, craved
(verb) If you crave something, you want it very much, e.g. *She craved luxury.*
craving (noun).
[from Old English *crafian* meaning 'to demand']

craven
(adjective; an old-fashioned word) cowardly.

crawl, crawls, crawling, crawled
1 (verb) When you crawl, you move forward on your hands and knees.
2 When a vehicle crawls, it moves very slowly.
3 (an informal use) If a place is crawling with people or things, it is full of them, e.g. *The building was crawling with reporters.*
4 (an informal use) If you crawl to someone, you try to please them to get some advantage for yourself.
5 (noun) The crawl is a swimming stroke done on your front, with first one arm swinging over your head, then the other.
crawler (noun).

crayfish
(noun) A crayfish is a small shellfish like a lobster. Crayfish live in rivers and ponds.
[from Old French *crevice* meaning 'crab']

crayon, crayons
(noun) A crayon is a coloured pencil or a stick of coloured wax.
[from French *crayon* meaning 'pencil']

craze, crazes
(noun) A craze is something that is very popular for a short time.

Similar words: fad, fashion, mania, cult, trend

crazy, crazier, craziest
1 (adjective) very strange or foolish, e.g. *They thought I was crazy... a crazy scheme.*

2 If you are crazy about something, you are very keen on it, e.g. *They are crazy about football.*
crazily (adverb), **craziness** (noun).

crazy paving
(noun) Crazy paving is irregular flat pieces of stone made into a path or terrace.

creak, creaks, creaking, creaked
1 (verb) If something creaks, it makes a harsh sound when it moves or when you stand on it.
2 (noun) A creak is a harsh squeaking noise.
creaky (adjective).

cream, creams
1 (noun) Cream is a thick, yellowish-white liquid taken from the top of milk.
2 Cream is also a substance women rub on their skin to make it soft.
3 (adjective) yellowish-white.
4 (noun) You can refer to the best people or things in a group as the cream, e.g. *They were the cream of their generation.*
creamy (adjective).

crease, creases, creasing, creased
1 (noun) Creases are irregular lines that appear on cloth or paper when it is crumpled.
2 Creases are also straight lines on something that has been pressed or folded neatly.
3 In cricket, the crease is a line in front of the wicket and parallel to it. In some situations, a batsman can be given out if he is not behind the crease.
4 (verb) To crease something means to make lines appear on it.
creased (adjective).

create, creates, creating, created
1 (verb) To create something means to cause it to happen or exist, e.g. *His work created enormous interest.*
2 When someone creates a new product or process, they invent it, e.g. *The industry created a new textile.*
creator (noun), **creation** (noun).
[from Latin *creare* meaning 'to produce' or 'to make']

creative
1 (adjective) Creative people are able to invent and develop original ideas.
2 Creative activities involve the inventing and developing of original ideas, e.g. *creative writing.*
creatively (adverb), **creativity** (noun).

creature, creatures
(noun) Any living thing that moves about can be referred to as a creature, e.g. *a large rat-like creature.*

creche, creches (pronounced **kresh**)
(noun) A creche is a place where small children are looked after while their parents are working.
[from Old French *crèche* meaning 'crib' or 'manger']

credence
(noun; a formal word) If something lends credence to a theory or story, it makes it easier to believe.
[from Latin *credere* meaning 'to believe']

credentials
1 (plural noun) Your credentials are your past achievements or other things in your background that make you qualified for something.
2 Credentials are also a letter or a certificate proving someone's identity or qualifications, e.g. *Didn't you ask for his credentials?*

credible
(adjective) If someone or something is credible, you can believe or trust them.
credibility (noun).

Similar words: believable, plausible

credit, credits, crediting, credited
1 (noun) If you are allowed credit, you can take something and pay for it later, e.g. *We bought the furniture on credit.*
2 (phrase) If someone or their bank account is in **credit**, their account has money in it.
3 (noun) If you get the credit for something good, people say you are responsible for it.
4 (verb) If you are credited with something good, people say you are responsible for it.
5 (phrases) If you say something **does someone credit** or **is to their credit**, you mean they should be praised or admired for it.
6 (verb; an old-fashioned use) If you cannot credit something, you cannot believe it.
7 (plural noun) The list of people who helped make a film, record, or television programme is called the credits.
[senses 1-2 are from Latin *creditum* meaning 'loan'; senses 3-7 are from Latin *credere* meaning 'to believe']

creditable
(adjective) satisfactory or fairly good, e.g. *She polled a creditable 44.8 per cent.*
creditably (adverb).

credit card, credit cards
(noun) A credit card is a card that allows someone to buy goods on credit.

creditor, creditors
(noun) Your creditors are the people you owe money to.

credulous
(adjective) Credulous people are too ready to believe what they are told and so are easily deceived.
credulity (noun).

creed, creeds
1 (noun) A creed is a religion.
2 You can refer to any set of beliefs as a creed, e.g. *the free enterprise creed.*
[from Latin *credere* meaning 'to believe']

creek, creeks
(noun) A creek is a narrow inlet where the sea comes a long way into the land.
[from Old Norse *kriki* meaning 'nook']

creep, creeps, creeping, crept
(verb) To creep means to move quietly and slowly, e.g. *She crept up to the door.*

Similar words: sneak, skulk, steal, tiptoe

creeper, creepers
(noun) A creeper is a plant with long stems that wind themselves round things.

creepy, creepier, creepiest
(adjective; an informal word) strange and frightening, e.g. *a creepy film.*

Similar words: spooky, eerie, scary, frightening

cremate, cremates, cremating, cremated
(verb) When someone is cremated, their dead body is burned during a funeral service.
cremation (noun).
[from Latin *cremare* meaning 'to burn']

crematorium, crematoriums or **crematoria**
(noun) A crematorium is a building in which the bodies of dead people are burned.

crenellated
(adjective) A crenellated building has walls with square indentations at the top, for example the battlements of a castle.

creole, creoles (pronounced **kree-ohl**)
(noun) A creole is a language that has developed from a mixture of different languages and has become the main language in a particular place.

creosote (pronounced **kree-o-sote**)
(noun) Creosote is a thick liquid made from coal tar used to preserve wood.

crepe (pronounced **krayp**)
1 (noun) Crepe is a thin ridged material made from cotton, silk, or wool.
2 Crepe is also a type of rubber with a rough surface.

crescendo, crescendos (pronounced krish-**en**-doe)
(noun) When there is a crescendo in a piece of music, the music gets louder.
[from Latin *crescere* meaning 'to grow']

crescent, crescents
(noun) A crescent is a curved shape that is wider in its middle than at the ends, which taper to a point.

cress
(noun) Cress is a plant with small, strong-tasting leaves. It is used in salads.

crest, crests
1 (noun) The crest of a hill or wave is its highest part.
2 A bird's crest is a tuft of feathers on top of its head.
3 A crest is also a small picture or design that is the emblem of a noble family, a town, or an organization.
crested (adjective).
[from Latin *crista* meaning 'tuft']

crestfallen
(adjective) Someone who is crestfallen looks sad and disappointed.

crevasse, crevasses (pronounced kriv-**vass**)
(noun) A crevasse is a deep crack, especially in a glacier.

crevice, crevices
(noun) A crevice is a narrow crack or gap in rock.
[from Latin *crepare* meaning 'to crack']

crew, crews
1 (noun) The crew of a ship, aeroplane, or spacecraft are the people who operate it.
2 Other people with special technical skills who work together are called crews, e.g. *the TV crew.*

crib, cribs, cribbing, cribbed
1 (verb; an informal use) If you crib, you copy what someone else has written and pretend it is your own work.
2 (noun; an old-fashioned use) A crib is a baby's cot.

cribbage
(noun) Cribbage is a card game in which the score is recorded by moving pegs in a wooden board.

crick, cricks, cricking, cricked
1 (noun) A crick in your neck or back is a pain caused by muscles becoming stiff.
2 (verb) If you crick your neck or back, you injure it so that it becomes stiff and sore.

cricket, crickets
1 (noun) Cricket is an outdoor game played by two teams who take turns at scoring runs by hitting a ball with a bat.
2 A cricket is a small jumping insect that produces sounds by rubbing its wings together.
cricketer (noun).
[sense 2 is from Old French *criquer* meaning 'to creak']

crime, crimes
(noun) A crime is an action for which you can be punished by law, e.g. *the crime of murder.*
[from Latin *crimen* meaning 'accusation']

Similar words: felony, misdemeanour, misdeed, wrongdoing, offence

criminal, criminals
1 (noun) A criminal is someone who has committed a crime.
2 (adjective) involving or related to crime, e.g. *a criminal offence.*
criminally (adverb).

Similar words: (sense 1) crook, felon, offender, wrongdoer

criminology
(noun) Criminology is the scientific study of crime and criminals.
criminologist (noun).

crimson
(noun and adjective) dark purplish-red.

cringe, cringes, cringing, cringed
(verb) If you cringe, you back away from someone or something because you are afraid or embarrassed.
[from Old English *cringan* meaning 'to yield in battle']

crinkle, crinkles, crinkling, crinkled
1 (verb) If something crinkles, it becomes slightly creased or folded.
2 (noun) Crinkles are small creases or folds.
crinkly (adjective).
[from Old English *crincan* meaning 'to bend']

crinoline, crinolines (pronounced **krin**-nol-lin)
(noun) A crinoline was a dress with a stiff petticoat worn by women in the nineteenth century.

cripple, cripples, crippling, crippled
1 (noun) A cripple is someone who cannot move their body properly because it is weak or affected by disease.
2 (verb) To cripple someone means to injure them severely so that they can never move properly again.
crippled (adjective), **crippling** (adjective).

Similar words: (sense 2) disable, lame

crisis, crises (pronounced **kry**-seez in the plural)
(noun) A crisis is a serious or dangerous situation.
[from Greek *krinein* meaning 'to decide']

crisp, crisper, crispest; crisps
1 (adjective) Something that is crisp is pleasantly fresh and firm, e.g. *a crisp lettuce.*
2 If the air or the weather is crisp, it is pleasantly fresh, cold, and dry, e.g. *a crisp morning.*
3 (noun) Crisps are thin slices of potato fried until they are hard and crunchy.

crispy, crispier, crispiest
(adjective) Crispy food is pleasantly hard and crunchy, e.g. *crispy bacon.*

crisscross
(adjective) A crisscross pattern or design has lines crossing each other.

criterion, criteria (pronounced kry-**teer**-ee-on)
(noun) A criterion is a standard by which you judge or decide something, e.g. *We must apply the same criteria in selecting staff at all levels.*

critic, critics
1 (noun) A critic is someone who writes reviews of books, films, plays, or musical performances.
2 A critic of a person or system is someone who criticizes them publicly, e.g. *critics of the EEC.*
[from Greek *kritēs* meaning 'a judge']

critical
1 (adjective) A critical time is one which is very important in determining what happens in the future, e.g. *a critical moment in his career.*
2 A critical situation is a very serious one, e.g. *the critical state of the economy.*
3 If you are critical, you examine and judge something carefully, e.g. *He looked at each picture with critical interest.*
4 If you are critical of something or someone, you criticize them.
critically (adverb).

Similar words: (sense 4) disparaging, censorious

criticism, criticisms
1 (noun) When there is criticism of someone or something, people express disapproval of them.
2 If you make a criticism, you point out a fault you think someone or something has.
3 Criticism of books, plays, and other works of art consists of serious examination and judgment of them, e.g. *literary criticism.*

criticize, criticizes, criticizing, criticized; also spelled **criticise**
(verb) If you criticize someone or something, you say what you think is wrong with them.

Similar words: knock, attack, find fault with

critique, critiques (pronounced krit-**teek**)
(noun; a formal word) A critique is a written examination and judgment of something, e.g. *a critique of our society.*

croak, croaks, croaking, croaked
1 (verb) When animals and birds croak, they make harsh, low sounds.
2 (noun) A croak is a harsh, low sound.
croaky (adjective).
[from Old Norse *kraka* meaning 'crow']

crochet (pronounced **kroh**-shay)
(noun) Crochet is a way of making clothes and household items out of thread using a needle with a small hook at the end.
[from French *crochet* meaning 'little hook']

crockery
(noun) Crockery is plates, cups, and saucers.
[from Old English *crocc* meaning 'pot']

crocodile, crocodiles
(noun) A crocodile is a large scaly meat-eating reptile which lives in tropical rivers.
[from Greek *krokodeilos* meaning 'lizard']

crocus, crocuses
(noun) Crocuses are yellow, purple, or white flowers that grow from corms in early spring.
[from Greek *krokos* meaning 'saffron']

croft, crofts
(noun) A croft is a small piece of land, especially in Scotland, which is farmed by one family.
crofter (noun).
[from Old English *croft* meaning 'enclosed field']

croissant, croissants (pronounced **krwus**-son)
(noun) A croissant is a light, crescent-shaped roll eaten at breakfast.
[from French *croissant* meaning 'crescent']

crone, crones
(noun) Crone is an offensive word for an old woman.
[from Old French *carogne* meaning 'carrion']

crony, cronies
(noun; an old-fashioned word) Your cronies are the friends you spend a lot of time with.
[from Greek *khronios* meaning 'long-lasting']

crook, crooks
1 (noun; an informal use) A crook is a criminal.
2 The crook of your arm or leg is the soft inside part where you bend your elbow or knee.
3 A crook is also a long pole with a large hook at the end.

[senses 2 and 3 are from Old Norse *krokr* meaning 'hook']

crooked (pronounced **kroo**-kid)
1 (adjective) bent or twisted.
2 Someone who is crooked is dishonest.

croon, croons, crooning, crooned
(verb) To croon means to sing or hum quietly and gently, e.g. *Emma was crooning to herself.*
[from Old Dutch *kronen* meaning 'to groan']

crop, crops, cropping, cropped
1 (noun) Crops are plants such as wheat and potatoes that are grown for food.
2 The plants collected at harvest time are called a crop, e.g. *They get two crops a year.*
3 (verb) To crop someone's hair means to cut it very short.
[from Old English *cropp* meaning 'something that comes up']

crop up
(phrasal verb; an informal use) If something crops up, it happens unexpectedly.

croquet (pronounced **kroh**-kay)
(noun) Croquet is a game in which the players use long-handled mallets to hit balls through metal arches pushed into a lawn.

cross, crosses, crossing, crossed; crosser, crossest
1 (verb) If you cross something such as a room or a road, you go to the other side of it.
2 Lines or roads that cross meet and go across each other.
3 If a thought crosses your mind, you think of it.
4 If you cross your arms, legs, or fingers, you put one on top of the other.
5 (noun) A cross consists of a vertical bar or line crossed by a shorter horizontal bar or line; also used to describe any object shaped like this.
6 The Cross is the cross-shaped structure on which Jesus Christ was crucified. A cross is also any symbol representing Christ's Cross.
7 A cross is also a written mark shaped like an X, e.g. *Indicate the answer with a cross or a tick.*
8 Something that is a cross between two things is neither one thing nor the other, but a mixture of both.
9 (adjective) Someone who is cross is rather angry.
crossly (adverb).
[from Latin *crux* meaning 'a cross']

Similar words: (sense 1) traverse, go across, span
(sense 2) intersect, crisscross
(sense 8) hybrid, crossbreed, mongrel

cross out
(phrasal verb) If you cross out words on a page, you draw a line through them because they are wrong or because you do not want people to read them.

crossbow, crossbows
(noun) A crossbow is a weapon consisting of a small bow fixed at the end of a piece of wood. Crossbows can fire arrows with great force.

cross-country
1 (noun) Cross-country is the sport of running across open countryside, rather than on roads or on a track.
2 (adverb and adjective) across country.

cross-examine, cross-examines, cross-examining, cross-examined
(verb) When someone is cross-examined during a trial in a law court, they are asked questions about evidence they have given.
cross-examination (noun).

cross-eyed
(adjective) A cross-eyed person has eyes that seem to look towards each other.

crossfire
(noun) Crossfire is gunfire crossing the same place from opposite directions.

crossing, crossings
1 (noun) A crossing is a place where you can cross a road safely.
2 A crossing is also a journey by ship to a place on the other side of the sea.

cross-legged
(adjective) If you are sitting cross-legged, you are sitting on the floor with your knees pointing outwards and your feet tucked under them.

cross-purposes
(plural noun) If people are at cross-purposes, they cannot understand each other because they are talking about different things without realizing it.

cross-reference, cross-references
(noun) A cross-reference is a note in a book that directs you to relevant information elsewhere in the book.

cross section, cross sections
1 (noun) A cross section of a group of people is a representative sample of them.
2 A cross section of an object is what you would see if you could cut it through the middle , e.g. *a cross section of the human brain.*

crossword, crosswords
(noun) A crossword or a crossword puzzle is a puzzle in which you work out the answers to clues and write them in the white squares of a pattern of black and white squares.

crotch, crotches
(noun) Your crotch is the part of your body between the tops of your legs.

crotchet, crotchets
(noun) A crotchet is a musical note equal to two quavers or half a minim.

crotchety
(adjective) Crotchety people are grumpy and easily irritated.

crouch, crouches, crouching, crouched
(verb) If you are crouching, you are leaning forward with your legs bent under you.

Similar words: huddle, hunch, squat

croup (pronounced **kroop**)
(noun) Croup is a disease which children

sometimes suffer from. It makes breathing difficult and causes coughing.

croupier, croupiers (pronounced **kroop**-ee-er)
(noun) A croupier is a person who collects bets and pays money to winners at a gambling table.

crouton, croutons (pronounced **kroo**-ton)
(noun) Croutons are small pieces of toasted or fried bread added to soup.
[from French *croute* meaning 'crust']

crow, crows, crowing, crowed
1 (noun) A crow is a large black bird which makes a loud, harsh noise.
2 (phrase) If a place is a certain distance away **as the crow flies**, that is how far it is when it is measured in a straight line.
3 (verb) When a cock crows, it utters a loud squawking sound.
4 If you crow about what you have achieved, you keep telling people about it.

crowbar, crowbars
(noun) A crowbar is a heavy iron bar used as a lever or for forcing things open.

crowd, crowds, crowding, crowded
1 (noun) A crowd is a large group of people gathered together.
2 (verb) When people crowd somewhere, they gather there close together or in large numbers.
[from Old English *crudan* meaning 'to push']

Similar words: (sense 1) flock, throng, mob, multitude, host, swarm

crowded
(adjective) A crowded place is full of people.

crown, crowns, crowning, crowned
1 (noun) A crown is a circular ornament worn on a royal person's head.
2 (verb) When a king or queen is crowned, a crown is put on their head during their coronation ceremony.
3 When something crowns an event, it is the final part of it, e.g. *The evening was crowned by a dazzling performance from Maria Ewing.*
4 (noun) The crown of something such as your head is the top part of it.
[from Latin *corona* meaning 'crown']

crucial (pronounced **kroo**-shl)
(adjective) If something is crucial, it is very important in determining how something else will be in the future, e.g. *a crucial issue.*
[from Latin *crux* meaning 'a cross']

Similar words: critical, decisive, pivotal, vital

crucible, crucibles (pronounced **kroo**-sib-bl)
(noun) A crucible is a pot in which substances are melted or heated to very high temperatures.
[from Latin *crucibulum* meaning 'night-lamp']

crucifix, crucifixes
(noun) A crucifix is a cross with a figure representing Jesus Christ being crucified on it.
[from Latin *crucifigere* meaning 'to crucify']

crucify, crucifies, crucifying, crucified
(verb) To crucify someone means to tie or nail them to a cross and leave them there to die.
crucifixion (noun).
[from Latin *crucifigere*]

crude, cruder, crudest
1 (adjective) rough and simple, e.g. *crude farm implements... crude methods.*
2 A crude person speaks or behaves in a rude and offensive way, e.g. *Do you have to be so crude?*
crudely (adverb), **crudeness** (noun), **crudity** (noun).
[from Latin *crudus* meaning 'raw' or 'rough']

Similar words: (sense 1) coarse, rough
(sense 2) gross, tasteless, coarse, smutty, vulgar, indelicate, ribald, rude

crude oil
(noun) Crude oil is oil in its natural state before it is processed.

cruel, crueller, cruellest
(adjective) Cruel people deliberately cause pain or distress to other people or to animals.
cruelly (adverb), **cruelty** (noun).
[from Latin *crudelis*]

Similar words: (sense 1) brutal, heartless, inhuman, vicious, merciless, hard

cruet, cruets (pronounced **kroo**-it)
(noun) A cruet is a container for holding pots of salt, pepper, and mustard.
[from Anglo-French *cruete* meaning 'little pot']

cruise, cruises, cruising, cruised
1 (noun) A cruise is a holiday in which you travel on a ship and visit places.
2 (verb) When a vehicle cruises, it moves at a constant moderate speed.
[from Dutch *kruisen* meaning 'to cross']

cruise missile, cruise missiles
(noun) A cruise missile is a missile which carries a nuclear warhead and is guided by a computer as it flies.

cruiser, cruisers
1 (noun) A cruiser is a motor boat with a cabin you can sleep in.
2 A cruiser is also a large, fast warship.

crumb, crumbs
(noun) Crumbs are very small pieces of bread or cake.

crumble, crumbles, crumbling, crumbled
1 (verb) When something crumbles, it breaks into small pieces.
2 (noun) A crumble is a pudding made of fruit topped with a crumbly mixture of flour, fat, and sugar.

crumbly
(adjective) Something crumbly easily breaks into small pieces.

crumpet, crumpets
(noun) A crumpet is a round, flat, breadlike cake which you eat toasted with butter.

crumple, crumples, crumpling, crumpled
(verb) To crumple paper or cloth means to squash it so that it is full of creases and folds.
[from Middle English *crump* meaning 'to bend']

Similar words: rumple, crease, crush

crunch, crunches, crunching, crunched
(verb) If you crunch something, you crush it noisily, for example between your teeth or under your feet.

crunchy, crunchier, crunchiest
(adjective) Crunchy food is hard or crisp and makes a noise when you eat it.

crusade, crusades
1 (plural noun) In the 11th to the 13th centuries, the Crusades were a number of expeditions by Christians who were attempting to recapture the Holy Land from the Muslims.
2 (noun) A crusade is a long and determined attempt to achieve something, e.g. *the great crusade to conquer cancer.*
crusader (noun).
[from Spanish *cruzar* meaning 'to take up the cross']

crush, crushes, crushing, crushed
1 (verb) To crush something means to destroy its shape by squeezing it.
2 To crush a substance means to turn it into liquid or powder by squeezing or grinding it.
3 To crush an army or political organization means to defeat it completely.
4 (noun) A crush is a dense crowd of people.
5 (an informal phrase) If you **have a crush** on someone, you are strongly attracted to them.

crust, crusts
1 (noun) The crust of a loaf is the hard outside part.
2 A crust is also a hard layer on top of something, e.g. *The snow had a fine crust on it.*
[from Latin *crusta* meaning 'rind' or 'shell']

crustacean, crustaceans (pronounced kruss-**tay**-shn)
(noun) A crustacean is a creature with a shell and several pairs of legs. Crabs, lobsters, and shrimps are crustaceans.

crusty, crustier, crustiest
1 (adjective) Something that is crusty has a hard outside layer.
2 Crusty people are impatient and irritable.

crutch, crutches
(noun) A crutch is a support like a long stick which you lean on to help you walk when you have an injured foot or leg.

crux
(noun) The crux of a problem or argument is the most important or difficult part.
[from Latin *crux* meaning 'a cross']

cry, cries, crying, cried
1 (verb) When you cry, tears appear in your eyes.
2 (noun) If you have a cry, you cry for a period of time.
3 (verb) To cry something means to shout it or say it loudly, e.g. *'Come on!' he cried.*

4 (noun) A cry is a shout or other loud sound made with your voice.
5 A cry is also a loud sound made by some birds, e.g. *the cry of a gull.*
6 (phrase) Something that is **a far cry** from something else is very different from it.
[from Latin *quiritare* meaning 'to call for help']

Similar words: (sense 1) bawl, weep, wail, sob

cry off
(phrasal verb) If you cry off, you change your mind and decide not to do something.

cry out for
(phrasal verb) If something is crying out for something else, it needs it very much.

crypt, crypts
(noun) A crypt is an underground room beneath a church, usually used as a burial place.
[from Greek *kruptein* meaning 'to hide']

cryptic
(adjective) A cryptic remark or message has a hidden meaning.
cryptically (adverb).

crystal, crystals
1 (noun) A crystal is a piece of a mineral that has formed naturally into a regular shape.
2 Crystal is a type of transparent rock, used in jewellery.
3 Crystal is also a kind of very high quality glass.
crystalline (adjective).
[from Greek *krustainein* meaning 'to freeze']

crystal ball, crystal balls
(noun) A crystal ball is a glass sphere in which fortune-tellers claim that they can see things that will happen in the future.

crystallize, crystallizes, crystallizing, crystallized; also spelled crystallise
1 (verb) If a substance crystallizes, it turns into crystals.
2 If an idea crystallizes, it becomes clear in your mind.
crystallization (noun).

cub, cubs
1 (noun) Some young wild animals are called cubs, e.g. *a lion cub.*
2 The Cubs is an organization for young boys before they join the Scouts.

Cuban, Cubans (pronounced kyoo-ban)
1 (adjective) belonging or relating to Cuba.
2 (noun) A Cuban is someone who comes from Cuba.

cubbyhole, cubbyholes
(noun) A cubbyhole is a small enclosed space.

cube, cubes, cubing, cubed
1 (noun) A cube is a three-dimensional shape with six equally-sized square surfaces.
2 If you multiply a number by itself twice, you get its cube.
3 (verb) To cube a number means to multiply it by itself twice.
[from Greek *kubos* meaning 'a die']

cube root, cube roots
(noun) The cube root of a number is another

number that makes the first number when it is multiplied by itself twice. For example, the cube root of 27 is 3.

cubic
(adjective) used in measurements of volume, e.g. *cubic centimetres... cubic yards.*

cubicle, cubicles
(noun) A cubicle is a small enclosed area in a place such as a sports centre, where you can dress and undress.
[from Latin *cubare* meaning 'to lie down'. Cubicles used to be parts of a dormitory]

cuckoo, cuckoos
(noun) A cuckoo is a grey bird with a two-note call that lays its eggs in other birds' nests.

cucumber, cucumbers
(noun) A cucumber is a long, thin, green-skinned vegetable eaten raw in salads.

cud
(noun) When cows or sheep chew the cud, they chew partly-digested food several times before swallowing it.

cuddle, cuddles, cuddling, cuddled
1 (verb) If you cuddle someone, you hold them affectionately in your arms.
2 (noun) If you give someone a cuddle, you hold them affectionately in your arms.

cuddly, cuddlier, cuddliest
(adjective) Cuddly people, animals, or toys are soft or pleasing in some way so that you want to cuddle them.

cudgel, cudgels
(noun) A cudgel is a short, thick stick for hitting people.

cue, cues
1 (noun) A cue is something said or done by a performer that is a signal for another performer to begin, e.g. *I nearly missed my first cue.*
2 In snooker and billiards, a cue is a long stick used to hit the balls.
[sense 1 is from Latin *quando?* meaning 'when?'; sense 2 is from French *queue* meaning 'pigtail']

cuff, cuffs, cuffing, cuffed
1 (noun) A cuff is the end part of a sleeve.
2 (phrase) If you are speaking **off the cuff**, you have not prepared what you are saying beforehand.
3 (verb) If you cuff someone, you hit them lightly with your hand.

cufflink, cufflinks
(noun) Cufflinks are small objects for holding shirt cuffs together.

cuisine (pronounced kwiz-**een**)
(noun) The cuisine of a region is the style of cooking that is typical of it.
[from French *cuisine* meaning 'kitchen']

cul-de-sac, cul-de-sacs (pronounced kul-des-sak)
(noun) A cul-de-sac is a road that does not lead to any other roads because one end is blocked off.
[from French *cul* + *de* + *sac* meaning 'bottom of the bag']

culinary
(adjective; a formal word) connected with the kitchen, food, or cooking.
[from Latin *culina* meaning 'kitchen']

cull, culls, culling, culled
1 (verb) If you cull things, you gather them from different places or sources, e.g. *ideas that I had culled from various books.*
2 (noun) When there is a cull, weaker animals are killed to reduce the numbers in a group.
[from Latin *colligere* meaning 'to collect']

culminate, culminates, culminating, culminated
(verb) To culminate in something means to finally develop into it, e.g. *The struggle between King and Parliament culminated in the Civil War.*
culmination (noun).
[from Latin *culmen* meaning 'peak' or 'top']

culpable
(adjective; a formal word) To be culpable means to be to blame for something harmful or wrong.
culpably (adverb), **culpability** (noun).
[from Latin *culpa* meaning 'fault']

culprit, culprits
(noun) A culprit is someone who has done something harmful or wrong, e.g. *The culprits were soon caught and punished.*
[from Anglo-French *culpable* meaning 'guilty' and *prit* meaning 'ready' (i.e. ready for trial)]

cult, cults
1 (noun) A cult is a religious group with special rituals, usually connected with the worship of a particular person.
2 Cult is used to refer to any situation in which someone or something is very popular with a large group of people, e.g. *the Boy George cult.*
[from Latin *cultus* meaning 'a refinement']

cultivate, cultivates, cultivating, cultivated
1 (verb) To cultivate land means to grow crops on it.
2 If you cultivate a feeling or attitude, you try to develop it in yourself or other people.
3 If you cultivate someone, you try to develop a friendship with them.
cultivation (noun).
[from Latin *cultivare* meaning 'to till']

cultivated
(adjective) Cultivated people are well-educated.

culture, cultures
1 (noun) Culture refers to the arts and to people's appreciation of them, e.g. *a man of culture.*
2 The culture of a particular society is its ideas, customs, and art, e.g. *Greek culture.*
3 In science, a culture is a group of bacteria or cells grown in a laboratory.
cultured (adjective), **cultural** (adjective).
[from Latin *cultura* meaning 'cultivation']

culvert, culverts
(noun) A culvert is a water pipe or sewer crossing under a road or railway.

cumbersome
(adjective) An object that is cumbersome is large and heavy and difficult to carry or handle.
[from Old French *combre* meaning 'barrier']

cumin or cummin
(noun) Cumin is a sweet spice used for flavouring in cooking, especially Indian cooking.

cumulative
(adjective) Something that is cumulative keeps being added to.

cumulus (pronounced **kyoom**-yul-luss)
(noun) Cumulus is fluffy white cloud formed when hot air rises quickly.
[from Latin *cumulus* meaning 'heap']

cunning
1 (adjective) Someone who is cunning uses clever and deceitful methods to get what they want.
2 (noun) Cunning is the ability to get what you want using clever and deceitful methods.
cunningly (adverb).
[from Old Norse *kunna* meaning 'to know']

Similar words: (sense 1) wily, sly, artful, crafty, subtle, foxy, sharp, knowing
(sense 2) guile, slyness, subtlety, wiles

cup, cups, cupping, cupped
1 (noun) A cup is a small, round container with a handle, which you drink out of.
2 A cup is also a large metal container with two handles, given as a prize.
3 (verb) If you cup your hands, you put them together to make a cuplike shape.
[from Latin *cupa* meaning 'cask']

cupboard, cupboards
(noun) A cupboard is a piece of furniture with doors and shelves.

cupidity
(noun; a formal word) Cupidity is greedy desire for money and possessions.
[from Latin *cupere* meaning 'to long for']

cupola, cupolas (pronounced **kyoo**-pol-la)
(noun) A cupola is a small dome, often with a spire in the middle.
[from Latin *cupula* meaning 'small cask']

curable
(adjective) If a disease or illness is curable, it can be cured.
curability (noun).

curate, curates
(noun) A curate is a Church of England clergyman who helps a vicar or rector.
curacy (noun).
[from Latin *cura* meaning 'care' or 'solicitude']

curative
(adjective) Curative describes something that can cure illnesses, e.g. *the curative power of herbal remedies.*

curator, curators
(noun) The curator of a museum or art gallery is the person in charge of its contents.

curb, curbs, curbing, curbed
1 (verb) To curb something means to keep it within definite limits, e.g. *proposals to curb the powers of the Home Secretary.*
2 (noun) If a curb is placed on something, it is kept within definite limits, e.g. *a curb on public spending.*

curdle, curdles, curdling, curdled
(verb) When milk curdles, it turns sour.

curds
(plural noun) Curds are the thick white substance formed when milk turns sour.

cure, cures, curing, cured
1 (verb) To cure an illness means to end it.
2 To cure a sick or injured person means to make them well.
3 (noun) A cure for an illness is something that cures it.
4 (verb) If something cures you of a habit or attitude, it stops you having it.
5 To cure food, tobacco, or animal skin means to treat it in order to preserve it.
[from Latin *curare* meaning 'to attend to' or 'to heal']

Similar words: (sense 1) heal
(sense 2) mend, remedy, restore

curfew, curfews
(noun) If there is a curfew, people must stay indoors between particular times at night.

curio, curios
(noun) A curio is a small, unusual ornament.

curiosity, curiosities
1 (noun) Curiosity is the desire to know about something or about many things.
2 A curiosity is something unusual and interesting.

Similar words: (sense 2) curio, objet d'art, oddity

curious
1 (adjective) Someone who is curious wants to know more about something.
2 Something that is curious is unusual and hard to explain, e.g. *a curious thing happened.*
curiously (adverb).
[from Latin *curiosus* meaning 'taking pains']

Similar words: (sense 1) nosey, inquisitive, prying, inquiring

curl, curls, curling, curled
1 (noun) Curls are lengths of hair shaped in tight curves and circles.
2 A curl is a curved or spiral shape, e.g. *curls of smoke.*
3 (verb) If something curls, it moves in a curve or spiral.
curly (adjective).

curl up
(phrasal verb) If you curl up, you sit or lie with your arms, legs, and head drawn in towards your stomach.

curler, curlers
(noun) Curlers are plastic or metal tubes that women roll their hair round to make it curly.

curlew, curlews (pronounced **kur**-lyoo)
(noun) A curlew is a large brown bird with a long curved beak and a loud cry.

currant, currants
1 (noun) Currants are small dried grapes often put in cakes and puddings.
2 A currant is a bush that produces blackcurrants or redcurrants.
3 Currants are also blackcurrants or redcurrants.
[sense 1 is from Middle English *rayson of Coraunte* meaning 'Corinth raisin']

currency, currencies
1 (noun) A country's currency is its coins and banknotes, or its monetary system generally, e.g. *foreign currency... a strong currency like the yen.*
2 If something such as an idea has currency, it is used a lot at a particular time.

current, currents
1 (noun) The current in a river or in the sea is a strong continuous movement of the water.
2 An air current is a flowing movement in the air.
3 An electric current is a flow of electricity through a wire or circuit.
4 (adjective) Something that is current is happening, being done, or being used now.
currently (adverb).
[from Latin *currere* meaning 'to run' or 'to flow']

current account, current accounts
(noun) A current account is a bank account that you can draw money out of at any time.

current affairs
(plural noun) Current affairs are political and social events discussed in newspapers and on television and radio.

curriculum, curriculums or **curricula**
(noun) The curriculum at a school or university consists of the different courses taught there.

curriculum vitae, curricula vitae (pronounced **vee**-tie)
(noun) Someone's curriculum vitae is a written account of their personal details, education, and work experience which they send when they apply for certain jobs.

curried
(adjective) Curried food has been flavoured with hot spices, e.g. *curried eggs.*

curry, curries, currying, curried
1 (noun) Curry is an Indian dish made with hot spices.
2 (phrase) To **curry favour** with someone means to try to please them by flattering them or doing things to help them.
[sense 1 is from Tamil *kari* meaning 'sauce'; sense 2 is from Old French *correer* meaning 'to make ready']

curse, curses, cursing, cursed
1 (verb) To curse means to swear because you are angry.
2 If you curse someone or something, you say angry things about them using rude words.
3 (noun) A curse is what you say when you curse.

4 A curse is also something supernatural that is supposed to cause unpleasant things to happen to someone.
5 A thing or person that causes a lot of distress can also be referred to as a curse, e.g. *the curse of loneliness.*
cursed (adjective).

cursive
(adjective) The letters in cursive writing or print are joined together.
[from Latin *cursivus* meaning 'running']

cursor, cursors
(noun) A cursor is an indicator on a computer monitor which indicates where the next letter or symbol is.
[from Latin *cursivus* meaning 'running']

cursory
(adjective) When you give something a cursory glance or examination, you look at it briefly without paying attention to detail.
cursorily (adverb).

curt, curter, curtest
(adjective) If someone is curt, they speak in a brief and rather rude way.
curtly (adverb), **curtness** (noun).
[from Latin *curtus* meaning 'cut short']

curtail, curtails, curtailing, curtailed
(verb; a formal word) To curtail something means to reduce or restrict it, e.g. *plans to curtail public expenditure.*
curtailment (noun).

curtain, curtains
1 (noun) A curtain is a hanging piece of material which can be pulled across a window for privacy or to keep out the light.
2 In a theatre, the curtain is a large piece of material which hangs in front of the stage until a performance begins.
[from Latin *cortina* meaning 'enclosed space']

curtsy, curtsies, curtsying, curtsied; also spelled **curtsey**
1 (verb) When a woman curtsies, she lowers her body briefly, bending her knees, to show respect.
2 (noun) A curtsy is the movement a woman makes when she curtsies, e.g. *She dropped him a curtsy.*

curvature
(noun) The curvature of something is its regular curved shape, e.g. *the curvature of the earth.*

curve, curves, curving, curved
1 (noun) A curve is a smooth, gradually bending line.
2 (verb) When something curves, it moves in a curve or has the shape of a curve, e.g. *The missile curved towards its target... The lane curved to the right.*
curved (adjective), **curvy** (adjective).
[from Latin *curvus* meaning 'bent']

cushion, cushions, cushioning, cushioned
1 (noun) A cushion is a soft object put on a seat to make it more comfortable.
2 (verb) To cushion something means to reduce its effect, e.g. *The snow cushioned his fall.*

cushy, cushier, cushiest
(adjective; an informal word) A cushy job or task is very easy.

custard
(noun) Custard is a sweet yellow sauce made from milk and eggs or milk and a powder.

custodian, custodians
(noun) The custodian of a collection in an art gallery or a museum is the person in charge of it.

custody
1 (noun) To have custody of a child means to have the legal right to keep it and look after it, e.g. *Divorce courts usually award custody to mothers.*
2 (phrase) Someone who is **in custody** is being kept in prison until they can be tried in a court.
custodial (adjective).
[from Latin *custos* meaning 'a guard']

custom, customs
1 (noun) A custom is a traditional activity, e.g. *an old English custom.*
2 A custom is also something usually done at a particular time or in particular circumstances by a person or by the people in a society, e.g. *It was his custom to take a walk before breakfast.*
3 Customs is the place at a border, airport, or harbour where you have to declare goods.
4 (a formal use) If a shop has your custom, you buy things there regularly, e.g. *I shall take my custom elsewhere.*

Similar words: (sense 1) convention, procedure (sense 2) practice, habit, way

customary
(adjective) usual, e.g. *She was rewarded in the customary way...Pippa was shaken out of her customary calm.*
customarily (adverb).

custom-built
(adjective) Something that is custom-built or custom-made is made to someone's special requirements.

customer, customers
1 (noun) A shop's or firm's customers are the people who buy its goods.
2 (an informal use) You can use customer to refer to someone when describing what they are like to deal with, e.g. *an awkward customer... a tough customer.*

Similar words: (sense 1) consumer, buyer, purchaser

customize, customizes, customizing, customized; also spelled customise
(verb) To customize a car means to alter its appearance to make it look unusual.

cut, cuts, cutting, cut
1 (verb) If you cut something, you use a knife, scissors, or some other sharp tool to mark it, damage it, or remove parts of it.
2 (noun) If you make a cut in something, you mark it with a knife or other sharp tool.
3 (verb) If you cut yourself, you injure yourself on a sharp object.

4 (noun) A cut is an injury caused by a sharp object.
5 (verb) If you cut the amount of something, you reduce it, e.g. *She cut her costs by half.*
6 (noun) A cut in something is a reduction in it, e.g. *a tax cut.*
7 (verb) When writing is cut, parts of it are not printed or broadcast.
8 (noun) A cut in something written is a part that is not printed or broadcast.
9 (adjective) Well cut clothes have been well designed and made, e.g. *a beautifully cut suit.*
10 (noun) A cut of meat is a large piece ready for cooking.
11 (phrase) Someone or something that is **a cut above** other people or things is better than they are.

Similar words: (sense 1) clip, lacerate, slit (sense 3) slit, lacerate, nick (sense 4) gash, slash, incision, laceration, slit

cut back
(phrasal verb) To cut back expenditure or cut back on it means to reduce it.

cut down
(phrasal verb) If you cut down on an activity, you do it less often, e.g. *Try to cut down on smoking.*

cut in
(phrasal verb) If you cut in, you interrupt.

cut off
1 (phrasal verb) To cut someone or something off means to separate them from things they are normally connected with, e.g. *We have cut ourselves off from the old ways of thinking.*
2 If a supply of something is cut off, you no longer get it, e.g. *Gas supplies were cut off.*
3 If your telephone or telephone call is cut off, it is disconnected.

cut out
1 (phrasal verb) If you cut out something you are doing, you stop doing it, e.g. *He's cut out the drinking.*
2 If an engine cuts out, it suddenly stops working.
3 If you are not cut out for a type of work, you do not have the right qualities for it.

cut-and-dried
(adjective; an informal use) A cut-and-dried answer or solution is clear and obvious.

cute, cuter, cutest
(adjective) pretty or attractive.

cut glass
(noun) Cut glass is glass with patterns cut into its surface.

cuticle, cuticles
(noun) Your cuticles are the pieces of skin that cover the base of your fingernails and toenails.
[from Latin *cuticula* meaning 'little skin']

cutlass, cutlasses
(noun) A cutlass was a curved sword used by sailors.
[from Latin *cultellus* meaning 'small knife']

cutlery
(noun) Cutlery is knives, forks, and spoons.
[from Latin *culter* meaning 'knife']

cutlet, cutlets
(noun) A cutlet is a small piece of meat which you fry or grill.
[from Old French *costelette* meaning 'little rib']

cutoff point, cutoff points
(noun) The cutoff point is the level or limit at which it is decided that something should stop.

cutout, cutouts
1 (noun) A cutout is an automatic device that turns off a motor if something goes wrong.
2 A cutout is also a shape cut out of card.

cut-price
(adjective) Cut-price articles are for sale at a reduced price.

cutthroat
(adjective) Cutthroat describes situations in which people compete for something without caring whether they harm each other, e.g. *cutthroat competition*.

cutting, cuttings
1 (noun) A cutting is something cut from a newspaper or magazine.
2 A cutting from a plant is a part cut from it and used to grow a new plant.
3 (adjective) A cutting remark is unkind and likely to hurt someone.

cuttlefish, cuttlefishes
(noun) A cuttlefish is a type of sea mollusc, similar to a squid.

CV an abbreviation for curriculum vitae.

cwt an abbreviation for 'hundredweights'.

cyanide (pronounced sigh-an-nide)
(noun) Cyanide is an extremely poisonous chemical.

cybernetics (pronounced sigh-ber-net-tiks)
(noun) Cybernetics is the study of systems of communication and control in electronic and mechanical devices, often in comparison with biological systems.
[from Greek *kubernētēs* meaning 'steersman']

cyclamen, cyclamens (pronounced sik-lam-men)
(noun) A cyclamen is a plant with white, pink, or red flowers whose petals turn back.

cycle, cycles, cycling, cycled
1 (verb) When you cycle, you ride a bicycle.
2 (noun) A cycle is a bicycle or a motorcycle.
3 A cycle is also a series of events which is repeated again and again in the same order, e.g. *the cycle of the seasons*.
4 A cycle in an electrical, electronic, mechanical, or organic process is a single complete series of movements or events.
5 A cycle of songs or poems is a series of them intended to be performed or read together.
[from Greek *kuklos* meaning 'ring' or 'wheel']

cyclic or cyclical
(adjective) happening over and over again in cycles, e.g. *a cyclical process*.

cyclist, cyclists
(noun) A cyclist is someone who rides a bicycle.

cyclone, cyclones
(noun) A cyclone is a violent tropical storm.
[from Greek *kukloein* meaning 'to revolve']

cygnet, cygnets (pronounced sig-net)
(noun) A cygnet is a young swan.
[from Latin *cygnus* meaning 'swan']

cylinder, cylinders
1 (noun) A cylinder is a regular three-dimensional shape with two equally-sized flat circular ends joined by a curved surface.
2 The cylinder in a motor engine is the part in which the piston moves backwards and forwards.
cylindrical (adjective).
[from Greek *kulindein* meaning 'to roll']

cymbal, cymbals
(noun) A cymbal is a circular brass plate used as a percussion instrument. Cymbals are clashed together or hit with a stick.
[from Greek *kumbē* meaning 'something hollow']

cynic, cynics (pronounced sin-nik)
(noun) A cynic is a cynical person.
[from Greek *kunikos* meaning 'dog-like']

cynical
(adjective) believing that people always behave selfishly or dishonestly.
cynically (adverb), cynicism (noun).

cypher another spelling of cipher.

cypress, cypresses
(noun) A cypress is a type of evergreen tree with small dark green leaves and round cones.

Cypriot, Cypriots (pronounced sip-ree-ot)
1 (adjective) belonging or relating to Cyprus.
2 (noun) A Cypriot is someone who comes from Cyprus.

cyst, cysts (pronounced sist)
(noun) A cyst is a growth containing liquid that can form under your skin or inside your body.
[from Greek *kustis* meaning 'bag' or 'bladder']

cystitis
(noun) Cystitis is an infection of the bladder.

czar another spelling of tsar.

czarina another spelling of tsarina.

czarist another spelling of tsarist.

Czech, Czechs (pronounced chek)
1 (adjective) belonging or relating to Czechoslovakia.
2 (noun) A Czech is someone who comes from Czechoslovakia, especially from Bohemia or Moravia.
3 Czech is one of the two main languages spoken in Czechoslovakia. The other one is Slovak.

Czechoslovak, Czechoslovaks (pronounced chek-oh-slow-vak)
1 (adjective) belonging or relating to Czechoslovakia.
2 (noun) A Czechoslovak is someone who comes from Czechoslovakia.

D

dab, dabs, dabbing, dabbed
1 (verb) If you dab something, you touch it with quick light strokes, e.g. *She dabbed the wound with TCP.*
2 (noun) A dab of something is a small amount that is put on a surface, e.g. *a dab of rouge.*
3 (an informal phrase) If you are a **dab hand** at something, you are very skilled at it.

dabble, dabbles, dabbling, dabbled
(verb) If you dabble in something, you work or play at it without being seriously involved in it, e.g. *a wealthy dilettante dabbling in science.*
dabbler (noun).

dace
(noun) A dace is a type of small freshwater fish.

dachshund, dachshunds (pronounced **daks**-hoond)
(noun) A dachshund is a small dog with a long body and very short legs.
[a German word meaning 'badger-dog']

dad, dads or **daddy,** daddies
(noun; an informal word) Your dad or your daddy is your father.

daddy-long-legs
(noun) A daddy-long-legs is a harmless flying insect with very long legs.

dado, dados or **dadoes** (pronounced **day**-doe)
(noun) A dado is the lower part of an interior wall, decorated differently from the top half.

daffodil, daffodils
(noun) A daffodil is an early spring flowering plant, with a yellow trumpet-shaped flower grown from a bulb.

daft, dafter, daftest
(adjective) foolish or slightly insane.
[from Old English *gedæfte* meaning 'gentle']

dagger, daggers
1 (noun) A dagger is a weapon like a short knife with a sharp pointed blade.
2 (phrase) If two people are **at daggers drawn**, they are openly hostile towards each other.
3 If you **look daggers** at someone, you glare or scowl angrily at them.

dahlia, dahlias (pronounced **dale**-ya)
(noun) A dahlia is a type of brightly coloured garden flower growing from a tuberous root. It is named after Anders Dahl, a Swedish botanist.

daily, dailies
1 (adjective) occurring every day.
2 (noun) A daily is a newspaper that is published every day except Sunday.
3 A daily is also someone employed to come every day to clean someone's home.

dainty, daintier, daintiest
(adjective) very delicate and pretty.
daintily (adverb), **daintiness** (noun).

dairy, dairies
1 (noun) A dairy is a shop or company that supplies milk and milk products.
2 (adjective) Dairy products are foods made from milk, such as butter, cheese, cream, and yoghurt.
3 A dairy farm is one which keeps cattle to produce milk and dairy products.

dais (pronounced **day**-is)
(noun) A dais is a raised platform, normally at one end of a hall and used by a speaker.

daisy, daisies
(noun) A daisy is a wild flower with a yellow centre surrounded by long white petals.
[from Old English *dæges eage* meaning 'day's eye', because the daisy opens in the daytime and closes at night]

daisywheel, daisywheels
(noun) A daisywheel is a small flat disc used for printing in some word processors.

dal
(noun) Dal is an Indian dish made from split pulses, usually lentils.
[from Sanskrit *dal* meaning 'to split']

dale, dales
(noun) A dale is a valley in the North of England.

dalliance
(noun; an old-fashioned word) Dalliance is flirtation.

dally, dallies, dallying, dallied
(verb; an old-fashioned word) To dally means to idly waste time or dawdle.
[from Old French *dalier* meaning 'to chat' or 'to gossip']

dalmatian, dalmatians
(noun) A dalmatian is a large dog with short smooth white hair and black or brown spots. Dalmatians are named after Dalmatia, a region of Yugoslavia.

dam, dams, damming, dammed
1 (noun) A dam is a barrier, often a concrete wall, built across a river to hold back water.
2 (verb) To dam a river means to build a dam across it.

damage, damages, damaging, damaged
1 (noun) Damage to something is injury or harm done to it.
2 (verb) To damage something means to harm or spoil it.
3 (noun) Damages is the sum of money claimed, or awarded by a court, to compensate someone for loss or harm.
damageable (adjective), **damaging** (adjective).
[from Latin *damnum* meaning 'injury' or 'loss']

damask
(noun) Damask is a type of cloth with a pattern woven into it.

dame, dames

1 Dame is the title given to a woman who has been awarded the OBE or one of the other British orders of chivalry.
2 (noun) The dame in pantomime is the role of a comic woman, normally played by a man.

damn, damns, damning, damned (pronounced dam)

1 (verb) To damn something or someone means to curse or condemn them.
2 'Damn' is a swearword.
damned (adjective).
[from Latin *damnare* meaning 'to injure']

damnable (pronounced dam-ni-bil)

(adjective; an old-fashioned word) very unpleasant or annoying.
damnably (adverb).

damnation (pronounced dam-nay-shun)

(noun) Damnation is everlasting punishment in Hell after death.

damning

(adjective) showing or proving someone's guilt, e.g. *damning evidence.*

damp, damper, dampest

1 (adjective) slightly wet.
2 (noun) Damp is slight wetness or moisture, especially in the air or in the walls of a building.
dampness (noun).
[from Old German *damp* meaning 'steam']

damp course, damp courses

(noun) A damp course or damp-proof course is a layer of waterproof material laid at the bottom of a wall to prevent dampness from rising.

dampen, dampens, dampening, dampened

1 (verb) If you dampen something, you make it slightly wet.
2 To dampen something also means to reduce its liveliness, energy, or strength, e.g. *The whole episode had somewhat dampened my spirits.*

damper, dampers

(an informal phrase) To **put a damper on** something means to stop it being enjoyable.

damsel, damsels

(noun; an old-fashioned or literary word) A damsel is a young unmarried woman.

damson, damsons

(noun) A damson is a small blue-black plum; also the tree that the fruit grows on.
[from Latin *prunum Damascenum* meaning 'Damascus plum']

dan

(noun) Dan is one of the grades of proficiency in a martial art such as judo; also the title given to the holder of such a grade.

dance, dances, dancing, danced

1 (verb) To dance means to move your feet and body rhythmically in time to music.
2 (noun) A dance is a series of rhythmical movements or steps in time to music.
3 A dance is also a social event where people dance with each other.
dancer (noun), **dancing** (noun).

dandelion, dandelions

(noun) A dandelion is a wild flower with yellow flowers which form a ball of fluffy seeds.
[from Old French *dent de lion* meaning 'lion's tooth', referring to the shape of the leaves]

dandruff

(noun) Dandruff is small, loose scales of dead skin in someone's hair.

dandy, dandies

(noun; an old-fashioned use) A dandy is a man who always dresses in smart clothes and is very concerned with his appearance.

Dane, Danes

(noun) A Dane is someone who comes from Denmark.

danger, dangers

1 (noun) Danger is the possibility that someone may be harmed or killed.
2 A danger is something or someone that can hurt or harm you.

Similar words: (sense 1) peril, jeopardy, hazard

danger money

(noun) If someone is paid danger money, they are paid extra for work which is considered to be particularly dangerous.

dangerous

(adjective) able to or likely to cause hurt or harm.
dangerously (adverb).

Similar words: unsafe, perilous, hazardous

dangle, dangles, dangling, dangled

(verb) When something dangles or when you dangle it, it swings or hangs loosely.

Danish

1 (adjective) belonging or relating to Denmark.
2 (noun) Danish is the main language spoken in Denmark.

dank, danker, dankest

(adjective) A dank place is unpleasantly damp and chilly.

daphnia

(noun) Daphnia is a type of water flea.

dapper

(adjective) neat and smart in appearance.
[from Old Dutch *dapper* meaning 'active' or 'nimble']

Similar words: natty, spruce

dappled

(adjective) marked with spots or patches of a different or darker shade.

dare, dares, daring, dared

1 (verb) To dare someone means to challenge them to do something in order to prove their courage.
2 To dare to do something means to have the courage to do it.
3 (noun) A dare is something done in response to a challenge as a proof of someone's courage.
[from Old English *durran* meaning 'to venture' or 'to be bold']

daredevil, daredevils
(noun) A daredevil is a person who is reckless and enjoys doing dangerous things.

daring
1 (adjective) bold and willing to take risks.
2 (noun) Daring is the courage required to do things which are dangerous.
daringly (adverb).

dark, darker, darkest
1 (adjective) If it is dark, there is not enough light to see properly.
2 (noun) The dark is where it is dark.
3 (adjective) Dark colours or surfaces reflect little light and therefore look deep-coloured or dull.
4 Dark is also used to describe thoughts, ideas, or looks which are sinister, unpleasant, or frightening.
5 (phrase) If you are **in the dark** about something, you don't know anything about it.
darkly (adverb), **darkness** (noun).

Similar words: (sense 1) gloomy, sombre, dim, murky

darken, darkens, darkening, darkened
(verb) If something darkens, or if you darken it, it becomes darker than it was.

dark horse, dark horses
(noun) If you say that someone is a dark horse, you mean that you suspect that they may have unexpected talents or abilities.

darkroom, darkrooms
(noun) A darkroom is a room from which daylight is excluded so that photographic film can be developed and processed.

darling, darlings
1 (noun) Someone who is lovable or a favourite may be called a darling.
2 (adjective) much admired or loved, e.g. *It was a darling little house.*

darn, darns, darning, darned
1 (verb) To darn a hole in a garment means to mend it with a series of interwoven stitches.
2 (noun) A darn is a part of a garment that has been darned.
darning (noun).

dart, darts, darting, darted
1 (noun) A dart is a small pointed arrow.
2 Darts is a game in which the players throw a number of darts at a dartboard.
3 A dart is also a small tapered fold sewn in a garment to make it fit more closely.
4 (verb) To dart about means to move quickly and suddenly from one place to another.

dartboard, dartboards
(noun) A dartboard is a circular wooden or cork board divided into numbered sections, with a bull's-eye at the centre. It is used as the target in the game of darts.

Darwinian
(adjective) The Darwinian theory of evolution, developed by Charles Darwin in the 19th century, describes the natural selection of plant and animal species.
Darwinism (noun).

dash, dashes, dashing, dashed
1 (verb) To dash somewhere means to rush there.
2 If something is dashed against something else, it strikes it or is thrown violently against it.
3 If hopes or ambitions are dashed, they are ruined or frustrated.
4 (noun) A dash is a sudden movement or rush.
5 A dash of something is a small quantity of it.
6 In writing, a dash is the punctuation mark (—) which shows a change of subject, or which may be used instead of brackets.

dashboard, dashboards
(noun) A dashboard is the instrument panel in a motor vehicle.

dashing
(adjective) stylish, and giving an impression of confidence, e.g. *a dashing young man.*

data
(noun) Data is information, usually in the form of facts or statistics.
[from Latin *data* meaning 'things given']

data base, data bases
(noun) A data base is a collection of information stored in a computer, that can easily be accessed and used by a computer operator.

data processing
(noun) Data processing is the series of operations carried out on data by a computer in order to obtain, present, or interpret information.

date, dates, dating, dated
1 (noun) A date is a particular day or year that can be named.
2 If you have a date, you have an appointment to meet someone; also used to refer to the person you are meeting.
3 (verb) If you date something, you find out the time or period when it began or was made.
4 If something dates from a particular time, that is when it happened or was made.
5 (phrase) If something is **out of date**, it is old-fashioned or no longer valid.
6 (noun) A date is a small dark-brown sticky fruit with a stone inside, which grows on palm trees in tropical countries.

dative
(noun and adjective) In the grammar of some languages, the dative is the form of a noun when it is the indirect object of a verb.

datum the singular form of data.

daub, daubs, daubing, daubed
(verb) If you daub a substance such as mud or paint on a surface, you smear it there.
[from Latin *dealbare* meaning 'to whitewash']

daughter, daughters
(noun) Someone's daughter is their female child.

daughter-in-law, daughters-in-law
(noun) Someone's daughter-in-law is the wife of their son.

daunt, daunts, daunting, daunted
(verb) If something daunts you, you feel afraid or worried about whether you can succeed in doing it, e.g. *He was daunted by the high quality of work they expected.*
daunting (adjective).
[from Latin *domitare* meaning 'to tame']

dauntless
(adjective) bold and not easily frightened or discouraged.

dauphin, dauphins (pronounced **doe**-fan)
(noun) The dauphin was the name given to the eldest son of the King of France from the 14th to the 19th century.

davenport, davenports
(noun) A davenport is a tall, narrow writing desk.

Davy lamp, Davy lamps
(noun) A Davy lamp was a miner's safety-lamp in which the flame was enclosed by a wire gauze. It was named after its inventor, Sir Humphrey Davy (1778-1829).

dawdle, dawdles, dawdling, dawdled
(verb) To dawdle means to walk slowly or lag behind.

dawn, dawns, dawning, dawned
1 (noun) Dawn is the same as daybreak.
2 The dawn of something is the beginning of it.
3 (verb) If day is dawning, morning light is beginning to appear.
4 If an idea or fact dawns on you, it gradually becomes apparent.

dawn chorus, dawn choruses
(noun) The dawn chorus is the singing of large numbers of birds at daybreak.

day, days
1 (noun) A day is one of the seven 24-hour periods of time in a week, measured from one midnight to the next.
2 Day is the period of light between sunrise and sunset.
3 You can refer to a particular day or days meaning a particular period in history, e.g. *in Shakespeare's day... these days.*
4 (phrase) If you **call it a day**, you decide to stop doing something and leave it to be finished later.
5 If something is **all in a day's work**, it is just part of the normal routine.
6 The person who **wins the day** is the most successful in a competition or struggle.

daybreak
(noun) Daybreak is the time in the morning when light first appears in the sky.

daycare
1 (noun) Daycare is the looking after of young children while their parents are at work.
2 Daycare is also the treatment, activities, and supervision provided for the mentally ill, handicapped, or elderly at a daycentre.

daycentre, daycentres
(noun) A daycentre is a building or room used by local councils, the health service, or voluntary organizations for providing daycare.

daydream, daydreams, daydreaming, daydreamed
1 (noun) A daydream is a pleasant, dreamlike fantasy, indulged in while you are awake.
2 (verb) When you daydream, you drift off into a daydream.

daylight
1 (noun) Daylight is the period during the day when it is light.
2 Daylight is also the light from the sun.

day nursery, day nurseries
(noun) A day nursery is a place where children who are too young to go to school are looked after while their parents are at work.

day release
(noun) Day release is a system in which workers spend one day a week studying at a college without loss of pay.

day-to-day
(adjective) happening every day as part of ordinary routine life.

day trip, day trips
(noun) A day trip is a journey for pleasure to a place and back again on the same day.

daze
(phrase) If you are **in a daze**, you are confused and bewildered.

dazed
(adjective) If you are dazed, you are stunned and unable to think clearly.

Similar words: stunned, stupefied

dazzle, dazzles, dazzling, dazzled
1 (verb) If a bright light dazzles you, it blinds you temporarily.
2 If someone or something dazzles you, you are extremely impressed by their brilliance.
dazzling (adjective).

dB an abbreviation for 'decibels'.

D-day
(noun) D-Day was 6 June 1944, the start of the Allied invasion of Europe in World War II. It is now used to mean the day chosen for the start of some important operation or event.

de-
(prefix) When de- is added to a noun or verb, it changes the meaning to its opposite, e.g. *decontaminate.*

deacon, deacons
1 (noun) In the Church of England or Roman Catholic Church, a deacon is a member of the clergy below the rank of priest.
2 In nonconformist churches, a deacon is a church official appointed to help the minister.
deaconess (noun).
[from Greek *diakonos* meaning 'servant' or 'messenger']

deactivate, deactivates, deactivating, deactivated
(verb) If something such as a bomb is deactivated, it is made harmless.

dead
1 (adjective) no longer living or supporting life.

2 no longer used or no longer functioning, e.g. *a dead language... The phone went dead.*
3 If part of your body goes dead, it loses sensation and feels numb.
4 complete or absolute, e.g. *dead silence.*
5 (adverb; an informal use) precisely or exactly, e.g. *It landed dead in the middle.*
6 (noun) The dead of night or of winter is the middle part of it, when it is most quiet and at its darkest or coldest.

deaden, deadens, deadening, deadened
(verb) To deaden something means to make it less intense, e.g. *The medicine deadened the pain.*

dead end, dead ends
(noun) A dead end is a street that is closed off at one end.

dead heat, dead heats
(noun) If a race ends in a dead heat, two or more competitors reach the finishing line first at the same time.

deadline, deadlines
(noun) A deadline is a time or date before which a job or activity must be completed.

deadlock, deadlocks
(noun) A deadlock is a situation in which neither side in a dispute is willing to give in.

Similar words: stalemate, impasse

deadly, deadlier, deadliest
1 (adjective) likely or able to cause death.
2 (adverb and adjective) Deadly is used to emphasize how serious or unpleasant a situation is, e.g. *He was deadly serious.*

deadpan
(adjective and adverb) showing no emotion or expression.

deaf, deafer, deafest
1 (adjective) partially or totally unable to hear.
2 refusing to listen or pay attention to something, e.g. *He was deaf to their complaints.*
deafness (noun).

deaf aid, deaf aids
(noun) A deaf aid is a small device fitted into the ear, which helps a deaf person to hear.

deafen, deafens, deafening, deafened
(verb) If you are deafened by a noise, it is so loud that you cannot hear anything else.
deafening (adjective), **deafeningly** (adverb).

deaf-mute, deaf-mutes
(noun) A deaf-mute is a person who is unable to hear or speak.

deal, deals, dealing, dealt
1 (noun) A deal is an agreement or arrangement, especially in business.
2 (verb) If you deal with something, you do what is necessary to sort it out, e.g. *I will deal with that problem tomorrow.*
3 If you deal in a particular type of goods, you buy and sell those goods.
4 If you deal someone or something a blow, you inflict or give it, e.g. *He dealt me a mighty blow.*

5 If you deal when playing cards, you give out the cards to the players.

dealer, dealers
(noun) A dealer is a person or firm whose business involves buying or selling things.

dealings
(plural noun) Your dealings with people are the relations you have with them or the business you do with them.

dean, deans
1 (noun) In a university or college, a dean is a person responsible for administration or for the welfare of students.
2 In the Church of England, a dean is a clergyman who is responsible for the administration of a cathedral or a group of parishes.
[from Latin *decanus* meaning 'someone in charge of ten people']

dear, dears; dearer, dearest
1 (noun) 'Dear' is used as a sign of affection, e.g. *How are you, dear?*
2 (adjective) much loved, e.g. *a very dear friend.*
3 Something that is dear is very expensive.
4 You use 'dear' at the beginning of a letter before the name of the person you are writing to.
dearly (adverb).

Similar words: (sense 3) costly, pricey, expensive

dearth (pronounced **derth**)
(noun) A dearth of something is a shortage of it.

death, deaths
1 (noun) Death is the end of the life of a person or animal.
2 The death of something is the end of it, e.g. *the death of democracy as we know it.*

deathly
(adjective) resembling death in some way.

death penalty
(noun) The death penalty is the punishment of execution for serious crimes, especially murder.

deathtrap, deathtraps
(noun) A deathtrap is a place that is so dangerous that it puts lives at risk, e.g. *This junction is a deathtrap.*

deathwatch beetle, deathwatch beetles
(noun) A deathwatch beetle is a type of beetle whose larvae tunnel into wood causing a lot of damage.

debacle, debacles (pronounced day-**bah**-kl)
(noun; a formal word) A debacle is a sudden disastrous failure.
[a French word]

debar, debars, debarring, debarred
(verb) If you are debarred from doing something, you are prevented from doing it by a rule or law.

debase, debases, debasing, debased
(verb) To debase something means to reduce its value or quality.
debasement (noun).

debatable
(adjective) not absolutely certain, e.g. *It's debatable how much he actually knows.*

Similar words: arguable, disputable, doubtful

debate, debates, debating, debated
1 (noun) Debate is argument or discussion, e.g. *There was a great deal of debate about the NHS.*
2 A debate is a formal discussion in which opposing views are expressed.
3 (verb) When people debate something, they discuss it in a fairly formal manner.
4 If you are debating whether or not to do something, you are considering it, e.g. *While I was debating what to do, the door opened.*

debauched (pronounced dee-**baw**-cht)
(adjective; a formal word) immoral or sexually corrupt.
debauchery (noun).

debilitate, debilitates, debilitating, debilitated
(verb) If something such as an illness debilitates you, it makes you very weak.
debilitating (adjective).

debility
(noun) Debility is weakness caused by illness or old age.

debit, debits, debiting, debited
1 (verb) To debit a person's bank account means to take money from it.
2 (noun) A debit is a record of the money that has been taken out of a person's bank account.
[from Latin *debitum* meaning 'debt']

debonair
(adjective) A debonair man is smartly dressed, polite, and charming.
[from Old French *de bon aire* meaning 'of good disposition']

debrief, debriefs, debriefing, debriefed
(verb) When someone such as a soldier, astronaut, or diplomat is debriefed, they are questioned by a senior officer about a particular mission or event.
debriefing (noun).

debris (pronounced **day**-bree)
(noun) Debris is fragments or rubble left after something has been destroyed, e.g. *volcanic debris.*
[from Old French *débrisier* meaning 'to shatter']

debt, debts (pronounced **det**)
1 (noun) A debt is money that is owed to one person by another.
2 Debt is the state of owing money, e.g. *He began getting deeper into debt.*
[from Latin *debitum*]

debtor, debtors
(noun) A debtor is a person who owes money.

debug, debugs, debugging, debugged
(verb) To debug a computer program means to remove the faults from it.

debut, debuts (pronounced **day**-byoo)
(noun) A performer's debut is his or her first public appearance.
[from French *débuter* meaning 'to begin the game']

debutante, debutantes (pronounced **deb**-yoo-tant)
(noun) A debutante is a girl from the upper classes who has started going to social events.

decade, decades
(noun) A decade is a period of ten years.
[from Greek *deka* meaning 'ten']

decadence
(noun) Decadence is a decline in standards of morality and behaviour.
decadent (adjective).
[from Latin *decadentia* meaning 'a falling away']

decaffeinated (pronounced dee-**kaf**-in-ate-ed)
(adjective) Decaffeinated coffee or tea has had most of the caffeine removed.

decamp, decamps, decamping, decamped
(verb) To decamp means to leave suddenly or secretly.
[from French *décamper* meaning 'to break camp']

decant, decants, decanting, decanted
(verb) To decant wine means to pour it from its bottle into another container, in order to serve it.
[from Latin *de-* meaning 'away from' and *canthus* meaning 'spout' or 'rim']

decanter, decanters
(noun) A decanter is a glass bottle with a stopper, from which wine and other drinks are served.

decapitate, decapitates, decapitating, decapitated
(verb) To decapitate someone means to cut off their head.
decapitation (noun).
[from Latin *caput* meaning 'head']

decathlon, decathlons (pronounced de-**cath**-lon)
(noun) A decathlon is a sports contest in which athletes compete in ten different events.
[from Greek *deka* meaning 'ten' and *athlon* meaning 'contest']

decay, decays, decaying, decayed
1 (verb) When things decay, they rot or deteriorate.
2 If an atomic nucleus decays, it disintegrates because of the effects of radioactivity.
3 (noun) Decay is the process of decaying.
[from Latin *decadere* meaning 'to fall away']

decease
(noun; a formal word) Decease is death.
[from Latin *decedere* meaning 'to depart']

deceased (a formal word)
1 (adjective) A deceased person is someone who has recently died.
2 (noun) The deceased is someone who has recently died.

deceit
(noun) Deceit is behaviour that is intended to mislead people into believing something that is not true.
deceitful (noun), **deceitfully** (adverb).

deceive, deceives, deceiving, deceived
(verb) If you deceive someone, you make them believe something that is not true, especially by lying or being dishonest.
[from Latin *decipere* meaning 'to ensnare' or 'to cheat']

decelerate, decelerates, decelerating, decelerated
(verb) If something decelerates, it slows down.
deceleration (noun).

December
(noun) December is the twelfth and last month of the year. It has 31 days.
[from Latin *December* meaning 'the tenth month']

decency
1 (noun) Decency is behaviour that is respectable and follows accepted moral standards.
2 Decency is also behaviour which shows kindness and respect towards people, e.g. *Not one of them had the decency to tell me!*

decent
1 (adjective) of an acceptable standard or quality, e.g. *Did you get a decent night's sleep?*
2 Decent people are honest and respectable, e.g. *decent, hard-working citizens.*
decently (adverb).

Similar words: (sense 2) respectable, seemly, decorous, proper

decentralize, decentralizes, decentralizing, decentralized; also spelled **decentralise**
(verb) To decentralize an organization means to reorganize it so that power is transferred from one main administrative centre to smaller local units.
decentralization (noun).

deception, deceptions
1 (noun) A deception is something that is intended to trick or deceive someone.
2 Deception is the act of deceiving someone.

deceptive
(adjective) likely to make people believe something that is not true.
deceptively (adverb).

Similar words: misleading, ambiguous, illusory

decibel, decibels
(noun) A decibel is a unit of the intensity of sound.

decide, decides, deciding, decided
1 (verb) If you decide to do something, you choose to do it.
2 If an event or fact decides a situation, it makes a particular result or choice absolutely certain, e.g. *This act decided what land could be claimed.*

Similar words: (sense 1) determine, settle, resolve (sense 2) determine

decided
1 (adjective) obvious and unmistakable, e.g. *There was a decided improvement.*

2 strong and definite, e.g. *She has decided views on abortion.*
decidedly (adverb).

deciduous
(adjective) Deciduous trees lose their leaves in the autumn every year.
[from Latin *decidere* meaning 'to fall down' or 'to fall off']

decimal, decimals
1 (adjective) The decimal system expresses numbers using all the digits from 0 to 9.
2 (noun) A decimal is a fraction in which a dot called a decimal point is followed by numbers representing tenths, hundredths, and thousandths. For example, 0.5 represents 5/10 (or 1/2); 0.05 represents 5/100 (or 1/20).
[from Latin *decima* meaning 'a tenth']

decimalize, decimalizes, decimalizing, decimalized; also spelled **decimalise**
(verb) To decimalize something means to change it to the decimal system.

decimate, decimates, decimating, decimated
(verb) To decimate a group of people or animals means to kill or destroy a large number of them.
decimation (noun).

decipher, deciphers, deciphering, deciphered
(verb) If you decipher a piece of writing or a message, you work out its meaning.

decision, decisions
(noun) A decision is a choice or judgment that is made about something, e.g. *the government's decision on the future of the railway.*

Similar words: conclusion, resolution

decisive (pronounced dis-**sigh**-siv)
1 (adjective) having great influence on the result of something, e.g. *This was the decisive campaign of the war.*
2 A decisive person is able to make decisions firmly and without unnecessary hesitation.
decisively (adverb), **decisiveness** (noun).

deck, decks, decking, decked
1 (noun) A deck is a floor or platform built into a ship, or one of the two floors on a bus.
2 A tape or record deck is the piece of equipment that carries the tape or record in a music system.
3 A deck of cards is a pack of them.
4 (verb) If you deck someone or something or deck them out, you decorate them, e.g. *The rooms had been decked with garlands and flowers.*
[from Old Dutch *dec* meaning 'a covering']

deckchair, deckchairs
(noun) A deckchair is a light portable folding chair, made from canvas and wood and used outdoors.

declaim, declaims, declaiming, declaimed
(verb) If you declaim, you make a speech or read something in public in a formal and dramatic way.
declamation (noun), **declamatory** (adjective).
[from Latin *de-* + *clamare* meaning 'to call out']

declaration, declarations
(noun) A declaration is a firm, forceful

statement, often an official announcement, e.g. *the Declaration of Independence.*

Similar words: affirmation, pronouncement, assertion

declare, declares, declaring, declared
1 (verb) If you declare something, you say it firmly and forcefully, e.g *He declared himself strongly in favour of the motion.*
2 To declare something means to announce it officially or formally, e.g. *War was declared.*
3 If you declare goods or earnings, you state what you have bought or earned, in order to pay tax or duty.
[from Latin *declarare* meaning 'to make clear']

Similar words: (sense 1) assert, aver, announce, affirm, pronounce

declassify, declassifies, declassifying, declassified
(verb) To declassify documents or information means to make them no longer secret, e.g. *Cabinet papers are declassified after 30 years.*

decline, declines, declining, declined
1 (verb) If something declines, it becomes smaller, weaker, or less important.
2 (noun) A decline is a gradual weakening or decrease, e.g. *the decline of the motor industry.*
3 (verb) If you decline something, you politely refuse to accept it or do it.
[from Latin *declinare* meaning 'to bend away']

decode, decodes, decoding, decoded
(verb) If you decode a coded message, you convert it into ordinary language.

decolletage (pronounced day-kol-**taj**)
(noun) A decolletage is a low cut neckline on a woman's dress or blouse.
[from French *décolleter* meaning 'to cut away the collar']

decompose, decomposes, decomposing, decomposed
(verb) If something decomposes, it decays through chemical or bacterial action.
decomposition (noun).

decompression
(noun) Decompression is a gradual reduction in air pressure.

decontaminate, decontaminates, decontaminating, decontaminated
(verb) To decontaminate an object or place means to remove or neutralize radioactivity or other dangerous substances in it.
decontamination (noun).

decor (pronounced **day**-kor)
(noun) The decor of a room or house is the style in which it is decorated and furnished.
[from French *décorer* meaning 'to decorate']

decorate, decorates, decorating, decorated
1 (verb) If you decorate something, you make it more attractive by adding some ornament or colour to it.
2 If you decorate a room or building, you paint or wallpaper it.
3 A person who is decorated is awarded a medal

or other honour, e.g. *He was decorated with the Military Cross for bravery.*

Similar words: (sense 1) adorn, garnish, deck, embellish, trim, ornament

decoration, decorations
1 (noun) Decorations are features or ornaments added to something to make it more attractive.
2 The decoration in a building or room is the style of the furniture, wallpaper, and ornaments.
3 A decoration is an official honour or medal awarded to someone.

decorative
(adjective) intended to look attractive.

decorator, decorators
(noun) A decorator is a person whose job is painting and wallpapering rooms and buildings.

decorous (pronounced **dek**-kor-uss)
(adjective) correct and polite, and unlikely to cause offence, e.g. *He gave her a decorous kiss.*
decorously (adverb).
[from Latin *decorus* meaning 'seemly']

decorum (pronounced **dik**-ore-um)
(noun) Decorum is polite and correct behaviour.
[from Latin *decorum* meaning 'propriety']

decoy, decoys, decoying, decoyed
1 (noun) A decoy is a person or object that is used to lead someone or something into danger.
2 (verb) To decoy someone or something means to lead them into a trap or away from the place where they are going, usually by means of a trick.

decrease, decreases, decreasing, decreased
1 (verb) If something decreases or if you decrease it, it becomes less in quantity, size, or strength.
2 (noun) A decrease is a lessening in the amount of something; also the amount by which something becomes less.
decreasing (adjective), **decreasingly** (adverb).

decree, decrees, decreeing, decreed
1 (verb) If someone decrees something, they state formally that it will happen.
2 (noun) A decree is an official decision or order, usually by governments or rulers.

decree absolute, decrees absolute
(noun) A decree absolute is the final order made by a court in a divorce case, which ends a marriage completely.

decree nisi, decrees nisi
(noun) A decree nisi is an order made by a court in a divorce case which states that the divorce will be made final after three months unless good reason is produced to prevent it.

decrepit
(adjective) broken or worn out by use or old age.
decrepitude (noun).
[from Latin *crepare* meaning 'to creak']

decry, decries, decrying, decried
(verb) If you decry something, you express disapproval of it or condemn it.

dedicate, dedicates, dedicating, dedicated
1 (verb) If you dedicate yourself to something, you devote your time and energy to it.
2 If you dedicate a book or piece of music to someone, you address it to them as a sign of respect or affection.
dedication (noun).
[from Latin *dedicare* meaning 'to announce']

Similar words: (sense 1) devote, commit

deduce, deduces, deducing, deduced
(verb) If you deduce something, you work it out from other facts that you know are true.
deducible (adjective).
[from Latin *deducere* meaning 'to lead away' or 'to derive']

Similar words: conclude, infer, surmise

deduct, deducts, deducting, deducted
(verb) To deduct an amount from a total amount means to subtract it from the total, e.g. *Tax is deducted automatically from your wages.*
deductible (adjective).
[from Latin *deducere* meaning 'to lead away']

deduction, deductions
1 (noun) A deduction is an amount which is taken away from a total.
2 A deduction is also a conclusion that you have reached because of other things that you know are true.
deductive (adjective).

deed, deeds
1 (noun) A deed is something that is done, e.g. *The deeds of Robin Hood live on in legend.*
2 A deed is also a legal document, especially concerning the ownership of land or buildings.

deed poll
(noun) A deed poll is a legal agreement made by one party only, especially one by which a person changes their name.

deem, deems, deeming, deemed
(verb; a formal use) If you deem something to be true, you judge or consider it to be true, e.g. *He was not deemed worthy of respect.*

deep, deeper, deepest
1 (adjective) situated or extending a long way down from the top surface of something, or a long way inwards, e.g. *a deep shelf.*
2 great or intense, e.g. *a matter of deep concern.*
3 low in pitch, e.g. *a deep voice.*
4 strong and fairly dark in colour, e.g. *The sky was a deep purple.*
5 totally absorbed, e.g. *deep in thought.*
6 (noun; a literary use) The deep is the sea, e.g. *monsters of the deep.*
deeply (adverb).

deepen, deepens, deepening, deepened
(verb) If something deepens or is deepened, it becomes deeper or more intense.

deepfreeze, deepfreezes
(noun) A deepfreeze is a freezer.

deer
(noun) A deer is a large, hoofed mammal that lives wild in parts of Britain. A male deer usually has antlers.
[from Old English *deor* meaning 'beast']

deface, defaces, defacing, defaced
(verb) If you deface something, you deliberately spoil its appearance or damage its surface, e.g. *Spray cans were used to deface the poster.*

de facto (pronounced day **fak**-toh)
(adjective; a formal word) true or existing in fact, even though not intended or recognized, e.g. *the de facto leader of the party.*

defamation
(noun) Defamation is the damaging of someone's reputation, e.g. *defamation of character.*
defamatory (adjective).

default, defaults, defaulting, defaulted
1 (verb) If you default on an obligation, you fail to do what you are supposed to do, e.g. *defaulting on a debt.*
2 (phrase) If something happens **by default**, it happens because something else which might have prevented it has failed to happen.

defeat, defeats, defeating, defeated
1 (verb) If you defeat someone or something, you win a victory over them, or cause them to fail.
2 (noun) Defeat is the state of being beaten or of failing, e.g. *He finally gave up in defeat.*
3 A defeat is an occasion on which someone is beaten or fails to achieve something, e.g. *The English team has suffered a series of defeats.*
[from Latin *disfacere* meaning 'to undo' or 'to mar']

defeatism
(noun) Defeatism is a way of thinking in which a person expects to be defeated, and therefore doesn't bother trying.
defeatist (noun and adjective).

defecate, defecates, defecating, defecated
(verb) To defecate means to get rid of waste matter from the bowels through the anus.
defecation (noun).

defect, defects, defecting, defected
1 (noun) A defect is a fault or flaw in something.
2 (verb) If someone defects, they leave their own country or organization and join an opposing one.
defection (noun), **defector** (noun).
[from Latin *deficere* meaning 'to desert' or 'to fail']

defective
(adjective) imperfect or faulty, e.g. *defective hearing.*

defence, defences
1 (noun) Defence is action that is taken to protect someone or something from attack.
2 A defence is any arguments, writing, or speech used in support of something that has been criticized or questioned, e.g. *He drew up a defence of his economic policy.*
3 In a court of law, the defence is the case presented by a lawyer for the person on trial; also the person on trial and his or her lawyers.
4 A country's defences are its military resources, such as its armed forces and weapons.

defend, defends, defending, defended
1 (verb) To defend someone or something means to protect them from harm or danger.
2 If you defend a person or their ideas and beliefs, you argue in support of them.
3 To defend someone in court means to represent them and argue their case for them.
4 In a game such as football or hockey, to defend means to try to prevent goals being scored by your opponents.
defender (noun).
[from Latin *defendere* meaning 'to ward off']

defendant, defendants
(noun) A defendant is a person who has been accused of a crime in a court of law.

defensible
(adjective) able to be defended or justified against criticism or attack.

defensive
1 (adjective) intended or designed for protection, e.g. *defensive weapons.*
2 Someone who is defensive feels unsure and threatened by other people's opinions and attitudes, e.g. *I was suspicious and defensive.*
defensively (adverb), **defensiveness** (noun).

defer, defers, deferring, deferred
1 (verb) If you defer something, you delay or postpone it until a future time.
2 If you defer to someone, you agree with them or do what they want because you respect them.

deference (pronounced **def**-er-ense)
(noun) Deference is polite and respectful behaviour.
deferential (adjective), **deferentially** (adverb).

defiance
(noun) Defiance is behaviour which shows that you are not willing to obey someone or behave in the expected way, e.g. *a gesture of defiance.*
defiant (adjective), **defiantly** (adverb).

deficiency, deficiencies
(noun) A deficiency is a lack of something, e.g. *vitamin deficiency.*
deficient (adjective).

deficit, deficits (pronounced **def**-iss-it)
(noun) A deficit is the amount by which money received by an organization is less than money spent.
[from Latin *deficit* meaning 'is lacking']

defile, defiles, defiling, defiled
(verb) To defile something precious or holy means to spoil or damage it, e.g. *The graves were defiled by vandals.*
[from Old French *defouler* meaning 'to trample']

Similar words: desecrate, profane

define, defines, defining, defined
(verb) If you define something, you say exactly what it is, e.g. *How would you define art?.*
[from Latin *definire* meaning 'to set limits to']

definite
1 (adjective) firm, clear, and unlikely to be changed, e.g. *There's a definite date for the wedding.*
2 certain or true rather than guessed or imagined, e.g. *There's no definite evidence.*
definitely (adverb).
[from Latin *definitus* meaning 'having fixed limits']

definition, definitions
1 (noun) A definition is a statement explaining the meaning of a word, expression, or idea.
2 Definition is the quality of being clear and distinct, especially in sound or image.

definitive
1 (adjective) final and unable to be questioned or altered, e.g. *a definitive verdict.*
2 most complete, or the best of its kind, e.g. *a definitive history of the First World War.*
definitively (adverb).

deflate, deflates, deflating, deflated
1 (verb) If you deflate something such as a tyre or balloon, you let out all the air or gas in it.
2 If you deflate someone, you take away their confidence or make them seem less important.
3 To deflate the economy means to reduce the level of prices, trade, and activity.

deflation
(noun) Deflation is a reduction in economic activity that leads to lower levels of industrial output, trade, investment, and prices.
deflationary (adjective).

deflect, deflects, deflecting, deflected
(verb) To deflect something means to turn it aside, divert it, or make it change direction.
deflection (noun).
[from Latin *deflectere* meaning 'to turn aside']

defoliate, defoliates, defoliating, defoliated
(verb) To defoliate plants and trees means to strip leaves off them by spraying them with a chemical substance.
[from Latin *folium* meaning 'leaf']

deforestation
(noun) Deforestation is the cutting down of all the trees in an area.

deform, deforms, deforming, deformed
(verb) To deform something means to put it out of shape or spoil its appearance, e.g. *Badly fitting shoes can deform the feet.*
deformed (adjective), **deformity** (noun).

Similar words: distort, twist, warp

defraud, defrauds, defrauding, defrauded
(verb) If you defraud someone, you cheat them out of money, property, or a right to something.

defray, defrays, defraying, defrayed
(verb) To defray costs or expenses means to provide money to cover those costs.

defrost, defrosts, defrosting, defrosted
1 (verb) If you defrost a freezer or refrigerator, you remove the ice from it.
2 If you defrost frozen food, you let it thaw out.

deft, defter, deftest
(adjective) Someone who is deft is quick and skilful in their movements.
deftly (adjective), **deftness** (noun).

defunct
(adjective) no longer existing or functioning.

defuse, defuses, defusing, defused
1 (verb) To defuse a dangerous or tense situation means to make it less dangerous or tense.
2 To defuse a bomb means to remove its fuse or detonator so that it cannot explode.

defy, defies, defying, defied
1 (verb) If you defy a person or a law, you openly resist and refuse to obey.
2 If something defies description or explanation, it is extremely difficult to describe or understand, e.g. *The vastness of space defies comprehension.*
3 (a formal use) If you defy someone to do something that you think is impossible, you challenge them to do it.

Similar words: (sense 1) challenge, dare, flout

degenerate, degenerates, degenerating, degenerated
1 (verb) If something degenerates, it becomes worse, e.g. *The conversation degenerated to a personal attack.*
2 (adjective) having low standards of morality.
3 (noun) A degenerate is someone whose standards of morality are so low that people find their behaviour shocking or disgusting.
degeneration (noun).
[from Latin *degener* meaning 'departing from its race or kind']

degradation
1 (noun) Degradation is a state of poverty and misery.
2 Degradation is also something that humiliates or corrupts a person.

degrade, degrades, degrading, degraded
1 (verb) If something degrades people, it humiliates or corrupts them.
2 In chemistry, when substances are degraded, they are broken into simpler structures.
degrading (adjective).
[from Latin *gradus* meaning 'rank' or 'degree']

Similar words: (sense 1) debase, demean

degree, degrees
1 (noun) A degree is an amount of a feeling or quality, e.g. *She admitted to a degree of prejudice.*
2 A degree is a unit of measurement of temperature; often written as ° after a number, e.g. *20°C.*
3 A degree is also a unit of measurement of angles in mathematics, and of latitude and longitude, e.g. *The yacht was 20° off course.*
4 A degree at a university or polytechnic is a course of study there; also the qualification obtained after passing the course.
5 (adjective) When 'degree' combines with numbers, it shows how serious something is, e.g. *third-degree burns.*
6 (phrase) If something happens **by degrees**, it happens very slowly and gradually.

dehydrate, dehydrates, dehydrating, dehydrated
(verb) If something is dehydrated, water is removed or lost from it.
dehydrated (adjective), dehydration (noun).

deify, deifies, deifying, deified
(verb; a formal word) If you deify someone or something, you consider them to be a god and treat them as an object of worship.
[from Latin *deus* meaning 'god' and *facere* meaning 'to make']

deign, deigns, deigning, deigned (pronounced **dane**)
(verb) If you deign to do something, you do it even though you think you are too important to do such a thing.

deity, deities
(noun) A deity is a god or goddess.

deja vu (pronounced **day**-ja **voo**)
(noun) Deja vu is the feeling that you have already experienced in the past exactly the same sequence of events as is happening now.
[from French *déjà vu* meaning 'already seen']

dejected
(adjective) miserable and unhappy.
dejectedly (adverb), dejection (noun).
[from Latin *de + jacere* meaning 'to throw down']

Similar words: downcast, despondent

delay, delays, delaying, delayed
1 (verb) If you delay doing something, you put it off until a later time.
2 If something delays you, it slows you down.
3 (noun) Delay is time during which something is delayed.

Similar words: (sense 1) postpone, defer, procrastinate, put off, suspend

delectable
(adjective) very pleasing or delightful.
delectably (adverb), delectation (noun).
[from Latin *delectare* meaning 'to delight']

delegate, delegates, delegating, delegated
1 (noun) A delegate is a person appointed to vote or to make decisions on behalf of a group of people.
2 (verb) If you delegate duties or power, you give them to someone who can then act on your behalf.
[from Latin *delegare* meaning 'to assign']

delegation, delegations
1 (noun) A delegation is a group of people chosen to represent a larger group of people.
2 Delegation is the giving of duties, responsibilities, or power to someone who can then act on your behalf.

delete, deletes, deleting, deleted
(verb) To delete something written means to rub it out or remove it.
deletion (noun).
[from Latin *delere* meaning 'to destroy']

Similar words: cancel, erase, cross out

deliberate, deliberates, deliberating, deliberated
1 (adjective) intentional or planned in advance,
e.g. *a deliberate policy to combat smoking.*
2 careful and unhurried in speech and action,
e.g. *He walked towards them at a deliberate
pace.*
3 (verb) If you deliberate about something, you
think about it seriously and carefully.
deliberately (adverb).

Similar words: (sense 1) intentional, knowing, wilful,
calculated, conscious

deliberation, deliberations
1 (noun) Deliberation is careful and often
lengthy consideration of a subject.
2 Deliberation is also slow, careful speech or
movement.

delicacy, delicacies
1 (noun) Delicacy is grace and attractiveness.
2 Something said or done with delicacy is said or
done carefully and tactfully so that nobody is
offended.
3 Delicacies are rare or expensive foods that are
considered especially nice to eat.

delicate
1 (adjective) fine, graceful, or subtle in
character, e.g. *a delicate floral design.*
2 fragile and needing to be handled carefully,
e.g. *delicate fabric.*
3 precise or sensitive, and able to notice very
small changes, e.g. *a delicate instrument.*
delicately (adverb).
[from Latin *delicatus* meaning 'giving pleasure']

delicatessen, delicatessens
(noun) A delicatessen is a shop selling unusual or
imported foods, such as cold meats, that are
already cooked or prepared.
[from German *Delikatessen* meaning 'delicacies']

delicious
(adjective) very pleasing, especially to taste.
deliciously (adverb).
[from Latin *delicere* meaning 'to entice']

Similar words: scrumptious, delectable,
mouthwatering, luscious, appetizing

delight, delights, delighting, delighted
1 (noun) Delight is great pleasure or joy.
2 (verb) If something delights you or if you are
delighted by it, it gives you a lot of pleasure.
delighted (adjective).
[from Latin *delicere* meaning 'to entice']

delightful
(adjective) very pleasant and attractive.
delightfully (adverb).

delimit, delimits, delimiting, delimited
(verb) To delimit something means to fix or
establish its limits.

delineate, delineates, delineating, delineated
(verb; a formal word) If you delineate an idea,
plan, or argument, you describe or define it.
delineation (noun).
[from Latin *delineare* meaning 'to sketch out']

delinquent, delinquents
(noun) A delinquent is a young person who
repeatedly commits minor crimes.
delinquency (noun).
[from Latin *delinquens* meaning 'offending']

delirious
1 (adjective) unable to speak or act in a rational
way because of illness or fever.
2 wildly excited and happy.
deliriously (adverb).

delirium
(noun) Delirium is a disorder of the mind causing
confused speech and behaviour.

deliver, delivers, delivering, delivered
1 (verb) If you deliver something to someone,
you take it somewhere and give it to them.
2 To deliver a lecture or speech means to give it.
3 If someone delivers a baby, they help at its
birth.
4 (a formal use) If someone delivers you from
something, they rescue you from it.
[from Latin *liberare* meaning 'to set free']

delivery, deliveries
1 (noun) Delivery or a delivery is the bringing of
letters, parcels, or goods to a person or firm.
2 Someone's delivery is the way in which they
give a speech.
3 Someone's delivery is also the way they bowl a
ball in cricket.
4 Delivery is the process of giving birth.

dell, dells
(noun; a literary word) A dell is a very small
wooded valley.

delphinium, delphiniums
(noun) A delphinium is a garden plant with long
spikes of blue, pink, or white flowers.

delta, deltas
(noun) A delta is a low, flat area at the mouth of
a river where silt has been deposited and where
the river has split into several branches to enter
the sea.

delude, deludes, deluding, deluded
(verb) To delude people means to deceive them
into believing something that is not true.

deluge, deluges, deluging, deluged
1 (noun) A deluge is a sudden, heavy downpour
of rain.
2 (verb) To be deluged with things means to be
overwhelmed by a great number of them.

delusion, delusions
(noun) A delusion is a mistaken or misleading
belief or idea.

de luxe (pronounced de **luks**)
(adjective) rich, luxurious, or of superior quality.
[from French *de luxe* meaning literally 'of
luxury']

delve, delves, delving, delved
(verb) If you delve into something, you seek out
more information about it.
[from Old English *delfan* meaning 'to dig']

demagogue, demagogues (pronounced **dem**-a-gog)
(noun) A demagogue is someone such as a

political leader who wins support through appealing to emotion and prejudice.
demagogy (noun).
[from Greek *dēmagōgos* meaning 'people's leader']

demand, demands, demanding, demanded
1 (verb) If you demand something, you ask for it forcefully and urgently.
2 If a job or situation demands a particular quality, it needs it, e.g. *The situation demands tact.*
3 (noun) A demand is a forceful request for something.
4 If there is a demand for something, a lot of people want to buy it or have it.

demanding
1 (adjective) requiring a lot of time, energy, or attention, e.g. *He has a demanding job.*
2 People who are demanding are difficult to please or satisfy.

Similar words: (sense 1) challenging, exacting, taxing

demarcation
(noun) Demarcation is the action of showing or stating exactly where two things are separated or are different.

demean, demeans, demeaning, demeaned
(verb) If you demean yourself, you do something which lowers your dignity and makes people have less respect for you.
demeaning (adjective).

demeanour
(noun) Your demeanour is the way you behave and the impression that this creates.

demented
(adjective) Someone who is demented behaves in a wild or violent way.

dementia (pronounced dee-**men**-sha)
(noun; a medical word) Dementia is serious illness resulting in emotional and mental deterioration.
[from Latin *dementia* meaning 'madness']

demi-
(prefix) Demi- means half.

demise (pronounced dee-**myz**)
(noun; a formal word) Someone's demise is their death.
[from Old French *demis* meaning 'dismissed']

demo, demos
(noun; an informal word) A demo is a demonstration.

demobilize, demobilizes, demobilizing, demobilized; also spelled **demobilise**
(verb) If someone is demobilized, they are released from military service.
demobilization (noun).

democracy, democracies
(noun) Democracy is a system of government in which the people choose their leaders by voting for them in elections.

democrat, democrats
(noun) A democrat is a person who believes in democracy, personal freedom, and equality.

democratic
1 (adjective) having representatives elected by the people.
2 favouring or supporting the idea that everyone should have equal rights and should be involved in making decisions that affect them.
democratically (adverb).
[from Greek *dēmos* meaning 'the people' and *kratos* meaning 'power']

demography
(noun) Demography is the study of the changes in the size and structure of populations.
demographic (adjective).

demolish, demolishes, demolishing, demolished
(verb) To demolish a building means to pull it down or break it up.
demolition (noun).

demon, demons
1 (noun) A demon is an evil spirit or devil.
2 (adjective) skilful, keen, and energetic, e.g. *She is a demon squash player.*
demonic (adjective).
[from Greek *daimōn* meaning 'spirit' or 'deity']

demonstrable
(adjective) able to be shown or proved to be true.
demonstrably (adverb).

demonstrate, demonstrates, demonstrating, demonstrated
1 (verb) To demonstrate a fact, theory, or principle means to prove or show it to be true.
2 If you demonstrate something to somebody, you show and explain it by using or doing the thing itself, e.g. *She demonstrated the art of bread-making.*
3 If people demonstrate, they take part in a march, meeting, or rally to show their opposition to something or their support for something.

demonstration, demonstrations
1 A demonstration is a talk or explanation to show how to do or use something.
2 Demonstration is proof that something exists or is true, e.g. *His arguments were a demonstration of the power of reason.*
3 A demonstration is also a public march, meeting, or rally in support of or opposition to something.
4 A demonstration of your feelings is a display or expression of them.
demonstrator (noun).

demonstrative
(adjective) People who are demonstrative openly show or express their feelings.

Similar words: unreserved, effusive, gushing

demoralize, demoralizes, demoralizing, demoralized; also spelled **demoralise**
(verb) If something demoralizes someone, it makes them feel depressed and lose their confidence.
demoralization (noun).

demote, demotes, demoting, demoted
(verb) A person who is demoted is reduced in rank or position, often as a punishment.
demotion (noun).

demur, demurs, demurring, demurred
(verb; a formal word) If you demur, you say that you do not agree with something or that you are unwilling to do something.
[from Latin *demorari* meaning 'to linger']

demure
(adjective) Someone who is demure is quiet, shy, and behaves very modestly.
demurely (adverb), **demureness** (noun).

den, dens
1 (noun) A den is the home of some wild animals such as lions or foxes.
2 A den is also a secret place where people meet, often for dishonest or immoral purposes.

denationalize, denationalizes, denationalizing, denationalized; also spelled **denationalise**
(verb) If a government denationalizes an industry, they transfer it to private ownership so that it is no longer owned and controlled by the state.
denationalization (noun).

denial, denials
1 (noun) A denial of something is a statement that it is untrue, e.g. *He made a denial of all charges against him.*
2 The denial of a request or something to which you have a right is the refusal of it, e.g. *the denial of civil liberties.*

denier (pronounced **den-ee-ay**)
(noun) Denier is a unit of measurement of the fineness of nylon or silk thread.

denigrate, denigrates, denigrating, denigrated
(verb) To denigrate someone or something means to criticize them in order to damage their reputation.
denigration (noun).
[from Latin *nigrare* meaning 'to blacken']

denim, denims
1 (noun) Denim is strong cotton cloth, usually blue, used for overalls, jeans, and other clothes.
2 (plural noun) Denims are clothes made from denim.
[from French *serge de Nîmes*, meaning 'serge (a type of cloth) from Nîmes']

denomination, denominations
1 (noun) A religious denomination is a particular group which has slightly different beliefs from other groups within the same faith.
2 A denomination is a unit in a system of weights, values, or measures, e.g. *Coins of small denomination will be withdrawn.*
denominational (adjective).

denominator, denominators
(noun) In maths, the denominator is the bottom part of a fraction.

denote, denotes, denoting, denoted
(verb) If one thing denotes another, it is a sign of it or it represents it, e.g. *His wrinkled brow denoted deep thought.*
[from Latin *denotare* meaning 'to mark']

denouement, denouements (pronounced day-**noo**-mon)
(noun) The denouement of a story is the explanation at the end of it of something that has previously been unclear or kept secret.
[from French *dénouement* meaning literally 'untying']

denounce, denounces, denouncing, denounced
1 (verb) If you denounce someone or something, you express very strong disapproval of them, e.g. *The government's policy was denounced by the opposition parties.*
2 If you denounce someone, you give information against them, e.g. *she denounced him as a traitor.*

dense, denser, densest
1 (adjective) thickly crowded or packed together, e.g. *pushing through the dense crowd.*
2 difficult to see through, e.g. *a dense fog.*
3 (an informal use) stupid or dull.
densely (adverb), **denseness** (noun).

density, densities
1 (noun) The density of something is the degree to which it is filled, concentrated, or occupied, e.g. *the high density of buildings in the city.*
2 The density of a substance is its compactness, measured by the relation of its mass to its volume.

dent, dents, denting, dented
1 (verb) To dent something means to damage it by hitting it and making a hollow in its surface.
2 (noun) A dent is a hollow in the surface of something.

dental
(adjective) relating to the teeth.
[from Latin *dens* meaning 'tooth']

dentine
(noun) Dentine is the hard tissue surrounding the pulp cavity of the tooth beneath the enamel.

dentist, dentists
(noun) A dentist is a person who is qualified to examine and treat people's teeth.

dentistry
(noun) Dentistry is the branch of medicine concerned with disorders of the teeth.

denture, dentures
(noun) Dentures are false teeth.

denude, denudes, denuding, denuded
(verb) To denude something means to make it bare or to uncover it.

denunciation, denunciations
(noun) A denunciation of someone or something is severe public criticism of them.

deny, denies, denying, denied
1 (verb) If you deny something that has been said, you state that it is untrue.
2 If you deny that something is the case, you refuse to believe it or accept it, e.g. *He denied the possibility of ghosts.*

3 If you deny someone something, you refuse to give it to them or you prevent them from having it, e.g. *They were denied access.*

Similar words: (sense 1) gainsay, contradict

---

deodorant, deodorants
(noun) A deodorant is a substance or spray used to hide or prevent the smell of perspiration.

depart, departs, departing, departed
1 (verb) When you depart, you leave.
2 If you depart from an accepted way of doing something, you do something different, e.g. *He departed from normal medical practice.*
departure (noun).

department, departments
(noun) A department is one of the sections into which an organization is divided, e.g. *the casualty department of the local hospital.*
departmental (adjective).

department store, department stores
(noun) A department store is a large shop selling many kinds of goods in different sections of the shop.

depend, depends, depending, depended
1 (verb) If you depend on someone or something, you trust them and rely on them.
2 If one thing depends on another, it is influenced or determined by it, e.g. *Success depends on hard work.*

Similar words: (sense 1) rely on, count on, bank on

---

dependable
(adjective) reliable and trustworthy.
dependability (noun).

Similar words: reliable, sure, trustworthy, trusty

---

dependant, dependants
(noun) A dependant is someone who relies on another person for financial support.

dependence
(noun) Dependence is a constant and regular need that someone has for something or someone in order to survive or operate properly, e.g. *His dependence on his mother lessened with the years.*

dependency, dependencies
(noun) A dependency is a country or province controlled by another country.

dependent
(adjective) reliant on someone or something.

Similar words: conditional, provisional, contingent on, subject to

---

depict, depicts, depicting, depicted
1 (verb) To depict someone or something means to represent them in painting or sculpture.
2 To depict someone or something also means to describe them in words, e.g. *His essay depicted the urban conditions in the last century.*
[from Latin *pingere* meaning 'to paint']

deplete, depletes, depleting, depleted
(verb) To deplete something means to reduce greatly the amount of it available.
depletion (noun).
[from Latin *deplere* meaning 'to empty']

deplorable
(adjective) shocking or regrettable, e.g. *deplorable lack of taste.*
deplorably (adverb).

deplore, deplores, deploring, deplored
(verb) If you deplore something, you condemn it because you feel it is wrong.
[from Latin *plorare* meaning 'to weep' or 'to lament']

deploy, deploys, deploying, deployed
(verb) To deploy troops or resources means to organize or position them so that they can be used effectively.
deployment (noun).

deport, deports, deporting, deported
1 (verb) If a government deports someone, it sends them out of the country because they have committed a crime or because they do not have the right to be there.
2 (a formal use) If you deport yourself in a particular way, you behave in that way, e.g. *She deported herself with great dignity.*
deportation (noun).
[from Latin *deportare* meaning 'to carry away' or 'to remove']

deportment
(noun; a formal word) A person's deportment is the way in which they stand or move.

depose, deposes, deposing, deposed
(verb) If someone is deposed, they are removed from office or from a position of power.
[from Latin *deponere* meaning 'to put down' or 'to put aside']

deposit, deposits, depositing, deposited
1 (verb) If something is deposited on a surface, a layer of it is left there as a result of chemical or geological action.
2 If you deposit something, you put it down or leave it somewhere.
3 If you deposit money or valuables, you put them somewhere for safekeeping.
4 (noun) A deposit is money given in part payment for goods or services.
[from Latin *deponere* meaning 'to put down']

deposition, depositions
1 (noun) Deposition is the geological process which causes layers of minerals to be formed in the ground over a period of time.
2 A deposition is a formal written statement of evidence, given under oath.

depot, depots (pronounced **dep**-oh)
(noun) A depot is a place where large supplies of materials or equipment may be stored.
[from Latin *depositum* meaning 'a deposit']

deprave, depraves, depraving, depraved
(verb) A person or thing that depraves someone

has a morally bad influence on them, e.g. *This book is likely to deprave youngsters.*
depraved (adjective), **depravity** (noun).
[from Latin *depravare* meaning 'to distort' or 'to corrupt']

deprecate, deprecates, deprecating, deprecated
(verb) If you deprecate something, you express disapproval of it.
deprecation (noun), **deprecating** (adjective).

depreciate, depreciates, depreciating, depreciated
(verb) If something depreciates, it loses some of its original value.
depreciation (noun).

depredation, depredations
(noun; a formal word) A depredation is an attack made in order to steal or destroy something.

depress, depresses, depressing, depressed
1 (verb) If something depresses you, it makes you feel sad and gloomy.
2 If wages or prices are depressed, their value is greatly reduced.
depressive (adjective and noun).
[from Latin *deprimere* meaning 'to press down']

depressant, depressants
(noun) A depressant is a drug which reduces nervous activity and so has a calming effect.

depressed
1 (adjective) unhappy and gloomy.
2 A place that is depressed has little economic activity and therefore low incomes and unemployment, e.g. *depressed areas of the North.*

Similar words: (sense 1) doleful, despondent, down

depression, depressions
1 (noun) Depression is a state of mind in which someone feels unhappy and has no energy or enthusiasm.
2 A depression is a time of industrial and economic decline.
3 A depression in the surface of something is a part which is lower than the rest.
4 In meteorology, a depression is a mass of air that has low pressure and often causes rain.

deprive, deprives, depriving, deprived
(verb) If you deprive someone of something, you take it away or prevent them from having it.
deprived (adjective), **deprivation** (noun).

depth, depths
1 (noun) The depth of something is the measurement or distance between its top and bottom, or between its front and back.
2 The depth of something such as emotion is its intensity, e.g. *the depth of his concern.*
3 (phrase) If you are **out of your depth**, you cannot understand or cope with something.

depth charge, depth charges
(noun) A depth charge is a type of bomb designed to explode underwater.

deputation, deputations
(noun) A deputation is a small group of people sent to speak or act on behalf of others.

depute, deputes, deputing, deputed
(verb) If you depute someone to do something, you appoint or ask them to do it on your behalf.

deputize, deputizes, deputizing, deputized; also spelled **deputise**
(verb) To deputize for someone means to stand in for them.

deputy, deputies
(noun) Someone's deputy is a person appointed to act in their place.

derail, derails, derailing, derailed
(verb) If a train is derailed, it comes off the tracks.
derailment (noun).

deranged
(adjective) mad, or behaving in a wild and uncontrolled way.
derangement (noun).

derby, derbies (pronounced **dar**-bee)
1 (noun) The Derby is a famous horse race held annually at Epsom. It is named after the 12th Earl of Derby, who founded it in 1780.
2 A local derby is a sporting event between two teams from the same area.

derelict, derelicts
1 (adjective) abandoned and falling into ruins.
2 (noun; a formal use) A derelict is a social outcast or tramp.

dereliction
(noun) Dereliction is deliberate or conscious neglect of something, e.g. *dereliction of duty.*

deride, derides, deriding, derided
(verb) To deride someone or something means to mock or jeer at them with contempt.

de rigueur (pronounced de-rig-**gur**)
(adjective) essential because of being very fashionable, e.g. *Calculators are now de rigueur for businessmen.*
[from French *de rigueur* meaning literally 'of strictness']

derision
(noun) Derision is an attitude of contempt or scorn towards something or someone.

derisive
(adjective) mocking or scornful, e.g. *a derisive smile.*
derisively (adverb).

derisory
(adjective) small and insufficient for its purpose and therefore not worth considering seriously.
e.g. *The budget of £1 million was said to be derisory by the opposition.*

derivation, derivations
(noun) The derivation of something is its origin or source.

derivative, derivatives
1 (noun) A derivative is something which has developed from an earlier source.
2 (adjective) not original, but based on or copied from something else, e.g. *the dullest and most derivative book he'd ever read.*

derive, derives, deriving, derived
1 (verb; a formal use) If you derive something from someone or something you get it from them, e.g. *I derive much fun from my grandchildren.*
2 (verb) If something derives from something else, it develops from it.

dermatitis
(noun) Dermatitis is inflammation of the skin, usually caused by an allergic reaction.

dermatology
(noun) Dermatology is the study of the skin and its diseases.
dermatological (adjective), **dermatologist** (noun).
[from Greek *derma* meaning 'skin']

derogatory
(adjective) critical and scornful, e.g. *He made derogatory remarks about her hat.*

derrick, derricks
1 (noun) A derrick is a simple crane used to move cargo on and off a ship. It is named after a 17th century hangman called Derrick.
2 A derrick is also a framework built over an oil well to raise and lower the drilling machinery.

derv
(noun) Derv is the fuel used by diesel vehicles. It gets its name from 'diesel engine road vehicle'.

desalinate, desalinates, desalinating, desalinated
(verb) To desalinate seawater means to remove salt from it to make it suitable for drinking or irrigation.
desalination (noun).

descant, descants
1 (noun) The descant to a tune is another tune played at the same time and at a higher pitch.
2 (adjective) A descant musical instrument is the highest one in a range of instruments, e.g. *a descant recorder.*

descend, descends, descending, descended
1 (verb) To descend means to move downwards.
2 If you descend on people or on a place, you arrive unexpectedly.
3 To descend to something means to behave in a way considered unworthy, e.g. *The discussion soon descended into insults.*

descendant, descendants
(noun) A person's descendants are the people in later generations who are descended from them.

descended
(adjective) If you are descended from someone who lived in the past, your family originally derived from them.

descent, descents
1 (noun) A descent is a movement or slope from a higher to a lower position or level.
2 Your descent is your family's origins.

describe, describes, describing, described
(verb) To describe someone or something means to give an account or a picture of them in words.
[from Latin *describere* meaning 'to write down']

description, descriptions
1 (noun) A description is an account or picture of something in words.

2 (phrase) **Of every description** means of every type or sort, e.g. *reptiles of every description.*
descriptive (adjective).

desecrate, desecrates, desecrating, desecrated
(verb) To desecrate something sacred or special means to damage or insult it, e.g. *The altar was desecrated by vandals.*
desecration (noun), **desecrator** (noun).

desegregate, desegregates, desegregating, desegregated
(verb) To desegregate a place, organization, or service means to stop keeping the people who use it in their separate racial groups.
desegregation (noun).

desert, deserts, deserting, deserted
1 (noun) A desert is a region of land with very little plant life, usually because of low rainfall.
2 (verb) To desert a person means to leave or abandon them, e.g. *He deserted his family.*
3 (phrase) If someone gets their **just deserts**, they are suitably punished.
desertion (noun).

deserter, deserters
(noun) A deserter is someone who leaves the army, navy, or air force without permission.

deserve, deserves, deserving, deserved
(verb) If you deserve something, you are entitled to it or earn it because of your qualities, achievements, or actions, e.g. *You deserve a good rest.*

Similar words: merit, warrant, justify, earn

deserving
(adjective) worthy of being helped, rewarded, or praised, e.g. *a deserving cause.*

Similar words: meritorious, worthy

deshabille (pronounced diss-ab-**eel**)
(noun; a literary word) Deshabille is the state of being only partly dressed.

desiccate, desiccates, desiccating, desiccated
(verb) To desiccate something means to remove most of the water from it.
desiccated (adjective), **desiccation** (noun).

design, designs, designing, designed
1 (verb) To design something means to plan it, especially by preparing a detailed sketch or drawings from which it can be built or made.
2 (noun) A design is a drawing or plan from which something can be built or made.
3 The design of something is its shape and style.
designer (noun).

designate, designates, designating, designated
(pronounced **dez**-ig-nate)
1 (verb) To designate someone or something means to formally label or name them, e.g. *The battlefield was designated a national monument.*
2 If you designate someone to do something, you appoint them to do it, e.g. *I was designated to take his place.*
3 (adjective) appointed to a position but not yet installed, e.g. *Attorney-General designate.*

designation, designations
(noun) A designation is a name or title.

designing
(adjective) crafty and cunning.

desirable
1 (adjective) very useful, necessary, or popular, e.g. *a desirable neighbourhood.*
2 sexually attractive.
desirability (noun).

desire, desires, desiring, desired
1 (verb) If you desire something, you want it very much.
2 (noun) A desire is a strong feeling of wanting something.
3 Desire for someone is a strong sexual attraction to them.

Similar words: (sense 1) crave, wish, hanker after (sense 2) appetite, hankering, stomach

desist, desists, desisting, desisted
(verb; a formal word) To desist from doing something means to stop doing it.

desk, desks
1 (noun) A desk is piece of furniture, often with drawers, designed for working at or writing on.
2 A desk is also a counter or table in a public building behind which a receptionist sits.
[from Latin *desca* meaning 'table']

desktop
(adjective) of a convenient size to be used on a desk or table, e.g. *a desktop computer.*

desolate, desolates, desolating, desolated
1 (adjective) deserted and bleak, e.g. *a desolate part of the country.*
2 lonely, very sad, and without hope, e.g. *She was left desolate and friendless.*
3 (verb) To desolate a place means to make it barren and empty.
desolated (adjective), **desolation** (noun).
[from Latin *desolare* meaning 'to leave alone']

despair, despairs, despairing, despaired
1 (noun) Despair is a total loss of hope.
2 (verb) If you despair, you lose hope, e.g. *I despaired of getting anything done.*
despairing (adjective), **despairingly** (adverb).
[from Latin *desperare* meaning 'to be without hope']

Similar words: (sense 1) hopelessness, desperation

despatch another spelling of **dispatch.**

desperate
1 (adjective) If you are desperate, you are so worried or frightened that you will try anything to improve your situation, e.g. *a desperate attempt to free herself.*
2 A desperate person is violent and dangerous.
3 A desperate situation is extremely dangerous, difficult, or serious.
desperately (adverb), **desperation** (noun).
[from Latin *desperare* meaning 'to be without hope']

despicable
(adjective) deserving contempt.

despise, despises, despising, despised
(verb) If you despise someone or something, you have a very low opinion of them and dislike them.
[from Latin *despicere* meaning 'to look down on']

despite
(preposition) in spite of, e.g. *Despite the difference in their ages they were close friends.*

Similar words: irrespective of, regardless of, notwithstanding, in spite of

despoil, despoils, despoiling, despoiled
(verb; a literary word) To despoil something means to destroy or ruin it.

despondent
(adjective) dejected and unhappy.
despondently (adverb), **despondency** (noun).

despot, despots
(noun) A despot is a ruler with total power, who uses it unfairly or cruelly.
despotic (adjective), **despotism** (noun).
[from Greek *despotēs* meaning 'lord' or 'master']

dessert, desserts (pronounced diz-ert)
(noun) A dessert is sweet food served after the main course of a meal.
[from French *desservir* meaning 'to clear the table after a meal']

destination, destinations
(noun) A destination is a place to which someone or something is going or is being sent.

destined
(adjective) meant or intended to happen, e.g. *She was destined to be famous.*

destiny, destinies
1 (noun) Your destiny is all the things that happen to you in your life, especially when they are considered to be outside human control.
2 Destiny is the force which some people believe controls everyone's life.

destitute
(adjective) without money or possessions, and therefore in great need.
destitution (noun).
[from Latin *destituere* meaning 'to abandon']

Similar words: down-and-out, penurious

destroy, destroys, destroying, destroyed
1 (verb) To destroy something means to damage it so much that it is completely ruined.
2 To destroy something means to put an end to it, e.g. *The argument destroyed our friendship.*

Similar words: (sense 1) annihilate, demolish, devastate, wreck, exterminate, obliterate

destroyer
(noun) A destroyer is a small fast warship.

destruction
(noun) Destruction is the act of destroying something or the state of being destroyed.

Similar words: annihilation, demolition, devastation, obliteration

destructive
(adjective) causing or able to cause great harm, damage, or injury.
destructively (adverb), **destructiveness** (noun).

desultory (pronounced **dez**-ul-tree)
(adjective) unplanned, disorganized, and without enthusiasm, e.g. *There were desultory attempts at conversation.*
desultorily (adverb), **desultoriness** (noun).

detach, detaches, detaching, detached
(verb) To detach something means to remove or unfasten it, e.g. *The handle can be detached.*
detachable (adjective).

detached
1 (adjective) separate or standing apart, e.g. *a detached house.*
2 having no real interest or emotional involvement in something, e.g. *He took a detached view of life in the country.*

detachment, detachments
1 (noun) Detachment is the feeling of not being personally involved with something, e.g. *She studied the blood stain with detachment.*
2 A detachment is a small group of soldiers sent to do a special job.

detail, details, detailing, detailed
1 (noun) A detail is an individual fact or feature of something, e.g. *He described it down to the smallest detail.*
2 A detail is also an item or fact that is considered to be unimportant, e.g. *The passengers' comfort was regarded as a detail.*
3 Detail is all the small features that make up the whole of something, e.g. *He has an eye for detail.*
4 (verb) If you detail something, you describe it fully.
5 To detail someone to do a job or task means to appoint them to do it.
detailed (adjective).
[from Old French *detailler* meaning 'to cut into pieces']

detain, detains, detaining, detained
1 (verb) To detain someone means to force them to stay, e.g. *They were detained in police cells.*
2 If you detain someone, you delay them, e.g. *I mustn't detain you any longer.*
detainment (noun).

detainee, detainees
(noun) A detainee is a person confined in prison, particularly because of political activities.

detect, detects, detecting, detected
1 (verb) If you detect something, you notice it, e.g. *I detected a note of sarcasm in her voice.*
2 To detect something means find it, e.g. *The submarine was detected by sonar.*
detectable (adjective).

detection
1 (noun) Detection is the act of noticing, discovering, or sensing something.
2 Detection is also the work of investigating crime.

detective, detectives
(noun) A detective is a person, usually a police officer, whose job is to investigate crimes.

detector, detectors
(noun) A detector is an instrument which is used to detect the presence of something, e.g. *a metal detector... a smoke detector.*

detente or détente (pronounced day-**tahnt**)
(noun) Detente is an improvement in a tense relationship between two countries.
[from French *détente* meaning literally 'a loosening']

detention
1 (noun) The detention of someone is their arrest or imprisonment.
2 Detention is a form of punishment in which a pupil is made to stay at school after the other children have gone home.

deter, deters, deterring, deterred
(verb) To deter someone means to discourage or prevent them from doing something by creating a feeling of fear or doubt, e.g. *I was deterred from speaking by the crowd's hostile reaction.*
[from Latin *deterrere* meaning 'to frighten away']

detergent, detergents
(noun) A detergent is a chemical substance used for washing or cleaning things.
[from Latin *detergens* meaning 'wiping off']

deteriorate, deteriorates, deteriorating, deteriorated
(verb) If something deteriorates, it gets worse, e.g. *His sight deteriorated.*
deterioration (noun).

determinant, determinants
(noun; a formal word) A determinant is something that controls or influences what will happen, e.g. *The determinant for hair colour is a gene.*

determination
1 (noun) Determination is great firmness, after you have made up your mind to do something, e.g. *Her determination to win was obvious.*
2 The determination of something is the act of deciding and settling it.

determine, determines, determining, determined
1 (verb) If something determines a situation or result, it causes it or controls it, e.g. *Economic factors determine society's progress.*
2 To determine something means to decide or settle it firmly, e.g. *The date is yet to be determined.*
3 To determine something means to find out or calculate the facts about it, e.g. *An x-ray determined that no bones were broken.*
4 (a formal use) If you determine to do something, you decide firmly to do it.
[from Latin *determinare* meaning 'to fix limits']

Similar words: (sense 2) establish, decide
(sense 3) ascertain, verify

determined

(adjective) firmly decided, e.g. *I was determined to find out what had happened.*
determinedly (adverb).

Similar words: firm, adamant, resolute, dogged

determinism

(noun) Determinism is the belief that human action and choice is not free, but is decided or controlled by past events.
determinist (noun and adjective).

deterrent, deterrents

(noun) A deterrent is something that prevents you from doing something by making you afraid of what will happen if you do it, e.g. *Imprisonment is supposed to be a deterrent.*
deterrence (noun).

detest, detests, detesting, detested

(verb) If you detest someone or something, you strongly dislike them.
detestation (noun), **detestable** (adjective).
[from Latin *detestari* meaning 'to curse']

detonate, detonates, detonating, detonated

(verb) To detonate a bomb or mine means to cause it to explode.
detonation (noun), **detonator** (noun).
[from Latin *detonare* meaning 'to thunder']

detour, detours

(noun) A detour is an alternative, less direct route.
[from French *détour* meaning 'change of direction']

detract, detracts, detracting, detracted

(verb) To detract from something means to make it seem less good, valuable, or impressive.
detraction (noun), **detractor** (noun).
[from Latin *detrahere* meaning 'to pull away']

detriment

(noun) Detriment is harm or disadvantage.
detrimental (adjective), **detrimentally** (adverb).

detritus (pronounced dit-**rye**-tuss)

(noun) Detritus is particles of rock and silt produced by erosion.
[from Latin *detritus* meaning 'a rubbing away']

de trop (pronounced de troh)

(adjective; a formal expression) unwanted or unwelcome, e.g. *felt I was de trop so I left.*
[a French expression meaning literally 'of too much']

deuce, deuces (pronounced joos)

(noun) In tennis, deuce is the score of forty all. To win the game, one of the players must win two points in succession.

devalue, devalues, devaluing, devalued

1 (verb) To devalue something means to lower its status, importance, or worth.
2 To devalue a country's currency means to reduce its value in relation to that of other currencies, usually in order to encourage exports and discourage imports, e.g. *The dollar was devalued by 10%.*
devaluation (noun).

devastate, devastates, devastating, devastated

(verb) To devastate an area or place means to damage it severely or destroy it, e.g. *The office was devastated by fire.*
devastation (noun).

devastated

(adjective) very shocked or upset, e.g. *I was devastated when I heard the news.*

devastating

1 (adjective) very destructive, e.g. *Modern farming has had devastating effects on wildlife.*
2 overwhelming or shocking, e.g. *a devastating piece of news.*
3 (an informal use) very effective or beautiful, e.g. *She looked devastating in her new dress.*
devastatingly (adverb).

develop, develops, developing, developed

1 (verb) When something develops or is developed, it grows or becomes more advanced, e.g. *The bud develops into a flower.*
2 To develop an area of land means to build on it.
3 To develop an illness or a fault means to become affected by it.
4 To develop photographs or film means to treat the film chemically in order to produce a visible image.
[from Old French *desveloper* meaning 'to unwrap']

developer, developers

1 (noun) A developer is a person or company that builds on land.
2 A developer is also a chemical used to treat film.

development, developments

1 (noun) Development is gradual growth or advancement.
2 The development of land or water is the process of making it more useful or profitable by the expansion of industry or housing, e.g. *the development of the North Sea.*
3 A development is a new stage in a series of events, e.g. *further developments in the industrial dispute.*
developmental (adjective).

deviant, deviants

1 (adjective) Deviant behaviour is unacceptable or different from what people consider as normal.
2 (noun) A deviant is someone whose behaviour or beliefs are different from what people consider to be acceptable.

deviate, deviates, deviating, deviated

(verb) To deviate means to differ or depart from what is usual or acceptable.
deviation (noun).

device, devices

1 (noun) A device is a machine or tool that is used for a particular purpose, e.g. *a device for getting stones out of horses' hooves.*
2 A device is also a plan or scheme, e.g. *He would stoop to any device to get her money.*
3 A device is also a design or figure used as an emblem, a sign on a coat of arms, or a trademark.

4 (phrase) If you **leave someone to their own devices**, you leave them alone to do as they wish.

devil, devils
1 (noun) In Christianity, the Devil is the spirit of evil and enemy of God.
2 A devil is any evil spirit.
3 (an informal use) You can use 'devil' to talk about people, e.g. *You lucky devil!*
[from Greek *diabolos* meaning 'slanderer', 'enemy', or 'devil']

devilish
(adjective) cruel or very unpleasant.

devilment
(noun) Devilment is the same as devilry.

devilry
(noun) Devilry is mischievous or bad behaviour.

devious
1 (adjective) insincere and dishonest.
2 A devious route or course of action is indirect.
deviously (adjective), **deviousness** (noun).
[from Latin *devius* meaning 'lying to one side of the road']

devise, devises, devising, devised
(verb) To devise something means to work it out, e.g. *I have devised a scheme for saving energy.*

devitalize, devitalizes, devitalizing, devitalized; also spelled **devitalise**
(verb) To devitalize something means to make it weak or lifeless.

devoid
(adjective) lacking in a particular thing or quality, e.g. *He was devoid of talent.*

devolution
(noun) Devolution is the transfer of power or authority from a central government or organization to smaller organizations or to local government departments.

devolve, devolves, devolving, devolved
(verb) To devolve a power, privilege, or duty means to transfer it, e.g. *Central government should devolve some of its powers to local councils.*

devote, devotes, devoting, devoted
(verb) If you devote yourself to something, you give all your time, energy, or money to it, e.g. *He devoted himself to his studies.*
[from Latin *devovere* meaning 'to vow']

devoted
(adjective) very loving and loyal.
devotedly (adverb).

devotee, devotees
(noun) A devotee of something is a fanatical or enthusiastic follower of it.

devotion, devotions
1 (noun) Devotion to someone or something is great love or affection for them.
2 Devotions are prayers or religious worship, e.g. *He spent three hours at his devotions.*
devotional (adjective).

devour, devours, devouring, devoured
(verb) If you devour something, you eat it hungrily or greedily.

devout
(adjective) deeply and sincerely religious, e.g. *a devout Catholic.*
devoutly (adverb), **devoutness** (noun).
[from Latin *devotus* meaning 'devoted']

dew
(noun) Dew is drops of moisture that form on the ground and other cool surfaces at night.

dewlap, dewlaps
(noun) Dewlaps are loose folds of skin that hang under the throats of some animals, such as cows and dogs.

dewy, dewier, dewiest
(adjective) moist with dew, or appearing to be so, e.g. *a dewy complexion.*

dewy-eyed
(adjective) innocent and trusting.

dexterity
(noun) Dexterity is skill or nimbleness in using your hands or mind, e.g. *It required great mental dexterity.*
dexterous or **dextrous** (adjective).

dextrose
(noun) Dextrose is a natural form of sugar found in fruits, honey, and in the blood of animals.

dhal another spelling of **dal**.

dhoti, dhotis (pronounced **doe-tee**)
(noun) A dhoti is a long loose covering for the lower part of the body, worn by Hindu men.
[a Hindi word]

diabetes (pronounced dy-a-**bee**-tiss)
(noun) Diabetes is a disease in which someone has too much sugar in their blood, because they do not produce enough insulin to absorb it.
diabetic (noun or adjective).

diabolic
(adjective) extremely wicked or cruel.
[from Greek *diabolos* meaning 'devil']

diabolical
1 (adjective; an informal use) dreadful and very annoying, e.g. *What a diabolical liberty!*
2 extremely wicked and cruel.
diabolically (adverb).

diadem, diadems
(noun) A diadem is a small jewelled crown or headband, usually worn by royalty.

diagnose, diagnoses, diagnosing, diagnosed
(verb) To diagnose an illness or problem means to identify exactly what is wrong.
[from Greek *diagignōskein* meaning 'to distinguish']

diagnosis, diagnoses
(noun) A diagnosis is the identification of what is wrong with someone who is ill.
diagnostic (adjective).

diagonal, diagonals
1 (adjective) in a slanting direction.
2 (noun) A diagonal in a four-sided shape is a straight line joining two of the opposite corners.
diagonally (adverb).
[from Greek *diagōnios* meaning 'from angle to angle']

diagram 198 **dictator**

diagram, diagrams

(noun) A diagram is a drawing that shows or explains something.
diagrammatic (adjective), **diagrammatically** (adverb).
[from Greek *diagraphein* meaning 'to mark out in lines']

dial, dials, dialling, dialled

1 (noun) A dial is the face of a clock or meter, with divisions marked on it so that a time or measurement can be recorded and read.
2 A dial is also the part on some equipment, such as a radio or time switch, by which the equipment is tuned or controlled.
3 (verb) To dial a telephone number means to press the number keys or move the circle to select the required number.

dialect, dialects

(noun) A dialect is a form of a language spoken in a particular geographical area.
dialectal (adjective).
[from Greek *dialektos* meaning 'speech' or 'discourse']

dialogue, dialogues

1 (noun) Dialogue is communication or discussion between people or groups of people, e.g. *The union sought dialogue with the council.*
2 In a novel, play, or film, dialogue is conversation.

dialysis

(noun) Dialysis is a treatment used for some kidney diseases, in which blood is filtered by means of a special machine to remove waste products.
[from Greek *dialuein* meaning 'to rip apart']

diameter, diameters

(noun) The diameter of a circle is the length of a straight line drawn across it through its centre.

diametrically

(adverb) Things that are diametrically opposed are absolutely and completely opposed.

diamond, diamonds

1 (noun) A diamond is a precious stone made of pure carbon. Diamonds are the hardest known substance in the world and are used for cutting substances and for making jewellery.
2 A diamond is also a shape with four straight sides of equal length forming two opposite angles less than 90 degrees and two opposite angles greater than 90 degrees.
3 Diamonds is one of the four suits in a pack of playing cards. It is marked by a red diamond-shaped symbol.
4 The diamond is the area between the four bases in the game of baseball.
5 (adjective) A diamond anniversary is the 60th anniversary of an event, e.g. *a diamond wedding.*

diaphanous

(adjective) Diaphanous cloth is very fine and almost transparent.

diaphragm, diaphragms (pronounced **dy**-a-fram)

(noun) In mammals, the diaphragm is the muscular wall that separates the lungs from the stomach.

diarrhoea (pronounced dy-a-**ree**-a)

(noun) Diarrhoea is a condition in which the faeces are more liquid and frequent than usual.
[from Greek *diarrhein* meaning 'to flow through']

diary, diaries

1 (noun) A diary is a book which has a separate space or page for each day of the year on which to keep a record of appointments.
2 (phrase) If you **keep a diary**, you regularly write your thoughts and experiences in a diary.
diarist (noun).
[from Latin *diarium* meaning 'daily allowance']

diastase (pronounced dy-ass-tayss)

(noun) Diastase is an enzyme that converts starch into sugar.

diastole (pronounced dy-**ass**-tol-ee)

(noun) The diastole is the rhythmical relaxation of the chambers of the heart during which they fill with blood.
[from Greek *diastellein* meaning 'to expand']

diatribe, diatribes

(noun) A diatribe is an angry, bitterly critical speech or written article.

dice, dices, dicing, diced

1 (noun) A dice is a small cube which has each side marked with dots representing the numbers one to six.
2 (verb) To dice food means to cut it into small cubes.
diced (adjective).

dicey, dicier, diciest

(adjective; an informal word) risky or uncertain.

dichotomy, dichotomies (pronounced dy-**kot**-tom-ee)

(noun; a formal word) A dichotomy is a division into two sharply divided or opposed parts, e.g. *the dichotomy between eastern and western cultures.*

Dickensian

(adjective) very old-fashioned or unpleasant, like the conditions described in many of Dickens' novels.

dicky, dickies; dickier, dickiest

1 (noun) A dicky is a false shirt front worn under a jacket.
2 (adjective; an informal use) unreliable, e.g. *He's got a dicky heart.*

dictate, dictates, dictating, dictated

1 (verb) If you dictate something, you say or read it aloud for someone else to write down.
2 To dictate something means to command or state what must happen, e.g. *Landlords can dictate their own conditions.*
3 (noun) A dictate is an order which has to be obeyed.
dictation (noun).
[from Latin *dictare* meaning 'to order']

dictator, dictators

(noun) A dictator is a ruler who has complete power in a country, especially one who has taken power by force.

Similar words: tyrant, autocrat, despot

dictatorial
(adjective) like a dictator.
dictatorially (adverb).

diction
(noun) Someone's diction is the clarity with which they speak or sing.
[from Latin *dictio* meaning 'phrase']

Similar words: pronunciation, enunciation, articulation

dictionary, dictionaries
(noun) A dictionary is a book in which words are listed alphabetically and explained or their equivalents in another language given.
[from Latin *dictio* meaning 'phrase' or 'word']

dictum, dicta or dictums
1 (noun) A dictum is a formal statement or pronouncement.
2 A dictum is also a popular saying, e.g. *His dictum was, 'If a job's worth doing, it's worth doing well.'*
[from Latin *dictum* meaning literally 'thing said']

didactic
(adjective; a formal word) intended to teach or instruct people.
didactically (adverb), **didacticism** (noun).

diddle, diddles, diddling, diddled
(verb; an informal word) To diddle someone means to cheat or swindle them.

die, dies, dying, died
1 (verb) When people, animals, or plants die, they stop living.
2 When things die or die out, they cease to exist, e.g. *That custom died out many years ago.*
3 When something dies, dies away, or dies down, it gradually fades away, e.g. *The smile died on his lips.*
4 (an informal use) If you are dying to do something, you are longing to do it.
5 (noun) A die is a specially shaped or patterned block of metal used to cut or mould other metal.
6 A die is also a dice.
7 (phrase) If the **die is cast**, a decision has been made, the consequences of which cannot be reversed.

Similar words: (sense 1) pass away, expire, decease, perish

die-cast, die-casts, die-casting, die-cast
(verb) To die-cast a metal or plastic object means to form it by forcing metal or plastic into a shaped mould.

diehard, diehards
(noun) A diehard is someone strongly opposed to change and new ideas.

diesel, diesels (pronounced **dee**-zel)
1 (noun) A diesel is a vehicle with a diesel engine.
2 Diesel or diesel oil is the heavy fuel used in diesel engines.

diesel engine, diesel engines
(noun) A diesel engine is an internal-combustion engine in which the fuel is ignited by hot air produced by compression in the cylinders. It is named after Rudolf Diesel, who invented it in 1892.

diet, diets
1 (noun) Someone's diet is the usual food that they eat, e.g. *a healthy diet.*
2 A diet is a special restricted selection of foods that someone eats to improve their health or regulate their weight.
dietary (adjective).
[from Greek *diaita* meaning 'mode of living']

dietetics
(noun) Dietetics is the scientific study of the composition and regulation of food and diets.
dietetic (adjective).

dietician, dieticians; also spelled dietitian
(noun) A dietician is someone trained to advise people about healthy eating.

differ, differs, differing, differed
1 (verb) If two or more things differ, they are unlike each other.
2 If people differ, they have opposing views or disagree about something.

difference, differences
1 (noun) The difference between things is the way in which they are unlike each other.
2 The difference between two numbers is the amount by which one is less than another.
3 A difference in someone or something is a significant change in them, e.g. *You wouldn't believe the difference in her.*
4 If people have a difference, they have an argument or disagreement.

Similar words: (sense 1) contrast, dissimilarity, disparity, discrepancy, distinction, variation

different
1 (adjective) unlike something else.
2 unusual and out of the ordinary.
3 distinct and separate, although of the same kind, e.g. *They had three different bank accounts.*
differently (adverb).

Similar words: (sense 1) contrasting, dissimilar, disparate, unlike
(sense 3) alternative, variant

differential, differentials
1 (noun) A differential is a difference between rates of pay for different types of work, different industries, or different groups of workers in the same industry or company.
2 (a technical use) In a vehicle, a differential is a gear mechanism which enables two shafts to rotate at different speeds.

differentiate, differentiates, differentiating, differentiated
1 (verb) To differentiate between things means to recognize or show how one is unlike the other.
2 Something that differentiates one thing from another makes it distinct and unlike the other.
differentiation (noun).

difficult
1 (adjective) not easy to do, understand, or solve.

2 hard to deal with or troublesome, especially because of being unreasonable or unpredictable, e.g. *a difficult child*.

Similar words: (sense 1) hard, laborious, knotty, thorny, tricky
(sense 2) awkward, perverse, trying

difficulty, difficulties
1 (noun) A difficulty is a problem, e.g. *The main difficulty is a shortage of time... he's in financial difficulties*.
2 Difficulty is the fact or quality of being difficult.

diffident
(adjective) timid and lacking in self-confidence.
diffidently (adverb), **diffidence** (noun).

diffract, diffracts, diffracting, diffracted
(verb) When rays of light or sound waves diffract, they break up after hitting an obstacle.
diffraction (noun).

diffuse, diffuses, diffusing, diffused (pronounced dif-**yooz**)
1 (verb) If something diffuses, it spreads out or scatters in all directions.
2 (adjective) spread out over a wide area.
3 vague and not easy to understand, e.g. *The book was diffuse and long-winded*.
diffusely (adverb), **diffusion** (noun).

dig, digs, digging, dug
1 (verb) If you dig, you break up soil or sand, especially with a spade or garden fork.
2 To dig something into an object means to push, thrust, or poke it in.
3 (noun) A dig is an archeological excavation.
4 A dig is also a prod or jab, especially in the ribs.
5 (an informal use) A dig at someone is a spiteful or unpleasant remark intended to hurt, anger, or embarrass them.
6 Digs are lodgings in someone else's house.

digest, digests, digesting, digested
1 (verb) To digest food means to break it down in the gut so that it can be easily absorbed and used by the body.
2 If you digest information or a fact, you understand it and take it in.
3 (noun) A digest is a shortened version of a report, article, or book.
digestible (adjective).
[from Latin *digerere* meaning 'to divide']

digestion, digestions
1 (noun) Digestion is the process of digesting food.
2 Your digestion is your ability to digest food, e.g. *His digestion had always been poor*.
digestive (adjective).

digit, digits (pronounced **dij**-it)
1 (noun; a formal use) Your digits are your fingers or toes.
2 (noun) A digit is a written symbol for any of the numbers from 0 to 9.

digital
(adjective) displaying information, especially

time, by numbers, rather than by a pointer moving round a dial, e.g. *a digital watch*.
digitally (adverb).

digital recording, digital recordings
(noun) A digital recording is a sound recording which uses a technique that breaks down the sound into thousands of very small signals.

dignified
(adjective) full of dignity.

dignify, dignifies, dignifying, dignified
(verb) If one thing dignifies another, it makes it impressive or grand, e.g. *A broad staircase dignified the front of the mansion*.

dignitary, dignitaries
(noun) A dignitary is a person who holds a high official position.

dignity
1 (noun) Dignity is behaviour which is serious, calm, and controlled, e.g. *Her quiet dignity impressed us all*.
2 The dignity of something is its quality of being worthy of respect.
3 Someone's dignity is their sense of self-importance.
4 (phrase) If something is **beneath your dignity**, you consider yourself too important to do it.
[from Latin *dignus* meaning 'worthy']

digress, digresses, digressing, digressed
(verb) If you digress when you are talking or writing, you move away from the main subject and talk about something else for a short time.
digression (noun).

dilapidated
(adjective) falling to pieces and generally in a bad condition, e.g. *A dilapidated house*.
[from Latin *dis-* meaning 'apart' and *lapides* meaning 'stones']

Similar words: broken down, run down, decrepit

dilate, dilates, dilating, dilated
(verb) To dilate means to become wider and larger, e.g. *The pupil of the eye dilates in the dark*.
dilated (adjective), **dilation** (noun).
[from Latin *dilatare* meaning 'to spread out']

dilatory (pronounced **dil**-la-tree)
(adjective) slow in acting or making up your mind.

dilemma, dilemmas
(noun) A dilemma is a situation in which a choice has to be made between alternatives that are equally difficult or unpleasant.
[from Greek *di-* meaning 'two' and *lemma* meaning 'assumption']

dilettante, dilettantes (pronounced dilly-**tahn**-tee)
(noun) A dilettante is someone who dabbles in a subject rather than having a serious or professional interest in it.
[from Italian *dilettare* meaning 'to delight']

diligent
(adjective) hard-working, and showing care and perseverance.
diligently (adverb), **diligence** (noun).

Similar words: industrious, assiduous

dill
(noun) Dill is a herb with yellow flowers, the seeds and leaves of which are used in cooking.

dilute, dilutes, diluting, diluted
1 (verb) To dilute a liquid means to add water or a thinner to it to make it less concentrated.
2 (adjective) Liquid that is dilute is thin or weakened because water has been added.
dilution (noun).

dim, dimmer, dimmest; dims, dimming, dimmed
1 (adjective) badly lit and lacking in brightness.
2 very vague and unclear in your mind, e.g. *a dim memory.*
3 (an informal use) stupid or mentally dull, e.g. *He is rather dim when it comes to maths.*
4 (verb) If lights dim or are dimmed, they become less bright.
dimly (adverb), **dimness** (noun).

dime, dimes
(noun) A dime is an American coin worth 10 cents.

dimension, dimensions
1 (noun) A dimension of a situation is an aspect or factor that influences the way you understand it, e.g. *Religion added another dimension to the problem.*
2 You can talk about the size or extent of something as its dimensions, e.g. *a problem of enormous dimensions.*
3 The dimensions of something are also its measurements, for example its length, breadth, height, or diameter.
[from Latin *dimensus* meaning 'measured out']

diminish, diminishes, diminishing, diminished
(verb) If something diminishes or if you diminish it, it becomes reduced in size importance, or intensity.

diminution
(noun) A diminution in something is a reduction in its size, importance, or intensity.

diminutive
(adjective) very small.

dimple, dimples
(noun) A dimple is a small hollow in someone's cheek or chin.
dimpled (adjective).

din, dins, dinning, dinned
1 (noun) A din is a loud and unpleasant noise.
2 (verb) To din something into someone means to teach it to them by constant and forceful repetition, e.g. *I had it dinned into me at school.*

dinar, dinars (pronounced **dee**-nar)
(noun) The dinar is a unit of currency in Yugoslavia and in several North African and Middle Eastern countries.

dine, dines, dining, dined
(verb; a formal use) To dine means to eat dinner in the evening, e.g. *We dine at eight.*

diner, diners
1 (noun) A diner is someone who is having dinner in a restaurant.
2 A diner is also a small restaurant or railway restaurant car.

ding-dong, ding-dongs
1 (noun) Ding-dong is used to represent the sound of bells, especially in songs or verse.
2 (an informal use) A ding-dong is a lively argument or quarrel.

dinghy, dinghies (pronounced **ding**-ee)
(noun) A dinghy is a small boat which is rowed, sailed, or powered by outboard motor.

dingo, dingoes
(noun) A dingo is an Australian wild dog.
[an Aboriginal word]

dingy, dingier, dingiest (pronounced **din**-jee)
1 (adjective) drab and rather depressing, e.g. *We drove through the town's dingiest streets.*
2 shabby, dirty, and discoloured, e.g. *dingy curtains.*

dinner, dinners
1 (noun) Dinner is the main meal of the day, eaten either in the evening or at lunchtime.
2 A dinner is a formal social occasion in the evening, at which a meal is served.

dinner dance, dinner dances
(noun) A dinner dance is a formal social occasion in the evening, with a dinner and dancing.

dinosaur, dinosaurs (pronounced **dy**-no-sor)
(noun) A dinosaur was a large reptile which lived in the Mesozoic era in prehistoric times.
[from Greek *deinos* + *sauros* meaning 'fearful lizard']

dint
(phrase) **By dint of** means by means of, e.g. *She passed the exams by dint of hard work.*

diocese, dioceses
(noun) A diocese is a district controlled by a bishop.
diocesan (adjective).
[from Greek *dioikein* meaning 'to keep house']

diode, diodes
(noun) A diode is an electrical device for converting alternating current into direct current.

dioxide
(noun) In chemistry, dioxide is any oxide containing two oxygen atoms per molecule, both of which are bonded to an atom of another element.

dip, dips, dipping, dipped
1 (verb) If you dip something into a liquid, you lower it or plunge it quickly into the liquid.
2 (noun) A dip is a rich creamy mixture which you scoop up with biscuits or raw vegetables and eat, e.g. *a cheese dip.*
3 (an informal use) A dip is also a swim.
4 (verb) If something dips, it slopes downwards

or goes below a certain level, e.g. *The land dips towards the river... Sales dipped in November.*
5 To dip also means to make a quick, slight downward movement, e.g. *The aeroplane dipped its wings.*
6 To dip headlights means to direct the beam downwards so that oncoming drivers are not dazzled.
7 To dip into a book means to glance at it or read only parts of it.
8 To dip sheep means to put them into a liquid containing disinfectant for a short time, in order to kill harmful insects and germs.
9 (noun) A dip is a liquid containing disinfectant for cleansing animals, e.g. *a sheep dip.*

diphtheria (pronounced dipth-**ear**-ee-a)
(noun) Diphtheria is a serious infectious bacterial disease causing fever and difficulty in breathing and swallowing.

diphthong, diphthongs
(noun) A diphthong is a vowel in which the speaker's tongue changes position while it is being pronounced, so that the vowel sounds like a combination of two other vowels.

diploma, diplomas
(noun) A diploma is a certificate awarded to a student who has successfully completed a course of study.
[from Greek *diploma* meaning 'folded paper' or 'letter of recommendation']

diplomacy
1 (noun) Diplomacy is the managing of relationships between countries.
2 Diplomacy is also skill in dealing with people without offending or upsetting them.
diplomatic (adjective), **diplomatically** (adverb),

diplomat, diplomats
(noun) A diplomat is an official who negotiates and deals with another country on behalf of his or her own country.

diplomatic immunity
(noun) Diplomatic immunity is the freedom from legal action and the paying of tax that diplomats have in the country in which they are working.

dipsomania
(noun) Dipsomania is a compulsive craving for alcohol.
dipsomaniac (noun).
[from Greek *dipsa* meaning 'thirst' and *-mania* meaning 'craving']

dire, direr, direst
(adjective) disastrous, urgent, or terrible, e.g. *dire warnings... people in dire need.*
[from Latin *dirus* meaning 'fearful']

direct, directs, directing, directed
1 (adjective) moving or aimed in a straight line or by the shortest route, e.g. *a direct flight.*
2 straightforward, and without delay or evasion, e.g. *a direct question.*
3 without anyone or anything intervening, e.g. *He has direct control over the workforce.*
4 exact, e.g. *the direct opposite.*

5 (verb) To direct something means to guide and control it.
6 To direct people or things means to send them, tell them, or show them the way.
7 To direct a film, a play, or a television or radio programme means to organize the way it is made and performed.
8 If you direct your attention or efforts towards someone or something, you turn your attention or efforts towards them.
[from Latin *dirigere* meaning 'to guide']

Similar words: (sense 2) forthright, matter-of-fact, frank, straightforward, straight

direct current
(noun) Direct current is a term used in physics to refer to an electric current that always flows in the same direction.

direction, directions
1 (noun) A direction is the general line that someone or something is moving or pointing in.
2 Direction is the controlling and guiding of something, e.g. *The department was under the firm direction of the manager.*
3 (plural noun) Directions are instructions that tell you how to do something or how to get somewhere.

directive, directives
(noun) A directive is an instruction that must be obeyed, e.g. *The EEC directives forced the government to act.*

directly
1 (adverb) in a straight line or immediately, e.g. *The sun was directly overhead... The door opened directly onto the street.*
2 very soon, e.g. *She will be here directly.*
3 (conjunction) Directly also means 'as soon as', e.g. *I left directly I heard the news.*

director, directors
1 (noun) A director is a member of the board of a company or institution.
2 A director is also the person responsible for the making and performance of a programme, play, or film.
directorial (adjective).

directorate, directorates
1 (noun) A directorate is a board of directors of a company or organization.
2 A directorate is also the position or work of a director.

directory, directories
(noun) A directory is a book which gives lists of facts, such as names and addresses, and is usually arranged in alphabetical order.

dirge, dirges
(noun) A dirge is a slow, sad, or mournful piece of music, sometimes played or sung at funerals.

dirt
1 (noun) Dirt is any unclean substance, such as dust, mud, or stains.
2 Dirt is also earth or soil.
[from Old Norse *drit* meaning 'excrement']

Similar words: (sense 1) filth, grime, muck, squalor

dirty, dirtier, dirtiest
1 (adjective) marked or covered with dirt.
2 unfair or dishonest, e.g. *a dirty trick.*
3 referring to sex in a way that many people find offensive, e.g. *a dirty book.*
4 Dirty weather is rough or squally.
5 (phrase) If you do someone's **dirty work**, you do something for them that is unpleasant and that they do not want to do themselves.
dirtily (adverb), **dirtiness** (noun).

Similar words: (sense 1) filthy, grimy, grotty, grubby, mucky

dis-
(prefix) Dis- is added to the beginning of words to form a word that means the opposite.

disability, disabilities
(noun) A disability is a physical or mental incapacity or illness that restricts someone's way of life.

disable, disables, disabling, disabled
(verb) If something disables someone, it injures or harms them so that they lose ability or power, especially of movement.
disablement (noun), **disabled** (adjective).

disabuse, disabuses, disabusing, disabused
(verb) If you disabuse someone of a false idea or belief, you convince them that it is untrue.

disadvantage, disadvantages
1 (noun) A disadvantage is an unfavourable or harmful circumstance.
2 (phrase) If you are **at a disadvantage**, you have a problem or difficulty that other people do not have, e.g. *Poor social conditions put the pupils at a disadvantage.*
disadvantaged (adjective), **disadvantageous** (adjective).

Similar words: (sense 1) drawback, hindrance, handicap, minus

disaffected
(adjective) If someone is disaffected with an idea or organization, they no longer believe in it or support it, e.g. *The new party gained disaffected socialists as members.*

disagree, disagrees, disagreeing, disagreed
1 (verb) If you disagree with someone, you have a different view or opinion from theirs.
2 If you disagree with an action or proposal, you disapprove of it and believe it is wrong, e.g. *I disagree with selling off national industries.*
3 If food or drink disagrees with you, it makes you feel unwell.
disagreement (noun).

Similar words: (sense 1) differ, dissent

disagreeable
(adjective) unpleasant or unhelpful and unfriendly, e.g. *a disagreeable job... a disagreeable person.*
disagreeably (adverb).

disallow, disallows, disallowing, disallowed
(verb) To disallow something means to refuse to accept or allow it because it is untrue, e.g. *The plea of insanity was disallowed by the judge.*

disappear, disappears, disappearing, disappeared
1 (verb) If something or someone disappears, they go out of sight or become lost.
2 To disappear also means to stop existing or happening, e.g. *The pain has disappeared.*
disappearance (noun).

Similar words: (sense 2) melt away, fade, pass away

disappoint, disappoints, disappointing, disappointed
(verb) If someone or something disappoints you, it fails to live up to what you expected of it.
disappointed (adjective), **disappointment** (noun).

disapprove, disapproves, disapproving, disapproved
(verb) To disapprove of something or someone means to believe they are wrong or bad, e.g. *I disapprove of smoking.*
disapproval (noun), **disapproving** (adjective), **disapprovingly** (adverb).

disarm, disarms, disarming, disarmed
1 (verb) To disarm means to get rid of weapons.
2 If someone disarms you, they overcome your anger or hostility, by charming or soothing you, e.g. *He was disarmed by her pleasant manner.*
disarming (adjective), **disarmingly** (adverb).

disarmament
(noun) Disarmament is the reducing or getting rid of military forces and weapons.

disarrange, disarranges, disarranging, disarranged
(verb) If something is disarranged, it is messed up or made untidy.

disarray
(noun) Disarray is a state of disorganization and confusion, e.g. *The nation was in disarray after the war.*

disassociate means the same as dissociate.

disaster, disasters
1 (noun) A disaster is an event or accident that causes great distress or destruction.
2 A disaster is also a complete failure.
disastrous (adjective), **disastrously** (adverb).

Similar words: (sense 1) catastrophe, cataclysm (sense 2) catastrophe, fiasco, debacle, calamity

disavow, disavows, disavowing, disavowed
(verb; a formal word) To disavow something means to deny any knowledge of it or connection with it.

disband, disbands, disbanding, disbanded
(verb) To disband means to break up or separate.

disbelieve, disbelieves, disbelieving, disbelieved
(verb) To disbelieve something means to refuse or be unable to accept that it is true, e.g. *There is no reason to disbelieve their story.*
disbelief (noun), **disbeliever** (noun).

disburse, disburses, disbursing, disbursed
(verb) To disburse money means to pay it out.
disbursement (noun).

disc, discs; also spelled **disk**
1 (noun) A disc is flat round object, e.g. *an identity disc... a compact disc.*
2 A disc is one of the thin circular pieces of cartilage which separate the bones in your spine.
[from Greek *diskos* meaning 'quoit' or 'discus']

discard, discards, discarding, discarded
(verb) To discard something means to get rid of it, because you no longer want it or find it useful.

Similar words: dispose of, ditch, dump, scrap

discern, discerns, discerning, discerned
(pronounced dis-**ern**)
(verb; a formal word) To discern something means to notice or understand it clearly, e.g. *I was unable to discern what was happening.*
[from Latin *discernere* meaning 'to separate' or 'to distinguish']

discernible
(adjective) able to be seen or recognized, e.g. *There was no discernible difference between the two prints.*

discerning
(adjective) having good taste and judgment.
discerningly (adverb), **discernment** (noun).

Similar words: discriminating, selective

discharge, discharges, discharging, discharged
1 (verb) If something discharges or is discharged, it is given or sent out, e.g. *oil discharged into the sea.*
2 To discharge someone from hospital means to allow to them to leave.
3 If someone is discharged from a job, they are dismissed from it.
4 (a formal use) If you discharge your duties or responsibilities, you carry them out.
5 (a formal use) To discharge your debts means to pay what you owe.
6 (noun) A discharge is a substance that is released from the inside of something, e.g. *a thick nasal discharge.*

disciple, disciples (pronounced dis-**sigh**-pl)
(noun) A disciple is a follower of someone or something.
[from Latin *discipulus* meaning 'pupil']

disciplinarian (pronounced dis-sip-lin-**air**-ee-an)
(noun) A disciplinarian is a person who believes in imposing strict rules.

discipline, disciplines, disciplining, disciplined
1 (noun) Discipline is the imposing of order by making people obey rules and punishing them when they break them.
2 Discipline is the ability to behave and work in a controlled way.
3 (verb) If you discipline yourself, you train yourself to behave and work in an ordered way.
4 To discipline someone means to punish them.

5 (noun; a formal use) A discipline is a particular area of academic study.
disciplinary (adjective), **disciplined** (adjective).
[from Latin *disciplina* meaning 'teaching']

disc jockey, disc jockeys
(noun) A disc jockey is someone who introduces and plays pop records on the radio or at a disco.

disclaim, disclaims, disclaiming, disclaimed
(verb) If you disclaim any knowledge of or responsibility for something, you deny that you know about it or are responsible for it.

disclaimer, disclaimers
(noun; a formal word) A disclaimer is a statement denying knowledge of or responsibility for something.

disclose, discloses, disclosing, disclosed
(verb) To disclose something means to make it known or allow it to be seen.
disclosure (noun).

disco, discos
(noun) A disco is a party or a club where young people go to dance to pop records played by a disc jockey.

discolour, discolours, discolouring, discoloured
(verb) To discolour something means to change or spoil its original colour.
discoloured (adjective), **discoloration** (noun).

discomfit, discomfits, discomfiting, discomfited
(verb; a literary word) If you are discomfited by something, it makes you feel slightly embarrassed or confused.
discomfiture (noun).

discomfort
1 (noun) Discomfort is distress or slight pain.
2 Discomfort is also a feeling of worry or embarrassment.
3 Discomforts are things that make you uncomfortable.

disconcert, disconcerts, disconcerting, disconcerted
(verb) If something disconcerts you, it makes you feel flustered or embarrassed.
disconcerting (adjective).

disconnect, disconnects, disconnecting, disconnected
1 (verb) To disconnect something means to detach it from something else.
2 If someone disconnects your telephone or supply of fuel, they cut you off.
disconnection (noun).

disconnected
(adjective) Disconnected ideas or thoughts are not joined together in a sensible way, e.g. *His sentences were rambling and disconnected.*

disconsolate
(adjective) unhappy and depressed, e.g. *Disconsolate passengers waited for hours in the airport.*
disconsolately (adverb).

discontent
(noun) Discontent is a feeling of dissatisfaction

with conditions or with life in general, e.g. *What are the causes of the current discontent?*
discontented (adjective), **discontentedly** (adverb).

discontinue, **discontinues, discontinuing, discontinued**
(verb) To discontinue something means to stop doing it.
discontinuation (noun).

discontinuity, **discontinuities**
(noun; a formal word) Discontinuity is a lack of smooth or unbroken development in something.
discontinuous (adjective).

discord, **discords**
1 (noun) Discord is an argument or unpleasantness between people.
2 A discord is a harsh and unattractive combination of musical notes.
[from Old French *descorder* meaning 'to disagree']

discordant
1 (adjective) Something that is discordant stands out as being unsuitable or ill-chosen in relation to its surroundings.
2 harsh and unpleasant sounding.
discordantly (adverb), **discordance** (noun).

discotheque, **discotheques** (pronounced **dis-ko-tek**)
(noun) A discotheque is a disco.
[from French *discothèque*]

discount, **discounts, discounting, discounted**
1 (noun) A discount is a reduction in the price of something.
2 (verb) If you discount an idea or theory, you reject it as being unsuitable or untrue, e.g. *This approach must be discounted as a way out of our difficulties.*

discourage, **discourages, discouraging, discouraged**
1 (verb) To discourage someone means to take away their enthusiasm or confidence to do something.
2 To discourage something means to make it less likely to happen, e.g. *This chemical solution will discourage rust.*
discouraging (adjective), **discouragement** (noun).

Similar words: (sense 1) deter, daunt, dishearten, dismay, dash, demoralize

discourse, **discourses, discoursing, discoursed** (a formal word)
1 (noun) A discourse is a formal talk or piece of writing intended to teach or explain something.
2 Discourse is serious conversation between people on a particular subject.
3 (verb) To discourse on a subject means to talk about it in an authoritative way.
[from Latin *discurrere* meaning 'to run to and fro']

discourteous (pronounced dis-**kur**-tee-uss)
(adjective) bad mannered and impolite.
discourteously (adverb), **discourtesy** (noun).

discover, **discovers, discovering, discovered**
(verb) When you discover something, you find it or find out about it, especially for the first time.
discovery (noun), **discoverer** (noun).

discredit, **discredits, discrediting, discredited**
1 (verb) To discredit someone means to damage their reputation.
2 To discredit an idea or theory means to cause it to be doubted or disbelieved.

discreditable
(adjective) shameful and wrong.

discreet
(adjective) careful to avoid embarrassment for other people, especially by tactful handling of personal secrets.
discreetly (adverb).

discrepancy, **discrepancies**
(noun) A discrepancy is a difference between two things which ought to be the same.
[from Latin *discrepare* meaning 'to sound different']

discrete
(adjective) separate and distinct, e.g. *The company was divided into several discrete units.*
[from Latin *discretus* meaning 'separated']

discretion
1 (noun) Discretion is the quality of behaving with care and tact so as to avoid embarrassment or distress to other people, e.g. *She is a woman of great discretion.*
2 Discretion is also freedom and authority to make decisions and take action according to your own judgment, e.g. *Doctors have no discretion over which patients they will treat.*
3 (phrase) If something is **at someone's discretion**, it can only happen if they give their permission.
discretionary (adjective).

discriminate, **discriminates, discriminating, discriminated**
1 (verb) To discriminate between things means to recognize and understand the differences between them, e.g. *He should be able to discriminate between right and wrong.*
2 To discriminate against a person or group means to treat them badly or unfairly, usually because of their race, colour, or sex.
3 To discriminate in favour of a person or group means to treat them more favourably than others.
discrimination (noun), **discriminatory** (adjective).

discriminating
(adjective) showing good taste and judgment, e.g. *a small but discriminating audience.*

discursive
(adjective; a formal word) moving from one topic to another in a rambling or unmethodical way.

discus, **discuses**
(noun) The discus is an athletics event in which contestants throw a heavy disc called a discus as far as they can.
[from Greek *diskos*]

discuss, discusses, discussing, discussed
(verb) When people discuss something, they talk about it in detail and consider different aspects of it.
[from Latin *discutere* meaning 'to investigate']

discussion, discussions
(noun) A discussion is a conversation or piece of writing in which a subject is considered in detail, from several points of view.

Similar words: debate, discourse, dialogue

disdain, disdains, disdaining, disdained
1 (noun) Disdain is a feeling of superiority over or contempt for someone or something, e.g. *They didn't hide their disdain for foreigners.*
2 (verb) If you disdain to do something, you refuse to do it because you think it is not worthy of you, e.g. *She disdained to answer.*
disdainful (adjective), **disdainfully** (adverb).
[from Latin *dedignari* meaning 'to reject as unworthy']

disease, diseases
(noun) A disease is an unhealthy condition in people, animals, or plants.
diseased (adjective).

disembark, disembarks, disembarking, disembarked
(verb) To disembark means to land or unload from a ship, aircraft, or bus, e.g. *Several passengers disembarked.*
disembarkation (noun).

disembodied
(adjective) separate from or existing without a body, e.g. *a disembodied skull.*

disenchanted
(adjective) disappointed with something, and no longer believing that it is good or worthwhile, e.g. *I soon became disenchanted with army life.*
disenchantment (noun).

disenfranchise, disenfranchises, disenfranchising, disenfranchised
(verb) To disenfranchise someone means to take away their right to vote.
disenfranchisement (noun).

disengage, disengages, disengaging, disengaged
1 (verb) If you disengage something, you release it from something else that it is attached to.
2 If two armies disengage, they stop fighting.
disengagement (noun).

disentangle, disentangles, disentangling, disentangled
(verb) If you disentangle something, you free it from other things that it has become mixed up with or wound round.

disestablish, disestablishes, disestablishing, disestablished
(verb; a formal word) To disestablish a Church means to break its official link with the State.
disestablishment (noun).

disfavour
(noun; a formal word) Disfavour is dislike or disapproval, e.g. *She viewed such practices with disfavour.*

disfigure, disfigures, disfiguring, disfigured
(verb) To disfigure something means to spoil its appearance, e.g. *Rubbish tips disfigured the countryside.*

disgorge, disgorges, disgorging, disgorged
1 (verb) If something disgorges its contents, it empties them out.
2 When a vehicle or building disgorges people, they get out of it.
[from French *gorge* meaning 'throat']

disgrace, disgraces, disgracing, disgraced
1 (noun) Disgrace is loss of approval and respect by people towards another person.
2 If something is a disgrace, it is unacceptable, e.g. *Your room is a disgrace!*
3 If someone is a disgrace to a group of people, their behaviour is unacceptable and makes the group feel ashamed, e.g. *You are a disgrace to the Regiment!*
4 (verb) If you disgrace yourself or disgrace someone else, you cause yourself or them to be strongly disapproved of by other people.

Similar words: (sense 1) discredit, dishonour, ignominy, shame, stigma, humiliation
(sense 4) discredit, dishonour, humiliate, shame

disgraceful
(adjective) If something is disgraceful, people disapprove of it strongly and think that those who are responsible for it should be ashamed.
disgracefully (adverb).

Similar words: shocking, shameful, scandalous, outrageous, reprehensible

disgruntled
(adjective) discontented or in a bad mood.
[from an old word *gruntle* meaning 'to complain']

disguise, disguises, disguising, disguised
1 (noun) A disguise is something you wear or something you do to alter your appearance so that you cannot be recognized by other people.
2 (verb) To disguise something means to change it so that people do not recognize it.
3 To disguise a feeling means to hide it, e.g. *She could not disguise her fear.*

disgust, disgusts, disgusting, disgusted
1 (noun) Disgust is the feeling aroused in you by something that is morally wrong, shameful, or very unpleasant.
2 (verb) To disgust someone means to make them feel sickened and disapproving.
disgusted (adjective).

Similar words: (sense 1) revulsion, loathing, repulsion
(sense 2) repel, sicken, put off

disgusting
(adjective) very unpleasant and offensive.
disgustingly (adverb).

Similar words: vile, repulsive, repugnant, revolting, foul, sickening

dish, dishes
1 (noun) A dish is a shallow container for cooking or serving food.

2 A dish is also food of a particular kind or food cooked in a particular way.

disharmony
(noun) Disharmony is disagreement between people causing an unpleasant atmosphere.

dishearten, disheartens, disheartening, disheartened
(verb) If you dishearten someone, you take away their hope and confidence in something.

dishevelled (pronounced dish-**ev**-ld)
(adjective) If someone looks dishevelled, their clothes or hair look disarranged and untidy.
[from Old French *chevel* meaning 'hair']

dishonest
(adjective) not truthful or able to be trusted.
dishonestly (adverb).

dishonesty
(noun) Dishonesty is behaviour which is meant to deceive people, either by not telling the truth or by cheating.

dishonour, dishonours, dishonouring, dishonoured
1 (noun; a formal word) Dishonour is a feeling of shame because people have lost respect for you, e.g. *He would prefer death to dishonour.*
2 (verb) If a bank dishonours a cheque, it refuses to pay because there is not enough money in the account.
dishonourable (adjective).

disillusion, disillusions, disillusioning, disillusioned
(verb) If something or someone disillusions you, you discover that you were mistaken about something you valued, and so you feel disappointed with it.
disillusion (noun), **disillusionment** (noun).

disillusioned
(adjective) If you are disillusioned with something, you are disappointed because it is not as good as you had expected it to be.

disincentive, disincentives
(noun) A disincentive is something that discourages you from doing something, or trying hard, e.g. *Low wages are a disincentive to work.*

disinclined
(adjective) If you are disinclined to do something, you do not want to do it.

disinfect, disinfects, disinfecting, disinfected
(verb) To disinfect something means to clean it with a chemical substance that kills germs.

disinfectant, disinfectants
(noun) A disinfectant is a chemical substance that kills germs.

disingenuous
(adjective) If someone is being disingenuous, they are being insincere and pretending to be more innocent or less knowledgeable than they really are.
disingenuously (adverb).

disinherit, disinherits, disinheriting, disinherited
(verb) If you disinherit someone, such as your child, you deliberately do not leave them your money or property in your will when you die.

disintegrate, disintegrates, disintegrating, disintegrated
1 (verb) If something disintegrates, it becomes weakened and breaks up, e.g. *Their marriage disintegrated under the stress of his job.*
2 If an object disintegrates, it shatters into many pieces and so is destroyed.
disintegration (noun).

disinterest
1 (noun) Disinterest is a lack of interest.
2 Disinterest is also a lack of personal involvement in a situation.

disinterested
(adjective) If someone is disinterested, they are not going to gain or lose from the situation they are involved in, and so can act in a way that is fair to both sides, e.g. *a disinterested judge.*
disinterestedly (adverb).

disjointed
(adjective) If thought or speech is disjointed, it jumps from subject to subject and so is difficult to follow or understand.

disk another spelling of **disc.**

dislike, dislikes, disliking, disliked
1 (verb) If you dislike something or someone, you think they are unpleasant and do not like them.
2 (noun) Dislike is a feeling that you have when you do not like someone or something.

Similar words: (sense 2) aversion, antipathy, distaste

dislocate, dislocates, dislocating, dislocated
1 (verb) To dislocate your bone or joint means to put it out of place, usually in an accident.
2 If something such as a routine is dislocated, it is put out of its usual order, so that it does not work smoothly.
[from Latin *dis-* meaning 'apart' and *locare* meaning 'to locate']

dislocation
(noun) Dislocation is a situation in which something has been changed or disturbed and so has been made worse, e.g. *Roadworks caused the dislocation of traffic on the A1.*

dislodge, dislodges, dislodging, dislodged
(verb) To dislodge something means to move it or force it out of place.

disloyal
(adjective) Someone who is disloyal does not remain firm in their friendship or support for someone or something.
disloyally (adverb), **disloyalty** (noun).

dismal (pronounced **diz**-mal)
(adjective) rather gloomy and depressing, e.g. *dismal weather.*
dismally (adverb).
[from Latin *dies mali* meaning 'evil days']

dismantle, dismantles, dismantling, dismantled
(verb) To dismantle something means to take it apart.
[from Old French *desmanteler* meaning 'to remove a cloak from']

dismay, dismays, dismaying, dismayed
1 (noun) Dismay is a feeling of fear and worry.
2 (verb) If someone or something dismays you, it fills you with alarm and worry.

dismember, dismembers, dismembering, dismembered
(verb; a formal word) To dismember a person or animal means to cut or tear their body into pieces.

dismiss, dismisses, dismissing, dismissed
1 (verb) If you dismiss something, you decide to ignore it because it is not important enough for you to think about.
2 To dismiss an employee means to ask that person to leave their job.
3 If someone in authority dismisses you, they tell you to leave.
4 If a judge dismisses a case in court, he or she states that there is no need for a trial, usually because there is not enough evidence.
dismissal (noun).

dismissive
(adjective) If you are dismissive of something or someone, you show that you think they are of little importance or value, e.g. *a dismissive smile of contempt.*

dismount, dismounts, dismounting, dismounted
(verb) To dismount from a horse or bicycle means to get off it.

disobedient
(adjective) If you are disobedient, you deliberately break a rule or law, or you do not do what someone tells you to do.
disobedience (noun), **disobediently** (adverb).

disobey, disobeys, disobeying, disobeyed
(verb) To disobey a person or an order means to deliberately refuse to do what you are told.

disobliging
(adjective) People who are disobliging are deliberately unhelpful.

disorder, disorders
1 (noun) Disorder is a state of untidiness.
2 Disorder is also a lack of organization, e.g. *The army retreated in some disorder.*
3 Disorder is violence or rioting in public.
4 A disorder is a disease, e.g. *a kidney disorder.*

Similar words: (sense 2) confusion, bedlam, mayhem, chaos, shambles, turmoil.

disorderly
1 (adjective) very untidy and confused, e.g. *Her bedroom was a disorderly mess.*
2 A person or group of people who are disorderly behave in an uncontrolled or violent way in public.

disorganize, disorganizes, disorganizing, disorganized; also spelled **disorganise**
(verb) To disorganize something means to upset its order or system, so that it becomes confused or less effective.
disorganized (adjective), **disorganization** (noun).

disorientate, disorientates, disorientating, disorientated
(verb) If something disorientates you, it confuses you so that you lose your sense of direction.
disorientated (adjective), **disorientation** (noun).

disown, disowns, disowning, disowned
(verb) To disown someone or something means to refuse to admit any connection with them or any responsibility for them.

disparage, disparages, disparaging, disparaged
(verb) If you disparage something or someone, you speak of them in a way that shows you have a poor opinion of them.
disparaging (adjective), **disparagement** (noun).

disparate
(adjective; a formal word) Things that are disparate are utterly and clearly different.
disparity (noun).
[from Latin *disparare* meaning 'to divide']

dispassionate
(adjective) If someone is dispassionate, they act without being influenced by their emotions.
dispassionately (adverb).

dispatch, dispatches, dispatching, dispatched; also spelled **despatch**
1 (verb) To dispatch someone or something to a particular place means to send them there for a special reason, e.g. *The cruiser dispatched boats to rescue the survivors.*
2 (noun) A dispatch is an official written message, often sent to an army or government headquarters.
3 A dispatch is also a story sent to a newspaper by a journalist who is based overseas.
4 (verb) To dispatch a person or animal means to kill them.
[from Old French *despeechier* meaning 'to set free']

dispel, dispels, dispelling, dispelled
(verb) To dispel fears or beliefs means to drive them away or to destroy them, e.g. *All doubts were dispelled by her presence.*
[from Latin *dispellere* meaning 'to scatter']

dispensable
(adjective) Someone or something dispensable is not really needed.

dispensary, dispensaries
(noun) A dispensary is a place where medicines are prepared and given out.

dispensation, dispensations
1 (noun) Dispensation is the issuing or giving out of something, especially by those in authority, e.g. *the dispensation of justice.*
2 Dispensation is also special permission to do something that is not normally allowed, e.g. *Dispensation was granted to the school to advertise.*

dispense, dispenses, dispensing, dispensed
1 (verb; a formal use) To dispense something means to give it out, e.g. *The charity dispensed the money as it saw fit.*
2 To dispense medicines means to prepare them and give them out, usually in a hospital or chemist's shop.
3 To dispense with something means to do

without it or do away with it, e.g. *We should dispense with all nuclear weapons.*
[from Latin *dispendere* meaning 'to weigh out']

dispenser, dispensers
(noun) A dispenser is a machine or container which provides an item or a quantity of something, either automatically or by the use of a lever or button, e.g. *a cash dispenser.*

disperse, disperses, dispersing, dispersed
1 (verb) When something disperses, it scatters over a wide area.
2 When people disperse or when someone disperses them, they move apart and go in different directions.
dispersion (noun).
[from Latin *dispergere* meaning 'to scatter']

dispirited
(adjective) depressed and having no enthusiasm for anything.
dispiritedly (adverb).

dispiriting
(adjective) Something dispiriting makes you depressed and unenthusiastic, e.g. *a dispiriting November day.*

displace, displaces, displacing, displaced
1 (verb) If one thing displaces another, it forces the thing out of its usual place or position and occupies that place itself.
2 To displace something means to move it from its correct position.
3 If people are displaced, they are forced to leave their home or country.

displacement
1 (noun) Displacement is the removal of something from its usual or correct place or position.
2 In physics, displacement is the weight or volume of liquid displaced by an object submerged or floating in it.

display, displays, displaying, displayed
1 (verb) If you display something, you show it or make it visible to people.
2 If you display something such as an emotion, you behave in a way that shows you feel it.
3 (noun) A display is an arrangement of things designed to attract people's attention.
4 A display by an animal or bird is behaviour designed to attract attention to itself.
[from Latin *displicare* meaning 'to unfold']

displease, displeases, displeasing, displeased
(verb) If someone or something displeases you, they make you annoyed, dissatisfied, or offended.
displeasing (adjective), **displeasure** (noun).

disposable
1 (adjective) designed to be thrown away after use, e.g. *disposable nappies.*
2 Disposable income is the amount of money left from someone's wage or salary after taxes have been deducted from it.

disposal
1 (noun) Disposal is the act of getting rid of something that is no longer wanted or needed.

2 (phrase) If you have something **at your disposal**, you can make use of it in whatever way you want.

dispose, disposes, disposing, disposed
1 (verb) To dispose of something means to get rid of it.
2 To dispose of a problem or question means to deal with it.
3 If you are not disposed to do something, you are not willing to do it.
4 If you are well disposed to someone, you like them and will oblige and help them if you can.
5 (a formal use) If things are disposed in a particular way, they are arranged in that way.
[from Latin *disponere* meaning 'to arrange']

disposition, dispositions
1 (noun; a formal word) Someone's disposition is their way of behaving and thinking, e.g. *a cheerful disposition.*
2 A disposition to do something is a tendency to do it, e.g. *She had a disposition to giggle.*
3 The disposition of something is the way it has been arranged.

dispossess, dispossesses, dispossessing, dispossessed
(verb) If you are dispossessed of something such as land or a building, it is taken away from you.

disproportionate
(adjective) Something that is disproportionate is out of proportion, being either too large or too small when compared with something else.
disproportionately (adverb).

disprove, disproves, disproving, disproved
(verb) If someone disproves an idea, belief, or theory, they show that it is not true.

dispute, disputes, disputing, disputed
1 (noun) A dispute is an argument.
2 (verb) To dispute a fact or theory means to question the truth of it.
3 When people dispute, they argue.

disqualify, disqualifies, disqualifying, disqualified
1 (verb) If someone is disqualified, their right to take part in a competition or activity is removed, e.g. *He was disqualified from driving for one year.*
2 If something disqualifies someone from taking part in an activity, it makes them unfit or unable to take part, e.g. *His inside knowledge disqualified him from the competition.*
disqualification (noun).

disquiet, disquiets, disquieting, disquieted
1 (noun) Disquiet is worry or anxiety.
2 (verb) If something disquiets you, it makes you feel anxious.
disquieting (adjective).

disregard, disregards, disregarding, disregarded
1 (verb) To disregard something means to pay little or no attention to it.
2 (noun) Disregard is a lack of attention or respect for something, e.g. *his disregard of the rules.*

disrepair
(phrase) If something is **in disrepair** or **in a state of disrepair**, it is broken or in poor condition.

disreputable
(adjective) not respectable or trustworthy.
disreputably (adverb), **disrepute** (noun).

disrespect
(noun) Disrespect is contempt or lack of respect, e.g. *They showed disrespect for the law.*
disrespectful (adjective), **disrespectfully** (adverb).

disrupt, disrupts, disrupting, disrupted
(verb) To disrupt something such as an event or system means to break it up or throw it into confusion, e.g. *The boys disrupted the new teacher's class.*
disruption (noun), **disruptive** (adjective).
[from Latin *dirumpere* meaning 'to smash to pieces']

dissatisfied
(adjective) not pleased or not contented.
dissatisfaction (noun).

dissect, dissects, dissecting, dissected
1 (verb) To dissect a plant or a dead body means to cut it up so that it can be scientifically examined.
2 To dissect a theory or piece of writing means to examine it carefully so that it can be better understood or its faults discovered.
dissection (noun).
[from Latin *dis-* meaning 'apart' and *secare* meaning 'to cut']

dissemble, dissembles, dissembling, dissembled
(verb) If someone dissembles, they hide their real thoughts and feelings.

disseminate, disseminates, disseminating, disseminated
(verb) To disseminate information means to spread it widely, e.g. *The news agency quickly disseminated the latest information on the crisis.*
dissemination (noun).

dissension, dissensions
(noun) Dissension is disagreement and argument.

dissent, dissents, dissenting, dissented
1 (noun) Dissent is strong difference of opinion, e.g. *The leader would tolerate no dissent from the members.*
2 (verb) When people dissent, they express a difference of opinion about something.
3 To dissent means to disagree with established rules or beliefs, especially of a Church.
dissenter (noun), **dissenting** (adjective).

dissertation, dissertations
1 (noun) A dissertation is a long essay, often one done as part of a degree or other qualification.
2 A dissertation is also a long formal speech.
[from Latin *dissertare* meaning 'to debate']

disservice
(noun) To do someone a disservice means to do something that harms them, especially when trying to help them.

dissident, dissidents
(noun) A dissident is someone who disagrees with and criticizes their government, especially when this is a dangerous thing to do.
dissidence (noun).
[from Latin *dis-* meaning 'apart' and *sedere* meaning 'to sit']

dissimilar
(adjective) If things are dissimilar, they are unlike each other.
dissimilarity (noun).

dissipate, dissipates, dissipating, dissipated
1 (verb; a formal word) When something dissipates or is dissipated, it completely disappears, e.g. *The fog dissipated in the sun.*
2 If someone dissipates time, money, or effort, they waste it.
dissipation (noun).

dissipated
(adjective) Someone who is dissipated overindulges in alcohol or other physical pleasures, e.g. *He led a dissipated life at college.*

dissociate, dissociates, dissociating, dissociated
1 (verb) If you dissociate yourself from something or someone, you show that you are not connected with or responsible for them.
2 To dissociate something from something else means to treat them as separate or unconnected, e.g. *I can't dissociate her from what she did.*
dissociation (noun).

dissolute
(adjective) Someone who is dissolute lives in a way that is considered immoral.
[from Latin *dissolutus* meaning 'loose']

dissolution
1 (noun) Dissolution is the act of officially breaking up an organization.
2 Dissolution is also the formal ending of a meeting or assembly, such as Parliament.
3 The dissolution of a formal agreement, such as a marriage, is the official end of it.
4 In chemistry, dissolution is the way in which something becomes weaker and then disappears.

dissolve, dissolves, dissolving, dissolved
1 (verb) If you dissolve something or if it dissolves in a liquid, it becomes mixed with and absorbed in the liquid.
2 To dissolve an organization or institution means to officially end it or break it up.
3 If something dissolves, it gradually disappears.
4 When scenes of a film dissolve, one is made to merge into the other.
5 If you dissolve into something such as tears or laughter, you cannot stop yourself from crying or laughing.
[from Latin *dis-* meaning 'apart' and *solvere* meaning 'to release' or 'to loosen']

dissonance
(noun) Dissonance is a lack of harmony between things such as colours or sounds.
dissonant (adjective).
[from Latin *dis-* meaning 'apart' and *sonare* meaning 'to sound']

dissuade, dissuades, dissuading, dissuaded
(pronounced dis-**wade**)

(verb) To dissuade someone from doing something or from believing something means to persuade them not to do it or not to believe it.

distance, distances, distancing, distanced
1 (noun) The distance between two points is how far it is between them.
2 Distance is the fact of being far away in space or time.
3 Distance is a reserve or aloofness in the way someone behaves.
4 (verb) If you distance yourself from someone or something or are distanced from them, you become less involved with them.

distant
1 (adjective) far away in space or time.
2 A distant relative is one who is not closely related to you.
3 Someone who is distant is cold and unfriendly.
distantly (adverb).
[from Latin *dis-* meaning 'apart' and *stare* meaning 'to stand']

Similar words: (sense 3) aloof, standoffish, unapproachable, withdrawn

distaste
(noun) Distaste is a dislike of something which you find offensive.

distasteful
(adjective) If you find something distasteful, you think it is unpleasant or offensive.

Similar words: displeasing, unpalatable, offensive

distemper
1 (noun) Distemper is a paint which dissolves in water and is used for decorating.
2 Distemper is also a dangerous and infectious disease which can affect young dogs.
[Sense 2 is from Latin *distemperare* meaning 'to disrupt the health']

distend, distends, distending, distended
(verb; a formal or medical word) If a part of a body distends, or if something distends it, it swells and becomes unnaturally large because of pressure from inside.
distended (adjective), **distension** (noun).
[from Latin *distendere* meaning 'to stretch apart']

distil, distils, distilling, distilled
(verb) When a liquid is distilled, it is heated until it evaporates and then cooled to enable purified liquid to be collected.
distillation (noun).
[from Latin *de-* meaning 'down' and *stillare* meaning 'to drip']

distillery, distilleries
(noun) A distillery is a place where whisky or other strong alcoholic drink is made, using a process of distillation.

distinct
1 (adjective) If one thing is distinct from another, it is recognizably different from it, e.g. *This word has three distinct meanings.*
2 If something is distinct, you can hear, smell, or

see it clearly and plainly, e.g. *There was a distinct smell of strawberries.*
3 If something such as a fact, idea, or intention is distinct, it is clear and definite, e.g. *There is a distinct possibility of rain.*
distinctly (adverb), **distinctness** (noun).
[from Latin *distinguere* meaning 'to distinguish' or 'to separate']

distinction, distinctions
1 (noun) A distinction is a difference between two things, e.g. *The distinction between an amateur and a professional is not always clear.*
2 Distinction is a quality of excellence and superiority, e.g. *a man of distinction.*
3 A distinction is also a special honour or favour, e.g. *I had the distinction of being invited to the opening night.*
4 A distinction is the highest level of achievement in an examination.

distinctive
(adjective) Something that is distinctive has a special quality which makes it recognizable, e.g. *a distinctive voice.*
distinctively (adverb), **distinctiveness** (noun).

distinguish, distinguishes, distinguishing, distinguished
1 (verb) To distinguish between things means to recognize the difference between them, e.g. *The child could not distinguish the letters 'p' and 'b'.*
2 To distinguish something means to make it out by seeing, hearing, or tasting it, e.g. *Few details could be distinguished in the photograph.*
3 If you distinguish yourself, you do something that makes people think highly of you.
distinguishable (adjective), **distinguishing** (adjective).
[from Latin *distinguere* meaning 'to separate' or 'to discriminate']

distinguished
1 (adjective) dignified in appearance or behaviour.
2 having a very high reputation e.g. *He was a distinguished professor.*

distort, distorts, distorting, distorted
1 (verb) If you distort a statement or an argument, you change it so as to give a wrong emphasis or interpretation to it.
2 If something is distorted, it is changed so that it seems strange or unclear, e.g. *His voice was distorted by the telephone.*
3 If an object is distorted, it is twisted or pulled out of shape.
distorted (adjective), **distortion** (noun).
[from Latin *dis-* meaning 'apart' and *torquere* meaning 'to twist']

distract, distracts, distracting, distracted
(verb) If something distracts you, your attention is taken away from what you are doing, e.g. *It distracted them from their work.*
distracted (adjective), **distractedly** (adverb), **distracting** (adjective).
[from Latin *dis-* meaning 'apart' and *trahere* meaning 'to drag']

Similar words: divert, side-track

distraction, distractions

1 (noun) A distraction is something that takes people's attention away from something.
2 A distraction is also an activity that is intended to amuse or relax someone.
3 (phrase) If someone or something **drives you to distraction**, it makes you very angry or distressed.

distraught

(adjective) so upset and worried that you cannot think clearly, e.g. *He was distraught at the news of the accident.*

distress, distresses, distressing, distressed

1 (noun) Distress is great suffering caused by pain, sorrow, or hardship.
2 Distress is also the state of needing help because of difficulties or danger.
3 (verb) To distress someone means to make them feel alarmed or unhappy, e.g. *I didn't mean to distress you by my question.*
[from Latin *districtus* meaning literally 'divided in mind']

Similar words: (sense 3) upset, harrow

distressing
(adjective) very worrying or upsetting.
distressingly (adverb).

Similar words: upsetting, harrowing, heart-rending

distribute, distributes, distributing, distributed

1 (verb) To distribute something such as leaflets means to hand them out or deliver them, e.g. *I'll get copies and distribute them to the staff.*
2 If things are distributed, they are spread throughout an area or space, e.g. *Gulls are distributed along the cliffs.*
3 To distribute something means to divide it and share it out among a number of people.
distributive (adjective).

Similar words: (sense 3) dispense, dole out, share out

distribution, distributions

1 (noun) Distribution is the delivering of something to various people or organizations, e.g. *the distribution of election addresses.*
2 Distribution is the sharing out of something, e.g. *distribution of wealth.*

distributor, distributors

1 (noun) A distributor is a person or company that supplies goods to other businesses who then sell them to the public.
2 In an internal-combustion engine, the distributor is the part that sends electric current to each spark plug in turn.

district, districts

(noun) A district is an area which has special or recognizable features, e.g. *a working-class district.*

district nurse, district nurses

(noun) A district nurse is a nurse employed by a Health Authority to visit and treat people in their own homes.

distrust, distrusts, distrusting, distrusted

1 (verb) If you distrust someone, you are suspicious of them because you are not sure whether they are honest.
2 (noun) Distrust is suspicion.
distrustful (adjective), **distrustfully** (adverb).

disturb, disturbs, disturbing, disturbed

1 (verb) If you disturb someone, you break their rest, peace, or privacy.
2 If something disturbs you, it makes you feel upset or worried.
3 If something is disturbed, it is moved out of position or meddled with.
disturbing (adjective).
[from Latin *disturbare* meaning 'to drive apart']

Similar words: (sense 2) agitate, fluster, unsettle, disconcert, ruffle

disturbance, disturbances

1 (noun) Disturbance is the state of being disturbed.
2 A disturbance is a violent or unruly incident in public.

disturbed

(adjective) Someone who is disturbed is so emotionally upset that they need special care or medical treatment.

disunity

(noun) Disunity is a lack of agreement among people which prevents them from working closely together.

disuse

(noun) Something that has fallen into disuse is neglected or no longer used.
disused (adjective).

ditch, ditches, ditching, ditched

1 (noun) A ditch is a channel at the side of a road or field, usually to drain away excess water.
2 (verb; an informal use) To ditch something means to get rid of it.
3 If an aircraft ditches in the sea, it makes an emergency landing.
[from Old English *dic* meaning 'dyke' or 'embankment']

dither, dithers, dithering, dithered

(verb) To dither means to be unsure and hesitant.

ditto

Ditto means 'the same'. In written lists, ditto is represented by a mark („) to avoid repetition.
[from Italian *detto* meaning 'said']

ditty, ditties

(noun; an old-fashioned word) A ditty is a short simple song or poem.
[from Old French *ditier* meaning 'to compose']

diuretic (pronounced dy-yoo-**ret**-ik)

(adjective) A diuretic drug is one that acts on the body to increase the flow of urine.

divan, divans

(noun) A divan is a low bed, or a couch without a back or arms.

dive, dives, diving, dived

1 (verb) To dive means to jump headfirst into water with your arms held straight above your head.

2 If you go diving, you go down under the surface of the sea or a lake using special breathing equipment.
3 If an aircraft or bird dives, it flies in a steep downward path, or drops sharply.
4 If you dive in a particular direction, you rush or leap in that direction.
diver (noun), **diving** (noun).

Similar words: (sense 3) plunge, plummet

diverge, diverges, diverging, diverged
1 (verb) If opinions or facts diverge, they differ, e.g. *Our views diverge on many political issues.*
2 If something diverges from the truth or from a course of action, it moves away from it.
3 If two things such as roads or paths which have been going in the same direction diverge, they separate and go off in different directions.
divergence (noun), **divergent** (adjective).
[from Latin *di-* meaning 'apart' and *vergere* meaning 'to bend']

diverse
1 (adjective) If a group of things is diverse, it is made up of different kinds of things, e.g. *the most diverse group of all animals, the insects.*
2 People, ideas, or objects that are diverse are very different from each other.
diversely (adverb), **diversity** (noun).
[from Latin *diversus* meaning 'contrary' or 'different']

diversify, diversifies, diversifying, diversified
(verb) To diversify means to increase the variety of something, e.g. *They wanted to diversify the company's products.*
diversification (noun).

diversion, diversions
1 (noun) A diversion is a special route arranged for traffic when the usual route is closed.
2 A diversion is something that takes your attention away from what you should be concentrating on, e.g. *A break for tea created a welcome diversion.*
3 A diversion is also a pleasant or amusing pastime or activity.
diversionary (adjective).

divert, diverts, diverting, diverted
1 (verb) To divert something means to change the course or direction it is following.
2 If something diverts you, it entertains or amuses you.
diverting (adjective).
[from Latin *di-* meaning 'apart' and *vertere* meaning 'to turn']

divest, divests, divesting, divested
1 (verb) If you divest yourself of a piece of clothing, you take it off, e.g. *She divested herself of her coat.*
2 To divest someone of something means to deprive them of it or take it away from them.
[from Latin *dis-* meaning 'apart' and *vestis* meaning 'a garment']

divide, divides, dividing, divided
1 (verb) When something divides or is divided, it is split up and separated into two or more parts.

2 If something divides two areas, it forms a barrier between them, e.g. *The Rio Grande divides Mexico from the USA.*
3 If people divide over something or if something divides them, it causes strong disagreement between them.
4 In mathematics, when you divide, you calculate how many times one number contains another.
5 (noun) A divide is a separation, e.g. *the North-South divide.*
divisible (adjective).

dividend, dividends
(noun) A dividend is a portion of a company's profits that is paid to shareholders.
[from Latin *dividendum* meaning 'what is to be divided']

divider, dividers
1 (noun) A divider is a barrier between people or areas of space, e.g. *a room divider.*
2 (plural noun) Dividers are an instrument with two pointed arms, used for measuring distances on paper.

divination
(noun) Divination is the foretelling of the future as though by supernatural power.

divine, divines, divining, divined
1 (adjective) having the qualities of a god or goddess.
2 (verb) To divine something means to discover it by guessing.
divinely (adverb), **diviner** (noun).
[Sense 1 is from Latin *divus* meaning 'god'; sense 2 is from Latin *divinare* meaning 'to foretell']

divinity, divinities
1 (noun) Divinity is the study of religion.
2 Divinity is the state of being a god, e.g. *The divinity of the Pharaoh was never doubted by the ancient Egyptians.*
3 A divinity is a god or goddess.

division, divisions
1 (noun) Division is the separation of something into two or more distinct parts.
2 Division is also the process of dividing one number by another.
3 A division is a difference of opinion that causes separation between ideas or groups of people, e.g. *There are considerable divisions in the Party.*
4 A division is also any one of the parts into which something is split, e.g. *The camera bag had divisions for each different lens.*
divisional (adjective), **divisible** (adjective).

divisive
(adjective) causing hostility between people so that they split into different groups, e.g. *A two-tier health service would be divisive.*
divisiveness (noun).

divisor, divisors
(noun) A divisor is a number by which another number is divided.

divorce, divorces, divorcing, divorced
1 (noun) Divorce is the formal and legal ending of a marriage.
2 (verb) When a married couple divorce, their marriage is legally ended.
divorced (adjective), **divorcee** (noun).
[from Latin *divertere* meaning 'to separate']

divulge, divulges, divulging, divulged
(verb) To divulge information means to reveal it.
[from Latin *divulgare* meaning 'to make public']

D.I.Y.
(noun) D.I.Y. is the activity of making or repairing things yourself, instead of buying things ready-made or paying someone else to do the work for you. D.I.Y. is an abbreviation for 'do-it-yourself'.

dizzy, dizzier, dizziest
(adjective) having or causing a whirling sensation.
dizzily (adverb), **dizziness** (noun).
[from Old English *dysig* meaning 'silly']

Similar words: giddy, light-headed, dazed

D.J., D.J.'s
(noun) A D.J. is a disc jockey.

DNA
(noun) DNA is deoxyribonucleic acid, a substance found in the cells of all living things. It determines the structure of every cell and is responsible for characteristics being passed on from parents to their children.

do, does, doing, did, done; dos
1 (verb) Do is an auxiliary verb, which is used to form questions, negatives, and to give emphasis to the main verb of a sentence.
2 If someone does a task, chore, or activity, they perform it and finish it, e.g. *We did a lot of work.*
3 If you ask what people do, you want to know what their job is, e.g. *What will you do when you leave school?*
4 If you do well at something, you are successful. If you do badly, you are unsuccessful.
5 If you do a subject, you study it.
6 If something will do, it is good enough in quality or quantity, e.g. *This pan will do.*
7 (noun; an informal use) A do is a party or other social event.

Similar words: (sense 2) carry out, effect, execute

do away with
(phrasal verb) To do away with something means to get rid of it.

do up
1 (phrasal verb) To do something up means to fasten it.
2 To do up something old means to repair and decorate it.

docile
(adjective) quiet, calm, and easily controlled.
docilely (adverb), **docility** (noun).
[from Latin *docilis* meaning 'easily taught']

dock, docks, docking, docked
1 (noun) A dock is an enclosed area in a harbour where ships go to be loaded, unloaded, or repaired.
2 (verb) When a ship docks, it is brought into dock at the end of its voyage.
3 If two spacecraft dock, they join together in space.
4 To dock someone's wages means to deduct an amount from the sum they would normally receive.
5 To dock an animal's tail means to cut part of it off.
6 (noun) In a court of law, the dock is the place where the accused person stands or sits.
7 A dock is a weed with broad leaves and a long root.
docker (noun).

docket, dockets, docketing, docketed
1 (noun) A docket is a label on a package or delivery which lists the contents and delivery instructions. It may also act as a receipt.
2 (verb) To docket a parcel or cargo means to fix a docket to it.

doctor, doctors, doctoring, doctored
1 (noun) A doctor is a person who is qualified in medicine and treats people who are ill.
2 A doctor of an academic subject is someone who has been awarded the highest academic degree, e.g. *He is a doctor of philosophy.*
3 (verb) To doctor something means to alter it in order to deceive people, e.g. *He doctored the figures in order to hide the mistake.*
4 To doctor an animal, especially a dog or cat, means to castrate or sterilize it.
[from Latin *doctor* meaning 'teacher']

doctorate
(noun) A doctorate is the highest university degree in any field of knowledge.
doctoral (adjective).

doctrinaire
(adjective) Someone who is doctrinaire stubbornly insists on using certain theories or ideas without considering whether they are practical.

doctrine, doctrines
(noun) A doctrine is a set of beliefs or principles held by a group.
doctrinal (adjective), **doctrinally** (adverb).
[from Latin *doctrina* meaning 'teachings']

document, documents, documenting, documented
1 (noun) A document is a piece of paper which provides an official record of something.
2 (verb) If you document something, you make a detailed record of it.
documentation (noun).
[from Latin *documentum* meaning 'lesson']

documentary, documentaries
1 (noun) A documentary is a radio or television programme, or a film, which provides information on a particular subject.
2 (adjective) Documentary evidence is made up of written or official records.

dodder, dodders, doddering, doddered
(verb) To dodder means to walk unsteadily or shakily because of old age.
doddery (adjective).

dodge, dodges, dodging, dodged
1 (verb) If you dodge or dodge something, you move suddenly to avoid being seen, hit, or caught.
2 If you dodge something such as an issue or accusation, you avoid dealing with it.
3 (noun) A dodge is a cunning trick.
dodger (noun).

dodgy
(adjective; an informal word) rather risky or unreliable, e.g. *This car's got a dodgy exhaust.*

dodo, dodos
(verb) A dodo was a large, flightless bird that lived in Mauritius and became extinct in the late seventeenth century.

doe, does
(noun) A doe is a female deer, rabbit, or hare.

does the third person singular of the present tense of **do.**

doff, doffs, doffing, doffed
(verb; an old-fashioned word) If someone doffs their hat or coat, they take it off.
[from Old English *don off* meaning 'to take off']

dog, dogs, dogging, dogged
1 (noun) A dog is a four-legged, meat-eating animal, kept as a pet or to guard or hunt things.
2 (verb) If you dog someone, you follow them very closely and never leave them.

dog collar, dog collars
(noun; an informal word) A dog collar is a white collar with no front opening worn by Christian clergy.

dog-eared
(adjective) A book that is dog-eared has been used so much that the corners of the pages are turned down or worn.

dogfight, dogfights
(noun) A dogfight is a fight between fighter planes flying very close to each other.

dogged (pronounced **dog**-ged)
(adjective) showing determination to continue with something, even if it is very difficult, e.g. *his dogged refusal to admit defeat.*
doggedly (adverb), **doggedness** (noun).

doggerel
(noun) Doggerel is funny or silly verse, often written quickly and not intended to be serious.
[from Middle English *dogerel* meaning 'worthless']

doggo
(an informal phrase) If you **lie doggo,** you keep still and hidden so that people cannot find you.

dogma, dogmas
(noun) A dogma is a belief or system of beliefs held by a religious or political group.
[from Greek *dogma* meaning 'opinion' or 'belief']

dogmatic
(adjective) Someone who is dogmatic about

something is convinced that they are right about it and will not consider other points of view.
dogmatically (adverb), **dogmatism** (noun).

dogsbody, dogsbodies
(noun) A dogsbody is someone who has to do all the unpleasant or boring jobs that no one else wants to do.

doily, doilies
(noun) A doily is a small decorative mat made from paper or lace. It is named after Doiley, an 18th century London draper.

dolby
(noun; a trademark) Dolby is a system used in recording sound which reduces unwanted noise. It is named after R. Dolby, its inventor.

doldrums
1 (plural noun) The doldrums is a region on either side of the equator where light winds and calm seas are common.
2 (an informal phrase) If you are **in the doldrums,** you are depressed or bored.

dole, doles, doling, doled
1 (noun) The dole is money given regularly by the government to people who are unemployed.
2 (verb) If you dole something out, you give a certain amount of it to each individual in a group.
[from Old English *dal* meaning 'share']

doleful
(adjective) miserable and depressed, e.g. *the music added to the doleful mood.*
dolefully (adverb), **dolefulness** (noun).
[from Latin *dolere* meaning 'to lament']

doll, dolls, dolling, dolled
1 (noun) A doll is a child's toy which looks like a baby or person.
2 (verb; an informal use) When a woman dolls herself up, she dresses up smartly.

dollar, dollars
(noun) The dollar is the main unit of currency in the USA, Canada, Australia, and some other countries. A dollar is worth 100 cents.

dollop, dollops
(noun) A dollop of food is an amount of it served casually in a lump.

dolly, dollies
(noun) A dolly is a doll.

dolomite
(noun) Dolomite is a type of limestone. It is named after Déodat de Dolomieu, a French mineralogist.

dolorous
(adjective; a literary word) sad or mournful.
dolorously (adverb), **dolour** (noun).

dolphin, dolphins
(noun) A dolphin is a mammal which lives in the sea and looks like a large fish with a long pointed snout.

dolt, dolts
(noun) Dolt is a name for a stupid person.

domain, domains
1 (noun) A domain is a particular area of activity

or interest, e.g. *This question comes into the domain of philosophy.*
2 A domain is also an area over which someone has control or influence, e.g. *His domain extended to New York.*

dome, domes
(noun) A dome is a round roof.
domed (adjective).
[from Latin *domus* meaning 'house']

domestic, domestics
1 (adjective) happening or existing within one particular country, e.g. *world and domestic news.*
2 involving or concerned with the home and family, e.g. *domestic chores.*
3 Domestic animals are not wild, but are tamed and kept for work, as pets, or for food.
[from Latin *domus* meaning 'house']

domesticate, domesticates, domesticating, domesticated
1 (verb) To domesticate wild animals means to bring them under control and use them for work, as pets, or for food.
2 If you domesticate someone, you get them used to helping with the tasks that need to be done around the house.
domesticated (adjective), **domestication** (noun).

domesticity
(noun; a formal word) Domesticity is life at home with your family.

domicile, domiciles
(noun; a legal or formal word) Your domicile is the place where you live.
domiciled (adjective), **domiciliary** (adjective).

dominance
1 (noun) Dominance is power or control.
2 If something has dominance over other similar things, it is more powerful, important, or noticeable than they are, e.g. *the dominance of economics in the social sciences.*
dominant (adjective).

dominate, dominates, dominating, dominated
1 (verb) If something or someone dominates a situation or event, they are the most powerful or important thing in it and have control over it, e.g. *These issues dominated the election.*
2 If a person or country dominates other people or places, they have power or control over them.
3 If something dominates an area, it towers over it, e.g. *The valley was dominated by the huge Benedictine abbey.*
dominating (adjective), **domination** (noun).
[from Latin *dominari* meaning 'to be lord over']

domineering
(adjective) Someone who is domineering tries to control other people, e.g. *domineering husbands.*

dominion, dominions
1 (noun) Dominion is control or authority that a person or a country has over other people, e.g. *They had dominion over a large part of India.*
2 A Dominion was one of the self-governing countries in the British Commonwealth.

domino, dominoes
(noun) Dominoes are small rectangular blocks marked with two groups of spots on one side, used for playing the game called dominoes.

don, dons, donning, donned
1 (noun) A don is a lecturer at a university, especially Oxford or Cambridge.
2 (verb; a literary use) If you don clothing, you put it on.

donate, donates, donating, donated
(verb) To donate something to a charity or organization means to give it as a gift.
donation (noun).
[from Latin *donare* meaning 'to give']

done the past participle of **do.**

donkey, donkeys
1 (noun) A donkey is an animal related to the horse, but smaller and with longer ears.
2 (an informal phrase) **Donkey's years** means a very long time, e.g. *I haven't seen her for donkeys years.*

donkey jacket, donkey jackets
(noun) A donkey jacket is a jacket made of thick warm navy-blue material with a waterproof panel along the shoulders.

donkey work
(noun) Donkey work is hard work which is not very interesting.

donor, donors
1 (noun) A donor is someone who gives their blood while they are alive or an organ after their death to be used for medical purposes, e.g. *a kidney donor.*
2 A donor is also someone who gives something such as money to a charity or other organization.
[from Latin *donare* meaning 'to give']

doodle, doodles, doodling, doodled
1 (noun) A doodle is a pattern or a drawing done when you are thinking about something else or when you are bored.
2 (verb) To doodle means to draw doodles.

doom
(noun) Doom is a terrible fate or event in the future which you can do nothing to prevent.

doomed
(adjective) If someone or something is doomed to an unpleasant or unhappy experience, they are certain to suffer it, e.g. *doomed to failure.*

doomsday
(noun) Doomsday is the end of the world.

door, doors
1 (noun) A door is a swinging or sliding panel for opening or closing the entrance to a building, room, or cupboard; also the entrance itself.
2 (phrase) If you **lay something at someone's door**, you blame them for it.

door-to-door
(adjective) Door-to-door activities involve going from one house to another along a street, often in order to try to sell something.

doorway, doorways
(noun) A doorway is an opening in a wall for a door.

dope, dopes, doping, doped
1 (noun) Dope is an illegal drug.
2 (verb) If someone dopes you, they put a drug into your food or drink.
3 (noun; an informal use) Dope is information or facts, e.g. *Give me the dope on the latest offer.*
[from Dutch *doop* meaning 'sauce']

dopey
1 (adjective; an informal word) sleepy, especially from taking drugs or alcohol.
2 Dopey also means silly or stupid.

dormant
1 (adjective) Something that is dormant is not active, growing, or being used, e.g. *The idea had lain dormant during the fifties.*
2 If a volcano is dormant, it is neither extinct nor erupting, but may possibly erupt in the future.
dormancy (noun).
[from Latin *dormire* meaning 'to sleep']

dormer, dormers
(noun) A dormer is a window that is built upright in a sloping roof.

dormitory, dormitories
1 (noun) A dormitory is a large bedroom where several people sleep.
2 (adjective) A dormitory town or dormitory suburb is one from which many of the residents travel to work in a nearby city or larger town.
[from Latin *dormire* meaning 'to sleep']

dormouse, dormice
(noun) A dormouse is a mouselike rodent with a furry tail which sleeps for several months a year.

dorsal
(adjective; a technical word) relating to the back of a fish or animal, e.g. *a dorsal fin.*

dosage, dosages
(noun) The dosage of a medicine or a drug is the amount of it that should be taken.

dose, doses, dosing, dosed
1 (noun) A dose of a medicine or drug is a measured amount of it.
2 A dose of something is an amount of it which you get whether you want it or not, e.g. *We got large doses of nationalism in the newspapers.*
3 (verb) If you dose someone, you give them a dose of medicine.
[from Greek *dosis* meaning 'giving' or 'gift']

doss, dosses, dossing, dossed
(verb; an informal word) If you doss or doss down somewhere, you sleep there.
dosser (noun).

dosshouse, dosshouses
(noun; an informal word) A dosshouse is a cheap lodging house.

dossier, dossiers (pronounced **doss**-ee-ay)
(noun) A dossier is a collection of papers containing information on a particular subject or person.
[from French *dossier* meaning 'file with a label on the back']

dot, dots, dotting, dotted
1 (noun) A dot is a very small, round mark.
2 (verb) If things dot an area, they are scattered all over it, e.g. *Fishing villages dot the coast.*
3 (phrase) If you arrive somewhere **on the dot**, you arrive there at exactly the right time.
[from Old English *dott* meaning 'head of a boil']

dotage (pronounced **doe**-tage)
(noun) If someone is in their dotage, they are very old and usually feeble-minded.

dote, dotes, doting, doted
(verb) If you dote on someone, you love them very much.
doting (adjective).
[from Old Dutch *doten* meaning 'to be silly']

dotty, dottier, dottiest
(adjective; an informal word) slightly mad.

double, doubles, doubling, doubled
1 (adjective) twice the usual size, e.g. *a double portion of chips.*
2 consisting of two parts, e.g. *double doors.*
3 (verb) If something doubles, it becomes twice as large.
4 To double as something means to have a second job or use as well as the main one, e.g. *The bedroom doubles as a study.*
5 (noun) Your double is someone who looks exactly like you.
6 Doubles is a game of tennis or badminton which two people play against two other people.
doubly (adverb).

double back
(phrasal verb) If you double back, you turn and go back in the direction you came from.

double up
(phrasal verb) If you double up with pain or laughter, you bend your body right over.

double agent, double agents
(noun) A double agent is someone who is a spy for two enemy countries at the same time.

double bass, double basses
(noun) The double bass is the largest instrument in the violin family.

double-cross, double-crosses, double-crossing, double-crossed
(verb) If someone double-crosses you, they cheat you by pretending they are doing what you had planned together, when in fact they are doing the opposite.

double-decker, double-deckers
1 (adjective) having two tiers or layers.
2 (noun) A double-decker is a bus with two floors.

double-edged
1 (adjective) having two cutting edges.
2 A double-edged comment can be understood in two ways.

double entendre, double entendres
(pronounced on-**ton**-dra)
(noun) A double entendre is a word or phrase that has two meanings, one of which is usually impolite or sexual.

double glazing
(noun) Double glazing is a second layer of glass fitted to windows to keep the building quieter or warmer.

double-jointed
(adjective) having flexible joints so that one's fingers or limbs bend easily both backwards and forwards.

doubt, doubts, doubting, doubted
1 (noun) Doubt is a feeling of uncertainty about whether something is true or possible.
2 (verb) If you doubt something, you think that it is probably not true or possible.
doubter (noun).
[from Latin *dubitare* meaning 'to hesitate']

Similar words: (sense 1) uncertainty, misgiving, qualm, dubiety, reservation

doubtful
1 (adjective) unlikely or uncertain.
2 If you are doubtful about something, you are unsure about it.
doubtfully (adverb).

doubtless
(adverb) Doubtless means probably or almost certainly, e.g. *Many species are known and doubtless more are still to be discovered.*
doubtlessly (adverb).

dough
1 (noun) Dough is a mixture of flour and water and sometimes other ingredients, used to make bread, pastry, or biscuits.
2 (an informal use) Dough is money.
doughy (adjective).

doughnut, doughnuts
(noun) A doughnut is a piece of sweet dough cooked in hot fat and usually covered with sugar.

dour (rhymes with poor)
(adjective) severe and unfriendly, e.g. *She faced me with her usual dour expression.*
dourly (adverb).

douse, douses, dousing, doused; also spelled dowse
(verb) If you douse a fire, you stop it burning by throwing water over it.

dove, doves
(noun) A dove is a bird like a small pigeon.

dovecote, dovecotes; also spelled dovecot
(noun) A dovecote is a shelter for doves.

dovetail, dovetails, dovetailing, dovetailed
1 (verb) If two things dovetail together, they fit together closely or neatly.
2 (adjective) A dovetail joint is a wedge-shaped joint used in carpentry for fitting two pieces of wood tightly together.

dowager, dowagers
1 (noun) A dowager is a grand-looking old lady.
2 A dowager is also a woman who has inherited a title from her dead husband, e.g. *the dowager Duchess.*

dowdy, dowdier, dowdiest
(adjective) wearing dull and unfashionable clothes.
dowdily (adverb), **dowdiness** (noun).

dowel, dowels
(noun) A dowel is a short, thin piece of wood or metal which is fitted into holes in larger pieces of wood or metal to join them together.
[from German *Dövel* meaning 'plug']

down, downs, downing, downed
1 (preposition and adverb) Down means towards the ground, towards a lower level, or in a lower place.
2 (adverb) If you put something down, you place it on a surface.
3 (preposition and adverb) If you go down a road or river, you go along it.
4 (adverb) If an amount of something goes down, it decreases.
5 If you feel down, you feel depressed.
6 (verb) If you down a drink, you drink it quickly.
7 (noun) Down is the small, soft feathers on young birds.
8 Down is also soft, fine hair.
9 (phrase) If someone **has a down on something or someone**, they feel hostile towards them.

down at heel
(adjective) shabby and in poor condition.

downcast
1 (adjective) feeling sad and dejected.
2 If your eyes are downcast, you are looking towards the ground.

downfall
1 (noun) The downfall of a successful or powerful person or institution is their failure.
2 Something that is someone's downfall is the thing that causes their failure, e.g. *Drink was his downfall.*

downgrade, downgrades, downgrading, downgraded
(verb) If you downgrade something, you give it less importance or make it less valuable.

downhearted
(adjective) feeling sad and discouraged.

downhill
1 (adverb) moving down a slope.
2 becoming worse, e.g. *Journalism is going downhill nowadays.*

down payment, down payments
(noun) A down payment is a sum of money paid as a deposit when you buy something. The remaining amount is paid later.

downpour, downpours
(noun) A downpour is a heavy fall of rain.

Similar words: deluge, cloudburst

downright
(adjective and adverb) You use downright to emphasize that something is extremely unpleasant or bad, e.g. *That's a downright lie.*

Down's syndrome
(noun) Down's Syndrome is a medical condition

caused by abnormal chromosomes, in which a baby is born with subnormal intelligence and develops a flattish face and sloping eyes. Down's syndrome is named after John Langdon-Down, a 19th century English physician.

downstairs
1 (adverb) going down a staircase towards the ground floor, e.g. *She ran downstairs.*
2 (adjective and adverb) on a lower floor or on the ground floor.

downstream
(adjective and adverb) Something that is downstream or moving downstream is nearer or moving nearer to the mouth of a river from a point further up.

down-to-earth
(adjective) sensible and practical, e.g. *his warm, down-to-earth manner.*

downtrodden
(adjective) People who are downtrodden are treated badly by those with power and do not have the energy or ability to fight back.

downturn, downturns
(noun) A downturn is a decline in the economy or in the success of a company or industry.

downwards or downward
1 (adverb and adjective) If you move or look downwards, you move or look towards the ground or towards a lower level, e.g. *It glided gently downwards... a downward glance.*
2 If an amount or rate moves downwards, it decreases.

downwind
(adverb) If something moves downwind, it moves in the same direction as the wind, e.g. *Sparks drifted downwind.*

downy, downier, downiest
1 (adjective) filled or covered with small, soft feathers, e.g. *downy feather beds.*
2 covered with fine, soft hairs, e.g. *the downy head of the sleeping baby.*

dowry, dowries
(noun) A woman's dowry is money or property which her father gives to the man she marries.

dowse, dowses, dowsing, dowsed
(verb) When someone dowses, they search for underground water or minerals using a divining rod.

doyen, doyens (pronounced doy-en)
(noun) The doyen or doyenne of a group or profession is the oldest or most experienced and respected member. 'Doyen' refers to a man and 'doyenne' to a woman.

doze, dozes, dozing, dozed
1 (verb) When you doze, you sleep lightly for a short period.
2 (noun) A doze is a short, light sleep.

dozen, dozens
(noun) A dozen things are twelve of them.

dozy, dozier, doziest
1 (adjective) feeling sleepy and not very alert.

2 (an informal use) If you call someone dozy, you think they are a bit stupid or slow to understand.

drab, drabber, drabbest
(adjective) dull and unattractive.
drabness (noun), **drably** (adverb).

Similar words: dingy, dismal, dreary, sombre

drachma, drachmas or drachmae (pronounced drak-ma)
(noun) The drachma is the unit of currency in Greece.

draconian
(adjective) Draconian laws, measures, or punishments are extremely harsh or severe.
[from *Draco*, a 7th century BC Athenian lawmaker who prescribed death for almost every offence]

draft, drafts, drafting, drafted
1 (noun) A draft of a document or speech is an early rough version of it.
2 (verb) When you draft a document or speech, you write the first rough version of it.
3 To draft people somewhere means to move them there so that they can do a specific job, e.g. *He hoped to draft in an extra 200 men to clear the backlog of work.*
4 (noun) A draft is a written order for payment of money by a bank.

drag, drags, dragging, dragged
1 (verb) If you drag a heavy object somewhere, you pull it slowly and with difficulty.
2 If you drag someone somewhere, you make them go although they may be unwilling.
3 If things drag behind you, they trail along the ground as you move along.
4 If an event or a period of time drags, it is boring and seems to last a long time.
5 When people drag a lake or river, they pull nets or hooks across the bottom to search for something, e.g. *The police dragged the river for the body.*
6 (noun) If something is a drag on the development of something, it slows it down.
7 Men in drag are male entertainers who wear women's clothing.

Similar words: (sense 1) haul, tug, pull, tow

dragon, dragons
(noun) In stories and legends, a dragon is a fierce animal like a large lizard with wings and claws that breathes fire.
[from Greek *drakōn* meaning 'serpent']

dragonfly, dragonflies
(noun) A dragonfly is a large, brightly-coloured insect with a long, thin body and two pairs of wings.

dragoon, dragoons, dragooning, dragooned
1 (noun) Dragoons are soldiers. Originally, they were mounted infantrymen.
2 (verb) If you dragoon someone into something, you force them to do it.

drain, drains, draining, drained
1 (verb) If you drain something or if it drains, liquid gradually flows out of it or off it.
2 If you drain a glass, you drink all its contents.
3 If something drains strength, energy, or resources, it gradually uses them up, e.g. *The project is already draining the charity's funds.*
4 If something drains you, it leaves you feeling physically and emotionally exhausted.
5 (noun) A drain is a pipe or channel that carries water or sewage away from a place.
6 A drain in a road is a metal grid through which rainwater flows.
7 (phrase) If you say that something goes **down the drain**, you mean that it is wasted or ruined.

drainage
1 (noun) Drainage is the system of pipes, drains, or ditches used to drain water or other liquid away from a place.
2 Drainage is also the process of draining water away, or the way in which a place drains, e.g. *Bad drainage caused flooding.*

drake, drakes
(noun) A drake is a male duck.

drama, dramas
1 (noun) A drama is a serious play for the theatre, television, or radio.
2 Drama is plays and the theatre in general, e.g. *modern drama.*
3 You can refer to the exciting events or aspects of a situation as drama, e.g. *the drama of village life.*
[from Greek *drama* meaning 'something performed']

dramatic, dramatics
1 (adjective) A dramatic change or event happens suddenly and is very noticeable, e.g. *dramatic improvements.*
2 lively, exciting, or impressive, e.g. *With a dramatic gesture he opened the lid.*
3 Dramatic art or writing is connected with plays and the theatre.
4 (noun) Dramatics is the performing of plays.
5 Exaggerated and emotional behaviour may be called dramatics, e.g. *George's dramatics irritated me.*
dramatically (adverb).

dramatis personae
(noun; a technical expression) The dramatis personae is the list of characters in a play.

dramatist, dramatists
(noun) A dramatist is a person who writes plays.

dramatize, dramatizes, dramatizing, dramatized; also spelled **dramatise**
1 (verb) To dramatize a book or story means to rewrite it as a play.
2 If you dramatize an event or situation, you try to make it seem more exciting, important, or serious than it really is, e.g. *The conflict has been dramatized in the newspapers.*
dramatization (noun).

drape, drapes, draping, draped
1 (verb) If you drape a piece of cloth, you arrange it so that it hangs down or covers something in loose folds.
2 (noun) Drapes are curtains, especially in American English.
[from Old French *drap* meaning 'cloth']

draper, drapers
(noun) A draper is a person who sells textiles.

drapery
(noun) Drapery is cloth and fabrics.

drastic
(adjective) A drastic course of action is very strong and severe and is usually taken urgently, e.g. *drastic measures to cut unemployment.*
drastically (adverb).
[from Greek *drastikos* meaning 'vigorous' or 'active']

Similar words: dramatic, extreme, radical

draught, draughts (pronounced **draft**)
1 (noun) A draught is a current of cold air.
2 A draught of liquid is an amount that you swallow.
3 The draught of a ship is the depth of water it needs to be able to float.
4 (adjective) Draught beer is served straight from barrels rather than in bottles.
5 A draught animal is one used for pulling heavy loads, e.g. *a draught horse.*
6 (noun) Draughts is a game for two people played on a chessboard with round pieces.

draughtsman, draughtsmen
(noun) A draughtsman is someone who prepares detailed drawings or plans.
draughtsmanship (noun).

draughty, draughtier, draughtiest
(adjective) A place that is draughty has currents of cold air blowing through it.

draw, draws, drawing, drew, drawn
1 (verb) When you draw, you use a pen, pencil, or crayon to make a picture or diagram.
2 To draw near means to move closer. To draw away or draw back means to move away.
3 If you draw something in a particular direction, you pull it there smoothly and gently, e.g. *He drew her towards him.*
4 If you draw a deep breath, you breathe in deeply.
5 If you draw the curtains, you pull them so that they cover the window.
6 If something such as money, water, or energy is drawn from a source, it is taken from it.
7 If you draw a conclusion, you arrive at it from the facts you know.
8 If you draw a distinction or a comparison, between two things, you point out that it exists.
9 If something draws people, it attracts them, e.g. *The play drew huge crowds.*
10 When characters in a play or story are drawn, they are described in words.
11 (noun) A draw is the result of a game or competition in which nobody wins.
12 (phrase) If something **draws to an end** or **draws to a close**, it finishes.

draw on
(phrasal verb) If you draw on something, you make use of it, e.g. *He drew on his vast reserves of energy.*

draw up
1 (phrasal verb) To draw up a plan, document, or list means to prepare it and write it out.
2 When a vehicle draws up at a place, it stops there.

drawback, drawbacks
(noun) A drawback is a problem that makes something less acceptable or desirable, e.g. *A major drawback of the system is that the funds are controlled centrally.*

drawbridge, drawbridges
(noun) A drawbridge is a bridge that can be pulled up or lowered.

drawer, drawers
1 (noun) A drawer is a sliding box-shaped part of a piece of furniture used for storage.
2 (plural noun; an old-fashioned use) Drawers are underpants.

drawing, drawings
1 (noun) A drawing is a picture made with a pencil, pen, or crayon.
2 Drawing is the skill or work of making drawings.

drawing pin, drawing pins
(noun) A drawing pin is a short nail with a broad, flat top.

drawing room, drawing rooms
(noun; an old-fashioned expression) A drawing room is a room in a house where people sit and relax or entertain guests.

drawl, drawls, drawling, drawled
(verb) If someone drawls, they speak slowly with long vowel sounds.

drawn
1 Drawn is the past participle of **draw.**
2 (adjective) If someone looks drawn, they look very tired, ill, or worried.

drawn-out
(adjective) Something that is drawn-out lasts longer than you would like.

dread, dreads, dreading, dreaded
1 (verb) If you dread something, you feel very worried and frightened about it, e.g. *I'm dreading the exams.*
2 (noun) Dread is a feeling of great fear or anxiety.
dreaded (adjective).

dreadful
(adjective) very bad or unpleasant.
dreadfully (adverb).

Similar words: terrible, abominable, abysmal, appalling, atrocious, monstrous, deplorable

dream, dreams, dreaming, dreamed or dreamt
1 (noun) A dream is a series of pictures or events that you experience in your mind while asleep.
2 A dream is a situation or event which you often think about because you would very much

like it to happen, e.g. *His dream of being champion was about to come true.*
3 (verb) When you dream, you see pictures and events in your mind while you are asleep.
4 When you dream about something happening, you often think about it because you would very much like it to happen.
5 If someone dreams up a plan or idea, they invent it.
6 If you say you would not dream of doing something, you are emphasizing that you would not do it, e.g. *I wouldn't dream of going without her.*
7 (adjective) beautiful or pleasing, e.g. *It was a dream house.*
dreamer (noun).

dreamy, dreamier, dreamiest
(adjective) Someone who is dreamy does things without concentrating, because they are thinking about something else.

dreary, drearier, dreariest
(adjective) dull or boring.
dreariness (noun), **drearily** (adverb).
[from Old English *dreorig* meaning 'gory' or 'grievous']

dredge, dredges, dredging, dredged
1 (verb) To dredge a harbour or river means to clear a channel for boats by removing silt or mud from the bed.
2 To dredge food means to sprinkle something over it, e.g. *dredge the dough with sugar.*
dredger (noun).

dregs
1 (plural noun) The dregs of a liquid are the last drops left at the bottom of a container, and any sediment left with it.
2 The dregs of society are the people who are thought to be the worst or most useless people in it.

drench, drenches, drenching, drenched
(verb) If you drench something or someone, you make them soaking wet.
[from Old English *drencan* meaning 'to cause to drink']

dress, dresses, dressing, dressed
1 (noun) A dress is a piece of clothing for women or girls made up of a skirt and top attached.
2 Dress is any clothing worn by men or women.
3 (verb) When you dress, you put clothes on.
4 If you dress for a special occasion, you put on formal clothes.
5 To dress a wound means to clean it up and treat it.
6 To dress a shop window means to arrange goods in it in an attractive way.
7 To dress food such as meat or fish means to prepare it ready for cooking or serving.

dressage (pronounced dres-ahj)
(noun) Dressage is the method of training horses to perform manoevres as a display of obedience.

dresser, dressers
(noun) A dresser is a piece of kitchen or dining room furniture with cupboards or drawers in the lower part and open shelves in the top part.

dressing, dressings
1 (noun) A dressing is a covering put on a wound to protect it while it heals.
2 A salad dressing is a sauce put on salad to enhance its flavour.

dressmaker, dressmakers
(noun) A dressmaker is a person who is paid to make clothes.

dribble, dribbles, dribbling, dribbled
1 (verb) When liquid dribbles down a surface, it trickles down it in drops or a thin stream.
2 If a person or animal dribbles, saliva trickles from their mouth.
3 (noun) A dribble of liquid is a small quantity of it flowing in a thin stream or drops.
4 (verb) In sport, to dribble a ball means to move it along by repeatedly tapping it with your hand, foot, or a stick.

drift, drifts, drifting, drifted
1 (verb) When something drifts, it is carried along by the wind or by water.
2 When people drift somewhere, they wander or move there gradually.
3 When people drift in life, they move without any aims from place to place or from one activity to another.
4 If you drift off to sleep, you gradually fall asleep.
5 (noun) A snow drift is a pile of snow heaped up by the wind.
6 The drift of an argument or speech is its main point.
drifter (noun).
[from Old Norse *drift* meaning 'snow drift']

drill, drills, drilling, drilled
1 (noun) A drill is any of various tools for making holes, e.g. *an electric drill.*
2 (verb) To drill into something means to make a hole in it using a drill.
3 Drill is a routine exercise or routine training, e.g. *fire drill.*
4 (verb) If you drill people, you teach them to do something by repetition.

drink, drinks, drinking, drank, drunk
1 (verb) When you drink, you take liquid into your mouth and swallow it.
2 To drink also means to drink alcohol, e.g. *He hardly ever drinks now.*
3 (noun) A drink is an amount of liquid suitable for drinking.
4 A drink is also an alcoholic drink.
5 (verb) If you drink in something such as a story, you are completely absorbed by it, e.g. *He drank in my every word.*
drinker (noun).

Similar words: (sense 1) quaff, swig, imbibe
(sense 2) booze, tipple, imbibe

drinkable
(adjective) nice enough to drink.

drip, drips, dripping, dripped
1 (verb) When liquid drips, it falls in small drops.
2 When an object drips, drops of liquid fall from it.

3 (noun) A drip is a drop of liquid falling from something.
4 (an informal use) If you call someone a drip, you mean they are weak or foolish.
5 A drip is also a device for allowing liquid food to enter the bloodstream of a person who cannot eat properly because they are ill.

drip-dry
(adjective) Drip-dry clothes or fabrics are designed to dry without creases if hung up when wet.

dripping
(noun) Dripping is the fat which comes from meat while it is cooking.

drive, drives, driving, drove, driven
1 (verb) To drive a vehicle means to operate it and control its movements.
2 To drive a group of people or animals means to guide them or force them to a place, e.g. *He drove the sheep into the next field.*
3 If something or someone drives you to do something, they force you to do it, e.g. *Losing his job drove him to suicide.*
4 If you drive a post or nail into something, you force it in by hitting it with a hammer.
5 If something drives a machine, it supplies the power that makes it work.
6 (noun) A drive is a journey in a vehicle such as a car.
7 A drive is also a private road that leads from a public road to a person's house.
8 Drive is energy and determination.
9 A drive is a special effort made by a group of people to achieve something.
10 (phrase) If you understand what someone is **driving at**, you understand what they are trying to say.
driver (noun), **driving** (noun).

drivel
(noun) Drivel is nonsense, e.g. *Her essay was absolute drivel.*
[from Old English *dreflian* meaning 'to dribble']

drizzle, drizzles, drizzling, drizzled
1 (verb) If it is drizzling, it is raining lightly.
2 (noun) Drizzle is light rain.
[from Old English *dreosan* meaning 'to fall']

droll (rhymes with **roll**)
(adjective) amusing in a quaint or strange way.

dromedary, dromedaries
(noun) A dromedary is a camel which has one hump.

drone, drones, droning, droned
1 (verb) If something drones, it makes a low, continuous humming noise.
2 If someone drones on, they keep talking or reading aloud in a boring way.
3 (noun) A drone is a male bee.

drool, drools, drooling, drooled
(verb) If someone drools, saliva dribbles from their mouth without them being able to stop it.

droop, droops, drooping, drooped
(verb) If something droops, it hangs or sags downwards with no strength or firmness.

[from Old Norse *drupa* meaning 'to hang one's head in sorrow']

drop, drops, dropping, dropped
1 (verb) If you drop something, you let it fall.
2 If something drops, it falls straight down.
3 If a level or amount drops, it becomes less.
4 If your voice drops, or if you drop your voice, you speak more quietly.
5 If you drop something that you are doing or dealing with, you stop doing it or dealing with it, e.g. *I dropped night classes last month.*
6 If you drop a hint, you give someone a hint in a casual way.
7 If you drop something or someone somewhere, you deposit or leave them there.
8 If you drop someone a line, you write them a short letter.
9 (noun) A drop of liquid is a very small quantity of it that forms or falls in a spherical shape.
10 A drop is a decrease, e.g. *a drop in prices.*
11 A drop is also the vertical distance between the top and bottom of something tall, such as a cliff or building, e.g. *a 30 metre drop.*

droplet, droplets
(noun) A droplet is a small drop.

droppings
(plural noun) Droppings are the faeces of birds and small animals.

dross
(noun) Dross is waste matter produced by smelting metal.
[from Old English *dros* meaning 'dregs']

drought, droughts (rhymes with **shout**)
(noun) A drought is a long period during which there is no rain.
[from Old English *drugath*]

drove, droves
1 Drove is the past tense of **drive**.
2 (noun) A drove is a herd of sheep, cattle, or other livestock being driven together.

drown, drowns, drowning, drowned
1 (verb) When someone drowns or is drowned, they die because they have gone under water and cannot breathe.
2 If a noise drowns a sound, it is louder than the sound and makes it impossible to hear it.

drowse, drowses, drowsing, drowsed (rhymes with **cows**)
(verb) If you drowse, you are almost asleep or just asleep.
drowsy (adjective), **drowsily** (adverb).

drudge, drudges
(noun) A drudge is a person who has to work hard at very uninteresting work.

drudgery
(noun) Drudgery is hard uninteresting work.

Similar words: chore, grind, donkey-work

drug, drugs, drugging, drugged
1 (noun) A drug is a chemical given to people to treat disease.
2 Drugs are chemical substances that some

people smoke, swallow, smell, or inject because of their stimulating effects.
3 (verb) To drug a person or animal means to give them a drug to make them unconscious.
4 To drug food or drink means to add a drug to it in order to make someone unconscious.
drugged (adjective).

druid, druids (pronounced **droo**-id)
(noun) A druid was a priest of an ancient pre-Christian religion in Gaul, Britain, and Ireland.

drum, drums, drumming, drummed
1 (noun) A drum is a musical instrument consisting of a skin stretched tightly over a round frame.
2 A drum is also any object shaped like a drum, e.g. *an oil drum.*
3 If something is drumming on a surface, it is hitting it regularly, making a continuous beating sound.
4 If you drum something into someone, you keep saying it to them until they understand it or remember it.

drum up
(phrasal verb) If you drum up support, you succeed in getting it.

drum major, drum majors
(noun) A drum major is an officer appointed to command a military band when it is marching.

drumstick, drumsticks
1 (noun) A drumstick is a stick used for beating a drum.
2 A chicken drumstick is the lower part of the leg of a chicken, when cooked and eaten.

drunk, drunks
1 Drunk is the past tense of **drink**.
2 (adjective) If someone is drunk, they have drunk so much alcohol that they cannot speak clearly or behave sensibly.
3 (noun) A drunk is a person who is drunk, or who often gets drunk.
drunken (adjective), **drunkenly** (adverb), **drunkenness** (noun).

Similar words: (sense 2) intoxicated, inebriated, drunken, tight, tipsy, sloshed

drunkard, drunkards
(noun) A drunkard is someone who often gets drunk.

dry, drier or **dryer, driest; dries, drying, dried**
1 (adjective) Something that is dry contains or uses no water or liquid.
2 (verb) When you dry something, or when it dries, it becomes dry.
3 (adjective) Dry bread or toast is eaten without jam, butter, or any other kind of topping.
4 Dry sherry, wine, or biscuits do not taste sweet.
5 Dry also means plain and sometimes boring, e.g. *the dry facts... a dry book.*
6 Dry humour is subtle and sarcastic.
dryness (noun), **drily** (adverb).

Similar words: (sense 1) arid, parched, dehydrated

dry up
1 (phrasal verb) If something dries up, it becomes completely dry.
2 If you dry up, you forget what you were going to say, or find that you have nothing left to say.

dry-clean, dry-cleans, dry-cleaning, dry-cleaned
(verb) When clothes are dry-cleaned, they are cleaned with a liquid chemical rather than with water.

dryer, dryers; also spelled drier
1 (noun) A dryer is any device for removing moisture from something by heating or by hot air, e.g. *a hair dryer*.
2 Dryer and drier are also the comparative forms of **dry**.

dual
(adjective) having two parts, functions, or aspects, e.g. *a dual-purpose gadget*.
[from Latin *duo* meaning 'two']

dub, dubs, dubbing, dubbed
1 (verb) If something is dubbed a particular name, it is given that name, e.g. *We dubbed our new car 'The Battleship'*.
2 If a film is dubbed, the voices on the soundtrack are not those of the actors, but those of other actors speaking in a different language.

dubiety (pronounced dyoo-by-it-ee)
(noun) Dubiety is the state of being doubtful.

dubious (pronounced dyoo-bee-uss)
1 (adjective) not entirely honest, safe, or reliable, e.g. *goods of dubious origin*.
2 doubtful, e.g. *dubious of the wisdom of the idea*.
dubiously (adverb).
[from Latin *dubius* meaning 'wavering']

Similar words: (sense 1) doubtful, questionable, suspect

duchess, duchesses
(noun) A duchess is a woman who has the same rank as a duke, or who is a duke's wife or widow.

duchy, duchies (pronounced dut-shee)
(noun) A duchy is the land owned and ruled by a duke or duchess.

duck, ducks, ducking, ducked
1 (noun) A duck is any of various waterbirds with short legs, webbed feet, a short neck, and a large flat bill.
2 (verb) If you duck, you move your head quickly downwards in order to avoid being hit by something.
3 If you duck a duty or responsibility, you avoid it.
4 To duck someone means to push them briefly under water.
5 (noun) In cricket, if a batsman scores a duck, he does not score any runs.
[from Old English *ducan* meaning 'to dive']

duckling, ducklings
(noun) A duckling is a young duck.

duct, ducts
1 (noun) A duct is a pipe, tube, or channel through which liquid or gas is sent.

2 A duct is also any bodily passage through which liquid such as tears or bile can pass.

ductile
(adjective) Material that is ductile can be easily shaped, moulded, or drawn out into threads.

dud, duds
(noun) A dud is something which does not function properly.

due, dues
1 (adjective) expected to happen or arrive, e.g. *The bus is due at 3.00 pm.*
2 If you give something due consideration, you give it the consideration that it needs.
3 (preposition) because of, e.g. *The fact that the letter arrived late was due to the postal strike.*
4 (adverb) Due means exactly in a particular direction, e.g. *The hills are due South, just beyond the river.*
5 (noun) Dues are sums of money that you pay regularly to an organization you belong to.
6 (phrase) If you say that something will happen **in due course**, you mean it will happen eventually, when the time is right.
7 You say **to give them their due** when you are saying something good about someone who has been criticized, e.g. *To give him his due, he has worked very hard.*

duel, duels, duelling, duelled
1 (noun) A duel is a prearranged fight between two people using deadly weapons, for the purpose of settling a quarrel.
2 Any contest or conflict between two people can be referred to as a duel.

duet, duets
(noun) A duet is a piece of music sung or played by two people.

duffel or duffle
(noun) Duffel is a rough heavy woollen material used especially to make coats. It is named after the Belgian town of Duffel.

duffer, duffers
(noun; an informal word) A duffer is a person who is slow to learn or not very good at doing things.

dug, dugs
1 Dug is the past tense of **dig**.
2 (noun) A female animal's dugs are its teats or breasts.

dugout, dugouts
1 (noun) A dugout is a canoe made by hollowing out a log.
2 (a military word) A dugout is also a shelter dug in the ground for protection.

duke, dukes
(noun) A duke is a nobleman with a rank just below that of a prince.
[from Latin *dux* meaning 'leader']

dukedom, dukedoms
(noun) A dukedom is the land owned or ruled by a duke.

dulcet (pronounced **dull**-sit)
(adjective; a literary word) gentle, pleasant, and soothing to listen to.
[from Latin *dulcis* meaning 'sweet']

dull, duller, dullest; dulls, dulling, dulled
1 (adjective) not at all interesting in any way.
2 slow to learn or understand.
3 not bright, sharp, or clear.
4 A dull day or dull sky is very cloudy.
5 Dull feelings are weak and not intense, e.g. *She had a dull throbbing in her head.*
6 (verb) If something dulls or is dulled, it becomes less bright, sharp, or clear.
dully (adverb), **dullness** (noun).
[from Old English *dol* meaning 'stupid']

Similar words: (sense 4) overcast, leaden, heavy

duly
1 (adverb; a formal use) If something is duly done, it is done in the correct way, e.g. *She was declared duly elected to Parliament.*
2 If something duly happens, it is something that you expected to happen, e.g. *He duly got into his car and drove to the office.*

dumb, dumber, dumbest
1 (adjective) unable to speak.
2 (an informal use) slow to understand or stupid.

Similar words: (sense 1) mute, speechless

dumbell, dumbells
(noun) Dumbells are weights for exercising the body, consisting of bars with heavy balls or discs at either end.

dumbfound, dumbfounds, dumbfounding, dumbfounded
(verb) If something or someone dumbfounds you, they surprise you to such an extent that you cannot speak.

dummy, dummies
1 (noun) A baby's dummy is a rubber teat which it sucks or bites on.
2 A dummy is also an imitation or model of something which is used for display.
3 (adjective) imitation or substitute.

dump, dumps, dumping, dumped
1 (verb) When unwanted waste matter is dumped, it is put somewhere where it can be left.
2 If you dump something, you throw it down or put it down somewhere in a careless way.
3 (noun) A dump is a place where rubbish is left.
4 A dump is also a storage place, especially used by the military for storing supplies.
5 (an informal use) You refer to a place as a dump when it is unattractive and unpleasant to live in.

dumpling, dumplings
(noun) A dumpling is a small lump of dough that is cooked and eaten with meat and vegetables.

dumpy, dumpier, dumpiest
(adjective) short and fat.

dun
(adjective) dull grey-brown.

dunce, dunces
(noun) A dunce is a person who cannot learn what someone is trying to teach them.

dune, dunes
(noun) A dune or sand dune is a hill of sand near the sea or in the desert.

dung
(noun) Dung is the faeces from large animals, sometimes called manure.

dungarees
(plural noun) Dungarees are trousers which have a bib covering the chest and straps over the shoulders. They are named after Dungri in India, where dungaree material was first made.

dungeon, dungeons (pronounced **dun**-jen)
(noun) A dungeon is an underground prison.

dunk, dunks, dunking, dunked
(verb) To dunk something means to dip it briefly into a liquid, e.g. *He dunked his biscuits in his tea.*

duo, duos
1 (noun) A duo is a pair of musical performers; also a piece of music written for two players.
2 Any two people doing something together can be referred to as a duo.

duodenum, duodenums (pronounced dyoo-o-**dee**-num)
(noun) The duodenum is the first part of the small intestine.
duodenal (adjective).

dupe, dupes, duping, duped
1 (verb) If someone dupes you, they trick you.
2 (noun) A dupe is someone who has been tricked.
[from Old French *de huppe* meaning 'of the hoopoe', a bird thought to be stupid]

duplicate, duplicates, duplicating, duplicated
1 (verb) To duplicate something means to make an exact copy of it.
2 (noun) A duplicate is something that is identical to something else.
3 (adjective) identical to or an exact copy of, e.g. *a duplicate set of keys.*
duplication (noun).

duplicator, duplicators
(noun) A duplicator is a machine which makes exact copies of writing or drawings.

duplicity
(noun; a formal word) Duplicity is deceitful or hypocritical behaviour.
[from Latin *duplicitas* meaning 'double']

durable
(adjective) strong and long-lasting.
durability (noun).
[from Latin *durare* meaning 'to last']

duration
(noun) The duration of something is the length of time during which it happens or exists.

duress (pronounced dyoo-**ress**)
(noun) If you do something under duress, you are forced to do it, and you do it very unwillingly.

during
(preposition) happening throughout a particular time or at a particular point in time.

dusk
(noun) Dusk is the time just before nightfall when it is not completely dark.
[from Old English *dox* meaning 'dark']

dusky, duskier, duskiest
(adjective) rather dark.

dust, dusts, dusting, dusted
1 (noun) Dust is dry fine powdery material such as particles of earth, dirt, or pollen.
2 (verb) When you dust furniture or other objects, you remove dust from them using a duster.
3 If you dust a surface with powder, you cover it lightly with the powder.
4 (phrase) When something **bites the dust**, it completely fails or stops working.

dustbin, dustbins
(noun) A dustbin is a large container for rubbish.

duster, dusters
(noun) A duster is a cloth used for removing dust from furniture and other objects.

dustjacket, dustjackets
(noun) A dustjacket is a paper cover put around a hardback book.

dustman, dustmen
(noun) A dustman is someone whose job is to collect the rubbish from people's houses.

dusty, dustier, dustiest
(adjective) covered with dust.

Dutch
1 (adjective) belonging or relating to Holland.
2 (noun) Dutch is the main language spoken in Holland.

Dutchman, Dutchmen
(noun) A Dutchman is a man who comes from Holland.
Dutchwoman (noun).

dutiful
(adjective) doing all you are expected to do.
dutifully (adverb).

duty, duties
1 (noun) Duties are things you ought to do or feel you should do, because it is your responsibility.
2 (plural noun) Your duties are the tasks which you do as part of your job.
3 (phrase) If an employed person is **on duty**, they are working. If they are **off duty**, they are not working.
4 (noun) Duty is tax paid to the government on some goods, especially imports.

Similar words: (sense 1) responsibility, obligation

duty-free
(adjective) Duty-free goods are goods which are not subject to customs duty and can be bought cheaply at airports or on planes and ships.

duvet, duvets (pronounced **doo**-vay)
(noun) A duvet is a bed cover consisting of a cotton quilt filled with feathers or other material, used in place of a sheet and blankets.
[a French word]

dwarf, dwarfs, dwarfing, dwarfed
1 (verb) If one thing dwarfs another, it is so much bigger that it makes it look very small.
2 (adjective) smaller than average.
3 (noun) A dwarf is a person who is much smaller than average size.

dwell, dwells, dwelling, dwelled or **dwelt**
1 (verb; a literary use) To dwell somewhere means to live there.
2 If you dwell on something or dwell upon it, you think, speak, or write about it a lot.

dwelling, dwellings
(noun; a formal word) Someone's dwelling is the house or other place where they live.

dwindle, dwindles, dwindling, dwindled
(verb) If something dwindles, it becomes less in size, strength, or number.

dye, dyes, dyeing, dyed
1 (verb) To dye something means to change its colour by applying coloured liquid to it.
2 (noun) Dye is a staining or colouring substance which is mixed into a liquid and used to change the colour of something such as cloth or hair.

dyke, dykes; also spelled **dike**
(noun) A dyke is a thick wall that prevents water flooding onto land from a river or the sea.

dynamic, dynamics
1 (adjective) A dynamic person is full of energy, ambition, personality, and new ideas.
2 (noun) In physics, dynamics is the study of the forces that change or produce the motion of bodies or particles.
3 (adjective) relating to energy or forces which produce motion.
4 (plural noun) The dynamics of a society or a situation are the forces that cause it to change.
dynamism (noun).
[from Greek *dunamis* meaning 'strength']

dynamite
(noun) Dynamite is an explosive made of nitroglycerine.

dynamo, dynamos
(noun) A dynamo is a device that converts mechanical energy into electricity.

dynasty, dynasties
(noun) A dynasty is a series of rulers of a country all belonging to the same family.
[from Greek *dunasteia* meaning 'power']

dysentery (pronounced **diss**-en-tree)
(noun) Dysentery is an infection of the bowel which causes severe diarrhoea.
[from Latin *dys-* meaning 'bad' and Greek *enteron* meaning 'intestine']

dyslexia (pronounced dis-**lek**-see-a)
(noun) Dyslexia is difficulty with reading caused by a slight disorder of the brain.
dyslexic (adjective and noun).
[from Latin *dys-* meaning 'bad' and Greek *lexis* meaning 'word']

E

each
(adjective or pronoun) every one taken separately, e.g. *Each building had a new roof... Each was wearing a hat.*

eager
(adjective) keen and full of enthusiasm.
eagerly (adverb), **eagerness** (noun).
[from Latin *acer* meaning 'sharp' or 'keen']

eagle, eagles
(noun) An eagle is a large bird which hunts and kills other animals for food.

ear, ears
1 (noun) Your ears are the parts of your body on either side of your head with which you hear sounds.
2 An ear of corn or wheat is the top part of the stalk which contains flowers or seeds.

eardrum, eardrums
(noun) Your eardrums are thin pieces of tightly stretched skin inside your ears which vibrate so that you can hear sounds.

earl, earls
(noun) An earl is a British nobleman, ranking between a marquis and a viscount.
[from Old English *eorl* meaning 'chieftain']

early, earlier, earliest
1 (adverb) before the usual, due, or expected time.
2 (adjective) near the beginning of a day, evening, or other period of time, e.g. *early evening... the early 1960s.*
3 happening a very long time ago, e.g. *Early Britain was very primitive.*

Similar words: (sense 1) premature, untimely

earmark, earmarks, earmarking, earmarked
(verb) If you earmark something for a special purpose, you keep it for that purpose.
[from identification marks on the ears of domestic or farm animals]

earn, earns, earning, earned
1 (verb) If you earn money, you get it in return for work that you do.
2 If something earns money, it brings it in as profit or interest, e.g. *My savings are earning 8% interest in the building society.*
3 If you earn something such as praise, you receive it because you deserve it.
earner (noun).

Similar words: (sense 1) make, bring in

earnest
1 (adjective) sincere in what you say or do, e.g. *My earnest wish is to make you happy.*
2 (phrase) If you are **in earnest** about something, you are serious about it, e.g. *She was in earnest about joining the army.*
earnestly (adverb), **earnestness** (noun).

earnings
(plural noun) Your earnings are money that you earn.

earphones
(plural noun) Earphones are small speakers which you wear on your ears to listen to a radio or cassette player without other people hearing it.

earring, earrings
(noun) Earrings are pieces of jewellery that you wear on your ear lobes.

earshot
(phrase) If you are **within earshot** of something, you can hear it.

earth, earths, earthing, earthed
1 (noun) The earth is the planet on which we live.
2 Earth is the dry land on the surface of the earth, especially the soil in which things grow.
3 An earth is a hole in the ground where an animal such as a fox lives.
4 The earth in a plug or piece of electrical equipment is the wire through which electricity can pass into the ground and so make the equipment safe for use.
5 (verb) If a piece of electrical equipment is earthed, it is fitted with an earth.

earthenware
(noun) Earthenware is pottery made of baked clay.

earthly
1 (adjective) concerned with life on earth rather than heaven or life after death.
2 (an informal use) If you say that there is no earthly reason for something, you are emphasizing that there is absolutely no reason.

earthquake, earthquakes
(noun) An earthquake is a series of vibrations along the surface of the earth caused by a build-up of pressure deep within the earth.

earthworm, earthworms
(noun) An earthworm is a common type of worm which breaks up the soil as it moves along.

earthy, earthier, earthiest
1 (adjective) looking or smelling like earth.
2 Someone who is earthy is open and direct, often in a crude way, e.g. *Her earthy language sometimes offended people.*
earthiness (noun), **earthily** (adverb).

earwig, earwigs
(noun) An earwig is a small, thin, brown insect which has a pair of pincers at the end of its body.
[from Old English *earwicga* meaning 'ear insect'; it was believed to creep into people's ears]

ease, eases, easing, eased
1 (noun) Ease is lack of difficulty, worry, or hardship, e.g. *He ran the last mile with ease.*
2 (verb) When something eases, or when you ease it, it becomes less, e.g. *She took an aspirin to ease her headache.*

3 If you ease something somewhere, you move it there slowly and carefully, e.g. *He eased the car into the small space.*

Similar words: (sense 1) facility, easiness
(sense 3) alleviate, assuage, relieve

easel, easels
(noun) An easel is an upright frame which supports a picture that someone is painting.
[from Dutch *ezel* meaning 'ass' or 'donkey']

easily
1 (adverb) without difficulty.
2 without a doubt, e.g. *She was easily the prettiest girl in the contest.*

east
1 (noun) East is the direction in which you look to see the sun rise.
2 The east of a place or country is the part which is towards the east when you are in the centre, e.g. *the east of England.*
3 (adverb and adjective) East means towards the east, e.g. *They got into the car and headed east.*
4 (adjective) An east wind blows from the east.
5 (noun) The East is the USSR and other Communist countries in the east of Europe. The East also refers to the countries in the south and east of Asia.

Easter
(noun) Easter is a Christian religious festival celebrating the resurrection of Christ.
[from Old English *Eostre*, a pre-Christian Germanic goddess whose festival was at the spring equinox]

easterly
1 (adjective) Easterly means to or towards the east.
2 An easterly wind blows from the east.

eastern
(adjective) in or from the east, e.g. *the eastern part of the country.*

eastward or **eastwards**
(adverb) towards the east.

easy, easier, easiest
1 (adjective) not difficult, e.g. *an easy task.*
2 comfortable and without any worries, e.g. *I want to make life easy for myself.*

Similar words: (sense 1) simple, straightforward, effortless

easy chair, easy chairs
(noun) An easy chair is a comfortable armchair.

easy-going
(adjective) not easily annoyed or worried.

Similar words: easy, laid-back, tolerant

eat, eats, eating, ate, eaten
1 (verb) To eat means to chew and swallow food.
2 When you eat, you have a meal, e.g. *We'll be eating at eight tonight.*
3 If something is eaten away, it is slowly destroyed, e.g. *Rust had eaten away the metal.*

eau-de-cologne (pronounced oh-de-kol-**own**)
(noun) Eau-de-cologne is weak perfume.
[a French expression meaning 'water of Cologne']

eaves
(plural noun) The eaves of a roof are the lower edges which jut out over the walls.

eavesdrop, eavesdrops, eavesdropping, eavesdropped
(verb) If you eavesdrop, you listen secretly to what other people are saying.
[from Old English *yfesdrype* meaning 'water dripping down from the eaves'; people were supposed to stand outside in the rain to hear what was being said inside the house]

ebb, ebbs, ebbing, ebbed
1 (verb) When the sea or the tide ebbs, it flows back.
2 If a person's feeling or strength ebbs, it gets weaker, e.g. *the strength ebbed from his body.*
3 (phrase) If someone or something is **at a low ebb**, they are very weak.

ebony
1 (noun) Ebony is the hard, dark-coloured wood of a tropical tree, used for making furniture.
2 (noun and adjective) very deep black.

ebullient
(adjective; a formal word) lively and full of enthusiasm.
ebulliently (adverb), **ebullience** (noun).
[from Latin *ebullire* meaning 'to boil over']

EC an abbreviation for 'European Community'.

eccentric, eccentrics (pronounced ik-**sen**-trik)
1 (adjective) having habits or opinions which are so different from other people's that you are thought to be odd or peculiar.
2 (noun) An eccentric is someone who is eccentric.
eccentricity (noun), **eccentrically** (adverb).
[from Greek *ekkentros* meaning 'off-centre']

Similar words: (sense 1) unconventional, cranky, quirky
(sense 2) oddball, crank

ecclesiastical (pronounced ik-leez-ee-**ass**-ti-kl)
(adjective) of or relating to the Christian church.
[from Greek *ekklēsia* meaning 'assembly' or 'church']

echelon, echelons (pronounced **esh**-el-on)
1 (noun) An echelon is a level of power or responsibility in an organization; also used of the group of people at that level.
2 An echelon is also a military formation in the shape of an arrowhead.
[from French *échelon* meaning 'rung of a ladder']

echo echoes, echoing, echoed
1 (noun) An echo is a sound which is caused by sound waves reflecting off a surface.
2 An echo is also a repetition or imitation of something, e.g. *The colours in the painting were an echo of the Antarctic.*
3 (verb) If a sound echoes, it is reflected off a surface so that you can hear it again after the original sound has stopped.

4 If you echo someone or something, you imitate them or repeat what they have said.

éclair, éclairs
(noun) An éclair is a finger-shaped cake made of light pastry, usually filled with cream and covered with chocolate.

eclipse, eclipses, eclipsing, eclipsed
1 (noun) An eclipse occurs when one planet passes in front of another and hides it from view for a short time.
2 (verb) When one planet eclipses another, it passes in front of it, blocking it from view for a short time.
3 (noun) The eclipse of a person or thing is their loss of importance, power, or fame.
4 (verb) If something eclipses something else, the first thing is so much better or more important that the second thing is no longer noticed.
[from Greek *ekleipsis* meaning 'abandoning']

ecology
(noun) Ecology is the relationship between plants, animals, people, and their environment; also used of the study of this relationship.
ecological (adjective), **ecologist** (noun).
[from Greek *oikos* meaning 'house']

economic
1 (adjective) concerning the management of the money, industry, and trade of a country.
2 concerning making a profit, e.g. *It is not economic to sell goods at too low a price.*

economical
1 (adjective) Something that is economical is cheap to use or operate.
2 Someone who is economical spends money carefully and sensibly.
economically (adverb).

economics
1 (noun) Economics is the study of the production and distribution of goods, services, and wealth in a society and the organization of its money, industry, and trade.
2 The economics of a country is the way that it organizes its money, production, and trade.

economist, economists
(noun) An economist is a person who studies or writes about economics.

economize, economizes, economizing, economized; also spelled **economise**
(verb) If you economize, you save money by being very careful about how you spend it.

economy, economies
1 (noun) The economy of a country is the system it uses to organize and manage its money, industry, and trade; also used of the wealth that a country gets from business and industry.
2 Economy is the careful use of things to save money, time, or energy, e.g. *His economy with words meant that the speech was soon over.*
3 (adjective) Economy goods or services are cheap, e.g. *Economy class flights are always cheaper than first class.*
[from Greek *oikonomia* meaning 'domestic management']

Similar words: (sense 2) thrift, frugality

ecosystem, ecosystems
(noun; a technical word) An ecosystem is the relationship between plants and animals and their environment.

ecstasy, ecstasies
(noun) Ecstasy is a feeling of extreme happiness.
ecstatic (adjective), **ecstatically** (adverb).
[from Greek *ekstasis* meaning 'trance']

Similar words: elation, euphoria, rapture, bliss

ecumenical (pronounced ee-kyoo-**men**-i-kl)
(adjective) Within Christianity, the ecumenical movement is the movement that is trying to unite all the various branches of the Church.
ecumenicism (noun), **ecumenism** (noun).
[from Greek *oikoumenē* meaning 'inhabited earth']

eczema (pronounced **ek**-sim-ma)
(noun) Eczema is a skin disease that causes the surface of the skin to become rough and itchy.
[from Greek *ekzein* meaning 'to boil over']

eddy, eddies, eddying, eddied
1 (noun) An eddy is a circular movement in water or air.
2 (verb) If water, wind, or smoke eddies, it moves around in small circles.

edge, edges, edging, edged
1 (noun) The edge of something is a border or line where it ends or meets something else.
2 The edge of a blade is its thin, sharp side.
3 An edge over someone or something is an advantage over them.
4 If something has edge, it has a keenness or sharpness, e.g. *Her experiences as a policewoman gave edge to her speech on crime.*
5 (verb) If you edge something, you make a border for it, e.g. *The handkerchief was edged with lace.*
6 To edge means to move very gradually, e.g. *She edged her way towards the front.*
7 (phrase) If you are **on edge**, you are nervous or tense about something.

Similar words: (sense 1) border, brink, margin, fringe

edgeways
1 (adverb) Edgeways means sideways, e.g. *They put the bookcase into the van edgeways.*
2 (an informal phrase) If you **cannot get a word in edgeways**, you do not get a chance to speak because someone else is talking so much.

edgy, edgier, edgiest
(adjective) nervous, anxious, and irritable.

edible
(adjective) safe and pleasant to eat.
[from Latin *edere* meaning 'to eat']

edict, edicts (pronounced **ee**-dikt)
(noun; a formal word) An edict is an official order or instruction issued by a government.
[from Latin *edictum* meaning 'something declared']

edifice, edifices (pronounced **ed**-if-iss)
(noun; a formal word) An edifice is a large and impressive building.

edify, edifies, edifying, edified
(verb; a formal word) If something edifies you, it makes you a better person by what it teaches you, e.g. *The sermon was intended to edify.*
edification (noun).
[from Latin *aedificare* meaning 'to build up']

edit, edits, editing, edited
1 (verb) If you edit a piece of writing, you examine it, correcting and improving it so that it is fit for publishing.
2 To edit a book means to collect pieces of writing by different authors and arrange them ready for publication.
3 To edit a film or a radio or television programme means to select different parts of it and arrange them in a particular order.
4 Someone who edits a newspaper or magazine is in charge of it.

edition, editions
1 (noun) An edition of a book, magazine, or newspaper is a particular version of it printed at one time; also the total number of copies printed at one time.
2 An edition of a television or radio programme is a single programme that is one of a series, e.g. *tonight's edition of Panorama.*
[from Latin *edere* meaning 'to give out']

editor, editors
1 (noun) An editor is a person who is responsible for the content of a newspaper or magazine.
2 An editor is also a person whose job is to check books and to make alterations and corrections to them before they are published.
3 An editor of a film or a radio or television programme is a person who selects different parts and arranges them in a particular order.
editorship (noun).
[from Latin *editor* meaning 'producer' or 'exhibitor']

editorial, editorials
1 (adjective) involved in preparing a newspaper, book, or magazine for publication.
2 involving the contents and the opinions of a newspaper or magazine, e.g. *editorial policy.*
3 (noun) An editorial is an article in a newspaper which gives the opinions of the editor or publisher on a particular topic.
editorially (adverb).

educate, educates, educating, educated
1 (verb) To educate someone means to teach them so that they acquire knowledge and understanding about something.
2 When parents educate their children, they provide schooling for them.
[from Latin *educere* meaning 'to lead out']

educated
(adjective) having a high standard of learning and culture.

education
1 (noun) Education is the process of acquiring knowledge and understanding through learning.

2 Education also refers to the system of teaching people at school, college, or university.

educational
(adjective) involving learning or teaching.
educationally (adverb), **educationalist** (noun).

EEC
(noun) The EEC is an organization of Western European countries which have agreed ways of dealing with matters like trade and agriculture. EEC is an abbreviation for 'European Economic Community'.

eel, eels
(noun) An eel is a long, thin, snakelike fish.

eerie, eerier, eeriest
(adjective) strange and frightening, e.g. *I had the eerie feeling that someone was watching me.*
eerily (adverb).

efface, effaces, effacing, effaced
(verb) If you efface something, you rub it out.
[from French *effacer* meaning 'to obliterate the face']

effect, effects, effecting, effected
1 (noun) An effect is a direct result of someone or something on another person or thing, e.g. *The effect of the drugs was to cause drowsiness.*
2 An effect that someone or something has is the overall impression or result that they have, e.g. *The effect of the colour was to give warmth.*
3 If something **takes effect**, it starts to happen or starts to produce results, e.g. *She fell asleep as the drugs began to take effect.*
4 (verb; a formal use) If you effect something, you achieve it or make it happen.
5 (plural noun) The effects in a film are the special sounds and scenery.
6 Someone's effects are their personal belongings.
[from Latin *efficere* meaning 'to accomplish']

effective
1 (adjective) working well and producing the intended results.
2 coming into operation or beginning officially, e.g. *The new tax becomes effective from today.*
3 producing a strong impression, e.g. *an effective style of acting.*
effectively (adverb), **effectiveness** (noun).

effectual
(adjective; a formal word) producing the intended results, e.g. *an effectual plan.*
effectually (adverb).

effeminate
(adjective) A man who is effeminate behaves, looks, or sounds like a woman.
effeminacy (noun).

effervescent
1 (adjective) An effervescent liquid is fizzy and gives off bubbles of gas.
2 Someone who is effervescent is lively and enthusiastic.
effervescence (noun), **effervesce** (verb).

effete (pronounced if-**feet**)
(adjective) feeble and powerless.

[from Latin *effetus* meaning 'having produced young', hence 'exhausted']

efficacious
(adjective; a formal word) successful in solving a problem or achieving a particular aim.
efficacy (noun).

efficient
(adjective) capable of doing something well without wasting time or energy.
efficiently (adverb), **efficiency** (noun).

Similar words: businesslike, capable, competent, well-organized

effigy, effigies (pronounced ef-**fij**-ee)
(noun) An effigy is a statue, carving, or other figure of a person.

effluent, effluents (pronounced ef-loo-ent)
(noun) Effluent is liquid waste that comes out of factories or sewage works.

effort, efforts
1 (noun) Effort is the physical or mental energy needed to do something.
2 An effort is an attempt or struggle to do something, e.g. *She made an effort in the exam.*
[from Latin *fortis* meaning 'strong']

Similar words: (sense 1) endeavour, exertion, pains, trouble

effortless
(adjective) done easily.
effortlessly (adverb).

effrontery, effronteries (pronounced if-**run**-ter-ee)
(noun; a formal word) Effrontery is bold, rude, or cheeky behaviour, e.g. *He had the effrontery to borrow the car without asking.*

effusive
(adjective) freely showing feelings of pleasure, gratitude, or approval.
effusively (adverb), **effusiveness** (noun).
[from Latin *effundere* meaning 'to pour out']

e.g.
e.g. means 'for example', and is abbreviated from the Latin expression 'exempli gratia'.

egalitarian
(adjective) favouring equality for all people, e.g. *an egalitarian society.*
[from French *égal* meaning 'equal']

egg, eggs, egging, egged
1 (noun) An egg is an oval or rounded object produced by female birds, reptiles, fishes, and insects. A new creature develops inside the egg.
2 An egg is also a hen's egg used as food.
3 In a female animal an egg is a cell produced in its body which can develop into a baby if it is fertilized.
4 (verb) If you egg someone on, you encourage them to do something, especially something foolish or daring.
[senses 1 to 3 are from Old Norse *egg*; sense 4 is from Old Norse *eggja* meaning 'to incite']

ego, egos (pronounced **ee**-goh)
1 (noun) Someone's ego is their self, the part of them which is able to distinguish who they are in relation to other people and things.
2 Your ego is also your opinion of what you are worth, e.g. *Failing the driving test was a blow to his ego.*
[from Latin *ego* meaning 'I']

egocentric
(adjective) only thinking of yourself and your own interests.

egoism or **egotism**
(noun) Egoism is behaviour and attitudes which show that you believe that you are more important than other people.
egoist or **egotist** (noun),
egoistic, egotistic, or **egotistical** (adjective).

Egyptian, Egyptians (pronounced ij-**jip**-shn)
1 (adjective) belonging or relating to Egypt.
2 (noun) An Egyptian is someone who comes from Egypt.

eiderdown, eiderdowns
(noun) An eiderdown is a thick bed covering that is filled with feathers.
[from the *eider* duck]

eight, eights
1 Eight is the number 8.
2 (noun) In rowing, an eight is the crew of a narrow racing boat, consisting of eight rowers.
eighth.

eighteen the number 18.
eighteenth.

eighty, eighties
the number 80.
eightieth.

eisteddfod, eisteddfods (pronounced eye-**sted**-fod)
(noun) An eisteddfod is an annual festival held in Wales, at which competitions in music, poetry, drama, and art are held.
[a Welsh word]

either
1 (determiner, pronoun or conjunction) one or the other of two possible alternatives, e.g. *Either pen will work... Either will do... You can go either Tuesday or Wednesday.*
2 (determiner) both one and the other, e.g. *The girls sat either side of him.*

ejaculate, ejaculates, ejaculating, ejaculated
1 (verb) When a man ejaculates, he discharges semen from his penis.
2 If you ejaculate, you suddenly say something.
ejaculation (noun).
[from Latin *jacere* meaning 'to throw']

eject, ejects, ejecting, ejected
(verb) If you eject something or someone, you forcefully push or send them out, e.g. *The pod was ejected from the spacecraft.*
ejection (noun).
[from Latin *ejicere* meaning 'to throw out']

Similar words: expel, throw out

eke, ekes, eking, eked (pronounced eek)
1 (verb) If you eke something out, you make it last as long as possible by using it sparingly.

2 If you eke out a living, you manage to survive in a difficult situation with very little money.
[from Old English *eacan* meaning 'to increase']

elaborate, elaborates, elaborating, elaborated
1 (adjective) carefully planned, detailed, and exact, e.g. *elaborate methods of concealment.*
2 highly decorated and complicated, e.g. *an elaborate tapestry.*
3 (verb) If you elaborate on something, you add more information or detail about it.
elaborately (adverb), **elaboration** (noun).
[from Latin *elaboratus* meaning 'produced by labour']

Similar words: (sense 3) expand, embellish, amplify

elapse, elapses, elapsing, elapsed
(verb) When time elapses, it passes by, e.g. *Very little time had elapsed since she fell asleep.*

elastic
1 (noun) Elastic is rubber material which stretches and returns to its original shape.
2 (adjective) able to stretch easily.
3 able to adapt to suit new circumstances and conditions when they arise, e.g. *an elastic policy.*
elasticity (noun).
[from Greek *elastikos* meaning 'pushing']

elation
(noun) Elation is a feeling of great happiness.
elated (adjective).

elbow, elbows, elbowing, elbowed
1 (noun) Your elbow is the joint between the upper part of your arm and your forearm.
2 (verb) If you elbow someone aside, you push them away with your elbow.
3 If you elbow your way through something, you push your way through with your elbows.

elder, eldest; elders
1 (adjective) Your elder brother or sister is older than you.
2 (noun) An elder is a senior member of a group who has influence or authority.
3 An elder is also a bush or small tree with white scented flowers and dark purple berries.

elderly
1 (adjective) An elderly person is rather old.
2 (noun) The elderly are people who are old, e.g. *The elderly need to be cared for.*

elect, elects, electing, elected
1 (verb) If you elect someone, you choose them, usually by voting, e.g. *She was elected captain.*
2 (a formal use) If you elect to do something, you choose to do it, e.g. *He elected to go to college.*
3 (adjective; a formal use) voted into a position, but not yet carrying out the duties of the position, e.g. *the vice-president elect.*
[from Latin *eligere* meaning 'to select']

election, elections
(noun) An election is the selection of one or more people for an official position by voting.
electoral (adjective).

electioneer, electioneers, electioneering, electioneered
(verb) Someone who electioneers works to persuade people to vote for a particular person or political party.

electorate, electorates
(noun) The electorate is all the people who have the right to vote in an election.

electric
1 (adjective) powered by, produced by, or carrying electricity.
2 very tense or exciting, e.g. *She gave an electric performance.*

electrical
(adjective) using, producing, or concerning electricity, e.g. *an electrical fault.*
electrically (adverb).

electric chair, electric chairs
(noun) The electric chair is a system of execution in the USA, in which criminals sit in the chair and are killed by a powerful electric current.

electrician, electricians
(noun) An electrician is a person whose job is to install, maintain, and repair electrical equipment.

electricity
(noun) Electricity is a form of energy used to provide power for machines, produced by means such as water, sun, coal, oil, and nuclear power. Electricity consists of the movement of charged particles such as electrons or ions.
[from Greek *ēlektron* meaning 'amber'; in early experiments, scientists rubbed amber in order to get an electrical charge]

electrify, electrifies, electrifying, electrified
1 (verb) If a piece of equipment is electrified, it is connected to a supply of electricity.
2 If an event electrifies you, it makes you feel very excited, e.g. *The film electrified her.*

electrocute, electrocutes, electrocuting, electrocuted
(verb) If someone is electrocuted, they are killed by touching something that is connected to electricity.
electrocution (noun).

electrode, electrodes
(noun) An electrode is a small piece of metal which allows an electric current to pass between a source of power and a piece of equipment.
[from *electric* and Greek *hodos* meaning 'way']

electrolysis (pronounced il-ek-**trol**-iss-iss)
(noun) Electrolysis is the process of passing an electric current through a substance in order to produce chemical changes in it.
[from *electric* and Greek *lysis* meaning 'loosening']

electromagnet, electromagnets
(noun) An electromagnet is a magnet made up of an iron or steel core with a coil of wire round it, through which an electric current is passed.
electromagnetic (adjective).

electron, electrons
(noun) In physics, an electron is a tiny particle of matter, which has a negative electrical charge and orbits the nucleus of an atom.

electronic
(adjective) having transistors, silicon chips, or valves which control an electric current.
electronically (adverb).

electronics
(noun) Electronics is the technology of electronic devices such as radios, televisions, and computers; also the study of how these devices work.

electroplate, electroplates, electroplating, electroplated
(verb) To electroplate something means to coat it with a thin layer of metal by dipping it in a special liquid through which an electric current is passed.

elegant
1 (adjective) pleasing and graceful in appearance, e.g. *an elegant dress.*
2 cleverly simple and clear, e.g. *an elegant speech... an elegant plan.*
elegantly (adverb), **elegance** (noun).
[from Greek *elegans* meaning 'choosing carefully']

elegiac (pronounced el-lij-**eye**-ak)
(adjective; a literary word) expressing or showing sadness.

elegy, elegies (pronounced **el**-lij-ee)
(noun) An elegy is a sad poem or song about someone who has died.
[from Greek *elegos* meaning 'lament sung to the flute']

element, elements
1 (noun) An element of something is a part which combines with others to make a whole.
2 The elements of a subject are the basic and most important points.
3 A particular element within a large group of people is a section of it which is similar, e.g. *the criminal element in society.*
4 An element of a quality is a small amount of it, e.g. *There was an element of sadness in the film.*
5 The element in an electric fire, water heater, or kettle is the metal part which heats up when electricity passes through it.
6 In chemistry, an element is a substance that is made up of only one type of atom.
7 The elements are the weather conditions, e.g. *He would never have survived the elements.*
8 In maths, an element is a number forming part of a sequence, for example in a matrix, or one of the figures which make up a set.
9 (phrase) If you are **in your element**, you are in a situation where you are happiest.
[from Latin *elementum* meaning 'principle' or 'rudiment']

elemental
(adjective; a formal word) simple and basic, but powerful, e.g. *outbursts of elemental rage.*

elementary
(adjective) simple, basic, and straightforward, e.g. *The elementary rules are easy to learn.*

elephant, elephants
(noun) An elephant is a very large mammal with thick leathery skin, a long trunk, and tusks. Elephants are found in Africa and India.

elephantine
(adjective) very large and rather clumsy.

elevate, elevates, elevating, elevated
1 (verb) To elevate someone to a higher status or position means to give them greater status or importance, e.g. *He was elevated to captain.*
2 To elevate something means to raise it up.

elevation, elevations
1 (noun) The elevation of someone or something is the raising of them to a higher level or position.
2 The elevation of a place is its height above sea level or above the ground.
3 In architecture, an elevation is a scale drawing of the outside face of a building.
[from Latin *levare* meaning 'to raise']

elevator, elevators
(noun) In American English, an elevator is a lift.

eleven, elevens
1 Eleven is the number 11.
2 (noun) An eleven is a team of cricket or football players.
eleventh.

elevenses
(noun) Elevenses is a small snack eaten in the middle of the morning about eleven o'clock.

eleventh hour
(noun) The eleventh hour is the last possible moment before doing something, e.g. *It was an eleventh-hour decision.*

elf, elves
(noun) In folklore, an elf is a small mischievous fairy.

elfin or elfish
(adjective) small and delicate and looking like an elf, e.g. *The little boy had elfin features.*

elicit, elicits, eliciting, elicited (pronounced il-**iss**-it)
1 (verb; a formal use) If you elicit information, you find it out by asking careful questions.
2 If you elicit a response or reaction, you make it happen, e.g. *Their entrance elicited cheers.*
[from Latin *elicere* meaning 'to lure forth']

elide, elides, eliding, elided
(verb; a technical word) If you elide a part of a word, you do not pronounce it when you speak.
[from Latin *elidere* meaning 'to knock']

eligible (pronounced **el**-lij-i-bl)
(adjective) suitable or having the right qualifications for something, e.g. *He was not eligible for unemployment benefit.*
eligibility (noun).
[from Latin *eligere* meaning 'to choose']

eliminate, eliminates, eliminating, eliminated
1 (verb) If you eliminate something, you get rid of it, e.g. *Poverty must be eliminated.*
2 If a team or a person is eliminated from a competition, they can no longer take part.
elimination (noun).
[from Latin *eliminare* meaning 'to turn out of the house']

elision
(noun) Elision is the leaving out of a sound when you pronounce a word.

elite, elites (pronounced ill-**eet**)
1 (noun) An elite is a group of the most powerful, rich, talented, or educated people in a society.
2 (adjective) the best of its kind, e.g. *an elite businessman's club.*
[from Old French *eslit* meaning 'chosen']

elitism
(noun) Elitism is the belief that society should be governed by a small group of people who are considered superior to everyone else.
elitist (adjective and noun).

elixir, elixirs (pronounced ill-**ik**-seer)
(noun) An elixir is a liquid believed to have magical powers, for example to cure any illness or to keep a person young.
[from Arabic *al iksir*]

Elizabethan, Elizabethans
1 (noun) An Elizabethan was a person who lived in the time of Elizabeth I (1558-1603).
2 (adjective) Someone or something that is Elizabethan lived or was made during the reign of Elizabeth I.

elk, elks
(noun) An elk is the largest type of deer, found in North Europe, Asia, and North America.

ellipse, ellipses
(noun) An ellipse is a regular oval shape, like a circle seen from an angle.

ellipsis, ellipses
(noun; a technical word) Ellipsis is the omission of parts of a sentence when the sentence can be understood without these parts. An example is 'You coming too?', where 'Are' has been omitted from the beginning of the question.
[from Greek *elleipsis* meaning 'omission']

elliptical
1 (adjective) shaped like an ellipse.
2 Elliptical writing or speech is difficult to understand because it is too condensed or too concise.

elm, elms
(noun) An elm is a tall deciduous tree with broad leaves. Its wood is used for timber and furniture.

elocution
(noun) Elocution is the art or study of speaking clearly or well in public with a standard accent.
[from Latin *elocutio* meaning 'a speaking out']

elongate, elongates, elongating, elongated
(verb) To elongate something means to make it longer.
elongation (noun).

elongated
(adjective) long and thin.

elope, elopes, eloping, eloped
(verb) If someone elopes, they run away secretly with their lover to get married.
elopement (noun).
[from medieval French *aloper* meaning 'to run away']

eloquent
(adjective) skilfully expressive and fluent in speech or writing, e.g. *an eloquent speech.*
eloquently (adverb), eloquence (noun).
[from Latin *eloquens* meaning 'speaking out']

else
1 (adverb) other than this or more than this, e.g. *Let's do something else... What else do you want?*
2 (conjunction) used to introduce a possibility or an alternative, e.g. *You've got to be very careful or else you'll miss the turning.*

elsewhere
(adverb) in or to another place or places, e.g. *I'd rather go elsewhere.*

elucidate, elucidates, elucidating, elucidated
(pronounced ill-**oo**-sid-ate)
(verb) If you elucidate something, you make it clear and understandable.
elucidation (noun).
[from Latin *elucidare* meaning 'to enlighten']

elude, eludes, eluding, eluded (pronounced ill-**ood**)
1 (verb) If a fact or idea eludes you, you cannot understand it or remember it.
2 If you elude someone or something, you avoid them or escape from them, e.g. *The murderer eluded the police every time.*
[from Latin *eludere* meaning 'to deceive']

elusive
(adjective) difficult to find, achieve, describe, or remember, e.g. *an elusive flavour.*

elves the plural of elf.

emaciated (pronounced im-**may**-see-ate-ed)
(adjective) extremely thin and weak, because of illness or lack of food.
emaciation (noun).
[from Latin *emacere* meaning 'to make thin']

emanate, emanates, emanating, emanated
(verb) If something emanates from a person or thing, it comes from them, e.g. *A strong smell emanated from the kitchen.*
emanation (noun).
[from Latin *emanare* meaning 'to flow out']

emancipate, emancipates, emancipating, emancipated
(verb) To emancipate someone means to free them from situations or restrictions which are unpleasant or harmful.
emancipation (noun).
[from Latin *emancipare* meaning 'to give independence to a son']

emasculate, emasculates, emasculating, emasculated
(verb) To emasculate someone or something means to remove their strength or power so that they become weak or ineffective.
emasculation (noun).
[from Latin *emasculare* meaning 'to castrate']

embalm, embalms, embalming, embalmed
(pronounced im-**bahm**)
(verb) If a dead body is embalmed, it is treated with chemicals to preserve it.
embalmer (noun).

embankment, embankments
(noun) An embankment is a man-made ridge built to support a road or railway or to prevent water from overflowing.

embargo, embargoes, embargoing, embargoed
1 (noun) An embargo is an order made by a government to stop trade with another country.
2 (verb) To embargo goods means to officially stop them going to another country.
[from Spanish *embargar* meaning 'to arrest']

embark, embarks, embarking, embarked
1 (verb) If you embark, you go onto a ship at the start of a journey.
2 If you embark on something, you start it, e.g. *He embarked upon a new career.*
embarkation (noun).
[from French *barque* meaning 'boat']

embarrass, embarrasses, embarrassing, embarrassed
(verb) If you embarrass someone, you make them feel shy, ashamed, or uncomfortable, e.g. *She was embarrassed by the expensive gift.*
embarrassed (adjective), **embarrassing** (adjective), **embarrassment** (noun).
[from Italian *imbarrazzare* meaning 'to impede']

embassy, embassies
(noun) An embassy is the building in which an ambassador and his or her staff work; also used of the ambassador and his or her staff.

embattled
(adjective) involved in conflicts and disagreements with people, e.g. *embattled politicians.*

embed, embeds, embedding, embedded
(verb) If something is embedded, it is fixed firmly and deeply, e.g. *The words are embedded in my memory.*

embellish, embellishes, embellishing, embellished
(verb) If you embellish something, you make it more beautiful or interesting by adding to it, e.g. *an embellished account of the event.*
embellishment (noun).
[from French *bel* meaning 'beautiful']

ember, embers
(noun) Embers are glowing or smouldering pieces of coal or wood from a dying fire.

embezzle, embezzles, embezzling, embezzled
(verb) To embezzle money means to steal it from an organization that you work for.
embezzlement (noun), **embezzler** (noun).
[from Old French *beseiller* meaning 'to make away with']

embitter, embitters, embittering, embittered.
(verb) If you are embittered by something, you feel angry or resentful because of it.
embitterment (noun).

emblazoned (pronounced im-**blaze**-nd)
(adjective) If something is emblazoned with designs, it is decorated with them, e.g. *a school jacket, emblazoned with a coat of arms.*
[originally a heraldic term from Old French *blason* meaning 'shield']

emblem, emblems
(noun) An emblem is an object or a design chosen to represent an organization or an idea, e.g. *the emblem of the Boy Scouts... an emblem of hope.*
emblematic (adjective).
[from Latin *emblema* meaning 'raised decoration' or 'mosaic']

embody, embodies, embodying, embodied
1 (verb) To embody a particular quality or idea means to contain it or express it, e.g. *He embodies strength and gentleness.*
2 If a number of things are embodied in one thing, they are contained in it, e.g. *These proposals were embodied in the Race Relations Act.*
embodiment (noun).

embolden, emboldens, emboldening, emboldened
(verb) If something or someone emboldens you, they give you confidence to do something.

embossed
(adjective) decorated with designs that stand up slightly from the surface, e.g. *embossed paper.*

embrace, embraces, embracing, embraced
1 (verb) If you embrace someone, you hug them when you greet them or to show affection.
2 (noun) An embrace is a hug.
3 (verb) If something embraces a group of people, things, or ideas, it includes them all, e.g. *The course embraces elements of chemistry, physics, and engineering.*
4 If you embrace an idea, religion, or political system, you accept it and believe in it.
[from Old French *embracier*, from *brace* meaning 'arms']

embrocation, embrocations
(noun; a formal word) An embrocation is an ointment that is rubbed into the skin to relieve sore and aching muscles.
[from Latin *embrocha* meaning 'poultice']

embroider, embroiders, embroidering, embroidered
1 (verb) If you embroider fabric, you sew a decorative design onto it.
2 If you embroider a story, you add details from your imagination to make it more interesting or exciting.

embroidery
(noun) Embroidery is decorative designs sewn onto fabric; also the art or skill of embroidery.

embroil, embroils, embroiling, embroiled
(verb) If someone is embroiled in an argument, conflict, or trouble, they become deeply involved in it and cannot get out of it, e.g. *This episode embroiled him in a major political storm.*
[from French *brouiller* meaning 'to mingle' or 'to confuse']

embryo, embryos (pronounced **em**-bree-oh)
1 (noun) An embryo is an animal or human being in the very early stages of development in the womb.
2 (phrase) If something is **in embryo**, it is in the very early stages of development.
embryonic (adjective).
[from Greek *embruon* meaning 'new-born animal']

emend, emends, emending, emended
(verb) If you emend a piece of writing, you correct it.
emendation (noun).

emerald, emeralds
1 (noun) An emerald is a bright green precious stone.
2 (noun and adjective) bright green.

emerge, emerges, emerging, emerged
1 (verb) If someone emerges from a place, they come out of it so that they can be seen.
2 If you emerge from a difficult or bad experience, you come to the end of it, e.g. *He emerged from the divorce a wiser man.*
3 If something emerges, it becomes known or begins to be recognized as existing, e.g. *Interesting facts emerged.*
emergence (noun), emergent (adjective).
[from Latin *emergere* meaning 'to rise up from']

emergency, emergencies
1 (noun) An emergency is an unexpected and serious event which needs immediate action to deal with it.
2 (adjective) Emergency equipment or supplies are intended to be used in an emergency.

Similar words: (sense 1) crisis, exigency

emery board, emery boards
(noun) An emery board is a strip of cardboard with a rough surface, used for filing fingernails.
[from Greek *smuris* meaning 'powder for rubbing']

emetic, emetics
(noun) An emetic is a substance that causes people to vomit.
[from Greek *emein* meaning 'to vomit']

emigrant, emigrants
(noun) An emigrant is a person who leaves their native country and goes to live permanently in another one.

emigrate, emigrates, emigrating, emigrated
(verb) If you emigrate, you leave your native country and go to live permanently in another one.
emigration (noun).

emigré, emigrés (pronounced **em**-ig-ray)
(noun) An emigré is a person who has left their country for political reasons.

eminence
1 (noun) Eminence is the quality of being well known and respected for what you do, e.g. *a chef of eminence.*
2 'Your Eminence' is a title of respect used to address a Roman Catholic cardinal.

eminent
(adjective) well known and respected for what you do, e.g. *an eminent doctor of physics.*
[from Latin *eminere* meaning 'to project' or 'to stand out']

eminently
(adverb; a formal word) very, e.g. *eminently sensible.*

emir, emirs (pronounced em-**eer**); also spelled **amir**
(noun) An emir is a Muslim ruler or nobleman.
[from Arabic *amir* meaning 'commander']

emissary, emissaries (pronounced **em**-iss-ar-ee)
(noun; a formal word) An emissary is an agent or messenger sent by a government or leader.

emission, emissions
(noun; a formal word) The emission of something such as gas or radiation is the release of it into the atmosphere.

emit, emits, emitting, emitted
(verb) To emit something means to give it out or release it, e.g. *The food emitted a strong smell.*
[from Latin *emittere* meaning 'to send out']

Similar words: exude, give off

emollient, emollients
(noun; a formal word) An emollient is a liquid or cream used to soften the skin.

emotion, emotions
(noun) An emotion is any strong feeling, such as love or fear.
[from Old French *émouvoir* meaning 'to move the feelings']

emotional
1 (adjective) causing strong feelings, e.g. *an emotional discussion... an emotional film.*
2 influenced by feelings rather than by thought, e.g. *He's always been an emotional person.*
3 to do with feelings rather than your physical condition, e.g. *She had emotional problems.*
4 showing your feelings openly, e.g. *She became very emotional and cried.*
emotionally (adverb).

emotive
(adjective) concerning emotions, or stirring up strong emotions, e.g. *He gave an emotive performance in the play... an emotive picture.*
emotively (adverb).

empathize, empathizes, empathizing, empathized; also spelled **empathise**
(verb) If you empathize with someone, you understand how they are feeling.
empathy (noun).
[from Greek *empatheia* meaning 'affection' or 'passion']

emperor, emperors
(noun) An emperor is a male ruler of an empire.
[from Latin *imperator* meaning 'commander-in-chief']

emphasis, emphases
(noun) Emphasis is special importance or extra stress given to something.
[from Greek *emphasis*, a term used in rhetoric meaning 'significant stress']

emphasize, emphasizes, emphasizing, emphasized; also spelled **emphasise**
(verb) If you emphasize something, you make it known that it is very important, e.g. *He emphasized how long the journey would be.*

emphatic
(adjective) expressed strongly and with force to

show how important something is, e.g. *John was emphatic about leaving college.*
emphatically (adverb).

emphysema (pronounced em-fiss-**ee**-ma)
(noun; a medical word) Emphysema is an illness caused by too much air or gas in an organ of the body, which makes breathing difficult and infections more likely.
[from Greek *emphusēma* meaning 'a swelling up']

empire, empires
1 (noun) An empire is a group of countries controlled by one country.
2 An empire is also a powerful group of companies controlled by one person.
[from Latin *imperium* meaning 'rule']

empirical
(adjective) based on practical experience rather than theories.
empirically (adverb).

empiricism (pronounced em-**pir**-iss-i-zm)
(noun) In philosophy, empiricism is the belief that everything we know is based on our experience.
[from Greek *empeiria* meaning 'experience']

employ, employs, employing, employed
1 (verb) If you employ someone, you pay them to work for you.
2 If you employ something for a particular purpose, you make use of it.
[from Latin *implicari* meaning 'to be involved in']

Similar words: (sense 1) hire, engage, take on

employee, employees
(noun) An employee is a person who is paid to work for another person or for an organization.

employer, employers
(noun) Someone's employer is the person or company that they work for.

employment
(noun) Employment is the position of having a paid job, or the recruiting of people for a job.

emporium, emporia or emporiums
(noun; an old-fashioned word) An emporium is a large shop which sells many different things.

empower, empowers, empowering, empowered
(verb) If you are empowered to do something, you have the authority or power to do it.

empress, empresses
(noun) An empress is a woman who rules an empire, or the wife of an emperor.

empty, emptier, emptiest; empties, emptying, emptied
1 (adjective) having nothing or nobody inside.
2 without purpose, value, or meaning, e.g. *She gave me an empty look... empty words.*
3 (verb) If you empty something, or empty its contents, you remove the contents.
emptily (adverb), **emptiness** (noun).

Similar words: (sense 2) blank, vacant, void
(sense 3) vacate, evacuate, void

emu, emus (pronounced **ee**-myoo)
(noun) An emu is a large greyish-brown Australian bird with long legs and three-toed feet. It can run fast, but cannot fly.
[from Portuguese *ema* meaning 'ostrich']

emulate, emulates, emulating, emulated
(verb) If you emulate someone or something, you imitate them because you admire them.
emulation (noun).
[from Latin *aemulare* meaning 'to compete with']

emulsify, emulsifies, emulsifying, emulsified
(verb) When two liquids of different thicknesses emulsify, or when something emulsifies them, they join together.
emulsification (noun), **emulsifier** (noun).

emulsion, emulsions
1 (noun) In photography, emulsion is a substance used to make photographic film sensitive to light.
2 Emulsion is also a water-based paint.

enable, enables, enabling, enabled
(verb) To enable something to happen means to make it possible.

enact, enacts, enacting, enacted
1 (verb) If a government enacts a law or bill, it officially passes it so that it becomes law.
2 If you enact a story or play, you act it out.
enactment (noun).

enamel, enamels, enamelling, enamelled
1 (noun) Enamel is a substance like glass, used to decorate or protect metal, glass, or china.
2 The enamel on your teeth is the hard, white substance that forms the outer part.
3 (verb) If you enamel something, you decorate or cover it with enamel.
enamelled (adjective).

enamoured (pronounced in-**am**-erd)
(adjective) If you are enamoured of someone or something, you like them very much.
[from French *amour* meaning 'love']

encamp, encamps, encamping, encamped
(verb) To encamp means to settle in a camp, e.g. *The army were encamped outside the city.*
encampment (noun).

encapsulate, encapsulates, encapsulating, encapsulated
(verb) If something encapsulates facts or ideas, it contains or represents them in a small space.

encase, encases, encasing, encased
(verb) To encase something means to surround or cover it with a substance, e.g. *encased in leather.*

enchant, enchants, enchanting, enchanted
1 (verb) If something or someone enchants you, they fascinate or charm you.
2 To enchant someone or something means to put a magic spell on them.
enchanted (adjective).
[from Latin *incantare* meaning 'to chant a spell']

enchanter, enchanters
(noun) An enchanter is a magician or wizard.

enchanting
(adjective) attractive, delightful, or charming,
e.g. *an enchanting smile.*
enchantingly (adverb).

encircle, encircles, encircling, encircled
(verb) To encircle something or someone means
to completely surround or enclose them.

enclave, enclaves
(noun) An enclave is a place that is surrounded
by areas that are completely different from it in
some important way, for example because the
people who live there are of a different race.
[from Old French *enclaver* meaning 'to enclose']

enclose, encloses, enclosing, enclosed
1 (verb) To enclose an object or area means to
surround it with something solid.
2 If you enclose something with a letter, you put
it in the same envelope.
enclosed (adjective).

enclosure, enclosures
(noun) An enclosure is an area of land
surrounded by a wall or fence and used for a
particular purpose.

**encompass, encompasses, encompassing,
encompassed**
1 (verb) To encompass a number of things means
to include all of those things, e.g. *The book
encompassed all aspects of maths.*
2 To encompass a place means to surround it.

encore, encores (pronounced **ong**-kor)
(noun) An encore is a short extra performance
given by an entertainer because the audience
asks for it.
[from French *encore* meaning 'again']

**encounter, encounters, encountering,
encountered**
1 (verb) If you encounter something, you meet it
or are faced with it, e.g. *She encountered many
problems in her new job.*
2 (noun) An encounter is a meeting, especially
when it is difficult or unexpected.

encourage, encourages, encouraging, encouraged
1 (verb) If you encourage someone, you give
them courage and confidence to do something.
2 If someone or something encourages a
particular activity, they support it, e.g.
Lunchtime clubs were encouraged at the school.
encouragingly (adverb), **encouragement** (noun).

Similar words: (sense 1) urge, egg on

encroach, encroaches, encroaching, encroached
(verb) If something encroaches on a place or on
your time or rights, it gradually takes up or
takes away more and more of it.
encroachment (noun).
[from French *encrochier* meaning 'to seize with
hooks']

encrusted
(adjective) covered with a crust or layer of
something, e.g. *clothes encrusted with jewels.*
encrustation (noun).

**encumber, encumbers, encumbering,
encumbered**
(verb) If something encumbers you, it prevents
you from moving or doing what you want, e.g.
passengers encumbered with parcels.

encumbrance, encumbrances
(noun) An encumbrance is something or someone
that prevents you from moving or doing what
you want.
[from Old French *combre* meaning 'barrier']

encyclopedia, encyclopedias
(pronounced en-sigh-klop-**ee**-dee-a); also spelled
encyclopaedia
(noun) An encyclopedia is a book or set of books
giving information and facts about many
different subjects, places, things, and people,
and usually arranged in alphabetical order.
[from Greek *enkuklios paideia* meaning 'general
education']

encyclopedic or **encyclopaedic**
(adjective) knowing or giving information about
many different things.

end, ends, ending, ended
1 (noun) The end of a period of time, an event, or
an experience is the last part.
2 The end of something is the farthest point of it.
3 An end is the purpose for which something is
done, e.g. *money used for political ends.*
4 (verb) If something ends or if you end it, it
comes to a finish.
5 (phrase) If you **make ends meet**, you have just
enough money to live on.
6 If you are **at a loose end**, you have nothing to
do.

Similar words: (sense 2) extremity, tip

endanger, endangers, endangering, endangered
(verb) To endanger something means to cause it
to be in a dangerous and harmful situation, e.g.
Insecticides can endanger wildlife.
endangered (adjective).

Similar words: imperil, jeopardize

endear, endears, endearing, endeared
(verb) If someone's behaviour endears them to
you, it makes you fond of them.
endearing (adjective), **endearingly** (adverb).

endearment, endearments
(noun) Endearments are words or phrases that
you use to show love or affection for someone.

**endeavour, endeavours, endeavouring,
endeavoured** (pronounced in-**dev**-er)
1 (verb; a formal word) If you endeavour to do
something, you try very hard to do it.
2 (noun) An endeavour is an effort to do or
achieve something.
[from Middle English *dever* meaning 'duty']

endemic
(adjective) found naturally or commonly in a
particular area, e.g. *Malaria was endemic in
Ceylon.*
[from Greek *endēmos* meaning 'native']

ending, endings
(noun) The ending is the final or concluding part
of something, especially of a film, play, or book.

endless
(adjective) having or seeming to have no end.

endocrine
(adjective; a medical word) The endocrine system is the system of glands that pass hormones directly into the bloodstream.

endorse, endorses, endorsing, endorsed
1 (verb) If you endorse someone or something, you give approval and support to them.
2 If you endorse a document, you write your signature or a comment on it, usually to show that you approve of it.
3 If a driving licence is endorsed, an official note is made on it that the person has been found guilty of a driving offence.
endorsement (noun).
[from Old French *endosser* meaning 'to put on the back']

endow, endows, endowing, endowed
(pronounced in-**dow**)
1 (verb) If someone is endowed with a quality or ability, they have it or are given it, e.g. *He has been endowed with a very sharp mind.*
2 If someone endows an institution, they provide it with money or with a permanent income.
endowment (noun).

endurance
(noun) Endurance is the ability to put up with a difficult situation for a period of time.

endure, endures, enduring, endured
1 (verb) If you endure a difficult or unpleasant situation, you put up with it calmly and patiently.
2 If something endures, it lasts or continues to exist.
enduring (adjective).
[from Latin *indurare* meaning 'to harden']

enema, enemas
(noun) An enema is a liquid that is put into a person's rectum in order to empty their bowels.
[from Greek *enienai* meaning 'to send in']

enemy, enemies
1 (noun) An enemy is a person or group that is hostile or opposed to another person or group.
2 (adjective) hostile or opposed to something or someone.
[from Latin *inimicus* meaning 'hostile']

Similar words: (sense 1) foe, adversary, opponent

energetic
(adjective) having or showing energy or enthusiasm.
energetically (adverb).

Similar words: lively, vigorous, dynamic, alive

energy, energies
1 (noun) Energy is the physical strength to do active things.
2 Energy is the power which drives machinery.
3 In physics, energy is the capacity of a body or system to do work. It is measured in joules.
[from Greek *energeia* meaning 'activity']

Similar words: (sense 1) verve, vigour, vitality, life, zest, go

enervate, enervates, enervating, enervated
(verb) If something enervates you, it takes away your strength or liveliness.
enervating (adjective), enervation (noun).

enfeebled
(adjective) extremely weak.

enfold, enfolds, enfolding, enfolded
(verb) To enfold something means to cover it or be wrapped round it, e.g. *Darkness enfolded us.*

enforce, enforces, enforcing, enforced
(verb) If you enforce a law or a rule, you make sure that it is obeyed.
enforceable (adjective), enforcement (noun)

enfranchise, enfranchises, enfranchising, enfranchised
(verb; a formal word) To enfranchise someone means to give them the right to vote in elections.
enfranchisement (noun).
[from Old French *enfranchir* meaning 'to set free']

engage, engages, engaging, engaged
1 (verb) To engage someone means to obtain their help, or services, e.g. *A new foreman was engaged.*
2 To engage someone's attention or interest means to gain it, e.g *They engaged her in conversation.*
3 If you engage in an activity, you take part in it.
4 When a part of a machine or other mechanism engages or is engaged, it locks with other parts and begins to operate, e.g. *She engaged first gear.*

engaged
1 (adjective) When two people are engaged, they have agreed to marry each other.
2 If someone or something is engaged, they are occupied or busy, e.g. *The phone was engaged.*
[from Old French *gage* meaning 'pledge']

engagement, engagements
1 (noun) An engagement is an appointment that you have with someone.
2 An engagement is also an agreement that two people have made with each other to get married.

engaging
(adjective) pleasant, charming, or interesting, e.g. *She spoke with an engaging honesty.*
engagingly (adverb).

engender, engenders, engendering, engendered
(pronounced in-**jen**-der)
(verb; a formal word) If someone or something engenders a particular feeling, atmosphere, or situation, they cause it to happen, e.g. *It is said that violent films engender violent behaviour.*
[from Latin *generare* meaning 'to beget']

engine, engines
1 (noun) An engine is any machine designed to convert heat or other kinds of energy into mechanical movement.
2 An engine is also a railway locomotive.
[from Latin *ingenium* meaning 'ingenious device']

engineer, engineers, engineering, engineered
1 (noun) An engineer is a person trained in designing and constructing machinery, engines, and electrical devices, or roads and bridges.
2 An engineer is also a person who repairs mechanical or electrical devices.
3 (verb) If you engineer an event or situation, you plan or cause it in a clever or devious way.

engineering
(noun) Engineering is the profession of designing and constructing machinery, engines, and electrical devices, or roads and bridges.

English
1 (adjective) belonging to or relating to England.
2 (noun) English is the main language spoken in the United Kingdom, the USA, Canada, Australia, and many other countries.

Englishman, Englishmen
(noun) An Englishman is a man who comes from England.
Englishwoman (noun).

engrave, engraves, engraving, engraved
1 (verb) To engrave means to cut marks, such as letters or designs, into a hard surface with a tool.
2 If paper is engraved, a design has been printed on it from an engraved plate.
3 If something is engraved on your mind, memory, or heart, it is fixed there permanently so that you feel that you will never forget it.

engraving, engravings
(noun) An engraving is a picture or design that has been cut into a hard surface; also, a print taken from such a picture or design.
engraver (noun).

engross, engrosses, engrossing, engrossed
(verb) If something or someone engrosses you, they hold all your attention, e.g. *She was engrossed in her book.*
engrossing (adjective).
[from French *en gros* meaning 'in quantity']

Similar words: absorb, immerse, involve

engulf, engulfs, engulfing, engulfed
(verb) To engulf something means to completely cover or surround it, e.g. *Flames engulfed them.*

enhance, enhances, enhancing, enhanced
(verb) To enhance something means to make it more valuable or attractive, e.g. *The herbs enhance the flavour of the meat.*
enhancement (noun).
[from Old French *haucier* meaning 'to raise']

enigma, enigmas
(noun) An enigma is anything which is puzzling or difficult to understand.
[from Greek *ainigma* meaning 'riddle']

enigmatic
(adjective) mysterious, puzzling, or difficult to understand, e.g. *an enigmatic smile.*
enigmatically (adverb).

enjoin, enjoins, enjoining, enjoined
(verb; a formal word) If you enjoin someone to do something, you order them to do it.

enjoy, enjoys, enjoying, enjoyed
1 (verb) If you enjoy something, you find pleasure and satisfaction in it.
2 If you enjoy something, you are lucky to have it or experience it, e.g. *They enjoyed good health.*

enjoyable
(adjective) giving pleasure or satisfaction.
enjoyably (adverb).

enjoyment
(noun) Enjoyment is the feeling of pleasure or satisfaction you get from something you enjoy.

enlarge, enlarges, enlarging, enlarged
1 (verb) When you enlarge something, it gets bigger.
2 If you enlarge on a subject, you give more details about it.

enlargement, enlargements
1 (noun) An enlargement of something is the action or process of making it bigger.
2 An enlargement is also something, especially a photograph, which has been made bigger.

enlighten, enlightens, enlightening, enlightened
(verb) To enlighten someone means to give them more knowledge or understanding of something.
enlightening (adjective), **enlightenment** (noun).

enlightened
(adjective) well-informed and willing to consider different opinions, e.g. *An enlightened approach.*

enlist, enlists, enlisting, enlisted
1 (verb) If someone enlists, they join the army, navy, or air force.
2 If you enlist someone's help, you persuade them to help you in something you are doing.

enliven, enlivens, enlivening, enlivened
(verb) To enliven something means to make it more lively or more cheerful.

en masse (pronounced on **mass**)
(adverb) If a group of people do something en masse, they do it together and at the same time.
[a French expression]

enmesh, enmeshes, enmeshing, enmeshed
(verb) If something is enmeshed, it is caught up or tangled in something.

enmity
(noun) Enmity is a feeling of anger or hatred for a person you strongly disagree with.

ennoble, ennobles, ennobling, ennobled
(verb) If something ennobles you, it makes you noble, honourable, or dignified.
ennoblement (noun).

ennui (pronounced on-wee)
(noun; a formal word) Ennui is a feeling of boredom and tiredness.
[from French *ennui* meaning 'apathy']

enormity, enormities
1 (noun) The enormity of a problem or difficulty is its great size and seriousness.
2 An enormity is something that is thought to be a terrible crime or offence.

enormous
(adjective) very large in size, amount, or degree.
enormously (adverb).

enough
1 (adjective and adverb) as much or as many as is needed, e.g. *Do you have enough money?... You've worked hard enough.*
2 (noun) Enough is the quantity necessary for something, e.g. *I've had enough, thank you.*
3 (adverb) very or fairly, e.g. *She was pleased enough to see me.*

enquire, enquires, enquiring, enquired; also spelled inquire
1 (verb) If you enquire about something or someone, you ask about them.
2 If you enquire into a crime, you investigate it.

enquiry, enquiries; also spelled inquiry
1 (noun) An enquiry is a question that you ask in order to find something out.
2 An enquiry is also an investigation into something that has happened and that needs explaining.

enrage, enrages, enraging, enraged
(verb) If something enrages you, it makes you very angry.
enraged (adjective).

enraptured
(adjective) filled with pleasure, joy, and fascination.

enrich, enriches, enriching, enriched
(verb) To enrich something means to improve the quality or value of it, e.g. *Travelling enriches one's experience of life.*
enriched (adjective), **enrichment** (noun).

enrol, enrols, enrolling, enrolled
(verb) If you enrol for something such as a course or a college, you sign your name on a list or register to join or become a member of it.
enrolment (noun).

en route (pronounced on **root**)
(adverb) If something happens en route to a place, it happens on the way there.
[a French expression]

ensconce, ensconces, ensconcing, ensconced
(verb) If you ensconce yourself or are ensconced in a particular place, you settle yourself there firmly and comfortably.
[from Old French *esconse* meaning 'hiding place']

ensemble, ensembles (pronounced on-**som**-bl)
1 (noun) An ensemble is a group of things or people considered as a whole rather than separately.
2 An ensemble is also a small group of musicians who play or sing together.
3 Someone who is wearing an ensemble is wearing a matching outfit of clothing.
[from French *ensemble* meaning 'together']

enshrine, enshrines, enshrining, enshrined
(verb) To enshrine something such as an idea or a thought means to cherish and keep it, e.g. *Memories of Julia were enshrined in his heart.*

ensign, ensigns
1 (noun) An ensign is a flag flown by a ship to show what country that ship belongs to.
2 An ensign is also the lowest ranking officer in

the American navy and formerly in the British army.
[from Latin *insignia* meaning 'badge of office']

enslave, enslaves, enslaving, enslaved
(verb) To enslave someone means to dominate them, e.g. *Her husband was enslaved by alcohol.*
enslaved (adjective), **enslavement** (noun).

ensnare, ensnares, ensnaring, ensnared
(verb) If you ensnare someone, you gain power over them, especially by dishonest or devious means.

ensue, ensues, ensuing, ensued (pronounced en-**syoo**)
(verb) If something ensues, it happens after another event, usually as a result of it, e.g. *Chaos ensued when the team walked off the pitch.*
ensuing (adjective).
[from Old French *ensuivre* meaning 'to follow after']

en suite (pronounced on **sweet**)
(adverb) If a bedroom has a bathroom en suite, it has a private bathroom that leads directly off it.
[from French *en + suite* meaning 'in sequence']

ensure, ensures, ensuring, ensured
(verb) To ensure that something happens means to make certain that it happens, e.g. *Please ensure that the oven is off before you go out.*

entail, entails, entailing, entailed
(verb) If one thing entails another, the second thing follows necessarily and inevitably from the first, e.g. *This job entails working long hours.*
[from Old French *taille* meaning 'limitation']

entangle, entangles, entangling, entangled
1 (verb) If something is entangled in something else, it is caught or tangled up in it.
2 If you are entangled in problems or difficulties, you are involved in them.
entanglement (noun).

entente, ententes (pronounced on-**tont**)
(noun) An entente is a friendly understanding or agreement between two or more countries.
[from French *entente cordiale* meaning 'friendly understanding']

enter, enters, entering, entered
1 (verb) To enter a place means to go into it.
2 If you enter an organization or institution, you join and become a member of it, e.g. *He entered the priesthood at an early age.*
3 If you enter a competition, race, or examination, you take part in it.

enterprise, enterprises
1 (noun) An enterprise is a project or task, especially one involving boldness and effort.
2 Enterprise is a readiness to start new projects.
3 An enterprise is a business or company.
[from French *entreprendre* meaning 'to undertake']

enterprising
(adjective) ready to start new projects and tasks and full of boldness and initiative, e.g. *an enterprising young architect.*

entertain, entertains, entertaining, entertained
1 (verb) If you entertain people, you keep them amused, interested, or attentive.
2 If you entertain guests, you receive them into your house and give them food and hospitality.
3 If you entertain an idea or suggestion, you think that it is possible or worth considering.

Similar words: (sense 1) amuse, divert, regale

entertainer, entertainers
(noun) An entertainer is someone whose job is to amuse and please audiences.

entertaining
1 (adjective) amusing and full of interest.
2 (noun) Entertaining is the hospitality that you give to guests, e.g. *She enjoys entertaining.*

entertainment, entertainments
1 (noun) Entertainment is anything that people watch for pleasure, such as shows and films.
2 Entertainment is the act or art of entertaining, or the state of being entertained.

enthral, enthrals, enthralling, enthralled
(pronounced in-**thrawl**)
(verb) If you enthral someone, you hold their attention and interest completely.
enthralling (adjective).
[from Old English *thræl* meaning 'slave']

enthuse, enthuses, enthusing, enthused
(pronounced inth-**yooz**)
(verb) If you enthuse about something, you talk about it with enthusiasm and excitement.

enthusiasm, enthusiasms
1 (noun) Enthusiasm is interest, eagerness, or delight for something that you enjoy.
2 An enthusiasm is an activity or subject that interests you a great deal.
[from Greek *enthousiasmos* meaning 'possessed or inspired by the gods']

Similar words: (sense 1) gusto, animation, zeal, zest, fervour

enthusiast, enthusiasts (pronounced inth-**yooz**-ee-ast)
(noun) An enthusiast is a person who is very interested in something.

enthusiastic
(adjective) showing a lot of excitement, eagerness, or approval about something, e.g. *enthusiastic applause.*
enthusiastically (adverb).

entice, entices, enticing, enticed
(verb) If you entice someone to do something, you tempt them to do it, e.g. *We tried to entice the mouse out of the hole.*
enticement (noun).

enticing
(adjective) extremely attractive and tempting.
enticingly (adverb).

entire
(adjective) all of something, e.g. *He painted the entire fence blue.*
[from Latin *integer* meaning 'whole']

entirely
(adverb) wholly and completely, e.g. *I was there entirely on my own.*

entirety (pronounced en-**tire**-it-tee)
(phrase) If something happens to something in its entirety, it happens to all of it, e.g. *The farm was sold in its entirety.*

entitle, entitles, entitling, entitled
1 (verb) If something entitles you to have or do something, it gives you the right to have or do it.
2 If a book, film, or painting is entitled, it is given a name, e.g. *She entitled her story 'Lost at Sea'.*
entitlement (noun).

entity, entities (pronounced **en**-tit-ee)
(noun) An entity is any complete thing that is not divided and not part of anything else.

entomology
(noun) Entomology is the study of insects.
entomologist (noun).
[from Greek *entomos* meaning 'cut up'; insects' bodies are in distinct sections]

entourage, entourages (pronounced **on**-too-rahj)
(noun) An entourage is the group of people who follow or travel with a famous or important person.
[from French *entourer* meaning 'to surround']

entrails
(plural noun) Entrails are the inner parts, especially the intestines, of people or animals.
[from Latin *intralia* meaning 'intestines']

entrance, entrances (pronounced **en**-trunss)
1 (noun) The entrance of a building or area is its doorway or gate.
2 A person's entrance is their arrival in a room or building, or the way in which they arrive, e.g. *She made a magnificent entrance.*

entrance, entrances, entrancing, entranced (pronounced **en**-trahnss)
(verb) If something entrances you, it gives you a feeling of wonder and delight.
entranced (adjective), **entrancing** (adjective).

Similar words: captivate, enthral, fascinate

entrant, entrants
(noun) An entrant is a person who officially enters a competition or an organization.

entreat, entreats, entreating, entreated
(verb) If you entreat someone to do something, you ask them very humbly and earnestly to do it.
entreaty (noun).

entrée, entrées (pronounced **on**-tray)
(noun) If you have an entrée to a place, you have the right to enter.

entrench, entrenches, entrenching, entrenched
(verb) If a belief, custom, or power is entrenched, it is firmly and strongly established.
entrenched (adjective).

entrenchment, entrenchments
(noun) An entrenchment is a series of trenches dug in the ground by soldiers for defence.

entrepreneur, entrepreneurs (pronounced on-tre-pren-**ur**)
(noun) An entrepreneur is a person who sets up business deals, especially ones in which risks are involved, in order to make a profit.
entrepreneurial (adjective).

entrust, entrusts, entrusting, entrusted
(verb) If you entrust something to someone, you give them the care and protection of it, e.g. *I'm entrusting you with my car while I'm away.*

entry, entries
1 (noun) Entry is an act of entering a place.
2 An entry is also any place through which you enter somewhere.
3 An entry is also anything which is entered or recorded, e.g. *He made an entry in his diary.*

Similar words: (sense 1) access, admission, admittance

entwine, entwines, entwining, entwined
(verb) If you entwine something, you twist or curl it around something else.

enumerate, enumerates, enumerating, enumerated
(verb) When you enumerate a list of things, you name each one in turn.
enumeration (noun).

enunciate, enunciates, enunciating, enunciated
(pronounced in-**un**-see-ate)
1 (verb) When you enunciate a word, you pronounce it clearly.
2 When you enunciate a thought, idea, or plan, you express it clearly and precisely.
enunciation (noun).
[from Latin *enuntiare* meaning 'to announce']

envelop, envelops, enveloping, enveloped
(verb) To envelop something means to cover, surround, or enclose it completely, e.g. *Flames enveloped the house.*
[from French *envelopper* meaning 'to wrap around']

envelope, envelopes
(noun) An envelope is a flat covering of paper with a flap that can be folded over to seal it, which is used to hold a letter.

enviable
(adjective) If you describe something as enviable, you mean that you wish you had it yourself.

envious
(adjective) full of envy.
enviously (adverb).

environment, environments
1 (noun) Your environment is the circumstances, things, and conditions that influence you, e.g. *Children need a secure environment.*
2 The environment is the natural world around us, e.g. *We need to protect the environment.*
environmental (adjective).
[from Old French *environer* meaning 'to surround']

environmentalist, environmentalists
(noun) An environmentalist is somebody who is concerned with the problems of the natural environment, such as pollution.

environs (pronounced in-**vie**-ronz)
(plural noun) The environs of a place are the surrounding districts, suburbs, or areas.

envisage, envisages, envisaging, envisaged
(verb) If you envisage a situation or state of affairs, you can picture it in your mind as being true or likely to happen.
[from French *envisager* meaning 'to look in the face']

envoy, envoys
1 (noun) An envoy is as a messenger, sent especially from one government to another.
2 An envoy is also a diplomat in an embassy who is immediately below the ambassador in rank.
[from French *envoyé* meaning 'sent']

envy, envies, envying, envied
1 (noun) Envy is a feeling of resentment you have when you wish you could have the same thing or quality that someone else has.
2 (verb) If you envy someone, you wish that you had the same things or qualities they have.

enzyme, enzymes
(noun) An enzyme is a chemical substance, usually a protein, produced by cells in the body.
[from Greek *enzumos* meaning 'leavened']

epaulette, epaulettes (pronounced ep-pol-et)
(noun) An epaulette is a piece of decorative material worn on the shoulder of a garment, especially a military uniform.
[from French *épaule* meaning 'shoulder']

ephemeral (pronounced if-**em**-er-al)
(adjective) lasting only a short time.

epic, epics
1 (noun) An epic is a long story of heroic events and actions in the form of a book, poem, or film.
2 (adjective) very impressive or ambitious, e.g. *an epic journey.*
[from Greek *epos* meaning 'speech' or 'song']

epicentre, epicentres
(noun) The epicentre of an earthquake is the place on the surface of the earth immediately above where the earthquake started.

epicure, epicures
(noun; a formal word) An epicure is a person who enjoys good food and wine. Epicurus was a Greek philosopher who taught that pleasure is the greatest good.

epidemic, epidemics
1 (noun) An epidemic is the occurrence of a disease in one area, spreading quickly and affecting many people.
2 An epidemic is a rapid development or spread of something, e.g. *an epidemic of unemployed young people.*
[from Greek *epi* + *dēmos* meaning 'upon the people']

epidermis (pronounced ep-pid-**der**-miss)
(noun) The epidermis is the top layer of skin.
epidermal (adjective).

epiglottis
(noun) The epiglottis is a piece of cartilage which covers the entrance to your windpipe during swallowing, preventing food from entering.

epigram, epigrams
(noun) An epigram is a short saying which expresses an idea in a clever and amusing way.
epigrammatic (adjective).
[from Greek *epigramma* meaning 'inscription']

epilepsy
(noun) Epilepsy is a condition of the brain which causes fits and periods of unconsciousness.
epileptic (noun or adjective).

epilogue, epilogues (pronounced **ep**-ill-og)
(noun) An epilogue is a passage added to the end of a book or play as a conclusion.

episcopal (pronounced ip-**piss**-kop-pl)
(adjective) relating to or involving the activities, duties, and responsibilities of a bishop.
[from Latin *episcopus* meaning 'bishop']

episode, episodes
1 (noun) An episode is an incident or event, e.g. *a most unfortunate episode.*
2 An episode is one of several parts of a novel or drama appearing for example on radio.
episodic (adjective).
[from Greek *epeisodion* meaning 'something added']

epistle, epistles (pronounced ip-**piss**-sl)
1 (noun; a formal word) An epistle is a letter.
2 The Epistles are the books in the New Testament originally written as letters.

epitaph, epitaphs (pronounced **ep**-it-ahf)
(noun) An epitaph is a short inscription on a gravestone about the person who has died.
[from Greek *epitaphios* meaning 'over a tomb']

epithet, epithets
(noun) An epithet is a word or short phrase used to describe some characteristic of a person.

epitome (pronounced ip-**pit**-om-ee)
(noun; a formal word) The epitome of something is the most typical example of its sort, e.g. *He was the epitome of politeness.*

epitomize, epitomizes, epitomizing, epitomized; also spelled epitomise
(verb) To epitomize something means to be a perfect or typical example of it.
[from Greek *epitemnein* meaning 'to summarize']

epoch, epochs (pronounced **ee**-pok)
(noun) An epoch is a long period of time.

eponymous (pronounced ip-**on**-im-uss)
(adjective; a formal word) The eponymous hero or heroine of a play, film, or book is the person whose name forms its title, e.g. *Hamlet, the eponymous hero of Shakespeare's play.*
[from Greek *eponumos* meaning 'given as a name']

equable (pronounced **ek**-wab-bl)
(adjective) always fair and reasonable, e.g *a very equable person.*
equably (adverb).

equal, equals, equalling, equalled
1 (adjective) having the same size, amount, value or standard.
2 (noun) Your equals are people who have the same ability, status, or rights as you.
3 (adjective) If you are equal to something, you have the necessary ability to deal with it.
4 (verb) If one thing equals another, it is as good or remarkable as the other, e.g. *Nobody can equal her skill on the piano.*
equally (adverb).
[from Latin *aequalis* meaning 'level' or 'even']

Similar words: (sense 4) match, parallel

equality
(noun) Equality is the same status, rights, and responsibilities for all members of a society, e.g. *There should be equality of opportunity for all.*

Similar words: equivalence, parity

equalize, equalizes, equalizing, equalized; also spelled equalise
(verb) To equalize something means to make it equal.
equalization (noun), **equalizer** (noun).

equanimity (pronounced ek-wan-**im**-it-ee)
(noun) Equanimity is a calm state of mind, e.g. *He accepted his loss with equanimity.*

equate, equates, equating, equated
(verb) If you equate a particular thing with something else, you believe that it is similar or equal, e.g. *He always equates holidays with expense.*

equation, equations
(noun) An equation is a mathematical formula stating that two amounts or values are the same.

equator (pronounced ik-**way**-tor)
(noun) The equator is an imaginary line drawn round the middle of the earth, lying halfway between the North and South poles.
equatorial (adjective).

equestrian (pronounced ik-**west**-ree-an)
(adjective) relating to or involving horses.
[from Latin *equus* meaning 'horse']

equidistant
(adjective) Things that are equidistant are at an equal distance from each other or from a central point, e.g. *The three houses are equidistant.*

equilateral
(adjective) An equilateral triangle has sides that are all the same length.

equilibrium, equilibria
1 (noun) Equilibrium is a state of balance or rest existing between different influences or aspects of a situation.
2 In chemistry, equilibrium is a state of balance in a chemical reaction where substances form at the same rate as they decompose.

equine
(adjective) relating to horses.
[from Latin *equus* meaning 'horse']

equinox, equinoxes
(noun) An equinox is one of the two days in the

year when the day and night are of equal length. The autumnal equinox occurs on about September 22, and the vernal (spring) equinox occurs on about March 21.
[from Latin *aequinoctium* meaning 'equal night']

equip, equips, equipping, equipped
(verb) If someone equips you with something, or if you equip yourself with it, you obtain it for a particular purpose, e.g. *You will be equipped for the journey... His training equipped him with all the qualities needed for the job.*
[from Old French *esciper* meaning 'to fit out a ship']

Similar words: (sense 1) outfit, rig, kit out

equipment
(noun) Equipment is all the things that are needed or used for a particular job or activity.

Similar words: kit, gear, apparatus, tackle, rig, paraphernalia

equitable
(adjective) fair and reasonable.
equitably (adverb).

equity
1 (noun) Equity is the quality of being fair and reasonable.
2 In law, equity is the principle which allows a fair judgment to be made in a case where the existing law does not give a reasonable answer to the problem.
3 In commerce, equity is the value of a company's shares.

equivalent, equivalents
1 (adjective) equal or nearly equal in use, size, value, or effect.
2 (noun) An equivalent is something that has the same use, size, value, or effect as something else, e.g. *A quilt is the equivalent of three blankets.*
equivalence (noun).

Similar words: (sense 2) counterpart, equal, parallel, match

equivocal
(adjective) deliberately vague and capable of many different interpretations.

equivocate, equivocates, equivocating, equivocated
(verb) If you equivocate, you deliberately use language which can be interpreted in different ways, to avoid speaking the truth.
equivocation (noun).
[from Latin *aequivocare* meaning 'to speak equally']

era, eras (pronounced **ear**-a)
(noun) An era is a period of time marked by a particular feature, e.g. *the post-war era.*
[from Latin *aera* meaning 'copper counters used for counting', hence for counting time]

Similar words: period, epoch, age

eradicate, eradicates, eradicating, eradicated
(verb) To eradicate something means to get rid of it or destroy it completely.
eradication (noun).
[from Latin *eradicare* meaning 'to uproot', from *radix* meaning 'root']

erase, erases, erasing, erased
(verb) To erase something means to remove it.

eraser, erasers
(noun) An eraser is anything which erases, especially a rubber used for rubbing out writing.

erect, erects, erecting, erected
1 (verb) To erect something means to put it up or construct it, e.g. *He erected the tent.*
2 (adjective) in a straight and upright position, e.g. *She stood on the stage, tall and erect.*
erectly (adverb).

Similar words: (sense 2) upright, vertical, straight

erection, erections
1 (noun) The erection of something is the process of erecting it.
2 An erection is anything which has been erected.
3 When a man has an erection, his penis is stiff, swollen, and in an upright position.

ergonomics
(noun) Ergonomics is the study of the organization of working conditions and the efficiency of the machines and equipment used.
ergonomic (adjective), **ergonomically** (adverb).
[from Greek *ergon* meaning 'work' + *economics*]

ermine, ermines
1 (noun) An ermine is a weasel whose brown fur turns white in winter.
2 Ermine is the white fur from the ermine.

erode, erodes, eroding, eroded
(verb) If something erodes or is eroded, it is gradually worn or eaten away and destroyed.
[from Latin *erodere* meaning 'to gnaw away']

erogenous
(adjective) The erogenous parts of the body are where feelings of sexual pleasure are aroused.
[from Greek *ēros* meaning 'love' and *-genos* meaning 'producing']

erosion
(noun) Erosion is the gradual wearing or eating away and destruction of something, e.g. *Soil erosion... the erosion of his authority.*

erotic
(adjective) relating to sexual desire and often intended to arouse feelings of sexual pleasure.
erotically (adverb), **eroticism** (noun).
[from Greek *erotikos* meaning 'of love']

erotica
(plural noun) Erotica are works of art or literature with a sexual theme that are often intended to arouse sexual feelings in the viewer or reader.

err, errs, erring, erred
(verb) If you err, you make a mistake.
[from Latin *errare* meaning 'to wander']

Similar words: miscalculate, slip up

errand, errands
(noun) An errand is a short trip you make in order to do a job for someone.
[from Old English *ar* meaning 'messenger']

erratic
(adjective) not following a regular pattern or a fixed course, e.g. *Her attendance is erratic.*
erratically (adverb).
[from Latin *errare* meaning 'to wander']

erroneous (pronounced ir-**rone**-ee-uss)
(adjective) Ideas, beliefs, or methods that are erroneous are incorrect or only partly correct.
erroneously (adverb).

error, errors
1 (noun) An error is a mistake or something which you have done wrong.
2 (phrase) If you are **in error**, you are mistaken.
[from Latin *errare* meaning 'to wander']

erudite (pronounced **eh**-roo-dite)
(adjective) having great academic knowledge.
[from Latin *eruditus* meaning 'polished']

erupt, erupts, erupting, erupted
1 (verb) When a volcano erupts, it violently throws out a lot of hot lava, ash, and steam.
2 When a situation erupts, it starts up suddenly and violently, e.g. *Fighting erupted in the city.*
eruption (noun).

escalate, escalates, escalating, escalated
(verb) If a situation escalates, it becomes greater in size, seriousness, or intensity.

escalator, escalators
(noun) An escalator is a mechanical moving staircase.

escalope, escalopes (pronounced **ess**-kal-op)
(noun) An escalope is a thin boneless cut of meat, especially of veal.
[from Old French *escalope* meaning 'shell']

escapade, escapades
(noun) An escapade is an adventurous or daring incident that causes trouble.

escape, escapes, escaping, escaped
1 (verb) To escape means to get free from a person, place, or thing.
2 If liquid, gas, or heat escapes, it gradually seeps out of the thing which contains it, e.g. *Water was escaping from the radiator.*
3 If something escapes you, it remains unknown, unnoticed, or forgotten, e.g. *She recognized the face, but the name escaped her completely.*
4 (noun) An escape is a situation or activity which distracts you from something unpleasant, e.g. *I read novels as an escape from boredom.*
5 An escape is an act of escaping from a particular place or situation, e.g. *They made their escape through the back door.*
6 An escape of gas or liquid is a leak of it from a pipe or container.

escapee, escapees (pronounced is-kay-**pee**)
(noun) An escapee is someone who has escaped, especially an escaped prisoner.

escapism
(noun) Escapism is the tendency to avoid the real and unpleasant things in life by thinking about pleasant or fantastic things, e.g. *Daydreaming is a form of escapism.*
escapist (adjective).

escarpment, escarpments
(noun) An escarpment is a wide, steep slope on a ridge or mountain.

eschew, eschews, eschewing, eschewed
(pronounced is-**chew**)
(verb; a formal word) If you eschew something, you deliberately avoid or keep away from it.

escort, escorts, escorting, escorted
1 (verb) If you escort someone, you go with them somewhere, especially in order to protect or guide them.
2 (noun) An escort is a person or vehicle that travels with another in order to protect or guide them.
3 An escort is also a person who accompanies another person of the opposite sex to a social event.

Eskimo, Eskimos
1 (noun) An Eskimo is a member of a group of people who live in Northern Canada, Greenland, Alaska, and Eastern Siberia.
2 Eskimo is the language spoken by Eskimos.

esoteric (pronounced ess-oh-**ter**-ik)
(adjective) Something that is esoteric is understood only by a small number of people, usually because they have special knowledge of it or have particular tastes and interests.

ESP an abbreviation for 'extrasensory perception'.

especial
(adjective) special or exceptional.
especially (adverb).
[from Latin *specialis* meaning 'individual']

espionage (pronounced **ess**-pee-on-ahj)
(noun) Espionage is the act of spying to get secret information, especially to find out military or political secrets.
[from French *espionner* meaning 'to spy']

esplanade, esplanades (pronounced ess-plan-**ade**)
(noun) An esplanade is a long open road for walking along, especially by the sea.
[from Italian *spianata* meaning 'made level']

espouse, espouses, espousing, espoused
(verb; a formal word) If you espouse a particular policy, cause, or plan, you give your support to it, e.g. *He espoused the cause with fervour.*
espousal (noun).
[from Old French *espouser* meaning 'to marry']

espresso
(noun) Espresso is strong coffee made by forcing steam or boiling water through ground coffee.
[from Italian *caffè espresso* meaning 'pressed coffee']

esprit de corps (pronounced ess-pree de **kor**)
(noun) Esprit de corps is a feeling of loyalty and pride in belonging to a particular group.
[a French phrase meaning 'team spirit']

espy, espies, espying, espied (pronounced is-**pie**)
(verb; an old-fashioned word) If you espy
something, you catch sight of it.

Esq.
Esq is a polite title for a man, which may be used
when you are addressing a letter. Esq. is a
written abbreviation for 'esquire', e.g. *P. Jones
Esq., 26 Mount Park Rd, London.*

essay, essays, essaying, essayed
1 (noun) An essay is a short piece of writing on a
particular subject.
2 (a formal use) An essay is also an attempt to do
something.
3 (verb; a formal use) If you essay something,
you try to do it, e.g. *She essayed a smile.*
[from French *essai* meaning 'attempt']

essence, essences
1 (noun) The essence of something is its most
basic part which gives it its identity.
2 The essence of something is also the perfect
form of it, e.g. *She was the essence of politeness.*
3 Essence is a concentrated liquid used for
flavouring food, e.g. *vanilla essence.*

Similar words: (sense 2) soul, spirit, quintessence

essential, essentials
1 (adjective) vitally important and absolutely
necessary.
2 very basic and important, e.g. *You should learn
the essential aspects of car maintenance.*
3 (noun) An essential is something that you
think is important or necessary for what you are
doing.
essentially (adverb).

establish, establishes, establishing, established
1 (verb) To establish something means to create
it or set it up in a permanent way.
2 If you establish that something is the case, you
find out that it is true, e.g. *They established
where the murder had taken place.*
established (adjective).
[from Latin *stabilire* meaning 'to make firm']

Similar words: (sense 1) found, institute, set up

establishment, establishments
1 (noun) The establishment of an organization or
system is the act of creating it or setting it up.
2 An establishment is a shop, business, or some
other sort of organization or institution.
3 The Establishment is the group of people in a
country who have power and influence.

estate, estates
1 (noun) An estate is a large area of privately
owned land in the country, together with all the
property on it.
2 An estate is also an area of land, usually in or
near a city, which has been developed for
housing or industry.
3 (a legal use) A person's estate consists of all
the possessions they leave behind when they die.
4 (a formal use) A person's estate is also their
circumstances or position in life or society.
[from Latin *status* meaning 'condition' or 'state']

estate agent, estate agents
(noun) An estate agent is someone who works for
a company that sells houses and land.

estate car, estate cars
(noun) An estate car is a car which has a long
body with a door at the back and luggage space
behind the back seats.

esteem, esteems, esteeming, esteemed
1 (noun) Esteem is admiration and respect that
you feel for another person.
2 (verb) If you esteem someone or something,
you regard them with great respect and
admiration.
esteemed (adjective).
[from Latin *aestimare* meaning 'to assess the
worth of']

esthete another spelling of **aesthete.**

esthetic another spelling of **aesthetic.**

estimate, estimates, estimating, estimated
1 (verb) If you estimate an amount or quantity,
you calculate it approximately.
2 If you estimate something, you make a
judgment about it from the evidence you have
available, e.g. *He estimated the size.*
3 (noun) An estimate is an approximate
calculation of an amount or quantity.
4 An estimate is also a judgment about a person
or situation based on available evidence.
5 An estimate is also a formal statement from a
company who may do some work for you, telling
you how much a particular job is likely to cost.
[from Latin *aestimare* meaning 'to assess the
worth of']

estimation, estimations
1 (noun) An estimation is an approximate
calculation of something that can be measured.
2 Your estimation of a person or situation is the
opinion or impression you have formed.

estrange, estranges, estranging, estranged
(verb) If you estrange someone, you cause them
to turn away from you and you lose their
affection and loyalty, e.g. *He estranged his
brother by his behaviour.*
estranged (adjective), **estrangement** (noun).
[from Latin *extraneare* meaning 'to treat as a
stranger']

estrogen
(noun) Estrogen is a female sex hormone which
regulates the reproductive cycle.

estuary, estuaries (pronounced **est**-yoo-ree)
(noun) An estuary is the wide part of a river
near where it joins the sea and where fresh
water mixes with salt water.

etc. a written abbreviation for **et cetera.**

et cetera (pronounced it **set**-ra)
Et cetera is used at the end of a list to indicate
that other items of the same type you have
mentioned could have been mentioned if there
had been time or space.
[from Latin *et cetera* meaning 'and other things']

etch, etches, etching, etched
1 (verb) If you etch a design or pattern on a

surface, you cut it into the surface by using acid or a sharp tool.
2 If something is etched on your mind or memory, it has made such a strong impression on you that you feel you will never forget it.
etched (adjective).

etching, etchings
(noun) An etching is a picture printed from a metal plate that has had a design cut into it.

eternal
(adjective) lasting forever, or seeming to last forever, e.g. *his eternal grumbling*.
eternally (adverb).

Similar words: perpetual, everlasting, endless

eternity, eternities
1 (noun) Eternity is time without end, or a state of existing outside time, especially the state some people believe they will pass into when they die.
2 An eternity is also a period of time which seems to go on for ever, e.g. *This winter seems to have lasted for an eternity!*

ether (pronounced **eeth**-er)
1 (noun) Ether is a colourless liquid that burns easily. It is used in industry as a solvent and in medicine as an anaesthetic.
2 (a literary or formal use) The ether is the air.

ethereal (pronounced ith-**ee**-ree-al)
(adjective) light and delicate, e.g. *her ethereal beauty*.

ethical
(adjective) in agreement with accepted principles of behaviour that are thought to be right, e.g. *That was a very ethical decision*.
ethically (adverb).

ethics
1 (noun) Ethics are moral beliefs about right and wrong, e.g. *The medical profession has a code of ethics... I don't agree with his business ethics*.
2 Ethics is also the study of questions about what is right and wrong.
[from Greek *ēthos* meaning 'custom']

Ethiopian, Ethiopians (pronounced eeth-ee-**oh**-pee-an)
1 (adjective) belonging to or relating to Ethiopia.
2 (noun) An Ethiopian is someone who comes from Ethiopia.

ethnic
1 (adjective) involving different racial groups of people, e.g. *ethnic minorities*.
2 relating to or characteristic of a particular racial or cultural group, e.g. *ethnic food*.
ethnically (adverb).
[from Greek *ethnos* meaning 'race']

ethnography
(noun) Ethnography is the study of different cultures.
ethnographic (adjective).

ethos (pronounced **eeth**-oss)
(noun) An ethos is a set of ideas and attitudes that is characteristic of a particular group of people, e.g. *an antigovernment ethos*.
[from Greek *ethos* meaning 'custom']

etiolated (pronounced **ee**-tee-oh-late-id)
(adjective) A plant that is etiolated has become pale and weak because of lack of sunlight and nutrients.

etiquette (pronounced et-ik-ket)
(noun) Etiquette is a set of rules for behaviour in a particular social situation.

Similar words: protocol, propriety, formalities

etymology (pronounced et-tim-**ol**-loj-ee)
(noun) Etymology is the study of the origin, development, and changes of form in words.
etymological (adjective), **etymologically** (adverb), **etymologist** (noun).

eucalyptus, eucalyptus or eucalyptuses
(noun) A eucalyptus is an evergreen tree grown, mostly in Australia, to provide timber, gum, and medicinal oil; also the wood and oil obtained from this tree.

Eucharist, Eucharists (pronounced **yoo**-kar-rist)
(noun) The Eucharist is a religious ceremony in which Christians remember and celebrate Christ's last meal with his disciples.
eucharistic (adjective).
[from Greek *eucharistia* meaning 'thanksgiving']

eugenics (pronounced yoo-**jen**-iks)
(noun) Eugenics is the study of how to improve the human race by the careful selection of parents and the control of genes.

eulogize, eulogizes, eulogizing, eulogized (pronounced **yoo**-loj-eyes); also spelled **eulogise** (verb; a formal word) If you eulogize something, you praise it highly.

eulogy, eulogies (pronounced **yoo**-loj-ee)
(noun) A eulogy is a speech or piece of writing that praises someone or something, e.g. *a eulogy about the Queen Mother*.
[from Greek *eulogia* meaning 'praise']

eunuch, eunuchs (pronounced **yoo**-nuk)
(noun) A eunuch is a man who has been castrated. Eunuchs were often employed in the past to guard women in Eastern countries.

euphemism, euphemisms
(noun) A euphemism is a polite word or expression that you can use instead of one that might offend or upset people, e.g. *To 'pass on' is a euphemism for 'to die'*.
euphemistic (adjective), **euphemistically** (adverb).
[from Greek *eu-* meaning 'pleasant' and *phēmē* meaning 'speech']

euphoria
(noun) Euphoria is a feeling of great happiness.
euphoric (adjective).

Eurasian, Eurasians (pronounced yoo-**ray**-shn)
(noun) A Eurasian is someone who has one Asian and one European parent.

eureka (pronounced yoo-**reek**-a)
(exclamation) Sometimes people say 'eureka'

when they have suddenly discovered something they have been looking for.

Europe
(noun) Europe is the second smallest continent. It has Asia on its eastern side, with the Arctic to the north, the Atlantic to the west, and the Mediterranean and Africa to the south.

European, Europeans
1 (adjective) belonging to or relating to Europe.
2 (noun) A European is someone who comes from Europe.

European Community
(noun) The group of countries who have joined together under the Treaty of Rome for economic and trade purposes are officially known as the European Community.

eustachian tube, eustachian tubes
(noun) In your ear, your eustachian tube is the tube that connects your middle ear to your throat and that helps keep the air pressure the same on either side of your eardrum. It was named after B. Eustachio, an 18th-century Italian anatomist.

euthanasia (pronounced yooth-a-**nay**-zee-a)
(noun) Euthanasia is the act of killing someone painlessly in order to stop their suffering when nothing can be done to help them, for example when they have an incurable illness.
[from Greek *eu-* meaning 'easy' and *thanatos* meaning 'death']

evacuate, evacuates, evacuating, evacuated
1 (verb) If someone is evacuated, they are removed from a place of danger to a place of safety, e.g. *Many children were evacuated to the countryside during the Second World War.*
2 If you evacuate a place, you move out of it for a period of time, usually because it is dangerous, e.g. *The entire building was evacuated.*
evacuation (noun), **evacuee** (noun).

evade, evades, evading, evaded
1 (verb) If you evade something or someone, you keep moving in order to keep out of their way, e.g. *She managed to evade his attentions.*
2 If you evade a problem or question, you avoid dealing with it.
3 If something evades you, you do not manage to achieve it, e.g. *Happiness evaded him all his life.*

evaluate, evaluates, evaluating, evaluated
(verb) If you evaluate something, you assess its quality, value, or significance.
evaluation (noun).

evanescent (pronounced ev-an-**ess**-nt)
(adjective; a formal or literary word) gradually disappearing from sight or memory.

evangelical (pronounced ee-van-**jel**-ik-kl)
(adjective) Evangelical beliefs are Christian beliefs that stress the importance of the gospels and a personal belief in Christ.

evangelist, evangelists (pronounced iv-**van**-jel-ist)
(noun) An evangelist is a person who travels from place to place preaching Christianity.
evangelize (verb), **evangelism** (noun).
[from Greek *evangelion* meaning 'good news']

evaporate, evaporates, evaporating, evaporated
1 (verb) When a liquid evaporates, it gradually becomes less and less because it has changed from a liquid into a gas.
2 If a substance has been evaporated, all the liquid has been taken out so that it is dry or concentrated.
evaporation (noun).
[from Latin *vapor* meaning 'steam']

evasion, evasions
(noun) Evasion is deliberately avoiding doing something, e.g. *tax evasion.*

evasive
(adjective) deliberately trying to avoid talking about or doing something, e.g. *I asked her if she liked my family, but she was very evasive.*

eve, eves
(noun) The eve of a particular event or occasion is the evening or day before it.

even, evens, evening, evened
1 (adjective) flat and level, e.g. *an even surface.*
2 regular and without variation, e.g. *an even heartbeat.*
3 calm and not easily excited, e.g. *John has an even temper.*
4 In maths, numbers that are even are exactly divisible by two, e.g. *4 is an even number.*
5 Scores that are even are exactly the same.
6 (adverb) in spite of, e.g. *Even if it rains I'd like to go.*
7 Even is used to suggest that something is unexpected or surprising, e.g. *Even a fool could do that.*
8 Even is also used to say that something is greater in degree than something else, e.g. *She's even better than Sue at swimming.*
9 (conjunction) **Even if** or **even though** is used to introduce something that seems to contradict the main part of the sentence, e.g. *She failed the exam, even though she was brilliant.*
10 (adverb) **Even so** is used to introduce a surprising statement, e.g. *They're a good team. Even so, they've lost all their games this season.*
evenly (adverb), **evenness** (noun).

Similar words: (sense 1) level, straight, horizontal (sense 5) level, equal, fifty-fifty

evening, evenings
(noun) Evening is the part of the day between late afternoon and the time you go to bed.

evening dress
(noun) Evening dress is formal clothes that people wear in the evening at formal occasions.

evensong
(noun) Evensong is the evening service in the Church of England.

event, events
1 (noun) An event is something that happens, especially when it is unusual or important.

2 An event is also one of the races or competitions that are part of an organized occasion, especially in sports.
3 (phrase) If you say **in any event**, you mean whatever happens, e.g. *In any event I'll see her.*
4 If you say **in the event of** something happening, you mean if a particular thing happens, e.g. *In the event of him missing his train, run him by car.*

Similar words: (sense 1) happening, occasion, occurrence, incident, episode

eventful
(adjective) full of interesting, exciting, and important events.

eventual
(adjective) happening or being achieved in the end, e.g. *The eventual outcome was good.*

eventuality, eventualities
(noun) An eventuality is a possible future event or result, e.g. *We're catering for all eventualities.*

eventually
(adverb) at last, e.g. *We eventually arrived.*

ever
1 (adverb) at any time, e.g. *Have you ever been to America?*
2 all the time, e.g. *Ever hopeful, she waited for him.*
3 Ever is used to give emphasis to what you are saying, e.g. *I don't ever want to see you again.*
4 (phrase; an informal use) **Ever so** means very, e.g. *I'm ever so glad you like it.*

evergreen, evergreens
(noun) An evergreen is a tree or bush which has green leaves all the year round.

everlasting
(adjective) never coming to an end.

evermore
(adverb; a literary word) for ever.

every
1 (determiner) Every is used to refer to all the members of a particular group, separately and one by one, e.g. *Every house was in bad repair.*
2 Every is used to mean the greatest or the best possible degree of something, e.g. *He has every chance of getting another job.*
3 Every is also used to indicate that something happens at regular intervals, e.g. *every three days.*
4 (phrase) **Every bit as** means equally, e.g. *Jane is every bit as good as you at sports.*
5 **Every other** means alternate, e.g. *every other day.*

everybody
1 (pronoun) all the people in a group.
2 all the people in the world, e.g. *Everybody knows that!*

everyday
(adjective) usual or ordinary, e.g. *a normal everyday life... my everyday routine.*

everyone
(pronoun) all the people in a group.

everything
1 (pronoun) all or the whole of something.
2 a great deal, especially of something very important, e.g. *You're everything to me.*

everywhere
(adverb) in all places or to all places.

Similar words: omnipresent, ubiquitous

evict, evicts, evicting, evicted
(verb) To evict someone means to officially force them to leave a place they are occupying.
eviction (noun).
[from Latin *evincere* meaning 'to conquer utterly']

Similar words: eject, throw out, kick out

evidence
1 (noun) Evidence is anything you see, experience, read, or are told which gives you reason to believe something.
2 Evidence is the information used in court to attempt to prove or disprove something.
3 (phrase) If something is **in evidence**, it is displayed and easily seen, e.g. *His trophies were in evidence all over the home.*

evident
(adjective) easily noticed or understood, e.g. *It was evident that Sue was happy.*
evidently (adverb).
[from Latin *evidens* meaning 'making itself seen']

evil, evils
1 (noun) Evil is a force or power that is believed to cause wicked or bad things to happen.
2 An evil is a very unpleasant or harmful situation or activity.
3 (adjective) Something that is evil is morally wrong or bad, e.g. *an evil plan.*
evilly (adverb).

evince, evinces, evincing, evinced
(verb; a formal word) If someone evinces a feeling or quality, they show it very clearly.

evocation, evocations
(noun; a formal word) An evocation is the evoking of an emotion, memory, or reaction.

evocative
(adjective) producing memories, emotions, and reactions in people, e.g. *an evocative song.*
evocatively (adverb).

evoke, evokes, evoking, evoked
(verb) To evoke an emotion, memory, or reaction means to cause it, e.g. *Her words evoked anger.*
[from Latin *evocare* meaning 'to call forth']

evolution (pronounced ee-vol-oo-shn)
1 (noun) Evolution is a process of gradual change and development over a period of time.
2 In biology, evolution is a process of gradual change taking place over many generations during which animals, plants, and insects slowly change as they adapt to different environments.

evolve, evolves, evolving, evolved
1 (verb) To evolve means to grow or develop gradually over a period of time.
2 When plants, animals, and insects evolve, they

gradually change and develop into different forms over a period of time.
[from Latin *evolvere* meaning 'to unfold']

ewe, ewes (pronounced **yoo**)
(noun) A ewe is a female sheep.

ewer, ewers (pronounced **yoo**-er)
(noun) A ewer is a large jug with a wide mouth.

ex-
(prefix) former, e.g. *her ex-husband.*

exacerbate, exacerbates, exacerbating, exacerbated (pronounced ig-**zass**-er-bate)
(verb) To exacerbate something means to make it worse.
[from Latin *exacerbare* meaning 'to irritate']

exact, exacts, exacting, exacted
1 (adjective) accurate and precise as opposed to approximate, e.g. *the exact amount.*
2 correct and complete in every detail, e.g. *The picture was an exact replica.*
3 operating with precision and allowing no deviation from a standard.
4 (verb) If you exact something from someone, you demand or obtain it from them, especially because you are in a more powerful position, e.g. *He exacted obedience from his employees.*

exacting
(adjective) demanding a great deal of hard work and care, e.g. *an exacting task.*

exactly
1 (adverb) with complete accuracy and precision.
2 You can use exactly to emphasize the truth of a statement, or a similarity or close relationship that one thing has with another, e.g. *That's exactly the same as mine.*

exaggerate, exaggerates, exaggerating, exaggerated
1 (verb) If you exaggerate, you say something which is more than the true facts.
2 To exaggerate also means to make more noticeable or important than usual, e.g. *Her clothes exaggerate her skinniness.*
exaggeration (noun).
[from Latin *exaggerare* meaning 'to heap up']

Similar words: (sense 2) magnify, overemphasize

exalt, exalts, exalting, exalted (pronounced ig-**zolt**)
1 (verb; a formal word) To exalt someone means to praise them highly.
2 To exalt someone means to raise them to a higher position in society, e.g. *They exalted him to vice chairman.*
[from Latin *exaltare* meaning 'to raise']

exaltation
1 (noun; a literary word) Exaltation is a feeling of great joy and excitement.
2 Exaltation is the act of praising someone or something very highly.

exam, exams
(noun) An exam is an official test set to assess your knowledge or skill in a subject.

examination, examinations
1 (noun) An examination is the same as an exam.

2 A medical examination is a physical inspection of someone in order to assess the state of their health or to diagnose disease.
3 An examination in law is a formal interrogation of a person on oath in a court.

examine, examines, examining, examined
1 (verb) If you examine something, you look carefully at it or inspect it in detail.
2 To examine someone means to assess their knowledge or skill in a particular subject by testing them.
[from Latin *examinare* meaning 'to weigh']

Similar words: (sense 1) inspect, analyse, check, test, scrutinize, study, peruse

examiner, examiners
(noun) An examiner is a person who sets or marks an exam.

example, examples
1 (noun) An example is something which represents or is typical of a group or set.
2 If you say someone or something is an example to people, you mean that people can imitate and learn from them.
[from Latin *exemplum* meaning 'pattern' or 'model']

Similar words: (sense 1) sample, specimen, illustration, instance

exasperate, exasperates, exasperating, exasperated
(verb) If someone or something exasperates you, they irritate you and make you angry.
exasperating (adjective), **exasperation** (noun).

excavate, excavates, excavating, excavated
1 (verb) To excavate means to remove earth from the ground by digging.
2 When archaeologists excavate objects, they carefully dig them up from the ground to discover information about the past.
excavation (noun), **excavator** (noun).
[from Latin *excavare* meaning 'to hollow out']

exceed, exceeds, exceeding, exceeded
(verb) To exceed something such as a limit means to go beyond it or to become greater than it, e.g. *Do not exceed the speed limit.*

exceedingly
(adverb) very much or extremely.

excel, excels, excelling, excelled
(verb) If someone excels in something, they are very good at doing it.
[from Latin *excellere* meaning 'to rise up']

Excellency, Excellencies
(noun) Excellency is a title used to address or refer to an official of very high rank, such as an ambassador or a governor.

excellent
(adjective) very good indeed.
excellence (noun), **excellently** (adverb)

Similar words: great, masterly, fine, pre-eminent, superb, outstanding, splendid

except, excepts, excepting, excepted
1 (preposition and conjunction) other than or apart from, e.g. *I'll eat anything except celery... I'd go with you except that I haven't got a babysitter.*
2 (verb) To except something means to regard it as not included in a general statement, judgment, or rule, e.g. *I dislike most of the people I work with, present company excepted.*
[from Old French *excepter* meaning 'to leave out']

exception, exceptions
1 (noun) An exception is someone or something that is not included in a general statement, judgment, or rule.
2 (phrase) If you **take exception to** something, you object to it because you feel offended or annoyed by it.

exceptionable
(adjective) causing offence and annoyance.

exceptional
1 (adjective) unusually talented, clever, or gifted.
2 unusual and only likely to happen very rarely.
exceptionally (adverb).

excerpt, excerpts
(noun) An excerpt is a short piece of writing or music which is taken from a larger piece.
[from Latin *excerptum* meaning 'something picked out']

excess, excesses
1 (noun) Excess is behaviour which goes beyond normal or permitted limits, e.g. *a life of excess.*
2 An excess is a larger amount of something than is needed, permitted, or usual, e.g. *The body should not have an excess of sugar.*
3 (adjective) more than is needed, permitted, or usual, e.g. *excess baggage.*
4 (phrase) **In excess of** a particular amount means more than that amount, e.g. *Her savings are in excess of 10,000 pounds.*
5 If you do something **to excess**, you do it too much, e.g. *He drinks to excess.*

excessive
(adjective) beyond the normal, permitted, or necessary extent or limit
excessively (adverb).

Similar words: extreme, overdone, immoderate

exchange, exchanges, exchanging, exchanged
1 (verb) To exchange things means to give or receive one thing in return for another, e.g. *They exchanged smiles... exchanging gifts.*
2 (noun) An exchange is the giving or receiving of something in return for something else; also the thing which is given or received.
3 An exchange is also a place where people trade and do business, e.g. *the stock exchange.*
4 A telephone exchange is a building where connections are made between telephone lines.
[from Latin *cambire* meaning 'to barter']

exchequer (pronounced iks-**chek**-er)
(noun) The exchequer is the department in the government which is responsible for money belonging to the state.

excise, excises, excising, excised
1 (noun) Excise is a tax put on goods produced for sale in the country that produces them.
2 (verb; a formal use) To excise something means to remove it completely.
[sense 2 is from Latin *excidere* meaning 'to cut out']

excitable
(adjective) easily excited.

excite, excites, exciting, excited
(verb) If someone or something excites you, they make you feel happy and nervous or interested and enthusiastic.
excited (adjective), **excitedly** (adverb), **exciting** (adjective), **excitement** (noun).

Similar words: thrill, electrify, exhilarate

exclaim, exclaims, exclaiming, exclaimed
(verb) When you exclaim, you cry out or speak suddenly or loudly because you are excited, shocked, or angry.

exclamation, exclamations
(noun) An exclamation is a word or phrase spoken suddenly to express a strong feeling such as surprise, pain, or anger.

exclamation mark, exclamation marks
(noun) An exclamation mark is a punctuation mark (!) used in writing to express shock, surprise, or anger.

exclude, excludes, excluding, excluded
1 (verb) If you exclude someone or something, you leave them out or do not consider them.
2 If you are excluded from a place or an activity, you are prevented from entering the place or taking part in the activity.
exclusion (noun).

exclusive
1 (adjective) belonging to or providing for a small, privileged group of people, e.g. *an exclusive night club.*
2 belonging to a particular individual or group and to nobody else, e.g. *They have exclusive use.*
3 separate and unable to exist together, e.g. *mutually exclusive.*
4 not including, e.g. *The rent is exclusive of bills.*
exclusively (adverb).

Similar words: (sense 1) private, select

excommunicate, excommunicates, excommunicating, excommunicated
(verb) If a person is excommunicated from the Church, they are no longer allowed to be a member.
excommunication (noun).

excrement (pronounced **eks**-krim-ment)
(noun) Excrement is the solid waste matter that is passed out of a person's or animal's body through their bowels.

excrescence, excrescences (pronounced iks-**kress**-ns)
(noun; a formal word) An excrescence is a lump or growth on the surface of an animal or plant.

[from Latin *excrescere* meaning 'to grow outwards']

excrete, excretes, excreting, excreted
(verb) When you excrete waste matter from your body, you get rid of it, for example by going to the lavatory or by sweating.
excretion (noun), **excretory** (adjective).

excruciating (pronounced iks-**kroo**-shee-ate-ing) (adjective) unbearably painful.
excruciatingly (adverb).
[from Latin *excruciare* meaning 'to torture']

excursion, excursions
1 (noun) An excursion is a short journey or outing.
2 An excursion is a diversion into something which you have not attempted before, e.g. *an excursion into politics.*

excusable
(adjective) deserving to be excused, e.g. *an excusable offence.*

excuse, exuses, excusing, excused
1 (noun) An excuse is a reason which you give to explain or defend something you have or have not done, or to avoid doing something.
2 (verb) If you excuse yourself, or someone else, you give reasons for doing something or you defend your actions or behaviour.
3 If you excuse someone for something wrong they have done, you forgive them for it.
4 If you excuse someone from a duty or responsibility, you free them from it.
5 If you ask someone to excuse you, you are asking them to allow you to leave.

execrable
(adjective; a formal word) extremely bad or unpleasant, e.g. *The food is execrable.*

execute, executes, executing, executed
1 (verb) To execute someone means to kill them as a punishment for a crime.
2 If you execute something such as a plan or an action, you carry it out or perform it.
3 To execute a legal document means to carry it into effect or enforce it, e.g. *executing a will.*
execution (noun).
[from Latin *exsequi* meaning 'to follow up,' 'carry out', or 'punish']

executioner, executioners
(noun) An executioner is a person whose job is to execute criminals.

executive, executives
1 (noun) An executive is a person who is employed by a company at a senior level.
2 (adjective) involved or concerned with making decisions and ensuring that they are carried out, e.g. *an executive committee.*
[from Latin *exsequi* meaning 'to carry out']

executor, executors (pronounced ig-**zek**-yoo-tor)
(noun) An executor is a person you appoint to carry out the instructions in your will.

exegesis, exegeses (pronounced eks-sij-**jee**-siss)
(noun; a formal word) An exegesis is an

explanation and interpretation of a piece of writing, especially a piece of religious writing.
[from Greek *exegeisthai* meaning 'to interpret']

exemplary
1 (adjective) being a good example and worthy of imitation, e.g. *exemplary behaviour.*
2 serving as a warning, e.g. *exemplary punishment.*
[from Latin *exemplum* meaning 'model']

exemplify, exemplifies, exemplifying, exemplified
1 (verb) To exemplify something means to be a typical example of it, e.g. *The monarchy exemplifies traditional English values.*
2 If you exemplify something, you give an example of it.
exemplification (noun).

exempt, exempts, exempting, exempted
1 (adjective) excused from a rule, duty, or obligation, e.g. *He was exempt from taxes.*
2 (verb) To exempt someone from a rule, duty, or obligation means to excuse them from it.
exemption (noun).
[from Latin *exemptus* meaning 'removed' or 'freed']

Similar words: (sense 2) absolve, relieve, let off

exercise, exercises, exercising, exercised
1 (noun) Exercise is any activity which you do to get fit or remain healthy.
2 Exercises are also activities which you do to practise and train for a particular skill, e.g. *piano exercises... mathematical exercises.*
3 Military exercises are operations performed by a section of the armed forces.
4 (verb) When you exercise, you do activities which help you to get fit and remain healthy.
5 If you exercise your authority, rights, or responsibilities, you use them.
[from Latin *exercere* meaning 'to keep busy' or 'to train']

Similar words: (sense 5) exert, use, wield

exert, exerts, exerting, exerted
1 (verb) To exert pressure means to apply it.
2 If you exert yourself, you make a physical or mental effort to do something.

exertion, exertions
(noun) Exertion is vigorous physical effort or exercise.

ex gratia (pronounced eks **gray**-sha)
(adjective) An ex gratia payment is given as a gift and not because it is legally necessary.
[from Latin *ex + gratia* meaning 'out of kindness']

exhale, exhales, exhaling, exhaled
(verb) When you exhale, you breathe out.
exhalation (noun).

exhaust, exhausts, exhausting, exhausted
1 (verb) To exhaust someone means to make them so tired that they have no energy left.
2 If you exhaust a supply of something such as money or food, you use it up completely.

3 If you exhaust a subject, you talk about it so much that there is nothing else to say about it.
4 (noun) An exhaust is a pipe which carries the gas or steam out of the engine of a vehicle.
5 Exhaust is the gas or steam produced by the engine of a vehicle.
exhaustion (noun).
[from Latin *exhaustus* meaning 'empty' or 'drained']

Similar words: (sense 1) fatigue, tire out, wear out, drain, weary

exhaustible
(adjective) existing only in a limited quantity.

exhaustive
(adjective) thorough and complete, e.g. *an exhaustive investigation*.
exhaustively (adverb).

exhibit, exhibits, exhibiting, exhibited
1 (verb) To exhibit things means to show them in a public place for people to see.
2 If you exhibit your feelings or abilities, you display them so that other people can see them.
3 (noun) An exhibit is anything which is put on show for the public to see.
[from Latin *exhibere* meaning 'to hold out']

exhibition, exhibitions
1 (noun) An exhibition is a public display of works of art, products, skills, or activities.
2 (phrase) If you **make an exhibition of yourself**, you behave stupidly in public so that people notice you.

exhibitionist, exhibitionists
(noun) Someone who is an exhibitionist tries to get people's attention all the time, especially by stupid behaviour or boasting.
exhibitionism (noun).

exhibitor, exhibitors
(noun) An exhibitor is a person whose work is being shown in an exhibition.

exhilarate, exhilarates, exhilarating, exhilarated
(pronounced ig-**zil**-ler-ate)
(verb) Something that exhilarates you makes you feel very happy and excited.
exhilarating (adjective), **exhilaration** (noun).
[from Latin *exhilarare* meaning 'to make cheerful']

exhort, exhorts, exhorting, exhorted
(pronounced ig-**zort**)
(verb) If you exhort someone to do something, you urge them or beg them to do it.
exhortation (noun).

exhume, exhumes, exhuming, exhumed
(verb) When a body is exhumed, it is dug up and taken out of the ground where it is buried.
[from Latin *ex* + *humus* meaning 'out of the ground']

exigency, exigencies
(noun; a formal word) The exigencies of a difficult situation or task are the problems that you have to deal with, e.g. *the exigencies of war*.

exile, exiles, exiling, exiled
1 (verb) If someone is exiled, they are sent from their own country and not allowed to return.
2 (noun) If someone lives in exile, they live in a foreign country because they cannot live in their own country, usually for political reasons.
3 An exile is someone who lives in exile.

exist, exists, existing, existed
(verb) If something exists, it is present in the world as a real or living thing.
[from Latin *exsistere* meaning 'to come forth' or 'appear']

existence
1 (noun) Existence is the state of being or existing.
2 An existence is a way of living or being, e.g. *He led a lonely existence*.

existential
(adjective; a formal word) involving human existence and experience.

existentialism (pronounced eg-ziss-**ten**-shall-izm)
(noun) Existentialism is a philosophical belief which emphasizes the importance of human experience and a person's freedom and responsibility in making his or her own decisions.
existentialist (noun and adjective).

exit, exits, exiting, exited
1 (noun) An exit is a way out of a place.
2 If you make an exit, you leave a place.
3 (verb) To exit means to go out.
[from Latin *exit* meaning 'he goes out']

exodus
(noun) An exodus is the departure of a large number of people from a place.

exonerate, exonerates, exonerating, exonerated
(verb; a formal word) To exonerate someone means to free them from blame or responsibility for something wrong that has happened.
exoneration (noun).
[from Latin *exonerare* meaning 'to free from a burden']

exorbitant
(adjective) much more extreme than is reasonable, e.g. *It was an exorbitant price*.

exorcize, exorcizes, exorcizing, exorcized; also spelled exorcise
(verb) To exorcize an evil spirit means to force it to leave a person or place by means of prayers.
exorcism (noun), **exorcist** (noun).

exoskeleton, exoskeletons
(noun) An exoskeleton is a hard covering around the outside of the bodies of creatures such as insects and shellfish.

exotic
1 (adjective) foreign, or coming from a foreign country, e.g. *an exotic flower*.
2 strange or very unusual, e.g. *exotic paintings*.
exotically (adverb).
[from Greek *exotikos* meaning 'foreign']

expand, expands, expanding, expanded
1 (verb) If something expands, or you expand it, it becomes larger in number or size.

2 If you expand on or expand upon something, you give more details about it.
expansion (noun).
[from Latin *expandere* meaning 'to spread out']

Similar words: (sense 2) amplify, embellish, enlarge on, expatiate, elaborate

expanse, expanses
(noun) An expanse is a very large or widespread area, e.g. *an expanse of sand and desert.*

Similar words: area, space, stretch, sweep

expansive
1 (adjective) Something that is expansive is very wide or extends over a very large area, e.g. *the expansive plains of North America.*
2 Someone who is expansive is friendly, open, or talkative.

expatiate, expatiates, expatiating, expatiated
(pronounced ik-**spay**-shee-ate)
(verb; a formal word) If you expatiate on a subject, you talk about it in great detail and at great length.
[from Latin *ex + spatiari* meaning 'to wander away']

expatriate, expatriates (pronounced eks-**pat**-ree-it)
(noun) An expatriate is someone who is living in a country which is not their own.
[from Latin *ex + patria* meaning 'out of your native land']

expect, expects, expecting, expected
1 (verb) If you expect something, you believe that it is going to happen or arrive.
2 If you expect something, you believe that it is your right to get it or have it, e.g. *I expect good behaviour from all of you.*

Similar words: (sense 1) anticipate, hope, bargain for, look forward to

expectancy
(noun) Expectancy is the feeling that something is about to happen, especially something exciting.

expectant
1 (adjective) If you are expectant, you believe that something is about to happen, especially something exciting.
2 An expectant mother or father is someone whose baby is going to be born soon.
expectantly (adverb).

expectation, expectations
(noun) Expectation is a strong belief or hope that something will happen or should happen.

expecting
(adjective; an informal use) A woman who is expecting is pregnant.

expectorate, expectorates, expectorating, expectorated
(verb; a formal word) To expectorate means to cough up or spit out matter from the throat.
[from Latin *expectorare* meaning 'to drive from the chest']

expedient, expedients (pronounced iks-**pee**-dee-ent)
1 (noun) An expedient is an action or plan that achieves the desired result but that may not be morally acceptable.
2 (adjective) Something that is expedient is useful or convenient in a particular situation.
expediency (noun).

expedite, expedites, expediting, expedited
(verb; a formal word) To expedite something means to make it happen faster.

expedition, expeditions
(noun) An expedition is an organized journey made for a special purpose, such as to explore; also the party of people who make such a journey, e.g. *The expedition set off at first light.*
expeditionary (adjective).

expeditious
(adjective; a formal word) quick and efficient.
expeditiously (adverb).

expel, expels, expelling, expelled
1 (verb) If someone is expelled from a school or club, they are officially told to leave because they have behaved badly.
2 If a gas or liquid is expelled from a place, it is forced out of it.
expulsion (noun).

expend, expends, expending, expended
(verb) To expend energy, time, or money means to use it up or spend it.
[from Latin *expendere* meaning 'to weigh out']

expendable
(adjective) no longer useful or necessary, and therefore able to be got rid of.

expenditure, expenditures
1 (noun) Expenditure is the total amount of money spent on something.
2 The expenditure of money, energy, or time is the use of it for a particular purpose.

expense, expenses
1 (noun) Expense is the money that something costs.
2 (plural noun) Someone's expenses are the money they spend while doing something connected with their work, which is paid back to them by their employers, e.g. *travelling expenses.*
3 (phrase) If you do something **at the expense of** someone or something else, you do it in a way that harms them, e.g. *Industry has flourished in the area at the expense of agriculture.*

Similar words: (sense 1) expenditure, outgoings, outlay

expense account, expense accounts
(noun) An expense account is an arrangement by which an employee is allowed to use their employer's money for matters connected with work.

expensive
(adjective) costing a lot of money.
expensively (adverb), **expensiveness** (noun).

experience, experiences, experiencing, experienced

1 (noun) An experience is something that happens to you, or something that you do, especially something new or unusual.
2 Experience consists of skills or knowledge gained through doing certain things.
3 (verb) If you experience a situation or feeling, it happens to you or you are affected by it.
[from Latin *experiri* meaning 'to test' or 'to prove']

Similar words: (sense 3) undergo, know, go through

experienced
(adjective) skilled or knowledgeable through doing something for a long time.

Similar words: seasoned, practised

experiment, experiments, experimenting, experimented
1 (noun) An experiment is the testing of something, either to find out its effect or to prove something.
2 (verb) If you experiment with something, you do a scientific test on it to prove or discover something.
3 To experiment also means to try out a new idea or method to see what effect it has.
experimentation (noun), **experimental** (adjective), **experimentally** (adverb), **experimenter** (noun).
[from Latin *experimentum* meaning 'trial' or 'test']

expert, experts
1 (noun) An expert is someone who is very skilled at doing something or very knowledgeable about a particular subject.
2 (adjective) Something that is expert is very well done.
expertly (adverb).
[from Latin *expertus* meaning 'known by experience']

Similar words: (sense 1) buff, authority, master, connoisseur, specialist, ace

expertise (pronounced eks-per-**teez**)
(noun) Expertise is special skill or knowledge.

expiate, expiates, expiating, expiated
(pronounced **eks**-pee-ate)
(verb; a formal word) If you expiate guilty feelings or bad behaviour, you do something to show that you are sorry for what you have done.
expiation (noun).

expire, expires, expiring, expired
1 (verb) When something expires, it reaches the end of the period of time for which it is valid, e.g. *My bus pass expires next week*.
2 (a literary use) When someone expires, they die.
expiry (noun), **expiration** (noun).

Similar words: (sense 1) lapse, run out

explain, explains, explaining, explained
(verb) If you explain something, you give details about it or reasons for it so that it can be understood.
explanation (noun), **explanatory** (adjective).

[from Latin *explanare* meaning 'to level out']

Similar words: elucidate, expound, interpret, illuminate, illustrate, clarify, spell out

expletive, expletives (pronounced ik-**splee**-tiv)
(noun) An expletive is an exclamation or swearword which expresses an emotional reaction.

explicable
(adjective) capable of being explained and understood.

explicit
(adjective) shown or expressed clearly, openly, and precisely, e.g. *explicit directions*.
explicitly (adverb), **explicitness** (noun).
[from Latin *explicitus* meaning 'unfolded']

explode, explodes, exploding, exploded
1 (verb) If something explodes, it bursts open with great violence, often causing damage.
2 When something increases suddenly and rapidly, it can be said to explode, e.g. *The population is exploding*.
3 If someone explodes, they react violently or angrily to something.
[from Latin *explodere* meaning 'to clap someone offstage', from *ex* meaning 'out of' + *plodere* meaning 'to clap']

exploit, exploits, exploiting, exploited
1 (verb) If someone exploits you, they unfairly use your work or ideas for their own ends.
2 If you exploit something such as a raw material, you make the best use of it, especially for profit.
3 (noun) An exploit is something brave or interesting that you have done.
exploitation (noun).
[sense 3 from French *exploit* meaning 'accomplishment']

explore, explores, exploring, explored
1 (verb) If you explore a place, you travel in it to find out what it is like.
2 If you explore an idea, you think about it carefully.
exploration (noun), **exploratory** (adjective), **explorer** (noun).

explosion, explosions
(noun) An explosion is a sudden violent burst of energy, for example one caused by a bomb.

explosive, explosives
1 (adjective) capable of exploding or likely to explode.
2 happening suddenly and making a loud noise.
3 An explosive situation is one which is likely to have serious or dangerous effects.
4 (noun) An explosive is a substance or device that can explode.

exponent, exponents
1 (noun) An exponent of an idea, theory, or plan is someone who puts it forward.
2 (a formal use) An exponent of a skill or activity is someone who is good at it.
3 In mathematics, an exponent is a number or symbol placed above and to the right of a

number, indicating how many times the number is to be multiplied by itself, e.g. 2^3 equals $2 \times 2 \times 2$.
[from Latin *exponere* meaning 'to set out']

exponential (pronounced eks-pon-**en**-shl) (adjective) growing or increasing rapidly.
exponentially (adverb).

export, exports, exporting, exported
1 (verb) To export goods means to sell them to another country and send them there.
2 (noun) Exports are goods which are sold and sent to another country.
exportation (noun), **exporter** (noun).
[from Latin *exportare* meaning 'to carry away']

expose, exposes, exposing exposed
1 (verb) To expose something means to uncover it and make it visible.
2 To expose a person to something dangerous means to put them in a situation in which it might harm them, e.g. *exposed to radiation*.
3 To expose a person or situation means to reveal the truth about them, especially when it involves dishonest or shocking behaviour.
4 To expose a film means to allow light to reach it.
[from Latin *exponere* meaning 'to set out']

Similar words: (sense 3) unmask, debunk, denounce, show up

exposé, exposés (pronounced eks-**poze**-ay) (noun) An exposé is a piece of writing which reveals the truth about a situation or a person.
[a French word]

exposition, expositions
(noun) An exposition is a detailed explanation of a particular subject.

expostulate, expostulates, expostulating, expostulated
(verb; a formal word) If you expostulate, you express strong disagreement with someone.
expostulation (noun).
[from Latin *expostulare* meaning 'to require']

exposure, exposures
1 (noun) Exposure is the exposing of something.
2 Exposure is the harmful effect on the body caused by very cold weather.
3 An exposure is the length of time a film is exposed to the light, resulting in a single photograph; also the photograph itself.

expound, expounds, expounding, expounded
(verb) If you expound an idea or opinion, you give a clear and detailed explanation of it.
[from Latin *exponere* meaning 'to set out']

express, expresses, expressing, expressed
1 (verb) When you express an idea or feeling, you show what you think or feel by saying or doing something.
2 If you express a quantity in a particular form, you write it down in that form, e.g. *Express that fraction as a decimal.*
3 (adjective) clearly stated and definite, e.g. *My express wish was that you go without me.*
4 very fast, e.g. *an express train.*

5 (noun) An express is a fast train or coach which stops at only a few places.
[from Latin *expressus* meaning 'squeezed out']

expression, expressions
1 (noun) An expression is a word or phrase used in communicating, e.g. *slang expressions.*
2 The expression of ideas or feelings is the showing of them through words, actions, or art.
3 Your expression is the look on your face which shows what you are thinking or feeling.

expressive
1 (adjective) showing feelings clearly.
2 full of expression.
expressively (adverb), **expressiveness** (noun).

expropriate, expropriates, expropriating, expropriated
(verb; a formal word) To expropriate something means to take it away from someone, especially for public use, e.g. *His property was expropriated by the army during the war.*
expropriation (noun).

expulsion, expulsions
(noun) Expulsion is the act of expelling.

expunge, expunges, expunging, expunged
(verb; a formal word) To expunge something means to wipe it out or destroy it.
[from Latin *expungere* meaning 'to blot out']

expurgate, expurgates, expurgating, expurgated
(verb; a formal word) If a book or text is expurgated, the parts in it which are obscene or offensive are removed.
expurgation (noun).
[from Latin *expurgare* meaning 'to clean out']

exquisite
1 (adjective) extremely beautiful and pleasing.
2 intense, but pleasant and satisfying, e.g. *the exquisite pleasure of the ice cold water.*
exquisitely (adverb), **exquisiteness** (noun).

extant
(adjective; a formal word) still existing.

extemporaneous
(adjective; a formal word) done without preparation, and in a temporary way.

extempore (pronounced eks-**tem**-por-ee) (adjective or adverb) without preparation.
[from Latin *ex tempore* meaning 'instantaneously']

extemporize, extemporizes, extemporizing, extemporized; also spelled **extemporise**
(verb) If you extemporize, you say or do something without having prepared or planned it.

extend, extends, extending, extended
1 (verb) If something extends for a distance, it continues and stretches into the distance.
2 If something extends from a surface or object, it sticks out from it.
3 If something extends over a period of time, it continues for that time.
4 If you extend something, you make it larger or longer, e.g. *She extended her visit by three weeks.*
5 (a formal use) If you extend a welcome or an invitation to someone, you offer it to them.

extension, extensions
1 (noun) An extension is a room or building which is added to an existing building.
2 An extension is an extra period of time for which something continues to exist or be valid.
3 An extension is also an additional telephone connected to the same line as another telephone.

extensive
1 (adjective) covering a large area.
2 very great in effect, e.g. *extensive damage*.
extensively (adverb).

extent, extents
(noun) The extent of something is its length, area, size, or scale.

extenuate, extenuates, extenuating, extenuated
(verb; a formal word) Something that extenuates a fault or offence makes it appear less serious.
extenuating (adjective), **extenuation** (noun).
[from Latin *extenuare* meaning 'to make thin']

exterior, exteriors
1 (noun) The exterior of something is its outside.
2 Your exterior is your outward appearance.
3 (adjective) situated or happening outside something or someone.

exterminate, exterminates, exterminating, exterminated
(verb) When animals or people are exterminated, they are deliberately killed.
extermination (noun).
[from Latin *exterminare* meaning 'to drive away']

external, externals
1 (adjective) existing or happening on the outside or outer part of something.
2 (plural noun) The externals of a situation are features that are not very important.
externally (adverb).

extinct
1 (adjective) An extinct species of animal or plant is no longer in existence.
2 An extinct volcano is no longer likely to erupt.
extinction (noun).

extinguish, extinguishes, extinguishing, extinguished
1 (verb) To extinguish a light or fire means to put it out.
2 (a literary use) To extinguish an idea or feeling means to destroy it completely, e.g. *All hope of ever getting back was extinguished*.
extinguisher (noun).
[from Latin *extinguere* meaning 'to quench']

extirpate, extirpates, extirpating, extirpated
(verb; a formal word) To extirpate something means to remove or destroy it completely.
[from Latin *exstirpare* meaning 'to root out', from *stirps* meaning 'root']

extol, extols, extolling, extolled
(verb) If you extol something you praise it highly.
[from Latin *extollere* meaning 'to raise up']

extort, extorts, extorting, extorted
(verb) To extort money or information from someone means to get it by using force or threats.
extortion (noun).
[from Latin *extorquere* meaning 'to wrench out']

extortionate
(adjective) more expensive than you consider to be fair.

extra, extras
1 (adjective) more than is usual, necessary, or expected.
2 (noun) An extra is anything which is additional.
3 An extra in a film is a person who is hired to play a very small and unimportant part in it.

Similar words: (sense 1) further, supplementary, additional

extra-
(prefix) Extra- means outside or beyond, e.g. *extracurricular activities*.
[from Latin *exterus* meaning 'outward']

extract, extracts, extracting, extracted
1 (verb) To extract something from a place means to take it out or get it out, often by force.
2 If you extract information from someone, you get it from them with difficulty.
3 (noun) An extract is a small section taken from a book, piece of music, play, or film.
[from Latin *extractus* meaning 'drawn forth']

extraction
1 (noun) Your extraction is the country or people that your family originally comes from, e.g. *She's of Irish extraction*.
2 Extraction is the process of taking or getting something out of a place.

extradite, extradites, extraditing, extradited
(verb) To extradite someone means to officially send them back to their own country to be tried for a crime of which they have been accused.
extradition (noun).
[from Latin *ex* meaning 'out' + *traditio* meaning 'handing over']

extramural
(adjective) Extramural courses in a college or university are those designed for part-time students.
[from Latin *extra* + *muri* meaning 'outside the walls']

extraneous (pronounced ik-**strain**-ee-uss)
(adjective) not relevant or essential to the situation or subject that you are talking about.
extraneously (adverb).
[from Latin *extraneus* meaning 'external']

extraordinary
(adjective) unusual or surprising.
extraordinarily (adverb).

Similar words: exceptional, phenomenal, remarkable, rare, unusual

extrasensory
(adjective) beyond the range and ability of the five senses.

extrasensory perception
(noun) Extrasensory perception is the ability to know or feel things without the use of the normal senses, e.g. *A clairvoyant uses extrasensory perception.*

extraterrestrial
(adjective) happening or existing beyond the earth's atmosphere.
[from Latin *extra* + *terra* meaning 'outside the earth']

extravagant
1 (adjective) spending or costing more money than is reasonable or affordable.
2 going beyond reasonable limits.
extravagantly (adverb), **extravagance** (noun).
[from Latin *extra* + *vagans* meaning 'wandering outside']

extravaganza, extravaganzas
(noun) An extravaganza is a very elaborate and expensive public activity or performance.
[from Italian *estravaganza* meaning 'extravagance']

extreme, extremes
1 (adjective) very great in degree or intensity, e.g. *unbearably extreme heat.*
2 going beyond what is usual or reasonable, e.g. *extreme behaviour.*
3 at the furthest point or edge of something, e.g. *the extreme edge of the cliff.*
4 (noun) An extreme is the highest or furthest degree of something.
extremely (adverb).
[from Latin *extremus* meaning 'outermost']

extremist, extremists
(noun) An extremist is a person who uses severe or unreasonable methods or behaviour, especially to bring about political change.
extremism (noun).

extremity, extremities
1 (noun) The extremities of something are its furthest ends or edges.
2 An extremity is a very serious situation.

extricate, extricates, extricating, extricated
(verb) To extricate someone from a place or a situation means to free them from it.
[from Latin *extricare* meaning 'to disentangle']

extrovert, extroverts
1 (noun) An extrovert is a person who is more interested in other people and the world around them than their own thoughts and feelings.
2 (adjective) active, lively, and sociable.
[from Latin *extra* meaning 'outwards' + *vertere* meaning 'to turn']

extrude, extrudes, extruding, extruded
(verb; a formal word) When something extrudes or is extruded, it is forced or squeezed out through a small opening.

exuberant
(adjective) full of energy and excitement.
exuberantly (adverb), **exuberance** (noun).
[from Latin *exuberans* meaning 'abundantly fruitful']

exude, exudes, exuding, exuded
1 (verb) If someone exudes a quality or feeling, they seem to have it to a great degree.
2 If something exudes a liquid or a smell, it is released from it or oozes out of it.
[from Latin *exsudare* meaning 'to sweat']

exult, exults, exulting, exulted
(verb) If you exult, you feel and show great happiness and pleasure because of a success.
exultant (adjective), **exultantly** (adverb), **exultation** (noun).
[from Latin *exsultare* meaning 'to jump for joy']

eye, eyes, eyeing or eying, eyed
1 (noun) The eye is the organ of sight.
2 If you have an eye for something, you can recognize it and make good judgments about it.
3 The eye of a needle is the small hole at the end through which you pass the thread.
4 The eye of a storm is the calm centre of it.
5 (verb) To eye something means to look at it carefully or suspiciously.
6 (phrase) If two people **see eye to eye**, they agree with each other.

eyeball, eyeballs
(noun) The eyeball is the whole of the ball-shaped part of the eye.

eyebrow, eyebrows
1 (noun) Your eyebrows are the lines of hair which grow on the ridges of bone above your eyes.
2 (phrase) If something causes you to **raise an eyebrow**, it causes you to feel surprised or disapproving.

eyelash, eyelashes
(noun) Your eyelashes are hairs that grow on the edges of your eyelids.

eyelet, eyelets
(noun) An eyelet is a small hole in a shoe or piece of material for a cord or lace to pass through.

eyelid, eyelids
(noun) Your eyelids are the muscular folds of skin which move to cover or expose your eyeballs.

eye-opener, eye-openers
(noun) If something you find out is an eye-opener, it is very surprising or revealing.

eye shadow
(noun) Eye shadow is a coloured substance that women put on their eyelids to make them look more attractive.

eyesight
(noun) Your eyesight is your ability to see.

eyesore, eyesores
(noun) Something that is an eyesore is extremely ugly.

eyewitness, eyewitnesses
(noun) An eyewitness is a person who has seen an event and can describe what happened.

eyrie, eyries (pronounced ear-ree)
(noun) An eyrie is the nest of an eagle or other bird of prey, usually built on a cliff or mountain.

F

F an abbreviation for **Fahrenheit**.

fable, fables
1 (noun) A fable is a story intended to teach a moral lesson, e.g. *Aesop's fables*.
2 A fable is also an unlikely story that is probably not true.
[from Latin *fabula* meaning 'story']

fabled
(adjective) well known because many stories have been told about it, e.g. *the fabled Timbuktu*.

fabric, fabrics
1 (noun) Fabric is cloth, e.g. *a crisp cotton fabric*.
2 The fabric of a building is its walls, roof, and other parts.
3 The fabric of a society or system is its structure, laws, and customs, e.g. *The priests upheld the fabric of Roman society*.
[from Latin *fabrica* meaning 'building work']

fabricate, fabricates, fabricating, fabricated
1 (verb) If you fabricate a story or an explanation, you invent it in order to deceive people.
2 To fabricate something means to make or manufacture it.
fabrication (noun).
[from Latin *fabricare* meaning 'to make' or 'to form']

fabulous
1 (adjective) wonderful or very impressive, e.g. *They missed a fabulous opportunity*.
2 not real, but happening or occurring in stories and legends, e.g. *fabulous animals and birds*.
fabulously (adverb).

façade, façades (pronounced fas-**sahd**)
1 (noun) A façade is the front outside wall of a building.
2 A façade is also a false outward appearance, e.g. *The unity of the party was just a façade*.
[a French word]

face, faces, facing, faced
1 (noun) Your face is the front part of your head from your chin to your forehead.
2 A face is the expression someone has or is making, e.g. *a puzzled face... Stop pulling faces!*
3 A face of something is a surface or side of it, especially the most important side, e.g. *the north face of Everest... the face of a watch*.
4 (verb) To face something or someone means to be opposite them or to look at them or towards them, e.g. *Most of the seats face forward*.
5 (noun) The face of something is its main aspect or general appearance, e.g. *The general face of industrial relations is changing*.
6 (verb) If you face something difficult or unpleasant, you have to deal with it, e.g. *Death is something that we all have to face*.
7 (phrase) If you try to **save face** or avoid **losing face**, you try to keep your good reputation or avoid looking silly.

8 **On the face of it** means judging by something's appearance or your initial reaction to it, e.g. *On the face of it, it sounds like a good idea*.
[from Latin *facies* meaning 'form' or 'appearance']

Similar words: (sense 1) countenance, visage

faceless
(adjective) without character or individuality, e.g. *faceless Civil Service bureaucrats*.

face-lift, face-lifts
1 (noun) A face-lift is an operation to tighten the skin on someone's face to make them look younger.
2 If you give something a face-lift, you clean it or improve its appearance.

face pack, face packs
(noun) A face pack is a thick substance which can be spread on the face, left for a while, and then removed, in order to cleanse the skin.

facet, facets (pronounced **fas**-it)
1 (noun) A facet of something is a single part or aspect of it, e.g. *one of the facets of his character*.
2 A facet is also one of the flat, cut surfaces of a diamond or other precious stone.
[from French *facette* meaning 'little face']

facetious (pronounced fas-**see**-shuss)
(adjective) witty or amusing but in a rather silly or inappropriate way, e.g. *facetious remarks*.
[from Latin *facetiae* meaning 'witty remarks']

facial, facials (pronounced **fay**-shal)
1 (adjective) Facial means appearing on or being part of the face, e.g. *facial hair*.
2 (noun) A facial is a beauty treatment for the face involving cleansing, toning, and massage.
facially (adverb).

facile (pronounced **fas**-sile)
(adjective) simple and obvious but without careful, serious thought, e.g. *facile generalizations about the economy*.
[from Latin *facilis* meaning 'easy']

facilitate, facilitates, facilitating, facilitated
(verb) To facilitate something means to make it easier for it to happen or be done, e.g. *legislation to facilitate the sale of businesses*.

facility, facilities
1 (noun) A facility is a service, opportunity, or piece of equipment which makes it possible to do something, e.g. *a hotel with sports facilities*.
2 A facility for something is an ability to do it easily or well, e.g. *a facility for languages*.

Similar words: (sense 1) amenity, service

facsimile, facsimiles (pronounced fak-**sim**-mil-ee)
(noun) A facsimile is an exact reproduction of a book or document.
[from Latin *facere* meaning 'to make' and *similis* meaning 'similar']

fact, facts
1 (noun) A fact is a piece of knowledge or information that is true or something that has actually happened.
2 (phrases) **In fact**, **as a matter of fact**, and **in point of fact** mean 'actually' or 'really' and are used for emphasis or when making an additional comment, e.g. *We were allowed, in fact expected, to write in French... As a matter of fact, these are the first zebras I've ever seen.*
factual (adjective), **factually** (adverb).
[from Latin *factum* meaning 'something done']

faction, factions
(noun) A faction is a small group of people belonging to a larger group, but differing from it in some aims or ideas.

fact of life, facts of life
1 (noun) The facts of life are details about sexual intercourse and how babies are conceived and born.
2 If you say that something is a fact of life, you mean that it is something that people expect to happen, even though they might find it shocking or unpleasant, e.g. *Economic difficulties are one of the facts of life in developing countries.*

factor, factors
1 (noun) A factor is something that helps to cause a result, e.g. *Youth unemployment is a major factor contributing to our inner city problems.*
2 The factors of a number are the whole numbers that will divide exactly into it. For example, 2 and 5 are factors of 10.
3 If something increases by a particular factor, it is multiplied that number of times, e.g. *The amount of energy used has increased by a factor of eight.*
[from Latin *factor* meaning 'doer']

Similar words: (sense 1) element, point, consideration

factorial, factorials
(noun) In maths, the factorial of a number is the product of all the whole numbers from 1 to that number. For example, factorial 3 is 1 x 2 x 3.

factory, factories
(noun) A factory is a building or group of buildings where goods are made in large quantities.

faculty, faculties
1 (noun) Your faculties are your physical and mental abilities, e.g. *He was in complete command of his faculties... the faculty of imagination.*
2 In some universities, a Faculty is a group of related departments, e.g. *the Arts Faculty.*
[from Latin *facultas* meaning 'ability']

fad, fads
(noun) A fad is an intense but temporary fashion or craze, e.g. *the skateboard fad.*

faddy, faddier, faddiest
(adjective) unreasonably fussy, especially about food.

fade, fades, fading, faded
1 (verb) If something fades, the intensity of its colour, brightness, or sound is gradually reduced.
2 To fade in or fade out a television picture or radio signal means to gradually alter the level of brightness or sound.

faeces or **feces** (pronounced **fee**-seez)
(noun) Faeces are the solid waste substances discharged from a person's or animal's body.
[from Latin *faeces* meaning 'dregs']

fag, fags
1 (noun; an informal use) A fag is a cigarette.
2 If you describe something as a fag, you mean that it is boring or tiring.
3 At some public schools, a fag is a younger boy who has to do jobs for an older boy.

fagged
(adjective; an informal word) really exhausted.

faggot, faggots
1 (noun) A faggot is a ball of chopped meat, bread, and herbs.
2 A faggot is also a bundle of sticks for firewood.
3 (an offensive use, mainly in American English) A faggot is also a homosexual man.

Fahrenheit (pronounced **far**-ren-hite)
(noun) Fahrenheit is a scale of temperature in which the freezing point of water is 32 degrees and the boiling point is 212 degrees. It was devised by Gabriel Fahrenheit, a German physicist.

fail, fails, failing, failed
1 (verb) If someone fails to achieve something, they are not successful.
2 If you fail an exam, your marks are too low and you do not pass.
3 (noun) In an exam, a fail is a piece of work that is not good enough to pass.
4 (verb) If you fail to do something that you should have done, you do not do it, e.g. *He failed to arrive.*
5 If something fails, it becomes less strong or effective or stops working properly, e.g. *The brakes failed... Her health is failing.*
6 (phrase) **Without fail** means definitely or regularly, e.g. *He comes every week without fail.*
[from Latin *fallere* meaning 'to deceive' or 'to let down']

Similar words: (sense 1) fall short, flop

failing
1 (noun) A failing is a fault or unsatisfactory feature in something or someone.
2 (preposition) used to introduce an alternative, e.g. *Failing that, we could always go to the pictures.*

fail-safe
(adjective) designed so that nothing dangerous can happen if part of a machine or system goes wrong.

failure, failures
1 (noun) Failure is a lack of success, e.g. *The attempt ended in failure.*
2 A failure is an unsuccessful person, thing,

action, or event, e.g. *The meeting was a complete failure.*
3 Your failure to do something is not doing something that you were expected to do, e.g. *His friends remarked on his failure to appear at the party.*

Similar words: (sense 2) flop, washout

fain
(adverb; an old-fashioned word) willingly or gladly.
[from Old English *fægen* meaning 'glad' or 'happy']

faint, fainter, faintest; faints, fainting, fainted
1 (adjective) A sound, colour, or feeling that is faint has little strength or intensity.
2 (verb) If you faint, you lose consciousness for a short time.
3 (adjective) If you feel faint, you feel weak, dizzy, and unsteady.
faintly (adverb), **faintness** (noun).
[from Old French *feint* meaning 'weak' or 'sluggish']

Similar words: (sense 2) pass out, black out, swoon, keel over

faint-hearted
(adjective) lacking courage and confidence.

fair, fairer, fairest; fairs
1 (adjective) reasonable or equal according to generally accepted ideas about what is right and just, e.g. *That's not fair!*
2 quite large, e.g. *She made a fair amount of money.*
3 moderately good or likely to be correct, e.g. *I had a pretty fair idea of the answer.*
4 having light coloured hair or pale skin.
5 (an old-fashioned use) attractive to look at, e.g. *this fair city of ours.*
6 with pleasant, dry, and fine weather, e.g *It promises to be fair.*
7 (noun) A fair is a form of open-air entertainment with stalls, sideshows, and machines to ride on.
8 A fair is also an exhibition of goods produced by a particular industry, e.g. *the Frankfurt Book Fair.*
fairly (adverb), **fairness** (noun).
[Senses 1-6 are from Old English *fæger* meaning 'lovely'; senses 7-8 are from Latin *feria* meaning 'festival']

Similar words: (sense 1) just, impartial, equitable, unbiased

fairway, fairways
(noun) On a golf course, the fairway is the area of trimmed grass between a tee and a green.

fairy, fairies
(noun) In stories, fairies are small, supernatural creatures with magical powers.
[from Old French *faerie* meaning 'fairyland']

fairy lights
(plural noun) Fairy lights are small, coloured electric lights used for decoration, for example on Christmas trees.

fairy tale, fairy tales
(noun) A fairy tale is a story of magical events.

fait accompli, faits accomplis (pronounced fate ak-**kom**-plee)
(noun) A fait accompli is something that has already been done and cannot be changed.
[a French expression meaning 'completed deed']

faith, faiths
1 (noun) Faith is a feeling of confidence, trust or optimism about something.
2 A faith is a particular religion.
3 (phrase) If you do something in **good faith**, your reasons are honest and sincere.
[from Latin *fides* meaning 'trust']

Similar words: (sense 1) confidence, conviction, trust

faithful
1 (adjective) loyal to someone or something and remaining firm in support of them.
2 accurate and truthful, e.g. *The film was faithful to the original book.*
faithfully (adverb), **faithfulness** (noun).

Similar words: (sense 1) steadfast, loyal, staunch

faith healing
(noun) Faith healing is the treatment of a sick person through prayer and the power of religious faith.
faith healer (noun).

faithless
(adjective) disloyal or dishonest.

fake, fakes, faking, faked
1 (noun) A fake is an imitation of something made to trick people into thinking that it is genuine.
2 (adjective) Fake means imitation and not genuine, e.g. *fake antiques.*
3 (verb) If you fake an emotion or feeling, you pretend that you are experiencing it.

Similar words: (sense 1) forgery, phoney, fraud, sham (sense 2) phoney, bogus, counterfeit, fraudulent, sham, false (sense 3) counterfeit

falcon, falcons
(noun) A falcon is a bird of prey that can be trained to hunt other birds or small animals.
[from Latin *falco* meaning 'hawk']

fall, falls, falling, fell, fallen
1 (verb) If someone or something falls or falls over, they drop towards the ground.
2 (noun) If you have a fall, you accidentally fall over.
3 A fall of snow, soot, or other substance is a quantity of it that has fallen to the ground.
4 (verb) If something falls somewhere, it lands there, e.g. *A shadow fell over her book.*
5 If something falls in amount or strength, it becomes less or weaker, e.g. *Oil consumption fell by 24%.*

6 (noun) A fall in something is a reduction in its amount or strength.
7 (verb) If a person or group in a position of power falls, they lose their position and someone else takes control.
8 Someone who falls in battle is killed.
9 If, for example, you fall asleep, fall ill, or fall in love, you change quite quickly to that new state.
10 If you fall for someone, you become strongly attracted to them and fall in love.
11 If you fall for a trick or lie, you are deceived by it.
12 If something falls into a particular classification or grouping, it is classified or grouped in that way, e.g. *My work really falls into three parts.*
13 Something that falls on a particular date occurs on that date.
14 (noun) In America, autumn is called the fall.

fall back
1 (phrasal verb) If you fall back, you retreat.
2 If you fall back on a particular solution, you use it when other solutions have failed because you know that it is easy or safe.

fall down
(phrasal verb) An argument or idea that falls down on a particular point is weak in that area and as a result will be unsuccessful.

fall in
1 (phrasal verb) If you fall in with a suggestion or system, you accept it without trying to change it.
2 When soldiers fall in, they take up their correct position in a formation.

fall out
(phrasal verb) If people fall out, they disagree and quarrel.

fall through
(phrasal verb) If an arrangement or plan falls through, it fails or is abandoned.

fallacy, fallacies (pronounced **fal**-lass-ee)
(noun) A fallacy is something false that is generally believed to be true.
[from Latin *fallacia* meaning 'deception']

fallible
(adjective) able or likely to make mistakes, e.g. *Economists, like other humans, are fallible.*
fallibility (noun).
[from Latin *fallibilis* meaning 'easily deceived']

fallopian tube, fallopian tubes (pronounced fal-**loh**-pee-an)
(noun) The fallopian tubes in a woman's body are the pair of tubes along which the eggs pass from the ovaries to the uterus. They are named after the Italian anatomist Gabriele Fallopio, who first described them in the 16th century.

fallout
(noun) Fallout is radioactive particles that fall to the earth after a nuclear explosion.

fallow
(adjective) Land that is fallow is not being used for crop growing so that it can regain its fertility.

false
1 (adjective) untrue, mistaken, or incorrect, e.g. *The accusation is false and unjust.*
2 not real or genuine but intended to seem real, e.g. *false teeth.*
3 unfaithful, disloyal, or deceitful.
falsely (adverb), **falseness** (noun), **falsity** (noun).
[from Latin *falsus*]

falsehood, falsehoods
1 (noun) Falsehood is the quality or fact of being untrue, e.g. *The enquiry must establish the truth or falsehood of the various rumours.*
2 A falsehood is a lie.

falsetto, falsettos
(noun) A falsetto is a man's very high-pitched speaking or singing voice.

falsify, falsifies, falsifying, falsified
(verb) If you falsify something, you change or misrepresent it in order to deceive people.
falsification (noun).

falter, falters, faltering, faltered
(verb) If someone or something falters, they hesitate or become unsure or unsteady, e.g. *His steps faltered.*

fame
(noun) Fame is the state of being very well known.
[from Latin *fama* meaning 'reputation']

Similar words: renown, eminence, glory, stardom

famed
(adjective) very well known, e.g. *The church is famed for its flower festivals.*

familiar, familiars
1 (adjective) well known or easy to recognize, e.g. *familiar faces... The name sounded familiar.*
2 knowing or understanding something well, e.g. *I am, of course, familiar with your work.*
3 too informal and friendly in behaviour towards someone, e.g. *I can't stand that familiar tone he uses with young women.*
4 (noun) A familiar is a cat or other animal, believed to live with a witch and share her magic power.
familiarity (noun), **familiarize** (verb).
[from Latin *familiaris* meaning 'known in the household']

Similar words: (sense 1) recognizable, well known (sense 2) conversant, au fait, well up on

family, families
1 (noun) A family is a group consisting of parents and their children; also all the people who are related to each other, including aunts and uncles, grandparents, and cousins.
2 A family is also a group of related species of animals or plants.
familial (adjective).
[from Latin *familia* meaning 'household']

family planning
(noun) Family planning is the practice of controlling the number of children you have, usually by using contraception.

family tree, family trees
(noun) A family tree is a chart showing all the people in a family and their relationship to others over many generations.

famine, famines
(noun) A famine is a serious shortage of food which may cause many deaths.
[from Latin *fames* meaning 'hunger']

famished
(adjective; an informal word) very hungry.

famous
(adjective) very well known.

Similar words: eminent, renowned, celebrated, legendary, illustrious, noted

famously
(adverb; an old-fashioned word) If people get on famously, they enjoy each other's company very much.

fan, fans, fanning, fanned
1 (noun) If you are a fan of someone or something, you like them very much and are very enthusiastic about them.
2 A fan is a hand-held or mechanical object which creates a draught of cool air when it moves.
3 (verb) To fan someone or something means to create a draught in their direction, e.g. *She was fanning her face with her programme.*
[Sense 1 is a short form of 'fanatic'; senses 2-3 are from Latin *vannus* meaning 'winnowing-fan']

Similar words: (sense 1) supporter, enthusiast

fan out
(phrasal verb) If things or people fan out, they move outwards from a point in different directions.

fanatic, fanatics
(noun) A fanatic is a person who is very extreme in their support for a cause or in their enthusiasm for a particular sport or activity.
fanaticism (noun).
[from Latin *fanaticus* meaning 'possessed by a god']

Similar words: devotee, extremist, zealot, diehard

fanatical
(adjective) If you are fanatical about something, you are very extreme in your enthusiasm or support for it.
fanatically (adverb).

Similar words: fervent, overenthusiastic, zealous, obsessive

fan belt, fan belts
(noun) A fan belt is a belt in an engine which drives the fan to cool the engine.

fancy, fancies, fancying, fancied; fancier, fanciest
1 (verb) If you fancy something, you want to have it or do it, e.g *She fancied a flat of her own.*
2 If you fancy someone, you feel sexually attracted to them.

3 (noun) A fancy is a liking or desire for something or someone.
4 (verb) If you fancy that something is the case, you imagine or think that it is so, e.g. *I fancied I could hear a baby screaming.*
5 (noun) Fancy is uncontrolled imagination, e.g. *a flight of fancy.*
6 (adjective) Something that is fancy is special and elaborate, e.g. *He prefers good, plain food, nothing fancy.*
fanciful (adjective).
[from Greek *phantasia* meaning 'imagination']

Similar words: (sense 6) elaborate, ornate, extravagant, fanciful, flowery

fancy dress
(noun) Fancy dress is clothing worn for a party at which people dress up to look like a particular character or animal.

fanfare, fanfares
(noun) A fanfare is a short, loud, musical introduction to a special event, usually played on trumpets.

fang, fangs
(noun) Fangs are long, pointed teeth.

fanlight, fanlights
(noun) A fanlight is a small window above a door.

fantasize, fantasizes, fantasizing, fantasized; also spelled **fantasise**
(verb) If you fantasize, you imagine pleasant but unlikely events or situations.

fantastic
1 (adjective) wonderful and very pleasing, e.g. *a fantastic film.*
2 extremely large in degree or amount, e.g. *We spend a fantastic amount of time on this.*
3 strange and difficult to believe, e.g. *The truth is scarcely less fantastic than the fable.*
fantastically (adverb).

Similar words: (sense 1) wonderful, fabulous, marvellous

fantasy, fantasies
1 (noun) A fantasy is an imagined story or situation.
2 Fantasy is uncontrolled imagination, e.g. *To a small child fantasy and reality are very close.*
[from Greek *phantasia* meaning 'imagination']

far, farther, farthest; further, furthest
1 (adverb) If something is far away from other things, it is a long distance away.
2 (adjective) Far means very distant, e.g. *in the far north.*
3 Far also describes the more distant of two things rather than the nearer one, e.g. *on the far side of the river.*
4 (adverb) Far also means very much or to a great extent or degree, e.g. *She's far better.*
5 (phrase) **By far** and **far and away** are used to say that something is the best, e.g. *She was by far the best swimmer.*
6 **Far from** is used to emphasize that something is definitely not true, e.g. *He was obviously far from happy.*

7 So far means up to the present moment, e.g. *So far, I haven't been able to contact her.*
8 As far as, so far as, and **in so far as** mean to the degree or extent that something is true, e.g. *As far as I know, he's not coming.*

Similar words: (sense 2) distant, remote (sense 4) decidedly, considerably, much

farce, farces
1 (noun) A farce is a humorous play in which ridiculous and unlikely situations occur.
2 A farce is also a disorganized and ridiculous situation.
farcical (adjective).

fare, fares, faring, fared
1 (noun) A fare is the amount charged for a journey on a bus, train, or plane.
2 (verb) How someone fares in a particular situation is how they get on, e.g. *They fared badly in the election.*
3 (noun; a rather old-fashioned use) The fare served in a restaurant is the range of food.
[from Old English *faran* meaning 'to go']

Far East
(noun) The Far East consists of the countries of East Asia, including China, Japan, and Malaysia.
Far Eastern (adjective).

farewell, farewells
1 (interjection) Farewell means goodbye.
2 (noun) A farewell is the act of saying goodbye and leaving, e.g. *Mr Partridge made his farewells and hurried off.*

far-fetched
(adjective) unlikely to be true.

farm, farms, farming, farmed
1 (noun) A farm is an area of land together with buildings, used for growing crops and raising animals.
2 (verb) Someone who farms uses land to grow crops and raise animals.
farmer (noun), **farming** (noun).
[from Old French *ferme* meaning 'rented land']

farmhouse, farmhouses
(noun) A farmhouse is the main house on a farm.

farmyard, farmyards
(noun) A farmyard is an area surrounded by farm buildings.

far-out
(adjective; an informal word) unusual or strange.

farrier, farriers
(noun) A farrier is a person who shoes horses.
[from Latin *ferrarius* meaning 'smith']

farrow, farrows, farrowing, farrowed
(verb) When a female pig farrows, she gives birth to piglets.
[from Old English *fearh* meaning 'piglet']

Farsi (pronounced **far**-see)
(noun) Farsi is the main language spoken in Iran. It is also known as Iranian.

fart, farts, farting, farted
(verb; a rude word) If someone farts, air is expelled from their anus, often producing a noise or smell.

farther, farthest the comparative and superlative forms of **far**.

farthing, farthings
(noun) A farthing is a coin that was worth a quarter of an old penny, before decimalization.

fascinate, fascinates, fascinating, fascinated
(verb) If something fascinates you, it interests and delights you so much that your thoughts concentrate on it and nothing else.
[from Latin *fascinare* meaning 'to bewitch']
fascinating (adjective).

Similar words: absorb, intrigue

fascism (pronounced **fash**-izm)
(noun) Fascism is an extreme right-wing political ideology or system of government with a powerful dictator and state control of most activities. Nationalism is encouraged and political opposition is not allowed.
fascist (noun or adjective).

fashion, fashions, fashioning, fashioned
1 (noun) A fashion is a style of dress or way of behaving that is popular at a particular time.
2 The fashion in which someone does something is the way in which they do it.
3 (phrase) Something that has been done **after a fashion** has not been done very well.
4 (verb) If you fashion something, you make it.
[from Latin *factio* meaning 'the making of something']

Similar words: (sense 1) trend, vogue, style, mode

fashionable
(adjective) Something that is fashionable is very popular with a lot of people at the same time.
fashionably (adverb).

Similar words: in, trendy, in vogue, up-to-date

fast, faster, fastest; fasts, fasting, fasted
1 (adjective and adverb) moving, doing something, or happening quickly or with great speed.
2 If a clock is fast, it shows a time that is later than the real time.
3 A fast film is very sensitive and can be used for taking photographs in low-light conditions.
4 A fast way of life involves a lot of enjoyable and expensive activities, e.g. *She wanted to move in the fast set.*
5 (adverb) Something that is held fast is firmly fixed.
6 (phrase) If you are **fast asleep**, you are in a deep sleep.
7 (adjective) Fast colours or dyes will not run or come out when wet.
8 (verb) If you fast, you eat no food at all for a period of time, usually for religious reasons.
9 (noun) A fast is a period of time during which someone does not eat food.

Similar words: (sense 1) quick, fleet, speedy, quickly, rapidly, swiftly

fast-breeder reactor, fast-breeder reactors
(noun) A fast-breeder reactor is a kind of nuclear reactor that produces more plutonium than it needs for the production of electricity.

fasten, fastens, fastening, fastened
1 (verb) To fasten something means to close it, do it up, or attach it firmly to something else.
2 If you fasten your hands or teeth around or onto something, you hold it tightly with them.
fastener (noun), **fastening** (noun).

Similar words: (sense 1) affix, attach, bind, lock, latch, secure, bolt

fast food
(noun) Fast food is hot food that is prepared and served quickly after you have ordered it.

fastidious
(adjective) extremely choosy and concerned about neatness and cleanliness.
fastidiously (adverb), **fastidiousness** (noun).
[from Latin *fastidium* meaning 'distaste']

fat, fatter, fattest; fats
1 (adjective) Someone who is fat has too much weight on their body.
2 (noun) Fat is the greasy, cream-coloured substance that animals and humans have under their skin, which is used to store energy and to help keep them warm.
3 Fat is also the greasy solid or liquid substance obtained from animals and plants and used in cooking.
4 (adjective) large or great, e.g. *a fat profit*.
fatness (noun), **fatty** (adjective).

Similar words: (sense 1) overweight, corpulent, podgy, roly-poly, rotund

fatal
1 (adjective) very important or significant and likely to have an undesirable effect, e.g. *I made the fatal mistake of accepting the offer*.
2 causing death, e.g. *a fatal accident*.
fatally (adverb).
[from Latin *fatum* meaning 'destiny']

Similar words: (sense 2) deadly, lethal, mortal, terminal

fatalism
(noun) Fatalism is a belief that people have no power to control or change events because they are predetermined by God or by Fate.
fatalist (noun), **fatalistic** (adjective).

fatality, fatalities
(noun) A fatality is a death caused by accident or violence.

fate, fates
1 (noun) Fate is a power that is believed to control events.
2 Someone's fate is what happens to them, e.g. *Several other companies suffered a similar fate*.
[from Latin *fatum* meaning 'destiny']

Similar words: (sense 1) destiny, providence

fated
(adjective) planned or controlled by fate, e.g. *She seemed fated to bring trouble wherever she went*.

fateful
(adjective) having an important, often disastrous, effect, e.g. *the fateful day of the election*.

father, fathers, fathering, fathered
1 (noun) A person's father is their male parent.
2 (verb) When a man fathers a child, he makes a woman pregnant.
3 (noun) The father of something is the man who invented or started it, e.g. *the founding fathers of the university*.
4 Father is used to address a priest in some Christian churches.
5 Father is another name for God.
fatherly (adjective), **fatherhood** (noun).

father-in-law, fathers-in-law
A person's father-in-law is the father of their husband or wife.

fathom, fathoms, fathoming, fathomed
1 (noun) A fathom is a unit for measuring the depth of water. It is equal to 6 feet or about 1.83 metres.
2 (verb) If you fathom something, you understand it after careful thought, e.g. *I couldn't fathom the reason for this change*.

fathomless
(adjective) too deep or difficult to measure or understand.

fatigue, fatigues, fatiguing, fatigued (pronounced fat-**eeg**)
1 (noun) Fatigue is extreme tiredness.
2 (verb) If you are fatigued by something, it makes you extremely tired.
3 (noun) Metal fatigue is a serious weakness caused by repeated stress or movement.
4 Fatigues are working clothes worn by soldiers for doing routine jobs.
[from Latin *fatigare* meaning 'to make tired']

fatten, fattens, fattening, fattened
(verb) If you fatten animals, you feed them so that they put on weight.

fatuous (pronounced **fat**-yoo-uss)
(adjective) showing no intelligence or thought, e.g. *a fatuous remark*.
[from Latin *fatuus* meaning 'foolish']

faucet, faucets (pronounced **faw**-sit)
(noun; used mainly in American English) A faucet is a tap.

fault, faults, faulting, faulted
1 (noun) If something bad is your fault, you are to blame for it.
2 (phrase) If you are **at fault**, you are mistaken or are to blame for something, e.g. *We failed to explain and are at fault in that*.
3 (noun) A fault in something or in someone's character is a weakness or imperfection in it.
4 (verb) If you cannot fault someone, you cannot criticize them for what they are doing because they are doing it so well.

5 (noun) A fault is a large crack in rock caused by movement of the earth's crust.
6 In tennis, a fault is an incorrect service.
faultless (adjective), **faulty** (adjective).

Similar words: (sense 3) defect, failing, shortcoming

fauna (pronounced **faw**-na)
(noun) The fauna of a particular area is all the animals found in that area, e.g. *the flora and fauna of Africa*.
[from Fauna, a minor Roman goddess of the countryside]

faux pas (pronounced foh **pah**)
(noun) A faux pas is an embarrassing mistake.
[a French expression, literally meaning 'false step']

favour, favours, favouring, favoured
1 (noun) If you regard someone or something with favour, you like or support them.
2 If you do someone a favour, you do something helpful for them.
3 (phrase) Something that is **in someone's favour** is a help or advantage to them, e.g. *The wind was in our favour... The umpire ruled in her favour.*
4 If you are **in favour of** something, you agree with it and think it should happen.
5 If someone is **out of favour**, they are not liked.
6 (verb) If you favour something or someone, you prefer that person or thing.
7 (a formal use) If you favour someone with your attention or presence, you give it to them, e.g. *The Minister favoured us with an interview.*
favourable (adjective), **favourably** (adverb).
[from Latin *favor* meaning 'goodwill']

favourite, favourites
1 (adjective) Your favourite person or thing is the one you like best.
2 (noun) Someone's favourite is the person or thing they like best.
3 In a race or contest, the favourite is the animal or person expected to win.

favouritism
(noun) Favouritism is behaviour in which you are unfairly more helpful or more generous to one person than to other people.

Similar words: favour, partiality

fawn, fawns, fawning, fawned
1 (noun and adjective) pale yellowish-brown.
2 (noun) A fawn is a very young deer.
3 (verb) To fawn on someone means to seek their approval by flattering them.
[Sense 2 is from Old French *faon* meaning 'young deer'; sense 3 is from Old English *fægnian* meaning 'to show delight']

fax, faxes
(noun) A fax is an exact copy of a document sent by a telegraphic system.

faze, fazes, fazing, fazed
(verb; an informal word) Something that fazes someone upsets or disturbs them.

FBI
(noun) The FBI is an agency of the American Department of Justice that investigates crimes in which American national law is broken. FBI is an abbreviation for 'Federal Bureau of Investigation'.

fear, fears, fearing, feared
1 (noun) Fear is an unpleasant feeling of danger.
2 (verb) If you fear someone or something, you are frightened of them.
3 If you fear something unpleasant, you are worried that it is likely to happen, e.g. *They feared that their independence might be lost.*
4 (noun) A fear is a thought that something undesirable or unpleasant might happen, e.g. *My fear is that he might give up.*
fearless (adjective), **fearlessly** (adverb).
[from Old English *fær* meaning 'danger']

Similar words: (sense 1) dread, terror, trepidation, fright, phobia

fearful
1 (adjective) afraid and full of fear.
2 extremely unpleasant or worrying, e.g. *the fearful risks of the operation.*
fearfully (adverb).

fearsome
(adjective) terrible or frightening, e.g. *The dog had a fearsome set of teeth.*

feasible
(adjective) possible and likely to be done or likely to happen, e.g. *Is this approach technologically feasible?*
feasibility (noun).
[from Old French *faisible* meaning 'able to be done']

feast, feasts, feasting, feasted
1 (noun) A feast is a large and special meal for many people.
2 (verb) To feast means to take part in a feast.
[from Latin *festum* meaning 'feast']

feat, feats
(noun) A feat is an impressive and difficult achievement, e.g. *an extraordinary feat of engineering.*
[from Old French *fait* meaning 'action']

feather, feathers, feathering, feathered
1 (noun) A feather is one of the light fluffy structures covering a bird's body.
2 (phrase) If someone **feathers their nest**, they collect possessions and money to make their life more comfortable, especially dishonestly.
feathery (adjective).

Similar words: (sense 1) plume, plumage

feature, features, featuring, featured
1 (noun) A feature of something is an interesting or important part or characteristic of it.
2 Someone's features are the various parts of their face, e.g. *He had very regular features.*
3 A feature is a special article or programme dealing with a particular subject or the main film in a cinema programme.
4 (verb) To feature something means to include it or emphasize it as an important part or subject.
featureless (adjective).

February

(noun) February is the second month of the year. It has 28 days, except in a leap year, when it has 29 days.
[from Februa, a Roman festival of purification]

feckless

(adjective) irresponsible and lacking determination or strength of character, e.g. *children with drunken or feckless parents.*
[from Middle English *feck* meaning 'value' or 'worth']

fecundity (pronounced fek-**kun**-dit-ee)

(noun; a formal word) Fecundity is great fertility.
[from Latin *fecundus* meaning 'fruitful']

fed the past tense and past participle of **feed.**

federal

(adjective) relating to a system of government in which a group of states is controlled by a central government, but each state has its own local powers, e.g. *a federal country like the USA.*

federation, federations

(noun) A federation is a group of organizations or states that have joined together for a common purpose.
[from Latin *foedus* meaning 'alliance']

fed up

(adjective; an informal expression) unhappy or bored.

fee, fees

(noun) A fee is a charge or payment for a job, service, or activity.

feeble, feebler, feeblest

(adjective) weak, ineffective, or lacking in power, strength, or influence, e.g. *The management was feeble and cowardly.*
[from Latin *flebilis* meaning 'pitiable' or 'pathetic']

feed, feeds, feeding, fed

1 (verb) To feed a person or animal means to give them food.
2 When an animal or baby feeds, it eats.
3 (noun) Feed is food for animals or babies.
4 (verb) To feed something means to supply what is needed for it to operate, develop, or exist, e.g. *Data is fed into the computer.*

feedback

1 (noun) Feedback is comments and information about the quality or success of something.
2 Feedback is also a condition in which some of the power, sound, or information produced by electronic equipment goes back into it, e.g. *Reduce the amount of feedback by moving the microphone.*

feel, feels, feeling, felt

1 (verb) If you feel an emotion or sensation, you experience it, e.g. *She felt close to tears.*
2 If you feel that something is the case, you believe it to be so, e.g. *He felt I was making a terrible mistake.*
3 If you feel something, you touch it.
4 If something feels warm or cold, for example, you experience its warmness or coldness through the sense of touch, e.g. *Does the water feel warm?*

5 (noun) The feel of something is how it feels to you when you touch it, e.g. *the cool feel of armchair leather.*
6 (verb) To feel the effect of something means to be affected by it, e.g. *The consequences of the computer revolution will be felt in the future.*
7 (phrase) If you **feel like** doing something, you want to do it.

Similar words: (sense 2) sense, perceive

feeler, feelers

(noun) An insect's feelers are the two thin antennae on its head with which it senses things around it.

feeling, feelings

1 (noun) A feeling is an emotion or reaction, e.g. *strong feelings of jealousy.*
2 A feeling is also a physical sensation, e.g. *a feeling of nausea.*
3 Feeling is the ability to experience the sense of touch in your body, e.g. *He has no feeling in his left arm.*
4 Your feelings about something are your general attitudes, impressions, or thoughts about it, e.g. *Americans have quite a different feeling about the press.*

Similar words: (sense 4) impression, notion, instinct

feet the plural of **foot.**

feign, feigns, feigning, feigned (rhymes with rain)

(verb) If you feign an emotion, feeling, or state, you pretend to experience it, e.g. *I feigned interest in his exam results.*
[from Latin *fingere* meaning 'to create' or 'to invent']

feint, feints, feinting, feinted (rhymes with paint)

1 (noun) A feint, especially in boxing, is a misleading movement intended to deceive the opponent.
2 (verb) To feint means to make a misleading movement.

felicitations

(noun; a formal word) Felicitations are congratulations, e.g. *I came along to offer you my felicitations.*

felicity, felicities

1 (noun; a formal word) Felicity is great happiness and pleasure.
2 A felicity is something that is appropriate and pleasing, e.g *a few architectural felicities amidst acres of monotony.*
felicitous (adjective).
[from Latin *felicitas* meaning 'good fortune']

feline (pronounced **fee**-line)

(adjective) belonging or relating to the cat family.
[from Latin *feles* meaning 'cat']

fell, fells, felling, felled

1 the past tense of **fall.**
2 (noun) A fell is a mountain or an area of high moorland in northern England.
3 (verb) To fell a tree means to cut it down.

4 (a literary use) To fell someone means to hit them so that they fall to the ground.
[Sense 2 is from Old Norse *fjall* meaning 'hill'; senses 3-4 are from Old English *fellan* meaning 'to cause to fall']

fellow, fellows
1 (noun; a rather old-fashioned informal use) A fellow is a man, e.g. *My dear fellow, I really am sorry!*
2 (adjective) You use fellow to describe people who have something in common with you, e.g. *You will soon feel at ease with your fellow students.*
3 (noun) A fellow is also a senior member of a learned society or a university college.
4 Your fellows are the people who share work or an activity with you.
[from Old Norse *felagi* meaning 'partner' or 'associate']

fellowship, fellowships
1 (noun) Fellowship is a feeling of friendliness that a group of people have when they are doing things together.
2 A fellowship is a society or other group of people that join together because they have interests in common, e.g. *the Women's Fellowship of the Methodist Church.*
3 A fellowship is also an academic post at a university which involves research work.

Similar words: (sense 1) camaraderie, fraternity, brotherhood

felon, felons
(noun; an old-fashioned legal word) A felon is a person guilty of a very serious crime such as murder or armed robbery.
felony (noun).

felt
1 the past tense and past participle of **feel.**
2 (noun) Felt is thick cloth made from woollen fibres matted closely together.

female, females
1 (noun) A female is a person or animal that belongs to the sex that can have babies or young.
2 (adjective) concerning or relating to females.
[from Latin *femina* meaning 'woman']

feminine
1 (adjective) relating to women or considered to be typical of women.
2 belonging to a particular class of nouns in some languages, such as French, German, and Latin.
femininity (noun).
[from Latin *femina* meaning 'woman']

feminism
(noun) Feminism is the belief that women should have the same rights, power, and opportunities as men.
feminist (noun and adjective).

femme fatale, femmes fatales (pronounced fam fat-**tal**)
(noun) A femme fatale is a mysterious and dangerously attractive woman.
[a French expression meaning 'deadly woman']

femur, femurs or **femora** (pronounced **fee**-mer)
(noun) Your femur is the large bone in the upper part of your leg.
[from Latin *femur* meaning 'thigh']

fen, fens
(noun) The fens are an area of low, flat, marshy land in the east of England.

fence, fences, fencing, fenced
1 (noun) A fence is a wooden or wire barrier between two areas of land.
2 (verb) To fence an area of land means to surround it with a fence.
3 (noun) A fence in horse racing or show jumping is a barrier or hedge for the horses to jump over.
4 (verb) When two people fence, they use special swords to fight each other as a sport.
5 In a discussion, if you fence, you answer evasively.
6 (noun; an informal use) A fence is also a person who receives and sells stolen property.

fencing
(noun) Fencing is a sport in which two people fight using special thin swords called foils.

fend, fends, fending, fended
1 (phrase) If you have to **fend for yourself**, you have to look after yourself.
2 (verb) If you fend off an attack or unwanted questions or attention, you defend and protect yourself.

fender, fenders
1 (noun) A fender is a low barrier round a fireplace to stop fuel from rolling out into the room.
2 A fender is also an old tyre or coil of rope hung over the side of a boat to protect it from bumps.

fennel
(noun) Fennel is a tall plant with feathery leaves and a bulbous lower stem. It is used as a herb for flavouring in cooking or as a vegetable.

feral (rhymes with **peril**)
(adjective) wild, especially after having existed in a domesticated state, e.g. *feral cats.*

ferment, ferments, fermenting, fermented
1 (verb) When wine, beer, or fruit ferments, a chemical change takes place in which the sugar in it is converted to alcohol and carbon dioxide, usually by the action of yeast.
2 (noun) Ferment is excitement and unrest caused by change or uncertainty.
fermentation (noun).
[from Latin *fermentum* meaning 'yeast']

fern, ferns
(noun) A fern is a plant with long feathery leaves, having no flowers and reproducing by spores.

ferocious
(adjective) violent and fierce, e.g. *a ferocious animal... ferocious fighting.*
ferociously (adverb), **ferocity** (noun).
[from Latin *ferox* meaning 'like a wild animal']

ferret, ferrets, ferreting, ferreted
1 (noun) A ferret is a small, white, fierce animal

related to the weasel and kept for hunting rats and rabbits.
2 (verb) If you ferret about for something, you search for it with determination.
[from Old French *furet* meaning 'little thief']

ferrous
(adjective) containing or relating to iron, e.g. *ferrous metals.*
[from Latin *ferrum* meaning 'iron']

ferry, ferries, ferrying, ferried
1 (noun) A ferry is a boat that carries people and vehicles across short stretches of water.
2 (verb) To ferry people or goods somewhere means to transport them there, usually on a short, regular journey.

fertile
1 (adjective) capable of producing strong, healthy plants, e.g. *fertile land.*
2 creative, e.g. *a fertile imagination.*
3 able to have babies or young.
fertility (noun).
[from Latin *fertilis* meaning 'fruitful']

fertilize, fertilizes, fertilizing, fertilized; also spelled **fertilise**
1 (verb) When an egg, plant, or female is fertilized, the process of reproduction begins by sperm joining with the egg, or by pollen coming into contact with the reproductive part of a plant.
2 To fertilize land means to put manure or chemicals onto it to feed the plants.

fertilizer, fertilizers; also spelled **fertiliser**
(noun) Fertilizer is a substance put onto soil to improve plant growth.

fervent
(adjective) showing strong, sincere, and enthusiastic feeling, e.g. *a fervent supporter of the EEC.*
fervently (adverb).
[from Latin *fervens* meaning 'heated' or 'fiery']

fervour
(noun) Fervour is a very strong feeling for or belief in something, e.g. *a tide of patriotic fervour.*
[from Latin *fervor* meaning 'heat']

fester, festers, festering, festered
(verb) If a wound festers it becomes infected and produces pus.
[from Latin *fistula* meaning 'ulcer']

festival, festivals
1 (noun) A festival is an organized series of events and performances, e.g. *the York Early Music festival.*
2 A festival is also a day or period of religious celebration.
[from Latin *festum* meaning 'festival']

Similar words: (sense 2) fiesta, carnival, celebration

---

festive
(adjective) full of happiness and celebration, e.g. *at Christmas or other festive occasions... a festive atmosphere.*
[from Latin *festum* meaning 'festival']

festivity, festivities
(noun) Festivity is celebration and happiness, e.g. *He enjoyed the wedding festivities.*

festoon, festoons, festooning, festooned
(verb) If you festoon something with decorations, you hang lots of decorations over it.

fetch, fetches, fetching, fetched
1 (verb) If you fetch something, you go to where it is and bring it back.
2 If something fetches a particular sum of money, it is sold for that amount, e.g. *Her works always fetch high prices.*

fetching
(adjective) attractive in appearance, e.g. *She looked remarkably fetching this evening.*

fete, fetes, feting, feted (rhymes with **date**)
1 (noun) A fete is an outdoor event with competitions, displays, and goods for sale, usually to raise money for charity.
2 (verb) Someone who is feted receives a public welcome or entertainment as an honour.
[from French *fête* meaning 'festival']

fetid
(adjective) having a strong, unpleasant smell.
[from Latin *foetidus* meaning 'stinking']

fetish, fetishes
(noun) A fetish is an object or activity that someone has an obsession about, e.g. *cleanliness is almost a fetish with her.*

fetlock, fetlocks
(noun) A horse's fetlock is the back part of its leg, just above the hoof.

fetter, fetters, fettering, fettered
1 (verb) If something fetters you, it prevents you from behaving freely and naturally, e.g. *We are being fettered with legal restrictions.*
2 (noun) A fetter is a chain fixed around a prisoner's ankle.

fettle
(phrase) Someone who is **in fine fettle** is in good health.

fetus another spelling of **foetus.**

feud, feuds, feuding, feuded (pronounced **fyood**)
1 (noun) A feud is a long-lasting and very bitter quarrel, especially between families.
2 (verb) When people feud, they take part in a feud.

feudalism
(noun) Feudalism is a social and political system that was common in the Middle Ages in Europe. Under this system, ordinary people were given land and protection by a lord, and in return they worked and fought for him.
feudal (adjective).

fever, fevers
1 (noun) Fever is a condition occurring during illness, in which the patient has a very high body temperature.
2 A fever is extreme excitement or agitation, e.g. *a fever of hugging and kissing.*

feverish
1 (adjective) in a state of extreme excitement or agitation, e.g. *a feverish race against time*.
2 suffering from a high body temperature.
feverishly (adverb).

Similar words: (sense 2) fevered, flushed, hot

few, fewer, fewest
1 (adjective and noun) used to refer to a small number of things, e.g. *I will do it in the next few days... A few of them came to see me*.
2 (phrases) **Quite a few** or **a good few** means quite a large number of things.

Similar words: (sense 1) some, scattering, handful

fey (rhymes with **day**)
(adjective) behaving in a vague, strange, and rather whimsical way.

fez, fezzes
(noun) A fez is a round red hat without a brim and usually with a tassel on top. It is named after the city of Fez in Morocco and used to be worn by men in Turkey and in some Arab countries.

fiancé, fiancés (pronounced fee-**on**-say)
(noun) A woman's fiancé is the man to whom she is engaged.
[from French *fiancier* meaning 'to betroth']

fiancée, fiancées
(noun) A man's fiancée is the woman to whom he is engaged.

fiasco, fiascos (pronounced fee-**ass**-koh)
(noun) A fiasco is an event or attempt that fails completely, especially in a ridiculous or disorganized way, e.g. *The meeting was a total fiasco*.

fiat, fiats
(noun; a formal word) A fiat is an official order given by someone in authority.
[from Latin *fiat* meaning 'let it be done']

fib, fibs, fibbing, fibbed
1 (noun) A fib is a small, unimportant lie.
2 (verb) If you fib, you tell a small lie.
fibber (noun).

fibre, fibres
1 (noun) A fibre is a thin thread of a substance used to make cloth.
2 Fibre is the material from which cloth is made, e.g. *artificial fibres*.
3 Fibre is also a part of plants that can be eaten but not digested; it helps food pass quickly through the body.
4 Moral fibre is strength of character and determination to do what is right.
fibrous (adjective).
[from Latin *fibra* meaning 'strand']

fibreglass
(noun) Fibreglass is a material made from thin threads of glass. It can be mixed with plastic to make boats, cars, and furniture, and is often used as an insulating material.

fibre optics
(noun) Fibre optics is the use of long, thin threads of glass to carry information in the form of light.

fibrin
(noun) Fibrin is a sticky, insoluble protein formed from fibrinogen when blood clots.

fibrinogen
(noun) Fibrinogen is a soluble protein in blood plasma which is converted to fibrin when the blood clots.

fibroid, fibroids
1 (adjective) made up of fibres.
2 (noun) A fibroid is a harmless tumour consisting of fibrous matter.

fibula, fibulae or fibulas
(noun) Your fibula is the outer and thinner of the two bones between your knee and your ankle.
[from Latin *fibula* meaning 'brooch' or 'clasp']

fickle
(adjective) A fickle person keeps changing their mind about who or what they like or want.
[from Old English *ficol* meaning 'treacherous' or 'deceitful']

fiction, fictions
1 (noun) Fiction is stories about people and events that have been invented by the author.
2 A fiction is something that is not true.
fictional (adjective), **fictitious** (adjective).
[from Latin *fictio* meaning 'creation' or 'invention']

fiddle, fiddles, fiddling, fiddled
1 (verb) If you fiddle with something, you keep moving it or touching it restlessly.
2 (an informal use) If someone fiddles something such as an account, they alter it dishonestly to get money for themselves.
3 (noun; an informal use) A fiddle is a dishonest action or scheme to get money.
4 A fiddle is also a violin.
5 (phrase) Someone who **plays second fiddle** is less important or powerful than another person.
fiddler (noun).

fiddly, fiddlier, fiddliest
(adjective) small and difficult to do, use, or handle, e.g. *It is a very fiddly job*.

fidelity
1 (noun) Fidelity is the quality of remaining firm in your beliefs, friendships, or loyalty to another person.
2 Fidelity is also the degree of accuracy in something such as a translation or sound reproduction.
[from Latin *fidelitas* meaning 'faithfulness']

fidget, fidgets, fidgeting, fidgeted
1 (verb) If you fidget, you keep changing your position because of nervousness or boredom.
2 (noun) A fidget is someone who is fidgeting.
fidgety (adjective).

field, fields, fielding, fielded
1 (noun) A field is an area of land where crops are grown or animals are kept.
2 A sports field is an area of land where sports are played, e.g. *a football field*.

3 A coal field, oil field, or gold field is an area where coal, oil, or gold is found.
4 A particular field is a subject or area of interest, e.g. *She is an expert in this field.*
5 (adjective) A field trip or a field study involves research or activity in the natural environment rather than theoretical or laboratory work.
6 In an athletics competition, the field events are the events such as the high jump and the javelin which do not take place on a running track.
7 (verb) In cricket, when you field the ball, you stop it after the batsman has hit it.
8 To field questions means to answer or deal with them skilfully.
9 (noun) A magnetic field or gravitational field is the area in which magnetism or gravity has an effect.
10 Your field of vision is the area that you can see without turning your head.
11 (verb) To field a number of people or things means to make use of them to achieve something, e.g. *We are fielding a good team this year.*
12 (phrase) If you have **a field day**, you have a very pleasant time doing something that you have been given the opportunity to do, e.g. *The local papers had a field day.*

Similar words: (sense 1) meadow, pasture

fielder, fielders
(noun) In cricket, the fielders are the players who stand at various parts of the pitch and try to get the batsmen out or to prevent runs from being scored.

field glasses
(plural noun) Field glasses are binoculars.

field marshal, field marshals
(noun) A field marshal is an army officer of the highest rank.

fieldwork
(noun) Fieldwork is direct study and observation of something in its natural environment.

fiend, fiends (pronounced **feend**)
1 (noun) A fiend is a devil or evil spirit.
2 A fiend is also a very wicked or cruel person.
3 (an informal use) You can describe someone who is very keen on a particular thing as a fiend, e.g. *He is a fresh air fiend.*
[from Old English *feond* meaning 'enemy']

fiendish
1 (adjective) very clever and imaginative, e.g. *a fiendish plan.*
2 very difficult and challenging.
fiendishly (adverb).

Similar words: (sense 1) ingenious
(sense 2) diabolical, tricky

fierce, fiercer, fiercest
1 (adjective) very aggressive or angry.
2 extremely strong or intense, e.g. *There will be fierce resistance... fierce heat.*
fiercely (adverb).
[from Old French *fiers* meaning 'brave']

Similar words: (sense 1) ferocious, violent, vicious, savage

fiery, fierier, fieriest
1 (adjective) involving fire or seeming like fire, e.g. *Johnny gulped down the fiery liquid.*
2 showing great anger, energy, or passion, e.g. *a fiery temper... a fiery speech.*

fiesta, fiestas
(noun) A fiesta is a time of public entertainment and religious celebrations, especially in Spain or Latin America.
[from Spanish *fiesta* meaning 'festival']

fife, fifes
(noun) A fife is a small high-pitched flute, used especially in military bands.
[from German *Pfeife* meaning 'pipe']

fifteen the number 15.
fifteenth.

fifth, fifths
1 The fifth item in a series is the one counted as number five.
2 (noun) A fifth is one of five equal parts.
3 In music, a fifth is the interval between two notes of a scale when there are three notes separating them.

fifth column, fifth columns
(noun) A fifth column is a group of hostile infiltrators into an organization. The expression originally referred to fascist sympathizers in Madrid during the Spanish Civil War when four armed columns were advancing to defeat the Republican government.

fifty, fifties
the number 50.
fiftieth.

fifty-fifty
1 (adverb) divided equally into two portions.
2 (adjective) just as likely not to happen as to happen, e.g. *It may have only a fifty-fifty chance of survival.*

fig, figs
(noun) A fig is a soft, sweet fruit full of tiny seeds. It grows in hot countries and is often eaten dried.

fight, fights, fighting, fought
1 (verb) When people fight, they take part in a battle, a war, a boxing match, or in some other attempt to hurt or kill someone.
2 (noun) A fight is a situation in which people hit or try to hurt each other.
3 (verb) To fight for something means to try in a very determined way to achieve it, e.g. *They will have to fight for their rights.*
4 (noun) A fight is a determined attempt to prevent or achieve something, e.g. *the fight against inflation.*
fighter (noun).

Similar words: (sense 1) come to blows, skirmish, tussle, brawl, scrap
(sense 2) scrap, brawl, scuffle, tussle, skirmish, free-for-all, scrimmage

figment, figments

(noun) A figment of the imagination is something nonexistent that someone has imagined.
[from Latin *figmentum* meaning 'something created or invented']

figurative

(adjective) If you use a word or expression in a figurative sense, you use it with a more abstract or imaginative meaning than its ordinary one.
figuratively (adverb).

figure, figures, figuring, figured

1 (noun) A figure is a written number or the amount expressed by a number.
2 A figure is a geometrical shape.
3 In written texts, a figure is a diagram or table.
4 In skating and dancing, a figure is a particular series of movements.
5 A figure is the shape of a person whom you cannot see clearly, e.g. *We could see three figures on the hill top.*
6 Your figure is the shape of your body, e.g. *She's got a lovely figure.*
7 A figure is also a person, e.g. *She is a major political figure... a father figure.*
8 (verb) To figure in something means to appear or be included in it, e.g. *Loneliness figures quite a lot in his conversation.*
9 (an informal use) If you figure that something is the case, you guess or conclude this, e.g. *He figured he had been awake now almost seventy-two hours.*
[from Latin *figura* meaning 'shape']

figurehead, figureheads

1 (noun) A figurehead is the leader of a movement or organization who has no real power.
2 A figurehead is also a large wooden model of a person, decorating the front of a sailing ship.

figure of speech, figures of speech

(noun) A figure of speech is an expression such as a simile or idiom in which the words are not used in their literal sense.

filament, filaments

1 (noun) A filament is a very fine wire or thread, especially the wire that produces light in a light bulb.
2 In a flower, the filament is the stalk of a stamen.

filch, filches, filching, filched

(verb) To filch something means to steal it.

file, files, filing, filed

1 (noun) A file is a box or folder in which a group of papers or records is kept; also used of the information kept in the file.
2 In computing, a file is a stored set of related data with its own name.
3 A file is a line of people one behind the other.
4 A file is also a long steel tool with a rough surface, used for smoothing and shaping hard materials.
5 (verb) When someone files a document, they put it in its correct place with similar documents.
6 A journalist who files a report or story sends it to a newspaper or broadcasting station.

7 When a group of people file somewhere, they walk one behind the other in a line.
8 If you file something, you smooth or shape it with a file.

filial (pronounced **fil**-yal)

(adjective) relating to the status or duties of a son or daughter.
[from Latin *filius* meaning 'son' and *filia* meaning 'daughter']

filibuster, filibusters, filibustering, filibustered

1 (verb) To filibuster means to prevent a law being passed by making prolonged speeches in parliament so that debating time runs out and a vote cannot be taken.
2 (noun) A filibuster is an act of filibustering.
[from Spanish *filibustero* meaning 'pirate']

filigree

(noun) Filigree is delicate ornamental designs made with silver or gold wire.

filings

(plural noun) Filings are shavings or particles removed by a file, e.g. *iron filings.*

Filipino, Filipinos (pronounced fil-ip-**pee**-noh)

1 (adjective) belonging or relating to the Philippines.
2 (noun) A Filipino is someone who comes from the Philippines.

fill, fills, filling, filled

1 (verb) If you fill something or if it fills up, it becomes full.
2 If something fills a need, it satisfies the need, e.g. *This book fills a major gap.*
3 To fill a job vacancy means to appoint someone to do that job.
4 (noun) If you have had your fill of something, you do not want any more.
[from Old English *fyllan* meaning 'to make full']

fill in

1 (phrasal verb) If you fill in a form, you write information in the appropriate spaces.
2 If you fill someone in, you give them information to bring them up to date.
3 If you fill in for someone, you do their job for them temporarily while they are away.

filler, fillers

(noun) Filler is a paste which hardens when it dries, used for filling in cracks or small holes.

fillet, fillets, filleting, filleted

1 (noun) Fillet is a strip of tender, boneless beef, veal, or pork.
2 A fillet of fish is a piece of fish with the bones removed.
3 (verb) To fillet meat or fish means to prepare it by cutting out the bones.

filling, fillings

1 (noun) The filling in a sandwich, cake, or pie is the soft food mixture inside it.
2 A filling is a small amount of metal or plastic put into a hole in a tooth by a dentist.

filling station, filling stations

(noun) A filling station is a place where petrol and oil for cars can be bought.

fillip, fillips
(noun) A fillip is a sudden improvement or increase in interest or energy, e.g. *The choice of films is wide and gives an added fillip to the lessons which follow.*

filly, fillies
(noun) A filly is a female horse or pony under the age of four.

film, films, filming, filmed
1 (noun) A film is a series of moving pictures projected onto a screen and shown at the cinema or on television.
2 A film is also a thin flexible strip of cellulose coated with photographic emulsion, used in a camera to record images when exposed to light.
3 (verb) If you film someone, you use a movie camera or a video camera to record their movements on film.
4 (noun) A film of powder or liquid is a very thin layer of it on a surface.
5 Plastic film is a very thin sheet of plastic used for wrapping things.
[from Old English *filmen* meaning 'membrane']

filmy, filmier, filmiest
(adjective) very thin, delicate, and almost transparent, e.g. *a filmy veil.*

filter, filters, filtering, filtered
1 (noun) A filter is a device that allows some substances, lights, or sounds to pass through it, but not others, e.g. *a water filter.*
2 (verb) To filter a substance means to pass it through a filter.
3 If something filters somewhere, it gets there slowly, gradually, or faintly, e.g. *Light filtered into the room.*
filtration (noun).
[from Old French *filtre* meaning 'felt']

filth
1 (noun) Filth is disgusting dirt and muck.
2 People often use the word filth to refer to excessively bad language or to sexual material that is thought to be crude and offensive.
filthy (adjective), **filthiness** (noun).
[from Old English *fylth* meaning 'pus' or 'corruption']

Similar words: (sense 1) grime, squalor

filtrate, filtrates
(noun) A filtrate is a liquid or gas that has been filtered.

fin, fins
(noun) A fin is a thin, angular structure on the body of a fish, used to help guide it and push it through the water.

final, finals
1 (adjective) last in a series or happening at the end of something.
2 A decision that is final cannot be changed or questioned.
3 (noun) A final is the last game or contest in a series which decides the overall winner.
4 (plural noun) Finals are the last and most important examinations of a university or college course.

[from Latin *finis* meaning 'end']

Similar words: (sense 1) closing, concluding, ultimate, last

finale, finales (pronounced fin-**nah**-lee)
(noun) The finale is the last section of a piece of music or show.

Similar words: climax, conclusion

finalist, finalists
(noun) A finalist is a person taking part in the final of a competition.

finality
(noun) If you say something with finality, it is clear that you do not intend to say anything more on the subject.

finalize, finalizes, finalizing, finalized; also spelled **finalise**
(verb) If you finalize something, you complete all the arrangements for it.

finally
1 (adverb) If something finally happens, it happens after a long delay.
2 You use the word finally to introduce a final point, question, or topic that you are talking or writing about.

Similar words: (sense 1) at last, eventually, in the end, ultimately
(sense 2) in conclusion, in summary, to conclude, lastly

finance, finances, financing, financed
1 (verb) To finance a project or a large purchase means to provide the money for it.
2 (noun) Finance for something is the money, loans, or grants used to pay for it.
3 Finance is also the management of money, loans, and investments.
[from Old French *finance* meaning 'final payment']

financial
(adjective) relating to or involving money.
financially (adverb).

Similar words: monetary, pecuniary, fiscal, economic

financial year, financial years
(noun) The financial year is a specific period of twelve months according to which budgets, profits, and other financial matters are planned and assessed. In Britain the main financial year starts on 5th April.

financier, financiers
(noun) A financier is a person who organizes and deals with the finance for large businesses.

finch, finches
(noun) A finch is a small bird with a short strong beak for crushing seeds.

find, finds, finding, found
1 (verb) If you find someone or something, you discover them, either as a result of searching or by coming across them unexpectedly.
2 If you find that something is the case, you become aware of it or realize it, e.g. *They found it impossible to get a bank loan.*

3 Something that is found in a particular place typically lives or exists there.
4 When a court or jury finds a person guilty or not guilty, they decide that the person is guilty or innocent, e.g. *He was found guilty of arson.*
5 (noun) If you describe something or someone as a find, you mean that you have recently discovered them and they are valuable, interesting, or useful.
finder (noun).

Similar words: (sense 1) come across, discover

find out
1 (phrasal verb) If you find out something, you learn or discover something that you did not know.
2 If you find someone out, you discover that they have been doing something they should not have been doing.

findings
(plural noun) Someone's findings are the conclusions they reach as a result of investigation.

fine, finer, finest; fines, fining, fined
1 (adjective) very good or very beautiful, e.g *It's a very fine film... fine houses.*
2 satisfactory or suitable, e.g *If you want to come too, that's fine.*
3 very narrow or thin, e.g. *My hair is too fine.*
4 A fine net or sieve has very small holes. Fine powder or dust consists of very small particles.
5 A fine detail, adjustment, or distinction is very delicate, exact, or subtle.
6 When the weather is fine, it is not raining and is bright or sunny.
7 (noun) A fine is a sum of money paid as a punishment.
8 (verb) Someone who is fined has to pay a specific sum of money as a punishment.

fine art
(noun) Fine art is painting, sculpture, and objects that are made to be admired rather than used.

finery
(noun) Finery is very beautiful clothing and jewellery.

finesse (pronounced fin-**ness**)
(noun) If you do something with finesse, you do it with skill, elegance, and subtlety.

finger, fingers, fingering, fingered
1 (noun) Your fingers are the four long jointed parts of your hands, sometimes including the thumbs.
2 (verb) If you finger something you feel it with your fingers.
3 (phrase) If you **put your finger on** a reason or problem, you identify it.
4 If you can **twist someone around your little finger**, they will do anything you ask.
5 If you are **all fingers and thumbs**, you are very clumsy with your hands.

fingernail, fingernails
(noun) Your fingernails are the hard coverings at the ends of your fingers.

fingerprint, fingerprints
(noun) A fingerprint is a mark made showing the pattern on the skin at the tip of a person's finger.

finicky
(adjective) extremely fussy, e.g. *He's very finicky about his food.*

finis
(noun) Finis means 'the end' in Latin. It is sometimes written at the end of a book or a play.

finish, finishes, finishing, finished
1 (verb) When you finish something, you reach the end of it and complete it.
2 When something finishes, it ends or stops.
3 (noun) The finish of something is the end or last part of it.
4 The finish that something has is the texture or appearance of its surface, e.g. *the gleaming finish of French polish on the woodwork.*
[from Latin *finis* meaning 'end']

Similar words: (sense 1) complete, conclude, wind up, wrap up, end, close
(sense 2) conclude, close, terminate
(sense 3) completion, conclusion, close, ending

finite (pronounced **fie**-nite)
(adjective) having a particular size or limit which cannot be increased, e.g. *The amount of land available for agriculture is finite.*
[from Latin *finitus* meaning 'finished']

Finn, Finns
(noun) A Finn is someone who comes from Finland.

Finnish
1 (adjective) belonging or relating to Finland.
2 (noun) Finnish is the main language spoken in Finland.

fiord another spelling of fjord.

fir, firs
(noun) A fir is a tall pointed evergreen tree that has thin needle-like leaves and produces cones.

fire, fires, firing, fired
1 (noun) Fire is the flames produced when something burns.
2 A fire is a pile or mass of burning material.
3 A fire is also a piece of equipment that is used as a heater, e.g. *an electric fire.*
4 (verb) If you fire a weapon you operate it so that the bullet or missile is released.
5 (noun) Shots fired from a gun are referred to as gun fire.
6 (phrase) If someone **opens fire**, they start shooting.
7 (verb) If you fire questions at someone, you ask them a lot of questions very quickly.
8 When an engine fires, an electrical spark is produced and the engine starts.
9 (an informal use) If an employer fires someone, he or she dismisses that person from their job.
10 To fire clay pots means to heat them to a very high temperature in a kiln to harden them.

Similar words: (sense 1) blaze
(sense 2) conflagration, inferno

firearm, firearms
(noun) A firearm is a gun.

firebrand, firebrands
(noun) A firebrand is someone who stirs up passionate political feelings, often causing trouble.

firebreak, firebreaks
(noun) A firebreak is an area of open land in a forest, which has been cleared in order to stop fire from spreading.

firebrick, firebricks
(noun) A firebrick is a heat-resistant brick used to line fireplaces.

fire brigade, fire brigades
(noun) The fire brigade is the organization which has the job of putting out fires.

firecracker, firecrackers
(noun) A firecracker is a firework which explodes with loud bangs.

fire drill, fire drills
(noun) A fire drill is a practice of what to do if there is a fire in the building.

fire engine, fire engines
(noun) A fire engine is a large vehicle that carries equipment for putting out fires.

fire escape, fire escapes
(noun) A fire escape is an emergency exit or staircase for use if there is a fire.

fire extinguisher, fire extinguishers
(noun) A fire extinguisher is a metal cylinder containing water or chemical foam for spraying onto a fire.

firefly, fireflies
(noun) A firefly is an insect belonging to the beetle family that glows in the dark.

fireguard, fireguards
(noun) A fireguard is a wire screen that can be put around a fire to prevent sparks or burns.

fire hydrant, fire hydrants
(noun) A fire hydrant is a pipe in the street used by firemen to obtain water.

fire irons
(plural noun) Fire irons are tools used for putting fuel on a fire and cleaning the hearth.

firelighter, firelighters
(noun) A firelighter is a small white block of solid fuel that is used to start a fire.

fireman, firemen
(noun) A fireman is a person whose job is to put out fires and rescue trapped people.

fireplace, fireplaces
(noun) A fireplace is the opening beneath a chimney where a domestic fire can be lit.

fireproof
(adjective) designed to be resistant to fire.

fire station, fire stations
(noun) A fire station is a building where fire engines are kept and where firemen wait to be called out.

fire trap, fire traps
(noun) A building that is described as a firetrap would be difficult to escape from in a fire.

firework, fireworks
(noun) A firework is a small container of gunpowder and other chemicals which explodes or produces coloured sparks or smoke when lit.

firing squad, firing squads
(noun) A firing squad is a group of soldiers ordered to shoot a person condemned to death.

firm, firmer, firmest; firms
1 (adjective) Something that is firm does not move easily when pressed, pushed, or shaken, or when weight is put on it.
2 A firm grasp or push is one with controlled force or pressure.
3 Firm information or a firm decision is definite.
4 Someone who is firm behaves with authority that shows they will not change their mind.
5 (noun) A firm is a business selling or producing something.
firmly (adverb), **firmness** (noun).
[from Latin *firmus* meaning 'fixed']

first, firsts
1 (adjective and adverb) happening, coming, or done before everything or everyone else.
2 (adjective) more important than anything else, e.g. *Her pig won first prize... The first duty of the state is to ensure law and order.*
3 (noun) A first is something that has never happened or been done before.
4 A first is also an honours degree of the highest standard.
firstly (adverb).

Similar words: (sense 1) initial, initially, firstly

first aid
(noun) First aid is medical treatment given to an injured person.

first-born
(noun and adjective; a literary word) Someone's first-born is their first child.

first class
1 (adjective) Something that is first class is of the highest quality or standard.
2 First-class accomodation on a train, aircraft, or ship is the best and most expensive type of accomodation.
3 First-class postage is quick but expensive.

first-hand
(adjective) First-hand knowledge or experience is gained directly rather than from books or other people.

First Lady
(noun) The First Lady of a country is the wife of a president.

first person
(noun) In English grammar, the first person is the 'I' or 'we' form of the pronoun or the verb.

first-rate
(adjective) excellent.

fiscal
(adjective) relating to or involving government or public money, especially taxes.
[from Latin *fiscus* meaning 'money-bag' or 'treasury']

fish, fishes, fishing, fished
The plural of the noun can be either **fish** or **fishes**, but is normally **fish**.
1 (noun) A fish is a cold-blooded creature living in water and having a spine, gills, fins, and a scaly skin.
2 Fish is the flesh of fish eaten as food.
3 (verb) To fish means to try to catch fish for food or sport.
4 If you fish for information, you try to get it in an indirect way.
fishing (noun), **fisherman** (noun).

fishcake, fishcakes
(noun) A fishcake is a mixture of fish and potato, formed into a flat round shape and fried.

fishery, fisheries
(noun) A fishery is an area of the sea where fish are caught commercially.

fish finger, fish fingers
(noun) A fish finger is a small oblong piece of chopped fish covered in breadcrumbs.

fishmonger, fishmongers
(noun) A fishmonger is a shopkeeper who sells fish; also the shop itself.

fish slice, fish slices
(noun) A fish slice is a kitchen tool with a broad, flat, slatted blade attached to a long handle.

fishwife, fishwives
(noun) If you refer to a woman as a fishwife, you mean she is coarse, and has a loud voice.

fishy, fishier, fishiest
1 (adjective) smelling of fish.
2 (an informal use) suspicious or doubtful, e.g. *Their explanation sounded a bit fishy somehow.*

fissile (rhymes with missile)
(adjective) capable of undergoing nuclear fission.

fission (rhymes with mission)
1 (noun) Fission is the splitting or breaking of something into parts.
2 Fission is also nuclear fission.
[from Latin *fissio* meaning 'a splitting']

fissure, fissures
(noun) A fissure is a deep crack in rock.

fist, fists
(noun) A fist is a hand with the fingers curled tightly towards the palm.

fisticuffs
(plural noun; an old-fashioned word) Fisticuffs is fighting in which people hit each other with their fists.

fit, fits, fitting, fitted; fitter, fittest
1 (verb) Something that fits is the right shape or size for a particular person or position.
2 If you fit something somewhere, you put it there carefully or securely, e.g. *I fitted locks on all the windows.*
3 If something fits a particular situation, person, or thing, it is suitable or appropriate, e.g. *That idea would fit the theory.*
4 (noun) The fit of something is how it fits, e.g. *The dress was a perfect fit.*
5 (adjective) good enough or suitable. e.g. *houses that are not fit for human habitation.*
6 Someone who is fit is healthy and has strong muscles as a result of regular exercise.
7 (noun) If someone has a fit, their muscles suddenly start contracting violently and they may lose consciousness.
8 A fit of laughter, coughing, anger, or panic is a sudden uncontrolled outburst.
fitness (noun).

Similar words: (sense 3) meet, match, suit
(sense 7) seizure, convulsion, spasm, paroxysm

fit out
(phrasal verb) To fit someone or something out means to provide them with the necessary equipment.

fitful
(adjective) happening at irregular intervals and not continuous, e.g. *a fitful sleep.*
fitfully (adverb).

fitter, fitters
(noun) A fitter is a person whose job is to assemble, adjust, or install machinery.

fitting, fittings
1 (adjective) right or suitable, e.g. *a fitting end to a wonderful day.*
2 (noun) A fitting is a small part that is fixed to a piece of equipment or furniture.
3 If you have a fitting, you try on a garment that is being made to see whether it fits properly.
4 A fitting is also a size in clothing or shoes, e.g. *I take a very narrow fitting.*

five, fives
1 Five is the number 5.
2 (noun) Fives is a ball game similar to squash, in which you hit the ball with your hand.

fix, fixes, fixing, fixed
1 (verb) If you fix something somewhere, you attach it or put it there firmly and securely.
2 If you fix something broken, you mend it.
3 If you fix your attention on something, you concentrate on it.
4 To fix a dye or photograph means to treat it with a chemical to make it permanent.
5 If you fix something, you make arrangements for it, e.g. *The meeting is fixed for the 11th.*
6 (an informal use) To fix something means to arrange the outcome unfairly or dishonestly.
7 (noun; an informal use) Something that is a fix has been unfairly or dishonestly arranged.
8 (an informal use) If you are in a fix, you are in a difficult situation.
9 A fix is an injection of a drug such as heroin.
fixed (adjective), **fixedly** (adverb).
[from Latin *fixus* meaning 'fastened']

Similar words: (sense 2) repair, mend

fixation, fixations
(noun) A fixation is an extreme and obsessive interest in something.

fixative, fixatives
(noun) Fixative is a liquid used to preserve the surface of a drawing.

fixity
(noun) The fixity of someone's gaze, concentration, or attitude is its steadiness.

fixture, fixtures
1 (noun) A fixture is a piece of furniture or equipment that is fixed into position in a house.
2 A fixture is also a sports event due to take place on a particular date.

fizz, fizzes, fizzing, fizzed
(verb) Something that fizzes makes a hissing sound.

fizzle, fizzles, fizzling, fizzled
(verb) Something that fizzles makes a weak hissing or spitting sound.

fizzy, fizzier, fizziest
(adjective) Fizzy drinks have carbon dioxide in them to make them bubbly.

fjord, fjords (pronounced fee-**ord**); also spelled **fiord**
(noun) A fjord is a long narrow inlet of the sea between very high cliffs, especially in Norway. [a Norwegian word]

flab
(noun) Flab is large amounts of surplus fat on someone's body.

flabbergasted
(adjective) extremely surprised.

flabby, flabbier, flabbiest
(adjective) Someone who is flabby is rather fat and unfit, with loose flesh on their body. **flabbiness** (noun).

Similar words: sagging, slack, flaccid

flaccid (pronounced **flass**-id)
(adjective) soft and loose or limp. [from Latin *flaccidus* meaning 'floppy']

flag, flags, flagging, flagged
1 (noun) A flag is a rectangular or square cloth of a particular colour and design which is used as the symbol of a nation, or as a signal.
2 A flag is also a flagstone.
3 (verb) If you or your spirits flag, you start to lose energy or enthusiasm.

Similar words: (sense 1) banner, standard, ensign, pennant

flag down
(verb) If you flag down a vehicle, you signal to the driver to stop.

flagellate, flagellates, flagellating, flagellated
(verb; a formal word) To flagellate someone means to beat or whip them. **flagellation** (noun). [from Latin *flagellum* meaning 'whip']

flagellum, flagella (pronounced flaj-**jel**-um)
(noun) Flagella are long thread-like parts of a

simple organism such as a bacterium, which it uses to help it move along. [from Latin *flagellum* meaning 'whip']

flagon, flagons
(noun) A flagon is a large wide bottle or jug for cider or wine.

flagrant (pronounced **flay**-grant)
(adjective) very shocking and bad in an obvious way, e.g. *a flagrant violation of human rights*. **flagrantly** (adverb). [from Latin *flagrans* meaning 'blazing']

flagship, flagships
1 (noun) A flagship is a ship carrying the commander of the fleet.
2 The flagship of an organization is its most modern or impressive product or asset.

flagstone, flagstones
(noun) A flagstone is a large flat rectangular piece of stone used for paving.

flail, flails, flailing, flailed
(verb) If someone's arms or legs flail about, they move in a wild, uncontrolled way. [from Old French *flaiel* meaning 'threshing implement']

flair
(noun) Flair is a natural ability to do something well or stylishly.

flak
1 (noun) Flak is anti-aircraft fire.
2 If you get flak for doing something, you get a lot of severe criticism. [from the first letters of the parts of German *Fliegerabwehrkanone* meaning 'anti-aircraft gun']

flake, flakes, flaking, flaked
1 (noun) A flake is a small thin piece of something.
2 (verb) When something such as paint flakes, small thin pieces of it come off. **flaky** (adjective), **flaked** (adjective).

flake out
(phrasal verb; an informal expression) If you flake out, you collapse, go to sleep, or lose consciousness.

flamboyant
(adjective) behaving in a very showy, confident, and exaggerated way. **flamboyance** (noun). [from French *flamboyer* meaning 'to blaze']

flame, flames, flaming, flamed
1 (noun) A flame is a flickering tongue or blaze of fire.
2 A flame of passion, desire, or anger is a sudden strong feeling.
3 (verb) Something that flames suddenly becomes bright red, e.g. *Sally's cheeks flamed*. **flaming** (adjective). [from Latin *flamma* meaning 'blazing fire']

flamenco
(noun) Flamenco is a type of very lively, fast Spanish dancing, accompanied by guitar music.

flamingo, flamingos or flamingoes
(noun) A flamingo is a long-legged wading bird with pink feathers and a long neck.

flammable
(adjective) likely to catch fire and burn easily.

flan, flans
(noun) A flan is an open sweet or savoury tart with a pastry or cake base.

flange, flanges (pronounced flanj)
(noun) A flange is a projecting edge on an object used for strengthening it or attaching it to another object.

flank, flanks, flanking, flanked
1 (noun) An animal's flank is its side between the ribs and the hip.
2 (verb) Someone or something that is flanked by a particular thing or person has them at their side, e.g. *an old-fashioned bed, flanked by marble tables.*

flannel, flannels
1 (noun) Flannel is a lightweight woollen fabric.
2 Flannels are men's trousers made of flannel.
3 A flannel is a small square of towelling, used for washing yourself.
4 (an informal use) Flannel is also indirect or evasive talk or explanations.

flannelette
(noun) Flannelette is a soft, thick cotton fabric.

flap, flaps, flapping, flapped
1 (verb) Something that flaps moves up and down or from side to side with a snapping sound.
2 (noun) A flap of something such as paper or skin is a loose piece that is attached at one edge.
3 A flap on an aircraft wing is a piece that can be raised or lowered to control the aircraft's movements.
4 (phrase) If you are in a flap, you are in a state of panic or agitation.

flapjack, flapjacks
(noun) A flapjack is a type of thick, chewy biscuit made from oats, butter, sugar, and syrup.

flapper, flappers
(noun) In the 1920s, flappers were young women who wore modern clothes and enjoyed going to parties and dances, and who sometimes led rather unconventional lives.

flare, flares, flaring, flared
1 (noun) A flare is a device that produces a brightly coloured flame, used especially as an emergency signal.
2 (verb) If a fire flares, it suddenly burns much more vigorously.
3 If violence or a conflict flares or flares up, it suddenly starts or becomes more serious.
4 Something that flares spreads outwards in a fan shape.

flash, flashes, flashing, flashed
1 (noun) A flash is a sudden short burst of light.
2 (verb) If a light flashes, it shines for a very short period, often repeatedly.
3 Something that flashes past moves or happens so fast that you almost miss it.
4 If you flash something, you show it briefly, e.g. *She flashed her identity card at the policeman.*
5 (phrase) Something that happens in a flash happens suddenly and lasts a very short time.
6 An achievement that is a flash in the pan is considered to be a fluke and not likely to be repeated.
7 (adjective; an informal use) Something that is flash looks very expensive and fashionable in a vulgar way.

flashback, flashbacks
(noun) A flashback is a scene in a film, play, or book that returns to events in the past.

flashbulb, flashbulbs
(noun) A flashbulb is a small bulb attached to a camera that produces a bright flash for taking photographs in dark conditions.

flash flood, flash floods
(noun) A flash flood is a sudden flood usually caused by a heavy storm.

flashlight, flashlights
(noun) A flashlight is a large, powerful torch.

flashy, flashier, flashiest
(adjective) expensive and fashionable in appearance, in a vulgar way, e.g. *a flashy car.*

flask, flasks
1 (noun) A flask is a long-necked glass bottle with a bowl-shaped base, used especially in laboratories.
2 A flask is also a small, flat bottle for carrying spirits such as brandy or whisky.

flat, flats; flatter, flattest
1 (noun) A flat is a self-contained set of rooms, usually on one level, for living in.
2 (adjective) Something that is flat is level and smooth.
3 A flat object is not very tall or deep.
4 A flat tyre or ball has not got enough air in it.
5 A flat drink has lost its fizziness.
6 A flat battery has lost its electrical charge.
7 Someone with flat feet has feet with very low arches.
8 A flat refusal or denial is complete and firm.
9 Something that is flat is without emotion, variety, or interest, e.g. *She spoke in a flat voice.*
10 A flat rate or price is fixed and the same for everyone whatever their circumstances, e.g. *All passengers pay a flat rate of 20p.*
11 A musical instrument or note that is flat is slightly too low in pitch.
12 (noun) In music, a flat is a note or key a semitone lower than that described by the same letter. It is represented by the symbol '♭'.
13 A flat is a punctured tyre.
14 A low area of marshland can be referred to as flats.
15 (adverb) Something that is done in a particular time flat, takes exactly that time, e.g. *It can reach the target in four minutes flat.*
flatly (adverb), **flatness** (noun).
[from Old Norse *flatr* meaning 'level']

Similar words: (sense 2) level, horizontal

flatfish
(noun) A flatfish is a sea fish with a wide flat body, such as a plaice or sole.

flatten, flattens, flattening, flattened
(verb) If you flatten something or if it flattens, it becomes flat or flatter.

flatter, flatters, flattering, flattered
1 (verb) If you flatter someone, you praise them in an exaggerated way, either to please them or to persuade them to do something.
2 If you are flattered by something, it makes you feel pleased and important, e.g. *I'm flattered to be invited.*
3 If you flatter yourself that something is the case, you believe, perhaps mistakenly, something good about yourself or your abilities.
4 Something that flatters you makes you appear more attractive.
flatterer (noun), **flattering** (adjective).

Similar words: (sense 1) butter up, cajole, sweet-talk

flattery
(noun) Flattery is flattering words or behaviour.

Similar words: blandishment, blarney, sweet-talk

flatulence
(noun) Flatulence is the uncomfortable state of having too much gas in your stomach or intestine.
[from Latin *flatus* meaning 'gust of wind']

flaunt, flaunts, flaunting, flaunted
(verb) If you flaunt your possessions or talents, you display them too obviously or proudly.

flautist, flautists
(noun) A flautist is someone who plays the flute.

flavour, flavours, flavouring, flavoured
1 (noun) The flavour of food is its taste.
2 (verb) If you flavour food with a spice or herb, you add it to the food to give it a particular taste.
3 (noun) The flavour of something is its distinctive characteristic or quality.
flavouring (noun), **flavourless** (adjective).

flaw, flaws
1 (noun) A flaw is a fault or mark in a piece of fabric, china, or glass, or in a decorative pattern.
2 A flaw is also a weak point or undesirable quality in a theory, plan, or person's character.
flawed (adjective), **flawless** (adjective).

Similar words: (sense 1) blemish, spot, mark (sense 2) blemish

flax
(noun) Flax is a blue-flowered plant, grown for its seeds which produce linseed oil, and its fibrous stem which is used for textile thread.

flaxen
(adjective) pale yellow in colour, e.g. *her flaxen hair.*

flay, flays, flaying, flayed
1 (verb) To flay a dead animal means to cut off its skin.
2 To flay someone means to criticize them severely.

flea, fleas
1 (noun) A flea is a small wingless jumping insect which feeds on blood.
2 (an informal phrase) If you send someone away **with a flea in their ear**, you firmly reject their suggestion and tell them off.

flea market, flea markets
(noun) A flea market is a market selling cheap second-hand or antique goods.

fleck, flecks
(noun) A fleck is a small coloured mark or particle.
flecked (adjective).

Similar words: speck, speckle, spot

fled the past tense and past participle of **flee**.

fledgling, fledglings
1 (noun) A fledgling is a young bird that is learning to fly.
2 (adjective) Fledgling means new, or young and inexperienced, e.g. *fledgling industries.*
[from Middle English *fledge* meaning 'having feathers']

flee, flees, fleeing, fled
(verb) To flee from someone or something means to run away from them.

fleece, fleeces, fleecing, fleeced
1 (noun) A sheep's fleece is its coat of wool.
2 (verb) To fleece someone means to overcharge or swindle them.
fleecy (adjective).

fleet, fleets
(noun) A fleet is a group of ships or vehicles owned by the same organization or travelling together.

fleeting
(adjective) lasting for a very short time.

Flemish
(noun) Flemish is a language spoken in many parts of Belgium.

flesh
1 (noun) Flesh is the soft part of the body.
2 The flesh of a fruit or vegetable is the soft inner part that you eat.
3 Flesh is the physical human body as opposed to the spirit or soul, e.g. *the comforts and pleasures of the flesh.*
4 (phrase) Your **own flesh and blood** are your relations.
fleshy (adjective).

fleur-de-lis, fleurs-de-lis (pronounced flur de **lee**)
(noun) A fleur-de-lis is a heraldic emblem consisting of three leaves or petals joined at the base; formerly the royal arms of France.
[from French *fleur de lis* meaning 'lily flower']

flew the past tense of **fly**.

flex, flexes, flexing, flexed
1 (noun) A flex is a length of wire covered in plastic, which carries electricity to an appliance.
2 (verb) If you flex your muscles, you bend and stretch them.
[from Latin *flexus* meaning 'bent']

flexible

1 (adjective) able to be bent easily without breaking.
2 able to adapt to changing circumstances.
flexibility (noun).
[from Latin *flexibilis*]

flexitime

(noun) Flexitime is a system allowing employees to vary the time that they start and finish work provided that the agreed total number of hours is completed.

flick, flicks, flicking, flicked

1 (verb) If something flicks somewhere, it moves with a short sudden movement, e.g. *Its huge tongue flicks in and out of its mouth.*
2 If you flick something, you move it sharply with your finger.
3 (noun) A flick is a sudden quick movement or sharp touch with the finger, e.g. *a quick upward flick of the arm.*
4 (an informal use) The flicks are the cinema, e.g. *What's on at the flicks?*

flicker, flickers, flickering, flickered

1 (verb) If a light or a flame flickers, it shines and moves unsteadily.
2 (noun) A flicker is a short unsteady light or movement of light, e.g. *a faint flicker of lightning.*
3 A flicker of emotion or feeling is a very brief experience of it, e.g. *a flicker of fear.*

flick knife, flick knives

(noun) A flick knife is a knife with a concealed blade that springs out when a button is pressed.

flight, flights

1 (noun) A flight is a journey made by aeroplane.
2 Flight is the action of flying or the ability to fly.
3 Flight is also the act of running away.
4 A flight of stairs or steps is a set running in a single direction.
5 A flight of fancy or imagination is an idea that is imaginative but not practical.
[from Old English *flyht*]

Similar words: (sense 2) flying, aviation

---

flight deck, flight decks

(noun) The flight deck of an aeroplane is the area where the pilot operates the controls.

flight lieutenant, flight lieutenants

(noun) A flight lieutenant is an RAF officer of the rank immediately above flying officer.

flight recorder, flight recorders

(noun) A flight recorder is an electronic device in an aircraft which records information about each flight. It may be used to determine the cause of a crash.

flighty, flightier, flightiest

(adjective) changeable and not very reliable or serious, e.g. *I thought her a flighty young minx.*

flimsy, flimsier, flimsiest

1 (adjective) made of something very thin or weak and not providing much protection.
2 not very convincing, e.g. *a flimsy excuse.*

flinch, flinches, flinching, flinched

(verb) If you flinch, you make a sudden small movement in fear or pain.
[from Old French *flenchir* meaning 'to turn aside']

Similar words: wince, blench, recoil

---

fling, flings, flinging, flung

1 (verb) If you fling something, you throw it with a lot of force.
2 (noun) A fling is a short period of unrestricted enjoyment and activity.

flint, flints

(noun) Flint is a hard greyish-black form of quartz. It produces a spark when struck with steel.

flinty

(adjective) hard and unkind, e.g. *flinty eyes.*

flip, flips, flipping, flipped

1 (verb) If you flip something, you turn or move it quickly and sharply, e.g. *flipping through the pages of the magazine.*
2 If you flip something, you hit it sharply with your finger or thumb.
3 (an informal use) If someone flips, they suddenly become very angry or upset.

flippant

(adjective) showing an inappropriate lack of seriousness, e.g. *a flippant remark.*
flippantly (adverb), **flippancy** (noun).

flipper, flippers

1 (noun) A flipper is one of the broad, flat limbs of sea animals, for example seals or penguins, used for swimming.
2 Flippers are broad, flat pieces of rubber that you can attach to your feet to help you swim.

flirt, flirts, flirting, flirted

1 (verb) If you flirt with someone, you behave as if you are sexually attracted to them but without serious intentions.
2 (noun) A flirt is someone who often flirts with people.
3 (verb) If you flirt with an idea, you consider it without seriously intending to do anything about it.
flirtation (noun), **flirtatious** (adjective).

Similar words: (sense 3) toy, dally

---

flit, flits, flitting, flitted

(verb) To flit somewhere means to fly or move there with quick, light movements.

float, floats, floating, floated

1 (verb) Something that floats is supported by water.
2 (noun) A float is a light object that floats and either supports something or someone or regulates the level of liquid in a tank or cistern.
3 (verb) Something that floats through the air moves along gently, supported by the air.
4 If a company is floated, shares are sold to the public for the first time and the company gains a listing on the stock exchange.
5 If a government floats its currency, it removes restrictions on the currency and its value is allowed to change in relation to other currencies.

6 (noun) A float is a decorated lorry that is part of a procession.
7 A float is also a small amount of coins that is used in a shop for change.

flock, flocks, flocking, flocked
1 (noun) A flock of birds, sheep, or goats is a group of them.
2 (verb) If people flock somewhere, they go there in large numbers.
3 (adjective) Flock wallpaper has a velvety raised pattern on it.
[Senses 1-2 are from Old English *flocc* meaning 'band of people'; sense 3 is from Latin *floccus* meaning 'tuft of wool']

floe, floes
(noun) A floe is an area of floating ice.
[from Norwegian *flo* meaning 'layer']

flog, flogs, flogging, flogged
1 (verb; an informal use) If you flog something, you sell it.
2 To flog someone means to beat them with a whip or stick.
flogging (noun).

flood, floods, flooding, flooded
1 (noun) A flood is a large amount of water covering an area that is usually dry.
2 (verb) If liquid floods an area, or if a river floods, the water or liquid overflows, covering the surrounding area.
3 (noun) A flood of something is a large amount of it suddenly occurring, e.g. *the flood of refugees*.
4 (verb) If people or things flood into a place, they come there in large numbers, e.g. *Calls for assistance flooded into the emergency services.*

Similar words: (sense 1) deluge, spate, torrent (sense 3) spate

floodgates
(phrase) To **open the floodgates** means suddenly to give a lot of people the opportunity to do something they could not do before.

floodlight, floodlights
(noun) A floodlight is a very powerful outdoor lamp used to illuminate public buildings and sports grounds.
floodlit (adjective).

floor, floors, flooring, floored
1 (noun) The floor of a room is the part you walk on.
2 A floor of a building is one of the levels in it, e.g. *on the third floor.*
3 The floor of a valley, forest, or the sea is the ground at the bottom.
4 In a large hall or place of entertainment, the floor is the main area, for example the dance area in a disco or the place where the audience sit in a public meeting.
5 (verb) If a remark or question floors you, you are completely unable to deal with it or answer it.
6 (phrase) In a debate, the person who **has the floor** is speaking or has the right to speak.

floorboard, floorboards
(noun) A floorboard is one of the long planks of wood from which a floor is made.

floor show, floor shows
(noun) The floor show in a nightclub is a performance of songs or dances, or a comedy act.

flop, flops, flopping, flopped
1 (verb) If someone or something flops, they fall loosely and rather heavily.
2 (an informal use) Something that flops fails.
3 (noun; an informal use) Something that is a flop is completely unsuccessful.

floppy, floppier, floppiest
(adjective) tending to hang downwards in a rather loose way, e.g. *a floppy straw hat*.
floppiness (noun).

Similar words: droopy, limp

floppy disk, floppy disks; also spelled **floppy disc**
(noun) A floppy disk is a small flexible magnetic disk on which computer data is stored.

flora
(noun) The flora of a particular area is the plants that grow there, e.g. *the flora and fauna of our countryside*.
[from Flora, a Roman flower goddess]

floral
(adjective) patterned with flowers or made from flowers, e.g. *floral wallpaper... a floral tribute*.
[from Latin *flores* meaning 'flowers']

floret, florets
(noun) A floret is a small individual flower or group of flowers forming part of a composite flower head, e.g. *cauliflower florets*.
[from Old French *florete* meaning 'little flower']

florid (rhymes with **horrid**)
1 (adjective) highly elaborate and extravagant, e.g. *florid verse... a spectacularly florid cast-iron hatstand*.
2 having a red face.
[from Latin *floridus* meaning 'flowery']

florist, florists
(noun) A florist is a person or shop selling flowers.

floss
(noun) Dental floss is soft silky threads or fibre which you use to clean between your teeth.
[from Old French *flosche* meaning 'down']

flotation, flotations
1 (noun) The flotation of a business is the issuing of shares in order to launch it or to raise money.
2 Flotation is the act of floating.

flotilla, flotillas (flot-til-la)
(noun) A flotilla is a small fleet or group of small ships.
[from Spanish *flotilla* meaning 'little fleet']

flotsam
(noun) Flotsam is rubbish or wreckage floating at sea or washed up on the shore.

flounce, flounces, flouncing, flounced
1 (verb) If you flounce somewhere, you walk there with exaggerated movements suggesting that you are feeling angry or impatient about something, e.g. *She flounced into the kitchen*.
2 (noun) A flounce is a big frill around the bottom of a dress or skirt.

flounder, flounders, floundering, floundered
1 (verb) To flounder means to struggle to move or stay upright, for example in water or mud.
2 If you flounder in a conversation or situation, you find it difficult to decide what to say or do.
3 (noun) A flounder is a type of edible flatfish.

flour
(noun) Flour is a powder made from finely ground grain, usually wheat, and used for baking and cooking.
floured (adjective), **floury** (adjective)

flourish, flourishes, flourishing, flourished
1 (verb) Something that flourishes continues, develops, or functions successfully or healthily.
2 If you flourish something, you wave or display it so that people notice it.
3 (noun) A flourish is a bold sweeping or waving movement.
[from Latin *florere* meaning 'to flower']

flout, flouts, flouting, flouted
(verb) If you flout a convention, law, or order, you deliberately disobey it.

flow, flows, flowing, flowed
1 (verb) If something flows, it moves, happens, or occurs in a steady continuous stream.
2 (noun) A flow of something is a steady continuous movement of it; also the rate at which it flows, e.g. *The blood flow is cut off... a good flow of information.*

flow chart, flow charts
(noun) A flow chart is a diagram showing the sequence of steps and choices that lead to various results and courses of action.

flower, flowers, flowering, flowered
1 (noun) A flower is the part of a plant containing the reproductive organs from which the fruit or seeds develop.
2 (verb) When a plant flowers, it produces flowers.
[from Latin *flos* meaning 'flower']

flowery
(adjective) Flowery language is full of elaborate literary expressions.

flown the past participle of **fly**.

flu
(noun) Flu is an illness similar to a very bad cold, which causes headaches, sore throat, weakness, and aching muscles. Flu is short for 'influenza'.

fluctuate, fluctuates, fluctuating, fluctuated
(verb) Something that fluctuates is irregular and changeable, e.g. *adjusting the supply to suit the fluctuating demand.*
fluctuation (noun).
[from Latin *fluctuare* meaning 'to toss about' or 'to waver']

flue, flues
(noun) A flue is a pipe which takes fumes and smoke away from a stove or boiler.

fluent
1 (adjective) able to speak a foreign language correctly and without hesitation.

2 able to express yourself clearly and without hesitation.
fluently (adverb).
[from Latin *fluens* meaning 'flowing']

Similar words: (sense 2) articulate, eloquent

fluff, fluffs, fluffing, fluffed
1 (noun) Fluff is soft, light, woolly threads or fibres bunched together.
2 (verb) If you fluff something out, you brush or shake it to make it seem larger and lighter, e.g. *birds fluffing their feathers out.*
fluffy (adjective).

fluid, fluids
1 (noun) A fluid is a liquid.
2 (adjective) Fluid movement is smooth and flowing.
3 A fluid arrangement, plan, or idea is flexible and without a fixed structure.
fluidity (noun).
[from Latin *fluidus* meaning 'flowing' or 'loose']

fluid ounce, fluid ounces
(noun) A fluid ounce is a unit of liquid volume equal to one twentieth of a pint or 28.4 millilitres.

fluke, flukes
(noun) A fluke is an accidental success or piece of good luck.

flummox, flummoxes, flummoxing, flummoxed
(verb) If you are flummoxed, you are confused and do not know what to do or say.

flung the past tense of **fling**.

flunk, flunks, flunking, flunked
(verb; an informal word) If you flunk a course or exam, you fail.

flunkey, flunkeys
(noun) A flunkey is a male servant in a large house.

fluorescent (pronounced floo-er-**ess**-nt)
1 (adjective) having a very bright appearance when light is shone on it, as if it is shining itself, e.g. *fluorescent paint.*
2 A fluorescent light is in the form of a tube and shines with a hard bright light.
fluorescence (noun).

fluoridation
(noun) The fluoridation of water is the addition of fluoride to the public water supply as a protection against tooth decay.

fluoride
(noun) Fluoride is a chemical compound containing fluorine.

fluorine
(noun) Fluorine is a chemical element which is a toxic, pungent, pale yellow gas. Its atomic number is 9 and its symbol is F.

fluorocarbon, fluorocarbons
(noun) Fluorocarbons are compounds derived by replacing all or some of the hydrogen atoms in hydrocarbons by fluorine atoms.

flurry, flurries
(noun) A flurry is a short rush of vigorous activity or movement.

flush, flushes, flushing, flushed

1 (noun) A flush is a rosy red colour, e.g. *A flush rose to her pallid cheeks.*
2 In cards, a flush is a hand all of one suit.
3 (verb) If you flush, your face goes red.
4 If you flush a toilet or something such as a pipe, you force water through it to clean it.
5 (adjective; an informal use) Someone who is flush has plenty of money.
6 Something that is flush with a surface is level with it or flat against it.

fluster, flusters, flustering, flustered

1 (verb) If someone flusters you, they make you confused and nervous by rushing you.
2 (noun) If you are in a fluster, you feel confused, nervous, and rushed.

flute, flutes

(noun) A flute is a musical wind instrument consisting of a long metal tube with holes and keys. It is held sideways to the mouth and played by blowing across a hole in its side.

fluted

(adjective) decorated with long upward curving grooves.

flutter, flutters, fluttering, fluttered

1 (verb) If something flutters, it flaps or waves with small, quick movements.
2 (noun) If you are in a flutter, you are excited and nervous.
3 (an informal use) If you have a flutter, you have a small bet.

fluvial (pronounced floo-vee-al)

(adjective; a technical word) produced by or relating to a river.
[from Latin *fluvius* meaning 'river']

flux

(noun) Flux is a state of constant change, e.g. *years of political flux and turmoil.*
[from *fluxus* meaning 'a flowing']

fly, flies, flying, flew, flown

1 (noun) A fly is an insect with two pairs of wings.
2 The front opening on a pair of trousers is the fly or the flies.
3 The fly or fly sheet of a tent is either a flap at the entrance or an outer layer providing protection from rain.
4 (verb) When a bird, insect, or aircraft flies, it moves through the air.
5 When a flag is flying, it is displayed at the top of a pole.
6 If someone or something flies, they move or go very quickly.
7 If you fly at someone or let fly at them, you attack or criticize them suddenly and aggressively.
flying (adjective and noun), **flyer** (noun).

Similar words: (sense 4) soar, flit

flyblown

(adjective) dirty or covered with marks, originally because of being infested with flies' eggs.

fly-by-night

(adjective) Someone who is fly-by-night is untrustworthy and likely to disappear without paying debts after having made money quickly.

fly-fishing

Fly-fishing is a method of fishing using imitation flies as bait.

flying buttress, flying buttresses

(noun) A flying buttress is an arch and vertical column that supports a wall from the outside.

flying fish, flying fishes

(noun) A flying fish is a type of tropical fish that has fins that enable it to move through the air.

flying officer, flying officers

(noun) A flying officer is an RAF officer of the rank immediately above pilot officer.

flying saucer, flying saucers

(noun) A flying saucer is a large disc-shaped spacecraft that has not been scientifically proven to exist.

flyleaf, flyleaves

(noun) A flyleaf is a blank page at the front of a book.

flyover, flyovers

(noun) A flyover is a structure carrying one road over another at a junction or intersection.

flywheel, flywheels

(noun) A flywheel is a heavy wheel that maintains a constant speed of rotation to control the speed at which a machine operates.

foal, foals, foaling, foaled

1 (noun) A foal is a young horse.
2 (verb) When a female horse foals, she gives birth.

foam, foams, foaming, foamed

1 (noun) Foam is a mass of tiny bubbles.
2 (verb) When something foams, it forms a mass of small bubbles.
3 (noun) Foam is light spongy material used, for example, in furniture or packaging.

Similar words: (sense 1) froth, spume

fob off, fobs off, fobbing off, fobbed off

(verb; an informal use) If you fob someone off, you provide them with something that is not very good or not adequate.

focus, focuses, focusing, focused

The plural of the noun is either **foci** or **focuses**.
1 (verb) If you focus your eyes or an instrument on an object, you adjust them so that the image is clear.
2 (noun) The focus of something is its centre of attention, e.g. *A shift in focus has occurred away from civil liberty.*
3 The focus of an earthquake is the point where it starts.
4 In physics, the focus of a number of rays is the point at which they meet.
focal (adjective).
[from Latin *focus* meaning 'hearth'. The hearth was seen as the centre of a Roman home]

fodder

(noun) Fodder is food for farm animals or horses.

foe, foes
(noun) A foe is an enemy.

foetus, foetuses; also spelled **fetus** (pronounced **fee**-tus)
(noun) A foetus is an unborn child or animal in the womb.
foetal (adjective).

fog, fogs, fogging, fogged
1 (noun) Fog is a thick mist of water droplets suspended in the air.
2 (verb) If glass fogs up, it becomes clouded with steam or condensation.
foggy (adjective).

fogey, fogeys (pronounced **foe**-gee)
(noun) If you call someone a fogey, you mean that they are boring and old-fashioned.

foghorn, foghorns
(noun) A foghorn is a loud horn used as a warning to ships in fog.

foible, foibles (pronounced **foy**-bl)
(noun) A foible is a minor eccentricity in a person's character.
[from French *faible* meaning 'feeble' or 'weak']

Similar words: peculiarity, idiosyncrasy, quirk

foil, foils, foiling, foiled
1 (verb) If you foil someone's attempt at something, you prevent them from succeeding.
2 (noun) Foil is thin, paper-like sheets of metal used to wrap food.
3 Something that is a good foil for something else contrasts with it and makes its good qualities more noticeable.
4 A foil is a thin, light sword with a button on the tip, used in fencing.

foist, foists, foisting, foisted
(verb) If you foist something on someone, you force or impose it on them.

fold, folds, folding, folded
1 (verb) If you fold something, you bend it so that one part lies over another.
2 (an informal use) If a business folds, it fails and closes down.
3 In cooking, if you fold one ingredient into another, you mix it in gently.
4 (noun) A fold in paper or cloth is a crease or bend.
5 A fold is a small enclosed area for sheep.

Similar words: (sense 1) crease, double over, tuck

-fold
-fold is used with a number to indicate that something has a certain number of parts or is multiplied by that number, e.g. *The problems were two-fold.*

folder, folders
(noun) A folder is a thin piece of folded cardboard for keeping loose papers together.

foliage
(noun) Foliage is leaves and plants.
[from Latin *folium* meaning 'leaf']

folk, folks
1 (noun) Folk or folks are people.

2 (adjective) Folk music, dance, or art is traditional or representative of the ordinary people of an area.
3 (noun) Folk or folks are your relatives.

folklore
(noun) Folklore is the traditional stories and beliefs of a community.

follicle , follicles
(noun) A follicle is a small sac or cavity in the body, e.g. *hair follicles.*

follow, follows, following, followed
1 (verb) If you follow someone, you move along behind them. If you follow a path or a sign, you move along in that direction.
2 Something that follows a particular thing happens after it.
3 Something that follows is true or logical as a result of something else being the case, e.g. *Just because they're old, it doesn't follow that they can't look after themselves.*
4 If you follow instructions or advice, you do what you are told.
5 If you follow an explanation or the plot of a story, you understand each stage of it.

Similar words: (sense 2) ensue, succeed

follow up
(verb) If you follow up a suggestion or discovery, you find out more about it or act upon it.

follower, followers
(noun) The followers of a person or belief are the people who support them.

Similar words: adherent, supporter, disciple

following
1 (noun) If a person or organization has a following, they have a group of supporters.
2 (adjective) coming afterwards or later.

folly, follies
(noun) Folly is a foolish act or foolish behaviour.

Similar words: foolishness, imprudence

foment, foments, fomenting, fomented
(verb) To foment trouble means to cause or encourage it.

fond, fonder, fondest
1 (adjective) If you are fond of someone or something, you like them.
2 A fond hope or belief is foolish because it is unlikely to happen.
fondly (adverb), **fondness** (noun).

Similar words: (sense 1) attached, devoted, doting

fondle, fondles, fondling, fondled
(verb) To fondle something means to stroke it affectionately.

fondue, fondues (pronounced **fon**-dyoo)
(noun) A fondue is a hot savoury sauce into which you dip small pieces of bread, vegetable, or meat at the table.
[from French *fondu* meaning 'melted']

font, fonts
(noun) A font is a large stone bowl in a church that holds the water for baptisms.
[from Latin *fons* meaning 'a spring']

food, foods
(noun) Food is any substance consumed by an animal or plant to provide energy.

Similar words: fare, foodstuff, nourishment, sustenance

food chain, food chains
(noun) A food chain is a series of living things which are linked because each one feeds on the next one in the series.

foodstuff, foodstuffs
(noun) A foodstuff is anything used for food.

fool, fools, fooling, fooled
1 (noun) Someone who is a fool behaves in a silly and unintelligent way.
2 A fool is also a dessert made from fruit, eggs, cream, and sugar whipped together.
3 (verb) If you fool someone, you deceive or trick them.

fool around
(phrasal verb) If you fool around, you behave in a silly way.

foolhardy
(adjective) foolish and involving too great a risk.

foolish
(adjective) very silly or unwise.
foolishly (adverb), **foolishness** (noun).

Similar words: injudicious, imprudent, unwise

foolproof
(adjective) Something that is foolproof is so well designed or simple to use that it cannot fail.

foot, feet; foots, footing, footed
1 (noun) Your foot is the part of your body at the end of your leg.
2 The foot of something is the bottom, base, or lower end of it, e.g. *the foot of the cliffs.*
3 A foot is a unit of length equal to 12 inches or about 30.5 centimetres.
4 In poetry, a foot is the basic unit of rhythm containing two or three syllables.
5 (adjective) A foot brake, pedal, or pump is operated by your foot.
6 (phrase) If you **foot the bill** for something, you pay for it.

footage
(noun) Footage is a length of film, e.g. *some spine-chilling footage of the fighting.*

foot-and-mouth disease
(noun) Foot-and-mouth disease is a serious infectious disease affecting cattle, sheep, pigs, and goats which causes swellings around the animal's hooves and mouth.

football, footballs
1 (noun) Football is a game played by two teams of eleven players kicking a ball in an attempt to score goals.
2 A football is a ball used in football.
footballer (noun).

foothill, foothills
(noun) Foothills are hills at the base of mountains.

foothold, footholds
1 (noun) A foothold is a place where you can put your foot when climbing.
2 A foothold is also a favourable position from which further progress can be made.

footing
1 (noun) Footing is a secure grip by or for your feet, e.g. *He lost his footing.*
2 A footing is the basis or nature of a relationship or situation, e.g. *We have to get this on an official footing.*

footlights
(plural noun) In a theatre, the footlights are the row of lights at the front of a stage.

footman, footmen
(noun) A footman is a male servant in a large house who wears uniform.

footnote, footnotes
(noun) A footnote is a note at the bottom of a page or an additional comment giving extra information.

footpath, footpaths
(noun) A footpath is a path for people to walk on.

footprint, footprints
(noun) A footprint is a mark left by a foot or shoe.

footstep, footsteps
(noun) A footstep is the sound or mark made by someone walking.

fop, fops
(noun; an old-fashioned word) A fop is a man who is very conscious of fashion and looking elegant.
foppish (adjective).

for
1 (preposition) intended to be given to or used by a particular person, or done in order to help or benefit them, e.g. *They bought it for me.*
2 For is used when explaining the reason, cause, or purpose of something, e.g. *Money is the primary reason for him leaving.*
3 You use 'for' to express a quantity, time, or distance, e.g. *I've known him for 11 years now... We drove on for another few miles.*
4 If you are for something, you support it or approve of it, e.g. *Are you for or against unilateral disarmament?*
5 (conjunction; an old-fashioned use) because, e.g. *They were surprised, for it was almost ten o'clock.*

forage, forages, foraging, foraged
(verb) When a person or animal forages, they search for food.

foray, forays
1 (noun) A foray is a brief attempt to do or get something.
2 A foray is also an attack or raid by soldiers.

forbear, forbears, forbearing, forbore, forborne
(verb; an old-fashioned word) If you forbear

from doing something, you restrain yourself and do not do it.
forbearance (noun).

forbid, forbids, forbidding, forbade, forbidden
(verb) If you forbid someone to do something, you order them not to do it.
forbidden (adjective).

forbidding
(adjective) severe and threatening in appearance or manner, e.g. *a rather forbidding woman.*

force, forces, forcing, forced
1 (verb) To force someone to do something means to make them do it.
2 To force something means to use violence or great strength to move, push, or open it.
3 (noun) The use of force is the use of violence or great strength.
4 The force of something is its strength or power, e.g. *The force of an earthquake can be measured accurately... She saw the force of his argument.*
5 A force is a person or thing that has considerable influence or effect, e.g. *Nationalism was rapidly becoming a dangerous force.*
6 A force is also an organized group of soldiers or police.
7 In physics, force is an influence that changes a body from a state of rest to one of motion, or changes its rate of motion, e.g. *The force acting on the particle is constant.*
8 (phrase) A law or rule that is in **force** is currently valid and must be obeyed.
[from Latin *fortis* meaning 'strong']

Similar words: (sense 1) bind, impel, compel, coerce, drive, make

forced
1 (adjective) A forced action is done only because there is no alternative, e.g. *a forced landing.*
2 Something that is forced is done with an effort and is not natural or spontaneous, e.g. *a forced smile.*

Similar words: (sense 2) contrived, strained, laboured

forceful
(adjective) powerful and convincing, e.g. *a forceful, able man... It made a forceful impression on me.*
forcefully (adverb).

forceps
(noun) Forceps are a pair of long tongs or pincers used by a doctor or surgeon.
[a Latin word]

forcible
1 (adjective) involving physical force or violence.
2 convincing and making a strong impression, e.g. *The riots were a forcible reminder of the continuing unrest.*
forcibly (adverb).

ford, fords, fording, forded
1 (noun) A ford is a shallow place in a river where it is possible to cross on foot or in a vehicle.

2 (verb) To ford a river means to cross it on foot or in a vehicle.

fore
1 (phrase) Someone or something that comes **to the fore** becomes important or popular.
2 (adjective) front, e.g. *the fore and hind wings of the dragonfly.*

forearm, forearms
(noun) Your forearm is the part of your arm between your elbow and your wrist.

forebear, forebears
(noun) Your forebears are your ancestors.

foreboding, forebodings
(noun) A foreboding is a strong feeling of approaching disaster.
[from 'fore' + Old English *bodian* meaning 'to announce']

forecast, forecasts, forecasting, forecast or **forecasted**
1 (noun) A forecast is a prediction of what will happen, especially a statement about what the weather will be like.
2 (verb) To forecast an event means to predict what will happen.

foreclose, forecloses, foreclosing, foreclosed
(verb) If a money-lending organization forecloses, it takes possession of goods or property, for example because regular payments have not been made.

forecourt, forecourts
(noun) A forecourt is an open area at the front of a petrol station or large building.

forefather, forefathers
(noun) Your forefathers are your ancestors.

forefinger, forefingers
(noun) Your forefinger is the finger next to your thumb.

forefront
(noun) The forefront of something is the most important and progressive part of it.

forego, foregoes, foregoing, forewent, foregone; also spelled **forgo**
(verb) If you forego something pleasant, you abstain from it or do without it.

foregoing
(a formal expression) You can say **the foregoing** when talking about something that has just been said, e.g. *How can they support ideas such as the foregoing?*

foregone conclusion, foregone conclusions
(noun) A foregone conclusion is an inevitable or predictable result or conclusion.

foreground
(noun) In a picture, the foreground is the part that seems nearest to you.

forehand, forehands
(noun and adjective) Forehand is a stroke in tennis, squash, or badminton made with the palm of your hand facing in the direction that you hit the ball.

forehead, foreheads
(noun) Your forehead is the area at the front of

your head, above your eyebrows and below your hairline.

foreign
1 (adjective) belonging to, relating to, or involving countries other than your own, e.g. *foreign holidays... foreign policy.*
2 unfamiliar or uncharacteristic, e.g. *Such doctrine seems foreign to our thought.*
3 Foreign matter or a foreign body is something that is in a place where it should not be and where it is likely to cause contamination or irritation, e.g. *a complaint about a foreign body in the food.*
foreigner (noun).

Similar words: (sense 2) alien, unfamiliar

foreknowledge
(noun) Foreknowledge is knowledge of an event before it actually happens.

forelock, forelocks
(noun) A forelock is a lock or tuft of hair hanging over the forehead.

foreman, foremen
1 (noun) A foreman is a person in charge of a group of workers, for example on a building site.
2 The foreman of a jury is the spokesman.

foremost
(adjective) The foremost of a group of things is the most important or the best.

forename, forenames
(noun) Your forename is your first name or your Christian name.

forensic
1 (adjective) relating to or involving the scientific examination of objects involved in a crime.
2 relating to or involving the legal profession.

forerunner, forerunners
(noun) The forerunner of something is the person who first introduced or achieved it, or the first example of it.

foresee, foresees, foreseeing, foresaw, foreseen
(verb) If you foresee something, you predict or expect that it will happen.
foreseeable (adjective).

foreshadow, foreshadows, foreshadowing, foreshadowed
(verb) Something that foreshadows an event suggests that it will happen.

foreshore, foreshores
(noun) The foreshore is the part of the shore between the points reached by the high and low tides.

foreshorten , foreshortens, foreshortening, foreshortened
(verb) Something that is foreshortened is reduced in length so that it appears to be in correct perspective.

foresight
(noun) Foresight is the ability to know what is going to happen in the future.

foreskin , foreskins
(noun) A man's foreskin is the fold of skin covering the end of his penis.

forest, forests
(noun) A forest is a large area of trees growing close together.

forestall, forestalls, forestalling, forestalled
(verb) If you forestall something, you prevent it from happening by taking action beforehand.

forestry
(noun) Forestry is the study and work of growing and maintaining forests.

foretaste, foretastes
(noun) A foretaste of something is a slight taste or experience of it in advance.

foretell, foretells, foretelling, foretold
(verb) If you foretell something, you predict that it will happen.

forethought
(noun) Forethought is careful thought and planning about future actions and consequences.

forever
(adverb) permanently or continually.

forewarn, forewarns, forewarning, forewarned
(verb) If you forewarn someone, you warn them in advance about something.

foreword, forewords
(noun) A foreword is an introduction in a book.

forfeit, forfeits, forfeiting, forfeited
1 (verb) If you forfeit something, you have to give it up as a penalty.
2 (noun) A forfeit is something that you have to give up or do as a penalty.
[from Old French *forfet* meaning 'offence']

forge, forges, forging, forged
1 (noun) A forge is a place where a blacksmith works making metal goods by hand.
2 (verb) To forge metal means to hammer and bend it into shape while hot.
3 To forge a relationship means to create a strong and lasting relationship.
4 Someone who forges money, documents, or paintings makes illegal copies of them.
5 To forge ahead means to progress quickly.

forgery, forgeries
(noun) Forgery is the crime of forging money, documents, or paintings; also something that has been forged.
forger (noun).

forget, forgets, forgetting, forgot, forgotten
1 (verb) If you forget something, you fail to remember or think about it.
2 If you forget yourself, you behave in an unacceptable, uncontrolled way.
forgetful (adjective).

forget-me-not, forget-me-nots
(noun) A forget-me-not is a small plant with tiny blue flowers.

forgive, forgives, forgiving, forgave, forgiven
(verb) If you forgive someone for doing

something bad, you stop feeling angry and resentful towards them.
forgiveness (noun), **forgiving** (adjective).

Similar words: pardon, absolve

forgo another spelling of **forego**.

fork, forks, forking, forked
1 (noun) A fork is a pronged instrument used for eating food.
2 A fork is also a large garden tool with three or four prongs.
3 (verb) To fork something means to move or turn it with a fork.
4 (noun) A fork in a road, path, river, or branch is a y-shaped junction or division.
[from Latin *furca* meaning 'pitchfork']

fork out
(phrasal verb; an informal use) If you fork out for something, you pay for it, often unwillingly.

fork-lift truck, fork-lift trucks
(noun) A fork-lift truck is a small vehicle with two horizontal movable arms at the front, used to move heavy loads in factories and warehouses.

forlorn
1 (adjective) lonely, unhappy, and uncared for.
2 desperate and without any expectation of success, e.g. *forlorn attempts to rescue the victims.*
forlornly (adverb).

form, forms, forming, formed
1 (noun) A particular form of something is a type or kind of it, e.g. *I never touch alcohol in any form.*
2 The form of something is its shape or pattern.
3 (verb) The things that form something are the things it consists of, e.g. *Her paintings will form the basis of a major exhibition.*
4 When someone forms something or when it forms, it is created, organized, or started.
5 (noun) A form is a sheet of paper with questions and spaces for you to fill in the answers.
6 In a school, a form is a class.
7 A form is also a long low bench.
[from Latin *forma* meaning 'shape']

formal
1 (adjective) correct, serious, and conforming to accepted conventions, e.g. *The letter was stiff and formal... formal dress.*
2 official and publicly recognized, e.g. *Formal approval has not yet been given.*
formally (adverb).

formaldehyde (pronounced for-**mal**-di-hide)
(noun) Formaldehyde is a soluble, poisonous, strong-smelling gas, used in the manufacture of plastics and for preserving biological specimens. Its formula is $HCHO$.

formalin
(noun) Formalin is a 40% solution of formaldehyde in water, used for preserving biological specimens or as a disinfectant.

formality, formalities
(noun) A formality is an action or process that is carried out as part of an official procedure.

formalize, formalizes, formalizing, formalized; also spelled **formalise**
(verb) If you formalize a plan or idea, you make it clear and official.

format, formats
(noun) The format of something is the way in which it is arranged or presented.

formation, formations
1 (noun) The formation of something is the process of developing and creating it.
2 A formation is the pattern or shape of something.
[from Latin *formare* meaning 'to shape' or 'to make']

formative
(adjective) having an important and lasting influence on character and development, e.g. *the formative years of a child's life.*

former
1 (adjective) happening or existing before now or in the past, e.g. *a former army officer.*
2 (noun) You use 'the former' to refer to the first of two things just mentioned, e.g. *If I had to choose between happiness and money, I would have the former.*
formerly (adverb).

Formica (pronounced for-**my**-ka)
(noun; a trademark) Formica is a hard plastic covering used for kitchen worktops and tables.

formidable
(adjective) very difficult to deal with or overcome, and therefore rather frightening or impressive, e.g. *a formidable task.*
[from Latin *formido* meaning 'terror']

Similar words: threatening, intimidating

formula, formulae or formulas
1 (noun) A formula is a group of letters, numbers, and symbols representing a mathematical or scientific rule.
2 A formula is also a list of quantities of substances that when mixed make another substance, for example in chemistry.
3 A formula is also a plan or set of rules for dealing with a particular problem, e.g. *a peace formula.*
formulaic (adjective).
[from Latin *formula* meaning 'set form of words']

formulate, formulates, formulating, formulated
(verb) If you formulate a plan or thought, you create it and express it in a clear and precise way.

fornication
(noun; a formal word) Fornication is the sin of having sex with someone when you are not married to them.

forsake, forsakes, forsaking, forsook, forsaken
(verb) To forsake someone or something means to desert, give up, or abandon them.

forsythia (pronounced for-**syth**-ee-a)
(noun) Forsythia is a garden shrub that produces yellow flowers before the leaves in spring. It is named after the 18th century botanist, William Forsyth.

fort, forts
1 (noun) A fort is a strong building built for defence.
2 (phrase) If you **hold the fort** for someone, you manage their affairs while they are away.
[from Latin *fortis* meaning 'strong']

Similar words: (sense 1) fortress, stronghold, citadel

forte, fortes (pronounced **for**-tay)
1 In music, forte is an instruction to play or sing something loudly.
2 (noun) If something is your forte, you are particularly good at doing it.

Similar words: (sense 2) speciality, metier, strong point, strength

forth
1 (adverb) out and forward from a starting place, e.g. *This tiny island sent forth her sons to conquer the world.*
2 into view, e.g. *He reached in and brought forth a blue file.*
3 from a particular point in time onwards, e.g. *From that day forth he was a marked man.*

forthcoming
1 (adjective) planned to happen soon, e.g. *the forthcoming election.*
2 given or made available, e.g. *The money will be forthcoming.*
3 willing to give information, e.g. *She was not forthcoming about the arrangements.*

forthright
(adjective) Someone who is forthright is direct and honest about their opinions and feelings.

fortification, fortifications
(noun) Fortifications are buildings, walls, and ditches used to protect a place.

fortify, fortifies, fortifying, fortified
1 (verb) To fortify a place means to strengthen it against attack.
2 If something fortifies you, it makes you feel stronger, more determined, or better prepared.
fortification (noun).

fortissimo
In music, fortissimo is an instruction to play or sing something very loudly.

fortitude
(noun) Fortitude is calm and patient courage.

fortnight, fortnights
(noun) A fortnight is a period of two weeks.
fortnightly (adverb and adjective).

fortress, fortresses
(noun) A fortress is a castle or well-protected town built for defence.

fortuitous (pronounced for-**tyoo**-it-uss)
(adjective) happening by chance or good luck, e.g. *a fortuitous discovery.*

fortunate
1 (adjective) Someone who is fortunate is lucky.
2 Something that is fortunate brings success or advantage.
fortunately (adverb).

fortune, fortunes
1 (noun) Fortune or good fortune is good luck.
2 (phrase) If someone **tells your fortune**, they predict your future.
3 (noun) A fortune is a large amount of money.

forty, forties
the number 40.
fortieth.

forum, forums
1 (noun) A forum is a place or meeting in which people can exchange ideas and discuss public issues.
2 In Roman towns, a forum was a square where people met to discuss business and politics.

forward, forwards, forwarding, forwarded
1 (adverb and adjective) Forward or forwards means in the front or towards the front, e.g. *The seats face forward.*
2 Forward means in or towards a future time, e.g. *forward planning.*
3 Forward or forwards also means developing or progressing, e.g. *We're no further forward.*
4 (adverb) If someone or something is put forward, they are suggested as being suitable for something.
5 (verb) If you forward a letter that you have received, you send it on to the person to whom it is addressed at their new address.
6 (noun) In a game such as football or hockey, a forward is a player in an attacking position.

Similar words: (sense 3) on, onwards, onward

fossil, fossils
(noun) A fossil is the remains or impression of an animal or plant of a previous geological age, preserved in rock.
fossilize (verb).
[from Latin *fossilis* meaning 'dug up']

foster, fosters, fostering, fostered
1 (verb) If someone fosters a child, they are paid to look after the child for a period, but do not become its legal parents.
2 If you foster something such as an activity or an idea, you help its development and growth by encouraging people to do or think it, e.g. *They intended to foster revolt.*
foster child (noun), **foster home** (noun), **foster parent** (noun).

fought the past tense of **fight**.

foul, fouler, foulest; fouls, fouling, fouled
1 (adjective) Something that is foul is very unpleasant, especially because it is dirty, wicked, or obscene.
2 (verb) To foul something means to make it dirty, especially with faeces, e.g. *Dogs must not be allowed to foul the pavement.*
3 If something fouls a mechanism, it becomes twisted around it and prevents it from functioning.

4 (noun) In sport, a foul is an act of breaking the rules.

found, founds, founding, founded
1 Found is the past tense and past participle of find.
2 (verb) If someone founds an organization or institution, they start it and set it up.
[from Latin *fundare* meaning 'to lay foundations']

foundation, foundations
1 (noun) The foundation of a belief or way of life is the basic ideas or attitudes on which it is built.
2 A foundation is a solid layer of concrete or bricks in the ground, on which a building is built to give it a firm base.
3 (noun) A foundation is also an organization set up by a legacy to provide money for research or charity.

founder, founders, foundering, foundered
1 (noun) The founder of an institution or organization is the person who sets it up.
2 (verb) If something founders, it fails.

foundry, foundries
(noun) A foundry is a factory where metal is melted and cast.
[from Latin *fundere* meaning 'to pour']

fountain, fountains
(noun) A fountain is an ornamental feature consisting of a jet of water forced into the air by a pump.
[from Latin *fontana*]

fountain pen, fountain pens
(noun) A fountain pen is a pen which is supplied with ink from a container inside the pen.

four, fours
1 Four is the number 4.
2 (phrase) If you are **on all fours**, you are on your hands and knees.

four-letter word, four-letter words
(noun) A four-letter word is a swear word.

four-poster, four-posters
(noun) A four-poster is a bed with a tall post at each corner supporting a canopy and curtains.

fourteen the number 14.
fourteenth.

fourth, fourths
1 The fourth item in a series is the one counted as number four.
2 (noun) In music, a fourth is the interval between two notes of a scale when there are two notes separating them.

fowl, fowls
(noun) A fowl is a bird such as chicken or duck that is kept or hunted for its meat or eggs.

fox, foxes, foxing, foxed
1 (noun) A fox is a dog-like wild animal with reddish-brown fur, a pointed face and ears, and a thick tail.
2 (verb) If something foxes you, it is too confusing or puzzling for you to understand.
foxy (adjective).

foxglove, foxgloves
(noun) A foxglove is a plant with a tall spike of purple or white trumpet-shaped flowers.

foxhound, foxhounds
(noun) A foxhound is a dog trained for hunting foxes.

foyer, foyers (pronounced **foy**-ay)
(noun) A foyer is a large area just inside the main doors of a cinema, hotel, or public building.

fracas (pronounced **frak**-ah)
(noun) A fracas is a rough noisy quarrel or fight.

fraction, fractions
1 (noun) In arithmetic, a fraction is a part of a whole number.
2 A fraction is a tiny proportion or amount of something, e.g. *I hesitated for a fraction of a second.*
fractional (adjective), **fractionally** (adverb).
[from Latin *frangere* meaning 'to break']

fractious
(adjective) When small children are fractious, they become upset or angry very easily, often because they are tired.
fractiously (adverb), **fractiousness** (noun).

fracture, fractures, fracturing, fractured
1 (noun) A fracture is a crack or break in something, especially a bone.
2 (verb) If something fractures, it breaks.

fragile
(adjective) easily broken or damaged, e.g. *fragile china... a fragile economy.*
fragility (noun).
[from Latin *fragilis* meaning 'breakable']

Similar words: brittle, delicate, frail, breakable

fragment, fragments, fragmenting, fragmented
1 (noun) A fragment of something is a small piece or part of it.
2 (verb) If something fragments, it breaks into small pieces or different parts.
fragmentation (noun), **fragmented** (adjective).

fragmentary
(adjective) made up of small or unconnected pieces, e.g. *fragmentary evidence.*

fragrance
(noun) A fragrance is a sweet or pleasant smell.

Similar words: aroma, pefume, scent

fragrant
(adjective) Something that is fragrant smells sweet or pleasant.
[from Latin *fragrans* meaning 'sweet-smelling']

frail, frailer, frailest
1 (adjective) Someone who is frail is not strong or healthy.
2 Something that is frail is easily broken or damaged.
frailty (noun).
[from Latin *fragilis* meaning 'breakable']

frame, frames, framing, framed
1 (noun) The frame of a door, window, or picture is the structure surrounding it.

2 A frame is also an arrangement of connected bars over which something is formed or built.
3 The frames of a pair of glasses are the wire or plastic parts that hold the lenses.
4 Your frame is your body, e.g. *his sturdy frame*.
5 A frame in snooker is the wooden triangle inside which the balls are arranged at the beginning of a game; also a single game in which all the balls are potted.
6 A frame in a cinema film is one of the many separate photographs of which it is made up.
7 (verb) To frame a picture means to put it into a frame, e.g. *a framed photograph*.
8 The language something is framed in is the language used to express it.

framework, frameworks
1 (noun) A framework is a structure acting as a support or frame.
2 A framework of rules, beliefs, or ideas is a set of them which you use to decide what to do.

franc, francs
(noun) The franc is the main unit of currency in France, Belgium, Switzerland, and some other countries. A franc is worth 100 centimes.

franchise, franchises
1 (noun) The franchise is the right to vote in an election, e.g. *the extension of the franchise to all the adult population*.
2 A franchise is the right given by a company to someone to allow them to sell its goods or services.
[from Old French *franc* meaning 'free']

frank, franker, frankest
(adjective) If you are frank, you say things in an open and honest way.
frankly (adverb), **frankness** (noun).
[from Old French *franc* meaning 'free']

Similar words: open, candid

frankfurter, frankfurters
(noun) A frankfurter is a type of sausage, originally a speciality of Frankfurt in Germany.

frantic
(adjective) If you are frantic, you behave in a wild, desperate way because you are anxious or frightened.
frantically (adverb).
[from Greek *phrenitikis* meaning 'delirious']

fraternal
(adjective) Fraternal is used to describe friendly actions and feelings between groups of people, e.g. *We send our fraternal greetings to our British comrades*.
[from Latin *frater* meaning 'brother']

fraternity, fraternities
1 (noun) Fraternity is friendship between groups of people.
2 You can refer to a group of people with something in common as a particular fraternity, e.g. *the banking fraternity*.

fraternize, fraternizes, fraternizing, fraternized; also spelled **fraternise**

(verb) To fraternize with someone means to associate with them in a friendly way.
fraternization (noun).

fraud, frauds
1 (noun) Fraud is the crime of getting money by deceit or trickery.
2 A fraud is something that deceives people in an illegal or immoral way.
3 Someone who is a fraud is not what they pretend to be.
[from Latin *fraus* meaning 'deception']

fraudulent
(adjective) dishonest or deceitful, e.g. *a fraudulent promise*.
fraudulently (adverb), **fraudulence** (noun).

fraught
(adjective) If something is fraught with problems or difficulties, it is full of them, e.g. *The way ahead is fraught with danger*.

fray, frays, fraying, frayed
1 (verb) If cloth or rope frays, its threads or strands become worn and it is likely to tear or break.
2 (noun) You can refer to a fight or argument as the fray.
[from French *frayer* meaning 'to rub']

freak, freaks
1 (noun) A freak is someone whose appearance or behaviour is very unusual.
2 (adjective and noun) A freak event is very unusual and unlikely to happen, e.g. *My mother died in a freak accident, struck by lightning*.

freakish
(adjective) very odd and unusual, e.g. *a freakish-looking man*.
freakishly (adverb), **freakishness** (noun).

freckle, freckles
(noun) Freckles are small, light brown spots on someone's skin, especially their face.
freckled (adjective).

free, freer, freest; frees, freeing, freed
1 (adjective) not restricted, controlled, or limited, e.g. *the free movement of labour... a free press*.
2 Someone who is free is no longer a prisoner, e.g. *Your husband is a free man*.
3 To be free of something unpleasant means not to have it, e.g. *The area is now free of pollution*.
4 If someone is free, they are not busy or occupied. If a place, seat, or machine is free, it is not occupied or not being used, e.g. *Are you free for lunch?*
5 If something is free, you can have it without paying for it.
6 (verb) If you free something that is fastened or trapped, you release it, e.g. *He managed to free his hands*.
7 When a prisoner is freed, he or she is released.

Similar words: (sense 2) liberated, at liberty, on the loose
(sense 5) complimentary, gratis, on the house
(sense 6) release
(sense 7) liberate, emancipate, turn loose, release

freedom

1 (noun) If you have the freedom to do something, you have the scope or are allowed to do it, e.g. *freedom of speech.*
2 When prisoners gain their freedom, they escape or are released.
3 When there is freedom from something unpleasant, people are not affected by it, e.g. *freedom from hunger.*

Similar words: (sense 2) liberty, release, emancipation

free-for-all, free-for-alls

(noun) A free-for-all is a disorganized fight, argument, or attempt to get something, which everyone joins in, e.g. *a free-for-all on wage bargaining.*

freehand

(adjective and adverb) A freehand drawing is done without instruments such as a ruler or compasses.

freehold, freeholds

(noun) The freehold of a house or piece of land is the right to own it for life without conditions.

freelance

(adjective and adverb) A freelance journalist or photographer is not employed by one organization, but is paid for each job he or she does.

freely

(adverb) Freely means without restriction, e.g. *Goods were allowed to move freely from one state to another.*

Freemason, Freemasons

(noun) A Freemason is a member of a large secret society whose members promise to help each other.
Freemasonry (noun).

free-range

(adjective) Free-range eggs are laid by hens that can move and feed freely on an area of open ground.

freesia, freesias

(noun) A freesia is a plant with brightly-coloured, sweet-scented tubular flowers.

freestyle

(noun) Freestyle refers to sports competitions, especially swimming, in which competitors can use any style or method.

free will

(phrase) If you do something **of your own free will**, you do it by choice and not because you are forced to.

freeze, freezes, freezing, froze, frozen

1 (verb) When a liquid freezes, it becomes solid because it is very cold.
2 If you freeze, you suddenly become still and quiet, because there is danger.
3 If you freeze food, you put it in a freezer to preserve it.
4 When wages or prices are frozen, they are officially prevented from rising.
5 (noun) A wage or price freeze is an official action taken to prevent wages or prices from rising.
6 A freeze is a period of freezing weather.

freezer, freezers

(noun) A freezer is a large refrigerator which runs at a specially low temperature in order to freeze and store food for a long time.

freezing

(adjective) extremely cold.

freight

(noun) Freight is goods moved by lorries, ships, or other transport; also the moving of these goods, e.g. *freight charges.*

freighter, freighters

(noun) A freighter is a ship or aeroplane that carries freight.

French

1 (adjective) belonging or relating to France.
2 (noun) French is the main language spoken in France, and is also spoken by many people in Belgium, Switzerland, and Canada.

French bean, French beans

(noun) French beans are green pods eaten as a vegetable, which grow on a climbing plant with white or mauve flowers.

French Canadian, French Canadians

(noun) A French Canadian is a Canadian whose main language is French. Most French Canadians live in the province of Quebec.

French horn, French horns

(noun) A French horn is a brass musical wind instrument consisting of a tube wound in a circle.

Frenchman, Frenchmen

(noun) A Frenchman is a man who comes from France.
Frenchwoman (noun).

french window, french windows

(noun) French windows are glass doors that lead into a garden or onto a balcony.

frenetic

(adjective) Frenetic behaviour is wild, excited, and uncontrolled.
frenetically (adverb).
[from Greek *phrenitikis* meaning 'delirious']

frenzy, frenzies

(noun) If someone is in a frenzy, their behaviour is wild and uncontrolled.
frenzied (adjective).

Similar words: fever, derangement

frequency, frequencies

1 (noun) The frequency of an event is how often it happens, e.g. *Serious disasters are happening with increasing frequency.*
2 The frequency of a sound or radio wave is the rate at which it vibrates.
3 In statistics, the frequency of a particular class is the number of individuals in it.

frequent, frequents, frequenting, frequented

1 (adjective) often happening, e.g. *His visits were frequent... They move at frequent intervals.*

2 (verb) If you frequent a place, you go there often.
frequently (adverb), **frequenter** (noun).
[from Latin *frequens* meaning 'occurring often']

fresco, frescoes
(noun) A fresco is a picture painted on a plastered wall while the plaster is still wet.
[from Italian *fresco* meaning 'fresh']

fresh, fresher, freshest
1 (adjective) A fresh thing replaces a previous one, or is added to it, e.g. *He poured himself a fresh drink... fresh instructions.*
2 Fresh food is newly made or obtained, and not tinned or frozen.
3 Fresh water is not salty, for example the water in a stream.
4 If the weather is fresh, it is fairly cold and windy.
5 If you are fresh from something, you have experienced it recently, e.g. *a young man fresh from university.*
freshly (adverb), **freshness** (noun).

freshen, freshens, freshening, freshened
(verb) To freshen something means to make it cleaner and more pleasant.

fresher, freshers
(noun) A fresher is a first-year student at university.

freshwater
1 (adjective) A freshwater lake or pool contains water that is not salty.
2 A freshwater creature lives in a river, lake, or pool that is not salty.

fret, frets, fretting, fretted
1 (verb) If you fret about something, you worry about it.
2 (noun) The frets on a stringed instrument, such as a guitar, are the metal ridges across its neck.
fretful (adjective), **fretfully** (adverb).
[from Old English *fretan* meaning 'to gnaw at']

fret saw, fret saws
(noun) A fret saw is a fine-toothed saw with a narrow blade for cutting designs in thin wood or metal.

Freudian slip, Freudian slips
(noun) A Freudian slip is something that you say or do that reveals your unconscious thoughts.

friar, friars
(noun) A friar is a member of a Catholic religious order.
[from Latin *frater* meaning 'brother'] ·

fricassee, fricassees (pronounced frik-a-**see**)
(noun) A fricassee consists of pieces of cooked meat served in a white sauce.

friction
1 (noun) Friction is the force that prevents things from moving freely when they rub against each other.
2 Friction between people is disagreement and quarrels.
frictional (adjective).
[from Latin *fricare* meaning 'to rub']

Friday, Fridays
(noun) Friday is the day between Thursday and Saturday.
[from Old English *Frigedæg* meaning 'Freya's day'. Freya was the Norse goddess of love]

fridge, fridges
(noun) A fridge is the same as a refrigerator.

friend, friends
(noun) Your friends are people you know well and like to spend time with.

Similar words: chum, pal, companion, crony

friendly, friendlier, friendliest
1 (adjective) If you are friendly to someone, you behave in a kind and pleasant way to them.
2 People who are friendly with each other like each other and enjoy spending time together.
friendliness (noun).

Similar words: (sense 1) genial, affable, amiable, amicable, cordial

friendship, friendships
1 (noun) Your friendships are the special relationships that you have with your friends.
2 Friendship is the state of being friends with someone.

Similar words: (sense 2) friendliness, camaraderie, closeness, amity

frieze, friezes
(noun) A frieze is a strip of decoration, carving, or pictures along the top of a wall.

frigate, frigates
(noun) A frigate is a small, fast warship.

fright
(noun) Fright is a sudden feeling of fear.

frighten, frightens, frightening, frightened
(verb) If something frightens you, it makes you afraid.
frightened (adjective), **frightening** (adjective).

frightful
(adjective) very bad or unpleasant, e.g. *The smell was frightful.*
frightfully (adverb).

frigid
(adjective) Frigid behaviour is cold and unfriendly, e.g. *She got a frigid reception.*
frigidly (adverb), **frigidity** (noun).
[from Latin *frigidus* meaning 'cold']

frill, frills
(noun) A frill is a strip of cloth with many folds, attached to something as a decoration.
frilly (adjective).

fringe, fringes
1 (noun) If someone has a fringe, their hair is cut to hang over their forehead.
2 A fringe is also a decoration on clothes and other objects, consisting of a row of hanging strips or threads.
3 The fringes of a place are the parts farthest from its centre, e.g. *the western fringe of London.*
4 The fringes of an activity or organization are

its most experimental or extreme elements, e.g.
the radical fringe of the Labour Party.
fringed (adjective).

frisk, frisks, frisking, frisked
1 (verb; an informal use) If someone frisks you,
they search you quickly with their hands to see
if you are hiding a weapon in your clothes.
2 When animals frisk, they run around in a
happy, energetic way, e.g. *His dogs frisked
around him.*
[Sense 2 is from Old French *frisque* meaning
'lively']

frisky, friskier, friskiest
(adjective) A frisky animal or child is energetic
and wants to have fun.
friskily (adverb), **friskiness** (noun).

fritter, fritter, frittering, frittered
1 (noun) Fritters consist of food dipped in batter
and fried, e.g. *banana fritters.*
2 (verb) If you fritter away your time or money,
you waste it on unimportant things.
[from Latin *frigere* meaning 'to fry']

frivolous
(adjective) Someone who is frivolous behaves in
a silly or light-hearted way, especially when
they should be serious or sensible.
frivolously (adverb), **frivolity** (noun).
[from Latin *frivolus* meaning 'trifling' or
'worthless']

Similar words: flighty, empty-headed

frizzy, frizzier, frizziest
(adjective) Frizzy hair has stiff, wiry curls.

frock, frocks
(noun; an old-fashioned word) A frock is a dress.

frog, frogs
(noun) A frog is a small amphibious creature
with smooth skin, prominent eyes, and long back
legs which it uses for jumping.

frogman, frogmen
(noun) A frogman is someone who works
underwater wearing rubber clothing and
breathing equipment.

frogmarch, frogmarches, frogmarching,
frogmarched
(verb) If you are frogmarched somewhere, you
are forced to walk there by two people, each
holding one of your arms.

frolic, frolics, frolicking, frolicked
(verb) When animals or children frolic, they run
around and play in a lively way.
frolicsome (adjective).
[from Dutch *vrolijk* meaning 'joyful']

Similar words: frisk, romp, caper, cavort, prance

from
1 (preposition) You use from to say what the
source, origin, or starting point of something is,
e.g. *smoke from a small fire... She came from
Ilford.*
2 If you take something from an amount, you
reduce the amount by that much, e.g. *This will be
deducted from your pension.*

3 You also use from when stating the range of
something, e.g. *The process takes from two to
three weeks.*

frond, fronds
(noun) Fronds are long feathery leaves.
[from Latin *frons* meaning 'leaf']

front, fronts, fronting, fronted
1 (noun) The front of something is the part that
faces forward.
2 In a war, the front is the place where two
armies are fighting.
3 In meteorology, a front is the line where a mass
of cold air meets a mass of warm air.
4 A front is an outward appearance, often one
that is false, e.g. *He put on a bold front... The
hotel is just a front for organized prostitution.*
5 (verb) If a building fronts something, it is next
to it and faces it, e.g. *This beach has two
restaurants fronting it.*
6 (phrase) **In front** means ahead or further
forward.
7 If you do something **in front of** someone, you do
it when they are present.
frontal (adjective).
[from Latin *frons* meaning 'forehead']

frontage, frontages
(noun) A frontage of a building is one of its walls
that faces a street.

frontier, frontiers
(noun) A frontier is a border between two
countries.

frontispiece, frontispieces
(noun) The frontispiece of a book is a picture
opposite the title page.

frost, frosts
(noun) When there is a frost, the temperature
outside falls below freezing.

frostbite
(noun) Frostbite is damage to your fingers, toes,
or ears caused by extreme cold.
frostbitten (adjective).

frosted
(adjective) Frosted glass has a rough surface
that you cannot see through.

frosty, frostier, frostiest
1 (adjective) If it is frosty, the temperature
outside is below freezing point.
2 If someone is frosty, they are unfriendly or
disapproving.
frostily (adverb).

froth, froths, frothing, frothed
1 (noun) Froth is a mass of small bubbles on the
surface of a liquid.
2 (verb) If a liquid froths, small bubbles appear
on its surface.
frothy (adjective).

frown, frowns, frowning, frowned
1 (verb) If you frown, you move your eyebrows
closer together, because you are annoyed,
worried, or concentrating.
2 (noun) A frown is a cross expression on
someone's face.

froze the past tense of **freeze.**

frozen

1 Frozen is the past participle of **freeze**.
2 (adjective) If you are frozen, you are extremely cold.

Similar words: (sense 2) icy, ice-cold

frugal

1 (adjective) Someone who is frugal spends very little money.
2 A frugal meal is small and cheap.
frugally (adverb), **frugality** (noun).
[from Latin *frugalis* meaning 'sparing']

Similar words: (sense 1) sparing; (sense 2) meagre

fruit, fruits

1 (noun) A fruit is the part of a plant that develops after the flower and contains the seeds. Many fruits are edible.
2 (plural noun) The fruits of something are its good results, e.g. *We can at last enjoy the fruits of our labours.*
[from Latin *fructus* meaning 'produce' or 'benefit']

fruitful

(adjective) Something that is fruitful has good and useful results, e.g. *a fruitful discussion.*
fruitfully (adverb), **fruitfulness** (noun).

fruition (pronounced froo-**ish**-on)

(noun; a formal word) When something comes to fruition, it has the results that were intended, e.g. *At last his efforts were coming to fruition.*

fruitless

(adjective) Something that is fruitless does not achieve anything, e.g. *their fruitless search.*
fruitlessly (adverb), **fruitlessness** (noun).

fruit machine, fruit machines

(noun) A fruit machine is a coin-operated gambling machine which pays out money when a particular series of symbols, usually fruit, appear on a screen.

fruity, fruitier, fruitiest

1 (adjective) Something that is fruity smells or tastes of fruit.
2 A fruity voice or laugh is pleasantly rich and deep.

frump, frumps

(noun) If you describe a woman as a frump, you mean that she dresses in a dull, old-fashioned way.
frumpish (adjective).

frustrate, frustrates, frustrating, frustrated

1 (verb) If something frustrates you, it prevents you doing what you want and makes you upset and angry, e.g. *The lack of money frustrated him.*
2 To frustrate something such as a plan means to prevent it, e.g. *They frustrated all changes of which they disapproved.*
frustrated (adjective), **frustrating** (adjective), **frustration** (noun).
[from Latin *frustrare* meaning 'to disappoint']

Similar words: (sense 2) foil, thwart, balk

fry, fries, frying, fried

1 (verb) When you fry food, you cook it in a pan containing hot fat or oil.
2 (noun) Fry are very small young fish.

fuchsia, fuchsias (pronounced fyoo-sha)

(noun) A fuchsia is a plant or small bush with pink, purple, or white flowers that hang downwards. It is named after the 16th century German botanist Leonhard Fuchs.

fuddled

(adjective) If you are fuddled, you are confused and cannot think clearly, e.g. *He was fuddled with drink.*

fuddy-duddy, fuddy-duddies

(noun; an informal word) A fuddy-duddy is someone who is very conservative and dull.

fudge, fudges, fudging, fudged

1 (noun) Fudge is a soft brown sweet made from butter, milk, and sugar.
2 (verb) If you fudge something, you avoid making clear or definite decisions or statements about it, e.g. *They're fudging the issue as usual.*

fuel, fuels, fuelling, fuelled

1 (noun) Fuel is a substance such as coal or petrol that is burned to provide heat or power.
2 (verb) A machine or vehicle that is fuelled by a substance works by burning the substance as a fuel, e.g. *boilers fuelled by coal.*

fug

(noun) A fug is an airless, smoky atmosphere.

fugitive, fugitives (pronounced fyoo-jit-tiv)

(noun) A fugitive is someone who is running away or hiding, especially from the police.
[from Latin *fugere* meaning 'to flee']

fugue, fugues (pronounced fyoog)

(noun) A fugue is a piece of music consisting of variations on a short melody.

fulcrum, fulcrums or fulcra

(noun) A fulcrum is the point at which something is balancing or pivoting.
[from Latin *fulcrum* meaning 'leg of couch']

fulfil, fulfils, fulfilling, fulfilled

1 (verb) If you fulfil a promise, hope, or duty, you carry it out or achieve it.
2 If something fulfils you, it gives you satisfaction.
fulfilling (adjective), **fulfilment** (noun).

full, fuller, fullest

1 (adjective) containing or having as much as it is possible to hold, e.g. *a full bottle of milk.*
2 complete or whole, e.g. *a return to full employment... my last full day in Warsaw.*
3 loose and made from a lot of fabric, e.g. *full sleeves... a full skirt.*
4 rich and strong, e.g. *a cheese with a good full flavour.*
5 (adverb) completely and directly, e.g. *The light was full upon me.*
6 (phrase) Something that has been done or described **in full** has been dealt with completely.
fullness (noun), **fully** (adverb).

Similar words: (sense 1) brimful, filled, chock-full, chock-a-block, replete, sated

full-blooded
1 (adjective) having great commitment and enthusiasm.
2 having ancestors of a single race or breed, e.g. *a full-blooded Cherokee Indian.*

full-blown
(adjective) complete and fully developed, e.g. *a full-blown military operation.*

full moon, full moons
(noun) The full moon is the moon when it appears as a complete circle.

full stop, full stops
(noun) A full stop is the punctuation mark (.) used at the end of a sentence and after an abbreviation or initial.

full-time
1 (adjective) involving work for the whole of each normal working week.
2 (noun) In games such as football, full time is the end of the match.

fully-fledged
(adjective) completely developed, e.g. *By the age of seventeen he was a fully-fledged atheist.*

fulminate, fulminates, fulminating, fulminated
(verb) If you fulminate against something, you criticize it angrily.
[from Latin *fulminare* meaning 'to send bolts of lightning']

fulsome
(adjective) exaggerated and elaborate, and often sounding insincere, e.g. *She fed his vanity with fulsome compliments and extravagant gifts.*

fumble, fumbles, fumbling, fumbled
(verb) If you fumble, you feel or handle something clumsily.

fume, fumes, fuming, fumed
1 (noun) Fumes are unpleasant-smelling gases and smoke, often toxic, that are produced by burning and by some chemicals.
2 (verb) If you are fuming, you are very angry.
[from Latin *fumus* meaning 'smoke']

fumigate, fumigates, fumigating, fumigated
(pronounced **fyoo**-mig-ate)
(verb) To fumigate a place means to use special smoke or gas to disinfect it.
fumigation (noun).

fun
1 (noun) Fun is pleasant, enjoyable and lighthearted activity or amusement.
2 (phrase) If you **make fun** of someone, you tease or ridicule them.

function, functions, functioning, functioned
1 (noun) The function of something is its purpose or role, e.g. *The main function of this committee is liaison.*
2 A function is a large formal dinner, reception, or party.
3 In maths, a function is a variable whose value

depends on the value of other independent variables. 'y is a function of x' is written y (x).
4 (verb) When something functions, it operates or works.
[from Latin *functus* meaning 'performed' or 'done']

functional
1 (adjective) relating to the way something works.
2 designed for practical use rather than for decoration or attractiveness, e.g. *functional modern furniture.*
3 working properly, e.g. *How long since the machine was functional?*

fund, funds, funding, funded
1 (noun) A fund is an amount of available money, usually for a particular purpose, e.g. *a disaster fund.*
2 A fund of something is a lot of it, e.g. *They have a fund of experience to draw on.*
3 (verb) Someone who funds something provides money for it, e.g. *schemes funded by the EEC.*
[from Latin *fundus* meaning 'estate']

Similar words: (sense 3) finance, support, sponsor, subsidize

fundamental, fundamentals
1 (adjective) basic and central, e.g. *the fundamental principles on which society is based... a fundamental error.*
2 (noun) The fundamentals of something are its most basic and important parts, e.g. *my inability to grasp the fundamentals of physics.*
[from Latin *fundamentum* meaning 'foundation' or 'base']

funeral, funerals (pronounced **fyoo**-ner-al)
(noun) A funeral is a religious service or ceremony for the burial or cremation of a dead person.
[from Latin *funus* meaning 'funeral']

funereal (pronounced few-**nee**-ree-al)
(adjective) depressing and gloomy.

fungicide, fungicides
(noun) A fungicide is a chemical used to kill or prevent fungus.

fungus, fungi or funguses
(noun) A fungus is a plant such as a mushroom or mould that does not have leaves and reproduces by spores.

funicular railway, funicular railways
(pronounced fyoo-**nik**-yoo-lar)
(noun) A funicular railway is a cable railway up a steep cliff or mountain side.
[from Latin *funiculus* meaning 'thin rope']

funk, funks, funking, funked
1 (verb; an old-fashioned informal use) If you funk something, you fail to do it because of fear.
2 (noun) Funk is a style of music with a strong rhythm based on jazz and blues.

funnel, funnels, funnelling, funnelled
1 (noun) A funnel is an open cone tapering to a narrow tube, used to pour substances into containers.

2 A funnel is also a metal chimney on a ship or steam engine.
3 (verb) If something is funnelled somewhere, it is directed through a narrow space into that place.
[from Latin *fundere* meaning 'to pour']

funny, funnier, funniest
1 (adjective) strange or puzzling, e.g. *It's funny that you met the same people.*
2 causing amusement or laughter, e.g. *a funny story.*
funnily (adverb).

Similar words: (sense 2) amusing, comical, comic, humorous, jocular, witty

funny bone, funny bones
(noun) Your funny bone is a sensitive area near your elbow which can give you a tingling sensation if you hit it accidentally.

fur, furs
1 (noun) Fur is the soft thick body hair of many animals.
2 A fur is a coat made from an animal's fur.
furry (adjective).

furbish, furbishes, furbishing, furbished
(verb) If you furbish something, you polish, paint, or repair it.

furious
1 (adjective) extremely angry.
2 involving great energy, effort, or speed, e.g. *the furious speed of technological development.*
furiously (adverb).
[from Latin *furiosus* meaning 'raving' or 'raging']

furl, furls, furling, furled
(verb) When you furl an umbrella or sail, you roll it up.

furlong, furlongs
(noun) A furlong is a unit of length equal to 220 yards or about 201.2 metres. Furlong originally referred to the length of the average furrow.

furnace, furnaces
(noun) A furnace is a container for a very large, hot fire used, for example, in the steel industry for melting ore.
[from Latin *furnus* meaning 'oven']

furnish, furnishes, furnishing, furnished
1 (verb) If you furnish a room, you put furniture into it.
2 (a formal use) If you furnish someone with something, you supply or provide it for them.

furnishings
(plural noun) The furnishings of a room or house are the furniture and fittings in it.

furniture
(noun) Furniture is movable objects such as tables, chairs and wardrobes.

Similar words: furnishings, effects

furore (pronounced fyoo-**roh**-ree)
(noun) A furore is an angry and excited reaction or protest.
[from Italian *furore* meaning 'rage']

furrier, furriers (rhymes with **worrier**)
(noun) A furrier is a person who makes or sells clothes made out of fur.

furrow, furrows, furrowing, furrowed
1 (noun) A furrow is a long, shallow trench made by a plough.
2 (verb) When someone furrows their brow, they frown.

further, furthers, furthering, furthered
1 a comparative form of **far**.
2 (adjective) additional or more, e.g. *A further five hundred pounds is needed.*
3 (verb) If you further something, you help it to progress, e.g. *This success will certainly further your career.*

Similar words: (sense 3) promote, advance, champion

further education
(noun) Further education is education at a college after leaving school, but not at a university or polytechnic. Compare **higher education**.

furthermore
(adverb; a formal use) used to introduce additional information, e.g. *There is no record of such a letter. Furthermore it is company policy never to send such letters.*

furthest a superlative form of **far**.

furtive
(adjective) secretive, sly and cautious, e.g. *a furtive glance.*
furtively (adverb).
[from Latin *furtum* meaning 'theft' or 'deceit']

fury
(noun) Fury is violent or extreme anger.
[from Latin *furia* meaning 'madness']

fuse, fuses, fusing, fused
1 (noun) In a plug or electrical appliance, a fuse is a safety device consisting of a piece of wire which melts to stop the electric current if a fault occurs.
2 In some types of simple bomb, a fuse is a long cord attached to the bomb which is lit to detonate it.
3 (verb) When an electrical appliance fuses, it stops working because the fuse has melted to protect it.
4 If two substances fuse, they join by melting together, e.g. *All they rescued were some gold coins that had fused together in the blaze.*
[from Latin *fundere* meaning 'to melt']

fuselage, fuselages (pronounced **fyoo**-zil-ahj)
(noun) The fuselage of an aeroplane or rocket is its main part.

fusillade (pronounced **fyoo**-zil-ade)
(noun) A fusillade of shots is a large number of them fired at the same time.

fusion
1 (noun) Fusion is what happens when two substances join by melting together.
2 Fusion is also nuclear fusion.

fuss, fusses, fussing, fussed
1 (noun) Fuss is unnecessarily anxious or excited behaviour.
2 (verb) If someone fusses, they behave with unnecessary anxiety and concern for unimportant things.

Similar words: (sense 1) to-do, commotion, bother, ado, palaver

fussy, fussier, fussiest
1 (adjective) likely to fuss a lot, e.g. *Feeling overanxious and fussy I began to question her further.*
2 with too much elaborate detail or decoration, e.g. *fussy lace curtains.*
fussily (adverb).

Similar words: (sense 1) finicky, pernickety, particular, choosy, faddy, fastidious

fusty, fustier, fustiest
(adjective) smelling stale and mouldy, e.g. *a small and fusty bachelor flat.*

futile
(adjective) having no chance of success, e.g. *It is futile to speculate.*
futility (noun).
[from Latin *futilis* meaning 'worthless']

Similar words: pointless, useless, vain, to no avail, unavailing, worthless

future, futures
1 (noun) The future is the period of time after the present.
2 Something that has a future is likely to succeed, e.g. *Does solar power have a future in Britain?*
3 (adjective) relating to or occurring at a time after the present, e.g. *What are your future plans?*
4 The future tense of a verb is the form used to express something that will happen in the future. [from Latin *futurum* meaning 'what is yet to be']

futuristic
(adjective) very modern and strange, as if belonging to a time in the future, e.g. *futuristic buildings.*

fuzz
1 (noun) Fuzz is short fluffy hair.
2 (an informal use) The fuzz are the police.

fuzzy, fuzzier, fuzziest
(adjective) A fuzzy picture or image is unclear or blurred.

G

g an abbreviation for 'grams'.

gabble, gabbles, gabbling, gabbled
1 (verb) If you gabble, you talk so fast that it is difficult for people to understand you.
2 (noun) Gabble is very fast talk that is difficult to understand.

gaberdine, gaberdines (pronounced gab-er-**deen**)
(noun) Gaberdine is thick, heavy cloth, used for making coats; also used of a coat made of this cloth.
[from Old French *gauvardine* meaning 'pilgrim's garment']

gable, gables
(noun) Gables are the triangular parts at the top of the outside walls at each end of a house.
gabled (adjective).

gad, gads, gadding, gadded
(verb) If you gad about, you go to lots of different places enjoying yourself.

gadget, gadgets
(noun) A gadget is a small machine or tool.
gadgetry (noun).

Similar words: appliance, contraption, device

Gaelic (pronounced **gay**-lik)
(noun) Gaelic is a language spoken in some parts of Scotland and Ireland.

gaffe, gaffes (pronounced **gaf**)
(noun) A gaffe is a social blunder or mistake.

gaffer, gaffers
(noun; an informal word) A gaffer is a boss.

gag, gags, gagging, gagged
1 (noun) A gag is a strip of cloth that is tied round or put inside someone's mouth in order to stop them speaking.
2 (verb) To gag someone means to put a gag round or in their mouth.
3 (noun; an informal use) A gag is also a joke told by a comedian.
4 (verb) If you gag, you choke and nearly vomit.

gaga (pronounced **gah**-gah)
(adjective; an informal word) senile, e.g. *I may be seventy-seven but I'm not completely gaga.*

gaggle, gaggles
1 (noun) A gaggle is a group of geese.
2 (an informal use) A gaggle is a noisy group, e.g. *a gaggle of schoolgirls.*
[from Old German *gagen* meaning 'to cry like a goose']

gaiety (pronounced **gay**-yet-tee)
(noun) Gaiety is liveliness and fun.

gaily
(adverb) in a happy and cheerful way.

gain, gains, gaining, gained
1 (verb) If you gain something, you get it gradually, e.g. *The speaker began to gain confidence.*
2 (noun) A gain is an increase, e.g. *a weight gain.*

3 (verb) If you gain from a situation, you get some advantage from it.
4 (noun) Gain is an advantage that you get for yourself, e.g. *He did it for financial gain.*
5 (verb) If a clock or watch gains, it is going too fast.
6 If you gain on someone, you gradually catch them up.

gainsay, gainsaying, gainsaid
(verb; a formal word) If there is no gainsaying something or if it cannot be gainsaid, it is true and cannot be denied.

gait, gaits
(noun) Someone's gait is their way of walking, e.g. *his unsteady gait.*

gaiter, gaiters
(noun) Gaiters are coverings, made of cloth or leather, for the lower part of the legs.

gala, galas
(noun) A gala is a special public celebration, entertainment, or performance, e.g. *a charity gala night at the Royal Opera House.*
[from Old French *galer* meaning 'to make merry']

galaxy, galaxies
(noun) A galaxy is an enormous group of stars that extends over many millions of miles. The galaxy to which the earth's solar system belongs is called the Milky Way.
galactic (adjective).
[from Greek *gala* meaning 'milk']

gale, gales
(noun) A gale is an extremely strong wind.

gall, galls, galling, galled (rhymes with **ball**)
1 (noun) If someone has the gall to do something, they have enough courage or impudence and daring to do it, e.g. *He had the gall to ask for another loan.*
2 (verb) If something galls you, it makes you extremely annoyed.

gallant
1 (adjective) brave and honourable, e.g. *They have put up a gallant fight for pensioners' rights.*
2 polite and considerate towards women.
gallantly (adverb), **gallantry** (noun).
[from Old French *galer* meaning 'to make merry']

gall bladder, gall bladders
(noun) Your gall bladder is an organ in your body which stores bile and which is next to your liver.

galleon, galleons
(noun) A galleon is a large sailing ship used by the Spanish in the fifteenth and sixteenth centuries.

gallery, galleries
1 (noun) A gallery is a building or room where works of art are exhibited.
2 In a theatre or large hall, the gallery is a raised area at the back or sides, e.g. *the public gallery at Parliament.*

galley, galleys
1 (noun) A galley is a kitchen in a ship or aircraft.
2 A galley is also a ship, propelled by oars and sometimes sails, which was used in ancient and medieval times.

Gallic (pronounced **gal**-lik)
(adjective; a formal or literary word) French.

gallivant, gallivants, gallivanting, gallivanted
(verb) If you go gallivanting, you go out to have fun.

gallon, gallons
(noun) A gallon is a unit of liquid volume equal to eight pints or about 4.55 litres.

gallop, gallops, galloping, galloped
1 (verb) When a horse gallops, it runs very fast, so that all four feet are off the ground at the same time.
2 (noun) A gallop is a very fast run.

gallows
(noun) A gallows is a framework on which criminals used to be hanged.

gallstone, gallstones
(noun) A gallstone is a small painful lump that can develop in your gall bladder.

Gallup poll, Gallup polls
(noun) A Gallup poll is a survey of the public's opinions, often used to predict the results of an election.

galore
(adjective) in very large numbers, e.g. *restaurants and clubs galore*.
[from Irish Gaelic *go leór* meaning 'to sufficiency']

galoshes
(plural noun) Galoshes are waterproof rubber shoes which you wear over your ordinary shoes to stop them getting wet.
[from Old French *galoche* meaning 'wooden shoe']

galvanize, galvanizes, galvanizing, galvanized; also spelled galvanise
(verb; a formal word) If something galvanizes you, it spurs you into action, e.g. *The country was galvanized by the new President into greater self-reliance*.

galvanized or galvanised
(adjective) Galvanized metal has been coated with zinc by an electrical process to protect it from rust. 'Galvanized' comes from the name of the Italian physiologist Luigi Galvani (1737-98).

gambit, gambits
1 (noun) In chess, a gambit is an opening move in which a piece, usually a pawn, is sacrificed in order to gain an advantage.
2 A gambit is also something which someone does to gain an advantage in a situation.
[from Italian *gambetto* meaning 'a tripping up']

gamble, gambles, gambling, gambled
1 (verb) When people gamble, they bet money or play games like roulette in order to try and win money.
2 (noun) If you take a gamble, you take a risk in the hope of gaining an advantage.

3 (verb) If you gamble something, you risk losing it in the hope of gaining an advantage, e.g. *The company gambled everything on the new factory*. **gambler** (noun).

Similar words: (sense 1) bet, wager
(sense 3) hazard, stake

---

gambol, gambols, gambolling, gambolled
(verb; a literary word) If children or animals gambol, they run and jump about playfully.

game, games
1 (noun) A game is an enjoyable activity with a set of rules which is played by individuals or teams against each other.
2 A game is also an enjoyable imaginative activity played by small children, e.g. *a game of cops and robbers*.
3 (plural noun) Games are sports played at school or in a competition.
4 You might describe a way of behaving as a game when it is designed to gain advantage as if in a sporting contest, e.g. *these games that politicians play*.
5 (adjective; an informal use) Someone who is game is willing to try something unusual or difficult.
6 (noun) Game is wild animals or birds that are hunted for sport or for food.
7 (phrase) To **give the game away** means to reveal a secret.
gamely (adverb).

Similar words: (sense 1) diversion, pastime

---

gamekeeper, gamekeepers
(noun) A gamekeeper is a person employed to look after game animals and birds on a country estate.

gamesmanship
(noun) Gamesmanship is the practice of trying to win a game by using methods which are slightly underhand but not against the rules.

gamete, gametes (pronounced **gam**-meet)
(noun) In biology, a gamete is a cell that can unite with another during reproduction to form a new organism.
[from Greek *gametē* meaning 'wife']

gamma-ray, gamma-rays
(noun) In physics, a gamma-ray is a form of radiation of shorter wavelength than an X-ray.

gammon
(noun) Gammon is cured meat from a pig, similar to bacon.

gamut (pronounced **gam**-mut)
(noun; a formal word) The gamut of something is the whole range of things that can be included in it, e.g. *a rich gamut of facial expressions*.

gander, ganders
(noun) A gander is a male goose.

gang, gangs, ganging, ganged
1 (noun) A gang is a group of people who join together for some purpose, for example to commit a crime.

2 (verb; an informal use) If people gang up on you, they join together to oppose you.

gangling
(adjective) A gangling person is tall, thin, and clumsy.

gangplank, gangplanks
(noun) A gangplank is a plank used for boarding and leaving a ship or boat.

gangrene (pronounced **gang**-green)
(noun) Gangrene is decay in the tissues of part of the body, due to inadequate blood supply.
gangrenous (adjective).
[from Greek *gangraina* meaning 'ulcer' or 'festering sore']

gangster, gangsters
(noun) A gangster is a violent criminal who is a member of a gang.

gangway, gangways
1 (noun) A gangway is a space between rows of seats for people to walk down, for example in a cinema or theatre.
2 A ship's gangway is a gangplank.

gannet, gannets
(noun) A gannet is a large seabird which dives steeply with wings closed to catch fish.

gantry, gantries
(noun) A gantry is a tall metal structure used to support a crane or a set of signs or lights over a road or railway.

gaol another spelling of **jail**.

gaoler another spelling of **jailer**.

gap, gaps
1 (noun) A gap is a space between two things or a hole in something solid.
2 A gap between things, people, or ideas is a great difference between them, e.g. *the gap between rich and poor*.
[from Old Norse *gap* meaning 'chasm']

Similar words: (sense 1) breach, break, cleft, hole, opening, space

gape, gapes, gaping, gaped
1 (verb) If you gape at someone or something, you stare at them with your mouth open in surprise.
2 Something that gapes is wide open, e.g. *a gaping wound*.

garage, garages
1 (noun) A garage is a building where a car can be kept.
2 A garage is also a place where cars are repaired and where petrol is sold.
[from French *garer* meaning 'to dock' or 'to park']

garb
(noun; a formal word) Someone's garb is their clothes, e.g. *a convict in striped prison garb*.

garbage
(noun) Garbage is rubbish, especially household rubbish.
[from Anglo-French *garbelage* meaning 'removal of discarded matter']

garbled
(adjective) Garbled messages are jumbled and the details may be wrong.

Similar words: distorted, confused

garden, gardens
1 (noun) A garden is an area of land next to a house, where flowers, fruit, or vegetables are grown.
2 (plural noun) Gardens are a type of park in a town or around a large house.
gardening (noun).
[from Old German *gart* meaning 'enclosure']

gardener, gardeners
(noun) A gardener is a person who looks after a garden either as a job or as a hobby.

gardenia, gardenias (pronounced gar-**deen**-ya)
(noun) A gardenia is a shrub with very large white or yellow sweet-smelling flowers.
Gardenia is based on the name of the naturalist Alexander Garden.

gargantuan (pronounced gar-**gan**-tyoo-an)
(adjective; a literary word) enormous, e.g. *a gargantuan meal*.
[based on the giant Gargantua, a character created by the 16th century French writer Rabelais]

gargle, gargles, gargling, gargled
(verb) When you gargle, you rinse the back of your throat by putting some liquid in your mouth, tilting your head back, and making a bubbling sound at the back of your throat without swallowing the liquid.
[from Old French *gargouille* meaning 'throat']

gargoyle, gargoyles
(noun) A gargoyle is a large stone carving under the roof of a building such as a church, in the shape of an ugly person or animal.

garish (pronounced **gair**-rish)
(adjective) bright and harsh to look at, e.g. *a garish yellow tie*.
garishly (adverb), **garishness** (noun).

garland, garlands
(noun) A garland is a circle of flowers and leaves which is worn around the neck or head.

garlic
(noun) Garlic is the small white bulb of an onion-like plant which has a strong taste and smell. Garlic is used for flavouring in cooking.

garment, garments
(noun) A garment is a piece of clothing.
[from Old French *garnement* meaning 'equipment']

garner, garners, garnering, garnered
(verb; a formal word) If you garner information, you collect it, usually with some difficulty.

garnet, garnets
(noun) A garnet is a type of gemstone, usually red in colour.

garnish, garnishes, garnishing, garnished
1 (noun) A garnish is something such as a wedge of lemon or a sprig of parsley, that is used in cooking for decoration.

2 (verb) To garnish food means to decorate it with a garnish.

garret, garrets
(noun) A garret is an attic.

garrison, garrisons
(noun) A garrison is a group of soldiers stationed in a town in order to guard it; also used of the buildings in which these soldiers live.
[from Old French *garir* meaning 'to defend']

garrotte, garrottes, garrotting, garrotted
(pronounced gar-**rot**); also spelled **garotte**
(verb) To garrotte someone means to strangle them with a piece of wire.

garrulous (pronounced **gar**-rul-luss)
(adjective) very talkative.
[from Latin *garrire* meaning 'to chatter']

garter, garters
(noun) A garter is a piece of elastic worn round the top of a stocking or sock to stop it slipping.
[from Old French *garet* meaning 'bend of the knee']

gas, gases, gasses, gassing, gassed
The form **gases** is the plural of the noun. The verb forms are spelled with a double 's'.
1 (noun) A gas is any airlike substance that is not liquid or solid, such as oxygen or hydrogen or the gas used as a fuel in heating.
2 In American English, gas is petrol.
3 (verb) To gas people or animals means to kill them with poisonous gas.
[from Greek *khaos* meaning 'atmosphere']

gas chamber, gas chambers
(noun) A gas chamber is a room in which people or animals are killed with poisonous gas.

gaseous (pronounced **gas**-see-uss)
(adjective) consisting of gas or like gas.

gash, gashes, gashing, gashed
1 (noun) A gash is a long, deep cut.
2 (verb) If you gash something, you make a long, deep cut in it.
[from Old French *garser* meaning 'to scratch']

gasket, gaskets
(noun) A gasket is a piece of rubber or other material used to seal joints in a pipe to prevent gas escaping.

gas mask, gas masks
(noun) A gas mask is a large mask with special filters attached which people wear over their face to protect them from poisonous gas.

gasoline
(noun) In American English, gasoline is petrol.

gasometer, gasometers (pronounced gas-**som**-mit-ter)
(noun) A gasometer is a huge metal container used for storing gas.

gasp, gasps, gasping, gasped
1 (verb) If you gasp, you quickly draw in your breath through your mouth because you are surprised, shocked, or in pain.
2 (noun) A gasp is a sharp intake of breath through the mouth.
[from Old Norse *geispa* meaning 'to yawn']

gassy, gassier, gassiest
(adjective) full of gas, e.g. *gassy beer.*

gastric
(adjective) occurring in the stomach or involving the stomach, e.g. *gastric flu.*
[from Greek *gastēr* meaning 'stomach']

gastroenteritis (pronounced gast-roh-en-ter-**eye**-tiss)
(noun) Gastroenteritis is an illness in which a person's stomach becomes inflamed.

gastronomy (pronounced gast-**ron**-nom-mee)
(noun) Gastronomy is knowledge about good food and enjoyment of it.
gastronomic (adjective).

gastropod, gastropods
(noun) Gastropods are creatures such as snails, limpets, and slugs, which have a slimy body, one central foot on which they slide about, and usually a shell.

gasworks
(noun) A gasworks is a factory in which coal gas is made.

gate, gates
1 (noun) A gate is a barrier which can open and shut and is used to close the entrance to a garden or field.
2 The gate at a sports event such as a football match is the total number of people who have attended it.
[from Old Norse *gat* meaning 'opening' or 'passage']

gateau, gateaux (pronounced **gat**-toe)
(noun) A gateau is a rich layered cake with cream in it.

gatecrash, gatecrashes, gatecrashing, gatecrashed
(verb) If you gatecrash a party, you go to it when you have not been invited.

gateway, gateways
1 (noun) A gateway is an entrance through a wall, fence, or hedge where there is a gate.
2 Something that is considered to be the entrance to a larger or more important thing can be described as the gateway to the larger thing, e.g. *Bombay, gateway to India.*

gather, gathers, gathering, gathered
1 (verb) When people gather, they come together in a group.
2 If you gather a number of things, you collect them or bring them together in one place.
3 If something gathers speed, momentum, or strength, it gets faster or stronger.
4 If you gather that something is true, you learn that it is true, often from what someone says.
5 (plural noun) Gathers are tiny pleats, for example at the waist of a skirt.
gathered (adjective).

Similar words: (sense 1) assemble, collect, group
(sense 2) amass, assemble, collect, group

gathering, gatherings
(noun) A gathering is a meeting of people who have come together for a particular purpose.

gauche (pronounced **gohsh**)
(adjective; a formal word) socially awkward.
[from French *gauche* meaning 'left-handed']

gaudy, gaudier, gaudiest (pronounced **gaw**-dee)
(adjective) very colourful in a vulgar way.
gaudily (adverb), **gaudiness** (noun).

Similar words: flamboyant, flashy, garish, loud

gauge, gauges, gauging, gauged (pronounced **gayj**)
1 (verb) If you gauge something, you estimate it
or calculate it, e.g. *gauging what the people of
America wanted*.
2 (noun) A gauge is a piece of equipment that
measures the amount of something, e.g. *a fuel
gauge*.
3 A gauge is also something that is used as a
standard by which you judge a situation, e.g. *The
poor attendance at the meeting is a gauge of the
public's indifference*.
4 On railways, the gauge is the distance between
the two rails on a railway line.

gaunt
1 (adjective) A person who looks gaunt is thin
and bony.
2 Something that looks gaunt is bare and
unattractive, e.g. *the gaunt outline of the house*.

gauntlet, gauntlets
1 (noun) Gauntlets are long thick gloves worn
for protection, for example by motorcyclists.
2 (phrase) If you **throw down the gauntlet**, you
challenge someone.
3 If you **run the gauntlet**, you have an unpleasant
experience in which you are attacked or
criticized by people.
[from French *gant* meaning 'glove']

gauze
(noun) Gauze is very fine cloth with lots of tiny
holes in it which is often used in bandages.

gauzy
(adjective) light, thin, and almost transparent.

Similar words: filmy, diaphanous, wispy, sheer

gave the past tense of **give**.

gavel, gavels
(noun) A gavel is a small wooden hammer that a
chairman bangs on the table at meetings in order
to get people's attention.

gawky, gawkier, gawkiest
(adjective) tall, thin, and bony, and usually
moving very clumsily, e.g. *a gawky schoolgirl*.

gawp, gawps, gawping, gawped
(verb; an informal word) If you gawp at
something, you stare at it in a rude or stupid way.

gay, gays; gayer, gayest
1 (adjective) Someone who is gay is homosexual.
2 (noun) A gay is a homosexual man.
3 (adjective; an old-fashioned use) Gay people or
places are lively and full of fun.

gaze, gazes, gazing, gazed
(verb) If you gaze at something, you look
steadily at it for a long time.

gazelle, gazelles
(noun) A gazelle is a small antelope found in
Africa and Asia.
[from Arabic *ghazal*]

gazette, gazettes
(noun) A gazette is an official newspaper or
other publication.

gazump, gazumps, gazumping, gazumped
(verb) To gazump someone who has agreed to
buy a house at a certain price means to make a
higher offer, which is accepted by the seller.

GB an abbreviation for 'Great Britain'.

GCE, GCEs
The GCE is an examination which used to be
taken at Ordinary Level when leaving school and
at Advanced Level before going to University. It
is now taken in Britain at Advanced Level only.
GCE is an abbreviation for 'General Certificate
of Education'.

GCSE, GCSEs
The GCSE is an examination introduced in
Britain to replace the GCE Ordinary Level
examination in 1988. GCSE is an abbreviation
for 'General Certificate of Secondary Education'.

GDR an abbreviation for 'German Democratic
Republic'.

gear, gears, gearing, geared
1 (noun) A gear is a piece of machinery which
controls the rate at which energy is converted
into movement. Gears in vehicles control the
speed and power of the vehicle.
2 The gear for an activity is the equipment and
clothes that you need for it.
3 (verb) If someone or something is geared to a
particular event or purpose, they are prepared
or organized for it.

gearbox, gearboxes
(noun) A gearbox is the metal box that contains
the gears of a vehicle.

geese the plural of **goose**.

geezer, geezers
(noun; an informal word) A geezer is a man.

Geiger counter, Geiger counters (pronounced
gy-ger)
(noun) A Geiger counter is a scientific
instrument used to detect and measure
radioactivity.

geisha, geishas (pronounced **gay**-sha)
(noun) A geisha is a Japanese woman whose job
is to entertain men, for example by dancing and
making conversation.

gel, gels, gelling, gelled
1 (noun) A gel is a smooth soft jelly-like
substance, e.g. *hair gel*.
2 (verb) If a liquid gels, it turns into a gel.
3 If a vague thought or plan gels, it becomes
more definite.

gelatin or **gelatine** (pronounced **jel**-lat-tin)
(noun) Gelatin is a clear tasteless substance
used to make liquids firm and jelly-like. It is
obtained from meat and bones, and used in
cooking, medicine, and photography.

gelding, geldings (pronounced **gel**-ding)
(noun) A gelding is a horse which has been castrated.
[from Old Norse *geldingr*]

gelignite (pronounced **jel**-lig-nite)
(noun) Gelignite is an explosive substance similar to dynamite.

gem, gems
1 (noun) A gem is a jewel or precious stone.
2 You can describe something or someone that is extremely good, pleasing, or beautiful as a gem, e.g. *a gem of wisdom*.
[from Latin *gemma* meaning 'jewel']

Gemini (pronounced **jem**-in-nye)
(noun) Gemini is the third sign of the zodiac, represented by a pair of twins. People born between May 21st and June 20th are born under this sign.

gemstone, gemstones
(noun) A gemstone is a precious or semiprecious stone, especially one that has been cut and polished for use in jewellery.

gen
(noun; an informal word) The gen on something is information about it.

gender, genders
(noun) Gender is the sex of a person or animal, e.g. *the female gender*.

gene, genes (pronounced **jeen**)
(noun) A gene is one of the parts of a living cell which controls the physical characteristics of an organism, for example its eye colour. Genes are passed on from one generation to the next.

genealogy, genealogies (pronounced jeen-nee-**al**-loj-ee)
(noun) Genealogy is the study of the history of families, or the history of a particular family.
genealogical (adjective), **genealogist** (noun).
[from Greek *genea* meaning 'race']

general, generals
1 (adjective) relating to the whole of something or to most things in a group, rather than to separate parts, e.g. *general household expenses*.
2 true, suitable, or relevant in most situations, e.g. *a general rule*.
3 including or involving a wide range of different things, e.g. *a general store*.
4 having complete responsibility over a wide area of work or a large number of people, e.g. *a general manager*.
5 (noun) A general is an army officer of the rank immediately above lieutenant-general and immediately below field marshal.
6 (phrase) **In general** means usually.
generally (adverb).

Similar words: (senses 1 and 2) broad, overall

general election, general elections
(noun) A general election is an election for a new government, which all the people of a country may vote in.

generality, generalities
(noun) Generalities are statements that are very general and not detailed.

generalize, generalizes, generalizing, generalized; also spelled **generalise**
(verb) To generalize means to say that something is true in most cases, ignoring minor details.
generalization (noun).

general practitioner, general practitioners
(noun) A general practitioner is a doctor who works in the community rather than in a hospital.

generate, generates, generating, generated
(verb) To generate something means to create or produce it, e.g. *methods of generating electricity... Tourism will generate new jobs*.

generation, generations
(noun) A generation is all the people of about the same age; also the period of time between one generation and the next, usually considered to be about 25-30 years.

generator, generators
(noun) A generator is a machine which produces electricity from another form of energy such as wind or water power.

generic
(adjective) A generic term is a name that applies to all the members of a group of similar things.

generous
1 (adjective) A generous person is very willing to give money, time, or gifts.
2 Something that is generous is very large, e.g. *a generous helping of pudding*.
generously (adverb), **generosity** (noun).

Similar words: (sense 1) lavish, liberal
(sense 2) abundant, lavish, liberal, bountiful

genesis
(noun; a formal word) The genesis of something is its beginning.

genetics
(noun) Genetics is the science of the way that characteristics are passed on from generation to generation by means of genes.
genetic (adjective), **genetically** (adverb), **geneticist** (noun).

genial
(adjective) cheerful, friendly, and kind.
genially (adverb), **geniality** (noun).

genie, genies (pronounced **jee**-nee)
(noun) In stories from Arabia and Persia, a genie is a magical being that obeys the wishes of the person who controls it.
[from Arabic *jinni* meaning 'demon']

genitals
(plural noun) The genitals are the reproductive organs. Technical name: **genitalia**.
genital (adjective).

genitive
(noun and adjective) In the grammar of some languages, the genitive is the form of a noun that is used to indicate possession or some other kind of association between two things.

genius, geniuses
1 (noun) A genius is a highly intelligent, creative, or talented person.
2 Genius is great intelligence, creativity, or talent, e.g. *a man of genius.*

genocide (pronounced **jen**-nos-side)
(noun; a formal word) Genocide is the systematic murder of all members of a particular race or group.
[from Greek *genos* meaning 'race' and Latin *caedere* meaning 'to kill']

genre, genres (pronounced **jahn**-ra)
(noun; a formal word) A genre is a particular style in art, literature, or music.
[from Latin *genus* meaning 'type' or 'kind']

genteel
(adjective) excessively polite and refined.
[from French *gentil* meaning 'well-born']

gentian, gentians (pronounced **jen**-shn)
(noun) A gentian is a mountain plant with blue flowers.

Gentile, Gentiles (pronounced **jen**-tile)
(noun) A Gentile is a person who is not Jewish.
[from Latin *gentilis* meaning 'of the same family, race, or nation']

gentility
(noun) Gentility is excessive politeness and refinement.

gentle, gentler, gentlest
(adjective) mild and calm; not violent or rough, e.g. *a gentle person... a gentle breeze...a gentle hint.*
gently (adverb), **gentleness** (noun).

gentleman, gentlemen
(noun) A gentleman is a man from the upper middle classes, or a man who is polite and well-educated. Gentleman is also a polite way of referring to any man.
gentlemanly (adjective).
[from French *gentil* meaning 'well-born']

gentry
(plural noun) The gentry are people from the upper classes.

gents
(noun; an informal word) The gents is a public toilet for men.

genuflect, genuflects, genuflecting, genuflected (pronounced **jen**-yoo-flekt)
(verb) To genuflect means to bend one or both knees, especially in church, as a sign of respect.

genuine (pronounced **jen**-yoo-in)
1 (adjective) real and not false or pretend, e.g. *genuine surprise... a genuine antique.*
2 A genuine person is sincere and honest.
genuinely (adverb), **genuineness** (noun).

genus, genera (pronounced **jee**-nuss)
(noun) In biology, a genus is a class of animals or closely related plants.

geography
(noun) Geography is the study of the physical features of the earth, together with the climate, natural resources and population in different parts of the world.
geographic or **geographical** (adjective), **geographically** (adverb), **geographer** (noun).
[from Greek *gē* meaning 'earth' and -*graphia* meaning 'writing']

geology
(noun) Geology is the study of the earth's structure, especially the layers of rock and soil that make up the surface of the earth.
geological (adjective), **geologist** (noun).

geometric or **geometrical**
1 (adjective) consisting of regular lines and shapes, such as squares, triangles, and circles, e.g. *geometric tower blocks.*
2 involving geometry.

geometry
(noun) Geometry is the branch of mathematics that deals with lines, angles, curves and spaces.
[from Greek *geōmetrein* meaning 'to measure the land']

geophysics
(noun) Geophysics is the study of the earth's structure and physical processes such as earthquakes, the weather, and ocean currents.
geophysical (adjective), **geophysicist** (noun).

Georgian
(adjective) belonging to or typical of the time from 1714 to 1830, when George I to George IV reigned in Britain.

geranium, geraniums
(noun) A geranium is a garden plant with strongly scented leaves and clusters of red, pink, or white flowers.

gerbil, gerbils
(noun) A gerbil is a small rodent with long back legs. Gerbils come from desert regions and are often kept as pets.

geriatrics (pronounced jer-ree-at-riks)
(noun) Geriatrics is the medical care of old people.
geriatric (adjective).
[from Greek *gēras* meaning 'old age' and *iatrikos* meaning 'of healing']

germ, germs
1 (noun) A germ is a micro-organism that causes disease.
2 (a formal use) The germ of an idea, plan, or theory is the beginning of it.
[from Latin *germen* meaning 'sprig', 'bud', or 'seed']

German, Germans
1 (adjective) belonging or relating to Germany.
2 (noun) A German is someone who comes from Germany.
3 German is the main language spoken in Germany and Austria and is also spoken by many people in Switzerland.

germane
(adjective; a formal word) very important and relevant to a particular subject, e.g. *issues germane to socialist policy.*

Germanic
1 (adjective) typical of Germany or the German people.
2 The Germanic group of languages includes English, Dutch, German, Danish, Swedish, and Norwegian.

germanium
(noun) Germanium is a chemical element used in transistors and for hardening and strengthening alloys. Its atomic number is 32 and its symbol is Ge.

German measles
(noun) German measles is a contagious disease that gives you a cough, sore throat, and red spots. It is dangerous to unborn babies if their mothers catch it.

germicide, germicides
(noun) A germicide is a substance that kills germs.

germinate, germinates, germinating, germinated
1 (verb) When a seed germinates, it starts to grow.
2 When an idea or plan germinates, it starts to develop.
germination (noun).

gestation (pronounced jes-**tay**-shn)
(noun; a technical word) Gestation is the time during which a fetus is growing inside its mother's womb.
[from Latin *gerere* meaning 'to carry']

gesticulate, gesticulates, gesticulating, gesticulated (pronounced jes-**stik**-yoo-late)
(verb) If you gesticulate, you move your hands and arms around while you are talking.
gesticulation (noun).
[from Latin *gestus* meaning 'action']

gesture, gestures, gesturing, gestured
1 (noun) A gesture is a movement of your hands or head that conveys a message or feeling.
2 (verb) If you gesture, you move your hands or head in order to convey a message or feeling.
3 (noun) A gesture is also an action symbolizing something, e.g. *a demonstration that was a gesture of defiance against the government.*

get, gets, getting, got
1 (verb) 'Get' often means the same as 'become', e.g. *She began to get suspicious.*
2 If you get into a particular situation, you put yourself in that situation, e.g. *He got into trouble with the police.*
3 If you get something done, you persuade someone to do it, e.g. *She finally got the door fixed.*
4 If you get somewhere, you go there, e.g. *They were trying to get through the window.*
5 If you get something, you fetch it, receive it, or are given it, e.g. *Get me a glass of water... He's trying to get a flat.*
6 If you get a joke or get the point of something, you understand it, e.g. *Do you get my meaning?*
7 If you get a train, bus, or plane, you travel on it, e.g. *I got the 9.18 to London.*

Similar words: (sense 1) become, grow
(sense 5) acquire, obtain, procure, secure

get across
(phrasal verb) If you get an idea across, you make people understand it.

get at
1 (phrasal verb) If someone is getting at you, they are criticizing you in an unkind way.
2 If you ask someone what they are getting at, you are asking them to explain what they mean.

get away with
(phrasal verb) If you get away with something dishonest or naughty, you are not found out or punished for doing it.

get by
(phrasal verb) If you get by, you have just enough money, food, and clothing to live on.

get on
1 (phrasal verb) If two people get on well together, they like each other's company.
2 If you get on with a job or task, you do it.
3 If someone is getting on, they are old.
4 (phrase) **Getting on for** means the same as nearly, e.g. *He's getting on for forty.*

get over with
(phrasal verb) If you want to get something unpleasant over with, you want it to be finished quickly.

get through
1 (phrasal verb) If you get through to someone, you make them understand what you are saying.
2 If you get through to someone on the telephone, you succeed in talking to them.

getaway, getaways
(noun) A getaway is an escape made by criminals.

get-together, get-togethers
(noun; an informal word) A get-together is an informal meeting or party.

get-up, get-ups
(noun; an informal word) A get-up is a set of clothes.

geyser, geysers (pronounced **gee**-zer)
1 (noun) A geyser is a spring through which hot water and steam gush up in spurts.
2 A geyser is also a gas-fired water heater.
[from Old Norse *geysa* meaning 'to gush']

Ghanaian, Ghanaians (pronounced gah-**nay**-an)
1 (adjective) belonging or relating to Ghana.
2 (noun) A Ghanaian is someone who comes from Ghana.

ghastly, ghastlier, ghastliest
(adjective) extremely horrible and unpleasant, e.g. *a ghastly massacre... ghastly curtains.*
[from Old English *gaste* meaning 'to terrify']

gherkin, gherkins
(noun) A gherkin is a small pickled cucumber.

ghetto, ghettoes or ghettos
(noun) A ghetto is a part of a city where many poor people of a particular race live.
[from Italian *borghetto* meaning 'settlement outside the city walls']

ghost, ghosts
1 (noun) A ghost is the spirit of a dead person, believed to haunt people or places.
2 A ghost of something is a faint trace of it, e.g. *a ghost of a smile.*
ghostly (adjective).

Similar words: (sense 1) apparition, phantom, spectre, spirit, wraith

ghost writer, ghost writers
(noun) A ghost writer is a person who writes a book for another person who is credited as the author.

ghoul, ghouls (pronounced **gool**)
(noun) A ghoul is an evil spirit or demon, believed by Muslims to eat dead bodies.

ghoulish
(adjective) very interested in unpleasant things such as death and murder.

GHQ an abbreviation for 'General Headquarters'.

GI, GIs
(noun) A GI is an ordinary soldier in the US army.

giant, giants
1 (noun) In stories and legends, a giant is a huge person who is very strong, and often very cruel or stupid.
2 (adjective) much larger than other similar things, e.g. *a giant doughnut... the giant panda.*
[from Latin *gigas* meaning 'giant']

gibber, gibbers, gibbering, gibbered (pronounced jib-ber)
(verb) To gibber means to talk very fast in a confused way.

gibberish
(noun) Gibberish is speech that makes no sense at all.

gibbet, gibbets (pronounced jib-bit)
1 (noun; an old-fashioned word) A gibbet was a structure like a gallows from which the bodies of executed criminals were hung for the public to see.
2 A gibbet was also the gallows itself.
[from Old French *gibet*]

gibbon, gibbons
(noun) A gibbon is an ape with very long arms. Gibbons live in forests in southern Asia.

gibe, gibes, gibing, gibed; also spelled jibe
1 (noun) A gibe is an insulting remark.
2 (verb) To gibe means to make insulting remarks.
[from Old French *giber* meaning 'to treat roughly']

giblets (pronounced jib-lits)
(plural noun) Giblets are the internal organs of a chicken or other bird, which are removed before the bird is cooked.
[from Old French *gibelet* meaning 'stew made from game birds']

giddy, giddier, giddiest
(adjective) If you feel giddy, you feel unsteady on your feet because you are ill, tired, or overexcited.
giddily (adverb), **giddiness** (noun).

[from Old English *gydig* meaning 'mad' or 'possessed']

gift, gifts
1 (noun) A gift is a present.
2 A gift is also a natural skill or ability, e.g. *a gift for languages.*
[from Old English *gift* meaning 'dowry']

gifted
(adjective) having a special ability, e.g. *a gifted actress.*

gig, gigs
1 (noun; an informal use) A gig is a rock or jazz concert.
2 A gig was an open two-wheeled carriage pulled by a horse.

gigantic
(adjective) extremely large.

giggle, giggles, giggling, giggled
1 (verb) To giggle means to laugh in a nervous or embarrassed way.
2 (noun) A giggle is a short, nervous laugh.
giggly (adjective).

gild, gilds, gilding, gilded
(verb) To gild something means to cover it with a thin layer of gold.

gill, gills
1 (noun; pronounced **gil**) The gills of a fish are the organs on its sides which it uses for breathing.
2 (pronounced **jil**) A gill is a unit of liquid volume equal to one quarter of a pint or about 0.142 litres.

gilt, gilts
1 (noun) Gilt is a thin layer of gold.
2 (adjective) covered with a thin layer of gold, e.g. *paintings in gilt frames.*
3 (plural noun) Gilts are gilt-edged stocks or securities.

gilt-edged
(adjective) Gilt-edged stocks or securities are issued by the government for a very safe investment.

gimlet, gimlets (pronounced **gim-lit**)
(noun) A gimlet is a small tool with a pointed screw end used for making holes in wood.

gimmick, gimmicks
(noun) A gimmick is a device that is not really necessary but is used to attract interest, e.g. *fancy gimmicks sell cars.*
gimmicky (adjective).

gin
(noun) Gin is a strong, colourless alcoholic drink made from grain and juniper berries.

ginger
1 (noun) Ginger is a plant root with a hot spicy flavour, used for flavouring in cooking, often in a powder form.
2 (adjective) bright orangey-brown, e.g. *ginger hair.*

ginger ale
(noun) Ginger ale is a fizzy, ginger-flavoured drink, often mixed with alcoholic drinks.

ginger beer
(noun) Ginger beer is a sweet, fizzy, ginger-flavoured drink, made with sugar and yeast.

gingerbread
(noun) Gingerbread is a sweet, ginger-flavoured cake.

gingerly
(adverb) If you move gingerly, you move cautiously, e.g. *She opened the door gingerly.*
[from Old French *gensor* meaning 'dainty']

gingham
(noun) Gingham is checked cotton cloth.
[from Malay *ginggang* meaning 'striped cloth']

gipsy another spelling of gypsy.

giraffe, giraffes
(noun) A giraffe is a tall, four-legged African mammal with a very long neck and dark patches on its skin.
[from Arabic *zarafah* meaning 'giraffe']

gird, girds, girding, girded
(phrase) If you gird up your loins, you prepare to do something difficult or dangerous.

girder, girders
(noun) A girder is a large metal beam used in the framework of a structure.

girdle, girdles
(noun) A girdle is a woman's corset.
[from Old German *gurtila* meaning 'waist belt']

girl, girls
(noun) A girl is a female child.
girlish (adjective), girlhood (noun).

girlfriend, girlfriends
(noun) Someone's girlfriend is the woman or girl with whom they are having a romantic or sexual relationship.

giro, giros (pronounced jie-roh)
1 (noun) Giro is a system of transferring money from one account to another through a bank or post office.
2 A giro is a cheque received regularly from the government by unemployed or sick people.

girth
(noun) The girth of something is the measurement round it.
[from Old Norse *gjörth* meaning 'belt']

gist (pronounced jist)
(noun) The gist of a piece of writing or speech is the general meaning or most important points in it.

give, gives, giving, gave, given
1 (verb) If you give someone something, you hand it to them or provide it for them, e.g. *I gave him some money... He gave me a good education.*
2 Give is also used to express physical actions and speech, e.g. *He gave the door a push... She gave a lecture on French impressionists.*
3 If you give a party or a meal, you are the host at it.
4 If something gives, it collapses under pressure.
5 (noun) If material has give, it will bend or stretch when pulled or put under pressure.

6 (phrase) You use give or take to indicate that an amount you are mentioning is not exact, e.g. *two hours, give or take a few minutes.*
7 If something gives way to something else, it is replaced by it.
8 If something gives way, it collapses
9 If you give way to someone, you allow them to do what they want even though you do not agree with it.
10 If someone gives way when they are driving, they allow other traffic to go first.

Similar words: (sense 1) bestow, confer, grant, impart, present, provide

give in
(phrasal verb) If you give in, you admit that you are defeated.

give out
(phrasal verb) If something gives out, it stops working, e.g. *The engine has finally given out.*

give up
1 (phrasal verb) If you give something up, you stop doing it, e.g. *giving up smoking.*
2 If you give up, you admit that you cannot do something.
3 If you give someone up, you let the police know where they are hiding.

given
1 the past participle of give.
2 (adjective) fixed or specified, e.g. *At a given moment we cheered.*
3 (preposition and conjunction) Given a particular fact means taking this fact into account, e.g. *Given his handicap, he did very well.*
4 (adjective) Someone who is given to doing something has a habit of doing it, e.g. *a boy given to stealing.*

gizzard, gizzards
(noun) The gizzard is a bird's second stomach, which grinds and digests food.
[from Latin *gigeria* meaning 'cooked poultry entrails']

glacé (pronounced glass-say)
(adjective) Glacé fruits are fruits soaked and coated with sugar, e.g. *glacé cherries.*
[from French *glacé* meaning 'iced']

glaciation (pronounced glay-see-ay-shn)
(noun) In geography, glaciation is the condition of being covered with sheet ice.

glacier, glaciers (pronounced glass-yer)
(noun) A glacier is a huge frozen river of slow-moving ice.
[from Old French *glace* meaning 'ice']

glad, gladder, gladdest
(adjective) happy and pleased, e.g. *I'm glad you can come... I'll be glad to help.*
gladly (adverb), gladness (noun).
[from Old Norse *glathr* meaning 'bright' or 'joyful']

gladden, gladdens, gladdening, gladdened
(verb) If something gladdens you, it makes you happy and pleased.

glade, glades
(noun) A glade is a grassy space in a forest.

gladiator, gladiators
(noun) At the time of the Roman Empire, gladiators were slaves trained to fight with various weapons, often to the death.
[from Latin *gladius* meaning 'sword']

gladiolus, gladioli
(noun) A gladiolus is a garden plant with spikes of brightly coloured flowers on a long stem.
[from Latin *gladius* meaning 'sword']

glamour
(noun) The glamour of a fashionable or attractive person or place is the charm and excitement that they have, e.g. *the glamour of Hollywood*.
glamorous (adjective).

glance, glances, glancing, glanced
1 (verb) If you glance at something, you look at it quickly.
2 If one object glances off another, it hits it at an angle and bounces away in another direction.
3 (noun) A glance is a quick look.

gland, glands
(noun) A gland is one of several organs in your body, such as the thyroid gland and the sweat glands, which either produce chemical substances for your body to use, or which help to get rid of waste products from your body.
glandular (adjective).

glandular fever
(noun) Glandular fever is an infectious disease which causes a fever and swollen lymph glands.

glare, glares, glaring, glared
1 (verb) If you glare at someone, you look at them angrily.
2 (noun) A glare is a hard, angry look.
3 Glare is extremely bright light.
[from Old Dutch *glaren* meaning 'gleam']

glaring
(adjective) Something that is glaring is very obvious, e.g. *a glaring inconsistency*.
glaringly (adverb).

glass, glasses
1 (noun) Glass is a hard, transparent substance that is easily broken, used to make windows and bottles.
2 A glass is a container for drinking out of, made from glass.

glasses
(plural noun) Glasses are two lenses in a frame, which some people wear over their eyes to improve their eyesight.

glasshouse, glasshouses
(noun) A glasshouse is a large greenhouse.

glassy
1 (adjective) smooth and shiny like glass, e.g. *glassy water*.
2 A glassy look shows no feeling or expression.
glassily (adverb).

glaze, glazes, glazing, glazed
1 (noun) A glaze on pottery or on food is a smooth shiny surface.
2 (verb) To glaze pottery or food means to cover it with a glaze.
3 To glaze a window means to fit a sheet of glass into a window frame.

glaze over
(phrasal verb) If your eyes glaze over, they lose all expression, usually because you are bored.

glazed
(adjective) Someone who has a glazed expression looks tired and bored.

glazier, glaziers (pronounced **glay**-zee-er)
(noun) A glazier is a person whose job is fitting glass into windows.

gleam, gleams, gleaming, gleamed
1 (verb) If something gleams, it shines and reflects light.
2 (noun) A gleam is a pale shining light.
3 A gleam of an emotion is a brief expression of it on someone's face, e.g. *a gleam of pride*.
[from Old German *glimo* meaning 'brightness']

glean, gleans, gleaning, gleaned
(verb) To glean information means to collect it from various sources.
[from Old French *glener*]

glee
(noun; an old-fashioned word) Glee is joy and delight.
gleeful (adjective), **gleefully** (adverb).
[from Old Norse *gly*]

glen, glens
(noun) A glen is a deep, narrow valley, especially in Scotland or Ireland.
[from Gaelic *gleann*]

glib
(adjective) speaking or spoken quickly and confidently but without sincerity, e.g. *glib promises*.
glibly (adverb), **glibness** (noun).
[from Old German *glibberich* meaning 'slippery']

Similar words: slick, smooth-tongued

glide, glides, gliding, glided
1 (verb) To glide means to move smoothly, e.g. *canoes gliding along the river*.
2 When birds or aeroplanes glide, they float on air currents.
[from Old German *glitan*]

glider, gliders
(noun) A glider is an aeroplane without an engine, which flies by floating on air currents.

glimmer, glimmers, glimmering, glimmered
1 (noun) A glimmer is a faint, unsteady light.
2 A glimmer of a feeling or quality is a faint sign of it, e.g. *a glimmer of hope*.
3 (verb) If something glimmers, it produces a faint, unsteady light.

glimpse, glimpses, glimpsing, glimpsed
1 (noun) A glimpse of something is a brief sight of it, e.g. *I caught a glimpse of a running figure*.
2 (verb) If you glimpse something, you see it very briefly.

glint, glints, glinting, glinted
1 (verb) If something glints, it reflects quick flashes of light.
2 (noun) A glint is a quick flash of light.
3 A glint in someone's eye is a brightness expressing some emotion, e.g. *a glint of envy*.

glisten, glistens, glistening, glistened
(pronounced **gliss**-sn)
(verb) If something glistens, it shines or sparkles.

glitter, glitters, glittering, glittered
1 (verb) If something glitters, it shines in a sparkling way, e.g. *glittering stars*.
2 (noun) Glitter is sparkling light.

gloat, gloats, gloating, gloated
(verb) If you gloat, you cruelly show your pleasure about your own success or someone else's failure, e.g. *They were gloating over my failure to win a medal*.

global
1 (adjective) concerning the whole world, e.g. *global issues... protests on a global scale*.
2 involving or relating to all the parts or aspects of a situation, e.g. *a global picture of a pupil's progress*.

globe, globes
1 (noun) A globe is a spherical object, especially one with a map of the earth on it.
2 You can refer to the world as the globe.
[from Latin *globus*]

globetrotter, globetrotters
(noun) A globetrotter is someone who travels all over the world.

globule, globules (pronounced **glob**-yool)
(noun) A globule of a liquid is a very small round drop of it.
globular (adjective).
[from Latin *globulus* meaning 'small globe']

glockenspiel, glockenspiels (pronounced **glok**-ken-shpeel)
(noun) A glockenspiel is a percussion instrument consisting of metal bars played with small hammers.
[from German *Glocken* meaning 'bells' and *Spiel* meaning 'play']

gloom
1 (noun) Gloom is darkness or dimness.
2 Gloom is also a feeling of unhappiness or despair.
gloomy (adjective), **gloomily** (adverb).

glorify, glorifies, glorifying, glorified
(verb) If you glorify someone or something, you make them seem better or more important than they really are, e.g. *His book glorifies the war*.
glorification (noun).

glorious
1 (adjective) beautiful and impressive to look at, e.g. *glorious architecture*.
2 very pleasant and giving a feeling of happiness, e.g. *glorious weather*.
3 involving great fame and success, e.g. *a glorious victory*.
gloriously (adverb).

glory, glories, glorying, gloried
1 (noun) Glory is fame and admiration for an achievement.
2 A glory is something considered splendid or admirable, e.g. *glories of Venice*.
3 (verb) If you glory in something, you take great delight in it.
[from Latin *gloria*]

gloss, glosses, glossing, glossed
1 (noun) Gloss is a bright shine on a surface.
2 Gloss is also an attractive appearance which may hide less attractive qualities, e.g. *He added gloss and glamour to the play*.
3 (verb) If you gloss a word or idea, you give an explanation of it.
4 If you gloss over a problem or fault, you try to ignore it or deal with it very quickly.

Similar words: (sense 1) lustre, sheen

glossary, glossaries
(noun) A glossary is a list of explanations of specialist words, usually found at the back of a book.

glossy, glossier, glossiest
1 (adjective) smooth and shiny, e.g. *glossy hair*.
2 Glossy magazines and photographs are produced on expensive, shiny paper.
glossily (adverb), **glossiness** (noun).

Similar words: (sense 1) lustrous, sleek

glove, gloves
(noun) Gloves are coverings which you wear over your hands for warmth or protection.

glow, glows, glowing, glowed
1 (verb) If something glows, it shines with a dull, steady light, e.g. *cigarettes glowing in the dark*.
2 (noun) A glow is a dull, steady light.
3 (verb) If you are glowing, you look very happy or healthy.
4 (noun) A glow is also a strong feeling of pleasure or happiness.

glower, glowers, glowering, glowered (rhymes with **shower**)
(verb) If you glower, you stare angrily.

Similar words: scowl, glare

glowing
(adjective) A glowing description praises someone or something very highly, e.g. *I read glowing reports of his book*.

glow-worm, glow-worms
(noun) A glow-worm is a beetle with special organs which produce a greenish light.

glucose
(noun) Glucose is a type of sugar found in plants and that animals and people make in their bodies from food. Glucose provides energy.
[from Greek *glukus* meaning 'sweet']

glue, glues, gluing or **glueing, glued**
1 (noun) Glue is a substance used for sticking things together.

2 (verb) If you glue one object to another, you stick them together using glue.
gluey (adjective).

glum, glummer, glummest
(adjective) miserable and depressed.
glumly (adverb), **glumness** (noun).

glut, gluts
(noun) A glut of things is a greater quantity than is needed.

glutinous (pronounced **gloo**-tin-nuss)
(adjective) thick and sticky, e.g. *glutinous mud*.

glutton, gluttons
1 (noun) A glutton is a person who eats too much.
2 If you are a glutton for something, such as punishment or hard work, you seem very eager for it.
gluttonous (adjective), **gluttony** (noun).
[from Latin *gluttus* meaning 'greedy']

glycerine (pronounced **gliss**-er-in)
(noun) Glycerine is a thick, sweet liquid used in making medicines and explosives.
[from Greek *glukus* meaning 'sweet']

glycogen (pronounced **gly**-koh-jen)
(noun) Glycogen is a type of carbohydrate found in the cells of humans and animals, which can easily be converted to glucose.

GMT an abbreviation for **Greenwich Mean Time.**

gnarled (pronounced **nar**-ld)
(adjective) old, twisted, and rough, e.g. *gnarled tree trunks*.

gnash, gnashes, gnashing, gnashed (pronounced **nash**)
(verb) If you gnash your teeth, you grind them together because you are angry or in pain.
[from Old Norse *gnastan* meaning 'gnashing of teeth']

gnat, gnats (pronounced **nat**)
(noun) A gnat is a tiny flying insect that bites.

gnaw, gnaws, gnawing, gnawed (pronounced **naw**)
1 (verb) To gnaw something means to bite at it repeatedly.
2 If a feeling gnaws at you, it keeps worrying you, e.g. *gnawing doubts*.

gnome, gnomes (pronounced **nome**)
(noun) A gnome is a dwarflike old man in fairy stories.

gnu, gnus (pronounced **noo**)
(noun) A gnu is a large African antelope.
[from *nqu*, an African word]

go, goes, going, went, gone
1 (verb) If you go somewhere, you move or travel there.
2 You can use go to mean 'become', e.g. *He's going grey*.
3 You can use go to describe the state that someone or something is in, e.g. *He went barefoot*.
4 If something goes well, it is successful. If it goes badly, it is unsuccessful.
5 If you are going to do something, you will do it.
6 If a machine or clock goes, it works and is not broken.

7 You use go before giving the sound something makes or before quoting a poem, song, or saying, e.g. *The bell went ding-dong*.
8 If something goes on something or to someone, it is allotted to them.
9 If one thing goes with another, they are appropriate or suitable together.
10 If one number goes into another, it can be divided into it.
11 If you go back on a promise or agreement, you do not do what you promised or agreed.
12 If you go for something, you like it very much.
13 If someone goes for you, they attack you.
14 If you go in for something, you decide to do it as your job.
15 If you go into something, you examine it or you describe it in detail.
16 If you go out with someone, you have a romantic relationship with them.
17 If you go over something, you think about it or discuss it carefully.
18 (noun) A go is an attempt at doing something.
19 (phrase) If someone is **making a go** of something, they are successful at it.
20 If someone is always **on the go**, they are always busy and active.
21 To go means remaining, e.g. *One exam down, three to go!*

go down
1 (phrasal verb) If something goes down well, people like it. If it goes down badly, they do not like it.
2 If you go down with an illness, you catch it.

go off
1 (phrasal verb) If you go off someone or something, you stop liking them.
2 If a bomb goes off, it explodes.

go on
1 (phrasal verb) If you go on doing something, you continue to do it.
2 If you go on about something, you keep talking about it in a rather boring way.
3 Something that is going on is happening.
4 If you go on a piece of information, you base an opinion on it.

go through
1 (phrasal verb) If you go through an unpleasant event, you experience it.
2 If a law, agreement, or decision goes through, it is approved and becomes official.
3 If you go through with something, you do it even though it is unpleasant.

go under
(phrasal verb) If someone goes under, they fail.

goad, goads, goading, goaded
(verb) If you goad someone, you encourage them to do something by making them angry or excited, e.g. *She was goaded into resigning*.

go-ahead
(noun) If someone gives you the go-ahead for something, they give you permission to do it.

goal, goals
1 (noun) In games like football or hockey, the

goal is the space into which the players try to get the ball in order to score a point.
2 A goal is an instance of this.
3 Your goal is something that you hope to achieve.

goalkeeper, goalkeepers
(noun) In games like football or hockey, the goalkeeper is the player who stands in the goal and tries to stop the other team from scoring.

goat, goats
(noun) A goat is an animal with shaggy hair, a beard, and horns. Goats live in mountainous areas, but are sometimes kept on farms for their milk or meat.
[from Old English *gat* meaning 'female goat']

gob, gobs
1 (noun; an informal use) Your gob is your mouth.
2 A gob of something is a thick mass of it.
[Sense 1 is from Gaelic *gob* meaning 'beak' or 'bill'; sense 2 is from Old French *gobe* meaning 'lump']

gobble, gobbles, gobbling, gobbled
1 (verb) If you gobble food, you eat it very quickly.
2 When a turkey gobbles, it makes a loud gurgling sound.

Similar words: (sense 1) bolt, gorge, guzzle, wolf, scoff, devour

gobbledygook or gobbledegook
(noun) Gobbledygook is language that is impossible to understand because it is so formal or complicated.

go-between, go-betweens
(noun) A go-between is someone who carries messages between two people or two groups.

goblet, goblets
(noun) A goblet is a glass with a long stem and a base.

goblin, goblins
(noun) A goblin is an ugly, mischievous creature in fairy stories.

go-cart, go-carts
(noun) A go-cart is a small, low vehicle with wheels, which children ride in.

god, gods
1 (noun) The name God is given to the being who is worshipped by Christians, Jews, and Muslims as the creator and ruler of the world.
2 A god is any of the beings that are believed in many religions to have power over an aspect of life or a part of the world.
3 If someone is your god, you admire them very much.
4 (plural noun) In a theatre, the gods are the highest seats farthest from the stage.

godchild, godchildren
(noun) If you are someone's godchild, they agreed to be responsible for your religious upbringing when you were baptized in a Christian church.
goddaughter (noun), **godson** (noun).

goddess, goddesses
(noun) A goddess is a female god.

godless
(adjective; used showing disapproval) not believing in God.

godly, godlier, godliest
(adjective) deeply religious, e.g. *a godly existence*.
godliness (noun).

godparent, godparents
(noun) A person's godparent is someone who agrees to be responsible for their religious upbringing when they are baptized in a Christian church.
godfather (noun), **godmother** (noun).

godsend, godsends
(noun) A godsend is something that comes unexpectedly and helps you very much.

goggle, goggles, goggling, goggled
1 (verb; an informal use) If you goggle at something, you stare at it in amazement.
2 (plural noun) Goggles are special glasses that fit closely round your eyes to protect them.

going
1 (noun) The going is the conditions that affect your ability to do something, e.g. *Let's get out while the going is good*.
2 (adjective) The going rate is the usual and expected rate.
3 (phrase) A business that is a **going concern** is operating successfully.

going-over, goings-over
(noun; an informal word) If you give something a going-over, you give it a thorough examination.

goings-on
(plural noun) Goings-on are strange, amusing, or improper activities.

goitre (pronounced **goy**-ter)
(noun) Goitre is a disease of the thyroid gland which makes your neck swell.
[from Latin *guttur* meaning 'throat']

go-kart, go-karts
(noun) A go-kart is a very small motor vehicle with four wheels, used for racing.

gold
1 (noun) Gold is a valuable, yellow-coloured metallic element. It is used for making jewellery and as an international currency. Its atomic number is 79 and its symbol is Au.
2 Gold is also used to mean things that are made of gold.
3 (adjective) bright yellow.

golden
1 (adjective) gold in colour, e.g. *golden hair*.
2 made of gold, e.g. *a golden bangle*.
3 excellent or ideal, e.g. *a golden opportunity*.

golden rule, golden rules
(noun) A golden rule is a very important rule to remember in order to be able to do something successfully.

golden wedding, golden weddings
(noun) Someone's golden wedding is their fiftieth wedding anniversary.

goldfinch, goldfinches
(noun) A goldfinch is a common small bird with yellow and black wings and a red, white, and black head.

goldfish
(noun) A goldfish is a small orange-coloured fish. Goldfish are often kept in ponds or bowls.

goldsmith, goldsmiths
(noun) A goldsmith is a person whose job is making jewellery and other objects out of gold.

golf
(noun) Golf is a game in which players use special clubs to hit a small ball into holes that are spread out over a large area of grassy land.
golfer (noun).

golf course, golf courses
(noun) A golf course is an area of grassy land where people play golf.

golliwog, golliwogs
(noun) A golliwog is a doll made of soft material, with a black face and black hair.

gonad, gonads (pronounced **goh**-nad)
(noun; a technical word) A gonad is an organ in the body that produces sex cells, such as a testis or an ovary.
[from Greek *gonos* meaning 'seed']

gondola, gondolas (pronounced **gon**-dol-la)
(noun) A gondola is a long narrow boat used in Venice, which is propelled with a long pole.

gondolier, gondoliers (pronounced gon-dol-**leer**)
(noun) A gondolier is a person who stands at the back of a gondola and propels it with a long pole.

gone the past participle of **go**.

gong, gongs
(noun) A gong is a flat, circular piece of metal that is hit with a hammer to make a loud sound, often as a signal for something.
[a Malay word]

gonorrhoea (pronounced gon-nor-**ee**-a)
(noun) Gonorrhoea is a sexually transmitted disease causing a thick discharge from the sex organs.

goo
(noun; an informal word) Goo is any thick, sticky substance like paste.
gooey (adjective).

good, better, best; goods
1 (adjective) pleasant, acceptable, or satisfactory, e.g. *good weather... good food.*
2 skilful or successful, e.g. *good at maths.*
3 kind, thoughtful, and loving, e.g. *She's always been good to me.*
4 well-behaved, e.g. *Have the children been good?*
5 used to emphasize something, e.g. *a good two hours.*
6 (noun) Good is moral and spiritual justice and rightness, e.g. *the forces of good and evil.*
7 Good also refers to anything that is desirable,

useful, or beneficial as opposed to harmful, e.g. *The exercise will do you good.*
8 (plural noun) Goods are objects that people own or that are sold in shops, e.g. *electrical goods.*
9 (phrase) **For good** means for ever.
10 **As good as** means almost, e.g. *She's as good as blind without her glasses.*
11 If someone **delivers the goods** they do what they are expected to do.

goodbye
You say 'Goodbye' when you are leaving someone or ending a telephone conversation.

Similar words: adieu, farewell

good-for-nothing, good-for-nothings
(noun) If you call someone a good-for-nothing, you mean that they are lazy and irresponsible.

Good Friday
(noun) Good Friday is the Friday before Easter, when Christians remember the crucifixion of Christ.

good-natured
(adjective) friendly, pleasant and even-tempered.

goodness
1 (exclamation) People say 'Goodness!' or 'My goodness!' when they are surprised.
2 (noun) Goodness is the quality of being kind.

good will
(noun) Good will is kindness and helpfulness, e.g. *a gesture of good will.*

goody, goodies; also spelled goodie
1 (noun; an informal word) Goodies are enjoyable things, often food.
2 You can call a hero in a film or book a goody.
3 (exclamation) Children sometimes say 'Goody' to express delight.

goose, geese
(noun) A goose is a fairly large bird with webbed feet and a long neck. Geese make a loud honking noise, and are sometimes kept on farms for their meat and eggs.
[from Old English *gos*]

gooseberry, gooseberries
(noun) A gooseberry is a round, green edible berry that grows on a bush and has a sharp taste.

goose flesh
(noun) If you have goose flesh or goose pimples, your skin is bumpy and the hairs are standing up, because you are cold or afraid.

gore, gores, goring, gored
1 (verb) If an animal gores someone, it wounds them badly with its horns or tusks.
2 (noun) Gore is clotted blood from a wound.
[sense 2 is from Old English *gor* meaning 'mud' or 'filth']

gorge, gorges, gorging, gorged
1 (noun) A gorge is a deep, narrow valley.
2 (verb) If you gorge yourself, you eat a lot of food greedily.
[from Old French *gorge* meaning 'throat']

gorgeous
(adjective) extremely pleasant or attractive, e.g. *gorgeous weather... a gorgeous girl.*
[from Old French *gorgias* meaning 'elegant' or 'stylish']

gorilla, gorillas
(noun) A gorilla is a very large, strong ape with very dark fur. Gorillas live in forests in central Africa.
[from *Gorillai*, the Greek name for an African tribe with hairy bodies]

gorse
(noun) Gorse is a dark green wild shrub that has sharp prickles and small yellow flowers.

gory, gorier, goriest
(adjective) Gory situations involve people being injured in horrible ways.

gosling, goslings (pronounced goz-ling)
(noun) A gosling is a young goose.
[from Old English *gos* + *ling* meaning 'little goose']

go-slow, go-slows
(noun) A go-slow is a protest in which workers deliberately work slowly.

gospel, gospels
1 (noun) The Gospels are the four books in the New Testament which describe the life and teachings of Jesus Christ.
2 A gospel is a set of ideas that someone strongly believes in, e.g. *spreading the pacifist gospel.*
3 (phrase) If you take something **as gospel** or **gospel truth**, you believe that it is true.
4 (adjective) Gospel music is a style of religious music popular among Black Christians in the United States.
[from Old English *god* + *spell* meaning 'good message']

gossamer
(noun; a literary word) Gossamer is very light, fine cobwebs. Very thin, fine cloth is sometimes described as gossamer.

gossip, gossips, gossiping, gossiped
1 (noun) Gossip is informal conversation, often concerning people's private affairs.
2 (verb) If you gossip, you talk informally with someone, especially about other people.
3 (noun) Someone who is a gossip enjoys talking about other people's private affairs.
[from Old English *godsibb* meaning 'godparent']

got
1 Got is the past tense of **get**.
2 You can use 'have got' instead of the more formal 'have' when talking about possessing things, e.g. *I have got a car.*
3 You can use 'have got to' instead of the more formal 'have to' when talking about something that must be done, e.g. *He's got to go.*

Gothic
1 (adjective) Gothic buildings have tall pillars, high vaulted ceilings, and pointed arches.
2 Gothic printing or writing has letters that are very ornate.

gouge, gouges, gouging, gouged (pronounced gowj)
1 (verb) If you gouge a hole in something, you make a hole in it with a pointed object.
2 If you gouge something out, you force it out of position with your fingers or a sharp tool.

goulash (pronounced goo-lash)
(noun) Goulash is a type of rich meat stew, originally from Hungary.

gourd, gourds (pronounced goord)
(noun) A gourd is a large fruit, similar to a marrow, which grows on a climbing plant.

gourmet, gourmets (pronounced goor-may)
(noun) A gourmet is a person who enjoys good food and drink and knows a lot about it.

gout
(noun) Gout is a disease which causes someone's joints to swell painfully, especially in their toes.

govern, governs, governing, governed
1 (verb) To govern a country means to control it.
2 Something that governs a situation influences it, e.g. *Poverty governed our behaviour.*
[from Latin *gubernare* meaning 'to steer' or 'to direct']

governess, governesses
(noun) A governess is a woman who is employed to teach the children in a family and who lives with the family.

government, governments
1 (noun) The government is the group of people who govern a country.
2 Government is the control and organization of a country.
governmental (adjective).

governor, governors
(noun) A governor is a person who controls and organizes a state or an institution.

gown, gowns
1 (noun) A gown is a long, formal dress.
2 A gown is also a special long, dark cloak worn by people such as judges and lawyers.
[from Latin *gunna* meaning 'fur garment' or 'leather garment']

GP an abbreviation for **general practitioner**.

grab, grabs, grabbing, grabbed
1 (verb) If you grab something, you take it or pick it up roughly.
2 If you grab an opportunity, you take advantage of it eagerly.
3 (an informal use) If an idea grabs you, it interests you or excites you.
4 (noun) A grab at an object is an attempt to grab it.
[from German *grabben* meaning 'to seize' or 'to scramble for']

Similar words: (senses 1 and 2) grasp, snatch, seize

grace, graces, gracing, graced
1 (noun) Grace is an elegant way of moving.
2 Grace is also a pleasant, kind way of behaving.
3 (verb) Something that graces a place makes it more attractive.

4 If someone important graces an event, they kindly agree to be present at it.
5 (noun) Grace is also a short prayer of thanks said before a meal.
6 Dukes and archbishops are addressed as 'Your Grace' and referred to as 'His Grace'.
7 (phrase) If you do something **with good grace**, you do it cheerfully and without complaining.
graceful (adjective), **gracefully** (adverb).
[from Latin *gratus* meaning 'pleasing']

Similar words: (sense 1) charm, elegance, poise

gracious
1 (adjective) kind, polite, and pleasant.
2 'Good gracious' is an exclamation of surprise.
graciously (adverb).

gradation, gradations
(noun) A gradation is one of a series of changes.

grade, grades, grading, graded
1 (verb) To grade things means to arrange them according to quality, size, or colour.
2 (noun) The grade of something is its quality.
3 A grade in an exam or piece of written work is the mark that you get for it.
4 Your grade in a company or organization is your level of importance or your rank.
[from Latin *gradus* meaning 'step']

gradient, gradients
(noun) A gradient is a slope or the steepness of a slope.

gradual
(adjective) happening or changing slowly over a long period of time rather than suddenly.

gradually
(adverb) happening or changing slowly over a long period of time.

graduate, graduates, graduating, graduated
1 (noun) A graduate is a person who has completed a first degree at a university or college.
2 (verb) When students graduate, they complete a first degree at a university or college.
3 To graduate from one thing to another means to progress gradually towards the second thing.
graduation (noun).
[from Latin *graduari* meaning 'to take a degree']

graffiti (graf-**fee**-tee)
(noun) Graffiti is slogans or drawings scribbled on walls, posters, trains, and buses.
[from Italian *graffiare* meaning 'to scratch a surface']

graft, grafts, grafting, grafted
1 (noun) A graft is a piece of healthy flesh or a healthy organ which is used to replace by surgery a damaged or unhealthy part of a person's body.
2 A graft is also a small part of a plant that is joined with an existing plant to form a new plant.
3 (verb) To graft one thing to another means to attach it.
4 (noun; an informal use) Graft is hard work.
5 Graft is also gaining money dishonestly by using your position of power.

grain, grains
1 (noun) Grain is a cereal plant, such as wheat or corn, that is grown as a crop and used for food.
2 Grains are seeds of a cereal plant.
3 A grain of sand or salt is a tiny particle of it.
4 A grain of a quality is a tiny amount of it.
5 The grain of a piece of wood is the pattern of lines made by the fibres in it.
6 (phrase) If something **goes against the grain**, you find it difficult to accept because it is against your principles.
[from Latin *granum* meaning 'corn' or 'grain']

Similar words: (senses 3 and 4) particle, speck, granule

grainy
(adjective) having a rough surface or texture.

gram, grams; also spelled **gramme**
(noun) A gram is a unit of weight equal to one thousandth of a kilogram.
[from Latin *gramma* meaning 'small weight']

grammar
(noun) Grammar is the rules of a language relating to the ways you can combine words to form sentences.
[from Greek *grammatikos* meaning 'concerning letters and writing']

grammar school, grammar schools
(noun) A grammar school is a secondary school for pupils of high academic ability.

grammatical
1 (adjective) relating to grammar, e.g. *grammatical rules.*
2 following the rules of grammar correctly, e.g. *He speaks grammatical English.*
grammatically (adverb).

gramophone, gramophones
(noun) A gramophone is an old-fashioned record player.

gran, grans
(noun; an informal word) Your gran is your grandmother.

granary, granaries
1 (noun) A granary is a building for storing grain.
2 (adjective) Granary bread contains whole grains of wheat.
[from Latin *granum* meaning 'grain']

grand, grander, grandest
1 (adjective) magnificent in appearance and size, e.g. *a grand palace.*
2 very important, e.g. *the grand plan.*
3 (an informal use) very pleasant or enjoyable, e.g. *We had a grand time.*
4 A grand total is the final complete amount.
5 (noun; an informal use) A grand is a thousand pounds or dollars.
grandly (adverb).
[from Latin *grandis* meaning 'great' or 'large']

Similar words: (sense 1) imposing, lofty, majestic, noble, stately

grandad, grandads
(noun; an informal word) Your grandad is your
grandfather.

grandchild, grandchildren
(noun) Someone's grandchildren are the children
of their son or daughter.

granddaughter, granddaughters
(noun) Someone's granddaughter is the daughter
of their son or daughter.

grandeur (pronounced **grand**-yer)
(noun) Grandeur is great beauty and
magnificence.

grandfather, grandfathers
(noun) Your grandfather is your father's father
or your mother's father.

grandfather clock, grandfather clocks
(noun) A grandfather clock is a clock in a tall
wooden case that stands on the floor.

grandiose (pronounced **gran**-dee-ose)
(adjective) intended to be very impressive, but
seeming ridiculous, e.g. *grandiose schemes.*

grandma, grandmas
(noun; an informal word) Your grandma is your
grandmother.

grandmother, grandmothers
(noun) Your grandmother is your father's
mother or your mother's mother.

grandparent, grandparents
(noun) Your grandparents are your parents'
parents.

grand piano, grand pianos
(noun) A grand piano is a large flat piano with
horizontal strings.

grandson, grandsons
(noun) Someone's grandson is the son of their
son or daughter.

grandstand, grandstands
(noun) A grandstand is a structure with a roof
and seats for spectators at a sports ground.

granite (pronounced **gran**-nit)
(noun) Granite is a very hard rock used in
building.
[from Italian *granito* meaning 'grained']

granny, grannies
(noun; an informal word) Your granny is your
grandmother.

grant, grants, granting, granted
1 (noun) A grant is an amount of money that the
government or local council gives to someone for
a particular purpose, e.g. *a research grant.*
2 (verb) If you grant something to someone, you
allow them to have it.
3 If you grant that something is true, you admit
that it is true.
4 (phrases) If you **take something for granted**,
you believe it without thinking about it. If you
take someone for granted, you accept their help
without being grateful.

granule, granules
(noun) A granule is a very small piece of
something, e.g. *coffee granules.*
granular (adjective).
[from Latin *granulum* meaning 'a small grain']

grape, grapes
(noun) A grape is a small green or purple fruit.
Grapes are eaten raw, dried to make raisins,
sultanas, and currants, or used to make wine.
[from Old French *grape* meaning 'bunch of
grapes']

grapefruit, grapefruits
(noun) A grapefruit is a large, round, yellow
citrus fruit with a thick skin and bitter taste.

grapevine, grapevines
1 (noun) A grapevine is a climbing plant which
grapes grow on.
2 If you hear some news on the grapevine, it has
been passed on from person to person.

graph, graphs
(noun) A graph is a diagram in which a straight,
curved, or zigzag line shows how two sets of
numbers or measurements are related.
[originally an abbreviation for 'graphic formula']

graphic, graphics
1 (adjective) A graphic description is very
detailed and lifelike.
2 relating to drawing or painting.
3 (plural noun) Graphics are drawings and
pictures composed of simple lines and strong
colours, e.g. *computer generated graphics.*
graphically (adverb).
[from Greek *graphein* meaning 'to write']

graphite
(noun) Graphite is a black form of carbon that is
used in pencil leads, as a lubricant, and in some
nuclear reactors.
[from Greek *graphein* meaning 'to write']

grapple, grapples, grappling, grappled
1 (verb) If you grapple with someone, you
struggle with them while fighting.
2 If you grapple with a problem, you try hard to
solve it.

grasp, grasps, grasping, grasped
1 (verb) If you grasp something, you hold it
firmly.
2 If you grasp an idea, you understand it.
3 (noun) A grasp is a firm hold.
4 Your grasp of something is your understanding
of it.
[from German *grapsen* meaning 'to seize']

grasping
(adjective) Someone who is grasping wants to get
and keep as much money as possible.

grass, grasses
1 (noun) Grass is the common green plant that
grows on lawns and in parks.
2 (an informal use) Grass is also marijuana.
grassy (adjective).

grasshopper, grasshoppers
(noun) A grasshopper is an insect with long back
legs which it uses for jumping and making a
high-pitched vibrating sound.

grassland, grasslands
(noun) Grassland is land covered with grass, especially grass that grows naturally.

grass roots
(plural noun) The grass roots of an organization or movement are the ordinary people involved in it, rather than the leaders.

grass snake, grass snakes
(noun) A grass snake is a type of harmless British snake with a green or brown body.

grate, grates, grating, grated
1 (noun) A grate is a framework of metal bars in a fireplace.
2 (verb) To grate food means to shred it into small pieces by rubbing it against a grater.
3 When something grates on something else, it rubs against it making a harsh sound.
4 If something grates on you, it irritates you.

grateful
(adjective) If you are grateful for something, you are glad you have it and want to thank the person who gave it to you.
gratefully (adverb).
[from Latin *gratus* meaning 'thankful']

Similar words: appreciative, indebted, obliged, thankful

grater, graters
(noun) A grater is a small metal tool used for grating food.

gratify, gratifies, gratifying, gratified
1 (verb) If you are gratified by something, you are pleased by it.
2 If you gratify a wish or feeling, you satisfy it.
[from Latin *gratificari* meaning 'to do a favour for']

grating, gratings
1 (noun) A grating is a metal frame with bars across it fastened over a hole in a wall or in the ground.
2 (adjective) A grating sound is harsh and unpleasant, e.g. *a grating voice.*

gratis (pronounced **grah**-tis)
(adverb and adjective) free, e.g. *I'll do it for you, gratis.*
[a Latin word]

gratitude
(noun) Gratitude is the feeling of being grateful.
[from Latin *gratus* meaning 'grateful']

Similar words: appreciation, gratefulness, thankfulness, thanks

gratuitous (pronounced grat-**yoo**-it-tuss)
(adjective) unnecessary, e.g. *gratuitous violence.*
gratuitously (adverb).

gratuity, gratuities (pronounced grat-**yoo**-it-tee)
(noun) A gratuity is a gift of money, such as a tip.
[from Latin *gratuitas* meaning 'gift']

grave, graves; graver, gravest
1 (noun) A grave is a place where a corpse is buried.
2 (adjective; a formal use) very serious, e.g. *You have made a grave mistake.*

[Sense 1 is from Old English *græf* meaning 'grave'; sense 2 is from Latin *gravis* meaning 'important']

grave (pronounced **grahv**)
(adjective) In French and some other languages, a grave accent is a downward-sloping line placed over a vowel to indicate a change in pronunciation, as in the word *lèvre.*

gravel
(noun) Gravel is small stones used for making roads and paths.

gravelly
1 (adjective) A place that is gravelly is covered with gravel.
2 A gravelly voice is low and rough.

gravestone, gravestones
(noun) A gravestone is a large stone placed over someone's grave, with their name and other information on it.

graveyard, graveyards
(noun) A graveyard is an area of land where corpses are buried.

gravitate, gravitates, gravitating, gravitated
(verb) When people gravitate towards something, they go towards it because they are attracted by it.

gravitation
(noun) Gravitation is the force which causes objects to be attracted to each other.
gravitational (adjective).

gravity
1 (noun) Gravity is the force that makes things fall when you drop them.
2 (a formal use) The gravity of a situation is its seriousness
[from Latin *gravitas* meaning 'weight']

gravy
(noun) Gravy is a brown sauce made from the juice that comes out of meat when you cook it.

gray an American spelling of **grey**.

graze, grazes, grazing, grazed
1 (verb) When animals graze, they eat grass.
2 If something grazes a part of your body, it scrapes against it, injuring you slightly.
3 (noun) A graze is a slight injury caused by something scraping against your skin.

grease, greases, greasing, greased
1 (noun) Grease is an oily substance used for lubricating machines.
2 Grease is also melted animal fat, used in cooking.
3 Grease is also an oily substance produced by your skin and found in your hair.
4 (verb) If you grease something, you lubricate it with grease.
greasy (adjective).

grease gun, grease guns
(noun) A grease gun is a device for putting grease into the moving parts of machines.

greasepaint
(noun) Greasepaint is a type of make-up used by actors in the theatre.

greaseproof paper
(noun) Greaseproof paper is a type of paper which grease cannot pass through. It is used in cooking and for wrapping food.

great, greater, greatest
1 (adjective) very large, e.g. *a great tree... a great change.*
2 very important, e.g. *a great writer.*
3 (an informal use) very good, e.g. *It's a great idea.*
greatly (adverb), **greatness** (noun).

Great Britain
(noun) Great Britain is the largest of the British Isles, consisting of England, Scotland, and Wales.

Great Dane, Great Danes
(noun) A Great Dane is a very large dog with short hair.

great-grandfather, great-grandfathers
(noun) Your great-grandfather is your father's or mother's grandfather.

great-grandmother, great-grandmothers
(noun) Your great-grandmother is your father's or mother's grandmother.

great tit, great tits
(noun) A great tit is a common small bird with a black and white head and a yellow and black breast.

grebe, grebes (pronounced greeb)
(noun) A grebe is a bird that lives near water and dives for its food.

greed
(noun) Greed is a desire for more of something, such as food, than you really need.

greedy, greedier, greediest
(adjective) wanting more of something, such as food, than you really need.
greedily (adverb), **greediness** (noun).

Similar words: avaricious, gluttonous, grasping, insatiable, voracious, mercenary

Greek, Greeks
1 (adjective) belonging or relating to Greece.
2 (noun) A Greek is someone who comes from Greece.
3 Greek is the main language spoken in Greece.
4 In etymologies in this dictionary, Greek refers to the language used by the ancient Greeks.

green, greener, greenest; greens
1 (adjective and noun) Green is a colour between yellow and blue on the spectrum.
2 (noun) A green is an area of grass in the middle of a village.
3 A putting green or bowling green is a grassy area on which putting or bowls is played.
4 In golf, a green is an area of smooth short grass around each hole on the course.
5 (plural noun) Greens are green vegetables.
6 (adjective) Green is used to describe political movements which are particularly concerned with environmental issues.
7 (an informal use) Someone who is green is young and inexperienced.

green belt, green belts
(noun) The green belt is the area of countryside round a city where people are not allowed to build houses and factories.

greenery
(noun) Greenery is a lot of trees, bushes, or other green plants together in one place.

greenfinch, greenfinches
(noun) A greenfinch is a common European bird with green and yellow plumage and a strong beak which it uses for cracking open seeds.

green fingers
(noun) If you say that someone has green fingers, you mean they are good at growing plants.

greenfly
(noun) Greenfly are small green insects that damage plants.

greengrocer, greengrocers
(noun) A greengrocer is a shopkeeper who sells vegetables and fruit.

greenhouse, greenhouses
(noun) A greenhouse is a glass building in which people grow plants that need to be kept warm.

Greenwich Mean Time (pronounced gren-itch)
(noun) Greenwich Mean Time is the standard time for Britain, used as a basis for calculating local times throughout the world.

greet, greets, greeting, greeted
1 (verb) If you greet someone, you say something friendly like 'hello' to them when you meet them.
2 If you greet something in a particular way, you react to it in that way, e.g. *His suggestion was greeted with laughter.*

Similar words: (sense 1) hail, salute

greeting, greetings
(noun) A greeting is something friendly that you say to someone when you meet them or when they arrive somewhere, e.g. *Greetings were exchanged.*

gregarious (pronounced grig-air-ee-uss)
(adjective; a formal word) Someone who is gregarious enjoys being with other people.
[from Latin *gregarius* meaning 'belonging to a flock']

grenade, grenades
(noun) A grenade is a small bomb, containing explosive or tear gas, which can be thrown by hand.
[from Spanish *granada* meaning 'pomegranate']

grew the past tense of grow.

grey, greyer, greyest; greys; greying
1 (adjective and noun) Grey is a colour between black and white.
2 (verb) If someone is greying, their hair is going grey.
greyness (noun).

greyhound, greyhounds
(noun) A greyhound is a thin dog with long legs

that can run very fast. People bet on greyhounds in races.

grid, grids
1 (noun) A grid is a pattern of lines crossing each other to form squares.
2 The grid is the network of wires and cables by which electricity is distributed throughout a country.

grief, griefs
1 (noun) Grief is extreme sadness.
2 A grief is something that causes extreme sadness.
3 (phrase) If someone or something **comes to grief**, they fail or are injured.
[from Latin *gravis* meaning 'concerned with important or sorrowful matters']

Similar words: (sense 1) anguish, mourning, sadness, sorrow, woe

grievance, grievances
(noun) A grievance is a reason for complaining.

grieve, grieves, grieving, grieved
1 (verb) If you grieve, you are extremely sad, especially because someone has died.
2 If something grieves you, it makes you feel very sad.

Similar words: (sense 1) bemoan, lament, mourn, sorrow

grievous
(adjective; a formal word) extremely serious, e.g. *a grievous mistake.*
grievously (adverb).

grill, grills, grilling, grilled
1 (noun) A grill is a part on a cooker where food is cooked by strong heat from above.
2 A grill is also a metal frame on which you cook food over a fire.
3 (verb) If you grill food, you cook it on or under a grill.
4 (noun) A grill is also a dish consisting of food that has been grilled, e.g. *a mixed grill.*
5 (verb; an informal use) If you grill someone, you ask them a lot of questions in a very intense way.

grille, grilles (rhymes with **pill**)
(noun) A grille is a metal framework over a window or piece of machinery, used for protection.

grim, grimmer, grimmest
1 (adjective) If a situation or piece of news is grim, it is very unpleasant and worrying, e.g. *The outlook is grim.*
2 Grim places are unattractive and depressing, e.g. *The streets were grim and sunless.*
3 If someone is grim, they are very serious, e.g. *Her expression was grim.*
grimly (adverb).

grimace, grimaces, grimacing, grimaced
(pronounced grim-**mace**)
1 (noun) A grimace is a twisted facial expression indicating annoyance, disgust, or pain.

2 (verb) When someone grimaces, they make a grimace.

grime
(noun) Grime is thick dirt which gathers on the surface of something.
grimy (adjective).

grin, grins, grinning, grinned
1 (verb) If you grin, you smile broadly.
2 (noun) A grin is a broad smile.
3 (phrase) If you **grin and bear it**, you accept a difficult situation without complaining.

grind, grinds, grinding, ground
1 (verb) If you grind something such as corn or pepper, you crush it into a fine powder.
2 If you grind your teeth, you rub your upper and lower teeth together.
3 (phrase) If something **grinds to a halt**, it stops, e.g. *The bus ground to a halt... The whole economy may grind to a halt.*
4 (noun; an informal use) The grind is routine work which is tiring or boring.

Similar words: (sense 1) crush, powder, pulverize

grip, grips, gripping, gripped
1 (verb) If you grip something, you hold it firmly.
2 (noun) A grip is a firm hold.
3 Your grip on a situation is your control over it.
4 (phrase) If you **get to grips with** a situation or problem, you start to deal with it effectively.
5 If you **are losing your grip**, you are becoming less able to deal with things.

gripping
(adjective) A story or film that is gripping is extremely interesting or exciting.

grisly, grislier, grisliest
(adjective) very nasty and horrible, e.g. *He described the accident in grisly detail.*
[from Old English *grislic* meaning 'causing horror']

grist
(phrase) Something that is **grist to the mill** is useful for a particular purpose.
[an Old English word meaning 'corn for grinding']

gristle (pronounced **gris**-sl)
(noun) Gristle is a tough, rubbery substance found in some meat.
gristly (adjective).
[from Old English *gristle* meaning 'cartilage between bones']

grit, grits, gritting, gritted
1 (noun) Grit consists of very small stones. It is put on icy roads to make them less slippery.
2 (verb) When workmen grit an icy road, they put grit on it.
3 (phrase) To **grit your teeth** means to decide to carry on in a difficult situation.
gritty (adjective).

grizzle, grizzles, grizzling, grizzled
(verb) If a baby or child grizzles, it keeps crying and whining.

grizzled
(adjective) Grizzled hair is grey. A grizzled person has grey hair.
[from French *gris* meaning 'grey']

grizzly bear, grizzly bears
(noun) A grizzly bear or a grizzly is a large, greyish-brown bear from North America.

groan, groans, groaning, groaned
1 (verb) If you groan, you make a long, low sound of pain, unhappiness, or disapproval.
2 (noun) A groan is the sound you make when you groan.

grocer, grocers
(noun) A grocer is a shopkeeper who sells many kinds of food and other household goods.

grocery, groceries
1 (noun) A grocery is a grocer's shop.
2 (plural noun) Groceries are the goods that you buy in a grocer's shop.

groggy, groggier, groggiest
(adjective) If you feel groggy, you feel dizzy and sick.

groin, groins
(noun) Your groin is the area where your legs join the main part of your body at the front.

groom, grooms, grooming, groomed
1 (noun) A groom is someone who looks after horses in a stable.
2 At a wedding, the groom is the bridegroom.
3 (verb) To groom an animal means to clean it.
4 If you groom someone for a particular job, you prepare them for it by teaching them the skills they will need.

groomed
(adjective) Someone who is well groomed is clean and smart.

groove, grooves
(noun) A groove is a deep line cut into a surface.
grooved (adjective).
[from Old Dutch *groeve* meaning 'furrow' or 'ditch']

Similar words: channel, hollow, rut

---

grope, gropes, groping, groped
1 (verb) If you grope for something you cannot see, you search for it with your hands.
2 If you grope for something such as the solution to a problem, you try to think of it.

gross, grosser, grossest; grosses, grossing, grossed
1 (adjective) extremely bad, e.g. *a gross miscarriage of justice.*
2 Gross speech or behaviour is very rude.
3 Gross things are ugly, e.g. *gross earrings.*
4 Someone's gross income is their total income before any deductions are made.
5 The gross weight of something is its total weight including the weight of its container.
6 (verb) If you gross an amount of money, you earn that amount in total.
7 (noun) A gross of things is 144 of them.
grossly (adverb).
[from Old French *gros* meaning 'large']

grotesque (pronounced groh-**tesk**)
1 (adjective) exaggerated and absurd, e.g. *The idea was simply grotesque.*
2 very strange and ugly, e.g. *a grotesque building.*
grotesquely (adverb).
[from Old Italian *pittura grottesca* meaning 'cave paintings']

grotto, grottoes or grottos
(noun) A grotto is a small cave that people visit because it is attractive.
[from Old Italian *grotta* meaning 'vault' or 'crypt']

grotty, grottier, grottiest
(adjective; an informal word) unattractive or of poor quality, e.g. *a grotty little flat.*

grouch, grouches, grouching, grouched
1 (verb) If you grouch, you complain in a bad-tempered way.
2 (noun) A grouch is someone who complains a lot in a bad-tempered way.
grouchy (adjective).

ground, grounds, grounding, grounded
1 (noun) The ground is the surface of the earth.
2 A ground is a piece of land that is used for a particular purpose, e.g. *a football ground.*
3 (noun) The ground covered by a book or course is the range of subjects it deals with.
4 (plural noun) The grounds of a large building are the land belonging to it and surrounding it.
5 (a formal use) The grounds for something are the reasons for it, e.g. *grounds for complaint.*
6 (verb; a formal use) If something is grounded in something else, it is based on it.
7 If an aircraft is grounded, it has to remain on the ground.
8 Ground is the past tense and past participle of **grind.**
9 (phrase) If you **gain ground**, you make progress.
10 If you **get something off the ground**, you get it started.

ground floor, ground floors
(noun) The ground floor of a building is the floor that is approximately level with the ground.

grounding
(noun) If you have a grounding in a skill or subject, you have had basic instruction in it.

groundless
(adjective) not based on reason or evidence, e.g. *a groundless fear.*
groundlessly (adverb).

groundnut, groundnuts
(noun) A groundnut is a peanut.

ground rules
(plural noun) Ground rules are the basic principles on which an activity is based.

groundsheet, groundsheets
(noun) A groundsheet is a large piece of waterproof material placed on the ground to sleep on when camping.

groundsman, groundsmen
(noun) A groundsman is someone whose job is to look after a sports ground or a park.

group, groups, grouping, grouped
1 (noun) A group of things or people is a number of them that are linked together in some way.
2 A group is also a number of musicians who perform pop music together.
3 (verb) When things or people are grouped together, they are linked together in some way.

Similar words: (sense 1) assembly, band, bunch, gang, gathering, party

group captain, group captains
(noun) A group captain is an RAF officer of the rank immediately above wing commander.

grouping, groupings
(noun) A grouping is a number of things or people that are linked together in some way.

grouse, grouses, grousing, groused
1 (noun) A grouse is a fat brown or grey bird. Grouse are shot for sport and can be eaten.
2 (verb) If you grouse, you complain.

grove, groves
(noun; a literary word) A grove is a group of trees growing close together.
[from Old English *græfa* meaning 'thicket']

grovel, grovels, grovelling, grovelled
(verb) If you grovel, you behave in an unpleasantly humble way towards someone you regard as important.
[from Middle English *on grufe* meaning 'lying on your belly']

grow, grows, growing, grew, grown
1 (verb) To grow means to increase in size, amount, or degree.
2 If a tree or plant grows somewhere, it is alive there.
3 When people grow plants, they plant them and look after them.
4 If a man grows a beard or moustache, he lets it develop by not shaving.
5 If you grow to have a particular feeling, you eventually have it.
6 If one thing grows from another, it develops from it.
7 (an informal use) If something grows on you, you gradually get to like it.
8 If you grow out of a type of behaviour, you stop behaving that way.

Similar words: (sense 1) enlarge, increase, multiply, rise, wax

grow up
(phrasal verb) When a child grows up, he or she becomes an adult.

growl, growls, growling, growled
1 (verb) When an animal growls, it makes a low rumbling sound, usually because it is angry.
2 (noun) A growl is the sound an animal makes when it growls.
3 (verb) If you growl something, you say it in a low, rough, rather angry voice.
[from Old French *grouller* meaning 'to grumble']

grown-up, grown-ups
1 (noun; an informal use) A grown-up is an adult.

2 (adjective) Someone who is grown-up is adult, or behaves like an adult.

growth, growths
1 (noun) When there is a growth in something, it gets bigger, e.g. *the growth in political opposition*.
2 Growth is the process by which something develops to its full size.
3 A growth is an abnormal lump on the outside or inside of a person, animal, or plant.

Similar words: (sense 1) increase, expansion, rise, increment

groyne, groynes
(noun) A groyne is a wall built from a beach into the sea to break the waves and prevent erosion.

grub, grubs
1 (noun) A grub is a wormlike insect that has just hatched from its egg.
2 (an informal use) Grub is food.

grubby, grubbier, grubbiest
(adjective) rather dirty.

grudge, grudges, grudging, grudged
1 (noun) If you have a grudge against someone, you resent them because they have harmed you in the past.
2 (verb) If you grudge someone something, you give it to them unwillingly, or are displeased that they have it.

grudging
(adjective) done or felt unwillingly, e.g. *grudging respect*.
grudgingly (adverb).

gruel
(noun) Gruel was oatmeal boiled in water or milk.

gruelling
(adjective) difficult and tiring, e.g. *gruelling work*.

Similar words: arduous, strenuous, exhausting

gruesome
(adjective) shocking and horrible, e.g. *a gruesome murder*.

gruff, gruffer, gruffest
(adjective) If someone's voice is gruff, it sounds rough and unfriendly.
gruffly (adverb).

grumble, grumbles, grumbling, grumbled
1 (verb) If you grumble, you complain in a bad-tempered way.
2 (noun) A grumble is a bad-tempered complaint.

grumpy, grumpier, grumpiest
(adjective) bad-tempered and fed-up.
grumpily (adverb), **grumpiness** (noun).

Similar words: irascible, gruff, ill-tempered, irritable, surly, testy, touchy, snappy

grunt, grunts, grunting, grunted
1 (verb) If a person or a pig grunts, they make a short, low, gruff sound.
2 (noun) A grunt is the sound a person or a pig makes when they grunt.

guarantee, guarantees, guaranteeing, guaranteed
1 (verb) If something or someone guarantees something, they make it certain that it will happen, e.g. *Freedom does not guarantee happiness.*
2 (noun) If something is a guarantee of something else, it makes it certain that it will happen.
3 A guarantee is also a written promise that if a product develops a fault within a specified period of time, it will be replaced or repaired free.
guarantor (noun).

Similar words: (sense 1) assure, ensure, warrant, secure
(sense 2) assurance, pledge, warranty

guard, guards, guarding, guarded
1 (verb) If you guard a person or object, you stay near to them either to protect them or to make sure they do not escape.
2 If you guard against something, you are careful to avoid it happening.
3 (noun) A guard is a person or group of people who guard a person, object, or place.
4 A guard is also a railway official in charge of a train.
5 Any object which covers and protects something can be called a guard, e.g. *a fire guard.*
[from Old French *garder* meaning 'to protect']

Similar words: (sense 1) defend, protect, safeguard, watch
(sense 3) sentry, protector, warden, watchman, lookout, sentinel

guarded
(adjective) not expressing any strong feelings or opinions, e.g. *His statements were guarded.*
guardedly (adverb).

guardian, guardians
1 (noun) A guardian is someone who has been legally appointed to look after an orphaned child.
2 A guardian of something is someone who protects it, e.g. *the guardians of morality.*
guardianship (noun).

guava, guavas (pronounced gwah-va)
(noun) A guava is a round, yellow tropical fruit with pink or white flesh and hard seeds.

guerrilla, guerrillas (pronounced ger-ril-la); also spelled guerilla
(noun) A guerrilla is a member of a small unofficial army fighting an official army.
[from Spanish *guerrilla* meaning 'little war']

guess, guesses, guessing, guessed
1 (verb) If you guess something, you form or express an opinion that it is the case, without having much information.
2 (noun) A guess is an attempt to give the correct answer to something without having much information.

Similar words: (sense 1) estimate, conjecture, surmise, speculate
(sense 2) speculation, supposition, conjecture

guest, guests
1 (noun) A guest is someone who stays at your home or who attends an occasion because they have been invited.
2 The guests in a hotel are the people staying there.
[from Old English *giest* meaning 'guest', 'stranger', or 'enemy']

guest house, guest houses
(noun) A guest house is a private house which has rooms where people can pay to stay and which usually provides some meals.

guest of honour, guests of honour
(noun) The guest of honour at a dinner or social occasion is the most important guest.

guffaw, guffaws, guffawing, guffawed
1 (verb) To guffaw means to laugh in a loud, coarse way.
2 (noun) A guffaw is a loud, coarse laugh.

guidance
(noun) Guidance is help and advice.

guide, guides, guiding, guided
1 (noun) A guide is someone who shows you round places, or leads the way through difficult country.
2 A guide is also a book which gives you information or instructions, e.g. *a guide to healthy living.*
3 A guide or a girl guide is a girl in the Girl Guides Association.
4 (verb) If you guide someone in a particular direction, you lead them in that direction.
5 If you are guided by something, it influences your actions or decisions.
[from Old French *guider* meaning 'to guide']

guidebook, guidebooks
(noun) A guidebook is a book which gives information about a place.

guided missile, guided missiles
(noun) A guided missile is a missile which is controlled from the ground during its flight.

guide dog, guide dogs
(noun) A guide dog is a dog that has been trained to lead a blind person.

guideline, guidelines
(noun) A guideline is a piece of advice about how something should be done.

guild, guilds
(noun) A guild is an organization of people who do the same job or have the same interest.

guile (rhymes with mile)
(noun) Guile is cunning and deceitfulness.
guileless (adjective).

guillemot, guillemots (pronounced gil-lim-mot)
(noun) A guillemot is a black-and-white diving sea bird with a long narrow bill.

guillotine, guillotines (pronounced gil-lot-teen)
1 (noun) In the past, the guillotine was a machine used for beheading people, especially in France. It was named after Joseph-Ignace Guillotin, who first recommended its use.
2 A guillotine is also a piece of equipment with a long sharp blade, used for cutting paper.

guilt
1 (noun) Guilt is an unhappy feeling of having done something wrong.
2 Someone's guilt is the fact that they have done something wrong, e.g. *He admitted his guilt.*

guilty, guiltier, guiltiest
1 (adjective) If you are guilty of doing something wrong, you did it, e.g. *He was guilty of murder.*
2 If you feel guilty, you are unhappy because you have done something wrong.
guiltily (adverb).

guinea, guineas (pronounced gin-ee)
(noun) A guinea is an old British unit of money, worth 21 shillings. Guinea coins were originally made of gold that came from Guinea in West Africa.

guinea fowl, guinea fowls
(noun) A guinea fowl is a large dark grey bird, originally from Africa, bred for its meat and eggs.

guinea pig, guinea pigs
1 (noun) A guinea pig is a small furry animal without a tail, often kept as a pet.
2 A guinea pig is also a person used in an experiment.

guise, guises (rhymes with prize)
(noun) A guise is a misleading appearance, e.g. *exploitation under the guise of helpfulness.*

guitar, guitars
(noun) A guitar is a musical instrument with six strings which are strummed or plucked with the fingers or a plectrum.
guitarist (noun).
[from Spanish *guitarra*]

Gujarati, Gujaratis (pronounced gooj-jer-rah-tee); also spelled Gujerati
1 (adjective) belonging or relating to Gujarat, a state in western India.
2 (noun) A Gujarati is someone who comes from Gujarat.
3 Gujarati is a language spoken in Gujarat.

gulf, gulfs
1 (noun) A gulf is a very large bay.
2 A gulf is a wide gap or difference between two things, people, or groups.
[from Italian *golfo*]

gull, gulls
(noun) A gull is a very common seabird with long wings, white and grey or black feathers, and webbed feet.
[from Welsh *gwylan*]

gullet, gullets
(noun) Your gullet is the tube that goes from your mouth to your stomach.
[from Latin *gula* meaning 'throat']

gullible
(adjective) easily tricked.
gullibility (noun).

Similar words: credulous, innocent, naive

gully, gullies
(noun) A gully is a long, narrow valley.

gulp, gulps, gulping, gulped
1 (verb) If you gulp food or drink, you swallow large quantities of it.
2 (noun) A gulp of food or drink is a large quantity of it swallowed at one time.
3 (verb) If you gulp, you swallow air, because you are nervous.

gum, gums, gumming, gummed
1 (noun) Gum is a soft flavoured substance that people chew but do not swallow.
2 Gum is also glue for sticking paper.
3 (verb) If you gum something, you stick it to something else using gum.
4 (noun) Your gums are the firm flesh in which your teeth are set.
[Senses 1-3 are from Latin *gummi*; sense 4 is from Old English *goma* meaning 'jaw']

gumboot, gumboots
(noun) Gumboots are long waterproof boots.

gun, guns
(noun) A gun is a weapon which fires bullets or shells.

gunboat, gunboats
(noun) A gunboat is a boat with large guns fixed on it.

gun dog, gun dogs
(noun) A gun dog is a dog that is trained to fetch birds and small animals that have been shot.

gunfire
(noun) Gunfire is the repeated firing of guns.

gunpowder
(noun) Gunpowder is an explosive powder made from a mixture of potassium nitrate and other substances.

gun-running
(noun) Gun-running is the activity of bringing guns illegally into a country.

gunshot, gunshots
(noun) A gunshot is the sound of a gun being fired.

gunwale, gunwales (pronounced gun-nl)
(noun) The gunwale is the upper edge of the hull of a boat.

guppy, guppies
(noun) A guppy is a small, brightly-coloured tropical fish. Guppies are often kept in aquariums.

gurgle, gurgles, gurgling, gurgled
1 (verb) To gurgle means to make a bubbling sound.
2 (noun) A gurgle is a bubbling sound.
[from Latin *gurgulio* meaning 'gullet' or 'throat']

guru, gurus (pronounced goo-rooh)
(noun) A guru is a spiritual leader and teacher, especially in India.
[from Sanskrit *guruh* meaning 'weighty' or 'of importance']

gush, gushes, gushing, gushed
1 (verb) When liquid gushes from something, it flows out of it in large quantities.

2 When people gush, they express admiration or pleasure in an exaggerated way.
gushing (adjective), **gushy** (adjective).

Similar words: (sense 1) cascade, flow, spout, spurt (sense 2) effuse, enthuse

gusset, gussets
(noun) A gusset is a piece of cloth sewn into a garment for strengthening or protection.
[from Old French *gousset* meaning 'piece of armour worn under armpit']

gust, gusts
1 (noun) A gust is a sudden rush of wind.
2 (a literary use) A sudden, intense feeling may be referred to as a gust, e.g. *a gust of anger.*
gusty (adjective).

gusto
(noun) Gusto is energy and enthusiasm, e.g. *We ate with gusto.*

gut, guts, gutting, gutted
1 (plural noun) Your guts are your internal organs, especially your intestines.
2 (verb) To gut a dead fish means to remove its internal organs.
3 (noun; an informal use) Guts is courage.
4 (verb) If a building is gutted, the inside of it is destroyed by fire.

Similar words: (sense 1) bowels, entrails, innards, intestines

gutter, gutters
1 (noun) A gutter is the edge of a road next to the pavement, where rain collects and flows away.
2 A gutter is also a channel fixed to the edge of a roof, where rain collects and flows away.
guttering (noun).

guttural (pronounced **gut**-ter-al)
(adjective) Guttural sounds are produced at the back of a person's throat and are often considered to be unpleasant.
[from Latin *guttur* meaning 'gullet']

guy, guys
1 (noun) A guy or guy rope is a rope or wire used to keep a pole or a tent fixed in position.
2 (an informal use) A guy is a man or boy.

guzzle, guzzles, guzzling, guzzled
(verb) To guzzle something means to drink or eat it quickly and greedily.

gym, gyms
1 (noun) A gym is a gymnasium.
2 Gym is gymnastics.

gymkhana, gymkhanas (pronounced jim-**kah**-na)
(noun) A gymkhana is an event in which people take part in horse-riding contests.
[from Hindi *gend-khana* literally meaning 'ball house', because it is where sports were held]

gymnasium, gymnasiums
(noun) A gymnasium is a room with special equipment for physical exercises.
[from Greek *gumnazein* meaning 'to exercise naked']

gymnast, gymnasts
(noun) A gymnast is someone who is trained in gymnastics.
gymnastic (adjective).

gymnastics
(noun) Gymnastics is physical exercises, especially ones using equipment such as bars and ropes.

gynaecology or **gynecology** (pronounced gie-nak-**kol**-loj-ee)
(noun) Gynaecology is the branch of medical science concerned with the female reproductive system.
gynaecologist (noun), **gynaecological** (adjective).
[From Greek *gunē* meaning 'woman' and *-logikos* meaning 'study']

gypsum
(noun) Gypsum is a soft white substance used to make plaster of Paris and some fertilizers.
[from Greek *gupsos* meaning 'chalk' or 'cement']

gypsy, gypsies; also spelled **gipsy**
(noun) A gypsy is a member of a race of people, originally from India but now found mainly in Europe, who travel around in caravans.
[from 'Egyptian', because people used to think gypsies came from Egypt]

gyrate, gyrates, gyrating, gyrated
(pronounced jy-**rate**)
(verb) To gyrate means to move round in a circle.
gyration (noun).
[from Latin *gyrus* meaning 'circle']

gyroscope, gyroscopes
(noun) A gyroscope is a piece of equipment that helps to keep an object steady by means of a rotation wheel which stays in the same position whenever the object moves.

H

ha an abbreviation for 'hectares'.

habeas corpus (pronounced **hay**-be-ass **kor**-puss)
(noun) Habeas corpus is a law stating that someone cannot be kept in prison without trial.
[from Latin *habeas corpus* meaning 'you may have the body']

haberdashery
(noun) Haberdashery refers to ribbons, needles, cotton, and other things used for sewing.

habit, habits
1 (noun) A habit is something that you do often, e.g. *I got into the habit of walking to work.*
2 A monk's or nun's habit is a garment like a loose dress.
habitual (adjective), **habitually** (adverb).
[from Latin *habitus* meaning 'custom']

habitable
(adjective) A house that is habitable is in a suitable state to be lived in.

habitat, habitats
(noun) The habitat of a plant or animal is its natural environment where it grows or lives.
[from Latin *habitare* meaning 'to inhabit']

habituate, habituates, habituating, habituated
(verb; a formal word) If you are habituated to something, you are used to it.

habitué, habitués (pronounced hab-**bit**-yoo-ay)
(noun) A habitué of a place is someone who often goes there.

hack, hacks, hacking, hacked
1 (verb) If you hack at something, you cut it using rough strokes.
2 (noun) A hack is a writer or journalist who produces work fast without worrying about quality.
3 (phrase) A **hacking cough** is a dry, painful cough with a harsh, unpleasant sound.

hacker, hackers
(noun; an informal word) A hacker is someone who uses a computer to break into the computer system of a company or government.

hackles
1 (plural noun) A dog's hackles are the hairs on the back of its neck that rise when it is angry.
2 (phrase) Something that **makes your hackles rise** makes you angry.

hackneyed
(adjective) A hackneyed phrase is meaningless because it has been used too often.

Similar words: clichéd, overworked

hacksaw, hacksaws
(noun) A hacksaw is a small saw with a narrow blade set in a frame. It is used for cutting metal.

haddock
(noun) A haddock is an edible sea fish.

haematite another spelling of **hematite.**

haematology or **hematology** (pronounced hee-mat-**ol**-loj-ee)
(noun) Haematology is the branch of medicine concerned with blood and diseases of the blood.
[from Greek *haima* + *logia* meaning 'study of blood']

haemoglobin or **hemoglobin** (pronounced hee-moh-**gloh**-bin)
(noun) Haemoglobin is a substance in red blood cells which carries oxygen round the body.

haemophilia or **hemophilia** (pronounced hee-moh-**fil**-lee-a)
(noun) Haemophilia is a disease in which a person's blood does not clot so they bleed for too long when they are injured.
haemophiliac (noun).

haemorrhage or **hemorrhage** (pronounced **hem**-er-rij)
(noun) A haemorrhage is serious bleeding especially inside a person's body.
[from Greek *haima* + *rhegnunai* meaning 'blood burst']

haemorrhoids or **hemorrhoids** (pronounced **hem**-er-roydz)
(plural noun) Haemorrhoids are painful lumps around the anus that are caused by swollen veins.
[from Greek *haimorrhois* meaning 'discharging blood']

hag, hags
(noun; an offensive word) A hag is an ugly old woman.

haggard
(adjective) A person who is haggard looks very tired and ill.

haggis, haggises
(noun) Haggis is a Scottish dish made of the internal organs of a calf or sheep, chopped up and boiled with oatmeal and spices in a skin.

haggle, haggles, haggling, haggled
(verb) If you haggle with someone, you argue with them, usually about the cost of something.

hail, hails, hailing, hailed
1 (noun) Hail is frozen rain.
2 (verb) When it is hailing, frozen rain is falling.
3 (noun) A hail of things is a lot of them falling together, e.g. *a hail of bullets... a hail of abuse.*
4 (verb) If someone hails you, they call to you to attract your attention or greet you.

hair, hairs
1 (noun) Hair consists of the long, threadlike strands that grow from the skin of animals and humans.
2 (phrase) If you **let your hair down**, you relax completely and enjoy yourself.
3 Someone who is **splitting hairs** is making distinctions that are too fine or unimportant.

4 A hair's breadth is a very small amount, e.g. *The bullet missed me by a hair's breadth.*

haircut, haircuts
(noun) A haircut is the cutting of someone's hair; also the style in which it is cut.

hairdo, hairdos
(noun) A hairdo is a hairstyle.

hairdresser, hairdressers
(noun) A hairdresser is someone who is trained to cut and style people's hair; also a shop where this is done.
hairdressing (noun and adjective).

hair-grip, hair-grips
(noun) A hair-grip is a thin metal clip, used to hold someone's hair firmly in place.

hairline, hairlines
1 (noun) Your hairline is the edge of the area on your forehead where your hair grows.
2 (adjective) A hairline crack is so fine that you can hardly see it.

hairpiece, hairpieces
(noun) A hairpiece is a piece of false hair worn to cover a bald patch or to make a person's own hair look thicker.

hairpin, hairpins
1 (noun) A hairpin is a U-shaped wire used to hold hair in position.
2 (adjective) A hairpin bend is a U-shaped bend in the road.

hair-raising
(adjective) very frightening or exciting.

hairspring, hairsprings
(noun) A hairspring is a very fine spring in a watch which helps to keep it ticking regularly.

hairstyle, hairstyles
(noun) Someone's hairstyle is the way in which their hair is arranged or cut.

hairy, hairier, hairiest
1 (adjective) covered in a lot of hair.
2 (an informal use) difficult, exciting, and rather frightening, e.g. *The ice on the road made driving a bit hairy.*

hake, hakes
(noun) A hake is a sea fish related to the cod.

halberd, halberds
(noun) A halberd is a 15th-century weapon consisting of a spear with an axe head fitted on the end.

halcyon (pronounced **hal**-see-on)
(adjective; a literary word) peaceful, gentle, and calm, e.g. *those halcyon days of her youth.*

half, halves
1 (noun, adjective, and adverb) Half refers to one of two equal parts that make up a whole, e.g. *the two halves of the brain... another half hour... The bottle was only half full.*
2 (adverb) You can use half to say that something is only partly true, e.g. *He half expected to see Davis there.*
3 (phrase) Someone who **never does things by halves** always does things thoroughly and completely.

half-baked
(adjective; an informal word) Half-baked ideas or plans have not been properly thought out.

half board
(noun) Half board at a hotel includes breakfast and an evening meal but not lunch.

half-brother, half-brothers
(noun) Your half-brother is a boy or man who has either the same mother or the same father as you.

half-caste, half-castes
(noun) Someone who is a half-caste has parents of different races.
[from Old English *healf* meaning 'half' and Portuguese *casta* meaning 'race']

half-cock
(noun; an informal expression) Something that goes off at half-cock is only partly successful.

half-hearted
(adjective) showing no real effort or enthusiasm.
half-heartedly (adverb).

half-life, half-lives
(noun) In physics, the half-life of a substance is the amount of time that it takes to lose half its radioactivity.

half-mast
(noun) A flag at half-mast is flying halfway down the pole, usually as a signal of mourning.

halfpenny, halfpennies (pronounced **hayp**-nee)
(noun) Until decimalization, a halfpenny was a small British coin worth half a penny.

half-sister, half-sisters
(noun) Your half-sister is a girl or woman who has either the same mother or the same father as you.

half-timbered
(adjective) A half-timbered building has a framework of wooden beams showing in the walls.

half-time
(noun) Half-time is a short break between two parts of a game when the players have a rest.

halftone, halftones
(noun) A halftone is a picture in a newspaper that has been photographed through a fine screen which breaks up the picture into tiny dots.

halfway
1 (adverb) at the middle of the distance between two points in place or time, e.g. *She was halfway up the stairs... halfway through the programme.*
2 (phrase) If you **meet someone halfway**, you change some of your own requests or opinions in order to come to an agreement with them.

halfwit, halfwits
(noun) A halfwit is a stupid person.
halfwitted (adjective).

halibut, halibuts
(noun) Halibut is a type of large edible flatfish.
[from Old English *halig* meaning 'holy' and Old Dutch *butte* meaning 'flat fish'; halibut was often eaten on holy days]

hall, halls
1 (noun) A hall is the small room just inside the front entrance of a house.
2 A hall is also a large room or building used for public meetings, concerts, plays, and exhibitions.

hallmark, hallmarks
1 (noun) A hallmark is an official mark on gold or silver indicating the quality of the metal.
2 The hallmark of a person, group, or organization is their most typical quality or feature, e.g. *The demonstration has become a hallmark of their political style.*
[from *Goldsmiths' Hall* where gold was marked for quality]

hall of residence, halls of residence
(noun) A hall of residence is accommodation designed for students.

hallowed (pronounced **hal**-lode)
(adjective) respected as being holy, e.g. *hallowed ground.*
[from Old English *halig* meaning 'holy']

Halloween
(noun) Halloween is October 31st, traditionally believed to be the night on which ghosts and witches can be seen.
[from Old English *halig* + *æfen* meaning 'holy evening', the evening before All Saints' Day]

hallucinate, hallucinates, hallucinating, hallucinated (pronounced hal-**loo**-sin-ate)
(verb) If you hallucinate, you see strange things in your mind because of illness or drugs.
hallucination (noun), **hallucinatory** (adjective).
[from Latin *alucinari* meaning 'to wander in thought']

hallucinogenic (pronounced hal-loo-sin-o-**jen**-ik)
(adjective) Hallucinogenic drugs cause hallucinations.
hallucinogen (noun).

halo, haloes or **halos**
(noun) A halo is a circle of light around the head of a holy figure.
[from Greek *halos* meaning 'disc shape of the sun or moon']

halogen (pronounced **hal**-o-jen)
(noun; a technical word) A halogen is any of the chemical elements fluorine, chlorine, bromine, iodine, and astatine. They form group VIII in the periodic table.
[from Greek *hals* + *genēs* meaning 'salt born']

halt, halts, halting, halted
1 (verb) To halt when moving means to stop.
2 To halt growth, development, or action means to stop it.

halter, halters
(noun) A halter is a strap fastened round a horse's head so that it can be led easily.

halting
(adjective) Halting speech is hesitating or uncertain.
[from Old English *healt* meaning 'lame']

halve, halves, halving, halved (pronounced hahv)
1 (verb) If you halve something, you reduce its size or amount by half.
2 To halve something also means to divide it into two equal parts.

halyard, halyards (pronounced **hal**-yard)
(noun; a nautical word) A halyard is a wire or rope used to raise or lower a sail.

ham, hams
1 (noun) Ham is meat from the hind leg of a pig, salted, cured, and usually bought ready-cooked.
2 A ham is an amateur radio enthusiast.
3 A ham is also a bad actor who exaggerates emotions and gestures.

hamburger, hamburgers
(noun) A hamburger is a flat disc of minced meat, seasoned and fried; often eaten in a bread roll.
[named after their city of origin *Hamburg* in Germany]

ham-fisted
(adjective) very clumsy or awkward.

hamlet, hamlets
(noun) A hamlet is a small village.
[from Old English *ham* meaning 'home' and -*let* meaning 'small']

hammer, hammers, hammering, hammered
1 (noun) A hammer is a tool consisting of a heavy piece of metal at the end of a handle, used for hitting nails into things.
2 (verb) If you hammer something, you hit it repeatedly, with a hammer or with your fist.
3 If you hammer an idea into someone, you keep repeating it and telling them about it.
4 (an informal use) If you hammer someone, you criticize, attack, or defeat them severely.
5 (noun) A hammer is also a device with a similar function to a hammer, such as the part of a piano that hits a string when you press a key.
6 In sport, a hammer is a heavy weight attached to a wire and thrown.

hammer out
(phrasal verb) To hammer out an agreement means to reach it after a long time discussing it.

hammerhead, hammerheads
(noun) A hammerhead is a fierce shark with a hammer-shaped head.

hammock, hammocks
(noun) A hammock is a piece of net or canvas hung between two supports and used as a bed.

hamper, hampers, hampering, hampered
1 (noun) A hamper is a rectangular wicker basket with a lid, used for carrying food.
2 (verb) If you hamper someone, you make it difficult for them to move or progress.

Similar words: (sense 2) impede, hinder, obstruct, limit, handicap, retard

hamster, hamsters
(noun) A hamster is a small furry rodent, with cheek-pouches for carrying grain.

hamstring, hamstrings, hamstringing, hamstrung
1 (noun) Your hamstring is a tendon behind your

knee joining your thigh muscles to the bones of
your lower leg.
2 (verb) If you hamstring someone, you make
|it| difficult for them to do something.

hand, hands, handing, handed
1 (noun) Your hand is the part of your body
beyond the wrist, with four fingers and a thumb.
2 Your hand is also your writing style.
3 In cards, your hand is the cards you are
holding.
4 The hands of a clock or watch are the pointers
that point to the numbers.
5 When an audience gives someone a big hand,
they applaud.
6 A hand is a worker doing a physical job, e.g.
All hands on deck!
7 A hand is also a measurement of four inches
(about ten centimetres), used to measure the
height of horses.
8 The hand of someone in a situation is their
influence or the part they play in it, e.g. *Maloney
had a hand in her death.*
9 If you give someone a hand, you help them to
do something.
10 (verb) If you hand something to someone, you
give it to them.
11 (phrases) Something that is **at hand**, **to hand**,
or **on hand** is available, close by, and ready for
use.
12 A situation that is **out of hand** is out of
control.
13 Someone who lives **from hand to mouth** has
very little food or money.
14 If you **force someone's hand**, you make them
take action.
15 If you **wash your hands of something**, you
refuse to have any more involvement with it.
16 If you **have the upper hand**, you have an
advantage over someone.
17 If you are **hand in glove** with someone, you
work very closely with them.
18 If you **win hands down**, you win very easily or
by a great amount.

hand down
(phrasal verb) Something that is handed down is
passed from one generation to another.

handbag, handbags
(noun) A handbag is a small bag used mainly by
women to carry money and other small items.

handbill, handbills
(noun) A handbill is a small printed notice
advertising an event or organization.

handbook, handbooks
(noun) A handbook is a book giving information
and instructions about something.

handcuff, handcuffs
(noun) Handcuffs are two metal rings linked by a
chain which are locked around a prisoner's
wrists.

handful, handfuls
1 (noun) A handful is a small quantity, e.g. *We
employ only a handful of workers.*
2 Someone who is a handful is difficult to
control, e.g. *He is a bit of a handful.*

handicap, handicaps, handicapping, handicapped
1 (noun) A handicap is a physical or mental
disability.
2 A handicap is also something that makes it
difficult for you to achieve something.
3 In sport or a competition, a handicap is a
disadvantage or advantage given to competitors
according to their skill, in order to equalize
people's chances of winning.
4 (verb) If something handicaps someone, it
makes it difficult for them to achieve something.
handicapped (adjective).

Similar words: (sense 1) disability, impediment,
impairment

handicraft, handicrafts
(noun) Handicrafts are activities such as
embroidery or pottery involving making things
with your hands; also the items produced.
[from Old English *hand* + *cræft* meaning 'hand
skill']

handiwork
(noun) Your handiwork is something that you
have done or made yourself.

handkerchief, handkerchiefs
(noun) A handkerchief is a small square of fabric
used for blowing your nose.

handle, handles, handling, handled
1 (noun) The handle of an object is the part by
which it is held or controlled.
2 (verb) If you handle an object, you hold it in
your hands to examine it.
3 If you handle something, you deal with it or
control it, e.g. *He handled the case very well.*
handler (noun).

handlebar, handlebars
(noun) Handlebars are the bar and handles at the
front of a bicycle, used for steering.

hand-me-down, hand-me-downs
(noun) A hand-me-down is a piece of clothing
which used to belong to older members of the
family, given to the younger ones to wear.

handout, handouts
1 (noun) A handout is a gift of food, clothing, or
money given to a poor person.
2 A handout is also a piece of paper giving
information about something.

hand-picked
(adjective) carefully chosen, e.g. *a hand-picked
team of men.*

handset, handsets
(noun) A handset is the part of a telephone that
is held in the hand and contains a transmitter
and receiver.

handshake, handshakes
(noun) A handshake is the grasping and shaking
of a person's hand by another person.

handsome
1 (adjective) very attractive in appearance.
2 large and generous, e.g. *a handsome pay rise.*
handsomely (adverb).

Similar words: (sense 1) attractive, good-looking

handstand, handstands
(noun) If you do a handstand, you balance
upside down on your hands with your body and
legs straight up in the air.

handwriting
(noun) Someone's handwriting is their style of
writing as it looks on the page.

handy, handier, handiest
1 (adjective) useful and convenient, e.g. *a handy
tool.*
2 skilful, e.g. *She's handy with a screwdriver.*

hang, hangs, hanging, hung
1 (verb) If you hang something somewhere, you
attach it to a high point. If it is hanging there, it
is attached by its top to something, e.g. *washing
hanging on the line.*
2 If a future event or possibility is hanging over
you, it worries or frightens you, e.g. *The threat
of deportation hung over me.*
3 When you hang wallpaper, you stick it onto a
wall.
4 (phrase) When you **get the hang of something**,
you understand it and are able to do it.
5 (verb) To hang someone means to kill them by
suspending them by a rope around the neck. For
this sense of 'hang', the past tense and past
participle is **hanged**.
hanging (noun).

Similar words: (sense 1) drape, suspend, dangle

hang about or **hang around**
1 (phrasal verb; an informal use) To hang about
or hang around means to wait somewhere.
2 To hang about or hang around with someone
means to spend a lot of time with them.

hang back
(phrasal verb) To hang back means to wait or
hesitate.

hang on
1 (phrasal verb) If you hang on to something,
you hold it tightly or keep it.
2 (an informal use) To hang on means to wait.

hang out
(phrasal verb; an informal use) If you hang out
somewhere, you live there or spend a lot of time
there.

hang up
(phrasal verb) When you hang up, you put down
the receiver to end a telephone conversation.

hangar, hangars
(noun) A hangar is a large building where
aircraft are kept.

hangdog
(adjective) ashamed or guilty, e.g. *a hangdog
expression.*

hanger, hangers
(noun) A hanger is a coat hanger.

hanger-on, hangers-on
(noun) A hanger-on is an unwelcome follower of
an important person.

hang-glider, hang-gliders
(noun) A hang-glider is an unpowered aircraft

consisting of a large frame covered in fabric,
from which the pilot is suspended in a harness.

hangnail, hangnails
(noun) A hangnail is a piece of torn skin around
your nail.
[from Old English *enge* + *nægl* meaning 'tight
nail']

hangover, hangovers
(noun) A hangover is a feeling of sickness and
headache after drinking too much alcohol.

hang-up, hang-ups
(noun) A hang-up about something is a continual
feeling of embarrassment or fear about it.

hank, hanks
(noun) A hank is a length of wool or thread
looped into a coil.
[from Old Norse *hanka* meaning 'to coil']

hanker, hankers, hankering, hankered
(verb) If you hanker after something, you
continually want it.
hankering (noun).

hanky, hankies
(noun) A hanky is a handkerchief.

hanky-panky
(noun) Hanky-panky is naughty or mischievous
behaviour, especially a casual sexual
relationship.

hansom cab, hansom cabs
(noun) A hansom cab was a two-wheeled
horse-drawn carriage with a fixed hood.
[named after their designer J A Hansom
(1803-1882)]

haphazard (pronounced hap-**haz**-ard)
(adjective) not organized or planned.
haphazardly (adverb).
[from Old Norse *hap* meaning 'chance' and
Arabic *az-zahr* meaning 'gaming dice']

hapless
(adjective; a literary word) unlucky.
[from Old Norse *happ* meaning 'chance' or 'good
luck' and Old English *leas* meaning 'without']

happen, happens, happening, happened
1 (verb) When something happens, it occurs or
takes place.
2 If you happen to do something, you do it by
chance.
happening (noun).

Similar words: (sense 1) occur, befall, transpire

happiness
(noun) Happiness is a feeling of great
contentment or pleasure.

happy, happier, happiest
1 (adjective) feeling, showing, or producing
contentment or pleasure, e.g. *a happy smile... a
happy place.*
2 satisfied that something is right, e.g. *I'm not
happy about this agreement.*
3 willing, e.g. *I'd be happy to help.*
4 fortunate or lucky, e.g. *a happy coincidence.*
happily (adverb).

Similar words: (sense 1) joyful, blissful, blithe, glad

happy-go-lucky
(adjective) carefree and unconcerned.

hara-kiri (pronounced ha-ra **kir**-ree)
(noun) Hara-kiri is a Japanese form of suicide by cutting open the stomach, traditionally regarded as an honourable way to avoid disgrace.
[from Japanese *hara* + *kiri* meaning 'belly cut']

harangue, harangues, haranguing, harangued
(pronounced har-**rang**)
1 (noun) A harangue is a long, forceful, passionate speech.
2 (verb) To harangue someone means to talk to them at length passionately and forcefully about something.
[from Old Italian *aringa* meaning 'public speech']

harass, harasses, harassing, harassed
(pronounced **har**-rass)
(verb) If someone harasses you, they trouble or annoy you continually.
harassed (adjective), **harassment** (noun).
[from Old French *harer* meaning 'to set a dog on']

harbinger, harbingers (pronounced **har**-bin-jer)
(noun) A harbinger of a future event is a person or thing that comes before it and is considered to be a sign of it.

harbour, harbours, harbouring, harboured
1 (noun) A harbour is a protected area of deep water where boats can be moored.
2 (verb) To harbour someone means to hide them secretly in your house.
3 If you harbour a feeling, you have it for a long time, e.g. *She still harbours a grudge against him.*
[from Old English *here* + *beorg* meaning 'army shelter']

hard, harder, hardest
1 (adjective or adverb) Something that is hard is firm, solid, or stiff, e.g. *a hard piece of cheese... The ground was baked hard.*
2 requiring a lot of effort, e.g. *hard work... Push hard.*
3 (adjective) difficult, e.g. *a hard problem.*
4 Someone who is hard has no kindness or pity, e.g. *Don't be hard on him... She's as hard as nails.*
5 A hard colour or voice is harsh and unpleasant.
6 Hard evidence or facts can be proved to be true.
7 Hard water contains a lot of lime, leaves a coating on kettles and does not easily produce a lather.
8 Hard drugs are very strong illegal drugs.
9 Hard drink is strong alcohol.
10 (adverb) An event that follows hard upon something takes place immediately afterwards.
hardness (noun).

Similar words: (sense 1) firm, solid, stiff, rigid, set

hard and fast
(adjective) fixed and not able to be changed, e.g. *hard and fast rules.*

hardback, hardbacks
(noun) A hardback is a book with a stiff cover.

hard-bitten
(adjective) tough and determined.

hardboard
(verb) Hardboard is wood fibres pressed together to form a flat sheet.

hard core
1 (noun) The hard core in an organization is the group of people who are most involved in it.
2 Hard core consists of pieces of broken stone used as a base for roads.

harden, hardens, hardening, hardened
(verb) To harden means to become hard or get harder.
hardening (noun), **hardened** (adjective).

hard-headed
(adjective) practical and determined, especially in business.

hardhearted
(adjective) unsympathetic and uncaring.

hard labour
(noun) Hard labour is physical work which is difficult and tiring. It is used in some countries as a punishment for a crime.

hardly
1 (adverb) almost not or not quite, e.g. *He had hardly any money.*
2 certainly not, e.g. *It's hardly surprising.*

hard-nosed
(adjective) tough, practical, and realistic.

hard of hearing
(adjective) not able to hear properly.

hard palate, hard palates
(noun) Your hard palate is the hard top part inside your mouth.

hardship, hardships
(noun) Hardship is a time or situation of suffering and difficulty.

hard shoulder, hard shoulders
(noun) The hard shoulder is the area at the edge of a motorway where a driver can stop in the event of a breakdown.

hard up
(adjective; an informal expression) having hardly any money.

hardware
1 (noun) Hardware is tools and equipment for use in the home and garden.
2 Hardware is also computer machinery rather than computer programs.

hard-wearing
(adjective) strong, well-made, and long-lasting.

hardwood, hardwoods
(noun) Hardwood is strong, hard wood from a tree such as an oak; also the tree itself.

hardy, hardier, hardiest
(adjective) tough and able to endure very difficult or cold conditions, e.g. *hardy sheep.*
hardiness (noun).
[from Old French *hardi* meaning 'bold']

hare, hares, haring, hared
1 (noun) A hare is an animal like a large rabbit, but with longer ears and legs.
2 (verb) To hare about means to run very fast, e.g. *He hared off down the corridor.*

harebrained
(adjective) foolish and likely to be unsuccessful, e.g. *harebrained ideas.*

harelip, harelips
(noun) Someone with a harelip was born with a cleft or split in their upper lip.

harem, harems (pronounced har-**reem**)
(noun) A harem is a group of wives or mistresses of one man, especially in Muslim societies; also the place where these women live.
[from Arabic *harim* meaning 'forbidden']

haricot bean, haricot beans (pronounced har-i-koh)
(noun) Haricot beans are small, pale beans, usually sold dried.

hark, harks, harking, harked
1 (verb; an old-fashioned use) To hark means to listen.
2 To hark back to something in the past means to refer back to it or recall it.

harlequin (pronounced **har**-lik-win)
(adjective) having many different colours.
[from the colourful costume of the character *Harlequin* in Italian comedy]

harlot, harlots
(noun; a literary word) A harlot is a prostitute, or a woman who looks or behaves like one.
[from Old French *herlot* meaning 'rascal']

harm, harms, harming, harmed
1 (verb) To harm someone or something means to injure or damage them.
2 (noun) Harm is injury or damage.
[from Old German *harm* meaning 'injury']

Similar words: (sense 1) hurt, injure, wound

harmful
(adjective) having a bad effect on something, e.g. *Too much salt can be harmful to your health.*

harmless
1 (adjective) safe to use or be near.
2 unlikely to cause problems or annoyance, e.g. *a harmless habit.*
harmlessly (adverb), **harmlessness** (noun).

Similar words: innocuous, inoffensive, safe

harmonic, harmonics
1 (adjective) using musical harmony.
2 (noun) A harmonic is an overtone of a musical note produced when that note is played, but not usually heard as a separate note.

harmonica, harmonicas
(noun) A harmonica is a small musical instrument which you play by blowing and sucking while moving it across your lips.

harmonious (pronounced har-**moh**-nee-uss)
1 (adjective) showing agreement, peacefulness, and friendship, e.g. *harmonious relationships.*
2 consisting of parts which blend well together making an attractive whole, e.g. *the harmonious design of the garden.*
harmoniously (adverb).

harmonium, harmoniums (pronounced har-**moh**-nee-um)
(noun) A harmonium is a musical keyboard instrument of the organ family. You work pedals which pump air through the reeds in order to produce sound.

harmonize, harmonizes, harmonizing, harmonized; also spelled **harmonise**
(verb) If things harmonize, they fit in with each other or interact in an agreeable way.

harmony, harmonies
1 (noun) Harmony is a state of peaceful agreement and cooperation, e.g. *working together in harmony.*
2 In music, harmony is the pleasant combination of two or more notes played at the same time.
[from Greek *harmonia* meaning 'agreement']

harness, harnesses, harnessing, harnessed
1 (noun) A harness is a set of straps and fittings fastened round a horse so that it can pull a vehicle, or fastened round someone's body to attach something, e.g. *a parachute harness.*
2 (verb) If you harness something, you bring it under control to use it, e.g. *harnessing the energy of the sun.*
[from Old French *herneis* meaning 'military equipment']

harp, harps, harping, harped
1 (noun) A harp is a musical instrument consisting of a triangular frame with vertical strings which you pluck with your fingers.
2 (verb) If someone harps on something, they keep talking about it, especially in a boring way.
harpist (noun).

harpoon, harpoons, harpooning, harpooned
1 (noun) A harpoon is a barbed spear attached to a rope, thrown or fired from a gun and used for catching whales or large sea fish.
2 (verb) To harpoon a whale or large sea fish means to catch it using a harpoon.

harpsichord, harpsichords
(noun) A harpsichord is a keyboard instrument in which the strings are plucked mechanically when the keys are pressed.

harrowing
(adjective) very upsetting or disturbing, e.g. *a harrowing experience.*

harry, harries, harrying, harried
(verb) If someone harries you, they try to get you to do something by repeatedly mentioning it.

harsh, harsher, harshest
(adjective) severe, difficult, and unpleasant, e.g. *a harsh winter... harsh treatment.*
harshly (adverb), **harshness** (noun).

Similar words: severe, hard, tough

harvest, harvests, harvesting, harvested
1 (noun) The harvest is the cutting and gathering of a crop; also the ripe crop when it is gathered and the time of gathering.

2 (verb) To harvest food means to gather it when it is ripe.
harvester (noun).
[from Old German *herbist* meaning 'autumn']

harvest festival, harvest festivals
(noun) A harvest festival is a Christian church service held to give thanks for the harvest.

has-been, has-beens
(noun; an informal expression) A has-been is a person who is no longer important or successful.

hash
1 (phrase) If you **make a hash of** a job, you do it badly.
2 (noun) Hash is a dish made of small pieces of meat and vegetables cooked together.
3 (an informal use) Hash is also hashish.
[from Old French *hacher* meaning 'to chop up']

hashish (pronounced **hash**-eesh)
(noun) Hashish is a drug made from the hemp plant. It is usually smoked, and is illegal in many countries.
[from Arabic *hashish* meaning 'hemp' or 'dried grass']

hasp, hasps
(noun) A hasp is a door fastening consisting of a metal plate with a slot in it which fits over a U-shaped piece and can be secured with a padlock.

hassle, hassles, hassling, hassled
1 (noun; an informal word) Something that is a hassle is difficult or causes trouble.
2 (verb) If you hassle someone, you annoy them by repeatedly asking them to do something.

hassock, hassocks
(noun) A hassock is a cushion for kneeling on in church.
[from Old English *hassuc* meaning 'matted grass']

haste
(noun) Haste is doing something quickly, especially too quickly.
[from Old English *hæst* meaning 'violence' or 'fury']

hasten, hastens, hastening, hastened
(pronounced **hay**-sn)
(verb) To hasten means to move quickly or do something quickly.

hasty, hastier, hastiest
(adjective) done or happening suddenly and quickly, often without enough care or thought.
hastily (adverb).

hat, hats
1 (noun) A hat is a covering for the head.
2 (phrase) If you say you'll **eat your hat** if something happens, you mean you do not believe it will happen.
3 If you do something **at the drop of a hat**, you do it straight away without hesitation.

hatch, hatches, hatching, hatched
1 (verb) When an egg hatches, or when a bird or reptile hatches, the egg breaks open and the young bird or reptile emerges.
2 To hatch a plot means to plan it.

3 (noun) A hatch is a covered opening in a floor, wall, or ceiling.

hatchback, hatchbacks
(noun) A hatchback is a car with a door at the back which opens upwards.

hatchet, hatchets
1 (noun) A hatchet is a small axe.
2 (phrase) To **bury the hatchet** means to resolve a disagreement and become friends again.
3 (adjective) A hatchet face is a long face with sharp features.
[from Old French *hachette* meaning 'little axe']

hate, hates, hating, hated
1 (verb) If you hate someone or something, you have a strong dislike for them.
2 (noun) Hate is a strong feeling of dislike.

Similar words: (sense 1) loathe, detest, abhor, abominate, despise

hateful
(adjective) extremely unpleasant, e.g. *Robert had just come from a hateful school.*

Similar words: abhorrent, abominable, loathsome, odious, detestable, despicable, obnoxious

hatred (pronounced **hay**-trid)
(noun) Hatred is an extremely strong feeling of dislike.

hat trick, hat tricks
(noun) In sport, a hat trick is a series of three achievements, for example when a footballer scores three goals in a match.

haughty, haughtier, haughtiest (rhymes with **naughty**)
(adjective) showing excessive pride, e.g. *He received it with haughty indifference.*
haughtily (adverb), **haughtiness** (noun).
[from Old French *haut* meaning 'high']

Similar words: disdainful, supercilious, high and mighty, proud, snooty

haul, hauls, hauling, hauled
1 (verb) To haul something somewhere means to pull it with great effort and difficulty.
2 (noun) A haul is a quantity of something obtained, e.g. *a good haul of fish... Thieves have made some spectacular hauls in this area.*
3 (phrase) Something that you describe as **a long haul** takes a lot of time and effort to achieve, e.g. *So women began the long haul to equality.*

haulage (pronounced **hawl**-lij)
(noun) Haulage is the business or cost of transporting goods by road.

haunches
(plural noun) Your haunches are your buttocks and the tops of your legs, e.g. *He squatted on his haunches.*

haunt, haunts, haunting, haunted
1 (verb) If a ghost haunts a place, it is seen or heard there regularly.
2 If a memory or a fear haunts you, it continually worries you.

3 (noun) A person's favourite haunt is a place they like to visit often.
[from Old French *hanter* meaning 'to visit']

haunted
1 (adjective) regularly visited by a ghost, e.g. *a haunted house.*
2 very worried or troubled, e.g. *a haunted expression.*

haunting
(adjective) extremely beautiful or sad so that it makes a lasting impression on you, e.g. *a haunting melody.*
hauntingly (adverb).

hauteur (pronounced owe-**ter**)
(noun) Hauteur is haughtiness.

have, has, having, had
1 (verb) Have is an auxiliary verb, used to form the past tense or to express completed actions, e.g. *People have already forgotten... I have lost it.*
2 If you have something, you own or possess it, e.g. *We have three cars.*
3 If you have something, you experience it, it happens to you, or you are affected by it, e.g. *I have an idea!... He has a bad cold.*
4 To have a child or baby animal means to give birth to it, e.g. *When is she having the baby?*
5 (phrases) If you **have to** do something, you must do it. If you **had better** do something, you ought to do it.
6 Something that has **had it** is a failure or is broken and cannot be repaired.
7 If you **have it in for someone**, you dislike them and are determined to cause them trouble.
8 If you are **having someone on**, you are teasing them by trying to deceive them.
9 If someone is **had up** for something, they are brought before a court for committing an offence.
10 If you **have been had**, you have been tricked.

haven, havens (pronounced **hay**-ven)
(noun) A haven is a safe place.
[from Old English *hæfen* meaning 'harbour']

haversack, haversacks (pronounced **hav**-er-sak)
(noun) A haversack is a light bag with straps, worn on your back or over your shoulders and used for carrying things when you are walking.
[from German *Habersack* meaning 'oat bag']

havoc
1 (noun) Havoc is disorder and confusion.
2 (phrase) To **play havoc** with something means to cause great disorder and confusion, e.g. *The anxiety had played havoc with his work.*
[from Old French *havot* meaning 'pillage']

hawk, hawks, hawking, hawked
1 (noun) A hawk is a large bird with a short, hooked bill, sharp claws and very good eyesight. Hawks hunt small birds and animals.
2 (verb) To hawk goods means to sell them by taking them around from place to place.
hawker (noun).

hawser, hawsers
(noun) A hawser is a large, heavy rope or cable used on a ship.
[from Old French *haucier* meaning 'to hoist']

hawthorn, hawthorns
(noun) A hawthorn is a small, thorny tree producing white blossom and red berries.
[from Old English *haguthorn* meaning 'hedge thorn']

hay
1 (noun) Hay is grass which has been cut and dried and is used as animal feed.
2 (phrase) To **make hay while the sun shines** means to do something while you have the opportunity to do it.

hay fever
(noun) Hay fever is an allergy to pollen and grass, causing sneezing, a blocked nose, and watering eyes.

haystack, haystacks
(noun) A haystack is a large, firmly built pile of hay, usually covered and left out in the open.

hazard, hazards, hazarding, hazarded
1 (noun) A hazard is something which could be dangerous to you.
2 (verb) If you hazard something, you put it at risk, e.g. *hazarding the health of his crew.*
3 (phrase) If you **hazard a guess**, you make a guess.
hazardous (adjective).
[from Arabic *az-zahr* meaning 'gaming dice']

haze
(noun) If there is a haze, you cannot see clearly because there is moisture, dust, or smoke suspended in the air.

hazel, hazels
1 (noun) A hazel is a small tree producing edible nuts.
2 (adjective) greenish brown in colour.

hazy, hazier, haziest
(adjective) dim or vague, e.g. *a hazy memory.*

H-bomb, H-bombs
(noun) An H-bomb is a hydrogen bomb.

he
(pronoun) He is used to refer to a man, boy, or male animal or to any person whose sex is not mentioned.

head, heads, heading, headed
1 (noun) Your head is the part of your body which has your eyes, brain, and mouth in it.
2 Your head is also your mind and mental abilities, e.g. *Use your head!*
3 The head of something is the top, start, or most important end, e.g. *at the head of the table.*
4 The head of a group or organization is the leader or person in charge.
5 (verb) To head a group or organization means to be the leader or be in charge, e.g. *Their car headed the procession.*
6 (noun) The head on beer is the layer of froth on the top.
7 The head on a tape-recorder is the part which touches the magnetic tape and transmits the

electronic signal to record onto or play from the tape.

8 (verb) To head in a particular direction means to move in that direction, e.g. *Unemployment was heading for 4 million.*

9 To head a ball means to hit it with your head.

10 (noun) When you toss a coin, the side called heads is the one with the head on it.

11 (phrase) If someone **bites** or **snaps your head off**, they speak to you sharply and angrily.

12 If you give some information **off the top of your head**, you give it from memory.

13 If you **lose your head**, you panic.

14 If you say that someone is **off their head**, you mean that they are mad or very stupid.

15 If you **give someone their head**, you let them take control or do what they want to do.

16 If something is **over someone's head**, it is too difficult for them to understand.

17 If you **can't make head nor tail of something**, you cannot understand it.

head off
(phrasal verb) If you head off someone or something, you make them change direction or prevent something from happening, e.g. *measures taken to head off possible unrest.*

headache, headaches
1 (noun) A headache is a pain in your head.

2 Something that is a headache is causing a lot of difficulty or worry, e.g. *The situation had become a real headache for the organizers.*

headdress, headdresses
(noun) A headdress is something that is worn on a person's head for decoration.

header, headers
(noun) A header in football is hitting the ball with your head.

head-hunter, head-hunters
(noun; an informal word) A head-hunter is a person who sets out to recruit someone from another company for a particular job.

heading, headings
(noun) A heading is a piece of writing that is written or printed at the top of a page.

headland, headlands
(noun) A headland is a narrow piece of land jutting out into the sea.

headlight, headlights
(noun) The headlights on a motor vehicle are the large powerful lights at the front.

headline, headlines
1 (noun) A newspaper headline is the title of a newspaper article printed in large, bold type.

2 The headlines are the main points of the radio or television news.

headmaster, headmasters
(noun) A headmaster is a man who is the head teacher of a school.

headmistress, headmistresses
(noun) A headmistress is a woman who is the head teacher of a school.

headphones
(plural noun) Headphones are a pair of small speakers which you wear over your ears to listen to music or speech without other people hearing.

headquarters
(noun) The headquarters of an organization is the main place or building from which it is run.

headroom
(noun) Headroom is the amount of space between the top of something and a roof or surface which it must pass under or fit under.

headstand, headstands
(noun) If you do a headstand, you balance upside down on your head and your hands with your body and legs straight up in the air.

headstone, headstones
(noun) A headstone is a large stone standing at one end of a grave and showing the name of the person buried there.

headstrong
(adjective) determined to do something in your own way and ignoring other people's advice.

head teacher, head teachers
(noun) The head teacher of a school is the teacher who is in charge of it.

headway
(phrase) If you are **making headway**, you are making progress.

headwind, headwinds
(noun) A headwind is a wind blowing in the opposite direction to the way you are travelling.

heady, headier, headiest
(adjective) extremely exciting, e.g. *the heady days of the sixties.*

heal, heals, healing, healed
(verb) If something heals or if you heal it, it becomes healthy or normal again, e.g. *His leg needs support while the bone is healing.*
healer (noun).

health
1 (noun) Health is the normally good condition of someone's body and the extent to which it is free from illness, e.g. *Smoking damages your health.*

2 (phrase) To **drink someone's health** means to drink to wish them good health and happiness. [from Old English *hælth* a toast drunk to a person's wellbeing]

Similar words: (sense 1) fitness, healthiness, soundness, wellbeing

health food, health foods
(noun) Health food is food which is free from added chemicals and is considered to be good for your health.

healthy, healthier, healthiest
1 (adjective) Someone who is healthy is fit and strong and does not have any diseases.

2 Something that is healthy is good for you and likely to make you fit and strong.

3 An organization or system that is healthy is successful, e.g. *a healthy economy.*
healthily (adverb), **healthiness** (noun).

Similar words: (sense 1) fit, robust, hearty, hale

heap, heaps, heaping, heaped
1 (noun) A heap of things is a pile of them.
2 (an informal use) Heaps of something means plenty of it, e.g. *We've got heaps of time.*
3 (verb) If you heap things, you pile them up.
4 To heap something such as praise on someone means to give them a lot of it.

Similar words: (sense 1) pile, stack, mound, mass

hear, hears, hearing, heard
1 (verb) When you hear sounds, you are aware of them because they reach your ears.
2 When you hear from someone, they write to you or phone you.
3 When a judge hears a case, he or she listens to it in court in order to make a decision on it.
4 (phrase) If you say that you **won't hear of** something, you mean you refuse to allow it.
5 'Hear, hear!' is sometimes said to show agreement with a speaker.

Similar words: (sense 1) listen to, perceive, catch

hear out
(phrasal verb) If you hear someone out, you listen to all they have to say without interrupting.

hearing, hearings
1 (noun) Hearing is the sense which makes it possible for you to be aware of sounds, e.g. *My hearing has deteriorated.*
2 (phrase) Someone who is **within hearing** is close enough to be heard or hear you.
3 (noun) A hearing is a court trial or official meeting to hear facts about an incident.
4 If someone gives you a hearing, they let you give your point of view and listen to you.

hearsay
(noun) Hearsay is information that you have heard from other people rather than something that you know personally to be true.

hearse, hearses (rhymes with **verse**)
(noun) A hearse is a large car that carries the coffin at a funeral.

heart, hearts
1 (noun) Your heart is the organ in your chest that pumps the blood around your body.
2 Heart is courage, determination, or enthusiasm, e.g. *People were losing heart.*
3 The heart of something is the most central and important part of it, e.g. *Get right to the heart of the matter... deep in the heart of the city.*
4 A heart is a shape similar to a heart, used especially as a symbol of love.
5 Hearts is one of the four suits in a pack of playing cards. It is marked by a red heart-shaped symbol.
6 (phrase) If you know something **by heart**, you can remember it all perfectly.
7 If you have a **change of heart**, you change your opinion about something.
8 Someone who is a person **after your own heart** shares your own opinions or interests.
9 If your **heart is in your mouth**, you are very frightened.

10 If you **take** what someone says **to heart**, you are very upset by it.
11 Someone who **wears their heart on their sleeve** openly shows their feelings.

heartache, heartaches
(noun) Heartache is very great sadness and emotional suffering.

heart attack, heart attacks
(noun) A heart attack is a serious medical condition in which the heart suddenly beats irregularly or stops completely. Death can result if medical attention is not given quickly.

heartbreak, heartbreaks
(noun) Heartbreak is great sadness and emotional suffering.
heartbreaking (adjective).

heartbroken
(adjective) very sad and emotionally upset, e.g. *She would be heartbroken if he died.*

heartburn
(noun) Heartburn is a painful burning sensation in your chest, caused by indigestion.

hearten, heartens, heartening, heartened
(verb) When something such as good news heartens someone, it encourages them and makes them cheerful.

heart failure
(noun) Heart failure is a serious condition in which someone's heart does not function as well as it should, sometimes stopping completely.

heartfelt
(adjective) sincerely and deeply felt, e.g. *a heartfelt prayer for the return of loved ones.*

hearth, hearths (pronounced **harth**)
(noun) A hearth is the floor of a fireplace.

heartless
(adjective) cruel and unkind.
heartlessly (adverb).

heart-rending
(adjective) causing great sadness and pity, e.g. *a heart-rending story.*

heart-throb, heart-throbs
(noun) A heart-throb is someone who is attractive to a lot of people.

heart-to-heart, heart-to-hearts
(noun) A heart-to-heart is a discussion in which two people talk about their deepest feelings.

hearty, heartier, heartiest
1 (adjective) cheerful and enthusiastic, e.g. *hearty applause... a hearty welcome.*
2 strongly felt, e.g. *a hearty dislike of animals.*
3 A hearty meal is large and satisfying.
heartily (adverb).

heat, heats, heating, heated
1 (noun) Heat is warmth or the quality of being hot; also the temperature of something that is warm or hot.
2 (verb) To heat something means to raise its temperature.
3 (noun) Heat is strength of feeling, especially of anger or excitement.
4 A heat is one of a series of contests in a

competition. The winners of a heat go forward to play in the next round of the competition.
5 (phrase) When a female animal is **on heat**, she is ready for mating.

heath, heaths
(noun) A heath is an area of open land covered with rough grass or heather.
[from Old German *heida* meaning 'heather']

heathen, heathens
(noun; an old-fashioned word) A heathen is someone who has no religion or who does not believe in one of the established religions.

heather
(noun) Heather is a low, spreading plant with small, spiky leaves and pink, purple, or white flowers. Heather grows wild on hills and moorland.

heating
(noun) Heating is the equipment used to heat a building; also the process and cost of running the equipment to provide heat.

heatwave, heatwaves
(noun) A heatwave is a period of time during which the weather is much hotter than usual.

heave, heaves, heaving, heaved
1 (verb) To heave something means to pull, push, or throw it with a lot of effort.
2 (noun) If you give something a heave, you pull, push, or throw it with a lot of effort.
3 (verb) If your stomach heaves, you vomit or suddenly feel sick.
4 If you heave a sigh, you sigh loudly.
[from Old German *heffen* meaning 'to raise']

heave to
(phrasal verb) When a ship heaves to, it stops moving.

heaven, heavens
1 (noun) Heaven is a place of happiness where God is believed to live and where good people are believed to go when they die.
2 If you describe a situation or place as heaven, you mean it is wonderful, e.g. *The cottage was just heaven.*
3 (a literary use) The heavens are the sky.
4 (phrase) You say '**Good heavens'** to express surprise.

heavenly
1 (adjective) relating to heaven, e.g. *heavenly spirits.*
2 (an informal use) wonderful, e.g. *a heavenly meal.*

heaven-sent
(adjective) unexpected but very welcome, e.g. *a heaven-sent opportunity.*

heavy, heavier, heaviest; heavies
1 (adjective) great in weight or force, e.g. *How heavy are you?... heavy rain.*
2 great in degree or amount, e.g. *There were heavy casualties.*
3 solid and thick in appearance, e.g. *glasses with heavy frames.*
4 using a lot of something quickly, e.g. *The van is heavy on petrol.*

5 serious and difficult to deal with or understand, e.g. *It all got a bit heavy when the police arrived... a heavy speech.*
6 Food that is heavy is solid and difficult to digest, e.g. *a heavy meal.*
7 When it is heavy, the weather is hot, humid, and still.
8 Someone with a heavy heart is very sad.
9 (noun; an informal use) A heavy is a large, strong man employed to protect someone or something.
heavily (adverb), **heaviness** (noun).

heavy-duty
(adjective) Heavy-duty equipment is strong and hard-wearing.

heavy-handed
(adjective) showing a lack of care or thought and using too much authority, e.g. *the government's heavy-handed intervention.*

heavy industry, heavy industries
(noun) Heavy industry is industry in which large machinery is used to produce raw materials such as steel, or large objects.

heavy metal
(noun) Heavy metal is a style of loud, fast rock music.

heavyweight, heavyweights
1 (noun) A heavyweight is a boxer in the heaviest weight group.
2 A heavyweight is also an important person with a lot of influence.

Hebrew, Hebrews (pronounced **hee**-broo)
1 (noun) Hebrew is an ancient language now spoken in Israel, where it is the official language.
2 In the past, the Hebrews were Hebrew-speaking Jews who lived in Israel.
3 (adjective) relating to the Hebrews and their customs.
[from Hebrew *ibhri* meaning 'one from beyond (the river)']

heckle, heckles, heckling, heckled
(verb) If members of an audience heckle a speaker, they interrupt and shout rude remarks.
heckler (noun).

hectare, hectares
(noun) A hectare is a unit for measuring areas of land. One hectare is equal to 10,000 square metres or about 2.471 acres.
[from Greek *hekaton* meaning 'one hundred' and *area* meaning 'piece of ground']

hectic
(adjective) involving a lot of rushed activity, e.g. *a hectic week.*
[from Greek *hektikos* meaning 'habitual']

hector, hectors, hectoring, hectored
(verb) To hector someone means to bully or torment them in an aggressive way.
[from the name of the Greek warrior *Hector*]

hedge, hedges, hedging, hedged
1 (noun) A hedge is a row of bushes forming a barrier or boundary.
2 A hedge against something unpleasant

happening is a way of protecting yourself from it, e.g. *a hedge against inflation*.
3 (verb) If you **hedge** against something unpleasant happening, you protect yourself.
4 If you hedge, you avoid answering a question or dealing with a problem.
5 (phrase) If you **hedge your bets**, you support two or more people or courses of action to avoid the risk of losing a lot.
6 If something is **hedged in** or **hedged around**, it has restrictions placed on its freedom or development, e.g. *The proposals were hedged in with legal niceties*.

hedgehog, hedgehogs
(noun) A hedgehog is a small, brown nocturnal animal with sharp spikes covering its back.

hedonism (pronounced **hee**-dn-izm)
(noun) Hedonism is the belief that gaining pleasure is the most important thing in life. **hedonistic** (adjective).
[from Greek *hēdonē* meaning 'pleasure']

heed, heeds, heeding, heeded
(verb) If you heed someone's advice, you pay attention to it.

Similar words: mark, mind, note

heedless
(adjective) without taking any notice of something, e.g. *She continued, heedless of his presence*.

heel, heels, heeling, heeled
1 (noun) Your heel is the back part of your foot.
2 The heel of a shoe or sock is the part covering or below the heel.
3 (verb) To heel a pair of shoes means to put a new piece on the heel.
4 (phrase) If you **take to your heels**, you run away.
5 If you **dig your heels in**, you refuse to be persuaded to do something.
6 If you are left **cooling** or **kicking your heels**, you are being kept waiting.
7 A person or place that looks **down at heel** looks untidy and in poor condition.

hefty, heftier, heftiest
(adjective) of great size, force, or weight, e.g. *a hefty profit... a hefty slap on the back*.

hegemony (pronounced hig-**gem**-on-ee)
(noun) Hegemony is the domination by one country over a group of others.

heifer, heifers (pronounced **hef**-fer)
(noun) A heifer is a young cow that has not yet had a calf.

height, heights
1 (noun) The height of an object is its measurement from the bottom to the top.
2 A height is a high position or place, e.g. *dropping from a height*.
3 The height of something is its peak, or the time when it is most successful or intense, e.g. *the height of the tourist season... It seemed the height of luxury*.

heighten, heightens, heightening, heightened
(verb) If something heightens a feeling or experience, it increases its intensity.

heinous (pronounced **hay**-nuss or **hee**-nuss)
(adjective) evil and terrible, e.g. *heinous crimes*.
[from Old French *haineus* meaning 'hateful']

heir, heirs (pronounced **air**)
1 (noun) A person's heir is the person who is entitled to inherit their property or title.
2 (phrase) If someone or something is **heir to** a particular quality or condition, it is passed on to them, e.g. *Graffiti is one of the many blights that the city is heir to*.
[from Greek *khēros* meaning 'bereaved']

heiress, heiresses (pronounced **air**-iss)
(noun) An heiress is a female with the right to inherit property or a title.

heirloom, heirlooms (pronounced **air**-loom)
(noun) An heirloom is something belonging to a family that has been passed from one generation to another.

helicopter, helicopters
(noun) A helicopter is an aircraft without wings, but with rotating blades above it which enable it to take off vertically, hover, and fly.
[from Greek *heliko* + *pteron* meaning 'spiral wing']

heliport, heliports
(noun) A heliport is an airport for helicopters.

helium (pronounced **hee**-lee-um)
(noun) Helium is an element which is a colourless inert gas. It occurs in some natural gases, and is used in air balloons. Its atomic number is 2 and its symbol is He.
[from Greek *hēlios* meaning 'sun', because helium was first discovered in the solar spectrum]

helix, helixes or **helices** (pronounced **hee**-liks)
(noun) A helix is a spiral or coil.

hell
1 (noun) Hell is the place where souls of evil people are believed to go to be punished after death.
2 (an informal use) If you say that something is hell, you mean it is very unpleasant.
3 Hell is also a swear word.
4 (phrase) If there will be **hell to pay**, there will be serious trouble.
5 If you **raise hell**, you protest angrily about something.
6 If you do something **for the hell of it**, you do it for fun.

hell-bent
(adjective) determined to do something whatever the consequences.

hellish
(adjective; an informal word) very unpleasant, e.g. *It's hellish being a student here*.
hellishly (adverb), **hellishness** (noun).

hello
You say 'Hello' as a greeting or when you answer the phone.

helm, helms
1 (noun) The helm on a boat is the position from which it is steered and the wheel or tiller.
2 (phrase) **At the helm** means in a position of leadership or control.

helmet, helmets
(noun) A helmet is a hard hat worn to protect the head.

help, helps, helping, helped
1 (verb) To help someone means to make something easier, better, or quicker for them.
2 (noun) If you have or need help, you have or need someone to help you.
3 A help is someone or something that helps you, e.g. *She's been a great help.*
4 (phrase) If you **help yourself** to something, you take it.
5 If you **can't help** something, you cannot control it or change it, e.g. *I can't help laughing.*
helper (noun).

Similar words: (sense 1) aid. assist, abet, oblige

(senses 2 and 3) aid, assistance

helpful
1 (adjective) If someone is helpful, they help you by doing something for you.
2 Something that is helpful makes a situation more pleasant or easier to tolerate.
helpfully (adverb), **helpfulness** (noun).

Similar words: (sense 1) accommodating, cooperative, obliging

helping, helpings
(noun) A helping is an amount of food that you get in a single serving.

helpless
(adjective) without power, strength, or protection, e.g. *a helpless child.*
helplessly (adverb), **helplessness** (noun).

helter-skelter, helter-skelters
1 (noun) A helter-skelter is a tall spiral-shaped slide, usually in a fairground.
2 (adverb and adjective) in a hurried and disorganized way.

hem, hems, hemming, hemmed
1 (noun) The hem of a garment is an edge which has been turned over and sewn in place.
2 (verb) To hem something means to make a hem on it.

hem in
(phrasal verb) If someone is hemmed in, they are surrounded and prevented from moving.

hematite or **haematite** (pronounced **hee**-mat-ite)
(noun) Hematite is a reddish-black mineral and is the main source of iron.
[from Greek *haimatites* meaning 'looking like blood']

hematology another spelling of **haematology**.

hemisphere, hemispheres (pronounced **hem**-iss-feer)
(noun) A hemisphere is one half of the earth, the brain, or a sphere.
hemispherical (adjective).

[from Greek *hemi-* + *sphaira* meaning 'half a globe']

hemlock
(noun) Hemlock is a poisonous plant with purple spotted stems and small white flowers.

hemoglobin another spelling of **haemoglobin**.

hemophilia another spelling of **haemophilia**

hemorrhage another spelling of **haemorrhage**

hemorrhoids another spelling of **haemorrhoids**

hemp
(noun) Hemp is a tall plant, originally grown in Asia. Some varieties of it are used to make rope, and others to produce the drug cannabis.

hen, hens
(noun) A hen is a female chicken; also any female bird.

hence
1 (adverb; a formal word) for this reason, e.g. *The computer has become cheaper and hence available to a greater number of people.*
2 from now or from the time mentioned, e.g. *A few hours hence they would be man and wife.*

henceforth
(adverb; a formal word) from this time onward, e.g. *You will henceforth put yourself at her disposal.*

henchman, henchmen
(noun) The henchmen of a powerful person are the people employed to do violent or dishonest work for that person.
[from Old English *hengest* meaning 'stallion', hence 'groom']

henna
(noun) Henna is a reddish-brown dye used especially for colouring hair. It is made from the leaves of a shrub from Asia and North Africa.
[from Arabic *hinna* meaning 'henna']

hen party, hen parties
(noun) A hen party is a party for women only.

henpecked
(adjective) A henpecked man is dominated by a woman, e.g. *henpecked husbands.*

hepatitis
(noun) Hepatitis is a serious infectious disease causing inflammation of the liver.
[from Greek *hepar* + *-itis* meaning 'liver inflammation']

heptagon, heptagons
(noun) A heptagon is a shape with seven straight sides.
heptagonal (adjective).
[from Greek *hepta* + *-gonos* meaning 'seven-angled']

heptathlon, heptathlons (pronounced hep-**tath**-lon)
(noun) A heptathlon is a sports contest in which athletes compete in seven different events.
[from Greek *hepta* meaning 'seven' and *athlon* meaning 'contest']

her
(pronoun and preposition) Her is used to refer to

a woman, girl or female animal that has already been mentioned, or to show that something belongs to a particular female.

herald, heralds, heralding, heralded
1 (noun) In the past, a herald was a messenger.
2 (verb) Something that heralds a future event is a sign of that event, e.g. *The 1933 Act heralded a new approach to child welfare.*

heraldry
(noun) Heraldry is the study of coats of arms and the histories of families.
heraldic (adjective).

herb, herbs
(noun) A herb is a plant whose leaves are used in medicine or to flavour food.
herbal (adjective), **herbalist** (noun).
[from Latin *herba* meaning 'grass']

herbivore, herbivores
(noun) A herbivore is an animal that eats only plants.
herbivorous (adjective).
[from Latin *herbivora* meaning 'grass-eaters']

herculean (pronounced herk-yoo-**lee**-an)
(adjective) requiring great strength or effort.
[from *Hercules*, the Greek hero who was famous for strength and determination]

herd, herds, herding, herded
1 (noun) A herd is a large group of animals.
2 (verb) To herd animals or people means to make them move together as a group.

here
1 (adverb) at, to, or in the place where you are, or the place mentioned or indicated.
2 (phrase) **Here and there** means in various unspecified places, e.g. *The shell was deep cream touched here and there with pink.*
3 When you are drinking a toast to someone, you can say, for example, '**Here's to Martin**'.

hereabouts
(adverb) near to you or in the same general area.

hereafter
(adverb; a formal word) after this time or point, e.g. *the South Australia Housing Trust (hereafter called the Trust).*

hereby
(adverb; a formal word) used in documents and statements to indicate that a declaration is official, e.g. *I hereby resign.*

hereditary
(adjective) passed on to a child from a parent, e.g. *a hereditary disease.*

heredity
(noun) Heredity is the process by which characteristics are passed from parents to their children through the genes.
[from Latin *hereditas* meaning 'inheritance']

herein
(adverb; a formal word) in this place or document.

hereinafter
(adverb; a formal word) after this point in this

document, e.g. *Redwood Travel Ltd, hereinafter called the Company.*

heresy, heresies (pronounced **herr**-ess-ee)
(noun) Heresy is belief or behaviour considered to be wrong because it disagrees with what is generally accepted, especially with regard to religion.
heretic (noun), **heretical** (adjective).
[from Greek *hairesis* meaning 'choice']

herewith
(adverb; a formal word) with this letter or document, e.g. *I herewith return your cheque.*

heritage
(noun) A heritage is the possessions, traditions, or conditions that have been passed from one generation to another.

hermaphrodite, hermaphrodites (pronounced her-**maf**-rod-ite)
(noun) A hermaphrodite is an animal or flower with male and female reproductive organs.
[from *Hermaphroditos*, the son of Greek gods Hermes and Aphrodite, who merged with a nymph to form one body]

hermetic (pronounced her-**met**-ik)
(adjective) tightly sealed and airtight.
hermetically (adverb).
[from *Hermes Trismegistus*, supposedly the inventor of a magic seal]

hermit, hermits
(noun) A hermit is a person who lives alone with a simple lifestyle, especially for religious reasons.
[from Greek *erēmitēs* meaning 'living in the desert']

hermit crab, hermit crabs
(noun) A hermit crab is a small type of crab that lives in the empty shells of other shellfish.

hernia, hernias (pronounced **her**-nee-a)
(noun) A hernia is a medical condition in which part of the intestine sticks through a weak point in the surrounding tissue. It is caused especially by muscular strain.

hero, heroes
1 (noun) A hero is the main male character in a book, film, or play.
2 A hero is also a person who has done something brave or good.

heroic
(adjective) brave, courageous, and determined.
heroically (adverb).

heroin (pronounced **herr**-oh-in)
(noun) Heroin is a powerful drug formerly used as an anaesthetic and now taken illegally by some people for pleasure.

heroine, heroines (pronounced **herr**-oh-in)
1 (noun) A heroine is the main female character in a book, film, or play.
2 A heroine is also a woman who has done something brave or good.

heroism (pronounced **herr**-oh-i-zm)
(noun) Heroism is great courage and bravery.

heron, herons
(noun) A heron is a wading bird with very long legs and a long beak and neck.

herpes (pronounced **her**-peez)
(noun) Herpes is a virus which causes painful red spots on the skin. There are several different types of herpes.
[from Greek *herpein* meaning 'to creep']

herring, herrings
(noun) A herring is a type of silvery fish that lives in large shoals in northern seas.

herringbone
(noun) Herringbone is a pattern consisting of long lines of V shapes, used, for example, in fabric and brickwork.

hers
(pronoun) Hers refers to something that belongs to or relates to a woman, girl, or female animal.

herself
1 (pronoun) Herself is used when the same woman, girl, or female animal does an action and is affected by it, e.g. *She stared at herself in the mirror.*
2 Herself is used to emphasize 'she'.

hertz
(noun) A hertz is a unit of frequency equal to one cycle per second. It is named after the German physicist H.R. Hertz (1857-1894).

hesitant
(adjective) If you are hesitant, you do not do something immediately because you are uncertain, worried, or embarrassed.
hesitantly (adverb), **hesitance** (noun), **hesitancy** (noun).

Similar words: uncertain, doubtful, wavering, irresolute, indecisive

hesitate, hesitates, hesitating, hesitated
(verb) To hesitate means to pause or show uncertainty.
hesitation (noun).
[from Latin *haesitare* meaning 'to be undecided']

Similar words: falter, waver, dither, vacillate

hessian
(noun) Hessian is a thick, rough fabric made from jute and used for making sacks.
[originally from the West German state of *Hesse*]

heterodox
(adjective) Beliefs or opinions that are heterodox are different from the accepted or official ones.
heterodoxy (noun).
[from Greek *heteros* + *doxa* meaning 'other opinion']

heterogeneous (pronounced het-ter-oh-**jee**-nee-uss)
(adjective; a formal word) consisting of many different types of things, e.g. *a heterogenous collection of European art.*
[from Greek *heteros* + *genos* meaning 'other type']

heterosexual, heterosexuals (pronounced het-roh-**seks**-yool)

1 (adjective) involving a sexual relationship between a man and a woman, e.g. *heterosexual couples.*
2 (noun) A heterosexual is a person who is sexually attracted to people of the opposite sex.
[from Greek *heteros* and Latin *sexus* meaning 'other sex']

het up
(adjective; an informal use) anxious, worried, or excited.

heuristic (pronounced hew-**riss**-tik)
(adjective; a formal word) involving thought and investigation as a method of learning, e.g. *a technique of heuristic problem solving.*
[from Greek *heuriskein* meaning 'to discover']

hew, hews, hewing, hewed or **hewn**
(verb) To hew stone or wood means to chop pieces from it.

hexagon, hexagons
(noun) A hexagon is a shape with six straight sides.
hexagonal (adjective).
[from Greek *hex* + *-gonos* meaning 'six-angled']

heyday (pronounced **hay**-day)
(noun) The heyday of a person or thing is the period when they are most successful, powerful, or popular, e.g. *Not even Hollywood in its heyday could match this.*

hi
'Hi!' is an informal greeting.

hiatus (pronounced high-**ay**-tuss)
(noun; a formal word) A hiatus is a pause or gap.
[from Latin *hiatus* meaning 'gaping']

hibernate, hibernates, hibernating, hibernated
(verb) Animals that hibernate spend the winter in a resting state in which their temperature, heartbeat, and breathing rate become very low.
hibernation (noun).
[from Latin *hibernare* meaning 'to spend the winter']

hibiscus, hibiscuses (pronounced hie-**bis**-kuss)
(noun) Hibiscus is a type of tropical shrub with very brightly coloured flowers.

hiccup, hiccups, hiccupping, hiccupped
(pronounced **hik**-kup); also spelled **hiccough**
1 (noun) Hiccups are short, uncontrolled choking sounds in your throat that you sometimes get if you have been eating or drinking too quickly.
2 (verb) When you hiccup, you make these little choking sounds.
3 (noun; an informal use) A hiccup is a minor problem.

hide, hides, hiding, hid, hidden
1 (verb) To hide something means to put it where it cannot be seen, or to prevent it from being discovered, e.g. *He couldn't hide his pleasure at the news.*
2 (noun) A hide is the skin of a large animal.

Similar words: (sense 1) conceal, obscure, stash, bury, mask

hidebound
(adjective) unwilling to change or accept new ideas.

hideous (pronounced **hid-ee-uss**)
(adjective) extremely ugly or unpleasant.
hideously (adverb).
[from Old French *hisdos* meaning 'fear']

hideout, hideouts
(noun) A hideout is a hiding place.

hiding, hidings
(noun; an informal word) To give someone a hiding means to beat them severely.

hierarchy, hierarchies (pronounced high-er-ar-kee)
(noun) A hierarchy is a system in which people or things are ranked or positioned according to how important they are.
hierarchical (adjective).
[from Greek *hieros* + *-arkhos* meaning 'sacred ruler']

hieroglyph, hieroglyphs (pronounced high-ra-gliff)
(noun) A hieroglyph is a picture or symbol used in the writing system of ancient Egypt.
[from Greek *hieros* + *gluphē* meaning 'sacred carving']

hieroglyphic, hieroglyphics (pronounced high-ra-gliff-ik)
(noun) Hieroglyphics are the same as hieroglyphs.

hi-fi, hi-fis
(noun) A hi-fi is a set of stereo equipment on which you can play records, tapes, and compact discs.

higgledy-piggledy
(adjective and adverb; an informal word) in a great muddle or disorder.

high, higher, highest; highs
1 (adjective and adverb) tall or a long way above the ground.
2 great in degree, quantity, or intensity, e.g. *high prices... times of high anxiety.*
3 towards the top of a scale of importance or quality, e.g. *high fashion.*
4 close to the top of a range of sound or notes, e.g. *a high voice.*
5 (adjective; an informal use) Someone who is high on a drug such as marijuana is affected by having taken it.
6 Food that is high has an unpleasant smell and is beginning to go bad.
7 (noun) A high is a high point or level, e.g. *Prices reached a record high last week.*
8 (an informal use) Someone who is on a high is in a very excited and optimistic mood.
9 (phrases) If it is **high time** that something was done, it should be done immediately.
10 If you are left **high and dry**, you have been abandoned in a difficult situation.
11 Someone whose behaviour is **high and mighty** is too confident and full of self-importance.

Similar words: (sense 1) tall, lofty, towering

highbrow
(adjective) concerned with serious, intellectual subjects.

higher education
(noun) Higher education is education at universities, colleges, and polytechnics. Compare **further education**.

high-fidelity
(adjective) High-fidelity recording equipment produces very high quality sound.

high-flown
(adjective) Expressions or ideas that are high-flown are very grand or elaborate.

high-handed
(adjective) using authority in an unnecessarily forceful way, e.g. *high-handed behaviour.*

high jump
1 (noun) The high jump is an athletics event involving jumping over a high bar.
2 (an informal phrase) If you are **for the high jump**, you are going to be in trouble.

highlands
(plural noun) Highlands are mountainous or hilly areas of land.

highlight, highlights, highlighting, highlighted
1 (verb) If you highlight a point or problem, you emphasize and draw attention to it.
2 (noun) The highlight of something is the most interesting part of it, e.g. *Seeing the palace was the highlight of the trip.*
3 A highlight is a lighter area of a painting, showing where light shines on things.
4 Highlights are also light-coloured streaks in someone's hair.

highly
1 (adverb) extremely, e.g. *It is highly improbable that they will accept.*
2 towards the top of a scale of importance, admiration, or respect, e.g. *She spoke highly of him... a highly regarded senior official.*

highly strung
(adjective) very nervous and easily upset.

high-minded
(adjective) Someone who is high-minded has strong moral principles.

Highness
Highness is used in titles and forms of address for members of the royal family other than a king or queen, e.g. *Her Royal Highness, Princess Alexandra.*

high-pitched
(adjective) A high-pitched sound or voice is high and often rather shrill.

high-rise
(adjective) High-rise buidings are very tall and modern.

high road, high roads
(noun) A high road is a main road.

high school, high schools
(noun) A high school is a secondary school, especially in America.

high sea, high seas
(noun) The high seas are the open seas of the world that are not controlled by any one nation.

high tea
(noun) High tea is a meal eaten in the early evening, often with tea to drink.

high technology
(noun) High technology is the development and use of advanced electronics, computers, and robots.

high tide
(noun) On a coast, high tide is the time, usually twice a day, when the sea is at its highest level.

highway, highways
(noun) A highway is a road along which vehicles have the right to pass, e.g. *He was charged with obstructing the highway.*

highwayman, highwaymen
(noun) In the past, highwaymen were robbers on horseback who used to rob travellers at gunpoint.

hijack, hijacks, hijacking, hijacked
(verb) If someone hijacks a plane or vehicle, they illegally take control of it by forcing the pilot or driver and any passengers to follow their instructions.
hijacker (noun), **hijacking** (noun).

hike, hikes, hiking, hiked
1 (noun) A hike is a long country walk.
2 (verb) To hike means to walk long distances in the country.
hiker (noun), **hiking** (noun).

Similar words: ramble, tramp, trek, walk

hilarious
(adjective) very funny.
hilariously (adverb).
[from Greek *hilaros* meaning 'cheerful']

Similar words: hysterical, uproarious, side-splitting

hilarity
(noun) Hilarity is great amusement and laughter, e.g. *His antics caused general hilarity.*

hill, hills
(noun) A hill is a rounded area of land higher than the land surrounding it.
hilly (adjective).

hillock, hillocks
(noun) A hillock is a very small hill.

hilt, hilts
(noun) The hilt of a sword, dagger, or knife is its handle.

him
(pronoun) You use him to refer to a man, boy, or male animal that has already been mentioned, or to any person whose sex is not known, e.g. *He asked if you'd ring him back.*

himself
1 (pronoun) Himself is used when the same man, boy, or male animal does an action and is affected by it, e.g. *He poured himself a whisky.*
2 Himself is used to emphasize 'he'.

hind, hinds (rhymes with blind)
1 (adjective) used to refer to the back part of an animal, e.g. *the hind legs.*
2 (noun) A hind is a female deer.

hinder, hinders, hindering, hindered
1 (verb; pronounced **hin**-der) If you hinder someone or something, you get in their way and make something difficult for them.
2 (adjective; pronounced **hine**-der) The hinder parts of an animal are the parts at the back.

Hindi (pronounced **hin**-dee)
(noun) Hindi is a language spoken in northern India.
[from Old Persian *Hindu* meaning 'the river Indus']

hindmost
(adjective) furthest back.

hindquarters
(plural noun) The hindquarters of an animal are its back parts and its two back legs.

hindrance, hindrances
1 (noun) Someone or something that is a hindrance causes difficulties or is an obstruction.
2 Hindrance is the act of hindering someone or something.

hindsight
(noun) Hindsight is the ability to understand an event or situation after it has actually taken place, e.g. *With hindsight, it was quite obvious that she had always hated city life.*

Hindu, Hindus (pronounced **hin**-doo)
(noun) A Hindu is a person who believes in Hinduism, an Indian religion which has many gods and teaches that people are reincarnated after death.

hinge, hinges, hinging, hinged
1 (noun) A hinge is the movable joint with which a door or window is attached to its frame.
2 (verb) Something that hinges on a situation or event depends entirely on that situation or event, e.g. *The success of our policies hinges on what happens to the United States economy.*

hint, hints, hinting, hinted
1 (noun) A hint is a suggestion, clue, or helpful piece of advice.
2 (verb) If you hint at something, you suggest it indirectly.

Similar words: (sense 1) clue, suggestion, intimation, insinuation, innuendo
(sense 2) suggest, allude, intimate, insinuate

hinterland, hinterlands
(noun) The hinterland of a coastline or a port is the area of land behind it or around it.
[from German *hinter* meaning 'behind']

hip, hips
(noun) Your hips are the two parts at the sides of your body between your waist and your upper legs.

hippie, hippies; also spelled hippy
(noun) A hippie is a person who has rejected conventional ideas and lives a life based on peace

and love. The hippie movement started and was most popular in the 1960's.

hippo, hippos
(noun; an informal word) A hippo is a hippopotamus.

hippopotamus, hippopotamuses or **hippopotami**
(noun) A hippopotamus is a large animal from tropical Africa with thick wrinkled skin. Hippopotamuses spend a lot of time in water. [from Greek *hippo* + *potamos* meaning 'river horse']

hire, hires, hiring, hired
1 (verb) If you hire something, you pay money to be able to use it for a period of time.
2 If you hire someone, you pay them to do a job for you.
3 (phrase) Something that is **for hire** is available for people to hire.

Similar words: (sense 1) rent, lease

hireling, hirelings
(noun) A hireling is someone who does not care what they do or who they work for as long as they are paid.

hire-purchase
(noun) Hire-purchase is a way of buying something by making regular payments over a period of time.

hirsute (pronounced **hir**-syoot)
(adjective; a formal word) hairy.
[from Latin *hirsutus* meaning 'shaggy']

his
(determiner or pronoun) His refers to something that belongs or relates to a man, boy, or male animal that has already been mentioned, or to any person whose sex is not known, e.g. *That's not mine, it's his.*

hiss, hisses, hissing, hissed
1 (verb) To hiss means to make a long 's' sound, especially to show disapproval or aggression.
2 (noun) A hiss is a long 's' sound.

histamine (pronounced **hiss**-tam-een)
(noun) Histamine is a substance released by the body in allergic reactions, and is also present in some insect and plant stings.

histogram, histograms
(noun) A histogram is a graph consisting of rectangles of varying sizes, that shows the frequency of values of a quantity.
[from Greek *histos* + *grammē* meaning 'web line']

historian, historians
(noun) A historian is a person who studies and writes about history.

historic
(adjective) important in the past or likely to be seen as important in the future, e.g. *this historic occasion when the Pope blessed our community.*

historical
1 (adjective) occurring in the past, or relating to the study of the past, e.g. *historical events... manuscripts of historical interest.*

2 describing or representing the past, e.g. *historical novels... historical costumes.*
historically (adverb).

history, histories
(noun) History is the study of the past. A history is a record of the past, e.g. *dramatic moments in Polish history...his medical history.*
[from Greek *historein* meaning 'to narrate a story']

histrionic, histrionics (pronounced hiss-tree-**on**-ik)
1 (adjective) Histrionic behaviour is very dramatic and full of exaggerated emotion, e.g. *He made a flamboyant, histrionic gesture.*
2 (noun) Histrionics are histrionic behaviour.
3 (adjective; a formal use) relating to drama and acting, e.g. *the greatest histrionic talent of the century.*
[from Latin *histrio* meaning 'actor']

hit, hits, hitting, hit
1 (verb) To hit someone or something means to strike or touch them forcefully, usually causing hurt or damage.
2 To hit a ball or other object means to make it move by hitting it with something.
3 If something hits you, it affects you badly and suddenly, e.g. *The sport has been badly hit by ticket price increases.*
4 If something hits a particular point or place, it reaches it, e.g. *The pound had hit a new low on the Stock Exchange.*
5 (noun) A hit is the action of hitting something, e.g. *Give it a good hard hit with the hammer.*
6 A hit is also a song, play, or film that is popular and successful.
7 (an informal phrase) If you **hit it off** with someone, you become friendly with them the first time you meet them.
8 (verb) If you hit on an idea or solution, you suddenly think of it.

Similar words: (sense 1) knock, strike, bash

hit and miss
(adjective) happening in an unplanned or unpredictable way.

hit-and-run
(adjective) A hit-and-run car accident is one in which the person who has caused the damage drives away without stopping.

hitch, hitches, hitching, hitched
1 (noun) A hitch is a slight problem or difficulty, e.g. *The whole thing went smoothly without a hitch... technical hitches.*
2 (verb; an informal use) If you hitch, you hitchhike, e.g. *We tried to hitch a lift to London.*
3 To hitch something somewhere means to hook it or fasten it there, e.g. *Each wagon was hitched onto the one in front.*
4 (an informal phrase) If you **get hitched**, you get married.

hitchhike, hitchhikes, hitchhiking, hitchhiked
(verb) To hitchhike means to travel by getting lifts from passing vehicles.
hitchhiker (noun), **hitchhiking** (noun).

hi tech
(adjective) designed using the most modern methods and equipment, especially electronic equipment.

hither (an old-fashioned word)
1 (adverb) used to refer to movement towards the place where you are.
2 (phrase) Something that moves **hither and thither** moves in all directions.

hitherto
(adverb; a formal word) until now, e.g. *This had hitherto escaped John's notice.*

hive, hives, hiving, hived
1 (noun) A hive is a beehive.
2 A place that is a hive of activity is very busy with a lot of people working hard.
3 (verb) If part of something such as a business is hived off, it is transferred to new ownership, e.g. *a proposal to hive off London Transport to the private sector.*

HM an abbreviation for 'Her Majesty's' or 'His Majesty's'; used in names for organizations and titles, e.g. *HM Customs and Excise.*

HMS an abbreviation for 'Her Majesty's ship'; used as part of the name of a Royal Navy ship, e.g. *HMS Cambridge.*

hoard, hoards, hoarding, hoarded
1 (verb) To hoard things means to save them even though they may no longer be useful.
2 (noun) A hoard is a store of things that has been saved or hidden.

Similar words: (sense 1) store, stockpile, stash
(sense 2) cache, store, stockpile, stash

hoarding, hoardings
(noun) A hoarding is a large advertising board by the side of the road.
[from Old French *hourd* meaning 'fence']

hoarfrost
(noun) Hoarfrost is frost consisting of ice crystals which form on the ground from dew freezing.
[from Old English *har* meaning 'old and grey']

hoarse, hoarser, hoarsest
(adjective) A hoarse voice sounds rough and unclear.
hoarsely (adverb), **hoarseness** (noun).

Similar words: rough, husky, croaky, gruff

hoary
(adjective) greyish white in colour; used especially of a person whose hair has gone grey with old age.

hoax, hoaxes, hoaxing, hoaxed
1 (noun) A hoax is a trick or an attempt to deceive someone.
2 (verb) To hoax someone means to trick or deceive them.
hoaxer (noun).

hob, hobs
(noun) A hob is a surface with a set of gas or electric cooking rings, either on top of a cooker or fitted into a work surface.

hobble, hobbles, hobbling, hobbled
1 (verb) If you hobble, you walk awkwardly because of pain or injury.
2 If you hobble an animal, you tie its legs together to restrict its movement.

hobby, hobbies
(noun) A hobby is something that you do for enjoyment in your spare time.

hobbyhorse, hobbyhorses
1 (noun) A subject that is someone's hobbyhorse is one about which they have strong feelings and which they discuss at every opportunity.
2 A hobbyhorse is also a toy consisting of a horse's head on a long stick.

hobnob, hobnobs, hobnobbing, hobnobbed
(verb; an informal word) To hobnob with someone means to chat and spend time with them.

hobo, hobos or hoboes (pronounced hoh-boh)
(noun) A hobo is a tramp.

Hobson's choice
(phrase) A situation is a case of Hobson's choice when it seems to offer alternatives but you actually have no choice. Thomas Hobson lived in the 17th century and hired out horses. Customers had to accept the horse offered to them or none at all.

hock, hocks
1 (noun) The hock of a horse or other animal is the angled joint in its back leg.
2 Hock is a type of white German wine from the Rhine region.
[sense 1 is from Old English *hohsinu* meaning 'heel sinew'; sense 2 is from German *Hochheimer Wein* meaning 'wine from Hochheim']

hockey
(noun) Hockey is an outdoor game for two teams of eleven players. They use long sticks with curved ends to try to hit a small ball into the other team's goal.

hocus-pocus (pronounced hoh-kus poh-kus)
(noun) Hocus-pocus is something said or done in an elaborate or mysterious way to trick or confuse someone.

hod, hods
1 (noun) A hod is a light, box-shaped container attached to a long pole, used for carrying bricks or mortar.
2 A hod is also a tall, narrow coal scuttle.
[from Old French *hotte* meaning 'basket']

hoe, hoes, hoeing, hoed
1 (noun) A hoe is a long-handled gardening tool with a small, flat, square blade, used to remove weeds and break up the soil.
2 (verb) To hoe the ground means to use a hoe on it.

hog, hogs, hogging, hogged
1 (noun) A hog is a castrated male pig.
2 (verb; an informal use) If you hog something, you take more than your share of it, or keep it for too long.
3 (an informal phrase) If you **go the whole hog,**

you do something completely or thoroughly in a bold or extravagant way.

Hogmanay (pronounced hog-man-**nay**)
(noun) Hogmanay is New Year's Eve in Scotland.

hoi polloi (pronounced hoy pol-**loy**)
(noun) The hoi polloi are ordinary people as opposed to the rich, well-educated, or upper class.
[from Greek *hoi polloi* meaning 'the many']

hoist, hoists, hoisting, hoisted
1 (verb) To hoist something means to lift it, especially using a crane or other machinery.
2 (noun) A hoist is a machine for lifting heavy things.

hoity-toity (pronounced hoy-tee-**toy**-tee)
(adjective; an informal word) too proud or haughty.

hold, holds, holding, held
1 (verb) To hold something means to carry, support, or keep it in place, usually with your hand or arms.
2 If something holds a certain amount, it can contain that amount, e.g. *a tub big enough to hold eight gallons... The theatre holds 150 people.*
3 Someone who holds power, office, or an opinion has it or possesses it.
4 If you hold something such as a meeting, a party, or an election, you arrange it and cause it to happen.
5 If something holds, it is still available, true, or valid, e.g. *The offer still holds... Your argument doesn't hold.*
6 If you hold someone responsible for something, you consider them responsible for it.
7 If you hold something such as theatre tickets, a telephone call, or the price of something, you keep or reserve it for a period of time, e.g. *The line is engaged — will you hold?*
8 If you don't hold with something, you do not approve of it, e.g. *You know I don't hold with all this permissiveness.*
9 To hold something down means to keep it or to keep it under control, e.g. *He'll never be able to hold down a proper job.*
10 If you hold on to something, you continue it or keep it even though it might be difficult, e.g. *Will you hold on to it for a couple of days?*
11 To hold something back means to prevent it, keep it under control, or not reveal it, e.g. *I tried to hold back the tears.*
12 (noun) If someone or something has a hold over you, they have power, control, or influence over you, e.g. *Black African nations wanted to destroy the white hold on South Africa.*
13 A hold is a way of holding something or the act of holding it, e.g. *Grab hold of that stick.*
14 The hold in a ship or plane is the place where cargo or luggage is stored.
15 (phrase) If you **hold your own**, you manage to resist a challenge or attack, especially in an argument.
16 If someone **holds forth**, they speak confidently for a long time.
holder (noun).

Similar words: *(sense 1)* grasp, grip, clasp, clutch *(sense 4)* have, run, conduct

hold off
(phrasal verb) To hold something off means to prevent or delay it, e.g. *Do you think the rain will hold off?*

hold out
(phrasal verb) If you hold out, you stand firm and manage to resist opposition in difficult circumstances, e.g. *The rebels could hold out for ten years.*

hold up
(phrasal verb) If something holds you up, it delays you.

holdall, holdalls
(noun) A holdall is a large, soft bag for carrying clothing.

holding, holdings
(noun) A holding is property owned by a person or organization, especially stocks and shares.

hold-up, hold-ups
1 (noun) A hold-up is a situation in which someone threatens people with a weapon in order to obtain money or valuables.
2 A hold-up is also a delay, e.g. *a traffic hold-up.*

hole, holes, holing, holed
1 (noun) A hole is an opening or hollow in something.
2 (an informal use) If you describe a place as a hole, you mean it is very unpleasant, e.g. *I need to get out of this hole and move to London.*
3 (an informal use) If you are in a hole, you are in a difficult situation.
4 In golf, a hole is one of the small holes into which you have to hit the ball.
5 (verb) When you hole the ball in golf, you hit the ball into one of the holes.
6 If a ship is holed, holes are made in it by a weapon or a collision.

Similar words: *(sense 1)* hollow, cavity

hole up
(phrasal verb; an informal use) If you hole up somewhere, you hide there.

hole-and-corner
(adjective) furtive and secretive.

holiday, holidays, holidaying, holidayed
1 (noun) A holiday is a period of time spent away from home for enjoyment.
2 A holiday is a time when you are not working or not at school or college.
3 (verb) When you holiday somewhere, you take a holiday there, e.g. *holidaying in the Bahamas.*
[from Old English *haligdæg* meaning 'holy day']

holidaymaker, holidaymakers
(noun) A holidaymaker is a person who is away from home on holiday.

holier-than-thou
(adjective) behaving in a self-righteous way as if you are superior to other people.

holiness

1 (noun) Holiness is the state or quality of being holy.
2 'Your Holiness' and 'His Holiness' are titles used to address or refer to the Pope or to leaders of some other religions.

hollow, hollows, hollowing, hollowed

1 (adjective) Something that is hollow has space inside it rather than being solid.
2 (noun) A hollow is a hole in something or a part of a surface that is lower than the rest, e.g. *hidden in a hollow in the tree trunk.*
3 (verb) To hollow means to make a hollow, e.g. *He hollowed out a small dip in the ground.*
4 (adjective) An opinion or situation that is hollow has no real value or worth, e.g. *His election optimism rang hollow... a hollow victory.*
5 A hollow sound is dull and has a slight echo, e.g. *the hollow sound of his footsteps on the stairs.*
[from Old English *holh* meaning 'hole' or 'cave']

holly

(noun) Holly is an evergreen tree or shrub with spiky leaves. It often has red berries in winter.

hollyhock, hollyhocks

(noun) A hollyhock is a flowering plant with tall spikes of brightly coloured flowers.

holmium (pronounced **hol**-mee-um)

(noun) Holmium is a silvery-white metallic element which forms magnetic compounds. Its atomic number is 67 and its symbol is Ho.

holocaust, holocausts (pronounced hol-o-kawst)

(noun) A holocaust is a large-scale destruction or loss of life, especially the result of war or fire.
[from Greek *holos* + *kaustos* meaning 'completely burnt']

hologram, holograms

(noun) A hologram is a three-dimensional photographic image created by laser beams.
[from Greek *holos* + *gramma* meaning 'something completely written or described']

holography

(noun) Holography is the science or practice of producing holograms.

holster, holsters

(noun) A holster is a holder for a pistol or revolver, worn at the side of the body or under the arm.

holy, holier, holiest

1 (adjective) relating to God or to a particular religion, e.g. *the holy book.*
2 Someone who is holy is religious and leads a pure and good life.

Similar words: (sense 1) divine, sacred
(sense 2) godly, pious, devout

Holy Communion

(noun) Holy Communion is a Christian religious service in which people share bread and wine in remembrance of the death and resurrection of Jesus Christ.

Holy Spirit

(noun) In Christianity, the Holy Spirit is one of the three aspects of God.

homage (pronounced **hom**-ij)

(noun) Homage is an act of respect and admiration, e.g. *The young soldiers gathered to pay homage to the new heroes.*

homburg, homburgs

(noun) A homburg is a type of man's felt hat, with a narrow brim and a long dent in the crown.
[from *Homburg*, the town in Germany where they were first made]

home, homes

1 (noun) Your home is the building, place, or country in which you live or feel you belong.
2 (adjective) connected with or involving your home or country, e.g. *home baked bread... The government is expanding the home market.*
3 (noun) A home is an institution in which elderly or ill people live and are looked after, e.g. *I wouldn't want to put my mother in a home.*
4 (phrase) If you feel **at home** somewhere or with a particular subject, you feel comfortable because it is familiar or easy to understand, e.g. *The otter is entirely at home in the water.*
5 If a situation or event **brings something home to you**, it makes you realize, often for the first time, how important or serious that thing is.
6 (adverb) If you press, drive, or hammer something home, you push it firmly into its correct position.
[from Old English *ham* meaning 'village']

Similar words: (sense 1) dwelling, residence, abode

home in

(phrasal verb) If something homes in on a target, it moves directly and quickly towards it.

Home Counties

(plural noun) The Home Counties are the counties surrounding London.

homeland, homelands

1 (noun) Your homeland is your native country.
2 The homelands are the regions which have been given by the South African government to the black population.

homeless

(adjective) having nowhere to live.
homelessness (noun).

homely

(adjective) simple, ordinary and comfortable, e.g. *The little hotel was a homely place.*

Similar words: cosy, comfortable, snug

homeopathy (pronounced home-ee-**op**-path-ee)

(noun) Homeopathy is a way of treating illness by means of minute amounts of a substance that would normally cause illness in a healthy person.
homeopathic (adjective), **homeopath** (noun).
[from Greek *homos* + *patheia* meaning 'same suffering']

homesick
(adjective) unhappy because of being away from home and missing family and friends.
homesickness (noun).

homespun
(adjective) simple and uncomplicated, e.g. *simple living and homespun virtues.*

homestead, homesteads
(noun) A homestead is a house and its land and other buildings, especially a farm.
[from Old English *ham* + *stede* meaning 'home place']

home truth, home truths
(noun) Home truths are unpleasant facts about yourself that you are told by someone else.

homeward or **homewards**
(adjective and adverb) towards home, e.g. *the homeward journey.*

homework
1 (noun) Homework is school work given to pupils to be done in the evening at home.
2 Homework is also research and preparation, e.g. *Aiken did his homework and worked out a convincing case.*

homicide, homicides
(noun) Homicide is the crime of murder.
homicidal (adjective).
[from Latin *homo* meaning 'man' and *caedere* meaning 'to kill']

homily, homilies (pronounced **hom**-il-lee)
(noun) A homily is a speech telling people how they should behave.
[from Greek *homilia* meaning 'sermon']

homing
(adjective) A homing device is able to guide itself to a target. An animal with a homing instinct is able to guide itself home.

homogeneous (pronounced hom-moh-**jeen**-ee-uss)
(adjective) having parts or members which are all the same.
homogeneity (noun).
[from Greek *homos* + *genos* meaning 'same type']

homogenized or **homogenised** (pronounced hom-**moj**-jen-eye-zd)
(adjective) Homogenized milk has been treated to distribute the cream evenly in the milk.

homogenous (pronounced hom-**moj**-jin-uss)
another word for **homogeneous.**

homo sapiens (pronounced hoh-moh **sap**-ee-enz)
(noun; a formal expression) Homo sapiens is the scientific name for human beings.
[from Latin *homo* meaning 'man' and *sapiens* meaning 'wise']

homosexual, homosexuals
1 (noun) A homosexual is a person who is sexually attracted to someone of the same sex.
2 (adjective) sexually attracted to people of the same sex, e.g. *a homosexual relationship.*
homosexuality (noun).
[from Greek *homos* meaning 'same' and Latin *sexus* meaning 'sex']

hone, hones, honing, honed
1 (verb) If you hone a tool, you sharpen it.
2 If you hone a quality or ability, you develop and improve it, e.g. *carefully honed techniques.*
[from Old English *han* meaning 'stone']

honest
(adjective) truthful and trustworthy.
honestly (adverb).
[from Latin *honos* meaning 'honour']

Similar words: truthful, honourable, above board, upright

honesty
1 (noun) Honesty is the quality of being truthful and trustworthy.
2 Honesty is also a plant with purple flowers. In autumn, it has flat silvery pods that people use in dried flower arrangements.

Similar words: (sense 1) integrity, truthfulness, trustworthiness, honour

honey
1 (noun) Honey is a sweet, edible, sticky substance produced by bees.
2 Honey means 'sweetheart' or 'darling', e.g. *Hi there honey!*

honeycomb, honeycombs
(noun) A honeycomb is a wax structure consisting of rows of six-sided cells made by bees for storage of honey and the eggs.

honeymoon, honeymoons
(noun) A honeymoon is a holiday taken by a couple who have just got married.

honeysuckle
(noun) Honeysuckle is a climbing plant with fragrant pink or cream flowers.

honk, honks, honking, honked
1 (noun) A honk is a short, loud sound like that made by a car horn or a goose.
2 (verb) When something honks, it makes a short, loud sound.

honorary
(adjective) An honorary title or job is given as a mark of respect or honour, and does not involve the usual qualifications, work, or payment, e.g. *They offered the President an honorary degree.*

Similar words: nominal, titular

honour, honours, honouring, honoured
1 (noun) Your honour is your good reputation and the respect that other people have for you, e.g. *the family honour.*
2 An honour is an award or privilege given as a mark of respect.
3 (phrase) If something is done **in your honour**, it is done specially for you, e.g. *The party was held in her honour.*
4 If you **do the honours**, you act as host or hostess by pouring drinks or giving out food.
5 (noun) Honours is a class of university degree which is higher than a pass or ordinary degree.
6 (verb) If you honour someone, you give them special praise or attention, or an award.
7 If you honour an agreement or promise, you do

what was agreed or promised, e.g. *The bank refused to honour the cheque.*

honourable
(adjective) worthy of respect or admiration, e.g. *He should do the honourable thing and resign.*
honourably (adverb).

hood, hoods
1 (noun) A hood is a loose covering for the head, usually part of a coat or jacket.
2 A hood is also a cover on a piece of equipment or vehicle, usually curved and movable, e.g. *a pram with the hood folded down.*
hooded (adjective).

hoodwink, hoodwinks, hoodwinking, hoodwinked
(verb) To hoodwink someone means to trick or deceive them.

hoof, hooves or **hoofs**
(noun) A hoof is the hard bony part of certain animals' feet.

hook, hooks, hooking, hooked
1 (noun) A hook is a curved piece of metal or plastic that is used for catching, holding, or hanging things, e.g. *curtain hooks.*
2 (verb) If you hook one thing onto another, you attach it there using a hook.
3 (noun) A hook is a curving movement, for example of the fist in boxing, or of a golf ball.
4 (phrase) If you are **let off the hook**, something happens so that you avoid punishment or a difficult situation.

hook up
(phrasal verb) To hook up electronic or electrical equipment means to link it to other equipment.

hooked
(adjective) addicted to something, e.g. *I tried it once and was hooked!... hooked on drugs.*

hooligan, hooligans
(noun) A hooligan is a noisy, destructive, and violent young person.
hooliganism (noun).

Similar words: delinquent, ruffian, lout

hoop, hoops
(noun) A hoop is a large ring, usually used as a toy.

hooray another spelling of **hurray.**

hoot, hoots, hooting, hooted
1 (verb) To hoot means to make a long 'oo' sound like an owl, e.g. *hooting with laughter.*
2 If a car horn hoots, it makes a loud honking noise.
3 (noun) A hoot is a sound like that made by an owl or car horn.

hooter, hooters
(noun) A hooter is a horn or siren.

hoover, hoovers, hoovering, hoovered
1 (noun; a trademark) A hoover is a vacuum cleaner.
2 (verb) When you hoover, you use a vacuum cleaner to clean the floor.

hooves a plural of **hoof.**

hop, hops, hopping, hopped
1 (verb) If you hop, you jump on one foot.
2 When animals or birds hop, they jump with two feet together.
3 (an informal use) If you hop into or out of something, you move there quickly and easily, e.g. *Hop in the car and we'll go.*
4 (noun) A hop is a jump on one leg.
5 (an informal use) A hop is also a dance.
6 (phrase) If you are **caught on the hop**, you are unprepared and surprised by something unexpected.
7 (noun) Hops are flowers of the hop plant, which are dried and used for making beer.

hope, hopes, hoping, hoped
1 (verb) If you hope that something will happen or hope that it is true, you want it to happen or be true.
2 (noun) Hope is a wish or feeling of desire and expectation, e.g. *Don't give up hope!*
hopeful (adjective), **hopefully** (adverb).

hopeless
1 (adjective) having no hope, e.g. *With a hopeless sigh, she turned away.*
2 certain to fail or be unsuccessful.
3 unable to do something well, e.g. *He's hopeless at games.*
hopelessly (adverb), **hopelessness** (noun).

hopper, hoppers
(noun) A hopper is a large, funnel-shaped container for storing things such as grain or sand.

hopscotch
(noun) Hopscotch is a game in which you throw a stone to land in one of a series of squares marked on the ground, and then hop over it to pick it up.

horde, hordes (rhymes with **bored**)
(noun) A horde is a large group or number of people, animals, or insects, e.g. *hordes of screaming children.*

horizon, horizons (pronounced hor-**eye**-zn)
1 (noun) The horizon is the distant line where the sky seems to touch the land or sea.
2 (phrase) **On the horizon** is used to refer to a time in the future, e.g. *On the horizon is a new type of drug.*
3 (noun) Your horizons are the limits of what you want to do or be involved in, e.g. *You need to broaden your horizons a bit.*
[from Greek *horizein* meaning 'to limit']

horizontal (pronounced hor-riz-**zon**-tl)
(adjective) flat and level with the ground or with a line considered as a base, e.g. *horizontal and vertical stripes.*
horizontally (adverb).

hormone, hormones
(noun) A hormone is a chemical made by one part of your body that stimulates or has a specific effect on another part of your body.
hormonal (adjective).
[from Greek *horman* meaning 'to stir up']

horn, horns
1 (noun) A horn is one of the hard, pointed growths on the heads of animals such as sheep and goats.

2 A horn is a musical instrument made of brass, consisting of a pipe or tube that is narrow at one end and wide at the other.
3 On vehicles, a horn is a warning device which makes a loud noise.

hornet, hornets
1 (noun) A hornet is a type of very large wasp.
2 (phrase) A situation described as **a hornet's nest** is very difficult to deal with and likely to cause trouble.

horoscope, horoscopes (pronounced hor-ros-kope)
(noun) A horoscope is a prediction about what is going to happen to someone, based on the position of the stars when they were born.
[from Greek *hora* + *skopos* meaning 'hour observer']

horrendous
(adjective) very unpleasant and shocking, e.g. *a horrendous murder*.

horrible
(adjective) causing dislike, shock, fear, or disgust, e.g. *It was a horrible colour*.
horribly (adverb).

Similar words: horrid, horrific, horrendous, gruesome, hideous

---

horrid
(adjective) very unpleasant indeed, e.g. *a horrid little flat... I didn't mean to be horrid to you*.

horrific
(adjective) so bad or unpleasant that people are horrified, e.g. *a horrific experience*.
horrifically (adverb).

horrify, horrifies, horrifying, horrified
(verb) If something horrifies you, it makes you feel dismay or disgust, e.g. *They were horrified at the proposal*.
horrifying (adjective), **horrifyingly** (adverb).

horror, horrors
1 (noun) Horror is a strong feeling of alarm, dismay, and disgust, e.g. *They shrank away in horror*.
2 If you have a horror of something, you dislike it very much, e.g. *She had a horror of violence*.
[from Latin *horrere* meaning 'to tremble']

hors d'oeuvre, hors d'oeuvres (pronounced or-durv)
(noun) Hors d'oeuvres are a variety of different foods, usually cold, eaten before the main course of a meal.
[from French *hors d'oeuvre* meaning literally 'outside the work']

horse, horses
1 (noun) A horse is a large animal with a mane and long tail, which is ridden for pleasure or hunting, or kept as a working animal.
2 In gymnastics, a horse is a piece of equipment with four legs or a solid base, used for jumping over.
3 (phrases) If you get information **straight from the horse's mouth**, the person directly involved tells you about it.

4 To look a gift horse in the mouth means to be critical of a gift or ungrateful for it.

horse-box, horse-boxes
(noun) A horse-box is a van or trailer used for transporting horses.

horse chestnut, horse chestnuts
(noun) A horse chestnut is a large tree with segmented leaves and tall clusters of white flowers in the spring. It produces a reddish brown nut called a conker in a green spiky case.

horseplay
(noun) Horseplay is rough or noisy play.

horsepower
(noun) Horsepower is a unit used for measuring how powerful an engine is, equal to about 746 watts.

horseradish
(noun) Horseradish is the white root of a plant made into a hot-tasting sauce, often served cold with beef.

horseshoe, horseshoes
(noun) A horseshoe is a U-shaped piece of metal, nailed to the hard surface of a horse's hoof to protect it; also anything of this shape, often regarded as a good luck symbol.

horsey or **horsy**
1 (adjective) very keen on horses and riding.
2 having a face similar to that of a horse.

horticulture
(noun) Horticulture is the study and practice of growing flowers, fruit, and vegetables.
horticultural (adjective).
[from Latin *hortus* + *cultura* meaning 'garden cultivation']

hosanna, hosannas (pronounced hoe-**zan**-na)
(noun) A hosanna is a shout of praise to God.
[from Hebrew *hoshi ah nna* meaning 'save now, we pray']

hose, hoses, hosing, hosed
1 (noun) A hose is a long flexible tube through which liquid or gas can be passed, e.g. *The water hose on the car is leaking*.
2 (verb) If you hose something, you wash or water it using a hose, e.g. *Hose down the path*.
3 (noun) Hose is an old-fashioned men's garment looking like tight trousers, e.g. *doublet and hose*.
4 Hose is also another word for **hosiery**.

hosiery (pronounced **hoze**-yer-ee)
(noun) Hosiery consists of tights, socks, stockings and similar items, especially in shops.

hospice, hospices (pronounced **hoss**-piss)
(noun) A hospice is a type of hospital which provides care for people who are dying.

hospitable
(adjective) friendly, generous, and welcoming to guests or strangers.
hospitably (adverb), **hospitality** (noun).
[from Latin *hospes* meaning 'guest']

hospital, hospitals
(noun) A hospital is a place where sick and injured people are treated and cared for.

[from Latin *hospitalis* meaning 'relating to a guest']

hospitalize, hospitalizes, hospitalizing, hospitalized; also spelled hospitalise
(verb) To hospitalize someone means to send or admit them to hospital.

host, hosts, hosting, hosted
1 (noun) The host of an event is the person or organization that welcomes guests or visitors and provides food or accommodation for them, e.g. *Charnwood Comprehensive are the hosts for this year's Schools Athletic Championships.*
2 (verb) To host an event means to organize it or act as host at it.
3 (noun) A host is a plant or animal with smaller plants or animals living on or in it.
4 A host of things is a large number of them, e.g. *We visited a whole host of places.*
5 In the Christian church, the Host is the consecrated bread used in Mass or Holy Communion.
[senses 1-3 are from Latin *hospes* meaning 'guest'; sense 4 is from Old French *hoste*; sense 5 is from Latin *hostia* meaning 'victim']

hostage, hostages
(noun) A hostage is a person who is illegally held prisoner and threatened with injury or death unless certain demands or conditions are met by other people.
[from Latin *obses* meaning 'hostage']

hostel, hostels
(noun) A hostel is a large building in which people can stay or live, e.g. *They spent the night in a Salvation Army Hostel.*

hostess, hostesses
(noun) A hostess is a woman who welcomes guests or visitors and provides food or accommodation for them.

hostile
1 (adjective) unfriendly, aggressive, and unpleasant, e.g. *a hostile attitude.*
2 relating to or involving the enemies of a country, e.g. *hostile territory.*
hostility (noun).
[from Latin *hostis* meaning 'enemy']

hot, hotter, hottest
1 (adjective) having a high temperature, e.g. *a hot day.*
2 very spicy and causing a burning sensation in your mouth, e.g. *a hot curry.*
3 new, recent, and exciting, e.g. *hot off the press.*
4 dangerous or difficult to deal with, e.g. *They're making it too hot for me — I'll have to leave.*
5 (phrase) Someone who has **a hot temper** gets very angry quickly and easily.
6 Someone who is **hot on something** is particularly concerned about it, e.g. *They're very hot on spelling mistakes.*
7 If you are **in hot water**, you are in trouble.
hotly (adverb), **hotness** (noun).

hotbed, hotbeds
(noun) A hotbed of some undesirable activity is a place that seems to encourage it, e.g. *The universities were hotbeds of unrest.*

hot-blooded
(adjective) quick to express anger, emotion, or passion.

hotchpotch
(noun) A hotchpotch of things is a jumbled or disorderly mixture of different things.

hot dog, hot dogs
(noun) A hot dog is a sausage served in a roll split lengthways.

hotel, hotels
(noun) A hotel is a building where people stay, paying for their room and meals.
[from Latin *hospitalis* meaning 'relating to a guest']

hotfoot
(adverb) quickly and eagerly, e.g. *The doctor went hotfoot to the rescue.*

hothead, hotheads
(noun) A hothead is someone who acts hastily without thinking about the consequences.
hot-headed (adjective).

hothouse, hothouses
1 (noun) A hothouse is a large heated greenhouse.
2 A hothouse is also a place or situation of intense intellectual or emotional activity.

hot line, hot lines
(noun) A hot line is a direct telephone line between heads of government in different countries by which they can contact each other in an emergency.

hotplate, hotplates
(noun) A hotplate is a heated metal surface on a cooker, used for cooking food in pans.

hot seat
(noun; an informal expression) Someone who is in the hot seat has to make difficult decisions for which they will be held responsible.

Hottentot, Hottentots
1 (noun) A Hottentot is a member of a group of people in southern Africa who are now almost extinct.
2 Hottentot is the language spoken by Hottentots.

hound, hounds, hounding, hounded
1 (noun) A hound is a dog, especially one used for hunting or racing.
2 (verb) If someone hounds you, they constantly pursue or trouble you.

hour, hours
1 (noun) An hour is a unit of time equal to 60 minutes. There are 24 hours in a day.
2 The hour for something is the time when it happens, e.g. *The hour for tea had arrived.*
3 An hour is also an important or difficult time, e.g. *The hour has come... She did not desert him in his hour of need.*
4 (plural noun) The hours that you keep are the times that you usually go to bed and get up.
hourly (adjective and adverb).
[from Greek *hora* meaning 'season' or 'time of day']

hourglass, hourglasses
(noun) An hourglass is a device for measuring an

hour. It has two glass sections containing sand and linked by a short, narrow tube. You turn it on one end and the sand takes an hour to flow from the top to the bottom section.

house, houses, housing, housed
1 (noun) A house is a building where a family, person, or small group of people lives.
2 A house is also a building used for a particular purpose, e.g. *a publishing house... the opera house.*
3 In a theatre or cinema, the house is the part where the audience sits; also the audience itself, e.g. *playing to packed houses.*
4 A house is also an important family and its ancestors, e.g. *the House of Windsor.*
5 (phrase) If someone is offered a drink or meal **on the house**, they do not have to pay for it.
6 (verb) To house something means to keep it, contain it, or shelter it, e.g. *The new wing will house the library.*

house arrest
(noun) Someone who is under house arrest is forbidden to go outside their home.

houseboat, houseboats
(noun) A houseboat is a small boat which people live on that is moored at a particular place on a river or canal.

housecoat, housecoats
(noun) A housecoat is a long garment like a dressing gown that some women wear in the house.

household, households
1 (noun) A household is all the people who live as a group in a house or flat.
2 (phrase) Someone who is **a household name** is very well known.
householder (noun).

housekeeper, housekeepers
(noun) A housekeeper is a person who is employed to cook, clean, and look after a house.

house martin, house martins
(noun) A house martin is a bird with white and blue-black feathers and a forked tail. House martins often build their nests under the eaves of houses.

House of Commons
(noun) The House of Commons is the more powerful of the two parts of parliament. Its members are elected by the public.

House of Lords
(noun) The House of Lords is the less powerful of the two parts of parliament. Its members have the right to belong because they come from noble families or hold a special office.

housewife, housewives
(noun) A housewife is a married woman who does the cooking, cleaning, and other chores in her home, and usually does not have a full time job outside the home.

housing
1 (noun) Housing is the buildings in which people live, e.g. *the housing shortage.*

2 Housing is also the job of providing houses for people, e.g. *the city housing department.*
3 The housing of a machine is the case or covering which protects it.

hovel, hovels
(noun) A hovel is a small hut or house that is dirty or badly in need of repair.

hover, hovers, hovering, hovered
1 (verb) When a bird, insect, or aircraft hovers, it stays in the same position in the air.
2 If someone hovers, they are uncertain and stay in the same place making indecisive movements, e.g. *A figure hovered uncertainly in the frame.*

hovercraft, hovercrafts
(noun) A hovercraft is a vehicle which can travel over water or land supported by a cushion of air.

how
1 (adverb) 'How' is used to ask about, explain, or refer to the way in which something is done, known, or experienced, e.g. *How did this happen?... This is how I make a curry.*
2 'How' is used to ask about or refer to a measurement or quantity, e.g. *How much is this?... I've forgotten how old he is.*
3 'How' is used to emphasize the following word or statement, e.g. *How I dislike that man!*

however
1 (adverb) You use 'however' when you are adding a comment that seems to contradict or contrast with what has just been said, e.g. *I had hoped to be offered the job. However, I didn't get it.*
2 You use 'however' to say that something makes no difference to a situation, e.g. *However we add that up, it does not make a dozen!*

howl, howls, howling, howled
1 (verb) To howl means to make a long, loud wailing noise such as that made by a dog when it is upset, e.g. *wolves howling in the distance... The wind howled through the deserted streets.*
2 (noun) A howl is a long, loud wailing noise.

howler, howlers
(noun; an informal word) A howler is a stupid mistake.

HQ an abbreviation for **headquarters.**

HRH an abbreviation for 'His Royal Highness' or 'Her Royal Highness'.

hub, hubs
1 (noun) The hub of a wheel is the centre part of it.
2 The hub of a place or organization is the central or most important, active part of it, e.g. *the village hall was the social hub of the district.*

hubbub
(noun) Hubbub is great noise, fuss, or confusion, e.g. *a hubbub of voices.*

huddle, huddles, huddling, huddled
1 (verb) If you huddle up or are huddled, you are curled up with your arms and legs close to your body.
2 When people or animals huddle together, they sit or stand close to each other, often for warmth.

3 (noun) A huddle of people or things is a small group of them.
4 (phrase) If you **go into a huddle**, you join closely with other people for a hurried discussion.

hue, hues
1 (noun; a literary use) A hue is a colour or a particular shade of a colour, e.g. *Her normally rosy face took on a deeper hue.*
2 (phrase) If people raise a **hue and cry**, they are very angry about something and protest.
[sense 1 is from Old English *hew* meaning 'colour' or 'beauty'; sense 2 is from Old French *huer* meaning 'to shout']

huff
(phrase) If you are **in a huff**, you are sulking or offended about something.
huffy (adjective), **huffily** (adverb).

hug, hugs, hugging, hugged
1 (verb) If you hug someone, you put your arms round them and hold them close to you.
2 (noun) If you give someone a hug, you hold them close to you.
3 (verb) To hug a surface while moving means to keep very close to it or in contact with it, e.g. *The car handles well, hugging the road nicely.*
[from Old Norse *hugga* meaning 'to comfort' or 'console']

Similar words: (senses 1 and 2) embrace, cuddle

huge, huger, hugest
(adjective) extremely large in amount, size, or degree, e.g. *a huge profit... a huge building.*
hugely (adverb).

Similar words: immense, enormous, colossal, gigantic, giant, mammoth, gargantuan, vast

hulk, hulks
1 (noun) A hulk is a large, heavy person or thing.
2 A hulk is also the body of a boat or ship that has been wrecked or abandoned.
hulking (adjective).
[from Greek *holkas* meaning 'barge']

hull, hulls, hulling, hulled
1 (noun) The hull of a boat is the main part of its body that sits in the water.
2 The hull on some fruit such as strawberries is the stalk and ring of leaves at the base.
3 (verb) To hull fruit means to prepare it by removing the hulls.

hullabaloo, hullabaloos
(noun) A hullabaloo is a lot of noise or fuss.

hum, hums, humming, hummed
1 (verb) To hum means to make a continuous low noise, e.g. *The air conditioners hummed.*
2 If you hum, you sing with your lips closed.
3 (noun) A hum is a continuous low noise, e.g. *She could hear the hum of the machine.*
4 (phrase) If someone **hums and haws**, they take a long time to say something because they feel awkward, uncertain, or embarrassed.

human, humans
1 (adjective) relating to, concerning, or typical of people, e.g. *meat that is not fit for human consumption... faults and weaknesses which are only human.*
2 (noun) A human is a person.
humanly (adverb).
[from Latin *homo* meaning 'man']

human being, human beings
(noun) A human being is a person.

humane
(adjective) showing kindness, thoughtfulness, and sympathy towards others, e.g. *working for a more humane society.*
humaneness (noun), **humanely** (adverb).

humanism
(noun) Humanism is the belief in mankind's ability to achieve happiness and fulfilment without the need for religion.

humanitarian, humanitarians
1 (noun) A humanitarian is a person who works for the welfare of mankind.
2 (adjective) concerned with the welfare of mankind, e.g. *liberal and humanitarian opinions.*
humanitarianism (noun).

humanities
(plural noun) The humanities are subjects such as literature, philosophy, and history, which are concerned with people rather than with science.

humanity
1 (noun) Humanity is people in general, e.g. *a triumph for humanity.*
2 Humanity is also the condition of being human, e.g. *They degraded the prisoners, denying them their humanity.*
3 Someone who has humanity is kind, thoughtful, and sympathetic.

humble, humbler, humblest; humbles, humbling, humbled
1 (adjective) A humble person is modest and thinks that he or she has very little value.
2 Something that is humble is small or not very important, e.g. *My humble filing system started with two cardboard boxes.*
3 (verb) To humble someone means to make them feel unimportant or humiliated.
4 (phrase) To **eat humble pie** means to behave humbly and admit that you are wrong.
humbly (adverb), **humbled** (adjective).
[from Latin *humilis* meaning 'low']

Similar words: (sense 1) modest, lowly, unassuming (sense 2) modest

humbug, humbugs
1 (noun) A humbug is a hard black and white striped sweet that tastes of peppermint.
2 Humbug is speech or writing that is obviously dishonest, untrue, or nonsense, e.g. *parliamentary humbug.*

humdrum
(adjective) ordinary, dull, and uninteresting, e.g. *their humdrum lives.*

humerus, humeri (pronounced **hyoo**-mer-us)
(noun) Your humerus is the long bone in the upper part of your arm.

humid
(adjective) If it is humid, the atmosphere feels damp, heavy, and warm.
[from Latin *umidus* meaning 'wet']

Similar words: clammy, muggy, sultry

humidity
(noun) Humidity is the amount of moisture in the atmosphere, or the state of being humid.

humiliate, humiliates, humiliating, humiliated
(verb) To humiliate someone means to make them feel ashamed or appear stupid to other people.
humiliation (noun).

Similar words: embarrass, shame, mortify, humble

humility
(noun) Humility is the quality of being modest and humble.

hummingbird, hummingbirds
(noun) A hummingbird is a very small brightly coloured bird with powerful wings that make a humming noise as they beat.

hummock, hummocks
(noun) A hummock is a very small hill or mound.

humorist, humorists
(noun) A humorist is a writer or entertainer who makes jokes and tells funny stories.

humour, humours, humouring, humoured
1 (noun) Humour is the quality of being funny, e.g. *The radio version loses all the humour of the original play.*
2 Humour is also the ability to be amused by certain things, e.g. *She's got a good sense of humour.*
3 Someone's humour is the mood they are in, e.g. *The work was done with good humour.*
4 (verb) If you humour someone, you are especially kind to them and do whatever they want.
humorous (adjective), **humorously** (adverb), **humourless** (adjective).

Similar words: (sense 1) comedy, wit

hump, humps, humping, humped
1 (noun) A hump is a small, rounded lump or mound, e.g. *a camel's hump.*
2 (verb; an informal use) If you hump something heavy, you carry or move it with difficulty.

humus (pronounced **hyoo**-muss)
(noun) Humus is a dark coloured substance in the soil, consisting of decayed plant and animal matter. Humus improves the fertility of the soil.
[from Latin *humus* meaning 'soil' or 'earth']

hunch, hunches, hunching, hunched
1 (noun) A hunch is a feeling or suspicion about something, not based on facts or evidence.
2 (verb) If you hunch your shoulders, you raise your shoulders and lean forwards.

hunchback, hunchbacks
(noun; an old-fashioned word) A hunchback is someone who has a large hump on their back.
hunchbacked (adjective).

hundred, hundreds
the number 100.
hundredth.

hundredweight, hundredweights
(noun) A hundredweight is a unit of weight equal to 112 pounds or about 45.36 kilograms.

Hungarian, Hungarians (pronounced hung-**gair**-ee-an)
1 (adjective) belonging or relating to Hungary.
2 (noun) A Hungarian is someone who comes from Hungary.
3 Hungarian is the main language spoken in Hungary.

hunger, hungers, hungering, hungered
1 (noun) Hunger is the need to eat or the desire to eat.
2 A hunger for something is a strong need or desire for it, e.g. *a hunger for power.*
3 (verb) If you hunger for something, you want it very much.

hunger strike, hunger strikes
(noun) A hunger strike is a refusal to eat anything at all, especially by prisoners as a form of protest.

hung over
(adjective; an informal expression) Someone who is hung over has a headache and feels sick because they drank too much alcohol the day before.

hungry, hungrier, hungriest
(adjective) needing or wanting to eat, e.g. *reports of children going hungry.*
hungrily (adverb).

hunk, hunks
(noun) A hunk of something is a large piece of it.

hunt, hunts, hunting, hunted
1 (verb) To hunt means to chase wild animals to kill them for food or for sport.
2 (noun) A hunt is a group of people who have met together to hunt foxes on horseback.
3 (verb) If you hunt for something, you search for it.
hunter (noun), **hunting** (adjective and noun).

hurdle, hurdles
1 (noun) A hurdle is one of the frames or barriers that you jump over in an athletics race called hurdles, e.g. *She won the four hundred metre hurdles.*
2 A hurdle is also a problem or difficulty, e.g. *Getting finance is one of the first hurdles that small businesses face.*

hurl, hurls, hurling, hurled
1 (verb) To hurl something means to throw it with great force.
2 If you hurl insults at someone, you insult them aggressively and repeatedly.

hurray or **hurrah** or **hooray**
an exclamation of excitement or approval.

hurricane, hurricanes
(noun) A hurricane is a violent wind or storm, usually force 12 or above on the Beaufort scale. [from Spanish *huracán*]

hurricane lamp, hurricane lamps
(noun) A hurricane lamp is a paraffin lamp which has glass round it so that the flame does not blow out in the wind.

hurry, hurries, hurrying, hurried
1 (verb) To hurry means to move or do something as quickly as possible, e.g. *They hurried to finish the work.*
2 To hurry something means to make it happen more quickly, e.g. *You can hurry up the defrosting by leaving the fridge door open.*
3 (noun) Hurry is the speed with which you do something quickly, e.g. *He had to leave in a great hurry.*
hurried (adjective), **hurriedly** (adverb).

Similar words: (sense 1) hasten, rush, fly, scurry (sense 3) bustle, rush

hurt, hurts, hurting, hurt
1 (verb) To hurt someone means to cause them physical pain.
2 If a part of your body hurts, you feel pain there.
3 If you hurt yourself, you injure yourself.
4 To hurt someone also means to make them unhappy by being unkind or thoughtless towards them, e.g. *I don't want to hurt his feelings.*
5 (adjective) If someone feels hurt, they feel unhappy because of someone's unkindness or thoughtlessness towards them, e.g. *He gave her a hurt look.*
hurtful (adjective).
[from Old French *hurter* meaning 'to knock against']

hurtle, hurtles, hurtling, hurtled
(verb) To hurtle means to move or travel very fast indeed, especially in an uncontrolled or violent way.

husband, husbands, husbanding, husbanded
1 (noun) A woman's husband is the man she is married to.
2 (verb; a formal use) To husband something means to manage it carefully and use it in an economical way, e.g. *the need for husbanding the nation's fuel resources.*
[from Old English *husbonda* meaning 'master of a house']

husbandry
1 (noun) Husbandry is the art or skill of farming.
2 Husbandry is also the art or skill of managing something carefully and economically.

hush, hushes, hushing, hushed
1 (verb) If you tell someone to hush, you are telling them to be quiet.
2 (noun) If there is a hush, it is quiet and still, e.g. *An expectant hush fell on the crowd.*
3 (verb) To hush something up means to keep it secret, especially something dishonest or disreputable involving important people, e.g. *The police hushed the matter up.*
hushed (adjective).

hush-hush
(adjective; an informal expression) secret, confidential, and not to be discussed in public.

hush money
(noun) Hush money is money given as a bribe to keep someone quiet.

husk, husks
(noun) Husks are the dry outer coverings of grain or seed.

husky, huskier, huskiest; huskies
1 (adjective) A husky voice is rough or hoarse.
2 (noun) A husky is a large, strong dog with a thick coat. Teams of huskies are used to pull sledges across snow.
huskily (adverb).

hussy, hussies
(noun; an old-fashioned word) 'Hussy' is a word for a girl or woman thought to behave in a sexually immoral or improper way.

hustings
(plural noun) Hustings are campaigns or speeches which take place before an election. [from Old Norse *husthing* meaning 'house assembly']

hustle, hustles, hustling, hustled
(verb) To hustle someone means to make them move by pushing and jostling them, e.g. *Anyone who protested was hustled out by the police.*
[from Dutch *husselen* meaning 'to shake']

hut, huts
(noun) A hut is a small, simple building, with one or two rooms.

hutch, hutches
(noun) A hutch is a wooden box with wire mesh at one side, in which rabbits, guinea pigs, or other small pets can be kept.

hyacinth, hyacinths (pronounced high-as-sinth)
(noun) A hyacinth is a spring flower which grows from a bulb and has many small, bell-shaped flowers grouped around the stem. [the flower supposedly first grew at the spot where the classical Greek character Hyacinthus was killed]

hyaena another spelling of **hyena**.

hybrid, hybrids
1 (noun) A hybrid is a plant or animal that has been bred from two different types of plant or animal.
2 A hybrid is also anything that is a mixture of two other things.
[from Latin *hibrida* meaning 'offspring of mixed parents']

hydra, hydras or **hydrae**
(noun) A hydra is a microscopic freshwater creature that has a slender tubular body and tentacles round the mouth.
[from Greek *hudra* meaning 'water serpent']

hydrangea, hydrangeas (pronounced
high-**drain**-ja)
(noun) A hydrangea is a garden shrub with large
clusters of pink or blue flowers.

hydrant, hydrants
(noun) A hydrant is an upright pipe attached to
a water main from which water can be obtained
in an emergency.

hydraulic (pronounced high-**drol**-lik)
(adjective) operated by water, oil, or other fluid
which is under pressure.
[from Greek *hudōr* + *aulos* meaning 'water pipe']

hydraulics
(noun) Hydraulics is the study and use of
systems that work using hydraulic pressure.

hydride, hydrides
(noun) A hydride is any combination of
hydrogen with another element.

hydrocarbon, hydrocarbons
(noun) A hydrocarbon is a chemical compound
that is a mixture of hydrogen and carbon.
[from Greek *hudōr* meaning 'water' and Latin
carbo meaning 'charcoal']

hydrochloric acid (pronounced
high-dro-**klor**-ik)
(noun) Hydrochloric acid is a very strong acid
used in chemical processes and in industry. It is a
solution of hydrogen chloride.

hydroelectric
(adjective) using or powered by energy
generated from the energy of running water.
hydroelectricity (noun).

hydrofoil, hydrofoils
(noun) A hydrofoil is a boat which has a pair of
fins like skis which raise the hull above the
water when it is moving at speed.

hydrogen
(noun) Hydrogen is the lightest gas and the
simplest chemical element. It is colourless and
odourless. Its atomic number is 1 and its symbol
is H.

hydrogen bomb, hydrogen bombs
(noun) A hydrogen bomb is a bomb in which
energy is released by the fusion of hydrogen
atoms to produce helium. The energy required is
provided by an atom bomb surrounded by a
substance containing hydrogen.

hydrolysis (pronounced high-**drol**-iss-iss)
(noun) In chemistry, hydrolysis is a process of
decomposition in which a compound reacts with
water to produce other compounds.

hydrophobia (pronounced high-dro-**foe**-bee-a)
(noun) Hydrophobia is an abnormal fear of
water, usually caused by the disease rabies.
[from Greek *hudōr* + *phobos* meaning 'water
fear']

hydroponics
(noun) Hydroponics is a method of growing
plants in water rather than in soil.
[from Greek *hudōr* meaning 'water' and *ponein*
meaning 'to labour']

hyena, hyenas (pronounced high-**ee**-na); also
spelled **hyaena**
(noun) A hyena is a doglike African and Asian
animal that hunts in packs.
[from Greek *huaina* meaning 'hog']

hygiene (pronounced high-jeen)
(noun) Hygiene is the practice of keeping
yourself and your surroundings clean, especially
in order to prevent the spread of disease.
hygienic (adjective), **hygienically** (adverb).
[from Greek *hugieinos* meaning 'healthful']

Similar words: cleanliness, sanitation

hymen, hymens
(noun) A woman's hymen is a piece of skin that
partly covers the vagina and that breaks before
puberty or when she has sex for the first time.
[from Greek *hymen* meaning 'membrane']

hymn, hymns
(noun) A hymn is a song in praise of God.

hyper-
(prefix) Hyper- means very much or excessive,
e.g. *She's hypercritical.*
[from Greek *huper* meaning 'over']

hyperactive
(adjective) A hyperactive person is unable to
relax and is always in a state of restless activity.
[from Greek *huper-* meaning 'over' and Latin
actus meaning 'performance']

hyperbola, hyperbolas (pronounced
high-**per**-bol-la)
(noun) In maths, a hyperbola is a smooth curve
that gets steeper or flatter at a constant rate.
hyperbolic (adjective).

hyperbole (pronounced high-**per**-bol-lee)
(noun) Hyperbole is a style of speech or writing
which uses exaggeration.
hyperbolic (adjective).

hypermarket, hypermarkets
(noun) A hypermarket is a very large
supermarket.

hypersensitive
(adjective) very sensitive indeed.

hypertension
(noun) Hypertension is a medical condition in
which a person has high blood pressure.

hyphen, hyphens
(noun) A hyphen is a punctuation mark used to
join together words or parts of words, as for
example in the word 'left-handed'.
hyphenate (verb), **hyphenation** (noun).
[from Greek *huphen* meaning 'together']

hypnosis (pronounced hip-**noh**-siss)
(noun) Hypnosis is the skill of hypnotizing
people.
[from Greek *hupnos* meaning 'sleep']

hypnotize, hypnotizes, hypnotizing, hypnotized;
also spelled **hypnotise**
(verb) To hypnotize someone means to put them
into a state in which they seem to be asleep but
can respond to questions and suggestions.
hypnotic (adjective), **hypnotism** (noun),
hypnotist (noun).

Similar words: mesmerize, entrance

hypochondriac, hypochondriacs (pronounced high-pok-**kon**-dree-ak)
(noun) A hypochondriac is a person who continually worries about their health, being convinced that they are ill when there is actually nothing wrong with them.
hypochondria (noun).

hypocrisy, hypocrisies
(noun) Hypocrisy is pretending to have beliefs, qualities, or feelings that you do not really have, so that you seem a better person than you are.
hypocritical (adjective), **hypocritically** (adverb), **hypocrite** (noun).
[from Greek *hupokrinein* meaning 'to pretend']

hypodermic, hypodermics
(noun) A hypodermic is a medical instrument consisting of a hollow needle attached to a cylinder and plunger. It is used for giving people injections.
[from Greek *hupo* + *derma* meaning 'under skin']

hypotenuse, hypotenuses (pronounced high-**pot**-tin-yooz)
(noun) In a right-angled triangle, the hypotenuse is the longest side and is opposite the right angle.

hypothermia
(noun) Hypothermia is a condition in which a person is very ill because their body temperature has been unusually low for a long time.

[from Greek *hupo* + *thermē* meaning 'under heat']

hypothesis, hypotheses
(noun) A hypothesis is an explanation or theory which has not yet been proved to be correct.
[from Greek *hupotithenai* meaning 'to suppose' or 'to propose']

hypothetical
(adjective) based on assumption rather than on fact or reality.
hypothetically (adverb).

hysterectomy, hysterectomies (pronounced his-ter-**rek**-tom-ee)
(noun) A hysterectomy is an operation to remove a woman's womb.
[from Greek *hustera* meaning 'womb' and *ektomos* meaning 'a slice cut out of']

hysteria (pronounced hiss-**teer**-ee-a)
(noun) Hysteria is a state of uncontrolled excitement, anger, or panic.

hysterical
1 (adjective) Someone who is hysterical is in a state of uncontrolled excitement, anger, or panic. **2** (an informal use) Something that is hysterical is extremely funny.
hysterically (adverb), **hysterics** (noun).

Similar words: (sense 1) overwrought, uncontrollable, frantic, beside yourself

I

I
(pronoun) A speaker or writer uses I to refer to himself or herself, e.g. *I like your dress.*

ice, ices, icing, iced
1 (noun) Ice is water that has frozen solid.
2 An ice is a portion of ice cream.
3 (verb) If something ices over or ices up, it becomes covered with a layer of ice.
4 If you ice cakes, you cover them with icing.
5 (phrase) If you do something to **break the ice**, you make people feel relaxed and comfortable.

ice age, ice ages
(noun) An ice age was a time in the past when a lot of the earth's surface was covered by ice for thousands of years.

iceberg, icebergs
(noun) An iceberg is a large, tall mass of ice floating in the sea.
[from Dutch *ijsberg* meaning 'ice mountain']

icebox, iceboxes
(noun) In American English, an icebox is a refrigerator.

icecap, icecaps
(noun) An icecap is a layer of ice and snow that permanently covers the North or South Pole.

ice cream, ice creams
(noun) Ice cream is a very cold sweet-tasting food made from frozen cream.

ice cube, ice cubes
(noun) Ice cubes are small cubes of ice put in drinks.

ice hockey
(noun) Ice hockey is a type of hockey played on ice, with two teams of six skaters.

Icelandic
(noun) Icelandic is the main language spoken in Iceland.

ice-skate, ice-skates, ice-skating, ice-skated
1 (noun) An ice-skate is a boot with a metal blade on the bottom, which you wear when skating on ice.
2 (verb) If you ice-skate, you move about on ice wearing ice-skates.

ichthyology (pronounced ik-thi-**ol**-lej-ee)
(noun) Ichthyology is the study of fish.
[from Greek *ikhthus* meaning 'fish']

icicle, icicles (pronounced **eye**-sikl)
(noun) An icicle is a piece of ice shaped like a pointed stick that hangs down from a surface.

icing
(noun) Icing is a mixture of powdered sugar and water or egg whites, used to decorate cakes.

icon, icons (pronounced **eye**-kon)
(noun) In the Orthodox Churches, an icon is a holy picture of Christ, the Virgin Mary, or a saint.
[from Greek *eikōn* meaning 'likeness' or 'image']

iconoclast, iconoclasts (pronounced eye-**kon**-i-klast)

(noun; a formal word) An iconoclast is someone who criticizes generally accepted beliefs.
iconoclastic (adjective), **iconoclasm** (noun).
[from Greek *eikōn* meaning 'image' and *klastēs* meaning 'breaker'. In the 8th and 9th centuries, members of a movement against using images in religious worship literally broke statues]

icy, icier, iciest
1 (adjective) An icy road has ice on it.
2 Something which is icy is very cold e.g. *an icy wind.*
3 An icy manner shows displeasure in a quiet, controlled way.
icily (adverb), **iciness** (noun).

idea, ideas
1 (noun) An idea is a plan, suggestion, or thought that you have after thinking about a problem.
2 An idea is also an opinion or belief, e.g. *He's got some really strange ideas about religion.*
3 An idea of something is what you know about it, e.g. *He had no idea of the time.*
[from Greek *idea* meaning 'model', 'pattern', or 'notion']

Similar words: (sense 1) notion, impression, inkling, feeling, hunch, thought
(sense 2) concept, notion, thought, image

ideal, ideals
1 (noun) An ideal is a principle or idea that seems perfect to you and so you try to achieve it.
2 Your ideal of something is the person or thing that seems the best example of it.
3 (adjective) The ideal person or thing is the best possible person or thing for the situation.

idealism (pronounced eye-**dee**-il-izm)
(noun) Idealism is the beliefs and behaviour of someone who bases their life on their ideals.
idealist (noun), **idealistic** (adjective).

idealize, idealizes, idealizing, idealized; also spelled **idealise**
(verb) If you idealize someone or something, you regard them as being perfect.
idealized (adjective), **idealization** (noun).

ideally
1 (adverb) If you say that ideally something should happen, you mean that you would like it to happen but you know that it is not possible.
2 Ideally means perfectly, e.g. *She's ideally suited for the job.*

identical
(adjective) exactly the same, e.g. *identical bags.*
identically (adverb).
[from Latin *idem* meaning 'the same']

identification
1 (noun) The identification of someone or something is the act of identifying them.
2 Identification is a document such as a driver's licence or passport, which proves who you are.

identify, identifies, identifying, identified
1 (verb) To identify someone or something means to recognize them or name them.
2 If you identify with someone, you understand their feelings and ideas.
3 If you identify one thing with another, you consider them to be the same.
identifiable (adjective).

identity, identities
(noun) Your identity consists of the characteristics that make you who you are.
[from Latin *idem* meaning 'the same']

identity parade, identity parades
(noun) An identity parade is a group of people shown to a witness to see if the witness recognizes any of them as having committed a crime.

ideology, ideologies
(noun) An ideology is a set of political beliefs.
ideological (adjective), **ideologically** (adverb).

idiocy, idiocies
(noun) Idiocy is total stupidity.

idiom, idioms
(noun) An idiom is a group of words whose meaning together is different from all the words taken individually. For example, 'It is raining cats and dogs' is an idiom.
[from Greek *idiōma* meaning 'special phraseology']

idiomatic (pronounced id-ee-om-**mat**-ik)
(adjective) Idiomatic language is natural, fluent, and often informal.
idiomatically (adverb).

idiosyncrasy, idiosyncrasies (pronounced id-ee-oh-**sing**-krassee)
(noun) Someone's idiosyncrasies are their own habits and likes or dislikes.
idiosyncratic (adjective), **idiosyncratically** (adverb).
[from Greek *idios* + *synkrasis* meaning 'personal mixture']

idiot, idiots
(noun) If you call someone an idiot, you mean that they are stupid or foolish.
[from Greek *idiōtēs* meaning 'ignorant person']

Similar words: fool, blockhead, nincompoop, nitwit, simpleton, moron, imbecile

idiotic
(adjective) extremely foolish or silly.
idiotically (adverb).

Similar words: stupid, fatuous, inane, dim, crass

idle, idles, idling, idled
1 (adjective) If you are idle, you are doing nothing.
2 Machines or factories that are idle are not being used.
3 If you describe a plan of action as idle, you mean that it is not useful, e.g. *It would be idle to search in the dark.*

4 (verb) An engine which is running slowly and is out of gear is idling.
idleness (noun), **idly** (adverb).
[from Saxon *idal* meaning 'worthless' or 'empty']

idol, idols (pronounced **eye**-doll)
1 (noun) An idol is a famous person who is loved, admired, and often imitated by fans.
2 An idol is also a picture or statue which is worshipped as if it were a god.
[from Greek *eidōlon* meaning 'image' or 'phantom']

idolatry
(noun) Idolatry is the worship of idols.
idolatrous (adjective).

idolize, idolizes, idolizing, idolized; also spelled **idolise**
(verb) If you idolize someone, you admire or love them very much.

idyll, idylls (pronounced **id**-ill)
(noun) An idyll is a situation which is pleasant, peaceful, and beautiful.
idyllic (adjective).
[from Greek *eidos* meaning 'picture']

i.e.
i.e. means 'that is', and is used before giving more information. It is an abbreviation for the Latin expression 'id est'.

if
1 (conjunction) on the condition that, e.g. *He'll go to Hull next year if he passes his exams.*
2 whether, e.g. *I asked her if I could help.*

igloo, igloos
(noun) An igloo is a dome-shaped house built out of blocks of snow by the Inuit, or Eskimo people.
[from *igdlu*, an Eskimo word meaning 'house']

igneous (pronounced **ig**-nee-uss)
(adjective; a technical word) Igneous rocks are formed by hot liquid rock cooling and going hard.
[from Latin *igneus* meaning 'fiery']

ignite, ignites, igniting, ignited
(verb) If you ignite something or if it ignites, it starts burning.
[from Latin *ignis* meaning 'fire']

ignition, ignitions
1 (noun) In a car, the ignition is the part of the engine where the fuel is ignited.
2 Ignition is the process by which a car engine is started.

ignoble
(adjective; a formal word) An ignoble person behaves in a dishonourable way.
ignobly (adverb).
[from *in-* and Latin *gnobilis* meaning 'noble']

ignominious
(adjective) shameful or morally unacceptable.
ignominiously (adverb), **ignominy** (noun).

ignoramus, ignoramuses (pronounced ig-nor-**ray**-muss)
(noun) An ignoramus is an ignorant person.
[from the character *Ignoramus*, an uneducated lawyer in a 17th-century play by Ruggle. In Latin, *ignoramus* means 'we do not know']

ignorant

1 (adjective) If you are ignorant of something, you do not know about it, e.g. *Prime Ministers are often ignorant of foreign affairs.*
2 Someone who is ignorant does not know about things in general, e.g. *How can he be so ignorant at his age?*
ignorantly (adverb), **ignorance** (noun).

Similar words: (sense 1) unaware, oblivious, unconscious, unwitting

ignore, ignores, ignoring, ignored

(verb) If you ignore someone or something, you deliberately do not take any notice of them.
[from Latin *ignorare* meaning 'to not know']

ill, ills

1 (adjective) unhealthy or sick.
2 harmful or unpleasant, e.g. *ill effects.*
3 (noun) Ills are difficulties or problems.
[from Norse *illr* meaning 'bad']

Similar words: (sense 1) sick, ailing, unwell, unhealthy, poorly, indisposed, off-colour

ill-advised

(adjective) not sensible or wise.

ill at ease

(phrase) If you feel **ill at ease**, you feel unable to relax.

ill-bred

(adjective) rude and having bad manners.

illegal

(adjective) forbidden by the law.
illegally (adverb), **illegality** (noun).

Similar words: illicit, unlawful, criminal

illegible (pronounced il-**lej**-i-bl)

(adjective) Writing which is illegible is unclear and difficult or impossible to read.
illegibly (adverb), **illegibility** (noun).

illegitimate (pronounced ili-**jit**-im-it)

(adjective) A person who is illegitimate was born to parents who were not married at the time.
illegitimately (adverb), **illegitimacy** (noun).

ill-fated

(adjective) doomed to end unhappily, e.g. *the ill-fated romance of Romeo and Juliet.*

ill-gotten gains

(plural noun) Ill-gotten gains are things that you have obtained dishonestly.

illicit (pronounced il-**liss**-it)

(adjective) not allowed by law or not approved of by society, e.g. *an illicit affair.*
[from *in-* + Latin *licitus* meaning 'permitted']

illiterate

(adjective) unable to read or write.
illiterately (adverb), **illiteracy** (noun).

illness, illnesses

1 (noun) Illness is the experience of being ill.
2 An illness is a particular disease, e.g. *colds, measles, and other illnesses.*

Similar words: (sense 2) sickness, ailment, complaint, indisposition, malady, disease

illogical

(adjective) An illogical feeling or action is not reasonable or sensible.
illogically (adverb).

ill-starred

(adjective) very unlucky, e.g. *an ill-starred scheme.*

ill-treat, ill-treats, ill-treating, ill-treated

(verb) If you ill-treat someone or something you hurt or damage them or treat them cruelly.
ill-treatment (noun).

illuminate, illuminates, illuminating, illuminated

1 (verb) To illuminate something means to shine light on it to make it easier to see.
2 If you illuminate something which is difficult to understand, you make it clearer, for instance by giving examples.
3 In medieval times, when monks illuminated books, they decorated them with small brightly-coloured pictures and designs.
[from Latin *lumen* meaning 'light']

illumination, illuminations

1 (noun) Illumination is lighting.
2 Illuminations are the coloured lights put up to decorate a town, especially at Christmas.

illusion, illusions

1 (noun) An illusion is a false belief which you think is true, e.g. *an illusion of freedom.*
2 An illusion is also something which you think you see clearly but in reality it is different or does not exist, e.g. *an optical illusion.*
[from Latin *illusio* meaning 'deceit']

illusory (pronounced ill-**yoo**-ser-ee)

(adjective) seeming to be true, but actually false, e.g. *illusory hopes that he would find a job.*

illustrate, illustrates, illustrating, illustrated

1 (verb) If you illustrate a point, you explain it or make it clearer, often by using examples.
2 If you illustrate a book, you supply it with pictures.
illustrator (noun), **illustrative** (adjective).
[from Latin *illustrare* meaning 'to make light']

illustration, illustrations

1 (noun) An illustration is an example or a story which is used to make a point clear.
2 An illustration in a book is a picture.
3 Illustration is the art of drawing pictures.

illustrious

(adjective) An illustrious person is famous and respected.
illustriously (adverb), **illustriousness** (noun).

ill will

(noun) Ill will is a feeling of hostility.

image, images

1 (noun) An image is a mental picture of someone or something.
2 An image is the public face of a person, group, or organization.
3 An image is a picture or feeling created by an author, musician, or artist in a work of art, which suggests a special meaning or theme.
[from Latin *imago* meaning 'copy' or 'representation']

imagery
(noun) The imagery of a poem or book is the descriptive language used.

imaginary
(adjective) Something that is imaginary exists only in your mind, not in real life.

imagination, imaginations
(noun) Your imagination is your ability to form new and exciting ideas, e.g. *a vivid imagination.*

imaginative
(adjective) Someone who is imaginative can easily form new or exciting ideas in their mind.
imaginatively (adverb).

imagine, imagines, imagining, imagined
1 (verb) If you imagine something, you form an idea of it in your mind, or you think you have seen or heard it but you have not really.
2 If you imagine that something is the case, you believe it is the case, e.g. *I imagine you are tired.*
imaginable (adjective).

Similar words: (sense 1) picture, conceive, envisage, visualize
(sense 2) think, fancy

imbalance, imbalances
(noun) If there is an imbalance between things, they are unequal, e.g. *the imbalance between rich and poor.*

imbecile, imbeciles (pronounced **im**-bis-seel)
(noun; an informal word) If you call someone an imbecile, you mean that they are stupid.
[from Latin *imbecillus* meaning 'physically or mentally feeble']

imbibe, imbibes, imbibing, imbibed
(verb; a formal word) To imbibe something means to drink it.
[from Latin *bibere* meaning 'to drink']

imitate, imitates, imitating, imitated
(verb) To imitate someone or something means to copy them.
imitator (noun), **imitative** (adjective).

Similar words: copy, ape, mimic, impersonate

imitation, imitations
(noun) An imitation is a copy of something else.

immaculate (pronounced im-**mak**-yoo-lit)
1 (adjective) completely clean and tidy, e.g. *The room was immaculate.*
2 without any mistakes at all, e.g. *Her playing was immaculate.*
immaculately (adverb).
[from Latin *im-* meaning 'not' and *macula* meaning 'blemish']

immaterial
(adjective) Something which is immaterial is not important.

immature
1 (adjective) Something that is immature has not finished growing or developing.
2 A person who is immature does not behave in a sensible adult way.
immaturity (noun).

immediate
1 (adjective) Something that is immediate happens or is done without delay.
2 Your immediate relatives and friends are the ones most closely connected or related to you.
immediacy (noun).

immediately
1 (adverb) If something happens immediately it happens right away.
2 Immediately means very near in time or position, e.g. *immediately behind the pub.*

immemorial
(adjective) If something has been happening from time immemorial, it has been happening longer than anyone can remember.

immense
(adjective) very large or huge.
immensely (adverb), **immensity** (noun).
[from Latin *im-* meaning 'not' and *mensus* meaning 'measured']

immerse, immerses, immersing, immersed
1 (verb) If you are immersed in an activity you are completely involved in it.
2 If you immerse something in a liquid, you put it into the liquid so that it is completely covered.
immersion (noun).
[from Latin *immergere* meaning 'to dip into']

immersion heater, immersion heaters
(noun) An immersion heater is an electric heater which provides hot water in the home.

immigrant, immigrants
(noun) An immigrant is someone who has come to live permanently in a new country.
immigrate (verb), **immigration** (noun).
[from Latin *immigrare* meaning 'to go into']

imminent
(adjective) If something is imminent, it is going to happen very soon.
imminently (adverb), **imminence** (noun).

Similar words: forthcoming, impending, looming, in the offing, prospective

immobile
(adjective) not moving.
immobility (noun).

immobilize, immobilizes, immobilizing, immobilized; also spelled immobilise
(verb) To immobilize someone or something means to stop them from moving.

immoderate
(adjective; a formal word) extreme or excessive.
immoderately (adverb).

immodest
1 (adjective) Someone who is immodest behaves in a way that some people consider rude or shocking.
2 If you boast a lot, you are immodest.
immodestly (adverb), **immodesty** (noun).

immoral
(adjective) If you describe someone or their behaviour as immoral, you mean that they do not

conform with generally accepted standards of what is morally right.
immorality (noun).

immortal
1 (adjective) Someone who is immortal will never die.
2 Something that is immortal is famous and will be remembered for a long time, e.g. *that immortal line from Shakespeare — 'If music be the food of love, play on.'*
immortality (noun).

immovable or immoveable
(adjective) Something that is immovable is fixed and cannot be moved.
immovably (adverb).

immune (pronounced im-**yoon**)
1 (adjective) If you are immune to a particular disease, you cannot catch it.
2 If someone or something is immune from something, they are able to avoid it or are not bound by it, e.g. *As a diplomat he was immune from prosecution.*
immunity (noun).

immunize, immunizes, immunizing, immunized;
also spelled **immunise**
(verb) To immunize a person or animal means to make them immune to a particular disease, usually by giving them an injection.
immunization (noun).

immutable (pronounced im-**yoot**-i-bl)
(adjective; a formal word) Something that is immutable will never change.

imp, imps
(noun) In fairy stories, an imp is a mischievous pixie.
impish (adjective).

impact, impacts
1 (noun) The impact that someone or something has is the impression that they make or the effect that they have.
2 Impact is the action of one object hitting another, usually with a lot of force, e.g. *The missile exploded on impact.*
[from Latin *impactus* meaning 'pushed against']

impair, impairs, impairing, impaired
(verb) To impair something means to damage it so that it stops working properly, e.g. *The explosion impaired his hearing.*
[from Old French *empeirer* meaning 'to make worse']

impale, impales, impaling, impaled
(verb) If you impale something, you pierce it with a sharp object.

impart, imparts, imparting, imparted
(verb; a formal word) To impart information to someone means to pass it on to them.
[from Latin *impartire* meaning 'to share']

impartial
(adjective) Someone who is impartial has a fair and unbiased view of something.
impartially (adverb), **impartiality** (noun).

Similar words: objective, detached, disinterested

impassable
(adjective) A road or path which is impassable cannot be travelled along because it is blocked or in bad condition.

impasse (pronounced am-pass)
(noun) An impasse is a difficult situation in which it is impossible to find a solution.
[from French *impasse* meaning 'dead end']

impassioned
(adjective) full of emotion, e.g. *an impassioned speech.*

impassive
(adjective) showing no emotion.
impassively (adverb).

impatient
1 (adjective) Someone who is impatient becomes annoyed easily or is quick to lose their temper when things go wrong, e.g. *He was impatient with students who could not follow him.*
2 If you are impatient to do something, you are eager and do not want to wait, e.g. *James was impatient to go inside.*
impatiently (adverb), **impatience** (noun).

impeach, impeaches, impeaching, impeached
(verb) If a government official is impeached, he or she is charged with serious crimes.
impeachable (adjective), **impeachment** (noun).
[from Latin *impedicare* meaning 'to entangle' or 'to catch']

impeccable (pronounced im-**pek**-i-bl)
(adjective) excellent, without any faults.
impeccably (adverb).
[from Latin *impeccabilis* meaning 'sinless']

impecunious (pronounced im-pek-**yoon**-ee-uss)
(adjective; a formal word) having very little or no money.
[from Latin *im-* meaning 'not' + *pecunia* meaning 'money']

impedance
(noun; a technical word) In an electrical circuit, an impedance is the resistance presented to an alternating current.

impede, impedes, impeding, impeded
(verb) If you impede someone, you make their progress difficult.
[from Latin *impedire* meaning 'to shackle the feet']

impediment, impediments
(noun) An impediment is something that makes it difficult to move, develop, or do something properly, e.g. *a speech impediment.*

impel, impels, impelling, impelled
(verb; a formal word) If you feel impelled to do something, you feel a strong emotional force urging you to do it.
[from Latin *impellere* meaning 'to push against']

impending
(adjective; a formal word) You use impending to describe something that is going to happen very soon, e.g. *an impending disaster.*
[from Latin *impendere* meaning 'to overhang']

impenetrable
(adjective) impossible to get through.
impenetrability (noun).

imperative
1 (adjective) Something that is imperative is extremely urgent or important.
2 (noun) In grammar, an imperative is a verb form that is used for giving orders.
[from Latin *imperare* meaning 'to command']

imperceptible
(adjective) so slight as to be almost unnoticed, e.g. *an imperceptible darkening of the sky.*
imperceptibly (adverb).

imperfect
1 (adjective) Something that is imperfect has faults or problems.
2 (noun) In grammar, the imperfect is a tense used to describe continuous or repeated actions which happened in the past.
imperfectly (adverb), **imperfection** (noun).

Similar words: (sense 1) faulty, flawed

imperial
1 (adjective) Imperial means relating to an empire or an emperor or empress, e.g. *the Imperial Palace.*
2 The imperial system of measurement is the British measuring system, using inches, feet, and yards, ounces and pounds, and pints and gallons.
[from Latin *imperium* meaning 'empire']

imperialism
(noun) Imperialism is a system of rule in which a rich and powerful nation controls other nations.
imperialist (adjective and noun), **imperialistic** (adjective).

imperil, imperils, imperilling, imperilled
(verb) If something is imperilled, it is in danger.

imperious
(adjective) proud and domineering, e.g. *the imperious presence of Uncle Joshua.*
imperiously (adverb), **imperiousness** (noun).

impermeable
(adjective) Something that is impermeable does not allow liquid to pass through it.
impermeability (noun).

impersonal
1 (adjective) Something that is impersonal makes you feel that individuals and their feelings do not matter, e.g. *a vast impersonal organization.*
2 An impersonal feeling or action does not relate to any particular person, e.g. *impersonal criticism of the firm.*
impersonally (adverb).

Similar words: (sense 2) dispassionate, clinical, detached, cold

impersonate, impersonates, impersonating, impersonated
(verb) If you impersonate someone, you pretend to be that person.
impersonation (noun), **impersonator** (noun).

impertinent
(adjective) disrespectful and rude, e.g. *impertinent remarks.*
impertinently (adverb), **impertinence** (noun).
[from Latin *im-* meaning 'not' + *pertinens* meaning 'relevant']

imperturbable
(adjective) Someone who is imperturbable stays calm, even in difficult situations.
imperturbably (adverb).

impervious
1 (adjective) If you are impervious to someone's actions or personality, you are not affected by them, e.g. *She was impervious to his charm.*
2 Something that is impervious to liquids or heat does not allow them to pass through, e.g. *Granite is an impervious rock.*

impetuous
(adjective) If you are impetuous, you act quickly without thinking, e.g. *an impetuous decision which he later regretted.*
impetuously (adverb), **impetuosity** (noun).
[from Latin *impetuosus* meaning 'violent']

impetus
1 (noun) An impetus is the stimulating effect that something has on a situation, which causes it to develop more quickly.
2 In physics, impetus is the force that starts an object moving and resists changes in speed or direction.
[from Latin *impetus* meaning 'attack']

impinge, impinges, impinging, impinged
(verb) If something impinges on your life, it has an effect on you and influences you, e.g. *Your politics will impinge on your private life.*
[from Latin *impingere* meaning 'to dash against']

impious (pronounced im-pee-uss)
(adjective) showing a lack of respect or religious reverence.

implacable (pronounced im-plak-a-bl)
(adjective) Someone who is implacable is being harsh and refuses to change their mind.
implacably (adverb), **implacability** (noun).

implant, implants, implanting, implanted
1 (verb) To implant something into a person's body means to put it there, usually by means of an operation.
2 If you implant an idea into someone's mind, you cause them to accept it as part of the way that they think.
3 (noun) An implant is something that has been implanted into someone's body.

implausible
(adjective) very unlikely, e.g. *an implausible story.*
implausibly (adverb), **implausibility** (noun).

implement, implements, implementing, implemented
1 (verb) If you implement something such as a plan, you carry it out, e.g. *The new traffic regulations will be implemented immediately.*
2 (noun) An implement is a tool.
implementation (noun).

implicate, implicates, implicating, implicated
(verb) If you are implicated in a crime, you are
shown to be involved in it.
[from Latin *im-* + *plicare* meaning 'to fold in']

implication, implications
1 (noun) An implication is something that is
suggested or implied but not stated directly.
2 The implication of someone in a crime is the act
of showing that they have been involved in it.

implicit (pronounced im-**pliss**-it)
1 (adjective) expressed in an indirect way, e.g.
implicit criticism.
2 If you have an implicit belief in something, you
have no doubts about it, e.g. *We had implicit
trust in his claims*.
implicitly (adverb).
[from Latin *implicatus* meaning 'interwoven']

implode, implodes, imploding, imploded
(verb) If an object implodes, it collapses inwards
because the pressure inside it is less than the
pressure outside it.
implosion (noun).

implore, implores, imploring, implored
(verb) If you implore someone to do something,
you beg them to do it.
imploring (adjective), **imploringly** (adverb).

imply, implies, implying, implied
1 (verb) If you imply that something is the case,
you suggest it in an indirect way.
2 If one situation implies another, then the
second situation must logically be true.

impolite
(adjective) rude and not polite.

imponderable
1 (adjective) impossible to assess.
2 (noun) Imponderables are things that are
impossible to assess, e.g. *Such imponderables as
power and knowledge*.

import, imports, importing, imported
1 (verb) If you import something from another
country, you bring it into your country or have it
sent there.
2 (noun) An import is a product that is made in
another country and sent to your own country
for use there.
importation (noun), **importer** (noun).
[from Latin *importare* meaning 'to carry in']

important
1 (adjective) Something that is important is very
valuable, necessary, or significant.
2 An important person has great influence or
power.
importantly (adverb), **importance** (noun).

Similar words: (sense 1) momentous, great, high,
portentous, weighty, salient, serious

importunate
(adjective; a formal word) Someone who is
importunate is very persistent in trying to get
what they want.
importunity (noun).
[from Latin *importunus* meaning 'tiresome']

importune, importunes, importuning, importuned
(verb; a formal word) If you importune someone,
you keep asking them to do something.

impose, imposes, imposing, imposed
1 (verb) If you impose something on people, you
force it on them, e.g. *OPEC imposed a huge oil
price increase*.
2 If someone imposes on you, they unreasonably
expect you to do something for them.
imposition (noun).
[from Latin *imponere* meaning 'to place upon']

Similar words: (sense 1) foist, enforce, inflict

imposing
(adjective) having an impressive appearance or
manner, e.g. *an imposing building*.

impossible
(adjective) Something that is impossible cannot
happen, be done, or be believed.
impossibly (adverb), **impossibility** (noun).

impostor, impostors; also spelled **imposter**
(noun) An impostor is a person who pretends to
be someone else in order to get things they want.
[from Latin *impostor* meaning 'deceiver']

impotent
1 (adjective) Someone who is impotent has no
power to influence people or events.
2 A man who is impotent is unable to have or
maintain an erection during sexual intercourse.
impotently (adverb), **impotence** (noun).

impound, impounds, impounding, impounded
(verb) If something you own is impounded, the
police or other officials take possession of it.

impoverish, impoverishes, impoverishing,
impoverished
(verb) To impoverish someone means to make
them poor.
impoverished (adjective), **impoverishment** (noun).

impracticable
(adjective) impossible to do.

impractical
(adjective) not practical, sensible, or realistic.

imprecation, imprecations
(noun; a formal word) An imprecation is a curse
or swearword.
[from Latin *imprecari* meaning 'to invoke evil']

impregnable
(adjective) A building or other structure that is
impregnable is so strong or so solid that it cannot
be broken into or captured.
[from Old French *im-* + *prenable* meaning 'not
able to be taken']

impregnate, impregnates, impregnating,
impregnated
1 (verb) If something is impregnated with a
substance, it has absorbed the substance so that
it spreads right through it, e.g. *paper
impregnated with chemicals*.
2 (a formal use) To impregnate a woman or
female animal means to make her pregnant.
[from Latin *impraegnare* meaning 'to make
pregnant']

impresario, impresarios (pronounced
im-pris-**sar**-ee-oh)
(noun) An impresario is a person who manages
theatrical or musical events or companies.

impress, impresses, impressing, impressed
1 (verb) If you impress someone, you do
something to make them admire or respect you.
2 If you impress something on someone, you
make them understand the importance of it.
[from Latin *impressio* meaning 'emphasis' or
'impression']

impression, impressions
1 (noun) An impression of someone or something
is the way they look or seem to you.
2 An impression of an object is a mark or shape
that it has left in something soft.
3 (phrase) If you are **under the impression** that
something is the case, you believe it to be true.
4 If you **make an impression,** you have a strong
effect on people you meet.

Similar words: (sense 2) imprint, stamp

impressionable
(adjective) easy to influence, e.g. *impressionable
teenagers.*

Similar words: suggestible, receptive

impressionism
(noun) Impressionism is a style of painting
which is concerned with the impressions created
by light and shapes, rather than with neat
realistic details. Impressionism was particularly
popular in France between 1870 and 1900,
especially with artists such as Monet and Renoir.
impressionist (noun).

impressive
(adjective) If something is impressive, it
impresses you, e.g. *an impressive group of
celebrities.*

imprint, imprints, imprinting, imprinted
1 (noun) If something leaves an imprint on your
mind, it has a strong and lasting effect.
2 (verb) If something is imprinted on your
memory, it is firmly fixed there.
3 (noun) An imprint is the mark left by the
pressure of one object on another.

imprison, imprisons, imprisoning, imprisoned
(verb) If you are imprisoned, you are locked up,
usually in a prison.
imprisonment (noun).

improbable
(adjective) not probable or likely to happen.
improbably (adverb), **improbability** (noun).

Similar words: unlikely, far-fetched, implausible,
unbelievable

impromptu (pronounced im-**prompt**-yoo)
(adjective) An impromptu action is one done
without planning or organization.
[from Latin *in promptu* meaning 'in readiness']

Similar words: improvised, off the cuff, extempore

improper
1 (adjective) rude or shocking, e.g. *improper
behaviour.*
2 illegal or dishonest, e.g. *improper business
dealings.*
3 not suitable or correct, e.g. *improper handling
of medicines.*
improperly (adverb).

impropriety
(noun; a formal word) Impropriety is improper
behaviour.

improve, improves, improving, improved
(verb) If something improves or if you improve
it, it gets better or becomes more valuable, e.g.
The home has been improved and extended.
improvement (noun).
[from Old French *en prou* meaning 'into profit']

Similar words: better, ameliorate, upgrade, enhance

improvident
(adjective; a formal word) Someone who is
improvident is wasteful and does not think about
the future.
improvidence (noun).

improvise, improvises, improvising, improvised
1 (verb) If you improvise something, you make
or do something without planning in advance,
and with whatever materials are available.
2 When musicians or actors improvise, they
make up the music or words as they go along.
improvised (adjective), **improvisation** (noun).
[from Latin *improvisus* meaning 'unforeseen']

imprudent
(adjective) not sensible, wise, or careful.

impudent
(adjective) If someone is impudent, they behave
or speak rudely or disrespectfully.
impudently (adverb), **impudence** (noun).
[from Latin *in-* + *pudens* meaning 'not modest']

impulse, impulses
1 (noun) An impulse is a strong urge to do
something, e.g. *I felt a sudden impulse to hit him.*
2 An impulse is also a short electrical signal that
is sent along a wire or nerve or through the air.
3 In physics, an impulse is the average
magnitude of a force multiplied by the time
during which it acts.
impulsion (noun).
[from Latin *impulsus* meaning 'pushing' or
'incitement']

impulsive
(adjective) If you are impulsive, you do things
suddenly, without thinking about them carefully.
impulsively (adverb).

impunity (pronounced imp-**yoon**-it-ee)
(noun) If you do something with impunity, you
are not punished for doing it even though it is
wrong or illegal.

impure
(adjective) Something which is impure contains
small amounts of other things, such as dirt.
impurity (noun).

impute, imputes, imputing, imputed (pronounced imp-**yoot**)
(verb; a formal word) If you impute something to someone, you say that they are responsible for it.
imputation (noun).
[from Latin *imputare* meaning 'to reckon' or 'to calculate']

in
1 (preposition and adverb) 'In' is used to indicate position, direction, time, and manner.
2 (adjective) Something that is in is fashionable.
3 (phrase) If you are **in for** something such as a shock or surprise, you are going to experience it.
4 If you are **in on** something, you are involved in it.

in-
1 (prefix) In- is added to the beginning of some words to form a word with the opposite meaning.
2 In- also means in, into, or in the course of.

inability
(noun) An inability is a lack of ability to do something.

inaccessible
(adjective) impossible or very difficult to reach.

inaccurate
(adjective) not accurate or correct.
inaccurately (adverb), **inaccuracy** (noun).

inactive
(adjective) not doing anything.
inactivity (noun), **inaction** (noun).

Similar words: dormant, quiescent

inadequate
1 (adjective) If something is inadequate, there is not enough of it, or it is not good enough in quality for a particular purpose.
2 If someone feels inadequate, they feel they do not possess the skills necessary to do a particular job or to cope with life in general.
inadequately (adverb), **inadequacy** (noun).

Similar words: (sense 1) insufficient, meagre, scant, poor, skimpy, sparse

inadvertent
(adjective) not intentional, e.g. *an inadvertent insult.*
inadvertently (adverb).
[from *in-* + Latin *advertare* meaning 'to see' or 'to notice']

inalienable
(adjective) An inalienable right is one that cannot be taken away.

inane
(adjective) silly or stupid.
inanely (adverb), **inanity** (noun).
[from Latin *inanis* meaning 'empty']

inanimate
(adjective) An inanimate object has no life.

inappropriate
(adjective) not suitable for a particular purpose or occasion, e.g. *My clothes were inappropriate for a formal dinner.*

inappropriately (adverb), **inappropriateness** (noun).

Similar words: unsuitable, incongruous, out of place, wrong

inarticulate
(adjective) If you are inarticulate, you are unable to express yourself well or easily in speech.
inarticulately (adverb).

inasmuch
(conjunction) 'Inasmuch as' means to the extent that, e.g. *I helped the victims inasmuch as I was able.*

inattentive
(adjective) not paying attention.

inaudible
(adjective) not loud enough to be heard.
inaudibly (adverb).

inaugurate, inaugurates, inaugurating, inaugurated (pronounced in-**awg**-yoo-rate)
1 (verb) To inaugurate a new scheme means to start it.
2 To inaugurate a new leader means to officially establish them in their new position in a special ceremony, e.g. *The President was inaugurated in January.*
inauguration (noun), **inaugural** (adjective).
[from Latin *inaugare* meaning 'to check the omens']

inauspicious (pronounced in-awe-**spish**-uss)
(adjective) Something that is inauspicious indicates that success is unlikely, e.g. *an inauspicious start to our holiday.*
inauspiciously (adverb).

inborn
(adjective) An inborn quality is one that you were born with.

inbred
1 (adjective) An inbred quality is one that you were born with, e.g. *an inbred fear of change.*
2 People who are inbred have ancestors who are closely related to one another.

inbreed, inbreeds, inbreeding, inbred
(verb) If a family inbreeds, close relatives marry and have children over several generations.
inbreeding (noun).

incalculable
(adjective) Something that is incalculable is too great to be counted or estimated.

incandescent
(adjective) Something which is incandescent gives out light when it is heated.
incandescence (noun).
[from Latin *candescere* meaning 'to glow white']

incantation, incantations
(noun) An incantation is a magic spell that is sung or chanted.
[from Latin *cantare* meaning 'to sing']

incapable
1 (adjective) Someone who is incapable of doing

something is not able to do it, e.g. *He is incapable of changing a fuse.*
2 An incapable person is weak and helpless.
incapability (noun).

incapacitate, incapacitates, incapacitating, incapacitated
(verb) If you are incapacitated by something such as illness, it weakens you so that you are unable to do certain things.

incapacity
(noun) Incapacity is an inability to do something.

incarcerate, incarcerates, incarcerating, incarcerated (pronounced in-**kar**-ser-rate)
(verb) To incarcerate someone means to lock them up.
incarceration (noun).
[from Latin *in* + *carcer* meaning 'in prison']

incautious
(adjective) not carefully thought out, e.g. *an incautious remark.*

incendiary (pronounced in-**send**-yer-ee)
(adjective) An incendiary weapon is one which sets fire to things, e.g. *incendiary bombs.*
[from Latin *incendere* meaning 'to kindle']

incense, incenses, incensing, incensed
1 (noun) Incense is a spicy substance which is burned to create a sweet smell, especially during religious services.
2 (verb) If you are incensed by something, it makes you extremely angry.
[from Latin *incendere* meaning 'to kindle']

incentive, incentives
(noun) An incentive is something that encourages you to do something.
[from Latin *incentivus* meaning 'the beginning of a song']

inception
(noun; a formal word) The inception of a project is the start of it.
[from Latin *incipere* meaning 'to take up' or 'to begin']

incessant
(adjective) continuing without stopping, e.g. *the incessant ringing of telephones.*
incessantly (adverb).

incest
(noun) Incest is the crime of two people who are closely related having sex with each other.
incestuous (adjective).
[from Latin *in-* + *castus* meaning 'not chaste']

inch, inches, inching, inched
1 (noun) An inch is a unit of length equal to about 2.54 centimetres.
2 (verb) To inch forward means to move forward slowly.
[from Latin *uncia* meaning 'twelfth part'; there are twelve inches to the foot]

incidence
(noun) The incidence of something is how often it occurs, e.g. *a high incidence of heart disease.*

incident, incidents
(noun) An incident is an event, e.g. *a shooting incident.*
[from Latin *incidere* meaning 'to fall into' or 'to happen']

incidental
(adjective) occurring as a minor part of something, e.g. *incidental music.*

incidentally
(adverb) You can say 'incidentally' when you are adding something that is not very important to what you are saying, e.g. *I lent him money, which incidentally he hasn't paid back.*

incinerate, incinerates, incinerating, incinerated
(verb) If you incinerate something, you burn it.
incineration (noun).

incinerator, incinerators
(noun) An incinerator is a furnace for burning rubbish.

incipient
(adjective) beginning to happen or appear, e.g. *incipient baldness.*

incision, incisions
(noun) An incision is a sharp cut, usually made by a surgeon operating on a patient.
[from Latin *incidere* meaning 'to cut into']

incisive
(adjective) clear and forceful.

incisor, incisors
(noun) An incisor is a flat tooth with a sharp cutting edge at the front of your mouth.

incite, incites, inciting, incited
1 (verb) If you incite someone to do something, you encourage them to do it by making them angry or excited.
2 If you incite trouble or violent behaviour, you encourage it by making people angry or excited.
incitement (noun).
[from Latin *incitare* meaning 'to excite']

Similar words: (sense 1) inflame, spur, goad
(sense 2) foment, stir up

inclement
(adjective; a formal word) Inclement weather is bad weather.

inclination, inclinations
(noun) If you have an inclination to do something, you want to do it.

incline, inclines, inclining, inclined
1 (noun) An incline is a slope.
2 (verb) If you are inclined to behave in a certain way, you often behave that way or you want to behave that way.
[from Latin *clinare* meaning 'to bend']

include, includes, including, included
(verb) If one thing includes another, it has the second thing as one of its parts.
included (adjective), **including** (preposition).
[from Latin *in-* + *claudere* meaning 'to shut in with']

Similar words: incorporate, encompass, embrace

inclusion
(noun) The inclusion of one thing in another is the act of making it part of the other thing.

inclusive
(adjective) A price that is inclusive includes all the goods and services that are being offered, e.g. *£68 inclusive of VAT.*

incognito (pronounced in-kog-**nee**-toe)
(adverb) If you are travelling incognito, you are travelling in disguise.
[from Latin *in-* + *cognitus* meaning 'not known']

incoherent
(adjective) If someone is incoherent, they are talking in an unclear or rambling way, e.g. *He was incoherent with rage.*
incoherently (adverb), **incoherence** (noun).

income, incomes
(noun) A person's income is the money they earn.

income tax
(noun) Income tax is a percentage of your salary which you pay regularly to the government.

incoming
(adjective) coming in, e.g. *incoming plane... the incoming government.*

incomparable
(adjective) Something that is incomparable is so good that it cannot be compared with anything else.
incomparably (adverb).

Similar words: inimitable, matchless, peerless, unequalled

incompatible
(adjective) Two things or people are incompatible if they are unable to live or exist together because they are completely different.
incompatibly (adverb), **incompatibility** (noun).
[from Latin *in-* + *compatibilis* meaning 'not in sympathy with']

incompetent
(adjective) Someone who is incompetent does not have the ability to do something properly.
incompetently (adverb), **incompetence** (noun).

incomplete
(adjective) not complete or finished.
incompletely (adverb).

incomprehensible
(adjective) not able to be understood.

inconceivable
(adjective) impossible to believe.

inconclusive
(adjective) not leading to a decision or to a definite result.

incongruous
(adjective) Something that is incongruous seems strange because it does not fit in to a place or situation.
incongruously (adverb), **incongruity** (noun).
[from *in-* + Latin *congruere* meaning 'to meet' or 'to agree']

inconsequential
(adjective) Something that is inconsequential is not very important, e.g. *inconsequential chat.*

inconsiderable
(adjective) If you describe something as not inconsiderable, you mean that it is large, e.g. *his not inconsiderable influence.*

inconsiderate
(adjective) If you are inconsiderate, you do not consider other people's feelings.
inconsiderately (adverb).

Similar words: insensitive, thoughtless

inconsistent
(adjective) Someone or something which is inconsistent is unpredictable and behaves differently in similar situations.
inconsistently (adverb), **inconsistency** (noun).

inconspicuous
(adjective) not easily seen or obvious.
inconspicuously (adverb).

incontinent
(adjective) Someone who is incontinent is unable to control their bladder or bowels.
[from *in-* + Latin *continere* meaning 'to hold' or 'to restrain']

incontrovertible
(adjective) If something is incontrovertible, it cannot be denied, e.g. *the incontrovertible truth.*
incontrovertibly (adverb).

inconvenience, inconveniences, inconveniencing, inconvenienced
1 (noun) If something causes inconvenience, it causes difficulty or problems.
2 (verb) To inconvenience someone means to cause them difficulty or problems.
inconvenient (adjective), **inconveniently** (adverb).

incorporate, incorporates, incorporating, incorporated
(verb) If something is incorporated into another thing, it becomes part of that thing.
incorporation (noun).
[from *in-* + Latin *corpus* meaning 'body']

incorrect
(adjective) wrong or untrue.
incorrectly (adverb).

incorrigible
(adjective) If someone is incorrigible, their bad behaviour will never change, e.g. *incorrigible criminals.*
incorrigibly (adverb).
[from Latin *in-* + *corrigibilis* meaning 'not set right']

increase, increases, increasing, increased
1 (verb) If something increases, it becomes larger in amount.
2 (noun) An increase is a rise in the number, level, or amount of something.
increasingly (adverb).

incredible
(adjective) totally amazing or impossible to believe.
incredibly (adverb).

Similar words: amazing, unbelievable

incredulous
(adjective) If you are incredulous, you are unable to believe something because it is very surprising or shocking.
incredulously (adverb), **incredulity** (noun).

increment, increments
(noun) An increment is the amount by which something increases, especially a regular increase in someone's salary.
incremental (adjective).
[from Latin *incrementum* meaning 'growth' or 'increase']

incriminate, incriminates, incriminating, incriminated
(verb) If something incriminates you, it suggests that you are involved in a crime.
[from Latin *incriminare* meaning 'to accuse']

incubate, incubates, incubating, incubated
(pronounced **in**-kyoo-bate)
(verb) When eggs incubate, they are kept warm until they are ready to hatch.
incubation (noun).
[from Latin *cubare* meaning 'to lie down']

incubator, incubators
(noun) An incubator is a piece of hospital equipment in which sick or weak newborn babies are kept warm.

inculcate, inculcates, inculcating, inculcated
(pronounced **in**-kull-kate)
(verb; a formal word) If you inculcate an idea into someone's mind, you fix it there by repeating it again and again.
[from Latin *inculcare* meaning 'to stamp in with the heel']

incumbent, incumbents (a formal word)
1 (adjective) If it is incumbent on you to do something, it is your duty to do it.
2 (noun) An incumbent is the person in a particular official position.

incur, incurs, incurring, incurred
(verb) If you incur something unpleasant, you cause it to happen.
[from Latin *incurrere* meaning 'to run into']

incurable
1 (adjective) An incurable disease is one which cannot be cured.
2 An incurable habit is one which cannot be changed, e.g. *an incurable romantic.*
incurably (adverb).

indebted
(adjective) If you are indebted to someone, you are grateful to them.
indebtedness (noun).

indecent
(adjective) Something that is indecent is shocking or rude, usually because it concerns nakedness or sex.
indecently (adverb), **indecency** (noun).

indecisive
(adjective) If you are indecisive, you find it difficult to make decisions.
indecision (noun).

indeed
(adverb) You use indeed to strengthen a point that you are making, e.g. *The possibility of rescue seems very remote indeed.*
[from Middle English *in dede* meaning 'in fact']

indefatigable (pronounced in-dif-**fat**-ig-abl)
(adjective) People who never get tired of doing something are indefatigable.

indefensible
(adjective) unable to be defended, e.g. *indefensible views... indefensible places.*

indefinite
1 (adjective) If something is indefinite, no time to finish has been decided, e.g. *an indefinite strike.*
2 Indefinite also means vague or not exact, e.g. *Milner advised him not to answer so indefinite a proposal.*
indefinitely (adverb).

indefinite article, indefinite articles
(noun) The indefinite article is the grammatical term for 'a' and 'an'.

indelible
(adjective) unable to be removed, e.g. *indelible writing... all the indelible memories of childhood.*
indelibly (adverb).
[from *in-* + Latin *delere* meaning 'to delete']

indelicate
(adjective) embarrassing or shocking, e.g. *a rather indelicate remark.*

indemnity
(noun; a formal word) If something provides indemnity, it gives insurance against damage or loss.
[from Latin *indemnis* meaning 'free from loss or hurt']

indent, indents, indenting, indented
1 (verb) In writing, when you indent a line, you start it further in from the margin than the other lines.
2 If you indent for goods, you order them using a special order form.

indentation, indentations
(noun) An indentation is a dent or a groove in a surface or on the edge of something.

independent
1 (adjective) Something that is independent happens or exists separately from other people or things, e.g. *They formed an independent organization outside the Labour Party.*
2 Someone who is independent does not need other people's help, e.g. *Their children are quite independent.*
independently (adverb), **independence** (noun).

Similar words: (sense 1) autonomous, self-sufficient

indescribable
(adjective) too intense or extreme to be

described, e.g. *The smell was indescribable... a feeling of indescribable pleasure.*
indescribably (adverb).

indestructible
(adjective) unable to be destroyed.

indeterminate
(adjective) not certain or definite, e.g. *He will be sent to prison for an indeterminate period.*

index, indices; indexes, indexing, indexed
1 (noun) An index is an alphabetical list at the back of a book, referring to items in the book.
2 An index is also a set of cards with information on them, arranged alphabetically.
3 In maths, an index is a small number placed to the right of another number to indicate the number of times the number is to be multiplied by itself.
4 (verb) To index a book or collection of information means to provide an index for it.
5 To index one thing to another means to arrange them so that they increase and decrease at the same rate, e.g. *the indexing of wages to inflation.*
[from Latin *index* meaning 'forefinger' or 'pointer']

index finger, index fingers
(noun) Your index finger is your first finger, next to your thumb.

Indian, Indians
1 (adjective) belonging or relating to India.
2 (noun) An Indian is someone who comes from India.
3 An Indian is also someone descended from the people who lived in North, South, or Central America before Europeans arrived.

Indian summer, Indian summers
(noun) An Indian summer is a period of warm, sunny weather in the autumn.

indicate, indicates, indicating, indicated
1 (verb) If something indicates something, it shows that it is true, e.g. *Evidence indicates that the experiments were unsuccessful.*
2 If you indicate something to someone, you point to it.
3 If you indicate a fact, you mention it.
4 If the driver of a vehicle indicates, they give a signal to show which way they are going to turn.
[from Latin *indicare* meaning 'to point out', from *dicare* meaning 'to proclaim']

Similar words: (sense 1) signify, denote, portent

---

indication, indications
(noun) An indication is a sign of what someone feels or what is likely to happen.

indicative
1 (adjective) If something is indicative of something else, it is a sign of that thing, e.g. *Their hesitation was indicative of their indecision.*
2 (noun) If a verb is used in the indicative, it is in the form used for making statements.

indicator, indicators
1 (noun) An indicator is something which tells

you what something is like or what is happening, e.g. *Price is not always an indicator of quality.*
2 A car's indicators are the lights at the front and back which are used to show when it is turning left or right.

indict, indicts, indicting, indicted (pronounced in-**dite**)
(verb; a formal word) To indict someone means to charge them officially with a crime.
indictment (noun), **indictable** (adjective).
[from Latin *indicare* meaning 'to proclaim']

indifferent
1 (adjective) If you are indifferent to something, you have no interest in it.
2 If something is indifferent, it is of a poor quality or low standard, e.g. *She was a gifted painter but an indifferent actor.*
indifferently (adverb), **indifference** (noun).

indigenous (pronounced in-**dij**-in-uss)
(adjective) If something is indigenous, it comes from the country in which it is found, e.g. *The elephant is indigenous to India.*
[from Latin *indi-* meaning 'within' and *gignere* meaning 'to beget']

indigestible
(adjective) Food that is indigestible cannot be digested easily, and may give you indigestion.

indigestion
(noun) Indigestion is a pain you get when you find it difficult to digest food.

indignant
(adjective) If you are indignant, you feel angry about something that you think is unfair.
indignantly (adverb).
[from Latin *indignari* meaning 'to disdain' or 'to be displeased with']

indignation
(noun) Indignation is anger about something that you think is unfair.

indignity, indignities
(noun) An indignity is something that makes you feel humiliated, e.g. *the indignity of slavery.*

indigo
(noun and adjective) dark violet-blue.

indirect
(adjective) Something that is indirect is not done or caused directly by a particular person or thing, but by someone or something else.
indirectly (adverb).

Similar words: roundabout, circuitous, oblique

---

indiscreet
(adjective) If you are indiscreet, you say or do things openly when you should have kept them secret, e.g. *an indiscreet remark.*
indiscreetly (adverb), **indiscretion** (noun).

indiscriminate
(adjective) not involving careful thought or choice, e.g. *indiscriminate police brutality.*
indiscriminately (adverb).

indispensable
(adjective) If something is indispensable, you

cannot do without it, e.g. *In my job, a telephone is indispensable.*

indisposed (a formal word)
1 (adjective) If you are indisposed, you are slightly ill.
2 If you are indisposed to do something, you are unwilling to do it.

indisposition, indispositions
(noun) An indisposition is a slight illness which prevents you from doing something.

indistinct
(adjective) not clear, e.g. *an indistinct mumble... an indistinct trail.*

individual, individuals
1 (adjective) relating to one particular person or thing, e.g. *individual tuition.*
2 Someone who is individual behaves quite differently from the way other people behave.
3 (noun) An individual is a person, different from any other person, e.g. *The freedom of the individual.*
individually (adverb).
[from Latin *in-* + *dividuus* meaning 'not divisible']

individualist, individualists
(noun) If you are an individualist, you like to do things in your own way.
individualistic (adjective).

individuality
(noun) If something has individuality, it is different from all other things, and very interesting and noticeable.

indoctrinate, indoctrinates, indoctrinating, indoctrinated
(verb) To indoctrinate someone means to teach them a particular belief in such a way that they will not accept any other belief.
indoctrination (noun).

indolent
(adjective; a formal word) lazy, e.g. *an indolent smile.*
indolence (noun).
[from Latin *indolens* meaning 'not suffering' or 'not feeling pain']

indomitable
(adjective; a formal word) impossible to overcome, e.g. *an indomitable spirit.*
[from Latin *indomitus* meaning 'untamable']

Indonesian, Indonesians (pronounced in-don-**nee**-zee-an)
1 (adjective) belonging or relating to Indonesia.
2 (noun) An Indonesian is someone who comes from Indonesia.
3 Indonesian is the official language of Indonesia.

indoor
(adjective) situated or happening inside a building, e.g. *an indoor swimming pool.*

indoors
(adverb) If something happens indoors, it takes place inside a building.

indubitable (pronounced ind-**yoo**-bit-a-bl)
(adjective; a formal word) definite and unable to be doubted, e.g. *indubitable signs of burglary.*
indubitably (adverb).
[from Latin *in-* + *dubitabilis* meaning 'not uncertain']

induce, induces, inducing, induced
1 (verb) To induce a state means to cause it, e.g. *Certain drugs induce sleep.*
2 If you induce someone to do something, you persuade them to do it.
3 To induce a birth means to cause labour to begin by the use of drugs.
[from Latin *in-* + *ducere* meaning 'to lead into']

inducement, inducements
(noun) An inducement is something offered to encourage someone to do something.

induction
1 (noun) Induction is a way of reasoning in which you use individual ideas or facts to reach a general conclusion.
2 In physics, induction is the process by which electricity or magnetism is passed between two objects without them touching each other.
3 An induction course is a course designed to help new students or people new to a job to become familiar with work they will be doing.

indulge, indulges, indulging, indulged
1 (verb) If you indulge in something, you allow yourself to do something that you enjoy.
2 If you indulge someone, you let them have or do what they want, often in a way that is not good for them.
[from Latin *indulgere* meaning 'to concede']

indulgence, indulgences
1 (noun) An indulgence is something you allow yourself to have because it gives you pleasure.
2 Indulgence is the act of indulging yourself or another person.

indulgent
(adjective) If you are indulgent, you treat someone with special kindness, e.g. *He was spoilt by an indulgent mother.*
indulgently (adjective).

industrial
(adjective) relating to industry.

industrial action
(noun) Industrial action is action taken by workers in protest over pay or working conditions.

industrialist, industrialists
(noun) An industrialist is a person who is very powerful in industry.

industrialize, industrializes, industrializing, industrialized; also spelled **industrialise**
(verb) When a place is industrialized, it develops a lot of industries.

industrious
(adjective) An industrious person works very hard.

industry, industries
1 (noun) Industry is the work and processes involved in manufacturing things in factories.

2 An industry is all the people and processes involved in manufacturing a particular thing.
[from Latin *industria* meaning 'diligence' or 'hard work']

inebriate (pronounced in-**nee**-bree-ate)
(adjective; a formal word) Someone who is inebriate drinks alcohol a lot and is regularly drunk.
[from Latin *ebrius* meaning 'drunk']

inebriated
(adjective) drunk.

inedible
(adjective) too nasty or poisonous to eat, e.g. *inedible school dinners... inedible plants.*

inefficient
(adjective) badly organized, wasteful, and slow, e.g. *inefficient farming.*
inefficiently (adverb), **inefficiency** (noun).

ineligible
(adjective) If you are ineligible for something, you are not qualified for it or not entitled to it.

inept
(adjective) without skill, e.g. *an inept politician.*
ineptitude (noun).
[from *in-* + Latin *aptus* meaning 'not joined on' or 'unfitting']

inequality
(noun) Inequality is a difference in size, status, wealth, or position, between different things, groups, or people.

inert
1 (adjective) Something that is inert does not move and appears lifeless, e.g. *We lifted his inert body on to the bed.*
2 In chemistry, an inert gas does not react with other substances.
[from Latin *iners* meaning 'unskilled' or 'inactive']

inertia (pronounced in-**ner**-sha)
(noun) If you have a feeling of inertia, you feel very lazy and unwilling to do anything.

inestimable
(adjective) very great or very valuable, e.g. *Your advice was inestimable.*

inevitable
(adjective) certain to happen.
inevitably (adverb), **inevitability** (noun).
[from Latin *in-* meaning 'not' and *evitare* meaning 'to avoid']

inexhaustible
(adjective) Something that is inexhaustible will never be used up, e.g. *an inexhaustible supply.*

inexorable
(adjective; a formal word) Something that is inexorable cannot be prevented from continuing, e.g. *The inexorable rise in house prices.*
inexorably (adverb).

inexpensive
(adjective) not costing much.

inexperienced
(adjective) lacking experience of a situation or activity, e.g. *an inexperienced swimmer.*
inexperience (noun).

Similar words: green, fresh, callow, raw, unaccustomed

inexplicable
(adjective) If something is inexplicable, you cannot explain it, e.g. *For some inexplicable reason he refused to see me.*
inexplicably (adverb).

inextricably
(adverb) If two or more things are inextricably linked, they cannot be separated.

infallible
(adjective) never wrong, e.g. *Teachers aren't infallible.*
infallibility (noun).

infamous (pronounced **in**-fe-muss)
(adjective) well known because of something bad or evil, e.g. *He was an infamous villain.*

infamy
(noun) Infamy is the state of being infamous.
[from Latin *infamis* meaning 'disreputable']

infant, infants
1 (noun) An infant is a baby or very young child.
2 (adjective) designed for young children, e.g. *infant school.*
infancy (noun), **infantile** (adjective).
[from Latin *infans* meaning 'unable to speak']

infantry
(noun) In an army, the infantry are soldiers who fight on foot rather than in tanks or on horses.
[from Italian *infante* meaning 'youth' or 'foot-soldier']

infatuated
(adjective) If you are infatuated with someone, you have such strong feelings of love or passion that you cannot think sensibly about them.
infatuation (noun).
[from Latin *fatuus* meaning 'foolish']

infect, infects, infecting, infected
(verb) To infect people, animals, plants, or food means to cause disease in them.
[from Latin *inficere* meaning 'to dip into' or 'to stain']

infection, infections
1 (noun) An infection is a disease caused by germs, e.g. *a chest infection.*
2 Infection is the state of being infected, e.g. *a high risk of infection.*

infectious
(adjective) spreading from one person to another, e.g. *an infectious disease... infectious laughter.*

Similar words: contagious, catching

infer, infers, inferring, inferred
(verb) If you infer something, you work out that

it is true on the basis of information that you already have.
inference (noun).
[from Latin *inferre* meaning 'to bring or carry in']

inferior
1 (adjective) having a lower position or worth less than something else, e.g. *an inferior model*.
2 (noun) Your inferiors are people in a lower position than you.
inferiority (noun).
[from Latin *inferus* meaning 'low']

Similar words: bad, poor, shoddy

inferiority complex
(noun) If you have an inferiority complex, you feel less important than other people.

infernal
1 (adjective) very unpleasant, e.g. *Stop that infernal noise!*
2 relating to hell.
[from Latin *infernus* meaning 'hell']

inferno, infernos
(noun) An inferno is a very large dangerous fire.
[from Latin *infernus* meaning 'hell']

infertile
1 (adjective) Infertile soil is of poor quality and plants cannot grow well in it.
2 Someone who is infertile cannot have children.
infertility (noun).

infest, infests, infesting, infested
(verb) When animals or insects infest something, they spread in large numbers over it or into it and cause damage, e.g. *My roses are infested with greenfly.*
infestation (noun).
[from Latin *infestus* meaning 'hostile']

infidelity, infidelities
(noun) Infidelity is the act of being unfaithful to your husband, wife, or lover.
[from Latin *in-* + *fidel* meaning 'not faithful']

infighting
(noun) Infighting is quarrelling or rivalry between members of the same organization.

infiltrate, infiltrates, infiltrating, infiltrated
(verb) If people infiltrate an organization, they gradually enter it in secret to spy on its activities.
infiltration (noun), **infiltrator** (noun).

infinite
(adjective) without any limit or end, e.g. *the infinite reaches of space.*
infinitely (adverb).

Similar words: boundless, endless, limitless

infinitesimal
(adjective) extremely small, e.g. *She was given infinitesimal amounts of the drug.*

infinitive
(noun) In grammar, the infinitive is the base form of the verb. It often has 'to' in front of it.

infinity
1 (noun) Infinity is a number that is larger than

any other number and can never be given an exact value.
2 Infinity is also an unreachable point, further away than any other point, e.g. *stars stretching away into infinity.*

infirm
(adjective) weak or ill, e.g. *old and infirm.*
infirmity (noun).

infirmary, infirmaries
(noun) Some hospitals are called infirmaries.

inflame, inflames, inflaming, inflamed
(verb) Something that inflames someone makes them very angry.

inflamed
(adjective) If part of your body is inflamed, it is red, hot, and swollen, usually because of infection.

inflammable
(adjective) An inflammable material burns easily.

inflammation
(noun) Inflammation is painful redness or swelling of part of the body.

inflammatory
(adjective) Inflammatory actions are likely to make people very angry or annoyed.

inflate, inflates, inflating, inflated
(verb) When you inflate something, you fill it with air or gas to make it swell.
inflation (noun), **inflatable** (adjective).
[from Latin *in-* + *flare* meaning 'to blow into']

inflation
(noun) Inflation is a general increase in the price of services and goods in a country, e.g. *Inflation is now running at 7%.*
inflationary (adjective).

inflect, inflects, inflecting, inflected
1 (verb) If you inflect your voice, you change the sound of it as you speak, for example to stress certain words.
2 In grammar, words inflect when their endings or forms change to show their grammatical function.
[from Latin *inflectere* meaning 'to curve round' or 'to alter']

inflection, inflections; also spelled inflexion
1 (noun) An inflection is the way you change the sound of your voice when you speak.
2 An inflection is also a change in the form of a word that shows its grammatical function, for example a change that makes a noun plural.

inflexible
(adjective) fixed and unable to be altered, e.g. *Banks have inflexible hours.*

inflict, inflicts, inflicting, inflicted
(verb) If you inflict something unpleasant on someone, you make them suffer it.
[from Latin *infligere* meaning 'to strike against']

influence, influences, influencing, influenced
1 (noun) Influence is power that a person has over other people.
2 An influence is also the effect that someone or

something has, e.g. *under the influence of alcohol.*
3 (verb) To influence someone or something means to have an effect on them.
[from Latin *influentia* meaning 'power flowing from the stars']

Similar words: (sense 1) pull, clout, weight

influential
(adjective) Someone who is influential has a lot of influence over people.

influenza
(noun; a formal word) Influenza is flu.

influx
(noun) An influx of people or things is a steady arrival of them, e.g. *a large influx of tourists.*
[from Latin *influere* meaning 'to flow into']

inform, informs, informing, informed
1 (verb) If you inform someone of something, you tell them about it.
2 If you inform on a person, you tell the police about a crime they have committed.
informant (noun).
[from Latin *in-* + *formare* meaning 'to give form to' or 'to describe']

Similar words: (sense 1) acquaint, apprise, notify, tell, enlighten
(sense 2) sneak, tell on, grass

informal
(adjective) relaxed and casual, e.g. *an informal interview... informal dress.*
informally (adverb), **informality** (noun).

information
(noun) If you have information on or about something, you know something about it.

Similar words: gen, intelligence, data, facts, word

informative
(adjective) Something that is informative gives you useful information.

informed
(adjective) having a lot of knowledge about something.

informer, informers
(noun) An informer is someone who tells the police that another person has committed a crime.

infrared
(adjective) Infrared light is below the colour red in the spectrum and cannot be seen, e.g. *infrared photography.*
[from Latin *infra* meaning 'below' + *red*]

infrequent
(adjective) If something is infrequent it does not happen often, e.g. *his infrequent letters.*
infrequently (adverb).

Similar words: occasional, rare

infringe, infringes, infringing, infringed
1 (verb) If you infringe a law, you break it.

2 To infringe people's rights means to not allow them the rights to which they are entitled.
infringement (noun).
[from Latin *infringere* meaning 'to break off']

infuriate, infuriates, infuriating, infuriated
(verb) If someone infuriates you, they make you very angry.
infuriating (adjective).

infuse, infuses, infusing, infused
1 (verb) If you infuse someone with a feeling such as enthusiasm or joy, you fill them with it.
2 If you infuse a substance such as a herb or medicine, you pour hot water onto it and leave it for the water to absorb the flavour.
infusion (noun).
[from Latin *infundere* meaning 'to pour into']

ingenious (pronounced in-**jeen**-yuss)
(adjective) very clever, involving new ideas or equipment, e.g. *an ingenious gadget.*
ingeniously (adverb), **ingeniousness** (noun).
[from Latin *ingenium* meaning 'natural ability']

ingenuity (pronounced in-jen-**yoo**-it-ee)
(noun) Ingenuity is cleverness and skill at inventing things or working out plans.

ingenuous (pronounced in-**jen**-yoo-uss)
(adjective) innocent, trusting, and incapable of deceiving anyone.
[from Latin *ingenuus* meaning 'virtuous']

ingot, ingots
(noun) An ingot is a brick-shaped lump of metal, especially gold.

ingrained
(adjective) If habits and beliefs are ingrained, they are difficult to change or destroy.

ingratiate, ingratiates, ingratiating, ingratiated (pronounced in-**gray**-shee-ate)
(verb) If you ingratiate yourself with people, you try to make yourself popular with them, for example by always agreeing with them.
ingratiating (adjective).
[from Latin *gratia* meaning 'favour']

Similar words: curry favour, insinuate yourself, toady

ingratitude
(noun) Ingratitude is a lack of gratitude for a gift or for something that has been done for you.

ingredient, ingredients
(noun) Ingredients are the elements that something is made from, especially in cookery.
[from Latin *ingrediens* meaning 'going into']

inhabit, inhabits, inhabiting, inhabited
(verb) If a place is inhabited, people live there, e.g. *It was a small town, inhabited by farmers.*
[from Latin *in-* + *habitare* meaning 'to dwell in']

inhabitant, inhabitants
(noun) The inhabitants of a place are the people who live there.

Similar words: resident, citizen, denizen, local

inhalant, inhalants
(noun) An inhalant is a substance that you

breathe in to help you breathe more easily, for example when you have a cold.

inhale, inhales, inhaling, inhaled
(verb) When you inhale, you breathe in.
[from *in-* + Latin *halare* meaning 'to breathe']

inhaler, inhalers
(noun) An inhaler is a container used for an inhalant.

inherent
(adjective) Inherent qualities or characteristics in something are a natural part of it, e.g. *her inherent laziness.*
inherently (adverb).
[from Latin *inhaerere* meaning 'to stick in']

inherit, inherits, inheriting, inherited
1 (verb) If you inherit money or property, you receive it from someone who has died.
2 If you inherit a quality or characteristic from someone, it is passed on to you genetically.
inheritance (noun), **inheritor** (noun).
[from Latin *inhereditare* meaning 'to appoint']

inhibit, inhibits, inhibiting, inhibited
1 (verb) If you inhibit someone from doing something, you prevent them from doing it.
2 To inhibit the growth of something means to slow its growth down.
[from Latin *inhibere* meaning 'to restrain']

inhibited
(adjective) People who are inhibited find it difficult to relax and to show their emotions.

inhibition, inhibitions
(noun) Inhibitions are feelings of fear or embarrassment that make it difficult for someone to relax and to show their emotions.

inhospitable
1 (adjective) An inhospitable place is unpleasant or difficult to live in.
2 If someone is inhospitable, they do not make people feel welcome when they visit them.

inhuman
(adjective) not human, e.g. *They looked weird and inhuman... inhuman atrocities.*

inhumane
(adjective) extremely cruel.
inhumanity (noun).

inimical
(adjective; a formal word) hostile and unfriendly.
[from Latin *in-* + *amicus* meaning 'not friendly']

inimitable
(adjective) If you have an inimitable characteristic, it is special to you, e.g. *his inimitable charm.*

iniquity, iniquities
(noun; a formal word) Iniquity is wickedness or injustice.
iniquitous (adjective).
[from Latin *in-* + *aequus* meaning 'not even or level']

initial, initials, initialling, initialled (pronounced in-**nish**-l)

1 (adjective) first, or at the beginning, e.g. *After my initial shock, I got used to his appearance.*
2 (noun) An initial is the first letter of a name.
3 (verb) When you initial something, you write your initials on it as a signature.
initially (adverb).

initiate, initiates, initiating, initiated (pronounced in-**nish**-ee-ate)
1 (verb) If you initiate something, you make it start or happen.
2 If you initiate someone into a group or club, you allow them to become a member of it, usually by means of a special ceremony.
initiation (noun).
[from Latin *initium* meaning 'beginning']

initiative, initiatives (pronounced in-**nish**-at-ive)
1 (noun) An initiative is an attempt to get something done.
2 If you have initiative, you decide what to do and then do it, without needing the advice of other people.
3 (phrase) If you **take the initiative,** you are the first person to do something.

inject, injects, injecting, injected
1 (verb) If a doctor or nurse injects you with a substance, they use a needle and syringe to put the substance into your body.
2 If you inject something new into a situation, you add it.
injection (noun).
[from Latin *in-* + *jacere* meaning 'to throw into']

injudicious
(adjective) showing poor judgment, e.g. *It was most injudicious of you to come here.*
injudiciously (adverb).

injunction, injunctions
(noun) An injunction is an order issued by a court of law to stop someone doing something.

injure, injures, injuring, injured
(verb) To injure someone means to damage part of their body.
injury (noun).
[from Latin *injuria* meaning 'injustice', from *jus* meaning 'right']

injurious
(adjective) harmful or damaging, e.g. *Cigarettes are injurious to your health.*

injustice, injustices
1 (noun) Injustice is unfairness and lack of justice.
2 If you do someone an injustice, you judge them too harshly.

ink
(noun) Ink is the coloured liquid used for writing or printing.
[from Greek *enkauston* meaning 'purple ink', from *enkaustos* meaning 'burnt in']

inkling, inklings
(noun) If you have an inkling of something, you have a vague idea about it.

inkwell, inkwells
(noun) An inkwell is a container for ink.

inlaid
(adjective) decorated with small pieces of wood, metal, or stone, e.g. *a table inlaid with gold.*
inlay (noun).

inland
(adverb and adjective) towards or near the middle of a country, away from the sea.

Inland Revenue
(noun) The Inland Revenue is the part of the government that collects tax from people.

in-law, in-laws
(noun) Your in-laws are members of your husband's or wife's family.

inlet, inlets
(noun) An inlet is a narrow bay.

inmate, inmates
(noun) An inmate is someone who lives in a prison or psychiatric hospital.

inmost
(adjective) deepest and most secret, e.g. *She read my inmost thoughts.*

inn, inns
(noun) An inn is a small old country pub or hotel.

innards
(plural noun) The innards of something are its inside parts.

innate
(adjective) An innate quality is one that you were born with, e.g. *an innate sense of tact.*
innately (adverb).
[from Latin *in-* + *nasci* meaning 'to be born in']

inner
(adjective) contained inside a place or object, e.g. *the inner courtyard.*

innermost
(adjective) deepest and most secret, e.g. *my innermost feelings.*

innings
(noun) In cricket, an innings is a period during which a particular team is batting.

innocent
1 (adjective) not guilty of a crime.
2 without experience of evil or unpleasant things, e.g. *innocent little children.*
innocently (adverb), **innocence** (noun).
[from Latin *in-* + *nocens* meaning 'not harming']

innocuous (pronounced in-**nok**-yoo-uss)
(adjective) not harmful, e.g. *The bottle of poison looked innocuous enough.*
[from Latin *innocuus* meaning 'harmless']

innovate, innovates, innovating, innovated
(verb) To innovate means to introduce new ideas or changes.
innovator (noun), **innovative** (adjective),
innovatory (adjective).
[from Latin *novus* meaning 'new']

innovation, innovations
(noun) An innovation is a completely new idea, product, or system of doing things.

innuendo, innuendos or **innuendoes** (pronounced in-yoo-**en**-doe)
(noun) An innuendo is an indirect reference to something rude or unpleasant.
[from Latin *innuendo* meaning 'by hinting', from *innuere* meaning 'to convey by a nod']

Innuit another spelling of **Inuit**.

innumerable
(adjective) too many to be counted, e.g. *innumerable stars in the night sky.*

inoculate, inoculates, inoculating, inoculated
(verb) To inoculate someone means to inject them with a weak form of a disease in order to protect them from that disease.
inoculation (noun).
[from Latin *inoculare* meaning 'to implant']

inopportune
(adjective) happening at an unsuitable time, and therefore causing difficulty or embarrassment, e.g. *You've called at an inopportune moment.*

inordinate
(adjective) excessive or extreme, e.g. *Colin spends an inordinate amount of time in the bathroom.*
inordinately (adverb).
[from Latin *inordinatus* meaning 'disordered']

inorganic
(adjective) Inorganic substances are substances which do not form part of living things and have no life of their own, for example rocks and water.

inorganic chemistry
(noun) Inorganic chemistry is the study of the elements and their compounds, except those containing carbon.

input, inputs, inputting, input
1 (noun) Input consists of all the money, information, and other resources that are put into a job, project, or company to make it work.
2 In computing, input is information which is fed into a computer.
3 (verb) To input information into a computer means to feed it in.

inquest, inquests
(noun) An inquest is an official inquiry to find out what caused a person's death.

inquire, inquires, inquiring, inquired; also spelled **enquire**
1 (verb) If you inquire about something, you ask for information about it.
2 If you inquire after someone, you ask for information about them, e.g. *Mr Jones inquired after her health.*
3 If you inquire into something, you investigate it carefully.
inquiring (adjective), **inquiringly** (adverb),
inquiry (noun).
[from *in-* + Latin *quarere* meaning 'to seek']

inquisition, inquisitions
1 (noun) An inquisition is an official investigation, especially one which is very thorough and uses harsh methods of questioning.
2 From 1232 to 1820, the Inquisition was a part of the Roman Catholic Church. It was founded to seek out and suppress heresy.

inquisitive
(adjective) Someone who is inquisitive likes finding out about things.
inquisitively (adverb), **inquisitiveness** (noun).

inroads
(plural noun) If something makes inroads on or into something, it starts affecting it or destroying it.

insane
(adjective) Someone who is insane is mad.
insanely (adverb), **insanity** (noun).

insanitary
(adjective) very dirty and unhygienic, e.g. *They were found to be living in insanitary conditions.*

insatiable (pronounced in-saysh-a-bl)
(adjective) A desire or urge that is insatiable is very great, e.g. *an insatiable curiosity.*
insatiably (adverb).
[from Latin *in-* meaning 'not' and *satis* meaning 'enough']

inscribe, inscribes, inscribing, inscribed
1 (verb) If you inscribe words on an object, you write or carve them on it.
2 If you inscribe a book, you write your name or a short message at the front.
[from Latin *inscribere* meaning 'to write upon']

inscription, inscriptions
(noun) An inscription is the words that are written or carved on something.

inscrutable (pronounced in-skroot-a-bl)
(adjective) Someone who is inscrutable does not show what they are really thinking.
[from Latin *in-* meaning 'not' and *scrutari* meaning 'to examine']

insect, insects
(noun) An insect is a small creature with six legs and a hard external skeleton. Most insects have wings.
[from Latin *insectum* meaning 'animal that has been cut into', because of its shape]

insecticide, insecticides
(noun) Insecticide is a poisonous chemical used to kill insects.

insectivorous
(adjective) An insectivorous animal eats insects.

insecure
1 (adjective) If you are insecure, you feel unsure of yourself and doubt whether other people like you.
2 Something that is insecure is not safe or well protected, e.g. *These knots look rather insecure.*
insecurity (noun).

inseminate, inseminates, inseminating, inseminated
(verb) To inseminate a female animal means to make her pregnant by means of male sperm.
insemination (noun).
[from Latin *in-* + *seminare* meaning 'to sow into']

insensible
1 (adjective) unconscious, e.g. *He was insensible, knocked unconcious by a blow on the head.*
2 unaffected by something, e.g. *He was insensible to ridicule.*

insensitive
(adjective) If you are insensitive, you do not notice when you are upsetting people.
insensitively (adverb), **insensitivity** (noun).

insert, inserts, inserting, inserted
1 (verb) If you insert an object into something, you put it inside.
2 (noun) An insert is something that is placed inside something, for example an advertisement on a loose piece of paper inside a book.
insertion (noun).
[from Latin *inserere* meaning 'to plant in']

inshore
(adjective) at sea but close to the shore.

inside, insides
1 (adverb, preposition, and adjective) Inside refers to the part of something which is surrounded by the main part and is often hidden, e.g. *Go inside when it starts raining... inside the house... an inside pocket.*
2 (an informal use) Someone who is inside is in prison.
3 (plural noun) Your insides are the parts inside your body.
4 (phrase) **Inside out** means with the inside part facing outwards.

insider, insiders
(noun) An insider is a person who is involved in a situation and who knows more about it than other people.

insidious
(adjective) Something that is insidious is unpleasant and develops slowly without being noticed, e.g. *an insidious disease.*
insidiously (adverb), **insidiousness** (noun).
[from Latin *insidiosus* meaning 'cunning']

insight, insights
(noun) If you gain insight into a problem, you gradually get a deep understanding of it.

insignia (in-sig-nee-a)
(noun) An insignia is a badge or a sign showing that you belong to a particular organization.
[from Latin *signum* meaning 'mark']

insignificant
(adjective) small and unimportant.
insignificantly (adverb), **insignificance** (noun).

insincere
(adjective) Someone who is insincere pretends to have feelings which they do not really have.
insincerely (adverb), **insincerity** (noun).

Similar words: two-faced, hypocritical, artificial, false, phoney, shallow

insinuate, insinuates, insinuating, insinuated
1 (verb) If you insinuate something unpleasant, you hint about it, e.g. *He insinuated I'd been cheating.*
2 If you insinuate yourself into a position of trust or responsibility, you slowly and cleverly get yourself into that position.
insinuation (noun).
[from Latin *insinuare* meaning 'to wind your way into', from *sinus* meaning 'curve']

insipid

1 (adjective) An insipid person or activity is dull and boring.
2 Food that is insipid has very little taste.
[from *in-* + Latin *sapidus* meaning 'full of flavour']

Similar words: (sense 1) spiritless, vapid, wishy-washy

insist, insists, insisting, insisted
(verb) If you insist on something, you demand it emphatically.
insistent (adjective), **insistence** (noun).

insole, insoles
(noun) An insole is a detachable inner sole for a boot or shoe.

insolent
(adjective) very rude and disrespectful.
insolently (adverb), **insolence** (noun).

insoluble (pronounced in-**soll**-yoo-bl)
1 (adjective) impossible to solve, e.g. *an insoluble mystery.*
2 unable to dissolve, e.g. *insoluble aspirin.*

insolvent
(adjective) unable to pay your debts.
insolvency (noun).

insomnia
(noun) Insomnia is difficulty in sleeping.
insomniac (noun).
[from *in-* + Latin *somnus* meaning 'sleep']

inspect, inspects, inspecting, inspected
(verb) To inspect something means to examine it carefully to check that everything is all right.
inspection (noun).
[from Latin *in-* + *specere* meaning 'to look into']

inspector, inspectors
1 (noun) An inspector is someone who inspects things.
2 In the police force, an Inspector is an officer just above a Sergeant in rank.

inspire, inspires, inspiring, inspired
1 (verb) If something inspires you, it gives you new ideas and enthusiasm to do something.
2 To inspire an emotion in someone means to make them feel this emotion.
inspired (adjective), **inspiring** (adjective), **inspiration** (noun).
[from Latin *in-* + *spirari* meaning 'to breathe in']

instability
(noun) Instability is the quality of being unstable, e.g. *political instability.*

install, installs, installing, installed
1 (verb) If you install a large object in a place, you place it there so it is ready to be used.
2 If you install yourself in a place, you settle there and make yourself comfortable.
3 To install someone in an important job means to officially give them that position.
installation (noun).

instalment, instalments
1 (noun) If you pay for something in instalments, you pay small amounts of money regularly over a period of time.

2 An instalment of a story or television series is one of the parts that appear regularly over a period of time.

instance, instances
1 (noun) An instance is a particular example or occurrence of an event, situation, or person, e.g. *an instance of negligence.*
2 (phrase) You use **for instance** to give an example of something you are talking about.

instant, instants
1 (noun) An instant is a moment or short period of time, e.g. *I'll be with you in an instant.*
2 (adjective) immediate and without delay, e.g. *The song was an instant success.*
instantly (adverb).
[from Latin *instans* meaning 'being present']

instantaneous
(adjective) happening immediately and without delay, e.g. *Death was instantaneous.*
instantaneously (adverb).

instead
(adverb) in place of something, e.g. *She expected him to shout but instead he began to cry... Use oil instead of butter.*
[from Middle English *in stead* meaning 'in place']

instep, insteps
(noun) Your instep is the middle part of your foot.

instigate, instigates, instigating, instigated
(verb) Someone who instigates a situation causes it to happen through their own efforts.
instigation (noun), **instigator** (noun).
[from Latin *instigare* meaning 'to stimulate']

instil, instils, instilling, instilled
(verb) If you instil an idea or feeling into someone, you make them feel or think it, usually gradually.
[from Latin *instillare* meaning 'to pour in a drop at a time']

instinct, instincts
(noun) An instinct is an unlearned natural tendency to behave in a certain way, e.g. *Babies have a natural instinct for swimming.*
instinctive (adjective), **instinctively** (adverb).
[from Latin *instinctus* meaning 'roused']

institute, institutes, instituting, instituted
1 (noun) An institute is an organization set up for teaching or research.
2 (verb; a formal use) If you institute a rule or system, you introduce it.
[from Latin *statuere* meaning 'to place' or 'to stand']

institution, institutions
1 (noun) An institution is a custom regarded as an old and important tradition within a society, e.g. *the institution of marriage.*
2 An institution is also a large, important organization, for example a university or bank.
institutional (adjective), **institutionally** (adverb), **institutionalize** or **institutionalise** (verb).

instruct, instructs, instructing, instructed
1 (verb) If you instruct someone to do something, you tell them to do it.

2 If someone instructs you in a subject or skill, they teach you about it.
instructor (noun), **instructive** (adjective), **instruction** (noun).
[from Latin *struere* meaning 'to build']

instrument, instruments
1 (noun) An instrument is a tool or device used for a particular job, especially for measuring something, e.g. *surgical instruments*.
2 A musical instrument is an object, such as a piano or flute, played to make music.
3 You can call a person, system, or organization an instrument when they are used to achieve a particular aim, e.g. *an instrument of change*.
[from Latin *instrumentum* meaning 'tool']

instrumental
1 (adjective) If you are instrumental in doing something, you help to make it happen.
2 Instrumental music is performed using only musical instruments, and not voices.

instrumentalist, instrumentalists
(noun) An instrumentalist is someone who plays a musical instrument.

insubordinate
(adjective; a formal word) disobedient, e.g. *He was punished for insubordinate behaviour.*
insubordination (noun).

insubstantial
(adjective) not very large, solid, or strong, e.g. *The insubstantial meal left us rather hungry.*

insufficient
(adjective) not enough for a particular purpose.
insufficiently (adverb).

insular (pronounced **inss**-yoo-lar)
(adjective) Someone who is insular is isolated and is unwilling to mix with others or to consider new ideas.
insularity (noun).
[from Latin *insula* meaning 'island']

insulate, insulates, insulating, insulated
1 (verb) If you insulate a person from harmful things, you protect them from those things, e.g. *insulated from the outside world.*
2 If materials such as feathers, fur, or foam insulate something, they keep it warm by covering it in a thick layer.
3 You insulate an electrical or metal object by covering it with rubber or plastic. This is to stop electricity passing through it and giving you an electric shock.
insulation (noun), **insulator** (noun).
[from Latin *insulatus* meaning 'made into an island']

insulin (pronounced **inss**-yoo-lin)
(noun) Insulin is a substance which controls the level of sugar in the blood. Diabetics do not produce insulin naturally and have to take regular doses of it.

insult, insults, insulting, insulted
1 (verb) If you insult someone, you offend them by being rude to them.

2 (noun) An insult is something rude said to you which offends you.
insulting (adjective).
[from Latin *insultare* meaning 'to jump upon']

Similar words: (sense 1) abuse, snub, offend
(sense 2) abuse, affront, indignity, offence

insuperable
(adjective) A problem that is insuperable cannot be dealt with successfully.

insure, insures, insuring, insured
1 (verb) If you insure something or yourself, you pay money regularly to a special company so that if there is an accident or damage, the company will pay for repairs or medical treatment.
2 If you do something to insure against something unpleasant happening, you do it in order to protect yourself if it does happen or to prevent it from happening.
insurance (noun).

insurgent, insurgents
(noun) Insurgents are people who are fighting against the government or army of their own country.
insurgency (noun).
[from Latin *insurgere* meaning 'to rise up']

insurrection, insurrections
(noun) An insurrection is a revolt against the rulers of a country.

intact
(adjective) complete, and not changed or damaged in any way, e.g. *They dug up some ancient pots, still intact.*
[from Latin *in-* + *tactus* meaning 'not touched']

intake, intakes
1 (noun) A person's intake of food, drink, or air is the amount they take in, e.g. *Oxygen intake.*
2 An intake is also the number of people accepted in an institution at a particular time.

intangible (pronounced in-**tan**-jibl)
(adjective) hard to define or explain, e.g. *a vast and intangible subject.*

integer, integers
(noun) In mathematics, an integer is any whole number.
[from Latin *integer* meaning 'intact' or 'entire']

integral
(adjective) If something is an integral part of a whole thing, it is an essential part.

integrate, integrates, integrating, integrated
1 (verb) If a person integrates into a group, they become part of it.
2 To integrate things means to combine them so that they become closely linked or form part of a whole idea or system, e.g. *The two railway systems were integrated.*
integration (noun).

Similar words: assimilate, incorporate

integrity
1 (noun) Integrity is the quality of being honest and morally firm.

2 The integrity of a group of people is the quality of their being united as one whole.

intellect, intellects
(noun) Intellect is the ability to understand ideas and information.
[from Latin *intellectus* meaning 'comprehension']

intellectual, intellectuals
1 (adjective) involving thought, ideas, and understanding, e.g. *intellectual stimulation.*
2 (noun) An intellectual is someone who spends a lot of time studying and thinking about complicated ideas and theories.
intellectually (adverb).

intelligence
(noun) A person's intelligence is their ability to understand and learn things quickly and well.
intelligent (adjective), **intelligently** (adverb).

Similar words: intellect, cleverness, brains

intelligentsia (pronounced in-telly-**jent**-sya)
(noun) The intelligentsia are intellectual people, considered as a group.

intelligible
(adjective) able to be understood, e.g. *His letters were barely intelligible.*

intemperate
(adjective; a formal word) Intemperate behaviour or opinions are too strong and uncontrolled, e.g. *Her criticisms were regarded as untimely and intemperate.*

intend, intends, intending, intended
1 (verb) If you intend to do something, you have decided or planned to do it, e.g. *I've already said more than I intended.*
2 If something is intended for a particular use, you have planned that it should have this use, e.g. *This room was intended as a bathroom.*
[from Latin *intendere* meaning 'to extend' or 'to direct']

intense
1 (adjective) very great in strength or amount, e.g. *intense heat... an intense love affair.*
2 If a person is intense, they take things very seriously and have very strong feelings.
intensely (adverb), **intensity** (noun).
[from Latin *intensus* meaning 'stretched']

intensify, intensifies, intensifying, intensified
(verb) To intensify something means to make it greater in strength or degree.

intensive
(adjective) involving a lot of energy or effort over a very short time, e.g. *intensive care... an intensive French course.*

intent, intents
1 (noun; a formal use) A person's intent is their purpose or intention.
2 (adjective) If you are intent on doing something, you are determined to do it.
3 (phrase) If you say to all intents and purposes, you mean that what you are saying is not exactly true, but is true in all important respects, e.g. *She was, to all intents and purposes, his wife.*
intently (adverb).

intention, intentions
(noun) If you have an intention to do something, you have a plan of what you are going to do.

inter, inters, interring, interred
(verb; a formal word) To inter a body means to bury it.
[from Latin *in-* meaning 'in' + *terra* meaning 'earth']

inter-
(prefix) Inter- means between, e.g. *an inter-school football match.*
[a Latin word]

interact, interacts, interacting, interacted
(verb) The way that two people or things interact is the way that they work together, communicate, or react with each other.
interaction (noun), **interactive** (adjective).

intercede, intercedes, interceding, interceded
(pronounced in-ter-**seed**)
(verb) If you intercede with a person or group, you talk to them and try to end a disagreement that they have had with another person or group.
[from *inter-* + *cedere* meaning 'to move']

intercept, intercepts, intercepting, intercepted
(pronounced in-ter-**sept**)
(verb) If you intercept someone or something, you stop them from reaching their destination.
interceptor (noun), **interception** (noun).
[from *inter-* + *capere* meaning 'to capture']

interchange, interchanges
(noun) An interchange is the act or process of exchanging things or ideas.
interchangeable (adjective).

intercom, intercoms
(noun) An intercom is a device consisting of a microphone and a loudspeaker, which you use to speak to people in another room.

intercourse
1 (noun) Intercourse or sexual intercourse is the act of sex.
2 (an old-fashioned use) Social intercourse is conversation between people.
[from Latin *intercursus* meaning 'business']

interest, interests, interesting, interested
1 (noun) If you have an interest in something, you want to learn or hear more about it.
2 Your interests are your hobbies.
3 Something that is of interest attracts your attention because it is exciting or unusual.
4 (verb) Something that interests you attracts your attention so that you want to learn or hear more about it.
5 (noun) If you have an interest in something being done, you want it to be done because it will benefit you.
6 Interest is a sum of money paid as a percentage of a larger sum of money which has been borrowed or invested.
interesting (adjective), **interestingly** (adverb), **interested** (adjective).
[from Latin *interest* meaning 'it concerns']

interface, interfaces
(noun; a formal word) The interface between two

subjects or systems is the area in which they interact with each other or are linked.

interfere, interferes, interfering, interfered
1 (verb) If you interfere in a situation, you try to influence it, although it does not really concern you.
2 Something that interferes with a situation has a damaging effect on it.
interference (noun), **interfering** (adjective).
[from Old French *s'entreferir* meaning 'to collide']

Similar words: (sense 1) meddle, tamper, poke your nose in

interim
(adjective) intended for use only until something permanent is arranged, e.g. *an interim report.*
[from Latin *interim* meaning 'meanwhile']

interior, interiors
1 (noun) The interior of something is the inside part of it.
2 (adjective) Interior means inside, e.g. *The interior walls need a coat of paint.*
[from Latin *inter* meaning 'within']

interior decorator, interior decorators
(noun) An interior decorator is someone whose job is to plan the decoration of the inside of a house.

interject, interjects, interjecting, interjected
(verb) If you interject something, you say something that interrupts someone who is speaking.
[from Latin *interjicere* meaning 'to place between']

interjection, interjections
(noun) An interjection is a word or phrase spoken suddenly to express a strong feeling such as surprise, pain, or anger.

interlock, interlocks, interlocking, interlocked
(verb) Things that interlock fit into each other so that they are firmly joined together.

interloper, interlopers
(noun) An interloper is a person who is in a place or situation that they are not supposed to be in.
[from *inter-* + Dutch *loopen* meaning 'to leap']

interlude, interludes (rhymes with **rude**)
(noun) An interlude is a short break from an activity.
[from *inter-* + *ludus* meaning 'game']

intermarry, intermarries, intermarrying, intermarried
(verb) When people from different social, racial, or religious groups intermarry, they marry each other.
intermarriage (noun).

intermediary, intermediaries (pronounced in-ter-**meed**-yer-ee)
(noun) An intermediary is someone who tries to get two groups of people to come to an agreement by negotiating with both sides.

intermediate
(adjective) An intermediate level occurs in the middle, between two other stages, e.g. *intermediate and advanced students.*

interminable
(adjective) If something is interminable, it goes on for a very long time, e.g. *interminable rows.*
interminably (adverb).

intermingle, intermingles, intermingling, intermingled
(verb) When things intermingle, they become mixed together.

intermission, intermissions
(noun) An intermission is an interval between two parts of a film or play.

intermittent
(adjective) happening only occasionally.
intermittently (adverb).

intern, interns, interning, interned
(verb) If someone is interned, they are imprisoned.
internment (noun), **internee** (noun).

internal
(adjective) happening inside a person, place, or object.
internally (adverb).

internal-combustion engine, internal-combustion engines
(noun) An internal-combustion engine is an engine with one or more cylinders, which creates energy by burning fuel inside the cylinders.

international, internationals
1 (adjective) involving different countries.
2 (noun) An international is a sports match between two countries.
internationally (adverb).

internecine (pronounced in-ter-**nee**-sine)
(adjective; a formal word) causing destruction to both sides in a conflict.
[from Latin *internecio* meaning 'slaughter']

interplay
(noun) The interplay between two things is the way they react with one another.

interpolate, interpolates, interpolating, interpolated
(verb; a formal word) If you interpolate a comment into a conversation or piece of writing, you add it.
interpolation (noun).

interpose, interposes, interposing, interposed
(verb) If you interpose something between two people or things, you put it between them.

interpret, interprets, interpreting, interpreted
1 (verb) If you interpret what someone says or does, you decide what it means.
2 If you interpret a foreign language that someone is speaking, you translate it.
interpretation (noun), **interpreter** (noun).

interrogate, interrogates, interrogating, interrogated
(verb) If you interrogate someone, you question them thoroughly to get information from them.
interrogation (noun), **interrogator** (noun).
[from *inter-* + Latin *rogare* meaning 'to ask']

Similar words: grill, cross-examine, quiz

interrogative, interrogatives
1 (adjective) An interrogative sentence is one that is in the form of a question.
2 (noun) An interrogative is a word such as 'who' or 'why' that is used to ask a question.

interrupt, interrupts, interrupting, interrupted
1 (verb) If you interrupt someone, you start talking while they are talking.
2 If you interrupt a process or activity, you stop it continuing for a time.
interruption (noun).
[from *inter-* + Latin *rumpere* meaning 'to break']

intersect, intersects, intersecting, intersected
(verb) When two roads intersect, they cross each other.
intersection (noun).
[from Latin *inter-* + *secare* meaning 'to cut between']

interspersed
(adjective) If something is interspersed with things, these things occur at various points in it.

interval, intervals
1 (noun) An interval is the period of time between two moments or dates.
2 An interval is also a short break during a play or concert.
3 In music, an interval is the difference in pitch between two musical notes.
4 (phrase) If something happens **at intervals**, it happens several times, but not necessarily regularly.
5 If things are placed **at intervals**, there is a certain amount of space between them.
[from Latin *intervallum* meaning 'space between ramparts']

Similar words: (sense 2) break, interlude, intermission, gap, pause

intervene, intervenes, intervening, intervened
1 (verb) If you intervene in a situation, you step in to prevent conflict between people.
2 If an event intervenes, it happens suddenly and so prevents something else from happening.
3 If time intervenes, it passes.
intervening (adjective), **intervention** (noun).
[from Latin *intervenire* meaning 'to come between']

Similar words: (sense 1) intercede, arbitrate, mediate

interview, interviews
1 (noun) An interview is a meeting at which someone asks you questions about yourself to see if you are suitable for a particular job.
2 An interview is a conversation in which a well-known person is asked questions by a newspaper, television, or radio reporter.
3 (verb) If you interview someone, you ask them questions about themselves.
interviewer (noun), **interviewee** (noun).

intestate (pronounced in-**tess**-tate)
(adjective; a legal word) having died without leaving a will.

intestine, intestines
(noun) Your intestines are a long tube which

carries food from your stomach through to your bowels, and in which the food is digested.
intestinal (adjective).
[from Latin *intestinus* meaning 'internal']

intimate, intimates, intimating, intimated
1 (adjective) If two people are intimate, they have a close relationship.
2 An intimate matter is very private and personal.
3 An intimate restaurant is small and cosy.
4 An intimate link between ideas or organizations is a very strong link between them.
5 An intimate knowledge of something is very deep and detailed.
6 (verb) If you intimate something, you hint at it, e.g. *She intimated her approval.*
intimately (adverb), **intimacy** (noun), **intimation** (noun).
[from Latin *intimus* meaning 'innermost' or 'deepest']

intimidate, intimidates, intimidating, intimidated
(verb) If you intimidate someone, you frighten them in a threatening way.
intimidated (adjective), **intimidating** (adjective), **intimidatory** (adjective), **intimidation** (noun).
[from Latin *timidus* meaning 'fearful']

into
1 (preposition) If something goes into something else, it goes inside it.
2 If you bump or crash into something, you hit it.
3 If someone changes into clothing, they put it on.
4 (an informal use) If you are into something, you like it very much, e.g. *He's into American football.*

intolerable
(adjective) If something is intolerable, it is so bad or extreme that it is difficult to bear.
intolerably (adverb).

intolerant
(adjective) not tolerant of people who are different from you in some way.
intolerance (noun).

intonation
(noun) Your intonation is the way that your voice rises and falls as you speak.

Similar words: cadence, modulation

intone, intones, intoning, intoned
(verb) If you intone something, you speak or sing it slowly and clearly.

intoxicated
1 (adjective) If someone is intoxicated, they are drunk.
2 If you are intoxicated with a feeling, you feel wild and excited.
intoxicating (adjective), **intoxication** (noun).

intra-
(prefix) Intra- means within or inside, e.g. *an intravenous injection.*
[from Latin *intra* meaning 'within']

intractable
(adjective; a formal word) stubborn and difficult to deal with or control.

intransigent
(adjective) If you are intransigent, you refuse to change your attitude.
intransigence (noun).
[from Spanish *los intransigentes* meaning 'the uncompromising ones', a 19th-century political party]

intransitive
(adjective) An intransitive verb is one that does not have a direct object.

intravenous (pronounced in-trav-**vee**-nuss)
(adjective) Intravenous foods or drugs are given to sick people through their veins.
intravenously (adverb).

intrepid
(adjective) brave, e.g. *intrepid explorers*.
intrepidly (adverb).
[from Latin *in-* + *trepidus* meaning 'not afraid']

intricate
(adjective) Something that is intricate has many fine details, e.g. *an intricate design*.
intricately (adverb), **intricacy** (noun).
[from Latin *intricatus* meaning 'tangled']

intrigue, **intrigues, intriguing, intrigued**
1 (noun) Intrigue is the making of secret plans that are often intended to harm other people, e.g. *financial intrigues*.
2 (verb) If something intrigues you, you are fascinated by it and curious about it.
intriguing (adjective).
[from Latin *intricare* meaning 'to entangle' or 'to perplex']

intrinsic
(adjective; a formal word) The intrinsic qualities of something are its basic qualities.
intrinsically (adverb).
[from Latin *intrinsecus* meaning 'inwardly']

introduce, **introduces, introducing, introduced**
1 (verb) If you introduce one person to another, you tell them each other's name so that they can get to know each other.
2 When someone introduces a radio or television show, they say a few words at the beginning to tell you about it.
3 If you introduce someone to something, they learn about it for the first time.
introductory (adjective).
[from Latin *introducere* meaning 'to bring inside']

introduction, **introductions**
1 (noun) The introduction of someone or something is the act of presenting them for the first time.
2 The introduction to a book is a piece of writing at the beginning of it, which usually discusses the book in some detail.

Similar words: (sense 2) preface, foreword, preamble

introspective
(adjective) examining your own feelings and desires, e.g. *He was in an introspective mood*.
introspection (noun).
[from Latin *introspicere* meaning 'to look within']

introvert, **introverts**
(noun) An introvert is someone who spends more time thinking about their private feelings than about the world around them, and who often finds it difficult to talk to others.
introverted (adjective).

intrude, **intrudes, intruding, intruded**
(verb) To intrude on someone or something means to disturb them, e.g. *I don't want to intrude on your family... Nothing could intrude on our happiness*.
intruder (noun), **intrusion** (noun),
intrusive (adjective).
[from Latin *intrudere* meaning 'to thrust in']

Similar words: barge in, gatecrash, trespass

intuition, **intuitions** (pronounced int-yoo-**ish**-n)
(noun) Your intuition is a feeling you have about something that you cannot explain, e.g. *My intuition warned me not to trust him*.
intuitive (adjective), **intuitively** (adverb).

Inuit, **Inuits;** also spelled **Innuit**
1 (noun) An Inuit is an Eskimo who comes from North America or Greenland.
2 Inuit is the language spoken by Inuits.

inundated
1 (adjective) If you are inundated by letters or requests, you receive so many that you cannot deal with them all.
2 If land is inundated, it becomes flooded with water.
inundation (noun).

inure, **inures, inuring, inured** (pronounced in-**yoor**)
(verb) If you become inured to something unpleasant, you become accustomed to it.
[from Middle English *enuren* meaning 'to accustom']

invade, **invades, invading, invaded**
1 (verb) If an army invades a country, it enters it by force.
2 If someone invades your privacy, they disturb you when you want to be alone.
invader (noun), **invasion** (noun).

invalid, **invalids** (pronounced **in**-va-lid)
(noun) An invalid is someone who is so ill that they need to be looked after by someone else.
[from Latin *invalidus* meaning 'infirm']

invalid (pronounced in-**val**-id)
1 (adjective) If an argument or result is invalid, it is not acceptable because it is based on a mistake.
2 If a law, marriage, or election is invalid, it is illegal because it has not been carried out properly.
invalidate (verb).
[from Latin *invalidus* meaning 'without legal force']

invalidity
1 (noun) Invalidity is the condition of being very ill for a very long time, e.g. *an invalidity pension*.
2 Invalidity is also the state of being invalid, e.g. *the invalidity of his argument*.

invaluable
(adjective) extremely useful, e.g. *A good map is invaluable if you're crossing London.*

invariable
(adjective) Something that is invariable always happens or never changes.
invariably (adverb).

invective
(noun; a formal word) Invective is abusive language used by someone who is angry.

invent, invents, inventing, invented
1 (verb) If you invent a machine, device, or process, you are the first person to think of it or to use it.
2 If you invent a story or an excuse, you make it up.
inventor (noun), **invention** (noun), **inventive** (adjective), **inventiveness** (noun).
[from Latin *invenire* meaning 'to find' or 'to come upon']

Similar words: devise, create

inventory, inventories
(noun) An inventory is a written list of all the objects in a place, e.g. *When the landlord checked the inventory, he found many items were missing.*

inverse
(adjective; a formal word) If there is an inverse relationship between two things, one decreases as the other increases.

invert, inverts, inverting, inverted
(verb) If you invert something, you turn it upside down or back to front.
inverted (adjective), **inversion** (noun).
[from *in-* + Latin *vertere* meaning 'to turn']

invertebrate, invertebrates
(noun; a technical word) An invertebrate is a creature which does not have a spine. Some invertebrates, for example crabs, have an external skeleton.

inverted comma, inverted commas
(noun) Inverted commas are the punctuation marks used to show where speech begins and ends.

invest, invests, investing, invested
1 (verb) If you invest money, you pay it into a bank or buy shares so that you will receive a profit.
2 If you invest money, time, or energy in something, you try to make it a success.
3 If you invest in something useful, you buy it because it will help you do something more efficiently.
4 To invest somebody with rights means to give them the rights formally, e.g. *A chairman is invested with great power.*
investor (noun), **investment** (noun).
[sense 4 is from Latin *investire* meaning 'to clothe']

investigate, investigates, investigating, investigated
(verb) To investigate something means to find out all the facts about it.
investigator (noun), **investigation** (noun).
[from Latin *investigare* meaning 'to search after', from *vestigium* meaning 'track']

Similar words: follow up, look into, make inquiries, explore, probe

inveterate
(adjective) having lasted for a long time and not likely to stop, e.g. *an inveterate womanizer.*
[from Latin *inveteratus* meaning 'having been made old']

invidious
1 (adjective) An invidious job is unpleasant because it can make you unpopular, e.g. *I had the invidious task of breaking the bad news.*
2 An invidious comparison is an unfair one because the two things are not similar enough to be compared properly.
[from Latin *invidiosus* meaning 'full of envy']

invigilate, invigilates, invigilating, invigilated
(pronounced in-**vij**-il-late)
(verb) When teachers invigilate an exam, they supervise it and check that everything is correct.
invigilator (noun).
[from Latin *invigilare* meaning 'to watch over']

invigorated
(adjective) energetic and refreshed.
invigorating (adjective).

invincible
1 (adjective) unable to be defeated, e.g. *Our local team are invincible.*
2 unable to be changed, e.g. *an invincible air of superiority.*
invincibly (adverb), **invincibility** (noun).
[from Latin *in-* meaning 'not' + *vincere* meaning 'to conquer']

Similar words: (sense 1) indomitable, insuperable

inviolable (pronounced in-**viol**-a-bl)
(adjective; a formal word) If a law is inviolable, you cannot break it, e.g. *the inviolable law of gravity.*

inviolate
(adjective; a formal word) unharmed or unaffected by something.

invisible
(adjective) If something is invisible, you cannot see it, because it is hidden, very small, or imaginary.
invisibly (adverb), **invisibility** (noun).

invite, invites, inviting, invited
1 (verb) If you invite someone to an event, you ask them to come to it.
2 If you invite someone to do something, you ask them to do it, e.g. *I was invited to speak first.*
3 If someone invites comment, they encourage you to comment on something.
4 If a situation invites trouble or danger, it makes trouble or danger more likely.
inviting (adjective), **invitation** (noun).

invoice, invoices
(noun) An invoice is a bill for services or goods.
[from Old French *envois* meaning 'messages']

invoke, invokes, invoking, invoked
1 (verb; a formal word) If you invoke a law, you use it to justify what you are doing.
2 If you invoke certain feelings, you cause someone to have these feelings.
[from Latin *invocare* meaning 'to call upon']

involuntary
(adjective) sudden and uncontrollable, e.g. *an involuntary smile.*
involuntarily (adverb).

involve, involves, involving, involved
1 (verb) If a situation involves someone or something, it includes them as a necessary part.
2 If you involve yourself in something, you take part in it.
3 If a film or a book involves you, it makes you feel that you are taking part in events.
involved (adjective), **involvement** (noun).
[from Latin *involvere* meaning 'to roll in' or 'to surround']

invulnerable
(adjective) unable to be hurt or damaged.
invulnerability (noun).

inward or **inwards**
1 (adjective) Your inward thoughts and feelings are private.
2 (adjective and adverb) If something moves inward or inwards, it moves towards the inside or centre of something.
inwardly (adverb), **inwardness** (noun).

iodine (pronounced **eye**-oh-deen)
(noun) Iodine is a bluish-black element whose compounds are used in medicine and photography. Its atomic number is 53 and its symbol is I.

ion, ions (pronounced **eye**-on)
(noun) Ions are electrically charged atoms.

iota, iotas
(noun) An iota is an extremely small amount, e.g. *He felt not an iota of guilt.*

IQ, IQs
(noun) Your IQ is your level of intelligence calculated from the results of a special test. IQ is an abbreviation for 'intelligence quotient'.

Iranian, Iranians (pronounced ir-**rain**-ee-an)
1 (adjective) belonging or relating to Iran.
2 (noun) An Iranian is someone who comes from Iran.
3 Iranian is the main language spoken in Iran. It is also known as Farsi.

Iraqi, Iraqis (pronounced ir-**ah**-kee)
1 (adjective) belonging or relating to Iraq.
2 (noun) An Iraqi is someone who comes from Iraq.

irascible (pronounced ir-**rass**-i-bl)
(adjective) very irritable and easily angered.

irate (pronounced eye-**rate**)
(adjective) very angry.
[from Latin *ira* meaning 'anger']

iridescent (pronounced irry-**dess**-ent)
(adjective; a formal word) Something that is iridescent has bright colours that seem to keep changing, e.g. *iridescent peacock feathers.*
iridescence (noun).

iridium (pronounced eye-**rid**-ee-um)
(noun) Iridium is a metallic element that occurs in platinum ores. It is used especially in alloys. Its atomic number is 77 and its symbol is Ir.

iris, irises (pronounced **eye**-riss)
1 (noun) The iris is the round, coloured part of your eye.
2 An iris is a tall plant with long leaves and large purple, blue, yellow, or white flowers.
[from Greek *iris* meaning 'rainbow' or 'coloured circle']

Irish
1 (adjective) belonging or relating to the Irish Republic, or to the whole of Ireland.
2 (noun) Irish or Irish Gaelic is a language spoken in some parts of Ireland.

Irishman, Irishmen
(noun) An Irishman is a man who comes from Ireland.
Irishwoman (noun).

irk, irks, irking, irked
(verb) If something irks you, it annoys you.
irksome (adjective).
[from Middle English *irken* meaning 'to grow weary']

iron, irons, ironing, ironed
1 (noun) Iron is a strong hard metallic element found in rocks. It is used in making tools and machines, and is also an important component of blood. Its atomic number is 26 and its symbol is Fe.
2 An iron is a device which heats up and which you rub over clothes to remove creases.
3 (verb) If you iron clothes, you use a hot iron to remove creases from them.
ironing (noun).

iron out
(phrasal verb) If you iron out difficulties, you solve them.

Iron Age
(noun) The Iron Age was a time about three thousand years ago when people first started to make implements out of iron.

Iron Curtain
(noun) The Iron Curtain is the border that separates the Soviet Union and its European allies from other European countries.

irony (pronounced **eye**-ronny)
1 (noun) Irony is a form of humour in which you say the opposite of what you really mean, e.g. *I detected a certain irony in her praise.*
2 The irony of a situation is when there is an unexpected connection between things or when factors combine in an odd or unusual way, e.g. *By a curious irony, both her husbands died of the same disease.*
ironic or **ironical** (adjective), **ironically** (adverb).

irradiate, irradiates, irradiating, irradiated
(verb) To irradiate something means to expose it to radiation.
irradiation (noun).

irrational
(adjective) Irrational feelings are not based on logical reasons, e.g. *an irrational fear of cats.*
irrationally (adverb), **irrationality** (noun).

irrefutable (pronounced ir-reff-**yoot**-i-bl)
(adjective; a formal word) A statement that is irrefutable cannot be denied or disproved.

irregular
1 (adjective) Something that is irregular is not smooth or straight, or does not form a regular pattern, e.g. *irregular marks on the photographs... feeding them at irregular intervals... an irregular surface.*
2 Irregular behaviour is unusual and strange.
irregularly (adverb), **irregularity** (noun).

Similar words: (sense 1) sporadic, spasmodic, erratic

irrelevant
(adjective) not directly connected with a subject, e.g. *The book was full of irrelevant information.*
irrelevance (noun), **irrelevancy** (noun).

irreparable (pronounced ir-**rep**-ir-a-bl)
(adjective) Irreparable damage is so bad that it cannot be put right again.

irreplaceable
(adjective) If something is irreplaceable, it is so special that it cannot be replaced if it is lost or destroyed.

irrepressible
(adjective) Someone who is irrepressible is lively, energetic, and never depressed.

irresistible
1 (adjective) unable to be controlled, e.g. *an irresistible urge to laugh.*
2 extremely attractive, e.g. *I find him irresistible.*
irresistibly (adverb).

irresolute (pronounced ir-**rez**-oll-yoot)
(adjective; a formal word) If you are irresolute, you cannot decide what to do.
irresolutely (adverb), **irresolution** (noun).

irrespective
(adjective) If you say something will be done irrespective of certain things, you mean it will be done without taking those things into account.

irresponsible
(adjective) An irresponsible person does things without considering the consequences, e.g. *an irresponsible driver.*
irresponsibly (adverb), **irresponsibility** (noun).

Similar words: thoughtless, feckless, reckless

irreverent
(adjective) not showing any respect, e.g. *irreverent humour.*
irreverently (adverb), **irreverence** (adverb).

irrevocable
(adjective) unable to be stopped or changed.
irrevocably (adverb).

irrigate, irrigates, irrigating, irrigated
(verb) To irrigate land means to supply it with water brought through pipes or ditches.
irrigated (adjective), **irrigation** (noun).
[from Latin *rigare* meaning 'to moisten']

irritate, irritates, irritating, irritated
1 (verb) If something irritates you, it annoys you.
2 If something irritates part of your body, it makes it tender, sore, and itchy.
irritable (adjective), **irritant** (noun),
irritation (noun).

Similar words: (sense 1) jar, chafe, grate

is the third person, present tense of **be.**

Islam (pronounced **iz**-lahm)
(noun) Islam is the Muslim religion, which teaches that there is only one God, Allah, and Mohammed is his prophet. The holy book of Islam is the Koran.
Islamic (adjective).
[from Arabic *islam* meaning 'surrender to God']

island, islands (pronounced **eye**-land)
(noun) An island is a piece of land entirely surrounded by water.
islander (noun).
[from Old English *ig* meaning 'island' + *land*]

isle, isles (rhymes with **mile**)
(noun; a literary word) An isle is an island.
[from Latin *insula* meaning 'island']

isobar, isobars (pronounced **eye**-so-bar)
(noun; a technical word) An isobar is a line on a map which joins places of equal air pressure.
[from Greek *isobarēs* meaning 'of equal weight']

isolate, isolates, isolating, isolated
1 (verb) If something isolates you or if you isolate yourself, you are physically or socially set apart from other people.
2 If you isolate something, you separate it from everything else.
isolated (adjective), **isolation** (noun).

isosceles (pronounced eye-**sossy**-leez)
(adjective) An isosceles triangle has two sides of the same length.
[from Greek *iso*- meaning 'equal' and *skelos* meaning 'leg']

isotherm, isotherms
(noun; a technical word) An isotherm is a line on a map which joins places of equal temperature.
[from Greek *iso* meaning 'equal' and *therme* meaning 'heat']

isotope, isotopes
(noun; a scientific word) An isotope is one of two or more atoms of the same atomic number that contain different numbers of neutrons.

Israeli, Israelis (pronounced iz-**rail**-ee)
1 (adjective) belonging or relating to Israel.
2 (noun) An Israeli is someone who comes from Israel.

issue, issues, issuing, issued (pronounced **ish**-yoo)
1 (noun) An issue is an important subject that people are talking about.

2 (phrase) If you **take issue** with someone, you disagree with something they have said.
3 (noun) An issue of a newspaper or magazine is a particular edition of it.
4 (verb) If you issue a statement or a warning, you say it formally and publicly.
5 If someone issues something, they officially supply it, e.g. *I was issued with a prison uniform.*
6 When a liquid, sound, or smell issues from something, it comes out of it.
[senses 3-6 from Latin *exuta* meaning 'something that has gone out']

Similar words: (sense 5) supply, distribute, give out

isthmus, isthmuses
(noun) An isthmus is a narrow strip of land connecting two larger areas.

it
1 (pronoun) It is used to refer to something that has already been mentioned, or to a situation or fact, e.g. *The council said it would pull the flats down... It's impossible to decide... It doesn't matter.*
2 It is used to refer to people or animals whose sex is not known, e.g. *Is it a little girl or a little boy?*
3 You use it to make statements about the weather, time, or date, e.g. *It snowed yesterday.*

Italian, Italians
1 (adjective) belonging or relating to Italy.
2 (noun) An Italian is someone who comes from Italy.
3 Italian is the main language spoken in Italy and is also spoken by some people in Switzerland.

italics
(plural noun) Italics are letters printed in a special sloping way, and are often used to emphasize something. All the examples in this dictionary are in italics.
italic (adjective).

itch, itches, itching, itched
1 (verb) When your skin itches, it has an unpleasant, irritated feeling and you want to scratch it.
2 (noun) An itch is an unpleasant, irritated feeling on your skin that you want to scratch.
3 (verb) If you are itching to do something, you are impatient to do it.
itchy (adjective).
[from Old English *giccean* meaning 'to itch']

item, items
1 (noun) An item is one of a collection or list of objects.
2 An item is a newspaper or magazine article.
[from Latin *item* meaning 'in like manner'; once used to introduce each item on a list]

Similar words: (sense 2) article, feature, piece

itemize, itemizes, itemizing, itemized; also spelled **itemise**
(verb) To itemize a number of things means to make a list of them.

itinerant
(adjective) travelling from place to place, e.g. *an itinerant farm hand.*
[from Latin *itinerari* meaning 'to travel', from *iter* meaning 'journey']

itinerary, itineraries
(noun) An itinerary is a plan of a journey, showing a route to follow and places to visit.

-itis
(suffix) -itis is added to the name of a part of the body to refer to disease or inflammation in that part, e.g. *appendicitis... tonsillitis.*

its
(determiner) 'Its' refers to something belonging to or relating to things, children, or animals that have already been mentioned, e.g. *The creature lifted its head.*

itself
1 (pronoun) 'Itself' is used when the same thing, child, or animal does an action and is affected by it, e.g. *It wraps its furry tail around itself.*
2 Itself is used to emphasize 'it'.

ivory
1 (noun) Ivory is the valuable creamy-white bone which forms the tusk of an elephant. It is used to make ornaments.
2 (noun and adjective) creamy-white.
3 (phrase) If you describe someone as living in an **ivory tower**, you mean that they keep themselves away from the problems of everyday life.
[from Latin *ebur* meaning 'ivory']

ivy
(noun) Ivy is an evergreen plant which creeps along the ground and up walls.

J

jab, jabs, jabbing, jabbed
1 (verb) To jab something means to poke at it roughly.
2 (noun) A jab is a sharp or sudden poke.
3 (an informal use) A jab is also an injection.

jabber, jabbers, jabbering, jabbered
(verb; an informal word) If people are jabbering, they are talking very fast and you cannot understand them.

jack, jacks, jacking, jacked
1 (noun) A jack is a piece of equipment for lifting heavy objects, especially for lifting a car when changing a wheel.
2 (verb) To jack up an object means to raise it, especially by using a jack.
3 (noun) In a pack of cards, a jack is a card with a picture of a man on it. It is more valuable than a ten and less valuable than a queen.
4 Jacks is a game in which you throw up and catch small criss-cross shaped objects.
[from the name *Jack*]

jackal, jackals
(noun) A jackal is a wild animal related to dogs. Jackals live in Africa and Asia.
[from Persian *shagal*]

jackboot, jackboots
(noun) A jackboot is a heavy, long boot that comes up to the knee.

jackdaw, jackdaws
(noun) A jackdaw is a bird like a small crow with black and grey feathers.

jacket, jackets
1 (noun) A jacket is a short coat.
2 A jacket is also an outer covering for something, e.g. *a book jacket.*
3 (adjective) Potatoes cooked in their skins in the oven are called jacket potatoes.

jackknife, jackknives; jackknifes, jackknifing, jackknifed
1 (noun) A jackknife is a knife with a blade that folds into the handle.
2 (verb) If an articulated truck jackknifes, the trailer skids and swings round out of control towards the cab.

jackpot, jackpots
1 (noun) In a gambling game, the jackpot is the top prize.
2 (an informal phrase) If you **hit the jackpot**, you win the top prize or have a stroke of good luck.

jade
(noun) Jade is a hard green stone used for making jewellery and ornaments.

jagged
(adjective) sharp and spiky.

Similar words: ragged, serrated, sharp, spiked

jaguar, jaguars
(noun) A jaguar is a large member of the cat family with spots on its back. Jaguars live in South and Central America.
[from *jaguara*, a South American Indian word]

jail, jails, jailing, jailed; also spelled **gaol**
1 (noun) A jail is a building where people convicted of a crime are locked up.
2 (verb) To jail someone means to lock them up in a jail.
[from Old French *jaiole* meaning 'cage']

Similar words: (sense 1) prison, clink, jug, penitentiary

jailer, jailers; also spelled **gaoler**
(noun) A jailer is a person who works in a jail and is in charge of the prisoners in it.

jam, jams, jamming, jammed
1 (noun) Jam is a food, made by boiling fruit and sugar together until it sets.
2 A jam is a situation where there are so many things or people that it is impossible to move, e.g. *a traffic jam.*
3 (an informal phrase) If someone is **in a jam**, they are in a difficult situation.
4 (verb) If people or things are jammed into a place, they are squeezed together so closely that they can hardly move.
5 To jam something somewhere means to push it there roughly, e.g. *Reporters jammed microphones into our faces.*
6 If something is jammed, it is stuck or unable to work properly.
7 To jam a radio or electric signal means to interfere with it and prevent it from being received clearly.

Similar words: (sense 3) fix, pickle, quandary

Jamaican, Jamaicans (pronounced jam-**may**-kn)
1 (adjective) belonging or relating to Jamaica.
2 (noun) A Jamaican is someone who comes from Jamaica.

jamb, jambs
(noun) A jamb is the upright part of a door or window frame.
[from French *jambe* meaning 'leg']

jamboree, jamborees
(noun) A jamboree is a party or a gathering of large numbers of people enjoying themselves.

jangle, jangles, jangling, jangled
1 (verb) If something jangles, it makes a harsh metallic ringing noise.
2 (noun) A jangle is the sound made by metal objects striking against each other.

janitor, janitors
(noun) A janitor is the caretaker of a building.

January
(noun) January is the first month of the year. It has 31 days.
[from Latin *Januarius* meaning 'the month of Janus', named after a Roman god]

Japanese
1 (adjective) belonging or relating to Japan.
2 (noun) A Japanese is someone who comes from Japan.
3 Japanese is the main language spoken in Japan.

jar, jars, jarring, jarred
1 (noun) A jar is a glass container with a wide top used for storing food such as jam.
2 (verb) if something jars on you, you find it unpleasant or annoying.
[sense 1 is from Arabic *jarrah* meaning 'large earthen container']

jardiniere, jardinieres (pronounced jar-din-**yair**)
(noun) A jardiniere is an ornamental container for displaying plants and flowers.
[from French *jardin* meaning 'garden']

jargon
(noun) Jargon consists of words or expressions that are used in special or technical ways by particular groups of people.

jasmine
(noun) Jasmine is a climbing plant with small sweet-scented white flowers.

jaundice
(noun) Jaundice is a condition in which the skin and the whites of the eyes become yellow, because of an illness affecting the liver.
[from French *jaune* meaning 'yellow']

jaundiced
(adjective) unenthusiastic and pessimistic, e.g. *He takes a rather jaundiced view of governments.*

jaunt, jaunts
(noun) A jaunt is a journey or trip you go on for pleasure.

jaunty, jauntier, jauntiest
(adjective) expressing cheerfulness and self-confidence, e.g. *a hat set at a jaunty angle.*
jauntily (adverb), **jauntiness** (noun).
[from Old French *gentil* meaning 'noble']

javelin, javelins
1 (noun) A javelin is a long spear that used to be thrown as a weapon.
2 The javelin is an athletics event in which contestants throw a javelin as far as they can.

jaw, jaws
1 (noun) A person's or animal's jaw is the bone in which the teeth are set.
2 A person's or animal's mouth and teeth are their jaws.

jay, jays
(noun) A jay is a large bird related to the crow.

jaywalking
Jaywalking is the act of crossing a road carelessly or dangerously.
jaywalker (noun).

jazz, jazzes, jazzing, jazzed
1 (noun) Jazz is a style of popular music with a forceful rhythm.
2 (verb; an informal use) To jazz something up means to make it more colourful or exciting.

jazzy, jazzier, jazziest
(adjective; an informal word) bright and showy.

jealous
1 (adjective) If you are jealous of someone, you feel bitterness and anger towards them because of something they possess or something they have achieved.
2 If you are jealous of something you have, you feel you must try to keep it from other people.
jealously (adverb), **jealousy** (noun).

Similar words: (sense 1) covetous, envious (sense 2) possessive

jeans
(plural noun) Jeans are casual denim trousers.

jeep, jeeps
(noun) A jeep is a small military road vehicle with four-wheel drive.

jeer, jeers, jeering, jeered
1 (verb) If you jeer at someone, you insult them in a loud, unpleasant way.
2 (noun) Jeers are rude and insulting remarks.
jeering (adjective).

Jehovah (pronounced ji-**hove**-ah)
Jehovah is the name of God in the Old Testament.
[from adding vowels to the Hebrew *JHVH*, the sacred name of God]

jejunum
(noun) The jejunum is the part of the small intestine between the duodenum and the ileum.

jell, jells, jelling, jelled
1 (verb) When a liquid jells, it sets like a jelly.
2 If an idea or plan jells, it becomes more definite.

jellied
(adjective) Jellied food is coated in jelly, e.g. *jellied eels.*

jelly, jellies
1 (noun) A jelly is a clear food made from gelatine and eaten as a dessert.
2 Jelly is a type of clear, set jam.
3 Jelly is also the clear rubbery substance formed when juices from cooked meat cool.

jellyfish, jellyfishes
(noun) A jellyfish is a sea animal with a clear soft body and tentacles which may sting.

jemmy, jemmies
(noun) A jemmy is a short metal bar that is curved at one end and used as a tool to force things open.

jeopardize, jeopardizes, jeopardizing, jeopardized (pronounced **jep**-par-dyz); also spelled **jeopardise**
(verb) To jeopardize something means to do something which puts it at risk, e.g. *I don't want to jeopardize my relationship with my boss.*

jeopardy
(noun) If someone or something is in jeopardy, they are at risk of failing or of being destroyed.

jerk, jerks, jerking, jerked
1 (verb) To jerk something means to give it a sudden, sharp pull.

2 If something jerks, it moves suddenly and sharply.
3 (noun) A jerk is a sudden sharp movement.
4 (an informal use) If you call someone a jerk, you mean they are stupid.
jerky (adjective), **jerkily** (adverb).

jerkin, jerkins
(noun) A jerkin is a short sleeveless jacket.

jeroboam, jeroboams (pronounced jer-ro-**boh**-am)
(noun) A jeroboam is a very large wine bottle, more than eight times the normal size.
[*Jeroboam* was 'a mighty man of valour' in the Bible (see 1 Kings 2)]

jerry-built
(adjective) cheaply and badly built.

jerry-can
(noun) A jerry-can is a metal or plastic flat-sided container for petrol or water.

jersey, jerseys
1 (noun) A jersey is a knitted garment for the upper half of the body.
2 Jersey is a type of knitted woollen or cotton fabric used to make clothing.
3 A Jersey is a type of small dairy cow that produces very rich high-quality milk.
[Both knitting and dairy products are industries in *Jersey*, one of the Channel Islands]

jest, jests, jesting, jested
1 (noun) A jest is a joke.
2 (verb) To jest means to speak jokingly.

jester, jesters
(noun) In the past, a jester was a man who was kept to amuse the monarch and court.

Jesuit, Jesuits (pronounced **jez**-yoo-it)
(noun) A Jesuit is a priest who is a member of the Roman Catholic Society of Jesus, founded in the sixteenth century by Ignatius Loyola. One of the main aims of the Society is missionary work.

jet, jets, jetting, jetted
1 (noun) A jet is a plane powered by a jet engine, out of which hot air and gases are forced, enabling the plane to fly very fast.
2 A jet is a stream of liquid, gas, or flame forced out under pressure; also the hole through which it is forced out.
3 (verb) To jet somewhere means to fly there in a plane, especially a jet.
4 (noun) Jet is a hard black stone, usually highly polished and used in jewellery and ornaments.
[senses 1-3 are from French *jeter* meaning 'to throw'; sense 4 is from *Gagai*, a town in Turkey]

jetlag
(noun) Jetlag is a feeling of intense tiredness or physical confusion experienced by air travellers after they have passed through several time zones.

jetsam
(noun) Jetsam is rubbish left floating on the sea or washed up on the seashore.
[shortened from *jettison*]

jetset
(noun) The jetset are rich and successful people who visit fashionable places around the world.

jettison, jettisons, jettisoning, jettisoned
(verb) If you jettison something, you throw it away because you no longer want it or need it.

jetty, jetties
(noun) A jetty is a wide stone wall or wooden platform at the edge of the sea or a river, where boats can be moored.
[from Old French *jetee* meaning 'something thrown out']

Jew, Jews (pronounced **joo**)
(noun) A Jew is a person who believes in and practises the religion of Judaism, or who is of Hebrew descent.
Jewish (adjective).
[from *Judah*, the name of a Jewish patriarch]

jewel, jewels
(noun) A jewel is a precious stone used to decorate valuable ornaments or jewellery.
jewelled (adjective).

Similar words: gem, gemstone

jeweller, jewellers
(noun) A jeweller is a person who makes jewellery or who buys, sells, and repairs jewellery and watches.

jewellery
(noun) Jewellery consists of ornaments that people wear, such as rings, bracelets, or necklaces, made of valuable metals and sometimes decorated with precious stones.

Jewess, Jewesses
(noun; a slightly old-fashioned word) A Jewess is a girl or woman who is Jewish.

jib, jibs, jibbing, jibbed
1 (noun) A jib is a small sail towards the front of a sailing boat.
2 (verb) If you jib at something, you show great reluctance or unwillingness to do it or accept it.

jibe another spelling of **gibe**.

jiffy
(noun) In a jiffy means very quickly, e.g. *I'll be back in a jiffy.*

jig, jigs, jigging, jigged
1 (noun) A jig is a type of lively folk dance; also the music that accompanies it.
2 (verb) If you jig, you dance or jump around in a lively bouncy manner.

jiggle, jiggles, jiggling, jiggled
(verb) If you jiggle something, you move it around with quick jerky movements.

jigsaw, jigsaws
(noun) A jigsaw is a puzzle consisting of a picture on cardboard or wood that has been cut up into small pieces, which have to be put together again.

jihad (pronounced jee-**had**)
(noun) A jihad is a Moslem holy war against those who reject the teachings of Islam.
[from Arabic *jihad* meaning 'conflict']

jilt, jilts, jilting, jilted
(verb) If you jilt someone, you suddenly break off your relationship with them.
jilted (adjective).

jingle, jingles, jingling, jingled
1 (noun) A jingle is a short, catchy phrase or rhyme set to music and used to advertise something on radio or television.
2 (verb) When something jingles, it makes a tinkling sound like small bells.
3 (noun) A jingle is also the sound of something jingling.

jingoism
(noun) Jingoism is overenthusiastic and unreasonable belief in the superiority of your own country.
jingoist (noun), **jingoistic** (adjective).
[from a 19th-century song with the refrain *By Jingo!*]

jinks
(noun) High jinks is boisterous and mischievous behaviour.

Similar words: fun and games, merrymaking

jinx, jinxes
(noun) A jinx is anything that is thought to bring bad luck; also the bad luck itself, e.g. *There must be a jinx on it.*

jitters
(plural noun; an informal word) If you have got the jitters, you are feeling very nervous.
jittery (noun).

jive, jives, jiving, jived
1 (noun) The jive is a lively, energetic dance that first became popular in the 1950s, and which is performed to rock music.
2 (verb) To jive means to dance the jive.

job, jobs
1 (noun) A job is the work that someone does to earn money.
2 A job is also a duty or responsibility, e.g. *It's your job to clean the windows.*
3 (phrase) If something is **just the job**, it is exactly right or exactly what you wanted.
4 If you **make the best of a bad job**, you do the best you can in difficult circumstances.
5 If you **give something up as a bad job**, you abandon it because you feel that you cannot do anything to improve it.

Similar words: (sense 1) occupation, employment, position, trade, profession, situation, work

jobbing
(adjective) not having regular work, but doing individual jobs when asked to, e.g. *a jobbing gardener.*

job centre, job centres
(noun) A job centre is a government office where people can find out about job vacancies.

jobless
(adjective) without any work.

job lot, job lots
(noun) A job lot is a collection of items, often cheap and of low quality, that are sold together.

jockey, jockeys, jockeying, jockeyed
1 (noun) A jockey is someone who rides a horse in a race.
2 (verb) To jockey for a position means to manoeuvre in order to gain an advantage over other people.

jockstrap, jockstraps
(noun) A jockstrap is a close-fitting piece of clothing worn under shorts to support the genitals of men or boys who are playing sports.
[from *jock* meaning 'penis']

jocose (pronounced jok-**kose**)
(adjective; an old-fashioned word) amusing or humorous.
jocosely (adverb).
[from Latin *jocus* meaning 'joke']

jocular
(adjective) Someone who is jocular is cheerful and often makes jokes.
jocularly (adjective), **jocularity** (noun).
[from Latin *joculus* meaning 'little joke']

jodhpurs (pronounced **jod**-purz)
(plural noun) Jodhpurs are close-fitting trousers worn when riding a horse.
[from *Jodhpur*, the name of a town in N. India]

jog, jogs, jogging, jogged
1 (verb) To jog means to run slowly and rhythmically, often as a form of exercise.
2 (noun) A jog is a slow run.
3 (verb) If you jog something, you knock it or nudge it slightly so that it shakes or moves.
4 If someone or something jogs your memory, they remind you of something.
jogger (noun), **jogging** (noun).

joggle, joggles, joggling, joggled
(verb) To joggle something means to shake it gently.

joie de vivre (pronounced jwa de **veev**-ri)
(noun) Joie de vivre is a feeling of happiness and enjoyment of life.
[a French phrase meaning 'joy of living']

join, joins, joining, joined
1 (verb) When two things join, or when one thing joins another, they come together.
2 If you join a club or organization, you become a member of it or start taking part in it.
3 To join two things means to fasten them.
4 (noun) A join is a place where two things are fastened together.
5 (phrase) If two people **join forces**, they work together to achieve a common aim.
[from Latin *jungere* meaning 'to yoke']

Similar words: (senses 1 and 3) link, connect, unite (sense 2) enlist, enrol, enter, sign up

join up
(phrasal verb) If someone joins up, they become a member of the armed forces.

joiner, joiners
(noun) A joiner is a person who makes wooden window frames, door frames, or doors.

joinery
(noun) Joinery is the work done by a joiner.

joint, joints, jointing, jointed
1 (adjective) shared by or belonging to two or more people, e.g. *a joint bank account.*
2 (noun) A joint is a part of the body where two bones meet and are joined together so that they can move, for example a knee or hip.
3 A joint is also a place where two things are fixed together.
4 (verb) To joint meat means to cut it into large pieces according to where the bones are.
5 (noun) A joint of meat is a large piece suitable for roasting.
6 (an informal use) A joint is any place of entertainment, such as a nightclub or pub.
7 A joint is also a cigarette containing cannabis.
jointly (adverb), jointed (adjective).

jointure, jointures (pronounced **joint**-cher)
(noun) A jointure is money set aside by a husband for his wife's income after his death.
[from Latin *junctura* meaning 'joining']

joist, joists
(noun) A joist is a large wooden, concrete, or metal beam used to support floors or ceilings.

joke, jokes, joking, joked
1 (noun) A joke is something that you say or do to make people laugh, such as a funny story.
2 A joke is also anything that you think is ridiculous and not worthy of respect, e.g. *This place is nothing but a joke.*
3 (verb) If you joke, you tell funny stories or say amusing things to make people laugh.
4 If you are joking, you are teasing someone, e.g. *Don't worry, I was only joking.*
jokingly (adverb).
[from Latin *jocus* meaning 'joke']

Similar words: (sense 1) jest, gag, hoax, trick, prank (sense 3) jest, kid, quip

joker, jokers
(noun) In a pack of cards, a joker is an extra card that does not belong to any of the four suits, but is used in some games.

jollity
(noun) Jollity is cheerful behaviour and high spirits, e.g. *an evening of fun and jollity.*

jolly, jollier, jolliest; jollies, jollying, jollied
1 (adjective) happy, cheerful, and pleasant.
2 (adverb; an informal use) Jolly also means very, e.g. *It was jolly decent of him.*
3 (verb) If you jolly someone along, you encourage them in a cheerful and friendly way.
jolliness (noun).

jolt, jolts, jolting, jolted
1 (verb) To jolt means to move or shake roughly and violently.
2 If you are jolted by something, it gives you an unpleasant shock or surprise.
3 (noun) A jolt is a sudden jerky movement.
4 A jolt is also an unpleasant shock or surprise.

jonquil, jonquils (pronounced **jong**-kwil)
(noun) A jonquil is a flowering spring bulb, which has clusters of sweet-scented white or yellow flowers.
[from Spanish *junquillo* meaning 'little reed']

Jordanian, Jordanians (pronounced jor-**dane**-ee-an)
1 (adjective) belonging or relating to Jordan.
2 (noun) A Jordanian is someone who comes from Jordan.

joss stick, joss sticks
(noun) A joss stick is a thin stick of incense, which burns slowly and fills the air with perfume.
[from pidgin English *joss* meaning 'god']

jostle, jostles, jostling, jostled
(verb) To jostle means to push or knock roughly against people in a crowd.

jot, jots, jotting, jotted
1 (verb) If you jot something down, you write it quickly in the form of a short informal note.
2 (noun) A jot means a very small amount.
jotting (noun).

jotter, jotters
(noun) A jotter is a pad or notebook.

joule, joules (rhymes with **school**)
(noun) A joule is a unit of energy or work. A watt is equal to one joule per second. The joule is named after the English physicist J.P. Joule (1818-1889).

journal, journals
1 (noun) A journal is a magazine which is published regularly and devoted to a particular subject, trade, or profession.
2 A journal is also a diary which someone keeps regularly.
[from Old French *jurnal* meaning 'daily']

journalism
(noun) Journalism is the work of collecting, writing, and publishing news in newpapers, magazines, and on television and radio.
journalist (noun), journalistic (adjective).

journey, journeys, journeying, journeyed
1 (noun) A journey is the act of travelling from one place to another.
2 (verb; a formal use) To journey somewhere means to travel there, e.g. *It got colder as he journeyed north.*
[from Old French *journee* meaning 'day' or 'a day's travelling']

Similar words: (sense 1) expedition, voyage

joust, jousts, jousting, jousted
1 (noun) In medieval times, a joust was a competition between knights fighting on horseback, using lances.
2 (verb) To joust means to fight in a joust.

jovial
(adjective) cheerful and friendly.
jovially (adverb), joviality (noun).
[from Latin *jovialis*, meaning 'of Jupiter']

jowl, jowls
1 (noun) Someone's jowls are the lower parts of their cheeks, over their jawbones.
2 (phrase) **Cheek by jowl** means very close together.

joy, joys
1 (noun) Joy is a feeling of great happiness.
2 (an informal use) Joy also means success or luck, e.g. *Any joy at the job centre?*
3 A joy is something that makes you happy or gives you pleasure.

joyful
1 (adjective) causing pleasure and happiness.
2 Someone who is joyful is extremely happy.
joyfully (adverb), **joyfulness** (noun).

joyless
(adjective) giving or experiencing no happiness or pleasure, e.g. *a joyless marriage.*

joyous
(adjective; a formal word) joyful.
joyously (adverb).

joyride, joyrides
(noun) A joyride is a drive in a stolen car for pleasure.
joyriding (noun), **joyrider** (noun).

joystick, joysticks
(noun) A joystick is a lever in an aircraft which the pilot uses to control height and direction.

JP an abbreviation for **Justice of the Peace.**

jubilant
(adjective) feeling or expressing great happiness or triumph.
jubilantly (adverb).
[from Latin *jubilans* meaning 'shouting for joy']

jubilation
(noun) Jubilation is a feeling of great happiness and triumph.

jubilee, jubilees
(noun) A jubilee is a special anniversary of an event such as a coronation, e.g. *the Queen's Silver Jubilee in 1977.*
[from Hebrew *yobhel* meaning 'ram's horn'; rams' horns were blown during festivals and celebrations]

Judaism (pronounced **joo**-day-i-zm)
(noun) Judaism is the religion of the Jewish people. It is based on a belief in one God, and draws its laws and authority from the Old Testament.
Judaic (adjective).

judder, judders, juddering, juddered
(verb) To judder means to shake and vibrate noisily and violently.

judge, judges, judging, judged
1 (noun) A judge is the person in a law court who has the power to decide how the law should be applied to people who appear in the court.
2 A judge is also someone who decides the winner in a contest or competition.
3 (verb) If you judge someone or something, you form an opinion about them based on the evidence or information that you have.

4 To judge a contest or competition means to decide on the winner.
judgment or **judgement** (noun).

Similar words: (sense 2) adjudicator, umpire, referee (sense 4) adjudicate, referee, umpire

judicial
(adjective) relating to judgment or to justice, e.g. *a judicial enquiry.*

judiciary
(noun) The judiciary is the branch of government concerned with justice and the legal system.

judicious
(adjective) sensible and showing good judgment.
judiciously (adverb).

judo
(noun) Judo is a sport in which two people try to force each other to the ground using special throwing techniques. It originated in Japan as a form of self-defence.
[from Japanese *ju do* meaning 'gentleness art']

jug, jugs
(noun) A jug is a container with a lip or spout used for holding or serving liquids.

juggernaut, juggernauts
(noun) A juggernaut is a large heavy lorry.
[from Hindi *Jagannath*, the name of a huge idol of the god Krishna, which every year is wheeled through the streets of Puri in India]

juggle, juggles, juggling, juggled
(verb) To juggle means to throw balls or other objects into the air, catching them in sequence, and tossing them up again so there are several in the air at one time.
juggler (noun).
[from Old French *jogler* meaning 'to perform as a jester']

jugular, jugulars
(noun) The jugular or jugular vein is one of the veins in the neck which carry blood from the head back to the heart.
[from Latin *jugulum* meaning 'throat']

juice, juices
1 (noun) Juice is the liquid that can be squeezed or extracted from fruit, vegetables, or meat.
2 Juices in the body are fluids, e.g. *gastric juices.*

juicy, juicier, juiciest
1 (adjective) Juicy food has a lot of juice in it.
2 Something that is juicy is interesting, exciting, or scandalous, e.g. *a juicy part for an actor... a juicy bit of news.*
juicily (adverb), **juiciness** (noun).

jujitsu (pronounced joo-jit-soo)
(noun) Jujitsu is a form of Japanese self-defence in which no weapons are used, and two opponents try to unbalance each other through strength and skill. Judo developed from jujitsu.
[from Japanese *ju jutsu* meaning 'gentleness art']

jukebox, jukeboxes
(noun) A jukebox is a large record player found in cafes and pubs which automatically plays a selected record when coins are inserted.

July
(noun) July is the seventh month of the year. It
has 31 days.
[from Latin *Julius*, the month of July, named
after Julius Caesar by the Romans]

jumble, jumbles, jumbling, jumbled
1 (noun) A jumble is an untidy muddle of things.
2 Jumble consists of articles for a jumble sale.
2 (verb) To jumble things means to mix them up
untidily.

jumble sale, jumble sales
(noun) A jumble sale is an event at which cheap
second-hand clothes and other articles are sold
to raise money, usually for a charity.

jumbo, jumbos
1 (noun) A jumbo or jumbo jet is a large jet
aeroplane that can carry several hundred
passengers.
2 (adjective) very large, e.g. *a jumbo packet of
soap powder.*
[from *Jumbo*, the name of a famous 19th-century
elephant]

jump, jumps, jumping, jumped
1 (verb) To jump means to spring off the ground
or some other surface using your leg muscles.
2 To jump something means to spring off the
ground and move over or across it.
3 If you jump at something such as an
opportunity, you accept it eagerly.
4 If you jump on someone, you criticize them
suddenly and forcefully.
5 If someone jumps, they make a sudden sharp
movement of surprise.
6 If people jump from one subject to another,
they stop talking about one thing and
unexpectedly start talking about something else.
7 If an amount or level jumps, it suddenly
increases.
8 (noun) A jump is a spring into the air,
sometimes over an object.
9 (an informal phrase) If you **jump down
someone's throat**, you say something angrily to
them, often in reply to something they have said.

Similar words: (senses 1 and 8) bound, gambol, leap,
spring
(sense 2) vault, hurdle, spring

jumped-up
(adjective) If you describe someone as
jumped-up, you mean that they are conceited
because they have risen from a low status or
position.

jumper, jumpers
(noun) A jumper is a knitted garment for the top
half of the body.

jump jet, jump jets
(noun) A jump jet is a jet aircraft that can take
off and land vertically.

jump lead, jump leads
(noun) A jump lead is a short cable used to make
an electrical connection between one terminal
and another.

jump suit, jump suits
(noun) A jump suit is a one-piece garment
combining both top and trousers.

jumpy, jumpier, jumpiest
(adjective) nervous and worried.
jumpily (adverb), **jumpiness** (noun).

junction, junctions
(noun) A junction is a place where roads or
railway lines meet, join, or cross.

junction box, junction boxes
(noun) A junction box is a box in which electrical
wires or cables are safely connected.

juncture, junctures
(noun) A juncture is a point in time which is
important to a process or series of events, e.g.
*Any move at this juncture would be interpreted
as weakness.*
[from Latin *jungere* meaning 'to join']

June
(noun) June is the sixth month of the year. It has
30 days.
[from Latin *Junius*, the month of June, probably
from the name of an important Roman family]

jungle, jungles
1 (noun) A jungle is a dense tropical forest.
2 A jungle is also a tangled mass of plants or
other objects.
[from Hindi *jangal* meaning 'wasteland']

junior, juniors
1 (adjective) Someone who is junior to other
people has a lower position in an organization.
2 Junior also means younger.
3 relating to childhood, e.g. *junior school.*
4 (noun) A junior is someone who holds an
unimportant position in an organization.
[from Latin *juvenis* meaning 'young']

juniper, junipers
(noun) A juniper is an evergreen shrub with
purple berries which may be used in cooking,
medicines, and in flavouring gin.

junk, junks
1 (noun) Junk is old or second-hand articles
which are sold cheaply or are discarded.
2 If you think something is junk, you think it is
worthless rubbish.
3 A junk is a Chinese sailing boat with a flat
bottom, high poop, and square sails.
[senses 1-2 are from Middle English *jonke*
meaning 'old rope'; sense 3 is from Javanese *jon*
meaning 'boat']

junket, junkets
1 (noun; an informal use) A junket is an official
trip or visit paid for with public money.
2 Junket is a dessert made of milk set with
rennet.
[from Old French *jonquette* meaning 'rush' or
'reed'; junkets were once served in rush baskets]

junk food
(noun) Junk food is food low in nutritional value
which is eaten as well as or instead of proper
meals.

junkie, junkies
(noun; an informal word) A junkie is a drug addict.

junta, juntas (pronounced **jun**-ter)
(noun) A junta is a political group, usually of military officers, which holds power in a country after gaining it by force and not through election. [from Spanish *junta* meaning 'council']

Jupiter
(noun) Jupiter is the largest planet in the solar system and the fifth from the sun.

jurisdiction
1 (noun; a formal word) Jurisdiction is the power or right of the courts to apply laws and make legal judgments, e.g. *The offender was removed from the jurisdiction of the Juvenile Court.*
2 Jurisdiction is power or authority, e.g. *The Governor had no jurisdiction over prices.*

jurisprudence
(noun; a formal word) Jurisprudence is the study of law and the principles on which laws are based.

jurist, jurists
(noun; a formal word) A jurist is a person who is an expert on law.

juror, jurors
(noun) A juror is a member of a jury.

jury, juries
1 (noun) A jury is a group of 12 people in a court of law who have been selected to listen to the facts of a case on trial, and to decide whether the accused person is guilty or not.
2 A jury is also a group of people chosen to judge the winner of a competition. [from Old French *jurer* meaning 'to swear']

just
1 (adjective) fair and impartial, e.g. *a just decision.*
2 morally right or proper, e.g. *a just reward.*
3 (adverb) If something has just happened, it happened a very short time ago.
4 If you just do something, you do it by a very small amount, e.g. *We only just won.*
5 simply or only, e.g. *We are just good friends.*
6 exactly, e.g. *It's just what I wanted.*
justly (adverb).

justice, justices
1 (noun) Justice is fairness and reasonableness.
2 The system of justice in a country is the way in which laws are maintained by the courts.
3 A justice is a judge or magistrate.
4 (phrase) If you **do yourself justice**, you do something as well as you are capable of doing it. [from Latin *justitia* meaning 'justice']

Justice of the Peace, Justices of the Peace
(noun) A Justice of the Peace or JP is a person who is appointed to act as an unpaid judge in a local court of law and to deal with the less serious crimes.

justify, justifies, justifying, justified
(verb) If you justify an action or idea, you prove or explain why it is reasonable or necessary.
justification (noun), **justifiable** (adjective).
[from Latin *justus* + *facere* meaning 'to make just']

jut, juts, jutting, jutted
(verb) If something juts out, it sticks out beyond or above a surface or edge.

Similar words: stick out, project, protrude

jute
(noun) Jute is a strong fibre made from the bark of an Asian plant, used to make rope and sacking. [from Bengali *jhuto*]

juvenile, juveniles
1 (adjective) suitable for young people.
2 childish and rather silly.
3 (noun) A juvenile is a young person not old enough to be considered an adult. [from Latin *juvenis* meaning 'young']

juvenile delinquent, juvenile delinquents
(noun) A juvenile delinquent is a young person guilty of a crime or of violent behaviour.
juvenile delinquency (noun).

juxtapose, juxtaposes, juxtaposing, juxtaposed
(verb) If you juxtapose things or ideas, you put them side by side or close together, often to emphasize the difference between them.
juxtaposition (noun).
[from Latin *juxta* meaning 'near to' + *position*]

K

K a symbol representing the number 1,000.

kaftan, kaftans; also spelled **caftan**
(noun) A kaftan is a long loose coat worn by men in some Eastern countries.
[from Turkish *qaftan*]

kale
(noun) Kale is a type of cabbage with large crinkled leaves.

kaleidoscope, kaleidoscopes (pronounced kal-**eye**-dos-skope)
(noun) A kaleidoscope is a toy consisting of a tube with a hole at one end. When you look through the hole and twist the other end of the tube, you can see a changing pattern of colours.
[from Greek *kalos* meaning 'beautiful', *eidos* meaning 'shape', and *skopein* meaning 'to look at']

kaleidoscopic
(adjective) colourful and constantly changing.

kamikaze
(noun) In the Second World War, a kamikaze was a Japanese pilot who performed a suicide mission by flying an aircraft loaded with explosives directly into an enemy target.

kangaroo, kangaroos
(noun) A kangaroo is a large Australian marsupial with very strong back legs which it uses for jumping.

kangaroo court, kangaroo courts
(noun) A kangaroo court is an unofficial court set up by a group of people, for example prisoners, to settle a dispute among themselves.

kaolin (pronounced **kay**-oh-lin)
(noun) Kaolin is a type of fine white clay used to make bone china and in some medicines, e.g. *kaolin and morphine mixture.*

kapok (pronounced **kay**-pok)
(noun) Kapok is a soft white fibre used for stuffing pillows, cushions, and sleeping bags.
[a Malay word]

karate (pronounced kar-**rat**-ee)
(noun) Karate is a sport in which people fight each other using only their hands, elbows, feet, and legs. Karate was originally a form of self-defence in Japan.
[from Japanese *kara* + *te* meaning 'empty hand']

kayak, kayaks (pronounced **ky**-ak)
(noun) A kayak is a covered canoe with a small opening for the person sitting in it, originally used by Eskimos.
[an Eskimo word]

kebab, kebabs
(noun) A kebab consists of pieces of meat or vegetable stuck on a stick and grilled.
[from Arabic *kabab* meaning 'roast meat']

kedgeree
(noun) Kedgeree is a cooked dish consisting of fish, rice, and eggs.
[from Hindi *khicari*]

keel, keels, keeling, keeled
1 (noun) The keel of a ship is the specially shaped bottom which supports the sides and sits in the water.
2 (verb) If someone or something keels over, they fall down sideways.

keen, keener, keenest
1 (adjective) Someone who is keen shows great eagerness and enthusiasm.
2 If you are keen on someone or something, you are attracted to or fond of them.
3 Keen senses let you see, hear, smell, and taste things very clearly or strongly.
4 A keen wind is very strong and cold.
keenly (adverb), **keenness** (noun).
[from Old English *cene* meaning 'fierce' or 'brave']

Similar words: (sense 1) eager, enthusiastic, zealous, ardent, avid

keep, keeps, keeping, kept
1 (verb) To keep someone or something in a particular condition means to make them stay in that condition, e.g. *We tried running around to keep warm.*
2 If you keep something, you have it and look after it.
3 If you keep doing something, you do it repeatedly or continuously, e.g. *He kept saying he didn't understand.*
4 If you keep a promise, you do what you promised to do.
5 If you keep a secret, you do not tell anyone else.
6 If you keep a diary, you write something in it every day.
7 If you keep someone from going somewhere, you delay them so that they are late.
8 To keep someone means to provide them with money, food, and clothing.
9 To keep something such as a shop means to own it and run it as a business.
10 If food keeps, it stays fresh.
11 (noun) Your keep is the cost of the food you eat, your housing, and your clothing, e.g. *My father gives me £20 a week towards my keep.*
12 A keep is the stronghold of a castle.

Similar words: (sense 1) retain, maintain, hold, preserve, store, uphold

keep in with
(phrasal verb) If you keep in with people, you make an effort to remain friendly with them.

keep up
(phrasal verb) If you keep up with other people, you move or work at the same speed as they do.

keeper, keepers
1 (noun) A keeper is a person whose job is to look after the animals in a zoo.
2 A keeper is also a goalkeeper in football or hockey.

keeping
1 (noun) If something is in your keeping, it has been given to you to look after for a while.
2 (phrase) If one thing is **in keeping with** another, the two things are suitable or appropriate together.

keepsake, keepsakes
(noun) A keepsake is something that someone gives you to remind you of a particular person or event.

Similar words: memento, souvenir

keg, kegs
(noun) A keg is a small barrel.

kelp
(noun) Kelp is a type of brown seaweed.

kelvin, kelvins
(noun) The kelvin is the SI unit of thermodynamic temperature. It is named after the British physicist Baron Kelvin (1824-1907).

kennel, kennels
1 (noun) A kennel is a shelter for a dog.
2 A kennels is a place where dogs can be boarded, or where they are bred.

Kenyan, Kenyans (pronounced **keen**-yan)
1 (adjective) belonging or relating to Kenya.
2 (noun) A Kenyan is someone who comes from Kenya.

kerb, kerbs
(noun) A kerb is the raised edge at the point where a pavement joins onto a road.

kernel, kernels
1 (noun) A kernel is the part of a nut that is inside the shell.
2 The kernel of a problem or issue is the most important aspect of it.

kerosene
(noun) Kerosene is the same as paraffin.

kestrel, kestrels
(noun) A kestrel is a type of small falcon that kills and eats other birds and small animals.

ketch, ketches
(noun) A ketch is a sailing ship with two masts.

ketchup
(noun) Ketchup is a cold sauce, usually made from tomatoes.
[from Chinese *koe* + *tsiap* meaning 'seafood sauce']

kettle, kettles
1 (noun) A kettle is a metal container with a spout, which you use to boil water in.
2 (phrase) If you call something **a different kettle of fish**, you mean that it is a completely different state of affairs.
[from Latin *catillus* meaning 'small cooking pot']

kettledrum, kettledrums
(noun) A kettledrum is a large drum with a curved bottom.

key, keys, keying, keyed
1 (noun) A key is a shaped piece of metal that fits into a hole so that you can unlock a door, wind a clockwork mechanism, or start a car.
2 The keys on a typewriter, piano, or cash register are the buttons that you press to use it.
3 In music, a key is a scale of notes.
4 A key is also an explanation of the symbols used in a map or diagram.
5 (verb) If you key in information on a computer keyboard, you type it.

keyboard, keyboards
(noun) A keyboard is a row of levers or buttons on a piano, organ, typewriter, or computer.

keystone, keystones
(noun) A keystone is the central stone in an arch, which keeps the other stones in place.

kg an abbreviation for 'kilograms'.

khaki (pronounced **kah**-kee)
1 (noun) Khaki is a strong yellowish-brown material, used especially for military uniforms.
2 (noun and adjective) yellowish-brown.
[from Urdu *kaki* meaning 'dusty']

Khoisan (pronounced **koy**-sahn)
(noun) Khoisan is the name of a group of languages, including Bushman and Hottentot, spoken in southern Africa.

kHz an abbreviation for 'kilohertz'.

kibbutz, kibbutzim (pronounced kib-**boots**)
(noun) A kibbutz is a place of work in Israel, for example a farm or factory, where the workers live together and share all the duties and income.
[from modern Hebrew *qibbus* meaning 'gathering']

kick, kicks, kicking, kicked
1 (verb) If you kick something, you hit it with your foot.
2 (noun) If you give something a kick, you hit it with your foot.
3 (an informal use) If you get a kick out of doing something, you enjoy doing it very much.

kick off
(phrasal verb) When players kick off, they start a football or rugby match.
kick-off (noun).

kid, kids, kidding, kidded
1 (noun; an informal use) A kid is a child.
2 A kid is also a young goat.
3 (verb) If you kid people, you tease them by deceiving them in fun.

kidnap, kidnaps, kidnapping, kidnapped
(verb) To kidnap somone means to take them away by force and demand a ransom in exchange for returning them.
kidnapper (noun), **kidnapping** (noun).
[from *kid* + *nap* meaning 'child stealing'; in the 17th century children were kidnapped to work on American plantations]

Similar words: abduct, snatch

kidney, kidneys
(noun) Your kidneys are two organs in your body that remove waste products from your blood.

kidney bean, kidney beans
(noun) Kidney beans are a type of edible dark red bean.

kill, kills, killing, killed
1 (verb) To kill a person, animal, or plant means to make them die.
2 If something is killing you, it is causing you severe pain or discomfort, e.g. *My shoes are killing me.*
3 (phrase) If you **kill time**, you do something unimportant while waiting.
4 (noun) The kill is the moment when a hunter kills an animal.

Similar words: (sense 1) butcher, murder, slay

kiln, kilns
(noun) A kiln is an oven for baking china or pottery until it becomes hard and dry.
[from Latin *culina* meaning 'kitchen' or 'cooking stove']

kilo, kilos
(noun) A kilo is a kilogram.

kilogram, kilograms
(noun) The kilogram is the SI unit of mass. One kilogram is equal to 1000 grams.

kilohertz
(noun) A kilohertz is a unit of frequency equal to one thousand cycles per second.

kilometre, kilometres
(noun) A kilometre is a unit of distance equal to one thousand metres.

kilowatt, kilowatts
(noun) A kilowatt is a unit of power equal to one thousand watts.

kilt, kilts
(noun) A kilt is a tartan skirt worn by men as part of Scottish Highland dress.
[from northern English *kilt* meaning 'to tuck up']

kimono, kimonos
(noun) A kimono is a long, loose garment with wide sleeves and a sash, worn in Japan.

kin
(plural noun) Your kin are your relatives.

Similar words: family, relations, kinsfolk

kind, kinds; kinder, kindest
1 (noun) A particular kind of thing is something of the same type or sort as other things.
2 (adjective) Someone who is kind is considerate and generous towards other people.
3 (phrase) If you pay someone **in kind**, you give them goods as payment instead of money.
kindly (adverb), **kindness** (noun).

Similar words: (sense 1) breed, genus, species, family, type
(sense 2) benevolent, magnanimous, kindhearted

kindergarten, kindergartens
(noun) A kindergarten is a school for children who are too young to go to primary school.

[from German *Kinder* + *Garten* meaning 'children's garden']

kindhearted
(adjective) considerate and sympathetic.

kindle, kindles, kindling, kindled
1 (verb) If you kindle a fire, you light it.
2 If something kindles a feeling in you, it causes you to have that feeling.

kindling
(noun) Kindling is bits of dry wood or paper that you use to start a fire.

kindred
1 (adjective) If you say that someone is a kindred spirit, you mean that they have the same interests or opinions that you have.
2 (noun; an old-fashioned use) Your kindred are your relatives.
[from Old English *cyn* meaning 'family']

kinetic, kinetics
1 (adjective; a technical use) relating to movement.
2 (noun) Kinetics is the scientific study of the way energy behaves when something moves.
[from Greek *kinein* meaning 'move']

kinetic energy
(noun) Kinetic energy is the energy that is produced when something moves.

king, kings
1 (noun) The king of a country is a man who is the head of state in the country, and who inherited his position from his parents.
2 In chess, the king is a piece which can only move one square at a time. When a king cannot move away from a position where it can be taken, the game is lost.
3 In a pack of cards, a king is a card with a picture of a king on it. It is more valuable than a queen and less valuable than an ace.

Similar words: (sense 1) monarch, sovereign, ruler

kingdom, kingdoms
1 (noun) A kingdom is a country that is governed by a king or queen.
2 The divisions of the natural world are called kingdoms, e.g. *the animal kingdom.*

kingfisher, kingfishers
(noun) A kingfisher is a brightly coloured bird that lives near water and feeds on fish.

kingpin, kingpins
(noun) The kingpin in a group or organization is the most important person in it.

king-size or king-sized
(adjective) larger than the normal size.

kink, kinks
(noun) A kink is a dent or curve in something which is normally straight.

kinky
(adjective; an informal word) having peculiar sexual tastes.

kinship
(noun) Kinship is a family relationship to other people.

kiosk, kiosks (pronounced **kee**-osk)
(noun) A kiosk is a covered stall on a street where you can buy sandwiches, newspapers, sweets, or cigarettes.
[from Turkish *kösk* meaning 'pavilion']

kip, kips, kipping, kipped (an informal word)
1 (noun) A kip is a period of sleep.
2 (verb) When you kip, you sleep.

kipper, kippers
(noun) A kipper is a smoked herring.

kirk, kirks
(noun) In Scottish English, a kirk is a church.

kiss, kisses, kissing, kissed
1 (verb) When you kiss someone, you touch them with your lips as a sign of love or affection.
2 (noun) When you give someone a kiss, you kiss them.

kiss of life
(noun) The kiss of life is a method of reviving someone by blowing air into their lungs.

kit, kits
1 (noun) A kit is a collection of things that you use for a sport or other activity.
2 A kit is also a set of parts that you put together to make something.

kitbag, kitbags
(noun) A kitbag is a long thin canvas bag often used by members of the armed forces.

kitchen, kitchens
(noun) A kitchen is a room used for cooking and preparing food.
[from Latin *coquere* meaning 'to cook']

kitchenette, kitchenettes
(noun) A kitchenette is a very small kitchen.

kite, kites
1 (noun) A kite is a frame covered with paper or cloth which is attached to a piece of string, and which you fly in the air.
2 A kite is also a large bird of prey with a long tail and long wings.

kith and kin
(noun) Your kith and kin are your friends and relations.

kitten, kittens
(noun) A kitten is a young cat.
[from Old French *chitoun* meaning 'small cat']

kitty, kitties
(noun) A kitty is a shared fund of money for common expenses.

kiwi, kiwis (pronounced kee-wee)
(noun) A kiwi is a type of bird found in New Zealand. Kiwis cannot fly.
[A Maori word]

kiwi fruit, kiwi fruits
(noun) A kiwi fruit is a fruit with a brown hairy skin and green flesh.

kleptomania
(noun) Kleptomania is an uncontrollable desire to steal things, occurring usually as a form of mental illness.

km an abbreviation for 'kilometres'.

knack
(noun) A knack is an ability to do something difficult with apparent ease, e.g. *He had the knack of always guessing the right answer.*

knapsack, knapsacks
(noun) A knapsack is a bag which is carried over the shoulder or on the back and is used for carrying food and belongings.
[from Old German *knapsack* meaning 'bag for food']

knave, knaves (an old-fashioned word)
1 (noun) A knave is a dishonest or mischievous man.
2 In card games, a knave is the same as a jack.
[from Old English *cnafa* meaning 'boy or male servant']

knead, kneads, kneading, kneaded
(verb) If you knead dough, you press it and squeeze it with your hands before baking it.

knee, knees
(noun) Your knee is the joint in your leg between your ankle and your hip.

kneecap, kneecaps
(noun) Your kneecaps are the bones at the front of your knees.

kneel, kneels, kneeling, knelt
(verb) When you kneel, you bend your legs and lower your body until your knees are touching the ground.
[from Old English *cneo* meaning 'knee']

knell, knells
(noun; a literary word) A knell is the sound of a bell rung to announce a death or at a funeral.

knickers
(plural noun) Knickers are underpants worn by women and girls.

knick-knacks
(plural noun) Knick-knacks are small objects that people enjoy looking at and playing with, for example ornaments.

knife, knives; knifes, knifing, knifed
1 (noun) A knife is a sharp metal tool that you use to cut things.
2 (verb) To knife someone means to stab them with a knife.

knight, knights, knighting, knighted
1 (noun) A knight is a man who has been given the title 'Sir' by the King or Queen.
2 In medieval Europe, a knight was a man who served a monarch or lord as a mounted soldier.
3 A knight is a chess piece that is usually in the shape of a horse's head.
4 (verb) To knight a man means to give him the title 'Sir'.
knighthood (noun).
[from Old English *cniht* meaning 'servant']

knit, knits, knitting, knitted or **knit**
1 (verb) If you knit a piece of clothing, you make it by working lengths of wool together, either using needles held in the hand, or with a machine.
2 If you knit your brows, you frown.
3 When broken bones knit, they heal.
[from Old English *cnyttan* meaning 'to knot']

knob, knobs
1 (noun) A knob is a round handle.
2 A knob of butter is a small amount of butter.

knock, knocks, knocking, knocked
1 (verb) If you knock on something, you strike it with your hand or fist.
2 If you knock a part of your body against something, you bump into it quite forcefully.
3 If a piece of machinery is knocking, it is making a repeated banging noise.
4 (an informal use) To knock someone means to criticize them.
5 (noun) A knock is a firm blow on something solid, e.g. *There were three knocks on the door.*

knock out
(phrasal verb) To knock someone out means to hit them so hard that they become unconscious.

knocker, knockers
(noun) A knocker is a metal lever attached to a door, which you use to knock on the door.

knockout, knockouts
1 (noun) A knockout is a punch in boxing which succeeds in knocking a boxer unconscious.
2 A knockout is also a competition in which competitors are eliminated in each round until only the winner is left.

knoll, knolls (rhymes with **roll**)
(noun; a literary word) A knoll is a gently sloping hill with a rounded top.

knot, knots, knotting, knotted
1 (noun) A knot is a fastening made by looping a piece of string around itself and pulling the ends tight.
2 A knot in a piece of wood is a small lump that is visible on the surface.
3 A knot of people is a small group of them.
4 (a technical use) A knot is a unit of speed used for ships and aircraft. One knot is equal to one nautical mile per hour.
5 (verb) If you knot a piece of string, you tie a knot in it.

know, knows, knowing, knew, known
1 (verb) If you know a fact, you have it in your mind and you do not need to learn it.
2 People you know are not strangers because you have met them and spoken to them.
3 (an informal phrase) If you are **in the know**, you are one of a small number of people who share a secret.

know-how
(noun) Know-how is the ability to do something that is quite difficult or technical.

knowing
(adjective) A knowing look is one that shows that you know or understand something that other people do not.
knowingly (adverb).

knowledge
(noun) Knowledge is all the information and facts that you know.

Similar words: learning, know-how

knowledgeable
(adjective) Someone who is knowledgeable knows a lot.

knuckle, knuckles
(noun) Your knuckles are the joints at the end of your fingers where they join your hand.

knuckle-duster, knuckle-dusters
(noun) A knuckle-duster is a piece of metal that fits over the knuckles and is used as a weapon.

koala, koalas
(noun) A koala is an Australian marsupial with grey fur and small tufted ears. Koalas live in trees and eat eucalyptus leaves.
[from Australian Aboriginal *kula*]

kookaburra, kookaburras
(noun) A kookaburra is a type of large Australian kingfisher, with a cackling cry.

Koran (pronounced kaw-**rahn**)
(noun) The Koran is the holy book of Islam.
[from Arabic *kara'a* meaning 'to read']

Korean, Koreans (pronounced kor-**ree**-an)
1 (adjective) relating or belonging to Korea.
2 (noun) A Korean is someone who comes from Korea.
3 Korean is the main language spoken in Korea.

kosher (pronounced **koh**-sher)
(adjective) Kosher food has been specially prepared to be eaten according to Jewish law.
[from Hebrew *kasher* meaning 'right' or 'proper']

kowtow, kowtows, kowtowing, kowtowed
(verb) If you kowtow to someone in authority, you behave very humbly and respectfully towards them.
[from Chinese *k'o + t'ou* meaning 'to knock the head'; from the custom of showing respect by touching the ground with the forehead]

krypton
(noun) Krypton is a whitish gas used in fluorescent lamps. It is a chemical element with the atomic number 36. Its symbol is Kr.

kudos (pronounced **kjoo**-doss)
(noun) Kudos is personal fame or glory.

kung fu (pronounced kung **foo**)
(noun) Kung fu is a Chinese style of fighting which involves using only your hands and feet.
[a Chinese expression]

Kurd, Kurds
(noun) The Kurds are a group of people who live mainly in eastern Turkey, northern Iraq, and western Iran.

Kurdish
1 (adjective) belonging or relating to the Kurds.
2 (noun) Kurdish is the language spoken by the Kurds.

kW an abbreviation for 'kilowatts'.

L

l an abbreviation for 'litres'.

lab, labs
(noun; an informal word) A lab is a laboratory.

label, labels, labelling, labelled
1 (noun) A label is a piece of paper or plastic attached to something as an identification.
2 (verb) If you label something, you put a label on it.

laboratory, laboratories
(noun) A laboratory is a place where scientific experiments are carried out.
[from Latin *laboratorium* meaning 'workshop']

laborious
(adjective) needing a lot of effort or time.
laboriously (adverb).

labour, labours, labouring, laboured
1 (noun) Labour is hard work.
2 The workforce of a country or industry is sometimes called its labour, e.g. *skilled labour*.
3 Labour or the Labour Party is one of the two main political parties in Britain. It believes in social equality.
4 Labour is also the last stage of pregnancy when a woman gives birth to a baby.
5 (verb; an old-fashioned use) To labour means to work hard.
6 (phrase) If you **labour a point**, you talk about it much longer than you need to.
7 If you **labour under a false impression**, you believe something which is not true.
labourer (noun).

Similar words: (sense 1) industry, toil, slog, travail (sense 5) slave, toil, slog, travail

labrador, labradors
(noun) A labrador is a large dog with short black or golden hair.

laburnum, laburnums
(noun) A laburnum is a small tree with poisonous flowers.

labyrinth, labyrinths (pronounced **lab**-er-inth)
(noun) A labyrinth is a complicated series of paths or passages.

lace, laces, lacing, laced
1 (noun) Lace is a very fine decorated cloth made with a lot of holes in it.
2 Laces are cords with which you fasten your shoes.
3 (verb) When you lace up your shoes, you tie a bow in the laces.
4 To lace someone's drink means to put some alcohol in it without their knowing.
lacy (adjective).

lacerate, lacerates, lacerating, lacerated
(pronounced **lass**-er-ate)
(verb) If something lacerates your skin, it cuts it very deeply.
laceration (noun).
[from Latin *lacerare* meaning 'to tear']

lachrymose (pronounced **lak**-rim-ohs)
(adjective; a formal word) Someone who is lachrymose has a tendency to cry very easily.

lack, lacks, lacking, lacked
1 (noun) If there is a lack of something, it is not present when or where it is needed.
2 (verb) If something is lacking, it is not present when or where it is needed.
3 If you lack something, you do not have it.

Similar words: (sense 1) absence, dearth, shortage, scarcity, want, paucity

lackadaisical (pronounced lakka-**day**-zikl)
(adjective) careless and half-hearted.

lackey, lackeys
(noun) If you call someone a lackey, you mean that they obey orders without question.

lacklustre (pronounced **lak**-luss-ter)
(adjective) dull and unexciting.

laconic (pronounced lak-**kon**-ik)
(adjective) using very few words.
[from Greek *Lakonikas* meaning 'Spartan'. The Spartans were famous for using few words]

lacquer, lacquers, lacquering, lacquered
(pronounced **lak**-er)
1 (noun) Lacquer is thin, clear paint that you put on wood to protect it and make it shiny.
2 (verb) If you lacquer wood, you paint it with lacquer.
[from Old French *lacre* meaning 'sealing wax']

lacrosse
(noun) Lacrosse is an outdoor ball game in which two teams try to score goals using long sticks with nets on the end of them.
[from Canadian French *la crosse* meaning 'the hooked stick']

lactate, lactates, lactating, lactated
(verb) When a female mammal lactates, she produces milk with which to feed her young.
lactation (noun).
[from Latin *lac* meaning 'milk']

lactose
(noun) Lactose is the natural sugar that occurs in milk. It is sometimes used for making medicines and baby food.

lad, lads
(noun) A lad is a boy or young man.

ladder, ladders, laddering, laddered
1 (noun) A ladder is a wooden or metal frame used for climbing which consists of horizontal steps fixed to two vertical poles.
2 A ladder is also a series of stages in someone's career.
3 If your stockings or tights have a ladder in them, they have vertical, ladder-like tear in them.
4 (verb) If you ladder your stockings or tights, you get a ladder in them.

laddie, laddies
(noun) In Scottish English a laddie is a boy.

laden (pronounced **lay**-den)
(adjective) To be laden with something means to be carrying a lot of it, e.g. *She was laden with books.*

la-di-da or **la-dih-dah**
(adjective; an informal expression) putting on an exaggeratedly genteel manner.

ladle, ladles, ladling, ladled
1 (noun) A ladle is a long-handled spoon with a deep, round bowl, which you use to serve soup.
2 (verb) If you ladle out food, you serve it with a ladle.

lady, ladies
1 (noun) A lady is a woman, especially one who is considered to be polite and socially correct.
2 Lady is a title used in front of the name of a woman from the nobility, such as a lord's wife.

ladybird, ladybirds
(noun) A ladybird is a small flying beetle with a round red body patterned with black spots.

lady-in-waiting, ladies-in-waiting
(noun) A lady-in-waiting is a woman from the upper classes who acts as companion to a queen or princess.

lady-killer, lady-killers
(noun; an informal word) A lady-killer is a man who attracts women, seduces them, and then leaves them to look for someone new.

ladylike
(adjective) behaving in a polite and socially correct way.

Ladyship, Ladyships
(noun) You address a woman who has the title 'Lady' as 'Your Ladyship'.

lag, lags, lagging, lagged
1 (verb) To lag behind means to make slower progress than other people or processes.
2 To lag pipes or water tanks means to wrap cloth round them to prevent the water inside freezing in cold weather.
3 (noun) A time lag is a period of time that passes between one event and another.

Similar words: (sense 1) trail, fall behind

lager, lagers
(noun) Lager is light-coloured beer.
[from German *Lagerbier* meaning 'beer for storing']

laggard, laggards
(noun; an old-fashioned word) A laggard is someone who is slower than other people.

lagging
(noun) Lagging is material that you wrap round pipes and water tanks to prevent the water freezing in cold weather.

lagoon, lagoons
(noun) A lagoon is an area of seawater separated from the sea by a reef or sandbank.
[from Latin *lacuna* meaning 'pond']

laid the past tense and past participle of **lay**.

lain the past participle of some meanings of **lie**.

lair, lairs
(noun) A lair is a place where a wild animal lives.

laird, lairds (rhymes with **dared**)
(noun) A laird is a landowner in Scotland.

laissez faire or **laisser faire** (pronounced less-ay **fare**)
(noun) A policy of laissez faire is one which allows people to trade and conduct business with very few government restrictions.
[from French *laissez faire* meaning 'let them act']

laity (pronounced **lay**-it-ee)
(noun; a formal word) The laity are all the people who are not members of a particular profession, especially people who belong to a church but are not members of the clergy.

lake, lakes
(noun) A lake is an area of fresh water surrounded by land.

lama, lamas
(noun) A lama is a Buddhist priest or monk.

lamb, lambs
1 (noun) A lamb is a young sheep.
2 Lamb is the meat from a lamb or a sheep.

lame, lames
1 (adjective) Someone who is lame has an injured leg and cannot walk easily.
2 A lame excuse is weak and unconvincing.
lamely (adverb), **lameness** (noun).

Similar words: (sense 2) feeble, thin, flimsy

lamé (pronounced **lah**-may)
(noun) Lamé is cloth that is shiny because it has gold or silver threads woven into it.

lament, laments, lamenting, lamented
1 (verb) To lament something means to express sorrow or regret about it.
2 (noun) A lament is an expression of sorrow or regret.
3 A lament is also a song or poem expressing grief at someone's death.

Similar words: (sense 1) bemoan, bewail

lamentable
(adjective) disappointing and regrettable.

laminated
(adjective) consisting of several thin sheets or layers stuck together, e.g. *laminated plastics.*
[from Latin *laminatus* meaning 'plated']

lamp, lamps
(noun) A lamp is a light that works by burning oil or gas, or by using electricity.
[from Greek *lampein* meaning 'to shine']

lampoon, lampoons, lampooning, lampooned
1 (verb) To lampoon someone means to ridicule them in a cartoon or piece of humorous writing.
2 (noun) A lampoon is a cartoon or piece of humorous writing that ridicules someone.

lamppost, lampposts
(noun) A lamppost is a tall column in a street, with a lamp at the top.

lamprey, lampreys (pronounced **lam**-pree)
(noun) A lamprey is an eel-like creature which attaches itself to other animals and feeds on them.

lampshade, lampshades
(noun) A lampshade is a decorative covering over an electric light bulb which prevents the bulb giving out too harsh a light.

lance, lances, lancing, lanced
1 (verb) To lance a boil or abscess means to stick a sharp instrument into it in order to release the fluid.
2 (noun) A lance is a long spear that used to be used by soldiers on horseback.

lance-corporal, lance-corporals
(noun) A lance-corporal is a noncommissioned officer of the lowest rank in the British army.

lancet, lancets
(noun) A lancet is a sharp double-edged knife used by doctors to cut into boils and abscesses.

land, lands, landing, landed
1 (noun) Land is an area of ground.
2 Land is also the part of the earth that is not covered by sea, lakes, or rivers.
3 A land is a country, e.g. *my native land.*
4 (verb) When a plane lands, it arrives back on the ground after a flight.
5 If you land something you have been trying to get, you succeed in getting it, e.g. *I finally landed a job with the BBC.*
6 To land a fish means to catch it while fishing.
7 If you land someone with something unpleasant, you cause them to have to deal with it.

landau, landaus (rhymes with **saw**)
(noun) A landau is a four-wheeled horse-drawn carriage used in former times. Landaus are named after Landau, the Bavarian town where they were first made.

landed
(adjective) owning a lot of land, e.g. *the landed gentry.*

landfall
(noun) Landfall is a first sighting of land made from a ship at the end of a voyage.

landing, landings
1 (noun) A landing is a flat area in a building at the top of a flight of stairs.
2 The landing of an aeroplane is its arrival back on the ground after a flight, e.g. *a safe landing.*
3 A landing is also a place where people get on and off boats.

landing gear
(noun) An aeroplane's landing gear is the wheels and supporting structure that are used when the aeroplane lands or is on the ground.

landing stage, landing stages
(noun) A landing stage is a platform at the edge of a river or lake where passengers can disembark or goods can be unloaded.

landlady, landladies
(noun) A landlady is a woman who owns a house or small hotel and who lets rooms to people.

landlocked
(adjective) A region or country that is landlocked is surrounded by land and has no sea coast.

landlord, landlords
(noun) A landlord is a man who owns a house or small hotel and who lets rooms to people.

landlubber, landlubbers
(noun; an old-fashioned word) A landlubber is a person who has no experience of sailing.

landmark, landmarks
1 (noun) A landmark is a noticeable feature in a landscape, which you can use to check your position.
2 A landmark is also an important stage in the development of something, e.g. *1832 was a landmark in the history of Parliament.*

land mine, land mines
(noun) A land mine is a bomb planted under the surface of the ground, which explodes when something heavy passes over it.

landscape, landscapes
1 (noun) The landscape is the view over an area of open land.
2 A landscape is a painting of the countryside.

landscape gardening
(noun) Landscape gardening is the art of designing and making gardens so that the new features look natural.

landslide, landslides
1 (noun) A landslide is loose earth and rocks falling down a mountainside.
2 In an election, a landslide is a victory won by a large number of votes.

lane, lanes
1 (noun) A lane is a narrow road, especially in the country.
2 A lane in a road is one of the strips marked with lines to guide drivers.

language, languages
1 (noun) A language is the system of words that the people of a country use to communicate with each other.
2 Your language is the style in which you express yourself, e.g. *The language of this essay is dull.*
3 Language is the study of the words and grammar of a particular language.
4 In computing, a language is a set of words or symbols that a computer will accept and which can be used in writing computer programs or giving instructions to the computer.
[from Latin *lingua* meaning 'tongue']

Similar words: (sense 2) speech, parlance, lingo, idiom

language laboratory, language laboratories
(noun) A language laboratory is a classroom equipped with tape recorders where students practise speaking and listening to a foreign language.

languid (pronounced **lang**-gwid)
(adjective) slow and lacking energy.
languidly (adverb).

languish, languishes, languishing, languished
(verb) If you languish, you endure an unpleasant
situation for a long time.

languor (pronounced **lang**-gur)
(noun; a literary word) Languor is inactivity and
unwillingness to do things.

lank
(adjective) Lank hair is straight and limp.

lanky, lankier, lankiest
(adjective) Someone who is lanky is tall and thin
and moves rather awkwardly.

Similar words: gangling, angular

lanolin or **lanoline**
(noun) Lanolin is a fatty substance found in
wool. It is used in making ointments and
cosmetics.
[from Latin *lana* meaning 'wool' and *oleum*
meaning 'oil']

lantern, lanterns
(noun) A lantern is a lamp in a metal frame with
glass sides.

lanthanide, lanthanides
(noun) A lanthanide is any element in the
lanthanide series.

lanthanide series
(noun) The lanthanide series is a class of 15
elements whose atomic numbers range from 57
to 71. They are also called rare-earth elements.

lanyard, lanyards
(noun) A lanyard is a piece of cord with a
whistle or knife attached to it, which is worn
round the neck, as part of a uniform.

lap, laps, lapping, lapped
1 (noun) Your lap is the flat area formed by your
thighs when you are sitting down.
2 A lap is one circuit of a running track or
racecourse.
3 (phrase) If you say that someone is living **in
the lap of luxury**, you mean they are rich and
have a very comfortable life.
4 (verb) When an animal laps up liquid, it drinks
using its tongue to get the liquid into its mouth.
5 If you lap someone in a race, you overtake
them when they are still on the previous lap.
6 When water laps against something, it gently
moves against it in little waves.

lapdog, lapdogs
(noun) A lapdog is a small dog kept as a pet.

lapel, lapels (pronounced lap-**el**)
(noun) A lapel is a flap which is joined on to the
collar of a jacket or coat.
[from Old English *læppa* meaning 'flap']

lapis lazuli
(noun) Lapis lazuli is a bright blue semiprecious
stone used in jewellery.

lapse, lapses, lapsing, lapsed
1 (noun) A lapse is a moment of bad behaviour
by someone who usually behaves well.
2 A lapse is also a slight mistake.
3 A lapse is also a period of time between two
events.
4 (verb) If you lapse into a different way of
behaving, you start behaving that way, e.g. *He
lapsed into an uneasy silence.*
5 If a legal document or contract lapses, it is not
renewed on the date when it expires.
[from Latin *lapsus* meaning 'error']

lapwing, lapwings
(noun) A lapwing is a black and white bird with
a crested head, often seen in flocks in fields.
Lapwings are also called peewits.

larceny
(noun) In law, larceny is the crime of stealing.

larch, larches
(noun) A larch is a deciduous tree which has
needle-shaped leaves and bears cones.

lard
(noun) Lard is fat from a pig, used in cooking.

larder, larders
(noun) A larder is a room in which you store
food, often next to a kitchen.

large, larger, largest
1 (adjective) Someone or something that is large
is much bigger than average.
2 (phrase) If a prisoner is **at large**, he or she has
escaped from prison.

largely
(adverb) to a great extent, e.g. *The story is
largely true.*

largess or **largesse** (pronounced lar-**jess**)
(noun; a formal word) Largess is great
generosity in giving money.

lark, larks, larking, larked
1 (noun) A lark is a small brown bird with a
distinctive song.
2 If you do something for a lark, you do it in a
high-spirited or mischievous way for amusement.
3 (verb) If you lark about, you enjoy yourself in
a high-spirited way.

larkspur, larkspurs
(noun) A larkspur is a plant with blue, pink, or
white spur-shaped flowers.

larva, larvae
(noun) A larva is an insect at the stage before it
becomes an adult. Larvae look like short, fat
worms.

laryngitis (pronounced lar-in-**jie**-tiss)
(noun) Laryngitis is an infection of the throat
which causes you to lose your voice.

larynx, larynxes or **larynges**
(noun) Your larynx is the part of your throat
containing the vocal cords, through which air
passes between your nose and lungs.

lasagne (pronounced laz-**zan**-ya)
(noun) Lasagne is an Italian dish made with wide
flat sheets of pasta, meat, and cheese sauce.
[from Latin *lasanum* meaning 'cooking pot']

lascivious (pronounced las-**siv**-ee-us)
(adjective) Someone who is lascivious shows an excessive interest in or desire for sex.

laser, lasers
(noun) A laser is a machine that produces a powerful concentrated beam of light which is used to cut very hard materials, in some kinds of surgery, and in modern telecommunications. [from the first letters of 'Light Amplification by Stimulated Emission of Radiation']

lash, lashes, lashing, lashed
1 (noun) Your lashes are the hairs growing on the edge of your eyelids.
2 A lash is a strip of leather at the end of a whip.
3 Lashes are blows struck with a whip.
4 (verb) To lash someone means to beat them with a whip.
5 If you lash things together, you tie them together.

lash out
(phrasal verb) To lash out at someone means to criticize them severely.

lashings
(plural noun) Lashings of something means a lot of it.

lass, lasses
(noun) A lass is a girl or young woman.

lassie, lassies
(noun) In Scottish English a lassie is a girl.

lassitude
(noun; a formal word) Lassitude is tiredness and unwillingness to become active.

lasso, lassoes or **lassos, lassoing, lassoed**
(pronounced las-**soo**)
1 (noun) A lasso is a length of rope with a noose at one end, used by cowboys to catch cattle and horses.
2 (verb) To lasso an animal means to catch it by throwing the noose of a lasso around its neck.

last, lasts, lasting, lasted
1 (adjective) The last thing or event is the most recent one, e.g. *last night... In the last lesson, we looked at the formation of crystals.*
2 The last thing that remains is the only one left after all the others have gone, e.g. *The last customers left at midnight.*
3 (adverb) If you last did something on a particular occasion, you have not done it since then, e.g. *I last saw him at Christmas.*
4 The thing that happens last in a sequence of events is the final one, e.g. *I always turn the lights out last.*
5 (verb) If something lasts, it continues to exist in sufficient quantity or quality, e.g. *These tomatoes won't last till Monday... a tradition that has lasted for over 400 years.*
6 (noun) A last is a piece of wood or metal in the shape of a foot, which is used to make or repair shoes.
7 (phrase) **At last** means after a long time, e.g. *At last it's stopped raining.*
lastly (adverb).

Similar words: (sense 5) endure, continue, hold out, survive

last-ditch
(adjective) A last-ditch attempt to do something is a final attempt to succeed when everything else has failed.

last post
(noun) The last post is a bugle call played at military funerals or to signal bedtime in military camps.

last rites
(plural noun) The last rites are a religious ceremony that priests administer to people who are about to die.

Last Supper
(noun) The Last Supper was the final meal Christ had with his disciples on the night before he was crucified.

latch, latches, latching, latched
1 (noun) A latch is a simple door fastening consisting of a metal bar which falls into a hook.
2 A latch is also a type of door lock which locks automatically when you close the door and which has to be opened with a key.
3 (verb; an informal use) If you latch onto someone or something, you become attached to them.
4 (phrase) If a door is **on the latch**, the lock has been set so that it does not automatically lock the door.

latchkey, latchkeys
(noun) A latchkey is a key which opens a door that has a latch.

late, later, latest
1 (adjective and adverb) Something that happens late happens towards the end of a period of time, e.g. *the late afternoon... late in the evening.*
2 If you arrive late, or do something late, you arrive or do it after the time you were expected to.
3 (adjective) A late event happens after the time when it usually takes place, e.g. *a late lunch.*
4 (a formal use) Late means dead, e.g. *the late Lord Stockton.*
5 (phrase) **Of late** means recently.

Similar words: (sense 2) belated, overdue, tardy

lately
(adverb) Events that happened lately happened recently.

latent
(adjective) A latent quality is hidden at the moment, but may emerge in the future, e.g. *She has, I am sure, a latent talent for music.* [from Latin *latere* meaning 'to lie hidden']

Similar words: potential, unrealized, dormant

latent heat
(noun) The latent heat of a substance is the heat it gives out or absorbs when it undergoes a physical change without changing its temperature.

lateral
(adjective) relating to the sides of something, or moving in a sideways direction.
[from Latin *latus* meaning 'side']

laterite
(noun) Laterite is a layer of hard, red soil formed through the washing out and depositing of iron and aluminium oxides by heavy rain in tropical regions.
[from Latin *later* meaning 'brick' or 'tile']

latex (pronounced **lay**-teks)
(noun) Latex is the milky white liquid taken from rubber trees and used to make rubber.
[from Latin *latex* meaning 'liquid' or 'fluid']

lath, laths (rhymes with **path**)
(noun) A lath is a thin strip of wood put on the inside of walls to give plaster something to stick to.

lathe, lathes
(noun) A lathe is a machine which holds and turns a piece of wood or metal against a tool in order to cut and shape it.

lather, lathers, lathering, lathered
1 (noun) Lather is the foam that you get when you rub soap in water.
2 (verb) If you lather something, you rub soap into it to create a lather in order to clean it.
[from Old English *leathor* meaning 'soap']

Latin, Latins
1 (noun) Latin is the language of ancient Rome.
2 (noun and adjective) Latins are people who speak languages closely related to Latin, such as French, Italian, Spanish, and Portuguese.
[from Latin *Latinus* meaning 'of Latium', a region of central Italy]

Latin America
(noun) Latin America consists of the countries in North, South, and Central America where Spanish or Portuguese is the main language.
Latin American (adjective).

latitude, latitudes
1 (noun) The latitude of a place is its distance north or south of the equator measured in degrees.
2 Latitude is the freedom to choose what you want to do or what you think.

latrine, latrines (pronounced lat-**reen**)
(noun) A latrine is a hole or trench in the ground used as a toilet at a camp.

latter
1 (adjective and noun) You use latter to refer to the second of two things that are mentioned, e.g. *the latter option... They found a hammer and a crowbar; the latter had been used to force a door.*
2 (adjective) Latter also describes the second or end part of something, e.g. *The latter half of July.*

latterly
(adverb; a formal word) Latterly means recently, e.g. *He has become more of a television personality, latterly on a chat show of his own.*

lattice, lattices
(noun) A lattice is a structure made of strips of wood interlaced in a diagonal pattern, used as a framework or decoration.

laud, lauds, lauding, lauded (rhymes with **broad**)
(verb; an old-fashioned word) To laud someone means to praise them.
[from Latin *laudare* meaning 'to praise']

laudable
(adjective; a formal word) deserving praise, e.g. *a laudable willingness to help.*
laudably (adverb).

laudanum (pronounced **lawd**-a-num)
(noun) Laudanum is a medicine made from opium, often used during the nineteenth century to help people to sleep.

laugh, laughs, laughing, laughed
1 (verb) When you laugh, you make a noise which shows that you are amused or happy.
2 (noun) A laugh is the noise you make when you laugh.
3 (phrase) If you **have the last laugh**, you succeed in a situation in which people had thought you were going to fail.
laughter (noun).

laughable
(adjective) quite absurd.
laughably (adverb).

laughing gas
(noun) Laughing gas is another name for nitrous oxide, which is used as an anaesthetic by dentists.

laughing stock
(noun) A laughing stock is someone who has been made to seem ridiculous.

launch, launches, launching, launched
1 (verb) To launch a ship means to send it into the water for the first time.
2 To launch a rocket means to send it into space.
3 When a company launches a new product, they have an advertising campaign to promote it as they start to sell it.
4 (noun) A launch is a motorboat.

launching pad, launching pads
(noun) A launching pad, or a launch pad, is the place from which space rockets take off.

launder, launders, laundering, laundered
(verb; an old-fashioned word) To launder clothes, sheets, or towels means to wash and iron them.
[from Latin *lavare* meaning 'to wash']

Launderette, Launderettes
(noun; a trademark) A Launderette is a place where you can take your clothes, sheets, and towels and wash them in coin-operated washing machines.

laundry, laundries
1 (noun) A laundry is a shop where you can take your clothes, sheets, and towels to be washed and ironed.
2 Laundry is also the dirty clothes, sheets, and towels that are being washed, or are about to be washed.

laurel, laurels
1 (noun) A laurel is an evergreen tree with shiny leaves.
2 (phrase) If you **rest on your laurels**, you do not make any more effort because you are satisfied with the success you have already had.

lava
(noun) Lava is the very hot liquid rock that comes shooting out of an erupting volcano, and solidifies as it cools.

lavatory, lavatories
(noun) A lavatory is a toilet.
[from Latin *lavare* meaning 'to wash']

lavender
1 (noun) Lavender is a small bush with bluish-pink flowers that have a strong, pleasant scent.
2 (adjective) bluish-pink.

lavish, lavishes, lavishing, lavished
1 (adjective) If you are lavish, you are very generous with your time, money, or gifts.
2 A lavish amount is a large amount.
3 (verb) If you lavish presents, money, or affection on someone, you are extremely generous to them.
lavishly (adverb).
[from Old French *lavas* meaning 'profusion']

law, laws
1 (noun) The law is the system of rules developed by the government of a country, which regulate what people may and may not do and deals with people who break these rules.
2 The law is also the profession of people such as lawyers and solicitors, whose job involves the application of the laws of a country.
3 A law is one of the rules established by a government or a religion, which tells people what they may or may not do.
4 A law is also a scientific fact which allows you to explain how things work in the physical world.
5 (an informal use) The police are sometimes called the law.
lawful (adjective), **lawfully** (adverb).

law-abiding
(adjective) obeying the law and not causing any trouble.

lawcourt, lawcourts
(noun) A lawcourt is a place where legal trials are held.

lawless
(adjective) having no regard for the law.
lawlessness (noun).

Law Lord, Law Lords
(noun) A Law Lord is a member of the House of Lords whose legal qualifications allow them to sit as judge when the House of Lords acts as a court of appeal.

lawn, lawns
1 (noun) A lawn is an area of cultivated grass.
2 Lawn is a fine linen or cotton material.

lawnmower, lawnmowers
(noun) A lawnmower is a machine for cutting grass.

lawn tennis
(noun) Lawn tennis is the official name for tennis played on grass or hard courts.

lawrencium (pronounced law-**ren**-see-um)
(noun) Lawrencium is an artificial radioactive element. Its atomic number is 103 and its symbol is Lr. It is named after the American physicist E.O. Lawrence.

lawsuit, lawsuits
(noun) A lawsuit is a civil court case between two people, as opposed to the police prosecuting someone for a criminal offence.

lawyer, lawyers
(noun) A lawyer is a person who is qualified in law, and whose job is to advise people about the law and represent them in court.

lax
(adjective) careless and not keeping up the usual standards, e.g. *Discipline is lax.*
[from Latin *laxus* meaning 'loose']

laxative, laxatives
(noun) A laxative is something that you eat or drink to stop you being constipated.

lay, lays, laying, laid
1 (verb) When you lay something somewhere, you put it down so that it lies there.
2 If you lay the table, you put cutlery on the table ready for a meal.
3 When a bird lays an egg, it produces the egg out of its body.
4 If you lay a trap for someone, you create a situation in which you will be able to catch them out.
5 If you lay emphasis on something, you refer to it in a way that shows you think it is very important.
6 If you lay odds on something, you bet that it will happen.
7 (adjective) Lay people are not officially ordained members of the clergy, e.g. *a lay preacher.*
8 Lay is the past tense of some senses of **lie**.

lay off
1 (phrasal verb) When workers are laid off, their employers tell them not to come to work for a while because there is a shortage of work.
2 (an informal use) If you tell someone to lay off, you want them to stop doing something annoying.

lay on
(phrasal verb) If you lay on a meal or entertainment, you provide it.

layabout, layabouts
(noun; an informal word) A layabout is someone who is lazy and does not work.

Similar words: idler, loafer, good-for-nothing

lay-by, lay-bys
(noun) A lay-by is an area by the side of a main road where motorists can stop for a short while.

layer, layers
(noun) A layer is a single thickness of something, e.g. *layers of clothing*.
layered (adjective).

Similar words: stratum, coat, sheet, seam

layette
(noun) A layette is the collection of clothes and bedding that people need when a baby is born.

layman, laymen
1 (noun) A layman is someone who does not have specialized knowledge of a subject, e.g. *electronics for the layman*.
2 A layman is someone who belongs to the church but is not a member of the clergy.

layout, layouts
(noun) The layout of something is the pattern in which it is arranged.

Similar words: design, format, arrangement

laze, lazes, lazing, lazed
(verb) If you laze, you relax and do no work, e.g. *lazing around in the garden*.

Similar words: lounge, loll, loaf, idle

lazy, lazier, laziest
(adjective) idle and unwilling to work.
lazily (adverb), **laziness** (noun).

Similar words: idle, indolent, slothful, shiftless

lb an abbreviation for 'pounds', e.g. *2lb of sugar*.

lbw
In cricket lbw is an abbreviation for 'leg before wicket', which is a way of dismissing a batsman when his legs prevent the ball from hitting the wicket.

leach, leaches, leaching, leached
(verb) When minerals are leached from rocks, they are dissolved by water which filters through the rock.

lead, leads, leading, led (rhymes with **feed**)
1 (verb) If you lead someone somewhere, you go in front of them in order to show them the way.
2 If one thing leads to another, it causes the second thing to happen.
3 A person who leads a group of people is in charge of them.
4 (noun) A dog's lead is a length of leather or chain attached to its collar, so that the dog can be kept under control.
5 If the police have a lead, they have a clue which might help them to solve a crime.
6 (phrase) If you **take the lead** in something, you are the first to do it.
leading (adjective).

Similar words: (sense 1) conduct, guide

lead (rhymes with **fed**)
(noun) Lead is a soft metallic element. Its atomic number is 82 and its symbol is Pb.

leaden (pronounced **led**-en)
1 (adjective) dark grey, e.g. *a leaden sky*.
2 heavy and slow-moving.

leader, leaders
1 (noun) A leader is someone who is in charge of a country, an organization, or a group of people.
2 In a race or competition, the leader is the person who is winning.
3 A leader in a newspaper is a leading article.

leadership
1 (noun) A group of people in charge of an organization may be referred to as the leadership.
2 Leadership is the ability to be a good leader.

leading article, leading articles
(noun) The leading article in a newspaper is an article which expresses the official views of the newspaper on a current news topic.

leading light, leading lights
(noun) A leading light is someone who is prominent or important in an organization or cause.

leaf, leaves; leafs, leafing, leafed
1 (noun) A leaf is the flat green growth on the end of a twig or branch of a tree or other plant.
2 In a book or newspaper, a leaf is a single sheet of paper.
3 The leaf of a table is an extra piece that you can pull out to make the surface larger.
4 (verb) If you leaf through a book, magazine, or newspaper, you turn the pages over quickly.
leafy (adjective).

leaflet, leaflets
(noun) A leaflet is a piece of folded paper with information or advertising printed on it.

league, leagues (pronounced **leeg**)
1 (noun) A league is an organization of people or groups who have joined together because they have a common interest.
2 A league was a unit of distance used in former times. In Britain, a league was equal to about 3 miles.
3 (phrase) If you are **in league with** someone, you are working together closely for a particular purpose.
[from Latin *ligare* meaning 'to bind']

leak, leaks, leaking, leaked
1 (verb) If a pipe or container leaks, it has a hole which lets gas or liquid escape.
2 If liquid or gas leaks, it escapes from a pipe or container.
3 If someone in an organization leaks information, they give the information to someone who is not supposed to have it, e.g. *The story was leaked to the media*.
4 (noun) If a pipe or container has a leak, it has a hole which lets gas or liquid escape.
5 If there is a leak in an organization, someone inside the organization is giving information to people who are not supposed to have it.
leaky (adjective).
[from Old Norse *leka* meaning 'to drip']

leakage, leakages
(noun) A leakage is an escape of gas or liquid from a pipe or container.

lean, leans, leaning, leant or **leaned; leaner leanest**
1 (verb) When you lean in a particular direction, you bend your body in that direction.
2 When you lean on something, you rest your body against it for support.
3 If you lean on someone, you depend on them.
4 If you lean towards particular ideas, you approve of them and follow them, e.g. *parents who lean towards strictness.*
5 (adjective) having little or no fat, e.g. *a lean figure... lean meat.*
6 A lean period is a time when food or money is in short supply.

leap, leaps, leaping, leapt or **leaped**
1 (verb) If you leap somewhere, you jump over a long distance or high in the air.
2 (noun) A leap is a jump over a long distance or high in the air.
3 (phrase) A leap forward or ahead is a great change, increase, or advance.

leapfrog
(noun) Leapfrog is a game in which you jump over people who are squatting with their backs bent.

leap year, leap years
(noun) A leap year is a year in which there are 366 days. Every fourth year is a leap year.

learn, learns, learning, learnt or **learned**
1 (verb) When you learn something, you gain knowledge or a skill through studying or training.
2 If you learn of something, you find out about it, e.g. *She learnt of his death from his sister.*
learner (noun).

Similar words: (sense 2) gather, discover, find, pick up

learned (pronounced **ler**-nid)
1 (adjective) A learned person has a lot of knowledge gained from years of study.
2 Learned books and journals are written about serious academic subjects.

Similar words: erudite, scholarly

learning
(noun) Learning is knowledge that has been acquired through serious study.

lease, leases, leasing, leased
1 (noun) A lease is an agreement under which someone is allowed to use a house or flat in return for rent.
2 (verb) To lease property to someone means to allow them to use it in return for rent.
3 (phrase) You can say someone has **a new lease of life** if they have been ill or unhappy but are now happier or healthier.

leash, leashes
(noun) A leash is a length of leather or chain attached to a dog's collar so that the dog can be controlled.

least
1 (noun) The least is the smallest possible amount of something.
2 (adjective and adverb) Least is a superlative form of **little.**
3 (phrase) You use **at least** to indicate that you

are referring to the minimum amount of something, and that you think the true amount is greater, e.g. *It'll cost at least ten pounds.*

Similar words: (sense 1) minimum, minimal, slightest

leather
(noun) Leather is the tanned skin of some animals, used to make shoes, bags, belts, and clothes.
leathery (adjective).

leatherjacket, leatherjackets
(noun) A leatherjacket is the larva of the cranefly or daddy longlegs.

leave, leaves, leaving, left
1 (verb) When you leave a place, you go away from it.
2 If you leave someone somewhere, they stay behind after you go away.
3 If you leave a job or organization, you stop being part of it, e.g. *I left school at 16.*
4 If someone leaves money or possessions to someone, they arrange for them to be given to them after their death.
5 In subtraction, when you take one number from another, it leaves a third number.
6 (noun) Leave is a period of holiday or absence from a job.
7 (phrase) If someone **gives you leave** to do something, they allow you to do it.

Similar words: (sense 1) go, depart, withdraw, exit, quit, retire

leave out
(phrasal verb) If you leave someone or something out, you do not include them.

leaven, leavens, leavening, leavened (rhymes with **heaven**)
1 (noun; an old-fashioned word) Leaven is a substance such as yeast which is added to dough to make bread rise.
2 (verb) To leaven dough means to add leaven to it.
[from Latin *levare* meaning 'to raise']

Lebanese
1 (adjective) belonging or relating to Lebanon.
2 (noun) A Lebanese is someone who comes from Lebanon.

lecherous
(adjective) constantly thinking about sex.
lecherously (adverb), **lechery** (noun).

lecithin (pronounced **les**-sith-in)
(noun) Lecithin is a substance found in some plants and in egg yolk, and is used as an emulsifier and stabilizer in foods.
[from Greek *lekithos* meaning 'egg yolk']

lectern, lecterns
(noun) A lectern is a sloping desk which people use to rest books or notes on.
[from Latin *lectrum*, the past participle of *legere* meaning 'to read']

lecture, lectures, lecturing, lectured
1 (noun) A lecture is a formal talk intended to teach people about a particular subject.

2 A lecture is also a talk intended to tell someone off.
3 (verb) Someone who lectures teaches in a college or university.

lecturer, lecturers
(noun) A lecturer is a teacher in a college or university.
lectureship (noun).

led the past tense and past participle of **lead**.

ledge, ledges
(noun) A ledge is a narrow shelf on the side of a cliff or rock face, or on the outside of a building, directly under a window.

ledger, ledgers
(noun) A ledger is a book in which accounts are kept.

lee
1 (noun) The lee of a place is the sheltered side of it, e.g. *the lee of the hill.*
2 (adjective) The lee side of a ship is the side away from the wind.
[from Old Norse *hle* meaning 'shelter']

leech, leeches
1 (noun) A leech is a small worm that feeds by sucking the blood from other animals. Leeches live in water.
2 If you call someone a leech, you mean that they try to live off other people.

leek, leeks
(noun) A leek is a long vegetable of the onion family, which is white at one end and has green leaves at the other. Leeks are sometimes used as the national symbol of Wales.

leer, leers, leering, leered
1 (verb) To leer at someone means to smile at them in an unpleasant or sexually suggestive way.
2 (noun) A leer is an unpleasant or sexually suggestive smile.

leery
(adjective) suspicious and mistrustful.

lees
(plural noun) The lees are the sediments found in the bottom of wine and other drinks.

leeward (pronounced **lee**-urd)
(adjective and adverb) towards or on the side of a ship protected from the wind.

leeway
(noun) If something gives you some leeway, it allows you more flexibility in your plans, for example by giving you time to finish an activity.

left
1 (noun) The left is one of two sides of something. For example, on a page, English writing begins on the left.
2 (adjective and adverb) Left means on or towards the left side of something, e.g. *We turned left down Bond Street.*
3 (noun) People and political groups who hold socialist or communist views are referred to as the Left.

4 Left is the past tense and past participle of **leave.**

left-handed
(adjective and adverb) Someone who is left-handed does things such as writing and painting with their left hand.

leftist, leftists
(noun and adjective) A leftist is someone who holds left-wing political views.

leftovers
(plural noun) The leftovers are the bits of uneaten food that remain at the end of a meal.

left wing
(adjective) believing more strongly in socialism, or less strongly in capitalism or conservatism, than other members of the same party or group.
left-winger (noun).

leg, legs
1 (noun) Your legs are the two limbs which stretch from your hips to your feet.
2 The legs of a pair of trousers are the parts that cover your legs.
3 The legs of an object such as a table are the parts which rest on the floor and support the object's weight.
4 A leg of a journey is one part of it.
5 (phrase) If you say that someone **does not have a leg to stand on**, you mean that they cannot justify or prove what they claim.
6 If you **pull someone's leg**, you tell them something untrue as a joke.
7 If you say something is **on its last legs**, you mean it is about to collapse or stop working.

legacy, legacies
1 (noun) A legacy is property or money that someone receives in the will of a person who has died.
2 A legacy is also something that exists as a result of a previous event or period of history, e.g. *a legacy of prewar unemployment.*

Similar words: (sense 1) inheritance, bequest,

legal
1 (adjective) relating to the law, e.g. *the British legal system.*
2 allowed by the law, e.g. *Is corporal punishment legal in your country?*
legally (adverb).
[from Latin *leges* meaning 'laws']

legal age
(noun) The legal age is the age at which a young person becomes legally responsible for their own actions. In Britain, the legal age is eighteen.

legal aid
(noun) Legal aid is a system which provides the services of a solicitor or lawyer free, or very cheaply, to people who cannot afford the full fees.

legality
(noun) The legality of an action concerns whether or not it is allowed by the law, e.g. *They disputed the legality of the rent increase.*

legalize, legalizes, legalizing, legalized; also spelled **legalise**
(verb) To legalize something that is illegal means to change the law so that it becomes legal.
legalization (noun).

legal tender
(noun; a formal word) Legal tender consists of the official coins and banknotes that are accepted as money in a particular country.

legate, legates (pronounced **leg**-it)
(noun; a formal word) A legate is an official representative of the Pope.

legation, legations
(noun; a technical word) A legation is a group of diplomats in a foreign country, led by a minister rather than an ambassador; also the building where they work.

legend, legends
1 (noun) A legend is an old story which was once believed to be true, but which is probably untrue.
2 A legend is also a caption.
3 If you refer to a person as a legend, you mean they are very famous, e.g. *John Lennon had become a legend by the time he was twenty-five.*
legendary (adjective).
[from Latin *legere* meaning 'to read']

leggings
1 (plural noun) Leggings are very close-fitting trousers made of stretch material, worn mainly by young women.
2 Leggings are also a waterproof covering worn over ordinary trousers to protect them.

leggy, leggier, leggiest
(adjective) having long legs.

legible
(adjective) Writing that is legible is clear enough to be read.
legibly (adverb), **legibility** (noun).

legion, legions
1 (noun) In ancient Rome, a legion was a military unit of between 3000 and 6000 soldiers.
2 A legion is a large military force, e.g. *the French Foreign Legion.*
3 Legions of people are large numbers of them.
4 (adjective; a formal use) If you say that certain things or people are legion, you mean that there are a lot of them, e.g. *Stories about him are legion.*

legionnaire, legionnaires
(noun) A legionnaire is a soldier who belongs to a legion.

legionnaire's disease
(noun) Legionnaire's disease is a serious lung disease caused by bacteria in contaminated water vapour from showers or air conditioners.

legislate, legislates, legislating, legislated
(verb; a formal word) When a government legislates, it creates new laws.

legislation
(noun) Legislation is a law or set of laws created by a government.

legislative
(adjective) relating to the making of new laws, e.g. *a legislative assembly.*

legislator, legislators
(noun; a formal word) A legislator is a person who is a member of a government or other law-making body.

legislature
(noun; a formal word) The legislature is the parliament or other official group in a country which is responsible for making new laws.

legitimate (pronounced lij-**it**-tim-it)
(adjective) Something that is legitimate is reasonable or acceptable according to existing laws or standards, e.g. *a legitimate business transaction... a legitimate complaint.*
legitimacy (noun), **legitimately** (adverb).

legitimize, legitimizes, legitimizing, legitimized; also spelled **legitimise**
(verb; a formal word) To legitimize something means to make it officially permissible or acceptable.

legume, legumes (pronounced **leg**-yoom)
(noun; a formal word) Legumes are vegetables such as peas or beans which grow inside a pod.
[from Latin *legumen* meaning 'bean']

leisure (rhymes with **measure**)
1 (noun) Leisure is time during which you do not have to work, and can do what you enjoy doing.
2 (phrases) If you do something **at leisure**, or **at your leisure**, you do it without hurrying.
[from Latin *licere* meaning 'to be allowed']

leisurely
(adjective and adverb) A leisurely action is done in an unhurried and calm way.

Similar words: unhurried, relaxed, slow

leitmotiv, leitmotivs (pronounced lite-moh-teef); also spelled **leitmotif**
(noun; a formal word) A leitmotiv is a theme that recurs throughout a piece of music or work of literature.
[from German *Leitmotiv* meaning 'leading motif']

lemming, lemmings
(noun) A lemming is a small rodent which lives in northern and arctic areas. Traditionally, lemmings are believed to jump off cliffs to their death in large numbers.

lemon, lemons
1 (noun) A lemon is a yellow citrus fruit with a sour taste.
2 (adjective) pale yellow.

lemonade
(noun) Lemonade is a clear, sweet, fizzy drink.

lemon curd
(noun) Lemon curd is a sweet paste made from sugar, butter, eggs, and lemons. It is used to spread on bread or as a filling in pies.

lemur, lemurs (pronounced lee-mur)
(noun) A lemur is a monkey-like, tree-dwelling mammal with a long tail. Lemurs live in Madagascar.
[from Latin *lemures* meaning 'ghost']

lend, lends, lending, lent
1 (verb) If you lend someone something, you give it to them for a period of time and then they give it back to you.
2 If a bank lends money, it gives the money to someone and the money has to be repaid in the future, usually with interest.
3 If you lend someone support, you help them in what they are trying to do.
4 If something lends a quality to a situation, it contributes that quality, e.g. *The portrait lent a gloomy air to the room.*
5 If something lends itself to a purpose, it is suitable for that purpose.
6 (phrase) If you **lend someone a hand**, you help them.
lender (noun).

length, lengths
1 (noun) The length of something is the horizontal distance from one end to the other.
2 The length of an event or activity is the amount of time it lasts for.
3 The length of something is also the fact that it is long rather than short, e.g. *Despite its length, it was a most enjoyable film.*
4 A length of something is a long piece of it.
5 (phrase) If someone does something **at length**, they do it for a long time.
6 If you **go to great lengths** to achieve something, you try very hard and do extreme things to achieve it, e.g. *She'll go to any lengths to get the job.*

lengthen, lengthens, lengthening, lengthened
(verb) To lengthen something means to make it longer.

Similar words: extend, stretch, elongate, prolong, protract

lengthways or **lengthwise**
(adverb) If you measure something lengthways, you measure the horizontal distance from one end to the other.

lengthy, lengthier, lengthiest
(adjective) Something that is lengthy lasts for a long time.

lenient
(adjective) If someone in authority is lenient, they are less severe than expected.
leniently (adverb), **leniency** or **lenience** (noun).
[from Latin *lenire* meaning 'to soothe']

lens, lenses
1 (noun) A lens is a curved piece of glass designed to focus light in a certain way, for example in a camera, telescope, or pair of glasses.
2 The lens in your eye is the part behind the iris, which focuses light.
[from Latin *lens* meaning 'lentil', because of its convex shape]

lent
1 the past tense and past participle of **lend**.
2 (noun) Lent is the period of forty days leading up to Easter, during which Christians fast or give up something they enjoy.

lenticel, lenticels (pronounced **len**-tis-sel)
(noun; a technical word) A lenticel is a pore in the stem of a woody plant that allows gases to pass between the outside and the interior of the plant.

lentil, lentils
(noun) Lentils are small dried red or brown seeds which are cooked and eaten in soups and curries.

Leo
(noun) Leo is the fifth sign of the zodiac, represented by a lion. People born between July 23rd and August 22nd are born under this sign.

leonine (pronounced **lee**-o-nine)
(adjective) resembling a lion.
[from Latin *leo* meaning 'lion']

leopard, leopards
(noun) A leopard is a large wild Asian or African animal of the cat family. Leopards have yellow fur and black or brown spots.

leotard, leotards (pronounced **lee**-eh-tard)
(noun) A leotard is a tight-fitting costume covering the body and legs, which is worn for dancing or exercise. It is named after a French acrobat called Jules Léotard.

leper, lepers
(noun) A leper is someone who has leprosy.
[from Greek *lepros* meaning 'scaly']

lepidopteran, lepidopterans or **lepidoptera** (pronounced lep-id-**dop**-ter-an)
(noun) Lepidopterans are an order of insects, for example, butterflies and moths, with two pairs of wings and caterpillars as larvae.

leprechaun, leprechauns (pronounced **lep**-rik-kawn)
(noun) In Irish mythology, leprechauns are mischievous elves who keep a hoard of treasure.
[from Old Irish *luchorpan* meaning 'small-bodied one']

leprosy
(noun) Leprosy is an infectious disease which attacks the skin and nerves, and which can lead to fingers or toes dropping off.
[from Greek *lepros* meaning 'scaly']

lesbian, lesbians
(noun) A lesbian is a homosexual woman.
lesbianism (noun).

lese-majesty (pronounced leez-**maj**-iss-tee)
(noun; a formal expression) Lese-majesty is a crime committed against the king or queen.
[from Latin *laesa majestas* meaning 'wounded majesty']

lesion, lesions (pronounced **lee**-shen)
(noun) A lesion is a wound or injury.
[from Latin *laesus* meaning 'hurt' or 'injured']

less
1 Less means a smaller amount, or not as much in quality, e.g. *I've got less than five pounds left... We're less worried now we've got the burglar alarm... I've had a lot less trouble with the new television.*

2 (adjective and adverb) Less is a comparative form of **little.**
3 (preposition) You use less to indicate that you are subtracting one number from another, e.g. *Eight less two leaves six.*

-less
(suffix) -less means without, e.g. *a colourless sky... He felt powerless.*

lessee, lessees
(noun) A lessee is someone renting property under the terms of a lease.

lessen, lessens, lessening, lessened
(verb) If something lessens, it is reduced in amount, size, or quality.

Similar words: abate, decline, decrease, dwindle, diminish, deplete, wane, reduce

lesser
(adjective) smaller in importance, degree, or amount than something else.

lesson, lessons
1 (noun) A lesson is a fixed period of time during which a class of pupils is taught by a teacher.
2 A lesson is also an experience that makes you understand something important which you had not realized before.

lessor, lessors
(noun) A lessor is a person who lets property to someone under the terms of a lease.

lest
(conjunction; an old-fashioned word) as a precaution in case something unpleasant or unwanted happens, e.g. *You'd better take some food lest you get hungry on the train.*

let, lets, letting, let
1 (verb) If you let someone do something, you allow them to do it.
2 If someone lets a house or flat that they own, they rent it out.
3 You can say 'let's' or 'let us' when you want to suggest doing something with someone else, e.g. *Let's go for a walk.*
4 If you let yourself in for something, you agree to do it although you do not really want to.
5 (phrase) If you say that something is not the case **let alone** something else, you mean that the second thing is even more unlikely than the first, e.g. *I've never been to France, let alone Greece.*

let down
(phrasal verb) If you let someone down, you fail to do something you had agreed to do for them.

let off
1 (phrasal verb) If someone in authority lets you off, they do not punish you for something you have done wrong.
2 If you let someone off a duty, you give them permission not to do it.
3 If you let off a firework or explosive, you light it or detonate it.

let on
(phrasal verb) not to let on about something means to keep it a secret.

let up
(phrasal verb) If something lets up, it stops or becomes less, e.g. *The heat did not let up.*

letdown, letdowns
(noun; an informal word) A letdown is a disappointment.

lethal (pronounced lee-thal)
(adjective) able to kill someone, e.g. *a lethal weapon.*
[from Latin *letum* meaning 'death']

lethargic (pronounced lith-**ar**-jik)
(adjective) If you feel lethargic, you have no energy or enthusiasm.
lethargically (adverb).

Similar words: languid, listless, torpid, sluggish

lethargy (pronounced **leth**-ar-jee)
(noun) Lethargy is a lack of energy and enthusiasm.

letter, letters
1 (noun) Letters are written symbols which go together to make words.
2 A letter is also a piece of writing addressed to someone, and usually sent through the post.

letter box, letter boxes
1 (noun) A letter box is an oblong gap in the front door of a house or flat, through which letters are delivered.
2 A letter box is also a large metal container in the street, into which letters are put to await collection.

letterhead, letterheads
(noun) A letterhead is the printed part at the top of a letter, giving the writer's address.

lettering
(noun) Lettering is writing, especially when you are describing the type of letters used, e.g. *bold lettering.*

letter of credit, letters of credit
(noun) A letter of credit is a document issued by a bank authorizing someone to withdraw up to a certain amount of money from its branches.

lettuce, lettuces
(noun) A lettuce is a vegetable with large green leaves eaten raw in salad.

leucocyte, leucocytes (pronounced **loo**-kos-site)
(noun) A leucocyte is a white blood cell.
[from Greek *leukos* meaning 'white']

leukaemia or **leukemia** (pronounced loo-**kee**-mee-a)
(noun) Leukaemia is a serious cancer-like disease in which too many white blood cells are produced by the body.
[from Greek *leukos* meaning 'white' and *haima* meaning 'blood']

levee, levees (pronounced **lev**-ee)
1 (noun) A levee is an embankment built beside a river or field to prevent flooding.
2 (a formal use) A levee is a formal reception held by a king or queen at their palace.
[from French *levée* meaning 'a raising' or 'a lifting'; a monarch would have a levee just after rising from bed]

level, levels, levelling, levelled
1 (adjective) A surface that is level is smooth, flat, and parallel to the ground.
2 (verb) To level a piece of land means to make it flat.
3 (noun) A level is a point on a scale which measures the amount, importance, or difficulty of something.
4 The level of a liquid is the height it comes up to in a container.
5 (adverb) If you draw level with someone, you get closer to them so that you are moving next to them.
6 (verb) If you level a criticism at someone, you say or write something critical about them.
7 To level with someone means to tell them the truth about something.

Similar words: (sense 3) grade, rank, step, stage, degree

level off or **level out**
(phrasal verb) If something levels off or levels out, it stops increasing or decreasing, e.g. *Economic growth is starting to level off.*

level crossing, level crossings
(noun) A level crossing is a place where road traffic is allowed to drive across a railway track.

level-headed
(adjective) Someone who is level-headed is sensible and calm in emergencies.

lever, levers
1 (noun) A lever on a machine is a handle that you pull in order to make the machine work.
2 A lever is also a long bar that you wedge underneath a heavy object. When you press down on the lever, it makes the object move.

leverage
1 (noun) Leverage is knowledge or influence that you can use to make someone do something.
2 Leverage is also the force you apply to a lever in order to make an object move.

leveret, leverets
(noun) A leveret is a young hare.
[from Old French *levre* meaning 'hare']

leviathan, leviathans (pronounced liv-**eye**-ath-an)
(noun; a literary word) A leviathan is anything that is very large or imposing.
[in the Bible, a leviathan was a huge monster]

levitate, levitates, levitating, levitated
(verb) To levitate means to rise into the air without any visible means of assistance, as if by magic.
levitation (noun).
[from Latin *levis* meaning 'lightweight']

levity
(noun) Levity is light-hearted or frivolous behaviour.

levy, levies, levying, levied (pronounced **lev**-ee)
1 (noun; a formal word) A levy is an amount of money that you pay in tax.
2 (verb) When a government levies a tax, it makes people pay the tax and organizes the collection of the money.

lewd (rhymes with **rude**)
(adjective) sexually coarse and crude.
lewdly (adverb), **lewdness** (noun).
[from Old English *læwde* meaning 'ignorant']

lexicography
(noun) Lexicography is the profession of writing dictionaries.
lexicographer (noun).
[from Greek *lexis* meaning 'word' and *graphein* meaning 'to write']

lexicon, lexicons
(noun) A lexicon is a dictionary, especially a dictionary of an ancient language such as Greek.

liability, liabilities
1 (noun) Someone's liability is their responsibility for something they have done wrong.
2 In business, a company's liabilities are the debts which it must pay.
3 (an informal use) If you describe someone as a liability, you mean that they cause a lot of problems or embarrassment.

liable
1 (adjective) If you say that something is liable to happen, you mean that you think it will probably happen.
2 If you are liable for something you have done, you are legally responsible for it.
[from Latin *ligare* meaning 'to bind']

liaise, liaises, liaising, liaised (pronounced lee-**aze**)
(verb) To liaise with someone or an organization means to cooperate with them and keep them informed.

liaison, liaisons (pronounced lee-**aze**-on)
1 (noun) Liaison is communication between two organizations or two sections of an organization.
2 (an old-fashioned use) If two people have a liaison, they have an illicit sexual relationship.

liana, lianas (pronounced lee-**ah**-na)
(noun) Liana is a climbing plant that grows in tropical forests.

liar, liars
(noun) A liar is a person who tells lies.

libation, libations
(noun) Libation is the act of pouring out wine to honour a god; also the drink itself.

libel, libels, libelling, libelled (pronounced **lie**-bel)
1 (noun) Libel is something written about someone which is not true, and for which the writer can be made to pay damages in court.
2 (verb) To libel someone means to write or say something untrue about them.
libellous (adjective).
[from Latin *libellus* meaning 'little book']

liberal, liberals
1 (noun) A liberal is someone who believes in political progress, social welfare, and individual freedom.
2 A liberal is a member or supporter of the Liberal Party, a political party supporting individual freedom. The Liberal Party merged with the Social Democratic Party in 1988 to form the Social and Liberal Democratic Party.

3 (adjective) Someone who is liberal is tolerant of a wide range of behaviour, standards, or opinions.
4 To be liberal with something means to be generous with it.
5 A liberal quantity of something is a large amount of it.
liberally (adverb), **liberalism** (noun).
[from Latin *liberalis* meaning 'of freedom']

liberalize, **liberalizes, liberalizing, liberalized**; also spelled **liberalise**
(verb) If a country liberalizes its laws or attitudes, it makes them less severe and allows more freedom.
liberalization (noun).

liberate, **liberates, liberating, liberated**
(verb) To liberate people means to free them from prison or from an unpleasant situation.
liberation (noun), **liberator** (noun).

liberty, **liberties**
1 (noun) Liberty is the freedom to choose how you want to live, without government restrictions.
2 (phrase) A criminal who is **at liberty** has not yet been caught or has escaped from prison.
3 If you are **not at liberty** to do something, you are not allowed to do it, e.g. *I'm not at liberty to give you the test results.*
4 Someone who **takes liberties** with someone is overfamiliar towards them.
[from Latin *liber* meaning 'free']

libidinous (pronounced lib-**bid**-in-uss)
(adjective) showing excessive sexual desire.

libido, **libidos** (pronounced lib-**bee**-doe)
(noun) Someone's libido is their sexual drive.
[from Latin *libido* meaning 'desire']

Libra
(noun) Libra is the seventh sign of the zodiac, represented by a pair of scales. People born between September 23rd and October 22nd are born under this sign.

librarian, **librarians**
(noun) A librarian is a person who is in charge of a library or who has been trained to do responsible work in a library.

library, **libraries**
1 (noun) A library is a building in which books are kept for people to come and read or borrow.
2 A library is also a personal collection of books, records, or videos.
[from Latin *librarius* meaning 'relating to books']

libretto, **librettos** or **libretti**
(noun) The libretto of an opera is the text which is sung.
[from Italian *libretto* meaning literally 'little book']

Libyan, **Libyans**
1 (adjective) belonging or relating to Libya.
2 (noun) A Libyan is someone who comes from Libya.

lice the plural of **louse.**

licence, **licences**
1 (noun) A licence is an official document which entitles you to carry out a particular activity, for example to drive a car or to sell alcohol.
2 Licence is the freedom to do what you want, especially when other people consider that it is being used irresponsibly.
[from Latin *licet* meaning 'it is allowed']

license, **licenses, licensing, licensed**
(verb) To license an activity means to give official permission for it to be carried out.

licentious (pronounced lie-**sen**-shuss)
(adjective; a formal word) Someone who is licentious behaves in a sexually immoral way.
[from Latin *licentiosus* meaning 'capricious']

lichen, **lichens** (pronounced **lie**-ken)
(noun) Lichen is a green, moss like growth on rocks or tree trunks.

lick, **licks, licking, licked**
1 (verb) If you lick something, you move your tongue over it.
2 (noun) A lick is the action of licking.
3 (phrase) If you **lick your lips**, you show eager anticipation of something.
4 If you **lick someone into shape**, you train them in something very quickly.
5 (an informal use) If you lick someone in a competition, you beat them easily.

licorice another spelling of **liquorice.**

lid, **lids**
(noun) The lid of a container is the top, which you open in order to reach what is inside.

lie, **lies, lying, lay, lain**
1 (verb) To lie somewhere means to rest there horizontally.
2 If you say where something lies, you are describing where it is, e.g. *The village lies midway between Norwich and Cromer.*
3 If you say that something lies ahead of you or behind you, you are referring to events that are likely to happen or that have already happened, e.g. *At the age of 90, his achievements now lie in the past.*
4 (an informal phrase) If you say that someone **will not take something lying down**, you mean that they will resist it strongly.

lie, **lies, lying, lied**
1 (verb) To lie means to say something that is not true.
2 (noun) A lie is something you say which is not true.

Similar words: (sense 1) fib, prevaricate
(sense 2) fib, falsehood, prevarication

---

lieder (pronounced **lee**-der)
(plural noun) Lieder are German romantic or lyrical songs.
[a German word meaning literally 'songs']

lie detector, **lie detectors**
(noun) A lie detector is a machine which notes a person's physical state as they answer questions. Any changes, such as a faster pulse rate, may indicate that they are lying.

liege (pronounced **leej**)
(noun) In a feudal society, your liege was the person you honoured and gave service to.

lieu (pronounced **lyoo**)
(phrase) If one thing happens in lieu of another, it happens instead of it.
[from French *lieu* meaning 'place']

lieutenant, lieutenants (pronounced lef-**ten**-ent)
(noun) A lieutenant is a junior officer in the army or navy.
[from Old French *lieutenant* meaning literally 'holding a place']

lieutenant colonel, lieutenant colonels
(noun) A lieutenant colonel is an army officer of the rank immediately above major.

lieutenant commander, lieutenant commanders
(noun) A lieutenant commander is a navy officer of the rank immediately above lieutenant.

lieutenant general, lieutenant generals
(noun) A lieutenant general is an army officer of the rank immediately above major general.

life, lives
1 (noun) Life is the quality of being able to grow and develop, which is present in people, plants, and animals.
2 Your life is your existence from the time you are born until the time you die.
3 The life of a machine is the period of time for which it is likely to work and be useful.
4 If you refer to the life in a place, you are talking about the amount of activity there, e.g. *There's no life in this town on Sundays.*
5 If criminals are sentenced to life, they are sent to prison for the rest of their lives, or until they are granted parole.

life assurance
(noun) Life assurance is an insurance which provides a sum of money in the event of the policy holder's death.

life belt, life belts
(noun) A life belt is a belt that you wear to keep afloat if you fall into water.

lifeblood
(noun) The lifeblood of something is the most essential part of it.

lifeboat, lifeboats
1 (noun) A lifeboat is a boat kept on shore, which is sent out to rescue people who are in danger at sea.
2 A lifeboat is also a small boat kept on a ship, which is used if the ship starts to sink.

life buoy, life buoys (rhymes with **toy**)
(noun) A life buoy is the same as a life belt.

life cycle, life cycles
(noun) The life cycle of an animal or plant is the series of changes it goes through during its life.

life expectancy, life expectancies
(noun) Your life expectancy is the number of years you can expect to live, based on statistical evidence.

lifeguard, lifeguards
(noun) A lifeguard is a person whose job is to rescue people who are in difficulty in the sea or in a swimming pool.

life jacket, life jackets
(noun) A life jacket is a sleeveless inflatable jacket that keeps you afloat in water.

lifeless
1 (adjective) Someone who is lifeless is dead.
2 If you describe a place or person as lifeless, you mean that they are dull and unexciting.

lifelike
(adjective) A picture or sculpture that is lifelike looks very real or alive.

lifeline, lifelines
1 (noun) A lifeline is something which helps you to survive or helps an activity to continue.
2 A lifeline is also a rope thrown to someone who is in danger of drowning.

lifelong
(adjective) existing throughout someone's life, e.g. *His lifelong passion was ballroom dancing.*

life peer, life peers
(noun) A life peer is a member of the House of Lords who has been given a title but who cannot pass the title on to their descendants.

lifer, lifers
(noun; an informal word) A lifer is a prisoner who is serving a term of life imprisonment.

life span, life spans
1 (noun) Someone's life span is the length of time during which they are alive.
2 The life span of a product or organization is the length of time it exists or is useful.

lifetime, lifetimes
(noun) Your lifetime is the period of time during which you are alive.

lift, lifts, lifting, lifted
1 (verb) To lift something means to move it to a higher position.
2 When fog or mist lifts, it clears away.
3 To lift a ban on something means to remove it.
4 (an informal use) To lift things means to steal them.
5 (noun) A lift is a machine like a large box which carries passengers from one floor to another in a building.
6 If something gives you a lift, it makes you feel happier.
7 If you give someone a lift, you drive them somewhere in a car or on a motorbike.

Similar words: (sense 1) elevate, hoist, raise, pick up

liftoff, liftoffs
(noun) Liftoff is the act of launching a rocket into space.

ligament, ligaments
(noun) A ligament is a piece of tough tissue in your body which connects your bones.
[from Latin *ligare* meaning 'to bind']

light, lights, lighting, lighted or lit; lighter, lightest
1 (noun) Light is brightness from the sun, moon, fire, or lamps, that enables you to see things.

2 A light is a lamp or other device that gives out brightness.
3 If you give someone a light, you give them a match or lighter to light their cigarette.
4 (adjective) A place that is light is bright because of the sun or the use of lamps.
5 A light colour is pale.
6 A light object does not weigh very much.
7 A light task is fairly easy.
8 Light books or music are entertaining and are not intended to be serious.
9 (verb) To light a place means to cause it to be filled with light.
10 To light a fire means to make it start burning.
11 To light upon something means to find it by accident.
12 (phrase) If something **comes to light**, it is discovered or becomes apparent.
13 In the light of something means taking that thing into consideration.
14 (plural noun) The lights of a sheep or pig are its lungs, used as food for animals or people.
lightly (adverb), **lightness** (noun).

Similar words: (sense 1) illumination, lighting (sense 10) kindle, ignite, set fire to

lighten, lightens, lightening, lightened
1 (verb) When something lightens, it becomes less dark.
2 To lighten a load means to make it less heavy.

lighter, lighters
1 (noun) A lighter is a device for lighting a cigarette.
2 A lighter is also a type of barge used to load and unload cargo from ships.

light-fingered
(adjective) Someone who is light-fingered steals things.

light-headed
(adjective) If you feel light-headed, you feel slightly dizzy or drunk.

light-hearted
(adjective) Someone who is light-hearted is cheerful and has no worries.
light-heartedly (adverb), **light-heartedness** (noun).

Similar words: carefree, blithe, happy-go-lucky

lighthouse, lighthouses
(noun) A lighthouse is a tower by the sea, which sends out a powerful light to guide ships and warn them of danger.

light industry, light industries
(noun) Light industry is industry in which only small items are made and which does not make use of heavy machinery.

lighting
(noun) The lighting in a room or building is the way that it is lit.

lightning
(noun) Lightning is the bright flashes of light in the sky which are produced by natural electricity during a thunder storm.

lightning conductor, lightning conductors
(noun) A lightning conductor is a metal rod fixed to a building, which runs into the earth in order to attract and direct lightning and so protect the building.

light pen, light pens
(noun) A light pen is a penlike device used to read bar codes electronically.

lightship, lightships
(noun) A lightship is a ship permanently moored in one place, which acts as a lighthouse.

lightweight, lightweights
1 (noun) A lightweight is a boxer in one of the lighter weight groups.
2 (adjective) Something that is lightweight does not weigh very much, e.g. *a lightweight suit.*

light year, light years
(noun) A light year is a unit of distance equal to the distance that light travels in a year.

lignite
(noun) Lignite is a brown sedimentary rock with a woody texture, which is burnt for fuel.
[from Latin *lignum* meaning 'wood']

likable or **likeable**
(adjective) Someone who is likable is very pleasant and friendly.

like, likes, liking, liked
1 (preposition) If one thing is like another, it is similar to it.
2 (noun) 'The like' means other similar things of the sort just mentioned, e.g. *cattle, pigs, goats, and the like.*
3 (adjective) If you refer to like things, you mean things of the same type, e.g. *nylon, terylene, and other like materials.*
4 (phrase) If you **feel like** something, you want to do it or have it, e.g. *I feel like a drink.*
5 (verb) If you like something or someone, you find them pleasant.

Similar words: (sense 5) care for, be fond of, enjoy, be keen on, be partial to

-like
(suffix) -like means resembling or similar to, e.g. *a balloonlike object.*

likelihood
(noun) If you say that there is a likelihood that something will happen, you mean that you think it will probably happen.

likely, likelier, likeliest
1 (adjective) Something that is likely will probably happen or is probably true.
2 Likely also means suitable or appropriate, e.g. *a likely candidate for promotion.*
3 (an informal phrase) If you describe what someone says as a **likely story**, you mean that you do not believe it.

liken, likens, likening, likened
(verb) If you liken one thing to another, you say that they are similar.

likeness, likenesses
1 (noun) If two things have a likeness to each other, they are similar in appearance.

2 (an old-fashioned use) A likeness is also a portrait of someone.

likewise
(adverb) Likewise means similarly, e.g. *She sat down and he did likewise.*

liking
1 (noun) If you have a liking for someone or something, you like them.
2 (phrase) If something is **to your liking**, you find it pleasant and suitable.

lilac
1 (noun) A lilac is a shrub with large clusters of sweet-smelling pink, white, or mauve flowers.
2 (adjective) pale mauve.

Lilliputian (pronounced lil-ee-**pyoo**-shen)
(adjective) extremely small. In 'Gulliver's Travels' by Jonathan Swift, Lilliput was an imaginary country of tiny people.

lilt, lilts
(noun) A lilt in someone's voice is a pleasant rising and falling sound in it.
lilting (adjective).

lily, lilies
(noun) A lily is a plant that produces trumpet-shaped flowers of various colours.

lily-livered
(adjective; an old-fashioned word) cowardly.

lily of the valley, lilies of the valley
(noun) A lily of the valley is a small plant with large leaves and clusters of small, fragrant, bell-shaped, white flowers.

limb, limbs
1 (noun) Your limbs are your arms and legs.
2 The limbs of a tree are its branches.
3 (phrase) If you have gone **out on a limb**, you have said or done something risky.

limber, limbers, limbering, limbered
1 (adjective) supple and agile, and able to move easily.
2 (verb) If you limber up, you stretch your muscles before doing a sport or exercise.

limbo
1 (noun) If you are in limbo, you are in an uncertain situation over which you feel you have no control.
2 The limbo is a West Indian dance in which the dancer has to pass under a low bar while leaning backwards.
[sense 1 is from Latin *in limbo* meaning 'on the border (of Hell)']

lime, limes
1 (noun) A lime is a small, green citrus fruit, rather like a lemon.
2 A lime tree is a large tree with pale green leaves, often planted in parks and along streets in towns.
3 Lime is a white powder with the chemical name calcium oxide. It is used in cement and other calcium compounds, in whitewash, and as a fertilizer.
[sense 1 is from Arabic *līmah*; sense 2 is from Old English *lind*; sense 3 is from Latin *limus* meaning 'slime']

limelight
(noun) If someone is in the limelight, they are getting a lot of attention.
[a limelight was a type of calcium light formerly used for stage lighting]

limerick, limericks
(noun) A limerick is an amusing nonsense poem of five lines, with special rules for the metre and rhyme. The first, second, and fifth lines rhyme with each other, while the third and fourth lines rhyme with each other using a different rhyme.

limestone
(noun) Limestone is a sedimentary rock composed of calcium carbonate from the shells and skeletons of sea creatures that died millions of years ago. It is used as a building stone and in making cement.

limey, limeys
(noun; an informal word) In American English, a limey is a British person.
[originally 'limeys' meant British sailors, who used to drink lime juice as a protection against scurvy]

limit, limits, limiting, limited
1 (noun) A limit is a boundary or an extreme beyond which something cannot go, e.g. *a speed limit of 40 mph.*
2 (verb) To limit something means to prevent it from becoming bigger, spreading, or making progress, e.g. *The government plans to limit military expenditure.*
3 If something limits you, it prevents you from doing what you want to do.
4 (phrase) If a place is **off limits**, you are not allowed to go there.
[from Latin *limes* meaning 'boundary']

Similar words: (sense 1) bound, boundary, extent

limitation, limitations
1 (noun) The limitation of something is the reducing or controlling of it.
2 If you talk about the limitations of a person or thing, you are talking about the limits of their capabilities.

limited
1 (adjective) Something that is limited is rather small in amount or extent, e.g. *a limited choice.*
2 A limited company is one in which the shareholders are responsible only to a limited extent for the company's debts and losses.

limousine, limousines (pronounced **lim**-o-zeen)
(noun) A limousine is a large, luxurious car, usually driven by a chauffeur.

limp, limps, limping, limped; limper, limpest
1 (verb) If you limp, you walk unevenly because you have hurt your leg or foot.
2 (noun) A limp is an uneven way of walking.
3 (adjective) Something that is limp is soft and floppy, and not stiff or firm, e.g. *a limp lettuce.*
limply (adverb), **limpness** (noun).

limpet, limpets
(noun) A limpet is a shellfish with a pointed shell, that attaches itself very firmly to rocks.

limpid
(adjective) very clear, e.g. *a limpid pool.*

linchpin, linchpins
(noun; a formal word) The linchpin of something is the most important person or thing involved in it.

linctus, linctuses
(noun) A linctus is a thick, syrupy medicine taken for a sore throat or cough.

line, lines, lining, lined
1 (noun) A line is a long, thin mark.
2 A line of people or things is a number of them positioned one behind the other.
3 A line is also a route along which someone or something moves, e.g. *a railway line.*
4 In a piece of writing, a line is a number of words together, e.g. *How does the next line go?... She forgot her lines.*
5 Someone's line of work is the kind of work they do.
6 The line someone takes is the attitude they have towards something, e.g. *He always takes a hard line.*
7 In a shop or business, a line is a type of product, e.g. *That line has been discontinued.*
8 (verb) To line something means to cover its inside surface or edge with something, e.g. *Line the drawers with paper... The streets were lined with cars.*
9 (phrase) If you **draw the line** at doing something, you refuse to do it.
10 If you **read between the lines**, you understand what someone really means, even though they do not say it openly.

line up
1 (phrasal verb) When people line up, they stand in a line.
2 When you line something up, you arrange it for a special occasion, e.g. *We've got a disco lined up for John's birthday.*

lineage, lineages (pronounced lin-ee-ij)
(noun) Someone's lineage is all the people from whom they are directly descended.

lineament, lineaments (lin-a-ment)
(noun) Someone's lineaments are the features of their face.

linear (pronounced lin-ee-ar)
(adjective) arranged in a line or in a strict sequence, or happening at a constant rate.
[from Latin *linearis* meaning 'by means of lines']

linen
1 (noun) Linen is a type of cloth made from a plant called flax.
2 Linen is also household goods made of cloth, such as sheets, teatowels, and tablecloths.
3 (phrase) If someone **washes their dirty linen in public**, they talk about personal and private things in front of other people.

liner, liners
(noun) A liner is a large passenger ship that makes long journeys.

linesman, linesmen
(noun) A linesman is an official at a sports match who watches the lines of the field or court and indicates when the ball goes outside them.

linger, lingers, lingering, lingered
(verb) To linger means to remain for a long time, e.g. *Her illness lingered on... We lingered over our meal.*
lingering (adjective).

lingerie (pronounced lan-jer-ee)
(noun) Lingerie is women's nightwear and underclothes.

lingo, lingoes
(noun; an informal word) A lingo is a foreign language.
[from Latin *lingua* meaning 'tongue']

lingua franca, lingua francas (pronounced ling-gwa frang-ka)
(a formal expression) A lingua franca is a language used between people who speak different native languages.

linguist, linguists
(noun) A linguist is someone who studies foreign languages or linguistics.

linguistic
(adjective) relating to language or to linguistics.

linguistics
(noun) Linguistics is the study of language and of how it works.

liniment
(noun) Liniment is a liquid which you rub into your skin to relieve stiffness and muscle pain.
[from Latin *linere* meaning 'to smear' or 'to anoint']

lining, linings
(noun) A lining is any material used to line the inside of something.

link, links, linking, linked
1 (noun) A link is a relationship or connection between two things, e.g. *the link between smoking and lung cancer.*
2 A link is also a physical connection between two things or places, e.g. *a rail link between London and Paris.*
3 A link is also one of the rings in a chain.
4 (verb) To link people, places, or things means to join them together.
linkage (noun).

links
(noun) A golf links is a golf course.

linnet, linnets
(noun) A linnet is a small songbird. The male has a pink chest and forehead.

lino
(noun) Lino is the same as linoleum.

linocut, linocuts
(noun) A linocut is a print made by a piece of lino with a design cut into it.

linoleum
(noun) Linoleum is a floor covering made from hessian or jute and treated with powdered cork, oil, and colouring.
[from Latin *linum* meaning 'flax' and *oleum* meaning 'oil']

linseed oil
(noun) Linseed oil is an extract from the seeds of flax, used in making oil paints.
[from Old English *lin* meaning 'flax' and *sæd* meaning 'seed']

lint
(noun) Lint is soft cloth made from linen, used to dress wounds.

lintel, lintels
(noun) A lintel is a horizontal beam over a door or a window.

lion, lions
(noun) A lion is a large member of the cat family which comes from Africa. Lions have light brown fur, and the male has a long mane. A female lion is called a lioness.

lionize, lionizes, lionizing, lionized; also spelled lionise
(verb; a formal word) To lionize someone means to treat them like a celebrity.

lip, lips
1 (noun) Your lips are the edges of your mouth.
2 The lip of a jug is the slightly pointed part through which liquids are poured out.
3 (phrase) Someone who has **a stiff upper lip** does not show emotion or fear in a difficult situation.

lip-read, lip-reads, lip-reading, lip-read
(verb) To lip-read means to watch someone's lips when they are talking in order to understand what they are saying. Deaf people often lip-read.
lip-reading (noun).

lip service
(noun) If you pay lip service to an idea, you say you are in favour of it but have no real intention of supporting it.

lipstick, lipsticks
(noun) Lipstick is a coloured substance which women wear on their lips.

liquefy, liquefies, liquefying, liquefied
(pronounced **lik**-wif-eye)
(verb) When something liquefies, it changes from a gas or solid into a liquid.
liquefication (noun).

liqueur, liqueurs (pronounced lik-**yoor**)
(noun) A liqueur is a strong sweet alcoholic drink, usually drunk with coffee after a meal.

liquid, liquids
1 (noun) A liquid is any substance which is not a solid or a gas, and which can be poured.
2 (adjective) Something that is liquid is in the form of a liquid, e.g. *liquid hydrogen*.
3 In commerce and finance a person's or company's liquid assets are the things that can be sold quickly to raise cash.

Similar words: (sense 2) fluid, runny, watery

liquidate, liquidates, liquidating, liquidated
1 (verb) To liquidate a company means to close it down and to use its assets to pay off its debts.
2 (an informal use) To liquidate a person means to murder them.
liquidation (noun), liquidator (noun).

liquidizer, liquidizers; also spelled liquidiser
(noun) A liquidizer is a kitchen machine with very sharp blades which you use to make food into a liquid or a pulp.
liquidize (verb).

liquid petroleum gas
(noun) Liquid petroleum gas is a mixture of gases formed during the refining of petroleum and stored under pressure to be used as a fuel.

liquor
(noun) Liquor is any strong alcoholic drink.

liquorice or licorice (pronounced lik-ker-iss)
(noun) Liquorice is a root used to flavour sweets; also the sweets themselves.

lira, lire
(noun) The lira is the unit of currency in Italy.

lisp, lisps, lisping, lisped
1 (noun) Someone who has a lisp pronounces the sounds 's' and 'z' like 'th'.
2 (verb) To lisp means to speak with a lisp.

lissom or lissome
(adjective) slim and graceful.

list, lists, listing, listed
1 (noun) A list is a set of words or items written one below the other.
2 (verb) If you list a number of things, you make a list of them.
3 (noun) If a ship has a list, it leans over to one side.

Similar words: (sense 1) catalogue, inventory (sense 2) itemize, catalogue, index

listed
(adjective) Listed buildings are protected by law from being demolished or altered because they are old or important.

listen, listens, listening, listened
(verb) If you listen to something, you hear it and pay attention to it.
listener (noun).

listless
(adjective) lacking energy and enthusiasm.
listlessly (adverb).
[from Old English *list* meaning 'desire']

lit a past tense and past participle of **light**.

litany, litanies
(noun) A litany is a part of a church service in which the priest says or chants a series of prayers and the people give a series of responses.
[from Greek *litaneia* meaning 'prayer']

literacy
(noun) Literacy is the ability to read and write.
literate (adjective).

literal
1 (adjective) The literal meaning of a word is its most basic meaning.
2 A literal translation from a foreign language is one that has been translated exactly word for word.
literally (adverb).

Similar words: (sense 2) verbatim, word for word

literary
(adjective) connected with literature, e.g. *a work of some literary merit.*

literature
1 (noun) Literature consists of novels, plays, and poetry.
2 The literature on a subject is everything that has been written about it.
[from Latin *litteratura* meaning 'writing']

lithe
(adjective) supple and graceful.

lithium
(noun) Lithium is a chemical element. It is the lightest known solid. Its atomic number is 3 and its symbol is Li.

lithograph, lithographs
(noun) A lithograph is a type of print made by taking an impression from a sheet of stone or metal which has been treated so that ink sticks to some parts of it and not to others.
lithography (noun).
[from Greek *lithos* meaning 'stone']

litigant, litigants
(noun; a legal word) A litigant is one of the parties in a legal case.

litigate, litigates, litigating, litigated
(verb) To litigate means to fight or defend a case in a civil court of law.
litigation (noun).
[from Latin *lis* meaning 'lawsuit' and *agere* meaning 'to carry on']

litmus
(noun) In chemistry, litmus is a substance that turns red under acid and blue under alkali conditions.

litre, litres
(noun) A litre is a unit of liquid volume equal to about 1.76 pints.

litter, litters, littering, littered
1 (noun) Litter is rubbish in the street and other public places.
2 Cat litter is a gravelly substance you put in a container where you want your cat to urinate and defecate.
3 A litter is a number of baby animals born at the same time to the same mother.
4 (verb) If things litter a place, they are scattered all over it.

little, littler, littlest; less, lesser, least
1 (adjective) small in size or amount.
2 (noun and adverb) A little is a small amount or degree, e.g. *a little milk... a little afraid.*
3 Little also means not much, e.g. *There is little to worry about... She ate little.*
4 (phrase) If something happens **little by little**, it happens gradually.

littoral
(noun) The littoral is the coastal area of a place.
[from Latin *litus* meaning 'shore']

liturgy, liturgies
(noun) A liturgy is an official form of public service in the Christian church.
liturgical (adjective).

live, lives, living, lived
1 (verb) If you live in a place, that is where your home is.
2 To live means to be alive.
3 (phrase) If you **live it up**, you have an exciting and enjoyable time, spending a lot of money.
4 (verb) If something lives up to your expectations, it is as good as you thought it would be.
5 (adjective) Live animals or plants are alive, rather than dead or artificial, e.g. *a live snake.*
6 (adjective and adverb) Live television or radio is broadcast while the event is taking place, e.g. *a live concert... This show is going out live.*
7 (adjective) Something is live if it is directly connected to an electricity supply, e.g. *Careful — those wires are live.*
8 Live bullets or ammunition have not yet been exploded.

Similar words: (sense 1) abide, dwell, inhabit, reside

live down
(phrasal verb) If you cannot live down a mistake or failure, you cannot make people forget it.

livelihood, livelihoods
(noun) Someone's livelihood is their job or the source of their income.

livelong (pronounced liv-long)
(phrase; a literary expression) If you say that something goes on **all the livelong day**, you mean that it goes on all day.

lively, livelier, liveliest
(adjective) full of life and enthusiasm, e.g. *lively children... a lively debate.*
liveliness (noun).

Similar words: active, brisk, frisky, perky, spirited

liven, livens, livening, livened
(verb) To liven things up means to make them more lively, cheerful, or interesting.

liver, livers
1 (noun) Your liver is a large organ in your body which cleans your blood and aids digestion.
2 Liver is also the liver of lambs, pigs, or cows, which may be cooked and eaten.
[from Greek *liparos* meaning 'fat']

liverish
1 (adjective) having a disorder of the liver.
2 bad-tempered and disagreeable.

livery, liveries
(noun) A livery is a uniform worn by some servants, hotel doormen, and chauffeurs.

livery stable, livery stables
(noun) A livery stable is a place where horses are looked after and hired out.

livestock
(noun) Livestock is farm animals.

live wire, live wires
(noun) A live wire is a bright, lively person.

livid
1 (adjective) extremely angry.
2 dark purple or bluish, e.g. *a livid bruise.*
[from Latin *livere* meaning 'to be black and blue']

living
1 (adjective) If someone is living, they are alive, e.g. *I have no living relatives.*
2 (noun) The work you do for a living is the work you do in order to earn money to live.

living room, living rooms
(noun) A living room is the room where people relax and entertain in their homes.

lizard, lizards
(noun) A lizard is a long, thin, dry-skinned reptile. Lizards live mainly in hot, dry countries.

llama, llamas
(noun) A llama is a South American animal related to the camel. It is used as a pack animal and provides wool, meat, and leather.
[a Spanish word]

load, loads, loading, loaded
1 (noun) A load is something being carried.
2 (an informal use) Loads means a lot, e.g. *loads of food.*
3 (verb) To load a vehicle or animal means to put a large number of things into it or onto it.
4 To load a gun means to put a bullet into it. To load a camera means to put a film into it.

loaded
1 (adjective) carrying a large number of things, e.g. *loaded with shopping.*
2 (an informal use) having a lot of money.
3 unfair, biased, or containing a hidden trap, e.g. *a loaded question.*

loaf, loaves; loafs, loafing, loafed
1 (noun) A loaf is a large piece of bread baked in a shape that can be cut into slices.
2 (verb) To loaf around means to be lazy and not do any work.
loafer (noun).

loam
(noun) Loam is rich, fertile soil containing sand, clay, and decaying organic matter.

loan, loans, loaning, loaned
1 (noun) A loan is a sum of money that you borrow.
2 A loan is also the act of borrowing or lending something, e.g. *a loan of a book.*
3 (verb) If you loan something to someone, you lend it to them.

Similar words: (sense 1) advance, credit
(sense 3) lend, advance

loath or loth (rhymes with both)
(adjective) If you are loath to do something, you are very unwilling to do it.

loathe, loathes, loathing, loathed
(verb) To loathe someone or something means to feel strong dislike or disgust for them.
loathing (noun), **loathsome** (adjective).

lob, lobs, lobbing, lobbed
1 (verb) If you lob something, you throw it high in the air.
2 (noun) In tennis, a lob is a stroke in which the player hits the ball high in the air.

lobby, lobbies, lobbying, lobbied
1 (noun) The lobby in a building is the main entrance area with corridors and doors leading off it.
2 A lobby is a group of people trying to persuade an organization that something should be done, e.g. *the antinuclear lobby.*
3 (verb) To lobby an MP or an organization means to try to persuade them to do something, for example by writing them lots of letters.

lobe, lobes
1 (noun) The lobe of your ear is the rounded soft part at the bottom.
2 A lobe is also any rounded part of something, e.g. *the frontal lobes of the brain.*

lobelia, lobelias (pronounced loh-**beel**-ee-a)
(noun) A lobelia is a low-growing plant with many small five-petalled flowers. It is named after the 16th century Flemish botanist Matthias de Lobel.

lobotomy, lobotomies
(noun) A lobotomy is an operation performed on the brain to treat severe mental disorders.

lobster, lobsters
(noun) A lobster is an edible shellfish with two front claws, eight legs, a long body, and a tail folded underneath.

local, locals
1 (adjective) Local means in, near, or belonging to the area in which you live, e.g. *the local newspaper.*
2 A local anaesthetic numbs only one part of your body and does not send you to sleep.
3 (noun) The locals are the people who live in a particular area.
4 (an informal use) Someone's local is the pub nearest their home.
locally (adverb).
[from Latin *locus* meaning 'place']

Similar words: (sense 1) district, neighbourhood, community, regional

locality, localities
(noun) A locality is an area of a country or city, e.g. *There are lots of schools in the locality.*

localized or localised
(adjective) existing or happening in only one place, e.g. *localized showers... localized pain.*

locate, locates, locating, located
1 (verb) To locate someone or something means to find out where they are.
2 If something is located in a place, it is in that place.

location, locations
1 (noun) A location is a place, or the position of something.
2 (phrase) If a film is made on **location**, it is made away from a studio.

Similar words: (sense 1) position, whereabouts

loch, lochs (pronounced lokh)
(noun) In Scottish English, a loch is a lake.

lock, locks, locking, locked
1 (verb) If you lock something, you close it and fasten it with a key.

2 If something locks into place, it moves into place and becomes firmly fixed there.
3 (noun) A lock is a device on something which fastens it and prevents it from being opened except with a key.
4 A lock on a canal is a place where the water level can be raised or lowered to enable boats to go between two parts of the canal which have different water levels.
5 A lock of hair is a small bunch of hair.

locker, lockers
(noun) A locker is a small cupboard for your personal belongings, for example in a changing room.

locket, lockets
(noun) A locket is a piece of jewellery consisting of a small case which you can keep a photograph in, and which you wear on a chain round your neck.

lockout, lockouts
(noun) When there is a lockout, an employer refuses to allow employees to enter their workplace unless they accept certain conditions.

locksmith, locksmiths
(noun) A locksmith is a person who makes or mends locks.

locomotion
(noun; a formal word) Locomotion is movement.

locomotive, locomotives
(noun) A locomotive is a railway engine.

locum, locums
(noun) A locum is a doctor or priest who takes over temporarily from another doctor or priest.
[from Latin *locum tenens* meaning 'holding (someone's) place']

locust, locusts
(noun) A locust is an insect similar to a large grasshopper. Locusts live in hot countries and usually travel in swarms, eating all the crops they find.

lodge, lodges, lodging, lodged
1 (noun) A lodge is a small house in the grounds of a large country house, or a small house used for holidays.
2 (verb) If you lodge in someone else's house, you live there and pay them rent.
3 If something lodges somewhere, it gets stuck there, e.g. *I got this bone lodged in my throat.*
4 If you lodge a complaint, you formally make it.

lodger, lodgers
(noun) A lodger is a person who lives in someone's house and pays rent.

lodgings
(noun) If you live in lodgings, you live in someone else's house and pay rent.

loft, lofts
(noun) A loft is the space immediately under the roof of a house, often used for storing things.

lofty, loftier, loftiest
1 (adjective) very high, e.g. *lofty treetops.*
2 very noble and important, e.g. *lofty ideals.*
3 proud and superior, e.g. *his lofty manner.*
loftily (adverb), **loftiness** (noun).

log, logs, logging, logged
1 (noun) A log is a thick branch or piece of tree trunk which has fallen or been cut down.
2 A log is also the captain's official record of everything that happens on board a ship.
3 A log is also a logarithm.
4 (verb) If you log something, you officially make a record of it, for example in a ship's log.
5 To log into a computer system means to gain access to it so that you can use it, usually by giving your name and password. To log out means to finish using the system, usually by typing 'logout'.

loganberry, loganberries
(noun) Loganberries are small purplish-red fruits that grow on prickly bushes.

logarithm, logarithms
(noun) In mathematics, every number has a logarithm to a particular base. Logarithms to the base 10 are arranged in tables to make calculations easier. For example, you can add or subtract the logarithms of two numbers instead of multiplying or dividing the numbers.
[from Greek *logos* meaning 'ratio' or 'reckoning' and *arithmos* meaning 'number']

logbook, logbooks
(noun) A logbook is a book in which you record the details of something, for example on a ship or in a car.

loggerheads
(phrase) If two people are **at loggerheads**, they disagree strongly with each other.

logic
1 (noun) Logic is a way of reasoning involving a series of statements, each of which must be true if the statement before it is true.
2 You can use logic to refer to any sensible thinking or reasonable decision.

logical
1 (adjective) A logical argument uses logic.
2 A logical course of action or decision is sensible or reasonable in the circumstances, e.g. *a logical conclusion.*
logically (adverb).

logistics
(noun; a formal word) The logistics of a complicated undertaking is the skilful organization of it.
logistic (adjective).

logo, logos (pronounced **loh**-goh)
(noun) The logo of an organization is a special design that is put on all its products.
[from Greek *logos* meaning 'word']

-logy
(suffix) -logy is used to form words that refer to the study of something, e.g. *biology... geology.*
[from Greek *logos* meaning 'reason', 'speech', or 'discourse']

loin, loins
1 (noun; an old-fashioned use) Your loins are the front part of your body between your waist and your thighs, especially your sexual parts.
2 (phrase) If you **gird up your loins**, you prepare to do something difficult or dangerous.
3 (noun) Loin is a piece of meat from the back or sides of an animal, e.g. *loin of pork.*

loincloth, loincloths
(noun) A loincloth is a piece of cloth worn by men in hot countries to cover their sexual parts.

loiter, loiters, loitering, loitered
(verb) To loiter means to stand about idly with no real purpose.

loll, lolls, lolling, lolled
1 (verb) If you loll somewhere, you sit or lie there in an idle, relaxed way.
2 If your head or tongue lolls, it hangs loosely.

lollipop, lollipops
(noun) A lollipop is a hard sweet on the end of a stick.

lolly, lollies
1 (noun) A lolly is a lollipop.
2 A lolly is also ice cream or water ice on a stick.
3 (an informal use) Lolly is money.

lone
(adjective) A lone person or thing is the only one in a particular place, e.g. *a lone figure.*

Similar words: single, solitary, sole, solo

lonely, lonelier, loneliest
1 (adjective) If you are lonely, you are unhappy because you are alone.
2 A lonely place is an isolated one which very few people visit, e.g. *a lonely windswept moor.*
loneliness (noun).

loner, loners
(noun) A loner is a person who likes to be alone.

lonesome
(adjective) lonely and sad.

long, longer, longest; longs, longing, longed
1 (adjective and adverb) continuing for a great amount of time, e.g. *a long time abroad... Our oil won't last much longer.*
2 (adjective) great in length or distance, e.g. *long hair... a long way.*
3 (phrase) If something **no longer** happens, it does not happen any more.
4 **Before long** means soon.
5 If one thing is true **as long as** another thing is true, it is true only if the other thing is true.
6 **So long** is an informal way of saying goodbye.
7 (verb) If you long for something, you want it very much.
longing (noun), **longingly** (adverb).

Similar words: (sense 1) lengthy, drawn-out, prolonged, protracted
(sense 7) yearn, wish, pine

longboat, longboats
(noun) Longboats were long, narrow boats which used to be carried by sailing ships.

longbow, longbows
(noun) A longbow was a very tall bow used to fire long arrows in medieval times.

longevity (pronounced lon-**jev**-it-ee)
(noun; a formal word) Longevity is long life.
[from Latin *longus* meaning 'long' and *aevum* meaning 'age']

longhand
(noun) If you write something in longhand, you do it in your own handwriting rather than using shorthand or a typewriter.

longitude, longitudes
(noun) The longitude of a place is its distance east or west of a line passing through Greenwich, measured in degrees.

long johns
(plural noun) Long johns are long underpants.

long jump
(noun) The long jump is an athletics event in which you jump as far as possible after taking a long run.

long-playing
(adjective) A long-playing record is about 12 inches in diameter, is played at $33^1/_3$ r p m, and has about 25 minutes of music on each side.

long-range
1 (adjective) able to be used over a great distance, e.g. *long-range missiles.*
2 extending a long way into the future, e.g. *a long-range weather forecast.*

long shot, long shots
1 (noun; an informal word) A long shot is a person, a bet, or an undertaking which has little chance of success.
2 (phrase) If someone has not finished **by a long shot**, they still have a lot to do.

long-sighted
(adjective) If you are long-sighted, you have difficulty seeing things that are close.

long-standing
(adjective) having existed for a long time, e.g. *a long-standing arrangement.*

long-suffering
(adjective) very patient, e.g. *his long-suffering wife.*

long-term
(adjective) extending a long way into the future, e.g. *a long-term commitment.*

long wave
(noun) Long wave is a radio wave with a wavelength of more than 1000 metres.

long-winded
(adjective) long and boring, e.g. *a long-winded speech.*

Similar words: rambling, verbose, wordy

loo, loos
(noun; an informal word) A loo is a toilet.

loofah, loofahs
(noun) A loofah is a long, rough, spongelike object, used for washing and scrubbing in the

bath. It consists of the dried and bleached interior of a gourd.

look, looks, looking, looked
1 (verb) If you look at something, you turn your eyes towards it so that you can see it.
2 If you look for someone or something, you try to find them.
3 If you look at a subject or situation, you study it, consider it, or judge it.
4 If you look down on someone, you think that they are inferior to you.
5 If you are looking forward to something, you want it to happen because you think you will enjoy it.
6 If you look up to someone, you admire and respect them.
7 If you describe the way that something looks, you are describing its appearance.
8 (noun) If you have a look at something, you look at it.
9 The look on your face is the expression on it.
10 If you talk about someone's looks, you are talking about how attractive they are.

Similar words: (sense 1) behold, view, regard, glance, peek, peep
(sense 8) glance, glimpse, peek, peep
(sense 9) appearance, aspect, countenance

look after
(phrasal verb) If you look after someone or something, you take care of them.

Similar words: tend, care for, nurse, mind

look out
(interjection) You say 'look out' to warn someone of danger.

look up
1 (phrasal verb) To look up information means to find it out in a book.
2 If you look someone up, you go to see them after not having seen them for a long time.
3 If a situation is looking up, it is improving.

lookalike, lookalikes
(noun) A lookalike is a person who looks very like someone else, e.g. *a Marilyn Monroe lookalike.*

look-in
(noun; an informal expression) If you do not get a look-in, you do not get the chance to do something, because too many other people are doing it.

lookout, lookouts
1 (noun) A lookout is someone who is watching for danger, or a place where they watch for danger.
2 (phrase) If you are on the lookout for something, you are watching for it or waiting expectantly for it.

loom, looms, looming, loomed
1 (noun) A loom is a machine for weaving cloth.
2 (verb) If something looms in front of you, it suddenly appears as a tall, unclear, and sometimes frightening shape.

3 If a situation or event is looming, it is likely to happen soon and is rather worrying.

loony, loonies (an informal word)
1 (adjective) People or behaviour can be described as loony if they are mad or eccentric.
2 (noun) A loony is a mad or eccentric person.
[from 'lunatic']

loop, loops, looping, looped
1 (noun) A loop is a curved or circular shape in something long such as a piece of string.
2 (verb) If you loop rope or string around an object, you place it in a loop around the object.

loophole, loopholes
(noun) A loophole is a small mistake or omission in the law which allows you to do something that the law really intends that you should not do.

loose, looser, loosest
1 (adjective) If something is loose, it is not firmly held, fixed, or attached.
2 (adverb) To set animals loose means to set them free after they have been tied up or kept in a cage.
3 (phrase) If you are at a loose end, you are bored and have nothing to do.
loosely (adverb), looseness (noun).

loosebox, looseboxes
(noun) A loosebox is a large stall for a horse.

loose-leaf
(adjective) Loose-leaf folders and binders can be opened and closed to allow pages to be put in or taken out.

loosen, loosens, loosening, loosened
(verb) To loosen something means to make it looser.

Similar words: undo, unfasten, slacken

loot, loots, looting, looted
1 (verb) To loot shops and houses means to steal money and goods from them during a battle or riot.
2 (noun) Loot is stolen money or goods.
[from Hindi *lut*]

Similar words: (sense 1) raid, ransack, plunder, pillage
(sense 2) booty, spoils, swag, haul

lop, lops, lopping, lopped
(verb) If you lop something off, you cut it off with one quick stroke.

lope, lopes, loping, loped
(verb) To lope means to run with long strides.

lopsided
(adjective) Something that is lopsided is uneven because its two sides are different sizes or shapes.
lopsidedly (adverb).

loquacious (pronounced lok-**way**-shuss)
(adjective; a literary word) very talkative.
[from Latin *loqui* meaning 'to speak']

lord, lords, lording, lorded
1 (noun) A lord is a nobleman.
2 Lord is a title used in front of the names of

some noblemen, and of bishops, archbishops, judges, and some high-ranking officials, e.g. *the Lord Mayor of London.*
3 In Christianity, 'Lord' is a name given to God and Jesus Christ.
4 (verb) If someone lords it over you, they act in a way that shows that they consider they are superior to you.

lordly
(adjective) proud and arrogant.

Lordship, Lordships
(noun) You address a lord, judge, or bishop as Your Lordship.

lore
(noun) The lore of a place, people, or subject is all the traditional knowledge and stories about it.

lorgnette, lorgnettes (pronounced lor-**nyet**)
(noun) A lorgnette is an old-fashioned pair of spectacles with a handle that someone holds to their eyes.
[from Old French *lorgne* meaning 'squinting']

lorry, lorries
(noun) A lorry is a large vehicle for transporting goods by road.

lose, loses, losing, lost
1 (verb) If you lose something, you cannot find it, or you no longer have it because it has been taken away from you, e.g. *He has lost the use of his legs.*
2 If you lose a relative or friend, they die, e.g. *She lost her father when she was six.*
3 If you lose a fight or an argument, you are beaten.
4 If a business loses money, it is spending more money than it is earning.
loser (noun).

loss, losses
1 (noun) The loss of something is the losing of it.
2 (phrase) If you are **at a loss**, you do not know what to do.

lost
1 (adjective) If you are lost, you do not know where you are.
2 If something is lost, you cannot find it.
3 If advice or a comment is lost on someone, they ignore it or do not understand it.
4 Lost is the past tense and past participle of **lose.**

Similar words: (sense 2) missing, astray, mislaid, misplaced

lot, lots
1 (noun) A lot of something, or lots of something, is a large amount of it.
2 A lot means very much or very often, e.g. *I like him a lot.*
3 A lot is an amount of something or a number of things, e.g. *You can have that lot for 50p.*
4 In an auction, a lot is one of the things being sold.
5 (phrase) You **draw lots** to decide who will do something by each person taking a straw or a

piece of paper from a container. The person who takes the straw or piece of paper that is different from the others is the one who is chosen.

Similar words: (sense 1) many, heaps, piles, oodles, loads, masses

loth another spelling of **loath.**

lotion, lotions
(noun) A lotion is a liquid that you put on your skin to protect or soften it, e.g. *suntan lotion.*

lottery, lotteries
(noun) A lottery is a type of gambling game in which numbered tickets are sold. Several tickets are selected and their owners win a prize.

lotus, lotuses
(noun) A lotus is a large water lily, found in Africa and Asia.

loud, louder, loudest
1 (adjective and adverb) A loud noise has a high volume of sound, e.g. *a loud bang.. He sang out loud.*
2 If you describe clothing as loud, you mean that it is too bright and tasteless, e.g. *a loud checked shirt.*
3 If you are loud in your support of something, you support it strongly and talk about it a lot.
loudly (adverb), **loudness** (noun).

Similar words: (sense 1) noisy, deafening, strident

loud-hailer, loud-hailers
(noun) A loud-hailer is a hand-held loudspeaker which contains its own microphone and amplifier.

loudspeaker, loudspeakers
(noun) A loudspeaker is a piece of equipment that makes your voice louder when you speak into a microphone connected to it.

lough, loughs (pronounced lokh)
(noun) In Irish English, a lough is a lake.

lounge, lounges, lounging, lounged
1 (noun) A lounge is a room in a house or hotel with comfortable chairs where people can relax.
2 In a pub or hotel, the lounge or lounge bar is the bar which is most comfortably furnished but where the drinks are more expensive.
3 (verb) If you lounge around, you lean against something or sit or lie around in a lazy and comfortable way.

lour, lours, louring, loured
1 (verb) If the weather or sky is louring, it is overcast and dark.
2 To lour means to scowl or frown.

louse, lice
(noun) Lice are small insects that live on people's bodies, e.g. *head lice.*

lousy, lousier, lousiest (an informal word)
1 (adjective) of bad quality or very unpleasant, e.g. *The hotels are lousy... lousy weather.*
2 ill or unhappy, e.g. *I feel really lousy.*

lout, louts
(noun) A lout is a boy or young man who behaves in an impolite or aggressive way.
loutish (adjective).

louvre, louvres (pronounced **loo**-ver)
(noun) Louvres are a set of slightly sloping slats in a door or window, designed originally to let in air in hot countries.
louvred (adjective).

lovable or **loveable**
(adjective) having very attractive qualities and therefore easy to love, e.g. *a lovable little puppy.*

love, loves, loving, loved
1 (verb) If you love someone, you have strong emotional feelings of affection for them.
2 If you love something, you like it very much, e.g. *I love chocolate cake.*
3 (noun) Love is a strong emotional feeling of affection for someone or something.
4 (verb) If you would love to do something, you want very much to do it, e.g. *I'd love to go to Paris.*
5 (noun) In tennis, love is a score of zero.
6 (phrase) If you are **in love** with someone, you feel strongly attracted to them romantically or sexually.
7 When two people **make love**, they have sex.
loving (adjective), **lovingly** (adverb).

Similar words: (sense 1) dote on, adore

love affair, love affairs
(noun) A love affair is a romantic and often sexual relationship between two people who are not married to each other.

lovebird, lovebirds
(noun) A lovebird is a type of small African parrot. Each pair of lovebirds keep very close together when perched.

love child, love children
(noun) A love child is the child of unmarried parents.

love life, love lives
(noun) A person's love life is their romantic and sexual relationships.

lovelorn
(adjective) miserable because of unreturned love or an unhappy love affair.

lovely, lovelier, loveliest
(adjective) very beautiful, attractive, and pleasant.
loveliness (noun).

lover, lovers
1 (noun) A person's lover is someone that they have a sexual relationship with but are not married to.
2 Someone who is a lover of something, for example art or music, is very fond of it.

low, lower, lowest
1 (adjective and adverb) Something that is low is close to the ground, or measures a short distance from the ground to the top, e.g. *a low wall.*
2 (adjective) Low means small in value or amount, e.g. *Temperatures will get lower soon.*
3 Low is used to describe people who are considered not respectable, e.g. *mixing with low company.*
4 A low sound is deep and quiet.
5 A light that is low is dim and not bright.
6 If you are low, you are depressed.
7 (noun) A low is a level or amount that is less than before, e.g. *output hit a new low.*

lowbrow
(adjective) of low intellectual standard or ability, e.g. *lowbrow music.*

lower, lowers, lowering, lowered
1 (verb) To lower something means to move it downwards or to make it less in value or amount.
2 (adjective) Lower describes people and things that are less important than other people and things.

Similar words: (sense 2) lesser, minor, subordinate, inferior

lower case
(adjective) Lower case letters are the small letters used in printing or on a typewriter.

Lower House
(noun) In Britain, the Lower House or Lower Chamber is the House of Commons.

lowest common denominator, lowest common denominators
(noun) In mathematics, the lowest common denominator is the smallest number which can be exactly divided by all the denominators of a group of fractions.

lowlands
(plural noun) Lowlands are an area of flat, low land.
lowland (adjective).

lowly, lowlier, lowliest
(adjective) low in importance, rank or status.

low profile
(noun) If you keep a low profile, you deliberately avoid publicity.

low tide
(noun) On a coast, low tide is the time, usually twice a day, when the sea is at its lowest level.

loyal
(adjective) firm in your friendship or support for someone or something.
loyally (adverb), **loyalty** (noun).

loyalist, loyalists
1 (noun) Loyalists are people who are loyal, particularly to the king or queen, in times of revolution or conflict.
2 In Ulster, a Loyalist is a Protestant who wishes Northern Ireland to remain part of the United Kingdom and not be joined to the Republic of Ireland.

lozenge, lozenges
1 (noun) A lozenge is a type of sweet with medicine in it, which you suck to relieve a sore throat or cough.
2 A lozenge is also a diamond shape.
[from Latin *lausa* meaning 'flat stone']

LP, LPs

(noun) An LP is a long-playing record. LP is short for 'long-playing record'.

LSD

(noun) LSD is a very powerful drug which causes hallucinations. LSD is an abbreviation for 'lysergic acid diethylamide'.

Ltd. an abbreviation for 'limited'; used after the names of limited companies.

lubricate, lubricates, lubricating, lubricated

(verb) To lubricate something such as a machine means to put oil or an oily substance onto it, so that it moves smoothly and friction is reduced.
lubrication (noun), **lubricant** (noun).
[from Latin *lubricus* meaning 'slippery']

lucerne (pronounced loo-**sern**)

(noun) Lucerne is a cereal crop grown for fodder. It is also known as alfalfa.

lucid

1 (adjective) Lucid writing or speech is clear and easy to understand.
2 Someone who is lucid after having been ill or delirious is able to think clearly again.
lucidly (adverb), **lucidity** (noun).
[from Latin *lucidus* meaning 'full of light']

Lucifer

(noun) In Christian mythology, Lucifer is the angel who led the revolt against God in heaven and then became known as Satan.

luck

1 (noun) Luck is anything that seems to happen by chance and not through your own efforts.
2 (phrase) If you are **in luck**, you are lucky or successful on one particular occasion.

Similar words: (sense 1) fortune, chance

luckless

(adjective; a literary or formal word) unsuccessful or unfortunate, e.g. *So our luckless hero went on his way.*

lucky, luckier, luckiest

1 (adjective) Someone who is lucky has a lot of good luck.
2 Something that is lucky happens by chance and has good effects or consequences.
luckily (adverb).

Similar words: (sense 1) fortunate
(sense 2) fortunate, fortuitous, auspicious, propitious

lucrative

(adjective) Something that is lucrative earns you a lot of money, e.g. *a lucrative arms deal.*

lucre

(noun) Lucre is another word for money and is often used humorously or sarcastically in the phrase 'filthy lucre'.
[from Latin *lucrum* meaning 'gain']

ludicrous

(adjective) completely foolish, unsuitable, or ridiculous.
ludicrously (adverb).
[from Latin *ludicrus* meaning 'done in sport']

lug, lugs, lugging, lugged

(verb) If you lug a heavy object around, you carry it with difficulty.

luggage

(noun) Your luggage is the bags and suitcases that you take with you when you travel.

lugubrious (pronounced loo-**goo**-bree-uss)

(adjective) very sad and dreary, e.g. *lugubrious hymns.*
lugubriously (adverb).
[from Latin *lugubris* meaning 'mournful']

lukewarm

1 (adjective) slightly warm, e.g. *Add 100ml of lukewarm water to this mixture.*
2 not very enthusiastic or interested, e.g. *My idea received a lukewarm response.*

lull, lulls, lulling, lulled

1 (noun) A lull is a pause in something, or a short time when it is quiet and nothing much happens, e.g. *There was a lull in the conversation.*
2 (verb) To lull someone means to send them to sleep or to make them feel safe and secure, e.g. *We had been lulled into a false sense of security.*

lullaby, lullabies

(noun) A lullaby is a song used for sending a baby or child to sleep.

lumbago

(noun) Lumbago is pain in the lower back.
[from Latin *lumbus* meaning 'loin']

lumbar

(adjective; a formal word) relating to or involving the lower half of your back, e.g. *pain in the lumbar region.*

lumber, lumbers, lumbering, lumbered

1 (noun) Lumber is wood that has been roughly cut up.
2 Lumber is also old unwanted furniture and other items.
3 (verb) If you lumber around, you move heavily and clumsily.
4 (an informal use) If you are lumbered with something, you are given it to deal with even though you do not want it, e.g. *I got lumbered with producing the end-of-term play.*

lumberjack, lumberjacks

(noun) A lumberjack is a man whose job is to chop down trees in forests.

lumen, lumens or lumina

(noun) A lumen is the derived SI unit of luminous flux.
[from Latin *lumen* meaning 'light']

luminance

(noun) Luminance is a measure of brightness of a point of light on a reflective surface.

luminary, luminaries

(noun; a literary word) A luminary is a person who is famous or an expert in a particular subject.

luminescence

(noun) Luminescence is the process of giving off light through some means other than burning, for example chemical action or fluorescence.
luminescent (adjective).

luminous
(adjective) Something that is luminous glows in the dark, usually because it has been treated with a special substance. e.g. *a luminous clock*. **luminously** (adverb), **luminosity** (noun).

lump, lumps, lumping, lumped
1 (noun) A lump of something is a solid piece of it, of any shape or size, e.g. *a big lump of clay*.
2 A lump is also a bump on the surface of something.
3 (verb) If you lump people or things together, you combine them into one group or consider them as being similar in some way.
4 (an informal phrase) If you **have to lump it**, you have to put up with something whether you like it or not.
lumpy (adjective), **lumpily** (adverb).

lump sum, lump sums
(noun) A lump sum is a large sum of money given or received all at once.

lunacy
1 (noun) Lunacy is extremely foolish or eccentric behaviour.
2 (an old-fashioned use) Lunacy is also severe mental illness.

lunar
(adjective) relating to the moon.
[from Latin *luna* meaning 'moon']

lunar month, lunar months
(noun) A lunar month is the time taken by the moon to make one complete revolution around the earth, measured from one new moon to the next. It is approximately 29.53 days.

lunatic, lunatics
1 (noun) If you call someone a lunatic, you mean that they are very foolish, stupid, and annoying, e.g. *Look at the way he drives — he's a lunatic!*
2 A lunatic is also someone who is insane.
3 (adjective) Lunatic behaviour is very stupid, foolish, or dangerous.

lunch, lunches, lunching, lunched
1 (noun) Lunch is a meal eaten in the middle of the day.
2 (verb) When you lunch, you eat lunch.

luncheon, luncheons (pronounced lun-shen)
(noun; a formal word) Luncheon is lunch.

lung, lungs
(noun) Your lungs are the two organs inside your ribcage with which you breathe.

lunge, lunges, lunging, lunged
1 (noun) A lunge is a sudden forward movement, e.g. *He made a lunge at me*.
2 (verb) To lunge means to make a sudden movement in a particular direction.
[from French *allonger* meaning 'to stretch out one's arm']

lupin, lupins
(noun) A lupin is a garden plant that has tall spikes of brightly coloured flowers and flattened seed-pods.

lurch, lurches, lurching, lurched
1 (verb) To lurch means to make a sudden, jerky movement.
2 (noun) A lurch is a sudden, jerky movement.
3 (phrase) If someone **leaves you in the lurch**, they leave you in a very difficult or dangerous situation, instead of helping you.

lure, lures, luring, lured
1 (verb) To lure someone means to attract them into going somewhere or doing something.
2 (noun) A lure is something that you find very attractive.

lurid (pronounced loo-rid)
1 (adjective) involving a lot of sensational detail, e.g. *lurid newspaper stories*.
2 very brightly coloured or patterned.
luridly (adverb).

lurk, lurks, lurking, lurked
(verb) To lurk somewhere means to remain there hidden from the person you are waiting for.

luscious
1 (adjective) very attractive, e.g. *a luscious car*.
2 very tasty, e.g. *a luscious peach*.
lusciously (adverb).

lush, lusher, lushest
1 (adjective) In a lush field or garden, the grass or plants are healthy and growing thickly.
2 If you describe a place as lush, you mean it is richly and luxuriously furnished, e.g. *lush apartments*.

lust, lusts, lusting, lusted
1 (noun) Lust is a very strong feeling of sexual desire for someone.
2 A lust for something is a strong desire to have it, e.g. *a lust for power*.
3 (verb) To lust for or after someone means to desire them sexually.
4 If you lust for or after something, you have a very strong desire to possess it, e.g. *They lusted after the gold of El Dorado*.

lustful
(adjective) feeling or expressing strong sexual desire.
lustfully (adverb).

Similar words: lecherous, prurient, salacious, lewd

lustre (pronounced lus-ter)
(noun) Lustre is soft shining light reflected from the surface of something, e.g. *the lustre of gold*.
lustrous (adjective).

lusty, lustier, lustiest
(adjective) strong, healthy, and full of energy, e.g *a strong and lusty boy*.
lustily (adverb).

lute, lutes
(noun) A lute is a stringed musical instrument which is plucked like a guitar. It is shaped like half a pear and was popular in the Middle Ages.

Lutheran, Lutherans
(noun) A Lutheran is a member of the Protestant church founded by Martin Luther.

luxuriant
(adjective) Luxuriant plants, trees, and gardens are large, healthy and growing strongly.
luxuriantly (adverb), **luxuriance** (noun).

luxuriate, luxuriates, luxuriating, luxuriated
(verb) If you luxuriate in something, you relax in it and enjoy it fully, e.g. *She luxuriated in the warm tropical waters.*

luxurious
(adjective) very expensive and full of luxury.
luxuriously (adverb).

Similar words: lavish, opulent, sumptuous

luxury, luxuries
1 (noun) Luxury is great comfort in expensive and beautiful surroundings, e.g. *a life of luxury.*
2 A luxury is something that you enjoy very much but do not have very often, usually because it is expensive.

Similar words: (sense 2) extra, treat, indulgence

lychee, lychees (pronounced **lie**-chee)
(noun) Lychees are a small Chinese fruit with firm reddish brown shells and smooth white flesh surrounding a stone.

lying
1 (noun) Lying is telling lies.
2 (adjective) A lying person often tells lies.
3 Lying is also the present participle of **lie**.

Similar words: (sense 2) mendacious, untruthful

lymph (pronounced **limf**)
(noun) Lymph is a fluid which contains white blood cells and transports them around the body.

lynch, lynches, lynching, lynched
(verb) If a crowd lynches someone, it kills them in a violent and unpleasant way without first holding a legal trial.

lynx, lynxes
(noun) A lynx is a wildcat with a short tail, tufted ears, and brown mottled fur. They are found in Europe, Africa and America and have very keen eyesight.

lyre, lyres
(noun) A lyre was a stringed instrument used in ancient Greece, which consisted of two curved arms and a sound-box.

lyrebird, lyrebirds
(noun) Lyrebirds are Australian pheasant-like birds. The male spreads his tail into the shape of a lyre during courtship dances.

lyric, lyrics
1 (adjective) Lyric poetry is written in a simple and direct style, and is usually about love.
2 (noun) The lyrics of a song are the words.
[from Greek *lura* meaning 'lyre']

lyrical
1 (adjective) poetic and romantic.
2 eager and enthusiastic, e.g. *He waxed lyrical about his new job.*
lyrically (adverb).

M

m an abbreviation for 'metres' or 'miles'.

MA, MAs
(noun) An MA is a higher university degree in a subject such as languages, literature, history, or a social science; also used to refer to someone who has such a degree. MA is an abbreviation for 'Master of Arts'.

mac, macs
(noun; an informal word) A mac is a mackintosh.

macabre
(adjective) A macabre event is strange and horrible, e.g. *a macabre murder story*.

macaroni
(noun) Macaroni is short hollow tubes of pasta. [an Italian word; from Greek *makaria* meaning 'food made from barley']

macaroon, macaroons
(noun) A macaroon is a sweet biscuit flavoured with almonds or coconut.

mace, maces
(noun) A mace is an ornamental pole carried by an official as a ceremonial symbol of authority.

Mach (pronounced **mak**)
(noun) Mach is a unit of measurement for very high speeds. If an aircraft is travelling at Mach 1, it is travelling at the speed of sound. Mach is named after Ernst Mach, an Austrian physicist.

machete, machetes (pronounced mash-**ett**-ee)
(noun) A machete is a large, heavy knife with a big blade.

machine, machines, machining, machined
1 (noun) A machine is a piece of equipment which uses electricity or power from an engine.
2 (verb) If you machine something, you make it or work on it using a machine.
3 (noun) A machine is also a well-controlled system or organization, e.g. *a war machine*.

Similar words: (sense 1) apparatus, device

machine-gun, machine-guns
(noun) A machine-gun is a gun that works automatically, firing bullets one after the other.

machinery
(noun) Machinery is machines in general.

machismo (pronounced mak-**kiz**-moe)
(noun) Machismo is exaggerated aggressive male behaviour.

macho (pronounced **mat**-shoh)
(adjective) A man who is described as macho behaves in an aggressively masculine way. [from Spanish *macho* meaning 'male']

mackerel, mackerels
(noun) A mackerel is a sea fish with blue and silver stripes.

mackintosh, mackintoshes
(noun) A mackintosh is a raincoat made from specially treated cloth. It is named after Charles Mackintosh, who invented it.

mad, madder, maddest
1 (adjective) Someone who is mad has a mental illness which often causes them to behave in strange ways.
2 If you describe someone as mad, you mean that they are very foolish, e.g. *You must be mad to go out there alone.*
3 (an informal use) Someone who is mad is angry, e.g. *She got pretty mad when she found out.*
4 If you are mad about someone or something, you like them very much, e.g. *She is mad about Michael Jackson.*
madness (noun), **madman** (noun).

Similar words: (sense 1) insane, demented, lunatic (sense 2) crazy, crackers

madam
'Madam' is a very formal way of addressing a woman. [from Old French *ma dame* meaning 'my lady']

madden, maddens, maddening, maddened
(verb) If something maddens you, it makes you very angry, irritated, or frustrated.
maddening (adjective), **maddeningly** (adverb).

madly
(adverb) If you do something madly, you do it in a fast, excited, and sometimes uncontrolled way.

madrigal, madrigals
(noun) A madrigal is a song for several people singing different parts, unaccompanied by instruments.

maelstrom (pronounced **male**-strome)
(noun; a formal word) You can refer to an extremely confused, violent, and destructive situation as a maelstrom.

Mafia
(noun) The Mafia is a large crime organization operating in Sicily, Italy, and the U.S.A.

magazine, magazines
1 (noun) A magazine is a weekly or monthly publication with articles, photographs, and advertisements.
2 The magazine of a gun is a compartment for cartridges. [from Arabic *makhzan* meaning 'storehouse']

magenta (pronounced maj-**jen**-ta)
(noun and adjective) dark reddish-purple.

maggot, maggots
(noun) A maggot is a creature that looks like a small worm and lives on things that are decaying. Maggots turn into flies.
maggoty (adjective).

magic
1 (noun) In fairy stories, magic is a special power that can make impossible things happen.
2 Magic is the art of performing tricks to entertain people.
3 The magic of something is a special quality

that makes it seem wonderful and exciting, e.g.
the magic of the theatre.
magical (adjective), **magically** (adverb).

Similar words: (sense 2) conjuring, illusion, trickery, sleight of hand

magician, magicians
1 (noun) A magician is a person who performs tricks as a form of entertainment.
2 In fairy stories, a magician is a man with magical powers.

magistrate, magistrates
(noun) A magistrate is an official who acts as a judge in a law court that deals with less serious crimes.

magma
(noun) Magma is a hot liquid within the earth's crust which forms igneous rock when it solidifies.

magnanimous
(adjective) generous and forgiving.
magnanimity (noun).
[from Latin *magnanimus* meaning 'great-souled']

magnate, magnates
(noun) A magnate is someone who is very rich and powerful in business.
[from Latin *magnus* meaning 'great']

magnesium
(noun) Magnesium is a metallic element which burns with a bright white flame. It is used in fireworks, flashbulbs, and flares. Its atomic number is 12 and its symbol is Mg.

magnet, magnets
(noun) A magnet is a piece of iron which attracts iron or steel towards it, and which points towards north if allowed to swing freely.
magnetic (adjective), **magnetically** (adverb), **magnetism** (noun), **magnetize** (verb).

magnetic north
(noun) Magnetic north is the direction that a compass needle points to.

magnetic tape
(noun) Magnetic tape is narrow plastic tape covered with a magnetic substance. It is used for recording sounds, images, or computer information.

magneto, magnetos (pronounced mag-**neet**-oh)
(noun) A magneto is an electrical generator that uses magnets, especially in the engine of a car or lorry.

magnificent
(adjective) extremely beautiful or impressive.
magnificently (adverb), **magnificence** (noun).
[from Latin *magnificus* meaning 'great in deeds']

magnify, magnifies, magnifying, magnified
1 (verb) When a microscope or lens magnifies something, it makes it appear bigger than it actually is.
2 To magnify something means to make it seem more important than it actually is, e.g. *You should not magnify the differences.*
magnification (noun).

magnifying glass, magnifying glasses
(noun) A magnifying glass is a lens which makes things appear bigger than they really are.

magnitude
(noun) The magnitude of something is its great size or importance.
[from Latin *magnus* meaning 'great']

magnolia, magnolias
(noun) A magnolia is a tree which has large white or pink flowers in spring.

magpie, magpies
(noun) A magpie is a large black and white bird with a long tail.

mahogany
(noun) Mahogany is a reddish brown wood used for making furniture.

maid, maids
(noun) A maid is a female servant.

maiden, maidens
1 (noun; a literary use) A maiden is a young woman.
2 (adjective) first, e.g. *a maiden voyage... a maiden speech.*
3 A maiden aunt is one who has never married.
maidenly (adjective).

maiden name, maiden names
(noun) A woman's maiden name is the surname she had before she married.

mail, mails, mailing, mailed
1 (noun) Your mail is the letters and parcels delivered to you by the post office.
2 (verb) If you mail a letter, you send it by post.
[from Old French *male* meaning 'bag']

mailing list, mailing lists
(noun) A mailing list is a list of names and addresses kept by an organization and used to send out information.

mail order
(noun) Mail order is a system of buying goods by post.

maim, maims, maiming, maimed
(verb) To maim someone means to injure them very badly for life.

main, mains
1 (adjective) most important, e.g. *main road.*
2 (noun) The mains are large pipes or wires that carry gas, water, electricity, or sewage.
mainly (adverb).

Similar words: (sense 1) chief, premier, major, head, principal, primary, prime

main clause, main clauses
(noun) In grammar, a main clause is a clause that can stand alone as a complete sentence.

mainframe, mainframes
(noun) A mainframe is a large computer which can be used by many people at the same time.

mainland
(noun) The mainland is the main part of a country in contrast to islands around its coast.

mainline, mainlines, mainlining, mainlined
(verb; an informal word) To mainline means to inject a drug into a vein.

mainsail, mainsails
(noun) On a ship, the mainsail is the largest sail on the tallest mast.

mainspring
(noun; a formal word) The mainspring of something is the most important reason for it or the thing that is essential to it, e.g. *Technology was the mainspring of economic growth.*

mainstay
(noun) The mainstay of something is the most important part of it.

mainstream
(noun) The mainstream is the most ordinary and conventional group of people or ideas in a society.

maintain, maintains, maintaining, maintained
1 (verb) If you maintain something, you keep it going or keep it at a particular rate or level, e.g. *an effort to maintain standards.*
2 If you maintain someone, you provide them regularly with money for what they need.
3 To maintain a machine or a building means to keep it in good condition.
4 If you maintain that something is true, you believe that it is true and say so.
[from Latin *manu tenere* meaning 'to hold in the hand']

maintenance
1 (noun) Maintenance is the process of keeping something in good condition.
2 Maintenance is also money that a person sends regularly to someone to provide for the things they need.

maisonette, maisonettes
(noun) A maisonette is a small flat on two floors of a larger building.

maize
(noun) Maize is a tall plant which produces sweetcorn.

majesty, majesties
1 You say 'His Majesty' when you are talking about a king, and 'Her Majesty' when you are talking about a queen.
2 (noun) Majesty is the quality of great dignity and impressiveness.
majestic (adjective), **majestically** (adverb).

major, majors
1 (adjective) more important or more serious or significant than other things, e.g. *He sustained major injuries in the accident.*
2 (noun) A major is an army officer of the rank immediately above captain.
3 (adjective) A major key is one of the two types of key in which most European music is written.

major-general, major-generals
(noun) A major-general is an army officer of the rank immediately above brigadier.

majority, majorities
1 (noun) The majority of people or things in a group is more than half of the group.

2 In an election, the majority is the difference between the number of votes gained by the winner and the number gained by the runner-up.

Similar words: (sense 1) bulk, best part

make, makes, making, made
1 (verb) To make something means to produce or construct it, or to cause it to happen.
2 To make something also means to do it, e.g. *to make a decision... to make a phone call.*
3 To make something means to prepare it, e.g. *She made a meal... I'll make the beds.*
4 If someone makes you do something, they force you to do it, e.g. *She makes us wash up.*
5 (noun) The make of a product is the name of the company that manufactured it, e.g. *'What make is your car?' — 'It's a Datsun.'*
6 (an informal phrase) If someone **makes it**, they are successful.
7 (phrase) If you **make do** with something, you use it only because you do not have anything better.
8 If you ask someone what they **make of** something, you are asking them what they think of it.

Similar words: (sense 1) create, form, fashion, manufacture, produce;
(sense 5) brand, type

make off with
(phrasal verb) To make off with something means to steal it.

make out
1 (phrasal verb) If you can make something out, you can see it, hear it, or understand it.
2 If you make out that something is true, you try to get people to believe it.
3 To make out a cheque means to write it.

make up
1 (phrasal verb) If a number of things make up something, they form that thing.
2 If you make up a story, you invent it.
3 If you make yourself up, you put make-up on.
4 If two people make it up, they become friends again after a quarrel.
5 To make up for something that you have done wrong means to put it right.
6 If you make up your mind, you come to a decision.

makeshift
(adjective) temporary and of poor quality, e.g. *The refugees were put into makeshift shelters.*

Similar words: temporary, provisional

make-up
1 (noun) Make-up is coloured creams and powders which women put on their faces to make themselves look more attractive. Actors also use make-up on the stage or in films.
2 Someone's make-up is their character or personality.

making
1 (noun) The making of something is the act or process of creating or producing it.

2 (phrase) When you describe someone as something **in the making**, you mean that they are gradually becoming that thing, e.g. *a president in the making*.
3 If something **is the making of** a person or thing, it is the reason for their success.

Similar words: (sense 1) creation, production

maladjusted
(adjective) A maladjusted person has psychological or behaviour problems.

maladroit (pronounced mal-la-**droyt**)
(adjective; a formal word) clumsy or awkward.

malady, maladies
(noun; an old-fashioned word) A malady is an illness.

malaise (pronounced mal-**laze**)
(noun; a formal word) Malaise is a feeling of dissatisfaction or unhappiness.

malaria (pronounced mal-**lay**-ree-a)
(noun) Malaria is a tropical disease caught from mosquitoes which causes periods of fever.
malarial (adjective).

Malay, Malays (pronounced mal-**lay**)
1 (noun) Malay is a language spoken by many people who live in Malaysia and Indonesia.
2 A Malay is a member of the group of people from Malaysia and Indonesia who speak Malay.

Malaysian, Malaysians
1 (adjective) belonging or relating to Malaysia.
2 (noun) A Malaysian is someone who comes from Malaysia.

male, males
1 (noun) A male is a person or animal belonging to the sex that cannot give birth or lay eggs.
2 (adjective) concerning or affecting men rather than women.
3 The male part of a plant fertilizes the part that will produce the fruit.
4 The male part of a device is the part that fits into the hole in the female part.

male chauvinist, male chauvinists
(noun) A male chauvinist is a man who thinks that men are better than women.

malevolent (pronounced mal-**lev**-oh-lent)
(adjective; a formal word) wanting or intending to cause harm.
malevolently (adverb), **malevolence** (noun).

Similar words: malign, malignant

malformed
(adjective) Something that is malformed has grown or been formed into the wrong shape.

malfunction, malfunctions, malfunctioning, malfunctioned
1 (verb) If a machine malfunctions, it fails to work properly.
2 (noun) A malfunction in a machine is when it fails to work properly.

malice
(noun) Malice is a desire to cause harm to people.

[from Latin *malus* meaning 'evil']

Similar words: malevolence, vindictiveness, ill will, spite

malicious
(adjective) Malicious talk or behaviour is intended to harm someone.
maliciously (adverb).

malign, maligns, maligning, maligned (a formal word)
1 (verb) To malign someone means to say unpleasant and untrue things about them.
2 (adjective) intended to harm someone.
[from Latin *malignus* meaning 'spiteful']

malignant
1 (adjective) harmful and cruel.
2 A malignant disease or tumour could cause death if it is allowed to continue.
malignancy (noun).

malinger, malingers, malingering, malingered
(verb) If you malinger, you pretend to be ill to avoid work.
[from French *malingre* meaning 'sickly']

mallard, mallards
(noun) A mallard is a kind of wild duck. The female is brown and the male has a green head.

malleable (a formal word)
1 (adjective) easily influenced by other people.
2 easily changed into a new shape, e.g. *a malleable dough*.
malleability (noun).

mallet, mallets
(noun) A mallet is a wooden hammer with a square head.
[from Latin *maleus* meaning 'hammer']

malnutrition
(noun) Malnutrition is not eating enough healthy food.

malpractice
(noun) If someone such as a doctor or lawyer breaks the rules of their profession, their behaviour is called malpractice.

malt
(noun) Malt is roasted grain, usually barley, that is used in making beer and whisky.

Maltese (pronounced moll-**teez**)
1 (adjective) belonging or relating to Malta.
2 (noun) A Maltese is someone who comes from Malta.
3 Maltese is the official language of Malta.

maltreat, maltreats, maltreating, maltreated
(verb) If people or animals are maltreated, they are treated cruelly or violently.
maltreatment (noun).

mammal, mammals
(noun) Animals that give birth to live babies and feed their young with milk from the mother's body are called mammals. Human beings, dogs, lions, and whales are all mammals.
mammalian (adjective).
[from Latin *mamma* meaning 'breast']

mammary
(adjective; a technical word) relating to the breasts, e.g. *the mammary gland.*

mammoth, mammoths
1 (adjective) very large indeed, e.g. *It's a mammoth task.*
2 (noun) A mammoth was a huge animal that looked like a hairy elephant with long tusks. Mammoths became extinct a long time ago.

man, men; mans, manning, manned
1 (noun) A man is an adult male human being.
2 (plural noun) Human beings in general are sometimes referred to as men, e.g. *All men are equal.*
3 The men in an army are the ordinary soldiers, not the officers.
4 (verb) To man something means to be in charge of it or operate it, e.g. *Who's manning the phones?*

Similar words: (sense 1) male, chap, guy, bloke, fellow, gentleman
(sense 2) humanity, mankind

manacle, manacles
(noun) Manacles are metal rings or clamps attached to a prisoner's wrists or ankles.
[from Latin *manus* meaning 'hand']

manage, manages, managing, managed
1 (verb) If you manage to do something, you succeed in doing it, e.g. *However did you manage to find me?*
2 If you manage an organization or business, you are responsible for controlling it.

Similar words: (sense 1) get by, cope, survive, contrive

manageable
(adjective) able to be dealt with.

management
1 (noun) The management of a business is the controlling and organizing of it.
2 The people who control an organization are called the management.

Similar words: (sense 1) administration, control, supervision, running

manager, managers
1 (noun) A manager is a person responsible for running a business or organization, e.g. *the bank manager.*
2 The manager of a star is the person who looks after the star's business interests.
3 The manager of a sports team is the person responsible for organizing and training it.

manageress, manageresses
(noun) A manageress is a woman responsible for running a business or organization.

managing director, managing directors
(noun) The managing director of a company is a director who is responsible for the way the company is managed.

mandarin, mandarins
(noun) A mandarin is a type of small orange which is easy to peel.

mandate, mandates
1 (noun; a formal word) A government's mandate is the authority it has to carry out particular policies as a result of winning an election.
2 A mandate is a task you are instructed to carry out, e.g. *My mandate was to find the best team.*

mandatory
(adjective) If something is mandatory, there is a law or rule stating that it must be done, e.g. *the mandatory wearing of seat-belts.*

mandible, mandibles (a technical word)
1 (noun) In mammals, the mandible is the lower, movable jaw.
2 In insects, the mandibles are the two mouthparts used for biting and crushing food.

mandolin, mandolins
(noun) A mandolin is a musical instrument like a small guitar with a deep, rounded body and four pairs of strings.

mane, manes
(noun) The mane of a lion or a horse is the long thick hair growing from its neck.

manfully
(adverb) If you do something manfully, you do it in a very determined way.

manganese
(noun) Manganese is a metallic element used in making steel. Its atomic number is 25 and its symbol is Mn.

manger, mangers
(noun) A manger is a feeding box in a barn or stable.
[from Old French *mangier* meaning 'to eat']

mangle, mangles, mangling, mangled
1 (verb) If something is mangled, it is crushed and twisted.
2 (noun) A mangle is an old-fashioned piece of equipment consisting of two large rollers which squeeze water out of wet clothes.

mango, mangoes or mangos
(noun) A mango is a sweet yellowish fruit which grows in tropical countries.

mangrove, mangroves
(noun) A mangrove is a tropical tree which has exposed roots. Mangroves grow along the coast.

mangy, mangier, mangiest (pronounced mane-jee)
(adjective) A mangy animal has lost a lot of hair through disease.

manhandle, manhandles, manhandling, manhandled
(verb) If you manhandle someone, you treat them roughly, e.g. *The kidnappers manhandled the boy into the car.*

manhole, manholes
(noun) A manhole is a covered hole in the ground leading to a drain or sewer.

manhood
(noun) Manhood is the state of being a man rather than a boy.

mania, manias
1 (noun) A mania for something is a strong liking for it, e.g. *a mania for cleanliness.*
2 A mania is also a mental illness.
[from Greek *mania* meaning 'madness']

maniac, maniacs
(noun) A maniac is a mad person who is violent and dangerous.

manic
(adjective) energetic and excited, e.g. *Weston finished his manic typing at last.*

manicure, manicures, manicuring, manicured
1 (verb) If you manicure your hands, you care for them by softening the skin and shaping and polishing the nails.
2 (noun) A manicure is a special treatment for the hands and nails.
manicurist (noun).
[from Latin *manus* meaning 'hand' and *cura* meaning 'care']

manifest, manifests, manifesting, manifested (a formal word)
1 (adjective) obvious or easily seen, e.g. *her manifest belief in God.*
2 To manifest something means to make people aware of it, e.g. *Fear can manifest itself in many ways.*
manifestly (adverb).

manifestation, manifestations
(noun; a formal word) A manifestation of something is a sign that it is happening or exists, e.g. *the first manifestations of the computer revolution.*

manifesto, manifestoes or manifestos
(noun) A political party's manifesto is a published statement of its aims and policies.

manifold
(adjective; a literary word) of many different kinds, e.g. *Her good works were manifold.*

Manila or Manilla
(noun) Manila is strong brown paper.

manipulate, manipulates, manipulating, manipulated
1 (verb) To manipulate people or events means to control or influence them to produce a particular result.
2 If you manipulate a piece of equipment, you control it in a skilful way.
manipulation (noun), **manipulator** (noun), **manipulative** (adjective).
[from Latin *manipulus* meaning 'handful']

mankind
(noun) You can refer to all human beings as mankind, e.g. *a service to mankind.*

manly, manlier, manliest
(adjective) having qualities that are typically masculine, e.g. *a strong, manly character.*
manliness (noun).

manna
(noun) If something appears like manna from heaven, it appears suddenly as if by a miracle and helps you in a difficult situation.

manner, manners
1 (noun) The manner in which you do something is the way in which you do it.
2 Your manner is the way in which you behave and talk, e.g. *The judge was impressed by his manner.*
3 (plural noun) If you have good manners, you behave and speak very politely.

Similar words: (sense 1) way, method, mode, system, fashion, style, technique
(sense 2) bearing, behaviour, attitude, approach, conduct, demeanour

mannerism, mannerisms
(noun) A mannerism is a gesture or a way of speaking which is characteristic of a person.

manoeuvre, manoeuvres, manoeuvring, manoeuvred (pronounced man-**noo**-ver)
1 (verb) If you manoeuvre something into a place, you skilfully move it there, e.g. *I manoeuvred the car into a tiny parking space.*
2 (noun) A manoeuvre is a clever move you make in order to change a situation to your advantage.
3 (phrase) If you have **room for manoeuvre**, you have the opportunity to change your plans if it becomes necessary or desirable.
4 (noun) When military manoeuvres take place, soldiers and equipment are moved around in a large area of countryside as a training exercise.
[from Latin *manuopera* meaning 'manual work']

manor, manors
(noun) A manor is a large country house with land.
[from Old French *maneir* meaning 'to dwell']

manpower
(noun) Workers can be referred to as manpower.

manqué (pronounced mong-**kay**)
(adjective) If you describe someone as an actor manqué or a writer manqué, for example, you mean that they never succeeded in becoming a writer or an actor, although they may have wanted to.
[from French *manqué* meaning 'having missed']

mansion, mansions
(noun) A mansion is a very large house.

manslaughter
(noun; a legal word) Manslaughter is the accidental killing of a person.

mantelpiece, mantelpieces
(noun) A mantelpiece is a shelf over a fireplace.

mantle, mantles
1 (noun; a literary word) To take on the mantle of something means to take on responsibility for it, e.g. *those who would inherit the mantle of office.*
2 A mantle of something is a layer covering a surface, e.g. *The earth bore a thick mantle of snow.*

manual, manuals
1 (adjective) Manual work involves physical strength rather than mental skill.
2 operated by hand rather than by electricity or by motor, e.g. *a manual typewriter.*

3 (noun) A manual is an instruction book which tells you how to use a machine.
manually (adverb).
[from Latin *manus* meaning 'hand']

manufacture, manufactures, manufacturing, manufactured
1 (verb) To manufacture goods means to make them in a factory.
2 (noun) The manufacture of goods is the making of them in a factory.
manufacturer (noun), **manufacturing** (noun).
[from Latin *manus* meaning 'hand' and *facere* meaning 'to make']

manure
(noun) Manure is animal faeces used to fertilize the soil.

manuscript, manuscripts
(noun) A manuscript is a handwritten or typed document, especially a version of a book before it is printed.
[from Latin *manus* meaning 'hand' and *scribere* meaning 'to write']

Manx
(adjective) belonging or relating to the Isle of Man.

many
1 (adjective) If there are many people or things, there are a large number of them.
2 You also use many to ask how great a quantity is or to give information about it, e.g. *How many brothers have you got?*
3 (pronoun) a large number of people or things, e.g. *Many are seated already.*

Maori, Maoris
1 (noun) A Maori is someone descended from the people who lived in New Zealand before Europeans arrived.
2 Maori is the language spoken by Maoris.

map, maps, mapping, mapped
1 (noun) A map is a detailed drawing of an area as it would appear if you saw it from above.
2 (verb) If you map out a plan, you work out in detail what you will do.
[from Latin *mappa* meaning 'cloth']

maple, maples
(noun) A maple is a tree that has large leaves with five points. Its wood is used for furniture.

maple syrup
(noun) Maple syrup is a very sweet syrup made from the sap of a type of maple.

mar, mars, marring, marred
(verb) To mar something means to spoil its appearance, e.g. *Graffiti marred the walls.*

marathon, marathons
1 (noun) A marathon is a race in which people run 26 miles (about 42 km) along roads.
2 (adjective) A marathon task is a large one that takes a long time.
[from Marathon, a place from which a messenger ran 20 miles to Athens bringing news of a victory in 490 BC]

marauder, marauders (pronounced mar-**raw**-der)
(noun) Marauders are people who go around looking for something to steal or kill.

marble, marbles
1 (noun) Marble is a very hard, cold stone which is often polished to show the coloured patterns in it. Marble is used to make statues and decorative features of houses.
2 Marbles is a children's game played with small coloured glass balls. These balls are also called marbles.
[from Greek *marmairein* meaning 'to gleam']

march, marches, marching, marched
1 (noun) March is the third month of the year. It has 31 days.
2 (verb) When soldiers march, they walk with quick regular steps in time with each other.
3 To march somewhere means to walk quickly in a determined way, e.g. *He slammed the door and marched out.*
4 (noun) A march is an organized protest in which a large group of people walk somewhere together.
5 The march of something is its steady development or progress, e.g. *the march of time.*

mare, mares
(noun) A mare is an adult female horse.

margarine (pronounced **mar**-jar-reen)
(noun) Margarine is a substance that is similar to butter but is made from vegetable oil and animal fats.

margin, margins
1 (noun) If you win a contest by a small margin, you win it by a small amount.
2 A margin is an extra amount that allows you more freedom of choice or action, e.g. *What is the margin of safety?*
3 The margin on a written or printed page is the blank space at each side.
4 The margin of something is the edge of it.
[from Latin *margo* meaning 'border']

marginal
1 (adjective) small and not very important, e.g. *These are marginal details.*
2 A marginal seat or constituency is a political constituency where the previous election was won by a very small majority.
marginally (adverb).

marigold, marigolds
(noun) A marigold is a type of yellow or orange garden flower.

marijuana (pronounced mar-rih-**hwan**-a)
(noun) Marijuana is an illegal drug which is smoked in cigarettes.

marina, marinas
(noun) A marina is a harbour for pleasure boats and yachts.

marinate, marinates, marinating, marinated; also spelled **marinade**
(verb) To marinate food means to soak it in a mixture of oil, wine, vinegar, herbs, and spices to flavour it before cooking.

marine, marines
1 (noun) A marine is a soldier who serves with the navy.
2 (adjective) relating to or involving the sea, e.g. *marine life*.
[from Latin *mare* meaning 'sea']

Similar words: (sense 2) maritime, nautical, oceanic

mariner, mariners
(noun; an old-fashioned word) A mariner is a sailor.

marital
(adjective) relating to or involving marriage, e.g. *What is your marital status?*

Similar words: conjugal, matrimonial

maritime
(adjective) relating to the sea and ships, e.g. *a maritime museum*.

marjoram
(noun) Marjoram is a herb which has small, rounded leaves and tiny, pink flowers. It is used for flavouring in cooking.

mark, marks, marking, marked
1 (noun) A mark is a small stain or damaged area on a surface, e.g. *I can't get these marks off the carpet*.
2 (verb) If something marks a surface, it damages it in some way.
3 (noun) A mark is also a written or printed symbol, e.g. *She made a few marks on the paper*.
4 (verb) If you mark something, you write a symbol on it or identify it in some other way.
5 (noun) The mark you get for homework or for an exam is a letter or number showing how well you have done.
6 (verb) When a teacher marks your work, he or she decides how good it is and gives it a mark.
7 (noun) When something reaches a particular mark, it reaches that stage, e.g. *Unemployment is well over the three million mark*.
8 A mark of something is a sign or typical feature of it, e.g. *They removed their hats as a mark of respect*.
9 (verb) To mark something means to be a sign of it, e.g. *The film marked a turning point in her career*.
10 (noun) The mark or Deutsche Mark is the main unit of currency in Germany. A mark is worth 100 pfennigs.
11 (verb) In football or hockey, if you mark your opposing player, you stay close to them, trying to prevent them from getting the ball.
12 (phrase) If you are **marking time**, you are doing something boring while waiting for something more interesting to happen.

marked
(adjective) very obvious, e.g. *a marked contrast*.
markedly (adverb).

market, markets, marketing, marketed
1 (noun) A market is a place where goods or animals are bought and sold.
2 A market is a place with many small stalls selling different goods.
3 The market for a product is the number of people who want to buy it, e.g. *There's not much of a market in this country for frogs' legs*.
4 (verb) To market a product means to sell it on a large scale and in an organized way.

Similar words: (sense 1) bazaar, mart

market garden, market gardens
(noun) A market garden is a small farm where vegetables and fruit are grown.

marketing
(noun) Marketing is the the part of a business concerned with the way a product is sold.

market research
(noun) Market research is research into what people want, need, and buy.

marksman, marksmen
(noun) A marksman is someone who can shoot very accurately.

marmalade
(noun) Marmalade is a jam made from citrus fruit, usually eaten at breakfast.
[from Latin *marmelo* meaning 'quince']

marmoset, marmosets
(noun) A marmoset is a type of small South American monkey.

maroon
(noun and adjective) dark reddish-purple.

marooned
(adjective) If you are marooned in a place, you cannot leave it.

marquee, marquees (pronounced mar-**kee**)
(noun) A marquee is a very large tent used at a fair or other outdoor entertainment.

marquis, marquises (pronounced **mar**-kwiss); also spelled **marquess**
(noun) A marquis is a male member of the nobility of the rank between duke and earl.

marriage, marriages
1 (noun) A marriage is the relationship between a husband and wife.
2 Marriage is the act of marrying someone.

Similar words: (sense 2) matrimony, wedlock

marrow, marrows
(noun) A marrow is a long, thick green vegetable with cream-coloured flesh.

marry, marries, marrying, married
1 (verb) When a man and a woman marry, they become each other's husband and wife during a special ceremony.
2 When a clergyman or registrar marries a couple, he or she is in charge of their marriage ceremony.
married (adjective).

Mars
(noun) Mars is the planet in the solar system which is fourth from the sun.

marsh, marshes
(noun) A marsh is an area of land which is permanently wet.

marshal, marshals, marshalling, marshalled
1 (verb) If you marshal things or people, you gather them together and organize them, e.g. *He hesitated, marshalling his thoughts.*
2 (noun) A marshal is an official who helps to organize a public event.

marshmallow, marshmallows
(noun) A marshmallow is a soft, spongy, pink or white sweet.

marsupial, marsupials (pronounced mar-**syoo**-pee-al)
(noun) A marsupial is an animal that carries its young in a pouch. Wombats, koala bears, and kangaroos are all marsupials.
[from Greek *marsupion* meaning 'purse']

martial (pronounced **mar**-shal)
(adjective) relating to or involving war or soldiers, e.g. *martial music.*

martial arts
(plural noun) The martial arts are the techniques of self-defence that come from the Far East, for example karate or judo.

Martian, Martians (pronounced **mar**-shan)
(noun) A Martian is an imaginary creature from the planet Mars.

martyr, martyrs, martyring, martyred
1 (noun) A martyr is someone who suffers or is killed rather than change their beliefs.
2 (verb) If someone is martyred, they are killed because of their beliefs.
martyrdom (noun).
[from Greek *martus* meaning 'witness']

marvel, marvels, marvelling, marvelled
1 (verb) If you marvel at something, it fills you with surprise or admiration, e.g. *We marvelled at the sheer size of the building.*
2 (noun) A marvel is something that makes you feel great surprise or admiration, e.g. *It's a marvel that we ever reached the top.*

marvellous
(adjective) wonderful or excellent.
marvellously (adverb).

Marxism
(noun) Marxism is a political philosophy based on the writings of Karl Marx. It states that society will develop towards communism through the struggle between different social classes.
Marxist (adjective and noun).

marzipan
(noun) Marzipan is a paste made of almonds, sugar, and egg. It is put on top of cakes or used to make small sweets.

mascara
(noun) Mascara is a substance that can be used to colour eyelashes and make them look longer.
[from Spanish *mascara* meaning 'mask']

mascot, mascots
(noun) A mascot is an animal or toy which is thought to bring good luck.

masculine
(adjective) typical of men, rather than women, e.g. *a heavy masculine way of walking.*
masculinity (noun).

mash, mashes, mashing, mashed
(verb) If you mash vegetables, you crush them after they have been cooked.

mask, masks, masking, masked
1 (noun) A mask is something you wear over your face for protection or disguise, e.g. *a surgical mask.*
2 (verb) If you mask something, you cover it so that it is protected or cannot be seen.
masked (adjective).

masochist, masochists (pronounced **mass**-o-kist)
(noun) A masochist is someone who gets pleasure from their own suffering.
masochism (noun).
[named after the Austrian novelist Leopold von Sacher Masoch (1836-95), who wrote about masochism]

mason, masons
1 (noun) A mason is a person who is skilled at making things with stone.
2 A mason is also a Freemason.

masonic
(adjective) relating to or involving the Freemasons.

masonry
(noun) Masonry is pieces of stone which form part of a wall or building.

masquerade, masquerades, masquerading, masqueraded (pronounced mass-ker-**raid**)
(verb) If you masquerade as something, you pretend to be it, e.g. *He masqueraded as her uncle.*
[from Spanish *mascara* meaning 'mask']

mass, masses, massing, massed
1 (noun) A mass of something is a large amount of it.
2 (adjective) involving a large number of people, e.g. *mass unemployment.*
3 (noun) The masses are the ordinary people in society considered as a group, e.g. *entertainment for the masses.*
4 (verb) When people mass, they gather together in a large group.
5 (noun) In physics, the mass of an object is the amount of physical matter that it has.
6 In the Roman Catholic Church, Mass is a religious service in which people share bread and wine in remembrance of the death and resurrection of Jesus Christ.

massacre, massacres, massacring, massacred (pronounced **mass**-ik-ker)
1 (noun) A massacre is the killing of a very large number of people in a violent and cruel way.
2 (verb) To massacre people means to kill large numbers of them in a violent and cruel way.

massage, massages, massaging, massaged
1 (verb) To massage someone means to rub their body in order to help them relax or to relieve pain.

2 (noun) A massage is treatment which involves rubbing the body.
[from French *masser* meaning 'to rub']

masseur, masseurs (pronounced mass-**ur**)
(noun) A masseur is someone whose job is to massage people.

masseuse, masseuses (pronounced mass-**uz**)
(noun) A masseuse is a woman whose job is to massage people.

massif, massifs (pronounced mass-**eef**)
(noun) A massif is a group of mountains forming part of a mountain range.
[from French *massif* meaning 'massive']

massive
(adjective) extremely large in size, quantity, or extent, e.g. *a massive task*.
massively (adverb).

mass media
(noun) Television, radio, newspapers, and other methods of giving information to many people at the same time are called the mass media.

mass-produce, mass-produces,
mass-producing, mass-produced
(verb) To mass-produce something means to make it in large quantities, e.g. *a contract for mass-producing cheap computers*.
mass-produced (adjective), **mass production** (noun).

mast, masts
1 (noun) The mast of a boat is the tall upright pole that supports the sails.
2 A radio or television mast is a very tall pole that acts as an aerial to transmit sound or television pictures.

mastectomy, mastectomies
(noun) A mastectomy is a surgical operation to remove a woman's breast.

master, masters, mastering, mastered
1 (noun) A master is a man who has authority over a servant.
2 If you are master of a situation, you have control over it, e.g. *He was master of his emotions*.
3 A master is also a male teacher at a school.
4 (verb) If you master a difficult situation, you succeed in controlling it.
5 If you master something, you learn how to do it properly, e.g. *He mastered the language*.
[from Latin *magister* meaning 'master']

masterful
(adjective) showing control and authority.

master key, master keys
(noun) A master key is a key that will open any of a particular set of locks.

masterly
(adjective) extremely clever or well done, e.g. *a masterly move*.

mastermind, masterminds, masterminding, masterminded
1 (verb) If you mastermind a complicated activity, you plan and organize it.

2 (noun) The mastermind behind something is the person responsible for planning it.

Master of Arts, Masters of Arts
(noun) A Master of Arts is a higher university degree in a subject such as languages, literature, history, or a social science; also used to refer to someone who has such a degree.

master of ceremonies, masters of ceremonies
(noun) The master of ceremonies at a formal occasion is the person who introduces speakers and controls the ceremonial order of events.

Master of Science, Masters of Science
(noun) A Master of Science is a higher university degree in a science subject; also used to refer to someone who has such a degree.

masterpiece, masterpieces
(noun) A masterpiece is an extremely good painting, novel, or other work of art.

mastery
(noun) Mastery of a skill or art is excellence in it.

masticate, masticates, masticating, masticated
(verb; a formal word) To masticate means to chew.
[from Greek *mastikhan* meaning 'to grind the teeth']

masturbate, masturbates, masturbating, masturbated
(verb) If someone masturbates, they stroke or rub their own genitals in order to get sexual pleasure.
masturbation (noun).

mat, mats
1 (noun) A mat is a small round or square piece of cloth, card, or plastic that is placed on a table in order to protect it from plates or glasses.
2 A mat is also a small piece of carpet or other thick material that is placed on the floor.

matador, matadors
(noun) A matador is a man who fights and tries to kill bulls in a bullfight.
[from Spanish *matar* meaning 'to kill']

match, matches, matching, matched
1 (noun) A match is an organized game of football, cricket, chess, or some other sport.
2 A match is also a small, thin stick of wood that produces a flame when you strike it against a rough surface.
3 (verb) If one thing matches another, the two things look the same or have similar qualities.
4 (phrase) If something is **no match for** something else, the first thing is inferior to the second, e.g. *He's no match for the prime minister*.
matched (adjective), **matching** (adjective), **matchless** (adjective).

matchmaker, matchmakers
(noun) Someone who tries to plan other people's relationships and marriages is called a matchmaker.

mate, mates, mating, mated
1 (noun; an informal use) Your mates are your friends.

2 (noun) The first mate on a ship is the officer who is next in importance to the captain.
3 An animal's mate is its sexual partner.
4 (verb) When a male and female animal mate, they come together sexually in order to breed.
mating (noun).

material, materials
1 (noun) Material is cloth.
2 A material is a substance from which something is made, e.g. *raw materials*.
3 The equipment for a particular activity can be referred to as materials, e.g. *writing materials*.
4 Material for a book, play, or film is the information or ideas on which it is based.
5 (adjective) involving possessions and money, e.g. *the material comforts of life*.
materially (adverb).
[from Latin *materia* meaning 'matter']

materialism
(noun) Materialism is an attitude held by people who think that money and possessions are the most important things in life.
materialist (noun), **materialistic** (adjective).

materialize, materializes, materializing, materialized; also spelled **materialise**
(verb) If something materializes, it actually happens or appears, e.g. *The predicted revolution did not materialize.*

maternal
(adjective) relating to or involving a mother, e.g. *maternal feelings*.
[from Latin *mater* meaning 'mother']

maternity
(adjective) relating to or involving pregnant women and birth, e.g. *maternity clothes*.

mathematics
(noun) Mathematics is the study of numbers, quantities, and shapes.
mathematical (adjective), **mathematically** (adverb), **mathematician** (noun).
[from Greek *mathēma* meaning 'a science']

maths
(noun) Maths is mathematics.

matinee, matinees (pronounced **mat**-in-nay); also spelled **matinée**
(noun) A matinee is an afternoon performance of a play or film.

matins
(noun) Matins is early morning prayers.
[from Latin *matutinas* meaning 'of the morning']

matriarch, matriarchs (pronounced **may**-tree-ark)
(noun) A matriarch is a woman who is the head of a family in a society in which power passes from mother to daughter.
matriarchy (noun), **matriarchal** (adjective).

matrices the plural of **matrix**.

matricide
(noun) Matricide is the crime of killing your own mother.
[from Latin *mater* meaning 'mother' and *cedere* meaning 'to murder']

matriculate, matriculates, matriculating, matriculated
(verb) To matriculate means to register as a student at a university.
matriculation (noun).
[from Latin *matriculare* meaning 'to register']

matrimony
(noun; a formal word) Matrimony is marriage.
matrimonial (adjective).

matrix, matrices (pronounced **may**-trix)
1 (noun; a formal use) A matrix is the framework in which something develops.
2 In maths, a matrix is a set of numbers or elements set out in rows and columns.
[from Latin *matrix* meaning 'womb']

matron, matrons
1 (noun) In a hospital, a senior nurse in charge of all the nursing staff used to be known as matron.
2 In a boarding school, the matron is the person who looks after the health of the children.

matronly
(adjective) A matronly woman is middle-aged and rather fat.

matt
(adjective) A matt surface is dull rather than shiny, e.g. *I prefer a matt finish on wood.*

matted
(adjective) Hair that is matted is tangled with the strands sticking together.

matter, matters, mattering, mattered
1 (noun) A matter is something that you have to deal with.
2 Matter is any substance, e.g. *The atom is the smallest divisible particle of matter.*
3 Books and magazines are reading matter.
4 (verb) If something matters to you, it is important.
5 (phrase) If you ask **What's the matter?**, you are asking what is wrong.

Similar words: (sense 1) affair, issue, concern, topic, subject, situation
(sense 4) count, signify, be important

---

matter-of-fact
(adjective) showing no emotion.

matting
(noun) Matting is thick woven material such as rope or straw, used as a floor covering.

mattress, mattresses
(noun) A mattress is a thick oblong pad filled with springs or feathers that is put on a bed to make it comfortable.

mature, matures, maturing, matured
1 (verb) When a child or young animal matures, it becomes an adult.
2 When something matures, it reaches a state of complete development.
3 (adjective) Mature means fully developed and balanced in personality and emotional behaviour.
4 Cheese or wine that is mature has been left for a time to allow its full flavour to develop.
maturely (adverb), **maturity** (noun).
[from Latin *maturus* meaning 'developed']

maudlin
(adjective) Someone who is maudlin is sad and sentimental when they are drunk.

maul, mauls, mauling, mauled
(verb) If someone is mauled by an animal, they are savagely attacked and badly injured by it.

Maundy Thursday
(noun) Maundy Thursday is the Thursday before Easter Sunday.

mausoleum, mausoleums (pronounced maw-sal-**lee**-um)
(noun) A mausoleum is a building which contains the grave of a famous person.

mauve (rhymes with **grove**)
(noun and adjective) pale purple.

maverick, mavericks
(noun) A maverick is someone with independent views who does not always do the same as the group he or she belongs to. Mavericks are named after Samuel Maverick, a Texan rancher who refused to brand his cattle.

mawkish
(adjective) showing too much feeling or emotion in a rather weak and silly way.

maxim, maxims
(noun) A maxim is a rule for good or sensible behaviour in the form of a short saying, e.g. *'Be prepared': that's my maxim.*

maximize, maximizes, maximizing, maximized; also spelled maximise
(verb) To maximize something means to make it as great or effective as possible, e.g. *The objective is to maximize profits.*

maximum
1 (adjective) The maximum amount is the most that is possible, e.g. *the maximum daily dosage.*
2 (noun) The maximum is the most that is possible, e.g. *a maximum of ten people.*

may
1 (verb) If something may happen, it is possible that it will happen, e.g. *We may have to wait.*
2 If someone may do something, they are allowed to do it, e.g. *Please may I have one?*
3 You can use 'may' when saying that, although something is true, something else is also true, e.g. *They may be silly, but they are clever.*
4 (a formal use) You also use 'may' to express a wish that something will happen, e.g. *May you both be very happy.*
5 (noun) May is the fifth month of the year. It has 31 days.

maybe
(adverb) You use 'maybe' when you are stating a possibility that you are not certain about, e.g. *I'll come on Tuesday or maybe Wednesday.*

mayhem
(noun) You can refer to a confused and chaotic situation as mayhem, e.g. *There was absolute mayhem in the dormitories.*
[from Old French *mahem* meaning 'injury']

mayonnaise (pronounced may-on-**nayz**)
(noun) Mayonnaise is a thick salad dressing made with egg yolks and oil.

mayor, mayors
(noun) The mayor of a town is a person who has been elected to lead and represent the people.
[from Latin *maior* meaning 'greater']

mayoress, mayoresses
(noun) The mayoress of a town is the wife of the mayor.

maze, mazes
(noun) A maze is a system of complicated passages which it is difficult to find your way through, e.g. *a maze of underground tunnels.*

MBE, MBEs
(noun) An MBE is an honour granted by the King or Queen. MBE is an abbreviation for 'Member of the Order of the British Empire', e.g. *Dr John Smith, MBE.*

MD an abbreviation for 'Doctor of Medicine' or 'Managing Director'.

me
(pronoun) A speaker or writer uses me to refer to himself or herself.

meadow, meadows
(noun) A meadow is a field of grass.

meagre (pronounced **mee**-ger)
(adjective) very small and poor, e.g. *They couldn't manage on his meagre wages.*
[from Old French *maigre* meaning 'poor' or 'lean']

meal, meals
(noun) A meal is an occasion when people eat, or the food they eat at that time.

mean, means, meaning, meant; meaner, meanest
1 (verb) If you ask what something means, you want it explained to you.
2 If you mean what you say, you are serious, e.g. *Don't laugh; I mean it.*
3 If something means a lot to you, it is important to you.
4 If one thing means another, it shows that the second thing is true or will happen, e.g. *Losing your wallet will mean a trip to the police station.*
5 If you mean to do something, you intend to do it, e.g. *Sorry, I meant to write before.*
6 If something is meant to be true, it is supposed to be true, e.g. *They're meant to be reliable cars.*
7 (adjective) Someone who is mean is unwilling to spend much money.
8 Someone who is mean is unkind or cruel, e.g. *Don't be mean to the new boys.*
9 (noun) A means of doing something is a method or object which makes it possible, e.g. *Scientists have a means of freezing the embryo.*
10 (plural noun) Someone's means are their money and income, e.g. *She's obviously a woman of means.*
11 (noun) In mathematics, the mean is the average of a set of numbers.
meanness (noun), **meanly** (adverb).

Similar words: (sense 5) intend, propose, purpose
(sense 7) stingy, miserly, parsimonious, niggardly, tight, tight-fisted

meander, meanders, meandering, meandered
(pronounced mee-**an**-der)

(verb) If a road or river meanders, it has a lot of bends in it.
[from *Maiandros*, the name of a Greek river]

meaning, meanings
1 (noun) The meaning of a word, expression, or gesture is what it refers to or expresses.
2 The meaning of what someone says, or of a book or a film, is the thoughts or ideas that it is intended to express.
3 If something has meaning, it seems to be worthwhile and to have real purpose.
meaningful (adjective), **meaningfully** (adverb), **meaningless** (adjective).

Similar words: (sense 2) significance, gist, content

meantime
(phrase) **In the meantime** means in the period of time between two events, e.g. *I'll call the doctor; in the meantime, you must sleep.*

meanwhile
1 (adverb) Meanwhile means while something else is happening.
2 (noun) Meanwhile also means the time between two events.

measles
(noun) Measles is an infectious illness in which you have red spots on your skin.
[from Germanic *masele* meaning 'spot on the skin']

measly
(adjective; an informal word) very small or inadequate, e.g. *She only gave me a measly serving of chips.*

measure, measures, measuring, measured
1 (verb) When you measure something, you find out how big it is by using an instrument such as a ruler or tape measure.
2 If something measures a particular distance, its length or depth is that distance, e.g. *This room measures nine feet wide.*
3 (noun) A measure of something is a certain amount of it, e.g. *a measure of agreement.*
4 A measure is a unit in which size, speed, or depth is expressed.
5 Something that is a measure of something else shows its standard, e.g. *It is a measure of their achievement that the system has lasted so long.*
6 Measures are actions carried out to achieve a particular result, e.g. *Measures have been taken to avoid delay.*
measurable (adjective), **measurement** (noun).

measured
(adjective) careful and deliberate, e.g. *walking at the same measured pace.*

measurement, measurements
1 (noun) A measurement is the result that you obtain when you measure something.
2 Measurement is the activity of measuring something.
3 Your measurements are the sizes of your chest, waist, and hips that you use to buy the correct size of clothes.

meat, meats
(noun) Meat is the flesh of animals that is cooked and eaten.
meaty (adjective).

mecca, meccas
(noun) If a place is a mecca for people of a particular kind, many of them go there because it is of special interest to them, e.g. *The United States is a mecca for film makers.*
[from *Mecca*, the holiest city of Islam, to which many Muslims make pilgrimages]

mechanic, mechanics
1 (noun) A mechanic is a person who repairs and maintains engines and machines.
2 (plural noun) The mechanics of something are the way in which it works or is done, e.g. *I'll try to explain the mechanics of the system.*
3 Mechanics is also the scientific study of movement and the forces that affect objects.

mechanical
1 (adjective) A mechanical device has moving parts and is used to do a physical task.
2 A mechanical action is done automatically without thinking about it, e.g. *She seemed distracted, and gave a mechanical smile.*
mechanically (adverb).

mechanism, mechanisms
1 (noun) A mechanism is a part of a machine that does a particular task, e.g. *The steering mechanism is broken.*
2 A mechanism is a way of getting something done within a system, e.g. *There's no mechanism for changing the decision.*
3 A mechanism is also part of your behaviour that is automatic, e.g. *your body's defence mechanism.*

mechanize, mechanizes, mechanizing, mechanized; also spelled mechanise
(verb) If a type of work is mechanized, machines are installed to do it, e.g. *The sorting operation has been mechanized.*
mechanized (adjective), **mechanization** (noun).

medal, medals
(noun) A medal is a small disc of metal given as an award for bravery or as a prize for sport.

medallion, medallions
(noun) A medallion is a round piece of metal worn as an ornament on a chain round the neck.

medallist, medallists
(noun) A medallist is a person who has won a medal in sport, e.g. *an Olympic medallist.*

meddle, meddles, meddling, meddled
(verb) To meddle means to interfere and try to change things without being asked.
meddler (noun), **meddlesome** (adjective).

media
(plural noun) You can refer to the television, radio, and newspapers as the media.
[from Latin *medius* meaning 'middle']

mediaeval another spelling of **medieval**.

median, medians (pronounced **mee**-dee-an)
1 (adjective) The median value of a set is the middle value when the set is arranged in order.

2 (noun) In geometry, a median is a straight line drawn from one of the angles of a triangle to the midpoint of the opposite side.

mediate, mediates, mediating, mediated
(verb) If you mediate between two groups, you try to settle a dispute between them.
mediation (noun), **mediator** (noun).
[from Latin *mediare* meaning 'to be in the middle']

medic, medics
(noun; an informal word) A medic is a doctor or a medical student.

medical, medicals
1 (adjective) relating to the prevention and treatment of illness and injuries.
2 (noun) A medical is a thorough examination of your body by a doctor.
medically (adverb).
[from Latin *medicare* meaning 'to heal']

medication, medications
(noun) Medication is a substance that is used to treat illness.

medicinal
(adjective) relating to the treatment of illness, e.g. *the medicinal qualities of herbs.*

medicine, medicines
1 (noun) Medicine is the treatment of illness and injuries by doctors and nurses.
2 A medicine is a substance that you drink or swallow to help cure an illness.

medieval or **mediaeval** (pronounced med-dee-**ee**-val)
(adjective) relating to the period between about 1100AD and 1500AD, especially in Europe.
[from Latin *medium aevum* meaning 'the middle age']

mediocre (pronounced meed-dee-**oh**-ker)
(adjective) of rather poor quality.
mediocrity (noun).

Similar words: so-so, indifferent

meditate, meditates, meditating, meditated
1 (verb) If you meditate on something, you think about it very deeply.
2 If you meditate, you remain in a calm, silent state for a period of time, often as part of a religious training.
meditation (noun).

meditative
(adjective) showing deep and careful thought, e.g. *They sat in meditative contemplation.*
meditatively (adverb).

Mediterranean
1 (noun) The Mediterranean is the large inland sea between southern Europe and northern Africa.
2 (adjective) relating to or typical of the Mediterranean or the European countries adjoining it.

medium, mediums or **media**
1 (adjective) If something is of medium size or degree, it is neither large nor small, e.g. *a medium sized jacket.*

2 (noun) A medium is a method or means by which something is done or expressed, e.g. *Sending messages through the medium of the printed word is becoming less common.*
3 A medium is also a person who claims to be able to speak to the dead and to receive messages from them.
[from Latin *medium* meaning 'middle' or 'midst']

medium wave
(noun) Medium wave is a radio wave with a wavelength of between 100 and 1000 metres.

medley, medleys
1 (noun) A medley of different things is a mixture of them creating an interesting effect.
2 A medley is also a number of different songs or tunes sung or played one after the other.
[from Old French *medler* meaning 'to mix']

meek, meeker, meekest
(adjective) A meek person is timid and does what other people say.
meekly (adverb), **meekness** (noun).

Similar words: submissive, mild

meet, meets, meeting, met
1 (verb) If you meet someone, you happen to be in the same place as them.
2 If you meet a visitor or if you meet their train, plane, or bus, you go to be with them when they arrive.
3 When a group of people meet, they gather together for a purpose.
4 If something meets a need, it is suitable to fulfil it, e.g. *a place large enough to meet our needs.*
5 If you meet a situation, attitude, or problem, you experience it, e.g. *I've never met such intolerance.*
6 If something meets with a particular reaction, it gets that reaction from people, e.g. *His appeal met with an icy glare.*

Similar words: (sense 1) encounter, come across, bump into

meeting, meetings
1 (noun) A meeting is an event in which people discuss proposals and make decisions together.
2 A meeting is what happens when you meet someone.

mega-
(prefix) very great.
[from Greek *megas* meaning 'huge' or 'powerful']

megahertz
(noun) A megahertz is a unit of frequency equal to 1000 kilohertz or one million cycles per second.

megalith, megaliths
(noun) A megalith is a large standing stone.
[from Greek *megas* + *lithos* meaning 'huge stone']

megalomaniac, megalomaniacs
(noun) Someone who is a megalomaniac is always seeking power and enjoys feeling important.

megaphone, megaphones
(noun) A megaphone is a cone-shaped device

that makes your voice sound louder when you speak into it.

megaton, megatons
(noun) A megaton is a unit for measuring the power of nuclear weapons. A one megaton bomb has the same power as one million tons of TNT.

meiosis (pronounced my-**oh**-siss)
(noun; a technical word) Meiosis is a method of cell division in which reproductive cells are produced, each containing half the chromosome number of the parent nucleus.

melancholy
(adjective and noun) If you feel melancholy, you feel sad.

Melanesia
(noun) Melanesia is one of the three groups into which the islands in the Pacific are divided. Fiji is in Melanesia.
Melanesian (adjective).

mêlée, mêlées (pronounced **mel**-lay)
(noun) If there are a lot of people rushing around, the situation is described as a mêlée. [a French word]

mellow, mellower, mellowest; mellows, mellowing, mellowed
1 (adjective) Mellow light is soft and golden.
2 A mellow sound is smooth and pleasant to listen to, e.g. *the mellow tone of the cello*.
3 (verb) If someone mellows, they become more pleasant or relaxed, e.g. *He has mellowed with age... the mellowing effect of wine.*

melodic
(adjective) relating to melody.

melodious
(adjective) pleasant to listen to, e.g. *a low melodious laugh.*

Similar words: mellifluous, sweet-sounding, dulcet

melodrama, melodramas
(noun) A melodrama is a story or play in which people's emotions are exaggerated.
[from Greek *melos* meaning 'song' and *drama* meaning 'action' or 'drama']

melodramatic
(adjective) behaving in an exaggerated, emotional way.

Similar words: dramatic, theatrical, histrionic

melody, melodies
(noun) A melody is a tune.
[from Greek *melōidia* meaning 'singing']

melon, melons
(noun) A melon is a large, juicy fruit with a green or yellow skin and many seeds inside.

melt, melts, melting, melted
1 (verb) When something melts or when you melt it, it changes from a solid to a liquid because it has been heated.
2 If something melts, it disappears, e.g. *Their differences melted away... She melted into the crowd.*

Similar words: (sense 1) dissolve, liquefy, thaw

melting pot, melting pots
(noun) A situation that is described as a melting pot is a mixture of many different kinds of things.

member, members
1 (noun) A member of a group is one of the people or things belonging to the group, e.g. *older members of the family.*
2 A member of an organization is a person who has joined the organization.
3 (adjective) A country belonging to an international organization is called a member country or a member state.
[from Latin *membrum* meaning 'limb']

Member of Parliament, Members of Parliament
(noun) A Member of Parliament is a person who has been elected to represent people in a country's parliament.

membership
1 (noun) Membership of an organization is the state of being a member of it.
2 The people who belong to an organization are its membership.

membrane, membranes
(noun) A membrane is a very thin piece of skin or tissue which connects or covers plant or animal organs or cells, e.g. *the throat membranes.*

memento, mementos
(noun) A memento is an object which you keep because it reminds you of a person or a special occasion, e.g. *I keep the badge as a memento of the last Presley concert.*

memo, memos
(noun) A memo is a note from one person to another within the same organization. Memo is short for 'memorandum'.

memoirs (pronounced **mem**-wahrz)
(plural noun) If someone writes their memoirs, they write a book about their life and experiences.

memorable
(adjective) If something is memorable, it is likely to be remembered because it is special or unusual, e.g. *a memorable evening.*
memorably (adverb).

memorandum, memorandums or memoranda
(noun) A memorandum is a memo.
[from Latin *memorandum* meaning 'something to be remembered']

memorial, memorials
1 (noun) A memorial is a structure built to remind people of a famous person or event, e.g. *a war memorial.*
2 (adjective) A memorial event or prize is in honour of someone who has died, so that they will be remembered.

memorize, memorizes, memorizing, memorized; also spelled memorise
(verb) If you memorize something, you learn it

thoroughly so you can remember it exactly, e.g.
We've got to memorize this poem for homework.

memory, memories
1 (noun) Your memory is your ability to
remember things.
2 A memory is something you remember about
the past, e.g. *childhood memories.*
3 A computer's memory is the part in which
information is stored.

Similar words: (sense 2) recollection, reminiscence

men the plural of **man.**

menace, menaces, menacing, menaced
1 (noun) A menace is someone or something that
is likely to cause serious harm, e.g. *Drunken
drivers are a menace on the road.*
2 Menace is the quality of being threatening, e.g.
a look of silent menace.
3 (verb) If someone or something menaces you,
they threaten to harm you.
menacing (adjective), **menacingly** (adverb).

menagerie, menageries (pronounced
men-**naj**-er-ree)
(noun) A menagerie is a collection of different
wild animals.
[from French *menagerie* meaning 'household
management', which used to include the care of
domestic animals]

mend, mends, mending, mended
1 (verb) If you mend something that is broken,
you repair it.
2 (phrase) If someone **mends their ways**, they
begin to behave better than before.

mendacious
(adjective; a formal word) untrue or untruthful,
e.g. *a mendacious report.*
mendacity (noun).
[from Latin *mendax* meaning 'untruthful']

menial
(adjective) Menial work is boring and tiring and
the people who do it have low status.

meningitis
(noun) Meningitis is a serious infectious illness
which affects your brain and spinal cord.

meniscus, menisci (pronounced
min-**niss**-kuss)
(noun; a technical word) The meniscus of a liquid
in a container is its curved upper surface, caused
by the surface tension.
[from Greek *mēniskos* meaning 'crescent']

menopause
(noun) The menopause is the time during which a
woman gradually stops menstruating. This
usually happens when she is about fifty.
[from Greek *mēn* meaning 'month' and *pausis*
meaning 'halt']

**menstruate, menstruates, menstruating,
menstruated**
(verb) When a woman menstruates, blood comes
from her womb. This normally happens once a
month.
menstruation (noun), **menstrual** (adjective).
[from Latin *mensis* meaning 'month']

mental
1 (adjective) relating to the process of thinking
or intelligence, e.g. *mental arithmetic.*
2 relating to the health of the mind, e.g. *a mental
disorder... a mental hospital.*
mentally (adverb).
[from Latin *mens* meaning 'mind']

mentality, mentalities
(noun) Your mentality is your attitude or way of
thinking, e.g. *He despised their narrow
mentality.*

menthol
(noun) Menthol is a substance that smells like
peppermint and is used in medicines and
cigarettes.
[from Latin *mentha* meaning 'mint']

mention, mentions, mentioning, mentioned
1 (verb) If you mention something, you talk
about it briefly.
2 (noun) A mention of someone or something is a
brief comment about them, e.g. *There was no
mention of James in the letter.*

Similar words: (sense 1) allude, bring up, refer to

mentor, mentors
(noun) Someone's mentor is a person who
teaches them and gives them advice, e.g. *my
friend and mentor, David Jones.*

menu, menus
1 (noun) A menu is a list of the foods you can eat
in a restaurant.
2 A menu is also a list of different options shown
on a computer screen which the user must choose
from.

MEP, MEPs
(noun) An MEP is a person who has been elected
to the European Parliament.

mercantile (pronounced **murk**-an-tile)
(adjective; a formal word) relating to trade and
commerce.

mercenary, mercenaries
1 (noun) A mercenary is a soldier who is paid to
fight for a foreign country.
2 (adjective) Someone who is mercenary is
mainly interested in getting money.
[from Latin *merces* meaning 'wages']

merchandise
(noun; a formal word) Merchandise is goods that
are sold, e.g. *a display of imported merchandise.*

Similar words: products, commodities, wares

merchant, merchants
(noun) A merchant is a trader who imports and
exports goods, e.g. *a textile merchant.*
[from Latin *mercari* meaning 'to trade']

Similar words: dealer, vendor, retailer, salesman,
trader

merchant bank, merchant banks
(noun) A merchant bank deals mainly with
businesses and investment.

merchant navy
(noun) The merchant navy is the shipping and seamen involved in carrying goods for trade.

merciful
1 (adjective) considered to be fortunate as a relief from suffering, e.g. *Death came as a merciful release.*
2 showing kindness and forgiveness.
mercifully (adverb).

Similar words: (sense 2) kind, humane, lenient, compassionate

merciless
(adjective) showing no kindness or forgiveness.
mercilessly (adverb).

Similar words: implacable, pitiless, remorseless, ruthless

mercurial
(adjective; a literary word) Someone who is mercurial frequently changes their mind or moods without warning, e.g. *a mercurial temperament.*

mercury
1 (noun) Mercury is a silver-coloured metallic element that is liquid at room temperature. It is used in thermometers. Its atomic number is 80 and its symbol is Hg.
2 Mercury is also the planet in the solar system which is nearest to the sun.

mercy, mercies
1 (noun) If you show mercy, you show kindness and forgiveness and do not punish someone as severely as you could.
2 If an event or situation is described as a mercy, it is fortunate, e.g. *What a mercy we weren't spotted.*
3 (phrase) If you are **at the mercy of** someone or something, they have complete power over you.

Similar words: (sense 1) compassion, clemency, pity, leniency

mere, merest
(adjective) used to emphasize how unimportant or small something is, e.g. *Our office lies a mere hundred yards from Leicester Square.*
merely (adverb).
[from Latin *merus* meaning 'pure']

meretricious (pronounced mer-it-**rish**-uss)
(adjective; a formal word) seeming attractive, but actually of little value, e.g. *Advertisements convey a somewhat meretricious impression of the importance of the goods.*
[from Latin *meretrix* meaning 'prostitute']

merge, merges, merging, merged
(verb) When two things merge, they combine together to make one thing, e.g. *If we merge with another company, we'll lose our identity.*
merger (noun).

meridian, meridians
(noun) A meridian is one of the lines drawn on a map running from the North Pole to the South Pole.

meringue, meringues (pronounced mer-**rang**)
(noun) A meringue is a type of crisp, sweet cake made with egg whites and sugar.

merit, merits, meriting, merited
1 (noun) If something has merit, it is good or worthwhile.
2 The merits of something are its advantages or good qualities.
3 (verb) If something merits a particular treatment, it deserves that treatment, e.g. *Your success merits a celebration.*

meritocracy, meritocracies
(noun) A meritocracy is a society in which people gain power as a result of hard work and ability rather than because of wealth or social status.

mermaid, mermaids
(noun) In stories, a mermaid is a woman with a fish's tail instead of legs, who lives in the sea. [from Middle English *mere* + *maid* meaning 'sea maiden']

merriment
(noun) Merriment is happiness, laughter, and fun.

Similar words: gaiety, jollity, glee, hilarity, mirth

merry, merrier, merriest
1 (adjective) happy and cheerful, e.g. *his merry smiling face.*
2 (an informal use) slightly drunk.
merrily (adverb).

merry-go-round, merry-go-rounds
(noun) A merry-go-round is a large rotating platform with models of animals or vehicles on it, on which children ride at a fair.

mesh, meshes, meshing, meshed
1 (noun) Mesh is threads of wire or plastic twisted together like a net, e.g. *a wire mesh fence.*
2 (verb) If two things mesh together, they fit together closely.

mesmerize, mesmerizes, mesmerizing, mesmerized; also spelled mesmerise
(verb) If you are mesmerized by something, you are so fascinated by it that you cannot think of anything else, e.g. *He stood perfectly still, mesmerized by the sound of the waterfall.*

mesolithic
(adjective) relating to the middle period of the Stone Age, roughly between 12000 BC and 3000 BC.

mess, messes, messing, messed
1 (noun) If something is a mess, it is untidy.
2 If a situation is a mess, it is full of problems and trouble.
3 A mess is a room or building in which members of the armed forces eat, e.g. *the officers' mess.*
4 (verb) If you mess about or mess around, you do things without any particular purpose.
5 If you mess something up, you spoil it or do it wrong.
messy (adjective), **messily** (adverb), **messiness** (noun).

message, messages

1 (noun) A message is a piece of information or a request that you send someone or leave for them.
2 A message is also an idea that someone tries to communicate to people, for example in a play or a speech, e.g. *His message was quite clear; we need to act now to protect the environment.*
[from Latin *missus* meaning 'sent']

messenger, messengers

(noun) A messenger is someone who takes a message to someone for someone else.

Similar words: emissary, envoy, courier

Messiah (pronounced miss-**eye**-ah)

1 (noun) For Jews, the Messiah is the king of the Jews who will be sent by God.
2 For Christians, the Messiah is Jesus Christ.
[from Hebrew *mashiach* meaning 'anointed']

Messrs (pronounced **mes**-serz)

Messrs is the plural of **Mr.** It is often used in the names of businesses, e.g. *Messrs Brown and Humberley, Solicitors.*
[from French *messieurs*]

met

1 the past tense and past participle of **meet.**
2 an abbreviation for **meteorological**, e.g. *a report from the Met Office.*

metabolism, metabolisms

(noun) Your metabolism is the chemical processes in your body that use food for growth and energy.
metabolic (adjective).
[from Greek *metabolē* meaning 'change']

metacarpal, metacarpals

(noun) The metacarpals are the bones in your hand joining your thumb and fingers to your wrist.

metal, metals

(noun) Metal is a chemical element such as iron, steel, copper, or lead. Metals are good conductors of heat and electricity and form positive ions.
metallic (adjective).
[from Latin *metallum* meaning 'mine']

metallurgy

(noun) Metallurgy is the study of the properties and uses of metals.
metallurgist (noun).

metamorphic

(adjective) Metamorphic rock is rock that has been altered from its original state by heat or pressure.

metamorphosis, metamorphoses (pronounced met-am-**mor**-fiss-iss)

(noun; a formal word) When a metamorphosis occurs, a person or thing changes into something completely different, e.g. *the metamorphosis of a caterpillar into a butterfly.*
metamorphose (verb).
[from Greek *meta-* meaning 'change' and *morphē* meaning 'form']

metaphor, metaphors

(noun) A metaphor is an imaginative way of describing something by saying that it has the typical qualities of something else. For example, if you wanted to say that someone is shy, you might say they are a mouse.
metaphorical (adjective), **metaphorically** (adverb).
[from Greek *metapherein* meaning 'to transfer']

metaphysics

(noun) Metaphysics is the area of philosophy concerned with existence and how we know that things exist.
metaphysical (adjective).

metatarsal, metatarsals

(noun) The metatarsals are the bones in your foot joining your toes to your ankle.

mete, metes, meting, meted

(verb; a formal word) To mete out a punishment means to order that someone should be punished, e.g. *Magistrates meted out heavy fines.*

meteor, meteors

(noun) A meteor is a piece of rock or metal that burns very brightly when it enters the earth's atmosphere from space.
[from Greek *meteōros* meaning 'lofty']

meteoric

(adjective) A meteoric rise to power or success happens very quickly.
meteorically (adverb).

meteorite, meteorites

(noun) A meteorite is a piece of rock from space that has landed on earth.

meteorological

(adjective) relating to or involving the weather or weather forecasting.
meteorologist (noun), **meteorology** (noun).

meter, meters

(noun) A meter is a device that measures and records something, e.g. *a gas meter.*
[from Old English *metan* meaning 'to measure']

methane (pronounced **mee**-thane)

(noun) Methane is a colourless gas with no smell that is found in coal gas and produced by decaying vegetable matter. It burns easily and can be used as a fuel.

method, methods

(noun) A method is a particular way of doing something, e.g. *These cakes are made by the creaming method.*

methodical

(adjective) Someone who is methodical does things carefully and in an organized way.
methodically (adverb).

Methodist, Methodists

(noun and adjective) A Methodist is someone who belongs to the Methodist Church, a Protestant church whose members worship God in a way begun by John Wesley and his followers.

methodology, methodologies

(noun) A methodology is a particular set of methods and principles for doing something, e.g. *a postgraduate course in research methodology.*

meths

(noun; an informal word) Meths is methylated spirits.

methylated spirits
(noun) Methylated spirits is a poisonous mixture of alcohol and chemicals. It is used for cleaning and as a fuel.

meticulous
(adjective) A meticulous person does things very carefully and with great attention to detail.
meticulously (adverb), **meticulousness** (noun).

métier, métiers (met-tee-ay)
(noun) Your métier is the type of work that you naturally do well and are good at.
[a French word]

metre, metres
1 (noun) The metre is the SI unit of length. One metre is equal to 100 centimetres.
2 In poetry, metre is the regular and rhythmic arrangement of words and syllables.
[from Greek *metron* meaning 'a measure']

metric
(adjective) relating to the system of measurement that uses metres, grams, and litres.

metrication
(noun) Metrication is the process of changing from measuring things in imperial units (such as feet, inches, pounds, and ounces) to measuring in metric units.

metro, metros
(noun) The metro is the underground railway system in some cities.

metronome, metronomes
(noun) A metronome is a device that produces a perfectly regular beat and which can be adjusted to work at different speeds. It is used by musicians when they want to make sure that they play or sing a piece of music at the correct speed.

metropolis, metropolises
(noun) A metropolis is a very large city.
[from Greek *mētēr + polis* meaning 'mother city']

metropolitan
(adjective) relating or belonging to a large, busy city, e.g. *metropolitan districts.*

mettle
(noun) If you are on your mettle, you are ready to do something as well as you can because you know you are being tested or challenged.

mew, mews, mewing, mewed
1 (verb) When a cat mews, it makes a short high-pitched noise.
2 (noun) A mew is the short high-pitched sound that a cat makes.
3 A mews is a quiet yard or street surrounded by houses.

Mexican, Mexicans
1 (adjective) belonging or relating to Mexico.
2 (noun) A Mexican is someone who comes from Mexico.

mg an abbreviation for 'milligrams'.

mHz an abbreviation for 'megahertz'.

mica (pronounced my-ka)
(noun) Mica is a hard mineral found in the form of crystals in rocks. It has great resistance to heat and electricity.
[from Latin *mica* meaning 'grain' or 'morsel']

mice the plural of **mouse.**

micro-
(prefix) very small.
[from Greek *micros* meaning 'small']

microbe, microbes
(noun) A microbe is a very small living thing which you can see only if you use a microscope.
[from Greek *mikros* meaning 'small' and *bios* meaning 'life']

microchip, microchips
(noun) A microchip is a small piece of silicon on which electronic circuits for a computer or calculator are printed.

microcomputer, microcomputers
(noun) A microcomputer is a small computer.

microcosm, microcosms
(noun) A place or event that is a microcosm of a larger one is a smaller version with all the same features.
[from Greek *mikros kosmos* meaning 'little world']

microelectronics
(noun) Microelectronics is the branch of electronics dealing with electronic circuits for computers.

microfiche, microfiches (pronounced my-kroh-feesh)
(noun) A microfiche is a small sheet of film on which information is stored in very small print. It is put into a machine which magnifies it for reading, e.g. *The catalogue is on microfiche.*

microfilm, microfilms
(noun) Microfilm is film used for photographing written information. The information is greatly reduced in size on the film.

micron, microns
(noun) A micron is a unit of length equal to one millionth of a metre.

Micronesia
(noun) Micronesia is one of the three groups into which the islands in the Pacific are divided. All the islands in Micronesia are very small.
Micronesian (adjective).

microorganism, microorganisms
(noun) A microorganism is a microbe.

microphone, microphones
(noun) A microphone is a device that is used to make sounds louder or to record them on a tape recorder.

microprocessor, microprocessors
(noun) A microprocessor is a microchip which can be programmed to do a large number of tasks or calculations.

microscope, microscopes
(noun) A microscope is a piece of equipment which magnifies very small objects so that you can study them.

microscopic

1 (adjective) very small indeed, e.g. *microscopic organisms*.
2 very detailed, e.g. *a microscopic study of medieval customs*.
microscopically (adverb).

microwave, microwaves, microwaving, microwaved

1 (noun) A microwave or microwave oven is a type of oven which cooks food very quickly by short-wave radiation.
2 (verb) If you microwave food, you cook it in a microwave.

mid-

(prefix) Mid- is used to form words that refer to the middle part of a place or period of time, e.g. *mid-Atlantic... the mid-80s*.

midday

(noun) Midday is twelve o'clock in the middle of the day.

middle, middles

1 (noun) The middle of something is the part furthest from the edges, ends, or outside surface.
2 (adjective) The middle one in a series or a row is the one that has an equal number of people or things each side of it, e.g. *a middle child*.
3 The middle course or way is a moderate course of action that lies between two opposite, extreme courses.
4 (phrase) If you are in the middle of doing something, you are busy doing it.

middle age

(noun) Middle age is the period of your life when you are between about 40 and 60 years old.
middle-aged (adjective).

Middle Ages

(plural noun) In European history, the Middle Ages were the period between about 1100 AD and 1500 AD.

middle class, middle classes

(noun) The middle classes are the people in a society who are not working class or upper class, for example managers, doctors, and lawyers.

Middle East

(noun) The Middle East consists of Iran and the countries in Asia to the west and south-west of Iran.
Middle Eastern (adjective).

Middle English

(noun) Middle English was the English language from about 1100 AD until about 1450 AD.

middleman, middlemen

(noun) A middleman is someone who buys goods from the producers and sells them to other people at a profit, e.g. *We could get it cheaper if we could cut out the middleman*.

middle-of-the-road

(adjective) Middle-of-the-road opinions are moderate.

middle school, middle schools

(noun) In Britain, a middle school is for children aged between about 8 and 12.

middling

(adjective) of average quality or ability.

midge, midges

(noun) A midge is a small flying insect which can bite people.

midget, midgets

(noun) A midget is a very short person.

midnight

(noun) Midnight is twelve o'clock at night.

midpoint, midpoints

(noun) In geometry, the midpoint of a line is the point on it that is the same distance from each of its ends.

midriff, midriffs

(noun) Your midriff is the middle of your body between your waist and your chest.
[from *mid-* meaning 'middle' and Old English *hrif* meaning 'belly']

midst

1 (noun) If you are in the midst of a crowd or an event, you are in the middle of it.
2 (a formal phrase) If you refer to someone as being **in our midst**, you are indicating that they are present as part of your group, e.g. *The President is in our midst tonight*.

midsummer

(adjective) relating to the period in the middle of summer, e.g. *a hot midsummer day in July*.

midway

(adverb) in the middle of a distance or period of time, e.g. *We stopped midway for a drink*.

midwife, midwives

(noun) A midwife is a nurse who is trained to help women at the birth of a baby.
midwifery (noun).

might

1 (verb) If you say something might happen, you mean that it is possible that it will happen, e.g. *I might go if I have time*.
2 If you say that someone might do something, you are suggesting that they do it, e.g. *You might write to thank them*.
3 Might is also the past tense of **may**.
4 (noun; a literary use) Might is power or strength, e.g. *They pulled with all their might*.

mightily

(adverb; a literary word) to a great degree or extent, e.g. *Things have changed mightily since then*.

mighty, mightier, mightiest (a literary word)

1 (adjective) very powerful or strong, e.g. *the mighty force of the empire*.
2 very large and impressive, e.g. *two of Asia's mightiest rivers*.

migraine, migraines (pronounced **mee**-grane)

(noun) A migraine is a severe headache that makes you feel very ill.
[from Latin *hemicrania* meaning 'pain in half the head']

migrate, migrates, migrating, migrated

1 (verb) If people migrate, they move from one place to another, especially to find work.

2 When birds or animals migrate, they move at a particular season to a different place, usually to breed or to find new feeding grounds, e.g. *Swallows migrate to Africa for the winter.* **migration** (noun), **migratory** (adjective), **migrant** (noun and adjective).

mike, mikes
(noun; an informal word) A mike is a microphone.

mild, milder, mildest.
1 (adjective) Something that is mild is not strong and does not have any powerful or damaging effects, e.g. *a mild detergent.*
2 Someone who is mild is gentle and kind.
3 Mild weather is warmer than usual, e.g. *We've had two mild winters.*
4 Mild qualities, emotions, or attitudes are not very great or extreme, e.g. *He raised an eyebrow in mild amazement.*
mildly (adverb).

Similar words: (sense 3) balmy, clement, temperate

---

mildew
(noun) Mildew is a soft white fungus that grows on things when they are warm and damp.
mildewed (adjective).

mile, miles
1 (noun) A mile is a unit of distance equal to 1760 yards or about 1.6 kilometres.
2 (phrase) If you are **miles away**, you are daydreaming, e.g. *Sorry, I was miles away.*
[from Latin *milia passuum* meaning 'a thousand paces']

mileage, mileages
1 (noun) Your mileage is the distance that you have travelled, measured in miles.
2 The amount of mileage that you get out of something is how useful it is to you.

milieu, milieus or **milieux** (pronounced **meel**-yoo)
(noun; a formal word) Your milieu is your surroundings and the people you live or work with.

militant, militants
1 (adjective) A militant person is very active in trying to bring about extreme political or social change, e.g. *militant party members.*
2 (noun) A militant is a person who tries to bring about extreme political or social change.
militantly (adverb), **militancy** (noun).

military
1 (adjective) related to or involving the armed forces of a country, e.g. *military leaders.*
2 (noun) The military are the armed forces of a country.
militarily (adverb).

militate, militates, militating, militated
(verb; a formal word) To militate against something means to make it less likely to happen or succeed.

militia, militias (pronounced mil-**lish**-a)
(noun) A militia is an organization that operates like an army but whose members are not professional soldiers.

milk, milks, milking, milked
1 (noun) Milk is the white liquid produced by female cows, goats, and some other animals to feed their young. People drink milk and use it to make butter, cheese, and yoghurt.
2 (verb) When someone milks a cow or a goat, they get milk from it by pulling its udders.
3 (noun) Milk is also the white liquid that a baby drinks from its mother's breasts.
4 (verb) If you milk a situation or place, you get as much personal gain from it as possible, e.g. *He's milked this company dry.*

milk shake, milk shakes
(noun) A milk shake is a cold, frothy drink made from milk, a flavouring, and sometimes ice cream.

milk tooth, milk teeth
(noun) Your milk teeth are your first teeth which fall out and are replaced by the permanent set.

milky, milkier, milkiest
1 (adjective) pale creamy white, e.g. *a milky opal stone.*
2 containing a lot of milk, e.g. *Don't make the coffee too milky.*

Milky Way
(noun) The Milky Way is a strip of stars clustered closely together, appearing as a pale band in the sky.

mill, mills, milling, milled
1 (noun) A mill is a building where grain is crushed to make flour.
2 A mill is also a factory for making materials such as steel, wool, or cotton.
3 A mill is also a small device for grinding coffee or spices into powder, e.g. *a pepper mill.*
4 (verb) To mill something means to crush and grind it in a mill.

millennium, millennia or **millenniums**
(noun; a formal word) A millennium is a period of 1000 years.
millennial (adjective).

millepede another spelling of **millipede**.

miller, millers
(noun) A miller is the person who operates a flour mill.

millet
(noun) Millet is a tall cereal grass cultivated for its grain.

milli-
(prefix) Milli- is added to some measurement words to form words that refer to measurements a thousand times smaller.
[from Latin *mille* meaning 'thousand']

milligram, milligrams
(noun) A milligram is a unit of weight equal to one thousandth of a gram.

millilitre, millilitres
(noun) A millilitre is a unit of liquid volume equal to one thousandth of a litre.

millimetre, millimetres
(noun) A millimetre is a unit of length equal to a tenth of a centimetre or one thousandth of a metre.

milliner, milliners
(noun) A milliner is someone who makes or sells women's hats.
millinery (noun).
[originally 'Milaner', meaning someone from Milan, a city famous for its fancy goods]

million, millions
the number 1,000,000.
millionth.

millionaire, millionaires
(noun) A millionaire is a very rich person who has property worth millions of pounds or dollars.

millipede, millipides (pronounced **mil**-lip-peed); also spelled **millepede**
(noun) A millipede is a small creature with a long, narrow body made of small segments each with two pairs of legs.
[from Latin *mille* meaning 'thousand' and *pedes* meaning 'feet']

millisecond, milliseconds
(noun) A millisecond is a unit of time equal to one thousandth of a second.

millstone, millstones
(phrase) If something is **a millstone round your neck**, it is an unpleasant problem or responsibility you cannot escape from.

mime, mimes, miming, mimed
1 (noun) Mime is the use of movements and gestures to express something or to tell a story without using speech.
2 (verb) If you mime something, you describe or express it using mime.
[from Greek *mimos* meaning 'imitator']

mimic, mimics, mimicking, mimicked
1 (verb) If you mimic someone's actions or voice, you imitate them in an amusing way.
2 (noun) A mimic is a person who can imitate other people.
mimicry (noun).

minaret, minarets
(noun) A minaret is a tall, thin tower on a mosque.

mince, minces, mincing, minced
1 (noun) Mince is meat which has been chopped into very small pieces in a mincer.
2 (verb) If you mince meat, you chop it into very small pieces using a mincer.
3 (phrase) If you **do not mince your words**, you tell someone something unpleasant in a very forceful and direct way.
4 (verb) To mince about means to walk with small quick steps in an affected, effeminate way.
mincing (adjective), **mincingly** (adverb).

mincemeat
(noun) Mincemeat is a sticky mixture of pieces of dried fruit, apples, and suet. It is used to make mince pies, especially at Christmas.

mincer, mincers
(noun) A mincer is a machine which cuts meat into small pieces using revolving blades.

mind, minds, minding, minded
1 (noun) Your mind is your ability to think, together with all the thoughts you have and your memory.
2 (phrase) If something is **on your mind**, you are worrying about it, e.g. *What's on your mind?*
3 If you **change your mind**, you change a decision that you have made or an opinion that you have.
4 (verb) If you do not mind something, you are not annoyed by it or bothered about it.
5 If you say that you wouldn't mind something, you mean that you would quite like it, e.g. *I wouldn't mind a holiday myself.*
6 If you mind a child or mind something for someone, you look after it for a while, e.g. *I'll mind your suitcase while you get the tickets.*

mindful
(adjective; a formal word) If you are mindful of something, you think about it carefully before taking action, e.g. *mindful of our responsibility.*

mindless
1 (adjective) Mindless actions are regarded as stupid and destructive, e.g. *mindless soccer hooliganism.*
2 A mindless job or activity is simple, repetitive, and boring.

mine, mines, mining, mined
1 (pronoun) Mine refers to something belonging or relating to the person who is speaking or writing, e.g. *a book of mine.*
2 (noun) A mine is a series of holes or tunnels in the ground dug in order to extract diamonds, coal, or other minerals, e.g. *a gold mine.*
3 (verb) To mine diamonds, coal, or other minerals means to obtain these substances from underneath the ground.
4 (noun) A mine is also a bomb hidden in the ground or underwater, which explodes when people or things touch it.
miner (noun), **mining** (noun).

minefield, minefields
(noun) A minefield is an area of land or water where mines have been hidden.

mineral, minerals
(noun) A mineral is a substance such as tin, salt, uranium, or coal that is formed naturally in rocks and in the earth, e.g. *rich mineral deposits.*

mineral water
(noun) Mineral water is water which comes from a natural spring.

minestrone (pronounced min-nes-**strone**-ee)
(noun) Minestrone is soup made from meat stock containing small pieces of vegetable and pasta.
[from Italian *minestrare* meaning 'to serve']

minesweeper, minesweepers
(noun) A minesweeper is a ship for clearing away underwater mines.

mingle, mingles, mingling, mingled
(verb) If things mingle, they become mixed together, e.g. *Her cries mingled with the wind.*

mini-
(prefix) Mini- is used to form nouns referring to something smaller or less important than similar things, e.g. *the Chancellor's mini-budget.*

miniature, miniatures (min-nit-cher)
1 (adjective) A miniature thing is a tiny copy of something much larger.
2 (noun) A miniature is a very small detailed painting, often of a person.
miniaturize (verb).

minibus, minibuses
(noun) A minibus is a van with seats in the back which is used as a small bus.

minim, minims
(noun) A minim is a musical note that has a time value equal to two crotchets.

minimal
(adjective) very small in quality, quantity, or degree, e.g. *a minimal knowledge of self-defence.*
minimally (adverb).

minimize, minimizes, minimizing, minimized; also spelled **minimise**
1 (verb) If you minimize something, you reduce it to the smallest amount possible, e.g. *Crop rotation helps to minimize the risk of disease.*
2 To minimize something also means to make it seem smaller or less important than it really is, e.g. *He minimized the importance of their contribution.*

minimum
1 (adjective) The minimum amount is the smallest amount that is possible, e.g. *A minimum deposit of £20 is required.*
2 (noun) The minimum is the smallest amount that is possible, e.g. *a minimum of ten minutes.*

minion, minions
(noun) A minion is a person who has an unimportant role or job and carries out other people's orders.

miniskirt, miniskirts
(noun) A miniskirt or a mini is a very short skirt.

minister, ministers, ministering, ministered
1 (noun) A minister is a person who is in charge of a particular government department, e.g. *the junior health minister.*
2 A minister in a Protestant church is a member of the clergy.
3 (verb) If you minister to people or their needs, you make sure they have everything that they need, e.g. *ministering to the poor.*
[from Latin *minister* meaning 'servant']

ministerial
(adjective) relating to a government minister or ministry, e.g. *ministerial duties.*

ministry, ministries
1 (noun) A ministry is a government department that deals with a particular area of work, e.g. *the Ministry of Education.*
2 The ministry of members of the clergy is their work.
3 Members of the clergy can be referred to as the ministry, e.g. *Her son is in the ministry.*

mink, minks
(noun) Mink is an expensive fur used to make coats or hats; also the animal from which the fur is obtained.

minnow, minnows
(noun) A minnow is a very small freshwater fish.

minor, minors
1 (adjective) not as important or serious as other things, e.g. *This is only a minor problem.*
2 A minor key is one of the keys in which most European music is written.
3 (noun; a formal use) A minor is a young person under the age of 18, e.g. *Alcohol may not be served to minors.*
[from Latin *minor* meaning 'less' or 'smaller']

minority, minorities
1 (noun) The minority of people or things in a group is a number of them forming less than half of the whole, e.g. *Only a minority were against the proposal.*
2 A minority is a group of people of a particular race or religion living in a place where most people are of a different race or religion, e.g. *ethnic minorities.*

minstrel, minstrels
(noun) A minstrel was a medieval singer and entertainer.

mint, mints, minting, minted
1 (noun) Mint is a herb used for flavouring in cooking.
2 A mint is a peppermint flavoured sweet.
3 The mint is the place where the official coins of a country are made.
4 (verb) When coins or medals are minted, they are made.
5 (adjective) If something is in mint condition, it is in very good condition, like new.
[senses 3-5 are from Old English *mynet* meaning 'coin']

minuet, minuets
(noun) A minuet is an 18th-century court dance.

minus
1 You use minus to show that one number is being subtracted from another, e.g. *Ten minus six equals four.*
2 (adjective) Minus is used when talking about temperatures below 0°C or 0°F.

minuscule (pronounced **min**-nus-kyool)
(adjective) very small indeed.

minute, minutes, minuting, minuted (pronounced **min**-nit)
1 (noun) A minute is a unit of time equal to sixty seconds.
2 The minutes of a meeting are the written records of what was said and decided.
3 (verb) To minute a meeting means to write the official notes of it.

minute (pronounced my-**nyoot**)
(adjective) extremely small, e.g. *The water contained minute amounts of fluoride.*
minutely (adverb).

minutiae (pronounced my-**nyoo**-shee-aye)
(plural noun; a formal word) Minutiae are small, unimportant details.

miracle, miracles
1 (noun) A miracle is a wonderful and surprising event, believed to have been caused by God.

2 Any very surprising and fortunate event can be called a miracle, e.g. *What a miracle! I've passed my exams.*
miraculous (adjective), **miraculously** (adverb).
[from Latin *mirari* meaning 'to wonder at']

mirage, mirages (pronounced mir-**ahj**)
(noun) A mirage is an image which you can see in the distance in very hot weather, but which does not actually exist.

mire
(noun; a literary word) Mire is swampy ground or mud.

mirror, mirrors, mirroring, mirrored
1 (noun) A mirror is a piece of glass which reflects light and in which you can see your reflection.
2 (verb) To mirror something means to reflect it or copy it, e.g. *The hills were mirrored in the lake.*

mirth
(noun; a literary word) Mirth is great amusement and laughter.

misadventure, misadventures
(noun; a formal word) A misadventure is an unfortunate incident, e.g. *The verdict was death by misadventure.*

misanthrope, misanthropes (pronounced miz-zan-thrope)
(noun; a formal word) A misanthrope is a person who does not like other people.
misanthropic (adjective).

misapprehension, misapprehensions
(noun) If you are under a misapprehension, you have a wrong idea or impression of something.

misappropriate, misappropriates, misappropriating, misappropriated
(verb; a formal word) To misappropriate money means to take it for personal use without permission, e.g. *The treasurer misappropriated the club funds.*
misappropriation (noun).

misbehave, misbehaves, misbehaving, misbehaved
(verb) If a child misbehaves, he or she is naughty or behaves badly.
misbehaviour (noun).

miscalculate, miscalculates, miscalculating, miscalculated
(verb) If you miscalculate, you make a wrong judgment or calculation, e.g. *He had badly miscalculated the time it would take.*
miscalculation (noun).

miscarry, miscarries, miscarrying, miscarried
1 (verb) If a woman miscarries, she gives birth to a baby before it is properly formed and it dies.
2 If a plan miscarries, it goes wrong and fails.
miscarriage (noun).

miscellaneous
(adjective) A miscellaneous group is made up of people or things that are different from each other.
miscellaneously (adverb).
[from Latin *miscellus* meaning 'mixed']

miscellany, miscellanies (pronounced mis-**sel**-lan-ee)
(noun) A miscellany is a collection of things that are very different from each other, e.g. *a miscellany of recipes.*

mischief
(noun) Mischief is eagerness to have fun by teasing people or playing tricks.
mischievous (adjective).

misconceived
(adjective) A misconveived plan or idea is based on a misunderstanding of the situation and therefore will not be successful.

misconception, misconceptions
(noun) A misconception is a wrong idea about something, e.g. *misconceptions about city life.*

misconduct
(noun) Misconduct is bad or unacceptable behaviour by a professional person, e.g. *He was struck off the medical register for misconduct.*

misconstrue, misconstrues, misconstruing, misconstrued
(verb; a formal word) To misconstrue a situation means to interpret it wrongly.

miscreant, miscreants
(noun; a formal word) A miscreant is a criminal or someone who does something wrong.

misdeed, misdeeds
(noun; a formal word) A misdeed is a bad or evil act.

misdemeanour, misdemeanours (pronounced miss-dem-**mee**-ner)
(noun; a formal word) A misdemeanour is an act that people consider shocking or unacceptable.

miser, misers
(noun) A miser is a person who enjoys saving money but hates spending it, e.g. *He's such a miser, he refuses to heat the house until it snows.*
miserly (adjective).
[from Latin *miser* meaning 'wretched']

miserable
1 (adjective) If you are miserable, you are very unhappy.
2 If a place or a situation is miserable, it makes you feel depressed, e.g. *a squalid, miserable little bed-sit.*
miserably (adverb).

Similar words: (sense 1) gloomy, disconsolate, wretched, woebegone, doleful, lugubrious (sense 2) gloomy, wretched

misery, miseries
(noun) Misery is great unhappiness.

misfire, misfires, misfiring, misfired.
(verb) If a plan misfires, it goes wrong.

misfit, misfits
(noun) A misfit is a person who is not accepted by other people because of being rather strange or eccentric.

misfortune, misfortunes
(noun) A misfortune is an unpleasant occurrence

that is regarded as bad luck, e.g. *I had the misfortune to lose my passport.*

misgiving, misgivings
(noun) If you have misgivings, you are worried or unhappy about something, e.g. *I was filled with misgiving about their marriage.*

misguided
(adjective) A misguided opinion or action is wrong because it is based on a misunderstanding or bad information.

mishap, mishaps (pronounced **miss**-hap)
(noun) A mishap is an unfortunate but not very serious accident.

misinform, misinforms, misinforming, misinformed
(verb) If you are misinformed, you are given wrong or inaccurate information.
misinformation (noun).

misinterpret, misinterprets, misinterpreting, misinterpreted
(verb) To misinterpret something means to understand it wrongly, e.g. *He misinterpreted her gesture and rose to leave.*

misjudge, misjudges, misjudging, misjudged
(verb) If you misjudge someone or something, you form an incorrect idea or opinion about them.
misjudgment (noun).

mislay, mislays, mislaying, mislaid
(verb) If you mislay something, you lose it because you have forgotten where you put it.

mislead, misleads, misleading, misled
(verb) To mislead someone means to make them believe something which is not true.
misleading (adjective), **misleadingly** (adverb).

mismanage, mismanages, mismanaging, mismanaged
(verb) To mismanage something means to organize or deal with it badly, e.g. *This company has been mismanaged for the past six years.*
mismanagement (noun).

misnomer, misnomers
(noun; a formal word) A misnomer is a word or expression that describes something wrongly or inaccurately.

misogynist, misogynists (pronounced mis-**soj**-jin-ist)
(noun) A misogynist is a man who hates women.

misplaced
(adjective) A misplaced feeling is inappropriate or directed at the wrong thing or person, e.g. *misplaced loyalties.*

misprint, misprints
(noun) A misprint is a mistake such as a spelling mistake in something that has been printed.

misquote, misquotes, misquoting, misquoted
(verb) To misquote someone means to repeat incorrectly something they have said or written.

misrepresent, misrepresents, misrepresenting, misrepresented
(verb) To misrepresent someone means to give

an inaccurate or misleading account of what they have said or done.
misrepresentation (noun).

miss, misses, missing, missed
1 (verb) If you miss something, you do not notice it, e.g. *He doesn't miss much.*
2 If you miss someone or something, you feel sad that they are no longer with you, e.g. *I miss the freedom of the bush in Africa.*
3 If you miss a chance or opportunity, you fail to take advantage of it.
4 If you miss a bus, plane, or train, you arrive too late to catch it.
5 If you miss something, you fail to hit it when you aim at it, e.g. *He missed the goal by an inch.*
6 (noun) A miss is an act of missing something that you were aiming at.
7 Miss is used before the name of an unmarried woman or girl as a form of address, e.g. *Miss Smith is the new French teacher.*

misshapen
(adjective) An object that is misshapen does not have a normal or natural shape.

missile, missiles
(noun) A missile is a weapon that moves long distances through the air and explodes when it reaches its target; also used of any object thrown as a weapon.

missing
(adjective) If someone or something is missing, you cannot find them, e.g. *He's been missing for four years... The aerial is missing.*

mission, missions
1 (noun) A mission is an important task that you have to do.
2 A mission is a group of people who have been sent to a foreign country to carry out an official task, e.g. *He's in charge of the Zambian mission.*
3 A mission is also a special journey made by a military aeroplane or space rocket.
4 If you have a mission, there is something that you believe it is your duty to try to achieve.
5 A mission is also the workplace of a group of Christians who are working for the Church, usually in a foreign country.
[from Latin *mittere* meaning 'to send']

missionary, missionaries
(noun) A missionary is a Christian who has been sent to a foreign country to work for the Church.

missive, missives
(noun; an old-fashioned word) A missive is a letter or message.

misspell, misspells, misspelling, misspelt or misspelled
(verb) If you misspell a word, you spell it wrongly.

misspend, misspends, misspending, misspent
(verb) If someone misspends time or money, they waste it or do not use it wisely, e.g. *my misspent youth.*

mist, mists, misting, misted
1 (noun) Mist consists of a large number of tiny

drops of water in the air, which make it hard to see things clearly.
2 (verb) If your eyes mist, you cannot see very far because there are tears in your eyes.
3 If glass mists over or mists up, it becomes covered with condensation so that you cannot see through it.

mistake, mistakes, mistaking, mistook, mistaken
1 (noun) A mistake is an action or opinion that is wrong or is not what you intended.
2 (verb) If you mistake someone or something for another person or thing, you wrongly think that they are the other person or thing, e.g. *I mistook your wife for your daughter.*
[from Old Norse *mistaka* meaning 'to take something by mistake']

Similar words: (sense 1) error, blunder, gaffe, faux pas, misunderstanding, slip

mistaken
1 (adjective) If you are mistaken about something, you are wrong about it.
2 If you have a mistaken belief or opinion, you believe something which is not true.
mistakenly (adverb).

mister
A man is sometimes addressed in a very informal way as 'mister', e.g. *Hey, mister, do you need your shoes cleaned?*

mistletoe (pronounced **mis**-sel-toe)
(noun) Mistletoe is a plant which grows on trees and has white berries on it. It is used as a Christmas decoration.

mistook the past tense of **mistake.**

mistreat, mistreats, mistreating, mistreated
(verb) To mistreat a person or animal means to treat them badly and make them suffer.

mistress, mistresses
1 (noun) A married man's mistress is a woman who is not his wife and who he is having a sexual relationship with.
2 A school mistress is a female teacher.
3 A servant's mistress is the woman who is the servant's employer.

mistrust, mistrusts, mistrusting, mistrusted
1 (verb) If you mistrust someone, you do not feel that you can trust them.
2 (noun) Mistrust is a feeling that you cannot trust someone.

misty, mistier, mistiest
(adjective) full of or covered with mist.

misunderstand, misunderstands, misunderstanding, misunderstood
(verb) If you misunderstand someone, you do not properly understand what they say or do, e.g. *He misunderstood my meaning.*

misunderstanding, misunderstandings
(noun) If two people have a misunderstanding, they have a slight quarrel or disagreement.

misuse, misuses, misusing, misused
1 (noun) The misuse of something is the incorrect, careless, or dishonest use of it, e.g. *the misuse of company funds.*

2 (verb) To misuse something means to use it incorrectly or dishonestly.

mite, mites
1 (noun; an old-fashioned use) A mite is a very small amount, e.g. *Anyone with a mite of common sense would have realized that!*
2 A mite is a very tiny creature that lives in the fur of animals.
3 A mite is also a small child, especially one you feel sorry for, e.g. *He was orphaned at six weeks, poor mite.*

mitigate, mitigates, mitigating, mitigated
(verb; a formal word) To mitigate something means to make it less unpleasant, serious, or painful, e.g. *an attempt to mitigate distress.*
mitigation (noun).
[from Latin *mitis* meaning 'mild' and *agere* meaning 'to make']

mitigating
(adjective; a formal word) Mitigating circumstances make a crime easier to understand, and perhaps justify it.

mitosis
(noun; a technical word) Mitosis is a method of cell division, in which the nucleus divides into daughter nuclei, each containing the same number of chromosomes as the parent.

mitre, mitres (pronounced **my**-ter)
(noun) A mitre is a tall, pointed hat worn by bishops and archbishops on ceremonial occasions.
[from Greek *mitra* meaning 'turban']

mitten, mittens
(noun) Mittens are gloves which have one section that covers your thumb and another section for the rest of your fingers together.

mix, mixes, mixing, mixed
(verb) If you mix things, you combine them or shake or stir them together.

Similar words: blend, amalgamate, mingle, merge

mix up
(phrasal verb) If you mix up two things or people, you confuse them, e.g. *I've often been mixed up with my sister and been given her mail.*

mixed
1 (adjective) consisting of several things of the same general kind, e.g. *mixed biscuits.*
2 involving people from two or more different races, e.g. *mixed marriages.*
3 Mixed education or accommodation is for both males and females, e.g. *a mixed comprehensive.*
4 Mixed feelings or reactions consist of some good and some bad feelings or reactions, e.g. *I've got mixed feelings about this job.*

mixed blessing, mixed blessings
(noun) Something that is described as a mixed blessing may be helpful in some ways but may also cause problems.

mixed up
1 (adjective) If you are mixed up, you are confused, e.g. *Could you repeat that? I got a bit mixed up.*

2 If you are mixed up in a crime or a scandal, you are involved in it.

mixer, mixers
(noun) A mixer is a machine used for mixing things together, e.g. *a food mixer*.

mixture, mixtures
1 (noun) A mixture of things consists of several different things together.
2 A mixture is a substance that consists of other substances which have been stirred or shaken together, e.g. *Whisk the ingredients together and spoon the mixture over the pastry.*

Similar words: (sense 1) blend, combination, compound, conglomeration, medley, amalgam

mix-up, mix-ups
(noun) A mix-up is a mistake in something that was planned, e.g. *a mix-up with the bookings.*

ml an abbreviation for 'millilitres'.

mm an abbreviation for 'millimetres'.

mnemonic, mnemonics (pronounced nim-**on**-nik)
(noun) A mnemonic is a word or rhyme that helps you to remember things such as scientific facts or spelling rules. 'i before e, except after c' is an example of a mnemonic.
[from Greek *mnēmōn* meaning 'mindful']

moan, moans, moaning, moaned
1 (verb) If you moan, you make a low, miserable sound because you are in pain or suffering.
2 (noun) A moan is a low cry of pain or misery.
3 (verb; an informal use) If you moan about something, you complain about it.

moat, moats
(noun) A moat is a wide, water-filled ditch around a building such as a castle.

mob, mobs, mobbing, mobbed
1 (noun) A mob is a large, disorganized crowd of people, e.g. *A violent mob attacked the embassy.*
2 (verb) If a lot of people mob someone, they crowd around the person in a disorderly way, e.g. *The pop star was mobbed by enthusiastic well-wishers.*
[from Latin *mobile vulgus* meaning 'the fickle public']

mobile, mobiles
1 (adjective) able to move or be moved freely and easily, e.g. *Antelopes are fully mobile as soon as they are born.*
2 If you are mobile, you are able to travel or move to another place, e.g. *a mobile workforce.*
3 (noun) A mobile is a decoration consisting of several small objects which hang from threads and move around when a breeze blows.
mobility (noun).

mobilize, mobilizes, mobilizing, mobilized; also spelled **mobilise**
1 (verb) If you mobilize a group of people, you organize them to do something, e.g. *We'll try to mobilize some volunteers.*
2 If a country mobilizes its armed forces, it prepares them to fight a war.
mobilization (noun).

moccasin, moccasins
(noun) Moccasins are soft leather shoes with a low heel and a raised seam above the toe.
[from *mocussin*, a North American Indian word meaning 'shoe']

mock, mocks, mocking, mocked
1 (verb) If you mock someone, you say something scornful or imitate their foolish behaviour.
2 (adjective) not genuine, e.g. *mock disapproval... mock Tudor houses.*
3 A mock examination is one that you do as a practice before the real examination.
mocking (adjective), **mockingly** (adverb).

Similar words: (sense 1) ridicule, deride, jeer, gibe, sneer, make fun of, scoff, taunt

mockery
1 (noun) Mockery is the expression of scorn for someone or ridicule of their foolish behaviour.
2 (phrase) If something **makes a mockery of** something else, it makes it appear foolish and worthless, e.g. *The judge's decision made a mockery of justice.*

Similar words: (sense 1) derision, jeering

mock-up, mock-ups
(noun) A mock-up of a building or a machine is a model of it for test purposes or display.

mode, modes
(noun) A mode of life or behaviour is a particular way of living or behaving.

model, models, modelling, modelled
1 (noun and adjective) A model is a physical representation that shows what something looks like or how it works, e.g. *a model railway.*
2 (noun) Something that is described as, for example, a model of clarity, is extremely clear or absolutely perfect.
3 (adjective) Someone who is described as, for example, a model wife or a model student is an excellent wife or student.
4 (verb) If you model yourself on someone, you copy their behaviour because you admire them.
5 (noun) A particular model of a machine is a version of it, e.g. *the latest model.*
6 A model is a person who poses for a painter or a photographer.
7 A model at a fashion show is a person who wears the clothes that are being displayed.
8 (verb) To model clothes means to display them by wearing them.
9 To model shapes or figures means to make them out of clay or wood.

Similar words: (sense 2) archetype, standard, epitome, ideal, paragon

modem, modems (pronounced **moe**-dem)
(noun) A modem is a piece of equipment that links a computer to the telephone system so that data can be transferred from one machine to another via the telephone line.
[from the first letters of 'modulator' and 'demodulator']

moderate, moderates, moderating, moderated
1 (adjective) Moderate views are not extreme, and usually favour gradual changes rather than major ones.
2 (noun) A moderate is a person whose political views are not extreme.
3 (adjective) A moderate amount of something is neither large not small.
4 (verb) If you moderate something or if it moderates, it becomes less extreme or violent, e.g. *The wind moderated.*
moderately (adverb), **moderation** (noun).
[from Latin *moderari* meaning 'to restrain']

moderation
1 (noun) Moderation is control of your behaviour that stops you acting in an extreme way, e.g. *He has not displayed the same moderation in his political behaviour as in his private life.*
2 (phrase) If you smoke or drink **in moderation**, you do not smoke or drink too much.

modern
1 (adjective) relating to the present time, e.g. *the social problems of modern society.*
2 new and involving the latest ideas and equipment, e.g. *modern technology.*
modernity (noun).
[from Latin *modo* meaning 'just recently']

Similar words: (sense 1) contemporary, present-day
(sense 2) up-to-date

modernize, modernizes, modernizing, modernized; also spelled **modernise**
(verb) To modernize something means to introduce new methods or equipment.

modest
1 (adjective) quite small in size or amount.
2 Someone who is modest does not boast about their abilities or possessions.
3 shy and easily embarrassed.
modestly (adverb), **modesty** (noun).

modicum
(noun; a formal word) A modicum of something is a small amount of it, e.g. *a modicum of good taste.*

modification, modifications
(noun) A modification to something is a small change made to improve it, e.g. *The new model has several modifications.*

modify, modifies, modifying, modified
(verb) If you modify something, you change it slightly in order to improve it.

modulate, modulates, modulating, modulated
(verb) If you modulate something, you adjust it to make it more suitable, e.g. *The actor carefully modulated his voice to suit the role.*
modulation (noun), **modulated** (adjective).

module, modules
1 (noun) A module is one of the parts which when put together form a whole unit or object, e.g. *Your course is made up of modules.*
2 A module is a part of a spacecraft which can do certain things independently from the main body, e.g. *the lunar module.*
modular (adjective).

modus operandi (pronounced **moh**-dus op-per-**and**-die)
(noun; a formal expression) A modus operandi is a method of doing something.

mohair
(noun) Mohair is very soft, fluffy wool obtained from angora goats.

moist, moister, moistest
(adjective) slightly wet.

moisten, moistens, moistening, moistened
(verb) If you moisten something, you make it slightly wet.

moisture
(noun) Moisture is tiny drops of water in the air or on the ground.

moisturizer, moisturizers; also spelled **moisturiser**
(noun) Moisturizer is a cream that can be used on dry skin to soften it and restore moisture.

molar, molars
(noun) Your molars are the large teeth at the back of your mouth.

mole, moles
1 (noun) A mole is a dark, slightly raised spot on your skin.
2 A mole is also a small animal with black fur. Moles live in tunnels underground.
3 (an informal use) A member of an organization who is working as a spy for a rival organization is called a mole.
4 (a technical use) The mole is the basic SI unit of amount of substance.

molecule, molecules
(noun) A molecule is the smallest amount of a substance that can exist.
molecular (adjective).

molehill, molehills
1 (noun) A molehill is a small pile of earth left by a mole that has been digging underground.
2 (phrase) If someone is **making a mountain out of a molehill**, they are exaggerating a problem.

molest, molests, molesting, molested
1 (verb) To molest a child means to touch the child in a sexual way. This is illegal.
2 If someone molests you, they annoy you and prevent you from doing something, especially by using physical violence.
molester (noun).

mollify, mollifies, mollifying, mollified
(verb) To mollify someone means to do something to make them less upset or angry.
[from Latin *mollis* + *facere* meaning 'to make soft']

mollusc, molluscs
(noun) A mollusc is an animal with a soft body and no backbone. Snails, slugs, clams, and mussels are all molluscs.
[from Latin *mollis* meaning 'soft']

mollycoddle, mollycoddles, mollycoddling, mollycoddled
(verb) To mollycoddle someone means to do too much to protect them and make them comfortable.

Molotov cocktail, Molotov cocktails
(noun) A Molotov cocktail is a home-made bomb consisting of petrol in a bottle with a rag in the bottle neck. It is named after the Soviet statesman V.M. Molotov (1890-1986).

molten
(adjective) Molten rock or metal has been heated to a very high temperature and has become a sticky liquid.

moment, moments
1 (noun) A moment is a very short period of time, e.g. *She hesitated for a moment.*
2 The moment at which something happens is the point in time at which it happens, e.g. *And at that precise moment, in walked Jamie.*
3 (phrase) If something is happening **at the moment**, it is happening now.
4 (a formal use) Something that is **of great moment** is very important.
5 (noun) In physics, moment is a tendency to produce rotation, especially about a point or axis.
6 A moment is the product of a physical quantity such as a force or mass, and its distance from a fixed point.

Similar words: (sense 1) minute, second, jiffy, instant

momentary
(adjective) Something that is momentary lasts for only a few seconds, e.g. *I caught a momentary glimpse of the Queen as the car sped past.*
momentarily (adverb).

momentous
(adjective; a formal word) very important, often because of its future effect, e.g. *a momentous decision.*
momentously (adverb), **momentousness** (noun).

momentum
1 (noun) Momentum is the ability that something has to keep developing, e.g. *The rebellion began to gather momentum.*
2 Momentum is also the ability that an object has to continue moving as a result of the speed it already has.
3 In physics, the momentum of an object is its mass multiplied by its velocity.

monarch, monarchs (pronounced **mon**-nark)
(noun) A monarch is a queen, king, or other royal person who reigns over a country.
[from Greek *mono-* meaning 'one' and *arch* meaning 'chief']

monarchist, monarchists
(noun) Monarchists are people who believe that their country should have a monarch.

monarchy, monarchies
(noun) A monarchy is a system in which a queen or king reigns in a country.

monastery, monasteries
(noun) A monastery is a building in which monks live.
monastic (adjective).
[from Greek *monāzein* meaning 'to live alone']

Monday, Mondays
(noun) Monday is the day between Sunday and Tuesday.
[from Old English *monandæg* meaning 'moon's day']

monetary (pronounced **mun**-net-tree)
(adjective; a formal word) relating to money, especially the total amount of money in a country, e.g. *the monetary system.*

money
1 (noun) Money is the coins or banknotes that you use to buy something.
2 (phrase) If you **make money**, you obtain it by earning it or making a profit.

Similar words: (sense 1) cash, capital, currency

moneyed another spelling of **monied**.

money-spinner, money-spinners
(noun; an informal word) Something that is described as a money-spinner makes a lot of money.

mongoose, mongooses
(noun) A mongoose is a small animal with a long tail. Mongooses lives in hot countries and kill snakes.

mongrel, mongrels
(noun) A mongrel is a dog with parents of different breeds.

monied or **moneyed**
(adjective) A monied person has a lot of money.

monitor, monitors, monitoring, monitored
1 (verb) If you monitor something, you regularly check its condition and progress, e.g. *His heartbeat is being monitored.*
2 (noun) A monitor is a machine used to check or record things.
3 A monitor is also the visual display unit of a computer.
4 A monitor is also a school pupil chosen to do special duties by the teacher.
[from Latin *monere* meaning 'to advise']

monk, monks
(noun) A monk is a member of a male religious community.

monkey, monkeys
(noun) A monkey is an animal which has a long tail and climbs trees. Monkeys live in hot countries.

mono
(adjective) used of a record or sound system in which all the sound is directed through one speaker only.

mono-
(prefix) Mono- is used at the beginning of nouns and adjectives that have 'one' as part of their meaning, e.g. *monosyllable... monochrome.*
[from Greek *monos* meaning 'single']

monochrome
1 (adjective) A monochrome painting is painted using only one colour in various shades.
2 A monochrome photograph or film is in black and white only.

monocle, monocles
(noun) A monocle is a glass lens worn in front of one eye only and held in place by the curve of the eye socket.
[from Greek *mono-* meaning 'one' and Latin *oculus* meaning 'eye']

monogamy
(noun; a formal word) Monogamy is the custom of being married to only one person at a time.
monogamous (adjective).

monogram, monograms
(noun) A monogram is a design based on someone's initials.
monogrammed (adjective).

monolith, monoliths
(noun) A monolith is a very large upright piece of stone.

monolithic
(adjective) very large and giving the impression that it will never change.

monologue, monologues (pronounced mon-nol-og)
(noun) A monologue is a long speech by one person during a play or a conversation.
[from Greek *monologos* meaning 'speaking alone']

monopolize, monopolizes, monopolizing, monopolized; also spelled monopolise
(verb) To monopolize something means to control it completely and prevent other people from having a share in it, e.g. *Our competitors have monopolized all the rail routes.*

monopoly, monopolies
(noun) A monopoly of an industry is control of most of it by one or a few large firms.
[from Greek *mono-* meaning 'one' and *pōlein* meaning 'to sell']

monorail, monorails
(noun) A monorail is a railway running on a single rail usually raised above ground level.

monosyllable, monosyllables
(noun) If someone speaks in monosyllables, they use only very short words such as 'yes' and 'no'.
monosyllabic (adjective).

monotone, monotones
(noun) A monotone is a tone which does not vary, e.g. *He droned on in a boring monotone.*

monotonous
(adjective) having a regular pattern which is very dull and boring, e.g. *monotonous chores.*
monotony (noun), **monotonously** (adverb).

monsoon, monsoons
(noun) In South-east Asia, the monsoon is the season of very heavy rain.

monster, monsters
1 (noun) A monster is a large, imaginary creature that looks very frightening.
2 (adjective) extremely large, e.g. *a monster computer.*
3 (noun) If you call someone a monster, you mean they are cruel, frightening, or evil.
[from Latin *monstrum* meaning 'omen' or 'warning']

monstrosity, monstrosities
(noun) Something that is described as a monstrosity is large and extremely ugly, e.g. *That new shopping precinct is a monstrosity.*

monstrous
(adjective) extremely shocking or unfair, e.g. *The judge's decision was absolutely monstrous.*
monstrously (adverb).

montage, montages (pronounced mon-**tajh**)
(noun) A montage is a picture or film consisting of a combination of several different items arranged to produce an unusual effect.
[a French word]

month, months
(noun) A month is one of the twelve periods that a year is divided into.

monthly, monthlies
1 (adjective) Monthly describes something that happens or appears once a month, e.g. *monthly staff meetings.*
2 (noun) A monthly is a magazine or publication produced once a month.

monument, monuments
(noun) A monument is a large stone structure built to remind people of a famous person or event, e.g. *a monument to Queen Victoria.*
[from Latin *monere* meaning 'to remind']

monumental
1 (adjective) A monumental building or sculpture is very large, impressive, and important.
2 very large or extreme, e.g. *The meal was a monumental disaster.*

moo, moos, mooing, mooed
(verb) When a cow moos, it makes a long, deep sound.

mooch, mooches, mooching, mooched
(verb; an informal word) If you mooch about, you walk about slowly with no particular purpose.

mood, moods
1 (noun) Your mood is the way you are feeling at a particular time, e.g. *I'm in a really good mood.*
2 If you are in a mood, you are angry, sulking, or impatient, e.g. *It's no good trying to persuade him, he's in one of his moods.*
3 The mood of a group of people is the way they think or feel about something, e.g. *A mood of pessimism grew amongst the delegates.*

Similar words: (sense 1) temper, frame of mind, humour
(sense 3) atmosphere, current, air

moody, moodier, moodiest
1 (adjective) Someone who is moody is depressed or unhappy, e.g. *He's been pretty moody since Sara left him.*
2 Someone who is moody often changes their mood for no apparent reason.
moodily (adverb).

Similar words: (sense 1) morose, petulant, sulky
(sense 2) temperamental

moon, moons
1 (noun) The moon is an object moving round the earth which you see as a shining circle or crescent in the sky at night. Some other planets have moons. For example, Mars has two moons.
2 (an informal phrase) If you are **over the moon** about something, you are very pleased about it.
3 Something that happens **once in a blue moon** happens very rarely.

moonlight, moonlights, moonlighting, moonlighted
1 (noun) Moonlight is the light that comes from the moon at night.
2 (verb; an informal use) If someone is moonlighting, they have a second job that they have not informed the tax office about.
moonlit (adjective).

moonshine
(noun) You can refer to foolish and unrealistic ideas as moonshine.

moor, moors, mooring, moored
1 (noun) A moor is a high area of open and uncultivated land.
2 (verb) If a boat is moored, it is attached to the land with a rope.
moorland (noun).

moorhen, moorhens
(noun) A moorhen is a a dark-coloured bird with a red bill. Moorhens live beside ponds, lakes, and canals.
[from Old English *mere* + *henn* meaning 'lake-hen']

mooring, moorings
(noun) A mooring is a place where a boat can be tied.

moose
(noun) A moose is a large North American deer with flat antlers.

moot, moots, mooting, mooted
(verb; a formal word) When something is mooted, it is suggested for discussion, e.g. *A holiday in France had been mooted earlier.*

moot point
(noun) A statement or idea that is a moot point is doubtful or debatable, e.g. *How serious he was about this is a moot point.*

mop, mops, mopping, mopped
1 (noun) A mop is a tool for washing floors, consisting of a sponge or string head attached to a long handle.
2 (verb) To mop a floor means to clean it with a mop.
3 To mop a surface means to wipe it with a dry cloth to remove liquid.
4 (noun) A mop of hair is a large amount of loose or untidy hair.

mop up
(phrasal verb) To mop up the remaining parts of a task means to deal with them to complete it.

mope, mopes, moping, moped
(verb) If you mope, you feel miserable and not interested in anything.

moped, mopeds (pronounced **moe**-ped)
(noun) A moped is a type of small motorcycle.
[from the first letters of *motor* and *pedal*]

moral, morals
1 (plural noun) Morals are values based on beliefs about the correct and acceptable way to behave.
2 (adjective) concerned with whether behaviour is right or acceptable, e.g. *moral standards.*
3 (noun) The moral of a story is the lesson it teaches about behaviour, e.g. *The moral was clear: never marry for money.*
4 (phrase) If you give **moral support** to someone, you encourage and support them in what they are doing.
morality (noun), **morally** (adverb).
[from Latin *moralis* meaning 'relating to customs']

morale (pronounced mor-**rahl**)
(noun) Morale is the amount of confidence and optimism that you have, e.g. *The morale of the troops was low after their recent defeat.*

moralist, moralists
(noun) A moralist is someone with strong ideas about right and wrong.

moralize, moralizes, moralizing, moralized; also spelled **moralise**
(verb) If someone is moralizing, they are telling another person what is right and wrong in a rather self-righteous way.

morass, morasses (pronounced mo-**rass**)
(noun) If a situation is described as a morass, it is very complicated or confused, e.g. *bogged down in a morass of paperwork.*
[a morass originally meant a swamp]

moratorium, moratóriums
(noun) A moratorium is the stopping of an activity for a period of time by official agreement.
[from Latin *mora* meaning 'delay']

morbid
(adjective) having too great an interest in unpleasant things, especially death.
morbidly (adverb).
[from Latin *morbus* meaning 'illness']

mordant, mordants
1 (noun) A mordant is a substance used to fix the colour when fabric is being dyed.
2 (adjective; a formal word) very sarcastic and critical, e.g. *The book sparkles with mordant wit.*

more
1 (determiner and pronoun) More means a greater number or amount than something else, e.g. *I've got more chips than you... I've got more than you.*
2 used to refer to an additional thing or amount of something, e.g. *I've got two more buyers here.*
3 (adverb) to a greater degree or extent, e.g. *I liked the second novel more than the first.*
4 You can use 'more' in front of adjectives and adverbs to form comparatives, e.g. *You look more beautiful than ever.*

moreover
(adverb) used to introduce a piece of information that supports or expands the previous· statement, e.g. *They have accused the government of corruption. Moreover, they have named names.*

mores (pronounced **maw**-rayz)
(plural noun; a formal word) The customs of a particular group can be referred to as its mores, e.g. *The last thirty years have seen great changes in social mores.*
[a Latin word]

morgue, morgues (pronounced **morg**)
(noun) A morgue is a building where dead bodies are kept before being buried or cremated.

moribund
(adjective) no longer having a useful function and about to come to an end, e.g. *moribund industries.*

morning, mornings
1 (noun) The morning is the early part of the day until lunchtime.
2 The part of the day between midnight and noon is also referred to as the morning, e.g. *I was born at two in the morning.*

morning sickness
(noun) Morning sickness is a feeling of sickness that affects some women during the first few months of pregnancy.

Moroccan, Moroccans (pronounced mor-**rok**-an)
1 (adjective) belonging or relating to Morocco.
2 (noun) A Moroccan is someone who comes from Morocco.

moron, morons
(noun; an informal word) If you describe someone as a moron, you mean they are very stupid.
moronic (adjective).
[from Greek *mōros* meaning 'foolish']

morose
(adjective) miserable and bad-tempered.
morosely (adverb).

morphine
(noun) Morphine is a drug which is used to relieve pain.
[from *Morpheus*, the Greek god of sleep and dreams]

Morse or **Morse code**
(noun) Morse or Morse code is a code used for sending messages in which each letter is represented by a series of dots and dashes. It is named after its American inventor, Samuel Morse.

morsel, morsels
(noun) A morsel of food is a small piece of it.

mortal, mortals
1 (adjective) unable to live forever, e.g. *All mortal beings fear death.*
2 (noun) You can refer to an ordinary person as a mortal.
3 (adjective) A mortal wound is one that results in death.
[from Latin *mors* meaning 'death']

mortality
1 (noun) Mortality is the fact that all people must die.
2 Mortality also refers to the number of people who die at any particular time, e.g. *Mortality has increased because of a measles outbreak.*

mortar, mortars
1 (noun) A mortar is a short cannon which fires missiles high into the air for a short distance.
2 Mortar is a mixture of sand, water, and cement used to hold bricks firmly together.

mortgage, mortgages, mortgaging, mortgaged (pronounced **mor**-gij)
1 (noun) A mortgage is a loan which you get from a bank or a building society in order to buy a house.
2 (verb) If you mortgage your house, you use it as a guarantee to a company in order to borrow money from them.
[from Old French *mort* meaning 'death' and *gage* meaning 'security']

mortify, mortifies, mortifying, mortified
(verb) If you are mortified, you feel great shame or embarrassment.
mortifying (adjective), **mortification** (noun).

mortuary, mortuaries
(noun) A mortuary is a special room in a hospital where dead bodies are kept before being buried or cremated.

mosaic, mosaics (pronounced moe-**zay**-yik)
(noun) A mosaic is a design made of small coloured stones or pieces of coloured glass set into concrete or plaster.

Moslem another spelling of **Muslim**.

mosque, mosques (pronounced **mosk**)
(noun) A mosque is a building where Muslims go to worship.
[from Arabic *masjid* meaning 'temple']

mosquito, mosquitoes or **mosquitos** (pronounced moss-**skee**-toe)
(noun) Mosquitoes are small insects which bite people in order to suck their blood.
[from Spanish *mosquito* meaning 'little fly']

moss, mosses
(noun) Moss is a soft, low-growing, green plant which grows on damp soil, wood, or stone.
mossy (adjective).

most
1 (determiner and pronoun) Most of a group of things or people means nearly all of them, e.g. *Most of us enjoyed the show.*
2 The most means a larger amount than anyone or anything else, e.g. *That was the most he would agree to.*
3 (adverb) You can use 'most' in front of adjectives or adverbs to form superlatives, e.g. *the most important reason for being here.*
4 (phrase) You say **at most** or **at the most** when stating the maximum number that is possible or likely, e.g. *There will only be ten people here at the most.*
5 If you **make the most of something**, you get the

maximum use or advantage from it, e.g. *Make the most of your talents.*

mostly
(adverb) Mostly is used to show that a statement is generally true, e.g. *The men at the party were mostly fairly young.*

MOT, MOTs
(noun) An MOT is an annual test for road vehicles to check that they are safe to drive, e.g. *My Mini failed the MOT again.*

motel, motels
(noun) A motel is a hotel providing overnight accommodation for people in the middle of a car journey.
[from *motor* and *hotel*]

moth, moths
(noun) A moth is an insect like a butterfly which usually flies at night.

moth-eaten
(adjective) Moth-eaten clothes look old and ragged with holes in them.

mother, mothers, mothering, mothered
1 (noun) Your mother is the woman who gave birth to you.
2 (verb) To mother someone means to look after them and bring them up.

motherhood
(noun) Motherhood is the state of being a mother.

mother-in-law, mothers-in-law
(noun) Someone's mother-in-law is the mother of their husband or wife.

motherly
(adjective) A motherly person shows warm, kind, and protective feelings.
motherliness (noun).

mother-of-pearl
(noun) Mother-of-pearl is a hard, smooth substance which forms on the inside of some shellfish. It is cream-coloured, but shines in various colours. Mother-of-pearl is used to make decorative things.

motif, motifs (pronounced moe-teef)
(noun) A motif is a design which is used as a decoration.

motion, motions, motioning, motioned
1 (noun) Motion is the process of continually moving or changing position, e.g. *the motion of the waves.*
2 A motion is an action, gesture, or movement, e.g. *He made stabbing motions with his spear.*
3 A motion at a meeting is a proposal which people discuss and vote on.
4 (verb) If you motion to someone, you make a movement with your hand in order to show them what they should do, e.g. *The teacher motioned us to fall into line.*
5 (phrase) If you **go through the motions**, you say or do something that is expected of you without being very sincere.
[from Latin *motio* meaning 'moving']

motionless
(adjective) not moving at all, e.g. *They froze and stayed motionless for a while.*

motivate, motivates, motivating, motivated
1 (verb) If you are motivated by something, it causes you to behave in a particular way, e.g. *people motivated by a lust for power and money.*
2 If you motivate someone, you make them feel determined to do something.
motivated (adjective), motivation (noun).

Similar words: (sense 1) inspire, prompt, move

motive, motives
(noun) Your motive for doing something is your reason or purpose, e.g. *a motive for the crime.*

motley
(adjective) A motley collection is made up of people or things of very different types.

motor, motors
1 (noun) A motor is a part of a vehicle or a machine that uses electricity or fuel to produce movement so that the machine can work.
2 (adjective) concerned with or relating to vehicles with a petrol or diesel engine, e.g. *the motor industry... a motor mechanic.*
[from Latin *motor* meaning 'mover']

motorcycle, motorcycles
(noun) A motorcycle is a two-wheeled vehicle with an engine.

motoring
(adjective) relating to cars and driving.

motorist, motorists
(noun) A motorist is a person who drives a car.

motorway, motorways
(noun) A motorway is a wide road specially built for fast travel over long distances.

mottled
(adjective) covered with patches of different colours, e.g. *a mottled camouflage jacket.*

motto, mottoes or mottos
(noun) A motto is a short sentence or phrase that expresses a rule for good or sensible behaviour.
[from Latin *muttum* meaning 'utterance']

mould, moulds, moulding, moulded
1 (verb) To mould someone or something means to influence and change them so they develop in a particular way.
2 To mould a substance means to make it into a particular shape, e.g. *clay moulded into pots.*
3 (noun) A mould is a container used to make something into a particular shape, e.g. *a rabbit-shaped jelly mould.*
4 If a person is cast in or fits into a particular mould, they are of that type.
5 Mould is a soft grey or green substance that can form on old food or damp walls.
mouldy (adjective).

moult, moults, moulting, moulted
(verb) When an animal or bird moults, it loses its hair or feathers to make way for new growth.

mound, mounds
1 (noun) A mound is a small man-made hill.

2 A mound of things is a large, untidy pile, e.g. *a mound of dirty washing.*

mount, mounts, mounting, mounted
1 (verb) To mount a campaign or event means to organize it and carry it out.
2 If something is mounting, it is increasing, e.g. *The temperature mounted rapidly.*
3 (a formal use) To mount something means to go to the top of it, e.g. *We mounted the steps.*
4 If you mount a horse, you climb on its back.
5 If you mount an object in a particular place, you fix it there to display it.
6 Mount is also used as part of the name of a mountain, e.g. *Mount Everest.*

mountain, mountains
1 (noun) A mountain is a very high piece of land with steep sides.
2 You can refer to a large amount of something as a mountain of it, e.g. *There are mountains of forms to fill in.*

mountaineer, mountaineers
(noun) A mountaineer is a person who climbs mountains.
mountaineering (noun).

mountainous
1 (adjective) A mountainous area has a lot of mountains.
2 very large or high, e.g. *mountainous waves.*

mourn, mourns, mourning, mourned
1 (verb) If you mourn for someone who has died, you are very sad and think about them a lot.
2 If you mourn something, you are sad because you no longer have it, e.g. *She mourned the passing of those happy days.*

mourner, mourners
(noun) A mourner is a person who attends a funeral.

mournful
(adjective) very sad.
mournfully (adverb).

mourning
(noun) If someone is in mourning, they wear special black clothes or behave in a special way because a member of their family has died.

mouse, mice
1 (noun) A mouse is a small rodent with a long tail.
2 A mouse is also a small device moved by hand on a special mat to control the position of the cursor on a computer screen.

mousse, mousses (pronounced **moos**)
(noun) Mousse is a light, fluffy food made from whipped eggs and cream.
[from French *mousse* meaning 'froth']

moustache, moustaches (pronounced mus-**stahsh**)
(noun) A man's moustache is hair growing on his upper lip.
[from Greek *mustax* meaning 'upper lip']

mousy
(adjective) Mousy hair is a dull, light brown colour.

mouth, mouths, mouthing, mouthed
1 (noun) Your mouth is your lips, or the space behind them where your tongue and teeth are.
2 The mouth of a cave or a hole is the entrance to it.
3 The mouth of a river is the place where it flows into the sea.
4 (verb) If you mouth something, you form words with your lips without making any sound.
mouthful (noun).

mouthpiece, mouthpieces
1 (noun) The mouthpiece of a telephone is the part you speak into.
2 The mouthpiece of a musical instrument is the part you put to your mouth.
3 The mouthpiece of an organization is the person who publicly states its opinions and policies.

mouth-watering
(adjective) Mouth-watering food looks or smells really delicious.

movable or **moveable**
(adjective) Something that is movable can be moved from one place to another.

move, moves, moving, moved
1 (verb) To move means to go to a different place or position. To move something means to change its place or position.
2 (noun) A move is a change from one place or position to another, e.g. *They had been watching his every move.*
3 (verb) If you move, or move house, you go to live in a different house.
4 (noun) You can refer to the act of moving house as a move.
5 (phrase) If you are **on the move**, you are going from one place to another.
6 (noun) A move is an action taken to achieve something, e.g. *Accepting that job was quite a good move.*
7 A move is also the act of putting a piece or counter in a game in a different position, e.g. *It's my move next.*
8 (verb) If something moves you, it causes you to feel a deep emotion, e.g. *The sight of the tiny coffin moved us all to tears.*
9 If you move a motion at a meeting, you propose it so that a vote can be taken.
moved (adjective).

Similar words: (sense 1) budge, shift, stir

movement, movements
1 (noun) Movement involves changing position or going from one place to another.
2 (plural noun; a formal use) Your movements are everything you do during a period of time, e.g.*Would you please describe your movements on the night of the 26th January.*
3 (noun) A movement is also a group of people who share the same beliefs or aims, e.g. *the women's movement.*
4 A movement is also one of the major sections of a piece of classical music.

moving
1 (adjective) Something that is moving causes you to feel deep sadness or emotion.
2 A moving part of a model or machine is a part which is able to move.
movingly (adverb).

mow, mows, mowing, mowed, mown
1 (verb) To mow grass means to cut it with a lawnmower.
2 To mow down a large number of people means to kill them all violently.

mower, mowers
(noun) A mower is a machine for cutting grass.

MP, MPs
(noun) An MP is a person who has been elected to represent people in a country's parliament. MP is an abbreviation for 'Member of Parliament'.

mpg an abbreviation for 'miles per gallon'.

mph an abbreviation for 'miles per hour'.

MPhil, MPhils
(noun) An MPhil is a higher university degree; also used to refer to someone who has such a degree. MPhil is an abbreviation for 'Master of Philosophy'.

Mr (pronounced **miss**-ter)
Mr is used before a man's name when you are speaking or referring to him.

Mrs (pronounced **miss**-iz)
Mrs is used before the name of a married woman when you are speaking or referring to her.

Ms (pronounced **miz**)
Ms is used before a woman's name when you are speaking or referring to her. Ms does not specify whether a woman is married or not.

MSc, MScs
(noun) An MSc is a higher university degree in a science subject; also used to refer to someone who has such a degree. MSc is an abbreviation for 'Master of Science'.

much
1 (adverb) You use much to emphasize that something is true to a great extent, e.g. *I feel much more confident.*
2 If something does not happen much, it does not happen very often.
3 If one thing is much the same as another, they are very similar.
4 (determiner and pronoun) You use 'much' to ask questions or give information about the size or amount of something, e.g. *How much string do you need?... There's not much left.*

muck, mucks, mucking, mucked
1 (noun; an informal use) Muck is dirt or some other unpleasant substance.
2 Muck is also manure.
3 (verb; an informal use) If you muck about, you behave stupidly and waste time.
4 To muck out farmyard buildings or stables means to clean them.
mucky (adjective).
[from Old Norse *myki* meaning 'dung']

mucus (pronounced **myoo**-kuss)
(noun) Mucus is a liquid produced in parts of your body, for example in your nose.

mud
(noun) Mud is wet, sticky earth.

muddle, muddles, muddling, muddled
1 (noun) A muddle is a state of disorder or untidiness, e.g. *My papers are all in a muddle.*
2 (verb) If you muddle things, you mix them up.
3 If you muddle someone, you confuse them.
muddled (adjective).
[from Dutch *moddelen* meaning 'to make muddy']

Similar words: (sense 2) jumble, confuse, mix up

muddy, muddier, muddiest
1 (adjective) covered in mud.
2 A muddy colour is dull and not clear, e.g. *a horrid muddy green colour.*

mudguard, mudguards
(noun) The mudguards on a bike are the parts above the tyres which prevent mud and water from being splashed up onto the rider.

muesli (pronounced **myooz**-lee)
(noun) Muesli is a mixture of chopped nuts, cereal flakes, and dried fruit that you can eat for breakfast with milk or yoghurt.

muffin, muffins
(noun) A muffin is a small, round, yeast cake which you eat hot.

muffle, muffles, muffling, muffled
(verb) If something muffles a sound, it makes it quieter and difficult to hear, e.g. *The snow muffled the sound of our footsteps.*
muffled (adjective).
[from Old French *emmouflé* meaning 'wrapped up']

mufti
(noun) If someone who normally wears a uniform is in mufti, they are wearing ordinary clothes.

mug, mugs, mugging, mugged
1 (noun) A mug is a large, deep cup with straight sides.
2 (verb; an informal use) If someone mugs you, they attack you in order to steal your money.
3 (noun; an informal use) Someone who is described as a mug is stupid and easily deceived.
mugging (noun), **mugger** (noun).

muggy, muggier, muggiest
(adjective) Muggy weather is unpleasantly warm and damp.

mulberry, mulberries
(noun) A mulberry is a tree with small black fruits rather like blackberries; also the fruit itself.

mulch, mulches, mulching, mulched
1 (noun) A mulch is a mixture of rotting plant material or compost put on the soil around plants in order to feed or protect them.
2 (verb) To mulch plants means to put a mulch around them.

mule, mules
(noun) A mule is the sterile offspring of a female horse and a male donkey.

mulish
(adjective) stubborn and obstinate.

mull, mulls, mulling, mulled
(verb) If you mull something over, you think about it for a long time before making a decision.

multi-
(prefix) Multi- is used to form words that refer to something that has many parts, forms, or aspects, e.g. *a multistorey car park*.
[from Latin *multus* meaning 'much' or 'many']

multifarious (pronounced mul-ti-**fare**-ee-uss)
(adjective; a formal word) of many different kinds, e.g. *pursuing their multifarious hobbies.*

multilateral
(adjective) involving more than two different countries or groups, e.g. *multilateral nuclear disarmament.*

multimillionaire, multimillionaires
(noun) Someone who is a multimillionaire has several million pounds or dollars.

multinational, multinationals
(noun) A multinational is a very large company with branches in many countries.

multiple, multiples
1 (adjective) having or involving many different functions or things, e.g. *There was a multiple accident in thick fog on the M1 today.*
2 (noun) The multiples of a number are other numbers that it will divide into exactly. For example, 6, 9, and 12 are multiples of 3.

multiple-choice
(adjective) In a multiple-choice test, you have to choose the correct answer from several possible answers listed on the question paper.

multiple sclerosis (pronounced skler-**roe**-siss)
(noun) Multiple sclerosis is a serious disease which attacks the nervous system, affecting your ability to move.

multiplication
1 (noun) Multiplication is the process of multiplying one number by another.
2 The multiplication of things is a large increase in their number, e.g. *a multiplication in the number of AIDS cases.*

multiplicity
(noun) If there is a multiplicity of things, there is a large number or variety of them.

multiply, multiplies, multiplying, multiplied
1 (verb) When something multiplies, it increases greatly in number, e.g. *The silkworms multiplied.*
2 When you multiply one number by another, you calculate the total you would get if you added the first number to itself the second number of times.
[from Latin *multus* meaning 'many' and *plicare* meaning 'to fold']

multitude, multitudes
(noun; a formal word) A multitude of things or people is a very large number of them.

mum, mums (an informal word)
1 (noun) Your mum is your mother.
2 (phrase) If you **keep mum** about something, you keep it secret.

mumble, mumbles, mumbling, mumbled
(verb) If you mumble, you speak very quietly and indistinctly.

mummified
(adjective) A mummified body is one that was preserved long ago with special oils and wrapped in cloth.

mummy, mummies
1 (noun; an informal use, used especially by children) Your mummy is your mother.
2 A mummy is a dead body which was preserved long ago by being rubbed with special oils and wrapped in cloth.
[sense 2 is from Persian *mum* meaning 'wax']

mumps
(noun) Mumps is a disease that causes painful swelling in the glands of the neck.

munch, munches, munching, munched
(verb) If you munch something, you chew it steadily and thoroughly.

mundane
(adjective) very ordinary and not at all interesting or unusual, e.g. *mundane chores.*

municipal (pronounced myoo-**nis**-si-pl)
(adjective) belonging to a city or town which has its own local government, e.g. *the municipal baths.*
[from Latin *municipium* meaning 'free town']

munificent
(adjective; a formal word) very generous.
[from Latin *munus* meaning 'gift' and *facere* meaning 'to make']

munitions
(plural noun) Munitions are bombs, guns, and other military supplies.

mural, murals
(noun) A mural is a picture painted on a wall.
[from Latin *murus* meaning 'wall']

murder, murders, murdering, murdered
1 (noun) Murder is the deliberate and unlawful killing of a person.
2 (verb) To murder someone means to kill them deliberately and unlawfully.
murderer (noun), **murderess** (noun).

Similar words: (sense 1) homicide, killing

murderous
1 (adjective) likely to murder someone, e.g. *murderous savages.*
2 (an informal use) very dangerous or difficult, e.g. *a murderous road.*

murky, murkier, murkiest
(adjective) dark or dirty and unpleasant, e.g. *We looked out into the murky streets.*
murk (noun).
[from Old Norse *myrkr* meaning 'darkness']

murmur, murmurs, murmuring, murmured
1 (verb) If you murmur, you say something very softly.
2 (noun) A murmur is an utterance which can hardly be heard.
3 A murmur is also a continuous, quiet, indistinct sound, e.g. *the murmur of waves on a beach.*

Similar words: (senses 1 and 2) mumble, mutter

muscle, muscles, muscling, muscled
1 (noun) Your muscles are pieces of flesh which you can expand or contract in order to move parts of your body.
2 (an informal use) If someone has muscle, they have power or influence.
3 (verb; an informal use) If you muscle in on something, you force your way into a situation in which you are not welcome.
[from Latin *musculus* meaning 'little mouse', because muscles were thought to look like mice]

muscular (pronounced **musk**-yool-lar)
1 (adjective) involving or affecting your muscles, e.g. *muscular dystrophy... muscular effort.*
2 Someone who is muscular has strong, firm muscles.

muse, muses, musing, mused
1 (verb; a literary use) To muse means to think about something for a long time.
2 (a formal use) A muse is an imaginary force which is believed to give people inspiration, e.g. *the poet's muse.*

museum, museums
(noun) A museum is a building where many interesting or valuable objects are kept and displayed.

mush
(noun) A mush is a thick, soft paste.

mushroom, mushrooms, mushrooming, mushroomed
1 (noun) A mushroom is a fungus with a short stem and a round top. Some types of mushroom are edible.
2 (verb) If something mushrooms, it appears and grows very quickly, e.g. *Self-help groups mushroomed overnight.*

mushroom cloud, mushroom clouds
(noun) A mushroom cloud is a large cloud of dust in the shape of a mushroom which rises after a nuclear explosion.

mushy, mushier, mushiest
1 (adjective) Mushy fruits or vegetables are too soft, e.g. *mushy, blackened bananas.*
2 (an informal use) Mushy stories are too sentimental.

music
1 (noun) Music is a pattern of sounds performed by people singing or playing instruments.
2 Music is also the written symbols that represent musical sounds, e.g. *I can't read music.*

musical, musicals
1 (adjective) relating to playing or studying music, e.g. *a musical career.*
2 A musical person has a natural ability in music.
3 Musical sounds are pleasant and tuneful.
4 (noun) A musical is a play or film that uses songs and dance to tell the story.
musically (adverb).

Similar words: (sense 3) harmonious, melodious

music hall, music halls
(noun) Music hall is entertainment consisting of a series of performances by singers, dancers, and comedians.

musician, musicians
(noun) A musician is a person who plays a musical instrument as their job or hobby.
musicianship (noun).

musk
(noun) Musk is a substance with a strong, sweet smell. It is used to make perfume.
musky (adjective).

musket, muskets
(noun) A musket is an old-fashioned gun with a long barrel.

muskrat, muskrats
(noun) A muskrat is a large North American rodent with brown fur, which lives near water.

Muslim, Muslims; also spelled Moslem
1 (noun) A Muslim is a person who believes in Islam and lives according to its rules.
2 (adjective) relating to Islam.

muslin
(noun) Muslin is a very thin cotton material.

musquash, musquashes
(noun) A musquash is a muskrat.

mussel, mussels
(noun) Mussels are a kind of shellfish with black shells.

must
1 (verb) If something must happen, it is very important or necessary that it happens, e.g. *You must clean your teeth... You mustn't worry.*
2 If you tell someone they must do something, you are suggesting that they do it, e.g. *You must come and stay with us.*
3 (noun) Something that is a must is absolutely necessary, e.g. *Sensible shoes are a must for the sightseer.*

mustang, mustangs
(noun) A mustang is a small breed of wild horse found in North America.

mustard
(noun) Mustard is a substance made from the small seeds of the mustard plant.

mustard gas
(noun) Mustard gas is an oily substance causing blindness, burns, and death, used as a chemical weapon.

muster, musters, mustering, mustered
1 (verb) If you muster energy, you gather it together in order to do something, e.g. *I hit him with all the force I could muster.*
2 When soldiers muster, they gather in one place to take action.
3 (phrase) If something **passes muster**, it is of an acceptable standard.

musty, mustier, mustiest
(adjective) smelling stale and damp, e.g. *musty old books.*

mutate, mutates, mutating, mutated
(verb; a technical word) If an animal or plant mutates, it develops different characteristics as the result of a change in its genes.
mutation (noun), **mutant** (noun and adjective).
[from Latin *mutare* meaning 'to change']

mute, mutes, muting, muted (a formal word)
1 (adjective) silent, e.g. *She remained mute, completely overwhelmed by the tragedy.*
2 (verb) To mute a sound means to make it quieter.
[from Latin *mutus* meaning 'silent']

muted
1 (adjective) Muted colours or sounds are soft and gentle.
2 A muted reaction is not very strong or intense.

mutilate, mutilates, mutilating, mutilated
1 (verb) If someone is mutilated, their body is badly injured, e.g. *victims mutilated in the blast.*
2 If you mutilate something, you deliberately damage or spoil it, e.g. *Almost every book had been mutilated in some way.*
mutilation (noun).

mutinous
(adjective) likely to disobey or rebel, e.g. *The crew were restive and mutinous.*

mutiny, mutinies, mutinying, mutinied
1 (verb) If a group of sailors or soldiers mutiny, they rebel against their officers.
2 (noun) A mutiny is a rebellion against someone in authority.
mutineer (noun).

mutter, mutters, muttering, muttered
(verb) To mutter means to speak in a very low and perhaps cross voice, e.g. *He muttered obscenities under his breath.*

mutton
(noun) Mutton is the meat of an adult sheep.

mutual
(adjective) used to describe something that two or more people do to each other or share, e.g. *I didn't like him and I was sure the feeling was mutual... They had a mutual interest in dance.*
[from Latin *mutuus* meaning 'reciprocal']

mutually
1 (adverb) Mutually describes a situation in which two or more people feel the same way about each other, e.g. *He enjoyed a mutually respectful relationship with them.*
2 (phrase) If two things are **mutually exclusive**, they cannot both be true or both exist at the same time.

Muzak (pronounced **myoo**-zak)
(noun; a trademark) Muzak is recorded music played in shops and restaurants.

muzzle, muzzles, muzzling, muzzled
1 (noun) The muzzle of an animal is its nose and mouth.
2 A muzzle is a cover or a strap for a dog's nose and mouth to prevent it from biting.
3 (verb) To muzzle a dog means to put a muzzle on it.
4 (noun) The muzzle of a gun is the open end through which the bullets come out.
[from Old French *musel* meaning 'little snout']

muzzy, muzzier, muzziest
(adjective) If you feel muzzy, you are unable to think clearly because you are ill or drunk.

my
(determiner) My refers to something belonging or relating to the person speaking or writing, e.g. *I closed my eyes.*

mynah bird, mynah birds
(noun) A mynah bird is a tropical bird which can mimic speech and sounds.

myopia (pronounced my-**oh**-pee-a)
(noun) Myopia is an inability to see clearly things that are far away.
myopic (adjective).
[from Greek *muein* meaning 'to blink' and *ōps* meaning 'eye']

myriad, myriads (pronounced **mir**-ree-ad)
(noun and adjective; a literary word) A myriad of people or things is a very large number of them.
[from Greek *murias* meaning 'ten thousand']

myrrh (rhymes with **purr**)
(noun) Myrrh is a fragrant resin used in perfume and incense. It is obtained from a shrub of the same name, found in Africa and Asia.

myself
1 (pronoun) Myself is used when the person speaking or writing does an action and is affected by it, e.g. *I will kill myself.*
2 Myself is also used to emphasize 'I'.

mysterious
1 (adjective) strange and not well understood.
2 secretive about something, e.g. *You've been very mysterious lately; what's going on?*
mysteriously (adverb).

Similar words: (sense 2) cryptic, enigmatic

mystery, mysteries
(noun) A mystery is something that is not understood or known about.
mystery (adjective).
[from Greek *mustērion* meaning 'secret rites']

mystic, mystics
1 (noun) A mystic is a religious person who spends long hours meditating.
2 (adjective) Mystic means the same as mystical.

mystical
(adjective) involving spiritual powers and influences, e.g. *mystical experiences.*
mysticism (noun).

mystify, mystifies, mystifying, mystified
(verb) If something mystifies you, you find it impossible to understand.

mystique (pronounced mis-**steek**)
(noun) Mystique is an atmosphere of mystery and importance associated with a particular person or thing.

myth, myths
1 (noun) A myth is an untrue belief or explanation.
2 A myth is also a story which was made up long ago to explain natural events and religious beliefs, e.g. *Greek myths and legends.*
[from Greek *muthos* meaning 'fable']

mythical
(adjective) imaginary, untrue, or existing only in myths, e.g. *mythical lands... They'd gone in search of mythical opportunities.*

mythology
(noun) Mythology refers to stories that have been made up about religion or natural events.
mythological (adjective).

myxomatosis (pronounced mik-soh-mat-**oh**-siss)
(noun) Myxomatosis is an infectious viral disease affecting rabbits.

N

nadir (pronounced **nay**-deer)
(noun; a formal word) The nadir of something is its least successful time, e.g. *The fortunes of the party reached their nadir.*

nag, nags, nagging, nagged
1 (verb) If you nag someone, you keep complaining to them about something.
2 If something nags at you, it keeps worrying you.

nail, nails, nailing, nailed
1 (noun) A nail is a small piece of metal with a sharp point at one end, which you hammer into objects to hold them together.
2 (verb) If you nail something somewhere, you fit it there using a nail.
3 (phrase) If you **hit the nail on the head**, you say something that expresses the point precisely.
4 (noun) Your nails are the hard coverings strengthening the ends of your fingers and toes.

naive or **naïve** (pronounced **ny**-eev)
(adjective) foolishly believing that things are easier or less complicated than they really are.
naively (adverb), **naivety** (noun).
[from Old French *naif* meaning 'native' or 'spontaneous']

naked
1 (adjective) not wearing any clothes or not covered by anything.
2 shown openly, e.g. *a look of naked anxiety.*
nakedness (noun).

name, names, naming, named
1 (noun) A name is a word that you use to identify a person, place, or thing.
2 (verb) If you name someone or something, you give them a name or you say their name.
3 If you name a price or a date, you say what you want it to be.
4 (noun) Someone's name is also their reputation, e.g. *She spoke out in public to clear his name.*
5 (phrase) If you do something **in the name of** an ideal or person, you do it because you believe in or represent that ideal or person.

name-dropping
(noun) Name-dropping is the habit of referring to famous people as though they were your friends, in order to impress people.

nameless
1 (adjective) You describe someone or something as nameless when you do not know their name, or when a name has not yet been given to them.
2 If you say that someone will remain nameless, you mean that you will not say their name, often so as not to embarrass them.

namely
(adverb) that is; used to introduce more detailed information about what you have just said, e.g. *three famous physicists, namely Simon, Kurte, and Mendelssohn.*

namesake, namesakes
(noun) Your namesake is someone with the same name as you.

Namibian (pronounced nah-**mib**-ee-an)
(adjective) belonging or relating to Namibia.

nanny, nannies
(noun) A nanny is a woman whose job is looking after young children.

nanny goat, nanny goats
(noun) A nanny goat is a female goat.

nap, naps, napping, napped
1 (noun) A nap is a short sleep.
2 The nap of a cloth, especially velvet, is the top surface of fibres lying smoothly in one direction.
3 (verb) When you nap, you have a short sleep.

napalm (pronounced **nay**-pahm)
(noun) Napalm is a kind of petrol used in bombs and flame-throwers.
[from the first letters of *naphthene* and *palmitate*]

nape, napes
(noun) The nape of your neck is the back of it.

naphthalene (pronounced **nahf**-thal-een)
(noun) Naphthalene is a white crystalline solid obtained from coal tar. It has a strong smell and is used in making dyes and mothballs.

napkin, napkins
(noun) A napkin is a small piece of cloth or paper used to wipe your hands and mouth after eating.

nappy, nappies
(noun) A nappy is a piece of towelling or paper worn round a baby's bottom.

narcissistic (pronounced nahr-siss-**siss**-tik)
(adjective; a formal word) extremely vain.
narcissism (noun).
[from *Narcissus*, a character in Greek mythology, who fell in love with his own reflection]

narcissus, narcissi (pronounced nahr-**siss**-suss)
(noun) A narcissus is any of several kinds of yellow or white flower, including daffodils.

narcotic, narcotics
(noun) A narcotic is a drug which makes you sleepy and unable to feel pain.
[from Greek *narkoun* meaning 'to make numb']

narrate, narrates, narrating, narrated
(verb) If you narrate a story, you tell it.
narration (noun), **narrator** (noun).
[from Latin *narrare*]

narrative, narratives (pronounced **nar**-rat-tiv)
(noun) A narrative is a story or an account of events.

narrow, narrows, narrowing, narrowed
1 (adjective) having a small extent from one side to the other, e.g. *a narrow street.*
2 (verb) To narrow means to become less wide, e.g. *The river narrowed.*

3 (adjective) concerned only with a few aspects of something and ignoring the important points, e.g. *I think you are taking too narrow a view.*
4 A narrow escape or victory is one that you only just achieve.
narrowly (adverb), **narrowness** (noun).

narrow boat, narrow boats
(noun) A narrow boat is a long thin boat specially built to be used on canals.

narrow-minded
(adjective) unwilling to consider new ideas or opinions.

Similar words: insular, parochial, narrow

nasal (pronounced **nay**-zal)
1 (adjective) relating to the nose, e.g. *the nasal passages.*
2 Nasal sounds are made by breathing out through your nose as you speak.
[from Latin *nasus* meaning 'nose']

nasturtium, nasturtiums (nas-**tur**-shum)
(noun) A nasturtium is a garden plant with red, yellow, or orange trumpet-shaped flowers.
[from Latin *nasus tortus* meaning 'twisted nose', because of its powerful smell]

nasty, nastier, nastiest
(adjective) very unpleasant, e.g. *a nasty smell.*
nastily (adverb), **nastiness** (noun).

natal
(adjective) relating to birth.

nation, nations
(noun) A nation is a large group of people sharing the same history and language and usually inhabiting a particular country.
[from Latin *natio* meaning 'tribe']

national, nationals
1 (adjective) relating to the whole of a country, e.g. *national newspapers.*
2 typical of a particular country, e.g. *dancers in national dress.*
3 (noun) A national of a country is a citizen of that country, e.g. *German nationals.*
nationally (adverb).

national anthem, national anthems
(noun) A country's national anthem is its official song.

national insurance
(noun) National insurance is a system by which the government collects money from employers and employees so that it can pay ill, unemployed, and retired people.

nationalism
1 (noun) Nationalism is a desire for the independence of a country; also a political movement aiming to achieve such independence.
2 Nationalism is also love of your own country.
nationalist (noun), **nationalistic** (adjective).

nationality, nationalities
(noun) Nationality is the fact of belonging to a particular country.

nationalize, nationalizes, nationalizing, nationalized; also spelled nationalise
(verb) To nationalize an industry means to bring it under the control and ownership of the state.
nationalized (adjective), **nationalization** (noun).

national park, national parks
(noun) A national park is an area of land protected by the government because of its natural beauty, which the public can visit.

national service
(noun) National service is a compulsory period of service in the armed forces.

nationwide
(adjective and adverb) happening all over a country, e.g. *a nationwide campaign.*

native, natives
1 (adjective) Your native country is the country where you were born.
2 Your native language is the language that you first learned to speak.
3 Animals or plants that are native to a place live or grow there naturally and have not been brought there by people.
4 (noun) A native of a place is someone who was born there.

Nativity
(noun) In Christianity, the Nativity is the birth of Christ or the festival celebrating this.

natter, natters, nattering, nattered
(verb; an informal word) If you natter, you talk about unimportant things.

natural, naturals
1 (adjective) normal and to be expected, e.g. *It's only natural that she should feel upset.*
2 not trying to pretend or hide anything, e.g. *talking in a relaxed, natural manner.*
3 existing or happening in nature, e.g. *natural disasters.*
4 A natural ability is one you were born with.
5 Your natural mother or father is your real mother or father and not someone who has adopted you.
6 (noun) A natural is someone who is born with a particular ability or talent, e.g. *He is a great craftsman, a natural.*
7 In music, a natural is a note that is not a sharp or a flat. It is represented by the symbol ' ♮ '.
8 (phrase) If someone dies of **natural causes**, they die because they are ill and not because they are killed or commit suicide.
naturally (adverb), **naturalness** (noun).

Similar words: (sense 4) inherent, innate, inborn, native

natural gas
(noun) Natural gas is a gas found underground or under the sea and used as a fuel.

natural history
(noun) Natural history is the study of animals and plants.

naturalist, naturalists
(noun) A naturalist is someone who studies animals and plants.

naturalized or **naturalised**
(adjective) A naturalized citizen is someone who

has legally become a citizen of a country that they were not born in.

natural number, natural numbers
(noun) In mathematics, a natural number is any whole number that is greater than zero.

natural science
(noun) Natural science is the study of biology, physics, and chemistry.

natural selection
(noun) Natural selection is Darwin's theory that only the species of animals and plants that are best suited to their environment survive and reproduce, while those that are less well suited die.

nature, natures
1 (noun) Nature is animals, plants, and all the other things in the world not made by people.
2 The nature of a person or thing is their basic character, e.g. *Rob had a very sweet nature... These problems are political in nature.*
[from Latin *natura* meaning 'birth']

naught
(noun; an old-fashioned word) nothing.

naughty, naughtier, naughtiest
1 (adjective) behaving badly.
2 rude or indecent, e.g. *a naughty film.*
naughtily (adverb), **naughtiness** (noun).

nausea (pronounced **naw**-zee-ah)
(noun) Nausea is a feeling in your stomach that you are going to be sick.
nauseous (adjective).
[from Greek *nausia* meaning 'seasickness']

nauseate, nauseates, nauseating, nauseated
(pronounced **naw**-zee-yate)
(verb) If something nauseates you, it makes you feel sick.

nautical (pronounced **naw**-tik-kl)
(adjective) relating to ships or navigation.
[from Greek *naus* meaning 'ship']

nautical mile, nautical miles
(noun) A nautical mile is a unit of distance used at sea, equal to 1852 metres.

naval
(adjective) relating to or having a navy, e.g. *U.S. naval forces... naval powers.*
[from Latin *navis* meaning 'ship']

Similar words: nautical, maritime

nave, naves
(noun) The nave of a church or cathedral is the long central part.

navel, navels
(noun) Your navel is the small hollow on the front of your body just below your waist.

navigable
(adjective) wide enough and deep enough to sail on, e.g. *navigable rivers.*

navigate, navigates, navigating, navigated
1 (verb) When someone navigates, they work out the direction in which a ship, plane, or car should go, using maps and sometimes instruments.

2 To navigate a stretch of water means to travel safely across it, e.g. *Until then no ship had been large enough to navigate the Atlantic.*
navigation (noun), **navigator** (noun).
[from Latin *navigare* meaning 'to drive a ship']

navvy, navvies
(noun; an old fashioned word) A navvy is a man employed to do hard physical work such as building roads or railways.
[from 'navigator', which used to mean 'builder of navigations (canals)']

navy, navies
1 (noun) A country's navy is the part of its armed forces that fights at sea.
2 (adjective) dark blue.
[from Latin *navis* meaning 'ship']

nay
(interjection; an old-fashioned word) no.

Nazi, Nazis (pronounced **naht**-see)
(noun) The Nazis were members of the National Socialist German Workers' Party, which was led for a time by Adolf Hitler.

NB
You write NB to draw attention to what you are going to write next. NB is an abbreviation for the Latin 'nota bene', which means 'note well'.

Neanderthal (pronounced nee-**an**-der-tahl)
(adjective) Neanderthal man was a primitive species of man who lived in Europe before 12,000 B.C. The name comes from Neandertal, a German valley where archaeological discoveries were made.

near, nearer, nearest; nears, nearing, neared
1 (preposition and adverb) not far from.
2 (adjective) You can also use near to mean almost, e.g. *a state of near chaos.*
3 (verb) When you are nearing something, you are approaching it and will soon reach it, e.g. *As they neared the harbour, it began to rain.*
nearness (noun).

nearby
(adjective or adverb) only a short distance away.

nearly
1 (adverb) not completely but almost.
2 (phrase) You use **not nearly** to emphasize that something is not the case, e.g. *not nearly enough.*

nearside
(noun) The nearside of a vehicle is the side nearest to the edge of the road when the vehicle is being driven normally.

neat, neater, neatest
1 (adjective) tidy and smart.
2 A neat alcoholic drink does not have anything added to it, e.g. *She takes her whisky neat.*
neatly (adverb), **neatness** (noun).
[from Latin *nitidus* meaning 'shining' or 'clean']

nebula, nebulas or nebulae
(noun) A nebula is an area of pale light consisting of gas and dust in the night sky.
[from Latin *nebula* meaning 'mist']

nebulous
(adjective) vague and unclear, e.g. *nebulous ideas.*

necessarily
(adverb) Something that is not necessarily the case is not always or inevitably the case.

necessary
1 (adjective) Something that is necessary is needed or must be done.
2 (a formal use) Necessary also means certain or inevitable, e.g. *There is no necessary connection between the two things.*
[from Latin *necessarius* meaning 'essential']

Similar words: (sense 1) needful, essential, required, requisite

necessitate, necessitates, necessitating, necessitated
(verb; a formal word) To necessitate something means to make it necessary, e.g. *The Government's action necessitated a by-election.*

necessity, necessities
1 (noun) Necessity is the need to do something, e.g. *She worked not from choice but necessity.*
2 Necessities are things needed in order to live.

neck, necks
1 (noun) Your neck is the part of your body which joins your head to the rest of your body.
2 The neck of a piece of clothing is the part that goes round your neck.
3 The neck of a bottle is the long narrow part at the top.
4 If you **stick your neck out**, you take a risk and do something that may be criticized or put you in danger.
5 If two competitors are **neck and neck**, they are level with each other.

necklace, necklaces
(noun) A necklace is a piece of jewellery which a woman wears around her neck.

neckline, necklines
(noun) A neckline is the shape or position of the neck of a dress or blouse.

necromancy (pronounced nek-rom-man-see)
(noun) Necromancy is communication with the dead in order to find out about the future.
necromancer (noun).
[from Greek *nekros* meaning 'corpse']

nectar
(noun) Nectar is a sweet liquid produced by flowers and attractive to insects.

nectarine, nectarines
(noun) A nectarine is a kind of peach with a smooth skin.

née (rhymes with **day**)
Née is used to indicate what a woman's surname was before she got married, e.g. *Jane Carmichael, née Byers.*
[from French *née*, the feminine past participle of *naître* meaning 'to be born']

need, needs, needing, needed
1 (verb) If you need something, you believe that you must have it or do it.
2 (noun) Your needs are the things that you need to have.
3 A need is also a strong feeling that you must have or do something, e.g. *She felt the need to speak.*
4 (phrase) If you are in **need of** something, you need it.

Similar words: (sense 2) necessity, requirement

needle, needles, needling, needled
1 (noun) A needle is a small thin piece of metal with a pointed end and a hole at the other for carrying thread, which is used for sewing.
2 Needles are also long thin pieces of steel or plastic, used for knitting.
3 The needle in a record player is the small pointed part that touches the record and picks up the sound signals.
4 The needle of a syringe is the part which a doctor or nurse sticks into your body.
5 The needle on a dial is the thin piece of metal or plastic which moves to show a measurement.
6 The needles of a pine tree are its leaves.
7 (verb; an informal use) If someone needles you, they annoy or provoke you.

needless
(adjective) unnecessary.
needlessly (adverb).

Similar words: uncalled for, gratuitous

needlework
(noun) Needlework is sewing or embroidery.

needy, needier, neediest
(adjective) very poor.

nefarious (pronounced nif-**fair**-ree-uss)
(adjective; a formal word) wicked, e.g. *a nefarious system which exploits people.*
[from Latin *nefas* meaning 'unlawful deed']

negate, negates, negating, negated
(verb; a formal word) To negate something means to make it useless and of no value.
negation (noun).
[from Latin *negare* meaning 'to say no']

negative, negatives
1 (adjective) A negative answer means 'no'.
2 Someone who is negative sees only problems and disadvantages, e.g. *He was very negative about my written work.*
3 If a medical or scientific test is negative, it shows that something has not happened or is not present, e.g. *a negative pregnancy test.*
4 A negative number is less than zero.
5 In physics, a negative electric charge has the same polarity as the charge of an electron.
6 (noun) A negative is the image that is first produced when you take a photograph.
negatively (adverb).

neglect, neglects, neglecting, neglected
1 (verb) If you neglect something, you do not look after it properly.
2 (a formal use) If you neglect to do something, you fail to do it, e.g. *I neglected to bring a gift.*
3 (noun) Neglect is failure to look after

something or someone properly, e.g. *buildings suffering from vandalism and neglect.*
neglectful (adjective).
[from Latin *neglegere* meaning 'to disregard']

negligee, negligees (pronounced **neg**-lij-jay); also spelled **négligée**
(noun) A negligee is a woman's dressing gown made of very thin material.

negligent
(adjective) not taking enough care, e.g. *He has been negligent in his duties.*
negligently (adverb), **negligence** (noun).

negligible
(adjective) very small and unimportant, e.g. *This would have a negligible effect.*

negotiable
(adjective) able to be changed or agreed by discussion, e.g. *The price is negotiable.*

negotiate, negotiates, negotiating, negotiated
1 (verb) When people negotiate, they have formal discussions in order to reach an agreement about something.
2 If you negotiate an obstacle, you manage to get over it or round it.
negotiation (noun), **negotiator** (noun).
[from Latin *negotiari* meaning 'to do business']

negro, negroes
(noun) A negro is a person with black skin who comes from Africa or whose ancestors came from Africa.
[from Spanish *negro* meaning 'black']

neigh, neighs, neighing, neighed (rhymes with day)
1 (verb) When a horse neighs, it makes a loud high-pitched sound.
2 (noun) A neigh is a loud sound made by a horse.

neighbour, neighbours
1 (noun) Your neighbour is someone who lives next door to you or near you.
2 Your neighbour is also someone standing or sitting next to you, e.g. *Rudolph turned his head towards his neighbour.*

neighbourhood, neighbourhoods
(noun) A neighbourhood is a district where people live, e.g. *a wealthy neighbourhood.*

neighbouring
(adjective) situated nearby, e.g. *Families came from neighbouring villages.*

neighbourly
(adjective) If people who live near you are neighbourly, they are kind and friendly.

neither
(determiner and pronoun) used to indicate that a negative statement refers to two or more things or people, e.g. *He spoke neither English nor French... Neither of us was having any luck.*

neo-
(prefix) new or modern, e.g. *neo-colonialism.*
[from Greek *neos* meaning 'new']

neolithic
(adjective) relating to the Stone Age period when people first started farming.
[from *neo-* + Greek *lithos* meaning 'stone']

neon (pronounced **nee**-yon)
(noun) Neon is a chemical element existing as a gas in very small amounts in the atmosphere. It is used in glass tubes to make bright electric lights and signs. Neon's atomic number is 10 and its symbol is Ne.

nephew, nephews
(noun) Someone's nephew is the son of their sister or brother.

nepotism
(noun) Nepotism is unfair use of your influence to get a job for another member of your family.
[from Italian *nepote* meaning 'nephew', because Popes used to grant favours to their nephews]

Neptune
(noun) Neptune is the planet in the solar system which is eighth from the sun.
[from *Neptune*, the Roman god of the sea]

nerve, nerves
1 (noun) A nerve is a long thin fibre that transmits messages between your brain and other parts of your body.
2 If you talk about someone's nerves, you are referring to how able they are to remain calm in a difficult situation, e.g. *She had strong nerves.*
3 Nerve is courage or impudence, e.g. *Nobody had the nerve to criticize him.*
4 (an informal phrase) If someone **gets on your nerves**, they irritate you.

nerve cell, nerve cells
(noun) A nerve cell is the same as a neuron.

nerve-racking
(adjective) making you feel very worried and tense, e.g. *a nerve-racking experience.*

nervous
1 (adjective) worried and frightened.
2 A nervous illness affects your emotions and mental health.
nervously (adverb), **nervousness** (noun).

Similar words: (sense 1) jittery, jumpy, edgy, on edge, uptight

nervous breakdown, nervous breakdowns
(noun) A nervous breakdown is an illness in which someone suffers from depression and worry and feels unable to cope with life.

nervous system, nervous systems
(noun) Your nervous system is the nerves in your body together with your brain and spinal cord.

nest, nests, nesting, nested
1 (noun) A nest is a place that a bird makes to lay its eggs in; also a place that some insects and other animals make to rear their young in.
2 (verb) When birds nest, they build a nest and lay eggs in it.

nestle, nestles, nestling, nestled (pronounced **ness**-sl)
(verb) If you nestle somewhere, you settle there

comfortably, often pressing up against someone else, e.g. *They nestled together on the sofa.*

nestling, nestlings
(noun) A nestling is a young bird that has not yet learned to fly and so has not left the nest.

net, nets, netting, netted
1 (noun) A net is a piece of material made of threads woven together with small spaces in between.
2 (verb) If you net something, you manage to get it, often by using skill, e.g. *He netted a fortune.*
3 (adjective) A net result or amount is final, after everything has been considered, e.g. *a net profit of just over 23%.*
4 The net weight of something is its weight without its wrapping.

netball
(noun) Netball is a game played by two teams in which each team tries to score goals by throwing a ball through a net at the top of a pole.

netting
(noun) Netting is material made of threads or metal wires woven together with small spaces in between.

nettle, nettles, nettling, nettled
1 (noun) A nettle is a wild plant covered with little hairs that sting.
2 (verb) If someone nettles you, they annoy you.

network, networks
1 (noun) A network is a large number of lines or roads which cross each other at many points, e.g. *the network of back streets.*
2 A network of people or organizations is a large number of them that work together as a system, e.g. *the public telephone network.*
3 A television network is a group of broadcasting stations that all transmit the same programmes at the same time.

neuralgia (pronounced nyoor-**ral**-ja)
(noun) Neuralgia is a severe pain along a nerve, especially in your head or face.
[from Greek *neuron* meaning 'nerve' and *algos* meaning 'pain']

neuritis (pronounced nyoor-**eye**-tiss)
(noun) Neuritis is an inflammation of a nerve.
[from Greek *neuron* meaning 'nerve' and *-itis* meaning 'inflammation']

neurology (pronounced nyoor-**rol**-loj-jee)
(noun) Neurology is the study of the nervous system.
neurological (adjective), **neurologist** (noun).

neuron, neurons
(noun) A neuron is a cell that is part of the nervous system and conducts messages to and from the brain.
[from Greek *neuron* meaning 'nerve']

neurone, neurones
(noun) A neurone is the same as a neuron.

neurosis, neuroses (pronounced nyoor-**roh**-siss)
(noun) Neurosis is mental illness which causes people to have strong and unreasonable fears and worries.

neurotic (pronounced nyoor-**rot**-ik)
(adjective) having strong and unreasonable fears and worries, e.g. *They are becoming neurotic about their careers.*
neurotically (adverb).

neuter, neuters, neutering, neutered (pronounced **nyoo**-ter)
1 (adjective) In some languages, a neuter noun or pronoun is one which is not masculine or feminine.
2 (verb) When an animal is neutered, its reproductive organs are removed.

neutral, neutrals
1 (adjective) People who are neutral do not support either side in a disagreement or war.
2 (noun) A neutral is a person or country that does not support either side in a disagreement or war.
3 Neutral is the position between the gears of a vehicle in which the gears are not connected to the engine and so the vehicle cannot move.
4 (adjective) The neutral wire in an electric plug is the one that is not earth or live.
5 A neutral colour is not definite or striking, for example pale grey.
6 In chemistry, a neutral substance is neither acid nor alkaline.
neutrality (noun).

neutralize, neutralizes, neutralizing, neutralized; also spelled **neutralise**
(verb) To neutralize something means to prevent it from working or taking effect, especially by doing or applying something that has the opposite effect.

neutron, neutrons
(noun) A neutron is an atomic particle that has no electrical charge.

neutron bomb, neutron bombs
(noun) A neutron bomb is a bomb that is designed to kill people by radiation and without destroying buildings.

never
(adverb) at no time in the past, present, or future.

nevertheless
(adverb) in spite of what has just been said, e.g. *She saw Clarissa immediately, but nevertheless pretended to look around for her.*

new, newer, newest
1 (adjective) recently made or created, e.g. *building new houses... a new idea.*
2 only recently discovered, e.g. *a new planet.*
3 not used or owned before, e.g. *He got a new job.*
4 different or unfamiliar, e.g. *a part of England completely new to him.*
newness (noun).

Similar words: (sense 1) brand-new, latest, novel

newborn
(adjective) born recently.

newcomer, newcomers
(noun) A newcomer is someone who has recently arrived in a place.

newfangled
(adjective) If you describe something as newfangled, you mean that you find it too modern and too complicated.

newly
(adverb) recently, e.g. *the newly married couple*.

new moon, new moons
(noun) The moon is a new moon when it is a thin crescent shape at the start of its four-week cycle.

news
1 (noun) News is information about things that have happened.
2 (phrase) If you say **that's news to me**, you mean that you did not know about it before.

newsagent, newsagents
(noun) A newsagent is a person or shop that sells newspapers and magazines.

newscaster, newscasters
(noun) A newscaster is someone who reads the news on the television or radio.

newsletter, newsletters
(noun) A newsletter is a printed sheet of paper containing information about an organization and sent regularly to its members.

newspaper, newspapers
(noun) A newspaper is a publication that is produced regularly and contains news, articles, and advertisements.

newsprint
(noun) Newsprint is the cheap rough paper on which newspapers are printed.

newt, newts
(noun) A newt is a small amphibious creature with a moist skin, short legs, and a long tail.
[from a mistaken division of Middle English *an ewt*]

New Testament
(noun) The New Testament is the second part of the Bible, which deals with the life of Jesus Christ and with the early Church.

newton, newtons
(noun) A newton is a unit of force. One newton causes one kilogram to have an acceleration of one metre per second. The newton is named after the English scientist Sir Isaac Newton (1643-1727).

New Year
1 (noun) New Year is the time when people celebrate the start of a year.
2 The New Year is the first few weeks of a year.

New Zealander, New Zealanders
(noun) A New Zealander is someone who comes from New Zealand.

next
1 (adjective and adverb) coming immediately after something else, e.g. *Stop at the next lay-by*.
2 (phrase) If one thing is **next to** another, it is at the side of it.

Similar words: (sense 1) subsequent, following

next door
(adjective and adverb) in the house next to yours.

next of kin
(noun) Your next of kin is your closest relative.

NHS an abbreviation for 'National Health Service'.

niacin (pronounced **nigh**-a-sin)
(noun) Niacin is a vitamin which is part of the vitamin B complex and is found in fresh meat and yeast.

nib, nibs
(noun) The nib of a pen is its pointed end.

nibble, nibbles, nibbling, nibbled
1 (verb) When you nibble something, you take small bites of it.
2 (noun) A nibble is a small bite of something.

nice, nicer, nicest
(adjective) pleasant or attractive.
nicely (adverb), **niceness** (noun).

nicety, niceties (pronounced **nigh**-se-tee)
(noun) A nicety is a small detail, e.g. *The niceties of etiquette must be observed.*

niche, niches (pronounced neesh)
1 (noun) A niche is a hollow area in a wall, e.g. *the little statue of the saint in his niche.*
2 If you say that you have found your niche, you mean that you have found a job or way of life that is exactly right for you.
[from Old French *nichier* meaning 'to nest']

nick, nicks, nicking, nicked
1 (verb) If you nick something, you make a small cut in its surface, e.g. *He nicked himself shaving.*
2 (noun) A nick is a small cut in the surface of something.
3 (verb; an informal use) To nick something also means to steal it.
4 (phrase) If something happens **in the nick of time**, it only just happens in time.
5 (an informal use) If something is **in good nick**, it is in good condition.

nickel, nickels
1 (noun) Nickel is a silver-coloured metallic element that is used in alloys. Its atomic number is 28 and its symbol is Ni.
2 A nickel is an American or Canadian coin worth five cents.

nickname, nicknames, nicknaming, nicknamed
1 (noun) A nickname is an informal name given to someone.
2 (verb) If you nickname someone, you give them a nickname.
[from Middle English *an ekename* meaning 'an additional name']

nicotine
(noun) Nicotine is an addictive substance found in tobacco. It is named after Jacques Nicot, who first brought tobacco to France.

niece, nieces
(noun) Someone's niece is the daughter of their sister or brother.

nifty
(adjective) neat and pleasing or cleverly done.

Nigerian, Nigerians (pronounced nie-**jeer**-ee-an)
1 (adjective) belonging or relating to Nigeria.

2 (noun) A Nigerian is someone who comes from Nigeria.

niggardly
(adjective) not generous, e.g. *a niggardly salary.*

niggle, niggles, niggling, niggled
1 (verb) If something niggles you, it worries you slightly.
2 If you niggle someone, you criticize them continually.
3 (noun) A niggle is a small worry that you keep thinking about.

night, nights
(noun) Night is the time between sunset and sunrise when it is dark.

nightcap, nightcaps
(noun) A nightcap is a drink, especially an alcoholic one, taken just before going to bed.

nightclub, nightclubs
(noun) A nightclub is a place where people go late in the evening to drink and dance.

nightdress, nightdresses
(noun) A nightdress is a loose dress that a woman or girl wears to sleep in.

nightfall
(noun) Nightfall is the time of day when it starts to get dark.

nightie, nighties
(noun; an informal word) A nightie is a nightdress.

nightingale, nightingales
(noun) A nightingale is a small brown European bird. The male nightingale sings very beautifully, especially at night.

nightly
(adjective and adverb) happening every night, e.g. *her nightly visits.*

nightmare, nightmares
(noun) A nightmare is a very frightening dream; also used of any very unpleasant or frightening situation, e.g. *My first day was a nightmare.*
nightmarish (adjective).
[from *night* + Middle English *mare* meaning 'evil spirit']

nil
(noun) Nil means zero or nothing.

nimble, nimbler, nimblest
1 (adjective) able to move quickly and easily.
2 able to think quickly and cleverly, e.g. *a nimble mind.*
nimbleness (noun), **nimbly** (adverb).

nimbus, nimbuses
(noun) A nimbus is a dark cloud bringing rain and snow.

nincompoop, nincompoops
(noun; an informal word) A nincompoop is a foolish person.

nine the number 9.
ninth.

nineteen the number 19.
nineteenth.

ninety, nineties
the number 90.
ninetieth.

nip, nips, nipping, nipped
1 (verb; an informal use) If you nip somewhere, you go there quickly.
2 (verb) To nip someone or something means to pinch, bite, or squeeze them slightly.
3 (noun) A nip is a light pinch.

nipper, nippers
(noun; an informal word) A nipper is a child.

nipple, nipples
1 (noun) Your nipples are the two small pieces of projecting flesh on your chest. Babies suck milk through the nipples on their mothers' breasts.
2 A nipple is also anything which is shaped like a nipple, or which functions as a nipple.

nippy
(adjective; an informal word) quite cold, e.g. *The air was nippy outside.*

nirvana (pronounced neer-**vah**-na)
(noun) Nirvana is the ultimate state of spiritual enlightenment which can be achieved in the Hindu and Buddhist religions.

nit, nits
1 (noun; an informal use) A nit is a stupid person.
2 (noun) Nits are the eggs of a kind of louse that sometimes lives in people's hair.

nitrate, nitrates
(noun) A nitrate is a chemical compound that includes nitrogen and oxygen. Nitrates are used as fertilizers in agriculture.

nitrogen
(noun) Nitrogen is a chemical element usually found as a gas. It forms about 78% of the earth's atmosphere. Nitrogen's atomic number is 7 and its symbol is N.

nitroglycerine
(noun) Nitroglycerine is a dense oily liquid used as an explosive.

nitty-gritty
(noun; an informal word) The most important facts about something can be referred to as the nitty-gritty.

no
1 (interjection) used to say that something is not true or to refuse something.
2 (determiner) none at all or not at all, e.g. *He gave no reason... She is no friend of mine.*
3 (adverb) used with a comparative to mean 'not', e.g. *no later than 31st August.*

no. a written abbreviation for **number.**

nobility
1 (noun) Nobility is the quality of being noble, e.g. *He had nobility in defeat.*
2 The nobility of a society are all the people who have titles and high social rank.

Similar words: (sense 2) aristocracy, upper classes, peers

noble, nobler, noblest; nobles
1 (adjective) honest and brave, and deserving admiration.
2 very impressive, e.g. *one of the noblest collections of art in England.*
3 (noun) A noble is a member of the nobility.
nobly (adverb).
[from Latin *nobilis* meaning 'well-known']

nobleman, noblemen
(noun) A nobleman is a man who is a member of the nobility.
noblewoman (noun).

nobody, nobodies
1 (pronoun) not a single person.
2 (noun) Someone who is a nobody is not at all important.

nocturnal
1 (adjective) happening at night, e.g. *a nocturnal tour of the city.*
2 active at night, e.g. *nocturnal animals.*

nocturne, nocturnes (pronounced **nok**-turn)
(noun) A nocturne is a short, gentle piece of music, often written for the piano.

nod, nods, nodding, nodded
1 (verb) When you nod, you move your head up and down, usually to show agreement.
2 If something nods, it moves gently up and down, e.g. *A little breeze made the poppies nod.*
3 (noun) A nod is a movement of your head up and down.

nod off
(phrasal verb) If you nod off, you fall asleep.

node, nodes
1 (noun) In biology, a node is the place on the stem of a plant from which a branch or leaf grows.
2 A node is also a point where two lines intersect.
[from Latin *nodus* meaning 'knot']

nodule, nodules (pronounced **nod**-yool)
(noun) A nodule is a small, rounded lump, especially one on the root of a plant.
[from Latin *nodus* meaning 'knot']

noise, noises
(noun) A noise is a sound, especially one that is loud or unpleasant.
[from Old French *noise* meaning 'disturbance']

Similar words: clamour, din, racket, row, sound

noiseless
(adjective) silent.

noisy, noisier, noisiest
(adjective) making a lot of noise or full of noise, e.g. *a noisy engine... The room was hot and noisy.*
noisily (adverb), **noisiness** (noun).

nomad, nomads
(noun) A nomad is a person who belongs to a tribe which travels from place to place rather than living in just one place.
nomadic (adjective).
[from Latin *nomas* meaning 'wandering shepherd']

nomenclature (pronounced nom-**men**-klat-yoor)
(noun; a formal word) The nomenclature of a particular subject is the system of naming things, e.g. *scientific nomenclature.*
[from Latin *nomenclatura* meaning 'list of names']

nominal
1 (adjective) Something that is nominal is supposed to have a particular identity or status, but in reality does not have it, e.g. *the nominal leader.*
2 A nominal amount of money is very small compared to the value of something, e.g. *They got the land at a nominal price.*
3 In grammar, nominal means relating to nouns.
nominally (adverb).
[from Latin *nomen* meaning 'name']

nominate, nominates, nominating, nominated
(verb) If you nominate someone for a job or position, you formally suggest that they have it.
nomination (noun).
[from Latin *nominare* meaning 'to call by name']

Similar words: propose, suggest, recommend

nominative
(noun and adjective) In the grammar of some languages, the nominative is the form of a noun when it is the subject of a verb.

non-
(prefix) not, e.g. *non-industrial societies.*

nonagenarian, nonagenarians (pronounced no-nej-jen-**air**-ee-an)
(noun) A nonagenarian is a person in their nineties.

nonaggression
(noun) Nonaggression is the idea or plan that countries should not attack each other, e.g. *They signed a nonaggression pact.*

nonaligned
(adjective) A country that is nonaligned is not part of any alliance.

nonchalant (pronounced **non**-shal-nt)
(adjective) seeming calm and not worried.
nonchalance (noun), **nonchalantly** (adverb).
[from Old French *nonchalant* meaning 'not concerned']

noncommissioned officer, noncommissioned officers
(noun) A noncommissioned officer is an officer such as a sergeant or corporal who has been appointed to that rank from the lower ranks, rather than by receiving a commission.

noncommittal
(adjective) not expressing any clear firm opinion, e.g. *He gave a noncommittal reply.*

noncompliance
(noun) Noncompliance is failure or refusal to agree to something or to do something.

nonconformist, nonconformists
1 (noun and adjective) A nonconformist is someone who behaves in an unusual or rebellious way.
2 A Nonconformist is a British Protestant who does not belong to the Church of England.
nonconformity (noun).

nondescript
(adjective) dull and uninteresting in appearance, e.g. *nondescript clothes.*

none
(pronoun) not a single thing or person, or not even a small amount of something.

nonentity, nonentities (pronounced non-**nen**-tit-tee)
(noun) Someone who is a nonentity is not important or special in any way.

nonexistent
(adjective) Something that is nonexistent does not exist.

nonfiction
(noun) Nonfiction is writing that gives facts and information rather than telling a story.

nonflammable
(adjective) not capable of burning.

nonplussed
(adjective) confused and unsure about how to react.
[from Latin *non plus* meaning 'no further']

nonsense
(noun) Nonsense is foolish and meaningless words or behaviour.
nonsensical (adjective).

Similar words: rubbish, rot

non sequitur, non sequiturs (pronounced non sek-kwit-ter)
(noun) A non sequitur is a remark that does not follow logically from what has just been said.
[from Latin *non sequitur* meaning 'It does not follow']

nonstick
(adjective) coated with a special substance to prevent food from sticking, e.g. *a nonstick frying pan.*

nonstop
(adjective and adverb) continuing without any pauses or breaks, e.g. *nonstop noise.*

noodle, noodles
(noun) Noodles are a kind of pasta shaped into long, thin pieces.

nook, nooks
(noun; a literary word) A nook is a small sheltered place.

noon
(noun) Noon is midday.

no-one or no one
(pronoun) not a single person.

noose, nooses
(noun) A noose is a loop at the end of a piece of rope, with a knot that tightens when the rope is pulled.

nor
(conjunction) used after 'neither' or after a negative statement, to add something else that the negative statement applies to, e.g. *Neither Margaret nor John was there.*

norm, norms
1 (noun) Norms are ways of behaving that are considered normal and acceptable, e.g. *the conventional norms of polite European society.*
2 If something is the norm, it is the usual and expected thing, e.g. *Working wives have been the norm for many years.*
[from Latin *norma* meaning 'carpenter's rule']

normal
(adjective) usual and ordinary, e.g. *Can she lead a normal life?*
normality (noun).

Similar words: natural, usual, typical

normally
1 (adverb) usually, e.g. *I don't normally drink at lunch.*
2 in a way that is normal, e.g. *The important thing is that she's eating normally.*

north
1 (noun) The north is the direction to your left when you are looking towards the place where the sun rises.
2 The north of a place or country is the part which is towards the north when you are in the centre.
3 (adverb and adjective) North means towards the north, e.g. *They were heading north.*
4 (adjective) A north wind blows from the north.

North America
(noun) North America is the third largest continent, consisting of Canada, the United States, and Mexico. It has the Pacific Ocean on its west side, the Atlantic on the east, and the Arctic to the north. North America is joined to South America by the Isthmus of Panama.
North American (adjective).

north-east
(noun, adverb, and adjective) North-east is halfway between north and east.

north-easterly
1 (adjective) North-easterly means to or towards the north-east.
2 A north-easterly wind blows from the north-east.

north-eastern
(adjective) in or from the north-east.

northerly
1 (adjective) Northerly means to or towards the north, e.g. *a northerly route.*
2 A northerly wind blows from the north.

northern
(adjective) in or from the north, e.g. *the mountains of northern Japan.*

North Pole
(noun) The North Pole is the most northerly point of the earth's surface.

northward or northwards
1 (adverb) Northward or northwards means towards the north, e.g. *They fled northwards.*
2 (adjective) The northward part of something is the north part.

north-west
(noun, adverb, and adjective) North-west is halfway between north and west.

north-westerly
1 (adjective) North-westerly means to or towards the north-west.
2 A north-westerly wind blows from the north-west.

north-western
(adjective) in or from the north-west.

Norwegian, Norwegians (pronounced nor-**wee**-jn)
1 (adjective) belonging or relating to Norway.
2 (noun) A Norwegian is someone who comes from Norway.
3 Norwegian is the main language spoken in Norway.

nose, noses, nosing, nosed
1 (noun) Your nose is the part of your face above your mouth which you use for smelling and breathing.
2 The nose of a car or plane is the front part of it.
3 (phrase) If you **pay through the nose** for something, you pay a very high price for it.
4 If someone **turns their nose up at** something, they reject it because they think it is not good enough for them.
5 (verb; an informal use) If someone noses into something, they try and find out about it when it is none of their business.

nosedive, nosedives
(noun) A nosedive is a sudden downward plunge by an aircraft.

nostalgia (pronounced nos-**tal**-ja)
(noun) Nostalgia is a feeling of affection for the past, and sadness that things have changed.
nostalgic (adjective), **nostalgically** (adverb).

nostril, nostrils
(noun) Your nostrils are the two openings in your nose which you breathe through.
[from Old English *nosu* meaning 'nose' and *thyrel* meaning 'hole']

nosy, nosier, nosiest; also spelled nosey
(adjective) trying to find out about things that do not concern you.

not
(adverb) used to make a sentence negative, to refuse something, or to deny something.

notable
(adjective) important or interesting, e.g. *With a few notable exceptions this trend has continued.*
notably (adverb).

notary, notaries
(noun) A notary is a person who has the authority to draw up and certify certain legal documents.
[from Latin *notarius* meaning 'clerk']

notation, notations
(noun) A notation is a set of written symbols, such as those used in music or mathematics.
[from Latin *notare* meaning 'to note']

notch, notches
1 (noun) A notch is a small V-shaped cut in a surface.
2 A notch is also a level on a scale, e.g. *My regard for her went up another notch.*

[from a mistaken division of Middle English *an otch*]

note, notes, noting, noted
1 (noun) A note is a short letter.
2 A note is also a written piece of information that helps you to remember something, e.g. *I'll make a note of that.*
3 A note is also a banknote.
4 In music, a note is a musical sound of a particular pitch, or a written symbol that represents it.
5 A note is also an atmosphere, feeling, or quality, e.g. *There was a note of triumph in her voice... This was a good note on which to end.*
6 (verb) If you note a fact, you become aware of it or you mention it, e.g. *His audience, I noted, were looking bored.*
7 If you note something down, you write it down so that you will remember it.
8 (phrase) If you **take note** of something, you pay attention to it, e.g. *I had started taking note of political developments.*
[from Latin *nota* meaning 'mark' or 'sign']

note down
(phrasal verb) If you note something down, you write it down so that you will remember it.

notebook, notebooks
(noun) A notebook is a small book for writing notes in.

noted
(adjective) well-known and admired, e.g. *a noted American writer.*

noteworthy
(adjective) interesting or significant, e.g. *a noteworthy fact.*

nothing
(pronoun) not anything, e.g. *There's nothing to worry about.*

Similar words: zero, nought, nil, naught

notice, notices, noticing, noticed
1 (verb) If you notice something, you become aware of it.
2 (noun) Notice is attention or awareness, e.g. *Many cases have come to my notice.*
3 A notice is a written announcement.
4 Notice is also advance warning about something, e.g. *She could have done it if she'd had a bit more notice.*
5 (phrase) If you **hand in your notice**, you tell your employer that you intend to leave your job after a fixed period of time.
[from Latin *notitia* meaning 'knowledge']

Similar words: (sense 1) note, observe, detect, perceive
(sense 2) attention, observation

noticeable
(adjective) obvious and easy to see, e.g. *The drug did not have any noticeable effect on her.*
noticeably (adverb).

noticeboard, noticeboards
(noun) A noticeboard is a board for notices.

notify, notifies, notifying, notified
(verb) To notify someone of something means to officially inform them of it, e.g. *He wrote to notify me that the cheque had arrived.*
notification (noun).
[from Latin *notificare* meaning 'to make known']

notion, notions
(noun) A notion is an idea or belief.

notorious
(adjective) well-known for something bad, e.g. *The area was notorious for murders.*
notoriously (adverb), **notoriety** (noun).
[from Latin *notorius* meaning 'well-known']

Similar words: disreputable, infamous

notwithstanding
(preposition; a formal word) in spite of, e.g. *Notwithstanding economic recessions, the future looks bright.*

nougat (pronounced **noo**-gah)
(noun) Nougat is a kind of chewy sweet containing nuts and sometimes fruit.
[from Provençal *noga* meaning 'nut']

nought the number 0.

noun, nouns
(noun) A noun is a word which refers to a person, thing, or idea. Examples of nouns are 'president', 'table', 'sun', and 'beauty'.
[from Latin *nomen* meaning 'name']

nourish, nourishes, nourishing, nourished
(pronounced **nur**-rish)
1 (verb) To nourish people or animals means to provide them with food.
2 (a literary use) To nourish a feeling or belief means to encourage it to grow.
[from Old French *norir* meaning 'to feed']

nourishing
(adjective) Food that is nourishing contains vitamins, protein, and other things that are necessary for growth and good health.

nourishment
(noun) Nourishment is food that your body needs in order to remain healthy, e.g. *The seeds are full of nourishment.*

nova, novas or novae
(noun) A nova is a star which suddenly becomes very bright for a short time.
[from Latin *nova stella* meaning 'new star']

novel, novels
1 (noun) A novel is a book that tells an invented story.
2 (adjective) new and interesting, e.g. *a novel experience.*
[from Old French *novelle* meaning 'new story']

novelist, novelists
(noun) A novelist is a person who writes novels.

novelty, novelties
1 (noun) Novelty is the quality of being new and interesting, e.g. *The novelty had worn off.*
2 A novelty is something new and interesting, e.g. *The car was still a novelty at that time.*

3 A novelty is also a small, unusual object sold as a gift or souvenir.
[from Latin *novellus* meaning 'new']

November
(noun) November is the eleventh month of the year. It has 30 days.
[from Latin *November* meaning 'the ninth month']

novice, novices
1 (noun) A novice is someone who is not yet experienced at something.
2 A novice is also someone who is preparing to become a monk or nun.

now
1 (adverb) at the present time or moment.
2 (conjunction) as a result or consequence of a particular fact, e.g. *I like him a lot now he's older.*
3 (phrase) **Just now** means very recently, e.g. *I was talking to him just now.*
4 If something happens **now and then**, it happens sometimes but not regularly.

nowadays
(adverb) at the present time, e.g. *Nowadays most babies are born in a hospital.*

nowhere
1 (adverb) not anywhere.
2 (phrase) If you are **getting nowhere**, you are not achieving anything.

noxious (pronounced **nok**-shus)
(adjective) harmful or poisonous, e.g. *a noxious gas.*
[from Latin *noxa* meaning 'injury']

nozzle, nozzles
(noun) A nozzle is a spout fitted onto the end of a pipe or hose to control the flow of a liquid.

nuance, nuances (pronounced **nyoo**-ahnss)
(noun) A nuance is a subtle difference in sound, colour, or meaning, e.g. *He could imitate every nuance of Hall's speech.*
[from French *nuer* meaning 'to show variations in light and shade']

nub, nubs
(noun) The nub of a situation, problem, or argument is the central and most basic part of it.

nubile (pronounced **nyoo**-bile)
(adjective) A woman who is nubile is physically well-developed and attractive but still young.
[from Latin *nubere* meaning 'to take a husband']

nuclear
1 (adjective) relating to the energy produced when the nuclei of atoms are split, e.g. *nuclear power... the nuclear industry.*
2 relating to weapons that explode using the energy released by atoms, e.g. *nuclear war.*
3 relating to the structure and behaviour of the nuclei of atoms, e.g. *nuclear physics.*

nuclear fission
(noun) Nuclear fission is the splitting of the nucleus of an atom to produce large amounts of energy or a nuclear explosion.

nuclear fusion
(noun) Nuclear fusion is a reaction in which two

atomic nuclei combine to form a nucleus, with a release of energy.

nuclear reactor, nuclear reactors
(noun) A nuclear reactor is a device which is used to obtain nuclear energy.

nucleus, nuclei (pronounced **nyoo**-klee-uss)
1 (noun) The nucleus of an atom is the central part of it. It is positively charged and is made up of protons and neutrons.
2 The nucleus of a cell is the part that contains the chromosomes and controls the growth and reproduction of the cell.
3 The nucleus of something is the basic central part of it to which other things are added.
[from Latin *nucleus* meaning 'kernel']

nude, nudes
1 (adjective) naked.
2 (noun) A nude is a picture or statue of a naked person.
nudity (noun).

nudge, nudges, nudging, nudged
1 (verb) If you nudge someone, you push them gently, usually with your elbow.
2 (noun) A nudge is a gentle push.

nudist, nudists
(noun) A nudist is a person who believes in wearing no clothes.

nugget, nuggets
(noun) A nugget is a small rough lump of something, especially gold.

nuisance, nuisances
(noun) A nuisance is someone or something that is annoying or inconvenient.

Similar words: pest, inconvenience, bother, drag

null
(phrase) **Null and void** means not legally valid, e.g. *The contract was declared null and void.*

nullify, nullifies, nullifying, nullified
(verb; a formal word) To nullify something means to make it useless or ineffective.
[from Latin *nullus* + *facere* meaning 'to make of no account']

numb, numbs, numbing, numbed
1 (adjective) unable to feel anything, e.g. *My leg had gone numb... numb with shock.*
2 (verb) If something numbs you, it makes you unable to feel anything, e.g. *His fingers were numbed by the frost.*
[from Middle English *nomen* meaning 'paralysed']

number, numbers, numbering, numbered
1 (noun) A number is a word or a symbol used for counting or calculating.
2 Someone's number is the series of numbers that you dial when you telephone them.
3 A number of things is a quantity of them, e.g. *There are large numbers of children in care.*
4 A number is also a song or piece of music.
5 (verb) If things number a particular amount, there are that many of them, e.g. *The force numbered almost a quarter of a million men.*
6 If you number something, you give it a number, e.g. *I numbered the pages.*

7 To be numbered among a particular group means to belong it, e.g. *She is numbered among the great musicians of our time.*
8 (phrase) If **someone's days are numbered**, they will not live much longer.

Similar words: (sense 1) figure, numeral, digit

numeral, numerals
(noun) A numeral is a symbol that represents a number, e.g. *a clock with Roman numerals.*

numerate (pronounced **nyoo**-mer-rit)
(adjective) able to do arithmetic.
numeracy (noun).

numerator, numerators
(noun) In maths, the numerator is the top part of a fraction.

numerical
(adjective) expressed in numbers or relating to numbers, e.g. *numerical data.*

numerous
(adjective) existing or happening in large numbers.

numismatics (pronounced nyoo-miz-**mat**-tiks)
(noun) Numismatics is the study of coins.
numismatist (noun).
[from Latin *nomisma* meaning 'coin']

nun, nuns
(noun) A nun is a woman who has taken religious vows and lives in a convent.

nuptials (pronounced **nupt**-shulz)
(noun; an old-fashioned word) Someone's nuptials are their wedding celebrations.

nurse, nurses, nursing, nursed
1 (noun) A nurse is someone whose job is to look after people who are ill.
2 (verb) If you nurse someone, you look after them when they are ill.
3 If you nurse a feeling, you feel it strongly for a long time, e.g. *He nursed a desire for revenge.*

nursery, nurseries
1 (noun) A nursery is a room in which young children sleep and play.
2 A nursery is also a place where young children are looked after while their parents are working.
3 A nursery is also a place where plants are grown and sold.

nursery rhyme, nursery rhymes
(noun) A nursery rhyme is a short poem or song for young children.

nursery school, nursery schools
(noun) A nursery school is a school for children from three to five years old.

nursing
(adjective) breastfeeding a baby, e.g. *nursing mothers.*

nursing home, nursing homes
(noun) A nursing home is a privately run hospital for people who are ill or convalescent.

nurture, nurtures, nurturing, nurtured
(verb; a formal word) If you nurture a young child or a plant, you look after it carefully.
[from French *nourir* meaning 'to nourish']

nut, nuts
1 (noun) A nut is a fruit with a hard shell and an edible centre that grows on certain trees.
2 A nut is also a piece of metal with a hole in the middle which a bolt screws into.
3 (an informal use) Someone who is a nut is mad or very foolish.

nutmeg
(noun) Nutmeg is the dried fruit of an East Indian tree, which is ground and used as a spice for flavouring in cooking.

nutrient, nutrients
(noun) Nutrients are substances that help plants or animals to grow, e.g. *the nutrients in the soil.*
[from Latin *nutrire* meaning 'to nourish']

nutrition
(noun) Nutrition is the food that you eat, considered from the point of view of how it helps you to grow and remain healthy, e.g. *Because of poor nutrition, he has grown weaker.*
nutritionist (noun).

nutritious
(adjective) containing substances that help you to grow and remain healthy.

nutty, nuttier, nuttiest
1 (adjective; an informal use) mad or very foolish.
2 tasting of nuts.

nuzzle, nuzzles, nuzzling, nuzzled
(verb) If you nuzzle someone, you gently cuddle up to them and rub your nose and mouth against them.

nylon, nylons
1 (noun) Nylon is a type of strong artificial material, e.g. *nylon stockings.*
2 Nylons are stockings or tights.

nymph, nymphs (pronounced **nimf**)
1 (noun) In Greek and Roman mythology, a nymph is a young goddess who lives in trees, rivers, or mountains.
2 In biology, a nymph is the immature form of an insect, such as a dragonfly, which becomes an adult without passing through the stage of being a pupa. The nymph looks like the adult, but cannot fly or reproduce.

O

oaf, oafs
(noun) An oaf is a clumsy and stupid person.
[from Old Norse *alfr* meaning 'elf']

Similar words: boor, lout

oak, oaks
(noun) An oak is a large deciduous tree which produces acorns. It has a hard wood which is often used to make furniture.

OAP, OAPs
(noun) An OAP is a man over the age of 65 or a woman over the age of 60 who receives a pension. OAP is an abbreviation for 'old age pensioner'.

oar, oars
(noun) An oar is a wooden pole used for rowing a boat.

oasis, oases (pronounced oh-**ay**-siss)
1 (noun) An oasis is a small area in a desert where water and plants are found.
2 An oasis is also a pleasant place or situation surrounded by unpleasant ones.

oast house, oast houses
(noun) An oast house is a building which contains an oven for drying hops.

oat, oats
(noun) Oats are a type of grain.

oath, oaths
1 (noun) An oath is a formal promise, especially a promise to tell the truth in a court of law.
2 (an old-fashioned use) An oath is also an offensive expression or a swearword.

Similar words: (sense 1) vow, pledge

oatmeal
(noun) Oatmeal is a coarse flour made from oats.

obdurate (pronounced **ob**-joor-it)
(adjective) stubborn and unwilling to change your mind, e.g. *his obdurate refusal to see me*.
obdurately (adverb), **obduracy** (noun).
[from Latin *ob-* + *durus* meaning 'very hard']

OBE, OBEs
(noun) An OBE is an honour granted by the King or Queen. OBE is an abbreviation for 'Officer of the Order of the British Empire', e.g. *Mark Lee, OBE*.

obedient
(adjective) doing what you are told to do.
obediently (adverb), **obedience** (noun).

obeisance (pronounced ob-**bay**-sense)
(noun; a formal word) Obeisance is a show of respect by bowing or curtsying.

obelisk, obelisks
(noun) An obelisk is a stone pillar built to commemorate a person or an event.

obese (pronounced oh-**bees**)
(adjective) extremely fat.
obesity (noun).

[from Latin *ob-* meaning 'much' and *edere* meaning 'to eat']

Similar words: gross, outsize

obey, obeys, obeying, obeyed
(verb) If you obey a person or an order, you do what you are told to do.

Similar words: follow, comply, abide by

obfuscate, obfuscates, obfuscating, obfuscated
(verb; a formal word) If you obfuscate something, you make it difficult to understand.
[from Latin *ob-* + *fuscus* meaning 'very dark']

obituary, obituaries
(noun) An obituary is a piece of writing about the life and achievements of someone who has just died.
[from Latin *obitus* meaning 'death']

object, objects, objecting, objected
1 (noun) An object is anything solid that you can touch or see, and that is not alive.
2 Someone's object is their aim or purpose.
3 The object of your feelings or actions is the person that they are directed towards.
4 In grammar, the object of a verb or preposition is the word or phrase which follows it and describes the person or thing affected.
5 (verb) If you object to something, you dislike it or disapprove of it.
[from Latin *objectus* meaning 'something thrown before (the mind)']

Similar words: (sense 5) oppose, protest, take exception, demur

objection, objections
(noun) If you have an objection to something, you dislike it or disapprove of it.

objectionable
(adjective) unpleasant and offensive.

objective, objectives
1 (noun) Your objective is your aim, e.g. *We shall never achieve our objectives.*
2 (adjective) If you are objective, you are not influenced by personal feelings or prejudices, e.g. *objective evidence.*
objectively (adverb), **objectivity** (noun).

object lesson, object lessons
(noun) An object lesson is an experience that demonstrates or exemplifies a moral or principle.

objet d'art, objets d'art (pronounced ob-jay **dar**)
(noun) An objet d'art is a small ornament of artistic value.
[from French *objet d'art* meaning literally 'object of art']

obligation, obligations
(noun) An obligation is something that you must do because it is your duty.

obligatory (pronounced ob-**lig**-a-tree)
(adjective) required by a rule or law, e.g. *It is not obligatory to answer.*

oblige, obliges, obliging, obliged
1 (verb) If you are obliged to do something, you have to do it.
2 If you oblige someone, you help them.
obliging (adjective).

oblique (pronounced o-**bleek**)
1 (adjective) An oblique remark is not direct, and therefore difficult to understand.
2 An oblique line slopes at an angle.

obliterate, obliterates, obliterating, obliterated
(verb) To obliterate something means to destroy it completely.
obliteration (noun).
[from Latin *oblitterare* meaning 'to erase']

oblivion
1 (noun) Oblivion is unconsciousness or complete unawareness of your surroundings.
2 Something that is in oblivion has been forgotten.
oblivious (adjective), **obliviously** (adverb).

oblong, oblongs
1 (noun) An oblong is a four-sided shape with two parallel short sides, two parallel long sides, and four right angles.
2 (adjective) shaped like an oblong.
[from Latin *oblongus* meaning 'oblong']

obnoxious (pronounced ob-**nok**-shuss)
(adjective) extremely unpleasant.
[from Latin *obnoxiosus* meaning 'exposed to harm']

oboe, oboes
(noun) An oboe is a woodwind musical instrument with a double reed.
oboist (noun).
[from French *haut bois* meaning literally 'high wood', a reference to the instrument's pitch]

obscene
(adjective) indecent and offensive, e.g. *obscene paintings.*
obscenely (adverb), **obscenity** (noun).

Similar words: filthy, foul, indecent, pornographic

obscure, obscures, obscuring, obscured
1 (adjective) Something that is obscure is known by only a few people, e.g. *obscure operas.*
2 Something obscure is difficult to see or to understand, e.g. *obscure points of theology... an obscure shape.*
3 (verb) To obscure something means to make it difficult to see or understand, e.g. *words that obscure the truth.*
obscurity (noun).
[from Latin *obscurus* meaning 'dark']

Similar words: (sense 2) abstruse, unclear, opaque, recondite

obsequious (pronounced ob-**see**-kwee-uss)
(adjective) Someone who is obsequious is too eager to please or to agree with people.
obsequiously (adverb), **obsequiousness** (noun).
[from Latin *obsequi* meaning 'to follow']

observance
(noun) The observance of a law or custom is the obeying or following of it.

observant
(adjective) Someone who is observant notices things that are not easy to see.

observation, observations
1 (noun) Observation is the act of watching something carefully, e.g. *She was put under observation in a nursing home.*
2 Observation is also the ability to notice things.
3 An observation is something that you have seen or noticed.
4 An observation is also a remark.

observatory, observatories
(noun) An observatory is a room or building containing telescopes and other equipment for studying the sun, moon, and stars.

observe, observes, observing, observed
1 (verb) To observe something means to watch it carefully.
2 To observe something also means to notice it.
3 If you observe that something is the case, you make a comment about it.
4 To observe a law or custom means to obey or follow it.
observer (noun), **observable** (adjective).
[from Latin *observare* meaning 'to watch']

obsession, obsessions
(noun) If someone has an obsession about something, they cannot stop thinking about that thing.
obsessional (adjective), **obsessed** (adjective), **obsessive** (adjective).
[from Latin *obsidere* meaning 'to sit down before']

Similar words: fixation, preoccupation

obsolete
(adjective) out of date and no longer used.
[from Latin *obsoletus* meaning 'worn out']

Similar words: defunct, passé

obstacle, obstacles
(noun) An obstacle is something which is in your way and makes it difficult to do something.
[from Latin *ob-* meaning 'against' and *stare* meaning 'to stand']

Similar words: hurdle, barrier, stumbling block

obstetrician, obstetricians
(noun) An obstetrician is a doctor who specializes in the care of women during pregnancy and childbirth.

obstetrics
(noun) Obstetrics is the branch of medicine concerned with pregnancy and childbirth.
[from Latin *obstetrix* meaning 'midwife']

obstinate

(adjective) Someone who is obstinate is stubborn and unwilling to change their mind.
obstinately (adjective), **obstinacy** (noun).

obstreperous

(adjective) behaving in an uncooperative, noisy, stubborn, and often aggressive way.
[from Latin *ob-* meaning 'against' and *strepere* meaning 'to roar']

obstruct, obstructs, obstructing, obstructed

1 (verb) If something obstructs a road or path, it blocks it.
2 To obstruct justice or progress means to prevent it from happening.
obstruction (noun), **obstructive** (adjective).
[from Latin *obstruere* meaning 'to build against']

obtain, obtains, obtaining, obtained

(verb) If you obtain something, you get it.
obtainable (adjective).
[from Latin *obtinere* meaning 'to take hold of']

obtrusive

(adjective) noticeable in an unpleasant way, e.g. *obtrusive graffiti.*
obtrusively (adverb).
[from Latin *ob-* meaning 'against' and *trudere* meaning 'to push forward']

obtuse

1 (adjective) Someone who is obtuse is stupid or slow to understand things.
2 An obtuse angle is between 90° and 180°.

obverse

(noun; a formal word) The obverse of an opinion or situation is its opposite.
[from Latin *obversus* meaning 'turn towards']

obviate, obviates, obviating, obviated

(verb; a formal word) To obviate something means to remove it or prevent it, e.g. *He destroyed the letter to obviate suspicion.*

obvious

(adjective) easy to see or understand.
obviously (adverb).

Similar words: blatant, apparent, evident, manifest, clear, conspicuous, overt, patent, plain, transparent

---

occasion, occasions, occasioning, occasioned

1 (noun) An occasion is a time when something happens, e.g. *I met him on only one occasion.*
2 An occasion is also an important event.
3 An occasion for doing something is an opportunity for doing it.
4 (verb; a formal use) To occasion something means to cause it, e.g. *deaths occasioned by police activity.*

occasional

(adjective) happening sometimes but not often, e.g. *an occasional trip to Aberdeen.*
occasionally (adverb).

Occident (pronounced ok-sid-dent)

(noun; a formal word) The Occident is countries or areas in the western hemisphere, such as Europe and America.
occidental (adjective and noun).

[from Latin *occident* meaning 'setting', 'sunset' or 'west']

occluded front, occluded fronts

(noun) In meteorology, an occluded front is the line where a cold front meets a warm front, forcing the warm air up and away from ground level.

occult

1 (noun) The occult is the knowledge and study of supernatural and magical forces, powers, or skills.
2 (adjective) Occult powers or experiences relate to the supernatural or magic.

occupancy

(noun) Someone's occupancy of a building is the fact that they live or work in it.

occupant, occupants

(noun) The occupants of a building are the people who live or work in it.

occupation, occupations

1 (noun) Your occupation is your job or profession.
2 An occupation is also a hobby or something you do for pleasure.
3 The occupation of a country is the act of invading it and taking control of it.
occupational (adjective).

occupational therapy

(noun) Occupational therapy is a type of therapy designed to help people who have been injured by exercising their minds and their muscles through handicrafts.

occupy, occupies, occupying, occupied

1 (verb) The people who occupy a building are the people who live or work there.
2 When people occupy a place, they move into it and take control of it, e.g. *The students occupied the Administration Block.*
3 To occupy a position in a system or plan means to have that position.
4 If something occupies you, you spend your time doing it, e.g. *That work occupied him all day.*
occupier (noun).
[from Latin *occupare* meaning 'to seize hold of']

occur, occurs, occurring, occurred

1 (verb) If something occurs, it happens or exists, e.g. *The attack occurred six days ago... Racism and sexism occur in all institutions.*
2 If something occurs to you, you suddenly think of it.

occurrence, occurrences

1 (noun) An occurrence is an event.
2 The occurrence of something is the fact that it happens or exists, e.g. *the occurrence of cancer.*

ocean, oceans

1 (noun; a literary use) The ocean is the sea.
2 The five oceans are the five very large areas of sea, e.g. *the Atlantic Ocean.*
oceanic (adjective).

oceanography (pronounced oh-shin-og-raf-ee)

(noun) Oceanography is the study of the sea.
oceanographer (noun).

ocelot, ocelots (pronounced **oss**-il-lot)
(noun) An ocelot is a wild cat with brown
spotted fur. Ocelots live in the forests of Central
and South America.
[from Aztec *ocelotl* meaning 'jaguar']

ochre (pronounced **oh**-kur)
1 (noun) Ochre is yellowish or reddish-brown
earth that is used for making paints and dyes.
2 (adjective and noun) yellowish-brown.
[from Greek *okhros* meaning 'pale yellow']

o'clock
(adverb) You use o'clock after the number of the
hour to say what the time is.

octagon, octagons
(noun) An octagon is a shape with eight straight
sides.
octagonal (adjective).
[from Greek *okto* + *gōnos* meaning 'eight angled']

octane
(noun) Octane is a chemical substance found in
petrol. It is used to measure and describe the
quality of the petrol.

octave, octaves
(noun) An octave is the musical interval between
the first note and the eighth note of a scale.
[from Latin *octo* meaning 'eight']

octet, octets
(noun) An octet is a group of eight musicians
who sing or play together; also a piece of music
written for eight instruments or singers.
[from Latin *octo* meaning 'eight']

October
(noun) October is the tenth month of the year. It
has 31 days.
[from Latin *october* meaning 'the eighth month']

octogenarian, octogenarians (pronounced
ok-toe-jin-**nair**-ee-an)
(noun) An octogenarian is a person in their
eighties.

octopus, octopuses
(noun) An octopus is a sea creature with eight
long tentacles which it uses to catch food.
[from Greek *okto* + *pous* meaning 'eight feet']

oculist, oculists
(noun) An oculist is a doctor who specializes in
eye problems.
ocular (adjective).
[from Latin *oculus* meaning 'eye']

odd, odder, oddest; odds
1 (adjective) Something odd is strange or
unusual.
2 Odd numbers are numbers that cannot be
divided exactly by two.
3 Odd things do not match each other, e.g. *odd
socks*.
4 (phrase) The **odd one out** in a group is the one
that is different from all the others.
5 (adverb) You use odd after a number to
indicate that it is approximate, e.g. *We met
twenty - odd years ago*.
6 (plural noun) In gambling, the probability of
something happening is referred to as the odds.

7 (phrase) If you are **at odds** with someone, you
disagree with them.
oddly (adverb), **oddness** (noun).

oddity, oddities
(noun) An oddity is something very strange.

oddment, oddments
(noun) Oddments are things that are left over
after other things have been used.

Similar words: remnants, odds and ends

odds and ends
(noun) You can refer to a collection of small
unimportant things as odds and ends.

ode, odes
(noun) An ode is a poem written in praise of
someone or something.
[from Greek *oidē* meaning 'song']

odious
(adjective) extremely unpleasant.

odour, odours
(noun; a formal word) An odour is a strong smell.
odorous (adjective).

odyssey, odysseys (pronounced od-i-see)
(noun) An odyssey is a long and exciting journey.
The name comes from Odysseus, the Greek hero
who wandered from adventure to adventure for
ten years.

oedema, oedemata (pronounced id-**eem**-ah)
(noun) Oedema is the condition of retaining too
much water in your body tissues.
[from Greek *oidein* meaning 'to swell']

Oedipus complex (pronounced **eed**-ee-puss)
(noun) An Oedipus complex is a condition in
which a boy becomes overattached to his mother
and feels jealous of his father. Oedipus was a
mythological Greek king who killed his father
and married his mother without realizing that
they were related.

oesophagus, oesophaguses (pronounced
ee-sof-fag-uss)
(noun) Your oesophagus is the tube that carries
food from your throat to your stomach.

oestrogen another spelling of **estrogen**.

of
1 (preposition) consisting of or containing, e.g. *a
collection of essays... a cup of tea*.
2 used when naming something or describing a
characteristic of something, e.g. *the village of
Keele... a boy of nineteen*.
3 belonging to or connected with, e.g. *an uncle of
mine... the sleeve of his jacket*.

off
1 (preposition and adverb) indicating movement
away from or out of a place, e.g. *He took his
hand off her arm... The train stopped and people
got off*.
2 indicating separation or distance from a place,
e.g. *two islands off the coast of China... The
railway was fenced off*.
3 not working, e.g. *Tonight is his night off*.
4 (preposition) not talking about a particular
subject, e.g. *She kept off the subject of marriage*.

5 not liking or not using something, e.g. *My father is off alcohol.*
6 (adverb and adjective) not switched on, e.g. *He turned the radio off... the off switch.*
7 (adjective) cancelled or postponed, e.g. *Tonight's match is off.*
8 Food that is off has gone sour or bad.

offal
(noun) Offal is liver, kidneys, and other edible organs of animals.

off chance
(phrase) If you do something **on the off chance**, you do it because there is a slight possibility that it will be successful or useful, e.g. *He went to the party on the off chance of seeing Susan.*

off colour
(adjective) feeling slightly ill.

offence, offences
1 (noun) An offence is a crime, e.g. *They were arrested for drug offences.*
2 (phrases) If something **gives offence**, it upsets people. If you **take offence**, you are upset by someone or something.

offend, offends, offending, offended
1 (verb) If you offend someone, you upset them.
2 (a formal use) To offend or to offend a law means to commit a crime.
offender (noun).
[from Latin *offendere* meaning 'to strike against']

offensive, offensives
1 (adjective) Something offensive is rude and upsetting, e.g. *an offensive remark.*
2 Offensive actions or weapons are used in attacking someone.
3 (noun) An offensive is an attack, e.g. *the enemy's air offensive.*
offensively (adverb).

offer, offers, offering, offered
1 (verb) If you offer something to someone, you ask them if they would like it, e.g. *He offered her his chair... She offered to take us home.*
2 (noun) An offer is something that someone asks if you would like, e.g. *She accepted the offer of a cigarette.*
3 An offer in a shop is a specially low price for a product, e.g. *This item is on special offer today.*
[from Latin *offere* meaning 'to present']

Similar words: (sense 1) tender, proffer, volunteer

offering, offerings
(noun) An offering is something that is offered or given to someone.

offhand
1 (adjective) If someone is offhand, they are unfriendly and slightly rude.
2 (adverb) If you know something offhand, you know it without having to think very hard, e.g. *Offhand, I can think of three examples.*

office, offices
1 (noun) An office is a room where people work at desks.
2 An office is also a government department

which deals with a particular area of administration, e.g. *your local education office.*
3 An office is also a place where people can go for information, tickets, or other services.
4 Someone who holds office has an important job or position in government or in an organization.
[from Latin *officium* meaning 'performance of a task']

officer, officers
(noun) An officer is a person holding a position of authority in the armed forces, the police, or a government organization.

official, officials
1 (adjective) approved by the government or by someone in authority, e.g. *the official figures.*
2 done or used by someone in authority as part of their job, e.g. *an official visit to Tanzania.*
3 (noun) An official is a person who holds a position of authority in an organization.
officially (adverb).

officialdom
(noun) You can refer to officials in government or other organizations as officialdom, especially when you find them unhelpful and unfriendly.

officiate, officiates, officiating, officiated
(verb) To officiate at a ceremony means to be in charge and perform the official part of the ceremony.

officious
(adjective) too eager to tell other people what to do, e.g. *officious interference by managers.*

offing
(phrase) If something is **in the offing**, it is likely to happen soon, e.g. *A wedding is in the offing.*

off-licence, off-licences
(noun) An off-licence is a shop which sells alcoholic drinks.

offset, offsets, offsetting, offset
(verb) If one thing is offset by another thing, its effect is reduced or cancelled out by that thing, e.g. *They argued that their wage increases would be offset by higher prices.*

offshoot, offshoots
(noun) If one thing has developed from another thing, you can say that it is an offshoot of that thing, e.g. *Afrikaans is an offshoot of Dutch.*

offshore
(adjective and adverb) towards or in the sea, e.g. *offshore breezes... offshore oil terminals.*

offside
1 (noun) The offside of a vehicle is the side that is furthest from the pavement.
2 (adjective) If a football, rugby, or hockey player is offside, they have broken the rules by moving too far forward.

offspring
(noun) A person's or animal's offspring are their children.

off the record
(adjective) confidential and not intended for publication.

often
(adverb) frequently or a lot of the time.

ogle, ogles, ogling, ogled (pronounced **oh-gl**)
(verb) To ogle someone means to stare at them in a way that indicates a sexual interest.

Similar words: leer, eye up

ogre, ogres (pronounced **oh-gur**)
(noun) An ogre is a cruel, frightening giant in a fairy story.

ohm, ohms (rhymes with **home**)
(noun) An ohm is a unit of electrical resistance. When the resistance is one ohm, each volt of electrical force produces one amp of current. The ohm is named after the German physicist G.S. Ohm (1787-1854).

oil, oils, oiling, oiled
1 (noun) Oil is a thick, sticky liquid used as a fuel and for lubrication.
2 Oil is also a thick greasy liquid made from plants or animals, e.g. *cooking oil... bath oil.*
3 Oils are oil paintings or oil paints.
4 (verb) If you oil something, you put oil in it or on it.
[from Latin *oleum* meaning '(olive) oil']

oilcloth
(noun) Oilcloth is cotton fabric treated with oil on one side to make it waterproof.

oil paint, oil paints
(noun) Oil paint is a thick paint used by artists, made from a coloured powder and linseed oil.

oil painting, oil paintings
(noun) An oil painting is a painting that has been painted with oil paints.

oilskin, oilskins
(noun) An oilskin is a piece of clothing made from a thick, waterproof material, worn especially by fishermen.

oily
1 (adjective) Something that is oily is covered with oil, or feels or looks like oil, e.g. *oily rags... an oily substance.*
2 An oily person behaves in an excessively flattering manner.

ointment, ointments
(noun) An ointment is a smooth thick substance that you put on sore skin to heal it.

Similar words: balm, salve, liniment

okay, okays, okaying, okayed; also spelled **OK**
1 (adjective or adverb; an informal word) Okay means all right, e.g. *Was the trip okay?*
2 (verb) To okay something means to agree to it officially, e.g. *The bank okayed my overdraft.*
3 (noun) To give the okay to something means to agree to it officially.

Similar words: (sense 1) passable, not bad

okra (pronounced **oh-kra**)
(noun) Okra is a tropical plant with long green edible pods.

old, older, oldest
1 (adjective) having lived or existed for a long time, e.g. *an old lady... an old joke.*
2 Old also means former, e.g. *Our old teacher.*
3 Old is used to give the age of someone or something, e.g. *She's about 50 years old.*

Similar words: (sense 1) age-old, ancient

old boy, old boys
(noun) An old boy of a school is a former male pupil of it.

olden
(phrase) **In the olden days** means long ago.

Old English
(noun) Old English was the English language from the fifth century A.D. until about 1100. Old English is also known as Anglo-Saxon.

old-fashioned
1 (adjective) Something which is old-fashioned is no longer fashionable, e.g. *old-fashioned shoes.*
2 Someone who is old-fashioned believes in the values and standards of the past.

Similar words: (sense 1) antiquated, archaic, outmoded, passé, fuddy-duddy

old flame, old flames
(noun) An old flame is a former boyfriend or girlfriend.

old girl, old girls
(noun) An old girl of a school is a former female pupil of it.

old hat
(adjective; an informal expression) out of date.

old maid, old maids
(noun) An old maid is an old woman who has never been married.

old man's beard
(noun) Old man's beard is a climbing plant which looks white and wispy in the winter.

old master, old masters
(noun) An old master is a famous painter of the past, or a painting by such a painter.

Old Norse
(noun) Old Norse was a language spoken in Scandinavia and Iceland from about 700 AD to about 1350 AD. Many English words are derived from Old Norse.

old school tie
(noun) The old school tie refers to the system by which people who knew each other at public school or university use their influence to help each other.

Old Testament
(noun) The Old Testament is the first part of the Christian Bible. It is also the holy book of the Jewish religion and contains writings which relate to the history of the Jews.

Old World
(noun) The Old World is the continents of Europe, Asia, and Africa, which were known before the discovery of the Americas.

oligarchy, oligarchies (pronounced ol-ig-gar-kee)
(noun) An oligarchy is a small group of people
who control and run a country, or a country that
is run in this way.
[from Greek *oligos* + *arkhē* meaning 'few rule']

olive, olives
1 (noun) An olive is a small Mediterranean green
or black fruit containing a stone. Olives are
usually pickled and eaten as a snack or crushed
to produce oil.
2 (adjective and noun) dark yellowish-green.
[from Latin *oliva* meaning 'olive']

olive branch, olive branches
(noun) If you offer someone an olive branch, you
show that you want to end a quarrel.

-ology
(suffix) -ology is used to form words that refer
to the study of something, e.g. *biology... geology*.
[from Greek *logos* meaning 'reason', 'speech', or
'discourse']

Olympian
(adjective) very large, powerful, or impressive,
e.g. *a catastrophe of Olympian proportions*.
[in Greek mythology, Mount Olympus was the
home of the gods]

Olympic Games (pronounced ol-lim-pik)
(plural noun) The Olympic games are a set of
sporting contests held in a different city every
four years. It originated in Ancient Greece where
a contest was regularly held in Olympia to
honour the god Zeus.

ombudsman, ombudsmen
(noun) The ombudsman is an official who
investigates complaints against the government
or a public organization.
[from Swedish *ombudsman* meaning
'commissioner']

omelette, omelettes (pronounced om-lit)
(noun) An omelette is a dish made by beating
eggs together and cooking them in a flat pan.

omen, omens
(noun) An omen is something that is thought to
be a sign of what will happen in the future, e.g. *It
was a good omen for the trip*.

Similar words: portent, sign

ominous
(adjective) suggesting that something unpleasant
is going to happen, e.g. *an ominous silence*.
ominously (adverb).

Similar words: forbidding, menacing, threatening,
unfavourable, sinister

omission, omissions
1 (noun) An omission is something that has not
been included or done, e.g. *The reports were full
of errors and omissions*.
2 Omission is the act of not including or not
doing something, e.g. *We deplore the omission of
women from these studies*.

omit, omits, omitting, omitted
1 (verb) If you omit something, you do not
include it.

2 (a formal use) If you omit to do something, you
do not do it.
[from Latin *ob-* meaning 'away' and *mittere*
meaning 'to send']

omnibus, omnibuses
1 (noun) An omnibus is a book containing a
collection of stories or articles by the same
author or about the same subject.
2 (adjective) An omnibus edition of a radio or
television show contains two or more
programmes that were originally broadcast
separately.
[from Latin *omnis* meaning 'all']

omnipotent (pronounced om-nip-pot-nt)
(adjective) having very great or unlimited
power, e.g. *an omnipotent deity*.
omnipotence (noun).
[from Latin *omnipotens* meaning 'all powerful']

omnipresent (pronounced om-ni-prez-nt)
(adjective) present in all places at the same time.
omnipresence (noun)
[from Latin *omni-* meaning 'all' and *scire*
meaning 'to know']

omniscient (pronounced om-niss-ee-nt)
(adjective) having unlimited knowledge, e.g. *an
omniscient God*.
omniscience (noun).

omnivore
(noun) An omnivore is an animal that eats all
kinds of food, including meat and plants.
omnivorous (adjective).
[from Latin *omni-* meaning 'all' and *vorare*
meaning 'to eat greedily']

on
1 (preposition) touching or attached to
something, e.g. *They were sitting on chairs*.
2 A book or talk on a particular subject is about
that subject.
3 If something is done on an instrument,
machine, or system, it is done using that
instrument, machine, or system, e.g. *a tune
played on the violin*.
4 If something happens on a particular day, that
is when it happens, e.g. *Come on Thursday*.
5 If you are on a bus, plane, or train, you are
inside it.
6 (adverb) If you have a piece of clothing on, you
are wearing it.
7 If an event is on, it is happening or taking
place, e.g. *The war was on then... What's on at
the Odeon?*
8 A machine or switch that is on is functioning.
9 (phrase) **On and off** means occasionally.
10 If you say that something is **not on**, you mean
that it is unacceptable or impossible.

once
1 (adverb) If something happens once, it
happens one time only.
2 If something was once true, it was true in the
past, but is no longer true.
3 (conjunction) If something happens once
another thing has happened, it happens
immediately afterwards.
4 (phrase) If you do something **at once**, you do it

immediately. If several things happen **at once**, they all happen at the same time.
5 Once and for all means completely or finally.

one, ones
1 One is the number 1.
2 (adjective) If you refer to the one person or thing of a particular kind, you mean the only person or thing of that kind, e.g. *Their one aim in life is to go to university.*
3 One also means 'a'; used when emphasizing something, e.g. *They had one hell of a row.*
4 (pronoun) One refers to a particular thing or person, e.g. *That's a difficult one to answer.*
5 One also means people in general, e.g. *One can eat well here.*
[from Greek *oinē* meaning 'ace']

oneness
(noun) Oneness is a feeling of being in complete agreement with someone else.

one-off
(noun) A one-off is something that happens or is made only once.

onerous (pronounced **ohn**-er-uss)
(adjective; a formal word) difficult or unpleasant, e.g. *his onerous duties.*
onerously (adverb).
[from Latin *onerosus* meaning 'burdensome']

oneself
(pronoun) Oneself is used when you are talking about people in general, e.g. *One should keep such thoughts to oneself.*

one-sided
1 (adjective) If a relationship or activity is one-sided, one of the people involved does a lot more than the other, e.g. *one-sided conversations.*
2 A one-sided argument or report considers the facts or a situation from only one point of view.

one-time
(adjective) One-time indicates that something used to be the case but is no longer, e.g. *a one-time farm worker.*

one-upmanship
(noun; an informal expression) One-upmanship is the art of gaining advantage over your rivals, often by underhand means.

one-way
1 (adjective) One-way streets are streets along which vehicles can drive in only one direction.
2 A one-way ticket is one that you can use to travel to a place, but not to travel back again.

ongoing
(adjective) continuing to happen, e.g. *an ongoing economic crisis.*

onion, onions
(noun) An onion is a small, round vegetable with a brown, papery skin and a very strong taste.

onlooker, onlookers
(noun) An onlooker is someone who is watching an event.

only
1 (adverb) You use only to indicate the one thing or person involved, e.g. *Only mother knows.*
2 You use only to emphasize that something is unimportant or small, e.g. *Don't worry, it's only a slight crack.*
3 (adjective) If you talk about the only thing or person, you mean that there are no others, e.g. *It was the only way out.*
4 If you are an only child, you have no brothers or sisters.
5 (conjunction) Only also means but or except, e.g. *Snake is just like chicken only tougher.*
6 (adverb) You can use only to introduce something which happens immediately after something else, e.g. *He broke off, only to resume almost at once.*
7 (phrase) **Only too** means extremely, e.g. *She remembered that night only too clearly.*

onomatopoeia (pronounced on-o-mat-o-**pee**-a)
(noun) Onomatopoeia is the use of words which sound like the thing that they represent. 'Hiss' and 'buzz' are examples of onomatopoeia.
[from Greek *onoma* meaning 'name' and *poiein* meaning 'to make']

onset
(noun) The onset of something unpleasant is the beginning of it, e.g. *the onset of war.*

onslaught, onslaughts (pronounced **on**-slawt)
(noun) An onslaught is a violent attack. [from Dutch *aan-* meaning 'on' and *slag* meaning 'blow' or 'stroke']

onto or on to
(preposition) If you put something onto an object, you put it on it.

onus (rhymes with **bonus**)
(noun; a formal word) If the onus is on you to do something, it is your duty to do it.

onwards or onward
1 (adverb) continuing to happen from a particular time, e.g. *From that time onwards he had never spoken to her again.*
2 travelling forwards, e.g. *We travelled from China to India, and onwards to Africa.*

onyx (pronounced **on**-iks)
(noun) Onyx is a semiprecious stone used for making ornaments and jewellery.
[from Greek *onux* meaning 'fingernail' or 'claw']

ooze, oozes, oozing, oozed
1 (verb) When a thick liquid oozes, it flows slowly, e.g. *Blood oozed from his wounds.*
2 (noun) Ooze is the fine mud found on the sea bed.
[sense 1 is from Old English *wos* meaning 'juice'; sense 2 is from Old English *wase* meaning 'mud']

opal, opals
(noun) An opal is a pale or whitish semiprecious stone used for making jewellery.
[from Sanskrit *upala* meaning 'precious stone']

opaque (pronounced oh-**pake**)
1 (adjective) If something is opaque, you cannot see through it, e.g. *opaque windows.*

2 Opaque also means difficult to understand, e.g. *Their intentions remained opaque.*
opacity or **opaqueness** (noun).

open, opens, opening, opened

1 (verb) When you open something, or when it opens, you move it so that it is no longer closed, e.g. *She opened the door.*
2 (adjective) Something that is open is not closed or fastened, e.g. *He tore open the envelope.*
3 If you have an open mind, you are willing to consider new ideas or suggestions.
4 Someone who is open is honest and frank.
5 (verb) When a shop or office opens, the people in it start working.
6 (adjective) When a shop or office is open, the people in it are working.
7 (verb) To open something also means to start it, e.g. *opening a new bank account.*
8 (adjective) An open area of sea or land is a large, empty area, e.g. *open country.*
9 (phrase) **In the open** means outside.
10 (adjective) If something is open to you, it is possible for you to do it, e.g. *We should use the opportunities now open to us.*
11 If a situation is still open, it is still being considered, e.g. *They left their options open.*
openly (adverb).

open-and-shut

(adjective) easily judged or decided, e.g. *an open-and-shut case.*

opencast

(adjective) An opencast mine is mined from the surface and not from underground.

open circuit, open circuits

(noun) An open circuit is an electrical circuit with a break in it which prevents the flow of electricity.

open-ended

(adjective) An open-ended activity does not specify the final result in advance, e.g. *an open-ended discussion.*

open-handed

(adjective) generous and unselfish.

opening, openings

1 (adjective) Opening means coming first, e.g. *the opening scene of the play.*
2 (noun) The opening of a book or film is the first part of it.
3 An opening is a hole or gap.
4 An opening is also an opportunity, e.g. *an opening into show business.*

Similar words: (sense 3) mouth, aperture, orifice

open-minded

(adjective) willing to consider new ideas and suggestions.

open-mouthed

(adjective) surprised or astonished.

open-plan

(adjective) An open-plan office or building has very few interior walls.

open verdict, open verdicts

(noun) In law, an open verdict does not specify the cause of death.

opera, operas

(noun) An opera is a play in which the words are sung rather than spoken.
operatic (adjective).
[from Latin *opera* meaning 'works']

operate, operates, operating, operated

1 (verb) To operate means to work, e.g. *the multinationals which operate in their country... We discussed how language operates.*
2 When you operate a machine, you make it work.
3 When surgeons operate, they cut open a patient's body to remove or repair a damaged part.
[from Latin *operari* meaning 'to work']

operation, operations

1 (noun) An operation is a complex, planned event, e.g. *a rescue operation... military operations.*
2 An operation is also a form of medical treatment in which a surgeon cuts open a patient's body to remove or repair a damaged part.
3 (phrase) If something is **in operation**, it is working or being used, e.g. *The plans were put into operation at once.*

operational

1 (adjective) working or able to be used, e.g. *We only have fifty operational warships.*
2 occurring while a plan is being carried out, e.g. *We had a few operational difficulties.*

operative, operatives

1 (adjective) Something that is operative is working or having an effect.
2 (noun) An operative is a worker, e.g. *each operative on a production line.*

operator, operators

1 (noun) An operator is someone who works at a telephone exchange or on a switchboard.
2 A machine operator is someone who operates a machine, e.g. *a computer operator.*
3 An operator is also someone who runs a business, e.g. *a tour operator.*

operetta, operettas

(noun) An operetta is a light-hearted opera, in which some of the words are spoken rather than sung.
[from Italian *operetta* meaning 'small opera']

ophthalmic (pronounced off-**thal**-mik)

(adjective) concerned with the medical care of your eyes, e.g. *an ophthalmic optician.*
[from Greek *ophthalmos* meaning 'eye']

opiate, opiates (pronounced **oh**-pee-it)

(noun) An opiate is a drug, especially one that contains opium, which reduces pain and makes you sleepy.

opinion, opinions

(noun) An opinion is a belief or view, e.g. *The students were eager to express their opinions.*
[from Latin *opinio* meaning 'belief']

Similar words: attitude, belief, view, estimation

opinionated
(adjective) Someone who is opinionated has strong views and refuses to accept that they might be wrong.

opium
(noun) Opium is a drug made from the seeds of a poppy. It is used in medicine to relieve pain.
[from Latin *opium* meaning 'poppy juice']

opossum, opossums
(noun) An opossum is a small animal which carries its young in a pouch on its body and has a long tail. Opossums are found in North and South America. They are famous for pretending to be dead when in danger.
[an American Indian word]

opponent, opponents
(noun) Your opponent is someone who is against you in an argument, a contest, or a game.

opportune
(adjective; a formal word) happening at a convenient time, e.g. *The call came at an opportune moment.*
[from Latin *opportunus* meaning 'towards harbour'; used to describe a favourable wind]

opportunism
(noun) Opportunism is the practice of taking advantage of any opportunity to gain money or power for yourself.
opportunist (noun).

opportunity, opportunities
(noun) An opportunity is a chance to do something, e.g. *an opportunity to meet people.*

oppose, opposes, opposing, opposed
(verb) If you oppose something, you disagree with it and try to prevent it.
[from Latin *ob-* meaning 'against' and *ponere* meaning 'to place']

opposed
1 (adjective) If you are opposed to something, you disagree with it, e.g. *I am opposed to hanging.*
2 Opposed also means opposite or very different, e.g. *Two bitterly opposed schools of thought.*
3 (phrase) If you refer to one thing **as opposed to** another, you are emphasizing that it is the first thing rather than the second which concerns you, e.g. *There's a need for technical colleges as opposed to universities.*

opposite, opposites
1 (preposition and adverb) If one thing is opposite another, it is facing it, e.g. *The hotel is opposite a railway station... the house opposite*
2 (adjective) The opposite part of something is the part farthest away from you, e.g. *on the opposite side of the street.*
3 If things are opposite, they are completely different, e.g. *the opposite direction... the opposite point of view.*
4 (noun) If two things are completely different, they are opposites.
[from Latin *ob-* meaning 'against' and *ponere*

meaning 'to place']

Similar words: (sense 4) antithesis, contrast, reverse, converse

opposite number, opposite numbers
(noun) Your opposite number is someone who does the same job as you, but in a different department or organization.

opposition
1 (noun) If there is opposition to something, people disagree with it and try to prevent it.
2 The political parties who are not in power are referred to as the Opposition.
3 In a game or sports event, the opposition is the person or team that you are competing against.

oppress, oppresses, oppressing, oppressed
1 (verb) To oppress people means to treat them cruelly or unfairly.
2 If something oppresses you, it makes you feel depressed and worried.
oppression (noun), **oppressor** (noun).
[from Latin *ob-* meaning 'against' and *premere* meaning 'to press']

Similar words: (sense 1) tyrannize, subjugate

oppressive
1 (adjective) If the weather is oppressive, it is hot and humid.
2 An oppressive situation makes you feel depressed or concerned, e.g. *The silence became oppressive.*
3 An oppressive system treats people cruelly or unfairly, e.g. *an oppressive regime.*
oppressively (adverb), **oppressiveness** (noun).

opprobrium (pronounced op-**pro**-bree-um)
(noun; a formal word) Opprobrium is the state of being disliked and criticized a lot for something you have done, e.g. *The opprobrium he incurred was caused by his outspokenness.*
[from Latin *ob-* meaning 'against' and *probrum* meaning 'shameful act']

opt, opts, opting, opted
(verb) If you opt for something, you choose it. If you opt out of something, you choose not to be involved in it.

optic
(adjective) relating to eyes, e.g. *the optic nerves.*
[from Greek *optos* meaning 'seen' or 'visible']

optical
1 (adjective) concerned with vision, light, or images, e.g. *an optical microscope.*
2 relating to the appearance of things, e.g. *an optical illusion.*

optician, opticians
(noun) An optician is someone who tests people's eyes, and makes and sells glasses and contact lenses.

optics
(noun) Optics is the study of vision, sight, and light.

optimism
(noun) Optimism is a feeling of hopefulness about the future.
optimist (noun), **optimistic** (adjective), **optimistically** (adverb).
[from Latin *optimus* meaning 'best']

optimum
(adjective) the best that is possible, e.g. *We were working in optimum conditions.*

option, options
(noun) An option is a choice between one or more things, e.g. *He had two options open to him.*
optional (adjective).
[from Latin *optare* meaning 'to choose']

opulent (pronounced op-yool-nt)
1 (adjective) very wealthy, e.g. *an opulent society.*
2 grand and expensive-looking, e.g. *an opulent marble altar.*
opulence (noun).
[from Latin *opes* meaning 'wealth']

opus, opuses or opera
1 (noun) An opus is a musical composition. 'Opus' is often used with a number, indicating its position in a series of published works by the same composer.
2 An opus is also a great artistic work, such as a piece of writing or a painting.
[from Latin *opus* meaning 'a work']

or
1 (conjunction) used to link alternatives, e.g. *He didn't know whether to laugh or cry.*
2 used to introduce a warning, e.g. *Don't put anything plastic in the oven or it will melt.*

oracle, oracles
1 (noun) An oracle was a priest or priestess in ancient Greece, who made predictions about the future by interpreting messages from the gods.
2 An oracle is also a prophecy made by a priest or other person with great authority or wisdom.
[from Latin *orare* meaning 'to pray']

oral, orals
1 (adjective) spoken rather than written, e.g. *an oral examination.*
2 Oral describes things that are used in your mouth or done with your mouth, e.g. *an oral antiseptic.*
3 (noun) An oral is an examination that is spoken rather than written.
orally (adverb).
[from Latin *oralis* meaning 'of the mouth']

Similar words: (sense 1) spoken, verbal

orange, oranges
1 (noun) An orange is a round citrus fruit that is juicy and sweet and has a thick reddish-yellow skin.
2 (adjective and noun) reddish-yellow.
[from Sanskrit *naranga* meaning 'orange']

orangeade
(noun) Orangeade is a drink made from, or flavoured with, oranges.

orang-utan, orang-utans; also spelled orang-utang
(noun) An orang-utan is a large ape with reddish-brown hair. Orang-utans come from the forests of Borneo and Sumatra.
[from Malay *orang* meaning 'man' and *hutan* meaning 'forest']

oration, orations
(noun; a formal word) An oration is a formal public speech.
[from Latin *oratio* meaning 'formal speech']

orator, orators
(noun) An orator is someone who is skilled at making speeches.

oratorio, oratorios
(noun) An oratorio is a piece of religious music written for singers and an orchestra.
[from the Church of the Oratory in Rome where musical services were held]

oratory
(noun) Oratory is the art and skill of making formal public speeches.
oratorical (adjective).
[from Latin *oratio* meaning 'formal speech']

orb, orbs
(noun; a literary word) An orb is something shaped like a ball, for example the sun or the moon.
[from Latin *orbis* meaning 'circle' or 'disc']

orbit, orbits, orbiting, orbited
1 (noun) An orbit is the curved path followed by an object going round a planet or the sun.
2 (verb) If something orbits a planet or the sun, it goes round and round it.
[from Latin *orbita* meaning 'course']

orbital
1 (adjective) Orbital means relating to the orbit of an object in space.
2 An orbital road goes all the way round a city.

orchard, orchards
(noun) An orchard is a piece of land on which fruit trees are grown.

orchestra, orchestras (pronounced or-kess-tra)
(noun) An orchestra is a large group of musicians who play musical instruments together.
orchestral (adjective).
[from Greek *orkhestra* meaning 'the area in a theatre reserved for musicians']

orchestrate, orchestrates, orchestrating, orchestrated
1 (verb) To orchestrate something means to organize it very carefully to produce a particular result.
2 To orchestrate a piece of music means to rewrite it so that it can be played by an orchestra.
orchestration (noun).

orchid, orchids (pronounced or-kid)
(noun) Orchids are plants with unusual flowers. Some varieties are rare and therefore expensive.

ordain, ordains, ordaining, ordained
1 (verb) When someone is ordained, they are made a member of the clergy.
2 (a formal use) To ordain something means to order it, e.g. *The law ordained her execution.*

ordeal, ordeals
(noun) An ordeal is a difficult and extremely unpleasant experience, e.g. *He described his terrible ordeal.*

Similar words: trial, tribulation, nightmare

order, orders, ordering, ordered
1 (phrase) If you do something **in order to** achieve a particular thing, you do it because you want to achieve that thing.
2 (noun) An order is a command given by someone in authority.
3 (verb) To order someone to do something means to tell them firmly to do it.
4 When you order something, you ask for it to be brought or sent to you.
5 (noun) An order is something that you ask to be brought to you or sent to you.
6 If things are arranged or done in a particular order, they are arranged or done in that sequence, e.g. *in alphabetical order.*
7 Order is a situation in which everything is in the correct place or done at the correct time.
8 (phrases) If a machine or device is **in working order**, it works and is not broken. If it is **out of order**, it is broken and does not work.
9 (noun) When people talk about a particular order, they mean the way society is organized at a particular time.
10 An order is also a group of monks or nuns who live according to certain rules.
11 If you refer to something of a particular order, you mean something of a particular quality or type, e.g. *a thinker of the highest order.*
12 (phrases) **In the order of** or **of the order of** means approximately, e.g. *Britain's contribution is something in the order of 5 per cent.*

Similar words: (sense 6) arrangement, grouping, array, sequence

orderly, orderlies
1 (adjective) Something that is orderly is well organized or arranged.
2 (noun) An orderly is an untrained male hospital attendant.
orderliness (noun).

Similar words: (sense 1) systematic, methodical

ordinal number, ordinal numbers
(noun) An ordinal number is a number such as 'third' or 'fifth', which tells you what position something has in a group or series.

ordinance, ordinances
(noun; a formal word) An ordinance is an official rule or order.
[from Latin *ordinare* meaning 'to set in order']

ordinarily
(adverb) If something ordinarily happens, it usually happens.

ordinary
1 (adjective) Ordinary means not special or different in any way.
2 (phrase) Something that is **out of the ordinary** is unusual or different.

Similar words: (sense 1) average, common, commonplace, mundane, everyday, pedestrian

ordination
(noun) When someone's ordination takes place, they are made a member of the clergy.

ordnance
(noun) Weapons and other military supplies are referred to as ordnance.

Ordnance Survey
(noun) The Ordnance Survey is the British government organization that produces detailed maps of Britain and Ireland.

ordure (pronounced **ord**-yoor)
(noun; a formal word) Ordure is excrement.
[from Old French *ord* meaning 'dirty']

ore, ores
(noun) Ore is rock or earth from which metal can be extracted.

oregano (pronounced or-rig-**ga**-no)
(noun) Oregano is a herb used for flavouring in cooking.

organ, organs
1 (noun) Your organs are parts of your body that have a particular function, for example your heart or lungs.
2 An organ is a large musical instrument with pipes of different lengths through which air is forced. It has various keyboards which are played like a piano.
3 You refer to a newspaper as an organ of an organization when the organization uses it as a means of informing or influencing people.
[from Greek *organon* meaning 'tool']

organdie
(noun) Organdie is a fine, slightly stiff, cotton fabric.

organic
1 (adjective) Something that is organic is produced by or found in plants or animals, e.g. *The rocks were searched for organic remains.*
2 Organic food is produced without the use of artificial fertilizers or pesticides.
organically (adverb).

organic chemistry
(noun) Organic chemistry is the branch of chemistry concerned with carbon compounds.

organism, organisms
(noun) An organism is any living animal or plant.

organist, organists
(noun) An organist is someone who plays the organ.

organization, organizations; also spelled organisation

1 (noun) An organization is any group, society, club, or business.
2 The organization of something is the act of planning and arranging it.
3 Organization is the ability to do things efficiently and in a well-planned and ordered way.
4 Organization is also the act of forming a trade union, e.g. *I'm in favour of widespread organization of labour.*
organizational (adjective).

Similar words: (sense 1) association, network, corporation

organize, organizes, organizing, organized; also spelled **organise**
1 (verb) If you organize an event, you plan and arrange it.
2 If you organize things, you arrange them in a sensible order.
3 When workers organize, they form a trade union.
organized (adjective), **organizer** (noun).

organza
(noun) Organza is a fine, stiff fabric made from cotton and silk or cotton and nylon.

orgasm, orgasms
(noun) An orgasm is the moment of greatest pleasure and excitement during sexual activity.
[from Greek *organ* meaning 'to swell']

orgy, orgies (pronounced **or**-jee)
1 (noun) An orgy is a wild, uncontrolled party involving a lot of drinking and sexual activity.
2 You can refer to a period of intense activity as an orgy of that activity, e.g. *an orgy violence.*
[from Greek *orgia* meaning 'nocturnal festival']

oriel
(noun) An oriel or oriel window is a bay window high up in a building.
[from Old French *oriol* meaning 'gallery']

orient, orients, orienting, oriented
1 (noun; a literary use) The Orient is eastern and south-eastern Asia.
2 (verb; a formal use) If you orient yourself to a new situation, you learn about and adjust to it.
[sense 1 is from Latin *oriens* meaning 'rising (sun)']

oriental, orientals
1 (adjective) relating to eastern or south-eastern Asia.
2 (noun; an old-fashioned use) People sometimes refer to a person who comes from eastern or south-eastern Asia as an Oriental.

orientate, orientates, orientating, orientated
1 (verb) When you orientate yourself, you find out where you are by looking at a map, or by looking around for familiar places.
2 If you orientate yourself to a new situation, you learn about it and adjust to it.
[sense 1 is from Old French *orienter* meaning 'to make to face east']

orientated
(adjective) If someone is interested in a particular thing, you can say that they are orientated towards it, e.g. *career-orientated women.*

orientation
1 (noun) You can refer to an organization's activities and aims as its orientation, e.g. *The party's revolutionary orientation.*
2 The orientation of an object is the direction it faces.

oriented
(adjective) Oriented means the same as orientated.

orienteering
(noun) Orienteering is a sport in which people run from one place to another in the countryside, using a map and compass to guide them.

orifice, orifices (pronounced **or**-i-fiss)
(noun; a formal word) An orifice is an opening or hole, for example, in your body.
[from Latin *os* meaning 'mouth' and *facere* meaning 'to make']

origami
(noun) Origami is the Japanese art of paper folding.
[from Japanese *ori* meaning 'a folding' and *kami* meaning 'paper']

origin, origins
1 (noun) You can refer to the beginning or cause of something as its origin or origins.
2 You can refer to someone's family background as their origin or origins, e.g. *a woman of Pakistani origin... His origins were humble.*
3 In mathematics, the origin is the point where two or more axes meet.
[from Latin *origo* meaning 'beginning' or 'birth']

Similar words: (sense 1) root, source

original, originals
1 (adjective) Original describes things that existed at the beginning, rather than being added later, or things that were the first of their kind to exist, e.g. *They will restore the house to its original state... the original steam engine.*
2 (noun) An original is a work of art or a document that is the one that was first produced, and not a copy.
3 (adjective) Original means imaginative and clever, e.g. *a daring and original idea.*
originally (adverb), **originality** (noun).

originate, originates, originating, originated
(verb) When something originates, or you originate it, it begins to happen or exist.
originator (noun).

Orlon
(noun; a trademark) Orlon is a crease-resistant acrylic fibre.

ormolu (pronounced **or**-mal-oo)
(noun) Ormolu is a gold-coloured alloy of copper, zinc, and tin, used to decorate furniture.
[from French *or* meaning 'gold' and *moulu* meaning 'ground']

ornament, ornaments, ornamenting, ornamented
1 (noun) An ornament is a small, attractive

object that you display in your home or that you wear in order to look attractive.
2 Ornament is decoration on a building, a piece of furniture, or a work of art.
3 (verb) If something is ornamented, it is decorated with attractive objects or patterns.
[from Latin *ornare* meaning 'to adorn']

ornamental
(adjective) designed to be attractive rather than useful, e.g. *an ornamental pond.*

ornamentation
(noun) Ornamentation is decoration on a building, a piece of furniture, or a work of art.

ornate
(adjective) Something that is ornate has a lot of decoration on it.

ornithology
(noun) Ornithology is the study of birds.
ornithologist (noun).
[from Greek *ornis* meaning 'bird' and *-logia* meaning 'study of']

orphan, orphans, orphaning, orphaned
1 (noun) An orphan is a child whose parents are dead.
2 (verb) If a child is orphaned, its parents die.

orphanage, orphanages
(noun) An orphanage is a place where orphans are looked after.

orthodontics
(noun) Orthodontics is the branch of dentistry concerned with straightening irregular teeth.
orthodontic (adjective), **orthodontist** (noun).
[from Greek *orthos* + *odous* meaning 'straight tooth']

orthodox
1 (adjective) Orthodox beliefs or methods are the ones that most people have or use and that are considered standard.
2 People who are orthodox believe in the older, more traditional ideas of their religion or political party.
3 The Orthodox church is the part of the Christian church which separated from the western European church in the 11th century and is the main church in Greece, the USSR, and some other countries.
orthodoxy (noun).
[from Greek *orthos* + *doxa* meaning 'correct belief']

orthography
(noun; a formal word) Orthography is the way words are spelled or should be spelled.
[from Greek *orthos* + *-graphos* meaning 'correct writing']

orthopaedics or orthopedics (pronounced orth-op-**pee**-diks)
(noun) Orthopaedics is the medical care of bones, especially the treatment of injuries or defects.
orthopaedic (adjective).
[from Greek *orthos* meaning 'straight' and *pais* meaning 'child']

oryx, oryx or oryxes
(noun) An oryx is a large African antelope with long, straight, nearly upright horns.

oscillate, oscillates, oscillating, oscillated (pronounced os-sil-late)
1 (verb; a formal word) If something oscillates, it moves repeatedly backwards and forwards.
2 If you oscillate between two moods, you keep changing from one to the other.
oscillation (noun), **oscillatory** (adjective).
[from Latin *oscillum* meaning 'swing']

oscilloscope, oscilloscopes (pronounced os-**sil**-los-scope)
(noun) An oscilloscope is a machine which shows the shape of a wave on a cathode-ray tube.
[from Latin *oscillum* meaning 'swing' and Greek *skopein* meaning 'to look at']

osier, osiers (pronounced oh-zee-er)
(noun) Osiers are willow trees whose twigs are used for making baskets.

osmosis (pronounced oz-**moh**-siss)
1 (noun; a technical use) Osmosis is the process by which a liquid moves through a semipermeable membrane from a weaker solution to a more concentrated one.
2 You can also refer to the way in which people seem to absorb new ideas gradually and without effort as osmosis.
[from Greek *ōsmos* meaning 'push']

osprey, ospreys (pronounced **oss**-pree)
(noun) An osprey is a large bird of prey which catches fish with its feet.

ossify, ossifies, ossifying, ossified
(verb) If you say that ideas or organizations ossify, you mean that they become fixed and difficult to change.

ostensible
(adjective; a formal word) The ostensible reason for something is the one that seems to be true, but which you have doubts about.
ostensibly (adverb).
[from Latin *ostendere* meaning 'to show']

ostentatious
1 (adjective) Something that is ostentatious is intended to impress people, for example by looking expensive, e.g. *an ostentatious ring.*
2 People who are ostentatious try to impress other people with their wealth or importance.
ostentatiously (adverb), **ostentation** (noun).

osteoarthritis (pronounced os-tee-oh-arth-**rite**-iss)
(noun) Osteoarthritis is inflammation of the joints, particularly the shoulder, knee, and hip joints, which gets progressively worse with age.
[from Greek *osteon* + *arthron* meaning 'bone joint']

osteopath, osteopaths
(noun) An osteopath is someone who treats illnesses by manipulating people's bones, especially the spine.
osteopathy (noun).
[from Greek *osteon* + *pathos* meaning 'bone suffering']

ostracize, ostracizes, ostracizing, ostracized
(pronounced **ost**-ras-size); also spelled **ostracise**
(verb) If you are ostracized, people deliberately
behave in an unfriendly way towards you and do
not let you join in with what they are doing.
ostracism (noun).

ostrich, ostriches
(noun) The ostrich is the largest bird in the
world. Ostriches live in Africa. They cannot fly,
have a long bare neck, long legs, and only two
toes on each foot.

other, others
1 (adjective and pronoun) Other people or things
are different people or things, e.g. *He had his
papers in one hand, his hat in the other... I shall
wait until the others come back.*
2 (phrases) **The other day** or **the other week**
means recently, e.g. *I saw him the other day.*
3 Other than means except, e.g. *She never
discussed it with anyone other than Derek.*
4 Every other day or **every other week** means
every alternate day or week.

otherwise
1 (adverb) You use otherwise to say a different
situation would exist if a particular fact or
occurrence was not the case, e.g. *Wash five times
a day. You're not really clean otherwise.*
2 Otherwise means apart from the thing
mentioned, e.g. *I'm tired but otherwise I'm fine.*
3 Otherwise also means in a different way, e.g.
He was incapable of acting otherwise.

otherworldly
(adjective) impractical or unrealistic.

otter, otters
(noun) An otter is a small, furry animal with a
long tail. Otters swim well and live on fish.

ottoman, ottomans
(noun) An ottoman is a long, low storage chest
with a hinged padded lid.

ouch
(interjection) You say ouch when you suddenly
feel pain.

ought (pronounced **awt**)
1 (verb) If you say that someone ought to do
something, you mean that they should do it, e.g.
She ought to see a doctor... I ought to have called.
2 If you say that something ought to be the case,
you mean that you expect it to be the case, e.g. *It
ought to be quite easy.*

ouija board, ouija boards (pronounced **wee**-ja)
(noun; a trademark) A ouija board is a board
marked with the letters of the alphabet. A
pointer or glass moves around the board,
supposedly directed by spiritual forces, to spell
out the answers to questions.
[from French *oui* meaning 'yes' and German *ja*
meaning 'yes']

ounce, ounces
1 (noun) An ounce is a unit of weight equal to
one sixteenth of a pound or about 28.35 grams.
2 An ounce of something is also a very small
amount of it, e.g. *an ounce of sense*

our
(determiner) Our refers to something belonging
or relating to the speaker or writer and one or
more other people, e.g. *the future of our society.*

ours
(pronoun) Ours refers to something belonging or
relating to the speaker or writer and one or more
other people, e.g. *a school such as ours.*

ourselves
1 (pronoun) Ourselves is used when the same
speaker or writer and one or more other people
do an action and are affected by it, e.g. *We
almost made ourselves ill...*
2 Ourselves is used to emphasize 'we'.

oust, ousts, ousting, ousted
(verb) If you oust someone, you force them out
of a job or a place, e.g. *a coup which ousted the
President.*
[from Latin *obstare* meaning 'to oppose']

out
1 (adverb) towards the outside of a place, e.g.
When he came into the room, she rushed out.
2 not at home, e.g. *He came when I was out.*
3 in the open air, e.g. *Many people slept out.*
4 no longer shining or burning, e.g. *The lights
went out.*
5 (adjective) on strike, e.g. *The men stayed out
for nearly a month.*
6 unacceptable or unfashionable, e.g. *Long skirts
are out this year.*
7 incorrect, e.g. *It's only a couple of degrees out.*

out-and-out
(adjective) entire or complete, e.g. *an
out-and-out villain.*

outback
(noun) In Australia, the outback is the remote
parts where very few people live.

outbid, outbids, outbidding, outbid or **outbidden**
(verb) If you outbid someone, you bid higher
than they do.

outboard motor, outboard motors
(noun) An outboard motor is a motor that can be
fixed to the back of a small boat.

outbreak, outbreaks
(noun) If there is an outbreak of something
unpleasant, such as war, it suddenly occurs.

outbuilding, outbuildings
(noun) Outbuildings are small buildings, such as
barns or stables, that are part of a larger
property.

outburst, outbursts
1 (noun) An outburst is a sudden, strong
expression of an emotion, especially anger, e.g. *I
apologize for my outburst just now.*
2 An outburst of violent activity is a sudden
occurrence of it, e.g. *an outburst of shooting.*

outcast, outcasts
(noun) An outcast is someone who is rejected by
other people.

outclass, outclasses, outclassing, outclassed
(verb) If you outclass someone, you are a lot
better than they are at a particular activity.

outcome, outcomes
(noun) The outcome of something is the result of it, e.g. *I predicted the outcome of the election.*

outcrop, outcrops
(noun) An outcrop is a large piece of rock that sticks out of the ground.

outcry, outcries
(noun) If there is an outcry about something, a lot of people are angry about it, e.g. *The experiments continued, despite the public outcry.*

outdated
(adjective) no longer in fashion.

outdistance, outdistances, outdistancing, outdistanced
(verb) If you outdistance someone, you progress faster than they do and leave them behind.

outdo, outdoes, outdoing, outdid, outdone
(verb) If you outdo someone, you do a particular thing better than they do.

outdoor
(adjective) happening or used outside, e.g. *outdoor activities.*

outdoors
(adverb) outside, e.g. *Classes were held outdoors.*

outer
(adjective) The outer parts of something are the parts furthest from the centre, e.g. *the building's outer walls.*

outermost
(adjective) furthest from the centre of something, e.g. *the outermost ring on the target.*

outer space
(noun) Outer space is everything beyond the Earth's atmosphere.

outfield
(noun) The outfield in cricket is the area furthest from the batsman.

outfit, outfits
1 (noun) An outfit is a set of clothes.
2 (an informal use) An outfit is also an organization.

outfitter, outfitters
(noun; an old-fashioned word) An outfitter or outfitters is a shop that sells men's clothes.

outflank, outflanks, outflanking, outflanked
(verb) If one army outflanks another, it manages to get round the side of it in order to attack it.

outgoing, outgoings
1 (adjective) Outgoing describes someone who is leaving a job or place, e.g. *the outgoing President.*
2 Someone who is outgoing is friendly and not shy.
3 (noun) Your outgoings are the amount of money that you spend.

outgrow, outgrows, outgrowing, outgrew, outgrown
1 (verb) If you outgrow a piece of clothing, you grow too big for it.
2 If you outgrow a way of behaving, you stop it because you have grown older and more mature.

outhouse, outhouses
(noun) An outhouse is a small building in the grounds of a house to which it belongs.

outing, outings
(noun) An outing is a pleasure trip.

outlandish
(adjective) very unusual or odd, e.g. *outlandish behaviour.*

outlast, outlasts, outlasting, outlasted
(verb) To outlast something means to live or exist longer than it does.

outlaw, outlaws, outlawing, outlawed
1 (verb) If something is outlawed, it is made illegal.
2 (noun) In the past, an outlaw was a criminal.

outlay, outlays
(noun) An outlay is an amount of money spent on something, e.g. *an initial outlay of £500.*

outlet, outlets
1 (noun) An outlet for your feelings or ideas is a way of expressing them.
2 An outlet is a hole or pipe through which water or air can flow away.
3 An outlet is also a shop which sells goods made by a particular manufacturer.

outline, outlines, outlining, outlined
1 (verb) If you outline a plan or idea, you explain it in a general way.
2 (noun) An outline is a general explanation or description of something.
3 (verb) You say that something is outlined when you can see its shape because there is a light behind it.
4 (noun) The outline of something is its shape.

Similar words: (sense 4) contour, profile

outlive, outlives, outliving, outlived
(verb) To outlive someone means to live longer than they do.

outlook
1 (noun) Your outlook is your general attitude towards life.
2 The outlook of a situation is the way it is likely to develop, e.g. *The economic outlook is bright.*

outlying
(adjective) Outlying places are far from cities.

outmanoeuvre, outmanoeuvres, outmanoeuvring, outmanoeuvred
(verb) If you outmanoeuvre someone, you gain an advantage over them by clever tactics.

outmoded
(adjective) old-fashioned and no longer useful, e.g. *outmoded techniques.*

outnumber, outnumbers, outnumbering, outnumbered
(verb) If there are more of one group than of another, the first group outnumbers the second.

out of
1 (preposition) If you do something out of a particular feeling, you are motivated by that feeling, e.g. *She did it out of spite.*

2 Out of also means from, e.g. *You can make petroleum out of coal.*
3 If you are out of something, you no longer have any of it, e.g. *We're out of milk again.*
4 If you are out of the rain, sun, or wind, you are sheltered from it.
5 You also use out of to indicate proportion. For example, one out of five means one in every five.

out of date
(adjective) old-fashioned and no longer useful.

out of doors
(adverb) outside, e.g. *eating out of doors.*

out-of-the-way
(adjective) remote and seldom visited.

outpace, outpaces, outpacing, outpaced
(verb) If you outpace someone, you go faster than they do.

outpatient, outpatients
(noun) Outpatients are people who receive treatment in hospital without staying overnight.

outplay, outplays, outplaying, outplayed
(verb) If you outplay someone, you play better than they do.

outpost, outposts
(noun) An outpost is a small settlement a long way from a main centre, e.g. *a trading outpost.*

outpouring, outpourings
(noun) An outpouring is a sudden, rapid, and uncontrolled rush of something, e.g. *an outpouring of ideas.*

output, outputs
1 (noun) Output is the amount of something produced by a person or organization.
2 The output of a computer is the information that it produces.

outrage, outrages, outraging, outraged
1 (verb) If something outrages you, it angers and shocks you, e.g. *I was outraged by his cruelty.*
2 (noun) Outrage is a feeling of anger and shock.
3 You can refer to something very shocking or violent as an outrage.
outrageous (adjective), **outrageously** (adverb).

outré (pronounced oo-tray)
(adjective) If something is outré, it is unusual and rather shocking, e.g. *her outré clothes.*
[from French *outrer* meaning 'to go beyond']

outrider, outriders
(noun) An outrider is someone on a motorcycle who rides near a vehicle as an escort or guard.

outrigger, outriggers
(noun) An outrigger is a boat with a framework which projects from its sides and floats on the water to increase its stability.

outright
1 (adjective) absolute, e.g. *an outright refusal.*
2 (adverb) in an open and direct way, e.g. *If I ask outright I will get nowhere.*
3 completely and totally, e.g. *The government has banned the drug outright.*

outset
(noun) The outset of something is the beginning of it, e.g. *You should tell him this at the outset.*

outshine, outshines, outshining, outshone
(verb) If you outshine someone, you perform better than they do.

outside
1 (noun) The outside of something is the part which surrounds or encloses the rest of it.
2 (adverb, adjective, and preposition) Outside means not inside, e.g. *a demonstration outside the Social Security office... let's go outside... an outside toilet.*
3 Outside also means not included in something, e.g. *outside office hours.*
4 (adjective) On a wide road, the outside lanes are the ones which are closest to its centre. You use the outside lanes for overtaking.

outsider, outsiders
1 (noun) An outsider is someone who does not belong to a particular group.
2 An outsider is also a competitor considered unlikely to win in a race.

outsize or **outsized**
(adjective) much larger than usual, e.g. *an outsized envelope.*

outskirts
(plural noun) The outskirts of a city or town are the parts around the edge of it.

outsmart, outsmarts, outsmarting, outsmarted
(verb; an informal word) If you outsmart someone, you cleverly get the better of them.

outspoken
(adjective) Outspoken people give their opinions openly, even if they shock other people.

outstanding
1 (adjective) extremely good, e.g. *an outstanding war record.*
2 Money that is outstanding is still owed, e.g. *There is fifty pounds outstanding.*

outstay, outstays, outstaying, outstayed
(phrase) If you **outstay your welcome**, you stay longer than your host wishes.

outstretched
(adjective) If your arms are outstretched, they are stretched out as far as possible.

outstrip, outstrips, outstripping, outstripped
(verb) If one thing outstrips another thing, it becomes bigger or more successful or moves faster than the other thing.

outward
1 (adjective) The outward feelings or qualities of someone are the ones they appear to have, rather than the ones they actually have, e.g. *I said it with outward calm.*
2 (adverb) Outward means away from a place or towards the outside, e.g. *Face outward.*
outwardly (adverb).

outwards
(adverb) away from a place or towards the outside, e.g. *The door opens outwards.*

outweigh, outweighs, outweighing, outweighed
(verb) If you say that the advantages of something outweigh its disadvantages, you mean that the advantages are more important than the disadvantages.

outwit, outwits, outwitting, outwitted
(verb) If you outwit someone, you cleverly get
the better of them.

outworn
(adjective; a formal word) old-fashioned and no
longer useful, e.g. *an outworn superstition.*

oval, ovals
1 (noun) An oval is a round shape, similar to a
circle but wider in one direction than the other.
2 (adjective) shaped like an oval, e.g. *an oval
mirror.*
[from Latin *ovalis* meaning 'egg shaped']

ovary, ovaries (pronounced oh-var-ree)
(noun) A woman's ovaries are the two organs in
her body that produce eggs.
[from Latin *ovum* meaning 'egg']

ovation, ovations
1 (noun) An ovation is a long burst of applause.
2 (phrase) If someone gets **a standing ovation**, the
audience stand up and applaud them.

oven, ovens
(noun) An oven is the part of a cooker that you
use for baking or roasting food in.

ovenware
(noun) Ovenware consists of heat-resistant
dishes that can be used in the oven for cooking.

over, overs
1 (preposition) Over something means directly
above it or covering it, e.g. *the picture over the
fireplace... Her hair hung down over her eyes.*
2 A view over an area is a view across that area,
e.g. *The windows look out over a park.*
3 If something is over a road or river it is on the
opposite side of the road or river.
4 Over indicates a topic which is causing
concern, e.g. *They are quarrelling over a woman.*
5 If something happens over a period of time, it
happens during that period, e.g. *He had flu over
Christmas.*
6 Something that is over a particular amount is
more than that amount.
7 (adverb) Over is used to indicate a position,
e.g. *over by the windows... Come over here.*
8 If something rolls or turns over, it is moved so
that its other side is facing upwards, e.g. *She
tipped the pan over.*
9 Something that is over is completely finished,
e.g. *His search was over.*
10 (adverb and preposition) If you lean over,
you bend your body in a particular direction, e.g.
*Pat leaned over and picked it up... bent over his
desk.*
11 (phrase) **All over** a place means everywhere in
that place, e.g. *I've been all over Austria.*
12 **Over and above** something means in addition
to it.
13 If something happens **over and over again**, it
happens many times, e.g. *I read it over and over
again.*
14 (noun) In cricket, an over is a set of six balls
bowled by a bowler from the same end of the
pitch.

over-
(prefix) to too great an extent or too much, e.g.

*an overconfident young man... My mother had
overprotected me.*

overabundance, overabundances
(noun) An overabundance of something is too
much of it.

overact, overacts, overacting, overacted
(verb) If you overact, you perform your part in
an exaggerated manner.

overage
(adjective) beyond the correct or required age.

overall, overalls
1 (adjective and adverb) Overall means taking
into account all the parts or aspects of
something, e.g. *The overall impression was of a
smoky industrial city... Overall, the prospects
are good.*
2 (plural noun) Overalls are a piece of clothing
that looks like trousers and a jacket combined.
You wear overalls to protect your other clothes
when you are working.
3 (noun) An overall is a piece of clothing like a
coat that you wear to protect your other clothes
when you are working.

overarm
(adverb) If you throw or hit a ball overarm, your
arm is raised above your shoulder and moves
forward and down.

overawe, overawes, overawing, overawed
(verb) If you are overawed by something, you
are very impressed by it and a little afraid of it.

overbearing
(adjective) trying to dominate other people, e.g.
her jealous, overbearing father.

overboard
1 (adverb) If you fall overboard, you fall over
the side of a ship into the water.
2 (an informal phrase) If you **go overboard**, you
are excessively enthusiastic.

**overburden, overburdens, overburdening,
overburdened**
(verb) If you are overburdened with something,
you have more of it than you can cope with.

overcast
(adjective) If it is overcast, the sky is covered by
cloud.

overcoat, overcoats
(noun) An overcoat is a thick, warm coat.

overcome, overcomes, overcoming, overcame
1 (verb) If you overcome a problem or a feeling,
you manage to deal with it or control it.
2 (adjective) If you are overcome by a feeling,
you feel it very strongly.

overcrowded
(adjective) If a place is overcrowded, there are
too many things or people in it.

overdo, overdoes, overdoing, overdid, overdone
(verb) If you overdo something, you do it too
much or in an exaggerated way, e.g. *Take some
gentle exercise, but don't overdo it.*

overdone
(adjective) If food is overdone, it has been
cooked for too long.

overdose, overdoses
(noun) An overdose is a larger dose of a drug than is safe.

overdraft
(noun) An overdraft is an amount of money that someone draws out of their bank account when they have no money in the account.

overdrawn
(adjective) If you are overdrawn, you have taken more money from your bank account than the account has in it.

overdressed
(adjective) dressed too elaborately.

overdrive
(noun) Overdrive is an extra, higher gear in a vehicle, which is used at high speeds to reduce engine wear and save petrol.

overdue
(adjective) If someone or something is overdue, they are late, e.g. *Tom is half an hour overdue... long overdue reforms.*

overestimate, overestimates, overestimating, overestimated
(verb) If you overestimate something, you think that it is bigger, more important, or better than it really is, e.g. *You are overestimating the problem.*

overflow, overflows, overflowing, overflowed, overflown
1 (verb) If a liquid overflows, it spills over the edges of its container. If a river overflows, it flows over its banks.
2 When people overflow a place, there are too many of them in it and some have to go outside.
3 If something is overflowing with things, it is full of them.
4 (noun) An overflow is a hole or pipe through which liquid can flow out of a container when it gets too full.

overgrown
(adjective) A place that is overgrown is covered with weeds because it has been neglected, e.g. *the overgrown path.*

overhang, overhangs, overhanging, overhung
1 (verb) If one thing overhangs another, it sticks out sideways above it, e.g. *a tree which overhung the lake.*
2 (noun) An overhang is a rock which sticks out over a cliff face below.

overhaul, overhauls, overhauling, overhauled
1 (verb) If you overhaul something, you examine it thoroughly and repair any faults.
2 (noun) If you give something an overhaul, you examine it and repair or improve it.

overhead, overheads
1 (adverb and adjective) Overhead means above you, e.g. *Seagulls were circling overhead.*
2 (plural noun) The overheads of a business are its regular and essential expenses.

overhear, overhears, overhearing, overheard
(verb) If you overhear someone's conversation, you hear what they are saying to someone else.

overjoyed
(adjective) extremely pleased, e.g. *Francis was overjoyed to see him.*

Similar words: jubilant, delighted, thrilled

overkill
1 (noun) You say that there is overkill when something is spoiled by being done too much, e.g. *the Media coverage amounts to overkill.*
2 Overkill is also the ability of nuclear weapons to destroy far more than would be necessary to achieve a victory.

overladen
(adjective) carrying too much.

overland
(adjective and adverb) travelling across land rather than going by sea or air, e.g. *an overland march... a trek overland.*

overlap, overlaps, overlapping, overlapped
1 (verb) If one thing overlaps another, one part of it covers part of the other thing.
2 (noun) If there is an overlap between two ideas or activities, they cover some of the same subjects or periods of time, e.g. *the overlap of responsibilities.*

overlay, overlays, overlaying, overlaid
1 (verb) To overlay something means to place something on top of it.
2 (noun) An overlay is something placed on top of another thing.

overleaf
(adverb) on the next page, e.g. *Some of the animals are illustrated overleaf.*

overload, overloads, overloading, overloaded
(verb) If you overload someone or something, you give them too much to do or to carry.

overlook, overlooks, overlooking, overlooked
1 (verb) If a building or window overlooks a place, it has a view over that place.
2 If you overlook something, you ignore it, do not notice it, or do not realize its importance, e.g. *They overlooked the enormous risks involved... I decided to overlook his unkindness.*

overlord, overlords
(noun) In the past, an overlord was a person who had power over many people.

overly
(adverb) excessively, e.g. *overly conscientious.*

overmuch
(adverb) too much, e.g. *It did not bother her overmuch.*

overnight
1 (adjective and adverb) during the night, e.g. *You can leave your bike here overnight.*
2 (adverb) sudden or suddenly, e.g. *an overnight success... The colonel became a hero overnight.*
3 (adjective) for use when you go away for one or two nights, e.g. *an overnight bag.*

overpower, overpowers, overpowering, overpowered
1 (verb) If you overpower someone, you seize them despite their struggles, because you are stronger than them.

2 If a feeling overpowers you, it affects you very strongly.
overpowering (adjective).

overprint, overprints, overprinting, overprinted
(verb) To overprint means to print on top of something which already has printing on it.

overrate, overrates, overrating, overrated
(verb) If you overrate something, you think that it is better or more important than it really is.
overrated (adjective).

overreach, overreaches, overreaching, overreached
(verb) If you overreach yourself, you try too hard to gain a particular goal, and in the end you fail.

overreact, overreacts, overreacting, overreacted
(verb) If you overreact, you react in an extreme way.

override, overrides, overriding, overrode, overridden
1 (verb) If one thing overrides other things, it is more important than them.
2 If you override someone, you change their decisions because you have more authority.

overrule, overrules, overruling, overruled
(verb) To overrule a person or their decisions means to decide that their decisions are incorrect.

Similar words: countermand, override

overrun, overruns, overrunning, overran, overrun
1 (verb) If an army overruns a country, it occupies it very quickly.
2 If animals or plants overrun a place, they spread quickly over it.
3 If an event overruns, it continues for longer than it was meant to.

overseas
1 (adjective and adverb) abroad, e.g. *an overseas market... travelling overseas.*
2 (adjective) from abroad, e.g. *overseas students.*

oversee, oversees, overseeing, oversaw, overseen
(verb) To oversee a job means to supervise it.
overseer (noun).

overshadow, overshadows, overshadowing, overshadowed
1 (verb) If one thing overshadows another, it is taller than it and so casts a shadow over it.
2 If something is overshadowed, it is made unimportant by something else that is better or more important.

overshoot, overshoots, overshooting, overshot
(verb) If you overshoot a place where you intended to stop, you go beyond it by mistake.

oversight, oversights
(noun) An oversight is something which you forget to do or fail to notice.

oversimplify, oversimplifies, oversimplifying, oversimplified
(verb) If you oversimplify something, you make it seem more simple than it really is.

oversize or **oversized**
(adjective) much bigger than usual.

oversleep, oversleeps, oversleeping, overslept
(verb) If you oversleep, you sleep for longer than you meant to.

overspill
(noun and adjective) Overspill refers to the rehousing of people from overcrowded cities in smaller towns, e.g. *Glasgow overspill... an overspill development.*

overstate, overstates, overstating, overstated
(verb) If you overstate something, you exaggerate its importance.

overstep, oversteps, overstepping, overstepped
(phrase) If you **overstep the mark**, you go too far and behave in an unacceptable way.

overt
(adjective) open and obvious, e.g. *overt hostility.*
overtly (adverb).
[from Old French *ovrir* meaning 'to open']

overtake, overtakes, overtaking, overtook, overtaken
1 (verb) If you overtake someone, you pass them because you are moving faster than them.
2 If an event overtakes you, it happens to you suddenly and unexpectedly.
3 If a feeling overtakes you, you feel it very strongly, e.g. *Utter weariness overtook me.*

overtax, overtaxes, overtaxing, overtaxed
(verb) If you are overtaxed, you are exhausted because you have done too much.

overthrow, overthrows, overthrowing, overthrew, overthrown
1 (verb) If a government is overthrown, it is removed from power by force.
2 If an idea or value is overthrown, it is replaced by another.

overtime
1 (noun) Overtime is time that someone works in addition to their normal working hours.
2 (adverb) If someone works overtime, they do work in addition to their normal working hours.

overtone, overtones
(noun) If something has overtones of an emotion or attitude, it suggests it without showing it openly, e.g. *The play has political overtones.*

overture, overtures
1 (noun) An overture is a piece of music that is the introduction to an opera or play.
2 If you make overtures to someone, you approach them because you want to start a friendly or business relationship with them.
[from Latin *apertura* meaning 'opening']

overturn, overturns, overturning, overturned
1 (verb) To overturn something means to turn it upside down or onto its side, e.g. *overturned lorries.*
2 If someone overturns a legal decision, they change it by using their higher authority.

overview, overviews
(noun) An overview of a situation is a general understanding or description of it.

overweening
(adjective; a formal word) excessive or extreme.

overweight
(adjective) too fat, and therefore unhealthy, e.g. *an overweight schoolgirl.*

overwhelm, overwhelms, overwhelming, overwhelmed
1 (verb) If you are overwhelmed by something, it affects you very strongly, e.g. *The horror of it all had overwhelmed me.*
2 If one group of people overwhelm another, they gain complete control or victory over them. **overwhelming** (adjective), **overwhelmingly** (adverb).

overwork, overworks, overworking, overworked
(verb) If you overwork, you work too hard.

overwrought (pronounced over-**rawt**)
(adjective) extremely upset, e.g. *I was tired and overwrought.*

oviduct, oviducts
(noun) The oviduct is the tube in a woman's or female animal's body along which the ova or eggs travel.
[from Latin *ovum* meaning 'egg' and *ducere* meaning 'to lead']

oviparous (pronounced oh-**vip**-par-russ)
(adjective) Animals that are oviparous produce eggs that hatch outside the mother's body. Fish, reptiles, and birds are oviparous.
[from Latin *ovum* meaning 'egg' and *parere* meaning 'to give birth']

ovulate, ovulates, ovulating, ovulated
(pronounced **ov**-yool-late)
(verb) When a woman or female animal ovulates, she produces ova or eggs from her ovary.

ovum, ova (pronounced **oh**-vum)
(noun) An ovum is a reproductive cell of a woman or female animal. The ovum is fertilized by a male sperm to produce young.
[a Latin word meaning 'egg']

owe, owes, owing, owed
1 (verb) If you owe someone money, they have lent it to you and you have not yet paid it back.
2 If you owe a quality or skill to someone, they are responsible for giving it to you, e.g. *She owed her technique entirely to his teaching.*
3 If you say that you owe someone gratitude, respect, or loyalty, you mean that they deserve it from you.
4 (phrase) **Owing to** something means because of that thing, e.g. *I was late owing to a traffic jam.*

owl, owls
(noun) Owls are birds of prey that hunt at night. They have large eyes and short, hooked beaks.

own, owns, owning, owned
1 (adjective) If something is your own, it belongs to you or is associated with you.
2 (phrase) **On your own** means alone, e.g. *She lived on her own.*
3 If you **get your own back** on someone, you pay them back for something unpleasant that they did to you.
4 (verb) If you own something, it belongs to you.

own up
(phrasal verb) If you own up to something, you admit that you did it.

owner, owners
(noun) The owner of something is the person it belongs to.

ownership
(noun) If you have ownership of something, you own it, e.g. *The desire for home ownership.*

ox, oxen
(noun) Oxen are cattle which are used for carrying or pulling things.

Oxbridge
(noun) Oxbridge is the name given to the universities of Oxford and Cambridge, considered together.

oxide, oxides
(noun) An oxide is a compound of oxygen and another chemical element.

oxidize, oxidizes, oxidizing, oxidized; also spelled oxidise.
(verb) When a substance oxidizes, it changes chemically by reacting with oxygen. **oxidation** (noun).

oxtail, oxtails
(noun) Oxtail is the skinned tail of an ox, which is used in making soups and stews.

oxygen
(noun) Oxygen is a chemical element in the form of a colourless gas. It makes up about 21% of the Earth's atmosphere. All animals and plants need oxygen to live, and things cannot burn without it. Oxygen's atomic number is 8 and its symbol is O.

oxygenate, oxygenates, oxygenating, oxygenated (pronounced **ok**-sij-jin-ate)
(verb) To oxygenate something means to mix or dissolve oxygen into it, e.g. *oxygenated water.*

oxygen tent, oxygen tents
(noun) An oxygen tent is a transparent tent placed over a patient into which oxygen is pumped in order to help the patient to breathe.

oyster, oysters
(noun) Oysters are large, flat shellfish. Some oysters can be eaten, and others produce pearls.
[from Greek *ostrakon* meaning 'shell']

oystercatcher, oystercatchers
(noun) Oystercatchers are large black-and-white wading birds with long red bills with which they catch and eat shellfish and worms.

oz an abbreviation for 'ounces'.

ozone
(noun) Ozone is a form of oxygen that is poisonous and has a strong smell. There is a layer of ozone high above the Earth's surface that absorbs ultraviolet rays from the sun.
[from Greek *ozein* meaning 'smell']

P

p
1 (noun) p is an abbreviation for 'pence'.
2 p is also a written abbreviation for 'page'. The plural is pp.

p.a.
p.a. means 'per year'. It is a written abbreviation for the Latin expression 'per annum', e.g. *salary starting at £8,500 p.a.*

PA, PA's
(noun) A PA is someone who does secretarial and administrative work for an important person. PA is an abbreviation for 'personal assistant'.

pace, paces, pacing, paced
1 (noun) The pace of something is the speed at which it moves or happens.
2 A pace is a step; also used as a measurement of distance.
3 (verb) If you pace up and down, you continually walk around because of anxiety or impatience.
[from Latin *passus* meaning 'a step']

pacemaker, pacemakers
(noun) A pacemaker is a small electronic device that controls someone's heartbeat. It is fitted in a special operation.

pachyderm, pachyderms (pronounced pak-kid-erm)
(noun) Pachyderms are a group of large thick-skinned animals. Elephants, rhinoceroses, and hippopotamuses are all pachyderms.
[from Greek *pakhus* meaning 'thick' and *derma* meaning 'skin']

Pacific (pronounced pas-**sif**-ik)
(noun) The Pacific is the ocean separating North and South America from Asia and Australia.

pacifist, pacifists
(noun) A pacifist is someone who is completely opposed to all violence and war.
pacifism (noun).
[from Latin *pax* meaning 'peace' and *facere* meaning 'to make']

pacify, pacifies, pacifying, pacified
(verb) If you pacify someone who is angry, you calm them.
pacification (noun), **pacifier** (noun).

Similar words: placate, mollify, conciliate, appease

---

pack, packs, packing, packed
1 (verb) If you pack, you put things neatly into a suitcase, bag, or box.
2 If people pack into a place, it becomes crowded with them.
3 (noun) A pack is a bag or rucksack carried on your back.
4 A pack of something is a packet or collection of it, e.g. *a pack of cigarettes.*
5 A pack of playing cards is a complete set.
6 A pack of dogs or wolves is a group of them.

7 (phrase) If you **send someone packing**, you send them away, perhaps angrily.

pack in
(phrasal verb; an informal use) If you pack something in, you stop doing it.

pack up
1 (phrasal verb; an informal use) If you pack up, you stop what you are doing.
2 If a machine packs up, it breaks down and stops working.

package, packages
1 (noun) A package is a small parcel.
2 A package is also a set of proposals to be considered as a single unit.
3 In computing, a package is a set of programs that allow the user to carry out several related operations.
packaged (adjective).

package holiday, package holidays
(noun) A package holiday is a complete holiday, including travel, that is bought from a travel company.

packaging
(noun) Packaging is the container or wrapping in which an item is sold or sent.

packed
(adjective) very full, e.g. *The room was absolutely packed.*

packet, packets
1 (noun) A packet is a thin cardboard box or paper container in which something is sold.
2 A packet or packet boat is a boat that transports goods, mail, or people on a short fixed route.

pack ice
(noun) Pack ice is a mass of floating ice consisting of smaller pieces packed together.

pact, pacts
(noun) A pact is a formal agreement or treaty.

pad, pads, padding, padded
1 (noun) A pad is a thick, soft piece of material.
2 (verb) If you pad something, you put a pad inside it or over it to protect it or change its shape.
3 (noun) The pads of an animal such as a cat or dog are the soft, fleshy underparts of its paws.
4 In cricket, pads are long pieces of soft material attached to the front of a batsman's or wicketkeeper's legs for protection.
5 (verb) If you pad around, you walk softly.
6 (noun) A pad of paper is a number of pieces of paper fixed together at one end.
7 A pad is also a flat surface from which helicopters take off or rockets are launched.
8 (an informal use) Someone's pad is the place where they live.
padding (noun).

paddle, paddles, paddling, paddled
1 (noun) A paddle is a short pole with a broad blade at one or both ends, used to move a small boat or a canoe.
2 (verb) If someone paddles a boat, they move it using a paddle.
3 If you paddle, you walk in shallow water.

paddle steamer, paddle steamers
(noun) A paddle steamer is a boat with large revolving wheels at each side powered by a steam engine. The wheels have flat boards attached to them, which push the boat through the water.

paddock, paddocks
(noun) A paddock is a small field.

paddy, paddies
1 (noun) A paddy or paddy field is an area in which rice is grown.
2 (an informal use) Someone who is in a paddy is angry or upset.

padlock, padlocks, padlocking, padlocked
1 (noun) A padlock is a detachable lock with a U-shaped bar that pivots at one end and snaps into the lock at the other.
2 (verb) If you padlock something, you lock it with a padlock.

padre, padres (pronounced **pah**-dray)
(noun) A padre is a priest, especially a chaplain to the armed forces.
[from Italian or Spanish *padre* meaning 'father']

paediatrician, paediatricians (pronounced pee-dee-ya-**trish**-n); also spelled **pediatrician.**
(noun) A paediatrician is a doctor who specializes in treating children.
[from Greek *pais* meaning 'child' and *iatros* meaning 'physician']

paediatrics or **pediatrics** (pronounced pee-dee-ya-**triks**)
(noun) Paediatrics is the area of medicine which deals with children's illnesses and diseases.
paediatric (adjective).

paeony another spelling of **peony.**

pagan, pagans (pronounced **pay**-gan)
1 (adjective) involving beliefs and worship outside the main religions of the world.
2 (noun) A pagan is someone who believes in a pagan religion.

page, pages, paging, paged
1 (noun) A page is one side of one of the pieces of paper in a book or magazine; also the sheet of paper itself.
2 (verb) To page someone means to call their name out on a loudspeaker system to give them a message.
3 (noun) In medieval times, a page was a young boy servant who was learning to be a knight.
4 A page is also a small boy who is one of the bride's attendants at a wedding.

pageant, pageants (pronounced **paj**-jent)
(noun) A pageant is a grand, colourful show or parade, especially one with a historical theme.
pageantry (noun).
[from Latin *pagina* meaning 'scene of a play']

paginate, paginates, paginating, paginated
(verb) To paginate a book or document means to number the pages in sequence.
pagination (noun).

pagoda, pagodas
(noun) A pagoda is a tall temple in China, Japan, and South-East Asia, elaborately decorated and having many storeys.

pail, pails
(noun) A pail is a bucket.

pain, pains, paining, pained
1 (noun) Pain is an unpleasant feeling of physical hurt or deep unhappiness.
2 (verb) If something pains you, it makes you very unhappy.
3 (phrase) If you **take pains** to do something, you are careful to do it properly.
4 (noun; an informal use) If you say that someone is a pain, you mean they are a nuisance.
painless (adjective), **painlessly** (adverb).
[from Latin *poena* meaning 'punishment']

Similar words: (sense 1) ache, hurt, pang, twinge

painful
(adjective) causing emotional or physical pain.
painfully (adverb).

painkiller, painkillers
(noun) A painkiller is a drug that relieves pain.

painstaking
(adjective) very careful and thorough.

paint, paints, painting, painted
1 (noun) Paint is a coloured liquid used to decorate buildings, or to make a picture.
2 (verb) If you paint something or paint a picture of it, you make a picture of it using paint.
3 When you paint something such as a wall, you cover it with paint.
painter (noun), **painting** (noun).

painter, painters
(noun) A painter is a rope attached to the bow of a small boat for tying it up.

pair, pairs, pairing, paired
1 (noun) You refer to two things as a pair when they are of the same type or do the same thing.
2 You use pair when referring to certain objects which have two main matching parts, e.g. *a pair of scissors.*
3 (verb) When people pair off, they become grouped in pairs.
4 If you pair up with someone, you agree to do something together.

pajamas another spelling of **pyjamas.**

Pakistani, Pakistanis (pronounced pah-kiss-**tah**-nee)
1 (adjective) belonging or relating to Pakistan.
2 (noun) A Pakistani is someone who comes from Pakistan.

pal, pals
(noun; an informal word) Your pal is your friend.

palace, palaces
(noun) A palace is a large, grand house, especially the official residence of a king or queen, or bishop.

palaeolithic (pronounced pal-lee-oh-**lith**-ik)
(adjective) belonging or relating to the period
about 2.5 to 3 million years ago when primitive
man emerged and was making unpolished
chipped stone tools.
[from Greek *palaios* meaning 'old' and *lithos*
meaning 'stone']

palaeontology (pronounced
pal-lee-on-**tol**-loj-ee)
(noun) Palaeontology is the study of fossils.

palatable
(adjective) Palatable food tastes pleasant.

palate, palates (pronounced **pall**-lat)
1 (noun) Your palate is the top of the inside of
your mouth.
2 Someone's palate is their ability to judge good
food and wine.

palatial (pronounced pal-**lay**-shal)
(adjective) large and splendid like a palace.

palaver (pronounced pal-**la**-ver)
(noun) Palaver is unnecessary fuss and bother.
[from Portuguese *palavra* meaning 'to talk']

pale, paler, palest
(adjective) rather white and without much
colour or brightness.

Palestinian, Palestinians
(noun) A Palestinian is an Arab from the region
formerly called Palestine situated between the
River Jordan and the Mediterranean.

palette, palettes
(noun) A palette is a flat piece of wood on which
an artist mixes colours.

palette knife, palette knives
(noun) A palette knife is a knife with a broad
flexible blade, used in cookery.

palindrome, palindromes
(noun) A palindrome is a word or phrase that is
the same whether you read it forwards or
backwards; for example the word 'refer'.

palings
(plural noun) Palings are a fence made of a series
of long, narrow, upright posts.
[from Latin *palus* meaning 'stake']

palisade, palisades
(noun) A palisade is a fence of upright posts to
protect people from attack.

pall, palls, palling, palled (rhymes with **fall**)
1 (verb) If something palls, it becomes
uninteresting or tedious, e.g. *a delight that never
palls... History began to pall on me.*
2 (noun) A pall of smoke is a thick cloud of it.
3 A pall is a cloth covering a coffin.

pallbearer, pallbearers
(noun) At a funeral, the pallbearers are the
people who help to carry the coffin.

pallet, pallets
1 (noun) A pallet is a narrow bed or straw
mattress.
2 A pallet is also a wooden platform on which
goods are stacked to be moved by a fork-lift
truck.
[sense 1 is from French *paille* meaning 'straw';

sense 2 is from Old French *pallette* meaning
'little spade']

palliative, palliatives (pronounced **pal**-lee-a-tiv)
(noun) A palliative is a drug or treatment that
relieves suffering without treating the cause.

pallid
(adjective) unnaturally pale.

pallor
(noun) Pallor is an unnatural paleness in
someone's face.

palm, palms, palming, palmed
1 (noun) A palm or palm tree is a tropical tree
with no branches and a crown of long leaves.
2 The palm of your hand is the flat surface
which your fingers bend towards.
3 (verb; an informal use) If you palm something
off on someone, you get them to accept it as a
way of getting rid of it.

palmate (pronounced **pal**-mate)
(adjective; a technical word) having five
segments that spread out from a central point,
e.g. *palmate leaves.*

palmistry (pronounced **pahm**-miss-tree)
(noun) Palmistry is the study of the lines on
people's hands to discover their future or their
characteristics.

Palm Sunday
(noun) Palm Sunday is the Sunday before Easter.

palpable
(adjective) obvious and easily sensed.
palpably (adverb).
[from Latin *palpabilis* meaning 'able to be
touched']

palpitate, palpitates, palpitating, palpitated
(verb) To palpitate means to tremble or beat
irregularly.
palpitation (noun).
[from Latin *palpitare* meaning 'to throb']

palsy (pronounced **pawl**-zee)
(noun; an old-fashioned word) Palsy is an illness
resulting in paralysis.

paltry (pronounced **pawl**-tree)
(adjective) A paltry sum of money is a very small
amount.

Similar words: worthless, trifling, wretched, sorry

pampas
(noun) The pampas is the area of extensive
grassland in South America.

pampas grass
(noun) Pampas grass is a kind of tall grass with
long feathery flowers.

pamper, pampers, pampering, pampered
(verb) If you pamper someone, you give them too
much kindness and comfort.

pamphlet, pamphlets
(noun) A pamphlet is a very thin book in paper
covers giving information about something.

pan, pans, panning, panned
1 (noun) A pan is a round metal container with a
long handle, used for cooking things in on top of
a cooker.

2 The pan on a set of scales is the dish for holding the substance to be weighed.
3 (verb) When a film camera pans, it moves in a wide sweep.
4 If someone pans for gold, they search for it in a river by washing mud or sand in a shallow metal dish.
5 (an informal use) To pan something means to criticize it strongly.

panacea, panaceas (pronounced pan-nass-**see**-ah)
(noun) A panacea is something that is supposed to cure everything.
[from Greek *panakeia* meaning 'healing everything']

panache (pronounced pan-**nash**)
(noun) Something that is done with panache is done confidently and stylishly.

pancake, pancakes
(noun) A pancake is a thin, flat round of cooked batter.

pancreas, pancreases (pronounced **pang**-kree-ass)
(noun) The pancreas is an organ in the body situated behind the stomach. It produces insulin and enzymes that help with digestion.

panda, pandas
(noun) A panda or giant panda is a large animal rather like a bear that lives in China. It has black fur with large patches of white.

panda car, panda cars
(noun) A panda car is a police patrol car.

pandemonium (pronounced pan-dim-**moan**-ee-um)
(noun) Pandemonium is a state of noisy confusion.
[from *Pandemonium*, the capital of Hell in Milton's 'Paradise Lost']

pander, panders, pandering, pandered
(verb) If you pander to someone, you do everything they want.

p & p a written abbreviation for 'postage and packing'.

pane, panes
(noun) A pane is a flat sheet of glass in a window or door.

panel, panels
1 (noun) A panel is a small group of people who are chosen to do something, e.g. *He was on the panel for 'Any Questions'*.
2 A panel is also a flat piece of wood forming part of a larger object, e.g. *door panels*.
3 A control panel is a surface containing switches and instruments to operate a machine.
panelled (adjective).

panelling
(noun) Panelling consists of rectangular pieces of wood covering an inside wall.

panellist, panellists
(noun) A panellist is a person who is part of a panel of people and speaks in public.

pang, pangs
(noun) A pang is a sudden strong feeling of sadness or pain.

panic, panics, panicking, panicked
1 (noun) Panic is an overwhelming feeling of fear or anxiety.
2 (verb) If you panic, you become so afraid or anxious that you cannot act sensibly.

panic-stricken
(adjective) unable to act sensibly because of fear or anxiety.

pannier, panniers
(noun) A pannier is one of two bags or baskets in which things are carried on either side of a bicycle or an animal.
[from French *panier* meaning 'basket']

panoply
(noun) A panoply of things is a magnificent collection or array of them.

panorama, panoramas
(noun) A panorama is an extensive view over a wide area of land.
panoramic (adjective).

pansy, pansies
(noun) A pansy is a small garden flower with large round petals.

pant, pants, panting, panted
(verb) If you pant, you breathe quickly and loudly through your mouth.

pantaloons
(plural noun) Pantaloons are baggy trousers gathered at the ankle.

pantechnicon, pantechnicons (pronounced pan-**tek**-nik-kon)
(noun) A pantechnicon is a large van used for moving equipment or furniture.

pantheism (pronounced **panth**-ee-izm)
(noun) Pantheism is the belief that God is in everything in nature and the universe.

panther, panthers
(noun) A panther is a large wild animal belonging to the cat family, especially the black leopard.

pantomime, pantomimes
(noun) A pantomime is a musical play, usually based on a fairy story and performed at Christmas.

pantry, pantries
(noun) A pantry is a small room where food is kept.
[from Old French *paneterie* meaning 'bread store']

pants
1 (plural noun) Pants are a piece of underwear with holes for your legs and elastic around the waist or hips.
2 In American English, pants are trousers.

pap
(noun) Pap is soft or liquid food for babies or invalids.

papacy (pronounced **pay**-pas-ee)
(noun) The papacy is the position and authority of the Pope.
papal (adjective).

papaya, papayas
(noun) A papaya is a fruit with sweet yellow flesh that grows in the West Indies.

paper, papers, papering, papered
1 (noun) Paper is a material made from wood pulp and used for writing on or wrapping things.
2 A paper is a newspaper.
3 (plural noun) Papers are official documents, for example, a passport, for identification.
4 (noun) A paper is part of a written examination.
5 A paper is also an article on a particular subject presented at a conference or in a journal.
6 (verb) If you paper a wall, you put wallpaper on it.
[from *papyrus*, the plant from which paper was made in ancient Egypt, Greece, and Rome]

Similar words: (sense 5) report, thesis, treatise, dissertation, article

paperback, paperbacks
(noun) A paperback is a book with a thin cardboard cover.

paperclip, paperclips
(noun) A paperclip is a small piece of bent wire, used to fasten papers together.

paperknife, paperknives
(noun) A paperknife is an object like a blunt knife, used for opening envelopes.

paperweight, paperweights
(noun) A paperweight is a small, heavy object placed on papers to keep them in place.

paperwork
(noun) Paperwork is the part of a job that involves dealing with letters, reports, and records.

papier-mâché (pronounced pap-yay **mash**-shay)
(noun) Papier-mâché is a hard substance made from mashed wet paper mixed with glue and moulded when moist to make things such as bowls and ornaments.
[from French *papier-mâché* meaning literally 'chewed paper']

paprika
(noun) Paprika is a red powdered pepper made from capsicums. It is used for flavouring in cooking.
[a Hungarian word]

papyrus (pronounced pap-**eye**-russ)
(noun) Papyrus was a type of paper made in ancient Egypt, Greece, and Rome from the stems of a tall water plant which is also called papyrus.

par
1 (phrase) Something that is **on a par** with something else is similar in quality or amount.
2 Something that is **below par** or **under par** is below its normal standard.
3 (noun) In golf, par is the number of strokes which it is thought a good player should take for a hole or all the holes on a particular golf course.
[from Latin *par* meaning 'equal']

parable, parables
(noun) A parable is a short story which makes a moral or religious point.

parabola, parabolas (pronounced par-**rab**-bol-la)
(noun) A parabola is a regular curve like the path of something that is thrown up in the air and comes down in a different place.
parabolic (adjective).

parachute, parachutes (pronounced **par**-rash-oot)
(noun) A parachute is a circular piece of fabric attached by lines to a person or package to enable them to fall safely to the ground from an aircraft.
parachuting (noun).

parade, parades, parading, paraded
1 (noun) A parade is a line of people or vehicles standing or moving together as a display.
2 (verb) When people parade, they walk together in a formal group as a display.

Paradise
(noun) According to some religions, Paradise is a wonderful place where good people go when they die.
[from Greek *paradeisos* meaning 'garden']

paradox, paradoxes
(noun) Something that is a paradox contains two ideas that seem to contradict each other.
paradoxical (adjective).

paraffin
(noun) Paraffin is a strong-smelling liquid obtained during the manufacture of petroleum. It is used as a fuel and as a solvent.

paragliding
(noun) Paragliding is the sport of being suspended from a parachute and towed along by a boat at high speed.

paragon, paragons
(noun) If you describe someone as a paragon, you mean that their behaviour is perfect in some way, e.g. *He was a paragon of honesty.*

paragraph, paragraphs
(noun) A paragraph is a section of a piece of writing. Paragraphs begin on a new line.

parakeet, parakeets
(noun) A parakeet is a small parrot with a long tail.

parallel, parallels, paralleling or **parallelling, paralleled** or **parallelled**
1 (noun) Something that is a parallel to something else has similar features to it.
2 (adjective) If two lines are parallel, they are the same distance apart along the whole of their length.
3 A parallel event or situation happens at the same time as another one or is similar to it.
4 (verb) If something parallels something else, it is as good as or similar to it.
[from Greek *parallēlos* meaning 'alongside one another']

parallelogram, parallelograms
(noun) A parallelogram is a four-sided shape in which each side is parallel to the opposite side.

paralyse, paralyses, paralysing, paralysed
(verb) If something paralyses you, it causes loss of feeling and movement in your body.

Similar words: immobilize, incapacitate, petrify, freeze, numb, transfix

paralysis (pronounced par-**ral**-liss-iss)
(noun) Paralysis is loss of the power to move.

paralytic, paralytics
(noun) A paralytic is someone who has paralysis.

paramedic, paramedics (pronounced par-ram-**med**-dik)
(noun) A paramedic is a person who does some types of medical work.

parameter, parameters (pronounced par-**ram**-met-ter)
(noun) A parameter is a factor or limit which affects the way something is done.

paramilitary
(noun) A paramilitary organization has a military structure but is not the official army of a country.

paramount
(adjective) more important than anything else.

paranoia (pronounced par-ran-**noy**-ah)
(noun) Paranoia is a mental illness in which someone believes that other people are trying to harm them.

paranoid (pronounced **par**-ran-noyd)
(adjective) Someone who is paranoid believes wrongly that other people are trying to harm them.

paranormal
(adjective) A paranormal event has no rational explanation and is thought to involve strange, unknown forces.

parapet, parapets
(noun) A parapet is a low wall along the edge of a bridge or roof.
[from Italian *parapetto* meaning 'chest-high wall']

paraphernalia (pronounced par-raf-fan-**ale**-yah)
(noun) Someone's paraphernalia consists of all their belongings or equipment.
[from Latin *parapherna* meaning 'personal property of a married woman']

paraphrase, paraphrases, paraphrasing, paraphrased
1 (noun) A paraphrase of a piece of writing or speech is the same thing said in a different way.
2 (verb) If you paraphrase what someone has said, you express it in a different way.

Similar words: (sense 2) reword, rephrase, restate

paraplegia (pronounced par-rap-**lee**-jya)
(noun) Paraplegia is paralysis of the lower half of the body.
paraplegic (noun and adjective).

parapsychology (pronounced par-rass-eye-**kol**-loj-ee)
Parapsychology is the study of unusual mental abilities such as telepathy that cannot be explained scientifically.

parasite, parasites
(noun) A parasite is a small animal or plant that lives on or inside a larger animal or plant.
parasitic (adjective).
[from Greek *parasitos* meaning 'someone who eats at someone else's table']

parasol, parasols
(noun) A parasol is an object like an umbrella that provides shelter from the sun.

paratroops or **paratroopers**
(plural noun) Paratroops are soldiers trained to be dropped by parachute.

parboil, parboils, parboiling, parboiled
(verb) If you parboil vegetables, you boil them until they are partly cooked.

parcel, parcels, parcelling, parcelled
1 (noun) A parcel is something wrapped up in paper.
2 (verb) If you parcel something up, you make it into a parcel.
3 If you parcel something out, you distribute it among several people.

parched
1 (adjective) If the ground is parched, it is very dry and in need of water.
2 If you are parched, you are very thirsty.

parchment
(noun) Parchment is thick yellowish paper of very good quality. Parchment was originally made from the dried skin of a sheep or goat.

pardon, pardons, pardoning, pardoned
1 You say **pardon** or **beg your pardon** to express surprise or apology, or when you have not heard what someone has said.
2 (verb) If you pardon someone, you forgive them for doing something wrong.

pardonable
(adjective) If you describe someone's bad behaviour as pardonable, you mean that you understand why they did it and think that they should be forgiven.

Similar words: excusable, forgivable, venial

pare, pares, paring, pared
1 (verb) When you pare fruit or vegetables, you cut off the skin.
2 To pare something means to reduce the amount of it, e.g. *This means paring food budgets.*

parent, parents
(noun) Your parents are your father and mother.
parental (adjective).

parentage
(noun) A person's parentage is their parents and ancestors.

parenthesis, parentheses (pronounced par-**renth**-iss-iss)
1 (noun) A parenthesis is a phrase or remark

inside brackets, dashes, or commas that is inserted into a piece of writing or speech.
2 Parentheses are a pair of brackets put round a word or phrase.
parenthetical (adjective).

par excellence (pronounced par ek-sel-**lons**)
You say par excellence to emphasize that something is the best possible example of its kind, e.g. *He is a lexicographer par excellence.*

pariah, pariahs (pronounced par-**eye**-ah)
(noun) A pariah is someone who is disliked and rejected by other people.

parish, parishes
(noun) A parish is an area with its own church and clergyman, and often its own elected council.

parishioner, parishioners
(noun) A clergyman's parishioners are the people who live in his parish and attend his church.

parity
(noun; a formal word) If there is parity between things, they are equal.
[from Latin *par* meaning 'equal']

park, parks, parking, parked
1 (noun) In a town, a park is a public area with grass and trees.
2 A park is also a private area of grass and trees around a large country house.
3 (verb) When someone parks a vehicle, they drive it into a position where it can be left.
parked (adjective), **parking** (noun).
[from Latin *parricus* meaning 'enclosure']

parka, parkas
(noun) A parka is a jacket with a quilted lining and fur round the hood.

parking meter, parking meters
(noun) A parking meter is a machine beside a parking space in which you put coins to pay for parking.

Parkinson's disease
(noun) Parkinson's disease is a disease that causes a person's limbs to shake and become uncontrollable. It is named after the surgeon James Parkinson, who first described it.

Parkinson's law
(noun) Parkinson's law is the idea that work expands to fill the amount of time available. It is named after C.N. Parkinson, who formulated it.

parlance
(noun; a formal word) A parlance is a way of speaking or type of language, e.g. *In common parlance, that's having your cake and eating it.*

parliament, parliaments
(noun) A country's parliament is the group of elected representatives who make its laws.
parliamentary (adjective).

parlour, parlours
(noun; an old-fashioned word) A parlour is a sitting room.
[from Old French *parleur* meaning 'room for talking to visitors (in a convent)']

parlous
(adjective; a formal word) Something that is in a parlous state is in a very bad state or condition.

parochial (pronounced par-**roe**-key-yal)
(adjective) concerned only with local matters.

parody, parodies, parodying, parodied
1 (noun) A parody is an amusing imitation of the style of an author or of a familiar situation.
2 (verb) If you parody something, you make a parody of it.

Similar words: (sense 1) send-up, take-off, spoof

parole
(noun) When prisoners are given parole, they are released early on condition that they behave well.
[from French *parole d'honneur* meaning 'word of honour']

paroxysm, paroxysms (pronounced par-rok-sizm)
(noun; a formal word) A paroxysm of rage or jealousy is a sudden strong feeling of it.

parquet (pronounced **par**-kay)
(noun) A parquet floor is made of small rectangular blocks of wood.

parrot, parrots
1 (noun) A parrot is a brightly coloured tropical bird with a curved beak.
2 (phrase) If you learn or repeat something **parrot fashion**, you do it accurately without understanding it or thinking about what it means.

parry, parries, parrying, parried
1 (verb) If you parry a question, you cleverly avoid answering it.
2 If you parry a blow, you push aside your attacker's arm to defend yourself.

parse, parses, parsing, parsed
(verb) If you parse a sentence, you decide the grammatical type of each word and clause.

parsimonious
(adjective; a formal word) very unwilling to spend money.

parsley
(noun) Parsley is a herb with curly leaves used for flavouring in cooking.

parsnip, parsnips
(noun) A parsnip is a long, pointed, cream-coloured root vegetable.

parson, parsons
(noun) A parson is a vicar or other clergyman.

part, parts, parting, parted
1 (noun) A part of something is one of the pieces, sections, or aspects that it consists of.
2 A part in a play is one of the roles in it, played by an actor or actress.
3 Someone's part in something is their involvement in it, e.g. *He was arrested for his part in the demonstration.*
4 (phrase) If you **take part** in an activity, you do it together with other people.
5 Something that is **part and parcel** of something else is an essential part of it.

6 (verb) If things that are next to each other part, they move away from each other.
7 If two people part, they leave each other.
[from Latin *partire* meaning 'to divide']

Similar words: (sense 1) component, element, member, constituent

partake, partakes, partaking, partook, partaken
(verb; a formal word) If you partake of food, you eat it.

partial
1 (adjective) not complete or whole, e.g. *I could give it only partial support... partial victory.*
2 liking something very much, e.g. *The vicar is very partial to roast pheasant.*
3 supporting one side in a dispute, rather than being fair and unbiased.
partially (adverb), **partiality** (noun).

participate, participates, participating, participated
(verb) If you participate in an activity, you take part in it.
participant (noun), **participation** (noun).

Similar words: partake, join in, share, engage in

participle, participles
(noun) In grammar, a participle is a form of a verb used in compound tenses and often as an adjective. English has two participles: the past participle and the present participle.

particle, particles
(noun) A particle is a very small piece of something.

particular, particulars
1 (adjective) relating or belonging to only one thing or person, e.g. *Each person had their own particular criticism.*
2 especially great or intense, e.g. *my particular concern.*
3 Someone who is particular demands high standards and is not easily satisfied.
4 (plural noun) Particulars are facts or details.
particularly (adverb).

parting, partings
1 (noun) A parting is an occasion when one person leaves another.
2 When someone combs two parts of their hair in opposite directions, the line dividing the parts is called a parting.

partisan, partisans
1 (adjective) favouring or supporting one person or group.
2 (noun) A partisan is a member of an unofficial armed force fighting to free their country from enemy occupation.

partition, partitions, partitioning, partitioned
1 (noun) A partition is a screen separating one part of a room or vehicle from another.
2 Partition is the division of a country into independent areas.
3 (verb) To partition something means to divide it into separate parts.

partly
(adverb) to some extent but not completely.

partner, partners, partnering, partnered
1 (noun) Someone's partner is the person they are married to or are having a sexual relationship with.
2 Your partner is the person you are doing something with, for example in a dance or a game.
3 Business partners are joint owners of their business.
4 (verb) If you partner someone, you are their partner for a game or social occasion.
partnership (noun).

part of speech, parts of speech
(noun) A part of speech is a particular grammatical class of word.

partook the past tense of **partake.**

partridge, partridges
(noun) A partridge is a brown game bird with a round body and a short tail.

part-time
(adjective) involving work for only a part of each normal working day or week.

party, parties
1 (noun) A party is a private social event held for people to enjoy themselves.
2 A political party is an organization whose members share the same political beliefs and campaign for election to government.
3 A party of people is a group who are doing something together.
4 (a formal use) A party in a legal agreement or dispute is one of the people involved.
5 (phrase) Someone who is **a party to** an agreement or activity is involved and partly responsible.
6 (adjective) A party wall or party fence between two houses is shared by them.

party line, party lines
1 (noun) The party line is the official view taken by a political party.
2 A party line is a telephone line shared by two or more houses.

pass, passes, passing, passed
1 (verb) To pass something means to move past it.
2 To pass in a particular direction means to move in that direction, e.g. *Slabs of toffee pass along the conveyor belt.*
3 If you pass something to someone, you hand it to them or transfer it to them.
4 If you pass a period of time doing something, you spend it that way, e.g. *The men pass their lives farming small plots of land.*
5 When a period of time passes, it happens and finishes.
6 If you pass a test, you are considered to be of an acceptable standard.
7 When a new law or proposal is passed, it is formally approved.
8 When a judge passes sentence on someone, the judge states what the punishment will be.

9 If you pass the ball in a ball game, you throw, kick, or hit it to another player in your team.
10 (noun) A pass in a ball game is the transfer of the ball to another player in the same team.
11 A pass is an official document that allows you to go somewhere.
12 A mountain pass is a narrow route between mountains.

Similar words: (sense 1) outstrip, overtake, exceed (sense 5) lapse, go by, elapse

pass away or **pass on**
(phrasal verb) Someone who has passed away has died.

pass out
(phrasal verb) If someone passes out, they faint.

pass up
(phrasal verb) If you pass up an opportunity, you do not take advantage of it.

passable
(adjective) of an acceptable standard.

passage, passages
1 (noun) A passage is a long, narrow corridor or space that allows movement between two areas.
2 A passage in a book or piece of music is a section of it.
3 Passage is the act of passing or moving, e.g. *the passage of gas through liquid.*
4 A passage is also a journey by ship.
[from Old French *passage* meaning 'act of passing']

passbook, passbooks
(noun) A building society passbook is a book containing a record of deposits and withdrawals.

passé (pronounced **pas**-say)
(adjective) no longer fashionable.

passenger, passengers
(noun) A passenger is a person travelling in a vehicle, aircraft, or ship.

passer-by, passers-by
(noun) A passer-by is someone who is walking past someone or something.

passing
(adjective) lasting only for a short time. e.g. *passing fashions.*

Similar words: fleeting, short-lived, transient, transitory, ephemeral, temporary

passion, passions
(noun) Passion is a very strong feeling, especially of sexual attraction.

Similar words: intensity, force, vehemence, fire, warmth, lust

passionate
(adjective) expressing very strong feelings about something.

Similar words: amorous, hot-blooded, fiery, impassioned, intense, vehement

passion fruit
(noun) A passion fruit is the small egg-shaped fruit of some kinds of tropical flowering plants.

passive
1 (adjective) remaining calm and showing no feeling when provoked.
2 (noun) In grammar, the passive or passive voice is the form of the verb in which the recipient of an action becomes the grammatical subject of the sentence. For example, the passive of *The committee rejected your application* is *Your application was rejected by the committee.*
passively (adverb), **passivity** (noun).

Similar words: (sense 1) inactive, submissive, compliant

Passover
(noun) The Passover is an eight day Jewish festival held in spring.

passport, passports
1 (noun) A passport is an official identification document which you need to show when you travel abroad.
2 Something that is a passport to success is the thing that makes success possible.

password, passwords
1 (noun) A password is a secret word known to only a few people. It allows people on the same side to recognize a friend.
2 A password is also a word you need to know to get into some computer files.

past
1 (noun) The past is the period of time before the present.
2 (adjective) Past things are things that happened or existed before the present.
3 (preposition and adverb) You use past when you are telling the time, e.g. *It is ten past six.*
4 If you go past something, you move towards it and continue until you are on the other side.
5 (preposition) Something that is past a place is situated on the other side of it.

pasta
(noun) Pasta is a dried mixture of flour, eggs, and water, formed into different shapes. Spaghetti and macaroni are types of pasta.

paste, pastes, pasting, pasted
1 (noun) Paste is a soft, rather sticky mixture that can be easily spread.
2 Paste is also a glassy substance used for making imitation jewellery.
3 (verb) If you paste something onto a surface, you stick it with glue.

pastel, pastels
1 (adjective) Pastel colours are pale and soft.
2 (noun) Pastels are small sticks of coloured crayon, used for drawing pictures.

pasteurized (pronounced **past**-yoor-ized); also spelled **pasteurised**
(adjective) Pasteurized milk has been treated with a special heating process to kill bacteria. It is named after the bacteriologist Louis Pasteur, who invented the process.

pastiche, pastiches (pronounced pass-**teesh**)
(noun; a formal word) A pastiche is a work of art
that contains a mixture of styles or that copies
the style of another artist.

pastille, pastilles (pronounced **pass**-till)
(noun) A pastille is a small, soft, round sweet
with a fruit flavour.

pastime, pastimes
(noun) A pastime is a hobby or something you do
just for pleasure.

Similar words: pursuit, interest, recreation, play

pastor, pastors
(noun) A pastor is a clergyman in charge of a
congregation.
[from Latin *pastor* meaning 'shepherd']

pastoral
1 (adjective) characteristic of peaceful country
life and landscape.
2 relating to the duties of the clergy in caring for
the needs of their parishioners.

past participle, past participles
(noun) In grammar, the past participle of a verb
is the form, usually ending in 'ed' or 'en', that is
used to make some past tenses and the passive.

pastry, pastries
1 (noun) Pastry is a mixture of flour, fat, and
water, rolled flat and used for making pies.
2 A pastry is a small cake.

past tense
(noun) In grammar, the past tense is the tense of
a verb that you use mainly to refer to things that
happened or existed before the time of writing or
speaking.

pasture, pastures
(noun) Pasture is an area of grass on which farm
animals graze.

pasty, pasties
1 (adjective; rhymes with **hasty**) Someone
who is pasty looks pale and unhealthy.
2 (noun; pronounced **pass**-tee) A pasty is a
small pie containing meat and vegetables.

pat, pats, patting, patted
1 (verb) If you pat something, you tap it lightly
with your hand held flat.
2 (noun) A pat of butter is a small lump of it.
3 (adjective) A pat answer sounds as if it has
been prepared in advance.

patch, patches, patching, patched
1 (noun) A patch is a piece of material used to
cover a hole in something.
2 (verb) If you patch something, you mend it by
fixing a patch over the hole.
3 (noun) A patch is an area of a surface that is
different in appearance from the rest, e g. *a
damp patch on the ceiling.*
4 (phrase) Something that is **not a patch on**
something else is not nearly as good.

patch up
(phrasal verb) If you patch something up, you
mend it hurriedly or temporarily.

patchwork
1 (adjective) A patchwork quilt is made from
many small pieces of material sewn together.
2 (noun) Something that is a patchwork is made
up of many different parts.

patchy, patchier, patchiest
(adjective) Something that is patchy is unevenly
spread or incomplete in parts.

pâté (pronounced **pa**-tay)
(noun) Pâté is a mixture of meat, fish, or
vegetables with various flavourings, blended
into a paste and eaten cold.

patella, patellae
(noun; a medical word) Your patella is your
kneecap.

patent, patents, patenting, patented
1 (noun) A patent is an official right given to an
inventor to be the only person or company
allowed to make or sell a new product.
2 (verb) If you patent something, you obtain a
patent for it.
3 (adjective) obvious, e.g. *This is patent
nonsense.*
4 (noun) Patent or patent leather is a leather
that has been coated with a very shiny surface.
patently (adverb).

paternal
(adjective) relating to a father.
[from Latin *pater* meaning 'father']

paternity
(noun) Paternity is the state or fact of being a
father.

path, paths
1 (noun) A path is a strip of ground for people to
walk on.
2 Your path is the area ahead of you and the
direction in which you are moving.
3 The path that you take to achieve something is
the way that you do it.

pathetic
(adjective) weak, inadequate, or helpless.
pathetically (adverb).
[from Greek *pathetikos* meaning 'sensitive']

Similar words: forlorn, pitiful, pitiable, plaintive,
moving, sorry

pathogen, pathogens
(noun) A pathogen is something that causes
disease.
pathogenic (adjective).
[from Greek *pathos* meaning 'suffering' and *-gen*
meaning 'producing']

pathological
(adjective) extreme and uncontrollable, e.g. *a
pathological liar.*
pathologically (adverb).

pathology
(noun) Pathology is the study of diseases and the
way they develop.
pathological (adjective), **pathologist** (noun).

pathos (pronounced **pay**-thoss)
(noun) Pathos is a quality in literature or art
that causes great sadness or pity.

pathway, pathways
(noun) A pathway is a path.

patience
1 (noun) Patience is the ability to stay calm in a difficult or irritating situation.
2 Patience is also a card game for one player.
[from Latin *patienta* meaning 'endurance']

Similar words: tolerance, stoicism

patient, patients
1 (adjective) If you are patient, you stay calm in a difficult or irritating situation.
2 (noun) A patient is a person receiving medical treatment from a doctor or in a hospital.
patiently (adverb).

patina
(noun; a formal word) The patina of an object is the surface that it develops through time.

patio, patios
(noun) A patio is a paved area close to a house.

patois (pronounced **pat**-twah)
(noun) A patois is an unwritten regional dialect, especially in France.

patriarch, patriarchs (pronounced **pay**-tree-ark)
1 (noun) A patriarch is the male head of a family or tribe.
2 In some Christian churches, especially the Eastern Orthodox Church, a patriarch is a bishop of high rank.
patriarchal (adjective).

patrician
(adjective; a formal word) belonging to a family of high rank.

patricide, patricides (a formal word)
1 (noun) Patricide is the crime of killing your father.
2 A patricide is someone who has killed his or her father.
[from Latin *pater* meaning 'father' and *caedere* meaning 'to kill']

patriot, patriots
(noun) A patriot is someone who loves their country and feels very loyal towards it.
patriotic (adjective), **patriotism** (noun).
[from Latin *patria* meaning 'native land']

patrol, patrols, patrolling, patrolled
1 (verb) When soldiers, police, or guards patrol an area, they walk or drive around to make sure there is no trouble.
2 (noun) A patrol is a group of people patrolling an area.
[from French *patouiller* meaning 'to flounder in mud']

patron, patrons
1 (noun) A patron is a person who supports or gives money to artists, writers, or musicians.
2 The patrons of a hotel, pub, or shop are the people who use it.
patronage (noun).
[from Latin *patronus* meaning 'protector']

patronize, patronizes, patronizing, patronized;
also spelled **patronise**
1 (verb) If someone patronizes you, they treat

you kindly, but in a way that suggests that you are less intelligent than them or inferior to them.
2 If you patronize a hotel, pub, or shop, you are a customer there.
patronizing (adjective).

patron saint, patron saints
(noun) The patron saint of a group of people, place, or activity is a saint who is believed to look after them.

patter, patters, pattering, pattered
1 (verb) If something patters on a surface, it makes quick, light, tapping sounds.
2 (noun) A patter is a series of light tapping sounds.
3 The patter of a salesperson or entertainer is a fast way of talking as part of their work.

pattern, patterns
1 (noun) The pattern of something is the way it is usually done or happens.
2 A pattern is a decorative design of repeated shapes.
3 A pattern is also a diagram or shape used as a guide for making something, for example clothes.
patterned (adjective).

paucity (pronounced **paw**-sit-tee)
(noun; a formal word) If there is a paucity of something, there is not enough of it.
[from Latin *paucus* meaning 'few']

paunch, paunches
(noun) If a man has a paunch, he has a fat stomach.

pauper, paupers
(noun; an old-fashioned word) A pauper is a very poor person.
[from Latin *pauper* meaning 'poor']

pause, pauses, pausing, paused
1 (verb) If you pause, you stop what you are doing for a short time.
2 (noun) A pause is a short period when you stop what you are doing.
3 A pause is also a short period of silence.

pave, paves, paving, paved
1 (verb) When an area of ground is paved, it is covered with flat, regular blocks of stone or concrete.
2 (phrase) If something **paves the way** for a change, it creates conditions which will help it to happen.

pavement, pavements
(noun) A pavement is a surfaced path at the side of a road.
[from Latin *pavimentum* meaning 'hard floor']

pavilion, pavilions
(noun) A pavilion is a building at a sports ground where players can wash and change.
[from Old French *pavillon* meaning 'tent' or 'canopy']

paw, paws, pawing, pawed
1 (noun) The paws of an animal such as a cat or bear are its feet with claws and soft pads.
2 (verb) If an animal paws something, it hits it or scrapes at it with its paws.

pawn, pawns, pawning, pawned
1 (verb) If you pawn something, you leave it with a pawnbroker as security for a loan. If you do not pay back the money within a certain time, the item will be sold.
2 (noun) In chess, a pawn is the smallest and least valuable playing piece.
3 Someone who is a pawn is being used for someone else's advantage.

pawnbroker, pawnbrokers
(noun) A pawnbroker is a dealer who lends money in return for personal property left with him, which may be sold if the loan is not repaid on time.

pawnshop, pawnshops
(noun) A pawnshop is a pawnbroker's shop.

pawpaw, pawpaws
(noun) A pawpaw is the same as a papaya.

pay, pays, paying, paid
1 (verb) When you pay money to someone, you give it to them because you are buying something or owe it to them.
2 (noun) Someone's pay is their salary or wages.
3 (verb) If it pays to do something, it is to your advantage to do it.
4 If you pay for something that you have done, you suffer as a result.
5 If you pay attention to something, you give it your attention.
6 If you pay a visit to someone, you visit them.

Similar words: (sense 1) settle, square up

payable
1 (adjective) An amount of money that is payable has to be paid or can be paid, e.g. *Fees are payable in advance.*
2 If a cheque is made payable to you, you are the person who should receive the money.

payee, payees
(noun; a formal word) The payee of a cheque is the person to whom the money will be paid.

payload, payloads
(noun) The payload of an aircraft or vehicle is the amount that it can carry.

payment, payments
1 (noun) Payment is the act of paying money.
2 A payment is a sum of money paid.

payroll, payrolls
(noun) Someone who is on an organization's payroll is employed and paid by them.

PC, PCs
1 (noun) A PC is a police constable.
2 A PC is also a personal computer.

PE
(noun) PE is a lesson in which gymnastics or sports are taught. PE is an abbreviation for 'physical education'.

pea, peas
(noun) Peas are small round green seeds that grow in pods and are eaten as a vegetable.

peace
1 (noun) Peace is a state of undisturbed calm and quiet.
2 When a country is at peace, it is not at war.
peaceable (adjective).

Similar words: (sense 1) harmony, concord, serenity, tranquillity, quiet, calm

peaceful
(adjective) quiet, calm, and free from disturbance.
peacefully (adverb).

Similar words: serene, tranquil

peach, peaches
1 (noun) A peach is a soft, round, juicy fruit with yellow flesh and a yellow and red skin.
2 (adjective) pale pinky-orange.

peacock, peacocks
(noun) A peacock is a large bird with green and blue feathers. The male has a long tail which it can spread out in a fan.

peahen, peahens
(noun) A peahen is a female peacock.

peak, peaks, peaking, peaked
1 (noun) The peak of an activity or process is the point at which it is strongest or most successful.
2 (verb) When something peaks, it reaches its highest value or its greatest level of success.
3 (noun) The peak of a mountain is its pointed top.
4 The peak of a cap is the part that sticks out over your eyes.
peaked (adjective).

Similar words: (sense 1) acme, apex, height, zenith, pinnacle, summit

peaky, peakier, peakiest
(adjective) looking pale and rather ill.

peal, peals, pealing, pealed
1 (noun) A peal of bells is the musical sound made by bells ringing one after another.
2 (verb) When bells peal, they ring one after the other.

peanut, peanuts
1 (noun) Peanuts are small oval nuts that grow under the ground.
2 (an informal use) If you describe an amount of money as peanuts, you mean that it is very small.

pear, pears
(noun) A pear is a fruit which is narrow at the top and wide and rounded at the bottom.

pearl, pearls
(noun) A pearl is a hard, round, creamy-white object used in jewellery. Pearls grow inside the shell of an oyster.

pearl barley
(noun) Pearl barley is small grains of barley ground smooth and used in making soup.

peasant, peasants
(noun) A peasant is a person who works on the land, especially in a poor country.

peat
(noun) Peat is dark-brown decaying plant material found in cool, wet regions. In some areas it is dug up, dried, and used as fuel.

pebble, pebbles
(noun) A pebble is a smooth, round stone.

pecan, pecans (pronounced **pee**-kan)
(noun) A pecan is an edible nut that grows on trees in the southern United States.

peccadillo, peccadillos or peccadilloes
(noun; an old-fashioned word) A peccadillo is a small sin or fault.
[a Spanish word]

peck, pecks, pecking, pecked
1 (verb) If a bird pecks something, it bites at it quickly with its beak.
2 If you peck someone on the cheek, you give them a quick kiss.
3 (noun) A peck is a quick bite by a bird.
4 A peck is also a quick kiss on the cheek.

peckish
(adjective; an informal word) If you are feeling peckish, you are hungry.

pectin
(noun) Pectin is a substance found in ripe fruit. It is used in jam-making to help the jam to set.

pectoral, pectorals
(noun) Your pectorals are the large chest muscles that help you to move your shoulders and arms.
[from Latin *pectus* meaning 'chest']

peculiar
1 (adjective) strange and perhaps unpleasant.
2 relating or belonging only to a particular person or thing, e.g. *a style of decoration peculiar to the 1920's.*
peculiarly (adverb), **peculiarity** (noun).

pecuniary (pronounced pek-**yoon**-yer-ee)
(adjective; a formal word) relating to or involving money.
[from Latin *pecunia* meaning 'money']

pedal, pedals, pedalling, pedalled
1 (noun) A pedal is a control lever on a machine or vehicle that you press with your foot.
2 (verb) When you pedal a bicycle, you push the pedals round with your feet to move along.

pedant, pedants
(noun) Someone who is a pedant is too concerned with unimportant details.
pedantic (adjective).

peddle, peddles, peddling, peddled
1 (verb) Someone who peddles illegal drugs sells them.
2 Someone who peddles an idea tries to persuade people to accept it.
peddler (noun), **pedlar** (noun).

pederast, pederasts
(noun) A pederast is a man who has homosexual relations with boys.
pederasty (noun).

pedestal, pedestals
(noun) A pedestal is a base on which a statue stands.

pedestrian, pedestrians
1 (noun) A pedestrian is someone who is walking.
2 (adjective) Pedestrian means ordinary and rather dull.
[from Latin *pedester* meaning 'on foot']

pedestrian crossing, pedestrian crossings
(noun) A pedestrian crossing is a place where you can cross the road safely.

pediatrician another spelling of **paediatrician.**

pediatrics another spelling of **paediatrics.**

pedicure, pedicures
(noun) Pedicure is treatment and care of the feet.
[from Latin *pedes* meaning 'feet' and *curare* meaning 'to care for']

pedigree, pedigrees
1 (adjective) A pedigree animal is descended from a single breed and its ancestors are known and recorded.
2 (noun) Someone's pedigree is their background or ancestry.

peek, peeks, peeking, peeked
1 (verb) If you peek at something, you have a quick look at it.
2 (noun) A peek is a quick look at something.

peel, peels, peeling, peeled
1 (noun) The peel of a fruit is the skin when it has been removed.
2 (verb) When you peel fruit or vegetables, you remove the skin.
3 If a surface is peeling, it is coming off in thin layers.
peelings (plural noun).

peep, peeps, peeping, peeped
1 (verb) If you peep at something, you have a quick look at it.
2 (noun) A peep at something is a quick look.
3 (verb) If something peeps out from behind something else, a small part of it becomes visible.
4 (noun) If you have not heard a peep out of someone, they have not said anything or made any noise.

peer, peers, peering, peered
1 (verb) If you peer at something, you look at it very hard.
2 (noun) A peer is a member of the nobility.
3 Your peers are the people who are of the same age and social status as yourself.

peerage, peerages
1 (noun) The peers in a country are called the peerage.
2 A peerage is also the rank of being a peer.

peerless
(adjective) so magnificent or perfect that nothing can equal it.

peeved
(adjective; an informal word) irritated and annoyed.

Similar words: put out, riled, sore, vexed

peevish
(adjective) irritable and complaining.

Similar words: complaining, querulous, plaintive

peewit, peewits
(noun) A peewit is a black and white bird with a crested head often seen in flocks in fields.

peg, pegs, pegging, pegged
1 (noun) A peg is a plastic or wooden clip used for hanging wet clothes on a line.
2 (verb) If you peg clothes on a line, you fix them there with pegs.
3 (noun) A peg is also a hook on a wall where you can hang things.
4 (verb) If a price is pegged at a certain level, it is fixed at that level.

pejorative (pronounced pej-**jor**-ra-tive)
(adjective) A pejorative word expresses criticism.
[from Latin *pejorare* meaning 'to make worse']

pekinese or **pekingese, pekineses**
(pronounced pee-kin-**eez**)
(noun) A pekinese is a small long-haired dog with a flat nose.

pelican, pelicans
(noun) A pelican is a large water bird with a pouch beneath its beak in which it stores fish.

pelican crossing, pelican crossings
(noun) A pelican crossing is a place where you can cross the road by pressing a button to operate traffic lights.

pellet, pellets
(noun) A pellet is a small ball of paper, lead, or other material.

pelmet, pelmets
(noun) A pelmet is a long piece of wood or fabric fixed above a window to hide the curtain rail.

pelt, pelts, pelting, pelted
1 (verb) If you pelt someone with things, you throw the things violently at them.
2 If you pelt along, you run very fast.
3 (noun) A pelt is the skin and fur of an animal.

pelvis, pelvises
(noun) Your pelvis is the wide framework of bones at hip-level at the base of your spine.
pelvic (adjective).
[from Latin *pelvis* meaning 'basin']

pen, pens, penning, penned
1 (noun) A pen is a long, thin instrument used for writing with ink.
2 (verb; a literary use) If someone pens a letter or article, they write it.
3 (noun) A pen is also a small fenced area in which farm animals are kept for a short time.
4 (verb) If you are penned up, you have to remain in an uncomfortably small area.
[from Latin *penna* meaning 'feather'; pens used to be made from feathers]

penal
(adjective) relating to the punishment of criminals.

penalize, penalizes, penalizing, penalized;
also spelled **penalise**
(verb) If you are penalized, you are made to suffer some disadvantage as a punishment for something.

penalty, penalties
(noun) A penalty is a punishment or disadvantage that someone is made to suffer.

penance
(noun) If you do penance, you do something unpleasant to show that you are sorry for something wrong that you have done.

pence a plural form of **penny**.

penchant (pronounced **pon**-shon)
(noun; a formal word) If you have a penchant for something, you have a particular liking for it.

pencil, pencils
(noun) A pencil is a long thin wooden instrument with a rod of graphite in the centre, used for drawing or writing.
[from Latin *pencillus* meaning 'painter's brush']

pendant, pendants
(noun) A pendant is a piece of jewellery attached to a chain and worn round the neck.
[from French *pendre* meaning 'to hang down']

pending (a formal word)
1 (adjective) Something that is pending is waiting to be dealt with or will happen soon.
2 (preposition) Something that is done pending a future event is done until the event happens.

pendulous
(adjective; a formal word) hanging loosely downwards.

pendulum, pendulums
(noun) A pendulum in a clock is a rod with a weight at one end which swings regularly from side to side to control the clock.
[from Latin *pendere* meaning 'to hang down']

penetrate, penetrates, penetrating, penetrated
(verb) To penetrate an area that is difficult to get into means to succeed in getting into it.
penetration (noun).

penetrating
1 (adjective) loud and high-pitched, e.g. *She has a penetrating voice.*
2 having or showing the ability to gain deep understanding, e.g. *a penetrating mind.*

pen friend, pen friends
(noun) A pen friend is someone living in a different place or country whom you write to regularly, although you may never have met each other.

penguin, penguins
(noun) A penguin is a black and white bird with webbed feet and small wings like flippers. Penguins are found mainly in the Antarctic.

penicillin
(noun) Penicillin is a powerful antibiotic obtained from the fungus penicillium and used to treat infections.

peninsula, peninsulas
(noun) A peninsula is an area of land almost surrounded by water.
[from Latin *paene* + *insula* meaning 'almost an island']

penis, penises
(noun) A man's penis is the part of his body that he uses when urinating or having sexual intercourse.

penitent
(adjective) Someone who is penitent is deeply sorry for having done something wrong.
penitence (noun).

penitentiary, penitentiaries
(noun) In America, a penitentiary is a prison.

penknife, penknives
(noun) A penknife is a small knife with a blade that folds back into the handle.

pen name, pen names
(noun) A pen name is a name used by a writer instead of his or her own name.

pennant, pennants
(noun) A pennant is a triangular flag, especially one used by ships as a signal.

penniless
(adjective) Someone who is penniless has no money.

penny, pennies or pence
(noun) The penny is a unit of currency in Britain and some other countries. In Britain, a penny is worth one-hundredth of a pound.

penny-farthing, penny-farthings
(noun) A penny-farthing is an old style of bicycle with a very large front wheel and a small back wheel.

pension, pensions (pronounced **pen**-shn)
(noun) A pension is a regular sum of money paid to an old, retired, or widowed person.
[from Latin *pensio* meaning 'a payment']

pension, pensions (pronounced **pon**-see-yon)
(noun) In many European countries, a pension is a small hotel.

pensioner, pensioners
(noun) A pensioner is an old retired person receiving a pension paid by the state.

pensive
(adjective) deep in thought.
[from French *penser* meaning 'to think']

Similar words: reflective, meditative, contemplative, thoughtful, dreamy

pentagon, pentagons
(noun) A pentagon is a shape with five straight sides.
pentagonal (adjective).
[from Greek *pente* meaning 'five' and *gōnus* meaning 'angled']

pentathlon, pentathlons (pronounced pen-**tath**-lon)
(noun) A pentathlon is a sports contest in which athletes compete in five different events.
[from Greek *pente* meaning 'five' and *athlon* meaning 'contest']

penthouse, penthouses
(noun) A penthouse is a luxurious flat at the top of a building.

pent-up
(adjective) Pent-up emotions have been held back for a long time without release.

Similar words: suppressed, bottled-up

penultimate
(adjective) The penultimate thing in a series is the one before the last.
[from Latin *paene* meaning 'almost' and *ultimus* meaning 'last']

penurious (pronounced pin-**yoor**-ree-uss)
(adjective; a formal word) having hardly any possessions or money.

penury (pronounced **pen**-yoo-ree)
(noun; a formal word) Penury is great poverty.

peony, peonies (pronounced **pee**-yon-ee); also spelled **paeony**
(noun) A peony is a garden plant with large pink, white, or red flowers.

people, peoples, peopling, peopled
1 (plural noun) People are men, women, and children.
2 (noun) A people is all the men, women, and children of a particular country or race.
3 (verb) If an area is peopled by a particular group, that group of people live there.

Similar words: (sense 1) folk, persons, human beings (sense 2) nation, race, population, public, populace

pepper, peppers, peppering, peppered
1 (noun) Pepper is a hot-tasting powdered spice made from ground peppercorns and used for flavouring in cooking.
2 A pepper is a hollow green, red, or yellow vegetable, with mild, sweet-flavoured flesh.
3 (verb) If something is being peppered with a lot of small things, they are hitting it.

peppercorn, peppercorns
(noun) Peppercorns are the small dried berries of an East Indian climbing plant. They are ground to produce pepper.

peppermint, peppermints
1 (noun) Peppermint is a variety of mint.
2 Peppermints are sweets flavoured with peppermint.

pep talk, pep talks
(noun; an informal expression) A pep talk is a speech intended to encourage people.

peptic ulcer, peptic ulcers
(noun) A peptic ulcer is an ulcer occurring in a person's digestive system.

per
(preposition) Per is used to mean 'each' when expressing rates and ratios, e.g. *The rent is £200 per month... travelling at 40 miles per hour.*

perambulator, perambulators
(noun; a formal word) A perambulator is a pram.
[from Latin *perambulare* meaning 'to walk across']

per annum
(adverb) A particular amount per annum means that amount each year.
[from Latin *per annum* meaning 'each year']

per capita
(adjective) The per capita income or output is the amount earned or produced by each person.
[from Latin *per capita* meaning 'for each head']

perceive, perceives, perceiving, perceived
(verb) If you perceive something that is not obvious, you see it or realize it.

Similar words: discern, make out, distinguish

per cent
(phrase) You use **per cent** to talk about amounts as a proportion of a hundred. An amount that is 10 per cent (10%) of a larger amount is equal to 10 hundredths of the larger amount, e.g. *Sixty per cent of Americans voted against.*
[from Latin *per* meaning 'each' and *centum* meaning 'hundred']

percentage, percentages
(noun) A percentage is a fraction expressed as a particular number of hundredths, e.g. *A high percentage of school children own calculators.*

perceptible
(adjective) Something that is perceptible can be seen, e.g. *a barely perceptible flicker of light.*

perception, perceptions
1 (noun) Someone who has perception realizes or notices things that are not obvious.
2 Your perception of something or someone is your understanding of them.
3 Perception is the recognition of things using the senses, especially the sense of sight.
perceptual (adjective).

perceptive
(adjective) Someone who is perceptive realizes or notices things that are not obvious.
perceptively (adverb).

Similar words: penetrating, percipient, perspicacious, observant

perch, perches, perching, perched
1 (verb) If you perch on something, you sit on the edge of it.
2 When a bird perches on something, it stands on it.
3 (noun) A perch is a short rod for a bird to stand on.
4 A perch is also an edible freshwater fish.

perchance
(adverb; an old-fashioned literary word). Perchance means the same as perhaps.
[from French *par chance* meaning 'by chance']

percipient
(adjective; a formal word) Someone who is percipient realizes or notices things that are not obvious.

percolate, percolates, percolating, percolated
1 (verb) To percolate coffee means to make it in a percolator.
2 If something percolates somewhere, it gradually spreads or passes through.
[from Latin *per* meaning 'through' and *colare* meaning 'to strain']

percolator, percolators
(noun) A percolator is a pot in which coffee is made by circulating boiling water up a central tube and over ground coffee beans.

percussion
(noun and adjective) Percussion instruments are musical instruments that you hit to produce sounds.
percussionist (noun).

perdition
(noun; a literary word) Perdition is a state of never-ending punishment after death.

peregrine, peregrines (pronounced **per**-reg-grin)
(noun) A peregrine or peregrine falcon is a type of large falcon.

peremptory
(adjective) indicating that immediate obedience is expected, e.g. *a peremptory demand.*

perennial, perennials
1 (adjective) continually occurring or never ending, e.g. *a perennial feature in politics.*
2 (noun) A perennial is a plant that lives for several years, dying back each winter and appearing again in spring.
[from Latin *per* + *annus* meaning 'through the years']

perfect, perfects, perfecting, perfected
1 (adjective) of the highest standard and without fault, e.g. *Her work was perfect.*
2 complete or absolute, e.g. *They were perfect strangers.*
3 In English grammar, the perfect tense of a verb is formed with the present tense of 'have' and the past participle of the main verb.
4 (verb) If you perfect something, you make it as good as it can possibly be.
perfectly (adverb), **perfection** (noun).

Similar words: (sense 1) faultless, flawless, immaculate, ideal, consummate
(sense 4) refine, polish, hone

perfectionist, perfectionists
(noun) Someone who is a perfectionist always tries to do everything perfectly.

perfidious
(adjective; a formal word) treacherous or untrustworthy.
perfidy (noun).
[from Latin *perfidius* meaning 'faithless']

perforated
(adjective) Something that is perforated has had small holes made in it.
perforation (noun).

perform, performs, performing, performed
1 (verb) To perform a task, action, or service means to do it.
2 To perform means to act, dance, or play music in front of an audience.
performer (noun).

performance, performances
1 (noun) A performance is an entertainment provided for an audience.

2 The performance of a task or action is the doing of it.
3 Someone's or something's performance is how successful they are, e.g. *Her performance in the exams was disappointing.*

perfume, perfumes
1 (noun) Perfume is a pleasant-smelling liquid which women put on their bodies.
2 The perfume of something is its pleasant smell.
perfumed (adjective).

perfunctory
(adjective) done quickly without interest or care, e.g. *a perfunctory glance.*
perfunctorily (adverb).

perhaps
(adverb) You use perhaps when you are not sure whether something is true, possible, or likely.

peril, perils
(noun; a formal word) Peril is great danger.
perilous (adjective), **perilously** (adverb).

perimeter, perimeters
(noun) The perimeter of an area or figure is the whole of its outer edge.

period, periods
1 (noun) A period is a particular length of time.
2 At school, a period is one of the parts the day is divided into.
3 A woman's period is the monthly bleeding from her womb.
4 In American English, a period is a full stop.
5 (adjective) relating to a historical period of time, e.g. *period costumes.*
periodic (adjective), **periodically** (adverb).
[from Greek *periodos* meaning 'circuit']

periodical, periodicals
(noun) A periodical is a magazine or journal.

periodic table
(noun) The periodic table is a table showing the chemical elements arranged according to their atomic numbers.

peripatetic (pronounced per-rip-at-**tet**-ik)
(adjective) travelling or working in different places, e.g. *a peripatetic music teacher.*
[from Greek *peripatein* meaning 'to pace to and fro']

peripheral (pronounced per-**rif**-fer-ral)
1 (adjective) of little importance in comparison with other things.
2 on or relating to the edge of an area.

periphery, peripheries
(noun) The periphery of an area is its outside edge.

periscope, periscopes
(noun) A periscope is a tube with mirrors which is used in a submarine to see above the surface of the water.
[from Greek *periskopein* meaning 'to look around']

perish, perishes, perishing, perished
1 (verb; a formal use) If someone or something perishes, they are killed or destroyed.
2 If fruit, rubber, or fabric perishes, it rots.
perishable (adjective).

peritonitis
(noun) Peritonitis is a painful inflammation of the inside of the abdomen.

perjury
(noun; a formal or legal word) If someone commits perjury, they tell a lie in court while under oath.
perjure (verb).
[from Latin *perjurium* meaning 'false oath']

perk, perks, perking, perked
1 (noun) A perk is an extra, such as a company car, offered by an employer in addition to a salary. Perk is an abbreviation for 'perquisite'.
2 (verb; an informal expression) When someone perks up, they become more cheerful.
perky (adjective).

perm, perms, perming, permed
1 (noun) If you have a perm, your hair is curled and treated with chemicals to keep the curls for several months. Perm is short for 'permanent wave'.
2 (verb) To perm someone's hair means to put a perm in it.

permafrost
(noun) Permafrost is land that is permanently frozen to a great depth.

permanent
(adjective) lasting for ever, or present all the time.
permanently (adverb), **permanence** (noun).

permeable (pronounced **per**-mee-a-bl)
(adjective; a formal word) If something is permeable, liquids are able to pass through it, e.g. *permeable rock.*

permeate, permeates, permeating, permeated
(verb) To permeate something means to spread through it and affect every part of it.
[from Latin *permeare* meaning 'to pass through']

Similar words: penetrate, suffuse, pervade, seep

permissible
(adjective) allowed by the rules.

Similar words: allowable, legitimate, admissible, permitted

permission
(noun) If you have permission to do something, you are allowed to do it.

Similar words: consent, dispensation, clearance, leave, licence, authorization

permissive
(adjective) A permissive society allows things which some people disapprove of, especially freedom in sexual behaviour.
permissiveness (noun).

permit, permits, permitting, permitted
1 (verb) To permit something means to allow it or make it possible.
2 (noun) A permit is an official document which says that you are allowed to do something.

Similar words: (sense 1) allow, authorize, let, grant

permutation, permutations
(noun) A permutation is one possible arrangement of a number of things.

pernicious
(adjective; a formal word) very harmful, e.g. *Many fear his pernicious influence.*
[from Latin *pernicies* meaning 'ruin']

pernickety
(adjective; an informal word) too concerned about unimportant details.

peroration, perorations
(noun; a formal word) A peroration is the summary or last part of a speech.

peroxide
(noun) Peroxide is a chemical used for bleaching hair or as an antiseptic.

perpendicular
(adjective) upright, or at right angles to a horizontal line.
[from Latin *perpendiculum* meaning 'plumb line']

perpetrate, perpetrates, perpetrating, perpetrated
(verb; a formal word) To perpetrate a crime means to commit it.
perpetrator (noun).

perpetual
(adjective) never ending.
perpetually (adverb), perpetuity (noun).

perpetuate, perpetuates, perpetuating, perpetuated
(verb) To perpetuate a situation or belief means to cause it to continue.
perpetuation (noun).

perplex, perplexes, perplexing, perplexed
(verb) If something perplexes you, it puzzles you because you do not understand it.
perplexed (adjective), perplexity (noun).
[from Latin *perplexus* meaning 'entangled']

perquisite, perquisites
(noun; a formal word) A perquisite is a perk.

per se (rhymes with **day**)
(adverb; a formal expression) used to emphasize that you are referring to something in terms of its basic characteristics or qualities, regardless of other factors.

persecute, persecutes, persecuting, persecuted
(verb) To persecute someone means to treat them with continual cruelty and unfairness.
persecution (noun), persecutor (noun).
[from Latin *persecutor* meaning 'pursuer']

Similar words: victimize, pick on

persevere, perseveres, persevering, persevered
(verb) If you persevere, you keep trying to do something and do not give up.
perseverance (noun).

Similar words: persist, carry on, keep going, stick at

Persian (pronounced **per**-shn) an old word for **Iranian**, used especially when referring to the older forms of the language.

persist, persists, persisting, persisted
1 (verb) If something undesirable persists, it continues to exist.
2 If you persist in doing something, you continue in spite of opposition or difficulty.
persistence (noun), persistent (adjective).

person, people or **persons**
1 (noun) A person is a man, woman, or child.
2 (phrase) If you do something **in person**, you do it yourself rather than getting someone else to do it for you.
3 (noun) In grammar, the first person is the speaker, the second person is the person being spoken to, and the third person is anyone else being referred to.
[from Latin *persona* meaning 'actor's mask']

Similar words: (sense 1) human being, individual, character

-person
used instead of '-man' or '-woman' in words such as 'spokesman' or 'chairwoman' when you want to refer to a person without indicating their sex, e.g. *CND chairperson Joan Ruddock.*

persona, personas or **personae** (pronounced per-**soh**-na)
(noun; a formal word) Your persona is the image of yourself and your character that you choose to present to other people.
[from Latin *persona* meaning 'actor's mask']

personable
(adjective) Someone who is personable has a pleasant appearance and character.

personage, personages
(noun) A personage is a famous or important person.

personal
1 (adjective) Personal means belonging or relating to a particular person rather than to people in general, e.g. *my personal opinion.*
2 If you give something your personal attention, you do it yourself rather than letting someone else do it.
3 Personal matters relate to your feelings, relationships, and health which you may not wish to discuss with other people.
4 Personal comments refer to someone's appearance or character in an offensive way, e.g. *She was getting very personal.*
personally (adverb).

Similar words: (sense 1) own, individual, private, exclusive

personality, personalities
1 (noun) Your personality is your character and nature.
2 You can refer to a famous person in entertainment or sport as a personality.

personalized or **personalised**
1 (adjective) designed specially for each individual person.
2 marked with the owner's initials.

persona non grata (pronounced per-**soh**-na non **grah**-ta)
(a formal expression) Someone who is persona non grata is unwelcome or unacceptable.

personify, personifies, personifying, personified
(verb) Someone who personifies a particular quality seems to be a living example of it, e.g. *She personifies British expertise.*
personification (noun).

personnel (pronounced per-son-**nell**)
(noun) The personnel of an organization are the people who work for it.

perspective, perspectives
1 (noun) A particular perspective is one way of considering something.
2 In art, perspective is a method by which things in the distance are made to look further away than things in the foreground.
3 (phrase) If you **get something into perspective**, you judge its importance rationally in comparison with other things.
[from Latin *perspicere* meaning 'to inspect carefully']

Perspex
(noun; a trademark) Perspex is a strong clear plastic that is sometimes used instead of glass.

perspicacious (pronounced per-spik-**ay**-shuss)
(adjective; a formal word) Someone who is perspicacious notices and understands things quickly.
perspicacity (noun).

perspiration
(noun) Perspiration is the moisture that appears on your skin when you are hot or frightened.
perspire (verb).

persuade, persuades, persuading, persuaded
(verb) If someone persuades you to do something or persuades you that something is true, they make you do it or believe it by giving you very good reasons.
persuasion (noun), **persuasive** (adjective).

Similar words: get, induce, prevail upon, win over

pert
(adjective) cheeky, e.g. *a pert grin.*
pertly (adverb).

pertain, pertains, pertaining, pertained
(verb; a formal word) Something that pertains to another thing belongs or relates to it, e.g. *documents pertaining to the Revolution.*

pertinacious
(adjective; a formal word) Someone who is pertinacious keeps doing something difficult and does not give up.
pertinacity (noun).

pertinent
(adjective) especially relevant to the subject being discussed, e.g. *That's a pertinent point.*

perturb, perturbs, perturbing, perturbed
(verb) If something perturbs you, it makes you worried.
perturbed (adjective).

peruse, peruses, perusing, perused (pronounced per-**ooz**)
(verb; a formal word) If you peruse something, you read it.
perusal (noun).

Peruvian, Peruvians (pronounced per-**roo**-vee-an)
1 (adjective) belonging or relating to Peru.
2 (noun) A Peruvian is someone who comes from Peru.

pervade, pervades, pervading, pervaded
(verb) Something that pervades a place is present and noticeable throughout it.
pervasive (adjective).
[from Latin *pervadere* meaning 'to go through']

perverse
(adjective) Someone who is perverse deliberately does things that are unreasonable or harmful.
perversely (adverb), **perversity** (noun).
[from Latin *perversus* meaning 'turned the wrong way']

pervert, perverts, perverting, perverted
1 (verb; a formal use) To pervert something means to interfere with it so that it is no longer what it should be, e.g. *They were conspiring to pervert the course of justice.*
2 (noun) A pervert is a person whose sexual behaviour is disgusting or harmful.
perversion (noun).
[from Latin *pervertere* meaning 'to turn the wrong way']

perverted
1 (adjective) Someone who is perverted has disgusting or unacceptable behaviour or ideas, especially sexual behaviour or ideas.
2 Something that is perverted is completely wrong, e.g. *his perverted sense of logic.*

Similar words: (sense 1) kinky, deviant, warped

peseta, pesetas (pronounced pes-**say**-ta)
(noun) The peseta is the main unit of currency in Spain. A peseta is worth 100 céntimos.

peso, pesos (pronounced **pay**-soh)
(noun) The peso is the main unit of currency in several South American countries.

pessary, pessaries
(noun) A pessary is a device or drug in solid form inserted into a woman's vagina, either as a medical treatment or as a contraceptive.

pessimism

(noun) Pessimism is the tendency to believe that bad things will happen.
pessimist (noun), **pessimistic** (adjective), **pessimistically** (adverb).
[from Latin *pessimus* meaning 'worst']

pest, pests

1 (noun) A pest is an insect or small animal which damages plants or food supplies.
2 Someone who is a pest keeps bothering or annoying you.
[from Latin *pestis* meaning 'plague']

pester, pesters, pestering, pestered

(verb) If you pester someone, you keep bothering them or asking them to do something.

Similar words: importune, harass, badger, hassle

pesticide, pesticides

(noun) Pesticides are chemicals sprayed onto plants to kill insects and grubs.

pestilence

(noun) Pestilence is a fast-spreading disease that kills large numbers of people.

pestle, pestles (pronounced pes-sl)

(noun) A pestle is a short stick with a rounded end. It is used for crushing spices or medicines in a bowl called a mortar.

pet, pets, petting, petted

1 (noun) A pet is a tame animal kept at home.
2 (adjective) Someone's pet theory or pet project is something that they particularly support or feel strongly about.
3 (verb) If you pet a person or animal, you stroke them affectionately.

petal, petals

(noun) The petals of a flower are the coloured outer parts.
[from Greek *petalon* meaning 'leaf']

petard

(phrase) If you try to harm someone and are **hoist with your own petard**, you only succeed in harming yourself.

peter, peters, petering, petered

(verb) If something peters out, it gradually comes to an end.

petite (pronounced pet-teet)

(adjective) A woman who is petite is small and slim.
[from French *petite*, the feminine form of *petit* meaning 'small']

petition, petitions, petitioning, petitioned

1 (noun) A petition is a document demanding official action and signed by a lot of people.
2 A legal petition is an application to a court for legal action to be taken.
3 (verb) If you petition someone in authority, you make a formal request to them.

petrel, petrels

(noun) A petrel is a long-winged seabird.

Petri dish, Petri dishes

(noun) A Petri dish is a flat, shallow dish used in laboratories. It is named after J. R. Petri (1852-1921), a German bacteriologist.

petrify, petrifies, petrifying, petrified

1 (verb) If something petrifies you, it makes you very frightened.
2 If something petrifies, it turns to stone or becomes fossilized.

petrochemical, petrochemicals

(noun) Petrochemicals are substances obtained from petroleum or natural gas.

petrol

(noun) Petrol is a liquid obtained from petroleum and used as a fuel.

petroleum

(noun) Petroleum is thick, dark oil found under the earth or under the sea bed. Many substances are obtained or made from it, including petrol, oil, and paraffin.
[from Latin *petra* meaning 'rock' and *oleum* meaning 'oil']

petticoat, petticoats

(noun) A petticoat is a piece of underclothing like a very thin skirt or dress.

petty, pettier, pettiest

1 (adjective) Petty things are small and unimportant.
2 Petty behaviour consists of doing small things which are selfish or unkind.

petty cash

(noun) Petty cash is money that is kept available for making small payments when necessary.

petty officer, petty officers

(noun) A petty officer is a noncommissioned officer in the navy.

petulant

(adjective) showing unreasonable and childish impatience or anger.
petulantly (adverb), **petulance** (noun).
[from Latin *petulans* meaning 'bold']

petunia, petunias (pronounced pit-yoon-nee-ah)

(noun) A petunia is a garden plant with large pink, white, or purple trumpet-shaped flowers.

pew, pews

(noun) A pew is a long wooden seat with a back, which people sit on in church.

pewter

(noun) Pewter is a silvery-grey metal made from a mixture of tin and lead, used especially for making tankards and plates.

pfennig, pfennigs (pronounced fen-nig)

(noun) The pfennig is a unit of currency in Germany. A pfennig is worth one-hundredth of a mark.

pH

(noun) The pH of a solution or of the soil is a measurement of how acid or alkaline it is. Acid solutions have a pH of less than 7 and alkaline solutions have a pH greater than 7. pH is an abbreviation for 'potential hydrogen'.

phalanx, phalanges or phalanxes (pronounced fal-lanks)

1 (noun; a formal word) A phalanx is a closely

packed group of people united for a particular purpose.
2 (a medical word) A phalanx is also one of the bones in your fingers or toes.

phallus, phalluses
(noun) A phallus is a penis or a symbolic model of a penis.
phallic (adjective).

phantom, phantoms
1 (noun) A phantom is a ghost.
2 (adjective) imagined or unreal, e.g. *a phantom pregnancy.*

pharaoh, pharaohs (pronounced **fair**-oh)
(noun) The pharaohs were kings of ancient Egypt.

Pharisee, Pharisees
1 (noun) The Pharisees were a group of Jews mentioned in the Bible who believed in strict obedience to the laws of Judaism.
2 Someone who is a pharisee pretends to be very moral or religious but in fact is not.

pharmaceutical (pronounced far-mass-**yoo**-tik-kl)
(adjective) connected with the industrial production of medicines.

pharmacist, pharmacists
(noun) A pharmacist is a person who is qualified to prepare and sell medicines.

pharmacology (pronounced far-mak-**kol**-oj-ee)
(noun) Pharmacology is the science or study of medicines.

pharmacy, pharmacies
1 (noun) A pharmacy is a shop where medicines are sold.
2 Pharmacy is the job of preparing medicines.
[from Greek *pharmakeia* meaning 'the making of drugs']

pharynx, pharynxes or pharynges (pronounced **far**-rinks)
(noun; a medical word) Your pharynx is the air passage connecting the back of your nose and mouth to your throat.
[from Greek *pharunx* meaning 'throat']

phase, phases, phasing, phased
1 (noun) A phase is a particular stage in the development of something.
2 (verb) To phase a change over a period of time means to cause it to happen gradually in stages.

PhD, PhDs
(noun) A PhD is a degree awarded to someone who has done advanced postgraduate research in a subject. PhD is an abbreviation for 'Doctor of Philosophy'.

pheasant, pheasants
(noun) A pheasant is a large, long-tailed game bird. The male has brightly coloured feathers.

phenomenal (pronounced fin-**nom**-in-nal)
(adjective) extraordinarily great or good.
phenomenally (adverb).

phenomenon, phenomena
(noun) A phenomenon is something that happens

or exists, especially something remarkable or something being considered in a scientific way.
[from Greek *phainomenon*]

phial, phials (pronounced **fy**-yel)
(noun) A phial is a tube-shaped glass bottle used for medicine.
[from Greek *phialē* meaning 'wide, shallow dish']

philanderer, philanderers
(noun; a formal word) A philanderer is someone who flirts a lot or who has a lot of casual affairs.

philanthropist, philanthropists (pronounced fil-**lan**-throp-pist)
(noun) A philanthropist is someone who freely gives help or money to people in need.
philanthropic (adjective), **philanthropy** (noun).
[from Greek *philanthropia* meaning 'love of mankind']

philately (pronounced fil-**lat**-tel-ee)
(noun) Philately is the collection and study of postage stamps.
philatelist (noun).

philistine, philistines
1 (noun) If you call someone a philistine, you mean that they do not like art, literature, or music.
2 The Philistines were a tribe of people in ancient Palestine.

philology
(noun) Philology is the study of the development of words in a language.
philologist (noun).
[from Greek *philologia* meaning 'love of language']

philosophical or **philosophic**
(adjective) Someone who is philosophical does not get upset when disappointing things happen.

philosophize, philosophizes, philosophizing
philosophized; also spelled **philosophise**
(verb) People who philosophize talk about important things in a boring, pretentious way.

philosophy, philosophies
1 (noun) Philosophy is the study or creation of theories about the nature of existence, knowledge, beliefs, or behaviour.
2 A philosophy is a set of beliefs that a person has.
philosopher (noun), **philosophical** (adjective).
[from Greek *philosophos* meaning 'lover of wisdom']

phlebitis (pronounced flib-**by**-tiss)
(noun) Phlebitis is an inflammation of the veins.

phlegm (pronounced **flem**)
(noun) Phlegm is a thick mucus secreted in your throat, especially when you have a cold.
[from Greek *phlegma* meaning 'inflammation']

phlegmatic (pronounced fleg-**mat**-tik)
(adjective) Someone who is phlegmatic remains calm in exciting or distressing situations.

phlox
(noun) Phlox is a garden plant with white, pink, or red flowers.
[from Greek *phlox* meaning 'flame']

phobia, phobias
(noun) A phobia is an abnormal, irrational fear or hatred of something, e.g. *She has a phobia about spiders.*
phobic (adjective).
[from Greek *phobos* meaning 'fear']

phoenix, phoenixes (pronounced **fee**-niks)
(noun) A phoenix is an imaginary bird which, according to myth, burns itself to ashes every five hundred years and rises from the fire again.

phone, phones, phoning, phoned
1 (noun) A phone is a piece of electronic equipment which allows you to speak to someone in another place by dialling their number.
2 (verb) If you phone someone, you dial their number and speak to them using a phone.

phone-in, phone-ins
(noun) A phone-in is a radio programme which broadcasts listeners' telephone calls to the programme.

phonetics
(noun) Phonetics is the study of speech sounds.
phonetic (adjective).
[from Greek *phonē* meaning 'sound' or 'voice']

phoney, phonier, phoniest; phoneys; also spelled phony (an informal word)
1 (adjective) false and intended to deceive.
2 (noun) Someone who is a phoney pretends to have qualities they do not possess.

phosphate, phosphates
(noun) A phosphate is a chemical compound containing phosphorus that is often used in fertilizers.

phosphorescent
(adjective) glowing with a soft light but giving out little or no heat.
phosphorescence (noun).

phosphorus
(noun) Phosphorus is a whitish, nonmetallic element that burns easily and is used in making fertilizers and matches. Its atomic number is 15 and its symbol is P.

photo, photos
(noun; an informal word) A photo is a photograph.

photocopier, photocopiers
(noun) A photocopier is a machine which makes instant copies of documents by photographing them.

photocopy, photocopies, photocopying, photocopied
1 (noun) A photocopy is a copy of a document produced by a photocopier.
2 (verb) If you photocopy a document, you make a copy of it using a photocopier.

photo finish, photo finishes
(noun) If the end of a race is a photo finish, competitors cross the finishing line so close together that a photograph has to be examined to decide the winner.

photogenic
(adjective) Someone who is photogenic always looks nice in photographs.

photograph, photographs, photographing, photographed
1 (noun) A photograph is a picture made using a camera.
2 (verb) When you photograph someone, you take a picture of them by using a camera.
photographer (noun), **photography** (noun).

photographic
1 (adjective) connected with photography.
2 Someone with a photographic memory can remember in detail things they have seen.

Photostat, Photostats
(noun; a trademark) A Photostat is a photocopy.

photosynthesis
(noun) Photosynthesis is the process by which the action of sunlight on the chlorophyll in plants produces the substances that keep the plants alive.

phrasal verb, phrasal verbs
(noun) A phrasal verb is a verb such as 'take over' or 'break in', which is made up of a verb and an adverb or preposition.

phrase, phrases, phrasing, phrased
1 (noun) A phrase is a group of words considered as a unit, especially a saying.
2 (verb) If you phrase something in a particular way, you choose those words to express it.
3 (noun) In music, a phrase is a group of notes forming a melodic unit.
[from Greek *phrasis* meaning 'speech']

phrase book, phrase books
(noun) A phrase book is a book which gives useful words and expressions in a foreign language together with their translations.

phraseology
(noun) A phraseology is a particular style of words chosen to express something.

phrenology
(noun) Phrenology is the study of the shape and size of the skull as a supposed indication of intelligence and character.
[from Greek *phrēn* meaning 'mind']

physical
1 (adjective) concerning the body rather than the mind.
2 relating to things that can be touched or seen, especially with regard to their size or shape.
3 concerning the laws of physics.
physically (adverb).
[from Greek *phusis* meaning 'nature']

physical education
(noun) Physical education consists of the sport, gymnastics, and athletics that you do at school.

physician, physicians
(noun) A physician is a doctor.

physics
(noun) Physics is the scientific study of the nature and properties of matter, energy, gravity, electricity, heat, and sound.
physicist (noun).

physiognomy (pronounced
fiz-zee-**yon**-nom-ee)

(noun; a formal word) Your physiognomy is your features or characteristic expression.

physiology
(noun) Physiology is the scientific study of the way the bodies of living things work.

physiotherapy
(noun) Physiotherapy is medical treatment which involves exercise and massage.
physiotherapist (noun).

physique, physiques (pronounced fiz-**zeek**)
(noun) A person's physique is the shape and size of their body and the tone of their muscles.

pi (rhymes with **fly**)
(noun) Pi is a number, approximately 3.142 and symbolized by the Greek letter π. Pi is the ratio of the circumference of a circle to its diameter.

pianissimo (pronounced pee-an-**iss**-sim-moh)
In music, pianissimo is an instruction to play or sing something very quietly.

piano, pianos
1 In music, piano is an instruction to play or sing something quietly.
2 (noun) A piano is a large musical instrument with a row of black and white keys. When the keys are pressed, little hammers hit wires to produce the different notes.
pianist (noun).
[originally called 'pianoforte', from Italian *gravecembalo col piano e forte* meaning 'harpsichord with soft and loud (sounds)']

piazza, piazzas (pronounced pee-**at**-sa)
(noun) A piazza is an open square in a town. [an Italian word]

piccolo, piccolos
(noun) A piccolo is a small, high-pitched wind instrument like a small flute.
[from Italian *piccolo* meaning 'small']

pick, picks, picking, picked
1 (verb) To pick something means to choose it.
2 If you pick a flower or fruit, or pick something from a place, you remove it with your fingers.
3 If you pick a fight or quarrel with someone, you deliberately start it.
4 If someone picks a lock, they open it with a piece of wire instead of a key.
5 If you pick your way across something, you move carefully, avoiding obstacles.
6 (noun) A pick is a pickaxe.

pick on
(phrasal verb) If you pick on someone, you criticize them unfairly or treat them unkindly.

pick out
(phrasal verb) If you pick out someone or something, you recognize them when they are difficult to see, or you choose them from among other things.

pick up
1 (phrasal verb) If you pick someone or something up, you collect them from the place where they are waiting.
2 When a radio or microphone picks up a signal, it receives it or detects it.
3 When things pick up, they improve.

4 (an informal use) If someone picks up another person, they start a romantic or sexual relationship with them.

pickaxe, pickaxes
(noun) A pickaxe is a tool consisting of a curved pointed iron bar attached in the middle to a long handle. It is used for breaking up cement or rock.

picket, pickets, picketing, picketed
1 (verb) When a group of people picket a place of work, they stand outside to persuade other workers to join or support a strike.
2 (noun) A picket is a group of people who are picketing a place.

pickings
(plural noun) Pickings are goods or money that can be obtained very easily.

pickle, pickles, pickling, pickled
1 (noun) Pickle or pickles consists of vegetables or fruit preserved in vinegar or salt water, often with additional flavouring.
2 (verb) To pickle food means to preserve it in vinegar or salt water.
3 (an informal phrase) If you are **in a pickle**, you are in a difficult situation.

pickled
(adjective; an informal word) Someone who is pickled is drunk.

pick-me-up, pick-me-ups
(noun) A pick-me-up is a drink intended to make you feel healthier.

pickpocket, pickpockets
(noun) A pickpocket is a thief who steals from people's pockets or handbags.

pick-up, pick-ups
(noun) A pick-up is a small truck with low sides.

picnic, picnics, picnicking, picnicked
1 (noun) A picnic is a meal eaten out of doors.
2 (verb) People who are picnicking are having a picnic.

pictorial
(adjective) relating to or using pictures.
pictorially (adverb).

picture, pictures, picturing, pictured
1 (noun) A picture of someone or something is a drawing, painting, or photograph of them.
2 (verb) If someone is pictured in a newspaper or magazine, a photograph of them is printed in it.
3 (plural noun) If you go to the pictures, you go to see a film at the cinema.
4 (noun) If you have a picture of something in your mind, you have an idea or impression of it.
5 (verb) If you picture something, you think of it and imagine it clearly.
[from Latin *pictura* meaning 'painting']

Similar words: (sense 1) illustration, sketch, figure

picturesque (pronounced pik-chur-**esk**)
(adjective) A place that is picturesque is very attractive and unspoiled.
[from Italian *pittoresco* meaning 'in the style of a painter']

pidgin, pidgins (pronounced **pij**-jin)
(noun) A pidgin is a simple language based on
two or more languages. Pidgins usually
developed as a means of communication between
traders from different countries.
[from the Chinese pronunciation of *business*]

pie, pies
(noun) A pie is a dish of meat, vegetables, or
fruit covered with pastry.

piebald
(adjective) A piebald animal has patches of two
different colours on it, usually black and white.

piece, pieces, piecing, pieced
1 (noun) A piece of something is a portion, part,
or section of it.
2 A piece is also something that has been written
or created, such as a work of art or a musical
composition, e.g. *It's a really beautiful piece.*
3 A piece is also a coin, e.g. *a ten pence piece.*
4 In board games such as chess, the pieces are
the objects which you move around the board.
5 (verb) If you piece together a number of things,
you gradually put them together to make
something complete.

pièce de résistance (pronounced pyess de
rez-**iss**-tans)
(noun) The pièce de résistance is the most
important or impressive thing in a series.
[a French expression]

piecemeal
(adverb and adjective) done gradually and at
irregular intervals.

piecework
(noun) If you do piecework, you are paid for the
amount of work you complete, rather than for
the number of hours you work.

pied-à-terre, pieds-à-terre (pronounced
pee-ay-de-**tair**)
(noun) A pied-à-terre is a small house or flat that
someone owns but uses only occasionally,
especially in a city.

pier, piers
(noun) A pier is a large structure which sticks
out into the sea at a seaside town, and which
people can walk along.

pierce, pierces, piercing, pierced
(verb) If a sharp object pierces something, it goes
through it, making a hole.

Similar words: penetrate, perforate, prick, puncture

piercing
1 (adjective) A piercing sound is high-pitched,
sharp, and unpleasant.
2 Someone with piercing eyes seems to look at
you very intensely.

Similar words: (sense 1) penetrating, shrill,
ear-splitting, sharp

piety (pronounced **pie**-it-tee)
(noun) Piety is strong and devout religious belief
or behaviour.

piffle
(noun; an informal word) Piffle is nonsense.

piffling
(adjective) unimportant and trivial.

pig, pigs
1 (noun) A pig is a farm animal kept for its meat.
It has pinkish skin, short legs, and a snout.
2 (an informal use) If you call someone a pig, you
mean they are greedy or unkind.
3 (phrase) If you **make a pig of yourself**, you eat
too much.
piggish (adjective), **piggery** (noun).

pigeon, pigeons
(noun) A pigeon is a plump bird with grey
feathers, often seen in towns and cities.

pigeonhole, pigeonholes
1 (noun) A pigeonhole is one of the sections in a
frame on a wall where letters can be left.
2 (verb) If you pigeonhole someone, you decide
that they belong to a particular class of person.

piggyback, piggybacks
(noun) If you give someone a piggyback, you
carry them on your back, supporting them under
their knees.

pig-headed
(adjective) Someone who is pig-headed is
stubborn and refuses to change their mind.

piglet, piglets
(noun) A piglet is a young pig.

pigment, pigments
(noun) A pigment is a substance that gives
something a particular colour.
pigmentation (noun).
[from Latin *pingere* meaning 'to paint']

pigsty, pigsties
1 (noun) A pigsty is a hut with a small enclosed
area where pigs are kept.
2 If you describe a room as a pigsty, you mean it
is very untidy and dirty.

pigtail, pigtails
(noun) A pigtail is a length of plaited hair.

pike, pikes
1 (noun) A pike is a large freshwater fish with
strong teeth and a flat snout.
2 A pike was a medieval weapon consisting of a
pointed metal blade attached to a long pole.

pilchard, pilchards
(noun) A pilchard is a small sea fish.

pile, piles, piling, piled
1 (noun) A pile of things is a quantity of them
lying one on top of another.
2 (verb) If you pile things somewhere, you put
them one on top of the other.
3 (noun) The pile of a carpet is its soft surface
consisting of many threads standing on end.
4 (plural noun) Piles are painful swellings that
appear in the veins inside or just outside a
person's anus.
[senses 1 and 2 are from Latin *pila* meaning
'pillar' or 'pier'; sense 3 is from Latin *pilus*
meaning 'hair']

pile-up, pile-ups
(noun; an informal word) A pile-up is a road
accident involving several vehicles.

pilfer, pilfers, pilfering, pilfered
(verb) Someone who pilfers steals small things over a period of time.
[from Old French *pelfre* meaning 'booty']

pilgrim, pilgrims
(noun) A pilgrim is a person who travels to a holy place for religious reasons.
pilgrimage (noun).

pill, pills
1 (noun) A pill is a small, round, hard tablet of medicine that you swallow without chewing.
2 The pill is a type of contraceptive tablet that some women take regularly to prevent them from becoming pregnant.
[from Latin *pilula* meaning 'little ball']

pillage, pillages, pillaging, pillaged
1 (noun) Pillage is the stealing of property in a violent way, usually by a group of people.
2 (verb) If a group of people pillage a place, they steal from it using violence.

pillar, pillars
1 (noun) A pillar is a tall, narrow, solid structure, usually supporting part of a building.
2 Someone who is described as a pillar of a particular group is an active and important member of it.

pillar box, pillar boxes
(noun) A pillar box is a red cylinder or box in which you post letters.

pillion
(adverb) Someone who is riding pillion on a motorcycle is sitting behind the person controlling it.

pillory, pillories, pillorying, pilloried
1 (verb) If someone is pilloried, they are criticized severely by a lot of people.
2 (noun) A pillory is a wooden frame with holes for a person's head and hands. In the Middle Ages, criminals were locked in a pillory as a punishment.

pillow, pillows
(noun) A pillow is a rectangular cushion which you rest your head on when you are in bed.

pillowcase, pillowcases
(noun) A pillowcase is a cover for a pillow which can be removed and washed.

pillowslip, pillowslips
(noun) A pillowslip is the same as a pillowcase.

pilot, pilots, piloting, piloted
1 (noun) A pilot is a person who is trained to fly an aircraft.
2 A pilot is also a person who goes on board ships to guide them through local waters to a port.
3 (verb) To pilot something means to control its movement or to guide it.
4 (adjective) A pilot study is a small test of a scheme or product. It is done to find out whether the scheme or product would be successful.

pilot light, pilot lights
(noun) A pilot light is a small flame in a gas boiler or cooker which burns continuously and lights the burner when the appliance is turned on.

pilot officer, pilot officers
(noun) A pilot officer is an RAF officer of the lowest commissioned rank.

pimp, pimps
(noun) A pimp is a man who finds clients for prostitutes and takes a large part of their earnings.

pimple, pimples
(noun) A pimple is a small spot on the skin.
pimply (adjective).

pin, pins, pinning, pinned
1 (noun) A pin is a thin, pointed piece of metal used to fasten together things such as pieces of fabric or paper.
2 (verb) If you pin something somewhere, you fasten it there with a pin or a drawing pin.
3 If someone pins you in a particular position, they hold you there so that you cannot move.
4 If you try to pin something down, you try to get or give a clear and exact description of them or statement about them.

pinafore, pinafores
(noun) A pinafore is a dress with no sleeves, worn over a blouse.

pinball
(noun) Pinball is a game in which you try to stop a small ball rolling to the bottom of a special table by getting it to bounce off various obstructions.

pince-nez (pronounced **pans**-nay)
(noun) Pince-nez are old-fashioned spectacles consisting of two lenses in a frame without parts over the ears.
[a French word meaning literally 'pinch-nose']

pincers
1 (plural noun) Pincers are a tool used for gripping and pulling things. They consist of two pieces of metal hinged in the middle.
2 The pincers of a crab or lobster are its front claws.

pinch, pinches, pinching, pinched
1 (verb) If you pinch something, you squeeze it between your thumb and first finger.
2 (noun) A pinch of something is the amount that you can hold between your thumb and first finger, e.g. *Add a pinch of salt.*
3 (verb; an informal use) If someone pinches something, they steal it.
4 (phrase; an informal use) **At a pinch** means if absolutely necessary.

pinched
(adjective) If someone's face is pinched, it looks thin and pale.

pincushion, pincushions
(noun) A pincushion is a very small cushion that you stick your pins and needles into, so that you can find them easily when you need them.

pine, pines, pining, pined
1 (noun) A pine or pine tree is an evergreen tree with very thin leaves.

2 (verb) If you pine for something, you are sad because you cannot have it.

pineapple, pineapples
(noun) A pineapple is a large, oval fruit with sweet, yellow flesh and a thick, tough, lumpy, pale brown skin.

ping-pong
(noun) Ping-pong is the same as table tennis.

pinion, pinions, pinioning, pinioned
(verb) If you pinion someone, you prevent them from moving by holding their arms.

pink, pinker, pinkest; pinks
1 (adjective) pale reddish-white.
2 (noun) Pinks are small garden plants with fragrant pink or white flowers and narrow leaves.

pin money
(noun) Pin money is small amounts of money that someone earns to buy small luxuries.

pinnacle, pinnacles
1 (noun) A pinnacle is a tall pointed piece of stone or rock.
2 The pinnacle of something is its best or highest level.
[from Latin *pinnaculum* meaning 'peak']

pinpoint, pinpoints, pinpointing, pinpointed
(verb) If you pinpoint something, you explain or discover exactly what or where it is.

pins and needles
(noun) If you get pins and needles, you feel sharp tingling pains in part of your body.

pinstripe
(adjective) Pinstripe cloth has very narrow vertical stripes.

pint, pints
(noun) A pint is a unit of liquid volume equal to one eighth of a gallon or about 0.568 litres.

pin-up, pin-ups
(noun) A pin-up is a picture of an attractive woman or man.

pioneer, pioneers, pioneering, pioneered
(pronounced pie-on-**ear**)
1 (noun) Someone who is a pioneer in a particular activity is one of the first people to develop it.
2 (verb) Someone who pioneers a new process or invention is the first person to develop it.

pious (pronounced pie-uss)
(adjective) very religious and moral.
piously (adverb).

pip, pips
1 (noun) Pips are the hard seeds in a fruit.
2 On the radio, the pips are a series of short sounds used as a time signal.

pipe, pipes, piping, piped
1 (noun) A pipe is a long, round, hollow tube through which liquid or gas can flow.
2 (verb) To pipe a liquid or gas somewhere means to transfer it through a pipe.
3 (noun) A pipe is an object used for smoking tobacco. It consists of a small hollow bowl attached to a tube.

4 A pipe is a tube that forms part of a musical instrument.

piped music
(noun) Piped music is recorded music played through loudspeakers in public places.

pipe dream, pipe dreams
(noun) A pipe dream is a hope or plan that you know is unlikely to happen.

pipeline, pipelines
1 (noun) A pipeline is a large underground pipe that carries oil or gas over a long distance.
2 (phrase) If something is **in the pipeline**, it is already planned or has begun.

piper, pipers
(noun) A piper is a person who plays the bagpipes.

pipette, pipettes
(noun) A pipette is a thin glass tube used for measuring or carrying small amounts of liquid.

piping
1 (noun) Piping consists of pipes and tubes.
2 Piping is a narrow tube of fabric used to decorate clothing and soft furnishings.

pipit, pipits
(noun) A pipit is a small bird, rather like a lark.

pippin, pippins
(noun) A pippin is a type of eating apple, e.g. *Cox's Orange Pippins*.
[from Old French *pepin* meaning 'seed']

piquant (pronounced pee-kant)
1 (adjective) having a pleasantly spicy taste.
2 interesting and exciting.
piquancy (noun).
[a French word, literally meaning 'pricking']

pique (rhymes with **leek**)
(noun) Pique is a feeling of resentment as a result of hurt pride.
piqued (adjective).
[from French *piquer* meaning 'to prick' or 'to sting']

piracy
1 (noun) Piracy is robbery carried out by pirates.
2 Piracy is also the illegal copying of videos and cassettes.

piranha, piranhas (pronounced pir-rah-nah)
(noun) A piranha is a small, fierce fish with sharp teeth, which lives in rivers in South America.
[a Portuguese word]

pirate, pirates, pirating, pirated
1 (noun) Pirates were sailors who attacked and robbed other ships.
2 (verb) Someone who pirates video tapes, cassettes, or books makes illegal copies for sale.
[from Greek *peiratēs* meaning 'attacker']

pirate radio
(noun) Pirate radio stations broadcast illegally without a licence.

pirouette, pirouettes (pronounced pir-roo-**et**)
(noun) In ballet, a pirouette is a fast spinning step done on the toes.

Pisces (pronounced **pie**-seez)
(noun) Pisces is the twelfth sign of the zodiac,
represented by two fish. People born between
February 19th and March 20th are born under
this sign.
[the plural of Latin *piscis* meaning 'a fish']

pistachio, pistachios (pronounced
pis-**tash**-ee-oh)
(noun) A pistachio is a nut with a green kernel
which grows on small trees in the Mediterranean
region.

pistol, pistols
(noun) A pistol is a small gun held in the hand.

piston, pistons
(noun) A piston is a cylinder or disc that slides
up and down inside a tube. Pistons in an engine
have rods attached to them, and their movement
causes other parts of the engine to move.

pit, pits, pitting, pitted
1 (noun) A pit is a large hole in the ground.
2 A pit in the surface of something is a small
hollow.
3 A pit is also a coal mine.
4 (plural noun) In motor racing, the pits are the
areas at the side of the track where drivers stop
for fuel and repairs.
5 (phrase) If you **pit your wits** against someone,
you compete against them.

pitch, pitches, pitching, pitched
1 (noun) A pitch is an area of ground marked out
for playing a game such as football.
2 The pitch of a sound is how high or low it is.
3 If an emotion or activity reaches a high pitch,
it reaches a high level or degree of intensity.
4 Pitch is a black substance used in road tar and
also for waterproofing boats and roofs.
5 (verb) If you pitch something somewhere, you
throw it with a lot of force.
6 If you pitch something at a particular level of
difficulty, you set it at that level.
7 When you pitch a tent, you put it in an upright
position and secure it to the ground.

pitcher, pitchers
(noun) A pitcher is a large jug.

pitchfork, pitchforks
(noun) A pitchfork is a long-handled fork used
for lifting hay.

piteous
(adjective) Something that is piteous is so sad or
weak that it makes you feel pity.
piteously (adverb).

pitfall, pitfalls
(noun) The pitfalls of a situation are its
difficulties or dangers.

pith
(noun) The pith of an orange or lemon is the
white substance between the outer skin and the
flesh.

pithy, pithier, pithiest
(adjective) A pithy remark is short, direct, and
full of meaning.

pitiable
(adjective) Someone or something that is pitiable

is in such a sad or weak situation that you feel
pity for them.

pitiful another word for **pitiable.**

pitiless
(adjective) having no feeling of pity or mercy.

pittance
(noun) If you receive a pittance, you receive only
a very small amount of money.
[from Old French *pietance* meaning 'ration']

pitted
(adjective) covered in small hollows, e.g. *his
pitted skin.*

pituitary gland, pituitary glands
(noun) In anatomy, the pituitary gland is a gland
at the base of the brain which produces
hormones affecting growth and sexual
development.

pity, pities, pitying, pitied
1 (verb) If you pity someone, you feel very sorry
for them.
2 (noun) Pity is a feeling of being sorry for
someone.
3 If you say that it is a pity about something, you
are expressing your disappointment about it.

pivot, pivots, pivoting, pivoted
1 (verb) If something pivots, it balances or turns
on a central point.
2 (noun) A pivot is the central point on which
something balances or turns.
pivotal (adjective).

pixie, pixies
(noun) A pixie is an imaginary little creature in
fairy stories.

pizza, pizzas (pronounced **peet**-sah)
(noun) A pizza is a flat piece of dough covered
with cheese, tomato, and other savoury food.

pizzicato (pronounced pit-sik-**kat**-oh)
(adverb) If a stringed instrument such as a violin
is played pizzicato, it is played by plucking the
strings.
[an Italian word, literally meaning 'pinched']

placard, placards
(noun) A placard is a large notice carried at a
demonstration or displayed in a public place.

placate, placates, placating, placated
(verb) If you placate someone, you stop them
feeling angry by doing something to please them.
[from Latin *placare* meaning 'to please']

place, places, placing, placed
1 (noun) A place is any point, building, or area.
2 You can refer to the position where something
belongs as its place.
3 A place at a table is a space set with cutlery
where one person can eat.
4 If you have a place in a group or at a college,
you are a member or are accepted as a student.
5 A place in a sequence of things is a particular
point or stage.
6 (phrase) When something **takes place**, it
happens.

7 (verb) If you place something somewhere, you put it there.
8 If you place an order, you order something.
9 If you cannot place someone, you cannot remember exactly who they are or where you met them before.
placement (noun).
[from French *place* meaning 'square' or 'courtyard']

Similar words: (sense 1) position, site, spot, situation, location, whereabouts

placebo, **placebos** (pronounced plas-**see**-boh)
(noun) A placebo is a harmless, inactive substance given to a patient in place of a drug, either as part of a controlled test or when the patient is not really ill.

placenta, **placentas** (pronounced plas-**sen**-tah)
(noun) In anatomy, the placenta is the organ that develops inside a mother's womb during pregnancy. It consists of a mass of veins and tissues which supply food and oxygen to the foetus from the mother's blood and remove waste products.

placid
(adjective) calm and not easily excited or upset.
placidly (adverb), **placidity** (noun).
[from Latin *placidus* meaning 'peaceful']

Similar words: phlegmatic, even-tempered

plagiarism (pronounced **play**-jer-rizm)
(noun) Plagiarism is the practice of copying someone else's work or ideas and pretending that it is your own.
plagiarist (noun), **plagiarize** (verb).
[from Latin *plagiarus* meaning 'plunderer']

plague, **plagues, plaguing, plagued**
(pronounced **playg**)
1 (noun) Plague is a very infectious disease that kills large numbers of people.
2 A plague of unpleasant things is a large number of them occurring at the same time.
3 (verb) If problems plague you, they keep causing you trouble.

plaice
(noun) A plaice is an edible flat fish.

plaid, **plaids** (pronounced **plad**)
(noun) Plaid is woven material with a tartan design.

plain, **plainer, plainest; plains**
1 (adjective) very simple in style with no pattern or decoration.
2 obvious and easy to recognize or understand.
3 You can use plain before a noun or adjective to emphasize it, e.g. *That was just plain mean.*
4 A person who is plain is not at all beautiful or attractive.
5 (noun) A plain is a large, flat area of land with very few trees.
6 Plain is the basic knitting stitch.
plainly (adverb).

Similar words: (sense 1) bare, stark, unadorned, basic, simple, natural

plain-clothes
(adjective) Plain-clothes police officers are wearing ordinary clothes instead of a uniform.

plaintiff, **plaintiffs**
(noun) In a court case, the plaintiff is the person who has brought the case against another person.

plaintive
(adjective) A plaintive sound is very sad.
[from Old French *plaintif* meaning 'complaining']

plait, **plaits, plaiting, plaited**
1 (verb) If you plait three lengths of hair or rope together, you twist them over each other in turn to make one thick length.
2 (noun) A plait is a length of hair that has been plaited.
[from Old French *pleit* meaning 'a fold']

plan, **plans, planning, planned**
1 (noun) A plan is a method of achieving something that has been worked out beforehand.
2 A plan of something that is going to be made is a detailed diagram or drawing of it.
3 (verb) If you plan something, you decide in detail what it is to be and how to do it.
4 If you are planning to do something, you intend to do it.

Similar words: (sense 1) scheme, ruse, strategy, design, formula, policy
(sense 3) design, devise, draft, formulate
(sense 4) mean, propose, intend

plane, **planes, planing, planed**
1 (noun) A plane is a vehicle with wings and engines that enable it to fly.
2 A plane is also a flat surface.
3 You can refer to a particular level of something as a particular plane, e.g. *She tried to lift the conversation onto a more elevated plane.*
4 A plane is a tool with a flat bottom with a sharp blade in it. You move it over a piece of wood to remove thin pieces from the surface.
5 (verb) If you plane a piece of wood, you smooth its surface with a plane.

planet, **planets**
(noun) A planet is a round body in space which moves around the sun or a star and is illuminated by light from it.
planetary (adjective).
[from Greek *planētēs* meaning 'wanderer']

planetarium, **planetariums**
(noun) A planetarium is a building with a domed ceiling on which images of the planets and stars are projected to show their movement.

plane tree, **plane trees**
(noun) A plane tree is a large tree with broad leaves that often grows in towns.

plank, **planks**
(noun) A plank is a long rectangular piece of wood.

plankton
(noun) Plankton is a layer of microscopic plants and animals that live just below the surface of a sea or lake.

plant, plants, planting, planted
1 (noun) A plant is a living thing that grows in the earth and has stems, leaves, and roots.
2 A plant is also a factory or power station.
3 Plant is large industrial machinery or equipment.
4 (verb) When you plant a seed or plant, you put it into the ground.
5 If you plant something somewhere, you put it there firmly, deliberately, or secretly.
6 If someone plants a weapon or drug on another person, they put it amongst the person's possessions to make it look as if that person has committed a crime.
7 If an organization plants an informer somewhere, they send the person there to spy.
[from Latin *planta* meaning 'shoot' or 'cutting']

plantain, plantains
1 (noun) A plantain is a large green banana-shaped fruit. The tree it grows on is also called a plantain.
2 A plantain is also a wild plant with broad leaves and a small head of tiny green flowers on a long stem.

plantation, plantations
1 (noun) A plantation is a large area of land where crops such as tea, cotton, or sugar are grown.
2 A plantation of trees is a large number of them being grown for their timber.

plaque, plaques (rhymes with **black**)
1 (noun) A plaque is a flat piece of metal which is fixed to a wall and has an inscription in memory of a famous person or event.
2 Plaque is a substance which forms around your teeth and consists of bacteria, saliva, and food. Plaque can damage your gums and teeth.

plasma (pronounced **plaz**-mah)
(noun) Plasma is the clear fluid part of blood in which the corpuscles and cells are suspended.

plaster, plasters, plastering, plastered
1 (noun) Plaster is a paste made of sand, lime, and water, which dries hard and is used to form a smooth surface for inside walls and ceilings.
2 (verb) To plaster a wall means to cover it with a layer of plaster.
3 (noun) A plaster is a strip of sticky material with a small pad, used for covering cuts on your body.
4 (phrase) If your arm or leg is **in plaster**, it is covered with plaster of Paris to protect a broken bone.
plasterer (noun).

plastered
1 (adjective) If something is plastered to a surface, it is stuck there.
2 If something is plastered with things, they are all over its surface.
3 (an informal use) If someone is plastered, they are very drunk.

plaster of Paris
(noun) Plaster of Paris is a white powder which hardens when mixed with water and is used for making moulds.

plastic, plastics
1 (noun) Plastic is a substance made by a chemical process that can be moulded when soft to make a wide range of objects.
2 (adjective) made of plastic.
3 soft and able to be moulded.
plasticity (noun).

Plasticine
(noun; a trademark) Plasticine is a soft coloured substance which can be used for modelling.

plastic surgery
(noun) Plastic surgery is surgery to replace or repair damaged skin or to improve a person's appearance by changing the shape of their features.

plate, plates
1 (noun) A plate is a flat round or oval dish used to hold food.
2 A plate is also a flat piece of metal, glass, or other rigid material used for various purposes in machinery or building.
3 Silver, pewter, and gold objects can be referred to as plate.
4 A dental plate is a shaped piece of plastic with false teeth attached to it.

plateau, plateaus or plateaux (rhymes with **snow**)
1 (noun) A plateau is a large area of high and fairly flat land.
2 If a process or activity reaches a plateau, it reaches a stage of no further change.

plated
(adjective) Metal that is plated is covered with a thin layer of silver or gold.

plate glass
(noun) Plate glass is thick glass made in large pieces for shop windows and doors.

platelet, platelets
(noun) Platelets are particles in the blood which help it to clot.

platform, platforms
1 (noun) A platform is a raised structure on which someone or something can stand.
2 The platform of a political party is their set of proposals and policies, with which they campaign in an election.

platinum
(noun) Platinum is a valuable silver-coloured metal. Its atomic number is 78 and its symbol is Pt.

platitude, platitudes
(noun) A platitude is a statement made as if it were significant but which has become meaningless or boring because it has been used so many times before.
[a French word, meaning literally 'flatness']

platonic
(adjective) A platonic relationship is simply one of friendship and does not involve sexual attraction.
[from the name of the Greek philospher Plato]

platoon, platoons
(noun) A platoon is a small part of a company of soldiers, commanded by a lieutenant.

platter, platters
(noun) A platter is a large serving plate.

platypus, platypuses
(noun) A platypus or duck-billed platypus is an Australian mammal which lives in rivers. It has brown fur, webbed feet, and a snout like a duck. Although it is a mammal, it lays eggs.
[from Greek *platus* meaning 'flat' and *pous* meaning 'foot']

plaudits
(plural noun; a formal word) If something receives people's plaudits, they express their admiration for it or approval of it.
[from Latin *plaudite* meaning 'applaud!']

plausible
(adjective) An explanation that is plausible seems likely to be true or valid.
plausibility (noun).

play, plays, playing, played
1 (verb) When children play, they take part in games or use toys.
2 When you play a sport or match, you take part in it.
3 (noun) A play is a piece of drama performed in the theatre or on television.
4 (verb) If an actor plays a character in a play or film, he or she performs that role.
5 If you play a musical instrument, you produce music from it.
6 If you play a record or tape, you listen to it.
7 When light plays on a surface, it moves about in an unsteady, flickering way.
player (noun).

play down
(phrasal verb) If you play something down, you make it seem less important than it really is.

play on or **play upon**
(phrasal verb) If you play upon people's feelings, you deliberately use them to get what you want.

play up
(phrasal verb) If something is playing up, it is not working or behaving as it should.

playboy, playboys
(noun) A playboy is a rich man who spends his time enjoying himself.

playful
1 (adjective) friendly and light-hearted, e.g. *She gave his hand a playful squeeze.*
2 lively, e.g. *a playful kitten.*
playfully (adverb).

playground, playgrounds
(noun) A playground is a special area for children to play in.

playgroup, playgroups
(noun) A playgroup is an informal kind of school for very young children where they learn by playing.

playing card, playing cards
(noun) Playing cards are cards printed with numbers or pictures which are used to play various games.

playing field, playing fields
(noun) A playing field is an area of grass where people play sports.

playpen, playpens
(noun) A playpen is a small structure with bars or a net round the sides in which a baby or young child can play safely.

plaything, playthings
(noun) A plaything is something that a child plays with.

playwright, playwrights
(noun) A playwright is a person who writes plays.

plaza, plazas (pronounced **plah**-za)
(noun) A plaza is an open square in a city.
[a Spanish word]

plea, pleas
1 (noun) A plea is an emotional request.
2 In a court of law, someone's plea is their statement that they are guilty or not guilty.

plead, pleads, pleading, pleaded
1 (verb) If you plead with someone, you ask them in an intense emotional way to do something.
2 If you plead someone's case, you speak in support of them.
3 When a person pleads guilty or not guilty, they state in court that they are guilty or not guilty of a particular crime.

pleasant
(adjective) enjoyable, likable, or attractive.
pleasantly (adverb).

Similar words: good, agreeable, pleasurable, pleasing, congenial, gracious, personable, enjoyable

pleasantry, pleasantries
(noun) Pleasantries are casual, friendly remarks which you say in order to be polite.

please, pleases, pleasing, pleased
1 You say please when you are asking someone politely to do something.
2 (verb) If something pleases you, it makes you feel happy and satisfied.
3 You use please in expressions such as 'as she pleases' or 'whatever you please' to indicate that someone can do whatever they want.
pleased (adjective).

Similar words: (sense 2) gladden, satisfy, suit, delight, gratify

pleasing
(adjective) attractive, satisfying, or enjoyable.

pleasure, pleasures
1 (noun) Pleasure is a feeling of happiness, satisfaction, or enjoyment.
2 A pleasure is an activity that you enjoy.
pleasurable (adjective).

pleat, pleats, pleating, pleated
1 (noun) A pleat is a permanent fold in fabric made by folding one part over another.

2 (verb) To pleat fabric means to make pleats in it.

plebeian, plebeians (a formal, offensive word)
1 (noun) A plebeian is a member of the lower classes.
2 (adjective) Something that is plebeian is connected with or typical of the lower classes.

plebiscite, plebiscites (pronounced **pleb**-iss-ite)
(noun; a formal word) A plebiscite is a vote on a matter of national importance in which all the voters in a country can take part.
[from Latin *plebiscitum* meaning 'decree of the people']

plectrum, plectrums
(noun) A plectrum is a small, flat piece of plastic or metal used for plucking the strings of an instrument such as a guitar.

pledge, pledges, pledging, pledged
1 (noun) A pledge is a solemn promise.
2 (verb) If you pledge something, you promise that you will do it or give it.

plenary (pronounced **pleen**-ar-ee)
(adjective) A plenary session or meeting is attended by everyone who has the right to attend.
[from Latin *plenus* meaning 'full']

plenipotentiary, plenipotentiaries
(noun; a formal word) A plenipotentiary is someone who has full authority to act as a representative of a country or organization.
[from Latin *plenus* meaning 'full' and *potentia* meaning 'power']

plentiful
(adjective) existing in large numbers or amounts and readily available.
plentifully (adverb).

plenty
(noun) If there is plenty of something, there is a lot of it.

plethora (pronounced **pleth**-thor-ah)
(noun) A plethora of something is an amount that is greater than you need.
[from Greek *plēthorē* meaning 'fullness']

pleurisy (pronounced **ploor**-ris-see)
(noun) Pleurisy is a serious illness in which a person's lungs become inflamed and breathing is difficult.

pliable
1 (adjective) If something is pliable, you can bend it without breaking it.
2 Someone who is pliable can be easily influenced or controlled.
[from French *plier* meaning 'to fold' or 'to bend']

Similar words: (sense 1) malleable, flexible, elastic

pliant
(adjective) Pliant means the same as pliable.

pliers
(plural noun) Pliers are a small tool with metal jaws for holding small objects and bending wire.

plight
(noun) Someone's plight is the very difficult or dangerous situation that they are in.

plimsoll, plimsolls
(noun) Plimsolls are canvas shoes with flat rubber soles.

Plimsoll line, Plimsoll lines
(noun) The Plimsoll line on a ship is a line painted on the outside to indicate how deep the ship can lie in the water when fully loaded. It is named after Samuel Plimsoll, who advocated it.

plinth, plinths
(noun) A plinth is a block of stone on which a statue or pillar stands.

plod, plods, plodding, plodded
1 (verb) If you plod somewhere, you walk there slowly and heavily.
2 If you plod through a piece of work, you work slowly without enthusiasm.

plonk, plonks, plonking, plonked
1 (verb) If you plonk something down, you put it down heavily and carelessly.
2 (noun; an informal use) Plonk is cheap wine.

plop, plops, plopping, plopped
1 (noun) A plop is a gentle sound made by something light dropping into a liquid.
2 (verb) If something plops into a liquid, it drops into it with a gentle sound.

plot, plots, plotting, plotted
1 (noun) A plot is a secret plan made by a group of people.
2 The plot of a novel or play is the story.
3 A plot of land is a small piece of it.
4 (verb) If people plot to do something, they plan it secretly.
5 If someone plots the course of a plane or ship on a map, or plots a graph, they mark the points in the correct places.

Similar words: (sense 1) conspiracy, intrigue, scheme, subterfuge, stratagem
(sense 4) conspire, scheme

plough, ploughs, ploughing, ploughed
1 (noun) A plough is a large farming tool that is pulled across a field to turn the soil.
2 (verb) When someone ploughs land, they use a plough to turn over the soil.
3 If you plough on, you continue moving or trying to complete something with a lot of effort.

plover, plovers (pronounced **pluv**-ver)
(noun) A plover is a bird with long wings and a short, straight beak. Plovers usually live on the seashore.

ploy, ploys
(noun) A ploy is a clever plan or way of behaving in order to get something that you want.

pluck, plucks, plucking, plucked
1 (verb) To pluck a fruit or flower means to remove it with a sharp pull.
2 To pluck a chicken or other dead bird means to pull its feathers out before cooking it.

3 When you pluck a stringed instrument, you pull the strings and let them go.
4 (noun) Pluck is courage.
5 (phrase) If you **pluck up courage** to do something frightening, you make an effort to do it.
plucky (adjective).

plug, plugs, plugging, plugged
1 (noun) A plug is a plastic object with metal prongs that can be pushed into a socket to connect an appliance to the electricity supply.
2 A plug is also a disc of rubber or metal with which you stop the hole in a sink or bath.
3 (verb) If you plug a hole, you block it with something.
4 (an informal use) If someone plugs a book or other product, they praise it in order to encourage people to buy it.

plug in
(phrasal verb) If you plug in an electrical appliance, you push its plug into the electricity socket.

plum, plums
1 (noun) A plum is a small fruit with a smooth red or yellow skin and a large stone in the middle.
2 (adjective; an informal use) A plum job is a very good one that everyone would like.

plumage (pronounced **ploom**-mage)
(noun) A bird's plumage is its feathers.
[from French *plume* meaning 'feather']

plumb, plumbs, plumbing, plumbed
(phrase) If you **plumb the depths** of an unpleasant emotion, you experience it intensely.

plumber, plumbers
(noun) A plumber is a person who connects and repairs water pipes, baths, and toilets.
[from Old French *plommier* meaning 'worker in lead']

plumbing
(noun) The plumbing in a building is the system of water pipes, sinks, baths, and toilets.

plumb line, plumb lines
(noun) A plumb line is a piece of string with a weight attached to the end, which is used to check that something is vertical.

plume, plumes
(noun) A plume is a large, brightly coloured feather.

plummet, plummets, plummeting, plummeted
(verb) If something plummets, it falls very quickly.

plump, plumper, plumpest; plumps, plumping, plumped
1 (adjective) rather fat.
2 (verb) If you plump a cushion, you shake it and push it back into a rounded shape.
3 (an informal use) When you plump for a particular thing, you choose it.

Similar words: (sense 1) chubby, portly, stout, tubby

plunder, plunders, plundering, plundered
(verb) If someone plunders a place, they steal things from it.

plunge, plunges, plunging, plunged
1 (verb) If something plunges, it falls suddenly.
2 If you plunge an object into something, you push it in quickly.
3 If you plunge into an activity or state, you suddenly become involved in it or affected by it.
4 (noun) A plunge is a sudden fall.

Similar words: (sense 1) dive, pitch, swoop

plunger, plungers
(noun) A plunger is a device for unblocking sinks. It consists of a rubber cup on a stick.

pluperfect
(noun) In grammar, the pluperfect is the tense of a verb used to describe actions that were completed before another event in the past happened. In English the pluperfect is formed using 'had' followed by the past participle, as in 'She had eaten them before I arrived'.

plural, plurals
(noun) The plural is the form of a word that is used to refer to two or more people or things, for example the plural of 'chair' is 'chairs', and the plural of 'mouse' is 'mice'.
[from Latin *pluralis* meaning 'concerning many']

plural noun, plural nouns
(noun) In this dictionary, 'plural noun' is the name given to a noun that is normally used only in the plural, for example 'scissors' or 'police'.

plus
1 You use plus to show that one number is being added to another, e.g. *Four plus three equals seven.*
2 (adjective) slightly more than the number mentioned, e.g. *my 25 years plus as an officer.*
3 (preposition) You can use plus when you mention an additional item, e.g. *Five people, plus Val, are missing.*
[from Latin *plus* meaning 'more']

plush
(adjective) very expensive and smart.

Pluto
(noun) Pluto is the smallest planet in the solar system and the furthest from the sun.

plutocracy (pronounced ploo-**tok**-rass-ee)
(noun) Plutocracy is the control of society by people who are very rich.
[from Greek *ploutokratia* meaning 'government by the rich']

plutonium
(noun) Plutonium is a radioactive element used in nuclear weapons and in the generation of nuclear power. Its atomic number is 94 and its symbol is Pu.

ply, plies, plying, plied
1 (verb) If you ply someone with things or questions, you keep giving them things or asking them questions.
2 If a boat plies somewhere, it makes regular journeys there.
3 To ply a trade means to do a particular job as your work.
4 (noun) Ply is the thickness of wool or thread,

measured by the number of strands it is made from.

plywood
(noun) Plywood is wooden board made from several thin sheets of wood glued together under pressure.

p.m.
used to specify times between 12 noon and 12 midnight, e.g. *I went to bed at 9 p.m.* It is an abbreviation for the Latin phrase 'post meridiem', which means 'after noon'.

pneumatic (pronounced new-**mat**-ik)
(adjective) operated by or filled with compressed air, e.g. *a pneumatic drill.*
[from Latin *pneumaticus* meaning 'of air or wind']

pneumonia (pronounced new-**moan**-ee-ah)
(noun) Pneumonia is a serious disease which affects a person's lungs and makes breathing difficult.
[from Greek *pneumōn* meaning 'lung']

poach, poaches, poaching, poached
1 (verb) If someone poaches animals from someone else's land, they illegally catch the animals for food.
2 When you poach food, you cook it gently in hot liquid.
poacher (noun).

P O Box
P O Box is used followed by a number as part of an address. The post office keeps the letters for collection by the customer who has paid for the service.

pocket, pockets, pocketing, pocketed
1 (noun) A pocket is a small bag or pouch that forms part of a piece of clothing.
2 A pocket of something is a small area of it, e.g. *small pockets of cloud.*
3 (verb) If someone pockets something that does not belong to them, they take it secretly.
4 (phrase) If you are **out of pocket**, you have less money than you should have.

pocketbook, pocketbooks
(noun) A pocketbook is a notebook.

pocket money
(noun) Pocket money is an amount of money given regularly to children by their parents.

pockmarked
(adjective) If a surface is pockmarked, it is covered with small hollow marks.

pod, pods
(noun) A pod is a long narrow seed container that grows on plants such as peas or beans.

podgy, podgier, podgiest
(adjective) Someone who is podgy is rather fat.

podium, podiums
(noun) A podium is a small platform, often one on which someone stands to make a speech.
[from Latin *podium* meaning 'platform' or 'balcony']

poem, poems
(noun) A poem is a piece of writing in which the words are arranged in short rhythmic lines, often with a rhyme.

poet, poets
(noun) A poet is a person who writes poems.

poetic
1 (adjective) very beautiful, expressive, and sensitive, e.g. *poetic language.*
2 relating to poetry.
poetically (adverb).

poetry
(noun) Poetry is poems, considered as a form of literature.

poignant (pronounced **poyn**-yant)
(adjective) Something that is poignant has a strong emotional effect on you, often making you feel sad, e.g. *a poignant story.*
poignancy (noun).

point, points, pointing, pointed
1 (noun) A point is an opinion or fact expressed by someone, e.g. *I want to make several points.*
2 A point is also a quality, e.g. *Your strong points are speed and accuracy.*
3 The point of something is its purpose, importance, or meaning, e.g. *You missed the point.*
4 A point is a position or time, e.g. *At some point, I must have dropped the key.*
5 A point in a competition is a single mark.
6 In tennis, a point is a stage in a game which begins when a player serves and ends when one player fails to return a shot successfully. The other player has then won the point.
7 The point of something such as a needle or knife is the thin, sharp end.
8 The points of a compass are the 32 directions indicated on it.
9 The decimal point in a number is the dot separating the whole number from the fraction.
10 On a railway track, the points are the levers and rails which enable a train to move from one track to another.
11 (verb) If you point at something, you stick out your finger to show where it is.
12 If something points in a particular direction, it faces that way.

point out
(phrasal verb) If you point something out to someone, you draw their attention to it by pointing to it or explaining it.

point-blank
1 (adverb) If you say something point-blank, you say it directly without explanation or apology.
2 (adjective) Something that is shot at point-blank range is shot with a gun held very close to it.

point duty
(noun) A policeman on point duty is controlling the traffic at a junction.

pointed
1 (adjective) A pointed object has a thin, sharp end.
2 Pointed comments express criticism.
pointedly (adverb).

pointer, pointers
(noun) A pointer is a piece of information which helps you to understand something, e.g. *We now have a few pointers to what happened.*

pointless
(adjective) Something that is pointless has no use, sense, or purpose.
pointlessly (adverb).

point of view, points of view
1 (noun) Your point of view is your opinion about something or your attitude towards it.
2 A point of view is also one aspect of something, e.g. *From the commercial point of view, they are of little value.*

poise
(noun) Someone who has poise is calm, self-controlled, and dignified.

poised
(adjective) If you are poised to do something, you are ready to do it at any moment.

poison, poisons, poisoning, poisoned
1 (noun) Poison is a substance that can kill people or animals if they swallow it or absorb it.
2 (verb) To poison someone means to try to kill them with poison.
poisonous (adjective).
[from Old French *puison* meaning 'potion']

Similar words: (sense 1) toxin, venom

poke, pokes, poking, poked
1 (verb) If you poke someone or something, you push at them quickly with your finger or a sharp object.
2 Something that pokes out of another thing appears from behind or underneath it.

Similar words: (sense 1) jab, prod, dig

poker, pokers
1 (noun) Poker is a card game in which the players make bets on the cards dealt to them.
2 A poker is a long metal rod used for moving coals or logs in a fire.

poky, pokier, pokiest
(adjective) A poky room or house is uncomfortably small.

polar
1 (adjective) relating to the area around the north and south poles.
2 (a formal use) completely opposite in character, quality, or type.
polarity (noun).

polar bear, polar bears
(noun) A polar bear is a large white bear which lives in the area around the North Pole.

polarize, polarizes, polarizing, polarized; also spelled polarise
(verb) If groups polarize, they form opposite opinions from each other.
polarization (noun).

Polaroid
(noun; a trademark) Polaroid is a type of plastic sheet used in sunglasses in order to reduce harsh brightness.

Polaroid camera, Polaroid cameras
(noun; a trademark) A Polaroid camera is a camera that can take, develop, and print a photograph in a few seconds.

polder, polders
(noun) A polder is a stretch of land reclaimed from the sea, especially in the Netherlands.

pole, poles
1 (noun) A pole is a long rounded piece of wood or metal.
2 The earth's poles are the two opposite ends of its axis.
3 The poles of a magnet are the two opposite ends where opposite magnetic forces are concentrated.
[senses 2 and 3 are from Greek *polos* meaning 'pivot' or 'axis']

Pole, Poles
(noun) A Pole is someone who comes from Poland.

poleaxe, poleaxes
(noun) A poleaxe is a very large axe used for killing or stunning animals.

polecat, polecats
(noun) A polecat is a small, fierce wild animal with a very unpleasant smell.

polemic, polemics (pronounced pol-lem-mik)
1 (noun; a formal word) A polemic is a speech or piece of writing that fiercely attacks or defends a belief or opinion.
2 Polemics is the skill of arguing passionately for or against a particular belief.
polemical (adjective).
[from Greek *polemikos* meaning 'relating to war']

pole vault
(noun) The pole vault is an athletics event in which contestants jump over a high bar using a long flexible pole to lift themselves into the air.

police, polices, policing, policed
1 (plural noun) The police are the people who are officially responsible for making sure that people obey the law.
2 (verb) To police an area means to preserve law and order there by means of the police or an armed force.

policeman, policemen
(noun) A policeman is a man who is a member of a police force.
policewoman (noun).

policy, policies
1 (noun) A policy is a set of plans used as a basis for action, especially in politics or business.
2 An insurance policy is a document which shows an agreement made with an insurance company.
[sense 1 is from Latin *politia* meaning 'administration'; sense 2 is from Old French *police* meaning 'certificate']

polio
(noun) Polio is an infectious disease that is caused by a virus and often results in paralysis. Polio is short for 'poliomyelitis'.

polish, polishes, polishing, polished
1 (verb) If you polish something, you put polish on it or rub it with a cloth to make it shine.
2 (noun) Polish is a substance that you put on an object to clean it and make it shine.
3 Something that has polish is elegant and of good quality.
polished (adjective).

Similar words: (sense 1) buff, burnish, rub, shine

polish off
(phrasal verb; an informal use) If you polish something off, you finish it completely.

Polish (pronounced **pole**-ish)
1 (adjective) belonging or relating to Poland.
2 (noun) Polish is the main language spoken in Poland.

polite
(adjective) Someone who is polite has good manners and behaves considerately towards other people.
politely (adverb), **politeness** (noun).
[from Latin *politus* meaning 'polished']

Similar words: gracious, courteous, well-behaved, well-mannered, respectful, civil

politic
(adjective; a formal word) If you say it would be politic to do something, you mean it would be a sensible thing to do.

politician, politicians
(noun) A politician is a person involved in the government of a country.

politics
1 (noun) Politics is the activity and planning concerned with achieving power and control in a country or organization.
2 (plural noun) Your politics are your beliefs about how a country ought to be governed.
political (adjective), **politically** (adverb).

polka, polkas
(noun) A polka is a fast dance in which couples dance together in circles around the room.

polka dot, polka dots
(noun) Polka dots are a pattern of spots printed on a piece of cloth.

poll, polls, polling, polled
1 (noun) A poll is a survey in which people are asked their opinions about something.
2 (verb) If you are polled on something, you are asked your opinion about it as part of a survey.
3 If a candidate in an election polls a particular number of votes, they get that number of votes.
4 (plural noun) A political election can be referred to as the polls.

pollen
(noun) Pollen is a fine yellow powder produced by flowers. Each grain is a male reproductive cell which can fertilize other flowers of the same species.
[from Latin *pollen* meaning 'powder']

pollen count, pollen counts
(noun) The pollen count is a measurement of the amount of pollen in the air at a particular time.

pollinate, pollinates, pollinating, pollinated
(verb) To pollinate a plant means to fertilize it with pollen.
pollination (noun).

polling station, polling stations
(noun) A polling station is a place where you go to vote in an election.

pollster, pollsters
(noun) A pollster is someone who conducts an opinion poll.

poll tax, poll taxes
(noun) A poll tax is a tax that every adult has to pay.

pollutant, pollutants
(noun) A pollutant is a substance that causes pollution.

pollute, pollutes, polluting, polluted
(verb) To pollute water or air means to make it dirty and dangerous to use or live in.
pollution (noun), **polluted** (adjective).

Similar words: taint, foul, sully

polo
(noun) Polo is a game played between two teams of players on horseback. The players use wooden hammers with long handles to hit a ball.

polo-necked
(adjective) A polo-necked jumper has a deep fold of material at the neck.

polonium
(noun) Polonium is a rare radioactive element. The isotope polonium 210 is used as a lightweight power source in satellites. Polonium's atomic number is 84 and its symbol is Po.

poltergeist, poltergeists (pronounced **pol**-ter-guyst)
(noun) A poltergeist is an invisible force which is believed to move objects or throw them around.
[a German word, from *poltern* meaning 'to make a noise' and *geist* meaning 'ghost']

poly-
(prefix) Poly- means many or much.
[from Greek *polus* meaning 'many' or 'much']

polyester
(noun) Polyester is a man-made fibre, used especially to make clothes.

polygamy (pronounced pol-**lig**-gam-ee)
(noun) Polygamy is the custom of having more than one wife at the same time.
polygamist (noun), **polygamous** (adjective).
[from Greek *polugamia*]

polygon, polygons
(noun) A polygon is any two-dimensional shape whose sides are all straight.

polyhedron, polyhedrons or **polyhedra**
(noun) A polyhedron is any three-dimensional shape whose edges are all straight and whose sides are all flat.

polymer, polymers
(noun) A polymer is a chemical compound with large molecules made up of many simple repeated units.

Polynesia
(noun) Polynesia is one of the three groups into which the islands in the Pacific are divided. Samoa and Tonga are in Polynesia.
Polynesian (adjective).

polyp, polyps (pronounced pol-lip)
1 (noun) A polyp is a tiny sea creature with a hollow, tubelike body. Coral is made up of polyps.
2 A polyp is also a small, unhealthy growth on a surface inside someone's body.

polystyrene
(noun) Polystyrene is a very light plastic substance, used especially as insulating material or to make containers.

polytechnic, polytechnics
(noun) A polytechnic is a college where you can study after leaving school.
[from Greek *polutekhnos* meaning 'skilled in many arts']

polythene
(noun) Polythene is a type of plastic that is used to make thin sheets or bags.

polyunsaturated
(adjective) Polyunsaturated oils and margarines are made mainly from vegetable fats and are considered to be healthier than saturated oils.

polyurethane (pronounced pol-lee-yoo-rath-ane)
(noun) Polyurethane is a plastic material used especially to make paint or types of foam.

pomegranate, pomegranates
(noun) A pomegranate is a round fruit with a thick reddish skin. It contains a lot of small seeds with juicy flesh around each one.
[from Latin *pomum granatum* meaning 'apple full of seeds']

pomp
(noun) Pomp is the use of ceremony, fine clothes, and decorations on special occasions.
[from Latin *pompa* meaning 'procession']

pom-pom, pom-poms
(noun) A pom-pom is a ball of woollen threads, usually used as a decoration.

pompous
(adjective) behaving in a way that is too serious and self-important.
pomposity (noun).

pond, ponds
(noun) A pond is a small, usually man-made area of water.

ponder, ponders, pondering, pondered
(verb) If you ponder, you think about something deeply.
[from Latin *ponderare* meaning 'to weigh' or 'to consider']

Similar words: muse, cogitate, mull over, ruminate

ponderous
(adjective) dull, slow, and serious, e.g. *a ponderous style of writing*.
ponderously (adverb), **ponderousness** (noun).
[from Latin *ponderosus* meaning 'weighty']

pong, pongs
(noun; an informal word) A pong is an unpleasant smell.

pontiff, pontiffs
(noun; a formal word) The pontiff is the Pope.

pontificate, pontificates, pontificating, pontificated
(verb) If someone pontificates, they state their opinions as if they are obviously correct.

Similar words: hold forth, expound

pontoon, pontoons
(noun) A pontoon is a floating platform.
[from French *ponton* meaning 'punt', from Latin *pons* meaning 'bridge']

pony, ponies
(noun) A pony is a small horse.

ponytail, ponytails
(noun) A ponytail is a hairstyle in which long hair is tied at the back of the head and hangs down like a tail.

ponytrekking
(noun) Ponytrekking is a leisure activity in which people ride across country on ponies.

poodle, poodles
(noun) A poodle is a type of dog with curly hair.

pool, pools, pooling, pooled
1 (noun) A pool is a small area of still water.
2 Pool is a game in which players try to hit coloured balls into pockets around the table using long sticks called cues.
3 A pool of people, money, or things is a group or collection used or shared by several people.
4 (verb) If people pool their resources, they gather together the things they have so that they can be shared or used by all of them.
5 (plural noun) The pools are a competition in which people try to guess the results of football matches.

poor, poorer, poorest
1 (adjective) Poor people have very little money and few possessions.
2 Poor places are inhabited by people with little money and show signs of neglect.
3 You use poor to show sympathy, e.g. *You poor thing!*
4 Poor also means of a low quality or standard, e.g. *books in a very poor condition*.
[from Latin *pauper* meaning 'poor']

Similar words: (sense 1) penniless, penurious, impoverished, needy

poorly
1 (adjective) feeling unwell or ill.
2 (adverb) badly, e.g. *It was poorly planned.*

pop, pops, popping, popped
1 (noun) Pop is modern music, especially songs, played and enjoyed by young people.

2 You can refer to fizzy, nonalcholic drinks as pop.
3 A pop is a short, sharp sound.
4 (verb) If something pops, it makes a sudden sharp sound.
5 If someone's eyes pop, they look very surprised.
6 If you pop something somewhere, you put it there quickly.
7 If you pop somewhere, you go there quickly.

popcorn
(noun) Popcorn is a snack consisting of grains of maize heated until they puff up and burst.

Pope, Popes
(noun) The Pope is the head of the Roman Catholic Church.
[from Latin *Papa* meaning 'bishop' or 'father']

poplar, poplars
(noun) A poplar is a type of tall thin tree.

poppadum, poppadums
(noun) A poppadum is a large circular crisp made of flour and spices and eaten with Indian food.

popper, poppers
(noun) A popper is a device for fastening clothes consisting of two pieces of metal or plastic that can be pressed together.

poppy, poppies
(noun) A poppy is a plant with a large delicate red flower on a hairy stem.

populace
(noun; a formal word) The populace of a country is its people.

popular
1 (adjective) enjoyed, approved of, or liked by a lot of people.
2 involving or intended for ordinary people, e.g. *the popular press.*
popularly (adverb), **popularity** (noun), **popularize** (verb).
[from Latin *popularis* meaning 'belonging to the people']

Similar words: (sense 1) in, fashionable, in favour, well-liked

populate, populates, populating, populated
(verb) The people or animals that populate an area live there.

population, populations
(noun) The population of a place is the people who live there, or the number of people living there.

populous
(adjective; a formal word) A populous area has a lot of people living in it.

porcelain
(noun) Porcelain is a delicate ceramic material used to make crockery and ornaments.

porch, porches
(noun) A porch is a covered area at the entrance to a building.
[from Latin *porticus* meaning 'portico']

porcupine, porcupines
(noun) A porcupine is a large rodent with long spines covering its body.
[from Old French *porc d'espins* meaning 'pig with spines']

pore, pores, poring, pored
1 (noun) The pores in your skin or on the surface of a plant are very small holes which allow moisture to pass through.
2 (verb) If you pore over a piece of writing or a diagram, you study it carefully.

pork
(noun) Pork is meat from a pig which has not been salted or smoked.
[from Latin *porcus* meaning 'pig']

pornography
(noun) Pornography refers to magazines and films that are designed to cause sexual excitement by showing naked people and sexual acts.
pornographic (adjective).
[from Greek *pornos* meaning 'prostitute' and *graphein* meaning 'to write']

porous
(adjective) containing many holes through which water and air can pass, e.g. *porous rock.*

porpoise, porpoises (pronounced por-pus)
(noun) A porpoise is a sea mammal related to the dolphin. It has a short, rounded snout.
[from Latin *porcus* meaning 'pig' and *piscis* meaning 'fish']

porridge
(noun) Porridge is a thick, sticky food made from oats cooked in water or milk.

port, ports
1 (noun) A port is a town or area which has a harbour or docks.
2 Port is a kind of sweet fortified red wine.
3 (adjective) The port side of a ship is the left side when you are facing the front.
[from Latin *portus* meaning 'harbour']

portable
(adjective) designed to be easily carried, e.g. *a portable television.*

portal, portals
(noun; a literary word) A portal is a large impressive entrance.
[from Latin *porta* meaning 'gate' or 'entrance']

portcullis, portcullises
(noun) A portcullis is a large metal gate above the entrance to a castle, which was lowered to keep out enemies.
[from Old French *porte coleice* meaning 'sliding gate']

portent, portents
(noun) A portent is something taken as a sign indicating what is going to happen in the future.
portentous (adjective).
[from Latin *portentum* meaning 'sign' or 'omen']

porter, porters
1 (noun) A porter is a person whose job is to be in charge of the entrance of a building, greeting and directing visitors.

2 A porter in a railway station, airport, or hospital is a person whose job is to carry or move things.
[sense 1 is from Latin *portarius* meaning 'gatekeeper'; sense 2 is from Latin *portator* meaning 'one who carries']

portfolio, portfolios
1 (noun) A portfolio is a thin, flat case for carrying papers.
2 A portfolio is also a group of selected duties, investments, or items of artwork.
[from Italian *portafoglio* meaning 'carrier for papers']

porthole, portholes
(noun) A porthole is a small window in the side of a ship or aircraft.

portico, porticoes or **porticos**
(noun; a formal word) A portico is a large covered area supported by pillars at the entrance to a building.
[an Italian word]

portion, portions
(noun) A portion of something is a part or amount of it.
[from Latin *portio* meaning 'portion' or 'share']

Similar words: helping, share

portly
(adjective) Portly people are rather fat.

portmanteau, portmanteaus or **portmanteaux**
(pronounced port-**man**-toe)
(noun) A portmanteau is a large, old-fashioned travelling case which opens into two compartments.
[from French *portmanteau* meaning 'cloak carrier']

portrait, portraits
(noun) A portrait is a picture or photograph of someone.

portray, portrays, portraying, portrayed
(verb) When an actor, artist, or writer portrays someone or something, they represent or describe them.
portrayal (noun).

Portuguese (pronounced por-tyoo-**geez**)
1 (adjective) belonging or relating to Portugal.
2 (noun) A Portuguese is someone who comes from Portugal.
3 Portuguese is the main language spoken in Portugal and Brazil.

pose, poses, posing, posed
1 (verb) If you pose for a photograph or painting, you stay in a particular position so that someone can photograph or paint you.
2 If you pose as someone else, you pretend to be that person in order to deceive people.
3 If something poses a problem, it is the cause of the problem.
4 (noun) Your pose is the way that you are standing, sitting, or lying.
5 A pose is also a way of behaving that is intended to impress or deceive people.
[from French *poser* meaning 'to put in place']

Similar words: (sense 4) posture, attitude

poser, posers; also spelled **poseur.**
1 (noun) A poser is someone who behaves or dresses in an exaggerated way in order to impress people.
2 A poser is also a difficult problem or question.

posh, posher, poshest
1 (adjective; an informal word) smart, fashionable, and expensive.
2 upper class.

position, positions, positioning, positioned
1 (noun) The position of someone or something is the place where they are.
2 When someone or something is in a particular position, they are sitting or lying in that way, e.g. *I helped her to a sitting position.*
3 A position in an organization is a job or post in it.
4 The position that you are in at a particular time is the situation that you are in, e.g. *You are in the fortunate position of having no cares.*
5 Your position with regard to a particular subject is your opinion or attitude towards it.
6 (verb) To position something somewhere means to put it there.

positive
1 (adjective) completely sure about something, e.g. *I'm positive she said she would come.*
2 confident and hopeful, e.g. *positive feelings.*
3 showing approval, agreement, or encouragement, e.g. *Public response was positive.*
4 providing definite proof of the truth or identity of something, e.g. *positive evidence.*
5 A positive number is greater than zero.
6 In physics, a positive electric charge has an opposite charge to that of an electron.
7 If a medical test is positive, it shows that something is present, e.g. *a positive pregnancy test.*
positively (adverb).
[from Latin *positivus* meaning 'positive' or 'agreed']

Similar words: (sense 4) affirmative, categorical, definite, certain

possess, possesses, possessing, possessed
1 (verb) If you possess something, you own it or have it.
2 If a feeling or belief possesses you, it strongly influences you.
possessor (noun).
[from Latin *possidere* meaning 'to own' or 'to occupy']

possession, possessions
1 (noun) If something is in your possession or if you are in possession of it, you have it.
2 Your possessions are the things that you own or that you have with you.

Similar words: (sense 2) property, belongings, chattels, effects

possessive
1 (adjective) A person who is possessive about

someone or something wants to keep them to themselves.
2 (noun) In grammar, the possessive is the form of a noun or pronoun used to show possession.

possibility, possibilities
(noun) A possibility is something that might be true or might happen.

Similar words: chance, likelihood, prospect

possible
1 (adjective) likely to happen or able to be done.
2 likely or capable of being true or correct.
possibly (adverb).
[from Latin *possibilis* meaning 'that may be', and from the verb *posse* meaning 'to be able']

Similar words: (sense 1) feasible, practicable, viable, workable

post, posts, posting, posted
1 (noun) The post is the system by which letters and parcels are collected and delivered.
2 (verb) If you post a letter, you send it to someone by putting it into a postbox.
3 (noun) A post in an organization is a job or official position in it.
4 (verb) If you are posted somewhere, you are sent by your employers to work there.
5 (noun) A post is a strong upright pole fixed into the ground.
postal (adjective).
[senses 1-4 are from Latin *posita* meaning 'something placed'; sense 5 is from Old English *post* meaning 'pole']

post-
(prefix) after a particular time or event, e.g. *the postwar years... a postelection survey.*
[from Latin *post* meaning 'after']

postage
(noun) Postage is the money that you pay to send letters and parcels by post.

postal order, postal orders
(noun) A postal order is a piece of paper representing a sum of money which you can buy at a post office.

postbox, postboxes
(noun) A postbox is a metal box with a hole in it which you put letters into for collection by the postman.

postcard, postcards
(noun) A postcard is a card, often with a picture on one side, which you write on and send through the post without an envelope.

postcode, postcodes
(noun) Your postcode is a short sequence of letters and numbers at the end of your address which helps the post office to sort the mail.

poster, posters
(noun) A poster is a large notice or picture that is stuck on a wall as an advertisement or for decoration.

posterior, posteriors
(noun; a humorous use) A person's posterior is their bottom.

posterity
(noun; a formal word) You can refer to the future and the people who will be alive then as posterity, e.g. *Such fine buildings should be preserved for posterity.*
[from Latin *posteritas* meaning 'future generations']

postgraduate, postgraduates
(noun) A postgraduate is a student with a first degree who is studying for a degree at a more advanced level.

posthumous (pronounced **poss**-tyum-uss)
(adjective) happening or awarded after a person's death, e.g. *a posthumous award for bravery.*
posthumously (adverb).

postman, postmen
(noun) A postman collects and delivers letters and parcels sent by post.

postmark, postmarks
(noun) A postmark is a mark printed on letters showing when and where they were posted.

postmaster, postmasters
(noun) A postmaster is a person in charge of a post office.
postmistress (noun).

postmortem, postmortems
(noun) A postmortem is a medical examination of a dead body to find out how the person died.
[from Latin *post mortem* meaning 'after death']

post office, post offices
1 (noun) The Post Office is the national organization responsible for postal services.
2 A post office is a building where you can buy stamps and post letters and parcels.

postpone, postpones, postponing, postponed
(verb) If you postpone an event, you arrange for it to take place at a later time than was originally planned.
postponement (noun).
[from Latin *postponere* meaning 'to put after']

Similar words: shelve, procrastinate, put off

postscript, postscripts
(noun) A postscript is an additional message at the end of a letter, after your signature.
[from Latin *post scriptum* meaning 'written after']

postulate, postulates, postulating, postulated
(verb; a formal word) If you postulate something, you assume or suggest it as the basis for a theory or calculation.
[from Latin *postulare* meaning 'to require']

posture, postures, posturing, postured
1 (noun) Your posture is the position or manner in which you hold your body.
2 (verb) Someone who is posturing is trying to give a particular impression to people.
[from Latin *positura* meaning 'position']

posy, posies
(noun) A posy is a small bunch of flowers.

pot, pots, potting, potted
1 (noun) A pot is a deep round container; also used to refer to its contents.
2 (an informal use) Pot is cannabis.
3 (verb) If you pot a plant, you plant it in a flowerpot.
4 If you pot a ball in snooker or billiards, you hit it into one of the pockets.

potash
(noun) Potash is a strong alkali, either potassium carbonate or potassium hydroxide, often used in fertilizers.

potassium
(noun) Potassium is a soft silver-coloured element used in making soap, detergents, fertilizers, and glass. Its atomic number is 19 and its symbol is K.

potato, potatoes
(noun) A potato is a white vegetable that has a brown or red skin and grows underground.

potbelly, potbellies
(noun) Someone who has a potbelly has a round fat stomach.
potbellied (adjective).

potboiler, potboilers
(noun) A potboiler is a novel that is written very quickly in order to earn money.

potent
(adjective) effective, powerful, or strong, e.g. *a potent drink*.
potency (noun).
[from Latin *potens* meaning 'able']

potentate, potentates
(noun) A potentate is a ruler who has direct and powerful control over people.
[from Latin *potentatus* meaning 'ruler']

potential
1 (adjective) capable of becoming the kind of thing mentioned, e.g. *a list of potential parliamentary candidates... potential sources of food production.*
2 (noun) Your potential is your ability to achieve a particular level of success in the future.
potentially (adverb).

Similar words: (sense 1) unrealized, dormant, latent

pothole, potholes
1 (noun) A pothole is a hole in the surface of a road caused by bad weather or traffic.
2 A pothole is also an underground cavern.

potholing
Potholing is the activity of exploring underground caverns.
potholer (noun).

potion, potions
(noun) A potion is a drink containing medicine, poison, or supposed magical powers.
[from Latin *potio* meaning 'a drink']

potluck
(noun) If you take potluck, you have whatever is available without being able to choose.

potpourri, potpourris (pronounced poh-**poor**-ee)
(noun) Potpourri is a mixture of dried petals and fragrant oil used to scent a room.
[from French *pot pourri* meaning literally 'rotten pot']

pot shot, pot shots
(noun) If someone takes a pot shot at something, they shoot at it without aiming carefully.

potted
1 (adjective) Potted meat or fish is cooked and put into a small sealed container to preserve it.
2 (an informal use) A potted account contains only the main facts in a simplified form.

potter, potters, pottering, pottered
1 (noun) A potter is a person who makes pottery.
2 (verb) If you potter about, you pass the time doing pleasant, unimportant things.

pottery, potteries
1 (noun) Pottery is pots, dishes, and other items made from clay and fired in a kiln.
2 Pottery is also the craft of making pottery.
3 A pottery is a workshop where pottery is made.

potty, potties; pottier, pottiest
1 (noun) A potty is a bowl which a small child can sit on and use instead of a toilet.
2 (adjective; an informal use) crazy or foolish.

pouch, pouches
1 (noun) A pouch is a small, soft container with a fold-over top, e.g. *a tobacco pouch.*
2 Marsupials such as kangaroos have a pouch, which is a pocket of skin in which they carry their young.
[from Old French *poche* meaning 'bag']

pouffe, pouffes (rhymes with **hoof**)
(noun) A pouffe is a low, soft piece of furniture used for sitting on or resting your feet on.

poultice, poultices
(noun) A poultice is a moist warm dressing that is treated with ointments and put over a swollen or sore part of a person's body.

poultry
(noun) Chickens, turkeys, and other birds kept for their meat or eggs are referred to as poultry.

pounce, pounces, pouncing, pounced
(verb) If an animal or person pounces on something, they leap forward and grab it.

pound, pounds, pounding, pounded
1 (noun) The pound is the main unit of currency in Britain and in some other countries.
2 A pound is also a unit of weight equal to·16 ounces or about 0.454 kilograms.
3 A pound is also a place where officially removed vehicles or stray dogs are held until they are claimed by their owners.
4 (verb) If you pound something, you hit it repeatedly with your fist.
5 If you pound a substance, you crush it into a powder or paste.
6 If your heart is pounding, it is beating very strongly and quickly.
7 If you pound somewhere, you run there with heavy noisy steps.

pour, pours, pouring, poured
1 (verb) If you pour a liquid out of a container, you make it flow out by tipping the container.
2 If something pours somewhere, it flows there quickly and in large quantities, e.g. *Sweat began to pour down his face.*
3 When it is raining heavily, you can say that it is pouring.

Similar words: (sense 3) teem, pelt, bucket, stream

pout, pouts, pouting, pouted
(verb) If you pout, you stick out your lip to show disappointment or annoyance.

poverty
(noun) Poverty is the state of being very poor.

Similar words: penury, necessity, privation, want

poverty-stricken
(adjective) very poor.

powder, powders, powdering, powdered
1 (noun) Powder consists of many tiny particles of a solid substance.
2 (verb) If you powder a surface, you cover it with powder.
powdery (adjective).

powder room, powder rooms
(noun) A powder room is a ladies' toilet.

power, powers, powering, powered
1 (noun) Someone who has power has a lot of control over people and activities.
2 Someone who has the power to do something has the ability to do it, e.g. *the power of speech.*
3 The power of something is the physical strength that it has to move things.
4 Power is energy obtained, for example, by burning fuel or using the wind or waves. Electricity is often referred to as power.
5 In maths, a power is the product of a number multiplied by itself a certain number of times.
6 In physics, power is the rate of doing work. It is measured in watts or horsepower.
7 (verb) Something that powers a machine provides the energy for it to work.
powerful (adjective), **powerfully** (adverb).

Similar words: (sense 3) force, potency, strength

power boat, power boats
(noun) A power boat is a large, extremely fast boat driven by a motor.

powerless
(adjective) unable to control or influence events.

Similar words: impotent, incapable, helpless

power station, power stations
(noun) A power station is a place where electricity is generated.

PR an abbreviation for **public relations** or **proportional representation.**

practicable
(adjective) If a task or plan is practicable, it can be carried out successfully.
practicability (noun).

practical, practicals
1 (adjective) The practical aspects of something are those that involve direct experience and real situations rather than ideas or theories.
2 Ideas, methods, tools, or clothes that are practical are sensible and likely to be effective.
3 Someone who is practical is able to deal effectively and sensibly with problems.
4 (noun) A practical is an examination in which you make or perform something.
practicality (noun).
[from Greek *praktikos* meaning 'fit for action']

Similar words: (sense 2) functional, utilitarian

practical joke, practical jokes
(noun) A practical joke is a trick that is intended to make someone look ridiculous.

practically
1 (adverb) almost but not completely or exactly, e.g. *The town was practically deserted.*
2 in a practical way, e.g. *practically minded.*

practice, practices
1 (noun) You can refer to something that people do regularly as a practice, e.g. *the former Japanese practice of binding the feet from birth.*
2 Practice is regular training or exercise.
3 A doctor's or lawyer's practice is his or her business.
4 (phrase) What happens **in practice** is what actually happens in contrast to what is supposed to happen.
[from Greek *praktikē* meaning 'practical work']

practise, practises, practising, practised
1 (verb) If you practise something, you do it regularly in order to improve.
2 People who practise a religion, custom, or craft take part in the activities associated with it.
3 Someone who practises medicine or law works as a doctor or lawyer.

practised
(adjective) Someone who is practised at doing something is very skilful at it.

practitioner, practitioners
(noun) You can refer to someone who works in a particular profession as a practitioner.

pragmatic
(adjective) based on practical considerations rather than theoretical ones.
pragmatically (adverb), **pragmatism** (noun).
[from Greek *pragma* meaning 'act' or 'deed']

prairie, prairies
(noun) A prairie is a large area of grassland, especially in North America.

praise, praises, praising, praised
1 (verb) If you praise someone or something, you express strong approval of their achievements.
2 (noun) Praise is what is said or written in approval of someone's qualities or achievements.

Similar words: (sense 1) commend, compliment, applaud, acclaim, extol, exalt, laud, glorify
(sense 2) compliment, tribute, commendation

praiseworthy
(adjective; a formal word) deserving praise, e.g.
His behaviour was considered praiseworthy.

pram, prams
(noun) A pram is a baby's cot on wheels. Pram is
short for 'perambulator'.

prance, prances, prancing, pranced
(verb) Someone who is prancing around is
walking with exaggerated bounding movements.

prank, pranks
(noun) A prank is a childish trick.

prattle, prattles, prattling, prattled
(verb) If someone prattles on, they talk a lot
without saying anything important.

prawn, prawns
(noun) A prawn is a small pink shellfish with a
long tail and two pairs of pincers.

pray, prays, praying, prayed
(verb) When someone prays, they speak to God
to give thanks or to ask for help.

prayer, prayers
1 (noun) Prayer is the activity of praying.
2 A prayer is the words said when someone
prays.

prayer book, prayer books
(noun) A prayer book is a book of prayers.

prayer rug, prayer rugs
(noun) A prayer rug or prayer mat is a small
carpet on which Muslims kneel to pray.

prayer shawl, prayer shawls
(noun) A prayer shawl is a white shawl worn by
Jewish men during religious ceremonies.

pre-
(prefix) before a particular time or event, e.g. *the
pre-Christmas period... a pre-school playgroup.*
[from Latin *prae* meaning 'before']

preach, preaches, preaching, preached
1 (verb) When someone preaches, they give a
short talk on a religious or moral subject as part
of a church service.
2 Someone who preaches a set of ideas tries to
persuade people to accept them.
preacher (noun).
[from Latin *praedicare* meaning 'to proclaim']

preamble, preambles (pronounced pree-**am**-bl)
(noun) A preamble is an introduction to
something that is said or written, e.g. *Without
any preamble he said, 'I need some money'.*
[from Latin *praeambulum* meaning 'walking
before']

prearranged
(adjective) arranged beforehand.

precarious
(adjective) Something that is precarious is likely
to fall because it is not well balanced or secured.
precariously (adverb).
[from Latin *precarius* meaning 'obtained by
begging']

Similar words: unstable, shaky, unsafe

precaution, precautions
(noun) A precaution is an action that is intended

to prevent something from happening, e.g. *As a
precaution, take your umbrella.*
precautionary (adjective).

Similar words: safety measure, safeguard

precede, precedes, preceding, preceded
1 (verb) Something that precedes another thing
happens or occurs before it.
2 If you precede someone somewhere, you go in
front of them.
preceding (adjective).

precedence (pronounced **press**-id-ens)
(noun) If something takes precedence over other
things, it is the most important thing and should
be dealt with first.

precedent, precedents
(noun) An action or decision that is regarded as a
precedent is referred to as a guide in taking
similar action or decisions later.

precept, precepts (pronounced **pree**-sept)
(noun) A precept is a general rule that helps you
decide how to behave.
[from Latin *praeceptum*]

precinct, precincts
1 (noun) A shopping precinct is a pedestrian
shopping area.
2 (plural noun) The precincts of a place are its
buildings and land.

precious
1 (adjective) Something that is precious is
valuable or very important and should be looked
after or used carefully.
2 A person who is described as precious behaves
in a formal and unnatural way.
3 (phrase) If there is **precious little** of something,
there is only a very small amount.
[from Latin *pretiosus* meaning 'valuable']

precipice, precipices (pronounced
press-sip-piss)
(noun) A precipice is a very steep rock face.

**precipitate, precipitates, precipitating,
precipitated**
1 (verb; a formal use) If something precipitates
an event or situation, it causes it to happen
suddenly.
2 (adjective; a formal use) happening or done
suddenly, e.g. *a precipitate marriage.*
3 (noun) A precipitate is a solid substance that
separates from a liquid during a chemical
reaction.
[from Latin *praecipitare* meaning 'to throw
down']

precipitation
(noun; a formal word) Precipitation is rain,
snow, or hail; used especially when stating the
amount that falls during a particular period.

precipitous
(adjective) high and with very steep sides, e.g.
precipitous hills.

précis (pronounced **pray**-see)
(noun) A précis is a short piece of writing which
summarizes the main points of a book or article.

precise
(adjective) exact and accurate in every detail.
precisely (adverb), **precision** (noun).
[from French *précis*]

preclude, precludes, precluding, precluded
(verb; a formal word) If something precludes an event or situation, it prevents it from happening, e.g. *This doesn't preclude other possibilities*.
[from Latin *praecludere* meaning 'to shut something up']

precocious
(adjective) Precocious children behave in a way that seems too advanced for their age.
[from Latin *praecox* meaning 'early maturing']

preconceived
(adjective) Preconceived ideas about something have been formed without any real experience or reliable information.
preconception (noun).

precondition, preconditions
(noun) If something is a precondition for another thing, it must happen before the second thing can take place.

precursor, precursors
(noun) A precursor of something that exists now is a similar thing that existed at an earlier time, e.g. *The pennyfarthing was a precursor of the modern bicycle*.
[from Latin *praecursor* meaning 'someone who runs in front']

predator, predators (pronounced **pred**-dat-tor)
(noun) A predator is an animal that kills and eats other animals.
predatory (adjective).

predecessor, predecessors
(noun) Someone's predecessor is a person who used to do their job in the past.

predestination
(noun) Belief in predestination is the belief that future events have already been decided by God or by fate.
predestined (adjective).

predetermined
(adjective) decided in advance or controlled by previous events rather than left to chance.

predicament, predicaments
(noun) If you are in a predicament, you are in a difficult situation.

Similar words: plight, dilemma, quandary

predicate, predicates
(noun) In traditional grammar, the predicate of a sentence is the part that is not the subject. In the sentence 'I decided what to do', 'decided what to do' is the predicate.

predicative
(adjective) In grammar, if an adjective is in predicative position, it comes after a verb.

predict, predicts, predicting, predicted
(verb) If someone predicts an event, they say that it will happen in the future.
prediction (noun).
[from Latin *praedicere* meaning 'to say

beforehand']

Similar words: forecast, foretell, prophesy, foresee

predilection, predilections (pronounced pree-dil-**lek**-shn)
(noun; a formal word) Someone who has a predilection for something likes it or prefers it.
[from Latin *praediligere* meaning 'to prefer']

predispose, predisposes, predisposing, predisposed
(verb; a formal word) If something predisposes you to do something, it influences you and makes you do it.
predisposed (adjective), **predisposition** (noun).

predominant
(adjective) more important or more noticeable than anything else in a particular set of people or things.

Similar words: prevailing, prevalent, dominant

predominate, predominates, predominating, predominated
(verb) If one type of person or thing predominates, it is the most common, frequent, or noticeable.
predominance (noun).

pre-eminent
(adjective) recognized as being the most important in a particular group, e.g. *the pre-eminent figure in economic policy*.
pre-eminence (noun).

pre-empt, pre-empts, pre-empting, pre-empted
(verb; a formal word) If you pre-empt something, you do something in advance which makes it pointless or impossible.

preen, preens, preening, preened
(verb) When a bird preens its feathers, it cleans them and arranges them using its beak.

prefab, prefabs
(noun) A prefab is a house built from large ready-made sections.
prefabricated (adjective).

preface, prefaces, prefacing, prefaced (pronounced **pref**-fiss)
1 (noun) A preface is an introduction at the beginning of a book explaining what the book is about or why it was written.
2 (verb) If you preface a remark or action with something else, you say or do this other thing first.
[from Latin *prae* + *fari* meaning 'to say before']

prefect, prefects
(noun) A prefect at a school is a pupil who has special duties.
[from Latin *praefectus* meaning 'someone put in charge']

prefer, prefers, preferring, preferred
(verb) If you prefer one thing to another, you like it better than the other thing.
preferable (adjective), **preferably** (adverb).

preference, preferences (pronounced **pref**-fer-enss)

1 (noun) If you have a preference for something, you like it more than other things.
2 When making a choice, if you give preference to one type of person or thing, you try to choose that type.

preferential
(adjective) A person who gets preferential treatment is treated better than others.

preferment
(noun; a formal word) Preferment is promotion to a better job.

prefix, prefixes
(noun) A prefix is a letter or group of letters added to the beginning of a word to make a new word, for example 'semi-', 'pre-', and 'un-'.

pregnant
1 (adjective) A woman who is pregnant has a baby developing in her womb.
2 A pregnant moment is full of special meaning or significance.
pregnancy (noun).
[from Latin *prae* meaning 'before' and *nasci* meaning 'to be born']

prehensile
(adjective; a technical word) able to curl around objects and grip them, e.g. *the prehensile tail of the South American monkey*.
[from Latin *prehendere* meaning 'to grasp']

prehistoric
(adjective) existing at a time in the past before anything was written down.

prejudge, prejudges, prejudging, prejudged
(verb) If someone prejudges a situation, they form an opinion before they have all the facts.

prejudice, prejudices, prejudicing, prejudiced
1 (noun) Prejudice is an unreasonable and unfair dislike of, or preference for, a particular type of person or thing, e.g. *racial prejudice*.
2 (verb) If someone or something prejudices your situation, they make your opportunities worse.
prejudicial (adjective).
[from Latin *prae* meaning 'before' and *judicium* meaning 'trial' or 'sentence']

prelate, prelates (pronounced **prel**-lit)
(noun) A prelate is a high-ranking clergyman such as a bishop or an archbishop.

preliminary, preliminaries
1 (adjective) Preliminary activities take place before something starts, in preparation for it.
2 (noun) You can refer to activities that take place before an event as preliminaries.

Similar words: (sense 1) prefatory, preparatory

prelude, preludes
1 (noun) Something that is an introduction to a more important event can be described as a prelude to that event.
2 A prelude is a piece of music, either a piece written for a keyboard instrument or one forming an introduction to a longer composition.

premature (pronounced prem-mat-**yoor**)
(adjective) happening too early, or earlier than expected, e.g. *a premature death*.
prematurely (adverb).
[from Latin *prae* + *maturus* meaning 'ripe in advance']

premeditated
(adjective) planned in advance, e.g. *Murder is usually a premeditated crime.*

premier, premiers
1 (noun) The leader of a government is sometimes referred to as the premier.
2 (adjective) considered to be the best or most important, e.g. *a new product to protect the company's premier position in the industry.*

premiere, premieres (pronounced **prem**-mee-er)
(noun) The premiere of a new play or film is its first public performance.
[from French *premier* meaning 'first']

premise, premises (pronounced **prem**-iss)
1 (plural noun) The premises of an organization are all the buildings it occupies on one site.
2 (noun) A premise is a statement which you suppose is true and use as the basis for an idea or argument.

premium, premiums
1 (noun) A premium is an extra sum of money that has to be paid.
2 A premium is also a sum of money that is paid regularly to an insurance company for insurance.
3 (phrase) If something is **at a premium**, it is being sold at a high price because it is in short supply.
[from Latin *praemium* meaning 'prize']

premium bond, premium bonds
(noun) Premium bonds are numbered tickets that you can buy at a post office. Each month a computer selects several numbers, and the people with those tickets win money.

premonition, premonitions (pronounced prem-on-**ishn**)
(noun) A premonition is a feeling that something unpleasant is going to happen.
[from Latin *prae* + *monere* meaning 'to warn before']

Similar words: foreboding, presentiment

prenatal
(adjective) occurring before birth or during pregnancy.

preoccupation, preoccupations
(noun) If you have a preoccupation with something, it is very important to you and you keep thinking about it.

preoccupied
(adjective) Someone who is preoccupied is deep in thought or totally involved with something.
preoccupy (verb).

preparatory
(adjective) Preparatory activities are done before doing something else in order to prepare for it.

preparatory school, preparatory schools
(noun) A preparatory school is a private school for children up to the age of 11 or 13.

prepare, prepares, preparing, prepared
(verb) If you prepare something, you make it ready for a particular purpose or event.
preparation (noun).

prepared
(adjective) If you are prepared to do something, you are willing to do it.

preponderance
(noun; a formal word) If there is a preponderance of one type of person or thing, there is more of that type than of any other.

preposition, prepositions
(noun) A preposition is a word such as 'by', 'for', 'into', or 'with', which usually has a noun as its object.
[from Latin *prae* + *positum* meaning 'placed before']

preposterous
(adjective) extremely unreasonable and ridiculous, e.g. *a preposterous story*.
[from Latin *praeposterus* meaning 'reversed']

prep school, prep schools
(noun; an informal expression) A prep school is a preparatory school.

prerequisite, prerequisites (pronounced pree-**rek**-wiz-zit)
(noun; a formal word) Something that is a prerequisite for another thing must happen or exist before the other thing is possible.

prerogative, prerogatives (pronounced prir-**rog**-at-tiv)
(noun; a formal word) Something that is the prerogative of a person is their special privilege or right.

presage, presages, presaging, presaged
(pronounced **press**-sij)
(verb; a formal word) Something that presages an event is a warning or sign of what is about to happen.

Presbyterian, Presbyterians
(noun and adjective) A Presbyterian is a member of the Presbyterian Church, a Protestant church in Scotland and Northern Ireland founded by John Knox.

presbytery, presbyteries
(noun) A presbytery is the house where a Roman Catholic priest lives.

prescribe, prescribes, prescribing, prescribed
1 (verb) When a doctor prescribes treatment, he or she states what treatment a patient should have.
2 If someone prescribes an order or duty, they state formally that it must be done.
[from Latin *prae* + *scribere* meaning 'to write before']

prescription, prescriptions
(noun) A prescription is a piece of paper on which the doctor has written the name of a medicine needed by a patient.

presence, presences
1 (noun) Someone's presence in a place is the fact of their being there, e.g. *His presence would not be welcome.*
2 Someone who has presence has an impressive appearance or manner.
3 A presence is something that you cannot see but that you are aware of.

present, presents, presenting, presented
1 (adjective) If someone is present somewhere, they are there.
2 A present situation is one that exists now rather than in the past or the future.
3 (noun) The present is the period of time that is taking place now.
4 A present is something that you give to someone for them to keep.
5 (verb) If you present someone with something, you give it to them.
6 Something that presents a difficulty or a challenge causes it or provides it.
7 The person who presents a radio or television show introduces each part or each guest.
8 If you present someone to another person, you formally introduce them to that person.
presentation (noun), **presenter** (noun).

Similar words: (sense 2) current, present-day, existing, contemporary

presentable
(adjective) neat or attractive and suitable for people to see.

present-day
(adjective) existing or happening now.

presentiment, presentiments
(noun; a formal word) A presentiment is a feeling that something unpleasant is about to happen.

presently
1 (adverb) If something will happen presently, it will happen soon, e.g. *He will be here presently.*
2 Something that is presently happening is happening now, e.g. *the oil rigs that are presently in operation.*

present participle, present participles
(noun) In grammar, the present participle of an English verb is the form that ends in '-ing'. It is used to form some tenses, and can be used to form adjectives and nouns from a verb.

present tense
(noun) In grammar, the present tense is the tense of a verb that you use mainly to talk about things that happen or exist at the time of writing or speaking.

preservative, preservatives
(noun) A preservative is a substance or chemical that prevents things from decaying.

preserve, preserves, preserving, preserved
1 (verb) If you preserve something, you take action to make sure that it remains as it is and is not changed, damaged, or ended.
2 If you preserve food, you treat it to prevent it from decaying so that it can be stored.
3 (noun) Preserves are foods such as jam or

chutney that have been made with a lot of sugar or vinegar which preserves the food.
[from Latin *prae* meaning 'before' and *servare* meaning 'to keep safe']

preside, presides, presiding, presided
(verb) A person who presides over a formal event is in charge of it or acts as chairperson.
[from Latin *praesidere* meaning 'to superintend']

president, presidents
1 (noun) In a country which has no king or queen, the president is the elected leader.
2 The president of an organization is the person who has the highest position.
presidency (noun), **presidential** (adjective).
[from Latin *praesidens* meaning 'ruler']

press, presses, pressing, pressed
1 (verb) If you press something, you push it or hold it firmly against something else.
2 If you press clothes, you iron them.
3 If you press for something, you try hard to persuade someone to agree to it.
4 If you press charges, you make an official accusation against someone which has to be decided in a court of law.
5 (noun) Newspapers and the journalists who work for them are called the press.
6 A printing press is a machine used for printing newspapers and books.

press on
(phrasal verb) If you press on, you continue with something in spite of difficulties or tiredness.

press conference, press conferences
(noun) When someone gives a press conference, they have a meeting to answer questions put by newspaper and television reporters.

pressing
(adjective) Something that is pressing needs to be dealt with immediately.

press release, press releases
(noun) A press release is a written statement given to the press about a matter of public interest.

press-up, press-ups
(noun) When you do press-ups, you lie with your face towards the floor and repeatedly raise your body by pushing down with your hands.

pressure, pressures, pressuring, pressured
1 (noun) Pressure is the force that is produced by pushing on something.
2 If you are under pressure, you have too much to do and not enough time, or someone is trying hard to persuade you to do something.
3 (verb) If you pressure someone, you try hard to persuade them to do something.

pressure cooker, pressure cookers
(noun) A pressure cooker is a large saucepan with a tightly-fitting lid, which you can use to cook food quickly using steam at high pressure.

pressure group, pressure groups
(noun) A pressure group is an organized group of people who are trying to persuade the authorities to change their policy on something.

pressurize, pressurizes, pressurizing, pressurized; also spelled pressurise
(verb) If you pressurize someone, you try hard to persuade them to do something.

pressurized or **pressurised**
1 (adjective) A pressurized container is in a state where the pressure inside is maintained at a different level from the pressure outside.
2 A pressurized liquid or gas has been compressed so that it is very compact.

prestige (pronounced **press**-teej)
(noun) If you have prestige, people admire you because of your position.
prestigious (adjective).

Similar words: status, stature, esteem, standing

presumably
(adverb) If you say that something is presumably the case, you mean you assume that it is.

presume, presumes, presuming, presumed
(pronounced priz-**yoom**)
(verb) If you presume something, you think that it is the case although you have no proof.
presumption (noun).
[from Latin *praesumere* meaning 'to anticipate']

Similar words: assume, presuppose, suppose, surmise

presumptuous
(adjective) Someone who behaves in a presumptuous way does things that they have no right to do.

presuppose, presupposes, presupposing, presupposed
(verb) If one thing presupposes another, the first thing cannot be true or exist unless the second is true or exists.

pretence, pretences
1 (noun) A pretence is a way of behaving that is false and intended to deceive people.
2 (phrase) If you do something **under false pretences**, you allow people to believe that your intentions are different from your real intentions.

pretend, pretends, pretending, pretended
(verb) If you pretend that something is the case, you try to make people believe that it is, although in fact it is not.
[from Latin *praetendere* meaning 'to put forward' or 'to claim']

Similar words: bluff, feign, simulate, sham

pretender, pretenders
(noun) A pretender to a throne or title is someone who claims it but whose claim is disputed.

pretension, pretensions
(noun) Someone with pretensions claims that they are more important than they really are.

pretentious
(adjective) Someone or something that is pretentious is trying to seem important or significant when in fact they are not.
pretentiousness (noun).

pretext, pretexts
(noun) A pretext is a false reason given to hide the real reason for doing something.

pretty, prettier, prettiest
1 (adjective) nice to look at and attractive in a delicate way.
2 (adverb; an informal use) quite or rather, e.g. *I thought it was pretty good.*
prettily (adverb), **prettiness** (noun).
[from Old English *prættig* meaning 'clever']

prevail, prevails, prevailing, prevailed
1 (verb) If something prevails in a particular place, it is normal or most common there, e.g. *the conditions that prevailed in India at that time.*
2 If someone or something prevails, they succeed in their aims, e.g. *Political arguments prevailed over economic sense.*
prevailing (adjective).
[from Latin *praevalere* meaning 'to be superior in strength']

prevalent
(adjective) very common or widespread, e.g. *Decayed teeth are less prevalent today.*
prevalence (noun).

prevaricate, prevaricates, prevaricating, prevaricated
(verb; a formal word) If you prevaricate, you avoid giving a direct or truthful answer.

prevent, prevents, preventing, prevented
(verb) If you prevent something, you stop it from happening or being done.
preventable (adjective), **prevention** (noun).
[from Latin *praevenire* meaning 'to come before' or 'hinder']

Similar words: avert, balk, preclude, stave off, stop

preventive or **preventative**
(adjective) intended to help prevent things such as disease or crime, e.g. *preventative medicine.*

preview, previews
(noun) A preview of something such as a film or exhibition is an opportunity to see it before it is shown to the public.

previous
(adjective) happening or existing before something else in time or position, e.g. *a previous marriage... the previous night.*
previously (adverb).
[from Latin *praevius* meaning 'leading the way']

Similar words: former, past, prior, old

prey, preys, preying, preyed (rhymes with **say**)
1 (noun) The creatures that an animal hunts and eats are called its prey.
2 (verb) An animal that preys on a particular kind of animal lives by hunting and eating it.

price, prices, pricing, priced
1 (noun) The price of something is the amount of money you have to pay to buy it.
2 (verb) To price something at a particular amount means to fix its price at that amount.

Similar words: (sense 1) charge, cost, rate

priceless
(adjective) Something that is priceless is so valuable that it is difficult to assess how much it is worth.

pricey, pricier, priciest
(adjective; an informal word) expensive.

prick, pricks, pricking, pricked
1 (verb) If you prick something, you stick a sharp pointed object into it.
2 (noun) A prick is a small, sharp pain caused when something pricks you.
3 (phrase) If you **prick up your ears**, you listen carefully.
[from Old English *prica* meaning 'point' or 'puncture']

prickle, prickles, prickling, prickled
1 (noun) Prickles are small sharp points or thorns on plants.
2 (verb) If your skin prickles, it feels as if a lot of sharp points are being stuck into it.
prickly (adverb).

pride, prides, priding, prided
1 (noun) Pride is a feeling of satisfaction you have when you have done something well.
2 Pride is also a feeling of being better than other people.
3 (verb) If you pride yourself on a quality or skill, you are proud of it.

Similar words: (sense 1) honour, self-respect, self-esteem, dignity

priest, priests
1 (noun) In the Christian church, a priest is a minister who has been ordained.
2 In many non-Christian religions, a priest is a man who has special duties and responsibilities in the place where people worship.
priestly (adjective).

priesthood
(noun) The priesthood is the position of being a priest.

prig, prigs
(noun) If you call someone a prig, you mean they are proud of their good behaviour and think they are better than other people.
priggish (adjective).

prim, primmer, primmest
(adjective) Someone who is prim always behaves very correctly and is easily shocked by anything rude.

Similar words: straight-laced, puritanical, staid

primacy (pronounced **pry**-mass-ee)
(noun; a formal word) Something that has primacy is the most important thing in a particular situation, e.g. *The development of American culture is based on the primacy of education.*

prima donna, prima donnas (pronounced **pree**-ma **don**-na)
1 (noun) A prima donna is a famous female opera singer, or the main female singer in a particular production of an opera.

2 (an informal use) Someone who is difficult to deal with because of their moody personality can also be called a prima donna.
[an Italian expression, meaning literally 'first lady']

primaeval another spelling of **primeval**.

prima facie (pronounced **pry**-ma **fay**-shee) (adjective; a formal or legal expression) Prima facie is used to describe something which seems to be true when considered for the first time, e.g. *prima facie evidence*.
[a Latin expression]

primal (adjective; a formal word) relating to the basic causes or origins of things, e.g. *primal truths*.
[from Latin *primus* meaning 'first']

primarily (adverb) You use primarily to indicate the main or most important feature of something, e.g. *The issue was primarily a political one*.

primary, primaries (adjective) Primary is used to describe something that is extremely important for someone or something, e.g. *One of Europe's primary requirements was minerals*.
[from Latin *primarius* meaning 'principal']

primary colour, primary colours
1 (noun) In physics, the primary colours are red, green, and blue, from which all other colours, including white, can be obtained by mixing.
2 In art, the primary colours are red, yellow, and blue, from which other colours can be obtained by mixing.

primary school, primary schools (noun) A primary school is for children between the ages of 5 and 11.

primate, primates
1 (noun) A primate is a member of the group of animals which includes humans, monkeys, and apes.
2 A primate is also an archbishop.

prime, primes, priming, primed
1 (adjective) main or most important, e.g. *a prime cause of industrial decline*.
2 of the best quality, e.g. *in prime condition*.
3 (noun) Someone's prime is the stage when they are at their strongest, most active, or most successful.
4 (verb) If you prime someone, you give them information about something in advance to prepare them.
5 To prime something means to prepare it for use.
[from Latin *primus* meaning 'first']

Similar words: (sense 3) bloom, heyday, height

Prime Minister, Prime Ministers (noun) The Prime Minister is the leader of the government.

prime number, prime numbers (noun) A prime number is a whole number greater than 1 that cannot be divided exactly by any whole number except itself and 1. 2,3,7, and 11 are prime numbers.

primer, primers
1 (noun) Primer is a special type of paint that is applied to bare wood, before the main paint.
2 A primer is a book for beginners that contains the basic facts about a subject.

primeval or **primaeval** (pronounced pry-**mee**-vl) (adjective) belonging to a very early period in the history of the world.
[from Latin *primaevus* meaning 'youthful']

primitive
1 (adjective) connected with a society that lives very simply without industries or a writing system.
2 very simple, basic, or old-fashioned, e.g. *The accommodation is somewhat primitive*.
[from Latin *primitivus* meaning 'earliest of its kind']

primordial (pronounced pry-**mor**-dee-al) (adjective; a formal word) existing at the beginning of time.

primrose, primroses (noun) A primrose is a small plant that has pale yellow flowers in spring.
[from Latin *prima rosa* meaning 'first rose']

Primus, Primuses (noun; a trademark) A Primus or Primus stove is a small paraffin-burning stove, often used in camping.

prince, princes (noun) A prince is a male member of a royal family, especially the son of a king or queen.
princely (adverb).
[from Latin *princeps* meaning 'chief' or 'ruler']

Prince of Wales (noun) The title Prince of Wales is given to the eldest son of a British monarch.

princess, princesses (noun) A princess is a female member of a royal family, usually the daughter of a king or queen, or the wife of a prince.

Princess Royal (noun) Princess Royal is a title sometimes given by the King or Queen to their eldest daughter.

principal, principals
1 (adjective) main or most important, e.g. *Women were the principal organizers of the campaign*.
2 (noun) The principal of a school or college is the person in charge of it.
principally (adverb).

principality, principalities (noun) A principality is a country ruled by a prince.

principle, principles
1 (noun) A principle is a belief you have about the way you should behave, e.g. *He stuck to his principles... a man of principle*.
2 A principle is also a general rule or scientific law which explains how something happens or works, e.g. *the principle of acceleration*.
3 (phrase) If you agree with something in principle, you agree with the idea but may be doubtful about the practical aspects.

Similar words: (sense 1) value, standard, ethic, ideal, moral

print, prints, printing, printed
1 (verb) To print a newspaper or book means to reproduce it in large quantities using a mechanical or electronic copying process.
2 (noun) The letters and numbers on the pages of a book or newspaper are referred to as the print.
3 (phrase) If a book is **out of print**, it is no longer available from the publisher.
4 (noun) A print is a photograph, or a printed copy of a painting.
5 A print is also a piece of material with a design printed on it.
6 Footprints and fingerprints can be referred to as prints.
7 (verb) If you print when you are writing, you do not join the letters together.
printable (adjective), **printer** (noun).

print-out, print-outs
(noun) A print-out is a printed copy of information from a computer.

prior
1 (preposition) Something that happens prior to a particular time or event happens before it.
2 (adjective) planned or done at an earlier time, e.g. *I have a prior engagement.*
3 of greater importance, e.g. *He feels a prior obligation to his job as a journalist.*
4 (noun) A prior is a monk in charge of a small group of monks in a priory.
prioress (noun).
[from Latin *prior* meaning 'previous']

priority, priorities
Something that is a priority is the most important thing and needs to be dealt with first.

priory, priories
(noun) A priory is a place where a small group of monks live under the charge of a prior.

prise, prises, prising, prised
(verb) If you prise something away from a surface, you force it away using a lever.

prism, prisms
1 (noun) A prism is an object made of clear glass with many flat sides. It separates light passing through it into the colours of the rainbow.
2 In maths, a prism is any polyhedron with two identical parallel ends and sides which are parallelograms.

prison, prisons
(noun) A prison is a building where criminals are kept in captivity.

prisoner, prisoners
(noun) A prisoner is someone who is kept in prison or held in captivity against their will.

pristine (pronounced **priss**-teen)
(adjective; a formal word) very clean or new and in perfect condition.

private, privates
1 (adjective) for the use of one person rather than people in general, e.g. *a private bathroom.*
2 owned or operated by individuals or companies rather than by the state.
3 taking place between a small number of people and kept secret from others, e.g. *private talks.*
4 (noun) A private is a soldier of the lowest rank.
privacy (noun), **privately** (adverb).
[from Latin *privatus* meaning 'belonging to one individual']

private enterprise
(noun) Private enterprise is industry and business owned by individuals and groups and not supported financially by the government.

private member's bill, private member's bills
(noun) A private member's bill is a proposal for a new law presented by an MP as an individual rather than as the policy of a political party.

private school, private schools
(noun) A private school is a school that is not supported financially by the government, and which parents pay for their children to attend.

privation, privations
(noun; a formal word) If you suffer privation, you are deprived of things that you need.

privatize, privatizes, privatizing, privatized; also spelled privatise
(verb) If the government privatizes a state-owned industry or organization, it allows it to be bought, owned, and controlled by a private individual or group.

privet
(noun) Privet is a type of evergreen shrub, commonly used to make hedges.

privilege, privileges
(noun) A privilege is a special right or advantage given to a person or group.
privileged (adjective).

privy, privies
1 (adjective; a formal use) If you are privy to something secret, you have been told about it.
2 (noun) A privy is an outside toilet.
[from Old French *privé* meaning 'something private']

prize, prizes, prizing, prized
1 (noun) A prize is a reward given to the winner of a competition or game.
2 (adjective) of the highest quality or standard, e.g. *His hobby is growing prize carnations.*
3 (verb) Something that is prized is wanted and admired for its value or quality, e.g. *Halibut and turbot are highly prized for their flavour.*

Similar words: (sense 1) award, trophy, jackpot, winnings, reward

pro, pros
1 (noun; an informal use) A pro is a professional.
2 (phrase) The **pros and cons** of a situation are its advantages and disadvantages.
[sense 2 is from Latin *pro* meaning 'for' and *contra* meaning 'against']

pro-
(prefix) supporting or in favour of, e.g. *pro-government newspapers.*
[from Latin *pro* meaning 'for' or 'on behalf of']

probability, probabilities
1 (noun) The probability of something happening is how likely it is to happen, e.g. *This would increase the probability of success.*
2 If something is a probability, it is likely to happen, e.g. *The probability is that they will find themselves in debt.*
3 (phrase) If something is true in **all probability**, it is very likely to be true, e.g. *He was, in all probability, the only white man they had seen.*

Similar words: (sense 1) likelihood, chance, odds

probable
(adjective) Something that is probable is likely to be true or correct, or likely to happen.

probably
(adverb) Something that is probably the case is likely but not certain.

probation
1 (noun) Probation is a period of time during which a person convicted of a crime is supervised by a probation officer instead of being sent to prison.
2 Probation is also a period of time during which someone's work is assessed before they are given a job permanently.
probationary (adjective), **probationer** (noun).

probe, probes, probing, probed
1 (verb) If you probe, you ask a lot of questions to discover the facts about something.
2 If you probe something, you gently push a long thin object into it, usually to find something.
3 (noun) A probe is a long thin instrument used by doctors and dentists when examining a patient.
4 A probe is also the same as a space probe.
[from Latin *probare* meaning 'to test']

problem, problems
1 (noun) A problem is an unsatisfactory situation that causes difficulties.
2 A problem is also a puzzle or question that you solve using logical thought or mathematics.
problematic (adjective).
[from Greek *problēma* meaning 'something put forward']

Similar words: (sense 1) hitch, snag, difficulty, drawback

proboscis, proboscises
(noun; a technical word) A proboscis is a long flexible tube that some insects have as a mouthpart.

procedure, procedures
(noun) A procedure is a way of doing something, especially the correct or usual way.
procedural (adjective).

proceed, proceeds, proceeding, proceeded
1 (verb) If you proceed to do something, you start doing it, or continue doing it, e.g. *He proceeded to explain.*
2 (a formal use) If you proceed in a particular direction, you move in that direction, e.g. *We were proceeding along the High Street.*

3 (plural noun) The proceeds from a fund-raising event are the money obtained from it.
[from Latin *pro + cedere* meaning 'to go onward']

proceedings
1 (plural noun) You can refer to an organized and related series of events as the proceedings, e.g. *We watched the proceedings from the balcony.*
2 Legal proceedings are legal action taken against someone.

process, processes, processing, processed
1 (noun) A process is a series of actions intended to achieve a particular result or change.
2 (phrase) If you are in **the process** of doing something, you have started doing it but have not yet finished.
3 (verb) When something such as food or information is processed, it is treated or dealt with.

procession, processions
(noun) A procession is a group of people moving in a line.

processor, processors
(noun) In computing, a processor is the central chip in a computer which controls its operations.

proclaim, proclaims, proclaiming, proclaimed
(verb) If someone proclaims something, they formally announce it or make it known.
proclamation (noun).
[from Latin *proclamare* meaning 'to shout out']

proclivity, proclivities
(noun; a formal word) A proclivity is a tendency to behave in a particular way, e.g. *Such people often display a proclivity for violence.*

procrastinate, procrastinates, procrastinating, procrastinated
(verb; a formal word) If you procrastinate, you put off doing something.
[from Latin *procrastinare* meaning 'to put off until tomorrow', from *cras* meaning 'tomorrow']

procreation
(noun; a formal word) Procreation is the process by which babies and young animals are conceived and born.

procure, procures, procuring, procured
(verb; a formal word) If you procure something, you obtain it.

prod, prods, prodding, prodded
(verb) If you prod something, you give it a push with your finger or with something pointed.

prodigal
(adjective; a literary word) Someone who is prodigal spends money freely and wastefully.

prodigious
(adjective; a formal word) amazingly large or great, e.g. *a prodigious store of information.*
prodigiously (adverb).

prodigy, prodigies (pronounced **prod**-dij-ee)
(noun) A prodigy is someone who shows an extraordinary natural ability at an early age.
[from Latin *prodigium* meaning 'unnatural happening']

produce, produces, producing, produced
1 (verb) To produce something means to make it or cause it, e.g. *artists producing works of great beauty... tensions produced by pressure.*
2 If you produce something from somewhere, you bring it out so it can be seen.
3 When someone produces a play, film, programme, or record, they organize it and decide how it will be done or made.
4 (noun) Produce is food that is grown to be sold.

producer, producers
(noun) The producer of a film or show is the person in charge of making it or putting it on.

product, products
1 (noun) A product is something that is made to be sold.
2 In maths, the product of two or more numbers or quantities is the result of multiplying them together.

production, productions
1 (noun) Production is the process of manufacturing or growing something in large quantities, e.g. *methods of production.*
2 Production is also the amount of goods manufactured or food grown by a country or company, e.g. *Production has fallen by over 20%.*
3 A production of a play, opera, or other show is a series of performances of it.

productive
1 (adjective) To be productive means to produce a large number of things, e.g. *Industry became more productive.*
2 If something such as a meeting is productive, good or useful things happen as a result of it.

Similar words: (sense 1) prolific, fruitful, fertile
(sense 2) fruitful, profitable, rewarding, useful, worthwhile

productivity
(noun) Productivity is the rate at which things are produced or dealt with.

profane
1 (adjective; a formal word) showing disrespect for a religion or religious things, e.g. *profane language.*
2 concerned with everyday life rather than with religious or spiritual matters.

profess, professes, professing, professed
1 (verb; a formal word) If you profess to do or have something, you claim to do or have it.
2 If you profess a feeling or opinion, you express it, e.g. *Many have professed disgust at this.*

profession, professions
1 (noun) A profession is a type of job that requires advanced education or training.
2 You can use profession to refer to all the people who have a particular profession, e.g. *the medical profession.*
[from Latin *professio* meaning 'taking of vows (when entering a religious order)']

professional, professionals
1 (adjective) Professional means relating to the work of someone who is qualified in a particular profession, e.g. *I sought professional advice.*
2 Professional also describes activities when they are done to earn money rather than as a hobby, e.g. *professional football.*
3 A professional piece of work is of a very high standard.
4 (noun) A professional is a person who has been trained in a profession.
5 A professional is also someone who plays a sport to earn money rather than as a hobby.

professor, professors
(noun) In a British university, a professor is the most senior teacher in a department.
professorial (adjective).

proffer, proffers, proffering, proffered
(verb; a formal word) If you proffer something to someone, you offer it to them.

proficient
(adjective) If you are proficient at something, you can do it well.
proficiency (noun).
[from Latin *proficere* meaning 'to make progress']

profile, profiles
1 (noun) Your profile is the outline of your face seen from the side.
2 A profile of someone is a short description of their life and character.
[from Italian *profilare* meaning 'to sketch lightly']

profit, profits, profiting, profited
1 (noun) When someone sells something, the profit is the amount they gain by selling it for more than it cost them to buy or make.
2 (verb) If you profit from something, you gain or benefit from it, e.g. *I profited from his advice.*
profitable (adjective).

Similar words: (sense 1) gains, proceeds, returns

profiteer, profiteers
(noun) A profiteer is someone who makes large profits by charging high prices for goods that are hard to get.
profiteering (noun).

profligate
(adjective; a formal word) extravagant and wasteful.
profligacy (noun).

profound
1 (adjective) great in degree or intensity, e.g. *She was in a state of profound shock.*
2 showing great and deep intellectual understanding, e.g. *a very profound question.*
profoundly (adverb), **profundity** (noun).
[from Latin *profundus* meaning 'deep']

profuse (pronounced prof-**yooss**)
(adjective) very large in quantity or number, e.g. *There were profuse apologies for his absence.*
profusely (adverb), **profusion** (noun).
[from Latin *profusus* meaning 'extravagant' or 'costly']

progeny (pronounced **proj**-jin-ee)
(noun; a formal word) You can refer to a person's children as their progeny.

progesterone
(noun) Progesterone is a hormone secreted in the ovaries of female mammals, which prepares the uterus for pregnancy.

prognosis, prognoses
(noun; a formal word) A prognosis is a prediction about the future course and outcome of something such as an illness.
[from Greek *prognosis* meaning 'knowledge beforehand']

prognosticate, prognosticates, prognosticating, prognosticated
(verb; a formal word) To prognosticate means to predict that certain things will happen.

program, programs, programming, programmed
1 (noun) A program is a set of instructions that a computer follows to perform a particular task.
2 (verb) When someone programs a computer, they write a program and put it into the computer.
programmer (noun).

programme, programmes
1 (noun) You can refer to a planned series of events as a programme, e.g. *They have embarked on a programme of modernization.*
2 A programme on television or radio is a particular piece presented as a unit, such as a play, show, or discussion.
3 A programme is a booklet giving information about a play, concert, or show that you are attending.
[from Greek *programma* meaning 'public notice']

Similar words: (sense 1) course, schedule, syllabus, curriculum

progress, progresses, progressing, progressed
1 (noun) Progress is the process of gradually improving or getting near to achieving something.
2 The progress of something is the way in which it develops or continues, e.g. *He followed the progress of the negotiations with impatience.*
3 (phrase) Something that is **in progress** is happening, e.g. *examinations in progress.*
4 (verb) If you progress, you become more advanced or skilful.
5 To progress also means to continue, e.g. *My impressions changed as the trip progressed.*
progression (noun).
[from Latin *progressus*, the past participle of *progredi* meaning 'to advance']

Similar words: (sense 1) advance, headway (sense 2) development, progression

progressive
1 (adjective) having modern ideas about how things should be done.
2 happening gradually, e.g. *the progressive industrialization of society.*
progressively (adverb).

prohibit, prohibits, prohibiting, prohibited
(verb) If someone prohibits something, they forbid it or make it illegal, e.g. *a bill to prohibit the use of lead in petrol.*
prohibition (noun).
[from Latin *prohibere*]

prohibitive
(adjective) If the cost of something is prohibitive, it is so high that people cannot afford it.

project, projects, projecting, projected
1 (noun) A project is a carefully planned attempt to achieve something or to study something over a period of time.
2 (verb) Something that is projected is planned or expected to happen in the future, e.g. *The population is projected to rise further.*
3 To project an image onto a screen means to make it appear there using equipment such as a projector.
4 If you project a particular impression or idea, you communicate it to other people, perhaps without realizing it, e.g. *City merchant banks still project the image of a gentleman's club.*
5 Something that projects sticks out beyond a surface or edge.
projection (noun).
[from Latin *proicere* meaning 'to throw down']

projectile, projectiles
(noun) A projectile is an object fired from a gun or thrown at something.

projector, projectors
(noun) A projector is a piece of equipment which produces a large image on a screen by shining light through a photographic slide or film strip.

proletariat
(noun; a formal word) Working-class people are sometimes referred to as the proletariat.
proletarian (adjective).

proliferate, proliferates, proliferating, proliferated
(verb) If things proliferate, they quickly increase in number.
proliferation (noun).
[from Latin *prolifer* meaning 'having children']

prolific
(adjective) producing a lot of something, e.g. *Blackcurrants are very prolific... a prolific writer.*

prologue, prologues
(noun) A prologue is a speech or section that introduces a play or book.

prolong, prolongs, prolonging, prolonged
(verb) If you prolong something, you make it last longer.
prolonged (adjective).
[from Latin *prolongare* meaning 'to extend']

prom, proms
1 (noun; an informal word) A prom is a promenade concert.
2 At a seaside resort, the prom is the promenade.

promenade, promenades (pronounced prom-min-**ahd**)
(noun) At a seaside resort, the promenade is a road or path next to the sea.

[a French word, from *se promener* meaning 'to go for a walk']

promenade concert, promenade concerts
(noun) A promenade concert is a concert at which some of the audience stand.

prominent
1 (adjective) Something that is prominent is very noticeable, e.g. *prominent landmarks*.
2 Prominent people are important, e.g. *US Senators and other prominent personalities*.
prominence (noun), **prominently** (adverb).
[from Latin *prominere* meaning 'to stick out']

promiscuous (pronounced prom-**misk**-yoo-uss)
(adjective) Someone who is promiscuous has sex with many different people.
promiscuity (noun).
[from Latin *promiscuus* meaning 'indiscriminate']

Similar words: wanton, loose, lewd

promise, promise, promising, promised
1 (verb) If you promise to do something, you say that you will definitely do it.
2 (noun) A promise is a statement made by someone that they will definitely do something.
3 (verb) Something that promises to have a particular quality shows signs that it will have that quality, e.g. *The next parliamentary session promised to be a particularly interesting one.*
4 (noun) Someone or something that shows promise seems likely to be very successful.
promising (adjective).

Similar words: (sense 1) assure, vow, pledge, swear (sense 2) assurance, pledge, vow, oath, word

promontory, promontories (pronounced prom-mon-tree)
(noun) A promontory is an area of high land sticking out into the sea.
[from Latin *promunturium*]

promote, promotes, promoting, promoted
1 (verb) If someone promotes something, they try to make it happen, increase, or become more popular, e.g. *The need to promote peace.*
2 If someone is promoted, they are given a more important job in the organization they work for.
promoter (noun), **promotion** (noun).

prompt, prompts, prompting, prompted
1 (verb) If something prompts someone to do something, it makes them decide to do it, e.g. *The article prompted him to call a meeting.*
2 If you prompt someone when they stop speaking, you tell them what to say next or encourage them to continue.
3 (adjective) A prompt action is done without any delay, e.g. *She received a prompt reply.*
4 (adverb) exactly at the time mentioned, e.g. *The meeting will start at 8 o'clock prompt.*
promptly (adverb).

promulgate, promulgates, promulgating, promulgated
(verb; a formal word) If someone promulgates an idea or plan, they announce it publicly and make it widely known.
promulgation (noun).

[from Latin *promulgare* meaning 'to bring to public knowledge']

prone
1 (adjective) If you are prone to something, you have a tendency to be affected by it or to do it, e.g. *Athletes are prone to muscle strains.*
2 If you are prone, you are lying flat and face downwards, e.g. *He lay prone on his bed.*
[from Latin *pronus* meaning 'bent forward']

Similar words: (sense 1) liable, tending, disposed, subject, inclined

prong, prongs
(noun) The prongs of a fork are the long, narrow, pointed parts.

pronoun, pronouns
(noun) In grammar, a pronoun is a word that is used to replace a noun. 'He', 'she', and 'them' are all pronouns.

pronounce, pronounces, pronouncing, pronounced
1 (verb) When you pronounce a word, you say it.
2 When someone pronounces a verdict or their opinion, they state or announce it formally.
[from Latin *pronuntiare* meaning 'to announce']

pronounced
(adjective) very noticeable.

pronouncement, pronouncements
(noun) A pronouncement is a formal statement.

pronunciation, pronunciations (pronounced pron-nun-see-**ay**-shn)
(noun) The pronunciation of a word is the way it is usually pronounced.

proof, proofs
1 (noun) If you have proof of something, you have evidence which shows that it happened, is true, or exists.
2 The proofs of a book or magazine are a first copy of the pages, printed so that they can be checked for mistakes.

Similar words: (sense 1) substantiation, evidence, authentication, corroboration

proofreading
Proofreading is the checking of proofs so that any mistakes can be found and corrected.
proofreader (noun).

prop, props, propping, propped
1 (verb) If you prop an object somewhere, you support it or rest it against something.
2 (noun) Someone or something that is described as a prop is the thing that strengthens an institution or system, e.g. *Discussing everything was the prop of their marriage.*
3 A prop is a stick or other object used to support something.
4 The props in a play are all the objects and furniture used by the actors.

propaganda
(noun) Propaganda is exaggerated or false information that is published or broadcast in order to influence people.
propagandist (noun).

propagate, propagates, propagating, propagated
1 (verb) If people propagate an idea, they spread it to try to influence many other people.
2 If you propagate plants, you grow more of them from an original one by, for example, taking cuttings or sowing seeds.
propagation (noun).

propane
(noun) Propane is a gas found in petroleum and used as a fuel for cooking and heating.

propel, propels, propelling, propelled
(verb) To propel something means to cause it to move in a particular direction.
[from Latin *pro* + *pellere* meaning 'to drive onwards']

propeller, propellers
(noun) A propeller on a boat or aircraft is a device with blades that is turned by the engine causing the boat or aircraft to move.

propensity, propensities
(noun; a formal word) A propensity is a tendency to behave in a particular way.
[from Latin *propensus* meaning 'inclined to']

proper
1 (adjective) real and satisfactory, e.g. *Why don't you get a proper job?*
2 correct or suitable, e.g. *in its proper place... It wasn't proper to show his emotions.*
3 actual, e.g. *This next street leads to the town proper.*
properly (adverb).
[from Latin *proprius* meaning 'special']

proper noun, proper nouns
(noun) A proper noun is the name of a person, place, or institution.

property, properties
1 (noun) A person's property is the things that belong to them.
2 A property is a building and the land belonging to it, e.g. *She arranged to rent the property.*
3 A property of something is a characteristic or quality that it has, e.g. *the properties of seeds.*
[from Latin *proprietas* meaning 'something personal']

prophecy, prophecies
(noun) A prophecy is a statement about what someone believes will happen in the future.

prophesy, prophesies, prophesying, prophesied
(verb) If someone prophesies something, they say it will happen.

prophet, prophets
(noun) A prophet is a person who predicts what will happen in the future.

prophetic
(adjective) correctly predicting what will happen, e.g. *These indeed were prophetic words.*

propitiate, propitiates, propitiating, propitiated
(pronounced prop-**pish**-ee-ate)
(verb; a formal word) If someone propitiates a person or god, they prevent them from becoming angry by doing something to please them.

propitious
(adjective; a formal word)

favourable and likely to lead to success, e.g. *Conditions were propitious for development.*

proponent, proponents
(noun) Someone who is a proponent of an idea or cause argues in favour of it.
[from Latin *proponere* meaning 'to propose']

proportion, proportions
1 (noun) A proportion of an amount or group is a part of it.
2 The proportion of one amount to another is its size in comparison with the other amount, e.g. *The proportion of workers to employers is large.*
3 (phrase) If one thing increases or decreases **in proportion** to or with another, it does so at the same rate or to the same degree, e.g. *Cities expanded in proportion with the growth of industry.*
4 If a part of something is **in proportion** to the whole, it is the correct size in comparison with the whole.
5 (noun) You can refer to the size of something as its proportions, e.g. *a cat of giant proportions.*

proportional or **proportionate**
(adjective) If one thing is proportional to another, it remains the same size in comparison with the other, e.g. *Suicide rates are generally proportional to the size of the city.*
proportionally (adverb), **proportionately** (adverb).

proportional representation
(noun) Proportional representation is a system of voting in elections in which the number of representatives of each party is in proportion to the number of people who voted for it.

proposal, proposals
1 (noun) A proposal is a plan that has been suggested.
2 When someone asks another person to marry them, this request is called a proposal.

propose, proposes, proposing, proposed
1 (verb) If you propose a plan or idea, you suggest it.
2 If you propose to do something, you intend to do it.
3 The person who proposes a motion in a debate is the person who introduces it and says why they believe it should be accepted.
4 When someone proposes a toast to a particular person, they ask people to drink a toast to that person.
5 If someone proposes to another person, they ask that person to marry them.
[from Latin *proponere* meaning 'to put forward']

proposition, propositions
1 (noun) A proposition is a statement expressing a theory or opinion, e.g. *The proposition is that man is basically selfish.*
2 A proposition is also an offer or suggestion, e.g. *I have a proposition to make.*

propound, propounds, propounding, propounded
(verb; a formal word) If you propound an idea or theory, you suggest it for people to consider.
[from Latin *proponere* meaning 'to put forward']

proprietary
(adjective) A proprietary substance or product is one that is sold under a trade name.
[from Latin *proprietarius* meaning 'owner']

proprietor, proprietors
(noun) The proprietor of a business is the owner.
proprietress (noun).

propriety
(noun; a formal word) Propriety is social or moral acceptability, e.g. *I slept here alone for reasons of propriety.*

propulsion
(noun) Propulsion is the power that moves something, e.g. *new ideas for rocket propulsion.*

pro rata (pronounced pro **rah**-ta)
(adjective; a formal expression) If you work part-time and are paid on a pro rata basis, you earn a proportion of a whole salary according to how much work you do.
[a Latin expression meaning 'in proportion']

prosaic (pronounced proh-**zay**-yik)
(adjective) dull and uninteresting.
prosaically (adverb).

proscenium, prosceniums (pronounced pro-**see**-nee-um)
(noun) In some theatres, the proscenium is an arch separating the audience from the stage. The area in front of this arch is also called the proscenium.

proscribe, proscribes, proscribing, proscribed
(verb; a formal word) If someone in authority proscribes something, they forbid it.
proscription (noun).
[from Latin *proscribere* meaning 'to put up a written public notice']

prose
(noun) Prose is ordinary written language in contrast to poetry.
[from Latin *prosa oratorio* meaning 'straightforward speech']

prosecute, prosecutes, prosecuting, prosecuted
(verb) If someone is prosecuted, they are charged with a crime and have to stand trial.
prosecutor (noun).

prosecution
(noun) The lawyers who try to prove that a person on trial is guilty are called the prosecution.

proselytize, proselytizes, proselytizing, proselytized (pronounced **pros**-sil-lit-eyez); also spelled **proselytise**
(verb; a formal word) Someone who proselytizes tries to persuade people to join their political party or religion.
[from Greek *proselutos* meaning 'recent arrival' or 'convert']

prospect, prospects, prospecting, prospected
1 (noun) If there is a prospect of something happening, there is a possibility that it will happen.
2 Someone's prospects are their chances of being successful in the future.

3 (verb) Someone who prospects for gold, oil, or some other valuable substance looks for it.
prospector (noun).
[from Latin *prospectus* meaning 'distant view']

Similar words: (sense 2) future, outlook

prospective
(adjective) Prospective is used to say that someone wants to be or is likely to be something. For example, the prospective owner of something is the person who wants to own it.

prospectus, prospectuses
(noun) A prospectus is a booklet giving details of something such as a college or a company.

prosper, prospers, prospering, prospered
(verb) When people or businesses prosper, they are successful and make a lot of money.
prosperous (adjective), **prosperity** (noun).
[from Latin *prosperare* meaning 'to succeed']

prostitute, prostitutes, prostituting, prostituted
1 (noun) A prostitute is a person, usually a woman, who has sex with men in exchange for money.
2 (verb) If people prostitute themselves, they use their talents for unworthy purposes, usually for money.
prostitution (noun).
[from Latin *prostituere* meaning 'to succeed']

prostrate, prostrates, prostrating, prostrated
1 (verb) If you prostrate yourself, you lie face downwards on the ground.
2 (adjective) lying face downwards on the ground.
[from Latin *prosternere* meaning 'to throw to the ground']

protagonist, protagonists (a formal word)
1 (noun) Someone who is a protagonist of an idea or movement is a leading supporter of it.
2 The protagonists in a play or story are the main characters.
[from Greek *protagonistes* meaning 'main actor in a play']

protect, protects, protecting, protected
(verb) To protect someone or something means to prevent them from being harmed or damaged.
protection (noun), **protective** (adjective).
[from Latin *protegere* meaning 'to cover']

protégé, protégés (pronounced **proh**-tij-ay)
(noun) Someone who is the protégé of an older, more experienced person is helped and guided by that person over a period of time.
[a French word, from *protéger* meaning 'to protect']

protein, proteins
(noun) Protein is a complex compound consisting of amino acid chains, found in many foods and essential for all living things.
[from Greek *proteios* meaning 'primary']

protest, protests, protesting, protested
1 (verb) If you protest about something, you say or demonstrate publicly that you disagree with it.
2 (noun) A protest is a demonstration or

statement showing that you disagree with
something.
[from Latin *protestari* meaning 'to make a formal
declaration']

Protestant, Protestants
(noun and adjective) A Protestant is a member of
one of the Christian churches which separated
from the Catholic church in the sixteenth
century.

protestation, protestations
(noun) A protestation is a strong declaration that
something is true or not true, e.g. *her vehement
protestations of innocence.*

protocol
(noun) Protocol is the system of rules about the
correct way to behave in formal situations.

proton, protons
(noun) A proton is a particle which forms part of
the nucleus of an atom and has a positive
electrical charge.
[from Greek *prōtos* meaning 'first']

protoplasm
(noun) Protoplasm is a colourless liquid forming
the living contents of a cell.

prototype, prototypes
(noun) A prototype is a first model of something
that is made so that the design can be tested and
improved.

protracted
(adjective) lasting longer than usual, e.g. *a
protracted lunch.*
[from Latin *protractum*, the past participle of
the verb *protrahere* meaning 'to prolong']

protractor, protractors
(noun) A protractor is a flat, semicircular piece
of plastic used for measuring angles.

protrude, protrudes, protruding, protruded
(verb; a formal word) If something is protruding
from a surface or edge, it is sticking out.
protrusion (noun).
[from Latin *protrudere* meaning 'to thrust
forward']

protuberance, protuberances
(noun; a formal word) A protuberance is a
rounded part that sticks out from something.

proud, prouder, proudest
1 (adjective) feeling pleasure and satisfaction at
something you own or have achieved, e.g. *They
were proud of their success.*
2 having great dignity and self-respect, e.g.
Don't be too proud to ask for advice.
proudly (adverb).

prove, proves, proving, proved, proven
1 (verb) To prove that something is true means
to provide evidence that it is definitely true.
2 If something proves to be the case, it becomes
clear that it is so, e.g. *I proved to be hopeless as a
teacher.*

Similar words: (sense 1) substantiate, verify,
authenticate, corroborate

provenance (pronounced **prov**-vin-nans)
(noun; a formal word) Something's provenance is
the place it originally came from.
[from Latin *provenire* meaning 'to originate']

Provençal
(noun) Provençal is a language which used to be
widely spoken in Provence in south-eastern
France, and is still spoken by a few people there.

proverb, proverbs
(noun) A proverb is a short sentence which gives
advice or makes a comment about life.
proverbial (adjective).

provide, provides, providing, provided
1 (verb) If you provide something for someone,
you give it to them or make it available for them.
2 If you provide for someone, you give them the
things they need.
3 If you provide for a future event, you make
arrangements to deal with it.

Similar words: (sense 1) cater for, supply, lay on,
purvey

provided or **providing**
(conjunction) If you say that something will
happen provided something else happens, you
mean that the first thing will happen only if the
second thing does.

providence
(noun) Providence is God or a force which is
believed to arrange the things that happen to us.

providential
(adjective) lucky and happening just at the right
time, e.g. *a providential coincidence.*
providentially (adverb).

province, provinces
1 (noun) A province is one of the areas into
which some large countries are divided, each
province having its own administration.
2 You can refer to the parts of a country which
are not near the capital as the provinces.
3 If you say that something is someone's
province, you mean they have special knowledge
of it or special responsibility for it.
[from Latin *provincia* meaning 'a conquered
territory']

provincial
1 (adjective) connected with the parts of a
country outside the capital, e.g. *provincial
newspapers.*
2 narrow-minded and unsophisticated, e.g. *She
found him dull and provincial.*

provision, provisions
1 (noun) The provision of something is the act of
making it available to people, e.g. *the provision
of unemployment pay for those out of work.*
2 (phrase) If you **make provision** for something,
you arrange for it to be dealt with or looked
after, e.g. *They have to make provision for their
children while they work.*
3 (plural noun) Provisions are supplies of food.
[from Latin *providere* meaning 'to provide']

provisional
(adjective) A provisional arrangement has not yet been made definite and so might be changed.

proviso, provisos (pronounced prov-**eye**-zoh)
(noun) A proviso is a condition in an agreement.
[from Latin *proviso quod* meaning 'provided that']

provocation, provocations
(noun) A provocation is an act done deliberately to annoy someone.

provocative
1 (adjective) intended to annoy people or make them react, e.g. *a provocative article on racism.*
2 intended to make someone feel sexual desire, e.g. *a provocative dance.*

provoke, provokes, provoking, provoked
1 (verb) If you provoke someone, you deliberately try to make them angry.
2 If something provokes an unpleasant reaction, it causes it.
[from Latin *provocare* meaning 'to call forth']

provost, provosts (pronounced **prov**-vost)
1 (noun) In some universities, a provost is the head of one of the university colleges.
2 In Scotland, a provost is the chief magistrate of a borough.

prow, prows
(noun) The prow of a boat is the front part.

prowess
(noun) Prowess is outstanding ability, e.g. *His prowess at sports earned their respect.*
[from Old French *proesce* meaning 'bravery']

prowl, prowls, prowling, prowled
(verb) If a person or animal prowls around, they move around quickly and secretly, as if hunting.

proximity
(noun; a formal word) Proximity is nearness to someone or something.
[from Latin *proximitas*]

proxy
(phrase) If you do something **by proxy**, someone else does it on your behalf, e.g. *If you cannot attend the meeting, you can vote by proxy.*

prude, prudes
(noun) If you call someone a prude, you mean they are too easily shocked by sex or nudity.
prudery (noun), **prudish** (adjective).
[from Old French *prode femme* meaning 'respectable woman']

prudent
(adjective) behaving in a sensible and cautious way, e.g. *It seemed prudent to keep quiet.*
prudence (noun), **prudently** (adverb).
[from Latin *prudens* meaning 'far-sighted']

prune, prunes, pruning, pruned
1 (noun) A prune is a dried plum.
2 (verb) When someone prunes a tree or shrub, they cut back some of the branches.

prurient
(adjective; a formal word) showing an unhealthy interest in sexual matters.
prurience (noun).
[from Latin *prurire* meaning 'to lust after']

pry, pries, prying, pried
(verb) If someone is prying, they are trying to find out about something secret or private.

PS
PS is written before an additional message at the end of a letter. PS is an abbreviation for 'postscript'.

psalm, psalms (pronounced **sahm**)
(noun) A psalm is one of the 150 songs, poems, and prayers which together form the Book of Psalms in the Bible.
[from Greek *psalmos* meaning 'song accompanied on the harp']

psephology (pronounced sif-**fol**-loj-ee)
(noun) Psephology is the study of how people vote in elections.
psephologist (noun).
[from Greek *psephos* meaning 'vote']

pseudo– (pronounced **syoo**-doh)
Pseudo- is used to form adjectives and nouns indicating that something is not what it is claimed to be, e.g. *a pseudo-democracy.*
[from Greek *pseudēs* meaning 'false']

pseudonym, pseudonyms (pronounced **syoo**-doe-nim)
(noun) A writer who uses a pseudonym uses another name as an author rather than their real name.
pseudonymous (adjective).
[from Greek *pseudōnumon* meaning 'false name']

psyche, psyches (pronounced **sigh**-kee)
(noun) Your psyche is your mind and your deepest feelings.
[from Greek *psukhē* meaning 'mind']

psychedelic (pronounced sigh-ked-**del**-lik)
1 (adjective) Psychedelic drugs are illegal drugs such as LSD which make you imagine that you are seeing strange things.
2 Psychedelic designs are brightly coloured with strange patterns.

psychiatry
(noun) Psychiatry is the branch of medicine concerned with mental illness.
psychiatrist (noun), **psychiatric** (adjective).
[from Greek *psukhē* meaning 'mind' and *iatros* meaning 'healer']

psychic
1 (adjective) having unusual mental powers such as the ability to read people's minds or predict the future.
2 relating to the mind, e.g. *psychic damage.*
[from Greek *psukhikos* meaning 'of the mind']

psychoanalysis
(noun) Psychoanalysis is the examination and treatment of someone who is mentally ill by encouraging them to talk about their feelings and

past events in order to discover the cause of the illness.
psychoanalyst (noun), **psychoanalyse** (verb).

psychology
1 (noun) Psychology is the scientific study of the mind and of the reasons for people's behaviour.
2 The psychology of a person is the kind of mind they have and the way they think.
psychological (adjective), **psychologist** (noun).

psychopath, psychopaths
(noun) A psychopath is a mentally ill person who behaves violently without feeling guilt.
psychopathic (adjective).

psychosis, psychoses (pronounced sigh-**koe**-siss)
(noun) A psychosis is a severe mental illness.
psychotic (adjective).

psychosomatic (pronounced sigh-koe-som-**mat**-tik)
(adjective) A psychosomatic illness is a physical disorder caused by a person's mental condition.
[from Greek *psukhē* meaning 'mind' and *somatikos* meaning 'of the body']

psychotherapy
(noun) Psychotherapy is the use of psychological methods to treat mental illness.
psychotherapist (noun).

PTA, PTAs
A PTA is an organization formed so that the parents of the children at a school can discuss school matters with the teachers. PTA is an abbreviation for 'Parent-Teacher Association'.

pterodactyl, pterodactyls (pronounced ter-rod-**dak**-til)
(noun) Pterodactyls were flying reptiles in prehistoric times.
[from Greek *pteron* meaning 'wing' and *daktulos* meaning 'finger']

PTO
PTO is an abbreviation for 'please turn over'. It is written at the bottom of a page to indicate that the writing continues on the other side.

pub, pubs
(noun) A pub is a building where people go to buy and drink alcoholic or soft drinks and talk with their friends.

puberty (pronounced **pyoo**-ber-tee)
(noun) Puberty is the stage when a person's body changes from that of a child into that of an adult.
[from Latin *pubertas* meaning 'maturity']

pubic (pronounced **pyoo**-bik)
(adjective) relating to the area around and above a person's genitals.

public
1 (noun) You can refer to people in general as the public.
2 (adjective) relating to people in general, e.g. *The campaign attracted public support.*
3 provided for everyone to use, or open to anyone, e.g. *public transport... public toilets.*
publicly (adverb).
[from Latin *poplicus* meaning 'of the people']

Similar words: (sense 3) civil, civic, communal, open, unrestricted

publican, publicans
(noun) A publican is a person who owns or manages a pub.

publication, publications
1 (noun) The publication of a book is the act of printing it and making it available.
2 A publication is a book or magazine.

public bar, public bars
(noun) A public bar is a room in a pub where the furniture is plain and the drinks are cheaper than in other bars.

public convenience, public conveniences
(noun) A public convenience is a toilet that anyone can use.

public house, public houses
(noun) A public house is the same as a pub.

publicity
(noun) Publicity is information or advertisements about an item or event.

publicize, publicizes, publicizing, publicized; also spelled **publicise**
(verb) When someone publicizes a fact or event, they advertise it and make it widely known.

public relations
(noun) Public relations is the effort an organization makes to give the public a good impression of what it does.

public school, public schools
(noun) In Britain, a public school is a school that is privately run and that charges fees for the pupils to attend.

public-spirited
(adjective) Someone who is public-spirited is eager to help their community.

publish, publishes, publishing, published
1 (verb) When a company publishes a book, newspaper, or magazine, they print copies of it and distribute it.
2 When someone publishes a book or article that they have written, they arrange to have it published.
publisher (noun), **publishing** (noun).
[from Latin *publicare* meaning 'to make public']

puce (pronounced **pyoos**)
(noun and adjective) dark purple.
[from Old French *couleur puce* meaning 'flea colour']

pucker, puckers, puckering, puckered
(verb) If something puckers, it becomes wrinkled or creased.

pudding, puddings
1 (noun) A pudding is a sweet cake mixture cooked with fruit or other flavouring.
2 You can refer to the sweet course of a meal as the pudding.

puddle, puddles
(noun) A puddle is a small shallow pool of liquid.

puerile (pronounced **pyoo**-rile)
(adjective) Puerile behaviour is silly and childish.
[from Latin *puerilis*, from *puer* meaning 'boy']

puff, puffs, puffing, puffed
1 (verb) To puff a cigarette or pipe means to smoke it.
2 If you are puffing, you are breathing loudly and quickly with your mouth open.
3 If something puffs out or puffs up, it swells and becomes larger and rounder.
4 (noun) A puff of air or smoke is a small amount that is released.

puffin, puffins
(noun) A puffin is a black and white sea bird with a large brightly-coloured striped beak.

pug, pugs
(noun) A pug is a small, short-haired dog with a flat nose.

pugnacious (pronounced pug-**nay**-shuss)
(adjective) aggressive and always ready to quarrel.
pugnacity (noun).
[from Latin *pugnare* meaning 'to fight']

puke, pukes, puking, puked
(verb; an informal word) If someone pukes, they vomit.

pull, pulls, pulling, pulled
1 (verb) When you pull something, you hold it and move it towards you.
2 When something is pulled by a vehicle or animal, it is attached to it and moves along behind it.
3 When you pull a curtain or blind, you move it so that it covers or uncovers the window.
4 If you pull a muscle, you injure it by stretching it too far or too quickly.
5 You say that something pulls people when it attracts their support or attention.
6 When a vehicle pulls away, pulls out, or pulls in, it moves in the direction indicated.
7 (noun) The pull of something is its attraction or influence.
8 A pull on a cigarette or pipe is a strong inward breath while smoking.

pull down
(phrasal verb) When a building is pulled down, it is deliberately destroyed.

pull off
(phrasal verb) If you pull something off, you succeed in doing it.

pull out
(phrasal verb) If you pull out of something, you withdraw from it or leave it, e.g. *You will lose your deposit if you decide to pull out.*

pull through
(phrasal verb) When someone pulls through, they recover from a serious illness.

pull together
1 (phrasal verb) When people pull together, they cooperate with each other to achieve something.
2 If someone tells you to pull yourself together, they are telling you to control yourself.

pull up
(phrasal verb) When a vehicle pulls up, it stops.

pullet, pullets
(noun) A pullet is a young hen which has just started to lay eggs.
[from Old French *poulet* meaning 'chicken']

pulley, pulleys
(noun) A pulley is a device for lifting heavy weights. It consists of a wheel or series of wheels over which a rope passes.

pullover, pullovers
(noun) A pullover is a woollen piece of clothing that covers the top part of your body.

pulmonary
(adjective; a formal word) relating to the lungs or to the veins and arteries carrying blood between the lungs and the heart.
[from Latin *pulmo* meaning 'lung']

pulp, pulps, pulping, pulped
1 (noun) If something is turned into a pulp, it is crushed until it is soft, smooth, and moist.
2 The pulp of a fruit or vegetable is the soft inner part.
3 Books or magazines that are considered to be of poor quality are sometimes referred to as pulp.
4 (verb) To pulp something means to crush it into a pulp.

pulpit, pulpits (pronounced **pool**-pit)
(noun) In a church, the pulpit is the small raised platform where a member of the clergy stands to preach.
[from Latin *pulpitum* meaning 'platform']

pulsar, pulsars
(noun) A pulsar is a small, extremely dense star which emits regular bursts of radio waves. Pulsar is short for 'pulsating star'.

pulsate, pulsates, pulsating, pulsated
(verb) If something is pulsating, it is moving in and out or vibrating regularly.
[from Latin *pulsare* meaning 'to push']

pulse, pulses, pulsing, pulsed
1 (noun) Your pulse is the regular beating of blood through your body, the rate of which you can feel at your wrists and elsewhere.
2 A pulse is a regular rhythmic movement or beat, e.g. *pulses of laser light.*
3 The seeds of beans, peas, and lentils are called pulses when they are used for food.
4 (verb) If something is pulsing, it is moving or vibrating with rhythmic, regular movements.

pulverize, pulverizes, pulverizing, pulverized; also spelled **pulverise**
(verb) To pulverize something means to crush it into very small pieces.
[from Latin *pulvus* meaning 'dust' or 'powder']

puma, pumas (pronounced **pyoo**-mah)
(noun) A puma is a wild animal belonging to the cat family. Pumas have brownish-grey fur and live in mountainous regions of America.

pumice (pronounced **pum**-miss)
(noun) Pumice stone is very light-weight grey stone that can be used to soften areas of hard skin.

pummel, pummels, pummelling, pummelled
(verb) If you pummel something, you beat it with your fists, e.g. *She pummelled the dough.*

pump, pumps, pumping, pumped
1 (noun) A pump is a machine that is used to force a liquid or gas to move in a particular direction.
2 (verb) To pump a liquid or gas somewhere means to force it to flow in that direction, using a pump.
3 (noun) Pumps are canvas shoes with flat soles which people wear for sport or leisure.
4 (verb) If you pump money into something, you put a lot of money into it.
5 If you pump someone about something, you ask them a lot of questions.

pumpernickel
(noun) Pumpernickel is dark brown bread made from rye.
[a German word]

pumpkin, pumpkins
(noun) A pumpkin is a very large, round, orange-coloured vegetable.

pun, puns
(noun) A pun is a clever and amusing use of words so that what you say has two different meanings.

punch, punches, punching, punched
1 (verb) If you punch someone, you hit them hard with your fist.
2 (noun) A punch is a hard blow with the fist.
3 A punch is also a tool used for making holes.
4 Punch is a drink made from a mixture of wine, spirits, fruit, sugar, and spices.

punch line, punch lines
(noun) The punch line of a joke is the last sentence which makes the joke funny.

punchy, punchier, punchiest
(adjective; an informal word) A punchy piece of writing is clear, brief, and forceful.

punctilious (pronounced punk-**til**-lee-uss)
(adjective; a formal word) always very correct and careful about small details.
[from Italian *puntiglio* meaning 'small detail']

punctual
(adjective) arriving at the correct time.
punctually (adverb), **punctuality** (noun).
[from Latin *punctualis* meaning 'of detail']

Similar words: prompt, timely, on time

punctuate, punctuates, punctuating, punctuated
1 (verb) Something that is punctuated by a particular thing is interrupted by it at intervals, e.g. *Her words were punctuated by coughs.*
2 When you punctuate a piece of writing, you put punctuation into it.

punctuation
(noun) The marks in writing such as full stops, question marks, and commas are called punctuation or punctuation marks.

puncture, punctures, puncturing, punctured
1 (noun) If a tyre has a puncture, a small hole has been made in it and it has become flat.

2 (verb) To puncture something means to make a small hole in it.
[from Latin *punctum* meaning 'little hole']

pundit, pundits
(noun) A pundit is someone who is an expert on a particular subject.
[from Hindi *pandit* meaning 'a learned Hindu']

pungent
1 (adjective) having a strong, unpleasant smell or taste, e.g. *the pungent, choking smell of sulphur.*
2 (a formal use) having a powerful, sharp effect and often severely critical, e.g. *a pungent attack on student obsession with computers.*
pungency (noun).
[from Latin *pungens* meaning 'piercing']

punish, punishes, punishing, punished
(verb) To punish someone who has done something wrong means to make them suffer because of it.
[from Latin *punire* meaning 'to punish']

Similar words: chastise, penalize

punishable
(adjective) If a crime is punishable in a particular way, anyone who commits it will be punished that way, e.g. *At that time, blasphemy was punishable by death.*

punishment, punishments
(noun) A punishment is something unpleasant done to someone because they have done something wrong.

punitive (pronounced **pyoo**-nit-tiv)
(adjective) harsh and intended to punish people, e.g. *the Government's punitive response to riots.*

Punjabi, Punjabis (pronounced pun-**jah**-bee)
1 (adjective) belonging or relating to the Punjab, a state in north-western India.
2 (noun) A Punjabi is someone who comes from the Punjab.
3 Punjabi is a language spoken in the Punjab.

punk, punks
1 (noun) Punk or punk rock is an aggressive style of rock music.
2 A punk is a young person who is a follower of punk music. Punks usually dress in black, decorate themselves with chains, and have brightly coloured, spiked hair.

punnet, punnets
(noun) A punnet is a very small, light box in which soft fruit is sold.

punt, punts
(noun) A punt is a long, flat-bottomed boat. You move it along by pushing a pole against the river bottom.

punter, punters
1 (noun) A punter is a person who bets money on horse races.
2 (an informal use) People sometimes refer to customers or members of the public as punters.

puny, punier, puniest
(adjective) very small and weak.

pup, pups
(noun) A pup is a young dog. Some other young animals such as seals are also called pups.

pupa, pupae (pronounced **pyoo**-pa)
(noun) A pupa is an insect that is at the stage of development between a larva and a fully developed adult.

pupil, pupils
1 (noun) The pupils at a school are the children who go there.
2 Your pupils are the small, round, black holes in the centre of your eyes.
[sense 1 is from Latin *pupillus* meaning 'orphan']

puppet, puppets
1 (noun) A puppet is a doll or toy animal that is moved by pulling strings or by putting your hand inside its body.
2 You can refer to someone as a puppet if their actions are controlled by someone else.
[from Old French *poupette* meaning 'little doll']

puppy, puppies
(noun) A puppy is a young dog.

purchase, purchases, purchasing, purchased
1 (verb) When you purchase something, you buy it.
2 (noun) A purchase is something you have bought.
purchaser (noun).

purdah (pronounced **pur**-dah)
(noun) Purdah is a Muslim or Hindu custom in which women avoid male strangers by remaining in a special part of the house or by covering their faces.
[from Hindi *parda* meaning 'veil']

pure, purer, purest
1 (adjective) Something that is pure is not mixed with anything else, e.g. *pure silk... pure white.*
2 Pure also means clean and free from harmful substances, e.g. *The advantage of breast feeding is that the milk is always pure.*
3 People who are pure have not done anything considered to be sinful.
4 Pure science or research is concerned only with theory and not with how it could be put into practice.
5 Pure also means complete, e.g. *pure chance.*
purity (noun).

Similar words: (sense 2) clean, spotless
(sense 3) virtuous, chaste, undefiled, unsullied, virginal

purée, purées (pronounced **pyoo**-ray)
(noun) A purée is a food which has been mashed or blended to a thick, smooth consistency.
[a French word]

purely
(adverb) involving only one feature and not including anything else, e.g. *purely practical.*

Purgatory
(noun) Roman Catholics believe that Purgatory is a place where spirits of the dead are sent to suffer for their sins before going to Heaven.

purge, purges, purging, purged
(verb) To purge something means to remove

undesirable things from it, e.g. *the campaign to purge the party of militants.*
[from Latin *purgare* meaning 'to purify']

purify, purifies, purifying, purified
(verb) To purify something means to remove all dirty or harmful substances from it.
purification (noun).
[from Latin *purificare* meaning 'to cleanse']

purist, purists
(noun) A purist is someone who believes that the traditional or pure form of a subject or art form should be maintained.

puritan, puritans
(noun) A puritan is someone who believes in strict moral principles and avoids physical pleasures.
puritanical (adjective).
[from Latin *puritas* meaning 'purity']

purl
(noun) Purl is one of the two main knitting stitches. You push the needle through the stitch so that the point comes towards you.

purloin, purloins, purloining, purloined
(pronounced pur-**loyn**)
(verb) If you purloin something, you take it without permission.

purple
(noun and adjective) reddish-blue.

purport, purports, purporting, purported
(pronounced pur-**port**)
(verb; a formal word) Something that purports to have a quality is claimed to have it, e.g. *cosmetics purporting to delay wrinkles.*

purpose, purposes
1 (noun) The purpose of something is the reason for it.
2 If you have a particular purpose, this is what you want to achieve, e.g. *Her only purpose in life was to get rich.*
3 (phrase) If you do something **on purpose**, you do it deliberately.
purposely (adverb), **purposeful** (adjective).

purr, purrs, purring, purred
(verb) When a cat purrs, it makes a low vibrating sound because it is contented.

purse, purses, pursing, pursed
1 (noun) A purse is a small leather or fabric container for carrying money.
2 In American English, a purse is a handbag.
3 (verb) If you purse your lips, you move them into a tight, rounded shape.
[from Latin *bursa* meaning 'bag']

purser, pursers
(noun) On a ship, the purser is the officer responsible for the accounts, the paperwork, and the welfare of passengers.

pursue, pursues, pursuing, pursued
1 (verb) If you pursue an activity, interest, or plan, you do it or make efforts to achieve it.
2 If you pursue someone, you follow them to try to catch them.
pursuer (noun), **pursuit** (noun).

purveyor, purveyors
(noun; a formal word) A purveyor of goods or services is a person who sells them or provides them.

pus
(noun) Pus is a thick yellowish liquid that forms in an infected wound.

push, pushes, pushing, pushed
1 (verb) When you push something, you press it using force in order to move it.
2 If you push someone into doing something, you force or persuade them to do it.
3 If you push something or push for it, you try hard to get it accepted or to increase its popularity, e.g. *He is pushing for secret balloting.*
4 (an informal use) Someone who pushes drugs sells them illegally.
5 (phrase; an informal use) If someone **is given the push**, they are dismissed from their job.
[from French *pousser*]

Similar words: (sense 1) shove, thrust, jog, jostle

push off
(phrasal verb; an informal expression) If you tell someone to push off, you are telling them rudely to go away.

push bike, push bikes
(noun; an informal expression) A push bike is a bicycle.

pushchair, pushchairs
(noun) A pushchair is a small folding chair on wheels in which a baby or toddler can be wheeled around.

pusher, pushers
(noun; an informal word) A pusher is someone who sells illegal drugs.

pushing
(adverb) Someone who is pushing a particular age is nearly that age, e.g. *pushing forty.*

pushover (an informal word)
1 (noun) Something that is a pushover is easy.
2 Someone who is a pushover is easily persuaded.

pushy, pushier, pushiest
(adjective; an informal word) behaving in a forceful and determined way.

pusillanimous (pronounced pyoo-sil-**lan**-nim-muss)
(adjective) afraid of taking risks.
[from Latin *pusillus* meaning 'weak']

pussy, pussies
(noun; an informal use) A pussy is a cat.

pussyfoot, pussyfoots, pussyfooting, pussyfooted
(verb; an informal word) Someone who is pussyfooting is behaving too cautiously because they are afraid to commit themselves.

put, puts, putting, put
1 (verb) When you put something somewhere, you move it into that place or position.
2 If you put an idea or remark in a particular way, you express it that way, e.g. *He didn't put it quite as crudely as that!*
3 To put someone or something in a particular state or situation means to cause them to be in it, e.g. *This puts me in a difficult position.*
4 You can use put to express an estimate of the size or importance of something, e.g. *The cost is now put at two billion pounds.*

Similar words: (sense 1) place, set, situate, lay

put across or **put over**
(phrasal verb) When you put something across, you describe or explain it to someone.

put away
(phrasal verb) If someone is put away, they are sent to prison or mental hospital for a long time.

put by
(phrasal verb) If you put something by, you save it for later use.

put down
1 (phrasal verb) If soldiers or police put down a rebellion, they stop it by using force.
2 To put someone down means to criticize them and make them appear foolish.
3 If an animal is put down, it is killed because it is very ill or dangerous.
4 If you put something down to a particular thing, you believe it is caused by that thing.

put forward
(phrasal verb) If you put someone or something forward, you suggest that they should be considered or chosen.

put in
1 (phrasal verb) If you put in an amount of time or effort, you spend that amount of time or effort.
2 If you put in a request or application, you make it.

put off
1 (phrasal verb) If you put something off, you delay doing it.
2 To put someone off means to discourage them.

put on
1 (phrasal verb) When people put on a show or exhibition, they arrange for it to take place.
2 (phrase) If someone is behaving or speaking in an artificial way, you can say that they **are putting it on.**

put out
1 (phrasal verb) If you put a fire out or put the light out, you make it stop burning or shining.
2 If you put your back, hip, or shoulder out, you injure it by dislocating a bone.
3 If you are put out, you are annoyed or upset.
4 If you put yourself out for someone, you go to a lot of trouble to help them.

put up
1 (phrasal verb) If you put up resistance to something, you argue or fight against it, e.g. *We had to put up a fierce struggle to save the building.*
2 If someone puts you up, you stay at their home for one or more nights.
3 If someone puts you up to something wrong or foolish, they encourage you to do it.

4 If you put up with something, you tolerate it even though you disagree with it or dislike it.

putative (pronounced **pyoo**-tat-tiv)
(adjective; a formal word) You use putative to say that something is generally thought to be a particular thing, e.g. *the putative father of her child.*
[from Latin *putativus* meaning 'supposed']

putrefy, putrefies, putrefying, putrefied
(pronounced **pyoo**-trif-fie)
(verb) When something putrefies, it rots, producing a disgusting smell.
putrefaction (noun), **putrescent** (adjective).
[from Latin *putrefacere* meaning 'to make rotten']

putrid (pronounced **pyoo**-trid)
(adjective) rotting and smelling disgusting.
[from Latin *putridus* meaning 'rotten']

putt, putts
In golf, a putt is a gentle stroke made when the ball is near the hole.

putting
(noun) Putting is a game played on a small grass course with no obstacles. You hit a ball gently with a club so that it rolls towards one of a series of holes around the course.

putty
(noun) Putty is a paste used to fix panes of glass into frames.

put-up job, put-up jobs
(noun) If something is a put-up job, it has been arranged beforehand in order to cheat someone.

puzzle, puzzles, puzzling, puzzled
1 (verb) If something puzzles you, it confuses you and you do not understand it.
2 If you puzzle over a problem or question, you try hard to think of an explanation for it.
3 (noun) A puzzle is a game, toy, or question that requires a lot of thought to complete or solve.
puzzled (adjective), **puzzlement** (noun).

Similar words: (sense 1) baffle, bamboozle, bemuse, bewilder, flummox, stump, confound, perplex

PVC
(noun) PVC is a plastic used for making clothing, pipes, and many other things. PVC is an abbreviation for 'polyvinyl chloride'.

pygmy, pygmies (pronounced **pig**-mee); also spelled **pigmy**
1 (adjective) Pygmy is used to describe the smallest of a group of related species, e.g. *the pygmy shrew.*

2 (noun) A pygmy is a very small person, especially one who belongs to a racial group in which all the people are small.
[from Greek *pugmaios* meaning 'undersized']

pyjamas
(noun) Pyjamas consist of loose trousers and a jacket or top that you wear in bed.
[from Persian *pay jama* meaning 'leg clothing']

pylon, pylons
(noun) Pylons are very tall metal structures which carry overhead electricity cables.
[from Greek *pulōn* meaning 'gateway']

pyramid, pyramids
1 (noun) A pyramid is a three-dimensional shape with a flat base and flat triangular sides sloping upwards to a point.
2 The Pyramids are ancient stone structures built over the tombs of Egyptian kings and queens. They are four-sided pyramids.
[from Greek *puramis*]

pyre, pyres
(noun) A pyre is a high pile of wood on which a dead body or religious offering is burned.
[from Greek *pura* meaning 'hearth']

Pyrex
(noun; a trademark) Pyrex is a type of glass used for making dishes that can withstand high temperatures.

pyromaniac, pyromaniacs (pronounced pie-roe-**main**-ee-ak)
(noun) A pyromaniac is someone who gets uncontrollable urges to set fire to things.
pyromania (noun).
[from Greek *pus* meaning 'fire' and *maniakos* meaning 'relating to madness']

pyrotechnics (pronounced pie-roe-**tek**-niks)
(noun) Pyrotechnics is the making or displaying of fireworks.

Pyrrhic victory, Pyrrhic victories (pronounced **pir**-rik)
(noun) A Pyrrhic victory is a success gained at such a great cost or sacrifice that it no longer seems worth achieving.
[named after *Pyrrhus*, who defeated the Romans at Asculum in 279 BC, but suffered very heavy losses]

python, pythons
(noun) A python is a large snake that kills animals by squeezing them with its body.
[from Greek *Python*, a huge mythical serpent]

Q

QC, QC's
(noun) A QC is a senior barrister. QC is an abbreviation for 'Queen's Counsel'.

quack, quacks, quacking, quacked
1 (verb) When a duck quacks, it makes the loud harsh sound that ducks typically make.
2 (noun) A quack is the sound made by a duck.
3 A quack is also a person who claims dishonestly to be able to cure people of illnesses.

quad, quads (pronounced **kwod**)
1 (noun) Quads are four children born at the same time to the same mother. Quad is an abbreviation for **quadruplet**.
2 A quad is a courtyard with buildings all round it. Quad is an abbreviation for **quadrangle**.

quadrangle, quadrangles (pronounced **kwod**-rang-gl)
1 (noun) A quadrangle is a courtyard with buildings all round it.
2 In geometry, a quadrangle is a four-sided figure.

quadrant, quadrants (pronounced **kwod**-rant)
1 (noun) A quadrant is a quarter of a circle, or a quarter of the circumference of a circle.
2 In the past, a quadrant was an instrument used in astronomy and navigation for measuring the altitude of stars.
[from Latin *quadrans* meaning 'quarter']

quadraphonic (pronounced kwod-raf-**fon**-ik)
(adjective) A quadraphonic hi-fi system reproduces sound using four independent speakers.

quadratic (pronounced kwod-**rat**-ik)
(adjective) A quadratic equation involves a variable raised to the power of two, but no higher.

quadri-
(prefix) Quadri- means four.
[a Latin word]

quadrilateral, quadrilaterals (pronounced kwod-ril-**lat**-ral)
(noun) A quadrilateral is a shape with four straight sides.
[from *quadri-* + Latin *latus* meaning 'side']

quadrille, quadrilles (pronounced kwod-**rill**)
(noun) A quadrille was an 18th- and 19th-century dance for four couples.
[from Spanish *cuadrilla* meaning 'little square']

quadruped, quadrupeds (pronounced **kwod**-roo-ped)
(noun) A quadruped is any animal with four legs.
[from Latin *quadri-* + *pes* meaning 'four feet']

quadruple, quadruples, quadrupling, quadrupled (pronounced kwod-**roo**-pl)
1 (verb) When an amount or number quadruples, it becomes four times as large as it was.
2 (adjective) Quadruple means four times as large as normal, e.g. *a quadruple measure of whisky.*

quadruplet, quadruplets (pronounced kwod-**roo**-plet)
(noun) Quadruplets are four children born at the same time to the same mother.

quaff, quaffs, quaffing, quaffed (pronounced **kwof**)
(verb; an old-fashioned word) If you quaff a drink, you drink it quickly in large gulps.

quagmire, quagmires (pronounced **kwag**-mire)
(noun) A quagmire is a soft, wet area of land which you sink into if you walk on it.

quail, quails, quailing, quailed
1 (noun) A quail is a type of small game bird with a round body and short tail.
2 (verb) If you quail, you feel or look afraid.

quaint, quainter, quaintest
(adjective) attractively old-fashioned or unusual, e.g. *quaint little houses... quaint ideas.*
quaintly (adverb), **quaintness** (noun).

quake, quakes, quaking, quaked
1 (verb) If you quake, you shake and tremble because you are very frightened.
2 (noun; an informal use) A quake is an earthquake.
[from Old English *cwacian*]

Quaker, Quakers
(noun) A Quaker is a member of a Christian group, the Society of Friends. Quakers have no priests or prayer books, and hold meetings at which any member can speak.

qualification, qualifications
1 (noun) Your qualifications are your skills and achievements, especially as officially recognized at the end of a course of training or study.
2 A qualification is also a detail or explanation that modifies or limits something already said, e.g. *Few people praise him without qualification.*

qualify, qualifies, qualifying, qualified
1 (verb) When you qualify, you pass the examinations that you need to pass to do a particular job, e.g. *I qualified as a doctor.*
2 If you qualify a statement, you add a detail or explanation to modify or limit it slightly.
3 If you qualify for something, you become eligible for it, e.g. *He didn't qualify for a pension.*
qualified (adjective).

qualitative
(adjective) relating to the quality of something.

quality, qualities
1 (noun) The quality of something is how good it is, e.g. *The quality of the photograph was poor.*
2 A quality is also a characteristic, e.g. *We look for certain qualities in a teacher.*
[from Latin *qualitas* meaning 'state' or 'nature']

qualm, qualms (pronounced **kwahm**)
(noun) If you have qualms about what you are doing, you worry that it might not be right.

quandary, quandaries (pronounced **kwon**-dree)
(noun) If you are in a quandary, you cannot decide what to do.

quantify, quantifies, quantifying, quantified
(verb) If you quantify something, you express it as a number or an amount.
quantifiable (adjective).
[from Latin *quantus* meaning 'how much' and *facere* meaning 'to make']

quantitative
(adjective) relating to the size or amount of something.

quantity, quantities
1 (noun) A quantity is an amount.
2 (phrase) **In quantity** means in large amounts.
3 (noun) Quantity is the amount of something that there is, e.g. *The food supply has declined in both quantity and quality.*
[from Latin *quantus* meaning 'how much']

quantity surveyor, quantity surveyors
(noun) A quantity surveyor is someone whose job is to estimate how much new buildings will cost to build.

quantum, quanta (pronounced **qwon**-tum)
1 (noun; a formal use) A quantum of something is an amount of it.
2 (adjective) Quantum is used to describe various theories in physics and mathematics which are concerned with the properties and behaviour of atomic particles.
3 A quantum leap is a very great advance.

quarantine, quarantines, quarantining, quarantined
(pronounced **kwor**-an-teen)
1 (noun) If an animal is in quarantine, it is kept away from other animals for a time because it might have an infectious disease.
2 (verb) If an animal is quarantined, it is kept in quarantine.
[from Italian *quarantina* meaning 'forty days']

quark, quarks
(noun) A quark is a hypothetical particle believed to be the fundamental unit of other particles.

quarrel, quarrels, quarrelling, quarrelled
1 (noun) A quarrel is an angry argument.
2 (verb) If people quarrel, they have an angry argument.
3 (noun) If you have no quarrel with something, you do not object to it.
4 (verb) To quarrel with something means to disagree with it, e.g. *I would quarrel with your suggestion that people do not care.*
[from Latin *queri* meaning 'to complain']

Similar words: (sense 1) fight, disagreement, altercation, tiff, dispute, squabble
(sense 2) fight, dispute, bicker, fall out, wrangle, squabble

quarrelsome
(adjective) often quarrelling, e.g. *His brothers were greedy and quarrelsome.*

Similar words: contentious, argumentative

quarry, quarries, quarrying, quarried
(pronounced **kwor**-ree)
1 (noun) A quarry is a place where stone is removed from the ground by digging or blasting.
2 (verb) To quarry stone means to remove it from a quarry by digging or blasting.
3 (noun) Your quarry is the animal or animals that you are hunting, e.g. *Move slowly or you will startle your quarry.*
[sense 3 is from Middle English *quirre* meaning 'entrails given to the hounds to eat']

quart, quarts (pronounced **kwort**)
(noun) A quart is a unit of liquid volume equal to two pints or about 1.136 litres.
[from Latin *quartus* meaning 'fourth'; there are four quarts to a gallon]

quarter, quarters
1 (noun) A quarter is one of four equal parts.
2 A quarter is also an American coin worth 25 cents.
3 You can refer to a particular area in a city as a quarter, e.g. *the Chinese quarter.*
4 You can use quarter to refer vaguely to a particular person or group of people, e.g. *Male prejudice still exists in certain quarters.*
5 (plural noun) A soldier's or a servant's quarters are the rooms that they live in.
6 (phrase) **At close quarters** means very close together.
7 (verb) To quarter something means to divide it into four equal parts.
8 (phrase) **To give no quarter** means to show no mercy.
[from Latin *quartarius* meaning 'a fourth part']

quarterly, quarterlies
1 (adjective or adverb) Quarterly means happening regularly every three months, e.g. *a salary paid quarterly.*
2 (noun) A quarterly is a magazine or journal published every three months.

quartermaster, quartermasters
(noun) A quartermaster is an army officer responsible for accommodation, food, and equipment.

quartet, quartets (pronounced kwor-**tet**)
(noun) A quartet is a group of four musicians who sing or play together; also a piece of music written for four instruments or singers.

quartz
(noun) Quartz is a kind of mineral. Quartz crystal is used in making electronic equipment and very accurate watches and clocks.

quasar, quasars (pronounced **kway**-sar)
(noun) A quasar is a starlike object in outer space which produces powerful radio waves and other forms of energy.
[an abbreviation of *quasi-stellar radio source*]

quash, quashes, quashing, quashed
(pronounced **kwosh**)
(verb) To quash a decision or judgment means to reject it officially, e.g. *Their prison sentences were quashed on appeal.*

quasi (pronounced **kway**-sie)
(prefix) Quasi means resembling something but

not actually being that thing, e.g. *a quasi-religious experience.*
[a Latin word meaning 'as if']

quatrain, quatrains (pronounced **kwot**-rain)
(noun) A quatrain is a verse of poetry with four lines.
[from Latin *quattuor* meaning 'four']

quaver, quavers, quavering, quavered
(pronounced **kway**-ver)
1 (verb) If your voice quavers, it sounds unsteady, usually because you are nervous.
2 (noun) A quaver is a musical note that has half the time value of a crotchet.
[from Middle English *quaven* meaning 'to tremble']

quay, quays (pronounced **kee**)
(noun) A quay is a place where boats are tied up and loaded or unloaded.

queasy, queasier, queasiest (pronounced **kwee**-zee)
(adjective) feeling slightly sick.
queasiness (noun).

queen, queens
1 (noun) A queen is a female monarch or a woman married to a king.
2 A queen is also a female bee or ant which can lay eggs.
3 In chess, the queen is the most powerful piece, which can move in any direction.
4 In a pack of cards, a queen is a card with a picture of a queen on it. It is more valuable than a jack and less valuable than a king.
queenly (adjective).
[from Old English *cwen*]

Queen Mother, Queen Mothers
(noun) A Queen Mother is the widow of a king and the mother of the reigning monarch.

queer, queerer, queerest
(adjective) Queer means very strange.

quell, quells, quelling, quelled
1 (verb) To quell a rebellion or riot means to put an end to it by using force.
2 If you quell a feeling such as fear or grief, you stop yourself from feeling it, e.g. *I was trying to quell a growing unease.*
[from Old English *cwellan* meaning 'to kill']

quench, quenches, quenching, quenched
1 (verb) If you quench your thirst, you have a drink so that you are no longer thirsty.
2 (an old-fashioned use) To quench a fire means to stop it burning.
[from Old English *acwencan* meaning 'to extinguish']

querulous (pronounced **kwer**-yoo-lus)
(adjective; a formal word) often complaining, e.g. *querulous children.*
[from Latin *queri* meaning 'to complain']

query, queries, querying, queried (pronounced **qweer**-ree)
1 (noun) A query is a question.
2 (verb) If you query something, you ask about it because you think it might not be right, e.g. *He queried the accuracy of the figures.*
[from Latin *quaerere* meaning 'to ask']

quest, quests
(noun) A quest is a long search for something.
[from Latin *quaesita* meaning 'thing sought for']

question, questions, questioning, questioned
1 (noun) A question is a sentence which asks for information.
2 (verb) If you question someone, you ask them questions.
3 If you question something, you express doubts about it, e.g. *Women are questioning their traditional role in society.*
4 (noun) If there is some question about something, there is doubt about it.
5 A question is also a problem that needs to be discussed, e.g. *His resignation raised the question of his successor.*
6 (phrase) If you **call something into question,** you express doubts about it.
7 If something is **out of the question,** it is impossible.
8 The time, place, or thing **in question** is the one that you have just been talking about, e.g. *Did you see him on the night in question?*

Similar words: (sense 1) query, inquiry
(sense 3) query, challenge

questionable
(adjective) possibly not true or not honest.

question mark, question marks
(noun) A question mark is the punctuation mark (?) which is used at the end of a question.

questionnaire, questionnaires
(noun) A questionnaire is a list of questions which asks for information for a survey.

queue, queues, queueing, queued
(pronounced **kyoo**)
1 (noun) A queue is a line of people or vehicles waiting for something.
2 (verb) When people queue, they stand in a line waiting for something.

quibble, quibbles, quibbling, quibbled
1 (verb) If you quibble, you argue about something unimportant.
2 (noun) A quibble is a minor objection.

quiche, quiches (pronounced **keesh**)
(noun) A quiche is a tart with a savoury filling.
[a French word, originally from German *Kuchen* meaning 'cake']

quick, quicker, quickest
1 (adjective) moving with great speed.
2 lasting only a short time, e.g. *a quick visit.*
3 happening without any delay, e.g. *You'll get a quicker reply if you telephone.*
4 intelligent and able to understand things easily.
quickly (adverb), **quickness** (noun).
[from Old English *cwicu* meaning 'alive']

quicksand, quicksands
(noun) A quicksand is an area of deep wet sand that you sink into if you walk on it.

quicksilver
1 (noun; an old-fashioned word) Quicksilver is the metal mercury.

2 (phrase) If something moves **like quicksilver**, it moves very quickly.

quickstep
(noun) The quickstep is a fast ballroom dance.

quid
(noun; an informal word) A quid is a pound.

quid pro quo, quid pro quos (pronounced kwid proh **kwo**)
(noun) A quid pro quo is a gift or advantage given in return for something.
[a Latin expression meaning 'something for something']

quiescent (pronounced kwee-**ess**-nt)
(adjective; a formal word) quiet and at rest.
[from Latin *quiescere* meaning 'to rest']

quiet, quieter, quietest
1 (adjective) Someone or something that is quiet makes very little noise or no noise at all.
2 Quiet also means peaceful, e.g. *She spent a quiet evening at home.*
3 (noun) Quiet is silence, e.g. *He demanded quiet.*
4 (adjective) A quiet event happens with very little fuss or publicity, e.g. *a quiet wedding.*
5 Quiet clothes or colours are not bright.
quietly (adverb), **quietness** (noun).
[from Latin *quies* meaning 'calm' or 'rest']

Similar words: (sense 1) soft, low

quieten, quietens, quietening, quietened
(verb) To quieten someone means to make them become quiet.

quill, quills
1 (noun) A quill is a pen made from a feather.
2 A bird's quills are the large feathers on its wings and tail.
3 A porcupine's quills are its spines.

quilt, quilts
(noun) A quilt is a cover for a bed, especially one that is padded.
[from Latin *culcita* meaning 'stuffed item of bedding']

quilted
(adjective) Quilted clothes are made of thick layers of material sewn together with diagonal stitching.

quin, quins
(noun) Quins are five children born at the same time to the same mother. Quin is an abbreviation for **quintuplet.**

quince, quinces
(noun) A quince is an acid-tasting fruit used for making jams and marmalades.

quinine (pronounced **kwin**-een)
(noun) Quinine is a drug used to treat fevers such as malaria.
[from Spanish *quina* meaning 'chinchona bark'; the drug is extracted from the bark of the chinchona tree]

quintessence (pronounced kwin-**tess**-sens)
(a formal word)

1 (noun) The quintessence of something is the most essential feature of it.
2 The quintessence of something is also the most perfect example of it, e.g. *She is the quintessence of sweetness.*
quintessential (adjective).

quintet, quintets (pronounced kwin-**tet**)
(noun) A quintet is a group of five musicians who sing or play together; also a piece of music written for five instruments or singers.
[from Italian *quinto* meaning 'fifth']

quintuplet, quintuplets (pronounced kwin-**tyoo**-plit)
(noun) Quintuplets are five children born at the same time to the same mother.
[from Latin *quintus* meaning 'fifth']

quip, quips, quipping, quipped
1 (noun) A quip is an amusing or clever remark.
2 (verb) To quip means to make an amusing or clever remark.

quirk, quirks
1 (noun) A quirk is an odd habit or characteristic, e.g. *Everyone has his little quirks.*
2 A quirk is also an unexpected event or development, e.g. *a quirk of fate.*
quirky (adjective).

quisling, quislings (pronounced **kwiz**-ling)
(noun) A quisling is a traitor who helps an enemy that is occupying his or her own country.
[from the name of *Vidkum Quisling*, a Norwegian major who collaborated with the Germans in Norway during World War II]

quit, quits, quitting, quit or quitted
1 (verb) If you quit something, you leave it or stop doing it, e.g. *I'm going to quit psychiatry.*
2 (an informal phrase) If two people **are quits**, neither of them owe the other anything.

quite
1 (adverb) fairly but not very, e.g. *quite young.*
2 completely, e.g. *I stood quite still.*
3 (phrase) You use **quite a** to emphasize that something is large or impressive, e.g. *It was quite a sight.*
4 (exclamation; a formal use) You can say 'quite' to agree with someone.

quiver, quivers, quivering, quivered
1 (verb) If something quivers, it trembles.
2 (noun) A quiver is a trembling movement, e.g. *Her whole body gave a slight quiver.*
3 A quiver is also a container for arrows.

quixotic (pronounced kwik-**sot**-ik)
(adjective) unrealistic and romantic.
[from the name of the character *Don Quixote* in the novel by Cervantes]

quiz, quizzes, quizzing, quizzed
1 (noun) A quiz is a game in which the competitors are asked questions to test their knowledge.
2 (verb) If you quiz someone, you question them closely about something.

quizzical (pronounced **kwiz**-ik-kl)
(adjective) amused and questioning, e.g. *a quizzical glance.*

quorum (pronounced **kwaw**-rum)
(noun) A quorum is the smallest number of
people required to make a meeting official.

quota, quotas
(noun) A quota is a number or quantity of
something which is officially allowed.
[from Latin *quot* meaning 'how many']

quotation, quotations
1 (noun) A quotation is an extract from a book or
speech which is quoted.
2 A quotation is also a statement of how much a
piece of work will cost.

quotation mark, quotation marks
(noun) Quotation marks are the punctuation
marks ('...') that show where a speech or
quotation begins and ends.

quote, quotes, quoting, quoted
1 (verb) If you quote something that someone
has written or said, you repeat their exact
words.

2 If you quote a fact, you state it because it
supports what you are saying.
3 To quote for a piece of work means to state
what it would cost to do it.
4 (noun) A quote is an extract from a book or
speech.
5 A quote is also an estimate of how much a
piece of work will cost.
[from Latin *quotare* meaning 'to mark passages
in a book with reference numbers or notes']

Similar words: (sense 2) cite, instance
(sense 4) citation, quotation

quoth (pronounced **kwohth**)
(verb; an old word) Quoth means the same as
'said', e.g. *Not I, quoth he.*

quotient, quotients (pronounced **kwoh**-shent)
(noun) A quotient is the number that you get
when you divide one number into another.
[from Latin *quotiens* meaning 'how often']

R

rabbi, rabbis (pronounced **rab**-by)
(noun) A rabbi is a Jewish religious leader.
[from Hebrew *rabh* + -*i* meaning 'my master']

rabbit, rabbits
(noun) A rabbit is a small animal with long ears.

rabble
(noun) A rabble is a noisy, disorderly crowd.

rabid
1 (adjective) used to describe someone with strong views that you do not approve of, e.g. *a rabid feminist*.
2 A rabid dog or other animal has rabies.

rabies (pronounced **ray**-beez)
(noun) Rabies is an infectious disease which causes people and animals, especially dogs, to go mad and die.
[from Latin *rabies* meaning 'madness']

raccoon, raccoons; also spelled **racoon**
(noun) A raccoon is a small North American animal with a long striped tail.

race, races, racing, raced
1 (noun) A race is a competition to see who is fastest, for example in running, swimming, or driving.
2 (verb) If you race someone, you compete with them in a race.
3 If you race something or if it races, it goes at its greatest rate, e.g. *He raced the engine... Her heart raced.*
4 If you race somewhere, you go there as quickly as possible, e.g. *She raced down the stairs.*
5 (noun) A race is also one of the major groups that human beings can be divided into according to their physical features.
racing (noun).

racecourse, racecourses
(noun) A racecourse is a grass track, sometimes with jumps, along which horses race.

racehorse, racehorses
(noun) A racehorse is a horse trained to run in races.

racial
(adjective) relating to the different races that people belong to, e.g. *racial discrimination*.
racially (adverb).

racism or **racialism**
(noun) Racism or racialism is the treatment of some people as inferior because of their race.
racist (noun and adjective).

rack, racks, racking, racked
1 (noun) A rack is a piece of equipment for holding things or hanging things on.
2 (verb) If you are racked by something, you suffer because of it, e.g. *She was racked by indecision.*
3 (an informal phrase) If you **rack your brains**, you try hard to think of or remember something.

rack-and-pinion
(noun and adjective) Rack-and-pinion is a system for converting rotary motion into linear motion using a rotating rod with teeth along its length which engage with a gearwheel.

racket, rackets
1 (noun) If someone is making a racket, they are making a lot of noise.
2 A racket is also an illegal way of making money.
3 Racket is another spelling of **racquet**.

racketeer, racketeers
(noun) A racketeer is someone who makes money in a dishonest way.

raconteur, raconteurs (pronounced rak-on-**tur**)
(noun) A raconteur is someone who tells stories in an amusing way.

racoon another spelling of **raccoon**.

racquet, racquets; also spelled **racket**
(noun) A racquet is a bat with strings across it used in tennis, squash, and badminton.
[from Arabic *rahat* meaning 'palm of the hand']

racy, racier, raciest
(adjective) lively, exciting, and slightly shocking, e.g. *a racy, romantic historical novel*.
racily (adverb).

rad, rads
(noun) A rad is a unit of energy absorbed from radiation. One rad is equal to 0.01 joule per kilogram of irradiated material.

radar
(noun) Radar is equipment used to track vehicles, ships, or aircraft that are out of sight by using radio signals that are reflected back from the object and shown on a screen.
[from *RA(dio) D(etecting) A(nd) R(anging)*]

radial, radials (pronounced **ray**-dee-al)
1 (adjective) Radial lines are all drawn from a central point but come out in different directions.
2 (noun) Radials are tyres that are strengthened inside by cords that point towards the centre of the wheel, giving the tyre more flexibility.
[from Latin *radius* meaning 'ray' or 'spoke']

radian, radians
(noun) A radian is a unit of measurement of angles. 2π radians are equal to 360 degrees.

radiant
1 (adjective) Someone who is radiant is so happy that it shows in their face.
2 glowing brightly.
radiantly (adverb), radiance (noun).
[from Latin *radiare* meaning 'to shine']

radiate, radiates, radiating, radiated
1 (verb) If things radiate from a place, they form a pattern like lines spreading out from the centre of a circle.
2 If you radiate a quality or emotion, it shows

clearly in your face and behaviour, e.g. *She radiated confidence.*

radiation
(noun) Radiation is the stream of particles given out by a radioactive substance.

radiator, radiators
1 (noun) A radiator is a hollow metal device for heating a room, usually connected to a central heating system.
2 A car's radiator is the part that is filled with water to cool the engine.

radical, radicals
1 (noun) Radicals are people who think there should be great changes in society, and try to make them happen.
2 (adjective) very significant, important, or basic, e.g. *a radical disagreement over policies.*
radically (adverb), **radicalism** (noun).
[from Latin *radicalis* meaning 'having roots']

radicle, radicles
(noun; a technical word) A radicle is the part of the embryo of a seed plant that develops into the main root.

radii the plural of radius.

radio, radios, radioing, radioed
1 (noun) Radio is a system of sending sound over a distance by electromagnetic waves.
2 Radio is also the broadcasting of programmes to the public by radio.
3 A radio is a piece of equipment for listening to radio programmes.
4 (verb) To radio someone means to send them a message by radio, e.g. *The pilot radioed for help.*
[a shortened form of *radiotelegraphy*]

radioactive
(adjective) giving off powerful and harmful rays.
radioactivity (noun).

radiocarbon
(noun) Radiocarbon is a type of radioactive carbon which decays very slowly and steadily. Its presence in an object can be measured to discover how old the object is.

radiography
(noun) Radiography is the process of taking X-rays.
radiographer (noun).

radiology
(noun) Radiology is the branch of medicine that uses radioactivity in the treatment of diseases.
radiological (adjective), **radiologist** (noun).

radio telescope, radio telescopes
(noun) A radio telescope is an instrument that can pick up radio waves from space and so detect things that cannot be seen using optical instruments.

radiotherapy
(noun) Radiotherapy is the treatment of diseases such as cancer using radiation.
radiotherapist (noun).

radish, radishes
(noun) A radish is a small salad vegetable with a red skin and white flesh and a strong, hot taste.
[from Latin *radix* meaning 'root']

radium
(noun) Radium is a radioactive element used in the treatment of cancer and other diseases. Its atomic number is 88 and its symbol is Ra. Radium was discovered in 1898 by Marie Curie.

radius, radii
(noun) The radius of a circle is the length of a straight line drawn from its centre to its circumference.
[from Latin *radius* meaning 'ray' or 'spoke']

radon
(noun) Radon is a chemical element in the form of a colourless radioactive gas. It is used in radiotherapy. Its atomic number is 86 and its symbol is Rn.

RAF an abbreviation for 'Royal Air Force'.

raffia
(noun) Raffia is a material made from palm leaves and used for making mats and baskets.

raffish
(adjective; a literary word) disreputable in a rather attractive way.

raffle, raffles, raffling, raffled
1 (noun) A raffle is a competition in which people buy numbered tickets and win a prize if they have the ticket that is chosen.
2 (verb) To raffle something means to hold a raffle with that thing as a prize.

raft, rafts
(noun) A raft is a floating platform made from long pieces of wood tied together.

rafter, rafters
(noun) Rafters are the sloping pieces of wood that support a roof.

rag, rags
1 (noun) A rag is a piece of old cloth used to clean or wipe things.
2 If someone is dressed in rags, they are wearing old torn clothes.
3 (an informal use) You can refer to a newspaper or magazine as a rag.

rage, rages, raging, raged
1 (noun) Rage is great anger.
2 (verb) To rage about something means to speak angrily about it.
3 If something such as a storm or battle is raging, it is continuing with great force or violence, e.g. *Outside the tempest raged.*
4 (an informal phrase) Something that is **the rage** is popular or fashionable.

Similar words: (sense 2) rant, rave, seethe, storm

ragged
1 (adjective) Ragged clothes are old and torn.
2 untidy and badly organized.

raglan
(adjective) A raglan sleeve is joined with a diagonal seam from under the arm to the neck. It is named after Lord Raglan (1788-1855).

ragtime
(noun) Ragtime is a kind of jazz that was popular in America in the early 1900s.

raid, raids, raiding, raided
1 (verb) To raid a place means to enter it by force to attack it or steal something.
2 (noun) A raid is the raiding of a building or a place, e.g. *The gang were planning a bank raid.*
[from Old English *rad* meaning 'military expedition']

rail, rails, railing, railed
1 (noun) A rail is a fixed horizontal bar used as a support or for hanging things on.
2 Rails are the steel bars which trains run along.
3 Rail is the railway considered as a means of transport, e.g. *I usually go by rail.*
4 (verb) To rail against something means to complain bitterly about it.

railing, railings
(noun) Railings are a fence made from metal bars.

railway, railways
(noun) A railway is a route along which trains travel on steel rails.

raiment
(noun; an old-fashioned word) Raiment is clothing.

rain, rains, raining, rained
1 (noun) Rain is water falling from the clouds in small drops.
2 (verb) When it is raining, rain is falling.
3 If something rains from above, it falls in large quantities, e.g. *Ash rained from the sky.*
rainy (adjective).

rainbow, rainbows
(noun) A rainbow is an arch of different colours that sometimes appears in the sky after it has been raining.

raincheck
(noun; an informal word) To take a raincheck means to postpone making a decision.

raincoat, raincoats
(noun) A raincoat is a waterproof coat.

raindrop, raindrops
(noun) A raindrop is a single drop of rain.

rainfall
(noun) Rainfall is the amount of rain that falls in a place during a particular period.

rainforest, rainforests
(noun) A rainforest is a dense forest of tall trees in a tropical area where there is a lot of rain.

rainwater
(noun) Rainwater is rain that has been stored.

raise, raises, raising, raised
1 (verb) If you raise something, you make it higher, e.g. *He tried to raise the window... We must raise our standards.*
2 If you raise your voice, you speak more loudly.
3 To raise money means to obtain it from several people or organizations.
4 To raise a child means to look after it until it is grown up.
5 If you raise a subject, you mention it.

raisin, raisins
(noun) Raisins are dried grapes.
[from French *raisin* meaning 'grape']

raison d'être, raisons d'être (pronounced ray-zon **detre**)
(noun) The raison d'être of something is the main purpose for its existence.

Raj
(noun) In Indian history, the Raj was the time when the British ruled India.

rajah, rajahs
(noun) A rajah is an Indian ruler or prince.
[from Sanskrit *rajan* meaning 'king']

rake, rakes, raking, raked
1 (noun) A rake is a garden tool with a row of metal teeth and a long handle.
2 (verb) To rake leaves or soil means to use a rake to gather the leaves or make the soil level.
3 (noun) A rake is also a man who behaves in rather an immoral way.

rake up
(phrasal verb) If you rake up something distressing or embarrassing from the past, you remind someone about it.

rakish
(adjective) If a hat is worn at a rakish angle, it is tilted in a confident, casual way.

rally, rallies, rallying, rallied
1 (noun) A rally is a large public meeting held to show support for something.
2 A rally is also a competition in which vehicles are raced over public roads.
3 In tennis or squash, a rally is a continuous series of shots exchanged by the players.
4 (verb) When people rally to something, they gather together to continue a struggle or to support something.
5 When sick people rally, they become stronger.
6 When people rally round, they work as a group to support someone at a difficult time.

ram, rams, ramming, rammed
1 (verb) If one vehicle rams another, it crashes into it.
2 To ram something somewhere means to push it there firmly, e.g. *He rammed tobacco in his pipe.*
3 (noun) A ram is an adult male sheep.

RAM
(noun) In computing, RAM is a temporary storage space which can be filled with data by the user but which loses its contents when the machine is switched off. RAM stands for 'random access memory'.

Ramadan
(noun) Ramadan is the ninth month of the Muslim year, during which Muslims eat and drink nothing during daylight.
[from Arabic *Ramadan* meaning literally 'the hot month']

ramble, rambles, rambling, rambled
1 (noun) A ramble is a long walk in the countryside.
2 (verb) To ramble means to go for a ramble.

3 To ramble also means to talk in a confused way, e.g. *I listened to him rambling.*
rambler (noun).

rambling
(adjective) A rambling building is large and spreads out in many directions.

ramification, ramifications
(noun) The ramifications of a decision or plan are all its consequences and effects.

ramp, ramps
(noun) A ramp is a sloping surface connecting two different levels.

rampage, rampages, rampaging, rampaged
1 (verb) To rampage means to rush about wildly causing damage.
2 (phrase) To **go on the rampage** means to rush about in a wild or violent way.

Similar words: (sense 1) go berserk, run amuck, run riot

rampant
(adjective) If something such as crime or disease is rampant, it is growing or spreading uncontrollably.
[from Old French *rampant* meaning 'crawling']

rampart, ramparts
(noun) Ramparts are earth banks, often with a wall on top, built to protect a castle or city.

ramrod
(noun) Someone who is as stiff as a ramrod is sitting or standing in a very stiff and upright way.

ramshackle
(adjective) A ramshackle building is in poor condition, and likely to fall down.

Similar words: rickety, tumbledown, dilapidated

ranch, ranches
(noun) A ranch is a large farm where cattle, sheep, or horses are reared, especially in the USA.
rancher (noun).
[from Mexican Spanish *rancho* meaning 'small farm']

rancid (pronounced **ran**-sid)
(adjective) Rancid food has gone bad.
[from Latin *rancere* meaning 'to stink']

rancour (pronounced **rang**-kur)
(noun; a formal word) Rancour is bitter hatred.
rancorous (adjective).

rand
(noun) The rand is the main unit of currency in South Africa.

random
1 (adjective) A random choice or arrangement is not based on any definite plan.
2 (phrase) If you do something **at random**, you do it without any definite plan, e.g. *He opened the book at random.*
randomly (adverb).

Similar words: (sense 1) arbitrary, haphazard, unplanned

range, ranges, ranging, ranged
1 (noun) The range of something is the maximum distance over which it can function, e.g. *We kept out of range of their guns.*
2 A range is a number of different things of the same kind, e.g. *a wide range of electrical goods.*
3 A range is also a set of values on a scale, e.g. *The age range is from six to seven.*
4 A range of mountains is a line of them.
5 A rifle range or firing range is a place where people practise shooting at targets.
6 (verb) When a set of things ranges between two points, they vary within these points on a scale. e.g. *increases ranging from £6 to £16 a week.*
[from Old French *range* meaning 'row']

Similar words: (sense 2) gamut, variety, scope, spectrum, sweep

rangefinder, rangefinders
(noun) A rangefinder is an instrument for measuring the distance of something you are photographing or shooting at.

ranger, rangers
(noun) A ranger is someone whose job is to look after a forest or park.

rank, ranks, ranking, ranked
1 (noun) Someone's rank is their official level in a job or profession.
2 The ranks are the ordinary members of the armed forces, rather than the officers.
3 The ranks of a group are its members, e.g. *the growing ranks of the unemployed.*
4 A rank is also a row of people or things.
5 (verb) To rank as something means to have that status or position on a scale, e.g. *The island ranks as one of the poorest in the region.*
6 (adjective) complete and absolute, e.g. *rank favouritism.*
7 having a strong, unpleasant smell, e.g. *Ken's clothes were rank with sweat.*

rank and file
(noun) The rank and file are the ordinary members of an organization rather than its leaders.

rankle, rankles, rankling, rankled
(verb) Something that rankles makes you angry or bitter.

ransack, ransacks, ransacking, ransacked
(verb) To ransack a room means to disturb everything, causing complete chaos, in order to search for or steal something.
[from Old Norse *rann* meaning 'house' and *saka* meaning 'to search']

ransom, ransoms
(noun) A ransom is money that is demanded to free someone who has been kidnapped.

rant, rants, ranting, ranted
(verb) To rant means to talk loudly in an excited or angry way.

rap, raps, rapping, rapped
1 (verb) If you rap something, you hit it with a series of quick blows.
2 (noun) A rap is a quick knock or blow on something, e.g. *There was a rap on the door.*
3 Rap is a style of poetry spoken to music with a strong rhythmic beat.

rap out
(phrasal verb) To rap out an order means to say it very sharply.

rapacious
(adjective; a formal word) Someone who is rapacious is very greedy for money.
rapaciously (adverb), **rapacity** (noun).

rape, rapes, raping, raped
1 (verb) If a man rapes a woman, he violently forces her to have sex with him against her will.
2 (noun) Rape is the act or crime of raping a woman, e.g. *a victim of rape.*
3 Rape is also a plant with yellow flowers that is grown as a farm crop to provide oil and fodder.
rapist (noun).
[senses 1 and 2 are from Latin *rapere* meaning 'to seize'; sense 3 is from Latin *rapum* meaning 'turnip']

rapid, rapids
1 (adjective) happening or moving very quickly, e.g. *rapid industrial expansion... He took a few rapid steps.*
2 (plural noun) An area of a river where the water moves extremely fast over rocks is referred to as rapids.
rapidly (adverb), **rapidity** (noun).

rapier, rapiers
(noun) A rapier is a long thin sword with a sharp point.

rapport (pronounced rap-**por**)
(noun; a formal word) If there is a rapport between two people, they find it easy to understand each other's feelings and attitudes.

Similar words: affinity, harmony, empathy

rapprochement (pronounced rap-**rosh**-mong)
(noun; a formal word) When there is a rapprochement between two countries, they become friendly again.
[a French word]

rapt
(adjective) If you are rapt, you are so interested in something that you are not aware of other things, e.g. *He listened in rapt silence.*
[from Latin *raptus* meaning 'carried away']

rapture
(noun) Rapture is a feeling of extreme delight.
rapturous (adjective), **rapturously** (adverb).

rare, rarer, rarest
1 (adjective) Something that is rare is not common or does not happen often, e.g. *rare wild flowers... Cases of smallpox are rare.*
2 Rare meat has been lightly cooked.
3 If the air is rare, it does not contain much oxygen, making it difficult to breathe.
rarely (adverb).

rarefied (pronounced **rare**-if-eyed)
(adjective) seeming to have little connection with ordinary life, e.g. *the rarefied world of the rich.*

raring
(adjective) If you are raring to do something, you are very eager to do it.

rarity, rarities
1 (noun) A rarity is something that is interesting or valuable because it is unusual.
2 The rarity of something is the fact that it is not common or does not happen often.

rascal, rascals
(noun) If you refer to someone as a rascal, you mean that they do bad or mischievous things.
rascally (adjective).
[from Old French *rascaille* meaning 'rabble']

rash, rashes
1 (adjective) If you are rash, you do something hasty and foolish.
2 (noun) A rash is an area of red spots that appear on your skin when you are ill or have an allergy.
3 A rash of events is a lot of them happening in a short time, e.g. *a rash of robberies.*
rashly (adverb), **rashness** (noun).

Similar words: (sense 1) foolhardy, impetuous, reckless, irresponsible

rasher, rashers
(noun) A rasher is a thin slice of bacon.

rasp, rasps, rasping, rasped
1 (verb) To rasp means to make a harsh unpleasant sound.
2 (noun) A rasp is a coarse file with rows of raised teeth, used for smoothing wood or metal.

raspberry, raspberries
(noun) A raspberry is a small soft red fruit that grows on a bush.

rat, rats
1 (noun) A rat is a long-tailed animal which looks like a large mouse.
2 If you call someone a rat, you are angry with them because they have done something disloyal.

ratafia (pronounced rat-taf-**fee**-a)
(noun) Ratafia is a flavouring essence made from almonds.

ratchet, ratchets
(noun) A ratchet is a wheel or bar with sloping teeth and a catch which allows the wheel to move only one way.

rate, rates, rating, rated
1 (noun) The rate of something is the speed or frequency with which it happens, e.g. *the rapid rate of change... the divorce rate.*
2 The rate of interest is its level, e.g. *Interest rates dropped to 6%.*
3 Rates are a local tax paid by people who own buildings. Rates will be replaced in 1989-90 by a community charge or poll tax.
4 (phrase) If you say **at this rate** something will

happen, you mean it will happen if things continue in the same way, e.g. *At this rate it'll all be over by Christmas.*
5 You say **at any rate** when you want to add to or amend what you have just said, e.g. *She must be what they want. At any rate, she got the job.*
6 (verb) The way you rate someone or something is your opinion of them, e.g. *Looks are never rated highly when people choose friends.*

ratepayer, ratepayers
(noun) A ratepayer is someone who pays rates.

rather
1 (adverb) Rather means to a certain extent, e.g. *He looked rather sad... I'm in rather a hurry.*
2 (phrase) If you **would rather** do a particular thing, you would prefer to do it.
3 If you do one thing **rather than** another, you choose to do the first thing instead of the second.
4 You use **or rather** to amend what you have just said or to make a contrast, e.g. *We walked, or rather staggered, home.*

Similar words: (sense 1) pretty, relatively, slightly (sense 2) preferably, sooner

ratify, ratifies, ratifying, ratified
(verb; a formal word) To ratify a written agreement means to approve it formally, usually by signing it.
ratification (noun).

rating, ratings
1 (noun) A rating is a score based on the quality or status of something.
2 The ratings are statistics showing how popular each television or radio programme is.
3 A rating is also a noncommissioned sailor.

ratio, ratios
(noun) A ratio is a relationship which shows how many times one thing is bigger than another, e.g. *a ratio of one teacher to eighteen pupils.*
[from Latin *ratio* meaning 'a reckoning']

Similar words: rate, proportion, relation

ration, rations, rationing, rationed
1 (noun) Your ration of something is the amount you are allowed to have.
2 (verb) When something is rationed, you are only allowed a limited amount of it, because there is a shortage.
3 (noun) Rations are the food supplied each day to a soldier or member of an expedition.
rationing (noun).

rational
(adjective) When people are rational, their judgments are based on reason rather than emotion.
rationally (adverb), **rationality** (noun).

rationale (pronounced rash-on-**nahl**)
(noun) The rationale for a course of action or for a belief is the set of reasons on which it is based.

rationalism
(noun) Rationalism is the belief that your life should be based on reason and not on emotions or on religion.
rationalist (noun and adjective).

rationalize, rationalizes, rationalizing, rationalized; also spelled **rationalise**
1 (verb) To rationalize something means to think of reasons to justify or explain it.
2 When a system or organization is rationalized, it is made more efficient.
rationalization (noun).

rat race
(noun) If you refer to a way of life as the rat race, you mean that it is fiercely competitive.

rattle, rattles, rattling, rattled
1 (verb) When something rattles, it makes short, regular knocking sounds.
2 (noun) A rattle is the noise something makes when it rattles.
3 A rattle is also a baby's toy which makes a noise when it is shaken.
4 (verb) If something rattles you, it upsets you, e.g. *His questions obviously rattled her.*

rattle off
(phrasal verb) If you rattle off a number of things, you say or produce them quickly and easily, e.g. *She rattled off a few names.*

rattlesnake, rattlesnakes
(noun) A rattlesnake is a poisonous American snake.

ratty, rattier, rattiest
(adjective; an informal word) cross and irritable, e.g. *All right, don't get ratty.*

raucous (pronounced **raw**-kuss)
(adjective) A raucous voice is loud and rough.
raucously (adverb).

ravage, ravages, ravaging, ravaged (a formal word)
1 (verb) To ravage something means to seriously harm or damage it, e.g. *a country ravaged by war.*
2 (noun) The ravages of something are its damaging effects, e.g. *the ravages of the weather.*
[from Old French *ravir* meaning 'to snatch away']

rave, raves, raving, raved
1 (verb) If someone raves, they talk in an angry, uncontrolled way, e.g. *He started raving about the brutality of war.*
2 (an informal use) If you rave about something, you talk about it very enthusiastically.
3 (adjective; an informal use) If something gets a rave review, it is praised enthusiastically.

raven, ravens
1 (noun) A raven is a large black bird with a deep, harsh call.
2 (adjective) Raven hair is black and shiny.

ravenous
(adjective) very hungry.
ravenously (adverb).

ravine, ravines
(noun) A ravine is a deep, narrow valley with steep sides.

raving, ravings
1 (adjective) If someone is raving, they are mad, e.g. *a raving lunatic.*
2 (noun) Someone's ravings are crazy things they write or say.

ravioli, (pronounced rav-ee-**oh**-lee)
(noun) Ravioli consists of small squares of pasta filled with meat and served with a sauce.

ravish, ravishes, ravishing, ravished
1 (verb) If you are ravished by something, it gives you great delight because it is very beautiful.
2 (an old-fashioned use) If a man ravishes a woman, he rapes her.
ravishing (adjective), **ravishingly** (adverb).

raw
1 (adjective) Raw food is uncooked.
2 A raw substance is in its natural state, e.g. *raw cotton.*
3 If part of your body is raw, the skin has come off or been rubbed away.
4 Someone who is raw is too young or too new in a job or situation to know how to behave.
5 Raw weather is unpleasantly cold.
6 (an informal phrase) If you have had a **raw deal**, you have been treated unfairly.

raw material, raw materials
(noun) Raw materials are the natural substances used to make something.

ray, rays
1 (noun) A ray is a beam of light or radiation.
2 A ray of hope is a small amount that makes an unpleasant situation seem slightly better.
3 A ray is also a large sea fish with eyes on the top of its body, and a long tail.

rayon
(noun) Rayon is a smooth synthetic material made from cellulose.

raze, razes, razing, razed
(verb) To raze a building, town, or forest means to completely destroy it, e.g. *Many villages were razed to the ground.*

razor, razors
(noun) A razor is an object used for shaving.

razor blade, razor blades
(noun) A razor blade is a small, sharp, flat piece of metal fitted into a razor for shaving.

re-
Re- is used to form nouns and verbs that refer to the repetition of an action or process. For example, to reread something means to read it again, and to remarry means to marry again.

reach, reaches, reaching, reached
1 (verb) When you reach a place, you arrive there.
2 When you reach for something, you stretch out your arm to it.
3 If something reaches a place or point, it extends as far as that place or point, e.g. *She wore a long skirt reaching to the ground.*
4 If something or someone reaches a stage, condition, or level, they get to it, e.g. *Unemployment has reached 3 million.*

5 To reach an agreement or decision means to succeed in achieving it.
6 (phrase) If a place is **within reach**, you can get there, e.g. *The shops are within easy reach of the house.*
7 If something is **out of reach**, you cannot get it by stretching out your arm, e.g. *Keep all medicines out of reach of children.*

react, reacts, reacting, reacted
1 (verb) When you react to something, you behave in a particular way because of it, e.g. *I wondered how he would react to this news.*
2 If one substance reacts with another, a chemical change takes place when they are put together.

reaction, reactions
1 (noun) Your reaction to something is what you feel, say, or do because of it, e.g. *My immediate reaction was one of revulsion.*
2 Your reactions are your ability to move quickly in response to something that happens, e.g. *an experiment to test their reactions.*
3 If there is a reaction against something, it becomes unpopular, e.g. *a reaction against privatization.*
4 In a chemical reaction, a chemical change takes place when two substances are put together.

Similar words: (sense 1) response
(sense 3) backlash

reactionary, reactionaries
1 (adjective) Someone who is reactionary tries to prevent political or social change.
2 (noun) Reactionaries are reactionary people.

reactor, reactors
(noun) A reactor is a device which is used to obtain nuclear energy.

read, reads, reading, read
1 (verb) When you read, you look at something written and follow it or say it aloud.
2 If you can read someone's moods or mind, you can judge what they are feeling or thinking.
3 When you read a meter or gauge, you look at it and record the figure on it.
4 If you read a subject at university, you study it.
5 (phrase) To **read between the lines** means to understand a meaning that is not expressed directly, e.g. *Reading between the lines, it is easy to see she was unhappy.*

reader, readers
1 (noun) The readers of a newspaper or magazine are the people who read it regularly.
2 At a university, a reader is a senior lecturer just below the rank of professor.

readership
(noun) The readership of a newspaper or magazine consists of the people who read it regularly.

readily
1 (adverb) willingly and eagerly, e.g. *She readily accepted the invitation.*
2 easily done or quickly obtainable, e.g. *Food was readily available.*

reading, readings
1 (noun) Reading is the activity of reading books.
2 A reading is the reading of something aloud to an audience, e.g. *a poetry reading.*
3 The reading on a meter or gauge is the figure or measurement it shows.

readjust, readjusts, readjusting, readjusted
(pronounced ree-aj-**just**)
1 (verb) If you readjust, you adapt to a new situation.
2 If you readjust something, you alter it to a different position.
readjustment (noun).

ready
1 (adjective) having reached the required stage, or prepared for action or use, e.g. *The crop was ready for harvesting... We were ready to leave.*
2 willing or eager to do something, e.g. *couples who are ready to move in order to find work.*
3 If you are ready for something, you need it, e.g. *We were ready for sleep.*
4 easily produced or obtained, e.g. *ready cash.*
readiness (noun).

ready-made
(adjective) already made and therefore able to be used immediately.

reaffirm, reaffirms, reaffirming, reaffirmed
(verb) To reaffirm something means to state it again, e.g. *He reaffirmed his commitment to European unity.*

reafforestation
(noun) Reafforestation is the planting of trees on land that used to be forested.

reagent, reagents
(noun) A reagent is a substance used in a chemical reaction.

real
1 (adjective) actually existing and not imagined or invented.
2 genuine and not imitation, e.g. *real gold.*
3 true or actual and not mistaken, e.g. *the real reason for his visit.*
4 (phrase) You use in **real terms** to refer to the actual value or cost of something. For example, if your pocket money rises by 5% but prices rise by 10%, in real terms you get less pocket money.

Similar words: (sense 2) actual, authentic, original

real estate
(noun) Real estate is property in the form of land and buildings rather than personal possessions.

realism
1 (noun) Realism is the recognition and acceptance of the true nature of a situation, e.g. *There is a new mood of realism in Britain.*
2 In paintings, novels, and films, realism is the representation of things and people as they are in real life, rather than in an idealized way.
realist (noun).

realistic
1 (adjective) recognizing and accepting the true nature of a situation.

2 representing things in a way that is true to real life, e.g. *a realistic impression of Viking life.*
realistically (adverb).

reality
1 (noun) Reality is the real nature of things, rather than the way someone imagines it, e.g. *He is out of touch with reality.*
2 If something has become reality, it actually exists or is actually happening.
3 (phrase) You use in **reality** to introduce a statement about the real nature of something, e.g. *They imagined that they made the rules but, in reality, they were mere puppets.*

Similar words: (sense 1) actuality, facts, truth

realize, realizes, realizing, realized; also spelled **realise**
1 (verb) If you realize something, you become aware of it.
2 (a formal use) If your hopes or fears are realized, what you hoped for or feared actually happens, e.g. *My worst fears were realized.*
3 To realize a sum of money means to receive it as a result of selling goods or shares.
realization (noun).

really
1 (adverb) used to add emphasis to what is being said, e.g. *It was really good.*
2 used to indicate that you are talking about the true facts about something, e.g. *I want to know what really happened.*

realm, realms (pronounced **relm**) (a formal word)
1 (noun) You can refer to any area of thought or activity as a realm, e.g. *Clearly, we are in the realm of imagination rather than fact.*
2 A realm is also a country with a king or queen, e.g. *the defence of the realm.*

ream, reams
(noun) If you write reams, you write a lot.

reap, reaps, reaping, reaped
1 (verb) To reap a crop such as corn means to cut and gather it.
2 When people reap benefits or rewards, they get them as a result of hard work or careful planning.
reaper (noun).

reappear, reappears, reappearing, reappeared
(verb) When people or things reappear, you can see them again, because they have come back, e.g. *The waiter reappeared... The mini-skirt reappeared for a time.*
reappearance (noun).

reappraisal, reappraisals
(noun; a formal word) If there is a reappraisal, people think about something and decide whether they want to change it, e.g. *a reappraisal of U.S. policy in the Middle East.*

rear, rears, rearing, reared
1 (noun) The rear of something is the part at the back.
2 (verb) To rear children or young animals means to bring them up until they are able to look after themselves.

3 When a horse rears, it raises the front part of its body, so that its front legs are in the air.

rear admiral, rear admirals
(noun) A rear admiral is a naval officer of the rank immediately above commodore.

rearguard
(phrase) To **fight a rearguard action** means to go on resisting something that can no longer be prevented.

rearm, rearms, rearming, rearmed
(verb) When a country rearms, it starts to build up a stock of weapons again.
rearmament (noun).

rearrange, rearranges, rearranging, rearranged
(verb) To rearrange something means to organize or arrange it in a different way.
rearrangement (noun).

reason, reasons, reasoning, reasoned
1 (noun) The reason for something is the fact or situation which explains why it happens or which causes it to happen.
2 If you have reason to believe or feel something, there are definite reasons why you believe it or feel it, e.g. *You had good reason to be annoyed!*
3 Reason is the ability to think and make judgments.
4 (verb) If you reason that something is true, you decide it is true after considering all the facts.
5 (phrase) If you reason with someone, you persuade them to accept something by using sensible arguments.

Similar words: (sense 1) cause, motive
(sense 3) logic, sense, judgment

reasonable
1 (adjective) Reasonable behaviour is fair and sensible.
2 If an explanation is reasonable, there are good reasons for thinking it is correct.
3 A reasonable amount is a fairly large amount.
4 A reasonable price is fair and not too high.
reasonably (adverb), **reasonableness** (noun).

reasoned
(adjective) A reasoned argument has been carefully thought out, e.g. *We must counter their propaganda with reasoned argument.*

reasoning
(noun) Reasoning is the process by which you reach a conclusion after considering all the facts.

reassemble, reassembles, reassembling, reassembled
(verb) To reassemble something means to put it back together after it has been taken apart.

reassert, reasserts, reasserting, reasserted
1 (verb) If someone reasserts their power or authority, they make it clear that they are in control again.
2 If something reasserts itself, it becomes noticeable again, e.g. *The urge to survive reasserted itself.*

reassess, reassesses, reassessing, reassessed
(verb) If you reassess something, you consider whether it still has the same value or importance.
reassessment (noun).

reassure, reassures, reassuring, reassured
(verb) If you reassure someone, you say or do things that make them less worried.
reassuring (adjective), **reassuringly** (adverb), **reassurance** (noun).

rebate, rebates
(noun) A rebate is money paid back to someone who has paid too much tax, rent, or rates.
[from Old French *rabattre* meaning 'to deduct']

rebel, rebels, rebelling, rebelled
1 (noun) Rebels are people who are fighting their own country's army in order to change the political system.
2 Someone who is a rebel rejects society's values and behaves differently from other people.
3 (verb) To rebel means to fight against authority and reject accepted values.
[from Latin *rebellis* meaning 'insurgent']

rebellion, rebellions
(noun) A rebellion is organized and often violent opposition to authority.

Similar words: insurrection, uprising, mutiny, revolt, revolution

rebellious
(adjective) unwilling to obey and likely to rebel against authority.
rebelliously (adverb).

rebound, rebounds, rebounding, rebounded
(verb) When something rebounds, it bounces or springs back after hitting a solid surface.

rebuff, rebuffs, rebuffing, rebuffed
1 (verb) If you rebuff someone, you reject what they offer, e.g. *His offer of help was rebuffed.*
2 (noun) A rebuff is a rejection of an offer.

rebuild, rebuilds, rebuilding, rebuilt
(verb) When a town or building is rebuilt, it is built again after being damaged or destroyed.

rebuke, rebukes, rebuking, rebuked (pronounced rib-**yook**)
(verb) To rebuke someone means to speak severely to them about something they have done.

rebut, rebuts, rebutting, rebutted
(verb) If you rebut a charge which is made against you, you prove that it is not true.
rebuttal (noun).

recalcitrant (pronounced rik-**kal**-sit-rent)
(adjective; a formal word) unwilling to obey orders or cooperate.
[from Latin *recalcitrare* meaning 'to kick backwards' (used of horses)]

recall, recalls, recalling, recalled
1 (verb) To recall something means to remember it.
2 If you are recalled to a place, you are ordered to return there.
3 If a company recalls products, it asks people to return them because they are faulty.

recant, recants, recanting, recanted
(verb; a formal word) When someone recants, they say publicly that they no longer have certain beliefs.

recap, recaps, recapping, recapped
(verb) To recap means to repeat and summarize the main points of an explanation or discussion.

recapitulate, recapitulates, recapitulating, recapitulated
(verb) Recapitulate means the same as recap. **recapitulation** (noun).

recapture, recaptures, recapturing, recaptured
1 (verb) When you recapture a pleasant feeling, you experience it again, e.g. *She failed to recapture her earlier mood.*
2 When soldiers recapture a place, they capture it from the people who took it from them.
3 When animals or prisoners are recaptured, they are caught after they have escaped.

recede, recedes, receding, receded
1 (verb) When something recedes, it moves away into the distance.
2 If a man's hair is receding, he is starting to go bald at the front.
[from Latin *recedere* meaning 'to go back']

receipt, receipts (pronounced ris-**seet**)
1 (noun) A receipt is a piece of paper confirming that money or goods have been received.
2 In a shop or theatre, the money received is often called the receipts, e.g. *Receipts are down this month.*
3 (a formal use) The receipt of something is the receiving of it, e.g. *We await the receipt of further information.*
[from Latin *recipere* meaning 'to receive']

receive, receives, receiving, received
1 (verb) When you receive something, someone gives it to you, or you get it after it has been sent to you.
2 To receive something also means to have it happen to you, e.g. *He received a kick on the shin.*
3 When you receive visitors or guests, you welcome them.
4 If something is received in a particular way, that is how people react to it, e.g. *Her latest novel has been very well received.*
[from Latin *recipere*]

received
(adjective; a formal word) The received opinion about something or the received way of doing something is the one that is generally accepted as correct.

receiver, receivers
1 (noun) The receiver is the part of a telephone you hold near to your ear and mouth.
2 A receiver is also a television or radio set.
3 The receiver of something is the person who receives it, e.g. *receivers of stolen goods.*
4 A receiver is also an official who is appointed to look after the affairs of a company that has been declared bankrupt.

recent
(adjective) Something recent happened a short time ago.
recently (adverb).
[from Latin *recens* meaning 'fresh']

receptacle, receptacles
(noun; a formal word) A receptacle is a container, e.g. *Put your cigarette ends in the receptacle provided.*
[from Latin *receptaculum* meaning 'store place']

reception, receptions,
1 (noun) In a hotel, office, or hospital, reception is the place near the entrance where appointments or enquiries are dealt with.
2 A reception is a formal party.
3 The reception someone or something gets is the way people react to them, e.g. *Butler received a hostile reception in Bristol.*
4 If your radio or television gets good reception, the sound or picture is clear.

receptionist, receptionists
(noun) The receptionist in a hotel, office, or surgery deals with people when they arrive, answers the telephone, and arranges reservations or appointments.

receptive
(adjective) Someone who is receptive to ideas or suggestions is willing to consider them.

recess, recesses
1 (noun) A recess is a period when no work is done by a committee or parliament, e.g. *the summer recess.*
2 A recess is a place where part of a wall has been built further back than the rest.
[from Latin *recessus* meaning 'retreat']

recession, recessions
(noun) A recession is a period when a country's economy is less successful and more people become unemployed.

Similar words: downturn, slump, decline

recharge, recharges, recharging, recharged
(verb) To recharge a battery means to charge it with electricity again after it has been used.

recherché (pronounced re-**sher**-shay)
(adjective; a formal word) very sophisticated and unusual, e.g. *a very recherché film.*

recidivist, recidivists (pronounced ris-**sid**-iv-ist)
(noun; a formal word) Someone who is a recidivist repeatedly commits crimes.

recipe, recipes (pronounced **res**-sip-ee)
1 (noun) A recipe is a list of ingredients and instructions for cooking something.
2 If something is a recipe for disaster or for success, it is likely to result in disaster or success.

recipient, recipients
(noun) The recipient of something is the person receiving it.

reciprocal
(adjective) A reciprocal agreement involves two people, groups, or countries helping each other

in a similar way, e.g. *a reciprocal agreement on deportation.*
[from Latin *reciprocus* meaning 'alternating']

reciprocate, reciprocates, reciprocating, reciprocated
(verb) If you reciprocate someone's feelings or behaviour, you feel or behave in the same way towards them.
reciprocity (noun).

recital, recitals
(noun) A recital is a performance of music or poetry, usually by one person.

recitative, recitatives (pronounced ress-it-at-**teev**)
(noun) Recitative is a type of singing in oratorios or operas, which is halfway between speaking and singing, and which reflects the natural rhythms of speech.

recite, recites, reciting, recited
(verb) If you recite a poem or something you have learnt, you say it aloud.
recitation (noun).

reckless
(adjective) showing a complete lack of care about danger or damage, e.g. *a reckless driver.*
recklessly (adverb), **recklessness** (noun).

reckon, reckons, reckoning, reckoned
1 (verb; an informal use) If you reckon that something is true, you think it is true, e.g. *I reckon he's lost.*
2 (an informal use) If someone reckons to do something, they claim or expect to do it, e.g. *They reckon to double their output each year.*
3 To reckon an amount means to calculate it.
4 If you reckon on something, you rely on it happening when making your plans, e.g. *He reckoned on getting a large reward.*
5 If you had not reckoned with something, you had not expected it and therefore were unprepared when it happened, e.g. *She had not reckoned with her father's disapproval.*
6 (phrase) If something is **to be reckoned with**, it has to be dealt with and will be difficult.

reckoning, reckonings
1 (noun) A reckoning is a calculation, e.g. *By his own reckoning, it had taken him three hours.*
2 (phrase) **The day of reckoning** is the time when someone has to account for their actions.

reclaim, reclaims, reclaiming, reclaimed
1 (verb) When you reclaim something, you collect it after leaving it somewhere or losing it.
2 To reclaim land means to make it suitable for use, for example by draining or clearing it.
reclamation (noun).

recline, reclines, reclining, reclined
(verb) To recline means to lie or lean back at an angle, e.g. *She was reclining in her chair.*

recluse, recluses
(noun) Someone who is a recluse lives alone and avoids other people.
reclusive (adjective).
[from Latin *recludere* meaning 'to shut away']

recognize, recognizes, recognizing, recognized; also spelled **recognise**
1 (verb) If you recognize someone or something, you realize that you know who or what they are, e.g. *I thought I recognized that perfume.*
2 To recognize something also means to accept and acknowledge it, e.g. *We recognize the need for controls... The new regime was recognized by China.*
recognition (noun), **recognizable** (adjective), **recognizably** (adverb).
[from Latin *recognoscere* meaning 'to know again']

Similar words: (sense 1) know, identify, place

recoil, recoils, recoiling, recoiled
(verb) To recoil from something means to draw back in shock or horror.

recollect, recollects, recollecting, recollected
(verb) If you recollect something, you remember it.
recollection (noun).

recommend, recommends, recommending, recommended
(verb) If you recommend something to someone, you praise it and suggest they try it.
recommendation (noun).

recompense
(noun) Recompense is something given as compensation for harm or trouble, e.g. *The boatman asked for recompense for the damage.*

reconcile, reconciles, reconciling, reconciled
1 (verb) To reconcile differing beliefs means to find a way of accepting both, e.g. *I asked how he could reconcile apartheid with Christianity.*
2 When people are reconciled, they become friendly again after a quarrel.
3 If you reconcile yourself to an unpleasant situation, you accept it.
reconciliation (noun).

recondite
(adjective; a formal word) unfamiliar and difficult to understand.

recondition, reconditions, reconditioning, reconditioned
(verb) To recondition a machine means to repair or replace all the worn or broken parts.

reconnaissance (pronounced rik-**kon**-iss-sanss)
(noun) Reconnaissance is the gathering of military information by sending out soldiers, planes, or satellites.

reconnoitre, reconnoitres, reconnoitring, reconnoitred (pronounced rek-on-**noy**-ter)
(verb) To reconnoitre a place means to explore it to see what is there.

reconsider, reconsiders, reconsidering, reconsidered
(verb) To reconsider something means to think about it again to decide whether to change it.
reconsideration (noun).

reconstitute, reconstitutes, reconstituting, reconstituted

1 (verb) To reconstitute an organization means to form it again in a different way.
2 To reconstitute dried food means to add water so that it can be cooked or eaten.
reconstitution (noun).

reconstruct, reconstructs, reconstructing, reconstructed
1 (verb) To reconstruct something that has been damaged means to build it again.
2 To reconstruct a past event means to obtain a complete description of it from small pieces of information.
reconstruction (noun).

Similar words: rebuild, reform, recreate

record, records, recording, recorded
1 (noun) If you keep a record of something, you keep a written account or store information in a computer, e.g. *medical records.*
2 (verb) If you record information, you write it down or put it into a computer.
3 To record sound means to put it on tape or record.
4 (noun) A record is a round, flat piece of black plastic on which music has been recorded.
5 A record is also an achievement which is the best of its type.
6 (adjective) higher, lower, better, or worse than ever before, e.g. *Unemployment was at a record high.*
7 (noun) Your record is what is known about your achievements or past activities, e.g. *He has a distinguished record... a police record.*
8 (phrase) Something that is said **off the record**, is said unofficially and is not intended to be published.
[from Latin *recordari* meaning 'to remember']

Similar words: (sense 1) annal, archive, chronicle (sense 2) log, register, enter, report

recorder, recorders
(noun) A recorder is a woodwind instrument that you play by blowing down one end while covering the holes with your fingers.

recording, recordings
(noun) A recording of something is a record, tape, or video of it.

record player, record players
(noun) A record player is a machine for playing records so that you can hear the words or music on them.

recount, recounts, recounting, recounted
1 (verb) If you recount a story, you tell it.
2 (noun) A recount is a second count of votes in an election when the result is very close.

recoup, recoups, recouping, recouped
(pronounced rik-**koop**)
(verb) If you recoup money that you have spent or lost, you get it back.

recourse
(noun; a formal word) If you have recourse to something, you use it to help you, e.g. *We need never have recourse to violence.*

recover, recovers, recovering, recovered
1 (verb) To recover from an illness or unhappy experience means to get well again or get over it.
2 If you recover a lost object or your ability to do something, you get it back.
recovery (noun).

Similar words: (sense 1) convalesce, recuperate (sense 2) recoup, regain, retrieve, reclaim, make good

recreate, recreates, recreating, recreated
(verb) To recreate something means to succeed in making it happen or exist again, e.g. *The museum recreates 18th-century village life.*

recreation, recreations
(noun) Recreation is all the things that you do for enjoyment in your spare time.
recreational (adjective).

recreation ground, recreation grounds
(noun) A recreation ground is a piece of public land where people can play sports and games.

recrimination, recriminations
(noun) Recriminations are accusations made by people about each other.
recriminate (verb), **recriminatory** (adjective).

recruit, recruits, recruiting, recruited
1 (verb) To recruit people means to get them to join a group or help with something.
2 (noun) A recruit is someone who has joined the army or some other organization.
recruitment (noun).
[from French *recrute* meaning 'new growth']

rectangle, rectangles
(noun) A rectangle is a four-sided shape with four right angles.
rectangular (adjective).
[from Latin *rectus* meaning 'straight' and *angulus* meaning 'angle']

rectify, rectifies, rectifying, rectified
(verb; a formal word) If you rectify something that is wrong, you put it right.
[from Latin *rectus + facere* meaning 'to make straight']

rectitude
(noun; a formal word) Rectitude is a quality of honesty and virtue.

rector, rectors
(noun) A rector is a Church of England priest in charge of a parish.
[from Latin *rector* meaning 'ruler' or 'guide']

rectory, rectories
(noun) A rectory is a house where a rector lives.

rectum, rectums
(noun; a medical word) Your rectum is the bottom end of the tube down which waste food passes out of your body.
rectal (adjective).
[from Latin *rectum intestinum* meaning 'straight intestine']

recumbent
(adjective; a formal word) lying down.

recuperate, recuperates, recuperating, recuperated

(verb) When you recuperate, you gradually recover after being ill or injured.
recuperation (noun), **recuperative** (adjective).
[from *re-* and Latin *capere* meaning 'to take']

recur, recurs, recurring, recurred
(verb) If something recurs, it happens or occurs again, e.g. *The symptoms may recur.*
recurrence (noun), **recurrent** (adjective).

recurring
(adjective) happening or occurring many times, e.g. *a recurring problem.*

recycle, recycles, recycling, recycled
(verb) To recycle used products means to process them so that they can be used again, e.g. *recycled paper.*

red, redder, reddest; reds
1 (noun and adjective) Red is the colour of blood or of a ripe tomato.
2 (adjective) Red hair is between orange and brown in colour.
3 (an informal phrase) If you **see red**, you get very angry.
4 If your bank account is **in the red**, you have spent more than you had in the account.
5 (noun) People with strong left wing views are sometimes called Reds.

red blood cell, red blood cells
(noun) Your red blood cells are the cells in your blood that carry oxygen, carbon dioxide, and haemoglobin to and from your tissues.

redbrick
(adjective) A redbrick university is one built in the late 19th or early 20th century.

Red Cross
(noun) The Red Cross is an international organization that helps people who are suffering because of war or a natural disaster.

redcurrant, redcurrants
(noun) Redcurrants are very small, bright red fruit that grow in bunches on a bush.

redden, reddens, reddening, reddened
(verb) When something reddens, it becomes red or more red.

redeem, redeems, redeeming, redeemed.
1 (verb) If a feature redeems an unpleasant thing or situation, it makes it seem less bad, e.g. *a terrible book with no redeeming qualities.*
2 If you redeem yourself, you do something that gives people a good opinion of you again.
3 If you redeem something, you get it back by paying for it.
4 In Christianity, to redeem someone means to free them from sin by giving them faith in Jesus Christ.
[from Latin *redimere* meaning 'to buy back']

redemption
(noun) Redemption is the state of being redeemed.

redeploy, redeploys, redeploying, redeployed
(verb) To redeploy forces or workers means to give them new positions or tasks.
redeployment (noun).

redevelop, redevelops, redeveloping, redeveloped
(verb) When part of a town is redeveloped, the buildings are knocked down and new ones are built.
redevelopment (noun).

red-handed
(phrase) To catch someone red-handed means to catch them doing something wrong.

red herring, red herrings
(noun) Something that is a red herring is irrelevant and distracts people's attention from what is important.

red-hot
(adjective) Red-hot metal has been heated to such a high temperature that it has turned red.

Red Indian, Red Indians
(noun; an old-fashioned expression) A Red Indian is someone descended from the people who lived in North America before Europeans arrived.

red-light district, red-light districts
(noun) A red-light district is an area in a city where prostitutes work.

redolent (a formal word)
1 (adjective) smelling strongly of something, e.g. *Her breath was redolent of gin.*
2 having features that remind you of something else, e.g. *written in language redolent of the Lakeland poets.*
[from Latin *redolens* meaning 'smelling of']

redouble, redoubles, redoubling, redoubled
(verb) If you redouble your efforts, you try much harder to achieve something.

redoubtable
(adjective; a formal word) A redoubtable person has a strong character and commands respect.

redress, redresses, redressing, redressed (a formal word)
1 (verb) To redress a wrong means to put it right.
2 (noun) If you get redress for harm done to you, you are compensated for it.
[from Old French *redrecier* meaning 'to set up again']

red tape
(noun) Red tape is official rules and procedures that seem unnecessary and cause delay. In the 18th century, red tape was used to bind official government documents.

reduce, reduces, reducing, reduced
1 (verb) To reduce something means to make it smaller in size or amount.
2 You can use reduce to say that someone or something is changed to a weaker or inferior state, e.g. *He was reduced to tears... The building was reduced to rubble.*
reducible (adjective).

Similar words: (sense 1) compress, condense, curtail, cut, dock, narrow, pare, trim

reduction, reductions
(noun) When there is a reduction in something, it is made smaller.

redundancy, redundancies
1 (noun) Redundancy is the state of being redundant.
2 The number of redundancies is the number of people made redundant.

redundant
1 (adjective) When people are made redundant, they lose their jobs because there is no more work for them or no money to pay them.
2 When something becomes redundant, it is no longer needed.
[from Latin *redundans* meaning 'overflowing']

redwood, redwoods
(noun) A redwood is an extremely tall tree that grows in California, often up to 100 metres in height; also the wood from this tree.

reed, reeds
1 (noun) Reeds are hollow stemmed plants that grow in shallow water or marshy ground.
2 A reed is a thin piece of cane or metal inside some wind instruments. The reed vibrates when air is blown over it.

reef, reefs
(noun) A reef is a long line of rocks or coral close to the surface of the sea.

reefer, reefers
1 (noun) A reefer or reefer jacket is a short, thick coat.
2 (an informal use) A reefer is also a cigarette containing marijuana.

reef knot, reef knots
(noun) A reef knot is a double knot that does not slip.

reek, reeks, reeking, reeked
1 (verb) To reek of something means to smell strongly and unpleasantly of it.
2 (noun) If there is a reek of something, there is a strong unpleasant smell of it.

reel, reels, reeling, reeled
1 (noun) A reel is a cylindrical object around which you wrap something; often part of a device which you turn as a control.
2 (verb) When someone reels, they move unsteadily as if they are going to fall.
3 If your mind is reeling, you are confused because you have too much to think about.
4 (noun) A reel is also a fast Scottish dance.

reel off
(phrasal verb) If you reel off information, you repeat it from memory quickly and easily.

re-elect, re-elects, re-electing, re-elected
(verb) When someone is re-elected, they win an election again and are able to stay in power.

refectory, refectories
(noun) In a university or monastery, the refectory is the dining hall.

refer, refers, referring, referred
1 (verb) If you refer to something, you mention it.
2 If you refer to a book, document, or record, you look at it to find something out.
3 (a formal use) If you refer someone to a source

of information, you tell them to look there, e.g. *I refer you to a paper by Sutherland.*
4 When a problem or issue is referred to someone, they are formally asked to deal with it, e.g. *Her case was referred a higher Court.*
[from Latin *referre* meaning 'to carry back']

referee, referees
1 (noun) The referee is the official who controls a football game or a boxing or wrestling match.
2 A referee is also someone who gives a reference to a person who is applying for a job.

reference, references
1 (noun) A reference to something or someone is a mention of them.
2 Reference is the act of referring to something or someone for information or advice, e.g. *a reference book.*
3 (noun) A reference is also a number or name that tells you where to obtain information or identifies a document.
4 If someone gives you a reference when you apply for a job, they write a letter about your character and abilities.

referendum, referendums or **referenda**
(noun) A referendum is a vote in which all the people in a country are officially asked whether they agree with a policy or proposal.

refine, refines, refining, refined
(verb) To refine a raw material such as oil or sugar means to process it to remove impurities.

refined
(adjective) very polite and well-mannered.

Similar words: civilized, cultured, genteel, polished

refinement, refinements
1 (noun) Refinements are minor improvements.
2 Refinement is politeness, good manners, and a dislike of anything vulgar.

refinery, refineries
(noun) A refinery is a factory where substances such as oil or sugar are refined.

reflationary
(adjective; a technical word) Reflationary economic activities cause an increase in the amount of money in circulation in a country.

reflect, reflects, reflecting, reflected
1 (verb) If something reflects an attitude or situation, it shows what it is like, e.g. *The choice of school reflected Dad's hopes for us.*
2 If something reflects light or heat, the light or heat bounces off it.
3 When something is reflected in a mirror or water, you can see its image in it.
4 When you reflect, you think about something.
reflective (adjective), **reflectively** (adverb).
[from Latin *reflectere* meaning 'to bend back']

reflection, reflections
1 (noun) If something is a reflection of something else, it shows what it is like, e.g. *Their behaviour was a reflection of their personalities.*
2 A reflection is an image in a mirror or water.
3 Reflection is the process by which light and heat are bounced off a surface.

4 Reflection is also thought, e.g. *On reflection, I suppose you are right.*

reflector, reflectors
(noun) A reflector is a piece of glass or plastic which glows when light shines on it.

reflex, reflexes
1 (noun) A reflex or reflex action is a sudden uncontrollable movement that you make as a result of pressure or a blow.
2 If you have good reflexes, you respond very quickly when something unexpected happens.
3 (adjective) A reflex angle is between 180° and 360°.

reflexive, reflexives
(adjective and noun) In grammar, a reflexive verb or pronoun is one that refers back to the subject of the sentence.

reform, reforms, reforming, reformed
1 (noun) Reforms are major changes to laws, systems, or institutions, e.g. *the reform of the divorce laws.*
2 (verb) When laws, systems, or institutions are reformed, major changes are made to them.
3 When people reform, they stop committing crimes or doing other unacceptable things.
reformer (noun).

Similar words: (sense 3) go straight, turn over a new leaf, mend your ways

Reformation
(noun) The Reformation was a religious and political movement in Europe in the 16th century that began as an attempt to reform the Roman Catholic Church, but ended in the establishment of the Protestant Churches.

refraction
(noun) Refraction is the bending of a ray of light, for example when it enters water or glass.
[from Latin *refractus* meaning 'broken up']

refractory
(adjective; a formal word) stubborn and difficult to deal with or control, e.g. *a refractory child.*

refrain, refrains, refraining, refrained
1 (verb; a formal use) If you refrain from doing something, you do not do it, e.g. *Kindly refrain from smoking.*
2 (noun) The refrain of a song is a short, simple part, repeated many times.
[from Latin *refrenare* meaning 'to restrain (a horse) with a bridle']

refresh, refreshes, refreshing, refreshed
1 (verb) If something refreshes you when you are hot or tired, it makes you feel cooler or more energetic, e.g. *a refreshing swim.*
2 (phrase) To **refresh someone's memory** means to remind them of something they had forgotten.

Similar words: (sense 1) invigorate, stimulate, revitalize

refresher course, refresher courses
(noun) A refresher course is a training course intended to bring people up to date with developments related to their job.

refreshing
(adjective) You say that something is refreshing when it is pleasantly different from what you are used to, e.g. *I found a refreshing absence of litter.*
refreshingly (adverb).

refreshment, refreshments
1 (noun) Refreshments are drinks and small amounts of food provided at an event.
2 (a literary use) Refreshment is food and drink, e.g. *We stopped for refreshment.*

refrigerate, refrigerates, refrigerating, refrigerated
(verb) To refrigerate food means to preserve it by keeping it very cold.
refrigeration (noun).
[from Latin *frigerare* meaning 'to make cool']

refrigerator, refrigerators
(noun) A refrigerator is an electrically cooled container in which you store food to keep it fresh.

refuel, refuels, refuelling, refuelled
(verb) When an aircraft or vehicle is refuelled, it is filled with more fuel.

refuge, refuges
1 (noun) A refuge is a place where you go for safety.
2 If you take refuge, you go somewhere for safety or behave in a way that will protect you, e.g. *We took refuge in a cave... She took refuge in silence.*
[from Latin *refugere* meaning 'to flee']

Similar words: (sense 1) asylum, haven, sanctuary, shelter

refugee, refugees
(noun) Refugees are people who have been forced to leave their country and live elsewhere.

refund, refunds, refunding, refunded
1 (noun) A refund is money returned to you because you have paid too much for something or because you have returned goods.
2 (verb) To refund someone's money means to return it to them after they have paid for something with it.

Similar words: (sense 2) reimburse, repay, pay back

refurbish, refurbishes, refurbishing, refurbished
(verb; a formal word) To refurbish a building means to decorate it and repair damage.
refurbishment (noun).

refusal, refusals
(noun) A refusal is when someone says firmly that they will not do, allow, or accept something.

refuse, refuses, refusing, refused
(pronounced rif-**yooz**)
1 (verb) If you refuse to do something, you say or decide firmly that you will not do it.
2 If someone refuses something, they do not allow it or do not accept it, e.g. *The council refused him a loan...I offered him wine but he refused it.*

refuse (pronounced **ref**-yoos)
(noun) Refuse is rubbish or waste.

refute, refutes, refuting, refuted
(verb; a formal word) To refute a theory or
argument means to prove that it is wrong.
refutation (noun).

regain, regains, regaining, regained
(verb) To regain something means to get it back.

regal
(adjective) very grand and suitable for a king or
queen, e.g. *a regal staircase*.
regally (adverb).
[from Latin *regalis*, from *rex* meaning 'king']

regale, regales, regaling, regaled
(verb) If someone regales you with stories or
jokes, they tell you a lot of them.
[from French *régaler* meaning 'to entertain']

regalia (pronounced rig-**gay**-lee-a)
(noun; a formal word) Regalia is all the
traditional clothes and objects worn or carried
by an official or monarch on ceremonial
occasions, e.g. *a Judge of the Supreme Court in
full regalia*.

regard, regards, regarding, regarded
1 (verb) To regard someone or something in a
particular way means to think of them in that
way or have that opinion of them, e.g. *I regard it
as one of my masterpieces... His colleagues
regarded him with envy.*
2 (noun) If you have a high regard for someone,
you have a very good opinion of them.
3 (verb; a literary use) To regard someone in a
particular way also means to look at them in that
way, e.g. *The cat regarded her malevolently.*
4 (phrases) **Regarding, as regards, with regard to,**
and **in regard to** are all used to indicate what you
are talking or writing about, e.g. *There was
always some question regarding education... As
regards the car, we have decided not to sell it.*
5 Regards is used in various expressions to
express friendly feelings, e.g. *Give my regards to
Andrew... With best regards, George.*
[from French *regarder* meaning 'to look']

regardless
(preposition and adverb) done or happening in
spite of something else, e.g. *We will continue
regardless of what the law says.*

regatta, regattas
(noun) A regatta is a race meeting for sailing or
rowing boats.

regency, regencies
(noun) A regency is a period when a country is
ruled by a regent.

**regenerate, regenerates, regenerating,
regenerated**
(verb; a formal word) To regenerate a place or
system means to develop and improve it after it
has been declining, e.g. *The main task is to
regenerate the inner cities.*
regeneration (noun).

regent, regents
(noun) A regent is someone who rules in place of
a king or queen who is ill or too young to rule.
[from Latin *regens* meaning 'ruling']

reggae
(noun) Reggae is a type of music, originally from
the West Indies, with a strong and distinctive
rhythm.

regime, regimes (pronounced ray-**jeem**)
(noun) A regime is a system of government, and
the people who are ruling a country, e.g. *a
socialist regime*.
[from Latin *regimen* meaning 'guidance']

regiment, regiments
(noun) A regiment is a large group of soldiers
commanded by a colonel.
regimental (adjective).
[from Latin *regimentum* meaning 'government']

regimented
(adjective) very strictly controlled, e.g. *the
tightly regimented life of the prison*.
regimentation (noun).

region, regions
1 (noun) A region is a large area of land.
2 You can refer to any area or part as a region,
e.g. *He has pains in the shoulder region*.
3 (phrase) **In the region of** means approximately,
e.g. *Temperatures in the region of 500°C*.
regional (adjective), **regionally** (adverb).

Similar words: (sense 1) district, province, territory

register, registers, registering, registered
1 (noun) A register is an official list or record of
things, e.g. *the electoral register*.
2 (verb) When something is registered, it is
recorded on an official list, e.g. *The car was
registered in my name*.
3 If an instrument registers a measurement, it
shows it.
4 If your face registers a feeling, it expresses it.
5 (noun; a technical use) A register is also a style
of speaking or writing used in particular
circumstances or social situations.
5 (noun; a technical use) A register is also a style
of speaking or writing used in particular
circumstances or social situations.
registration (noun).

registered
(adjective) If you send a letter by registered
post, you pay extra to insure it in case it is not
delivered.

registrar, registrars
1 (noun) A registrar is a person who keeps
official records of births, marriages, and deaths.
2 At a college or university, the registrar is a
senior administrative official.
3 A registrar is also a senior hospital doctor.

registration number, registration numbers
(noun) The registration number of a motor
vehicle is the sequence of letters and numbers on
the front and back that identify it.

registry, registries
(noun) A registry is a place where official records are kept.

registry office, registry offices
(noun) A registry office is a place where births, marriages, and deaths are recorded, and where people can marry without a religious ceremony.

regress, regress, regresses, regressing
(verb; a formal word) To regress means to return to a worse condition.
regression (noun), **regressive** (adjective).
[from Latin *regressus* meaning 'a retreat']

regret, regrets, regretting, regretted
1 (verb) If you regret something, you are sorry that it happened.
2 (noun) If you have regrets, you are sad or sorry about something.
3 (verb) You can say that you regret something as a way of apologizing, e.g. *We regret any inconvenience to passengers.*
regretful (adjective), **regretfully** (adverb).

Similar words: (sense 1) rue, repent

---

regrettable
(adjective) unfortunate and undesirable, e.g. *a regrettable error.*
regrettably (adverb).

regular, regulars
1 (adjective) even and equally spaced, e.g. *He could hear her deep, regular breathing.*
2 Regular events or activities happen often and according to a pattern, for example each day or each week, e.g. *regular Sunday concerts.*
3 If you are a regular customer or visitor somewhere, you go there often.
4 (noun) People who go to a place often are known as its regulars.
5 (adjective) usual or normal, e.g. *It's way past his regular bedtime... Who's your regular doctor?*
6 having a well balanced appearance, e.g. *his regular features.*
regularly (adverb), **regularity** (noun), **regularize** (verb).

Similar words: (sense 1) even, steady, uniform

---

regulate, regulates, regulating, regulated
(verb) To regulate something means to control the way it operates, e.g. *a well regulated system... How do you regulate the boiler?*
regulator (noun).
[from Latin *regulare* meaning 'to control']

regulation, regulations
1 (noun) Regulations are official rules.
2 Regulation is the control of something, e.g. *regulation of the money supply.*

regurgitate, regurgitates, regurgitating, regurgitated (pronounced rig-**gur**-jit-tate)
(verb) To regurgitate food means to bring it back from your stomach before it is digested.
regurgitation (noun).
[from *re-* and Latin *gurgitare* meaning 'to flood']

rehabilitate, rehabilitates, rehabilitating, rehabilitated
(verb) To rehabilitate someone who has been ill or in prison means to help them lead a normal life.
rehabilitation (noun).
[from *re-* and Latin *habilitas* meaning 'skill']

rehash, rehashes
(noun) A rehash is a piece of writing or other material which is a rearrangement of earlier work.

rehearsal, rehearsals
(noun) A rehearsal is a practice of a performance in preparation for the actual event.

rehearse, rehearses, rehearsing, rehearsed
(verb) To rehearse a performance means to practise it in preparation for the actual event.

rehouse, rehouses, rehousing, rehoused
(verb) To rehouse people means to provide them with new homes.

reign, reigns, reigning, reigned (pronounced rain)
1 (verb) When a king or queen reigns, he or she rules a country.
2 (noun) The reign of a king or queen is the period during which he or she reigns.
3 (verb) You can say that something reigns when it is a noticeable feature of a situation or period of time, e.g. *Peace reigned in Europe.*
[from Latin *regnum* meaning 'kingdom']

reimburse, reimburses, reimbursing, reimbursed
(verb) To reimburse someone means to pay them back money they have spent.
reimbursement (noun).
[from *re-* and Latin *imbursare* meaning 'to put into a moneybag']

rein, reins
1 (noun) Reins are the thin leather straps which you hold when you are riding a horse or controlling it.
2 (phrase) To **keep a tight rein on** someone or something means to control them firmly.

reincarnation
(verb) People who believe in reincarnation believe that when you die, you are born again as another creature.

reindeer
(noun) Reindeer are deer with large antlers, that live in northern areas of Europe, Asia, and America.

reinforce, reinforces, reinforcing, reinforced
1 (verb) To reinforce something means to strengthen it, e.g. *reinforced helmets.*
2 If something reinforces an idea or claim, it provides evidence to support it.

reinforced concrete
(noun) Reinforced concrete has pieces of metal inside to make it stronger.

reinforcement, reinforcements
1 (noun) Reinforcements are additional soldiers sent to join an army in battle.
2 Reinforcement is the reinforcing of something.

reinstate, reinstates, reinstating, reinstated
1 (verb) To reinstate someone means to give them back a position they have lost.

2 To reinstate something means to bring it back, e.g. *reinstating capital punishment.*
reinstatement (noun).

reiterate, reiterates, reiterating, reiterated
(pronounced ree-**it**-er-ate)
(verb; a formal word) If you reiterate something, you say it again.
reiteration (noun).
[from *re-* and Latin *iterare* meaning 'to do again']

reject, rejects, rejecting, rejected
1 (verb) If you reject a proposal or request, you do not accept it or agree to it.
2 If you reject a belief, political system, or way of life, you decide that it is not for you.
3 (noun) A reject is a product that cannot be used, because there is something wrong with it.
rejection (noun).
[from Latin *reicere* meaning 'to throw back']

Similar words: (sense 1) repudiate, rebuff
(sense 2) discard, shun, repudiate, spurn

rejoice, rejoices, rejoicing, rejoiced
(verb; a literary word) To rejoice means to be very pleased about something, e.g. *We rejoiced in his success.*
rejoicing (noun).

rejoin, rejoins, rejoining, rejoined
(verb) If you rejoin someone, you go back to them soon after leaving them, e.g. *He rejoined his friends in the pub.*

rejoinder, rejoinders
(noun; a formal word) A rejoinder is a reply, e.g. *a swift rejoinder from the Prime Minister.*

rejuvenate, rejuvenates, rejuvenating, rejuvenated
(verb) To rejuvenate someone means to make them feel young again.
rejuvenation (noun).
[from *re-* and Latin *juvenis* meaning 'young']

relapse, relapses, relapsing, relapsed
1 (verb) To relapse into an undesirable way of behaving means to start behaving that way again, e.g. *He relapsed into silence.*
2 (noun) If a sick person has a relapse, their health suddenly gets worse after improving.
[from Latin *relabi* meaning 'to slip back']

relate, relates, relating, related
1 (verb) If something relates to something else, it is connected or concerned with it, e.g. *the way the words relate to each other.*
2 If you can relate to someone, you can understand their thoughts and feelings.
3 To relate a story means to tell it.

related
1 (adjective) If two things are related, they are connected in some way.
2 People who are related belong to the same family.

relation, relations
1 (noun) If there is a relation between two things, they are similar or connected in some

way, e.g. *The official account bears no relation to what actually happened.*
2 Your relations are the members of your family.
3 Relations between people are their feelings and behaviour towards each other, e.g. *an improvement in East-West relations.*

Similar words: (sense 1) correspondence, relationship

relationship, relationships
1 (noun) The relationship between two people or groups is the way they feel and behave towards each other.
2 A relationship is a close friendship, especially one involving romantic or sexual feelings.
3 The relationship between two things is the way in which they are connected, e.g. *the relationship between language and thought.*

relative, relatives
1 (adjective) compared to other things or people of the same kind, e.g. *I prefer the relative peace of my home village... He is a relative newcomer.*
2 You use relative when comparing the size or quality of two things, e.g. *the relative naval strengths of Britain and Japan.*
3 (noun) Your relatives are the members of your family.

relatively
(adverb) fairly or quite, e.g. *relatively easy.*

relativity
(noun) The theory of relativity is Einstein's theory about space, time, and motion.

relax, relaxes, relaxing, relaxed
1 (verb) If you relax, you become calm and your muscles lose their tension.
2 If you relax your hold, you hold something less tightly.
3 To relax something also means to make it less strict or controlled, e.g. *The rules were relaxed.*
relaxation (noun), **relaxed** (adjective),
relaxing (adjective).
[from *re-* and Latin *laxare* meaning 'to loosen']

Similar words: (sense 1) unwind, rest, loosen up
(sense 2) slacken, loose, ease

relay, relays, relaying, relayed
1 (noun) A relay race or relay is a race between teams, with each team member running one part of the race.
2 (verb) To relay a television or radio signal means to send it on.
3 If you relay information, you tell it to someone else.

release, releases, releasing, released
1 (verb) To release someone or something means to set them free or remove restraints from them.
2 (noun) When the release of someone or something takes place, they are set free.
3 (verb) To release something also means to issue it or make it available, e.g. *The Ministry released a statement last night.*
4 (noun) A press release or publicity release is an official written statement given to reporters.
5 A new release is a new record or video that has just become a available.

relegate, relegates, relegating, relegated
(verb) To relegate something or someone means
to give them a less important position or status.
relegation (noun).

Similar words: demote, downgrade

relent, relents, relenting relented
(verb) If someone relents, they agree to
something they had previously not allowed.

relentless
(adjective) never stopping and never reducing in
severity, e.g. *the relentless beating of the sun.*
relentlessly (adverb), **relentlessness** (noun).

Similar words: unrelenting, unyielding,
uncompromising

relevant
(adjective) If something is relevant, it is
connected with and is appropriate to what is
being discussed, e.g. *Please bring all relevant
documents.*
relevance (noun).

Similar words: germane, applicable, apposite,
pertinent

reliable
1 (adjective) Reliable people and things can be
trusted to do what you want.
2 If information is reliable, you can assume that
it is correct.
reliably (adverb), **reliability** (noun).

reliant
(adjective) If you are reliant on someone or
something, you need them and depend on them,
e.g. *They are reliant on government funds.*
reliance (noun).

relic, relics
1 (noun) Relics are objects or customs that have
survived from an earlier time.
2 A relic is also an object regarded as holy
because it is thought to be connected with a
saint.
[from Latin *reliquiae* meaning 'remains']

relief
1 (noun) If you feel relief, you are glad and
thankful because a bad situation is over or has
been avoided.
2 Relief is also money, food, or clothing provided
for poor or hungry people.
3 (phrase) A design that is done **in relief** is raised
from a surface.

relief map, relief maps
(noun) A relief map shows the shape of
mountains and hills by shading.

relieve, relieves, relieving, relieved
1 (verb) If something relieves an unpleasant
feeling, it makes it less unpleasant, e.g. *They
gave me an injection to relieve the pain.*
2 (a formal use) If you relieve someone, you do
their job or duty for a period.
3 If someone is relieved of their duties, they are
dismissed from their job.
4 If you relieve yourself, you urinate.

relieved
(adjective) glad and thankful.

religion, religions
1 (noun) Religion is the belief in a god or gods
and all the activities connected with such beliefs.
2 A religion is a system of religious belief.

Similar words: (sense 2) cult, creed, sect

religious
1 (adjective) connected with religion, e.g.
religious practices.
2 Someone who is religious has a strong belief in
a god or gods.

Similar words: (sense 2) devout, pious

religiously
(adverb) If you do something religiously, you do
it regularly as a duty, e.g. *Every morning she
religiously scrubbed the doorstep.*

**relinquish, relinquishes, relinquishing,
relinquished** (pronounced ril-**ling**-kwish)
(verb; a formal word) If you relinquish
something, you give it up.

relish, relishes, relishing, relished
1 (verb) If you relish something, you enjoy it,
e.g. *He relished arguments.*
2 (noun) Relish is enjoyment, e.g. *He watched
with obvious relish.*
3 Relish is also a savoury sauce or pickle.

relive, relives, reliving, relived
(verb) If you relive a past experience, you
remember it and imagine it happening again.

relocate, relocates, relocating, relocated
(verb) If people or businesses are relocated, they
are moved to a different place.
relocation (noun).

reluctant
(adjective) If you are reluctant to do something,
you are unwilling to do it.
reluctance (noun).
[from Latin *reluctari* meaning 'to resist']

reluctantly
(adverb) If you do something reluctantly, you do
it although you do not want to.

rely, relies, relying, relied
1 (verb) If you rely on someone or something,
you need them and depend on them, e.g. *She is
forced to rely on social security money.*
2 If you can rely on someone to do something,
you can trust them to do it, e.g. *She can always
be relied on to liven things up.*
[from Old French *relier* meaning 'to fasten
together']

remain, remains, remaining, remained
1 (verb) If you remain in a particular place or
state, you stay there or stay the same and do not
change, e.g. *Suzie remained adamant.*
2 Something that remains still exists or is left
over, e.g. *This custom remains today.*
3 (plural noun) The remains of something are the
parts that are left after most of it has been
destroyed, e.g. *the scarred remains of the city.*

4 You can refer to a dead body as remains, e.g. *Human remains were found in a shallow grave.*
remaining (adjective).
[from Latin *remanere* meaning 'to stay behind']

Similar words: (sense 3) debris, remnants, traces, vestiges

remainder
(noun) The remainder of something is the part that is left, e.g. *Pay the remainder next month.*

remand, remands, remanding, remanded
1 (verb) If a judge remands someone who is accused of a crime, the trial is postponed and the person is ordered to come back at a later date.
2 (phrase) If someone is **on remand**, they are in prison waiting for their trial to begin.

remark, remarks, remarking, remarked
1 (verb) If you remark on something, you mention it or comment on it, e.g. *He remarked on the absence of women at the meeting.*
2 (noun) A remark is something you say, often in a casual way.

Similar words: (sense 1) comment, observe (sense 2) observation, comment

remarkable
(adjective) impressive and unexpected, e.g. *You've made remarkable progress.*
remarkably (adverb).

Similar words: noteworthy, singular, notable, uncommon, significant, outstanding

remarry, remarries, remarrying, remarried
(verb) If someone remarries, they get married again.

remedial
1 (adjective) Remedial activities are to help someone improve their health after they have been ill.
2 Remedial exercises are designed to improve someone's ability in something, e.g. *I've put her in the remedial reading group.*

remedy, remedies, remedying, remedied
1 (noun) A remedy is a way of dealing with a problem, e.g. *a good remedy for a sore throat.*
2 (verb) If you remedy something that is wrong, you correct it, e.g. *Can we remedy the fault?*

remember, remembers, remembering, remembered
1 (verb) If you can remember someone or something from the past, you can bring them into your mind or think about them.
2 If you remember to do something, you do it when you intended to, e.g. *Remember to send off the application forms.*
3 If you ask someone to remember you to a person, you are asking them to send your greetings to that person, e.g. *Remember me to your parents.*
[from Latin *rememorari*]

Similar words: (sense 1) recollect, recall, reminisce, commemorate

remembrance
(noun) If you do something in remembrance of a dead person, you are showing that they are remembered with respect and affection.

remind, reminds, reminding, reminded
1 (verb) If someone reminds you of a fact, they say something to make you think about it, e.g. *Remind me to phone Pete later, will you?*
2 If someone reminds you of another person, they look similar and make you think of them.

reminder, reminders
1 (noun) If one thing is a reminder of another, the first thing makes you think of the second, e.g. *a reminder of happier days.*
2 A reminder is a note sent to tell someone they have forgotten to do something.

reminisce, reminisces, reminiscing, reminisced
(pronounced rem-in-**niss**)
(verb) If you reminisce about the past, you think, write, or talk about it with pleasure.
reminiscence (noun).

reminiscent
(adjective) Something that is reminiscent of something else reminds you of it.

remiss
(adjective; a formal word) careless about doing things which ought to be done, e.g. *That was very remiss of him.*

remission
(noun) When prisoners get remission for good behaviour, their sentences are reduced.

remit, remits, remitting, remitted (a formal word)
1 (verb) To remit money to someone means to send it to them in payment for something.
2 (noun) The remit of a person or committee is the subject or task they are responsible for, e.g. *Lord Scarman's remit for the enquiry is confined to Brixton.*

remittance, remittances
(noun; a formal word) A remittance is payment for something sent through the post.

remnant, remnants
(noun) A remnant is a small part of something left after the rest has been used or destroyed.
[from Old French *remenant* meaning 'remaining']

remonstrate, remonstrates, remonstrating, remonstrated
(verb; a formal word) If you remonstrate with someone, you protest to them about something.

remorse
(noun; a formal word) Remorse is a strong feeling of guilt.
remorseful (adjective), **remorsefully** (adverb).
[from Latin *remorsus* meaning 'a gnawing']

Similar words: repentance, penitence, contrition, self-reproach, regret

remorseless
1 (adjective) unkind and showing no pity or regret.
2 continuing in an unpleasant and persistent way.
remorselessly (adverb).

remote, remoter, remotest
1 (adjective) Remote areas are far away from places where most people live.
2 far away in time, e.g. *the remote past.*
3 If you say a person is remote, you mean they do not want to be friendly, e.g. *He seems a silent, remote sort of chap.*
4 If there is only a remote possibility of something happening, it is unlikely to happen.
remoteness (noun).
[from Latin *remotus* meaning 'distant']

remote control
(noun) Remote control is a system of controlling a machine or vehicle from a distance using radio or electronic signals.

remotely
(adverb) used to emphasize a negative statement, e.g. *I've never seen anything remotely like it.*

remould, remoulds
(noun) A remould is a used tyre that has been given a new surface.

removal
1 (noun) The removal of something is the act of taking it away.
2 A removal company transports furniture from one building to another, e.g. *The removal men will pack boxes for you.*

remove, removes, removing, removed
1 (verb) If you remove something from a place, you take it off or away.
2 If you are removed from a position of authority, you are not allowed to continue your job.
3 If you remove an undesirable feeling or attitude, you get rid of it, e.g. *Publication would remove suspicion.*
4 (noun) A remove is a stage or step away from close association with something, e.g. *We remained at one remove from the reality of war.*
removable (adjective).

Similar words: (sense 1) withdraw, extract, obviate, eliminate, purge, weed out

removed
(adjective) If an idea or situation is far removed from something, it is very different from it, e.g. *Your dreams are far removed from reality.*

remuneration, remunerations (pronounced rim-yoo-ner-**ray**-shn)
(noun; a formal word) Remuneration is pay for work that has been done.
remunerate (verb), **remunerative** (adjective).
[from Latin *remunerari* meaning 'to reward']

Renaissance (pronounced ren-**nay**-sonss)
(noun) The Renaissance was a period from the 14th to 16th centuries in Europe when there was a great revival in art, literature, and learning.
[a French word, meaning literally 'rebirth']

renal
(adjective; a technical word) concerning the kidneys, e.g. *renal failure.*

rename, renames, renaming, renamed
(verb) If you rename something, you give it a new name.

render, renders, rendering, rendered
1 (verb) You can use render to say that something is changed into a different state, e.g. *The bomb was quickly rendered harmless.*
2 (a formal use) If you render someone assistance, you help them.
3 To render an outside wall means to cover it with a protective layer of cement or plaster.

rendezvous (pronounced **ron**-day-voo)
1 (noun) A rendezvous is a meeting, e.g. *a lovers' midnight rendezvous.*
2 A rendezvous is also a place where you have arranged to meet someone, e.g. *at a secret rendezvous near the river.*
[a French word, meaning literally 'present yourselves!']

rendition, renditions
(noun; a formal word) A rendition of a play, poem, or piece of music is a performance of it.

renegade, renegades
(noun) A renegade is someone who abandons their original beliefs to accept opposing beliefs.
[from Latin *renegare* meaning 'to renounce']

renege, reneges, reneging, reneged (pronounced rin-**nayg**)
(verb; a formal word) If someone reneges on an agreement, they fail to keep it.

renew, renews, renewing, renewed
1 (verb) To renew an activity or relationship means to begin it again.
2 To renew a licence or contract means to extend the period of time for which it is valid.
renewed (adjective), **renewable** (adjective), **renewal** (noun).

rennet
(noun) Rennet is a substance obtained from a calf's stomach which is used to thicken milk for cheese-making.

renounce, renounces, renouncing, renounced
(verb; a formal word) If you renounce something, you reject it or give it up.
renunciation (noun).

renovate, renovates, renovating, renovated
(verb) If you renovate an old building or machine, you repair it and restore it to good condition.
renovation (noun).
[from Latin *renovare* meaning 'to renew']

renowned
(adjective) well known for something good, e.g. *The people are renowned for their hospitality.*
renown (noun).

rent, rents, renting, rented
1 (verb) If you rent something, you pay the owner a regular sum of money in return for being able to use it.
2 (noun) Rent is the amount of money you pay regularly to rent accommodation or land.
rented (adjective).

rental

1 (adjective) concerned with the renting out of goods and services, e.g. *a car rental service*.
2 (noun) Rental is the amount of money you pay when you rent something.

reorganize, reorganizes, reorganizing, reorganized;
also spelled **reorganise**
(verb) To reorganize something means to organize it in a new way in order to make it more efficient or acceptable.

rep, reps (an informal word)
1 (noun) A rep is a travelling salesperson. Rep is an abbreviation for **representative**.
2 (phrase) When actors work **in rep**, they are working with a repertory company.

repair, repairs, repairing, repaired
1 (noun) A repair is something you do to mend something that is damaged or broken.
2 (verb) If you repair something, you mend it.
3 If you repair something wrong or harmful that has been done, you do something to correct it.
[from Latin *reparare*]

reparation, reparations
(noun; a formal word) To make reparation for harm done means to pay money or do something else to compensate for it.

repartee
(noun) Repartee is quick, witty comments and replies.

repast, repasts
(noun; a literary word) A repast is a meal.

repatriate, repatriates, repatriating, repatriated
(verb; a formal word) If someone is repatriated, they are sent back to their own country.
repatriation (noun).
[from *re-* and Latin *patria* meaning 'fatherland']

repay, repays, repaying, repaid
1 (verb) To repay money means to give it back to the person who lent it.
2 If you repay a favour, you do something to help the person who helped you.
repayment (noun).

repeal, repeals, repealing, repealed
(verb) If the government repeals a law, it cancels it so that it is no longer valid.

repeat, repeats, repeating, repeated
1 (verb) If you repeat something, you say, write, or do it again.
2 If you repeat what someone has said, you tell someone else about it, e.g. *Please don't repeat what I've just told you.*
3 (noun) A repeat is something which is done or happens again, e.g. *The BBC was criticized for showing too many repeats.*
repeated (adjective), **repeatedly** (adverb).

repel, repels, repelling, repelled
1 (verb) If something repels you, you find it horrible and disgusting.
2 When soldiers repel an attacking force, they successfully defend themselves against it.
3 When a magnetic pole repels an opposite pole, it forces the opposite pole away.

[from Latin *repellere* meaning 'to drive away']

Similar words: (sense 2) repulse, ward off

repellent, repellents
1 (adjective; a formal use) horrible and disgusting, e.g. *He found it repellent.*
2 (noun) Repellents are chemicals used to keep insects or other creatures away.

repent, repents, repenting, repented
(verb; a formal word) If you repent, you are sorry for something bad you have done.
repentance (noun), **repentant** (adjective).

repercussion, repercussions
(noun) The repercussions of an event are the effects it has at a later time.

repertoire, repertoires (pronounced rep-et-twar)
(noun) A performer's repertoire is all the pieces of music or dramatic parts he or she has learned and can perform.

repertory
(noun) Repertory is the practice of performing a small number of plays in a theatre for a short time, using the same actors in each play.
[from Latin *repertorium* meaning 'storehouse']

repetition, repetitions
(noun) If there is a repetition of something, it happens again, e.g. *I don't want a repetition of yesterday's disaster.*

repetitious
(adjective) Repetitious means the same as repetitive.

repetitive
(adjective) A repetitive activity involves a lot of repetition and is boring, e.g. *a repetitive job.*
repetitively (adverb).

replace, replaces, replacing, replaced
1 (verb) When one thing replaces another, the first thing takes the place of the second.
2 If you replace something that is damaged or lost, you get a new one.
3 If you replace something, you put it back where it was before, e.g. *He replaced the receiver.*
replacement (noun).

Similar words: (sense 1) supplant, supersede

replacement, replacements
(noun) The replacement for someone or something is the person or thing that takes their place.

replay, replays, replaying, replayed
1 (verb) If a match is replayed, the teams play it again.
2 (noun) A replay is a match that is played for a second time.
3 (verb) If you replay a tape or film, you play it again, e.g. *Can you replay that last track?*

replenish, replenishes, replenishing, replenished
(verb; a formal word) If you replenish something, you make it full or complete again.
replenishment (noun).
[from Old French *replenir*]

replete
(adjective; a formal word) pleasantly full of food and drink.

replica, replicas
(noun) A replica is an accurate copy of something, e.g. *a plaster replica of the sculpture.*
replicate (verb).
[from Italian *replica* meaning 'a reply']

reply, replies, replying, replied
1 (verb) If you reply to something, you say or write an answer.
2 (noun) A reply is what you say or write when you answer someone.

report, reports, reporting, reported
1 (verb) If you report that something has happened, you tell someone about it or give an official account of it, e.g. *He rushed back to report the news.*
2 (noun) A report is an account of an event, a situation, or a person's progress.
3 (verb) To report someone to an authority means to make an official complaint about them.
4 If you report to a person or place, you go there and say you have arrived.
[from Old French *reporter* meaning 'to carry back']

Similar words: (sense 2) account, statement, write-up

reporter, reporters
(noun) A reporter is someone who writes news articles or broadcasts news reports.
reporting (noun).

repose, reposes, reposing, reposed (a formal word)
1 (noun) Repose is a state in which you are resting and feeling calm.
2 (verb) To repose somewhere means to be lying or resting there.

repository, repositories
(noun; a formal word) A repository is a place where something is kept safely, e.g. *All legal documents were locked in a repository.*

repossess, repossesses, repossessing, repossessed
(verb) If a shop or company repossesses goods that have not been paid for, they take them back.

reprehensible
(adjective; a formal word) Reprehensible behaviour is very bad and morally wrong.

represent, represents, representing, represented
1 (verb) If you represent someone, you act on their behalf, e.g. *lawyers representing the victims of the disaster.*
2 If a sign or symbol represents something, it stands for it.
3 To represent something in a particular way means to describe it in that way, e.g. *Does the budget represent a change of policy?*

Similar words: (sense 3) depict, portray, render

representation, representations
1 (noun) Representation is the state of being represented by someone, e.g. *There is no student representation on the committee.*
2 You can describe a picture or statue of someone as a representation of them.
3 Representations are formal requests or complaints, e.g. *Following representations, the Government have agreed to the proposals.*

Similar words: (sense 2) portrait, profile

representative, representatives
1 (noun) A representative is a person chosen to act on behalf of another person or a group.
2 (adjective) A representative selection is typical of the group it belongs to, e.g. *a representative cross section of the community.*

repress, represses, repressing, repressed
1 (verb) If you repress a feeling, you succeed in not showing or feeling it, e.g. *I bit my lip, repressing my anger.*
2 To repress people means to restrict their freedom and control them by force.
repression (noun).

repressive
(adjective) Repressive governments use force and unjust laws to restrict and control people.

reprieve, reprieves, reprieving, reprieved
(pronounced rip-**preev**)
1 (verb) If someone who has been sentenced to death is reprieved, their sentence is changed and they are not killed.
2 (noun) A reprieve is a delay before something unpleasant happens, e.g. *a slight reprieve before the major ordeal.*
3 A reprieve is also an official order cancelling a death sentence.

reprimand, reprimands, reprimanding, reprimanded
1 (verb) If you reprimand someone, you officially tell them that they should not have done something.
2 (noun) A reprimand is something said or written by a person in authority when they are reprimanding someone.

reprint, reprints, reprinting, reprinted
1 (verb) If a book is reprinted, further copies are printed because the others have been sold.
2 (noun) A reprint of a book is a copy which has been reprinted.

reprisal, reprisals
(noun) Reprisals are violent actions taken by one group of people against another group that has harmed them.

reproach, reproaches, reproaching, reproached
(a formal word)
1 (noun) If you express reproach, you show that you feel sad and angry about what someone has done, e.g. *a long letter of reproach.*
2 (verb) If you reproach someone, you tell them, rather sadly, that they have done something wrong.
reproachful (adjective), **reproachfully** (adverb).

reprobate, reprobates
(noun; an old-fashioned word) A reprobate is someone whose behaviour is unacceptable.

reproduce, reproduces, reproducing, reproduced
1 (verb) To reproduce something means to make a copy of it.
2 When people, animals, or plants reproduce, they produce more of their own kind, e.g. *Bacteria reproduce by splitting into two.*

reproduction, reproductions
1 (noun) A reproduction is a modern copy of a painting or piece of furniture.
2 The reproduction of sound, art, or writing is the copying of it, e.g. *Compact discs give marvellous reproduction.*
3 Reproduction is the process by which a living thing produces more of its kind, e.g. *We're studying human reproduction in Biology.*

reproductive
(adjective) relating to the reproduction of living things, e.g. *the reproductive organs.*

reproof, reproofs
(noun; a formal word) A reproof is a comment expressing disapproval and criticism.

reprove, reproves, reproving, reproved
(verb) If you reprove someone, you tell them that they have behaved wrongly or foolishly.
reproving (adjective), **reproval** (noun).

reptile, reptiles
(noun) A reptile is a cold-blooded animal which has scaly skin and lays eggs. Snakes and lizards are reptiles.
reptilian (adjective).
[from Latin *reptilis* meaning 'creeping']

republic, republics
(noun) A republic is a country which has a president rather than a king or queen.
republican (noun and adjective),
republicanism (noun).
[from Latin *res publica* meaning literally 'public thing']

repudiate, repudiates, repudiating, repudiated
(pronounced rip-**yoo**-dee-ate)
(verb; a formal word) If you repudiate something, you reject it and do not want to have anything to do with it.
repudiation (noun).

repugnant
(adjective; a formal word) horrible and disgusting.
repugnance (noun).
[from Latin *repugnans* meaning 'resisting']

repulse, repulses, repulsing, repulsed
1 (verb) If you repulse someone who is being friendly, you put them off by behaving coldly towards them, e.g. *He repulses friendly advances.*
2 To repulse an attacking force means to fight it and cause it to retreat.
3 If something repulses you, you find it horrible and disgusting and you want to avoid it.

repulsive
(adjective) horrible and disgusting.
repulsively (noun).

reputable
(adjective) known to be good and reliable, e.g. *A reputable company should give a guarantee.*
reputably (adjective).

reputation, reputations
(noun) The reputation of something or someone is the opinion that people have of them, e.g. *She had built up a reputation as a creative designer.*

Similar words: repute, name, honour

repute
(noun; a formal word) Someone or something of repute is known to be honest and trustworthy.

reputed
(adjective) If something is reputed to be true, some people say that it is true, e.g. *The buildings were reputed to be haunted.*
reputedly (adverb).

request, requests, requesting, requested
1 (verb) If you request something, you ask for it politely or formally.
2 (noun) If you make a request for something, you request it.

Similar words: (sense 2) appeal, petition, entreaty

requiem, requiems (pronounced **rek**-wee-em)
1 (noun) A requiem or requiem mass is a mass celebrated for someone who has recently died.
2 A requiem is also a piece of music for singers and an orchestra, originally written for a requiem mass, e.g. *Fauré's Requiem.*
[from Latin *requies* meaning 'rest']

require, requires, requiring, required
1 (verb) If you require something, you need it.
2 If you are required to do something, you have to do it because someone says you must, e.g. *Children are required to study religion at school.*

requirement, requirements
(noun) A requirement is something that you must have or must do, e.g. *O level maths is a requirement for entry.*

requisite (a formal word)
1 (adjective) necessary for a particular purpose, e.g. *the requisite number of staff.*
2 (noun) A requisite is something that is necessary for a particular purpose.
[from Latin *requisitus* meaning 'sought after']

requisition, requisitions, requisitioning, requisitioned
(verb) If someone in authority requisitions something, they formally demand it for their own use, e.g. *My car's been requisitioned by the Captain.*

reroute, reroutes, rerouting, rerouted
(verb) If traffic is rerouted, it is directed along a different road.

rescind, rescinds, rescinding, rescinded
(pronounced ris-**sind**)
(verb; a formal word) If a law or agreement is rescinded, it is officially withdrawn.

rescue, rescues, rescuing, rescued
1 (verb) If you rescue someone, you save them from a dangerous or unpleasant situation.
2 (noun) Rescue is help which saves someone from a dangerous or unpleasant situation.
rescuer (noun).

research, researches, researching, researched
1 (noun) Research is work that involves studying something and trying to find out facts about it.
2 (verb) If you research something, you try to discover facts about it.
researcher (noun).

resemblance
(noun) If there is a resemblance between two things, they are similar to each other, e.g. *The dog bore a striking resemblance to his master.*

Similar words: likeness, similarity

resemble, resembles, resembling, resembled
(verb) To resemble something means to be similar to it.
[from Old French *resembler*]

resent, resent, resenting, resented
(verb) If you resent something, you feel bitter and angry about it.
resentment (noun).

resentful
(adjective) bitter and angry, e.g. *He felt very resentful about being dropped from the team.*
resentfully (adverb).

reservation, reservations
1 (noun) If you have reservations about something, you are not sure that it is right.
2 If you make a reservation, you book a place in advance.
3 A reservation is an area of land that is kept separate for a group of people to live on.

reserve, reserves, reserving, reserved
1 (verb) If something is reserved for a particular person or purpose, it is kept specially for them.
2 (noun) A reserve is a supply of something for future use.
3 In sport, a reserve is someone who is available to play in case one of the team is unable to play.
4 A nature reserve is an area of land where animals, birds, or plants are officially protected.
5 If someone shows reserve, they keep their feelings hidden.
reserved (adjective).
[from Latin *reservare* meaning 'to save up']

Similar words: (sense 1) withhold, save, preserve, set aside, earmark

reservoir, reservoirs (pronounced **rez**-ev-wahr)
1 (noun) A reservoir is a lake used for storing water before it is supplied to people.
2 A reservoir of something is a large quantity of it that is available for use.
[from French *réservoir*; from *réserver* meaning 'to keep']

reshuffle, reshuffles
(noun) A reshuffle is a reorganization of people or things.

reside, resides, residing, resided (pronounced riz-**zide**)
(verb; a formal word) If a quality resides in something, the quality is in that thing.

residence, residences (a formal word)
1 (noun) A residence is a house.
2 (phrase) If you **take up residence** somewhere, you go and live there.

resident, residents
(noun and adjective) A resident of a house or area is someone who lives there.

residential
1 (adjective) A residential area contains mainly houses rather than offices or factories.
2 providing accommodation, e.g. *a residential home for the elderly.*

residue, residues
(noun) A residue is a small amount of something that remains after most of it has gone, e.g. *Residues of pesticide build up in the soil.*
residual (adjective).
[from Latin *residere* meaning 'to stay behind']

resign, resigns, resigning, resigned
1 (verb) If you resign from a job, you formally announce that you are leaving it.
2 If you resign yourself to an unpleasant situation, you realize that you have to accept it.
resigned (adjective).

resignation, resignations
1 (noun) Someone's resignation is a formal statement of their intention to leave a job.
2 Resignation is the reluctant acceptance of an unpleasant situation or fact.

resilient
(adjective) able to recover quickly from unpleasant or damaging events.
resiliently (adverb), **resilience** (noun).

resin, resins
1 (noun) Resin is a sticky substance produced by some trees.
2 Resin is also a substance produced chemically and used to make plastics.
resinous (adjective).

resist, resists, resisting, resisted
1 (verb) If you resist something, you refuse to accept it and try to prevent it, e.g. *He resisted all attempts to modernize the system.*
2 If you resist someone, you fight back against them.
[from Latin *resistere* meaning 'to remain standing']

Similar words: (sense 1) oppose, withstand

resistance, resistances
1 (noun) Resistance to something such as change is a refusal to accept it.
2 Resistance to an attack consists of fighting back, e.g. *The invaders met with little resistance.*
3 Resistance of your body to germs or disease is its power to remain unharmed by them.
4 Resistance is also the power of a substance to resist the flow of an electrical current through it.

resistant

1 (adjective) opposed to something and wanting to prevent it, e.g. *resistant to change*.
2 If something is resistant to a particular thing, it is not harmed or affected by it, e.g. *Certain insects are resistant to this spray*.

resistor, resistors

(noun) A resistor is a device which is designed to increase the resistance in an electrical circuit.

resolute (pronounced rez-ol-loot)

(adjective; a formal word) Someone who is resolute is determined not to change their mind. **resolutely** (adverb), **resoluteness** (noun).

resolution, resolutions

1 (noun) Resolution is determination.
2 If you make a resolution, you promise yourself to do something.
3 A resolution is a formal decision taken at a meeting.
4 (a formal use) The resolution of a problem is the solving of it.

resolve, resolves, resolving, resolved

1 (verb) If you resolve to do something, you firmly decide to do it.
2 (noun) Resolve is absolute determination.
3 (verb) If you resolve a problem, you find a solution to it.

resonance, resonances

1 (noun) Resonance is sound produced by an object vibrating as a result of another sound nearby.
2 Resonance is also a deep, clear, and echoing quality of sound.

resonant

(adjective) A resonant sound is deep and strong.

Similar words: rich, sonorous

resonate, resonates, resonating, resonated

(verb) If something resonates, it vibrates and produces a deep, strong sound.

resort, resorts, resorting, resorted

1 (verb) If you resort to a course of action, you do it because you have no alternative.
2 (phrase) If you do something as a last resort, you do it because you can find no other way of solving a problem.
3 (noun) A resort is a place where people spend their holidays.

resound, resounds, resounding, resounded

(verb; a literary word) If a place resounds, it is filled with a loud noise.

resounding

1 (adjective) loud and echoing, e.g. *a resounding cheer*.
2 A resounding success is a great success.

resource, resources

(noun) The resources of a country, organization, or person are the materials, money, or skills they have available for use.

resourceful

(adjective) A resourceful person is good at finding ways of dealing with problems. **resourcefulness** (noun), **resourcefully** (adverb).

respect, respects, respecting, respected

1 (verb) If you respect someone, you have a good opinion of their character or ideas.
2 (noun) If you have respect for someone, you respect them.
3 (verb) If you respect someone's rights or wishes, you do not do things that they would not like, or would consider wrong, e.g. *We respected Muslim customs*.
4 (phrase) You can say in this respect to refer to a particular feature, e.g. *We are behind in this respect*.
5 To pay your last respects to someone who has just died means to show respect by visiting their body or grave.
respected (adjective).

respectable

1 (adjective) considered to be acceptable and morally correct, e.g. *respectable families*.
2 adequate or reasonable, e.g. *a respectable amount of work*.
respectability (noun), **respectably** (adverb).

respectful

(adjective) showing respect for someone, e.g. *He followed the Queen at a respectful distance*. **respectfully** (adverb).

respective

(adjective) belonging or relating individually to the people or things just mentioned, e.g. *He drove them to their respective homes*.

respectively

(adverb) in the same order as the items just mentioned, e.g. *Harvard and MIT are fourth and fifth respectively*.

respiration

(noun; a technical word) Your respiration is your breathing.
[from Latin *respirare* meaning 'to exhale']

respirator, respirators

1 (noun) A respirator is a device worn over your mouth and nose to allow you to breathe when surrounded by smoke or poisonous gas.
2 A respirator is also a device which helps someone to breathe when they are ill or injured.

respiratory

(adjective; a technical word) relating to breathing, e.g. *respiratory infections*.

respite

(noun; a formal word) A respite is a short rest from something unpleasant.

resplendent

(adjective; a formal word) very impressive.

respond, responds, responding, responded

(verb) When you respond to something, you react to it by doing or saying something.
[from Latin *respondere* meaning 'to return like for like']

respondent, respondents

1 (noun) A respondent is a person who answers a questionnaire or a request for information.
2 In a court case, the respondent is the defendant.

response, responses
(noun) Your response to an event is your reaction or reply to it, e.g. *There has been no response from the Ministry yet.*

responsibility, responsibilities
1 (noun) If you have responsibility for something, it is your duty to deal with it or look after it, e.g. *The garden is Paul's responsibility.*
2 If you accept responsibility for something that has happened, you agree that you caused it or were to blame, e.g. *The company will not accept responsibility for any loss or damage.*

Similar words: (sense 2) obligation, liability

responsible
1 (adjective) If you are responsible for something, it is your duty to deal with it and you are to blame if it goes wrong.
2 If you are responsible to someone, that person is your boss and tells you what you have to do.
3 A responsible person behaves properly and sensibly without needing to be supervised.
4 A responsible job involves making careful judgments about important matters.
responsibly (adverb).

Similar words: (sense 1) accountable, answerable, culpable, liable

responsive
1 (adjective) quick to show interest and pleasure.
2 taking notice of events and reacting in an appropriate way, e.g. *Industry is highly responsive to consumer demand.*
responsiveness (noun).

rest, rests, resting, rested
1 (noun) The rest of something is all the remaining parts of it.
2 (verb) If you rest, you relax and do not do anything active for a while.
3 (noun) If you have a rest, you sit or lie quietly and relax.
4 A rest is an object used to support something.
rested (adjective).

Similar words: (sense 3) breather, stop, lull, respite, break, time off

restaurant, restaurants (pronounced **rest**-rong)
(noun) A restaurant is a place where you can buy and eat a meal.
[a French word; from *restaurer* meaning 'to restore']

restaurateur, restaurateurs (pronounced rest-er-a-**tur**)
(noun) A restaurateur is someone who owns or manages a restaurant.

restful
(adjective) Something that is restful helps you feel calm and relaxed.

restitution
(noun; a formal word) Restitution is the returning of something that has been lost or stolen, or payment for damage.
[from Latin *restituere* meaning 'to rebuild']

restive
(adjective) impatient, discontented, and disobedient.
restively (adverb), **restiveness** (noun).

restless
(adjective) finding it difficult to remain still or relaxed as a result of boredom or impatience.
restlessness (noun), **restlessly** (adverb).

Similar words: jumpy, restive, unsettled, fidgety

restore, restores, restoring, restored
1 (verb) To restore something means to cause it to exist again or to return to its previous state.
e.g. *You've restored my faith in human nature.*
2 To restore an old building or work of art means to clean and repair it.
restoration (noun), **restorative** (adjective).

Similar words: (sense 2) refurbish, renovate, do up

restrain, restrains, restraining, restrained
(verb) To restrain someone or something means to hold them back or prevent them from doing what they want to.
[from Latin *restringere* meaning 'to draw back tightly']

Similar words: curb, check, inhibit, hold back

restrained
(adjective) behaving in a controlled way.

restraint, restraints
1 (noun) Restraints are rules or conditions that limit something, e.g. *price restraints.*
2 Restraint is calm, controlled behaviour.

restrict, restricts, restricting, restricted
1 (verb) If you restrict something, you prevent it becoming too large or varied.
2 To restrict people or animals means to limit their movement or actions.
restrictive (adjective).

Similar words: (sense 2) cramp, hem in, inhibit

restriction, restrictions
(noun) A restriction is a rule or situation that limits what you can do, e.g. *traffic restrictions.*

Similar words: limitation, constraint

result, results, resulting, resulted
1 (noun) The result of an action or situation is the situation that is caused by it, e.g. *I went the unmarked way and got lost as a result.*
2 (verb) If something results in a particular event, it causes that event to happen, e.g. *The cutbacks resulted in widespread poverty.*
3 If something results from a particular event, it is caused by that event.
4 (noun) The result is also the final marks, figures, or situation at the end of a contest, examination, experiment, or calculation, e.g. *football results... What do you make the result?*
resultant (adjective).
[from Latin *resultare* meaning 'to rebound']

Similar words: (sense 1) aftereffect, aftermath, consequence, outcome, upshot, repercussion

resume, resumes, resuming, resumed
(pronounced riz-**yoom**)
(verb) If you resume an activity or position, you return to it again after a break.
resumption (noun).
[from Latin *resumere* meaning 'to take up again']

résumé, résumés (pronounced **rez**-yoo-may)
(noun) A résumé is a summary.
[a French word]

resurgence
(noun) If there is a resurgence of an attitude or activity, it reappears and grows stronger.
resurgent (adjective).
[from Latin *resurgere* meaning 'to rise again']

resurrect, resurrects, resurrecting, resurrected
(verb) If you resurrect something, you cause it to exist again after it has disappeared or ended.
resurrection (noun).

Resurrection
(noun) In Christian belief, the Resurrection is the coming back to life of Jesus Christ three days after he had been killed.

resuscitate, resuscitates, resuscitating, resuscitated (pronounced ris-**suss**-it-tate)
(verb) If you resuscitate someone, you make them conscious again after an accident.
resuscitation (noun).
[from Latin *resuscitare*]

retail, retails, retailing, retailed
1 (noun) The retail price is the price at which something is sold in the shops.
2 (verb) To retail goods means to sell them to the public.
retailer (noun).

retain, retains, retaining, retained
(verb) To retain something means to keep it.
retention (noun).

retainer, retainers
1 (noun) A retainer is a fee paid to someone to keep them available for work when required.
2 A person's retainers are their servants.

retaliate, retaliates, retaliating, retaliated
(verb) If you retaliate, you do something to harm, annoy, or upset someone because they have already acted in a similar way against you.
retaliation (noun), **retaliatory** (adjective).

retard, retards, retarding, retarded
(verb) To retard a process means to delay it or make it happen more slowly.
retardation (noun).
[from Latin *retardare* meaning 'to delay' or 'to impede']

retarded
(adjective) If someone is retarded, their mental development is much less advanced than average.

retch, retches, retching, retched
(verb) If you retch, you stomach moves as if you were vomiting.

retention
(noun) The retention of something is the keeping of it, e.g. *They voted for the retention of the death penalty.*

retentive
(adjective) able to keep or remember things, e.g. *a retentive memory.*

rethink, rethinks, rethinking, rethought
(verb) If you rethink something, you think about how it should be changed, e.g. *The government should rethink their policies.*

reticent
(adjective) Someone who is reticent is unwilling to tell people about things.
reticence (noun).
[from re- and Latin *tacere* meaning 'to be silent']

retina, retinas
(noun) The retina is the light-sensitive membrane at the back of your eyeball, which receives an image and sends it to your brain.
retinal (adjective).

retinue, retinues
(noun) A retinue is a group of helpers or friends travelling with an important person.

retire, retires, retiring, retired
1 (verb) When older people retire, they give up work.
2 (a formal use) If you retire, you leave to go into another room, or to bed, e.g. *She had retired early with a good book.*
retired (adjective), **retirement** (noun).

retiring
(adjective) A retiring person is shy and avoids meeting other people.

retort, retorts, retorting, retorted
1 (verb) To retort means to reply angrily.
2 (noun) A retort is a short, angry reply.
3 A retort is also a glass container with a long neck and a round bulb that is used in laboratories, especially for distilling substances.

retouch, retouches, retouching, retouched
(verb) If you retouch a painting or photograph, you improve it by painting over parts of it.

retrace, retraces, retracing, retraced
(verb) If you retrace your steps, you go back along the same route to where you started.

retract, retracts, retracting, retracted
1 (verb) If you retract something you have said, you say that you did not mean it.
2 When something is retracted, it moves inwards or backwards, e.g. *The tortoise was retracting into its shell.*
retraction (noun), **retractable** (adjective).

Similar words: (sense 1) withdraw, take back, recant

retread, retreads
(noun) A retread is an old tyre which has been given a new surface.

retreat, retreats, retreating, retreated
1 (verb) To retreat means to move backwards away from something or someone.
2 (noun) If an army moves away from the enemy, this is referred to as a retreat.
3 (verb) If you retreat from something difficult or unpleasant, you avoid doing it.
4 (noun) A retreat is a quiet, secluded place that you go to in order to rest or do things in private.

retrenchment
(noun; a formal word) Retrenchment is the process of reducing the amount of money that a person or organization spends.

retribution
(noun; a formal word) Retribution is punishment, e.g. *divine retribution.*
[from Latin *retribuere* meaning 'to give back']

retrieval
(noun) The retrieval of something is the process of getting it back.

retrieve, retrieves, retrieving, retrieved
1 (verb) If you retrieve something, you get it back.
2 If you retrieve a bad situation, you do something to improve it.
[from *re-* and French *trouver* meaning 'to find']

retriever, retrievers
(noun) A retriever is a large dog often used by hunters to bring back birds and animals which have been shot.

retroactive
(adjective) taking effect from a date in the past.

retrograde
(adjective; a formal word) A retrograde step is something which makes a situation worse instead of better.
[from Latin *retro* meaning 'backwards' and *gradi* meaning 'to walk']

retrospect
(noun) When you consider something in retrospect, you think about it afterwards and often have a different opinion from the one you had at the time, e.g. *I was heartbroken, but in retrospect I see it was all for the best.*
[from Latin *retro* meaning 'backwards' and *specere* meaning 'to look']

retrospective
1 (adjective) concerning things that happened in the past.
2 taking effect from a date in the past.
retrospectively (adverb).

return, returns, returning, returned
1 (verb) When you return to a place, you go back after you have been away.
2 (noun) Your return is your arrival back at a place.
3 (verb) If you return something to someone, you give it back to them.
4 When you return a ball during a game, you hit it back to your opponent.
5 When a judge or jury returns a verdict, they announce it.
6 (noun) The return on an investment is the profit or interest you get from it.
7 A return is a ticket for the journey to a place and back again.
8 (phrase) If you do something **in return** for a favour, you do it to repay the favour.
9 You say **many happy returns** to wish someone a happy birthday.
10 To reply **by return** means to send a reply immediately in the next post.

returning officer, returning officers
(noun) The returning officer is the person in charge of an election who announces the result.

reunion, reunions
(noun) A reunion is a party or meeting for people who have not seen each other for a long time.

reunite, reunites, reuniting, reunited
(verb) If people are reunited, they meet again after they have been separated for some time.

rev, revs, revving, revved (an informal word)
1 (verb) When you rev the engine of a vehicle, you press the accelerator to increase the engine speed.
2 (noun) The speed of an engine is measured in revolutions per minute, referred to as revs.

Rev or Revd abbreviations for Reverend.

revalue, revalues, revaluing, revalued
(verb) To revalue something means to adjust its price or value.
revaluation (noun).

revamp, revamps, revamping, revamped
(verb) To revamp something means to improve or repair it.

reveal, reveals, revealing, revealed
1 (verb) To reveal something means to tell people about it, e.g. *Police revealed his name.*
2 If you reveal something that has been hidden, you uncover it.
[from Latin *revelare* meaning 'to unveil']

Similar words: (sense 1) disclose, divulge, leak, let slip, unfold

revealing
1 (adjective) A revealing statement or action tells you something you did not know.
2 Revealing clothes allow more of someone's body to be seen than usual.

reveille (pronounced riv-val-ee)
(noun) Reveille is a short tune played on a trumpet to signal the time when soldiers have to get up in the morning.
[from French *réveillez!* meaning 'wake up!']

revel, revels, revelling, revelled
(verb) If you revel in a situation, you enjoy it very much.
reveller (noun), revelry (noun).

Similar words: luxuriate, relish, thrive on

revelation, revelations
1 (noun) A revelation is a surprising or interesting fact made known to people.
2 If an experience is a revelation, it makes you realize or learn something.

revenge, revenges, revenging, revenged
1 (noun) Revenge involves hurting someone who has hurt you.
2 (verb) If you revenge yourself on someone who has hurt you, you hurt them in return.
revengeful (adjective).

Similar words: (sense 1) reprisal, retaliation, retribution, vengeance
(sense 2) avenge, vindicate, even the score

revenue, revenues
(noun) Revenue is money that a government, company, or organization receives, e.g. *the government's tax revenues.*

reverberate, reverberates, reverberating, reverberated
(verb) When a loud sound reverberates, it echoes loudly around.
reverberation (noun).
[from *re-* + Latin *verberare* meaning 'to beat']

revere, reveres, revering, revered
(verb; a formal word) If you revere someone, you respect and admire them.
revered (adjective).
[from *re-* + Latin *vereri* meaning 'to fear']

reverence
(noun) Reverence is a feeling of great respect.

Reverend
Reverend is a title used before the name of a member of the clergy, e.g. *the Reverend Alnut.*
[from Latin *reverendus* meaning 'venerable']

reverent
(adjective) showing great respect.
reverently (adverb).

reverie, reveries (pronounced **rev**-er-ee)
(noun) A reverie is a pleasant daydream.

revers (pronounced riv-**veer**)
(noun) A revers is part of a garment that is turned back, for example, a lapel.
[from French *revers* meaning 'reverse']

reversal, reversals
1 (noun) If there is a reversal of a process or policy, it is changed to the opposite process or policy.
2 If there is a reversal of two things, each one acquires the position or function of the other.

reverse, reverses, reversing, reversed
1 (verb) When someone reverses a process, they change it to the opposite process, e.g. *We can't reverse our decision now.*
2 If you reverse the order of things, you arrange them in the opposite order.
3 When you reverse a car, you drive it backwards.
4 (noun) The reverse is the opposite of what has just been said or done.
5 (adjective) Reverse means opposite to what is usual or to what has just been described.
[from Latin *revertere* meaning 'to turn back']

reversible
(adjective) Reversible clothing can be worn with either side on the outside.

revert, reverts, reverting, reverted
(verb; a formal word) To revert to a former state, system, or type of behaviour means to go back to it.
reversion (noun).

review, reviews, reviewing, reviewed
1 (noun) A review is an article or an item on television or radio, giving an opinion of a new book or play.
2 (verb) To review a play or book means to write an account expressing an opinion of it.

3 (noun) When there is a review of a situation or system, it is examined to decide whether changes are needed.
4 (verb) To review something means to examine it to decide whether changes are needed.
reviewer (noun).

Similar words: (sense 3) evaluation, examination, judgment
(sense 4) criticize, evaluate

revise, revises, revising, revised
1 (verb) If you revise something, you alter, improve or correct it.
2 When you revise for an examination, you go over your work to learn things thoroughly.
revision (noun).
[from Latin *revisere* meaning 'to look back at']

revitalize, revitalizes, revitalizing, revitalized; also spelled **revitalise**
(verb) To revitalize something means to make it more active or lively.

revive, revives, reviving, revived
1 (verb) When a feeling or practice is revived, it becomes active or popular again.
2 When you revive someone who has fainted, they become conscious again.
revival (noun).
[from Old French *revivre* meaning 'to live again']

revoke, revokes, revoking, revoked
(verb; a formal word) When somebody in authority revokes a licence or order, they cancel it, e.g. *Planning permission was revoked.*

revolt, revolts, revolting, revolted
1 (noun) A revolt is a violent attempt by a group of people to change their country's political system.
2 (verb) When people revolt, they fight against the authority that governs them.
3 If something revolts you, it is so horrible that you feel disgust.

revolting
(adjective) horrible and disgusting, e.g. *a revolting smell of rotten vegetables.*

revolution, revolutions
1 (noun) A revolution is a violent attempt by a large group of people to change the political system of their country.
2 A revolution is also an important change in an area of human activity, e.g. *the Industrial Revolution... the computer revolution.*
3 A revolution is one complete turn in a circle.

revolutionary, revolutionaries
1 (adjective) involving great changes, e.g. *revolutionary changes in the design of cars.*
2 (noun) A revolutionary is a person who takes part in a revolution.

revolutionize, revolutionizes, revolutionizing, revolutionized; also spelled **revolutionise**
(verb) To revolutionize an activity means to cause great changes in the way that it is done.

revolve, revolves, revolving, revolved
1 (verb) If something revolves round something

else, it centres on that as the most important thing, e.g. *Her life revolves around his family.*
2 When something revolves, it turns in a circle around a central point, e.g. *The earth revolves round the sun.*
revolving (adjective).
[from Latin *revolvere* meaning 'to roll back']

revolver, **revolvers**
(noun) A revolver is a small gun held in the hand.

revue, **revues**
(noun) A revue is a theatrical show with songs, dances, and jokes about recent events.
[a French word]

revulsion
(noun) Revulsion is a strong feeling of disgust or disapproval.
[from Latin *revulsio* meaning 'a pulling away']

reward, **rewards**, **rewarding**, **rewarded**
1 (noun) A reward is something you are given because you have done something good.
2 (verb) If you reward someone, you give them a reward.

rewarding
(adjective) Something that is rewarding gives you a lot of satisfaction.

rewind, **rewinds**, **rewinding**, **rewound**
(verb) If you rewind a tape on a tape recorder or video, you make the tape go backwards.

rewrite, **rewrites**, **rewriting**, **rewrote**
(verb) If you rewrite a piece of writing, you write it again in a different way.

rhapsodic
(adjective) expressing great delight or enthusiasm for something.

rhapsody, **rhapsodies** (pronounced **rap**-sod-ee)
(noun) A rhapsody is a short piece of music, irregular in form, but very passionate and flowing.
[from Greek *rhaptein* meaning 'to sew together' and *ōidē* meaning 'song']

rhea, **rheas** (pronounced **ree**-a)
(noun) A rhea is a type of South American bird rather like a small ostrich.

rheostat, **rheostats**
(noun) A rheostat is a device which varies the resistance in an electric circuit.

rhesus, **rhesuses** (pronounced **ree**-suss)
(noun) A rhesus or rhesus monkey is a small short-tailed monkey from northern India, often used in medical research.

rhesus factor
(noun) The rhesus factor (or Rh factor) is an antigen that is often present in blood. Blood containing this factor is called rhesus positive, and blood without it is called rhesus negative.

rhetoric
(noun) Rhetoric is fine-sounding speech or writing that is intended to impress people.

rhetorical
1 (adjective) A rhetorical question is one which is asked in order to make a statement rather than to get an answer.

2 Rhetorical language is intended to be grand and impressive.
rhetorically (adverb).

rheumatism (pronounced **room**-at-izm)
(noun) Rheumatism is an illness that makes your joints and muscles stiff and painful.
rheumatic (adjective).
[from Latin *rheumatismus* meaning 'catarrh']

rhino, **rhinos**
(noun; an informal word) A rhino is a rhinoceros.

rhinoceros, **rhinoceroses**
(noun) A rhinoceros is a large African or Asian animal with one or two horns on its nose.
[from Greek *rhin* meaning 'of the nose' and *keras* meaning 'horn']

rhizome, **rhizomes** (pronounced **rye**-zome)
(noun) A rhizome is a thick underground stem, whose buds develop into new plants. Plants such as mint and irises develop from rhizomes.
[from Greek *rhiza* meaning 'root']

rhodium (pronounced **rode**-ee-um)
(noun) Rhodium is a hard silvery-white metallic element similar to platinum. It does not corrode easily and is used in alloys. Its atomic number is 45 and its symbol is Rh.

rhododendron, **rhododendrons**
(noun) A rhododendron is an evergreen bush with large coloured flowers.
[from Greek *rhodon* + *dendron* meaning 'rose tree']

rhombus, **rhombuses** or **rhombi**
(noun) A rhombus is a shape with four equal sides and no right angles.

rhubarb
(noun) Rhubarb is a plant with long red stems which can be cooked with sugar and eaten.

rhyme, **rhymes**, **rhyming**, **rhymed**
1 (verb) If two words rhyme, they have a similar sound, e.g. *Sally rhymes with valley.*
2 (noun) A rhyme is a word that rhymes with another.
3 A rhyme is a short poem with rhyming lines.

rhythm, **rhythms**
1 (noun) Rhythm is a regular movement or beat.
2 A rhythm is a regular pattern of changes, for example, in the seasons.
rhythmic (adjective), **rhythmically** (adverb).

Similar words: (sense 1) tempo, pulse, time, beat

rib, **ribs**
1 (noun) Your ribs are the curved bones that go from your backbone to your chest.
2 A rib is a long, curved piece of wood forming part of the structure of a roof or boat.
3 Rib is a method of knitting that makes a raised pattern of vertical parallel lines.
ribbed (adjective).

ribald (pronounced **rib**-ld)
(adjective) Ribald remarks refer to sex in a humorous way and are considered rather rude.
ribaldry (noun).

ribbon, ribbons
1 (noun) A ribbon is a long, narrow piece of cloth used for decoration.
2 A typewriter ribbon is a long, narrow piece of cloth containing a special ink for printing letters.

riboflavin (pronounced ry-boe-**flay**-vin)
(noun) Riboflavin is a vitamin belonging to the B group. It occurs in green vegetables, milk, fish, eggs, liver, and kidney.

rice
(noun) Rice is a tall grass that produces edible grains. Rice is grown in warm countries on wet ground.

rice paper
(noun) Rice paper is an edible paper made from the straw of rice plants.

rich, richer, richest; riches
1 (adjective) Someone who is rich has a lot of money and possessions.
2 Something that is rich in something contains a large amount of it, e.g. *The sea bed is rich in minerals.*
3 Rich food contains a large amount of fat, oil, or sugar.
4 Rich colours, smells, and sounds are strong and pleasant.
5 (plural noun) Riches are valuable possessions or desirable qualities and substances, e.g. *the riches of the East.*
richness (noun).

richly
1 (adverb) If someone is richly rewarded, they are rewarded well with something valuable.
2 If you feel strongly that someone deserves something, you can say it is richly deserved.

rick, ricks, ricking, ricked
1 (noun) A rick is a large pile of hay or straw.
2 (verb) If you rick your neck or back, you hurt it by twisting it.

rickets
(noun) Rickets is a disease that affects children if they do not get enough Vitamin D. It causes softening of the bones and enlargement of the liver and spleen.

rickety
(adjective) likely to collapse or break, e.g. *a rickety bridge.*

rickshaw, rickshaws
(noun) A rickshaw is a hand-pulled cart used in Asia for carrying passengers.

ricochet, ricochets, ricocheting or ricochetting, ricocheted or ricochetted (pronounced rik-osh-ay)
(verb) When a bullet ricochets, it hits a surface and bounces away from it.

rid, rids, ridding, rid
1 (phrase) When you **get rid** of something you do not want, you remove or destroy it.
2 (verb; a formal use) To rid a place of something unpleasant means to succeed in removing it.

Similar words: (sense 2) relieve, unburden, free, purge

riddance
(an informal phrase) If you say **good riddance** when someone leaves, you mean you are glad they have gone.

riddle, riddles
1 (noun) A riddle is a puzzle which seems to be nonsense, but which has an entertaining solution.
2 Something that is a riddle puzzles and confuses you.

Similar words: (sense 2) conundrum, puzzle, poser

riddled
(adjective) full of something undesirable, e.g. *This sideboard's riddled with woodworm.*
[from Old English *hriddel* meaning 'sieve']

ride, rides, riding, rode, ridden
1 (verb) When you ride a horse or a bike, you sit on it and control it as it moves along.
2 When you ride in a car, you travel in it.
3 (noun) A ride is a journey on a horse or bike or in a vehicle.
4 (an informal phrase) To **take someone for a ride** means to deceive them.

rider, riders
1 (noun) A rider is a person riding on a horse or bicycle.
2 A rider is also an additional statement which changes or puts a condition on what has already been said.

ridge, ridges
1 (noun) A ridge is a long, narrow piece of high land.
2 A ridge is also a raised line on a flat surface.
3 In meteorology, a ridge of high pressure is a line of high pressure from an anticyclone.

ridicule, ridicules, ridiculing, ridiculed
1 (verb) To ridicule someone means to make fun of them in an unkind way.
2 (noun) Ridicule is unkind laughter and mockery.

ridiculous
(adjective) very foolish.
ridiculously (adverb).
[from Latin *ridere* meaning 'to laugh']

rife
(adjective; a formal word) very common.

riffle, riffles, riffling, riffled
(verb) If you riffle through the pages of a book, you flick through them quickly.

riffraff
(noun) You can refer to worthless, badly-behaved people as riffraff.

rifle, rifles, rifling, rifled
1 (noun) A rifle is a gun with a long barrel.
2 (verb) When someone rifles something, they make a quick search through it to steal things.

rift, rifts
1 (noun) A rift between friends is a serious quarrel that damages their friendship.
2 A rift is also a split in something solid, especially in the ground.

rig, rigs, rigging, rigged
1 (verb) If someone rigs an election or contest,

they dishonestly arrange for a particular person to succeed.
2 (noun) A rig is a large structure used for extracting oil or gas from the ground or sea bed.

rig up
(phrasal verb) If you rig up a device or structure, you make it quickly and fix it in place, e.g. *We rigged up a makeshift tent.*

rigging
(noun) The rigging of a sailing ship is the ropes supporting its mast and sails.

right, rights, righting, righted
1 (adjective and adverb) correct and in accordance with the facts, e.g. *Is that clock right?... Did I pronounce that right?*
2 (adjective) The right choice, action, or decision is the best or most suitable one.
3 The right people or places are those that have influence or are socially admired, e.g. *You've got to know the right people to get on.*
4 The right side of something is the side intended to be seen and to face outwards.
5 (noun) Right is used to refer to principles of morally correct behaviour, e.g. *the development of a sense of right and wrong.*
6 If you have a right to do something, you are morally or legally entitled to do it.
7 The right is one of the two sides of something. For example, when you look at the word 'to', the 'o' is to the right of the 't'.
8 (adjective and adverb) Right means on or towards the right side of something.
9 (noun) The Right refers to people who support the political ideas of capitalism and conservatism rather than socialism.
10 (adverb) Right is used to emphasize a precise place, e.g. *I'm staying right here.*
11 Right means immediately, e.g. *I'll be right back.*
12 (verb) If you right something, you correct it or put it back in an upright position.
rightly (adverb).

Similar words: (sense 2) just, proper
(sense 6) privilege, prerogative

right angle, right angles
(noun) A right angle is an angle of 90°.

righteous
(adjective) Righteous behaviour is morally good, religious, and praiseworthy.
righteousness (noun).

rightful
(adjective) Someone's rightful possession is one which they have a moral or legal right to.
rightfully (adverb).

right-handed
(adjective and adverb) Someone who is right-handed does things such as writing and painting with their right hand.

right-hand man, right-hand men
(noun) Someone's right-hand man is the person who helps them most in their work.

rightist, rightists
(noun and adjective) A rightist is someone who holds right-wing political views.

right of way, rights of way
1 (noun) When a vehicle has right of way, all other traffic must stop for it.
2 A right of way is a public path across private land.

right-wing
(adjective) believing more strongly in capitalism or conservatism, or less strongly in socialism, than other members of the same party or group.
right-winger (noun).

rigid
1 (adjective) Rigid laws or systems cannot be changed and are considered severe.
2 A rigid object is stiff and does not bend easily.
rigidly (adverb), **rigidity** (noun).
[from Latin *rigere* meaning 'to be stiff']

Similar words: (sense 1) inflexible, stiff, unyielding

rigmarole, rigmaroles
(noun; an informal word) A rigmarole is a series of actions or statements that seems unnecessarily complicated.

rigor mortis
(noun) Rigor mortis is stiffening of the body in a dead person or animal.
[a Latin expression meaning 'rigidity of death']

rigorous
(adjective) very careful and thorough.
rigorously (adverb).

rigour, rigours
(noun; a formal word) The rigours of a situation are the things which make it hard or unpleasant, e.g. *the rigours of a city winter.*

rile, riles, riling, riled
(verb; an informal word) If someone riles you, they make you angry.

rim, rims
(noun) The rim of an object such as a wheel or a cup is the outside or top edge.
rimmed (adjective).

rind, rinds
(noun) Rind is the thick outer skin of fruit, cheese, or bacon.

ring, rings, ringing, rang, rung
1 (verb) If you ring someone, you phone them.
2 When a bell rings, it makes a clear, loud sound.
3 (noun) A ring is the sound made by a bell.
4 (phrase) If a statement **rings true**, it sounds likely to be true.
5 (noun) A ring is also a small circle of metal worn on your finger.
6 A ring is also an object or group of things in the shape of a circle.
7 At a boxing match, show jumping contest, or circus, the ring is the place where the performance takes place.
8 A ring is also an organized group of criminals, e.g. *The police have uncovered a drugs ring.*
9 (verb) To ring something means to draw a circle around it.

10 If something is ringed with something else, it has that thing all the way around it, e.g. *The lake was ringed with trees.*

Similar words: (senses 2 and 3) knell, chime, peal, toll, clang
(sense 5) band, circle

ring finger, ring fingers
(noun) Your ring finger is the third finger of your hand.

ringleader, ringleaders
(noun) The ringleader is the leader of a group of troublemakers or criminals.

ringlet, ringlets
(noun) Ringlets are long, hanging curls of hair.

ringmaster, ringmasters
(noun) The ringmaster in a circus is the person who introduces the different acts.

ring road, ring roads
(noun) A ring road is a road that goes round the edge of a town, avoiding the centre.

ringworm
(noun) Ringworm is a fungal infection of the skin that causes itching circular patches.

rink, rinks
(noun) A rink is a large indoor area for ice-skating or roller-skating.

rinse, rinses, rinsing, rinsed
1 (verb) When you rinse something, you wash it in clean water.
2 (noun) A rinse is a liquid you can put on your hair to give it a different colour.

riot, riots, rioting, rioted
1 (noun) When there is a riot, a crowd of people behave noisily and violently.
2 (verb) To riot means to behave noisily and violently.
3 (phrase) To **run riot** means to behave in a wild and uncontrolled way.

riotous
(adjective) enthusiastic and rather wild, e.g. *The children gave him a riotous welcome.*

rip, rips, ripping, ripped
1 (verb) When you rip something, you tear it violently.
2 If you rip something away, you remove it quickly and violently.
3 (noun) A rip is a long split in cloth or paper.

rip off
(phrasal verb; an informal expression) If someone rips you off, they cheat you by overcharging you.

RIP
RIP is an abbreviation often written on gravestones, meaning 'rest in peace'.

ripcord, ripcords
(noun) A ripcord is the cord that you pull to open a parachute.

ripe, riper, ripest
1 (adjective) When fruit or grain is ripe, it is fully developed and ready to be eaten.

2 If a situation is ripe for something to happen, it is ready for it.
3 If someone lives to a ripe old age, they live to be very old.
ripeness (noun).

ripen, ripens, ripening, ripened
(verb) When crops ripen, they become ripe.

rip-off, rip-offs
(noun; an informal word) If you say that something you bought was a rip-off, you mean it was not worth what you paid.

riposte, ripostes (pronounced rip-**posst**)
(noun) A riposte is a quick and clever reply.

ripple, ripples, rippling, rippled
1 (noun) Ripples are little waves on the surface of calm water.
2 (verb) When the surface of water ripples, little waves appear on it.
3 (noun) If there is a ripple of laughter or applause, people laugh or applaud gently for a short time.

rise, rises, rising, rose, risen
1 (verb) If something rises, it moves upwards.
2 (a formal use) When you rise, you stand up.
3 To rise also means to get out of bed.
4 When the sun rises, it first appears.
5 The place where a river rises is where it begins.
6 If land rises, it slopes upwards.
7 If a sound or wind rises, it becomes higher or stronger.
8 If an amount rises, it increases.
9 (noun) A rise is an increase.
10 (verb) If you rise to a challenge or a remark, you respond to it rather than ignoring it, e.g. *I like teasing her; she always rises to the bait.*
11 When people rise up, they start fighting against people in authority.
12 (noun) Someone's rise is the process by which they become more powerful or successful, e.g. *her rise to fame.*
13 (phrase) To **give rise to** something means to cause it to happen, e.g. *The infection can give rise to hair loss.*
rising (adjective).

Similar words: (sense 1) soar, ascend, mount

riser, risers
(noun) An early riser is someone who likes to get up early in the morning.

rising damp
(noun) If a building has rising damp, moisture is getting in from the ground and is moving upwards, damaging the walls.

risk, risks, risking, risked
1 (noun) A risk is a chance that something unpleasant or dangerous might happen.
2 (verb) If you risk something unpleasant, you do something knowing that the unpleasant thing might happen as a result, e.g. *If you don't play, you risk losing your place in the team.*
3 If you risk someone's life, you put them in a dangerous situation in which they might be killed.
risky (adjective).

[from Italian *rischiare* meaning 'to be in danger']

Similar words: (senses 1 and 2) chance, venture, gamble

risotto, risottos
(noun) Risotto is an Italian dish of rice cooked with vegetables and meat.

risqué (pronounced **riss**-kay)
(adjective) Risqué jokes or stories are considered rather rude because they refer to sex.
[a French word]

rissole, rissoles
(noun) Rissoles are flat, round patties made of finely chopped savoury food.

rite, rites
(noun) A rite is a religious ceremony.
[from Latin *ritus*]

ritual, rituals
1 (noun) A ritual is a series of actions carried out according to the custom of a particular society or group, e.g. *the rituals of greeting.*
2 (adjective) Ritual activities happen as part of a tradition or ritual, e.g. *ritual sacrifices.*
ritualism (noun), ritualistic (adjective).

rival, rivals, rivalling, rivalled
1 (noun) Your rival is the person you are competing with.
2 (verb) If something rivals something else, it is of the same high standard or quality, e.g. *Nothing can rival the first sight of Venice.*

Similar words: (sense 1) competitor, opponent, contender

rivalry, rivalries
(noun) Rivalry is active competition between people.

Similar words: opposition, competition, contention

river, rivers
(noun) A river is a natural feature consisting of water flowing for a long distance between two banks.

rivet, rivets, riveting, riveted
1 (verb) If you are riveted by something, it fascinates you and holds your attention.
2 (noun) A rivet is a short, round pin with a flat head which is used to fasten sheets of metal together. The other end of the rivet is hammered flat when it is in place.
riveting (adjective).
[from Old French *river* meaning 'to fix']

rivulet, rivulets (pronounced riv-yoo-lit)
(noun; a formal word) A rivulet is a small stream.

RN an abbreviation for 'Royal Navy'.

roach
(noun) A roach is a European fresh water fish.

road, roads
1 (noun) A road is a long piece of hard ground specially surfaced so that people and vehicles can travel along it easily.
2 (phrase) If you are on the road, you are travelling by road.

3 If someone is on the road to something, they are likely to achieve it, e.g. *He's well on the road to success.*

roadblock, roadblocks
(noun) A roadblock is a barrier erected across a road by the police or army to stop and check all vehicles.

roadworks
(noun) Roadworks are repairs being done on a road.

roadworthy
(adjective) A roadworthy car is in good condition.

roam, roams, roaming, roamed
(verb) If you roam around, you wander around without any particular purpose, e.g. *Young lads roamed around the streets at night.*

roan, roans
(noun) A roan is a black or brown horse with some white hairs mixed in.

roar, roars, roaring, roared
1 (verb) If something roars, it makes a very loud noise.
2 (noun) A roar is a very loud noise.
3 (verb) To roar with laughter or anger means to laugh or shout very noisily.
4 When a lion roars, it makes a loud, angry sound.

roaring
1 (adjective) A roaring fire is very hot with big flames.
2 (phrase) When someone is doing a roaring trade, they are selling a lot of goods.

roast, roast, roasting, roasted
1 (verb) When you roast meat, you cook it in a small amount of fat in an oven or over a fire.
2 If you roast nuts or coffee beans, you heat them to a high temperature, e.g. *We roasted chestnuts in the fire.*
3 (adjective) Roast meat has been roasted.
4 (noun) A roast is a piece of meat that has been roasted.

roasting, roastings (an informal word)
1 (noun) If you give someone a roasting, you tell them off or criticize them.
2 (adjective) Roasting means very hot indeed.

rob, robs, robbing, robbed
1 (verb) If someone robs you, they steal your possessions.
2 If you rob someone of something they need or deserve, you deprive them of it, e.g. *He's robbed me of every opportunity to express my opinion.*

robber, robbers
(noun) Robbers are people who steal money or property using force or threats, e.g. *bank robbers.*
robbery (noun).

robe, robes
(noun) A robe is a long, loose piece of clothing which covers the body, e.g. *priests in ceremonial robes.*

robin, robins
(noun) A robin is a small bird with a red breast.

robot, robots
(noun) A robot is a machine which is programmed to move and perform tasks automatically.
[from Czech *robota* meaning 'work']

robust
(adjective) very strong and healthy.
robustly (adverb), **robustness** (noun).
[from Latin *robur* meaning 'oak' or 'strength']

rock, rocks, rocking, rocked
1 (noun) Rock is the hard mineral substance that forms the surface of the earth.
2 A rock is a large piece of rock, e.g. *I sat down on a rock.*
3 (verb) When something rocks or when you rock it, it moves regularly backwards and forwards or from side to side, e.g. *She gently rocked the cradle.*
4 If something rocks people, it shocks and upsets them.
5 (noun) Rock or rock music is music with simple tunes and a very strong beat.
6 Rock is also a sweet shaped into long, hard sticks, sold in holiday resorts.
7 (phrase) If you have a drink **on the rocks**, you have it with lumps of ice.
8 If someone's marriage or relationship is **on the rocks**, it is unsuccessful and about to end.

rock and roll
(noun) Rock and roll is a style of music with a strong beat that was especially popular in the 1950s.

rock-bottom
(adjective) at the lowest price or level, e.g. *videos at rock-bottom prices.*

rocker, rockers
1 (noun) A rocker is a rocking chair.
2 (an informal phrase) If you say that someone is **off their rocker**, you mean they are mad.

rockery, rockeries
(noun) A rockery is a raised area of garden built of rocks and soil, where small plants are grown.

rocket, rockets, rocketing, rocketed
1 (noun) A rocket is a space vehicle, usually shaped like a long pointed tube.
2 A rocket is also an explosive missile, e.g. *Rebels fired anti-tank rockets for three nights.*
3 A rocket is also a firework that explodes when it is high in the air.
4 (verb) If prices rocket, they increase very quickly.
5 (noun; an informal use) If someone gives you a rocket, they tell you off angrily.

rocking chair, rocking chairs
(noun) A rocking chair is a chair on two curved pieces of wood that rocks backwards and forwards when you sit in it.

rocking horse, rocking horses
(noun) A rocking horse is a toy horse for children that can be made to rock backwards and forwards.

rock salmon
(noun) Rock salmon is a name used for various kinds of coarse fish when it is sold as fish and chips.

rocky
(adjective) covered with rocks.

rod, rods
(noun) A rod is a long, thin pole or bar, usually made of wood or metal, e.g. *a fishing rod.*

rodent, rodents
(noun) A rodent is a small mammal with sharp front teeth used for gnawing. Mice, rats, and squirrels are rodents.
[from Latin *rodere* meaning 'to gnaw']

rodeo, rodeos
(noun) A rodeo is a public entertainment in which cowboys show different skills.

roe
(noun) Roe is the eggs of a fish.

roe deer
(noun) A roe deer is a small, graceful deer with short antlers and a reddish-brown summer coat.

roentgen, roentgens (pronounced **ront**-gn); also spelled **röntgen**
(noun) A roentgen is a unit of dose of radiation. It is named after the German physicist W.K. Roentgen (1845-1923).

rogue, rogues
1 (noun) You can refer to a man who behaves dishonestly as a rogue.
2 (adjective) A rogue animal is a vicious animal that lives apart from its herd or pack.

roguish
(adjective) mischievous.
roguishly (adverb).

role, roles; also spelled **rôle**
1 (noun) Someone's role is their position and function in a situation or society.
2 An actor's role is the character that he or she plays, e.g. *She played the leading role.*

roll, rolls, rolling, rolled
1 (verb) When something rolls or when you roll it, it moves along a surface, turning over and over.
2 When vehicles roll along, they move, e.g. *The bus rolled to a stop.*
3 If you roll your eyes, you make them turn up or go from side to side.
4 If you roll something flexible into a cylinder or ball, you wrap it several times around itself, e.g. *She rolled up the poster.*
5 (noun) A roll of paper or cloth is a long piece of it that has been rolled into a tube, e.g. *a roll of velvet... a roll of film.*
6 A roll is also a small, rounded, individually baked piece of bread.
7 A roll is also an official list of people's names, e.g. *the electoral roll.*
8 A roll on a drum is a long, rumbling sound made on it.

roll in
(phrasal verb) If something rolls in, it arrives in large quantities, e.g. *Applications are rolling in.*

roll up

1 (phrasal verb) If you roll up something flexible, you wrap it several times around itself.
2 If you roll up your sleeves or trousers, you fold them over from the bottom to make them shorter.
3 (an informal use) If you roll up, you arrive.

roll-call, roll-calls

(noun) If you take a roll-call, you call a register of names to see who is present.

roller, rollers

1 (noun) A roller is a cylinder that turns round in a machine or piece of equipment.
2 Rollers are tubes which you can wind your hair around to make it curly.

roller-coaster, roller-coasters

(noun) A roller-coaster is a pleasure ride at a funfair, consisting of a small railway that goes up and down very steep slopes.

roller-skate, roller-skates, roller-skating, roller-skated

1 (noun) Roller-skates are shoes with four small wheels underneath.
2 (verb) If you roller-skate, you move over a flat surface wearing roller-skates.

rolling

1 (adjective) Rolling hills have gentle slopes.
2 (an informal phrase) If someone is **rolling in it**, they are very rich.

rolling pin, rolling pins

(noun) A rolling pin is a wooden cylinder used for rolling pastry dough to make it flat.

rolling stock

(noun) Rolling stock is the engines and carriages used on a railway.

roly-poly

(adjective) pleasantly fat and round.

ROM

(noun) In computing, ROM is a storage device that holds data permanently and cannot be altered by the programmer. ROM stands for 'read only memory'.

Roman alphabet

(noun) The Roman alphabet is the alphabet used for writing most European languages.

Roman Catholic, Roman Catholics

1 (adjective) relating or belonging to the branch of the Christian church that accepts the Pope in Rome as its leader.
2 (noun) A Roman Catholic is someone who belongs to the Roman Catholic church.
Roman Catholicism (noun).

romance, romances

1 (noun) A romance is a relationship between two people who are in love with each other.
2 Romance is the pleasure and excitement of doing something new and unusual, e.g. *the romance of living in a houseboat.*
3 A romance is also a novel about a love affair.
4 (adjective; a technical use) Romance languages are the ones which derive from Latin. French, Italian, and Spanish are Romance languages.

Romanian, Romanians (pronounced roe-**may**-nee-an); also spelled **Rumanian**

1 (adjective) belonging or relating to Romania.
2 (noun) A Romanian is someone who comes from Romania.
3 Romanian is the main language spoken in Romania.

Roman numeral, Roman numerals

(noun) Roman numerals are the letters used by the Romans in ancient times to write numbers. For example, V means five, VI means six, X means ten, and IX means nine.

romantic, romantics

1 (adjective and noun) A romantic person has ideas that are not realistic, for example about love or about ways of changing society, e.g. *a romantic idealist.*
2 (adjective) connected with sexual love, e.g. *a romantic attachment.*
3 Romantic music or literature is imaginative and more concerned with feelings than form.
romantically (adverb), **romanticism** (noun), **romanticize** (verb).

Romany, Romanies (pronounced **rom**-an-ee)

1 (noun) Romanies are gypsies.
2 Romany is the language spoken by gypsies.

romp, romps, romping, romped

(verb) When children romp around, they play and jump around in a happy, noisy way.
[from Old French *ramper* meaning 'to crawl' or 'to climb']

rompers

(noun) Rompers are a piece of babies' clothing consisting of trousers and a top joined together.

rondo, rondos

(noun) In classical music, a rondo is a piece in which the main tune is repeated several times.

röntgen another spelling of **roentgen**.

roof, roofs

1 (noun) The roof of a building or car is the covering on top of it.
2 The roof of your mouth or of a cave is the highest part.
3 (an informal phrase) If someone **hits the roof** or **goes through the roof**, they get very angry indeed.
roofed (adjective).

roofing

(noun) Roofing is material used for covering roofs.

roof rack, roof racks

(noun) A roof rack is a frame placed on top of a car and used for carrying objects.

rooftop, rooftops

(noun) The rooftop is the outside part of the roof of a building.

rook, rooks

1 (noun) A rook is a large black bird.
2 In chess, a rook is a piece which can move any number of squares in a straight but not diagonal line.

rookery, rookeries
(noun) A rookery is a place in a group of trees where many rooks have their nests.

room, rooms
1 (noun) A room is a separate section in a building, divided from other rooms by walls.
2 If there is plenty of room, there is a lot of space, e.g. *Have you room for a passenger?*
3 If there is room for a particular kind of activity, people are able to do it, e.g. *There ought to be room for more research.*

room service
(noun) In a hotel, room service is a service by which meals or drinks are brought to a guest's room.

roost, roosts, roosting, roosted
1 (noun) A roost is a place where birds rest or build their nests.
2 (verb) When birds roost, they settle somewhere for the night.
3 Someone who **rules the roost** has authority over the people in a particular place.

rooster, roosters
(noun) A rooster is an adult male chicken.

root, roots, rooting, rooted
1 (noun) The roots of a plant are the parts that grow under the ground.
2 The root of a hair is the part beneath the skin.
3 You can refer to the place or culture that you grew up in as your roots.
4 The root of something is its original cause or basis, e.g. *We traced the root of the problem.*
5 (verb) To root through things means to search through them, pushing them aside, e.g. *The pigs are trained to root for truffles.*
6 (phrase) If things **take root**, they start to grow or develop.

root out
(phrasal verb) If you root something or someone out, you find them and force them out, e.g. *She was determined to root out corruption.*

rooted
1 (adjective) developed from or strongly influenced by something, e.g. *His methods are rooted in years of experience.*
2 (phrase) If you are **rooted to the spot**, you are unable to move away.

rope, ropes, roping, roped
1 (noun) A rope is a thick, strong length of twisted cord.
2 (verb) If you rope one thing to another, you tie them together with rope.
3 (phrase) If someone **knows the ropes**, they are experienced and know how a job should be done.

rope in
(phrasal verb) If you rope someone in to do something, you persuade them to help.

ropey, ropier, ropiest
(adjective; an informal word) not of very good quality, e.g. *That was a ropey performance.*

rosary, rosaries
(noun) A rosary is a string of beads that Catholics use for counting prayers.

rose, roses
1 (noun) A rose is a large garden flower, often having many petals and a pleasant smell. Roses grow on bushes with thorny stems.
2 (noun and adjective) reddish-pink.
3 A rose is also a device with very small holes fitted onto the spout of a watering can, so that the water comes out in a fine spray.

rosé (pronounced **roe**-zay)
(adjective) Rosé wine is pale pink in colour.
[from French *rosé* meaning 'pink']

rosemary
(noun) Rosemary is a herb with thin, spiky, greyish-green leaves and a tangy smell, used for flavouring in cooking.

rosette, rosettes
(noun) A rosette is a large badge made of coloured ribbons gathered into a circle, which is worn as a prize in a competition or to support a sports team or political party.
[from Old French *rosette* meaning 'little rose']

rosewood
(noun) Rosewood is a hard, dark-coloured wood from a tropical tree, used to make furniture.

roster, rosters
(noun) A roster is a list of people who take it in turn to do a particular job, e.g. *You'd better check the duty roster; I think it's your turn next week.*

rostrum, rostrums or rostra
(noun) A rostrum is a raised platform on which someone stands to speak to an audience or conduct an orchestra.
[from Latin *rostrum* meaning 'ship's prow'; Roman orators' platforms were decorated with the prows of captured ships]

rosy, rosier, rosiest
1 (adjective) reddish-pink.
2 If a person looks rosy, they have pink cheeks and look healthy.
3 If a situation seems rosy, it is likely to be good or successful.

rot, rots, rotting, rotted
1 (verb) When food or wood rots, it decays and can no longer be used.
2 (noun) Rot is the condition that affects things when they rot, e.g. *Destroy bulbs affected by rot.*
3 (verb) When something rots another substance, it causes it to decay, e.g. *Bleach can rot fabric.*

Similar words: (sense 1) moulder, decay, decompose, perish, putrefy
(sense 2) mould, decay, canker

rota, rotas
(noun) A rota is a list of people who take turns to do a particular job.
[from Latin *rota* meaning 'wheel']

rotary
(adjective) moving in a circular direction, e.g. *a rotary dryer.*

rotate, rotates, rotating, rotated
1 (verb) When something rotates, it turns with a

circular movement, e.g. *Two drums rotate in opposite directions.*
2 When you rotate a group of things, you use each one of them in turn, beginning with the first again when you reach the end.
rotation (noun).

rote
1 (adjective) involving repetition or routine rather than careful thought, e.g. *rote learning.*
2 (phrase) If you learn something **by rote**, you memorize it without really understanding it.

rotor, rotors
1 (noun) The rotor is the part of a machine that turns.
2 The rotors or rotor blades of a helicopter are the four long flat pieces of metal on top of it which rotate and lift it off the ground.
[short for 'rotator']

rotten
1 (adjective) decayed and no longer of use, e.g. *The fabric was rotten and fell to pieces.*
2 (an informal use) of very poor quality, e.g. *What a rotten song!*
3 (an informal use) very unfair, unkind, or unpleasant, e.g. *You're being rotten to me!*
4 (an informal use) If you feel rotten, you feel ill.

rotund
(adjective; a formal word) round and fat, e.g. *a rotund, jovial little man.*

rouble, roubles (pronounced roo-bl)
(noun) The rouble is the main unit of currency in the Soviet Union.
[In Russian, *rubl* means literally 'silver bar']

rouge (pronounced rooj)
(noun) Rouge is a red powder or cream put on the cheeks to give more colour.
[from French *rouge* meaning 'red']

rough, rougher, roughest; roughs, roughing, roughed
1 (adjective) uneven and not smooth.
2 not using enough care or gentleness, e.g. *Don't be so rough or you'll break it.*
3 difficult or unpleasant, e.g. *Steve's having a rough time in his new job.*
4 approximately correct, e.g. *about sixty, at a rough guess.*
5 If the sea is rough, there are big waves because of bad weather.
6 A rough town or area has a lot of crime or violence.
7 (noun and adjective) A rough or a rough sketch is a drawing or description that shows the main features but does not show the details.
8 If you have to **rough it**, you have to live without the comforts and possessions you normally have.
9 On a golf course, the rough is the part of the course next to a fairway where the grass is untrimmed.
roughly (adverb), **roughness** (noun).

Similar words: (sense 5) squally, choppy, turbulent, stormy

roughage
(noun) Roughage is the fibre in food that makes digestion easier and helps your bowels work properly.

roughcast
(noun) Roughcast is a mixture of plaster and small stones used to cover outside walls.

roughen, roughens, roughening, roughened
(verb) To roughen the surface of something means to make it less smooth.

roulette (pronounced roo-let)
(noun) Roulette is a gambling game in which a ball is dropped onto a revolving wheel with numbered holes in it.
[from French *roue* meaning 'wheel']

round, rounder, roundest; rounds
1 (adjective) Something round is shaped like a ball or a circle.
2 complete or whole, e.g. *round numbers.*
3 (preposition and adverb) If something is round something else, it surrounds it.
4 The distance round something is the length of its circumference or boundary, e.g. *It measures fifteen feet round the trunk.*
5 You can refer to an area near a place as the area round it, e.g. *There's not a lot else round here.*
6 (preposition) If something moves round you, it keeps moving in a circle with you in the centre.
7 When someone goes to the other side of something, they have gone round it.
8 (adverb) If you turn or look round, you turn so you are facing in a different direction.
9 (adverb and preposition) If you go round a place, you go to different parts of it to look at it, e.g. *We went round the castle.*
10 (adverb) When someone comes round, they visit you, e.g. *The Smiths are coming round.*
11 (noun) A round is one of a series of events, e.g. *out in the first round.*
12 If you buy a round of drinks, you buy a drink for each member of the group you are with.
13 A round of ammunition is the bullets released when a gun is fired.
14 A round is also a song which several people sing together, each starting after the other.

Similar words: (sense 1) globular, spherical

round up
(verb) If you round up people or animals, you gather them together.

roundabout, roundabouts
1 A roundabout is a meeting point of several roads with a circle in the centre which vehicles have to travel around.
2 (noun) A roundabout is also a circular platform which rotates and which children can ride on in a park or playground.
3 A roundabout is also the same as a merry-go-round.

rounded
(adjective) curved in shape, without any points or sharp edges.

rounders
(noun) Rounders is a game played by two teams, in which a player scores points by hitting a ball and running around four sides of a square pitch.

roundly
(adverb) If you say something roundly, you say it very forcefully.

round-the-clock
(adjective) happening continuously.

roundup, roundups
1 (noun) A news roundup on television or radio is a summary of the news.
2 If there is a roundup of people or animals, they are gathered together.

roundworm, roundworms
(noun) A roundworm is a type of parasitic worm that lives in the intestines of dogs and cats.

rouse, rouses, rousing, roused
1 (verb) If someone rouses you, they wake you up.
2 If you rouse yourself to do something, you make yourself get up and do it.
3 If something rouses you, it makes you feel very emotional and excited.
rousing (adjective).

rout, routs, routing, routed (rhymes with out)
(verb) To rout your opponents means to defeat them completely and easily.

rout out
(phrasal verb) To rout someone out from somewhere means to search for them and force them to come out.

route, routes
(noun) A route is a way from one place to another.

routine, routines
1 (adjective) Routine activities are done regularly.
2 (noun) A routine is the usual way or order in which you do things.
3 A routine is also a boring repetition of tasks.
routinely (adverb).
[from Old French *route* meaning 'usual way']

roux (pronounced roo)
(noun) A roux is a brownish mixture of fat and flour that is cooked for a short time before adding liquid to make a sauce.
[from French *roux* meaning 'brownish']

rove, roves, roving, roved
(verb; a literary word) To rove around an area means to wander around it.

row, rows, rowing, rowed (rhymes with snow)
1 (noun) A row of people or things is several of them arranged in a line.
2 (verb) When you row a boat, you use oars to make it move through the water.
rowing (noun).

Similar words: (sense 1) column, line, rank

row, rows, rowing, rowed (rhymes with now)
1 (noun) A row is a serious argument.
2 (verb) If people are rowing, they are quarrelling noisily.

3 (noun) If someone is making a row, they are making too much noise.

rowan, rowans (pronounced roe-an)
(noun) A rowan is a tree with small leaves arranged in pairs, and red berries.

rowdy, rowdier, rowdiest
(adjective) rough and noisy.
rowdily (adverb).

Similar words: obstreperous, stroppy, unruly

rowing boat, rowing boats
(noun) A rowing boat is a small boat that you move through the water using oars.

rowlock, rowlocks (pronounced rol-luk)
(noun) Rowlocks are the U-shaped pieces of metal on the sides of a rowing boat that hold the oars in position.

royal
1 (adjective) belonging to or involving a queen, a king, or a member of their family.
2 Royal is used in the names of organizations appointed or supported by a member of a royal family.
3 (noun; an informal use) Members of the royal family are sometimes referred to as the royals.
royally (adverb).

Similar words: (sense 1) regal, imperial, sovereign

royal blue
(noun and adjective) deep, bright blue.

royalist, royalists
(noun) A royalist is someone who supports their country's royal family.

royal jelly
(noun) Royal jelly is a substance made by bees and fed to larvae that develop into queens.

royalty, royalties
1 (noun) The members of a royal family are sometimes referred to as royalty.
2 Royalties are payments made to authors and musicians from the sales of their books or records.

rpm an abbreviation for 'revolutions per minute'.

RSVP
RSVP is an abbreviation for the French expression 'répondez s'il vous plaît' which means 'please reply'. It is often put at the end of invitations.

rub, rubs, rubbing, rubbed
1 (verb) If you rub something, you move your hand or a cloth backwards and forwards over it.
2 If two things rub together they move backwards and forwards, pressing against each other.
3 (phrase) If you rub someone up the wrong way, you unintentionally annoy or offend them.

rub out
(phrasal verb) To rub out something written means to remove it by rubbing it with a rubber or a cloth.

rubber, rubbers
1 (noun) Rubber is a strong, elastic substance

made from the sap of a tropical tree or produced chemically.
2 (adjective) made of rubber.
3 (noun) A rubber is a small piece of rubber used to rub out pencil mistakes.
4 A rubber is also a series of games played between the same two people or teams.

rubber stamp, rubber stamps, rubber stamping, rubber stamped
1 (noun) A rubber stamp is a small device with a name or date on it, used to stamp a document.
2 (verb) When someone in authority rubber stamps something, they agree to it without properly thinking about it.

rubbery
(adjective) soft and elastic, like rubber.

rubbish
1 (noun) Rubbish is unwanted things or waste material.
2 You can refer to nonsense or something of very poor quality as rubbish.

Similar words: (sense 1) junk, trash, garbage, litter, refuse, waste
(sense 2) rot, nonsense, trash, piffle, twaddle

rubble
(noun) Bits of old brick and stone are referred to as rubble.

rubella (pronounced roo-**bell**-a)
(noun; a medical word) Rubella is German measles.
[from Latin *rubellus* meaning 'reddish']

rubidium
(noun) Rubidium is a silvery-white metallic element that ignites in air. It is used in photocells and in the manufacture of vacuum tubes. Its atomic number is 37 and its symbol is Rb.

rubric, rubrics (pronounced **roo**-brik)
(noun; a formal word) A rubric is a set of instructions at the beginning of an official document.

ruby, rubies
(noun) A ruby is a type of red jewel.
[from Latin *ruber* meaning 'red']

rucksack, rucksacks
(noun) A rucksack is a bag with shoulder straps for carrying things on your back.

ruction, ructions
(noun) If there are ructions about something, there is a row about it.

rudder, rudders
(noun) A rudder is a vertical piece of metal attached to the stern of a boat below water level or at the back of an aeroplane, and used for steering.

ruddy, ruddier, ruddiest
1 (adjective; a literary use) reddish, e.g. *ruddy cheeks*.
2 (adjective) Ruddy is also a swearword.

rude, ruder, rudest
1 (adjective) not polite.

2 embarrassing or offensive because of reference to sex or other bodily functions, e.g. *rude jokes*.
3 unexpected and unpleasant, e.g. *a rude awakening*.
4 (a literary use) very simply or roughly made, e.g. *a rude wooden bench*.
rudely (adverb), **rudeness** (noun).

Similar words: (sense 1) impolite, discourteous, uncivil, unmannerly

rudimentary
(adjective; a formal word) very basic and undeveloped, e.g. *I have only a rudimentary understanding of computer technology.*

rudiments
(plural noun) When you learn the rudiments of something, you learn only the simplest and most basic things about it.
[from Latin *rudimentum* meaning 'beginning']

rueful
(adjective) expressing sorrow or regret in a quiet and gentle way, e.g. *a rueful smile.*
ruefully (adverb).

ruff, ruffs
1 (noun) A ruff is a stiff circular collar with many pleats in it, worn especially in the 16th century.
2 A ruff is also a thick band of fur or feathers around the neck of a bird or animal.

ruffian, ruffians
(noun) A ruffian is a rough or violent person.

ruffle, ruffles, ruffling, ruffled
1 (verb) If you ruffle someone's hair, you move your hand quickly backwards and forwards over their head.
2 If something ruffles you, it makes you annoyed or upset.
3 (noun) Ruffles are small folds made in a piece of material for decoration.

rug, rugs
1 (noun) A rug is a small, thick carpet.
2 A rug is also a blanket which you can use to cover your knees or for sitting on outdoors.

rugby
(noun) Rugby is a game played by two teams, who try to kick and throw an oval ball to their opponents' end of the pitch. Rugby League is played by professionals with 13 players in each side. Rugby Union is for amateurs with 15 players in each side. The game is named after the public school at Rugby where it was first played.

rugged
1 (adjective) rocky, wild, and unsheltered, e.g. *the rugged Cornish coastline.*
2 having strong features, e.g. *a rugged face.*
3 honest, determined, and tough.

rugger
(noun) Rugger is the same as rugby.

ruin, ruins, ruining, ruined
1 (verb) If you ruin something, you destroy or spoil it completely.
2 (noun) Ruin is the state of being destroyed or completely spoilt.

3 A ruin or the ruins of something refers to the parts that are left after it has been severely damaged, e.g. *the ruins of a Norman castle.*
4 (verb) If someone is ruined, they have lost all their money.
5 (phrase) If something is **in ruins**, it is completely spoilt.
ruined (adjective).

ruination
(noun; a formal word) Ruination is the act or process of ruining something.

ruinous
(adjective) costing far more than you can afford, e.g. *the ruinous expense of the wedding.*
ruinously (adverb).

rule, rules, ruling, ruled
1 (noun) Rules are statements which tell you what you are allowed to do.
2 (verb) To rule a country or group of people means to have power over it and be in charge of its affairs.
3 (a formal use) When someone in authority rules on a particular matter, they give an official decision about it.
4 To rule lines means to draw them with a ruler.
5 (phrase) If something is **the rule**, it is the normal state of affairs, e.g. *One room dwellings are the rule in these areas.*
6 As a rule, means usually or generally, e.g. *We have lunch, as a rule, around one o'clock.*
ruling (adjective).

Similar words: (sense 1) law, regulation, principle, canon, code, ordinance, tenet

rule out
1 (phrasal verb) If you rule out an idea or course of action, you reject it.
2 If one thing rules out another, it prevents it from happening or being possible, e.g. *The music was so loud it completely ruled out conversation.*

ruler, rulers
1 (noun) A ruler is a person who rules a country.
2 A ruler is also a long, flat piece of wood or plastic with straight edges marked in centimetres or inches, used for measuring or drawing straight lines.

rum, rummer, rummest
1 (noun) Rum is a strong alcoholic drink made from sugar cane juice.
2 (adjective; an informal use) rather strange.

Rumanian (pronounced roo-**may**-nee-an) another spelling of **Romanian**.

rumble, rumbles, rumbling, rumbled
1 (verb) If something rumbles, it makes a continuous low noise, e.g. *The traffic rumbled past constantly.*
2 (noun) A rumble is a continuous low noise, e.g. *a rumble of thunder.*
3 (verb; an informal use) If you rumble someone, you find out about something that they have been concealing.

ruminant, ruminants (pronounced **roo**-min-ant)
(noun) A ruminant is an animal such as a cow

that returns partly digested food from its stomach to its mouth to be chewed again.
[from Latin *ruminare* meaning 'to chew the cud']

ruminate, ruminates, ruminating, ruminated
(verb; a formal word) If you ruminate about something, you think about it carefully.

rummage, rummages, rummaging, rummaged
(verb) If you rummage somewhere, you search for something, moving things about carelessly.

rummy
(noun) Rummy is a card game.

rumour, rumours
1 (noun) A rumour is a story that people are talking about, which may or may not be true.
2 (verb) If something is rumoured, people are suggesting that it is has happened.
[from Latin *rumor* meaning 'common talk']

Similar words: (sense 1) hearsay, gossip, report

rump, rumps
1 (noun) An animal's rump is its rear end.
2 Rump or rump steak is meat cut from the rear end of a cow.
3 The rump of a group is the members who remain after the rest have left.

rumple, rumples, rumpling, rumpled
(verb) If you rumple something, you make it untidy or creased.
rumpled (adjective).

rumpus
(noun) A rumpus is a lot of noise or argument.

run, runs, running, ran
1 (verb) When you run, you move quickly, leaving the ground during each stride.
2 If you run away from a place, you leave it suddenly and secretly.
3 (noun) If you go for a run, you run for pleasure or exercise.
4 (verb) If you say that a road or river runs in a particular direction, you are describing its course.
5 If you run your hand or an object over something, you move it over it.
6 If someone runs in an election, they stand as a candidate, e.g. *He ran for President in 1988.*
7 If you run a business or an activity, you are in charge of it.
8 If you run an experiment, a computer program, or tape, you start it and let it continue, e.g. *We'll have to run the data through again.*
9 To run a car means to have it and use it.
10 If you run someone somewhere in a car, you drive them there, e.g. *Could you run Maggie home?*
11 (noun) A run is a journey somewhere, e.g. *It's a fair run up to Glasgow.*
12 (verb) If you run water, you turn on a tap to make it flow, e.g. *I'm going to run my bath.*
13 If your nose is running, it is producing a lot of mucus.
14 If the dye in something runs, the colour comes out when it is washed.
15 If a feeling runs through your body, it affects you quickly and strongly.

16 If a newspaper runs a particular story, it publishes it.
17 If an amount is running at a particular level, it is at that level, e.g. *Unemployment is currently running at 48%.*
18 If someone or something is running late, they have taken more time than was planned.
19 If a play, event, or contract runs for a particular time, it lasts for that time.
20 (noun) If a play or show has a run of a particular length of time, it is on for that time.
21 A run of success or failure is a series of successes or failures.
22 In cricket or baseball, a player scores one run by running between marked places on the pitch after hitting the ball.

Similar words: (sense 1) dash, sprint, bolt (sense 2) flee, fly, abscond

run down
1 (phrasal verb) To run someone down means to criticize them strongly.
2 To run down an organization means to reduce its size and activity.

run into
(phrasal verb) To run into someone or something means to meet or find them suddenly and unexpectedly.

run off
(phrasal verb) To run off copies of a document means to make the copies on a printer or photocopier.

run out
(phrasal verb) If you run out of something, you have no more left.

run over
(phrasal verb) If someone is run over, they are hit by a moving vehicle.

run through
(phrasal verb) To run through something means to rehearse or practise it.

runaway, runaways
(noun) A runaway is a person who has escaped from a place or left it secretly and hurriedly.

Similar words: fugitive, escapee

rundown
1 (adjective) tired and not well.
2 neglected and in poor condition.
3 (noun; an informal use) If you give someone the rundown on a situation, you tell them the basic, important facts about it.

rung, rungs
(noun) The rungs on a ladder are the wooden or metal bars that form the steps.

runner, runners
1 (noun) A runner is a person who runs, especially as a sport.
2 A runner is also a person who takes messages or runs errands.
3 A runner on a plant such as a strawberry is a long shoot from which a new plant develops.

4 The runners on drawers, sledges, and ice skates are the thin strips on which they move.

runner bean, runner beans
(noun) Runner beans are long green pods eaten as a vegetable, which grow on a climbing plant with red flowers.

runner-up, runners-up
(noun) A runner-up is a person or team that comes second in a race or competition.

running
1 (adjective) continuing without stopping over a period of time, e.g. *a running commentary on the match.*
2 Running water is flowing rather than standing still.
3 (phrase) If someone is **in the running** for something, they have a good chance of getting it, e.g. *He's in the running for a gold medal.*

runny, runnier, runniest
1 (adjective) more liquid than usual, e.g. *a runny mixture of flour and milk.*
2 If someone's nose or eyes are runny, liquid is coming out of them.

runt, runts
(noun) The runt of a litter of animals is the smallest and weakest.

runway, runways
(noun) A runway is a long strip of ground used by aeroplanes for taking off or landing.

rupee, rupees (pronounced roo-pee)
(noun) The rupee is the main unit of currency in India, Pakistan, and some other countries.

rupture, ruptures, rupturing, ruptured
1 (noun) A rupture is a severe injury in which part of your body tears or bursts open, e.g. *a ruptured appendix.*
2 (verb) To rupture part of the body means to cause it to tear or burst.
[from Latin *ruptura* meaning 'a breaking']

rural
(adjective) relating to or involving the countryside.
[from Latin *ruralis*, from *rus* meaning 'the country']

Similar words: rustic, pastoral

ruse, ruses
(noun; a formal word) A ruse is an action which is intended to deceive someone.
[from Old French *ruse* meaning 'trick']

rush, rushes, rushing, rushed
1 (verb) To rush means to move fast or do something quickly.
2 If you rush someone into doing something, you make them do it without allowing them enough time to think.
3 (noun) If you are in a rush, you are busy and do not have enough time to do things.
4 If there is a rush for something, there is a sudden increase in demand for it, e.g. *There has been a mad rush for tickets today.*

5 Rushes are plants with long, thin stems that grow near water.
rushed (adjective).

rush hour, rush hours
(noun) The rush hour is one of the busy parts of the day when most people are travelling to or from work.

rusk, rusks
(noun) A rusk is a hard, dry biscuit given to babies.

russet
(noun and adjective) reddish-brown.

Russian, Russians
1 (adjective) belonging or relating to the Soviet Union.
2 (noun) A Russian is someone who comes from the Soviet Union.
3 Russian is the main language spoken in the Soviet Union.

rust, rusts, rusting, rusted
1 (noun) Rust is a reddish-brown flaky oxide coating that forms on iron or steel by the action of oxygen with moisture.
2 (verb) When a metal object rusts, it becomes covered in rust.
3 (noun) Rust is also a plant disease caused by a fungus that produces a reddish-brown discoloration on stems and leaves.
4 (noun and adjective) reddish-brown.

rustic
(adjective) simple in a way considered to be typical of the countryside, e.g. *a rustic stone wall.*
rustically (adverb).
[from Latin *rus* meaning 'the country']

rustle, rustles, rustling, rustled
(verb) When something rustles, it makes soft sounds as it moves.
rustling (adjective and noun).

rusty, rustier, rustiest
1 (adjective) affected by rust, e.g. *a rusty old bicycle.*
2 If someone's knowledge is rusty, it is not as good as it used to be because they have not used it for a long time, e.g. *My French is a bit rusty nowadays.*

rut, ruts
1 (noun) A rut is a deep, narrow groove in the ground made by the wheels of a vehicle.
2 (phrase) If someone is **in a rut**, they have become fixed in their way of doing things.

ruthless
(adjective) very harsh or cruel, e.g. *ruthless military commanders.*
ruthlessness (noun), **ruthlessly** (adverb).

rye
(noun) Rye is a type of grass that produces light brown grain. Bread and whisky are made from rye.

S

Sabbath
(noun) The sabbath is the day of the week when members of some religious groups, especially Jews and Christians, do not work.
[from Hebrew *shabbath* meaning 'to rest']

sabbatical, sabbaticals
(noun) A sabbatical is a period of time during which a teacher or lecturer leaves their work and spends time studying or travelling.

sable, sables
(noun) Sable is a very expensive fur used for making coats and hats; also the wild animal from which this fur is obtained.

sabotage, sabotages, sabotaging, sabotaged
(pronounced **sab**-ot-ahj)
1 (noun) Sabotage is the deliberate damaging of things such as machinery and railway lines.
2 (verb) If something is sabotaged, it is deliberately damaged.
saboteur (noun).
[from French *saboter* meaning 'to spoil through clumsiness']

sabre, sabres
1 (noun) A sabre is a heavy curved sword.
2 A sabre is also a light sword used in fencing.

sac, sacs
(noun) A sac is a small part of an animal's body, shaped like a little bag, containing air or liquid.

saccharine or saccharin (pronounced sak-er-rine)
(noun) Saccharine is a chemical used instead of sugar to sweeten things.
[from Greek *sakkharon* meaning 'sugar']

sachet, sachets (pronounced sash-ay)
(noun) A sachet is a small closed plastic or paper packet, containing a small amount of something such as sugar or shampoo.
[from Old French *sachet* meaning 'little bag']

sack, sacks, sacking, sacked
1 (noun) A sack is a large bag made of rough material used for carrying or storing goods.
2 (verb; an informal use) If someone is sacked, they are dismissed from their job.
3 (an informal phrase) If someone **gets the sack**, they are sacked by their employer.
4 (verb; an old-fashioned use) If soldiers sack a place, they destroy it and take away all the valuable things in it.

Similar words: (sense 2) fire, discharge, dismiss

sackcloth
(noun) Sackcloth is a rough material used for making sacks.

sacrament, sacraments
(noun) A sacrament is an important Christian ceremony such as communion, baptism, or marriage.

sacred (pronounced say-krid)
(adjective) holy, or connected with religion or religious ceremonies, e.g. *sacred music*.
sacredness (noun).
[from Latin *sacer* meaning 'holy']

sacrifice, sacrifices, sacrificing, sacrificed
(pronounced **sak**-riff-ice)
1 (verb) If you sacrifice something valuable or important, you give it up.
2 To sacrifice an animal means to kill it as an offering to a god or gods.
3 (noun) A sacrifice is the killing of an animal as an offering to a god or gods.
sacrificial (adjective).

Similar words: (sense 1) forego, forfeit, give up

sacrilege (pronounced sak-ril-ij)
(noun) Sacrilege is behaviour that shows great disrespect for something holy.
sacrilegious (adjective), **sacrilegiously** (adverb).

sacristy, sacristies
(noun) A sacristy is a room in a church where sacred objects are kept.

sacrosanct (pronounced sak-roe-sangkt)
(adjective) regarded as too important to be criticized or changed, e.g. *These ideas were considered sacrosanct.*

sad, sadder, saddest
1 (adjective) If you are sad, you feel unhappy.
2 Something sad makes you feel unhappy, e.g. *sad news*.
sadly (adverb), **sadness** (noun).

Similar words: (sense 1) glum, unhappy, melancholy, down in the dumps

sadden, saddens, saddening, saddened
(verb) If something saddens you, it makes you feel sad.

saddle, saddles, saddling, saddled
1 (noun) A saddle is a leather seat that you sit on when you are riding a horse.
2 The saddle on a bicycle is the seat.
3 (verb) If you saddle a horse, you put a saddle on it.
4 To saddle someone with a problem means to give it to them to deal with.

saddlebag, saddlebags
(noun) A saddlebag is a bag fastened to the saddle of a horse, bicycle, or motorcycle.

saddler, saddlers
(noun) A saddler is someone who makes and sells saddles and other equipment for horses.

saddlery
(noun) Saddlery is equipment for horses.

sadism (pronounced say-diz-m)
(noun) Sadism is the obtaining of pleasure,

especially sexual pleasure, from making people suffer pain or humiliation.
sadist (noun), **sadistic** (adjective),
sadistically (adverb).
[from the Marquis de Sade (1740-1814), who got his pleasure in this way]

s.a.e. an abbreviation for 'stamped addressed envelope', an envelope with a stamp and your own address on it.

safari, safaris
(noun) A safari is an expedition for hunting or observing wild animals, especially in East Africa.
[from Swahili *safari* meaning 'journey']

safari park, safari parks
(noun) A safari park is a large park where wild animals such as lions and elephants roam freely and do not live in cages.

safe, safer, safest; safes
1 (adjective) Something that is safe does not cause harm or danger.
2 If you are safe, you are not in any danger.
3 If it is safe to say something, you can say it with very little risk of being wrong.
4 (noun) A safe is a strong metal box with special locks, in which you can keep valuable things.
safely (adverb), **safety** (noun).
[from Latin *salvus* meaning 'uninjured' or 'healthy']

Similar words: (sense 2) unharmed, unhurt, unscathed, secure, safe and sound

safeguard, safeguards, safeguarding, safeguarded
1 (verb) To safeguard something means to protect it.
2 (noun) A safeguard is a rule or law designed to protect something or someone.

safekeeping
(noun) If something is given to you for safekeeping, it is given to you to look after.

safety belt, safety belts
(noun) A safety belt is a strap fixed to an aeroplane or car seat which you fasten round you when you are travelling.

safety catch, safety catches
(noun) The safety catch on a gun is a catch that stops the gun from being fired accidentally.

safety pin, safety pins
(noun) A safety pin is a pin that has the point protected by a cover.

saffron
1 (noun) Saffron is a yellowish-orange spice used in cooking to colour and flavour food.
2 (adjective and noun) yellowish-orange.

sag, sags, sagging, sagged
(verb) When something sags, it hangs down loosely or sinks downwards in the middle.
sagging (adjective).

saga, sagas (pronounced **sah**-ga)
(noun) A saga is a very long story, usually with many different adventures, e.g. *the Norse sagas.*
[from Old Norse *saga* meaning 'story']

sagacious (pronounced sag-**gay**-shuss)
(adjective; a formal word) wise or sensible, e.g. *sagacious remarks.*
sagaciously (adverb), **sagacity** (noun).
[from Latin *sagire* meaning 'to be astute']

sage, sages
1 (noun; a literary use) A sage is a very wise person.
2 Sage is a herb used for flavouring in cooking.
sagely (adverb).
[sense 1 is from Latin *sapere* meaning 'to be wise'; sense 2 is from Latin *salvus* meaning 'healthy', because of the supposed medicinal properties of the plant]

Sagittarius (pronounced saj-it-**tair**-ee-uss)
(noun) Sagittarius is the ninth sign of the zodiac, represented by a creature half-horse, half-man holding a bow and arrow. People born between November 22nd and December 21st are born under this sign.
[from Latin *sagittarius* meaning 'archer']

sago (pronounced **say**-go)
(noun) Sago is a starchy substance obtained from palm trees. It is used for making puddings and for thickening sauces.

sail, sails, sailing, sailed
1 (noun) Sails are large pieces of material attached to a ship's mast. The wind blows against the sail and moves the ship.
2 (verb) When a ship sails, it moves across water.
3 If you sail somewhere, you go there by ship.
4 (noun) The sails on a windmill are the long arms that move round in the wind.

sailboard, sailboards
(noun) A sailboard is a board like a surfboard with a mast and sail attached, used for windsurfing.

sailor, sailors
(noun) A sailor is a member of a ship's crew.

saint, saints
(noun) Saints are people honoured after their death by the Church because of their holiness.
[from Latin *sanctus* meaning 'holy']

saintly
(adjective) behaving in a very good or holy way.

sake, sakes
1 (phrase) You use **for the sake of** to say why you are doing something, e.g. *I usually check from time to time, just for safety's sake.*
2 If you do something **for someone's sake**, you do it to help or please them.

salacious (pronounced sal-**lay**-shuss)
(adjective) concerned with sex in an unnecessarily detailed way, e.g. *a salacious novel.*
salaciously (adverb), **salaciousness** (noun).

salad, salads
1 (noun) A salad is a mixture of raw vegetables served as a meal or as a side dish.
2 A fruit salad is a mixture of pieces of different fruits served in a juice as a dessert.

[from Old Provençal *salar* meaning 'to season with salt']

salamander, salamanders
(noun) A salamander is an amphibian that looks rather like a lizard.

salami (pronounced sal-**lah**-mee)
(noun) Salami is a kind of spicy sausage.

salary, salaries
(noun) A salary is a regular monthly payment to an employee.
salaried (adjective).
[from Latin *salarium* meaning 'money given to soldiers to buy salt']

sale, sales
1 (noun) The sale of goods is the selling of them.
2 (plural noun) The sales of a product are the numbers that are sold.
3 (noun) A sale is an occasion when a shop sells things at reduced prices.
4 A sale is also an auction.

saleable
(adjective) easy to sell or suitable for being sold.

salesman, salesmen
(noun) A salesman is someone who sells products for a company.

salient (pronounced **say**-lee-ent)
(adjective; a formal word) The salient points or facts are the important ones.

saline (pronounced **say**-line)
(adjective) containing salt, e.g. *a saline solution*.
[from Latin *sal* meaning 'salt']

saliva (pronounced sal-**live**-a)
(noun) Saliva is the watery liquid in your mouth that helps you chew and digest food.

sallow
(adjective) Sallow skin is pale and unhealthy.

sally, sallies
(noun; a literary word) Sallies are witty remarks.

salmon (pronounced **sam**-on)
(noun) A salmon is a large edible silver-coloured fish with pink flesh. It is considered to be a luxury.

salmonella (pronounced sal-mon-**nell**-a)
(noun) Salmonella is any of several bacteria which cause severe food poisoning.

salon, salons
(noun) A salon is a place where hairdressers or beauticians work.
[from French *salon* meaning 'reception room']

saloon, saloons
1 (noun) A saloon is a car with a fixed roof and a separate boot.
2 In America, a saloon is a building or bar where alcoholic drinks are sold and drunk.
3 On a passenger ship, a saloon is a large public room.
[sense 2 is from French *salon* meaning 'reception room']

saloon bar, saloon bars
(noun) The saloon bar in a pub or hotel is a comfortable bar where the drinks are slightly more expensive.

salt, salts
1 (noun) Salt is a white substance found naturally in sea water. It is used to flavour and preserve food.
2 A salt is a chemical compound formed from an acid base.
3 (phrase) If you **take something with a pinch of salt**, you do not believe it completely.
[from Latin *sal* meaning 'salt']

salt cellar, salt cellars
(noun) A salt cellar is a small container for salt.

saltpetre (pronounced salt-**peet**-er)
(noun) Saltpetre is potassium nitrate. It is used in making gunpowder, matches, and fertilizers, and in preserving meat.

salty, saltier, saltiest
(adjective) containing salt or tasting of salt.

salubrious (pronounced sal-**loo**-bree-uss)
(adjective; a formal word) good for your health.
[from Latin *salus* meaning 'health']

salutary (pronounced **sal**-yoo-tree)
(adjective; a formal word) A salutary experience is unpleasant but is actually good for you.
[from Latin *salutaris* meaning 'beneficial']

salutation, salutations
(noun; a formal word) A salutation is a greeting.

salute, salutes, saluting, saluted
1 (noun) A salute is a formal sign of respect. In the armed forces, soldiers give a salute by raising their right hand to their forehead.
2 (verb) If you salute someone, you give them a salute.
[from Latin *salutare* meaning 'to greet']

salvage, salvages, salvaging, salvaged
1 (verb) If you salvage things, you save them, for example from a wrecked ship or a destroyed building.
2 (noun) You refer to things saved from a wrecked ship or destroyed building as salvage.
[from Latin *salvare* meaning 'to save']

salvation
1 (noun) When someone's salvation takes place, they are saved from harm or evil.
2 To be someone's salvation means to save them from harm or evil.
[from Latin *salvare* meaning 'to save']

Similar words: (sense 1) deliverance, redemption

Salvation Army
(noun) The Salvation Army is a Christian organization whose members wear uniforms and have military ranks.

salve, salves, salving, salved
1 (verb) If you salve your conscience, you do something that makes you feel less guilty.
2 (noun) Salve is an ointment that soothes and heals sore skin, e.g. *lip salve*.

salver, salvers
(noun) A salver is a tray, usually made of silver.

salvo, salvos or **salvoes**
(noun) A salvo is the firing of several guns or missiles at the same time.

Samaritan, Samaritans

1 (noun) A Samaritan is someone who helps a person in difficulty.
2 The Samaritans are a voluntary organization that listens and gives sympathy to people in distress over the telephone.
[from the story of the Good Samaritan in the Bible]

samba, sambas

(noun) The samba is a lively Brazilian dance.
[a Portuguese word]

same

1 (adjective and pronoun) If two things are the same, they are identical.
2 Same means just one thing and not two different ones, e.g. *We come from the same place.*
3 (phrase) **All the same** means in spite of what has just been said, e.g. *He wasn't listening, but she went on all the same.*

samizdat (pronounced sam-iz-dat)

(noun) Samizdat is the secret printing in the USSR of banned books and magazines.
[from Russian *samizdat* meaning 'self-published']

samosa, samosas

(noun) A samosa is a small pastry case filled with a spicy meat or vegetable mixture, eaten as a snack.

samovar, samovars

(noun) A samovar is a decorated metal urn used in the USSR for making tea.

sampan, sampans

(noun) A sampan is a small boat with oars used in China.
[from Chinese *san* + *pan* meaning 'three board']

sample, samples, sampling, sampled

1 (noun) A sample of something is a small amount of it that you can try or test, e.g. *free samples of shampoo.*
2 A sample of people is a small number of them used in a test or survey.
3 (verb) If you sample something, you try it, e.g. *Next he sampled the roast beef.*
[from Latin *exemplum* meaning 'example']

sampler, samplers

(noun) A sampler is a piece of cloth embroidered to show someone's skill at needlework.

samurai (pronounced sam-oor-eye)

(noun) A samurai was a member of an ancient Japanese warrior class.
[a Japanese word]

sanatorium, sanatoriums or sanatoria

(noun) A sanatorium is an institution that provides medical treatment and rest for people who have been very ill.
[from Latin *sanare* meaning 'to heal']

sanctify, sanctifies, sanctifying, sanctified

(verb) To sanctify something means to make it holy.
[from Latin *sanctus* meaning 'holy' and *facere* meaning 'to make']

sanctimonious (pronounced sank-tim-moan-ee-uss)

(adjective) pretending to be very religious and virtuous.
sanctimoniously (adverb).

sanction, sanctions, sanctioning, sanctioned

1 (verb) To sanction something means to officially approve of it or allow it.
2 (noun) Sanction is official approval of something.
3 A sanction is a severe punishment or penalty intended to make people obey the law. Sanctions are sometimes taken by countries against a country that has broken international law.
[from Latin *sancire* meaning 'to decree']

sanctity

(noun) If you talk about the sanctity of something, you are saying that it should be respected because it is very important, e.g. *the sanctity of human life.*

sanctuary, sanctuaries

1 (noun) A sanctuary is a place where you are safe from harm or danger.
2 A sanctuary is also a place where wildlife is protected, e.g. *a bird sanctuary.*
[from Latin *sanctus* meaning 'holy']

sand, sands, sanding, sanded

1 (noun) Sand consists of tiny pieces of stone. Deserts and beaches are made of sand.
2 (verb) If you sand something, you rub sandpaper over it to make it smooth.

sandal, sandals

(noun) Sandals are light shoes with straps. They are worn in warm weather.

sandalwood

(noun) Sandalwood is the sweet-smelling wood of an Asian tree; also a perfumed oil extracted from this wood.

sandbag, sandbags

(noun) A sandbag is a sack filled with sand and used as a protection against floods or explosives.

sandbank, sandbanks

(noun) A sandbank is a bank of sand in the sea or a river.

sandpaper

(noun) Sandpaper is strong paper with a coating of sand on it. It is used for rubbing wooden or metal surfaces to make them smooth.

sandstone

(noun) Sandstone is a type of rock formed from compacted sand. It is often used for building.

sandwich, sandwiches, sandwiching, sandwiched

1 (noun) A sandwich is two slices of bread with a filling between them.
2 (verb) If one thing is sandwiched between two others, it is in a narrow space between them, e.g. *shacks sandwiched between flats.*
[sense 1 is named after the 4th Earl of Sandwich (1718-92), for whom they were invented so that he could eat and gamble at the same time]

sandwich board, sandwich boards

(noun) A sandwich board is a pair of boards hung over a person's shoulders to display advertisements.

sandwich course, sandwich courses
(noun) A sandwich course is a course of study between periods of work in industry or business.

sandy, sandier, sandiest
1 (adjective) A sandy area is covered with sand.
2 Sandy hair is light orange-brown.

sane, saner, sanest
1 (adjective) If someone is sane, they have a normal and healthy mind.
2 A sane action is sensible and reasonable, e.g. *It was the only sane thing to do.*
[from Latin *sanus* meaning 'healthy']

sang-froid (pronounced sahng-**frwah**)
(noun; a formal word) Sang-froid is calmness and coolness in a difficult situation, e.g. *He faced the attack with amazing sang-froid.*
[a French expression meaning literally 'cold blood']

sanguinary (pronounced **sang**-gwin-ar-ee)
(adjective; a formal word) A sanguinary event involves a lot of violence and bloodshed.
[from Latin *sanguis* meaning 'blood']

sanguine (pronounced **sang**-gwin)
(adjective; a formal word) cheerful and confident.

sanitary
(adjective) Sanitary means concerned with keeping things clean and hygienic, e.g. *Sanitary conditions in the hospitals had deteriorated.*
[from Latin *sanitas* meaning 'health']

sanitary towel, sanitary towels
(noun) Sanitary towels are pads of thick, soft material which women wear during their periods.

sanitation
(noun) Sanitation is the process of keeping places clean and hygienic, especially by providing a sewage system and clean water supply.

sanity
(noun) Your sanity is your ability to think and act normally and reasonably.

Sanskrit
(noun) Sanskrit is an ancient language of India, now used only for religious purposes.

sap, saps, sapping, sapped
1 (verb) If something saps your strength or confidence, it gradually weakens and destroys it.
2 (noun) Sap is the watery liquid in plants.

sapling, saplings
(noun) A sapling is a young tree.

sapphire, sapphires
(noun) A sapphire is a blue precious stone.

sarcastic
(adjective) saying or doing the opposite of what you really mean in order to mock or insult someone, e.g. *a sarcastic smile.*
sarcasm (noun), **sarcastically** (adverb).
[from Greek *sarkazein* meaning 'to tear the flesh']

sarcophagus, sarcophagi or **sarcophaguses**
(pronounced sar-**kof**-fag-uss)
(noun) A sarcophagus is a stone coffin used in ancient times.

sardine, sardines
(noun) A sardine is a small edible sea fish.

sardonic
(adjective) mocking or scornful, e.g. *a sardonic chuckle.*
sardonically (adverb).

sari, saris (pronounced **sah**-ree)
(noun) A sari is a piece of clothing worn especially by Indian women. It consists of a long piece of material folded around the body.
[a Hindi word]

sarong, sarongs (pronounced sar-**rong**)
(noun) A sarong is a piece of clothing worn by Malaysian men and women. It consists of a long piece of material attached round the waist or under the armpits.
[a Malay word]

sartorial
(adjective; a formal word) relating to clothes, e.g. *People's sartorial habits have changed.*
[from Latin *sartor* meaning 'tailor']

sash, sashes
(noun) A sash is a long piece of cloth worn round the waist or over one shoulder.
[from Arabic *shash* meaning 'muslin']

sash window, sash windows
(noun) A sash window is a window consisting of two frames, one above the other. You open the window by sliding one frame over the other.

Satan
(noun) Satan is the Devil.
[from Hebrew *satan* meaning 'to plot against']

satanic (pronounced sa-**tan**-ik)
(adjective) caused by or influenced by Satan, e.g. *a satanic cult.*

satchel, satchels
(noun) A satchel is a bag with a long strap used by children for carrying school books.

sated
(adjective; a formal word) If you are sated with something, you have had as much as you can enjoy at one time.

satellite, satellites
1 (noun) A satellite is an object sent into orbit round the earth to collect information or as part of a communications system.
2 A satellite is also a natural object in space that moves round a planet or star.
3 You can refer to a country as a satellite when it has no real power of its own, but is dependent on a larger, more powerful country.

satiate, satiates, satiating, satiated (pronounced **say**-she-ate)
(verb; a formal word) If a pleasure satiates you, you have so much of it that you get tired of it.
[from Latin *satiare* meaning 'to satisfy']

satin, satins
(noun) Satin is a kind of smooth, shiny silk.

satire, satires
1 (noun) Satire is the use of mocking or ironical

humour, especially in literature, to show how foolish or wicked some people are.
2 A satire is a play, novel, or poem containing satire.
satirical (adjective), **satirically** (adverb).

satirist, satirists (pronounced **sat**-tir-ist)
(noun) A satirist is a writer who uses satire.

satirize, satirizes, satirizing, satirized
(pronounced **sat**-tir-rize); also spelled **satirise**
(verb) If you satirize people, you criticize them by using satire in a play, novel, or poem.

satisfaction
1 (noun) Satisfaction is the feeling of pleasure you get when you do something you wanted or needed to do.
2 (phrase) If you do something **to someone's satisfaction**, they are happy with the way you have done it.
[from Latin *satis* meaning 'enough' and *facere* meaning 'to make']

satisfactory
(adjective) acceptable or adequate, e.g. *He found these answers satisfactory.*
satisfactorily (adverb).

satisfy, satisfies, satisfying, satisfied
1 (verb) To satisfy someone means to give them enough of something to make them pleased or contented.
2 To satisfy someone that something is the case means to convince them of it.
3 To satisfy the requirements for something means to fulfil them.
satisfied (adjective).

Similar words: (sense 1) indulge, gratify

satisfying
(adjective) Something that is satisfying gives you a feeling of pleasure and fulfilment.

Similar words: fulfilling, rewarding, enriching

satsuma, satsumas (pronounced sat-**soo**-ma)
(noun) A satsuma is a fruit like a small orange.

saturated
1 (adjective) very wet.
2 If a place is saturated with things, it is completely full of them.
3 In chemistry, if a liquid is saturated with a substance, the maximum amount possible of the substance has been dissolved in the liquid.
saturation (noun).

saturation point
(noun) In chemistry, the saturation point of a substance is the point at which it can absorb no more of another substance.

Saturday, Saturdays
(noun) Saturday is the day between Friday and Sunday.
[from Latin *Saturni dies* meaning 'day of Saturn']

Saturn
(noun) Saturn is the planet in the solar system which is sixth from the sun.
[named after the Roman god of agriculture and plants]

saturnine (pronounced **sat**-tur-nine)
(adjective; a literary word) gloomy and unfriendly.

sauce, sauces
(noun) A sauce is a liquid eaten with food.
[from Latin *salsus* meaning 'salted']

saucepan, saucepans
(noun) A saucepan is a deep metal cooking pot with a handle and a lid.

saucer, saucers
(noun) A saucer is a small curved plate for a cup.
[from Old French *saussier* meaning 'a container for sauce']

saucy, saucier, sauciest
(adjective) cheeky in an amusing way.

Saudi, Saudis (rhymes with **cloudy**)
1 (adjective) belonging or relating to Saudi Arabia.
2 (noun) A Saudi is someone who comes from Saudi Arabia.

sauerkraut (pronounced **sour**-krowt)
(noun) Sauerkraut is finely shredded and pickled cabbage. It is eaten mainly in Germany.
[from German *sauer* + *Kraut* meaning 'sour cabbage']

sauna, saunas (pronounced **saw**-na)
(noun) If you have a sauna, you go into a very hot room in order to sweat, then have a cold bath or shower.
[a Finnish word]

saunter, saunters, sauntering, sauntered
1 (verb) To saunter somewhere means to walk there slowly and casually.
2 (noun) A saunter is a slow, casual walk.

sausage, sausages
(noun) A sausage is a mixture of minced meat and herbs formed into a tubular shape and served cooked.

sausage roll, sausage rolls
(noun) A sausage roll is a small piece of sausage meat covered with pastry and cooked.

sauté, sautés, sautéing or sautéeing, sautéed
(pronounced **soh**-tay)
(verb) To sauté food means to fry it quickly in a small amount of oil or butter.
[from French *sauté* meaning 'tossed']

savage, savages, savaging, savaged
1 (adjective) cruel and violent, e.g. *two weeks of savage rioting.*
2 (noun) If you call someone a savage, you mean that they are cruel, violent, and uncivilized.
3 (verb) If a dog or other animal savages you, it attacks you and bites you.
4 To savage someone means to criticize them severely.
savagely (adverb).

Similar words: (sense 1) bloodthirsty, murderous, brutal, uncivilized, barbarous

savagery
(noun) Savagery is cruel and violent behaviour.

savanna, savannas (pronounced sav-**van**-a);
also spelled **savannah**
(noun) The savanna is an area of open, flat
grassland in Africa.

save, saves, saving, saved
1 (verb) If you save someone, you rescue them or
help to keep them safe, e.g. *She saved him from
drowning.*
2 If you save something, you keep it so that you
can use it later, e.g. *They had saved enough
money to buy a house.*
3 To save time, money, or effort means to
prevent it from being wasted, e.g. *You could save
yourself a lot of work with a computer.*
4 (preposition; a formal use) Save means except,
e.g. *The stage was empty save for a few pieces of
furniture.*

Similar words: (sense 1) rescue, redeem

saving, savings
1 (noun) A saving is a reduction in the amount of
time or money used.
2 Your savings are the money you have saved.

saviour, saviours
1 (noun) If someone saves you from danger, you
can refer to them as your saviour.
2 In Christianity, the Saviour is Jesus Christ.

savoir-faire (pronounced sav-wahr-**fare**)
(noun; a formal word) Someone who has
savoir-faire knows what to do in social
situations.
[a French expression meaning literally 'knowing
how to do']

savour, savours, savouring, savoured
(verb) If you savour something, you take your
time with it and enjoy it fully, e.g. *I savoured
every mouthful of breakfast.*
[from Latin *sapere* meaning 'to taste']

savoury
1 (adjective) Savoury is salty or spicy.
2 Something that is not very savoury is not very
pleasant or respectable, e.g. *the less savoury
episodes in her past.*

saw, saws, sawing, sawed, sawn
1 Saw is the past tense of **see.**
2 (noun) A saw is a tool for cutting wood. It has
a blade with sharp teeth along one edge.
3 (verb) If you saw something, you cut it with a
saw.

sawdust
(noun) Sawdust is the fine powder produced
when you saw wood.

sawmill, sawmills
(noun) A sawmill is a factory in which wood is
sawn up into planks.

saxophone, saxophones
(noun) A saxophone is a curved metal wind
instrument often played in jazz bands.
[named after Adolphe Sax (1814-1894), who
invented the instrument]

say, says, saying, said
1 (verb) When you say something, you speak
words.

2 Say is used to give an example, e.g. *Compare,
say, a Michelangelo painting with a Van Gogh.*
3 (noun) If you have a say in something, you can
give your opinion and influence decisions.
4 (phrase) You use **that is to say** to express the
same idea in a different way, e.g. *She had angina
pectoris, that is to say, heart trouble.*
5 If something **goes without saying**, it is obvious.

Similar words: (sense 1) utter, remark, comment

saying, sayings
(noun) A saying is a well-known sentence or
phrase that tells you something about human life.

Similar words: adage, axiom, motto, proverb, maxim

scab, scabs
1 (noun) A scab is a hard, dry covering that
forms over a wound.
2 (an offensive use) Scabs are people who work
when their colleagues are on strike.
scabby (adjective).

scabbard, scabbards
(noun) A scabbard is a cover for a sword.

scabies (pronounced **skay**-beez)
(noun) Scabies is an infectious skin disease
caused by a parasite.

scaffold, scaffolds
(noun) A scaffold is a platform on which
criminals used to be hanged or beheaded.

scaffolding
(noun) Scaffolding is a temporary structure
erected around buildings being built or repaired.

scald, scalds, scalding, scalded (pronounced
skawld)
1 (verb) If you scald yourself, you burn yourself
with very hot liquid or steam.
2 (noun) A scald is a burn caused by scalding.
[from Latin *excaldare* meaning 'to wash in warm
water']

scale, scales, scaling, scaled
1 (noun) The scale of something is its size or
extent, e.g. *The scale of change is enormous.*
2 A scale is a set of levels or numbers used for
measuring things.
3 The scale of a map is the ratio of
measurements on the map to measurements in
the real world, e.g. *a scale of 1:50,000.*
4 A scale is also an upward or downward
sequence of musical notes.
5 (verb) If you scale something high, you climb it.
6 (noun) The scales of a fish or reptile are the
small pieces of hard skin covering its body.
7 Scales are a piece of equipment used for
weighing things.
[senses 2-5 are from Latin *scala* meaning 'ladder']

scaled-down
(adjective) A scaled-down version of something
is a smaller version of it.

scalene
(adjective) A scalene triangle has sides which
are all of different lengths.

scallop, scallops
(noun) Scallops are edible shellfish with two flat fan-shaped shells.
[from Old French *escalope* meaning 'shell']

scalp, scalps, scalping, scalped
1 (noun) Your scalp is the skin under the hair on your head.
2 (verb) To scalp someone means to remove the skin and hair from their head in one piece. This was sometimes done by North American Indians as a sign of victory.
3 (noun) A scalp is the piece of skin and hair removed when someone is scalped.

scalpel, scalpels
(noun) A scalpel is a knife with a thin, sharp blade. Scalpels are used by surgeons.
[from Latin *scalper* meaning 'a knife']

scaly
(adjective) covered with scales.

scamper, scampers, scampering, scampered
(verb) To scamper means to move quickly and lightly.

scampi
(noun) Scampi consists of large prawns often eaten fried in batter.

scan, scans, scanning, scanned
1 (verb) If you scan something, you look at all of it carefully, e.g. *lifeguards scanning the sea for shark fins.*
2 If a machine scans something, it examines it quickly by means of a beam of light or x-rays.
3 (noun) A scan is a search or examination by a scanner, e.g. *a liver scan.*
4 (verb) If the words of a poem scan, they fit into a regular, rhythmical pattern.

scandal, scandals
(noun) A scandal is a situation or event that people think is shocking and immoral.
scandalous (adjective), **scandalously** (adverb).

scandalize, scandalizes, scandalizing, scandalized; also spelled **scandalise**
(verb) If you are scandalized, you are shocked and horrified by something.

Scandinavia (pronounced skan-din-**nay**-vee-a)
(noun) Scandinavia is the name given to a group of countries in Northern Europe, including Norway, Sweden, Denmark, and sometimes Finland and Iceland.
Scandinavian (adjective).

scanner, scanners
(noun) A scanner is a machine that examines things by means of a beam of light or x-rays. Scanners are used in hospitals, airports, and research laboratories.

scansion
(noun) Scansion is the analysis of the rhythmic arrangement of syllables in lines of poetry.

scant
(adjective) If something receives scant attention, it does not receive enough attention.

scanty, scantier, scantiest
(adjective) small in size or amount, e.g. *a rather scanty audience.*
scantily (adverb).

scapegoat, scapegoats
(noun) If someone is made a scapegoat, they are blamed for something, although it may not be their fault.

scapula, scapulas (pronounced **skap**-yoo-la)
(noun; a medical word) Your scapula is your shoulder blade.

scar, scars, scarring, scarred
1 (noun) A scar is a mark left on your skin after a wound has healed.
2 (verb) If an injury scars you, it leaves a permanent mark on your skin.
3 If an unpleasant experience scars you, it has a permanent effect on you.
4 (noun) A scar is also a permanent effect on someone's mind that results from a very unpleasant experience, e.g. *the scars of poverty.*
[from Greek *eskhara* meaning 'scab']

scarce, scarcer, scarcest
1 (adjective) If something is scarce, there is not very much of it.
2 (phrase) If you **make yourself scarce**, you leave quickly.
scarcity (noun).

scarcely
(adverb) Scarcely means hardly, e.g. *They were scarcely ever apart.*

scare, scares, scaring, scared
1 (verb) If something scares you, it frightens you.
2 (noun) If something gives you a scare, it scares you.
3 If there is a scare about something, a lot of people are afraid or worried about it, e.g. *a rabies scare.*
scared (adjective).

Similar words: (sense 1) frighten , alarm, startle

scarecrow, scarecrows
(noun) A scarecrow is an object shaped like a person put in a field to scare birds away.

scarf, scarfs or scarves
(noun) A scarf is a piece of cloth worn round your neck or head to keep you warm.

scarlet
(noun and adjective) bright red.

scarlet fever
(noun) Scarlet fever is an infectious disease causing a sore throat, high temperature, and red rash.

scarp, scarps
(noun) A scarp is a steep slope.

scarper, scarpers, scarpering, scarpered
(verb; an informal word) To scarper means to run away.

scary, scarier, scariest
(adjective; an informal word) frightening.

scathing (pronounced **skayth**-ing)
(adjective) harsh and scornful, e.g. *a scathing article about lady novelists.*
scathingly (adverb).

Similar words: vitriolic, caustic, virulent, withering

scatter, scatters, scattering, scattered
1 (verb) To scatter things means to throw or drop them all over an area.
2 If people scatter, they suddenly move away in different directions.

Similar words: (sense 1) sprinkle, strew
(sense 2) disperse

scattering
(noun) A scattering of things is a small number of them spread over a large area, e.g. *a scattering of stars.*

scatty, scattier, scattiest
(adjective; an informal word) rather absent-minded, e.g. *a scatty but charming girl.*

scavenge, scavenges, scavenging, scavenged
(verb) If you scavenge for things, you search for them among waste and rubbish.
scavenger (noun).

scenario, scenarios (pronounced sin-**nar**-ee-oh)
(noun) The scenario of a film or play is a summary of its plot.
[an Italian word]

scene, scenes
1 (noun) A scene is part of a play, film, or book in which a series of events happen in one place.
2 Pictures and views are sometimes called scenes, e.g. *a village scene.*
3 The scene of an event is the place where it happened.
4 A scene is also an area of activity, e.g. *the business scene.*
5 (phrase) If you **make a scene**, you embarrass people by losing your temper in public.
6 If something happens **behind the scenes**, it happens in secret.
[from Latin *scena* meaning 'theatrical stage']

scenery
1 (noun) In the countryside, you can refer to everything you see as the scenery.
2 In a theatre, the scenery is the painted cloth and structures on the stage which represent the place where the action is happening.

scenic
(adjective) A scenic place or route has nice views.

scent, scents, scenting, scented
1 (noun) A scent is a smell, especially a pleasant one.
2 Scent is perfume.
3 (verb) When an animal scents something, it becomes aware of it by smelling it.
[from Old French *sentir* meaning 'to sense']

sceptic, sceptics (pronounced **skep**-tik)
(noun) A sceptic is someone who has doubts about things that other people believe.

sceptical (pronounced **skep**-tik-kl)
(adjective) If you are sceptical about something, you have doubts about it, e.g. *He was sceptical about hypnotism.*
sceptically (adverb), **scepticism** (noun).

sceptre, sceptres (pronounced **sep**-ter)
(noun) A sceptre is an ornamental rod carried by a king or queen as a symbol of power.

schedule, schedules, scheduling, scheduled (pronounced **shed**-yool)
1 (noun) A schedule is a plan that gives a list of events or tasks, together with the times at which each thing should be done.
2 (verb) If something is scheduled to happen, it has been planned and arranged, e.g. *A meeting had been scheduled for that day.*

schema, schemata (pronounced **skee**-ma)
(noun; a technical word) A schema is an outline of a plan or theory.

schematic (pronounced skim-**mat**-ik)
(adjective) A schematic representation or diagram shows in a simple way how something works.
schematically (adverb).

scheme, schemes, scheming, schemed
1 (noun) A scheme is a plan or arrangement, e.g. *the State Pension Scheme.*
2 (verb) When people scheme, they make secret plans.
scheming (adjective).
[from Greek *skhēma* meaning 'form']

schism, schisms (pronounced **sizm**)
(noun) A schism is a split or division within a group or organization.
[from Greek *skhizein* meaning 'to split']

schizophrenia (pronounced skit-soe-**free**-nee-a)
(noun) Schizophrenia is a serious mental illness which prevents someone relating their thoughts and feelings to what is happening around them.
schizophrenic (noun and adjective).
[from Greek *skhizein* meaning 'to split' and *phren* meaning 'mind']

schnapps (pronounced **shnaps**)
(noun) Schnapps is a strong alcoholic drink made from potatoes.
[from German *Schnaps*]

scholar, scholars
1 (noun) A scholar is a person who studies an academic subject and knows a lot about it.
2 A scholar is also a pupil or student who has a scholarship.

scholarly
(adjective) having or showing a lot of knowledge.

scholarship, scholarships
1 (noun) If you get a scholarship to a school or university, your studies are paid for by the school or university or by some other organization.
2 Scholarship is academic study and knowledge.

scholastic
(adjective) Your scholastic ability is your ability to study and learn things at school.

school, schools, schooling, schooled
1 (noun) A school is a place where children are educated.
2 University departments and colleges are sometimes called schools, e.g. *an art school.*
3 (verb) When someone is schooled in something, they are taught it, e.g. *She was schooled in charm by her mother.*
4 (phrase) A **school of thought** is a theory or opinion shared by a group of people.
5 (noun) You can refer to a large group of dolphins or fish as a school.
[senses 1-4 are from Latin *schola* meaning 'school'; sense 5 is from Old English *scolu* meaning 'shoal']

schoolchild, schoolchildren
(noun) Schoolchildren are children who go to school.
schoolboy (noun), **schoolgirl** (noun).

schooling
(noun) Your schooling is the education you get at school.

school-leaver, school-leavers
(noun) School-leavers are young people who have just left school.

schooner, schooners
1 (noun) A schooner is a sailing ship.
2 A schooner is also a tall glass for sherry.

sciatica (pronounced sigh-**at**-tik-ka)
(noun) Sciatica is a severe pain in a nerve in your hips or legs.

science, sciences
1 (noun) Science is the study of nature and natural phenomena and the knowledge obtained about them.
2 A science is a branch of science, for example physics or biology.
[from Latin *scientia* meaning 'knowledge']

science fiction
(noun) Stories about events happening in the future or in other parts of the universe are called science fiction.

scientific
1 (adjective) relating to science or to a particular science, e.g. *scientific instruments.*
2 done in a systematic way, using experiments or tests, e.g. *a scientific study of language.*
scientifically (adverb).

scientist, scientists
(noun) A scientist is an expert in one of the sciences who does work connected with it.

scimitar, scimitars (pronounced **sim**-mit-ar)
(noun) A scimitar is a curved sword used in the past in some Eastern countries.

scintillating (pronounced **sin**-til-late-ing)
(adjective) lively and witty, e.g. *scintillating personalities.*

scion, scions (pronounced **sigh**-on)
(noun; a literary word) A scion of a rich or famous family is one of its younger members.

scissors
(plural noun) Scissors are a cutting tool with two sharp blades.

scoff, scoffs, scoffing, scoffed
1 (verb) If you scoff, you speak in a scornful, mocking way about something.
2 (an informal use) If you scoff food, you eat it quickly and greedily.

scold, scolds, scolding, scolded
(verb) If you scold someone, you tell them off.

Similar words: castigate, chastise, chide, tick off, reprove, admonish, reproach, rebuke, reprimand

scone, scones (pronounced **skone** or **skon**)
(noun) Scones are small cakes made from flour and fat and usually eaten with butter.

scoop, scoops, scooping, scooped
1 (verb) If you scoop something up, you pick it up using a spoon or the palm of your hand.
2 (noun) A scoop is an object like a large spoon which is used for picking up food such as ice cream or flour.
3 A scoop is also an important news story reported in one newspaper before it appears elsewhere.
[from Old Dutch *schope* meaning 'vessel for baling']

scooter, scooters
1 (noun) A scooter is a small, light motorcycle.
2 A child's scooter is a simple cycle which the child rides by standing on it and pushing the ground with one foot.

scope
1 (noun) If there is scope for doing something, the opportunity to do it exists.
2 The scope of something is the whole subject area which it deals with or includes.

scorch, scorches, scorching, scorched
(verb) To scorch something means to burn it slightly.

scorched-earth
(adjective) When soldiers carry out a scorched-earth policy, they deliberately destroy things such as food that could be used by the enemy.

scorching
(adjective) extremely hot, e.g. *a scorching day.*

score, scores, scoring, scored
1 (verb) If you score in a game, you get a goal, run, or point.
2 (noun) The score in a game is the number of goals, runs, or points obtained by the two teams.
3 (verb) To score in a game also means to record the score obtained by the players.
4 If you score a success or victory, you achieve it.
5 If you score over someone, you gain an advantage over them.
6 (noun) Scores of things means very many of them, e.g. *We received scores of letters.*
7 (an old-fashioned use) A score is twenty.
8 (verb) To score a surface means to cut a line into it.
9 (noun) The score of a piece of music is the written version of it.
scorer (noun).

[from Old Norse *skor* meaning 'notch', 'tally', or 'twenty']

scorn, scorns, scorning, scorned
1 (noun) Scorn is great contempt, e.g. *This suggestion was greeted with scorn.*
2 (verb; a formal use) If you scorn something, you refuse to accept it.

scornful
(adjective) showing contempt, e.g. *scornful laughter.*
scornfully (adverb).

Similar words: mocking, sardonic, contemptuous, supercilious, disdainful

Scorpio
(noun) Scorpio is the eighth sign of the zodiac, represented by a scorpion. People born between October 23rd and November 21st are born under this sign.
[from Latin *scorpio* meaning 'scorpion']

scorpion, scorpions
(noun) A scorpion is a small tropical animal which looks like a large insect. It has a long tail with a poisonous sting on the end.

Scot, Scots
1 (noun) A Scot is a person who comes from Scotland.
2 (adjective) Scots means the same as Scottish.

scotch, scotches
(noun) Scotch is whisky made in Scotland. A scotch is a glass of scotch.

scot-free
(adverb) If you get away scot-free, you get away without being punished.
[from Old English *scot* meaning 'payment'; hence 'payment-free']

Scotsman, Scotsmen
(noun) A Scotsman is a man who comes from Scotland.
Scotswoman (noun).

Scottish
(adjective) belonging or relating to Scotland.

scoundrel, scoundrels
(noun; an old-fashioned word) A scoundrel is a man who cheats and deceives people.

scour, scours, scouring, scoured
1 (verb) If you scour a place, you look all over it in order to find something, e.g. *Traders were scouring the villages for family treasures.*
2 If you scour something such as a pan, you clean it by rubbing it with something rough.
[from Latin *excurare* meaning 'to cleanse']

scourge, scourges (rhymes with **urge**)
1 (noun) A scourge is something that causes a lot of suffering, e.g. *Smallpox was the scourge of the Western world.*
2 In the past, a scourge was a whip used to punish people.

scout, scouts, scouting, scouted
1 (noun) A scout is a boy who is a member of the Scout Association, an organization for boys

which aims to develop character and responsibility.
2 A scout is also someone who is sent to an area to find out the position of an enemy army.
3 (verb) If you scout around for something, you look around for it.
[from Old French *ascouter* meaning 'to listen to']

scowl, scowls, scowling, scowled
1 (verb) If you scowl, you frown because you are angry, e.g. *I scowled at him.*
2 (noun) A scowl is an angry expression.

scrabble, scrabbles, scrabbling, scrabbled
1 (verb) If you scrabble at something, you scrape at it with your hands or feet.
2 (noun; a trademark) Scrabble is a word game played with letters on a board.
[from Old Dutch *schrabbelen* meaning 'to scrape repeatedly']

scraggy, scraggier, scraggiest
(adjective) thin and bony, e.g. *a scraggy neck.*

scram
(interjection) If you tell someone to scram, you want them to go away quickly.

scramble, scrambles, scrambling, scrambled
1 (verb) If you scramble over something, you climb over it using your hands to help you.
2 To scramble a radio or telephone transmission means to interfere with it so that it can only be understood using special equipment.
3 (noun) A scramble is a motorcycle race over rough ground.

scrambled egg, scrambled eggs
(noun) Scrambled egg is a dish consisting of eggs mixed with milk and cooked in a pan.

scrap, scraps, scrapping, scrapped
1 (noun) A scrap of something is a very small piece of it, e.g. *a scrap of paper... There was not a scrap of evidence against him.*
2 (plural noun) Scraps are pieces of leftover food.
3 (verb) If you scrap something, you get rid of it, e.g. *The existing system should be scrapped.*
4 (adjective and noun) Scrap metal or scrap is metal from old machinery or cars that can be re-used.
5 (noun; an informal use) A scrap is also a fight.

scrapbook, scrapbooks
(noun) A scrapbook is a book in which you stick things such as pictures or newspaper articles.

scrape, scrapes, scraping, scraped
1 (verb) If you scrape something off a surface, you remove it by pulling a knife over it, e.g. *She scraped the mud off her boots.*
2 If something scrapes, it makes a harsh noise by rubbing against something, e.g. *Her chair scraped.*
3 If you scrape, you spend as little money as possible, e.g. *People scraped and saved to get their boys into private schools.*
4 (noun; an old-fashioned use) If you are in a scrape, you are in a difficult situation.

scrappy, scrappier, scrappiest
(adjective) badly organized or done.

scratch, scratches, scratching, scratched
1 (verb) To scratch something means to make a small cut on it accidentally, e.g. *His knees were scratched by thorns.*
2 (noun) A scratch is a small cut.
3 (verb) If you scratch, you rub your skin with your nails because it is itching.
4 (an informal phrase) If you do something **from scratch**, you do it from the beginning, without making use of anything that has been done before.
5 If something is **up to scratch**, it is satisfactory.

scrawl, scrawls, scrawling, scrawled
1 (verb) If you scrawl something, you write it in a careless and untidy way.
2 (noun) You can refer to careless and untidy writing as a scrawl.

scrawny, scrawnier, scrawniest
(adjective) thin and bony, e.g. *scrawny cattle.*

scream, screams, screaming, screamed
1 (verb) If you scream, you shout or cry in a loud, high-pitched voice.
2 (noun) A scream is a loud, high-pitched cry.
3 (an informal use) You can say that someone is a scream when you think they are very funny.

Similar words: (senses 1 and 2) cry, screech, shriek

scree
(noun) Scree is a mass of loose stones on the side of a mountain.
[from Old English *scrithan* meaning 'to slip']

screech, screeches, screeching, screeched
1 (verb) To screech means to make an unpleasant high-pitched noise, e.g. *'You'll be sorry you did that!' she screeched.*
2 (noun) A screech is an unpleasant high-pitched noise.

screen, screens, screening, screened
1 (noun) A screen is a flat vertical surface on which a picture is shown, e.g. *a television screen.*
2 (verb) To screen a film or television programme means to show it.
3 (noun) A screen is also a vertical panel used to separate different parts of a room or to protect something.
4 (verb) If you screen someone, you put something in front of them to protect them.
5 When an organization screens people, it investigates them to make sure they are not likely to be disloyal.
6 To screen people for a disease means to examine them to make sure they have not got it, e.g. *Women were screened for breast cancer.*

screenplay, screenplays
(noun) The screenplay of a film is the script.

screw, screws, screwing, screwed
1 (noun) A screw is a small, sharp piece of metal used for fixing things together or for fixing something to a wall.
2 (verb) If you screw things together, you fix them together using screws.
3 If you screw something onto something else, you fix it there by twisting it round and round, e.g. *He screwed the lid onto the jar.*

screw up
1 (phrasal verb) If you screw something up, you twist it or squeeze it so that it no longer has its proper shape, e.g. *She screwed up her eyes as she faced the sun.*
2 (an informal use) To screw something up means to spoil it, e.g. *That screws up all my arrangements.*

screwdriver, screwdrivers
(noun) A screwdriver is a tool for turning screws.

scribble, scribbles, scribbling, scribbled
1 (verb) If you scribble something, you write it quickly and roughly.
2 To scribble also means to make meaningless marks, e.g. *Someone's scribbled all over the wall.*
3 (noun) You can refer to something written or drawn quickly and roughly as a scribble.

scribe, scribes
(noun) In the past, a scribe was someone who made copies of manuscripts.
[from Latin *scriba* meaning 'clerk']

scrimp, scrimps, scrimping, scrimped
(verb) If you scrimp, you live cheaply and spend as little money as you can.

script, scripts
1 (noun) The script of a play, film, or television programme is the written version of it.
2 A script is also a system of writing, e.g. *Arabic script.*
[from Latin *scriptum* meaning 'something written']

scripture, scriptures
(noun) Scripture refers to sacred writings, especially the Bible.
scriptural (adjective).
[from Latin *scriptura* meaning 'written material']

scriptwriter, scriptwriters
(noun) A scriptwriter is someone who writes scripts for films or for radio or television.

scroll, scrolls
(noun) A scroll is a long roll of paper or parchment with writing on it.

scrotum, scrota or scrotums (pronounced skroe-tum)
(noun) A man's scrotum is the bag of skin that contains his testicles.

scrounge, scrounges, scrounging, scrounged
(verb; an informal word) If you scrounge something, you get it by asking for it rather than by earning or buying it.
scrounger (noun).

Similar words: cadge, sponge

scrub, scrubs, scrubbing, scrubbed
1 (verb) If you scrub something, you clean it with a stiff brush and water.
2 (noun) If you give something a scrub, you scrub it.
3 (verb; an informal use) If you scrub an idea or a plan, you cancel it.
4 (noun) Scrub consists of low trees and bushes.

scruff
(noun) The scruff of your neck is the back of your neck or collar.

scruffy, scruffier, scruffiest
(adjective) dirty and untidy, e.g. *a scruffy child.*

Similar words: tatty, unkempt

scrum, scrums
(noun) When rugby players form a scrum, they form a group and push against each other with their heads down in an attempt to get the ball.

scruple, scruples (pronounced skroo-pl)
(noun) Scruples are moral principles that make you unwilling to do something that seems wrong, e.g. *He had no scruples about borrowing money.*

scrupulous
1 (adjective) always doing what is honest or morally right.
2 paying very careful attention to detail, e.g. *She has a reputation for scrupulous scholarship.*
scrupulously (adverb).

scrutinize, scrutinizes, scrutinizing, scrutinized; also spelled scrutinise
(verb) If you scrutinize something, you examine it very carefully.
[from Latin *scrupulosus* meaning 'punctilious']

scrutiny
(noun) If something is under scrutiny, it is being studied or observed very carefully.
[from Latin *scrutinium* meaning 'investigation']

scuba diving
(noun) Scuba diving is the sport of swimming underwater with tanks of compressed air on the back.
[from *S(elf)-C(ontained) U(nderwater) B(reathing) A(pparatus)*]

scud, scuds, scudding, scudded
(verb; a literary word) If clouds scud, they move quickly and smoothly.

scuff, scuffs, scuffing, scuffed
1 (verb) If you scuff your feet, you drag them along the ground when you are walking.
2 If you scuff your shoes, you mark them by scraping or rubbing them.

scuffle, scuffles, scuffling, scuffled
1 (noun) A scuffle is a short, rough fight.
2 (verb) When people scuffle, they fight roughly.

scull, sculls, sculling, sculled
1 (noun) Sculls are small oars.
2 (verb) To scull means to row a boat using sculls.

scullery, sculleries
(noun) A scullery is a small room next to a kitchen where washing and cleaning is done.

sculpt, sculpts, sculpting, sculpted
(verb) When something is sculpted, it is carved or shaped in stone, wood, or clay.
[from Latin *sculpere* meaning 'to carve']

sculptor, sculptors
(noun) A sculptor is someone who makes sculptures.

sculpture, sculptures
1 (noun) A sculpture is a work of art produced by carving or shaping stone, wood, or clay.
2 Sculpture is the art of making sculptures.
sculptured (adjective).
[from Latin *sculptura* meaning 'carving']

scum
1 (noun) Scum is a layer of a dirty substance on the surface of a liquid.
2 People regarded as worthless are referred to as scum.

scupper, scuppers, scuppering, scuppered
(verb; an informal word) To scupper something means to ruin or destroy it, e.g. *Any chance of a compromise was scuppered.*

scurf
(noun) Scurf is dandruff.

scurrilous (pronounced skur-ril-luss)
(adjective) abusive and damaging to someone's good name, e.g. *scurrilous gossip.*
[from Latin *scurrilis* meaning 'derisive']

scurry, scurries, scurrying, scurried
(verb) To scurry means to run quickly with short steps.

scurvy
(noun) Scurvy is a disease caused by a lack of vitamin C.

scuttle, scuttles, scuttling, scuttled
1 (verb) To scuttle means to run quickly.
2 To scuttle a ship means to sink it deliberately by making holes in the bottom.
3 (noun) A scuttle is a container for coal.

scythe, scythes
(noun) A scythe is a tool with a long handle and a curved blade used for cutting grass or grain.

sea, seas
1 (noun) The sea is the salty water that covers much of the earth's surface.
2 (phrase) If you are at sea, you are baffled.
3 (noun) A sea of people or things is a very large number of them, e.g. *a sea of faces.*

sea anemone, sea anemones
(noun) A sea anemone is a sea animal that lives fixed to a rock. It has tentacles to trap food.

seaboard, seaboards
(noun) The seaboard of a country is the land along its coastline.

seafaring
(adjective) working as a sailor or travelling regularly on the sea, e.g. *a seafaring life.*
seafarer (noun).

seafront, seafronts
(noun) The seafront is the part of a seaside town next to the sea or beach.

seagull, seagulls
(noun) Seagulls are common white, grey, and black birds that live near the sea.

seahorse, seahorses
(noun) A seahorse is a small fish which swims upright. Its head resembles a horse's head.

seal, seals, sealing, sealed
1 (noun) A seal is an official mark on a document which shows that it is genuine.
2 A seal is also a piece of wax fixed over the opening of a container. The container cannot be opened without the seal being broken.
3 (verb) If you seal an envelope, you stick down the flap.
4 If you seal an opening, you cover it securely so that air, gas, or liquid cannot get through.
5 (phrases) To **put the seal** or **set the seal** on something means to confirm it, e.g. *The experience set the seal on their friendship.*
6 If you give something your **seal of approval**, you say officially that you approve of it.
7 (noun) A seal is also a large mammal with flippers. Seals eat fish and live partly on land and partly in the sea.
[senses 1-6 are from Latin *sigillum* meaning 'little picture'; sense 7 is from Old English *seolh*]

sea level
(noun) Sea level is the average level of the surface of the sea in relation to the land.

sealing wax
(noun) Sealing wax is a substance used for putting seals on documents and letters.

sea lion, sea lions
(noun) A sea lion is a type of large seal found in the Pacific Ocean.

seam, seams
1 (noun) A seam is a line of stitches joining two pieces of cloth.
2 A seam of coal is a long, narrow layer of it beneath the ground.

seaman, seamen
1 (noun) A seaman is a sailor.
2 Leading seaman, able seaman, ordinary seaman, and junior seaman are the four lowest ranks in the navy.

seamed
(adjective) wrinkled or cracked on the surface, e.g. *His brown face was seamed and wrinkled.*

seamstress, seamstresses (pronounced sem-striss)
(noun) A seamstress is a woman whose job is sewing.

seamy, seamier, seamiest
(adjective) sordid and unpleasant, e.g. *the seamy side of life.*

seance, seances (pronounced say-ahnss); also spelled séance
(noun) A seance is a meeting in which people try to communicate with the spirits of dead people.
[from French *séance* meaning 'sitting']

sear, sears, searing, seared
(verb) To sear something means to burn its surface.
[from Old English *sear* meaning 'withered']

search, searches, searching, searched
1 (verb) If you search for something, you look for it in several places.
2 If a person is searched, for instance by the police, their body and clothing is examined to see if they are hiding anything.
3 (noun) A search is an attempt to find something.
[from Latin *circare* meaning 'to go around']

Similar words: (sense 1) comb, scour, hunt, look for, seek, sift through
(sense 3) quest, pursuit, hunt

searching
(adjective) intended to discover the truth about something, e.g. *searching questions.*

searchlight, searchlights
(noun) A searchlight is a powerful light whose beam can be turned in different directions to look for people or things.

search warrant, search warrants
(noun) A search warrant is an official document giving the police permission to search a building.

searing
(adjective) A searing pain is very sharp.

seashore
(noun) The seashore is the land along the edge of the sea.

seasick
(adjective) feeling sick because of the movement of a boat.
seasickness (noun).

seaside
(noun) The seaside is an area next to the sea.

season, seasons, seasoning, seasoned
1 (noun) A season is a period of the year that has particular climatic characteristics. The seasons are spring, summer, autumn, and winter.
2 A season is also a period of the year when something usually happens, e.g. *the football season... the holiday season.*
3 (phrase) If fruits and vegetables are **in season**, they are ready for eating and available in the shops.
4 (verb) If you season food, you add salt, pepper, or spices to it.
[from Latin *satio* meaning 'sowing' (of crops)]

seasonable
(adjective) Seasonable weather occurs at the time of year when you would expect it.
seasonably (adverb).

seasonal
(adjective) happening during one season or one time of the year, e.g. *seasonal work.*

seasoned
(adjective) very experienced, e.g. *a seasoned traveller.*

seasoning
(noun) Seasoning is flavouring such as salt and pepper.

season ticket, season tickets
(noun) A season ticket is a train or bus ticket that you can use as many times as you like within a certain period.

seat, seats, seating, seated
1 (noun) A seat is something you can sit on.

2 The seat of a piece of clothing is the part that covers your bottom.
3 (verb) If you seat yourself somewhere, you sit down.
4 If a place seats a particular number of people, it has enough seats for that number, e.g. *The hall seats four hundred.*
5 (noun) If someone wins a seat in parliament, they are elected.
6 The seat of something, such as a government, is the place where it is based.

seat belt, seat belts
(noun) A seat belt is a strap that you fasten across your body for safety when travelling in a car or an aircraft.

seating
(noun) The seating in a place is the number or arrangement of seats there.

sea urchin, sea urchins
(noun) A sea urchin is a small sea animal with a round hard spiny shell.

seaward or **seawards**
(adjective and adverb) Seaward or seawards means moving or facing towards the sea.

seaweed
(noun) Plants that grow in the sea are called seaweed.

seaworthy
(adjective) A seaworthy ship is in good condition and can go to sea safely.
seaworthiness (noun).

sebaceous glands (pronounced sib-**bay**-shuss)
(plural noun) Sebaceous glands are small glands in the skin which provide oil for the skin and hair.
[from Latin *sebum* meaning 'tallow' or 'fat']

secateurs (pronounced sek-at-**turz**)
(plural noun) Secateurs are small shears for pruning garden plants.
[from Latin *secare* meaning 'to cut']

secede, secedes, seceding, seceded
(pronounced siss-**seed**)
(verb; a formal word) To secede from a group or country means to break away from it and become independent.
[from Latin *secedere* meaning 'to withdraw']

secluded
(adjective) quiet and hidden from view, e.g. *secluded beaches.*
seclusion (noun).
[from Latin *secludere* meaning 'to shut off']

second, seconds, seconding, seconded
1 The second item in a series is the one counted as number two.
2 (noun) A second is an SI unit of time. There are sixty seconds in a minute.
3 Seconds are goods that are sold cheaply because they are slightly faulty.
4 In music, a second is the interval between two notes of a scale when they are next to each other on the scale.
5 In a boxing match, a second is an attendant who looks after one of the boxers.

6 (verb) If you second a proposal, you formally agree with it so that it can be discussed or voted on.
7 If you are seconded somewhere, you are sent there temporarily to work.
secondly (adverb).
[from Latin *secundus*]

secondary
1 (adjective) Something that is secondary is less important than something else.
2 Secondary education is education for pupils between the ages of eleven and eighteen.

secondary school, secondary schools
(noun) A secondary school is a school for pupils between the ages of eleven and eighteen.

second childhood
(noun) When old people are in their second childhood, they are confused and tend to talk or behave like small children.

second-class
1 (adjective) Second-class things are regarded as less important than other things of the same kind, e.g. *There can be no second-class citizens in a free society.*
2 (adjective or adverb) Second-class services are cheaper and therefore slower or less comfortable than first-class ones.
3 (adjective) A second-class degree is a good or average university degree.

second cousin, second cousins
(noun) Your second cousins are the children of your parents' cousins.

second-hand
1 (adjective or adverb) Something that is second-hand has already been owned by someone else, e.g. *second-hand clothes.*
2 If you hear a story second-hand, you hear it indirectly, rather than from the people involved.

second nature
(noun) If something is second nature to you, you have done it so often that you do it without thinking about it.

second-rate
(adjective) of poor quality, e.g. *a second-rate department store.*

second thoughts
(plural noun) If you have second thoughts about something you have said or done, you have doubts about it and wonder if it was right.

secret, secrets
1 (adjective) Something that is secret is told to only a small number of people and hidden from everyone else, e.g. *secret negotiations.*
2 (noun) A secret is a fact told to only a small number of people and hidden from everyone else.
secretly (adverb), **secrecy** (noun).
[from Latin *secretus* meaning 'concealed']

Similar words: (sense 1) classified, confidential, covert, hush-hush

secret agent, secret agents
(noun) A secret agent is a spy.

secretariat, secretariats
(noun) A secretariat is a department responsible for the administration of a government or an international political organization.

secretary, secretaries
1 (noun) A secretary is a person employed by an organization to keep records, write letters, and do other office work.
2 Ministers in charge of some government departments are also called secretaries, e.g. *the Foreign Secretary*.
secretarial (adjective).
[from Latin *secretarius* meaning 'confidential officer']

secrete, secretes, secreting, secreted
(pronounced sik-**kreet**)
1 (verb) When part of a plant or animal secretes a liquid, it produces it.
2 (a formal use) If you secrete something somewhere, you hide it.
secretion (noun).

secretive
(adjective) Secretive people tend to hide their feelings and intentions.

Similar words: furtive, clandestine, stealthy, close, surreptitious

secret service
(noun) A country's secret service is the government department in charge of espionage and counterespionage.

sect, sects
(noun) A sect is a religious or political group which has broken away from a larger group.
[from Latin *secta* meaning 'faction' or 'following']

sectarian (pronounced sek-**tair**-ee-an)
(adjective) strongly supporting a particular sect, e.g. *sectarian violence*.

section, sections
1 (noun) A section of something is one of the parts it is divided into, e.g. *the first-class section of the train*.
2 A section is also a cross-section.
[from Latin *secare* meaning 'to cut']

Similar words: (sense 1) portion, segment

sectional
(adjective) concerned with the interests of only one group within a community or country.

sector, sectors
1 (noun) A sector of something, especially a country's economy, is one part of it, e.g. *the private sector*.
2 A sector of a circle is one of the two parts formed when you draw two straight lines from the centre to the circumference.
[from Latin *sector* meaning 'cutter']

secular
(adjective) having no connection with religion, e.g. *secular education*.
secularize or **secularise** (verb).

secure, secures, securing, secured
1 (verb; a formal use) If you secure something,

you manage to get it, e.g. *He secured only 526 votes*.
2 If you secure a place, you make it safe from harm or attack.
3 To secure something also means to fasten it firmly, e.g. *A plastic box was secured to the wall*.
4 (adjective) If a place is secure, it is tightly locked or well protected.
5 If an object is secure, it is firmly fixed in place.
6 If you feel secure, you feel safe and confident.
7 Secure also means certain not to be lost, e.g. *a secure job*.
securely (adverb).
[from Latin *securus* meaning 'free from care']

security, securities
1 (noun and adjective) Security means all the precautions taken to protect a place, e.g. *Security forces were patrolling the streets*.
2 (noun) A feeling of security is a feeling of being safe.
3 If you promise something as security, you promise to give it to someone if you fail to pay them back the money that they are lending you, e.g. *The bank may ask for security if you want an overdraft*.
4 Securities are stocks, shares, bonds or other certificates that you buy as an investment.

sedan chair, sedan chairs (pronounced sid-**dan**)
(noun) A sedan chair is a small cabin with a chair in it carried on poles by two men. Sedan chairs were used in the 17th and 18th centuries.

sedate, sedates, sedating, sedated (pronounced sid-**date**)
1 (adjective) quiet, calm, and dignified.
2 (verb) To sedate someone means to give them a drug to calm them down or make them sleep.
sedately (adverb).
[from Latin *sedare* meaning 'to soothe']

sedative, sedatives (pronounced **sed**-at-tiv)
1 (noun) A sedative is a drug that calms you down or makes you sleep.
2 (adjective) having a calming or soothing effect, e.g. *This drink has sedative properties*.
sedation (noun).

sedentary (pronounced **sed**-en-tree)
(adjective) A sedentary occupation is one in which you spend most of your time sitting down.
[from Latin *sedere* meaning 'to sit']

sedge
(noun) Sedge is a grasslike plant that grows on marshy ground.

sediment
(noun) Sediment is solid material that settles at the bottom of a liquid.
[from Latin *sedimentum* meaning 'settling']

Similar words: deposit, dregs, lees

sedimentary
(adjective) Sedimentary rocks are formed from fragments of shells or rocks that have become compressed. Sandstone and limestone are sedimentary rocks.

sedition
(noun) Sedition is speech or action which encourages rebellion against the government, e.g. *They were charged with sedition.*
seditious (adjective).

seduce, seduces, seducing, seduced
1 (verb) To seduce someone means to persuade them to have sex.
2 If you are seduced into doing something, you are persuaded to do it because it seems very attractive.
[from Latin *seducere* meaning 'to lead apart']

seductive
1 (adjective) A seductive person is sexually attractive.
2 Something seductive is very attractive and tempting.
seductively (adverb).

see, sees, seeing, saw, seen
1 (verb) If you see something, you are looking at it or you notice it.
2 If you see someone, you visit them or meet them, e.g. *You ought to see a doctor.*
3 If you see someone to a place, you accompany them there.
4 To see something also means to realize or understand it, e.g. *I see what you mean.*
5 If you ask what someone sees in a person, you want to know why they like them.
6 If you see through someone, you can tell what they are really thinking even though they are trying to hide it.
7 If you say you will see what is happening, you mean you will find out.
8 If you say you will see if you can do something, you mean you will try to do it.
9 If you see that something is done, you make sure that it is done.
10 If you see to something, you deal with it.
11 See is used to say that an event takes place during a particular period of time, e.g. *The following year saw a return to full employment.*
12 (phrases; an informal use) **Seeing that** or **seeing as** means because, e.g. *Seeing that you're the guest, you can decide where we're going.*
13 (noun) A bishop's see is his diocese.

Similar words: (sense 1) spy, espy, catch sight of, spot, sight, perceive

see off
(phrasal verb) If you see someone off, you go with them to the station or airport they are leaving from and say goodbye to them there.

seed, seeds, seeding, seeded
1 (noun) The seeds of a plant are the small, hard parts from which new plants can grow.
2 The seeds of a feeling or process are its beginning or origins, e.g. *The seeds of doubt had been sown.*
3 A seed is also a tennis player who is ranked according to his or her ability.
4 (verb) When tennis players are seeded, they are ranked according to their ability, e.g. *He was seeded number two.*

seedling, seedlings
(noun) A seedling is a young plant grown from a seed.

seedy, seedier, seediest
(adjective) untidy and shabby, e.g. *The photographic studio was a seedy, run-down place.*

seek, seeks, seeking, sought (a formal word)
1 (verb) To seek something means to try to find it, obtain it, or achieve it, e.g. *Both countries are seeking peace.*
2 If you seek to do something, you try to do it, e.g. *The government sought to reduce inflation.*

seem, seems, seeming, seemed
(verb) If something seems to be the case, it appears to be the case or you think it is the case, e.g. *It seemed like a good idea... The experiments seem to prove that sugar is bad for you.*

seeming
(adjective) appearing to be real or genuine, e.g. *his seeming willingness to participate.*
seemingly (adverb).

seemly
(adjective; a formal word) right and proper, e.g. *seemly conduct.*
[from Old Norse *sœmiligr* meaning 'fitting' or 'proper']

seep, seeps, seeping, seeped
(verb) If a liquid or gas seeps through something, it flows through very slowly.

seer, seers
(noun) A seer is a person who is supposed to be able to see into the future.

seersucker
(noun) Seersucker is a cotton fabric with a crinkled surface.
[from Persian *shir o shakkar* meaning 'milk and sugar']

seesaw, seesaws
(noun) A seesaw is a long plank supported in the middle. Two children sit on it, one on each end, and they move up and down in turn.

seethe, seethes, seething, seethed
1 (verb) If you seethe, you feel very angry but do not show it, e.g. *I seethed with secret rage.*
2 If a place is seething with people, there are a lot of them moving about.

segment, segments
1 (noun) A segment of something is one part of it.
2 The segments of an orange or grapefruit are the sections which you can divide it into.
3 A segment of a circle is one of the two parts formed when you draw a straight line across it.
[from Latin *secare* meaning 'to cut']

segmentation
(noun) Segmentation is the dividing of something into segments.

segregate, segregates, segregating, segregated
(verb) To segregate two groups of people means to keep them apart from each other.
segregated (adjective), **segregation** (noun).
[from Latin *se* meaning 'apart' and *grex* meaning 'flock']

seismic (pronounced **size**-mik)
(adjective; a technical word) happening as part of an earthquake or as the result of an earthquake, e.g. *seismic activity*.
[from Greek *seismos* meaning 'earthquake']

seismograph, seismographs (pronounced **size**-moh-grahf)
(noun) A seismograph is an instrument for measuring the strength of earthquakes.
[from Greek *seismos* meaning 'earthquake' and *graphein* meaning 'to write']

seismology (pronounced size-**mol**-loj-ee)
(noun) Seismology is the scientific study of earthquakes.
[from Greek *seismos* meaning 'earthquake' + -*ology*]

seize, seizes, seizing, seized
1 (verb) If you seize something, you grab it firmly, e.g. *I seized him by the collar*.
2 To seize a place or to seize control of it means to take control of it quickly and suddenly.
3 If you seize an opportunity, you take advantage of it.
4 If you seize on something, you immediately show great interest in it, e.g. *The press seized on these rumours*.

seize up
1 (phrasal verb) If a part of your body seizes up, it becomes stiff and painful.
2 If an engine seizes up, it becomes jammed and stops working.

seizure, seizures (pronounced **seez**-yer)
1 (noun) A seizure is a sudden violent attack of an illness, especially a heart attack or a fit.
2 If there is a seizure of power, a group of people suddenly take control using force.

seldom
(adverb) not very often, e.g. *It seldom rains there*.

select, selects, selecting, selected
1 (verb) If you select something, you choose it.
2 (adjective) of good quality, e.g. *a select New England school*.
selector (noun).
[from Latin *seligere* meaning 'to choose']

selection, selections
1 (noun) Selection is the choosing of people or things, e.g. *She stood little chance of selection*.
2 A selection of people or things is a set of them chosen from a larger group.
3 The selection of goods in a shop is the range of goods available, e.g. *They have a good selection*.

selective
(adjective) choosing things carefully, e.g. *They are very selective in their television watching*.
selectively (adverb).

self, selves
(noun) Your self is your basic personality or nature, e.g. *Soon she was her normal self again*.

self-
1 (prefix) done to yourself or by yourself, e.g. *self-pity... self-induced catastrophes*.

2 doing something automatically, e.g. *self-locking doors*.

self-addressed
(adjective) A self-addressed envelope is one on which you have written your own name and address.

self-assured
(adjective) behaving in a way that shows confidence in yourself.

self-catering
(adjective) In self-catering accommodation, you provide your own meals.

self-centred
(adjective) thinking only about yourself and not about other people.

self-confessed
(adjective) admitting to having bad habits or unpopular opinions, e.g. *a self-confessed racist*.

self-confident
(adjective) confident of your own abilities or worth.
self-confidence (noun).

self-conscious
(adjective) nervous and easily embarrassed, and worried about what other people think of you.
self-consciously (adverb), **self-consciousness** (noun).

self-contained
(adjective) Self-contained living accommodation has all its own facilities.

self-control
(noun) Self-control is the ability to restrain yourself and not show your feelings.

self-defence
1 (noun) Self-defence is the use of violence or special physical techniques to protect yourself when someone attacks you.
2 (phrase) If you say something in **self-defence**, you say it to justify your behaviour.

self-determination
(noun) Self-determination is the right of a country to be independent and to choose its own form of government.

self-employed
(adjective) working for yourself and organizing your own finances, rather than working for an employer.

self-esteem
(noun) Your self-esteem is your good opinion of yourself.

self-evident
(adjective) Self-evident facts are completely obvious and need no proof or explanation.

self-indulgent
(adjective) allowing yourself to do or have things you enjoy, especially as a treat.

self-interest
(noun) If you do something out of self-interest, you do it for your own benefit rather than to help other people.

selfish
(adjective) caring only about yourself, and not about other people.
selfishly (adverb), **selfishness** (noun).

selfless
(adjective) putting other people's interests before your own.
selflessly (adverb), **selflessness** (noun).

self-made
(adjective) rich and successful through your own efforts, e.g. *a self-made millionaire.*

self-possessed
(adjective) calm, confident, and restrained.

self-raising
(adjective) Self-raising flour contains baking powder to make it rise.

self-reliant
(adjective) able to do things by yourself rather than depending on other people.
self-reliance (noun).

self-respect
(noun) Self-respect is a feeling of confidence and pride in your own abilities and worth.

self-righteous
(adjective) convinced that you are better or more virtuous than other people.
self-righteousness (noun).

Similar words: priggish, sanctimonious

self-sacrifice
(noun) Self-sacrifice is giving up things for the sake of other people.

selfsame
(adjective) Selfsame is used to emphasize that a person or thing is the same as one mentioned earlier, e.g. *This was the selfsame woman I'd met on the train.*

self-satisfied
(adjective) feeling smug and satisfied with yourself.

self-seeking
(adjective) interested only in things that will benefit you.

self-service
(adjective) A self-service shop or restaurant is one where you serve yourself.

self-sufficient
1 (adjective) producing or making everything you need, and so not needing to buy things.
2 able to live in a way in which you do not need other people.

self-willed
(adjective) stubborn and obstinate.

sell, sells, selling, sold
1 (verb) If you sell something, you let someone have it in return for money.
2 If a shop sells something, it has it available for people to buy, e.g. *Do you sell flowers?*
3 If something sells, people buy it, e.g. *These little books sell for 95p each.*
4 (an informal use) If you sell someone an idea, you convince them that it is a good idea.

5 If you sell yourself, you present yourself well, so that people have confidence in your ability, e.g. *You've got to sell yourself at the interview.*
seller (noun).
[from Old English *sellan* meaning 'to lend' or 'to deliver']

Similar words: (sense 2) market, peddle, retail

sell out
(phrasal verb) If a shop has sold out of something, it has sold it all.

sell up
(phrasal verb) If you sell up, you sell everything you have because you need the money.

Sellotape
(noun; a trademark) Sellotape is a transparent sticky tape.

sellout
(an informal word)
1 (noun) If an event is a sellout, all the tickets for it have been sold.
2 You describe someone's behaviour as a sellout when they have betrayed you or their principles in order to gain an advantage or benefit.

selvage, selvages
(noun) The selvage of a length of cloth is the edge of it which has been finished so that it will not fray.

semantic
(adjective; a formal use) concerned with the meaning of words, e.g. *semantic confusions.*
[from Greek *sēmantikos* meaning 'having significance']

semantics
(noun) Semantics is the study of the meanings of words.

semaphore (pronounced **sem**-ma-for)
(noun) Semaphore is a system of sending messages using two flags. You hold the flags in different positions to represent the different letters of the alphabet.
[from Greek *sēma* + *-phoros* meaning 'signal bearing']

semblance
(noun) If there is a semblance of something, it seems to exist, although it might not really exist, e.g. *By this time some semblance of order had been established.*
[from Old French *sembler* meaning 'to seem']

semen (pronounced **see**-men)
(noun) Semen is the liquid containing sperm produced by a man's or male animal's sex organs.
[from Latin *semen* meaning 'seed']

semester, semesters (pronounced sim-**mess**-ter)
(noun) A semester is one of the two periods into which the year is divided at American universities and colleges.
[from Latin *semestris* meaning 'six-monthly']

semi-
(prefix) half or partly, e.g. *semiskilled workers.*
[from Latin *semi-* meaning 'half' or 'partly']

semibreve, semibreves
(noun) A semibreve is a musical note with a time value equal to four crotchets.

semicircle, semicircles
(noun) A semicircle is a half of a circle, or something with this shape.
semicircular (adjective).

semicolon, semicolons
(noun) A semicolon is the punctuation mark (;), used to separate different parts of a sentence or to indicate a pause.

semiconductor, semiconductors
(noun) A semiconductor is a substance used in electronics whose ability to conduct electricity increases with greater heat.

semidetached
(adjective) A semidetached house is joined to another house on one side.

semifinal, semifinals
(noun) The semifinals are the two matches in a competition played to decide who plays in the final.
semifinalist (noun).

seminal (pronounced **sem**-in-al)
(adjective; a formal word) extremely influential and important, e.g. *This experience had a seminal influence on his political development.*

seminar, seminars
(noun) A seminar is a meeting of a small number of university students or teachers to discuss a particular topic.

seminary, seminaries
(noun) A seminary is a college where priests are trained.

semiprecious
(adjective) Semiprecious stones are stones such as opals or turquoises that are used in jewellery. They are less valuable than precious stones.

Semitic
1 (adjective) The Semitic languages are a group of languages that includes Arabic and Hebrew.
2 Semitic means Jewish.
[from Latin *semita* meaning 'descendant of Shem', one of Noah's sons in the Bible story]

semitone, semitones
(noun) A semitone is the smallest interval between two notes, for example from F to F sharp. Two semitones are equal to one tone.

semolina
(noun) Semolina consists of the hard parts of wheat grains that are left after flour is made. Semolina is often used for making puddings.
[from Italian *semola* meaning 'bran']

SEN, SENs
(noun) An SEN is a nurse who has successfully completed a two-year practical course in nursing. SEN is an abbreviation for 'State Enrolled Nurse'.

senate, senates
1 (noun) The Senate is the smaller, more important of the two councils in the government of some countries, for example the U.S.A.

2 In ancient Rome, the Senate was the governing council.
[from Latin *senatus* meaning 'council of the elders']

senator, senators
(noun) A senator is a member of a senate, for example in the U.S.A.

send, sends, sending, sent
1 (verb) If you send something to someone, you arrange for it to be delivered to them.
2 To send a radio signal or message means to transmit it.
3 If you send someone somewhere, you tell them to go there or arrange for them to go.
4 If you send for someone, you send a message asking them to come and see you.
5 If you send off for something, you write and ask for it to be sent to you.
6 To send things in a particular direction means to make them move in that direction, e.g. *The noise sent them racing towards the bush.*

Similar words: (sense 1) dispatch, remit, consign, direct, transmit, forward

send up
(phrasal verb) If you send someone or something up, you imitate them and make fun of them.

senile
(adjective) If old people become senile, they become confused and cannot look after themselves.
senility (noun).
[from Latin *senex* meaning 'old man']

senior, seniors
1 (adjective) The senior people in an organization or profession have the highest and most important jobs.
2 (noun) Someone who is your senior is older than you.
3 At a school or college, the seniors are the older pupils or students.
seniority (noun).
[from Latin *senior* meaning 'older']

senior citizen, senior citizens
(noun) A senior citizen is someone receiving an old-age pension.

sensation, sensations
1 (noun) A sensation is a feeling, especially a physical feeling.
2 If something is a sensation, it causes great excitement and interest.

sensational
1 (adjective) causing great excitement and interest.
2 (an informal use) extremely good, e.g. *a sensational evening.*
sensationally (adverb).

sensationalism
(noun) Sensationalism is writing in which certain things are deliberately exaggerated in order to shock or excite people.
sensationalist (adjective).

sense, senses, sensing, sensed
1 (noun) Your senses are your ability to see, hear, smell, touch, and taste.
2 (verb) If you sense something, you become aware of it.
3 (noun) A sense is also a feeling, e.g. *a sense of failure... She has a strong sense of justice.*
4 A sense of a word is one of its meanings.
5 Sense is the ability to think and behave sensibly.
6 (phrase) If something **makes sense**, you can understand it or it seems sensible, e.g. *It made sense to adopt labour-saving methods.*
[from Latin *sentire* meaning 'to feel']

senseless
1 (adjective) A senseless action has no meaning or purpose, e.g. *a senseless act of cruelty.*
2 If someone is senseless, they are unconscious.
senselessly (adverb), **senselessness** (noun).

sense of humour
(noun) Your sense of humour is your ability to find certain things funny.

sensibility, sensibilities
(noun) Your sensibility is your ability to experience deep feelings, e.g. *a writer of high sensibility.*

sensible
(adjective) showing good sense and judgment.
sensibly (adverb).

Similar words: practical, judicious, logical, wise, prudent, politic, pragmatic, realistic, sound, rational, balanced, level-headed

sensitive
1 (adjective) If you are sensitive to other people's feelings, you understand them.
2 If you are sensitive about something, you are worried or easily upset about it, e.g. *You mustn't be so sensitive about your accent.*
3 A sensitive subject or issue needs to be dealt with carefully because it can make people angry or upset.
4 Something that is sensitive to a particular thing is easily affected or harmed by it.
5 A sensitive piece of equipment can measure very small changes.
sensitively (adverb), **sensitivity** (noun).

sensitize, sensitizes, sensitizing, sensitized; also spelled sensitise
1 (verb) If people are sensitized to a problem, they are made aware of it.
2 If a material is sensitized to light or touch, it is made sensitive to it.

sensor, sensors
(noun) A sensor is an instrument which reacts to physical conditions such as light or heat.

sensory
(adjective) relating to the physical senses.

sensual (pronounced **senss**-yool)
1 (adjective) showing or suggesting a liking for sexual pleasures, e.g. *plump sensual lips.*
2 giving pleasure to your physical senses rather than to your mind, e.g. *the sensual rhythms of the drums.*
sensuality (noun).

Similar words: (sense 1) sensuous, voluptuous, sultry

sensuous
(adjective) giving pleasure through the senses.
sensuously (adverb).

sentence, sentences, sentencing, sentenced
1 (noun) A sentence is a group of words which, when written down, begins with a capital letter and ends with a full stop.
2 In a law court, a sentence is a punishment given to someone who has been found guilty.
3 (verb) When a guilty person is sentenced, they are told officially what their punishment will be.
[from Latin *sententia* meaning 'feeling', 'opinion', or 'judgment']

sententious
(adjective; a formal word) making pompous remarks about morality and correct behaviour.
sententiously (adverb).

sentient (pronounced **sen**-tee-ent)
(adjective; a formal word) capable of experiencing things through the physical senses, e.g. *sentient creatures.*
[from Latin *sentiens* meaning 'feeling']

sentiment, sentiments
1 (noun) A sentiment is a feeling, attitude, or opinion, e.g. *These sentiments were echoed by other speakers.*
2 Sentiment consists of feelings such as tenderness, romance, or sadness, e.g. *He scorns sentiment and emotion.*
[from Latin *sentire* meaning 'to feel']

sentimental
1 (adjective) feeling or expressing tenderness, romance, or sadness to an exaggerated extent, e.g. *sentimental songs.*
2 relating to a person's emotions, e.g. *She kept the ring for sentimental reasons.*
sentimentality (noun), **sentimentally** (adverb).

Similar words: (sense 1) maudlin, mawkish, emotional, nostalgic, soppy, sloppy

sentimentalize, sentimentalizes, sentimentalizing, sentimentalized; also spelled sentimentalise
(verb) If you sentimentalize something, you make it seem sentimental or you think about it in a sentimental way.

sentinel, sentinels
(noun; an old-fashioned word) A sentinel is a sentry.
[from Old Italian *sentina* meaning 'watchfulness']

sentry, sentries
(noun) A sentry is a soldier who keeps watch and guards a camp or building.

separable
(adjective) able to be separated, e.g. *There are some parts that seem separable from the whole.*

separate, separates, separating, separated
1 (adjective) If something is separate from something else, the two things are not connected.
2 (verb) To separate people or things means to cause them to be apart from each other.
3 If people or things separate, they move away from each other.
4 If a married couple separate, they decide to live apart.
separately (adverb), **separation** (noun), **separated** (adjective).

Similar words: (sense 2) dissociate, alienate, segregate, sunder
(sense 3) part, diverge, part company, divide

sepia (pronounced **see**-pee-a)
(adjective and noun) deep brown, like the colour of old photographs.
[from Latin *sepia* meaning 'cuttlefish', because the brown dye is obtained from this fish]

September
(noun) September is the ninth month of the year. It has 30 days.
[from Latin *September* meaning 'the seventh month']

septic
(adjective) If a wound becomes septic, it becomes infected with poison.
[from Greek *sēpein* meaning 'to rot']

septicaemia or **septicemia** (pronounced sep-tiss-**see**-mee-a)
(noun; a medical word) Septicaemia is an infection of the blood which develops in a wound.

septic tank, septic tanks
(noun) A septic tank is a large underground tank into which faeces, urine, and other waste matter are sent through pipes to be treated chemically.

septuagenarian, septuagenarians (pronounced sept-yoo-a-jin-**nair**-ee-an)
(noun) A septuagenarian is a person in their seventies.
[from Latin *septuaginta* meaning 'seventy']

sepulchral (pronounced sip-**pul**-kral)
(adjective; a literary word) gloomy and solemn.

sepulchre, sepulchres (pronounced **sep**-pul-ka)
(noun; a literary word) A sepulchre is a large tomb.

sequel, sequels
1 (noun) A sequel to a book or film is another book or film which continues the story.
2 The sequel to an event is a result or consequence of it, e.g. *There was an amusing sequel to this incident.*

sequence, sequences
1 (noun) A sequence of events is a number of them coming one after the other, e.g. *the strange sequence of events that led up to the murder.*
2 The sequence in which things are arranged is the order in which they are arranged, e.g. *paintings exhibited in chronological sequence.*
[from Latin *sequi* meaning 'to follow']

sequential (pronounced sik-**kwen**-shal)
(adjective; a formal word) happening in a fixed order or sequence.
sequentially (adverb).

sequestrate or **sequester, sequestrates, sequestrating, sequestrated** (pronounced sik-**kwess**-trate)
(verb; a formal word) When property is sequestrated, it is officially taken away from someone until they have paid off their debts.
sequestration (noun).
[from Latin *sequestrare* meaning 'to surrender for safekeeping']

sequin, sequins
(noun) Sequins are small, shiny, coloured discs sewn on clothes to decorate them.

seraph, seraphs or **seraphim** (pronounced **ser**-raf)
(noun) In Christianity, a seraph is one of the highest order of angels.

Serbo-Croat (pronounced ser-boh-**kroh**-at)
(noun) Serbo-Croat is the main language spoken in Yugoslavia.

serenade, serenades, serenading, serenaded
1 (verb) If you serenade someone you love, you sing or play music to them outside their window.
2 (noun) A serenade is a song sung outside a woman's window by a man who loves her.

serendipity (pronounced ser-en-**dip**-it-ee)
(noun; a formal word) Serendipity is the ability to find interesting or valuable things by accident.
[coined by Horace Walpole in the 18th century from the story 'The Three Princes of Serendip' who have this ability]

serene
(adjective) peaceful and calm, e.g. *a serene expression.*
serenely (adverb), **serenity** (noun).

serf, serfs
(noun) Serfs were a class of people in medieval Europe who had to work on their master's land and could not leave without his permission.
serfdom (noun).
[from Latin *servus* meaning 'slave']

serge
(noun) Serge is a type of strong woollen cloth used to make coats and suits.

sergeant, sergeants
1 (noun) A sergeant is a noncommissioned officer of middle rank in the army or air force.
2 A sergeant is also a police officer just above a constable in rank.
[from Latin *serviens* meaning 'serving']

sergeant major, sergeant majors
(noun) A sergeant major is a noncommissioned army officer of the highest rank.

serial, serials
(noun) A serial is a story which is broadcast or published in a number of parts over a period of time, e.g. *a television serial.*

serialize, serializes, serializing, serialized; also spelled **serialise**
(verb) When a book is serialized, it is broadcast

or published in a number of parts over a period of time.

serialization (noun).

serial number, serial numbers

(noun) An object's serial number is a number you can see on it which identifies it and distinguishes it from other objects of the same kind.

series

1 (noun) A series of things is a number of them coming one after the other, e.g. *a series of lectures on American politics.*
2 A radio or television series is a set of programmes with the same title.
[from Latin *serere* meaning 'to link']

Similar words: (sense 1) succession, sequence, string, chain

serious

1 (adjective) A serious problem or situation is very bad and worrying.
2 Serious matters are important and should be thought about carefully.
3 Serious work or writing involves thinking about things deeply and thoughtfully, e.g. *We had a serious political discussion.*
4 If you are serious about something, you are sincere about it, e.g. *You can't be serious!*
5 People who are serious are thoughtful, quiet, and slightly humourless.
seriously (adverb), **seriousness** (noun).

Similar words: (sense 1) grave, grievous, severe, critical
(sense 5) solemn, sober, sombre, stern, grim

seriously

1 (adverb) You say seriously to emphasize that you mean what you say, e.g. *Seriously, I have no intentions of leaving.*
2 (phrase) If you **take something seriously**, you regard it as important.

sermon, sermons

(noun) A sermon is a talk on a religious or moral subject given as part of a church service.
[from Latin *sermo* meaning 'talk']

sermonize, sermonizes, sermonizing, sermonized; also spelled sermonise

(verb) When someone sermonizes, they tell people what they think is right or wrong, especially when their opinion was not asked for.

serpent, serpents

(noun; a literary word) A serpent is a snake.
[from Latin *serpere* meaning 'to creep']

serpentine

(adjective; a literary word) twisting or winding in shape, like a moving snake.

serrated

(adjective) having a row of V-shaped points along the edge, like a saw, e.g. *serrated leaves.*
[from Latin *serratus* meaning 'saw-shaped']

serried

(adjective; a literary word) closely crowded or pressed together, e.g. *The soldiers marched in serried ranks.*

serum, serums (pronounced seer-um)

(noun) A serum is a liquid injected into someone's blood to protect them against a poison or disease. It is produced from the blood of an animal that is immune to that poison or disease.
[from Latin *serum* meaning 'watery fluid']

servant, servants

(noun) A servant is someone who is employed to work in another person's house.
[from Old French *servir* meaning 'to serve']

serve, serves, serving, served

1 (verb) If you serve a country, an organization, or a person, you do useful work for them.
2 To serve as something means to act or be used as that thing, e.g. *I failed to see what purpose this could serve.*
3 If something serves people in a particular place, it provides them with something they need, e.g. *There were five water taps to serve all thirty camps.*
4 If you serve food or drink to people, you give it to them or help them to it.
5 To serve customers in a shop means to help them and provide them with what they want.
6 To serve a legal order on someone means to officially send or present it to them.
7 To serve a prison sentence or an apprenticeship means to spend time doing it.
8 When you serve in tennis or badminton, you throw the ball or shuttlecock into the air and hit it over the net to start playing.
9 (noun) A serve is the act of serving in tennis or badminton.
10 (phrase) If you say that something unpleasant **serves someone right**, you mean that it is their own fault and they deserve it.
[from Latin *servus* meaning 'slave']

server, servers

(noun) A server is a spoon or fork used for serving food, e.g. *salad servers.*

service, services, servicing, serviced

1 (noun) A service is a system organized to provide something for the public, e.g. *the postal service.*
2 Some government organizations are called services, e.g. *the diplomatic service.*
3 The services are the army, the navy, and the air force.
4 If you give your services to a person or organization, you work for them or help them in some way, e.g. *He was knighted for his services to television.*
5 In a shop or restaurant, service is the process of being served.
6 (phrase; a formal use) To be **of service** to someone means to help them in some way, e.g. *May I be of service to you?*
7 If a vehicle or piece of equipment is **in service**, it is being used or is available for use, e.g. *New weapons were now coming into service.*
8 (verb) When a machine or vehicle is serviced, it is examined, adjusted, and cleaned so that it will continue working efficiently.
9 (noun) A service is also a religious ceremony.

10 A dinner service or tea service is a set of plates and other pieces of china.

11 Motorway services consist of a garage, restaurant, shop, and toilets.

12 When it is your service in a game of tennis or badminton, it is your turn to serve.

[from Latin *servus* meaning 'slave']

Similar words: (sense 8) overhaul, recondition

serviceable
(adjective) strong and durable, e.g. *I wore serviceable boots.*

service charge
(noun) A service charge is an amount added to your bill in a restaurant to pay for the service provided by the waiter or waitress.

serviceman, servicemen
(noun) A serviceman is a man in the army, navy, or air force.

service station, service stations
(noun) A service station is a garage that sells petrol, oil, spare parts, and snacks.

serviette, serviettes
(noun) A serviette is a square of cloth or paper used when you are eating to protect your clothes or to wipe your mouth.

[from Old French *serviette* meaning 'small towel']

servile
(adjective) too eager to obey people.
servility (noun).

Similar words: ingratiating, obsequious, sycophantic, subservient, unctuous, smarmy

serving, servings
1 (noun) A serving is a helping of food.
2 (adjective) A serving spoon or dish is used for serving food.

servitude
(noun) Servitude is slavery.

sesame (pronounced **sess**-am-ee)
(noun) Sesame seeds are the seeds of a tropical plant. They are used in cooking and to make an oil.

session, sessions
1 (noun) A session is a meeting of an official group, e.g. *an emergency session of the Council.*
2 A session is also a period during which meetings are held regularly, e.g. *the 1966-67 parliamentary session.*
3 The period during which an activity takes place can also be called a session, e.g. *a recording session.*

[from Latin *sessio* meaning 'sitting']

set, sets, setting, set
1 (noun) Several things make a set when they belong together or form a group, e.g. *a set of encyclopaedias.*
2 In maths, a set is a collection of numbers or other things which are treated as a group.
3 (verb) If something is set somewhere, that is where it is, e.g. *The house is set back from the road.*
4 When the sun sets, it goes below the horizon.

5 When you set the table, you prepare it for a meal by putting plates and cutlery on it.
6 When you set a clock or a control, you adjust it to a particular point or position.
7 If you set a time, price, or level, you decide what it will be.
8 If you set a precedent, standard, or example, you establish it for other people to follow.
9 If you set someone a piece of work or a target, you give it to them to do or to achieve.
10 To set a poem to music means to write music for it.
11 When something such as jelly or cement sets, it becomes firm or hard.
12 (adjective) Something that is set is fixed and not varying, e.g. *a set charge.*
13 A set book must be studied by the students taking a course.
14 If you are set to do something, you are ready or likely to do it.
15 If you are set on doing something, you are determined to do it.
16 If a play, film, or story is set at a particular time or in a particular place, the events in it take place at that time or in that place.
17 (noun) A television set is a television.
18 The set for a play or film is the scenery or furniture on the stage or in the studio.
19 In tennis, a set is a group of six or more games. There are usually several sets in a match.

[senses 1 and 2 are from Latin *secta* meaning 'sect'; senses 3 and 4 are from Old English *settan* meaning 'to cause to sit' or 'to place']

Similar words: (sense 7) fix, arrange, schedule (sense 12) fixed, rigid, inflexible

set about
(phrasal verb) If you set about doing something, you start doing it.

set aside
(phrasal verb) If you set something aside, you keep it so that you can use it later.

set back
1 (phrasal verb) If something sets back a project or scheme, it delays it.
2 (an informal use) If something sets you back a large amount of money, it costs you that much money.

set in
(phrasal verb) If something unpleasant sets in, it begins and seems likely to continue.

set off
1 (phrasal verb) When you set off, you start a journey.
2 To set something off means to cause it to start.

set out
1 (phrasal verb) When you set out, you start a journey.
2 If you set out to do something, you start trying to do it.
3 If you set out facts or opinions, you state them in a clear, organized way.

set up
1 (phrasal verb) If you set something up, you

make all the necessary preparations for it, e.g. *It took a long time to set up the experiment.*
2 If you set up somewhere, you establish yourself there in a new home or business.
3 (an informal use) If someone sets you up, they make it seem that you have done something wrong when you have not.

setback, setbacks
(noun) A setback is something that delays or hinders you.

set square, set squares
(noun) A set square is a triangular piece of plastic or metal used for drawing angles and lines.

settee, settees
(noun) A settee is a long comfortable seat for two or three people to sit on.

setter, setters
(noun) A setter is a long-haired breed of dog originally used in hunting.

set theory
(noun) Set theory is a branch of mathematics concerned with the properties of sets and the relations between sets.

setting, settings
1 (noun) The setting of something is its surroundings or circumstances, e.g. *The castle provided the perfect setting for a horror story.*
2 The settings on a machine are the different positions to which the controls can be adjusted.
3 A place setting is an arrangement of cutlery on a table for one person.

settle, settles, settling, settled
1 (verb) To settle an argument means to put an end to it, e.g. *The strike was finally settled.*
2 If something is settled, it has all been decided and arranged.
3 If you settle on something or settle for it, you choose it, e.g. *He settled for hamburgers.*
4 When you settle a bill, you pay it.
5 If you settle in a place, you make it your permanent home.
6 If you settle yourself somewhere, you sit down and make yourself comfortable.
7 If something settles, it sinks slowly down and comes to rest, e.g. *The dust was settling.*
8 When birds or insects settle on something, they land on it.
9 To settle money on someone means to formally give it to them, for example in a will.

settle down
1 (phrasal verb) When someone settles down, they start living a quiet life in one place, especially when they get married.
2 To settle down means to become quiet or calm.

settle up
(phrasal verb) When you settle up, you pay a bill.

settlement, settlements
1 (noun) A settlement is an official agreement between people who have been involved in a conflict, e.g. *The chance for a peaceful political settlement has disappeared.*

2 A settlement is also a place where people have settled and built homes.

settler, settlers
(noun) A settler is someone who settles in a new country, e.g. *The first White settlers in South Africa were Dutch.*

seven the number 7.

seventeen the number 17.
seventeenth.

seventh, sevenths
1 The seventh item in a series is the one counted as number seven.
2 (noun) A seventh is one of seven equal parts.
3 In music, a seventh is the interval between two notes of a scale when there are five notes separating them.

seventy, seventies
the number 70.
seventieth.

sever, severs, severing, severed
1 (verb) To sever something means to cut it off or cut right through it.
2 If you sever a connection with someone, you end it completely, e.g. *She severed all ties with her parents.*
[from Latin *separare* meaning 'to separate']

several
(adjective or pronoun) Several people or things means a small number of them.

severance pay
(noun) Severance pay is money that a firm pays its employees when it makes them redundant.

severe
1 (adjective) extremely bad or unpleasant, e.g. *The blast caused severe damage.*
2 stern and harsh, e.g. *I hope the Magistrate has not been too severe with him.*
severely (adverb), **severity** (noun).
[from Latin *severus* meaning 'stern' or 'harsh']

sew, sews, sewing, sewed, sewn (pronounced **so**)
(verb) When you sew things together, you join them using a needle and thread.
sewing (noun).

sewage
(noun) Sewage is dirty water and waste matter which is carried away in sewers.

sewer, sewers
(noun) A sewer is a large underground channel that carries sewage to a place where it is treated to make it harmless.
[from Old French *essever* meaning 'to drain']

sewerage
(noun) Sewerage is the system by which sewage is carried away in sewers and treated.

sex, sexes
1 (noun) The sexes are the two groups, male and female, into which people and animals are divided.
2 The sex of a person or animal is their characteristic of being either male or female.

3 Sex is the physical activity by which people and animals produce young.

sexism
(noun) Sexism is discrimination against the members of one sex, usually women.
sexist (adjective and noun).

sexless
(adjective) having or showing no sexual feelings.

sextant, sextants
(noun) A sextant is an instrument used in navigation for measuring angles, for example the angle between a planet and the horizon. This information can help calculate a ship's or aeroplane's position.
[from Latin *sextans* meaning 'one sixth of a unit', because the instrument contains an arc which is a sixth of a circle]

sextet, sextets
(noun) A sextet is a group of six musicians who sing or play together; also a piece of music written for six instruments or singers.
[from Latin *sex* meaning 'six']

sexton, sextons
(noun) A sexton is a person who looks after a church and its graveyard.

sextuplet, sextuplets
(noun) Sextuplets are six children born at the same time to the same mother.

sexual
1 (adjective) connected with the act of sex or with people's desire for sex, e.g. *sexual attraction.*
2 relating to the difference between males and females, e.g. *sexual equality.*
3 relating to the biological process by which people and animals produce young, e.g. *sexual reproduction.*
sexually (adverb).

sexual intercourse
(noun) Sexual intercourse is the physical act of sex between a man and a woman.

sexuality (pronounced seks-yoo-**al**-it-ee)
(noun) A person's sexuality is their ability to experience sexual feelings.

sexy, sexier, sexiest
(adjective) sexually attractive or exciting, e.g. *her sexy brown eyes.*

shabby, shabbier, shabbiest
1 (adjective) old and worn in appearance, e.g. *shabby clothes.*
2 dressed in old, worn-out clothes, e.g. *shabby children.*
3 behaving in a mean or unfair way, e.g. *What a shabby way to treat your friends!*
shabbily (adverb).
[from Old English *sceabb* meaning 'scab']

Similar words: (sense 1) threadbare, worn, faded

shack, shacks
(noun) A shack is a small hut.

shackle, shackles, shackling, shackled
1 (noun) In the past, shackles were two metal rings joined by a chain fastened around a prisoner's wrists or ankles.
2 (verb) To shackle someone means to put shackles on them.
3 (a literary use) If you are shackled by something, it restricts or hampers you.
4 (noun; a literary use) Shackles are circumstances that restrict or hamper you, e.g. *the shackles of colonial rule.*
[from Old English *sceacel* meaning 'fetter']

shade, shades, shading, shaded
1 (noun) Shade is an area of darkness and coolness which the sun does not reach, e.g. *There are no trees or bushes to give shade.*
2 (verb) If a place is shaded by trees or buildings, they prevent the sun from shining on it.
3 If you shade your eyes, you put your hand in front of them to protect them from a bright light.
4 (noun) A shade is a lampshade.
5 The shades of a colour are its different forms. For example, olive green is a shade of green.
6 (verb) When one thing shades into another, there is no clear division between them, e.g. *reds shading into pinks... innocence shading into ignorance.*

shadow, shadows, shadowing, shadowed
1 (noun) A shadow is the dark shape made when an object prevents light from reaching a surface.
2 Shadow is darkness caused by light not reaching a place.
3 (phrase) If someone is **a shadow of their former self**, they are much weaker than they used to be.
4 (verb) To shadow someone means to follow them and watch them closely.
[from Old English *sceadu* meaning 'shade']

Shadow Cabinet
(noun) The Shadow Cabinet consists of the leaders of the main opposition party, each of whom is concerned with a particular policy.

shadowy
1 (adjective) A shadowy place is dark and full of shadows.
2 A shadowy figure or shape is difficult to see because it is dark or misty.
3 Shadowy also means not well known or understood, e.g. *the shadowy world of espionage.*

shady, shadier, shadiest
1 (adjective) A shady place is sheltered from sunlight by trees or buildings.
2 (an informal use) Shady people and activities are slightly dishonest and not to be trusted.

shaft, shafts
1 (noun) A shaft is a vertical passage, for example one for a lift or one in a mine.
2 A shaft in a machine is a rod which revolves and transfers movement in the machine, e.g. *the drive shaft.*
3 A shaft of light is a beam of light.

shaggy, shaggier, shaggiest
(adjective) Shaggy hair or fur is long and untidy.
[from Old English *sceacga* meaning 'rough hair' or 'wool']

Shah, Shahs
(noun) The ruler of Iran used to be called the Shah.
[from Persian *shah* meaning 'king']

shake, shakes, shaking, shook, shaken
1 (verb) To shake something means to move it quickly from side to side or up and down.
2 (noun) If you give something a shake, you shake it.
3 (verb) If something shakes, it moves from side to side or up and down with small, quick movements.
4 If your voice shakes, it trembles because you are nervous or angry.
5 If something shakes you, it shocks and upsets you.
6 If something shakes your beliefs, it makes you doubt them.
7 When you shake your head, you move it from side to side in order to say 'no'.
8 (phrase) When you **shake hands** with someone, you grasp their hand as a way of greeting them.

Similar words: (sense 3) quake, quiver, tremble, shudder, tremor, shiver

shake-up, shake-ups
(noun) A shake-up is a major set of changes in an organization or system.

shaky, shakier, shakiest
(adjective) rather weak and unsteady, e.g. *a company with very shaky financial prospects.*
shakily (adverb).

shale
(noun) Shale is a smooth soft rock, which breaks easily into flakes.
[from Old English *scealu* meaning 'shell']

shall
1 (verb) If I say I shall do something, I mean that I intend to do it.
2 If I say something shall happen, I am emphasizing that it will definitely happen, or I am ordering it to happen, e.g. *No more drink shall be drunk tonight.*
3 Shall is also used in questions when you are asking what to do, or making a suggestion, e.g. *Shall I shut the door?... Shall we go to a film?*

shallot, shallots (pronounced shal-**lot**)
(noun) A shallot is a kind of small onion.

shallow, shallower, shallowest; shallows
1 (adjective) Shallow means not deep.
2 Shallow also means not involving serious thought or sincere feelings, e.g. *This kind of life is shallow and trivial.*
3 If your breathing is shallow, you take only short breaths.
4 (noun) The shallows are the shallow part of a river or lake.
shallowness (noun).

sham, shams
1 (noun) Something that is a sham is not real or genuine.
2 (adjective) not real or genuine, e.g. *a sham fight.*

shamble, shambles, shambling, shambled
1 (noun) If an event is a shambles, it is confused and badly organized, e.g. *The rehearsal was a shambles.*
2 (verb) If you shamble, you walk clumsily, dragging your feet.
[sense 1 is from Old English *shamble* meaning 'meat-seller's table'; sense two is from *shamble legs* meaning 'legs like a meat-seller's table']

shame, shames, shaming, shamed
1 (noun) Shame is the feeling of guilt or embarrassment you get when you know you have done something wrong or foolish.
2 To bring shame on someone means to make people lose respect for them, e.g. *Don't bring shame on the family.*
3 (verb) If something shames you, it makes you feel ashamed.
4 If you shame someone into doing something, you force them to do it by making them feel ashamed not to, e.g. *Father was shamed into helping them.*
5 (noun) If you say something is a shame, you mean that you are sorry about it, e.g. *It's a shame he didn't come.*

shamefaced
(adjective) guilty or embarrassed.
shamefacedly (adverb).

shameful
(adjective) If someone's behaviour is shameful, they ought to be ashamed of it.
shamefully (adverb).

shameless
(adjective) behaving in an indecent or unacceptable way, but showing no shame or embarrassment, e.g. *a shameless hussy.*
shamelessly (adverb).

Similar words: brazen, barefaced, wanton

shampoo, shampoos, shampooing, shampooed
1 (noun) Shampoo is a soapy liquid used for washing your hair.
2 (verb) When you shampoo your hair, you wash it with shampoo.
[from Hindi *champna* meaning 'to knead']

shamrock, shamrocks
(noun) A shamrock is a plant with three round leaves on each stem. The shamrock is the national emblem of Ireland.
[from Irish Gaelic *seamrog* meaning 'little clover']

shandy, shandies
(noun) Shandy is a drink made by mixing beer and lemonade.

shank, shanks
1 (noun) The shank of an object is the long, thin, straight part of it, e.g. *the shank of a hook.*
2 Your shanks are the parts of your legs between your knees and your ankles.

shanty, shanties
1 (noun) A shanty is a small, rough hut.
2 A sea shanty is a song sailors used to sing.
[sense 1 is from Canadian French *chantier* meaning 'cabin built in a lumber camp'; sense 2 is from French *chanter* meaning 'to sing']

shanty town, shanty towns
(noun) A shanty town is a collection of small rough huts which poor people live in.

shape, shapes, shaping, shaped
1 (noun) The shape of something is the form or pattern of its outline, for example whether it is round or square.
2 A shape is something with a definite form, for example a circle, square, or triangle.
3 The shape of something such as an organization is its structure and size.
4 (verb) If you shape an object, you form it into a particular shape, e.g. *He began to shape the dough into rolls.*
5 To shape something means to cause it to develop in a particular way, e.g. *It was the Greeks who shaped the thinking of Western Man.*
6 (phrase) **In good shape** means in good condition or in a good state of health.
[from Old English *gesceap* meaning 'creation' or 'form']

Similar words: (sense 1) form, formation, contour, line, mould, configuration

shape up
(phrasal verb) The way that something is shaping up is the way that it is developing.

shapeless
(adjective) not having a definite shape.

shapely, shapelier, shapeliest
(adjective) A shapely woman has an attractive figure.

Similar words: voluptuous, buxom, curvaceous

shard, shards
(noun) A shard is a small fragment of pottery, glass, or metal.

share, shares, sharing, shared
1 (verb) If two people share something, they both use it, do it, or have it, e.g. *He shared a room with his brother.*
2 If you share an idea or a piece of news with someone, you tell it to them.
3 (noun) A share of something is a portion of it.
4 The shares of a company are the equal parts into which its ownership is divided. People can buy shares as an investment.
shared (adjective).
[from Old English *scearu* meaning 'cutting' or 'division']

Similar words: (sense 3) allocation, allotment, quota, ration, lot, cut, portion

share out
(phrasal verb) If you share something out, you distribute it equally among a group of people.

shareholder, shareholders
(noun) A shareholder is a person who owns shares in a company.

shark, sharks
1 (noun) Sharks are large, powerful fish with sharp teeth. They sometimes attack people.
2 A shark is also a person who cheats people out of money.

sharp, sharper, sharpest; sharps
1 (adjective) A sharp object has a fine edge or point that is good for cutting or piercing things.
2 A sharp outline or distinction is easy to see.
3 A sharp person is quick to notice or understand things.
4 A sharp change is sudden and significant, e.g. *sharp increases in food prices.*
5 A sharp action or movement is done quickly and firmly.
6 If you say something in a sharp way, you say it firmly and rather angrily.
7 A sharp sound is short, sudden, and quite loud.
8 A sharp pain is sudden and painful.
9 A sharp taste is slightly sour.
10 (adverb) If something happens at a certain time sharp, it happens at that time precisely, e.g. *His train came in at eight sharp.*
11 (noun) In music, a sharp is a note or key a semitone higher than that described by the same letter. It is represented by the symbol ' ♯ '.
12 (adjective) A musical instrument or note that is sharp is slightly too high in pitch.
sharply (adverb), **sharpness** (noun).

Similar words: (sense 3) keen, acute

sharpen, sharpens, sharpening, sharpened
1 (verb) To sharpen an object means to make its edge or point sharper.
2 If your senses or abilities sharpen, you become quicker at noticing or understanding things.
3 If you voice sharpens, you begin to speak more angrily or harshly.
4 If something sharpens the disagreements between people, it makes them greater.

sharpener, sharpeners
(noun) A sharpener is a device for sharpening things.

shatter, shatters, shattering, shattered
1 (verb) If something shatters, it breaks into a lot of small pieces.
2 If something shatters your hopes or beliefs, it destroys them completely.
3 If you are shattered by an event or piece of news, you are shocked and upset by it.

shattered
(adjective; an informal word) completely exhausted, e.g. *I'm shattered after a day's work.*

shattering
1 (adjective) making you feel shocked and upset, e.g. *a shattering experience.*
2 making you very tired, e.g. *Sunday had been a shattering day.*

shave, shaves, shaving, shaved
1 (verb) When a man shaves, he removes hair from his face with a razor.
2 (noun) When a man has a shave, he shaves.
3 If you shave off part of a piece of wood, you cut very thin pieces from it.
4 (an informal phrase) A **close shave** is a narrow escape.

shaven
(adjective) If part of someone's body is shaven, it has been shaved, e.g. *his shaven head.*

shaver, shavers
(noun) A shaver is an electric razor.

shavings
(plural noun) Shavings are small, very thin pieces of wood which have been cut from a larger piece.

shawl, shawls
(noun) A shawl is a large piece of woollen cloth worn round a woman's head or shoulders or used to wrap a baby in.
[from Persian *shal* meaning 'shawl']

she
(pronoun) 'She' is used to refer to a woman or girl whose identity is clear. 'She' is also used to refer to a country, a ship, or a car.

sheaf, sheaves
1 (noun) A sheaf of papers is a bundle of them.
2 A sheaf of corn is a bundle of ripe corn tied together.

shear, shears, shearing, sheared, shorn
1 (verb) To shear a sheep means to cut the wool off it.
2 (plural noun) Shears are a tool like a large pair of scissors, and used especially for cutting hedges.

shear off
(phrasal verb) If a piece of metal shears off, it breaks because it is too weak or under too much strain.

sheath, sheaths
1 (noun) A sheath is a covering for the blade of a knife.
2 A sheath is also a condom.

sheathe, sheathes, sheathing, sheathed (rhymes with breathe)
(verb) When you sheathe a knife, you put it in its sheath.

shed, sheds, shedding, shed
1 (noun) A shed is a small building used for storing things.
2 (verb) When an animal sheds hair or skin, some of its hair or skin drops off. When a tree sheds its leaves, its leaves fall off.
3 (a formal use) To shed something also means to get rid of it, e.g. *2000 workers are due to be shed by the company.*
4 If a lorry sheds its load, the load falls off the lorry onto the road.
5 If you shed tears, you cry.
6 To shed blood means to kill people violently.
7 (phrase) If something **sheds light** on a problem, it makes it clearer by giving more information about it.
[senses 2-7 are from Old English *sceadan* meaning 'to drop', 'to spill', or 'to separate']

sheen
(noun) A sheen is a gentle brightness on the surface of something.

sheep
(noun) A sheep is a farm animal with a thick woolly coat. Sheep are kept for meat and wool.

sheepdog, sheepdogs
(noun) A sheepdog is a breed of dog often used for controlling sheep.

sheepish
(adjective) If you look sheepish, you look embarrassed because you feel shy or foolish.
sheepishly (adverb).

sheepskin
(noun) Sheepskin is the skin and wool of a sheep, used for making rugs and coats.

sheer, sheerest
1 (adjective) Sheer means complete and total, e.g. *The hotel was sheer luxury.*
2 A sheer cliff or drop is vertical.
3 Sheer fabrics are very light and delicate.

sheet, sheets
1 (noun) A sheet is a large rectangular piece of cloth used to cover a bed.
2 A sheet of paper is a rectangular piece of it.
3 A sheet of glass, metal, or wood is a large, flat piece of it.

sheet anchor, sheet anchors
(noun) A sheet anchor is a large, strong anchor used when a boat is in difficulties.

sheet lightning
(noun) Sheet lightning is lightning which appears to flash across a large area of sky at once.

sheik, sheiks (pronounced shake); also spelled sheikh
(noun) A sheik is an Arab chief or ruler.
[from Arabic *shaykh* meaning 'old man']

shelf, shelves
(noun) A shelf is a flat piece of wood, metal, or glass fixed to a wall and used for putting things on.
[from Old English *scylfe* meaning 'partition' or 'compartment']

shelf life
(noun) The shelf life of a product is the length of time it can be kept in a shop before it becomes too old or stale to sell.

shell, shells, shelling, shelled
1 (noun) The shell of an egg or nut is its hard covering.
2 The shell of a tortoise, snail, or crab is the hard protective covering on its back.
3 (verb) If you shell peas or nuts, you remove their natural covering.
4 (noun) The shell of a building or other structure is its frame, e.g. *the burned-out shell that had once been their home.*
5 A shell is also a container filled with explosives that can be fired from a gun.
6 (verb) To shell a place means to fire large explosive shells at it.

shellfish
(noun) A shellfish is a small sea creature with a shell.

shell shock
(noun) Shell shock is an illness affecting the mind or nerves of soldiers, caused by the frightening experiences of war.

shelter, shelters, sheltering, sheltered
1 (noun) A shelter is a small building made to protect people from bad weather or danger.
2 If a place provides shelter, it provides protection from bad weather or danger.
3 (verb) If you shelter in a place, you stay there and are safe.
4 If you shelter someone, you provide them with a place to stay when they are in danger.

sheltered
1 (adjective) A sheltered place is protected from wind and rain.
2 If you lead a sheltered life, you do not experience unpleasant or upsetting things.
3 Sheltered accommodation is accommodation designed for old or handicapped people. It consists of a group of individual houses or flats with a caretaker to provide supervision and help.

shelve, shelves, shelving, shelved
(verb) If you shelve a plan, you decide to postpone it for a while.

shepherd, shepherds, shepherding, shepherded
1 (noun) A shepherd is a person who looks after sheep.
2 (verb) If you shepherd someone somewhere, you accompany them there.
[from Old English *scep* meaning 'sheep' and *hierde* meaning 'keeper of a herd']

shepherdess, shepherdesses
(noun) A shepherdess is a woman who looks after sheep.

shepherd's pie, shepherd's pies
(noun) Shepherd's pie is a dish of minced meat covered with mashed potatoes and baked.

sherbet
(noun) Sherbet is a sweet fizzy powder used in sweets and drinks.
[from Arabic *sharbah* meaning 'drink']

sheriff, sheriffs
1 (noun) In America, a sheriff is a person elected to enforce the law in a county.
2 In Scotland, a sheriff is the senior judge of a county or district.
3 In England and Wales, a sheriff is a person appointed by the king or queen to carry out various ceremonial duties in a county.
[from Old English *scir* meaning 'shire' and *gerefa* meaning 'reeve', an official]

sherry, sherries
(noun) Sherry is a kind of fortified wine, often drunk before a meal.
[from the Spanish town *Jerez* where it was first made]

Shetland pony, Shetland ponies
(noun) A Shetland pony is a kind of very small, strong pony.

shield, shields, shielding, shielded
1 (noun) A shield is a large piece of metal or leather that soldiers used to carry to protect themselves.
2 If something is a shield against something, it gives protection from it.

3 (verb) To shield someone means to protect them from something.

shift, shifts, shifting, shifted
1 (verb) If you shift something, you move it. If something shifts, it moves, e.g. *He shifted the chair closer to the bed.*
2 (noun) A shift in an opinion or situation is a slight change.
3 (verb) If an opinion or situation shifts, it changes slightly.
4 (noun) A shift is also a set period during which people work in a factory, e.g. *the night shift.*

shift key, shift keys
(noun) The shift key on a typewriter is the key you press to type a capital letter.

shiftless
(adjective) lazy and lacking ambition.

shifty, shiftier, shiftiest
(adjective) looking sly and deceitful.
shiftiness (noun).

shilling, shillings
(noun) A shilling was a unit of money equivalent to 5p, used in Britain until 1971.

shillyshally, shillyshallies, shillyshallying, shillyshallied
(verb) If you shillyshally, you hesitate a lot and cannot make a decision.
[from an 18th century expression '*to go, shill I, shall I*' meaning 'shall I or shan't I go']

shimmer, shimmers, shimmering, shimmered
1 (verb) If something shimmers, it shines with a faint, flickering light.
2 (noun) A shimmer is a faint, flickering light.

shin, shins, shinning, shinned
1 (noun) Your shin is the front part of your leg between your knee and your ankle.
2 (verb) If you shin up a tree or pole, you climb it quickly by gripping it with your hands and legs.

shindig, shindigs
(noun; an informal word) A shindig is a large, noisy party.

shine, shines, shining, shone
1 (verb) When something shines, it gives out or reflects a bright light, e.g. *The sun shone all day... His eyes shone like stars.*
2 If you shine a torch or lamp somewhere, you point it there.
3 If you shine at something, you are very good at it, e.g. *He shines at amateur theatricals.*

shingle, shingles
1 (noun) Shingle consists of small pebbles on the seashore.
2 Shingles are small wooden roof tiles.
3 Shingles is a disease that causes a painful red rash, especially around the waist.
[sense 2 is from Latin *scindula* meaning 'split piece of wood'; sense 3 is from Latin *cingulum* meaning 'belt']

shining
1 (adjective) Shining things are very bright, usually because they are reflecting light, e.g. *a row of shining glasses.*
2 A shining achievement is extremely good.

Similar words: (sense 1) incandescent, phosphorescent, refulgent, glowing, gleaming

shiny, shinier, shiniest
(adjective) Shiny things are bright and look as if they have been polished, e.g. *shiny black shoes.*

ship, ships, shipping, shipped
1 (noun) A ship is a large boat which carries passengers or cargo.
2 (verb) If people or things are shipped somewhere, they are transported there.

shipboard
(noun) Something that happens on shipboard happens on board a ship.

shipment, shipments
1 (noun) A shipment is a quantity of goods that are transported somewhere, e.g. *They sent him a shipment of tobacco.*
2 The shipment of goods is the transporting of them.

shipping
1 (noun) Shipping is the transport of cargo on ships.
2 You can also refer to ships generally as shipping, e.g. *Attention all shipping!*

shipshape
(adjective) If a place is shipshape, it is neat and tidy.

shipwreck, shipwrecks, shipwrecking, shipwrecked
1 (noun) When there is a shipwreck, a ship is destroyed in an accident at sea, e.g. *The whole family perished in a shipwreck.*
2 (verb) If someone is shipwrecked, they survive a shipwreck and manage to reach land.

shipyard, shipyards
(noun) A shipyard is a place where ships are built and repaired.

shire, shires
1 (noun; an old-fashioned use) A shire is a county.
2 The Shires are the Midland counties of England.
[from Old English *scir* meaning 'county']

shire horse, shire horses
(noun) A shire horse is a breed of large, strong horse used for pulling loads.

shirk, shirks, shirking, shirked
(verb) To shirk a task means to avoid doing it.

shirt, shirts
(noun) A shirt is a piece of clothing worn on the upper part of the body. It has a collar, sleeves, and buttons down the front.

shirty
(adjective; an informal word) bad-tempered.

shish kebab (pronounced sheesh kib-**bab**)
(noun) Shish kebab is a dish consisting of small pieces of meat and sometimes vegetables put on a thin metal rod and grilled.
[from Turkish *sis* meaning 'skewer' and Arabic *kebab* meaning 'roast meat']

shiver, shivers, shivering, shivered
1 (verb) When you shiver, you tremble slightly because you are cold or frightened.
2 (noun) A shiver is a slight trembling caused by cold or fear.

shivery
(adjective; an informal word) If you are shivery, you cannot stop shivering.

shoal, shoals
(noun) A shoal of fish is a large group of them swimming together.

shock, shocks, shocking, shocked
1 (noun) If you have a shock, you have a sudden upsetting experience.
2 Shock is a person's emotional and physical condition when something very unpleasant or upsetting has happened to them.
3 In medicine, shock is a serious physical condition in which the blood cannot circulate properly because of an injury.
4 A shock is also a slight movement in something when it is hit by something else, e.g. *The padding should absorb any sudden shocks.*
5 (verb) If something shocks you, it upsets you because it is unpleasant and unexpected, e.g. *She was deeply shocked by her husband's death.*
6 You can say that something shocks you when it offends you because it is rude or immoral.
7 (noun) A shock of hair is a thick mass of it.
shocked (adjective).
[senses 1-6 are from Old French *choquier* meaning 'to make violent contact with']

Similar words: (sense 5) traumatize (sense 6) appal, scandalize

shock absorber, shock absorbers
(noun) Shock absorbers are devices fitted near the wheels of a vehicle. They help to prevent the vehicle from bouncing up and down.

shocking
1 (adjective; an informal use) very bad, e.g. *His liver was in a shocking state.*
2 rude or immoral, e.g. *a shocking book.*

shoddy, shoddier, shoddiest
(adjective) badly made or done, e.g. *shoddy work.*

shoe, shoes, shoeing, shod
1 (noun) Shoes are things worn on your feet. They are usually made of leather, and cover most of your foot, but not your ankle.
2 (verb) To shoe a horse means to fix horseshoes onto its hooves.

shoehorn, shoehorns
(noun) A shoehorn is a curved piece of metal, plastic, and, in the past, horn, that you put in the back of your shoe so your foot will go in more easily.

shoestring
(noun) If you do something on a shoestring, you do it using very little money.

shoo, shoos, shooing, shooed
(verb) If you shoo a person or animal away, you

make them go away by waving your arms at them and saying 'shoo'.

shoot, shoots, shooting, shot

1 (verb) To shoot a person or animal means to kill or injure them by firing a gun at them.
2 (noun) A shoot is an occasion when people hunt animals or birds with guns.
3 (verb) To shoot an arrow means to fire it from a bow.
4 If something shoots in a particular direction, it moves there quickly and suddenly, e.g. *She shot back into the room.*
5 When a film is shot, it is filmed, e.g. *Most of the film was shot in Spain.*
6 In games such as football or hockey, to shoot means to kick or hit the ball towards the goal.
7 (noun) A shoot is also a plant that is beginning to grow, or a new part growing from a plant.

shoot up

(phrasal verb) If something shoots up, it grows or increases very quickly, e.g. *The inflation rate shot up to 48%.*

shooting, shootings

(noun) A shooting is an incident in which someone is shot.

shooting star, shooting stars

(noun) A shooting star is a meteor.

shop, shops, shopping, shopped

1 (noun) A shop is a place where things are sold.
2 (verb) When you shop, you go to the shops to buy things.
3 (noun) A shop is also a place where things are manufactured, e.g. *a metalwork shop.*
4 (verb; an informal use) To shop someone means to inform on them.
5 (phrase) When people **talk shop**, they talk about their work, especially at a social occasion.
shopper (noun).
[from Old French *eschoppe* meaning 'stall' or 'booth']

shop around

(phrasal verb) If you shop around, you compare goods in several shops before you buy them.

shop floor

(noun) You can refer to all the workers in a factory as the shop floor.

shopkeeper, shopkeepers

(noun) A shopkeeper is someone who owns or manages a small shop.

shoplifting

(noun) Shoplifting is stealing goods from shops.
shoplifter (noun).

shopping

(noun) Your shopping is the goods you have bought from the shops.

shopsoiled

(adjective) Shopsoiled goods are slightly dirty or damaged because they have been in a shop for a long time.

shop steward, shop stewards

(noun) A shop steward is a trade union member elected to represent the workers in a factory or office.

shore, shores, shoring, shored

1 (noun) The shore of a sea, lake, or wide river is the land along the edge of it.
2 (verb) If you shore something up, you reinforce it or strengthen it, e.g. *Action is needed to shore up economic links with American suppliers.*
[from Old Dutch *schore*]

shoreline, shorelines

(noun) The shoreline is the edge of a sea, lake, or wide river.

shorn

1 Shorn is the past participle of **shear**.
2 (adjective) Grass or hair that is shorn is cut very short.

short, shorter, shortest; shorts

1 (adjective) not lasting very long.
2 small in length, distance, or height, e.g. *Her hair was cut short... the shortest way home.*
3 If you are short with someone, you speak to them crossly.
4 If you have a short temper, you lose it easily.
5 If you are short of something, you do not have enough of it.
6 If a name is short for another name, it is a short version of it.
7 (noun) Shorts are trousers with short legs.
8 (adverb) If you stop short of a place, you do not quite reach it.
9 (phrase) **Short of** is used to say that a level or amount has not quite been reached, e.g. *He was only a year short of fifty.*
10 If something is **cut short**, it is stopped before it has finished.
11 If you **stop short**, you suddenly stop what you are doing because something has surprised you.

Similar words: (sense 3) terse, curt, abrupt

shortage, shortages

(noun) If there is a shortage of something, there is not enough of it.

shortbread or shortcake

(noun) Shortbread is a crumbly biscuit made from flour and butter.
[from an old-fashioned use of *short* meaning 'crumbly']

short circuit, short circuits

(noun) A short circuit is a fault in an electrical system. It happens when two points accidentally become connected and the electricity travels directly between them rather than through the complete circuit.

shortcoming, shortcomings

(noun) Shortcomings are faults or weaknesses.

shortcrust

(adjective) Shortcrust pastry is made with a lot of fat and crumbles very easily.

shortcut, shortcuts

1 (noun) A shortcut is a quicker way of getting somewhere than the usual route.
2 A shortcut is also a quicker way of doing something, e.g. *Parents of twins simply have to find shortcuts in housework.*

shorten, shortens, shortening, shortened
(verb) If you shorten something or if it shortens, it becomes shorter, e.g. *The colonel had a plan to shorten the war.*

shortfall, shortfalls
(noun) If there is a shortfall in something, there is less than you need.

shorthand
(noun) Shorthand is a way of writing in which signs represent words or syllables. It is used to write down quickly what someone is saying.

short-handed
(adjective) If a firm is short-handed, it does not have enough workers to do all the work.

short-list, short-lists, short-listing, short-listed
1 (noun) A short-list is a list of people selected from a larger group, from which one person is finally selected for a prize or job.
2 (verb) If someone is short-listed for a job or prize, they are put on a short-list.

short-lived
(adjective) not lasting very long.

shortly
1 (adverb) Shortly means soon, e.g. *She's going to London shortly.*
2 If you speak to someone shortly, you speak to them in a cross and impatient way.

short-sighted
1 (adjective) If you are short-sighted, you cannot see things clearly when they are far away.
2 A short-sighted decision does not take account of the way things may develop in the future.

short-staffed
(adjective) If a firm is short-staffed, it does not have enough workers to do all the work.

short-tempered
(adjective) Someone who is short-tempered loses their temper easily.

short-term
(adjective) happening or having an effect within a short time or for a short time.

short wave
(noun) Short wave is a radio wave with a wavelength of between 10 and 100 metres.

shot, shots
1 Shot is the past tense and past participle of **shoot.**
2 (noun) A shot is the act of firing a gun.
3 Someone who is a good shot can shoot accurately.
4 In football, golf, and tennis, a shot is the act of kicking or hitting the ball.
5 A shot is also a photograph or short film sequence, e.g. *The film contained some shots of the university.*
6 (an informal use) If you have a shot at something, you try to do it.
7 (an informal use) A shot of a drug is an injection of it.
8 (phrase; an informal use) If you do something **like a shot**, you do it quickly and eagerly.

shotgun, shotguns
(noun) A shotgun is a gun that fires a lot of small pellets all at once.

shot put
(noun) In athletics, the shot put is an event in which the contestants throw a heavy metal ball called a shot as far as possible.
shot putter (noun).

should
1 (verb) You use 'should' to say that something ought to happen, e.g. *Crimes should be punished... She should have won.*
2 You also use 'should' to say that you expect something to happen, e.g. *We should be there by dinner... They should have heard the news by now.*
3 (a formal use) You can use 'should' to announce that you are about to do or say something, e.g. *I should like to say a few words.*
4 'Should' is used in conditional sentences, e.g. *If we should be seen together, they might get suspicious.*
5 'Should' is sometimes used in 'that' clauses, e.g. *It's strange that you should come today.*
6 If you say that you should think something, you mean that it is probably true, e.g. *I should think it was about twelve years ago.*

shoulder, shoulders, shouldering, shouldered
1 (noun) Your shoulders are the parts of your body between your neck and the tops of your arms.
2 The shoulders of a piece of clothing are the parts that cover your shoulders.
3 (phrase) If someone needs **a shoulder to cry on**, they need someone to listen to them sympathetically.
4 If you **rub shoulders** with famous people, you meet them and talk to them.
5 (verb) If you shoulder something heavy, you put it across one of your shoulders to carry it.
6 If you shoulder the responsibility or blame for something, you accept it.

shoulder blade, shoulder blades
(noun) Your shoulder blades are the two large, flat, triangular bones in the upper part of your back, below your shoulders.

shout, shouts, shouting, shouted
1 (noun) A shout is a loud call or cry.
2 (verb) If you shout something, you say it very loudly, e.g. *She shouted at us for spoiling her evening.*

Similar words: call, cry, yell, roar, bellow, bawl

shout down
(phrasal verb) If you shout someone down, you prevent them from being heard by shouting at them.

shove, shoves, shoving, shoved
1 (verb) If you shove someone or something, you push them roughly, e.g. *He shoved the man through the door.*
2 (noun) A shove is a rough push.
[from Old English *scufan* meaning 'to push']

shove off
(phrasal verb; an informal use) If you tell someone to shove off, you are telling them angrily and rudely to go away.

shovel, shovels, shovelling, shovelled
1 (noun) A shovel is a tool like a spade, used for moving earth, coal, or snow.
2 (verb) If you shovel earth, coal, or snow, you move it with a shovel.

show, shows, showing, showed, shown
1 (verb) To show that something exists or is true means to prove it, e.g. *The postmortem shows that death was due to natural causes.*
2 If a picture shows something, it represents it, e.g. *The painting shows four athletes bathing.*
3 If you show someone something, you let them see it, e.g. *Let me show you the garden.*
4 If you show someone to a room or seat, you lead them there.
5 If you show someone how to do something, you demonstrate it to them.
6 If something shows, it is visible.
7 If something shows a quality or characteristic, you can see that it has it, e.g. *The sketch shows a lot of talent.*
8 If you show your feelings, you let people see them, e.g. *She was feeling sad and didn't want to show it.*
9 If you show affection or mercy, you behave in an affectionate or merciful way, e.g. *She often showed me kindness.*
10 (noun) A show of a feeling or attitude is behaviour in which you show it, e.g. *a show of defiance.*
11 A show is a form of light entertainment at the theatre or on television.
12 (verb) To show a film or television programme means to let the public see it.
13 (noun) A show is also an exhibition, e.g. *a flower show.*
14 (phrase) If something is **on show**, it is being exhibited for the public to see.
15 If something is done **for show**, it is done to give a good impression.

Similar words: (sense 1) demonstrate, reveal
(sense 2) exhibit, reveal
(sense 7) demonstrate, reveal, display
(sense 8) reveal
(sense 13) exhibit, exhibition, spectacle, pageant, pageantry, performance, presentation, display

show off
1 (phrasal verb; an informal use) If someone is showing off, they are trying to impress people.
2 If you show something off, you show it to a lot of people because you are proud of it, e.g. *He was eager to show off the new car.*

Similar words: (sense 2) flaunt, vaunt, parade

show up
1 (phrasal verb; an informal use) If you show up, you arrive at a place where you are expected.
2 If something shows up, it can be seen clearly, e.g. *Dark colours will not show up against a dark background.*

3 (an informal use) If someone shows you up, they embarrass you by behaving badly.

show business
(noun) Show business is entertainment in the theatre, films, and television.

showcase, showcases
1 (noun) A showcase is a glass container in which valuable objects are exhibited.
2 A showcase for something is a situation or setting in which it is shown to its best advantage.

showdown, showdowns
(noun; an informal word) A showdown is a major argument or conflict intended to end a dispute.

shower, showers, showering, showered
1 (noun) A shower is a device which sprays you with water so that you can wash yourself.
2 If you have a shower, you wash yourself by standing under a shower.
3 (verb) If you shower, you have a shower.
4 (noun) A shower is also a short period of rain.
5 You can refer to a lot of things falling at once as a shower.
6 (verb) If you are showered with a lot of things, they fall on you.

showery
(adjective) If the weather is showery, there are showers of rain.

showing, showings
(noun) A showing of a film or television programme is a presentation of it so that the public can see it.

showjumping
(noun) Showjumping is a horse-riding competition in which the horses jump over a series of high walls and fences.

show-off, show-offs
(noun; an informal word) A show-off is someone who tries to impress people with their knowledge or skills.

showplace, showplaces
(noun) A showplace is a place or building that is beautifully designed or well-equipped, and usually intended to be shown to the public.

showroom, showrooms
(noun) A showroom is a shop where goods such as cars or electrical appliances are displayed.

showy, showier, showiest
(adjective) large or bright and intended to impress people, e.g. *a showy bracelet.*

Similar words: loud, flashy, garish, ostentatious, gaudy, flamboyant

shrapnel
(noun) Shrapnel consists of small pieces of metal scattered from an exploding shell.
[named after General Henry *Shrapnel* (1761-1842), who invented it]

shred, shreds, shredding, shredded
1 (verb) If you shred something, you cut or tear it into very small pieces.
2 (noun) A shred of paper or material is a small, narrow piece of it.

3 If there is not a shred of something, there is absolutely none of it, e.g. *There is no shred of evidence to support this theory.*

shrew, shrews (pronounced **shroo**)
1 (noun) A shrew is a small mouse-like animal with a long pointed nose.
2 A shrew is also a bad-tempered woman.

shrewd, shrewder, shrewdest
(adjective) Someone who is shrewd is intelligent and makes good judgments.
shrewdly (adverb), **shrewdness** (noun).

Similar words: acute, astute, canny, keen, knowing, perceptive

shriek, shrieks, shrieking, shrieked
1 (noun) A shriek is a high-pitched scream.
2 (verb) If you shriek, you make a high-pitched scream.

shrift
(noun) If you give someone or something short shrift, you pay very little attention to them.
[from Old English *scrift* meaning 'confession'; 'short shrift' referred to the short time allowed to prisoners before they were put to death to make their confession]

shrill, shriller, shrillest
(adjective) A shrill sound is unpleasantly high-pitched and piercing.
shrilly (adverb).

shrimp, shrimps
(noun) A shrimp is a small edible shellfish with a long tail and many legs.

shrine, shrines
(noun) A shrine is a place of worship associated with a sacred person or object.
[from Latin *scrinium* meaning 'bookcase'; originally it referred to a container of sacred relics]

shrink, shrinks, shrinking, shrank, shrunk
1 (verb) If something shrinks, it becomes smaller.
2 If you shrink from something, you move away from it because you are afraid of it.
3 (noun; an informal use) A shrink is a psychiatrist.
shrinkage (noun).

shrivel, shrivels, shrivelling, shrivelled
(verb) When something shrivels, it becomes dry and withered.

shroud, shrouds, shrouding, shrouded
1 (noun) A shroud is a cloth in which a dead body is wrapped before it is buried.
2 (verb) If something is shrouded in darkness or fog, it is hidden by it.
3 If something is shrouded in mystery, very little is known about it.
[from Old English *scrud* meaning 'garment']

shrub, shrubs
(noun) A shrub is a low, bushy plant.

shrubbery, shrubberies
(noun) A shrubbery is part of a garden where there are a lot of shrubs.

shrug, shrugs, shrugging, shrugged
1 (verb) If you shrug your shoulders, you raise them slightly as a sign of indifference.
2 (noun) If you give a shrug of your shoulders, you shrug them.

shrug off
(phrasal verb) If you shrug something off, you ignore it or treat it as unimportant, e.g. *The Chairman shrugs off any criticism of their methods.*

shrunken
(adjective; a formal use) Something that is shrunken has become smaller than it used to be, e.g. *a shrunken old man.*

shudder, shudders, shuddering, shuddered
1 (verb) If you shudder, you tremble with fear or horror.
2 (noun) A shudder is a shiver of fear or horror.
3 (verb) If a machine or vehicle shudders, it shakes violently.
[from Old German *schoderen* meaning 'to shake']

shuffle, shuffles, shuffling, shuffled
1 (verb) If you shuffle, you walk without lifting your feet properly off the ground.
2 (noun) A shuffle is the way someone walks when they shuffle.
3 (verb) If you shuffle about, you move about and fidget because you feel uncomfortable or embarrassed.
4 If you shuffle a pack of cards, you mix them up before you begin a game.

shun, shuns, shunning, shunned
(verb) If you shun someone or something, you deliberately avoid them.

shunt, shunts, shunting, shunted
(verb; an informal word) If you shunt people or things to a place, you move them there, e.g. *the sound of desks being shunted across the room.*

shut, shuts, shutting, shut
1 (verb) If you shut something, you close it.
2 (adjective) If something is shut, it is closed.
3 (informal phrases) If someone tells you to **shut your mouth** or **shut your face**, they are telling you rudely to stop talking.
4 (verb) When a shop or pub shuts, it is closed and you can no longer go into it.

shut down
(phrasal verb) When a factory or business is shut down, it is closed permanently.
shutdown (noun).

shut up
(phrasal verb; an informal expression) If you shut up, you stop talking.

shutter, shutters
1 (noun) Shutters are hinged wooden or metal covers fitted on the outside or inside of a window.
2 The shutter in a camera is the part which opens to allow light through the lens when a photograph is taken.

shuttle, shuttles
1 (adjective) A shuttle service is an air, bus, or

train service which makes frequent journeys between two places.

2 (noun) A shuttle is a plane used in a shuttle service.

3 A shuttle is also the part of a loom which takes a thread backwards and forwards over other threads in order to weave cloth.
[from Old English *scytel* meaning 'bolt' or 'dart', from the shape and movement of the shuttle of a loom]

shuttlecock, shuttlecocks
(noun) A shuttlecock is the feathered object used as a ball in the game of badminton.

shy, shyer, shyest; shies, shying, shied
1 (adjective) A shy person is nervous and uncomfortable in the company of other people.
2 (verb) When a horse shies, it moves away suddenly because something has frightened it.
3 If you shy away from doing something, you avoid doing it because you are afraid or nervous.
shyly (adverb), **shyness** (noun).

Similar words: (sense 1) timid, mousy, diffident, retiring, bashful

SI
(adjective) The SI system is an international system of metric units. The seven basic SI units are the metre, kilogram, second, ampere, kelvin, candela, and mole. SI is an abbreviation for 'Système International'.

Siamese cat, Siamese cats
(noun) A Siamese cat is a breed of cat with short cream or brown fur and blue eyes.

Siamese twins
(plural noun) Siamese twins are twins who are born joined to each other by a part of their bodies.
[from a pair of twins born in Siam, now Thailand, in the 19th century who were joined in this way]

sibilant, sibilants (a formal word)
1 (adjective) making a hissing noise, e.g. *There was a little sibilant whispering.*
2 (noun) Sibilants are speech sounds in which you make a hissing noise, for example 's' and 'z'.
[from Latin *sibilare* meaning 'to hiss']

sibling, siblings
(noun; a formal word) Your siblings are your brothers and sisters.
[from Old English *sibling* meaning 'relative']

sic
You write sic in brackets after quoting a written mistake to show that you are quoting accurately, e.g. *February Fun Raising (sic).*
[from Latin *sic* meaning 'thus' or 'so']

sick, sicker, sickest
1 (adjective) If you are sick, you are ill.
2 If you feel sick, you feel as if you are going to vomit. If you are sick, you vomit.
3 (phrase) If something **makes you sick**, it makes you angry.
4 (adjective; an informal use) If you are sick of doing something, you feel you have been doing it too long.

5 (an informal use) A sick joke or story deals with death or suffering in an unpleasantly frivolous way.
sickness (noun).

Similar words: (sense 2) queasy, nauseous, squeamish

sick bay, sick bays
(noun) A sick bay is an area, for example on a ship, where people who are ill can receive treatment.

sickbed, sickbeds
(noun) Your sickbed is the bed you are lying on while you are ill.

sicken, sickens, sickening, sickened
1 (verb) If something sickens you, it makes you feel disgusted.
2 (an old-fashioned use) If you sicken, you become ill.
sickening (adjective).

sickle, sickles
(noun) A sickle is a tool with a short handle and a curved blade used for cutting grass or grain.
[from Latin *secare* meaning 'to cut']

sickly, sicklier, sickliest
1 (adjective) A sickly person or animal is weak and unhealthy.
2 Sickly also means very unpleasant to smell, taste, or look at.

side, sides, siding, sided
1 (noun) Side refers to a position to the left or right of something, e.g. *Standing on either side of him were two younger men.*
2 The sides of a boundary or barrier are the two areas it separates, e.g. *on the other side of the border.*
3 Your sides are the parts of your body from your armpits down to your hips.
4 The sides of something are its outside surfaces, especially the surfaces which are not its front or back.
5 The sides of a hill or valley are the parts that slope.
6 (adjective) situated on a side of a building or vehicle, e.g. *the side door.*
7 A side road is a small road leading off a larger one.
8 (noun) The two sides in a war, argument, or relationship are the two people or groups involved.
9 The two sides of your family are your mother's family and your father's family.
10 A particular side of something is one aspect of it, e.g. *They wanted to emphasize the political side of the play.*
11 (verb) If you side with someone in an argument, you support them.
12 (adjective) A side issue is an issue that is less important than the main one.
13 (phrase) If you do some work **on the side**, you do it in addition to your main work.
14 If you keep **on the right side** of someone, you stay on good terms with them. If you get **on the**

wrong side of someone, you annoy them and make them dislike you.

sideboard, sideboards
1 (noun) A sideboard is a long, low cupboard for plates and glasses.
2 (plural noun) A man's sideboards are areas of hair growing on his cheeks in front of his ears.

sideburns
(plural noun) A man's sideburns are his sideboards.
[from a 19th century US army general called *Burnside* who wore his whiskers like this]

sidecar, sidecars
(noun) A sidecar is a small vehicle attached to the side of a motorcycle for carrying passengers.

side dish, side dishes
(noun) A side dish is a dish served to accompany a main dish.

side effect, side effects
(noun) The side effects of a drug are the effects it has in addition to its main effects.

sidekick, sidekicks
(noun; an informal word) Someone's sidekick is their close friend who spends a lot of time with them.

sidelight, sidelights
(noun) The sidelights on a vehicle are the small lights at the front.

sideline, sidelines
1 (noun) A sideline is an extra job in addition to your main job.
2 The sidelines are the lines marking the sides of a football pitch or other sports area.

sidelong
(adverb and adjective) out of the corner of your eye, e.g. *a sidelong look*.

sideshow, sideshows
(noun) Sideshows are stalls at a fairground.

sidestep, sidesteps, sidestepping, sidestepped
(verb) If you sidestep a difficult problem or question, you avoid dealing with it.

sidetrack, sidetracks, sidetracking, sidetracked
(verb) If you are sidetracked, you forget what you are supposed to be doing or saying and start doing or talking about something else.

sidewalk, sidewalks
(noun) In American English, a sidewalk is a pavement.

sideways
(adverb) from or towards the side of something or someone.

siding, sidings
(noun) A siding is a short railway track beside the main tracks, where engines and carriages are left when not in use.

sidle, sidles, sidling, sidled
(verb) If you sidle somewhere, you walk there cautiously and slowly, as if you do not want to be noticed.

siege, sieges (pronounced **seej**)
(noun) A siege is a military operation in which

an army surrounds a place and prevents food or help from reaching the people inside.

siesta, siestas (pronounced see-ess-ta)
(noun) A siesta is a short sleep in the afternoon.

sieve, sieves, sieving, sieved (pronounced **siv**)
1 (noun) A sieve is a kitchen implement used for sifting or straining things. It consists of a net attached to a ring of metal or plastic.
2 (verb) If you sieve a powder or liquid, you pass it through a sieve.

sift, sifts, sifting, sifted
1 (verb) If you sift a powdery substance, you pass it through a sieve to remove lumps.
2 If you sift through something such as evidence, you examine it all thoroughly.

sigh, sighs, sighing, sighed
1 (verb) When you sigh, you let out a deep breath.
2 (noun) A sigh is the breath you let out when you sigh.

sight, sights, sighting, sighted
1 (noun) Sight is the ability to see, e.g. *Her sight is failing.*
2 A sight is something you see, e.g. *It was an awe-inspiring sight.*
3 Sights are interesting places which tourists visit.
4 (verb) If you sight someone or something, you see them briefly or suddenly, e.g. *The missing woman has been sighted in Birmingham.*
5 (phrases) If something is **in sight**, you can see it. If it is **out of sight**, you cannot see it.
6 If you **set your sights** on something, you decide you want it and try hard to get it.

sighted
(adjective) Someone who is sighted is not blind.

sighting, sightings
(noun) A sighting of something rare or unexpected is an occasion when it is seen.

sightless
(adjective) Someone who is sightless is blind.

sight-read, sight-reads, sight-reading, sight-read
(verb) If you can sight-read, you can play or sing music from a printed sheet without practising it.

sightseeing
(noun) Sightseeing is visiting the interesting places that tourists usually visit.
sightseer (noun).

sign, signs, signing, signed
1 (noun) A sign is a mark or symbol that always has a particular meaning, for example in mathematics or music.
2 A sign is also a gesture with a particular meaning.
3 A sign can also consist of words, a picture, or a symbol giving information or a warning.
4 If there are signs of something, there is evidence that it exists or is happening.
5 (verb) If you sign a document, you write your name on it, e.g. *Sign here to acknowledge receipt.*
[from Latin *signum* meaning 'mark']

Similar words: (sense 2) cue, signal, gesticulation

sign on
1 (phrasal verb) If you sign on for a job or course, you officially agree to do it by signing a contract.
2 When people sign on, they officially state that they are unemployed and claim benefit from the state.

sign up
(phrasal verb) If you sign up for a job or course, you officially agree to do it by signing a contract.

signal, signals, signalling, signalled
1 (noun) A signal is a gesture, sound, or action intended to give a message to someone.
2 (verb) If you signal to someone, you make a gesture or sound to give them a message.
3 (noun) A railway signal is a piece of equipment beside the track which tells train drivers whether to stop or not.
4 A signal is also a series of radio waves, light waves, or electrical impulses which carry information.
5 (adjective; a formal use) very important, e.g. *a signal triumph for the Labour Party*.
signally (adverb).
[from Latin *signum* meaning 'sign' or 'mark']

signatory, signatories
(noun; a formal word) The signatories of a document are the people who sign it.

signature, signatures
(noun) If you write your signature, you write your name the way you usually write it.
[from Latin *signare* meaning 'to sign']

signature tune, signature tunes
(noun) A signature tune is the tune which is always played at the beginning or end of a television or radio programme.

signboard, signboards
(noun) A signboard is a piece of wood with writing or a picture on it giving information, directions, or a warning.

signet ring, signet rings
(noun) A signet ring is a ring with a pattern, drawing, or letters carved into the front.
[from Latin *signetum* meaning 'little seal', because originally they were used to stamp documents]

significant
1 (adjective) A significant amount is a large amount.
2 Something that is significant is important, e.g. *a significant discovery*.
3 A significant action or gesture has a special meaning, e.g. *With a significant look at her husband, she went out*.
significance (noun), **significantly** (adverb).

signify, signifies, signifying, signified
(verb) A sign or gesture that signifies something has a particular meaning, e.g. *Leggett gave a long wheeze to signify disgust*.
[from Latin *significare* meaning 'to mean']

sign language
(noun) Sign language is a way of communicating using your hands, used especially by the deaf.

signpost, signposts
(noun) A signpost is a road sign with information on it such as the name of a town and how far away it is.

Sikh, Sikhs (pronounced **seek**)
(noun) A Sikh is a person who believes in Sikhism, an Indian religion which separated from Hinduism in the sixteenth century. Sikhs believe that there is only one God.
[from Hindi *sikh* meaning 'disciple']

silage (pronounced **sigh**-lij)
(noun) Silage is a fodder crop which is harvested when it is green and then partially fermented.

silence, silences, silencing, silenced
1 (noun) Silence is quietness.
2 Someone's silence about something is their failure or refusal to talk about it.
3 (verb) To silence someone or something means to stop them talking or making a noise.

Similar words: (sense 3) muffle, gag, hush, muzzle

silencer, silencers
(noun) A silencer is a device on a car exhaust or a gun which makes it quieter.

silent
1 (adjective) If you are silent, you are not saying anything.
2 If you are silent about something, you do not tell people about it.
3 When something is silent, it makes no noise.
4 A silent film has only pictures and no sound.
[from Latin *silere* meaning 'to be quiet']

Similar words: (sense 1) mute, tacit, dumb

silhouette, silhouettes (pronounced sil-loo-**ett**)
(noun) A silhouette is the outline of a dark shape against a light background.
silhouetted (adjective).

silica
(noun) Silica is a mineral containing silicon which is found in sand, quartz, and flint. It is used to make glass.
[from Latin *silex* meaning 'flint']

silicon
(noun) Silicon is an element found in sand, clay, and stone. It is used to make glass and also to make parts of computers. Its atomic number is 14 and its symbol is Si.

silicone
(noun) Silicone is a tough artificial substance containing silicon. It is used to make things such as paints and protective sprays.

silk, silks
(noun) Silk is a fine, soft cloth made from a substance produced by silkworms.
[from Chinese *ssu* meaning 'silk']

silken
(adjective; a literary word) smooth and soft, e.g. *silken hair*.

silkworm, silkworms
(noun) Silkworms are the larvae of a particular kind of moth. They produce a substance which is used to make silk.

silky, silkier, silkiest
(adjective) smooth and soft.

sill, sills
(noun) A sill is a ledge at the bottom of a
window.

silly, sillier, silliest
(adjective) foolish or childish.

Similar words: daft, senseless, witless

silo, silos (pronounced **sigh**-low)
1 (noun) A silo is a tall metal tower on a farm in
which silage is stored.
2 A silo is also a place underground where a
nuclear missile is kept ready to be launched.
[from Greek *siros* meaning 'pit to store corn in']

silt, silts, silting, silted
1 (noun) Silt is fine sand or soil which is carried
along by a river.
2 (verb) If a river or lake silts up, it becomes
blocked with silt.

silver
1 (noun) Silver is a valuable greyish-white
metallic element used for making jewellery and
ornaments. Its atomic number is 47 and its
symbol is Ag.
2 Silver is also coins made from silver or from
silver-coloured metal, e.g. *five pounds in silver.*
3 In a house, the silver is all the things made
from silver, especially the cutlery.
4 (adjective and noun) greyish-white.

silver birch, silver birches
(noun) A silver birch is a tree with a
greyish-white trunk.

silver jubilee, silver jubilees
(noun) A silver jubilee is the 25th anniversary of
an important event.

silver medal, silver medals
(noun) A silver medal is a medal made from
silver awarded to the competitor who comes
second in a competition.

silver paper
(noun) Silver paper is thin metal foil used for
wrapping things.

silver wedding, silver weddings
(noun) A couple's silver wedding is the 25th
anniversary of their wedding.

silvery
(adjective) having the appearance or colour of
silver, e.g. *silvery hair.*

simian (pronounced **sim**-ee-an)
(adjective; a formal word) relating to or
resembling monkeys or apes.
[from Latin *simia* meaning 'ape']

similar
1 (adjective) If one thing is similar to another, or
if two things are similar, they are like each other.
2 In maths, two triangles are similar if the angles
in one correspond exactly to the angles in the
other.
similarly (adverb).

similarity, similarities
(noun) If there is a similarity between things,
they are similar in some way.

Similar words: likeness, resemblance

simile, similes (pronounced **sim**-ill-ee)
(noun) A simile is an expression in which a
person or thing is described as being similar to
someone or something else. Examples of similes
are *She runs like a deer* and *He's as white as a
sheet.*
[from Latin *simile* meaning 'something similar']

simmer, simmers, simmering, simmered
(verb) When food simmers, it cooks gently at just
below boiling point.

simper, simpers, simpering, simpered
1 (verb) If you simper, you smile in a rather silly
way.
2 (noun) A simper is a rather silly smile.

simple, simpler, simplest
1 (adjective) Something that is simple is
uncomplicated and easy to understand or do.
2 Simple also means plain and not elaborate in
style, e.g. *a simple brown dress.*
3 A simple way of life is uncomplicated.
4 Someone who is simple is mentally retarded.
5 You use 'simple' to emphasize that what you
are talking about is the only important thing, e.g.
*Simple fear of death is often what turns people
to religion.*
simplicity (noun).
[from Latin *simplex* meaning 'plain']

simple-minded
(adjective) naive and unsophisticated, e.g. *the
simple-minded view people have about robots.*

simpleton, simpletons
(noun; an old-fashioned word) A simpleton is a
person with very low intelligence.

simplify, simplifies, simplifying, simplified
(verb) To simplify something means to make it
easier to do or understand.
simplification (noun).
[from Latin *simplus* meaning 'simple' and *facere*
meaning 'to make']

simplistic
(adjective) too simple or naive, e.g. *a simplistic
analysis of the situation.*

simply
1 (adverb) Simply means merely, e.g. *It's simply
a question of hard work.*
2 You use 'simply' to emphasize what you are
saying, e.g. *I simply can't believe it.*
3 If you say or write something simply, you do it
in a way that makes it easy to understand.

simulate, simulates, simulating, simulated
(verb) To simulate something means to imitate it,
e.g. *The wood is carved to simulate hair... They
simulated illness.*
[from Latin *simulare* meaning 'to copy']

simulation, simulations
1 (noun) Simulation is the process of simulating
something or the result of simulating it.
2 (a technical use) A simulation is an attempt to

solve a problem by representing it mathematically, often on a computer.

simulator, simulators
(noun) A simulator is a device designed to reproduce actual conditions, for example in order to train pilots or astronauts.

simultaneous
(adjective) Things that are simultaneous happen at the same time.
simultaneously (adverb).
[from Latin *simul* meaning 'at the same time']

sin, sins, sinning, sinned
1 (noun) Sin is wicked and immoral behaviour.
2 (verb) To sin means to do something wicked and immoral.
3 (an old-fashioned phrase) If an unmarried couple **are living in sin**, they are living together as if they were married.
[from Old English *synn* meaning 'wrongdoing']

Similar words: (sense 1) iniquity, evil, transgression (sense 2) err, transgress, lapse

since
1 (preposition, conjunction, and adverb) Since means from a particular time until now, e.g. *I've been wearing glasses since I was three.*
2 (adverb) Since also means at some time after a particular time in the past, e.g. *He used to be an art student. He has since become a lawyer.*
3 (conjunction) Since also means because, e.g. *Noise is a problem since we're close to Heathrow.*
[from Old English *siththan* meaning 'after that']

sincere
(adjective) If you are sincere, you say things that you really mean, e.g. *The apology was sincere.*
sincerity (noun).
[from Latin *sincerus* meaning 'genuine']

Similar words: genuine, heartfelt

sincerely
1 (adverb) If you say or feel something sincerely, you mean it or feel it genuinely.
2 (phrase) You write **yours sincerely** before your signature at the end of a formal letter.

sine, sines
(noun) In mathematics, a sine is a function of an angle. If B is the right angle in a right-angled triangle ABC, the sine of the angle at A is BC divided by AC.

sinecure, sinecures (pronounced **sigh-ni-kyoor**)
(noun; a formal word) A sinecure is a job that involves very little work.
[from Latin *sine* + *cura* meaning 'without care']

sinew, sinews (pronounced **sin-yoo**)
(noun) A sinew is a tough, fibrous cord in your body that connects a muscle to a bone.

sinewy
(adjective) lean and muscular, e.g. *his sinewy brown arms.*

sinful
(adjective) wicked and immoral.

sing, sings, singing, sang, sung
1 (verb) When you sing, you make musical sounds with your voice, usually producing words that fit a tune.
2 (phrase) If you **sing someone's praises**, you praise them enthusiastically.
3 (verb) When birds or insects sing, they make pleasant sounds.
singer (noun).

singe, singes, singeing, singed
1 (verb) To singe something means to burn it slightly so that it goes brown but does not catch fire.
2 (noun) A singe is a slight burn.

Singhalese (pronounced sing-al-**leez**) another spelling of **Sinhalese**.

single, singles, singling, singled
1 (adjective) Single means only one and not more, e.g. *We heard a single shot.*
2 People who are single are not married.
3 A single bed or bedroom is for one person.
4 A single ticket is a one-way ticket.
5 (noun) A single is a small gramophone record with one song on each side.
6 Singles is a game of tennis, badminton, or squash between just two players.
7 (phrase) If a group of people walk in **single file**, they walk in a line, one behind the other.
[from Latin *singulus* meaning 'individual']

single out
(phrasal verb) If you single someone out from a group, you give them special treatment, e.g. *Three people were singled out for praise.*

single-handed
(adverb) If you do something single-handed, you do it on your own, without any help.

single-minded
(adjective) A single-minded person has only one aim and is determined to achieve it.

singles bar, singles bars
(noun) A singles bar is a bar where single people go to drink and meet other people.

singlet, singlets
(noun) A singlet is a sleeveless vest.

singly
(adverb) If people do something singly, they do it on their own or one by one.

singsong, singsongs
(noun) When people have a singsong, they sing songs together for pleasure.

singular
1 (noun) In grammar, the singular is the form of a word that refers to just one person or thing.
2 (adjective; a formal use) unusual and remarkable, e.g. *a lady of singular beauty.*
singularity (noun), **singularly** (adverb).

Sinhalese (pronounced sin-hal-**leez**); also spelled **Singhalese**
1 (noun) Sinhalese is the main language spoken in Sri Lanka.
2 A Sinhalese is a member of the group of people from Sri Lanka who speak Sinhalese.

sinister
(adjective) seeming harmful or evil, e.g. *A sinister figure appeared.*
[from Latin *sinister* meaning 'left-hand side', because the left side was considered unlucky]

sink, sinks, sinking, sank, sunk
1 (noun) A sink is a basin with taps supplying water, usually in a kitchen or bathroom.
2 (verb) If something sinks, it moves slowly downwards, especially through water, e.g. *The boat sank to the bottom of the lake.*
3 To sink a ship means to cause it to sink by attacking it.
4 If an amount or value sinks, it decreases.
5 If your voice sinks, it becomes quieter.
6 If you sink into an unpleasant state, you gradually pass into it, e.g. *I sank further into debt.*
7 To sink something sharp into an object means to make it go deeply into it, e.g. *He sank his teeth into an apple.*

sink in
(phrasal verb) When a fact sinks in, you fully understand it or realize it, e.g. *It took a moment for her words to sink in.*

sinner, sinners
(noun) A sinner is someone who has committed a sin.

Sino-
(prefix) between China and another country, e.g. *Sino-Soviet relations.*
[from Latin *Sinae* meaning 'the Chinese']

sinuous (pronounced sin-yoo-uss)
(adjective; a literary word) having a lot of smooth twists and curves, e.g. *sinuous dances.*
[from Latin *sinuosus* meaning 'winding']

sinus, sinuses
(noun) Your sinuses are the air passages in the bones of your skull, just behind your nose.

sinusitis (pronounced sigh-nus-**sigh**-tiss)
(noun) Sinusitis is inflammation of the sinuses.

sip, sips, sipping, sipped
1 (verb) If you sip a drink, you drink it by taking a small amount at a time.
2 (noun) A sip is a small amount of drink that you take into your mouth.

siphon, siphons, siphoning, siphoned (pronounced sigh-fn); also spelled syphon
1 (verb) If you siphon off a liquid, you draw it out of a container through a tube and transfer it to another place.
2 (noun) A siphon is a tube used for siphoning.
3 A siphon is also the same as a **soda siphon.**
[from Greek *siphōn* meaning 'tube']

sir
1 Sir is a polite, formal way of addressing a man.
2 Sir is also the title used in front of the name of a knight or baronet.
[from Latin *senior* meaning 'an elder']

sire, sires, siring, sired
1 (verb; an old-fashioned use) When a man sires a child, the child is born and the man is its father.

2 (noun; a technical use) The sire of an animal such as a dog or horse is its father.

siren, sirens
1 (noun) A siren is a warning device, for example on a police car or ambulance, which makes a loud, wailing noise.
2 (a literary use) A siren is also an attractive woman who is dangerous to men.
[the Sirens in Greek mythology were sea nymphs who had beautiful voices and sang in order to lure sailors to their deaths on the rocks where the nymphs lived]

sirloin
(noun) Sirloin is a prime cut of beef from the lower part of a cow's back.
[from Old French *sur* meaning 'above' and *longe* meaning 'loin']

sisal (pronounced **sigh**-sl)
(noun) Sisal is a plant grown in the West Indies, South America, and Africa. Sisal fibres are used to make rope.
[named after the port *Sisal* in Mexico]

sissy, sissies; also spelled cissy
(noun; an informal word) A sissy is a weak, cowardly boy.

sister, sisters
1 (noun) Your sister is a girl or woman who has the same parents as you.
2 A sister is a member of a female religious order.
3 In a hospital, a sister is a senior nurse who supervises a ward.
4 (adjective) Sister means closely related to something or very similar to it, e.g. *Her sister ship was sunk by a torpedo.*

sisterhood
(noun) Sisterhood is a strong feeling of companionship between women.

sister-in-law, sisters-in-law
(noun) Your sister-in-law is the wife of your brother, the sister of your husband or wife, or the woman married to your wife's or husband's brother.

sisterly
(adjective) A woman's sisterly feelings are her feelings of affection for her sister or brother.

sit, sits, sitting, sat
1 (verb) If you are sitting, your weight is supported by your buttocks rather than your feet.
2 When you sit or sit down somewhere, you lower your body until you are sitting.
3 If you sit an examination, you take it.
4 If you sit on a committee, you are a member of it.
5 If you sit in on a meeting, you attend it and watch but do not take part.
6 (a formal use) When a parliament, law court, or other official body sits, it meets and officially carries out its work.
7 (phrase) If you **sit tight**, you remain where you are, do nothing, and wait.

sit back
(phrasal verb) If you sit back, you relax and do not become involved in something.

sitar, sitars (pronounced sit-**tar**)
(noun) A sitar is an Indian musical instrument with strings that are plucked.
[from Hindi *sitar* meaning 'three-stringed']

sitcom, sitcoms
(noun; an informal word) A sitcom is a television comedy series which shows characters in amusing situations that are similar to everyday life.
[shortened from *situation comedy*]

site, sites, siting, sited
1 (noun) A site is a piece of ground where a particular thing happens or is situated, e.g. *a caravan site... the site of the murder.*
2 (verb) If something is sited in a place, it is built or positioned there.
[from Latin *situs* meaning 'situation']

sit-in, sit-ins
(noun) A sit-in is a protest in which people sit in a public place for a long time.

sitting, sittings
1 (noun) A sitting is one of the times when a meal is served.
2 A sitting is also one of the occasions when a parliament, law court, or other official body meets and carries out its work.

sitting room, sitting rooms
(noun) A sitting room is a room in a house where people sit and relax.

sitting tenant, sitting tenants
(noun) A sitting tenant is a person who officially rents a house or flat and is entitled to remain there if the ownership changes.

situated
(adjective) If something is situated somewhere, that is where it is, e.g. *The control centre is situated many miles away.*
[from Latin *situare* meaning 'to position']

situation, situations
1 (noun) A situation is what is happening in a particular place at a particular time, e.g. *the economic situation.*
2 The situation of a building or town is its location and surroundings.
3 (an old-fashioned use) A situation is also a job, e.g. *It's not so easy to find another situation.*

Similar words: (sense 1) circumstances, position, state, condition

situation comedy
(noun) A situation comedy is the same as a sitcom.

six, sixes
1 Six is the number 6.
2 (phrase) To be at **sixes and sevens** means to be completely disorganized.

sixpence, sixpences
(noun) A sixpence was a small silver coin worth 2½p. It was used in Britain until the 1970s.

sixteen the number 16.
sixteenth.

sixth, sixths
1 The sixth item in a series is the one counted as number six.
2 (noun) A sixth is one of six equal parts.
3 In music, a sixth is the interval between two notes of a scale when there are four notes separating them.

sixth sense
(noun) You say that someone has a sixth sense when they know something instinctively, without having any evidence of it.

sixty, sixties
the number 60.
sixtieth.

sizable or sizeable
(adjective) fairly large, e.g. *a sizable sum of money.*

size, sizes, sizing, sized
1 (noun) The size of something is how big or small it is, e.g. *The population increased in size.*
2 The size of something is also the fact that it is very large, e.g. *The world overwhelms us by its sheer size.*
3 A size is one of the standard graded measurements of clothes and shoes.

Similar words: (sense 1) dimension, proportions, measurement, magnitude

size up
(phrasal verb) If you size up people or situations, you look at them carefully and make a judgment about them.

sizzle, sizzles, sizzling, sizzled
(verb) If something sizzles, it makes a hissing sound like the sound of frying food.

skate, skates, skating, skated
1 (noun) Skates are ice skates or roller skates.
2 (verb) If you skate, you move about on ice wearing ice skates.
3 (noun) A skate is also a flat edible sea fish.
4 (verb) If you skate round a difficult subject, you avoid discussing it.

skateboard, skateboards
(noun) A skateboard is a narrow board on wheels which people stand on and ride for pleasure.
skateboarder (noun), **skateboarding** (noun).

skein, skeins (pronounced **skane**)
(noun) A skein is a loosely coiled length of wool or thread.

skeletal
1 (adjective) relating to skeletons.
2 extremely thin, e.g. *skeletal children.*

skeleton, skeletons
1 (noun) Your skeleton is the framework of bones in your body.
2 (phrase) If someone has **a skeleton in the cupboard**, there is something scandalous or embarrassing in their private life which they are keeping secret.

3 (adjective) A skeleton staff is the smallest number of staff necessary to run an organization. [from Greek *skeleton* meaning 'dried up']

skeleton key, skeleton keys
(noun) A skeleton key is a key which has been specially made to fit a lot of different locks.

sketch, sketches, sketching, sketched
1 (noun) A sketch is a quick, rough drawing.
2 (verb) If you sketch something, you draw it quickly and roughly.
3 If you sketch a situation or an incident, you give a brief description of it.
4 (noun) A sketch of a situation or incident is a brief description of it.
5 A sketch is also a short, humorous piece of acting, usually forming part of a comedy show.
[from Latin *schedius* meaning 'hastily made']

sketchy, sketchier, sketchiest
(adjective) giving only a rough description or account, e.g. *his sketchy lecture notes.*

skew or **skewed** (pronounced **skyoo**)
(adjective) in a slanting position, rather than straight or upright.

skewer, skewers, skewering, skewered
1 (noun) A skewer is a long metal pin used to hold pieces of food together during cooking.
2 (verb) If you skewer something, you push a skewer through it.

ski, skis, skiing, skied
1 (noun) Skis are long pieces of wood, metal, or plastic that you fasten to your boots so you can move easily on snow.
2 (verb) When you ski, you move on snow wearing skis, especially as a sport.
[from Old Norse *skith* meaning 'snowshoes']

skid, skids, skidding, skidded
(verb) If a vehicle skids, it slides sideways or forwards in an uncontrolled way, for example because the road is wet or icy.

skiff, skiffs
(noun) A skiff is a small, light boat.

skilful
(adjective) If you are skilful at something, you can do it very well.
skilfully (adverb).

Similar words: able, adroit, skilled, deft, dexterous, expert, proficient, adept, consummate

skill, skills
1 (noun) Skill is the knowledge and ability that enables you to do something well.
2 A skill is a type of work or technique which requires special training and knowledge.
[from Old Norse *skil* meaning 'distinction' or 'knowledge']

Similar words: (sense 1) ability, artistry, craft, dexterity, proficiency, prowess, expertise

skilled
1 (adjective) A skilled person has the knowledge and ability to do something well.
2 Skilled work is manual work which can only be done by people who have had special training.

skillet, skillets
(noun) A skillet is a small frying pan.

skim, skims, skimming, skimmed
1 (verb) If you skim something from the surface of a liquid, you remove it.
2 If something skims a surface, it moves along just above it, e.g. *birds skimming the water.*

skimmed milk
(noun) Skimmed milk has had the cream removed.

skimp, skimps, skimping, skimped
(verb) If you skimp on a task, you do it carelessly or using less material than you should.

Similar words: stint, scrimp

skimpy, skimpier, skimpiest
(adjective) inadequate in size or amount, e.g. *skimpy cotton frocks.*

skin, skins, skinning, skinned
1 (noun) Your skin is the natural covering of your body. An animal skin is the skin and fur of a dead animal.
2 The skin of a fruit or vegetable is its outer covering.
3 A skin is also a solid layer which forms on the surface of a liquid.
4 (verb) If you skin a dead animal, you remove its skin.
5 If you skin a part of your body, you accidentally graze it.
6 (phrase) If you do something **by the skin of your teeth**, you only just manage to do it.
[from Old English *scinn* meaning 'skin']

skin diving
(noun) Skin diving is the sport of swimming underwater using breathing apparatus.
skin-diver (noun).

skinflint, skinflints
(noun; an informal word) A skinflint is a person who is very mean with money.

skinhead, skinheads
(noun) A skinhead is one of a group of youths who wear heavy boots and have their hair closely shaved.

skinny, skinnier, skinniest
(adjective) extremely thin.

skint
(adjective; an informal word) If you are skint, you have no money.

skip, skips, skipping, skipped
1 (verb) If you skip along, you move along jumping from one foot to the other.
2 (noun) Skips are the movements you make when you skip.
3 (verb) If you skip something, you miss it out or avoid doing it, e.g. *I decided to skip lunch.*
4 (noun) A skip is also a large metal container for holding rubbish and old bricks.

skipper, skippers
(noun; an informal word) The skipper of a ship or boat is its captain.
[from Old Dutch *schipper* meaning 'shipper']

skipping

(noun) Skipping is a game in which you jump over a rope being twirled either by yourself or by two other people standing on either side of you.

skirmish, skirmishes, skirmishing, skirmished

1 (noun) A skirmish is a short, rough fight.
2 (verb) When soldiers skirmish, they have a short, rough fight.

skirt, skirts, skirting, skirted

1 (noun) A woman's skirt is a piece of clothing which fastens at her waist and hangs down over her legs.
2 (verb) Something that skirts an area is situated around the edge of it.
3 If you skirt something, you go around the edge of it, e.g. *They skirted round a bus.*
4 If you skirt a problem, you avoid dealing with it or talking about it, e.g. *The President had skirted the issue.*
[from Old Norse *skyrta* meaning 'shirt']

skirting, skirtings

(noun) A skirting or skirting board is a narrow strip of wood running along the bottom of a wall in a room.

skit, skits

(noun) A skit is a short piece of humorous or satirical acting.

skittish

(adjective) very excitable and lively.

skittle, skittles

(noun) Skittles is a game in which players roll a ball and try to knock down wooden objects called skittles.

skive, skives, skiving, skived

(verb; an informal word) If you skive, you avoid working by staying away from a place.

skulk, skulks, skulking, skulked

(verb) If you skulk in a place, you stay there quietly because you do not want to be noticed.

skull, skulls

(noun) Your skull is the bony part of your head which encloses your brain.

skullcap, skullcaps

(noun) A skullcap is a close-fitting cap worn on the top of the head.

skunk, skunks

(noun) A skunk is a small black and white animal from North America which gives off an unpleasant smell when it is frightened.
[a North American Indian word]

sky, skies

(noun) The sky is the space around the earth which you can see when you look upwards.
[from Old Norse *sky* meaning 'cloud']

skydiving

(noun) Skydiving is the sport of jumping from an aeroplane and falling freely for a while before opening the parachute.
skydiver (noun).

skylight, skylights

(noun) A skylight is a window in a roof or ceiling.

skyline, skylines

(noun) The skyline is the line where the sky meets buildings or the ground, e.g. *the impressive Manhattan skyline.*

skyscraper, skyscrapers

(noun) A skyscraper is a very tall building.

slab, slabs

(noun) A slab is a thick, flat piece of something.

slack, slacker, slackest; slacks

1 (adjective) Something that is slack is loose and not firmly stretched or positioned.
2 (noun) The slack in a rope is the part that hangs loose.
3 (adjective) A slack period is one in which there is not much work to do.
4 If you are slack in your work, you do not do it properly or thoroughly.
5 (plural noun; an old-fashioned use) Slacks are casual trousers.
slackly (adverb), **slackness** (noun).

slacken, slackens, slackening, slackened

1 (verb) If something slackens, it becomes slower or less intense, e.g. *The rain began to slacken.*
2 To slacken also means to become looser, e.g. *The grip on his wrist did not slacken.*

slag, slags, slagging, slagged

1 (noun) Slag is the waste material left when ore has been melted down to remove the metal, e.g. *a slag heap.*
2 (verb; an informal use) To slag someone off means to criticize them in an unpleasant way, usually behind their back.

slake, slakes, slaking, slaked

(verb; a literary word) If you slake your thirst, you drink something so that you no longer feel thirsty.

slalom, slaloms (pronounced slah-lom)

(noun) A slalom is a skiing competition in which the competitors have to twist and turn quickly to avoid a series of obstacles.
[from Norwegian *slad + lom* meaning 'sloping path']

slam, slams, slamming, slammed

1 (verb) If you slam a door or if it slams, it shuts noisily and with great force.
2 If you slam something down, you throw it down violently, e.g. *He slammed the money on the table.*
3 (an informal use) If you slam a person or an idea, you criticize them severely, e.g. *The proposals were slammed by the opposition.*

slander, slanders, slandering, slandered

1 (noun) Slander is something untrue and malicious said about someone.
2 (verb) To slander someone means to say untrue and malicious things about them.
slanderous (adjective).
[from Latin *scandalum* meaning 'cause of offence']

Similar words: (sense 1) calumny, vilification, slur, smear

slang
(noun) Slang consists of very informal words and expressions.

slanging match, slanging matches
(noun) A slanging match is an angry quarrel in which people insult each other.

slant, slants, slanting, slanted
1 (verb) If something slants, it slopes, e.g. *The old wooden roof slanted a little.*
2 (noun) A slant is a slope.
3 (verb) If news or information is slanted, it is presented in a biased way.
4 (noun) A slant on a subject is one way of looking at it, especially a biased one.

slap, slaps, slapping, slapped
1 (verb) If you slap someone, you hit them with the palm of your hand.
2 (noun) If you give someone a slap, you slap them.
3 (verb) If you slap something onto a surface, you put it there quickly and noisily.
[from German *Schlappe* an imitation of the sound]

slapdash
(adjective) done quickly and carelessly, e.g. *My cooking is rather slapdash.*

slapstick
(noun) Slapstick is rough, boisterous comedy.

slash, slashes, slashing, slashed
1 (verb) If you slash something, you make a long, deep cut in it.
2 If you slash at something, you hit at it with a swinging movement, e.g. *He slashed at the ball.*
3 (an informal use) To slash money means to reduce it greatly, e.g. *a plan to slash taxes.*
4 (noun) A slash is a diagonal line that separates letters, words, or numbers, for example in the number 340/21/K.

slat, slats
(noun) Slats are the narrow pieces of wood, metal, or plastic in things such as Venetian blinds.
slatted (adjective).
[from Old French *esclat* meaning 'splinter']

slate, slates, slating, slated
1 (noun) Slate is a dark grey rock that splits easily into thin layers.
2 Slates are small, flat pieces of slate used for covering roofs.
3 (verb) If critics slate a play, film, or book, they criticize it severely.
[from Old French *esclat* meaning 'fragment' or 'splinter']

slattern, slatterns
(noun; an old-fashioned word) A slattern is a dirty, untidy woman.

slaughter, slaughters, slaughtering, slaughtered
1 (verb) To slaughter a large number of people means to kill them unjustly or cruelly.
2 (noun) Slaughter is the killing of many people.
3 (verb) To slaughter farm animals means to kill them for meat.

Similar words: (sense 2) carnage, massacre

slaughterhouse, slaughterhouses
(noun) A slaughterhouse is a place where farm animals are killed for meat.

slave, slaves, slaving, slaved
1 (noun) A slave is someone who is owned by another person and must work for them.
2 If you are a slave to something, you are completely dominated by it.
3 (verb) If you slave for someone, you work very hard for them.
slavery (noun).
[from Latin *Sclavus* meaning 'a Slav', because the Slavonic races were frequently conquered and made into slaves]

slave-driver, slave-drivers
(noun; an informal word) A slave-driver is someone who makes people work very hard.

slaver, slavers, slavering, slavered (pronounced **slav**-ver)
(verb) If a person or animal slavers, saliva drips from their mouth.

slavish (pronounced **slay**-vish)
(adjective) Slavish means imitating or copying something exactly and not being at all original, e.g. *a slavish adherence to things of the past.*
slavishly (adverb), **slavishness** (noun).

slay, slays, slaying, slew, slain
(verb; a literary word) To slay someone means to kill them.

sleazy, sleazier, sleaziest
(adjective) A sleazy place looks dirty, run-down, and not respectable.

sled, sleds
(noun) A sled is a sledge.

sledge, sledges
(noun) A sledge is a vehicle on runners used for travelling over snow.

sledgehammer, sledgehammers
(noun) A sledgehammer is a large, heavy hammer.
[from Old English *slecg* meaning 'large hammer']

sleek, sleeker, sleekest
1 (adjective) Sleek hair is smooth and shiny.
2 Someone who is sleek looks rich and dresses elegantly.

sleep, sleeps, sleeping, slept
1 (noun) Sleep is the natural state of rest in which your eyes are closed and you are inactive and unconscious.
2 (verb) When you sleep, you rest in a state of sleep.
3 (noun) If you have a sleep, you sleep for a while, e.g. *You'll feel better for a little sleep.*
4 (verb) If a house sleeps a particular number of people, it has beds for that number.
5 (phrase) If a sick or injured animal **is put to sleep**, it is painlessly killed.

Similar words: (sense 3) doze, snooze, nap, slumber, forty winks

sleeper, sleepers

1 (noun) You use sleeper to say how deeply someone sleeps, e.g. *I'm a light sleeper.*
2 A sleeper is a bed on a train.
3 A sleeper is also a train with beds on it.
4 Railway sleepers are the large, heavy beams that support the rails of a railway track.

sleeping bag, sleeping bags

(noun) A sleeping bag is a large, warm bag for sleeping in, especially when you are camping.

sleeping pill, sleeping pills

(noun) A sleeping pill or a sleeping tablet is a pill which you take to help you sleep.

sleepwalk, sleepwalks, sleepwalking, sleepwalked

(verb) If you sleepwalk, you walk around while you are asleep.
sleepwalker (noun).

sleepy, sleepier, sleepiest

1 (adjective) tired and ready to go to sleep.
2 A sleepy town or village is very quiet.
sleepily (adverb), **sleepiness** (noun).

Similar words: (sense 1) drowsy, dozy, somnolent

sleet, sleets, sleeting, sleeted

1 (noun) Sleet is a mixture of rain and snow.
2 (verb) If it is sleeting, sleet is falling.
[from Old German *sloten* meaning 'hail']

sleeve, sleeves

1 (noun) The sleeves of a piece of clothing are the parts that cover your arms.
2 A record sleeve is the stiff envelope in which a record is kept.
sleeveless (adjective).

sleigh, sleighs (pronounced **slay**)

(noun) A sleigh is a sledge.
[from Old Dutch *slee* meaning 'sledge']

sleight of hand (pronounced **slite**)

(noun) If you do something by sleight of hand, you do it using quick skilful movements of your hands which other people cannot see.
[from Old Norse *slægr* meaning 'sly']

slender

1 (adjective) attractively thin and graceful.
2 small in amount or degree, e.g. *slender prospects of promotion.*

Similar words: (sense 1) willowy, svelte, slim

sleuth, sleuths (pronounced **slooth**)

(noun; an old-fashioned word) A sleuth is a detective.
[a shortened form of *sleuthhound*, a tracker dog, from Old Norse *sloth* meaning 'track']

slew, slews, slewing, slewed

1 Slew is the past tense of **slay**.
2 (verb) If a vehicle slews, it slides or skids, e.g. *A bus slewed across the road.*

slice, slices, slicing, sliced

1 (noun) A slice of cake, bread, or other food is a piece of it cut from a larger piece.
2 A slice is also a kitchen tool with a broad, flat blade, e.g. *a fish slice.*

3 (verb) If you slice food, you cut it into thin pieces.
4 To slice through something means to cut or move through it quickly, like a knife, e.g. *The shark's fin sliced through the water.*
5 (noun) In tennis, a slice is a stroke in which the player makes the ball go to one side, rather than straight ahead.
[from Old French *esclice* meaning 'piece split off']

slick, slicker, slickest; slicks

1 (adjective) A slick book or film is well-made and attractive, but superficial or insincere.
2 A slick action is done quickly and smoothly, e.g. *a relay race with slick baton-changing.*
3 A slick person speaks easily and persuasively but is not sincere, e.g. *a slick salesman.*
4 (noun) An oil slick is a layer of oil floating on the surface of the sea or a lake.

slide, slides, sliding, slid

1 (verb) When something slides, it moves smoothly over or against something else.
2 If you slide into a way of behaving, you change to it gradually and unintentionally, e.g. *He felt himself sliding into apathy.*
3 (noun) A slide is a small piece of photographic film which can be projected onto a screen so that you can see the picture.
4 A slide is also a small piece of glass on which you put something that you want to examine through a microscope.
5 In a playground, a slide is a structure with a steep, slippery slope for children to slide down.

slide rule, slide rules

(noun) A slide rule is a mathematical instrument. It looks like a ruler and has a middle part which you slide backwards and forwards to calculate numbers.

sliding scale, sliding scales

(noun) A sliding scale is a system for calculating something such as wages, in which the amounts paid vary when other things vary.

slight, slighter, slightest; slights, slighting, slighted

1 (adjective) Slight means small in amount or degree, e.g. *He had a slight German accent.*
2 (phrase) **Not in the slightest** means not at all, e.g. *My tennis hadn't improved in the slightest.*
3 (adjective) A slight person has a slim body.
4 (verb) If you slight someone, you insult them by behaving rudely towards them.
5 (noun) A slight is rude or insulting behaviour.
slightly (adverb).

slim, slimmer, slimmest; slims, slimming, slimmed

1 (adjective) A slim person is attractively thin.
2 (verb) If you are slimming, you are trying to lose weight.
3 (adjective) A slim object is thinner than usual, e.g. *a slim book.*
4 If there is only a slim chance that something will happen, it is unlikely to happen.
slimmer (noun), **slimness** (noun).

slime

(noun) Slime is an unpleasant, thick, slippery substance.
[from Old English *slim* meaning 'soft sticky mud']

slimy, slimier, slimiest

1 (adjective) covered in slime.
2 Slimy people are friendly and pleasant in an insincere way, e.g. *a slimy politician*.

sling, slings, slinging, slung

1 (verb; an informal use) If you sling something somewhere, you throw it there.
2 If you sling a rope between two points, you attach it so that it hangs loosely between them.
3 (noun) A sling is a device made of ropes or cloth used for carrying things, e.g. *Mothers carry their babies around in slings*.
4 A sling is also a piece of cloth tied round a person's neck to support a broken or injured arm.

slink, slinks, slinking, slunk

(verb) If you slink somewhere, you move there in a slow, quiet, secretive way.
[from Old English *slincan* meaning 'to creep']

slinky, slinkier, slinkiest

(adjective) Slinky clothes are tight-fitting and usually shiny, e.g. *a slinky dress*.

slip, slips, slipping, slipped

1 (verb) If you slip, you accidentally slide and lose your balance.
2 If something slips, it slides out of place accidentally, e.g. *It slipped from his fingers*.
3 If you slip somewhere, you go there quickly and quietly, e.g. *She slipped out of the room*.
4 If you slip something somewhere, you put it there quickly and quietly.
5 If something slips to a lower level or standard, it falls to that level or standard, e.g. *Industrial production has slipped by 12 per cent in a year*.
6 (phrase) If something **slips your mind**, you forget about it.
7 If you **let slip** information, you tell someone about it without intending to.
8 If you **give someone the slip**, you manage to escape from them when they have been following you.
9 (noun) A slip is a small mistake.
10 A slip of paper is a small piece of paper.
11 A slip is also a piece of underclothing worn under a dress or skirt.

slip up

(phrasal verb; an informal expression) If you slip up, you make a mistake.
slip-up (noun).

slipped disc, slipped discs

(noun) A slipped disc is a painful condition in which one of the discs in your spine has moved out of its proper position.

slipper, slippers

(noun) Slippers are loose, soft shoes that you wear indoors.

slippery

1 (adjective) smooth, wet, or greasy, and difficult to hold or walk on.

2 You describe a person as slippery when they cannot be trusted.

slip road, slip roads

(noun) A slip road is a narrow road by which you join or leave a motorway.

slipshod

(adjective) done in a careless or untidy way, e.g. *a slipshod piece of research*.
[originally meant wearing slippers or loose shoes; hence carelessly dressed]

slipstream, slipstreams

(noun) The slipstream of a car or plane is the flow of air directly behind it.

slipway, slipways

(noun) A slipway is a platform sloping down into the water, on which ships are built and from which they are launched.

slit, slits, slitting, slit

1 (verb) If you slit something, you make a long, narrow cut in it.
2 (noun) A slit is a long, narrow cut or opening.
[from Old English *slitan* meaning 'to slice']

slither, slithers, slithering, slithered

(verb) To slither somewhere means to move there by sliding along the ground in an uneven way, e.g. *A huge snake slithered under my bed*.
[from Old English *slidan* meaning 'to slide']

sliver, slivers

(noun) A sliver is a small, thin piece of something.
[from Middle English *sliven* meaning 'to split']

slob, slobs

(noun; an informal word) A slob is a lazy, untidy person.

slobber, slobbers, slobbering, slobbered

(verb) If someone slobbers, they dribble.
[from Old German *slubberen* meaning 'to slaver']

slobbery

(adjective) A slobbery mouth or kiss is very wet.

sloe, sloes (rhymes with go)

(noun) A sloe is a small, sour fruit with a dark purple skin. Sloes grow on blackthorn bushes and are used to make alcoholic drinks.

slog, slogs, slogging, slogged (an informal word)

1 (verb) If you slog at something, you work hard and steadily at it, e.g. *slogging away at revision*.
2 If you slog somewhere, you move along with difficulty, e.g. *slogging through the snow*.

slogan, slogans

(noun) A slogan is a short, easily-remembered phrase used in advertising or by a political party.
[from Gaelic *sluagh-ghairm* meaning 'war cry']

Similar words: watchword, catchphrase, motto

sloop, sloops

(noun) A sloop is a small sailing ship with one mast.

slop, slops, slopping, slopped

1 (verb) If a liquid slops, it spills over the edge of a container in a messy way.
2 (plural noun) You can refer to dirty water or liquid waste as slops.

slope, slopes, sloping, sloped
1 (noun) A slope is a flat surface that is at an angle, so that one end is higher than the other.
2 (verb) If a surface slopes, it is at an angle.
3 If something slopes, it leans to one side rather than being upright, e.g. *sloping handwriting*.
4 (noun) The slope of something is the angle at which it slopes, e.g. *a slope of ten degrees*.
[from Old English *aslope* meaning 'slanting']

Similar words: (sense 1) incline, tilt, slant
(sense 4) inclination, gradient

sloppy, sloppier, sloppiest (an informal word)
1 (adjective) very messy or careless, e.g. *a sloppy piece of work*.
2 foolishly sentimental, e.g. *sloppy letters*.
sloppily (adverb), **sloppiness** (noun).

slosh, sloshes, sloshing, sloshed
(verb; an informal word) If a liquid sloshes it moves or splashes around in a messy way.

sloshed
(adjective; an informal word) drunk.

slot, slots, slotting, slotted
1 (noun) A slot is a narrow opening in a machine or container, for example for putting coins in.
2 (verb) When you slot something into something else, you put it into a space where it fits.
3 (noun) A slot is also a place in a schedule, scheme, or organization, e.g. *Students get only two slots in the week for private study*.

sloth, sloths (pronounced **slowth**)
1 (noun; a formal use) Sloth is laziness.
2 A sloth is an animal that lives in Central or South America. Sloths move very slowly and hang upside down from the branches of trees.
slothful (adjective).

slot machine, slot machines
(noun) A slot machine is a machine which you operate by putting in coins.

slouch, slouches, slouching, slouched
(verb) If you slouch, you stand or sit with your shoulders and head drooping forwards.

slough, sloughs, sloughing, sloughed (pronounced **sluff**)
1 (verb) When an animal such as a snake sloughs off its skin, it sheds it.
2 (a literary use) If you slough off something you no longer need, you get rid of it.

slovenly (pronounced **sluv-ven-lee**)
(adjective) untidy and careless.

slow, slower, slowest; slows, slowing, slowed
1 (adjective) moving, happening, or doing something with very little speed, e.g. *slow music... slow changes*.
2 (verb) If something slows, slows down, or slows up, it moves or happens more slowly.
3 (adjective) Someone who is slow is not very clever.
4 If a clock or watch is slow, it shows a time earlier than the correct one.
slowly (adverb), **slowness** (noun).
[from Old English *slaw* meaning 'sluggish']

slowcoach, slowcoaches
(noun; an informal word) If you call someone a slowcoach, you mean they do things very slowly.

slow motion
(noun) Slow motion is movement which is much slower than normal, especially in a film, e.g. *I dreamed I was falling off a cliff in slow motion*.

slow-witted
(adjective) not very clever.

slowworm, slowworms
(noun) A slowworm is a small legless lizard which looks and moves like a snake.

sludge
(noun) Sludge is thick mud or sewage.

slug, slugs, slugging, slugged
1 (noun) A slug is a small, slow-moving creative with a slimy body, like a snail without a shell.
2 (an informal use) A slug of an alcoholic drink such as whisky is a mouthful of it.
3 (verb; an informal use) If you slug someone, you hit them hard.
4 (noun) A slug is also a bullet.

sluggish
(adjective) moving slowly and without energy, e.g. *the sluggish water of East Canal*.
sluggishly (adverb).

sluice, sluices, sluicing, sluiced
1 (noun) A sluice is a channel which carries water. It has an opening called a sluicegate which can be opened or closed to control the flow of water.
2 (verb) If you sluice something, you wash it by pouring water over it, e.g. *We sluiced out the trough*.
[from Latin *exclusa aqua* meaning 'water shut out']

slum, slums, slumming, slummed
1 (noun) A slum is a poor, run-down area of a city.
2 (verb) If you are slumming, you are living in conditions poorer than the ones you are used to.
slummy (adjective).

slumber, slumbers, slumbering, slumbered (a literary word)
1 (noun) Slumber is sleep.
2 (verb) When you slumber, you sleep.
[from Old English *sluma* meaning 'sleep']

slump, slumps, slumping, slumped
1 (verb) If an amount or a value slumps, it falls suddenly by a large amount.
2 (noun) A slump is a sudden, severe drop in an amount or value, e.g. *a slump in oil demand*.
3 A slump is also a time when there is economic decline and high unemployment.
4 (verb) If you slump somewhere, you fall or sit down heavily, e.g. *She slumped against the wall*.

slur, slurs, slurring, slurred
1 (noun) A slur is an insulting remark.
2 (verb) When people slur their speech, they do not pronounce their words clearly, often because they are drunk or ill.

slurp, slurps, slurping, slurped
(verb) If you slurp a drink, you drink it noisily.
[from Old Dutch *slorpen* meaning 'to sip']

slurry (rhymes with **curry**)
(noun) Slurry is a watery mixture of something such as mud, cement, or clay.

slush
1 (noun) Slush is wet melting snow.
2 (an informal use) You can refer to sentimental love stories as slush.
slushy (adjective).

slut, sluts
(noun; an offensive word) A slut is a dirty, untidy woman, or one considered to be immoral.

sly, slyer or **slier, slyest** or **sliest**
1 (adjective) A sly expression or remark shows that you know something other people do not know, e.g. *a sly smile.*
2 A sly person is cunning and good at deceiving people.
slyly (adverb).
[from Old Norse *slægr* meaning 'clever' or 'cunning']

Similar words: (sense 2) sneaky, devious, underhand, shifty

smack, smacks, smacking, smacked
1 (verb) If you smack someone, you hit them with your open hand.
2 (noun) If you give someone a smack, you smack them.
3 A smack is a loud, sharp noise, e.g. *The book hit the floor with a smack.*
4 (phrase) If you **smack your lips**, you open and close your mouth noisily to show you are enjoying your food or looking forward to it.
5 (verb) If something smacks of something else, it reminds you of it, e.g. *Any literature other than romantic novels smacked to her of school.*
6 (noun; an informal use) Smack is heroin.
7 A smack is also a small fishing boat.
[senses 1-4 are from Old German *smacken* an imitation of the sound; senses 5 and 6 are from Old English *smæc* meaning 'flavour'; sense 7 is from Old German *smack* meaning 'ship']

small, smaller, smallest; smalls
1 (adjective) Small means not large in size, number, or amount.
2 Small means not important or significant, e.g. *small changes.*
3 (noun) The small of your back is the narrow part where your back curves slightly inwards.
4 (plural noun; an old-fashioned, informal use) Smalls are items of underwear.
smallness (noun).

Similar words: (sense 1) little, petite, slight
(sense 2) minor, trivial, unimportant, slight

small ad, small ads
(noun) A small ad is a short advertisement in a newspaper which advertises something such as an object for sale or a room to let.

small change
(noun) Coins of low value are small change.

small fry
(plural noun) You can refer to people who are unimportant as small fry, e.g. *Being small fry they had done what they were told.*

smallholding, smallholdings
(noun) A smallholding is a very small area of land used for farming.
smallholder (noun).

small hours
(plural noun) If something happens in the small hours, it happens in the early morning, after midnight, e.g. *We talked until the small hours.*

smallish
(adjective) fairly small.

small-minded
(adjective) having a narrow, selfish attitude.

smallpox
(noun) Smallpox is a serious contagious disease that causes a fever and a rash.

small print
(noun) The small print of a legal document is the details, often printed in small letters but sometimes very important.

small-scale
(adjective) A small-scale event or organization is limited in extent.

small talk
(noun) Small talk is conversation about unimportant things.

smarmy
(adjective; an informal word) unpleasantly polite and flattering, e.g. *a smarmy little man.*

smart, smarter, smartest; smarts, smarting, smarted
1 (adjective) A smart person is clean and neatly dressed.
2 Smart means clever, e.g. *a smart idea.*
3 A smart place or event is connected with wealthy and fashionable people.
4 A smart movement is quick and sharp.
5 (verb) If a wound smarts, it stings.
6 If you are smarting from criticism or unkindness, you are feeling upset by it.
smartly (adverb), **smartness** (noun).

smarten, smartens, smartening, smartened
(verb) If you smarten something up, you make it look neater and tidier.

smash, smashes, smashing, smashed
1 (verb) If you smash something, you break it into a lot of pieces by hitting it or dropping it.
2 To smash through something such as a wall means to go through it by breaking it.
3 To smash against something means to hit it with great force, e.g. *The sea smashed the boat against the rocks.*
4 (an informal use) If people smash something such as a political system, they destroy it.
5 (noun; an informal use) If a play or film is a smash or a smash hit, it is very successful.
6 A smash is also a car crash.
7 In tennis, a smash is a stroke in which the player hits the ball downwards very hard.

smashed
(adjective; an informal word) extremely drunk.

smashing
(adjective; an informal word) If you describe something as smashing, you mean you like it very much.

smattering
(noun) A smattering of knowledge or information is a very small amount of it, e.g. *Jane spoke Spanish and a smattering of Greek.*

smear, smears, smearing, smeared
1 (noun) A smear is a dirty, greasy mark on a surface, e.g. *a smear of blue paint.*
2 (verb) If something smears a surface, it makes dirty, greasy marks on it, e.g. *The windows were all smeared.*
3 If you smear a surface with a greasy or sticky substance, you spread a layer of the substance over the surface.
4 (noun) A smear is also an untrue and malicious rumour.
[from Old English *smierwan* meaning 'to anoint' or 'to rub with grease or oil']

smear test, smear tests
(noun) A smear test is a medical test in which a tiny amount of the coating of a woman's cervix is removed and analysed to see if there are any cancer cells present.

smell, smells, smelling, smelled or smelt
1 (noun) The smell of something is a quality it has which you perceive through your nose, e.g. *the smell of fresh bread.*
2 (verb) If something smells or if you can smell it, it has a quality you can perceive through your nose, e.g. *The papers smelled musty and stale.*
3 (noun) Your sense of smell is your ability to smell things.
4 (verb) If you can smell something such as danger or trouble, you feel it is present or likely to happen.

Similar words: (sense 1) odour, whiff

smelling salts
(plural noun) Smelling salts are a chemical substance with a strong smell which were used in the past to revive someone who had fainted.

smelly, smellier, smelliest
(adjective) having a strong, unpleasant smell.

smelt, smelts, smelting, smelted
(verb) To smelt a metal ore means to heat it until it melts, so that the metal can be extracted.

smile, smiles, smiling, smiled
1 (verb) When you smile, the corners of your mouth move outwards and slightly upwards because you are pleased or amused.
2 (noun) A smile is the expression you have when you smile.

smirk, smirks, smirking, smirked
1 (verb) When you smirk, you smile in a sneering or sarcastic way, e.g. *'That's where you're wrong,' said Ellen, smirking.*
2 (noun) A smirk is a sneering or sarcastic smile.
[from Old English *smearcian* meaning 'to smile']

smite, smites, smiting, smote, smitten
(verb; an old-fashioned word) To smite something means to hit it hard.

smith, smiths
(noun) A smith is someone who makes things out of iron, gold, or another metal.
[from Old English *smith* meaning 'craftsman']

smithy, smithies
(noun) A smithy is a place where a blacksmith works.

smock, smocks
(noun) A smock is a loose garment like a long blouse.

smog
(noun) Smog is a mixture of fog and smoke which occurs in some industrial cities.
[from a combination of *smoke* and *fog*]

smoke, smokes, smoking, smoked
1 (noun) Smoke is a mixture of gas and small particles sent into the air when something burns.
2 (verb) If something is smoking, smoke is coming from it.
3 When someone smokes a cigarette, cigar, or pipe, they suck smoke from it into their mouth and blow it out again.
4 To smoke fish or meat means to hang it over burning wood so that the smoke preserves it and gives it a pleasant flavour, e.g. *smoked salmon.*
smoker (noun), **smoking** (noun).

smokeless
(adjective) Smokeless fuel burns without producing smoke.

smokescreen, smokescreens
(noun) A smokescreen is something intended to hide the truth about someone's activities or intentions, e.g. *Working at the embassy was just a smokescreen for his work as a spy.*

smoky, smokier, smokiest
1 (adjective) A smoky place is full of smoke.
2 You can also describe something as smoky when it looks like smoke, e.g. *a smoky-blue scarf.*

smooth, smoother, smoothest; smooths, smoothing, smoothed
1 (adjective) A smooth surface has no roughness and no holes in it.
2 A smooth liquid or mixture has no lumps in it.
3 (verb) If you smooth something, you move your hands over it to make it smooth and flat.
4 (adjective) A smooth movement or process happens evenly and steadily, e.g. *the smooth flow of his speech.*
5 Smooth also means successful and without problems, e.g. *Cooperation is essential if you are going to lead a smooth existence in the office.*
6 If you say that a man is smooth, you mean that he is smart, confident, and polite in a way you find rather unpleasant.
smoothly (adverb), **smoothness** (noun).

Similar words: (sense 6) debonair, suave, slick, urbane

smother, smothers, smothering, smothered
1 (verb) If you smother a fire, you cover it with something to put it out.

2 To smother a person means to cover their face with something so that they cannot breathe.
3 To smother someone also means to give them too much love and protection, e.g. *Parents should love their children without smothering them.*
4 If you smother an emotion, you control it so that people do not notice it, e.g. *I turned away and tried to smother my sobs.*
[from Old English *smorian* meaning 'to suffocate']

smothered
(adjective) completely covered with something, e.g. *The pear tree was smothered in ivy.*

smoulder, smoulders, smouldering, smouldered
1 (verb) When something smoulders, it burns slowly, producing smoke but no flames.
2 If a feeling is smouldering inside you, you feel it very strongly but do not show it, e.g. *Inside he smouldered with anger.*

smudge, smudges, smudging, smudged
1 (noun) A smudge is a dirty or blurred mark or a smear on something.
2 (verb) If you smudge something, you make it dirty or messy by touching it or marking it.

smug, smugger, smuggest
(adjective) Someone who is smug is very pleased with how good or clever they are.
smugly (adverb), **smugness** (noun).

smuggle, smuggles, smuggling, smuggled
(verb) To smuggle things or people into or out of a place means to take them there illegally or secretly.

smuggler, smugglers
(noun) A smuggler is someone who smuggles goods illegally into a country.

smut, smuts
1 (noun) People refer to remarks, stories, or pictures as smut when they are offended by them because they are to do with sex or nudity.
2 Smuts are particles of dirt which make dark marks on something.
smutty (adjective).

snack, snacks
(noun) A snack is a light, quick meal.

snack bar, snack bars
(noun) A snack bar is a place where you can buy snacks and drinks.

snag, snags, snagging, snagged
1 (noun) A snag is a small problem or disadvantage, e.g. *This stuff is really good. The only snag is it dissolves plastics.*
2 (verb) If you snag your clothing, you damage it by catching it on something sharp.
3 (noun) A snag is a small hole in clothing caused by catching it on something sharp.

snail, snails
1 (noun) A snail is a small, slow-moving creature with a long, shiny body and a shell on its back.
2 (phrase) If you do something **at a snail's pace,** you do it very slowly.

snake, snakes, snaking, snaked
1 (noun) A snake is a long, thin, scaly reptile with no legs.

2 (verb) Something that snakes moves in long winding curves, e.g. *The river snaked through the valley.*

snake charmer, snake charmers
(noun) A snake charmer is a person who entertains people by controlling the behaviour of a snake, for example by playing music and causing the snake to rise out of a basket.

snap, snaps, snapping, snapped
1 (verb) If something snaps or if you snap it, it breaks with a sharp cracking noise.
2 (noun) A snap is the sound of something snapping.
3 (verb) If you snap something into a particular position, you move it there quickly with a sharp sound.
4 If an animal snaps at you, it shuts its jaws together quickly as if to bite you.
5 If someone snaps at you, they speak in a sharp, unfriendly way.
6 (adjective) A snap decision or action is taken suddenly without careful thought.
7 (verb) If you snap someone, you take a quick photograph of them.
8 (noun; an informal use) A snap is a photograph taken quickly and casually.
9 Snap is a simple card game played by children.
[from Old German *snappen* meaning 'to seize']

snapdragon, snapdragons
(noun) A snapdragon is a common garden plant with small colourful flowers.

snappy, snappier, snappiest
(adjective) Someone who is snappy speaks to people in a sharp, unfriendly way.

snapshot, snapshots
(noun) A snapshot is a photograph taken quickly and casually.

snare, snares, snaring, snared
1 (noun) A snare is a trap for catching birds or small animals.
2 (verb) To snare an animal or bird means to catch it using a snare.

snarl, snarls, snarling, snarled
1 (verb) When an animal snarls, it bares its teeth and makes a fierce growling noise.
2 (noun) A snarl is the noise an animal makes when it snarls.
3 (verb) If you snarl, you say something in a fierce, angry way.

snarled up
(adjective) When something such as traffic is snarled up, it has become blocked or disorganized and cannot move or continue.

snarl-up, snarl-ups
(noun; an informal word) A snarl-up is a confused, disorganized situation.

snatch, snatches, snatching, snatched
1 (verb) If you snatch something, you reach out for it quickly and take it.
2 (noun) If you make a snatch at something, you reach out for it quickly to try to take it.
3 (verb) If you snatch an amount of time or an opportunity, you quickly make use of it.

4 (noun) A snatch of conversation or song is a very small piece of it.

snazzy, snazzier, snazziest
(adjective; an informal word) bright, stylish, and attractive.

sneak, sneaks, sneaking, sneaked
1 (verb) If you sneak somewhere, you go there quickly trying not to be seen or heard.
2 If you sneak something somewhere, you take it there secretly.
3 If you sneak a look at something or someone, you secretly have a quick look at them.
4 (noun; an informal use) A sneak is someone who tells people in authority that someone else has done something naughty or wrong.
[from Old English *snican* meaning 'to creep']

sneaker, sneakers
(noun) Sneakers are casual shoes with rubber soles.

sneaking
(adjective) If you have a sneaking feeling about something or someone, you have this feeling rather reluctantly, e.g. *I have a sneaking suspicion you're right.*

sneaky, sneakier, sneakiest
(adjective; an informal word) Someone who is sneaky does things secretly rather than openly.
sneakily (adverb).

sneer, sneers, sneering, sneered
1 (verb) If you sneer at someone or something, you show by your expression and your comments that you think they are stupid or inferior.
2 (noun) A sneer is the expression on someone's face when they sneer.

sneeze, sneezes, sneezing, sneezed
1 (verb) When you sneeze, you suddenly take in breath and blow it down your nose noisily, because there is a tickle in your nose as you have a cold.
2 (noun) A sneeze is an act of sneezing.
3 (an informal phrase) If you say that something is **not to be sneezed at**, you mean that it is worth having.

snicker, snickers, snickering, snickered
1 (verb) If you snicker, you laugh quietly and disrespectfully, especially at something rude or at someone's misfortune.
2 (noun) A snicker is a quiet, disrespectful laugh.

snide
(adjective) A snide comment or remark criticizes someone in a nasty and unfair way.

sniff, sniffs, sniffing, sniffed
1 (verb) When you sniff, you breathe in air through your nose hard enough to make a sound.
2 If you sniff something, you smell it by sniffing.
3 (noun) A sniff is the noise you make when you sniff.
4 A sniff of something is a smell of it, e.g. *Have a sniff of my new aftershave.*
5 (verb) You can say that a person sniffs at something when they do not think very much of it, e.g. *She sniffed at the idea of leaving London.*

6 When someone sniffs around, they look around a place to try and find out things, e.g. *The police have been sniffing around all morning.*

sniffle, sniffles, sniffling, sniffled
1 (verb) If you sniffle, you sniff a lot, for example because you have a cold.
2 (noun) A sniffle is a slight cold.

snigger, sniggers, sniggering, sniggered
1 (verb) If you snigger, you laugh quietly and disrespectfully, e.g. *They all sniggered as Mr Hart fell over.*
2 (noun) A snigger is a quiet, disrespectful laugh.

snip, snips, snipping, snipped
1 (verb) If you snip something, you cut it with scissors or shears in a single quick action.
2 (noun) A snip is a small cut made by scissors or shears.
3 (an informal use) If something for sale is a snip, it is cheap and good value.
[from Old German *snippen* an imitation of the sound]

snipe, snipes, sniping, sniped
1 (verb) To snipe at someone means to shoot at them from a hiding place.
2 To snipe at someone also means to keep making critical remarks to them.
3 (noun) A snipe is a bird with a very long beak, which usually lives in marshy areas.
sniper (noun).

snippet, snippets
(noun) A snippet of something such as information or news is a small piece of it.

snivel, snivels, snivelling, snivelled
(verb) When someone snivels, they cry and sniff in an irritating way.

snob, snobs
1 (noun) A snob is someone who admires upper-class people and looks down on lower-class people.
2 A snob is also someone who believes that they are better than other people.
snobbery (noun), **snobbish** (adjective).

snooker
(noun) Snooker is a game played on a large table covered with smooth green cloth. Players score points by hitting different coloured balls into side pockets using a long stick.

snoop, snoops, snooping, snooped
(verb; an informal word) Someone who is snooping is secretly looking round a place to find out things.
snooper (noun).
[from Dutch *snoepen* meaning 'to eat furtively']

snooty, snootier, snootiest
(adjective; an informal word) A snooty person behaves as if they are better than other people.

snooze, snoozes, snoozing, snoozed (an informal word)
1 (verb) If you snooze, you sleep lightly for a short time, especially during the day.
2 (noun) A snooze is a short, light sleep.

snore, snores, snoring, snored
1 (verb) When a sleeping person snores, they make a loud noise each time they breathe.
2 (noun) A snore is the noise someone makes when they snore.

snorkel, snorkels, snorkelling, snorkelled
1 (noun) A snorkel is a tube you can breathe through when you are swimming just under the surface of the sea.
2 (verb) To snorkel means to swim underwater using a snorkel.
snorkelling (noun).
[from German *Schnorchel*, originally an air pipe for a submarine]

snort, snorts, snorting, snorted
1 (verb) When people or animals snort, they force breath out through their nose in a noisy way, e.g. *My sister snorted with laughter*.
2 (noun) A snort is the noise you make when you snort.

snot
(noun; an informal word) Snot is mucus.
snotty (adjective).

snout, snouts
(noun) An animal's snout is its nose.

snow, snows, snowing, snowed
1 (noun) Snow consists of flakes of ice crystals which fall from the sky in cold weather.
2 (verb) When it snows, snow falls from the sky.
3 (phrase) If you are **snowed in** or **snowed up**, you cannot go anywhere because of heavy snow.
4 If you are **snowed under** with work, you have a lot of it to deal with.

snowball, snowballs, snowballing, snowballed
1 (noun) A snowball is a ball of snow.
2 (verb) When something such as a project snowballs, it grows rapidly.

snowdrift, snowdrifts
(noun) A snowdrift is a deep pile of snow formed by the wind.

snowdrop, snowdrops
(noun) A snowdrop is a small white flower which appears in early spring.

snowfall, snowfalls
1 (noun) A snowfall is a fall of snow.
2 The snowfall in a region is the amount of snow that falls there during a particular period.

snowfield, snowfields
(noun) A snowfield is a large area which is always covered in snow.

snow line
(noun) The snow line is the height on a mountain above which there is snow all the time.

snowman, snowmen
(noun) A snowman is a large mound of snow moulded into the shape of a person.

snowplough, snowploughs
(noun) A snowplough is a vehicle which is used to push snow off roads or railway lines.

snowshoe, snowshoes
(noun) Snowshoes are oval frames with a strong

net stretched across them which you fasten to your boots for walking over soft snow.

snub, snubs, snubbing, snubbed
1 (verb) To snub someone means to behave rudely towards them, especially by making an insulting remark or ignoring them.
2 (noun) A snub is an insulting remark or a piece of rude behaviour.
3 (adjective) A snub nose is short and turned-up.
[senses 1 and 2 are from Old Norse *snubba* meaning 'to scold']

Similar words: (sense 2) rebuff, rejection, slight, affront

snuff, snuffs, snuffing, snuffed
1 (noun) Snuff is powdered tobacco which people take by sniffing it up their noses.
2 (verb) If you snuff a candle, you put it out.
[sense 1 is from Dutch *snuftabak* meaning 'tobacco for sniffing']

snuffle, snuffles, snuffling, snuffled
1 (verb) When people or animals snuffle, they make sniffing noises.
2 (noun) A snuffle is a sniffing noise.
snuffly (adjective).

snug, snugger, snuggest
1 (adjective) A snug place is warm and comfortable. If you are snug, you are warm and comfortable.
2 If something is a snug fit, it fits very closely.
snugly (adverb).
[from an old use which describes a ship made secure and ready for a storm]

snuggle, snuggles, snuggling, snuggled
(verb) If you snuggle somewhere, you cuddle up more closely to something or someone.

so
1 (adverb) So is used to refer back to what has just been mentioned, e.g. *Do you like reading? If so, try this*.
2 So is used to mean also, e.g. *Sue smiled, and so did Jane*.
3 (conjunction) 'So that' and 'so as' are used to introduce the reason for doing something, e.g. *They went on foot, so as not to be heard*.
4 (adverb) So can be used to mean 'therefore', e.g. *I had no money, so I couldn't pay*.
5 So is used when you are talking about the degree or extent of something, e.g. *Don't go so fast*.
6 So is used before words like 'much' and 'many' to say that there is a definite limit to something, e.g. *a friend with only so long to live*.

soak, soaks, soaking, soaked
1 (verb) To soak something or leave it to soak means to put it in a liquid and leave it there.
2 When a liquid soaks something, it makes it very wet.
3 When a liquid soaks through something, it goes right through it.
4 When something soaks up a liquid, the liquid is drawn up into it.

Similar words: (sense 2) drench, saturate

soaked
(adjective) extremely wet.

soaking
(adjective) If something is soaking, it is very wet.

soap, soaps, soaping, soaped
1 (noun) Soap is a substance made of natural oils and fats and used for washing yourself.
2 (verb) If you soap yourself, you rub soap on your body to wash yourself.
soapy (adjective).

soap opera, soap operas
(noun) A soap opera is a popular television drama serial about people's daily lives.

soar, soars, soaring, soared
1 (verb) If an amount soars, it quickly increases by a great deal, e.g. *Property prices soared.*
2 If something soars into the air, it quickly goes up into the air.
soaring (adjective).

sob, sobs, sobbing, sobbed
1 (verb) When someone sobs, they cry in a noisy way, breathing in short breaths.
2 (noun) A sob is the noise made when you cry.

sober, soberer, soberest; sobers, sobering, sobered
1 (adjective) If someone is sober, they are not drunk.
2 Sober also means serious and thoughtful.
3 Sober colours are plain and rather dull.
4 (verb) To sober up means to become sober after being drunk.
soberly (adverb).

sobering
(adjective) Something which is sobering makes you serious and thoughtful, e.g. *His words had a sobering effect on us all.*

sobriety (soe-bry-et-tee)
(noun; a formal word) Sobriety is serious and thoughtful behaviour.

sob story, sob stories
(noun) A sob story is a story you tell someone about something that has happened to you so that you get their sympathy, especially as an excuse for not doing something.

so-called
(adjective) You use so-called to say that the name by which something is called is incorrect or misleading, e.g. *her so-called friends.*

soccer
(noun) Soccer is the same as football.
[formed from *Association Football*]

sociable
(adjective) Sociable people are friendly and enjoy talking to other people.
sociability (noun).

Similar words: gregarious, outgoing, convivial, cordial

---

social
1 (adjective) to do with society or life within a society, e.g. *children from different social backgrounds.*
2 to do with leisure activities that involve meeting other people.
socially (adverb).
[from Latin *socialis* meaning 'companionable']

socialism
(noun) Socialism is the political belief that the state should own industries on behalf of the people and that everyone should be equal.
socialist (adjective and noun).

socialite, socialites
(noun) A socialite is a person who goes to many fashionable, upper-class social events.

socialize, socializes, socializing, socialized; also spelled socialise
(verb) When people socialize, they meet other people socially, for example at parties.

social science, social sciences
(noun) Social science is the scientific study of society. The social sciences are the different areas of social science.

social security
(noun) Social security is a system by which the government pays money regularly to people who have no other income or only a very small income. The money paid can also be called social security, e.g. *Are you claiming social security?*

social services
(plural noun) The social services are the services provided by a local authority to help people who have social and financial problems.

social work
(noun) Social work involves giving help and advice to people with serious financial or family problems.
social worker (noun).

society, societies
1 (noun) Society is the people in a particular country or region, e.g. *Women must have equal status in society.*
2 A society is an organization for people who have the same interest or aim.
3 Society is also rich, upper-class, fashionable people.
[from Latin *societas* meaning 'companion']

Similar words: (sense 1) culture, community, civilization

Society of Friends
(noun) The Society of Friends is the Christian sect to which Quakers belong.

sociology
(noun) Sociology is the study of human societies and the relationships between groups in these societies.
sociological (adjective), **sociologist** (noun).
[from Latin *socius* meaning 'companion' + *-ology*]

sock, socks
(noun) Socks are pieces of clothing covering your foot and ankle.
[from Old English *socc* meaning 'light shoe']

socket, sockets
1 (noun) A socket is a place on a wall or on a

piece of electrical equipment into which you can put a plug or bulb.
2 Any hollow part or opening into which another part fits can be called a socket, e.g. *eye sockets*.

sod
(noun; a literary use) The sod is the surface of the ground, together with the grass and roots growing in it.

soda, sodas
1 (noun) Soda is the same as soda water.
2 Soda is also sodium in the form of crystals or a powder. It is used for baking or cleaning.
[from Latin *sodanum* meaning 'barilla', a plant that was burned to obtain sodium carbonate]

soda siphon, soda siphons
(noun) A soda siphon is a bottle containing soda water under pressure. When you press a lever, the soda water shoots out from a tube at the top.

soda water, soda waters
(noun) Soda water is fizzy water used for mixing with alcoholic drinks or fruit juice.

sodden
(adjective) soaking wet.

sodium
(noun) Sodium is a silvery-white chemical element which combines with other chemicals. Salt is a sodium compound. Sodium's atomic number is 11 and its symbol is Na.

sofa, sofas
(noun) A sofa is a long comfortable seat with a back and arms for two or three people.
[from Arabic *suffah* meaning 'an upholstered raised platform']

soft, softer, softest
1 (adjective) Something soft is not hard, stiff, or firm.
2 Soft also means very gentle, e.g. *a soft breeze*.
3 A soft sound or voice is quiet and not harsh.
4 A soft colour or light is not bright.
5 If you say that someone is soft, you mean they are weak and rather cowardly.
6 You can also say that someone is soft when you think they are not strict enough.
softly (adverb).

soft drink, soft drinks
(noun) A soft drink is any cold, nonalcoholic drink.

soften, softens, softening, softened
1 (verb) If something is softened or softens, it becomes less hard, stiff, or firm.
2 If you soften, you become more sympathetic and less critical, e.g. *She gradually softened towards me.*

soft focus
(noun) Something in a photograph or film that is in soft focus has been made to look slightly blurred.

soft furnishings
(plural noun) Soft furnishings are cushions, curtains, lampshades, and furniture covers.

soft palate, soft palates
(noun) Your soft palate is the soft top part of the inside of your mouth, near your throat.

soft sell
(noun) Soft sell is a gentle and persuasive method of selling something.

software
(noun) Computer programs are known as software.

softwood
(noun) Softwood is wood that you can saw easily. It comes from trees that grow quickly.

soggy, soggier, soggiest
(adjective) unpleasantly wet or full of water.
[from American dialect *sog* meaning 'marsh']

soil, soils, soiling, soiled
1 (noun) Soil is the top layer on the surface of the earth in which plants grow.
2 (verb) If you soil something, you make it dirty.
soiled (adjective).
[sense 1 is from Anglo-French *soil* meaning 'land']

Similar words: (sense 1) loam, earth, land

soiree, soirees (pronounced **swah**-ray)
(noun; an old-fashioned formal word) A soiree is a small social gathering in the evening.
[from French *soir* meaning 'evening']

sojourn, sojourns (pronounced **soj**-jurn)
(noun; a literary word) A sojourn is a stay for a short time in a place that is not your home.

solace
(noun; a literary word) Solace is something that makes you feel less sad, e.g. *He found solace in prayer.*
[from Latin *solatium* meaning 'comfort']

solar
1 (adjective) relating or belonging to the sun.
2 using the sun's light and heat as a source of energy, e.g. *a solar-heated swimming pool*.
[from Latin *sol* meaning 'sun']

solar cell, solar cells
(noun) A solar cell is a device that produces electricity from the sun's rays.

solarium, solaria or solariums
(noun) A solarium is a place where people go to get a suntan, usually from sun lamps.

solar plexus
(noun) The part of the stomach beneath the ribs is known as the solar plexus.

solar system
(noun) The solar system is the sun and all the planets, comets, and asteroids that orbit round it.

solder, solders, soldering, soldered
1 (verb) To solder two pieces of metal together means to join them with molten metal.
2 (noun) Solder is the soft metal used for soldering.
[from Latin *solidare* meaning 'to join together']

soldering iron, soldering irons
(noun) A soldering iron is a tool used to solder things together.

soldier, soldiers, soldiering, soldiered
1 (noun) A soldier is a person in an army.
2 (verb) A person who soldiers serves in an army as a soldier.
[from Old French *soude* meaning 'army pay']

soldierly
(adjective) behaving or looking like a soldier.

sole, soles, soling, soled
1 (adjective) The sole thing or person of a particular type is the only one of that type.
2 (noun) The sole of your foot or shoe is the underneath part.
3 (verb) When a shoe is soled, a sole is fitted to it.
4 (noun) A sole is a flat sea-water fish which you can eat.
[sense 1 is from Latin *solus* meaning 'alone'; senses 2 to 4 are from Latin *solea* meaning 'sandal'; the fish is called this because of its shape]

solecism, solecisms (pronounced **sol**-liss-izm)
(noun; a formal word) A solecism is a minor grammatical mistake in speech or writing.
[from Greek *soloikos* meaning 'speaking incorrectly']

solely
(adverb) If something involves solely one thing, it involves that thing and nothing else.

solemn
(adjective) Solemn means serious rather than cheerful or humorous.
solemnly (adverb), **solemnity** (noun).

solicit, solicits, soliciting, solicited
1 (verb) To solicit money, help, or an opinion from someone means to ask them for it, e.g. *We had to solicit contributions to pay off her debt.*
2 When prostitutes solicit, they offer to have sex with men in return for money.
soliciting (noun).
[from Latin *sollicitare* meaning 'to harass']

solicitor, solicitors
(noun) A solicitor is a lawyer who gives legal advice and prepares legal documents and cases.

solicitous
(adjective) showing anxious or eager concern for someone.
solicitously (adverb), **solicitude** (noun).

solid, solids
1 (adjective) A solid substance or object is hard or firm, and not in the form of a liquid or gas.
2 (noun) A solid is a solid substance or object.
3 (adjective) You say that something is solid when it is not hollow, e.g. *solid rock.*
4 You say that a structure is solid when it is strong and not likely to fall down, e.g. *It looks pretty solid to me.*
5 If you describe someone as solid, you mean that they are very reliable.
6 You use solid to say that something happens for a period of time without interruption, e.g. *two hours' solid revision.*
solidly (adverb).

solidarity
(noun) If a group of people show solidarity, they show unity and support for each other.

solidify, solidifies, solidifying, solidified
(verb) When a liquid solidifies, it becomes solid.

solid-state
(adjective) Solid-state electronic equipment is made using transistors or silicon chips rather than valves or mechanical parts.

soliloquy, soliloquies (pronounced sol-lill-ok-wee)
(noun) A soliloquy is a speech in a play made by a character who is alone on the stage.
soliloquize or **soliloquise** (verb).
[from Latin *solus* meaning 'alone' and *loqui* meaning 'to speak']

solitaire, solitaires
1 (noun) Solitaire is a game for one person that is played by moving pegs to different positions on a board with the aim of having one peg left at the end of the game.
2 A solitaire is a single diamond or other jewel set on its own in a piece of jewellery.
[from Old French *solitaire* meaning 'solitary']

solitary
1 (adjective) A solitary activity is one that you do on your own.
2 A solitary person or animal spends a lot of time alone.
3 If there is a solitary person or object somewhere, there is only one.
[from Latin *solus* meaning 'alone']

solitary confinement
(noun) A prisoner in solitary confinement is being kept alone in a prison cell.

solitude
(noun) Solitude is the state of being alone.

Similar words: seclusion, isolation, loneliness

solo, solos
1 (noun) A solo is a piece of music played or sung by one person alone.
2 (adjective) A solo performance or activity is done by one person alone, e.g. *a solo flight.*
3 (adverb) Solo means alone, e.g. *the boat in which he sailed solo around the world.*
[from Latin *solus* meaning 'alone']

soloist, soloists
(noun) A soloist is a person who performs a solo.

solstice, solstices
(noun) A solstice is one of the two times in the year when the sun is furthest away from the equator.
[from Latin *sol* meaning 'sun' and *sistere* meaning 'to stand still']

soluble
1 (adjective) A soluble substance is able to dissolve in liquid.
2 A soluble problem can be solved.
[from Latin *solvere* meaning 'to dissolve']

solute, solutes
(noun) In chemistry, the solute is the substance which dissolves in a liquid to form a solution.

solution, solutions
1 (noun) A solution is a way of dealing with a problem or difficult situation, e.g. *The only solution is to all go in the same car.*
2 The solution to a riddle or a puzzle is the answer.
3 A solution is also a liquid in which a solid substance has been dissolved.

solve, solves, solving, solved
(verb) If you solve a problem or a question, you find a solution or answer to it.

Similar words: answer, decipher, unravel, resolve, crack, work out, get to the bottom of

solvent, solvents
1 (adjective) If a person or company is solvent, they have enough money to pay all their debts.
2 (noun) A solvent is a liquid that can dissolve other substances.
solvency (noun).
[from Latin *solvere* meaning 'to dissolve', 'to loosen', or 'to free from debt']

Somali, Somalis
1 (adjective) belonging or relating to Somalia.
2 (noun) The Somalis are a group of people who live in Somalia.
3 Somali is the language spoken by Somalis.

sombre
1 (adjective) Sombre colours are dark and dull.
2 A sombre person is serious, sad, or gloomy.
sombrely (adverb).
[from Latin *sub* + *umbra* meaning 'under shade']

sombrero, sombreros
(noun) A sombrero is a pointed hat with a very wide brim which is worn mainly in Mexico.
[from Spanish *sombrero de sol* meaning 'shade from the sun']

some
1 You use some to refer to a quantity or number when you are not stating the quantity or number exactly, e.g. *Please may I have some cake?*
2 You use some to emphasize that a quantity or number is fairly large, e.g. *I haven't seen him for some days.*
3 (adverb) You use some in front of a number to show that it is not exact, e.g. *The bookshelves were some eight metres high.*

somebody
(pronoun) Somebody means someone.

some day
(adverb) Some day means at a date in the future that is unknown or that has not yet been decided.

somehow
1 (adverb) You use somehow to say that you do not know how something was done or will be done, e.g. *We'll manage somehow.*
2 You use somehow to say that you do not know the reason for something, e.g. *Somehow it didn't seem important any more.*

someone
(pronoun) You use someone to refer to a person without saying exactly who you mean.

somersault, somersaults, somersaulting, somersaulted
1 (noun) A somersault is a forwards or backwards roll in which the head is placed on the ground and the body is brought over it.
2 (verb) To somersault means to perform a somersault.
[from Old Provençal *sobre* meaning 'over' and *saut* meaning 'jump']

something
1 (pronoun) You use something to refer to anything that is not a person without saying exactly what you mean.
2 Something also means a little or to some degree, e.g. *Profits fell by something over 35%.*

sometime
1 (adverb) at a time in the future or the past that is unknown or that has not yet been fixed, e.g. *Can I come and see you sometime?*
2 (adjective; a formal use) Sometime is used to say that a person had a particular job or role in the past, e.g. *...a sometime president of the Students' Union.*

sometimes
(adverb) occasionally, rather than always or never.

somewhat
(adverb) to some extent or degree, e.g. *I found, somewhat to my surprise, that I enjoyed myself.*

somewhere
1 (adverb) Somewhere is used to refer to a place without stating exactly where it is, e.g. *There's a pen around somewhere.*
2 Somewhere is used when giving an approximate amount, number, or time, e.g. *I'll meet you somewhere between 1.00 and 1.15.*

somnambulism
(noun; a formal word) Somnambulism is sleepwalking.
somnambulist (noun).
[from Latin *somnus* meaning 'sleep' and *ambulare* meaning 'to walk']

somnolent
(adjective; a formal word) sleepy.
somnolence (noun).

son, sons
(noun) Someone's son is their male child.

sonar
(noun) Sonar is equipment on a ship which calculates the depth of the sea or the position of an underwater object using sound waves.
[from *So(und) Na(vigation) R(anging)*]

sonata, sonatas
(noun) A sonata is a piece of classical music written for the piano or for a piano and one other instrument.
[from Italian *sonare* meaning 'to sound']

song, songs
1 (noun) A song is a piece of music with words that are sung to the music.
2 (phrase) If you buy something **for a song**, you buy it very cheaply.

songbird, songbirds
(noun) A songbird is a bird that produces musical sounds like singing.

sonic
(adjective; a technical word) involving or producing sound.
[from Latin *sonus* meaning 'sound']

sonic boom, sonic booms
(noun) A sonic boom is the loud noise caused by an aircraft travelling faster than the speed of sound.

son-in-law, sons-in-law
(noun) Someone's son-in-law is the husband of their daughter.

sonnet, sonnets
(noun) A sonnet is a poem with 14 lines, in which lines rhyme according to fixed patterns.
[from Old Provençal *sonet* meaning 'little poem']

sonorous
(adjective) A sonorous sound is deep and rich, e.g. *his deep sonorous voice.*
sonorously (adverb), **sonority** (noun).
[from Latin *sonorus* meaning 'loud']

soon, sooner, soonest
(adverb) If something is going to happen soon, it will happen in a very short time.

soot
(noun) Soot is black powder which rises in the smoke from a fire. It contains carbon, sulphur, and hydrocarbons.
sooty (adjective).

soothe, soothes, soothing, soothed.
1 (verb) If you soothe someone who is angry or upset, you make them calmer.
2 Something that soothes pain makes the pain less severe.
soothing (adjective).

soothsayer, soothsayers
(noun; an old-fashioned word) A soothsayer is a person who forecasts the future.
[from Old English *sooth* meaning 'truth']

sop, sops, sopping, sopped.
1 (noun) A sop is something small given to a person who is dissatisfied to stop them getting angry or causing trouble.
2 (verb) Material that sops liquid up soaks it up like a sponge.
[from Old English *sopp* meaning 'piece of bread dipped in liquid']

sophisticated
1 (adjective) Sophisticated people have refined or cultured tastes or habits.
2 A sophisticated machine or device is made using advanced and complicated methods.
sophistication (noun).

Similar words: (sense 1) cosmopolitan, urbane, suave

sophistry, sophistries
(noun) A sophistry is a clever argument that sounds convincing but is in fact false.
[from Greek *sophisma* meaning 'clever trick' or 'argument']

soporific
(adjective) Something soporific makes you feel sleepy, e.g. *Her teaching style is rather soporific.*
[from Latin *sopor* meaning 'deep sleep']

sopping
(adjective) soaking wet.

soppy, soppier, soppiest
(adjective; an informal word) silly or foolishly sentimental.

soprano, sopranos
1 (noun) A soprano is a woman, girl, or boy with a singing voice in the highest range of musical notes.
2 (adjective) A soprano instrument has a range of notes higher than most instruments of its kind, e.g. *a soprano saxophone.*
[from Italian *sopra* meaning 'above']

sorbet, sorbets (pronounced **sor**-bay)
(noun) Sorbet is water ice made from fruit.
[from Turkish *serbet* meaning 'sherbet']

sorcerer, sorcerers (pronounced **sor**-ser-er)
(noun) A sorcerer is a person who performs magic by using the power of evil spirits.
[from Latin *sors* meaning 'lot', because a sorcerer was someone who cast lots]

sorceress, sorceresses
(noun) A sorceress is a female sorcerer.

sorcery
(noun) Sorcery is magic that uses the power of evil spirits.

sordid
1 (adjective) dishonest or immoral, e.g. *How did you get involved in this sordid business?*
2 dirty, unpleasant, or depressing, e.g. *sordid backstreets.*
[from Latin *sordere* meaning 'dirty']

Similar words: (sense 2) squalid, sleazy, seedy

sore, sorer, sorest; sores
1 (adjective) If part of your body is sore, it causes you pain and discomfort.
2 (noun) A sore is a painful place where your skin has become infected.
3 (adjective) 'Sore' is used to emphasize something, e.g. *She was in sore need of a good meal.*
sorely (adverb), **soreness** (noun).

Similar words: (sense 1) raw, tender, sensitive, painful

sorrel
(noun) Sorrel is a herb with bitter-tasting leaves which are used in salads and sauces.
[from Old French *sur* meaning 'sour']

sorrow, sorrows, sorrowing, sorrowed
1 (noun) Sorrow is deep sadness or regret.
2 Sorrows are things that cause sorrow, e.g. *You don't want to hear all about my sorrows.*
3 (verb; a literary use) Someone who sorrows about something feels deep sadness about it.

sorrowful
(adjective) showing or causing deep sadness.
sorrowfully (adverb).

sorry, sorrier, sorriest
1 (adjective) If you are sorry about something, you feel sadness, regret, or sympathy because of it, e.g. *I'm sorry to hear that you failed the exam.*
2 'Sorry' is used to describe people and things that are in a bad physical or mental state, e.g. *I've never seen him in such a sorry state.*

Similar words: (sense 1) apologetic, contrite, remorseful, penitent, repentent

sort, sorts, sorting, sorted
1 (noun) The different sorts of something are the different types of it.
2 (phrase) You use **of sorts** to say that something is not a very good example of a particular type of thing, e.g. *He was a salesman of sorts.*
3 If you are **out of sorts**, you are upset, annoyed, or unwell.
4 (verb) To sort things means to arrange them into different groups or sorts.
sorter (noun).

Similar words: (sense 1) form, variety, ilk, quality

sort out
(phrasal verb) If you sort out a problem or misunderstanding, you deal with it and find a solution to it.

sortie, sorties (pronounced sor-tee)
(noun) A sortie is a raid into enemy territory.
[from French *sortie* meaning 'going out']

SOS
(noun) An SOS is a signal that you are in danger and need help.

so-so
(adjective) neither good nor bad, e.g. *'What's the food like?'—'So-so.'*

sotto voce (pronounced sot-toe **voe**-chee)
(adverb) If you say something sotto voce, you say it in a soft voice.
[from Italian *sotto voce* meaning 'under one's voice']

soufflé, soufflés (pronounced **soo**-flay); also spelled souffle
(noun) A soufflé is a light, fluffy food made from beaten egg whites and other ingredients.
[from French *souffler* meaning 'to blow']

sought the past tense and past participle of seek.

soul, souls
1 (noun) A person's soul is the spiritual part of them that is supposed to continue after their body is dead.
2 People also use 'soul' to refer to a person's mind, character, thoughts, and feelings.
3 'Soul' can be used to mean person, e.g. *She's a happy soul... not a soul in sight.*
4 (phrase) If someone is **the soul of** a particular quality, they have a lot of this quality, e.g. *She is the soul of kindness.*
5 (noun) Soul is a type of pop music.

soul-destroying
(adjective) Something soul-destroying is so tedious that it makes your life miserable, e.g. *a soul-destroying job.*

soulful
(adjective) expressing deep feelings, e.g. *large soulful eyes.*
soulfully (adverb).

soulless
(adjective) lacking in human qualities and unable to produce deep feelings, e.g. *a soulless environment.*

sound, sounds, sounding, sounded; sounder, soundest
1 (noun) Sound is everything that can be heard.
2 A particular sound is something that you hear.
3 (verb) If something sounds or if you sound it, it makes a noise.
4 (noun) The sound of something is the impression you have of it, e.g. *I don't like the sound of computer science.*
5 (adjective) in good condition, e.g. *My teeth are sound.*
6 reliable and sensible, e.g. *He put forward some very sound arguments.*
7 (verb) To sound something deep, such as a well or the sea, means to measure how deep it is using a weighted line or sonar.
soundly (adverb), **soundness** (noun).
[senses 1-4 are from Old French *soner* meaning 'to make a sound'; senses 5 and 6 are from Old English *gesund* meaning 'whole' or 'uninjured'; sense 7 is from Old French *sonde* referring to a line used to measure the depth of water]

sound out
(phrasal verb) If you sound someone out, you question them to find out their opinion on something.

sound barrier
(noun) The sound barrier is the sudden increase in the force of the air against an aircraft that occurs as it passes the speed of sound.

soundbox, soundboxes
(noun) The soundbox of a stringed instrument is the hollow part that increases the sound of the vibration of the strings.

sound effect, sound effects
(noun) Sound effects are sounds created artificially to make a play more realistic, especially a radio play.

sounding board, sounding boards
(noun) If you use someone as a sounding board, you discuss your ideas with them while you are working them out.

soundless
(adjective) not making a sound.
soundlessly (adverb).

soundproof, soundproofs, soundproofing, soundproofed
1 (adjective) If a room is soundproof, sound cannot get into it or out of it.
2 (verb) To soundproof something means to make it soundproof.

soundtrack, soundtracks
(noun) The soundtrack of a film is the part you hear.

sound wave, sound waves
(noun) A sound wave is a wave on which sound is carried.

soup, soups
(noun) Soup is liquid food made by boiling meat, fish, or vegetables in water.

soupçon (pronounced **soop**-song)
(noun) A soupçon of something is a very small amount of it.
[a French word]

soup kitchen, soup kitchens
(noun) A soup kitchen is a place where soup or other food is served to poor or homeless people.

sour, sours, souring, soured
1 (adjective) If something is sour, it has a sharp, acid taste.
2 Sour milk has an unpleasant taste because it is no longer fresh.
3 A sour person is bad-tempered and unfriendly.
4 (verb) If a friendship, situation, or attitude sours or if something sours it, it becomes less friendly, enjoyable, or hopeful.

source, sources
1 (noun) The source of something is the person, place, or thing that it comes from, e.g. *They're trying to trace the source of the trouble.*
2 A source is a person or book that provides information for a news story or for research.
3 The source of a river or stream is the place where it begins.
[from Old French *sourdre* meaning 'to spring forth']

sour grapes
(noun) You describe someone's behaviour as sour grapes when they say something is worthless but secretly want it and cannot have it.

souse, souses, sousing, soused (rhymes with mouse)
(verb) To souse something or someone means to drench them with a liquid.

south
1 (noun) The south is the direction to your right when you are looking towards the place where the sun rises.
2 The south of a place or country is the part which is towards the south when you are in the centre.
3 (adverb and adjective) South means towards the south, e.g. *We headed south... the south wall of the church.*
4 (adjective) A south wind blows from the south.

South America
(noun) South America is the fourth largest continent. It has the Pacific Ocean on its west side, the Atlantic on the east, and the Antarctic to the south. South America is joined to North America by the Isthmus of Panama.
South American (adjective).

south-east
(noun, adverb, and adjective) South-east is halfway between south and east.

south-easterly
1 (adjective) South-easterly means to or towards the south-east.
2 A south-easterly wind blows from the south-east.

south-eastern
(adjective) in or from the south-east.

southerly
1 (adjective) Southerly means to or towards the south.
2 A southerly wind blows from the south.

southern
(adjective) in or from the south.

South Pole
(noun) The South Pole is the place on the surface of the earth that is farthest towards the south.

southward or **southwards**
1 (adverb) Southward or southwards means towards the south, e.g. *They travelled southwards.*
2 (adjective) The southward part of something is the south part, e.g. *The shore was badly eroded on its southward side.*

south-west
(noun, adverb, and adjective) South-west is halfway between south and west.

south-westerly
1 (adjective) South-westerly means to or towards the south-west.
2 A south-westerly wind blows from the south-west.

south-western
(adjective) in or from the south-west.

souvenir, souvenirs
(noun) A souvenir is something you acquire and keep to remind you of a holiday, place, or event.
[from French *se souvenir* meaning 'to remember']

sou'wester, sou'westers
(noun) A sou'wester is a waterproof hat with a wide brim at the back to keep your neck dry.

sovereign, sovereigns (pronounced **sov**-rin)
1 (noun) A sovereign is a king, queen, or royal ruler of a country.
2 (adjective) A sovereign state or country is independent and not under the authority of any other country.
3 (noun) In the past, a sovereign was a gold coin worth £1.

sovereignty (pronounced **sov**-rin-tee)
(noun) Sovereignty is the political power that a country has to govern itself.

Soviet, Soviets (pronounced **soe**-vee-et)
1 (adjective) belonging or relating to the Soviet Union.
2 (noun) The Soviet people and their government are sometimes referred to as the Soviets, e.g. *The Soviets have put a man into space.*

sow, sows, sowing, sowed, sown (pronounced soh)
1 (verb) To sow seeds or sow an area of land with seeds means to plant them in the ground.
2 To sow undesirable feelings or attitudes means

to cause them, e.g. *sowing doubt and
uncertainty.*

sow, sows (rhymes with **now**)
(noun) A sow is an adult female pig.

soya
(noun) Soya flour, margarine, oil, and milk are
made from soya beans.
[from Chinese *chiang yu* meaning 'paste sauce']

soya bean, soya beans
(noun) Soya beans are a type of edible Asian
bean.

spa, spas
(noun) A spa is a place where water containing
minerals bubbles out of the ground. People drink
or bathe in the water to improve their health.
[from the Belgian town *Spa* where there are
mineral springs]

space, spaces, spacing, spaced
1 (noun) Space is the area that is empty or
available in a place, building, or container.
2 Space is the area beyond the earth's
atmosphere surrounding the stars and planets.
3 A space is a gap between two things, e.g. *The
door had spaces at the top and bottom.*
4 Space can also refer to a period of time, e.g. *It
happened twice in the space of three weeks.*
5 (verb) If you space a series of things, you
arrange them with gaps between them.

space capsule, space capsules
(noun) A space capsule is the part of a
spacecraft which astronauts travel in.

spacecraft
(noun) A spacecraft is a rocket or other vehicle
that can travel in space.

spaceman, spacemen
(noun; an old-fashioned word) A spaceman is
someone who travels in space.

space probe, space probes
(noun) A space probe is a small spacecraft sent
into space to transmit information about space.

spaceship, spaceships
(noun) A spaceship is a spacecraft that carries
people through space.

space shuttle, space shuttles
(noun) A space shuttle is a spacecraft designed
to be used many times for travelling out into
space and back again.

space station, space stations
(noun) A space station is a large satellite that
orbits the earth and is used as a base by
astronauts or scientists.

spacesuit, spacesuits
(noun) A spacesuit is a protective suit covering
the whole of an astronaut's body.

spacious
(adjective) having or providing a lot of space,
e.g. *a very spacious dining room.*
spaciousness (noun).

Similar words: roomy, capacious, commodious,
expansive

spade, spades
1 (noun) A spade is a tool with a flat metal blade
and a long handle used for digging.
2 Spades is one of the four suits in a pack of
playing cards. It is marked by a black symbol in
the shape of a heart-shaped leaf with a stem.

spadework
(noun) Spadework is uninteresting work done as
preparation for a project or activity.

spaghetti (pronounced spag-**get**-ee)
(noun) Spaghetti consists of long, thin pieces of
pasta. It is usually served with a sauce.
[from Italian *spago* meaning 'string']

spake an old form of the past tense of **speak.**

span, spans, spanning, spanned
1 (noun) A span is the period of time during
which something exists or functions, e.g. *in the
short span that man has been on earth.*
2 (verb) If something spans a particular length
of time, it lasts throughout that time, e.g. *His
career spanned half a century.*
3 (noun) The span of something is the total
length of it from one end to the other.
4 (verb) A bridge that spans something stretches
right across it.

spangle, spangles, spangling, spangled
1 (verb) If something is spangled with small,
bright objects, the objects are scattered over it
and make it sparkle.
2 (noun) Spangles are small sparkling pieces of
metal or plastic used to decorate clothing or hair.

Spaniard, Spaniards (pronounced **span**-yard)
(noun) A Spaniard is someone who comes from
Spain.

spaniel, spaniels
(noun) A spaniel is a gundog with long drooping
ears and a silky coat.
[from Old French *espaigneul* meaning 'Spanish
dog']

Spanish
1 (adjective) belonging or relating to Spain.
2 (noun) Spanish is the main language spoken in
Spain, and is also spoken by many people in
Central and South America.

spank, spanks, spanking, spanked
(verb) If a child is spanked, it is punished by
being slapped, usually on its leg or bottom.

spanner, spanners
(noun) A spanner is a tool with a specially
shaped end that fits round a nut to turn it.

spar, spars, sparring, sparred
1 (verb) When boxers spar, they hit each other
with light punches for exercise or practice.
2 To spar with someone also means to argue with
them, but not in an unpleasant or serious way.
3 (noun) A spar is a strong pole that a sail is
attached to on a yacht or ship.
[senses 1 and 2 are from Old English *sperran*
meaning 'strike with your feet or weapon'; sense
3 is from Old Norse *sperra* meaning 'beam']

spare, spares, sparing, spared
1 (adjective) extra to what is needed, e.g. *I have
lots of spare time.*

2 (noun) A spare is anything that is extra to what is needed.
3 (verb) If you spare something for a particular purpose, you make it available, e.g. *Nowadays less land can be spared to graze cattle.*
4 If someone is spared an unpleasant experience, they are prevented from suffering it, e.g. *He was spared the shame of being told off.*
5 (phrase) If you **spare no expense** in doing something, you do it as well as possible, without trying to save money.
[from Old English *sparian* meaning 'to refrain from injuring or using']

sparerib, spareribs
(noun) Spareribs are pork ribs with most of the meat trimmed off.

sparing
(adjective) If you are sparing with something, you use it in very small quantities.
sparingly (adverb).

spark, sparks, sparking, sparked
1 (noun) A spark is a tiny, bright piece of burning material thrown up by a fire.
2 A spark also is a small flash of light caused by electricity.
3 A spark of feeling is a small amount of it, e.g. *A faint spark of pleasure came into his eyes.*
4 (verb) If something sparks, it throws out sparks.
5 If one thing sparks another thing off, it causes the second thing to start happening, e.g. *The letter sparked off a friendship between them.*

sparkle, sparkles, sparkling, sparkled
1 (verb) If something sparkles, it shines with a lot of small, bright points of light.
2 (noun) Sparkles are small, bright points of light.
3 (verb) Someone who sparkles is lively, intelligent, and witty.
sparkling (adjective).

Similar words: (sense 1) glisten, glitter, scintillate, twinkle

sparkler, sparklers
(noun) A sparkler is a small firework you can hold in your hand.

spark plug, spark plugs
(noun) A spark plug is a device in the engine of a motor vehicle that makes the electric sparks that ignite the fuel.

sparrow, sparrows
(noun) A sparrow is a very common, small bird with brown and grey feathers.

sparrowhawk, sparrowhawks
(noun) A sparrowhawk is a hawk that preys on smaller birds.

sparse, sparser, sparsest
(adjective) small in number or amount and spread out over an area, e.g. *sparse white hair.*
sparsely (adverb).
[from Latin *spargere* meaning 'to scatter']

spartan
(adjective) A spartan way of life is very simple with no luxuries, e.g. *spartan accommodation.*
[from *Sparta*, a city in Ancient Greece, whose inhabitants were famous for their discipline, military skill, and stern and plain way of life]

spasm, spasms
1 (noun) A spasm is a sudden tightening of the muscles.
2 A spasm is also a sudden, short burst of something, e.g. *a spasm of anger.*
[from Greek *spasmos* meaning 'cramp']

spasmodic
(adjective) happening suddenly for short periods of time at irregular intervals, e.g. *spasmodic bursts of energy.*
spasmodically (adverb).

spastic, spastics
1 (adjective) A spastic person is born with a disability which makes it difficult for them to control their muscles.
2 (noun) A spastic is a spastic person.
[from Greek *spasmos* meaning 'cramp' or 'convulsion']

spate
(noun) A spate of things is a large number of them that happen or appear in a rush, e.g. *a spate of new books about the Royal Family.*

spatial (pronounced spay-shl)
(adjective) to do with size, area, or position.
spatially (adverb).

spats
(plural noun) Spats are specially shaped pieces of cloth which were worn by men in the past over their ankles and the front of their shoes.

spatter, spatters, spattering, spattered
1 (verb) If something spatters a surface, it covers the surface with drops of liquid.
2 (noun) A spatter of something is a small amount of it in drops or tiny pieces.
spattered (adjective).

spatula, spatulas
(noun) A spatula is a knife-like object with a wide, flat blade. Spatulas are used in cooking and by doctors.
[from Latin *spatha* meaning 'flat wooden implement']

spawn, spawns, spawning, spawned.
1 (noun) Spawn is a jelly-like substance containing the eggs of fish or amphibians.
2 (verb) When fish or amphibians spawn, they lay their eggs.
3 If something spawns something else, it causes it, e.g. *Unemployment has spawned an increase in violence.*
[from Old French *spandre* meaning 'to spread out']

spay, spays, spaying, spayed
(verb) When a female animal is spayed it has its ovaries removed so that it cannot become pregnant.
[from Old French *espeer* meaning 'to cut with a sword']

speak, speaks, speaking, spoke, spoken
1 (verb) When you speak, you use your voice to say words.
2 If you speak a foreign language, you know it and can use it.
3 If you speak for a group of people, you give their opinion on their behalf.
4 (phrase) If something **is spoken for**, it is reserved.

Similar words: (sense 1) talk, discourse, converse

speak out
(phrasal verb) To speak out about something means to publicly state an opinion about it.

speaker, speakers
1 (noun) A speaker is a person who is speaking, especially someone making a speech.
2 A speaker on a radio or hi-fi is a loudspeaker.
3 In Parliament, the Speaker is a member of the House of Commons who is elected to control the meetings.

speaking clock
(noun) The speaking clock is a telephone service which gives you the correct time.

spear, spears, spearing, speared
1 (noun) A spear is a weapon consisting of a long pole with a sharp point.
2 (verb) To spear something means to push or throw a spear or other pointed object into it.

spearhead, spearheads, spearheading, spearheaded
(verb) If someone spearheads a campaign, they lead it.

spearmint, spearmints
1 (noun) Spearmint is a mint-flavoured herb which is used as a flavouring.
2 Spearmints are spearmint-flavoured sweets.

spec, specs (an informal word)
1 (plural noun) Someone's specs are their glasses.
2 (phrase) If you do something **on spec**, you do it hoping for a result but without any certainty, e.g. *They just turned up on spec.*
[sense 1 is a shortened form of *spectacles*; sense 2 is a shortened form of *speculation*]

special
1 (adjective) Something special is more important or better than other things of its kind.
2 Special describes someone who is officially appointed, or something that is needed or intended for a particular purpose, e.g. *You need special permission to marry a foreigner.*
3 Special also describes something that belongs or relates to only one particular person, group, or place, e.g. *the special needs of children with learning difficulties.*
[from Latin *specialis* meaning 'individual']

Special Branch
(noun) The Special Branch is the department of the police concerned with political security. It deals with such things as terrorism.

specialist, specialists
1 (noun) A specialist is someone who has a particular skill or who knows a lot about a particular subject, e.g. *an eye specialist.*
2 (adjective) having a skill or knowing a lot about a particular subject, e.g. *a specialist teacher of mathematics.*
specialism (noun).

speciality, specialities
(noun) A person's speciality is something they are especially good at or know a lot about, e.g. *Work with children is their speciality.*

specialize, specializes, specializing, specialized; also spelled specialise
(verb) If you specialize in something, you make it your speciality, e.g. *a shop specializing in camping equipment.*
specialization (noun).

specialized or specialised
(adjective) developed for a particular purpose or trained in a particular area of knowledge, e.g. *highly specialized staff.*

specially
(adverb) If something has been done specially for a particular person or purpose, it has been done only for that person or purpose.

species (pronounced spee-sheez)
(noun) A species is a class of plants or animals whose members have the same characteristics and are able to breed with each other.

specific
1 (adjective) particular, e.g. *Education should not be restricted to any one specific age group.*
2 precise and exact, e.g. *Try to be more specific.*
specifically (adverb).

Similar words: precise, exact, certain

specification, specifications
1 (noun) Specification is the specifying of something.
2 A specification is a detailed description of what is needed for something, such as the necessary features in the design of something, e.g. *ships built to merchant ship specifications.*

specific gravity, specific gravities
(noun) The specific gravity of a substance is the ratio of the density of the substance to the density of water at a particular temperature, usually 15°.

specify, specifies, specifying, specified
(verb) To specify something means to state or describe it clearly and precisely, e.g. *Please specify what it is you want.*

specimen, specimens
(noun) A specimen of something is an example or small amount of it which gives an idea of what the whole is like, e.g. *a specimen of his work.*
[from Latin *specimen* meaning 'mark' or 'evidence']

specious
(adjective) A specious argument appears to be true or valid, but is in fact untrue or invalid.
speciously (adverb), **speciousness** (noun).
[from Latin *speciosus* meaning 'plausible']

speck, specks
1 (noun) A speck is a very small stain or mark.
2 A speck is also a very small piece of a powdery substance.

speckle, speckles, speckling, speckled
(verb) If something speckles a surface, it covers it with very small marks or spots.

spectacle, spectacles
1 (plural noun) Someone's spectacles are their glasses.
2 (noun) A spectacle is a strange or interesting sight or scene, e.g. *a tragic spectacle.*
3 A spectacle is also a grand and impressive event or performance.
[from Latin *spectaculum* meaning 'a show']

spectacular, spectaculars
1 (adjective) Something spectacular is very impressive or dramatic.
2 (noun) A spectacular is a grand and impressive show or performance.

Similar words: (sense 1) breathtaking, dazzling, stunning, sensational

spectator, spectators
(noun) A spectator is a person who is watching something.
[from Latin *spectare* meaning 'to watch']

Similar words: observer, watcher, viewer, onlooker

spectra the plural of **spectrum.**

spectral
1 (adjective) like a ghost or related to ghosts.
2 to do with a spectrum.

spectre, spectres
1 (noun) A spectre is a ghost.
2 A spectre is also a frightening idea or image, e.g. *the spectre of another world war.*
[from Latin *spectrum* meaning 'appearance']

spectrum, spectra or spectrums
1 (noun) The spectrum is the range of different colours produced when light passes through a prism or a drop of water. A rainbow shows the colours in a spectrum.
2 A spectrum of opinions or emotions is a range of them.
[from Latin *spectrum* meaning 'appearance' or 'image']

speculate, speculates, speculating, speculated
1 (verb) If you speculate about something, you think about it and form opinions about it based on the information available to you.
2 If someone speculates financially, they buy goods and shares in the hope of being able to sell them at a profit.
speculation (noun).
[from Latin *speculari* meaning 'to spy out']

speculative
1 (adjective) A speculative piece of information is based on guesswork and opinions rather than known facts.
2 Someone with a speculative expression seems to be trying to guess something, e.g. *He had an oddly speculative glint in his eyes.*

3 Speculative activities involve buying goods or shares in the hope of selling them at a profit.

speculator, speculators
(noun) A speculator is a person who speculates financially.

speech, speeches
1 (noun) Speech is the ability to speak or the act of speaking.
2 A speech is a formal talk given to an audience.
3 In a play, a speech is a group of lines spoken by one of the characters.
4 The speech of a country or region is the language or dialect spoken there.
[from Old English *spec* meaning 'speech']

Similar words: (sense 2) oration, address

speechless
(adjective) Someone who is speechless is temporarily unable to speak because something has shocked them.

speed, speeds, speeding, sped or speeded
1 (noun) The speed of something is the rate at which it moves, travels, or happens.
2 Speed is very fast movement or travel.
3 (verb) If you speed somewhere, you move or travel there quickly.
4 Someone who is speeding is driving a vehicle faster than the legal speed limit.
[from Old English *sped* meaning 'success']

Similar words: (sense 1) pace, rate, tempo, velocity (sense 2) rapidity, alacrity

speedboat, speedboats
(noun) A speedboat is a small, fast motorboat.

speed limit, speed limits
(noun) The speed limit is the maximum speed at which vehicles are legally allowed to drive on a particular road.

speedometer, speedometers
(noun) A speedometer is an instrument in a vehicle which shows how fast the vehicle is moving.

speed trap, speed traps
(noun) A speed trap is a section of a road along which the police check the speed of passing vehicles.

speedway
(noun) Speedway is the sport of racing lightweight motorcycles on special tracks.

speedy, speedier, speediest
(adjective) done very quickly.
speedily (adverb).

spell, spells, spelling, spelled or spelt
1 (verb) When you spell a word, you name or write its letters in order.
2 When letters spell a word, they form that word when put together in a particular sequence.
3 If something spells a particular result, it suggests that this will be the result, e.g. *Nuclear war would spell the end of civilization.*
4 (noun) A spell of something is a short period of it, e.g. *a spell of mild weather.*

5 A spell is a word or sequence of words used to perform magic.
6 (phrase) If you are **under someone's spell**, you are so fascinated by them that you cannot think about anything else.
[senses 1-3 are from Old French *espeller* meaning 'to spell'; sense 4 is from Old English *spelian* meaning 'to take the place of someone for a short time'; senses 5 and 6 are from Old English *spell* meaning 'speech']

spell out
(phrasal verb) If you spell something out, you explain it in detail, e.g. *Do I have to spell it out to you?*

spellbound
(adjective) so fascinated by something that you cannot think about anything else, e.g. *We were all spellbound as we listened to her.*

spelling, spellings
(noun) The spelling of a word is the correct order of letters in it.

spend, spends, spending, spent
1 (verb) When you spend money, you buy things with it.
2 To spend time or energy means to use it.
spending (noun), **spender** (noun).
[from Latin *expendere* meaning 'to spend']

spendthrift, spendthrifts
(noun) A spendthrift is a person who spends money in a wasteful or extravagant way.

spent
1 (adjective) Spent describes things which have been used and therefore cannot be used again, e.g. *spent matches.*
2 If you are spent, you are exhausted and have no energy left.

sperm, sperms
(noun) A sperm is a cell produced in the sex organ of a male animal which can enter a female animal's egg and fertilize it.
[from Greek *sperma* meaning 'seed']

spermatozoon, spermatozoa (pronounced spur-mat-toe-**zoe**-on)
(noun) A spermatozoon is the same as a sperm.

sperm whale, sperm whales
(noun) A sperm whale is a large whale which is hunted for the oil contained in a large cavity in its head.

spew, spews, spewing, spewed
1 (verb) When things spew from something or when it spews them out, they come out of it in large quantities.
2 (an informal use) To spew up means to vomit.
[from Latin *spuere* meaning 'to spit out' or 'to vomit']

sphere, spheres
1 (noun) A sphere is a perfectly round object, such as a ball.
2 An area of activity or interest can be referred to as a sphere of activity or interest.
spherical (adjective).
[from Latin *sphaera* meaning 'globe']

sphinx, sphinxes (pronounced **sfingks**)
1 (noun) Sphinxes are huge stone statues built by the ancient Egyptians. Each one has the head of a man and the body of a lion.
2 A person who seems mysterious or puzzling can be called a sphinx.

spice, spices, spicing, spiced
1 (noun) Spice is powder or seeds from a plant added to food to give it flavour.
2 (verb) To spice food means to add spice to it.
3 (noun) Spice is something which makes life more exciting, e.g. *Variety is the spice of life.*
4 (verb) If you spice something up, you make it more exciting or lively.
spiced (adjective).
[from Old French *espice* meaning 'spice']

spick and span
(adjective) very clean and tidy.

spicy, spicier, spiciest
(adjective) strongly flavoured with spices.

spider, spiders
(noun) A spider is a small insect-like creature with eight legs. Most spiders spin webs in which they catch insects for food.
[from Old English *spinnan* meaning 'to spin']

spidery
(adjective) composed of long crooked lines or strands, like a spider's legs, e.g. *spidery handwriting.*

spike, spikes, spiking, spiked
1 (noun) A spike is a long pointed piece of metal.
2 The spikes on a sports shoe are the pointed pieces of metal attached to the sole.
3 Some other long pointed objects are called spikes, e.g. *The plant has spikes of greenish flowers.*
4 (verb) If you spike something, you drive a spike or other pointed piece of metal into it.
spiked (adjective).

spiky, spikier, spikiest
1 (adjective) Something spiky has sharp points.
2 (an informal use) A spiky person is bad-tempered and easily irritated.

spill, spills, spilling, spilled or **spilt**
1 (verb) If you spill something or if it spills, it accidentally falls or runs out of a container.
2 If people or things spill out of a place, they come out of it in large numbers.
3 (an informal use) To spill information means to tell it to someone.
[from Old English *spillan* meaning 'to destroy']

spillage, spillages
(noun) A spillage is the spilling of something, or something that has been spilt, e.g. *an oil spillage.*

spin, spins, spinning, spun
1 (verb) If something spins, it turns quickly around a central point.
2 (noun) A spin is a rapid turn around a central point, e.g. *Try to put a spin on the ball.*
3 (verb) When spiders spin a web, they give out a sticky substance and make it into a web.
4 When people spin, they make thread by twisting together pieces of fibre using a machine.

5 If your head is spinning, you feel dizzy or confused.

spin out
(phrasal verb) If you spin something out, you make it last longer than it otherwise would.

spina bifida (pronounced spy-na **biff**-id-a)
(noun) Spina bifida is a congenital condition of the spine which some people are born with. It sometimes causes paralysis.
[from Latin *spina* + *bifidus* meaning 'spine split into two parts']

spinach (pronounced **spin**-ij)
(noun) Spinach is a vegetable with large green leaves.

spinal
(adjective) to do with the spine.

spinal column, spinal columns
(noun) Your spinal column is your spine.

spinal cord, spinal cords
(noun) Your spinal cord is a bundle of nerves inside your spine which connects your brain to nerves in the rest of your body.

spindle, spindles
1 (noun) A spindle is a rod in a machine around which another part of the machine turns.
2 A spindle is also a pointed rod around which thread or wool is wound for sewing or spinning.

spindly
(adjective) long, thin, and weak-looking.

spin-dry, spin-dries, spin-drying, spin-dried
(verb) To spin-dry clothes means to get most of the water out of them by spinning them in a machine.

spin dryer, spin dryers; also spelled **spin drier**
(noun) A spin dryer is a machine for spinning the water out of wet clothes.

spine, spines
1 (noun) Your spine is your backbone.
2 The spine of a book is the narrow, stiff part that holds the pages together.
3 Spines are long, sharp points on an animal's body or on a plant.

spine-chilling
(adjective) A spine-chilling story or film makes you feel very frightened.
spine-chiller (noun).

spineless
(adjective) A spineless person behaves in a cowardly way.

spinet, spinets (pronounced spin-**net**)
(noun) A spinet is a small harpsichord.

spinney, spinneys
(noun) A spinney is a small wood.
[from Old French *espine* meaning 'thorn']

spinning wheel, spinning wheels
(noun) A spinning wheel is a wooden machine for spinning flax or wool. It has a wheel, operated by a treadle, which makes the spindle turn round.

spin-off, spin-offs
(noun) A spin-off is something useful that unexpectedly results from an activity.

spinster, spinsters
(noun) A spinster is a woman who has never married.
[originally a person whose occupation was spinning; later, the official label of an unmarried woman]

spiny
(adjective) covered with spines.

spiral, spirals, spiralling, spiralled
1 (noun) A spiral is a continuous curve which winds round and round, with each curve above or outside the previous one.
2 (adjective) in the shape of a spiral, e.g. *a spiral staircase.*
3 (verb) If something spirals, it moves up or down in a spiral curve, e.g. *The leaves came spiralling down.*
4 If an amount or level spirals, it rises or falls quickly at an increasing rate, e.g. *Prices had continued to spiral.*
5 (noun) The rapid rise or fall of a level or amount can be referred to as a spiral, e.g. *a wage and price spiral.*
[from Latin *spira* meaning 'coil']

spire, spires
(noun) The spire of a church is the tall cone-shaped structure on top.
[from Old English *spir* meaning 'blade']

spirit, spirits, spiriting, spirited
1 (noun) Your spirit is the part of you that is not physical and that is connected with your deepest thoughts and feelings.
2 The spirit of a dead person is a nonphysical part that is believed to remain alive after death.
3 A spirit is a supernatural being, such as a ghost.
4 Spirit is liveliness, energy, and self-confidence, e.g. *a performance full of spirit and originality.*
5 'Spirit' can refer to an attitude, e.g. *the pioneering spirit.*
6 The spirit of a law is the way it was originally intended to be interpreted.
7 (plural noun) 'Spirits' can describe how happy or unhappy someone is, e.g. *in high spirits.*
8 Spirits are strong alcoholic drinks such as whisky and gin.
9 (verb) If you spirit someone or something into or out of a place, you get them in or out quickly and secretly.
[from Latin *spiritus* meaning 'breath' or 'spirit']

spirited
(adjective) showing energy and courage.

spirit level, spirit levels
(noun) A spirit level is a device for finding out if a surface is level. It consists of a bubble of air sealed in a tube of liquid in a wooden or metal frame.

spiritual, spirituals
1 (adjective) to do with people's thoughts and beliefs, rather than their bodies and physical surroundings.
2 to do with people's religious beliefs, e.g. *a book of spiritual instruction.*

3 (noun) A spiritual is a religious song originally sung by Black slaves in America.
spiritually (adverb), **spirituality** (noun).

spiritualism
(noun) Spiritualism is the belief that the spirits of dead people can communicate with the living.
spiritualist (noun).

spit, spits, spitting, spat
1 (noun) Spit is saliva.
2 (verb) If you spit, you force saliva or some other substance out of your mouth.
3 When it is spitting, it is raining very lightly.
4 (noun) A spit is a long stick made of metal or wood which is pushed through a piece of meat so that it can be hung over a fire and cooked.
5 A spit is also a long, flat, narrow piece of land sticking out into the sea.
[senses 1-3 are from Old English *spittan* meaning 'to spit'; senses 4 and 5 are from Old English *spitu* meaning 'long pointed rod used for roasting meat']

spite, spites, spiting, spited
1 (phrase) **In spite of** is used to introduce a statement which makes the rest of what you are saying seem surprising, e.g. *In spite of poor health, my father was always cheerful.*
2 (verb) If you do something to spite someone, you do it deliberately to hurt or annoy them.
3 (noun) If you do something out of spite, you do it to spite someone.

spiteful
(adjective) A spiteful person does or says nasty things to people deliberately to hurt them.
spitefully (adverb).

Similar words: malicious, vicious, mean, nasty, vindictive, catty, bitchy

spitting image
(noun) If someone is the spitting image of someone else, they look just like them.

spittle
(noun) Spittle is saliva.
[from Old English *spætl* meaning 'saliva']

spittoon, spittoons
(noun) A spittoon is a bowl for spitting into.

splash, splashes, splashing, splashed
1 (verb) If you splash around in water, your movements disturb the water in a noisy way.
2 If liquid splashes something, it scatters over it in a lot of small drops.
3 (noun) A splash is the sound made when something hits or falls into water.
4 A splash of liquid is a small quantity of it that has been spilt on something.
5 A splash of colour is an area of bright colour that contrasts with duller colours around it.

splash down
(phrasal verb) When a space vehicle splashes down, it lands in the sea at the end of a space flight.
splashdown (noun).

splash out
(phrasal verb) To splash out on something means to spend a lot of money on it.

splatter, splatters, splattering, splattered
(verb) When something is splattered with a substance, the substance is splashed all over it.

splay, splays, splaying, splayed
(verb) If things are splayed or if they splay out, their ends spread away from each other.

spleen, spleens
1 (noun) Your spleen is an organ near your stomach which controls the quality of your blood.
2 (a formal use) Spleen is violent and spiteful anger, e.g. *In an unusual burst of spleen, Rob wrote me a furious letter.*

splendid
1 (adjective) very good indeed, e.g. *I think it's a splendid idea.*
2 beautiful and impressive, e.g. *a splendid Victorian building.*
splendidly (adverb).

Similar words: (sense 2) magnificent, grand, glorious

splendour, splendours
1 (noun) If something has splendour, it is beautiful and impressive.
2 (plural noun) The splendours of something are its beautiful and impressive features.

splice, splices, splicing, spliced
(verb) To splice two pieces of rope, film, or tape together means to join them neatly so that they make one long continuous piece.

splint, splints
(noun) A splint is a long piece of wood or metal fastened to a broken limb to hold it in place.

splinter, splinters, splintering, splintered
1 (noun) A splinter is a thin, sharp piece of wood or glass which has broken off a larger piece.
2 (verb) If something splinters, it breaks into thin, sharp pieces.

splinter group, splinter groups
(noun) A splinter group is a group of people who have broken away from a larger group.

split, splits, splitting, split
1 (verb) If something splits or if you split it, it divides into two or more parts.
2 If something such as wood or fabric splits, a long crack or tear appears in it.
3 (noun) A split in a piece of wood or fabric is a crack or tear.
4 A split between two things is a division or difference between them, e.g. *the split between the rich and the poor.*
5 (verb) If people split something, they share it between them.
6 (phrase) If two people **split the difference**, they agree on a figure halfway between two figures that have been mentioned.
[from Old Dutch *splitten* meaning 'to break up']

Similar words: (sense 1) cleave, divide
(sense 4) cleft, division, rift, schism

split infinitive, split infinitives
(noun) A split infinitive is an infinitive with a word between the 'to' and the verb, as in 'to boldly go'. This is often thought to be incorrect.

split pea, split peas
(noun) Split peas are dried peas cut in half and used as a vegetable in soups and casseroles.

split personality
(noun) Someone with a split personality has moods which change so much that they seem to have two different personalities.

split second
(noun) A split second is an extremely short period of time.

splitting
(adjective) A splitting headache is very painful.

splodge, splodges
(noun; an informal word) A splodge is a large messy mark or stain.

splurge, splurges, splurging, splurged
(verb; an informal word) To splurge on something means to spend a lot of money on it, especially when you do not really need it.

splutter, splutters, spluttering, spluttered
1 (verb) If someone splutters, they speak in a confused way because they are embarrassed.
2 If something splutters, it makes a series of short, sharp sounds.

spoil, spoils, spoiling, spoiled or spoilt
1 (verb) If you spoil something, you prevent it from being successful or satisfactory.
2 To spoil children means to give them everything they want, with harmful effects on their character.
3 To spoil someone also means to give them something nice as a treat.
4 (plural noun) Spoils are valuable things obtained during war or as a result of violence, e.g. *the spoils of war*.
5 (verb) If you are spoiling for a fight, you are eager to have one.
[from Latin *spoliare* meaning 'to strip' or 'to plunder']

Similar words: (sense 1) mar, ruin, wreck, scupper (sense 2) pamper, indulge, cosset, mollycoddle, pet

spoilsport, spoilsports
(noun) A spoilsport is someone who spoils people's fun.

spoke, spokes
(noun) The spokes of a wheel are the bars which connect the hub to the rim.

spokesperson, spokespersons
(noun) A spokesperson is someone who speaks on behalf of another person or a group.
spokesman (noun), **spokeswoman** (noun).

sponge, sponges, sponging, sponged
1 (noun) A sponge is a sea creature with a porous body made up of many cells.
2 A sponge is also part of the very light skeleton of a sponge, used for bathing and cleaning.
3 A sponge or sponge cake is a very light cake.

4 (verb) If you sponge something, you clean it by wiping it with a wet sponge.
5 Someone who sponges off other people gets money from them without giving anything in return.
sponger (noun).
[from Greek *spongia*]

spongy
(adjective) soft and squashy, like a sponge.

sponsor, sponsors, sponsoring, sponsored
1 (verb) To sponsor something, such as an event or someone's training, means to support it financially, e.g. *My trip was sponsored by ICI.*
2 If you sponsor someone who is doing something for charity, you agree to give them a sum of money for the charity if they manage to do it.
3 If you sponsor a proposal or suggestion, you officially put it forward and support it, e.g. *Two Labour MPs sponsored the Bill.*
4 (noun) A sponsor is a person or organization sponsoring something or someone.
sponsorship (noun).
[from Latin *spondere* meaning 'to promise solemnly']

spontaneous
1 (adjective) Spontaneous acts are not planned or arranged, but are done because you feel like it.
2 A spontaneous event happens because of processes within something rather than being caused by things outside it, e.g. *a spontaneous explosion.*
spontaneously (adverb), **spontaneity** (noun).
[from Latin *sponte* meaning 'voluntarily']

spoof, spoofs
(noun) A spoof is something such as an article or television programme that seems to be about a serious matter but is actually a joke.

spook, spooks
(noun; an informal word) A spook is a ghost.
[a Dutch word]

spooky, spookier, spookiest
(adjective) eerie and frightening.

spool, spools
(noun) A spool is a cylindrical object onto which thread, tape, or film can be wound.

spoon, spoons
(noun) A spoon is an object shaped like a small shallow bowl with a long handle, used for eating, stirring, and serving food.

spoonerism, spoonerisms
(noun) A spoonerism is a mistake made when speaking in which the first sounds of two words are changed over. For example, you might say, 'I saw her fighting a liar' when you meant to say, 'I saw her lighting a fire'.
[named after a clergyman W. A. *Spooner* (1844-1930), who made frequent slips of this kind]

spoon-feed, spoon-feeds, spoon-feeding, spoon-fed
1 (verb) To spoon-feed someone means to do everything for them or to tell them everything

they need to know, so that they never have to
think or act for themselves.
2 To spoon-feed a baby means to feed it using a
spoon.

spoonful, spoonfuls or **spoonsful**
(noun) A spoonful is the amount held by a spoon.

spoor, spoors
(noun) The spoor of an animal is the visible trail
it leaves as it moves along.
[from Afrikaans *spoor* meaning 'trail']

sporadic
(adjective) happening at irregular intervals, e.g.
*Sporadic attacks continued throughout the
night.*
sporadically (adverb).
[from Greek *sporas* meaning 'scattered']

spore, spores
(noun; a technical word) Spores are cells
produced by bacteria and nonflowering plants
such as fungi which develop into new bacteria or
plants.
[from Greek *spora* meaning 'sowing']

sporran, sporrans
(noun) A sporran is a large purse made of leather
or fur, worn on a belt by a Scotsman over a kilt.
[from Scottish Gaelic *sporan* meaning 'purse']

sport, sports, sporting, sported
1 (noun) Sports are games and other enjoyable
activities which need physical effort and skill.
2 You say that someone is a sport when they
accept defeat or teasing cheerfully, e.g. *Be a
sport, Madeleine.*
3 (verb) If you sport something noticeable or
unusual, you wear it, e.g. *He sported a beard.*
[from Middle English *disport* meaning 'to amuse
oneself']

sporting
1 (adjective) relating to sport.
2 behaving in a fair and decent way.
3 (phrase) If there is **a sporting chance** that
something will happen, it is quite likely to
happen.

sports car, sports cars
(noun) A sports car is a low, fast car, usually
with room for only two people.

sports jacket, sports jackets
(noun) A sports jacket is a man's jacket made of
tweed and worn on informal occasions.

sportsman, sportsmen
(noun) A sportsman is a man who takes part in
sports and is good at them.

sportsmanship
(noun) Sportsmanship is the behaviour and
attitudes of a good sportsman, for example
fairness, generosity, and cheerfulness when
losing.

sportswear
(noun) Sportswear is clothes worn for sport.

sportswoman, sportswomen
(noun) A sportswoman is a woman who takes
part in sports and is good at them.

sporty, sportier, sportiest
1 (adjective) A sporty car is fast and flashy.
2 A sporty person is good at sports.

spot, spots, spotting, spotted
1 (noun) Spots are small, round, coloured areas
on a surface.
2 Spots on a person's skin are small lumps,
usually caused by an infection or allergy.
3 A spot of something is a small amount of it, e.g.
spots of rain... How about a spot of lunch?
4 A place can be called a spot, e.g. *It's a lovely
spot for a picnic.*
5 A spot in a television show is a part regularly
reserved for a particular performer or type of
entertainment.
6 (verb) If you spot something, you notice it.
7 (phrase) If you do something **on the spot**, you
do it immediately.
8 If you put someone **on the spot**, you put them
in a situation where they have to answer a
difficult question or make a difficult decision.

spot check, spot checks
(noun) A spot check is a random examination of
one of a group of things.

spotless
(adjective) perfectly clean.
spotlessly (adverb).

Similar words: immaculate, pristine, impeccable

spotlight, spotlights, spotlighting, spotlit or
spotlighted
1 (noun) A spotlight is a powerful light which
can be directed to light up a small area.
2 (verb) If something spotlights a situation or
problem, it draws the public's attention to it, e.g.
*The event is designed to spotlight the needs of the
handicapped.*

spot-on
(adjective; an informal expression) exactly
correct or accurate.

spotted
(adjective) Something spotted has a pattern of
spots on it.

spotter, spotters
(noun) A spotter is a person whose hobby is
looking out for things of a particular kind, e.g. *a
train spotter.*

spotty, spottier, spottiest
(adjective) Someone who is spotty has spots or
pimples on their skin, especially on their face.

spouse, spouses
(noun) Someone's spouse is the person they are
married to.

spout, spouts, spouting, spouted
1 (verb) When liquid or flame spouts out of
something, it shoots out in a long stream.
2 When someone spouts what they have learned,
they say it in a boring way.
3 (noun) A spout is a tube with a lip-like end for
pouring liquid, e.g. *the spout of a kettle.*

sprain, sprains, spraining, sprained
1 (verb) If you sprain a joint, you accidentally
damage it by twisting it violently.

2 (noun) A sprain is the injury caused by spraining a joint.

sprat, sprats
(noun) A sprat is a very small European sea fish related to the herring.

sprawl, sprawls, sprawling, sprawled
1 (verb) If you sprawl somewhere, you sit or lie there with your legs and arms spread out.
2 A place that sprawls is spread out over a large area, e.g. *The village sprawls along the coastline.*
3 (noun) A sprawl is anything that spreads in an untidy and uncontrolled way, e.g. *London's urban sprawl.*
sprawled (adjective), **sprawling** (adjective).

spray, sprays, spraying, sprayed
1 (noun) Spray consists of many drops of liquid splashed or forced into the air, e.g. *Drenching spray splashed over the deck.*
2 Spray is also a liquid kept under pressure in a can or other container, e.g. *hair spray.*
3 (verb) To spray a liquid over something means to cover it with drops of the liquid.
4 (noun) A spray is a piece of equipment for spraying liquid, e.g. *a garden spray.*
5 A spray of flowers or leaves consists of several of them on one stem or branch.
[senses 1-4 are from Old Dutch *spraien* meaning 'spray']

spray gun, spray guns
(noun) A spray gun is a device that sprays fluid such as paint or insecticide evenly over an area.

spread, spreads, spreading, spread
1 (verb) If you spread something out, you open it out or arrange it so that it can be seen or used easily, e.g. *He spread the map over the table.*
2 If you spread a substance on a surface, you put a thin layer on the surface.
3 If something spreads, it gradually reaches or affects more people, e.g. *News of the wreck spread quickly.*
4 If something spreads over a period of time, it happens regularly or continuously over that time, e.g. *The breeding period is spread over five months.*
5 If something such as work is spread, it is distributed evenly, e.g. *You are advised to spread the workload.*
6 (noun) The spread of something is the extent to which it gradually reaches or affects more people, e.g. *the spread of higher education.*
7 A spread of ideas, interests, or other things is a wide variety of them.
8 A spread is soft food put on bread.

spread-eagled
(adjective) Someone who is spread-eagled is lying with their arms and legs spread out.

spree, sprees
(noun) A spree is a period of time spent doing something enjoyable, e.g. *a shopping spree.*

sprig, sprigs
(noun) A sprig is a small twig with leaves on it.

sprightly, sprightlier, sprightliest
(adjective) lively and active.

spring, springs, springing, sprang, sprung
1 (noun) Spring is the season between winter and summer.
2 A spring is a coil of wire which returns to its natural shape after being pressed or pulled.
3 A spring is also a place where water comes up through the ground.
4 (verb) To spring means to jump upwards or forwards, e.g. *She sprang to her feet.*
5 If something springs in a particular direction, it moves suddenly and quickly, e.g. *The door sprang open.*
6 (noun) A spring is an act of springing, e.g. *With a spring he had opened the door.*
7 (verb) If one thing springs from another, it is the result of it, e.g. *These problems spring from different causes.*
8 (phrase) If a boat or container **springs a leak**, water starts coming in through a crack.
9 (verb) If you spring some news or a surprise on someone, you tell them something unexpected.

springboard, springboards
1 (noun) A springboard is a flexible board on which a diver or gymnast jumps to gain height.
2 If something is a springboard for an activity or enterprise, it makes it possible for it to begin.

springbok, springboks
(noun) A springbok is a small South African antelope which moves in leaps.
[from Dutch *springen* meaning 'to leap' and *bok* meaning 'goat' or 'antelope']

spring-clean, spring-cleans, spring-cleaning, spring-cleaned
(verb) To spring-clean something, especially a house, means to thoroughly clean it throughout.

spring onion, spring onions
(noun) A spring onion is a small onion with long green shoots, often eaten raw in salads.

springy
(adjective) Something springy returns quickly to its original shape after being pressed.

sprinkle, sprinkles, sprinkling, sprinkled
(verb) If you sprinkle a liquid or powder over something, you scatter it over it.

sprinkler, sprinklers
(noun) A sprinkler is a device used to spray water, especially to water lawns or put out fires.

sprinkling, sprinklings
(noun) A sprinkling of something is a small quantity of it, e.g. *Add a sprinkling of salt.*

sprint, sprints, sprinting, sprinted
1 (noun) A sprint is a short, fast race.
2 (verb) To sprint means to run fast over a short distance.

sprinter, sprinters
(noun) A sprinter is an athlete who runs fast over short distances.

sprite, sprites
(noun) A sprite is a type of fairy.
[from Latin *spiritus* meaning 'spirit']

sprocket, sprockets
(noun) A sprocket is a wheel with teeth that fit

into the holes in a chain, reel of film, or tape in order to turn it.

sprout, sprouts, sprouting, sprouted
1 (verb) When something sprouts, it grows.
2 If things sprout up, they appear rapidly, e.g. *Small towns sprouted up all over the country.*
3 (noun) Sprouts are vegetables like small cabbages.
4 A sprout is also a new shoot on a plant.

spruce, spruces; sprucer, sprucest; spruces, sprucing, spruced
1 (noun) A spruce is an evergreen tree with needle-like leaves.
2 (adjective) Someone who is spruce is very neat and smart.
3 (verb) To spruce something up means to make it neat and smart.

spry, spryer, spryest
(adjective) A spry old person is lively and active, e.g. *Now, at eighty, he was as spry as ever.*
spryly (adverb)

spud, spuds
(noun; an informal word) A spud is a potato.

spume
(noun) Spume is white foam on the sea.

spunk
(noun; an old-fashioned informal word) Spunk is courage.

spur, spurs, spurring, spurred
1 (verb) If something spurs you to do something or spurs you on, it encourages you to do it.
2 (noun) Something that acts as a spur encourages a person to do something.
3 (phrase) If you do something **on the spur of the moment**, you do it suddenly, without planning it.
4 (noun) Spurs are sharp metal points attached to the heels of a rider's boots and used to urge a horse on.
5 A spur is a short or stunted branch of a tree.
6 A spur is also a ridge projecting from a mountain or hillside.

spurious (pronounced **spyoor**-ee-uss)
(adjective) not genuine or real.
spuriously (adverb), **spuriousness** (noun).
[from Latin *spurius* meaning 'illegitimate']

spurn, spurns, spurning, spurned
(verb) If you spurn something, you refuse to accept it, e.g. *You spurned my friendship.*
[from Old English *spurnan* meaning 'to kick']

spurt, spurts, spurting, spurted
1 (verb) When a liquid or flame spurts out of something, it comes out quickly in a thick, powerful stream.
2 (noun) A spurt of liquid or flame is a thick powerful stream of it, e.g. *a spurt of blood.*
3 A spurt of activity or effort is a sudden, brief period of it.

sputnik, sputniks (pronounced **spoot**-nik)
(noun) A sputnik is a Russian satellite used for space research.
[a Russian word literally meaning 'fellow traveller']

sputter, sputters, sputtering, sputtered
(verb) To sputter means to make hissing and popping sounds, e.g. *The engine sputtered.*

sputum (pronounced **spyoo**-tum)
(noun; a formal word) Sputum is spittle or phlegm.
[from Latin *spuere* meaning 'to spit out']

spy, spies, spying, spied
1 (noun) A spy is a person sent to find out secret information about a country or organization.
2 (verb) Someone who spies tries to find out secret information about another country or organization.
3 If you spy on someone, you watch them secretly.
4 If you spy something, you notice it.
[from Old French *espier* meaning 'to espy']

squabble, squabbles, squabbling, squabbled
1 (verb) When people squabble, they quarrel about something trivial.
2 (noun) A squabble is a quarrel.

squad, squads
(noun) A squad is a small group chosen to do a particular activity, e.g. *the drugs squad.*
[from Old Spanish *escuadra* meaning 'square', because of the square formation used by soldiers]

squad car, squad cars
(noun) A squad car is a police car.

squadron, squadrons
(noun) A squadron is a section of one of the armed forces, especially the air force.
[from Italian *squadrone* meaning 'soldiers drawn up in a square formation']

squadron leader, squadron leaders
(noun) A squadron leader is an RAF officer of the rank immediately above flight lieutenant.

squalid
1 (adjective) dirty, untidy, and in bad condition.
2 Squalid activities are unpleasant and often dishonest.
squalidly (adverb), **squalidness** (noun).
[from Latin *squalidus* meaning 'rough' or 'dirty']

squall, squalls, squalling, squalled
1 (noun) A squall is a brief, violent storm.
2 (verb) To squall means to make a harsh, unpleasant cry.

squalor
(noun) Squalor consists of bad or dirty conditions or surroundings.

squander, squanders, squandering, squandered
(verb) To squander money or resources means to waste them, e.g. *He squandered all his money on clothes and entertainment.*
squanderer (noun).

square, squares, squaring, squared
1 (noun) A square is a shape with four equal sides and four right angles.
2 In a town or city, a square is a flat, open place, bordered by buildings or streets.
3 (adjective) shaped like a square, e.g. *He has rather a square face.*
4 (noun) The square of a number is the number

multiplied by itself. For example, the square of
3, written 3^2, is 3 x 3.
5 (adjective) Square is used before units of
length when talking about the area of something.
For example, an area 2 metres wide and 4 metres
long has an area of 8 square metres, written $8m^2$.
6 Square is used after units of length when you
are giving the length of each side of something
square, e.g. *a silicon chip less than a centimetre
square.*
7 (verb) If you square a number, you multiply it
by itself.
8 (adjective) parallel with something else, e.g.
Make sure the table is square with the wall.
9 (verb) When you square two different
situations or ideas with each other or when they
square, they seem compatible.
[from Latin *quadra* meaning 'square']

square up
(phrasal verb) If you square up with someone,
you pay them the money you owe them.

square dance, square dances
(noun) A square dance is performed in a set way
by couples arranged in a square or other pattern.

squarely
1 (adverb) Squarely means directly rather than
indirectly or at an angle, e.g. *She looked him
squarely in the face and told him she was
leaving.*
2 If you approach a subject squarely, you
consider it fully, without trying to avoid difficult
or unpleasant aspects of it.

square root, square roots
(noun) A square root of a number is a number
that makes the first number when it is multiplied
by itself. For example, the square roots of 25 are
5 and –5.

squash, squashes, squashing, squashed
1 (verb) If you squash something, you press it, so
that it becomes flat or loses its shape.
2 To squash a difficult or troubling situation
means to stop it, often by force.
3 (noun) If there is a squash in a place, there are
a lot of people squashed in it.
4 Squash is a game in which two players hit a
small rubber ball against the walls of a court
using rackets.
5 Squash is also a drink made from fruit juice,
sugar, and water.
[from Latin *quassare* meaning 'to shatter']

squashy, squashier, squashiest
(adjective) soft and able to be squashed easily.

**squat, squats, squatting, squatted; squatter,
squattest**
1 (verb) If you squat down, you crouch,
balancing on your feet with your legs bent.
2 A person who squats in an unused building
lives there as a squatter.
3 (noun) A squat is a building used by squatters.
4 (adjective) short and thick.
[from Old French *esquater* meaning 'to crouch']

squatter, squatters
(noun) A squatter is a person who lives in an

unused building without permission and without
paying rent.

squaw, squaws
(noun; an offensive word) A squaw is a North
American Indian woman.
[a North American Indian word]

squawk, squawks, squawking, squawked
1 (verb) When a bird squawks, it makes a loud,
harsh noise.
2 (noun) A squawk is a loud, harsh noise made
by a bird.

squeak, squeaks, squeaking, squeaked
1 (verb) If something squeaks, it makes a short
high-pitched sound.
2 (noun) A squeak is a short, high-pitched sound.
squeaky (adjective).

squeal, squeals, squealing, squealed
1 (verb) When things or people squeal, they
make long, high-pitched sounds.
2 (noun) A squeal is a long, high-pitched sound.

squeamish
(adjective) easily upset by unpleasant sights or
situations.

squeeze, squeezes, squeezing, squeezed
1 (verb) When you squeeze something, you press
it firmly from two sides.
2 (noun) If you give something a squeeze, you
squeeze it, e.g. *He gave her hand a soft squeeze.*
3 If getting into something is a squeeze, it is just
possible to fit into it, e.g. *We all got into the lift,
but it was rather a squeeze.*
4 (verb) If you squeeze something into a small
amount of time or space, you manage to fit it in.
5 If you squeeze something out of someone, you
persuade them to give it to you, e.g. *I managed to
squeeze £5 out of John.*
[from Middle English *queysen* meaning 'to press']

squelch, squelches, squelching, squelched
1 (verb) To squelch means to make a wet,
sucking sound.
2 (noun) A squelch is a wet, sucking sound.

squib, squibs
1 (noun) A squib is a small firework that makes a
loud bang.
2 (phrase) A **damp squib** is an event or
performance that is expected to be good, but
fails miserably, e.g. *The party was a damp squib.*

squid, squids
(noun) A squid is a sea creature with a long soft
body and many tentacles. Squids can be anything
from 10cm to 16.5 metres long.

squiggle, squiggles
(noun) A squiggle is a wriggly line.

squint, squints, squinting, squinted
1 (verb) If you squint at something, you look at it
with your eyes screwed up.
2 (noun) If someone has a squint, their eyes look
in different directions from each other.

squire, squires
1 (noun) In a village, the squire was a gentleman
who owned a large house with a lot of land.
2 In medieval times, a squire was a young

nobleman who served a knight as part of his training for his own knighthood.
[from Latin *scutarius* meaning 'shield-bearer']

squirm, squirms, squirming, squirmed
(verb) If you squirm, you wriggle and twist your body about, usually because you are nervous, embarrassed, or uncomfortable.

squirrel, squirrels
(noun) A squirrel is a small furry animal with a long bushy tail. Squirrels live in trees.
[from Greek *skia* meaning 'shadow' and *oura* meaning 'tail']

squirt, squirts, squirting, squirted
1 (verb) If a liquid squirts, it comes out of a narrow opening in a thin, fast stream.
2 (noun) A squirt is a thin, fast stream of liquid.

Sri Lankan, Sri Lankans (pronounced sree-**lang**-kan)
1 (adjective) belonging or relating to Sri Lanka.
2 (noun) A Sri Lankan is someone who comes from Sri Lanka.

SRN, SRNs
(noun) An SRN is a fully qualified nurse. SRN is an abbreviation for 'State Registered Nurse'.

stab, stabs, stabbing, stabbed
1 (verb) To stab someone means to wound them by pushing a knife into their body.
2 To stab at something means to push at it sharply with your finger or with something long and narrow.
3 (phrase; an informal use) If you **have a stab** at something, you try to do it.
4 If you say that someone **has stabbed you in the back**, you mean that they have done something unpleasant to you when you thought you could trust them.
5 (noun) You can refer to a sudden unpleasant feeling as a stab of something, e.g. *a stab of fear.*
[from Middle English *stabbe* meaning 'stab wound']

stable, stables
1 (adjective) not likely to change or come to an end suddenly, e.g. *a stable marriage.*
2 firmly fixed or balanced and not likely to move, wobble, or fall.
3 (noun) A stable is a building in which horses are kept.
stability (noun), **stabilize** (verb).
[from Latin *stabilis* meaning 'steady']

staccato (pronounced stak-**kah**-toe)
(adjective) consisting of a series of short, sharp, separate sounds.
[from Italian *staccare* meaning 'to separate']

stack, stacks, stacking, stacked
1 (noun) A stack of things is a pile of them, one on top of the other.
2 (verb) If you stack things, you arrange them one on top of the other in a pile.
3 (plural noun; an informal use) If someone has stacks of something, they have a lot of it.
[from Old Norse *stakkr* meaning 'haystack']

stadium, stadiums
(noun) A stadium is a sports ground with rows of seats around it.
[from Greek *stadion* meaning 'racecourse']

staff, staffs, staffing, staffed
1 (noun) The staff of an organization is the people who work for it.
2 (verb) To staff an organization means to find and employ people to work in it.
3 If an organization is staffed by particular people, they are the people who work for it.
staffing (noun).

stag, stags
(noun) A stag is an adult male deer.

stage, stages, staging, staged
1 (noun) A stage is a part of a process that lasts for a period of time.
2 In a theatre, the stage is a raised platform where the actors or entertainers perform.
3 You can refer to the profession of acting as the stage.
4 (verb) If someone stages a play or event, they organize it and present it or take part in it.
5 (phrase) To **set the stage** for something means to prepare the right conditions for it to happen.
[from Old French *estage* meaning 'position']

Similar words: (sense 1) point, juncture

stagecoach, stagecoaches
(noun) A stagecoach is a large carriage pulled by horses which used to carry passengers and mail.

stage fright
(noun) Stage fright is fear or nervousness in front of an audience.

stage-manage, stage-manages, stage-managing, stage-managed
(verb) To stage-manage an event means to organize it and control it.

stagger, staggers, staggering, staggered
1 (verb) If you stagger, you walk unsteadily because you are ill or drunk.
2 If something staggers you, it amazes you.
3 If events are staggered, they are arranged so that they do not all happen at the same time.
staggered (adjective), **staggering** (adjective).
[from Old Norse *staka* meaning 'to push']

Similar words: (sense 1) reel, totter, lurch

stagnant
1 (adjective) Stagnant water is not flowing and is unhealthy and dirty.
2 If business or society is stagnant, there is a lack of activity or development.
[from Latin *stagnum* meaning 'pool']

stagnate, stagnates, stagnating, stagnated
(verb) If a business or society stagnates, it becomes inactive or unchanging.
stagnation (noun).

stag night, stag nights
(noun) A stag night is a party for a man who is about to get married, which only men can attend.

staid
(adjective) serious and dull.

stain, stains, staining, stained

1 (noun) A stain is a mark on something that is difficult to move.
2 (verb) If a substance stains something, the thing becomes marked or coloured by it.
[from Old French *desteindre* meaning 'to discolour']

stained glass

(noun) Stained glass is coloured pieces of glass held together with strips of lead.

stainless steel

(noun) Stainless steel is a metal made from steel and chromium which does not rust.

stair, stairs

(noun) Stairs are a set of steps inside a building going from one floor to another.

staircase, staircases

(noun) A staircase is a set of stairs.

stairway, stairways

(noun) A stairway is a set of stairs.

stairwell, stairwells

(noun) A stairwell is the part of a building that contains a staircase.

stake, stakes, staking, staked

1 (phrase) If something is **at stake**, it might be lost or damaged if something else is not successful, e.g. *We must fight to save the company — there are thousands of jobs at stake.*
2 (plural noun) The stakes involved in something are the things that can be lost or gained.
3 (verb) If you say you would stake your money, life, or reputation on the success or truth of something, you mean you would risk it, e.g. *I wouldn't like to stake my life on that assertion.*
4 (noun) If you have a stake in something such as a business, you own part of it and its success is important to you.
5 (plural noun) You can use 'stakes' to refer to something you are considering as a contest, e.g. *This gives you an advantage in the promotion stakes.*
6 (phrase) If you **stake a claim** to something, you state that it is or should be yours.
7 (noun) A stake is a pointed wooden post that can be hammered into the ground and used as a support.
[sense 7 is from Old English *staca* meaning 'pin']

stalactite, stalactites

(noun) A stalactite is a piece of rock like a huge icicle hanging from the roof of a cave.
[from Greek *stalaktos* meaning 'dripping']

stalagmite, stalagmites

(noun) A stalagmite is a large pointed piece of rock sticking up from the floor of a cave.
[from Greek *stalagmos* meaning 'dripping']

stale, staler, stalest

1 (adjective) Stale food or air is no longer fresh.
2 If you feel stale, you have no new ideas and are bored.

Similar words: (sense 1) musty, fusty

stalemate

1 (noun) Stalemate is a situation in which neither side in an argument or contest can win.
2 In chess, stalemate is a situation in which a player cannot make any move permitted by the rules, so that the game ends and no-one wins.

stalk, stalks, stalking, stalked (pronounced stawk)

1 (noun) The stalk of a flower or leaf is its stem.
2 (verb) To stalk a person or animal means to follow them quietly in order to catch, kill, or observe them.
3 If someone stalks into a room, they walk in a stiff, proud, or angry way.
[sense 1 is from Old English *stalu* meaning 'upright piece of wood'; senses 2 and 3 are from Old English *bestealcian* meaning 'to walk stealthily']

stall, stalls, stalling, stalled

1 (noun) A stall is a large table containing goods for sale or information.
2 (plural noun) In a theatre, the stalls are the seats at the lowest level, in front of the stage.
3 (verb) When a vehicle stalls, the engine suddenly stops.
4 If you stall when someone asks you to do something, you try to avoid doing it until a later time.
[senses 1-3 are from Old English *steall* meaning 'place for standing'; sense 4 is from Anglo-French *estale* meaning 'bird used as a decoy', hence 'avoidance']

stallion, stallions

(noun) A stallion is an adult male horse that can be used for breeding.

stalwart (pronounced stawl-wort)

(adjective) loyal and hard-working.
[from Old English *stælwirthe* meaning 'serviceable']

stamen, stamens

(noun) The stamens of a flower are the small delicate stalks which grow inside the blossom and produce pollen.
[from Latin *stamen* meaning 'thread', because stamens resemble the upright threads in weaving]

stamina

(noun) Stamina is the physical or mental energy needed to do something for a very long time.

stammer, stammers, stammering, stammered

1 (verb) When someone stammers, they speak with difficulty, repeating words and sounds and hesitating awkwardly.
2 (noun) Someone who has a stammer tends to stammer when they speak.

stamp, stamps, stamping, stamped

1 (noun) A stamp is a small piece of gummed paper which you stick on a letter or parcel before posting it.
2 A stamp is also a small block with a pattern cut into it. You press it onto an inky pad and make a mark with it on paper. The mark is also called a stamp.

3 (verb) If you stamp a piece of paper, you make a mark on it using a stamp.
4 If you stamp, you lift your foot and put it down hard on the ground.
5 (noun) If something bears the stamp of a particular quality or person, it shows clear signs of that quality or of the person's style or characteristics.

stamp out
(phrasal verb) To stamp something out means to put an end to it, e.g. *They are determined to stamp out fraud.*

stampede, stampedes, stampeding, stampeded
1 (verb) When a group of animals stampede, they run in a wild, uncontrolled way.
2 (noun) A stampede is a group of animals stampeding.
[from Spanish *estampida* meaning 'crash' or 'din']

stance, stances
1 (noun) Your stance on a particular matter is your attitude and way of dealing with it, e.g. *his rigid stance on nonviolence.*
2 Your stance is also the way you stand.
[from Italian *stanza* meaning 'place for standing']

stand, stands, standing, stood
1 (verb) If you are standing, you are upright, your legs are straight, and your weight is supported by your feet. When you stand up, you get into a standing position.
2 If something stands somewhere, that is where it is, e.g. *In the square stands a splendid Victorian building.*
3 If you stand something somewhere, you put it there in an upright position, e.g. *He stood the bottle on the bench beside him.*
4 If a decision or offer stands, it is still valid, e.g. *Fifty years later, the ruling still stands.*
5 You can use 'stand' when describing the state or condition of something. e.g. *Unemployment stands at 38 per cent.*
6 If a letter stands for a particular word, it is an abbreviation for that word.
7 (phrase) If you ask someone **where they stand** on a particular issue, you are asking what their attitude to it is.
8 (verb) If you say you will not stand for something, you mean you will not tolerate it.
9 If you stand by someone who is in trouble, you continue to give them support.
10 If you stand by an earlier decision or promise, you continue to keep to it.
11 If something can stand a situation or test, it is good enough or strong enough not to be damaged by it.
12 If you cannot stand something, you cannot bear it, e.g. *I couldn't stand his nagging any longer.*
13 If you stand to gain or lose something, you are likely to gain or lose it.
14 If you stand in an election, you are one of the candidates.
15 (phrase) If it **stands to reason** that something is the case, it is obvious and logical.
16 When someone **stands trial**, they are tried in a court of law.

17 (noun) A stand is a stall or very small shop outdoors or in a large public building.
18 A stand is a piece of furniture designed to hold something, e.g. *an umbrella stand.*
19 (phrases) If you **make a stand** or **take a stand**, you defend your beliefs or ideas against criticism.
[from Latin *stare* meaning 'to stand']

stand by
1 (phrasal verb) If you stand by to provide help or take action, you are ready to do it if necessary.
2 If you stand by while something happens, you do nothing to stop it.

stand down
(phrasal verb) If someone stands down, they resign from their job or position.

stand in
(phrasal verb) If you stand in for someone, you take their place while they are ill or away.

stand out
(phrasal verb) If something stands out, it can be easily noticed or is more important than other similar things.

stand up
1 (phrasal verb) If something stands up to rough treatment, it remains undamaged or unharmed.
2 If you stand up to someone who is criticizing or attacking you, you defend yourself.
3 If evidence stands up, it is accepted as being true after careful examination, e.g. *The evidence will never stand up in a court of law.*
4 (an informal use) If a boyfriend or girlfriend stands you up, they fail to keep an arrangement to meet you.

standard, standards
1 (noun) A standard is a level of quality or achievement that is considered acceptable, e.g. *His work is below the standard required.*
2 (plural noun) Standards are moral principles of behaviour.
3 (adjective) usual, normal, and correct, e.g. *There is a standard procedure for recording errors.*
4 A standard work or text is the book most widely read and recommended on a particular subject.

standardize, standardizes, standardizing, standardized; also spelled **standardise**
(verb) To standardize things means to change them so that they all have a similar set of features, e.g. *We have decided to standardize our equipment.*

standard lamp, standard lamps
(noun) A standard lamp is a tall electric light that has a large shade and stands on the floor.

standard of living, standards of living
(noun) The standard of living in a country or a family is the level of comfort and wealth.

stand-by, stand-bys
1 (noun) A stand-by is something available for use when you need it, e.g. *Eggs are a great stand-by in the kitchen.*

2 (adjective) A stand-by ticket is a cheap ticket that you buy just before a theatre performance or a flight if there are any seats left.

stand-in, stand-ins
(noun) A stand-in is someone who takes a person's place while the person is ill or away.

standing
1 (adjective) permanently in existence or used regularly, e.g. *a standing joke.*
2 (noun) A person's standing is their status and reputation.
3 Standing is used to say how long something has existed, e.g. *a member of twenty-five years' standing.*

standing order, standing orders
(noun) A standing order is an instruction to a bank to pay a fixed amount of money to someone at regular times.

standoffish
(adjective) behaving in a formal and rather unfriendly way.

standpipe, standpipes
(noun) A standpipe is a vertical pipe connected to the water supply in a street for use in an emergency.

standpoint, standpoints
(noun) If you consider something from a particular standpoint, you consider it from that point of view, e.g. *The proposal was perfect from a business standpoint.*

standstill
(noun) If something comes to a standstill, it stops completely.

stanza, stanzas
(noun) A stanza is a verse of a poem.
[from Italian *stanza* meaning 'stopping place']

staple, staples, stapling, stapled
1 (noun) Staples are small pieces of wire that hold sheets of paper firmly together. You insert them with a stapler.
2 (verb) If you staple sheets of paper, you fasten them together with staples.
3 (adjective) A staple food forms a regular and basic part of someone's everyday diet.
[senses 1 and 2 are from Old English *stapol* meaning 'prop'; sense 3 is from Old Dutch *stapel* meaning 'warehouse']

stapler, staplers
(noun) A stapler is a long rectangular device used for inserting staples into sheets of paper.

star, stars, starring, starred
1 (noun) A star is a large ball of burning gas in space that appears as a point of light in the sky at night.
2 A star is also a shape with four, five, or more points sticking out in a regular pattern.
3 Famous actors, sports players, and musicians are referred to as stars.
4 (verb) If an actor or actress stars in a film or if the film stars that person, he or she has one of the most important parts in it.
5 (plural noun) The horoscope in a newspaper or magazine can be referred to as the stars, e.g. *What do the stars say today?*

starboard
(adjective and noun) The starboard side of a ship is the right-hand side when you are facing the front.
[from Old English *steorbord* meaning 'steering side', because boats were formerly steered with a paddle over the right-hand side]

starch, starches, starching, starched
1 (noun) Starch is a substance used for stiffening fabric such as cotton and linen.
2 (verb) To starch fabric means to stiffen it with starch.
3 (noun) Starch is a carbohydrate found in foods such as bread, potatoes, and rice.

stare, stares, staring, stared
1 (verb) If you stare at something, you look at it for a long time.
2 (noun) A stare is a long fixed look at something.

Similar words: gape, gawk, gaze, goggle

starfish
(noun) A starfish is a flat, star-shaped sea creature with five limbs.

stark, starker, starkest
1 (adjective) harsh, unpleasant and plain, e.g. *Those are the stark facts.*
2 (phrase) If someone is **stark-naked**, they have no clothes on at all.
[from Old English *stearc* meaning 'stiff']

starling, starlings
(noun) A starling is a common European bird with shiny dark feathers.

starry
(adjective) lit by many stars, e.g. *a starry night.*

starry-eyed
(adjective) Someone who is starry-eyed is so full of dreams and hopes that they cannot see the reality of a situation.

start, starts, starting, started
1 (verb) To start means to begin. To start doing something means to begin doing it, e.g. *The meeting starts at 7 o'clock... Ralph started to run.*
2 (noun) The start of something is the point or time at which it begins.
3 (verb) If you start a machine or car, you operate the controls to make it work.
4 If you start, you body suddenly jerks because of surprise or fear.
5 (noun) If you do something with a start, you do it with a sudden jerky movement because of surprise or fear, e.g. *He awoke with a start.*

starter, starters
1 (noun) A starter is a small quantity of food served as the first part of a meal.
2 The starter of a vehicle is the device that starts the engine.

startle, startles, startling, startled
(verb) If something sudden and unexpected

startles you, it surprises you and makes you slightly frightened.
startled (adjective), **startling** (adjective).
[from Old English *steartlian* meaning 'to stumble']

starve, starves, starving, starved
1 (verb) If people are starving, they are suffering from a serious lack of food and are likely to die.
2 To starve a person or animal means to prevent them from having any food.
3 (an informal use) If you say you are starving, you mean you are very hungry.
4 If someone or something is starved of something they need, they are suffering because they are not getting enough of it, e.g. *Our research is being starved of funds.*
starvation (noun).
[from Old English *steorfan* meaning 'to die']

stash, stashes, stashing, stashed
(verb; an informal word) If you stash something away in a secret place, you store it there to keep it safe.

state, states, stating, stated
1 (noun) The state of something is its condition, what it is like, or its circumstances.
2 (phrase) If you are **in a state**, you are nervous or upset and unable to control your emotions.
3 (noun) Countries are sometimes referred to as states, e.g. *the state of Denmark.*
4 Some countries are divided into regions called states which make some of their own laws, e.g. *New York State.*
5 You can refer to the government or administration of a country as the state.
6 (adjective) A state ceremony involves the ruler or leader of a country.
7 (verb) If you state something, you say it or write it, especially in a formal way.
[from Latin *status* meaning 'standing' or 'condition']

stateless
(adjective) A stateless person is not a citizen of any country and therefore has no nationality.

stately, statelier, stateliest
(adjective) impressive, graceful, and dignified.

stately home, stately homes
(noun) A stately home is a very large old house which belongs to an aristocratic family. Many stately homes can be visited by the public.

statement, statements
1 (noun) A statement is something you say or write when you give facts or information in a formal way.
2 A statement is also a document provided by a bank showing all the money paid into and out of an account during a period of time.

state of affairs, states of affairs
(noun) The state of affairs is the general situation and circumstances concerning something or someone at a particular time.

state of mind, states of mind
(noun) Your state of mind is your mood and the way you are thinking at a particular time.

state school, state schools
(noun) A state school is a school maintained and financed by the local authority and government.

statesman, statesmen
(noun) A statesman is an important and experienced politician.

static
1 (adjective) never moving or changing, e.g. *the static quality of village life.*
2 (noun) Static is an electrical charge caused by friction. It builds up in metal objects and can also be produced by brushing your hair.
[from Greek *statikos* meaning 'causing to stand']

station, stations, stationing, stationed
1 (noun) A railway station is a building and platforms where trains stop for passengers.
2 A bus or coach station is a building or area where buses start their journeys or collect long-distance passengers.
3 A radio station is the frequency on which a particular company broadcasts.
4 (an old-fashioned use) A person's station is their position or rank in society.
5 (verb) Someone who is stationed somewhere is sent there to work or do a particular job, e.g. *I was stationed at Tangmere during the war.*
[from Latin *statio* meaning 'a standing still']

stationary
(adjective) not moving, e.g. *stationary vehicles.*

Similar words: immobile, motionless, static, standing

stationer, stationers
(noun) A stationer is someone who sells paper, pens, and other writing equipment. A stationer's is a shop which sells these things.
[from Latin *stationarius* meaning 'shopkeeper'; used especially of a bookseller]

stationery
(noun) Stationery is paper, pens, and other writing equipment.

stationmaster, stationmasters
(noun) A stationmaster is the official in charge of a railway station.

statistic, statistics
1 (noun) Statistics are facts obtained by analysing numerical information.
2 Statistics is the branch of mathematics that deals with the analysis of numerical information.
statistical (adjective), **statistically** (adverb).
[from Latin *statisticus* meaning 'concerning state affairs']

statistician, statisticians (pronounced stat-iss-**tish**-an)
(noun) A statistician is a person who studies or works with statistics.

statue, statues
(noun) A statue is a sculpture of a person.
[from Latin *statua* meaning 'statue' or 'image']

stature

1 (noun) Someone's stature is their height and size.
2 Someone's stature is also their importance and reputation, e.g. *His stature as a world-class cricketer is diminishing.*
[from Latin *stare* meaning 'to stand']

status, statuses (pronounced **stay**-tuss)
1 (noun) A person's status is their position and importance in society.
2 Status is also the official classification given to someone or something, e.g. *What is the status of this document—is it confidential?*
[from Latin *status* meaning 'posture' or 'position']

Similar words: (sense 1) rank, standing, rating

status quo (pronounced stay-tuss **kwoh**)
(noun) The status quo is the situation that exists at a particular time, e.g. *He argued for maintaining the status quo.*
[a Latin expression, meaning literally 'the state in which']

status symbol, status symbols
(noun) A status symbol is something that someone owns that shows their wealth and importance.

statute, statutes
(noun) A statute is a law.
statutory (adjective).
[from Latin *statuere* meaning 'to set up' or 'to decree']

staunch, stauncher, staunchest; staunches, staunching, staunched
1 (adjective) A staunch supporter is a strong and loyal supporter, e.g. *Berry's staunchest ally.*
2 (verb) If you staunch blood, you stop it from flowing out of a wound.
[from Old French *estanche* meaning 'watertight']

stave, staves, staving, staved
1 (noun) In music, a stave is the five lines used for recording musical notation.
2 (verb) If you stave something off, you try to delay or prevent it.

stay, stays, staying, stayed
1 (verb) If you stay in a place, you do not move away from it, e.g. *We stayed on the beach all day.*
2 If you stay at a hotel or a friend's house, you spend some time there as a guest or visitor.
3 If you stay in a particular state, you continue to be in it, e.g. *I stayed awake half the night.*
4 (phrase) If you **stay put**, you remain in the same place.
5 (noun) A stay is a short time spent somewhere, e.g. *my stay in Germany.*

Similar words: (sense 1) remain, linger, tarry

stead
(noun) Something that will stand someone in good stead will be useful to them in the future.

steadfast
(adjective) If you are steadfast in your beliefs or opinions, you refuse to change them because you are convinced they are right.
steadfastly (adverb), **steadfastness** (noun).

steady, steadier, steadiest; steadies, steadying, steadied
1 (adjective) continuing or developing gradually without major interruptions or changes, e.g. *a steady rise in prices.*
2 firm and not shaking or wobbling, e.g. *He held it with a steady hand.*
3 A steady look or voice is calm and controlled.
4 Someone who is steady is sensible and reliable.
5 (verb) When you steady something, you hold on to prevent it from shaking or wobbling.
6 When you steady yourself, you control and calm yourself.

Similar words: (sense 2) firm, secure, sure, fixed

steak, steaks
1 (noun) Steak is a good-quality beef without much fat.
2 A fish steak is a large thick piece of fish.
[from Old Norse *steik* meaning 'roast']

steal, steals, stealing, stole, stolen
1 (verb) To steal something means to take it without permission and without intending to return it.
2 To steal somewhere means to move there quietly and secretively.

Similar words: (sense 1) filch, thieve, pilfer, pinch, purloin, snaffle, nick, knock off

stealth (rhymes with **health**)
(noun) If you do something with stealth, you do it quietly and secretively.
stealthy (adjective), **stealthily** (adverb).

steam, steams, steaming, steamed
1 (noun) Steam is the hot vapour formed when water boils.
2 (adjective) Steam engines are operated using steam as a means of power.
3 (verb) If something steams, it gives off steam.
4 To steam food means to cook it in steam.
5 (an informal phrase) If you **let off steam**, you get rid of your energy or emotions by behaving noisily or energetically.
6 If you **run out of steam**, you have no more energy or enthusiasm left to do something.
steamy (adjective).

steamed up
(adjective; an informal use) If you are steamed up about something, you are very annoyed.

steam-engine, steam-engines
(noun) A steam-engine is any engine that uses the energy of steam to produce mechanical work.

steamer, steamers
1 (noun) A steamer is a ship powered by steam.
2 A steamer is a container with small holes in the bottom in which you steam food.

steamroller, steamrollers
(noun) A steamroller is a very heavy vehicle with wide solid metal wheels. Steamrollers are used to flatten the surface of new roads.

steed, steeds
(noun; a literary word) Someone's steed is their horse.
[from Old Englsih *steda* meaning 'stallion']

steel, steels, steeling, steeled
1 (noun) Steel is a very strong metal containing mainly iron with a small amount of carbon.
2 (verb) To steel yourself means to prepare to deal with something unpleasant.

steel band, steel bands
(noun) A steel band is a group of people who play music on special metal drums.

steel wool
(noun) Steel wool is a mass of fine threads of steel, used for cleaning surfaces.

steelworks
(noun) A steelworks is a factory where steel is made.

steely
1 (adjective) having a hard, greyish colour.
2 determined, hard, and strong in nature, e.g. *a steely determination to succeed.*

steep, steeper, steepest; steeps, steeping, steeped
1 (adjective) A steep slope rises sharply and is difficult to go up.
2 A steep increase is large and sudden.
3 (verb) To steep something in a liquid means to soak it thoroughly.
steeply (adverb).
[senses 1 and 2 are from Old English *steap* meaning 'high' or 'towering'; sense 3 is from Old English *stepan* meaning 'soak in liquid']

Similar words: (sense 1) precipitous, sheer

steeped
(adjective) If a person or place is steeped in a particular quality, they are deeply affected by it, e.g. *The house is steeped in history.*

steeple, steeples
(noun) A steeple is a tall pointed structure on top of a church tower.

steeplechase, steeplechases
(noun) A steeplechase is a long horse race in which the horses jump over obstacles such as hedges and water jumps.
[originally a race with a church steeple in sight as the goal]

steeplejack, steeplejacks
(noun) A steeplejack is a person who climbs up very high buildings to repair or paint them.

steer, steers, steering, steered
1 (verb) To steer a vehicle or boat means to control it so that it goes in the right direction.
2 To steer someone towards a particular course of action means to influence and direct their behaviour or thoughts.
3 (noun) A steer is a castrated bull.

Similar words: (sense 1) pilot, guide, direct

stellar
(adjective) relating to the stars.
[from Latin *stella* meaning 'star']

stem, stems, stemming, stemmed
1 (noun) The stem of a plant is the long thin central part above the ground that carries the leaves and flowers.
2 The stem of a glass is the long narrow part connecting the bowl to the base.
3 The stem of a smoker's pipe is the long narrow part through which the smoke is sucked.
4 (verb) If a problem stems from a particular situation, that situation is the original starting point or cause of the problem.
5 If you stem the flow of something, you restrict it or stop it from spreading, e.g. *stemming the flow of illegal drugs.*
[senses 1-4 are from Old English *stemn* meaning 'stem' or 'stalk'; sense 5 is from Middle English *stemmen* meaning 'to stop the flow']

stench, stenches
(noun) A stench is a very strong, unpleasant smell.

stencil, stencils, stencilling, stencilled
1 (noun) A stencil is a piece of card or metal with a design cut out of it. You rest the stencil on a surface and put paint or ink over the cut-out area to create a pattern on the surface.
2 (verb) To stencil a design on a surface means to create it using a stencil.
[from Middle English *stanselen* meaning 'to decorate with bright colours']

stentorian
(adjective; a formal word) A stentorian voice is very loud and strong.

step, steps, stepping, stepped
1 (noun) If you take a step, you lift your foot and put it down somewhere else.
2 (verb) If you step in a particular direction, you move your foot in that direction.
3 (phrase) If someone tells you to **watch your step**, they are warning you about your behaviour.
4 (noun) A step is one of a series of actions that you take in order to achieve something.
5 A step is also a raised flat surface, usually one of a series that you can walk up or down.
6 (phrase) If people are walking **in step**, they are moving their feet at exactly the same time as each other.
7 (verb) If someone steps down or steps aside from an important position, they resign.

step in
(phrasal verb) If you step in, you become involved in a difficult situation in order to help to resolve it.

step up
(phrasal verb) If you step up the rate of something, you increase it.

stepbrother, stepbrothers
(noun) Someone's stepbrother is a son of their stepmother or stepfather.

stepchild, stepchildren
(noun) Someone's stepchild is their stepdaughter or stepson.

stepdaughter, stepdaughters
(noun) Someone's stepdaughter is a daughter their husband or wife had by an earlier marriage.

stepfather, stepfathers
(noun) Someone's stepfather is the man who is

married to their mother but who is not their natural father.

stepladder, stepladders
(noun) A stepladder is a ladder consisting of two parts that are hinged at the top so that it stands on its own when opened out.

stepmother, stepmothers
(noun) Someone's stepmother is the woman who is married to their father but who is not their natural mother.

steppe, steppes (pronounced **step**)
(noun) A steppe is a large area of open grassland with no trees, especially in the USSR.
[from Old Russian *step* meaning 'lowland']

stepping stone, stepping stones
1 (noun) Stepping stones are a line of large stones that you walk on to cross a shallow river.
2 A stepping stone is a job or event that is regarded as a stage in your progress, especially in your career.

stepsister, stepsisters
(noun) Someone's stepsister is a daughter of their stepmother or stepfather.

stepson, stepsons
(noun) Someone's stepson is a son their husband or wife had by an earlier marriage.

stereo, stereos
1 (adjective) A stereo record or music system is one in which the sound is directed through two speakers.
2 (noun) A stereo is a piece of equipment that reproduces sound from records, tapes, or CDs directing the sound through two speakers.

stereophonic
(adjective) Stereophonic means the same as stereo.
[from Greek *stereos* + *phōnē* meaning 'solid sound']

stereotype, stereotypes, stereotyping, stereotyped
1 (noun) A stereotype is a fixed image or set of characteristics that people consider to represent a particular type of person or thing, e.g. *the stereotype of the woman's role in the home.*
2 (verb) If you stereotype someone, you assume they are a particular type of person and will behave in a particular way.

sterile
1 (adjective) Sterile means completely clean and free from germs.
2 A sterile person or animal is unable to have or produce babies.
3 A sterile situation lacks new ideas and enthusiasm.
sterility (noun).
[from Latin *sterilis* meaning 'barren' or 'unfruitful']

Similar words: (sense 1) antiseptic, aseptic, disinfected

---

sterilize, sterilizes, sterilizing, sterilized; also spelled **sterilise**
1 (verb) To sterilize something means to make it completely clean and free from germs, usually by boiling it or treating it with an antiseptic.
2 If a person or animal is sterilized, they have an operation that makes it impossible for them to have babies.

sterling
1 (noun) Sterling is the money system of Great Britain.
2 (adjective) excellent in quality, e.g. *a man of sterling character*

sterling silver
(noun) Sterling silver is an alloy containing not less than 92.5% of silver.

stern, sterner, sternest; sterns
1 (adjective) very serious and strict, e.g. *stern parents... a stern warning.*
2 (noun) The stern of a boat is the back part.
[sense 1 is from Old English *styrne* meaning 'severe' or 'harsh'; sense 2 is from Old Norse *stjorn* meaning 'steering']

sternum, sternums or **sterna**
(noun) Your sternum is the flat bone in the centre of your chest that is joined to your ribs.
[from Greek *sternon* meaning 'breastbone']

steroid, steroids
(noun) Steroids are organic compounds that occur naturally in your body, for example as hormones. They are sometimes prescribed by a doctor as a medical drug.

stertorous
(adjective) Stertorous breathing is very noisy, like snoring.

stethoscope, stethoscopes
(noun) A stethoscope consists of earpieces connected to a hollow tube and a small disc. A doctor uses a stethoscope to listen to a patient's heart and breathing.
[from Greek *stēthos* meaning 'chest' and *skopein* meaning 'to look at']

stetson, stetsons
(noun) A stetson is a hat with a wide brim that is worn especially by cowboys.

stevedore, stevedores
(noun) In American English, a stevedore is a person who loads and unloads ships.

stew, stews, stewing, stewed
1 (noun) A stew consists of small pieces of savoury food cooked together slowly in a liquid.
2 (verb) To stew meat, vegetables, or fruit means to cook them slowly in a liquid.
3 (an informal phrase) If you **let someone stew**, you deliberately leave them to worry rather than giving them information that would stop them worrying.
[from Middle English *stuen* meaning 'to take a very hot bath']

steward, stewards
1 (noun) A steward is a man who works on a ship or plane looking after passengers and serving meals.
2 A steward is also a person who helps to direct the public at a race, march, or other event.

[from Old English *stigweard* meaning 'hall protector']

stewardess, stewardesses
(noun) A stewardess is a woman who works on a ship or plane looking after passengers and serving meals.

stick, sticks, sticking, stuck
1 (noun) A stick is a long, thin piece of wood.
2 A stick of something is a long, thin piece of it, e.g. *sticks of dynamite*.
3 (verb) If you stick a long or pointed object into something, you push it in.
4 If you stick one thing to another, you attach it with glue or sticky tape.
5 If one thing sticks to another, it becomes attached and is difficult to remove.
6 If a movable part of something sticks, it becomes fixed and will no longer move or work properly, e.g. *If the zip sticks, see if a thread has caught in it.*
7 (an informal use) If you stick something somewhere, you put it there.
8 If you stick by someone, you continue to help and support them.
9 If you stick to something, you keep to it and do not change to something else, e.g. *They stuck to the agreement.*
10 If you stick with something or someone, you do not change or move to something or someone else.
11 When people stick together, they stay together and support each other.
12 (phrase) If someone gets **the wrong end of the stick**, they completely misunderstand a situation. [senses 1, 2, and 12 are from Old English *sticca* meaning 'rod'; senses 3-11 are from Old English *stician* meaning 'to stab']

stick out
1 (phrasal verb) If something sticks out, it projects from something else.
2 To stick out also means to be very noticeable.
3 (an informal use) If someone in a difficult position sticks it out, they do not leave or give up.
4 If you stick out for something, you continue to demand it and do not accept anything less.

stick up
1 (phrasal verb) If something sticks up, it points upwards from a surface.
2 (an informal use) If you stick up for a person or principle, you support or defend them.

sticker, stickers
(noun) A sticker is a small piece of paper or plastic with writing or a picture on it, that you stick onto a surface.

sticking plaster, sticking plasters
(noun) A sticking plaster is a small piece of fabric that you stick over a cut or sore to protect it.

stick insect, stick insects
(noun) A stick insect is an insect with a long cylindrical body and long legs, which looks like a twig.

stick-in-the-mud, stick-in-the-muds
(noun; an informal word) A stick-in-the-mud is someone who does not like doing anything new.

stickler, sticklers
(noun) Someone who is a stickler for something always insists on it, e.g. *He's a stickler for punctuality.*

sticky, stickier, stickiest
1 (adjective) A sticky object is covered with a substance that can stick to other things, e.g. *sticky hands.*
2 Sticky paper or tape has glue on one side so that you can stick it to a surface.
3 (an informal use) A sticky situation is difficult or embarrassing to deal with.
4 Sticky weather is unpleasantly hot and humid.
5 (an informal phrase) If someone **comes to a sticky end**, they die in an unpleasant way.

stiff, stiffer, stiffest
1 (adjective) Something that is stiff is firm and not easily bent.
2 If you feel stiff, your muscles or joints ache when you move.
3 Stiff behaviour is formal and not friendly or relaxed.
4 Stiff also means difficult or severe, e.g. *Competition is stiff.*
5 A stiff drink contains a large amount of alcohol.
6 A stiff breeze is blowing strongly.
7 (adverb; an informal use) If you are bored stiff or scared stiff, you are very bored or very scared.
stiffly (adverb), **stiffness** (noun).

stiffen, stiffens, stiffening, stiffened
1 (verb) If you stiffen, you suddenly stop moving and your muscles become tense, e.g. *Tom stiffened with alarm.*
2 If your joints or muscles stiffen, they become sore and difficult to bend or move.
3 If attitudes stiffen, they become stronger and are less likely to change.
4 If fabric or material is stiffened, it is made firmer so that it does not bend easily.

stifle, stifles, stifling, stifled (pronounced sty-fl)
1 (verb) To stifle something means to stop it from happening or continuing, e.g. *She put her hand over her mouth to stifle her laughter.*
2 If the atmosphere stifles you, you feel you cannot breathe properly.
stifling (adjective).
[from Old French *estouffer* meaning 'to smother']

stigma, stigmas or stigmata
1 (noun) If something has a stigma attached to it, people consider it unacceptable or a disgrace, e.g. *the stigma of failure.*
2 The stigma of a flower is the part which receives the pollen.
[from Greek *stigma* meaning 'mark' or 'brand']

stile, stiles
(noun) A stile is a step on either side of a wall or fence to enable you to climb over.

stiletto, stilettos
(noun) Stilettos are women's shoes with very high, narrow heels.
[from Italian *stilo* meaning 'dagger', because of the shape of the heels]

still, stiller, stillest; stills
1 (adverb) If a situation still exists, it has continued to exist and it exists now.
2 If something could still happen, it might happen although it has not happened yet.
3 'Still' emphasizes that something is the case in spite of other things, e.g. *You might not like him, but he's still your brother.*
4 (adverb and adjective) Still means staying in the same position without moving, e.g. *Try to keep still... the still water of the lagoon.*
5 (adjective) A still place is quiet and peaceful with no signs of activity, e.g. *Around them, the forest was very still.*
6 (noun) A still is a photograph taken from a cinema film or video.
stillness (noun).

stillborn
(adjective) A stillborn baby is dead when it is born.

still life, still lifes
(noun) A still life is a painting or drawing of a group of objects such as fruit or pots.

stilt, stilts
1 (noun) Stilts are long upright poles on which a building is built, for example on marshy land.
2 Stilts are also two long pieces of wood or metal on which people balance and walk.
[from Middle English *stilte* meaning 'crutch' or 'handle of a plough']

stilted
(adjective) formal, unnatural, and rather awkward, e.g. *After some stilted efforts at conversation, he gave up.*

Similar words: wooden, stiff

stimulant, stimulants
(noun) A stimulant is a drug or other substance that makes your body work faster, increasing your heart rate and making it difficult to sleep.

stimulate, stimulates, stimulating, stimulated
1 (verb) To stimulate something means to encourage it to begin or develop, e.g. *Rising prices will stimulate demands for higher wages.*
2 If something stimulates you, it gives you new ideas and enthusiasm.
stimulating (adjective), **stimulation** (noun).

Similar words: (sense 1) animate, inspire, arouse, kindle, enliven, whet, rouse, excite

stimulus, stimuli
1 (noun) A stimulus is something that causes a process or event to begin or develop.
2 Stimulus is something which causes energy and enthusiasm, e.g. *all the stimulus and excitement that battle brought.*
[from Latin *stimulus* meaning 'spur' or 'incentive']

sting, stings, stinging, stung
1 (verb) If a creature or plant stings you, it pricks your skin and injects a substance which causes pain.
2 (noun) A creature's sting is the part it stings you with.
3 (verb) If a part of your body stings, you feel a sharp tingling pain there.
4 If someone's remarks sting you, they make you feel upset and hurt.

Similar words: (sense 3) smart, tingle, nip

stingy, stingier, stingiest (pronounced **stin**-jee)
(adjective; an informal word) very mean.

stink, stinks, stinking, stank, stunk
1 (verb) Something that stinks smells very unpleasant.
2 (noun) A stink is a very unpleasant smell.
3 (verb; an informal use) If you say that a situation stinks, you mean there is something very unpleasant or suspicious about it.

Similar words: (sense 2) stench, reek, pong

stinking
(adjective; an informal word) A stinking cold is a very bad one.

stint, stints
(noun) A stint is a period of time spent doing a particular job, e.g. *She's doing a three-month stint as a lecturer.*

stipend, stipends (pronounced **sty**-pend)
(noun) A stipend is a regular sum of money paid as a salary or as living expenses.
[from Latin *stipendium* meaning 'tax' or 'pay of a soldier']

stipulate, stipulates, stipulating, stipulated
(verb) If you stipulate that something must be done, you state clearly that it must be done.
stipulation (noun).

stir, stirs, stirring, stirred
1 (verb) When you stir a liquid, you move it around using a spoon or a stick.
2 To stir means to move slightly.
3 If something stirs you, it makes you feel strong emotions, e.g. *The music stirred him profoundly.*
4 (noun) If an event causes a stir, it causes general excitement or shock, e.g. *Her latest speech has caused a huge stir.*

stir up
1 (phrasal verb) If something stirs up mud in water, it causes it to rise up and swirl around.
2 To stir up trouble or emotion means to cause it.

stir-fry, stir-fries, stir-frying, stir-fried
(verb) To stir-fry meat or vegetables means to fry small pieces of them quickly in oil over a high heat.

stirring, stirrings
1 (adjective) causing excitement, emotion, and enthusiasm, e.g. *a stirring speech.*
2 (noun) If there is a stirring of emotion, people begin to feel it.

stirrup, stirrups
(noun) Stirrups are two metal loops hanging by leather straps from a horse's saddle, which you put your feet in when riding.
[from Old English *stig* meaning 'step' and *rap* meaning 'rope']

stitch, stitches, stitching, stitched
1 (verb) When you stitch pieces of material together, you use a needle and thread to sew them together.
2 (noun) A stitch is one of the pieces of thread that can be seen where material has been sewn.
3 (verb) To stitch a wound means to use a special needle and thread to hold the edges of skin together.
4 (noun) A stitch is one of the pieces of thread that can be seen where a wound has been stitched, e.g. *I had to have three stitches.*
5 If you have a stitch, you feel a sharp pain at the side of your abdomen, usually because you have been running or laughing.
6 (phrase; an informal use) Someone who is **in stitches** is laughing and cannot stop.

stoat, stoats
(noun) A stoat is a wild animal with a long body, brown fur, and a black tip to its tail.

stock, stocks, stocking, stocked
1 (noun) Stocks are shares bought as an investment in a company; also the amount of money raised by the company through the issue of shares.
2 (verb) A shop that stocks particular goods keeps a supply of them to sell.
3 (noun) A shop's stock is the total amount of goods it has for sale.
4 (phrases) If goods are **in stock** in a shop, they are available for sale. If they are **out of stock**, they have all been sold and are temporarily unavailable.
5 (verb) If you stock a shelf or cupboard, you fill it with food or other things.
6 (noun) If you have a stock of things, you have a supply ready for use.
7 The stock an animal or person comes from is the type of animal or person they are descended from, e.g. *He came from sturdy peasant stock.*
8 Stock is a liquid made from boiling meat, bones, or vegetables together in water. Stock is used as a base for soups, stews, and sauces.
9 (adjective) A stock expression or way of doing something is one that is commonly used.
10 (phrase) If you **take stock**, you pause and think about a situation before deciding what to do next.

stock up
(phrasal verb) If you stock up with something, you buy a supply of it.

stockbroker, stockbrokers
(noun) A stockbroker is a person whose job is to buy and sell shares for people who want to invest money.

stock car, stock cars
(noun) A stock car is an old car made suitable for racing on tracks where the cars often collide.

stock exchange, stock exchanges
(noun) A stock exchange is a place where there is trading in stocks and shares, e.g. *Prices on the London stock exchange fell heavily today.*

stocking, stockings
(noun) Stockings are long pieces of clothing that cover a woman's legs. They are often held up by suspenders.

stockinged
(adjective) Someone who is in their stockinged feet is wearing socks or stockings, but no shoes.

stock in trade
(noun) Someone's stock in trade is their usual behaviour or work, e.g. *Cynicism was his stock in trade.*

stock market, stock markets
(noun) The stock market is the organization and activity involved in buying and selling stocks and shares.

stockpile, stockpiles, stockpiling, stockpiled
1 (verb) If someone stockpiles something, they store large quantities of it for future use.
2 (noun) A stockpile is a large store of something.

stock-still
(adverb) If you stand stock-still, you do not move at all.
[from Old English *stock* meaning 'tree trunk' or 'log' plus *still*]

stocktaking
(noun) Stocktaking is the counting and checking of all a shop's or business's goods.

stocky, stockier, stockiest
(adjective) A stocky person is rather short, but broad and solid-looking.

stodgy, stodgier, stodgiest
(adjective) Stodgy food is very solid and makes you feel very full.

stoic or stoical (pronounced stoe-ik)
(adjective; a formal word) accepting difficulties and worries without complaining or getting upset.
stoically (adverb), **stoicism** (noun).
[the Stoics were philosophers in Ancient Greece who believed that virtue and happiness could only be obtained by accepting anything that happened]

stoke, stokes, stoking, stoked
1 (verb) To stoke a fire means to put more fuel onto it.
2 To stoke an emotion or conflict means to make it stronger or worse.
[from Old Dutch *stoken* meaning 'to push' or 'to poke']

stolid
(adjective) not showing much emotion, e.g. *He was stolid and dependable.*
stolidly (adverb).
[from Latin *stolidus* meaning 'dull']

stoma, stomata
(noun) In botany, stomata are pores in the outer layer of cells in a plant which control the passage of gases into and out of the plant.

stomach, stomachs, stomaching, stomached
1 (noun) Your stomach is the organ inside your body where food is digested.
2 You can refer to the front part of your body below your waist as your stomach.
3 (verb) If you cannot stomach something, you strongly dislike it and cannot accept it.

Similar words: (sense 1) abdomen, tummy, belly, gut

stomp, stomps, stomping, stomped
(verb; an informal word) If you stomp around, you walk with heavy steps, often because you are angry.

stone, stones, stoning, stoned
1 (noun) Stone is the hard solid substance found in the ground and used for building.
2 A stone is a small piece of rock.
3 You can refer to a jewel as a stone, e.g. *a gold ring with three stones.*
4 The stone in a fruit such as a plum or cherry is the large seed in the centre.
5 (verb) To stone something or someone means to throw stones at them.
6 (noun) A stone is also a unit of weight equal to 14 pounds or about 6.35 kilograms.

Stone Age
(noun) The Stone Age is the earliest known period of human history when people used stone to make weapons and tools. The Stone Age is often divided into three periods: the Palaeolithic, the Mesolithic, and the Neolithic.

stone-cold
(adjective) completely without warmth.

stoned
1 (adjective; an informal word) affected by drugs.
2 (an old-fashioned use) very drunk.

stone-deaf
(adjective) completely deaf.

stonewall, stonewalls, stonewalling, stonewalled
(verb) To stonewall means to put difficulties in the way of something so that it takes longer to achieve.

stoneware
(noun) Stoneware is pottery that has been fired at a very high temperature.

stony, stonier, stoniest
1 (adjective) Stony ground is rough and contains a lot of stones or rocks.
2 If someone's behaviour or expression is stony, it shows no friendliness or sympathy.

stooge, stooges
(noun; an informal word) A stooge is someone who is used by another person to do unpleasant or dishonest tasks.

stool, stools
1 (noun) A stool is a seat with legs but no back or arms.
2 A stool is also a lump of faeces.

stoop, stoops, stooping, stooped
1 (verb) If you stoop, you stand or walk with your shoulders bent forwards.

2 If you would not stoop to something, you would not disgrace yourself by doing it.
[from Old English *stupan* meaning 'to bow down']

stop, stops, stopping, stopped
1 (verb) If you stop doing something, you no longer do it.
2 If an activity or process stops, it comes to an end or no longer happens.
3 If a machine stops, it no longer functions or it is switched off.
4 To stop something means to prevent it.
5 (phrase) To **put a stop to** something means to prevent it from happening or continuing.
6 (verb) If people or things that are moving stop, they no longer move.
7 (noun) A stop is a place where a bus, train, or other vehicle stops during a journey.
8 If something that is moving comes to a stop, it no longer moves.
9 (verb) If you stop somewhere, you stay there for a short while.
10 If you stop someone's pay or a cheque, you give instructions that it should not be paid.

Similar words: (sense 1) cease, desist, discontinue, quit, leave off, pack in

stop off
(phrasal verb) If you stop off somewhere on a journey, you stay there for a short while.

stop up
(phrasal verb) If you stop up a hole or gap in something, you fill it.

stopcock, stopcocks
(noun) A stopcock is a tap or valve on a pipe which is used to stop or start the flow of liquid.

stopgap, stopgaps
(noun) A stopgap is something that serves a purpose for a short time but is soon replaced with something more suitable.

stopover, stopovers
(noun) A stopover is a short stay during a journey.

stoppage, stoppages
(noun) If there is a stoppage, people stop work because of a disagreement with their employer.

stopper, stoppers
(noun) A stopper is a piece of glass, plastic, or cork that fits into the neck of a jar or bottle.

stop press
(noun) The stop press is the latest news inserted into a special section of a newspaper after the rest has been printed.

stopwatch, stopwatches
(noun) A stopwatch is a watch that can be started and stopped by pressing buttons. Stopwatches are used to time events.

storage
(noun) The storage of something is the keeping of it somewhere until it is needed.

storage heater, storage heaters
(noun) A storage heater is a heater containing special bricks that can store heat. The heater

uses cheaper electricity and radiates heat gradually.

store, stores, storing, stored
1 (noun) A store is a shop.
2 (verb) When you store something somewhere, you keep it there until it is needed.
3 (noun) A store of something is a supply kept for future use.
4 A store is also a place where things are kept while they are not used.
5 (phrase) Something that is **in store for** you is going to happen to you in the future.
6 If you **set great store** by something, you think it is very important.
[from Latin *instaurare* meaning 'to restore' or 'to renew']

Similar words: (sense 3) reserve, stockpile, stock, reservoir, supply

storehouse, storehouses
(noun) A storehouse is a large building where goods are stored.

storekeeper, storekeepers
(noun) A storekeeper is a person who owns or manages a shop.

storeroom, storerooms
(noun) A storeroom is a room where things are kept until they are needed.

storey, storeys
(noun) A storey of a building is one of its floors or levels.

stork, storks
(noun) A stork is a very large white and black bird with long red legs and a long bill. Storks live mainly near water in Eastern Europe and Africa.

storm, storms, storming, stormed
1 (noun) When there is a storm, there is heavy rain, a strong wind, and often thunder and lightning.
2 If something causes a storm, it causes an angry or excited reaction, e.g. *The decision provoked a storm of criticism from opposition MPs.*
3 (verb) If someone storms out, they leave quickly, noisily, and angrily.
4 To storm means to say something in a loud, angry voice, e.g. *'This is disgraceful!' the professor stormed.*
5 If people storm a place, they attack it.
stormy (adjective).

story, stories
1 (noun) A story is a description of imaginary people and events written or told to entertain people.
2 The story of something or someone is an account of the important events that have happened to them, e.g. *her life story.*
[from Latin *historia* meaning 'narrative' or 'history']

Similar words: (sense 1) yarn, anecdote, tale, narrative, saga

stout, stouter, stoutest
1 (adjective) rather fat.
2 thick, strong, and sturdy, e.g. *stout shoes.*
3 determined, firm, and strong, e.g. *We must put up the stoutest possible resistance.*
stoutly (adverb).
[from Old French *estout* meaning 'bold']

stove, stoves
(noun) A stove is a piece of equipment which provides heat for a room or for cooking.

stow, stows, stowing, stowed
1 (verb) If you stow something somewhere or stow it away, you store it until it is needed.
2 If someone stows away in a ship or plane, they hide in it to go somewhere secretly without paying.
[from Old English *stowian* meaning 'to keep back from' or 'to hold back from']

stowaway, stowaways
(noun) A stowaway is someone who hides in a ship or plane in order to go somewhere secretly without paying.

straddle, straddles, straddling, straddled
1 (verb) If you straddle something, you stand or sit with one leg on either side of it.
2 If something straddles a place, it crosses it, linking different parts together, e.g. *A viaduct straddles the River Wye.*

straggle, straggles, straggling, straggled
1 (verb) If people straggle somewhere, they move slowly in irregular and disorganized groups.
2 If something straggles over an area, it spreads over it in an untidy way, e.g. *Her hair was straggling over her eyes.*
straggly (adjective), **straggler** (noun).

straight, straighter, straightest
1 (adjective and adverb) continuing in the same direction without curving or bending, e.g. *a straight road... The car came straight at me.*
2 upright or level rather than sloping or bent, e.g. *Keep your back straight.*
3 (adverb) immediately and directly, e.g. *Go straight to bed.*
4 (adjective) neat and tidy, e.g. *I must get the house straight this weekend.*
5 honest, frank, and direct, e.g. *Give me a straight answer... I'll be straight with you.*
6 A straight choice involves only two options.
7 (phrase) To **get something straight** means to understand it properly and correctly.
8 To **keep a straight face** means to manage not to laugh.
9 A criminal who is **going straight** is no longer involved in crime.
[from Middle English *streccan* meaning 'to stretch']

straightaway
(adverb) If you do something straightaway, you do it immediately.

straighten, straightens, straightening, straightened
1 (verb) To straighten something means to remove any bends or curves from it.

2 To straighten something also means to make it neat and tidy.
3 To straighten out a confused situation means to organize and deal with it.

straightforward
1 (adjective) easy and involving no problems.
2 honest, open, and frank.

strain, strains, straining, strained
1 (noun) If a strain is put on something, it is affected by a strong force which may damage it.
2 (verb) To strain something means to force it or use it more than is reasonable or normal.
3 If you strain a muscle, you injure it by moving awkwardly.
4 (noun) Strain is worry and nervous tension.
5 You can refer to an aspect of someone's character as a strain.
6 You can refer to distant sounds of music as strains of music.
7 (verb) To strain food means to pour away the liquid from it.
8 (noun) A particular strain of plant is a variety of it, e.g. *high-yielding strains of wheat.*
[senses 1 to 7 are from Old French *estreindre* meaning 'to press together']

Similar words: (sense 2) tax, overexert, overwork
(sense 7) sieve, sift, filter

strained
1 (adjective) worried and anxious.
2 If a relationship is strained, people feel unfriendly and do not trust each other.

strait, straits
1 (noun) You can refer to a narrow strip of sea as a strait or the straits, e.g. *the Straits of Gibraltar.*
2 (plural noun) If someone is in a bad situation, you can say they are in difficult straits, e.g. *The company is in dire financial straits.*
[from Old French *estreit* meaning 'tight']

straitjacket, straitjackets
(noun) A straitjacket is a special jacket used to tie the arms of a violent person tightly around their body.

strait-laced
(adjective) having a very strict and serious attitude to moral behaviour.

strand, strands
1 (noun) A strand of thread or hair is a single long piece of it.
2 You can refer to a part of a situation or idea as a strand of it, e.g. *How do we merge these two strands of industrial policy?*

stranded
(adjective) If someone or something is stranded somewhere, they are stuck and cannot leave.

strange, stranger, strangest
1 (adjective) unusual or unexpected.
2 not known, seen, or experienced before, e.g. *Adapting to a strange culture can be difficult.*
strangely (adverb), **strangeness** (noun).
[from Latin *extraneus* meaning 'foreign']

Similar words: (sense 1) peculiar, odd, queer, curious, uncanny, funny, zany, freakish
(sense 2) new, unfamiliar, alien, foreign, exotic

stranger, strangers
1 (noun) A stranger is someone you have never met before.
2 If you are a stranger to a place or situation, you have not been there or experienced it before.

strangle, strangles, strangling, strangled
1 (verb) To strangle someone means to kill them by squeezing their throat.
2 To strangle something means to prevent it from developing.
strangulation (noun).
[from Greek *straggein* meaning 'to draw tight' or 'to squeeze']

strangled
(adjective) A strangled sound is unclear and muffled.

stranglehold, strangleholds
(noun) To have a stranglehold on something means to have control over it and prevent it from developing.

strap, straps, strapping, strapped
1 (noun) A strap is a narrow piece of leather or cloth, used to fasten or hold things together.
2 (verb) To strap something means to fasten it with a strap.

strapping
(adjective) tall, strong, and healthy-looking.

strata the plural of stratum.

stratagem, stratagems
(noun) A stratagem is a plan or tactic.

strategic (pronounced strat-**tee**-jik)
1 (adjective) planned or intended to achieve something or to gain an advantage, e.g. *I took up a strategic position near the exit.*
2 Strategic weapons are long-range weapons targeted to destroy the enemy's industry, economy, or military bases.
strategically (adverb).

strategy, strategies
1 (noun) A strategy is a plan for achieving something.
2 Strategy is the skill of planning the best way to achieve something, especially in war.
strategist (noun).
[from Greek *stratēgia* meaning 'the function of a general']

stratified
(adjective) divided into different layers or levels.
stratification (noun).

stratosphere
(noun) The stratosphere is the layer of the earth's atmosphere which lies between 10 and 50 kilometres above the earth.

stratum, strata
1 (noun) The strata in the earth's surface are the different layers of rock.
2 The different levels or classes in society can be referred to as strata.

[from Latin *stratum* meaning 'something laid down']

straw, straws
1 (noun) Straw is the dry, yellowish stalks from cereal crops.
2 A straw is a hollow tube of paper or plastic which you use to suck a drink into your mouth.
3 (phrase) If you are **clutching at straws**, you are trying unusual or unlikely ideas because all other ideas have failed.
4 If something is **the last straw**, it is the latest in a series of bad events and makes you feel you cannot stand any more.

strawberry, strawberries
(noun) A strawberry is a small red fruit with tiny seeds in its skin.

straw poll, straw polls
(noun) A straw poll is a quick unofficial vote taken to get an indication of people's opinion.

stray, strays, straying, strayed
1 (verb) When people or animals stray, they wander away from where they should be.
2 (adjective) A stray dog or cat is one that has wandered away from home.
3 (noun) A stray is a stray dog or cat.
4 (verb) If your thoughts stray, you stop concentrating.
5 (adjective) Stray things are separated from the main group of things of their kind, e.g. *A hen was pecking around for stray grains of corn.*

streak, streaks, streaking, streaked
1 (noun) A streak is a long mark or stain.
2 (verb) If something is streaked with a colour, it has lines of the colour in it.
3 (noun) If someone has a particular streak, they have that quality in their character.
4 (verb) To streak somewhere means to move there very quickly.
5 (noun) A lucky or unlucky streak is a series of successes or failures.
streaky (adjective).
[from Old English *strica* meaning 'mark' or 'stroke of a pen']

streaker, streakers
(noun) A streaker is someone who runs somewhere in public with no clothes on.

stream, streams, streaming, streamed
1 (noun) A stream is a small river.
2 You can refer to a steady flow of something as a stream, e.g. *She blew out a stream of smoke.*
3 (verb) To stream somewhere means to move in a continuous flow in large quantities, e.g. *Tears streamed down his face.*
4 (noun) In a school, a stream is a group of children of the same age and ability.

streamer, streamers
(noun) A streamer is a long, narrow strip of coloured paper used for decoration.

streamline, streamlines, streamlining, streamlined
1 (verb) To streamline a vehicle, aircraft, or boat means to improve its shape so that it moves more quickly and efficiently.

2 To streamline an organization means to make it more efficient by removing parts of it.

street, streets
1 (noun) A street is a road in a town or village, usually with buildings along it.
2 (phrase) Someone who is **streets ahead** has made much more progress than others.
3 If something is **right up your street**, you are very interested in it or know a lot about it.
[from Latin *via strata* meaning 'paved way']

strength, strengths
1 (noun) Your strength is your physical energy and the power of your muscles.
2 Strength can refer to the degree of someone's confidence or courage.
3 You can refer to power or influence as strength, e.g. *Pacifist movements gathered strength in Norway.*
4 Someone's strengths are their good qualities and abilities.
5 The strength of an object is the degree to which it can stand rough treatment.
6 The strength of a substance is the amount of other substances that it contains, e.g. *Make sure you mix the spray to the correct strength.*
7 The strength of a feeling or opinion is the degree to which it is felt or supported.
8 The strength of a relationship is its degree of closeness or success.
9 The strength of a group is the total number of people in it.
10 (phrase) If people do something **in strength**, a lot of them do it together, e.g. *By Easter, the tourists were arriving in strength.*
11 If you do something **on the strength of** a fact or situation, this provides a basis or reason for your action, e.g. *The bank agreed to a loan on the strength of last year's sales figures.*

Similar words: (sense 1) might
(sense 3) force, intensity, muscle
(sense 6) potency
(sense 7) force, intensity

strengthen, strengthens, strengthening, strengthened
1 (verb) To strengthen something means to give it more power, influence, or support and make it more likely to succeed.
2 To strengthen an object means to improve it or add to its structure so that it can withstand rough treatment.

Similar words: fortify, reinforce, bolster, toughen

strenuous (pronounced **stren**-yoo-uss)
(adjective) involving a lot of effort or energy.
strenuously (adverb).
[from Latin *strenuus* meaning 'brisk']

stress, stresses, stressing, stressed
1 (noun) Stress is worry and nervous tension.
2 Stresses are strong physical forces applied to an object.
3 (verb) If you stress a point, you emphasize it and draw attention to its importance.
4 (noun) Stress is emphasis put on a word or part

of a word when it is pronounced, making it slightly louder.
stressful (adjective).
[shortened form of *distress*]

Similar words: (sense 1) strain, pressure, tension
(sense 3) accentuate, emphasize, highlight, underline
(sense 4) accent, emphasis

stretch, stretches, stretching, stretched
1 (verb) Something that stretches over an area extends that far.
2 (noun) A stretch of land or water is an area of it.
3 A stretch of time is a period of time.
4 (verb) When you stretch, you hold out part of your body as far as you can.
5 To stretch something soft or elastic means to pull it to make it longer or bigger.
6 If someone's money or resources are stretched, they hardly have enough for their needs.

stretcher, stretchers
(noun) A stretcher is a long piece of material with a pole along each side, used to carry an injured person.

strew, strews, strewing, strewed, strewn
(verb) If things are strewn about, they are scattered about untidily.
[from Old English *streowian* meaning 'to scatter']

stricken
(adjective) severely affected by something unpleasant.

strict, stricter, strictest
1 (adjective) Someone who is strict controls other people very firmly.
2 A strict rule must always be obeyed absolutely.
3 The strict meaning of something is its precise and accurate meaning.
4 You can use strict to describe someone who never breaks the rules or principles of a particular belief, e.g. *a strict vegetarian.*
[from Latin *stringere* to draw tight]

Similar words: (sense 1) rigorous, severe
(sense 2) stringent

strictly
1 (adverb) Strictly means only for a particular purpose, e.g. *This meeting is strictly for members only.*
2 (phrase) You say **strictly speaking** to correct a statement or add more precise information, e.g. *This is my friend Paul — well, strictly speaking, he's my sister's friend.*

stride, strides, striding, strode, stridden
1 (verb) To stride along means to walk quickly with long steps.
2 (noun) A stride is a long step; also the length of a step.
3 (phrase) To **make strides** means to make rapid progress.
4 To **take a problem in your stride** means to deal with it calmly.

strident (pronounced **stry**-dent)
(adjective) loud, harsh, and unpleasant.
stridently (adverb).

[from Latin *stridere* meaning 'to make a grating sound']

strife
(noun) Strife is trouble, conflict, and disagreement.

strike, strikes, striking, struck
1 (noun) If there is a strike, people stop working as a protest.
2 A hunger strike is a refusal to eat anything as a protest. A rent strike is a refusal to pay rent.
3 (verb) To strike someone or something means to hit them.
4 If an illness, disaster, or enemy strikes, it suddenly affects or attacks someone.
5 (noun) A strike is a military attack, e.g. *They carried out air strikes on selected targets.*
6 (verb) If a thought strikes you, it comes into your mind.
7 If you are struck by something, you are impressed by it.
8 When a clock strikes, it makes a sound to indicate the time.
9 To strike a deal with someone means to come to an agreement with them.
10 If someone strikes oil or gold, they discover it in the ground.
11 If you strike a match, you rub it against something to make it burst into flame.
12 (phrase) To **strike a balance** means to compromise between two extremes.
13 If you **strike lucky**, you have good luck.

strike off
(phrasal verb) If a professional person is struck off for bad behaviour, their name is removed from an official register and they are not allowed to practise their profession.

strike out
(phrasal verb) If someone strikes out, they go off to do something different on their own.

strike up
1 (phrasal verb) To strike up a conversation or friendship means to begin it.
2 When musicians strike up, they start to play.

striker, strikers
1 (noun) Strikers are people who are refusing to work as a protest.
2 In football, a striker is a player whose function is to attack and score goals rather than to defend.

striking
(adjective) very noticeable because of being unusual or very attractive.
strikingly (adverb).

string, strings, stringing, strung
1 (noun) String is thin cord made of twisted threads.
2 You can refer to a row or series of similar things as a string of them, e.g. *a string of islands... the latest in a string of disasters.*
3 The strings of a musical instrument are tightly stretched lengths of wire or nylon which vibrate to produce the notes.
4 (plural noun) The section of an orchestra consisting of stringed instruments is called the strings.

5 (phrase; an informal use) If someone **pulls strings**, they use their influence with powerful people to achieve something.
6 If something is offered with **no strings attached**, it is offered without any conditions.

string along
1 (phrasal verb; an informal use) To string someone along means to deceive them.
2 To string along with someone means to go with them and do what they are doing for a while.

string out
1 (phrasal verb) If things are strung out, they are spread out in a long line.
2 To string something out means to make it last longer than necessary.

stringed
(adjective) A stringed instrument is one with strings, such as a guitar or violin.

stringent
(adjective) Stringent laws, rules, or conditions are very severe or are strictly controlled, e.g. *a stringent review of public expenditure*.
stringently (adverb), **stringency** (noun).

stringy, stringier, stringiest
1 (adjective) Stringy food is tough and fibrous.
2 Stringy hair is thin and rough.

strip, strips, stripping, stripped
1 (noun) A strip of something is a long, narrow piece of it.
2 If you strip, you take off all your clothes.
3 To strip something means to remove whatever is covering its surface.
4 To strip someone of their property or rights means to officially take them away from them.
5 (noun) A comic strip is a series of drawings which tell a story.
6 A football team's strip is the clothes worn by the team when playing a match.
7 (phrase; an informal use) To **tear someone off a strip** means to scold them severely.
[sense 1 is from Old Dutch *stripe* meaning 'stripe'; senses 2-4 are from Old English *bestriepan* meaning 'to plunder']

strip club, strip clubs
(noun) A strip club is a club where people go to watch striptease.

stripe, stripes
1 (noun) Stripes are long, thin lines, usually of different colours.
2 Stripes are also narrow bands of material sewn onto a uniform to indicate someone's rank.
striped (adjective).

strip lighting
(noun) Strip lighting is in the form of a long tube rather than a light bulb.

stripling, striplings
(noun; an old-fashioned word) A stripling is someone who is not yet fully grown.

stripper, strippers
(noun) A stripper is an entertainer who does striptease.

striptease
(noun) Striptease is a form of entertainment in which someone takes off their clothes gradually to music.

strive, strives, striving, strove, striven
(verb) If you strive to do something, you make a great effort to achieve it.

strobe lighting
(noun) Strobe lighting is high-intensity flashing light produced by a perforated disc rotating in front of a light source.
[from Greek *strobos* meaning 'twisting' or 'spinning']

stroke, strokes, stroking, stroked
1 (verb) If you stroke something, you move your hand smoothly and gently over it.
2 (noun) If someone has a stroke, they suddenly lose consciousness as a result of a blockage or rupture in a blood vessel in the brain. A stroke can result in damage to speech and paralysis.
3 The strokes of a brush or pen are the movements that you make with it.
4 When you swim or row, the strokes are the movements you make with your arms or the oars.
5 A swimming stroke is a particular style of swimming.
6 In games such as tennis, a stroke is a particular way of hitting the ball.
7 The strokes of a clock are the sounds that indicate the hour.

stroll, strolls, strolling, strolled
1 (verb) To stroll along means to walk slowly in a relaxed way.
2 (noun) A stroll is a slow, pleasurable walk.

Similar words: amble, saunter, promenade, walk

strong, stronger, strongest
1 (adjective) Someone who is strong has powerful muscles.
2 You also say that someone is strong when they are confident and have courage.
3 Strong objects are able to withstand rough treatment.
4 Strong also means great in degree or intensity, e.g. *a strong wind... a strong smell*.
5 A strong argument or theory is supported by a lot of evidence.
6 If a group or organization is strong, it has a lot of members or influence.
7 You can use strong to say how many people there are in a group, e.g. *Troops nearly 50,000 strong were stationed in Germany*.
8 Your strong points are the things you are good at.
9 A strong competitor or candidate is likely to win or succeed.
10 A strong relationship is close and successful.
11 A strong economy or currency is financially stable and successful.
12 A strong liquid or drug contains a lot of a particular substance.
13 (adverb) If someone or something is still going strong, they are still healthy or working well after a long time.

Similar words: (sense 1) mighty, muscular, powerful (sense 4) intense, acute, keen, extreme

stronghold, strongholds
(noun) A stronghold of an attitude or belief is a place in which the attitude or belief is strongly held.

strongroom, strongrooms
(noun) A strongroom in a bank is a reinforced room with a special security door in which money and valuables are kept.

strontium
(noun) Strontium is a soft, silvery-white metallic element used in making fireworks. Strontium-90 is used in generating nuclear power and is one of the dangerous fall-out products after a nuclear explosion. Strontium's atomic number is 38 and its symbol is Sr.
[from *Strontian* the area in Scotland where it was first discovered]

stroppy, stroppier, stroppiest
(adjective; an informal word) bad-tempered or annoyed.

structure, structures, structuring, structured
1 (noun) The structure of something is the way it is made, built, or organized.
2 A structure is something that has been built or constructed.
3 If something has structure, it is properly organized, e.g. *We need to give these ideas some structure.*
4 (verb) To structure something means to arrange it into an organized pattern or system.
structural (adjective), **structurally** (adverb).
[from Latin *structura* meaning 'building', 'construction', or 'arrangement']

Similar words: (sense 1) composition, make-up, construction, constitution

struggle, struggles, struggling, struggled
1 (verb) If you struggle to do something, you try hard to do it in difficult circumstances.
2 (noun) Something that is a struggle is difficult to achieve and takes a lot of effort.
3 (verb) When people struggle, they twist and move violently during a fight.
4 (noun) A struggle is a fight.

strum, strums, strumming, strummed
(verb) To strum a guitar means to play it by moving your fingers backwards and forwards across all the strings.

strut, struts, strutting, strutted
1 (verb) To strut means to walk in a stiff, proud way with your chest out and your head high.
2 (noun) A strut is a piece of wood or metal which strengthens or supports part of a building or structure.
[from Old English *strutian* meaning 'to walk stiffly']

Similar words: (sense 1) swagger, parade

strychnine (pronounced **strik**-neen)
(noun) Strychnine is a strong poison.
[from Greek *strukhnos* meaning 'nightshade'. Strychnine actually comes from a different plant]

stub, stubs, stubbing, stubbed
1 (noun) The stub of a pencil or cigarette is the short piece that remains when the rest has been used.
2 The stub of a cheque or ticket is the small part that you keep.
3 (verb) If you stub your toe, you hurt it by accidentally kicking something.
[from Old English *stubb* meaning 'stump']

stub out
(phrasal verb) To stub out a cigarette means to put it out by pressing the end against something.

stubble
1 (noun) The short stalks remaining in the ground after a crop is harvested are called stubble.
2 If a man has stubble on his face, he has very short hair growing there because he has not shaved recently.
[from Latin *stipula* meaning 'stalk' or 'stem']

stubborn
1 (adjective) Someone who is stubborn is determined not to change their opinion or course of action.
2 A stubborn stain is difficult to remove.
stubbornly (adverb), **stubbornness** (noun).

Similar words: (sense 1) obstinate, intransigent, obdurate, persistent, tenacious, refractory, pig-headed

stubby, stubbier, stubbiest
(adjective) short and thick, e.g. *stubby fingers.*

stucco (pronounced **stuck**-koe)
(noun) Stucco is a type of plaster used for covering or decorating walls.
[from Italian *stucco* meaning 'plaster']

stuck
1 (adjective) If something is stuck in a particular position, it is fixed or jammed and cannot be moved, e.g. *The lift is stuck between the second and third floors.*
2 If you are stuck, you are unable to continue what you were doing because it is too difficult.
3 If you are stuck somewhere, you are unable to get away.

stuck-up
(adjective; an informal word) proud and conceited.

stud, studs
1 (noun) A stud is a small piece of metal fixed into something.
2 A male horse or other animal that is kept for stud is kept for breeding purposes.
3 A stud or a stud farm is a place where horses are kept and bred.
[sense 1 is from Old English *studu* meaning 'post' or 'nail head'; senses 2 and 3 are from Old English *stod* meaning 'establishment for breeding horses']

studded
(adjective) decorated with small pieces of metal or precious stones.

student, students
(noun) A student is a person studying at university or college.
[from Latin *studens* meaning 'diligent']

studentship, studentships
(noun) A studentship is a scholarship to study at a university or college.

studied
(adjective) A studied action or response has been carefully planned and is not natural, e.g. *With studied casualness he mentioned his departure.*

studio, studios
1 (noun) A studio is a room where a photographer or painter works.
2 A studio is also a room containing special equipment where records, films, or radio or television programmes are made.
[from Italian *studio* meaning 'study']

studious (pronounced styoo-dee-uss)
(adjective) spending a lot of time studying.
[from Latin *studiosus* meaning 'eager' or 'diligent']

studiously
(adverb) carefully and deliberately, e.g. *They studiously avoided talking to me.*

study, studies, studying, studied
1 (verb) If you study a particular subject, you spend time learning about it.
2 (noun) Study is the activity of studying a subject, e.g. *a room set aside for quiet study.*
3 Studies are subjects which are studied, e.g. *the Department of European Studies.*
4 (verb) If you study something, you look at it carefully, e.g. *I studied the map for a while.*
5 (noun) A study is a piece of research on a particular subject, e.g. *She has made a close study of male drinking habits.*
6 A study by an artist or composer is a drawing or composition done in preparation for a larger work.
7 A study in a house is a room used for writing, reading, and studying.
[from Latin *studere* meaning 'to study']

stuff, stuffs, stuffing, stuffed
1 (noun) You can refer to a substance or group of things as stuff.
2 (verb) If you stuff something somewhere, you push it there quickly and roughly.
3 If you stuff something with a substance or objects, you fill it with the substance or objects.
[from Old French *estoffer* meaning 'to furnish' or 'to provide']

stuffing
(noun) Stuffing is a mixture of small pieces of food put inside poultry or a vegetable before it is cooked.

stuffy, stuffier, stuffiest
1 (adjective) very formal and old-fashioned.
2 If it is stuffy in a room, there is not enough fresh air.

Similar words: (sense 2) fusty, airless, close

stultify, stultifies, stultifying, stultified
(verb) To stultify someone means to be so boring or repetitive as to destroy their natural interest or prevent their development, e.g. *The regular use of calculators can stultify a child's capacity to do mental arithmetic.*
stultifying (adjective).
[from Latin *stultus* meaning 'stupid' and *facere* meaning 'to make']

stumble, stumbles, stumbling, stumbled
1 (verb) If you stumble while you are walking or running, you trip and almost fall.
2 If you stumble when speaking, you make mistakes when pronouncing the words.
3 If you stumble across something or stumble on it, you find it unexpectedly.

stumbling block, stumbling blocks
(noun) A problem or obstacle that prevents you from achieving something can be referred to as a stumbling block.

stump, stumps, stumping, stumped
1 (noun) A stump is a small part of something that is left when the rest has been removed, e.g. *the stump of an old tree.*
2 In cricket, the stumps are the three upright wooden sticks that support the bails, forming the wicket.
3 (verb) If a question or problem stumps you, you cannot think of an answer or solution.

stumpy, stumpier, stumpiest
(adjective) short and thick.

stun, stuns, stunning, stunned
1 (verb) If you are stunned by something, you are very shocked by it.
2 To stun a person or animal means to knock them unconscious with a blow to the head.
[from Old French *estoner* meaning 'to daze']

stunning
(adjective) very beautiful or impressive, e.g. *The film is visually stunning... a stunning victory.*

stunt, stunts, stunting, stunted
1 (noun) A stunt is an unusual or dangerous and exciting action that someone does to get publicity or as part of a film.
2 (verb) To stunt the growth or development of something means to prevent it from developing as it should.

stunt man, stunt men
(noun) A stunt man is a man whose job is to do dangerous things in films in place of an actor.

stupefied (pronounced styoo-piff-eyed)
(adjective) completely unable to think because of being very tired, bored, or surprised.
[from Latin *stupefacere* meaning 'to stun']

stupendous
(adjective) very large or impressive, e.g. *stupendous sums of money.*
stupendously (adverb).
[from Latin *stupere* meaning 'to be amazed']

stupid, stupider, stupidest
(adjective) showing lack of good judgment or intelligence and not at all sensible.
stupidity (noun).
[from Latin *stupidus* meaning 'senseless']

Similar words: dull, dim, dumb, obtuse, simple

stupor, stupors
(noun) Someone who is in a stupor is completely unable to think clearly and is almost unconscious, e.g. *a drunken stupor*.
[from Latin *stupor* meaning 'senselessness']

sturdy, sturdier, sturdiest
(adjective) strong and firm and unlikely to be damaged or injured, e.g. *a sturdy oak table*.

sturgeon (pronounced **stur**-jon)
(noun) A sturgeon is a large edible fish. Its eggs are also eaten and are known as caviar.

stutter, stutters, stuttering, stuttered
1 (noun) Someone who has a stutter finds it difficult to speak smoothly and often repeats sounds through being unable to complete a word.
2 (verb) When someone stutters, they hesitate or repeat sounds when speaking.

sty, sties
1 (noun) A sty is the same as a pigsty.
2 A sty or stye is an infection in the form of a small red swelling on a person's eyelid.
[sense 1 is from Old English *stig* meaning 'pig pen'; sense 2 is from Old English *stigend* meaning 'swelling' and *ye* meaning 'eye']

style, styles, styling, styled
1 (noun) The style of something is the general way in which it is done or presented, often showing the attitudes of the people involved.
2 A person or place that has style is smart, elegant, and fashionable.
3 The style of something is its design, e.g. *I don't like that style of dress*.
4 (verb) To style a piece of clothing or a person's hair means to design and create its shape.
5 (noun) In botany, the style is the slender part of a flower which comes out of the ovary and is tipped by the stigma.
[from Latin *stilus* meaning 'writing implement', hence types and styles of writing]

Similar words: (sense 2) flair, elegance, stylishness, panache

stylish
(adjective) smart, elegant, and fashionable.
stylishly (adverb).

Similar words: chic, smart

stylistic
(adjective) relating to the methods, techniques, and principles of design used in creating a piece of writing, music, or art.

stylized or **stylised**
(adjective) using a particular artistic or literary form as a basis rather than being natural or spontaneous, e.g. *a stylized picture of a Japanese garden*.

stylus, styluses
(noun) A stylus is the pointed object on a record player that picks up the sound signals on the records.

stymie, stymies, stymieing, stymied (pronounced **sty**-mee)
(verb; an informal word) If something stymies you, it prevents you from succeeding.

suave (pronounced **swahv**)
(adjective) charming, polite, and confident, e.g. *a suave young man*.
[from Latin *suavis* meaning 'sweet' or 'agreeable']

sub-
1 (prefix) Sub- is used at the beginning of words that have 'under' as part of their meaning.
2 Sub- is also used to form nouns that refer to the parts into which something is divided, e.g. *Subsection 1(b) of the report... the subgroups of society*.
[from Latin *sub* meaning 'under' or 'below']

subatomic
(adjective) A subatomic particle is a particle which is part of an atom.

subconscious
1 (noun) Your subconscious is the part of your mind that can influence you without your being aware of it.
2 (adjective) happening or existing in someone's subconscious and therefore not directly realized or understood by them, e.g. *He had a subconscious desire to punish himself*.
subconsciously (adverb).

subcontinent, subcontinents
(noun) A subcontinent is a large mass of land, often consisting of several countries, and forming part of a continent, e.g. *the Indian subcontinent*.
subcontinental (adjective).

subcontract, subcontracts, subcontracting, subcontracted
(verb) If one company subcontracts part of its work to another company, it pays the other company to do it.

subcontractor, subcontractors
(noun) A subcontractor is a company that has agreed to do part of a job for another company.

subculture, subcultures
(noun) A subculture is the way of life, ideas, and art of a particular group within a society.

subdivide, subdivides, subdividing, subdivided
(verb) To subdivide a part of something means to divide it again into smaller parts.

subdivision, subdivisions
(noun) A subdivision is an area which is part of a larger area.

subdue, subdues, subduing, subdued
1 (verb) If soldiers subdue a group of people, they bring them under control by using force, e.g. *Troops were sent to subdue the rebels*.
2 To subdue a colour, light, or emotion means to make it less bright or strong.

Similar words: (sense 1) quell, suppress, repress

subdued
1 (adjective) rather quiet and sad.
2 not very noticeable or bright.

subject, subjects, subjecting, subjected
1 (noun) The subject of writing or a conversation is the thing or person being discussed.
2 In grammar, the subject is the word or words representing the person or thing doing the action expressed by the verb. For example, in the sentence 'My cat keeps catching birds', 'my cat' is the subject.
3 A subject is an area of study.
4 (verb) To subject someone to something means to make them experience it, e.g. *I'm sorry to have to subject you to all these tests.*
5 (noun) The subjects of a country are the people who live there.
6 (adjective) Subject peoples and countries are controlled by the government of another country.
7 Someone or something that is subject to something is affected by it, e.g. *These earnings will be subject to tax.*
[from Latin *subjectus* meaning 'brought under']

subjective
(adjective) influenced by personal feelings and opinion rather than based on fact or rational thought.

sub judice (pronounced sub **joo**-diss-ee)
(adjective; a legal expression) If something is sub judice, newspapers and broadcasters are not allowed to comment on it because it is the subject of a trial taking place in a court of law.
[a Latin expression meaning 'before a judge']

subjugate, subjugates, subjugating, subjugated
(pronounced **sub**-joo-gate; a formal word)
1 (verb) To subjugate people means to defeat them and take control of them.
2 If your wishes are subjugated to something else, they are treated as less important.
subjugation (noun).
[from Latin *subjugare* meaning 'to subdue']

subjunctive
(noun) In grammar, the subjunctive or subjunctive mood is one of the forms a verb can take. It is used to express attitudes such as wishing and doubting.

sublet, sublets, subletting, sublet
(verb) If you are renting a house and you sublet it to someone, you let it to them and they pay rent to you.

sublime, sublimer, sublimest
(adjective) Something that is sublime is wonderful and affects people emotionally, e.g. *a sublime moment.*
[from Latin *sublimis* meaning 'lofty' or 'exalted']

subliminal
(adjective) affecting your mind without your being aware of it, e.g. *subliminal messages in advertising.*
[from Latin *sub-* + *limen* meaning 'below the threshold', hence unnoticed]

sub-machine-gun, sub-machine-guns
(noun) A sub-machine-gun is a light portable machine-gun.

submarine, submarines
(noun) A submarine is a ship that can travel beneath the surface of the sea.

submerge, submerges, submerging, submerged
1 (verb) To submerge means to go beneath the surface of a liquid.
2 If you submerge yourself in an activity, you become totally involved in it.
submerged (adjective).
[from Latin *submergere* meaning 'to plunge under' or 'to sink']

submission, submissions
1 (noun) Submission is a state in which someone accepts the control of another person, e.g. *They brought the trade unions into submission.*
2 The submission of a proposal or application is the act of sending it for consideration.

submissive
(adjective) behaving in a quiet, obedient way.

submit, submits, submitting, submitted
1 (verb) If you submit to something, you accept it because you are not powerful enough to resist it.
2 If you submit an application or proposal, you send it to someone for consideration.
[from Latin *submittere* meaning 'to place under']

subnormal
(adjective) Someone who is subnormal has less intelligence than a normal person of their age.

subordinate, subordinates, subordinating, subordinated
1 (noun) A person's subordinate is someone who is in a less important position than them.
2 (adjective) If one thing is subordinate to another, it is less important, e.g. *All other questions are subordinate to this one.*
3 (verb) To subordinate one thing to another means to treat it as being less important.
[from Latin *subordinare* meaning 'below in rank']

subordinate clause, subordinate clauses
(noun) In grammar, a subordinate clause is a clause which adds details to the main clause of a sentence.

subpoena, subpoenas, subpoenaing, subpoenaed
(pronounced sub-**pee**-na)
1 (noun) A subpoena is a document ordering a person to attend a court of law as a witness.
2 (verb) To subpoena someone means to issue them with a subpoena.
[a Latin phrase meaning 'under penalty']

subscribe, subscribes, subscribing, subscribed
1 (verb) If you subscribe to a particular belief or opinion, you support it or agree with it.
2 If you subscribe to a magazine, you pay to receive regular copies.
3 If you subscribe to a charity or campaign, you send money to it regularly.
subscriber (noun).
[from Latin *subscribere* meaning 'to write underneath']

subscription, subscriptions
(noun) A subscription is a sum of money that you

pay regularly to belong to an organization or to receive regular copies of a magazine.

subsequent
(adjective) happening or coming into existence at a later time than something else, e.g. *Subsequent research has provided even better results.*
subsequently (adverb).
[from Latin *subsequi* meaning 'to follow after']

subservient
1 (adjective) Someone who is subservient does whatever other people want them to do.
2 If one thing is subservient to another, it is treated as less important or less urgent than it.
[from Latin *subservire* meaning 'to comply with']

subset, subsets
(noun) A subset of a larger set or group is a smaller set or group contained within it.

subside, subsides, subsiding, subsided
1 (verb) To subside means to become less intense or quieter, e.g. *The pain subsided.*
2 If water or the ground subsides, it sinks to a lower level.
[from Latin *subsidere* meaning 'to settle down' or 'to sink down']

subsidence
(noun) If a place is suffering from subsidence, parts of the ground have sunk to a lower level.

subsidiary, subsidiaries (pronounced sub-**sid**-yer-ee)
1 (adjective) treated as being of less importance and additional to another thing, e.g. *I tried to discuss this and some subsidiary questions.*
2 (noun) A subsidiary is a company which is part of a larger company.

subsidize, subsidizes, subsidizing, subsidized; also spelled **subsidise**
(verb) To subsidize something means to provide part of the cost of it, e.g. *Many governments subsidize their railways.*
subsidized (adjective).

subsidy, subsidies
(noun) A subsidy is a sum of money paid to help support a company or provide a public service.

subsist, subsists, subsisting, subsisted
(verb) If people are subsisting on a particular food, they are just managing to stay alive by eating it.
subsistence (noun).
[from Latin *subsistere* meaning 'to stand firm']

subsoil
(noun) The subsoil is the layer of rather infertile soil lying between the surface soil and the rock below.

substance, substances
1 (noun) Anything which is a solid, a powder, a liquid, or a paste can be referred to as a substance.
2 If something has substance, it consists of matter and can be touched and not just heard, seen, or imagined, e.g. *They had no more substance than shadows.*
3 If a speech or piece of writing has substance, it

is meaningful, important, or significant, e.g. *There isn't anything of substance in the book.*
[from Latin *substantia* meaning 'substance' or 'property']

Similar words: (sense 1) matter, stuff, material, fabric

substandard
(adjective) below a required standard and therefore unacceptable.

substantial
1 (adjective) very large in degree or amount, e.g. *a substantial increase... substantial damage.*
2 large and strongly built, e.g. *a substantial timber building.*

substantially
(adverb) Something that is substantially true is generally or mostly true.

substantiate, substantiates, substantiating, substantiated
(verb) To substantiate a claim or account of something means to provide proof that it is true.

substantive
(adjective; a formal word) effective, real, and significant, e.g. *Substantive measures were needed.*

substitute, substitutes, substituting, substituted
1 (verb) To substitute one thing for another means to use it instead of the other thing or to put it in the other thing's place.
2 (noun) If one thing is a substitute for another, it is used instead of it or put in its place.
substitution (noun).
[from Latin *substituere* meaning 'to set in place']

Similar words: (sense 1) replace
(sense 2) replacement, stand-in, surrogate

subsume, subsumes, subsuming, subsumed
(verb; a formal word) To subsume something within a group means to include it in that group.
[from Latin *subsumere* meaning 'to take under']

subterfuge, subterfuges (pronounced sub-ter-fyooj)
(noun) Subterfuge is the use of devious or dishonest methods.
[from Latin *subterfugere* meaning 'to escape by stealth']

subterranean (pronounced sub-ter-**rain**-ee-an)
(adjective) A subterranean river or passage is underground.
[from Latin *subterraneus* meaning 'under the earth']

subtitle, subtitles
(noun) A film with subtitles has a printed translation of the dialogue at the bottom of the screen.

subtle, subtler, subtlest (pronounced **sut**-tl)
1 (adjective) very fine, delicate, or small in degree, e.g. *a subtle change... subtle forms of racism.*
2 using indirect methods to achieve something.
subtly (adverb), **subtlety** (noun).
[from Latin *subtilis* meaning 'finely woven']

subtract, subtracts, subtracting, subtracted
(verb) If you subtract one number from another,
you take away the first number from the second.
subtraction (noun).
[from Latin *subtrahere* meaning 'to draw away']

subtropical
(adjective) relating to areas of the world
between the tropical and the temperate regions.

suburb, suburbs
(noun) A suburb is an area of a town or city that
is away from its centre.
[from Latin *suburbium* meaning 'close to a city']

suburban
1 (adjective) relating to a suburb or suburbs.
2 dull and conventional.

suburbia
(noun) You can refer to the suburbs of a city as
suburbia.

subversive
1 (adjective) intended to destroy or weaken a
political system, e.g. *subversive literature*.
2 (noun) Subversives are people who try to
destroy or weaken a political system.
subversion (noun).

subvert, subverts, subverting, subverted
(verb; a formal word) To subvert something
means to cause it to weaken, fail, or be
destroyed, e.g. *Conflict and division subvert the
foundations of society*.
[from Latin *subvertere* meaning 'to overturn']

subway, subways
1 (noun) A subway is a footpath that goes
underneath a road.
2 In American English, a subway is an
underground railway.

succeed, succeeds, succeeding, succeeded
1 (verb) To succeed means to achieve the result
you intend.
2 To succeed someone means to be the next
person to have their job.
3 If one thing succeeds another, it comes after it
in time, e.g. *The first demand would be
succeeded by others*.
succeeding (adjective).
[from Latin *succedere* meaning 'to follow after']

Similar words: (sense 1) manage, prosper, thrive,
flourish, do well

---

success, successes
1 (noun) Success is the achievement of
something you have been trying to do.
2 Someone who is a success has achieved an
important position or made a lot of money.
successful (adjective), **successfully** (adverb).

succession, successions
1 (noun) A succession of things is a number of
them occurring one after the other.
2 (phrase) If something happens a number of
weeks, months, or years **in succession**, it happens
that number of times without a break, e.g. *She
went to Rome for the third year in succession*.
3 (noun) When someone becomes the next person
to have an important position, you can refer to

this event as their succession to this position,
e.g. *his succession to the peerage*.

successive
(adjective) occurring one after the other without
a break, e.g. *On two successive Saturdays the car
broke down*.

successor, successors
(noun) Someone's successor is the person who
takes their job when they leave.

succinct (pronounced suk-**singkt**)
(adjective) expressing something clearly and in
very few words.
succinctly (adverb).
[from Latin *succinctus* meaning 'brief']

succour (pronounced **suk**-kur)
(noun; a formal word) To give someone succour
when they are suffering means to give them
help.
[fromLatin *succurrere* meaning 'to hasten to
help']

succulent
(adjective) Succulent food is juicy and delicious.
[from Latin *sucus* meaning 'juice']

succumb, succumbs, succumbing, succumbed
(verb) If you succumb to something, you are
unable to resist it any longer, e.g. *He finally
succumbed to temptation and ate the chocolate*.
[from Latin *succumbere* meaning 'to be
overcome']

such
1 (determiner or pronoun) You use 'such' to refer
to the person or thing you have just mentioned,
or to someone or something similar, e.g. *It was
Brighton or Bournemouth or some such place*.
2 (phrase) You can use **such as** to introduce an
example of something, e.g. *a game of chance
such as roulette*.
3 (determiner) 'Such' can be used for
emphasizing, e.g. *It was such a lovely day*.
4 (phrase) You can use **such as it is** to indicate
that something is not great in quality or
quantity, e.g. *Dinner's on the table, such as it is*.
5 You can use **such and such** when you want to
refer to something that is not specific, e.g. *You
always have to consider carefully — have I
taken such and such into account?*

suchlike
(determiner and pronoun) used to refer to things
similar to those already mentioned, e.g.
*artichokes, smoked salmon, and suchlike
delicacies*.

suck, sucks, sucking, sucked
1 (verb) If you suck something, you hold it in
your mouth and pull at it with your cheeks and
tongue, usually to get liquid out of it.
2 To suck something in a particular direction
means to draw it there with a powerful force.
3 (an informal use) To suck up to someone means
to do things to please them in order to obtain
praise or approval.

sucker, suckers
1 (noun; an informal use) If you call someone a

sucker, you mean that they are easily fooled or cheated.

2 Suckers are pads on the bodies of some animals and insects which they use to cling to a surface.

3 A sucker on a plant is a new shoot that grows from an underground stem or root.

suckle, suckles, suckling, suckled
(verb) When a mother suckles a baby, she feeds it with milk from her breast.

sucrose (pronounced **syoo**-kroze)
(noun; a technical word) Sucrose is sugar in crystalline form found in sugar cane and sugar beet.

suction
1 (noun) Suction is the force involved when a substance is drawn or sucked from one place to another.
2 Suction is the process by which two surfaces stick together when the air between them is removed, e.g. *You press the pads onto the side of the bath and they are held there by suction.*
[from Latin *suctio* meaning 'sucking']

Sudanese (pronounced soo-dan-**neez**)
1 (adjective) belonging or relating to the Sudan.
2 (noun) A Sudanese is someone who comes from the Sudan.

sudden
(adjective) happening quickly and unexpectedly, e.g. *a sudden drop in temperature.*
suddenly (adverb), **suddenness** (noun).
[from Latin *subitus* meaning 'unexpected']

suds
(plural noun) Suds are the bubbles that form on the surface of soapy water.

sue, sues, suing, sued
(verb) To sue someone means to start a legal case against them, usually to claim money from them.
[from Latin *sequi* meaning 'to follow']

suede (pronounced **swayd**)
(noun) Suede is leather with a soft, roughened surface.
[from French *gants de Suède* meaning 'gloves from Sweden']

suet (pronounced **soo**-it)
(noun) Suet is hard fat from around the kidneys and loins of an animal, often used in cooking.
[from Latin *sebum* meaning 'fat' or 'suet']

suffer, suffers, suffering, suffered
1 (verb) If someone is suffering pain, or suffering as a result of an unpleasant situation, they are badly affected by it.
2 If something suffers as a result of neglect or an unfavourable situation, its condition or quality becomes worse, e.g. *His studies are suffering.*
sufferer (noun), **suffering** (noun).
[from Latin *sufferre* meaning 'to bear']

sufferance
(noun) If you are allowed to do something on sufferance, you can do it, although you know that the person who gave you permission would prefer that you did not do it.

suffice, suffices, sufficing, sufficed
(verb; a formal word) If something suffices, it is enough or adequate for a purpose.

Similar words: serve, be sufficient, do

sufficiency
(noun; a formal word) If there is a sufficiency of something, there is enough of it.

sufficient
(adjective) If a supply or quantity is sufficient for a purpose, there is enough of it available.
sufficiently (adverb).
[from Latin *sufficiens* meaning 'supplying the needs of']

suffix, suffixes
(noun) A suffix is a group of letters which is added to the end of a word to form a new word, for example '-ology' or '-itis'.
[from Latin *suffigere* meaning 'to fasten' or 'to fix below']

suffocate, suffocates, suffocating, suffocated
(verb) To suffocate means to die as a result of having too little air or oxygen to breathe.
suffocation (noun).
[from Latin *suffocare* meaning 'to strangle']

suffrage
(noun) Suffrage is the right to vote in political elections.
[from Latin *suffragium* meaning 'vote']

suffragette, suffragettes
(noun) A suffragette was a woman who, at the beginning of this century, was involved in the campaign for women to be given the right to vote.

suffuse, suffuses, suffusing, suffused
(verb; a literary word) If something is suffused with light or colour, light or colour spreads gradually over or through it.
suffusion (noun).
[from Latin *suffusus* meaning 'overspread with']

sugar
(noun) Sugar is a sweet substance used to sweeten food or drinks. Sugar is obtained from sugar cane or sugar beet.
[from Arabic *sukkar*]

sugar beet
(noun) Sugar beet is a plant with white roots from which sugar is obtained.

sugar cane
(noun) Sugar cane is a tall tropical plant with thick stems from which sugar is obtained.

suggest, suggests, suggesting, suggested
1 (verb) If you suggest a plan or idea to someone, you mention it as a possibility for them to consider.
2 If something suggests a particular thought or impression, it makes you think in that way or gives you that impression, e.g. *The evidence suggests high unemployment.*
[from Latin *suggerere* meaning 'to bring up']

Similar words: (sense 1) propose, recommend, advocate, advance, move
(sense 2) imply

suggestion, suggestions
1 (noun) A suggestion is a plan or idea that is mentioned as a possibility for someone to consider.
2 A suggestion of something is a very slight indication or faint sign of it, e.g. *He replied with the merest suggestion of a smile.*
3 In psychology, suggestion is the process of getting someone to accept an idea by associating it with other ideas.

Similar words: (sense 1) motion, proposition, proposal, recommendation

suggestive
1 (adjective) Something that is suggestive of a particular thing gives a slight hint or sign of it.
2 Suggestive remarks or gestures make people think about sex.
suggestively (adverb).

Similar words: (sense 2) smutty, risqué, naughty, saucy, racy

suicidal
1 (adjective) People who are suicidal want to kill themselves.
2 Suicidal behaviour is so dangerous that it is likely to result in death, e.g. *a suicidal attack.*
suicidally (adverb).

suicide, suicides
1 (noun) People who commit suicide deliberately kill themselves.
2 If you say that to do something would be suicide, you mean that it would ruin someone's career or future.
[from Latin *sui* meaning 'of oneself' and *caedere* meaning 'to kill']

suit, suits, suiting, suited
1 (noun) A suit is a matching jacket and trousers or skirt.
2 (verb) If a situation or course of action suits you, it is appropriate or acceptable for your purpose.
3 If a piece of clothing or a colour suits you, you look good when you are wearing it.
4 If you do something to suit yourself, you do it because you want to and without considering other people.
5 (noun) In a court of law, a suit is a legal action taken by one person against another.
6 A suit is one of four different types of card in a pack of playing cards. The four suits are hearts, clubs, diamonds, and spades.
7 (phrase) To **follow suit** means to do what someone else has just done, e.g. *He bowed his head. Mother and Jenny followed suit.*
[from Old French *sieute* meaning 'set of things']

suitable
(adjective) right or acceptable for a particular purpose or occasion.
suitability (noun), **suitably** (adverb).

Similar words: fitting, appropriate, apt, fit, due, proper

suitcase, suitcases
(noun) A suitcase is a case in which you carry your clothes when you are travelling.

suite, suites (pronounced **sweet**)
1 (noun) In a hotel, a suite is a set of rooms.
2 A suite is a set of matching furniture or bathroom fittings.
[from Old French *sieute* meaning 'set of things']

suited
(adjective) right or appropriate for a particular purpose or person, e.g. *ideally suited for the job.*

suitor, suitors
(noun; an old-fashioned word) A woman's suitor is a man who wants to marry her.

sulk, sulks, sulking, sulked
(verb) Someone who is sulking is showing their annoyance by being silent and moody.
sulky (adjective).

sullen
(adjective) behaving in a bad-tempered and disagreeably silent way, e.g. *a sullen boy.*
sullenly (adverb).

sully, sullies, sullying, sullied
(verb) To sully something means to spoil it or make it dirty.

sulphate, sulphates
(noun) A sulphate is a salt or compound containing sulphuric acid.

sulphur
(noun) Sulphur is a pale yellow nonmetallic element which burns with a very unpleasant smell. Its atomic number is 16 and its symbol is S.

sulphur dioxide
(noun) Sulphur dioxide is a strong-smelling soluble gas produced by burning sulphur. It is used as a preservative and in the manufacture of bleach, disinfectant, and sulphuric acid.

sulphuric acid (pronounced sul-**fyoo**-rik)
(noun) Sulphuric acid is a colourless, oily, highly corrosive acid.

sultan, sultans
(noun) In some Muslim countries, the ruler of the country is called the sultan.
[from Arabic *sultan* meaning 'rule']

sultana, sultanas
1 (noun) Sultanas are dried grapes.
2 A sultana is also the wife of a sultan.

sultry, sultrier, sultriest
1 (adjective) Sultry weather is unpleasantly hot and humid.
2 A sultry woman has a manner which suggests hidden passion.
sultriness (noun).

sum, sums, summing, summed
1 (noun) A sum is an amount of money.
2 In arithmetic, a sum is a calculation.
3 The sum of something is the total amount of it.
4 (verb) If you sum something up, you briefly describe its main points.
[from Latin *summus* meaning 'highest' or 'total']

summarize, summarizes, summarizing, summarized; also spelled **summarise**

(verb) To summarize something means to give a short account of its main points.

summary, summaries
1 (noun) A summary of something is a short account of its main points.
2 (adjective) A summary action is done without delay or careful thought, e.g. *Mass arrests and summary executions.*
summarily (adverb).

Similar words: (sense 1) abstract, outline, synopsis, precis, résumé, rundown, recapitulation

summation, summations
(noun; a formal word) A summation is a summary of what someone has done or said.
[from Latin *summare* meaning 'to total']

summer, summers
(noun) Summer is the season between spring and autumn.

summer school, summer schools
(noun) A summer school is an educational course run at a university or college during the summer.

summit, summits
1 (noun) The summit of a mountain is its top.
2 A summit is a meeting between leaders of different countries to discuss particular issues.

summon, summons, summoning, summoned
1 (verb) If someone summons you, they order you to go to them.
2 If you summon up strength or energy, you make a great effort to be strong or energetic.
[from Latin *summonere* meaning 'to remind discreetly']

summons, summonses, summonsing, summonsed
1 (noun) A summons is an official order to appear in court.
2 A summons is an order to go to someone, e.g. *I waited for a summons from the boss.*
3 (verb) If someone is summonsed, they are officially ordered to appear in court.

sump, sumps
(noun) The sump is the part underneath an engine which holds the engine oil.

sumptuous
(adjective) Something that is sumptuous is magnificent and obviously very expensive.
sumptuously (adverb), **sumptuousness** (noun).
[from Latin *sumptuosus* meaning 'expensive']

sum total
(noun) The sum total of a number of things is all of them added or considered together.

sun, suns, sunning, sunned
1 (noun) The sun is the star providing heat and light for the planets revolving around it in our solar system.
2 You refer to heat and light from the sun as sun, e.g. *plenty of sun and fresh air.*
3 (verb) If you sun yourself, you sit in the sunshine.

sunbathe, sunbathes, sunbathing, sunbathed
(verb) If you sunbathe, you sit in the sunshine to get a suntan.

sunbeam, sunbeams
(noun) A sunbeam is a ray of light from the sun.

sunburn
(noun) Sunburn is sore red skin on someone's body due to too much esposure to the rays of the sun.

sunburnt
(adjective) Someone who is sunburnt has sore, red skin because they have spent too much time in the sun.

sundae, sundaes (pronounced **sun**-day)
(noun) A sundae is a dish of ice cream with cream and fruit or nuts.

Sunday, Sundays
(noun) Sunday is the day between Saturday and Monday.
[from Old English *sunnandæg* meaning 'day of the sun']

Sunday school, Sunday schools
(noun) Sunday school is a special class held on Sundays to teach children about Christianity.

sun deck, sun decks
(noun) A sun deck is a flat area, especially a deck on a ship, where people can sit or lie in the sun.

sundial, sundials
(noun) A sundial is a device used for telling the time, consisting of a pointer which casts a shadow on a flat base marked with the hours.

sundown
(noun) In American English, sundown is sunset.

sundry
1 (adjective) Sundry is used to refer to several things or people of various sorts, e.g. *The pilot pressed sundry switches.*
2 (phrase) **All and sundry** means everyone.
[from Old English *syndrig* meaning 'separate']

sunflower, sunflowers
(noun) A sunflower is a tall plant with very large yellow flowers. The seeds are edible and are used to make cooking oil.

sunglasses
(plural noun) Sunglasses are spectacles with dark lenses that you wear to protect your eyes from the sun.

sunken
1 (adjective) having sunk to the bottom of the sea, a river, or lake, e.g. *a sunken battleship.*
2 A sunken object or area has been constructed below the level of the surrounding area, e.g. *a sunken garden... a sunken bath.*
3 curving inwards, e.g. *His cheeks were white and sunken.*

sun lamp, sun lamps
(noun) A sun lamp is a lamp which gives out ultraviolet rays to make people's skin suntanned.

sunlight
(noun) Sunlight is the bright light produced when the sun is shining.
sunlit (adjective).

sunny, sunnier, sunniest
(adjective) When it is sunny, the sun is shining.

sunrise, sunrises
(noun) Sunrise is the time in the morning when the sun first appears, and the colours produced in the sky at that time.

sunroof, sunroofs
(noun) A sunroof is an opening part in the roof of a car.

sunset, sunsets
(noun) Sunset is the time in the evening when the sun disappears below the horizon, and the colours produced in the sky at that time.

sunshade, sunshades
(noun) A sunshade is anything which is used as a protection from the sun, such as a parasol.

sunshine
(noun) Sunshine is the bright light produced when the sun is shining.

sunspot, sunspots
(noun) Sunspots are dark cool patches that appear on the surface of the sun. Sunspots have a strong magnetic field.

sunstroke
(noun) Sunstroke is an illness caused by spending too much time in hot sunshine.

suntan, suntans
(noun) If you have a suntan, the sun has tanned your skin brown.
suntanned (adjective).

sup, sups, supping, supped
1 (verb) If you sup something, you drink it, especially in small sips.
2 (an old-fashioned use) If you sup, you eat dinner in the evening.
[sense 1 is from Old English *supan* meaning 'to drink by taking small quantities at a time']

super
1 (adjective) very nice or very good, e.g. *We had a super holiday.*
2 Super is used to describe something that is larger or better than similar things, e.g. *a super plastic that is resistant to high temperatures.*
[from Latin *super* meaning 'above']

superable
(adjective; a formal word) A problem that is superable can be solved or overcome.

superabundance
(noun; a formal word) If there is a superabundance of something, there is more of it than is needed.
superabundant (adjective).

superannuation
(noun) Superannuation is money that people pay regularly into a fund organized by their employer to provide them with a retirement pension.
[from Latin *superannatus* meaning 'aged more than one year']

superb
(adjective) very good indeed.
superbly (adverb).
[from Latin *superbus* meaning 'distinguished']

supercharger, superchargers
(noun) A supercharger is a device which increases the amount of air drawn into an engine to improve its performance.
supercharge (verb).

supercilious (pronounced soo-per-**sill**-ee-uss)
(adjective) If you are supercilious, you behave in a scornful way towards other people because you think they are inferior to you.
superciliously (adverb), **superciliousness** (noun).

superconductivity
(noun) Superconductivity is a physical property that some substances have, by which there is almost no electrical resistance at temperatures close to absolute zero.

superego
(noun; a technical word) Your superego is the part of your mind that controls your ideas of right and wrong and produces feelings of guilt.

superficial
1 (adjective) involving only the most obvious or most general aspects of something, e.g. *superficial knowledge.*
2 not having a deep, serious, or genuine interest in anything, e.g. *She's always been superficial.*
3 Superficial wounds are not very deep or severe.
superficially (adverb).

superfluous (pronounced soo-**per**-floo-uss)
(adjective; a formal word) unnecessary or no longer needed.
superfluity (noun), **superfluously** (adverb).
[from Latin *superfluus* meaning 'overflowing']

superhuman
(adjective) having much greater power or ability than is normally expected of humans, e.g. *superhuman strength.*

superimpose, superimposes, superimposing, superimposed
(verb) To superimpose one image on another means to put the first image on top of the other so that they are seen as one image.

superintend, superintends, superintending, superintended
(verb) If you superintend someone or an activity, you make sure that something is done properly.
[from Latin *superintendere* meaning 'to oversee']

superintendent, superintendents
1 (noun) A superintendent in the police force is an officer above the rank of inspector.
2 A superintendent is a person whose job is to be responsible for a particular thing, e.g. *He is the Superintendent of Buildings at the college.*

superior, superiors
1 (adjective) better or of higher quality than other similar things.
2 in a position of higher authority than another person.
3 showing too much pride and self-importance, e.g. *'You wouldn't understand,'* Clarissa said in a superior way.
4 (noun) Your superiors are people who are in a

higher position than you in society or an organization.
[from Latin *superus* meaning 'higher']

superlative, superlatives (pronounced soo-**per**-lat-tiv)
1 (noun) In grammar, the superlative is the form of an adjective which indicates that the person or thing described has more of a particular quality than anyone or anything else. For example, **quickest, best,** and **easiest** are all superlatives.
2 (adjective; a formal use) very good indeed, e.g. *She is a superlative actress.*
[from Latin *superlatus* meaning 'extravagant']

supermarket, supermarkets
(noun) A supermarket is a shop selling food and household goods arranged so that you can help yourself and pay for everything at a till by the exit.

supernatural
1 (adjective) Something that is supernatural, for example ghosts or witchcraft, cannot be explained by normal scientific laws.
2 (noun) You can refer to supernatural things as the supernatural.

supernova, supernovae or **supernovas**
(noun) A supernova is a star that explodes and for a few days becomes very much brighter than the sun.

superpower, superpowers
(noun) A superpower is a very powerful and influential country such as the U.S.A. or the U.S.S.R.

supersede, supersedes, superseding, superseded
(pronounced soo-per-**seed**)
(verb) If something supersedes another thing, it replaces it because it is more modern.
[from Latin *supersedere* meaning 'to sit above']

supersonic
(adjective) A supersonic aircraft can travel faster than the speed of sound.
[from Latin *super- + sonus* meaning 'above sound']

superstar, superstars
(noun) You can refer to a very famous entertainer or sports player as a superstar.

superstition, superstitions
(noun) Superstition is a belief in things like magic and powers that bring good or bad luck.
superstitious (adjective).
[from Latin *superstitio* meaning 'dread of the supernatural']

superstructure, superstructures
1 (noun) The superstructure of a ship is the part above its main deck.
2 The superstructure of a bridge, building, or other structure is the part supported above the ground on pillars or foundations.

supervise, supervises, supervising, supervised
(verb) To supervise someone means to check and direct what they are doing to make sure that they do it correctly.
supervision (noun), **supervisor** (noun).

[from Latin *super-* meaning 'above' or 'over' and *videre* meaning 'to see']

Similar words: preside, superintend

supine (pronounced **soo**-pine)
(adjective; a formal word) Someone who is supine is lying flat on their back.
[from Latin *supinus* meaning 'bent backwards']

supper, suppers
(noun) Supper is a meal eaten in the evening or a snack eaten before you go to bed.
[from Old French *soper*]

supplant, supplants, supplanting, supplanted
(verb; a formal word) To supplant someone or something means to take their place, e.g. *Electric cars may one day supplant petrol-driven ones.*
[from Latin *supplantare* meaning 'to overthrow']

supple
(adjective) able to bend and move easily, e.g. *Polish leather regularly to keep it supple.*
[from Latin *supplex* meaning 'bowed']

supplement, supplements, supplementing, supplemented
1 (verb) To supplement something means to add something to it to improve it, e.g. *There should be no need to supplement your diet with vitamins.*
2 (noun) A supplement is something that is added to something else to improve it.
3 A newspaper or magazine supplement is a separate extra part of it.

Similar words: (sense 1) augment, boost, complement, top up

supplementary
(adjective) added to something else to improve it, e.g. *You could claim a supplementary pension.*

supplicant, supplicants
(noun; a formal word) A supplicant is a person who humbly asks for help.

supplicate, supplicates, supplicating, supplicated
(verb; a formal word) To supplicate means to humbly ask for help.
supplication (noun).
[from Latin *supplicare* meaning 'to beg on bended knees']

supplier, suppliers
(noun) A supplier is a firm which provides particular goods.

supply, supplies, supplying, supplied
1 (verb) To supply someone with something means to provide it or send it to them.
2 (noun) A supply of something is an amount available for use, e.g. *a hot water supply.*
3 (plural noun) Supplies are food and equipment for a particular purpose.
4 (noun) In economics, supply is the amount of something that can be made available, e.g. *an economy controlled by supply and demand.*
[from Latin *supplere* meaning 'to complete']

support, supports, supporting, supported
1 (verb) If you support someone, you agree with their aims and want them to succeed.

2 If you support someone who is in difficulties, you are kind, encouraging, and helpful to them.
3 If something supports an object, it is underneath it and holding it up.
4 (noun) A support is an object that is holding something up.
5 (verb) To support someone or something means to prevent them from falling by holding them.
6 (noun) Financial support is money that is provided for someone or something.
7 (verb) To support someone financially means to provide them with money.
8 If a fact supports a theory, it helps to show that the theory is correct.
supporter (noun), **supportable** (adjective).
[from Latin *supportare* meaning 'to bring']

supportive
(adjective) A supportive person is kind, encouraging, and helpful to someone who is in difficulties.

suppose, supposes, supposing, supposed
1 (verb) If you suppose that something is the case, you think that it is likely, e.g. *He supposed that they would come tomorrow.*
2 (phrase) You can say **I suppose** when you are not entirely certain or enthusiastic about something, e.g. *We could take him with us, I suppose.*
3 (conjunction) You can use 'suppose' or 'supposing' when you are considering or suggesting a possible situation or action, e.g. *Suppose something goes wrong — what then?*
4 (phrase) If something **is supposed** to be done, it should be done, e.g. *You are supposed to report it to the police.*
5 If something **is supposed** to happen, it is planned or expected to happen, e.g. *The party was supposed to be tonight.*
6 Something that **is supposed** to be the case is generally believed or thought to be so, e.g. *It's supposed to be the best hairdresser's in town.*

supposed
(adjective) Supposed is used to express doubt about something that is generally believed, e.g. *the supposed benefit of privatization.*
supposedly (adverb).

supposition, suppositions
(noun) A supposition is something that is believed or assumed to be true, e.g. *That argument rests on the supposition that equality is possible.*

suppository, suppositories
(noun) A suppository is a medicine in solid form that is inserted into the rectum or vagina where it dissolves.

suppress, suppresses, suppressing, suppressed
1 (verb) If an army or government suppresses an activity, it prevents people from doing it.
2 If someone suppresses a piece of information they prevent it from becoming generally known.
3 If you suppress your feelings, you stop yourself expressing them.
suppression (noun).

Similar words: (sense 1) repress, quash, stamp out

suppurate, suppurates, suppurating, suppurated
(pronounced **sup**-yoo-rate)
(verb; a formal word) If a wound suppurates, pus forms inside it because of infection.
suppuration (noun).

supremacy (pronounced soo-**prem**-mass-ee)
(noun) If a group of people has supremacy over others, it is more powerful than the others.

supreme
1 (adjective) Supreme is used as part of a title to indicate the highest level of an organization or system, e.g. *the Supreme Court.*
2 Supreme is used to emphasize the greatness of something, e.g. *a supreme achievement.*
supremely (adverb).
[from Latin *supremus* meaning 'highest']

Similar words: (sense 2) superlative, paramount, foremost

surcharge, surcharges
(noun) A surcharge is an additional charge.

sure, surer, surest
1 (adjective) If you are sure about something, you have no doubts about it.
2 If you are sure of yourself, you are very confident.
3 If something is sure to happen, it will definitely happen.
4 (phrase) If you **make sure** about something, you check it or take action to see that it is done.
5 (adjective) Sure means reliable or accurate, e.g. *Those holes are a sure sign of woodworm.*
6 (interjection) Sure is an informal way of saying 'yes', e.g. *'Can I come too?' — 'Sure.'*
[from Latin *securus* meaning 'secure']

surely
1 (adverb) Surely is used to emphasize the belief that something is the case, e.g. *He didn't do it on purpose, surely!*
2 (phrase) If something is happening **slowly but surely**, it is happening gradually and cannot be stopped.

surety
(noun; a formal or legal word) A person who acts as surety for another person agrees to be responsible for that person's debts or behaviour.
[from Latin *securitas* meaning 'security']

surf
(noun) Surf is the white foam that forms on the top of waves when they break near the shore.

surface, surfaces, surfacing, surfaced
1 (noun) The surface of something is the top or outside area of it.
2 The surface of a situation is what can be seen easily rather than what is hidden or not immediately obvious.
3 (verb) If someone surfaces, they come up from under water to the surface.
4 If a piece of news or a feeling surfaces, it becomes known.
5 (an informal use) When someone who has been

sleeping surfaces, they appear, especially later than expected.
6 To surface an area means to give it a surface, e.g. *They've been surfacing the road all morning.* [from French *sur* meaning 'on' and *face* meaning 'face' or 'side']

surface mail
(noun) Surface mail is mail sent by land or sea.

surfboard, surfboards
(noun) A surfboard is a long narrow lightweight board used for surfing.

surfeit (pronounced **sur**-fit)
(noun) If there is a surfeit of something, there is too much of it.
[from Old French *sourfaire* meaning 'to overdo']

surfing
(noun) Surfing is a sport which involves riding towards the shore on the top of a large wave while standing on a surfboard.

surge, surges, surging, surged
1 (noun) A surge is a sudden great increase in the amount of something, e.g. *a surge of jealousy.*
2 (verb) If an emotion surges in you, you feel it suddenly and strongly.
3 If something surges, it moves suddenly and powerfully, e.g. *The crowd surged forwards.*
surging (adjective).
[from Latin *surgere* meaning 'to rise']

surgeon, surgeons
(noun) A surgeon is a doctor who performs operations.

surgery, surgeries
1 (noun) Surgery is medical treatment involving cutting open part of the patient's body to treat the damaged part.
2 The room or building where a doctor or dentist works is called a surgery.
3 A period of time during which a doctor is available to see patients is called surgery, e.g. *I'll be in for morning surgery at nine.*

surgical
(adjective) used in or involving a medical operation, e.g. *surgical instruments.*
surgically (adverb).

surgical spirit
(noun) Surgical spirit is a type of methylated spirit which is used for sterilizing medical instruments.

surly, surlier, surliest
(adjective) rude and bad-tempered.
surliness (noun).

surmise, surmises, surmising, surmised
(verb; a formal word) To surmise something means to guess it, e.g. *The French, for reasons which could only be surmised, opposed the idea.*
[from Old French *surmettre* meaning 'to accuse']

surmount, surmounts, surmounting, surmounted
1 (verb) To surmount a difficulty means to manage to solve it.
2 (a formal use) If something is surmounted by a particular thing, that thing is on top of it, e.g. *The column is surmounted by a statue.*

[from Old French *sur* meaning 'on' and *monter* meaning 'to climb']

surname, surnames
(noun) Your surname is your last name which you share with other members of your family.

surpass, surpasses, surpassing, surpassed
(verb; a formal word) To surpass someone or something means to be better than them.

Similar words: eclipse, exceed, outstrip, excel, outdo, outclass, transcend

surplice, surplices (pronounced **sur**-pliss)
(noun) A surplice is a loose garment worn over a long robe by priests and members of the choir in some churches.
[from Latin *super-* meaning 'over' and *pellicium* meaning 'coat of fur'. They were worn over fur clothing in church]

surplus, surpluses
(noun) If there is a surplus of something there is more of it than is needed.
[from Latin *super-* meaning 'over' and *plus* meaning 'more']

Similar words: glut, surfeit, excess, overabundance, plethora, superfluity

surprise, surprises, surprising, surprised
1 (noun) A surprise is an unexpected event.
2 Surprise is the feeling caused when something unexpected happens.
3 (verb) If something surprises you, it gives you a feeling of surprise.
4 If you surprise someone, you do something they were not expecting.
5 (phrase) If something **takes you by surprise**, it was unexpected and you were not prepared for it.
surprising (adjective).
[from Old French *surprendre* meaning 'to overtake']

surreal
(adjective) very strange and dreamlike.

surrealism
(adjective) Surrealism began in the 1920s. It involves the putting together of strange images and things that are not normally seen together.
surrealist (adjective), **surrealistic** (adjective).
[from French *surréalisme* meaning 'beyond realism']

surrender, surrenders, surrendering, surrendered
1 (verb) To surrender means to stop fighting and agree that the other side has won.
2 (noun) Surrender is a situation in which one side in a fight agrees that the other side has won and gives in.
3 (verb) If you surrender to a temptation or feeling, you let it take control of you.
4 To surrender something means to give it up to someone else, e.g. *The United States would never surrender this territory.*
[from Old French *surrendre* meaning 'to yield']

Similar words: (sense 1) cede, concede, yield
(sense 2) capitulation, submission
(sense 3) capitulate, succumb, submit, give in
(sense 4) forfeit, relinquish, give up

---

surreptitious (pronounced sur-rep-**tish**-uss)
(adjective) A surreptitious action is done
secretly or so that no-one will notice, e.g.
*surreptitious visits to betting shops... a
surreptitious glance.*
surreptitiously (adverb).
[from Latin *surrepticius* meaning 'furtive']

surrogate, surrogates
1 (adjective) acting as a substitute for someone
or something.
2 (noun) A surrogate is a person or thing that
acts as a substitute.
[from Latin *surrogare* meaning 'to substitute']

surrogate mother, surrogate mothers
(noun) A surrogate mother is a woman who
agrees to conceive and give birth to a baby for
another woman who is not able to have children
of her own.

surround, surrounds, surrounding, surrounded
1 (verb) To surround someone or something
means to be situated all around them.
2 (noun) The surround of something is its outside
edge or border.
[from Old French *suronder* meaning 'to
overflow']

Similar words: (sense 1) circle, encircle, enclose,
envelop

---

surrounding, surroundings
1 (adjective) The surrounding area of a
particular place is the area around it, e.g. *the
surrounding countryside.*
2 (plural noun) You can refer to the area and
environment around a place or person as their
surroundings, e.g. *We used to live in nice
surroundings.*

Similar words: (sense 2) environment, habitat,
element, milieu

---

surtax, surtaxes
(noun) A surtax is an additional tax on incomes
that exceed a particular level.

surveillance (pronounced sur-**vay**-lanss)
(noun) Surveillance is the close watching of a
person's activities by the police or army.
[from French *surveiller* meaning 'to watch over']

survey, surveys, surveying, surveyed
1 (verb) To survey something means to look
carefully at the whole of it.
2 To survey a building or piece of land means to
examine it carefully in order to make a report or
plan of its structure and features.
3 (noun) A survey of something is a detailed
examination or investigation of it, often in the
form of a report.
[from Old French *surveoir* meaning 'to oversee']

Similar words: (sense 1) view, scan, look over

---

surveyor, surveyors
(noun) A surveyor is a person whose job is to
survey buildings or land.

survival, survivals
1 (noun) Survival is being able to continue living
or existing in spite of great danger or difficulties,
e.g. *What are the chances of survival?*
2 Something that is a survival from an earlier
time continues to exist in the present.

survive, survives, surviving, survived
(verb) To survive means to continue to live or
exist in spite of a great danger or difficulties, e.g.
Very few people survived the explosion.
survivor (noun).

susceptible
(adjective) If you are susceptible to something,
you are likely to be influenced or affected by it,
e.g. *We are all susceptible to advertising.*
susceptibility (noun).
[from Latin *suscipere* meaning 'to take up']

suspect, suspects, suspecting, suspected
1 (verb) If you suspect something, you think that
it is likely or is probably true, e.g. *They
suspected that a secret deal had been made.*
2 If you suspect something, you have doubts
about its reliability or trustworthiness, e.g. *I
have my reasons for suspecting these reports.*
3 If you suspect someone of doing something
wrong, you think that they have done it.
4 (noun) A suspect is someone who is thought to
be guilty of a crime.
5 (adjective) If something is suspect, it cannot be
trusted or relied upon, e.g. *Their military titles
were a little suspect.*
[from Latin *suspicere* meaning 'to mistrust']

suspend
1 (verb) If something is suspended, it is hanging
from somewhere, e.g. *A model aeroplane was
suspended above the stage.*
2 To suspend an activity or event means to delay
it or stop it for a while.
3 If someone is suspended from their job, they
are prevented from doing it for a period of time,
usually as a punishment.
4 If small bits of solid material are suspended in
air or a liquid, they float there and remain still.
[from Latin *sub-* meaning 'under' and *pendere*
meaning 'hang']

suspender, suspenders
(noun) Suspenders are fastenings which hold up
a woman's stockings.

suspense
(noun) Suspense is a state of excitement or
anxiety caused by having to wait for something.

suspension
1 (noun) The suspension of something is the
delaying or stopping of it.
2 A person's suspension is their removal from a
job for a period of time, usually as a punishment.
3 The suspension of a vehicle consists of springs
and shock absorbers which provide a smooth
ride.
4 A suspension is a liquid mixture in which very

small bits of a solid material are contained and are not dissolved.

suspension bridge, suspension bridges
(noun) A suspension bridge is a bridge that is supported from above by cables attached to towers.

suspicion, suspicions
1 (noun) Suspicion is the feeling of not trusting someone or the feeling that something is wrong.
2 A suspicion is a feeling that something is likely to happen or is probably true, e.g. *I have a suspicion that I am not going to enjoy this.*

Similar words: (sense 1) distrust, scepticism

suspicious
1 (adjective) If you are suspicious of someone, you do not trust them.
2 Suspicious is used to describe things that make you think that there is something wrong with a situation, e.g. *Several suspicious aircraft were spotted.*
suspiciously (adverb).

Similar words: (sense 2) fishy, shady, doubtful, dubious, suspect, questionable

sustain, sustains, sustaining, sustained
1 (verb) To sustain something means to continue it or maintain it for a period of time, e.g. *They do not have enough money to sustain a strike.*
2 If something sustains you, it gives you energy and strength, e.g. *They had had nothing to sustain them except two cups of coffee.*
3 (a formal use) To sustain an injury or loss means to suffer it.
[from Latin *sustinere* meaning 'to hold up']

sustenance
(noun; a formal word) Sustenance is food and drink.

suture, sutures (pronounced **soo**-cher)
(noun; a medical word) A suture is a stitch holding together the edges of a wound.
[from Latin *sutura* meaning 'seam']

svelte (pronounced **svelt**)
(adjective) slim and elegant, e.g. *a svelte young woman.*

swab, swabs, swabbing, swabbed
1 (noun) A swab is a small piece of cotton wool used for cleaning a wound.
2 (verb) To swab something means to clean it using a large mop and a lot of water.
3 To swab a wound means to clean it or take specimens from it using a swab.
[from Old Dutch *swabbe* meaning 'mop']

swagger, swaggers, swaggering, swaggered
1 (verb) To swagger means to walk in a proud, exaggerated way.
2 (noun) A swagger is an exaggerated walk.
swaggeringly (adverb).

Swahili (pronounced swa-**hee**-lee)
(noun) Swahili is a language spoken by many people in eastern Africa. It is an official language in Kenya and Tanzania.

swallow, swallows, swallowing, swallowed
1 (verb) If you swallow something, you make it go down your throat and into your stomach.
2 When you swallow, you move your throat muscles as if you were swallowing something, especially when you are nervous.
3 To swallow a story or explanation means to believe it.
4 To swallow an unkind or unfair remark means to accept it without protest.
5 If you swallow your feelings, you stop yourself from showing them.
6 (noun) A swallow is a bird with a long forked tail. It is dark blue in colour with a creamy white chest.

swamp, swamps, swamping, swamped
1 (noun) A swamp is an area of permanently wet land.
2 (verb) If something is swamped, it is covered or filled with water.
3 If you are swamped by things, you have more than you are able to deal with, e.g. *We've been swamped with applications.*
swampy (adjective).

swan, swans
(noun) A swan is a large bird with a very long neck. Swans are usually white and live on rivers or lakes.

swanky, swankier, swankiest
(adjective; an informal word) smart, fashionable, and expensive.

swan song
(noun) A famous person's swan song is their last performance or work of art before they retire or die.
[from the legend that swans sing just before they die]

swap, swaps, swapping, swapped (rhymes with **stop**); also spelled **swop**
(verb) To swap one thing for another means to replace the first thing with the second, often by making an exchange with another person, e.g. *He swapped a dozen marbles for eight stamps.*

Similar words: exchange, interchange, switch, trade

swarm, swarms, swarming, swarmed
1 (noun) A swarm of insects is a large group of them flying together.
2 (verb) When bees or other insects swarm, they fly together in a large group.
3 If people swarm somewhere, a lot of people go there quickly and at the same time, e.g. *On bank holidays, crowds of people swarm to the coast.*
4 If a place is swarming with people, there are a lot of people there.

Similar words: (sense 4) seethe, teem

swarthy, swarthier, swarthiest
(adjective) A swarthy person has a dark complexion.
swarthiness (noun).

swashbuckling
(adjective) Swashbuckling is used to describe

people who have the exciting behaviour or appearance of pirates.
[from Middle English *swashbuckling* meaning 'making a noise by striking your sword against a shield']

swastika, swastikas (pronounced **swoss**-tik-ka)
(noun) A swastika is a symbol in the shape of a cross with each arm bent over at right angles. It was the official symbol of the Nazis in Germany, but in India it is a good luck sign.
[from Sanskrit *svasti* meaning 'prosperity']

swat, swats, swatting, swatted
1 (verb) To swat an insect means to hit it sharply with something in order to kill it.
2 (noun) A swat is a sharp hit with something.

swathe, swathes (rhymes with **bathe**)
1 (noun) A swathe is a long strip of cloth that is wrapped around something, e.g. *balconies strewn with swathes of silk.*
2 A swathe of land is a long strip of it.
[sense 1 is from Old English *swathian* meaning 'wrapping'; sense 2 is from Old English *swæth* meaning 'width of grass cut with one stroke of a scythe']

swathed
(adjective) If someone is swathed in something, they are wrapped in it, e.g. *She was swathed in bandages from head to foot.*

sway, sways, swaying, swayed
1 (verb) To sway means to lean or swing slowly from side to side.
2 If something sways you, it influences your judgment.
3 (noun; a literary use) Sway is the power to influence people, e.g. *He was coming under the sway of new ideas.*

swear, swears, swearing, swore, sworn
1 (verb) To swear means to say words that are considered to be very rude or blasphemous.
2 If you swear to something, you state solemnly that you will do it or that it is true.
3 If you swear by something, you firmly believe that it is a reliable cure or solution, e.g. *He swears by herbal teas to cure colds.*

swear in
(phrasal verb) When someone is sworn in to a new position, they solemnly promise to fulfil the duties and are officially appointed.

swearword, swearwords
(noun) A swearword is a word which is considered to be rude or blasphemous, which people use when they are angry.

sweat, sweats, sweating, sweated
1 (noun) Sweat is the salty liquid produced by your sweat glands when you are hot or afraid.
2 (verb) When you sweat, sweat comes through the pores in your skin in order to lower the temperature of your body.
3 (noun; an informal use) You can refer to hard work as sweat.

sweater, sweaters
(noun) A sweater is a knitted piece of clothing covering your upper body and arms.

sweat gland, sweat glands
(noun) Your sweat glands are the organs under your skin that produce sweat.

sweat shirt, sweat shirts
(noun) A sweat shirt is a piece of clothing made of thick fleecy cotton, covering your upper body and arms.

sweaty
(adjective) covered or soaked with sweat.

swede, swedes
(noun) A swede is a large round root vegetable with yellow flesh and a brownish-purple skin.
[from *Swedish turnip* because it was introduced from Sweden in the 18th century]

Swede, Swedes
(noun) A Swede is someone who comes from Sweden.

Swedish
1 (adjective) belonging or relating to Sweden.
2 (noun) Swedish is the main language spoken in Sweden, and is also spoken by many people in Finland.

sweep, sweeps, sweeping, swept
1 (verb) If you sweep the floor, you use a brush to gather up dust or rubbish from it.
2 To sweep things off a surface means to push them all off with a quick, smooth movement.
3 If something sweeps from one place to another, it moves there very quickly, e.g. *Cold winds sweep over the plain... She was swept out to sea.*
4 If an attitude or new fashion sweeps a place, it spreads rapidly through it, e.g. *The camping craze that is currently sweeping America.*
5 (noun) A sweep is a wide open area, e.g. *a sweep of road.*
6 A sweep is a chimney sweep.
7 (phrase) To **sweep something under the carpet** means to prevent it from becoming generally known.

sweeping
1 (adjective) A sweeping curve or movement is long and wide.
2 A sweeping statement is based on a general assumption rather than on careful thought.
3 affecting a lot of people to a great extent, e.g. *The government has made sweeping cuts.*

sweet, sweeter, sweetest; sweets
1 (adjective) containing a lot of sugar, e.g. *a cup of sweet tea.*
2 (noun) Things such as toffees, chocolates, and mints are sweets.
3 A sweet is a dessert.
4 (adjective) pleasant and satisfying, e.g. *The sweet experience of success.*
5 A sweet smell is soft and fragrant.
6 A sweet sound is gentle and tuneful.
7 attractive and delightful, e.g. *Oh! Isn't that kitten sweet!*
sweetly (adverb), **sweetness** (noun).

Similar words: (sense 7) adorable, cute

sweetbread, sweetbreads
(noun) Sweetbreads are meat obtained from the pancreas of a calf or lamb.

sweet corn
(noun) Sweet corn is a long stalk covered with juicy yellow seeds that can be eaten as a vegetable.

sweeten, sweetens, sweetening, sweetened
(verb) To sweeten food means to add sugar, honey, or another sweet substance to it.

sweetener, sweeteners
(noun) A sweetener is a very sweet, artificial substance that can be used instead of sugar.

sweetheart, sweethearts
1 (noun) You can call someone who you are very fond of 'sweetheart'.
2 A young person's sweetheart is their boyfriend or girlfriend.

sweetmeat, sweetmeats
(noun; an old-fashioned word) Sweetmeats are small delicacies preserved in sugar.

sweet pea, sweet peas
(noun) Sweet peas are delicate, very fragrant climbing flowers.

sweet potato, sweet potatoes
(noun) A sweet potato is a root vegetable with a reddish coloured skin and yellow flesh.

sweet tooth
(noun) If you have a sweet tooth, you like sweet food very much.

sweet william
(noun) Sweet william is a small garden plant with round clusters of coloured flowers.

swell, swells, swelling, swelled, swollen
1 (verb) If something swells, it becomes larger and rounder, e.g. *Joan's foot began to swell.*
2 If an amount swells, it increases in number.
3 If a sound or feeling swells, it becomes more intense.
4 (noun) The regular up and down movement of the waves at sea can be called a swell.

swelling, swellings
1 (noun) A swelling is an enlarged area on your body as a result of injury or illness.
2 The swelling of something is the increase in its size.

swelter, swelters, sweltering, sweltered
(verb) If you swelter, or are sweltering, you are very uncomfortable because it is so hot.
[from Old English *sweltan* meaning 'to die']

swerve, swerves, swerving, swerved
(verb) To swerve means to suddenly change direction to avoid colliding with something.

Similar words: veer, swing, sheer

swift, swifter, swiftest; swifts
1 (adjective) happening or moving very quickly, e.g. *a swift decision.*
2 (noun) A swift is a bird with narrow crescent-shaped wings, which can fly very fast.
swiftly (adverb), **swiftness** (noun).

[from Old English *swifan* meaning 'to turn' or 'to move with a sweeping motion']

swig, swigs, swigging, swigged (an informal word)
1 (verb) To swig a drink means to drink it in large mouthfuls, usually from a bottle.
2 (noun) If you have a swig of a drink, you take a large mouthful of it.

swill, swills, swilling, swilled
1 (verb) To swill something means to pour water over it to clean it, e.g. *Go and swill the bucket out.*
2 (noun) Swill is a liquid mixture containing waste food that is fed to pigs.
[from Old English *swilian* meaning 'to wash out']

swim, swims, swimming, swam, swum
1 (verb) To swim means to move through water using various movements with parts of the body.
2 (noun) If you go for a swim, you go into water to swim for pleasure.
3 (verb) If things are swimming, it seems as if everything you see is moving and you feel dizzy.
swimmer (noun).

swim bladder, swim bladders
(noun) The swim bladder of a fish is a sac filled with air that controls the fish's buoyancy at different depths.

swimming
(adjective) If something is swimming in a liquid, there is too much liquid around it.

swimming bath, swimming baths
(noun) A swimming bath is a public swimming pool.

swimming costume, swimming costumes
(noun) A swimming costume is the clothing worn by a woman when she goes swimming.

swimming pool, swimming pools
(noun) A swimming pool is a large hole that has been tiled and filled with water for swimming.

swimming trunks
(plural noun) Swimming trunks are shorts worn by a man when he goes swimming.

swimsuit, swimsuits
(noun) A swimsuit is a swimming costume.

swindle, swindles, swindling, swindled
1 (verb) To swindle someone means to deceive them to obtain money or property.
2 (noun) A swindle is a deception in which someone is cheated out of money or property.
swindler (noun).
[from German *Schwindler* meaning 'cheat']

swine, swines
1 (noun; an old-fashioned use) Swine are pigs.
2 (an informal use) If you call someone a swine, you mean they are nasty and spiteful.
[from Old English *swin* meaning 'pig']

swing, swings, swinging, swung
1 (verb) If something swings, it moves repeatedly from side to side from a fixed point.
2 If someone or something swings in a particular direction, they turn quickly or move in a sweeping curve in that direction.
3 To swing at someone means to hit them.

4 (noun) A swing is a seat hanging from a frame or a branch, which moves backwards and forwards when you sit on it.
5 A swing in opinion is a significant change in people's opinion.
6 (verb) If opinions or situations swing in a particular direction, they change in that way.
7 (phrase) If something is **in full swing**, it is operating fully and no longer in its early stages.
8 (an informal use) If you get **into the swing** of something, you become familiar with it and understand what you are doing.

swipe, swipes, swiping, swiped
1 (verb) To swipe at something means to try to hit it making a curving movement with the arm.
2 (noun) To take a swipe at something means to swipe at it.
3 (verb; an informal use) To swipe something means to steal it.

swirl, swirls, swirling, swirled
(verb) To swirl means to move quickly in circles, e.g. *bath water swirling down the plughole.*

swish, swishes, swishing, swished
1 (verb) To swish means to move quickly through the air making a soft sound, e.g. *The curtains swished back.*
2 (noun) A swish is the sound made when something swishes.

Swiss
1 (adjective) belonging or relating to Switzerland.
2 (noun) A Swiss is someone who comes from Switzerland.

switch, switches, switching, switched
1 (noun) A switch is a small control for an electrical device or machine.
2 (verb) To switch to a different task or topic means to change to it.
3 (noun) A switch is a change, e.g. *a switch in policy.*
4 (verb) If you switch things, you exchange one for the other.

switch off
1 (phrasal verb) To switch off a light or machine means to stop it working by pressing a switch.
2 (an informal use) If you switch off, you stop paying attention.

switch on
(phrasal verb) To switch on a light or machine means to start it working by means of a switch.

switchback, switchbacks
(noun) A switchback is something, such as a mountain road, which rises and falls sharply many times or which has many sharp bends.

switchboard, switchboards
(noun) The switchboard in an organization is the part where all telephone calls are received and connected.

swivel, swivels, swivelling, swivelled
1 (verb) To swivel means to turn round on a central point.
2 (adjective) A swivel chair or lamp is made so

that you can move the main part of it while the base remains in a fixed position.
[from Old English *swifan* meaning 'to turn']

swollen
(adjective) something that is swollen has swelled up.

Similar words: bloated, distended, puffy

swoon, swoons, swooning, swooned
(verb; a literary word) To swoon means to faint as a result of strong emotion or shock.
[from Old English *geswogen* meaning 'insensible']

swoop, swoops, swooping, swooped
1 (verb) To swoop means to move downwards through the air in a fast curving movement, e.g. *Planes swoop low over the village.*
2 (phrase) If you do something in **one fell swoop**, you achieve it in a single action.
[from Old English *swapan* meaning 'to sweep' or 'to move in a curving movement']

swop another spelling of **swap.**

sword, swords
1 (noun) A sword is a weapon consisting of a very long blade with a short handle.
2 (phrase) To **cross swords** with someone means to have a disagreement with them.

swordfish, swordfishes or **swordfish**
(noun) A swordfish is a large sea fish with a long upper jaw.

sworn
(adjective) If you make a sworn statement, you swear that everything in it is true.

swot, swots, swotting, swotted (an informal word)
1 (verb) To swot means to study or revise very hard.
2 (noun) A swot is someone who spends too much time studying.
3 (verb) If you swot up on a subject you find out as much about it as possible in a short time.

sycamore, sycamores (pronounced **sik**-am-mor)
(noun) A sycamore is a tree that has large leaves with five points. Its seed cases have two wings which spin as they fall.

sycophant, sycophants (pronounced **sik**-off-ant)
(noun; a formal word) A sycophant is someone who praises important people in order to gain some advantage.
sycophantic (adjective).

syllable, syllables
(noun) A syllable is part of a word that contains a single vowel sound and is pronounced as a unit. For example, 'book' has one syllable and 'reading' has two.
syllabic (adjective).

syllabus, syllabuses or **syllabi**
(noun) The subjects that are studied for a particular course or examination are called the syllabus.

sylph, sylphs (pronounced **silf**) (a literary word)

1 (noun) You can refer to a slender, graceful girl as a sylph.
2 A sylph is an imaginary creature believed to live in the air.

sylvan
(adjective; a literary word) relating to woods.
[from Latin *silva* meaning 'wood']

symbiosis (pronounced sim-bee-**oh**-siss)
(noun; a formal word) Symbiosis is a relationship between two organisms which benefits both.
symbiotic (adjective), **symbiotically** (adverb).
[from Greek *sumbiōsis* meaning 'living together']

symbol, symbols
(noun) A symbol is a shape, design, or idea that is used to represent something, e.g. *Huey Newton was an important symbol of Black militancy.*
[from Greek *sumbolon* meaning 'mark' or 'token']

Similar words: emblem, token, sign, logo

symbolic
(adjective) Something that is symbolic has a special meaning that is considered to represent something else, e.g. *The communion wine is symbolic of Christ's blood.*

Similar words: figurative, metaphorical, allegorical

symbolize, symbolizes, symbolizing, symbolized; also spelled **symbolise**
(verb) If a shape, design, or idea symbolizes something, it is regarded as being a symbol of it, e.g. *a dancer in a red robe symbolizing the sun.*
symbolism (noun).

symmetrical
(adjective) If something is symmetrical, it has two halves which are exactly the same, except that one half is the mirror image of the other.
symmetrically (adverb).

symmetry
(noun) Something that has symmetry is symmetrical.
[from Greek *summetria* meaning 'proportion']

sympathetic
1 (adjective) A sympathetic person shows kindness and understanding to other people.
2 If you are sympathetic to a proposal or an idea, you approve of it.

sympathize, sympathizes, sympathizing, sympathized; also spelled **sympathise**
(verb) To sympathize with someone who is in difficulties means to show them understanding and care.

sympathizer, sympathizers; also spelled **sympathiser**
(noun) People who support a particular cause can be referred to as sympathizers.

sympathy, sympathies
1 (noun) Sympathy is kindness and understanding towards someone who is in difficulties.
2 If you have sympathy with someone's ideas or actions, you agree with them.
3 (phrase) If you do something **in sympathy** with

someone, you do it to show your support for them.
[from Greek *sumpathēs* meaning 'sharing a feeling']

Similar words: (sense 1) commiseration, compassion, condolence

symphonic poem, symphonic poems
(noun) A symphonic poem is an orchestral composition based on a work of literature.

symphony, symphonies
(noun) A symphony is a piece of music for an orchestra, usually in four movements.
symphonic (adjective).
[from Greek *sumphōnos* meaning 'harmonious']

symposium, symposiums or **symposia**
(pronounced sim-**poze**-ee-um)
(noun) A symposium is a conference at which experts discuss a particular subject.
[from Greek *sumpinein* meaning 'to drink together and have conversation']

symptom, symptoms
1 (noun) A symptom is something wrong with your body that is a sign of an illness.
2 Something that is considered to be a sign of a bad situation can be referred to as a symptom of it, e.g. *Hunger is chiefly a symptom of poverty.*
symptomatic (adjective).

synagogue, synagogues (pronounced sin-a-gog)
(noun) A synagogue is a building where Jewish people meet for worship and religious instruction.
[from Greek *sunagōgē* meaning 'meeting']

synapse, synapses (pronounced **sigh**-naps)
(noun; a technical word) A synapse is the point at which a nerve impulse is relayed from one nerve cell to another.

synchromesh (pronounced **sing**-kroe-mesh)
(noun) In a gearbox, synchromesh is a system which allows a smooth change of gear by making the gears spin at the same speed before engaging them.

synchronize, synchronizes, synchronizing, synchronized (pronounced **sing**-kron-nize);
also spelled **synchronise**
1 (verb) To synchronize two actions means to do them at the same time and speed.
2 To synchronize watches means to set them to show exactly the same time as each other.
synchronization (noun).

synchronous (pronounced **sing**-kron-nuss)
(adjective) happening at the same time as or during the same phase as something.
[from Greek *sun-* meaning 'together' and *khronos* meaning 'time']

syncopated (pronounced **sing**-ko-pay-ted)
(adjective) A syncopated rhythm is one in which the weak beats are stressed instead of the usual strong ones.
syncopation (noun).
[from Greek *suncopē* meaning 'cutting off']

syndicate, syndicates
(noun) A syndicate is an association of business people formed to carry out a particular project.

syndrome, syndromes
1 (noun) A syndrome is a medical condition characterized by a particular set of symptoms, e.g. *Down's syndrome*.
2 You can refer to a typical set of characteristics as a syndrome, e.g. *The capitalist syndrome of growth, profits, competition*.
[from Greek *sun-* meaning 'together' and *dramein* meaning 'to run']

synergy (sin-er-jee)
(noun) Synergy is a situation in which things work much more effectively together than they would if they were used separately.
[from Greek *sun-* meaning 'together' and *ergon* meaning 'work']

synod, synods
(noun) A synod is a council of church leaders which meets regularly to discuss religious and moral issues.
[from Greek *sunodos* meaning 'meeting']

synonym, synonyms
(noun) If two words have the same or a very similar meaning, they are synonyms.

synonymous
1 (adjective) Two words that are synonymous have the same or very similar meanings.
2 If two thing are closely associated, you can say that one is synonymous with the other, e.g. *The symbol is synonymous with high-quality produce*.
synonymously (adverb).

synopsis, synopses
(noun) A synopsis is a summary of a book, play, or film.

syntax
(noun) The syntax of a language is its grammatical rules and the way its words are arranged.
syntactic (adjective).
[from Greek *suntassein* meaning 'to arrange']

synthesis, syntheses
1 (noun) A synthesis of different ideas or styles is a blended combination of them, e.g. *A synthesis of Jewish theology and Greek philosophy*.
2 The synthesis of a substance is its production by means of a chemical reaction, e.g. *We need sunlight for the synthesis of vitamin D*.
synthesize (verb).
[from Greek *suntithenai* meaning 'to put together']

synthesizer, synthesizers; also spelled **synthesiser**
(noun) A synthesizer is an electronic machine that creates music or speech sounds from electronic signals rather than by playing a prerecorded tape or disc.

synthetic
1 (adjective) made from artificial substances rather than natural ones.
2 not sincere or genuine, e.g. *a synthetic smile*.

syphilis (pronounced **siff**-ill-iss)
(noun) Syphilis is a type of venereal disease.

syphon another spelling of **siphon**.

Syrian, Syrians (pronounced **sirr**-ee-an)
1 (adjective) belonging or relating to Syria.
2 (noun) A Syrian is someone who comes from Syria.

syringe, syringes, syringing, syringed
(pronounced **sir**-inj)
1 (noun) A syringe is a hollow tube with a plunger and a fine hollow needle. Syringes are used for injecting or extracting liquids.
2 (verb) To syringe part of the body means to clean it by extracting a substance with a syringe, e.g. *He needs to go to have his ears syringed*.
[from Greek *surinx* meaning 'pipe' or 'tube']

syrup, syrups
(noun) Syrup is a thick sweet liquid made by boiling sugar with water.
syrupy (adjective).
[from Arabic *sharab* meaning 'drink']

system, systems
1 (noun) A system is an organized way of doing or arranging something according to a fixed plan or set of rules.
2 People sometimes refer to the government and administration of the country as the system.
3 You can also refer to a set of equipment as a system, e.g. *a stereo system*.
4 In biology, a system of a particular kind is the set of organs that perform that function, e.g. *the digestive system*.
[from Greek *sustēma* meaning 'organized whole']

Similar words: (sense 1) process, procedure, routine

systematic
(adjective) following a fixed plan and done in an efficient way, e.g. *a systematic search*.
systematically (adverb).

systematize, systematizes, systematizing, systematized; also spelled **systematise**
(verb) To systematize things means to organize them according to a system.

systems analysis
(noun) In computing, systems analysis is analysis of methods used so that a more efficient system can be designed.
systems analyst (noun).

T

tab, tabs
1 (noun) A tab is a small piece of paper or cloth that is attached to something, especially a garment.
2 (an informal phrase) If you **keep tabs** on someone, you make sure that you always know where they are and what they are doing.

tabby, tabbies
(noun) A tabby is a cat whose fur has grey, brown, or black stripes.
[from Old French *tabis* meaning 'striped silk cloth']

tabernacle, tabernacles (pronounced tab-er-nak-kl)
1 (noun) A tabernacle is a place of worship used by some religious groups including the Mormons.
2 A tabernacle is also an ornamental box or cupboard in which the bread and wine for the Christian service of Holy Communion is kept.
[from Latin *tabernaculum* meaning 'tent']

table, tables, tabling, tabled
1 (noun) A table is a piece of furniture with a flat horizontal top supported by one or more legs.
2 A table is a set of facts or figures arranged in rows or columns.
3 (phrase) If you **turn the tables** on someone, you change the situation completely, so that they have the problems they were causing you.
4 (verb) If you table something such as a proposal, you say formally that you want it to be discussed.

tableau, tableaux or tableaus (pronounced tab-loh)
(noun) A tableau is a scene from history or a legend, represented by actors in costumes.
[short for French *tableau vivant*, meaning 'living picture']

tablecloth, tablecloths
(noun) A tablecloth is a cloth used to cover a table and keep it clean.

table d'hôte (pronounced tah-bl dote)
(noun) In a restaurant, the table d'hôte is a meal consisting of a set number of courses with a limited choice of dishes at a fixed price.
[a French expression, meaning literally 'the host's table']

tablespoon, tablespoons
1 (noun) A tablespoon is a large spoon used for serving food.
2 A tablespoon or tablespoonful is the amount that a tablespoon contains.

tablet, tablets
1 (noun) A tablet is any small, round pill made of powdered medicine.
2 A tablet of soap is a flattish block of it.
3 A stone tablet is a slab of stone with words cut into it.

table tennis
(noun) Table tennis is a game for two or four people in which you use bats to hit a small hollow ball over a low net across a table.

tableware
(noun) Tableware is the crockery and cutlery that you use when you eat a meal.

tabloid, tabloids
(noun) A tabloid is a newspaper with small pages, short news stories, and lots of photographs.

taboo, taboos
1 (noun) A taboo is a religious custom that forbids people to do something.
2 A taboo is a social custom that some words, subjects, or actions must be avoided because they are considered embarrassing or offensive, e.g. *the old taboo against talking about death*.
3 (adjective) forbidden or disapproved of, e.g. *a taboo subject*.

tabor, tabors (pronounced tay-bor)
(noun) A tabor was a small medieval drum that was struck with one hand.

tabular
(adjective) arranged in the form of a table or list.

tabulate, tabulates, tabulating, tabulated
(verb) If you tabulate information, you arrange it in columns or rows.
tabulation (noun).

tabulator, tabulators
(noun) A tabulator is a device on a typewriter that moves the carriage quickly to a particular place on the line.

tachometer, tachometers (pronounced tak-kom-it-er)
(noun) A tachometer is a device for measuring speed, especially the number of revolutions per minute of the engine of a car.

tacit (pronounced tass-it)
(adjective) understood or implied without actually being said or written.
tacitly (adverb).
[from Latin *tacere* meaning 'to be silent']

taciturn (pronounced tass-it-urn)
(adjective) Someone who is taciturn does not talk very much and so seems unfriendly.
taciturnly (adverb), **taciturnity** (noun).

tack, tacks, tacking, tacked
1 (noun) A tack is a short nail with a broad, flat head.
2 (verb) If you tack something to a surface, you nail it there with tacks.
3 (noun) A tack is also a long, loose stitch used in dressmaking.
4 (verb) If you tack a piece of fabric, you sew it with long loose stitches.
5 In sailing, when you tack, you steer the boat in a series of zigzags to take advantage of the wind.

6 (noun) If you change tack, you start to use a different method for dealing with something.
7 Tack is the equipment used for horseriding.
[senses 1-6 are from Middle English *tak* meaning 'nail'; sense 7 is short for 'tackle']

tackle, tackles, tackling, tackled
1 (verb) If you tackle a difficult task, you start dealing with it in a determined way.
2 If you tackle someone in a game such as football, you try to get the ball away from them.
3 (noun) A tackle in sport is an attempt to get the ball away from your opponent.
4 (verb) If you tackle someone about something, you talk to them about it in order to get something changed or dealt with.
5 (noun) Tackle is the equipment used for fishing.

Similar words: (sense 1) undertake, take on

tacky, tackier, tackiest
1 (adjective) slightly sticky to touch, e.g. *the paint was still tacky.*
2 (an informal use) badly made and unpleasant, e.g. *tacky furniture.*

tact
(noun) Tact is the ability to see when a situation is difficult or delicate and to handle it without upsetting or offending people.
tactful (adjective), **tactfully** (adverb),
tactless (adjective), **tactlessly** (adverb).

Similar words: discretion, diplomacy, delicacy, sensitivity

tactic, tactics
1 (noun) Tactics are the methods you use to achieve what you want.
2 Tactics are also the ways in which troops and equipment are used in order to win a battle.

tactical
(adjective) Tactical weapons are used over fairly short distances.
tactically (adverb).

tactician, tacticians (pronounced tak-**tish**-shn)
(noun) A tactician is a person who is skilled in using tactics in war.

tactile
(adjective) involving the sense of touch.
[from Latin *tactilis* meaning 'able to be touched']

tadpole, tadpoles
(noun) Tadpoles are the larvae of frogs and toads. They are black with round heads and long tails and live in water.
[from Middle English *tadde* meaning 'toad' and *pol* meaning 'head']

taffeta (pronounced **taf**-fit-a)
(noun) Taffeta is a stiff, shiny fabric made of silk, nylon, or rayon.
[from Persian *taftah* meaning 'spun']

tag, tags, tagging, tagged
1 (noun) A tag is a small label made of cloth, paper, plastic, or leather.
2 (verb) If you tag something, you attach a tag to it.

3 (noun) Tag is a children's game in which one child chases the others and tries to touch them.
4 (verb) If you tag along with someone, you go with them or behind them.

tail, tails, tailing, tailed
1 (noun) The tail of an animal, bird, or fish is the part extending beyond the end of its body.
2 Tail can be used to mean the end or concluding part of something, e.g. *the tail of the storm.*
3 (plural noun) If a man is wearing tails, he is wearing a formal jacket which has two long pieces hanging down at the back.
4 (verb; an informal use) If you tail someone, you follow them in order to find out where they go and what they do.
5 (adjective and adverb) The tails side of a coin is the side which does not have a person's head.

tail off
(phrasal verb) If something tails off, it becomes gradually less.

tailback, tailbacks
(noun) A tailback is a long queue of traffic stretching back from whatever is blocking the road.

tailboard, tailboards
(noun) A tailboard is a large door at the back of a lorry which can be removed or let down on a hinge.

tailgate, tailgates
(noun) A tailgate is the same as a tailboard.

taillight, taillights
(noun) A taillight is a red light at the back of a car or lorry that lights up when the headlights are on.

tailor, tailors, tailoring, tailored
1 (noun) A tailor is a person who makes, alters, and repairs clothes, especially for men.
2 (verb) If something is tailored for a particular purpose, it is specially designed for it.
tailored (adjective).
[from Old French *tailleur* meaning 'cutter']

tailor-made
(adjective) suitable for a particular person or purpose, or specifically designed for them.

tailwind, tailwinds
(noun) A tailwind is a wind blowing in the same direction as a vehicle is travelling.

taint, taints, tainting, tainted
1 (verb) To taint something means to spoil it by adding something undesirable to it.
2 (noun) A taint is an undesirable quality in something which spoils it.
tainted (adjective).
[from Old French *teindre* meaning 'to dye']

take, takes, taking, took, taken
1 (verb) Take is used to show what action or activity is being done, e.g. *She took a bath... What exams are you taking?... She took an interest in us.*
2 If something takes a certain amount of time, or a particular quality or ability, it requires it, e.g. *It took a lot of effort to get him to come.*
3 If you take something, you put your hand

round it and hold it or carry it, e.g. *Here, let me take your luggage for you.*
4 If you take someone somewhere, you drive them there by car or lead them there.
5 If you take something that is offered to you, you accept it, e.g. *She took the job.*
6 If you take the responsibility or blame for something, you accept responsibility or blame.
7 If you take something that does not belong to you, you steal it.
8 If you take pills or medicine, you swallow them.
9 If you can take something painful, you can bear it, e.g. *I can't take her criticism.*
10 If you take someone's advice or orders, you do what they say you should do.
11 If you take a person's temperature or pulse, you measure it.
12 If you take a car or train, or a road or route, you use it to go from one place to another.
13 (noun) In filming, a take is a short piece of action filmed without stopping the camera.

take after
(phrasal verb) If you take after someone in your family, you look or behave like them.

take down
(phrasal verb) If you take down what someone is saying or has written, you write it down.

take in
1 (phrasal verb) If someone is taken in, they are deceived.
2 If you take something in, you understand it.

take off
1 (phrasal verb) When an aeroplane takes off, it leaves the ground and begins to fly.
2 To take time off means to stay away from work.
3 (an informal use) If you take someone off, you imitate them in an amusing way to make people laugh.
takeoff (noun).

take on
1 (phrasal verb) If you take on a job or responsibility, you accept it.
2 To take someone on means to employ them.
3 If you take on a person, you fight them or compete against them.

take over
(phrasal verb) To take something over means to start controlling it.
takeover (noun).

take to
1 (phrasal verb) If you take to someone or something, you like them immediately.
2 If you take to doing something, you begin to do it regularly, e.g. *She took to eating oranges daily.*

takeaway, takeaways
1 (noun) A takeaway is a shop or restaurant that sells hot cooked food to be eaten elsewhere.
2 A takeaway is a hot cooked meal bought from a takeaway.

takings
(plural noun) Takings are the money that a shop,

theatre, or cinema gets from selling its goods or tickets.

talc
1 (noun) Talc is a white, grey, or pale green mineral used to make talcum powder.
2 Talc is also talcum powder.
[a Persian word]

talcum powder
(noun) Talcum powder is a soft perfumed powder made of purified talc and used for absorbing moisture on the body.

tale, tales
(noun) A tale is a story.

talent, talents
(noun) Talent is the natural ability to do something well.
talented (adjective).

Similar words: knack, gift, flair

talent scout, talent scouts
(noun) A talent scout is someone whose job is to find and employ talented people, especially in show business.

talisman, talismans (pronounced **tal**-iz-man)
(noun) A talisman is an object which you believe has magic powers to protect you or bring luck.
[from Greek *telesma* meaning 'holy object']

talk, talks, talking, talked
1 (verb) When you talk, you say things to someone.
2 If people talk, especially about other people's private affairs, they gossip about them, e.g. *We mustn't be seen together or people will talk.*
3 (noun) Talk is discussion or gossip.
4 (verb) If you talk on or about something, you make an informal speech about it.
5 (noun) A talk is an informal speech about something.

talk down
(phrasal verb) If you talk down to someone, you talk to them in a way that shows that you think you are more important or clever than them.

talkative
(adjective) talking a lot.

Similar words: garrulous, loquacious, chatty, voluble

talking-to
(noun; an informal expression) If you give someone a talking-to, you tell them off about something they have done wrong.

tall, taller, tallest
1 (adjective) of more than average or normal height.
2 having a particular height, e.g. *She was five feet tall.*
3 (phrase) If you say that a task is **a tall order**, you mean that it will be difficult to do.
4 If you describe something as **a tall story**, you mean that it is difficult to believe because it is so unlikely.

tallboy, tallboys
(noun) A tallboy is a tall chest of drawers made in two sections placed on top of one another.

tallow
(noun) Tallow is the melted fat of animals such as cattle and sheep, which is used for making soap, candles, and some foods.

tally, tallies, tallying, tallied
1 (noun) A tally is an informal record of amounts which you keep adding to as you go along, e.g. *Are you keeping a tally of the score?*
2 (verb) If numbers or statements tally, they are exactly the same or they give the same results or conclusions.

Talmud (pronounced **tal**-mood)
(noun) The Talmud consists of the books containing the ancient Jewish ceremonies and civil laws.
[a Hebrew word meaning literally 'instruction']

talon, talons
(noun) Talons are sharp, hooked claws, especially of a bird of prey.
[from Latin *talus* meaning 'heel']

tamarind, tamarinds (pronounced **tam**-ar-ind)
(noun) A tamarind is a type of tropical evergreen tree; also the fruit and wood of this tree.
[from Arabic *tamr hindi* meaning 'Indian date']

tambourine, tambourines
(noun) A tambourine is a percussion instrument made up of a skin stretched tightly over a circular frame with small round pieces of metal around the edge.
[from Old French *tambourin* meaning 'little drum']

tame, tamer, tamest; tames, taming, tamed
1 (adjective) A tame animal or bird is not afraid of people and is not violent towards them.
2 Something that is tame is uninteresting and lacks excitement or risk, e.g. *It was a tame film.*
3 (verb) If you tame people or things, you bring them under control.
4 To tame a wild animal or bird means to train it to be obedient and live with humans.
tamely (adverb), **tameness** (noun).

Tamil, Tamils
1 (noun) Tamil is a language spoken in the state of Tamil Nadu in southern India and in Sri Lanka.
2 A Tamil is a member of the group of people from Tamil Nadu and Sri Lanka who speak Tamil.

tamper, tampers, tampering, tampered
(verb) If you tamper with something, you interfere or meddle with it.

tampon, tampons
(noun) A tampon is a firm, specially shaped piece of cotton wool that a woman places inside her vagina to absorb the blood during her period.
[from French *tampon* meaning 'plug']

tan, tans, tanning, tanned
1 (noun) If you have a tan, your skin is darker than usual because you have been in the sun.
2 (verb) When you tan, your skin becomes darker because it is exposed to a lot of sun.
3 To tan an animal's hide means to turn it into leather by treating it with tannin or other chemicals.

4 (adjective) Something that is tan is of a light yellowish-brown colour, e.g. *tan shoes.*
tanned (adjective).

tandem, tandems
(noun) A tandem is a bicycle designed for two riders sitting one behind the other.

tandoori (pronounced tan-**doo**-ree)
(noun) Tandoori is an Indian method of cooking meat in a clay oven.
[an Urdu word]

tang, tangs
(noun) A tang is a strong, sharp smell or flavour, e.g. *This sauce has a real tang to it.*
tangy (adjective).

tangent, tangents
1 (noun) A tangent of a curve is any straight line that touches the curve at one point only.
2 A tangent is also a function of an angle. If B is the right angle in a right-angled triangle ABC, the tangent of the angle at A is BC divided by AB.
3 (phrase) If you **go off at a tangent**, you start talking or thinking about something that is not completely relevant to what has gone before.
[from Latin *tangere* meaning 'to touch']

tangential (pronounced tan-**jen**-shal)
1 (adjective) involving a tangent.
2 not completely relevant to what has gone before.

tangerine, tangerines
1 (noun) A tangerine is a type of small sweet orange with a loose rind. It is named after Tangier in Morocco.
2 (noun and adjective) reddish-orange.

tangible (pronounced **tan**-jib-bl)
(adjective) clear or definite enough to be easily seen, felt, or noticed, e.g. *tangible evidence.*
tangibly (adverb).
[from Latin *tangere* meaning 'to touch']

tangle, tangles, tangling, tangled
1 (noun) A tangle is a mass of things such as hairs, lines, or fibres knotted or coiled together and difficult to separate.
2 (verb) If you are tangled in wires or ropes, you are caught or trapped in them so that it is difficult to get free.
3 (noun) A complicated problem or a state of disorder and confusion can be called a tangle.

tango, tangos, tangoing, tangoed
1 (noun) A tango is a Latin American dance using long gliding steps and sudden pauses; also a piece of music composed for this dance.
2 (verb) To tango means to dance a tango.

tank, tanks
1 (noun) A tank is a large container for storing liquid or gas.
2 A tank is also an armoured military vehicle which moves on tracks and is equipped with guns or rockets.

tankard, tankards
(noun) A tankard is a large metal mug used for drinking beer.

tanker, tankers
(noun) A tanker is a ship, lorry, or aeroplane

designed to carry large quantities of gas or liquid, e.g. *an oil tanker.*

tanner, tanners
(noun) A tanner is a person who makes leather from animal skins.

tannery, tanneries
(noun) A tannery is a place where animal skins are made into leather.

tannin
(noun) Tannin is a brown or yellow substance found in plants and used in making leather.

tantalize, tantalizes, tantalizing, tantalized; also spelled **tantalise**
(verb) If something or someone tantalizes you, they tease you by making you feel hopeful and excited and then do not allow you to have what you want.
tantalizing (adjective), **tantalizingly** (adverb).

tantamount
(adjective) If you say that something is tantamount to something else, you mean that it is almost the same as it, e.g. *His statement was tantamount to lies.*
[from Anglo-French *tant amunter* meaning 'to amount to as much']

tantrum, tantrums
(noun) A tantrum is a noisy and sometimes violent outburst of temper, especially by a child.

Tanzanian, Tanzanians (pronounced tan-zan-**nee**-an)
1 (adjective) belonging or relating to Tanzania.
2 (noun) A Tanzanian is someone who comes from Tanzania.

tap, taps, tapping, tapped
1 (noun) A tap is a device that you turn in order to control the flow of liquid or gas from a pipe or container.
2 (phrase) If something is **on tap**, it is ready to be used immediately.
3 (verb) If you tap a resource or situation, you make use of it by getting what you want from it.
4 If a telephone is tapped, a device is fitted to it so that someone can listen secretly to the calls.
5 If you tap something or tap on it, you hit it lightly.
6 (noun) A tap is the action of hitting something lightly; also the sound that this action makes.

tap-dancing
(noun) Tap-dancing is a type of dancing in which the dancers wear special shoes with pieces of metal on the toes and heels. The shoes make clicking noises as the dancers move their feet.
tap-dance (verb), **tap-dancer** (noun).

tape, tapes, taping, taped
1 (noun) Tape is plastic ribbon covered with a magnetic substance and used to record sounds, pictures, and computer information.
2 A tape is a cassette or spool with magnetic tape wound round it.
3 (verb) If you tape music, sounds, or television pictures, you record them using a tape recorder or a video recorder.

4 (noun) Tape is a long, thin strip of fabric that is used for binding or fastening.
5 In a race, the tape is a ribbon stretched across the finishing line and broken by the winner.
6 Tape is also a strip of sticky plastic which you use for sticking things together.
7 (verb) If you tape one thing to another, you attach them using sticky tape.

tape deck, tape decks
(noun) A tape deck is a part of a hi-fi system that contains all the equipment necessary for the playing and recording of tapes.

tape measure, tape measures
(noun) A tape measure is a strip of plastic, cloth, or metal that is marked off in inches or centimetres and used for measuring things.

taper, tapers, tapering, tapered
1 (verb) Something that tapers gradually becomes thinner towards one end.
2 Something that tapers off becomes gradually smaller, e.g. *The baby boom is tapering off.*
3 (noun) A taper is a thin candle.

tape recorder, tape recorders
(noun) A tape recorder is a machine used for recording sounds onto magnetic tape, and for reproducing these sounds.
tape recording (noun).

tapestry, tapestries
(noun) A tapestry is a piece of heavy cloth with designs embroidered on it.
[from Old French *tapisserie* meaning 'carpeting']

tapeworm, tapeworms
(noun) A tapeworm is a type of flat parasitic worm which lives in the intestines of some animals.

tapioca (pronounced tap-ee-**oh**-ka)
(noun) Tapioca is a starchy substance obtained from dried cassava root. It looks like tiny beads and is used in puddings and soups.
[an American Indian word]

tapir, tapirs (pronounced **tay**-per)
(noun) A tapir is a large piglike mammal from South and Central America and south east Asia. It has a long snout and short legs.

tappet, tappets
(noun) A tappet is a lever in an engine that moves up and down, transferring movement from one part of the engine to another.

taproot, taproots
(noun) The taproot of a plant is the main root.

tar, tars, tarring, tarred
1 (noun) Tar is a thick, black, sticky substance which comes from distilling coal, wood, or peat.
2 To tar something means to coat it in tar.
tarred (adjective).

taramasalata (pronounced tar-ram-as-sal-**lah**-ta)
(noun) Taramasalata is a Greek fish pâté made of smoked cod's roe.

tarantula, tarantulas (pronounced tar-**rant**-yoo-la)

(noun) A tarantula is a large, hairy poisonous spider found in Southern Europe and America.

tardy, tardier, tardiest
(adjective; a literary word) happening later or more slowly than expected.
tardily (adverb), **tardiness** (noun).

target, targets
1 (noun) A target is something which you aim at when firing weapons.
2 The target of an action or remark is the person or thing at which it is directed, e.g. *Her brother was always the target for her sarcasm.*
3 Your target is the result that you are trying to achieve.
[from Old French *targette* meaning 'little shield']

tariff, tariffs
1 (noun) A tariff is a tax that a government collects on imported goods.
2 A tariff is any list of prices or charges.
[from Arabic *tarifa* meaning 'to notify']

tarmac
(noun) Tarmac is a material used for making road surfaces. It consists of crushed stones mixed with tar.
[short for *tarmacadam*, from the name of John McAdam, the Scottish engineer who invented it]

tarn, tarns
(noun) A tarn is a small mountain lake or pool.

tarnish, tarnishes, tarnishing, tarnished
1 (verb) If metal tarnishes, it becomes stained and loses its shine.
2 If something tarnishes your reputation, it spoils it and causes people to lose their respect for you.
tarnished (adjective).

tarot (pronounced **tar**-roh)
(noun) A tarot card is one of a special pack of cards used for fortune-telling.

tarpaulin, tarpaulins
(noun) A tarpaulin is a sheet of heavy waterproof material used as a protective covering.

tarragon
(noun) Tarragon is a herb with narrow green leaves used in cooking.

tarry, tarries, tarrying, tarried
(verb; an old-fashioned word) To tarry means to wait, or to stay somewhere for a little longer.

tarsus
(noun) Your tarsus consists of all the bones in your ankle and heel.
[from Greek *tarsos* meaning 'instep']

tart, tarts; tarter, tartest
1 (noun) A tart is a pastry case with a sweet filling.
2 (adjective) Something that is tart is sour or sharp to taste.
3 A tart remark is unpleasant and cruel.
[sense 1 is from Old French *tarte*; senses 2 and 3 are from Old English *teart* meaning 'rough']

tartan, tartans
(noun) Tartan is a woollen fabric from Scotland

with checks of various colours and sizes, depending on which clan it belongs to.

tartar, tartars
1 (noun) Tartar is a hard, crusty deposit on the teeth, made up of saliva, food, and mineral salts.
2 (an old-fashioned use) A tartar is a frightening or cruel person.
[sense 1 is from Latin *tartarum*; sense 2 is from the name of the *Tartars*, Genghis Khan's fierce warriors]

task, tasks
(noun) A task is any piece of work which has to be done.

Similar words: chore, assignment, mission, undertaking

task force, task forces
1 (noun) A task force is a small section of the army, navy, or air force that is sent out on a particular mission.
2 A task force is also any group set up to carry out a particular task.

taskmaster, taskmasters
(noun) Someone who is a hard taskmaster gives people a lot of difficult or tiring work.

tassel, tassels
(noun) A tassel is a tuft of loose threads tied by a knot and used for decoration.

taste, tastes, tasting, tasted
1 (noun) Your sense of taste is your ability to recognize the flavour of things in your mouth.
2 The taste of something is its flavour.
3 If you have a taste of food or drink, you have a small amount of it to see what it is like.
4 (verb) When you can taste something in your mouth, you are aware of its flavour.
5 If you taste food or drink, you have a small amount of it to see what it is like.
6 If food or drink tastes of something, it has that flavour.
7 (noun) If you have a taste for something, you enjoy it, e.g. *He had a taste for the high life.*
8 If you have a taste of something, you experience it, e.g. *She's had a taste of work.*
9 A person's taste is their choice in the things they like to buy or have around them, e.g. *His taste in clothes is appalling.*

Similar words: (sense 6) savour, smack (sense 7) relish

taste bud, taste buds
(noun) Your taste buds are very small oval-shaped sensory organs on the surface of your tongue which enable you to taste things.

tasteful
(adjective) attractive and elegant.
tastefully (adverb).

tasteless
1 (adjective) vulgar and unattractive.
2 A tasteless remark or joke is offensive.
3 Tasteless food has very little flavour.
tastelessly (adverb).

tasty, tastier, tastiest
(adjective) having a pleasant flavour.

tatter, tatters
(noun) A tatter is any torn piece of fabric hanging loose.
tattered (adjective).

tatting
(noun) Tatting is a type of lace.

tattle, tattles, tattling, tattled
1 (verb) To tattle means to gossip about other people or to reveal their secrets.
2 (noun) Tattle is gossip.

tattoo, tattoos, tattooing, tattooed
1 (verb) If someone tattoos you or tattoos a design on you, they draw it on your skin by pricking little holes and filling them with coloured dye.
2 (noun) A tattoo is a picture or design tattooed on someone's body.
3 If you beat a tattoo, you hit something quickly and repeatedly.
4 A tattoo is also a public military display of exercises and music.

tatty, tattier, tattiest
(adjective) worn out or untidy and rather dirty.

taught the past tense and past participle of
teach.

taunt, taunts, taunting, taunted
1 (verb) To taunt someone means to speak offensively to them about their weaknesses or failures in order to make them angry or upset.
2 A taunt is an offensive remark intended to make a person angry or upset.

Taurus
(noun) Taurus is the second sign of the zodiac, represented by a bull. People born between April 20th and May 20th are born under this sign.
[from Latin *taurus* meaning 'bull']

taut
(adjective) stretched very tight, e.g. *a taut rope.*

tauten, tautens, tautening, tautened
(verb) To tauten something means to make it become very tight or tense.

tautology, tautologies
(noun) Tautology is using different words to say the same thing twice in the same sentence.
tautological (adjective).

tavern, taverns
(noun; an old-fashioned word) A tavern is a pub.
[from Latin *taberna* meaning 'hut' or 'stall']

tawdry, tawdrier, tawdriest (pronounced taw-dree)
(adjective) cheap, gaudy, and of poor quality.

tawny
(noun and adjective) brownish-yellow.

tax, taxes, taxing, taxed
1 (noun) Tax is an amount of money that citizens have to pay to the government so that it can provide public services such as health care and education.
2 (verb) If a sum of money is taxed, a proportion of it has to be paid to the government.

3 If goods are taxed, a proportion of their price has to be paid to the government.
4 If a person or company is taxed, they have to pay a proportion of their income to the government.
5 If something taxes you, it makes heavy demands on you, e.g. *The climb had taxed his strength.*
6 (a formal use) If you tax someone with something, you accuse them of it or blame them for it.
taxing (adjective), **taxable** (adjective),
taxation (noun).

Similar words: (sense 1) duty, excise, levy, tariff

tax-free
(adjective) Tax-free goods or services are those on which you do not have to pay tax.

taxi, taxis, taxiing, taxied
1 (noun) A taxi or taxicab is a car with a driver which you hire to take you to where you want to go.
2 (verb) When an aeroplane taxis, it moves slowly along the runway before taking off or after landing.

taxidermist, taxidermists (pronounced tak-sid-der-mist)
(noun) A taxidermist is a person who preserves and stuffs animal skins.
taxidermy (noun).
[from Greek *taxis* meaning 'arrangement' and *derma* meaning 'skin']

taxpayer, taxpayers
(noun) Taxpayers are people who pay a proportion of their income to the government as tax.

tea, teas
1 (noun) Tea is the dried leaves of an evergreen shrub found in Asia.
2 Tea is a drink made by brewing the leaves of the tea plant in hot water; also a cup of this.
3 Tea is also any drink made with hot water and leaves or flowers, e.g. *mint tea.*
4 Tea is a meal taken in the late afternoon or early evening.

tea bag, tea bags
(noun) A tea bag is a small paper bag with tea leaves in it which is placed in boiling water to make tea.

teacake, teacakes
(noun) A teacake is a type of large currant bun that is often split in half and toasted.

teach, teaches, teaching, taught
1 (verb) If you teach someone something, you give them instructions so that they know about it or know how to do it.
2 If you teach a subject, you help students learn about a subject at school, college, or university.
3 If you teach someone to think or behave in a certain way, you persuade them to think or behave in that way, e.g. *We are taught to respect our elders.*
teacher (noun), **teaching** (noun).

teak
(noun) Teak is a hard wood which comes from a large Asian tree.

teal, teals
(noun) A teal is a type of small duck.

team, teams, teaming, teamed
1 (noun) A team is a group of people who play together against another group in a sport or game.
2 Any group of people who work together can be called a team, e.g. *a team of engineers*.
3 (verb) If you team up with someone, you join them and work together with them.

Similar words: (sense 2) company, crew, squad

team spirit
(noun) Team spirit is a willingness to work together as a team.

teamwork
(noun) Teamwork is the ability of a group of people to work well together.

teapot, teapots
(noun) A teapot is a round pot with a handle, a lid, and a spout.

tear, tears (rhymes with **peer**)
(noun) Tears are the drops of salty liquid that come out of your eyes when you cry.

tear, tears, tearing, tore, torn (rhymes with **hair**)
1 (verb) If you tear something, it is damaged by being pulled so that a hole appears in it.
2 (noun) A tear in something is a hole that has been made in it.
3 (verb) If you tear something from somewhere, you remove it roughly and violently, e.g. *He tore the book out of her hands.*
4 If you tear somewhere, you rush or race there, e.g. *He tore out of the house.*

Similar words: (sense 2) rend, rip, rupture

tear away
(phrasal verb) If you tear yourself away from somewhere, you come away very reluctantly.

tearaway, tearaways
(noun) A tearaway is someone who is wild and uncontrollable.

teardrop, teardrops
(noun) A teardrop is a single tear that falls from your eye.

tearful
(adjective) about to cry or crying gently.
tearfully (adverb), **tearfulness** (noun).

tear gas
(noun) Tear gas is a gas that causes your eyes to sting and water. It is used by the police or the army to control crowds in riots.

tear-jerker, tear-jerkers
(noun; an informal expression) A tear-jerker is a play or film that is very sad and makes people cry.

tease, teases, teasing, teased
1 (verb) If you tease someone, you deliberately make fun of them or embarrass them because it amuses you.
2 (noun) Someone who is a tease enjoys teasing people.
teasing (adjective and noun).

teaspoon, teaspoons
(noun) A teaspoon is a small spoon used for stirring drinks; also the amount that a teaspoon holds.

teat, teats
1 (noun) A teat is a nipple on a female animal.
2 A teat is also a piece of rubber or plastic that is shaped like a nipple and fitted to a baby's feeding bottle.

tech, techs (pronounced **tek**)
(noun; an informal word) A tech is a technical college.

technical
1 (adjective) involving machines, processes, and materials used in industry, transport, and communications.
2 skilled in practical and mechanical things rather than theories and ideas.
3 involving a specialized field of activity, e.g. *the technical jargon of computer science.*
[from Greek *tekhnē* meaning 'art' or 'skill']

technical college, technical colleges
(noun) A technical college is a college where you can study subjects to GCSE and 'A' level, usually as part of the qualifications and training required for a particular job.

technicality
1 (noun) The technicalities of a process or activity are the detailed methods used to do it.
2 A technicality is a point that is based on a strict interpretation of a law or a set of rules.

technically
(adverb) If something is technically true or correct, it is true or correct when you consider only the facts, rules, or laws, but may not be important or relevant in a particular situation, e.g. *Technically, you are breaking the law.*

technician, technicians
(noun) A technician is someone who is employed in a laboratory or technical college and whose job involves skilled practical work with scientific equipment.

Technicolor
(noun; a trademark) Technicolor is a process of making colour films by putting different colour film of the same scene on top of each other to obtain the final colour.

technique, techniques
1 (noun) A technique is a particular method of doing something, e.g. *The different techniques of printing.*
2 Technique is skill and ability in an activity which is developed through training and

practice, e.g. *Her swimming technique was perfect.*

technologist, technologists
(noun) A technologist is an expert in technology.

technology, technologies
1 (noun) Technology is the study of the application of science and scientific knowledge for practical purposes in industry, farming, medicine, or business.
2 A technology is a particular area of activity that requires scientific methods and knowledge, e.g. *industrial technology.*
technological (adjective), **technologically** (adverb).

tectonic
(adjective) relating to or involving the geological forces that shape the earth's crust.

teddy, teddies
(noun) A teddy or teddy bear is a stuffed toy that looks something like a friendly bear. [named after the American President Theodore (Teddy) Roosevelt, who hunted bears]

tedious (pronounced **tee**-dee-uss)
(adjective) boring and lasting for a long time, e.g. *a rather tedious history lesson.*
tediously (adverb).

tedium (pronounced **tee**-dee-um)
(noun) Tedium is the quality of being boring and lasting for a long time, e.g. *the tedium of waiting.*

tee, tees, teeing, teed
1 (noun) A tee is a level area of ground from which a golfer hits their first ball.
2 A tee is also the small wooden or plastic peg on which the golf ball is placed.
3 (verb) To tee off means to hit the golf ball from the tee, or to start a round of golf.

teem, teems, teeming, teemed
1 (verb) If it teems, it rains very heavily, e.g. *It's teeming down.*
2 If a place is teeming with people, there are a lot of them moving about.
teeming (adjective).

teenage
1 (adjective) aged between thirteen and nineteen.
2 typical of people aged between thirteen and nineteen, e.g. *teenage music.*
teenager (noun).

teens
(plural noun) Your teens are the period of your life when you are between thirteen and nineteen years old.

teenybopper, teenyboppers
(noun; an informal word) A teenybopper is a young teenager who is very interested in pop music and fashion.

tee shirt another spelling of **T-shirt.**

teeter, teeters, teetering, teetered
(verb) To teeter means to shake or sway slightly in an unsteady way and seem about to fall over.

teeth the plural of **tooth.**

teethe, teethes, teething, teethed
(rhymes with **breathe**)

(verb) When babies are teething, their teeth are starting to come through, usually causing them pain.
teething (noun).

teething troubles
(noun) Teething troubles are problems which arise at the beginning of a project or when something is new.

teetotal (pronounced tee-**toe**-tl)
(adjective) Someone who is teetotal never drinks alcohol.
teetotaller (noun).

Teflon
(noun; a trademark) Teflon is a tough, waxy plastic which is used on objects which need a nonstick surface, e.g. *a Teflon frying pan.*

telecommunications
(noun) Telecommunications is the science and activity of sending signals and messages over long distances using electronic equipment.

telegram, telegrams
(noun) A telegram is a message sent by telegraph.

telegraph, telegraphs, telegraphing, telegraphed
1 (noun) The telegraph is a system of sending messages over long distances by means of electrical or radio signals.
2 (verb) If you telegraph someone, you send them a message by telegraph.
telegraphic (adjective), **telegraphy** (noun). [from Greek *tele* meaning 'far' and *graphein* meaning 'to write']

telegraphist, telegraphists
(noun) A telegraphist is a person whose job is to send messages by telegraph.

telekinesis (pronounced tel-ik-in-**nee**-siss)
(noun) Telekinesis is the movement of objects by means of thought or willpower. [from Greek *tele* meaning 'far' and *kinēsis* meaning 'motion']

telepathy (pronounced til-**lep**-ath-ee)
(noun) Telepathy is direct communication between people's minds.
telepathic (adjective).

telephone, telephones, telephoning, telephoned
1 (noun) A telephone is an electrical device for talking directly to someone who is in a different place. It consists of a microphone and receiver mounted on a handset.
2 (verb) If you telephone someone, you speak to them using a telephone.
telephonic (adjective).

telephone box, telephone boxes
(noun) A telephone box is a type of small shelter in the street where there is a public telephone.

telephone exchange, telephone exchanges
(noun) A telephone exchange is a building where telephone calls are connected.

telephonist, telephonists (pronounced til-**lef**-on-ist)
(noun) A telephonist is someone who works in a

telephone exchange or whose job it is to answer the telephone for a business.

telephoto
(adjective) A telephoto lens is a lens attached to a camera which makes distant objects larger and clearer.

teleprinter, teleprinters
(noun) A teleprinter is a device with a keyboard which sends or receives messages by telegraph.

telescope, telescopes, telescoping, telescoped
1 (noun) A telescope is a long tubelike instrument with lenses in it which make distant objects appear larger and nearer.
2 (verb) If you telescope something, such as a book or a report, you shorten it but keep all the important parts.
3 If a device telescopes, it can become longer or shorter because it is made in movable sections which slide inside each other.

telescopic (pronounced tel-liss-**kop**-ik)
1 (adjective) making things seem larger or nearer, e.g. *a telescopic lens.*
2 having sections that fit or slide into each other like those in a telescope.

teletext
(noun) Teletext is an electronic system that broadcasts pages of information onto a television set.

televise, televises, televising, televised
(verb) If an event is televised, it is filmed and shown on television.

television, televisions
1 (noun) A television is a piece of electronic equipment which receives pictures and sounds by electrical signals over a distance.
2 Television is the business or industry of making and broadcasting television programmes, e.g. *She has always wanted to get into television.*
3 Television is also all the programmes that you can watch on television.

telex, telexes, telexing, telexed
1 (noun) Telex is a system of sending written messages by teleprinter.
2 A telex is a machine that sends and receives telex messages; also a message sent by telex.
3 (verb) If you telex a message, you send it by means of a telex machine.
[short for *teleprinter exchange*]

tell, tells, telling, told
1 (verb) If you tell someone something, you let them know about it.
2 If you tell someone to do something, you order, instruct, or advise them to do it.
3 If you can tell something, you are able to judge correctly what is happening or what the situation is, e.g. *I could tell she was unhappy.*
4 If an unpleasant or tiring experience begins to tell, it begins to have a serious effect, e.g. *The strain was beginning to tell.*

Similar words: (sense 1) narrate, recount, relate

teller, tellers
(noun) A teller is a person who receives or gives out money in a bank.

telling
1 (adjective) important or effective, e.g. *He made a very telling speech on unemployment.*
2 If something you do or say is telling, it reveals thoughts or feelings that you are trying to hide.

telltale, telltales
1 (noun) A telltale is a person who reveals something that is meant to be secret.
2 (adjective) A telltale sign reveals information, e.g. *The car was beginning to show telltale signs of needing repair.*

telly, tellies
(noun; an informal word) A telly is a television.

temerity (pronounced tim-**mer**-it-ee)
(noun) Temerity is rashness or boldness, e.g. *He had the temerity to use the car without asking.*

temp, temps
(noun; an informal word) A temp is a secretary who works for short periods of time in different places.
[short for *temporary*]

temper, tempers, tempering, tempered
1 (noun) Your temper is the frame of mind or mood you are in.
2 A temper is a sudden outburst of anger.
3 (phrase) If you **lose your temper**, you become very angry.
4 (verb) To temper something means to make it more acceptable or suitable, e.g. *Discipline must be tempered with kindness.*
5 When metal is tempered, it is strengthened or hardened by being heated and then cooled quickly.

tempera
(noun) Tempera is a type of artists' paint, usually consisting of colouring and egg yolk.
[an Italian word]

temperament, temperaments (pronounced **tem**-pra-ment)
(noun) Your temperament is your nature or personality, shown in the way you react towards people and situations, e.g. *She has a very cheerful temperament.*

temperamental
1 (adjective) Someone who is temperamental has moods that change often and suddenly.
2 Temperamental means involving or relating to a person's temperament.
temperamentally (adverb).

temperance
1 (noun; a formal use) Temperance is behaviour that is very self-controlled.
2 Temperance is the habit of not drinking alcohol.
[from Latin *temperare* meaning 'to be moderate']

Similar words: (sense 2) abstinence, abstemiousness

temperate
(adjective) A temperate place has weather that is neither extremely hot nor extremely cold.

temperature, temperatures
1 (noun) The temperature of something is how hot or cold it is.
2 Your temperature is the temperature of your body.
3 (phrase) If you **have a temperature**, the temperature of your body is higher than it should be, usually because you are ill.

tempest, tempests
(noun; a literary word) A tempest is a violent storm.

tempestuous (pronounced tem-**pest**-yoo-uss) (adjective) violent, e.g. *a tempestuous argument.* **tempestuously** (adverb).

template, templates
(noun) A template is a shape or pattern cut out in wood, metal, plastic, or card which you draw or cut around to reproduce that shape or pattern.

temple, temples
1 (noun) A temple is a building used for the worship of a god in various religions, e.g. *a Hindu temple.*
2 Your temples are the flat parts on each side of your forehead.

tempo, tempos or **tempi**
1 (noun) The tempo of something is the speed at which it happens, e.g. *Life moves at a very fast tempo in the city.*
2 (a technical use) The tempo of a piece of music is its speed.
[from Italian *tempo* meaning 'time']

temporal
1 (adjective) If you describe things as temporal, you are talking about how they change or last over a period of time.
2 Temporal matters are to do with the present physical world rather than spiritual matters.
[from Latin *tempus* meaning 'time']

temporary
(adjective) lasting for only a short time.
temporarily (adverb).

temporize, temporizes, temporizing, temporized; also spelled **temporise**
(verb; a formal word) If you temporize, you do something else in order to gain time or delay something, e.g. *'Ask your mother,' he temporized.*

tempt, tempts, tempting, tempted
1 (verb) If you tempt someone, you try to persuade them to do something by offering them something they want.
2 If you are tempted to do something, you want to do it but you think it might be wrong or harmful, e.g. *I was tempted to walk out.*
tempting (adjective), **tempter** (noun).

Similar words: (sense 1) lure, entice, lead on

temptation, temptations
1 (noun) Temptation is the state you are in when you want to do or have something, even though you know it might be wrong or harmful.
2 A temptation is something that you want to do or have, even though you know it might be

wrong or harmful, e.g. *It was such a temptation to leave.*

ten the number 10.
tenth.

tenable
1 (adjective) An argument or point of view that is tenable is reasonable and able to be defended.
2 A job or position that is tenable is meant to be kept by someone for a particular length of time, e.g. *This post is tenable for three years.*
[from French *tenir* meaning 'to hold']

tenacious (pronounced tin-**nay**-shuss) (adjective) determined and not giving up easily.
tenaciously (adverb), **tenacity** (noun).

tenant, tenants
(noun) A tenant is someone who pays rent for the place they live in, or for land or buildings that they use.
tenancy (noun).

tench
(noun) A tench is a freshwater fish with a thick dark-greenish body.

tend, tends, tending, tended
1 (verb) If something tends to happen, it happens usually or often.
2 If you tend someone or something, you look after them.
[sense 1 is from Latin *tendere* meaning 'to stretch'; sense 2 is short for *attend*]

Similar words: (sense 1) be liable to, lean towards, be disposed to, be prone to

tendency, tendencies
(noun) A tendency is a habit, trend, or type of behaviour that happens very often, e.g. *He has a tendency to become irritated.*

Similar words: bias, inclination, liability, leaning, disposition, liability, proclivity, penchant, predilection, propensity

tendentious (pronounced ten-**den**-shuss) (adjective; a formal word) strongly expressing an opinion or point of view, especially one that many people disagree with.

tender, tenderest; tenders, tendering, tendered
1 (adjective) Someone who is tender has gentle and caring feelings.
2 If someone is at a tender age, they are young and do not know very much about life.
3 Tender meat is easy to cut or chew.
4 If a part of your body is tender, it is painful and sore.
5 (verb) If someone tenders an apology or their resignation, they formally offer it.
6 (noun) A tender is a formal offer to supply goods or to do a job for a particular price.
tenderness (noun), **tenderly** (adverb).

Similar words: (sense 1) affectionate, loving

tendon, tendons
(noun) A tendon is a strong cord of tissue which joins a muscle to a bone.

tendril, tendrils
(noun) Tendrils are short, thin stems which grow on climbing plants and attach them to walls.

tenement, tenements (pronounced **ten**-em-ent)
(noun) A tenement is a large house or building divided into many flats.

tenet, tenets
(noun) The tenets of a theory or belief are the main ideas it is based upon.
[from Latin *tenere* meaning 'to hold']

tenner, tenners
(noun; an informal word) A tenner is a ten-pound note.

tennis
(noun) Tennis is a game played by two or four players on a rectangular court in which a ball is hit by players over a central net.

tenon, tenons
(noun) A tenon is a part of a piece of wood that has been cut so that it fits into a rectangular slot in another piece of wood.

tenor, tenors
1 (noun) A tenor is a man who sings the second lowest part in four-part harmony.
2 (adjective) A tenor recorder, saxophone, or other musical instrument has a range of notes of a fairly low pitch.
3 (noun) The tenor of something is the general meaning or mood that it expresses, e.g. *The tenor of the message was that they will be late.*

tense, tenser, tensest; tenses, tensing, tensed
1 (adjective) If you are tense, you are worried and nervous and cannot relax.
2 A tense situation or period of time is one that makes people nervous and worried.
3 If your body is tense, your muscles are tight.
4 (verb) If you tense, or if your muscles tense, your muscles become tight and stiff.
5 (noun) The tense of a verb is the form which shows whether you are talking about the past, present, or future.
[senses 1-4 are from Latin *tensus* meaning 'stretched'; sense 5 is from Latin *tempus* meaning 'time']

Similar words: (sense 1) strained, uptight, keyed up, overwrought

tensile
(adjective; a technical word) The tensile strength of something is its ability to withstand stress or pressure without breaking.

tension, tensions
1 (noun) Tension is the feeling of nervousness or worry that you have when something difficult, dangerous, or important is happening.
2 The tension in a rope or wire is how tightly it is stretched.

tent, tents
(noun) A tent is a shelter made of canvas or nylon held up by poles and pinned down with pegs and ropes.

tentacle, tentacles
(noun) The tentacles of an animal such as an octopus are the long, thin parts that it uses to feel and hold things.
[from Latin *tentare* meaning 'to feel']

tentative
(adjective) acting or speaking cautiously because of being uncertain or afraid.
tentatively (adverb).

tenterhooks
(plural noun) If you are on tenterhooks, you are nervous and excited about something that is going to happen.
[from the hooks called *tenterhooks* which were used to stretch cloth tight while it was drying]

tenuous (pronounced **ten**-yoo-uss)
(adjective) If an idea, connection, or relation is tenuous, it is so slight and weak that it may not really exist or may easily cease to exist, e.g. *He kept in tenuous contact with his family.*
tenuously (adverb).

tenure (pronounced **ten**-yoor)
1 (noun) Tenure is the legal right to live in a place or to use land or buildings for a period of time.
2 Tenure is the period of time during which someone holds an important job, e.g. *His tenure ends next month.*

tepee, tepees (pronounced **tee**-pee)
(noun) A tepee is a cone-shaped tent of animal skins used by North American Indians.
[from an American Indian word meaning 'dwelling']

tepid
(adjective) Tepid liquid is only slightly warm.

tequila (pronounced tik-**keel**-a)
(noun) Tequila is an alcoholic drink made in Mexico from a cactus-like plant and often used as a base for cocktails. It is named after Tequila, a district of Mexico.

tercentenary, tercentenaries (pronounced ter-sen-**teen**-er-ee)
(noun) A tercentenary is the 300th anniversary of something.

term, terms, terming, termed
1 (noun) A term is a fixed period of time, e.g. *His term of office lasts one year.*
2 A term is one of the periods of time that each year is divided into at a school or college.
3 A term is a name, expression, or word used for a particular thing.
4 (plural noun) The terms of an agreement are the conditions that have been accepted by the people involved in it.
5 If you express something in particular terms, you express it using a particular type of language or in a way that clearly shows your attitudes, e.g. *She spoke in glowing terms.*
6 (phrase) If you talk about something **in terms of** a particular thing, you are saying which part of it or whose view of it you are talking about, e.g. *It has been bad in terms of business.*
7 If you **come to terms with** something difficult or unpleasant, you learn to accept it.

8 (verb) To term something means to give it a name or to describe it, e.g. *The committee meeting was termed a disaster.*

terminal, terminals
1 (adjective) A terminal illness or disease cannot be cured and causes death gradually.
2 Terminal means positioned or happening at the end of something.
3 (noun) A terminal is a place where vehicles, passengers, or goods begin or end a journey.
4 A terminal is also one of the parts of an electrical device through which electricity enters or leaves.
5 A computer terminal is a keyboard and a visual display unit that is used to put information into or get information out of a computer.
terminally (adverb).
[from Latin *terminus* meaning 'end']

terminal velocity
(noun) The terminal velocity of something is the maximum speed that it reaches when falling from a height.

terminate, terminates, terminating, terminated
(verb) When you terminate something or when it terminates, it stops or ends.
termination (noun).

terminology, terminologies
(noun) The terminology of a subject is the set of special words and expressions used in it.

terminus, terminuses (pronounced ter-min-uss)
(noun) A terminus is a place where a bus or train route ends.

termite, termites
(noun) Termites are small white tropical insects that feed on wood.
[from Latin *termes* meaning 'woodworm']

tern, terns
(noun) A tern is a small black and white seabird with long wings and a forked tail.

terrace, terraces
1 (noun) A terrace is a row of houses joined together by their side walls.
2 A terrace is a flat area of stone next to a building where people can sit.
3 A terrace is one of a series of flat areas of ground built like steps so that crops can be grown there.
terraced (adjective).
[from Old French *terrasse* meaning 'platform']

terracotta
(noun) Terracotta is a type of reddish-brown unglazed pottery.
[from Italian *terra cotta* meaning 'baked earth']

terrain
(noun) The terrain of an area is the type of land there, e.g. *rocky, dry terrain.*

terrapin, terrapins
(noun) A terrapin is a type of small North American freshwater turtle.
[an American Indian word]

terrestrial
(adjective) involving the earth or land.

terrible
1 (adjective) serious and unpleasant, e.g. *a terrible accident.*
2 (an informal use) very bad or of poor quality, e.g. *The weather was terrible.*

terribly
(adverb) very or very much, e.g. *He was a terribly good dancer.*

terrier, terriers
(noun) A terrier is a small, short-bodied dog.
[from Old French *chien terrier* meaning 'earth dog']

terrific
1 (adjective; an informal use) very pleasing or impressive, e.g. *We had a terrific holiday.*
2 great in amount, degree, or intensity, e.g. *There was a terrific explosion.*
terrifically (adverb).

terrify, terrifies, terrifying, terrified
(verb) If something terrifies you, it makes you feel extremely frightened.
terrifying (adjective), **terrified** (adjective).
[from Latin *terrificare*]

territorial
(adjective) involving or relating to the ownership of a particular area of land or water.

territory, territories
1 (noun) The territory of a country is the land that it controls.
2 An animal's territory is an area which it regards as its own and defends when other animals try to enter it.

terror, terrors
1 (noun) Terror is great fear or panic.
2 A terror is something that makes you feel very frightened.

terrorism
(noun) Terrorism is the use of violence for political reasons.
terrorist (noun and adjective).

terrorize, terrorizes, terrorizing, terrorized; also spelled **terrorise**
(verb) If someone terrorizes you, they frighten you by threatening you or being violent to you.

terry
(noun) Terry is a type of material which has lots of tiny loops on each side.

terse, terser, tersest
(adjective) A terse comment or statement is short and rather unfriendly.
tersely (adverb).
[from Latin *tersus* meaning 'neat' or 'precise']

tertiary (pronounced ter-shar-ee)
1 (adjective) third in order or importance.
2 Tertiary education is education at university or college level.

Terylene (pronounced ter-ril-een)
(noun; a trademark) Terylene is a man-made fabric used for clothes.

tessellated
(adjective) made out of lots of small square

pieces of coloured stone or pottery, e.g. *a tessellated Roman pavement.*
[from Latin *tessella* meaning 'small stone cube']

test, tests, testing, tested
1 (verb) When you test something, you try it to find out what it is, what condition it is in, or how well it works.
2 If you test someone, you ask them questions to find out how much they know.
3 (noun) A test is a deliberate action or experiment to find out whether something works or how well it works.
4 A test is also a set of questions or tasks given to someone to find out what they know or can do.

testament, testaments
1 (noun; a legal use) A testament is the same as a will.
2 A testament is also a copy of either the Old or the New Testament of the Bible.
[from Latin *testari* meaning 'to bear witness']

test case, test cases
(noun) A test case is a legal case that becomes an example for deciding other similar cases.

testicle, testicles
(noun) A man's testicles are the two sex glands that produce sperm.

testify, testifies, testifying, testified
1 (verb) When someone testifies, they make a formal statement, especially in a court of law, e.g. *Three witnesses testified against him.*
2 To testify to something means to show that it is likely to be true, e.g. *Her thoughtful actions testified to her love for him.*

testimonial, testimonials (pronounced tess-tim-**moh**-nee-al)
(noun) A testimonial is a statement saying how good someone or something is.

testimony, testimonies
(noun) A person's testimony is a formal statement they make, especially in a court of law.

testing
(adjective) Testing situations or problems are very difficult to deal with, e.g. *The death of his son was a testing time for him.*

test match, test matches
(noun) A test match is one of a series of international cricket or rugby matches.

testosterone (pronounced tess-**toss**-ter-rone)
(noun) Testosterone is a male hormone that produces male characteristics.

test tube, test tubes
(noun) A test tube is a small cylindrical glass container that is used in chemical experiments.

test-tube baby, test-tube babies
(noun) A test-tube baby is a baby that develops from an egg that has been removed from the mother's body, fertilized, and then replaced in her womb.

testy, testier, testiest
(adjective) impatient and easily irritated.
testily (adverb).

tetanus (pronounced **tet**-nuss)
(noun) Tetanus is a painful infectious disease caused by germs getting into wounds. It causes muscular spasms and convulsions.
[from Greek *tetanos* meaning 'stretched']

tetchy, tetchier, tetchiest
(adjective) cross and irritable.
tetchily (adverb), **tetchiness** (noun).

tête-à-tête, tête-à-têtes (pronounced tate-a-**tate**)
(noun) A tête-à-tête is a private conversation between two people.
[a French expression, meaning literally 'head to head']

tether, tethers, tethering, tethered
1 (verb) If you tether an animal, you tie it to a post.
2 (noun) A tether is a rope or chain used to tie an animal to a post.
3 (phrase) If you are **at the end of your tether**, you are extremely tired and have no more patience or energy left to deal with your problems.

tetrahedron, tetrahedrons or **tetrahedra** (pronounced tet-ra-**hee**-dron)
(noun) A tetrahedron is any three-dimensional shape with six straight edges and four flat sides.

Teutonic (pronounced tyoo-**tonn**-ik)
(adjective; a formal word) involving or related to German people.
[from *Teutoni*, the Latin name for an ancient Germanic people]

text, texts
1 (noun) The text of a book is the main written part of it, rather than the pictures or index.
2 Text is any written material.
3 A text is a book or other piece of writing used for study or an exam at school or college.
textual (adjective).
[from Latin *textus* meaning 'something woven or composed']

textbook, textbooks
(noun) A textbook is a book about a particular subject that is intended for students to use.

textile, textiles
(noun) A textile is a woven cloth or fabric.
[from Latin *texere* meaning 'to weave']

texture, textures
(noun) The texture of something is the way it feels when you touch it.

Similar words: feel, consistency, constitution

Thai, Thais
1 (adjective) belonging or relating to Thailand.
2 (noun) A Thai is someone who comes from Thailand.
3 Thai is the main language spoken in Thailand.

thalidomide
(noun) Thalidomide is a type of tranquillizer. It was withdrawn from use after it was discovered to cause abnormalities in unborn babies if taken by pregnant women.

than

1 (preposition and conjunction) You use 'than' to link two parts of a comparison, e.g. *She is older than me.*
2 You use 'than' to link two parts of a contrast, e.g. *He'd rather do things by himself than ask for help.*

thank, thanks, thanking, thanked

(verb) When you thank someone, you show that you are grateful for something, usually by saying 'thank you'.

thankful

(adjective) happy and relieved that something has happened.
thankfully (adverb).

thankless

(adjective) A thankless job or task involves doing a lot of hard work that other people do not notice or are not grateful for, e.g. *Housework is a thankless task.*

thanks

1 (plural noun) When you express your thanks to someone, you tell or show them how grateful you are for something.
2 (phrase) If something happened **thanks to** someone or something, it happened because of them, e.g. *Thanks to you I'm going to be late.*
3 (interjection) You say 'Thanks' to show that you are grateful for something.

thanksgiving

1 (noun) Thanksgiving is an act of thanking God, especially in prayer or in a religious ceremony.
2 In the United States, Thanksgiving is a public holiday in the autumn.

thank you

You say 'thank you' to show that you are grateful to someone for something.

that, those

1 (determiner and pronoun) 'That' or 'those' is used to refer to things or people already mentioned or known about, e.g. *That film came out years ago.*
2 (conjunction) 'That' is used to introduce a clause, e.g. *She suggested that I wrote to him.*
3 (pronoun) 'That' is also used to introduce a relative clause, e.g. *I opened the door that led to the basement.*
4 (phrase) You use **that is** or **that is to say** when you are giving further details about something, e.g. *We deal with social matters; that is, everything from housing to education.*

thatch, thatches, thatching, thatched

1 (noun) Thatch is straw and reeds used to make roofs.
2 (verb) To thatch a roof means to cover it with thatch.
[from Old English *theccan* meaning 'to cover']

thaw, thaws, thawing, thawed

1 (verb) When snow or ice thaws, it melts.
2 (noun) A thaw is a period of warmer weather in winter when snow or ice melts.
3 (verb) When you thaw frozen food, or when it thaws, it becomes unfrozen.

4 When people who are unfriendly thaw, they begin to be more friendly and relaxed.

the

(determiner) The definite article 'the' is used when you are talking about something that is known about, that has just been mentioned, or that you are going to give details about.

theatre, theatres (pronounced **theer**-ter)

1 (noun) A theatre is a building where plays and other entertainments are performed on a stage.
2 Theatre is work such as writing, producing, and acting in plays, e.g. *She was really happy working in the theatre.*
3 A lecture theatre is a large room or hall with a raised platform and tiered seats for an audience.
4 An operating theatre is a room in a hospital designed and equipped for surgical operations.
[from Greek *theatron* meaning 'viewing place']

theatrical (pronounced thee-**at**-rik-kl)

1 (adjective) involving the theatre or performed in a theatre, e.g. *a theatrical production.*
2 Theatrical behaviour is exaggerated, unnatural, and done for effect.
theatrically (adverb).

thee

(pronoun; an old-fashioned word) Thee means you.

theft, thefts

(noun) Theft is the crime of stealing.

Similar words: robbery, larceny

their

(determiner) Their refers to something belonging or relating to people or things, other than yourself or the person you are talking to, which have already been mentioned e.g. *the car companies and their workers.*

theirs

(pronoun) Theirs refers to something belonging or relating to people or things, other than yourself or the person you are talking to, which have already been mentioned, e.g. *It was his fault, not theirs.*

them

(pronoun) Them refers to things or people, other than yourself or the people you are talking to, which have already been mentioned, e.g. *He took off his glasses and put them in his pocket.*

thematic (pronounced thim-**mat**-ik)

(adjective; a formal word) concerned with or involving particular subjects or topics, e.g. *thematic teaching.*

theme, themes

1 (noun) A theme is a main idea or topic which is expressed or developed in writing, painting, film, or music, e.g. *The theme of the poem is love.*
2 A theme is also a tune, especially one played at the beginning and end of a television or radio programme.
[from Latin *thema* meaning 'something laid down']

theme park, theme parks

(noun) A theme park is an area in which

displays, buildings, and activities on a particular subject have been set up which people pay to visit.

theme song, theme songs
(noun) A theme song is a song or tune which is played several times in a film or a musical.

themselves
1 (pronoun) Themselves is used when people, other than yourself or the person you are talking to, do an action and are affected by it, e.g. *They tried to persuade themselves that it had been a mistake.*
2 Themselves is used to emphasize 'they'.

then
1 (adverb) at a particular time in the past or future, e.g. *I'll never get there by then.*
2 in that case, e.g. *If you haven't got the money, then don't buy it.*

thence
(adverb; a formal word) from that place, time, or event.

theodolite, theodolites (pronounced thee-**od**-dol-lite)
(noun) A theodolite is an instrument used in surveying for measuring angles.

theologian, theologians (pronounced thee-ol-**loe**-jee-an)
(noun) A theologian is someone who studies religion and the nature of God.

theology
(noun) Theology is the study of religion and God.
theological (adjective), **theologically** (adverb).

theorem, theorems (pronounced **thee**-rem)
(noun) A theorem is a statement in mathematics that can be proved to be true by reasoning.
[from Greek *theōrēma* meaning 'something to be looked at']

theoretical
1 (adjective) based on or to do with ideas of a subject rather than the practical aspects.
2 not proved to exist or be true.
theoretically (adverb).

theorist, theorists
(noun) A theorist is someone who develops ideas about a particular subject in order to explain it.

theorize, theorizes, theorizing, theorized; also spelled theorise
(verb) If you theorize about something, you develop ideas about it to try to explain it.

theory, theories
1 (noun) A theory is an idea or set of ideas that is meant to explain something, e.g. *Darwin's theory of evolution.*
2 Theory is the set of rules, principles, and ideas that a particular subject or skill is based upon.
3 (phrase) You use **in theory** to say that although something is supposed to happen, it may not in fact happen, e.g. *In theory, the car should start.*
[from Greek *theōria* meaning 'speculation']

Similar words: (sense 1) hypothesis, conjecture

therapeutic (pronounced ther-ap-**yoo**-tik)
1 (adjective) If something is therapeutic, it helps you to feel happier and more relaxed, e.g. *Music can be very therapeutic.*
2 In medicine, therapeutic treatment is designed to treat a disease or to improve a person's health.
[from Greek *therapeuein* meaning 'to treat medically']

therapy
(noun) Therapy is the treatment of mental or physical illness, often without the use of drugs or operations.
therapist (noun).

there
1 (adverb) in, at, or to that place, point, or case, e.g. *I'm going there... I agree with you there.*
2 (pronoun) There is used to say that something exists or does not exist, or to draw attention to something, e.g. *There were no buses yesterday because of the strike.*

thereby
(adverb; a formal word) as a result of the event or action mentioned, e.g. *She cheated in the exam and thereby failed.*

therefore
(adverb) as a result.

therm, therms
(noun; a technical word) A therm is a measurement of heat.

thermal
1 (adjective) to do with or caused by heat, e.g. *thermal energy.*
2 Thermal clothes are specially designed to keep you warm in cold weather.
[from Greek *thermē* meaning 'heat']

thermo-
(prefix) related to, caused by, or measuring heat.

thermodynamics
(noun) Thermodynamics is the branch of physics concerned with the relationship between heat and other forms of energy.
thermodynamic (adjective).

thermometer, thermometers
(noun) A thermometer is an instrument for measuring the temperature of a room or a person's body.

thermonuclear
(adjective) involving nuclear reactions that take place at very high temperatures, for example nuclear fusion.

thermoplastic
(adjective) A thermoplastic material becomes soft when heated and hard again when cooled.

Thermos, Thermoses
(noun; a trademark) A Thermos or Thermos flask is a container which is used to keep drinks either hot or cold by means of a vacuum.

thermostat, thermostats
(noun) A thermostat is a device used to control temperature, for example on a central heating system.

thesaurus, thesauruses (pronounced
this-**saw**-russ)
(noun) A thesaurus is a reference book in which
words with similar meanings are grouped
together.
[from Greek *thēsauros* meaning 'treasure']

these the plural of **this**.

thesis, theses (pronounced **thee**-siss)
(noun) A thesis is a long piece of writing, based
on research, that is done as part of a university
degree.

they
1 (pronoun) They refers to people or things,
other than you or the people you are talking to,
that have already been mentioned, e.g. *They ran
the company while he was in hospital... They
found the body in a dustbin.*
2 They is sometimes used instead of 'he' or 'she'
where the sex of the person is unknown or
unspecified. Some people consider this to be
incorrect, e.g. *I was going to stay with a friend,
but they were ill.*

thiamine (pronounced **thigh**-a-meen)
(noun) Thiamine is a soluble vitamin that is part
of the B group of vitamins and is essential for
carbohydrate metabolism. It occurs in the outer
coat of rice and other grains.

thick, thicker, thickest
1 (adjective) Something thick has a large
distance between its two opposite surfaces.
2 If something is a particular amount thick, it
measures that amount between its two sides.
3 Thick means growing or grouped closely
together and in large quantities, e.g. *thick
undergrowth.*
4 Thick liquids contain little water and do not
flow easily, e.g. *thick soup.*
5 Thick smoke or fog is difficult to see through.
6 A thick accent is very strong, e.g. *She spoke
with a thick Yorkshire accent.*
7 (an informal use) A thick person is stupid or
slow to understand things.
thickly (adverb), **thickness** (noun).

thicken, thickens, thickening, thickened
(verb) If something thickens, it becomes thicker,
e.g. *The fog thickened.*
thickener (noun), **thickening** (noun).

thicket, thickets
(noun) A thicket is a small group of trees
growing closely together.
[from Old English *thicce* meaning 'thick']

thickset
(adjective) Someone who is thickset is broad and
heavy with a solid-looking body.

thief, thieves
(noun) A thief is a person who steals.

thieving
(noun) Thieving is the act of stealing.

thigh, thighs
(noun) Your thighs are the top parts of your legs,
between your knees and your hips.

thimble, thimbles
(noun) A thimble is a small metal or plastic cap

that you put on the end of your finger to protect
it when you are sewing.
[from Old English *thuma* meaning 'thumb']

thin, thinner, thinnest; thins, thinning, thinned
1 (adjective) Something that is thin is much
narrower than it is long.
2 A thin person or animal has very little fat on
their body.
3 Thin liquids contain a lot of water.
4 (verb) If you thin something such as paint or
soup, you add water or other liquid to it.
thinness (noun), **thinly** (adverb).

Similar words: (sense 2) skinny, scrawny, scraggy,
lean, spindly, spare

thing, things
1 (noun) A thing is an object, rather than a plant,
an animal, a human being, or something abstract.
2 (plural noun) Your things are your clothes or
possessions.
3 (an informal phrase) If you **have a thing** about
someone or something, you have very strong
feelings about them, e.g. *He's got a thing about
motor racing.*

Similar words: (sense 1) item, article, object

think, thinks, thinking, thought
1 (verb) When you think about ideas or
problems, you use your mind to consider them.
2 If you think something, you have the opinion
that it is true or the case, e.g. *I think dogs are
more friendly than cats as pets.*
3 If you think of something, you remember it or
it comes into your mind.
4 If you think to do something, you remember to
do it, e.g. *I didn't think to bring the car.*
5 If you think a lot of someone or something, you
admire them or think they are good.
thinking (noun and adjective).

Similar words: (sense 1) meditate, cogitate, muse,
consider, regard
(sense 2) believe, feel, deem, consider, reckon, count,
suppose

third, thirds
1 The third item in a series is the one counted as
number three.
2 (noun) A third is one of three equal parts.
3 In music, a third is the interval between two
notes of a scale when there is one note
separating them.
thirdly (adverb).

third degree
(noun; an informal expression) If you give
someone the third degree, you question them in
great detail and for a long time about something.

third party, third parties
1 (noun) A third party is a person who is not
directly involved in a business agreement or
legal case, but is affected by it or is asked to take
part in a minor way.
2 (adjective) If someone has third party
insurance and they cause an accident, the
insurance company will pay money only to other

people who are hurt or whose property is damaged, and not to them.

Third World
(noun) The poorer countries of Africa, Asia, and South America can be referred to as the Third World.

thirst, thirsts, thirsting, thirsted
1 (noun) If you have a thirst, you feel a need to drink something.
2 (verb) If you thirst for something, you have a very strong desire for it, e.g. *He thirsted for knowledge.*
thirsty (adjective), **thirstily** (adverb).

thirteen the number 13.
thirteenth.

thirty, thirties
the number 30.
thirtieth.

this, these
1 (determiner and pronoun) This is used to refer to something or someone that is nearby or has just been mentioned, e.g. *This is David.*
2 This is used to refer to the present time or place, e.g. *Are you going out this morning?*

thistle, thistles
(noun) A thistle is a wild plant with prickly-edged leaves and purple flowers.

thong, thongs
(noun) A thong is a long narrow strip of leather.

thorax, thoraxes or **thoraces** (pronounced **thor**-raks)
1 (noun) In a human or animal, the thorax is the part of the body enclosing the ribs.
2 In an insect, the thorax is the part of the body between the head and the abdomen where the wings and legs are.
[from Greek *thōrax* meaning 'chest' or 'breastplate']

thorium
(noun) Thorium is a soft silvery-white metallic element. It is radioactive and is used in electronic equipment and as a nuclear power source. Its atomic number is 90 and its symbol is Th.

thorn, thorns
(noun) A thorn is one of many sharp points growing on some plants and trees.

thorny, thornier, thorniest
1 (adjective) covered with thorns.
2 A thorny subject or question is difficult to discuss or answer.

thorough (pronounced **thur**-ruh)
1 (adjective) done very carefully and completely, e.g. *a thorough examination.*
2 A thorough person is very careful and methodical in what they do.
thoroughly (adverb), **thoroughness** (noun).

thoroughbred, thoroughbreds
(noun) A thoroughbred is a purebred animal, especially a racehorse.

thoroughfare, thoroughfares
(noun) A thoroughfare is a main road in a town.

those the plural of **that.**

thou
(pronoun; an old-fashioned word) Thou means you, when you are talking to only one person.

though
1 (conjunction) despite the fact that, e.g. *She arrived on time, even though she'd missed her bus.*
2 if, e.g. *He looked as though he'd just got up.*

thought, thoughts
1 Thought is the past tense and past participle of **think.**
2 (noun) A thought is an idea that you have in your mind.
3 Thought is the activity of thinking, e.g. *lost in thought.*
4 Thought is a particular way of thinking or a particular set of ideas, e.g. *political thought in the early sixties.*
5 If you give thought to something, you give it your attention and consideration.

Similar words: (sense 3) consideration, contemplation, cogitation, reflection, thinking

thoughtful
1 (adjective) When someone is thoughtful, they are quiet and serious because they are thinking about something.
2 A thoughtful person remembers what other people want or need, and tries to be kind to them.
thoughtfully (adverb).

Similar words: (sense 1) meditative, pensive, contemplative, reflective
(sense 2) caring, considerate, solicitous

thoughtless
(adjective) A thoughtless person forgets or ignores what other people want, need, or feel.
thoughtlessly (adverb), **thoughtlessness** (noun).

thousand, thousands
the number 1000.
thousandth.

thrash, thrashes, thrashing, thrashed
1 (verb) To thrash someone means to beat them by hitting them with something.
2 To thrash someone in a game, contest, or fight means to defeat them completely.
3 If you thrash around, you twist and turn your body violently because you are afraid or in pain.
4 To thrash out a problem or an idea means to discuss it in detail until a solution is reached.
thrashing (noun).

thread, threads, threading, threaded
1 (noun) A thread is a long, fine piece of cotton, silk, nylon, or wool.
2 The thread on something such as a screw or the top of a container is the raised spiral line of metal or plastic round it.
3 The thread of an argument or story is an idea or theme that connects the different parts of it.
4 (verb) When you thread something, you pass thread, magnetic tape, or cord through it.
5 If you thread your way through people or

things, you carefully make your way through them.

threadbare
(adjective) Threadbare cloth or clothing is old and thin.

threat, threats
1 (noun) A threat is a statement that someone will harm you, especially if you do not do what they want.
2 Anything or anyone that seems likely to harm you can be called a threat.
3 If there is a threat of something unpleasant happening, it is very possible that it will happen.

threaten, threatens, threatening, threatened
1 (verb) If you threaten to harm someone or threaten to do something that will upset them, you say that you will do it.
2 If someone or something threatens a person or thing, they are likely to harm them.
threatened (adjective), **threatening** (adjective).

Similar words: (sense 2) intimidate, menace

three the number 3.

three-dimensional
1 (adjective) solid rather than flat.
2 lifelike or real, e.g. *The characters were not really three-dimensional.*

three-ply
(adjective) having three layers or thicknesses, e.g. *three-ply tissues.*

three-point turn, three-point turns
(noun) A three-point turn is a way of turning a car in a road by driving backwards and forwards across it three times.

threesome, threesomes
(noun) A threesome is a group of three.

thresh, threshes, threshing, threshed
(verb) When people thresh corn, wheat, or rice, they beat it in order to separate the grains from the rest of the plant.
thresher (noun), **threshing** (noun).

threshold, thresholds (pronounced **thresh-hold**)
1 (noun) The threshold of a building or room is the doorway, or the floor in the doorway.
2 The threshold of something is the lowest amount, level, or limit at which something happens or changes, e.g. *The tax threshold is £445.*
3 (phrase) Someone who is **on the threshold of** something is about to do it or experience it.

thrice
(adverb; an old-fashioned word) If you do something thrice, you do it three times.

thrift
(noun) Thrift is the practice of saving money and not wasting things.
[from an Old Norse word meaning 'prosperity']

thrifty, thriftier, thriftiest
(adjective) A thrifty person saves money and does not waste things.

thrill, thrills, thrilling, thrilled
1 (noun) A thrill is a sudden feeling of great excitement, pleasure, or fear; also any event or experience that gives you such a feeling.
2 (verb) If something thrills you, or you thrill to it, it gives you a feeling of great pleasure and excitement.
thrilled (adjective), **thrilling** (adjective).
[from Old English *thyrlian* meaning 'to pierce']

Similar words: (sense 1) buzz, kick

thriller, thrillers
(noun) A thriller is a book, film, or play that tells an exciting story about dangerous, frightening, or mysterious events.

thrive, thrives, thriving, thrived or **throve**
(verb) When people or things thrive, they are healthy, happy, successful, or strong.
thriving (adjective).

throat, throats
1 (noun) Your throat is the back of your mouth and the top part of the passages inside your neck.
2 Your throat is also the front part of your neck.

throaty, throatier, throatiest
(adjective) A throaty voice is hoarse and husky.
throatily (adverb), **throatiness** (noun).

throb, throbs, throbbing, throbbed
1 (verb) If a part of your body throbs, you feel a series of strong beats or dull pains.
2 If something throbs, it vibrates and makes a loud, rhythmic noise, e.g. *The engine throbbed.*

throes
1 (plural noun) Throes are a series of violent pangs, pain, or convulsions, e.g. *death throes.*
2 (phrase) If you are **in the throes of** something, you are deeply involved in it.

thrombosis, thromboses (pronounced **throm-boe-siss**)
(noun) A thrombosis is a blood clot which blocks the flow of blood in the body. Thromboses are dangerous and often fatal.
[from Greek *thrombōsis* meaning 'curdling' or 'clotting']

throne, thrones
1 (noun) A throne is a ceremonial chair used by a King or Queen on important official occasions.
2 The throne is a way of referring to the position of being King or Queen.

throng, throngs, thronging, thronged
1 (noun) A throng is a large crowd of people.
2 (verb) If people throng somewhere or throng a place, they go there in great numbers, e.g. *Supporters thronged to the football ground.*

throttle, throttles, throttling, throttled
1 (verb) To throttle someone means to kill or injure them by squeezing their throat.
2 (noun) On a car, the throttle is the device which controls the amount of fuel going into the engine.
[from Middle English *throte* meaning 'throat']

through
1 (preposition) moving all the way from one side

of something to the other, e.g. *a path through the garden.*
2 because of, e.g. *She failed the exam through lack of study.*
3 during, e.g. *We keep the heating on through the winter.*
4 If you go through an experience, it happens to you, e.g. *I never want to go through another exam like that again.*
5 If you achieve something through particular methods, you use those methods to achieve it.
6 (adjective) If you are through with something, you have finished doing it or using it.

throughout
1 (preposition) during, e.g. *She fidgeted throughout the film.*
2 (adverb) happening or existing through the whole of a place, e.g. *carpeted throughout.*

throve the past tense of **thrive.**

throw, throws, throwing, threw, thrown
1 (verb) When you throw something you are holding, you move your hand quickly and let it go, so that it moves through the air.
2 If you throw yourself somewhere, you move there suddenly and with force, e.g. *He threw himself onto the floor.*
3 To throw someone into an unpleasant situation means to put them there, e.g. *He always throws me into confusion.*
4 If something throws light or shadow on something else, it makes that thing have light or shadow on it.
5 If you throw yourself into an activity, you become actively and enthusiastically involved in it.
6 If you throw a fit or tantrum, you suddenly begin behaving in an uncontrolled way.
7 (an informal use) If something such as a remark or an experience throws you, it confuses or surprises you because it is unexpected, e.g. *Your phone call really threw me.*

Similar words: (sense 1) bowl, hurl, fling, cast, catapult, chuck, pelt, pitch

throwaway
(adjective) A throwaway remark is made casually in a way that suggests that you do not expect a response.

throwback, throwbacks
(noun) A throwback is something which has the characteristics of something that existed a long time ago, e.g. *Some of today's music is a throwback to the sixties.*

thrush, thrushes
1 (noun) A thrush is a small brown songbird.
2 Thrush is a fungal disease of the mouth or of the vagina.

thrust, thrusts, thrusting, thrust
1 (verb) If you thrust something somewhere, you push or move it there quickly with a lot of force.
2 (noun) A thrust is a sudden forceful movement.
3 (verb) If you thrust your way somewhere, you move along, pushing between people or things.

4 (noun) The main thrust of an activity or idea is the most important part of it, e.g. *The main thrust of the debate was pay increases.*

thud, thuds, thudding, thudded
1 (noun) A thud is a dull sound, usually made by a solid, heavy object hitting something soft.
2 (verb) If something thuds somewhere, it makes a dull sound, usually by hitting something else.
[from Old English *thyddan* meaning 'to strike']

thug, thugs
(noun) A thug is a very rough and violent person.
[from Hindi *thag* meaning 'thief']

thumb, thumbs, thumbing, thumbed
1 (noun) Your thumb is the short, thick finger on the side of your hand.
2 (verb) If someone thumbs a lift, they stand at the side of the road and stick out their thumb until a driver stops and gives them a lift.

thumbnail, thumbnails
1 (noun) Your thumbnail is the nail on your thumb.
2 (adjective) A thumbnail sketch or account is a very short description of an event, idea, or plan which gives only the main details.

thump, thumps, thumping, thumped
1 (verb) If you thump someone or something, you hit them hard with your fist.
2 If something thumps somewhere, it makes a fairly loud, dull sound, usually when it hits something else.
3 When your heart thumps, it beats strongly and quickly.
4 (noun) A thump is a hard hit.
5 A thump is also a fairly loud, dull sound.

thunder, thunders, thundering, thundered
1 (noun) Thunder is a loud cracking or rumbling noise caused by expanding air which is suddenly heated by lightning.
2 (verb) When it thunders, a loud cracking or rumbling noise occurs in the sky after a flash of lightning.
3 (noun) Thunder is any loud rumbling noise, e.g. *the thunder of the underground trains.*
4 (verb) If something thunders, it makes a loud continuous noise, e.g. *The traffic thundered by.*
5 If you thunder, you say something loudly and angrily.

thunderbolt, thunderbolts
(noun) A thunderbolt is a flash of lightning, accompanied by thunder.

thunderous
(adjective) A thunderous noise is very loud.

thunderstruck
(adjective) completely amazed.

thundery
(adjective) Thundery weather has a lot of thunder.

Thursday, Thursdays
(noun) Thursday is the day between Wednesday and Friday.
[from Old English *Thursdæg* meaning 'Thor's day'; Thor was the Norse god of thunder]

thus (a formal word)
1 (adverb) in this way, e.g. *You tie the knot thus.*
2 therefore, e.g. *He failed. Thus he must reapply.*

thwack, thwacks, thwacking, thwacked
1 (verb) If you thwack someone or something, you hit them, especially with something flat, e.g. *He thwacked the ball over the boundary.*
2 (noun) A thwack is a blow with something flat.

thwart, thwarts, thwarting, thwarted
(verb) To thwart someone or their plans means to prevent them from doing or getting what they want.
[from Old English *thweorh* meaning 'crooked' or 'perverse']

thy
(determiner; an old-fashioned word) Thy means your.

thyme (pronounced **time**)
(noun) Thyme is a bushy herb with very small leaves used for flavouring in cooking.

thymus (pronounced **thigh**-muss)
(noun) Your thymus is a gland just below your thyroid gland. It is quite large in children, when it produces white blood cells for the immune system, and almost nonexistent in adults.
[from Greek *thumos* meaning 'sweetbread']

thyroid gland, thyroid glands
(noun) Your thyroid gland is situated at the base of your neck. It releases hormones which control your growth and your metabolism.
[from Greek *thyreoeidēs* meaning 'shield-shaped']

tiara, tiaras (pronounced tee-**ah**-ra)
(noun) A tiara is a semicircular crown of jewels worn by a woman on formal occasions.

Tibetan, Tibetans
1 (adjective) belonging or relating to Tibet.
2 (noun) A Tibetan is someone who comes from Tibet.

tibia, tibias
(noun) Your tibia is the inner and thicker of the two bones in your leg below your knee.

tic, tics
(noun) A tic is a twitching of a group of muscles, especially the muscles in the face.

tick, ticks, ticking, ticked
1 (noun) A tick is a written mark to show that something is correct or has been dealt with.
2 (verb) To tick something written on a piece of paper means to put a tick next to it.
3 When a clock ticks, it makes a regular series of short sounds as it works.
4 (noun) The tick of a clock is the series of short sounds it makes when it is working.
5 (verb) If you talk about what makes someone tick, you are talking about what makes them behave the way they do.
6 (noun) A tick is also a type of blood-sucking arachnid, that usually lives on the bodies of people or animals.
ticking (noun).

tick off
(phrasal verb; an informal expression) If you tick someone off, you speak angrily to them because they have done something wrong.

tick over
(phrasal verb) Something that is ticking over is working or operating steadily.

ticket, tickets
1 (noun) A ticket is a piece of paper or card which shows that you have paid for a journey or have paid to enter a place of entertainment.
2 When drivers get a ticket, they are given an official piece of paper which says that they have committed a driving or parking offence.
[from Old French *estiquier* meaning 'to stick on']

ticking
(noun) Ticking is a type of very strong fabric used to cover pillows and mattresses.

tickle, tickles, tickling, tickled
1 (verb) When you tickle someone, you move your fingers lightly over their body in order to make them laugh.
2 If something tickles you, it amuses you or gives you pleasure, e.g. *I was tickled by her remark.*

ticklish
1 (adjective) If someone is ticklish, they are very sensitive to being tickled.
2 A ticklish problem or situation is difficult and needs to be dealt with carefully.

tidal
(adjective) to do with or produced by tides, e.g. *tidal energy.*

tidal wave, tidal waves
(noun) A tidal wave is a very large wave, often caused by an earthquake, that comes over land and destroys things.

tiddler, tiddlers
(noun) A tiddler is a very small fish, such as a stickleback or minnow.

tiddly, tiddlier, tiddliest
(adjective) slightly drunk.

tiddlywinks
(noun) Tiddlywinks is a game in which players try to flick small plastic discs into a cup.

tide, tides, tiding, tided
1 (noun) The tide is the regular change in the level of the sea on the shore, caused by the gravitational pull of the sun and the moon.
2 The tide of opinion or fashion is what the majority of people think or do at a particular time.
3 A tide of things is a large quantity of them, e.g. *The rising tide of the unemployed.*
[from Old English *tid* meaning 'time']

tide over
(phrasal verb) If something will tide someone over, it will help them through a difficult period of time.

tidings
(plural noun; a formal word) Tidings are news.
[from Old English *tidan* meaning 'to happen']

tidy, tidier, tidiest; tidies, tidying, tidied
1 (adjective) Something that is tidy is neat and arranged in an orderly way.

2 Someone who is tidy always keeps their things neat and arranged in an orderly way.
3 (verb) To tidy a place means to make it neat by putting things in their proper place.
4 (adjective; an informal use) A tidy amount of money is a fairly large amount of it.

Similar words: (sense 1) neat, trim, orderly, uncluttered, shipshape, spick and span
(sense 3) neaten, clear, straighten, spruce up

tie, ties, tying, tied
1 (verb) If you tie one thing to another or tie it in a particular position, you fasten it using cord of some kind.
2 If you tie a knot or a bow in a piece of cord or cloth, you fasten the ends together to make a knot or bow.
3 (noun) A tie is a long, narrow piece of cloth worn around the neck under a shirt collar and tied in a knot at the front.
4 (verb) Something or someone that is tied to something else is closely linked with it, e.g. *He's very tied to his work.*
5 (noun) A tie is a connection or feeling that links you with a person, place, or organization, e.g. *This company has strong ties with Germany.*
6 (verb) If you tie with someone in a competition or game, you have the same number of points.

Similar words: (sense 1) bind, rope, tether, lash

tie up
1 (phrasal verb) If you tie up money or resources, you do something with it so that it is not available for other people or for other purposes, e.g. *All his money is tied up in property.*
2 To tie up with something means to be closely linked with it, e.g. *That ties up with my idea.*

tiebreak, tiebreaks
(noun) In tennis, a tiebreak is a method of getting a result in a set when each player has won six games. It involves playing a further game for the best of twelve points with each player serving two points alternately.

tiebreaker, tiebreakers
(noun) A tiebreaker is the same as a tiebreak.

tied up
(adjective) If you are tied up, you are busy.

tier, tiers
(noun) A tier is one of a number of rows or layers of something, e.g. *a wedding cake of four tiers.* [from Old French *tire* meaning 'rank']

tiff, tiffs
(noun) A tiff is a small unimportant quarrel.

tiger, tigers
(noun) A tiger is a large carnivorous animal of the cat family. It comes from Asia and has an orange coloured coat with black stripes.

tight, tighter, tightest
1 (adjective) fitting closely, e.g. *These shoes are too tight.*
2 firmly fastened and difficult to move, e.g. *a tight knot.*

3 stretched or pulled so as not to be slack, e.g. *a tight cord.*
4 (adverb) held firmly and securely, e.g. *She held him tight.*
5 (adjective) A tight plan or arrangement allows only the minimum time or money needed to do something, e.g. *I have a very tight schedule.*
6 A tight rule or system of control is very strict.
tightly (adverb), **tightness** (noun).

Similar words: (sense 3) taut, tense

tighten, tightens, tightening, tightened
1 (verb) If you tighten your hold on something, you hold it more firmly.
2 If you tighten a rope or chain, or if it tightens, it is stretched or pulled until it is straight.
3 When you tighten a fastening, you move it so that it is more firmly in place or holds something more firmly.
4 If someone tightens a rule or system, they make it stricter or more efficient.

tightrope, tightropes
(noun) A tightrope is a tightly-stretched rope on which an acrobat balances and performs tricks.

tights
(plural noun) Tights are a piece of clothing made of thin stretchy material that fit closely round a person's hips, legs, and feet. Tights are worn by women, ballet dancers, and acrobats.

tilde, tildes (pronounced tild-a)
(noun) In Spanish and some other languages, a tilde is a curly line placed over a letter to indicate a change in pronunciation, as in the word *señor.*

tile, tiles, tiling, tiled
1 (noun) A tile is a small flat square piece of something, for example, slate, carpet, or cork, that is used to cover surfaces.
2 (verb) To tile a surface means to fix tiles to it.
tiled (adjective).

till, tills, tilling, tilled
1 (preposition and conjunction) Till means the same as until.
2 (noun) A till is a drawer or box in a shop where money is kept, usually in a cash register.
3 (verb) To till the ground means to plough it for raising crops.

tiller, tillers
(noun) In a boat, the tiller is the handle fixed to the top of the rudder for steering.

tilt, tilts, tilting, tilted
1 (verb) If you tilt an object or it tilts, it changes position so that one end or side is higher than the other.
2 (noun) A tilt is a position in which one end or side of something is higher than the other.

Similar words: (sense 1) heel, list, lean

timber, timbers
1 (noun) Timber is wood that has been cut and prepared ready for building and making furniture.

2 The timbers of a ship or house are the large pieces of wood that have been used to build it.

timbre (pronounced **tam**-ber)
(noun) The timbre of a sound is the particular characteristic or quality that it has.
[from Old French *timbre* meaning 'bell']

time, times, timing, timed
1 (noun) Time is what is measured in hours, days, and years, e.g. *What time is it?*
2 Time is used to mean a particular period or point, e.g. *I enjoyed my time in France.*
3 If you say it is time for something or it is time to do it, you mean that it ought to happen or be done now, e.g. *'Time for bed,' said Mother.*
4 Time is used after numbers to indicate how often something happens, e.g. *I play squash three times a week.*
5 Time is used after numbers when you are saying how much bigger, smaller, better, or worse one thing is compared to another, e.g. *It would cost me four times as much.*
6 Times is used in arithmetic to link numbers that are multiplied together, e.g. *3 times 4 is 12.*
7 (verb) If you time something for a particular time, you plan that it should happen then, e.g. *He timed his visit for 11.00 am.*
8 If you time an activity or action, you measure how long it lasts.
9 (phrase) Someone who is **behind the times** is old-fashioned.
10 If you **have no time for** something or someone, you do not like them and cannot put up with them.

Similar words: (sense 1) span, spell, stretch, phase, term, period, space, interval

time bomb, time bombs
(noun) A time bomb is a bomb with a device to make it explode at a set time.

time-honoured
(adjective) A time-honoured way of doing something has been used for a very long time.

time-lag
(noun) A time-lag is a period of time between two connected events.

timeless
(adjective) Something timeless is so good, beautiful, or perfect that it cannot be affected by the passing of time or by changes in fashion.

timely
(adjective) happening at just the right time.

Similar words: well-timed, opportune, propitious

timepiece, timepieces
(noun; an old-fashioned word) A timepiece is a clock or watch.

timer, timers
(noun) A timer is a device that measures time, especially one that is part of a machine, e.g. *I've set the timer on the cooker.*

timescale, timescales
(noun) The timescale of an event is the length of time during which it happens.

time signature, time signatures
(noun) A time signature is a sign at the beginning of a line of music showing the number of beats in a bar.

timetable, timetables
1 (noun) A timetable is a plan of the times when particular activities or jobs should be done.
2 A timetable is a list of the times when particular trains, boats, buses, or aeroplanes arrive and depart.

timid
(adjective) shy and having no courage or self-confidence.
timidly (adverb), **timidity** (noun).
[from Latin *timere* meaning 'to fear']

Similar words: cowardly, timorous, faint-hearted, pusillanimous

timing
1 (noun) Someone's timing is their skill in judging the right moment at which to do something.
2 The timing of an event is when it actually happens.

timorous
(adjective; a literary word) frightened and nervous.

timpani (pronounced **tim**-pan-ee)
(plural noun) Timpani are kettledrums that are played in an orchestra.
[an Italian word]

timpanist, timpanists
(noun) A timpanist is someone who plays the timpani in an orchestra.

tin, tins
1 (noun) Tin is a soft silvery-white metallic element used in alloys. Its atomic number is 50, and its symbol is Sn.
2 A tin is a metal container which is filled with food and then sealed in order to preserve the food.
3 A tin is a small metal container which may have a lid, e.g. *a baking tin... the biscuit tin.*

tincture, tinctures (pronounced **tingt**-chur)
(a formal word)
1 (noun) A tincture is a medicine consisting of alcohol and a small amount of a drug.
2 A tincture of something is a tint, colour, or tinge of it.
[from Latin *tinctura* meaning 'a dyeing']

tinder
(noun) Tinder is small pieces of something dry, especially wood or grass, that burns easily and can be used for lighting a fire.

tine, tines
(noun; a technical word) The tines of a fork or rake are the long pointed parts.

tinfoil
(noun) Tinfoil is sheet aluminium as thin as paper, used for wrapping and covering food.

tinge, tinges, tingeing, tinged
1 (noun) A tinge of something is a small amount of it, e.g. *a tinge of blue... a tinge of sadness.*

2 (verb) To tinge something with a particular colour means to colour it very slightly.
tinged (adjective).
[from Latin *tingere* meaning 'to colour']

tingle, tingles, tingling, tingled
1 (verb) When a part of your body tingles, you feel a slight prickling feeling in it.
2 (noun) A tingle is a slight prickling feeling.
tingling (noun and adjective).

tinker, tinkers, tinkering, tinkered
1 (noun) A tinker is a person who travels from place to place mending metal pots and pans or doing other small repair jobs.
2 (verb) If you tinker with something, you make a lot of small adjustments to it in order to repair or improve it, e.g. *He's tinkering with the car.*

tinkle, tinkles, tinkling, tinkled
1 (verb) If something tinkles, it makes a sound like a small bell ringing.
2 (noun) A tinkle is a sound like that of a small bell ringing.

tinned
(adjective) Tinned food has been preserved by being sealed in a tin.

tinnitus (pronounced tin-**nie**-tuss)
(noun) Tinnitus is ringing in the ears.
[from Latin *tinnire* meaning 'to ring']

tinny, tinnier, tinniest
1 (adjective) A tinny sound has an unpleasant high-pitched quality.
2 If something such as a car is tinny, it is made of thin metal and is of poor quality.

tinpot
(adjective; an informal word) A tinpot country, government, or organization is thought to be inferior and unimportant.

tinsel
(noun) Tinsel is long threads with strips of shiny paper attached, used as a decoration at Christmas.

tint, tints, tinting, tinted
1 (noun) A tint is a small amount of a particular colour, e.g. *Your hair has a tint of auburn in it.*
2 A tint is also a weak dye used for changing the colour of a person's hair.
3 (verb) If a person tints their hair, they change its colour by adding a weak dye to it.
tinted (adjective).

tiny, tinier, tiniest
(adjective) extremely small.

Similar words: minuscule, miniature, diminutive, infinitesimal, Lilliputian

tip, tips, tipping, tipped
1 (noun) The tip of something long and thin is the end of it, e.g. *a fingertip.*
2 (verb) If you tip an object, you move it so that it is no longer horizontal or upright.
3 If you tip something somewhere, you pour it there quickly or carelessly.
4 (noun) A tip is a place where rubbish is dumped.
5 If you give someone such as a waiter a tip, you give them some money to thank them for their services.
6 A tip is also a useful piece of advice or information.
tipped (adjective).

tipple, tipples
(noun) A person's tipple is the alcoholic drink that they normally drink.

tipsy, tipsier, tipsiest
(adjective) slightly drunk.

tiptoe, tiptoes, tiptoeing, tiptoed
(verb) If you tiptoe somewhere, you walk there very quietly on your toes.

tirade, tirades (pronounced tie-**rade**)
(noun) A tirade is a long, angry speech in which you criticize someone or something.
[from Italian *tirata* meaning 'volley of shots']

tire, tires, tiring, tired
1 (verb) If something tires you, it makes you use a lot of energy so that you want to rest or sleep.
2 If you tire of something, you become bored with it.
tired (adjective), **tiredness** (noun).

Similar words: (sense 1) weary
(sense 2) flag, weary

tireless
(adjective) Someone who is tireless has a lot of energy and never seems to need a rest.

tiresome
(adjective) A person or thing that is tiresome makes you feel irritated or bored.

tiring
(adjective) Something that is tiring makes you tired.

tissue, tissues (pronounced **tiss**-yoo)
1 (noun) The tissue in plants and animals consists of cells that are similar in appearance and function, e.g. *scar tissue left by a wound.*
2 Tissue is thin paper that is used for wrapping breakable objects.
3 A tissue is a small piece of soft paper that you use as a handkerchief.
4 (phrase) A story which is completely untrue can be called **a tissue of lies**.
[from Old French *tissu* meaning 'woven cloth']

tit, tits
(noun) A tit is a small European bird that eats insects and seeds, e.g. *a blue tit.*

titanic
(adjective) very big or important.
[in Greek legend, the *Titans* were a family of giants]

titanium (pronounced tie-**tane**-ee-um)
(noun) Titanium is a strong white metallic element used in making lightweight alloys for machine parts. Its atomic number is 22 and its symbol is Ti.

titbit, titbits
(noun) A titbit is a small, tasty piece of food.

tithe, tithes
(noun) A tithe was a fixed amount of money or

goods that people used to give regularly to support churches and charities.
[from Old English *teogoth* meaning 'tenth part']

titian (pronounced **tish**-en)
(adjective) Titian hair is reddish-gold. The Italian painter *Titian* often painted red-haired people

titillate, titillates, titillating, titillated
(verb) If something titillates someone, it pleases and excites them, especially in a sexual way. **titillation** (noun).

titivate, titivates, titivating, titivated
(verb) To titivate something means to smarten it up, e.g. *I'll just titivate my hair before we go out.*

title, titles
1 (noun) The title of a book, play, or piece of music is its name.
2 Someone's title is a word that describes their rank, status, or job, e.g. *His title is Area Manager.*
3 A title in a sports competition is the position of champion, e.g. *He's won the heavyweight title.*
4 Title is the legal ownership of something, especially land or property, e.g. *The landlord has title to the property.*

titled
(adjective) Someone who is titled has a high social rank and has a title such as 'Princess', 'Lord', 'Lady', or 'Sir'.

title deed, title deeds
(noun) A title deed is a document that gives a person the legal ownership of something, especially land or property.

titter, titters, tittering, tittered
(verb) If you titter, you laugh in a way that shows you are nervous or embarrassed.

tittle-tattle
(noun) Tittle-tattle is gossip.

titular (pronounced **tit**-yoo-lar)
(adjective) A titular job or position has a name that makes it seem important, although the person has no real power, e.g. *the titular head of state.*

tizz or **tizzy**
(noun; an informal word) If you get into a tizz, you get excited, worried, or nervous.

TNT
(noun) TNT is a type of powerful explosive. It is an abbreviation for 'trinitrotoluene'.

to
1 (preposition) 'To' is used to indicate the place that someone or something is moving towards or pointing at, e.g. *Jill's going with us to London.*
2 'To' is used to indicate the limit of something, e.g. *Goods to the value of £3,000 were stolen.*
3 'To' is used in ratios and rates when saying how many units of one type there are for each unit of another, e.g. *It does 40 miles to the gallon.*
4 (adverb) If you push or shut a door to, you close it but do not shut it completely.
5 (phrase) When you **come to**, you regain consciousness after fainting.

toad, toads
(noun) A toad is an amphibian that looks like a frog but has a drier skin and lives less in the water.

toadstool, toadstools
(noun) A toadstool is a type of poisonous fungus.

toady, toadies, toadying, toadied
1 (noun) A toady is someone who flatters important people in the hope of getting some advantage out of them.
2 (verb) To toady means to flatter important people in the hope of getting some advantage out of them.

toast, toasts, toasting, toasted
1 (noun) Toast is slices of bread made brown and crisp by cooking at a high temperature.
2 (verb) If you toast bread, you cook it at a high temperature so that it becomes brown and crisp.
3 If you toast yourself, you sit in front of a fire so that you feel pleasantly warm.
4 (noun) To drink a toast to someone means to drink an alcoholic drink in honour of them.
5 (verb) To toast someone means to drink an alcoholic drink in honour of them.
[from Latin *tostus* meaning 'parched']

toaster, toasters
(noun) A toaster is a piece of electrical equipment used for toasting bread.

tobacco
(noun) Tobacco is the dried leaves of the tobacco plant which people smoke in pipes, cigarettes, and cigars.
[from Spanish *tabaco*]

tobacconist, tobacconists
(noun) A tobacconist is a person who runs a shop that sells tobacco, cigarettes, and cigars; also the shop itself.

toboggan, toboggans, tobogganing, tobogganed
1 (noun) A toboggan is a flat seat with two wooden or metal runners, used for sliding over the snow.
2 (verb) To toboggan means to ride a toboggan.
[an American Indian word]

toby jug, toby jugs
(noun) A toby jug is a beer mug or jug in the shape of a fat man wearing a three-cornered hat and smoking a pipe.

today
1 (adverb and noun) Today means the day on which you are speaking or writing.
2 Today also means the present period of history, e.g. *Today we have very efficient means of transport.*

toddle, toddles, toddling, toddled
(verb) To toddle means to walk in short, quick steps, as a very young child does.

toddler, toddlers
(noun) A toddler is a small child who has just learned to walk.

toddy, toddies
(noun) A toddy is a drink made from alcohol, hot water, sugar, and sometimes lemon juice.
[from Hindi *tari* meaning 'palm juice']

to-do, to-dos
(noun) A to-do is a situation in which people are very agitated, confused, or annoyed, e.g. *There was an awful to-do about her leaving college.*

toe, toes, toeing, toed
1 (noun) Your toes are the five moveable parts at the end of your foot.
2 The toe of a shoe or sock is the part that covers the end of your foot.
3 (phrase) If you **toe the line**, you behave in the way that people in authority expect you to.

toehold, toeholds
(noun) A toehold is a small crack or ledge in a cliff where climbers can place their feet when climbing.

toff, toffs
(noun; an informal, old-fashioned word) A toff is an upper-class or rich person.

toffee, toffees
(noun) Toffee is a sticky, chewy sweet made by boiling sugar and butter together with water.

toga, togas
(noun) In ancient Rome, a toga was a long loose robe.

together
1 (adverb) If people do something together, they do it with each other.
2 If two things happen together, they happen at the same time.
3 If things are joined or fixed together, they are joined or fixed to each other.
4 If things or people are together, they are very near to each other.

Similar words: (sense 1) jointly, collectively
(sense 2) simultaneously, contemporaneously

togetherness
(noun) Togetherness is a feeling of closeness and friendship.

toggle, toggles
(noun) A toggle is a fastener consisting of a small rod which is pushed through a loop or hole.

togs
(plural noun; an informal word) Togs are clothes.

toil, toils, toiling, toiled
1 (verb) When people toil, they work hard doing unpleasant, difficult, or tiring tasks or jobs.
2 If you toil up a slope or along a road, you move slowly and with difficulty, especially when you are very tired.
3 (noun) Toil is unpleasant, difficult, or tiring work.

toilet, toilets
1 (noun) A toilet is a large bowl, connected by a pipe to the drains, which you use when you want to get rid of urine or faeces.
2 A toilet is a small room containing a toilet.
3 (an old-fashioned use) Your toilet is the activity of washing and dressing yourself.
[from French *toilette* meaning 'dress']

toiletries
(plural noun) Toiletries are the things you use when cleaning and taking care of your body, such as soap and deodorant.

toilet water, toilet waters
(noun) Toilet water is a very lightly scented liquid which may be used as a perfume.

token, tokens
1 (noun) A token is a piece of paper or card that is worth a particular amount of money and can be exchanged for goods, e.g. *book tokens.*
2 Tokens are flat round pieces of metal or plastic that can sometimes be used instead of money, for example in a juke-box.
3 If you give something to someone as a token of your feelings for them, you give it to them as a way of showing those feelings.
4 (adjective) If something is described as token, it shows that there is something required but it is not being treated as important, e.g. *a token payment.*
5 (phrase) **By the same token** means that what follows is true for the same reasons that were given for a previous statement.

told
1 Told is the past tense and past participle of **tell**.
2 (phrase) You use **all told** when you want to emphasize that everything has been counted, e.g. *There are five of us all told going to the play.*

tolerable
1 (adjective) able to be borne or put up with.
2 fairly satisfactory or reasonable.

Similar words: (sense 1) bearable, endurable, supportable
(sense 2) acceptable, adequate

tolerance
1 (noun) A person's tolerance is their ability to accept or put up with something which may not be enjoyable or pleasant for them.
2 Tolerance is the quality of allowing other people to have their own attitudes or beliefs, or to behave in a particular way, even if you do not agree or approve, e.g. *religious tolerance.*
tolerant (adjective).

tolerate, tolerates, tolerating, tolerated
1 (verb) If you tolerate things that you do not approve of or agree with, you allow them.
2 If you can tolerate something, you accept it, even though it is unsatisfactory or unpleasant.
toleration (noun).
[from Latin *tolerare* meaning 'to endure']

Similar words: bear, suffer, endure, put up with, stand, stick, stomach

toll, tolls, tolling, tolled
1 (verb) When someone tolls a bell, it is rung slowly, often as a sign that someone has died.
2 (noun) The death toll in an accident is the number of people who have died in it.
3 (phrase) If something **takes its toll**, it has a serious effect and causes a lot of suffering, e.g. *Working nights was beginning to take its toll.*
4 (noun) A toll is a sum of money that you have to pay in order to use a particular bridge or road.
[senses 2-4 are from Greek *telos* meaning 'tax']

tom, toms
(noun) A tom is a male cat.

tomahawk, tomahawks
(noun) A tomahawk is a small, light axe used by North American Indians.

tomato, tomatoes
(noun) A tomato is a small round red fruit, used as a vegetable and often eaten raw in salads. [from Spanish *tomate*]

tomb, tombs
(noun) A tomb is a large grave for one or more corpses.

Similar words: crypt, vault, mausoleum, sepulchre

tombola
(noun) Tombola is a game in which you buy a ticket with a number on it and can win a prize if this number is chosen.

tomboy, tomboys
(noun) A tomboy is a girl who likes playing rough or noisy games.

tome, tomes
(noun; a formal word) A tome is a very large heavy book.

tomfoolery
(noun) Tomfoolery is childish, playful behaviour.

tommy, tommies
(noun; an old-fashioned, informal word) Tommy is a name for a British soldier.
[short for *Thomas Atkins*, an imaginary soldier referred to in army regulations]

tomorrow
1 (adverb and noun) Tomorrow means the day after today.
2 You can refer to the future, especially the near future, as tomorrow.

tom-tom, tom-toms
(noun) A tom-tom is an African or Asian drum played by hand.
[from Hindi *tamtam*]

ton, tons
1 (noun) A ton is a unit of weight equal to 2240 pounds or about 1016 kilograms.
2 (plural noun; an informal use) If you have tons of something, you have a lot of it.

tonal
(adjective) involving the quality or pitch of a sound or of music.

tone, tones, toning, toned
1 (noun) Someone's tone is a quality in their voice which shows what they are thinking or feeling.
2 The tone of a musical instrument or a singer's voice is the kind of sound it has.
3 The tone of a piece of writing is its style and the ideas or opinions expressed in it, e.g. *The tone of the newspaper article was offensive.*
4 A tone is a lighter, darker, or brighter shade of the same colour, e.g. *You need to match the skirt with a blouse of a darker tone.*

tone down
(phrasal verb) If you tone down something, you make it more moderate.

tone-deaf
(adjective) unable to sing in tune or to recognize different tunes.

tone poem, tone poems
(noun) A tone poem is a piece of orchestral music which is based on a poem, folk tale, or scene.

tongs
(plural noun) Tongs consist of two long narrow pieces of metal joined together at one end. You press the pieces together to pick an object up.

tongue, tongues
1 (noun) Your tongue is the soft part in your mouth that you can move and use for tasting, licking, and speaking.
2 A tongue is also a language.
3 Tongue is the cooked tongue of an ox.
4 The tongue of a shoe or boot is the piece of leather underneath the laces.
5 (phrase) If you **have your tongue in your cheek**, you are not being sincere or serious, although you may appear to be.
6 A **slip of the tongue** is a small mistake that you make when you are speaking.

tongue twister, tongue twisters
(noun) A tongue twister is a sentence that is very difficult to say properly, especially when you are saying it quickly.

tonic, tonics
1 (noun) Tonic or tonic water is a colourless, fizzy drink that has a slightly bitter flavour and is often mixed with alcoholic drinks.
2 A tonic is a medicine that makes you feel stronger, healthier, and less tired.
3 You can refer to anything that makes you feel stronger or more cheerful as a tonic, e.g. *That holiday was a real tonic for her.*
4 (a technical use) The tonic of a musical scale is its first note.

Similar words: (sense 3) pick-me-up, stimulant, boost

tonight
(adverb and noun) Tonight is the evening or night that will come at the end of today.

tonnage (pronounced **tun**-nij)
1 (noun) The tonnage of a ship is its size or the amount of cargo it can carry.
2 Tonnage is the total number of tons that something weighs, or the total amount of something measured in tons.

tonne, tonnes (pronounced **tun**)
(noun) A tonne is a unit of weight equal to 1000 kilograms.

tonsil, tonsils
(noun) Your tonsils are the two small, soft lumps in your throat at the back of your mouth.

tonsillitis (pronounced ton-sil-**lie**-tiss)
(noun) Tonsillitis is a painful swelling of your tonsils caused by an infection.

tonsure, tonsures (pronounced **ton**-sher)
(noun) A tonsure is a shaved area on a man's

head surrounded by hair. Some monks have a tonsure.
[from Latin *tonsura* meaning 'a clipping']

too
1 (adverb) also or as well, e.g. *You come too.*
2 more than a desirable, necessary, or acceptable amount, e.g. *There's too much salt in the rice.*

tool, tools
1 (noun) A tool is any hand-held instrument or piece of equipment that you use to help you do a particular kind of work.
2 A tool is an object, skill, or idea that is needed or used for a particular purpose, e.g. *Textbooks are one of the essential tools of the student.*
3 You refer to someone as a tool when they are in someone else's power and are used by them, especially to do unpleasant or dishonest things.

Similar words: (sense 1) implement, utensil

toot, toots, tooting, tooted
1 (verb) If a car horn toots, it produces a short sound.
2 (noun) A toot is a short sound made by a car horn, e.g. *He gave two toots on the horn.*

tooth, teeth
1 (noun) Your teeth are the hard enamel-covered objects in your mouth that you use for biting and chewing food.
2 The teeth of a comb, saw, or zip are the parts that stick out in a row on its edge.
3 (phrase) If you do something **in the teeth of** a difficulty or danger, you do it in spite of the difficulty or danger.

toothpaste
(noun) Toothpaste is a substance which you use to clean your teeth.

top, tops, topping, topped
1 (noun) The top of something is its highest point, part, or surface.
2 (adjective) The top thing of a series of things is the highest one, e.g. *He was on the top step.*
3 (noun) The top of a bottle, jar, or tube is its cap or lid.
4 A top is a piece of clothing worn on the upper half of your body.
5 A top is a toy with a pointed end on which it spins.
6 (verb) If someone tops a poll or popularity chart, they do better than anyone else in it, e.g. *The band has topped the charts for three weeks.*
7 If something tops a particular amount, it is greater than that amount, e.g. *Money raised by the marathon topped five thousand.*
8 If you top a remark or action, you follow it with a better or more impressive one, e.g. *He topped my joke with a better one.*

Similar words: (sense 1) crest, crown (sense 3) cover, stopper, lid, cap

top hat, top hats
(noun) A top hat is a tall hat with a narrow brim that men wear on special occasions.

top-heavy
(adjective) larger or heavier at the top than at the bottom.

topiary (pronounced **toe**-pee-ar-ee)
(noun) Topiary is the art of cutting hedges and bushes into different shapes.
[from Latin *topia* meaning 'ornamental gardening']

topic, topics
(noun) A topic is a particular subject that you write about or discuss.

topical
(adjective) involving or related to events that are happening at the time you are speaking or writing.

topmost
(adjective) The topmost thing in a group of things is the one that is highest or nearest the top.

topnotch
(adjective; an informal word) excellent.

topography, topographies
1 (noun) Topography is the study and description of the physical features of an area, for example the hills, valleys, or rivers.
2 The topography of a particular area is its physical shape.
[from Greek *topos* meaning 'place' and *graphein* meaning 'to write']

topping, toppings
(noun) A topping is food that is put on top of other food in order to decorate it or add to its flavour.

topple, topples, toppling, toppled
(verb) If something topples, it becomes unsteady and falls over.

top-secret
(adjective) meant to be kept completely secret.

topsoil
(noun) Topsoil is the layer of soil nearest the surface of the ground.

topsy-turvy
(adjective) in a confused state, e.g. *Her room was all topsy-turvy.*

tor, tors
(noun) A tor is a bare, rocky hill.

torch, torches
1 (noun) A torch is a small electric light carried in the hand and powered by batteries.
2 A torch is also a long stick with burning material wrapped around one end.
[from Old French *torche* meaning 'handful of twisted straw']

toreador, toreadors (pronounced **tor**-ee-a-dor)
(noun) A toreador is a bullfighter.
[a Spanish word]

torment, torments, tormenting, tormented
1 (noun) Torment is extreme pain or unhappiness.
2 A torment is something that causes extreme pain and unhappiness, e.g. *His new job was a torment to him.*

3 (verb) If something torments you, it causes you extreme unhappiness.
4 If someone torments you, they annoy you in a playful and rather cruel way, e.g. *Jan is always tormenting her younger sister.*
[from Latin *tormentum* meaning 'torture']

Similar words: (sense 2) bane, blight, scourge, plague

tormentor, tormentors
(noun) A tormentor is someone who deliberately causes pain or unhappiness to another person.

torn
1 Torn is the past participle of **tear.**
2 (adjective) If you are torn between two or more things, you cannot decide which one to choose and this makes you unhappy, e.g. *He was torn between his job and his family.*

tornado, tornadoes or **tornados** (pronounced tor-**nay**-doh)
(noun) A tornado is a violent storm with strong circular winds around a funnel-shaped cloud.

torpedo, torpedoes, torpedoing, torpedoed
(pronounced tor-**pee**-doh)
1 (noun) A torpedo is a tube-shaped bomb that travels underwater and explodes when it hits a target.
2 (verb) If a ship is torpedoed, it is hit, and usually sunk, by a torpedo.

torpid
(adjective) mentally or physically inactive.
[from Latin *torpere* meaning 'to be stiff' or 'to be numb']

torpor
(noun) Torpor is the state of being torpid.

torrent, torrents
1 (noun) When a lot of water is falling very rapidly, it can be said to be falling in torrents.
2 A torrent of speech is a lot of it directed continuously at someone, e.g. *a torrent of speech.*
[from Latin *torrens* meaning 'burning']

torrential
(adjective) Torrential rain pours down very rapidly and in great quantities.

torrid
1 (adjective) Torrid weather is very hot and dry.
2 A torrid love affair is one in which people show very strong emotions.

torso, torsos
(noun) Your torso is the main part of your body, excluding your head, arms, and legs.
[an Italian word]

tortilla, tortillas (pronounced tor-**tee**-a)
(noun) A tortilla is a Mexican pancake made from corn and eggs.

tortoise, tortoises
(noun) A tortoise is a slow-moving reptile with a large hard shell over its body into which it can pull its head and legs for protection.

tortoiseshell
(noun) Tortoiseshell is the hard brown and yellow shell from the sea turtle. It is often polished and used to make jewellery and ornaments.

tortuous
1 (adjective) A tortuous road is full of bends and twists.
2 A tortuous piece of writing is long and complicated.

torture, tortures, torturing, tortured
1 (noun) Torture is great pain that is deliberately caused to someone in order to punish them or get information from them.
2 (verb) If someone tortures another person, they deliberately cause that person great pain in order to punish them or get information.
3 To torture someone also means to cause them to suffer mentally, e.g. *Why do you have to torture me by talking about mother's death?*
torturer (noun).

Tory, Tories
(noun) A Tory is a member or supporter of the Conservative Party.
[from Irish *toraidhe* meaning 'outlaw']

toss, tosses, tossing, tossed
1 (verb) If you toss something somewhere, you throw it there lightly and carelessly.
2 If you toss your head, you move it suddenly backwards, especially when you are angry, annoyed, or want your own way.
3 If you toss a coin, you decide something by throwing a coin into the air and guessing which side will face upwards when it lands.
4 To toss means to move repeatedly from side to side, e.g. *He tossed restlessly in his sleep.*
5 (noun) A toss is an act of tossing.

Similar words: (sense 1) lob, flip, flick

toss-up
(noun; an informal expression) If a situation is a toss-up, either of two possible results seems equally likely.

tot, tots, totting, totted
1 (noun) A tot is a very young child.
2 A tot of strong alcohol such as whisky is a small amount of it.
3 (verb) To tot up numbers means to add them together.

total, totals, totalling, totalled
1 (noun) A total is the number you get when you add several numbers together.
2 (verb) When you total a set of numbers or objects, you add them all together.
3 If several numbers total a certain figure, that is the figure you get when all the numbers are added together, e.g. *The cost totalled £3.*
4 (adjective) Total means complete, e.g. *The trip was a total disaster.*
totally (adverb).

Similar words: (sense 1) sum, totality, whole, aggregate

totalitarian (pronounced toe-tal-it-**tair**-ee-an)
(adjective) A totalitarian political system is one

in which one political party controls everything and does not allow any other parties to exist. **totalitarianism** (noun).

totality
(noun) The totality of something is the whole of it.

tote, totes, toting, toted (an informal word)
1 (noun) The tote is a system of betting money on horses at a racetrack, in which all the money is divided among the people who have bet on the winning horses. Tote is an abbreviation for 'totalizator'.
2 (verb) To tote a gun means to carry it.

totem, totems
(noun) A totem is an object that is regarded as a symbol by a particular group of people who treat it with great respect.
[an American Indian word]

totem pole, totem poles
(noun) A totem pole is a long wooden pole with symbols and pictures carved and painted on it. Totem poles are made by some North American Indians.

totter, totters, tottering, tottered
(verb) When someone totters, they walk in an unsteady way.

toucan, toucans (pronounced **too**-kan)
(noun) A toucan is a large tropical fruit-eating bird with a very large beak.

touch, touches, touching, touched
1 (verb) If you touch something, you put your fingers or hand on it.
2 When two things touch, their surfaces come into contact, e.g. *the wires are touching.*
3 (noun) Your sense of touch is your ability to tell what something is like by touching it.
4 A touch is a detail which is added to improve something, e.g. *finishing touches.*
5 The way someone does something can be called their touch, e.g. *He hasn't got your touch, David, when it comes to being a parent.*
6 A touch of something is a small amount of it, e.g. *'Milk?' — 'Just a touch.'*
7 (verb) If you are touched by something, you are emotionally affected by it, e.g. *I was touched by her kind words.*
8 (phrase) If you are **in touch** with someone, you are in contact with them.
9 If something is **touch and go**, it is uncertain whether it will happen or succeed.
10 (noun) In games such as football, touch is the area just outside the touchlines, e.g. *The ball went into touch.*

touch down
(phrasal verb) When an aircraft touches down, it lands.

touch on
(phrasal verb) To touch on something means to mention it briefly.

touchdown, touchdowns
(noun) Touchdown is the landing of an aircraft.

touché (pronounced too-**shay**)
(exclamation) You say touché to admit to

someone in an argument that they have made a good point against you. [a French expression meaning literally 'touched', used in fencing to acknowledge a hit]

touching
(adjective) causing feelings of sadness and sympathy.

Similar words: moving, poignant, affecting

touchline, touchlines
(noun) In games such as football, the touchline is either of the lines marking the side of the pitch.

touchpaper, touchpapers
(noun) A touchpaper is a piece of paper coated with potassium nitrate, which is used as a slow-burning fuse for fireworks.

touchstone, touchstones
(noun) A touchstone is a feature of something which is used as a test by which its quality can be judged.

touch-type, touch-types, touch-typing, touch-typed
(verb) To touch-type means to type without looking at the keys.

touchy, touchier, touchiest
1 (adjective) If someone is touchy, they are easily upset, offended, or irritated.
2 A touchy subject is one that needs to be dealt with carefully, because it might upset or offend people.

tough, tougher, toughest
1 (adjective) A tough person is strong and independent and able to put up with hardship.
2 A tough substance is difficult to break.
3 A tough task, problem, or way of life is difficult or full of hardship, e.g. *One of the toughest problems is unemployment.*
4 Tough policies or actions are strict and firm, e.g. *We need tough measures to combat crime.*
toughly (adverb), **toughness** (noun), **toughen** (verb).

Similar words: (sense 2) durable, sturdy, resilient

toupee, toupees (pronounced **too**-pay)
(noun) A toupee is a small wig worn by a man to cover a bald patch on his head.
[from French *toupet* meaning 'tuft of hair']

tour, tours, touring, toured
1 (noun) A tour is a long journey during which you visit several places.
2 A tour is a short trip round a place such as a city or famous building.
3 (verb) If you tour a place, you go on a journey or a trip round it.
[from French *tour* meaning 'a turn']

tour de force, tours de force (pronounced toor de **forss**)
(noun) A tour de force is a brilliant and skilful action or theatrical performance.
[a French expression, meaning literally 'feat of strength']

tourism
(noun) Tourism is the business of providing

services for people on holiday, for example hotels, sightseeing trips, and leisure activities.

tourist, tourists
(noun) A tourist is a person who visits places for pleasure or interest.

tournament, tournaments
(noun) A tournament is a sports competition in which players who win a match play further matches, until just one person or team is left.
[from Old French *tourneier* meaning 'to fight on horseback']

tourniquet, tourniquets (pronounced **toor-nik-kay**)
(noun) A tourniquet is a strip of cloth tied tightly round a wound in order to stop it bleeding.
[a French word]

tousled
(adjective) Tousled hair is untidy.

tout, touts, touting, touted
1 (verb) If someone touts something, they try to sell it.
2 (noun) A tout is someone who sells tickets outside a sports ground or theatre, charging more than the original price.
3 (verb) If someone touts for business or custom, they try to obtain it in a very direct way, e.g. *He went from door to door touting for custom.*

tow, tows, towing, towed
1 (verb) If a vehicle tows another vehicle, it pulls it along behind it.
2 (noun) To give a vehicle a tow means to tow it.
3 (phrase) If you have someone **in tow**, they are with you because you are looking after them, e.g. *He came late, his younger brother in tow.*

towards
1 (preposition) in the direction of, e.g. *He saw his mother running towards him.*
2 about or involving, e.g. *I never understood her feelings towards me.*
3 as a contribution for, e.g. *Dad gave me £20 towards my new bike.*
4 near to, e.g. *We sat towards the back.*

towbar, towbars
(noun) A towbar is a metal bar or frame used by one vehicle to tow another.

towel, towels
1 (noun) A towel is a piece of thick, soft cloth that you use to dry yourself with.
2 (verb) If you towel yourself, you dry yourself with a towel.

towelling
(noun) Towelling is thick, soft cloth that is used for making towels.

tower, towers, towering, towered
1 (noun) A tower is a tall, narrow building, sometimes attached to a larger building such as a castle or church.
2 (phrase) Someone who is **a tower of strength** gives help and support.
3 (verb) Someone or something that towers over other people or things is much taller than them.
towering (adjective).

towheaded
(adjective) having blond or yellowish hair.
[from *tow*, the straw-coloured fibre of flax]

town, towns
1 (noun) A town is a place with many streets and buildings where people live and work.
2 Town is the central shopping and business part of a town rather than the suburbs, e.g. *We went into town to do some Christmas shopping.*
3 (phrase) If you **go to town on** an activity, you put a lot of effort and enthusiasm into it.

township, townships
1 (noun) A township is a small town in South Africa where only Black people or Coloured people are allowed to live.
2 A township is a small area of local government in the United States or Canada, especially a town and the land surrounding it.

towpath, towpaths
(noun) A towpath is a path along the side of a canal or river.

toxic
(adjective) poisonous.
[from Greek *toxikon* meaning 'poison used on arrows' from *toxon* meaning 'arrow']

toxicity
(noun) Toxicity is the strength of a poison.

toxicology
(noun) Toxicology is the study of poisons.

toxin, toxins
(noun) A toxin is a poison, especially one produced by bacteria and very harmful to plants, people, and other living creatures.

toy, toys, toying, toyed
1 (noun) A toy is any object made to play with.
2 (verb) If you toy with an idea, you consider it without being very serious about it, e.g. *We both toyed with the idea of joining the Air Force.*
3 If you toy with an object, you fiddle with it, e.g. *She toyed with the pencil as she spoke.*

trace, traces, tracing, traced
1 (verb) If you trace something, you find it after looking for it, e.g. *They were trying to trace the missing child.*
2 To trace the development of something means to find out or describe how it developed.
3 If you trace a drawing or a map, you copy it by covering it with a piece of transparent paper and drawing over the lines underneath.
4 (noun) A trace is a sign which shows you that someone or something has been in a place, e.g. *There was no trace of the car or its owner.*
5 A trace of something is a very small amount of it.
tracing (noun).

trace element, trace elements
(noun) A trace element is any of various chemical elements that are necessary for normal animal and plant growth but are needed only in very small amounts.

tracery
(noun) Tracery is a decorative pattern of

interlacing bars, as on the upper part of a stained glass window.

trachea, tracheas (pronounced trak-**kee**-a)
(noun; a medical word) Your trachea is your windpipe.
[from Greek *arteria trakheia* meaning 'rough artery']

tracing paper
(noun) Tracing paper is transparent paper that you use to make tracings.

track, tracks, tracking, tracked
1 (noun) A track is a narrow road or path.
2 A railway track is a strip of ground with rails on it that a train travels along.
3 A track is also a piece of ground, shaped like a ring, which horses, cars, or athletes race around.
4 (adjective) In an athletics competition, the track events are the races on a running track.
5 (plural noun) Tracks are marks left on the ground by a person or animal, e.g. *The fox didn't leave any tracks.*
6 (verb) If you track animals or people, you find them by following their footprints or other signs that they have left behind.
7 (noun) A track on a record or tape is one of the songs or pieces of music on it.

track down
(phrasal verb) If you track down someone or something, you find them by searching for them.

track record, track records
(noun) The track record of a person or a company is their past achievements or failures, e.g. *He has a very good track record.*

tracksuit, tracksuits
(noun) A tracksuit is a loose, warm suit of trousers and a top, worn for outdoor sports.

tract, tracts
1 (noun) A tract is a pamphlet which expresses a strong opinion on a religious, moral, or political subject.
2 A tract of land or forest is a large area of it.
3 A tract is a system of organs and tubes in an animal's or person's body that has a particular function, e.g. *the digestive tract.*
[sense 1 is from Latin *tractatus* meaning 'treatment'; senses 2 and 3 are from Latin *tractus* meaning 'a stretching out']

tractable
(adjective) easily controlled or dealt with, e.g. *He has a calm and tractable nature.*
[from Latin *tractare* meaning 'to manage']

traction
1 (noun) Traction is a form of medical treatment given to an injured limb which involves pulling it gently for long periods of time using a system of weights and pulleys.
2 Traction is the pulling of something using a particular form of power.
3 Traction is the grip that the wheels of a vehicle have on the ground, e.g. *Four wheel drive gives improved traction in rain, snow, and ice.*
[from Latin *tractum*, the past participle of *trahere* meaning 'to drag']

traction engine, traction engines
(noun) A traction engine is a large, heavy vehicle powered by steam that was used in the past for pulling heavy loads.

tractor, tractors
(noun) A tractor is a vehicle with large rear wheels that is used on a farm for pulling machinery, trailers, and other heavy loads.

trade, trades, trading, traded
1 (noun) Trade is the activity of buying, selling, or exchanging goods or services between people, firms, or countries.
2 (verb) When people, firms, or countries trade, they buy, sell, or exchange goods or services.
3 (noun) Someone's trade is the kind of work they do, especially when it requires special training in practical skills.
4 (verb) If you trade things, you exchange them, e.g. *They traded ideas about the church.*

Similar words: (sense 1) commerce
(sense 2) bargain, barter, haggle, deal

trade in
(phrasal verb) If a person trades in something such as a car, they give it to a dealer when they buy a new one to get a reduction on the price.

trademark, trademarks
(noun) A trademark is a name or symbol that a manufacturer always uses on its products. Trademarks are usually protected by law so that no-one else can use them.

trader, traders
(noun) A trader is a person whose job is to trade in goods, e.g. *market traders.*

tradesman, tradesmen
(noun) A tradesman is a person, for example a shopkeeper, whose job is to sell goods.

trade union, trade unions
(noun) A trade union is an organization of workers that tries to improve the pay and conditions in a particular industry.

trade wind, trade winds
(noun) The trade winds are the northeast and southeast winds which blow regularly and form part of the planetary wind system.
[from an old sense of *trade* meaning 'track']

tradition, traditions
(noun) A tradition is a custom or belief that has existed for a long time without changing.
[from Latin *traditio* meaning 'a handing down']

Similar words: custom, convention

traditional
1 (adjective) Traditional customs or beliefs have existed for a long time without changing, e.g. *The bride is dressed in traditional costume.*
2 A traditional organization or institution is one in which older methods are used rather than modern ones, e.g. *a very traditional school.*
traditionally (adverb)

Similar words: (sense 2) orthodox, conventional, conservative

traditionalist, traditionalists
(noun) A traditionalist is someone who supports the established customs and beliefs of their society, and does not want to change them.

traduce, traduces, traducing, traduced
(pronounced trad-**yoos**)
(verb; a formal word) To traduce someone means to deliberately say unpleasant things about them that are not true.
[from Latin *traducere* meaning 'to lead (prisoners) in a procession to be jeered at']

traffic, traffics, trafficking, trafficked
1 (noun) Traffic is the movement of vehicles or persons along a route at a particular time.
2 Traffic in something such as drugs is an illegal trade in them.
3 (verb) Someone who traffics in drugs or other goods buys and sells them illegally.
[from Italian *traffico* meaning 'trade']

traffic light, traffic lights
(noun) Traffic lights are the set of red, amber, and green lights at a road junction which control the flow of traffic.

traffic warden, traffic wardens
(noun) A traffic warden is a person whose job is to make sure that cars are not parked in the wrong place or for longer than is allowed.

tragedy, tragedies (pronounced **traj**-id-ee)
1 (noun) A tragedy is an event or situation that is disastrous or very sad.
2 A tragedy is a serious story or play, that usually ends with the death of the main character.
3 Tragedy is a type of literature, especially drama, that is serious and sad and that often ends with the death of the main character.
[from Greek *tragoidia*]

tragic
1 (adjective) Something tragic is very sad because it involves death, suffering, or disaster, e.g. *He had a tragic accident and lost both legs.*
2 Tragic films, plays, and books are sad and serious, e.g. *a tragic love story.*
tragically (adverb).

tragicomedy, tragicomedies
(noun) A tragicomedy is a play or other written work that is both sad and funny.
tragicomic (adjective).

trail, trails, trailing, trailed
1 (noun) A trail is a rough path across open country or through forests.
2 A trail is a series of marks or other signs left by someone or something as they move along.
3 (verb) If you trail something or it trails, it drags along behind you as you move, or it hangs down loosely, e.g. *She trailed her fingers through the water.*
4 If someone trails along, they move slowly, without any energy or enthusiasm, e.g. *I used to trail around after him like a child.*
5 If a voice trails away or trails off, it gradually becomes more hesitant until it stops completely.
[from Latin *trahere* meaning 'to drag']

trailer, trailers
1 (noun) A trailer is a small vehicle which can be loaded with things and pulled behind a car.
2 A trailer for a film or a television or radio programme is a set of short extracts from it, which are shown or broadcast in order to advertise it.

train, trains, training, trained
1 (noun) A train is a number of carriages or trucks which are pulled by a railway engine.
2 A train of thought is a connected series of thoughts, e.g. *My train of thought was interrupted by the phone ringing.*
3 The train of a formal dress is a long part at the back of it that rests on the ground.
4 A train of vehicles or people is a line or group following behind something or someone, e.g. *The Pope was followed by a train of bodyguards.*
5 (verb) If you train, you learn how to do a particular job, e.g. *She is trained as a nurse.*
6 If you train for a sports match or a race, you prepare for it by doing exercises.
training (noun).

trainee, trainees
(noun) A trainee is someone who is being taught how to do a job, e.g. *a trainee accountant.*

trainers
(plural noun) Trainers are special shoes worn for running or jogging.

traipse, traipses, traipsing, traipsed
(verb; an informal word) If you traipse along, you go slowly and aimlessly, often because you are tired.

trait, traits
(noun) A trait is a particular characteristic, quality, or tendency, e.g. *Certain personality traits made her unpopular.*

traitor, traitors
(noun) A traitor is someone who betrays their country or the group which they belong to.
traitorous (adjective), **traitorously** (adverb).
[from Latin *traditor*]

trajectory, trajectories (pronounced traj-**jek**-tor-ee)
(noun) The trajectory of an object moving through the air is the curving path that it follows.
[from *trans-* and Latin *jacere* meaning 'to throw across']

tram, trams
(noun) A tram is a vehicle which runs on rails along the street and is powered by electricity from an overhead wire.

trammel, trammels, trammelling, trammelled (a formal word)
1 (verb) If you are trammelled by something, you are prevented from acting freely by something that is outside your control, e.g. *She was trammelled by her children and the chores.*
2 (noun) A trammel is anything that trammels you.
[from Old French *tramail* meaning 'three-mesh net']

tramp, tramps, tramping, tramped
1 (noun) A tramp is a person who has no home, no job, and very little money.
2 (verb) If you tramp from one place to another, you walk with slow, heavy footsteps.
3 (noun) A tramp is also a long country walk, e.g. *They went for a tramp over the hills.*

trample, tramples, trampling, trampled
1 (verb) If you trample on something, you tread heavily on it so that it is damaged.
2 If you trample on someone or on their rights or feelings, you behave in a way that shows you don't care about them.

trampoline, trampolines
(noun) A trampoline is a piece of gymnastic apparatus consisting of a large piece of strong cloth held taut by springs in a frame.

trance, trances
(noun) A trance is a mental state in which someone seems to be asleep but is conscious enough to be aware of their surroundings and to respond to questions and commands.
[from Old French *transir* meaning 'to faint']

tranquil (pronounced **trang**-kwil)
(adjective) calm and peaceful, e.g. *a lake of tranquil blue water... a tranquil sleep.*
tranquilly (adverb), **tranquillity** (noun).

tranquillize, tranquillizes, tranquillizing, tranquillized; also spelled **tranquillise**
(verb) If people or animals are tranquillized, they are given a drug to make them become calm, sleepy, or unconscious.

tranquillizer, tranquillizers; also spelled **tranquilliser**
(noun) A tranquillizer is a drug that makes people feel less anxious or nervous.

trans-
(prefix) Trans means across, through, or beyond, e.g. *transatlantic.*

transact, transacts, transacting, transacted
(verb) To transact business means to start it and carry on with it until it is finished.
transaction (noun).

transceiver, transceivers
(noun) A transceiver is a radio set that is able to both transmit and receive radio waves.

transcend, transcends, transcending, transcended
(verb) If one thing transcends another, it goes beyond it or is superior to it, e.g. *The holiday transcended our wildest dreams.*
[from Latin *transcendere* meaning 'to climb over']

transcendent
(adjective; a formal word) going beyond or existing outside normal limits or boundaries, e.g. *the transcendent unity of all religions.*
transcendence (noun).

transcendental
(adjective) A transcendental experience or idea is based on things that are beyond the practical experience of ordinary people, and cannot be discovered or understood by ordinary reasoning.

transcendental meditation
(noun) Transcendental meditation is a type of meditation derived from Hinduism, in which people relax mentally by silently repeating over and over again a special form of words.

transcribe, transcribes, transcribing, transcribed
(verb) If you transcribe something that is spoken or written, you write it down, copy it, or change it into a different form of writing, e.g. *He transcribed recordings of conversations.*

transcript, transcripts
(noun) A transcript of something that is spoken is a written copy of it.

transcription, transcriptions
1 (noun) Transcription of a piece of text or music is the process of transcribing it.
2 A transcription is a written text that has been made from a tape recording or from notes.

transept, transepts
(noun) A transept in a cathedral or church is a wing at right angles to the main part of the building.
[from *trans-* and Latin *saeptum* meaning 'enclosure']

transfer, transfers, transferring, transferred
1 (verb) If you transfer something from one place to another, you move it, e.g. *She transferred her savings to a special account.*
2 (noun) The transfer of something is the movement of it from one place to another.
3 (verb) If you transfer to a different place or job, or are transferred to it, you move to a different place or job within the same organization.
4 (noun) A transfer is also a piece of paper with a design on one side which can be ironed or pressed onto cloth, paper, or china.
transferable (adjective), **transference** (noun).

transfiguration, transfigurations
(noun) A transfiguration is a change in appearance.

transfigure, transfigures, transfiguring, transfigured
(verb) If something transfigures you or if you are transfigured, the appearance of your face changes because something has made you very happy, e.g. *Their faces were transfigured with joy.*
[from *trans-* and Latin *figura* meaning 'appearance']

transfix, transfixes, transfixing, transfixed
1 (verb) If you are transfixed by something, you are so impressed, fascinated, or frightened by it that you do not move, e.g. *She was transfixed throughout the whole performance of Swan Lake.*
2 To transfix a person or an animal means to stick a long pointed object through them, e.g. *a wild animal transfixed by a spear.*

transform, transforms, transforming, transformed
(verb) If something is transformed, it is changed

completely, e.g. *Her appearance was transformed when she had her hair permed.*
transformation (noun).

transformer, transformers
(noun) A transformer is a piece of electrical equipment which changes the voltage of a current.

transfusion, transfusions
(noun) A transfusion or blood transfusion is a process in which blood from a healthy person is injected into the body of another person who is badly injured or ill.
transfuse (verb).
[from *trans-* and Latin *fundere* meaning 'to pour']

transgress, transgresses, transgressing, transgressed
(verb; a formal word) When someone transgresses, they break a moral law or rule of behaviour, e.g. *If you transgress the law, you will be punished.*
transgression (noun), **transgressor** (noun).

transient (pronounced **tran**-zee-ent)
(adjective) Something transient does not stay or exist for very long, e.g. *transient happiness.*
transiently (adverb), **transience** (noun).

transistor, transistors
1 (noun) A transistor is a small electrical device in something such as a television or radio which uses a small electrical current or voltage to control a larger electrical current or voltage.
2 A transistor or a transistor radio is a small portable radio.

transit
1 (noun) Transit is the carrying of goods or people by vehicle from one place to another.
2 (phrase) People or things that are **in transit** are travelling or being taken from one place to another, e.g. *The parcel had been lost in transit.*
3 (adjective) A transit area or building is an area or building where people wait or where goods are kept between different stages of a journey, e.g. *a transit camp for refugees.*
[from Latin *transire* meaning 'to pass over']

transition, transitions
(noun) A transition is a change from one form or state to another, e.g. *We made the transition from grammar to comprehensive school.*

transitional
(adjective) A transitional period or stage is one during which something changes from one form or state to another.

transition series
(noun) The transition series is a class of 44 elements with atomic numbers between 21 and 30, 39 and 48, and 57 and 80. Transition elements tend to have more than one valency and to form complexes.

transitive
(adjective) In grammar, a transitive verb is a verb which has an object.

transitory
(adjective) lasting for only a short time.

translate, translates, translating, translated
1 (verb) To translate something that someone has said or written means to say it or write it in a different language.
2 If one thing is translated into another, it is changed or converted into it.
translation (noun), **translator** (noun).
[from Latin *translatus* meaning 'transferred']

translucent
(adjective) If something is translucent, light passes through it so that it seems to glow, e.g. *The beech leaves are translucent in the sunlight.*
translucently (adverb), **translucence** (noun).
[from *trans-* and Latin *lucere* meaning 'to shine']

transmigrate, transmigrates, transmigrating, transmigrated
(verb) To transmigrate means to move from one place, especially via a country, to another place.
transmigration (noun).

transmission, transmissions
1 (noun) The transmission of something involves passing or sending it to a different place or person, e.g. *the transmission of diseases.*
2 The transmission of television or radio programmes is the broadcasting of them.
3 A transmission is a broadcast.

transmit, transmits, transmitting, transmitted
1 (verb) When a message or an electronic signal is transmitted, it is sent by radio waves.
2 To transmit something to a different place or person means to pass it or send it to the place or person, e.g. *a way of transmitting energy.*
transmitter (noun).
[from *trans-* and Latin *mittere* meaning 'to send']

transmute, transmutes, transmuting, transmuted
(verb; a formal word) If something is transmuted into a different form, it is changed to that form.
transmutable (adjective), **transmutation** (noun).

transparency, transparencies
1 (noun) A transparency is a small piece of photographic film which can be projected onto a screen.
2 Transparency is the quality that an object or substance has if you can see through it.

transparent
1 (adjective) If an object or substance is transparent, you can see through it.
2 If something such as a statement, situation, or feeling is transparent, it is easily understood or recognized.
transparently (adverb).
[from *trans-* and Latin *parere* meaning 'to appear']

Similar words: (sense 1) clear, limpid, pellucid, see-through

transpiration
(noun; a technical word) Transpiration is the loss of water vapour from plants, especially through their leaves.

transpire, transpires, transpiring, transpired
1 (verb; a formal use) When it transpires that something is the case, people discover that it is

the case, e.g. *It transpired that he had been lying
all along.*
2 When something transpires, it happens, e.g.
Nobody knows what transpired at the meeting.

transplant, transplants, transplanting,
transplanted
1 (noun) A transplant is the process of removing
something from one place and putting it in
another, e.g. *He's had a liver transplant.*
2 A transplant is also something which has been
transplanted.
3 (verb) When something is transplanted, it is
moved to a different place.

transport, transports, transporting, transported
1 (noun) Vehicles that you travel in are referred
to as transport, e.g. *public transport.*
2 Transport is the moving of goods or people
from one place to another, e.g. *High transport
costs make foreign goods too expensive.*
3 (verb) When goods or people are transported
from one place to another, they are moved there.
[from *trans-* and Latin *portare* meaning 'to
carry']

Similar words: (sense 3) ferry, shuttle, convey, carry

transportation
(noun) Transportation is the transporting of
people and things from one place to another.

transpose, transposes, transposing, transposed
1 (verb; a formal use) If you transpose
something to a different place or position, you
move it there.
2 To transpose something also means to alter it
to a different form, while keeping its essential
features, e.g. *The piece was transposed to the key
of E flat.*
transposition (noun).
[from *trans-* and Latin *ponere* meaning 'to place']

transubstantiation (pronounced
tran-sub-stan-shee-**ay**-shun)
(noun; a formal word) Transubstantiation is the
changing of one substance into another.

transverse
(adjective; a technical word) Transverse is used
to describe something that is at right angles to
something else, e.g. *the transverse muscles run
from side to side.*

transvestite, transvestites
(noun) A transvestite is a person who enjoys
wearing clothes normally worn by people of the
opposite sex.
transvestism (noun).
[from *trans-* and Latin *vestitus* meaning 'clothed']

trap, traps, trapping, trapped
1 (noun) A trap is a piece of equipment or a hole
that is carefully positioned in order to catch
animals or birds.
2 A trap is a trick that is intended to catch or
deceive someone.
3 (verb) Someone who traps animals catches
them using traps.
4 If you trap someone, you trick them so that
they do or say something which they did not
want to.

5 If you are trapped somewhere, you cannot
move or escape because something is blocking
your way or holding you down.
6 If you are trapped, you are in an unpleasant
situation that you cannot easily change, e.g. *She
hated being unemployed; she felt so trapped.*
7 (noun) A trap is an unpleasant situation that
cannot easily be changed, e.g. *the poverty trap.*

Similar words: (sense 3) snare, ensnare, net
(sense 4) ambush

trap door, trap doors
(noun) A trap door is a small horizontal door in a
floor, ceiling, or stage.

trapeze, trapezes
(noun) A trapeze is a bar of wood or metal
hanging from two ropes on which acrobats and
gymnasts swing and perform skilful movements.

trapezium, trapeziums or **trapezia** (pronounced
trap-**pee**-zee-um)
(noun) A trapezium is a four-sided shape with
two sides parallel to each other.

trapper, trappers
(noun) A trapper is a person who traps animals,
especially for their fur.

trappings
(plural noun) The trappings of a particular rank,
position, or state are the clothes or equipment
that go with it.

trash
1 (noun) Trash is rubbish, e.g. *The pavement was
littered with trash.*
2 If you say that something such as a book,
painting, or film is trash, you mean that it is not
very good.

trashy, trashier, trashiest
(adjective) of very poor quality.

trauma, traumas (pronounced **traw**-ma)
1 (noun) A trauma is a very upsetting
experience, e.g. *the trauma of having their
parents arrested.*
2 Trauma is great stress and unhappiness, e.g.
Moving house now will create trauma for her.
[from Greek *trauma* meaning 'wound']

traumatic
(adjective) A traumatic experience is very
upsetting.

travail (pronounced **trav**-ale)
(noun; an old-fashioned word) Travail is difficult
or painful work.
[from Old French *travaillier* meaning 'to work
hard']

travel, travels, travelling, travelled
1 (verb) To travel means to go from one place to
another.
2 (noun) Travel is the act of travelling, e.g. *air
travel.*
3 (plural noun) Someone's travels are the
journeys that they make to places a long way
from their home, e.g. *She told us all about her
travels abroad.*
4 (verb) When something reaches one place from

another, you say that it travels there, e.g. *News travels fast... The ball travelled through the air.*
traveller (noun), **travelling** (adjective).

Similar words: (sense 1) journey, commute, go

traveller's cheque, traveller's cheques
(noun) Traveller's cheques are cheques for use abroad. You buy them at your bank and then exchange them when you are abroad for foreign currency.

travelogue, travelogues (pronounced trav-el-log)
(noun) A travelogue is a talk, film, or brochure about travel or particular travels.

traverse, traverses, traversing, traversed
(verb; a formal word) If you traverse an area of land or water, you go across it or over it, e.g. *I traversed the rest of the slope at a run.*

travesty, travesties
(noun) A travesty of something is a very bad or ridiculous representation or imitation of it, e.g. *The film was a travesty of the original story.*
[from French *travestir* meaning 'to disguise']

trawl, trawls, trawling, trawled
1 (verb) When fishermen trawl, they drag a wide net behind a ship in order to catch fish.
2 (noun) A trawl or trawl net is the wide net that fishermen use in trawling.

trawler, trawlers
(noun) A trawler is a fishing boat that is used for trawling.

tray, trays
(noun) A tray is a flat object with raised edges which is used for carrying food or drinks.

treacherous
1 (adjective) A treacherous person is likely to betray you and cannot be trusted, e.g. *He was a cruel and treacherous man.*
2 The ground or the sea can be described as treacherous when it is dangerous or unreliable, e.g. *The currents are treacherous.*
treacherously (adverb).

Similar words: (sense 1) perfidious, traitorous

treachery
(noun) Treachery is behaviour in which someone betrays their country or a person who trusts them.
[from Old French *trechier* meaning 'to cheat']

treacle
(noun) Treacle is a thick, sweet, sticky syrup obtained by refining sugar, e.g. *treacle tart.*

treacly
(adjective) thick and sticky.

tread, treads, treading, trod, trodden
1 (verb) If you tread on something, you walk on it or step on it.
2 If you tread something into the ground or into a carpet, you crush it in by stepping on it, e.g. *Don't tread mud into the carpet.*
3 (noun) A person's tread is the sound they make with their feet as they walk, e.g. *She could hear the light tread of footsteps on the carpet.*

4 The tread of a tyre or shoe is the pattern of ridges on it that stops it slipping.

treadle, treadles
(noun) A treadle is a lever on something such as a sewing machine that you work with your foot to turn a wheel in the machine.

treadmill, treadmills
1 (noun) A treadmill is a large wheel attached to a machine by various shafts and levers. People or animals used to walk inside the wheel in order to make the machine work.
2 Any task or job that you must keep doing even though it is unpleasant or tiring can be referred to as a treadmill, e.g. *the treadmill of housework.*

treason
(noun) Treason is the crime of betraying your country, for example by helping its enemies.

treasonable
(adjective) A treasonable activity or act is a serious offence against your country and is intended to help your country's enemies.

treasure, treasures, treasuring, treasured
1 (noun) Treasure is a collection of gold, silver, jewels, or other precious objects, especially one that has been hidden, e.g. *buried treasure.*
2 Treasures are valuable works of art, e.g. *the sale of art treasures.*
3 (verb) If you treasure something, you are very pleased that you have it and regard it as very precious, e.g. *I treasure my memories.*
4 (noun) If you call someone a treasure, you mean that they are very helpful to you.
treasured (adjective).

treasurer, treasurers
(noun) A treasurer is a person who is in charge of the finance and accounts of an organization.

treasure-trove
(noun) Treasure-trove is a large amount of money or valuable objects which has been found somewhere and nobody knows who it belongs to.

treasury, treasuries
1 (noun) The Treasury is the government department that deals with the country's finances.
2 A treasury is a place where funds are kept and paid out.

treat, treats, treating, treated
1 (verb) If you treat someone in a particular way, you behave that way towards them.
2 If you treat something in a particular way, you deal with it that way or see it that way, e.g. *Did he treat it as some sort of joke?*
3 When a doctor treats a patient or an illness, he or she gives them medical care and attention.
4 If something such as wood or cloth is treated, a special substance is put on it in order to protect it or give it special properties, e.g. *The floorboards have been treated for woodworm.*
5 (noun) If you give someone a treat, you buy or arrange something special for them which they will enjoy, e.g. *They took her out for a meal as a birthday treat.*
6 (verb) If you treat someone, you buy or

arrange something special for them which they will enjoy.
treatment (noun).
[from Latin *tractare* meaning 'to manage']

treatise, treatises (pronounced **tree**-tiz)
(noun) A treatise is a long formal piece of writing about a particular subject.

treaty, treaties
(noun) A treaty is a written agreement between countries in which they agree to do something or to help each other.
[from Latin *tractatus*]

treble, trebles, trebling, trebled
1 (verb) If something trebles or is trebled, it becomes three times greater in number or amount.
2 (adjective) Treble means three times as large or three times as strong as previously, e.g. *The price is treble the amount it was last year.*
3 (noun) A treble is a boy with a singing voice in the highest range of musical notes. Trebles sing the highest part in four-part harmony.
4 In music, a treble is an instrument which uses a high range of musical notes, e.g. *a treble recorder.*

tree, trees
(noun) A tree is a large plant with a hard woody trunk, branches, and leaves.

tree line
(noun) The tree line is a limit beyond which trees will not grow, because the land beyond is too high, too far north, or too far south.

trefoil (pronounced **tref**-foil)
1 (noun) Trefoil is a plant such as clover whose leaves are each divided into three smaller leaves.
2 (adjective) Trefoil leaves are divided into three smaller leaves.
[from Latin *trifolium* meaning 'three-leaved herb']

trek, treks, trekking, trekked
1 (verb) If you trek somewhere, you go on a long and difficult journey.
2 (noun) A trek is a long and difficult journey.
[an Afrikaans word]

trellis, trellises
(noun) A trellis is a frame made of horizontal and vertical strips of wood or metal and used to support climbing plants.

tremble, trembles, trembling, trembled
1 (verb) If you tremble, you shake slightly, usually because you are frightened or cold.
2 If something trembles, it shakes slightly.
3 If your voice trembles, it sounds unsteady, usually because you are frightened or upset.
4 (noun) A tremble is an act of trembling.
trembling (adjective).

tremendous
1 (adjective) large or impressive, e.g. *The film was a tremendous success.*
2 (an informal use) very good or pleasing, e.g. *We had a tremendous holiday.*
tremendously (adverb).

tremolo, tremolos
(noun) In music, tremolo is the rapid repetition of a note on a stringed instrument.
[an Italian word]

tremor, tremors
1 (noun) A tremor is a shaking movement of your body which you cannot control.
2 A tremor is an unsteady quality in your voice, for example when you are upset.
3 A tremor is also a small earthquake.

tremulous (pronounced **trem**-yoo-luss)
(adjective) If someone's smile or voice is tremulous, it is unsteady because they are nervous, uncertain, or unhappy.
tremulously (adverb).

trench, trenches
(noun) A trench is a long narrow channel dug into the ground.

trenchant (pronounced **trent**-shent)
(adjective) Trenchant writing or comments are bold and firmly expressed.
trenchantly (adverb).

trench coat, trench coats
(noun) A trench coat is a type of raincoat with pockets and a belt, especially one that looks like a long coat worn by a soldier.

trend, trends
(noun) A trend is a change towards doing or being something different, e.g. *the trend towards equal opportunities for men and women.*

trendy, trendier, trendiest
(adjective; an informal word) Trendy things or people are fashionable.
trendily (adverb), **trendiness** (noun).

trepidation
(noun; a formal word) Trepidation is fear or anxiety, e.g. *I approached the headmaster with trepidation.*

trespass, trespasses, trespassing, trespassed
1 (verb) If you trespass on someone's land or property, you go onto it without their permission.
2 If you trespass upon someone's generosity or friendship, you take advantage of them by asking or expecting too much from them, e.g. *I won't trespass upon your hospitality any longer.*
trespasser (noun).
[from Old French *trespasser* meaning 'to pass through']

tress, tresses
(noun; an old-fashioned word) A woman's tresses are her long flowing locks of hair.

trestle, trestles
(noun) A trestle is a wooden or metal structure that is used as one of the supports for a table.

tri-
(prefix) three.

triad, triads (pronounced **try**-ad)
1 (noun; a formal use) A triad is a group of three similar things, e.g. *a patriotic triad of red, white, and blue.*
2 (a technical use) In music, a triad is a chord of

three notes consisting of the tonic and the third and fifth above it.

trial, trials
1 (noun) A trial is the legal process in which a judge and jury decide whether a person is guilty of a particular crime after listening to all the evidence about it.
2 A trial is also an experiment in which something is tested, e.g. *After many trials the new drug has proved to be successful.*
3 (phrase) If you do something **by trial and error**, you try different methods of doing it until you find one that works well.
4 (noun) The trials that a person has are the unpleasant things they experience, e.g. *the trials of growing up.*

triangle, triangles
1 (noun) A triangle is a shape with three straight sides.
2 A triangle is also a percussion instrument consisting of a thin steel bar bent in the shape of a triangle. It is hit with a small steel rod.
triangular (adjective).
[from *tri-* and Latin *angulus* meaning 'corner']

triangulation
(noun) Triangulation is a method of surveying land, in which the land is divided into triangles and the areas of the triangles are calculated.
triangulate (verb).

triathlon, triathlons (pronounced tri-**ath**-lon)
(noun) A triathlon is a sports contest in which athletes compete in three different events.
[from *tri-* and Greek *athlon* meaning 'contest']

tribe, tribes
1 (noun) A tribe is a group of people of the same race, who have the same customs, religion, language, or land, especially when they are thought to be primitive.
2 A tribe is a group of related animals, especially ones that live or hunt together.
3 A tribe is also a group of people who do the same activities or the same job, e.g. *There was a tribe of schoolchildren coming up the path.*
tribal (adjective).
[from Latin *tribus* meaning 'division of the (Roman) people']

tribulation, tribulations
(noun; a formal word) Tribulation is trouble or suffering, e.g. *Life is full of tribulation.*
[from Latin *tribulare* meaning 'to afflict']

tribunal, tribunals (pronounced try-**byoo**-nl)
(noun) A tribunal is a special court or committee appointed to deal with particular problems, e.g. *An industrial tribunal.*

tribune, tribunes
(noun) In ancient Rome, a tribune was an officer elected by the ordinary people in order to protect their interests.

tributary, tributaries
1 (noun) A tributary is a stream or river that flows into a larger river.
2 (adjective) A tributary road, river, or path joins another more important road, river, or path.

tribute, tributes
1 (noun) A tribute is something said or done to show admiration and respect for someone, e.g. *Mrs Thatcher paid tribute to the soldiers.*
2 If one thing is a tribute to another, it is the result of the other thing and shows how good it is, e.g. *Her cure is a tribute to modern medicine.*
3 Tribute is a payment of goods or money that a country is forced to give to another country or ruler in return for peace or protection.

trice
(noun) If someone does something in a trice, they do it very quickly.

triceps (pronounced **try**-seps)
(noun) Your triceps is the large muscle at the back of your upper arm that straightens your arm.

trick, tricks, tricking, tricked
1 (verb) If someone tricks you, they deceive you.
2 (noun) Tricks are clever or skilful actions done in order to entertain people, e.g. *magic tricks.*
3 A trick is also a clever way of doing something, e.g. *The trick is not to let the milk boil.*
4 In card games, a trick is a batch of cards, one from each player, which is won by the person who plays the card with the highest value.
5 (adjective) Trick devices and methods are intended to deceive people for a joke or for entertainment, e.g. *trick photography.*

trickery
(noun) Trickery is deception, e.g. *The old man suspected trickery.*

trickle, trickles, trickling, trickled
1 (verb) When a liquid trickles somewhere, it flows slowly in a thin stream.
2 When people or things trickle somewhere, they move there slowly in small groups or amounts.
3 (noun) A trickle of liquid is a thin stream of it.
4 A trickle of people or things is a small number or quantity of them.

trickster, tricksters
(noun) A trickster is a person who deceives or cheats people.

tricky, trickier, trickiest
(adjective) difficult to do or deal with.

tricolour, tricolours
(noun) A tricolour is a flag with three equal stripes in different colours, especially the French or Irish national flag.

tricycle, tricycles
(noun) A tricycle is a vehicle similar to a bicycle but with two wheels at the back and one at the front.
[from *tri-* and Greek *kyklos* meaning 'wheel']

trident, tridents
(noun) A trident is a three-pronged spear, especially the one carried by the sea god Neptune in Greek mythology.
[from *tri-* and Latin *dentes* meaning 'teeth']

triennial, triennials (pronounced try-**en**-ee-al)
(adjective) happening every three years.
[from *tri-* and Latin *annus* meaning 'year']

trifle, trifles, trifling, trifled
1 (verb) If you trifle with someone or something,
you treat them in a disrespectful way, as if you
did not think they were important, e.g. *He is not
a person to be trifled with.*
2 (noun) Trifles are things that are not very
important or valuable.
3 A trifle is a cold pudding made of layers of
sponge cake, fruit, jelly, and custard.
4 A trifle also means a little, e.g. *She was a trifle
overweight.*

trifling
(adjective) small and unimportant.

trigger, triggers, triggering, triggered
1 (noun) The trigger of a gun is the small lever
which is pulled in order to fire it.
2 (verb) If something triggers an event or
triggers it off, it causes it to happen.
3 (noun) A trigger is also anything which causes
an event to happen.
[from Dutch *trekken* meaning 'to pull']

trigonometry (pronounced trig-gon-**nom**-it-ree)
(noun) Trigonometry is the branch of
mathematics that is concerned with calculating
the angles of triangles or the lengths of their
sides.
trigonometric (adjective).
[from Greek *trigonon* meaning 'triangle']

trilby, trilbies
(noun) A trilby is a man's hat made of felt with a
dent along the top from front to back.

trill, trills, trilling, trilled
1 (noun) In music, a trill is the rapid repetition
one after the other of a pair of notes a tone or
semitone apart.
2 (verb) If a bird trills, it sings with short
high-pitched repeated notes.
[from Italian *trillo*]

trillion, trillions
(noun; an informal word) Trillions of things
means an extremely large number of them.
Formerly, a trillion meant a million million
million.

trilogy, trilogies
(noun) A trilogy is a series of three books or
plays that have the same characters or are on
the same subject.
[from Greek *trilogia* meaning 'group of three
tragedies']

trim, trimmer, trimmest; trims, trimming, trimmed
1 (adjective) neat, tidy, and attractive.
2 (verb) To trim something means to clip small
amounts off it, e.g. *to trim a hedge.*
3 (noun) If something is given a trim, it is cut a
little, e.g. *His beard needs a trim.*
4 (verb) If you trim off parts of something, you
cut them off because they are not needed, e.g.
Trim the fat off the meat.
5 (noun) A trim on something is a decoration on
it, especially along its edges, e.g. *a lace trim.*
trimly (adverb), **trimmed** (adjective).

trimaran, trimarans (pronounced **try**-mar-ran)
(noun) A trimaran is a fast sailing boat with
three parallel hulls joined above the water.
[from *tri-* and *catamaran*]

trimming, trimmings
(noun) Trimmings are extra parts added to
something for decoration or as a luxury, e.g.
Tonight it was turkey with all the trimmings.

trinitrotoluene (pronounced
try-ny-troh-**tol**-yoo-een)
(noun) Trinitrotoluene is the full name for TNT,
a yellow solid used as an explosive.

trinity
1 (noun) In the Christian religion, the Trinity is
the joining of God the Father, God the Son, and
God the Holy Spirit.
2 (a literary use) A trinity is a group of three
things or people.
[from Latin *trinus* meaning 'triple']

trinket, trinkets
(noun) A trinket is a cheap ornament or piece of
jewellery.

trio, trios
1 (noun) A trio is a group of three musicians who
sing or play together; also a piece of music
written for three instruments or singers.
2 Any group of three things or people together
can be referred to as a trio.
[an Italian word]

trip, trips, tripping, tripped
1 (noun) A trip is a journey made to a place.
2 (verb) If you trip, you catch your foot on
something and fall over.
3 If you trip someone, you make them fall over
by making them catch their foot on something.
4 (an old-fashioned use) If you trip along, you
walk lightly and quickly.
5 (noun; an informal use) A trip is also a strange
experience, usually involving hallucinations,
caused by taking drugs.

Similar words: (sense 1) jaunt, outing, excursion

tripartite
(adjective) having three parts or involving three
groups of people.

tripe
1 (noun) Tripe is the stomach lining of a pig,
cow, or ox, which is cooked and eaten.
2 (an informal use) Tripe is also anything that
you consider to be silly or worthless, e.g. *I wish
you wouldn't read tripe like that.*

triple, triples, tripling, tripled
1 (adjective) consisting of three things or three
parts, e.g. *a triple somersault.*
2 (verb) If you triple something or if it triples, it
becomes three times greater in number or size.

triple jump
(noun) The triple jump is an athletics event in
which you do a hop, step, and jump after taking
a long run.

triplet, triplets
1 (noun) Triplets are three children born at the
same time to the same mother.

2 In music, a triplet is a sequence of three notes played in the time of two or four notes.

triplicate
(noun) If a document is in triplicate, there are three identical copies of it.

tripod, tripods (pronounced **try**-pod)
(noun) A tripod is a stand with three legs used to support something like a camera or telescope.
[from *tri-* and Greek *podes* meaning 'feet']

tripper, trippers
(noun) A tripper is a tourist or someone on an excursion.

triptych, triptychs (pronounced **trip**-tik)
(noun) A triptych is a set of three pictures or panels, usually hinged together.
[from *tri-* and Greek *ptux* meaning 'plate']

trite
(adjective) dull and unoriginal, e.g. *a very trite film.*
tritely (adverb), **triteness** (noun).
[from Latin *tritus* meaning 'worn down']

triumph, triumphs, triumphing, triumphed
1 (noun) A triumph is a great success or achievement.
2 Triumph is a feeling of great satisfaction when you win or achieve something.
3 (verb) If you triumph, you win a victory or succeed in overcoming something.

triumphal
(adjective) done or made to celebrate a victory or great success, e.g. *his triumphal return.*

triumphant
(adjective) Someone who is triumphant feels very happy because they have won a victory or have achieved something, e.g. *triumphant soldiers... a triumphant shout.*

triumvirate, triumvirates (pronounced try-**um**-vir-it)
(noun) A triumvirate is a group of three people who together are in charge of something.
[from Latin *trium virorum* meaning 'of three men']

trivet, trivets
(noun) A trivet is a metal stand on which hot dishes are placed on a table.
[from Latin *tripes* meaning 'three-footed']

trivia
(plural noun) Trivia are unimportant or uninteresting things, e.g. *the trivia of gossip.*

trivial
(adjective) Something trivial is unimportant.
[from Latin *trivialis* meaning 'found everywhere']

triviality, trivialities
1 (noun) Trivialities are unimportant things.
2 The triviality of something is its unimportance, e.g. *conversations of unbelievable triviality.*

trivialize, trivializes, trivializing, trivialized; also spelled **trivialise**
(verb) To trivialize something important means to make it seem unimportant.

troglodyte, troglodytes (pronounced **trog**-lod-ite)
(noun; a technical word) A troglodyte is someone who lives in a cave.
[from Greek *troglē* meaning 'hole']

troika, troikas (pronounced **troy**-ka)
(noun) A troika is a Russian vehicle drawn by three horses abreast.

Trojan
(noun) If you call someone a Trojan, you mean that they are hard-working and determined.
[the Trojans were the people of ancient Troy, who defended it bravely in the Trojan War]

troll, trolls
(noun) A troll is an imaginary creature in Scandinavian mythology that lives in caves or mountains and is believed to turn to stone when exposed to daylight.

trolley, trolleys
1 (noun) A trolley is a small table on wheels.
2 A trolley is a small cart on wheels used for carrying heavy objects, e.g. *supermarket trolleys.*

trolley bus, trolley buses
(noun) A trolley bus is a public transport vehicle powered by overhead electricity wires.

trollop, trollops
(noun; an old-fashioned and offensive word) A trollop is an immoral woman.

trombone, trombones
(noun) A trombone is a brass wind instrument with a U-shaped slide which you move to produce different notes.
[an Italian word]

troop, troops, trooping, trooped
1 (noun) Troops are soldiers.
2 A troop of people or animals is a group of them.
3 (verb) If people troop somewhere, they go there in a group.

trooper, troopers
1 (noun) A trooper is a low-ranking soldier in the cavalry.
2 (an informal phrase) If someone **swears like a trooper**, they swear a lot.

trophy, trophies
1 (noun) A trophy is a cup or shield given as a prize to the winner of a competition.
2 A trophy is something you keep to remember a success or victory.
[from Greek *tropē* meaning 'defeat of the enemy']

tropical
(adjective) belonging to or typical of the tropics, e.g. *a tropical downpour.*

tropics
(plural noun) The tropics are the hottest parts of the world between two lines of latitude, the Tropic of Cancer, 23½° north of the equator, and the Tropic of Capricorn, 23½° south of the equator.

tropism (pronounced **troe**-pizm)
(noun; a technical word) Tropism is a change in

the growth of something that is caused by an outside stimulus, such as light.

trot, trots, trotting, trotted
1 (verb) When a horse trots, it moves at a speed between a walk and a canter, lifting its feet quite high off the ground.
2 (noun) When a horse breaks into a trot, it starts trotting.
3 (verb) If you trot, you run or jog using small quick steps.
4 (noun) A trot is a run or jog using small quick steps.
5 (phrase) If things happen **on the trot**, they happen one after the other.

trot out
(phrasal verb) If you trot out information or ideas, you repeat them in a boring way, e.g. *They trot out all the old reasons for failure.*

troth (rhymes with **both**)
(an old-fashioned phrase) When lovers **plight their troth**, they promise their love to each other or promise to marry.

Trotskyism
(noun) Trotskyism is a theory of communism invented by Leon Trotsky (1879-1940), in which he called for immediate worldwide revolution by the workers.
Trotskyite or **Trotskyist** (noun and adjective).

trotter, trotters
(noun) A pig's trotters are its feet.

troubadour, troubadours (pronounced troo-bad-door)
(noun) In medieval times, a troubadour was a travelling poet or singer, especially in Italy and France.
[from Provençal *trobar* meaning 'to write verses']

trouble, troubles, troubling, troubled
1 (noun) Troubles are difficulties or problems.
2 (phrase) If you are **in trouble**, you are in a situation where you may be punished because you have done something wrong.
3 (noun) If there is trouble, people are quarrelling or fighting, e.g. *He's the sort of person who always makes trouble.*
4 (phrase) If you **take the trouble** to do something, you do it although it requires time and effort.
5 (verb) If something troubles you, it makes you feel worried or anxious.
6 If you trouble someone for something, you disturb them in order to ask them for it, e.g. *I'm sorry to trouble you, but do you have the time?*
troubling (adjective), **troubled** (adjective).

Similar words: (sense 1) affliction, inconvenience, bother
(sense 6) bother, inconvenience

troublesome
(adjective) causing problems or difficulties, e.g. *She has a very troublesome aunt.*

trough, troughs (pronounced **troff**)
1 (noun) A trough is a long, narrow container from which animals drink or feed.

2 A trough is also the area between two large waves on the sea.
3 In weather forecasting, a trough of low pressure is a long, narrow area of low air pressure.

trounce, trounces, trouncing, trounced
(verb) If you trounce someone, you defeat them completely.

troupe, troupes (pronounced **troop**)
(noun) A troupe is a group of actors, singers, or dancers who work together and often travel around together.

trousers
(plural noun) Trousers are a piece of clothing covering the body from the waist down, enclosing each leg separately.
[from Gaelic *triubhas*]

trousseau, trousseaux or **trousseaus** (pronounced **troo**-soh)
(noun; an old-fashioned word) A trousseau is the clothes and household linen a bride collects for her marriage.
[an Old French word meaning literally 'little bundle']

trout
(noun) A trout is a type of freshwater fish.

trowel, trowels
1 (noun) A trowel is a small garden tool with a curved, pointed blade used for planting or weeding.
2 A trowel is a small tool with a flat diamond-shaped blade used for spreading cement or plaster.
[from Latin *trulla* meaning 'ladle']

truant, truants
1 (noun) A truant is a child who stays away from school without permission.
2 (phrase) If children **play truant**, they stay away from school without permission.
truancy (noun).

truce, truces
(noun) A truce is an agreement between two people or groups to stop fighting for a short time.

truck, trucks
1 (noun) A truck is a large motor vehicle used for carrying heavy loads.
2 A truck is an open vehicle used for carrying goods on a railway.
3 (phrase) If you say that you will **have no truck with** someone, you mean that you refuse to be involved with them.

truculent (pronounced **truk**-yoo-lent)
(adjective) bad-tempered and aggressive.
truculently (adverb), **truculence** (noun).

trudge, trudges, trudging, trudged
1 (verb) If you trudge, you walk with slow, heavy steps.
2 (noun) A trudge is a slow tiring walk, e.g. *They set off before dawn for the long trudge home.*

true, truer, truest
1 (adjective) A true story or statement is based on facts and is not made up.

2 (phrase) If something **comes true**, it actually happens.
3 (adjective) True is used to describe things or people that are genuine, e.g. *He's a true friend.*
4 True feelings are sincere and genuine, e.g. *We often try to hide our true feelings.*
5 If an object is true, it is perfectly straight and level, e.g. *The window frame isn't quite true.*
truly (adverb).

Similar words: (sense 1) veracious, veritable

truffle, truffles
1 (noun) A truffle is a soft, round sweet flavoured with chocolate or rum.
2 A truffle is also a round mushroom-like fungus which grows underground and is considered very good to eat.

truism, truisms
(noun) A truism is a statement that is obviously true.

trump, trumps, trumping, trumped
1 (noun) In a game of cards, trumps is the suit with the highest value.
2 A trump is a card that belongs to the suit that is trumps.
3 (phrase) Your **trump card** is the most powerful thing that you can use or do to gain an advantage.
4 (verb) To trump a card means to beat it by playing a trump.
[from *triumph*]

trump up
(phrasal verb) If charges are trumped up against someone, they are made up and are not true.
trumped-up (adjective).

trumpet, trumpets, trumpeting, trumpeted
1 (noun) A trumpet is a brass wind instrument with a narrow tube ending in a bell-like shape.
2 (verb) When an elephant trumpets, it makes a sound like a very loud trumpet.
3 (noun) A trumpet is also an elephant's cry.
4 (verb) If you trumpet something, you state it publicly in a forceful way, e.g. *The results of the election were trumpeted all over the news.*
trumpeter (noun).
[from French *trompette*]

truncate, truncates, truncating, truncated
(verb) To truncate something means to make it shorter.
truncated (adjective).
[from Latin *truncare* meaning 'to lop']

truncheon, truncheons (pronounced **trunt**-shn)
(noun) A truncheon is a short, thick stick that policemen carry as a weapon.
[from Old French *tronchon* meaning 'stump']

trundle, trundles, trundling, trundled
(verb) If you trundle something or it trundles somewhere, it moves or rolls along slowly.

trunk, trunks
1 (noun) The trunk of a tree is the main stem from which the branches and roots grow.

2 Your trunk is the main part of your body, excluding your head, neck, arms, and legs.
3 An elephant's trunk is its long flexible nose.
4 A trunk is a large, strong case or box with a hinged lid used for storing things.
5 (plural noun) A man's trunks are his bathing pants or shorts.
[from Latin *truncus* meaning 'lopped']

trunk call, trunk calls
(noun; an old-fashioned expression) A trunk call is a long-distance telephone call within a country.

trunk road, trunk roads
(noun) A trunk road is a main road, especially one that is suitable for heavy vehicles.

truss, trusses, trussing, trussed
1 (verb) To truss someone or truss them up means to tie them up so that they cannot move.
2 (noun) A truss is a supporting belt with a pad worn by a man with a hernia.

trust, trusts, trusting, trusted
1 (verb) If you trust someone, you believe that they are honest and will not harm you.
2 If you trust someone to do something, you believe they will do it successfully or properly.
3 If you trust someone with something, you give it to them or tell it to them, e.g. *She's not a person I can trust with this sort of secret.*
4 If you do not trust something, you feel that it is not safe or reliable, e.g. *I don't trust old cars.*
5 (noun) Trust is the responsibility you are given to deal with or look after important, valuable, or secret things, e.g. *To be school librarian is a position of trust.*
6 (phrase) If you **take something on trust**, you believe it without checking it.
7 (noun) A trust is a financial arrangement in which an organization looks after and invests money for someone.
trustful (adjective), **trusting** (adjective).

trustee, trustees
(noun) A trustee is someone who is allowed by law to control money or property they are keeping or investing for another person.

trustworthy
(adjective) A trustworthy person is reliable and responsible and can be trusted.

trusty, trustier, trustiest
(adjective) Trusty things and animals are considered to be reliable because they have always worked well in the past, e.g. *I put on my trusty old wellington boots.*

truth, truths
1 (noun) The truth is the facts about something, rather than things that are imagined or made up, e.g. *I think he's telling the truth.*
2 A truth is an idea or principle that is generally accepted to be true, e.g. *It's a book that contains important truths.*

Similar words: (sense 1) verity, actuality, veracity, fact

truthful
(adjective) A truthful person is honest and tells the truth.
truthfully (adverb), **truthfulness** (noun).

try, tries, trying, tried
1 (verb) To try to do something means to make an effort to do it.
2 (noun) A try is an attempt to do something.
3 (verb) If you try for something, you make an effort to get it or achieve it, e.g. *She wanted to try for university.*
4 If you try something, you use it, do it, or experience it in order to test how useful, effective, or enjoyable it is, e.g. *Have you ever tried painting?*
5 (noun) A try of something is a test of it, e.g. *We can always give it a try.*
6 In rugby, a try is scored when someone carries the ball over the goal line of the opposing team and touches the ground with it.
7 (verb) When a person is tried, they appear in court and a judge and jury decide if they are guilty after hearing the evidence.

Similar words: (sense 1) attempt, endeavour, strive, bid, essay
(sense 2) go, shot, endeavour, bid, essay

trying
(adjective) Something or someone trying is difficult to deal with and makes you feel impatient or annoyed.

tryst, trysts (pronounced **trist**)
(noun) A tryst is an appointment or meeting, especially between lovers in a quiet, secret place.
[from Old French *triste* meaning 'lookout post']

tsar, tsars (pronounced **zar**); also spelled **czar**
(noun) A tsar was a Russian emperor or king between 1547 and 1917.

tsarina, tsarinas (pronounced zah-**ree**-na); also spelled **czarina**
(noun) A tsarina was a female tsar or the wife of a tsar.

tsarist, tsarists (pronounced **zar**-ist); also spelled **czarist**
(noun) belonging to or believing in the system of government by a tsar.

tsetse fly, tsetse flies (pronounced **tset**-tsee)
(noun) A tsetse fly is an African fly that feeds on blood and causes serious diseases in people and animals it feeds off.
[from an African word]

T-shirt, T-shirts; also spelled **tee shirt**
(noun) A T-shirt is a simple short-sleeved cotton shirt with no collar.

T-square, T-squares
(noun) A T-square is a T-shaped ruler used for drawing parallel or perpendicular lines.

tub, tubs
(noun) A tub is a wide circular container.

tuba, tubas
(noun) A tuba is a large brass musical instrument that can produce very low notes.
[an Italian word]

tubby, tubbier, tubbiest
(adjective) rather fat.

tube, tubes
1 (noun) A tube is a round, hollow pipe.
2 A tube is a soft metal or plastic cylindrical container with a screw cap at one end, e.g. *a tube of toothpaste.*
3 The Tube is the London underground railway.
tubing (noun).

tuber, tubers
(noun) A tuber is a swollen and fleshy root of a plant such as a potato.
tuberous (adjective).

tubercular
(adjective) relating to, causing, or suffering from tuberculosis.
[from Latin *tuber* meaning 'swelling']

tuberculosis (pronounced tyoo-ber-kyoo-**low**-siss)
(noun) Tuberculosis is a serious infectious disease affecting mainly the lungs.

tubular
(adjective) in the shape of a tube.

TUC an abbreviation for 'Trades Union Congress', which is an association of trade unions.

tuck, tucks, tucking, tucked
1 (noun) A tuck in a piece of clothing is a small pleat in it.
2 (verb) If you tuck a piece of fabric into or under something, you push the loose ends inside or under it to make it tidy.
3 If you tuck something somewhere, you put it there so that it is safe or comfortable, e.g. *He tucked the books under his arm.*
4 If you tuck away something, you store it in a safe place, e.g. *She had money tucked away.*
5 If something is tucked away, it is in a quiet place where few people go, e.g. *a pretty cottage tucked away in the hills.*

tuck shop, tuck shops
(noun) A tuck shop is a small shop in a school that sells snacks and sweets to the pupils.

Tudor, Tudors
1 (noun) Tudor was the family name of the British monarchs who reigned from 1485 to 1603.
2 (adjective) relating to or made in the Tudor period of history.

Tuesday, Tuesdays
(noun) Tuesday is the day between Monday and Wednesday.
[from Old English *tiwesdæg* meaning 'Tiw's day'; Tiw was the Scandinavian god of war and the sky]

tufa (pronounced **tyoo**-fa)
(noun) Tufa is a soft porous rock consisting of calcium carbonate.

tuft, tufts
(noun) A tuft of something such as hair is a bunch of it growing closely together.
tufted (adjective), **tufty** (adjective).

tug, tugs, tugging, tugged
1 (verb) To tug something means to give it a quick, hard pull.
2 (noun) A tug is a quick, hard pull, e.g. *Tom felt a tug at his sleeve.*
3 A tug is also a small, powerful boat which tows large ships.

tug of war
(noun) A tug of war is a sport in which two teams test their strength by pulling against each other on opposite ends of a rope.

tuition
(noun) Tuition is the teaching of a subject, especially to one person or to a small group.
[from Latin *tuitio* meaning 'guarding']

tulip, tulips
(noun) A tulip is a brightly-coloured spring flower shaped like an upside-down bell.
[from Turkish *tulbend* meaning 'turban', because of its shape]

tulle (pronounced **tyool**)
(noun) Tulle is a soft nylon or silk netlike material used for making evening dresses and veils. It is named after Tulle, a city in France.

tumble, tumbles, tumbling, tumbled
1 (verb) To tumble means to fall with a rolling or bouncing movement.
2 (noun) A tumble is a fall.
3 (verb) If you tumble to something, you suddenly understand it or realize what is happening, e.g. *What if he tumbles to what's going on?*

tumbledown
(adjective) A tumbledown building is in a very bad condition and is partly falling down.

tumble dryer, tumble dryers
(noun) A tumble dryer is a machine that dries washing.

tumbler, tumblers
1 (noun) A tumbler is a drinking glass with straight sides.
2 A tumbler is an acrobat who performs on the ground, often with other members of a group.

tumbrel, tumbrels; also spelled tumbril
(noun; an old-fashioned word) A tumbrel is a farm cart which can be tilted backwards to empty its load.

tumescent (pronounced tyoo-**mess**-ent)
(adjective) swollen, or becoming swollen.
tumescence (noun).

tummy, tummies
(noun; an informal word) Your tummy is your stomach.

tumour, tumours (pronounced **tyoo**-mur)
(noun) A tumour is a mass of diseased or abnormal cells that has grown in a person's or animal's body.

tumult (pronounced **tyoo**-mult)
(noun; a formal word) A tumult is a lot of noise and disturbance caused by a crowd of people.

tumultuous
1 (adjective) A tumultuous event or welcome is very noisy because people are happy or excited.
2 Tumultuous feelings and events are very exciting or confusing.
tumultuously (adverb).

tumulus, tumuli (pronounced **tyoo**-myoo-luss)
(noun) A tumulus is a mound of earth and stones covering a prehistoric grave.

tun, tuns
(noun) A tun is a large beer barrel.

tuna (pronounced **tyoo**-na)
(noun) Tuna are large fish that live in warm seas and are caught for food.

tundra
(noun) The tundra is a vast treeless Arctic region with permanently frozen subsoil.
[a Russian word]

tune, tunes, tuning, tuned
1 (noun) A tune is a series of musical notes arranged in a particular way.
2 (verb) To tune a musical instrument means to adjust it so that it produces the right notes.
3 To tune an engine or machine means to adjust it so that it works well.
4 If you tune to a particular radio or television station you turn or press the controls to select the station you want to listen to or watch.
5 (phrase) If your voice or an instrument is **in tune**, it produces the right notes.
6 To the tune of means to the amount of, e.g. *He brings home wages to the tune of £1,000.*

tune in
(phrasal verb) To tune in to a radio station means to set the controls to that station.

tuneful
(adjective) having a pleasant and easily remembered tune.

tuner, tuners
1 (noun) The tuner in a radio or television set is the part that receives the radio or television signals.
2 A piano tuner is a person whose job it is to tune pianos.

tungsten
(noun) Tungsten, also known as wolfram, is a greyish-white metallic element used for electric light filaments and cutting tools. Its atomic number is 74 and its symbol is W.

tunic, tunics
(noun) A tunic is a sleeveless garment covering the top part of the body and reaching to the hips, thighs, or knees.

tuning fork, tuning forks
(noun) A tuning fork is a two-pronged metal fork that when struck vibrates at a set pitch. It is used to tune musical instruments correctly.

Tunisian, Tunisians (pronounced tyoo-**niz**-ee-an)
1 (adjective) belonging or relating to Tunisia.
2 (noun) A Tunisian is someone who comes from Tunisia.

tunnel, tunnels, tunnelling, tunnelled
1 (noun) A tunnel is a long underground passage.
2 (verb) To tunnel means to make a tunnel.

tunny another word for **tuna**.

tuppence, tuppences
(noun) Tuppence is two old pence.

turban, turbans
(noun) A turban is a head-covering worn by a Hindu, Muslim, or Sikh man consisting of a long piece of cloth wound round his head.
[from Turkish *tulbend*]

turbid
(adjective; a literary word) Turbid water is cloudy with mud.

turbine, turbines
(noun) A turbine is a machine or engine in which power is produced when a stream of air, gas, water, or steam pushes the blades of a wheel and makes it turn round.
[from Latin *turbo* meaning 'whirlwind']

turbo, turbos
(noun) A turbo is a fan in an engine that improves its performance.

turbogenerator, turbogenerators
(noun) Turbogenerators are electrical generators powered by steam turbines.

turbojet, turbojets
1 (noun) A turbojet engine is a gas turbine whose exhaust gases propel an aircraft.
2 A turbojet is an aircraft propelled by a turbojet engine.

turboprop, turboprops
1 (noun) A turboprop is a gas turbine which drives an aircraft propellor.
2 A turboprop is also an aircraft driven by turboprops.

turbot (pronounced **tur**-bot)
(noun) A turbot is a large, flat fish that lives in European seas and is caught for food.

turbulent
1 (adjective) A turbulent period of history is one where there is much confusion, uncertainty, and possibly violent change.
2 Turbulent air or water currents make sudden changes of direction.
turbulence (noun), **turbulently** (adverb).

tureen, tureens (pronounced tur-**reen**)
(noun) A tureen is a large dish with a lid for serving soup.
[from French *terrine* meaning 'earthenware vessel']

turf, turves; turfs, turfing, turfed
1 (noun) Turf is short thick even grass and the layer of soil beneath it.
2 (verb) To turf an area of ground means to lay turf on it.
3 (noun) The turf refers to a track where horseracing takes place.

turf out
(phrasal verb; an informal expression) To turf someone out means to force them to leave a place.

turf accountant, turf accountants
(noun) A turf accountant is the formal name for a bookmaker.

turgid (pronounced **tur**-jid)
1 (adjective; a literary word) A turgid mass, especially of water, is swollen and thick.
2 A turgid play, film, or piece of writing is difficult to understand and rather boring.

Turk, Turks
(noun) A Turk is someone who comes from Turkey.

turkey, turkeys
(noun) A turkey is a large bird kept for food; also the meat of this bird.

Turkish
1 (adjective) belonging or relating to Turkey.
2 (noun) Turkish is the main language spoken in Turkey.

Turkish bath, Turkish baths
1 (noun) A Turkish bath is a type of bath where the bather sits in a very hot steamy room then has a wash, massage, and a cold shower or swim.
2 A Turkish bath is a place where people can have a Turkish bath.

Turkish delight
(noun) Turkish delight is a jelly-like sweet covered with powdered sugar or chocolate.

turmeric (pronounced **tur**-mer-ik)
(noun) Turmeric is a spice used in Indian cookery to flavour and colour food.

turmoil
(noun) Turmoil is a state of confusion, disorder, or great anxiety, e.g. *The city was in turmoil.*

turn, turns, turning, turned
1 (verb) When you turn, you move so that you are facing or going in a different direction.
2 When you turn something or when it turns, it moves or rotates so that it faces in a different direction or is in a different position.
3 (noun) A turn is an act of turning something so that it faces in a different direction or is in a different position.
4 (verb) If you turn your attention or thoughts to someone or something, you start thinking about them or discussing them.
5 If you turn to someone, you ask for their help or advice.
6 When something turns or is turned into something else, it becomes something different, e.g. *If you apply heat, water turns into steam.*
7 When someone turns a wooden object they are making, they shape it on a lathe.
8 (noun) A turn is a change in the way something is happening or being done, e.g. *She took a turn for the worse.*
9 If it is your turn to do something, you have the right, chance, or duty to do it.
10 (phrase) If you do someone **a good turn**, you do something that helps or benefits them.
11 **In turn** is used to refer to people, things, or actions that are in sequence one after the other.

Similar words: (sense 9) shift, spell, stint, stretch

turn down
1 (phrasal verb) If you turn down someone's request or offer, you refuse or reject it.
2 If you turn down a radio or heater, you adjust the controls and reduce the sound or heat.

turn up
1 (phrasal verb) If someone or something turns up, they arrive or appear somewhere.
2 If something turns up, it is found or discovered.
3 If you turn up a radio or heater, you adjust the controls and increase the sound or heat.

turnabout, turnabouts
(noun) A turnabout is a change or reversal of opinions or attitudes.

turncoat, turncoats
(noun) A turncoat is a person who leaves one political party or group for an opposing one.

turning, turnings
(noun) A turning is a road which leads away from the side of another road.

turning point, turning points
(noun) A turning point is the moment when decisions are taken and events start to move in a different direction.

turnip, turnips
(noun) A turnip is a round root vegetable with a white or yellow skin.

turnkey, turnkeys
(noun; an old-fashioned word) A turnkey is a jailer or prison officer.

turnout, turnouts
1 (noun) The turnout at an event is the number of people who go to it.
2 Someone's turnout is how they are dressed.
3 If you have a turnout, you sort through things and throw away the unwanted ones.

turnover, turnovers
1 (noun) The turnover of people in a particular organization or group is the rate at which people leave it and are replaced by others.
2 The turnover of a company is the value of the goods or services sold during a particular period.
3 A turnover is a small piece of pastry filled with fruit or jam, folded over, and baked.

turnpike, turnpikes
(noun; an old-fashioned word) A turnpike is a road which you have to pay a toll to use.
[from Middle English *turnepike* meaning 'revolving spiked barrier']

turnstile, turnstiles
(noun) A turnstile is a revolving mechanical barrier at the entrance to places like football grounds or zoos.

turntable, turntables
1 (noun) A turntable is the flat round part of a record player on which the record is put.
2 A turntable is also a large flat metal area onto which a railway engine can be driven and then turned round to face in a different direction.

turn-up, turn-ups
(noun) The turn-ups on a pair of trousers are the ends of the trouser legs which are folded upwards on the outside.

turpentine
(noun) Turpentine is a strong-smelling colourless liquid used for cleaning and for thinning paint. It is distilled from the resin and oil of pine trees.
[from Latin *terebinthus* meaning 'turpentine tree']

turps
(noun) Turps is turpentine.

turquoise (pronounced tur-kwoyz)
1 (noun and adjective) light bluish-green.
2 (noun) Turquoise is a bluish-green stone used in jewellery.
[from Old French *turqueise* meaning 'Turkish']

turret, turrets
1 (noun) A turret is a small narrow tower on top of a larger tower or other buildings.
2 A turret is also a revolving structure on tanks and warships, on which guns are mounted.

turtle, turtles
(noun) A turtle is a large reptile with a thick shell covering its body and flippers for swimming. It lays its eggs on land but lives the rest of its life in the sea.

turtledove, turtledoves
(noun) A turtledove is a type of brown speckled dove.
[from Latin *turtur*, from the noise they make]

turtleneck, turtlenecks
(noun) A turtleneck is a round, high close-fitting neck on a sweater.

tusk, tusks
(noun) The tusks of an elephant, wild boar, or walrus are the pair of long curving pointed teeth it has.

tussle, tussles, tussling, tussled
1 (noun) A tussle is an energetic fight, struggle, or argument between two people, especially about something they both want.
2 (verb) If two people tussle over something, they argue about it.

tussock, tussocks
(noun) A tussock is a thick clump of grass.

tutelage (pronounced tyoo-til-lij)
(noun; a formal word) If you have someone under your tutelage, you guide and look after them.

tutor, tutors, tutoring, tutored
1 (noun) A tutor is a teacher at a college or university.
2 A tutor is a private teacher.
3 (verb) If someone tutors a person or subject, they teach that person or subject.
[from Latin *tueri* meaning 'to watch over']

tutorial, tutorials
(noun) A tutorial is a regular meeting in which a tutor and a small group of students discuss a subject as part of the students' course.

tutu, tutus (pronounced too-too)
(noun) A tutu is a short stiff skirt made of tulle and worn by female ballet dancers.

tuxedo, tuxedos (pronounced tuk-**see**-doe)
(noun; an American word) A tuxedo is a black or white jacket that men wear with a bow tie at formal social events.

TV, TVs
1 (noun) TV is television.
2 A TV is a television set.

twaddle (pronounced twod-dl)
(noun) Twaddle is meaningless or silly talk or writing.

twain
(noun; an old-fashioned word) Twain means two.

twang, twangs, twanging, twanged
1 (noun) A twang is a sound like the one made by pulling and then releasing a tight wire.
2 (verb) If a tight wire or string twangs or you twang it, it makes a sound as it is pulled and then released.
3 (noun) A twang is a nasal quality in a person's voice.

tweak, tweaks, tweaking, tweaked
1 (verb) If you tweak something, you twist it or pull it.
2 (noun) A tweak of something is a short twist or pull of it.

twee
(adjective) sweet and pretty but in bad taste or sentimental.

tweed, tweeds
1 (noun) Tweed is a thick woollen cloth, often woven from different coloured threads.
2 Someone wearing tweeds is wearing a tweed suit.

tweet, tweets, tweeting, tweeted
1 (verb) When a small bird tweets, it makes a short, high-pitched sound.
2 (noun) A tweet is a short high-pitched sound made by a small bird.

tweezers
(plural noun) Tweezers are a small tool with two arms, used for pulling out hairs or picking up small objects.

twelve the number 12.
twelfth.

twenty, twenties
the number 20.
twentieth.

twice
(adverb) Twice means two times.

twiddle, twiddles, twiddling, twiddled
(verb) To twiddle something means to twist it or turn it quickly.

twig, twigs, twigging, twigged
1 (noun) A twig is a very small thin branch growing from a main branch of a tree or bush.
2 (verb; an informal use) If you twig, you realize or understand something.

twilight (pronounced **twy**-lite)
1 (noun) Twilight is the time after sunset when it is just getting dark.

2 The twilight of something is the final stages of it, e.g. *the twilight of the campaign.*
[from Old English *twi-* meaning 'half' and *light*]

twill
(noun) Twill is cloth woven in a way which produces diagonal lines or ridges across it.
[from Old English *twilic* meaning 'having a double thread']

twin, twins, twinning, twinned
1 (noun) If two people are twins, they have the same mother and were born on the same day.
2 Twin is used to mean double, e.g. *a small twin-engined plane.*
3 (verb) A town that is twinned with another town in a different country has agreed to exchange visits of groups of citizens.

twine, twines, twining, twined
1 (noun) Twine is strong smooth string.
2 (verb) If you twine one thing round another, you twist or wind it round, e.g. *a long scarf twined around her neck.*

twinge, twinges
(noun) A twinge is a sudden, unpleasant feeling, e.g. *a twinge of fear... I've got a twinge in my leg.*

twinkle, twinkles, twinkling, twinkled
1 (verb) If something twinkles, it sparkles or seems to sparkle with an unsteady light, e.g. *The lights twinkled... Her eyes twinkled.*
2 (noun) A twinkle is a sparkle or brightness that something has.

twinset, twinsets
(noun) A twinset is a matching cardigan and jumper.

twirl, twirls, twirling, twirled
(verb) If something twirls, or if you twirl it, it spins or twists round and round.

twist, twists, twisting, twisted
1 (verb) When you twist something you turn one end of it in one direction while holding the other end or turning it in the opposite direction.
2 (noun) A twist is a twisting action or motion.
3 (verb) When something twists or is twisted, it moves or bends into a strange shape.
4 If you twist a part of your body, you injure it by turning it too sharply or in an unusual direction, e.g. *She twisted her wrist.*
5 (phrase) If you **twist someone's arm**, you persuade them to do something.
6 (verb) If you twist something that someone has said, you change the meaning slightly.
7 (noun) A twist in a story or film is an unexpected development or event, especially at the end, e.g. *There was an odd twist to the plot.*

Similar words: (sense 1) wind, coil
(sense 3) contort, kink

twisted
1 (adjective) Something twisted has been bent or moved into a strange shape, e.g. *They were trapped under the twisted steel girders.*
2 If someone's mind or behaviour is twisted, it is unpleasantly abnormal, e.g. *He has become bitter and twisted.*

twister, twisters
(noun) A twister is someone who is dishonest and deliberately deceives people.

twisty
(adjective) having a lot of sharp bends and corners, e.g. *a twisty road.*

twit, twits
(noun; an informal word) A twit is a silly person.

twitch, twitches, twitching, twitched
1 (verb) If you twitch, you make little jerky movements which you cannot control.
2 If you twitch something, you give it a little jerk in order to move it.
3 (noun) A twitch is a little jerky movement.

twitter, twitters, twittering, twittered
1 (verb) When birds twitter, they make short high-pitched sounds.
2 If someone twitters, they speak very fast in a high-pitched voice.

two the number 2.

two-faced
(adjective) A two-faced person is not honest in the way they behave towards other people, e.g. *a two-faced liar.*

twofold
(adjective) Something twofold has two equally important parts or reasons, e.g. *Their targets were twofold: inflation and unemployment.*

twosome, twosomes (pronounced **too**-sum)
(noun) A twosome refers to two people or things that are usually seen together.

two-step
(noun) The two-step is a traditional ballroom dance, or the music for that type of dance.

two-stroke
(adjective) A two-stroke engine has a piston which makes two strokes for every explosion.

two-time, two-times, two-timing, two-timed
(verb; an informal expression) If you two-time your lover or friend, you deceive them, usually by having a romantic relationship with someone else without telling them.

tycoon, tycoons
(noun) A tycoon is a person who is successful in business and has become rich and powerful.
[from Chinese *ta* + *chun* meaning 'great ruler']

tyke, tykes; also spelled **tike**
(noun; an informal word) A tyke is a mischievous child.
[from Old Norse *tik* meaning 'bitch']

type, types, typing, typed
1 (noun) A type of something is a class of it that has common features and belongs to a larger group of related things, e.g. *What type of cheese would you prefer?*
2 A particular type of person has a particular appearance or quality, e.g. *He's one of these quiet, intellectual types.*
3 (verb) If you type something, you use a typewriter or word processor to write it.

4 (noun) Type is the printing used in a book or newspaper, e.g. *The headlines were in bold type.*
[from Greek *tupos* meaning 'image']

typecast, typecasts, typecasting, typecast
(verb) If an actor or actress is typecast, they keep being given the same type of roles to play.

typeface, typefaces
(noun) A typeface is a particular design of letters and characters.

typescript, typescripts
(noun) A typescript is a typed copy of a piece of writing.

typeset, typesets, typesetting, typeset
(verb) To typeset something means to prepare the type for printing.

typewriter, typewriters
(noun) A typewriter is a machine with a keyboard whose individual keys you press to produce letters and numbers on a page.

typewritten
(adjective) Something typewritten has been typed on a typewriter or word processor.

typhoid (pronounced **tie**-foyd)
(noun) Typhoid, or typhoid fever, is an infectious disease caused by contaminated water or food. It produces fever and can kill.

typhoon, typhoons
(noun) A typhoon is a very violent tropical storm.
[from Chinese *tai fung* meaning 'great wind']

typhus
(noun) Typhus is an infectious disease transmitted by lice or mites. It results in fever, severe headaches, and a skin rash.
[from Greek *tuphos* meaning 'fever']

typical
(adjective) showing the most usual characteristics or behaviour.
typically (adverb).

Similar words: characteristic, standard, classic, conventional

typify, typifies, typifying, typified
1 (verb) If something typifies a situation or thing, it is characteristic of it or a typical example of it, e.g. *These old houses typify the architecture of the early 19th century.*
2 If someone typifies a particular type of person or attitude, they show all the most usual characteristics of that person or attitude.

Similar words: (sense 1) characterize, distinguish, embody, epitomize, incarnate

typing
(noun) Typing is the work or activity of producing something on a typewriter.

typist, typists
(noun) A typist is a person who types, especially as part of their job.

typography
(noun) Typography is the planning, choosing, and setting of type for printing.

tyrannize, tyrannizes, tyrannizing, tyrannized;
also spelled **tyrannise**
(verb) If someone tyrannizes you, they behave in
a cruel and unjust way towards you, e.g. *He used
to tyrannize his younger brother.*

tyrannosaurus, tyrannosauruses (pronounced
tir-ran-oh-**saw**-russ)
(noun) The tyrannosaurus was a very large
meat-eating dinosaur which walked upright on
its hind legs and was common in North America.
[from Greek *turannos* meaning 'tyrant' and Latin
saurus meaning 'lizard']

tyranny, tyrannies
1 (noun) A tyranny is cruel and unjust rule of
people by a person or group, e.g. *They came here
to escape political tyranny.*

2 You can refer to harsh inhuman force as
tyranny, e.g. *the tyranny of the assembly line.*
tyrannical (adjective), **tyrannically** (adverb).

tyrant, tyrants
(noun) A tyrant is a person who treats the people
he or she has authority over cruelly and
unjustly.
[from Greek *turannos*]

tyre, tyres
(noun) A tyre is a thick ring of rubber fitted
round each wheel of a vehicle and filled with air.

tyro, tyros (pronounced **tie**-roh); also spelled **tiro**
(noun; a formal word) A tyro is a beginner at
something.
[from Latin *tiro* meaning 'recruit']

U

ubiquitous (pronounced yoo-**bik**-wit-tuss)
(adjective) Something that is ubiquitous seems
to be everywhere at the same time, e.g. *the
ubiquitous white dust of Athens.*
[from Latin *ubique* meaning 'everywhere']

UCCA (pronounced uk-ah)
(noun) UCCA is the organization in Britain that
deals with applications from people wanting to
go to university. UCCA is an abbreviation for
'Universities Central Council on Admission'.

udder, udders
(noun) A cow's udder is the baglike organ that
hangs below its body and produces milk.

UFO, UFOs
(noun) A UFO is a strange object seen in the sky,
which some people believe to be a spaceship
from another planet. UFO is an abbreviation for
'unidentified flying object'.

Ugandan, Ugandans (pronounced yoo-**gan**-dan)
1 (adjective) belonging or relating to Uganda.
2 (noun) A Ugandan is someone who comes from
Uganda.

ugly, uglier, ugliest
1 (adjective) very unattractive in appearance.
2 An ugly situation is very unpleasant and often
involves anger or violence.
[from Old Norse *uggligr* meaning 'terrifying']

Similar words: (sense 1) unsightly, hideous,
unattractive

UHF
(noun) UHF is a radio frequency of between
3000 and 300 megahertz, which produces
high-quality sound reproduction. UHF is an
abbreviation for 'ultrahigh frequency'.

UHT
(adjective) UHT milk has been treated at a very
high temperature so that it will keep in a sealed
carton for a long time. UHT is an abbreviation
for 'ultra-heat-treated'.

UK an abbreviation for **United Kingdom.**

ukulele, ukuleles (pronounced yoo-kel-**lay**-lee);
also spelled **ukelele**
(noun) A ukelele is a small guitar with four
strings.
[A Hawaiian word]

ulcer, ulcers
(noun) An ulcer is a sore area on the skin or
inside the body, which takes a long time to heal,
e.g. *stomach ulcers.*
ulcerous (adjective).
[from Latin *ulcus* meaning 'sore']

ulna, ulnas or ulnae
(noun; a technical word) The ulna is the inner
and longer bone in the lower part of your arm.
[from Latin *ulna* meaning 'elbow']

ulterior (pronounced ul-**teer**-ee-or)
(adjective) If you have an ulterior motive for
doing something, you have a hidden reason for it.
[from Latin *ulterior* meaning 'further']

ultimate
1 (adjective) final or eventual, e.g. *the ultimate
success of the revolution.*
2 most important or powerful, e.g. *the ultimate
authority.*
3 (noun) You can refer to the best or most
advanced example of something as the ultimate,
e.g. *This car is the ultimate in luxury.*
ultimately (adverb).
[from Latin *ultimus* meaning 'last']

ultimatum, ultimatums (pronounced
ul-tim-**may**-tum)
(noun) An ultimatum is a warning stating that
unless someone meets your conditions, you will
take action against them.

ultra-
(prefix) Ultra- is used to form adjectives
describing something as having a quality to an
extreme degree, e.g. *ultra-sophisticated
equipment... an ultra-modern building.*
[from Latin *ultra* meaning 'beyond']

ultramarine
(noun and adjective) bright blue.
[from Latin *ultramarinus* meaning 'beyond the
sea', because the pigment was imported from
abroad]

ultrasonic
(adjective) An ultrasonic sound has a very high
frequency that cannot be heard by the human
ear.

ultraviolet
(adjective) Ultraviolet light is not visible to the
human eye. It is a form of radiation that causes
your skin to darken after exposure to sunlight.

umber
(noun and adjective) yellowish or reddish brown.
[from *Umbria* the name of the Italian region
where the pigment was obtained]

umbilical cord, umbilical cords (pronounced
um-**bil**-lik-kl)
(noun) The umbilical cord is the tube of blood
vessels which connects an unborn baby to its
mother and through which the baby receives
nutrients and oxygen.
[from Latin *umbilicus* meaning 'navel']

umbrage
(noun) If someone takes umbrage at something,
they are offended or upset by it.

umbrella, umbrellas
(noun) An umbrella is a device that you use to
protect yourself from the rain. It consists of a
folding frame covered in cloth attached to a long
stick.

umlaut, umlauts (pronounced **oom**-lout)
(noun) In German and some other languages, an

umlaut is a mark consisting of two dots placed over a vowel ' to indicate a change in pronunciation, as in the word *für*, which means 'four'.
[a German word]

umpire, umpires, umpiring, umpired
1 (noun) The umpire in cricket or tennis is the person who makes sure that the game is played according to the rules and who makes a decision if there is a dispute.
2 (verb) If you umpire a game, you are the umpire.

umpteen
(adjective; an informal word) very many, e.g. *I've told you umpteen times before!*
umpteenth (adjective).

UN an abbreviation for **United Nations.**

un-
(prefix) un- is added to the beginning of many words to form a word with the opposite meaning, e.g. *an uncomfortable chair... He regretted his unkindness... He unlocked the door... The hedges remained uncut.*

unabashed
(adjective) not ashamed, embarrassed, or discouraged by something, e.g. *She seemed completely unabashed.*

unabated
(adjective and adverb) continuing without any reduction in intensity or amount, e.g. *They continued with unabated enthusiasm.*

unable
(adjective) If you are unable to do something, you cannot do it.

unacceptable
(adjective) very bad or of a very low standard.

unaccompanied
(adjective) alone.

unaccountable
1 (adjective) without any sensible explanation, e.g. *For some unaccountable reason I put it in the wrong envelope.*
2 Someone who is unaccountable does not have to justify their actions to other people, e.g. *Many decision-makers are unaccountable to the public.*
unaccountably (adverb).

unaccounted
(adjective) If something is unaccounted for, you do not know what has happened to it.

unaccustomed
(adjective) If you are unaccustomed to something, you are not used to it, e.g. *They were unaccustomed to wearing suits and ties.*

unacquainted
(adjective) If you are unacquainted with something, you do not know about it, e.g. *people who are unacquainted with feminist ideas.*

unadulterated
(adjective) completely pure, with nothing added, e.g. *unadulterated spring water.*

unaffected
1 (adjective) not changed in any way by a particular thing, e.g. *Jobs would be largely unaffected by automation.*
2 behaving in a natural and genuine way, e.g. *He was simple, unaffected, and obviously sincere.*

unaided
(adverb and adjective) without help, e.g. *The baby was sitting up unaided.*

unalterable
(adjective) Something that is unalterable cannot be changed.

unaltered
(adjective) still in the original form, e.g. *The Great Hall survives relatively unaltered.*

unambiguous
(adjective) An unambiguous statement has only one meaning.

unanimous (pronounced yoon-**nan**-nim-mus)
(adjective) When people are unanimous, they all agree about something.
unanimously (adverb), **unanimity** (noun).
[from Latin *unanimus* meaning 'of one mind']

unannounced
(adjective) happening unexpectedly and without advance warning.

unapproachable
(adjective) An unapproachable person is difficult to talk to and not very friendly.

unarmed
(adjective) not carrying any weapons.

unassuming
(adjective) modest and quiet.

unattached
(adjective) An unattached person is not married and is not having a steady relationship.

unattended
(adjective) not being watched or looked after, e.g. *unattended baggage.*

unauthorized or **unauthorised**
(adjective) done without official permission.

unavoidable
(adjective) unable to be prevented or avoided.

unaware
(adjective) If you are unaware of something, you do not know about it.

unawares
(adverb) If something catches you unawares, it happens when you are not expecting it.

unbalanced
1 (adjective) slightly mad.
2 An unbalanced account of something is an unfair one because it emphasizes some things and ignores others.

unbearable
(adjective) Something unbearable is so unpleasant or upsetting that you feel unable to tolerate it, e.g. *The pain was unbearable.*
unbearably (adverb).

Similar words: intolerable, unacceptable

unbeatable
(adjective) Something that is unbeatable is the best thing of its kind.

unbelievable
1 (adjective) extremely good or surprising, e.g. *an unbelievable apartment.*
2 so unlikely that you cannot believe it.
unbelievably (adverb).

Similar words: fantastic, incredible, astonishing, staggering

unbeliever, unbelievers
(noun) An unbeliever is someone who does not believe in a particular religion.

unborn
(adjective) not yet born.

unbridled
(adjective) Unbridled feelings or behaviour are not controlled.

unbroken
(adjective) continuous or complete, e.g. *The sky was an unbroken sheet of grey.*

unburden, unburdens, unburdening, unburdened
(verb) If you unburden yourself to someone, you tell them about something which you have been secretly worrying about.

unbutton, unbuttons, unbuttoning, unbuttoned
(verb) When you unbutton something, you undo the buttons on it.
unbuttoned (adjective).

uncalled-for
(adjective) A remark that is uncalled-for is unkind and unjustified.

uncanny
(adjective) strange and difficult to explain, e.g. *an uncanny resemblance between the two men.*
[from Scottish *uncanny* meaning 'unreliable' or 'not safe to deal with']

unceasing
(adjective) continuing without stopping, e.g. *Miss Crabbe's unceasing conversation continued.*
unceasingly (adverb).

unceremonious
1 (adjective) relaxed and informal, e.g. *She treated him with unceremonious friendliness.*
2 sudden and rude, e.g. *an unceremonious dismissal.*
unceremoniously (adverb).

uncertain
1 (adjective) not knowing what to do, e.g. *She hesitated, uncertain whether to continue.*
2 doubtful or not known, e.g. *The cause of death remains uncertain.*
uncertainty (noun).

unchallenged
(adjective) accepted without any questions being asked, e.g. *Her decisions went unchallenged.*

uncharacteristic
(adjective) not typical or usual, e.g. *He jumped out of the car with uncharacteristic agility.*

uncharitable
(adjective) unkind or unfair, e.g. *I hope I'm not being uncharitable, but he really is very boring.*

uncivil
(adjective) Uncivil behaviour is rude and impolite.

uncivilized or **uncivilised**
1 (adjective) unacceptable, for example by being very cruel or rude, e.g. *the uncivilized behaviour of football hooligans.*
2 (phrase) If you do something **at an uncivilized hour,** you do it very early in the morning.

uncle, uncles
(noun) Your uncle is the brother of your mother or father or the husband of your aunt.
[from Latin *avunculus* meaning 'mother's brother']

unclean
(adjective) dirty and likely to cause disease, e.g. *the dangers of drinking unclean water.*

unclear
(adjective) confusing and not obvious.

uncomfortable
1 (adjective) If you are uncomfortable, you are not physically relaxed and feel slight pain or discomfort.
2 Uncomfortable also means slightly worried or embarrassed.
uncomfortably (adverb).

uncommitted
(adjective) not supporting either side in a dispute, e.g. *their uncommitted position in the war.*

uncommon
1 (adjective) not happening often or not seen often.
2 unusually great, e.g. *He showed an uncommon understanding of children.*
uncommonly (adverb).

uncomprehending
(adjective) not understanding what has been said or done, e.g. *She turned to her uncomprehending husband and explained.*

uncompromising
(adjective) determined not to change an opinion or aim in any way, e.g. *He was an uncompromising opponent of the war.*
uncompromisingly (adverb).

unconcerned
(adjective) not interested in something or not worried about it, e.g. *He tried to act unconcerned.*
unconcernedly (adverb).

unconditional
(adjective) with no conditions or limitations, e.g. *They offered unconditional support.*
unconditionally (adverb).

unconscionable (pronounced un-**kon**-shon-a-bl)
(adjective; a literary word) If something is unconscionable, the person responsible should be ashamed of it, e.g. *He took an unconscionable time to answer my letter.*
unconscionably (adverb).

[the opposite of the obsolete word *conscionable* meaning 'conscientious' or 'scrupulous']

unconscious
1 (adjective) Someone who is unconscious is in a state similar to sleep as a result of a shock, accident, or injury.
2 If you are unconscious of something, you are not aware of it.
3 (noun) Your unconscious is the part of your mind that contains feelings which you are not aware of and cannot control.
unconsciously (adverb).

unconsidered
(adjective) Unconsidered thoughts and actions have not been carefully thought out.

unconstitutional
(adjective) against the rules of an organization or political system, e.g. *sanctions against unofficial unconstitutional strikers.*

unconventional
(adjective) not behaving in the same way as most other people.

unconvinced
(adjective) not at all certain that something is true or right, e.g. *I remain unconvinced.*

uncooperative
(adjective) An uncooperative person makes no effort to help or work with other people.

uncoordinated
(adjective) Uncoordinated movements are jerky and not controlled.

uncouth (pronounced un-**kooth**)
(adjective) bad-mannered and unpleasant.
[from Old English *uncuth* meaning 'unfamiliar' or 'unusual']

Similar words: boorish, loutish, unrefined, coarse

uncover
1 (verb) If you uncover a secret, you find it out.
2 To uncover something means to remove the cover or lid from it.

uncritical
(adjective) unable or unwilling to judge whether something is good or bad, e.g. *an admiring and uncritical audience.*

unction (pronounced **ungk**-shn)
(noun; a formal word) In religious ceremonies, unction is the act of anointing a person with oil.
[from Latin *unguere* meaning 'to anoint']

unctuous
(adjective; a formal word) An unctuous person is not sincere in their flattery.

undaunted
(adjective) If you are undaunted by something disappointing, you are not discouraged by it.

undecided
(adjective) If you are undecided, you have not yet made a decision about something.

undemanding
(adjective) not difficult to do or deal with, e.g. *The pay was adequate, the work undemanding.*

undemonstrative
(adjective) An undemonstrative person does not show their feelings.

undeniable
(adjective) certainly true, e.g. *It was undeniable that they were still fond of each other.*
undeniably (adverb).

Similar words: incontrovertible, indubitable, irrefutable

under
1 (preposition) below or beneath.
2 You can use 'under' to say that a person or thing is affected by a particular situation, condition, or state, e.g. *The company is under pressure to act quickly... under difficult circumstances.*
3 If someone studies or works under a particular person, that person is their teacher or their boss.
4 Someone who uses a different name as an author writes under that name.
5 You use under to say what section of a book or system of classification something is in, e.g. *You'll find it under O in the dictionary.*
6 less than, e.g. *under £10... under sixteen years old.*
7 (phrase) **Under way** means already started, e.g. *Preparations for the trial were under way.*

under-
(prefix) Under- is used in words that describe something as not being provided to a sufficient extent or not having happened to a sufficient extent.

underachieve, underachieves, underachieving, underachieved
(verb) If you underachieve, you do not perform as well as you could.
underachiever (noun).

underarm
1 (adjective) under your arm, e.g. *an underarm deodorant.*
2 Underarm actions, such as throwing a ball, are those in which you do not raise your arm over your shoulder.

underbrush
(noun) Underbrush is undergrowth.

undercarriage, undercarriages
(noun) The undercarriage of an aircraft is the part, including the wheels, that supports the aircraft when it is on the ground.

underclothes
(plural noun) Your underclothes are the clothes that you wear under your other clothes and next to your skin.

undercover
(adjective) involving secret work to obtain information, e.g. *undercover police work.*

undercurrent, undercurrents
(noun) An undercurrent is a weak, partially hidden feeling that may become stronger later.

undercut, undercuts, undercutting, undercut
1 (verb) To undercut someone's prices means to sell a product more cheaply than they do.
2 If something undercuts your attempts to

achieve something, it prevents them from being effective.

underdeveloped
(adjective) An underdeveloped country does not have modern industries, and usually has a low standard of living.

underdog, underdogs
(noun) The underdog in a competitive situation is the person who seems likely to lose.

underdone
(adjective) not cooked for long enough.

underestimate, underestimates, underestimating, underestimated
(verb) If you underestimate something or someone, you do not realize how large, great, or capable they are.

underfed
(adjective) not getting enough to eat, e.g. *Underfed children are more open to infection.*

underfelt
(noun) Underfelt is thick felt laid between floorboards and carpet for comfort and insulation.

underfoot
1 (adjective and adverb) under your feet, e.g. *the grass underfoot... The ground was spongy underfoot.*
2 (phrase) To be **trampled underfoot** means to be trodden on.

undergo, undergoes, undergoing, underwent, undergone
(verb) If you undergo something unpleasant, it happens to you.

undergraduate, undergraduates
(noun) An undergraduate is a student who is studying for a first degree.

underground
1 (adjective) below the surface of the ground.
2 secret, unofficial, and usually illegal.
3 (noun) The underground is a railway system in which trains travel in tunnels below ground.

undergrowth
(noun) Small bushes and plants growing under trees are called the undergrowth.

underhand
(adjective) secret and dishonest.

underlay
(noun) Underlay is a thick material that you place between a carpet and the floor.

underlie, underlies, underlying, underlay, underlain
(verb) The thing that underlies a situation is the cause or basis of it.
underlying (adjective).

underline, underlines, underlining, underlined
1 (verb) If something underlines a feeling or a problem, it emphasizes it.
2 If you underline a word or sentence, you draw a line under it.

underling, underlings
(noun) An underling is someone who is inferior in rank or status to someone else.

undermine, undermines, undermining, undermined
(verb) To undermine an idea, feeling, or system means to make it less strong or secure.
[from the practice in warfare of digging tunnels under enemy fortifications in order to make them collapse]

Similar words: sabotage, subvert

underneath
1 (preposition) below or beneath.
2 (adjective) The underneath part of something is the part that touches or faces the ground.
3 (adverb and preposition) Underneath describes feelings and qualities that do not show in your behaviour, e.g. *Underneath, he is rather shy.*

undernourished
(adjective) weak and ill because of not eating enough food.

underpants
(plural noun) Underpants are a piece of clothing worn by men and boys under their trousers.

underpass, underpasses
(noun) An underpass is a road or footpath that goes under a road or railway.

underpin, underpins, underpinning, underpinned
(verb) If something underpins something else, it helps it to continue by supporting and strengthening it.

underprivileged
(adjective) Underprivileged people have much less money and fewer opportunities than other people in their society.

underrate, underrates, underrating, underrated
(verb) If you underrate someone, you do not realize how clever or valuable they are.

underscore, underscores, underscoring, underscored
(verb) To underscore something means to underline it.

undersized
(adjective) smaller than is usual or normal.

understand, understands, understanding, understood
1 (verb) If you understand what someone says, you know what they mean.
2 If you understand a situation, you know what is happening and why.
3 If you say that you understand that something is the case, you mean that you have heard that it is the case, e.g. *I understand you're new here.*

Similar words: (sense 1) know, comprehend, grasp, fathom, follow, perceive

understandable
(adjective) If something is understandable, people can easily understand it.
understandably (adverb).

Similar words: intelligible, comprehensible, lucid, clear

understanding, understandings
1 (noun) If you have an understanding of something, you have some knowledge about it.

2 (adjective) kind and sympathetic, e.g. *Thank you for being so understanding.*
3 (noun) An understanding is an informal agreement between people.

Similar words: (sense 1) comprehension, grasp, insight, perception, perspicacity

understate, understates, understating, understated
(verb) If you understate something, you describe it as being less important or significant than it really is.

understatement, understatements
(noun) An understatement is a statement that does not fully express the extent to which something is true, e.g. *'You must be exhausted!'* — *'That's an understatement.'*

understudy, understudies
(noun) An understudy is someone who has learnt a part in a play so that they can act it if the main actor or actress is ill.

undertake, undertakes, undertaking, undertook, undertaken
(verb) When you undertake a task or job, you agree to do it.
undertaking (noun).

undertaker, undertakers
(noun) An undertaker is someone whose job is to prepare bodies for burial and arrange funerals. [from *funeral-undertaker* meaning 'someone who undertakes funeral arrangements']

undertone, undertones
1 (noun) If you say something in an undertone, you say it very quietly.
2 If something has undertones of a particular kind, it indirectly suggests ideas of this kind.

undervalue, undervalues, undervaluing, undervalued
(verb) If you undervalue something, you think it is less important than it really is.

underwater
1 (adverb and adjective) beneath the surface of the sea, a river, or a lake.
2 (adjective) designed to work in water, e.g. *an underwater camera.*

underwear
(noun) Your underwear is the clothing that you wear under your other clothes, next to your skin.

underwent the past tense of **undergo**.

underworld
(noun) You can refer to organized crime and the people who are involved in it as the underworld.

underwrite, underwrites, underwriting, underwrote, underwritten
(verb; a formal word) Someone who underwrites an activity agrees to provide money to cover any losses or special costs.
underwriter (noun).

undesirable
(adjective) unwelcome and likely to cause harm, e.g. *Cuts in education are very undesirable.*

undeveloped
1 (adjective) An undeveloped country is not industrialized and does not use modern farming methods.
2 Undeveloped land has not yet been built on.

undid the past tense of **undo**.

undignified
(adjective) foolish and embarrassing.

undisguised
(adjective) shown openly, e.g. *He looked at her with undisguised admiration.*

undisputed
(adjective) definite and without any doubt, e.g. *the undisputed leader.*

undistinguished
(adjective) without any really good qualities or features, e.g. *an undistinguished political career.*

undivided
(adjective) If you give something your undivided attention, you concentrate on it totally.

undo, undoes, undoing, undid, undone
1 (verb) If you undo something that is fastened, you unfasten it.
2 If you undo something that has been done, you reverse the effect of it.

undoing
(noun) If something is someone's undoing, it is the cause of their failure.

undoubted
(adjective) You use undoubted to emphasize something, e.g. *The play was an undoubted success.*
undoubtedly (adverb).

undress, undresses, undressing, undressed
(verb) When you undress, you take off your clothes.

undue
(adjective) greater than is reasonable, e.g. *She put undue pressure on clients.*
unduly (adverb).

undulate, undulates, undulating, undulated
(pronounced **un**-dyool-ate)
(verb; a formal word) Something that undulates has gentle curves or moves gently up and down. [from Latin *unda* meaning 'wave']

undying
(adjective) lasting forever, e.g. *Daniel's undying love for his wife.*

unearth, unearths, unearthing, unearthed
(verb) If you unearth something that is hidden, you discover it.

unearthly
1 (adjective) strange and unnatural.
2 If you do something at an unearthly hour, you do it very late at night.

uneasy
(adjective) If you are uneasy, you feel worried that something may be wrong.
unease (noun), **uneasily** (adverb), **uneasiness** (noun).

uneconomic or uneconomical

(adjective) Something uneconomic produces little profit or wastes time or energy, e.g. *arguments over the closure of uneconomic coal mines.*

unemotional

(adjective) not showing any feelings.

unemployed

1 (adjective) without a job, e.g. *a training scheme for unemployed young people.*
2 (noun) The unemployed are all the people who are without a job.

unemployment

(noun) Unemployment is the state of being without a job.

unending

(adjective) Something unending has continued for a long time and seems as if it will never stop, e.g. *the unending debate about tobacco.*

unenviable

(adjective) An unenviable situation is one that you would not like to be in.

unequal

1 (adjective) An unequal society does not offer the same opportunities and privileges to all people.
2 Unequal things are different in size, strength, or ability.

unequivocal (pronounced un-ik-**wiv**-vok-kl)

(adjective; a formal word) having a completely clear meaning, e.g. *an unequivocal refusal.*
unequivocally (adverb).

unerring

(adjective) Someone who has an unerring ability to do something can always do it.
unerringly (adverb).

unethical

(adjective) Unethical behaviour is morally wrong.
unethically (adverb).

uneven

1 (adjective) not regular or consistent, e.g. *John's short, uneven breathing.*
2 An uneven surface is not level or smooth.
unevenly (adverb).

uneventful

(adjective) During an uneventful occasion or period of time nothing interesting happens.

unexpected

(adjective) Something unexpected is surprising because it was not expected.
unexpectedly (adverb).

unfailing

(adjective) continuous and not weakening as time passes, e.g. *I could not have succeeded without the unfailing support of my staff.*

unfair

(adjective) not right, fair, or just.
unfairly (adverb).

unfaithful

(adjective) If someone is unfaithful to their lover or the person they are married to, they have a sexual relationship with someone else.

unfamiliar

(adjective) If something is unfamiliar to you, or if you are unfamiliar with it, you have not seen or heard it before.

unfasten, unfastens, unfastening, unfastened

(verb) If you unfasten something, you undo its buttons, straps, or clips.

unfeeling

(adjective) An unfeeling person shows no sympathy for people who are suffering.

unfettered

(adjective) completely free and not controlled or limited by anything, e.g. *They are young and still unfettered by families.*

unfit

1 (adjective) If you are unfit, your body is not in good condition because you have not been taking regular exercise.
2 Something that is unfit for a particular purpose is not suitable for that purpose, e.g. *This meat is unfit for human consumption.*

unfold, unfolds, unfolding, unfolded

1 (verb) When a situation unfolds, it develops and becomes known.
2 If you unfold something that has been folded, you open it out so that it is flat.

unforeseen

(adjective) happening unexpectedly.

unforgettable

(adjective) Something unforgettable is so good or so bad that you are unlikely to forget it.
unforgettably (adverb).

unforgivable

(adjective) Something unforgivable is so bad or cruel that it can never be forgiven or justified.
unforgivably (adverb).

unfortunate

1 (adjective) Someone who is unfortunate is unlucky.
2 If you describe an event as unfortunate, you mean that it is a pity that it happened, e.g. *an unfortunate remark.*
unfortunately (adverb).

unfounded

(adjective) Something that is unfounded has no evidence to support it, e.g. *The court decided that the charge against him was unfounded.*

unfulfilled

(adjective) If a hope or desire is unfulfilled, the thing that you wanted has not happened.

unfurnished

(adjective) containing no furniture.

ungainly

(adjective) awkward or clumsy.
[from Old Norse *ungegn* meaning 'not straight']

ungodly

(adjective; an informal word) Something that is ungodly seems unreasonable and unpleasant, e.g. *Stop that ungodly noise!*

ungovernable

(adjective) Ungovernable feelings cannot be controlled, e.g. *in an ungovernable rage.*

ungracious
(adjective) If you are ungracious, you are impolite or unfriendly towards someone who is being kind to you.

ungrateful
(adjective) Someone who is ungrateful is not thankful for something that has been done for them or given to them.

unguarded
1 (adjective) Something that is left unguarded is left without anyone to look after it, e.g. *Never leave luggage unguarded at airports.*
2 An unguarded moment is one in which you are careless about what you say and when you reveal a secret unintentionally.

unhappy, unhappier, unhappiest
1 (adjective) sad and depressed.
2 not pleased or satisfied, e.g. *Parents were unhappy about the lack of information.*
3 If you describe a situation as an unhappy one, you regret that it exists, e.g. *an unhappy state of affairs.*
unhappily (adverb), unhappiness (noun).

unhealthy
1 (adjective) likely to cause illness, e.g. *the unhealthy life we lead in the cities.*
2 An unhealthy person is often ill.
3 Unhealthy attitudes are regarded as being extreme or unnatural, and possibly harmful.

unheard-of
(adjective) never having happened before and therefore surprising or shocking.

unheeded
(adjective) If something goes unheeded, it is ignored.

unheralded
(adjective) If something is unheralded, there is no indication that it is going to happen.

unhinge, unhinges, unhinging, unhinged
(verb) If an experience unhinges someone, it affects them so deeply that they become mentally ill.

unicellular
(adjective) consisting of only one cell.

unicorn, unicorns
(noun) A unicorn is an imaginary animal that looks like a white horse with a straight horn growing from its forehead.
[from Latin *unicornis* meaning 'having one horn']

unicycle, unicycles
(noun) A unicycle is a cycle with one wheel and no handlebars.

unidentified
(adjective) You say that someone or something is unidentified when nobody knows who or what they are.

uniform, uniforms
1 (noun) A uniform is a special set of clothing worn by some people at work or school, or by members of a group such as Guides or Scouts.

2 (adjective) Something that is uniform does not vary but is even and regular throughout.
uniformity (noun).
[from Latin *uniformis* meaning 'of one kind']

unify, unifies, unifying, unified
(verb) If you unify a number of things, you bring them together to form a single unit.
unification (noun).
[from Latin *unificare* meaning 'to make one']

unilateral
(adjective) A unilateral decision or action is one made or done by only one of several groups involved in a particular situation.
unilaterally (adverb).

unilateral disarmament
(noun) Unilateral disarmament is the process or policy by which a country gets rid of its nuclear weapons without waiting for other countries to agree to do the same.

unimaginable
(adjective) impossible to imagine or understand properly, e.g. *the unimaginable vastness of space.*

unimaginative
(adjective) rather dull and without any imagination, e.g. *unimaginative teachers.*

unimportant
(adjective) having very little significance or importance.

Similar words: insignificant, inconsequential, marginal, negligible, trivial, petty, slight

uninhabited
(adjective) An uninhabited place is a place where nobody lives.

uninhibited
(adjective) If you are uninhibited, you behave freely and naturally and show your true feelings.

Similar words: abandoned, liberated

uninitiated (pronounced un-in-**nish**-ee-ay-tid)
(plural noun) You can refer to people who have no knowledge of a particular thing as the uninitiated.

uninspired or uninspiring
(adjective) dull, and not likely to cause interest or excitement.

unintelligible
(adjective; a formal word) impossible to understand.
unintelligibly (adverb).

unintentional
(adjective) not done deliberately.

uninterested
(adjective) If you are uninterested in something, you are not interested in it.

uninterrupted
(adjective) continuing without breaks or interruptions, e.g. *uninterrupted views.*

uninvited
(adjective) arriving or doing something without being asked, e.g. *He sat down uninvited.*

union, unions
1 (noun) A union is an organization of workers that aims to improve the working conditions, pay, and benefits of its members.
2 When the union of two things takes place, they are joined together to become one thing.
[from Latin *unus* meaning 'one']

unique (pronounced yoo-**neek**)
1 (adjective) being the only one of its kind.
2 If something is unique to one person or thing, it concerns or belongs to that person or thing only, e.g. *These problems are unique to nuclear power.*
uniquely (adverb), **uniqueness** (noun).
[from Latin *unicus* meaning 'one and only']

unisex
(adjective) designed to be used by both men and women, e.g. *a unisex hairdresser's... unisex jeans.*

unison
(noun) If a group of people do something in unison, they all do it together at the same time.
[from Latin *unisonus* meaning 'making the same musical sound']

unit, units
1 (noun) If you consider something as a unit, you consider it as a single complete thing.
2 A unit is a group of people who work together at a particular job, e.g. *the intensive-care unit.*
3 A unit is also a machine or piece of equipment which has a particular function, e.g. *a waste-disposal unit... kitchen units.*
4 A unit of measurement is a fixed standard that is used for measuring things. The metre, the litre, and the gram are all units, e.g. *the units of electricity used during a three-month period.*
[from Latin *unus* meaning 'one']

unite, unites, uniting, united
(verb) If a number of people unite, they join together and act as a group.
[from Latin *unire* meaning 'to form into one']

United Kingdom
(noun) The United Kingdom consists of Great Britain and Northern Ireland.

United Nations
(noun) The United Nations is an international organization which tries to encourage peace, cooperation, and friendship between countries.

United Reformed Church
(noun) The United Reformed Church is a nonconformist Protestant church in England and Wales.

unit trust, unit trusts
(noun) A unit trust is an organization which invests money in many different businesses and offers units of shares for sale to the public as an investment.

unity
(noun) Where there is unity, people are in agreement and act together for a particular purpose.
[from Latin *unitas* meaning 'oneness']

universal
1 (adjective) concerning or relating to everyone or every part of the world or universe.
2 A universal truth is something that is equally true at all times and in all situations.
universally (adverb).

universe, universes
(noun) The universe is the whole of space, including all the stars and planets.
[from Latin *universum* meaning 'whole world']

university, universities
(noun) A university is an institution where students study for degrees and where academic research is done.
[from Latin *universitas* meaning 'group of scholars']

unjust
(adjective) not fair or reasonable.
unjustly (adverb).

unjustifiable
(adjective) An unjustifiable action is wrong and unfair and cannot be excused.

unjustified
(adjective) If a belief or action is unjustified, there is no good reason for it.

unkempt
(adjective) untidy and not looked after properly, e.g. *unkempt flower borders.*
[from Old English *uncembed* meaning 'not combed']

unkind
(adjective) unpleasant and rather cruel.
unkindly (adverb), **unkindness** (noun).

Similar words: nasty, uncharitable

unknown
1 (adjective) If someone or something is unknown, people do not know about them or have not heard of them.
2 (noun) You can refer to the things that people in general do not know about as the unknown.

unlawful
(adjective) not legal, e.g. *unlawful business activities.*

unleash, unleashes, unleashing, unleashed
(verb) When a powerful or violent force is unleashed, it is released.

unless
(conjunction) You use unless to introduce the only circumstances in which something will not take place or is not true, e.g. *You can't get into that club unless you are a member.*

unlike
1 (preposition) If one thing is unlike another, the two things are different.
2 If you describe someone's behaviour as being unlike them, you mean that it is not typical of their normal behaviour.

unlikely
1 (adjective) If something is unlikely, it is probably not true or probably will not happen.
2 strange and unexpected, e.g. *They make an unlikely couple.*

unlimited
(adjective) If a supply of something is unlimited, you can have as much as you want or need.

unlit
1 (adjective) An unlit fire has not yet been lit.
2 An unlit place is dark because there are no lights switched on.

unload, unloads, unloading, unloaded
1 (verb) If you unload things from a container or vehicle, you remove them.
2 If you unload a problem or worry onto someone, you tell them about it.

unlock, unlocks, unlocking, unlocked
(verb) If you unlock a door or container, you open it by turning a key in the lock.

unlucky
1 (adjective) Someone who is unlucky has bad luck.
2 Something that is unlucky is thought to cause bad luck.
unluckily (adverb).

Similar words: (sense 1) unfortunate, luckless, hapless, wretched
(sense 2) inauspicious, ill-fated

unmade
(adjective) An unmade bed has not had the bedclothes straightened after it was last slept in.

unmanageable
(adjective) difficult or impossible to use, deal with, or control, e.g. *unmanageable hair.*

unmanly
(adjective) Unmanly behaviour is thought to be not suitable for a man.

unmanned
(adjective) An unmanned spacecraft has no people inside it.

unmarked
1 (adjective) with no marks of damage or injury.
2 with no signs or marks of identification, e.g. *unmarked police cars.*

unmentionable
(adjective) too embarrassing or unpleasant to talk about.

unmistakable or unmistakeable
(adjective) Something unmistakable is so obvious that it cannot be mistaken for something else.
unmistakably (adverb).

unmitigated
(adjective) You use unmitigated to describe a situation or quality that is completely bad, e.g. *an unmitigated disaster.*

unmoved
(adjective) not emotionally affected, e.g. *He was unmoved by her distress.*

unnatural
1 (adjective) strange and rather frightening because it is not usual, e.g. *the hard and unnatural light that comes before a storm.*
2 artificial and not typical, e.g. *Her voice sounded strained and unnatural.*
unnaturally (adverb).

unnerve, unnerves, unnerving, unnerved
(verb) If something unnerves you, it frightens you or makes you lose courage.
unnerving (adjective).

unobserved
(adjective) If you do something unobserved, you do it without being seen.

unobtrusive
(adjective) Something that is unobtrusive does not draw attention to itself.
unobtrusively (adverb).

unoccupied
(adjective) If a house is unoccupied, there is nobody living in it.

unofficial
(adjective) without the approval or authorization of a person in authority, e.g. *an unofficial strike.*
unofficially (adverb).

unorthodox
(adjective) unusual and not generally accepted, e.g. *unorthodox styles of living... unorthodox medicine.*

unpack, unpacks, unpacking, unpacked
(verb) When you unpack, you take everything out of a suitcase or bag.

unpaid
1 (adjective) If you do unpaid work, you do not receive any money for doing it.
2 An unpaid bill has not yet been paid.

unpalatable
1 (adjective) Unpalatable food is so unpleasant that you can hardly eat it.
2 An unpalatable idea is so unpleasant that it is difficult to accept.

unparalleled
(adjective) better than anything else of its kind, e.g. *The specialist library is unparalleled.*

unparliamentary
(adjective) Unparliamentary language or behaviour is not suitable for Parliament, usually because it is too rude or abusive.

unpick, unpicks, unpicking, unpicked
(verb) To unpick a piece of sewing means to remove the stitches from it.

unpleasant
1 (adjective) Something unpleasant causes you to have bad feelings, for example by making you uncomfortable, upset, or frightened.
2 An unpleasant person is unfriendly or rude.

unplug, unplugs, unplugging, unplugged
(verb) If you unplug an electrical appliance, you take the plug out of the socket.

unpopular
(adjective) disliked by most people, e.g. *an unpopular idea.*

unprecedented (pronounced
un-**press**-id-en-tid)
(adjective; a formal word) Something that is
unprecedented has never happened before or is
the best of its kind so far.

unpredictable
(adjective) If someone or something is
unpredictable, you never know how they will
behave or react.

unpremeditated
(adjective) Something unpremeditated has not
been thought about or planned in advance.

unprepared
(adjective) If you are unprepared for something,
you are not ready for it and are therefore
surprised or at a disadvantage when it happens.

unpresentable
(adjective) in a poor condition and therefore not
fit to be seen.

unproductive
(adjective) not producing anything useful.

Similar words: fruitless, unprofitable

unprofitable
(adjective) An unprofitable company or product
does not make enough profit.

unprovoked
(adjective) An unprovoked attack is one that is
made without any cause.

unqualified
1 (adjective) having no qualifications or not
having the right qualifications for a particular
job, e.g. *unqualified childminders.*
2 total, e.g. *an unqualified success.*

unquestionable
(adjective) so obviously true or real that nobody
can doubt it, e.g. *His skill is unquestionable.*
unquestionably (adverb).

unquestioned
(adjective) accepted by everyone without doubt
or disagreement.

unquestioning
(adjective) Unquestioning describes beliefs and
attitudes that people have without thinking
about them or doubting them in any way, e.g.
with unquestioning obedience.

unquiet
(adjective) restless and uneasy.

unravel, unravels, unravelling, unravelled
1 (verb) If you unravel something such as a
twisted and knotted piece of string, you untie
and unwind it so that it is straight.
2 If you unravel a mystery, you work out the
answer to it.
[from Dutch *ravelen* meaning 'to unpick']

unreal
(adjective) so strange that you find it difficult to
believe.

unrealistic
1 (adjective) An unrealistic person does not face
the truth about something or deal with it in a
practical way.

2 Something unrealistic is not true to life, e.g.
The plot of the film was completely unrealistic.
unrealistically (adverb).

unreasonable
(adjective) unfair and difficult to deal with or
justify, e.g. *an unreasonable request.*
unreasonably (adverb).

unreasoning
(adjective) Unreasoning feelings or beliefs are
not logical, sensible, or controlled.

unrefined
1 (adjective) An unrefined substance is in its
natural state and has not been processed in any
way.
2 Unrefined people have coarse manners.

unrelated
(adjective) Things that are unrelated have no
connection with each other.

unrelenting
(adjective) continuing in a determined way
without caring about any hurt that is caused, e.g.
waging an unrelenting barrage of insults.
unrelentingly (adverb).

unreliable
(adjective) If people, machines, or methods are
unreliable, you cannot rely on them.

unremarkable
(adjective) ordinary and not particularly
attractive, interesting, or exciting.

unremitting
(adjective) continuing without stopping.
[from *un-* + Latin *remittere* meaning 'not to
slacken off']

unrepentant
(adjective) If someone is unrepentant, they are
not sorry for their behaviour.

unresolved
(adjective) If a difficulty or problem is
unresolved, no solution has been found for it.

unresponsive
(adjective) not reacting, e.g. *The audience was
unresponsive.*

unrest
(noun) If there is unrest, people are angry and
dissatisfied.

unrivalled
(adjective) better than anything else of its kind,
e.g. *an unrivalled collection of modern art.*

unroll, unrolls, unrolling, unrolled
(verb) If you unroll a roll of cloth or paper, you
open it up and make it flat.

unruffled
(adjective) calm and not affected by something
surprising or frightening.

unruly
(adjective) difficult to control, organize, or keep
tidy, e.g. *unruly children... unruly hair.*
[from *un-* meaning 'not' and the obsolete word
ruly meaning 'orderly']

unsatisfactory
(adjective) not good enough.

unsavoury
(adjective) unpleasant or distasteful, e.g. *an unsavoury character... an unsavoury district.*

unscathed
(adjective) not injured or harmed as a result of a dangerous experience.
[from *un-* meaning 'not' and Old German *skado* meaning 'injury' or 'harm']

unscrew, unscrews, unscrewing, unscrewed
1 (verb) If you unscrew a lid, you remove it by turning it.
2 If you unscrew something that is attached to a surface, you take it off it by removing the screws that are holding it.

unscrupulous
(adjective) willing to behave dishonestly in order to get what you want.
unscrupulously (adverb).

unseal, unseals, unsealing, unsealed
(verb) To unseal something means to open it.

unseasonable
(adjective) Unseasonable weather, clothing, or food is unusual or inappropriate for the time of year.
unseasonably (adverb).

unseat, unseats, unseating, unseated
(verb) When a person in an important position is unseated, they are removed from that position.

unseemly
(adjective) Unseemly behaviour is not suitable for a particular situation and shows a lack of control and good manners, e.g. *an unseemly public squabble over his salary.*
[from *un-* meaning 'not' and Old Norse *sœmiligr* meaning 'fitting' or 'honourable']

unseen
(adjective) You use unseen to describe things that you cannot see or have not seen.

unselfish
(adjective) Someone who is unselfish is concerned about other people's wishes and needs rather than their own.
unselfishly (adverb).

unsettle, unsettles, unsettling, unsettled
(verb) If something unsettles you, it makes you restless, dissatisfied, or rather worried.

unshakable or **unshakeable**
(adjective) An unshakable belief is so strong that it cannot be destroyed or altered.
unshakably (adverb).

unshaven
(adjective) If a man is unshaven, he has not shaved recently.

unsightly
(adjective) very ugly, e.g. *unsightly steel pylons.*
unsightliness (noun).

unskilled
(adjective) Unskilled work does not require any special training.

unsociable
(adjective) An unsociable person does not enjoy meeting and talking to other people.

unsolicited
(adjective) given or happening without being asked for.

unsophisticated (pronounced un-sof-**fist**-tik-kay-tid)
1 (adjective) An unsophisticated person has simple tastes and does not have a lot of experience or knowledge.
2 An unsophisticated method or device is simple and basic.

unsound
1 (adjective) If a conclusion or method is unsound, it is based on ideas that are likely to be wrong.
2 An unsound building is likely to collapse.

unspeakable
(adjective) very unpleasant.

unspecified
(adjective) You say that something is unspecified when you are not told exactly what it is, e.g. *at some unspecified point in the future.*

unspoken
(adjective) An unspoken wish or feeling is one that is not mentioned to other people.

unstable
1 (adjective) likely to change suddenly and create difficulty or danger, e.g. *the unstable political situation in the Middle East.*
2 not firm or fixed properly and likely to wobble or fall.

unsteady
1 (adjective) having difficulty in controlling the movement of your legs or hands, e.g. *unsteady on her feet... an unsteady hand.*
2 not held or fixed securely and likely to fall over.
unsteadily (adverb).

unstructured
(adjective) not organized in a complete and detailed way.

unstuck
1 (adjective) If something comes unstuck, it becomes separated from the thing that it was stuck to.
2 (an informal use) If someone or something comes unstuck, they fail.

unsubstantiated
(adjective) not yet proved to be true, e.g. *unsubstantiated reports.*

unsuccessful
(adjective) If you are unsuccessful, you do not succeed in what you are trying to do.
unsuccessfully (adverb).

unsuitable
(adjective) not right or appropriate for a particular purpose.
unsuitably (adverb).

unsuited
(adjective) not appropriate for a particular task or situation, e.g. *vehicles that are unsuited for use in the desert.*

unsung
(adjective) You use unsung to describe someone who is not appreciated for their good work, e.g. *heroic but unsung volunteers.*
[from the custom of celebrating in song the exploits of heroes]

unsure
(adjective) uncertain or doubtful.

unsuspecting
(adjective) having no idea of what is happening or going to happen, e.g. *leopards pouncing on unsuspecting young baboons.*

untangle, untangles, untangling, untangled
(verb) If you untangle something that is twisted together, you undo the knots and twists.

untapped
(adjective) An untapped supply has not yet been used, e.g. *an untapped oil supply.*

untenable
(adjective) A theory, argument, or position that is untenable cannot be successfully defended.

unthinkable
(adjective) so shocking or awful that you cannot imagine it to be true.

unthinking
(adjective) Someone who is unthinking does not consider the effects of their behaviour.

untidy, untidier, untidiest
(adjective) not neat or well arranged.

untie, unties, untying, untied
(verb) If you untie something, you undo the knots in the string or rope round it.

until
1 (preposition and conjunction) If something happens until a particular time, it happens before that time and stops at that time, e.g. *I stayed until midnight... He kept working until he had finished.*
2 If something does not happen until a particular time, it does not happen before that time and only starts happening at that time, e.g. *We didn't arrive until ten... I can't leave until Jill returns.*

untimely
(adjective) happening too soon or sooner than expected, e.g. *his untimely death.*

unto
(preposition; an old-fashioned word) Unto means the same as to, e.g. *Do unto others as you would have them do unto you.*

untold
(adjective) You use untold to emphasize how great or extreme something is, e.g. *The war has brought untold suffering upon the population.*
[from Old English *unteald* meaning 'immense' or 'uncountable']

untouched
1 (adjective) not changed, moved, or damaged, e.g. *a Norman chapel, untouched since the twelfth century.*
2 If a meal is untouched, none of it has been eaten.

untoward
(adjective) unexpected and causing difficulties, e.g. *Nothing untoward has happened.*
[from *un-* meaning 'not' and Old English *toweard* meaning 'favourable']

untried
(adjective) not yet used, done, or tested.

untroubled
(adjective) not affected or worried by something.

untrue
1 (adjective) not true.
2 If someone is untrue to another person, they are unfaithful or lie to that person.

untruth, untruths
(noun; a formal word) An untruth is a lie.

untruthful
(adjective) Someone who is untruthful tells lies.

untutored
(adjective; a formal word) not educated or knowledgeable.

unused
1 (adjective; pronounced un-**yoozd**) not yet used.
2 (pronounced un-**yoost**) If you are unused to something, you have not often done or experienced it.

unusual
(adjective) Something that is unusual does not occur very often.
unusually (adverb).

Similar words: abnormal, anomalous, irregular

unveil, unveils, unveiling, unveiled
1 (verb) When in a special ceremony someone unveils a new statue or plaque, they draw back a curtain that is covering it.
2 If someone unveils something that has been secret, they make it known for the first time.

unwarranted
(adjective; a formal word) not justified or not deserved, e.g. *Our fears proved unwarranted.*

unwary (rhymes with **scary**)
(adjective) not careful or cautious and therefore likely to be harmed.

unwelcome
(adjective) not wanted, e.g. *an unwelcome visitor... unwelcome news.*

unwell
(adjective) If you are unwell, you are ill.

unwieldy
1 (adjective) difficult to move or carry because of being large or an awkward shape.
2 large and badly organized, e.g. *the country's unwieldy banking system.*
[from *un-* meaning 'not' and Old English *wielde* meaning 'manageable' or 'capable of easy movement']

unwilling
(adjective) If you are unwilling to do something, you do not want to do it.
unwillingly (adverb).

unwind, unwinds, unwinding, unwound
1 (verb) When you unwind after working hard, you relax.
2 If you unwind something that is wrapped round something else, you undo it.

unwise
(adjective) foolish or not sensible.

unwitting
(adjective) Unwitting describes someone who becomes involved in something without realizing what is really happening, e.g. *I became the unwitting instrument of that unscrupulous man.*
unwittingly (adverb).
[from Old English *unwitende* meaning 'not knowing']

unwonted
(adjective) Something that is unwonted is unusual or has not often been experienced before, e.g. *We ate breakfast in unwonted silence.*

unworkable
(adjective) A plan that is unworkable cannot be made to work.

unworldly
(adjective) not interested in having a lot of money or possessions.

unworthy
(adjective; a formal word) Someone who is unworthy of something does not deserve it.

unwrap, unwraps, unwrapping, unwrapped
(verb) When you unwrap something, you take off the paper or covering round it.

unwritten
(adjective) An unwritten law is one which is generally understood and accepted without being officially laid down.

up
1 (adverb and preposition) towards or in a higher place, e.g. *I carried the case up the stairs... up in the hills.*
2 towards or in the north, e.g. *Why did you come up to Edinburgh?*
3 (preposition) If you go up a road or river, you go along it.
4 (adverb) If an amount of something goes up, it increases.
5 (adjective) If you are up, you are not in bed.
6 If a period of time is up, it has come to an end.
7 (preposition) You use 'up to' to say how large something can be or what level it has reached, e.g. *up to a metre wide... The work isn't up to the required standard.*
8 If you feel up to doing something, you feel well enough or have enough energy to do it.
9 If it is up to someone to do something, it is their responsibility.
10 (an informal use) If someone is up to something, they are secretly doing something they should not be doing.
11 (an informal use) If something **is up**, something is wrong.

up-and-coming
(adjective) Up-and-coming people are likely to be successful.

upbringing
(noun) Your upbringing is the way that your parents have taught you to behave.

update, updates, updating, updated
(verb) If you update something, you make it more modern or incorporate new information into it, e.g. *Our records are regularly updated.*

upend, upends, upending, upended
(verb) If you upend something, you turn it upside down.

upgrade, upgrades, upgrading, upgraded
(verb) If a person or their job is upgraded, they are given more responsibility or status and usually more money.

upheaval, upheavals
(noun) An upheaval is a big change which causes a lot of trouble.

uphill
1 (adverb) If you go uphill, you go up a slope.
2 (adjective) An uphill task requires a lot of effort and determination.

uphold, upholds, upholding, upheld
(verb) If someone upholds a law or a decision, they support and maintain it.

upholstery
(noun) Upholstery is the soft covering on chairs and sofas that makes them comfortable.
upholstered (adjective).

upkeep
(noun) The upkeep of something is the continual process and cost of keeping it in good condition.

upland, uplands
1 (adjective) An upland area is an area of high land.
2 (noun) Uplands are areas of high land.

uplifted
(adjective) If people's faces or arms are uplifted, they are holding them upwards.

uplifting
(adjective) making you feel happy and good.

up-market
(adjective) sophisticated and expensive.

upon
1 (preposition; a formal use) Upon means on, e.g. *sitting with the cat upon her knee.*
2 You use 'upon' when mentioning an event that is immediately followed by another, e.g. *Upon entering the cabin, she sat down.*
3 If an event is upon you, it is about to happen, e.g. *The festive season is upon us.*

upper, uppers
1 (adjective) referring to something that is above something else, or the higher part of something, e.g. *an upper shelf... the upper half of his face.*
2 (phrase) If you have **the upper hand** in a situation, you have an advantage over others.
3 (noun) The upper of a shoe is the top part.

upper case
(adjective) Upper case letters are the capital letters used in printing or on a typewriter.

upper class, upper classes
(noun) The upper classes are people who belong to the highest social class of wealthy or aristocratic people.

Upper House
(noun) In Britain, the Upper House or Upper Chamber is the House of Lords.

uppermost
1 (adjective and adverb) on top or in the highest position, e.g. *the uppermost leaves... Hold your hand with the thumb uppermost.*
2 (adjective) most important, e.g. *Political motives were uppermost.*

upright
1 (adjective and adverb) standing or sitting up straight, rather than bending or lying down.
2 very respectable and moral.

uprising, uprisings
(noun) If there is an uprising, a large group of people begin fighting against the existing government to bring about political changes.

uproar
(noun) If there is uproar or an uproar, there is a lot of shouting and noise, often because people are angry.
[from Dutch *oproer* meaning 'revolt']

Similar words: babel, hubbub, furore, commotion, pandemonium, rumpus, tumult

uproarious
(adjective) very loud, e.g. *uproarious laughter.*
uproariously (adverb).

uproot, uproots, uprooting, uprooted
1 (verb) If someone is uprooted, they have to leave the place where they have lived for a long time.
2 If a tree is uprooted, it is pulled out of the ground.

upset, upsets, upsetting, upset
1 (adjective) unhappy and disappointed.
2 (verb) If something upsets you, it makes you feel worried or unhappy.
3 If someone upsets a procedure or state of affairs, they cause things to go wrong.
4 If you upset something, you turn it over or spill it accidentally.
5 (noun) A stomach upset is a slight stomach illness caused by an infection or by something you have eaten.

upshot
(noun) The upshot of a series of events is the final result.
[from the term used for the final shot in an archery contest]

upside down
1 (adjective and adverb) the wrong way up.
2 (phrase) If you **turn a place upside down**, you make it untidy by moving everything.

upstage, upstages, upstaging, upstaged
(verb) If someone upstages you, they draw

people's attention away from you by being more attractive or interesting.

upstairs
1 (adverb) If you go upstairs in a building, you go up to a higher floor.
2 (noun) The upstairs of a building is its upper floor or floors.

upstanding
(adjective; a formal word) very respectable and moral.

upstart, upstarts
(noun) If you call someone an upstart, you mean that they have risen too quickly to an important position and are too arrogant.

upstream
(adverb) towards the source of a river, e.g. *He was making his way upstream.*

upsurge
(noun) An upsurge of something is a sudden large increase in it, e.g. *a massive upsurge of interest.*

uptake
(noun) You can say that someone is quick on the uptake if they understand things quickly.
[from Scottish *uptake* meaning 'to understand']

uptight
(adjective; an informal word) tense or annoyed.

up-to-date
1 (adjective) being the newest thing of its kind.
2 having the latest information.

up-to-the-minute
(adjective) Up-to-the-minute information is the latest available information.

upturn, upturns
(noun) An upturn in a situation is an improvement in it.

upturned
1 (adjective) pointing upwards, e.g. *the upturned face of the youngest child.*
2 upside down, e.g. *an upturned bucket.*

upwards
1 (adverb) towards a higher place, e.g. *He happened to glance upwards.*
2 (adverb) to a higher level or point on a scale, e.g. *The world population is rocketing upwards.*
3 (phrase) **Upwards of** a particular number means more than that number.
upward (adjective).

uranium (pronounced yoo-**ray**-nee-um)
(noun) Uranium is a radioactive metallic element used in the production of nuclear power and weapons. Its atomic number is 92 and its symbol is U.

Uranus
(noun) Uranus is the planet in the solar system which is seventh from the sun.
[named after the Greek god *Ouranos* who ruled the universe]

urban
(adjective) relating to a town or city, e.g. *urban development.*
[from Latin *urbs* meaning 'city']

urbane
(adjective) well-mannered, relaxed, and comfortable in social situations.

urchin, urchins
(noun) You can refer to a young child who is dirty and poorly dressed as an urchin.
[from Latin *ericius* meaning 'hedgehog']

Urdu (pronounced **oor**-doo)
(noun) Urdu is the official language of Pakistan. It is also spoken by many people in India.

ureter, ureters
(noun) The ureter is the tube in the body that carries urine from the kidney to the bladder.

urethra, urethras
(noun) The urethra is the tube in the body that carries urine from the bladder out of the body.

urge, urges, urging, urged
1 (noun) If you have an urge to do something, you have a strong wish to do it.
2 (verb) If you urge someone to do something, you try hard to persuade them to do it.
from Latin *urgere* meaning 'to insist']

Similar words: (sense 1) compulsion, impulse (sense 2) exhort, press

urgent
1 (adjective) needing to be dealt with as soon as possible.
2 If you say something in an urgent way, you show that you are anxious for someone to take notice or do what you say.
urgently (adverb), **urgency** (noun).
[from Latin *urgens* meaning 'pressing' or 'insistent']

Similar words: (sense 1) pressing, immediate

urinal, urinals (pronounced yoor-**rye**-nl)
(noun) A urinal is a bowl or trough fixed to the wall in a men's public toilet for men to urinate in.

urinate, urinates, urinating, urinated
(pronounced **yoor**-rin-ate)
(verb) When you urinate, you go to the toilet and get rid of urine from your body.

urine (pronounced **yoor**-rin)
(noun) Urine is the waste liquid that you get rid of from your body when you go to the toilet.
[from Latin *urina*]

urn, urns
1 (noun) An urn is a decorated container that is used to hold the ashes of a person who has been cremated.
2 A tea urn is a large container in which tea can be made and kept hot.
[from Latin *urna* meaning 'pitcher' or 'jug']

us
(pronoun) A speaker or writer uses us to refer to himself or herself and one or more other people, e.g. *Why didn't you tell us?*

US or **USA** an abbreviation for 'United States of America'.

usage
1 (noun) Usage is the way in which words are actually used, e.g. *a guide to English usage.*
2 Usage is also the degree to which something is used, or the way in which it is used.

use, uses, using, used
1 (verb) If you use something, you do something with it in order to do a job or achieve something, e.g. *He wants to use the phone.*
2 If you use someone, you take advantage of them by making them do things for you.
3 (noun) The use of something is the act of using it, e.g. *the use of fertilizers.*
4 If you have the use of something, you have the ability or permission to use it.
5 If you find a use for something, you find a purpose for it.
6 (phrase) Something that is **of use** is useful.
7 If you say it's **no use** doing something or **what's the use** of doing it, you are saying that it is pointless and will not succeed.
usable or **useable** (adjective),
user (noun).

Similar words: (sense 1) apply, employ, utilize (sense 3) appliance, application, utilization, employment, usage

use up
(phrasal verb) If you use up a supply of something, you use it until it is finished.

Similar words: exhaust, expend, drain, spend

used
1 (verb; pronounced **yoost**) Something that used to be done or used to be true was done or was true in the past.
2 (phrase) If you are **used to** something, you are familiar with it and have often experienced it.
3 (adjective; pronounced **yoozd**) A used object has had a previous owner.

useful
(adjective) If something is useful, you can use it in order to do something or to help you in some way.
usefully (adverb), **usefulness** (noun).

useless
1 (adjective) If something is useless, you cannot use it because it is not suitable or helpful.
2 If a course of action is useless, it will not achieve what is wanted.
3 (an informal use) Someone who is useless at something is very bad at it.

usher, ushers, ushering, ushered
1 (verb) If you usher someone somewhere, you show them where to go by going with them.
2 (noun) An usher is a person who shows people where to sit at a wedding or a concert.
[from Latin *ostiarius* meaning 'doorkeeper']

usherette, usherettes
(noun) An usherette is a woman who shows people where to sit in a cinema or theatre.

USSR an abbreviation for 'Union of Soviet Socialist Republics'.

usual
1 (adjective) happening, done, or used most often, e.g. *He sat in his usual chair.*

2 (phrase) If you do something **as usual**, you do it in the way that you normally do it.
usually (adverb).
[from Latin *usualis* meaning 'ordinary']

Similar words: (sense 1) general, accustomed, habitual, customary, routine

usurp, usurps, usurping, usurped (pronounced yoo-**zerp**)
(verb; a formal word) If someone usurps another person's job, title, or position, they take it when they have no right to do so.
[from Latin *usurpare* meaning 'to seize for use']

utensil, utensils (pronounced yoo-**ten**-sil)
(noun) Utensils are tools, e.g. *cooking utensils.*
[from Latin *utensilis* meaning 'available for use']

uterus, uteruses (pronounced **yoo**-ter-russ)
(noun; a formal word) A woman's uterus is her womb.
[a Latin word]

utilitarian
1 (adjective) intended to produce the greatest benefit for the greatest number of people, e.g. *He had not entered science for utilitarian purposes.*
2 designed to be useful rather than beautiful.

utility, utilities
1 (noun) The utility of something is its usefulness.
2 A utility is a service, such as water or gas, that is provided for everyone.
[from Latin *utilis* meaning 'useful']

utilize, utilizes, utilizing, utilized; also spelled **utilise**
(verb; a formal word) To utilize something means to use it.
utilization (noun).

utmost
1 (adjective) used to emphasize a particular quality, e.g. *I have the utmost respect for her.*

2 (noun) If something is done to the utmost, it is done to the greatest possible degree or extent.
[from Old English *utemest* meaning 'outermost' or 'furthest part']

Utopia, Utopias (pronounced yoo-**toe**-pee-a)
(noun) A Utopia is a perfect social system in which everyone is happy. It is named after the book 'Utopia' by Sir Thomas More which described a perfectly governed republic.
utopian (adjective).
[from Greek *ou* + *topos* meaning 'no place']

utter, utters, uttering, uttered
1 (verb) When you utter sounds or words, you make or say them.
2 (adjective) Utter means complete or total, e.g. *Judith is an utter fool.*
utterly (adverb).
[Sense 1 is from Dutch *uiteren* meaning 'to speak' or 'to make known'; sense 2 is from Old English *utera* meaning 'outer' or 'extreme']

utterance, utterances
(noun) An utterance is something that is said, e.g. *The children copied my every utterance.*

U-turn, U-turns
1 (noun) When a vehicle does a U-turn, it turns half a circle to face in the opposite direction.
2 If a government or organization does a U-turn, it abandons a policy and does something completely different.

uvula, uvulas or **uvulae** (pronounced yoo-**vyoo**-la)
(noun; a technical word) Your uvula is the small piece of flesh that hangs down above the back of your tongue.
[from Latin *uva* meaning 'grape']

V

v

v is used to indicate that two people or teams are competing against each other. It is an abbreviation for 'versus'.

vacant

1 (adjective) If something is vacant, it is not occupied or being used.
2 If a job or position is vacant, no-one holds it at present.
3 A vacant look suggests that someone does not understand something or is not very intelligent.
vacancy (noun), vacantly (adverb).
[from Latin *vacare* meaning 'to be empty']

vacate, vacates, vacating, vacated
(verb) If you vacate a room or job, you leave it and it becomes available for someone else.

vacation, vacations

1 (noun) A vacation is the period between academic terms at a university or college, e.g. *the summer vacation.*
2 In American English, a vacation is a holiday.

vaccinate, vaccinates, vaccinating, vaccinated
(pronounced **vak**-sin-ate)
(verb) To vaccinate someone means to give them a vaccine, usually by injection, to protect them against a disease.
vaccination (noun).

vaccine, vaccines (pronounced **vak**-seen)
(noun) A vaccine is a substance made from the germs that cause a disease and is given to people to make them immune to that disease.
[from Latin *vacca* meaning 'cow', because smallpox vaccine is based on cowpox]

vacillate, vacillates, vacillating, vacillated
(pronounced **vas**-sil-late)
(verb; a formal word) If you vacillate, you keep changing your opinion about something.
vacillation (noun).

vacuole, vacuoles (pronounced **vak**-yoo-ole)
(noun) In biology, a vacuole is the area in a cell containing air, fluid, or partially digested food.
[from French *vacuole* meaning 'little vacuum']

vacuous
(adjective) showing no sign of intelligence or understanding, e.g. *a vacuous look.*

vacuum, vacuums, vacuuming, vacuumed
(pronounced **vak**-yoom)
1 (noun) A vacuum is a space containing no air, gases, or other matter.
2 If someone or something creates a vacuum, they leave a place or position which must be filled, e.g. *the power vacuum left by the departing British.*
3 (verb) If you vacuum something, you clean it using a vacuum cleaner.
[from Latin *vacuum* meaning 'empty space']

vacuum cleaner, vacuum cleaners
(noun) A vacuum cleaner is an electric machine which cleans by sucking up dirt.

vacuum flask, vacuum flasks
(noun) A vacuum flask is the same as a Thermos.

vagabond, vagabonds
(noun) A vagabond is a person who travels from place to place and has no fixed home or job.
[from Latin *vagabundus* meaning 'wandering']

vagary, vagaries (pronounced **vay**-gar-ee)
(noun; a formal word) Vagaries are unpredictable changes in a situation or in someone's behaviour, e.g. *the vagaries of the British climate.*

vagina, vaginas (pronounced vaj-**jie**-na)
(noun) A woman's vagina is the passage that connects her outer sex organs to her womb.
[from Latin *vagina* meaning 'sheath']

vagrant, vagrants
(noun) A vagrant is a person who moves from place to place, and has no home or regular job.
vagrancy (noun).

vague, vaguer, vaguest (pronounced **vayg**)
1 (adjective) If something is vague, it is not expressed or explained clearly, or you cannot see or remember it clearly, e.g. *vague instructions... a vague memory of my first home.*
2 Someone looks or sounds vague if they are not concentrating or thinking clearly.
vaguely (adverb), vagueness (noun).

Similar words: (sense 1) indefinite, nebulous, woolly, indeterminate

---

vain, vainer, vainest
1 (adjective) A vain action or attempt is one which is not successful, e.g. *the teacher's vain plea for silence.*
2 A vain person is very proud of their looks, intelligence, or other qualities.
3 (phrase) If you do something **in vain**, you do not succeed in achieving what you intend.
vainly (adverb).

vale, vales
(noun; a literary word) A vale is a valley.

valedictory (pronounced val-lid-**dik**-tree)
(adjective; a formal word) A valedictory speech or letter is one in which you say goodbye to someone.
valediction (noun).
[from Latin *valedicere* meaning 'to say farewell']

valence
(noun; a technical word) Valence is the same as valency.

valency
(noun; a technical word) The valency of an atom or chemical group is the number of atoms it has available to combine with atoms of hydrogen and so form compounds.

valentine, valentines
1 (noun) Your valentine is someone you love and send a card to on Saint Valentine's Day, February 14th.

2 A valentine or a valentine card is the card you send to the person you love on Saint Valentine's Day.
[Saint Valentine was a 3rd century martyr]

valet, valets (pronounced **val**-lit)
(noun) A valet is a male servant who is employed to look after another man, particularly caring for his clothes.
[from Latin *vassus* meaning 'servant']

Valhalla (pronounced val-**hal**-la)
(noun) In Norse mythology, Valhalla was the place where heroes killed in battle went.
[from Old Norse *valr* + *höll* meaning 'slain warriors' hall']

valiant
(adjective) very brave.
valiantly (adverb).

valid
1 (adjective) Something that is valid is based on sound reasoning.
2 A valid ticket or document is one which is officially accepted.
validly (adverb), **validity** (noun).

validate, validates, validating, validated
(verb) If something validates a statement or claim, it proves that it is true or correct.

valise, valises (pronounced val-**eez**)
(noun; an old-fashioned word) A valise is a small suitcase.

Valium
(noun; a trademark) Valium is a drug which is given to people to calm their nerves.

valley, valleys
(noun) A valley is a long stretch of land between hills, often with a river flowing through it.

valour
(noun) Valour is great bravery.

valuable, valuables
1 (adjective) Something that is valuable has great value.
2 (noun) Valuables are things that you own that cost a lot of money, for example jewellery.

Similar words: (sense 1) prized, valued, precious, invaluable

---

valuation, valuations
(noun) A valuation is a judgment about how much money something is worth or how good it is.

value, values, valuing, valued
1 (noun) The value of something is its importance or usefulness, e.g. *the value of sincerity.*
2 The value of something you own is the amount of money that it is worth.
3 The values of a group or a person are the moral principles and beliefs that they think are important, e.g. *the traditional values of politeness and good manners.*
4 (verb) If you value something, you think it is important and you appreciate it.

5 When experts value something, they decide how much money it is worth.
valued (adjective), **valuer** (noun).

value-added tax
(noun) Value-added tax is the same as VAT.

value judgment, value judgments
(noun) A value judgment is a personal opinion about something based on the beliefs of the person giving the opinion, and not on facts which can be checked or proved.

valve, valves
1 (noun) A valve is a part attached to a pipe or tube which controls the flow of gas or liquid.
2 A valve is a small flap in your heart or in a vein which controls the flow and direction of blood.
3 A valve is a closed tube through which electrons move in a vacuum.
[from Latin *valva* meaning 'folding door']

vamp, vamps
(noun; an informal word) A vamp is an attractive woman who seduces men.

vampire, vampires
(noun) In horror stories, vampires are corpses that come out of their graves at night and suck the blood of living people.
[from Hungarian *vampir*]

vampire bat, vampire bats
(noun) A vampire bat is a tropical American bat which feeds off the blood of animals.

van, vans
(noun) A van is a covered vehicle larger than a car but smaller than a lorry, used for carrying goods.

vanadium (pronounced van-**nay**-dee-um)
(noun) Vanadium is a metallic element used to toughen steel. Its atomic number is 23 and its symbol is V.

Van Allen belt
(noun) In astronomy, the Van Allen belt is the name used to describe either of two belts of charged particles which surround the Earth. They are named after the American physicist, J.A. Van Allen (1914 -), who discovered them.

vandal, vandals
(noun) A vandal is someone who deliberately damages or destroys things, particularly public property.
vandalize or **vandalise** (verb),
vandalism (noun).
[from the Germanic tribe the *Vandals* who sacked Rome in 455 AD]

vane, vanes
(noun) A vane is a flat blade that is part of a mechanism for using the energy of the wind or water to drive a machine.

vanguard (pronounced van-gard)
(noun) If someone is in the vanguard of something, they are in the most advanced part of it.
[from Old French *avant-* meaning 'fore-' and *garde* meaning 'guard']

vanilla
(noun) Vanilla is a flavouring for food such as ice cream, which comes from the pods of a tropical plant.
[from Spanish *vainilla* meaning 'pod']

vanish, vanishes, vanishing, vanished
(verb) If something vanishes, it disappears or ceases to exist, e.g. *The car vanished from sight... protection of vanishing species.*

vanity
(noun) Vanity is a feeling of excessive pride about your looks or abilities.

vanquish, vanquishes, vanquishing, vanquished
(pronounced **vang**-kwish)
(verb; a literary word) To vanquish someone means to defeat them completely.

vantage point, vantage points
(noun) A vantage point is a place from which you have a wide or clear view of something.

vapid
(adjective) dull and uninteresting.

vaporize, vaporizes, vaporizing, vaporized; also spelled vaporise
(verb) When a liquid vaporizes, it changes into a vapour.
vaporizer (noun), **vaporization** (noun).

vapour
(noun) Vapour is a mass of tiny drops of water or other liquids in the air, which looks like mist.
[from Latin *vapor* meaning 'steam']

variable, variables
1 (adjective) Something that is variable is likely to change at any time.
2 (noun) In any situation, a variable is something in it that can change.
3 In maths, a variable is a symbol such as x which can represent any value or any one of a set of values.
variability (noun).

variance
(noun) If one thing is at variance with another, the two seem to contradict each other.

variant, variants
1 (noun) A variant of something has a different form from the usual one, for example *gaol* is a variant of *jail.*
2 (adjective) alternative or different.

variation, variations
1 (noun) A variation is a change from the normal or usual pattern.
2 A variation is a change in level, amount, or quantity, e.g. *a large variation in demand.*
3 In music, a variation is the repetition of a simple tune with the addition of new harmonies or a change in rhythm.

varicose veins
(plural noun) Varicose veins are swollen painful veins in the legs.

varied
(adjective) of different types, quantities, or sizes.

variegated (pronounced **vair**-ig-ay-tid)
(adjective) marked with different patches or lines of colour.

variety, varieties
1 (noun) If something has variety, it consists of things which are not all identical.
2 A variety of things is a number of different kinds of them, e.g. *for a whole variety of reasons.*
3 A variety of something is a particular type of it, e.g. *a new variety of dahlia.*
4 Variety is a form of entertainment consisting of short unrelated acts, such as singing, dancing, and comedy.

Similar words: (sense 2) assortment, array, miscellany, medley

various
(adjective) Various means of several different types, e.g. *drugs of various kinds.*
variously (adverb).

Similar words: varied, sundry, diverse, miscellaneous

varnish, varnishes, varnishing, varnished
1 (noun) Varnish is a liquid which when painted onto a surface gives it a hard clear shiny finish.
2 (verb) If you varnish something, you paint it with varnish.
[from Latin *veronix* meaning 'fragrant resin']

vary, varies, varied, varying
1 (verb) If things vary, they change, e.g. *The fees vary a lot.*
2 If you vary something, you introduce changes in it, e.g. *He varied his daily routine.*
varied (adjective).

vascular
(adjective) relating to tubes or ducts that carry blood or sap within animals or plants.

vase, vases
(noun) A vase is a glass or ceramic jar for flowers.

vasectomy, vasectomies (pronounced vas-**sek**-tom-ee)
(noun) A vasectomy is an operation to sterilize a man by cutting the tube that carries the sperm.
[from Latin *vas* meaning 'vessel' and *-ectomia* meaning 'surgical removal']

Vaseline
(noun; a trademark) Vaseline is a type of thick white oily cream obtained from petroleum and used as a base for ointments and as a lubricant.
[from German *Wasser* meaning 'water' and Greek *elaion* meaning 'oil']

vassal, vassals
(noun) In medieval times, a vassal was a person who gave service to his lord in exchange for land or protection.
[from Latin *vassus* meaning 'servant']

vast
(adjective) extremely large.
vastly (adverb), **vastness** (noun).

vat, vats
(noun) A vat is a large container for liquids.

VAT

(noun) VAT is a tax which is added to the costs of making or providing goods and services.

vault, vaults, vaulting, vaulted (rhymes with salt)

1 (noun) A vault is a strong secure room, often underneath a building, where valuables are stored, or underneath a church where people are buried.

2 A vault is an arched roof, often found in churches.

3 (verb) If you vault over something, you jump over it using your hands or a pole to help.

VCR an abbreviation for 'video cassette recorder'.

VD an abbreviation for **venereal disease.**

VDU, VDUs

(noun) A VDU is a monitor screen attached to a computer or word processor. VDU is an abbreviation for 'visual display unit'.

veal

(noun) Veal is the meat from a calf.
[from Latin *vitellus* meaning 'little calf']

vector, vectors

(noun) In maths, a vector is a quantity, such as a force, which has magnitude and direction.

veer, veers, veering, veered

(verb) If something which is moving veers in a particular direction, it suddenly changes course, e.g. *The plane seemed to veer off to one side.*

vegan, vegans (pronounced **vee**-gn)

(noun) A vegan is someone who does not eat any food made from animal products, such as meat, eggs, cheese, or milk.
veganism (noun).

vegetable, vegetables

1 (noun) Vegetables are edible roots or leaves such as carrots or cabbage.

2 (adjective) Vegetable is used to refer to any plants in contrast to animals or minerals, e.g. *vegetable matter.*
[from Latin *vegetabilis* meaning 'enlivening']

vegetarian, vegetarians

(noun) A vegetarian is a person who does not eat meat.
vegetarianism (noun).

vegetate, vegetates, vegetating, vegetated

(verb) If you vegetate, you live in a dull and boring way with little to stimulate your mind.

vegetation

(noun) Vegetation is the plants in a particular area.

vehement (pronounced **vee**-im-ent)

(adjective) Someone who is vehement has strong feelings or opinions and expresses them forcefully, e.g. *With a vehement gesture he threw the book away.*
vehemence (noun), **vehemently** (adverb).

vehicle, vehicles (pronounced **vee**-ik-kl)

1 (noun) A vehicle is a machine, often with an engine, used for transporting people or goods.

2 A vehicle is something used to achieve a particular purpose or as a means of expression, e.g. *The newspaper was a vehicle for explaining government policies.*
vehicular (adjective).

veil, veils (rhymes with **male**)

(noun) A veil is a piece of cloth worn by women as part of a hat or headdress, or to cover their face.
veiled (adjective).
[from Latin *vela* meaning 'sails' or 'curtains']

vein, veins (rhymes with **rain**)

1 (noun) Your veins are the tubes in your body through which your blood flows to your heart.

2 Veins are the thin lines on leaves or on insects' wings.

3 A vein of a metal or a mineral is a layer of it in rock.

4 Something that is in a particular vein is in that style or mood, e.g. *in a lighter vein.*

veld or **veldt** (pronounced **felt**)

(noun) The veld is flat high grassland in Southern Africa.
[an Afrikaans word]

vellum

(noun) Vellum is fine parchment made from the skin of calves, lambs, or kids.

velocity, velocities

(noun) Velocity is the speed at which something is moving in a particular direction.
[from Latin *velox* meaning 'swift']

velour or **velours**

(noun) Velour or velours is a silk or cotton cloth similar to velvet.

velvet

(noun) Velvet is a very soft material which has a thick layer of fine short threads on one side.
velvety (adjective).
[from Latin *villus* meaning 'shaggy hair']

venal

(adjective) Someone who is venal will accept bribes in return for acting dishonestly or unfairly.
venally (adverb), **venality** (noun).

vendetta, vendettas

(noun) A vendetta is a long-lasting bitter quarrel which results in people or organizations trying to harm each other.
[from Latin *vindicare* meaning 'to avenge']

vending machine, vending machines

(noun) A vending machine is a machine which provides things such as drinks, sweets, or cigarettes when you put money in it.

vendor, vendors

(noun) A vendor is a person who sells something.

veneer

1 (noun) You can refer to a superficial quality that someone has as a veneer of that quality, e.g. *a veneer of exaggerated politeness.*

2 Veneer is a thin layer of wood or plastic used to cover a surface.
[from Old French *fournir* meaning 'to furnish']

venerable
1 (adjective) A venerable person is someone you treat with respect because they are old and wise.
2 Something that is venerable is impressive because it is old or important historically.

venerate, venerates, venerating, venerated
(verb; a formal word) If you venerate someone, you feel great respect for them.
veneration (noun).

venereal disease, venereal diseases
(pronounced vin-**ear**-ee-al)
(noun) A venereal disease is one that is passed on by sexual intercourse.
[from Latin *venus* meaning 'sexual love']

Venetian blind, Venetian blinds (pronounced vin-**nee**-shn)
(noun) A Venetian blind is a window blind made of thin horizontal overlapping strips which can be adjusted to let in more or less light.

vengeance
1 (noun) Vengeance is the act of harming someone because they have harmed you.
2 (phrase) If something happens **with a vengeance**, it happens to a much greater extent than was expected, e.g. *The hurricane struck the coast with a vengeance.*

vengeful
(adjective; a literary word) If you are vengeful, you feel a great desire for revenge.

venial
(adjective; a formal word) A venial sin or fault is easily excused or forgiven because it is not very serious.

venison
(noun) Venison is the meat from a deer.
[from Latin *venatio* meaning 'hunting']

Venn diagram, Venn diagrams
(noun) In mathematics, a Venn diagram is a drawing which uses circles to show the relationships between different sets. Venn diagrams are named after the English logician John Venn (1834-1923), who invented them.

venom
1 (noun) The venom of a snake, scorpion, or spider is its poison.
2 Venom is a feeling of great bitterness or spitefulness towards someone, e.g. *'What a filthy trick,' she said, with unexpected venom.*
venomous (adjective), **venomously** (adverb).
[from Latin *venenum* meaning 'love potion' or 'poison']

venous (pronounced **vee**-nuss)
(adjective) relating to the veins, or the blood carried through the veins.

vent, vents, venting, vented
1 (noun) A vent is a hole in something through which gases and smoke can escape and fresh air can enter, e.g. *air vents.*
2 (verb) If you vent strong feelings, you express them, e.g. *He vented his rage on Bernard.*
3 (phrase) If you **give vent** to strong feelings, you express them, e.g. *She gave vent to her rage.*

ventilate, ventilates, ventilating, ventilated
(verb) To ventilate a room means to allow fresh air into it.
ventilated (adjective), **ventilation** (noun).

ventilator, ventilators
(noun) A ventilator is a device which allows fresh air into a building and lets stale air out.

ventricle, ventricles
1 (noun) A ventricle is a chamber of the heart that pumps blood to the arteries.
2 A ventricle is also one of the four main cavities of the brain.
[from Latin *ventriculus* meaning 'small belly']

ventriloquist, ventriloquists (pronounced ven-**trill**-o-kwist)
(noun) A ventriloquist is an entertainer who can speak without moving their lips so that the words seem to come from another place.
ventriloquism (noun).
[from Latin *venter* meaning 'belly' and *loqui* meaning 'to speak']

venture, ventures, venturing, ventured
1 (noun) A venture is something new which involves the risk of failure or of losing money, e.g. *a new scientific venture.*
2 (verb) If you venture something such as an opinion, you say it cautiously or hesitantly because you are afraid it might be foolish or wrong, e.g. *Mrs Harris ventured to speak.*
3 If you venture somewhere that might be dangerous, you go there.

Similar words: (sense 1) enterprise, endeavour, project, undertaking

venue, venues (pronounced **ven**-yoo)
(noun) The venue for an event is the place where it will happen.

Venus
(noun) Venus is the planet in the solar system which is second from the sun.
[named after the Roman goddess of love]

veracious (pronounced ver-**ray**-shuss)
(adjective; a formal word) Someone who is veracious always tells the truth.

veracity
(noun; a formal word) Veracity is the quality or habit of telling the truth.

veranda, verandas (pronounced ver-**ran**-da); also spelled verandah
(noun) A veranda is a platform with a roof attached to an outside wall of a house at ground level.

verb, verbs
(noun) In grammar, a verb is a word that expresses actions and states, for example 'be', 'become', 'take', 'run', and 'like'.

verbal
1 (adjective) You use verbal to describe things connected with words and their use, e.g. *a contest of verbal skills.*
2 Verbal describes things which are spoken

rather than written, e.g. *a written exam paper followed by verbal questioning.*
3 Verbal also means relating to verbs.
verbally (adverb).

verbatim (pronounced ver-**bay**-tim)
(adverb and adjective) If you repeat something verbatim, you use exactly the same words.

verbiage (pronounced **ver**-be-ij)
(noun; a formal word) Verbiage is the use of too many words.

verbose
(adjective) using more words than is necessary.
verbosely (adverb), **verbosity** (noun).

verdant
(adjective; a literary word) green and fresh, and covered with grass, trees, and plants.

verdict, verdicts
1 (noun) In a law court, a verdict is the decision which states whether a prisoner is guilty or not guilty.
2 If you give a verdict on something, you give your opinion after thinking about it.

Similar words: judgment, finding, conclusion

verge, verges, verging, verged
1 (noun) The verge of a road is the narrow strip of grassy ground at the side.
2 (phrase) If you **are on the verge** of something, you are going to do it soon or it is likely to happen soon, e.g. *on the verge of starvation.*
3 (verb) Something that verges on something else is almost the same as it, e.g. *distrust verging on panic.*

verger, vergers
(noun) In the Anglican Church, a verger is an official who looks after a church building and its contents.
[from Latin *virga* meaning 'rod', because they used to carry one]

verify, verifies, verifying, verified
(verb) If you verify something, you check that it is true, e.g. *evidence that could be verified.*
verifiable (adjective), **verification** (noun).

verisimilitude (pronounced ver-iss-im-**mil**-it-yood)
(noun) If something has verisimilitude, it seems to be true or real.

veritable
(adjective) You use veritable to emphasize that something is really true, even if it seems as if you are exaggerating, e.g. *He was a veritable liar.*

verity, verities
(noun) The verities of something are all the things that are believed to be true about it.

vermicelli (pronounced ver-mich-**chell**-ee)
(noun) Vermicelli is long, thin threads of pasta.
[from Italian *vermicelli* meaning 'little worms']

vermilion
(noun and adjective) vivid red.

vermin
(plural noun) Vermin are small animals or insects, such as rats and cockroaches, which carry disease and damage crops or food.

vernacular, vernaculars (pronounced ver-**nak**-yoo-lar)
(noun) The vernacular of a particular country or district is the language widely spoken there.
[from Latin *vernaculus* meaning 'belonging to a household slave', because slaves only spoke one language]

verruca, verrucas (pronounced ver-**roo**-ka)
(noun) A verruca is a small hard infectious growth rather like a wart. It most commonly occurs on the feet.

versatile
(adjective) If someone is versatile, they have many different skills.
versatility (noun).

verse, verses
1 (noun) Verse is another word for poetry.
2 A verse is one part of a poem, song, or chapter of the Bible.

versed
(adjective) If you are versed in something, you know a lot about it.

version, versions
1 (noun) A version of something is a form of it in which some details are different from earlier or later forms, e.g. *from first draft to final version.*
2 Someone's version of an event is their personal description of what happened.

versus
(preposition) Versus is used to indicate that two people or teams are competing against each other.

vertebra, vertebrae (pronounced **ver**-tib-bra)
(noun) Vertebrae are the small bones which form a person's or animal's backbone.

vertebrate, vertebrates
(noun) Vertebrates are any creatures which have a backbone.

vertex, vertexes or **vertices**
(noun) The vertex of something such as a triangle or pyramid is the point opposite the base.

vertical
(adjective) Something that is vertical points straight up and forms a ninety-degree angle with the surface on which it stands.
vertically (adverb).

vertigo
(noun) Vertigo is a feeling of dizziness caused by looking down from a high place.
[from Latin *vertigo* meaning 'whirling around']

verve
(noun) Verve is lively and forceful enthusiasm.
[from Latin *verba* meaning 'words' or 'chatter']

very
1 (adjective and adverb) Very is used before words to emphasize them, e.g. *a very small child... the very top of the hill.*
2 (phrase) You use **not very** to mean that something is the case only to a small degree, e.g. *'Is it difficult?' — 'No, not very.'*

Similar words: (sense 1) highly, extremely,
exceedingly, really, terribly, truly

very high frequency
(noun) Very high frequency is the same as VHF.

vespers
(noun) Vespers is a service held in a Christian
church in the evening.
[from Latin *vesper* meaning 'evening star']

vessel, vessels
1 (noun) A vessel is a ship or large boat.
2 A vessel is also any bowl or container in which
a liquid can be kept.
3 A vessel is also a thin tube along which liquids
such as blood or sap move in animals and plants.

vest, vests
1 (noun) A vest is a piece of underclothing worn
for warmth on the top half of the body.
2 In American English, a vest is a waistcoat.
[from Latin *vestis* meaning 'clothing']

vested interest, vested interests
(noun) If someone has a vested interest in
something, they have a strong reason for acting
in a particular way, for example to protect their
own money, power, or reputation.

vestibule, vestibules (pronounced **vest**-ib-yool)
(noun) A vestibule is an enclosed area between
the outside door of a building and the rooms.
[from Latin *vestibulum* meaning 'entrance hall']

vestige, vestiges (pronounced **vest**-ij)
(noun; a formal word) If there is not a vestige of
something, then there is not even a little of it
left, e.g. *the last vestige of political freedom.*

vestment, vestments
(noun) Vestments are the special clothes worn by
priests during church ceremonies.

vestry, vestries
(noun) The vestry is the part of the church
building where a priest or minister changes into
his official clothes.

vet, vets, vetting, vetted
1 (noun) A vet is a doctor for animals.
2 (verb) If you vet someone or something, you
check them carefully to see if they are
acceptable, e.g. *He was vetted by security.*

vetch
(noun) Vetch is a climbing or creeping plant
found in temperate climates. Some kinds of vetch
are used to feed cattle.

veteran, veterans
1 (noun) A veteran is someone who has served in
the armed forces, particularly during a war.
2 A veteran is also someone who has been
involved in a particular activity for a long time,
e.g. *a veteran of the civil rights movement.*
3 (adjective) A veteran car is one made before
1918.
[from Latin *vetus* meaning 'old']

veterinary (pronounced **vet**-er-in-ar-ee)
(adjective) Veterinary is used to describe the
work of a vet and the medical treatment of
animals.

[from Latin *veterinae* meaning 'animals used for
pulling carts and ploughs']

veterinary surgeon, veterinary surgeons
(noun) A veterinary surgeon is the same as a vet.

veto, vetoes, vetoing, vetoed
1 (verb) If someone in authority vetoes
something, they reject or forbid it.
2 (noun) Veto is the right that someone in
authority has to reject or forbid something, e.g.
the Sovereign's power of veto.
[from Latin *veto* meaning 'I forbid']

vex, vexes, vexing, vexed
(verb; an old-fashioned word) If something vexes
you, it makes you annoyed, worried, or puzzled.
vexed (adjective), **vexation** (noun).

VHF
(noun) VHF is a range of high radio frequencies
between 300 and 30 megahertz, which is used for
transmissions over short distances. VHF is an
abbreviation for 'very high frequency'.

via
1 (preposition) If you go to one place via
another, you travel through that place to your
destination, e.g. *to Glasgow via Carlisle.*
2 Via also means done or achieved by making use
of a particular thing or person, e.g. *television
pictures via satellite.*
[from Latin *via* meaning 'way' or 'road']

viable (pronounced **vy**-a-bl)
(adjective) Something that is viable is capable of
doing what it is intended to do without extra
help or financial support, e.g. *a viable project.*
viably (adverb), **viability** (noun).

viaduct, viaducts
(noun) A viaduct is a long high bridge that
carries a road or railway across a valley.
[from Latin *via* meaning 'road' and *ducere*
meaning 'to bring']

vial, vials
(noun; a formal word) A vial is a small bottle of
something such as perfume or medicine.

vibes
(plural noun; an informal word) Vibes are the
emotional reactions that you feel a person has
towards you, or the atmosphere that a place has.

vibrant
(adjective) Something or someone that is vibrant
is full of life, energy, and enthusiasm.
vibrantly (adverb), **vibrancy** (noun).

vibrate, vibrates, vibrating, vibrated
(verb) If something vibrates, it moves a tiny
amount backwards and forwards very quickly.
vibration (noun).

vibrato
(noun) Vibrato is the rapid slight variation in the
pitch of a musical note.

vicar, vicars
(noun) A vicar is a priest in the Church of
England.
[from Latin *vicarius* meaning 'deputy'; in
medieval times, vicars were bishops'
representatives]

vicarage, vicarages
(noun) A vicarage is a house where a vicar lives.

vicarious
(adjective) A vicarious pleasure or feeling is one that you experience by watching, listening to, or reading about other people doing something rather than by doing it yourself.
vicariously (adverb).

vice, vices
1 (noun) A vice is a serious moral fault in someone's character, such as greed, or a weakness, such as smoking.
2 Vice is criminal activities connected with drugs, prostitution, pornography, or gambling.
3 A vice is a tool with a pair of jaws that hold an object tightly while it is being worked on.
[senses 1 and 2 are from Latin *vitium* meaning 'defect'; sense 3 is from Old French *vis* meaning 'screw']

vice-
(prefix) Vice- is used before a title or position to show that the holder is the deputy of the person with that title or position, e.g. *vice-chairman*.

vice admiral, vice admirals
(noun) A vice admiral is a naval officer of the rank immediately below admiral and immediately above rear admiral.

vice chancellor, vice chancellors
(noun) A vice chancellor is the head of academic and administrative matters in a British university.

viceroy, viceroys
(noun) A viceroy is someone who has been appointed to govern a place as a representative of a monarch.
[from *vice* + French *roy* meaning 'king']

vice squad, vice squads
(noun) The vice squad is a section of the police force which deals with crime relating to pornography, prostitution, drugs, and gambling.

vice versa
Vice versa is used to indicate that the reverse of what you have said is also true, e.g. *Wives criticize their husbands, and vice versa.*
[from Latin *vice versa* meaning 'relations being reversed']

vicinity (pronounced vis-**sin**-it-ee)
(noun) If something is in the vicinity of a place, it is in the surrounding or nearby area.
[from Latin *vicus* meaning 'village']

vicious
(adjective) cruel and violent.
viciously (adverb), **viciousness** (noun).

vicious circle, vicious circles
(noun) A vicious circle is a situation in which a difficulty leads to a new difficulty which then causes the original difficulty to occur again.

vicissitude, vicissitudes (pronounced vis-**siss**-sy-tyood)
(noun; a literary word) Vicissitudes are the changes in circumstances at different times in the life of someone or in the development of something.

victim, victims
(noun) A victim is someone who has been harmed or injured by someone or something.

victimize, victimizes, victimizing, victimized; also spelled **victimise**
(verb) If someone is victimized, they are deliberately treated unfairly.
victimization (noun).

victor, victors
(noun) The victor in a fight or contest is the person who wins.

Victorian
(adjective) Victorian describes things that happened or were made during the reign of Queen Victoria.

Victoriana (pronounced vik-tor-ee-**ah**-na)
(noun) Objects made during the reign of Queen Victoria are referred to as Victoriana.

victory, victories
(noun) A victory is a success in a battle or competition.
victorious (adjective), **victoriously** (adverb).

Similar words: conquest, win, triumph

victuals (pronounced **vit**-telz)
(plural noun; an old-fashioned word) Victuals are food and drink.

video, videos, videoing, videoed
1 (noun) Video is the recording and showing of films and events using a video recorder, video tape, and a television set.
2 A video is a sound and picture recording which can be played back on a television set.
3 A video is also a video recorder.
4 (verb) If you video something, you record it on magnetic tape for later viewing.
[from Latin *videre* meaning 'to see']

video recorder, video recorders
(noun) A video recorder or video cassette recorder is a machine for recording and playing back programmes from television.

video tape, video tapes
(noun) Video tape is magnetic tape that can be used to record sound and pictures.

vie, vies, vying, vied
(verb; a formal word) If you vie with someone, you compete to do something sooner than or better than they do, e.g. *They vied with each other for the best positions.*
[from Old French *envier* meaning 'to challenge']

Vietnamese (pronounced vyet-nam-**meez**)
1 (adjective) belonging or relating to Vietnam.
2 (noun) A Vietnamese is someone who comes from Vietnam.
3 Vietnamese is the main language spoken in Vietnam.

view, views, viewing, viewed
1 (noun) Your views are your personal opinions, e.g. *He went to jail for his political views.*
2 (verb) If you view something in a particular way, you think of it in that way, e.g. *He viewed the future with gloom.*

3 (noun) A view is everything you can see from a particular place.
4 (phrase) You use **in view of** to specify the main fact or event influencing your actions or opinions, e.g. *In view of the fact that the rest of the group are going, I think you should go too.*
5 If something is **on view**, it is being shown or exhibited to the public.

Similar words: (sense 3) aspect, prospect, landscape, scene, panorama

viewer, viewers
1 (noun) Viewers are the people who watch television.
2 A viewer is a boxlike object with a magnifying lens for looking at photographic slides.

viewfinder, viewfinders
(noun) A viewfinder is a small square of glass in a camera that you look through so that you can see what you are about to photograph.

viewpoint, viewpoints
1 (noun) Your viewpoint is your attitude towards something.
2 A viewpoint is a place from which you get a good view of an area or event.

Similar words: (sense 1) outlook, point of view, standpoint, perspective, position, stance

vigil, vigils (pronounced **vij-jil**)
(noun) A vigil is a period of time, especially at night, when you stay quietly in one place because you are, for example, looking after someone, making a political protest, or praying.
[from Latin *vigilia* meaning 'watch before a religious festival']

vigilant
(adjective) careful and alert to danger or trouble.
vigilance (noun), **vigilantly** (adverb).

vigilante, vigilantes (pronounced vij-il-**ant**-ee)
(noun) Vigilantes are unofficially organized groups of people who try to protect their community and catch and punish criminals.
[from Latin *vigilare* meaning 'to be watchful']

vignette, vignettes (pronounced vin-**yet**)
(noun) A vignette is a short description or piece of writing about a particular subject or thing, e.g. *a fascinating vignette of family life.*
[from French *vignette* meaning 'little vine', because vine leaves were used to decorate texts]

vigorous
(adjective) energetic or enthusiastic.
vigorously (adverb), **vigour** (noun).

Viking, Vikings
(noun) The Vikings were groups of seamen from Scandinavia who attacked villages in parts of north-western Europe from the 8th to the 11th centuries.

vile, viler, vilest
(adjective) unpleasant or disgusting, e.g. *vile weather... vile language.*
vilely (adverb), **vileness** (noun).

vilify, vilifies, vilifying, vilified
(verb; a formal word) To vilify someone means to say or write unpleasant things about them.
vilification (noun).

villa, villas
(noun) A villa is a house, especially a pleasant holiday home in a country with a warm climate.

village, villages
(noun) A village is a collection of houses and other buildings in the countryside.
villager (noun).
[from Old French *ville* meaning 'farm']

villain, villains
(noun) A villain is someone who harms others or breaks the law.
villainous (adjective), **villainy** (noun).
[from Old French *vilein* meaning 'serf']

Similar words: knave, scoundrel, rogue, blackguard

villus, villi (pronounced **vil-lus**)
(noun) Villi are the small finger-like projections lining the small intestine of most animals, which absorb digested food.
[from Latin *villus* meaning 'shaggy hair']

vinaigrette (pronounced vin-nay-**gret**)
(noun) Vinaigrette is a salad dressing made by mixing oil, vinegar, salt, pepper, and herbs.
[from French *vinaigre* meaning 'vinegar']

vindicate, vindicates, vindicating, vindicated
(verb; a formal word) If someone is vindicated, their views or ideas are proved to be right, e.g. *His gloomy forecasts have been vindicated.*
vindication (noun).

vindictive
(adjective) Someone who is vindictive is deliberately hurtful towards someone, often as an act of revenge.
vindictively (adverb), **vindictiveness** (noun).

vine, vines
(noun) A vine is a trailing or climbing plant which winds itself around and over a support, especially one which produces grapes.

vinegar
(noun) Vinegar is a sharp-tasting liquid made from sour wine, beer, or cider, which is used for salad dressing and pickling.
[from French *vin* meaning 'wine' and *aigre* meaning 'sour']

vineyard, vineyards
(noun) A vineyard is an area of land where grapes are grown.

vintage, vintages
1 (adjective) A vintage wine is a good quality wine which was made in a particular year.
2 Vintage describes something which is the best or most typical of its kind, e.g. *vintage Beatles music.*
3 (noun) A vintage is a grape harvest of one particular year and the wine produced from it.
4 (adjective) A vintage car is one made between 1918 and 1930.
[from Old French *vendage* meaning 'grape harvest']

vinyl
(noun) Vinyl is a strong plastic used to make things such as furniture and floor coverings.

viol, viols
(noun) A viol is a medieval stringed instrument with six strings. It is played with a curved bow.

viola, violas (pronounced vee-**oh**-la)
(noun) A viola is a musical instrument with four strings. It is similar to a violin, but larger and with a lower pitch.

violate, violates, violating, violated
1 (verb) If you violate an agreement, law, or promise, you break it.
2 If you violate someone's peace or privacy, you disturb it.
3 If you violate a place, especially a holy place, you treat it with disrespect or violence.
violation (noun), **violator** (noun).

violence
1 (noun) Violence is behaviour which is intended to hurt or kill people.
2 If you do or say something with violence, you use a lot of energy in doing or saying it, often because you are angry.
3 (phrase) To **do violence** to someone or something means to hurt or damage them.

violent
1 (adjective) If someone is violent, they try to hurt or kill people.
2 A violent event happens unexpectedly and with great force.
3 Something that is violent is said, felt, or done with great force.
violently (adverb).

violet, violets
1 (noun) A violet is a plant with dark purple flowers similar to but smaller than a pansy.
2 (noun and adjective) bluish purple.

violin, violins
(noun) A violin is a musical instrument with four strings which is held under the chin and played with a bow.
violinist (noun).
[from Italian *violino* meaning 'little viola']

VIP, VIPs
(noun) VIPs are famous or important people. VIP is an abbreviation for 'very important person'.

viper, vipers
(noun) Vipers are poisonous snakes found in Europe, Africa, and Asia.

virgin, virgins
1 (noun) A virgin is someone who has never had sexual intercourse.
2 (adjective) Something that is virgin is fresh and unused, e.g. *virgin land.*
3 (noun) The Virgin, or the Blessed Virgin, is a name given to Mary, the mother of Jesus Christ.
virginity (noun).

virginal, virginals
1 (noun) The virginal was a keyboard instrument in an oblong case without legs, popular in the 16th and 17th centuries. It was also called 'the virginals'.
2 (adjective) Someone who is virginal looks young and innocent.
3 Something that is virginal is fresh and clean and looks as if it has never been used.

Virgo
(noun) Virgo is the sixth sign of the zodiac, represented by a girl. People born between August 23rd and September 22nd are born under this sign.
[from Latin *virgo* meaning 'virgin']

virile
(adjective) A virile man has all the qualities that a man is traditionally expected to have, such as strength, forcefulness, and sexuality.
virility (noun).
[from Latin *virilis* meaning 'manly']

virtual (pronounced **vur**-tyool)
(adjective) Virtual means that something has all the characteristics of a particular thing, but it is not formally recognized as being that thing, e.g. *The strike led to the virtual closure of the factory.*
virtually (adverb).

virtue, virtues
1 (noun) Virtue is thinking and doing what is morally right and avoiding what is wrong.
2 A virtue is a good quality in someone's character.
3 A virtue of something is an advantage, e.g. *the plan has the virtue of simplicity.*
4 (a formal phrase) **By virtue of** means because of, e.g. *dominating its surroundings, by virtue of its size.*

Similar words: (sense 1) goodness, integrity, morality, probity

virtuoso, virtuosos or virtuosi (pronounced vur-tyoo-**oh**-zoh)
(noun) A virtuoso is someone who is exceptionally good at something, particularly playing a musical instrument.
[from Italian *virtuoso* meaning 'skilled']

virtuous
(adjective) behaving with or showing moral virtue.
virtuously (adverb).

Similar words: good, moral, righteous, upright

virulent (a formal word)
1 (adjective) Virulent feelings, actions, or speeches are extremely bitter and hostile.
2 A virulent disease or poison is extremely powerful and dangerous.
virulence (noun), **virulently** (adverb).

virus, viruses (pronounced **vie**-russ)
1 (noun) A virus is a kind of germ, smaller than a bacterium, that can only multiply in living cells. Many viruses cause disease.
2 The disease caused by a virus may also be called a virus.
viral (adjective).
[from Latin *virus* meaning 'slime' or 'poisonous liquid']

visa, visas
(noun) A visa is an official stamp, usually put in your passport, that allows you to visit a particular country.
[from Latin *visa* meaning 'things seen']

visage, visages (pronounced **viz**-ij)
(noun; a formal and old-fashioned word) Your visage is your face, e.g. *his grim visage*.
[from Latin *visus* meaning 'appearance']

vis-à-vis (pronounced veez-a-**vee**)
(preposition) Vis-à-vis means in relation to or in comparison with, e.g. *His position vis-à-vis the budget was unknown.*
[a French phrase literally meaning 'face to face']

viscera (pronounced **vis**-sera)
(plural noun) Viscera are the large organs inside the body, such as the heart, liver, and stomach.
visceral (adjective).

viscose
(noun) Viscose is a thick liquid made from cellulose, used for making some fabrics and wrappings.

viscosity
(noun) The viscosity of a liquid is the degree to which it is thick and sticky.

viscount, viscounts (pronounced **vie**-kount)
(noun) A viscount is a British nobleman who is above a baron and below an earl in rank.
viscountess (noun).
[from *vice-* + Latin *comes* meaning 'count']

viscous (pronounced **viss**-kuss)
(adjective) Something which is viscous is thick and sticky and does not flow easily, e.g. *viscous lava*.

visibility
(noun) You use visibility to say how far or how clearly you can see in particular weather conditions.

visible
1 (adjective) able to be seen.
2 noticeable or evident, e.g. *a period of little visible advance*.
visibly (adverb).

vision, visions
1 (noun) Vision is the ability to see clearly.
2 A vision is a mental picture, in which you imagine how things might be different, e.g. *his vision of the New China*.
3 Vision is also imaginative insight, e.g. *a leader of great vision*.
4 A vision is also a mental picture or hallucination that someone has as a result of divine inspiration, madness, or drugs.
visionary (noun and adjective).

visit, visits, visiting, visited
1 (verb) If you visit someone, you go to see them and spend time with them.
2 If you visit a place, you go to see it.
3 (noun) A visit is a trip to see a person or place.
visitor (noun).

visitation, visitations
1 (noun) A visitation is the appearance or arrival of a supernatural or divine being.

2 (a formal use) A visitation is also an official visit, especially for a formal inspection.

visor, visors (pronounced **vie**-zor)
(noun) A visor is a transparent movable shield attached to a helmet, which can be pulled down to protect the eyes or face.

vista, vistas (a literary word)
1 (noun) A vista is a beautiful view.
2 A vista is also a range of exciting new ideas or possibilities, e.g. *a whole new vista of hope*.
[from Italian *vista* meaning 'view']

visual
(adjective) relating to sight, e.g. *visual jokes*.
visually (adverb).

visual aid, visual aids
(noun) Visual aids are things you look at to help you learn and remember things, for example, maps, slides, and films.

visualize, visualizes, visualizing, visualized (pronounced **viz**-yool-eyes); also spelled **visualise**
(verb) If you visualize something, you form a mental picture of it.

vital
1 (adjective) necessary or very important, e.g. *vital repair work*.
2 energetic, exciting, and full of life, e.g. *a modern vital parliament*.
vitally (adverb).
[from Latin *vita* meaning 'life']

Similar words: (sense 1) essential, crucial, imperative, indispensable

vitality
(noun) People who have vitality are energetic and lively.

vital statistics
(plural noun) A woman's vital statistics are her bust, waist, and hip measurements.

vitamin, vitamins
(noun) Vitamins are organic compounds which you need in order to remain healthy. They occur naturally in food.

vitiate, vitiates, vitiating, vitiated (pronounced **vish**-ee-ate)
(verb; a formal word) If something is vitiated, it is spoiled, weakened, or made less effective.

vitreous
(adjective) Something that is vitreous is made of or looks like glass.

vitriol (pronounced **vit**-ree-ol)
1 (noun) Vitriol is sulphuric acid.
2 (a literary use) Vitriol is also angry and bitter speech or writing.

vitriolic
(adjective; a formal word) Vitriolic language or behaviour is full of bitterness and hate.
[from Old French *vitriol* meaning 'sulphuric acid']

viva, vivas (pronounced **vie**-va)
(noun) A viva is a spoken examination in which you are asked questions about your studies.
[from Latin *viva voce* meaning 'living voice']

vivacious (pronounced viv-**vay**-shuss)
(adjective) A vivacious person is attractively
lively and high-spirited.
vivaciously (adverb), **vivaciousness** (noun),
vivacity (noun).

Similar words: animated, sparkling, exuberant,
effervescent, lively

vivid
(adjective) very bright in colour or clear in
detail, e.g. *a vivid green dress... a vivid dream.*
vividly (adverb), **vividness** (noun).

Similar words: graphic, descriptive, powerful

viviparous (pronounced viv-**vip**-par-uss)
(adjective) Viviparous animals give birth to live
and fully-formed young, rather than to eggs.
[from Latin *vivus* meaning 'alive' and *parere*
meaning 'to bear']

vivisection
(noun) Vivisection is the act of cutting open
living animals for medical research.
vivisect (verb), **vivisectionist** (noun).
[from Latin *vivus* meaning 'living' and *secare*
meaning 'to cut']

vixen, vixens
(noun) A vixen is a female fox.
[from Old English *fyxe* meaning 'female fox']

vocabulary, vocabularies
1 (noun) Someone's vocabulary is the total
number of words they know in a particular
language.
2 The vocabulary of a language is all the words
in it.

vocal
1 (adjective) You say that someone is vocal if
they express their opinions strongly and openly.
2 Vocal means involving the use of the human
voice, especially in singing.
vocalist (noun), **vocally** (adverb).

vocal cords or **vocal chords**
(plural noun) Your vocal cords are the part of
your larynx which can be made to vibrate when
you breathe out, making the sounds you use for
speaking.

vocation, vocations
1 (noun) A vocation is a strong wish to do a
particular job, especially one such as nursing,
which involves serving other people.
2 A vocation is also a profession or career.

vocational
(adjective) Vocational is used to describe the
skills needed for a particular job or profession,
e.g. *vocational training.*

vocative
(noun and adjective) In the grammar of some
languages, the vocative is the form of a noun or
name used when the person it refers to is being
spoken or written to.

vociferous (pronounced voe-**sif**-fer-uss)
(adjective) Someone who is vociferous speaks a
lot, or loudly, because they want to make a point
strongly, e.g. *vociferous supporters.*
vociferously (adverb).

vodka, vodkas
(noun) Vodka is a strong clear spirit made from
rye or other vegetable products, which originally
came from Russia.
[from Russian *vodka* meaning 'little water']

vogue (pronounced **vohg**)
(phrase) If something is **the vogue** or **in vogue**, it
is stylish and popular, e.g. *Flowery carpets
became the vogue... Miniskirts were not in vogue.*
[from Italian *voga* meaning 'fashion']

voice, voices, voicing, voiced
1 (noun) Your voice is the sounds produced by
your vocal cords, or the ability to make such
sounds.
2 Voice also means someone's opinion on a
particular topic and what they say about it, e.g.
The only dissenting voice was Mr Foot's.
3 If you have a voice in something, you have the
right to express an opinion on it.
4 (verb) If you voice an opinion or an emotion,
you say what you think or feel, e.g. *They voiced
their anger.*

void, voids
1 (noun) A void is a situation which seems empty
because it has no interest, excitement, or value,
e.g. *Tending her mother had filled the void for a
time.*
2 A void is also a large empty hole or space, e.g.
the gaping void at his feet.
3 (adjective; a technical use) In law, something
that is void has no legal authority.

volatile
1 (adjective) liable to change often and
unexpectedly, e.g. *The situation is extremely
volatile... Judy was as volatile as ever.*
2 A volatile liquid has a low boiling point and
turns easily from a liquid to a vapour.

vol-au-vent, vol-au-vents (pronounced
vol-o-vong)
(noun) A vol-au-vent is a small light pastry case
filled with a sauce containing chopped meat,
fish, or vegetables.
[from French *vol-au-vent* literally meaning
'flight in the wind']

volcanic
1 (adjective) A volcanic region has many
volcanoes or was created by volcanoes.
2 In geology, volcanic rocks are igneous rocks
which cooled and hardened on or close to the
earth's surface.

volcano, volcanoes
(noun) A volcano is a hill or mountain with an
opening through which lava, gas, and ash are
expelled from inside the earth's crust onto the
surface.
[named after *Vulcan*, the Roman god of fire]

vole, voles
(noun) Voles are small animals like mice with
short tails. They live in fields and near rivers.

[shortened form of *volemouse*; from Old Norse *vollr* + *mus* meaning 'fieldmouse']

volition
(noun; a formal word) If you do something of your own volition, you do it because you have decided for yourself, without being persuaded by others, e.g. *She didn't go there of her own volition.*

volley, volleys
1 (noun) A volley of shots or gunfire is a lot of shots fired at the same time.
2 In tennis, a volley is a stroke in which the player hits the ball before it bounces.
[from French *volée* meaning 'flight']

volleyball
(noun) Volleyball is a game in which two teams hit a large ball back and forth over a high net with their hands. The ball is not allowed to bounce on the ground.

volt, volts
(noun) A volt is a unit of electrical force. One volt produces one amp of electricity when the resistance is one ohm. The volt is named after the Italian physicist Count Alessandro Volta (1745-1827).

voltage, voltages
(noun) The voltage of an electric current is its force measured in volts.

voltameter, voltameters (pronounced vol-**tam**-mit-er)
(noun) A voltameter is an instrument for measuring an electric current.

voltmeter, voltmeters
(noun) A voltmeter is an instrument for measuring potential difference in volts.

voluble
(adjective) A voluble person talks a lot with great energy or enthusiasm.
volubly (adverb), **volubility** (noun).

volume, volumes
1 (noun) A volume is a book, or one of a series of books.
2 The volume of something is the amount of space it contains or occupies.
3 The volume of something is also the amount of it that there is.
4 The volume of a radio, TV, or record player is the strength of the sound that it produces.
[from Latin *volumen* meaning 'roll' or 'book']

voluminous (pronounced vol-**loo**-min-uss)
(adjective) very large or full in size or quantity, e.g. *a voluminous pink dress.*

voluntary
1 (adjective) Voluntary actions are ones that you do because you choose to do them and not because you have been forced to do them.
2 Voluntary work is done by people who are not paid for what they do.
voluntarily (adverb).
[from Latin *voluntas* meaning 'will']

volunteer, volunteers, volunteering, volunteered
1 (noun) A volunteer is someone who does work

for which they are not paid, e.g. *volunteer work at the hospital.*
2 A volunteer is also someone who chooses to join the armed forces, especially during wartime.
3 (verb) If you volunteer to do something, you offer to do it rather than being forced into it.
4 If you volunteer information, you give it without being asked.

voluptuous (pronounced vol-**lupt**-yoo-uss)
(adjective) A voluptuous woman has a figure which is considered to be sexually exciting.
voluptuously (adverb), **voluptuousness** (noun).

vomit, vomits, vomiting, vomited
1 (verb) If you vomit, food and drink comes back up from your stomach and out through your mouth.
2 (noun) Vomit is partly digested food and drink that has come back up from someone's stomach and out through their mouth.

voodoo
(noun) Voodoo is a form of magic practised in the Caribbean, especially in Haiti.

voracious (pronounced vor-**ray**-shuss)
(adjective; a literary word) If you say that someone is voracious or that they have a voracious appetite for something, you mean that they want a lot of it.
voraciously (adverb), **voraciousness** (noun).

vortex, vortexes or **vortices**
(noun) A vortex is a mass of wind or water which spins round so fast that it pulls objects into its empty centre.
[from Latin *vortex* meaning 'whirlpool']

vote, votes, voting, voted
1 (noun) Someone's vote is their choice in an election, or at a meeting where decisions are taken.
2 When a group of people have a vote, they make a decision by allowing each person in the group to say what they would prefer.
3 In an election, the vote is the total number of people who have made their choice, e.g. *Labour increased its total vote by a million.*
4 (verb) When people vote, they indicate their choice or opinion, usually by writing on a piece of paper or by raising their hand.
5 (noun) If people have the vote, they have the legal right to vote in an election.
6 (verb) If you vote that a particular thing should happen, you are suggesting it should happen, e.g. *I vote we all go to the cinema.*
voter (noun).

vouch, vouches, vouching, vouched
1 (verb) If you say that you can vouch for someone, you mean that you are sure that you can guarantee their good behaviour or support, e.g. *He said you'd vouch for him.*
2 If you say that you can vouch for something, you mean that you have evidence from your own experience that it is true or correct.

voucher, vouchers
(noun) A voucher is a piece of paper that can be used instead of money to pay for something.

vouchsafe, vouchsafes, vouchsafing, vouchsafed
(verb; an old-fashioned word) To vouchsafe
something means to give it, often in a gracious or
condescending way.

vow, vows, vowing, vowed
1 (verb) If you vow to do something, you make a
solemn promise to do it, e.g. *She vowed never to
let it happen again.*
2 (noun) A vow is a solemn promise.
[from Latin *votum* meaning 'solemn promise']

vowel, vowels
(noun) A vowel is a sound made without your
tongue touching the roof of your mouth or your
teeth, or one of the letters a, e, i, o, u, which
represent such sounds.

voyage, voyages, voyaging, voyaged
1 (noun) A voyage is a long journey on a ship or
in a spacecraft.
2 (verb; an old-fashioned use) To voyage means
to go on a voyage.
voyager (noun).
[from Latin *viaticus* meaning 'concerning a
journey']

voyeur, voyeurs (pronounced vwie-**yur**)
(noun) A voyeur is someone who gets sexual
pleasure from secretly watching other people
having sex or from watching them undress.
voyeurism (noun).
[from French *voyeur* meaning literally 'one who
sees']

vulcanite
(noun) Vulcanite is a hard black substance made
by heating rubber with sulphur.

vulcanize, vulcanizes, vulcanizing, vulcanized;
also spelled **vulcanise**
(verb) To vulcanize rubber means to treat it with
sulphur under heat and pressure to improve its
elasticity or to produce vulcanite.
vulcanization (noun).
[named after *Vulcan*, the Roman god of fire]

vulgar
1 (adjective) socially unacceptable or offensive,
e.g. *vulgar remarks.*
2 lacking taste and behaving in a socially
unacceptable way, e.g. *She's an incredibly
vulgar woman.*
vulgarity (noun), **vulgarly** (adverb).

vulnerable
(adjective) weak and without protection.
vulnerably (adverb), **vulnerability** (noun).

Similar words: susceptible, defenceless, unprotected

vulture, vultures
(noun) A vulture is a large bird which lives in
hot countries and eats the flesh of dead animals.

vulva, vulvas or **vulvae**
(noun) The vulva is the outer part of a woman's
sexual organs.

vying the present participle of **vie.**

W

wacky, wackier, wackiest
(adjective; an informal word) odd or crazy, e.g. *a wacky new comedy.*

wad, wads
1 (noun) A wad of papers or banknotes is a thick bundle of them.
2 A wad of something is a lump of it, e.g. *a wad of tobacco.*

wadding
(noun) Wadding is soft material used for stuffing things or packing round things to protect them.

waddle, waddles, waddling, waddled
(verb) When a duck or a fat person waddles, they walk with short, quick steps, swaying slightly from side to side.

wade, wades, wading, waded
1 (verb) If you wade through water or mud, you walk slowly through it.
2 If you wade through a book or document, you spend a lot of time and effort reading it because you find it dull or difficult.

wader, waders
1 (noun) A wader is a long-legged and long-necked bird that lives near water and feeds on fish.
2 Waders are long waterproof rubber boots commonly worn by fishermen.

wadi, wadis (pronounced **wod**-ee)
(noun) A wadi is a river in North Africa which is dry except in the rainy season.
[an Arabic word]

wafer, wafers
1 (noun) A wafer is a thin, crisp, sweet biscuit often eaten with ice cream.
2 A wafer is also a thin disc of special bread used in the Christian service of Holy Communion.
[from Old French *waufre*]

wafer-thin
(adjective) extremely thin.

waffle, waffles, waffling, waffled (pronounced **wof**-fl)
1 (verb) When someone waffles, they talk or write a lot without being clear or without saying anything of importance.
2 (noun) Waffle is vague and wordy speech or writing.
3 A waffle is a thick, crisp pancake with squares marked on it often eaten with syrup poured over it.

waft, wafts, wafting, wafted (pronounced **wahft**)
(verb) If a sound or scent wafts or is wafted through the air, it moves gently through it.

wag, wags, wagging, wagged
1 (verb) If you wag your finger, you move it repeatedly up and down.
2 When a dog wags its tail, it shakes it repeatedly from side to side.
3 (an informal phrase) When **tongues wag,**
people are gossiping, e.g. *He dared not visit her, because tongues might wag.*
4 (noun; an old-fashioned use) A wag is someone who tells or plays jokes.
[senses 1-3 are from Old English *wagian* meaning 'to shake']

wage, wages, waging, waged
1 (noun) A wage or wages is the regular payment made to someone each week for the work they do, especially for manual or unskilled work.
2 (verb) If a person or country wages a campaign or war, they start it and carry it on over a period of time.
[from Old French *wagier* meaning 'to pledge']

wage-packet, wage-packets
(noun) A wage-packet is the envelope containing someone's wages that they are given each week.

wager, wagers
(noun) A wager is a bet.

waggle, waggles, waggling, waggled
(verb) If you waggle something or if it waggles, it moves up and down or from side to side with short, quick movements, e.g. *He waggled his eyebrows.*

wagon, wagons; also spelled **waggon**
1 (noun) A wagon is a strong four-wheeled vehicle for carrying heavy loads, usually pulled by a horse or tractor.
2 Wagons are also the containers for freight pulled by a railway engine.
[from Dutch *wagen*]

wagtail, wagtails
(noun) A wagtail is a small bird with a long tail which moves up and down as the bird walks.

waif, waifs (pronounced **wayf**)
(noun) A waif is a young, thin person, especially a child, who looks hungry and homeless.

wail, wails, wailing, wailed
1 (verb) To wail means to cry loudly with sorrow or pain.
2 (noun) A wail is a long, unhappy cry.

wain, wains
(noun; a literary word) A wain is a cart or wagon.

wainscot, wainscots
(noun) A wainscot is a wooden panel running round the lower half of the walls of a room, especially in old houses.

waist, waists
1 (noun) Your waist is the middle part of your body where it narrows slightly above your hips.
2 The waist of a piece of clothing is the part of it covering the middle of your body.

waistband, waistbands
(noun) A waistband is a narrow piece of material sewn on to the waist of a skirt or pair of trousers in order to strengthen it.

waistcoat, waistcoats
(noun) A waistcoat is a sleeveless piece of clothing, often worn under a suit or jacket, which buttons up the front.

waistline, waistlines
(noun) Your waistline is an imaginary line round your waist which you use as a way of measuring how fat you are.

wait, waits, waiting, waited
1 (verb) If you wait, you spend time, usually doing little or nothing, before something happens.
2 If something can wait, it is not urgent and can be dealt with later.
3 (noun) A wait is a period of time before something happens.
4 (phrase) If you **can't wait** to do something, you are very excited and eager to do it.
5 (verb) If you wait on people in a restaurant, it is your job to serve them food.
6 If you wait on someone hand and foot, you do everything for them.

wait up
(phrasal verb) If you wait up, you do not go to bed until someone arrives or something happens.

waiter, waiters
(noun) A waiter is a man who works in a restaurant, serving people with food and drink.

waiting list, waiting lists
(noun) A waiting list is a list of people who have asked for something which cannot be given to them immediately, for example medical treatment or housing.

waiting room, waiting rooms
(noun) A waiting room is a room in a place such as a railway station or doctor's surgery, where people can sit and wait.

waitress, waitresses
(noun) A waitress is a woman who works in a restaurant, serving people with food and drink.

waive, waives, waiving, waived (pronounced **wave**)
(verb) If someone waives something such as a rule or a right, they decide not to insist on it being enforced.

wake, wakes, waking, woke, woken
1 (verb) When you wake or when something wakes you, you become conscious again after being asleep.
2 (noun) The wake of a boat or other object moving in water is the track of waves it leaves behind it.
3 A wake is a gathering of people who mourn together and watch over a dead body the night before a funeral. It is also the party after the funeral.
4 (phrase) If one thing follows **in the wake of** another, it follows it as a result of it, or in imitation of it, e.g. *Famine came in the wake of the floods.*

Similar words: (sense 1) arouse, awake, waken, stir

wake up
1 (phrasal verb) When you wake up or something wakes you up, you become conscious again after being asleep.
2 If you wake up to a dangerous situation, you become aware of it.

wakeful
1 (adjective) unable to sleep for very long.
2 (a formal use) awake and alert, e.g. *This alarmed her and made her more wakeful.*
wakefully (adverb), **wakefulness** (noun).

waken, wakens, wakening, wakened
(verb; a literary word) When you waken someone, you wake them up.

walk, walks, walking, walked
1 (verb) When you walk, you move along by putting one foot in front of the other on the ground.
2 If you walk away with or walk off with something such as a prize, you win it or achieve it easily.
3 (an informal use) If someone walks off with something, they take it without asking the person who owns it.
4 (noun) Your walk is the way you walk, e.g. *her distinctive walk.*
5 A walk is a journey made by walking, e.g. *He went for a long walk.*
6 A walk is also a path.
[from Old English *wealcan*]

walk out
1 (phrasal verb) If workers walk out, they go on strike.
2 If you walk out on someone, you leave them suddenly.

walkabout, walkabouts
(noun) A walkabout is an informal walk amongst crowds in a public place by royalty or by some other well-known person.

walker, walkers
(noun) A walker is a person who walks, especially for pleasure or to keep fit.

walkie-talkie, walkie-talkies
(noun) A walkie-talkie is a small portable radio used for sending and receiving messages.

walking stick, walking sticks
(noun) A walking stick is a wooden stick which people can lean on while walking.

Walkman, Walkmans
(noun; a trademark) A Walkman is a small cassette player with lightweight headphones, which people carry around so that they can listen to music while they are doing something like walking.

walk of life, walks of life
(noun) The walk of life that you come from is the position you have in society and the kind of job you have.

walk-on
(adjective) A walk-on part in a play is a very small one that usually does not involve speaking.

walkout, walkouts
(noun) A walkout is a strike.

walkover, walkovers
(noun; an informal word) A walkover is a very easy victory in a competition or contest.

walkway, walkways
(noun) A walkway is a passage between two buildings for people to walk along.

wall, walls
1 (noun) A wall is one of the vertical sides of a building or a room.
2 A wall is a long, narrow vertical structure made of stone or brick that surrounds or divides an area of land.
3 A wall is also a lining or membrane enclosing a bodily cavity or structure, e.g. *the abdominal wall*.
4 (phrase) If you are **banging your head against a brick wall**, you are not making any progress in something you are trying to do.
5 If a person or a business **goes to the wall**, they fail.
6 If someone **has their back to the wall**, they are in a difficult situation, and can see no way out.
[from Old English *weall*]

wallaby, wallabies
(noun) A wallaby is an animal like a small kangaroo which lives in Australia and New Guinea.
[from *wolaba*, an Australian aboriginal word]

wallet, wallets
(noun) A wallet is a small, flat case made of leather or plastic, used for keeping paper money and sometimes stamps or credit cards.

wallflower, wallflowers
(noun) A wallflower is a garden plant with sweet-smelling yellow, red, orange, or purple flowers.

wallop, wallops, walloping, walloped (an informal word)
1 (verb) If you wallop someone, you hit them very hard.
2 In a competition or contest, if one person or team wallops another, they beat them easily.
[from Old French *galoper* meaning 'to gallop']

wallow, wallows, wallowing, wallowed
1 (verb) If you wallow in an unpleasant feeling or situation, you allow it to continue longer than is reasonable or necessary because you are getting a kind of enjoyment from it, e.g. *I just wanted to wallow in my misery.*
2 When an animal wallows in mud or water, it lies or rolls about in it slowly for pleasure.
[from Old English *wealwian* meaning 'to roll (in mud)']

wallpaper, wallpapers, wallpapering, wallpapered
1 (noun) Wallpaper is thick coloured or patterned paper for pasting onto the walls of rooms in order to decorate them.
2 (verb) To wallpaper a room means to cover its walls with wallpaper.

Wall Street
(noun) Wall Street is a street in New York where the Stock Exchange and large banks are, and where the most important financial business takes place.

walnut, walnuts
1 (noun) A walnut is an edible nut with a wrinkled shape and a hard, round, light-brown shell.
2 Walnut is wood from the walnut tree which is often used for making expensive furniture.
[from Old English *walh-hnutu* meaning 'foreign nut']

walrus, walruses
(noun) A walrus is an animal which lives in the sea and which looks like a large seal with a tough skin, coarse whiskers, and two tusks. Walruses live mainly in the Arctic.

waltz, waltzes, waltzing, waltzed
1 (noun) A waltz is a piece of music with a rhythm of three beats to the bar, which people can dance to.
2 A waltz is a ballroom dance in which two people hold each other and move around the floor in time to music.
3 (verb) If you waltz with someone, you dance a waltz with them.
4 (an informal use) If you waltz somewhere, you walk there in a relaxed and confident way.
[from Old German *walzen* meaning 'to revolve']

wan (rhymes with **on**)
(adjective) pale and tired-looking.
wanly (adverb).

wand, wands
(noun) A wand is a long, thin rod that magicians wave when they are performing tricks and magic.

wander, wanders, wandering, wandered
1 (verb) If you wander in a place, you walk around in a casual way.
2 If your mind wanders or your thoughts wander, you lose concentration and start thinking about other things.
wanderer (noun).
[from Old English *wandrian*]

Similar words: (sense 1) ramble, meander, stray, roam, rove

wanderlust
(noun) Wanderlust is a great desire to travel.

wane, wanes, waning, waned
1 (verb) If a condition, attitude, or emotion wanes, it becomes gradually weaker.
2 When the moon wanes, it shows a smaller area of its face each day as it changes from a full moon to a new moon.
3 (phrase) If something is **on the wane**, it is becoming weaker.
[from Old English *wanian* meaning 'lessen']

wangle, wangles, wangling, wangled
(verb; an informal word) If you wangle something that you want, you manage to get it by being crafty or persuasive.

wankel engine, wankel engines
(noun) A wankel engine is a type of internal-combustion engine.

want, wants, wanting, wanted

1 (verb) If you want something, you feel a desire to have it or a need for it to happen.
2 (an informal use) If something wants doing, there is a need for it to be done, e.g. *The grass wants cutting.*
3 If someone is wanted, the police are searching for them, e.g. *He is wanted for murder.*
4 (noun; a formal use) A want of something is a lack of it.
5 (phrase) If you do something **for want of** something else, you do it because the other thing is not available or not possible.
[from Old Norse *vanta* meaning 'to be lacking']

wanting

(adjective) If you find something wanting or if it proves wanting, it is not as good in some way as you think it should be.

wanton

1 (adjective) deliberately causing harm without any reason or without being provoked, e.g. *wanton destruction.*
2 wild or without restraint, e.g. *wanton spending.*
wantonly (adverb), **wantonness** (noun).
[from Old English *wan-* meaning 'un-' and *togen* meaning 'brought up']

war, wars, warring, warred

1 (noun) A war is a period of fighting between countries or states when weapons are used and many people may be killed.
2 A war is also competition between groups of people, or a campaign against something, e.g. *a price war... the war against drugs.*
3 (an informal phrase) If you say someone has been **in the wars**, you mean they look as if they have been in a fight.
4 (verb) When two countries war with each other, they are fighting a war against each other.
warring (adjective).
[from French *guerre*]

Similar words: (sense 1) fray, battle, warfare, conflict
(sense 4) battle, contend, combat, wage war

---

warble, warbles, warbling, warbled

(verb) When a bird warbles, it sings with high notes and many variations.

warbler, warblers

(noun) A warbler is one of several kinds of small songbird.

ward, wards, warding, warded

1 (noun) A ward is a room in a hospital which has beds for several people who need similar treatment.
2 A ward is an area or district which forms a separate part of a political constituency or local council.
3 A ward or a ward of court is a child who is officially put in the care of an adult or a court of law, because their parents are dead or because they need protection.
4 (verb) If you ward off a danger or an illness, you do something to prevent it from affecting or harming you.

-ward or -wards

-ward and -wards form adverbs or adjectives that show the way something is moving or facing, e.g. *skyward... homewards.*
[from Old English *-weard* meaning 'towards']

warden, wardens

1 (noun) A warden is a person in charge of a building or institution such as a youth hostel or prison.
2 A warden is an official who makes sure that certain laws or rules are obeyed, e.g. *traffic wardens.*

warder, warders

(noun) A warder is a person who works in a prison and is in charge of prisoners.

wardrobe, wardrobes

1 (noun) A wardrobe is a tall cupboard in which you can hang your clothes.
2 Someone's wardrobe is their collection of clothes.
3 The wardrobe in a theatre company is the part of the company in charge of the making, hiring, or storing of the costumes.
[from Old French *garder* + *robes* meaning 'to guard robes']

wardroom, wardrooms

(noun) The wardroom is the room on board a warship where the officers sleep or eat.

ware, wares

1 (noun) Ware is manufactured goods of a particular kind, e.g. *kitchenware... glassware.*
2 Someone's wares are the things they sell, usually in the street or in a market.

warehouse, warehouses

(noun) A warehouse is a large building where raw materials or manufactured goods are stored.

warfare

(noun) Warfare is the activity of fighting a war.

warhead, warheads

(noun) A warhead is the front end of a bomb or missile, where the explosives are carried.

warlock, warlocks

(noun) A warlock is a male witch.
[from Old English *wærloga* meaning 'oath breaker']

warm, warmer, warmest; warms, warming, warmed

1 (adjective) Something that is warm has some heat, but not enough to be hot, e.g. *a warm day.*
2 Warm clothes or blankets are made of a material which protects you from the cold.
3 Warm colours or sounds are pleasant and make you feel comfortable and relaxed.
4 A warm person is friendly and affectionate.
5 (verb) If you warm something, you heat it up gently so that it stops being cold.
6 If you warm to a person, you become fond of them. If you warm to an idea, you become more interested in it.
warmly (adverb).
[from Old English *wearm*]

warm up

1 (phrasal verb) If you warm up for an event or

an activity, you practise or exercise gently to prepare for it.
2 When a machine or engine warms up, it becomes ready for use a little while after being switched on or started.

warm-blooded
1 (adjective) An animal that is warm-blooded has a relatively high body temperature which remains constant and does not change with the surrounding temperature.
2 If you describe a person as warm-blooded, you mean that they are passionate.

warm front, warm fronts
(noun) When there is a warm front, warm air near the ground is pushing up into cold air above.

warm-hearted
(adjective) friendly and affectionate.

warmonger, warmongers (pronounced wor-mung-ger)
(noun) A warmonger is a person, such as a politician or a newspaper editor, who encourages people to start a war.
warmongering (noun).

warmth
1 (noun) Warmth is a moderate amount of heat.
2 The warmth of material or clothes is their ability to protect you from the cold.
3 Someone who has warmth is friendly and affectionate.

warm-up, warm-ups
(noun) A warm-up is preparation done just before an activity, such as gentle exercising.

warn, warns, warning, warned
1 (verb) If you warn someone about a possible problem or danger, you tell them about it in advance so that they are aware of it, e.g. *I did warn you it was expensive.*
2 If you warn someone not to do something, you advise them not to do it, in order to avoid possible danger or punishment, e.g. *I warned him not to lose his temper.*
[from Old English *wearnian*]
warningly (adverb).

Similar words: (sense 1) forewarn, caution, alert, give notice, tip off

warn off
(phrasal verb) If you warn someone off, you tell them to go away or to stop doing something.

warning, warnings
(noun) A warning is something said or written to tell people of a possible problem, danger, or other unpleasant thing that might happen.

warp, warps, warping, warped
1 (verb) If something warps or is warped, it becomes bent, often because of the effect of heat or water.
2 If something warps someone's mind or character, it makes them abnormal or corrupt.
3 (noun) A warp in time or space is an imaginary break or sudden change in normal experience.

4 The warp in a piece of cloth is the stronger lengthwise threads.
[from Old English *wearp* meaning 'a throw']

warpath
(noun) If someone is on the warpath, they are angry and are getting ready for a fight or argument.

warrant, warrants, warranting, warranted
1 (verb; a formal use) If something warrants a particular action, it makes the action seem necessary, e.g. *The case warrants further investigation.*
2 (noun) A warrant is an official document signed by a judge or magistrate, which gives permission to the police to do something such as search someone's house, e.g. *A warrant was issued for his arrest.*

warrant officer, warrant officers
(noun) A warrant officer is a non-commissioned officer of the highest rank in the army or the RAF.

warranty, warranties
(noun) A warranty is a guarantee, e.g. *The car is under warranty.*
[from Old French *guarantir* meaning 'to guarantee']

warren, warrens
1 (noun) A warren is a group of holes under the ground connected by tunnels, which rabbits live in.
2 A place where many people live in crowded conditions may also be called a warren.

warrior, warriors
(noun) A warrior is a fighting man or soldier, especially in former times.

warship, warships
(noun) A warship is a ship built with guns and used for fighting in wars.

wart, warts
1 (noun) A wart is a small, hard piece of skin which can grow on someone's face or hands.
2 (phrase) If someone or something is described **warts and all**, there is no attempt to conceal any faults or defects.
[from Old English *wearte*]

wart hog, wart hogs
(noun) A wart hog is a large wild pig with two tusks and wart-like bumps on its face. Wart hogs live in Africa.

wartime
(noun) Wartime is a period of time during which a country is at war.

wary, warier, wariest
(adjective) cautious and on one's guard, e.g. *They were understandably wary of the new military government.*
warily (adverb), **wariness** (noun).

wash, washes, washing, washed
1 (verb) If you wash something, you clean it with water and soap or detergent.
2 (noun) The wash is all the clothes and bedding that are washed together at one time, e.g. *the average weekly wash.*

3 (verb) If you wash or if you wash part of your body, you clean yourself or part of your body using soap and water.
4 If something is washed somewhere, it is carried there gently by water, e.g. *The body was washed ashore.*
5 (noun) The wash in water is the disturbance and waves produced at the rear of a moving boat.
6 A wash is a thin layer of something such as a liquid or a colour, e.g. *He first painted a blue wash over the canvas.*
7 (phrase) If you **wash your hands of** something, you refuse to have anything more to do with it.
8 (an informal use) If you say that something will **come out in the wash**, you mean it will become known or obvious in time.
[from Old English *wæscan*]

wash down
(phrasal verb) If you wash down food, you drink while you are eating it or drink just after you have eaten it.

wash up
1 (phrasal verb) If you wash up, you wash the dishes, pans, and cutlery used in preparing and eating a meal.
2 If something is washed up on land, it is carried by a river or sea and left there, e.g. *A body was washed up on the beach.*

washable
(adjective) able to be washed without being damaged.

washbasin, washbasins
(noun) A washbasin is a deep bowl, usually fixed to a wall, with taps for hot and cold water.

washed-out
1 (adjective) Something that looks washed-out is faded or pale and dull in colour.
2 If someone looks washed-out, they look very tired and pale.

washer, washers
(noun) A washer is a thin, flat ring of metal or plastic which is placed over a bolt before the nut is screwed on, in order to make a tighter connection.

washing
(noun) Washing consists of clothes and bedding which need to be washed or are in the process of being washed and dried.

washing machine, washing machines
(noun) A washing machine is a machine for washing clothes in.

washing powder, washing powders
(noun) Washing powder is powdered soap or detergent that is used to wash clothes.

washing-up
(noun) If you do the washing-up, you wash the dishes, pans, and cutlery which have been used in the cooking and eating of a meal.

washout, washouts
(noun; an informal word) If an event or project is a washout, it is a complete disaster or failure.

washy, washier, washiest
(adjective) watery or weak.

wasp, wasps
(noun) A wasp is an insect with yellow and black stripes across its body, which can sting like a bee but does not produce honey.

waspish
(adjective) bad-tempered or speaking sharply.
waspishly (adverb), **waspishness** (noun).

wastage
1 (noun) Wastage is loss and misuse of something, e.g. *a wastage of talent among the young.*
2 (phrase) **Natural wastage** of a workforce is a reduction in its size, because of workers retiring or resigning rather than by being made redundant.

waste, wastes, wasting, wasted
1 (verb) If you waste time, money, or energy, you use too much of it on something that is not important or necessary.
2 If you waste an opportunity, you do not take advantage of it when it is available.
3 If you say that something is wasted on someone, you mean that it is too good, too clever, or too sophisticated for them, e.g. *Fine clothes are wasted on her — she's a tomboy!*
4 (noun) If an activity is a waste of time, money, or energy, it uses too much of it and is not important or necessary.
5 Waste is the use of more money or some other resource than is necessary.
6 Waste is also material that has been used and is no longer wanted, or material left over from a useful process, e.g. *radioactive waste.*
7 (adjective) unwanted and unusable in its present form, e.g. *waste paper.*
8 Waste land is land which is not used or looked after by anyone.
9 (noun) Wastes are large areas of land in which there is very little evidence of life, e.g. *the polar wastes.*
10 (phrase) If something **goes to waste**, it is unused, goes bad, or is thrown away.
11 (a literary phrase) If something is **laid waste**, it is completely destroyed.
[from Latin *vastus* meaning 'empty']

Similar words: (sense 1) fritter, squander, dissipate (sense 5) prodigality, profligacy, wastage, dissipation, extravagance, squandering

waste away
(phrasal verb) If someone is wasting away, they are becoming very thin and weak because they are ill or not eating properly.

wasted
(adjective) unnecessary, e.g. *a wasted journey.*

wasteful
(adjective) extravagant or causing waste by using resources in a careless and inefficient way.
wastefully (adverb), **wastefulness** (noun).

Similar words: improvident, spendthrift, profligate, prodigal

wasteland, wastelands
1 (noun) A wasteland is land which is of no use because it is infertile or has been misused.
2 (a literary use) A wasteland is also a situation in which there is little hope of improvement or development, e.g. *The Royal Academy Summer Show may be largely a wasteland.*

wasting
(adjective) A wasting disease is one that gradually reduces the strength and health of the body.

watch, watches, watching, watched
1 (noun) A watch is a small clock usually worn on a strap on the wrist or attached to a chain and carried in a pocket.
2 (verb) If you watch something, you look at it for some time and pay close attention to what is happening.
3 If you watch a situation, you pay attention to it or are aware of it, e.g. *I'll watch her progress with interest.*
4 If you watch over someone or something, you care for them.
5 (noun) A watch is a period of time during which a guard is kept over something.
[from Old English *wæccan* meaning 'to be awake']

watch out
1 (phrasal verb) If you watch out for something, you look and wait for it carefully because you do not want to miss it, e.g. *Watch out for the Perth turn-off.*
2 If you tell someone to watch out, you are warning them to be very careful because something unpleasant might happen.

watchdog, watchdogs
1 (noun) A watchdog is a dog used to guard property.
2 You use watchdog to refer to a person or a committee whose job is to make sure that people or organizations do not act illegally, inefficiently, or irresponsibly.

watchful
(adjective) careful to notice everything that is happening, e.g. *The police keep a watchful eye on lawbreakers.*
watchfully (adverb), **watchfulness** (noun).

watchman, watchmen
(noun) A watchman is a person whose job is to guard property.

watchword, watchwords
(noun) A watchword is a word or phrase that sums up the way a particular group of people think or behave, e.g. *The watchword in education today is 'learn through play'.*

water, waters, watering, watered
1 (noun) Water is a clear, colourless, tasteless, and odourless liquid that is necessary for all plant and animal life.
2 You use water or waters to refer to a large area of water, such as a lake or sea, e.g. *coastal waters.*
3 (verb) If you water a plant or an animal, you give it water to drink.

4 If your eyes water, you have tears in them because they are hurting.
5 If your mouth waters, it produces extra saliva, usually because you think of or can smell something appetizing.
6 (plural noun) A pregnant woman's waters are the liquid, also called amniotic fluid, which surrounds the baby in her womb.
7 (phrase) When you **pass water**, you urinate.
8 If you say that an event or incident is **water under the bridge**, you mean that it is past and done with and cannot now be changed.
9 If you **pour** or **throw cold water on** an idea or suggestion, you discourage it or show that you do not think it is a very good one.

water down
(phrasal verb) If you water something down, you make it weaker.
watered-down (adjective).

water bed, water beds
(noun) A water bed is a waterproof mattress filled with water.

water biscuit, water biscuits
(noun) A water biscuit is a thin, crisp, unsweetened biscuit which is usually eaten with butter or cheese.

waterborne
(adjective) carried or passed on by water.

water buffalo, water buffaloes or **water buffalos**
(noun) A water-buffalo is a large buffalo from the swampy regions of south Asia. Water buffaloes are often used as work animals.

water butt, water butts
(noun) A water butt is a large barrel for collecting rainwater as it flows down a drainpipe off the roof.

water cannon, water cannons
(noun) A water cannon is a machine which shoots powerful jets of water. Water cannons are used by the police to break up crowds of people.

water chestnut, water chestnuts
(noun) A water chestnut is the thick bottom part of the stem of an aquatic plant that grows in China. Water chestnuts are used in Chinese cooking.

watercolour, watercolours
1 (noun) Watercolours are paints for painting pictures, which are diluted with water or put on the paper using a wet brush.
2 A watercolour is a picture which has been painted using watercolours.

watercourse, watercourses
(noun) A watercourse is the channel that a stream or river flows along.

watercress
(noun) Watercress is a small plant which grows in streams and pools. Its hot-tasting leaves are eaten raw in salads or used as a garnish.

waterfall, waterfalls
(noun) A waterfall is water from a river or stream as it flows over the edge of a steep cliff in hills or mountains and falls to the ground below.

waterfront, waterfronts
(noun) A waterfront is a street or piece of land next to an area of water such as a river or harbour.

water hole, water holes
(noun) A water hole is a pond or pool in a desert or other dry area where animals can find water to drink.

water ice
(noun) Water ice is a type of ice cream made with fruit juice, sugar, and water.

watering can, watering cans
(noun) A watering can is a bucket-shaped container with a handle on one side and a long spout on the other, which you use to water plants.

watering hole, watering holes
1 (noun; an informal use) A watering hole is a bar or café where people go to drink.
2 A watering hole is also a place where animals drink.

water jump, water jumps
(noun) A water jump is a fence with a pool of water on the far side of it, over which people or horses jump as part of a race.

water lily, water lilies
(noun) A water lily is a plant with large leaves and showy, colourful flowers that float on the surface of ponds and lakes.

water line, water lines
(noun) A water line is a line painted round the side of a ship's hull to mark the level that the water will reach when the ship floats.

waterlogged
1 (adjective) Land that is waterlogged is so wet that the soil cannot contain any more water, so that some water remains on the surface of the ground.
2 A waterlogged boat is so full of water that it may soon sink.

water main, water mains
(noun) A water main is a large underground pipe used for supplying water to houses and factories.

watermark, watermarks
1 (noun) A watermark is a design put into paper as it is being made, which is only visible when held up to the light. Banknotes have a watermark to prove they are genuine.
2 A watermark is a mark or line which shows the highest or lowest level reached by the water in a river or harbour.

watermelon, watermelons
(noun) A watermelon is a large, round fruit which has a hard green skin and red juicy flesh with a lot of black seeds.

waterproof, waterproofs, waterproofing, waterproofed
1 (adjective) not letting water pass through, e.g. *waterproof trousers*.
2 (noun) A waterproof is a coat which keeps water out.

3 (verb) To waterproof something means to make it waterproof.

water rate, water rates
(noun) Water rates are the charges made for the use of water obtained from a public water supply.

watershed, watersheds
1 (noun) A watershed is an event or period which is important because it acts as a turning point or marks the beginning of a new way of life, e.g. *The Vietnam War was one of the great watersheds of modern history.*
2 A watershed is an area of high ground, such as a ridge, which divides two river systems, so that they flow in different directions.

waterside
(noun) The waterside is an area of land next to a river, canal, or lake.

water-skiing
Water-skiing is the sport of skimming over the water on skis while being pulled by a boat.

water softener, water softeners
(noun) A water softener is a substance or a device which can be added to water in order to remove minerals and reduce the water's hardness.

water-soluble
(adjective) able to dissolve in water.

waterspout, waterspouts
(noun) A waterspout is a whirlwind over the sea, which causes a tall column of water and mist to be formed between the surface of the water and the clouds above.

water table, water tables
(noun) The water table is the level below the surface of the ground at which water can be found.

watertight
1 (adjective) Something that is watertight does not allow water to pass through because it is tightly sealed.
2 An agreement or an argument that is watertight has been so carefully put together that nobody should be able to find a fault in it.

water tower, water towers
(noun) A water tower is a large tank of water raised above the ground so that the pressure of the flow of water to surrounding buildings can be kept steady.

water vapour
(noun) Water vapour is steam formed by water when it boils.

waterway, waterways
(noun) A waterway is a canal, river, or narrow channel of sea which ships or boats can sail along.

waterworks
1 (noun) A waterworks is the system of pipes, filters, and tanks where the public supply of water is stored and cleaned, and from where it is distributed.
2 (an informal use) Waterworks is used to

describe the parts in someone's body which form their urinary system, e.g. *He's had trouble with his waterworks.*
3 (an informal phrase) If someone **turns on the waterworks**, they start crying.

watery
1 (adjective) pale or weak, e.g. *a watery smile.*
2 Watery food or drink contains a lot of water or is thin like water, e.g. *watery milk.*

watt, watts (pronounced **wot**)
(noun) A watt is a unit of power equal to 1 joule per second. It is named after James Watt (1736-1819), the inventor of the modern steam engine.

wattage, wattages
(noun) The wattage of a piece of electrical equipment is the amount of electrical power, expressed in watts, which it uses or generates.

wattle, wattles (pronounced **wot**-tl)
1 (noun) Wattle is a frame of branches woven together with thin twigs and used for making fences and walls.
2 A wattle is the fold of skin, often brightly coloured, that hangs from the neck or throat of some birds and lizards.

wave, waves, waving, waved
1 (verb) If you wave your hand, you move it from side to side, usually to say hello or goodbye.
2 If you wave someone somewhere or wave them on, you make a movement with your hand to tell them which way to go.
3 If you wave something, you hold it up and move it from side to side, e.g. *He waved the photographs in the air.*
4 (noun) A wave is a ridge of water on the surface of the sea caused by wind or by tides.
5 A wave in someone's hair is part of the hair that forms a gently curving shape.
6 A wave is the form in which some types of energy such as heat, light, or sound travel through a substance.
7 A wave of sympathy, alarm, or panic is a steady increase in it which spreads through you or through a group of people.
8 A wave is an increase in a type of activity or behaviour, e.g. *a wave of crime against banks.*

Similar words: (sense 3) brandish, flourish

wave aside
(phrasal verb) If you wave aside an idea or an argument, you decide it is not important enough to be used or considered.

wave down
(phrasal verb) To wave down a vehicle means to wave at the driver as a signal to stop.

waveband, wavebands
(noun) A waveband is a group of radio waves of similar length which are used for particular types of radio transmission.

wavelength, wavelengths
1 (noun) A wavelength is the distance between the same point on two adjacent waves of energy.
2 A wavelength is the size of radio wave which a

particular radio station uses to broadcast its programmes.
3 (phrase) If two people are **on the same wavelength**, they have a lot in common and get on very well together.

waver, wavers, wavering, wavered
1 (verb) If you waver or if your confidence or beliefs waver, you are no longer as firm, confident, or sure in your beliefs, e.g. *Her love for him never wavered.*
2 If you waver, you hesitate and are uncertain about a decision you have to make, e.g. *After some wavering, I accepted his view.*
3 If something wavers, it moves or changes slightly, e.g. *The temperature wavered between freezing and thawing.*
[from Old Norse *vafra* meaning 'to flicker']

wavy, wavier, waviest
(adjective) having waves or regular curves, e.g. *wavy hair... a wavy line.*
wavily (adverb), **waviness** (noun).

wax, waxes, waxing, waxed
1 (noun) Wax is a solid, slightly shiny substance made of fat or oil and used to make candles and polish.
2 Wax is also the sticky yellow substance in your ears.
3 (verb) If you wax a surface, you treat it or cover it with a thin layer of wax, especially in order to polish it.
4 (a formal use) If you wax eloquent or wax lyrical, you talk in an eloquent or lyrical way.
5 (phrase) If something **waxes and wanes** it increases and then decreases over a period of time, e.g. *My feelings for him wax and wane.*
[senses 1 to 3 are from Old English *weax* meaning 'wax'; senses 4 and 5 are from Old English *weaxan* meaning 'to become larger']

waxen
(adjective) A waxen face is pale and unhealthy-looking.

wax paper or **waxed paper**
(noun) Wax paper or waxed paper is paper that is made waterproof by a thin layer of wax coating the surface.

waxwork, waxworks
1 (noun) A waxwork is a model of a famous person made out of wax.
2 A waxworks is a place where wax models of famous people are displayed for the public to look at.

waxy, waxier, waxiest
(adjective) looking or feeling like wax.

way, ways
1 (noun) A way of doing something is how you can do it or the manner of doing it, e.g. *different ways of cooking fish.*
2 The ways of a person or group are their customs or their normal behaviour, e.g. *Their ways were very different from ours.*
3 The way you feel about something is your attitude to it or your opinion about it.
4 If you have a way with people or things, you are very skilful at dealing with them.

5 The way to a particular place is the route that you take to get there.
6 If you go or look a particular way, you go or look in that direction, e.g. *She looked the other way.*
7 (phrase) If something or someone is **in the way**, they prevent you from moving freely or seeing clearly.
8 (noun) If you divide something a number of ways, you divide it into that number of parts.
9 Way is used with words such as 'little' or 'long' to say how far off in distance or time something is, e.g. *I can swim quite a long way.*
10 (phrase) If you say that something **goes a long way** towards doing a particular thing, you mean it helps to achieve that thing.
11 You say **by the way** when adding something to what you are saying, e.g. *We're having fish tonight. Do you like fish, by the way?*
12 If you **go out of your way** to do something, you make a special effort to do it.
13 (an informal phrase) If someone is **in a bad way**, they are in a poor state of health or state of mind.

Similar words: (sense 5) course, path, road, route

wayfarer, wayfarers
(noun; an old-fashioned word) A wayfarer is a traveller who walks from place to place.
wayfaring (noun and adjective).

waylay, waylays, waylaying, waylaid
1 (verb) If you waylay someone, you stop them when they are going somewhere, in order to talk to them.
2 (an old-fashioned use) To waylay someone also means to ambush them in order to attack them.

way-out
(adjective; an informal word) unusual, odd, or very modern.

wayside, waysides
1 (noun; an old-fashioned use) The wayside is the side or edge of the road.
2 (phrase) If someone or something **falls by the wayside**, they fail in what they are trying to do, or become forgotten and ignored.

wayward
(adjective) difficult to control and likely to change suddenly, e.g. *a wayward child.*

WC, WCs
(noun) A WC is a toilet. WC is an abbreviation for 'water closet'.

we
(pronoun) A speaker or writer uses we to refer to himself or herself and one or more other people, e.g. *We could hear the birds singing.*

weak, weaker, weakest
1 (adjective) not having much strength, e.g. *weak from hunger... a weak voice.*
2 If something is weak, it is likely to break or fail, e.g. *a weak link in the system.*
3 If you describe someone as weak, you mean they are easily influenced by other people.
4 If someone is weak in a particular subject, they

do not have much ability, skill, or information on that subject, e.g. *I was weak in maths.*
weakly (adverb).
[from Old English *wac* meaning 'soft' and 'miserable']

Similar words: (sense 1) feeble, puny, infirm, weedy

weaken, weakens, weakening, weakened
1 (verb) If someone weakens something, they make it less strong, powerful, or certain.
2 If something weakens you, it causes you to lose some of your physical strength and energy.
3 If someone weakens, they become less certain about something that they had previously decided.

Similar words: (sense 2) debilitate, sap

weak-kneed
(adjective) Someone who is weak-kneed is not able or willing to make their own decisions or stand up for themselves.

weakling, weaklings
(noun) A weakling is a person who lacks physical strength or who is weak in character or health.

weakness, weaknesses
1 (noun) Weakness is lack of moral or physical strength.
2 If you have a weakness for something, you have a great liking for it, e.g. *a weakness for chocolate.*

weal, weals
(noun) A weal is a raised mark made on someone's skin by a blow, especially from something sharp or thin such as a whip or stick.
[from Old English *walu* meaning 'ridge of land']

wealth
1 (noun) Wealth is the large amount of money, property, or other valuable things which someone owns.
2 If someone has a wealth of something, they have a lot of it, e.g. *a wealth of knowledge.*

Similar words: (sense 1) affluence, fortune, opulence, wealthiness, riches, prosperity

wealthy, wealthier, wealthiest
(adjective) having a large amount of money, property, or other valuable things.

Similar words: affluent, well-to-do, prosperous, rich, well-off

wean, weans, weaning, weaned
1 (verb) To wean a baby or animal means to start feeding it food other than its mother's milk.
2 If you wean someone from something, you help them to gradually stop doing it.
[from Old English *wenian* meaning 'to accustom']

weapon, weapons
1 (noun) A weapon is an object used to kill or hurt people in a fight or war.
2 A weapon is anything which can be used to get

the better of an opponent, e.g. *His wit was his best weapon.*

weaponry (noun).

wear, wears, wearing, wore, worn
1 (verb) When you wear something such as clothes, make-up, or jewellery, you have them on your body or face.
2 If you wear a particular expression, it shows on your face.
3 (noun) You can refer to clothes that are suitable for a particular time or occasion as a kind of wear, e.g. *evening wear.*
4 (verb) If something wears, it becomes thinner, weaker, or worse in condition.
5 (noun) Wear is the amount or type of use that something has and which causes damage or change to it, e.g. *signs of wear.*

wear down
(phrasal verb) If you wear people down, you weaken them by being more persistent than they are.

wear off
(phrasal verb) If a feeling such as pain wears off, it gradually disappears.

wear on
(phrasal verb) If time wears on, it seems to pass very slowly or boringly.

wear out
1 (phrasal verb) When something wears out or when you wear it out, it is used so much that it becomes thin, weak, and no longer usable.
2 (an informal use) If you wear someone out, you make them feel extremely tired.

wear and tear
(noun) Wear and tear is the damage caused to something by normal use.

wearing
(adjective) Someone or something that is wearing makes you feel extremely tired.

wearisome
(adjective) tiring and boring or frustrating, e.g. *a wearisome meeting.*

weary, wearier, weariest; wearies, wearying, wearied
1 (adjective) very tired.
2 (verb) If you weary of something, you become tired of it and lose your enthusiasm for it.
wearily (adverb), **weariness** (noun).
[from Old English *werig*]

weasel, weasels
(noun) A weasel is a small wild animal with a long, thin body and short legs. Weasels are related to stoats and ferrets and are carnivorous.

weather, weathers, weathering, weathered
1 (noun) The weather is the condition of the atmosphere at any particular time.
2 (verb) If something such as rock or wood weathers, it changes colour or shape as a result of being exposed to the wind, rain, or sun.
3 If you weather a problem or difficulty, you come through it safely and continue normally after it is over.
4 (phrase) If you say that someone is making

heavy weather of doing something, you mean they are making it much more difficult for themselves than it needs to be.
5 If you are under the weather, you feel slightly ill.
[from Old English *weder*]

weather-beaten
1 (adjective) If skin is weather-beaten, it is brown, rough, and lined because of exposure to the weather.
2 Something that is weather-beaten is rough or damaged because of being outside for a long time.

weathercock, weathercocks
(noun) A weathercock is a metal object, often in the shape of a cockerel, which is fixed to the roof of a building so that it can turn round as the wind blows and so show the direction of the wind.

weather forecast, weather forecasts
(noun) A weather forecast is a statement saying what the weather will be like the next day or for the next few days.
weather forecaster (noun).

weatherproof
(adjective) able to keep out or resist wind and rain.

weather vane, weather vanes
(noun) A weather vane is the same as a weathercock.

weave, weaves, weaving, wove, woven
1 (verb) To weave cloth means to make it by crossing threads over and under each other, especially by using a machine called a loom.
2 (noun) The weave of cloth is the way in which the threads are arranged and the pattern that they form, e.g. *a tight, firm weave.*
3 (verb) If you weave your way somewhere, you go there by moving from side to side through and round the obstacles.
4 (an informal phrase) If you tell someone to get weaving, you are telling them to hurry up and start what that they are supposed to be doing.
[from Old English *wefan*]

weaver, weavers
(noun) A weaver is a person who weaves cloth.

web, webs
1 (noun) A web is a fine net of threads that a spider makes from a sticky substance which it produces in its body.
2 A web is a complicated structure or pattern, e.g. *a web of lies.*
3 A web is a piece of skin which connects the toes on the feet of water birds such as ducks, and which helps them to swim well.
[from Old English *webb* meaning 'cobweb' or 'woven fabric']

webbed
(adjective) Webbed feet have the toes connected by a piece of skin.

webbing
(noun) Webbing is strong material woven in strips and used to make belts or straps, or used

in seats to support the springs, e.g. *canvas webbing.*

wed, weds, wedding, wedded or **wed**
(verb; an old-fashioned word) If you wed someone or if you wed, you get married.
[from Old English *weddian*]

wedded
(adjective; a formal word) If you are wedded to an idea or system, you support it strongly.

wedding, weddings
(noun) A wedding is a marriage ceremony.

wedge, wedges, wedging, wedged
1 (verb) If you wedge something, you force it to remain there by holding it there tightly, or by fixing something next to it to prevent it from moving, e.g. *Wedge the door open with a book.*
2 (noun) A wedge is a piece of something such as wood, metal, or rubber with one pointed edge and one thick edge which is used to wedge something.
3 A wedge is a piece of something that has a thick triangular shape, e.g. *a wedge of cake.*
4 (phrase) If someone **drives a wedge between** people or groups, they create bad feelings between them in order to weaken their relationship.
5 If you describe something as **the thin end of the wedge**, you mean that it appears to be unimportant at the moment, but you think it could be the beginning of something greater and more harmful.

wedlock
(noun; an old-fashioned word) Wedlock is the state of being married.

Wednesday, Wednesdays
(noun) Wednesday is the day between Tuesday and Thursday.
[from Old English *Wodnes dæg* meaning 'Woden's day']

wee, weer, weest
(adjective; a Scottish word) very small.

weed, weeds, weeding, weeded
1 (noun) A weed is a wild plant that grows in gardens or fields and prevents cultivated plants from growing properly.
2 (verb) If you weed a place, you remove the weeds from it.
3 (noun; an informal use) If you call someone a weed, you mean they are physically weak or have a weak character.
weedy (adjective).

weed out
(phrasal verb) If you weed out unwanted things, you get rid of them.

week, weeks
1 (noun) A week is a period of seven days, especially one beginning on a Sunday and ending on a Saturday.
2 A week is also the number of hours you spend at work during a week, e.g. *a 40-hour week.*
3 The week can refer to the part of a week that

does not include Saturday and Sunday, e.g. *I don't go out during the week.*
[from Old English *wice*]

weekday, weekdays
(noun) A weekday is any of the days of the week except Saturday and Sunday.

weekend, weekends
(noun) A weekend is Saturday and Sunday.

weekly, weeklies
1 (adjective and adverb) happening or appearing once a week.
2 (noun) A weekly is a newspaper or magazine that is published once a week.

weep, weeps, weeping, wept
1 (verb) If someone weeps, they cry.
2 If something such as a wound weeps, it oozes blood or other liquid.

weeping
(adjective) A weeping tree has long drooping branches.

weepy, weepies
1 (adjective) sad and likely to cry.
2 (noun; an informal use) A weepy is a film or story which is full of sad events that make people want to cry.

weevil, weevils
(noun) A weevil is a type of beetle which eats grain, seeds, or plants.
[from Old English *wifel* meaning 'beetle']

weft
(noun) The weft of a piece of woven material is the threads which are passed sideways in and out of the threads held in a loom.

weigh, weighs, weighing, weighed
1 (verb) If something weighs a particular amount, that is how heavy it is.
2 If you weigh something, you measure how heavy it is using scales.
3 If you weigh facts or words, you think about them carefully before coming to a decision or before speaking.
4 If a problem weighs on you or weighs upon you, it makes you very worried.

weigh down
1 (phrasal verb) If a load weighs you down, it stops you moving easily by making you heavier.
2 If you are weighed down by a difficulty, it is making you very worried or depressed.

weigh up
(phrasal verb) If you weigh up a person or a situation, you make an assessment of them.

weighbridge, weighbridges
(noun) A weighbridge is a machine for weighing vehicles by means of a metal platform set into the road surface.

weigh-in, weigh-ins
(noun) A weigh-in is the checking of a competitor's weight shortly before a boxing match or horse race.

weight, weights, weighting, weighted
1 (noun) The weight of something is its heaviness.

2 A weight is a metal object which has a certain known heaviness. Weights are used with sets of scales in order to weigh things.
3 You can refer to any heavy object as a weight.
4 (verb) If you weight something or weight it down, you make it heavier, often so that it cannot move.
5 (noun) The weight of something is its large amount or importance which makes it hard to fight against or contradict, e.g. *The weight of evidence was against me.*
6 If you feel a weight on you, you have a problem or a responsibility that causes you a lot of worry.
7 (phrase) If you **pull your weight**, you do your work just as hard as other people involved in the same activity.
8 If you **throw your weight about**, you act in an aggressive or bossy way.

weighted
(adjective) A system that is weighted in favour of a particular person or group is organized in such a way that this person or group will have an advantage.

weighting
(noun) A weighting is an advantage that a group of people receive, such as an extra payment to compensate for a high cost of living, e.g. *a London weighting of £1000.*

weightless
(adjective) Something that is weightless has no weight or very little weight, for example because it is in space and not affected by the Earth's gravity.
weightlessness (noun).

weightlifting
(noun) Weightlifting is the sport of lifting heavy weights in competition or for exercise.
weightlifter (noun).

weighty, weightier, weightiest
(adjective) serious or important, e.g. *weighty matters.*

weir, weirs (rhymes with **near**)
(noun) A weir is a low dam which is built across a river to raise the water level, control the flow of water, or change its direction.
[from Old English *wer* meaning 'river-dam' or 'enclosure for fish']

weird, weirder, weirdest (pronounced **weerd**)
(adjective) strange or bizarre.
weirdly (adverb), **weirdness** (noun).
[from Old English *wyrd* meaning 'destiny']

Similar words: grotesque, outlandish

weirdo, weirdos (pronounced **weer**-doe)
(noun; an informal word) If you call someone a weirdo, you mean they behave in a strange way.

welcome, welcomes, welcoming, welcomed
1 (verb) If you welcome a visitor, you greet them in a friendly way when they arrive.
2 'Welcome' can be said as a greeting to a visitor who has just arrived.

3 (noun) A welcome is a greeting to a visitor, e.g. *a warm welcome.*
4 (adjective) If someone is welcome at a place, they will be warmly received there.
5 If something is welcome, it brings pleasure or is accepted gratefully, e.g. *a welcome gift.*
6 If you tell someone they are welcome to something or welcome to do something, you mean you are willing for them to have or to do it.
7 (phrase) **You're welcome** is used to acknowledge thanks.
8 (verb) If you welcome something, you approve of it and support it, e.g. *I welcomed his proposal.*
welcoming (adjective).
[from Old English *wilcuma* meaning 'welcome guest']

weld, welds, welding, welded
1 (verb) To weld two pieces of metal together means to join them by heating their edges and fixing them together so that when they cool they harden into one piece.
2 (a formal use) If you weld people into a group, you form them into a close and united organization.
3 (noun) A weld is a joint where two pieces of metal have been welded together.
welder (noun).
[from Old English *weallan* meaning 'to boil' or 'melt']

welfare
1 (noun) The welfare of a person or group is their general state of health, comfort, and prosperity.
2 Welfare is used to describe activities concerned with the health, living conditions, and financial problems of people in society, e.g. *welfare workers.*

welfare state
(noun) The welfare state is a system in which the government uses money from taxes to provide health care and education services, and to give benefits to people who are old, unemployed, or sick.

well, better, best; wells, welling, welled
1 (adverb) If something goes well, it happens in a satisfactory way, e.g. *The party went well.*
2 in a good, skilful, or pleasing way, e.g. *She plays the violin well.*
3 thoroughly and completely, e.g. *well established.*
4 kindly, e.g. *They treated me well.*
5 If something may well or could well happen, it is likely to happen.
6 (adjective) If you are well, you are healthy.
7 (adverb) You use well to emphasize an adjective, adverb, or phrase, e.g. *I'm well aware of that... They stood well back.*
8 (phrase) **As well** means 'also', e.g. *You'll be late as well.*
9 As well as means 'in addition to', e.g. *Women, as well as men, have certain rights.*
10 If you say you **may as well** or **might as well** do something, you mean you will do it although you are not keen to do it.

11 (noun) A well is a hole drilled in the ground from which water, oil, or gas is obtained.
12 (verb) If tears well or well up, they appear in someone's eyes.
[senses 1 to 10 are from Old English *wel* meaning 'well'; senses 11 and 12 are from Old English *weallan* meaning 'to boil' or 'to melt']

well-advised
(adjective) sensible or wise, e.g. *You would be well-advised to leave.*

well-appointed
(adjective) equipped to a high standard, e.g. *a well-appointed kitchen.*

well-balanced
(adjective) sensible and without serious emotional problems, e.g. *He is mature and well-balanced.*

wellbeing
(noun) Someone's wellbeing is their health and happiness.

well-bred
(adjective) having good manners.

well-disposed
(adjective) sympathetic or friendly towards someone or something.

well-earned
(adjective) thoroughly deserved.

well-established
(adjective) successful, and having been in existence for a long time, e.g. *a well-established local firm.*

well-founded
(adjective; a formal word) based on facts, e.g. *a well-founded complaint.*

well-groomed
(adjective) neat and tidy in appearance.

well-heeled
(adjective; an informal word) wealthy.

well-informed
(adjective) having a great deal of knowledge about a subject or subjects.

wellington, wellingtons
(noun) Wellingtons or wellington boots are long waterproof rubber boots. Long boots were popularized by the 1st Duke of Wellington.

well-intentioned
(adjective) Something that is well-intentioned is meant to be helpful but often has unfortunate results.

well-meaning
(adjective) A well-meaning person tries to be helpful but is often unsuccessful.

well-nigh
(adverb; a formal word) almost.

well-off
(adjective; an informal word) quite wealthy.

well-oiled
(adjective; an informal word) drunk.

well-thought-of
(adjective) admired and respected.

well-to-do
(adjective) quite wealthy.

well-worn
1 (adjective) A well-worn expression or saying has been used too often and has become boring.
2 A well-worn object or piece of clothing has been used and worn so much that it looks old and shabby.

welly, wellies
(noun; an informal word) Wellies are wellingtons.

welsh, welshes, welshing, welshed; also spelled **welch**
(verb; an informal word) If you welsh on a debt, you fail to pay what you owe.

Welsh
1 (adjective) belonging or relating to Wales.
2 (noun) Welsh is a language spoken in parts of Wales.

Welshman, Welshmen
(noun) A Welshman is a man who comes from Wales.
Welshwoman (noun).

Welsh rarebit or **Welsh rabbit**
(noun) Welsh rarebit is a savoury food made of melted seasoned cheese served on hot buttered toast.

welt, welts
1 (noun) A welt is a raised mark on someone's skin made by a blow from something like a whip or a stick.
2 A welt is a raised or strengthened seam or edge sewn onto a garment.
3 The welt of a shoe is the strip of leather put between the sole and the upper part of the shoe.

welter
(noun; a formal word) A welter of things is a large number of them that appear together in a state of confusion, e.g. *a welter of blood and bullets.*

wench, wenches
(noun; an old-fashioned word) A wench is a woman or young girl, especially a servant.
[from Old English *wencel* meaning 'child']

wend, wends, wending, wended
(verb; a literary word) If you wend your way in a particular direction, you walk slowly in that direction.
[from Old English *wendan* meaning 'to turn' or 'go']

wept the past tense and past participle of **weep**.

werewolf, werewolves
(noun) In horror stories, a werewolf is a person who sometimes changes into a wolf.
[from Old English *wer* + *wulf* meaning 'man wolf']

west
1 (noun) The west is the direction in which you look to see the sun set.
2 The west of a place or country is the part which is towards the west when you are in the centre, e.g. *the west of Ireland.*

3 (adverb and adjective) West means towards the west.
4 (adjective) A west wind blows from the west.
5 (noun) The West refers to the countries of North America and western and southern Europe.

westerly
1 (adjective) Westerly means to or towards the west, e.g. *The harbour has a westerly outlook.*
2 A westerly wind blows from the west.

western, westerns
1 (adjective) in or from the west.
2 coming from or associated with the countries of North America and western and southern Europe, e.g. *western-style housing.*
3 (noun) A western is a book or film about life in the west of America in the nineteenth century.
westerner (noun).

westernize, westernizes, westernizing, westernized; also spelled westernise
(verb) To westernize a society or system means to introduce into it ideas and behaviour which are commonly practised in Europe and North America.
westernization (noun).

West Indian, West Indians
(noun) A West Indian is someone who comes from the West Indies.

West Indies
(noun) The West Indies are a large group of islands lying between North and South America and adjoining the Caribbean Sea and the Atlantic Ocean.

westward or westwards
1 (adverb) Westward or westwards means towards the west, e.g. *The reef stretches westwards from Florida.*
2 (adjective) The westward part of something is the west part.

wet, wetter, wettest; wets, wetting, wet or wetted
1 (adjective) If something is wet, it is covered in water, rain, or another liquid.
2 If the weather is wet, it is raining.
3 If something such as paint, ink, or cement is wet, it is not yet dry or solid.
4 (an informal use) If you say someone is wet, you mean they are weak and lack enthusiasm, energy, or confidence, e.g. *Don't be so wet!*
5 (noun) A Wet is a Conservative politician who supports moderate political policies.
6 (verb) To wet something means to put water or some other liquid over it.
7 If people wet themselves or wet their beds, they urinate in their clothes or bed because they cannot control their bladder.
8 (an informal phrase) If someone is **wet behind the ears,** they are immature or inexperienced.
wetness (noun).

wet blanket, wet blankets
(noun; an informal expression) A wet blanket is a person whose lack of enthusiasm has a depressing effect on others.

wet nurse, wet nurses
(noun) In the past, a wet nurse was a woman who was paid to breast-feed another woman's baby.

wet suit, wet suits
(noun) A wet suit is a close-fitting rubber suit which a diver or someone taking part in water sports wears to keep his or her body warm.

whack, whacks, whacking, whacked
1 (verb) If you whack someone or something, you hit them hard.
2 (noun) A whack is a hard blow.
3 (an informal use) If someone gets their whack of something, they get their fair share of it.
4 (an informal phrase) If you **have a whack** at doing something, you attempt it.

whacked
(adjective; an informal word) extremely tired, e.g. *By nine o'clock, I was whacked.*

whacking
(adjective; an informal word) very big.

whale, whales
1 (noun) A whale is a very large sea mammal which breathes out water through a blowhole on the top of its head. Whales are hunted for their oil and flesh.
2 (an informal phrase) If you say that you had a **whale of a time**, you mean that you enjoyed yourself very much.

whalebone
(noun) Whalebone is a hard elastic material taken from the mouth of a whale. It was often used in the past to stiffen material in garments such as corsets.

whaling
(noun) Whaling is the work of hunting and killing whales for oil or food.

wham
(interjection) You can use wham to indicate the force of a kick, punch, or other blow.

wharf, wharves or wharfs (pronounced worf)
(noun) A wharf is a platform built of stone or wood along the side of a river or the sea, where ships may be tied up to load or unload.
[from Old English *hwearf* meaning 'heap']

wharfage
(noun) Wharfage is the accommodation for ships at a wharf, or the fee charged for this.

what
1 (pronoun) What is used in questions when asking for information about something, e.g. *What is your name?*
2 What is used in indirect questions and statements about knowing or telling things, e.g. *I don't know what to do.*
3 What can be used at the beginning of a clause to refer to something with a particular quality, e.g. *He mixes what is real with what is unreal.*
4 (determiner) What can be used at the beginning of a clause to show that you are talking about the whole amount that is available to you, e.g. *I've spent what money I had.*
5 You say 'what' to emphasize an opinion or

reaction, especially in exclamations, e.g. *What rubbish!*

6 (phrase) You say **what about** at the beginning of a question when you are making a suggestion or offer, e.g. *What about lunch?*

7 (an informal phrase) **What's what** means the important things that need to be known about a situation, e.g. *There'll be a meeting to find out what's what.*

whatever

1 (pronoun) You use whatever to refer to anything or everything of a particular type, e.g. *I'll do whatever I can to help.*

2 (conjunction) You use whatever to mean no matter what, e.g. *I have to bring my family back whatever happens.*

3 (adverb) You use whatever to emphasize a negative statement or a question, e.g. *There is no evidence whatever to support such a view... Whatever is the matter?*

4 (pronoun) You use whatever when you do not know the precise nature of something, e.g. *Whatever it is, I don't like it.*

whatsoever

(adverb) You use whatsoever to emphasize a negative statement, e.g. *There is no proof whatsoever.*

wheat

(noun) Wheat is a cereal plant grown for its grain which is used to make flour.

wheaten (adjective).

[from Old English *hwǣte*]

wheat germ

(noun) Wheat germ is the middle part of a grain of wheat. It is rich in vitamins and is often added to other food.

wheatmeal

(noun) Wheatmeal is a brown flour made from wheat grains.

wheedle, wheedles, wheedling, wheedled

(verb) If you wheedle someone into doing something, you gently and cleverly persuade them to do it.

wheel, wheels, wheeling, wheeled

1 (noun) A wheel is a circular object which turns on a rod attached to its centre. Wheels are fixed underneath vehicles so that they can move along.

2 The wheel of a car is its steering wheel.

3 (verb) If you wheel something such as a bicycle, you push it.

4 If something wheels, it moves round in the shape of a circle, e.g. *The birds wheeled back and forth in the sky.*

5 If you wheel round, you turn round to face someone or something.

wheelbarrow, wheelbarrows

(noun) A wheelbarrow is a small cart with a single wheel at the front, used for carrying things in the garden.

wheelbase, wheelbases

(noun) The wheelbase of a vehicle is the distance between its front and back wheels.

wheelchair, wheelchairs

(noun) A wheelchair is a chair with wheels in which sick, injured, or disabled people can move around. Wheelchairs are propelled mechanically or by hand.

wheeler-dealer, wheeler-dealers

(noun; an informal word) A wheeler-dealer is someone who uses deception and unfair methods in business to try and get what they want.

wheelwright, wheelwrights (pronounced weel-rite)

(noun) A wheelwright is someone who makes and repairs wooden wheels and other wooden things such as carts and gates.

wheeze, wheezes, wheezing, wheezed

1 (verb) If someone wheezes, they breathe with difficulty, making a whistling sound, usually because they have a chest complaint such as asthma.

2 (noun; an old-fashioned, informal use) A wheeze is a clever idea, often a joke or trick.

wheezy (adjective).

whelk, whelks

(noun) A whelk is a snail-like shellfish with a strong shell and a soft edible body.

whelp, whelps, whelping, whelped

(verb; an old-fashioned word) When a female dog whelps, she gives birth to pups.

when

1 (adverb) You use when to ask what time something happened or will happen, e.g. *When are you getting married?*

2 (conjunction) You use when to refer to a time in the past, e.g. *I first met him when I was twenty.*

3 You use when to introduce the reason for an opinion, comment, or question, e.g. *When I can't read or write, how can I get a job?*

4 When is used to mean although, e.g. *You describe this policy as rigid, when in fact it has been extremely flexible.*

[from Old English *hwanne*]

whence

(adverb and conjunction; an old-fashioned word) Whence means from where.

whenever

(conjunction) Whenever means at any time, or every time that something happens, e.g. *I avoid conflict whenever possible.*

where

1 (adverb) You use where to ask which place something is in, is coming from, or is going to, e.g. *Where is Jane?*

2 (conjunction) You use where to refer to the place in which something is situated or happening, e.g. *I know where we are.*

3 (conjunction, pronoun and adverb) You use where when asking about or referring to a situation, a stage in something, or an aspect of something, e.g. *I wouldn't know where to start... a situation where unemployment is rising... I want, where possible, to keep costs down.*

4 (conjunction) Where can introduce a clause that contrasts with the other part of the

sentence, e.g. *Sometimes a teacher will be listened to, where a parent might not.*
[from Old English *hwær*]

whereabouts
1 (noun) The whereabouts of a person or thing is the place where they are.
2 (adverb) You use whereabouts when you are asking more precisely where something is, e.g. *Whereabouts in Spain will you be going?*

whereas
(conjunction) Whereas introduces a comment that contrasts with the other part of the sentence, e.g. *Humans are capable of error whereas the computer is not.*

whereby
(pronoun; a formal word) Whereby means by which or by what, e.g. *a system whereby we work more overtime.*

whereupon
(conjunction; a formal word) Whereupon means at which point, e.g. *His department was shut down, whereupon he returned home.*

wherever
1 (conjunction) Wherever means in every place or situation, e.g. *Wherever you go, you see poverty.*
2 You use wherever to show what you do not know where a place or person is, e.g. *in Royston, wherever that is.*

wherewithal
(noun) If you have the wherewithal to do something, you have enough money to do it.

whet, whets, whetting, whetted
1 (verb; an old-fashioned use) To whet a blade means to sharpen it.
2 (phrase) To **whet someone's appetite** for something, means to increase their desire for it.
[from Old English *hwettan* meaning 'sharpen']

whether
(conjunction) You use whether when you are talking about two or more alternatives, e.g. *I can't tell whether he loves me or not.*

whetstone, whetstones
(noun) A whetstone is a stone used for sharpening blades and tools.

whey (rhymes with **day**)
(noun) Whey is the watery liquid that is separated from the curds in sour milk when cheese is made.
[from Old English *hwæg*]

which
1 (adjective and pronoun) You use which to ask about alternatives or to refer to a choice between alternatives, e.g. *I don't know which team she played for... Which of the two do you prefer?*
2 (pronoun) Which at the beginning of a clause identifies the thing you are talking about or gives more information about it, e.g. *the awful conditions which exist in our prisons.*

whichever
1 (adjective and pronoun) You use whichever to say that it does not matter which of several alternatives happens or is chosen, e.g. *He would*

do justice to whichever role he played... *Write or phone, whichever you prefer.*
2 You use whichever to say which possibility is the right one or which one is the one you mean, e.g. *Use whichever soap powder is recommended... Ask whichever of the children is the brightest.*

whiff, whiffs
1 (noun) A whiff of something is a slight smell of it.
2 A whiff is also a slight sign or trace of something, e.g. *at the first whiff of danger.*

while, whiles, whiling, whiled
1 (conjunction) If something happens while something else is happening, the two things happen at the same time.
2 While also means whereas, e.g. *Fred gambled his money while Julia spent hers on clothes.*
3 (noun) A while is a period of time, e.g. *a little while ago.*
4 (phrase) If an action or activity is **worth your while**, it will be helpful or useful to you if you do it.

while away
(phrasal verb) If you while away the time in a particular way, you idly pass the time that way because you are waiting for something or because you have nothing else to do.

whilst
(conjunction) Whilst means the same as while.

whim, whims
(noun) A whim is a sudden desire or fancy.

Similar words: quirk, caprice, vagary, notion

whimper, whimpers, whimpering, whimpered
1 (verb) When children or animals whimper, they make soft, low, unhappy sounds.
2 If you whimper something, you say it in an unhappy or frightened way, as if you are about to cry, e.g. *'Let me go,' she whimpered.*

whimsical
(adjective) unusual and slightly playful, e.g. *whimsical images of birds and beasts.*
whimsically (adverb).

whimsy, whimsies; also spelled whimsey
(noun) Whimsy is unusual and slightly playful behaviour.

whine, whines, whining, whined
1 (verb) To whine means to make a long, high-pitched noise, especially one which sounds sad or unpleasant.
2 (noun) A whine is the noise made by something or someone whining.
3 If someone whines about something, they complain about it in an annoying way.

whinge, whinges, whinging or whingeing, whinged
(verb) If someone whinges about something, they complain about it in an annoying way.
[from Old English *hwinsian* meaning 'to whine']

whinny, whinnies, whinnying, whinnied
1 (verb) When a horse whinnies, it neigh

2 (noun) A whinny is the noise a horse makes when it whinnies.

whip, whips, whipping, whipped
1 (noun) A whip is a thin piece of leather or rope attached to a handle, which is used for hitting people or animals.
2 (verb) If you whip a person or animal, you hit them with a whip.
3 When the wind whips something, it strikes it.
4 If you whip something out or off, you take it out or off very quickly, e.g. *He whipped off the mask to reveal his identity.*
5 If you whip cream or eggs, you beat them until they are thick and frothy or stiff.
6 (phrase) If you **have the whip hand** in a situation, you are in control or have power over people.

Similar words: (sense 2) flay, flog, scourge, lash

whip up
(phrasal verb) If you whip up a strong emotion, you deliberately make people feel it, e.g. *His speech whipped up the audience into a frenzy of rage.*

whiplash injury, whiplash injuries
(noun) A whiplash injury is a neck injury caused by your head suddenly jerking forwards and then back again, for example in a car accident.

whippet, whippets
(noun) A whippet is a small, thin dog used for racing.

whipping boy, whipping boys
(noun) When someone is made a whipping boy, they are blamed for other people's mistakes.

whip-round, whip-rounds
(noun; an informal word) When people have a whip-round, money is collected from each person, often to help someone in trouble or to buy them a present.

whir, whirs, whirring, whirred; also spelled whirr
1 (verb) When something such as a machine whirrs, it makes a series of low sounds so fast that it sounds like one continuous sound.
2 (noun) A whir is the noise made by something whirring.

whirl, whirls, whirling, whirled
1 (verb) When something whirls, or when you whirl it round, it turns round very fast.
2 (noun) You can refer to a lot of intense activity as a whirl of activity.
3 (verb) If you say that your head or mind is whirling, you mean you are very confused or excited by something.
[from Old Norse *hvirfla* meaning 'to turn about']

whirlpool, whirlpools
(noun) A whirlpool is a small circular area in a river or the sea where the water is moving quickly round and round so that objects floating near it are pulled into its centre.

whirlwind, whirlwinds
1 (noun) A whirlwind is a tall column of air which spins round and round very fast while moving across the land or sea.

2 (adjective) more rapid than usual, e.g. *a whirlwind romance.*

whisk, whisks, whisking, whisked
1 (verb) If you whisk someone or something somewhere, you take them there quickly, e.g. *I was whisked into hospital.*
2 If you whisk eggs or cream, you stir air into them quickly.
3 When an animal whisks its tail, it makes quick sweeping movements with it.
4 (noun) A whisk is a kitchen tool used for quickly stirring air into eggs or cream.
[from Old Norse *visk* meaning 'wisp']

whisker, whiskers
1 (noun) The whiskers of an animal such as a cat or mouse are the long, stiff hairs near its mouth.
2 You can refer to the hair on a man's face, especially on his cheeks, as his whiskers.
3 (an informal phrase) **By a whisker** means by a very small amount.

whisky, whiskies; also spelled whiskey
(noun) Whisky is a strong alcoholic drink made from grain such as barley or rye.
[from Scottish Gaelic *uisge beatha* meaning 'water of life']

whisper, whispers, whispering, whispered
1 (verb) When you whisper, you talk to someone very quietly, using your breath and not your throat, so that other people cannot hear what you are saying.
2 (noun) If you talk in a whisper, you whisper.
3 A whisper is also a low, quiet sound which can only just be heard, e.g. *the whisper of wind in the trees.*
whispered (adjective).

whist
(noun) Whist is a card game for four players in which one pair of players tries to win more tricks than the other pair.

whist drive, whist drives
(noun) A whist drive is a social event at which people play whist.

whistle, whistles, whistling, whistled
1 (verb) When you whistle a tune or whistle, you produce a clear musical sound by forcing your breath out between your lips.
2 If something whistles, it makes a loud, high sound, e.g. *The kettle whistled... Bullets whistled past his head.*
3 (noun) A whistle is the sound something or someone makes when they whistle.
4 A whistle is also a small metal tube that you blow into to produce a whistling sound.
whistler (noun).

whit
1 (noun; a formal use) You say 'not a whit' or 'no whit' to emphasize that something is not the case at all, e.g. *He hadn't improved a whit since the doctor last saw him.*
2 Whit is the same as Whitsun.

white, whiter, whitest; whites
1 (noun and adjective) White is the lightest

possible colour. A white surface reflects more light than any other coloured surface.
2 Someone who is white has a pale skin and is of European origin.
3 (adjective) If someone goes white, their face becomes very pale because they are afraid, shocked, or ill.
4 White coffee contains milk or cream.
5 White wine is pale yellowish in colour.
6 (noun) The white of an egg is the transparent liquid surrounding the yolk.
whiteness (noun).
[from Old English *hwit*]

whitebait
(noun) Whitebait are very small young herrings or sprats that are eaten fried.

white blood cell, white blood cells
(noun) Your white blood cells are the cells in your blood that cannot carry oxygen.

white-collar
(adjective) White-collar workers work in offices rather than doing manual work, e.g. *a white-collar union*.

white elephant, white elephants
(noun) A white elephant is an expensive but useless possession.
[from the pale-coloured elephants of parts of South Asia which are regarded as sacred]

Whitehall
(noun) Whitehall is a London street in which and near which there are many government offices. The word Whitehall is often used to refer to the government itself.

white horses
(plural noun) White horses are waves in the sea or on a lake which are blown by the wind so that their tops appear white.

white-hot
(adjective) extremely hot.

white lie, white lies
(noun) A white lie is a harmless lie, especially one told to prevent someone's feelings from being hurt.

white light
(noun) White light is the technical term given to ordinary daylight, which contains all the wavelengths of the spectrum.

whiten, whitens, whitening, whitened
(verb) When something whitens or when you whiten it, it becomes white or paler in colour.

white paper, white papers
(noun) A white paper is an official report published by the British Government, which gives the policy of the Government on a particular subject.

white spirit
(noun) White spirit is a colourless liquid made from petrol and used, for example, to thin paint or clean surfaces.

whitewash, whitewashes, whitewashing, whitewashed

1 (noun) Whitewash is a mixture of lime and water used for painting walls white.
2 (verb) To whitewash something means to cover or whiten it with whitewash.
3 (noun; an informal use) Whitewash is also used to refer to attempts to hide the unpleasant facts about someone or something.

whither
(adverb and conjunction; an old-fashioned word) Whither means to what place.

whiting
(noun) A whiting is a sea fish related to the cod.

Whitsun
(noun) Whitsun is the seventh Sunday after Easter. The week following that Sunday is also called Whitsun.
[from Old English *hwita sunnandæg* meaning 'white Sunday', probably because of the wearing of white robes after baptism]

whittle, whittles, whittling, whittled
(verb) If you whittle a piece of wood, you shape it by shaving or cutting small pieces off it.
[from Middle English *thwittle* meaning 'large knife']

whittle away or **whittle down**
(phrasal verb) To whittle away at something or to whittle it down means to make it less effective or smaller over a period of time, e.g. *The Government whittled away at civil liberties*.

whizz, whizzes, whizzing, whizzed; also spelled **whiz** (an informal word)
1 (verb) If you whizz somewhere, you move there quickly, e.g. *The cars whizzed by*.
2 (noun) If you are a whizz at something, you are very good at it.

whizz-kid, whizz-kids; also spelled **whiz-kid**
(noun; an informal word) A whizz-kid is a fairly young person who is very good at their job and extremely successful for their age.

who
1 (pronoun) You use who when you are asking about someone's identity, e.g. *Who was that lady I saw you with last night?*
2 Who at the beginning of a clause identifies the person or people you are talking about or gives more information about them, e.g. *Joe, who was always early, was already there.*

whoa (pronounced **woh**)
Whoa is a command used to slow down or stop a horse.

whodunit, whodunits; also spelled **whodunnit**
(noun) A whodunit is a book, film, or play about a murder, in which the identity of the murderer is not revealed until the end.

whoever
1 (pronoun) Whoever means the person who, e.g. *Whoever discovers the body should contact the doctor.*
2 Whoever also means no matter who, e.g. *Whoever you vote for, prices will go on rising.*
3 Whoever is used in questions as an emphatic form of who, e.g. *Whoever is that at the door?*

whole, wholes
1 (noun and adjective) The whole of something is all of it, e.g. *the whole of Europe... the whole thing... You must understand each part before you can understand the whole.*
2 (adverb) in one piece, e.g. *He swallowed a plum whole.*
3 (phrase) You use **as a whole** to emphasize that you are talking about all of something, e.g. *Is that just in India, or in the world as a whole?*
4 You say **on the whole** to mean that something is generally true, e.g. *On the whole, I hated school.*
wholeness (noun).

wholefood, wholefoods
(noun) Wholefoods are foods which have been refined as little as possible, do not contain additives, and are eaten in their natural state.

wholehearted
(adjective) enthusiastic and totally sincere, e.g. *She had the wholehearted support of her staff.*
wholeheartedly (adverb).

wholemeal
(adjective) Wholemeal flour is made from the complete grain of the wheat plant, including the husk.

whole number, whole numbers
(noun) A whole number is an exact number such as 1, 5, 12, or 300, rather than a fraction or a decimal.

wholesale
1 (adjective and adverb) Wholesale refers to the activity of buying goods cheaply in large quantities and selling them again, especially to shopkeepers, e.g. *A rise in wholesale prices will soon be reflected in the shops.*
2 (adjective) Wholesale also means done to an excessive extent, e.g. *the wholesale slaughter of whales.*
wholesaler (noun).

wholesome
(adjective) good and likely to improve your life, behaviour, or health, e.g. *a wholesome attitude.*

whole-wheat
(adjective) Whole-wheat means wholemeal.

wholly (pronounced **hoe**-lee)
(adverb) completely.

whom
(pronoun) Whom is the object form of 'who'.

whoop, whoops, whooping, whooped
1 (verb) If you whoop, you shout loudly in a happy or excited way.
2 (noun) A whoop is a loud cry of happiness or excitement, e.g. *There were whoops of delight.*

whoopee
People sometimes shout 'whoopee!' when they are excited or happy.

whooping cough (pronounced **hoop**-ing)
(noun) Whooping cough is an acute infectious disease which makes people cough violently and produce a loud sound when they breathe.

whopper, whoppers (an informal word)
1 (noun) A whopper is an unusually large example of something, e.g. *Look at this potato! What a whopper!*
2 If you tell whoppers, you tell lies.

whopping
(adjective; an informal word) unusually large.

whore, whores (pronounced **hore**)
(noun; an offensive word) A whore is a prostitute, or a woman believed to act like a prostitute.

whorl, whorls (pronounced **wurl**)
(noun) A whorl is a spiral shape, such as the coiled lines that make up a fingerprint.

whose
1 (pronoun) You use whose to ask who something belongs to, e.g. *Whose car is this?*
2 You use whose at the beginning of a clause which gives information about something relating or belonging to the thing or person you have just mentioned, e.g. *Barbara, whose father had just died, did not want to come.*

whosoever
(pronoun; a formal or old-fashioned word) Whosoever means the same as whoever.

why
1 (adverb and pronoun) You use why when you are asking about the reason for something, or talking about it, e.g. *Why did it happen?... He explained why he couldn't come.*
2 People say 'why!' to express surprise, shock, or indignation, e.g. *Why, he's only just learned to swim himself!*

whys and wherefores (pronounced **ware**-forz)
(plural noun) The whys and wherefores of something are the reasons for it.

WI an abbreviation for **Women's Institute**.

wick, wicks
1 (noun) The wick of a candle is the cord in the middle, which you set alight.
2 The wick of a lamp or cigarette lighter is the part which supplies fuel to the flame.
3 (an informal phrase) If someone **gets on your wick**, they irritate you.

wicked
1 (adjective) very bad, e.g. *the wicked witch... a wicked crime.*
2 mischievous in an amusing or attractive way, e.g. *her wicked wit.*
wickedly (adverb), **wickedness** (noun).
[from Old English *wicce* meaning 'witch']

Similar words: (sense 1) iniquitous, heinous

wicker
(adjective) A wicker basket or chair is made of wickerwork.
[from Swedish *vika* meaning 'bend']

wickerwork
(noun) Wickerwork is used to make baskets and furniture and is made by weaving twigs, canes, or reeds together.

wicket, wickets
1 (noun) In cricket, the wicket is one of the two

sets of stumps and bails at which the bowler aims the ball.

2 The grass between the wickets on a cricket pitch is also called the wicket.

3 A wicket is also a small gate or door, especially one that is part of a larger one.

wicketkeeper, wicketkeepers
(noun) In cricket, the wicketkeeper is the player who stands behind the wicket and stops balls missed by the batsman.

wide, wider, widest
1 (adjective) measuring a large distance from one side to the other.
2 (adverb) If you open or spread something wide, you open it to its fullest extent.
3 (adjective) If there is a wide variety, range, or selection of something, there are many different kinds of it, e.g. *a wide range of books.*
4 Wide means relating to the most important or general parts of a situation, rather than to the smaller details, e.g. *the wider context of world events.*
5 (adverb) If something goes wide, it goes far from the desired point or mark, e.g. *The bullet went wide.*
widely (adverb).

Similar words: (sense 3) general, catholic, broad, extensive, wide-ranging

wide-angle lens, wide-angle lenses
(noun) A wide-angle lens is a lens which allows you to photograph a wider view than with a normal camera lens.

wide-awake
(adjective) completely awake.

wide-eyed
1 (adjective) with eyes more open than usual, especially because of surprise or fear.
2 inexperienced and innocent, e.g. *I was a wide-eyed American, abroad for the first time.*

widen, widens, widening, widened
1 (verb) If something widens or if you widen it, it becomes wider in area or scope, e.g. *They could widen their experience by going on a course.*
2 If a gap or difference widens, it becomes more extreme, e.g. *The gulf between them widened.*

wide-ranging
(adjective) extending over a variety of different things or over a large area, e.g. *a wide-ranging interview.*

widespread
(adjective) existing or happening over a large area or to a great extent, e.g. *a widespread belief.*

Similar words: general, rife, rampant

widow, widows
1 (noun) A widow is a woman whose husband has died and who has not remarried.
2 (an informal use) Widow is also used jokingly to describe a woman whose husband leaves her alone for long periods while he takes part in a sport or other activity, e.g. *a golf widow.*

widowed
(adjective) If someone is widowed, their husband or wife has died.

widower, widowers
(noun) A widower is a man whose wife has died and who has not remarried.

widowhood
(noun) Widowhood is the state of being a widow, or the time during which a woman is a widow.

width, widths
(noun) The width of something is the distance from one side or edge to the other.

wield, wields, wielding, wielded (pronounced **weeld**)
1 (verb) If you wield a weapon or tool, you carry it and use it.
2 If someone wields power, they have it and are able to use it, e.g. *The unions wielded enormous power over their members.*

wife, wives
(noun) A man's wife is the woman he is married to.
wifely (adjective).
[from Old English *wif* meaning 'woman']

wig, wigs
(noun) A wig is a false head of hair worn to cover someone's own hair or to hide their baldness.
[short for *periwig* from Italian *perrucca* meaning 'wig']

wigging, wiggings
(noun; an informal word) A wigging is a telling-off.

wiggle, wiggles, wiggling, wiggled
1 (verb) If you wiggle something, you move it up and down or from side to side with small jerky movements.
2 (noun) A wiggle is a small jerky movement or line.
wiggly (adjective).
[from Old German *wiggelen*]

wigwam, wigwams
(noun) A wigwam is a dwelling used by North American Indians, especially one made of bark or skins stretched over a frame of arched poles lashed together.
[from American Indian *wikwam* meaning 'their house']

wild, wilder, wildest; wilds
1 (adjective) Wild animals, birds, and plants live and grow in natural surroundings and are not looked after by people.
2 (noun) The wild is a free and natural state of living, e.g. *Zoo-bred animals could not survive in the wild.*
3 (adjective) Wild land is natural and uncultivated, e.g. *the wilder parts of Scotland.*
4 (noun) The wilds are remote areas where few people live, far away from towns.
5 (adjective) Wild weather or sea is stormy and rough.

6 Wild behaviour is excited and uncontrolled, e.g. *He struck at me in wild fury.*
7 A wild idea or scheme is original and crazy.
8 A wild guess is made without much thought and is unlikely to be right.
9 (an informal use) If you are not wild about something, you do not like it very much.
wildly (adverb).

wildcat, wildcats
(noun) A wildcat is a kind of large, fierce cat which lives in mountains and forests.

wildcat strike, wildcat strikes
(noun) A wildcat strike is a strike begun suddenly and not officially approved by a trade union.

wildebeest (pronounced **wil**-dee-beest)
(noun) A wildebeest is a large African antelope with a hairy tail, short curved horns, and hair under its neck like a beard. Wildebeest live in large herds and are also called gnu.
[an Afrikaans word meaning literally 'wild beast']

wilderness, wildernesses
1 (noun) A wilderness is a desert or other area of land where there are very few plants or animals.
2 An area where grass or plants grow thickly in a confused, uncontrolled mass can also be called a wilderness, e.g. *The garden's turned into a wilderness.*
[from Old English *wildeor* + *nes* meaning 'wild animal state' or 'wild animal condition']

wildfire
(noun) If something spreads like wildfire, it spreads very quickly, e.g. *The news spread like wildfire round the college.*

wildfowl
(noun) Wildfowl are birds such as ducks, pheasants, and quails which are hunted and shot.

wild-goose chase, wild-goose chases
(noun) A wild-goose chase is a hopeless or useless search for something you have little chance of finding.

wildlife
(noun) Wildlife means wild animals and plants.

Wild West
(noun) The Wild West was the western part of the United States when it was first being settled by Europeans. Films and stories about the Wild West are often about cowboys, American Indians, gunfights, and lawbreaking.

wiles
(plural noun) Wiles are clever or crafty tricks used to persuade people to do something.
[from Old Norse *vel* meaning 'craft']

wilful
1 (adjective) Wilful actions or attitudes are deliberate and often intended to hurt someone, e.g. *wilful destruction.*
2 Someone who is wilful is obstinate and determined to get their own way, e.g. *a wilful child.*
wilfully (adverb).

Similar words: (sense 2) headstrong, wayward

will, wills, willing, willed
1 (verb) You use will to form the future tense, e.g. *She will turn up soon.*
2 You use will to say that you intend to do something, e.g. *I will never betray you.*
3 You use will when inviting someone to do or have something, e.g. *Will you have another scone?*
4 You use will when asking or telling someone to do something, e.g. *Will you do me a favour?... You will do as I say.*
5 You use will to say that you are assuming something to be the case, e.g. *You will have gathered I don't like her.*
6 (noun) Will is the determination to do something, e.g. *the will to succeed.*
7 If something is the will of a person or group, they want it to happen, e.g. *the will of the people.*
8 (phrase) If you can do something **at will**, you can do it whenever you want.
9 (verb) If you will something to happen, you try to make it happen by mental effort, e.g. *I willed my legs to walk a bit further.*
10 (noun) A will is a legal document in which you say what you want to happen to your money and property when you die.
11 (verb) If you will something to someone, you leave it to them when you die, e.g. *She willed all she had to the dogs' home.*

willies
(noun; an informal word) If something gives you the willies, it makes you nervous and uncomfortable.

willing
1 (adjective) agreeable to do something, e.g. *I am willing to get married right now.*
2 eager and enthusiastic, e.g. *a willing helper.*
willingly (adverb), **willingness** (noun).

Similar words: (sense 1) game, ready, prepared

will-o'-the-wisp, will-o'-the-wisps
1 (noun) A will-o'-the-wisp is a pale, flickering light seen over marshy ground at night.
2 A will-o'-the-wisp is also a person or thing that keeps disappearing or that is impossible to catch or reach.
[from *Will with the wisp* meaning 'William with a bundle of straw used as a torch']

willow, willows
(noun) A willow or willow tree is a tree with long, thin branches and narrow leaves that often grows near water. Its wood is used for making baskets and cricket bats.

willow pattern
(noun) Willow pattern is a traditional Chinese design, usually blue on a white background, used on pottery and porcelain.

willowy
(adjective) A willowy person is tall, slim, and graceful.

willpower
(noun) Willpower is a strong determination to do something and the mental strength to control

one's actions, e.g. *She stayed calm by sheer willpower.*

willy-nilly
(adverb) whether you like it or not, e.g. *All the children were taken willy-nilly on a guided tour of the town.*

wilt, wilts, wilting, wilted
1 (verb) If a plant wilts, it gradually droops downwards and becomes weak because it needs more water or is dying.
2 If someone wilts, they gradually lose strength or confidence, e.g. *I wilted under her glare.*
3 If something stiff wilts, it becomes limp or floppy.

wily, wilier, wiliest (pronounced wie-lee)
(adjective) clever and cunning.
wiliness (noun).

wimp, wimps
(noun; an informal word) If you call someone a wimp, you mean they are feeble and timid.
wimpish (adjective).

wimple, wimples
(noun) In medieval times, a wimple was a piece of cloth wrapped round a woman's head so that only her face could be seen. Wimples are still worn by some nuns.

win, wins, winning, won
1 (verb) If you win a fight, game, or argument, you defeat your opponent.
2 (noun) A win is a victory in a game or contest.
3 (verb) If you win a prize, you get it as a reward for succeeding in something.
4 If you win something you want, such as approval or support, you succeed in getting it.
5 (an informal phrase) If you say that someone **can't win** in a situation, you mean they are certain to fail or to suffer in some way whatever they do.

win over or win round
(phrasal verb) If you win someone over or win them round, you persuade them to support you or agree with you.

wince, winces, wincing, winced
(verb) When you wince, the muscles of your face tighten suddenly because of pain, fear, or distress.

winceyette (pronounced win-see-ett)
(noun) Winceyette is a soft cotton fabric.

winch, winches, winching, winched
1 (noun) A winch is a machine used to lift heavy objects. It consists of a cylinder around which a rope or chain is wound.
2 (verb) If you winch an object or person somewhere, you lift, lower, or pull them using a winch.
[from Old English *wince* meaning 'pulley']

wind, winds (rhymes with tinned)
1 (noun) A wind is a current of air moving across the earth's surface.
2 Your wind is the ability to breathe easily, e.g. *I regained my wind and carried on running.*
3 Wind is air swallowed with food or drink, or

gas produced in your stomach, which causes discomfort.
4 The wind section of an orchestra is the group of musicians who play wind instruments.
5 (an informal phrase) If you **get wind of** something, you begin to suspect it or become aware of it.
6 If something **takes the wind out of your sails**, it makes you much less confident about what you are doing.

wind, winds, winding, wound (rhymes with mind)
1 (verb) If a road or river winds in a particular direction, it twists and turns in that direction.
2 When you wind something round something else, you wrap it round it several times.
3 When you wind a clock or machine or wind it up, you turn a key or handle several times to make it work.
[from Old English *windan*]

wind up
1 (phrasal verb) When you wind up something such as an activity or a business, you finish it or close it.
2 If you wind up in a particular place, you end up there.
3 (an informal use) If you wind someone up, you deliberately annoy or tease them.

windbag, windbags
(noun; an informal word) A windbag is someone who talks too much.

windbreak, windbreaks
(noun) A windbreak is something such as a line of trees which gives protection against the wind.

winded
(adjective) out of breath because of vigorous exercise or because you have been hit in the stomach.

windfall, windfalls
1 (noun) A windfall is a sum of money that you receive unexpectedly.
2 A windfall is also a fruit, usually an apple, that has been blown from a tree by the wind.

wind instrument, wind instruments
(noun) A wind instrument is an instrument you play by using your breath, for example a flute, an oboe, or a trumpet.

windlass, windlasses
(noun) A windlass is a machine for pulling or moving heavy objects. It consists of a crank or motor operating a revolving cylinder around which a rope or chain is wound.
[from Old Norse *vinda* meaning 'to wind' and *ass* meaning 'pole']

windmill, windmills
(noun) A windmill is a machine for grinding grain or pumping water. It is driven by vanes or sails turned by the wind.

window, windows
1 (noun) A window is a space in a wall or roof or in the side of a vehicle, usually with glass in it so that light can pass through and people can see in or out.
2 A window is also any opening or structure that

looks like or acts like a window, such as the transparent panel on an envelope through which the address can be seen.
[from Old Norse *vindauga* meaning 'wind eye']

window box, window boxes
(noun) A window box is a long, narrow container on a windowsill in which plants are grown.

window-dressing
1 (noun) Window-dressing is the arranging of goods attractively in a shop window.
2 Window-dressing is also an attempt to hide the unpleasant nature of something by presenting some aspect of it in an attractive way.
window-dresser (noun).

window-shopping
If you go window-shopping, you spend time looking in shop windows without actually buying anything.

windowsill, windowsills
(noun) A windowsill is a ledge along the bottom of a window, either on the inside or outside of a building.

windpipe, windpipes
(noun) Your windpipe is the tube which carries air into your lungs when you breathe. The technical name for windpipe is **trachea**.

windscreen, windscreens
(noun) The windscreen of a vehicle is the glass at the front through which the driver looks.

windscreen wiper, windscreen wipers
(noun) A windscreen wiper is an electrically operated blade with a rubber edge that wipes rain from the windscreen of a vehicle.

windsock, windsocks
(noun) A windsock is a cut-off cone of material flown from a mast, especially at airports, to show the local wind direction.

windsurfing
Windsurfing is the sport of moving along the surface of the sea or a lake standing on a sailboard equipped with a mast, sail, and boom.
windsurfer (noun).

windswept
1 (adjective) A windswept place is exposed to strong winds, e.g. *a windswept hillside*.
2 A windswept person has untidy hair blown about by the wind.

wind tunnel, wind tunnels
(noun) A wind tunnel is a tunnel-like chamber in which air currents of various speeds are produced to test the effects of wind on aircraft.

windward
(adjective and adverb) facing the direction from which the wind is blowing, or moving in that direction.

windy, windier, windiest
1 (adjective) If it is windy, there is a lot of wind.
2 Windy speech or writing is long-winded and self-important.
3 (an informal use) If someone gets windy, they become nervous or worried about something.

wine, wines
(noun) Wine is the red or white alcoholic drink which is normally made by fermenting grapes, but which can be made from other fruits and vegetables.
[from Latin *vinum* meaning 'wine']

wing, wings
1 (noun) A bird's or insect's wings are the parts of its body that it uses for flying.
2 An aeroplane's wings are the long, flat parts on each side that support it while it is in the air.
3 A wing of a building is a part which sticks out from the main part or which has been added later.
4 A wing of an organization, especially a political party, is a group within it with a particular role or particular beliefs, e.g. *the political wing of the IRA*.
5 (plural noun) The wings in a theatre are the sides of the stage which are hidden from the audience by curtains or scenery.
6 (noun) In football or hockey, the wing is the left or right edge of the pitch.
7 A car's wings are the parts around and above its wheels.
8 (phrase) To **clip someone's wings** means to restrict their freedom.
9 If someone **is waiting in the wings**, they are ready to act if necessary.
10 If you **spread your wings**, you do something new in order to make full use of your abilities or skills.
11 If you **take someone under your wing**, you help and guide them.
winged (adjective).
[from Old Norse *vængir*]

wing commander, wing commanders
(noun) A wing commander is an RAF officer of the rank immediately above squadron leader.

winger, wingers
(noun) In football or hockey, the wingers are attacking players who play mainly on the far right or left of the pitch.

wing nut, wing nuts
(noun) A wing nut is a threaded nut which is tightened by hand by means of two flat lugs or wings projecting from its centre.

wingspan
(noun) The wingspan of a bird, insect, or aeroplane is the distance from the end of one wing to the end of the other.

wink, winks, winking, winked
1 (verb) When you wink, you close one eye briefly, often as a signal that something is a joke or a secret.
2 (noun) A wink is the closing of your eye when you wink.
3 (verb) If a light winks, it shines in short flashes.
4 (an informal phrase) If you have **forty winks**, you sleep for a short while.
5 If you **tip someone the wink**, you give them a hint or a piece of important information.
6 (verb) To wink at something means to pretend

not to notice it, e.g. *The authorities winked at small-scale corruption.*
[from Old English *wincian* meaning 'to close your eyes']

winkle, winkles, winkling, winkled
1 (noun) A winkle is a small hard-shelled sea-snail with a soft edible body.
2 (verb) If you winkle information out of someone, you get them to give it to you.

winkle-picker, winkle-pickers
(noun) Winkle-pickers are shoes or boots with long pointed toes, popular in the 1950s.

winner, winners
(noun) The winner of a prize, race, or competition is the person or thing that wins it.

Similar words: victor, champion, champ

winning
1 (adjective) The winning team or entry in a competition is the one that has won.
2 (plural noun) Your winnings are the money you have won in a competition or by gambling.
3 (adjective) attractive and charming, e.g. *a winning smile.*

winnow, winnows, winnowing, winnowed
(verb) To winnow grain means to separate the chaff by means of a wind or current of air.
[from Old English *windwian* meaning 'to winnow']

wino, winos (pronounced **why**-no)
(noun) A wino is someone who is an alcoholic, especially someone with nowhere to live and no job.

winsome (pronounced **win**-sum)
(adjective; a literary word) charming and attractive, e.g. *a winsome smile.*
[from Old English *wynn* meaning 'joy' and *-sum* meaning '-some']

winter, winters, wintering, wintered
1 (noun) Winter is the season between autumn and spring.
2 (verb; a formal use) To winter somewhere means to spend the winter there.

wintry
1 (adjective) Something wintry has features that are typical of winter, e.g. *a cold wintry sky.*
2 If you describe a person's behaviour or expression as wintry, you mean they seem cold and unfriendly, e.g. *a wintry smile.*

wipe, wipes, wiping, wiped
1 (verb) If you wipe something, you rub its surface lightly to remove dirt or liquid.
2 If you wipe dirt or liquid off something, you remove it using a cloth or your hands, e.g. *He wiped the tears from his eyes.*
3 If you wipe a tape, you remove the sounds or pictures recorded on it.
4 (an informal phrase) If you **wipe the floor with** someone, you defeat them totally.

wipe out
(phrasal verb) To wipe out people or places means to destroy them completely.

wire, wires, wiring, wired
1 (noun) Wire is metal in the form of a long, thin, flexible thread which can be used to make or fasten things or to conduct an electric current.
2 (verb) If you wire one thing to another, you fasten them together using wire.
3 If you wire something or wire it up, you connect it so that electricity can pass through it.
4 (an informal phrase) If someone **gets their wires crossed**, they become confused and misunderstand something.
5 (noun) If you send someone a wire, you send them a telegram.
wired (adjective).

wireless, wirelesses
(noun; an old-fashioned word) A wireless is a radio.

wiretapping
Wiretapping involves making a secret connection in order to listen to someone's telephone conversations.

wire wool
(noun) Wire wool consists of very thin wire twisted together and used to clean metal objects, especially kitchen equipment.

wiring
(noun) The wiring in a building is the system of wires that supply electricity to the rooms.

wiry, wirier, wiriest
1 (adjective) Wiry people are thin but with strong muscles.
2 Wiry things are stiff and rough to the touch, e.g. *wiry black hair.*

wisdom
1 (noun) Wisdom is the ability to use experience and knowledge in order to make sensible decisions and judgments.
2 Wisdom is also the store of knowledge that a society or culture has collected over a long period of time.
3 If you talk about the wisdom of an action or a decision, you are talking about how sensible it is.
[from Old English *wis* + *-dom* meaning 'wise state' or 'wise condition']

wisdom tooth, wisdom teeth
(noun) Your wisdom teeth are the four molar teeth at the back of your mouth which grow much later than other teeth.

wise, wiser, wisest
1 (adjective) Someone who is wise can use their experience and knowledge to make sensible decisions and judgments.
2 If you say that someone is **none the wiser** or **no wiser**, you mean that they know no more about something than they did before, e.g. *I read the article, but I'm none the wiser.*
3 (an informal phrase) If you **get wise** to a situation, you find out about it.

Similar words: (sense 1) sage, sagacious

-wise
1 (prefix) -wise means behaving like someone or something, e.g. *I edged crabwise to my seat.*
2 -wise can also indicate that one aspect of

something is true, e.g. *We're all Socialists vote-wise.*

wisecrack, wisecracks
(noun) A wisecrack is a clever remark, intended to be amusing but often unkind, e.g. *He made some wisecrack about her clothes.*

wish, wishes, wishing, wished
1 (noun) A wish is a longing or desire for something, often something difficult to achieve or obtain.
2 A wish is something desired or wanted, e.g. *his last wish.*
3 (plural noun) Good wishes are expressions of hope that someone will be happy or successful, e.g. *My parents send their best wishes.*
4 (verb) If you wish to do something, you want to do it, e.g. *We wish to marry next month.*
5 If you wish something were the case, you would like it to be the case, but know it is not very likely, e.g. *I often wish I were wealthy.*
6 (phrase) If you say you **would not wish something on** someone, you mean you would not want them to have to suffer it, e.g. *I would not wish this illness on my worst enemy.*
[from Old English *wyscan* meaning 'to have a desire for']

wishbone, wishbones
(noun) A wishbone is a V-shaped bone above the breastbone in most birds. The bone is sometimes pulled apart by two people after the meat has been eaten, and the person with the longer part makes a wish.

wishful thinking
(noun) If someone's hope or wish is wishful thinking, it is unlikely to come true.

wishy-washy
(adjective; an informal word) feeble and half-hearted, e.g. *They supported us in a rather wishy-washy way.*

wisp, wisps
1 (noun) A wisp of grass or hair is a small, thin, untidy bunch of it, e.g. *birds carrying wisps of hay in their beaks.*
2 A wisp of smoke is a long, thin streak of it.
wispy (adjective).

wisteria (pronounced wiss-**teer**-ee-a)
(noun) Wisteria is a woody climbing plant with blue, purple, or white flowers in large drooping clusters.
[named after Casper *Wistar* (1761-1818), an American anatomist]

wistful
(adjective) sadly thinking about something, especially something you want but cannot have, e.g. *She had a last wistful look around the flat.*
wistfully (adverb), **wistfulness** (noun).

wit, wits
1 (noun) Wit is the ability to use words or ideas in an amusing and clever way.
2 If someone does something sensible and practical, you can say they had the wit to do it, e.g. *No-one had the wit to bring a bottle-opener.*
3 (plural noun) Your wits are the ability to think

and act quickly in a difficult situation, e.g. *She used her wits to outsmart the enemy.*
4 (phrase) If someone is **at their wits' end**, they are so worried and exhausted by problems or difficulties that they do not know what to do.
5 (a formal, old-fashioned use) **To wit** means that is to say, e.g. *We speak in a language they don't know: to wit, English.*

witch, witches
(noun) A witch is a woman claimed to have magic powers and to be able to use them for good or evil.
[from Old English *wicca* meaning 'witch']

witchcraft
(noun) Witchcraft is the skill or art of using magic powers, especially evil ones.

Similar words: wizardry, sorcery, black magic

witch doctor, witch doctors
(noun) A witch doctor is a man in some societies, especially in Africa, who appears to have magic powers which he can use to cure sickness and sometimes to harm people.

witch hazel, witch hazels
1 (noun) A witch hazel is a winter-flowering garden shrub.
2 Witch hazel is a liquid made from the bark and leaves of the witch hazel shrub. It is put onto bruised or sore skin to heal it.

witch-hunt, witch-hunts
(noun) A witch-hunt is a campaign to find, expose, or punish people who hold unpopular or unusual views while claiming that the aim of the campaign is to protect the interests of the public.
witch-hunting (noun).

with
1 (preposition) With someone means in their company, e.g. *Walk home with me.*
2 With is used to show who your opponent is in a fight or competition, e.g. *at war with France.*
3 With can mean using or having, e.g. *Eat with a knife and fork... a man with a beard.*
4 With is used to show how someone does something or how they feel, e.g. *He looked at her with surprise... This left him quaking with fear.*
5 With can mean concerning, e.g. *a problem with maternity allowance.*
6 If you do something with something happening, you do it while it is happening, e.g. *He put his hat on with Perkins watching him.*
7 With can introduce a factor that affects something, e.g. *With all the traffic jams, it wouldn't be economic.*
8 With is used to show support, e.g. *I'm with the Government on this.*
9 (an informal phrase) **With it** means fashionable and up-to-date.

withdraw, withdraws, withdrawing, withdrew, withdrawn
1 (verb) If you withdraw something, you remove it or take it out, e.g. *I withdrew all my money from the account.*
2 If you withdraw to another place, you leave

where you are and go there, e.g. *He withdrew into his office.*
3 If you withdraw from an activity, you back out of it, e.g. *She withdrew from the argument.*
4 If you withdraw a remark, you say that you wish to change or deny it.

withdrawal, withdrawals
1 (noun) The withdrawal of something is the act or process of removing it or taking it away, e.g. *the withdrawal of troops.*
2 The withdrawal of a statement is the act of saying formally that you wish to change or deny it.
3 Withdrawal is behaviour in which someone does not want to have anything to do with other people, e.g. *He has periods of withdrawal.*
4 A withdrawal is an amount of money you take from your bank or building society account.

withdrawal symptoms
(noun) Withdrawal symptoms are the unpleasant effects suffered by someone who has suddenly stopped taking a drug to which they are addicted.

withdrawn
1 Withdrawn is the past participle of **withdraw.**
2 (adjective) unusually shy or quiet.

wither, withers, withering, withered
1 (verb) When something withers or withers away, it becomes weaker until it no longer exists.
2 If a plant withers, or if heat or lack of water withers it, it wilts or shrivels up and dies.
3 (plural noun) A horse's withers are the highest part of its back behind its neck.

Similar words: (senses 1 and 2) shrivel, atrophy

withering
(adjective) A withering look or remark makes you feel ashamed, stupid, or inferior.

withhold, withholds, withholding, withheld
(verb; a formal word) If you withhold something that someone wants, you do not let them have it.

within
1 (preposition and adverb) Within means in or inside.
2 (preposition) Within can mean not going beyond certain limits, e.g. *Keep within your budget.*
3 Within can mean before a period of time has passed, e.g. *Within weeks the trees budded.*

without
1 (preposition) Without means not having, feeling, or showing, e.g. *She was without ambition.*
2 Without can mean not using, e.g. *He did it without a screwdriver.*
3 Without can mean not in someone's company, or not living or working with someone, e.g. *He couldn't face life without her.*
4 Without can indicate that something does not happen when something else happens, e.g. *I knocked twice, without reply.*
5 (preposition and adverb; an old-fashioned use) Without means outside, e.g. *without the city walls.*

withstand, withstands, withstanding, withstood
(verb) When something or someone withstands a force or action, they survive it or do not give in to it, e.g. *The walls had to withstand high winds.*

witless
(adjective; a formal word) stupid or silly.

witness, witnesses, witnessing, witnessed
1 (noun) A witness is someone who has seen an event such as an accident and can describe what happened.
2 A witness is also someone who appears in a court of law to say what they know about a crime or other event.
3 A witness is also someone who writes their name on a document that someone else has signed, to confirm that it is really that person's signature.
4 (verb; a formal use) If you witness an event, you see it.
5 If you witness someone's signature, you write your own name near to it to confirm that it is really their signature.
6 (a formal phrase) If something **bears witness to** something, it shows that it exists or happened.
[from Old English *witan* meaning 'to know']

Similar words: (sense 1) bystander, onlooker, eyewitness

witness-box, witness-boxes
(noun) The witness-box in a court of law is the place where people stand to give evidence.

witter, witters, wittering, wittered
(verb; an informal word) If you say that someone is wittering on about something, you mean they are saying a lot of silly and boring things.

witticism, witticisms (pronounced **wit**-tiss-izm)
(noun) A witticism is a clever and amusing remark or joke.

wittingly
(adverb; a formal word) deliberately or knowingly, e.g. *Wittingly or not, he had ruined the plan.*

witty, wittier, wittiest
(adjective) amusing in a clever way.
wittily (adverb).

wives the plural of **wife.**

wizard, wizards
1 (noun) A wizard is a man with magic powers, usually in a fairy story.
2 A wizard is also an expert at something, e.g. *a financial wizard.*

wizardry
(noun) Wizardry is something that is very cleverly done, e.g. *technological wizardry.*

wizened (pronounced **wiz**-nd)
(adjective) having a wrinkled skin, especially with age, e.g. *a wizened little man.*
[from Old English *wisnian* meaning 'dry up']

woad
(noun) Woad was a blue dye used by the ancient Britons to paint their bodies.
[from Old English *wad*, the plant from which the dye was obtained]

wobble, wobbles, wobbling, wobbled
1 (verb) If something wobbles, it shakes or moves from side to side because it is loose or unsteady, e.g. *She wobbled and then fell.*
2 If your voice wobbles, it trembles or shakes.
[from German *wabbeln* meaning 'waver']

wobbly
1 (adjective) unsteady, e.g. *a wobbly chair.*
2 If you feel wobbly, you feel weak and shaky, because you are ill, afraid, or shocked.

wodge, wodges
(noun; an informal word) A wodge is a large amount or thick lump of something, e.g. *I cut myself a wodge of cheese.*

woe, woes (a literary word)
1 (noun) Woe is great unhappiness or sorrow.
2 (plural noun) Someone's woes are their problems or misfortunes.

woebegone (pronounced woe-bee-gon)
(adjective; a formal word) looking sad or miserable.

woeful (a formal word)
1 (adjective) very sad, e.g. *the lovers' woeful farewell.*
2 very bad or deplorable, e.g. *a woeful standard of work.*
woefully (adverb).

wok, woks
(noun) A wok is a large bowl-shaped metal pan used for Chinese-style cooking.
[a Chinese word]

woke the past tense of wake.

woken the past participle of wake.

wolf, wolves; wolfs, wolfing, wolfed
1 (noun) A wolf is a wild animal related to the dog that hunts in packs and kills other animals for food.
2 (verb; an informal use) If you wolf food or wolf it down, you eat it up quickly and greedily.
3 (phrase) If someone **cries wolf**, they ask for help so often when they do not need it that people do not believe them when they really are in danger or trouble.
4 If you **keep the wolf from the door**, you manage to provide food and other necessary things for yourself or your family.
5 A **wolf in sheep's clothing** is someone who appears to be nice or harmless, but is in fact rather dangerous.
wolfish (adjective).

wolfhound, wolfhounds
(noun) A wolfhound is a very large dog used in the past to hunt wolves.

wolf-whistle, wolf-whistles
(noun) A wolf-whistle is a whistle usually made by a man to show he likes a woman's appearance.

woman, women
1 (noun) A woman is an adult female human being.
2 Woman can refer to women in general, e.g. *man's inhumanity to woman.*
womanliness (noun).

[from Old English *wifmann* meaning 'woman human being']

womanhood
1 (noun) Womanhood is the state of being a woman rather than a girl, e.g. *She was on the threshold of womanhood.*
2 You can refer to women in general as womanhood, e.g. *a perfect specimen of English womanhood.*

womanish
(adjective) Womanish is used to describe a man who is thought to be weak and unmanly.

womanizer, womanizers; also spelled womaniser
(noun) A womanizer is a man who has many casual sexual affairs with women.
womanizing (noun).

womankind
(noun) Womankind means all women in general.

womanly
(adjective) having qualities such as warmth and gentleness that are thought to be typical of a woman or suitable for a woman.

womb, wombs (pronounced woom)
(noun) A woman's womb is the part inside her body where her unborn baby grows. Womb is a non-technical word for uterus.

wombat, wombats (pronounced wom-bat)
(noun) A wombat is a short-legged furry Australian animal which makes burrows and eats plants.

Women's Institute, Women's Institutes
(noun) The Women's Institute is an organization for women in towns and villages throughout England and Wales.

Women's Liberation
(noun) Women's Liberation is the ideal that women should have the same social and economic rights and privileges as men.

wonder, wonders, wondering, wondered
1 (verb) If you wonder about something, you think about it with curiosity or doubt.
2 If you wonder at something, you are surprised and amazed at it, e.g. *I wondered at her strength.*
3 (noun) A wonder is something or someone that surprises and amazes people, e.g. *the wonders of modern technology.*
4 Wonder is a feeling of surprise and amazement.
5 (adjective) extremely clever or skilful, e.g. *the wonder boy of snooker.*
wonderingly (adverb).

Similar words: (sense 3) marvel, miracle, phenomenon, prodigy

wonderful
1 (adjective) making you feel very happy and pleased, e.g. *It was wonderful to breathe fresh air again.*
2 very impressive, e.g. *Heart transplants are wonderful things.*
wonderfully (adverb).

Similar words: (sense 2) miraculous, marvellous, wondrous

wonderland, wonderlands

1 (noun) Wonderland is an imaginary land of marvels and wonders.
2 You can refer to a place as a wonderland when it seems unusually beautiful, e.g. *a winter wonderland.*

wonderment

(noun) Wonderment is amazement and admiration, e.g. *I stood shaking my head in wonderment.*

wondrous

(adjective; a literary word) amazing and impressive.

wonky, wonkier, wonkiest (an informal word)

1 (adjective) shaky or unsteady, e.g. *a wonky table.*
2 unreliable and likely to break down, e.g. *My knee's wonky.*
[from Old English *wancol* meaning 'wavering' or 'unsteady']

wont (rhymes with **don't**)

1 (adjective; an old-fashioned word) If someone is wont to do something, they do it often, e.g. *They were wont to take long walks in the evening.*
2 (phrase) If you say that someone is doing something **as is their wont**, you mean it is something they usually do, e.g. *They were all talking, as is their wont, about cars.*
[from Old English *gewunian* meaning 'to be accustomed to']

woo, woos, wooing, wooed

1 (verb) If you woo people, you try to get them to help or support you, e.g. *She hoped to woo the voters in her ward.*
2 (an old-fashioned use) When a man woos a woman, he tries to make himself seem attractive to her, because he wants to marry her.

wood, woods

1 (noun) Wood is the substance which forms the trunks and branches of trees.
2 A wood is a large area of trees growing near each other.
3 (phrase) If you **can't see the wood for the trees**, you are so involved with the details of a situation or activity that you cannot see or understand its general purpose or important features.
4 If you say that someone is **not out of the woods yet**, you mean they are still involved in a difficult or dangerous situation.

Similar words: (sense 2) woodland, copse, thicket

woodcock

(noun) A woodcock is a game bird like a large snipe.

woodcut, woodcuts

(noun) A woodcut is a print made from an engraved design cut into a block of wood.

wooded

(adjective) covered in trees, e.g. *a wooded valley.*

wooden

1 (adjective) made of wood, e.g. *a wooden box.*
2 Behaviour which is wooden is stiff and shows little life or vigour, e.g. *His performances have become wooden and dull.*
woodenly (adverb).

wooden spoon, wooden spoons

(phrase) If a person or team **gets the wooden spoon**, it means they come last in a competition.

woodland, woodlands

(noun) Woodland is land that is mostly covered with trees.

woodlouse, woodlice

(noun) A woodlouse is a very small grey creature that looks rather like an insect. It has seven pairs of legs and lives in damp places.

woodpecker, woodpeckers

(noun) A woodpecker is a climbing bird with a long, sharp beak that it uses to drill holes into trees to find insects.

wood pulp

(noun) Wood pulp is wood that has been crushed to a pulp in order to be used to make paper.

woodwind

(adjective) Woodwind instruments are musical instruments such as flutes, oboes, clarinets, and bassoons, that are played by being blown into.

woodwork

1 (noun) Woodwork refers to the parts of a house, such as stairs, doors or window-frames, that are made of wood.
2 Woodwork is the craft or skill of making things out of wood.

woodworm, woodworm or woodworms

1 (noun) Woodworm are the larvae of a kind of beetle. They make holes in wood by feeding on it.
2 Woodworm is damage caused to wood by woodworm making holes in it.

woody, woodier, woodiest

1 (adjective) Woody plants have hard tough stems.
2 A woody area has a lot of trees in it.

woof, woofs

1 (noun) The woof is the crosswise yarns in a piece of woven cloth.
2 A woof is the sound that a dog makes when it barks.

wool, wools

1 (noun) Wool is the hair that grows on sheep and some other animals.
2 Wool is also yarn spun from the wool of animals which is used to knit, weave, and make such things as clothes, blankets, and carpets.
3 (phrase) If you **pull the wool over someone's eyes**, you deliberately tell them something that is not true in order to deceive them.

woolgathering

(noun) Woolgathering is absentminded daydreaming.

woollen, woollens

1 (adjective) made wholly or partly from wool.
2 (noun) Woollens are clothes made of wool.

woolly, woollies; woollier, woolliest
1 (adjective) made of wool or looking like wool,
e.g. *a woolly cap.*
2 (noun) A woolly is a woollen garment,
especially a pullover.
3 (adjective) If you describe people or their ideas
and thoughts as woolly, you mean that they
seem confused and unclear.

woolsack
(noun) The woolsack is the seat of the Lord
Chancellor in the House of Lords.

woozy, woozier, wooziest
(adjective; an informal word) dazed, unsteady,
and unable to think clearly.

word, words, wording, worded
1 (noun) A word is a single unit of language in
speech or writing which has a meaning.
2 A word can mean something brief said, such as
a remark, statement, or conversation, e.g. *a word
of warning... Can we have a word?*
3 A word can also be a message, e.g. *The word
got out that he was leaving.*
4 Your word is a promise that you make to
someone, e.g. *I give you my word.*
5 A word can mean a command, e.g. *Give the
word, and I'll go.*
6 (verb) When you word something, you choose
your words in order to express your ideas
accurately or acceptably, e.g. *How would you
word the advertisement?*
7 (plural noun) The words of a play or song are
the spoken or sung text.
8 (noun) In Christianity, the Word or the Word
of God, is the message and teachings of the Bible.
9 (phrase) If you **have words** with someone, you
have an argument with them.
10 If someone **has the last word** in an argument
or discussion, they make the final comment that
settles the issue.
11 If something is **the last word** in something
such as comfort or fashion, it is the finest
example or the latest in design, e.g. *The car was
the last word in luxury.*

wording
(noun) The wording of a piece of writing or a
speech is the words used in it, especially when
these words have been carefully chosen to have
a certain effect.

word-perfect
(adjective) If you are word-perfect, you are able
to repeat from memory the exact words of
something you have learned.

wordplay
(noun) Wordplay is the making of jokes by clever
use of words.

word processing
(noun) Word processing is the production,
storage, and organization of documents, letters,
and other written material by means of an
electronic word processor.

word processor, word processors
(noun) A word processor is an electronic
machine which has a keyboard and a visual
display unit and which is used to produce, store,
and organize printed material.

wordy, wordier, wordiest
(adjective) using too many words, e.g. *a rather
wordy essay.*

work, works, working, worked
1 (verb) People who work have a job which they
are paid to do, e.g. *He was working in a shop.*
2 (noun) People who have work or who are in
work have a job which they are paid to do, e.g. *I
can't find work.*
3 Work is the tasks that have to be done.
4 (verb) When you work, you do the tasks that
your job involves or that the situation demands.
5 (noun) A work is something done or made
as a result of effort, e.g. *a work of art.*
6 (verb) To work the land means to cultivate it.
7 If someone works a machine, they control or
operate it.
8 If metal or other material is worked, it is
shaped or formed in a particular way.
9 If a machine works, it operates properly and
effectively, e.g. *The clock won't work.*
10 If something such as an idea or a system
works, it is successful, e.g. *Does democracy
really work?*
11 If something works its way into a particular
position, it gradually moves there, e.g. *the rope
worked loose.*
12 To work someone into a state of emotion
means to arouse or provoke that emotion in
them, e.g. *She worked herself into a rage.*
13 (noun) A works is a place where a number of
people are employed to make something or
where an industrial process is carried out, e.g.
the gas works.
14 (plural noun) Works are large scale building,
digging, or general construction activities, e.g.
Civil engineering works caused a traffic jam.
15 (noun) In physics, work is transfer of energy.
It is calculated by multiplying a force by the
distance through which its point of application
moves. Work is measured in joules.

Similar words: (sense 7) drive, handle
(sense 9) go, function, run

work off
(phrasal verb) If you work off a feeling, you
gradually overcome it by doing something
energetic or violent, e.g. *He worked off his anger
by chopping wood all afternoon.*

work out
1 (phrasal verb) If you work out a solution to a
problem, you find the solution.
2 If a situation works out in a particular way, it
happens in that way.
3 If you work out, you practise physical
exercises or do athletic training.

work up
1 (phrasal verb) If you work up to something,
you gradually progress towards it.
2 If you work yourself up or work someone else
up, you make yourself or the other person very
upset or angry about something.

3 If you work up a feeling, you develop it, e.g. *I worked up a healthy appetite.*
worked up (adjective).

workable
(adjective) Something workable can operate successfully or can be used for a particular purpose, e.g. *Is it a workable system?*

workaday
(adjective) ordinary and quite usual, e.g. *a quiet workaday man.*

workaholic, workaholics
(noun) A workaholic is a person who finds it difficult to stop working and do other things.

workday, workdays
(noun) A workday is a day on which work is done, usually for an agreed number of hours.

worker, workers
1 (noun) A worker is a person employed in a particular industry or business and who has no responsibility for it.
2 A worker is also someone who does a particular kind of job, e.g. *a research worker.*
3 A worker is a female member of a colony of ants, bees, or wasps that cannot produce any young but searches for food and cares for the colony's larvae.

workforce, workforces
(noun) The workforce is the number of people who work in a particular industry, company, region, or country.

workhorse, workhorses
1 (noun) A workhorse is a horse used for a particular job.
2 (an informal use) A workhorse is a person who regularly takes on a large amount of work.

workhouse, workhouses
(noun) In the past a workhouse was a building to which very poor people were sent and made to work in return for food and shelter.

working, workings
1 (adjective) Working people have jobs which they are paid to do.
2 A working day or week is the number of hours that are worked during a day or a week.
3 A person's working life is the period of their life in which they have a job or are of a suitable age to have a job.
4 Working conditions or practices are those which are found in a job or place of work.
5 Working can mean sufficient to be useful or to achieve what is required, e.g. *A working majority.*
6 (noun) The working of a mathematical calculation is a record of the steps by which the solution is reached, e.g. *Show all working on your answer paper.*
7 The workings of a piece of equipment, an organization, or a system are the ways in which it operates, e.g. *The workings of Wall Street are analyzed by the students.*

working class, working classes
(noun) The working class or working classes are the group of people in society who do not own

much property and who do jobs which involve physical rather than intellectual skills.

working party, working parties
(noun) A working party is a committee set up to study and report on a specific issue or problem.

workload, workloads
(noun) The workload of a person or a machine is the amount of work that they have to do.

workman, workmen
(noun) A workman is a man whose job involves using physical rather than intellectual skills.

workmanlike
(adjective) showing efficiency, skill, and hard work.

workmanship
(noun) Workmanship is the skill with which something is made or a job completed.

workmate, workmates
(noun) Someone's workmate is the fellow worker with whom they do their job.

workout, workouts
(noun) A workout is a session of physical exercise or training.

workshop, workshops
1 (noun) A workshop is a room or building that contains tools or machinery used for making or repairing things, e.g. *an engineering workshop.*
2 A workshop on a particular subject is a period of discussion or practical work in which a group of people learn about the subject, e.g. *a voice workshop.*

workshy
(adjective) not wanting to work.

work-to-rule
(noun) A work-to-rule is a form of industrial action in which workers stop doing any extra work and follow all the working rules with the aim of slowing down production.

world, worlds
1 (noun) The world is the earth, the planet we live on.
2 You can use world to refer to people generally, e.g. *in the eyes of the world.*
3 The world refers to all the societies and ways of life of people living on this planet, e.g. *The world seems a smaller place now.*
4 Someone's world is the life they lead and the things they experience, e.g. *We're in different worlds now, you and I.*
5 World can also mean social and public life, e.g. *the world beyond the village.*
6 (adjective) World is used to describe someone or something that is one of the best or most important of its kind, e.g. *a world power.*
7 (noun) A world is a division or section of the earth, its history, or its people, such as the Arab World, or the Ancient World.
8 A particular world is a field of activity and the people involved in it, e.g. *the world of television.*
9 (phrase) If you **think the world** of someone, you like or admire them very much.
10 If someone has **gone** or **come up in the world,**

they are richer and have a higher social status than they used to have.
[from Old English *weorold* from *wer* meaning 'man' and *ald* meaning 'age']

worldly, worldlier, worldliest
1 (adjective) relating to the ordinary activities of life rather than spiritual things, e.g. *put aside worldly things.*
2 experienced and knowledgeable about life.
worldliness (noun).

worldly-wise
(adjective; a formal or literary word) sophisticated, experienced, and knowledgeable about life.

world war, world wars
(noun) A world war is a war that involves countries all over the world.

worldwide
(adjective) throughout the world, e.g. *a worldwide economic depression.*

worm, worms
1 (noun) A worm is a small, boneless, legless animal with a long, thin body which lives in the soil or off other creatures.
2 A worm is an insect such as a beetle or moth at a very early stage in its life, e.g. *The apples had worms in them.*
3 (verb) If you worm an animal, you give it medicine in order to kill the worms that are living as parasites in its intestines.
4 (phrase) If you **worm your way** somewhere, you move there slowly and with difficulty.
5 If you **worm your way into** someone's confidence or affection, you gradually make them trust or like you, often in order to gain some advantage.
wormy (adjective).

worm out
(phrasal verb) If you worm information out of someone, you gradually find it out from them by constant questioning, even though they had wanted to keep it secret.

wormcast, wormcasts
(noun) A wormcast is a small coil of earth or sand produced by a worm and left on the surface of the ground.

worm-eaten
(adjective) damaged and holed by insects, e.g. *an old, worm-eaten piece of furniture.*

wormwood
(noun) Wormwood is a woody plant with a very bitter taste which is used in making medicines and alcoholic drinks.

worn
1 Worn is the past participle of **wear**.
2 (adjective) damaged or thin because of long use.
3 looking old or exhausted, e.g. *He looked pinched and worn.*

worn-out
1 (adjective) used until it is too thin or too damaged to be of further use, e.g. *a worn-out old sofa.*

2 extremely tired, e.g. *Sit down, you look worn-out.*

worried
(adjective) unhappy and anxious about a problem or about something unpleasant that might happen.
worriedly (adverb).

Similar words: perturbed, uneasy, concerned, apprehensive, anxious

worrier, worriers
(noun) A worrier is someone who spends a lot of time thinking about problems and unpleasant things that might happen.

worry, worries, worrying, worried
1 (verb) If you worry, you feel anxious, fearful, and uneasy about a problem or about something unpleasant that might happen.
2 If something worries you, it causes you to feel uneasy or fearful, e.g. *It worried him to think that Kay was alone.*
3 If you worry someone with a problem, you disturb or bother them by telling them about it, e.g. *don't worry me with details.*
4 If a dog worries sheep or other animals, it frightens or harms them by chasing them, or by biting and shaking them.
5 (noun) Worry is a feeling of unhappiness and unease caused by a problem or by thinking of something unpleasant that might happen, e.g. *Housing was their main source of worry.*
6 A worry is a person or thing that causes you to feel anxious or uneasy, e.g. *The cost of fuel is a major worry for many old people.*
worrying (adjective).
[from Old English *wyrgan* meaning 'strangle']

Similar words: (sense 1) agonize, fret
(sense 2) bother, alarm, concern, perturb, trouble
(sense 5) anxiety, apprehension, concern

worry beads
(noun) Worry beads are a string of beads that are supposed to calm or relax you when you play with or finger them. Worry beads originated in the Middle East or Greece.

worse
1 (adjective) Worse is the comparative form of **bad** and **badly**.
2 If someone who is ill gets worse, they become more ill than before.
3 (phrase) If someone or something is **none the worse** for something, they have not been harmed by it, e.g. *He was none the worse for his fall.*

worsen, worsens, worsening, worsened
(verb) If a situation worsens or if something worsens it, it becomes more difficult, unpleasant, or unacceptable, e.g. *Oil pollution seems to be worsening.*

Similar words: deteriorate, decline, degenerate, aggravate, compound, exacerbate

worse off
1 (adjective) having less money than before or

than someone else, e.g. *The budget made the elderly worse off.*
2 in a more unfavourable or unpleasant situation than before or than someone else.

worship, worships, worshipping, worshipped
1 (verb) If you worship a god, you show your love and respect by praying or singing hymns.
2 If you worship someone or something, you love them or admire them very much so that often you do not notice their faults or weaknesses.
3 (noun) Worship is the feeling of respect, love, or admiration you feel for something or someone.
worshipful (adjective), **worshipper** (noun).
[from Old English *weorth* meaning 'worth' and *-ship* meaning 'condition', 'rank', or 'position']

Similar words: (sense 2) adore, idolize, venerate, revere
(sense 3) adoration, adulation, homage, veneration, reverence

worst
1 (adjective and adverb) Worst is the superlative of **bad** and **badly, e.g.** *the worst thing that happened... the worst affected areas.*
2 (phrase) You use **at worst** to show that you are looking at a situation in the most unfavourable way, e.g. *At best he is forceful, at worst ruthless.*
3 If you say that something might happen **if the worst comes to the worst**, you mean that it might happen if the situation develops in the most unfavourable way, e.g. *If the worst comes to the worst, I'll have to sell the house.*

worsted (pronounced **wus**-tid)
(noun) Worsted is a fine woollen cloth used to make jackets, trousers, and skirts.

worth
1 (preposition) If something is worth a sum of money, it has that value, e.g. *It's worth £50,000.*
2 If something is worth doing or worth having, it deserves to be done or deserves to be had.
3 (noun) A particular amount of money's worth of something is the quantity of it that you can buy for that money, e.g. *£5's worth of sweets.*
4 Someone's worth is the value, usefulness, or importance they are considered to have.
[from Old English *weorth*]

worthless
1 (adjective) having no real value or use, e.g. *The goods were worthless when they finally arrived.*
2 without skills or qualities, e.g. *He was worthless as a painter.*
worthlessness (noun).

worthwhile
(adjective) important enough or valuable enough to justify the time, money, or effort spent on it, e.g. *A trip to London is always worthwhile.*

worthy, worthier, worthiest
1 (adjective) If someone or something is worthy of something, they deserve it because they have the qualities or abilities required, e.g. *He was a worthy winner.*
2 A worthy person deserves people's respect or admiration.
worthily (adverb), **worthiness** (noun).

would
1 (verb) You use would to say what someone thought was going to happen, e.g. *I felt confident that everything would be all right.*
2 You use would when you are referring to the result or effect of a possible situation, e.g. *If you can manage to help I would be very grateful.*
3 You use would when referring to someone's willingness to do something, e.g. *I wouldn't go on holiday with him if you paid me.*
4 You use would in polite questions, e.g. *Would you like a drink?*

would-be
(adjective) wanting to be or claiming to be, e.g. *a would-be writer.*

wound, wounds, wounding, wounded
1 (noun) A wound is an injury to part of your body, especially a cut in your skin and flesh, which is caused by a knife, gun, or other weapon.
2 (verb) If someone wounds you, they damage your body using a gun, knife, or other weapon.
3 If you are wounded by what someone says or does, your feelings are hurt.
4 (noun) A wound is also great unhappiness or damage to a person's mind which is caused by an upsetting experience.
5 (phrase) Something that **opens old wounds** reminds someone about an upsetting experience in the past which they would prefer to forget.
wounded (adjective), **wounding** (adjective).

wow
1 (exclamation) Wow is an expression of admiration or surprise.
2 (noun; an informal use) If you describe someone or something as a wow, you think they are amazingly successful or attractive.

WPC, WPCs
(noun) A WPC is a female member of the police force. WPC is an abbreviation for 'woman police constable'.

wpm
wpm is the written abbreviation for 'words per minute' and is usually used to show the speed at which a person can type or take shorthand.

WRAC
(noun) The WRAC is a branch of the army which only women can join. WRAC is an abbreviation for 'Women's Royal Army Corps'.

WRAF
(noun) The WRAF is a branch of the Air Force which only women can join. WRAF is an abbreviation for 'Women's Royal Air Force'.

wraith, wraiths (pronounced **rayth**)
(noun; a literary word) A wraith is a ghost or apparition.
[a Scottish word]

wrangle, wrangles, wrangling, wrangled
(verb) If you wrangle with someone, you argue noisily or angrily, often about something unimportant.
wrangle (noun), **wrangling** (noun).
[from German *wrangeln*]

wrap, wraps, wrapping, wrapped
1 (verb) If you wrap something or wrap something up, you fold a piece of paper or cloth tightly around it to cover or enclose it.
2 If you wrap paper or cloth round something, you put or fold the paper round it.
3 If you wrap your arms, fingers, or legs round something, you coil them round it.
4 (noun) A wrap is a shawl worn round your shoulders.
5 (phrase) If you **keep something under wraps**, you keep it secret.

wrap up
1 (verb) If you wrap up, you put warm clothes on, e.g. *Wrap up well. It's cold today.*
2 (an informal use) If you wrap up something such as an agreement, you complete it in a satisfactory way.

wrapped up
(adjective; an informal use) If you are wrapped up in a person or thing, you give that person or thing all your attention.

wrapper, wrappers
(noun) A wrapper is a piece of paper, plastic, or foil which covers and protects something that you buy, e.g. *A sweet wrapper.*

wrapping, wrappings
(noun) Wrapping is the material used to cover and protect something.

wrath (pronounced **roth**)
(noun; a literary word) Wrath is great anger, e.g. *The wrath of God.*

wreak, wreaks, wreaking, wreaked (pronounced **reek**)
1 (verb) To wreak havoc or damage means to cause it.
2 (a literary use) If you wreak vengeance on someone, you inflict it on them.
[from Old English *wrecan*]

wreath, wreaths (pronounced **reeth**)
1 (noun) A wreath is an arrangement of flowers and leaves, often in the shape of a circle, which is put on a grave as a sign of remembrance for the dead person.
2 A wreath is also a circle of leaves or flowers worn round the head or neck as decoration or as an honour, e.g. *a laurel wreath for the winner.*
[from Old English *writha* meaning 'coil' or 'twisted band']

wreathe, wreathes, wreathing, wreathed (rhymes with **breathe**)
(verb; a literary word) If something is wreathed in something else, it is surrounded by it, e.g. *The sun rose wreathed in mist.*

wreck, wrecks, wrecking, wrecked
1 (verb) If someone wrecks something, they break it, destroy it, or spoil it completely.
2 If a ship is wrecked, it is has been so badly damaged that it can no longer sail.
3 (noun) A wreck is a ship, car, plane, or other vehicle which has been badly damaged in an accident.
4 If you say someone is a wreck, you mean that they are in a very poor physical or mental state

of health and cannot cope with life, e.g. *You'll end up a wreck if you don't rest.*
wrecked (adjective), **wrecker** (noun).

wreckage
(noun) Wreckage is what remains after something has been badly damaged or destroyed.

wren, wrens
(noun) A wren is a very small brown songbird.

WREN
(noun) The WRENs are a branch of the navy which only women can join. WREN is an abbreviation for 'Women's Royal Naval Service'.

wrench, wrenches, wrenching, wrenched
1 (verb) If you wrench something, you give it a sudden and violent twist or pull, especially to remove it from what it is attached to, e.g. *I wrenched the door off its hinges.*
2 If you wrench a limb or a joint, you twist and injure it.
3 (noun) A wrench is a metal tool with parts which can be adjusted to fit around nuts or bolts to loosen or tighten them.
4 If a parting from someone or something is a wrench, it is a painful parting to make.
[from Old English *wrencan* meaning 'turn' or 'twist']

wrest, wrests, wresting, wrested (pronounced **rest**)
(verb; a formal word) If you wrest something from someone else you take it from them violently or with effort, e.g. *He wrested the knife from her.*

wrestle, wrestles, wrestling, wrestled
1 (verb) If you wrestle someone or wrestle with them, you fight them by holding or throwing them, but not hitting them.
2 When you wrestle with a problem, you try to deal with it.
wrestler (noun).

Similar words: grapple, struggle

wrestling
(noun) Wrestling is a sport in which two people fight and try to win by throwing or pinning their opponent to the ground.

wretch, wretches
(noun; an old-fashioned word) A wretch is someone who is thought to be wicked or very unfortunate, e.g. *The wretch in the cell groaned.*
[from Old English *wrecca* meaning 'exile' or 'despised person']

wretched (pronounced **ret**-shid)
1 (adjective) very unhappy or unfortunate, e.g. *How that wretched woman suffered.*
2 very bad or of very poor quality, e.g. *Poverty meant she had a wretched diet.*
3 (an informal use) You use wretched to describe something or someone you feel angry about or dislike, e.g. *a wretched nuisance.*

wriggle, wriggles, wriggling, wriggled
1 (verb) If someone wriggles, they twist and turn their body or a part of their body using quick movements, e.g. *They wriggled their toes.*

2 If you wriggle somewhere, you move there by twisting and turning, e.g. *We had to wriggle under the fence.*
3 If you wriggle out of doing something that you do not want to do, you manage to avoid doing it.
[from Old German *wriggelen* meaning 'to wriggle a lot']

-wright, -wrights (pronounced **rite**)
(suffix) -wright is used to form nouns that refer to a person who creates, builds, or repairs something, e.g. *a playwright.*
[from Old English *wryhta* meaning 'craftsman']

wring, wrings, wringing, wrung
1 (verb) When you wring a wet cloth or wring it out, you squeeze the water out of it by twisting it.
2 If you wring something from someone or from a situation, you manage to get it with a lot of effort, e.g. *Wring the information out of her.*
3 If you wring your hands, you hold them together and twist and turn them, usually because you are worried or upset.
4 If someone wrings a bird's neck, they kill the bird by twisting and breaking its neck.
[from Old English *wringan*]

wrinkle, wrinkles, wrinkling, wrinkled
1 (noun) Wrinkles are lines in someone's skin, especially on the face, which form as they grow old.
2 (verb) If something wrinkles or if something wrinkles it, folds or lines develop on it, e.g. *New paint shouldn't wrinkle or peel.*
3 When you wrinkle your nose, forehead, or eyes, you tighten the muscles in your face so that the skin folds into several lines.
wrinkled (adjective), **wrinkly** (adjective).
[from Old English *wrinclian* meaning 'to wind around']

Similar words: (sense 1) crease, fold

wrist, wrists
(noun) Your wrist is the part of your body between your hand and your arm which bends when you move your hand.

wristwatch, wristwatches
(noun) A wristwatch is a watch with a strap or a band which you wear round your wrist.

writ, writs
1 (noun) A writ is a legal document that orders a person to do or not to do a particular thing.
2 (a formal phrase) If something is **writ large**, it is very obvious or in an exaggerated form, e.g. *This was the new Toryism writ large.*

write, writes, writing, wrote, written
1 (verb) When you write something, you use a pen or pencil to form letters, words, or numbers on a surface.
2 If you write something such as a poem, a book, or a piece of music, you create it.
3 When you write to someone or write them a letter, you give them information, ask them something, or express your feelings in a letter.
4 When someone writes something such as a cheque, they put the necessary information on it and sign it.

[from Old English *writan* meaning 'to scratch marks in wood']

write down
(phrasal verb) If you write something down, you record it on a piece of paper.

write into
(phrasal verb) If a detail is written into a contract or agreement, it is included in it.

write off
1 (phrasal verb) If you write off for something, you write and ask for it.
2 If you write off an amount of money or a debt, you accept that you are not going to get the money back.
3 (an informal use) If you write off a vehicle, you damage it so badly in a crash that it is not worth repairing.

write up
(phrasal verb) If you write up something, you write a full account of it, often using notes that you have previously made.

write-off, write-offs
(noun; an informal word) A write-off is anything that is so badly damaged or so badly done that it is not worth keeping.

writer, writers
1 (noun) A writer is a person who writes books, stories, or articles as a job.
2 The writer of something is the person who wrote it.

write-up, write-ups
(noun) A write-up is an article in a newspaper or magazine which describes or gives an opinion on something such as a play, film, or new product.

writhe, writhes, writhing, writhed (pronounced rie-th)
(verb) If you writhe, you twist and turn your body, often because you are in pain.

writing, writings
1 (noun) Writing is something that has been written or printed, e.g. *Get an offer in writing.*
2 Your writing is way you write with a pen or pencil.
3 Writing is also a piece of written work, especially the style of language used, e.g. *The book contains some very witty writing.*
4 An author's writings are his or her written works.

written
1 Written is the past participle of **write.**
2 (adjective) taken down in writing, e.g. *written evidence.*

wrong, wrongs, wronging, wronged
1 (adjective) not working properly or unsatisfactory, e.g. *There was nothing wrong with his eyesight.*
2 not correct or truthful, e.g. *the wrong answer.*
3 bad or immoral, e.g. *It is wrong to steal.*
4 (noun) A wrong is an unjust action or situation, e.g. *Two wrongs do not make a right.*
5 (verb) If someone wrongs you, they treat you in an unfair or unjust way.

6 (adjective) The wrong side of a piece of cloth is the side which is not meant to be seen.
wrongly (adverb).
[from Old English *wrang* meaning 'injustice']

Similar words: (sense 2) false, inaccurate, incorrect, erroneous

wrongdoer, wrongdoers (pronounced rong-doo-er)
(noun; a formal word) A wrongdoer is a person who does things that are illegal or immoral.
wrongdoing (noun).

wrong-foot, wrong-foots, wrong-footing, wrong-footed
1 (verb) If you wrong-foot your opponent in a sports game, you cause them to be off balance.
2 If you wrong-foot someone, you take them by surprise and put them in an embarrassing or difficult situation.

wrongful
(adjective) illegal, unfair or immoral, e.g. *wrongful arrest*.
wrongfully (adverb).

wrong-headed
(adjective) foolishly stubborn in making wrong decisions.

wrought (pronounced **rawt**)
1 (verb; a literary use) If something has wrought a change, it has caused it.
2 (adjective) decorated or made into a delicate shape, e.g. *wrought silver*.
[from Old English *worht* meaning 'worked']

wrought iron
(noun) Wrought iron is a pure type of iron that is formed into decorative shapes.

WRVS
(noun) The WRVS is a voluntary branch of the army which provides support services for people in need. WRVS is an abbreviation for 'Women's Royal Voluntary Service'.

wry
1 (adjective) A wry expression shows that you find a situation slightly amusing because you know more about it than other people.
2 A wry expression is also rather strange or twisted, usually showing that you dislike something.
wryly (adverb), **wryness** (noun).
[from Middle English dialect *wry* meaning 'to twist']

Similar words: (sense 1) dry, ironic

X

X, x

1 X is used to represent the name of an unknown or secret person or place, e.g. *She was referred to as Miss X during the trial.*
2 In algebra, x is used as a symbol to represent a number whose value is not known.
3 People sometimes write X on a map to mark a precise position.
4 X is used to represent a kiss at the bottom of a letter, a vote on a ballot paper, or the signature of someone who cannot write.

X chromosome, X chromosomes

(noun) In biology, an X chromosome is one of an identical pair of chromosomes found in a woman's cells, or one of a nonidentical pair found in a man's cells. X chromosomes are associated with female characteristics.

xenon (pronounced zen-non)

(noun) Xenon is a chemical element in the form of a colourless, odourless gas found in very small quantities in the atmosphere. It is used in radio valves and in some lamps. Its atomic number is 54 and its symbol is Xe.
[from Greek *xenon* meaning 'something strange']

xenophobia (pronounced zen-nof-foe-bee-a)

(noun) Xenophobia is a fear or strong dislike of people from other countries, e.g. *They are nationalists to the point of xenophobia.*
xenophobic (adjective).
[from Greek *xenos* meaning 'stranger' and *phobos* meaning 'fear']

xerophyte, xerophytes (pronounced zee-rof-fite)

(noun) A xerophyte is a plant, such as a cactus, which is adapted to live in very dry conditions.
xerophytic (adjective).
[from Greek *xēros* + *phuton* meaning 'dry plant']

Xerox, Xeroxes (pronounced zeer-roks) (a trademark)

1 (noun) A Xerox is a machine that makes photographic copies of sheets of paper with writing or printing on them.
2 A Xerox is also a copy made by a Xerox machine.

Xhosa (pronounced kohs-sa)

1 (noun) The Xhosa are a group of black people in southern Africa who live mainly by rearing cattle.
2 Xhosa is the language spoken by the Xhosa.

Xmas

(noun; an informal word) Xmas means the same as Christmas.
[in Greek *X* is the first letter of *Christos* meaning 'Christ']

X-ray, X-rays, X-raying, X-rayed

1 (noun) An X-ray, or a Röntgen ray, is a stream of electromagnetic radiation of very short wavelength that can pass through some solid materials. X-rays are used by doctors to examine the bones or organs inside a person's body.
2 An X-ray is a picture made by sending X-rays through someone's body in order to examine the inside of their body.
3 (verb) If you are X-rayed, a picture is made of the inside of your body by passing X-rays through it.

xylem (pronounced zy-lem)

(noun; a technical word) Xylem is a plant tissue that conducts water and mineral salts from the roots, provides support to a plant, and forms the wood in trees and shrubs.

xylophone, xylophones (pronounced zy-lo-fone)

(noun) A xylophone is a musical instrument made of a row of wooden bars of different lengths. It is played by hitting the bars with special hard-headed hammers.
[from Greek *xulon* + *phōnē* meaning 'wood sound']

Y

y
In algebra, y is used as a symbol to represent a number whose value is not known.

yacht, yachts (pronounced **yot**)
(noun) A yacht is a boat with sails or an engine, used for racing or for pleasure trips.

yachting
(noun) Yachting is the sport or activity of sailing a yacht.

yachtsman, yachtmen
(noun) A yachtsman is a man who sails a yacht.
yachtswoman (noun).

yak, yaks, yakking, yakked
1 (noun) A yak is a type of long-haired long-horned ox found mainly in the mountains of Tibet. Yaks are kept as work animals or to provide meat and milk.
2 (verb; an informal use) Someone who is yakking is talking noisily about nothing of importance.
[sense 1 is from Tibetan *gyag*]

Yale lock, Yale locks
(noun; a trademark) A Yale lock is a type of door lock with a cylinder which is opened with a grooved key.

yam, yams
(noun) A yam is a root vegetable which grows in tropical regions. It is also called a sweet potato.
[from Portuguese *inhame*]

yank, yanks, yanking, yanked
1 (verb) If you yank something, you pull or jerk it suddenly with a lot of force.
2 (noun; an informal use) A Yank is an American.

Yankee, Yankees
(noun) A Yankee is the same as a Yank.

yap, yaps, yapping, yapped
(verb) If a dog yaps, it barks a lot with a high-pitched sound.

yard, yards
1 (noun) A yard is a unit of length equal to 36 inches or about 91.4 centimetres.
2 A yard is also an enclosed area that is usually next to a building and is often used for a particular purpose, e.g. *a builder's yard.*
[sense 1 is from Old English *gierd* meaning 'twig' or 'rod'; sense 2 is from Old English *geard* meaning 'enclosure']

yardstick, yardsticks
(noun) If you use someone or something as a yardstick, you use them as a standard against which to judge other people or things, e.g. *The yardstick for success is exam achievement.*

yarn, yarns
1 (noun) Yarn is thread used for knitting or making cloth.
2 (an informal use) A yarn is a story that someone tells, often with invented details to make it more interesting or exciting.

yashmak, yashmaks
(noun) A yashmak is a veil that some Muslim women wear over their faces when they are in public.
[an Arabic word]

yaw, yaws, yawing, yawed
(verb) If a ship or an aircraft yaws, it turns to one side or from side to side as it is moving.

yawn, yawns, yawning, yawned
1 (verb) When you yawn, you open your mouth wide and take in more air than usual. You often yawn when you are tired or bored.
2 A gap or opening that yawns is large and wide, e.g. *A great gap yawned between the rocks.*
yawning (adjective).

yaws
(noun) Yaws is an infectious tropical skin disease.

Y chromosome, Y chromosomes
(noun) In biology, a Y chromosome is the single chromosome in a man's cells which will produce a male baby if it joins with an X chromosome during reproduction.

ye (an old word)
1 (pronoun) Ye used to mean 'you'.
2 (determiner) Ye also used to mean 'the'.

yea (rhymes with **day**)
(an old word) Yea used to mean 'yes'.

yeah
(an informal word) Yeah means 'yes'.

year, years
1 (noun) A year is a period of twelve months or 365 days (366 days in a leap year), which is the time taken for the earth to make one revolution around the sun.
2 A year is also a period of twelve consecutive months on which administration or organization is based, e.g. *The school year ends in July.*
3 (phrase) If something happens **year in, year out**, it happens every year, e.g. *They went to Blackpool in September year in, year out.*
yearly (adjective and adverb).

yearbook, yearbooks
(noun) A yearbook is a reference book that is published once a year and contains up-to-date information about a particular subject.

yearling, yearlings
(noun) A yearling is an animal between one and two years old.

yearn, yearns, yearning, yearned (rhymes with **learn**)
(verb) If you yearn for something, you want it very much indeed, e.g. *She yearned to go home.*
yearning (noun).

yeast, yeasts
(noun) Yeast is a kind of fungus which is used to make bread rise, and to make liquids ferment in order to produce alcohol.

yell, yells, yelling, yelled
1 (verb) If you yell, you shout loudly, usually because you are angry, excited, or in pain.
2 (noun) A yell is a loud shout.

yellow, yellower, yellowest; yellows, yellowing, yellowed
1 (noun and adjective) Yellow is the colour of buttercups, egg yolks, or lemons.
2 (verb) When something yellows or is yellowed, it becomes yellow, often because it is old.
3 (adjective; an informal use) If you say someone is yellow, you mean they are cowardly.
yellowish (adjective).

yellow fever
(noun) Yellow fever is a serious infectious viral disease that is transmitted by mosquitoes in tropical countries. It causes fever and jaundice.

yellow pages
(plural noun) The yellow pages are a telephone directory or part of a directory in which businesses are listed under headings describing the kind of goods or service provided.

yelp, yelps, yelping, yelped
1 (verb) When people or animals yelp, they give a sudden, short cry.
2 (noun) A yelp is a sudden, short cry.

yen
1 (noun) The yen is the main unit of currency in Japan.
2 (an informal use) If you have a yen to do something, you have a strong desire to do it, e.g. *He had a yen to hike through Canada.*
[sense 1 is from Japanese *en* meaning 'round thing' or 'dollar']

yeoman, yeomen (pronounced **yoe**-man)
(noun) In the past, a yeoman was a man who owned and farmed his own land.

Yeoman of the Guard, Yeomen of the Guard
(noun) Yeomen of the Guard, or beefeaters, were formerly bodyguards to the king or queen. Now they only have a ceremonial role.

yes
You use yes to agree with someone, to say that something is true, or to accept something.

yes-man, yes-men
(noun) If you call someone a yes-man, you mean that they always agree with their superior.

yesterday
1 (noun and adverb) Yesterday is the day before today.
2 You also use yesterday to refer to the past, e.g. *The worker of today is different from the worker of yesterday.*

yet
1 (adverb) If something has not happened yet, it has not happened up to the present time, e.g. *Have you had your lunch yet?*
2 If something should not be done yet, it should not be done now, but later, e.g. *Don't open the door yet.*
3 Yet can mean there is still a possibility that something can happen, e.g. *We'll make a footballer of you yet.*

4 You can use yet when you want to say how much longer a situation will continue, e.g. *It will not be dark for half an hour yet.*
5 (conjunction) You can use yet to introduce a fact which is rather surprising, e.g. *Everything was blown to pieces, yet he escaped unharmed.*
6 (adverb) Yet can be used for emphasis, e.g. *I am sorry to bring up this subject yet again.*

yeti, yetis (pronounced **yet**-tee)
(noun) A yeti, or 'abominable snowman', is a large hairy apelike animal which some people believe exists in the Himalayas.
[a Tibetan word]

yew, yews
(noun) A yew is an evergreen tree with bright red berries. Its wood is sometimes used for furniture.

Yiddish
(noun) Yiddish is a language derived mainly from German, which many Jewish people of European origin speak. It is written in Hebrew characters.
[from German *jüdisch* meaning 'Jewish']

yield, yields, yielding, yielded
1 (verb) If you yield to someone or something, you stop resisting and give in to them, e.g. *He yielded to public pressure.*
2 If you yield something that you have control of or responsibility for, you surrender it, e.g. *They yielded fifteen kilometres to the enemy.*
3 If something yields, it breaks or gives way, e.g. *Any lock will yield to brute force.*
4 To yield something means to produce it, e.g. *One acre yielded only 500 pounds of rice.*
5 (noun) A yield is an amount of food, money, or profit produced from a given area of land or from an investment.

yippee
(exclamation) 'Yippee!' is an exclamation of happiness or excitement.

yob, yobs
(noun; an informal word) A yob is a noisy, badly behaved boy or young man.

yodel, yodels, yodelling, yodelled (pronounced **yoe**-dl)
(verb) When someone yodels, they sing normal notes with high quick notes in between. This style of singing is associated with the Swiss and Austrian Alps.
yodeller (noun).
[from German *jodeln*]

yoga (pronounced **yoe**-ga)
(noun) Yoga is a Hindu method of mental and physical exercise or discipline.
[from Sanskrit *yoga* meaning 'union']

yoghurt, yoghurts; also spelled yoghourt or yogurt (pronounced **yog**-gurt)
(noun) Yoghurt is a slightly sour thick liquid made from milk that has had bacteria added to it.
[a Turkish word]

yogi, yogis
(noun) A yogi is a person who has spent many years practising or teaching yoga.

yoke, yokes
1 (noun) A yoke is a wooden bar attached to two collars which is laid across the necks of animals such as oxen to hold them together, and to which a plough or other tool may be attached.
2 (a literary use) If people are under a yoke of some kind, they are being oppressed, e.g. *They threw off the yoke of tyranny.*
3 A yoke of a dress or skirt is the fitted part, onto which a fuller part of the garment is attached.

yokel, yokels (pronounced **yoe**-kl)
(noun) If you call someone a yokel, you mean they live in the country, and you think they are rather slow-witted and old-fashioned.

yolk, yolks (rhymes with **joke**)
(noun) The yolk of an egg is the yellow part in the middle of the egg. It provides food for the developing embryo.
[from Old English *geoloca*, from *geolu* meaning 'yellow']

Yom Kippur (pronounced yom kip-**poor**)
(noun) Yom Kippur is an annual Jewish religious holiday, which is a day of fasting and prayers. It is also called the Day of Atonement.
[from Hebrew *yom* meaning 'day' and *kippur* meaning 'atonement']

yon (an old word)
(determiner) Yon means that or those.

yonder
(adverb or determiner; an old word) over there, e.g. *over that hill yonder.*

yore
(an old-fashioned or literary phrase) Of yore means existing a long time ago, e.g. *Where are the palaces of yore?*

Yorkshire pudding, Yorkshire puddings
(noun) Yorkshire pudding is a kind of baked batter made of flour, milk, and eggs, and usually eaten with roast beef.

you
1 (pronoun) You refers to the person or group of people that a person is speaking or writing to.
2 You also refers to people in general, e.g. *You can get freezers with security locks.*

young, younger, youngest
1 (adjective) A young person, animal, or plant has not lived very long and is not yet mature.
2 (noun) 'The young' is used to refer to people who are young, e.g. *This area teems with the young, especially students.*
3 The young of an animal are its babies.

Similar words: (sense 1) youthful, juvenile
(sense 3) offspring, progeny, issue

youngster, youngsters
(noun) A youngster is a child or young person.

your
1 (determiner) Your means belonging or relating to the person or group of people that someone is speaking to, e.g. *Where's your father?*
2 Your is used to show that something belongs or relates to people in general rather than to a particular person, e.g. *The system is geared to taking your GCSE when you're 16.*

yours
(pronoun) Yours refers to something belonging or relating to the person or group of people that someone is speaking to, e.g. *Our swimming pool is better than yours.*

yourself, yourselves
1 (pronoun) Yourself is used when the person being spoken to does the action and is affected by it, e.g. *You'll have to do it yourself.*
2 Yourself is used to emphasize 'you', e.g. *You yourself said you wanted to go.*

youth, youths
1 (noun) Someone's youth is the period of their life before they are a fully mature adult.
2 Youth is the quality or condition of being young and often inexperienced.
3 A youth is a boy or young man.
4 The youth are young people thought of as a group, e.g. *the youth of today.*
youthful (adjective), **youthfully** (adverb).

youth hostel, youth hostels
(noun) A youth hostel is a place where young people can stay cheaply when they are on holiday.

yowl, yowls, yowling, yowled
1 (noun) A yowl is a loud wailing noise made by an animal or person.
2 (verb) To yowl means to wail loudly.

yo-yo, yo-yos
(noun) A yo-yo is a round wooden or plastic toy attached to a piece of string. You play by making the yo-yo rise and fall on the string.

yucca, yuccas
(noun) A yucca is a tropical plant with spiky leaves and white flowers.
[from American Spanish *yuca*]

Yugoslav, Yugoslavs (pronounced yoo-goe-slahv)
1 (adjective) belonging or relating to Yugoslavia.
2 (noun) A Yugoslav is someone who comes from Yugoslavia.

Yule
(noun; an old word) Yule means Christmas.
[from Old English *geola* a pagan winter feast]

yummy, yummier, yummiest
(adjective; an informal word) delicious or tasty.

yuppie, yuppies
(noun) If you say people are yuppies, you think they are young, middle-class, and earn a lot of money which they spend on themselves. Yuppie stands for 'Young urban professional'.

Z

Zambian, Zambians (pronounced **zam**-bee-an)
1 (adjective) belonging or relating to Zambia.
2 (noun) A Zambian is someone who comes from Zambia.

zany, zanier, zaniest
(adjective) odd and ridiculous, e.g. *his zany wit*.
[from Italian *zanni* meaning 'clown']

zap, zaps, zapping, zapped (an informal word)
1 (verb) To zap someone means to kill them, usually by shooting, e.g. *That guy got zapped later on the same day*.
2 To zap also means to do something, or go somewhere quickly.

zeal
(noun) Zeal is very great enthusiasm.
zealous (adjective), **zealously** (adverb).
[from Greek *zēlos*]

zealot, zealots (pronounced **zel**-lot)
(noun) A zealot is a person who acts with very great enthusiasm, especially in following a political or religious cause.

zebra, zebras
(noun) A zebra is a type of African wild horse with black and white stripes over its body.

zebra crossings, zebra crossings
(noun) A zebra crossing is a place where people can cross the road safely. The road is marked with black and white stripes.

zebu, zebus (pronounced **zee**-boo)
(noun) A zebu is an Asian ox with a humped back and long horns.

Zen or **Zen Buddhism**
(noun) Zen is a form of Buddhism that concentrates on learning through meditation and intuition.
[a Japanese word]

zenith
1 (noun; a literary use) The zenith of something is the time when it is at its most successful or powerful, e.g. *at the zenith of his career*.
2 The zenith is the highest point in the heavens directly above you.
[from Old French *cenit* meaning 'point of the sky directly overhead']

zephyr, zephyrs (pronounced **zef**-fer)
(noun; a literary word) A zephyr is a gentle breeze.
[from Greek *zephuros* meaning 'west wind']

zero, zeros or **zeroes, zeroing, zeroed**
1 Zero is the number 0.
2 Zero is freezing point, 0° Centigrade.
3 (adjective) Zero means there is none at all of a particular thing, e.g. *Its running costs were zero*.
4 (verb) To zero in on a target means to aim at or to move towards it, e.g. *The missile zeroed in on the tank*.
[from Arabic *sifr* meaning 'cipher' or 'empty']

zero hour
(noun) Zero hour is the time at which something is planned to begin, for example a military operation.

zest
1 (noun) Zest is a feeling of pleasure and enthusiasm, e.g. *zest for life*.
2 Zest is a quality which adds extra flavour, interest, or charm to something, e.g. *Her presence gave zest to the occasion*.
3 The zest of an orange or lemon is the outside of the peel which is used to flavour food or drinks.
zestful (adjective), **zestfully** (adverb).

zigzag, zigzags, zigzagging, zigzagged
1 (noun) A zigzag is a line which has a series of sharp, angular turns to the right and left in it, like a continuous series of 'W's.
2 (verb) To zigzag means to move forward by going at an angle first right and then left, e.g. *We zigzagged up the hill*.

Zimbabwean, Zimbabweans (pronounced zim-**bahb**-wee-an)
1 (adjective) belonging or relating to Zimbabwe.
2 (noun) A Zimbabwean is someone who comes from Zimbabwe.

zinc
(noun) Zinc is a bluish-white metallic element used in alloys and to coat other metals to stop them rusting. Its atomic number is 30 and its symbol is Zn.

zing
(noun; an informal word) Zing is a quality in something that makes it lively or interesting, e.g. *White wine gave extra zing to the recipe*.

Zionism (pronounced **zie**-on-izm)
(noun) Zionism is a political movement which was originally concerned with the establishment of a state in Palestine for Jewish people. It is now concerned with the development of the modern state of Israel.
Zionist (noun).
[*Zion* is the name of the hill on which Jerusalem is built]

zip, zips, zipping, zipped
1 (noun) A zip is a long narrow fastener with two rows of teeth that are closed or opened by a small clip pulled between them.
2 (verb) When you zip something or zip it up, you fasten it using a zip.

zip code, zip codes
(noun; an American word) A zip code is the same as a postcode.

zipper, zippers
(noun) A zipper is the same as a zip.

zircon
(noun) Zircon is a hard mineral used in industry and as a gem for jewellery.

zither, zithers
(noun) A zither is a musical instrument

consisting of strings stretched over a flat box and plucked to produce musical notes.
[from Greek *kithara*]

zodiac (pronounced **zoe**-dee-ak)
1 (noun) The zodiac is an imaginary belt in the sky which contains the planets and stars which astrologers think are important influences on people.
2 The zodiac is a diagram used by astrologers to represent the positions of the planets and stars. It is divided into 12 sections, each with a special name and symbol.
[from Greek *zōidiakos kuklos* meaning 'circle of signs']

zombie, zombies
1 (noun; an informal use) If you refer to someone as a zombie, you mean that they seem to be unaware of what is going on around them and to act without thinking about what they are doing.
2 In voodoo, a zombie is a dead person who has been brought back to life by witchcraft.
[from an African word *zumbi* meaning 'good-luck charm']

zone, zones
(noun) A zone is an area that has particular features or properties, e.g. *a nuclear-free zone*.
zonal (adjective).
[from Latin *zona* meaning 'belt']

zoo, zoos
(noun) A zoo is a place where live animals are kept so that people can look at them.

zoology (pronounced zoo-**ol**-loj-jee)
(noun) Zoology is the scientific study of animals.'
zoological (adjective), **zoologically** (adverb), **zoologist** (noun).
[from Greek *zōion* meaning 'animal' and *-logy* meaning 'study of']

zoom, zooms, zooming, zoomed
1 (verb) To zoom means to move very quickly, e.g. *They zoomed down on their bikes*.
2 If a camera zooms in on something, it gives a close-up picture of it.

zoom lens, zoom lenses
(noun) A zoom lens on a camera is a lens that allows the photographer to make the details of a picture larger or smaller and still remain in focus.

zoophyte, zoophytes (pronounced **zoe**-af-ite)
(noun) A zoophyte is any animal which resembles a plant, such as a sea anemone.
zoophytic (adjective).
[from Greek *zōion* + *phuton* meaning 'animal plant']

zucchini (pronounced zoo-**keen**-nee)
(plural noun) Zucchini are courgettes.
[an Italian word]

Zulu, Zulus (pronounced **zoo**-loo)
1 (noun) The Zulus are a group of black people who live in southern Africa.
2 Zulu is the language spoken by the Zulus.